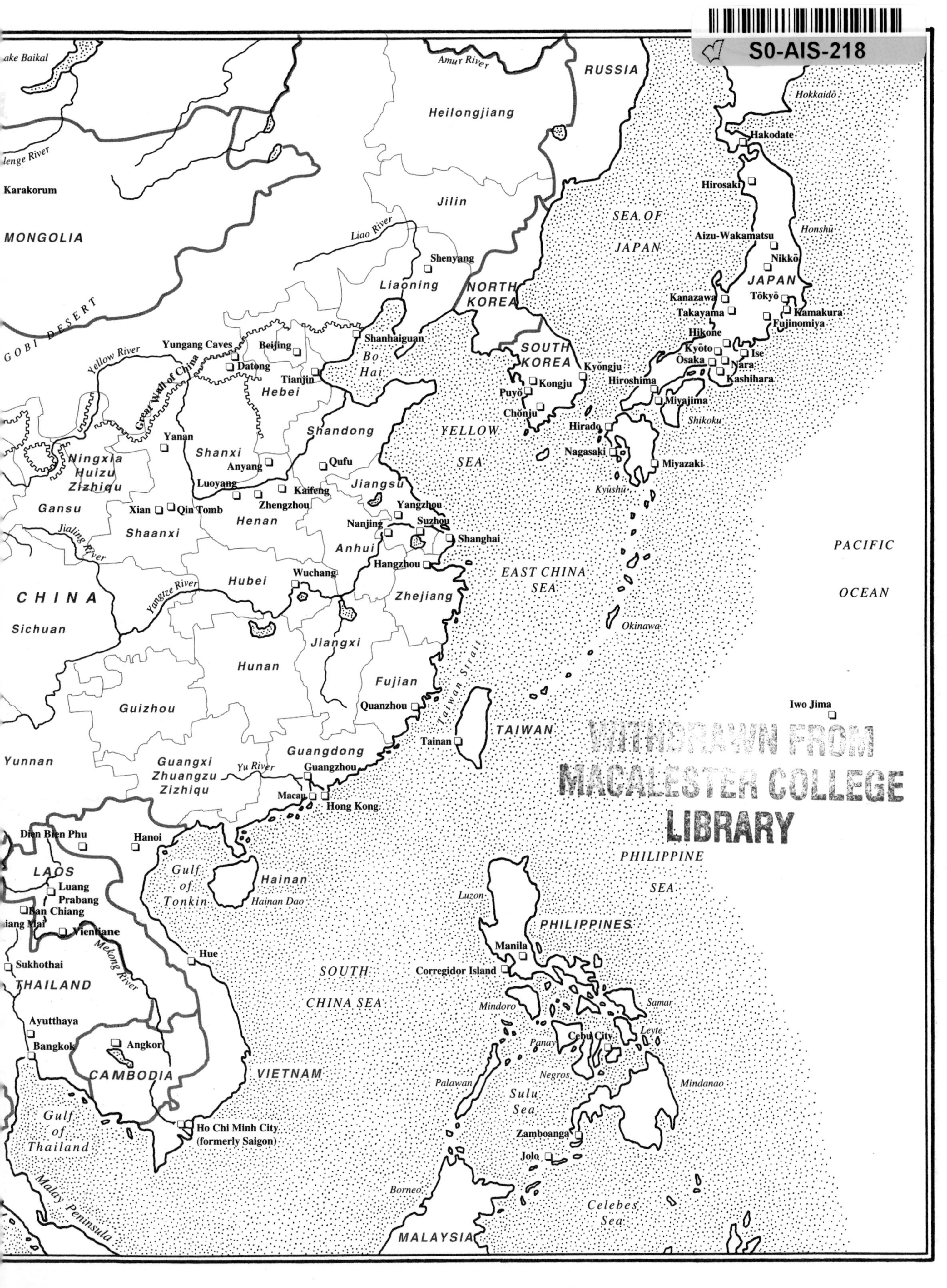

Lake Baikal
Selenge River
Karakorum
MONGOLIA
GOBI DESERT
RUSSIA
Amur River
Heilongjiang
Jilin
Liao River
Shenyang
Liaoning
NORTH KOREA
SOUTH KOREA
SEA OF JAPAN
Hokkaidō
Hakodate
Hirosaki
Honshū
Aizu-Wakamatsu
Nikkō
JAPAN
Kanazawa
Tōkyō
Takayama
Kamakura
Fujinomiya
Hikone
Kyōto
Ōsaka
Ise
Nara
Kashihara
Kyŏngju
Hiroshima
Miyajima
Shikoku
Kongju
Puyŏ
Chŏnju
Hirado
Nagasaki
Miyazaki
Kyūshū
Yungang Caves
Beijing
Datong
Shanhaiguan
Bo Hai
Tianjin
Hebei
Yellow River
Great Wall of China
Shandong
YELLOW SEA
Yanan
Shanxi
Anyang
Qufu
Ningxia Huizu Zizhiqu
Luoyang
Kaifeng
Jiangsu
Gansu
Xian
Qin Tomb
Zhengzhou
Yangzhou
Henan
Nanjing
Suzhou
Shaanxi
Shanghai
Jialing River
Anhui
Hangzhou
EAST CHINA SEA
PACIFIC OCEAN
Wuchang
Hubei
CHINA
Yangtze River
Zhejiang
Sichuan
Okinawa
Jiangxi
Hunan
Fujian
Taiwan Strait
Guizhou
Quanzhou
Iwo Jima
TAIWAN
Tainan
Guangdong
Yunnan
Guangxi Zhuangzu Zizhiqu
Yu River
Guangzhou
Macau
Hong Kong
Dien Bien Phu
Hanoi
PHILIPPINE SEA
LAOS
Luang Prabang
Gulf of Tonkin
Hainan
Hainan Dao
Luzon
Ban Chiang
Chiang Mai
Vientiane
PHILIPPINES
Mekong River
Manila
Sukhothai
Hue
SOUTH CHINA SEA
Corregidor Island
THAILAND
Mindoro
Samar
Ayutthaya
Leyte
Panay
Cebu City
Bangkok
Angkor
CAMBODIA
VIETNAM
Negros
Palawan
Sulu Sea
Mindanao
Gulf of Thailand
Ho Chi Minh City (formerly Saigon)
Zamboanga
Jolo
Malay Peninsula
Borneo
Celebes Sea
MALAYSIA

INTERNATIONAL DICTIONARY OF
HISTORIC PLACES

INTERNATIONAL DICTIONARY OF HISTORIC PLACES

VOLUME 1	AMERICAS
VOLUME 2	NORTHERN EUROPE
VOLUME 3	SOUTHERN EUROPE
VOLUME 4	MIDDLE EAST AND AFRICA
VOLUME 5	ASIA AND OCEANIA

INTERNATIONAL DICTIONARY OF

HISTORIC PLACES

VOLUME 5

ASIA AND OCEANIA

Editors
PAUL E. SCHELLINGER
ROBERT M. SALKIN

Photo Editors
CHRISTOPHER HUDSON
SHARON LA BODA

Commissioning Editors
K.A. BERNEY
TRUDY RING

FITZROY DEARBORN PUBLISHERS
CHICAGO AND LONDON

For information, write to:
FITZROY DEARBORN PUBLISHERS
70 East Walton Street
Chicago, Illinois 60611
U.S.A.
or
11 Rathbone Place
London W1P 1DE
England

Library of Congress Cataloging-in-Publication Data:

International dictionary of historic places / editor, Paul E. Schellinger; editor, Robert M. Salkin.
p. cm.
Essays on the history of 1,000 historic places.
Includes bibliographical references and index.
Contents: v. 1. Americas — v. 2. Northern Europe — v. 3. Southern Europe — v. 4. Middle East and Africa — v. 5 Asia and Oceania.

ISBN 1-884964-05-2 (set): $125 (per vol.) — ISBN 1-884964-00-1 (v. 1). — ISBN 1-884964-01-X (v. 2). — ISBN 1-884964-02-8 (v. 3). — ISBN 1-884964-03-6 (v. 4). — ISBN 1-884964-04-4 (v. 5).
1. Historic sites. I. Schellinger, Paul E., 1962– II. Salkin, Robert M., 1965–.
CC135.I585 1996
973—dc20 94-32327
CIP

British Library Cataloguing-in-Publication Data

International Dictionary of Historic Places, Volume 5—Asia and Oceania
I. Schellinger, Paul E. II. Salkin, Robert M.
970

ISBN 1-884964-04-4

First published in the U.S.A. and U.K. 1996
Typeset by Acme Art, Inc.
Printed by Braun-Brumfield, Inc.

Cover photograph: Torana arch, near Jaisalmer, India
Photo courtesy of Christopher Turner
Cover designed by Peter Aristedes, Chicago Advertising and Design

Frontispiece and endpaper maps by Tom Willcockson, Mapcraft

CONTENTS

Historic Places by Country or Location xi
Editors' Note xv
Contributors xvii
The Dictionary:
Āgra 1
Ahmadābād 6
Aizu-Wakamatsu 10
Ajanta 14
Ajmer 20
Amber 24
Amritsar 27
Angkor 31
Anuradhapura 35
Anyang 40
Ayers Rock 44
Ayodhyā 47
Ayutthaya 52
Bago 60
Bali 65
Balkh 71
Ballarat 75
Bāmiān 79
Ban Chiang 82
Banda 87
Bangalore 92
Bangkok 96
Banten 101
Beijing: Forbidden City 105
Beijing: Tiananmen Square 109
Bengkulu 113
Bhopāl 117
Bhubaneswar 121
Bijāpur 125
Bīkaner 129
Bishnupur 134
Bodh Gayā 138

Bombay . . . 142
Borobudur . . . 147
Botany Bay . . . 153
Brunei Darussalam . . . 158
Bukhara . . . 163
Buxar . . . 168
Calcutta . . . 172
Cebu City . . . 177
Chiang Mai . . . 182
Chittagong . . . 186
Chittaurgarh . . . 191
Chŏnju . . . 195
Colombo . . . 199
Corregidor Island . . . 204
Darwin . . . 208
Datong . . . 212
Delhi . . . 218
Dhākā . . . 225
Dien Bien Phu . . . 230
Dunedin . . . 234
Dunhuang: Dunhuang Town . . . 239
Dunhuang: Mogao Caves . . . 242
Easter Island . . . 247
Elephanta Island . . . 252
Ellora . . . 256
Fatehpur Sīkri . . . 260
Fiji . . . 264
Fujinomiya . . . 269
Galle . . . 272
Gayā . . . 276
Ghaznī . . . 279
Goa . . . 284
Golconda . . . 290
Great Wall . . . 293
Guadalcanal . . . 298
Guangzhou . . . 302
Guwāhāti . . . 308
Gwalior . . . 312
Hakodate . . . 317
Hami . . . 321
Hangzhou . . . 325
Hanoi . . . 329

Herāt .333
Hikone .338
Hirado .340
Hirosaki .345
Hiroshima .349
Ho Chi Minh City .353
Hong Kong .358
Hue .362
Hyderābād, India .366
Hyderābād, Pakistan .371
Ise .374
Iwo Jima .379
Jaipur .383
Jaisalmer .388
Jakarta .395
Jodhpur .399
Jolo .403
Junāgadh .408
Kābul .414
Kaifeng .420
Kamakura .426
Kanazawa .431
Kānchipuram .435
Kandahār .439
Kandy .443
Karāchi .448
Karakorum .451
Kashgar .456
Kashihara .460
Kāthmāndu .464
Khajurāho .468
Khyber Pass .473
Konārak .478
Kongju and Puyŏ .482
Kot Diji .489
Krakatau .493
Kuching .497
Kumbakonam .501
Kurukshetra .505
Kyŏngju .509
Kyōto .515
Lahore .522

Lhasa 526
Luang Prabang 530
Lucknow 534
Luoyang 538
Macau 542
Madras 547
Mahābalipuram 552
Mandalay 556
Māndu 561
Manila 565
Mathurā 572
Mazār-i-Sharīf 578
Melaka 582
Miyajima 587
Miyazaki 592
Mohenjo-daro 595
Mount Ābu 600
Mount Everest 603
Multān 608
Nagasaki 612
Nanjing 616
Nara 621
Nāsik 625
Niah Caves 629
Nikkō 632
Norfolk Island 639
Nouméa 644
Ōsaka 648
Pagan 653
Paharpur 657
Palembang 661
Penang 665
Peshāwar 669
Pitcairn Island 673
Plassey 679
Polonnaruwa 684
Port Arthur 688
Prambanan 692
Puri 697
Qin Tomb 701
Quanzhou 704
Qufu 707

Quilon .710
Rāmeswaram .714
Samarkand .718
Samoa (Western Samoa and American Samoa) .723
Sānchi .727
Shanghai .732
Shanhaiguan .739
Shenyang .744
Shigatse .750
Sīgiriya .754
Singapore .757
Somnāth .762
Srīnagar .767
Sukhothai .771
Suzhou .776
Sydney .781
Tahiti .785
Tainan .790
Takayama .795
Takht-i-Bahi .798
Tatta .801
Taxila .805
Thanjāvūr .809
Tianjin .813
Tokelau .818
Tōkyō .822
Tonga .827
Tongariro .832
Ujjain .835
Ujung Pandang .839
Vanuatu .843
Vārānasī .847
Vientiane .851
Vijayanagara .855
Waitangi .859
Windsor .863
Wuchang .866
Xian .870
Yanan .874
Yangon .879
Yangzhou .884
Yogyakarta .888

Yungang Caves 893
Zamboanga 897
Zhengzhou 901
Index 907
Notes on Contributors 951

HISTORIC PLACES BY COUNTRY OR LOCATION

AFGHANISTAN
Balkh
Bāmiān
Ghaznī
Herāt
Kābul
Kandahār
Khyber Pass
Mazār-i-Sharīf

AUSTRALIA
Ayers Rock
Ballarat
Botany Bay
Darwin
Norfolk Island
Port Arthur
Sydney
Windsor

BANGLADESH
Chittagong
Dhākā
Paharpur

BRUNEI DARUSSALAM

CAMBODIA
Angkor

CHILE
Easter Island

CHINA
Anyang
Beijing: Forbidden City
Beijing: Tiananmen Square
Datong
Dunhuang: Dunhuang Town
Dunhuang: Mogao Caves
Great Wall
Guangzhou
Hami
Hangzhou
Kaifeng
Kashgar
Lhasa
Luoyang
Nanjing
Qin Tomb
Quanzhou
Qufu
Shanghai
Shanhaiguan
Shenyang
Shigatse
Suzhou
Tianjin
Wuchang
Xian
Yanan
Yangzhou
Yungang Caves
Zhengzhou

FIJI

FRENCH POLYNESIA
Tahiti

HONG KONG

INDIA
Āgra
Ahmadābād
Ajanta
Ajmer
Amber
Amritsar
Ayodhyā
Bangalore
Bhopāl
Bhubaneswar
Bijāpur
Bīkaner
Bishnupur
Bodh Gayā
Bombay
Buxar
Calcutta
Chittaurgarh
Delhi
Elephanta Island
Ellora
Fatehpur Sīkri
Gayā
Goa
Golconda
Guwāhāti
Gwalior
Hyderābād
Jaipur
Jaisalmer
Jodhpur

Junāgadh
Kānchipuram
Khajurāho
Konārak
Kumbakonam
Kurukshetra
Lucknow
Madras
Mahābalipuram
Māndu
Mathurā
Mount Ābu
Nāsik
Plassey
Puri
Quilon
Rāmeswaram
Sānchi
Somnāth
Srīnagar
Thanjāvūr
Ujjain
Vārānasī
Vijayanagara

INDONESIA
Bali
Banda
Banten
Bengkulu
Borobudur
Jakarta
Krakatau
Palembang
Prambanan
Ujung Pandang
Yogyakarta

JAPAN
Aizu-Wakamatsu
Fujinomiya
Hakodate
Hikone
Hirado
Hirosaki
Hiroshima
Ise
Iwo Jima
Kamakura
Kanazawa
Kashihara
Kyōto
Miyajima
Miyazaki
Nagasaki
Nara
Nikkō
Ōsaka
Takayama
Tōkyō

LAOS
Luang Prabang
Vientiane

MACAU

MALAYSIA
Kuching
Melaka
Niah Caves
Penang

MONGOLIA
Karakorum

MOUNT EVEREST

MYANMAR
Bago
Mandalay
Pagan
Yangon

NEPAL
Kāthmāndu

NEW CALEDONIA
Nouméa

NEW ZEALAND
Dunedin
Tokelau
Tongariro
Waitangi

PAKISTAN
Hyderābād
Karāchi
Kot Diji
Khyber Pass
Lahore
Mohenjo-daro
Multān
Peshāwar
Takht-i-Bahi
Tatta
Taxila

PHILIPPINES
Cebu City
Corregidor Island
Jolo
Manila
Zamboanga

PITCAIRN ISLANDS
Pitcairn Island

SAMOA ISLANDS

SINGAPORE

SOLOMON ISLANDS
Guadalcanal

SOUTH KOREA
Chŏnju
Kongju and Puyŏ
Kyŏngju

SRI LANKA
Anuradhapura
Colombo
Galle
Kandy
Polonnaruwa
Sigiriya

TAIWAN
Tainan

THAILAND
Ayutthaya
Ban Chiang
Bangkok
Chiang Mai
Sukhothai

TONGA

UZBEKISTAN
Bukhara
Samarkand

VANUATU

VIETNAM
Dien Bien Phu
Hanoi
Ho Chi Minh City
Hue

EDITORS' NOTE

Fitzroy Dearborn Publishers' *International Dictionary of Historic Places* is designed to provide detailed and accurate information on the world's most important cities and sites. The dictionary's five volumes cover nearly 1,000 sites worldwide. Volume 1 is devoted to the Americas, Volume 2 to Northern Europe, Volume 3 to Southern Europe, Volume 4 to Africa and the Middle East, and Volume 5 to Asia and Oceania. The dictionary is intended for the use of students, teachers, librarians, historians, and anyone interested in historic places.

Each entry contains an essay that provides an historical overview of the site as well as information about what the site offers to contemporary visitors. Headnotes for each essay provide that site's geographic location, a concise description of the site, and the address of an information office there, or, when no such office is available, the address of a central contact for the area. We expect this information to assist persons who are traveling to any of the places, as well as those who wish to write or call any of the sites to request material. Each entry closes with some suggestions for further reading—a selective listing of relevant published works recommended by the author of the essay.

The entries for Volume 5 were compiled from publicly available sources, including books, magazine and newspaper articles, and, in some cases, material supplied by the site offices. We thank those site offices that provided us with such material and with illustrations. The site offices' assistance in no way constitutes their endorsement of the facts presented. Our contributors and editors, however, have made every effort to ensure the accuracy of each entry.

For their editorial, research, and proofreading assistance and/or their expertise in Asian languages and history, the editors wish to thank Marijke Rijsberman, Paula Pyzik Scott, Trudy Ring, Mary F. McNulty, Randall J. Van Vynckt, Monica Cable, Shome Chowdhury, Taka Fukunaga, Dorothy O'Shea, Dorothy Kachouh, and Cynthia Crippen.

CONTRIBUTORS

S. A. M. Adshead
David Arnold
Andrew Beattie
Bernard A. Block
Elizabeth Brice
Elizabeth E. Broadrup
A. E. Brown
Holly E. Bruns
Neville Buch
Monica Cable
Dilip K. Chakrabarti
Sappho Charney
Maria Chiara
Shome Chowdhury
Denise Coté
Robert Cribb
Sina Dubovoy
Jeffrey Felshman
Graham Field
David Flood
Lynn Gelfand
Lawrence F. Goodman
Jackie Griffin
Patrick Heenan
Pam Hollister
Christopher A. Hoyt
John Keay
Robert Kellerman
Beverly Kingston
Rion Klawinski
Lee Kottner
Monique Lamontagne
Anthony Levi
Clarissa Levi
Claudia Levi
Kit S. Liew
Christine Ann Longcore
Jean L. Lotus
Adam Yuen-chung Lui
Mary F. McNulty
Caterina Mercone Maxwell
Sue Montgomery
L. R. Naslund
L. J. Newby
Ngai-ha Ng Lun
Terence Daniel O'Leary
Erik Olssen
M. N. Pearson
Tim Pepper
Linda Pollak
Bob Reece
Marijke Rijsberman
Trudy Ring
Robert M. Salkin
Charles Savile
June Skinner Sawyers
Paula Pyzik Scott
Kenneth R. Shepherd
Sarva Daman Singh
Joseph M. Siracusa
Naomi Standen
Martin Stuart-Fox
James Sullivan
Hilary Collier Sy-Quia
Nicholas Tarling
Karen Terry
Christopher Turner
A. Vasudevan
Richard White
Lulu Wilkinson
Thomas Wiloch

INTERNATIONAL DICTIONARY OF

HISTORIC PLACES

Āgra (Uttar Pradesh, India)

Location: Southwest corner of Uttar Pradesh state, north India, 115 miles south-southeast of Delhi.

Description: The third city in size and importance of Uttar Pradesh, Āgra is renowned for its fort and great mausoleums, which include the world-famous Tāj Mahal; all were built during the period of the Mughal Empire (1526–1761).

Site Office: Government of India Tourist Office
191, the Mall
Āgra 282 001
Uttar Pradesh
India
363377 or 363959

The earliest reference to Āgra dates from the first quarter of the twelfth century and is contained in a poem that refers to the capture of its ancient Hindu fort by Sultan Mas'ad III in 1115. Apparently, the sultan permitted the city's previous occupants—the Rājputs—to remain, albeit under his suzerainty. Almost 400 years were to pass before the city reappears in the historical record.

Sikandar Lodī, sultan of Delhi, reestablished the city between 1492 and 1502 and rebuilt its fort in brick. Toward the end of this period he left Delhi for Āgra, which became his new capital and was renamed Sikandarābād. The prime reason for this move appears to be Sikandar's wish to subdue the Rājputs in what is now Rājasthān, an area much more accessible from Āgra than from Delhi. Sikandar, however, appears to have preferred to reside outside the city walls, to the north, in a town still known as Sikandra, where he built the Bayadari Palace. This two-story building, now somewhat dilapidated, later became home to the Tomb of Mariam, the mother of the Mughal emperor Jahāngīr, who died in the seventeenth century and was buried here. It became an orphanage in 1838, and the part of it that housed the tomb later accommodated a printing press; all is now protected by the government.

Ibrāhīm Lodī, who succeeded Sikandar following his death in 1517, remained at Āgra, but his harshness made him unpopular and many of his erstwhile supporters schemed to dethrone him. They sought the assistance of Ẓahīr-ud-Dīn Muḥammad, better known as Bābur, the Mughal leader of Afghanistan, whose troops, provided with gunpowder, defeated Ibrāhīm, first at Lahore in 1526, and again two years later at Pānīpat, fifty miles north of Delhi, where Ibrāhīm was killed. The Delhi sultanate had ended, and 350 years of Mughal rule began.

Immediately following his victory, Bābur sent his son Humāyūn to Āgra Fort, as it was rumored that the Lodī jewels were guarded within; not only did this prove true, but, as a bonus, members of the mahārāja of Gwalior's family had taken refuge in the fort with their own jewels. In order to gain Humāyūn's favor, it is said that they presented him with the Koh-i-Noor diamond, now a feature of the Crown Jewels of England.

Although Bābur made Āgra his capital, he spent little time there owing to his involvement in campaigns against the Rājputs, whom he finally defeated in 1528. His victory and proclamation as Emperor of Hindustan were celebrated at Āgra Fort. During Bābur's four-year rule, he appears to have built little, although it is said that a palace was constructed for him on the east bank of the Yamuna. No remnants of buildings in Āgra have been connected with Bābur, but his Rām Bāgh garden, laid out in formal Persian *charbagh* style, may still be seen to the north of the city, much in need of restoration; Rām Bāgh is a corruption of Aram Bāgh (Garden of Repose). It is alleged that, following Bābur's death in 1530, he was initially buried in this garden; his body was later transferred to Kābul, Afghanistan, where it was laid in a simple grave, in accordance with the teachings of the Koran. A similar garden nearby, the Zahara Bāgh, is also believed to have been the work of Bābur, and may have been built even earlier.

Humāyūn, after inheriting the throne from his father, immediately began the reconstruction of Āgra Fort. He also built a small mosque, dated 1630, which lies immediately behind the Tāj Mahal, on the opposite bank of the river; this mosque is the only building that survives in Āgra from Humāyūn's reign. In 1533, he began the construction of a new citadel at Delhi, known as Dinapanah (Asylum of Faith). Within seven years, Shēr Shāh of Sūr, an Afghan who ruled the northeastern provinces of Bengal and Bihār, contested Mughal dominance, for a lack of resolution, combined with fraternal uprisings, had made Humāyūn's position appear fragile. Shēr Shāh's army defeated the Mughals in battle in 1539 and 1540, and the fifteen-year Sūr interregnum began in 1540. The new ruler replaced Humāyūn's citadel at Dinapanah with his own new city of Shērgarh, and it is not clear how much time he or his descendants spent at Āgra. However, it may be that a small structure within its fort, known as the Salimgarh Kiosk, was built during their period of rule.

After the death of Shēr Shāh in 1545, the dynasty gradually weakened, and Humāyūn returned from his exile in Persia, taking both Āgra and Delhi in 1555 with a reorganized force led by his outstanding general, Bayram Khān. Within a year Humāyūn was killed in an accident at Delhi, and his fourteen-year-old son Akbar ruled the Mughal Empire from Āgra, guided initially by Bayram Khān, who acted as regent. Within three years, Āgra had regained its preeminence, and the fort was rebuilt in greatly enlarged form. Only the walls,

Fort at Āgra
Photo courtesy of Christopher Turner

gates, and one pavilion remain of Akbar's work in the fort, the remainder having been replaced by his grandson, Shāh Jahān. Of particular interest is the interior of the pavilion, which is now known as the Jahangiri Mahal because its exterior was remodeled by Akbar's son Jahāngīr after his father's death. Akbar completed the interior in 1570; its traditional Muslim architectural features were replaced almost entirely by Hindu versions, possibly to emphasize both Akbar's great religious tolerance and his wish to unify his Muslim and Hindu subjects.

In 1569, a Muslim saint, Shaik Salīm, who lived in seclusion on a ridge to the west of Āgra, prophesied that Akbar, then twenty-six years of age, would at last father a son who would survive infancy. Prince Salīm (later Emperor Jahāngīr), named after the saint by his grateful father, was duly born, and Akbar decided to build a great new city on the ridge in tribute to the saint. This was called Fatehpur Sīkri, and the emperor transferred his court there from Āgra in the early 1570s. The move was short-lived, as Akbar left his new city in 1585 to fight campaigns in the Punjab, transferring his base to Lahore. In 1599, Akbar returned not to Fatehpur Sīkri but to Āgra, where he died in 1605; Jahāngīr was enthroned in Āgra Fort the same year.

The only structure known for certain to have been erected by Akbar after his return to Āgra is the inner archway of the fort's Delhi Gate, which is dated 1600. Nevertheless, it seems likely that Akbar's great tomb at Sikandra was initially planned, and possibly begun, during its occupant's lifetime. Jahāngīr apparently disliked the existing design of the large mausoleum, altering it as work progressed, even possibly, as some allege, demolishing a third of it in 1607. The result is an architectural hybrid, but the gateway to the complex is a superb composition of red sandstone inlaid with colorful mosaics. Minarets at the four corners of the gateway were entirely faced with marble (for the first time in India) and are reminiscent of the Tāj Mahal's minarets, both in placement and style. The gateway was built in 1608, and it would therefore appear that Jahāngīr was responsible for commissioning its design.

Three years later, Jahāngīr married Mehron-Nesā, who became known first as Nūr Mahal (Light of the Palace) and later Nūr Jahān (Light of the World). Allegedly, it was for her that the emperor remodeled and extended the Jahangiri Mahal within Āgra Fort; as the palace obviously lay within the *zenana* (the area designated for females), this theory may well be true. Jahāngīr was unhappy at both Āgra and Fatehpur

The Tāj Mahal, Āgra
Photo courtesy of Christopher Turner

Sīkri, and in 1618, four years after finally establishing Mughal suzerainty over the Sīsōdias of Udaipur, he left Āgra for good, dividing his time between Lahore and Srīnagar in Kashmir. Jahāngīr, who shared Bābur's passion for gardening, could pursue that interest with greater rewards in the cooler, less arid north.

Jahāngīr also carried on another family tradition; like his grandfather Humāyūn, he was addicted to opium, and also to alcohol (two of his brothers had similar problems). As a result of his addictions, his wife Nūr Jahān, together with her father, Itimad-ud-Dawlah, and her brother Asaf Khān, assumed increasing responsibility for administering the empire.

The parents of Nūr Jahān died in 1622, within a short time of each other, and their daughter immediately commissioned an important mausoleum for them at Āgra on the east bank of the Yamuna. It was the first building in India to be entirely clad in white marble, although most of its external surfaces are exuberantly decorated with inlay work in floral and geometric patterns. The mausoleum of Itimad-ud-Dawlah was not completed until 1628, a year after Jahāngīr had died in Lahore. The emperor's widow then built a similar tomb for her husband at Shāhdara, a short distance from Lahore. Henceforth, most of the important buildings erected by the Mughals would be entirely faced with white marble.

Jahāngīr had rebelled against his father Akbar toward the end of his reign, but was forgiven, and the same situation occurred with Jahāngīr's own son Khurram, who was to succeed him. It was Khurram's military ability that finally earned his father's approval, although as Emperor Shāh Jahān (Ruler of the World), he is best remembered for the exquisite buildings erected during his reign.

At Āgra, the full flowering of Mughal architecture occurred. Although Muslim buildings in India from the very beginning had incorporated Hindu features, these always had retained a separate identity. Not until Shāh Jahān began to build at Āgra were Hindu and Muslim details fused, to create a unique style. The style is characterized by simplified forms and by the almost exclusive use of white (or whitish) marble, taken from the Makrāna quarries in Rājasthān, as a cladding material. A further unifying factor was the extensive decoration of the surfaces, achieved by inlaying semiprecious stones in colorful floral and geometric patterns.

Shāh Jahān was enthroned at Āgra in 1628, but four years of campaigning lay ahead before he could settle in his capital, which he was to enrich with architectural master-

Tomb of Itimad-ud-Dawlah, Āgra
Photo courtesy of Christopher Turner

pieces. Upon his return, the new emperor immediately began work at Āgra Fort and, apart from the Jahangiri Mahal already mentioned, he rebuilt all its pavilions; there is no clear record of what was replaced, although it seems likely that most had been Akbar's work. As was the custom, the pavilions providing the royal accommodation were set in a straight line overlooking the Yamuna in order to take advantage of the river breezes. A major interruption to building at Āgra Fort occurred in 1631 with the death of Mumtāz Mahal, Shāh Jahān's favorite wife, after which most workers were transferred to the construction of the Tāj Mahal, her great mausoleum. Nevertheless, the project did not come to a complete halt; the Khas Mahal (House Palace) and Dīwān-i-Khas (Private Audience Chamber) were completed in 1636 and 1637 respectively.

Shāh Jahān's chief minister, Alami Afzal Khan Shīrāzi, of Persian origin, died at Lahore in 1639 but was buried at Āgra, near Bābur's Rām Bāgh garden. His mausoleum, in severe Persian style, survives, albeit in poor condition. It is the only building in India ever to be completely clad with glazed ceramic tiles (fragments of which may still be seen), which have given the building its name, Chini Ka Rauza.

Of course, Āgra has come to be associated most closely with the Tāj Mahal, the mausoleum built by Shāh Jahān to accommodate the bodies of his favorite wife and himself. Originally his wife had been known as Arūjmand Bānū Baygam, but upon her husband's accession to the throne, she became known as Mumtāz Mahal (Greatest Ornament of the Palace); the corruption of Mumtāz to Tāj has given this extraordinary building its name. Work began immediately following the death of Mumtāz Mahal in 1631, indicating that the structure was planned well in advance. Mumtāz had died in her fortieth year, while giving birth to her fourteenth child, and Shāh Jahān was distraught. It is said that the project's workforce initially consisted of 20,000 laborers, who lived in a small town known as Mumtāzābād that sprang up around the enclosure. The mausoleum was completed in 1653, and the body of Mumtāz was immediately transferred to it from the surrounding garden. There is no clear record of who the Tāj Mahal's designer was, but the building is very Persian in style, suggesting an architect from that country. According to legend, when the Tāj Mahal was completed, Shāh Jahān cut off the architect's hands and plucked out his eyes so that the artist would never design a building to rival it. A French traveler reported that Shāh Jahān had planned to build an "echo" of the Tāj Mahal in black marble on the opposite side of the river, and that the two buildings were to be linked by bridges. However, no other evidence corroborates this report, and certainly no such structure was ever built.

In 1648, the great gateway to the enclosure was finished, and work on Āgra's Jāma Masjid (Friday Mosque) was begun for Shāh Jahān's daughter Jahanara, who had become the First Lady of the Mughal Empire. Later that year, Shāh Jahān moved to his new city of Shāhjahānābād in Delhi, although Āgra officially remained the capital. Building work at Āgra Fort continued in the emperor's absence; its Moti Masjid (Pearl Mosque) was not completed until 1653.

Shāh Jahān became ill four years after moving to Delhi, and it was thought that he would die. His least-favored, but most able son, Aurangzeb, rebelled against his father and elder brother Dārā Shukōh and triumphed. Dārā Shukōh was put to death, and Shāh Jahān, who had fully recovered his health, was placed under house arrest at Āgra Fort, where he remained for the last eight years of his life, accompanied by his faithful daughter Jahanara. Aurangzeb, upon taking the throne (and the imperial name 'Ālamgīr), immediately transferred the capital to Delhi, and Āgra's long period of decline began.

A devout Muslim, 'Ālamgīr would not tolerate other religions as his great grandfather, Akbar, had done. This stance earned him the hatred of his Hindu and Sikh subjects, and on his death in 1707, the Mughal Empire went into decline. Within 100 years Āgra had become a pawn in the struggle between the Hindu Jāts and Marāṭhās, each of whom controlled the city for alternating periods. Finally, in 1803, General Gerard Lake took Āgra for the British East India Company, and it became the capital city of the North West Provinces between 1803 and 1859. A great deal of fighting took place at Āgra during the Indian Mutiny of 1857, and some damage occurred to its fort; however, there was less subsequent desecration of its buildings by the British than occurred at Delhi's Red Fort. The greatest destruction was suffered in Āgra by the Jāma Masjid; when the new railway line was laid between the Jāma Masjid and the fort, the mosque's great courtyard and Naubat Khana (Musician's Gateway) were demolished to accommodate it.

Cemeteries and the Anglican Church of St. George, built in 1826, are the locations of chief interest in the otherwise undistinguished area of the former British cantonment to the south. In the Anglican cemetery lies the tomb of Elizabethan envoy John Mildenhall, who died at Āgra in 1614.

Today, Āgra is almost equally divided between the ancient city of narrow, winding streets and the much more spacious British cantonment, laid out in the nineteenth century. Apart from Āgra Fort, no secular buildings of historic or architectural importance have survived in the old city, and the great mausoleums all lie on its periphery. But in the old city's narrow streets, Āgra's craftsmen continue their traditional trades of marble carving, stone setting, embroidery with gold and silver threads, carpet manufacture, and shoemaking.

The only extensive restoration of Āgra's monuments occurred during the vice regal administration of Lord Curzon early in the twentieth century, following years of neglect. These monuments are now jeopardized by pollution from chemical works located on the banks of the Jumma River. Although international attention has focused on this problem and a campaign has emerged to initiate preservation measures, questions remain as to whether authorities are prepared to act firmly or quickly enough to stop the discoloration and cracking of marble at the Tāj Mahal, among other structures.

Some idea of the lost splendors of Āgra can be gained from the English traveler Ralph Fitch, who wrote in his diary of 1584, "Āgra and Fetepore (Fatehpur Sīkri) are two very great cities, either of them much greater than London. Between, all the way is a market."

Further Reading: *The Great Moghuls* by Bamber Gascoigne (London: Cape, and New York: Harper and Row, 1971) is a well-illustrated book dealing with the history of the Mughals from Bābur to 'Ālamgīr. It was the basis for a BBC television series of the same name. *Mughal India* by G. H. R. Tillotson (London: Viking, and New York: Chronicle Books, 1990), part of the Architectural Guides for Travellers series, provides excellent plans and illustrations of leading Mughal buildings. *Penguin Guide to the Monuments of India,* volume 2, by Philip Davies (London and New York: Viking, 1989) includes plans and descriptions of Āgra's leading buildings. *Taj Mahal* by M. C. Josh (New York: Abbeville, 1993) is primarily a photographic record, supported by informative text.

—Christopher Turner

Ahmadābād (Gujarāt, India)

Location: The premier city of Gujarāt state in western India, on the banks of the Sābarmati River, 62 miles north of the head of the Gulf of Cambay and 290 miles north of Bombay.

Description: Founded in 1411 by a Muslim ruler of Gujarāt, Ahmadābād has played an important role in Indian history, first as capital of the independent sultanate of Gujarāt, then as the capital of the Mughal Indian province of the same name, and since 1947 as one of the main industrial cities of independent India.

Site Office: Tourism Corporation of Gujarāt
H. K. House
Ashram Road
Ahmadābād, Gujarāt
India
(44) 9683

The city of Ahmadābād is located in the fertile lowlands of Gujarāt, in western India. For centuries a major production area in India, Gujarāt is especially known for the indigo dye found near Ahmadābād at Sarkhej, for saltpeter, an ingredient once used in making gunpowder, and most importantly for the cotton and silk cloths produced there. The area includes several major ports on the Gulf of Cambay—at different times Cambay, Broach, Diu, and Sūrat—that act as entrepôts not only for Gujarāt but for northern India in general. Not surprisingly, then, the region has prospered for many centuries. Indeed, the first great civilization in India, the Indus Valley civilization (c. 2500–1700 B.C.), extended as far as the important port of Lothal, at the head of the Gulf of Cambay.

The area around modern Ahmadābād was the location of several major cities during the period that Hindus ruled Gujarāt. From the tenth century the area was subjected to raids from Muslim armies based in Sind, in modern Pakistan, and later in Delhi. These raids caused considerable destruction. Their objective often was to plunder the very rich Hindu temples in the area. In 1298 Muslim armies defeated a Hindu kingdom whose capital was Pātan, about sixty-five miles north of the future Ahmadābād. From this time Gujarāt was ruled by Muslims, although the bulk of the population remained Hindu, with an important Jain minority.

The control of the Muslim rulers of Delhi, who in the fourteenth century included Gujarāt as one of their provinces, weakened late in that century. The coup de grace was the invasion and plunder of Delhi by the great conqueror Timur (Tamerlane) in 1398. Central control was now ended, and in 1407 the governor of Gujarāt, Zafar Khan, declared his independence and proclaimed himself to be sultan Muzaffar Shāh. This independent Muslim dynasty lasted until 1573, and among its greatest achievements was the founding of the city of Ahmadābād.

There are five major periods in the history of Ahmadābād. From 1411 to 1573 it was ruled by the independent Muslim sultanate of Gujarāt. Next came rule from Delhi by the Mughal Empire, which ended in the 1750s when the Hindu Marāṭhā rulers took over the town. In 1817 they in turn were replaced by the British. When India became independent in 1947, Ahmadābād and Gujarāt were part of the state of Mahārāshtra, centered on Bombay. In 1960 Ahmadābād became the capital of the newly created state of Gujarāt, and remains the most important town, although the capital was moved to the new city of Gāndhīnagar, eighteen miles to the northeast, in 1970.

Aḥmad Shāh I came to the throne of Gujarāt in 1410 on the death of his grandfather, Muzaffar Shāh. A devout Muslim, Aḥmad was anxious to move his capital from Pātan, for it had been the Hindu capital. Legend has it that he consulted his spiritual adviser, who recommended a site on the left bank of the Sābarmati River, which site became Ahmadābād. In 1411 building commenced, beginning with the Bhadra fort or citadel, with its famous triple gateway. Enclosed in this area is the mosque of Aḥmad Shāh, founded in the year of the creation of the city. In the 1420s he built a great congregational mosque, the Jāmi Masjid; many other mosques and tombs from the fifteenth and sixteenth centuries are to be seen today in the town. Many of the early buildings are notable for their blending of Hindu and Muslim materials and motifs; indeed, many of these Muslim buildings were erected on the sites of Hindu temples and used some of their materials. The period of the independent Muslim sultanate produced most of the finest buildings in Ahmadābād.

Ahmadābād's golden age under the sultans was based on its status as capital of this wealthy region, for it received lavish royal patronage to make it a showcase for the dynasty. However, the town's prosperity was also based on its strategic economic location. It was well placed to act as the focus and transshipment center for very far-flung trade routes. These stretched as far as Rājasthān, Delhi, and northern India to the north, east to Mālwa and central India, and west to Sind and what is now Pakistan. Ahmadābād was also well situated to service the great ports of the Gulf of Cambay, of which in this period Diu, Broach, and Cambay were most important.

Additionally, Ahmadābād was the center of thriving export industries, of which indigo, saltpeter, and handicrafts were important, but were far outweighed by cotton and silk textiles. Modern Ahmadābād contains numerous textile factories, but long before industrial development it was the center of a huge cotton and silk spinning, weaving, and dyeing area. Before the nineteenth century, production was dispersed into thousands of households in the surrounding countryside,

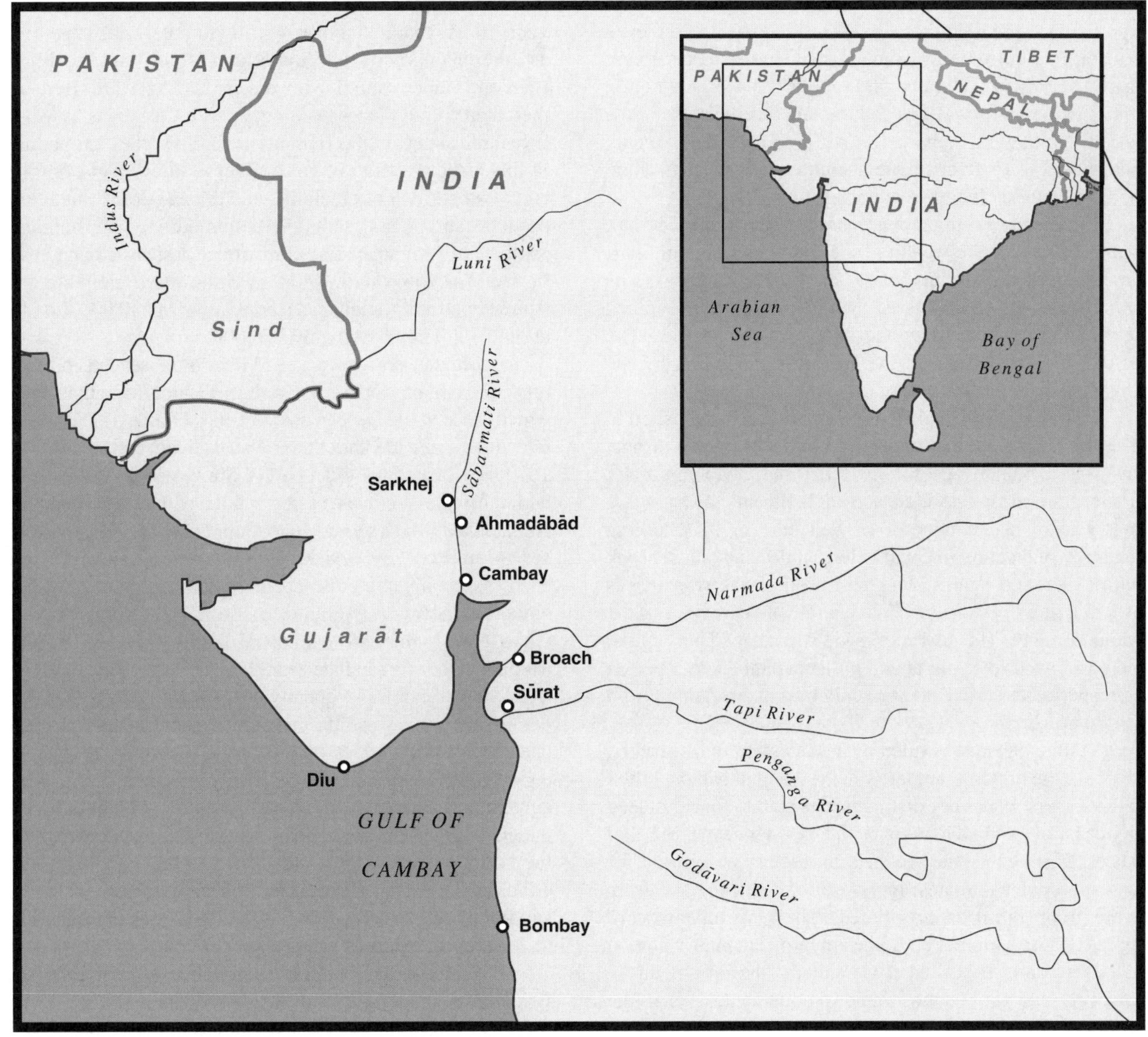

Map showing the position of Ahmadābād within the Mughal Indian province of Gujarāt
Illustration by Tom Willcockson

where peasant families undertook the whole production process in domestic surroundings. During the fourteenth to eighteenth centuries, Gujarātī cloth, in a bewildering range of colors, styles, fineness, and quality, was India's major export, along with the cloth of the two other major production areas of Bengal and Coromandel. These cloths were exported to countries all around the Indian Ocean shore, from East Africa to the Middle East and Southeast Asia. From the sixteenth century they also found a ready market in Europe. The prosperity of Gujarāt, and of Ahmadābād, was based squarely on this industry.

The sultanate of Gujarāt had two strong and long-lived rulers, and many less powerful ones. Aḥmad Shāh I ruled from 1410 to 1442, and Maḥmūd from 1459 to 1511. Both were great conquerors, expanding the sultanate into the surrounding Hindu-ruled areas. However, after the death of Maḥmūd, Gujarāt and Ahmadābād entered a period of decline. While the economy remained buoyant and most of the population was little affected by political changes, there was considerable instability at the top; this continued until Mughal rule in 1573 restored stability. During this period the nobles often became virtually independent, refusing to send revenue to the capital and the sultan. The city suffered as a result.

It was also during this period that Ahmadābād was first visited by Europeans, although any European dominance or control was far in the future. The Portuguese had arrived in India in 1498 and soon became aware that Asian trade was dominated by two main products, spices and cloth. Textiles in particular were ubiquitous in Asian trade, being used even as a form of currency in some areas. Thus the Portuguese desired access to Gujarāt's vast supplies of silk and cotton cloth. They built forts at Diu and Damān, on either side of the Gulf of Cambay, but their main role in Gujarāt in the sixteenth century was to buy very large quantities of textiles in Sūrat and take them to Goa for reexport.

The early Portuguese accounts of Ahmadābād go into great detail about the wealth of the town, its fine buildings, and the skill and probity of its merchants. Indeed, some Portuguese were so impressed that they deserted and joined the sultan's army, providing valuable artillery expertise. The Portuguese also witnessed the conquest of Gujarāt by the Mughals.

The Mughal Empire in India had been established in 1526. In 1556 the great emperor Akbar came to the throne. This was a golden age for his territories, with important artistic, cultural, and political accomplishments. Akbar was a great warrior and conqueror as well, and in 1572, taking advantage of disunity in Gujarāt, he invaded and quickly took control. A revolt against Mughal rule in the next year was easily put down, and from 1573 Gujarāt was a province of the Mughal Empire. The governor made Ahmadābād his capital. There followed for Gujarāt and for its capital another period of prosperity and peace, marred only by a major famine from 1630 to 1632.

Ahmadābād was ruled by a succession of governors, subject to the imperial authority in the Mughal capital. Often the governors were very distinguished grandees, and indeed on occasion Ahmadābād was the residence of Mughal princes. Despite this, the Mughals' preference was always for drier and cooler climates, like those of Central Asia, from where their families originated. Their attitude toward Ahmadābād is summed up in the emperor Jahāngīr's pun on the city's name: he called it Gardabad, "the city of dust." However, several of its most famous monuments, such as the mosques and tombs of Sardar Khan and Shuja'at Khan, two Mughal grandees, date from this period, although not much else has survived. The Mughals also were great creators of gardens, and they and their nobles developed several in Ahmadābād, such as the Shāhi Bāgh, but these either have been greatly altered over the centuries or have not survived at all.

The Mughals generally were tolerant rulers, with little discrimination against the majority Hindu and Jain population of Ahmadābād. In particular, Ahmadābād's very wealthy merchant community had considerable autonomy in the town, and indeed Mughal nobles were often in debt to them. As one of the most productive provinces in Mughal India, Gujarāt flourished and participated fully in the prosperity of Mughal India in the late sixteenth and seventeenth centuries.

This prosperity attracted more Europeans to the area. The English and the Dutch had entered the Indian Ocean late in the sixteenth century, and early in the next century they began to establish trading posts, called factories, in Gujarāt, including Ahmadābād. In 1613 one of the first Englishmen to visit Ahmadābād, Nicholas Withington, described the town as "the chiefest city of Gujarāt and is very near as big as London, walled round with a very strong wall. Here are merchants of all places residing, as well Christians as Moors [Muslims] and Gentiles [Hindus and Jains]. The commodities of this place are cloth of gold, silver tissue, velvets, taffetas, and other stuffs [cotton cloths] and diverse drugs [medicinal products and plants] with other commodities." Withington's estimate of Ahmadābād's population as less than London's is in fact far too small. Modern authorities estimate that Ahmadābād at its height had a population of 250,000. London around 1600 numbered only 170,000.

Mughal power weakened late in the seventeenth century. Their main opponents were the Hindu Marāṭhā power, which arose in the Deccan area of central India. The Marāṭhās raided far and wide under their leader Śivajī, and in 1664 and 1670 they sacked the great port of Sūrat, which was the main outlet for the products of the whole of Gujarāt, including Ahmadābād. Marāṭhā raids into Gujarāt continued later in the seventeenth century, and Mughal power was gravely weakened, especially after the death of the last strong Mughal emperor, 'Ālamgīr (Aurangzeb), in 1707. From this time Gujarāt was subjected to frequent battles between the local Mughal authorities and the Marāṭhās. To add to the confusion, rival Mughal nobles frequently clashed with each other, thus easing the way for Marāṭhā incursions. Ahmadābād was threatened by Marāṭhā forces on numerous occasions in the early eighteenth century, and was besieged by them in 1736–37. An agreement was made for the Marāṭhās and the Mughals to share the government of Ahmadābād, but this soon collapsed; from the 1750s Ahmadābād was ruled by the Marāṭhās alone. Nevertheless, the city was still subjected to frequent raids by the surviving Mughal nobles; this was indeed a time of troubles for the once great and prosperous city.

While Indian peoples fought among themselves, the British were making inroads into their country. Two parallel processes were at work. First, the collapse of the central Mughal power in India rendered the country vulnerable to invasion from outside, for the various successor states of the eighteenth century lacked the size and power of the Mughal Empire. Second, economic progress in England in the second half of the century, spurred by a series of technological and industrial developments that became known as the Industrial Revolution, gave the English a decisive advantage over Indian rulers. These factors made possible the slow conquest of India, and Ahmadābād participated in this process. In the 1750s and 1760s, the English acquired control over Bengal, and in 1759 Gujarāt's main port, Sūrat, was placed under British authority. The Marāṭhās were the last major Indian power to confront them, and little by little they too were overcome. One of the last stages of this process was England's taking possession of Ahmadābād from its Marāṭhā rulers in 1817. Ahmadābād thus entered a period of 130 years of rule by foreigners. By this time its population had fallen to about 80,000.

British rule had far-reaching effects. On the one hand, it brought in a most welcome period of peace and order after the tumult of the eighteenth century. However, despite the resulting revival of trade and traditional industry, the city remained something of a backwater until the later nineteenth century, as British attention in western India was concentrated on Bombay. More generally, British rule over India meant that machine-made English cotton cloth was freely imported into the colony, eventually undercutting the traditional handicraft industry that had for so long been the foundation of the city's prosperity. Production of cheap coarse cloth continued, but the finer varieties were totally displaced by imports. The population thus failed to recover fully, and the outer suburbs declined or disappeared. In 1872 the total population was fewer than 120,000. British rule had less effect on Ahmadābād than it had on many other Indian cities. Ahmadābād's social cohesion enabled it to retain its autonomy and character largely unaffected by alien rule. Unlike Bombay, Calcutta, or Delhi, Ahmadābād has few large buildings or monuments dating from the British period.

Ahmadābād revived as a result of the development of its own factory-based cotton textile industry similar to those that had emerged in the West. Even today it is the textile mills, along with the monuments, that the visitor will note in the city. The founders of these mills were usually Jain traders and financiers. The industry began to develop in the 1880s and expanded rapidly. In 1891 nine mills employed about 7,500 workers; by 1910 fifty-two mills employed more than 30,000, while the municipal population by then had risen to more than 210,000, many of them underpaid mill workers living in appalling conditions. World War I created a boom for the mills, as imports from Britain were stopped.

Meanwhile, opposition to British rule in India was growing, and Ahmadābād played a central role in this during the period between the world wars. Mohandas Karamchand Gandhi (known as Mahatma Gandhi), a native of Gujarāt, emerged as the leader of the Freedom Movement during World War I. Although he traveled constantly, and spent long periods in jail, his main base was in Ahmadābād; several of that town's mill owners, whose workers participated in the movement more or less directly, were among Gandhi's principal financial supporters. In April 1919 major riots broke out in the city after Gandhi had been arrested, and many government buildings were destroyed. Even before this, in 1915, Gandhi had established an ashram at Ahmadābād, a center for community living in which caste restrictions were ignored. The more famous Sābarmati Ashram, founded in 1917 on the west bank of the Sābarmati River, remained Gandhi's headquarters until 1933. It was from here in 1930 that he started his famous Dandi salt march, the supreme example of his technique of nonviolent resistance to British rule. The ashram continues functioning today and houses a small museum.

India became independent in 1947. For a time Gujarāt was included in the state of Mahārāshtra, but in 1960 a partition was made along linguistic lines, and Ahmadābād became the capital of the new state. Soon after, construction began on a new capital for the state, Gāndhīnagar, located eighteen miles northeast of the city. This new city, designed in part by the French architect Le Corbusier, became fully operational in 1970, but Ahmadābād remains the dominant city in the state. Along with the rest of India it has suffered various setbacks and difficulties. Among these is a population explosion: between 1961 and 1991 the city's size trebled from 1.1 million to 3.3 million. The level of air and water pollution in Ahmadābād is extreme even by Indian standards. Even more worrisome, the traditional tolerance of its residents toward people of different religions has on several occasions broken down. There were major riots between Hindus and Muslims in 1969, and these have been repeated with distressing frequency since then. Nevertheless, Ahmadābād remains one of India's premier cities: a center of industry, a historical site of great interest, a city with a deep association with the Mahatma, and a vibrant, complex, challenging metropolis of the late twentieth century.

Further Reading: By far the best introduction to the history of Ahmadābād is a monograph by Kenneth Gillion: *Ahmedābād: A Study in Indian Urban History* (Berkeley and Los Angeles: University of California Press, 1968). More detailed and specialized is a volume in the official series of Indian state gazetteers, *Gujarāt State Gazetteers: Ahmadābād District Gazetteer* by S. B. Rajyagor et al. (Ahmadābād: Government of Gujarāt, 1984). Much more readable, and with excellent color illustrations, is a comprehensive introduction to Ahmadābād's history and culture, *Ahmadābād*, edited by George Michell and Snehal Shah (Bombay: Marg, and Columbia, Missouri: Southeast Asia Books, 1988).

—M. N. Pearson

Aizu-Wakamatsu (Fukushima, Japan)

Location: Aizu-Wakamatsu stands 718 feet above sea level at the heart of the Aizu Basin, between the Echigo Mountains to the west and the hills around Lake Inawashiro to the east. It is in the Fukushima prefecture, in the northeast of Honshū (the main island of Japan), 165 miles north of Tōkyō.

Description: A castle town, formerly the headquarters of the powerful Matsudaira family, noted for its traditional buildings and crafts.

Site Office: Tourist Information Center
1-1 Ekimae-machi
Aizu-Wakamatsu, Fukushima
Japan
(0242) 32-0688

Like many other ancient cities, the origins and early development of Aizu-Wakamatsu are obscure, except for scraps of legend. The word "Aizu" itself, which is written with two Chinese characters meaning "meeting" and, puzzlingly, "harbor," refers to a legendary event said to have taken place near the present site of the city in 88 B.C. This meeting was between Ohiko and Takenukawa-wake, two famous generals who were sent to Tohoku by the equally legendary Emperor Sujin; the generals were given the job of establishing peace after the completion of their campaigns against the rebellious people of the region. The name now refers not only to the city itself but also to the area around it, which was governed from the city by a series of feudal lords over a period of approximately 700 years. Like other centers of population in the outlying regions of Japan, far from the more complex social and economic developments of central Honshū, Aizu-Wakamatsu was for centuries a sort of military outpost; amid frequent conflict, it was a city of warriors, and of merchants subordinate to them, who exercised their power over the farmers of the surrounding countryside. Unfortunately, little is known for certain about this relatively remote area before 1192, when Minamoto Yoritomo established the first of a series of military regimes, the *shōgunates*, which were to govern Japan almost uninterruptedly until 1868. Aizu, like other settlements that became domainal centers, probably existed as a market town and strategic base for regional warlords several centuries before Yoritomo's rule.

When Yoritomo came to power, he granted the domain of Aizu to the *samurai* Suwara Yoshitsura, a member of the Miura clan. Suwara's descendants would take the family name Ashina and one of them, Morinori, began the construction of the first castle in the city in 1384. Soon afterward both the castle and the city that expanded around it became known as Kurokawa (Black River). It was not until two centuries later, during the long and complex civil wars that disrupted Japan between 1477 and 1600, and following the death of the lord Ashina Moritaka in 1583, that they fell from power. At that time, the castle was seized by the forces of the Satake family, who had long been rivals of the Ashina. One of their number, a twelve-year-old boy, was renamed Ashina Morishige and declared lord of Aizu. The leading retainers of the original Ashina family regained control of the domain in 1589, but they were aided by one of the most powerful military leaders of the period, Date Masamune. He in turn took over the castle, only to surrender it in 1590 to Toyotomi Hideyoshi, who would achieve greater fame as the effective reunifier of the country. Toyotomi granted the domain of Aizu to Gamō Ujisato, a close ally. In 1592 Gamō began construction of a new castle at the site and gave both castle and town the new name Wakamatsu (Young Pine), although the castle alone is also known as the Tsuruga-jō (Castle of the Crane).

However, Gamō Ujisato did not control Aizu for much longer than had the false Ashina lord. Gamō died in battle in 1596 and by 1600, after a series of local struggles, the domain passed into the hands of Uesugi Kagekatsu, who was appointed in that year to the council of regents that ruled Japan after Toyotomi Hideyoshi's death in 1598. Fellow-regent Tokugawa Ieyasu accused him of gathering troops at Aizu in order to seize greater power for himself, and ordered Date Masamune and other allies to move against Uesugi. Meanwhile, the numerous *daimyō* (lords) became more and more sharply divided; some supported Toyotomi Hideyoshi's young son Hideyori, while others followed Tokugawa Ieyasu, the most powerful among the regents. Ieyasu's decisive victory over his enemies at the battle of Sekigahara, also in 1600, sealed the fate of Uesugi and of Aizu. Gamō Ujisato's descendants were reconfirmed in their claim to Aizu after Ieyasu's establishment, in 1603, of a new *shōgunate*. They were regarded as *fudai daimyō* (attached lords), who could be trusted to defend the area against the much less reliable tozama daimyō (outside lords), comprised mostly of those who had been defeated at the battle of Sekigahara and who were given domains far away from the Tokugawa capital of Edo (now Tōkyō). This connection with the *shōgunate* was reinforced in 1643, when Wakamatsu castle and the Aizu domain passed by inheritance to Hoshina Masayuki (or Masanobu), a half-brother of Iemitsu, the third of the Tokugawa *shōgūns*.

Like other *shimpan daimyō*, lords who were blood relatives of the ruling dynasty, Hoshina Masayuki and his descendants were given the right to use the family name Matsudaira (originally that of Ieyasu, the founder of the Tokugawa line) and the *kamon* (family crest) of three hollyhock leaves in a circle, which was shared by all branches of the Tokugawa and Matsudaira families. The Aizu

Tsuruga-jō Castle
Photo courtesy of Japan National Tourist Organization

Matsudaira family was steadfastly loyal to their distant relatives, the Tokugawa *shōguns*, up to and beyond the resignation of the last *shōgun* in 1868. The daimyō and the leading officials of the domain alternated their residence between the Aizu *yashiki* (a headquarters building in Edo), and their home city. There, the Matsudaira lords sponsored the creation of a formal garden, the Onyaku-en, which contained a pavilion for their use as well as some 200 different medicinal plants, and the Kyū Aizu-han Gohonjin (also known as the Takizawa Honjin), the domain's principal garrison. Both the garden and the garrison, a large thatch-roofed building constructed between 1668 and 1679, still stand in the city today. Under the Tokugawa system, which was a unique type of feudal federation, Aizu became the capital not only of the domain that was historically associated with it, but also of an additional neighboring area, nearly four times larger. These lands were formally owned by the Tokugawa family but were administered by the Aizu Matsudaira on their behalf. These formed the largest such *azukarichi* (entrusted lands) in Japan.

The power and wealth of these mighty Aizu lords and that of the officials and merchants who served them derived partly from their privileged connection with the national government, partly from their involvement in the developing trade in their region. During the middle of the sixteenth century, Japan began expanding in population and production; thus, what had been a relatively isolated highland garrison town rapidly became a point of interchange in new nationwide networks of trade for both basic commodities and luxury goods. The Ashina had already steadily reduced freight charges and eased the burden of taxes on merchants in order to encourage trade with such larger cities as Kyōto, Ise, and Edo, and the Matsudaira continued this policy of favoring commerce. Two products in particular made Aizu well known throughout the country and brought prosperity to merchants and farmers alike: lacquerware and sake. Approximately one in ten of the craftsmen living in the city were makers of lacquerware, Aizu's chief export. These craftsmen used lacquer sold to them by the domain government. The lacquer itself was collected as a tax in kind from the local farmers' magnolia and beech trees, and the government eventually planted numerous additional trees as demand for lacquerware products increased. The city also became a leading center for the brewing of sake, the traditional alcoholic drink that is often misleadingly called rice wine in English. This industry also used a material that was collected as tax in kind: rice. In Tokugawa Japan, rice was the main form of stipend for the *samurai*, who, in Aizu as elsewhere in the country, were only too happy to sell it to dealers. There are now two museums in the city devoted to the history of the sake industry, the Aizu Shuzō Rekishikan (literally, the Sake-Brewing History Building), and the Aizu Shuzō Hakubutsukan (the Sake-Brewing Museum), the latter operated by the Kōno family, which has brewed sake for at least twelve generations.

With enhanced economic growth and product exchange, Aizu-Wakamatsu experienced a greater degree of cultural interaction with other parts of Japan. The closeness of the links between the warriors and officials of Aizu-Wakamatsu and the heartland of Japanese culture far away in the Kinki region (around the cities of Kyōto and Ōsaka) is strikingly expressed in the Sazae-dō, the Conch Shell Hall (1796). This six-sided tower, approximately 190 feet high, stands in the grounds of Entsu-ji, one of the main Buddhist temples of the city. Inside the tower, a pair of curved staircases lead visitors through depictions of the thirty-three temples of Kannon, the Buddhist goddess of mercy (Avalokitesvara in Sanskrit), which form a traditional pilgrimage route in the Kinki region. The wealth and sophistication of the leading warriors may also be gauged by the reconstruction (completed in 1978) of the estate of Saigō Tanomo at the Buke-Yashiki (the Warrior Mansion), which includes his elegant house, a rice mill, and a farmhouse. The site also features a tea house brought from elsewhere in the city, as well as exhibits of pottery and lacquerware inside traditional warehouses.

Tokugawa and Matsudaira descendants would attempt to secure peace and order of a more permanent kind for Japan. Matsudaira Katamori, who was to be the ninth and last *daimyō* of Aizu, was born the younger son of the fourteenth Tokugawa shōgun and was adopted into the Aizu Matsudaira family in childhood. He proved his devotion to his double legacy in 1863 when, aged only eighteen, he directed the forces that suppressed a rebellion that originated in the Chōshū domain, one of the *tozama* areas of Kyūshū in the far southwest; Chōshū officials and warriors had attempted to seize control of Kyōto, where the symbolically important emperor still resided. Only five years later, Katamori found himself leading part of the resistance to the new imperial army, created by the Chōshū and their allies in support of a new regime replacing the Tokugawa system. The so-called Meiji Restoration, which brought the new regime to power, was inaugurated by soldiers from Chōshū and two other *tozama* domains, Satsuma and Tosa, on January 3, 1868, when they captured the imperial palace in Kyōto. The thirty-year-old *shōgun* Tokugawa Yoshinobu (or Keiki), who had taken office in 1866, had already agreed in November of 1867 to share power with the leading *daimyō*, but now submitted to the new government of Kyōto courtiers and rebellious *samurai*. However, many of his allies and supporters did not. A brief but bloody conflict followed, which has come to be known as the Boshin Civil War. Separate armies loyal to the dynasty fought losing battles at Toba-Fushimi, near Kyōto, and at Ueno, in Edo.

In April, Katamori led his retainers back to Aizu-Wakamatsu and made its castle the headquarters for the remaining pro-Tokugawa forces. During the following summer months, approximately 1,500 warriors loyal to Katamori were driven back across the mountains by 10,000 troops of the imperial army, a process culminating on August 23 in a battle at the pass between the city and Lake Inawashiro. After the fighting ended in victory for the Chōshū and Satsuma warriors, the surviving contingents from Aizu moved in closer to the city, making their last stand in the battle of Tonokuchihara on October 8. The most famous event of the entire brief civil war followed their defeat, the suicide by *hara-kiri* (stomach-slitting) of nineteen young warriors, survivors of the battle who were members of the domain's Byakkotai (the White Tiger Brigade). This reserve force of Aizu retainers' sons had been hastily created in March. Gathered on Iimoriyama, a forested hill overlooking the city, they committed their final act of defiance in sight of what they thought was the burning castle. The warriors' deaths were in fact pointless, based on a misunderstanding, for it was not the castle that was on fire but a few houses in front of it. In the end, the soldiers remaining inside the castle were bombarded and starved out a month later and the Aizu domain formally surrendered to the imperial government on November 6. After the surrender, both the castle and the city of Aizu-Wakamatsu were largely destroyed by the victorious imperial troops. The columns and doors of the Kyū Aizu-han Gohonjin still bear bullet holes and sword markings, but the castle site was cleared in 1874; the concrete replica that stands there now was built in 1965.

The transformation of Aizu-Wakamatsu from a feudal garrison town to a modern provincial center was officially marked in 1899 when it was granted city status and the local assembly and administration along European lines was established. When Japan stumbled deeper into its destructive and disastrous military adventure in China, the legend of the Byakkotai was popularized. These heroic figures were incorporated into the state ideology, regardless of the fact that they had resisted the creation of the regime that now sought to honor them. They are now commemorated on Iimoriyama, bizarrely enough, by a white marble column bearing a bronze eagle, donated by the Fascist government of Italy in 1928, and by a small black marble block donated during the 1930s "by one German man," as the inscription claims, but on behalf of the Nazi regime he had served as military attaché in Tōkyō. The name of the brigade was also borrowed by one of the Japanese regiments that fought the British in Burma between 1942 and 1945. Following Japan's defeat at the end of World War II, the Byakkotai once again fell out of official favor. In response to the wishes of the Allied Occupation authorities, the inscriptions on both of the Iimoriyama monuments were removed, only to be restored soon after the Occupation ended in 1952. It remains a puzzle why any Japanese government after 1868 should ever have honored soldiers who fought to retain the Tokugawa shōgunate.

It is less puzzling, of course, that the city's tourist authorities now emphasize the story of the Byakkotai in their campaigns to attract visitors to the city. Aizu-Wakamatsu now has a population of approximately 115,000, and its principal industries still include the brewing of sake (by twenty-three of the original fifty breweries) and the production of lacquerware. The city has also become a supplier of implements for Buddhist worship, producing half of all those sold in Japan. The Aizu Matsudaira, among the richest and most powerful of the *daimyō* of Tokugawa Japan, are long gone, but the local culture that they sponsored is still reflected in these activities, in the annual festivals associated with them, and in many of the buildings and streets in the historic center of the city.

Further Reading: Regrettably, Tōhoku and Aizu-Wakamatsu have been somewhat neglected by writers in English, who have typically focused on Tōkyō and the Kinki region. However, both are well treated in Jan Brown's *Exploring Tohoku: A Guide to Japan's Back Country* (New York: Weatherhill, 1982) and in two general guide books that are outstanding in their attention to history and their wealth of detail: June Kinoshita and Nicholas Palevsky's *Gateway to Japan* (Tōkyō and New York: Kodansha International, 1990; second edition, 1992) and Jay, Sumi, and Garet Gluck's *Japan Inside Out* (second edition, Ashiya, Japan: Personally Oriented Limited, 1992).

—Patrick Heenan

Ajanta (Mahārāshtra, India)

Location: In Aurangābād district of Mahārāshtra state in western India; approximately 220 miles northeast of Bombay.

Description: Ajanta is home to thirty-one caves excavated into an almost perpendicular rockface, in a semicircular curve about 100 feet above a glen, into which the Waghorā River descends in a cascading tumble from the southwestern end of the arc. The caves are famous for their Buddhist rock-cut architecture and sculpture but especially celebrated for their wall paintings, dating as early as the second century B.C.

Contact: Government of India Tourist Office
Krishna Vilas
Station Road
Aurangābād 431 005, Mahārāshtra
India
31217

The imposing rock-cut chambers of Ajanta were created by the tireless, innovative industry of ancient Indian sculptors. The first Europeans to stumble upon the caves were officers of the Madras army in 1819; Lieutenant James Alexander, who visited the caves in 1824, was the first to publish an account, in the 1829 *Transactions* of the Royal Asiatic Society. He was impressed by the caves' sculpture but astonished by their wall-paintings. In 1836, James Prinsep published in the Asiatic Society's *Journal* the notes of a Mr. Ralph detailing his visit to the caves and describing how a Dr. Bird "contrived to peel off four painted figures" from a wall "notwithstanding protestations about defacing monuments." Sadly, many later visitors did the same, including an unscrupulous caretaker who gave visitors a fragment as a memento for a paltry payment.

Dismayed by the rampant vandalism and neglect of the priceless paintings when he visited Ajanta about 1839, James Fergusson mounted a vigorous campaign to save the fragile artwork. The first to recognize their Buddhist origin, Fergusson dated the work from approximately 200 B.C. to approximately A.D. 650. "I numbered them like houses in a street," he wrote, and his numerical order established their accepted nomenclature.

At Fergusson's insistence, in 1844 Major Robert Gill began producing replicas of these glorious wall paintings in order to bring them to the attention of the scholarly world; he would eventually dedicate more than twenty years of his life to the project. Gill's oil reproductions of the murals were exhibited at the Crystal Palace in London, only to be destroyed—without having been photographed—in a disastrous fire in 1866. The stoic major returned to Ajanta to begin again but died there a year later.

In 1872, John Griffiths of the Bombay School of Art took up Gill's work, and his copies of the Ajanta murals were displayed, again in London, at the Victoria and Albert Museum. They, too, perished in a fire, but fortunately not before they were photographed. Griffiths' copies were published in 1896–97; those by Lady Herringham in 1915. As author Benjamin Rowland stated, they were "far less adequate" than those painted by Gill. But they did make the world aware of the legacy of Ajanta.

Gill had applied a thick coat of varnish to protect the sadly mutilated, crumbling paintings from the creeping moisture of monsoons and to make their colors more vivid. This process blurred the original brushwork, however, and in 1871 Clements Markham declared that the varnish had done irreparable damage to the fast-fading murals. The nizām of Hyderābād, the state in which Ajanta resided, was persuaded to have the paintings restored by two famous Italian specialists, Professor Cecconi and Count Orsini. These two worked at Ajanta from 1920 to 1922, delicately removing the old varnish, dirt, and smoke from the surfaces, with breathtaking results. The *Burlington Magazine* called the paintings "perhaps the greatest artistic wonder of Asia." "One of the Wonders of the East," said Sir John Marshall in his introduction to some reproductions in the *Illustrated London News,* timed to coincide with the performance of the *Ajanta Ballet* by the celebrated Anna Pavlovna Pavlova at London's Covent Garden in 1923. Postures and hand gestures imitating those represented in the Ajanta paintings informed the choreography of this ballet.

Ajanta had exerted powerful influence over other regions' artistic production long before the *Ajanta Ballet* appeared in the West: the beginnings of Buddhist painting in Tibet, Nepal, Central Asia, China, and Japan all can be traced to the inspiration of Ajanta. Indeed, Ajanta is unique in its scope, combining painting, sculpture, and architecture, and illustrating the development of Buddhism over the centuries of the caves' excavation. It is a Buddhist site that thrived in a Brahmanical world, and at the zenith of its artistic achievement it represented the pervasive classical culture of the Gupta age (c. A.D. 320–c. 540). No strict dynastic designation of this art is possible, however; the monks also received patronage from the Śaka (c. 80 B.C. to second century A.D.), Ābhīra (second century B.C. to tenth century A.D.), and Ikṣvāku (third to fifth centuries A.D.) rulers, and from ministers and vassals of the Vākāṭakas (c. A.D. 250–470). Furthermore, commoners, merchants, and ministers joined with royalty to provide funds for monasteries and monuments. Not infrequently, monks and nuns are named as donors. They gave money before their ordination, or passed on what was given to them by lay followers.

Scarcity of evidence makes precise dating of the caves exceedingly difficult. Their consecutive numbering

Exterior, Ajanta Caves
Photo courtesy of Air India Library, New York

from east to west bears no relation to the sequence of their excavation. How long did it take to excavate them? Who excavated them? Who were the creators of the sculptural adornment? Who painted the magnificent murals? We do not even know if the sculptors and painters were themselves Buddhists.

Many of the caves were excavated only partially. Author Sheila L. Weiner has hypothesized that the artists worked on a number of caves at the same time, moving from one to another following the natural light of the sun at varying hours of the day. We may speculate about the length of time taken to excavate a specific prayer hall or monastery. The artists' dependence on natural light would help explain why they did not complete their work in some of the caves; the time taken to bring a specific *caitya* (prayer hall) or *vihara* (residence quarter) to completion would explain the presence of different periodic styles within it.

Although some writings found at Ajanta yield information about donors, dates, and customs during the period of their inscription, archaeologists are unable with certainty to establish a cumulative chronology of the caves even with additional insights furnished by stylistic variations of the sculptures and paintings. Scholars generally date them between the second or first century B.C. and seventh century A.D. Walter Spink assigns all the later caves to the late fifth century A.D.—a period, he claims, marked by unusual spiritual fervor translated into artistic activity. Using the broader of the two theorized time lines, Caves 9, 10, 12, 13, and 30 may be assigned to the beginning of the first century B.C.; 16 and 17 to approximately A.D. 500; and 19 and 26 to the late fifth century A.D. Caves 7 and 2, assigned by Spink to the late fifth century A.D., are dated to the first half of the seventh century A.D. by A. K. Coomaraswamy and others, together with Caves 3 through 5 and 21 through 26.

The excavation of every cave must have been based on the plan of a master builder-sculptor, who directed the labor of a number of excavators. They knew where to leave an exact number of blocks standing, to be carved later into pillars, and they knew the exact height and width of the roof they needed to create. As they excavated into the mountainside, their methods of measurement ensured perfect alignment of the columns, as also their uniformity, and their mutual correspondence on both sides of a nave. They cut from the top downward, as illustrated by the unfinished Cave 5, the floor of which was never reached. The caves vary considerably in their dimensions: Cave 10 measures 95 by 41 feet;

Entrance to Cave 19, Ajanta
Photo courtesy of Air India Library, New York

Cave 9 is approximately 45 by 23 feet; and the main pillared hall of Cave 1 is 64 feet on each side.

Of the fully excavated caves, 9, 10, 19, and 26 are *caityas;* the others are *viharas.* The caves carry profuse sculptural embellishment on their roofs, pillars, doorways, and facades. The most important sculptures at Ajanta are cult images of the Buddha and the Bodhisattvas. Narrative themes generally form the subject matter of paintings. Caves, 1, 2, and 17 have shrines with substantial images of the Buddha, the oldest seated shrine images in India. The Buddha figure portrayed at Ajanta expresses in its suppleness and simplicity the serene purity of the Buddha principle.

Ajanta is, however, best known for its wall paintings, which represent the pinnacle of an ancient tradition; even the earliest among them is marked by refinement of style and technique. The ancient Indian epics, the *Rāmāyaṇa* and the *Mahābhārata,* refer to painted palaces and pavilions. The *Viṣṇudharmottaram* describes paintings appropriate to temples, palaces, and private houses, connects painting to the theory of *rasa* (Indian aesthetic theory as expressed in Sanskrit poetics) and emphasizes the rendering of life-movement (*cetanā*) in any composition. The painter should be able to depict the dead without cetanā, but he should endow a sleeping figure with it. The expression of emotion in painting also requires a knowledge of the postures and gestures of dance. Indeed, painting was considered an essential component of the fine arts. The *Kāmasūtra* refers to the practice of painting by gentlemen and enumerates six limbs, or principles, of painting: *rūpabheda* (knowledge of appearances), *pramāṇa* (correct perception), *bhāva* (the effect of feeling on forms), *lāvaṇyayojana* (the injection of grace), *sādṛśya* (resemblance to natural objects instead of literal imitation), and *varṇikabhaṇga* (the proper manner of using brushes and colors).

From very early times, Indian painters used shading to produce the effects of relief, and the wash and stipple methods are clearly recognizable at Ajanta, together with the suggestion of relief through the varying thickness of outline. The technique of Indian wall painting throughout Asia differs considerably from that of the Western fresco. Indian and Asian murals were generally painted on dry walls. Benjamin Rowland describes the process as follows:

> At Ajanta the rough surface of the rock wall was covered with a layer of earth or cow-dung, mixed with chopped straw or animal hair as a binding medium, to a thickness of an inch or an inch and a half. When this surface had been completely smoothed off, it was covered with a thin layer of finely sieved gypsum or lime plaster, and it was upon this surface that the actual painting was done. The composition was first entirely outlined in cinnabar red. There followed an underpainting corresponding to the terra-verde of mediaeval Italian practice. The various local colours were then applied and the painting finished by an overall strengthening of outlines, dark accents and highlights. A final burnishing process gave a lustrous finish to the whole surface.

Cave 10 is perhaps the earliest of the rock-cut halls at Ajanta. Its paintings date from the first century B.C. to the first century A.D. The subject matter of these illustrations is provided by the Jātaka tales, which describe the sacrifices of the Buddha in his previous lives. The paintings appear in the form of a long frieze, the narration proceeding from one incident to the next. Initially, the painting unfolded within a single narrative band, but in succeeding centuries it covered the entire surface of the walls. Human and animal life is intertwined in the depiction of these stories. Intuitive spontaneity in the painting of both plant and animal life stresses the closeness of Buddha and Buddhism to all forms of nature. Conventional landscape or stage props provide the setting for the unfolding story; and the human and animal images are stylized rather than strict imitations of nature.

The Śyāma Jātaka painting on the right wall of Cave 10 portrays rows of hunters in a manner somewhat similar to the sculptures of Bhārhut and Sānchi. The Chaḍdanta Jātaka, also illustrated on the right wall of Cave 10, impresses the onlooker with the neat elegance of its composition. The disposition of complex groups displays an easy assurance of style further enhanced by the suggestion of movement, reminiscent of the best sculptures of the Sānchi gateways. Cave 9, created at about the same time as Cave 10, also contains two remarkable sets of paintings. The frieze of animals and herdsmen is especially noteworthy for its realistic depiction of natural grace and movement. These early murals display the same homogeneity of tradition that characterizes the art of Bhārhut, Bodh Gayā, Sānchi, and Bhājā.

The later murals of Ajanta mirror the artistic culture of the Gupta age. The Guptas' conquest of the south created a mighty domain, the cultural influences of which extended far beyond their borders. Under the Guptas occurred a marvelous renaissance of poetry, drama, architecture, sculpture, and painting; the greatest artistic heights were scaled at Ajanta between the fourth and sixth centuries. An overwhelming wave of *bhakti,* or devotion, had already replaced Theravāda (Hinayana) doctrines with the popular principles of theistic Mahāyāna, or the Greater Vehicle. Buddha was now the great savior, whose grace would deliver humanity from its sorrows. Since any anthropomorphic portrayal would detract from his transcendental state beyond the flux to which ordinary mortals are subject, early Buddhist art represented the Buddha only through symbols. His apotheosis in Mahāyāna evoked his physical image as a necessary corollary of devotion, petition, and prayer.

Mahāyāna also emphasized the primacy of *karuṇā* (compassion) over *prajnā* (wisdom), an emphasis embodied in the person of the Bodhisattva, who delays his entry into nirvana to help others achieve liberation, takes upon himself the afflictions and sufferings of others, and transfers his own merit to others. The Jātaka stories demonstrate the altruistic activity of the Bodhisattva, not to be seen in the solitary life of the monk engaged in the pursuit of nirvana. Indeed, the Bodhisattva ideal became accessible to every human being grounded in the Buddha's Body of Essence that pervades the cosmos. No wonder that the Bodhisattva became the supreme statement and popular icon of the concept of compassion in Mahāyāna Buddhism. This Mahāyāna spirit informed and inspired the greatest paintings of Ajanta.

The porch of Cave 17, created around A.D. 500, illustrates a scene from the Viśvantara Jātaka, in which the prince, seated in a pillared pavilion, tells his wife of his banishment from his father's kingdom. She swoons in his arms, and her limp limbs and tilted head dramatize her distress. The painting triumphs in the portrayal of emotion through pose, gesture, and form. The entire composition is characterized by a pervasive expression of anxiety seen in the eyes of the attendants turned toward the prince. At the left of the composition, the portrait of a beggar with a bowl and a crooked staff immediately arrests the viewer's attention with its true-to-life delineation. The scheme of continuous narration suggests the movement of figures across the stage, while their expressive gestures convey a sense of their emotional animation. The palace setting reflects the nature of contemporary architecture, and the easy elegance of the forms corresponds with the gracious ambience of the aristocratic setting. The figure of the prince stands out from the others in its idealization of beauty.

The seemingly weightless ease and grace of the god Indra and his musicians in the vestibule of Cave 17, suggested by their bent legs and strands of jewels swaying backward in their flight, is painted with a felicity characteristic of contemporary sculpture. Distinguished from his entourage by his heroic stature, light complexion, and impressive crown, Indra exemplifies the wonderful touch of the painter's brush. A flying *apsara* (a female fairy) in Indra's train, with her tiny mouth and oval face, the heavy pendants of her wondrous necklace swaying to the right as she flies, like the jewels in her hair, charms the visitor with the warm glow of her beauty and vivacity. The fluid brushstrokes imbue the figures with a vitality that defies age. Abstract shading added to outlines of varying thickness makes them stand out from the painted surface.

Cave 19, with its beautiful facade marked by a pillared portico, provides an excellent example of a Mahāyāna *caitya* of the late fifth century. This cave contains some of Ajanta's finest sculpture. Close to the entrance on the right, a towering image of the Buddha offers his son Rāhula the promise of Bodhi as his inheritance; and on the left, a similar Buddha figure makes a similar gesture. On either side of the door, facing inward, the figures seem to offer the same promise to every devotee entering the cave. In their gracious postures, as in the simplicity of their physical contours, the figures display a clear affinity with the Sārnāth and Mathurā images of the period. Another remarkable sculpture on the facade is that of Nāgarāja accompanied by his consorts, exuding stately grace with the promise of his protective presence. The stupa inside is an elongated structure with a triple-tiered parasol and the figure of the standing Buddha adorning its front. Among the paintings in Cave 10, one of Buddha Sakyamuni is perhaps the most striking, for the sweet serenity of its expression.

Cave 26 of the late fifth century represents the apogee of Mahāyāna *caitya* architecture at Ajanta. Much larger and more elaborate than Cave 19, it makes a marked impression on the visitor with its carved Buddhas and Bodhisattvas. The Buddha sits in the so-called European pose in the pillared niche on the stupa's front. In the ambulatory passage rests a twenty-three-foot-long image of the reclining Buddha surrounded by mourners.

Cave 1 consists of two painted panels of enormous size at the back of the hall, containing two great images of the Bodhisattva Avalokiteśvara, with a sculpted image of the Buddha in the center. The great Bodhisattva holding a blue lotus in his hands is the epitome of the cult image of Mahāyāna Buddhism. He portrays perfection as prescribed in the tests; the human figure is idealized and serves merely as a metaphorical vehicle for the projection of the abstract attributes of calm and compassion. The half-closed eyes and the smooth glow of the skin, the linear precision of drawing and the softness of shading, the unbroken planes of the body that eschew any suggestion of muscular or bony structure, the thoughtful serenity of the face, the posture of the body and the gestures of hands, all convey a sense of the vibrant rhythm hidden beneath the tranquil exterior.

Although images of the great Bodhisattva dominate the paintings of Cave 1, the Jātaka tales are not forgotten. A depiction of the Mahājanaka Jātaka, for instance, shows the prince leaning toward the queen with his hands in *dharmacakra* gesture, suggestive here of his imminent renunciation. The painter excels in portraying the emotions of the queen and her attendants stirred by the statement of his intent. The voluptuousness of the female forms contrasts with the canonical economy of the Bodhisattva's contours.

The Ajanta paintings also provide wonderful glimpses of the material culture of India in the Gupta-Vākāṭaka period. A great variety of textiles and jewelry, fruits and flowers, and plant and animal motifs are displayed in the various paintings on the walls, pillars, and ceilings.

The Gupta paintings and sculptures of Ajanta have had an abiding influence both in India and abroad. In the words of the scholar Ananda K. Coomaraswamy, "almost all that belongs to the common spiritual consciousness of Asia, the ambient in which its diversities are reconcilable, is of Indian origin in the Gupta period." The entire importance of Ajanta today lies in this legacy. Propped by the charity of kings and commoners, Buddhist monastic life hummed in an environment of artistic creativity from the second century B.C. to the seventh century A.D. The demise of Buddhism in the region consigned Ajanta to historical oblivion until its rediscovery in the early nineteenth century. A tiny place with a very small population, the sleepy village of Ajanta has no real relationship with the site, except for the fact that some of the local residents find employment in the tourist trade generated by the caves. Even though the sculptures and the murals may no longer have a direct religious affiliation with the current beliefs of these people, the residents now understand the site's significance to the wider world. The goat-track that once provided access to Ajanta is now a road open to automobiles. The caves and their art are preserved and maintained by the Archaeological Survey of India, whose officers and guides provide informed assistance to the visitor.

Further Reading: The earliest illustrated texts on Ajanta are John Griffiths's *The Paintings in the Buddhist Cave Temples of Ajanta* (2 vols., London: Griggs, 1896–97) and Lady Herringham's and others' *Ajanta Frescoes* (London and New York: Oxford University Press, 1915). Ghulam Yazdani's *Ajanta: Colour and Monochrome Reproductions of the Ajanta Frescoes Based on Photography* (4 vols., London: Oxford University Press, 1930–55) was the official publication patronized by the nizām of Hyderābād. Other valuable publications are Ananda K. Coomaraswamy's *History of Indian and Indonesian Art* (Leipzig: Hiersemann, New York: Weyhe, and London: Goldston, 1927; reprint, New York: Dover, 1965); Benjamin Rowland's and Ananda K. Coomaraswamy's *The Wall Paintings of India, Central Asia, and Ceylon* (Boston: Merrymount, 1938); and Benjamin Rowland's *The Ajanta Caves: Early Buddhist Paintings from India* (London: Collins, 1963); Sheila L. Weiner's *Ajanta: Its Place in Buddhist Art* (Berkeley and London: University of California Press, 1977); and Susan Huntington's *The Art of Ancient India* (New York: Weatherhill, 1985).

—Sarva Daman Singh

Ajmer (Rājasthān, India)

Location: In a semi-arid region in the Aravālli hills, in the center of northwestern India's Rājasthān state, 225 miles southwest of Delhi.

Description: Founded in the seventh century by Rāja Ajai Pal Chauhān, Ajmer became the chief town of a prominent Rājput principality. Late in the twelfth century, Ajmer was pillaged by Muhammad of Ghūr and was annexed to the Slave Dynasty. Akbar the Great took the city in 1556. Strategically located at the center of Rājput territory, Ajmer served as a Mughal military stronghold until falling to the Marāṭhās in 1770. The city was ceded to the British in 1818. Ajmer has long been one of India's most important places of pilgrimage for Muslims, who visit the Dargah, the tomb of a Sufi saint. It is also famous for its ancient mosques, the fortified palace of Akbar, a Jain temple, and the Mayo Rajkumar College.

Contact: Government of India Tourist Office
State Hotel, Khasa Kothi
Jaipur 302 001, Rājasthān
India
372200

Hemmed in by barren hills in the heart of Northwestern India's Rājasthān state, Ajmer stands on the shore of Anā Sāgar Lake, occupying the lower slopes of Tārāgarh Hill. The city was founded in the seventh century A.D. by Rāja Ajai Pal Chauhān and became the chief town in the Rājput principality of Sāmbhar.

The Rājputs (meaning "sons of kings") belonged to warrior clans thought to have descended from Central Asian tribes. In the seventh century, these warlike Hindu horsemen conquered a large part of northern India and divided the land into petty kingdoms. Ajmer was one of these. For some five centuries, the Chauhān line of Rājputs controlled the city, and in the eleventh and twelfth centuries they played a prominent role in the ultimately futile Hindu resistance to the Muslim conquest of India.

Rājput control was first threatened by Maḥmūd of Ghaznī, ruler of the Turkish Muslim kingdom of Ghaznī (now in Afghanistan) from 997 to 1030. From his home base, Maḥmūd led more than twenty devastating expeditions into India between 1001 and 1027, destroying Hindu temples and carrying off enormous riches and thousands of captives. Ajmer was one of the cities that suffered great losses at his hands. In the first of these expeditions, Maḥmūd viciously defeated Rāja Jaipal of Bathindah (now in the Patiala State). In response, Jaipal's son organized a league of Hindu rājas. Their armies, which were placed under the supreme command of the Chauhān Rāja Visala-Deva of Ajmer, soon took to the battlefield on the plain of Peshāwar. The Hindu forces were defeated and suffered enormous losses when, reportedly, an elephant turned and fled, causing the Hindus to break in disorder. However, following Maḥmūd's death in 1030, the Rājputs recouped their losses and held on to Rājasthān for another 150 years.

The Chauhāns of Ajmer expanded their territories in the twelfth century under Vigraharāja IV, who captured Delhi. Although Delhi was not very important at the time, Ajmer's strength was clearly building. But the Chauhāns made an even more lasting impression on Hindu literature. Vigraharāja, himself a noted patron of Sanskrit literature, has been credited with the composition of a drama, fragments of which have been preserved on stone tablets at Ajmer. His nephew and successor, the gallant Prithvīrāja, was immortalized in bardic songs both for his romantic exploits and his military leadership. Around 1175, for instance, Prithvīrāja famously carried off the daughter of the most powerful Indian prince of the time, Jaichand of Benares. Declining to appear at the princess's *swayamvara*—a traditional ceremony at which suitors formally presented themselves—Prithvīrāja entered the assembly on horseback and rode off with the princess without observing any of the formalities honor demanded. The incident engendered bitter enmity between northern India's two leading forces and became a popular poetic subject. Prithvīrāja is still a popular folk hero in northern India, and his daring, honor, and heroism form the subject of many songs and epics in the vernacular literature. The most celebrated of these epics, the *Chand Rāisā,* was composed by Prithvīrāja's own court poet, Chand Bardāī. The poem, originally written in archaic Hindi, has been endlessly altered and added to in the oral tradition. Some versions are believed to comprise as many as 125,000 verses.

Prithvīrāja's military accomplishments commemorated in these epic poems include his victory over the Chandēl Rāja, Parmāb, in 1182 and his capture of the important fortress of Mahoba. He found a more formidable opponent in Muhammad of Ghūr, who was the leader of a new invasion from Ghaznī. In 1191, Prithvīrāja commanded the contingents of all the leading powers of northern India against the sultan of Ghaznī. The Hindu host, meeting its Muslim foes at Tarāin (Tarāorī, in modern Karnal district), was initially victorious. However, Muhammad returned in 1192 with reinforcements, challenging the Hindu forces on the same ground. One of India's most decisive military encounters, the second battle of Tarāin pitted Prithvīrāja's forces against 10,000 mounted archers. His men ignominiously fled from

Ahdai-din-ka-jhonpra Mosque, Ajmer
Photo courtesy of Christopher Turner

the field, and the Rājput king was captured and executed, passing from defeat into romantic immortality.

Prithvīrāja has since been celebrated as the paragon of Rājput chivalry, and his Queen's final speech became a rallying cry in later years: "O Sun of the Chauhāns, none has drunk so deeply of both glory and pleasure as thou. Life is an old garment; what matters if we throw it off? To die well is life immortal." Accompanied by her attendants, the woman Prithvīrāja had carried away from the court of a rival then followed him into the afterlife, entering the flames of a funeral pyre.

The Muslim victory at Tarāin opened the way to Prithvīrāja's capital. Ajmer was sacked, its people were enslaved or killed, and its transformation into a Muslim city was begun with the razing of the Hindu temples. However, given its isolation within the desert, Ajmer was not yet considered a secure residence for a Muslim conquerer. Govindarāja, Prithvīrāja's illegitimate son, was appointed governor of Ajmer after he paid tribute to his new overlords. According to Muslim chroniclers, the new rāja was distasteful to his subjects because of his illegitimacy, although other sources indicate that difficulties arose because he was a minor and thus unable to contend successfully with his enemies. As a result, the boy's uncle, Prithvīrāja's brother, usurped the throne and once again challenged the Muslims, but to no effect. He committed suicide after suffering two defeats at the hands of Muhammad of Ghūr's lieutenant and faithful slave, Quṭb-ud-Dīn-Aybak.

When Muhammad of Ghūr was assassinated on the banks of the Indus River in 1206, the territories he had conquered in northern India passed to his slave-lieutenant, Quṭb-ud-Dīn-Aybak. Aybak, accepted as overlord by the Muslim governors, assumed the title of Sultan of Delhi, founding what became known as the Slave Dynasty. Apart from founding a dynasty, Aybak did not leave much of a mark on Ajmer, since he died in a polo accident a few years after his accession. He was succeeded by an ineffectual son, who was quickly replaced by Iltutmish, Aybak's son-in-law, who ruled from 1211 to 1236.

Under Iltutmish, the Ahdai-din-ka-jhonpra mosque was completed. The structure was originally a Jain college built in 1153, and for the mosque a new screen facade was added—in a mere two-and-a-half days, legend insists. The screen contained an arcade of Persian arches with forty columns, all of a different design. The building materials were taken from Hindu temples, as if to underscore the subjugation of the Hindu faith. The mosque is now in an advanced state of disrepair, but the ruins of two small fluted minarets still give an impression of the building's former grandeur.

The Dargah complex, now one of Ajmer's principal architectural glories, was begun shortly after the completion of the Ahdai-din-ka-jhonpra Mosque. It is centered on the tomb of a Sufi saint who came to Ajmer the year it fell to the invading Muslims and who lived in the city in exemplary saintliness for more than fifty years. At his death in 1146, a white marble tomb was erected at the foot of a hill in the old town of Ajmer. Over the centuries, the shrine has grown into a huge complex, as generations of Muslim faithful have made it the object of their pilgrimages.

The city of Ajmer once again changed hands in the sixteenth century, this time passing to the Mughals. The Mughal Dynasty was founded after a successful invasion of India in 1525 by Bābur, a Turkish Muslim who traced his ancestry back to the famous Mongol chieftain Genghis Khan. (The designation Mughal is supposed to be a corruption of Mongol.) Bābur's grandson, Akbar the Great (reigned 1556–1605), annexed Ajmer at his accession in 1556, and his reign unexpectedly brought a degree of reconciliation between Muslims and Hindus in the region. In 1561 a local rāja carried out an ill-conceived attack on Akbar. Poised to destroy the upstart rāja, Akbar heeded a court order enjoining his forbearance and accepted the rāja's daughter in marriage instead. This marriage and the subsequent loyalty of the Rājputs led to an eventual repeal of the discriminatory taxation imposed on Akbar's Hindu subjects.

Akbar maintained his primary imperial residence at Āgra, which lies some 300 miles to the east, but he visited Ajmer at least once a year when he made a pilgrimage to the Dargah. He improved the road from Āgra to Ajmer to underscore the importance of these journeys. Trees were planted along the road, and inns were constructed at regular intervals as were milestones in the form of brick towers decorated with antlers of stags that Akbar himself had killed in the hunt. Akbar's father, Humāyūn, had been responsible for the construction of several buildings at the Dargah complex, and Akbar constructed a mosque in the courtyard as an offering of thanks for being granted a son. The emperor discontinued his annual pilgrimages to the Dargah after 1579, however.

Akbar eventually gained control of all of Rājasthān, or Rajwarra, as it was called in Rājasthānī, through a series of military victories on the one hand and marriages to Rājput princesses on the other. After taking Chitor (Chittaurgarh) in 1568 and Ranthambor in 1569, he designated Rajwarra a province, or *suba,* with its capital at Ajmer. The province became an important source of revenue for the Mughals: scholarly calculations suggest that it was one of the richest regions in the empire. Agriculturally poor, Rajwarra has a wealth of natural resources, including zinc, copper, salt, and marble, all of which were mined and quarried during Mughal times.

Ajmer itself was also valuable for its strategic location. Throughout the Mughal period, the city was the key to controlling Rajwarra. Situated at the approximate midpoint of the Aravālli Mountain range, Ajmer commanded the plains on either side. Shortly after the city was made a provincial capital, Akbar began construction of his fortified palace. The building now houses a museum with a sculpture collection and military exhibits, but throughout the Mughal period it held a garrison meant to remind the Rājputs that rebellion would be met with force. From 1605, when Akbar died, until 1608, Ajmer functioned as the imperial capital under the new emperor, Jahāngīr. The court at Ajmer remained important even after the city ceased to be Jahāngīr's capital.

Jahāngīr died in 1627 and was succeed by his son Shāh Jahān, who ruled from 1628 to 1658 and became famous for commissioning the Tāj Mahal. Shāh Jahān also made architectural contributions to Ajmer, embellishing the shores of Anā Sāgar Lake with five marble pavilions in 1637. He also built a white marble mosque in an inner courtyard of the Dargah. This beautiful structure has eleven arches and a Persian inscription running the full length of the building. Rajwarra was prosperous and quiet for most of Shāh Jahān's reign, but disputes over the succession shook the region in the late 1650s. Three of Shāh Jahān's four sons formed a pact against the crown prince, Dārā Shukōh. When Shāh Jahān fell ill in 1657, the bloody War of Succession broke out.

At the beginning of the conflict, Dārā went to Ajmer to gather his Hindu supporters. In the end, however, he was betrayed by the Rājputs, so that he was hopelessly outnumbered by the forces of his brother Aurangzeb ('Ālamgīr) in the Battle of Deorai, four-and-a-half miles south of Ajmer. After three days of fighting, Dārā, his son, and a dozen men fled, while his army dispersed in all directions. Having anticipated defeat, Dārā had appointed troop escorts and eunuchs to keep guard over his harem and treasury on the shores of Ajmer's Anā Sāgar Lake, where he was to meet them. But in the panic of escape, he missed the crucial rendez-vous. As the eunuchs prepared to lead the party to safety, the troop escorts robbed the women of their valuables and made off into the desert hills.

In the wake of Dārā's defeat, Ajmer was looted by camp followers of both armies. Government and military stores vanished, while wounded soldiers were stripped naked and left to wander the hills in agony. All except one of Dārā's high ranking officers lingered behind in Ajmer to ensure the safety of their families and property, after which they joined Aurangzeb's ranks. Dārā was harbored by a chieftain whose life he had saved some years earlier, but after a few days the crown prince was betrayed and handed over to Aurangzeb. After being paraded through the streets of Delhi, dressed in rags, on the back of a dirty elephant, Dārā was executed on a trumped-up charge of heresy. Aurangzeb had already disposed of the brothers who had been in league with him, and he next imprisoned his father in the Āgra fort (where he died in 1666). His kin thus out of the way, Aurangzeb declared himself emperor and took the name 'Ālamgīr.

The Mughal Dynasty began to crumble after 'Ālamgīr's death in 1707, and their overlordship in Rajwarra was challenged later in the century by the Marāṭhās, a Hindu warrior clan from Mahārāshtra. Ajmer fell to the Marāṭhās in 1770. The following decades were marked by almost continuous fighting between the Marāṭhās and various Rājput princes. By this time, the British were making inroads into the northwestern regions of India, and they proved too powerful for the beleaguered Marāṭhās. Prince Sindhia ceded Ajmer to Lord Hastings in 1818. Under the British, the land of the Rājputs was controlled from Ajmer and continued as a collection of princely states known as Rājputāna, each with its own mahārāja. In 1956, independent India combined these principalities to create the state of Rājasthān.

The modern city of Ajmer is noted for its wide streets and educational institutions, especially Mayo Rajkumar College, which was established in 1875 for the education of the sons of the nobility. Major road and rail routes now run through the city, which serves as a trade center for salt, mica, fabrics, and agricultural products. Corn, wheat, millet, oilseed, cotton, and onions are the chief crops traded through Ajmer. The city's industries include oilseed mills, railway workshops, and pharmaceutical companies. The Dargah still attracts numerous Muslim pilgrims each year during the fast of Ramadan. One of Ajmer's most notable modern architectural structures is a nineteenth-century Jain temple known as the Nasiyan, or Red, Temple, which houses a remarkable collection of wooden sculptures representing figures from Jain mythology.

Further Reading: An excellent, concise, general history of India is to be found in *A History of India from the Earliest Times to the Present Day* by Michael Edwardes (London: Thames and Hudson, and New York: Farrar Straus, 1961; revised edition, London: New English Library, 1967). *The Great Moghuls* by Bamber Gascoigne with photographs by Christina Gascoigne (New York: Harper and Row, and London: Cape, 1971) brings the Mughal period to life with hundreds of vibrant photographs and engaging prose. Sir Wolsely Haig's *The Cambridge History of India: Volume III, Turks and Afghans* (New York: Macmillan, and Cambridge: Cambridge University Press, 1928) and Vincent Smith's *The Oxford History of India: From the Earliest Times to the End of 1911* (Oxford: Clarendon Press, 1919; fourth edition, edited by Percival Spear, New York and Oxford: Oxford University Press, 1981) are indispensible general resources. *The Rajput Rebellion against Aurangzeb: A Study of the Mughal Empire in Seventeenth-Century India* by Robert C. Hallissey (Columbia: University of Missouri Press, 1977) is a well-written volume packed with detailed descriptions of Rajwarra and the province of Ajmer during the Mughal reign. *The Peacock Throne: The Drama of Mogul India* by Waldemar Hansen (New York: Holt Rinehart, 1972; London: Weidenfeld and Nicholson, 1973) is a very engaging account of Mughal imperial life that contains much more information on Ajmer than indicated by its index.

—Caterina Mercone Maxwell and Marijke Rijsberman

Amber (Rājasthān, India)

Location: In east Rājasthān, seven miles northeast of Jaipur.

Description: Amber was the original fortress stronghold of the Khachchawa clan, who were later to become mahārājas of Jaipur. Generally regarded as the most outstanding Rājput fortress in Rājasthān, the hilltop complex is now owned and maintained by the state.

Contact: Government of India Tourist Office
State Hotel, Khasa Kothi
Jaipur 302 001, Rājasthān
India
372200

The site of Amber has been inhabited for one thousand years. The Sasawat Minas are known to have occupied a small fortress on the ridge overlooking Amber in the tenth century. Around 1150, the Khachchawa Rājputs deposed them but, surprisingly, permitted the Minas to remain there as their vassals. The earlier history of the Khachchawas is a mystery, although a local myth links their origin directly with the sun.

Equally uncertain are the origins of the name Amber. Ambikashwara is a local name for the god Siva, and Amba Mata an alternative for Siva's consort Pārvatī, in her dreaded form of Durgā; either could have been the source. The city's name might also have derived from that of King Ambarisha of Ayodhyā.

The Khachchawas proved to be a resilient clan, maintaining undisturbed their position of regional authority for 600 years. They accomplished this through political astuteness rather than fighting pointless battles against vastly superior opponents; the Khachchawas established amicable relations both with the Mughal emperors and, later, the British colonizers.

In January 1562, Mughal emperor Akbar rested at Amber on his return to Āgra from Ajmer, where he had made his first pilgrimage, on foot, to the shrine of the Muslim saint Khwāja Muīn-ud-dīn Chishtī. The Khachchawas had already acknowledged Akbar's suzerainty, and Mahārāja Bihar Mal, who ruled from approximately 1548 to 1574, attended the emperor's encampment. The two groups established good relations, and the mahārāja's daughter was presented to Akbar in marriage, the first of Akbar's many Hindu wives. Later known as Mariam-uz-Zamani (Mary of the Age), she is believed to have converted to Christianity; her son, Salīm, would become the emperor Jahāngīr.

Bihar Mal had adopted a grandson, Mān Singh, and the youth enthusiastically joined Akbar's army. He proved to be a successful military leader and gained enormous wealth from the spoils acquired during his campaigns. Mān Singh was the nephew of a close friend of Akbar, Bhagwan Das, whom he succeeded as mahārāja in 1592 as Mān Singh I. Almost immediately, the new mahārāja decided to spend a substantial amount of his fortune on rebuilding Amber Fort. No doubt he was influenced by the splendor of Akbar's palaces at Āgra and Fatehpur Sīkri, both of which he must have seen.

The fort occupies a precisely rectangular site oriented along a north-south axis; it is more than four times as long as it is wide. Most accommodations are located at an upper level, while the public areas nestle below. No traces of earlier forts have survived. Mān Singh I's buildings, ranged around a large courtyard, were adapted to form the *zenana* (female quarters) by enclosing the balconies. Although the ranges are now in a dilapidated condition, they never appear to have approached the sumptuous quality of the buildings later added to the fort by Jai Singh I (reigned 1621–67), for which Amber is renowned.

Mān Singh I, however, did add one further building of great importance, which still survives just outside the entrance to the palace. In 1604, he returned from a successful campaign as Akbar's commander in chief in Jessore, East Bengal, bringing with him a black marble idol of Kālī, the most terrible incarnation of the goddess Pārvatī. Mān Singh I then built a temple at Amber for private family worship, in which the figure would be venerated. Known as the Shila Devi (or Kālī) Temple, it is the only building in the palace complex to remain in the possession of the Khachchawa family. Traditionally, each mahārāja of Amber, upon inheriting the title, would worship in the temple and sacrifice a live goat to Kāli; this practice continued into the twentieth century. Mān Singh II, the last mahārāja of Jaipur, carried on the tradition shortly before World War II. Mān Singh II had survived an air crash in 1939, and his grateful wife commissioned the present doors of solid silver, which she presented to the temple as a votive offering. Among the more interesting architectural features of the temple are its columns, carved in the shape of palm trees. Constructed of expensive white Carrara marble imported from Italy, they were, surprisingly, each painted green.

The remaining two-thirds of the palace is, with the possible exception of the Ganesh Pol (Elephant Gate), the work of Mahārāja Jai Singh I. This sector is even more influenced by Mughal designs, particularly in its sunken gardens and Dīwān-i-Am (Public Audience Hall).

Entry to the walled palace enclosure is via the Jai Pol (Victory Gate), alternatively known as the Surya Pol (Sun Gate) because it faces the rising sun; the name may also be an allusion to the mythical solar origins of the Khachchawa clan. Jaleb Chowk, an extensive public courtyard, offers splendid views down to the Kadmi Palace, which provided accommodation for the mahārājas before the present Amber Fort was constructed.

View into the courtyard at Amber Fort, with the Jaigarh Fort above it
Photo courtesy of Christopher Turner

Singh Pol (Lion Gate), in double-archway form, provides entrance to the complex of royal buildings. The Dīwān-i-Am, the first pavilion one sees upon entering the complex, was likely among the last built. (Jai Singh's buildings were constructed from the south of the complex to the north.) Columns set in pairs are typical Mughal features and, combined with Hindu brackets and *chajjas* (broad, sloping eaves), the building echoes Akbar's work at Fatehpur Sīkri. Apparently, the Dīwān-i-Am was so highly regarded that Emperor Jahāngīr became jealous, and Jai Singh plastered over the structure to avoid further annoying him.

Ganesh Pol, a colorful ceremonial structure, divides the private from the public areas of the fort's palace. Originally built by Jai Singh I, it may well have been remodeled in the eighteenth century by Jai Singh II (ruled 1699–1744). Vibrant mosaics and sculptures decorate the gateway, and a figure of Ganesh, the popular elephant-headed god, surmounts the archway. Forming a second story to the structure is the Sohag Mandir, its *jalis* (latticed screens) indicating that the pavilion served as a viewing platform for the royal ladies.

Ahead lie the most important buildings in the palace, set in Hindu-style ranges around a Mughal-style sunken garden. To the west is the Sukh Niwas (Pleasure Hall), renowned for its ingenious air-cooling systems, whereby the walls are arranged at different heights and angles specifically to create air currents that are then conducted over water to cool before being filtered into the palace. A water channel runs through each room to further reduce temperatures. Delicate pastel colors are used for the decor, and the popular theme of stylized flower vases recurs throughout. The Mughal influence here is obvious.

Facing the Sukh Niwas is the Jai Mandir (Hall of Victory), the private apartments of Jai Singh I, possessing the finest interiors of any Rājasthān fort. Murals in the hall contain exquisite representations of flowers, as well as hunting and battle scenes done in delicate colors. It is believed that their excellent state of preservation owes to the high quality of the top coat of plaster, allegedly composed of ground eggshells, marble, and pearls. On the ground floor lies the Dīwān-i-Khas (Private Audience Hall) and the Sheesh Mahal (Mirror Hall), both of which are lined with examples of the mirror work for which the Jaipur region is renowned. It is said that the Sheesh Mahal was used by the mahārāja as his bedroom. The Jas Mandir (Hall of Glory) forms the upper floor and is decorated with further mirrored glass. Full-length windows, screened by intricate *jalis* of alabaster, provide delightful views of Lake Maota below, in which the fort is reflected.

The military capabilities of the mahārājas of Amber appear to have been passed down to succeeding generations; the last great Mughal emperor, 'Ālamgīr (Aurangzeb), a religious zealot and persecutor of non-Muslims, was sufficiently impressed by the valor of Jai Singh II to award the Khachchawas the title Sawah Mahārāja (One and One-quarter Mahārāja) toward the end of the seventeenth century. To emphasize his new rank, Jai Singh II immediately increased the size of his banner by one-quarter. When the hated 'Ālamgīr died in 1707, Jai Singh II refused to accept his successor Bahādur Shāh I as emperor, and after a series of battles, the Mughals, now divided and weakened, were forced to end their suzerainty in Amber.

Without the stability of Mughal dominance, northern India became a battleground for warring parties intent on their own expansion. To strengthen the defenses of Amber Fort, Jai Singh II in 1726 rebuilt and expanded a small existing fort perched above it. The fort, renamed Jaigarh, had long served as the treasury of the mahārājas, and the five-key lock to the treasury may still be seen in the armory collection.

To the south of the fort's enclosure stands Jaivan, a cannon claimed to be the world's largest, which was made for Jai Singh II in 1720. On test (the only time it has ever been fired), the cannon ball was dispatched a distance of twenty-four miles. Guns have been produced at this fort for centuries; the foundry, built in 1584, still exists. At that time, the Mughals believed that they were the only ones in India who knew how to produce gunpowder; apparently, they were none too pleased to discover that the Khachchawas had discovered the secret direct from Afghanistan. Jaigarh Fort, opened to visitors in 1983, remains the property of the former mahārāja's family.

Just one year after rebuilding Jaigarh Fort, Jai Singh II, by then immensely wealthy, laid the foundation stone of his new city, named Jaipur to commemorate him. By 1733 the most important buildings, including the royal palace, were ready, and the court was transferred there from Amber.

Of all the Rājput forts, Amber is superseded in magnificence only by Gwalior. Certainly, no other fort in Rājasthān is its equal. Below the fort, the city of Amber once contained many Hindu temples, but few have survived; most of the population moved to Jaipur when the new city's water supply was connected in 1735.

Once a great city, now only a small town survives beneath the fort. Even the elephants, which transport tourists there, are quartered in nearby Jaipur. The fortress/palace has become state property, serving as a museum, although the small Jaigarh Fort, which overlooks it, remains in the possession of the Khachchawa family, the former rulers who have, since India became independent in 1947, occupied part of Jaipur Palace.

Further Reading: A comprehensive description of Amber's architecture is to be found in *Rājput Palaces: The Development of an Architectural Style 1450–1750* by G. H. R. Tillotson (New Haven, Connecticut, and London: Yale University Press, 1987). For historical treatment, the most authoritative source is *A History of Jaipur c. 1503–1938* by Jadunath Sarkar (Hyderābād, India: Longman, 1984), which includes a discussion of Amber. General works touching upon the subject include *The Royal Palaces of India* by George Michell (London: Thames and Hudson, 1994) and the monumental *New Cambridge History of India*, edited by Gordon Johnson, C. A. Bayly, and John F. Richards (29 vols., Cambridge and New York: Cambridge University Press, 1987–).

—Christopher Turner

Amritsar (Punjab, India)

Location: In the Punjab, in northwestern India, approximately 30 miles from the Indian-Pakistani border and 250 miles northwest of Delhi.

Description: Founded in 1577 as a holy site of the Sikh religion, Amritsar is the spiritual capital of the Sikh world. The principal Sikh temple, known as the Harimandir or Golden Temple, dominates the city. Amritsar developed as a center of trade soon after its founding and is now a major commercial city owing to the relative prosperity of the grain-producing Punjab. In the twentieth century, Amritsar has seen a great deal of bloodshed, with the Jalliānwālla Bāgh Massacre in 1919, the violent upheavals of India's Partition in 1947, and a bloody repression of Sikh separatist forces in 1984. Because of the violence that plagues the Punjab, special entry permits to the area are often required.

Site Office: Temple Administration Office
City Center
Amritsar, Punjab
India

Amritsar is a relatively young city, founded in 1577 by the fourth *gurū* of the brotherhood of Sikhs, Rām Dās. Hearing reports of the miraculous healing of a crippled man who had taken a bath in a pool named Amrita Saras, the Sikh leader declared the pool a holy site and had it enclosed. The Mughal emperor Akbar, who then controlled the area and was known for his religious tolerance, granted the surrounding land to the Sikhs. Despite the imperial grant, Rām Dās is reported to have compensated the local owners for the loss of their land. A town sprang up around the pool to serve the visiting pilgrims. Rām Dās also encouraged traders to settle in the town, where local farmers and craftsmen soon began to bring their goods to market. Amritsar is still known for its locally produced and woven blankets.

At that time, the Sikh religion was less than a century old and had not yet acquired its militant character. Emerging from the Hindu population in the Punjab region late in the fifteenth century, Sikhism, a monotheistic religion, was in fact an attempt to reconcile Islam and Hinduism. The founding *gurū* refused to recognize the caste system so fundamental to Hindu culture and spoke out against superstition, idolatry, and abuses of the clergy. He proclaimed a universal brotherhood of men and women, regardless of birth or religious background. Until early in the seventeenth century, the brotherhood remained a peaceful community despite occasional difficulties with the temporal authorities.

The original Sikh temple at Amritsar was built under the leadership of the fifth *gurū,* Arjun. Constructed on a small island in the middle of the holy pool, the building was finished in 1601. Upon its completion, the temple became the repository of the Sikh holy book, the *Ādi Granth,* which contains the writings of the early *gurūs*. Part of the temple was dedicated to the continuous reading of the *Ādi Granth,* a tradition still carried on today, although now the reader's voice is amplified and broadcast throughout the temple complex. Another important section of the temple was given over to the kitchens and refectory: the injunction to feed all comers has been observed at the temple from its first days. The pool itself was made neatly rectangular, its edges clad with tiles.

Arjun did not live long after the completion of the temple. With Sikh egalitarianism appealing to poor Hindus and Muslims alike, the growing Sikh community posed a serious threat to the authority of Mughal emperor Jahāngīr, who succeeded his father Akbar and was far less tolerant toward non-Muslims. In 1606, when Arjun sided in a political struggle with a rebellious prince, Jahāngīr had the *gurū* seized and tortured to death for sedition.

The sixth *gurū*, Hargobind, began to transform the Sikhs from a peaceful community of believers to a warrior church. Hargobind, who was *gurū* from 1606 to 1645, allowed the Sikhs to wear swords, although he did not authorize their use except as defensive weapons. He showed his willingness to defend the faithful by fortifying Amritsar, building a nearly circular wall around the town in anticipation of further conflict with the Mughals. The defensive wall no longer exists, but the Circular Road around the old city follows its outline, and one of the original gates survives.

Hargobind also transformed the *gurū's* purely spiritual leadership role, adding to it a secular dimension. At his installation ceremony, he himself wore two swords, to symbolize both his spiritual and worldly authority. These symbols of militancy became increasingly prominent in the Sikh religion, eventually finding their way into the Sikh crest, which bears an emblem of crossed swords. In the Akāl Takht, or Immortal Throne, a smaller domed temple on the west side of the main temple complex at Amritsar, Hargobind established a court, similar to those of local chiefs and princes. From there he oversaw the worldly affairs of the community. The Akāl Takht has not always been the center of Sikh worldly governance, but over the centuries the building has repeatedly been transformed into a military headquarters until its almost complete destruction in 1984.

The gradual militarization of the Sikh community was taken to a new level under the last *gurū*, Gobind Singh, who acceded to the office after the death of his father, Gurū Tegh Bahādur, in 1675. Aurangzeb ('Ālamgīr), then Mughal em-

Golden Temple, Amritsar
Photo courtesy of Air India Library, New York

peror, had launched a full-scale persecution of non-Muslims. He seized Tegh Bahādur and, when the *gurū* refused to embrace Islam, had him publicly beheaded. Gobind Singh, although only nine years old at the time, assumed leadership of the Sikh community. Vowing revenge on the Mughals, he focused all his energies on military organization. He created the initiation rite that admits Sikhs to the community. Known as the Ceremony of the Sword, the rite involves a great deal of military symbolism. Gobind Singh also established the symbols that mark modern Sikhs—the uncut hair wound around a large comb, the sword, the short trousers, the bracelet on the right wrist, and the common names of Singh (Lion) and Sardar (Chieftain). Each of these distinguishing marks is meant to remind everyone of the readiness, prowess, and nobility of the warrior Sikhs.

Adherents to this form of Sikhism are known as Khālsā Sikhs. They form the majority of Sikhs and enjoy the leadership positions in the Sikh community. However, there are those who consider themselves Sikh but do not subscribe to the various initiation rules and customs of appearance of the Khālsās. Most Khālsās consider the Sahajdhārīs (as those who did not join the Khālsā order came to be known) as non-Sikh, or Hindu. The Sahajdhārīs, however, contest this marginalization and proudly proclaim their Sikhism. The division between these orders of Sikhism exists to this day.

Gobind Singh separated himself from the spiritual focus of the Sikh religion, abolishing the office of the *gurū*, for instance. Determining that the *Ādi Granth* would henceforward fulfill the office, he bestowed the new name of *Gurū Granth Sahib* on the holy writings. He also removed his headquarters from Amritsar in 1699, reestablishing himself at Anandpur and further weakening the organization's link with its spiritual antecedents. After waging war in the Punjab for decades, Gobind Singh eventually made peace with the Mughals, and for this reconciliation with the Muslim authorities he was assassinated by a Hindu in 1708.

Gobind Singh's death left the Sikhs without a strong leader. For a while, Amritsar, as the home of the principal Sikh temple, once again became the center of Sikh activity. But by the middle of the eighteenth century, the Sikh community was called to military action again when the Punjab and other parts of India were invaded by the Afghans. In 1757, Amritsar fell prey to Afghan troops led by Aḥmad Shāh Durrāni, who occupied the city and desecrated the temple. The Sikhs managed to drive out the invaders but were unable to prevent their return in 1761. On that occasion, Durrāni swept through the Punjab, sacked Amritsar, and leveled the temple.

Rebuilding of the temple began immediately. The new building consists of three floors, all three of which are dedicated to perpetual readings or chantings of the *Gurū Granth Sahib*. In addition, the ambulatory surrounding the tank contains shrines to Sikh saints who figured prominently in the history of Amritsar. Bāba Deep Singh, for instance, was working in the temple, copying out the *Gurū Granth Sahib*, when Durrāni invaded Amritsar in 1757. The story tells that Deep Singh immediately threw himself into the fighting. When his head was severed from his body, he held it on his shoulders with one hand while continuing to fight with the other. In this manner, he managed to make his way back to the hallowed ground of the temple before he fell down dead. Other shrines include the *jubi* tree where the original crippled pilgrim is believed to have taken his miraculous bath and a special building housing a copy of the *Gurū Granth Sahib*. Outside the tank walls are the administrative buildings of the temple as well as housing and a dining hall for pilgrims who visit the site.

Following the destruction of the temple, the Sikhs held their ground in the Punjab against the Afghans. In fact, under the leadership of Ranjit Singh, "the Lion of the Punjab," who ruled from 1799 to 1839, separate Sikh chiefdoms were united into a single realm, and territories controlled by the Sikhs were greatly expanded. Using a large mercenary army that eventually numbered 40,000 infantry and 12,000 cavalry, Ranjit Singh captured Lahore in 1799 and established his capital there, once again leaving Amritsar as the purely spiritual focus of the Sikh nation. In 1809, Ranjit Singh fought the British to a standstill and negotiated the Treaty of Amritsar with them. This treaty required the Sikhs to aid the British in the event of a foreign attack, in exchange for Sikh sovereignty in the greater part of the Punjab. By the end of Ranjit Singh's life, most of the Punjab and large parts of Kashmir were in Sikh hands. The Sikhs also controlled the trade routes running through northern India, connecting Central Asia, western Asia, and Iran.

Ranjit Singh was also responsible for an important change in the appearance of the Amritsar temple. In 1830, he donated 220 pounds of pure gold to the temple trust, and this gold, as a symbol of celestial light, was used to gild both the exterior and interior of the building from the roof almost to the ground. Only at the lower levels is the white marble of the walls still exposed. Since it received its golden covering, the temple has been known as the Golden Temple.

Sikh fortunes shifted after Ranjit Singh's death. In 1845, after the British were defeated by the Afghans at Kābul, the Sikhs launched an ill-advised invasion of British India. They suffered a defeat and lost their Kashmir territories to the British. However, the Sikh army rallied for another offensive in 1848 with Afghan support in what became known as the Second Afghan War. Although the Sikhs won a famous victory at Chilianwālla, they were decisively defeated at Gujarāt in February of 1849. In March of that year the Sikh nation surrendered, and the state, including Amritsar, was annexed to the British Raj.

Amritsar became infamous in the early twentieth century as the site of the Jalliānwālla Bāgh Massacre. In the aftermath of World War I, Indian nationalist sentiment ran high, particularly in the Punjab. Hundreds of thousands of Sikh soldiers had fought in the British army, and the country as a whole had made tremendous financial and personnel contributions to the war effort. India expected a move toward Indian self-government and perhaps even independence, but it soon became clear that the British had no intention of granting these wishes. Amritsar, one of the most volatile towns in the Punjab, saw rioting early in April 1919. Five Englishmen died in these disturbances. One incident that was perceived by the British as a particularly galling act of provocation involved an assault on a female English missionary.

Despite a ban on public meetings, political activists continued to hold rallies. On April 13, 1919, a large crowd assembled in the Jalliānwālla Bāgh, a sunken garden that had been converted to a public square. The square was surrounded by high walls, and its single exit was a narrow passageway. While the crowd was listening to a speech on the subject of liberty and independence, a squadron of armed men, led by English officers, entered the Jalliānwālla Bāgh. Without warning, the soldiers began firing into the crowd. Six minutes later, the shooting stopped—only because ammunition had run out, one soldier later acknowledged. The British left the bloodbath they had created without tending to the wounded. While exact figures have never been available, official British estimates put the number of dead at 379 and the wounded at 1,200.

The massacre sparked mixed reactions both in India and in Britain. The officer who had commanded the troops, Brigadier General Reginald Dyer, was forced to resign his commission, but nevertheless the House of Lords commended him for his actions. The governor of the Punjab approved the massacre as a necessary antisubversive measure and declared martial law in the province shortly thereafter. In addition to imposing martial law, the governor ordered a number of public floggings (among other humiliations), in the futile attempt to drive home Dyer's message that resistance to British authority would not be tolerated. The massacre served to radicalize many Indians who had until then been supportive of the British. However, the keepers of the Golden Temple listed Dyer's name in the rolls of the Brotherhood of Sikhs.

Amritsar witnessed another tragedy during the Partition of 1947, when Muslim Pakistan was hastily created. Across India, communities of Hindus and Muslims, who had lived together as neighbors for centuries, exploded in violence. The upheavals were particularly intense and bloody in the Punjab, which had been split down the middle with little forethought. Amritsar saw some of the most severe violence; in one series of incidents, trains filled mostly with unarmed Muslim refugees headed for Pakistan pulled into the Amritsar station and were met by bands of militant Sikhs. When the trains pulled out of the station, they carried many dismembered bodies and few survivors. Later, when the attacks became known in Delhi, trains were ordered through Amritsar without stopping, but the Sikhs then ambushed them farther down the line. Many of the Muslim inhabitants of Amritsar were killed and their houses razed before they could flee.

The violence finally came to an end when the Sutlej River overflowed its banks and washed away large sections of the city. However, in the six weeks between the beginning of August and the middle of September 1947, approximately 750,000 Indians—Muslim, Hindu, and Sikh—died. The Sikhs, caught in the middle of the land division, suffered the highest number of casualties of any population group.

Partition left Amritsar the principal city of the Indian Punjab, and since 1947 it has grown into a major commercial center. With its relatively reliable water supply and subtropical climate, the Punjab quickly became the granary of India. Much of the local produce is traded through Amritsar, which has also undergone some industrial development. Political stability, however, has proved elusive. Since the first days of Indian independence, calls have gone up for an autonomous Sikh homeland in the Punjab. As a partial answer to these demands, the Punjab was divided, in 1966, into the state of Haryāna, which contains most of the Hindi-speaking areas, and a Punjābī-speaking state called Punjab, harboring the majority of the Sikh community. The two states have a joint capital at Chandīgarh in Haryāna.

Although it is a victory to the Sikh community that they now live in a state whose official language is Punjābī, several radical nationalist factions continued to agitate for Sikh autonomy. These separatist forces, headquartered at Amritsar and led by the fundamentalist Sikh preacher Jarnail Singh Bhindranwale, have engaged in acts of terrorism against Hindus and more moderate Sikhs since the early 1980s. They ensconced themselves in the Akāl Takht at the Golden Temple, parts of which they fortified. On June 5, 1984, the Indian army launched "Operation Blue Star," attacking the terrorist strongholds to dislodge Bhindranwale and his followers from the temple complex. When the army unexpectedly met with resistance, tanks were called in and the Akāl Takht was bombarded by order of Prime Minister Indira Gandhi. By day's end, the Akāl Takht was reduced to rubble and the main temple complex seriously damaged. Bhindranwale was dead, as were many of his followers. About a hundred army soldiers lost their lives. Unfortunately, this was not the end of the story. Indira Gandhi was assassinated shortly afterward by her Sikh bodyguards, who were bent on revenge. The assassination, in turn, sparked acts of violence against Sikhs living outside the Punjab.

The Golden Temple has been restored, although bullet holes still mark its walls. In addition, permanent security measures, including mandatory body searches for all who enter the complex, have changed the atmosphere at the temple. Rooms that might serve as a refuge to terrorists have been permanently sealed off. By the late 1990s, disorder and violence were still a regular feature of life in the Punjab, and the future of Amritsar remained uncertain.

Further Reading: Two fine volumes of Indian history are W. H. Moreland and Atul Chandra Chatterjee's *A Short History of India* (London and New York: Longmans, 1936; fourth edition, New York: McKay, 1966) and A. L. Basham's *The Wonder That Was India: A Survey of the Culture of the Indian Sub-continent before the Coming of the Muslims* (New York: Grove, and London: Sidgwick and Jackson, 1954). Alistair Shearer's *The Traveler's Key to Northern India: A Guide to the Sacred Places of Northern India* (New York: Knopf, 1983) focuses mainly on the Golden Temple, but also gives a brief, concise history of the Sikhs and the role they played in Amritsar's history. A brief but detailed description of the Jalliānwālla Bāgh massacre can be found in James Morris's *Farewell the Trumpets: An Imperial Retreat* (New York: Harcourt Brace, and London: Faber, 1978), the third volume of that author's history of the British Empire. A very thorough and readable eyewitness account of the Indian army's 1984 attack on the Golden Temple is available in Mark Tully and Satish Jacob's *Amritsar: Mrs. Gandhi's Last Battle* (London: Cape, 1985).

—Kenneth R. Shepherd and Marijke Rijsberman

Angkor (Siem Reap, Cambodia)

Location: In the dense jungle of northwest Cambodia, 200 miles north of the capital of Phnom Penh in Siem Reap province, about 4 miles from the town of Siem Reap and near the Tonle Sap, a huge lake into which the surrounding river network flows.

Description: The ruined city of Angkor is the ancient capital of the great Khmer Empire, which flourished from the ninth to the fifteenth centuries. There are more than 100 temples within the vast complex, but the most famous is the huge and magnificent temple of Angkor Wat. Less than a mile away stands the old city of Angkor Thom, at the center of which is the Bayon Temple. Despite warfare and the encroachment of the surrounding jungle, Angkor Wat is in a generally good state of preservation and remains one of humanity's most magnificent architectural achievements.

Site Office: Angkor Tourism Desk
Grand Hotel d'Angkor
Siem Reap, Siem Reap
Cambodia

Angkor was established as the seat of the Khmer Empire at the end of the ninth century, but the surrounding region has a heritage that predates this great civilization. The earliest inhabited portion of northwestern Cambodia was Loang Spean, which was occupied in the fourth millennium B.C. Recent archaeological evidence suggests that there were early settlements on the summits of hills surrounding Angkor. A civilized society developed there by the first century A.D. The area was part of a state called Funan by the third-century Chinese traders, who left the earliest written records of the region. Although Funan also encompassed much of what is now southern Vietnam, the inhabitants were effectively the predecessors of the Khmers. By the sixth century Funan, shaken by civil wars, was absorbed by the new state of Chenla (also written as Zhenla). Funan and Chenla apparently were the most important of many states in early Cambodia.

By the beginning of the ninth century, Chenla had become a vassal of the Sailendra Dynasty of Java. In 802 a young Khmer prince, Jayavarman II, declared his independence from Java and made himself king. He made his capital at Mount Mahendrapura (Phnom Kulen), about twenty-five miles northeast of Angkor. He unified the Khmer lands and established the belief system by which Khmer kings were seen as gods incarnate. He identified himself with the Hindu god Siva, the Khmers having adopted Hinduism through contact with Indian traders. His successor, Indravarman I, began development of irrigation works, including artificial lakes, which helped the empire prosper.

After an intermediate move of the capital to Roluos, the seat of government was shifted to Angkor during the reign of Yaśovarman I, who ascended the throne in 889. What would become Angkor began as the city of Yaśodharapura, founded by Yaśovarman on the hill that is now known as Phnom Bakheng. The hill, only a short distance from Angkor Wat, was the first "temple mountain" at Angkor. (The name Angkor, meaning "city" or "capital," was applied to the city by westerners.) The Khmer pyramid temples differ from other, similar structures around the world because of their degree of symbolism. The temple mountain represents Mount Meru, which, according to Hindu mythology, is the cosmic mountain and the axis of the universe. The summit of Mount Meru with its five peaks is the home of the celestial gods. The representation of Mount Meru in the architectural form of a temple symbolically created a home for the gods on earth. Later Khmer kings elaborated on this symbolism; temples built at the center of *barays* (lakes) represented the cosmic ocean that surrounded Mount Meru.

The temple at Phnom Bakheng originally had 109 towers: 5 on the upper terrace, representing the 5 peaks of Mount Meru; 12 on each of the 5 tiers of the base; and 44 surrounding the base. Many of the towers are now missing. The number of levels in the structure—ground, tiers, and terrace—totaled seven, representing the seven heavens of Hinduism. The temple was carved from rock and faced with sandstone.

The Khmer kings, once established, began to extend the borders of their empire. King Rajendravarman, who reigned from 944 to 968, invaded the rival Cham heartland and captured a golden statue as a trophy in 950. The Chams, who occupied the central region of Vietnam, were archrivals of the Khmers. An inscription states that Rajendravarman's "brilliance burned the enemy kingdoms, beginning with Champa." Rajendravarman also built temples with funerary associations, such as Pre Rup, constructed about 961. Its name derives from words describing cremation rituals. One of the easternmost of the Angkor temples, the three-tiered pyramid is surmounted by five brick towers, again representing the five peaks of Mount Meru. Rajendravarman also was responsible for another temple, the East Mebon, which was built slightly earlier than Pre Rup and which served as a model for the later structure. The East Mebon was constructed in 952 and stands in the middle of the Eastern Baray, a man-made lake. The pyramidal structure also has the symbolic five towers, made of sandstone and laterite. The staircases leading to the top are adorned with carved lions and monolithic elephants.

The reign of Suryavarman I (1010–50) saw major territorial expansion of the Khmer Empire. A series of successful wars extended its boundaries into the Menam and

Angkor Wat
Photo courtesy of the Embassy of Cambodia, Washington, D.C.

Mekong Valleys and as far south as the Gulf of Siam. With this increase in territory came a need for regional control. Suryavarman I established regional capitals at Sukhothai and Phimai, both in what is now Thailand. A complex road network connected the empire.

Territorial expansion also brought increased prosperity, which in turn stimulated further temple building during the reign of Suryavarman I. The temple of Phimeanakas, later enclosed within the palace of Angkor Thom, probably was completed at this time, having been begun by either of Suryavarman's two immediate predecessors, Jayavarman V or Udayadityavarman I. The temple is rather plain, but once had a golden tower at its top. Rituals associated with the golden tower were described by the Chinese emissary Zhou Daguan:

> Out of the palace rises a golden tower, to the top of which the ruler ascends nightly to sleep. It is common belief that in the tower dwells a genie, formed like a serpent with nine heads, which is Lord of the entire kingdom. Every night this genie appears in the shape of a woman, with whom the sovereign couples. . . . Should the spirit fail to appear for a single night, it is a sign that the King's death is at hand.

As the only reliable contemporaneous source of information on Angkor, Zhou's writings are invaluable. He recorded the daily events at the court of the king, at which he was a guest in 1296 and 1297.

Ta Keo, the first temple to have been built completely of sandstone, was patronized by Suryavarman I. Surrounded by a moat (now dry), the pyramid rises to an impressive 200 feet. Unfortunately, the temple never was finished, and there is a distinct absence of carved decoration on the roughly hewn sandstone blocks. This temple still is an important milestone in Khmer history, as it marks the transition of architecture from brick or laterite to the more durable and carvable material of sandstone.

Suryavarman I's successor Udayadityavarman II (reigned 1050–66) created the Khmers' largest irrigation project in the middle of the eleventh century. The Western Baray, a reservoir one and one-half miles wide and eight miles long, was created by the construction of huge earthen dikes. The project was so successful that it still is used to irrigate twenty-eight square miles today. Udayadityavarman II also was responsible for building the Baphuon, a magnificent temple that had a bronze tower even higher than the golden tower of Phimeanakas; sadly, Baphuon today is in a poor state of repair.

After the time of Udayadityavarman II, Khmer history is quiet until the rise of the great Suryavarman II, who reigned from 1113 to 1150. His reign was marked by wars with the Chams of Vietnam and with the Siamese, but, more importantly, by the Khmers' most significant architectural achievement, the building of the magnificent Angkor Wat (*wat* means "temple" in Thai). Angkor Wat is built on such a huge scale that it truly can be appreciated only from the air. Estimated to have taken thirty years to complete, the temple complex, encompassing 500 acres, is a gigantic representation of Mount Meru. Five towers made of stylized lotuses rise from the center, with the innermost tower soaring to a staggering 699 feet, about the same height as Notre Dame Cathedral in Paris. The sanctuary of this tower once contained a sacred image of Vishnu, to whom the temple was dedicated. The five central towers are surrounded by numerous courtyards, galleries, enclosures, and still more towers. The outermost towers are not as well preserved as the central five and are missing their topmost portions.

Angkor Wat is surrounded by a moat, measuring 1,400 by 1,600 yards and representing the ocean surrounding the world. A causeway stretches across the moat to the temple complex; a stone balustrade along the edge of the causeway is in the form of a snake. At various intervals the scaled body of the snake rears up to form a fan of five or seven snake heads. The snake fans are a distinctive feature of Khmer architecture and a hallmark of Khmer temples of this period.

In the outer galleries of Angkor Wat is the largest relief sculpture in the world, stretching one-half mile around an interior wall. The beautifully executed sculpture depicts scenes from the Hindu legends of the *Mahābhārata* and *Rāmāyaṇa,* as well as depictions of heaven and hell. Along the eastern gallery is the most remarkable of the tableaux, portraying the Hindu creation myth, the Churning of the Sea of Milk. In this story, the elixir of immortality was lost in the cosmic ocean. To retrieve it, the gods and demons broke off the peak of Mount Meru to use as a pivot around which the serpent-king Vāsuki wrapped himself. The gods and demons pulled at the serpent to rotate the peak and churn the Sea of Milk for 1,000 years until they retrieved all that had been lost. In the process of churning, celestial nymphs, known as *apsaras,* were born. The depiction of this tale constitutes perhaps the most enchanting and famous piece of Khmer sculpture.

Unlike most other Khmer temples, Angkor Wat is oriented to the west rather than to the east, stimulating a debate as to its function. Its orientation suggests funerary purposes, since the west, the direction of the setting sun, symbolizes death. Although a deep shaft was found at the center of the temple, it held only treasure and was not a tomb. As yet, no tomb has been found at Angkor Wat.

In 1177 the Khmer capital was devastated by a surprise attack from the Chams. Although much of the city was destroyed, most of the temples were spared. Jayavarman VII (reigned 1181–1219) expelled the Chams and stabilized the empire. His victories over the Chams are portrayed in the sculptural reliefs in the Bayon Temple, in the heart of the new city he built, Angkor Thom. Despite the fact that Jayavarman VII was sixty when he ascended the throne, he not only built this new city but also was responsible for the construction of a large number of temples, including Banteay Srei, Srah Srang, Prah Khan, and Ta Prohm. Unlike earlier temples, these are not Hindu but Buddhist, reflecting Jayavarman VII's conversion to Mahāyāna Buddhism.

The Bayon always has impressed foreign visitors with its beauty and grandeur. More than 200 faces are carved on the 54 towers that crown the structure. The magnificence and serenity of these huge faces was described by Pierre Loti in 1912: "They had such superhuman proportions, these sculpted masks high above, that it takes some time to understand them. They smile under their great broad noses and keep their eyes half-closed. . . ." The serene smile on each of the faces has come to be known as the "smile of Angkor." There has been much debate as to whom the faces represent, either Jayavarman himself or perhaps the Lokeśvara, a bodhisattva, an enlightened being who chooses to remain on earth.

Leading to the entrance gateways of Angkor Thom are further sculptural representations of the Churning of the Sea of Milk. A line of fifty-four carved gods stands along one side of the walk and along the other stands the same number of demons. Both are carved in a stance of churning the sea of milk and have their arms wrapped around the body of the serpent. The serpent spreads out into a fan of nine heads at the end of the walk. Many of the heads have been damaged and lost, so there are several reproductions in place today. The towers at the end of the walk have smiling faces like those of the Bayon, as well as depictions of three-headed elephants. The elephant motif is used frequently in Angkor Thom, along with many other animal forms on the appropriately named Elephant Terrace.

The Khmer Empire was frequently under attack by the Thais after the reign of Jayavarman VII. The Thais continued to apply pressure until they sacked Angkor in 1353. Although the Khmers recaptured the city, ferocious warfare continued between the two kingdoms until Angkor Thom was devastated in 1431. The Khmers then left Angkor and moved their capital to Phnom Penh. The Khmer rulers returned to Angkor for brief periods in the sixteenth and seventeenth centuries, but finally deserted it altogether.

After Angkor's abandonment, the jungle encroached upon it and eventually covered it completely. It was not until 1860 that Angkor again became famous, thanks to the efforts of French naturalist Henri Mouhot. Mouhot, however, was not, as he claimed, the first foreigner to discover Angkor; numerous visitors, both European and Asians, came to Angkor before Mouhot, but their accounts were not as well publicized as his. Since Mouhot's time, numerous explorers, archaeologists, and tourists have come to see the magnificent temples in the jungle.

The importance of preserving the monuments was recognized early. The bulk of the restoration work has been done since 1933. Cambodia was a French colony at this time, as it had been since 1863. After it became independent in 1954, French archaeologists were invited to continue their work. Angkor Wat is the best preserved of the temples because it has been maintained and occupied by an order of Theravāda Buddhist monks. Since the early twentieth century there have been organized tours of Angkor. Increased foreign awareness of Angkor has had both positive and negative results. Tourist spending has been welcomed, but the theft of statues and other artifacts has become a serious problem. The first visitors simply helped themselves and thought nothing of it, and theft has continued to the present day, with organized trade occurring over the Thai border, despite the presence of armed guards. The sheer size of the ruins and their location in the jungle has made Angkor difficult to protect.

Angkor was made off-limits to foreign visitors after warfare commenced in 1970 with Lon Nol's military coup against Prince Sihanouk. Battles between Lon Nol's army and the communist Khmer Rouge, whose stronghold was in the jungle around Angkor, threatened the monuments in the early 1970s. The Vietnamese invasion in 1978 plunged the country into further chaos. In 1991 the United Nations negotiated a peace agreement among the various factions and sent in troops to enforce it, but Cambodia has remained a dangerous place. The Khmer Rouge still dominate the country around Angkor and sporadically take foreign hostages. But despite the warfare that raged around the temples for two decades, the monuments of Angkor have survived remarkably well. There are a few bullet holes, but all parties agreed that Angkor should be spared. Restoration work by archaeologists even continued throughout the war amid shells and rockets.

Today the jungle is the greatest threat to the monuments; as it rapidly encroaches, the roots of huge strangler fig trees tear apart the stone buildings. The monuments are again open for tourists to visit, and a large airport is planned for Siem Reap. Angkor is currently under the jurisdiction of UNESCO, which has created a program to preserve Angkor for the future.

Further Reading: *Angkor: The Hidden Glories* by Michael Freeman and Roger Warner (Boston: Houghton Mifflin, 1990), combining Warner's well-researched text with Freeman's evocative photographs, is possibly the best book on Angkor. *Angkor: An Introduction to the Temples* by Dawn Rooney (Hong Kong: Odyssey, and Sevenoaks, England: Hodder Headline, 1994) is a very informative book on the monuments of Angkor, with a section on historical background. Despite being a guidebook, it is soundly researched. It also is illuminated by the photographs of Michael Freeman. *Angkor: Heart of an Asian Empire* by Bruno Dagens (London: Thames and Hudson, and New York: Abrams, 1995; originally published as *Angkor, la forêt de pierre,* Paris: Gallimard, 1989) focuses on the foreign visitors to Angkor and includes descriptions of the monuments, but no Khmer history. *Travels in the Central Parts of Indo-China, Cambodia and Laos during the Years 1858–1861* by Henri Mouhot (London: Murray, 1864; as *Henri Mouhot's Diary: Travels in the Central Parts of Siam, Cambodia and Laos during the Years 1858–1861,* edited by Christopher Pym, London: Oxford University Press, 1966) is an interesting diary, enlightened by recent editing, of Mouhot's experiences of Angkor.

—Charles Savile

Anuradhapura (Sri Lanka)

Location: In north-central Sri Lanka (formerly Ceylon), on the Aruvi Aru River; approximately 100 miles north of the Sri Lankan capital city of Colombo, at an intersection of main east-west and north-south roads.

Description: Ancient capital of the Sinhalese kings of the Greater and Lesser Dynasties, from the fourth century B.C. until the Sinhalese abandoned the city in the tenth century A.D. The site lay undisturbed until British colonialists reinvigorated the town in the early nineteenth century. An archaeological preserve that occupies about fifteen square miles of the old city contains the ruins from Anuradhapura's glory days: monumental, bell-shaped Buddhist shrines called *dagabas;* Buddhist temples and monasteries; palaces; and delicate Sinhalese sculpture. The preserved city also contains the legendary Bo-tree, reportedly planted from a branch of the pipal tree under which Siddhārtha Gautama attained perfect enlightenment. The surrounding region's extensive irrigation system allowed the cultivation of rice on a grand scale in arid northern Sri Lanka. The modern city of 37,000 residents serves as capital of the Anuradhapura administrative district, as headquarters of the Archaeological Survey of Ceylon, and as a Buddhist pilgrimage site.

Contact: Ceylon Tourist Board
78 Steuart Place
P. O. Box 1504
Colombo 3
Sri Lanka
(43) 7059 or (43) 7060

Time and legend shroud the beginnings of the city of Anuradhapura. The *Mahāvaṃsa,* an epic record of the history of the Sinhalese that begins with their legendary arrival on the island of Sri Lanka in the fourth century A.D., provides the main account of the city's earliest years. Probably composed during the sixth century A.D., the *Mahāvaṃsa* derives from the records of Buddhist *bhikkhus*, or monks. The chronicle's blend of legend and fact, however, compromises its reliability in terms of strict historical accuracy.

Sinhalese invaders from northern India who arrived on the northern coast of Sri Lanka during the sixth century B.C. most likely settled Anuradhapura. These newcomers probably migrated from a water culture, for they quickly developed the first stages of a huge irrigation system, a necessity in the arid northern region for the water-intense cultivation of rice, the island staple. King Vijaya, who founded what has come to be called the Great Dynasty of Sri Lanka, and his immediate successors built the earliest reservoirs of this system during the sixth and fifth centuries B.C. Throughout the centuries, Anuradhapura's rulers created a complex system of reservoirs (often called tanks), dams, sluice gates, and canals to transport water from mountain and highland rivers to the hundreds of square miles of rice paddies upon which the city depended almost wholly for sustenance. The construction, enlargement, and maintenance of this system—one of the major engineering achievements of the ancient world—were so critical to the kingdom's survival that even war did not slow progress.

During the fourth century B.C., the Sinhalese king Pāṇḍukhābhaya made Anuradhapura his capital. With just one brief interlude, the city served as capital of the Sinhalese kingdom for the next 1,500 years. The kingdom ruled from Anuradhapura comprised the northern third of the island and became known as Rājarata (King's Country). The principality of Ruhuna controlled the southern part of the island, while Malayadeśa covered the mountainous central region, during ancient times sparsely populated and politically unimportant.

More accurate historical records regarding Anuradhapura begin in approximately 247 B.C., with the introduction of Buddhism to the island. The Sinhalese ruler at that time, Devānampiyatissa, dispatched emissaries from Anuradhapura to the court of the Mauryan king Aśoka, whose vast domain extended from present-day Bengal to Madras on the Indian subcontinent. In return, Aśoka sent his son (possibly his brother) Mahinda to Anuradhapura to expose the Sinhalese to the teachings of the Buddha, which Aśoka's court followed. Four "noble truths" support the tenets of Buddhism: from birth to death, life equals suffering; human desire causes this suffering; suffering can end only when one conquers human desire; and one may attain the spiritual goal, nirvana, once righteous behavior and thought have eliminated all desire.

Mahinda succeeded in converting Devānampiyatissa and the entire court to Buddhism, and the remainder of the Sinhalese population soon followed. At about the same time, a Buddhist nun (probably Mahinda's sister Saṅghamitthā) planted at Anuradhapura a branch of the famous Bo-tree, under which Siddhārtha Gautama had achieved perfect enlightenment, or Buddhahood. Anuradhapura's enthusiastic reception of Buddhism resulted in a city that not only housed numerous Buddhist shrines and monasteries but that also served as headquarters of the Sangha, the order of Buddhist *bhikkhus*. These first links that led to Buddhism ultimately becoming the Sinhalese state religion brought Anuradhapura under the unofficial suzerainty of the Mauryan Empire.

In addition to his substantial contributions to the irrigation network—the 400-acre Tissawewa Reservoir at the

The sacred Bo-tree, Anuradhapura
Photo courtesy of Mr. Herath Navaratne, Information Officer, Embassy of Sri Lanka, Washington, D.C.

Detail of a makara, *foliated scroll railing, Anuradhapura*
Photo courtesy of Mr. Herath Navaratne, Information Officer, Embassy of Sri Lanka, Washington, D.C.

edge of town, for example—Devānampiyatissa ordered the construction of Anuradhapura's first *dagaba*, the Thūpārāmā. *Dagabas* (stupas in Sanskrit) commemorate the Buddha's attainment of perfect enlightenment. In contrast to other religious structures that have enclosed interior spaces designed to be occupied for worship, *dagabas* are solid to the core—usually solid brick in the case of those at Anuradhapura. Some of the *dagabas* at Anuradhapura varied from the traditional shape of a huge bell rising to a point: instead of the usual practice of burying the relic associated with a particular *dagaba* inside the core of the bell, a chamber atop the dome housed the revered object. The Thūpārāmā, forty feet in diameter, rose to a height of sixty-three feet. Forty columns, the tallest of them twenty-six feet tall, formed four concentric circles of diminishing height to support the *dagaba*'s wooden dome, originally of the conical, "paddy-heap" type. The Thūpārāmā's basic composition—a dome mounted on a series of stepped, circular platforms, with pillars around the periphery—served as the prototype for the later circular relic houses known as *vatadages*.

Despite their avowed acceptance of Buddhist principles, Sinhalese monarchs at Anuradhapura created a tumultuous history replete with war, hunger for power, conquest, murder, and deceit, both from within the dynasty and from external forces. After the death of King Aśoka in 235 B.C., the Mauryan Empire fell into dissolution. The vacuum left by Aśoka's death corresponded with the emergence of the Tamil, a people indigenous to South India who spoke a Dravidian language and practiced Hinduism. Tamil invasions of the Sinhalese island from the mainland increased toward the end of the third century B.C., introducing the linguistic, cultural, racial, and religious differences that have continued to plague Sri Lanka to the present day.

Soon after Devānampiyatissa's reign, two Tamils from South India named Sena and Guttika assassinated the Sinhalese monarch and seized the throne, becoming the first Dravidian monarchs to rule at Anuradhapura. After approximately two decades, they too were deposed and murdered, and a Sinhalese king reclaimed the throne. Less than a decade later, Prince Elara of the Tamil kingdom of Coḷa landed on the shores of northern Sri Lanka with a major Tamil invasion force. This incursion so severely disrupted the Sinhalese kingdom that even work on the irrigation system came to a halt—the only such occurrence in the island's history. After capturing Anuradhapura and slaying the Sinhalese ruler, Elara declared himself king in 205 B.C. Although Elara apparently governed fairly and impartially, Sinhalese resentment simmered throughout his forty-year reign.

In 161 B.C. a Sinhalese prince from the province of Ruhuna, Duṭṭhagāmanī Abhaya (popularly known as Duṭugümuṇu), mounted a campaign to overthrow Elara. Sinhalese lore emphasizes Duṭugümuṇu's great personal heroism during his fight to recapture Anuradhapura. Astride his war elephant, Duṭugümuṇu faced a series of grave challenges as he led his army over the mountains and onto the northern plains. In one close encounter, his forces had to storm the Tamil fortress at Vijitapura, near Anuradhapura, before they could even approach the capital. At the gate of Anuradhapura, Duṭugümuṇu and Elara engaged in single combat atop their respective war elephants, and the king fell to the prince's spear. Duṭugümuṇu assumed the throne, and for the first time a Sinhalese king ruled over a united Sri Lanka from Anuradhapura.

The *Mahāvaṃsa* celebrates Duṭugümuṇu's prowess as warrior and statesman; the Sinhalese consider him both a champion of Sinhalese nationalism and the ideal defender of Buddhism, for it was he who irrevocably committed the Great Dynasty to Buddhism. Duṭugümuṇu's reign began a sixty-year period of peace and prosperity that fostered the building of some of Anuradhapura's largest *dagabas*. He also built the Lohapasada Monastery in approximately 150 B.C. The monastery's Brazen Palace, so called for its metal cladding, contained 1,000 rooms in its nine stories. Despite a number of renovations throughout the centuries, only the monastery's stone foundation pillars remain—1,600 of them. Duṭugümuṇu decorated his temples, reliquaries, gardens, ponds, and pavilions with elaborate bas reliefs, carved friezes, and other elegant ornamentation.

Duṭugümuṇu ended his reign with two colossal constructions, the Mirisavati Dagaba, measuring 168 feet in diameter, and the even larger Ruwanvelisaya Dagaba (137 B.C.), with a diameter at the ground of 300 feet. Also known as the Mahāthupa (Grand Stupa), the Ruwanvelisaya required that its foundation, made of stone reinforced with iron and copper, be excavated to a depth of more than 100 feet to support the massive brick dome that soared 270 feet above the base. A later restoration added the 500 sculptural brick elephants, spaced around the circumference less than twenty-four inches apart, that appear to support the vast platform above the *dagaba*'s lower levels.

As peaceful as Duṭugümuṇu's reign seemed, the internal struggle for power continued, as did external pressure on the Sinhalese monarchy from the Tamils. The succession of rule at Anuradhapura describes a never-ending tale of assassination, suicide, usurpation, and war. In 104 B.C. the Tamils again took Anuradhapura, and for fifteen years a succession of five Tamil princes ruled Sri Lanka from the city. When Vatagamani reestablished Sinhalese rule in approximately 89 B.C., he built the largest of all *dagabas* in Anuradhapura, the legendary Abhayagiri Dagaba. The Abhayagiri may have sprawled over eight acres and towered 450 feet above the city, perhaps the largest Buddhist shrine ever constructed in Sri Lanka.

Events following the death of the Sinhalese robber-king Choranaga typify the violently unpredictable chronicle of succession at Anuradhapura. His successor, Kudatissa, was poisoned by his own wife, Anula, who became Anuradhapura's first female ruler. In less than a decade, she married, enthroned, and poisoned as many as five consorts. A son of Kudatissa assumed the throne only after murdering Anula.

The first great reservoirs—actually lowland areas dammed into artificial lakes controlled by sluice gates—were built by King Vasabha during the first century A.D. Truly massive, the perimeter of these great tanks measured up to three miles. Vasabha also probably constructed the thirty-mile-long Giant's Canal. In the late third century A.D., King Mahāsena built the Minneriya Reservoir, which covered an area of 4,670 acres. Mahāsena, the last king recounted in the *Mahāvaṃsa* chronicle of the Great Dynasty, died in 302.

Some sixty-two kings of the Lesser Dynasty ruled Anuradhapura from 352 until the beginning of the eleventh century, with only a few of note. As in previous centuries, the internal feuds and struggles continued, as did the Tamil invasions from India. In 432 the Tamils again gained the throne at Anuradhapura, but a new Sinhalese leader, Dhātusena, expelled them and was declared king in 459. In his first year of rule, Dhātusena built the Kalawewa, an inland lake measuring forty miles in circumference that resulted from the damming of an entire river system. The Kalawewa became Anuradhapura's main source of water.

This period also marked the beginning of what has been called a golden age of Sri Lankan art. The so-called moonstone design, a semicircular pavement usually found at the bottom of a flight of stairs, especially distinguished shrines of this period, which ended in the tenth century. Typically comprising a half-lotus expanding outward in concentric circles intricately carved with natural motifs—including foliage, sacred geese, flames, and processions of lions, elephants, horses, and bulls—the moonstones represent the Buddhist concept of the universe.

King Dhātusena reigned for eighteen years but eventually fell victim to the court's violent intrigues. Migara, commander in chief of the army and son-in-law of the king, conspired with Kāśyapa, Dhātusena's eldest son, to stage a coup d'état. Kāśyapa seized the throne in 478 and, in a particularly vicious act, had his father walled up alive. Dhātusena's second son, Mogalla, fled to India to escape assassins sent by his older brother. Kāśyapa, unpopular and fearful of reprisals from his brother, removed the capital of the kingdom from Anuradhapura to the rocky fortress of Sigiriya, a more secure location where he created a splendid bastion for himself.

Kāśyapa's downfall came in 495 at the hands of Mogalla, who, supported by the opportunistic Migara, returned to Sri Lanka and defeated his brother's forces. Perhaps unable to face Mogalla's certain revenge, Kāśyapa committed suicide. Crowned king in the same year, Mogalla returned the capital to Anuradhapura, from where he ruled until 513. After

Mogalla's death, the royal succession became even more anarchic. Fourteen subsequent rulers at Anuradhapura were deposed or murdered. Finally, in 993, an invading Tamil army from the Coḷa Kingdom captured, looted, and burned the city. The Sinhalese abandoned Anuradhapura as their capital in favor of Polonnaruwa, a less vulnerable city about thirty-three miles to the southwest.

Except for a few Buddhist monks who stayed to maintain the shrines as best they could, Anuradhapura was left to crumble in the encroaching jungle. King Parākramabāhu the Great (ruled 1153–86), an ambitious builder who ruled Sri Lanka from Polonnaruwa, ordered the restoration of several large *dagabas* at Anuradhapura; as well, his efforts to restore the Brazen Palace of the Lohapasada Monastery resulted in the present arrangement of forty parallel rows of forty columns each. Parākramabāhu's successors possessed neither the resources nor the zeal to renovate further Anuradhapura's deteriorating monuments, and the once-glorious capital passed several more centuries in oblivion.

Beginning in the sixteenth century, a succession of European powers controlled Sri Lanka. The Portuguese arrived first, having discovered the route around Africa into the Indian Ocean. They soon became involved in Sri Lanka's internal political struggles, eventually wresting control of most of the island for themselves. The Portuguese ruled for about 150 years before being supplanted by the increasingly ambitious Dutch in the mid–seventeenth century; the Dutch, too, governed Sri Lanka for 150 years.

Meanwhile, the British had begun their own colonial forays into the Indian subcontinent and surrounding territories. In 1802 the British took control of Sri Lanka and unified the administration of the entire island as the Crown Colony of Ceylon (from Sinhala, meaning Lion Race). British travelers to Ceylon in the early nineteenth century reported that, with the exception of a few shrines, the jungle had reclaimed all of Anuradhapura. Although the Thūpārāmā received a new, hemispherical dome in 1842, the site as a whole received little notice. As late as 1873, one visitor reported that "it was not possible to see twenty yards ahead." The British initiated archaeological excavations in Ceylon during the 1870s, but not until 1890 did a systematic survey of the ruins at Anuradhapura begin, under the direction of government archaeologist H. C. P. Bell.

The city's revival since the nineteenth century under British guidance ultimately led to a slight relocation of modern Anuradhapura in the mid–twentieth century to preserve the remaining ruins of the ancient capital. Appropriately, the Archaeological Survey of Ceylon maintains its headquarters in Anuradhapura. Owing to the religious significance of its many monuments, Anuradhapura once again enjoys the distinction of being a major pilgrimage destination for Buddhists. The huge Bo-tree—perhaps the oldest living tree of which there is historical record—continues to flourish and cannot, by tradition, be pruned or plucked; the Ruwanvelisaya Dagaba still dominates the ancient precinct of Anuradhapura.

Unfortunately, the conflict between the Tamil and the Sinhalese continues. Violence again escalated between the two factions following a 1983 ambush of a Sri Lankan army patrol by Tamil secessionists operating in the north of the island, and in May 1985 in Anuradhapura, approximately 150 people, mostly Sinhalese, were massacred by Tamil forces.

Further Reading: *Sri Lanka: A Travel Survival Kit* by Tony Wheeler, John Noble, and Susan Forsyth (fifth edition, Hawthorn, Victoria, and Berkeley, California: Lonely Planet, 1993) deals with the practical aspects of traveling in Sri Lanka. The guide contains a concise history of the country and a description and map of present-day Anuradhapura. *Ceylon* by S. A. Pakeman (New York: Praeger, and London: Benn, 1964) contains a chapter on ancient and medieval Sri Lanka but is, in large part, devoted to the period of British colonization of Ceylon and its independence since 1948. *A History of Sri Lanka* by K. M. De Silva (London: Hurst, and Berkeley and Los Angeles: University of California Press, 1981) is a comprehensivehistory of Sri Lanka from ancient times to the twentieth century. The first section of the book is devoted to the settlement, political history, and structure of the kingdom of Anuradhapura. The influence of Buddhism on Anuradhapura is also discussed.

—Rion Klawinski

Anyang (Henan, China)

Location: In the far north of the central Chinese province of Henan, just south of the Henan/Hebei border; approximately 300 miles south-southeast of Beijing.

Description: The town of Anyang is the site of a rich archaeological find: the remains of the Shang Dynasty capital of Yin. Since its rediscovery in the late nineteenth century, excavations at Anyang have given concrete proof of the existence of the early empire of the Shang (traditional dates, 1766–1122 B.C.). The highly developed bronze artifacts and bone fragments containing early Chinese characters suggest that this is the site of China's oldest civilization.

Contact: Henan Tourism Bureau
16 Jinshui Avenue
450003 Zhengzhou, Henan
China
(371) 5952707

The small town of Anyang was once the site of a Shang Dynasty capital called Yin. Archaeological excavations have uncovered the remains of tombs, palaces, and temples, as well as bronze vessels and bone fragments that have established the Shang Dynasty (1766–1122 B.C.) as the oldest documented Chinese civilization. The area was, however, probably settled well before the Shang, in the days of the Long Shan around 2000 B.C.

Such knowledge of Anyang's history was obscured until the late nineteenth century, when these Shang artifacts were rediscovered. Prior understanding of the dynasty was based on Chinese mythical creation stories. According to tradition, Chinese civilization began with the Three August Ones: Fu Xi, Zhu Zhong, and Shen Nong. These forefathers of the Chinese were followed by Five Sovereigns, among these being Huang Di, the famous Yellow Emperor. These individual god-like figures are the forebears of the first Chinese dynasty, that of the Xia, who are purported to have ruled from 2205 to 1766 B.C. The Three August Ones and the Five Sovereigns are mentioned in several early Chinese historical accounts, but are generally regarded as mythical figures by archaeologists and historians alike. The existence of the Xia, however, is more convincing. Although no archaeological digs have unearthed any substantial evidence in their favor, experts remain unconvinced that the Xia were pure fiction.

The shadowy Xia were overthrown sometime between the nineteenth and the sixteenth centuries B.C. by the onslaught of a warrior people who swept into the Yellow River valley. These new victors ruled the region beginning in 1766 B.C., under the name of Shang (later known as Yin), thus forming the first historically proven unified state of China. Details of the Shang conquest remain a confusing mixture of historical fact and traditional myth. Experts, however, believe their territory existed in modern-day western Henan, and that their first capital was established near what is now the city of Luoyang.

The Shang were an advanced civilization, and their capitals were large cities divided into areas dedicated to religious and administrative activities. The site of Ao, near modern Zhengzhou, is believed to have been the Shang's second capital; it has the remains of an impressive four-and-one-half-mile city wall of pounded earth, some thirty feet high and ranging from sixty-five to one hundred feet wide. The most fantastic remains of the Shang, however, are to be found near Anyang, at a place once called Yin. Historians believe the Shang moved their capital to Yin around 1384 B.C., where it remained until their defeat at the hands of the Western Zhou in 1122 B.C.

The ancient wonders at Anyang lay buried for some 2,000 years, until A.D. 1079. That year, a terrible storm hit the city, driving the residents out of town in search of shelter. When the storm subsided and the people returned, they were astonished to find that a large mound near the city had partially caved in, revealing its hidden contents: a spectacular tomb complete with human remains, splendid bronze vessels, chariots, and the bones of horses. The citizens of Anyang took the bronzes and sold them to collectors, and in A.D. 1092, a Chinese archaeologist recorded the find at the "Mounds of Yin." Not long after these events, the entire site slipped back into obscurity.

The Anyang artifacts resurfaced during the late nineteenth century, when townspeople again began exploiting the mounds as a source of curios to be sold for profit. This time, strange fragments of bones and turtle shells were found, covered with oddly shaped cracks and scratch marks. Sold to a local pharmacist as dragon bones, these fragments were touted as a cure for numerous illnesses. Word of the dragon bones reached the Qing imperial court, and scholars flocked to Anyang to study them. Scholars theorized that the strange scratchings and figures found on the shells and bones might be an early form of Chinese characters. Word of these findings traveled to the West, drawing two foreigners from America and England to the site. They purchased numerous fragments and installed them in the British Museum, as well as museums in Scotland and Chicago.

The archaeological free-for-all was finally stopped in 1927 when China's Academia Sinica claimed the site and began organized excavations. Archaeologists and historians quickly determined that the odd mound outside the town was the fabulous tomb of a Shang Dynasty king, filled with spectacular examples of the earliest known bronze art in the

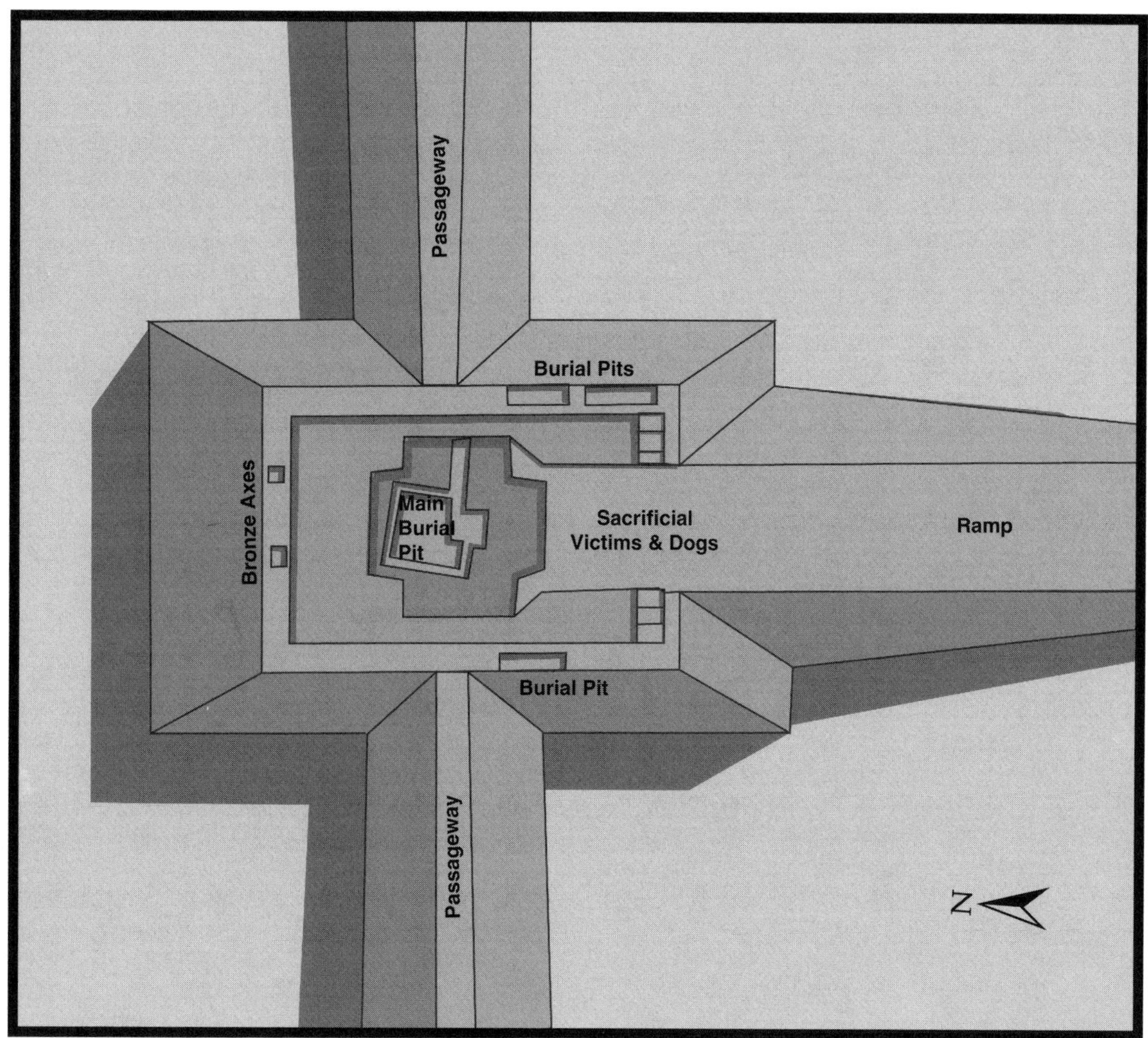

Plan of Shang-era tomb near Anyang
Illustration by Tom Willcockson

country and fragments of the oldest examples of Chinese writing, found on fragments of shell and bone.

The discoveries made at Anyang are staggering; eleven royal tombs have been uncovered, each of tremendous proportions. Located in pits situated some thirty feet below the surface, the tombs range from forty to sixty feet in diameter. To provide access to the pit, each area is reached by two to four ramps, sloping down some one hundred feet. Similar to the royal burial sites of ancient Egypt, the mounds at Anyang are littered with the remains of soldiers and workmen, placed in the tomb perhaps to guard the king in the afterlife, or to keep the location of the site a secret. The sheer size of the tombs and the numbers of the servants accompanying the ruler into the afterlife are indications of the power of the Shang and their ability to command the labor of their subjects, even to the latters' ultimate death.

The bronzes found at the Shang capital of Yin figure among the site's crowning glories. Experts hypothesize that the finely cast vessels were used primarily for ritualistic purposes, such as sacrifices to the dynastic ancestors and gods. Some vessels, however, may have been used to signify the bestowing of royal favor upon a family, such as the appointment of a noble or the granting of lands to a clan.

Many of the vessels found at Anyang bear striking resemblance to the pottery of the earlier Neolithic civilizations, particularly that known as the Long Shan culture. Recent excavations at Anyang have even found remains of Long Shan pottery in the layers of dirt between those containing traces of the city of Yin; the lower and older layers are marked by the even older Yang Shao pottery culture. Further finds of grey Shang Dynasty pottery shards in the layers above black Long Shan shards indicate that Anyang was probably settled long before the Shang arrived, as far back as the Neolithic period of the Long Shan around 2000 B.C.

Owing to the high quality of the bronzes found around Anyang, researchers first believed that bronze casting originated in western Asia and made its way to ancient China, where it was further refined. Recent excavations, however, have uncovered thinner and more primitive bronze artifacts. These less dignified bronzes suggest that bronze casting was independently initiated and refined in China and perfected by the craftsmen of the Shang era. In fact, the bronze work done by the Shang is unequaled by any other Bronze Age society. Numerous tools and weapons have been unearthed at Anyang, but the greatest treasures are the ceremonial pieces that vary in size from small goblets to huge cauldrons weighing over 1,500 pounds. Cast from clay molds and decorated with geometric designs, the bronze pieces that remain are outstanding examples of this highly advanced art.

Other bronze artifacts found in the tombs at Yin include spears and axes, which may have been used in the ceremonial decapitation of the people buried in the tombs with the Shang rulers. These victims, usually in groups of ten, are believed to have been Shang prisoners of war or captives from outlying nomadic tribes. The wooden chariots found in several of the Shang burial mounds have fine bronze fittings for both the chariot itself and the horses' harnesses. Although no bows have actually been found at the Anyang site (bows made of wood or horn would have decayed long ago), etchings on bronze vessels portray these Shang weapons to be compound in style. A powerful compound bow used in conjunction with the chariots known to exist at the time would have helped make the Shang a formidable military force. One weapon found in particularly large numbers is the Chinese ge, or halberd. The halberd consisted of a blade mounted on a shaft. Both military halberds and ceremonial ones made with jade blades have been found in the Yin mounds.

Possibly the most exciting discovery made at the ancient Shang capital, however, has been the so-called "dragon bones," now known to have been an integral part of the ancient divination process known as scapulimancy. The practice of scapulimancy in China is thought to date back even earlier, perhaps as early as 6000 B.C. Seeking to know the future, early Chinese priests took animals' bones, primarily the scapulas (shoulder blades), and applied intense heat to points along the bones. They then read the cracks that resulted from the heat in order to foretell the future.

By the time of the Shang some several thousand years later, the practice of divination using bones had changed slightly. The Shang used both shoulder-blade bones and the lower halves of tortoise shells (plastrons), cutting a slight hollow into one side of the fragment. A question was posed, and then heat was applied to the fragment using a sharp bronze point. The bone or shell then cracked, generally one long line with a smaller crack heading off the larger line at an angle. This cracking pattern is reflected in the Chinese character bu (卜), meaning to divine or foretell. Despite the thousands of fragments that remain, experts are uncertain as to how the cracks were interpreted and what angles indicated favorable or negative responses.

The fragments remaining from pre-Shang scapulimancy bear only the resulting cracks. With the advent of Shang civilization, however, characters were inscribed on the surface of the fragments, briefly indicating the question posed by the priest. Occasionally, the script provides the result of the divination, and still more rarely the actual outcome of the event in question. Since the king was the only person empowered to interpret the cracks, it is not surprising that these accounts almost always assert the accuracy of the forecast.

The questions given to the oracles dealt primarily with crops, military battles, rain, and royal concerns. From the thousands of remaining oracle bones with inscriptions detailing questions about sacrifices to ancestors, historians have been able to verify the lineage of Shang kings. The names of the Shang rulers had long been known as part of China's quasi-mythical past, but the artifacts at Anyang lent credibility to their existence. An integral part of Chinese religious practices has always been the worship of ancestral spirits, treating the dead like an all-knowing deity. Bones with inscriptions asking if a sacrifice will be acceptable to an ancestral spirit have served to corroborate the historical list of Shang rulers, even showing that the capital at Anyang itself was founded by the Shang king Pan Geng.

With the extensive excavations at Anyang, archaeologists have unearthed some 100,000 bone and shell fragments used in scapulimancy. Of this number, some 15,000 have been studied in detail, resulting in the identification of approximately 5,000 different Chinese characters used by the Shang. Unfortunately, only about 1,500 of these known characters have been decoded. Massive reforms under the Legalist Li Si during the Qin Dynasty (221–206 B.C.) radically altered the Chinese writing system, effectively erasing the meaning of numerous Shang inscriptions. They remain, however, as evidence of a highly evolved system of writing, which indicates that the Shang were the first literate people in Eastern Asia.

Many of the mounds surrounding Anyang had been plundered during the centuries between their construction by the Shang, their discovery in the eleventh century, and their rediscovery in the late nineteenth century. Although the items taken from the tombs are a great loss to historians, the artifacts that remain have helped archaeologists and historians piece together life as it must have been under the Shang. Similar to later dynasties, the Shang were feudal in nature, partitioning the empire into small fiefs ruled by lords and powerful families. The economy was based primarily on agriculture and the production of wheat, millet, and rice. Animals were kept, but their contribution to the society was minimal. Although they were hunters, the Shang appear to have hunted as much for sport and maintaining military prowess as to supplement the diet of the people.

The dynasty's rulers were often engaged in conflict with the tribes of barbarians (as non-Chinese were referred to) who inhabited adjacent lands. The Shang forces were armed with powerful compound bows and numerous chariots, used primarily to transport troops to the battlefields. Records indicate that the dynastic ruler frequently conscripted thousands of men to fight for the Shang, allowing the dynasty to maintain its territory along the Yellow River in modern-day Henan perhaps as far as the Yangtze River basin.

This ability to command the Shang people, in battle, in labor (such as the building of elaborate tombs), and in the practice of accompanying the king in death, was perhaps the dynasty's greatest accomplishment. The worship of ancestors was a powerful mechanism used to maintain a cohesive society; the dynasty used this religion to define a cultural system based on dependency and obligation. Without this central strength, it is doubtful that the Shang would have made such great technical and cultural advances.

The remains of the Shang capital at Yin (modern-day Anyang) have proven to be a truly remarkable find. The beautiful bronzework and thousands of shards left from a mysterious system of divination have given historical and archaeological evidence as to the actual existence of the ancient Shang, once thought to be only a mythical people in China's shadowy and extensive past.

Further Reading: For information on the ancient empires of China, see Leonard Cottrell's *The Tiger of Ch'in: The Dramatic Emergence of China as a Nation* (New York: Holt Rinehart, 1962; with subtitle *How China Became a Nation,* London: Evans, 1962). William Watson's *China: Before the Han Dynasty* (New York: Praeger, and London: Thames and Hudson, 1961) provides an account of early China emphasizing archaeological finds. Books detailing China's extensive past include Robert Silverberg's *The Great Wall of China* (Philadelphia: Chilton, 1965); *The Chinese: Their History and Culture* by Kenneth Scott Latourette (2 vols., New York: Macmillan, 1934; fourth edition, 1964); and Charles O. Hucker's brief but concise *China to 1850: A Short History* (Stanford, California: Stanford University Press, 1978). Additional information on China's rich cultural heritage may be found in Scott Morton's *China: Its History and Culture* (New York: Lippincott and Crowell, 1980; third edition, New York: McGraw-Hill, 1995).

—Monica Cable

Ayers Rock (Northern Territory, Australia)

Location: The Ayers Rock resort is in the township of Yulara on the edge of Uluru National Park in the Northern Territory in Australia's vast Outback. Permits are required in order to visit Aboriginal lands in this part of the country.

Description: An immense rock formation, important in Aboriginal lore and one of the most sacred Aboriginal sites.

Site Office: Ayers Rock Resort
P. O. Box 46
Yulara, Northern Territory 0872
Australia
(89) 546 2144

Australia is one of the world's oldest continents, and Ayers Rock one of its most unusual formations. With its eerie and otherworldly shapes and its immense physical presence, Ayers Rock, or Uluru, often is called the spiritual heart of Australia. Thousands of people from all over the world visit it each year. For both Aborigine and non-Aborigine it is a special place of pilgrimage.

Ayers Rock is one of the most sacred of Aboriginal sites. According to Aboriginal myth, it was the scene of great battles, from which great heroes emerged. The most important struggle took place between the Liru, or poisonous snake people, and the Kunia, or carpet snake people. This battle, so Aboriginal legend goes, resulted in the creation of the rock. The story of the battle is part of the body of Aboriginal creation mythology known as the Dreaming.

The Dreaming refers to a time before people had arrived on the continent. The Sky Heroes, the greatest of Aboriginal heroes, created all the natural features of the earthly landscape. In their time, the desert that is now the vast Australian Outback was a fertile garden, with rivers trailing through what are now dry beds. Eventually, the heroes came down from their home in the gum trees, attracted as they were by the green landscape that they saw below. The pillar-like gum trees, however, held up the sky, and when the heroes climbed down from their berths, the trees disappeared.

Where the gum trees had been, there was left a small hole in the sky that became larger and larger. The land was racked alternately by floods and droughts. The time of plenty was over, and the early inhabitants had to learn how to adapt to a harsh, dry climate.

Two of the groups of Sky Heroes were the Kunia and the Mala, or hare-wallaby people, who occupied, respectively, what are now the shady and sunny sides of Ayers Rock (which did not exist at this time). Both groups were invited to attend a youth initiation ceremony by the Mulga, or seed people, who lived far to the west in the Petermann Mountains. The Kunia set out for the Petermanns, and on the first night of their journey they rested at a waterhole that is now a deep basin on the summit of the rock. Here they met and were attracted to a group of women, known as the Sleepy Lizard Women. They decided to settle down and marry these women and forgo the trip to the Mulga's ceremony.

The Mulga began to wonder about the Kunia's whereabouts; furthermore, they needed the Kunia's assistance in their ceremony. They sent Panpanpalana, the bell bird, to find them. The Kunia, however, did not want to leave their new wives. Meanwhile, the Mala had declined to attend the Mulga's ceremony because they were busy with initiation rites of their own, and they reiterated this to the bell bird. Offended, the Mulga decided that both the Mala and the Kunia should be punished. They sent a devil-dog to attack and kill the Mala and sent another group of Sky People, the Liru, to make war upon the Kunia. The Liru defeated the Kunia in a tremendous battle in which both groups' leaders were killed, and then set fire to the home of the Sleepy Lizard Women. The survivors among the Kunia all committed suicide by the rather unusual method of singing themselves to death. These events caused such great disruptions in the earth that Uluru, or Ayers Rock, rose from the ashes of the Lizard Women's camp.

Many of the physical features of Ayers Rock are said to represent events in the battle. Three holes high on the rock, so the legend goes, mark the spot where Ungata, the Kunia leader, bled to death. Rainwater that fills them now is believed to be his transubstantiated blood. A formation at the head of Mutitjilda Gorge represents the severed nose of Kulikitjeri, the Lira leader. Three cuts into the rock's eastern face recall the wounds given Kulikitjeri by Ungata. Not far from them is a cave identified as the womb of a woman who gave birth during the battle; a stone at the entrance symbolizes her child.

These legendary associations gave Ayers Rock profound significance for Australia's Aborigines. The Rainbow Snake, an intermediary between the earthly and the divine, is believed to sleep in Mutitjilda Gorge. According to an Aboriginal belief identifying the continent with the human body, the rock is the navel—the center of the universe.

Tribal and territorial, the Aborigines encountered a great deal of misunderstanding among the whites who began to settle in Australia in the late eighteenth century, when the British established penal colonies there. The Aborigines were divided into innumerable tribes, and they had no king or formal system of government, at least not one that Europeans understood. Rather, each tribe was united by language, religion, and a body of myths and rituals. The tribes were no-

Ayers Rock, Australia
Photo courtesy of Australian Tourist Commission, Los Angeles

madic and did not have a Western conception of property ownership; the land belonged more to their legendary ancestors than to anyone in the modern era. This attitude, unfortunately, opened the door to wholesale confiscation of Aboriginal lands by the new white settlers.

The area around Ayers Rock has long been inhabited by the Anangu, one of the most isolated of the Aboriginal tribes. They managed to avoid contact with whites for many years. William Gosse was the first white explorer to visit Ayers Rock. Gosse arrived on July 19, 1873. and gave the rock its name, honoring Sir Henry Ayers, governor of South Australia. Gosse called Ayers Rock "the most wonderful natural feature I have ever seen." The prominent explorer Earnest Giles came a year later. Others would soon follow in their footsteps—day laborers, prospectors searching for gold, scientists, anthropologists, government officials, and, inevitably, tourists.

In 1894 Baldwin Spencer, a professor of biology at Melbourne University, took the first full photographic view of the rock. He described it as "a huge dome-shaped monolith, brilliant venetian red in colour . . . that rises precipitously to a height of eleven hundred feet above the plain . . . ."

By 1900 gold was discovered not far from the rock, around Alice Springs. Over the next several decades prospectors came from all over Australia to find the elusive substance. A prospector named Harold Lasseter led an expedition in 1930 that took him to Ayers Rock. Leaving his party and setting out on his own, he wandered west of the rock but found no gold. Instead he collapsed and died near a creek. Eventually his body and diary were recovered.

In the meantime, the relationship between Aboriginal and European cultures became increasingly strained as more white immigrants settled in what were once Aboriginal lands. The new arrivals also brought with them Western diseases, such as smallpox, measles, and venereal disease, that brought suffering and death to the native population. Frequent violent skirmishes broke out between the Aborigines and the settlers, especially during the 1880s and as recently as the early twentieth century. The battles ultimately failed to help the Aborigines' cause.

Government policy regarding Aboriginal issues has changed frequently over the years. Around the beginning of the twentieth century, Aborigines were segregated into reserves—one of which included Ayers Rock—and their rights to own property and seek employment were restricted. After World War II, the government pursued an assimilation policy. Aborigines were forced to move to townships where, presumably, acclimation to the majority culture would lead to a smoother and faster transition. Unfortunately, assimilation often meant the subjugation of their own ancient traditions and dependence on the state.

Gradually, however, conditions in the Aboriginal communities began to improve. In 1969 Aborigines were given the right to vote and, for the first time in Australian history, they were counted in the federal census as full-fledged Australian citizens. Assimilation officially ended and was replaced by a policy that encouraged self-determination for Aborigines, who began to assume control of the reserve lands. Some white interests, particularly mining companies, are still in conflict with the Aborigines over certain lands, and Aborigines continue to meet resistance when they attempt to assert their rights. Yet, the Aboriginal rights movement has gathered strength in the late twentieth century.

Ayers Rock has changed possession a few times. In the late 1950s the Rock and nearby lands were removed from the Aboriginal reserve and turned into a national park. The "handback," as it was called, of Ayers Rock to the traditional owners did not actually occur until 1985. At that point Ayers Rock became known by its Aboriginal name, Uluru. Aborigines and non-Aborigines now jointly manage the national park. Today more than 30 percent of land in the vast Northern Territory belongs to the Aborigines.

One of the most famous incidents at the rock in modern times involved the death of Azaria Chamberlain, the infant daughter of Lindy and Michael Chamberlain, who were camping in the park in August 1980. One night a dingo, the wild dog that is indigenous to Australia, entered the Chamberlains' tent and carried the baby into the night. The Chamberlains were convicted of murdering their daughter in a trial that became a national obsession. Ultimately, however, a Royal Commission overturned the verdict.

Ayers Rock has remained one of the most popular of Australian sites—tourists flock to it by the thousands every year. But it also continues to be the most sacred of Aboriginal sites. Both Aborigines and non-Aborigines acknowledge its immense presence and the special place it holds in Australian history.

Further Reading: James G. Cowan, *The Elements of the Aborigine Tradition* (Rockport, Massachusetts: Element, 1994) explores Aboriginal heritage, myth, and culture. Barry Hill's *The Rock: Travelling to Uluru* (St. Leonards, New South Wales: Allen and Unwin, 1994) is a perceptive combination of travel guide and cultural exploration. Although Hill tells the story of Uluru from an Aboriginal perspective, commenting on modern Aboriginal culture and lore, he is not afraid to offer his own opinions on the changes that have taken place within the community around the rock. For another personal view of Aboriginal culture, see Bruce Chatwin's *The Songlines* (Franklin Center, Pennsylvania: Franklin Library, New York: Viking, and London: Cape, 1987). The definitive study of early Australia is *The Fatal Shore: A History of the Transportation of Convicts to Australia, 1787–1868* by Robert Hughes (New York: Knopf, 1986; London: Collins Harvill, 1987) a detailed, compelling account of Australia's convict past.

—June Skinner Sawyers

Ayodhyā (Uttar Pradesh, India)

Location: On the south bank of the Ghāghara River, a tributary of the Ganges, in the state of Uttar Pradesh in India; adjacent to the city of Faizābād.

Description: A modern city, better known as the traditional birthplace of Rāma, the hero of the ancient Indian Sanskrit epic *Rāmāyaṇa,* and thus a major center of pilgrimage for the Hindus. Also, a large early historic city site with clear archaeological and literary references taking its history of occupation to at least 600 B.C.

Contact: Government of India Tourist Office
15B, The Mall
Vārānasī, Uttar Pradesh 221 002
India
43744

Ayodhyā is a holy city of the Hindus. Traditionally it has been considered the birthplace of Rāma, the hero of the Sanskrit epic *Rāmāyaṇa,* which was set down as a text between the late centuries B.C. and the early centuries A.D. Rāma's divine status springs from the tradition that he was an incarnation of Vishnu, one of the three principal gods (the other two being Brahmā and Siva) upholding the Hindu universe. Traditionally Ayodhyā was also the capital of the mythical Ikshvaku Dynasty, which in turn belonged to the Solar Race of the Hindu cosmogony. Rāma's father, Daśaratha, was an Ikshvaku king who sent his eldest son, Rāma, into exile for fourteen years to keep his promise to one of his three queens (who wanted the kingdom to go to her own son) that he would grant her whatever she asked for. Rāma was accompanied into exile by his wife, Sītā, and one of his stepbrothers, Lakṣmaṇa. Sītā was abducted by the ten-headed king of Lanka (generally identified with modern Sri Lanka), and to get her back Rāma was helped by an army of monkeys under the great monkey-hero Hanumān, who as a supreme devotee of Rāma enjoys divine status in modern Hinduism. The *Rāmāyaṇa* revolves around the story of Rāma's battle against Rāvaṇa, his triumph and recovery of Sītā, and eventual return to and reign in Ayodhyā.

Ayodhyā is prominent in the Buddhist and Jain texts as well. In the early Buddhist literature, dating from approximately 600 to 200 B.C., Ayodhyā—or to be accurate, the ancient city of Sāketa, which has been identified with Ayodhyā—is mentioned as a place where the Buddha spent some time, and in the tradition of the Jains a few *Tīrthankaras,* or preceptors with divine status, have been associated with the site. Finally, Ayodhyā contains some mosques and burial grounds of a few Muslim saints, and thus is important to Muslims as well.

Ayodhyā's importance extends beyond religion, however. Its location on the network of early historic trade routes of the Ganges Valley, especially on the bank of a major river such as the Ghāghara and in the same geographical zone as two other major contemporary cities, Sravasti (modern Saheth-Maheth, about fifty miles to the north) and Kashi (modern Vārānasī, downstream on the Ganges, which is joined by the Ghāghara), helped it to emerge as a major commercial and administrative center of early northern India. It is primarily in this capacity that Sāketa or Ayodhyā is known in the early Buddhist literature. This literature also tells us that Sāketa was the earlier capital of the kingdom of Kośala, the later one being Sravasti.

In any complex historical situation of this kind, sources and traditions are not always coherent. Two issues that immediately confront scholars are whether the ancient Buddhist city of Sāketa and Rāma's birthplace Ayodhyā refer to the same place, and whether Ayodhyā, as described in the *Rāmāyaṇa,* was really an earthly city and not a mythical or heavenly one. With regard to the first problem, the early Buddhist literature makes fifty-four references to Sāketa, compared to only three references to Ayodhyā. Most of those who have examined the related historical and geographical issues agree that these places were the same. In any case, it is probable that only after the consolidation of Rāma worship in Hinduism, which must have been a long historical process, the name Ayodhyā came to be applied to the modern Faizābād-Ayodhyā area as a whole. Two promontories jut out into the Ghāghara at this point; now one is called Faizābād and the other Ayodhyā. There is no reason to assume that the total area of these two adjacent promontories could not have been considered a single locality during the ancient period.

The second issue is more complex and stems from the mention of Ayodhyā in a text that is earlier than either the early Buddhist literature or the epic *Rāmāyaṇa*. The *Taittiriya Āranyaka,* part of the Vedic prose literature, describes Ayodhya as a celestial city with nine gates, eight circular enclosures, and a pool of nectar. The description in the *Rāmāyaṇa* (sixth canto of Book I), on the other hand, more accurately reflects a real city. The earlier description as a celestial city notwithstanding, Ayodhyā need not be considered a mythical city.

The earliest non-mythological description of the site occurs in the early Buddhist literature. As Sāketa it figures as the older capital of the kingdom of Kośala and one of the six great cities of India during the time of the Buddha. Sāketa lay on the Ganges trade route between eastern India and the northwestern portion of the subcontinent, and also on one particular route between the Ganges Valley and the Deccan. The Buddha is said to have stayed in two groves near the city, one with a deer park attached to it. That not everything about

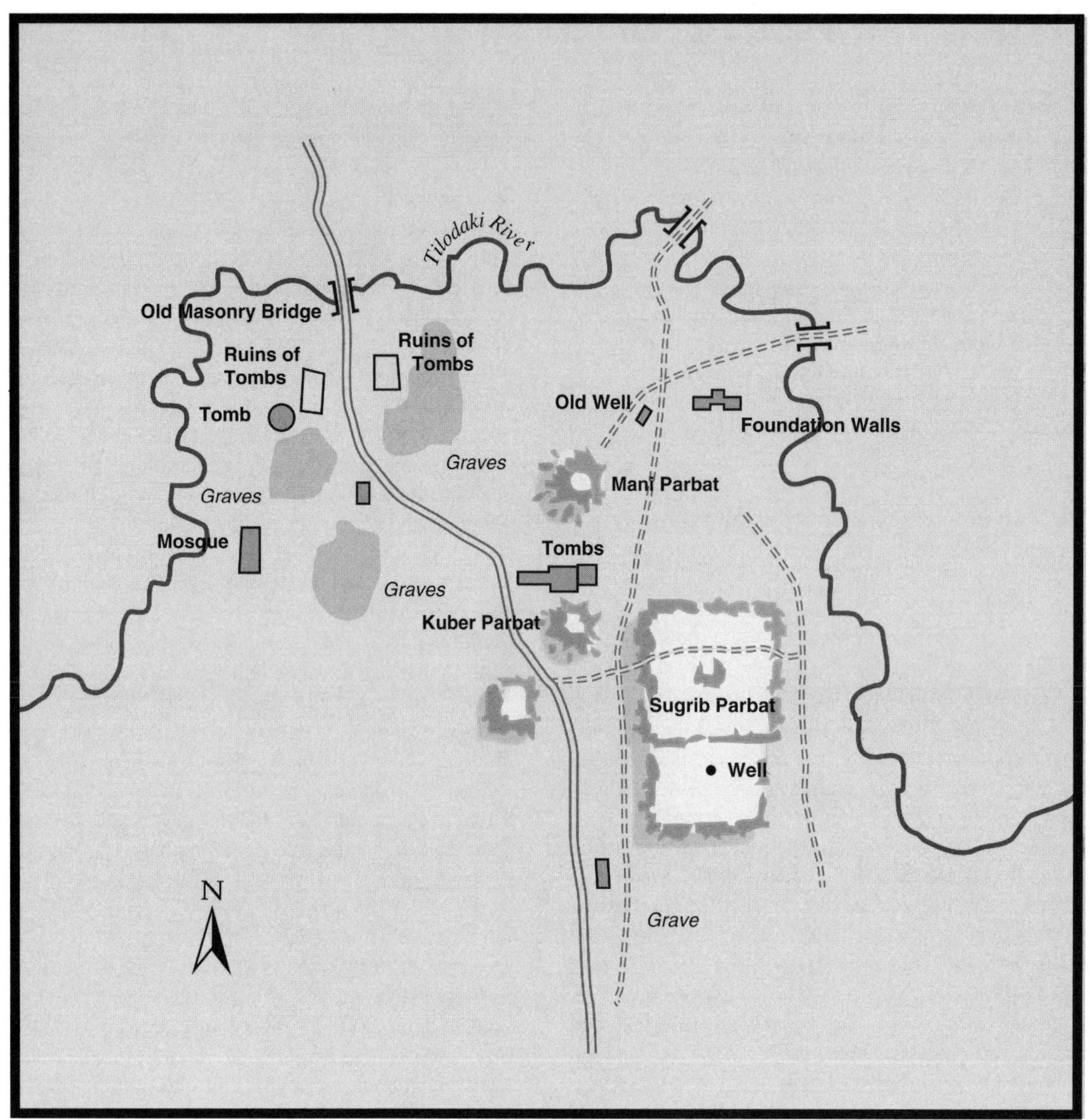

Site plan of the area around the Buddhist mounds, Ayodhyā
Illustration by Tom Willcockson

ancient Sāketa was holy is suggested by an allusion to the introduction of alcohol there soon after the substance was discovered.

Archaeology has substantially filled in the general picture of an early historic city at the site of modern Ayodhyā. The earliest evidence goes back to the period known as that of the Northern Black Polished Ware in the Ganges Valley archaeological sequence, the beginning of which in this region is now placed in the seventh century B.C. This was the time of the first phase of urban growth in India, and although any direct archaeological evidence of the period from Ayodhyā is scanty, the size of the site itself demonstrates that it was a major city, thus confirming the early Buddhist record in this case. The old ruins here have a circuit of two and one-half to three miles, rising in places to the imposing height of about 30 feet from the level of the surrounding plain. In the available maps of the site appears a large mound segment known as Ramkot (roughly 3,000 by 2,500 feet), which likely covered an area of approximately 200 acres. To the south of this area, across the Tilodaki stream that joins the Ghāghara downstream of Ayodhyā, a cluster of ancient but much smaller mounds are interspersed with Muslim tombs and at least one mosque. These mounds are locally known as Mani Parbat (more than 65 feet high), Kuber Parbat (about 30 feet high), and Sugrib Parbat (about 10 feet high). The first two mounds represented Buddhist stupas (shrines), whereas the third one could be a Buddhist monastery. The image of a large city site during the Buddhist period is complete—a large residential, commercial, and administrative complex with some stupa and monastic ruins outside the urban limits.

Although excavations have been conducted in as many as fourteen portions of the modern settlement of Ayodhyā, these have been attempts to determine only the vertical sequence of occupation at the site. Thus archaeology has not contributed substantially to the history of the site from phase to phase. The earliest phase, as previously noted, dates to the seventh century B.C. and consists of only wattle-and-daub and mud and mud-brick houses. A massive wall of burned bricks belonging to this phase and discovered in the western part of the Ramkot mound may be tentatively identified with the ancient fortification wall of the city. Mud-brick houses found immediately below this wall strongly suggest that the fortification wall was built sometime after the site was occupied. A deep ditch was cut into the natural clay outside the fortification wall.

The post-fortification phase of the site began during the third century B.C. and continued up to the fourth century A.D. and later. One excavator contends the site was deserted between the fifth and eleventh centuries A.D., but this is unlikely because all other known major Ganges Valley settlements have been occupied continuously and because the excavation trenches in this case were laid in an area that, according to some earlier reports, had been thoroughly plundered for bricks; vertical trenches laid in brick-robbed mounds cannot tell the complete story of habitation. The antiquities found in the early historic levels comprise a few inscribed terra-cotta seals, about seventy coins, and more than 100 terra-cotta sculptures, including one of a Jain monk. Coming from the fourth-century B.C. level, this may be the earliest representation of a Jain monk. One of the inscribed terra-cotta sealings belongs to King Dhanadeva of Ayodhyā, who reigned during the second century B.C., and one of the coins belongs to the Ayodhyan king Mūladeva of the same general period. The variety of terra-cotta types is similar to that found in other Ganges Valley sites, but a notable find from the first century A.D. is that of some Rouletted Ware shards that are associated with the Indo-Roman trade. This is the first time that these shards have been found so far inland, thus providing evidence of the commercial importance of the site as mentioned in the early Buddhist records.

The rest of the information up to the end of the ancient period in the history of Ayodhyā does not come from archaeological excavations but partly from coins, partly from inscriptions, and largely from literary allusions.

The coins found at random fall into three classes. The first and earliest class consists of three types. The first type has a plain reverse but a flower on the obverse and may even be an ornament. There is a swastika sign on the obverse of the second type, which bears on the reverse a stylized flower motif. The third type of this class of coins shows on its obverse a swastika sign over a fish and on the reverse a crescent or taurine symbol shown along with an axe or steelyard. The steelyard sign indicates that these were local coins, not dynastic or royal issues. All three types of coin in this category, apparently the earliest issued in Ayodhyā, are believed to date to the third century B.C.

The two other classes of Ayodhyā coins were issued by two different dynasties. The coins of the rulers of the first dynasty, who have their names inscribed on these coins—Mūladeva, Vāyudeva, Viśākhadeva, Dhanadeva, Śivadatta and Naradatta—are broadly similar: silver, square in shape, with a bull or occasionally an elephant on the obverse and a group of five or six symbols on the reverse. These coins are believed to come from the first two centuries B.C. The coins of the presumably later dynasty—probably from the first two centures A.D.—are round die-struck pieces of silver, generally with a bull before a standard or a spear on the obverse and a bird or palm tree by a river on the reverse. The rulers who issued these coins were Satyamitra, Aryamitra, Samghamitra, Vijayamitra, Kumudasena, Ajavarman, and Devamitra. The coins indicate that the city did not lose its significance during the period from the end of the fortification phase in the third century B.C. to the beginning of the dynastic period of the Guptas in the beginning of the fourth century A.D. If one of the coins is truly a city coin, as one hypothesis holds, Ayodhya may even have gained economic importance, since only a major commercial city would have issued its own coins. Moreover, that Ayodhyā was the capital of a succession of regional kings means that the site preserved a distinctive identity even after the Ganges Valley came under the influence of the better known and much stronger dynasties of the Suṇgas, Kanvas, and Kushāns between the second century B.C. and the second century A.D.

In addition to coins, a significant find is a two-line inscription on a stone slab, discovered near modern Ayodhyā, that belongs to the time of Pushyamitra, founder of the Suṇga Dynasty in the second century B.C. The inscription records the erection of a shrine or some other memorial in honor of Phalgudēva, the father of Dhana, who is mentioned as the lord of the kingdom of Kośala and the sixth son of Pushyamitra. Another clear record is the mention of Ayodhyā or Sāketa as "Sagoda" (the Greek version of Sāketa) in Ptolemy's *Geography* of the second century A.D. This classical reference fits in with the find of the Rouletted Ware shards related to the Indo-Roman trade in the first-century A.D. level of the site.

According to one tradition, early in the second half of the fifth century A.D. the Gupta monarch Skanda Gupta shifted his dynastic capital from Patna to Ayodhyā. This tradition is not corroborated by other sources, but even if Ayodhyā did not become the capital of the Guptas from the reign of Skanda Gupta onward, it certainly was an important administrative center of the Gupta Empire. Fa Xian, a Chinese Buddhist pilgrim in India in the early fifth century A.D., mentions Ayodhyā as Sha-Chi, and describes some of its stupas, but a more detailed record is available in the account of another Chinese Buddhist pilgrim, Xuan Zang, who visited India in the seventh century A.D. The kingdom of which Ayodhyā was capital during Xuan Zang's time was prosperous, and the city itself contained 100 Buddhist monasteries, 3,000 Buddhist priests, and 10 Hindu temples. He refers to a stupa and a monastery built by the Mauryan king Aśoka of the third century B.C., and another stupa built over the Buddha's relics. He also mentions a mango grove to the northwest where Asanga, the elder brother of the famous fifth-century A.D. Buddhist teacher Vasubandhu, lived and taught, and a monastery associated with Vasubandhu himself.

For several centuries after the end of the Gupta period in the sixth century A.D., Ayodhyā languished in obscurity. Its political role was taken over by the new city of Kanauj, which became the capital of the numerous minor kingdoms that ruled the area. Ayodhyā was alternately under the control of these minor monarchs or local chieftains. It remained an important religious center, however, and enjoyed a period of renewed growth as part of the new Hindu kingdom of Kanauj during the second half of the eleventh century. The area at this time was attracting Muslim invaders, and Quṭb-ud-Dīn-Aybak conquered Ayodhyā in the late twelfth century. Ayodhyā became capital of the province of Oudh. The city and province were under the control of a succession of Muslim rulers for the next several centuries. During the second half of the fourteenth century, however, Ayodhyā lost its importance to the neighboring Jaunpur, which became the center of a ruling group for some time.

In the first half of the sixteenth century, Ayodhyā and Oudh were contested between the Afghan nobility, who had gained the area through marriage and inheritance, and a rising new power, the Mughals. The Mughals did not gain permanent control of Ayodhyā until 1559, but during a period of temporary possession of the city, in 1528, the first Mughal emperor, Bābur, had a mosque built at the spot traditionally considered to be the birthplace of Rāma. During the reign of Akbar (1556–1605), Ayodhyā was a Mughal mint-town and formed part of a Mughal administrative province. Akbar occasionally had to put down uprisings by rebellious subordinates who governed Ayodhyā, but he managed to maintain control of the city and province. The later Mughal records say little about Ayodhyā, which no doubt continued to be the provincial capital.

With the Mughal Empire in decline by the beginning of the eighteenth century, a new independent kingdom of Oudh emerged with Lucknow as its principal center of government. Faizābād, the locality or town that is adjacent to Ayodhyā, was built by a ruler of this kingdom, Safdar Jang, who died in 1754. His son Shujā-'ud-Dawlah made Faizābād his permanent residence, but after his death in 1775 the capital of Oudh permanently shifted to Lucknow. Faizābād was given to a lady of the royal family. After her death in 1818, Faizābād declined in importance until 1856, when Oudh was annexed by the British and Faizābād became their headquarters. With the takeover of Oudh, Ayodhyā, now administratively joined to Faizābād, also came under British rule. Ayodhyā-Faizābād formed a major center of the Indian Mutiny of 1857–58, when Indian troops rebelled against the British; the garrison there maintained possession of the area for several months before the British reclaimed it. After the revolt was put down, little of note occurred in Ayodhyā until the beginning of the controversy leading to the demolition of the mosque built by Bābur on December 6, 1992.

This controversy had its roots in Ayodhyā's central role in the worship of Rāma. The Rāma cult was well established by the middle of the second century A.D. Even during Ayodhyā's period of historical obscurity in the early Middle Ages, the city remained an important Hindu pilgrimage center, a role that may even have intensified during this era. Evidence of this is found in a Sanskrit text, *Ayodhyāmahatmyam,* which describes the religious glories of ancient Hindu pilgrim spots; the earliest available version of this text dates from at least as far back as the thirteenth century. Moreover, King Chandradeva of the Gāhaḍavāla Dynasty visited Ayodhyā and worshiped Vishnu in the eleventh century, and a temple in honor of Vishnu was constructed here by another Gāhaḍavāla king a century later. An inscription originally set in the walls of the temple it describes but recovered recently from the demolished walls of Bābur's mosque provides further evidence that there was a temple dedicated to Vishnu, incarnated as Rāma, on the same site as the mosque.

The demolition of this mosque by the Hindus on December 6, 1992, was the culmination of a lengthy dispute between India's Hindus and Muslims. The existence of a mosque at this Hindu sacred place was a bone of contention between the two communities during British rule, a particularly virulent episode of which was recorded in 1855. Up to the period of the 1857 rebellion, both Hindus and Muslims worshiped in the same building, but after 1857 an outer enclosure was put up for the Hindus to use, and the inner enclosure was now reserved for Muslims.

Bitterness between these two groups continued into the twentieth century, especially after India won its independence in 1947. Hindu idols were placed under the central dome of the mosque on December 23, 1949. The very next day, to maintain peace, the premises were attached by the government under a provision of the Indian Criminal Procedure Act. In January 1950, a civil judge passed interim orders preventing the removal of Hindu idols or interfering with their worship. Then in April 1955, these orders were confirmed by the High Court. Legal disputes between Muslims and Hindus over the property continued into the 1980s and 1990s, but the courts generally upheld the Hindus' right to worship there. In October 1991, Hindus unsuccessfully tried to begin construction of a temple on a plot of adjacent land acquired by the provincial government of Uttar Pradesh. On December 6, 1992, the mosque was torn down by a Hindu mob, even though their right to use the property had won legal sanction. The federal government has since promised to rebuild the mosque and put up a Hindu shrine adjacent to it, but how this aspect of the history of Ayodhyā develops in the future remains an open question.

Further Reading: The most useful introduction is *Ayodhyā* by Hans Bakker (Groningen: Egbert Forsten, 1986). Bakker is more at home among Sanskrit texts than history or archaeology, but his book carries an excellent set of maps of the site. For archaeology, see *An Encyclopaedia of Indian Archaeology,* volume 2, edited by A. Ghosh (Delhi: Munshiram Manoharlal Publishers, 1989). For general historical notes, see K. T. S. Sarao's *Urban Centres and Urbanisation as Reflected in the Pāli Vinaya and Sutta Piṭakas* (Delhi: Vidyanidhi, 1990). The basic data regarding the Muslim and British periods have been incorporated in H. R. Nevill's *Fyzabad: A Gazetteer, Being Volume XLIII of the District Gazetteers of the United Provinces of Agra and Oudh* (Allahabad: Government Press, United Provinces, 1905). For an assessment of the Rama situation, see A. M. Shastri's "Ayodhyā and God Rāma" in *Puratattva: Bulletin of the Indian Archaeological Society* (New Delhi), No. 23 (1992–93).

—Dilip K. Chakrabarti

Ayutthaya (Ayutthaya, Thailand)

Location: In central Thailand, approximately forty-five miles north of Bangkok, on an island encircled by three conjoined rivers: the Chao Phraya, the Pa Sak, and the Lopburi.

Description: Capital of an early Thai state, the kingdom of Ayutthaya (later called Siam) from 1350 to 1767. Ayutthaya's first king, Ramathibodi, founded the city in 1350 as the capital of his new Thai kingdom. By 1438, Ayutthaya emerged as a major Southeast Asian power after extending control over the rival Thai state of Sukhothai. Conflict with its western neighbor Burma (modern Myanmar) erupted in the mid–sixteenth century, and the city fell under Burmese rule until it won independence at the Battle of Nong Sarai in 1592. The rejuvenated kingdom attracted European traders to the city, where a considerable foreign population resided. Burma renewed attacks on Ayutthaya in 1765 and captured the city in 1767, destroying ancient religious monuments and taking residents prisoner. Siam's capital transferred downriver to Bangkok. Today Ayutthaya has grown into a modest provincial city whose surviving ruins and restored temples attract visitors seeking Thailand's *Krung Kao* (Ancient Capital).

Site Office: Tourism Authority of Thailand (TAT)
Si Sanphet Road.
Amphoe Phra Nakhon Si Ayutthaya
Phra Nakhon Si Ayutthaya 13000
Thailand
(35) 246 076 7

Ayutthaya preceded Bangkok as the capital of the Thai kingdom that would become Siam. Formally known as Phra Nakhon Si Ayutthaya (Sacred City of Ayutthaya), the city flourished for 400 years, from its founding in 1350 to its near destruction by invading Burmese in 1767. During this period, Ayutthaya reigned as Siam's preeminent city: it was an architectural showplace, a bustling center of international trade, and home to the royal court. Although the city lost its capital status to Bangkok after the Burmese conquest, Ayutthaya continues to symbolize a glorious period of economic, military, and artistic achievement in Thai history.

The Thai people established themselves in Southeast Asia over several centuries before Ayutthaya emerged as the first true Thai empire and the seed of the modern Thai nation. Scholars have concluded that the Thais originally migrated to present-day Thailand from southern China's Yunnan region. By the mid–thirteenth century, groups of Thais had settled an area from the Yunnan plateau to Southeast Asia's lower river valleys. In the hilly uplands, Thai villages banded together in small political units whose concerns centered chiefly on internal affairs and conflicts with neighboring Thai rulers. As Thais expanded farther southward into the Menam and Chao Phraya River valleys, they mixed with and eventually conquered the area's Mon-Khmer inhabitants. These lower river valleys where the Mon-Khmers lived comprised the western provinces of the Angkorian empire of Cambodia in the thirteenth century.

As Angkorian control over its western territory weakened in the mid–thirteenth century, Thai aggressiveness sparked an overthrow of Angkorian rule in at least two major Khmer outposts: Sukhothai and Lopburi. Sukhothai, located 150 miles north of Ayutthaya, served Angkor as an outpost on the central Chao Phraya plain until the 1240s. Under Thai leadership, Sukhothai successfully rebelled against Angkorian rule and soon became the nucleus of an early Thai state. By the late thirteenth century, its king Ramkamhaeng asserted control over a formidable territory, from Luang Prabang on the upper Mekong River to Nakhon Si Thammarat on the Malay Peninsula. Although the kingdom of Sukhothai remained viable for less than a century, the artistic and religious culture that developed there is the first to be credited as distinctively Thai or Siamese. King Ramkamhaeng's kingdom, which he had assembled largely through personal allegiances, disintegrated soon after his death in 1298, and the surviving Sukhothai state, which later clashed with Ayutthaya, became a small regional power.

Angkor also lost control of Lopburi, its Mon-Khmer administrative center on the lower Chao Phraya plain, in the mid–thirteenth century. The Thai role in Lopburi's independence was less direct than at Sukhothai; however, the Thai success at Sukhothai, as well as the increasingly strong Thai population in the lower Chao Phraya Valley, certainly influenced Lopburi's revolt against Angkor. By the end of the thirteenth century, Sukhothai asserted control over principalities in the western Chao Phraya Valley, while Lopburi claimed allegiance from the eastern part of the valley, signaling the decline of Angkorian authority and the rise of Thai power in the region.

This growing Thai influence in the lower Chao Phraya Valley provided a strong local impetus for the emergence of Ayutthaya in the mid–fourteenth century. Another influence, however, came from foreign shores. As Angkorian control waned and Thai rule stabilized, Chinese merchants were attracted by the Chao Phraya Valley's new potential for commercial activity. International trade between China and India could increase significantly if stable market towns on the route through Southeast Asia could be maintained. The Chinese also saw potential profit from Southeast Asia's own natural resources; China had demand for the region's precious

Temple ruins, Ayutthaya Historical Park
Photo courtesy of Tourism Authority of Thailand, Chicago

metals, jewels, cotton textiles, and betel nut, while India sought to import its tin, spices, gold, and ivory. With these products in mind, Chinese diplomats, merchants, and even craftsmen migrated to the lower Chao Phraya Valley; the Chinese presence in this area eventually contributed to the founding of Ayutthaya.

The exact circumstances of Ayutthaya's beginnings remain unclear. Historical records are fragmentary and perhaps mythical. Historians, however, consistently attribute Ayutthaya's founding to one man: U Thong, "Prince Golden Cradle." U Thong is thought to have been born in 1314, the son of a prominent Chinese merchant family. During this period in the lower Chao Phraya Valley, no strong political leader existed to unify the Thais as King Ramkamhaeng had done at Sukhothai. A few towns, such as Lopburi and Suphanburi, became minor centers of political power, but neither exerted the influence necessary to unite Thais throughout the region. U Thong became such a leader in 1350. The key to his political achievement was the power he commanded through personal alliances. U Thong apparently took at least two wives: one was a princess from the ruling family of Lopburi, and the other was a princess from Suphanburi. Through these marriages, U Thong gained the military support of Suphanburi Thais as well as the skilled administrative support of Lopburi Mon-Khmers. U Thong's own background in the Chinese merchant community gave him financial support and a strong understanding of the commercial potential in the area.

Capitalizing on these impressive alliances, U Thong founded a new kingdom called Ayutthaya in 1351, uniting Suphanburi and Lopburi under his rule. U Thong chose an island in the Chao Phraya River for the site for his capital; located twenty-five miles south of Lopburi, it was also just thirty miles east of Suphanburi on a river with direct access to the Gulf of Siam. To what extent the island was settled prior to U Thong's arrival is unclear. Some sources suggest that the island housed a Khmer outpost, while others describe it as an old port city with an established international trade. Whatever the case, U Thong transformed the island into a royal capital called Ayutthaya and himself into its first king, Ramathibodi. Soon a royal palace and temples were erected on the island; living quarters for foreigners, particularly Chinese traders, were built outside the walled royal compound.

From the kingdom's inception, Ramathibodi organized Ayutthaya's government as a bureaucracy based on an Angkorian model. Recognizing their administrative skills, the king recruited former Khmerized officials from Lopburi and other eastern Chao Phraya plain towns for his own government. As a result, many of his court officers, including chamberlains, physicians, astrologers, and scribes, spoke Khmer. Ramathibodi established this bureaucracy to exert strict control over Ayutthaya and its surrounding provinces. The main tenet of this establishment was the ruling class's claim on freemen in the kingdom. By law, each freeman was required annually to devote six months of labor to the king, whether in military service or on public works projects. This system proved relatively unpopular, for it usurped the more flexible traditional relationship between Thai freemen and the patrons for whom they worked. Some freemen actually left the kingdom or sold themselves into debt slavery to avoid their governmental obligation, a problem that would plague Ayutthaya in future centuries. In the mid–fourteenth century, however, Ayutthaya could still rely on the strength of its manpower in conflicts with neighboring Angkor.

During his reign of almost twenty years, Ramathibodi's chief military aim was to fortify Ayutthaya's eastern border against Angkor. His campaigns were largely successful: records indicate that his forces resettled a sizable group of borderland inhabitants to Ayutthaya territory, thereby boosting his subject population and potential manpower. Evidence suggests that Ramathibodi's armies may even have occupied Angkor for a time.

Although Ayutthaya strengthened its status as a new regional power in its conflicts with Angkor, the young kingdom was weakened by internal rivalries and succession disputes. When he first took power, Ramathibodi had split the duty of ruling outer provinces among family members. He dispatched his queen's brother to govern in that family's ancestral home, Suphanburi. The king sent his oldest son Ramesuan to rule in Lopburi. Upon Ramathibodi's death in 1369, a crisis of succession exposed a Suphanburi-Lopburi rivalry that would rage for forty years. Prince Ramesuan left Lopburi to inherit the throne from his father, but he ruled for only a year. In 1370 his uncle Borommaracha led an army from Suphanburi to the palace in Ayutthaya, forcing Ramesuan's abdication. As King Borommaracha I, the sixty-three-year-old warrior from Suphanburi directed Ayutthaya's military forces against the northern state of Sukhothai. By defeating Sukhothai, he hoped to win allegiance from that kingdom's former vassal states (of which Suphanburi was one). Despite intensive efforts, Borommaracha failed to subdue Sukhothai.

When Borommaracha died in 1388, his nephew Ramesuan exacted his revenge. The prince, who had returned to Lopburi after his forced abdication in 1370, attacked the royal palace in Ayutthaya and ordered Borommaracha's young son and heir, Thong Chan, executed. Ramesuan took the throne for the second time and renewed his father's military campaign against Angkor, which the Lopburi faction perceived as a greater threat to Ayutthaya than Sukhothai. Ramesuan's troops may have occupied Angkor for the second time since his father's invasion.

Ramesuan's son Ramaracha, who reigned from 1395 to 1409, may have felt pressure from his Suphanburi Thai subjects to again face the threat from their northern rival Sukhothai. Ramaracha's forces succeeded in imposing Ayutthaya's legal system on Sukhothai and its vassal states in 1397. Sukhothai fought back, however, and regained control of Nakhon Sawan in 1400. This city, located halfway between Ayutthaya and Sukhothai, had been seized by Ayutthaya under King Borommaracha in 1378, and its loss brought disgrace to King Ramaracha. Less than ten years later, the king lost his throne in a coup. Although the reasons are not clear, some historians believe that the Suphanburi faction's push for a stronger policy toward Sukhothai precipitated his fall from power. Some of the royal ministers allied themselves with Nakhon In, Borommaracha I's younger son from Suphanburi. Nakhon In's forces marched to Ayutthaya from Suphanburi and exiled Ramaracha; Nakhon In subsequently assumed the throne as King Intharacha.

The coup of 1409 brought the disruptive Suphanburi-Lopburi rivalry to an end. Intharacha quieted Lopburi by placing it under direct administrative control of the throne. He then turned his full attention to the conflict with Sukhothai, where his policy of aggression brought swift results. By 1412 an Ayutthaya official was posted in Sukhothai as "chief resident," even as Sukhothai's King Mahathammaracha III accepted the reduced status of vassal ruler. By 1438 Sukhothai relinquished all independence and became a province of Ayutthaya.

Ayutthaya's next major military initiative was a renewed campaign against Angkor, carried out by Intharacha's successor, his son King Borommaracha II. Borommaracha II came to the throne despite his status as the king's third son. Upon their father's death in 1424, the two oldest princes waged a battle for succession in a duel that occured on elephant back. Neither prince survived the fight, and their younger brother ascended to the throne. Borommaracha II took up the struggle against Angkor that the Lopburi kings had begun in the late fourteenth century. By the 1420s, Angkorian power had weakened considerably, as it was beset by raids from both Ayutthaya in the west and the Chams in the east. Borommaracha II invaded the capital city of Angkor in 1431–32 and installed his son as its vassal ruler. The last of the Khmer kings deserted the city soon thereafter, escaping to the region of Phnom Penh.

After incorporating Sukhothai and reducing Angkor to a vassal state, Borommaracha II sought to expand Ayutthaya's territory north of Sukhothai. His aim was Lan Na, a rival Thai kingdom in the hilly uplands whose capital lay at Chiang Mai. Borommaracha II initiated warfare against Lan Na in 1442 but died during an offensive in 1448. His son, King Borommatrailokanat (called Trailok), continued his father's quest to expand the kingdom. Seeking to manage the northern campaign more effectively, Trailok moved his capital temporarily from Ayutthaya to Phitsanulok, a northern city just east of Sukhothai. Phitsanulok held capital status from 1463 to 1488 through warfare in which neither side could claim victory.

King Trailok sought to strengthen the kingdom of Ayutthaya not only with territorial expansion but also with

Temple ruins, Ayutthaya Historical Park
Photo courtesy of Tourism Authority of Thailand, Chicago

administrative reform. Beginning with the first ruler, Ramathibodi I, Ayutthaya's kings had exercised their prerogative to issue both civil and criminal legislation. King Trailok issued two influential pieces of legislation: the Law of the Civil Hierarchy, and the Law of the Military and Provincial Hierarchies. The Law of the Civil Hierarchy created an exhaustively detailed system by which every resident of Ayutthaya received a numerical designation *(sakdi na)* according to his or her perceived importance in the society. This order of value ranged from slave (5) to freeman (25) to bureaucratic nobility (400), and even rated the minister of state (10,000) and the heir-apparent (100,000). Criminal punishments were then determined based on the rank of the victim; thus, a crime against a government official incurred a much harsher penalty than a crime against a freeman, peasant wife, or monk. This law reinforced the social order in Ayutthaya, in which the king was paramount, on the assumption of inherent human inequality. Moreover, this inequality legitimized the king's right to call on his subjects for enforced labor and military service.

Trailok also issued the Law of the Military and Provincial Hierarchies, which assigned specific duties to different divisions of government. Accordingly, Trailok separated his government into a military division, headed by the minister of the Kalahom, and a civilian division, headed by the minister of the Mahatthai. The civilian division encompassed four ministries: capital, palace, agriculture, and treasury. The treasury ministry (Phrakhlang) administered foreign trade and the immigrant trading communities located in Ayutthaya. In regulating foreign commercial activities through his bureaucracy, King Trailok exerted control over one of Ayutthaya's most dynamic assets: its potential to profit from international trade.

The relative stalemate with Lan Na stalled Ayutthaya's expansion in the north, but the kingdom continued to assert its control southward on the Malay Peninsula. Trailok pursued a policy of direct access to the Bay of Bengal and Indian Ocean by annexing two cities on the west side of the peninsula: Tenasserim (in the 1460s) and Tavoy (1488). These acquisitions increased Ayutthaya's trade opportunities during the reigns of Trailok's sons, Intharacha II (1488–91) and Ramathibodi II (1491–1529). International trade grew exponentially during the fifteenth and sixteenth centuries, benefitting the Ayutthaya kings directly. Tradition dictated that kings enjoyed a monopoly on international commerce; the king asserted first rights to buy any import, at his own price. In addition, his subjects could not purchase staple goods from any trader until the king's tax-generated supply had been sold, again at the price he dictated. Obviously, this policy filled the king's coffers, at the same time reducing foreign and resident merchants' opportunity for profit. The rules limiting the sale of staple goods also deprived farmers of a substantial market for their produce. This situation further eroded peasant freemen's loyalty to the crown. King Trailok, obviously enamored of bureaucracy, assigned government officials to monitor and enforce the laws of public service that so vexed freemen in Ayutthaya. This system eventually failed, however, and freemen's loyalty to their kingdom diminished greatly through the mid–sixteenth century, leaving Ayutthaya vulnerable to invasion.

Burma, Ayutthaya's western rival, exploited the kingdom's manpower weakness with a series of debilitating attacks. The first invasion, in 1548, ended abruptly (within two years) after the murder of the Burmese king. However, his successor, Bayinnaung, upheld the conquest of Ayutthaya as his goal. The formidable Burmese army launched another campaign against the Kingdom of Ayutthaya in 1563–64. Overwhelmed by the invaders, Ayutthaya's King Chakkraphat lost control of his northern provinces, including Phitsanulok, and pledged fealty to Burma, offering his son as a hostage. King Chakkraphat suffered further humiliation in 1564 when rebels from the southern Malay Peninsula managed briefly to occupy his palace, once an impregnable sanctuary. The king's effort to redeem himself as ruler in 1568 failed miserably; his troops recaptured Phitsanulok but quickly lost it and retreated to Ayutthaya's island capital. Seizing this opportunity, an enormous Burmese army marched directly on the capital city, where Ayutthaya's serious manpower crisis was now shockingly obvious. The king's call to rally Ayutthaya's freemen roused few loyal defenders. Many freemen from the city and its surrounding provinces escaped duty by fleeing to the forests. Only local rulers and their personal retinues came to the king's aid. This meager force managed to defend the moated city from January to August 1569, when Thai treachery and Burmese trickery combined to give the attackers access to the city. Burmese troops won control of the city on August 8, looted and destroyed buildings, captured reigning King Mahin (son of Chakkraphat), and appointed Maha Thammaracha vassal ruler of Ayutthaya.

Burma retained its hold on Ayutthaya for more than a decade, during which time Ayutthaya's population continued to decline. Burma's victory in 1569 did not involve extensive slaughter; instead, according to Southeast Asian custom, the king ordered massive transfers of Ayutthaya residents (whether noble or common) to Burma as prisoners. This forced immigration weakened the vanquished state while boosting the subject population of the victor. Burma left only a small military garrison to support its vassal ruler in Ayutthaya. With its own manpower depleted and few Burmese troops to defend it, Ayutthaya suffered repeated attacks and population raids from the Khmers between 1570 and 1587. With Burma's permission, Ayutthaya began rebuilding its devastated city walls as a means of self-defense in 1580. In fact, this reconstruction also signified an incipient movement against Burmese rule; this movement would mature under Prince Naresuan, the son of vassal ruler Maha Thammaracha and grandson of former King Chakkraphat.

Naresuan earned a place in history as one of Thailand's legendary heroes. Under his leadership, Ayutthaya shed its vassal status and reasserted itself as a major Southeast Asian empire. Born in 1555, Naresuan was taken as a captive to Burma during the 1564 conflict. When he returned to Ayutthaya as sixteen-year-old heir-apparent *(uparat),* he was granted rule of Phitsanulok under Burmese authority. During this period, Naresuan performed admirably in conflicts with the Khmers and cultivated an allegiance among local soldiers. Naresuan's abilities drew Burmese attention and enmity. In 1584, Naresuan foiled a Burmese ambush planned for his murder. Outraged, he and his numerous followers set out for Ayutthaya, where they reinforced the island city's defensive capabilities. The Burmese retaliated by direct attacks on the city from 1585 to 1587, none of which overcame Naresuan's forces.

Burma made a final, massive attack on its rebellious vassal late in 1592. Heading a highly coordinated offensive, the Burmese crown prince led his army from Martaban on the Burmese coast southeast through the mountainous Three Pagodas Pass. His plan to attack Ayutthaya from the west was not fulfilled, for Naresuan (now established as king) met the advancing Burmese at Nong Sarai, some fourteen miles northwest of Suphanburi. The battle, waged there on January 18, 1593, changed the course of history for the Ayutthaya Kingdom. Naresuan's frontlines could not withstand the Burmese onslaught, but he and his younger brother, Ekathotsarot, held their men firm behind the crumbling frontlines. At a crucial point, the immense battle became personal: King Naresuan challenged the Burmese crown prince to an elephant-back duel for the honor of his kingdom. The clash lasted only minutes before Naresuan killed the prince in swordplay. The leaderless Burmese army immediately retreated, ceding victory. Naresuan had won Ayutthaya's independence from Burma.

Following this victory, King Naresuan began rebuilding his kingdom through vigorous territorial expansion. In 1594, just one year after the Battle of Nong Sarai, Naresuan sent forces over his eastern border to the Khmer capital of Lovek; eventually all of Cambodia would fall to Ayutthaya. In the mid–1590s, ethnic alliances in Burma crumbled, plunging the kingdom into crisis. Naresuan seized this opportunity to regain Tenasserim and Tavoy on the Bay of Bengal. Continued attacks won Burma's entire southeast coast north to Martaban. Before the end of the century, Naresuan had also brought Lan Na, the rival northern Thai kingdom based in Chiang Mai, under Ayutthaya's control. By the time he died in 1605, King Naresuan had extended Ayutthaya's realm across a vast section of Southeast Asia, regaining the kingdom's former prestige. His vision of Siam as a unified

Temple ruins, Ayutthaya Historical Park
Photo courtesy of Tourism Authority of Thailand, Chicago

Thai nation, with a role to play in international politics and trade, greatly influenced his successors.

The dawn of the seventeenth century brought increased economic prosperity and international attention to Ayutthaya. The city had long been a busy port of trade for Asian nations. Ayutthaya exported products including rice, spices, deer hides, and rainforest woods to China, Japan, and India. This activity naturally created interest among the European nations. Portugal won the right to trade in Ayutthaya in 1518, becoming the first European country given that privilege. Ayutthaya granted the request in exchange for firearms and ammunition. European guns, a novelty in Asia, gave their possessors an advantage by adding the power of explosives to traditional Asian fighting tactics. Numerous Portuguese settled in Ayutthaya's foreign quarters and eventually gained the king's permission to erect Siam's first Christian church. By the early seventeenth century, European interest in trading at Ayutthaya was booming. The first Dutch trading ships docked at Ayutthaya in 1604, bringing merchants who hoped to gain access to Chinese and Japanese markets. Ayutthaya's King Ekathotsarot, Naresuan's brother, welcomed the Dutch as a potential ally against the Portuguese, whose presence in the Bay of Bengal threatened Ayutthaya's territory. English traders followed the Dutch in 1612 and established a trading station from which to sell English manufactured goods. Disappointed with their sales, the English left Ayutthaya eleven years later. Even Denmark's East India Company joined Ayutthaya's trading community in 1620.

Ayutthaya's kings encouraged European involvement in the city's trade for more than economic reasons. These European nations commanded military might that could bolster Ayutthaya's own forces. When revolts broke out in the Malay Peninsula in the 1630s, King Prasat Thong received Dutch naval aid in exchange for a monopoly on hide exports. The Dutch also provided support in Ayutthaya's struggles to quell uprisings at Songkhla, on the Malay Peninsula, between 1647 and 1655. However, a succession dispute following Prasat Thong's death in 1656 ended the Netherlands' favored status. King Narai won Ayutthaya's throne despite a rejection of support from the Dutch. As king, he sought to diminish Dutch power by courting England's return to Ayutthaya. The English reopened their Ayutthaya facility in 1661, having been persuaded by the king that it would provide a foothold in the Japanese market, which was dominated by the Dutch.

Ayutthaya not only relied on foreigners for outside military support and political leverage; it also utilized foreigners internally, within the government bureaucracy. As King Trailok had decreed, Ayutthaya's government was divided into military and civilian departments. The Phrakhlang (ministry of finance and foreign affairs) oversaw all international trade arrangements and transactions. To give his government best advantage, the king hired those most skilled in trade: foreign merchants, particularly Chinese and Persian. One foreigner, a Greek named Constantine Phaulkon, arrived in Siam with English merchants in 1678. His skills in translation and accounting won him a job in the Phrakhlang, from which he quickly ascended to the highest position in the Mahatthai (the Siamese civil administration). Phaulkon had earned King Narai's trust and was acknowledged as a close advisor. Within ten years, however, anti-foreign sentiment violently ended his career.

Phaulkon used his influence to suggest a new international ally for Siam: France. Recently converted to Catholicism by Ayutthaya's community of French Jesuits, Phaulkon embarked on a grand scheme to convert the Buddhist king and his Buddhist kingdom to Christianity. (The Persians had similar designs; they sought to establish Islam as Ayutthaya's state religion.) Phaulkon encouraged the French in 1685 to send a mission to accomplish this goal. The French received trade concessions and agreed to station troops at rebellious Songkhla, but achieved no conversion; a subsequent French mission in 1687 ended similarly.

Opposition steadily grew among Thais to what they saw as an undue foreign influence in their government, personified by Phaulkon and his attempts at national religious conversion. Driven by anti-foreign sentiment, in 1688 King Narai's foster brother, Phra Phetracha, devised a plan to remove Phaulkon and claim the throne upon Narai's death, which seemed imminent. Like-minded bureaucrats convinced the dying king to name Phra Phetracha as his heir. Phra Phetracha immediately ordered Phaulkon arrested for treason and executed. He also briefly jailed French missionaries and requested the departure of French troops from their garrison at Bangkok.

The degree to which foreigners influenced Siamese kings also appeared to alienate the general Thai population. Despite the efforts of Ayutthaya kings to maintain tight control over their subjects, many freemen had lost faith in the king's authority and saw no reason to serve him as laborer or soldier. A serious loss of manpower resulted as early as the 1630s. Freemen evaded service in several ways: refusing to register, entering personal agreements with individual noblemen, or even trading exportable commodities in exchange for exemption from service. By 1758 Siam's chronic manpower shortage again severely undermined Ayutthaya's ability to defend itself.

The kingdom's manpower problems proved disastrous. Energized by an ambitious new ruler, Burma attacked Ayutthaya in 1760. The Burmese ruler Alaunghpaya ravaged Ayutthaya's territory on the Bay of Bengal (Martaban, Tenasserim, and Tavoy) and proceeded to Ayutthaya, where a small, ill-prepared group of soldiers stood in defense. The siege backfired, however, when a gun exploded and injured Burma's leader, forcing the Burmese to retreat. Ayutthaya was spared major conflict with Burma until 1765. In that year the Burmese implemented a two-pronged attack on Ayutthaya, with one force assuming control (and taking prisoners) in the upland provinces and another crossing the Malay Peninsula into the lower river valleys. With their ranks swelled by hostages and insurgents, the two Burmese armies came together and began a massive siege on Ayutthaya's capital city in February 1766. Although the Siamese might have learned from the 1760 attack and prepared for future onslaughts, they had apparently wasted their opportunity. When Burmese forces arrived at the city in 1766, they caught the Siamese unprepared, undermanned, and unable to seek assistance from the conquered northern provinces. During the siege, an insufficient food supply led to famine and disease in the city. A huge fire destroyed 10,000 homes early in 1767. Realizing the bleak prospects for victory, King Suriyamarin proposed his submission to the Burmese as a vassal ruler. Bent on total surrender, the Burmese refused his offer and attacked the city walls until they broke through, claiming victory at Ayutthaya on April 7, 1767.

The jubilant Burmese devastated Ayutthaya in the war's aftermath. Splendid ancient buildings were looted, burned, and destroyed. Revered Buddha icons were robbed of gold coatings. Ayutthaya's population suffered rape, robbery, murder, and capture; tens of thousands were marched to Burma as prisoners. After enjoying their victory and its spoils, the Burmese withdrew from the ruined city. Within several years, however, Siam began to rebuild, moved its capital down the Chao Phraya River to Bangkok, and entered a new age of expansion and prosperity.

The Age of Ayutthaya lasted more than 400 years, establishing a sound, resilient foundation on which modern Thailand grew. Ayutthaya's rulers transformed their kingdom from a small regional power to an international trading partner and political ally. Perhaps more importantly, Ayutthaya fostered a new sense of Thai unity in a disparate confederation of ethnic Asians. Today Thais regard this ancient capital city dotted with aging ruins as a symbolic cornerstone of modern Thailand.

Ayutthaya's fame now stems from the visible remnants of its past. While much of the city was destroyed in Burma's 1767 attack, many of Ayutthaya's royal and religious edifices survive as ruins. The city has grown into a modest provincial capital and commercial center, but its economy relies most heavily on tourism. Therefore, the modern city has adapted itself to accommodate the island's historic sites. Although crumbling or sometimes overgrown, these ancient temples and palaces echo Ayutthaya's former grandeur.

Buddhist temples *(wats)* comprise a majority of Ayutthaya's ruins. The kings' royal temple stands in the ancient palace grounds in the island's northwestern corner. Wat Phra Si Sanphet once contained a standing Buddha (fifty-two and one-half feet high) covered with gold. When the Burmese broke into the royal complex in 1767, they set fire to the image, melting the gold and destroying the figure. Still standing are three *chedis* (pagodas) holding the ashes of King Trailok and his sons, Intharacha II and Ramathibodi II. These *chedis,* built in the classic Ayutthaya style, incorporate bell-shaped domes influenced by Ceylon architecture and elongated, ringed spires inspired by Burmese models.

Little remains of Wat Maha That, built in the late fourteenth century near a lake in the island's center. The temple's Khmer-influenced *prang* (tower) once rose 165 feet into the air. Visitors now find only the *prang's* base, a multi-layered structure with a bullet-like shape. Government repairs in 1956 revealed a Buddha relic buried in a golden casket at the site. Early in the fifteenth century, King Borommaracha II ordered construction of Wat Ratburana just north of Wat Maha That. The king built the temple to honor his two older brothers, who killed each other in an elephant-back duel over succession to the throne.

Several of Ayutthaya's ancient temples boast restored Buddhas. Constructed in 1357 during the reign of King Ramathibodi I, Wat Yai Chai Mongkon stands across the Pa Sak River southeast of the city proper. Buddhist monks returning with new teachings from Ceylon (Sri Lanka) inspired the king to build this temple. Today the temple's huge *chedi* houses a reclining Buddha whose form draws on Ceylon types. A monastery located south of the ancient palace complex contains one of Thailand's largest Buddha images. Visitors come to Wihan Phra Mongkon Bopit to admire its enormous bronze Buddha with mother-of-pearl eyes. Damaged in 1767, the idol was restored in the twentieth century with support from the Burmese. Two other temples feature figurative sculpture: Wat Phra Ram (1369) includes mythical statues, and Wat Thammik Rat displays lion sculptures.

Ayutthaya has transferred many of its cultural and religious treasures to its two major museums. Chao Sam Phraya Museum holds a collection of stone and bronze Buddhas from Ayutthaya's historic period. The second museum, Chandrakasem Palace, was originally built by King Maha Thammaracha for his son Prince Naresuan. Demolished by the Burmese conquerors, it was rebuilt by King Mongkut (1851–68).

Further Reading: Accounts of Ayutthaya's history range from the general to the minutely detailed. A solid, scholarly overview of Ayutthaya's role in Thai history can be obtained from volume one of *The Cambridge History of South East Asia,* edited by Nicholas Tarling (2 vols., Cambridge, New York, and Victoria, Australia: Cambridge University Press, 1992). For an in-depth study of Thai history, David K. Wyatt offers an impressively detailed, authoritative account in his *Thailand: A Short History* (New Haven, Connecticut and London: Yale University Press, 1984).

—Elizabeth E. Broadrup

Bago (Myanmar)

Location: Lower Myanmar (formerly Burma); Bago (formerly Pegu) lies fifty miles northeast of the capital city of Yangon.

Description: Port on the Bago River settled by the Mon (Talaing) people in approximately A.D. 825. Bago prospered as a trade center and bastion of Theravada Buddhism; site of important Buddhist shrines, most notably the 180-foot reclining Buddha and the highly venerated Shwe Mawdaw Pagoda. Bago gained political importance during the fourteenth and fifteenth centuries as capital of the independent Mon kingdom of Bago, covering much of Lower Myanmar; from 1539 to 1635, it served as national capital for Burman rulers from Upper Myanmar. The site was periodically destroyed and rebuilt after earthquakes and military invasions. The city's name was changed to Bago in 1989, when military government changed the country's name from Burma to Myanmar. Bago, also the name of a modern political division, generally denoted all of Lower Myanmar prior to British takeover in the nineteenth century.

Contact: Ministry of Hotels and Tourism
77-91 Sule Pagoda Street
Kyauktada Township
Yangon
Myanmar
(1) 77966 or (1) 75328

Buddhist records suggest that two Mon nobles, the brothers Thamala and Wimala, left the Mon center in Thaton when they were passed over in the line of succession and founded Bago in A.D. 825. The Mon people, probably resident in southern Myanmar for more than 1,000 years, apparently brought the Theravada form of Buddhism to the country. The establishment of Bago was said to fulfill a prophecy by Siddhārtha Gautama (the historic Buddha). Ibn Khurrdāhbih, an Arab geographer, first recorded Bago's existence during the mid–ninth century; he called it Ramaññadesa (Rmen or Mon land). The chiefs of Hanthawaddy (as the Mon called Bago) maintained the Mon presence there for centuries, occasionally attaining mastery over neighboring states.

A moat and wall enclosing a square of six miles in perimeter protected the early Mon settlement. In the manner of all Buddhist cities, the Mon built a pagoda to house relics of the Buddha. According to Buddhist legend, the Shwe Mawdaw Pagoda (Pagoda of the Great Golden God), one of the most revered shrines in Myanmar, houses several hairs of the Buddha that two traveling merchants brought to Bago. Successive monarchs donated other relics, such as teeth of the Buddha, and embellished the monument's architecture. In approximately 994 a sculptor called Migadippa created Bago's most famous icon, the colossal Shwethalyaung Buddha. Measuring a formidable 180 feet long by 53 feet high, the reclining statue presents one of the most naturalistic images of the Buddha, reputedly depicting him just before he attained nirvana.

Two centuries of subservience to the northern kingdom of Pagan began in 1057 when the Burman king Anawrahta (ruled 1044–77) swept into southern Myanmar and conquered the Mon kingdom. Traditionally, the Burmans had practiced the Mahāyāna form of Buddhism. After a monk from the southern region converted Anawrahta to the Theravāda (or Hinayana) religion practiced by the Mon, the Burman king determined to obtain the three Pali canons of scripture that form the basis of Theravada Buddhism. Anawrahta destroyed Bago in order to steal the closely guarded scriptures and ordered the transfer of 30,000 Mon to Pagan, the first of several depopulations to cripple Bago throughout its history. The exodus from Bago included numerous artisans who worked on pagodas and other religious shrines throughout Upper Myanmar. Anawrahta's forceful initiative in promoting the Theravada tenets dramatically changed the practice of Buddhism throughout Myanmar.

The Mongols vanquished the kingdom of Pagan in 1287, in a series of incursions from China that enabled the Mon to reclaim Bago from the Burmans. The Chinese recognized Bago's autonomy in 1298, although they considered the Mon state to be a vassal, the Mon chief merely serving as China's resident governor. A casual arrangement of tribute to the Chinese emperor, with no further interference, seemed to suit both parties well into the seventeenth century. During the early period of the Mon kingdom, the city was known by its traditional Mon name, Hanthawaddy.

As with any of the states in the region at the time, the Mon kingdom faced continual aggression from its rivals. One of the chief contenders for control of Mon territory was Ayutthaya, in the region of what is now Thailand. In 1363 the Siamese threat forced Binnya U (ruled 1353–85) to abandon his palace at the port of Martaban in favor of the more secure Donwun; ultimately, in response to continued threats of rebellion, he repaired the walls at Bago and relocated his capital there in 1369.

Binnya U's son Razadarit (ruled 1385–1423), engaged from Dagon (Yangon) in feuds within the extended royal family, finally seized Bago for his capital. He staved off repeated Burman assaults from the north and subdued local rebellions, providing a legacy of rare stability for his heirs, Binnyadammayaza (ruled 1423–26) and Binnyaran I (ruled 1426–46). Their reigns ushered in a century of civility and prosperity at Bago, which attracted a multitude of foreign

Shwethalyaung Buddha, Bago
Photo courtesy of Embassy of the Union of Myanmar, Washington, D.C.

traders and entrepreneurs. One Russian traveler reported in approximately 1470 on the preponderance of Indians involved in the busy port's thriving mercantile activities.

Razadarit's daughter Shin Saw Bu (ruled 1453–72) continued the era of relative peace; significantly, she chose to retire to religious pursuits at Dagon during the latter part of her reign, relinquishing power to a Buddhist monk named Dhammazedi, whom she married to her daughter. The devout Dhammazedi (ruled 1460–92) revolutionized Bago's government—and ultimately that of greater Myanmar—by purifying the Sangha (Buddhist monastic order) and inspiring a Buddhist revival throughout the region. He sent twenty-two monks to Sri Lanka, traditional bastion of Theravada Buddhism, to receive orders at the esteemed Mahavihara monastery. These devout emissaries returned to Bago to perform specially sanctioned mass ordinations in Bago and throughout Lower Myanmar. In 1476 Dhammazedi commissioned the Kalyani Sima, the first hall in Myanmar built specifically to accommodate the sacred ordination rites. The Kalyani Sima holds ten original stone pillars inscribed with the consecration ceremony. Set in both the Pali and the Mon languages, the pillars relate the history of early Buddhism.

Binnyaran II (ruled 1492–1526) continued his father's policies of peace and benevolence, but during the early sixteenth century, the Toungoo Dynasty based far upriver at Ava sought to acquire the wealthy, sophisticated Mon kingdom. The Portuguese, seizing the opportunities of the new sea routes, arrived in Bago in 1511. They settled mostly in Martaban, a major seaport serving the inland capital. Bago prospered as a commercial center handling wares from all over Southeast Asia. Europeans such as the Venetian merchant Caesar Frederick fondly described Bago's moat of crocodiles, imposing fortifications, stunning palaces, golden, bejeweled shrines, and lavish processions.

Binnyaran II's son Takayutpi (ruled 1529–39), a weak administrator, nearly lost Bago when the Toungoo ruler Tabinshweti (ruled 1531–50) marched on the capital in 1535. Although the Burmans routed the Mon flotilla of war canoes and gained control over parts of the Mon kingdom, Tabinshweti repeatedly failed to capture the city of Bago itself. Eventually, he took advantage of Takayutpi's death in 1539 to gain control of Bago and Lower Myanmar. Tabinshweti, who was crowned in Bago as King of Lower Burma in 1542 and proclaimed himself King of All Burma in 1546, chose Bago over Toungoo or Ava—Myanmar's other political strongholds—as the capital of his unified kingdom; while courting his Mon subjects by adopting their customs and their capital, Tabinshweti secured Bago as a strategic base for incursions into the rival kingdom of Ayutthaya, a perennial Myanmarese target. Tabinshweti's reign heralded two centuries of political prestige and economic prosperity for Bago; for most of the next 100 years, Bago served as capital for the adventuresome Myanmarese monarchs. Tabinshweti himself lapsed into insanity, however, emboldening Bago's Mon population to expel their Burman masters upon the king's death in 1550. They installed the Mon official Smim Sawhtut as king of Bago, but he soon was murdered; Smim Htaw succeeded to the throne at Bago.

The ambitious Toungoo warrior prince Bayinnaung (ruled 1551–81), dispossessed of Tabinshweti's realm by rival brothers, fought to reclaim Bago, which he planned to transform into a suitably luxurious capital for the prosperous kingdom. Bayinnaung sacked the city, and the execution of Smim Htaw ended the Mon royal lineage at Bago. Once Bayinnaung had secured Bago, he advanced promptly on Upper Myanmar and Siam. His conquests greatly enriched Bago's culture, as he routinely deported skilled craftsmen, artists, dancers, and musicians from areas such as Ayutthaya. Between 1555 and 1559 Bayinnaung expanded Bago's hegemony to include the staunchly independent Shan states of Upper Myanmar. Despite his military prowess, the court continually faced revolts at the local level. Bago suffered multiple calamities in 1564. The Mon peasantry took advantage of Bayinnaung's frequent military campaigns to besiege and burn the king's grand capital in his absence. Some 20,000 Shan and Siamese war slaves contributed enthusiastically to the effort. Only the Buddhist monks could restrain Bayinnaung from carrying out mass slaughter in retribution. A major earthquake that year compounded the destruction at Bago.

Despite Bayinnaung's grand embellishments of Bago—notably his palace and the new city gates that each of twenty vassal provinces built as tribute—his neglect of administrative duties during his three decades of rule seriously compromised the quality of life in Bago. The city suffered a devastating famine in 1567, because the manpower needed to cultivate the rice paddies was engaged in one of Bayinnaung's sorties to Siam. The king continued to deplete the country's resources with such costly forays as the siege of Ayutthaya in 1568. At the same time, Bayinnaung sought to serve as a model Buddhist monarch, generously embellishing the country's pagodas in the wake of each murderous campaign. He promoted the faith by distributing copies of the Pali scriptures, building monasteries, and conducting mass ordinations at the Kalyani Sima. He contributed one of Bago's chief Buddhist shrines, the Mahazedi Pagoda.

His son Nandabayin (ruled 1581–99) nearly brought Bago to ruin as a result of his excessive purges of the court and exhausting military failures. Indeed, his war-weary subjects invited invasions from neighboring rival kingdoms. The Siamese turned the tables on Nandabayin, sending the Burmans on a bloody retreat when they tried to take Ayutthaya. Ayutthaya subsequently raided the countryside around Bago and besieged the city in 1595. Another famine that desolated Lower Myanmar in 1596 only compounded the Bago citizenry's hostility toward the king. Toungoo sought the assistance of the Arakanese—across the mountains to the west of Bago—in ending the Bago scourge in 1599. Together the two states besieged the city; when Toungoo's forces withdrew to deal with other conflicts, the Arakanese burned Bago to the ground, looting the palaces that Bayinnaung had furnished with booty from his numerous conquests. To ensure that Bago would not soon rise from the ashes, the Arakanese deported thousands of the city's residents.

The Portuguese had become increasingly active in Southeast Asian trade throughout the sixteenth century, and one Portuguese opportunist succeeded in filling the political void in Lower Myanmar that followed Nandabayin's chaotic regime and the demise of Bago. Much of Lower Myanmar spent ten years under the rule of Philip de Brito Nicote—originally a ship's cabin boy—who in 1603 proclaimed himself king of Lower Myanmar and held court at Syriam, Bago's main seaport. The Burman king Anaukpetlun (ruled 1605–28) controlled Bago, however, rebuilding it as his capital and even plotting the requisite raids on Ayutthaya. But de Brito enjoyed the backing of many Mon and Burmans in the delta. His persistence in converting his subjects to Christianity, however, ultimately offended them; his pillaging of Buddhist relics, including a treasured bell from the Shwe Dagon Pagoda in Yangon that had been donated by the revered king Dhammazedi, earned him a dramatic death by impalement at the hands of the Burmans.

The silting up of Bago's river by the end of the sixteenth century compounded the city's troubles. Despite the high regard in which the Europeans held Bago (an efficient, upstanding team of eight brokers handled all trade for the port), the drastically curtailed access to the sea caused economic activity to migrate increasingly toward the delta ports of Syriam and Martaban. Bago desperately courted foreign commercial interests during the early seventeenth century, negotiating with Southeast Asia's new trading operations, the English East India Company and the Dutch East India Company. These companies established factories at Bago in 1627, but the country's instability hindered the facilities' profitability. The Dutch and English ceased most of their activity at Bago in 1677. Meantime, Thalun (ruled 1629–48) ended Bago's reign as Myanmar's administrative capital when he removed the court in 1635 from the increasingly vulnerable Mon city to the Burmans' traditional capital at Ava, securely inaccessible far to the north. Bago remained under the Burman king's jurisdiction but languished in its depopulated state.

During the course of the following century, however, the Mon steadily repopulated Lower Myanmar. In 1740 the independent-minded Mon waged a bloody revolt to oust the Burmans. Following historic precedent, the Mon resurrected Bago as their capital. But the reigns of the Hanthawaddy chiefs Smim Htaw Buddhaketi (ruled 1740–47) and Binnyadala (ruled 1747–57) marked the last period of Mon rule at Bago. Indeed, the invasion of the Mon kingdom in 1747 and the destruction of Bago in 1756–57 by Alaungpaya, an official from Shwebo bent on establishing his own dynasty, presaged the demise of the Mon during the ensuing decades. He burned the Mon palace and tore down the city wall, although he left many of the religious shrines intact. He held Binnyadala captive for seventeen years before executing him during a period of political upheaval. Alaungpaya did indeed establish Myanmar's last native dynasty, the Konbaung Dynasty, but Bago's days as a suitable capital for such a dynasty had come to an end.

The centuries of warfare had debilitated Bago's population, and by 1795 the city's inhabitants numbered fewer than 6,000. Bodawpaya (ruled 1782–1819), Alaungpaya's son, attempted to rebuild the city, but his efforts proved futile. He did, however, continue the royal Buddhist tradition of embellishing the many shrines, increasing the Shwe Mawdaw Pagoda's height by thirteen feet in 1796, and donating his crown jewels for the creation of new *hti,* the characteristic umbrellas that grace the top of the pagoda's spire.

The English, meanwhile, figured more prominently in Lower Myanmar as they aggressively assembled their Indian empire. Indeed, the imperial administrators referred to the independent territories east of India as Further India. During the nineteenth century, the British sought to acquire parts of Myanmar, including Bago, through treaties with the country's native rulers. The Myanmarese could not conceive of giving up any of their homelands in such a manner, and war inevitably followed. The British acquired some Myanmarese properties during the First Anglo-Burmese War in 1824, but Bago had retained its autonomy.

During the Second Anglo-Burmese War in 1852, the British occupied Lower Myanmar and annexed Bago officially on January 20, 1853. At first the British based their operations in Bago, under the first commissioner appointed for the region, Major Arthur Purvis Phayre. A decade later, however, upon the creation of the province of British Burma as part of British India, the British moved the capital to Yangon. Bago enjoyed a commercial revival, however, as the city's proximity to Myanmar's bountiful teak forests enabled the British to develop the city as a major teak export center. They drained the swamps and introduced an irrigation system that fostered rice cultivation, transforming the desolate Bago district once again into the country's major exporter of the vital staple. In 1886 the British concluded their conquest of Myanmar, having wrested Upper Myanmar from the Myanmarese after the Third Anglo-Burmese War. For the next fifty years, Bago functioned as a British colonial outpost.

A major earthquake that rocked Lower Myanmar in 1930 destroyed much of Bago. Rebuilding of the city and its Buddhist shrines took place during the next twenty-five years. Meanwhile, Myanmar became a British crown colony in 1935.

During World War II, the Japanese occupied Myanmar; they succeeded in evicting the British from Bago in March 1942. When Allied forces moved to retake the country in May 1945, the penultimate battle before the storming of Yangon occurred at Bago. The British Fourteenth Army under General William Slim captured Bago on May 2 before moving on to Yangon. The War Cemetery at Htaukkyan on the road linking Bago and Yangon, a memorial to the 27,000 Allied troops who died in Myanmar during the war, attests to the intense warfare that plagued the region.

After the war, Myanmar achieved independence (January 4, 1948), only to struggle with abject poverty and military repression. Civil war ensued as various factions within the country vied for control of the fledgling nation. The national government moved quickly to squelch the rebels, but even so, Bago district ended up split between the central government and the PVO. The communists, who had been marshaling support mainly in Bago district, boasted enough followers by April to wage assaults on police stations, occupy small towns, and sabotage communications. As well, in 1949 insurgents from Myanmar's hill-dwelling Karen tribes planned to capture both Bago and Yangon in their bid for a stake in the government. The much-contended Bago district remained under martial law until February 1951.

A military junta in 1962 shut Myanmar off from the rest of the world for a quarter of a century. Until 1972, Bago district covered approximately the same area as had the ancient Mon kingdom, but the government separated the region around the capital into the Yangon Division. The country resurfaced internationally in 1988 when popular demonstrations for democracy resulted in mass murder by government troops. Although most of the recent turmoil centered in Yangon and Mandalay, the upheaval inevitably has affected cities near the capital, including Bago.

In spite of its diminished status, Bago continues as a center of Buddhism. Many of the sacred structures built during the fifteenth and sixteenth centuries—heyday of Bago's Buddhist revival—survive, despite frequent alterations throughout the centuries. The city's most famous shrine, the giant, reclining Shwethalyaung Buddha—which disappeared during Alaungpaya's invasion—has remained just west of the city since the British recovered it from the jungle in 1881. So arresting is the Buddha's size that signs posted around it list the measurements of its various parts: the ear, fifteen feet; the sole of the foot, twenty-five feet; the big toe, six feet; and the eyelid, seven and one-half feet. The octagonal-based Shwe Mawdaw Pagoda, toppled in the 1930 earthquake, then reconstructed by 1954, has a diamond-studded *hti*; the stupa bears one and one-half tons of gold. Large temple lions called *clinthes* stand guard at the stairways, each holding a seated Buddha in its mouth. A museum within the pagoda houses the Buddha images that survived the earthquake. Also destroyed in the 1930 earthquake and rebuilt by the early 1950s, the Kalyani Sima, with its sacred inscriptions, evokes the tradition of Bago's rulers fortifying the Buddhist presence in atonement for their transgressions

Further Reading: Historical information on Bago can be gleaned from general sources on Myanmar. G. E. Harvey's *History of Burma* (London: Cass, 1925; New York: Octagon, 1983), although archaic in style, provides a wealth of historical detail amid copious lore about Bago and its rulers. Broader histories of Southeast Asia also contain some excellent scholarship about Bago and Myanmar's other historic capitals. Exemplary is D. G. E. Hall's exhaustive history of Myanmar and Indochina, *A History of Southeast Asia* (New York: St. Martin's, 1955), which contains chapters on Myanmar's various dynastic periods and the British hegemony. D. J. M. Tate's multi-volume *The Making of Modern South-East Asia* (Kuala Lumpur and Singapore: Oxford University Press, 1971) offers a more contemporary view of Bago in its regional context. Although essentially a travel guide, the *Thailand and Burma Handbook* (fourth edition, Bath, England: Trade and Travel, and Lincolnwood, Illinois: Passport, 1995) provides a useful overview of Myanmar's history. For a discussion of the Mon influence on Buddhism in Myanmar, see *World Religions: From Ancient History to the Present,* edited by Geoffrey Parrinder (New York and Bicester, England: Facts on File, 1971).

—Mary F. McNulty

Bali (Bali, Indonesia)

Location: The westernmost of the chain of Lesser Sunda Islands between the South China Sea and the Indian Ocean, Bali lies a little over a mile east of Java, eight degrees south of the equator.

Description: The only surviving Hindu society in Indonesia, Bali is known for its rich cultural life. Independent for most of its history, Bali at first maintained close cultural ties with eastern Java but later developed independently. The island fell to the Dutch early in the twentieth century but was spared most of the dislocations usually associated with colonialism. Bali joined the independent Republic of the United States of Indonesia in 1949, and in 1956 it became one of the twenty-six provinces of the Republic of Indonesia.

Site Office: Kanwil Depparpostel X Bali
Komplex Niti Mandala
Jl. Raya Puputan, Renon
80235 Denpasar, Bali
(361) 225649

Little is known of Bali's prehistory, since archaeological excavations have yielded nothing but a smattering of Stone Age tools. It is clear, however, that by the Bronze Age the island had a sizable population of hunter-gatherers of Mongoloid origin. Historians speculate that Bali, like other Indonesian islands, was colonized by separate groups of Proto-Malays, seafaring people who gradually made their way south and east out of China, through the Malay Peninsula, and into the Indonesian Archipelago, Polynesia, Australia, and other parts of the South Pacific. Balinese legend, however, does not recall an ocean-borne arrival. Long ago, the stories say, in the time when rugged and desolate Bali was still joined to Java by an isthmus, a pious Javanese king sent his wicked son into exile there. To make sure that the young man would not return to disgrace his father again, the king drew a line in the sand, and immediately the ocean flowed across the isthmus, separating Bali from Java forever. In truth, Bali was once a part of Java and today is separated from it by a very narrow strait.

If indeed the Balinese are of distant seafaring origin, they have decisively turned their backs on this element of their heritage—turned their backs, in fact, on the ocean itself. Balinese life is oriented, instead, toward the mountains. The island's chain of peaks, some of them still active volcanoes, are thought to be the home of the Hindu gods, while the ocean is considered evil, a haven of demons and spirits hostile to human endeavor. The Balinese sail graceful outrigger canoes, from which they do some fishing on a very modest scale. But unlike other Indonesian ethnic groups, who played a major role in Southeast Asian trade for many centuries, they have never been traders. On the whole, Bali is an agricultural society solidly based on wet-rice cultivation, much like the traditional inland economies of Java.

Although no records exist to give an insight into Balinese history before the eleventh century A.D., historians surmise that the village functioned as the chief unit of social organization. Links between villages would occasionally arise when resources had to be shared, and such intervillage connections may have formed the basis for small and probably rather unstable princedoms. Most likely, the courts of such local rulers formed the points of entry of Hinduism to Bali. Although it was formerly thought that Indian traders introduced the Hindu faith to the Indonesian Archipelago, historians now suspect that traveling Hindu scholars settled at the courts of local rulers on Java and Bali, where religious thought was characterized by animism. The Hindus were well received because they consolidated the authority and enhanced the prestige of the princes by promulgating the idea that the rulers stood closer to the gods or even were incarnations of Siva. By the seventh century A.D., Bali was largely Hinduized to the extent that elements of Hindu belief were grafted onto the earlier animist customs, many of which, nevertheless, have survived in altered form, particularly the cult of ancestor worship. Shamanistic elements of ancient Balinese culture also were assured of a continued existence because they were to some extent congruent with Tantric influences emanating from India. Balinese syncretism is also hospitable to Buddhist impulses, but whether these derive directly from India or indirectly from Javanese Buddhism is unclear.

Although Hinduism strengthened the position of local rājas, village life was also influenced by Hindu social organization, particularly the caste system, which exists on Bali in simplified form. Nine out of ten Balinese belong to the Śūdra caste, and there are no "untouchables" as in the Hindu system on the Indian subcontinent. In everyday life, Low Balinese, a Malayo-Polynese dialect, is used except when a Śūdra addresses a member of a higher caste. Such a situation calls for the use of High Balinese, which is not a fully developed language but rather a fairly limited collection of Old Javanese and Sanskrit words transplanted into a Balinese grammatical system. While High Balinese gives some indication of Bali's ancient cultural connections, it must be emphasized that the island has developed independently for many centuries. Bali's connection with India dissolved late in the first millenium, although it maintained close ties with Java until the advent of Islam under Java's maritime kingdoms during the sixteenth century.

In fact, the first documentary evidence of Balinese history concerns its relationship with Java. An internal rebel-

Besakih Temple, Bali
Photo courtesy of Indonesia Tourist Promotion Office, Los Angeles

Stairway, Besakih Temple, Bali
Photo courtesy of Indonesia Tourist Promotion Office, Los Angeles

lion toppled one of the more powerful eastern Javanese kingdoms in 1016. The king's son-in-law, Airlangga, the son of a Balinese princess, managed in the course of the next three decades to reestablish royal authority and recoup its territories, laying the basis for the later kingdom of Kaḍiri. The intermarriages between Balinese and Javanese royal families indicate an already well-established relationship between the two islands. During Airlangga's reign, contact between Java and Bali intensified, and it is possible that Bali became part of a unified kingdom, on an equal footing with the Javanese territories. Javanese cultural influences became more marked as some Javanese nobility settled on Bali. Late in the eleventh century, these connections dissolved again during the struggle over Airlangga's succession, but the cultural influence continued to make itself felt.

In 1284 the last king of the maritime kingdom of Singhasāri on Java captured Bali, but the island regained its independence with the death of the king in 1292 and the subsequent dissolution of the kingdom. Some fifty years later, with the rise of the Majapahit Empire, the eastern Javanese made another attempt to bring Bali into their sphere of influence, this time more successfully. Bali, then under the rule of Beda Ulu, fell to Majapahit forces in 1343. Local legend remembers Beda Ulu as a king who used his magical powers to assert his dominance over his awed and frightened subjects. Having the ability to reattach severed limbs, Beda Ulu is reported to have cut off his own head and reattach it whenever his subjects needed reminding of his privileged standing with the gods. Tired of being thus manipulated, the bystanders one day handed Beda Ulu a pig's head rather than his own, which was thrown into a deep river never to be found again. Thus reduced, Beda Ulu could no longer command the same degree of respect and allegiance from his subjects; nor did he impress the Majapahits, which decided forthwith to subjugate the Balinese.

Whatever Beda Ulu's role in Bali's capitulation, the island received a Javanese governor, who held court in Gelgel, near the southeastern coast. Bali remained subordinate to Majapahit, whose territories included the coastal regions of most of the archipelago's major islands, until late in the fifteenth century. At that time, the locus of power on Java shifted to the port cities, where Muslim traders built up competing kingdoms. As the Majapahit empire began to crumble and Java underwent a gradual process of Islamization, many of Java's Hindu nobility took refuge on Bali, where they were able to continue their customary way of life. Although various Muslim Javanese principalities fought over Bali, Islam never made significant inroads there, perhaps in part because Bali did not develop any major ports along the international trade routes.

By the mid–sixteenth century, Bali was once again independent and had recovered sufficiently to make some territorial conquests of its own. The island was then under the rule of Batu Renggong, who took the title of Dewa Agung (Divine Ruler) and held court at the former gubernatorial seat at Gelgel. The Dewa Agung transformed the ruins of the Majapahit administration into the first strongly centralized kingdom Bali had known, and in this way he was able to marshal the necessary resources for an aggressively expansionist policy. Bali made a fairly short-lived conquest of Balambangan on Java, just across the Bali Strait. More permanent gains were made on Lombok and Sumbawa, to the east. These islands remained in Balinese hands until the late nineteenth century, when the Dutch massacred the residing Balinese nobility and incorporated the islands themselves into the Dutch colonial empire.

Around the same time that Bali began to expand its dominion to nearby islands, European explorers first penetrated to these parts of Southeast Asia. Although it is possible that Portuguese and English ships briefly put in at Bali in the course of the sixteenth century, the first attempt to establish an outpost on Bali came from the Portuguese in 1588. A Portuguese ship with soldiers and building materials was dispatched to the island, but it shipwrecked not far from its destination. The few survivors were graciously received by the Dewa Agung, who, according to local custom, considered the salvage of shipwrecks his by right and refused to let the Portuguese depart.

The first reliably documented European visit was made in 1600 by Cornelis de Houtman, an explorer in the service of the Dutch V.O.C. (Vereenigde Oostindische Compagnie, or United East India Company). The expedition reports that the island was then governed by Rāja Bekung, a benevolent ruler much beloved of his people. Dutch descriptions of his resplendent court at Gelgel are tinged with awe. The population was estimated at about 300,000, but it is unclear how these calculations were made or how reliable they are. Income from Lombok and Sumbawa undoubtedly contributed to the impressive style of the Dewa Agung's reign. In the following year, 1601, Jacob van Heemskerck, an emissary of the V.O.C., received permission to establish trade links with Bali. Whether this grant was more than a graceful gesture on the Dewa Agung's part is doubtful, but in any event the Dutch concentrated their efforts on eastern Java and threw themselves into securing monopolies in the spice trade. As a consequence, Bali was bypassed and continued free of European intervention for several centuries.

In 1639, however, the newly-consolidated Javanese kingdom of Mataram invaded Bali and took Balambangan, Lombok, and Sumbawa. Mataram was unable to establish a permanent presence on Bali, and Lombok and Sumbawa were subsequently recovered. But the brief invasion undermined the authority of Di Made, the reigning Dewa Agung. In the eyes of the local rājas, he had lost face as the divine protector of his island society, and they began to steer their own course on their home turf. Matters were not helped when Di Made had the rāja of Karangasem assassinated sometime in the mid–seventeenth century. The reported cause of this atrocity was that the ascetic rāja neglected his physical hygiene to such a degree as to give great offense to his overlord. In response, the murdered rāja's sons publicly renounced their allegiance to the Dewa Agung. As this action went unpunished, it set an example for the Dewa Agung's other vassals, and the centralized kingdom broke up into twelve local principalities that paid only nominal obeisance to the central ruler. Eventually, only eight of these princely states survived in the competition for dominance, and these form the eight districts into which Bali is now divided.

Di Made's son and successor, Gusti Sideman, moved the court from Gelgel to nearby Klungkung, building another magnificent *puri* (palace compound) there. But he was unable to reunify the island, which gradually fell prey to rivalries between the different princely states. One of the results of these internal conflicts was the rise of a soldier class, which sometimes found employment with one or another of the local rājas and sometimes provided for its own upkeep by plunder on Bali and even on Java. In 1717 and 1718, for instance, roving bands of Balinese laid waste to several towns on east Java and Madura (an island immediately to the northeast), and the V.O.C. army was called upon to expel them. (Javanese rulers more than once turned to the Dutch to resolve such local conflicts, often forfeiting a degree of their autonomy in return for aid. The Balinese wisely abstained from such a policy.)

Buleleng, comprising the fertile northern plateau and the only settlement that maintained regular contact with international traders, was the first Balinese principality to assert its dominance, beginning in the late seventeenth century. Although Buleleng became powerful enough to ignore or even defy the Dewa Agung, its authority remained too localized to put down the continuing conflicts among the other rājas. By the end of the eighteenth century, Buleleng itself had to cede the dominant role on the island to Karangasem, in the southeast. The latter owed much of its local influence and prestige to family connections with the reigning nobility on Lombok.

European contacts at this time appear to have been limited to the British, who were selling opium and weapons to the Balinese while buying slaves, principally through Buleleng—or so, at least, the Dutch thought. The extent of the British opium running and slave and arms trading remains unknown since no account of these illicit activities has been located.

Meanwhile, the Dewa Agung's court, although marginal in political developments on the island, had remained the center of religious and cultural expression. By the end of the eighteenth century, even that position became more tenuous as the rāja of Gianyar built a *puri* that eventually surpassed that of the Dewa Agung in cultural affairs in the course of the nineteenth century.

As the focus of Dutch efforts in Indonesia had shifted from the monopoly trade in spices to an outright policy of colonial control and agricultural exploitation in a variety of staple goods, Bali once again became highly desirable in the nineteenth century. Its plentiful rice crop was particularly attractive to the Dutch colonial empire. Several missions were sent to the island early in the century to try to force from the Balinese a recognition of Dutch sovereignty. Trading rights granted long ago to Jacob van Heemskerck formed the basis of the slender Dutch claim to overlordship. As these missions returned to Jakarta (or Batavia, as the Dutch had named their stronghold in western Java) empty-handed, the Dutch found an excuse for military intervention in the time-honored Balinese custom of salvaging wrecks off its shores and appropriating whatever valuables were recovered.

In 1841 a foundered Dutch ship was plundered by subjects of the rāja of Buleleng, and the Dutch sent a mission to demand restitution and recognition of Dutch sovereignty. They were met by Gusti Ktut Jelantik, the rāja's brother, who refused to enter into negotiations. As the Dutch left, Jelantik began to prepare for war, building fortifications at Buleleng and requesting arms from the British at Singapore. He also forged an alliance with Buleleng's erstwhile rival Karangasem; the remaining rājas and the Dewa Agung refused to become involved in the conflict. The reprisal did not come until 1846, when an expeditionary force of fifty-eight ships anchored off Buleleng, which was taken in short order. In the wake of Buleleng's defeat, a treaty was negotiated that arranged for reparations and the upkeep of a Dutch garrison to be stationed at Buleleng. Whether Jelantik ever had any intention of honoring the treaty we do not know, but certainly no payments were ever made.

Jelantik's troops repelled a renewed attack on Buleleng in 1848, although at the cost of heavy casualties. The following year, the Dutch sent an expeditionary force large enough to brook no more resistance, consisting as it did of 100 ships, carrying 3,000 sailors and 5,000 well-armed and highly trained soldiers. Dutch troops first marched on Buleleng and neighboring Singarāja, and the clash came at the fort of Jagaraga. Once the Balinese defenders realized their position was hopeless, they committed the first *puputan,* or mass suicide, that the Dutch were to provoke in the course of their Balinese expeditions. The fighting continued into 1850, as an attack on Klungkung was repelled and a temporary stalemate resulted. Dutch troops, already worn down by the tropical climate and jungle terrain, were decimated by disease, and for a moment it looked as if Bali might prevail. However, the Dutch managed to create an alliance with an anti-Balinese faction on Lombok, and a raiding party from Lombok ambushed the Buleleng military leadership, killing both Jelantik and the Buleleng rāja. These developments broke the back of Balinese resistance, and a new treaty was negotiated by which the principalities of Buleleng and Jembrana, in the west, passed into Dutch hands. By 1855, a new government structure headed by an indigenous regent and supervised by a Dutch *controleur* was in place in these areas. The Dutch administration was headquartered at Singarāja.

Not long after the first Dutch inroads on Bali had become a reality, local conflicts again came to a head. Warring among the still independent southern princely states reached a new level as the Dewa Agung forged an alliance against Gianyar. In 1868, however, Gianyar demonstrated its dominance by inflicting an ignominious defeat on Klungkung, relegating the Dewa Agung to an even more marginal position. No further Dutch military action took place on Bali for the remainder of the nineteenth century, however, although in 1894 the colonial regime sent a punitive expedition to Lombok to chastise that island's rulers, who were mostly Balinese, for their persecution of the Muslim population. The expedition was ambushed, and in response Dutch troops devastated the island and killed most of the Balinese nobility there.

However, continued looting of shipwrecks caused friction between Dutch authorities and local rulers on Bali itself. In 1904, a wrecked Chinese ship salvaged by subjects of the Badung rāja again formed an excuse for a major military expedition. Troops landed in 1906 and had as their principal objective the subjugation of Badung, in the south. Dutch soldiers marching on the Badung *puri* at Denpasar were met by the entire royal household arrayed in their burial clothes. A *puputan* followed. The rāja of nearby Pemacutan almost immediately followed suit. When the Dutch next advanced on the princely state of Tabanan, they provoked a massive *puputan* there as well. Their hands thus steeped in blood, the Dutch attempted to provoke the Dewa Agung to defend himself, but he instead chose to submit to Dutch demands. The remaining princely states silently followed the Dewa Agung in acknowledging defeat.

All of Bali was now a possession of the Dutch Crown, but the bloodshed was not yet over. In 1908 the Dewa Agung gave refuge to a group of Balinese from Gelgel who were wanted by the colonial authorities. Preparations for defense were made at the Klungkung *puri*, but apparently the Dewa Agung relied primarily on a prophecy that his family's holy *kris* (a dagger with a long and wavy blade), thrown into the ground at the feet of the colonial troops, would open a chasm to swallow them up. As the ruler performed this ceremonial act of defiance, he was shot and killed. His entire household threw itself into another *puputan*.

Colonial rule on Bali was unusually respectful of the traditional society it had subjugated. A substantial part of revenues in fact went into the provision of public services, such as health care and education. The colonial army was replaced by a police force. The indigenous government structure was left untouched, although it was placed under the supervision of a Dutch resident. Foreign enterprise was prohibited, and on the whole Bali became more peaceful than it had been during previous centuries. Traditional culture was reinvigorated, while a few anthropologists and artists settled on the island and began to broadcast its cultural riches. Tourism made a modest beginning as a Dutch freightliner began to reserve passenger berths on its ships and built a hotel in Denpasar.

During World War II, Bali was occupied by Japanese forces, and a local resistance movement under the leadership of Gusti Ngurai Rai came into being. The movement armed itself against both the Japanese and the Dutch, who had no intention of giving up their colonial holdings in Indonesia following the anticipated Japanese surrender. In August 1945, the resistance movement immediately installed an interim government in Denpasar, but the returning Dutch expelled them from office. A group of resistance fighters hid out in the mountainous interior, but in 1946 the Dutch colonial army forced a confrontation that resulted in the final *puputan* in the history of Bali's resistance to colonial power. The Dutch established Bali as a province of the Republic of East Indonesia, with a puppet government controlled by the Hague, in an effort to stem the postwar independence movement and confine it to Java. Indonesia's nationalist forces under Sukarno eventually won the war, however, and in 1949 Bali joined the independent federation that made up the Republic of the United States of Indonesia. Following the reorganization of the federation in 1956, the island became a province of the Republic of Indonesia.

Since that time, Bali has enjoyed virtually continuous prosperity, a booming tourist trade, and a flourishing international reputation for its arts and crafts. Balinese music, dance, and painting, in particular, are recognized the world over for their variety, inventiveness, and technical accomplishment. The island's art undoubtedly also receives a great deal of attention for its communal nature and its integration into the islanders' everyday life—conditions of artistic production that still hold out a promise of an earthly paradise to alienated Westerners.

Further Reading: *Bali,* with a text by Star Black and Willard A. Hanna (fourteenth edition, Singapore: APA, and New York: Prentice Hall, 1989), provides the best general description of the island, including a highly readable section devoted to its history. *Indonesia Bali Plus* by Sarita J. Newson (Bali: Bali Tourism Promotion Board, 1987) offers a detailed guide to the island's attractions and accommodations. The best general history of Indonesia in English is M. C. Ricklefs' *A History of Modern Indonesia: 1300 to the Present* (Bloomington: Indiana University Press, and London: Macmillan, 1981).

—Elizabeth Brice and Marijke Rijsberman

Balkh (Balkh, Afghanistan)

Location: Balkh (ancient Bactra), in the Amu Darya (Oxus) Basin, is approximately nine miles west of Mazār-i-Sharīf and forty-six miles south of the Amu Darya River.

Description: Once fabled as a town of ancient splendors, Balkh retains few relics of its rich history to attract the attention of the casual visitor. The old town is now mostly in ruins, with only the Green Mosque, a few decaying buildings, and the crumbling remnants of walls from which to reconstruct the epic of past greatness and catastrophic reverses. The clue lies in the sheer size and scale of these ruins. The new town lies at a short distance from the old, on the right bank of the Balkh River, a dried-up tributary of the Amu Darya.

Contact: Embassy of the Republic of Afghanistan
2341 Wyoming Avenue N.W.
Washington, D.C. 20008
U.S.A.
(202) 234-3770

In his introduction to the Penguin edition of Robert Byron's *The Road to Oxiana,* Bruce Chatwin recounts a conversation he had in 1962: "In Balkh, the Mother of Cities, I asked a fakir the way to the shrine of Hadji Piardeh [Hajji Piyade]. 'I don't know it,' he said, 'It must have been destroyed by Genghiz'." The destruction wrought by Genghis Khan and his 100,000 Mongol horsemen was horrific, but it had taken place in 1220, and it says much about Balkh that the atrocity seemed relatively recent and occupied a prominent place in residents' minds even in 1962.

The shrine about which Chatwin inquired, Hajji Piyade, also known locally as Kob el Akhbar or Nouh Gumbad, still exists in partly ruined state, and Chatwin succeeded in getting to it. It was discovered and described by the outstanding Russian authority G. A. Pugachenkova in the 1960s and subsequently has attracted much attention from art historians. After some dispute, historians finally have agreed that it was built in the second half of the ninth century during the period of rule by the Islamic ʿAbbāsid Dynasty. The story of Hajji Piyade nonetheless underlines the extent of what remains to be investigated and the need for prolonged specialized study of sites across Central Asia.

Balkh's history is long and rich. The city's position in the fertile Amu Darya Valley and on one of the river's tributaries, as well as on the most important trade route to cross southern Central Asia to the north of the Himalayas, must have made it an important site as early as the second millennium B.C.

Its origins as a prosperous settlement, like those of later Silk Road towns such as Mary and Samarkand, may have derived from its development as a staging post at which merchandise was sold for transport across the desert to northern China, crossing Chinese Turkistan south of the Takla Makan Desert to the north of Tibet. The trade initially would have been chiefly in lapis lazuli, possibly found in Tibet but known to have been mined in Badakhshān in northeastern Afghanistan, destined for Mesopotamia and the eastern Mediterranean ports. Balkh was known in ancient times as Bactra; considering that the surrounding region was known as Bactria, Bactra was probably its leading town.

By the end of the second millennium B.C., although neither written records nor archaeological remains can verify it, Balkh had perhaps attained the size, importance, and prosperity of Babylon, Nineveh, and Ecbatana (Hamadan) at their zeniths. It was a merchant center rather than a military fortress. Herodotus, the fifth-century B.C. historian, believed the Bactrians to be of Persian origin, and it is to be presumed that Bactra (the name by which Balkh was known throughout most of the period during which Bactria was an important regional kingdom) was already an established settlement even earlier, in the second millennium B.C., when the Bactrian and Persian Indo-European invaders together pushed through the Hindu Kush and obliterated all trace of the Dravidian early Indus Valley civilization centered on Mohenjodaro and Harappā. Balkh was certainly an important center under the Persian Empire inaugurated in 550 B.C., when Cyrus rebelled against the king of the Medes, Astyages, to found the Achaemenid Empire of twenty tribute-paying satrapies, noted for the efficiency of its central administration and postal service.

Balkh surrendered to Alexander the Great without a struggle after he had destroyed the Persian army at Gaugamela in 331 B.C. On Alexander's death in 323 B.C., Bactria was taken by his general, Seleucus I Nicator, who founded the Seleucid Empire. Bactria did not break away from this empire until the middle of the third century B.C., when it formed the Greco-Bactrian kingdom under Euthydemus, a Greek who had killed Diodotus II, the Seleucid satrap. It is normally assumed that Balkh must have developed full Greek political and administrative forms, with council, assembly, and magistrates proposed by the council and elected by the people. The city no doubt also had been fortified and walled by this time.

Much of the missing information about the relationships of the peoples who lived between the Mediterranean and the Indus Valley during the first millennium of recorded history can be revealed only by major archaeological investigations. Such investigations, however, would be so complex and on such a large scale that they are unlikely to occur. In particular, more archaeological evidence is needed for the history of Balkh, crucial for an understanding of the history

Shrine of Hajji Piyade, Balkh
Photo courtesy of Mr. Rashid Uddin, Park Travel Agency, Chicago

of Central Asia as a whole. A French archaeological mission of 1923 was allowed to sink a trench, but dug to a stratum representing nothing earlier than the fifteenth century. The ruin mounds around Balkh extend for fifteen miles and almost certainly conceal important information about the Greek presence in Bactria.

It is known that about 130 B.C. Bactria fell to a large group of raiding nomads or former nomads known as the Yüeh-Chi. The Yüeh-Chi were not a tribe per se. They were homogeneous only linguistically, not ethnically, and as time passed they absorbed other groups and shed splinter bands. One of these groups, the Kushāns, emerged to establish a dynasty at Balkh; they had taken control of the city by 128 B.C., at which time a Chinese envoy named Chang Kien visited there. He found Balkh undamaged, its mercantile life unhindered. It remained the capital of Bactria, having no doubt negotiated terms for surrender. Eventually, in the middle of the third century A.D., the Kushāns became vassals of the Persian Sāsānians.

As a result of the city's location on important trade routes and its repeated conquest by diverse invaders, Balkh was exposed over the centuries to a variety of religions, many of which took firm hold there. The rise of the Achaemenids' Persian Empire saw the spread of two very different forms of worship. One was the cult of Anahita, the water deity who acquired Babylonian characteristics to become a goddess of fertility. The other was Zoroastrianism, which scholars generally acknowledge to have become the official religion of the Achaemenid Empire. Balkh is said to have played a significant role in the development of Zoroastrianism. Ancient sources claim that Balkh was the birthplace of Zoroaster (c. 628–551 B.C.), founder of the religion, but recent scholarship indicated that he was more likely to have been born in northwestern Iran. The tenth-century *Shāh-nāma,* drawing on a mixture of lost Sāsānian sources, claims that the prophet died at Balkh. The city was also home, at least temporarily, to several items mentioned in the Zoroastrian *Avesta,* including a statue of Anāhitā wearing a crown of eight gold sunrays and a hundred stars, and a cloak of thirty beaver skins presented by Artaxerxes of Persia in the early fourth century B.C.; both items were noted by Alexander the Great in 329 B.C. Written descriptions have also survived of a great Zoroastrian fire altar in the city's largest temple. The alternative ancient name for the city, Zariaspa, may allude specifically to this temple, or possibly to a section of the city.

Buddhism also seems to have thrived at Balkh. The religion most likely spread to the city, and to the other trading posts of the Amu Darya Valley, via the Silk Road from China. Little is known about Buddhist life at Balkh, and the scant information we have comes from the travel reports of the seventh-century Buddhist monk Xuan Zang, which are not necessarily reliable. Although he castigates the monks of Balkh for their apathy and the city's inhabitants for their lack of religious devotion, Xuan Zang describes a sizeable Buddhist community there, including approximately 100 convents, 3,000 worshipers, and a number of stupas. One of the stupas measured over 200 feet, and one convent, the Nau Bahar (New Convent), had a notably expensive statue of Buddha.

Other religions found adherents in Balkh as well. Balkh was a metropolitan Nestorian Christian bishopric from as early as the late fifth century until at least the thirteenth, and it was from Balkh that Christians and Jews reached China. The coexistence of these varied religions in Balkh is more a testament to the city's primary concern with trade than an indication of its ideological or ethnic diversity.

In 651 Balkh surrendered to the Islamic Arab advance as readily as it had to Alexander and the Yüeh-Chi. The rise of Islam, with its aversion to images of live animals and the human form, must have hastened the decline of Buddhist art, which thrived on such representations, and it is for its Islamic glories, however decayed, that Balkh is chiefly remembered. The Arabs conferred on Balkh the title Mother of Cities, a phrase that suggested—and still today denotes—Balkh's size and importance as a center of commerce, religion, culture, and scholarship.

The Hajji Piyade shrine discovered by Pugachenkova is the earliest surviving Muslim religious monument in Afghanistan and the easternmost example of a building in its style. It is 65 feet square and contains thick pillars of bricks measuring 12 by 12 by 2 inches. Scholars believe that curtain walls once stretched between the pillars, only four of which are still standing. Massive arches once joined the pillars to the coupled columns attached to the walls, and there was a semidome in the middle of the southwest wall serving as the hood of the *mihrab* (prayer niche). The roof must have consisted of a series of brick domes, and the interior consisted of nine equal-sized squares. The columns supported arcades that rose into the walls of the barrel vaults covering the corridors. The architectural idiom was imported from the Middle East, but it was related to pre-Islamic traditions. Stucco carvings of grape leaves, vine scrolls, palms, and fir cones almost completely fill the available space and, with the other decoration, reveal the survival of Sāsānian styles, making the Balkh mosque an important indication of the way in which Islamic decorative patterns and techniques incorporated and built upon those dating from earlier centuries.

Balkh is reported by early Islamic writers to have been the greatest city in all Khorāsān, a label at that date understood to indicate the eastern quarter of the Sāsānian Empire but which today corresponds to northeastern Iran. The city was renowned for its beauty as early as the seventh century, and reports mention that it had three concentric walls with thirteen gates; pottery found in the surviving walls, however, dates them to the fifteenth century, the last period of the city's importance. The walls, like local houses, were made of sundried bricks.

Very early in the eleventh century Balkh became part of the territory amassed by Maḥmūd of Ghaznī, son of Sebüktigin, founder of the Ghaznavid Empire, which came to encompass Afghanistan, Iran, and the Punjab. Then in 1220 Genghis Khan mounted his atrocious assault on Balkh, site of the worst slaughter he was to inflict on Afghanistan. During the raid he leveled much of the city, including one-third of its great mosque, in a fruitless search for hidden treasure. Balkh was still in ruins when Marco Polo passed through in 1275, although Polo described it as a "noble city." It was apparently still unreconstructed in the early fourteenth century.

Finally, under Timur (Tamerlane), who captured Balkh later in the fourteenth century, the city's walls and fortress were rebuilt. Timur, however, did not succeed in reestablishing the city's reputation for culture and trade. He extended the town westward from its original square, and some of the walls he erected are relatively well preserved. Balkh's greatest monument, the Green Mosque, is the ruin of the green-tiled shrine erected to the memory of the theologian Khvājeh Abū Naṣr Pārṣā, who died in 1597. The western dome, which is all that remains, was built to an octagonal plan, with wings attached to four of the sides. The dome is framed between two twisted dark blue pillars, veneered, like the magnificent front, in faience, and the drum on top of the octagon, covered with mosaic, is accompanied by two still-standing minarets. The dome, architecturally reminiscent of the Gūr-e Amīr at Samarkand, has a ribbed turquoise exterior. In the walls the niches and balconies are white, decorated in green. Inside, the dome has cobalt ribs, yellow and green flowers, and a *mihrab*. Additions were made later to the building, and at the eastern end of the square an empty gateway to the *medrese* (theological school) still stands. It was built in the late seventeenth century by Sayid Subhān Kūlī Khān; the decoration was inspired by that found at Herāt. The tiles were stripped in the 1860s for use at Mazār-i-Sharīf. The discovery of the tomb of ʿAli, the prophet Muḥammad's son-in-law, in the latter city in the late fifteenth century meant that Mazār-i-Sharīf soon outstripped Balkh in significance.

Except for brief periods of rule by Bābur, by the Ṣafavids under Shāh Ismaīl, and by the Mughals (the latter from 1641–47), Balkh remained mostly in Uzbek hands from the early sixteenth century until 1736, the year the Persian Nāder Shāh overthrew the Ṣafavid Dynasty prior to capturing Delhi, destroying Mughal power, and severing Afghanistan from the Indian monarchy for good. In 1737 Nāder Shāh suppressed a revolt against his rule by the Uzbeks of Balkh. After his death, Balkh passed briefly back into Uzbek hands before submitting to Ahmad Shāh Durrāni and the Afghans in approximately 1752. Afghanistan gradually became independent under the two branches of the Durrāni family, one of which furnished the shahs, the other the emirs. Balkh, by now in decline, was taken by Shah Murah of Kundūz in 1820. For a time it was subject to the khan of Bukhara. It was annexed to Afghanistan again in 1850 and subsequently remained under Afghan rule.

A new town of Balkh, also known as Wazīrābād, was laid out from 1919 to 1929. It is still only a small village. The archaeological wonders of the ancient city yet remain to be explored. Despite the withdrawal of Soviet forces in 1989 and the establishment of a new government in 1992, northern Afghanistan has continued to be torn by factional fighting and has remained dangerous even for official teams of archaeologists.

Further Reading: The complete history of Balkh has not been written. It is therefore necessary to consult histories of regions and periods. Of general interest is Peter Levi's *The Light Garden of the Angel King: Journeys in Afghanistan* (London: Collins, and Indianapolis: Bobbs Merrill, 1972). Levi accompanied Bruce Chatwin and describes the 'Abbāsid Mosque. More technical, and with a full bibliography, is *The Archeology of Afghanistan from Earliest Times to the Timurid Period,* edited by F. Raymond Allchin and Norman Hammond (London and New York: Academic Press, 1978). For the earlier period, the indispensable study remains W. W. Tarn's *The Greeks in Bactria and India* (Cambridge: Cambridge University Press, 1938; third edition, Chicago: Ares, 1985). No modern guidebook offers significant information on the region.

—Anthony Levi

Ballarat (Victoria, Australia)

Location: Approximately sixty miles west-northwest of Melbourne, Victoria's capital, along the Western Freeway.

Description: During the gold rush of the 1850s, Ballarat boasted one of the richest alluvial gold deposits in the world. It was the site of the Eureka Stockade of 1854, a turning point in Australian history. A brief and bloody battle erupted on December 3, 1854, between miners and police after months of growing tension regarding the unpopular licence tax and the broader issue of miners' rights. This event marked the first and only instance of Australian civil conflict on domestic soil.

Contact: Ballarat Tourist Information Centre
Sturt and Albert Streets
North Ballarat 3350, Victoria
Australia
(53) 32 2694

Ballarat is Australia's largest inland city in the southern region of Victoria's central highlands. Recorded history indicates that this area originally formed part of the territory of the aboriginal Kulin tribe. The Kulin people named the district Ballaarat, which literally translates as "reclining on an elbow," or a good place to rest. European encroachment into the area began in the late 1830s, when settlers established sheep stations there. In 1851 the discovery of gold in Bunninyong, on the southern outskirts of Ballarat, caused a large rush of Australians and foreigners to the region. It soon became clear that the easily accessible Ballarat flats, creeks, and flood plains were rich in deposits of alluvial gold.

A British observer noted in 1853 that any remnants of aristocratic feeling or sympathy with the old country were annihilated on the goldfields of Victoria. Another commentator noted, "Nothing indeed can have a more levelling effect on society than the power of digging gold, for it can be done, for a time at least, without any capital but that of health and strength; and the man innured to toil, however ignorant, is on more equal terms with the educated and refined in a pursuit involving so much personal hardship." The gold rush in Victoria happened in a society where physical activity and industry were the highest standards of judgment, a feature still evident in contemporary Australian society. Certainly the gold rush brought drastic changes to Victorian society. Between 1851 and 1854, the state's population increased fourfold. In 1854 the population on the goldfields was close to 61,000, one quarter that of the entire colony.

The population density added to the already harsh conditions of life on the goldfields. Individual prospectors battled dysentery and other diseases, faced cramped and unhygienic living conditions, and contended with the dry and windy climate. Work on the goldfields was hazardous: miners were crushed by earthfalls, murdered for their find, or killed by equipment; some even committed suicide (records indicate twenty-five accounts of suicide in 1853). As deposits of alluvial gold became exhausted, miners began to work the deeper quartz reefs in groups, usually of four. Two miners were required to cut timber for shaft props, one to dig, and another to winch the buckets of rock to the surface. The average Ballarat mine site measured about forty square feet. Sinking the deep, narrow mineshafts in quartz was dangerous, time consuming, and expensive work that often produced little or no reward. Later, larger shafts were sunk to work deeper underground. This method employed many workmen and used heavy, sophisticated machinery. It was usually done by companies and reaped rich rewards. The gold nuggets unearthed in the 1850s using this method were among the heaviest ever found in Australia.

As company mining began to replace the individual digger and more people flocked to exploit the limited resources on the Ballarat goldfields, discontent and frustration heightened, often erupting in outbreaks of crime and violence. The situation worsened when Captain Sir Charles Hotham, governor of Victoria, envisaged the goldfields in 1854 as a potential source of revenue to assist in the financial burdens of running the colony.

In 1851 Governor FitzRoy proclaimed the crown's right of common law to all the gold in New South Wales and threatened to prosecute anybody who dug for it without authorization. When gold was discovered in the recently separated Victorian colony, the government introduced a licencing system that cost miners thirty shillings per month. Victorian governor Joseph LaTrobe was concerned over the response of the miners to this new tax in his under-policed state. LaTrobe proposed several compromises to appease the disgruntled miners, all of which were rejected by the Legislative Council in Whitehall. LaTrobe suggested an export tax on gold that would tax a miner in proportion to his earnings. This plan, finally introduced after the Eureka Stockade, may have averted the conflict had London officials agreed to it initially. They had opposed LaTrobe's plan, however, arguing that gold would be smuggled out through Sydney and Adelaide.

In May 1854 LaTrobe was recalled to England and replaced by Vice-Admiral Sir Charles Hotham. Under pressure from London, Hotham in turn increased the pressure on the miners. The colony was in debt to the bank for more than £400,000, and Hotham was determined that the miners help reduce this. He devised a divide-and-rule policy on the goldfields by increasing searches for miners without licences, condoning police brutality, and planting spies and agitators who

Town Hall, Ballarat
Photo courtesy of Tourism Victoria, Melbourne

forced miners into a state of rebellion. The miners would then be blamed for initiating the violence. Bob O'Brien, author of a recent book on the violence at Eureka, argues that the ambitious Vice-Admiral Hotham had his orders from Whitehall to pick a fight with the miners, and that there was "absolutely nothing the miners could have done to avoid the clash."

By this time, the scarcity of gold for individual prospectors had drawn their attention to what they perceived as a division between, on the one hand, the equality and mateship on the goldfields, and on the other the political and social privileges they were denied in the world around them. This was best illustrated, they argued, in the enforced administration of the licences required by miners to work the diggings. Police enforced the licence fee, which many described as too costly considering the unpredictable nature of their work. Miners also complained of the difficulty in obtaining the licences, which often required them to walk miles and wait for hours before being interviewed. Raffaello Carboni, one of the diggers' leaders, commented in 1855, "I think the practical miner, who had been hard at work, night and day, for the last four or six months, . . . objected to the tax itself, because he could not possibly afford to pay it. And was it not atrocious to confine this man in the lousy lock-up at the Camp, because he had no luck?"

The government's severe enforcement of the licence fee constituted another of the miners' major grievances. Hotham ordered police to conduct brutal "on person" inspections on the goldfields up to twice a week. Armed bands of police would pounce on one area, demanding licences, and, after dealing severely with miners who could not produce a licence, marched them to the nearest magistrate where they would be fined or imprisoned. Evidence of the famous Australian egalitarian legacy is seen with the introduction of a plan understood among the miners to elude police. If a group of police was seen approaching, miners would raise a cry of "Joe! Joe!" The miners would continue the cry down the gully, and all defaulters would automatically head for safety. William Kelly in 1859 recalled a "digger raid" he witnessed in Ballarat: "I heard the swelling uproar and the loud chorus of 'Joes!' from every side. Everybody was in commotion, diggers lowering down their mates without licences; others cursing the system; some 'stealing away' like hares; and others running up the hill-sides to spread to the neighbouring gullies the commencement of the police foray." While many managed to escape the police prosecution, the fierce enforcement tactics and the miner's licence was a constant source of irritation and indignation.

The miner's licence, however, soon became only the foremost of several issues the miners wanted redressed. By 1854 miners saw that the gap between themselves and the upper social classes had became more pronounced. The colonial government was seen as corrupt and unjust. Governor Hotham did little to appease the growing miner population. This situation became critical on October 6, 1854. Late that evening, James Scobie, a miner, was murdered on the goldfields of Ballarat. The proprietor of the nearby Eureka Hotel, James Bentley, along with his wife and his associate John Ferrell, were charged with the murder. The magistrate, John d'Ewes, acquitted all three of the charge. The miners, suspecting corruption and bribery in the acquittal, organized a protest meeting, after which the Eureka Hotel was burned to the ground. Three men were charged and convicted of riot and arson. Bentley was rearrested and convicted of manslaughter, and magistrate d'Ewes was dismissed. Yet the incident had proven to be the breaking point for the miners. They rallied together, organizing a list of demands upon which they insisted the government act.

Recent events attracted other grievances that were aired throughout November. Suddenly the issues under discussion expanded beyond the licence fee to include the general rights of miners, their political rights, and the conditions on the goldfields. Many called for the government to improve roads, the postal service, and amenities, and to provide military escorts for gold. Throughout 1854, the stump orators, speakers who commented on public affairs at meetings, had discerned three major grievances. It was beyond the capacity of miners, they argued first, to pay the overbearing licence fee, and the police were overtly tyrannical in their searches. Second, the government provided little opportunity for lucky miners to invest their money in land; miners found that acquiring land on reasonable terms was impossible. Finally, the lack of political rights became an important concern for miners. They considered themselves contributors to the economic wealth of the government without participating in its administration.

As these concerns became more focused, greater numbers of miners began to discuss issues and demand justice. On November 11, 1854, a mass meeting of 10,000 diggers met on Bakery Hill and formed the Ballarat Reform League, which argued that "taxation without representation [was] tyranny." The league also threatened corrupt and dishonest officials with the "people's prerogatives" and committed itself to the immediate abolition of the miner's licence and reorganization of the goldfields. It asserted its five major aims: full and fair representation; manhood suffrage; abolition of property qualification for members of the Legislative Council; payment of members; and short duration of parliaments. A notice advertising the league's meeting stated, "All who claim the right to a voice in the framing of the laws under which they should live, are solemnly bound to attend the meeting, and further its objects to the utmost extent of their power." However, as many no doubt predicted, Hotham and his government were less than attentive to the miners' concerns.

In response to the demands of the Ballarat Reform League, Hotham dispatched more troops to the goldfields and organized and intensified licence hunts. On Wednesday, November 29, 4,000 men met on Bakery Hill for a mass meeting, many burning their licences in a huge bonfire. The next day Hotham retaliated by intensifying licence searches, resulting in several fights between miners and police. Miners again met on Bakery Hill. They elected as their leader an Irishman named Peter Lalor, who promised, "If once I pledge my hand to the diggers, I will neither defile it with treachery, nor render it contemptible by cowardice." Hundreds of diggers enrolled into military companies and adopted a rebel flag, the Southern Cross, which was blue with a white cross upon it. A newspaper reporter from the Melbourne *Argus* described the ceremony: "The leader . . . mounted the stump, called upon all present to swear allegiance to the flag that waved over them, and to acknowledge no other. This ceremony being gone through, nearly every one present then went to the stump and signed a large document of some kind."

By the weekend, a stockade had been erected on Eureka Hill. On Saturday night, only 150 men, not expecting an attack on a Sunday, remained on guard. However, the officer commanding the reinforcement troops sent from Melbourne decided to act quickly to disarm the diggers. At 4:00 on the morning of December 3, the commander led his 400 troops to Eureka Hill. When the diggers refused to surrender, he ordered the troops to charge. A brief and bloody battle ensued. It took less than fifteen minutes for the crudely constructed and underguarded stockade at Eureka to fall. In that brief time, 25 diggers were killed and 30 wounded, compared to 1 officer and 3 privates killed and 11 privates wounded. The ringleader, Peter Lalor, lost his arm in the battle but still managed to escape. One hundred diggers were taken into custody, and no further attempt was made to challenge the government.

Thirteen miners faced charges of high treason for their role in the rebellion, but Melbourne juries refused to convict them. A general amnesty was extended to all who participated in the uprising. Lalor came out of hiding in 1855 to become a member of parliament. His selection as a candidate indicated community approval of his leadership at Eureka. The "miner's right" was introduced to replace the licence tax. It cost each miner one pound sterling per year and allowed the holder to dig for gold, vote at elections, and stand for the Legislative Assembly. An export duty such as had been proposed by Joseph LaTrobe was at last implemented to cover goldfield administration costs. Wardens replaced commissioners as the administrators of the goldfields, which were incorporated into the electoral district. More ground was allotted to each miner working on the fields. While it is debatable whether some of these results were the direct consequence of the Eureka Stockade, it would seem the Eureka rebellion moved the process along.

Today the city of Ballarat stands as a monument to the diggers and their cause. The Sovereign Hill Historical Park is a sixty-two acre living museum that was opened in 1970 on the site of the former Sovereign Hill Quartz Mining Co. It is an accurate recreation of life in the gold rush era of the 1850s. The restored town buildings overlook the tents and slab huts of the prospectors, with tourists invited to try their own luck. A recent addition to the Sovereign Hill Park is an evening sound and light show, "Blood on the Southern Cross," which graphically stages the events that culminated in the Eureka Stockade. Ballarat's Gold Museum hosts a world-class collection of alluvial gold and nuggets as well as coins and artifacts of the era. Bentley's Eureka Hotel can be visited, as can the original Eureka flag, housed at the Ballarat Art Gallery. These attractions have made Ballarat a popular tourist spot that has provided a lucrative asset to its economy.

Ballarat, and the sacrifice of its miners in December 1854, has a lasting place in Australian history. The Eureka Stockade looms large in Australian culture as a symbol of rugged freedom and egalitarian independence of spirit. Yet Eureka has been subject to different interpretations. Conservatives have seen it as a misguided adventure achieving little that would not have occurred otherwise. In fact, for many years the Eureka Stockade was reduced to a faint moment in Australia's turbulent history. Less than one year after the rebellion, Peter Lalor stated that he was "free to confess that it was a rash act" in which he had participated at Eureka. Australians were led to believe that the battle was a revolt by "foreign" miners against the authority of Queen Victoria. Yet it was not their loyalty to the queen that was in question, but their loyalty to the corrupt administration in Ballarat.

More recently, however, a favorable view of Eureka has been adopted in Australia. On the fiftieth anniversary of the conflict, the *Ballarat Star* reported, "The blood of the patriots had not been shed in vain. . . . Young Victoria owes a debt of gratitude to the men of '54. The peace, protection and unfettered liberty we now enjoy were baptised with the blood of the martyr patriots who fell at Eureka." With the abolition of the licence tax, many argued that while the military had won the battle at Eureka Hill, the miners won the war. Eureka brought Irish, English, and a score of other nationalities together under a shared cause and a common flag. A writer for the Melbourne *Argus* in December 1854 showed incredible foresight when describing the miners' revolt on Bakery Hill: "There is a degree of wild romance about the proceedings, which, connected with the cause that called them into operation, must form an important picture in the future history of Australia."

Further Reading: For recent texts dedicated to the Eureka Stockade, see *Eureka* by John Molony (Ringwood, Victoria: Viking, 1984), *Eureka: Rebellion beneath the Southern Cross*, edited by Geoffrey Gold (Adelaide, South Australia: Rigby in association with Widescope, 1977), and *Massacre at Eureka: The Untold Story* by Bob O'Brien (Kew, Victoria: Australian Scholarly Publishing, 1992). For Raffaello Carboni's eyewitness account see *The Eureka Stockade* (Carlton, Victoria: Melbourne University Press, 1975). Weston Bate's *Life After Gold: Twentieth Century Ballarat* (Carlton, Victoria: Melbourne University Press, 1993) provides an insight into modern-day Ballarat. For life on the Victorian goldfields see David Goodman's *Gold Seeking: Victoria and California in the 1850s* (Sydney: Allen and Unwin, 1994; Stanford, California: Stanford University Press, 1995).

—Joseph M. Siracusa

Bāmiān (Bāmiān, Afghanistan)

Location: Bāmiān, capital of the province of the same name, is eighty miles west-northwest of Kābul, nestling near the Bāmiān River in the now-irrigated high valley of the Kundūz River among an intricate series of mountain passes through the Hindu Kush.

Description: Virtually a museum of ancient Buddhist culture, Bāmiān was a former stopping place on the main trade route between India and central Asia. The Bāmiān Valley is lined with high cliffs into which Buddhist monks once carved cave dwellings and niches for the giant Buddha figures that still stand there.

Contact: Embassy of the Republic of Afghanistan
2341 Wyoming Avenue N.W.
Washington, D.C. 20008
U.S.A.
(202) 234-3770

One Dr. Gerard, describing the site of Bāmiān in the nineteenth century, wrote, "Desolation is not the word for this place; the surface of the hills is actually dead; no vegetable trace is to be seen. . . . Such is the horrid aspect." This was not always the case. Bāmiān was once a crucial site on the bustling trade route between India, Central Asia, and China. The Bāmiān Pass connected the Indus Valley to the Amu Darya (Oxus) Valley by providing a route through the Hindu Kush range, thereby connecting India and Afghanistan to Central Asia along the East-West Silk Road to China. The steady stream of trade caravans that traveled through the Bāmiān Pass brought with them one import that was to have a particularly large and lasting impact on the town: Buddhism. By the sixth century, a thriving Buddhist community had developed at Bāmiān. Today, the site is known chiefly for the splendid caves and statues that this community created.

The early history of Bāmiān is somewhat hazy. Very little is known of the city's founding. Some ten miles to the south of the Bāmiān Valley is a mound, as yet not properly excavated, of Shahr-I-Gholghola, on which once stood the citadel guarding the city's approaches. It is an isolated rock on which the ruins of the acropolis can still be found. The actual site of the old city is still marked by mounds and remains of walls, but the chronology of the city and the Buddhist relics cannot be established without the proper excavation, of which, for the moment, there is little prospect. Pottery fragments at Shahr-I-Gholghola indicate a Ghūrid occupation, Ghūr being the medieval and local modern term for the region of highlands east of Herāt, but they probably date from the fifteenth century or later. All the existing settlements were burned down by the Mongols under Genghis Khan in 1221.

There is also a triple series of fortifications at the cliff castle of Shahr-I-Zohak, called the Red City after the color of the cliff, near the confluence of the Bāmiān, Hajjigak, and Kundūz Rivers. The ruins are of red clay brick, and the cliff has been deliberately sheared off below the castle, leaving the river 100 yards beneath. Record was made of a courtyard here in 1928, but it has been destroyed. One of the three sets of fortifications encircled a castle, its longest side about 400 feet of crenellated walls and towers. The other buildings, with better views of the pass to the south, presumably served only military purposes.

The whole fortified area lies on rock to the east of the main valley, covering an area of about 1,000 by 650 feet, with the top of one of the rocks supporting the fortified buildings as much as 500 feet above the valley. To the west of the ruined fortifications are huge mountains of barren rock on the other side of the Bāmiān Valley. It has been estimated, based on little more than archaeologically inspired guesswork, that the brick fortress of Shahr-I-Zohak dates from the same period as the Hunter King wall painting at nearby Kakrak, generally assigned to the period between the fifth and the seventh centuries. Some have suggested that Shahr-I-Zohak was renovated during the period of Islamic rule in the region, starting in the eighth century, but there is little to support this theory. At Shahr-I-Gholghola the rebuilding is from the period of Mongol rule from 1220 to 1506, and the population of the Bāmiān region today is still predominantly of Mongol origin.

The relics of Buddhism at Bāmiān are on the whole late, probably dating from no earlier than the fifth century A.D. The mixture of Sāsānian, Indian, and Greek decorative elements in the painting and sculpture at Bāmiān reinforces the theory that these relics date from the sixth or seventh century, although huge Buddha figures continued to be erected in cliff niches in China as late as the fourteenth century.

The difficulty of dating derives partly from the need for much more systematic fieldwork than has been undertaken, but also from the fact that Bāmiān could have continued its practice of Buddhism uninterrupted from the time it arrived there. This certainly had occurred by the sixth century A.D. and probably much earlier; Buddhism survived at least until Maḥmūd established his power center at Ghaznī in the eleventh century, and perhaps beyond. In fact, Bāmiān might well have escaped any Islamic incursion prior to Genghis Khan's raid in 1221. True, scholars believe that the Hepthalite princes who conquered Bāmiān in the seventh century converted to Islam 100 years later, and that the town was captured in 871 by Ya'qūb ebn Leys, founder of the Islamic Ṣaffārid Dynasty; nevertheless, there is no physical evidence for any Arab or Islamic presence at Bāmiān. Its Buddhist paintings and sculptures, offensive to Islamic sensibilities, were left

Buddha statue cut into a mountain face, Bāmiān
Photo courtesy of Mr. Rashid Uddin, Park Travel Agency, Chicago

unharmed. Furthermore, there were Buddhist kings of Bāmiān in the late ninth and again in the late tenth centuries, well after the regions to the north and south of the mountains had been taken by the Arabs and had become strongly Islamic. Bāmiān might have escaped early Islamic conquests because it was no longer an attractive target; by the eighth century, the increasing popularity of East-West sea trade and the growing political instability in Central Asia and Asia Minor had made the overland Silk Road network unsafe and little-used. It would not revive until the time of the Mongols.

Surprisingly little that is commonly assumed about the history of Bāmiān actually rests on evidence. One of the first reliable written accounts of the town was recorded in the fifth century by Fa Xian, the famed Buddhist pilgrim from China. Fa Xian happened to be at Bāmiān when the king was due to summon there the quinquennial assembly of the monks. He recorded his impressions as follows: "Their place of session is grandly decorated. Silken streamers and canopies are hung out in it, and water-lilies in gold and silver are made and fixed over the places where the chief of them are to sit. . . . The king waits on them himself . . . uttering vows at the same time as all his ministers." The same pilgrim records avalanches and landslides in the mountains, and snow in both winter and summer. Since Bāmiān and its valley have long been free from snow in summer, this is one of a number of facts that point to a perceptible and progressive cooling of at least central Asia around the time of the late Roman Empire. This climatic change is not ordinarily mentioned in history books, but it must have been of determining importance in the historical development of mining, travel, and transport during the Middle Ages.

Xuan Zang, another famous Buddhist pilgrim from China, passed through Bāmiān in the seventh century A.D. By this time, the caves monastery and the huge Buddha carvings were already in place, but the best days of the Buddhist settlement apparently were over. Xuan Zang records that the purest forms of Buddhist devotion had decayed, that the manners of the people were "hard and uncultivated," that superstition flourished, and that the Buddhist community had declined.

During the late twelfth century, after Maḥmūd's time, Bāmiān was ruled by the Ghūrid Dynasty from the Amu

Darya Valley. It was besieged by the Mongols in 1221, and Genghis's favorite grandchild was killed by an arrow from the fortress at Shahr-I-Zohak during the siege. Genghis destroyed the fortress, overran the Bāmiān Valley, and massacred its inhabitants. There is archaeological evidence of a Timurid repopulation and rebuilding in the fifteenth century, after which again very little is known until 1840, when a British force routed Afghan ruler Dōst Moḥammad Khān in the First Anglo-Afghan War.

The monastery at Bāmiān consists of several colonies of several hundreds of cells cut into the rock of a cliff face. The caves monastery is a honeycomb of grotto cells and passages cut into the south-facing cliffs to the north of the modern city and of Shahr-I-Gholghola, from which the best panoramic view is to be had. Other cell complexes cut into cliff faces are known, but none is so large or so intricate as this, with its several hundred cells. Some of the painted stucco survives in the shrines and hermitages, and at least one chapel still contains blue and white roundels of striking intensity. Writer Peter Levi describes the complex as follows: "There were single round domes and systems of multiple domes in the rock, in one place a lantern roof carved into rock beams, tall, steep stairs like mine-shafts, and at least one absolutely night-dark chapel with no outlet except on to the dark stairs."

Three huge Buddhas survive, tucked into their niches. The two more famous ones are on the cliff face, and one stands to the east of the village in the Kakrak Valley, about one mile from the confluence of the Bāmiān and Kakrak Rivers. This third figure is smaller than the others. Ancient reports described an even larger recumbent figure, 1,000 feet in length showing the historic Buddha entering *nirvana,* but it has not been observed by any modern traveler; most likely it was made of plastered rubble and, like other such figures elsewhere, washed away over time.

The larger of the two main figures is an unbelievable 173 feet high, and the smaller is about 112 feet. Xuan Zang writes of the larger one, "On the declivity of the hill to the northeast of the capital was a standing image of Buddha made of stone, 140 or 150 feet high, of a brilliant golden color and resplendent with ornamentation of precious substances." The Buddhas were originally red and gold, although they are now the same color as the mountain cliff. Their faces, heavily built and stylized into impassivity, have been removed during the process of restoration, yielding expressionless, robotic, and menacing figures. Both statues have been damaged by what appears to have been cannon fire. Like the smaller, earlier figure, the larger Buddha is carved of stone and finished with stucco and clay plaster. The appearance of folds in a cloak covering the figures was obtained by nailing ropes to the stone with wooden pegs and modeling plaster around the ropes. On each side of the niche are staircases leading to a chamber near the head, once elaborately decorated with azure and gilding.

The niches, like the Buddhas, were painted, and it has been possible to reproduce the general outline of the figure filling the dome above the larger Buddha and some of the figures surrounding the central one, but the detail is insufficient to precisely identify the symbolism, and the inscription above the niche of the greater Buddha has not yet been interpreted. In the cave complex there is an octagonal room; one of its eight walls is almost totally taken up by the entrance, which is nearly four feet wide. The whole fits into a square with sides of fifteen feet, and the roof is a particularly complex series of concentric geometrical figures, eight-sided, sixteen-sided, circular, and square. On top of the cliffs, ruined towers still stand, and some of the caves are again inhabited, as are ancient cells that are not part of the cliff-face complex. The chambers near the Buddhas' heads have been used for grain storage.

Bāmiān never regained its former importance after Genghis Khan's raid. Today it is a small village with an economy based on agriculture and metalworking. The number of travelers coming to see the caves has prompted the building of a hotel and tourist facilities in recent years; a small airstrip provides access. However, the ongoing civil conflict in Afghanistan makes travel hazardous.

Further Reading: Valuable introductions to Bāmiān can be found in Peter Levi's *The Light Garden of the Angel King: Journeys in Afghanistan* (London: Collins, and Indianapolis: Bobbs Merrill, 1972) and a more technical work, *The Archaeology of Afghanistan from Earliest Times to the Timurid Period,* edited by F. Raymond Allchin and Norman Hammond (London and New York: Academic Press, 1978). A small guidebook, Nancy Hatch Dupree's *The Valley of Bāmiān* (Kabul: Afghan Tourist Organization, 1963; third edition, 1967), while useful, will most likely be available only in large university collections.

—Anthony Levi

Ban Chiang (Udon Thani, Thailand)

Location: On the Khorat Plateau of northeastern Thailand, thirty-six miles east of the town of Udon Thani, in the province of Udon Thani.

Description: An important archaeological site beneath a modern village, Ban Chiang has provided evidence of a highly developed ancient culture in an area once thought to be a backwater. Inhabited from the fourth millennium B.C. until the early or mid–first millennium A.D., the ancient settlement of Ban Chiang made advances in agriculture, metallurgy, and pottery-making. Excavations have been going on at Ban Chiang since the late 1960s.

Site Office: Tourism Authority of Thailand
c/o Provincial Education Office
Phosi Road
Amphoe Muang
Udon Thani 41000
Thailand
(42) 241 968

The discovery of unusual ancient pottery at Ban Chiang transformed the obscure Thai village into an important archaeological site. Shards of distinctive red-on-buff painted pottery had been collected locally for years before they drew widespread notice in the 1960s. At that time, the discovery of a perfectly intact vessel, as well as escalating sales of potsherds to foreign tourists, turned the Thai government's attention to the village. Archaeological investigations at Ban Chiang, begun in 1967, revealed remnants of a prehistoric settlement that was established in the fourth millennium B.C. and survived until perhaps the fourth century A.D. Excavated objects, including human and animal bones, pottery shards, and bronze and iron fragments, signify the considerable advances in agriculture, metallurgy, and ceramic craft made by Ban Chiang's prehistoric people.

These discoveries precipitated decades of debate, during which scholars revised their theories about the early development of human settlements in Asia. Traditionally, scholars viewed prehistoric Southeast Asia as a backward region, with little cultural life prior to the arrival of influences from China and India. Results from the excavations at Ban Chiang strongly challenged this notion. Evidence of early animal domestication, rice cultivation, and metal use forced scholars to devise a new chronology for the region by dating excavated bones and metal fragments. Initial dating of artifacts estimated that bronze was produced in the region as early as 3500 B.C., thus predating bronze use in the Indus Valley and China. Early estimates of iron use at Ban Chiang were dated tentatively to 1600–1200 B.C., a time when the metal was unknown to the nearby Indian civilization. Some scholars even proposed the possibility that iron was developed indigenously, without influence from other cultures, in prehistoric Thailand. Although these findings have been since revised to a more conservative estimate, Ban Chiang's importance as one of Southeast Asia's earliest developed cultures remains unquestioned.

Modern Ban Chiang (population 4,500) is a rural village built on a high mound well above flood stage on the Khorat Plateau. Since 1967, archaeologists have conducted the majority of their excavations on the outskirts of the village. Evidence from these investigations generally can be classified into three main periods of civilization: early (Neolithic), middle (Bronze Age), and late (Iron Age). Although the approximate dates for these periods are still a matter of debate, scholars agree that a settlement existed at Ban Chiang from the fourth millennium B.C. to the early first millennium A.D. Archaeological finds from the major chronological periods have proven essential in documenting Ban Chiang's prehistoric cultural development.

Ban Chiang's earliest period of settlement has been classified by scholars as "Neolithic." This term implies a society that practices agriculture but utilizes no metal, relying instead on such tools as stone adzes. Ban Chiang's Neolithic period offers scholars a unique opportunity for study; as of the early 1990s, it remained the only excavated site in northeastern Thailand with a purely agricultural, pre-metal age base layer of exposed strata.

The date at which Ban Chiang originally was settled has not been conclusively resolved. Some early estimates fixed the date at 3600 B.C. More recent scholarship, while it de-emphasizes such specific dating, concurs that an agricultural society existed at Ban Chiang by 3000 B.C. The question of *who* first settled Ban Chiang remains less certain. Apparently, the floodplains of the Khorat Plateau, where Ban Chiang stands, were largely uninhabited before the arrival of a migrant people during the fourth millennium B.C. These people brought with them an understanding of agriculture and the ability to create stone tools. Neolithic artifacts found at Ban Chiang bear a resemblance to contemporaneous objects found in southern China and Vietnam. This fact prompted the theory that Ban Chiang's settlers migrated from coastal southern China and northern Vietnam. A competing theory, however, suggests that the Neolithic people left an early population center at the head of the Gulf of Thailand and moved inland to found villages such as Ban Chiang.

Although the geographic origin of Ban Chiang's first inhabitants is still unknown, scholars have used archaeological evidence to gain insight into their Neolithic society. Ban Chiang in 3000 B.C. was most likely a small village, encompassing an area anywhere from eight and one-half to twenty

Excavation site at Ban Chiang
Photo courtesy of Tourism Authority of Thailand, Chicago

acres. Little is known about the dwellings built by the settlers. Any post-hole patterns left by the presumably wooden structures have not survived in Thailand's tropical climate. Burial sites, however, offer more information. Bones of both adults and children have been excavated at Ban Chiang. Infants were interred in pottery jars of a cord-marked or incised style. The bodies of adults were buried in either an extended (laid-out) or flexed (crouching) position, often alongside grave goods such as cord-marked pottery. The uniformity of objects placed in graves indicates that Ban Chiang's Neolithic population was not divided into classes or social rankings.

The bones of animals found at Ban Chiang provide insight into the society's dietary practices. Skeletal remains reveal that Ban Chiang's early residents had domesticated chickens, cattle, pigs, and dogs. Bones of other animals, including shellfish, turtles, crocodiles, and rhinoceros, suggest that Ban Chiang residents also hunted for meat. The major agricultural crop for which evidence exists at Ban Chiang is rice. Scholars have suggested that the village's Neolithic inhabitants practiced an early form of wet-field rice cultivation. In this method, rice grains are propagated into shoots in seed beds before being planted in wet soil. The soil is flooded, by natural or artificial means, and eventually drained to permit harvesting. At Ban Chiang, rice probably was grown in swamps or low-lying, seasonally flooded fields. This wet-field method was a forerunner of the highly complex, man-made rice terrace systems used in Southeast Asia today.

Although rice was cultivated for food, a by-product of the crop proved useful to Neolithic craftspeople. Potsherds dating from the fourth millennium B.C. at Ban Chiang show that pottery was tempered with rice chaff (husks). Pottery created during this period was often "cord-marked," reflecting a classic style of prehistoric East Asian pottery. Vessels made in this way were beaten on the outside by a wooden paddle wrapped with cord or basketry. The resulting linear surface patterns served both aesthetic and functional purposes, since the distressed surface offered an easier grip. Although cord-marked pottery predominated during Ban Chiang's Neolithic period, it was supplanted in succeeding eras by the red-painted pottery for which Ban Chiang is famed.

The appearance of bronze in the archaeological record of northeastern Thailand marks the end of the Neolithic era and the beginning of the Bronze Age, also called the Early Metal Age (approximately 2000–300 B.C.). According to

Early cord-marked vessels, Ban Chiang
Photo courtesy of Tourism Authority of Thailand, Chicago

recent scholarship, the first use of bronze at Ban Chiang came early in the second millennium B.C. The evolution of bronze in northeastern Thailand is not clear; two distinct theories have been proposed. Knowledge of metallurgy may have come to the area through contact with established prehistoric cultures in China, Mesopotamia, or the Indus Valley. Some scholars, however, have suggested that the invention of bronze metallurgy occured independently in Thailand.

Whatever its origins, bronze was in common use at Ban Chiang by 1500 B.C. The metal, an alloy of copper and tin, was fashioned into objects for a variety of uses. Practical objects made from bronze included socketed axes, fish hooks, bowls, and spearheads. Other bronze artifacts, such as bracelets, beads, rings, and bells, were purely decorative. Based on evidence obtained at other prehistoric sites on the Khorat Plateau, scholars surmise that bronze was produced from tin and pre-smelted copper. Craftsmen used open-hearth furnaces to melt the alloy in crucibles, which were made from rice-chaff-tempered clay. The liquid bronze then was poured from the crucible and cast by either the lost-wax technique or bivalve molds of stone or baked clay.

Although little is known of Ban Chiang's contact with other communities or cultures during the Neolithic period, the appearance of bronze proves that by 1500 B.C. Ban Chiang had developed at least a rudimentary trade network. No mineral deposits exist at Ban Chiang, so the copper and tin needed to produce bronze must have come from elsewhere. Scholars have theorized that Ban Chiang established trade with western mineral-rich regions such as Nong Khai on the Mekong River (a source of copper) and northwestern Thailand or Laos (possible sources of tin).

Pottery vessels (crucibles and molds) were integral to bronze production and other functions of daily life. Even though it was highly utilitarian, Bronze Age pottery also evolved aesthetically. Neolithic pottery often bore a distinctive cord-marked or incised linear pattern. This pattern persisted into the second millennium B.C., with a major change: the addition of color. Bronze Age potters produced red pigment by mixing hematite and resin. At first this color was applied within linear surface patterns. Later, however, the red pigment was painted in tightly drawn triangular or curvilinear patterns on a smooth buff-colored base. The Bronze Age also produced a variety of vessel shapes. Some rested on a round bottom, while others incorporated footrim stands.

Despite the introduction of metal-producing technology, Ban Chiang remained primarily agricultural throughout the Bronze Age. Villagers continued to raise domesticated pigs, cattle, and fowl and to produce rice using wet-field techniques. These Bronze Age farmers appear to have devised a way to control water flow in their seasonally flooded fields by building bunds, or embankments—a first step toward modern controlled irrigation methods.

An example of the red-on-buff pottery found at Ban Chiang
Photo courtesy of Tourism Authority of Thailand, Chicago

The Bronze Age ended with the ascension of iron, tentatively dated at about 300 B.C. in northeastern Thailand. Excavations at Ban Chiang reveal that iron, like bronze, served both practical and decorative purposes for villagers. Iron weaponry included spearheads and knives; iron jewelry included bracelets and neck rings. One particular group of iron artifacts, however, has puzzled archaeologists: the so-called "rollers," iron spheres or ovoids, pierced through the long axis, with designs carved over their entire surfaces. While some scholars argue that the rollers were used for decorating cloth or in systems of accounting, others suggest that they were purely decorative, meant to be strung and worn as jewelry.

Ironically, the most celebrated artifacts produced at Ban Chiang during the Iron Age were not made of metal. During the first millennium B.C., Ban Chiang's distinctive red-on-buff painted pottery reached an apex of fine craftsmanship and beautiful design. Potters at Ban Chiang had begun their practice of painting clay vessels with red pigment during the Bronze Age (second millennium B.C.). At that time, paint was applied within incised patterns or was used to color tightly constructed geometric designs. By the Iron Age, the designs loosened into more flowing, curvilinear patterns of red whorls or spirals snaking across the cream-colored surface, free of linear boundaries. The predominant shape of the clay vessels evolved, too, from the large, round-bottomed globes of the Bronze Age to smaller, more refined vase-like shapes with ring feet. It is this remarkable pottery, which appeared on the international antiquities market in the 1970s, that brought international attention to Ban Chiang's significance as a prehistoric cultural site.

Agriculture also underwent significant changes during the Iron Age. Ban Chiang farmers had sought to control crop growth and harvesting during the Bronze Age by bunding (or damming) naturally flooded rice fields. During the Iron Age, they continued to assert greater control over crop production by constructing more permanent cultivation sites and working them more intensively. The harnessing of water buffaloes for trampling and, possibly, plowing, certainly helped farmers increase their efficiency.

The pressures that forced Ban Chiang's farmers to increase their efficiency and yield suggest a growth in northeastern Thailand's population during the first millennium B.C. As Ban Chiang and other Khorat Plateau settlements grew, their social structures changed fundamentally. Once a small nuclear village with no discernible social classes, Ban Chiang in the Iron Age probably became a community of highly defined social rankings and uneven divisions of wealth and political power. This social restructuring occurred in settlements throughout the region, creating a new class of political rulers who appear to have united local villages into a loose confederation under their control. Such a union was antithetical to the villages' traditional independence; the stark differences in pottery styles from neighboring settlements on the Khorat Plateau suggest that, until the first millennium B.C., contact between them was limited. The archaeological record also indicates that Ban Chiang developed contacts with cultures beyond northeastern Thailand during this period. Beads of glass and precious stones excavated at Ban Chiang indicate that trade with India began around 200 B.C. and became fairly common in the first century A.D. Bimetallic artifacts also suggest outside contact. Such objects as spearheads with iron blades and bronze sockets, and daggers with iron blades and copper or bronze hilts, have been discovered across southern and eastern Asia. Two bimetallic spearheads were excavated at Ban Chiang. From this finding, scholars deduce that the knowledge of metallurgy was spread throughout Asia by contact between different cultural groups. The theory that prehistoric northeastern Thailand may have developed iron metallurgy independently now seems unlikely.

The record of prehistoric life at Ban Chiang ends sometime in the early or mid–first millennium A.D. The village was abandoned, for an unknown reason, perhaps around A.D. 300. The site was not home to another settlement until 1827, when a group of people called the "Thai Puan" migrated from Chieng Kwang in southern Laos to Ban Chiang. This new group of settlers made the site their home; Ban Chiang's modern residents are descendants of the Thai Puan.

Below the rural village of modern Ban Chiang lies a site whose discovery, made only decades ago, has transformed the world's understanding of ancient Southeast Asia. Prehistoric Ban Chiang's achievements in agriculture, metallurgy, and pottery refuted notions of the region as a cultural backwater. Excavations at Ban Chiang continue, and the archaeological investigations they have inspired throughout northeast Thailand promise to increase knowledge of prehistoric Southeast Asia in decades to come.

Further Reading: Archaeological work continues at Ban Chiang, and new information continually revises or refutes earlier studies. The most recent scholarship is, therefore, the most reliable. Volume 1 of *The Cambridge History of South East Asia,* edited by Nicholas Tarling (2 vols., Cambridge, New York, and Victoria, Australia: Cambridge University Press, 1992), is an excellent source of up-to-date scholarship. Older and less comprehensive, although still highly detailed, sources include Peter S. Bellwood's *Man's Conquest of the Pacific: The Prehistory of Southeast Asia and Oceania* (Auckland, New Zealand: Collins, 1978; New York: Oxford University Press, 1979) and *Early South East Asia: Essays in Archaeology, History, and Historical Geography,* edited by R. B. Smith and William Watson (New York: Oxford University Press, 1979).

—Elizabeth E. Broadrup

Banda (Maluku, Indonesia)

Location: In the Banda Sea, itself an eastward extension of the Java and Flores Seas; 150 miles southeast of Ambon and 600 miles north of Darwin, Australia.

Description: Clustered around a modest but active volcano, the Banda Archipelago's six diminutive islands rise steeply in humps of tousled forest ringed by coral reefs. For many years the world's only source of nutmeg and mace, their approximately forty square miles were once the most sought after in the Spice Islands.

Contact: Diparda (Provincial Tourist Service) Tk.I Maluku
Jl. Pattimura
P.O. Box 113
Ambon 97124
Maluku
Indonesia
(911) 52471

Bitterly contested and ruthlessly exploited by a succession of European maritime powers, the minuscule Banda Archipelago epitomized the romance and the tragedy of the spice trade. A historical landmark as well as an ecological curiosity, its cartographically insignificant specks of land witnessed the genesis of both the Dutch and British Empires. The golden-fruited nutmeg trees, Banda's precious and at one time exclusive bounty, still grow beside the gaunt fortresses of the conquistadores and the verandaed mansions of their colonial successors. In what was once one of the busiest anchorages in the East, a forlorn esplanade links the governor's offshore belvedere to his porticoed residence, while a wisp of smoke strays from the shattered volcano on whose enriching dustings the islands' unique vegetation depends.

The earliest mention of the Spice Islands and their produce is found in Chinese annals dating to 200 B.C. They may have been known in India even earlier, and they had been the subject of much conjecture in Europe since spices began to reach the Mediterranean via Arab middlemen during Roman times. It is not known whether Arab, Chinese, and Indian shipping actually visited the Spice Islands or whether their produce was collected exclusively by Malay shipping agents and carried to Java and Sumatra for further sale. Certainly the former seems to have been the case by the thirteenth century, when the declining Srivijaya Kingdom in Sumatra was heavily involved in the westward trade. To this period is also dated the coming to the Spice Islands of Islam, which quickly established there what was and still is its most easterly bastion.

It was to discover and appropriate the wealth of the spice-producing Indies that European navigators first undertook transoceanic voyages in the sixteenth century. Christopher Columbus, sailing west, mistakenly thought that in the Caribbean he had reached them; it remained for Ferdinand Magellan to complete Spain's westward push and pioneer the Pacific route to the Spice Islands. Meanwhile, in 1497, Portugal's eastward endeavors proved successful when Vasco da Gama rounded the African coast and crossed the Indian Ocean. His successors pushed farther east, reaching Malacca (near Singapore) in 1511 and the Moluccas, including Banda, in 1512.

The exotic cornucopia known to da Gama and his followers as "spices" included all manner of oriental flavorings, preservatives, and medicines and was soon found not to be the product of a single island group. Ginger and cardamon were obtainable from growers in India, cinnamon from Sri Lanka, and pepper from India, Sumatra, and Java. Only cloves, nutmeg, and mace came from the Moluccas or Spice Islands proper. They became all the more desirable, and therefore valuable, owing to their remote and exclusive provenance; and it was to engross the supply of cloves that the Portuguese concentrated on the north Moluccan islands of Ternate and Tidore, where Spanish rivals menaced their monopoly. For nutmegs and mace they relied on regional traders making annual voyages to the Banda Islands. Unthreatened by the Spanish, the Bandas rarely necessitated Portuguese expeditions, although toward the end of the sixteenth century a fort was built on Ambon, a day's voyage to the northwest, to protect this trade.

It was a timely move; in 1599 and 1601 challengers more formidable than the Spanish made their debut in the Indies when vessels of the second Dutch fleet to the East and then merchants of the first English fleet anchored in Banda's waters. Both would soon assail and eliminate Portugal's domination of the north Moluccas. But cloves were obtainable elsewhere in the Moluccas, whereas nutmeg and mace (the former the kernel of a peach-like fruit, the latter its lacy aril or membrane) grew only in the tiny Banda Archipelago. A world monopoly of the two most prized preservatives awaited whichever power could enforce its authority over the six islets and their inhabitants.

The cosmopolitan character of the archipelago's population and their conversion (possibly in the fourteenth century) to Islam attested to the importance of the spice trade in earlier times. The islanders were far from guileless savages. They understood that multilateral trading relations could alone guarantee a good price for their nutmegs and that unrestricted access was essential for the import of the foodstuffs on which they depended. New bidders for their produce were not, therefore, unwelcome. Jacob van Heemskerck, commander of the first Dutch ships, was permitted to leave behind twenty-two of his fellow countrymen, and the English were similarly obliged with a residential concession.

Gunung Api, Banda Islands
Photo courtesy of Indonesia Tourist Promotion Office, Los Angeles

Indeed, until 1605 the Bandanese enjoyed some success in playing one European nation against another. But in that year the Dutch effectively eliminated Portuguese competition when they took the fortress of Ambon. Four years later they commandeered the main port in the Banda Islands and constructed Fort Nassau, now a mildewed ruin near the shoreline of Bandanaira, the islands' capital. This prompted a bloody uprising by the Bandanese and even more sanguinary reprisals by the Dutch, who now elicited the cession of Bandanaira, which thus became, in the words of scholar Willard A. Hanna, "the first piece of real estate in the Indies to which the Dutch formally claimed sovereign rights." In 1611 Fort Nassau was superseded in favor of a more commanding site, on which was built Fort Belgica, a veritable castle with lofty bastions and cavernous dungeons. Much restored since, it continues to brood over Bandanaira and today is still the largest structure on the islands.

Bandanaira, with the township of Bandanaira; Great Banda (or Lonthor), with the largest nutmeg yield; and Gunung Api (Fire Mountain), the virtually uninhabited volcano island, comprised the archipelago's central island cluster and combined to form the three sides of its triangular anchorage. Here, by 1612, vessels of the V.O.C. (Vereenigde Oostindische Compagnie, the Dutch East India Company) were well protected by the cannon of Fort Belgica; hence V.O.C. representatives endeavored to enforce their assumed monopoly of the islands' priceless export.

But farther afield, in the archipelago's outlying islands of Ai and Run, respectively nine and eighteen miles to the west, agents of the infant English East India Company continued to defy Dutch claims. Their shipping sporadic and their defenses unimpressive, they posed no threat to the Bandanese, who enthusiastically supplied them with provisions and nutmegs. In 1616, after a decade and a half of continuous association and much ingenious trading, the Bandanese of Ai and Run, menaced by Dutch offensives, formally acknowledged English sovereignty and invited English protection of their islands. In accepting this offer, the English acquired their first territorial possessions in Asia. Considering the islands' economic potential, one East India Company agent made no mistake that they would prove quite as valuable to King James I as did Scotland. He was thinking of the nutmegs, the Bandanese having pledged their loyalty with two tiny seedlings rooted in Bandanese soil, a token of profound trust: mischievously planted elsewhere, such seedlings could destroy the archipelago's monopoly.

However, this courageous gesture failed to save Ai from coming under Dutch control. In 1616, in its second attempt, a Dutch force of more than 1,000 men commanded by Governor General Jan Dirksen t'Lam stormed the island and dislodged or killed most of the islanders. A makeshift fort erected by the English was strengthened by the Dutch, renamed Fort Revenge, and permanently garrisoned. Meanwhile, those of Ai's distraught population who had escaped made their way to Run, now the last stronghold of English influence in the Spice Islands.

Three miles long and less than one mile wide, with no fresh water for most of the year and only fish, bananas, and nutmegs to eat, Run had little to recommend it as a site for prolonged resistance. Yet for the next four years (1616–20), it witnessed an unrivaled, but largely forgotten, saga of survival and defiance. In command of the small English force and numerous Bandanese allies was Nathaniel Courthope, who arrived on Run in December 1616 and immediately signified his intent to stay there: according to his account, the English "spread [the flag of] St. George upon the island and shott off most of [their] ordinance." The cannon from his two ships were then landed and aligned behind hastily rigged fortifications to command the island's main anchorage. Snooping Dutch vessels were warned off.

His two ships—Courthope's best guarantee of provisions—were both lost within the first few months: the *Swan* fell into Dutch hands when visiting Great Banda for water, and the *Defence* mysteriously drifted from its mooring. Their crews, interned in the dungeons of Fort Belgica, bombarded Courthope with appeals to forego further resistance and secure their release. The Dutch even offered to return the ships with a full loading of nutmegs if only Courthope would evacuate Run.

Courthope would not relent. To do so would be treason to his king and a complete betrayal of his Bandanese allies. Instead he smuggled through the Dutch blockade appeals for help directed to his superiors in Java. These paid off in March 1618 when, heralded by an eruption of Gunung Api, two English vessels were seen approaching from the west. Courthope's now-ragged band lined the rocks and primed their guns for a mighty welcome. But the first shots came from four Dutch vessels that slipped out of Bandanaira and began maneuvering to cut off the heavily laden relief force. When dusk fell, the issue was still in doubt. The next morning Courthope woke to see both English ships being escorted to Bandanaira by their Dutch captors.

In a further appeal to Java, Courthope described his force as reduced to thirty-eight men, "our wants extreame." The Dutch had ten ships, "all fitted to come against us," and perhaps 1,000 men. "I look daily and howerly for them." Indeed he longed for the attack "being not so much able to stand out [against them] as to make them pay deare." This he did in June 1618, when a Dutch assault was repulsed. But 1619 passed with no more relief fleets, only a message to "proceed in your resolution." That was all very well, but as Courthope reported, "we have rubbed off the skinne alreadie and if we rub any longer we shall rub to the bone."

In Europe the English and Dutch governments had in fact persuaded their respective East India Companies to collaborate. But word of this pact would make little difference to the jealous rivals in the Banda Islands, and it may not even have reached them when, in October 1620, Courthope's heroics came to an abrupt end. While returning from Great Banda with fresh water, his native prahu (a small Malay boat) was ambushed and overwhelmed. Courthope seems to have fought and then have been knocked into the sea. His body, recovered on Ai by the Dutch, was there buried "so stately and honestly as ever we could"; it was, said his adversaries, "only fitting for such a man."

A year later, emboldened rather than restrained by the pact with the English, the Dutch introduced their final solution for the Banda Islands. The brainchild of V.O.C. governor general Jan Pieterszoon Coen, the founder of Dutch empire and a man whose vision, according to Hanna, "was exceeded only by his violence," this plan involved another massive offensive against the Bandanese, followed by a judicious mixture of deportations and butchery that would be tantamount to genocide. The offensive, initially against the Bandanese of Great Banda, where two stone strongholds (Forts Hollandia and Concordia) attest his ruthless repression, was soon extended to all the islands. Even Run, although still technically English, was not spared. As well as dispersing its population, Coen also caused most of its nutmeg trees to be destroyed, thus rendering the island worthless. Of the archipelago's supposed population of about 5,000 in 1620, fewer than 500 remained by the end of the decade.

Nor were the English, now ostensibly allies of the Dutch, spared. In 1623 fifteen employees of the English Company were arrested in Ambon and charged by the Dutch with plotting to take its fort (the erstwhile Portuguese stronghold that, as Fort Victoria, today houses units of the Indonesian army). All hideously tortured, ten of the accused were eventually executed along with nine Japanese mercenaries in what became known as the Amboina Massacre. The charges were almost certainly fabricated and the torture crude even for the times. The whole affair provoked outrage in London and was to be much invoked whenever Anglo-Dutch relations faltered. But it served its purpose in ending English involvement in the Spice Islands. The last English agents were withdrawn from the Bandas and the English Company turned, not without relief, to less fraught commercial opportunities in India. Run was not forgotten, but for the time being Holland's monopoly of the spice trade went unchallenged.

To exploit this monopoly, it was necessary to reorganize and repopulate the nutmeg forests. Great Banda, Ai, and Bandanaira were divided into sixty-eight *perken,* or plantations, and sold or leased to Dutch *perkeniers,* who were usually former employees of the V.O.C. The company itself undertook to supply them with the imported slave labor to farm their *perkens* and to purchase from them as much mace and nutmeg as they could produce. But the extent of each *perken,* the terms under which it was held, and the prices paid for its crop occasioned endless and acrimonious debate. With a pound of prime nutmeg commonly costing half a *stuiver* in the Bandas and selling for sixty-one *stuivers* in Amsterdam, the *perkeniers* claimed with some reason that it was they who were being exploited. But their luxuries, their extravagant lifestyle, and their apparent fortunes, subjects of frequent remark by visitors, not to mention the handsome villas that stand to this day, suggest otherwise. No less telling is the record of mutilations and executions meted out to slaves. Perhaps the Bandas had never fulfilled their promise of paradise, yet seldom can so idyllic a spot have harbored such rank injustice.

Meanwhile Run, denuded, depopulated, and now ignored by the V.O.C., continued to trouble patriotic Englishmen. Courthope's protracted defiance was not quite forgotten; nor was that pledge of allegiance by the Bandanese. Since the English Company's original charter did not empower it to assume territorial obligations, the Bandanese Islands had been accepted on behalf of the crown. James I had thus been acknowledged "King of England, Scotland, Ireland, France [an empty boast], Puloway [Island of Ai] and Puloroon [Island of Run]"; and his successors, including Oliver Cromwell, continued solicitous for their far-flung possessions and their now nonexistent subjects. The Dutch government, repeatedly reminded of the English claim, eventually conceded it, and twice in the 1630s English claimants made abortive efforts to resettle the island. In 1648 a Cromwellian initiative might well have succeeded had not war with the Dutch broken out just as the *London*, laden with psalter-waving settlers, was about to sail for the Bandas. Instead, the ship was redirected to the island of St. Helena in mid-Atlantic, which thus became the East India Company's first overseas settlement.

Further schemes during the 1660s came to nothing, and thus few tears were shed when under the 1667 Treaty of Breda Charles II finally ceded all claims in the Bandas to the Dutch. Part of a comprehensive settlement, the treaty also adjusted Anglo-Dutch claims in the Americas, including the award of New Amsterdam, plus its island of Manhattan, to the English. Hence the claim that the almost-valueless real estate of Run was traded for what promptly became New York, a woeful misrepresentation of the treaty.

Thereafter, notwithstanding occasional slumps, frequent alarms, and continuous scandals, the Bandas fulfilled their role of offsetting the exorbitant cost of Dutch expansion in the Indies. The halcyon days lasted until the late eighteenth century, when three events conspired to consign the islands to an oblivion that their appeal as tourist destinations is only now beginning to dispel.

With the volcano of Gunung Api forever smoldering in their midst, the islanders were not unfamiliar with natural disasters; scarcely a decade passed without an eruption, although for the most part the effects were not serious. With the volcano rising straight from the sea, its lava flowed harmlessly onto the submerged coral, while its dust settled on the adjacent islands, thereby enriching the soil and ensuring a good nutmeg harvest. But on April 2, 1778, an earthquake hit the islands, triggering not only a massive eruption but also a typhoon and a tidal wave. In barely an hour's time, thousands of the massive Kanari trees that provided essential shade and shelter for the delicate nutmeg came crashing to the ground. The nutmeg harvest fell from approximately 800,000 pounds in 1777 to 30,000 in 1778.

The harvest had still not fully recovered by 1795, when the V.O.C. was declared bankrupt, and in 1796 the Dutch lost the Bandas when a gloating English East India Company returned to the Spice Islands for a belated encore. In Europe and elsewhere the enemy was now Napoleonic France. But, as the Batavian Republic, Holland had become a Napoleonic satellite and its colonial possessions therefore potential French bases. It was to preempt this possibility and to deny the enemy profits from the spice trade that British ships began taking control of the Moluccas. They encountered minimal resistance, and although the islands were restored to Holland in 1803, the British again commandeered them from 1810 until 1817.

As a result of these changes in the islands' allegiance, nutmegs found their way to new markets, and nutmeg seedlings, at last, to new plantations. The Dutch had experimented with nurseries outside the Bandas, and an ingenious Frenchman with the apt name of Pierre Poivre (whose surname translates into English as "pepper") had successfully introduced both cloves and nutmegs in Madagascar and Réunion. But it was the British, with ample opportunity during their Moluccan sojourn, with no fond memories of the spice monopoly, and with promising prospects in Malaya and Sumatra, who finally ended the Bandas' exclusive command of nutmeg production.

Despite brief revivals during the nineteenth century, the saga of the Bandas and their nutmeg *perkens* has since been one of fitful decline. Slavery was abolished in 1860, and the official monopoly of all nutmeg production ended in 1873. In the 1930s the islands served as a place of exile for political undesirables, most notably Sutan Sjahrir and Mohammad Hatta, later respectively prime minister and vice president of independent Indonesia. They lived in some style in two of the already superfluous *perkeniers'* mansions; the buildings' spreading roofs and paved halls, hung with chandeliers and fading portraits, still lend to Bandanaira a gracious air quite out of keeping with the island's spectacular riot of tropical vegetation.

Further Reading: Willard A. Hanna's *Indonesian Banda: Colonialism and its aftermath in the Nutmeg Islands* (Philadelphia: Institute for the Study of Human Issues, 1978) was the first attempt to piece together a history of the islands. Highly readable, it also summarizes most of the main Dutch language sources and has a useful bibliography. Many of the journals of the English East India Company's early voyages to the Spice Islands were published as extracts in Samuel Purchas's *His Pilgrimes* (London, 1625; available in a variety of editions). Some of these journals have also been published, with annotations, by the Hackluyt Society of London. For more accessible summaries of these journals and of the company's voluminous correspondence with its agents in the Moluccas, see William Forster's *England's Quest of Eastern Trade* (London: Black, 1933) or John Keay's *The Honourable Company: A History of the English East India Company* (London: HarperCollins, 1991; New York: Macmillan, 1994). The best guidebook is Kal Muller's *Spice Islands: The Moluccas* (Berkeley, California: Periplus, 1990; as *Indonesian Spice Islands,* Singapore: Periplus, 1993).

—John Keay

Bangalore (Karnātaka, India)

Location: In the center of southern India, almost equidistant from Madras on the east coast (183 miles away) and Mangalore on the west.

Description: Perhaps the most westernized of all Indian cities, Bangalore was founded as a fortress town in the sixteenth century and became the center of a fiefdom ruled by Hyder Ali in the eighteenth century, and as such played a significant role in the Mysore Wars. It was the headquarters of the British rulers of the former Indian state of Mysore from 1831 to 1881; today the capital of the modern state of Karnātaka, it is a center of industry and commerce, noted for its progressive attitudes and its varied cultural and social life.

Site Office: Government of India Tourist Office
KFC Building
48 Church Street
Bangalore, Karnātaka 560 001
India
5585417

Founded in the sixteenth century, Bangalore is a relatively young city. Yet the surrounding region—the former Indian state of Mysore, now the state of Karnātaka—has been inhabited much longer: artifacts dating to the Stone Age have been unearthed there. From ancient times through the Middle Ages the area was ruled by a succession of Hindu dynasties, and it became the center of the Hindu Vijayanagar Empire in the fourteenth century and remained so until the rise of Muslim power 200 years later. Legend has it that the name "Bangalore" originated when a Vijayanagar king who was wandering in a forest, lost and without food, was saved from starvation by an old woman who gave him some boiled beans. He called the spot where this happened "Bendakalooru," meaning "town of boiled beans"; this was corrupted to "Bangalore."

A Vijayanagar emperor donated the land on which Bangalore was built to a minor chieftain named Kempe Gowda in the 1530s. He constructed a mud-brick fortress there and built four watchtowers, which were meant to mark the town's future boundaries. The city actually has grown far beyond them. The fort was replaced by a stone structure in the eighteenth century, but that is now in a ruined state, and is not consistently open to the public. Another building from Kempe Gowda's era that has survived much better is a Hindu temple called the Bull Temple, which features a magnificent monumental sculpture of Nandi, a bull belonging to the Hindu god Siva. The bull, made of gray granite that is polished so as to appear nearly black, is more than sixteen feet high and nineteen feet long. Each autumn, local farmers make an offering of their first harvest to Nandi. Unlike some Hindu temples, the Bull Temple is open to non-Hindus.

In the seventeenth century, the rulers of the Muslim kingdom of Bijāpur captured Bangalore from Kempe Gowda's descendants. A Bijāpur administrator, Shāhji (father of Śivājī, founder of the Marāṭhā dynasty), lived for a time at Bangalore, one of several garrison towns under his charge. Supported by a well-trained army, Shāhji set up a state centered on Bangalore. There he received visits from his estranged wife and son, Śivājī. The rulers of Bijāpur, who found Shāhji too independent for their liking and suspected him of assisting Śivājī in his raids against their territory, had Shāhji arrested and imprisoned in 1648. He was freed after a few years, but he was not given control of Bangalore again until 1658. Toward the end of his life, Shāhji tried to mediate between Bijāpur's rulers and his son Śivājī, who was still in rebellion against Bijāpur. Shāhji died in a hunting accident in 1664.

Bangalore passed into the hands of another of Shāhji's sons, Venkaji, who found the town too isolated to be secure in the unsettled political climate of the time. In 1687 he negotiated the sale of Bangalore to the rāja of Mysore. Before the transaction could be completed, an army sent by the Mughal ruler 'Ālamgīr (Aurangzeb) entered Bangalore and captured it without resistance. The commanding general, Kasim Khan, did not see Bangalore as valuable, so he agreed to sell the town to Mysore at the price that had been set by Venkaji.

In the eighteenth century Hyder Ali, a Mysore general who had conducted several successful military campaigns and found favor with powerful government ministers, received Bangalore as a fief. About 1761, with Mysore weakened by financial problems, Hyder Ali overthrew Mysore's rāja and prime minister and made himself ruler. At this time he rebuilt Kempe Gowda's old mud-brick fort, replacing it with a stone edifice. He also began the construction of a palace, still standing but in poor condition, and the development of the still-magnificent Lāl Bagh Gardens, among the loveliest botanical gardens in India, filled with rare plants and with a Glass House, modeled on London's Crystal Palace, at the center; both projects were completed by his son, Tippu Sultan.

Hyder Ali soon found matters other than public works to occupy his time, however, as his power was challenged by the Marāṭhās and other Indian rulers, as well as the British, who saw Hyder Ali as a threat to their own designs on India. The British, in fact, did not wish to see any Indian ruler gain a great deal of power, and the contest for supremacy in central India resulted in four wars, known as the Mysore Wars, between the British and the forces of Hyder Ali and Tippu Sultan from 1767 to 1799. Hyder Ali at times had the aid of the French; some

Gomateswara in Shravanabelagola, near Bangalore
Photo courtesy of Air India Library, New York

Glass House at Lāl Bagh Gardens, Bangalore
Photo courtesy of Air India Library, New York

historians believe that if the French had been more consistently helpful, Hyder Ali might have prevailed over the British. At any rate, he was a capable soldier, his outnumbered forces often beaten but rarely routed. The thirty-two years of sporadic warfare were marked by bloody battles and broken treaties; some of the actions involved Bangalore directly. A British Army officer, Sir David Baird, is said to have been imprisoned in the Bangalore fort in 1780. The cell, which Baird shared with another, less famous, captive, was very small—estimated at twelve to fifteen square feet—with a ceiling so low a man could barely stand up.

Hyder Ali died suddenly in 1782, during a lull in the fighting, but the wars for Mysore continued under Tippu Sultan. Tippu was said to be extremely cruel. He reportedly executed criminals by having them thrown from a cliff, with a sheer drop of 2,000 feet, near his summer palace in the Nandi Hills, thirty-seven miles from Bangalore. He also is said to have starved a prisoner to death on a meager diet of rice and milk; the prisoner's bones, still in the iron cage that had been his cell, were exhibited in the Bangalore bazaar. Tippu's cruelties may have been exaggerated by the British to justify their actions against him. Tippu was ultimately unsuccessful in his fight to retain Mysore. Although a capable civil administrator, he did not possess his father's military skill; moreover, reforms in the British administration of India enabled its forces to fight much more vigorously against him than they had against his father. The British, led by Lord Cornwallis, stormed and captured Bangalore in 1791, and a year later the Treaty of Seringapatam forced Tippu to give up half his territory. When hostilities flared between Tippu and the British again in 1799, he was killed in battle in Seringapatam, and his forces surrendered to the British.

Hyder Ali and Tippu Sultan today are considered to have been capable rulers, enlightened for their time, dedicated to civic improvements, and unable to accept rule by the British. Both Muslims, they were tolerant of the Hindu faith; that they were less so toward Christianity owes more to their enmity toward the British than to any religious reasons. In any case, they did leave significant marks on Bangalore, with their buildings and gardens still standing out amid the modern architecture of the twentieth-century city.

After the death of Tippu Sultan, the British made Mysore a protectorate and restored the Mysore rāja, Krishnarāja Wodeyar, to the throne. Krishnarāja was at the time an infant, and when he grew old enough to perform his duties on his own, he proved an incompetent ruler. Therefore, the British took over direct administration of the Mysore realm in 1831 and moved its capital from the city of Mysore to Bangalore. They improved Bangalore by developing parks, churches, and museums along wide, tree-lined streets. Cubbon Park, laid out by Lord Cubbon, viceroy of India, in 1864, is still one of Bangalore's major attractions. It covers nearly 300 acres and contains numerous government buildings—including the High Court and the State

Central Library—and museums in addition to the expected green spaces.

The British returned the state of Mysore to its rāja in 1881, but maintained a military presence and civil administration in Bangalore, with a section of the city reserved for this purpose, until India became independent in 1947. The Mysore royals were generally progressive rulers and were so well liked by their subjects that their mahārāja became the first governor of the Indian state of Mysore after independence. (The state was renamed Karnātaka in 1973.) The Bangalore Palace of the Mysore mahārāja was built in the late nineteenth century and remains a tourist attraction; it shows obvious British influence in its resemblance to Windsor Castle.

In the twentieth century Bangalore has developed into a prosperous and cosmopolitan city. The city and the surrounding suburban area have a combined population exceeding 4 million. Bangalore's prosperity is based on a wide range of industries, some run by the state or federal government, some privately owned. Products manufactured there include aircraft, machine tools, porcelain, soap, leather goods, textiles, pharmaceuticals, farm equipment, and watches. Newspaper and magazine publishing are major businesses there, too, and Bangalore is the headquarters of a large regional radio station. People from all over India, and many other countries, come to Bangalore in search of employment. At the same time, it is a popular place for retirement, as the climate is milder than that of many other Indian cities, and the bustle of industry is balanced by the peacefulness of the city's many parks and gardens. Bangalore has been nicknamed "The Garden City."

The city also is home to Bangalore University, founded in 1964 as the successor institution to a branch of Mysore University, which was established in 1916. The University of Agricultural Sciences opened in 1964 as well. Other educational and research institutions in Bangalore include the Indian Institute of Science, the Raman Research Institute, the National Aeronautical Research Laboratory, and the National Power Research Institute.

Bangalore is intellectually and politically liberal, indeed one of the most liberal cities in India. While the citizens of Bangalore are by no means agreed on all issues, they are generally tolerant toward a variety of lifestyles and opinions. Moreover, rigid social rules, including Hindu caste distinctions, often are ignored. Numerous immigrants, including a significant Tibetan community, give Bangalore great ethnic diversity.

Bangalore's vibrant social life takes place in numerous high-quality restaurants and fashionable coffeehouses and nightclubs, many of them quite westernized. In many parts of India, only men are allowed in bars; in Bangalore, however, women are equally welcome. The citizens of Bangalore also display great interest in culture, evident in a wealth of excellent bookshops and cinemas. Bangalore also has numerous museums. In Cubbon Park stands the Government Museum, established in 1886, one of the oldest in India. Its varied collection includes relics from Mohenjo-daro, the great prehistoric city in Pakistan, and some items from the Vijayanagar Dynasty. Adjacent to it are the Visvesvaraya Industrial and Technological Museum and the Venkatappa Art Gallery.

Most of Bangalore's buildings are modern, but its few historic ones are notable, including the Bull Temple and the remains of the Hyder Ali–Tippu Sultan Palace and Kempe Gowda's fort. The ruins of Kempe Gowda's watchtowers are visible approximately 400 yards west of the temple. Also of note is the Gangadhareshwara Cave Temple, built by Kempe Gowda near the Bull Temple. The cave temple is situated so that on January 14 and 15 of each year, a ray of sunlight passes precisely through the horns of a bull statue in front of the temple and shines on the goddess statue inside. One of the most impressive buildings in Bangalore, however, is of relatively recent origin—1956—but designed so as to emulate the ancient Dravidian style of architecture. This is the Vidhana Soudha, where the state legislature meets. Built almost completely of dressed granite from the Bangalore area, it is ornately and colorfully decorated, and has an enormous central dome.

From "town of boiled beans" to "The Garden City," from isolated fortress to sophisticated metropolitan area, Bangalore has had a history of remarkable growth and development, while maintaining awareness of its past. Kempe Gowda, who is memorialized in a statue in front of the city government offices, and whose name is borne by Bangalore's main street, would be amazed by the twentieth-century appearance of the city he founded. Bangalore's vitality is such that further growth and change seems inevitable.

Further Reading: An important new general source for Indian history is *The New Cambridge History of India,* edited by Gordon Johnson, C. A. Bayly, and John F. Richards (29 vols., Cambridge and New York: Cambridge University Press, 1987–); more than half of its projected volumes have been published to date. Until that work is complete, a useful source remains Vincent A. Smith's *The Oxford History of India: From the Earliest Times to the End of 1911* (Oxford: Clarendon Press, 1919; fourth edition, edited by Percival Spear, New York and Oxford: Oxford University Press, 1981). Sinharaja Tammita-Delgoda's *A Traveller's History of India* (Moreton-in-Marsh, Gloucestershire: Windrush, and Brooklyn, New York: Interlink, 1994) is also to be recommended.

—Clarissa Levi and Trudy Ring

Bangkok (Thailand)

Location: In southern Thailand, in the Chao Phraya (Menam) River Delta, a few miles inland from the Bight of Bangkok, which itself opens out into the Gulf of Thailand.

Description: Bangkok is the name used by foreigners for Krung Thep, City of Angels, the capital of the former Siam, now Thailand, and the most important Thai port. Established in 1782, Bangkok now also includes Thonburi, an earlier Siamese capital. The old royal enclave, known as Ko Ratanakosin, and a wealth of old Buddhist temples coexist with the concrete, chrome, and steel of the highrises that have sprung up in every corner of the modern cosmopolitan city.

Site Office: Tourist Authority of Thailand (TAT)
372 Bamrung Nuang Road
Bangkok 10100
Thailand
(2) 226 0060, (2) 226 0072, (2) 226 0085, or (2) 226 0098

From the fourteenth to the mid–eighteenth century, the kingdom of Siam had maintained its capital at Ayutthaya, a city on an island in the Chao Phraya River, often referred to by Westerners as the Menam River. Throughout a protracted war with neighboring Burma (modern Myanmar), the city had seemed impregnable, and the royal forces had successfully beaten back a number of attacks. But in 1767, the Burmese scaled the walls and laid waste to the city within. Of the more than 1 million inhabitants, only 10,000 survived the devastation. Siam was nearly wiped out in one stroke. Not a member of the royal family survived, and the sorry remnant of the army was left in complete disorganization. Almost all of the kingdom's cultural and religious institutions were razed, at the same time that much of the artwork was carried off by the victors. Burma annexed large parts of the kingdom, and former vassal states to the east in the Laotian and Cambodian territories capitalized on this chance for independence. Several rival Thai leaders appropriated different parts of the remaining territories and proclaimed themselves successors to the throne.

As Siam teetered on the brink of dissolution, an army general, Phraya Taksin, made his way to Thonburi, a prosperous trading settlement at the mouth of the Chao Phraya River. Thonburi was also the site of a fort built by the French, before the ignominious expulsion of all Europeans from Siam in 1688. Taksin rallied some of the scattered elements of the Siamese army and set out to recreate Siam. A great deal of luck united with his military acumen, and he was able to recover all of Siam's former territories in a little over a decade. Burma was forced to turn its attention to British expansionist efforts within its own borders, permanently eliminating the Burmese threat to the regenerating Siamese kingdom. No efforts were made to reconstruct Ayutthaya, since Taksin's priorities were primarily military in nature. Thonburi quietly began to take on the character of the new Siamese capital, and the residence of the former town governor did service as Taksin's headquarters.

Once the reconquest of Siam was accomplished, Taksin had himself coronated as the new king of Siam, but shortly after his installation, in 1781, a palace revolt broke out. Taksin had apparently lost command of his senses, and his paranoid reprisals against imagined conspirators exceeded the bounds of his courtiers' tolerance. Taksin was taken prisoner and executed in the fashion reserved for royalty, who by Siamese tradition ruled by divine right and so assumed the mantle of divinity themselves. He was put into a velvet sack and clubbed to death, so that the royal blood would not be defiled by the earth. One of Taksin's generals, Thong Duang, was recalled from a campaign and crowned king in 1782 by consensus of the court. The new king, who took the title of Ramathibodi, became the founder of the Chakkri Dynasty, which still supplies the now largely ceremonial royal office with the nominal rulers of modern Thailand.

The kingdom's borders were securely established by 1782, and the new capital enjoyed growing prosperity with an upsurge in trade to China. These factors enabled Ramathibodi to focus his energies on rebuilding Siam's shattered cultural heritage. One of his first acts was to move his court across the Chao Phraya River to Bangkok (Village of the Kok, or Plum-Olive), a small settlement of Chinese traders. The village had first come into existence in the early sixteenth century, when a canal, a little over a mile long, had been dug between different sections of the Chao Phraya near the sea. The canal afforded the Chinese traders a strategic if modest position along Siam's main artery of traffic. Eventually, the river carved out its bed through the canal, so that Bangkok found itself on the river bank. In 1782, however, the Chinese had to make way for the Siamese king, who wished to use the land to recreate the ancient city of Ayutthaya.

A system of canals was dug to form an island that would set apart the royal palace, government offices, and the principal temple of the kingdom. As at Ayutthaya, a further network of canals, or *klongs,* served to carry the bulk of Bangkok's traffic, instead of roads and streets. Work crews were sent to the old capital to dismantle any surviving buildings and carry the material back to Bangkok for use in the city's fortifications. Thus a physical link was established between the old and the new seat of Siamese power. Survivors

Grand Palace, Bangkok
Photo courtesy of Tourism Authority of Thailand, Chicago

of the sack of Ayutthaya were sought out for their memories of its physical appearance, to aid in the effort to construct at Bangkok as close a copy as possible of Ayutthaya's most glorious features.

Shortly after dawn on April 21, 1782—a moment singled out by court astrologers as particularly auspicious—the building campaign at Bangkok was officially begun with the erection of a column dedicated to the Hindu god Siva. Defensive needs were first attended to with the building of more than six miles of wall around the planned outer city. Two of the fourteen watchtowers stationed along the wall survive, together with sections of the original earth-and-brick barrier. Work on the royal enclave also was begun with construction of a crenellated wall around the royal island. The first building to be erected there was the Wat Phra Kaew, a Buddhist temple, which was to house the kingdom's most revered religious icon, the Emerald Buddha, which Ramathibodi had brought back with him from a raid on Vientiane, in Laos. Magical properties of all sorts are ascribed to this jade image of the Buddha, but it is thought in particular to bring blessings to the entire nation, giving it prosperity and protecting it from enemies. It is for this reason that the Emerald Buddha is still closely associated with the center of the country's political power. The Wat Phra Kaew is a complex of richly decorated temples and slender stupas (*chedi* in Thai) covered in gold. When the buildings were finished in 1784, construction of the royal palace was begun.

By 1785 work on the palace had advanced far enough for the king to take up residence there. On that occasion, Ramathibodi also dedicated the new capital, giving it a long ceremonial name that is habitually shortened to Krung Thep, or City of Angels. The renaming, however, has made no impression on foreigners, who still refer to the city by the rather incongruous name of its most humble predecessor, Bangkok. Construction of the royal complex continued far into the nineteenth century, and some of the later buildings attempt a reconciliation of traditional Thai architecture with Western neoclassicism, emulating French models in particular. The Chakkri Maha Prasad, which was finished in 1882 by King Chulalongkorn and still dominates the royal enclave, looks at first sight like an eighteenth-century French palace, outlandishly topped with a colorful and elaborately decorated Thai roof.

However, the reconstruction of Siam involved more than the rebuilding of its capital. During the sack of Ayutthaya, virtually all the nation's written texts had been lost. As a consequence, the legal codes had to be rewritten,

Wat Phra Kaew, Temple of the Emerald Buddha, Bangkok
Photo courtesy of Tourism Authority of Thailand, Chicago

a task not finished until 1805. The elaborate court ceremonial, which played a pivotal role in traditional Siamese court life, had to be reconstructed from memory when possible and reinvented when memory fell short. Sacred texts had to be recreated to reinvigorate Siam's official religion: a form of Buddhism with rich admixtures of Hinduism and, to a lesser extent, of the more ancient rituals of animism. By the king's orders, the ancient Buddhist canon was recreated during a five-month conference of 250 monks and laymen. The most important Hindu text, the Thai version of the *Rāmāyṇa,* the *Ramakien,* was also painstakingly rewritten.

All of these labors of cultural and literary reconstruction continued into the reign of Ramathibodi's successor, Isarasuntorn, who ascended the throne in 1805. Presiding over an era of peace and plenty, the new king was free to devote himself primarily to the arts. Himself an accomplished woodcarver, Isarasuntorn is also remembered for having revived classical Thai dance. Isarasuntorn was responsible for Bangkok's enchanting Garden of the Night, a complex of islands and bridges on a lake, which became the site of numerous performances and receptions. Although he did not live to see it completed, he also commissioned the construction of Wat Arun, a resplendent temple on the Thonburi side of the river.

Isarasuntorn was succeeded in 1824 by King Chesda, an extremely devout man who turned his attention away from the arts and toward religion. Chesda was responsible for the building of Wat Po, the Temple of the Reclining Buddha, one of the foremost institutes of learning in Thailand and one of its most popular temples. It houses a gigantic image of the Buddha, 160 feet long and some 40 feet high. The figure is built of brick and cement and entirely covered in gold leaf. The soles of his feet are decorated with mother-of-pearl inlay work, depicting scenes from the life of the Buddha. The temple also contains a series of marble reliefs that were recovered from Ayutthaya, as well as 394 sitting Buddhas and some notable Buddhist murals.

But Chesda's reign was not as uncomplicated as his predecessor's. Territorial gains were made in all directions, the most significant being expansions on the Malay Peninsula. However, the French were preying on Siam's vassal states in Laos and Cambodia, while the British, having subdued Burma, also turned their attention to Siam. In 1826,

Chesda reluctantly concluded a treaty with a British delegation, which gave the British trading rights in Siam in return for a promise not to bring opium into the country. The royal house remained wary of European influence, but undoubtedly the fate of colonized Burma reminded Chesda of the value of flexibility and negotiation. Vientiane, meanwhile, must have expected Siam to follow in Burma's tragic footsteps and revolted against Siamese overlordship. In 1829, a force from Vientiane, in an access of overconfidence, attacked Bangkok but retreated when the Siamese army returned to defend the capital. The Vientianese were massacred on their retreat, and their leader was ignominiously displayed in a cage in Bangkok until he died of a fever. The vassal states were thus secured for a while longer.

Bangkok itself had grown considerably, in part as a result of Chinese immigration. By the end of Chesda's rule, 15,000 Chinese entered Siam each year. Since most of these newcomers were traders, commercial relations with China increased rapidly. Sugar, tin, and rice were Siam's principal export products; rubber was added to this list later on. The Bangkok port became busier than ever, and canals were built and rivers widened to accommodate the increased flow of commercial traffic. The growth of the city brought serious public health problems, however. Sanitation was extremely rudimentary, and as the city became more crowded, smallpox, cholera, and dysentery became more and more widespread. A cholera epidemic in 1849, toward the end of Chesda's reign, wiped out a significant part of Bangkok's population. Royal insistence on tradition, however, stood in the way of modern measures that could have reduced the threat of major epidemics.

Chesda's successor, Mongkut, who acceded to the throne in 1851, began to pursue a new policy of greater openness to Western influence. In 1855, a new treaty with Britain established free trade, again on the assurance that Siam be kept free of opium. Consulates of the major Western powers were built in Bangkok, and merchant houses of many nationalities opened offices in the city. Banks soon followed. In a matter of years, Bangkok became an international city of considerable standing in Southeast Asia as a result of the decision to open the country to trade with the West. The king himself began learning Latin and English and provided English governesses for his children. One of these, Anna Leonowens, wrote a rather fatuous memoir of her experience at the Siamese court. Her memoir was turned into an even worse novel, which in turn was dramatized by Hollywood under the title *The King and I.* The movie, banned in Thailand, infantilizes Mongkut, a highly intelligent and learned man, who was generally far too busy to take much notice of Anna Leonowens. Besides encouraging the study of Western science, Mongkut also initiated a series of modernizations that finally took Siam beyond the glory days of Ayutthaya. He established a Western-style mint, imported printing presses, and welcomed other technological advances brought to Siam by foreign visitors.

Chulalongkorn, who succeeded Mongkut in 1868 at the age of fifteen, continued his father's policies. He oversaw a reorganization of the centralized government, establishing more efficient connections between Bangkok and the provincial administrations. He also instituted two government bodies somewhat similar in organization to a bicameral parliamentary system; these bodies were to advise him and take over some of his executive functions. Since Chulalongkorn retained absolute power, this attempt to revamp the monarchy died a quiet death within a few years. With more success, he abolished slavery and the corvée labor system, instituted a network of educational institutions, and established a postal service. He also built railroads and a system of land routes. In Bangkok itself, Chulalongkorn had many of the canals filled in to create more conventional streets. One of the last areas to be modernized, however, was the public health infrastructure in the city. In 1873, another serious cholera epidemic had broken out, but it was not until the 1910s, when Chulalongkorn's successor built a waterworks for the city, that any real progress was made in the control of infectious diseases.

Chulalongkorn also continued to foster a generally friendly relationship with the British, while relations with the French were frequently strained. In the second half of the nineteenth century, France had managed to wrest control of large stretches of Siam's vassal territories in a piecemeal fashion. In 1893, the French demanded all Siamese holdings east of the Mekong River, and Chulalongkorn refused. In response, the French sailed up the mouth of the Chao Phraya River and attacked the Paknam Fort outside Bangkok. Although this was not a large-scale assault or even a well-orchestrated operation, Siam was not in a position to rebuff the French when they brandished their guns. Bangkok ceded its Laotian and Cambodian territories without further incident.

Chulalongkorn died in 1910. The reigns of his successors were clouded by growing challenges to the absolute monarchy. Siam entered World War I in 1917 on the side of the Allies (an unpopular decision at home); a serious flood that same year seriously damaged the rice harvest. Bangkok's economy suffered, and the government was seriously in debt, in part through the extravagance of the royal house. Discontent gathered in the city, particularly among Thais educated in Europe, but it was not until 1932 that Bangkok saw a coup d'état carefully orchestrated by the People's Party, an alliance of intellectuals and army officers. Bangkok's garrison was marched unarmed to Dusit Palace, ostensibly for a parade. The soldiers, met by the revolutionaries in tanks, joined the coup without demur. The king's bodyguards never received orders to fight and apparently had no interest in doing so of their own accord. The conspirators seized radio communications networks, the royal princes were arrested, and one of them was made to read an announcement to the Bangkok citizenry urging them to remain quiet and acquiesce in the takeover. King Prajadhipok, apparently weary of the stresses of absolute kingship, refused to interrupt his golf game at a country estate when he was informed of the takeover.

In the wake of the coup, Siam was reorganized as a constitutional monarchy with a democratic parliamentary system, but over time the military began to take a more and more dominant role. As the 1930s wore on, the army, under the leadership of General Pibul, began to adopt a fascist stance in emulation of both Germany and Japan. A growing nationalist outlook also led to the official name change from Siam to Thailand. Nevertheless, the country attempted to remain neutral in World War II, until Japan forced the government's hand in December of 1940, announcing its intention to march Japanese troops into Bangkok with or without Thai consent. Pibul opted for expediency, welcoming the Japanese into the city and thus entering the conflict on the side of the Axis. Today, the military still maintains a conspicuous presence in all reaches of public life both in Bangkok and in the provinces.

After World War II, Bangkok shared in the economic upsurge of Southeast Asia, and the city has undergone a process of rapid growth and modernization. More and more of the trappings of modern Western culture have appeared in Bangkok, but traditional ways of life flourish in the midst of highrises, traffic congestion, neon lights, and a steamy night life. With its diverse mix of ostentation and practicality, advanced technology and traditional customs, Bangkok offers the visitor a unique version of late-twentieth-century cosmopolitanism.

Further Reading: *Bangkok: The Story of a City* by Alec Waugh (Boston: Little Brown, and London: Allen, 1971) is a highly readable account of the ups and downs of the Thai royal house and gives considerable insight into the history of Bangkok as well. *Thailand: Aspects of Landscape and Life* by Robert L. Pendleton (New York: Duell, Sloan and Pearce, 1962) contains a brief but informative history of the Bangkok region. *A Concise History of Southeast Asia* by Nicholas Tarling (New York: Praeger, 1966; as *Southeast Asia Past and Present,* Melbourne: Cheshire, 1966) includes some helpful background information on the development of Siam. Steve van Beek's *Insight City Guides: Bangkok* (Singapore: APA, 1988) contains both an excellent historical overview and detailed information on architectural monuments and other attractions.

—James Sullivan and Marijke Rijsberman

Banten (West Java, Indonesia)

Location: On the north coast of western Java in the Malay Archipelago.

Description: Major Islamic port city in Indonesia during the sixteenth and seventeenth centuries.

Contact: Diparda Jawa Barat
Jl Cipaganti 151-153
Bandung, West Java
Indonesia
(22) 81490

The two centuries from approximately 1450 to 1650 were a time of intense commercial activity in Southeast Asia. Spurred by the growth of markets in China, India, and the West, a host of port cities sprang up along the coasts of western Indonesia. For a brief interlude in the sixteenth century, the greatest of these was Banten. Facing north to the Java Sea but close to the Sunda Strait, one of Indonesia's two main maritime gateways to the West, Banten owed its prominence both to temporarily favorable conditions and to the energy of its founders.

The Dutch form of the city's name, Bantam, is shared by a diminutive breed of fowl, but although the jungle fowl of Java is probably the ancestor of all domestic fowl, no historical record exists to link bantams with Banten. Rather, the city's fortunes were built on pepper.

True, or black, pepper is native to India. Even after the spread of chili peppers from the Americas following the Columbus voyages, black pepper was the main ingredient used by Old World cooks to add spice to their dishes. In the sixteenth century, culinary fashion in both Europe and China put a high premium on pepper, and large tracts of land in the Malay Archipelago were cleared for growing the vine. By the middle of the sixteenth century, an estimated 2,000 metric tons of pepper reached Europe every year, most of it from the archipelago.

The town of Banten first appears in the historical record as a port for the shadowy Hindu-Buddhist kingdom of Pajajaran, whose capital, Pakuan, was situated in the foothills some distance from the coast. Archaeological research has shown that the settlement of Banten Girang, about six miles from the mouth of the Banten River, was a trading center as early as the eleventh century; it was to this port that Portuguese vessels came in the early sixteenth century in search of pepper.

Trade in pepper had allowed the rulers of Banten to become increasingly independent of Pajajaran, but the rulers themselves faced a growing threat from the Javanese state of Demak, farther east in what is now Central Java. Demak was one of a number of trading states to emerge on the north coast of Central and East Java in the fifteenth century after the decline of the Hindu-Javanese empire of Majapahit. Sometime in the late fifteenth century, Demak converted to Islam, partly through the efforts of Muslim missionaries, partly for commercial reasons. Not only did the increasing number of Muslim traders in the Malay Archipelago prefer to use Muslim ports, but for traders of all faiths Islamic law provided a more stable legal regime than Hinduism.

By the beginning of the sixteenth century, Demak was a powerful state with hegemony over much of central Java and imperialist ambitions abroad. The rising power of Banten attracted its attention, both as a rival and as a potential area for imperial expansion. Demak's influence arrived first in the form of Islam: a prominent missionary, Sunan Gunung Jāti, settled in the town, won local converts and, in 1527, seized power with the help of forces from Demak. The sultan of Demak then installed Gunung Jāti's son, Hasanudīn, as vassal king in Banten. Since this time, the Banten region has been ethnically mixed; the former dominance of the indigenous Sundanese was eroded in the coastal regions by settlers from the Javanese regions farther east. Demak's control, however, was never solid and Hasanudīn was able to develop Banten as a major kingdom in its own right. His most important achievement was to extend Banten's hegemony over the pepper-producing regions of southern Sumatra. The Lampung and Bengkulu regions had traditionally been loosely subject to states based on the Sumatran city of Palembang, but Palembang was weak in the sixteenth century. Hasanudīn also extended Banten's territory on Java, although it was probably not until the reign of his son and successor Maulana Yūsup that the last remnants of Pajajaran fell and Banten was able to claim the mountain regions nearly as far as the borders of Java proper.

The reigns of Hasanudīn and Yūsup represented Banten's golden age. Hasanudīn moved his court downstream to the coast for better management of trade. In formal Javanese style, he constructed a city according to a square plan, with each side facing one point of the compass. Within brick ramparts six feet thick and stretching around a circumference of nearly five miles, he built a large palace, a great mosque, and extensive residential quarters (foreigners—never fully trusted—had to live outside the walls). By the end of the sixteenth century, Banten was one of the great cities of Asia. A throng of merchants from three continents bustled about its docks and warehouses, and a well-managed system of canals linked the city to its agricultural hinterland.

Under the rule of Hasanudīn and Yūsup, Banten had benefitted from the single-minded determination of rulers who were both chief warrior and chief merchant. In times of less despotic rule, however, severe political tensions arose in the kingdom between the older aristocratic and bureaucratic elite

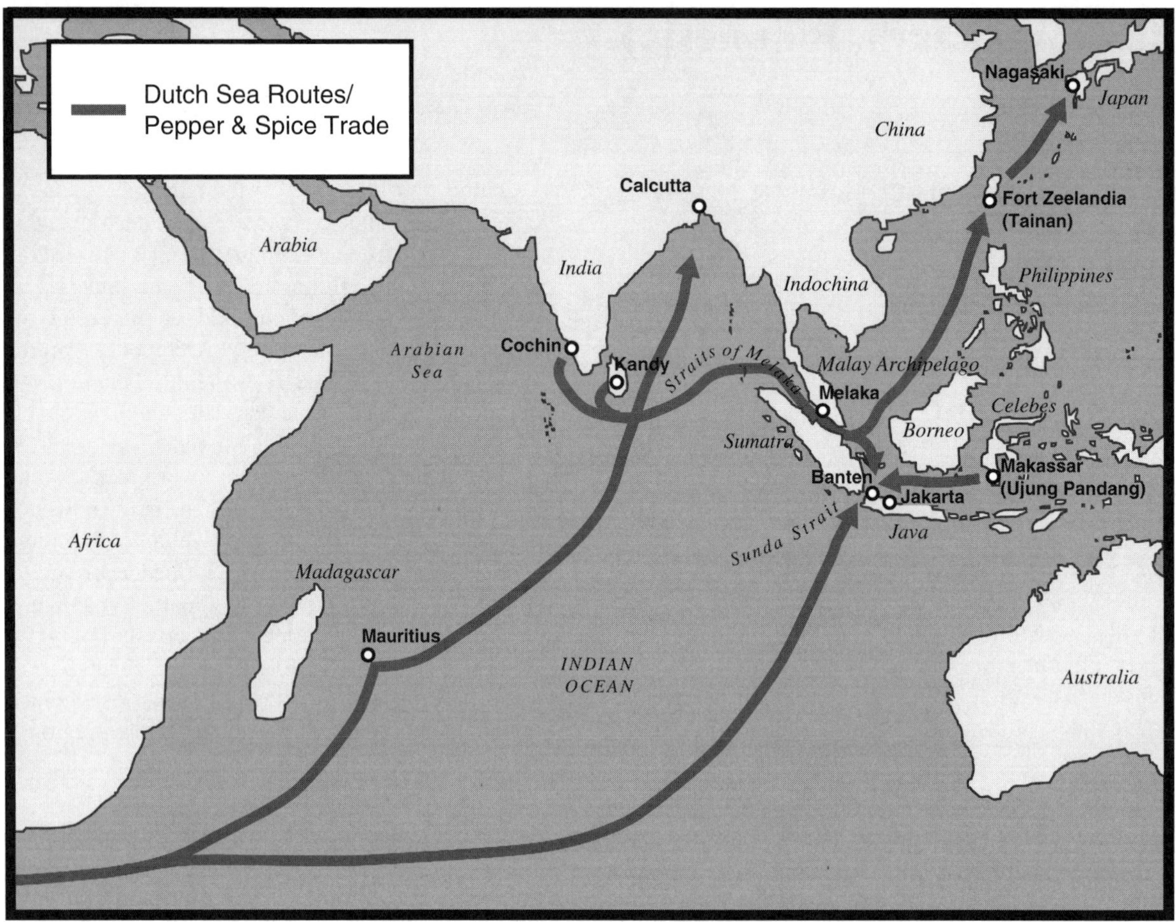

Map showing the convergence of Dutch trade routes on Banten
Illustration by Tom Willcockson

and the newer class of powerful merchants, who were simply referred to as *orang kaya* (rich people). Whereas the latter favored freedom of trade, the former not only saw benefits for themselves in heavier commercial taxes but distrusted the power of the merchants. This conflict reached its peak after 1596, when Yūsup's son and heir was killed in battle against Palembang, culminating in a destructive civil war from 1602 to 1609.

The civil war weakened Banten at a critical moment in Southeast Asian history. The first Dutch trading expedition had reached Banten in 1596, and in 1602 the various Dutch trading ventures were amalgamated into the Dutch East Indies Company or V.O.C. (Vereenigde Oostindische Compagnie). The internal structure of the V.O.C. made it one of the most advanced corporations of its era, but it also commanded the best in European military and naval technology, which it used ruthlessly to establish monopolies in lucrative sectors of the economy of the archipelago. Banten had a clear view of Dutch power in 1601, when a V.O.C. fleet utterly destroyed a Portuguese force in the Bay of Banten. The Dutch and their northern European rivals, the British, both established factories, or trading posts, in Banten and soon showed themselves to be difficult to control. They drank heavily, fought in the streets, and on one occasion even fired a cannon at the palace. Their presence almost certainly strengthened the convictions of those who argued that too much free trade was not in Banten's interests.

Increasingly aware that they were not welcome in Banten, the Dutch began to develop the idea of creating their own secure trading center and administrative headquarters in the archipelago. With the Portuguese still firmly established in what had been the preeminent port city of Melaka, and with the newly powerful Javanese state of Mataram already victorious over Demak and other Javanese coastal states, the V.O.C. chose the Banten region as the most favorable site. They established a post at the port of Jayakarta, on the coast a little to the east of Banten and in 1619 transformed it into their Asian headquarters with the name Batavia (now Jakarta).

The close proximity of such a powerful rival was fatal for Banten's commercial interests. Determined to channel as much trade as possible through Batavia, the V.O.C. blockaded Banten, and the economy went into crisis. An emergency meeting of the Great Council was called and the members decided to take desperate measures. Recognizing that the Dutch could not be beaten, the Council decided to abandon pepper production in the hope that the Europeans would leave Banten alone. A drastic order was issued that all pepper vines should be uprooted. The merchants exhibited considerable resistance to the new policy, which was nevertheless implemented with enough vigor to take Banten for a time out of the ranks of the major pepper producers of the archipelago.

In retrospect, the Great Council's decision was wise, although less because it mitigated Dutch hostility than because it forced the Banten economy to diversify. Instead of focusing on a single, high-value crop, Banten turned increasingly to the production of sugar and rice, two commodities whose main market was in Southeast Asia itself rather than in distant Europe. By so doing, Banten put itself into a position to benefit from the growth of Batavia as a supplier of agricultural produce.

The scale of this agricultural development was massive. Coconut plantations were established stretching over thousands of acres. Extensive irrigation works were developed to open up land for rice cultivation, and some 30,000 people were resettled to provide labor for the new fields. Sugar production, on the other hand, was predominantly in the hands of Chinese entrepreneurs, who sponsored large estates and funded the construction of mills to process the cane. Pepper production remained important, too. International pepper prices fell dramatically in the 1650s, but the crop remained a valuable one and Banten's colonies in southern Sumatra remained among the world's most important production areas. Like the Dutch, however, the rulers of Banten could make pepper most profitable only by enforcing a rigid system of monopoly over sale and distribution.

Banten's second era of prosperity was also the result of international factors. The kingdom of Mataram remained the dominant power on Java, and its rulers were both profoundly hostile to the Dutch presence and keen to establish hegemony over Banten, which they had already stripped of its eastern provinces in the Priangan hills. The V.O.C. did not go so far as make a formal alliance with Banten against Mataram, but it saw no immediate advantage in eliminating a state that shared its fear of Javanese expansionism. Banten's other advantage came from the English, who were making a last effort to carve out a sphere of commercial influence in the archipelago after the Dutch had brutally expelled them from the Moluccas.

Although a treaty with the V.O.C. in 1659 put some restrictions on Banten's freedom of trade, the rulers of Banten soon found enough opportunities to turn their city once more into a great trading port and the largest city in the Malay Archipelago. While the Dutch concentrated on exploiting their monopolies from Batavia, Banten launched imaginative trading ventures. It set up a regular link with Spanish Manila, which had become a lucrative source of silver coin from the mines of the Americas. It even set up something close to a trading company on the model of the Dutch and English, commissioning the construction of ships according to the most advanced techniques, and sending them with expert crews and trading teams to the ports of the archipelago and beyond to China and India. At its peak, the Bantenese trade network stretched from Arabia to Japan.

That the two most powerful trading states of the Malay Archipelago, however, had their capitals on the same coastline less than sixty miles apart represented an inherently unstable situation, especially as Banten's dynamic Sultan Ageng also had territorial ambitions in the region. In 1661, Banten extended its overseas sphere of influence to the diamond-producing state of Landak in western Borneo (West Kalimantan), and in the 1670s it took advantage of civil war in Mataram to reassert its control over the Priangan hills and even to establish a brief hegemony over the port of Cirebon. With the Dutch now confidently manipulating dynastic politics in Mataram, however, the V.O.C. had no wish to see its Batavia headquarters surrounded by a resurgent Banten, and in a brief war the Bantenese were forced back.

The defeat crystallized divisions within the Banten elite over the best way of handling the Dutch. Ageng's ambitious policy of expansion was now questioned by his son and heir, Sultan Haji, who favored accommodation with the V.O.C. and who used the opportunity of his father's defeat to gain power in a palace coup in 1680. Haji's position, however, proved to be very weak. His Dutch sympathies alienated him from the military and Islamic elites of the kingdom, while the V.O.C.'s ill-disguised determination to break Banten's commercial power had little to appeal to the commercial elites. Beleaguered and desperate, Haji turned directly to the Dutch, asking for their assistance and agreeing in return to sign a treaty renouncing Banten's territorial ambitions on Java and excluding other Europeans from his ports.

Dutch assistance arrived just in time. By March 1682, Ageng and his supporters had burned the city to the ground, leaving Haji besieged in his palace. Dutch artillery turned the tide of battle, and Ageng was forced to flee into the hills. He surrendered a year later and was exiled in Batavia, where he died. His more determined followers were shipped by the V.O.C. as far away as possible to the Dutch colony at the Cape of Good Hope, where they became the core of what eventually became known as the Cape Malay community. Meanwhile, Banten's remaining fortifications were torn down and a Dutch fortress, Fort Speelwijk, was built to house a permanent garrison.

Banten remained a nominally independent state in alliance with the V.O.C., but its power was now utterly gone. European traders were excluded from its port, few facilities remained for Asian traders, and the agricultural production of the interior had been set back by the war. Symbolically, the center of administration was shifted from Banten to the inland town of Serang. Banten itself declined to something less than a village, with only the Great Mosque and the scattered ruins of once impressive buildings to indicate its former existence.

During the next seventy years, the V.O.C. shaved a series of thin slices of territory from Banten's eastern border, taking Dutch territory steadily closer to the Banten capital. In 1752, the sultan formally acknowledged Dutch sovereignty, but this was more a pretext for Dutch annexation of Banten's former territories in Sumatra and Borneo than a sign of real change in the status of the sultanate. In 1808, under the reforming colonial government of Marshal H. W. Daendels, the Dutch formally annexed the fertile coastal districts of the north, leaving the sultan only the impoverished southern hills until they, too, were taken from him in 1813. The sultan was exiled in 1832.

Banten's experience under colonialism was grim. In the first years of colonial rule, significant areas along the northern coast were distributed to supporters of the Dutch as private estates. The lords of these estates, granted what amounted to feudal rights over the inhabitants, enjoyed a legal freedom from government supervision that led to their quasi-sovereign position. Elsewhere in Banten, encouraged by the agricultural expansion programs of the sultans, the Dutch began experiments with new, potentially lucrative crops such as indigo, cinnamon, tobacco, and cochineal. In order to create the large plantations needed to make these ventures profitable, however, they seized still more land from local farmers and demanded labor services from almost all the population.

The Dutch found few collaborators among the indigenous elite in the region who were willing to join them in this systematic exploitation, and they were forced to introduce instead aristocratic administrators from the more pliant Priangan regions. Seen as outsiders by both the Javanese-speaking Bantenese of the north and the Sundanese speakers of the south, these aristocrats were extremely unpopular, and the region was wracked by revolt after revolt during the nineteenth century. The aristocrats themselves made use of their power to extract all they could from the peasants. One of the most savage nineteenth–century liberal Dutch denunciations of colonial practice drew on Banten for its arguments. This was the semi-autobiographical novel *Max Havelaar*, written by Eduard Douwes Dekker under the pseudonym Multatuli (I have suffered much), which presented a depressing picture of conniving, murderous aristocratic administrators in league with weak and venal Dutch colonial officials.

Colonial reforms in the late nineteenth and early twentieth centuries may have mitigated the immediate hardship for the Bantenese, but they were insufficient to assuage the deeply rooted hatred of the Dutch and the colonial elites. In 1926 three groups, the influential rural Islamic teachers or *ulama*, the powerful Banten gang leaders or *jawara*, and a new nationalist stream concentrated in the Indonesian communist party, came together to stage an uprising against colonialism. The rebellion was easily crushed by colonial forces, but its ferocity so alarmed the Dutch that they jailed and exiled several hundred people accused of involvement in the movement.

Small wonder, then, that the Japanese forces that landed in Banten in March 1942 were hailed by the Bantenese as liberators. Japanese propaganda led people to believe that the Japanese would grant immediate independence, but in fact they subjected the people of Banten to extortionate demands for rice as well as the forced recruitment of laborers for Japanese projects; tens of thousands died as a result. Banten, therefore, was one of the first regions in Indonesia to seize the opportunity to declare independence when the Japanese surrendered in August 1945. During most of the revolution, which raged from 1945 to 1949, Banten was a virtually independent region, ruled by a nationalist-Islamic coalition; for a time it even issued its own currency. Recalling the ferocity of Bantenese anti-colonialism, the Dutch left Banten unmolested until their final attempt to crush the rebel Indonesian Republic in the last days of 1948, and even then they never again established control outside the larger towns.

During the first years of Indonesian independence, Banten remained a backwater. Only recently has industrial development begun to transform the region. Banten has also benefitted from its position along a corridor connecting Jakarta to Sumatra.

Further Reading: The most important work on Banten at the height of its powers is *The Sultanate of Banten* by Claude Guillot (Jakarta: Gramedia, 1990). *Expansion and Crisis*, volume two of *Southeast Asia in the Age of Commerce 1450–1680* by Anthony Reid (New Haven, Connecticut, and London: Yale University Press, 1993) makes frequent reference to Banten in the context of broader developments in Southeast Asian history. For the turbulent nineteenth century, Sartono Kartodirdjo's *The Peasants' Revolt of Banten in 1888, Its Conditions, Course and Sequel: A Case Study of Social Movements in Indonesia* (The Hague: Martinus Nijhoff, 1966) is valuable, while Michael Charles Williams' two studies, *Communism, Religion, and Revolt in Banten* (Athens: Ohio University Center for International Studies, 1990) and "Banten: Rice Debts Will Be Repaid with Rice, Blood Debts with Blood," in *Regional Dynamics of the Indonesian Revolution: Unity from Diversity* (Honolulu: University of Hawaii Press, 1985), cover the twentieth century.

—Robert Cribb

Beijing (China): Forbidden City

Location: In the historic center of the Chinese capital.

Description: Residence of the Chinese emperors and headquarters of their government from 1420 to 1911, now open to the public as the Palace Museum, displaying numerous imperial treasures.

Site Office: Beijing Tourism Bureau
28 Jianguo Menwai Avenue
100022 Beijing
China
(1) 5158252

The palace complex known to the West as the Forbidden City still physically dominates much of the heart of the modern city of Beijing, capital of the People's Republic of China, and serves as a constant reminder of China's past development as a feudal empire over thousands of years. Yet, ironically, the palace itself is relatively new in Chinese terms, having been begun as recently as the fifteenth century. Throughout its history, its successive expansion, decline, and preservation have depended on the changing fortunes of Beijing itself and of the political forces that have variously controlled, abandoned, or invaded the city. The tranquility of the palace buildings in their present state is by no means characteristic of their past.

A number of different palaces and government buildings had existed in what is now Beijing long before the Forbidden City itself was established. Beijing originated more than 2,000 years ago as a frontier garrison on the edge of the North China Plain. Over the centuries, the map of northern China was frequently altered as various kingdoms grew more powerful or faded away, so that even such an initially remote settlement sometimes served as a royal capital, at other times as a market town or as a fortress, with consequent changes of name and layout. By the twelfth century, what is now Beijing was known as Zhongdu and was the capital of the Jin Dynasty, which controlled the northern half of China and devoted much of its wealth to expanding the city; the capital was overthrown in 1215 when the Mongols, led by Genghis Khan, managed to break through the Great Wall and other defenses and burn Zhongdu to the ground.

The city was refounded after this disaster, not by the Chinese but by their new Mongol overlords. In 1271 the city was granted its enduring status as the capital of the whole of China by Genghis's grandson, Kublai Khan, the first Mongol emperor of China and founder of the Yuan Dynasty. It was his regime that rebuilt the city, giving it the Mongol name Khanbaliq, although among ordinary Chinese it became known simply as Dadu (Great Capital). China was once more united and Khanbaliq, which may have had a population of more than 400,000, prospered for a century as an imperial city, attracting such foreign visitors as Marco Polo, who arrived there in 1275. Under the Yuan Dynasty, city walls were built and the water supply was improved by the emperor's engineers, who restored and extended the network of canals and drains. However, the dynasty's palaces, notably the Danei (Great Within), have not survived, and controversy continues over the extent to which they were prototypes for the Forbidden City. Perhaps the most enduring legacy of the 108 years of Yuan rule is the grid or checkerboard layout that still characterizes the central area around the palace complex today.

During the fourteenth century, Chinese rebel forces gathered in Central China, gradually pushed the dynasty's armies back into the north and, in 1368, took control of Khanbaliq (Dadu) and overthrew the Yuan. Their leader Zhu Yuanzhang declared himself emperor, taking the name Hongwu and establishing the Ming Dynasty. At first the new regime was based at what is now Nanjing (Southern Capital), while Khanbaliq was renamed Beiping (Northern Peace) and reduced in size, but in 1421 Zhudi, a son of Zhu Yuanzhang who had become the third Ming emperor in 1403 under the name of Yongle, moved the capital back from Nanjing to Beiping. The city was renamed once more, as Beijing (Northern Capital), and considerably enlarged, eventually consisting of walled cities within cities, among which the Imperial City or Inner City was developed in the northern part of the capital as a complex of residences for government officials, imperial food warehouses, and other imperial buildings. (Many of the Ming walls from this period were destroyed during the Communist regime's "Great Leap Forward" campaign in 1958.)

Within the Inner City was the main complex of palaces, known in Chinese as the Zijincheng, which literally means "purple forbidden city" (or, reflecting the historic origins of most Chinese capitals, fortress). In Chinese traditional symbolism the color purple represents the Zi, the North Star, which is said to be the center of the universe where the deity has his palace. Since the emperor was believed to be the "Son of Heaven" it was necessary that he, too, should have a sacred palace and that it should be "forbidden," that is, arranged so that ordinary eyes could not look upon the members of the imperial family. A total of 9,999 rooms were built within the Forbidden City, one fewer than the 10,000 rooms in the mythical palace of the deity: among these were not only the living quarters for the emperor and his extensive entourage but also the main offices of the enormous imperial bureaucracy.

The construction of the Forbidden City began in 1406 and was completed fourteen years later. It is likely that more

The Taihedian (Hall of Supreme Harmony), Forbidden City, Beijing
Photo courtesy of Marvin Weinstein

than 200,000 men were put to work on the project. The red walls that still surround the complex are about 32 feet high and run for about 2,500 feet from east to west and approximately 3,150 feet from north to south, enclosing an area of roughly 183 acres. A three-story watchtower stands at each corner of the rectangular enclosure, which is surrounded by a moat 168 feet wide and crossed by seven bridges, originally allocated to different ranks within the imperial hierarchy. Within these formidable defenses the complex is laid out in three main sections: the Outer Court to the south, in front of the main palace buildings, entered through four enormous gatehouses; the main palace buildings in the center, consisting of three halls where official and ritual business was conducted, and, to the north, the Inner Court, which contains the residences of the emperor, his family, his concubines, and his personal servants. The uniform north/south axis on which the whole of the Forbidden City is laid out was known as the meridian line and divided the entire city of Beijing into eastern and western halves.

The seventy-five buildings still standing within the imperial walls are the finest examples of Ming architecture in China today. Each feature, whether it was the color and design of the roof tiles or the details in the design of the bridges, was planned and executed to illustrate rankings within the imperial court, and the position, appearance, and name of each structure was devised to fit within the elaborate traditional symbology considered suitable to a complex that represented the summit of Chinese political and religious life. Thus, among the five Outer Gold Water Bridges or Marble Bridges to the south, the middle bridge, known as the Yuluqiao (Bridge of the Imperial Way), was used only by the emperor; the two bridges on each side were for the imperial family; and the outer two were for the elite military and government officials permitted to enter the complex.

Beyond the bridges, the ceremonial entrance consists of a series of gates, beginning with the Tiananmen (Gate of Heavenly Peace) and the Duanmen (Gate of Correct Demeanor). Tiananmen, originally known as Chiengtianmen (Gate of Receiving Orders From Heaven), has a roof decorated with mythological animals, believed to ward off evil spirits, and five separate openings, of which the middle one was again reserved for the emperor. The rooms in the gatehouse above these openings were used as quarters for court officials as well as for such ceremonies as the public proclamation of imperial edicts.

The third gate in the series is the Wumen (Meridian Gate), which, because of its decoration, is also known as the Wufenglou (Five Phoenix Tower). This horseshoe-shaped structure of three blocks linking five towers was used for public ceremonies such as reviews of the imperial troops and the annual announcement of the ritual details of the lunar calendar, and was also the place where officials were flogged for infringements of the emperor's dignity or other offenses against court ritual. In later centuries, under the Qing Dynasty, it was used for the ceremonial meeting of the emperor and his officials each morning. Again, only the emperor could pass through the middle of this gate, while others were required to use the openings to either side.

The large courtyard lying beyond the Meridian Gate, like others within the Forbidden City, is made primarily of gray bricks but has a central marble path, known as the Imperial Way, which was reserved for members of the imperial family. The stream that flows through a marble channel across the middle of this courtyard is crossed by way of the Inner Golden Water Bridges, five small, beautifully decorated marble bridges that lead to the final gate, the Taihemen (Gate of Supreme Harmony), which was rebuilt in 1890. It is a raised, porch-like structure with large red-lacquered pillars, in front of which are two bronze lions, a female with a cub under her paw, and a male holding a sphere, both symbolizing the strength of the emperor and his subjects' obedience.

Next is the courtyard known as the Sea of Flagstone, which was built to accommodate more than 90,000 people during imperial ceremonies. In the center of this courtyard is the largest building in the Forbidden City, the Taihedian (Hall of Supreme Harmony). For centuries this wooden structure, 123 feet high, was the tallest building in Beijing, since anyone was forbidden to build a structure higher than the emperor's palace. It is reached by a three-tier staircase decorated with such motifs as dragons among clouds, representing the emperor in heaven. In the middle of the forty-four steps extends a carved stone ramp reserved for the emperor. Both the exterior and the interior of the hall are decorated with the highest ranking color (yellow) and in an extremely ornate style, for it contained the main throne room and was the most important building in the complex. Its fifty-five rooms were used for conducting the main business of the state and such important ceremonies as the enthronement of new emperors, the celebration of emperors' birthdays, the crucial rituals welcoming the New Year, and the announcement of the names of successful candidates in the imperial examinations.

The many treasures displayed in the hall today include the throne and its platform, both beautifully carved with clouds and dragons, and surrounded by six golden lacquered pillars carved with coiled dragons; a screen depicting nine dragons, placed behind the throne; and such objects as jade musical chimes and animal-shaped incense burners. Behind the Taihedian, and aligned on the same axis, are, first, the Zhonghedian (The Hall of Complete Harmony), restored in 1627 and 1765, where less important state business was conducted and where the emperor was dressed for his ceremonial appearances in the Taihedian; and, farther north, the Baohedian (Hall of Preserving Harmony), where the examinations for the imperial bureaucracy were held each year.

The Inner Court, the residential quarter in the section of the complex that lay farthest from the commoners' streets and homes when it was first built, contains three main buildings, the Qianqinggong (Palace of Heavenly Purity), restored in 1797, the Jiaotaidian (Hall of Heavenly and Earthly Union), restored in 1655, and the Kunninggong (Palace of Earthly Peace). The latter, painted entirely in red, the color of joy, was traditionally the place where each emperor spent his wedding night, even in later centuries when the imperial family had moved to live in less ceremonial buildings at the edges of the complex (although in 1922—ten years after he had abdicated—the last emperor, Puyi, was apparently so put off by the red color that he returned to his old rooms). Other smaller buildings in the Inner Court were built at various times for the imperial family, concubines, government officials, and the thousands of eunuchs who composed the imperial household. According to records for 1572, for example, the Ming emperor Wanli (Zhu Yijun) had approximately 9,000 women and 70,000 eunuchs living in the Forbidden City. Behind their quarters are several imperial gardens, where some of the trees planted during the 1420s still survive today.

The Ming Dynasty, which founded and elaborated this extraordinary sacred and imperial settlement, came to an end in 1644, when Beijing first passed into the control of a peasant army led by Li Zicheng, and then, forty-three days later, was conquered by an army from Manchuria to the northeast. The Forbidden City was badly damaged by fire during fierce battles between the Manchu forces and Li's troops, who were at least nominally loyal to the Ming. The victorious Manchu established a new dynasty, known as the Qing (pure) and marked their triumph by having the Chiengtianmen gate rebuilt, a project completed in 1651, and renamed Tiananmen. Throughout the Qing era, which lasted for 267 years, no expense was spared on repairs and improvements to the Forbidden City and to Beijing as a whole.

By the middle of the nineteenth century, China's isolation from the outside world was being forcibly brought to an end. The Opium Wars with Britain (1840–42 and 1858–60) culminated in the occupation of Beijing by British and French troops, who destroyed and looted parts of the city but left the palace complex untouched. Subsequently, the various great powers of Europe, along with Japan, gained control of large parts of the Chinese Empire, and a growing economic crisis, owing partly to the large war indemnities imposed on the imperial government, eventually led to widespread revolts. Meanwhile, effective power over the Forbidden City and therefore over those parts of China that remained under its control passed into the hands of the xenophobic and corrupt Empress Dowager Cixi, who had entered the court as a minor concubine in 1852 and then manipulated her way to supreme power as regent from 1861 to 1908.

Anti-foreign sentiment reached its height during the Boxer Rebellion of 1900, when a group that called itself the Society of the Righteous and Harmonious Fists, but which was nicknamed the Boxers by Europeans because its members exercised by shadow-boxing, took to the streets and attacked Chinese Christians and foreigners. The Empress Dowager, who privately supported the Boxers but publicly dissociated herself from them, escaped from the capital, which by the end of July was under occupation by a joint force of French, British, American, and Japanese troops. After her departure, the sanctity of the Forbidden City was violated for the first time since 1644, as buildings were burned down and many jade objects, jewels, silks, and furs were taken by foreign troops and even by the families of foreign diplomats and missionaries. A fragile peace returned to China in 1901, and the Empress Dowager reentered the Forbidden City in 1902.

The accession in 1908 of the infant Puyi to an increasingly powerless throne did nothing to stop the tide of republicanism that swept through China and reached its height with demonstrations in front of the Forbidden City, in what is now Tiananmen Square. A revolutionary movement led by Sun Yat-sen took power in 1912 and forced Puyi, the last emperor, to abdicate. China was declared a republic, with Nanjing as its capital. Supporters of the constitutional monarchy, however, still considered Beijing the capital, a status it maintained until 1928, when Nanjing became the official capital. The Outer Court of the Forbidden City, closed to ordinary Chinese for centuries, was opened to the public, while Puyi, the imperial family, and a staff of eunuchs, reduced in number from 3,000 to about 1,500, were allowed to remain within the Forbidden City but restricted to the buildings of the Inner Court.

Factional conflicts continued among the civilian and military leaders of the republic, and during the course of yet another upheaval in 1917, three small bombs were dropped on the Forbidden City, which was believed to harbor groups who favored an imperial restoration. By 1922, when Puyi was married and yet another political movement, the Communist Party, was beginning to add to the general chaos of the country, conditions inside the complex were such that Puyi himself sold some of his dynasty's treasures to boost his income, while unknown to him the eunuchs were also looting the palace, selling off up to 6,000 priceless objects for their own gain. Their activities were discovered by Puyi's British tutor, Sir Reginald Johnston, and more than 1,000 of them were dismissed. In 1925 the last emperor was forced to leave by the latest military faction to seize control of Beijing; he went on to become puppet ruler of the Japanese colony of Manchukuo, and ended up working as a gardener in Beijing until his death in 1967. The Forbidden City was formally renamed the Palace Museum at this time (although it is still best known to the Chinese themselves as the Gugong, the Ancient Palace). However, because of the civil war that plagued China for more than a decade and then the Japanese occupation of Beijing between 1937 and 1945, the Palace Museum was neglected and fell into disrepair.

On October 1, 1949, after winning the most recent of China's civil wars, the communist leader Mao Zedong announced from a rostrum on top of the Tiananmen the foundation of the People's Republic of China, with Beijing as capital. Mao and his colleagues rejected proposals to reestablish the Forbidden City as a government center because it was not as secure as the Zhongnanhai, the presidential compound that had been used by Sun Yat-sen in 1911, and instead had the complex restored and the treasures it still contained organized into formal exhibits. The Palace Museum was reopened to the public and in 1961 was officially declared a major national treasure. After Mao's death twenty-five years later, a portrait of him was hung from the Tiananmen, overlooking the massive square where, in June 1989, the communist regime, now led by Deng Xiaoping, confronted thousands of demonstrators rallying for democracy and human rights. The official government denounced the students' movement as a "counter-revolutionary insurrection," and an undetermined number of people were killed. Within a year of the incident, Chinese and foreign tourists alike were flocking back to the capital of the world's most powerful remaining Stalinist state.

Many visitors are attracted by what they have seen of the Forbidden City in Bernardo Bertolucci's film *The Last Emperor,* much of which was shot inside the complex in 1986; most of them are no doubt impressed by the peaceful atmosphere of the Forbidden City, which can seem a world away from the busy metropolis beyond its walls. With the aged Deng no longer appearing in public, his colleagues scheming for the succession, and the country being rapidly transformed by the introduction of free markets and the growth of foreign investment, it is an open question whether this superficial tranquility might not again be disturbed by political protest, social upheaval, or even another change of dynasty.

Further Reading: A detailed description of the Forbidden City (Palace Museum) can be found in Liu Junwen's *Beijing: China's Ancient and Modern Capital* (Beijing: Foreign Languages Press, and San Francisco: China Books, 1982). The life of the last emperor, Puyi, including the many ancient rituals in which he continued to take part until 1925, is evocatively described by Sir Reginald Johnston in *Twilight in the Forbidden City* (London: Gollancz, and New York: Appleton-Century, 1934). David Bonavia's *Peking* (Alexandria, Virginia, and London: Time-Life, 1978), although outdated in some respects, remains one of the most interesting accounts of the Chinese capital, including the Forbidden City.

—Monique Lamontagne

Beijing (China): Tiananmen Square

Location: Tiananmen Square lies in the center of Beijing, bounded by the Forbidden City on the north and the large Qianmen Gate on the south.

Description: Possibly the largest public square in the world, Tiananmen Square is capable of holding 1 million people. Since its creation during the Qing Dynasty, Tiananmen Square has been the site of several important popular demonstrations, including those of the influential May Fourth movement and the ill-fated democracy movement of 1989.

Site Office: Beijing Tourism Bureau
28 Jianguo Menwai Avenue
100022 Beijing
China
(1) 5158252

Lying at the very heart of China's capital city of Beijing is the vast Tiananmen Guangchang (Tiananmen Square). Flanked on the north by the imposing Forbidden City and on the south by the majestic Qianmen gate, the Square of Heavenly Peace measures some 1,600 feet by 2,600 feet and has the capacity to hold 1 million people. Probably the largest public square in the world, Tiananmen Square has played a significant role in modern Chinese history.

Beijing and its environs have been settled for thousands of years. Indeed, the famous Peking Man (whose fossilized remains were discovered there by archaeologists) lived in caves near Zhoukoudian, on the southwestern edge of what is now Beijing, some 500,000 years ago. The city of Beijing was founded more than 2,000 years ago under the name Ji. During the Warring States period (403–221 B.C.), the kingdom of Yan made the city its capital, and it was known as Yanjing (Capital of Yan)—a name still used occasionally today.

By the time of the Qin (221–206 B.C.), the city's name had reverted to Ji, and it became the imperial military base, governed by the Qin capital at Xianyang (just outside what is now Xian). After the demise of the Qin and the rise of the Eastern Han (A.D. 25–220), Beijing continued to be an important military base used to defend the region against hostile nomadic tribes. During the Tang (618–907), the city was renamed Youzhou and was overshadowed by the Tang's fantastic metropolitan capital at Xian, then called Chang'an.

It was not until the foreign-ruled Liao Dynasty (907–1125) that Beijing regained some of its former importance. While conquering the Tang, the Khitan people had destroyed Youzhou, but they promptly built their own city on the site. This new city was called Nanjing, or Southern Capital (not to be confused with the city of Nanjing in Jiangsu province) and was the dynasty's second city, after the Liao capital in Manchuria. When the Jürchens conquered the region in 1153, Beijing was declared the capital of their Jin Empire (1115–1234) and was renamed Zhongdu, or Middle Capital.

The Jin took pride in Zhongdu and used hundreds of thousands of workers to enhance the city, building both fortifications and royal palaces. When the Mongols overthrew the Jin in the thirteenth century, the capital was destroyed. The Mongols chose the site of Beijing as the seat of their dynasty, the Yuan (1234–1368), and the city was renamed Khanbaliq (City of Khan); it was most commonly known, however, as Dadu (Great Capital). As the capital of the Yuan, the city was rebuilt in grand style. The great traveler Marco Polo spent some time there in 1275, and he described at length the "wonders of the city."

When the Chinese regained control of their own country and the Ming Dynasty (1368–1644) rose to power, the imperial capital was moved south to Nanjing (in Jiangsu province) and Beijing was renamed Beiping (Northern Peace). The third Ming emperor, Yongle, however, returned the imperial capital north to Beijing in the early fifteenth century; under Yongle, the city was given its current name, Beijing (Northern Capital). The layout of Beijing and many of the city's well-known monuments date from the time of the Ming.

Qianmen, or Outer Gate, standing at the southern end of Tiananmen Square, dates to Ming rule. At the time of construction in 1421, Qianmen was one of the gates in Beijing's Imperial City Wall, built during the rule of Yongle. According to imperial protocol, only the emperor could pass through the gate's central passageway—lesser officials and ordinary citizens were required to use smaller side passageways built for everyday use. Qianmen was damaged by fire in 1780 and 1849 and was nearly destroyed during the Boxer Rebellion in 1900. Careful rebuilding in the twentieth century has restored Qianmen to its former magnificence.

Tiananmen Square was designed in 1651, during the Qing Dynasty (1644–1912). A gate bearing the same name, Tiananmen (Gate of Heavenly Peace), forms the northern boundary of the square and also was constructed in 1651. Positioned in front of the Forbidden City and standing more than 100 feet high, the gate and its five passageways were reserved for ceremonial uses. As with Qianmen, only the emperor was allowed to use the central passage.

The square's central location in front of the Forbidden City and near modern-day government buildings in the Chinese capital has made it the site of several important demonstrations. The first such incidents, during what commonly is called the May Fourth Movement, resulted from China's dissatisfaction with decisions reached by the Allies at the Versailles peace conference after World War I. In May 1919,

Gate of Heavenly Peace, facing Tiananmen Square, Beijing
Photo courtesy of China National Tourist Office, New York

word from the conference reached China that Japan was to be given control of formerly German-controlled territory in the province of Shandong.

Frustrated by the Western powers' treatment of China and angered by the warlord government's acquiescence to such a treaty, Chinese students and intelligentsia in Beijing met May 4, 1919, to discuss the situation. This meeting produced a list of five resolutions: to protest the Shandong decision in no uncertain terms, to make China's citizens aware of the country's treatment by the Allied powers, to bring the people of Beijing together to discuss the situation, to form a union for Beijing's many students, and to demonstrate against the Versailles Treaty that very afternoon.

Despite government orders prohibiting the demonstration, 3,000 students gathered in Tiananmen Square. The students began to march toward the foreign settlement in the city, but after being turned back by police and guards, they moved instead toward the homes of Chinese officials known to be sympathetic to the Japanese. By the end of the day, one Chinese diplomat had been beaten severely and another's house had been destroyed.

The May Fourth Movement of 1919 ultimately succeeded in implementing several of the original points. Student unions were formed in Beijing and other cities, and the Chinese political consciousness was raised significantly. Opposition to warlord government and exploitation by foreign powers became widespread. The movement was not able to effect political change immediately, but it inspired a good deal of hope in the Chinese people.

The May Fourth Movement also produced another wave of change: the cultural movement sometimes referred to as the Chinese Renaissance. For centuries, all serious literary efforts had been written in classical Chinese, known only to the educated elite. To make literature more accessible to the majority of Chinese—who, the intellectuals reasoned, would be better political participants if their cultural awareness were raised—the American-educated Hu Shi and other members of the intelligentsia urged that writers use colloquial Chinese, the language as it was spoken. Despite some opposition, the colloquial style took root and held. The demonstration in Tiananmen Square produced a movement that brought lasting change to Chinese literature.

Since its construction, Tiananmen Gate had been used by emperors to issue imperial edicts. At such a time, the edict would be lowered from the top of the gate in a golden, phoenix-shaped box into the hands of a waiting official. The gate also has been used for important announcements from Chinese leaders in modern times. On October 1, 1949, Chinese Communist Party leader Mao Zedong used the gate as the setting for his announcement of the founding of the People's Republic of China.

Since then, the Tiananmen Gate has been used by numerous leaders and officials to review troops and to watch parades held on China's national day (in 1949 the square was opened and the gate was rebuilt expressly for these purposes). During the Cultural Revolution of the late 1960s, Mao often stood atop the gate to review and encourage the thousands of Red Guards—members of radical Chinese youth groups—who assembled in Tiananmen Square below. Begun as a movement to refine Communist ideology and instill a new revolutionary fervor in young people, the Cultural Revolution actually brought political and economic instability, along with persecution and purges of those not considered ideologically correct. At the height of this chaotic period, huge crowds of the fanatic guards would amass in the square, waving their copies of Mao's "Little Red Book" and chanting quotations from him.

Across from the gate in Tiananmen Square stands the 118-foot-high Monument to the People's Heroes, commemorating the people and events vital in establishing the People's Republic. Dedicated in 1958, the monument bears the inscription "The People's Heroes are Immortal," written in Mao's own calligraphy. Other modern attractions surrounding the square are the Museum of Chinese History, Museum of the Chinese Revolution, the Mao Zedong Memorial Hall—where Mao's preserved body is displayed in a crystal coffin—and the Great Hall of the People, where China's parliament meets.

In 1976 the square was the site of what has become known as the Tiananmen Incident. On April 4—the day before China's Qingming festival, during which people pay homage to the dead—thousands of people clustered around the Monument to the People's Heroes, laying wreaths and flowers to honor the recently deceased premier Zhou Enlai. Zhou and Vice Premier Deng Xiaoping had been noted as moderates who opposed the more radical aspects of the Cultural Revolution. Both were respected by the majority of the Chinese people, although their views were opposed by many other Communist leaders. The memorials to Zhou in the square were accompanied by messages of support for Deng, considered his heir as the voice of reason in China. The fact that Deng was falling from favor with party officials made such a display controversial, so when the crowds returned to the square the morning of April 5, they found the previous day's offerings had been removed by the police. Angered at official interference, the crowd protested, an act that quickly led to violence between police and civilians.

As the incident escalated, some 100,000 people poured into the square and surrounding government buildings. Although most of those gathered had gone home by evening, a small group of protesters remained. At 10:00 that night, they were forcibly removed by police and militia estimated to number in the tens of thousands. According to the official count, 388 people were arrested, but many Chinese believe the total to have been much higher. Those arrested either were put through a mass trial or were sent to prison camps for "reform."

Two years later, in the fall of 1978, China seemed to begin to open up, both in terms of its relationship with the West and in terms of intellectual privilege and freedom of expression. Those found guilty of crimes against the state in the Tiananmen Incident of 1976 had their verdicts reversed. Even more surprising, though, was the willingness of people to put their thoughts in writing (China traditionally was not a safe environment for self-expression). Many people wrote essays that were posted on a long segment of wall near the Forbidden City. A large number of the essays contained a bold call for freedom and democracy in China.

The Democracy Wall, as the long stretch of posters was called, quickly sparked further protests against the Chinese government. On December 17, 1978, twenty-eight youths gathered in Tiananmen Square to express their dissatisfaction with living and working conditions in the southern province of Yunnan. Although their number was nearly negligible, the group claimed to represent 50,000 others still in Yunnan.

This period of protest continued into January 1979, when thousands of people sent into the countryside around Beijing to do public works (a practice held over from the massive "reeducation" policy of the Cultural Revolution, which sent millions of intellectuals and city dwellers into the countryside to do manual labor) held a demonstration in the capital, complete with banners calling for human rights and democracy. Later that same month, another 30,000 workers who had been sent to the country massed outside the Beijing railway station to protest their treatment. The frigid weather caused at least eight deaths among the demonstrators. Similar protests took place in other cities around the country.

With a severity that would continue in the coming years, the Chinese government began in mid-January 1979 to crack down on protesters in Tiananmen Square and other areas around the country. The posting of essays on the Democracy Wall was forbidden, and people who had expressed ideas contrary to those of the Communist Party were gathered and jailed.

Another wave of discontent washed through China in the mid-1980s, a period marked by a nearly universal feeling of self-doubt among the Chinese and cynicism about their leaders, who had reformed electoral laws but had not created a truly representative government. The renowned scientist Fang Lizhi was one of the movement's primary leaders. Fang put the popular feeling into words, blaming the "unethical behavior by Party leaders" for "the social malaise in [China] today." In December 1986, some 30,000 students in Anhui province demonstrated against the rigged elections held in the city of Hefei and at the local university.

The wave swept out from Hefei and quickly reached the country's capital, where posters reminiscent of those on the Democracy Wall started appearing on university campuses, all calling for better living conditions and a more open, democratic society. As demonstrations began in the metropolitan areas of Shanghai and Tianjin, the Communist Party banned the protests and condemned the movement's leaders. After a huge student rally held in Tiananmen Square in January 1987, the government began a massive crackdown on both the organizers of the dissent and those figures held in esteem by the movement. The two most notable figures criticized and demoted by the communists were Fang Lizhi, for his role in inciting the students, and Hu Yaobang, the Communist Party secretary-general. Hu's denouncement came as a direct result of his vocal insistence that China needed speedy reform and his condemnation of the excesses of the former Maoist regime.

Hu's death on April 15, 1989, was one of the sparks for what the Chinese now call Liu Si (June Fourth), an event watched in horror by much of the world. The atmosphere in the spring of 1989 was already tense: it was the seventieth anniversary of the May Fourth Movement and the fortieth anniversary of the People's Republic, and popular leaders such as Fang Lizhi were taking the opportunity to encourage the government to move toward democracy and social freedom. Hu's death saddened the students, who had idolized him during the democracy movement of 1986, and they came together to call for his posthumous reinstatement to power and to bring the issues of the 1986 movement back to national attention.

On April 17, thousands of students gathered in Tiananmen Square for a rally held both to honor Hu and to protest the corruption of the present government. The following day, a sit-in was held near the Great Hall of the People next to the square; sit-ins were held that night as well at the residences of several senior party officials. On the day of Hu Yaobang's funeral, April 22, all demonstrations were forbidden, but students rose early and occupied the square before the police could enforce the rule, and a large but peaceful demonstration took place.

Up to this point, the government had largely ignored the students and refused to hear their requests. In late April, students were enraged at an editorial in the official *People's Daily* newspaper that criticized their efforts as a "planned conspiracy" and threatened anyone who took part in the movement with arrest. This hard-line approach led defiant industrial workers, journalists, and other citizens to join the students in criticizing the government and calling for democracy. On May 4, the anniversary of the 1919 demonstrations, 100,000 people marched peacefully through Beijing.

Although the march was not disruptive, it received international coverage from the numerous journalists gathered in Beijing for a mid-May summit between China and the Soviet Union. By the time of the proposed summit, some 3,000 protesters had begun a hunger strike in an attempt to emphasize their calls for governmental reform. As increasing numbers of demonstrators poured into Beijing, they turned Tiananmen Square into a tented camp. By mid-May, the number of demonstrators in and near the square exceeded 1 million.

Embarrassed by the demonstration's international coverage, the government declared martial law, and several Chinese officials urged the students to empty the square and return to their own universities. By the end of May, the student leaders themselves began to encourage the protesters to leave the garbage-strewn square. While some students did return home, their places were taken by thousands of others who flooded into Beijing to show their support.

Determined to put an end to the situation, hard-liners in the Chinese government brought in the People's Liberation Army (PLA). Some of the troops were reluctant to guard the square and refused to enforce martial law, but they soon were replaced by well-armed units complete with tanks and armored personnel carriers.

To the shock of both the Chinese people and the international community, the army moved in on Tiananmen Square in the early hours of June 4, 1989. They fired into crowds and at anyone who approached them. The students debated at length whether to stay or leave, but finally admitted defeat and began to file out of the square, only to be shot by soldiers or crushed by huge tanks. Numerous students, other civilians, and soldiers were wounded and killed. The Chinese government claims that civilian deaths took place only after mobs of protesters had attacked and wounded the PLA soldiers sent to keep peace.

According to the official Chinese account of the events, there was no bloodbath in Tiananmen Square. The government claimed 200 civilians had died, 36 of them students, a number far smaller than estimates by outside sources. Because much of the debris left in the square was burned by the PLA, it probably never will be known exactly how many people died in their quest for democracy.

Further Reading: Dun J. Li's *The Ageless Chinese* (New York: Scribner, 1965; third edition, New York: Macmillan, 1978) provides a detailed look at Chinese history from the country's quasi-mythical prehistory up to the modern era. Another exhaustive look at China is Jonathan D. Spence's *The Search for Modern China* (New York and London: Norton, 1990). Spence's account of China since the time of the late Ming is rich in both historical and cultural insight. Readers interested in visiting Beijing and Tiananmen Square will find John Summerfield's *Fodor's China* (New York: Fodor, 1994) and *China: A Travel Survival Kit* by Alan Samagalski, Robert Strauss, and Michael Buckley (second edition, South Yarra, Victoria, and Berkeley, California: Lonely Planet, 1988) invaluable for their historical and practical information.

—Monica Cable

Bengkulu (Bengkulu, Indonesia)

Location: On the mountainous southwest coast of Sumatra, almost 200 miles southwest of Palembang and 50 miles west of Gunung Dempo, an active volcano.

Description: A provincial city, formerly known as Bencoolen or Bengkoelen, that gained its importance in the pepper trade rivalry between the Dutch and the British during the eighteenth and nineteenth centuries. In the twentieth century the Indonesian independence leader Sukarno was exiled there.

Site Office: Diparda Tk.I Bengkulu
Jl. Pembangunan 14
Bengkulu
Indonesia
(736) 21272

Bengkulu owes its place in world history to the commercial rivalries of European traders in Southeast Asia during the seventeenth, eighteenth, and nineteenth centuries. But even before that time, the story of Bengkulu and its inhabitants, who form a distinct ethnic group known as the Bengkulunese and speak a Malay dialect known as Bahasa Bengkulu, was a tale of long periods of foreign domination. The town has been of minor importance for centuries as the port for the pepper-producing hinterland, and it was subject to various Southeast Asian trading empires before the arrival of the British and the Dutch.

The island of Sumatra rose in importance with the beginning of trade between China and India in the early centuries A.D. The India-China trade route passed through the Straits of Melaka (Malacca), giving rise to local trading empires on both the eastern and western shores of the straits. Spices produced in what is now the Indonesian Archipelago and traded westward also passed through the Straits of Melaka, further bolstering the kingdoms that controlled this waterway. Sumatra, which forms the western shore of the straits, produced several maritime empires that dominated the island at various times. Sumatra also was the point of entry for the Hindu, Buddhist, and Islamic influences that have shaped the cultures of the Indonesian Archipelago.

Probably the first trading empire to which Bengkulu was subject was the Srivijaya Kingdom, based in Palembang in southeastern Sumatra. Srivijaya, a Buddhist state, controlled not only Sumatra, but much of the Malay Peninsula and the coastal areas of Java from the seventh through the ninth centuries. Neither these Buddhist Sumatrans nor the Buddhist Javanese of the Shailendra Kingdom who succeeded Srivijaya as overlords in the area have left any trace of their centuries-long dominion. Early in the thirteenth century, the Hindu-Buddhist Singosari Kingdom of East Java made a bid for control of the Straits of Melaka and captured territories in the Malay Peninsula and on Sumatra. Whether Singosari gained a foothold on Sumatra's western coast, however, remains unclear. The Singosari state, in turn, was ousted from the straits later in the same century by the maritime empire of Majapahit, a Hindu-Buddhist state based in Central Java. Contemporary chronicles indicate that Majapahit controlled only the eastern coast of Sumatra, leaving Bengkulu in peace.

During the time of Majapahit's ascendancy, several states along the Straits of Melaka converted to Islam. The first Sumatran state to become Muslim was Aceh (Atjeh), at the far northern tip of the island. From there the religion spread rapidly south across Sumatra, to Java and the eastern archipelago. The Bengkulu region, relatively remote, seems initially to have remained untouched by Islam. However, early in the fifteenth century, Bengkulu was subjugated by Banten, a Muslim city-state on the far western edge of Java, which imposed its religion on the vassal city. Today, Bengkulu is still exclusively Muslim, with the exception of a small contingent of Chinese. Banten held on to Bengkulu for a considerable period, even though by the mid-fifteenth century the kingdom of Melaka, also Muslim, came to control much of the territory on either side of the straits.

Melaka in turn was the first victim of European penetration into Southeast Asia, falling to the Portuguese in 1511. The Portuguese had two goals: to establish monopolies in the spice trade, including the Sumatran pepper trade, and to convert the local populations to Christianity. With respect to the second goal, the Portuguese ran into intense local resistance, and their influence certainly never reached as far as Bengkulu. As for their hope of monopolizing the spice trade, they soon found that the Islamic local traders diverted the trade route from the Straits of Melaka, sailing along Sumatra's western coast instead, entering the eastern archipelago and making for China by way of the Sunda Straits between Sumatra and Java. In this way they successfully evaded Portuguese control. One consequence of the altered trade route was that Bengkulu became a port of call. All of its pepper was sold to Banten, strategically located just off the Sunda Straits.

Although the Portuguese managed to hold (ill-enforced) monopolies in the spice trade for a brief period, European competitors soon appeared on the scene. Much better equipped and better funded, the Dutch V.O.C. (Vereenigde Oostindische Compagnie, or United East India Company) wrested all trade monopolies from the Portuguese by the early seventeenth century. After the Portuguese lost Melaka to the Dutch in 1641, they ceased to play a major role in the European trade rivalries of the seventeenth and eighteenth centuries. The British, however, made a sustained

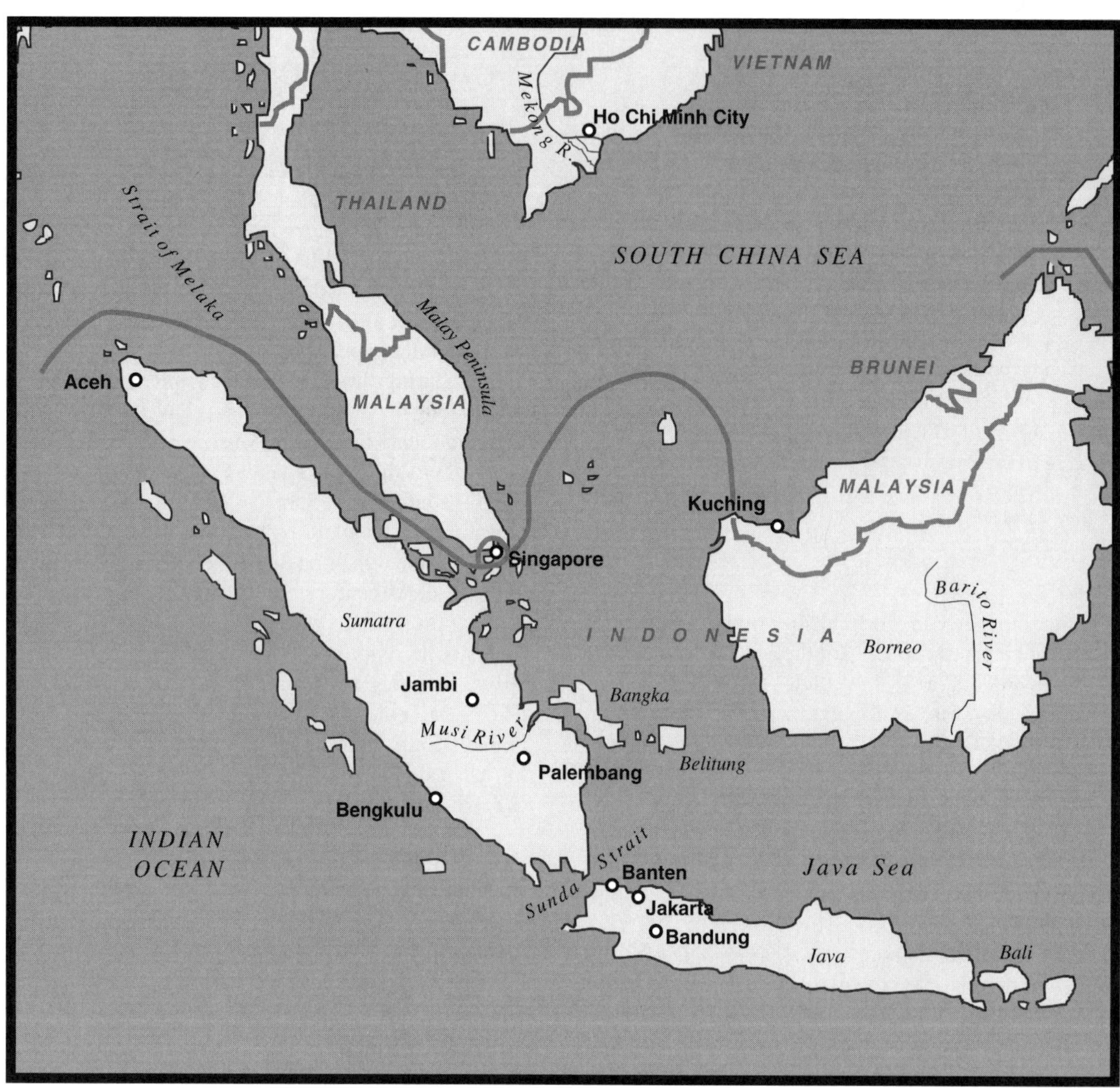

Map of western Indonesia, showing the position of Bengkulu
Illustration by Tom Willcockson

attempt to break the Dutch monopoly on the profitable pepper trade, and it was they who first brought Bengkulu into the network of European settlements. The British had established a so-called factory, or settlement, at Banten, on Java, not far from the primary base of the V.O.C. at Jacatra (renamed Batavia by the Dutch, now Jakarta). However, the sultan of Banten, embroiled in a conflict with Javanese rivals, called on the Dutch, who in return for their good offices required the sultan to expel the English from their Banten settlement in 1682.

The British withdrew to Sumatra, resettling at Bengkulu, for reasons that are not entirely clear. Some sources allege they retired to Bengkulu at the invitation of local *rajas* (rulers). Others suggest they chose Bengkulu with permission from the sultan of Banten, which still controlled Bengkulu and imported all the pepper traded through the Bengkulu port. To be sure, areas north of Bengkulu were mostly under the control of Aceh, while other potentially threatened cities had already made common cause with the Dutch to escape Acehnese overlordship. Several other outposts along Sumatra's west coast, even more precarious than Bengkulu, were also occupied by the British.

A treaty with local rulers gave the British the exclusive right to buy the local pepper crop. This treaty also guaranteed that determined amounts of pepper would be delivered into British hands. In addition to trading in pepper, the British traded opium, armaments, and other goods to the eastern archipelago from Bengkulu. In 1685, the British built their first fortified factory, called York, just north of the natural harbor of Bengkulu. Later, from 1709 to 1719, they constructed Fort Marlborough, which still stands today, on the heights just south of the harbor. Fort Marlborough was one of the largest fortresses built by the British in the East, even though Bengkulu was a relatively insignificant, and always precariously held, outpost. The fort is now one of the principal tourist attractions of Bengkulu.

The British did not fare well at Bengkulu. Malaria devastated the garrison to such an extent that at one point slaves brought in from Madagascar had to be used to hold the fort. In addition, the local pepper crop regularly fell short of the amounts stipulated by the treaty, in large part because the prices offered by the British were so low that local growers stopped cultivating pepper. Little could be done about the crop shortfalls: although the British organized surveys to ensure that local farmers had the requisite number of plants under cultivation, these surveys proved unsuccessful in stimulating local pepper production. Not only did British soldiers encounter great difficulties traveling inland to the pepper lands; they did not have reliable records of the population and so could not effectively track cultivation.

Failing in their efforts to stimulate pepper production, the British in the end harvested nothing but rebellion. Joseph Collet, the British governor of Bengkulu from 1712 to 1716, privately admitted that the British were corrupt and that they used the local inhabitants most shamefully. He was apparently unable to improve the situation, and a year after his departure the Bengkulunese revolted. They succeeded in driving away the garrison and burning Fort Marlborough, which had just then been completed. In 1724, the British concluded a new treaty with the local rulers that was much more favorable to the pepper farmers, and they were finally able to return to their stronghold.

Despite its impressive size, Fort Marlborough again proved insufficient protection for the British settlement several decades later when the French captured the fortress under Admiral d'Estaing in 1760. The French also managed to wrest from the British two outposts farther north along Sumatra's west coast, those at Natal and Tapanoeli. Since the French had little interest in establishing a trading network in Southeast Asia, they offered the outpost factories to the Dutch at Batavia (Jakarta). The Dutch declined the offer, but the V.O.C. did proceed to build its own fortresses at Natal and Tapanoeli. Bengkulu was left alone, however. In 1763 the British returned to their coastal settlements and managed to push the V.O.C. out of the trade it had just begun to establish with the indigenous people.

While the British settlement at Bengkulu went unchallenged for approximately fifty years following the temporary French ouster, it did not flourish. Even though the V.O.C. was financially in dire straits as the result of mismanagement and corruption, its hold on the pepper trade was unassailable. In 1772, several outposts were added to the British holdings when the local *rajas* revolted against the Dutch, but the British were unable to increase significantly their share in the pepper trade or to extend their control inland from the coastal settlements at Bengkulu and elsewhere. Furthermore, difficulties with the Bengkulunese population continued to threaten the security of the Bengkulu settlement.

In 1807 the British governor of Bengkulu was murdered, either by the townspeople or by his own Buginese officers. By that time, Fort Marlborough was manned by an officer corps of Buginese, a people hailing from southern Sulawesi (Celebes), who often engaged in piracy or hired themselves out as mercenary soldiers. Parr, the British governor, tried to dismiss the Bugis at Fort Marlborough, thus provoking their wrath. He also made himself unpopular with the Bengkulunese by forcing them to cultivate coffee, a commodity for which the farmers were very ill paid. By this time, sugar and tobacco had been added as cash crops that the local farmers, to their chagrin, were to deliver to the British settlers at fixed prices. Which of Parr's policies cost him his head is unclear, but one night in September 1807 either the Buginese officers or the irate Bengkulunese stabbed him to death and then decapitated him.

From 1811 to 1816 all Dutch holdings in the Indonesian Archipelago—which by then belonged to the Dutch crown, the V.O.C. having gone bankrupt in 1799—passed into British hands. Napoléon Bonaparte occupied the Netherlands at this time, and the Dutch were unable to administer their East Indian possessions. Thomas Stamford Raffles, governing Britain's newly acquired colonies from Batavia, attempted to curb the extortionate taxes imposed by indigenous rulers on the common people—without diminishing profits for the colonial rulers. While Stamford Raffles meant to improve the lot of common farmers throughout the Indonesian Archipelago, in the end his reforms burdened them still further. Famines resulted because farmers were forced to devote even more of their land and time to growing crops and performing services for the Europeans and the indigenous rulers. When the British reluctantly surrendered control of the former Dutch settlements and territories in 1818, Stamford Raffles was posted to Bengkulu.

The new governor hoped to retake control from the Dutch and build a British trade empire in the Indonesian Archipelago from this very modest base on Sumatra. One of his first actions was to support the sultan of Palembang in a revolt against the Dutch in 1819, which came to nought, although it took the Dutch two years to force Palembang to its knees. Nevertheless, when religious ferment in the Minangkabau provinces of central Sumatra brought further requests for British aid from indigenous leaders opposing their own kings, Stamford Raffles declined to intervene. At Bengkulu he also pushed through a series of reforms, freeing slaves and improving relations with the local rulers.

By 1824 Stamford Raffles's dream of a British East Indian colony was effectively dead. The British and the Dutch concluded the Treaty of London, by which all settlements on Sumatra, including Bengkulu, passed into Dutch hands, while the British gained uncontested control of the Malay Peninsula. Thus ended British efforts to break into the spice monopolies in Southeast Asia. Stamford Raffles's legacy to Bengkulu was a statue honoring the murdered Parr, which still stands across from Fort Marlborough. An ardent amateur botanist and the first president of the London Zoological Society, he also bestowed his name on the rafflesia plant, an insect-"eating" plant that carries the world's largest flower and is found in the jungle around Bengkulu.

Following the Dutch takeover of the settlement, Bengkulu became a quiet backwater of the colonial territories on Sumatra. The Dutch concentrated on capturing the remaining independent kingdoms across the island during the second half of the nineteenth century, finally completing their aims with the conclusion of the Aceh War in the first decade of the twentieth century. On the eve of World War II, the city had become so remote from the political ferment brewing elsewhere that the Dutch exiled Sukarno—who was later to be one of the principal engineers of Indonesian independence and the unified republic—to Bengkulu in 1938. Sukarno's house is still open to visitors, as is the mosque he designed during the years of his exile on Sumatra. Sukarno was freed with the Japanese occupation of the Indonesian Archipelago in 1942. The only other event of note associated with Bengkulu also took place in 1942, when British submarines sank a ship carrying 7,000 Japanese prisoners of war just off the Bengkulu coast. More than 5,000 Japanese drowned in this greatest of all maritime disasters.

Bengkulu has seen considerable growth and modernization since the early 1960s, when it boasted ten cars and one traffic light. Tourism is now the main industry of the town, which has a relatively pleasant climate in spite of the heavy rainfall it receives virtually every day of the year. Bengkulu's principal attraction apart from the few historic monuments, however, is its access to the beautiful jungles and mountains that lie just behind the coastal plains.

Further Reading: Most of the English-language histories of Sumatra focus on Aceh, Palembang, or Minangkabau, so that the reader interested in Bengkulu must resort to general histories of Indonesia. The best and most readable of these is M. C. Ricklefs' *A History of Modern Indonesia: 1300 to the Present* (Bloomington: Indiana University Press, and London: Macmillan, 1981). Ailsa Zainu'ddin's *A Short History of Indonesia* (London: Cassell, 1969; New York and Washington, D.C.: Praeger, 1970) is also worth consulting and more readily available. *The Contest for North Sumatra: Atjeh, the Netherlands and Britain, 1858–1898* by Anthony Reid (London and New York: Oxford University Press, 1969) is informative about the end of British involvement on Sumatra. John Bastin's *The Native Policies of Sir Stamford Raffles in Java and Sumatra: An Economic Interpretation* (Oxford: Clarendon Press, 1957) discusses Raffles' intended reforms in colonial government.

—Marijke Rijsberman

Bhopāl (Madhya Pradesh, India)

Location: The capital city of India's largest state, Bhopāl lies at the heart of the subcontinent, on the arid Mālwa Plateau, some 375 miles south of Delhi and about 425 miles northeast of Bombay.

Description: Capital of the ancient principality of Bhopāl, the city is now heavily industrialized, and it is a major rail junction between Bombay and Delhi. A massive gas leak at a Union Carbide plant in 1984 became the world's worst nonnuclear industrial accident.

Contact: Government of India Tourist Office
Near Western Group of Temples
Khajurāho 471 606, Madhya Pradesh
India
2047, 2048

The Union Carbide disaster of 1984 made the world aware of Bhopāl's existence, but in fact the city is almost 1,000 years old and has a rich history. Archaeological evidence points to human habitation at sites near Bhopāl as far back as the late Paleolithic Era (around 10,000 B.C.). At Bhīmbetka, approximately thirty miles southeast of Bhopāl, archaeologists have discovered one of the world's largest collections of prehistoric rock art. Some 1,000 caves in a cliff six miles long have been surveyed, and about half of these hold paintings. Carbon dating has revealed that the oldest of these paintings were executed as long ago as 10,000 B.C.; others were painted as late as the Middle Ages.

In comparison to the age of numerous sites in its vicinity, Bhopāl is relatively young. In fact, the city was founded in the eleventh century by Rāja Bhoj of the Paramāra Dynasty. The Paramāras were the rulers of Mālwa, a broad region in central India, from the ninth through the twelfth century. Local legend alleges that the Paramāras were born from the fire-pit of Mount Ābu, and in fact they were not native to the area; they belonged to the warlike Rājput caste of foreign descent. Rāja Bhoj had a reputation as a brilliant scholar, a liberal advocate of Sanskrit learning, and a patron of the arts. He is also credited with the creation of the lakes around which Bhopāl is built. He ordered the construction of a dam, or *pal,* across the Betwa River and a smaller nearby stream, and he built a fortified city, called Bhojapal, on a ridge overlooking the two large lakes formed by the dam. But the new settlement remained of modest importance because Bhoj maintained his capital at Dhār.

Bhoj also built a dam at Bhojpūr, some eighteen miles southeast of Bhopāl, creating another huge lake. This dam was destroyed several centuries later and the land reclaimed for cultivation. However, Bhoj's remarkable, though unfinished, temple to Siva still stands at Bhojpūr. Built on a simple square plan, the temple is noteworthy most of all for its richly carved, soaring dome, which is supported by four massive, tapered pillars. Its imposing *liṇgam,* a monolithic phallic symbol representing the male principle in the universe and a common feature of Hindu temples, is an unusual seven and one-half feet in height and eighteen feet in circumference.

In 1060 Bhoj suffered a military defeat at the hands of the Chandelās, who ruled over a neighboring princely state. Following Bhoj's defeat and death, the Paramāras slowly sank into insignificance and Mālwa was fractured. Bhopāl suffered a series of invasions that ultimately reduced it to little more than a village. Thus it remained for about six centuries. The Muslim invasions that began in the fourteenth century had little or no effect on Bhopāl or its immediate vicinity. The powerful Mughal empire that dominated much of India after the fifteenth century was apparently not much interested in the humble settlement and ignored it for many years.

It was not until the early eighteenth century that the city experienced a rebirth with the arrival of Dōst Moḥammad Kāhn, a former general of the Mughal emperor 'Ālamgīr (Aurangzeb). Dōst Moḥammad, a Warkzai Afghan noble from the Indo-Afghan border area, came to Mālwa in 1708 and began acquiring land in the area of Bhopāl by a variety of means. He illegally appropriated the estate of a deceased local chieftain and bought property from another. Mostly, though, he added to his growing state by military conquest. By 1722, having built himself into a formidable regional power, Dōst Moḥammad looked for a suitable capital for the new state he had created.

Taken by the beauty of its lakeside location, he settled on Bhopāl and began construction of additional fortifications. His wife, Fateh Bi Begum, who reputedly had accompanied him on all his military campaigns, was involved in the planning of the construction. It was after her that the new fort, Fatehgarh, was named. Fatehgarh incorporated Bhoj's eleventh-century defenses, now called the Old Fort. In addition, Dōst Moḥammad built a wall to encompass the city proper, which evolved to include lakes, parks, gardens, broad avenues, monuments, and mausoleums. The newly reconstructed city attracted a host of artists and musicians, whose presence further added to its growth and improvement.

Although Dōst Moḥammad Khān had made himself a major power in central India, the political instabilities plaguing the subcontinent involved him in a conflict that ultimately set his family against itself. Throughout much of India, the divisions of the Mughal Empire and the Hindu princely states frequently engaged in territorial struggles with each other and among themselves. Networks of ever-shifting alliances, based on estimates of relative military might, dominated the

Union Carbide plant, December 1984, Bhopāl
Photo courtesy of A.P. / Wide World Photos, New York

court life of all Indian rulers. Dōst Moḥammad made a miscalculation in the choice of one of his allies, or rather, in the choice of one of his enemies. Having been offered an alliance by the Nizām-al-Mulk, Dōst Moḥammad threw in his lot with the nizām's enemy instead, contributing a regiment to the forces that engaged the nizām in battle. Unexpectedly, the nizām emerged victorious, a dangerous enemy. To appease him, Dōst Moḥammad gave up his eldest son, Yar Moḥammad Khān, as a hostage.

The young man remained at the nizām's court until his father's death in 1728, when his younger brother, Sultan Moḥammad Khān, was installed as the new ruler of Bhopāl. With the nizām's approval (and massive military support), Yar Moḥammad returned to Bhopāl. Although he suffered his brother to remain the nabob, or chief, in name, he asserted himself as the de facto ruler of the state of Bhopāl. One of his first acts was to move his capital to Islamnagarh. Bhopāl lost some of its former glory as a result, but its fortifications remained of strategic importance. In fact, some ten years later Bhopāl suffered a brief but devastating siege as the nizām and his army took refuge from an army of the Marāṭhās, a Rājput family who were gradually conquering Mālwa. The city was quickly surrounded, and all supply lines were cut. Faced with inevitable starvation, the nizām and his men surrendered after no more than a week's siege. A peace treaty was then signed that recognized the Marāṭhās as the legitimate rulers of Mālwa and granted them monetary compensation for losses sustained in the conflict.

These developments put an end to the nizām's power in central India and diminished the influence of his protégé, Yar Moḥammad, who died four years later, in 1742. Upon Yar Moḥammad's death, Sultan Moḥammad Khān, who still held the title of nabob, was proclaimed the official ruler at Bhopāl. However, the army championed Yar Moḥammad's son, Faiz Moḥammad Khān, who has gone down in history with the reputation of being a religious recluse with no interest in government. The conflict was finally settled in a fierce battle fought just outside the city's gates. Sultan Moḥammad was put to rout, but in the end he was given a section of the state of Bhopāl. The most notable aspect of Faiz's colorless rule was his friendliness to the British East India Company. In 1771, he allowed the British army, on its way to Mālwa to push back the troublesome Marāṭhās, safe passage through the state.

Faiz was succeeded in 1778 by his son Hayat Moḥammad Khān, who seems to have taken after his father with respect to his lack of interest in governing the state. He gave a free hand to his four tyrannical adopted sons, whom he appointed to high positions in his administration. Generally, Hayat was extremely unfortunate in his choice of ministers, and for the greater part his reign was marked by factional strife, intrigues, sieges, palace coups, and even attempts to give away fortified Bhopāl to the Marāṭhās in return for military support.

By the end of Hayat's reign, in the early years of the nineteenth century, actual power resided in the hands of Wazīr Moḥammad Khān, who, however, had used up all his resources in putting down his enemies at court. Meanwhile, the Marāṭhās were pressing at the borders. Left with few other options, Wazīr began courting the British and attempted to conclude a treaty with them in 1811 and again in 1814, both times without success. Bhopāl's situation, meanwhile, was deteriorating alarmingly. In fact, the Marāṭhās had mounted a major attack in 1812, and Bhopāl was saved only because the Marāṭhā high command began fighting one another. Wazīr died in 1816, and his successor, Nazar Moḥammad Khān, finally found a willing ear with the British.

In 1818, Nazar and the British East India Company signed the Treaty of Raisen and established an amicable relationship that would last for nearly 150 years. The Treaty of Raisen (which set up the Bhopāl Agency as a subdivision of the British Central India Agency and comprised the former princely states of Bhopāl, Rājgarh, Narsinghgarh, and several others) consisted of eleven articles specifying the rules according to which the parties would conduct all future affairs for the mutual benefit of both. The first three articles of the treaty were of great significance. Article 1 called for perpetual friendship and declared that from that time forward all friends or enemies of one party would be friends or enemies of both. Article 2 assured Bhopāl that the British government would protect it against all enemies. And Article 3 decreed that upon execution of the treaty the nabob of Bhopāl and his heirs and successors would act in subordinate cooperation with the British government and would not make affiliations with other chiefs or states.

Within months of signing the treaty, Nazar, then twenty-eight years old, was killed in an accident. His eight-year-old brother-in-law, Faujdar Moḥammad Khān, drew a pistol from Nazar's belt and, while playing with the weapon, inadvertently discharged it. The bullet penetrated Nazar's skull, and he died instantly. Since Nazar left no male heirs, his wife Gohar Begum—better known as Qudsia III—would act as regent until the marriage of her daughter, Sikandar Jahān Begum. The regency of Qudsia III, which began when she was only seventeen and lasted eighteen years, ushered in a period of relative peace and staunch loyalty to the British. Qudsia was known for her charity, and she made many civil improvements during her regency, building a waterworks and many gardens at the city of Bhopāl. She also built the famous mosque of Jāma Masjid on the site of a former Hindu temple. Its minarets still mark the Bhopāl skyline.

In 1835 Qudsia officially relinquished power to her son-in-law, Jahāngīr Moḥammad Khān, after mediation by the British. However, she effectively continued to rule Bhopāl behind the scenes, so much so that Jahāngīr revolted in 1836. Sikandar Begum sided with her mother in this conflict rather than her husband, from whom she became permanently estranged. Again the British intervened and persuaded Qudsia to retire, enabling Jahāngīr to take the reins in 1837. His was not a long reign; the young nabob met an untimely death in 1844. The chief accomplishment of his government was the removal of the Bhopāl garrison from the city, to quarters on the other side of the lakes. He died without male heirs, leaving only an infant daughter, Shāh Jahān Begum.

Upon Jahāngīr's death, the British government recognized the succession of Shāh Jahān in the same way that, on the death of Nazar Moḥammad Khān, it had recognized the entitlement of Sikandar. However, in this case the British did not appoint the mother as the regent. Her maternal uncle, Faujdar Moḥammad Khān, who as a child had accidentally discharged the fatal pistol, was selected to hold the regency, while Sikandar was limited to an advisory role. The arrangement became unworkable when the paternal grandfather of Shāh Jahān Begum attempted to seize power. The British determined that there would be no hope for peace until the power structure was more clearly delineated, and Faujdar Moḥammad was forced to resign. Sikandar was placed at the head of the state's administration as regent during the period of her daughter's minority.

Sikandar continued her mother's policies and public works programs. In addition, she undertook extensive government reforms, rationalizing the administration at every level. The entire state was surveyed, official boundaries were established, and districts were demarcated. A new system of revenue collection was implemented to the general satisfaction of the citizenry. Courts of justice were improved, and a code of laws was instituted to prevent crime and protect the rights of the people. The state armed forces were reorganized, and its arsenal was updated. State debts were paid and mortgaged lands redeemed.

Sikandar Begum also continued in her mother's loyalty to the British. During the uprising of 1857 that is known in British histories as the Mutiny, Sikandar proved herself a valuable protégé of the colonial rulers. As a revolt of native soldiers in the British army spread across the subcontinent, drawing popular support of Hindu and Muslim civilians in large numbers, groups of citizens in Bhopāl began to join the rebellion. Large numbers of soldiers in the Bhopāl army were recruited by Fazil Moḥammad and Ādil Moḥammad Khān, the local rebel leaders. The object of the leadership was to take part in a major confrontation with the British at Sehore, the headquarters of the Bhopāl Agency. Sikandar Begum, unmoved by nationalist demands, continued to pledge her loyalty to the British and made strenuous efforts to keep peace within her own territories. She provided shelter to British officers and supplied provisions and troops to help suppress the revolt in Saugor (Sāgar) and Bundelkhand.

In January 1858 British forces under the command of Hugh Rose captured and executed Nabob Fazil Moḥammad Khān and a large number of his followers at Rahatgarh. Ādil Moḥammad managed to escape, and for the next twenty months he and his growing band of rebels continued to organize successfully in and around Bhopāl. However, the rebel forces were no match for the British, and in September 1859 the exhausted men under Ādil Moḥammad surrendered to the British. Ādil Moḥammad himself once again managed to escape and was never apprehended.

When British authority was firmly reestablished and order restored in the region of Bhopāl, Sikandar requested that her administrative claim be modified from regent to ruling chief of Bhopāl, on the basis of her loyal efforts and support during the uprising. She asserted that the recognition of her late husband as nabob had been technically incorrect and that she and her daughter were the legitimate heirs to the throne. The British government approved her request, and Sikandar Begum was formally inaugurated in March 1860 as chief of Bhopāl. In that same year she requisitioned the construction of the Moti Masjid, a mosque smaller than but similar in style to the Jāma Masjid of Delhi. It remains one of the distinguishing landmarks of Bhopāl.

Nabob Shāh Jahān Begum succeeded her mother in November 1868 and continued the reform program that Sikander had begun. She played a major role in the creation of railway links with neighboring territories. She also built and endowed the Lady Lansdowne Hospital, which offered health care to women. Her most memorable architectural contribution to Bhopāl is the Tāj-ul-Masajid, which was begun in 1887 and left unfinished at her death. This mosque, which has two massive white-domed minarets and three white domes over the main structure, is one of the largest in India. Shāh Jahān was succeeded in 1901 by her daughter, Sultan Jahān Begum, who ruled over Bhopāl until her death in 1926.

Following Indian independence in 1949, Bhopāl became a chief commissioner's province of India. In 1952 the first elected ministry took office. The state of Bhopāl was merged with Madhya Pradesh, India's largest state, in 1956, and Bhopāl was named the capital.

Following Bhopāl's incorporation into Madhya Pradesh, the government encouraged major industrial development in the city, without, however, providing the necessary infrastructure. The most obvious effects of this policy were tremendous overcrowding and vast stretches of shantytowns. These conditions contributed significantly to the devastating proportions of the Union Carbide accident in 1984. As a result of layoffs of maintenance workers and neglect of safety precautions, a routine cleaning operation went awry at the pesticide plant. In the early morning hours of December 3, tons of poisonous gases, including methyl isocyanate and cyanide, were released over the slums across the street.

Emergency relief and civil defense efforts were slow and disorganized. Nobody knew which gases had leaked or how victims should be treated. Confusion and hysteria reigned. Instead of being advised to lie on the ground with their faces covered by wet cloths, people living in the shantytowns were urged to flee the area. By sunrise, thousands of lifeless bodies and animal carcasses littered sidewalks, streets, railway platforms, bus stands, and the narrow alleyways and slum dwellings that bordered the industrial complex. At the end of the week almost 3,000 people were dead, 7,000 were critically injured, and more than 300,000 had experienced adverse reactions to the exposure.

Industrial practices around the world have come under increased scrutiny in the wake of the Bhopāl calamity, and safety measures have been mandated in an attempt to avoid such disasters in the future. The pesticide plant in Bhopāl has been permanently closed, and city emergency services have been revamped. Union Carbide has been forced to make some monetary compensation to victims. But the tragedy is not yet over. It is still unclear what the long-term medical, financial, and psychological consequences of the nightmare will be. Medical studies indicate a range of continuing, often disabling, symptoms among victims of exposure. Possibly the most serious of the adverse health consequences are increases in spontaneous abortions, stillbirths, and birth defects. Bhopāl will live with the consequences of the accident for many years to come.

Further Reading: Kamla Mittal's *History of Bhopal State: Development of Constitution, Administration, and National Awakening 1901–1949* (New Delhi: Munshiram Manoharlal, 1990) gives a detailed account of the private and political lives of the imperial dynasty that descended from Dōst Moḥammad Khān. Its readability leaves something to be desired, however. Many accounts of the Union Carbide accident are available. *Bhopal: Anatomy of a Crisis* by Paul Shrivastava (Cambridge, Massachusetts, Ballinger, 1987; second edition, London, Paul Chapman, 1992) is one of the most thorough of these studies.

—Holly E. Bruns and Marijke Rijsberman

Bhubaneswar (Orissa, India)

Location: Bhubaneswar lies in the district of Puri along the coast of eastern Orissa, on the Bay of Bengal. This district is the most fertile and densely populated area in the state of Orissa.

Description: Although Bhubaneswar became the capital of Orissa in 1948, the city had rarely been known as a commercial or political center. Rather, Bhubaneswar has been revered as a temple city by Hindu pilgrims. Others celebrate the architectural significance of the city's temples, most of which were built between the seventh and thirteenth centuries A.D.

Site Office: Government of India Tourist Office
B-20 Kaplana Area
Bhubaneswar 751 014, Orissa
India
54203

Known as the Temple City of India, Bhubaneswar's fame rests on thirty temples of medieval origin that still serve as sites of Hindu pilgrimage. Excavations have revealed that Bhubaneswar was once home to several thousand small shrines and temples dating from roughly the seventh to the thirteenth centuries. The remains of 500 of these structures still stand, most around the Bindu Sagara Lake, which sits in the middle of the Old Town. The twelve large pools formed from Bindu Sagara's waters are believed to possess powers of physical and spiritual healing and have attracted pilgrims for centuries. According to legend, the goddess Pārvatī (consort of Siva) departed the famous Saivite temple city, Benares (Vārānasī), to come to Bhubaneswar, where she created a holy lake by collecting droplets from every sacred body of water in India. Eventually she enticed Siva to join her in Bhubaneswar. The temples that sprang up along the shores of this holy lake profited greatly from the spiritual significance the lake had achieved.

Bhubaneswar largely avoided the waves of Muslim conquest and plunder that destroyed many other religiously significant Hindu cities between the thirteenth and eighteenth centuries. This good fortune spared Bhubaneswar's major temples and allowed the city to become one of the most revered sites of pilgrimage and worship in northern India. The temples of Bhubaneswar rival those in Vārānasī as the most holy Saivite places in India. Today, four main temple complexes exist in the Old Town. The most famous and magnificent complex, which houses the Lingarāja Temple, is the focal point of the Old Town. The Lingarāja Temple was originally a Saivite temple solely, but the infusion of Vaisnava beliefs between the eleventh and fifteenth centuries added Vaisnava elements to the complex. Thus, the Lingarāja complex has become a Vaisnava and Saivite pilgrimage destination. This sort of religious syncretism may be witnessed in the various complexes and temples of the area. Buddhist and Jain influences on these complexes, from ancient times and from the monastic influences still current, have diversified Bhubaneswar's religious culture, broadening the scope of pilgrimage and contributing greatly to the popularity of the town. Its popularity as a pilgrimage site increased further with the creation of a rail network that connected the town to the predominantly Hindu south and the Hindu population of Bengal. In addition, during the British period, Bhubaneswar became a center for Bengali vacationers from Calcutta, who came to enjoy the cool shore breezes and to escape the overcrowded city.

Although best known for the period of temple construction beginning in the seventh century A.D., Bhubaneswar's history began much earlier. Archaeological excavations have unearthed remains in the area dating to the third century B.C. Information specifically focused on Bhubaneswar prior to the era of temple building is somewhat scant, but the town's history may be inferred from the broader historical narratives of eastern India. References to Kalinga, the name used in ancient sources to identify the principal kingdom in what is today the state of Orissa, surface sporadically starting in the fifth century B.C. Although the boundaries of the Kalingan Kingdom fluctuated over the centuries, it mainly encompassed the eastern coastal section of Orissa, which included Bhubaneswar, Puri, Jagannātha and Cuttack. The *Padmā Purāṇa* (from the fourth to eighth centuries A.D.) refers to thirty-two kings ruling over an independent Kalinga kingdom in the fifth and fourth century B.C. Known at the time as Toshali, Bhubaneswar served as the capital of this powerful kingdom. Mahāpadmā Nanda, the last great ruler of the Nanda Dynasty, ended this period of independence by conquering the kingdom in the middle of the fourth century B.C.

From the fall of the Nanda Dynasty until the reign of the Mauryan emperor Aśoka (272–235 B.C.), the kingdom of Kalinga was virtually independent. When Aśoka attacked Kalinga in 261 B.C., he met with fierce resistance. The devastation and cost of this war, which killed tens of thousands, deeply affected Aśoka, convincing him to convert to Buddhism and adhere to a nonviolent and tolerant philosophy. Aśoka recorded the history of his conversion and the precepts of his enlightened ruling philosophy by ordering the inscription of edicts on stones throughout his domain. Aśoka commissioned edicts in Dhauli, five miles to the south of Toshali, which he made the provincial capital of Kalinga. As a result, the Kalinga campaign and Toshali featured prominently in the history of the Mauryan Empire.

The death of Aśoka in 235 B.C. and the disintegration of the Mauryan Empire once again placed the independent king-

Lingarāja Temple, Bhubaneswar
Photo courtesy of Air India Library, New York

dom of Kalinga in a position of historical obscurity. According to inscriptions at the Elephant Cave (Hathigumpha) near present-day Bhubaneswar, Khāravela, the most famous and successful ruler of the Cedi Dynasty, became the ruler of an independent Kalinga kingdom in the second or first century B.C.; damage to the inscriptions has rendered the dates of his reign ambiguous. Little is known about Khāravela beyond his impressive military exploits (he extended the kingdom to include all of modern-day Orissa) and his devout adherence to Jainism.

Between Khāravela's reign and the beginnings of Gupta rule around A.D. 330, the history of Kalinga has remained obscure. Evidence indicates that after Khāravela's death the Sātavāhannas may have included Kalinga in their realm. The Murundas, Buddhists from Central Asia, came to rule in the area around the third century A.D. upon the gradual decline of the Sātavāhanna Dynasty. Thus, from the era of Aśoka's reign until the rise of the Guptas in the fourth century A.D., the Kalinga Kingdom came under the rule of both Jain and Buddhist rulers. Although Buddhism and Jainism enjoyed lavish royal patronage under Kalinga rulers during this period, a great majority of people in the kingdom adhered to Hindu practices and worship that had been part of the local religious landscape as early as the pre-Mauryan era.

The beginning of Gupta rule marked the onset of the first truly brahmanical Hindu empire in India. From the Gupta era until the fall of the area to Muslim forces in the late sixteenth century, Hindu rulers reigned over Kalinga almost wholly uninterrupted. Thus, Bhubaneswar's reputation as a devoutly Hindu town should rightly begin with Samudra Gupta's conquest of the area around 335. The Gupta era in Kalinga did not last long, however. Within sixty years, Kalinga was under the independent rule of the Mathara Dynasty. Little is known about the Mathara Dynasty or their successors, the Vāśistha Dynasty, except that these indigenous Hindu rulers reigned from the end of the fourth until the beginning of the seventh century.

The seventh century is perhaps the most significant period in Bhubaneswar's history because the Saivite religious tradition, although existent prior to this period, for the first time assumed the predominant position in the cultural and religious affairs of the kingdom, hitherto dominated by Buddhist and Jain patronage. The Saivite tradition was supposedly initiated by King Śaśānka, who ruled in the region in the early seventh century. A devout Saivite and fierce enemy of Buddhists, he is said to have built several Saivite temples on the ruins of Buddhist monuments in the Bhubaneswar region.

None of the monuments created under his rule have survived, but legend credits him with commissioning the famous Tribhuvanesvara Temple from which the city took its name. Derived from the Sanskrit words *ishvara* (lord) and *bhuvana* (universe), Bhubaneswar translates as Lord of the Universe, the title commonly attributed to Siva. The eleventh-century Lingarāja Temple is said to have been built on the ruins of Śaśānka's temple.

After Śaśānka's death around 619, Kalinga briefly fell under the rule of King Harshavardharna of Kanauj (Kānpur). King Harsha, perhaps the last powerful Buddhist empire builder in India, briefly interrupted the Hindu hold over the area. Upon his death, the Bhauma-Kara Dynasty regained Kalinga and returned the region to Hindu hands. Eighteen Bhauma-Kara kings and queens ruled over Kalinga until the tenth century. Originally Mahāyāna Buddhists, the Bhauma-Karas eventually adopted Saivism, undoubtedly influenced by their heavily Saivite surroundings. They never completely abandoned Buddhism, however, and the mix of Buddhist and Saivite traditions was reflected in the cultural achievements of their era. The Bhauma-Karas and their successors, the Soma Dynasty (known also as the Kesari kings), served as great patrons of the Saivite temple tradition in Bhubaneswar. Brahmanical rather than Buddhist from the beginning, the Somas encouraged Saivite worship among the local population not only by constructing many temples, but also by sponsoring religious festivals and encouraging the migration of brahmans to the region from north India. The Bhauma-Karas and Somas established their capitals in the Bhubaneswar area, making explicit the connection between religious and spiritual authority.

The architectural tradition of this period serves not only as a model of Oriyan architecture but as the prototypical example of *nāgara* (north Indian) temple style. According to this style, a sanctum enshrining the main image forms the focal center of the temple. In most of the temples in Bhubaneswar, a representation of Siva or a Siva *liṇgam* (phallic symbol) serves as the main image. The exterior of the sanctum is richly decorated while the interior is plain, focusing attention on the god's image. A vestibule adjoining the sanctum is also a standard feature of this temple style. Rising from the roof of the sanctum and the vestibule are pyramidal superstructures, the vestibule's superstructure being the shorter of the two. The pyramidal structure can be of two types, *latina* (a curvilinear spire) or *phamsana* (a rectilinear spire).

The gradual development of the *nāgara* temple style can be traced through the major temples in Bhubaneswar. The Parasurameśvara Temple, built during the Bhauma-Kara Dynasty in the late seventh and early eighth centuries, consists of a single sanctum with a *latina* spire without the elaborate halls (*maṇḍapas*) and vestibule of the later temples. The exterior walls of this temple are richly carved, but the interior is plain, setting the standard that most other temple decorations would follow. The Mukteśvara Temple, constructed in the early tenth century, expanded upon this earlier simplicity by adding a *phamsana* spire on the vestibule to accompany the *latina* spire of the sanctum, thus combining the two major roof styles of north Indian temple architecture. Standing side by side, these towers are the most striking feature of the exterior and can be seen from a great distance.

The Lingarāja Temple, built in the early eleventh century by the Soma king Yayati, is the ultimate expression of the *nāgara* temple style in Bhubaneswar, combining all the elements of its predecessors and surpassing them in size and elaborateness. For example, its *latina* spire is over 125 feet high. Within the sanctum, a rough stone Siva *liṇgam* over eight feet in diameter serves as the focus of worship. An audience hall (*jagamohana*), dance hall (*natamandira*), and dining hall (*bhogamaṇḍapa*) are all part of the vast complex. Because of its architectural importance and its role as the main temple in this city of temples, the Lingarāja Temple has become one of the most popular and celebrated pilgrimage sites in all of India. Ironically, however, this temple marks the end of the heyday of medieval temple construction in Bhubaneswar.

The vacuum created by the fall of the Somas around the middle of the eleventh century was filled by the Gaṅgas, who introduced into the region the religious creed of Vaisnavism, the other major sect of the Hindu belief system. The Gaṅgas' adherence to Vaisnavism shifted the focus of temple construction away from Siva's city, Bhubaneswar, and toward Vaishnavite centers of worship. Bhubaneswar did see limited benefits from the new religious tradition, particularly the incorporation of Vaisnava elements to the Lingarāja Temple between the eleventh and fifteenth centuries, which opened the complex to Vishnu worshipers. The resurgence of Saivite rulers in the area during the Sūrya Dynasty of the fifteenth century briefly refocused royal patronage on Saivite centers such as Bhubaneswar, but the era of Hindu temple building had virtually come to a close. The Kapileśwar Temple, constructed by Kapilendradeva of the Sūrya Dynasty in the mid–fifteenth century, is considered the last of Bhubaneswar's medieval temples.

Muslim forces, which had conquered other Hindu sites centuries earlier, began to make their presence felt around Bhubaneswar at the end of the sixteenth century. Throughout this period, the independent sultanate of Bengal battled with the Mughal Empire for supremacy in eastern India. Suleiman Kurrani, the independent sultan of Bengal, captured the area in 1568. When he died in 1572, the contest for the region escalated. Mughal emperor Akbar officially annexed Bengal in 1592. Upon the death of Emperor 'Ālamgīr (Aurangzeb) in 1707, the empire fell into disarray, spurring the development of independent kingdoms throughout India. Murshid Qulī Khān, the former Mughal governor of what are now Bengal and Orissa, declared the area independent.

Periodically threatened by Marāṭhā and British invasion, Bhubaneswar finally became British territory when Robert Clive defeated Nabob Sirāj-ud-Dawlah, thereby annexing Bengal and the eastern tracts of modern Orissa in 1757. The Marāṭhās disturbed British power in the area periodically during the late eighteenth century, but for the most part Bhubaneswar remained in British hands until Indian independence. In 1936, the British government finally acquiesced to Oriyans' demands that their territory be recognized as a separate province with a unified linguistic identity.

The boundaries of Orissa set in 1936 were not altered when India achieved independence in 1947, but the appearance and function of Bhubaneswar changed significantly after it was named the state's capital in 1948. This decision to make Bhubaneswar the Oriyan capital launched a heated debate over designs to renovate the city, which at the time lacked the infrastructure necessary for its new administrative role. The crux of the debate—whether the new city should recall its temple town tradition or whether it should embark upon a wholly modern and secular civic plan—was seen by many as the defining question facing the new nation. As a result, the development of Bhubaneswar acquired national significance.

Historically, Bhubaneswar had served as the capital of Kalinga in the pre-Mauryan era, during the reign of Aśoka, in the period of Khāravela's rule, and finally again during the Bhauma-Kara and Soma Dynasties. But even during those periods, Bhubaneswar never really emerged as a commercial or political center. Its identity continued to be linked primarily to the religious traditions and institutions of the area. Buddhist, Jain, Saivite, and Vaisnavite monastic establishments were the most prominent institutions in the Old Town. Some estimates show that even up to the late nineteenth century, priests and those serving the priests and temples constituted well over half the population of the Old Town.

Koenigsberger, the architect hired to design the New Capital, wanted to break with this tradition. The Old Town, he believed, represented a divided and unequal society created by the institutions of religious culture. He wanted the new Bhubaneswar to become a modern city embodying egalitarian, secular beliefs. The city was to be a monument now to India's future, as evidenced by the prominent memorials to leaders of India's independence movement, such as Mohandas Karamchand Gandhi (the Mahatma), Gopabandhu Das, and Madhusudhan Das. The political order of the day, however, both locally and nationally, was to reconnect with and revive India's cultural legacy. Opposition to Koenigsberger's vision was voiced loudly by the Oriyan government architect Julius Vaz, who proposed to place the center of the New Capital in direct eye-line with the Old Town and to construct buildings to reflect Bhubaneswar's traditional architectural heritage. Even though some of the architecture in the New Capital does reflect Vaz's vision, his plan as a whole did not win out. Koenigsberger's modern vision triumphed.

Ironically, Koenigsberger planned to break with the tradition of hierarchy and inequality by creating a "double town" that left the old section of the city intact while concentrating new construction efforts in the region of the New Capital. Critics argued that the "double town" would create unequal standards of living and housing, turning the Old Town into a parasitic slum of the New Capital. Koenigsberger himself recognized and warned against these problems, which nevertheless have plagued the city. Slums have cropped up in the space between the two towns, and the Old Town has failed to become an independent, self-sustaining community. Inhabited by a socio-economically lower class, the Old Town has become a somewhat neglected dependent of the New Capital. With attention focused on the development of the New Capital as a separate entity, the necessary interactions and connections between the two populations were overlooked. In order to survive and flourish, the Old Town needed to attract an educated professional community from the capital and develop a strong patronage relationship. Some of the educated professionals of the capital have become patrons of the monastic and temple traditions, but few have chosen the Old Town as a place to live.

Still, the creation of the New Capital has in some measure aided the temple culture of the Old Town. The construction of the New Capital has made the Old Town a more accessible and convenient tourist and pilgrimage site. The growth in tourist income and pilgrimage patronage has been a boon to both the capital and the temples. Tourist interest in the temples has fostered their preservation and renovation, to some extent counterbalancing the lack of local patronage. Since Bhubaneswar has become a capital city, two divergent civic identities have emerged: temple town and capital city. Reconciling this split and addressing the inequalities it has produced will be the tasks of the future.

Further Reading: For a complete history of Bhubaneswar, from its ancient origins to its modern role as a capital city, the most recent and thorough work is *Bhubaneswar: From a Temple Town to a Capital City* by Ravi Kalia (Delhi and Oxford: Oxford University Press, and Carbondale: Southern Illinois University Press, 1994). A descriptive tour of Bhubaneswar's temple complexes can be found in *Bhubaneswar and Its Environs* by R. K. Das (Puri: Sri, 1982). An excellent source for the monastic culture of Bhubaneswar is *Hindu Monastic Life: The Monks and Monasteries of Bhubaneswar* by David M. Miller and Dorothy C. Wertz (Montreal: McGill-Queen's University Press, 1976). *Encyclopedia of India* by P. K. V. Kaimal (New Delhi: Rima, 1992) contains a section that deals more generally with the history of Orissa and the kingdom of Kalinga. Two surveys of Indian history that discuss the history of Orissa in the context of larger political movements are *A History of India, Vol. I*, by Romila Thapar (Harmondsworth, Middlesex, and Baltimore, Maryland: Penguin, 1966) and *A New History of India* by Stanley Wolpert (New York: Oxford University Press, 1977; fourth edition, 1993). For a more scholarly look into Indian history turn to *The New Cambridge History of India*, edited by Gordon Johnson, C. A. Bayly, and John F. Richards (29 vols., Cambridge and New York: Cambridge University Press, 1987–).

—Shome Chowdhury

Bijāpur (Karnātaka, India)

Location: In western India, 245 miles southeast of Bombay, on the north slope of a ridge between the Krishna and Bhīma Rivers.

Description: Former capital of the independent Islamic state of Bijāpur, ruled by the 'Ādil Shāhī Dynasty from 1489 to 1686, Bijāpur is the site of many mosques, gardens, and other Muslim structures.

Contact: Government of India Tourist Office
3-6-369 / A-30, Sandozi Building
Second Floor, 26 Himayat Nagar
Hyderābād 500 029
Andhra Pradesh
India
660037

From the fifteenth to the seventeenth century, Bijāpur was the capital of the independent Islamic state of Bijāpur, one of the five states in the Deccan, the western Islamic provinces of India. Eventually, Bijāpur came to rule over a large area of central India spanning both coasts, and is said to have contained nearly 1 million inhabitants and some 1,600 mosques. Throughout the city's long reign as a capital city, its sultans built an array of mosques, gardens, palaces, battlements, and mausoleums. Accordingly, it is well known today for its impressive range of late medieval Islamic architecture, including more than fifty mosques, twenty tombs, and twenty palaces.

Bijāpur first appears in the historical record in A.D. 1074 under the name Vijayapura (City of Victory); at the time, the city formed part of the Western Chāḷukya Empire. From 973 to 1190, the Hindu Western Chāḷukya Empire sprawled over the entire western half of the Deccan Plateau from the upper Godāvari Basin to the upper Cauvery region, thus linking Mahārāshtra in the north politically with Karnātaka in the south. In 1190 a Marāthī-speaking family, the Yādava Dynasty, broke off from the Chāḷukya power by declaring full authority over the northern, Marāthī-speaking portion of the empire including the Bijāpur Plateau and the city of Bijāpur itself. Shortly after the Yādava Dynasty proclaimed its rule in the north, the Kannada Kingdom under the Hoysala Dynasty likewise established its rule over the southern, Kannada-speaking portion of the former Chāḷukya Empire. During the Yādava period, Bijāpur served as the southernmost provincial seat of that dynasty's realm. Thus, Bijāpur straddled the cultural and political line between the Yādava and Hoysala Dynasties, the north and the south, Mahārāshtra and Karnātaka. Historically and culturally, the Bijāpur Plateau and the city itself sat directly in the middle of these two zones, never completely belonging to either. Perhaps that is why Islam, and particularly Sufism, emerged so powerfully in the region, presenting a third cultural system as an alternative. In approximately 1290 the Khaljīs of the Delhi sultanate began making raids into the plateau. By 1311, all of the former Chāḷukya Empire became tributary regions of the Delhi sultanate. Delhi directly annexed Bijāpur in 1318 and ruled it until 1347, when the city fell to the Bahmanī Kingdom.

The Bahmanī Dynasty reigned from 1347 to 1518 and had its original capital at Gulbarga. Bijāpur became an important city in its own right when five provincial governors rebelled and declared their independence from their Bahmanī rulers. One of those five, Yūsuf 'Ādil Khān, established Bijāpur as the capital of his independent state in 1489 and, in doing so, founded the 'Ādil Shāhī Dynasty, which lasted nearly 200 years until 1686. Yūsuf 'Ādil Khān's arrival in the Deccan is the subject of speculation among historians. Some believe that he was born a slave in Russian Georgia and was later purchased by a minister to the Bahmanī sultan. Others adhere to the legend that he was, in fact, the son of Sultan Murād II of Turkey and was whisked away to Persia as a child to avoid being killed when his older brother assumed the throne; when he was seventeen years old Persia became unsafe, and he was sold into slavery, eventually becoming the property of the Bahmanī minister. Both accounts agree that he flourished under the tutelage of that minister and soon rose in the Bahmanī court, eventually becoming governor of Bijāpur.

The first rulers of Bijāpur followed the Shi'ite branch of Islam (perhaps the result of Yūsuf's childhood in Persia, if that account is to be believed), but with the ascension of Ibrāhīm 'Ādil Shāh to the throne in 1535, the province took up the Sunni practice, more common in the region. He and his successor, Alī 'Ādil Shāh, ushered in an era of religious intolerance. Even so, Alī was willing to put aside his religious differences with the other Muslim independent states; he joined with the sultanates of Bīdar, Ahmadnagar, and Golconda to defeat the Hindu armies to the south in the Battle of Tālikota, which took place on January 23, 1565. This battle was one of the most decisive in Indian history: it broke the power of the Hindu empire to the south, assured that the Deccan would remain Muslim territory, and gave Bijāpur the opportunity to extend its land holdings.

Bijāpur's rise to political prominence sparked its architectural development. Yūsuf began the building of the city walls and Alī finished them. Just over six miles in circumference, they include five gates to the city, each of which features two huge circular towers with a doorway reinforced with spikes and studs. This wall encloses only the central fort of the city; the city itself once encompassed an area thirty miles in circumference.

Gōl Gumbaz, Bijāpur
Photo courtesy of Milton Mann

Alī also built the principal mosque complex of the city, the Jāmi Masjid, begun in the late sixteenth century but not completed until 1686. The complex includes fountains and a reservoir in the inner courtyard, and the dome of its mosque is especially well designed. The floor pavement of the mosque is divided into 2,250 regular spaces designed to look like prayer rugs, and the mosque itself can accommodate 5,000 worshipers. In 1561, Alī built the Gagan Mahal (Heavenly Palace), its facade formed by a large central arch with two narrower arches on either side.

The next sultan of Bijāpur, Ibrāhīm 'Ādil Shāh II, ascended the throne in 1580 and ruled until 1626. Recognized as perhaps the ablest ruler of the 'Ādil Shāhī Dynasty, he is remembered not only for his policy of religious tolerance but also for the fine architecture that he left in Bijāpur, including most of the monuments for which the city is today known. The most important of these is a group of buildings known as the Ibrāhīm Rawza, built in 1626 to the west of the city. This complex includes the tombs of Ibrāhīm 'Ādil Shāh II, his queen, his mother, his daughter, and two sons. One unusual architectural feature of the tomb itself is its hanging ceiling, made of stone slabs apparently supported only by the structure's strong mortar. The complex also includes a mosque, and together the buildings are noted for their beautiful Islamic ornamentation.

Ibrāhīm 'Ādil Shāh II also began construction on the Anand Mahal (Palace of Delight) in 1589, but it remained unfinished at the time of his death, and its design was weakened by later additions. The Jhanjiri Mosque (constructed approximately 1600), with its delicate tracery and rich facade, is also attributed to his rule.

Bijāpur's wealth and power throughout this period is attested by the fact that sultans of all the surrounding territory considered it a prize worth having. Early in the reign of Ibrāhīm 'Ādil Shāh II, the Mughal emperors took a strong interest in Bijāpur. In 1590 Emperor Akbar sent envoys to Bijāpur to pressure the sultanate into recognizing his sovereignty and paying tribute. Although Ibrāhīm 'Ādil Shāh II received the emissaries cordially, he refused to grant formal allegiance to the Mughals. Akbar then began preparations for war in 1593, but the campaign went nowhere. In 1635, Akbar's grandson Shāh Jahān resumed plans for conquest of the Deccan states, and especially of Bijāpur, which was still a largely independent kingdom under 'Ādil Shāh II, son of Ibrāhīm 'Ādil Shāh II. In 1631 his forces began a policy of ravaging the province. Bijāpur sought to resist the Mughal forces but was unable to do so; although the city itself was not taken, the rest of the province was laid to waste. In 1636, a treaty was signed requiring the 'Ādil Shāhī sultan to pay allegiance—and tribute—to the Mughal conqueror.

Although Muhammad 'Ādil Shāh II had capitulated to the Mughals, the treaty allowed him the security to greatly expand his territory, which soon spanned both shores of the peninsula and included a naval fleet in Goa. Furthermore, he paid tribute to the Mughals more in theory than in practice, much to the consternation of Prince Aurangzeb (later to become the emperor 'Ālamgīr), son of Shāh Jahān and Mughal viceroy of the Deccan.

Muhammad 'Ādil Shāh II used his new power and wealth to glorify his capital. His single greatest architectural contribution was the Gōl Gumbaz, the largest and most famous structure in Bijāpur. The building, his mausoleum, was constructed in 1659, most likely by famed architect Yaqut of Dabul, and today is recognized as one of India's great buildings. The tomb's immense dome covers an area of 18,109 square feet, the largest space enclosed by any single dome in the world; the dome's diameter is 124 feet, second only to that of St. Peter's Basilica at Rome, which is 15 feet larger. Gōl Gumbaz makes use of pendentives, groined vaults that rise from corbels (support columns) to support the dome by counteracting its outer thrust. The acoustics of the rather bare interior are such that any sound is repeated twelvefold. On the exterior, the structure beneath the dome is shaped like a huge square block and faced with plaster; at each of its four corners stands a domed, seven-story octagonal tower.

With the death of Muhammad 'Ādil Shāh II in November 1656, his eighteen-year-old son Alī 'Ādil Shāh II became sultan of Bijāpur. The local nobility would not unite behind the youthful new ruler, however, and much political infighting ensued. These events were not lost on Mughal viceroy Aurangzeb; he had, in fact, long been planning to take advantage of the death of the old sultan, and had already acquired the support of many local nobles and military commanders nominally under Bijāpur authority. As political turmoil spread following the death of the old sultan, Aurangzeb attacked. By the end of the summer of 1657, Alī 'Ādil Shāh II was forced to sign a new treaty giving the Mughals much of the territory his father had conquered and requiring the payment of a larger annual tribute. Once again, however, the treaty did not prove particularly binding—at least in the short term. Soon after Aurangzeb's victory, his attentions were diverted by more pressing matters: the struggle for the Mughal throne. While Aurangzeb was busy fighting his three brothers for the right to succeed the ailing Shāh Jahān, Bijāpur and the other Deccan states were given a temporary reprieve from Mughal domination.

Unfortunately, they were not able to enjoy their relative freedom. Perhaps as early as 1655, the territory had been under attack from forces commanded by Śivājī, a young Marāṭhā chieftain from the south. Śivājī had once been in the employ of the Bijāpur government, but he soon organized bands of horsemen to attack the sultanate. Such raids proved successful, and in 1674 Śivājī established the independent Marāṭhā kingdom.

During this period, Alī 'Ādil Shāh II added to the splendors of his capital. Among these additions is his unfinished tomb, originally designed to outdo the Gōl Gumbaz, just as that building had been designed to surpass the Ibrāhīm Rawza. The base of Alī's tomb encloses an area over 45,000 square feet (the Gōl Gumbaz encloses under 25,000 square feet) and was to have supported an even more massive dome. Today all that remains of the complex is the outer arcade.

In 1681 Aurangzeb, having won the contest for succession and assumed the name 'Ālamgīr, returned to the Deccan in hopes of finally conquering the independent sultanates. Following an extended siege, the city of Bijāpur surrendered to the Mughal forces in October 1686, and the young sultan, Sikandar, became a prisoner for life. With the Mughals victorious, the 'Ādil Shāhī Dynasty came to an end, and the independent state of Bijāpur was no more.

Although he mutilated some of the city's buildings, 'Ālamgīr also added to the city's architecture. He had mosques built, including one for his own personal use in the city palace, for which he laid some of the stones himself as a sign of piety. He also ordered construction of a garden and water tank in the vicinity of the city. Bijāpur is in fact noted for its many gardens and water tanks, including the Tāj Bauri (built approximately 1620), the largest in the city, and its waterworks, the sophistication of which attests to the engineering ability of Islamic architects.

Although 'Ālamgīr had long dreamed of conquering Bijāpur and the other independent Deccan sultanates, his completion of this goal brought with it new problems. The Marāṭhās now faced greatly reduced resistance to their raids, and they soon pushed increasingly farther north. In 1760, Bijāpur was ceded to the Marāṭhās, and soon thereafter the city was abandoned. Its buildings became quarries for distant construction projects.

The forest all but swallowed the city in the ensuing decades, and it was not until the British turned the site into its military headquarters in 1883 that large-scale reconstruction took place.

Further Reading: D. C. Verma's *History of Bijāpur* (New Delhi: Kumar Brothers, 1974) covers the city throughout the Mughal era, focusing on the political aspects of the reigning dynasties. Originally a thesis, this work is very detailed and scholarly. Coverage of India during the Muslim period may be found in Vincent A. Smith's *The Oxford History of India: From the Earliest Times to the End of 1911* (Oxford: Clarendon Press, 1919; fourth edition, edited by Percival Spear, New York and Oxford: Oxford University Press, 1981). In addition, two volumes of *The New Cambridge History of India*, edited by Gordon Johnson, C. A. Bayly, and John F. Richards (29 vols., Cambridge and New York: Cambridge University Press, 1987–) provide information about Bijāpur: John F. Richard's *The Mughal Empire* (volume 1, part 5, 1993) and Catherine B. Asher's *Architecture of Mughal India* (volume 1, part 4, 1992). *The Penguin Guide to the Monuments of India*, volume 2, *Islamic, Rajput, European* by Philip Davies (London and New York: Viking, 1989) describes important structures in Bijapur. Richard Eaton's *Sufis of Bijāpur: 1300–1700* (Princeton, New Jersey: Princeton University Press, 1978) provides a thorough and engaging cultural and religious history of the 'Ādil Shāhī Dynasty.

—Robert Kellerman

Bīkaner (Rājasthān, India)

Location: In northwestern Rājasthān state, in the Thar Desert, approximately 225 miles west-southwest of Delhi.

Description: Bīkaner is an oasis city; its walled settlement, with ruins of the original fort, survives. Outside the wall stands Junāgarh Fort, surrounded by the modern sector. The city includes superb Jain and Hindu temples and intricately carved mansions (*havelis*).

Contact: Government of India Tourist Office
State Hotel, Khasa Kothi
Jaipur 302 001, Rājasthān
India
372200

Bīkaner, the fourth largest city in the Indian state of Rājasthān, was founded by Rao Bīka, who acquired the extensive but arid northern region of Rājasthān in 1472. He was the second son of Jodhpur's founder, the Rathor clan leader Mahārāja Rāo Jodha, and therefore had little prospect of inheriting his father's title. It appears that Bīka deliberated for some time before choosing the site of Bīkaner for his base, because he did not build a stone fort there until sixteen years later. In spite of its arid appearance, Bīkaner is an oasis in the Thar Desert, provided with an adequate supply of spring water. Its elevated location (760 feet above sea level) and strategic position on the trading route between the Gujarāt coast and Delhi were additional advantages. It may be presumed that both the former Rājput state and its capital derived their names from Bīka.

Only the ruins of Bīka's fort have survived, as Rāo Singh appears to have demolished most of it a century later when he built a new stronghold, Junāgarh Fort, outside the city wall. Bīkaner's earliest complete structures are Jain and Hindu temples dating from the late fifteenth century, many of which were grouped around the original fort. Although most buildings in Bīkaner were constructed of local red sandstone, gold sandstone from Jaisalmer was introduced for many of the temples; when red sandstone was used, it often was covered with whitewash. The name of the Bhandasar Temple (Jain) commemorates its patron, who began construction in the late fifteenth century, but did not complete the building until 1514. Unusually, the temple combines red and gold sandstone, all now whitewashed—presumably in the interest of uniformity. The *maṇḍapa* hall and porches are seventeenth–century additions; the former displays rather garish, recently executed murals. The more restrained decor in the sanctuary dates from the eighteenth century.

Dating from the same period is the Laksmināth Temple (Hindu), with its large, marble courtyard; here again, most of the building has been whitewashed. Completed in 1535, the Nemināth Temple (one of the city's twenty-seven Jain temples) commemorates its patron, the brother of Bhandasar, and is generally regarded as the finest of Bīkaner's temples. Particularly outstanding is the exquisite and intricate carving, a hallmark of Jain temples and the reason they took so long to complete. A lofty *śikhara* tower is a distinguishing feature of the building. Two other temples outside the complex are of importance. The Chintamani Temple, like the Nemināth Temple, was completed in 1535; built of red sandstone, it replaced an earlier gold sandstone structure. The Adināth Temple of 1583 appears to be a smaller version of the Chintamani Temple, although its ceiling paintings are modern.

Almost as impressive as Bīkaner's temples are its splendid mansions, known as *havelis*, most of which were owned by wealthy Marwari merchants. (The Marwari are a linguistically and ethnically distinct group from western Rājasthān who have a reputation as entrepreneurs and traders.) The *havelis* are multi-story buildings with relatively narrow street frontages of profusely carved red sandstone; the richness of the carving indicated the prestige of the owner. Some date to the fifteenth and sixteenth centuries, including the noteworthy Shri Krishnan Das Haveli. However, the finest survivors are relatively modern, dating from the late nineteenth and early twentieth centuries; they include the Rampuria, Bohar Niwas, and Kothari Havelis.

It was not until a century after its foundation that Bīkaner's importance and wealth reached their zenith. Mahārāja Rāo Singh (ruled 1571–1611), a descendant of Bīka, accepted the suzerainty of the Mughals and cooperated fully with Emperor Akbar, who appointed him a general in his army. Since only the Mughals possessed gunpowder in India, his military success was virtually guaranteed, and Rāo Singh was rewarded not only by the spoils of war but also by Akbar's personal munificence.

Accumulated wealth enabled Rāo Singh to build his own fortress-palace complex, on a much grander scale than the city's original fort, between 1588 and 1593. Such was the Mahārāja's confidence that the new site was chosen outside of the protection of the city wall. Nevertheless, massive ramparts were constructed, and Junāgarh Fort never fell to an aggressor in battle. Although it is built on flat ground, the fort still presents a picturesque scene; its wall, stretching some 1,000 yards, and gateways have survived intact from Rāo Singh's period. Within, however, virtually all the original palace has been replaced by later buildings. It seems likely that pride rather than convenience led successive mahārājas to replace or modify their predecessors' buildings, for only a marginal difference in architectural styles is noticeable; a similar practice was followed in Muslim palaces throughout

Courtyard within Bīkaner Fort, Bīkaner
Photo courtesy of Christopher Turner

Part of the temple complex, Bīkaner
Photo courtesy of Christopher Turner

India. In some Rājput palaces, the Mughal preference for relatively small, separate pavilions constructed around courtyards had some influence on architectural planning, but not at Bīkaner, where the traditional Hindu system of large ranges containing numerous linked chambers was maintained. These activities were not interrupted by the introduction of British rule in India; the princes of Rājasthān signed a treaty with the British in 1818, accepting a new suzerainty. This arrangement made it all the easier for Bīkaner's mahārājas to lavish their attention and revenues on renovating the fort.

Visitors to the palace must pass through a series of gateways that, as was usual in Indian forts, provided a defense against attackers. The first of these gates, Karan Prole, is fitted with iron spikes at a level that prohibited the use of elephants' heads as battering rams. Following this, at right angles, is Daulat Prole; a red-painted handprint beside it signifies that one of the Bīkaner mahārājas' wives committed *satī* by immolation on her husband's funeral pyre. Two further gates—making five in all—stand before the main entrance, Suraj Prole. Suraj Prole (Sun Gate) is so named because from it the morning sun can be seen to rise, which is considered a lucky omen. The gate is built of golden sandstone, a rare example at Junāgarh Fort, most of which is constructed of red sandstone. This gate also has been fitted with elephant spikes and displays additional symbolic satī prints. Elephants and their mahout riders are painted on both sides of the structure. Suraj Prole formerly served as the place where musicians announced the arrival of important visitors from a gallery surmounting the gateway, which is now blocked.

A courtyard follows, providing an open area between the main gateway to the fortress and the palace buildings, but yet another gate, the Tripolia Prole, must be entered to gain access to the princely quarters. To its left lies a small temple, the Har Mandīr, which was reserved for worship by the mahārāja and his family. In the next courtyard, a central pavilion has been built of white Carrara marble imported from Italy. It features a pool, which is still filled with water during the summer months. In the same courtyard, now seen through a protective glass screen, is the Karan Mahal, which served as the Dīwān-i-Am (Public Audience Hall) of its builder, Karan Singh (reigned 1631–69) and his successors until the twentieth century. Under Mughal suzerainty, Rājput princes still held a great degree of autonomy in their own states and could dispense justice as they wished; the mahārāja even retained the power of granting life or death to a convicted criminal. All citizens were permitted to attend the ruler's deliberations and air their grievances in the Dīwān-i-Am. Much of the present decoration of the Karan Mahal is the work of Anup Singh and was produced in the late seventeenth century.

Floors above the Karan Mahal were added by later mahārājas: the first by Gaj Singh in the eighteenth century and the second by Dungar Singh in the late nineteenth century. Known as the Gaj Mandīr, the five-room suite, which forms the first story, is the most renowned section of Junāgarh Fort. Four interlinked rooms surround a central, slightly raised hall, which is decorated with blue ceramic tiles imported from Persia. Displayed within the hall, which can be entered from only one of the rooms, is a Krishna swing, an object of Hindu veneration. Of the surrounding rooms, the decor of the Shish Mahal is the most important, comprised of mirror glass, stained glass, and gold leaf gilding. The top story, known as Chattar Niwas, consists of a single chamber containing a nineteenth-century Rājput bed and an "early warning system" mirror, which has been positioned so that an occupant of the bed could see if an enemy was approaching. It was usual for a Rājput to keep his sword within easy reach beside a low bed.

Anup Singh (reigned 1669–98) rebuilt much of the palace toward the close of his reign, including the female quarters (zenana) at the west end. His most important achievement at Junagarh was the Anup Mahal, added in 1690 to provide the Dīwān-i-Khas (Private Audience Hall) of the mahārājas. However, most of its rich interior decor, of glass and vibrant paintwork, is the late-eighteenth-century work of Surat Singh (reigned 1787–1828). It was Gaj Singh (reigned 1746–87), the predecessor of Surat Singh, who added the sumptuously decorated Chandra Mahal (Moon Palace). In the late nineteenth century, Dungar Singh (reigned 1872–87) built the Badal Mahal (Weather Palace), thereby replacing the seventeenth-century structure of Anup Singh. In the entrance is a painting of falling rain—a rare event in Bīkaner—which gives the pavilion its name. It would appear that Dungar Singh was impressed by the blue Persian tiles in the Gaj Mandīr, but for some reason did not obtain more for the Badal Mahal; instead, blue paintwork was used to give a trompe l'oeil effect of tiles.

The great Ganga Niwas, built by Ganga Singh (reigned 1887–1943), towers over the entrance courtyard. Its architect was Colonel Samuel Swinton Jacob, who began work in 1902. Jacob had recently designed the Albert Hall at Jaipur, where he combined Indian and European styles; Gothic Revival was selected at Jaipur, while at Bīkaner, neo-Classicism prevailed. Outside of India, Ganga Singh was the best known of all the Indian princes; the esteem in which he was held by the British king George V was reflected in the succession of honors awarded to the prince, who became General H. H. Mahārāja and Sir Ganga Singh Bahādur; he carried numerous other honorary titles as well. Ganga Singh inherited the title of mahārāja in 1877, at the age of seven, and did not rule personally until attaining his sixteenth birthday. In 1911 he was appointed Knight Commander of the Star of India, a personal gift of George V. Serving as a member of India's War Cabinet, Ganga Singh gained international attention when he represented his country at the Imperial (First World) War Conferences and the British Empire at the Versailles Peace Conference. He lived long enough to see the tide turn in World War II, dying in 1943.

It was specified that the Ganga Niwas should include separate public and private audience halls to replace the functions of the existing Dīwān-i-Am and Dīwān-i-Khas. In addition to providing a new Dīwān-i-Am, the larger hall had to be able to accommodate durbars (large formal receptions). In 1937, Ganga Singh celebrated his Golden Jubilee in the hall, which is now a museum. Exhibits include the imperial throne of sandalwood, made specifically for the hall, and Ganga Singh's elephant howdah.

The modern city of Bīkaner evolved around the fort, which must originally have stood in splendid isolation. To the north, Ganga Singh commissioned Swinton Jacob to build him a new palace, Bīkaner's third, which was named in honor of Lal Singh, Ganga's father. It was habitable by 1902, and the mahārāja moved to Lalgarh Palace immediately from Junāgarh Fort; however, work continued, and the building as it stands today was not completed for another quarter of a century. Built entirely of red sandstone, the palace owes less to European styles than to the architect's other buildings in India. In 1976 the Shri Sadul Museum was opened within the palace as a tribute to the son of Ganga Singh, who died in 1950. The complex is now one of India's palace hotels. Many of the original furnishings remain, and the palace's Shiv Bilas dining room, seating 400, now accommodates hotel guests. Also converted to a hotel is the former summer palace of Bīkaner's mahārājas, Gajner Palace, located by its eponymous lake, twenty miles west of the city on the main road to Jaisalmer.

Only five miles distant from Bīkaner are the cenotaph *chattris* of the royal family. They are grouped together in a walled enclosure above a small lake, Devi Kund Sagar, which almost dries up in the summer. The oldest cenotaph is that of Rāo Kalyan (1572); room also was found to commemorate Sadal Singh in 1950, but no space remains for further additions. Most impressive are the marble *chattris,* particularly that of Surat Singh, who died in 1828.

Twenty miles south of Bīkaner lies the undistinguished village of Deshnok, which is famous for its Karni Matra Temple, inhabited by hundreds of rats. Karni Matra, in her own lifetime, was believed to be an incarnation of Durgā, the fierce and dark aspect of Siva's consort, Pārvatī. By tradition, Yama, who holds dominion over the dead, was unable to return a relative of Karni Matra to life, and therefore the god decreed that all members of Karni's minstrel caste (Charan) would hence be reincarnated as rats. Members of the caste built this temple to Karni Matra as a refuge for the animals. Holes are drilled in the walls to encourage rats to live in the temple. It is probable that the first temple was built here in the sixteenth century, to be replaced with an enlarged structure in later years. A tradition that Karni Matra had given Rāo Bīka her blessing prior to his victory at Bīkaner in 1472 led to the mahārājas giving the temple their patronage; in the twentieth century, Ganga Singh provided it with silver entrance doors.

Today Bīkaner supports various trades and is the administrative center for the surrounding district. Between 1925 and 1927 the Gaṇgā Canal was constructed, which has greatly facilitated irrigation in the Bīkaner region, where water is rarely found at a depth of less than 150 feet. Agriculture and, surprisingly, sheep farming, which produces fine quality wool, are important to Bīkaner, as is the breeding of camels. Marwari merchants still trade in the city, which is gradually becoming more dependent on tourism. All titles were abolished in India shortly after the 1947 independence, but the descendants of the mahārājas continue to live in a suite at the Lalgarh Palace Hotel. Junāgarh Fort is an unoccupied museum. All of these changes show how the once isolated town of Bīkaner has become part of modern India.

Further Reading: The definitive history of Bīkaner is *The Art and Architecture of Bīkaner State* by Hermann Goetz (Oxford: B. Cassiver, 1950), but copies will be found only in specialist libraries. More biographical in nature is *India and Its Native Princes: Travels in Central India and in the Presidencies of Bombay and Bengal* by Louis Rousselet (London: Chapman and Hall, 1875; reprint, 1983), but this work is equally difficult to locate. The *Penguin Guide to the Monuments of India* (London and New York: Viking, 1989) in two volumes—volume 1 by George Michell covering Buddhist and Hindu sites, and volume 2 by Philip Davies dealing with Islamic and European sites—is readily available and particularly useful for plans and photographs.

—Christopher Turner

Bishnupur (West Bengal, India)

Location: Bishnupur lies approximately 100 miles northeast of Calcutta between the Ganges River and Chota Nāgpur Plateau, just south of the Dhalkisor River.

Description: Situated in the district of Bānkura, with a population of about 40,000, Bishnupur (or Vishnupur, as it is also known) was the capital of the Mallabhūm kings for approximately 1,000 years and is still the site of many fine Hindu and Jain temples erected during their tenure. A bazaar town and seat of administration, Bishnupur is also a frequent pilgrimage and festival site, known for its fine silk textiles, brass work, and terra-cotta statuary.

Contact: Government of India Tourist Office
4 Shakespeare Sarani
Calcutta 700 071, West Bengal
India
2421402, 2421475, or 2425813

Bishnupur is best known today as a center of religious temples and festivals, and its earliest history is entwined with the lives of gods and goddesses, pilgrims and holy men. Although Bishnupur probably originated as a market town inhabited by indigenous non-Aryans and, later, Aryan immigrants from northern India, local legend ties its founding to a miraculous vision of the goddess Durgā. According to the story, Jagat (or Jay) Malla, nineteenth king of the Mallabhūm Dynasty, came upon the site while hunting in A.D. 994. A skilled falconer, he one day sent his hawk after a heron, only to have the heron kill it. With this occurrence, Durgā revealed herself to Jagat Malla and commanded him to establish a place for her worship on that spot and to move his capital there from the city of Laugram.

For the next 800 years the history of Bishnupur was inextricably tied to the fortunes of the Mallabhūm Dynasty. The Mallabhūm rulers traced their origin to the seventh century, when a Rājput prince on pilgrimage to a shrine in Puri abandoned his pregnant wife in the jungle when she went into labor. The infant was taken home by a local Bagdi woman to grow up among the lower caste, where he became a superior wrestler or *mal,* from which the dynasty takes its name. After the appearance of several miraculous signs that revealed him to be the son of a king, the young man, Adi Malla, was granted a small fief from which he and his descendants carved out a substantial kingdom in eastern India, one that endured until well into the eighteenth century.

As the new capital of the Mallabhūm Kingdom, Bishnupur became a center of worship for both Jains and Hindus, a site of religious festivals, and the home to lavishly decorated temples. The first temple to the goddess Durgā was not so spectacular, however, consisting merely of a mud hut in which her image rested on a mud platform. It is said that each attempt to build a more imposing temple was foiled by Ma Durgā, who does not like elaborate buildings. The present temple on this spot was built in the twentieth century, and even this required a show of divine approval. According to legend, the temple walls fell whenever workers tried to raise them to the level of the tree branches on which Durgā's heron had first shown itself; only after a local holy man convinced Durgā to miraculously raise the branches could the temple be completed.

The earliest completed temple still standing in Bishnupur is Rāsa Mancha, built near the end of the sixteenth century by the greatest Mallabhūm king, Bīr Hambīr. Bīr Hambīr's court was acclaimed for its artists, musicians, scholars, and holy men, and under his rule Bishnupur became known as the most beautiful city in Bengal. It was also Bīr Hambīr who helped introduce the worship of Vishnu and Krishna to Bishnupur. The most widely practiced religion in north India had previously been Jainism, which eventually gave way to Buddhism under the Palas (c. 700–c. 1000), and then to Brahmin Hinduism under the Senas (1095–1245). Some of the oldest temples in the district and town of Bishnupur display the iconography of Jainism on the outside walls while housing Hindu statues within.

It is said that before his conversion to Vaishnavism (the worship of Vishnu), Bīr Hambīr was a cruel tyrant. According to legend, one day he hijacked two cart-loads of valuables and manuscripts from the care of two devotees. Later he received in his court one of the two holy men (the other had died of a broken heart following the theft) and heard the texts explicated; Bīr Hambīr was so moved that he immediately converted and gave himself over to worship and temple building.

Rāsa Mancha dates from this time, and it was in this temple that all of Bishnupur's sacred images were exhibited during the annual Rāsa festival. The temple itself is a domed sanctuary surrounded by a vaulted veranda and dominated by a stepped masonry pyramid, a unique feature among the city's temples.

The majority of the local religious architecture is built in the Pratihāra or *rekha* style. This consists of a spire rising from the shrine and carrying through the lower projections, as well as a porch or colonnade on some structures. Clusters of towers, sometimes as many as twenty-five, crowned with curved, domed roofs and cornices may also rise from the corners of the veranda or central shrine. These curved roofs are an indigenous style originally modeled on the local thatch roofs; the name of the style reflects this: *Jor Bāṅgla* means "pair of bungalows." Keshta Raya temple, built in 1655 by Raghunath Singh, is the best example of this particular style,

Rāsa Mancha, Bishnupur
Photo courtesy of Dilip K. Chakrabarti

consisting of two vaulted chambers displaying curved cornices and a domed central chamber surrounded by vaulted verandas. Typically, Bānkura temples utilized laterite quarried outside the area and stucco, or they were built of local brick and terra-cotta.

Bishnupur's temples feature some of the finest of the terra-cotta plaques for which the region is known. Such decorations from this period typically display a lively, flowing, and rhythmic style using mostly Krishna iconography. Rāsa Mancha contains the city's oldest surviving examples of such decorations, and the temple of Shyam Rai, built in 1643 by Raghunath Singh, contains the richest collection of terra-cotta plaques in all of Bengal. Shyam Rai's plaques show Krishna embracing Rādhā, playing his flute to her, or standing between two *gopīs* (cowherding young women with whom Krishna played as a child); they also depict dancers, celebrants, devotees, and musicians. The porch plaques depict the ten incarnations of Vishnu and other gods and goddesses, such as Siva, Brahmā, Kālī, Ganesh, Chinamosta, and, of course, Durgā. Inside are imposing images of Siva and Narasiṃha, epic and mythic battles between the gods and heros, as well as contemporary battles and depictions of the rāja himself in his state palanquin. The plaques have their share of delicate floral and foliage designs as well as the more unusual giant, elephant-eating ostriches and winged lions.

The terra-cotta decorations of Keshta Raya, built twelve years later, display similar subject matter with a bolder and more ordered hand, but the tiles themselves are unique in size and distribution. The detail on the friezes ranges from mythic Purāṇic themes to battles carved in great period detail, numerous animal scenes, and a woman massaging her husband's legs. In the following century six more temples were built in this unusual style with similar plans and decorations. Although Hindu temples built under the Guptas (A.D. 320–c. 540) and Buddhist temples built under the Palas had both exhibited terra-cotta decorations, the Bishnupuri plaques were an outgrowth of Muslim terra-cotta decoration common at that time in surrounding regions. With their cultured and independent court, it is no surprise that the Bishnupur rājas in their heyday were comfortable acquiring a decorative craft from the surrounding Muslims and encouraging its development into a distinctive, elaborate art form.

Bishnupur was, in fact, the capital of one of the largest Hindu kingdoms in a mostly Muslim state. Eastern Bengal had been under Muslim rule intermittently since 1338, but the Mallabhūm Kingdom remained a Hindu stronghold well into the eighteenth century. Even when the Mughals, a particularly powerful Muslim dynasty, entered the region in the sixteenth century, the Mallas continued to be independent. They did not acknowledge Mughal suzerainty until 1590, soon after which they formed an agreement whereby the Mallabhūm rājas were left largely to their own devices so long as they paid the revenues assessed against their estates. Even then, however, their obedience seemed to depend on the personality and strength of the current Mughal ruler; the stronger he was, the readier Bishnupur's rājas were to pay their assessments.

The decline of Bishnupur's power and independence apparently began during the reign of Raghunath Singh II (1694–1720), a rāja most remembered for his patronage of Indian classical music. It was the reign of Raghunath's successor, Gopal Singh (1720–45 or c. 1758), however, that marked the steepest decline in the city's fortunes. A devout Hindu, Gopal apparently spent more time tending to the spiritual well-being of his subjects than administering his realm. More importantly, it was Gopal who invited the Marāṭhās into his territory.

During this period, the Mallabhūmis owed direct obedience to the Muslim kings of Bengal, a former Mughal dependency. When Bengali rule turned oppressive under the reign of the nabob Alivardi, who attained the throne in 1740, Gopal Singh decided to move against him. Unfortunately, he did so by allying Bishnupur with the Marāṭhās. In league with the rāja of Bīrbhūm and the Mughal emperor at Delhi, Gopal Singh allowed the Marāṭhās to enter his territory without a struggle, ostensibly to collect revenues owed to the Mughals. The Marāṭhās advanced against Alivardi through Burdwān, but Alivardi managed to halt their progress. The Marāṭhās then turned toward Bishnupur, burning and plundering on the way. The fighting continued for nine years through the districts of Bānkura, Bīrbhūm, Burdwān, and Midnapur, leaving the countryside decimated.

A contemporary chronicle, the *Riyāzu-s-Salātin*, describes the Marāṭhā raids:

> Sacking the villages and towns of the surrounding tracts, and engaging in slaughter and captures, they set fire to granaries and spared no vestige of fertility. . . . Those murderous freebooters drowned in the rivers a large number of the people, after cutting off their ears, noses and hands. Tying sacks of dirt to the mouths of others, they mangled and burnt them with indescribable tortures.

According to legend, Bishnupur was once saved from total destruction at the hands of the Marāṭhās by its then-principal deity, Madanmohan. Upon the Marāṭhās' advance, Gopal Singh gathered the townspeople into the city fortress and directed them all to pray, rather than mount a defense of any sort. In answer to their prayers, Madanmohan took charge of the city's defense himself, striding the ramparts of the fort with a cannon under each arm, firing at the invaders who, inevitably, scattered. One of these cannon is still preserved in the remains of the fort and is known as Dalmardan (Slayer of the Invading Hordes). A more likely explanation of Bishnupur's survival is the strength of its moated fortress, built under the reign of Bīr Singh II (c. 1656–77) to protect against raids by Afghans, Pathans, and Mughals. The structure most likely would have proven impenetrable to Marāṭhā cavalry, who were armed only with light artillery.

Nevertheless, a decade of raids, depredations, and weak rulership took its toll on Bishnupur and the surrounding countryside, leaving it vulnerable to the British East India Company's political and economic maneuvering. The British first arrived in Bengal in 1681, but, as had been the case with the Mughals, their presence originally had little effect on Bishnupur. With the weakened state of Mallabhūm rule, however, British influence soon increased. In 1760 the rāja of Bishnupur, Chaitanya Singh, was deposed by his relative Damodar Singh and reinstated only with the help of the British. Bishnupur finally came under the direct control of the East India Company in 1765, when Shāh Ālam, the largely titular emperor at Delhi, gave the region to the British in a land grant that included the Dīwāni of Bengal, Bihār, and Orissa. Revenues were fixed and collected by local *amils* (fiscal or financial officers). Unlike their arrangement with the Mughals, however, the rulers of Bishnupur were given little flexibility in making their payments to the British. The system established by the British aimed at the extraction of maximum revenues, regardless of the long-term effects on the populous or the land's future productivity.

By now Bishnupur was suffering from a number of distinct but related causes: the cumulative effects of Marāṭhā raids; the rising power of neighboring rulers; continued military operations carried out by the British East India Company, the nabob of Bengal, and others; and its own ineptitude and greed in dealing with the company's traders. When the region experienced repeated droughts and crop failures beginning in 1768, the local economy collapsed utterly. Starvation became so widespread that one-third of the population had died by 1770; the jungle soon reclaimed one-third of the arable land. Despite this, net land revenues exacted by the British hardly fluctuated as a result of greater burdens imposed on the living. To make matters even worse, company officials often became profiteers, exercising monopolies on grain and seed.

Following hard on these disasters was an increase in raids by freebooters, who often were joined by the local inhabitants when the targets were British. This alliance did not last long, however, and the British stepped into the changed political climate, winning some local favor. Such intervention was, of course, costly both monetarily and politically to the rāja of Bishnupur. For a time Chaitanya Singh was held in debtors prison, and in 1799 his lands were sold in arrears of revenue to the mahārāja of Burdwān. His sons raised a small army to fend off the seizure, but the action was ultimately carried out in 1806.

Bishnupur's importance then shifted from the realms of religion and politics to that of economics. Although Bishnupur remained an important center of worship, temple building and decoration came to a virtual standstill without the patronage of the royal house. At the same time, the East India Company accelerated trade in silks, cotton, and dyes. Reflecting this change, the nature of unrest in the area shifted from violent uprisings to somewhat more peaceful economic and political confrontation. Much of the unrest can be attributed to the introduction of indigo plantations to the area. Oppressive methods of forcing its cultivation upon the residents surrounding Bishnupur made the British more than usually unpopular and led to boycotts and court cases, but little actual violence.

The area remained largely peaceful until the independence movement of the mid–twentieth century, when residents of Bishnupur participated in Mohandas Karamchand (Mahatma) Gandhi's noncooperation, civil disobedience movement by withholding taxes, disrupting the census, setting up national schools, and boycotting the law courts. Violence was limited to a few cases of arson. Even when violence broke out elsewhere in Bānkura district, Bishnupur remained quiet, with only rumblings of discontent and such peaceful yet defiant displays of nationalism as hoisting the Indian national flag on the court building.

The 1960s and 1970s were far more politically restive than preceding decades had been in Bishnupur. In the 1970s, corruption in many of the local artisans' cooperatives spurred demonstrations and hunger strikes that brought government ministers to the city to listen to demands for reforms. In the late 1960s and early 1970s, an armed uprising in north Bengal, known as the Naxalite Movement, in which landless laborers seized surplus and fallow land from a tea plantation, spread to Bishnupur, where educated urban youths raided police stations and eliminated "class enemies." Among their most notorious acts was the murder of a policeman on Ekhan Sikar day, part of a four-day harvest festival often celebrated quite wildly: the fourth day of the festival, the Day of the Hunt, when the kings used to lead the people on a hunt into the jungle, sometimes still involves blood sacrifices. The significance was not lost on the citizens of Bishnupur. Even in its modern politics, Bishnupur remembers its gods and goddesses. The unrest of the 1970s left a legacy in the numerous political organizations headquartered in Bishnupur today.

Although Bānkura's economy remains largely agrarian, Bishnupur is also a thriving center of cottage handicrafts and industries, closely connected with other market towns in the district as well as with Calcutta. The region produces fine silk textiles, bell metal, and brass; it also remains a center for the production of terra-cotta ware, continuing the long tradition begun centuries ago with the decorations of the city's many temples. The population is largely Hindu, with a Muslim minority dating from the Mughal invasions of the sixteenth century.

Modern Bishnupur has many faces: bazaar town, political and administrative center, college campus, and site of an annual festival of music and dance, but its temples and *pujas* (religious rites) still dominate the town's psyche and recall its former status as a royal city. It is said 1,000 places of worship stood throughout the district in the nineteenth century, and hundreds of shrines and temples remain today in the town itself. About thirty of these are seventeenth- and eighteenth-century Hindu temples sheltering great metal images of Krishna and other gods consecrated by the Mallabhūm kings.

The city still attracts pilgrims and tourists who come to participate in or just observe the numerous religious festivals. Nearly every day a religious festival is being held somewhere in the city, and at least one major festival occurs each month; the annual Durgāpuja is the city's largest. Often the same *puja* is performed in several parts of town in different social contexts related to caste and economic station. In the days of the Mallabhūm kings, the organization and production of such festivals was a royal prerogative and duty, but the honor has now passed to the descendants of royal priests and to the people themselves.

Further Reading: The most comprehensive English-language historical outline of both the Bānkura district and Bishnupur is *West Bengal District Gazetteers,* volume 2, *Bānkura* by Amiya Kumar Banerji (Calcutta: State Editor, West Bengal District Gazetteers, 1957–1970). A brief history is also given in Tara Sankar Panigrahi's *The British Rule and the Economy of Rural Bengal: A Study of the Mallabhūm from 1757–1833* (New Delhi: Marwah, 1982), although this is primarily a study of the region's economics. Bishnupur's temples receive a brief treatment in *The Penguin Guide to the Monuments of India,* volume 1, by George Michell (London and New York: Viking, 1989). For a detailed discussion of the art and architecture of Bishnupur's temples, see David McCutchion's *The Temples of Bānkura District* (Calcutta: Writer's Workshop, 1967). Two fascinating and quite readable sociological studies of the religious and political life of Bishnupur have been written by Ákōs Őstőr: *Culture and Power: Legend, Ritual, Bazaar, and Rebellion in a Bengali Society* (New Delhi: Sage, 1984), and *The Play of the Gods: Locality, Ideology, Structure and Time in the Festivals of a Bengali Town* (Chicago: University of Chicago Press, 1980).

—Lee Kottner

Bodh Gayā (Bihār, India)

Location: Central Bihār state, northeastern India, seven miles south of Gayā.

Description: Holiest of all Buddhist sites; where Siddhārtha Gautama attained enlightenment seated beneath the Bo-tree 2,500 years ago. With a major temple—the Mahābodhi—and several monasteries in the vicinity, it is considered a hallowed place of pilgrimage and worship for both Buddhists and Hindus, but in recent years has been the subject of dispute between the two religions.

Site Office: Bihār Tourism Development Corporation
Shop No. 34-35
Mahābodhi Temple Market Complex
Bodh Gayā, Bihār
India

Bodh Gayā (alternately spelled Buddh Gayā, Buddha Gayā, Bodhi Gayā, Bodhgayā), considered by many the seat of Buddhism, is the most sacred Buddhist pilgrimage site in the world. Here, under the sacred *Bodhi-druma* (Tree of Enlightenment), Gautama sat in meditation until he received enlightenment, that is, an understanding of all the mysteries of the universe. For twenty-five centuries, this tree has been as important to Buddhists as the cross is to Christians. Pilgrims have journeyed from all parts of eastern Asia to worship there, and the surrounding area has been glorified with monasteries and temples built by kings of India, as well as those as far away as Burma and Sri Lanka.

Many historians now date the birth of Siddhārtha Gautama to 563 B.C. According to Buddhist tradition, a soothsayer proclaimed at his birth that Gautama would either become a universal ruler or, upon witnessing the inescapable conditions of mankind, retire from the world and become a Buddha, an enlightened being whose wisdom would save humanity. His father, a minor king, surrounded Gautama with material comforts in hope of deterring him from choosing a life of poverty. But as he wandered outside the palace gates, Gautama was distressed by the suffering he witnessed, and he realized that all worldly things were ephemeral. At age twenty-nine, he renounced his privileged birth, abandoned home and family, and began a regimen of solitary meditation in a neighboring forest in search of true wisdom.

Gautama visited the area around Gayā as a Hindu ascetic and passed some time on the Gayaśīrṣa Hill, now called Brahmjūnī; then he and five fellow ascetics traveled on to the village of Uruvelā, near Bodh Gayā. Here he and his companions spent six years pursuing a course of extreme self-denial until, near death, he became convinced that asceticism was not the path to gain the knowledge he sought. He turned to begging to support himself. His companions, seeing this as an abandonment of his principles, deserted Gautama, who wandered forth seeking the place where he should obtain perfect knowledge.

Along the way he met a grass-cutter, who gave him some grass to spread under a neighboring pipal tree (a type of fig, Ficus religiosa). Seated on the grass under this tree, also called a Bo-tree, Gautama took a vow: "Never from this seat will I stir, until I have attained the supreme and absolute wisdom." Māra, the demon of delusions, and his legions attempted to divert Gautama from his purpose. Gautama remained steadfast, however, and Māra's efforts failed. The demons left at sunset, and that night, while meditating, Gautama received the revelation he desired. He became the Buddha, "the enlightened one."

Grass-and-mud platforms similar to the one used by the Buddha continue to be built today around the largest pipal tree in each village of northern India. The platforms provide settings for religious discussions among each village's spiritual leaders. The Buddha's seat came to be called the Bodhimanda, or "Seat of Enlightenment" and, later, the Vajrāsana, or "Adamantine Throne." It was perceived to be the center of the universe.

According to tradition, the Buddha remained in Bodh Gayā for seven weeks after receiving enlightenment, then ventured out to spread his doctrine. He taught that individuals could achieve spiritual salvation not by sacrificial rituals or by the efforts of priests, but through one's own efforts of self-discipline, purity of thought, and ethical conduct. Bodh Gayā became the holiest of the four most important sites associated with the Buddha's life. The others are Kapilavastu, attributed as his birthplace; Sārnāth, near Vārānasī, where he preached his first sermon after his enlightenment; and Kusinārā, where he died.

A sacred pipal tree still grows at Bodh Gayā; it shades a stone platform (identified as the Vajrāsana) beneath it. A relatively short-lived species, the tree that stands today could not possibly be the one under which Buddha sat. There is credible evidence, however, that it descends directly from the original Bo-tree, the subject of numerous legends. According to one, the third-century B.C. emperor Aśoka, before embracing Buddhism, destroyed and burned the sacred tree or its descendant, condemning tree-worship as foolish and unproductive. Miraculously, it regenerated from the ashes. Aśoka prayed so fervently in remorse for his actions that he forgot to return home. His angry queen had the tree destroyed again that night, but it came to life once more. Another legend states that Aśoka, having embraced Buddhism in his remorse over his wars of conquest and the suffering he had caused, often would visit the Bo-tree to pay homage. His second wife, resentful of her husband's frequent absences, uprooted the

Mahābodhi Temple, Bodh Gayā
Photo courtesy of Milton Mann

tree. Grief-stricken, the emperor tended the root with great care and built a huge temple there.

Still another story states that when Aśoka sent his son Mahendra and his daughter Saṅghamitrā to Sri Lanka, they brought with them a sapling of the original tree; it grew into a tree that now flourishes in Anurādhapura. Centuries later, when the original tree was burned by a hostile king, a sapling from Sri Lanka was returned to Bodh Gayā, producing the tree that grows today. According to one other account, in the sixth century A.D. King Śaśāṅka dug up the ground where the Bodhi-druma stood and saturated the earth with sugar-cane juice to prevent the tree from growing again. Through the pious deeds of King Pūrṇavarmā, last descendant of Aśoka, the tree was renewed again and a wall constructed around it; this wall was observed by the Chinese Buddhist pilgrim Xuan Zang, who first visited India around 635 A.D. In 1811, a British antiquarian reported the tree to be healthy, but not more than 100 years old. In 1862, another British archaeologist, Alexander Cunningham, found the pipal tree nearly decayed with only a single healthy stem; in 1876, its last vestiges were blown down in a storm. Shortly thereafter, in the same spot, a seedling from this tree was planted to produce the tree that is venerated today.

Next to the Bodhi-tree, between 259 and 241 B.C., Emperor Aśoka built a small temple, or *vihar,* known as the Vajrāsana Mulagandhakuti Vihāra. It contained a stone slab, the Vajrāsana, commemorating the place where the Buddha sat, surrounded by pillars. The remains of the slab lie between the present temple and the Bo-tree. Aśoka also built a cloister over the path near the Bo-tree where Gautama was said to have walked while debating revealing his message to the world; as he walked, flowers grew beneath his feet. The Chankramana, or Holy Walk, now in ruins, runs along the northern side of the present temple, and is carved with lotus flowers to commemorate the real ones that are said to have appeared in the Buddha's wake. It is also known as the Jewel Walk. Little else now remains of Aśoka's temple except fragments of the entrance and foundation.

Just east of the sacred pipal stands the impressive Mahābodhi Temple (Temple of the Great Enlightenment). Several theories exist concerning the temple's construction, but it was most likely built in the sixth century A.D. The temple, said to have been inspired by a vision, was described by Xuan Zang in the seventh century:

> The building is of blue tiles covered with chunam (lime). The four sides of the temple are covered with impressive ornamental decorations which contribute to the overall impression of poise and balance. The eastern face adjoins a storeyed pavlion, the projecting caves of which rise one above the other to the height of three distinct chambers; its projecting caves, pillars, beams, doors and windows are decorated with gold and silver ornamented work, with pearls and gems. All the niches in the different storeys contain golden figures.

The massive temple found by Cunningham, although devoid of gold and silver adornment, corresponds almost exactly in size and appearance to the one Xuan Zang described. Much renovated, it still stands at the site. It is approximately 170 feet high and 50 feet square at its base, with an elaborately ornamented stone spire surrounded by four smaller towers, one at each corner of the square base. The smaller spires are believed to have been added by Burmese Buddhists in the fourteenth century. Cunningham detected a bluish tint to the temple's dark red brick exterior and noticed traces of plaster all over it. The archaeologist also saw that the exterior walls were ornamented with eight tiers of niches, many still holding figures of Buddha. Inside the temple sits a colossal gilded image of the Buddha, his finger touching the earth in the classic pose of enlightenment; an upper chamber holds a statue of Queen Māyā, his mother.

Surrounding the temple are railings, originally attributed to Aśoka, but now dated to the later Suṅga period (184–72 B.C.). Some of the carvings adorning the railings narrate the story of the Buddha while others portray graceful, animated scenes from everyday life. No matter who was responsible for them, the railings are among the oldest and best-preserved sculptured monuments in India. Some parts of them have been removed to museums in Calcutta and London.

A Burmese inscription at Bodh Gayā, dated A.D. 948, ascribes the temple to Amara Deva, said to be an important member of the court of King Vikrāmaditya. This fact serves to identify him with the historical figure Amara Simha and places him at about A.D. 500 (another record indicates that an Amara Deva built a large temple around that date). Moreover, Fa Xian, a Chinese pilgrim who visited Bodh Gayā in the early fifth century, 200 years before Xuan Zang's journey, made no mention of the larger temple, although he mentioned the earlier Aśokan construction. Therefore, the Mahābodhi Temple must have been constructed between the two pilgrims' visits.

Buddhism began to decline in India, ironically, about the time the Mahābodhi Temple was built. The religion's problems included political persecution from without and a loss of vitality from within. Hinduism gained more adherents, in the process absorbing some of Buddhism's characteristics, with Hindus regarding Buddha as an incarnation of Vishnu, one of the three major Hindu deities. In the Middle Ages, Bodh Gayā became a site of worship for Hindus. At this time Buddhism, although it had become the major religion of eastern Asia, was further eclipsed in India by the growth of Islam. All the same, Buddhist pilgrims continued to journey to Bodh Gayā, where the temple and its surroundings went through various periods of decay and renovation.

During the early period of British rule in India, the Bodh Gayā area attracted the attention of historians. Soon after the temple was found buried in debris in 1774, excavation and reconstruction efforts were undertaken. In 1876, the king of Burma sent a mission to make repairs, but this group worked without regard for archaeological accuracy, prompting the government of Bengal to ask a celebrated Sanskrit scholar, Rājendralāla Mitra, to visit the area and report on the activity. Consequently, Bengal assumed responsibility for the restoration, which was completed in 1894 under the supervision of Cunningham and Mitra.

Because of a general rise in the land level, the temple now sits in the middle of a large sunken courtyard dotted with numerous shrines of varying sizes, from actual temples to tiny models. These represent only a small portion of those excavated since limitations of space would not allow for more. Before their removal was prohibited, hundreds were taken away as souvenirs. Buddhist monasteries have been built here by the Japanese, Thai, Chinese, Burmese, and Tibetans, each in their own architectural style. A Hindu temple and monastery also are nearby, as is the Buddha Archaeological Museum, housing ancient and rare Buddhist sculpture.

Since the site's restoration, Buddhists and Hindus both have continued to lay claim to Bodh Gayā. Hindu priests had run the temple since the sixteenth century, but in 1947 Buddhists gained a role through the Bodh Gayā Temple Management Act, passed by the Bihar state assembly. It established a committee made up of equal numbers of Hindus and Buddhists, with the chairmanship (and decisive vote) going to the Gayā district magistrate, providing that person was a Hindu; if not, another Hindu official would be deputized.

The arrangement has not had the wholehearted support of Buddhists, who see it as another effort by the Hindus to reassimilate them into their religion. Hindu priests have fixed a Sivaliṅgam (a representation of the Hindu god Siva) in front of the golden Buddha inside the temple, positioned their own idols in adjacent buildings, and adorned other statues of the Buddha with the robes of Hindu deities. This is particularly distressing to the many who have converted to Buddhism as a means to escape the stigma associated with their caste. Indian Buddhists now wish for full control of the temple and its grounds, but local Hindus insist that because they consider Buddha an incarnation of Vishnu, the site should be open to Hindu deities and ceremonies as well. On May 16, 1992, the anniversary of the Buddha's enlightenment, the dispute reached a peak: Buddhist pilgrims and Hindu priests engaged in vociferous argument and even a bit of physical violence in the temple, leading Buddhist priests to demand complete administrative control of the site. As of this writing, no resolution had been reached, and both Buddhists and Hindus continue to worship at Bodh Gayā in an uneasy coexistence.

Further Reading: *Archaeological Survey of India: Four Reports Made during the Years 1862–65*, volume 1, by Alexander Cunningham (Calcutta: C. B. Lewis, 1863–64; Delhi and Varanasi, Indological Book House, 1972) contains the preeminent archaeologist's first-hand, detailed report of the structures found in the Gayā area and his conclusions regarding their history supported by the contributions of previous scholars. *Buddha Gayā Temple, Its History* by Dipak K. Barua (Bodh Gayā: Bodh Gayā Temple Management Committee, 1975) chronicles the temple's history and art, recent activities, the Temple Act and by-laws, and contains a section that presents both the Buddhist and Hindu points of view. *The Bodhgayā Temple* by Tarapada Bhattacharyya (second edition, Calcutta: Firma K. L. Mukhopadhya, 1966) aims to justify the Hindu claim to Bodh Gayā. *Buddhagayā Temple and the Hindu-Buddhist Conflict* by M. P. Chowdhury (Calcutta: Cultural Heritage of Pakistan and Bangladesh Series, 1982) is a treatise written to urge the protection of the temple as a Buddhist historical and cultural site. *Encyclopaedia of Religion and Ethics*, volume 6, edited by James Hastings (13 vols., Edinburgh: Clark, and New York: Scribner, 1908–27) presents a well-rounded historical overview of the Bodh Gayā area.

—Linda Pollak

Bombay (Mahārāshtra, India)

Location: On the Arabian Sea on the west coast of India; once a group of seven islands, Bombay was linked by land reclamation in the nineteenth century and has now expanded on the mainland.

Description: The principal commercial and financial city of India, Bombay is the country's second largest city (after Calcutta) and one of the largest in the world, noted for its vital industries (including textiles, finance, and filmmaking) as well as for the extreme poverty of many of its residents. Once known as the Gateway to India, its port still handles half of the nation's foreign trade. Although its site has been inhabited since prehistoric times, the city of Bombay dates only to the arrival of the British in the seventeenth century. The years of British rule are evident in many historic buildings of Bombay.

Site Office: Government of India Tourist Office
123 Maharishi Karve Road
Bombay 400 200, Mahārāshtra
India
(20) 32932, (20) 33144, (20) 33145, or (20) 36054

Although Bombay did not begin to develop as a city until the seventeenth century, its site has been occupied since the Stone Age, as evidenced by the presence of stone tools in the surrounding area. By 1,000 B.C. the region was heavily involved in seaborne commerce with Egypt and Persia. In the third century B.C. the settlement here was part of the realm of Aśoka, whose Mauryan Empire covered much of present-day India. From the sixth to the eighth centuries A.D. the site was dominated by the Cāḷukyas, a people who left their mark on nearby Elephanta Island (then known as the fortified settlement of Ghārāpuri) in the form of Hindu cave temples. A group of Buddhist caves, probably used as retreats by monks, is at Kāṇheri, twenty-six miles north of Bombay, and dates from roughly the same era.

The settlement of Mahikavati (Māhīm) was founded on Bombay Island in 1294 by the Yādava Kingdom in response to raids on their capital at Deogiri (modern Daulatābād) by the Khaljī sultan of Delhi. Many of Bombay's current residents trace their ancestry to this settlement; many of the place names on the island originated at this time as well. In 1348 Muslim forces conquered the region and incorporated it into the Kingdom of Gujarāt. In 1507 the Portuguese tried but failed to conquer Māhīm; but in 1534 Sultan Bahādur Shāh, the ruler of Gujarāt, ceded (in the Treaty of Bassein) the seven islands to the Portuguese, who divided the land among a variety of religious orders and individuals either on a rental basis or as a reward for military service. At this time the islands still were marshy, malarial, and largely undeveloped. Their principal inhabitants were fishermen known as Kolis, from whose name the word "coolie" derives; many of their descendants found work in low-skill service jobs as Bombay grew. Also in 1534, Bassein, across the river that separates the mainland from Bombay Island, was captured by the Portuguese and developed into a fortified city complete with cathedral, churches, and palaces. Today most of Bassein is in ruins, the result of its conquest by the Marāṭhās in 1739; the same fate befell another Portuguese settlement, Chaul, south of Bombay, which was in Portuguese hands from 1522 to 1739.

In 1626, Māhīm came under attack from British and Dutch forces, and although many buildings were destroyed by fire, the Portuguese managed to retain control of the islands. In 1661 Bombay Island was ceded to Britain as part of the marriage agreement between King Charles II of England and Catherine of Braganza, sister of King Peter II of Portugal. In 1664 the British Crown officially took possession of the island; in 1668 the Crown leased it to the British East India Company, which set up headquarters on the island in 1672. The company previously had maintained a base farther north along the coast at Surat. The company reformed taxation, established courts, built fortifications, and enacted rules providing for freedom of trade and religion. This marked the beginning of the development of modern Bombay, which had a population of 50,000 by century's end. Even so, Samuel Pepys called the place "a poor little island" and wrote that the king had been duped as to the true value of the site. The name the British gave the city derived from a combination of native and Portuguese sources. The natives knew the site as Mumba Devi, named for the local goddess Mumba, an incarnation of Pārvatī, the consort of Siva. The Portuguese called the site Bombaim, taken from their words *buan bahai,* meaning "good bay." "Bombay" appears to be a British combination of the two names for the area.

About the time of the British takeover, in the 1670s, the Parsis (or Parsees) came to live in Bombay. Parsis are adherents of Zoroastrianism, a religion founded in Persia (hence the name given to its followers) by the prophet Zoroaster in the seventh or sixth century B.C. As Islam spread in Persia, many Zoroastrians fled to northwestern India. Today Bombay is one of the three important Parsi centers remaining in the world, along with Karachi, in Pakistan, and Shīrāz, in Iran. Zoroastrianism was one of the first religions to claim the existence of an omnipotent and invisible god; this god is known as Ahura Mazdā, the god of light, and is symbolized by fire. Parsis believe in the sanctity of earth, air, fire, and water, so they will not cremate or bury their dead; instead, they leave them on top of Towers of Silence, where the corpses are consumed by vultures. The first Tower of Silence

Rājabāī Tower, University of Bombay
Photo courtesy of Air India Library, New York

in Bombay was built in 1675, and today there are a number on the summit of Malabar Hill, in the western part of the city; they are well shielded from public view.

The Parsis also established a shipbuilding industry that was the basis of Bombay's economy until the nineteenth century. The Parsis, the British, and a substantial community of Sephardic Jews generally worked well together and developed Bombay into a sophisticated, tolerant city. Such cooperation was necessary for survival, as Bombay at this time was largely isolated from the rest of India, both because of geographical features such as the Western Ghāts mountains and political ones such as warfare by the Marāṭhās of central India.

The first British governor of Bombay was Gerald Aungier, a charismatic figure who usually had his meals preceded by trumpet fanfares and accompanied by music. During his tenure trade increased and English institutions began to supersede Portuguese ones. An important monument dating from this time is the Cathedral of St. Thomas, begun during the governorship of Aungier in 1672 and opened in 1718. In the nineteenth century marble sculptures—many by the same sculptors who had designed similar works for the interior of St. Paul's Cathedral in London—were installed in the interior. Toward the end of the seventeenth century, Calcutta was founded, and it soon eclipsed Bombay as the most important administrative and commercial city of British India. Nevertheless, the development of Bombay continued during the eighteenth century. The Temple of Walkeshwar, an important Hindu pilgrimage site, dates from this time. According to the epic poem *Rāmāyaṇa,* Prince Rāma, the hero of the story, rested at this site on his way from Ayodhyā to Lanka to rescue the princess Sita from the clutches of the evil King Ravanna. The original temple was built approximately 1,000 years ago; the current temple dates from 1715 and is located on Malabar Point.

Communication links with mainland India and with Europe were strengthened continuously during the eighteenth and nineteenth centuries. A fire destroyed much of Bombay in 1803, but the city was rebuilt and improved. The early part of the nineteenth century also saw the abolition of the East India Company's trade monopoly and the gradual pacification of the Marāṭhās (achieved only after the British waged three separate wars with them between 1775 and 1818), both factors that encouraged the growth of commerce in Bombay. In the middle of the century, Bombay entered a period of rapid development. In 1847, St. John's Church (also known as the

Afghan Church) was built in the southern part of the Colaba Peninsula; it was dedicated to soldiers who died in the Sind campaign in 1838 and the First Afghan War in 1843. In 1854 a railway link was established between Bombay and other Indian cities, and later the Victoria Terminus and Churchgate Station were opened; after the Indian Mutiny of 1857, Bombay was portrayed as a safe place to live and work in comparison to the northern cities that had suffered insurrections. In the 1850s the first spinning and weaving mill was established in Bombay, and the city became a cotton milling center, a role it continues to occupy. The fledgling industry received a boost during the U.S. Civil War, when cotton exports from the United States were cut off, and Bombay began supplying cotton to Britain and elsewhere. This led to a massive growth of business and industry, which continued even after the war's end. In 1862, a major land reclamation project drained the areas between the islands and joined them into one piece of land. The governor at the time, Sir Bartle Frere, demolished the walls of the old fort and encouraged new construction. By 1864 Bombay's population exceeded 800,000 and was continuing to grow. In 1869 the Flora Fountain (now renamed Hutatma Chowk) was built in honor of Frere and his role in the city's economic development. The area around the fountain is still the center of Bombay's business district, home to major banks and numerous corporate headquarters.

After 1869, with the opening of the Suez Canal and the establishment of trade routes from India to England through the Mediterranean rather than around the Cape of Good Hope, Bombay prospered even more. It became the subcontinent's leading port and was dubbed the Gateway to India. During the second half of the nineteenth century, many civic and public buildings were constructed in Bombay in Victorian Gothic style. Examples of buildings in this style include the Secretariat (1874), the Council Hall (1876), and Elphinstone College (1890). The buildings of the university are in Victorian Gothic style and are dominated by the 260-foot-high Rājabāī Clock Tower, which rises above the university library. Beyond the university is the High Court building, topped by statues of Justice and Mercy and completed in 1878. The most impressive example of Victorian Gothic, however, is the Victorian Terminus, the massive railroad station completed in 1887, Queen Victoria's Golden Jubilee Year. Its huge central dome is surmounted by a statue personifying Progress; it was carved by Thomas Earp, who also produced the statues of the lion (symbol of the British Empire) and tiger (symbol of India) that adorn the station's gate. The building was constructed during a time of debate over whether Britain should impose its architectural designs, believed to convey the superiority of Western culture, on India or help develop native styles. The building is evidence of the victory by supporters of Western design, but its decorative motifs show some concessions to native Indian styles. Another late-nineteenth-century project was the Hanging Gardens, developed in 1881 on Malabar Hill atop reservoirs that supply Bombay with water. The gardens are distinguished by a number of hedges cut into animal shapes. Malabar Hill today is one of Bombay's wealthier residential areas; its elevation makes it cooler than the lower-lying parts of the city, and the hill offers the further advantage of excellent views.

Bombay's late-nineteenth-century development, in addition to its natural beauty, impressed its visitors. In the 1870s the British writer Edward Lear wrote of Bombay Harbor's "extreme beauty" and expressed "violent and amazing delight at the wonderful variety of life and dress here." There was another side to the city's development, however. As its population grew, so did its slums, which were marked by dire poverty and squalid living conditions. There was a plague epidemic in 1896. The City Improvement Trust, established at this time, partially alleviated the problems by constructing new housing for the artisan classes, but poverty continued to grow as people moved to the city in ever-increasing numbers.

Landmark buildings continued to be constructed in Bombay. According to legend, in the late nineteenth century the industrialist Jamshetji Nusserwanji Tata, an important Parsi businessman and the founder of the Indian steel industry, was thrown out of Watson's, at that time the leading hotel in Bombay. In response he created the Tāj Mahal Hotel, the grandest in the city, which opened in 1903 and featured an electric laundry, a post office, a pharmacy and medical office, and Turkish baths. For a long time the hotel was unique in that it accepted Indian guests. It is still regarded as one of the most magnificent hotels in the world; like the Raffles Hotel in Singapore, it has attracted prominent guests from all over the world. The original hotel is a huge edifice of crenellated towers, battlements, and domes; adjacent is a modern, high-rise wing. In 1926 Aldous Huxley wrote that "the gigantic Tāj combines the style of the South Kensington Natural History Museum with that of an Indian pavilion at an International Exhibition."

In 1923 the Prince of Wales Museum of Western India was opened in palatial buildings opposite the Council Hall, near the harbor. It was built to commemorate the visit of King George V to India in 1905, when he was still Prince of Wales. The museum has sections devoted to art, paintings, archaeology, and natural history, and includes the Jahāngīr Art Gallery. In 1924 Bombay's most famous landmark, the Gateway of India, was officially opened; it is a gigantic triumphal archway that still dominates the harborside next to the Tāj Mahal Hotel. It was built to commemorate the visit of King George V and Queen Mary in 1911.

While these buildings commemorating British rule of India were being constructed, the movement for Indian self-government was developing. Support for greater Indian autonomy had been growing since the 1850s, when the coming of the railways facilitated communications between Bombay and the other large cities of India. All these cities had a fair number of proponents of self-rule, drawn largely from the middle and upper classes of native Indians. With improvements in transportation they could meet, exchange ideas, and develop plans for reform. In 1885 Bombay hosted

Victoria Terminus, Bombay
Photo courtesy of Air India Library, New York

the first meeting of the Indian National Congress; this organization initially was formed with the stated goal of strengthening the British Empire in India, but it evolved into a movement for independence. The congress met annually, changing cities each year. By the time it met at Bombay again in 1889, it had 1,000 delegates, compared with 71 in 1885. Bombay also hosted the congress in 1904, 1915, 1918, and 1934, with 1918 being a particularly important year. At that meeting the Indian nationalists, who had come to dominate the congress, rejected as inadequate British plans, as spelled out in the Montagu-Chelmsford Report, for limited provincial autonomy and direct popular election of legislators. The British enacted the reforms anyway. Many of the more moderate members of the congress, who wanted to accept the reform package, resigned. Within two years the congress endorsed the goal of complete self-rule and rallied behind a charismatic new leader, Mohandas Karamchand Gandhi (also known as the Mahatma). Britain finally granted India its independence in 1947, and the last British troops left the country from the Gateway of India arch in 1948.

Since independence Bombay has continued to be India's leading commercial and industrial city. The stock exchange is here, and the business district has a skyline rivaling Manhattan's. Bombay resembles another U.S. community as well; as the center of Indian film production, it is the country's version of Hollywood, and indeed is second only to Hong Kong in film production worldwide. Many Indian movie stars live in the Malabar Hill area. Bombay has become quite Westernized and is a city of great vitality despite the dire poverty of many of its inhabitants.

This poverty and the accompanying squalor, however, are often the features most noted by observers. The writer Arthur Koestler, visiting Bombay in 1960, wrote that the "sewers of Bombay had been opened by mistake . . . the damp heat, impregnated by their stench invaded the air-conditioned cabin . . . I had the sensation that a wet, smelly diaper was being wrapped around my head by some abominable joker." In his work *India: A Wounded Civilization* (1977), V. S. Naipaul wrote about the plight of the 1,500 people who moved into Bombay each day. In the shanty towns, he wrote, "we walked without speaking, picking our way between squirts and butts and twists of human excrement. It was unclean to clean; it was unclean even to notice." A different side to Bombay was noted by Naipaul's brother Shiva Naipaul in *Beyond the Dragon's Mouth* (1984). Writing about the variety of life and business in the teeming city, Naipaul remarked that

> A walk along any stretch of pavement will reveal a hundred minute specializations of function, a hundred strategies for survival. You can hawk anything; water, nuts, cheap pens, toys, peacock feathers, religious bric-a-brac, plastic flowers, aphrodisiacs, quack medicines, lottery tickets, hard-luck stories . . . you can grind lenses, repair broken locks, stitch leather, sell cage birds, charm snakes, read palms, interpret dreams, clean out the ears of passers-by; you can parade your dancing monkey, display your acrobatic skills, pick pockets. The will to live is capable of infinite articulation. When life is hard, a man will do anything.

In the late twentieth century, the government of Bombay and that of the state of Mahārāshtra (of which Bombay has been capital since the partition of Bombay state in 1960) have taken steps to ease the city's overcrowding. In the 1990s a twin city was being developed on the mainland across from the original island site of Bombay, and other developments were being built in the southern part of Bombay to attract people from the more crowded north. Additionally, the state government has sought to encourage industry to locate in less congested areas.

Further Reading: Philip Ward's *Western India: Bombay, Maharashtra, Karnataka* (Cambridge: Oleander, 1991) is a detailed practical and personal book on Bombay and the surrounding area, part travelogue and part practical guide. A good general history of India is *A Traveller's History of India* by Sinharaja Tammita-Delgoda (Moreton-in-Marsh, Gloucestershire: Windrush, 1994; Brooklyn, New York: Interlink, 1995). V. S. Naipaul wrote about the condition of modern India in *An Area of Darkness* (London: Deutsch, 1964; New York: Macmillan, 1965) and *India: A Wounded Civilization* (London: Deutsch, and New York: Knopf, 1977). The *Penguin Guide to the Monuments of India* (London and New York: Viking, 1989) is in two volumes: volume 1 by George Michell covers Buddhist and Hindu sites, and volume 2 by Philip Davies deals with Islamic and European sites. *India: A Literary Companion* by Bruce Palling (London: John Murray, 1992) contains a number of first-hand accounts written by travelers.

—Andrew Beattie and Trudy Ring

Borobudur (Central Java, Indonesia)

Location: On the Kedu Plain in Central Java, near the town of Magelang.

Description: Massive Buddhist temple constructed between A.D. 760 and 830 but soon neglected with the rise of Hinduism and later Islam; restored successively since 1907. The Borobudur complex includes the smaller, related temples of Mendut and Pawon.

Contact: Direktorat Pariwisata Daerah Jawa Tengah
Jl Veteran
Semarang, Central Java
Indonesia
(24) 24146

The Kedu plain of Central Java is one of the most fertile agricultural regions of the world. Abundantly watered by tropical monsoons and fertilized by ash from surrounding volcanoes, Kedu was an early center of population in the Indonesian archipelago and became the center of a rich ancient Javanese civilization that began to emerge during the sixth century A.D.

Nothing definite is known of Javanese society before this time, but it seems that local lords, controlling the intricate irrigation systems that were the basis of the economy, delivered rice to the trading economies of maritime Southeast Asia and received in return not just trade goods—especially cloth and metalwork from India and China—but also Indian ideas of kingship. Hindu-Buddhist cosmology exalted rulers to the status of incarnations of the gods or of the Buddha and provided an appealing rationale for the growing social difference between rulers and ruled, which became more and more marked as trading wealth concentrated in rulers' hands. Although Buddhism was a minority religion in its native India, it spread widely in Southeast Asia, thanks in part to active Buddhist missionaries.

To mark and consolidate their new status and power, the lords of central Java began building a series of religious monuments, both Hindu and Buddhist, in Kedu and on the nearby Prambanan Plain. There is some evidence that the Hindu and Buddhist monuments were constructed by rival dynasties, the Hindu Sanjaya clan and the Buddhist Śailendras. However, the doctrinal distinctions between Hinduism and Buddhism in this era were not pronounced, and rulers may well have sponsored construction for both religions as part of a policy of religious inclusiveness. The era of temple building in central Java largely ended in the tenth century, when an unknown calamity struck the region and the centers of power moved to the eastern part of the island.

Borobudur is the largest of the central Java temples. It was constructed over a period of about sixty years using more than a million blocks of volcanic rock, each weighing approximately 220 pounds, collected from nearby rivers and fitted tightly together—without the use of mortar—to form a dome-shaped structure on the foundation of an existing small hill; the entire structure is about 3.2 acres in area. The many galleries were then intricately carved to illustrate Buddhist doctrine. Finally, the structure was covered with white plaster (now all but gone) on which still greater detail was painted and incised. The construction is a remarkable testimony both to the capacity of the Kedu lords to mobilize their people on a long-term project that had no direct economic value, and to the priority that early Javanese society placed on religious observance. No secular building from the era has been found to compare remotely in scale to Borobudur and the other temples: religious edifices, not palaces, were the main signifier of glory for the early Javanese rulers. The scale of the carving, too, is evidence of well-established artistic traditions in early Java.

Nothing definite is known about the specific religious rituals for which Borobudur was used, although there is archaeological evidence of both a Buddhist monastery and a secular village in the vicinity of the temple. Scholars are divided over whether all parts of the monument were open to all believers or whether some parts may have been restricted to people of higher religious status. Such restrictions were becoming widespread in Buddhism at the time of Borobudur's construction, but there is no evidence from the structure that any part was closed to the general public. Most scholars believe that Borobudur was a place of both instruction and religious observance. Although the monument is capacious, it has no single space to accommodate a large crowd; thus religious activity there was probably conducted individually or in small groups.

The Borobudur complex includes the two much smaller temples of Mendut and Pawon located slightly less than two miles to the east, in direct line with the temple's main entrance. Although they were built at about the same time as Borobudur and were almost certainly a part of the same pilgrimage route, they are architecturally distinct. Both have inner chambers that can be entered through narrow doorways, and Mendut contains a massive statue of the Buddha flanked by two bodhisattvas.

Borobudur is a complex monument: intricate symbolism may be discerned in the profile of the structure as a whole, in the layout of its parts, and in the detail of the delicately carved panels that line the galleries. This meaning comes mainly from Buddhist cosmology, but archaeological excavation during the restoration has shown that Borobudur was built on top of an older pre-Buddhist structure of three massive stone terraces, suggesting that the site, if not the actual form, of the temple may have been influenced by earlier beliefs.

A view of the temple at Borobudur
Photo courtesy of Indonesia Tourist Promotion Office, Los Angeles

Borobudur was constructed as a raised cap on an existing hill, and its form was intended to be that of a mountain. In pre-Buddhist Javanese cosmology, mountains were places of special spiritual power, and this belief easily blended with the Mahayana Buddhist reverence for mountains as reflections of the cosmic Mount Sumeru (or Meru), which lies at the heart of the cosmos, surrounded by concentric rings of mountain ranges and oceans. For the early Javanese, mountains and symbolic representations of mountains gave access to the power of the cosmos. Constructing and controlling a spiritually perfect representation of Mount Sumeru was one sure way of accumulating cosmic power.

On the slopes of Mount Sumeru and in the sky above it, according to Buddhist cosmology, are twenty-eight heavens representing stages in the Buddhist search for release from worldly passion. These stages are reflected in the character of the terraces that comprise Borobudur. The lower terraces are rectilinear, with high outer balustrades and many ninety-degree corners. Ornately carved with stories from the lives of the Buddha and illustrations of other Buddhist texts, these terraces represent the stage of human life in which the distractions of the world prevail. The details of the carvings attract human attention, while the high balustrades and sharp corners keep one's vision focused on the immediate environment; only glimpses of Borobudur's commanding view of the Kedu Plain are possible on these levels. Steep stairs between the levels reflect the effort needed to make spiritual progress.

The three uppermost terraces, by contrast, are circular and completely unadorned except for seventy-two bell-shaped stupas or reliquaries, each containing a statue of the seated Buddha visible through stone latticework. The panorama of forest, mountain, and ricefield visible from these levels symbolizes the insight that Buddhists achieve at higher levels of meditation. At the center of the temple is a single, larger stupa, originally crowned with a pillar (now lost) at the top of which was a thirteen-tiered umbrella, the Indian symbol of divine royalty. Borobudur is now only 103 feet high (an early archaeologist described it with some disappointment as resembling a badly-risen cake), but in its original form it appeared much higher. Just what purpose the stupas served remains unclear since any relics they might once have housed were removed by plunderers well before the restoration. Nevertheless, they certainly represent the peaks of the cosmic mountain in the overall form of the temple.

Buddha images are found not only in the stupas but on the balustrades of the lower terraces. All are seated, but they have been carved with their hands in various positions, or *mudras,* symbolizing different points of Buddhist philoso-

Relief sculptures at Borobudur temple
Photo courtesy of Indonesia Tourist Promotion Office, Los Angeles

phy. The Buddhas represented inside the stupas touch the tip of the index finger of their left hands with the tip of the ring finger of their right. This *dharmacakra* (the turning of the wheel of doctrine) *mudra* represents the role of the Buddha's teaching in starting the process of salvation. On the eastern flank of the temple, ninety-two statues display the *bhumisparsa* (touching the earth) *mudra,* which represents the Buddha's struggle with the demon Mara. To the south, another ninety-two statues hold their right hands with palm up in the *vara mudra,* which symbolizes charity. On the west, ninety-two right hands rest contemplatively in ninety-two left hands, all palms facing upward in the meditative *dhyani mudra,* while the northern statues—again ninety-two in number—hold their right hands up, palms outward, to quell fear in the *abhaya mudra.* The topmost Buddha statues on each side, sixty-four in all, hold their hands in the *vitarka mudra,* symbolizing preaching.

The most detailed message of Borobudur, however, lies in its carvings. In all, 1,460 panels adorn the walls and balustrades of the terraces, forming a wonderful treasury of artistic work. The panels illustrate five Buddhist scriptures with different roles in Buddhist doctrine. Each series begins at the temple's eastern stairway and leads the pilgrim clockwise around the monument. In general, the lower panels provide simple, concrete messages, while the panels on the upper galleries present more abstract doctrine. Some of the panels correspond to no known version of the scriptures (the artists who carved Borobudur were presumably working from texts that have since been lost), and scholars disagree on the meaning of every panel.

The carvings around the base of Borobudur, representing the Visions of Worldly Desire, were visible to pilgrims without their actually having to enter the temple, and offered simple moral precepts, showing the rewards and punishments that follow good or evil acts. Killers of sheep, for instance, are shown having their heads sawn through. Only a few of these panels are now visible. Soon after the construction of Borobudur, the architects found that they needed to strengthen the structure by building a broad platform around the base. There is no reason to believe the apocryphal story that the panels were covered because their depiction of sin and punishment was too graphic. The panels were rediscovered and photographed in the late nineteenth century, but the platform was then restored and they have not been seen since, except for a small section left uncovered as a sample.

The lowest of the four main galleries shows four series of reliefs, two on either side, and there is evidence that pilgrims were expected to pass along this gallery at least twice. The Jataka stories recount earlier lives of the Buddha, most of them showing the Buddha's outstanding compassion: incarnated as a hare, for instance, he flings himself into a fire to provide food for a wandering priest; in another sequence that echoes a fable of Aesop, the Buddha as a bird generously removes a bone from the throat of a tiger. The Avadana stories simply tell moral tales of selflessness and its spiritual rewards. The upper series of panels on the main wall of the first gallery tells the story of the Buddha himself, from his descent to earth to be born, his youth as a pampered prince, his renunciation of that life and search for truth, his enlightenment, and finally his first sermon, in which the fundamental truths of Buddhism were at last set out clearly for humans, who could then begin the long process of seeking salvation. This is the moment symbolized by the *dharmacakra mudra* of the Buddha statues on the topmost terraces.

The balustrade of the second gallery continues the Jataka and Avadana stories, but the rest of the three upper galleries tell the long story of a young man named Sudhana and his search for wisdom. The panels chart Sudhana's journey from teacher to teacher until he reaches the palace of the Maitreya Buddha (Mahayana Buddhism's Buddha-to-come), where he finally receives the highest wisdom. The story of Sudhana is much more difficult to follow in the panels than are the relatively straightforward narratives depicted in the lower gallery; these panels assume that the visitor is already thoroughly familiar with the story. At each stage of Sudhana's journey, "good friends" impart elements of wisdom and understanding to him, the message being both that the path to enlightenment is long and that the compassion and assistance of others is necessary to traverse it. Once in the Maitreya's palace, Sudhana learns more both from the direct example of the Maitreya and from visions of many kinds.

The carvings of Borobudur are important not only for their artistry and their explication of Buddhist doctrine, but for the insights they provide about life in early ninth-century Java. In particular, the carvings confirm the antiquity of many elements of Javanese culture known from later eras. The instruments of the distinctive gamelan orchestra, including gongs, cymbals, lutes, and trumpets, are seen in several places. Houses, on the other hand, resemble styles still found in Sumatra but long gone from Java. A large outrigger vessel sails the ocean, typical of the seacraft that Javanese traders took to China and India in the great age of Southeast Asian commerce before the European arrival in the sixteenth century. Ploughing and harvesting grain are shown in intricate detail; so is fishing and hunting. For the most part, both men and women are unclothed above the waist, as was still common on Bali until the nineteenth century. Realistic elephants appear many times, suggesting that, although they were not indigenous to Java, they may have been imported, perhaps from Sumatra, for warfare and display.

With the shift of political power from central to eastern Java during the tenth century and the gradual penetration of Islam from the fourteenth century, Borobudur was neglected. The temple seems to have remained a site of pilgrimage for some time, but by the nineteenth century it was overgrown with jungle and partly buried in the ash of volcanic eruptions. For the local Javanese, Borobudur was little more than a hill of some spiritual power where a visitor could see famous images such as the stone "warrior in a cage." Only in 1814, on the initiative of Sir Thomas Stamford Raffles, who was briefly British lieutenant governor of Java during the Napoleonic Wars, were the first efforts made to clear the monument of vegetation and soil. Scholars recognized at once that this was a major archaeological discovery, and debate began over the identity of the monument's builders. For many years the view prevailed that the Javanese could never have created such a work of art, and that Borobudur must have been built by colonists from India. This opinion, which has been laid to rest by more detailed archaeological work carried out since the early twentieth century, is still occasionally given by poorly informed sources.

Considerable damage was done to the ruins during the nineteenth century. The temple became once more a destination for pilgrims and tourists, whose unsupervised activities put pressure on the fragile fabric of the temple. Further damage was done by looters who hoped to find hidden treasures in the stonework. In 1896, moreover, the Dutch colonial government marked the visit of the Buddhist monarch of Siam, King Rama V (better known as Chulalongkorn), by presenting him with eight cartloads of reliefs and sculptures from the monument. On top of this, weathering had begun to cause serious damage to the exposed stone, while seepage through the cracks between the stones had eroded the loose foundation of the monument, leaving parts of it vulnerable to collapse. By the turn of the century, Borobudur was in a sorry state indeed.

Early in the twentieth century, fortunately, the colonial government realized the need to preserve and restore Borobudur, and in 1907 restoration work began under the direction of a young military engineer, Thadeus van Erp. Van Erp's restoration, which lasted three years, involved reconstructing the stupas on the upper terraces, which had suffered most from excavation by treasure-hunters, sealing the gallery floors with cement to limit seepage, and restoring displaced stones as far as possible to their original positions. In retrospect, we can say that van Erp's reconstruction was more important for attracting attention to Borobudur's form and structure than for preservation; seepage and erosion continued almost unabated.

The Great Depression, World War II, Indonesia's national revolution, and the political turmoil that followed all militated against providing further protection for Borobudur, although both colonial and independent Indonesian governments realized that something needed to be done if Borobudur were not to suffer serious and permanent damaged.

Finally, in 1971, at the initiative of Dr R. Soekmono, head of the Indonesian Archaeological Service, a major res-

Stupas at Borobudur temple
Photo courtesy of Indonesia Tourist Promotion Office, Los Angeles

toration program was launched. The program used the most advanced technologies then available in Indonesia and abroad, including detailed aerial photography and analysis of rock types and structure. Borobudur's galleries were completely dismantled so that a new, earthquake-proof foundation could be installed, along with a hidden drainage system to prevent further water damage. The project, costing $25 million—about a quarter of it from foreign aid—was finally completed in 1983.

Since 1973, Borobudur has been closed to organized religious observance. The annual Vaisak festival—held at Borobudur until the latest restoration was begun there—has been transferred to nearby Mendut. In recent years Borobudur's status as the preeminent symbol of Java's pre-Islamic heritage has made it the occasional target of radical Muslim hostility.

Further Reading: The best general work on Borobudur is John Miksic's *Borobudur: Golden Tales of the Buddhas* (Berkeley, California, and Singapore: Periplus, and London: Bamboo, 1990). The text is comprehensive, readable, and reliable and is accompanied by exquisite color photographs and helpful line drawings and maps. For architectural and other interpretation of the monument, Jacques Dumarçay's *Borobudur,* edited and translated by Michael Smithies (Oxford and New York: Oxford University Press, 1978) is still useful. A. J. Bernet Kempers's *Ageless Borobudur* (Wassenaar, Netherlands: Servire, 1976), although less readable than Miksic's book and illustrated only in black and white, provides a more detailed analysis of both the temple and its inscriptions. *Barabudur: History and Significance of a Buddhist Monument,* edited by Luis O. Gómez and Hiram W. Woodward Jr. (Berkeley, California: Berkeley Buddhist Studies, 1981) is a useful collection on the philosophy of Borobudur.

—Robert Cribb

Botany Bay (New South Wales, Australia)

Location: Botany Bay is a large inlet on the east coast of Australia about five miles south of Sydney. Two rivers, the Georges River and the Cooks River, drain into the bay, which is now surrounded by Sydney's southern suburbs.

Description: Busy port serving adjacent industrial complexes, including oil refineries and chemical works. Runways for Sydney's major domestic and international air terminals extend far into the bay. The Kurnell Peninsula on the southern part of Botany Bay was the site of the first European landfall on the east coast of Australia on April 29, 1770, and its northern shore was chosen as the site of the first European settlement in Australia in 1788. Thus Botany Bay was the site of early and sustained encounters between Aboriginal cultures and the Europeans who settled Australia toward the end of the eighteenth century.

Site Office: The Discovery Centre
Captain Cook's Historic Landing Place
Botany Bay National Park
Kurnell 2231, NSW
Australia
(2) 668 9111

It is thought that Botany Bay was formed as the sea rose to its present level approximately 6,000 years ago, although the bay was probably larger then. It is a relatively shallow, oval-shaped inlet approximately seven and one-half by five and one-half miles. The headlands guarding either side of the entrance, separated by slightly less than a mile, were named Cape Banks (the northern side) and Cape Solander (the southern) by Captain James Cook for the two botanists accompanying his ship, the *Endeavour*. Two rivers drain into the bay, the Cook's River to the northwest and the Georges River to the southwest, both carrying considerable quantities of silt. Notwithstanding extensive dredging operations (about twenty-five percent of Sydney's sand for building and other purposes has long been obtained from this source), the area of the bay has diminished considerably in the past 200 years owing to the encroachment of massive man-made constructions, including parallel runways for Sydney Kingsford Smith Airport and berthing facilities for a number of oil refineries and chemical works.

In 1770 Botany Bay was inhabited by the Eora people, who lived mainly by fishing. Its mangroves and shallow waters yielded plenty of shellfish such as oysters, cockles, whelks, and abalone, as well as snapper, bream, catfish, flathead, and groper. Fishhooks were constructed from turban shells *(ninella torquata)*, and stone was imported from a considerable distance to make weapons and other implements. The bones of some land mammals such as kangaroo, wallaby, potoroo, possum, and bandicoot have been found among the shells and fishbones in middens (piles of refuse), while grinding stones discovered there suggest that rhizomes of bracken and tubers of bullrush and waterlily vegetables may have been eaten along with berries and seeds. An occcasional stranded whale provided inhabitants with a great feast.

At 3:00 P.M. on April 29, 1770, a 368-ton, three-masted former Whitby coal ship, renamed *Endeavour* for an exploratory expedition to the South Pacific under the command of then-Lieutenant James Cook, anchored in the bay in the lee of its southern shore. That evening Cook recorded in his log "gentle breezes" and "settled weather" at the *Endeavour*'s first landfall since sighting the east coast of Australia on April 19. He also noted "several of the natives" on either side of the bay, and a few "hutts, women and children" on the north shore opposite. A musket shot sent most of the natives running off, except for two men who "seemed resolved to oppose our landing." In an attempt to gain their consent, "nails, beeds etc." were thrown ashore, but the natives responded by throwing a large stone and then two darts at the landing party. Two or three muskets loaded with small shot were then fired and the natives "took to the woods." They were not seen again. Cook and his party found huts there, too, in which children were hiding. They left "some strings of beeds, etc." and then went in search of water, which they found only by digging a hole in the sand. The landing place now known as Kurnell is in fact the sheltered and wooded side of a huge sand dune, neither very fertile nor well watered. It was there on May 1 that the body of one of Cook's seamen, Forby Sutherland, who died of tuberculosis, was buried; another headland was named Cape Sutherland in his memory (the southern shore of the bay is now called Sutherland Shire).

Still searching for water, Cook decided to row over to the northern shore. Again the natives fled when they saw the white men coming. Here there was fresh water that, Cook wrote, "came trinkling down and stood in pools among the rocks," but it was "troublesome to get at" so they ended up digging more wells in the sand at Kurnell. The expedition then spent six days charting the bay and collecting as much as possible of the local fauna and flora. Some 3,000 plant specimens representing more than 200 unknown species were gathered from around the shores of the bay by Joseph Banks and Daniel Solander, the naturalists appointed by the London Royal Society to accompany the expedition, while the official artist, Sydney Parkinson, made rapid drawings with color-coded sections of as many of the specimens as possible before they faded. Cook had initially named the bay Sting-Rays

Harbour, but he later changed this to Botanists Harbour, then Botanists Bay, and finally Botany Bay.

During their stay in Botany Bay, both Cook and Banks were greatly preoccupied with the Aborigines (the Indians as Banks described them) and with attempts to make contact, although it seemed communication was quite impossible. Not surprisingly, the Tahitian named Tupia (Tupaia), who had accompanied them across the Pacific, was unable to understand their language any better than the Englishmen. Cook remarked wistfully, "all they seem'd to want was for us to be gone." Apart from charting the bay, marking sources of water, and compiling elaborate instructions for finding the channel at the entrance, neither Cook nor Banks said much about what the country was really like. Both noted the prevalence of sandy soil and tufted grass, although there was some confusion about the rest of the vegetation, perhaps because of geological variations that have historically given rise to several different plant communities.

Near the coast were probably good stands of cabbage tree palm, which still grow in sheltered gullies along this coast. Stumps of the large *eucalyptus botryoides,* which may have been the oak-like tree Cook described, have been uncovered with *banksia integrifolia* in old swamp areas. These, too, are found along the coast where the native vegetation has been better preserved. There were also some stands of the casuarina common to this type of coastal scenery. Away from the shore and following the rivers inland some distance, patches of good black soil appear to have supported low scrub (or maybe the land had been burned by the Aborigines)—what Cook described as lawns "free from underwood." Banks could not have collected so many specimens had there not been some well-wooded areas; indeed, the *banksia serrata* (old man banksia), which became one of the highlights of his collection, is also characteristic of the tangle of coastal scrub. The expedition designated the grassy areas along the northern shore "Banksmeadow." It is now thought that nineteenth-century timber collecting and grazing were mostly responsible for destroying the coastal vegetation as it existed when the first Europeans saw it, causing subsequent severe erosion and leaving the sand dunes as the dominant feature of the landscape.

On the basis of these observations and largely due to Banks's advocacy, Botany Bay was later chosen as the site for a British settlement to compensate for the loss of the American colonies in 1776, to alleviate some of the overcrowding in British jails, and to help forestall the imperial ambitions of other European powers—particularly France—in the South Pacific. On May 13, 1787, a fleet consisting of two Admiralty vessels, (the frigate *Sirius* and the armed tender *Supply*), six convict transports, and three storeships carrying in all about 1,450 men and women, about half of them convicts, were dispatched from Portsmouth, England. The expedition's commander, Arthur Phillip, a former Royal Navy captain who had some experience transporting convicts across the Atlantic, brought the *Supply* into Botany Bay on January 18, 1788. Within three days the whole fleet was anchored in the bay.

In the harsh light of mid-summer, Botany Bay appeared very different from the benign late April impressions of it left by Cook and Banks. But Phillip was unimpressed by the site for other reasons: he thought the land surrounding the bay too swampy for a settlement; he found the water supply unsatisfactory; but his greatest objection was to the lack of a deep-water anchorage basin that would be well sheltered from the sea. He immediately began looking for a more suitable harbor, and by January 26 the settlement had been relocated northward to Port Jackson and named Sydney. Botany Bay became a backwater, the haunt of fishermen, oyster gatherers, limeburners, and timbergetters, and a haven for Aboriginal people displaced from the settlement at Sydney. Its name remained in use, however, and for many years the convict settlement on the east coast of Australia was known as Botany Bay. The bay also held the most sought after and highly promoted product of the Australian colonies: the finest grade of merino wool.

On the very day the convict fleet was withdrawing to Sydney Cove, two French ships, *La Boussole* and *L'Astrolabe,* under the command of Jean-François de La Pérouse, were observed trying to enter Botany Bay, thus confirming Phillip's fear of the shallow channel during adverse winds, still a problem for tankers wishing to berth at Port Botany in heavy weather. La Pérouse was engaged in exploration and also seeking land for a possible French settlement in the South Pacific. He camped for several weeks on the northern arm of the bay, which now bears his name; the naturalist accompanying him, Father Le Receveur, died and was buried there. Later, in the 1820s, because of the fear of invasion, a watchtower was erected, and nearby Bare Island was fortified in 1885. Today these sites are protected within the Botany Bay National Park. An elegant late-nineteenth-century telegraph station has been transformed into a fine museum honoring the French explorers.

The northern shore of the bay was most accessible from Sydney—little more than an hour's walk for the market gardeners who began to take up land there in the 1840s—and it attracted industry and settlement long before the southern or western shores. Simeon Lord established a fellmongery (a place for removing hair or wool from hides in preparation for leather making), using ponds near the mouth of the Cooks River in 1815. From the 1850s to the 1880s, this area was the main source of Sydney's water, which was pumped from Lord's ponds to reservoirs nearer the city. During this time development was discouraged by those who saw the need to maintain the quality of the water catchment, but this did not prevent recreational use of the waters by weekend visitors and daytrippers. There had been an inn at Banksmeadow and a small village at Botany from the 1840s. By 1850, the inn, now the Sir Joseph Banks Hotel, had become a popular resort with a zoo, a ballroom, and facilities for picnics, boating, fishing, and footracing. It was claimed that 5,000 visitors came there on Boxing Day 1852. Races attracted international competi-

Captain Cook Landing Place, Kurnell, Botany Bay
Photo courtesy of Tourism New South Wales

tion, and the games held annually on St. Patrick's Day became a regular attraction. By 1884 the village of Botany had a post office, a savings bank, a Mechanics Institute, a library, and two public schools with 212 children in attendance. The Seven Mile Beach running along the western shore of the bay between the mouths of the two rivers (renamed Lady Robinson's Beach in honor of the wife of the governor of New South Wales in the 1870s) also became popular with vacationers when Thomas Saywell built the New Brighton Hotel, with swimming baths, a racecourse, and a tramway to link his resort to the railway. Beachside villages bearing names like Brighton-le-Sands, Sandringham, Ramsgate, and Sans Souci were marked out, but they remained holiday places until the arrival of the motor car, which made possible the suburban development of the bay's western shore and its hinterland.

The southern Kurnell Peninsula was more difficult to reach, and thus development there did not occur. From the 1860s, most of the land there was in the hands of a colorful entrepreneur and politician named Thomas Holt, who cut out the timber and then tried to revegetate the sandhills thus created with buffalo grass. He ran sheep, tried mining for coal, and in 1870 marked the centenary of Captain Cook's landing by enclosing the site and erecting a new memorial. (There had been a plaque set on the cliff face as early as 1823 by the Philosophical Society of Australasia, but Holt's action secured the site, which was later incorporated in the Botany Bay National Park.)

In the 1880s Sydney's water supply moved from Botany Bay to the Nepean River, so that once more Botany Bay water was available for commercial use. Trades that had been discouraged in Sydney moved south toward Botany. Market gardens, many of them worked by the Chinese, flourished on human excrement carried out of the city. A sewage farm was established near the mouth of the Cooks River. The fellmongers returned, as did other trades associated with the wool industry, including tanneries, leatherworks, wool stores, a gelatin factory, and fertilizers. Other industries such as a paper mill required water as well. Sydney's outcasts found homes at Botany Bay. An infectious diseases hospital was established at Little Bay near La Pérouse. The main prison was moved to Long Bay nearby. From the 1880s, Aborigines were accommodated in a mission at La Pérouse.

Much of the now-degraded sandy scrub was cleared for factories or neat rows of modest cottages to house a convenient workforce. Model workers' housing estates developed by Labor governments became the new suburbs of Daceyville, Hillsdale, and Matraville. Some of them were ready just in time to house servicemen returned from World War I. While the area developed quickly with a strong working-class character (where employment, industry, and politics were closely intertwined), it still had plenty of available space. During the Depression of the 1930s, waste land at La Pérouse attracted the unemployed and the homeless. In 1933, when Frederick Davies was looking for a site to establish an Australian Hollywood with clear air, plenty of sunshine, and no intrusive noise or industrial interference (yet still a short distance from Sydney), he discovered his twenty-two-acre site at Pagewood, a new suburb that had been developed on the old market gardens of Botany.

A wharf had been built at Botany Bay in the 1880s for unloading coal. In 1927–28 a new electric power station was built at Bunnerong, and for fifty years its smokestacks dominated the Botany Bay skyline. Now, however, the skyline is lurid with the flares of the oil refineries on either side of the bay, and aircraft come and go with monotonous regularity. Botany Bay's modern era began in 1919, when Nigel B. Love set up Australian Aircraft and Engineering Company, Limited, and chose as the site of his airfield an area known since 1911 as Mascot, near the mouth of the Cooks River. In 1921 additional land for an airport was purchased by the Australian Civil Aviation authority from the Kensington Racing Club. Eventually it became necessary to retake adjacent recreational land, redirect the course of the Cooks River, and reclaim land in the bay to expand the airport, named Sydney Kingsford Smith in honor of one of the pioneers of Australian aviation. The airport's north-south runway has been gradually lengthened into the bay. In 1994 a second runway was built parallel to the first, reclaiming yet more of the northwestern area of the bay.

The airfield at Mascot encouraged the establishment of a fuel depot there in 1930 and the building of a small refinery at Matraville in 1948. In 1955 another refinery was established at Kurnell, necessitating a long wharf reaching into the bay within sight of Captain Cook's landing place. The refinery also needed undersea pipelines connecting to storage facilities on the other side of the bay at Banksmeadow. There were local protests, but these were overridden by economic considerations. In 1962 local authorities decided to develop Botany Bay as a major port to handle crude oil, chemicals, and general bulk cargoes. The shallow northern shore of the bay by Banksmeadow has now been completely transformed by dredging and the construction of a one and one-quarter mile breakwater. Some 618 acres of land have been reclaimed from the bay in connection with container wharves and storage facilities of Port Botany. Transport has been improved by the construction of a freeway on the foreshore, also on reclaimed land. The combined requirements of the airport runways and the terminal at Port Botany have changed the northwestern configuration of the bay beyond all recognition, and many fear the effects of such changes on the ecology of Botany Bay. Changing currents, disturbed breeding grounds for marine and birdlife, and various forms of pollution have all been cause for concern.

A backwater for most of the nineteenth century, Botany Bay is now vital to modern Sydney. In addition to the airport and industrial complexes, its beaches and river frontages have become popular alternatives to the older harborside locations for the homes of the rich and successful. The bay's historic associations confer a sense of distinction and now attract growing numbers of tourists. With so many monuments, both to the history of European exploration and settlement and to modern industry and commerce, Botany Bay is symbol of some of Australia's most poignant encounters between past and present, while the survival of a significant Aboriginal community at La Pérouse has added great strength to the meaning of commemorative celebrations held regularly since 1938. With each anniversary, the memory of the first European settlement, clouded though it must be by reminders of Aboriginal dispossession, becomes more significant. But so does the foreboding sense of environmental catastrophe in the thick yellow-brown smog blotting out the bay, especially on days of settled weather and gentle breezes.

Further Reading: The first accounts of Botany Bay are to be found in explorers' journals such as *The Journals of Captain James Cook on His Voyages of Discovery,* volume 1, *The Voyage of the Endeavour 1768–1771* (Cambridge: Cambridge University Press, 1955) and *The Endeavour Journal of Joseph Banks 1768–1771,* volume 2 (Sydney: Trustees of the Public Library of New South Wales in association with Angus and Robertson, 1962), both edited by J. C. Beaglehole. A lively modern account of first European contacts is *The Fatal Shore: A History of the Transportation of Convicts to Australia, 1787–1868* by Robert Hughes (New York: Knopf, 1986; London: Collins Harvill, 1987). Of the several local histories, *The History of Botany, 1788–1963* by Frederick A. Larcombe (Botany Bay: Council of the Municipality of Botany, 1963) is the most useful. While no truly comprehensive study of the development of the bay exists, a useful if dated overview is *The Botany Bay Project: A Handbook of the Botany Bay Region,* edited by D. J. Anderson (Botany Bay: The Botany Bay Project Committee, 1973).

—Beverley Kingston

Brunei Darussalam

Location: In the South China Sea, between the Philippines and Malaysia, northwest of Borneo; bordered by Sarawak to the east, west, and south, and by the South China Sea to the north.

Description: Malay Islamic Monarchy, 5,765 square miles in area, ruled by the Sultan of Brunei, the second-richest man in the world. Once Brunei controlled most of Borneo; today Borneo is divided between three countries: the Malaysian-controlled Sarawak and Sabah, Indonesian-controlled Kalimantan, and the independent state of Brunei. Brunei is separated into two sections by Sarawak.

Site Office: Tourism Section
Economic Development Board
Ministry of Finance
Bandar Seri Begawan 2011
Brunei Darussalam

The name of Brunei Darussalam means Abode of Peace. Situated in the northwest of the lovely island of Borneo, Brunei is the site of enormous reserves of oil and natural gas, which allow its people a high standard of living. In 1993 the average per capita income was $19,000. The people of Brunei also benefit from state-provided health care, education, and pensions all provided without the need for taxation.

The population of Brunei encompasses a wide range of races and religions. Approximately 68 percent of the people are of Malay extraction; 18 percent are Chinese; approximately 5 percent are indigenous peoples or descendants of early tribal colonizers, such as the Dusuns, Ibans, Dyaki, and Punans; and the rest are expatriates. Although Brunei is officially Muslim, other religions are tolerated.

Human habitation at Brunei can be traced back thousands of years. Archaeologists have found human remains dating from 50,000 to 250 B.C. in limestone caves some 100 miles west of modern Brunei. From such objects and remains, they have been able to reconstruct the way in which these ancient societies lived. The ancient inhabitants were agrarian and used a system of shifting cultivation, whereby one area of the heavily forested landscape was cleared and cultivated until it became exhausted, after which the community would move and clear another area for cultivation. This system is still used today in some areas of Brunei.

The Malay population reached Brunei around the fifth century A.D. The Sumatran Malays traveled from Johor, near Singapore, through Sarawak to Brunei. As they traveled, the Malays built forts and towns on the rivers and estuaries. They also brought with them Buddhism.

Brunei became a center of trade very early. Indian merchants appear to have traveled there by the second century A.D., and Chinese merchants followed. A Chinese manuscript dating from the sixth century makes reference to a site that historians believe to be Brunei. The manuscript describes "a country with 10,000 people in its capital and over 100 fighting men who wore armor and carried swords in battle." The discovery of Tang Dynasty-era coins and ceramic fragments near the capital of Bandar Seri Begawan suggests that China was actively trading with Brunei as early as the seventh century. In 977 and 1082, Brunei paid tribute to the Song emperor. Brunei soon took advantage of its location on the trade routes between China, Melaka, and India and gained control over much of the South China Sea traffic. It became a major supply station for trade ships, as well as a port of trade for such local items as beeswax, camphor, rattan, and brass work.

According to Chinese manuscripts, Islam reached the island in 1371, but some historians believe that Brunei had contact with the Arabic-speaking world even earlier. An Arabic book, *A jaibal-Hind (The Wonders of the Indies),* written in approximately A.D. 950, makes a reference to Sribuza, which historian Robert Nicoll believes to have been located in Brunei Bay. Early in the fifteenth century, the ruler of Brunei, Awang Alak Be Takar, abducted a Muslim princess, Ratu Johar of Malacca, and converted to Islam after marrying her. The present sultan of Brunei is descended from this union.

When Europeans arrived in Southeast Asia in the early sixteenth century, the Brunei sultanate was at the height of its power. Its empire encompassed nearly the entire island of Borneo and extended into the Philippines. In 1521 Antonio Pigafetta, a member of Ferdinand Magellan's expedition, became the first European to visit the country. He was quite impressed by the wealth of the city and the sophistication of the royal court. Brunei soon began to trade with Portugal, buying arms and cloth in exchange for sago, pepper, rice, and low-quality gold. A 1559 sea chart labels all of Borneo as Brune, from which we derive the name Brunei. Trade with China continued, meanwhile, and the Chinese community increased. By 1578, when Spain invaded Brunei, its population was composed of Chinese, Vietnamese, Cambodian, Javan, Malay, Sumatran, and Moluccan traders. Spain controlled Brunei for one year; in 1579, the Brunei fleet drove the Spanish out of their kingdom.

By the end of the sixteenth century, Brunei's reputation had spread as far as England. In 1599, Sir Francis Drake reported to Elizabeth I that Brunei "abounded in great wealth and riches and neither the Portuguese nor Spanish possessed any castle or fort, blockhouse or commandment there." Accordingly, the British East India Company was formed to take

Jame' Asr Hassanil Bolkiah Mosque, Brunei
Photo courtesy of Malaysian Tourism Promotion Board, New York

advantage of the possibilities the region held out. The British built a trading station at Bandjermasir, on the southern coast of the island. The Dutch, however, keen to increase their trading area, attacked Bandjermasir and expelled British traders in 1612.

Unlike most of its Southeast Asian neighbors, Brunei remained comparatively untouched by European colonialism until the nineteenth century. This lack of foreign intervention owed in no small part to the stability of the sultanate and the royal court's diplomatic prowess. However, Brunei's commercial and trade relations were affected by the extension of European power nearby. Brunei lost its traditional markets in the Spanish-dominated Philippines and in Dutch-controlled areas of China and islands in Southeast Asia. Brunei also lost territory during the period of European expansion. The Philippine island of Sulu declared its independence from Brunei in 1578, the year of Spanish occupation, and was never recovered. In 1622, the sultan of Brunei gave his holdings in northern Borneo to the sultan of Sulu in exchange for his help in suppressing a rebellion. (This agreement was later disputed, for northern Borneo possessed abundant natural resources.) In time, Sulu also became an important aggressive power, as the home of the infamous Balanini pirates, who terrorized the Borneo coast. Gradually, the loss of markets and the increased pirate activity led to the decline of Brunei's economy—a fact shown by the drop in population from 40,000 in 1750 (when the sultanate had a substantial Chinese trading community) to 10,000 in 1830. Political instability followed, as well; when the sultan proved unable to counter incursions by Sulu forces and Balanini pirates, chieftains of outlying areas took note of his weakness and asserted increasing independence.

Throughout much of its history, Brunei had maintained its independence by playing one foreign power against another. Now, faced with the possible dissolution of its empire, the sultanate was forced to turn to a single outside nation for support. It chose Great Britain. Initially, these requests for aid went unanswered; the sultan asked the British East India Company for protection in both 1774 and 1804 to no avail. Finally in 1839, following a revolt in Sarawak, the British intervened in Brunei's affairs. Unfortunately for the sultan, this intervention proved far more costly than he had imagined.

The revolt in Sarawak was being led by local chiefs who had grown resentful of the high taxes imposed on mineral deposits mined under their jurisdiction. Initially the sultan had sent his uncle, Raja Muda Hasim, to mediate, but Hasim proved ineffective. Hasim, in turn, sought the aid of James Brooke, a retired English cavalry officer. Brooke happened to be in Sarawak on a diplomatic mission from the British governor of Singapore, who wished to thank Hasim for saving the lives of several British sailors.

Brooke had long advocated an enlarged British presence in Southeast Asia, and he jumped at the chance to advance this goal—and, in the process, greatly enrich himself. He managed to suppress the rebellion and in return was granted a large quantity of antimony from the local mines and authority over the Sarawak River district. In November 1841, he was made raja and governor of Sarawak. Following the murder of Hasim and his brothers by court members who resented the increased European presence, the sultan of Brunei was forced to give Brooke tenure of Sarawak in perpetuity. Brooke's cause was helped by the presence of the Royal Navy, which aimed its guns at the sultan's palace. The sultan further ceded the island of Labuan to Britain, and in 1842 signed a treaty agreeing not to cede any further land without British approval.

Under Brooke's governorship, Sarawak increased in territory at the expense of Brunei. By 1853 Sarawak had doubled its size by moving the border east to Kabong. In 1861 it expanded an additional 200 miles, and the border was changed again, to Bintulu. Often these land grabs were justified on the pretext of driving out local pirates. When Brooke died in 1868, he was succeeded by his nephew Charles, who ten years later increased Sarawak's size by adding 100 miles of coastline, which brought it to its present border with Brunei.

Understandably, the sultans of Brunei were concerned about the increasing size of Sarawak. Their response to these territorial incursions was somewhat surprising, however: once again, they sought the protection of the British. Apparently they felt many of the same commercial and political threats to the survival of the empire as had their predecessors in the eighteenth century, and they reached the same conclusion about how to combat these threats. Unfortunately, they also met the same indifference from the British. When it became clear that Britain was not opposed to the expansion of Sarawak—and might, in fact, have favored it—they returned to the more familiar game of playing the major powers against one another.

In 1850 Sultan Hashim signed a Treaty of Friendship and Commerce with the United States of America; in so doing, he introduced a new player into the region and threatened Britain's hold over the area, which pressured Britain to protect its interests there more actively. Sultan Abdul Mumin upped the ante by leasing a tract of land occupying the approximate region of modern-day Sabah to the American consul, Charles Lee Moses. Moses established the American Trading Company, with backing from Chinese and American businessmen, and created a commercial and agricultural settlement at Kimanis, sixty miles north of Brunei Town, the capital. The settlement failed, however, as conflicts and disease plagued its inhabitants.

Ten years after its establishment, the American Trading Company was bought by Baron von Overbeck (the Austrian consul) and the British-born Alfred Dent. In 1877 the sultan granted them sovereignty over Sabah for an annual payment. In 1881 Dent bought out von Overbeck, and the British government, fearful of foreign presence in northern Borneo, granted Dent a charter to form the British North Borneo Company (BNBC).

These dealings were a dangerous gamble for Brunei: far from leading to immediate British protection for Brunei, the formation of the BNBC created intense competition between Dent and the Brooke family for new territory. Piece by piece, they began to carve away Brunei's holdings, all with the formal consent of the British government. In 1882 Britain approved Charles Brooke's annexation of the Baram Basin, and two years later the acquisition of the Tuscan Valley. The gamble ultimately yielded the long-sought prize for Brunei, however; concerned that the weakened and reduced sultanate of Brunei would prove a tempting target for European powers such as Germany and Spain (which had conquered Sulu in 1882), Britain established a protectorate over Brunei, as well as Sarawak and North Borneo, in 1888.

Unfortunately, Brunei soon discovered that its new relationship with Britain offered far less protection than its name implied. In 1890, Sarawak annexed the district around the Limbang River, splitting Brunei in two. Not only did the British do nothing to stop the annexation, they formally recognized its legality. This was a major affront to the sultan and the court at Brunei, and one still keenly felt today. In the ensuing years, Sarawak repeatedly applied heavy pressure to annex all of Brunei; the latter managed to maintain its independence by bombarding Britain with letters, appeals, and diplomatic visits to defend its status. In this they were eventually aided by the administrators of North Borneo, who wished Brunei to remain as a buffer state between itself and Sarawak.

Only in 1906 did the British sign a Supplementary Agreement with Brunei, whereby the Crown guaranteed the permanent existence of Brunei in return for the introduction of a British Resident, who would assume most of the nation's political authority (the sultan retained authority only over Islamic and Malay law and custom). Finally, after more than a century of calculated risks, complex diplomatic intrigues, and a steady erosion of territory leaving only two tiny strips of land, each of which is surrounded by a foreign nation, Brunei received the protection it had sought. The gamble of the sultans paid off: the same ruling family has governed Brunei uninterrupted since 1579.

Great Britain's ultimate goodwill was not wholly the result of the sultan's public opinion campaign, for the British had a new interest to protect in Brunei: oil. Petroleum reserves had been discovered in Miri, Sarawak, very near the western border of Brunei in 1895. In 1913, exploration for oil began in earnest in Brunei, at Tutong, Labi, and Jerudong. Sixteen years later, substantial amounts of oil were discovered at Seria, in the Belait district. In 1940, Seria was producing 17,000 barrels of oil a day. Although Seria was partially destroyed by the Japanese during World War II, it began to operate again after the war. In 1956 Shell Oil initiated further explorations, yielding four more fields that effectively established Brunei's wealth. More than 80 percent of Brunei's oil comes from offshore sites. Most of the oil is exported to Japan, Singapore, Thailand, and the Philippines.

During the 1950s and 1960s, Brunei's position in the world again came into question. In 1957–58 the governors of Sarawak and North Borneo suggested the formation of a northern Borneo federation comprising British North Borneo, Brunei, and Sarawak. The sultan, Omar Ali Saifuddien, was opposed to this scheme, not least because he felt it would reduce Brunei's international status and affect its oil revenues. However, Brunei's people's party, the Party Rakyat Brunei (PRB), supported the action. The idea of a federation lost momentum as Brunei became embroiled in a larger scheme to form the Federation of Malaysia; Sabah and Sarawak were also invited to participate. The sultan and the PRB came into conflict again over this issue. Eventually, the struggle resulted in the Brunei Revolt in December 1962, which spilled into northern Sarawak and southern Sabah. After three days of heavy fighting, the Tentara National Kalimantan Utara (TNKU), which supported the PRB, was suppressed by the combined efforts of the Brunei police and British troops brought to Brunei specifically to help put down the uprising. Consequently the PRB was banned in Brunei. Although Brunei remained independent following the formation of the Federation of Malaysia, it continued to suffer from guerilla activity along its borders until August 1966, when a new treaty was signed between Indonesia and Malaysia. In 1967 the sultan abdicated, and his son, Paduka Seri Baginda Sultan Haji Hassanal Bolkiah Muizzadin Waddaulah, the present sultan of Brunei, succeeded him.

Brunei's friendly relationship with Britain continued. In 1971, the new sultan agreed to a limited British military presence in his country. During the 1970s the sultan negotiated with the British government, and in 1979 Brunei signed a friendship treaty with Britain whereby it became essentially independent. Five years later, on New Year's Day, it became the 169th sovereign state; in the same year it became a member of the Commonwealth.

Today Brunei is divided into two parts separated by Sarawak. West Brunei is approximately three times the size of East. The capital, Bandar Seri Begawan, and the oil fields are situated in the West. East Brunei is more remote, predominantly agrarian, and is less populated. The total population of Brunei is approximately 260,000.

The sultan of Brunei is an absolute monarch who is also the prime minister and defense minister. Two of his brothers are ministers of finance and foreign affairs. The sultan has been called the richest man in the world, his income predominantly derived from Brunei's oil and natural gas reserves. The substantial income generated by Brunei's oil allows its population to enjoy free education and health care, among other benefits. However, the country does have stringent citizenship requirements, including a minimum residency requirement of thirty continuous years and difficult Malay language tests, which have resulted in a considerable loss in status for Brunei's Chinese community. It is estimated that over 40,000 Chinese residents have been denied official Brunei citizenship. In 1985 the sultan agreed to the establishment of the Brunei National Democratic Party (BNDP); leading officials of the BNDP tend to have links to the sultan's family, however.

The capital city, Bandar Seri Begawan, or BSB/Bandar as it is also known, is a modern town that owes much to the discovery of oil nearby. Known as Brunei Town until 1970, its name was changed to honor the former sultan Omar Ali Saifuddien, who took the name Seri Begawan following his abdication in 1967. Today the city is situated on the north bank of the Brunei River. The Kampung Ayer/Air, a water village opposite the new city, was the original capital and main business center until the British persuaded the sultan of Brunei to move to a new palace on dry land in 1909. Today Kampung Air is still densely populated, although the government is trying to persuade people to move from their stilt houses.

Until the discovery of oil, Brunei's capital was a small village. The wealth generated from the sale of oil and natural gas has brought great change to the city. Most of the development came in the 1970s when shopping malls, hotels, bank complexes, and new housing were built. Dominated by the Omar Ali Saifuddien Mosque, Bandar lacks the atmosphere, smells, sounds, and colors of most other Asian capitals. The Istana Nurul Iman, the sultan's palace, is the largest palace in the world. It has 1,788 rooms and is open to the public on the second, third, and fourth days of Hari Raya, at the end of Ramadan. It contains impressive art collections. This palace, more than any other building in Brunei, shows the effect of the discovery of oil on this country and its leaders.

Further Reading: *Let's Visit Brunei* by S. and P. J. Hassall (London: Macmillan, 1988) is a very useful, informative exploration of Brunei that examines the country's history from ancient times to the present. *Short History of Malaysia, Singapore and Brunei* by C. M. Turnbull (Stanmore, New South Wales: Cassell Australia, 1979) is a dense but detailed history of these countries, suited to people interested in a reliable, factual account of the development of this area. *Brunei, 1839–1983: Problems of Political Survival* by D. S. Ranjit Singh (Singapore and New York: Oxford University Press, 1984) is a very interesting and readable history of Brunei during its contact with European colonial powers and its emergence into modern Brunei. *East Malaysia and Brunei* (Singapore: Periplus, and Lincolnwood, Illinois: Passport, 1993), like other books in the Periplus series, gives concise and important information on both these countries. *Brunei: The Modern Southeast Asian Islamic Sultanate* by David Leake Jr. (Jefferson, North Carolina: McFarland, 1989) is a straightforward analysis of Brunei, its sultan, and the effect of oil on the country.

—A. Vasudevan and Robert M. Salkin

Bukhara (Bukhara, Uzbekistan)

Location: In the lower valley of the Zeravshan River, a tributary of the Amu Darya (Oxus); about 140 miles west of Samarkand.

Description: Bukhara is an old oasis city of Central Asia, Iranian in origin but progressively Turkified from the Mongol invasions. Its chief significance was as a seat of Islamic learning and in particular as the birthplace and headquarters of the Naqshbandī order, the most widely diffused of Muslim *tarikats* (dervish orders). In addition, Bukhara was the capital of the Uzbek polity and of one of its three successor states. Its considerable monuments reflect its role as a religious and political capital.

Contact: Intourist Service Bureau
Hotel Samarkand
University Boulevard
Samarkand
Uzbekistan
(35) 8812 or (35) 1880

Bukhara was never as blessed with natural resources or commerce as its Central Asian oasis neighbors Herāt or Mary. Unlike those towns, Bukhara did not have sole access to its river; its source of water for irrigation was the Zeravshan, which it had to share with Samarkand upriver. Bukhara therefore only received what Samarkand did not want. Militarily, too, Bukhara was more exposed and less defensible than Samarkand, and its citadel was built on an artificial mound. And although located on the central Eurasian land route, Bukhara's trade was generally less flourishing than that of Samarkand or Kokand, particularly with respect to the long-distance trade between China and the West. The location itself was unhealthy: travelers frequently described the Guinea worm, which was widely prevalent. Bukhara's moments of eminence in Central Asian, indeed world, history were a triumph of culture—and specifically of religious culture—over nature.

Unlike Herāt and Samarkand, Bukhara is not mentioned in Ptolemy's *Geography.* Though an Indo-European Neolithic site, it only became an urban center in later antiquity, perhaps as a result of the spread of Buddhism. It has been suggested that the name Bukhara derives from a Sanskrit term, *vihara,* which denotes a Buddhist monastery. In any event, Bukhara was early a center of religious activity. Remains of a Christian church have been found outside the eastern gates; this may be the cathedral of the bishop of Bukhara. As early as the council of Seleucia-Ctesiphon in 424, mention is made of bishops from Neyshabur, Herāt, and Mary, and subsequently an archbishopric of Samarkand was established, to whom, no doubt, the bishop of Bukhara was subordinate.

In 709, Islam and the overlordship of the caliphate were brought to Bukhara by the forces of Qutaybah ibn Muslim, but the local ruler, the Bukkar Khudat, continued to coexist alongside the caliph's emir. He, like other rulers in the region then known as Transoxiana, sent emissaries to Siking (Xian) to solicit aid against the caliphate from Tang China, then in its period of maximum expansion under emperor Hsuan Tsung. A rivalry between China and the caliphate soon developed and was resolved only by the defeat of Tang viceroy Kao Hsien-chih by Ziyad ibn Salih at the Talas River in 751. By that time, the 'Abbāsids from Khorāsān were in power in the region, but Bukhara remained restive. One of the villages of its oasis was the headquarters of the prophet Hashim ibn Hakim, known as al-Muqanna' (The Veiled One), who led a revolt in the 770s, claimed personal divinity, and perhaps aspired to found a new religion.

With the decline of the 'Abbāsid caliphate after 850, Bukhara came under the rule first of the Ṭāhirids of Mary and then of the Sāmānids, former Zoroastrians from Balkh, who made it their capital. It was under the Sāmānids in the tenth century that Bukhara began to enjoy fame in the Muslim world as a seat of Islamic learning. The Sāmānids united Arabic and Persian culture, began extending this culture to their Turkish slaves, and gave patronage to the physician-philosopher Razi (Rhazes), the scientist-philosopher (and Bukhara native) Ibn Sina (Avicenna), and the poet Firdawsi. According to the contemporary historian Narshakhi, Bukhara already possessed the typical Central Asian three-fold character it has today: citadel, or *arg,* often the seat of alien rulers or their garrison; walled native city, or *shahristan,* the home of the local notables, or *sadr,* and their servants and craftspeople; and commercial suburbs, or *rabad,* the locus of caravansaries and long-distance trade. The principal monument of this period is the domed, four-square mausoleum of Isma'il Samani to the west of the citadel.

After the beneficent rule of the Sāmānids, Bukhara passed successively under the suzerainty of the Karakhanid Ilek khans of Kashgar, the first Turkish dynasty in Islam, and then of the Seljuks, who diffused Turkish power much more widely. In 1141, however, the Seljuk sultan Sanjar was defeated at the battle of Qatawan by Yeh-lü Ta-shih, formerly of the Liao Dynasty in north China, who had become ruler of a new realm called Karakitai in Central Asia. Bukhara remained under non-Muslim rule until revolts by Muslims in Transoxiana and by Buddhists in Kashgaria led to the collapse of Karakitai in 1210. Bukhara then became part of the far-flung but precarious empire of Khiva. The historian Juvaini describes the city at this time:

View of Bukhara
Photo courtesy of A.P. / Wide World Photos, New York

> In the Eastern countries it is the Cupola of Islam and is in those regions like unto the City of Peace (Baghdad). Its environs are adorned with the brightness of the light of doctors and jurists and its surroundings embellished with the rarest of high attainments. Since ancient times it has in every age been the place of assembly of the great savants of every religion.

Bukhara fell to Genghis Khan in 1220 in the first wave of his attack. It fell, indeed, before Samarkand because Genghis made an encircling movement through the Kyzyl Kum desert to attack the shah's capital from the rear. Consequently, Bukhara offered little resistance, suffered less destruction, and recovered more quickly than the cities of Khorāsān. Marco Polo did not visit Bukhara himself, but his uncles had spent time there on their first expedition to Cathay (China) in 1263. In his prologue, Polo described it as "a large and splendid city called Bukhara," part of the Chagatai khanate ruled by Genghis Khan's descendants, and noted that, "It was the finest city in all Persia."

Even before this degree of economic recovery, Bukhara had made a contribution of another kind to the post-Mongol world. In his *History of the World Conqueror,* Juvaini tells the story of Mahmud Tarabi, a sieve maker from the Bukhara oasis, who, encouraged by a dervish, led a lower-class uprising in 1238–39 against the Mongols and their upper-class collaborators. The revolt was crushed, inevitably, but it required a Mongol army corps to do so. Moreover, Tarabi's brief gesture foreshadowed that wider movement of urban protest by people known as *sarbadars* (gibbetmen), a movement that, in conjunction with nomad secessions from the ruling oligarchy, led to far-reaching changes in the Chagatai khanate in the fourteenth century.

These changes provided the context for Bukhara's most significant citizen, the fourteenth-century religious leader Bahā' ad-Dīn Naqshband, whose tomb to the northeast of the city has been called the holiest place in Central Asia. He was significant because he was the founder of the Naqshbandīyah, the most important of the dervish orders or *tarikats*, which sought both to maintain the purity of Islam in the face of infidel or lukewarm rulers and to champion the townspeople against the Chagatai state. Bahā' ad-Dīn wrote little, and except for two pilgrimages to Mecca and a visit to Herāt, never left Bukhara. However, he believed in itinerant preaching to both Persian and Turkish speakers and became known as a spiritual adviser. His order practiced *dhikr-i khafī* (silent meditation or mental prayer), a solitude within society before action against it. Conservative in religion, radical in politics, the order had an illuminist dimension (referring to an esoteric school of philosophy in Islam), not unlike that of the Mawlawīyah (Whirling Dervishes) of Jalāl ad-Dīn ar-Rūmī, whose writings became very popular in Central Asia. In the lifetime of Bahā' ad-Dīn, Chagatai government broke down under the simultaneous and sometimes allied attacks of alienated townspeople and secessionist nomads. Its successor, the government of Timur (Tamerlane) and the Timurids, sought a reconciliation between court, townspeople, and nomads through a policy of war abroad and peace at home: war was meant to reactivate the transcontinental trade routes and thereby finance urban renewal and social rehabilitation on the home front. Tamerlane's policy produced a brilliant cultural flowering at Samarkand and Herāt, but while he posed as the champion of the *sarbadars* and the friend of dervishes, his government never embraced the Naqshbandī order, which increasingly became the framework for opposition to the regime.

The order was at first only of local significance. It was extended to other parts of Transoxiana by its second major proponent, Khoja Ahrar, originally from Tashkent, who became the leading religious figure at Samarkand in the reign of Abu Sa'id (1451–69). Khoja Ahrar was highly political. He aimed at a theocracy and, by allying his townspeople with the nomad Uzbeks, he virtually achieved it in Samarkand. By the time of his death in 1490, he had reduced Timurid rule to a nullity, driven princes who refused to be his puppets to Khorāsān or Kābul, and prepared the way for the Uzbek conquest of Herāt in 1507. At the same time, Khoja Ahrar began to look beyond Central Asia. While the story of his presence at the Ottoman capture of Constantinople in 1453 is legend, he both received disciples from and sent them to the Ottoman Empire in the second half of the fifteenth century. Another disciple, Mawlana Khwajagi Amgangi, undertook pioneer missionary expeditions to India and Southeast Asia.

Under the Uzbeks, who made Bukhara the capital of their confederacy, the Naqshbandīyah reached new heights of political power and religious influence. By the middle of the sixteenth century, the khans were enthroned not by their four regent beys, as in the past, but by four leading dervishes. Although Muhammad Shaybānī, the founder of Uzbek rule in Bukhara, distrusted theocracy and executed the sons of Khoja Ahrar, the Naqshbandī organization was reconstituted under his successors by its third major leader, the Fergana-born Khoja Ahmad Kasani (1461–1542), better known as the Makhdum-i Azam (Grand Master). During his long life, he traveled widely in the Islamic world, to such destinations as Herāt, Egypt, Mecca, India, and Kābul, before settling at Samarkand, where his leadership was accepted by Khoja Ahrar's direct successors, the Juybari sheikhs at Bukhara. A pupil of the poet and mystic Jami at Herāt and a friend of Mughal rulers Bābur and Humāyūn in India, the Grand Master, it may be supposed, stressed the more liberal and inclusive aspects of Naqshbandī teaching: its illuminism rather than its religious traditionalism or political radicalism. The Makhdum-i Azam made the Naqshbandīyah a major force in Islamdom.

After the Grand Master's death, the order divided into a number of streams that nevertheless retained a common resemblance and still looked to their common source. In Transoxiana, the Juybari sheikhs under Khoja Islam reasserted the leadership of Bukhara and the place of the movement's founder. The sons and grandsons of the Makhdum-i Azam founded two rival lines, the Ishaniyah and the Ishakiyah, both of which directed their activities to eastern Turkistan and the Kansu panhandle. A sub-branch of the Ishaniyah, the Afaqi Makhdumzadas, established themselves in the late seventeenth century as the predominant power in Kashgaria, a position they retained until the Qing conquest of 1759. In India, a Naqshbandī sheikh, Aḥmad Sirhindī, was a prominent opposition leader under Emperor Jahāngīr. Sirhindī's son had two associates from Bukhara, one of whom subsequently went to the Ottoman Empire and founded the Naqshbandī hostel at Eyub at the head of the Golden Horn, from which further branches were founded, at Sarajevo in one direction and at Damascus in another. In the Ottoman Empire, the order took a prominent part in the administration of religious trusts, *waqf* or *evkaf*, major institutions of later Ottoman society. All these branches and sub-branches had some feeling of affiliation to Bukhara, which functioned as one of the poles of the Sunni Muslim world.

There is an account of Bukhara in its age of expansion from Anthony Jenkinson, the agent of the Muscovy Company, who, in 1558, became probably the first Englishman to visit the city. The previous year, the city had been captured by Abd Allah ibn Iskandar (1577–98), the strongest of the early Uzbek rulers. Jenkinson writes:

> So upon the 23rd day of December we arrived at the citie of Boghar in the land of Bactria . . . the citie is very great, and the houses for the most part of earth, but there are also many houses, temples and monuments of stone sumptuously builded and gilt. . . . There is a Metropolitan in this Boghar, who causeth this lawe to be so straightly kept, and he is more obeyed than the king and will depose the king and place another at his will and pleasure. . . . There is yeerely great resort of Marchants to

> this citie of Boghar, which travel in great caravans from the countries thereabout adjoining as India, Persia, Balkh, Russia and divers others, and in times past from Cathay, when there was passage . . . .

Jenkinson admitted, however, that the trade, especially to China, was much interrupted. Numerous monuments from this era are still extant in Bukhara: the Gaukushan complex, the mosque of which was built by the Juybari sheikh Khoja Kalon in 1598; the Kalyan complex, of which the Mir-i Arab *medrese* (religious school) was built by the spiritual adviser to Uzbek prince Abdullah I (1512–39), brother of Ubaidulla Khan; the Chor Bakr complex of 1558, which contains the necropolis of the Juybari sheikhs; the Kukeldush *medrese* of 1568; the mid-sixteenth-century Bahā' ad-Dīn tomb complex; and the Abdul-Aziz *medrese* of 1654, the last major Uzbek building. By this time, however, the prosperity of Bukhara was being subverted by the weakness of the khanate, civil disorder, the decline of international trade as part of the seventeenth-century depression, demographic contraction, and eventually deurbanization. Resources for building were no longer available.

Following the capture of Bukhara by Nāder Shāh in 1740, the Uzbek khanate was replaced by three city-states: the khanates of Khiva and Kokand and the emirate of Bukhara. Under the Manghit emirs, Bukhara recovered a limited prosperity and enjoyed a modest cultural renaissance. The emirs worked closely with the dervishes. Shah Murad, the most successful of them, had been a *medrese* student in his youth and as ruler continued to wear dervish dress and lead his troops on a pony rather than a charger. By 1834, there were sixty *medrese* of various sizes in the city, although Muslim students from outside Transoxiana were beginning to find their teaching ossified and overly traditional. Agriculture was revived by the use of slave labor on royal and *waqf* estates. East-West trade expanded with the Qing conquest of Eastern Turkistan, and additional links with Russia developed via the Tatar community of Kazan. Bukhariot merchants became well known in the cities of Siberia, particularly those trading in salt and rhubarb, although some of them were probably from Altishahr or even Hsi-ning rather than Bukhara itself. Sir Alexander Burnes, the second Englishman to visit Bukhara, was impressed. The city had a population of 150,000, and it was growing: the "country is flourishing, trade prospers, and property is protected," he observed. Moreover, the atmosphere was cosmopolitan. Visitors from all over Asia could be seen, and there was a Jewish community of 4,000. Everything could be bought in the market: European cutlery, Chinese tea, Indian sugar, and spices from Manila. Of this prosperity, the most notable extant monument is the Chor Minor, or four minarets, the gatehouse to a *medrese* built in 1807.

This prosperous period was not long-lived. Beginning in 1840, partly as a result of Britain's invasion of Afghanistan, the emir turned xenophobic; he executed two English East India Company officers, Charles Stoddart and Arthur Conolly, who sought to renew Burnes's intelligence work. The Hungarian Orientalist Arminius Vámbéry, who visited the city in 1863, disguised as a Turkish dervish, was much less impressed than his predecessors. Nevertheless, he admitted that, "The man that has wandered about through the deserts of Central Asia will still find in Bukhara, in spite of all its wretchedness, something of the nature of a metropolis." Dervishism, moreover, linked Bukhara to a wider world. Vámbéry visited the tomb of Bahā' ad-Dīn on arrival and on departure, as was customary, and noted the presence of pilgrims from China. Chinese-speaking Muslims, known as Tungans, were experiencing a religious revival at this time, indeed were on the eve of a major revolt. The revival and revolt were based on a new branch of the Naqshbandīyah known to the Chinese as the *hsin-chiao*, or new sect. It was so named because, in contrast to the older branches of the order, it practiced *dhikr-i jahri,* prolonged vocal prayer, rather than *dhikr-i khafi,* silent meditation. At the same time, however, it returned to the political radicalism of the founder. Indeed, all over the Islamic world at this time, branches of the Naqshbandī order were taking a politically radical turn: at Yemen, Dagestan, Circassia, Indonesia, and Kurdistan. Muslim militancy looked to Bukhara rather than to Constantinople. The Naqshbandī order was not centralized, but, through the *haj* and common veneration for Bahā' ad-Dīn, these currents maintained contact with each other.

In 1868, the emir, having fought an unsuccessful war against the Russians, was forced to accept a czarist protectorate and to cede part of his territory, including Bukhara, to direct Russian rule. Until 1917, Bukhara continued in this status, which resembled that of one of the greater princely states in British India. The railway came, some modernization was accomplished, and the ideas of the Jadids, Muslim modernists from Kazan and the Crimea, began to take hold. During the period of the Russian Revolution, the emir sought but failed to assert greater independence and in 1920 was compelled to withdraw to Afghanistan. Following the suppression of the Basmachi revolt, many of whose local leaders were Naqshbandī dervishes, Bukhara became part of Soviet Uzbekistan ruled by a typical *korenizatsia* regime at Tashkent. Its limited powers were further circumscribed by the determination of Gosplan (Soviet State Planning Committee) in Moscow to turn all Uzbekistan into a cotton plantation. Religion was from time to time severely repressed. The dervish orders were suppressed, but they continued in the form of clandestine, so-called Parallel Islam, and even developed new expressions such as the greater involvement of women, especially in running primary education. The shrine of Bahā' ad-Dīn was converted into a museum of atheism in 1965, but by 1985, it was again a place of pilgrimage. The Mir-i Arab *medrese* was reopened in 1945 as an institution of Official Islam. Soon it had students coming from all over the Soviet Union, some of whom completed their training in the Muslim universities of the Middle East, even before the fall of the Soviet Union in 1991. Bukhara today retains its character as a religious center, an interface between Arabic, Persian, and Turkish cultures, and as the emotionally charged birthplace of an order whose influence is still felt, not only in Central Asia, but in Bosnia, Turkey, and the Caucasus.

Further Reading: A survey of Bukhara's monuments is contained in *Bukhara: A Museum in the Open* (Tashkent: Gafur Gulyam, 1991). The medieval city is covered in R. N. Frye's *Bukhara: The Medieval Achievement* (Norman: University of Oklahoma Press, 1965). For information on the Naqshbandīyah, see Hamid Algar's "The Naqshbandī Order: A Preliminary Survey of its History and Significance" in *Studia Islamica* (Paris), volume 46, 1975–76, and *Les ordres mystique dans l'Islam,* edited by A. Popovic and G. Veinstein, (Paris: Éditions de L'École des Hautes Études en Sciences Sociales, 1986), especially the article by Joseph Fletcher. Bukhara in the nineteenth century is detailed in Arminius Vámbéry's *Sketches of Central Asia* (London: Allen, 1868). For more recent history, see Alexandre Bennigsen and S. Enders Wimbush's *Muslims of the Soviet Empire* (Bloomington: Indiana University Press, and London: Hurst, 1986); Pierre Julien's "In Quest of the Holiest Place in Central Asia" in *Central Asian Survey* (Abingdon, Oxfordshire), volume 4, number 1, 1985; and Glenda Fraser's "Alim Khan and the Fall of the Bukharan Emirate in 1920" in *Central Asian Survey* (Abingdon, Oxfordshire), volume 7, number 4, 1988.

—S. A. M. Adshead

Buxar (Bihār, India)

Location: On the south bank of the Ganges River and the main rail line from Patna to Vārānasī and Allahābād. Buxar lies 62 miles east of Vārānsasī and 75 miles west of Patna.

Description: Buxar is a large village in what was formerly the district of Shāhābād in west Bengal. With fewer than 50,000 inhabitants and generally considered of little interest to visitors, Buxar's historical significance derives entirely from the Battle of Buxar (1764), which guaranteed the future establishment of British control over the entire Indian subcontinent. A small dismantled fort, once significant for its commanding position over the Ganges, remains there.

Contact: Bihār State Tourist Office
Frazer Road
Patna
India
25 295

The Battle of Buxar was fought during the morning of October 23, 1764, between British East India Company forces under Major Hector Munro and an allied Indian force under Mīr Qāsim (the company's client nabob of Bengal), Shujā-ud-Dawlah (the wazir of Awadh), and Shāh 'Ālam (titular Mughal emperor). The British victory at Buxar was the culmination of a long struggle, the principal single episode of which was the victory at Plassey on June 23, 1757, of Lieutenant Colonel Robert Clive over Sirāj-ud-Dawlah, then nabob of Bengal. Plassey finally demonstrated the East India Company's effective sovereignty throughout the richest part of what remained of the old Mughal Empire; the company's handling of the spoils of this victory produced antagonisms that led to the Battle of Buxar.

Clive had been sent to the area to retake Calcutta following that city's capture by Sirāj-ud-Dawlah in 1756. Clive successfully negotiated with the nabob in February 1757 what seemed a generous restoration of the company's valuable trading privileges, but at the same time he entered into secret negotiations with Mīr Ja'far, husband of the nabob's aunt. According to the terms of the deal, Mīr Ja'far was to be made viceroy of Bengal, Bihār, and Orissa; Clive was promised full compensation and increased privileges for the company, along with a personal fortune for himself, his officers, and the company servants. Despite orders to return to Madras, Clive struck the deal on June 4, 1757. It involved the forging of his admiral's signature on a document committing the British to pay 2 million rupees demanded by a Sikh banker who had brokered the conspiracy but then threatened to divulge it unless his silence was bought. Clive's troops then moved upriver toward Murshidābād, deliberately forcing Sirāj-ud-Dawlah into a pitched battle at Plassey, knowing that the forces controlled by Mīr Ja'far would desert the nabob as soon as the battle began. Sirāj-ud-Dawlah fled but was betrayed, caught, and hacked to death on the orders of Mīr Ja'far's son.

As a result of the battle, Clive was enormously enriched, his officers made wealthy, and the company given landowner's rights over a large tract of country south of Calcutta, the annual dues otherwise payable to the nabob to go to Clive until his death, at which point they would revert to the company. Others offered cash benefits included the British and Indian inhabitants of Calcutta and its Armenian merchants. Despite his new position of power, Mīr Ja'far grew to resent his dependence on British intervention, and the company reached an agreement with his son-in-law, Mīr Qāsim, by which Mīr Ja'far would be forced to yield power to him, and the territory demanded by the company would be ceded to it. When Mīr Ja'far refused, the company deposed him in October 1760, placing Mīr Qāsim in power. The resulting situation led directly to the Battle of Buxar.

The territories demanded by the company were the very rich *zamindar* of Burdwān, already assigned to it, and the districts of Midnapur in west Bengal and Chittagong, in what is now Bangladesh. The company established its authority over the three districts, using force in Burdwān, and Mīr Qāsim took possession of the rest of Bengal and Bihār. Although he may have been willing to abandon south Bengal to the British, he apparently intended to establish a territory independent of them much higher up the Ganges, with links to north India and a new capital without a British resident at Monghyr. The British probably overestimated Mīr Qāsim's revenues, and certainly underestimated the shortfall in their own, but the greatest tension was caused by private commercial interests trespassing into areas and commodities hitherto not considered the province of Europeans. European salt trading was particularly contentious, as it deprived Mīr Qāsim of a huge excise tax. The company, feeling that a principle was at stake, decided to defend the private European trading interests.

Fighting broke out in July 1763. Mīr Qāsim was immediately driven out of Bihār into the territory of Shujā-ud-Dawlah, the wazir of Awadh (Oudh), whose intention it was to exploit Mīr Qāsim in a personal attempt to gain control of Bengal. In 1764, supported by the wazir and the titular Mughal emperor Shāh 'Ālam, whose followers no longer constituted an army, and transporting his personal wealth, Mīr Qāsim returned to Bihār across the Karamnasa, entrusting himself to the alliance which Shujā-ud-Dawlah had offered and inscribed on the flyleaves of a copy of the Koran. The agreement was that Mīr Qāsim would pay Shujā-ud-Dawlah

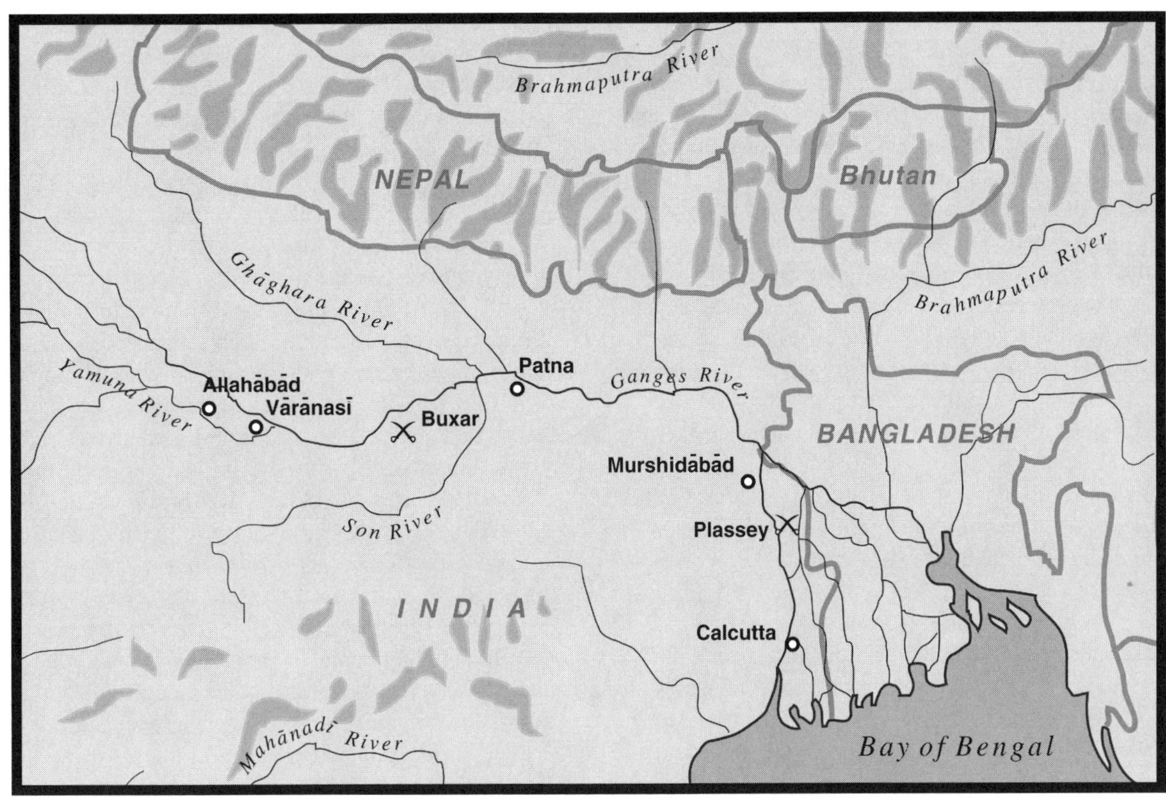

Map showing Buxar's position relative to Plassey and Calcutta
Illustration by Tom Willcockson

1,100,000 rupees per month beginning the day his army crossed the Ganges, in return for which Bengal would be restored to Mīr Qāsim, who would also pay a tribute to the emperor and maintain troops to aid Shujā-ud-Dawlah if necessary. The property of the English and Mīr Ja'far, reinstated by the British when they drove out Mīr Qāsim, was to be divided between Mīr Qāsim, Shujā-ud-Dawlah, and the emperor. The combined armies then set out, reaching Vārānasī on March 7, 1764.

Everything on the company's side was primed to go wrong. The command was in the hands of an experienced artillery officer, Captain Jennings, but he knew that his appointment was temporary and he was not interested in long-term strategies. Jennings had been wrongly assured by his superiors that Mīr Qāsim would receive no help from Shujā-ud-Dawlah. Two-thirds of Jennings's force was composed of unreliable mercenaries, among whom the withholding of a bounty promised by Mīr Ja'far to the company's army had caused serious unrest and nearly led to mass desertion to Mīr Qāsim. In the end, fewer than 200 went over to Mīr Qāsim, but rumblings of trouble continued when a first bounty payment was distributed; six rupees were given to European soldiers for every rupee to Indians of equivalent rank. There was nearly a battle between the two groups, and the bounty paid to the lowest ranking Indian troops was tripled.

On March 5 Major Carnac, notoriously incompetent and avaricious and assuming a semiregal lifestyle, arrived to take command. His camp was to the rear, and decisions were delegated to subordinates. He was later responsible for a major disaster in the west. His army consisted of 750 European infantrymen, 150 artillerymen, 70 European cavalry, 300 Indian cavalry, and 7 battalions of Indian infantry—about 6,000 in all. Both Indian and European reinforcements were on the way. Carnac moved his private tent across a river to the camp of Mīr Ja'far, having reports dealt with by subordinates in his own camp. On March 12 the order to move was given, and on March 17 the army reached Buxar.

On March 24 the company's nonmilitary council in Calcutta ordered Carnac to cross the Karamnasa, but he procrastinated, alleging a shortage of grain. On April 3, Carnac received another command to attack, but he eluded it by calling a council of war, which was persuaded to advise waiting even longer. G. B. Malleson, the author of an 1883 military history of India, writes witheringly of Carnac's repeated dithering and the failures of his intelligence reports (for which he had paid unprecedented sums to obtain).

Meanwhile, the Bengali alliance of Mīr Qāsim, Shujā-ud-Dawlah, and Shāh 'Ālam had reached Vārānasī on March 7 and thrown a bridge of boats over the Ganges. The bridge collapsed with only half the force across, but their army finished crossing on April 2. With Bengali forces now uncomfortably close, Carnac's council of war recommended a retreat seventy-five miles to Patna, for which they departed on April 4. Bengali forces were close behind. After he reached

Buxar on April 9, Shujā-ud-Dawlah tried to cut off Carnac's retreat. On April 17 and 18 he crossed Son River. A chance encounter with an East India Company patrol on April 22 misled Shujā-ud-Dawlah, however, and he decided to abandon the attempt to cut off Carnac. The British reached Patna on April 25 and dug in. When the troops of the Bengali alliance arrived—now 40,000 strong, over half in calvary—they took up a position opposite Carnac's trenches, which were protected by the guns of Patna's fortifications.

Carnac now sent his European cavalry, about seventy men, to engage the enemy and then to withdraw so that the Bengalis would pursue them into an ambush. Unfortunately, when the cavalry followed these orders, withdrawing with the enemy in pursuit, they found no ambush and were lucky to escape.

On May 2, Shujā-ud-Dawlah decided to attack before Carnac received further reinforcements, known to be on the way. Mīr Qāsim failed to send reinforcements, however, and the naked Bengali troops were either slaughtered or forced to flee; the attack, which began at midday, was repulsed by 2:30 P.M. One further attack seemed for a moment to have a chance of success, but Shujā-ud-Dawlah was forced to withdraw, sending a contemptuous message to his ally Mīr Qāsim. Carnac would not allow his troops to pursue. Malleson strongly hints that Carnac was negotiating financially with Shujā-ud-Dawlah and personally profited more that way than he could have by winning a battle. The approach of the rains forced Shujā-ud-Dawlah to break camp, and he fell back to Buxar. On June 28 Carnac was dismissed by the British East India Company's London court of directors.

He was succeeded by Hector Munro, who arrived in Calcutta at the end of May. Munro held discussions with the council, with Carnac, and also with Mīr Ja'far before joining the army—which again was strengthened by fresh reinforcements—on August 13. Munro clearly wished to assert firm leadership immediately. On the day of his arrival, he gathered together a company that had mutinied and placed them in front of his own loyal troops. The mutineers' commander then picked out twenty-four ringleaders, who were condemned to the old Mughal execution of being blown out of guns. Four additional mutineers volunteered to join those condemned, and their offer was accepted. Twenty-four men were blown out of guns on the spot, and the remaining four in front of different troops elsewhere.

On October 6 Munro advanced, his various groups uniting as planned, although not without incident. He split the army into three divisions and advanced again on October 13. When one advanced scouting party was ambushed, Munro became more cautious. He reached the plain of Buxar on October 22, confronting the enemy for an hour before they retreated. The Bengali leadership, meanwhile, was doing some housecleaning of its own. Disdainful of Mīr Qāsim's performance at Patna, Shujā-ud-Dawlah had bribed Mīr Qāsim's troops. He then had Mīr Qāsim robbed, imprisoned, and, the day after Munro arrived at Buxar, turned loose on a lame elephant. Mīr Qāsim found a protector, but the protector died and Mīr Qāsim ended his life in extreme poverty at Delhi. Throughout all this, Emperor Shāh 'Ālam was virtually a prisoner, so that the Bengali alliance was effectively reduced to a single leader, Shujā-ud-Dawlah, entrenched with 40,000 troops under his command.

When the English did not attack on October 22, Shujā-ud-Dawlah resolved to leave his position and attack the next day. Munro, meanwhile, had held a council of war that resolved to rest on the twenty-third and attack on the twenty-fourth, with a feint on the twenty-third to the enemy's left. Munro was alerted to the nabob's attack early on the twenty-third, however, and his army prepared to take up the formation they had practiced if attacked by cavalry. His front line was in four block: right and left center, and right and left flank, interspersed with six six-pounder guns and a twelve-pounder. In the second line, 200 European troops occupied the center, with two battalions of Indian troops on either side, and four six-pounders. Two divisions of cavalry protected the baggage. The army, exclusive of officers and sergeants, comprised 857 Europeans, 5,297 Indian infantry, and 918 Indian cavalry, making in all 7,072 soldiers with 28 guns. In front of the British left was an unfordable marsh and a village. On the right, toward the Ganges, was a grove and the village of Buxar, both occupied by Bengali forces.

Shujā-ud-Dawlah advanced until he was within range, then opened fire with his heavy guns in the center. Since Munro's guns had a shorter range, he ordered an advance. The marsh was successfully bypassed and the left-wing troops formed the practiced formation when attacked by the enemy cavalry. Only the baggage was taken. The critical moment, on which the fate of three provinces of Bengal, Bihar, and Orissa hinged, came when Munro, to avoid discouragement in his army, ordered the taking of the village of Buxar on his right. Everything now depended on action at the grove, which Munro realized he had to take to be victorious. He put his whole strength into the thrust, the success of which was assisted by a mistake of the enemy commander on his left. The Bengali commander, mistakenly believing that the grove had been held, made a frontal assault that was repulsed, giving Munro the now-irreversible advantage.

Shujā-ud-Dawlah succeeded in retreating across the Karamnasa River with his money, jewels, and regular brigades, and then ordered the destruction of the bridge of boats just under two miles from the battle site, leaving men, camels, elephants, horses, and bullocks to drown or be slaughtered. The battle had lasted a mere three hours, from nine A.M. until noon. Of the Bengali casualties, 2,000 drowned and another 2,000 were otherwise killed; the British losses were considered heavy at just under 900 killed and wounded. After the battle, Munro is said to have called the destruction of the boat bridge "the best piece of generalship Shujā-ud-Dawlah showed that day, because if I had crossed the rivulet with the army, I should either have taken or drowned his whole army in the Karamnasa, and come up with his treasure and jewels, and Qāsim Ali Khan's (Mīr Qāsim's) jewels, which I was informed amounted to between two and three millions."

The Buxar victory was the last major military event that guaranteed eventual British control over the entire subcontinent, duly achieved over the following half century. The British reinstated Mīr Ja'far, but insisted that he derive his authority from them, not from the emperor. They made that insistence even clearer when, upon Mīr Ja'far's death in 1765, the British appointed Muhammad Reza Khan his successor as deputy nabob. As Robert Clive wrote, "Either the princes of the country must, in a great measure, be dependent on us, or we totally so on them." After Plassey, Clive had returned home in February 1760 to be made a member of the Irish peerage, which, although it did not give him a seat in the House of Lords, left him eligible as a commoner to be a member of the House of Commons, which he duly arranged. After Buxar, he was immediately called on by the directors of the British East India Company to return to India and reintroduce order into company affairs. He arrived at Calcutta on May 3, 1765, effectively reduced the indigenous rulers to pensioners by the Treaty of Allahābād on August 12, 1765, disbanded the Indian armies, and regulated the private trading by which company officials were expected to supplement their salaries. Technically, the company became the Mughal emperor's *diwan* for the provinces of Bengal, Bihar, and Orissa, and in the immediate wake of Buxar the dividing line between Mughal and British Bengal was established.

Further Reading: A narrative of the battle is to be found in G. B. Malleson's *The Decisive Battles of India from 1746 to 1849 Inclusive* (London: Allen, 1883; third edition, New Delhi: Sagar, 1969). On the pressures leading to the battle of Buxar, the battle itself, and its consequences, historical atlases such as *The Times Atlas of World History,* edited by Geoffrey Barraclough (London: Guild, 1984), together with general histories of India and British colonial expansion in the eighteenth century, are often helpful. Most important are the relevant volumes of *The New Cambridge History of India,* edited by Gordon Johnson, C. A. Bayly, and John F. Richards (29 vols., Cambridge and New York: Cambridge University Press, 1987–), in particular P. J. Marshall's *Bengal: The British Bridgehead: Eastern India, 1740–1828* (1987).

—Claudia Levi

Calcutta (West Bengal, India)

Location: On the Hooghly (Hūgli) River, eighty-five miles from the Bay of Bengal.

Description: Capital city of the British Empire in India from 1774 to 1912, now capital of the state of West Bengal; one of the largest cities in the world, noted for the extreme poverty of many of its citizens.

Site Office: Government of India Tourist Office
4 Shakespeare Sarani
Calcutta, West Bengal 700 071
India
2421402, 2421475, or 2425813

Greater Calcutta (or Kalkatar) is now the largest city in India, containing at least 11 million people and spreading thirty miles along the Hooghly (or Hūgli) River, its prosperous districts intermingled with the *bustees,* the officially registered slums, and other areas inhabited by some of the poorest people in the world. At its heart lies the historic city of Calcutta, founded by the British in 1690, its architecture and many of its institutions still recalling 257 years of British rule.

Before 1690, the area comprised several farming villages, subject to the Mughal Empire based at Delhi. Among these was Kalikshetra, to which Hindu pilgrims came in order to worship at its Kālīghāt, a temple dedicated to the goddess Kālī (wife of Siva), one of whose toes was said to have fallen onto the spot after her corpse was cut into pieces by Vishnu. The temple has given its name to the modern city. But although Calcutta began as a producer of rural goods, its origins have less to do with Bengal's indigenous development of silk, indigo, rice, and other products than with the commercial rivalry among the European powers such development inspired. The Portuguese were the first to arrive, founding a trading post on the river in 1537. The city that grew up around it, twenty-five miles north of Kalikshetra, became a settlement named Hooghly. The Dutch followed, trading out of Chinsura, one mile south of Hooghly, which they owned until 1825 (the two locations have since merged as Hooghly-Chinsura). The French then arrived in 1673, founding Chandannagar, twenty miles from Kalikshetra, which remained under their control until 1950. The English, operating through the East India Company established in 1600, had already begun trading along the river in 1651, but thirty-nine years later the company sent gunboats, commanded by Admiral Nicholson, up the coast from Madras to help persuade the reluctant Mughal officials to sell Kalikshetra and two other villages to the company's local representative, Job Charnock, who had been in India since 1655 and whose mausoleum is the oldest structure now remaining in Calcutta.

From 1700 Calcutta was the headquarters of the company's Bengal Presidency, controlled from the company's offices in the Writers Building and from Fort William, named for King William III and built in 1707. This dual commercial and military function, incidentally, gave rise to the term "civil servant," used to distinguish the company's "writers" (clerks) from the troops. Meanwhile, the company's Indian employees settled in a separate area, known to the British as "Black Town." In 1717 the East India Company was granted trading rights throughout the rest of Bengal, along with possession of another thirty-eight villages after one of its physicians had cured the Mughal emperor Farruksiyar of a venereal disease. But the company's presence in and around Calcutta was resented by the hereditary nabobs (imperial deputies) of Bengal, and relations often broke down, most notably in June 1756, when a new nabob, Sirāj-ud-Dawlah, denounced earlier agreements and attacked the settlement. A number of captured British residents (some accounts say 64, others 146) were imprisoned in the brig at Fort William, where many of them died after being suffocated or exhausted in what became known as the Black Hole of Calcutta. Their deaths provided the pretext for a military campaign against the nabob, led by Robert Clive, which ended in 1757 with the British victory at the Battle of Plassey, with the installation of a rival nabob, Mīr Ja'far, and with Clive's seizure of the Portuguese base at Hūgli. The British Indian Empire is often said to have begun with this triumph, although the other European powers maintained their footholds; indeed, Denmark set up a trading post at Serampore, only thirteen miles from Calcutta, as late as 1755. The Danes sold this post to the British ninety years later.

Mīr Ja'far is believed to have given the extraordinary amount of approximately 4.7 million pounds in cash, jewels, and other presents to Clive and other prominent Britons in Calcutta. Then, in 1765, Clive persuaded the Mughal emperor Shāh 'Alam II to grant the company tax-gathering rights, and therefore also opportunities for corruption on a massive scale, for the whole of Bengal. Trade continued to grow both with Europe through official company channels and, through the "country trade," which the East India Company's staff were allowed to conduct for themselves, with the rest of India, as well as with Arabia, China, and Southeast Asia. The wealthiest merchants, including Clive, who was to become a member of the British Parliament, a landowner, and an opium addict before his suicide in 1774, came to be known as nabobs (a term borrowed from the earlier Mughal nabobs, from Urdū "Nawab"), while many *banians,* local Indian merchants, were able to make considerable fortunes in joint ventures with them. Bengal soon came to supply approximately three-fifths of all goods imported into Britain from the whole of Asia. Meanwhile, poorer Bengalis continued to suffer from spo-

Victoria Memorial, Calcutta
Photo courtesy of Air India Library, New York

radic epidemics and famines, as, for example, in 1770, when perhaps 76,000 people starved to death in Calcutta itself, while thousands more died in the surrounding countryside.

A new and larger Fort William was completed in 1770, to the south of its predecessor. It is still a military headquarters (now for the Eastern Region of the Indian Army), and still the centerpiece of the Maidan, an open space originally created to give British troops clear lines of fire, now an enormous park rivaling in area Central Park in New York or Phoenix Park in Dublin. Only three years later the East India Company, desperate for a loan from the Bank of England, had to accept intervention from the British Parliament, in the form of an act stipulating, first, that those of its officials who had tax-gathering or judicial powers must withdraw from the country trade and, second, that British residents must not accept any more gifts such as those Mīr Jaf'ar had offered. Warren Hastings, governor of Bengal and, from 1774, the first governor-general of the company's Indian possessions, aroused enmity by trying to enforce these rules, but also gained supporters, partly by sponsoring the construction of a new Writers Building in 1780. Hastings was eventually tried for corruption by parliament after his retirement in 1785, but was acquitted, mainly because his prosecutors failed to include his illegal dealings in silk, opium, and diamonds among the charges.

By this time the British quarter of Calcutta was being referred to as a "city of palaces" because of its impressive offices, mansions, and public buildings. These included several churches, notably St. John's (opened in 1787), with its cemetery laid out around Charnock's mausoleum, its fittings including a painting of the Last Supper by Johan Zoffany, who used leading members of the British community as models for the disciples of Jesus. But the most magnificent building of this period is the administrative complex then known as Government House, which was completed in 1802. This domed, brick structure, covered with plaster, is a copy of Kedleston Hall, a stately home in England. Now known as the Raj Bhavan, it is the official residence of the governor of West Bengal.

Another important new complex was Fort William College, founded in 1800, where prospective company writers were to be trained both by their British seniors and by Bengali scholars. There the first Christian missionaries in India began to preach and publish; there also the literary and political movement known as the Bengali Renaissance was initiated. In 1813 this movement found an additional home at the Hindu College, established in that year; as Presidency College, it is now part of the University of Calcutta, founded in 1857. The British capital of India thus became the capital of the *bhadralok,* the Bengali elite, many of them absentee landlords of the poor peasants in the surrounding countryside. The *bhadralok* took from these and other educational institutions a number of important lessons in modern science and scholarship, as well as in developing a national identity. This elite's early leaders included Raja Rajendra Mullick Bahadur, whose Marble Palace, completed in 1835, is still used to display the numerous Indian and European paintings and other art objects that he and his family collected; and Rammohan Roy, an influential thinker who was among the first to advocate such reforms as abolishing *satī* (or suttee), the ancient Hindu custom requiring widows to join their dead husbands on the funeral pyre.

According to the first census taken in Calcutta in 1821, the city contained at least 120,000 Hindus and 48,000 Muslims—all excluded, along with the small number of Indian Christian converts, from political power of any kind, which resided with Calcutta's 13,000 British residents. Even the bhadralok lacked any direct influence over, for example, Lord William Bentinck, governor-general from 1828 to 1835 and the first to be called governor-general of India (from 1834). Bentinck abolished *satī* and suppressed the Thugs, worshippers of Kālī who ritually strangled travelers (and whose name has passed, mispronounced, into the English language). He also inaugurated the Grand Trunk Road, which would eventually link Calcutta to Delhi and help to alter patterns of communication and settlement across northern India.

Calcutta was not directly involved in the Indian Mutiny that erupted across the northern provinces in 1857, but the savage punishments meted out to mutineers, real or suspected, in Calcutta and elsewhere during 1858 went beyond the effective control of Viscount Canning, governor-general from 1856, and marked the beginning of organized anti-British sentiment in the city. Another result of the mutiny was that Canning became the first viceroy of India in 1858, when the British government took direct control of the country. For fifty-four years Calcutta would be the capital of by far the largest single body of British subjects, in a "Raj" that covered approximately two-thirds of the Indian subcontinent, dominated the activities of the 562 traditional rulers in the other one-third, and also supervised British interests in the Persian Gulf and in Burma (now Myanmar). All this vast territory officially became an empire in 1877, when Queen Victoria was proclaimed Kaisar-i-Hind (Empress of India).

Calcutta was now home to a large, stratified British community, whose leading members cemented their business and political relationships through the Bengal Club (founded in 1827), the Tollygunge Club (founded in 1895), and other exclusive societies. Much of this population's wealth came from the city's jute mills after British investors and managers, most of them Scots, seized the opportunity offered by the disappearance of Russian jute from European markets during the Crimean War, which began in 1854. Jute and other products made Calcutta the leading center of manufacturing in the subcontinent and gave it economic dominance over neighboring provinces, which supplied it in turn with food, tea, iron ore, and coal. (Most of the tea, from Darjeeling, Assam, and elsewhere, had in fact been developed by East India Company officials at the city's Botanical Gardens, founded in 1787.)

The British enhanced their city with still more imposing public buildings, which may be seen as outstanding examples of Victorian architecture, as unpleasant relics of imperialism, or, without stretching the imagination too much, as both at once. St. Paul's Cathedral, for example, had been built in 1847; since the 1940s it has been graced with a tower based on the Bell Harry Tower of Canterbury Cathedral in England. The domed and colonnaded General Post Office was built in 1868, on the site of the older Fort William; the Gothic High Court complex, based on the Cloth Hall in Ypres, Belgium, and on the Rathaus in Hamburg, Germany, was completed in 1872; the enormous and eclectic Indian Museum was founded in 1875; and a grandiose terra-cotta facade was added to the Writers Building in 1880.

The cityscape was also improved by the increasingly influential leaders of the Indian population of Calcutta, most of whom lived along unpaved streets on the mudflats beyond the British center of the city. The Kālīghat had already been rebuilt and expanded in 1809, but in 1847 the twelve-towered Dakshineswar Kālī Temple, with its twelve subtemples, was built elsewhere in the city to honor Kālī, Siva, and other deities popular among Bengali Hindus. Between 1835 and 1843, three new mosques—known respectively as Ghulam-Muḥammad's, Shahbani Begum's, and Tipu Sultan's—were opened for the city's Muslim population. Each mixed Islamic and European traditions of architecture; each was financed respectively by the first two named and by descendants of the third named, Tipu Sultan (or Tipu Sahib), one of the greatest military opponents of British rule, who had been defeated and killed at Seringapatam in 1799.

Two events took place in Calcutta in 1898 that symbolize perhaps better than any others the extremes of imperial rule. In the first, Ronald Ross, experimenting with mosquitoes at the Presidency General Hospital, determined how malaria was spread; in the second, Captain Bertie Clay, working at the military barracks in Dum Dum (now the site of Calcutta's international airport), perfected the soft-nosed lethal objects still known to the British as "dum-dum bullets." By then the city had expanded to the opposite bank of the Hooghly to take in Haora (or Howrah) and other older settlements, so that Calcutta had become the second largest city in the British Empire, with a population of more than 1 million. Among the non-British population, nationalist feeling was steadily growing.

In 1905, those opposing British rule in Calcutta found two local issues on which to focus: the transfer of city government from the elected Indian council to an appointed committee with a British majority; and the proposal to partition Bengal into two separate provinces, Western Bengal, with Calcutta at its heart, and Eastern Bengal. Mass protests, which included a boycott of British goods in favor of swadeshi, or Indian, products, along with resignations by Bengali officials and university teachers, secured the removal of Lord Curzon of Kedleston, the viceroy who had made these unwelcome changes. However, his successor, the Earl of Minto, maintained both policies in the face of bombings and demonstrations organized by a variety of groups, notably the new Muslim League and the internally divided but increasingly radical Indian National Congress (usually referred to simply as "Congress"). Caught between these groups' hostility and the distrust of the British business community, which looked to him to impose repressive measures, the Earl of Minto introduced greater Indian representation in government bodies. After he departed in 1910, his successor, Baron Hardinge of Penshurst, began preparing his officials for two new decisions: first, to redivide the province into three—a reunited but smaller Bengal for the Bengali people, and two smaller provinces, Bihār and Orissa, for non-Bengalis; and second, to remove the capital to Delhi. The departure from Calcutta was kept secret until December 1911, when King George V, visiting Delhi for a Durbar (a celebration of his coronation), announced that Calcutta would cease to be the capital on April 1, 1912. A simultaneous announcement was made in Calcutta, where the resident British community greeted the news with dismay and anger.

Meanwhile, Curzon had left behind him plans for the Victoria Memorial in Calcutta, which was eventually completed in 1921. This elaborate white marble conglomeration of Italian Renaissance and Mughal styles dwarfs any such memorial in Britain. It contains twenty-five galleries, displaying records and pictures of British Calcutta, and is adorned, not just with two different statues of the Queen-Empress herself, one of bronze in the open air and one of marble inside, but also with figures of such characteristic Victorian abstractions as Motherhood, Prudence, Art, Justice, and, perching atop yet another dome, a Winged Victory. By the time the memorial was officially opened, Calcutta was moving decisively away from such British triumphalism. Wealthier Indians were beginning to achieve some financial independence: Indian investors, for example, now owned about one-half the shares in the city's jute companies. Poorer Indians were becoming ever more divided along religious lines, especially in Bengal, where Muslims formed a majority in the countryside but minorities in the cities, and where intercommunal riots occurred in Calcutta in 1918, 1924, and 1926. The possible directions in which Calcutta, and India, might proceed during the twentieth century were to many observers indicated by the contrasting careers of two great Bengalis of the period.

Rabindranath Tagore (1861–1941) is perhaps the one Calcutta intellectual known throughout the world. His poems and plays brought him the Nobel Prize for literature in 1913, the first to be awarded to an Asian, making him one of the first prominent Indians to be taken up, somewhat patronizingly, by Europeans and Americans. His political activities, culminating in his retirement in 1921 after he had broken with what he saw as the excessive anti-Westernism of the nationalist leaders, brought him many followers but had little effect on independent India, although one of his songs became the national anthem and his humanist theories of education are still practiced at the Rabindra Bharati University in Calcutta, which he founded.

Subhas Chandra Bose (1897–1945) represented a very different type of bhadralok. After studying at the universities of Calcutta and Cambridge, he was appointed chief executive of the Calcutta Corporation, the city's government, in 1924, when the nationalist Swaraj Party won a majority of its seats. The British promptly jailed him as a "terrorist." Bose alternately spent time in prison, served as mayor of Calcutta, and made propaganda trips to Europe until 1938, when he became president of Congress. In 1941 he left Calcutta, just before yet another trial, and reappeared in Hitler's Berlin, where he remained until 1943, when he flew to Tokyo to place his "Indian National Army" under Japanese protection. In October 1943 his 25,000 troops entered India through Burma but were beaten back. After several more defeats, Bose died of injuries suffered in a plane crash in Taiwan in August 1945. One of the main avenues of Calcutta is now named for him, and there are two statues of him in the city, one of them on the Maidan near the Raj Bhavan.

As it turned out, however, neither Tagore's mystical humanism nor Bose's military adventurism was to lead India to independence. During the period between Tagore's death and Bose's invasion, Calcutta, along with the rest of Bengal, suffered a famine that, following a series of bad rice harvests, devastated the province during 1943 and led to the deaths of at least 2 million people. The British, who had been quick to criticize, for example, the Soviet Union when famine broke out there, did little until the autumn of 1943, when a new viceroy, Lord Wavell of Cyrenaica, visited Calcutta and directed the army to organize relief supplies.

The famine was followed by a renewal of intercommunal unrest as the city's Hindus and Muslims were turned against each other by their political leaders. In 1946 the Muslim League's national leader, Mohammed Ali Jinnah, announced a day of "direct action" to support demands for a separate homeland, Pakistan. The announcement set off riots in Calcutta that left approximately 4,000 people dead, and murders and disturbances continued even after August 1947, when India and Pakistan became independent. Mahatma Gandhi, who withdrew to Calcutta rather than join in the independence celebrations in New Delhi, appears to have brought some calm to the situation for at least a few weeks.

Tagore, Bose, and Gandhi alike had opposed plans for the partition of the subcontinent, but the mutual distrust of Congress and the Muslim League, and the hasty departure of the British, made such partition inevitable. At least 5 million people were exchanged, many by force or in desperation, between the two new nation-states, while in Bengal Curzon's plan was effectively revived, with Eastern Bengal becoming East Pakistan, an enclave surrounded by Indian territory apart from its southern coast, and the remainder, around Calcutta, becoming the Indian state of West Bengal. These changes also had a lasting impact on the economy of the city, which was effectively deprived of its supplies of raw jute by the breakdown in commercial relations between India and Pakistan from 1949 onward. More than 3 million people, including thousands of Hindu refugees from what had become East Pakistan, were now living in a city with increasingly inadequate supplies of water, electricity, and other utilities, under a government that was so embarrassingly incompetent, corrupt, and close to bankruptcy that a report on its activities, commissioned by the new government of West Bengal, was withheld from official publication. Conditions became worse for most of the city's residents during the 1950s and 1960s, although some alleviation was offered by the Missionaries of Charity, a Catholic order that had been founded in 1940 by Mother Teresa and set up the first of its nearly 300 homes and refuges in 1952.

In 1967, however, the voters of Calcutta made it clear that they wanted, and needed, more than places to die and Christian prayers over their corpses. In that year, for the first time since independence, the Congress was outnumbered in the state assembly of West Bengal by a variety of communist and other leftist parties, which overcame their mutual suspicions to form a coalition government, dedicated above all to land reform. The ensuing confrontation with the Congress government of India led to the dismissal of the coalition in 1969 and its replacement by direct rule from New Delhi. This arrangement lasted for more than a year before giving way to another fragile United Front government in 1970.

Meanwhile, after the Communist Party of India—which, Marxist in orientation, called itself CPI(M)—expelled those of its members in the rural Naxalbari district who had taken land reform to mean arranging armed warfare between peasants and police, the dissidents created the terrorist Naxalite movement and proclaimed a new Communist Party of India (now with a Marxist-Leninist emphasis) at a rally on the Maidan. By doing so they inadvertently enabled the authorities to blame them for all the murders, kidnappings, riots, and other troubles that were making Calcutta ungovernable, although they were just one of several radical groups operating in the city, as in the countryside. The main parties in the United Front turned against each other, the coalition collapsed, and rule by the national government was imposed once again, this time with martial law throughout the city. The leftists assembled again, briefly, for the unveiling of a statue of Lenin on the centenary of his birth, in April 1970.

During 1971, the Naxalites and many others suspected of having ties to them were suppressed, often brutally, by the army and the police, and a new Congress-led coalition was elected to power. This body was immediately confronted with a new crisis over the Pakistan Civil War that began in March 1971 and quickly became a war of independence for Bangladesh, the former East Pakistan or Eastern Bengal. Some 10 million refugees entered West Bengal during that year, and although most returned home during 1972, many joined the poor of Calcutta. The state government tried to take direct relief measures, abolishing the Calcutta Corporation in 1972, but was itself placed under severe limits during the national state of emergency proclaimed by Indira Gandhi in 1975. One event during these years offered some hope: in 1975 the Hooghly, which had long been so silted up that the salinity of the city's drinking water frequently rose to dangerous levels, was freshened and cleaned with water diverted from the Ganges by a national government scheme that was, in fact, a revival of plans made in the 1850s. The number of oceangoing vessels reaching Calcutta rose to a level not seen since the nineteenth century, and the city's commerce and industry began to revive.

In 1977, after the state of emergency ended, the CPI(M) came to power in West Bengal as the leading party in a Left Front coalition that remains in office, under chief minister Jyoti Basu, in the mid-1990s. The new government marked its victory with the symbolic removal of the sixteen statues of British statesmen and other heroes then still standing on the Maidan. During the 1980s, the government invested in a subway system for the city, the first in India, and in a new suspension bridge over the Hooghly. Further, following the example set by the Indian national government from 1991 onward, the West Bengal Marxists have begun to liberalize the economy, in order to attract foreign investment and encourage free-market capitalism, while continuing to promote the development of ports, roads, and air services and to seek some way to sustain the jute industry, which has long been in decline relative to its competition in Bangladesh.

The British monuments in the historic center of Calcutta continue to decay, the population goes on rising, and chronic poverty is still the lot of most of the people of Calcutta (even while thousands of better-placed individuals are benefiting from the government's abandonment of its revolutionary program). The only city in the world to contain statues of both Queen Victoria and Lenin, Calcutta has gained much and suffered much from its encounters with the West these figures represent. Still, it has yet to find either the harmony between native and foreign traditions envisaged by Tagore, or the social justice Bose demanded and for which, rather than for his disastrous choice of allies, he is honored in the city today.

Further Reading: Geoffrey Moorhouse's *Calcutta* (New York: Harcourt Brace, and London: Weidenfeld and Nicolson, 1971) is a fascinating and affectionate description of the city's past and present, although the author occasionally leans over backward to find still more aspects of British rule to praise.

—Patrick Heenan

Cebu City (Cebu, Philippines)

Location: On the eastern coast of Cebu Island in the Visayas, south-central Philippines, 367 miles southeast of Manila.

Description: Cebu City, oldest and one of the largest cities in the Philippines, is a thriving center for trade and commerce. The city and its harbor are protected on the inland by the Cordillera Central range and offshore by Mactan Island. The Portuguese navigator Ferdinand Magellan landed in Cebu in 1521, paving the way for what was to be four centuries of Spanish rule in the Philippines.

Site Office: Department of Tourism
3/F GMC Plaza Building
Legaspi Street, 6000
Cebu City
Philippines
(32) 91503 or 96518

The Philippine Archipelago is made up of more than 7,000 islands. The central cluster of these are known as the Visayas and are located south of Luzon, which is home to the capital Manila, and north of Mindanao. Cebu is the point of entry to the Visayas and is in many ways the second Philippine city after Manila. Many Manila firms maintain branches in Cebu City, where interisland commodities such as fish, sugar, timber, abaca, and copra are shipped to Manila and throughout the country. The local economy is also based on the manufacture of textiles, chemicals, and furniture, as well as pearl and aquamarine jewelry.

It was in Cebu that the Spaniards first landed in the Philippines, and there is still extensive evidence of the city's long Hispanic history. Furthermore, preserved in the accounts of some of the first European visitors to the island is evidence of life in the settlement before the arrival of the Spanish. The most important of these accounts is that of Antonio Pigafetta, chronicler of Ferdinand Magellan's expedition and emissary to the natives encountered on the way.

In the sixteenth century Spain and Portugal were vying for control over the spice trade and over the newly discovered New World. Threatened with Portuguese supremacy in the spice trade, the Spanish crown commissioned a Portuguese navigator, Ferdinand Magellan, to captain a Spanish expedition to the Moluccas via the Atlantic and the Spanish colonies in America. This entailed sailing around the southern tip of South America and then crossing the Pacific. The journey was arduous and perilous: it took Magellan and his men eighteen months to reach the easternmost Philippine Islands, off the coast of Samar. After another seven months of negotiating their way between the central and southern Philippine Islands, they reached the Spice Islands. Of the entire expedition, only one ship returned to Seville in 1522, able to claim to have been the first ship to circumnavigate the globe.

Magellan, however, was not on that returning ship. He lost his life in Cebu. The chieftain Kolambu of Samar, the first Filipino with whom Magellan's men made contact, had directed the party to Cebu, where they might find food and fresh water. According to Pigafetta, the first natives the Spaniards saw must have made a deep impression. Pigafetta described Kolambu's brother Siaui as

> the finest looking man that we saw among those people. His hair was exceedingly black, and hung to his shoulders. He had a covering of silk on his head, and wore two large golden earrings fastened in his ears. He wore a cotton cloth all embroidered with silk, which covered him from the waist to the knees. At his side hung a dagger, the shaft of which was somewhat long and all of gold, and its scabbard of carved wood. He had three spots of gold on every tooth and his teeth appeared as if bound with gold. He was perfumed with storax and benzoin. He was tawny and painted [i.e., tattooed] all over.

The Spaniards sailed into Cebu harbor as if for battle, firing their guns to intimidate the natives. Magellan then sent a message to the chieftain, saying that this welcome was to "honor the king of the village."

Cebu was already a center of trade for Chinese, Thai, and Arabian ships, and the chieftain Humabon refused to exempt the Spaniards from the docking tax required of these other countries' ships. Magellan, however, refused to pay—hardly an auspicious start to relations between the Cebuanos and the Spanish. Yet Humabon did grant his hospitality to the Spanish delegation, giving them the opportunity to see the riches from China and elsewhere that the chieftain and his family had in their households. During this visit, the Spanish were told that trade with China came through the northern island of Luzon; a later Spanish expedition under Miguel López de Legazpi set out to control that trading center, Manila, in 1571.

Magellan invited Humabon to serve the Spanish king and to adopt the Christian faith, itself a useful tool for gaining subservience. Although Humabon had claimed to be the most important chieftain in Cebu, it soon became clear that he did not exercize complete authority. Indeed, he used the existence of many other dissenting chieftains as an excuse to avoid this unwelcome "invitation." Eventually Humabon and his family submitted to Spanish rule, promising to pay a tribute to the

Magellan's Cross, Cebu City
Photo courtesy of Philippine Consulate General

Fort San Pedro, Cebu City
Photo courtesy of Philippine Consulate General

king of Spain. In part they may have been influenced by the reports of foreign traders, who told them of Portuguese control over parts of India and the inevitability of such submission. As a sign of their recognition of the new order, Humabon's entire family was baptized. Thereupon Magellan presented Humabon's wife with a statue of the child Jesus, which was later discovered by members of the Legazpi expedition and now recognized as the oldest Catholic relic in the Philippines, housed in the Augustinian church in Cebu.

Some of the other chieftains were less pliant, especially when Magellan insisted that all other chieftains in the region now pay homage to Humabon, according to the terms of the new "friendship" between Humabon and the Spanish. One in particular, Chieftain Lapu-lapu, refusing to recognize either the supremacy of his rival Humabon or the overall sovereignty of the Spanish invaders, caused Magellan to launch an attack on his kingdom, the island of Mactan, opposite Cebu. Magellan went well prepared, accompanied by sixty well-armed soldiers, but even so the Spanish forces were no match for Lapu-lapu's army of 1,500 warriors, armed with bows and arrows and metal-tipped spears. Having set fire to the village, the Spaniards only saw their adversary more determined to overwhelm and rout them. Magellan and several members of his party lost their lives that day in hand-to-hand combat, vividly described by Pigafetta.

As was clear to Pigafetta, who described the deceased Magellan as "our mirror, our light, our comfort, our true guide," the loss of their leader was a major setback for the Spanish expedition. Most importantly it meant that the newly subdued Cebuanos under Humabon no longer harbored quite the same awe for the Spanish as before. The Spanish threat now seemed somewhat hollow. In fact, Humabon soon afterward proved a treacherous ally when he invited several of the Spaniards to attend a banquet during which he had them mercilessly killed. Those remaining on board the Spanish vessels heard the outcry and abandoned any surviving comrades to their fate, setting sail immediately.

It was not until 1564 that another Spanish expedition set sail for the Philippines. In the meantime Spain and Portugal had signed the treaty of Zaragoza in 1530, by which the Spanish ceded all claims to the Moluccas and all territory west of "a line drawn pole to pole . . . 296 1/2 leagues east" of those islands in exchange for 350,000 ducats. While this meant that their claim on the Philippines was disputable, the Spanish were still eager to establish a foothold in Southeast Asia and saw the Philippines, or "Las Islas del Poniente" (the Western Isles), as an opportunity for just such a venture. Moreover, the Spanish authorities, haunted by the idea of Spanish men stranded during the ignominious withdrawal of Magellan's expedition from Cebu in 1521, resolved to return to find them if they were still alive. This time, however, the expedition was to set sail from the Spanish colony of Nueva España, or Mexico, which significantly reduced the length and the danger of the voyage.

The king himself corresponded with the Mexican viceroy, Don Luis de Velasco, to arrange the expedition, urging him to instruct the captain that he was on a voyage of "discovery of the Islands of the West in the region of the Moluccas" but to avoid any action that might be interpreted as an infringement on the Treaty of Zaragoza. An Augustinian friar, Father Andrés Urdaneta, was appointed navigator of the expedition, together with Velasco's kinsman, Miguel López de Legazpi, as commander of the fleet. It was Urdaneta's view that the expedition be justified solely as a rescue operation for the stranded Spaniards left in the islands in 1521. In the midst of this diplomatic confusion, Velasco died and the expedition was placed under the control of the Mexican Audiencia (Supreme Court). Owing to the great delays in any correspondence between the New World and the Spanish Peninsula, further clarification from the king was not sought. Instead, the Audiencia instructed Legazpi to set out for the Western Islands with commercial and missionary intentions. Thus left with considerable control over his own expedition, Legazpi hoped to colonize the islands while recognizing the limitations of his small expeditionary force and the unknown challenges of the Philippines, so far from the rest of the Spanish Empire. All that the Audiencia asked was that Father Urdaneta, a trusted and revered navigator, should return to Mexico across the Pacific, thus charting a new route and opening the way for the galleon trade between Manila and Acapulco in the seventeenth century.

Finally, five years after King Philip II's first instructions, the Legazpi expedition left the Mexican port of Navidad on November 21, 1564. It took three months to cross the Pacific, and in February 1565 it cast anchor off the island of Samar, just as Magellan had done. Legazpi's men spent the next few months exploring the Visayas and the coast of Mindanao. Everywhere they went they claimed to have taken possession of the territories, meeting with no resistance from the inhabitants. This proved to be an empty victory, however, for the *indios* or native Filipinos had simply retreated inland with all their provisions. It was not until May that Legazpi's expedition arrived in Cebu, by this time badly in need of fresh water and food.

On the basis of their various exploratory trips, Legazpi's men concluded that Cebu not only had an excellent harbor in which the Spanish vessels could be safely anchored, but also that the island seemed to be well populated, both in the coastal regions and further inland. Desperate now for food and provisions, Legazpi resolved to offer Cebu Spanish friendship in return for these supplies; failing that, he would take what he needed by force, perhaps by taking the chieftain hostage until food was released to his men. Legazpi justified a more aggressive approach to Cebu on the grounds that its inhabitants had committed treason against their first Spanish friends, the Magellan party.

By 1569 reports began to reach the Mexican authorities of activities in Cebu not worthy of the Spanish name; some claimed that local inhabitants were being abused and exploited by Legazpi's expeditionary force. Although the military authorities protested that such reports, given by friars returning from the Philippines, were exaggerated, they were not able to refute the fundamental allegations. This situation arose with Legazpi's arrival in Cebu in April 1565 and continued as an inevitable result of the unwelcome nature of their conquest of Cebu the following month. After their experiences with Spanish "friendship" forty years before, the Cebuanos were hardly receptive to Legazpi's proposals of vassalage to the Spanish king. Remembering the hollow claim of Spanish invincibility, they armed themselves, ready to resist any Spanish use of force. Once again, however, the sound of Spanish cannon fired from the fleet sitting in Cebu harbor left a strong impression on the *indios,* who decided against a confrontation and instead retreated inland with all the food and supplies they were able to carry, burning whatever they could not take with them.

All attempts to establish some kind of exchange, however illusory, for the food so urgently needed by the demoralized Spanish soldiers were then abandoned, and looting and violence followed as the only means the Spanish could see of sustaining themselves. Even after Legazpi had succeeded in meeting Chief Tupa of Cebu and exacting from him an agreement to submit to Spanish rule, the invaders met with no greater measure of collaboration or assistance, and in fact many of the island's inhabitants simply fled to neighboring islands and the rule of a different chief. Thus Legazpi's first few years in the Philippines were marked by constant battle to maintain control over the native population, if only in sufficient measure to feed his men, as well as to stem the tide of mutiny among his own ranks of disillusioned and demoralized soldiers. All the time he awaited further orders from Spain or from Mexico, as well as relief in the form of a subsequent fleet, after the successful return of his flagship, with Father Urdaneta on board, to Mexico in 1565.

The following year an expedition was indeed sent out from Mexico, although it barely survived the Pacific crossing and thus gave no relief to Legazpi's men when it finally arrived, exhausted, in October 1566. As Cebu was proving a tough outpost for the Spanish conquerors, Legazpi sent his second in command, Martín de Goiti, to explore and try to take Manila in 1570. The full force of Legazpi's expeditionary fleet was required to accomplish that task the following year, after which the Spanish colonizers moved their headquarters to Manila, where they were able to benefit from trade with Chinese junks.

Cebu remained the main Spanish colonial outpost and Catholic mission in the southern Philippines, however, and it retains much of this historic flavor today. The oldest street in the Philippines is Colon Street, now in the center of downtown Cebu City. Many Chinese mestizos fled Manila, especially after the massacre of 1603, and settled in Cebu, the second trading center of the Philippines. As in Manila, there is a Chinese Parian district, where the Mestizo de Sangley, as the Chinese mestizos were called by the Spanish, lived in the sixteenth and seventeenth centuries; it later became home to the professional, merchant, and land-owning classes of Cebu. In this district there is a restored nineteenth-century Spanish house, now open to the public, that was home to the Gorordo family, one member of which, Juan Gorordo (1862–1934), became the first Filipino bishop of Cebu. The house was acquired by this Spanish family shortly after Cebu was declared open to foreign trade in 1860. Another earlier testimony to the Spanish presence in the city can be found in Fort San Pedro, the oldest and the smallest fort in the Philippines, built by Legazpi's expeditionary fort soon after they settled in Cebu and named after his flagship.

The Basilica Minore del Santo Niño occupies a special place in the history of the Catholic missionaries to the Philippines. It houses the statue of the child Jesus that Magellan presented to Chief Humabon's wife as a baptismal gift, rediscovered by a member of Legazpi's expedition undamaged after forty years of neglect and a fire in 1565. Taking these circumstances as an omen, the Augustinians constructed a church on the spot where the statue was rediscovered. Although this first church was destroyed by another fire in 1568, it was rebuilt in 1602 and remains standing today. The venerated relic is now swathed in robes encrusted with jewels and encased in glass to the right of the altar. Outside the City Hall, inside a small kiosk and incorporated into a more recent wooden cross are the remains of Magellan's Cross, placed on the shore of Cebu harbor and torn down in rage by the Cebuanos. It is claimed as the oldest European relic in the Philippines.

Further Reading: General introductions to the Philippines include *The Philippines: A Singular and a Plural Place* by David Joel Steinberg (Boulder, Colorado: Westview Press, 1982); *The Filipino Nation: The Philippines: Lands and Peoples, A Cultural Geography* by Eric S. Casiño (Manila: Grolier International Philippines, 1982); and *The Filipino Nation: A Concise History of the Philippines* by Helen R. Tubangui, Lesie E. Bauzon, Marcelino A. Foronda Jr., and Luz U. Ausejo (Manila: Grolier International Philippines, 1982). The history of the Philippines in the context of Southeast Asia, that is, sharing traits with Thailand, Laos, Cambodia, Malaysia and Indonesia, Burma, China, and Annam, is given a fascinating account in *The Philippines in the World of Southeast Asia* by E. P. Patañne (n.p.: Enterprise Publications, Philippines, 1972). For specific information regarding recent Philippine history, including the overthrow of the Marcos regime and the considerable problems now faced by the country, see *Impossible Dream* by Sandra Burton (New York: Warner Books, 1989), *Imelda Marcos* by Carmen Navarro Pedrosa (London: Weidenfeld and Nicholson, and New York: St. Martin's, 1987), and "The Snap Revolution" by James Fenton in *Granta* (Cambridge), volume 18, Spring 1986.

—Hilary Collier Sy-Quia

Chiang Mai (Chiang Mai, Thailand)

Location: Northwestern Thailand, on the Ping River, near the center of a fertile valley. Average elevation is 1,100 feet.

Description: Historically Chiang Mai served as the royal residence and the capital of the independent kingdom of Lan Na. Now this city serves as the religious, economic, cultural, educational, and transportation center for northern Thailand and parts of adjacent Myanmar (Burma). The city also has strong cultural ties to Laos.

Site Office: Tourism Authority of Thailand
105/1 Chiang Mai-Lamphun Road
Amphoe Muang
Chiang Mai 50000
Thailand
(53) 248 604 or (53) 248 607

Chiang Mai, Thailand's third-largest city and capital of the northern region, is situated 430 miles north of Bangkok on the banks of the Ping River. The ancient settlement sits in a broad, fertile region known as the Chiang Mai Valley. The valley, approximately twenty-five miles long and twelve miles wide (at its broadest point), is bordered on the east and west by jungle-covered mountain ridges. The area's seclusion accounts for the independent historical and cultural development of this 700-year-old community.

The history of Chiang Mai dates back more than 1,000 years, when a group of peoples known as the Lua occupied the valley. This civilization later was forced into the surrounding highlands by more powerful and advanced newcomers. Next to occupy the valley were the Mon, whose central kingdom was located in the Chao Phraya River basin near present-day Bangkok. The more advanced Mon civilization was known for its accomplishments in the arts and in architecture. The Mon were ruled by Chama Devi, an illustrious queen who, in 660, established her capital at Haripunchai (now Lamphun) fifteen miles south of Chiang Mai. For several centuries, Haripunchai dominated the area, controlling both the fertile Chiang Mai Valley and the strategic Ping River, which was important for travel, trade, and communication. By the thirteenth century, the nearby highland valleys had been organized into small city-states by bands of Tai peoples who probably originated in southwestern China and began migrating southward into Thailand, Laos, and portions of Burma (now called Myanmar). These city-states of northern Thailand were governed overall by a state power based at Chiang Saen, located on the Mekong River beyond the mountains north of the Chiang Mai Valley.

In 1259 King Mangrai succeeded his father, King Lao Meng, as ruler of Chiang Saen. Upon assuming power, Mangrai gathered several small tribes and began moving south in a crusade to capture Tai principalities. In 1262 he established a temporary capital at Chiang Rai north of the Chiang Mai Valley. Twelve years later, he crossed over the rugged mountains west of his capital and settled in Fang, a narrow river valley north of Chiang Mai; the acquisition of Fang allowed access to the Chiang Mai Valley. The king's goal, however, was to capture the powerful city of Haripunchai. He planted an agent named Ai Fa, who procured a post at the court of the king of Haripunchai. During seven years of scheming, Ai Fa laid the foundation for a successful coup by Mangrai in 1281. Upon seizing the throne, Mangrai named his new kingdom Lan Na (A Million Rice Fields). In 1287 he established amicable alliances with the neighboring states of Phayao to the east and Sukhothai to the south. Phayao later was merged with Lan Na. Mangrai, searching for a suitable location for the capital of the newly unified state, established a temporary base at Kum Kam near Chiang Mai.

Mangrai's final decision to establish his capital at Chiang Mai in 1291 is told in a legend. On a hunting trip along the Ping River, the king sighted a pair of white barking deer, a pair of white sambar deer, and a white mouse with a litter of five. The king regarded this menagerie as a fortunate sign and ordered that his capital be built upon the site.

Before any building could begin at Chiang Mai, however, Mangrai had to stave off the expansion-minded Mongols, who, commanded by Kublai Khan, had overthrown the neighboring empire of Burma in 1287. Fighting never broke out, however, and in 1296 approximately 90,000 workers began construction on the new capital. To formulate a design for the royal city, Mangrai collaborated with his allies, the kings of Sukhothai and Phayao. The new city was to be called Nopphaburi Si Nakhonping Chiangmai, a blending of Sanskrit and Thai that translates roughly as "new city, city of the Ping, new city." Wat Chiang Man, a temple that still stands, was the residence of King Mangrai and the focal point of the original city.

Mangrai's sixty-year reign ended in 1317, when he allegedly was struck by lightning. For the next thirty-five to forty years, Lan Na was plagued by weak administration and internal conflict. It was not until 1355, when King Ku Na's reign (1355–85) commenced, that the state's affairs began to improve. Ku Na was both intelligent and skillful as an administrator. He persuaded an esteemed monk named Sumana to establish the Singhalese Buddhist order in the capital city, and Ku Na had a temple, the Wat Suan Dork, built for him. Significantly, the Buddhists provided a sense of cultural leadership and fostered a more regional identity by encouraging centralization of the kingdom.

Wat Phra That, Chiang Mai
Photo courtesy of Tourism Authority of Thailand, Chicago

Chiang Mai's most famous landmark, a magnificent temple called Wat Phra That, was built on Mount Suthep during Ku Na's reign. Buddhists, attempting to locate an appropriate sanctuary for relics of the Buddha, turned loose an elephant carrying the sacred objects to wander at will. After climbing Mount Suthep, the elephant is said to have trumpeted, turned around three times and knelt at the place where the temple was to be built. The monastery's spired pagoda is believed to be the sacred chamber where the relics are housed.

During the fourteenth century, Lan Na thrived. Chiang Mai, as the capital city, officiated over the regions known today as Lamphun, Lampang, Mae Hong Son, Chiang Rai, Phrae, Nan, Phayao, and lands extending as far south as the neighboring, allied state of Sukhothai. In the Chao Phraya basin near what is now Bangkok, the Ayutthaya Kingdom (Siam) was prospering as well. As Ayutthaya grew in power and size, the Sukhothai Kingdom south of Lan Na became a target of hostile interest. This greatly concerned Lan Na, because if Sukhothai were to fall to Ayutthaya, the Lan Na Kingdom would find its own borders seriously threatened. It was in Lan Na's interest then, not only as an ally of Sukhothai but for its own security, to provide troops during the confrontation between the two warring states. Despite these defensive maneuvers, Ayutthaya defeated Sukhothai in 1378, one more step in the rapid development of a unified Siamese nation. The king of Siam, Boromaraja I of Ayutthaya, conducted two intense campaigns against Lan Na following his capture of Sukhothai, but they were unsuccessful. After his death in 1388, Ayutthaya made no further large-scale attempts to annex Lan Na, although skirmishes continued to occur frequently, and relations between the two kingdoms remained volatile for many years.

During the mid–fifteenth century, a period known as the Golden Age, Chiang Mai and the Lan Na Kingdom flourished under King Tilokaraja, who ruled from 1442 to 1487. Tilokaraja, a devout Buddhist and an advocate of the arts, ordered the construction of numerous temples and requisitioned elaborate religious sculptures. In 1477 he arranged for Chiang Mai to host the prestigious Eighth World Buddhist Council.

Intermittent warfare between Lan Na and Ayutthaya persisted, and, gradually—as the Golden Age waned and the Mangrai Dynasty began to lose strength—it appeared Ayutthaya would conquer its northern adversary after all. Yet it was a new enemy from the west, the Burmese, who finally overpowered and took control of Lan Na in 1557. For the next two centuries, Lan Na was governed either by puppet rulers installed by the Burmese at Chiang Mai or by direct control from Burma. Lan Na principalities occasionally struggled for independence from Burma but also had to thwart Ayutthaya's continued raids along the southern border.

In 1767, two centuries after the Burmese had seized Lan Na, their powerful forces finally defeated Ayutthaya. Burma briefly controlled nearly all of Thailand. The city of Thon Buri, in the south near the present city of Bangkok, became a new, temporary capital for the besieged Siamese when the Burmese invaded and ravaged the capital at Ayutthaya. It was at Thon Buri that General Taksin, who had escaped the Burmese when they demolished the Ayutthayan capital, established a base where insurgents could plan a revolt. Within a few years, Taksin's forces had succeeded in evicting the Burmese, driving them back to the north.

Burmese officials then deployed Lan Na troops to check the advance of the Ayutthayan forces led by Taksin, who had become the new Siamese king. The Lan Na soldiers rebelled, however, and joined their former Ayutthayan enemies to expel the Burmese. The Siamese finally recovered Chiang Mai in 1774. Burma counterattacked a year later but was unsuccessful in winning the city back. The years of fighting, however, had taken a great toll on Chiang Mai: the significantly diminished population, impoverished both morally and financially, decided to abandon the city altogether. King Taksin moved the remaining citizens southeast to Lampang, leaving Chiang Mai deserted for the next twenty years.

Revitalization at Chiang Mai began in 1796 during the reign of King Rama I, who had established a new Thai capital at Bangkok. The king appointed Chao Kavila as governor-prince of the northern territory, which was to function as a vassal state of Siam. Kavila devoted himself to the restoration of Lan Na, the reconstruction of Chiang Mai, and the establishment of a new line of hereditary rulers. The *chao,* or princes, of Chiang Mai continued to govern the "Northern Circle" of the Siamese nation with relative autonomy until the early twentieth century.

Foreign influence began to be felt at Chiang Mai as early as the late nineteenth century, when Christian missionaries and "teak wallahs" (who came to harvest wood from the region's teak forests) established their northern bases there. McKean Rehabilitation Institute, a leper colony on a small island in the Ping River south of Chiang Mai, and McCormick Hospital, the first hospital to open outside of Bangkok, were planned and developed by medical missionaries.

By 1913 the railway from Bangkok extended as far as Den Chai, a city approximately 125 miles southeast of Chiang Mai. The completion in 1922 of the 467-mile Bangkok–Chiang Mai rail connection, reducing the travel time between the two cities from weeks to hours, enabled outside influences to penetrate the isolated valley much more rapidly than before. The geographical barriers that had served to isolate and nourish a distinctive culture in the north no longer were insurmountable. In 1935, when the last governor-prince at Chiang Mai died, administration of the northern region of Thailand was consolidated with the central government at Bangkok.

Today, despite the influx of foreign influences, the food, dress, language, and cultural traditions of Chiang Mai still differ notably from those of Bangkok or southern Thailand. Chiang Mai's residents continue to refer to themselves as "Lan Na" people, and the pace of life is leisurely by comparison. Unlike many overcrowded Asian cities, Chiang Mai appears clean, peaceful, and spacious. It is a center for

Thai art and handicrafts, and nearby villages specialize in traditional silver work, teak carving, and silk weaving. Even the introduction of modern architecture has not obliterated the ancient charm of Chiang Mai: the ruins of many thirteenth- and fourteenth-century temples can be found on the west bank of the Ping River within an eighteenth-century walled settlement. One notable survivor is the Wat Phra Sing, built in 1345, which houses the Phra Sing, the most revered Buddha figure of the north. And just outside the city, high on the slopes of Mount Suthep, the temple complex of Wat Phra That remains one of Thailand's most renowned pilgrimage sites.

Further Reading: *Chiang Mai, The Tranquil Valley* (Bangkok: Artasia, 1989), with text by John Hoskin and photographs by John Everingham, is a beautifully illustrated book with straightforward text that outlines the history and culture of Chiang Mai.

—Holly E. Bruns

Chittagong (Chittagong, Bangladesh)

Location: Southeastern Bangladesh, on the coast of the Indian Ocean about 12 miles north of the Karnaphuli River and 164 miles southeast of Dhākā.

Description: The second-largest manufacturing city in Bangladesh, Chittagong has a natural harbor that is Bangladesh's primary port. Occupied by Muslims in the fourteenth century, Chittagong was subsequently home to Portuguese pirates and Arakanese conquerors before passing into Mughal dominion in 1666 and British rule a century later.

Contact: Bangladesh Parjatan Corporation
National Tourism Organization
233 Airport Road
Tejgaon, Dhākā 1215
Bangladesh
325155 9

The earliest known inhabitants of the Chittagong region were probably of Mongoloid, Austric, or Dravidian origin. It is believed that more than 2,000 years before the Common (Christian) Era, these people lived in a sophisticated society whose wealth, commerce, and arts paralleled those of Egypt. Sometime around 2000 B.C. the Aryan invasions began, destroying this civilization and laying the foundation of much of contemporary society on the Indian subcontinent; Vedic Hinduism was introduced, as was the caste system. The Aryan newcomers, who left records in Sanskrit, referred to the native peoples as *dasayus* or Namaśūdras; many historians believe that the Namaśūdras were descendants of the original residents of Bangladesh.

The Namaśūdras gradually were assimilated into the dominant Aryan society, and the region is believed to have been fairly stable, despite the influx of Scythians from about 1000 to 200 B.C., until Western invaders began arriving. Alexander the Great, fresh from conquering Afghanistan, arrived in 327 B.C. prepared to sweep through the Indian subcontinent, beginning with the region that is now Bangladesh. He was met at the Beās River (in modern-day Pakistan) by an enormous army and was persuaded—both by the size of the opposing forces and the exhaustion of his own men—to retreat without battle.

Alexander indirectly altered the government of the region nonetheless: his former ally Candra Gupta Maurya remained in Bihār and ousted the existing Nanda leadership. Thus, the Mauryan Empire arose; its most notable leader was Aśoka, who became a Buddhist and established this religion throughout northeast India. The *Tibetan Chronicles* tells of a Buddhist monument, Pandit Vihara, in what is now Chittagong, but no traces of it remain today. The Buddhist warriors who came to Chittagong gave the area its name: *tsi-tsi-gong* is Arakanese for "that war should never be fought."

At this time the area around Chittagong was just emerging from a jungle environment into rice-growing land. Accessible to other parts of India by the Bay of Bengal, the region was known for weaving the cotton grown in western and central India and producing fine silk; it also was beginning to trade with Southeast Asia and Indonesia. In the second century A.D., the Greek geographer Ptolemy noted that Chittagong was among the most impressive ports in the East. The seventh-century A.D. Chinese traveler Xuan Zang declared it a "sleeping beauty emerging out of the misty water." Much later, Marco Polo was to be similarly awed by the harbor and lush landscape.

In the ninth century A.D., Chittagong met with new forces from outside the region. Buddhism began to decline in favor of a new form of Hinduism that emphasized a personal god. Arabs arrived in the harbor (which they called Samunda) to trade goods, and they became so powerful that for a time they controlled the port. By the twelfth century Buddhists were an oppressed minority in the area, and many took refuge in Chittagong, which at the time was in the kingdom of Samatata, ruled by the Hindu Sena Dynasty. Chittagong was one of the main seaports of the Sena rulers. Renowned for its textiles and rice, Chittagong was the point of departure for ships loaded with fruit, spices, lead, and jute. In addition to exports, the area was known for its banking and seafaring industries.

Sena rule was relatively brief, however. Led by Baktiar, Muslim invaders arrived in Bangladesh at the beginning of the thirteenth century and occupied Chittagong in 1299. Conversion to Islam became extremely popular in the region, perhaps due to the concentration of *śūdras,* or lowest-level caste members, in the area. With its promise of an afterlife, its echoes of the discipline and self-restraint of Buddhism, and its gentler treatment of women, Islam was very appealing to the farmers and members of the military who lived around Chittagong.

The lure of the new religion may also have been pragmatic: just after the Muslims arrived in India, the Ganges shifted course from one tributary to another, causing a tremendous economic upheaval. It has been suggested that some rural residents were converted from animism by the offer of land, suddenly fertile with the new flow of the Ganges, for the cultivation of rice. In Chittagong and other eastern Bengal seaports, Arab traders had been preparing the ground for Islam for some time; local hagiography in Chittagong describes the Sunni saint Pīr Badr as having traveled in Bengal during the Buddhist period of the ninth century. For whatever reason, a majority of people in Chittagong converted to Islam during this time.

A church at Jamal Khan Road, Chittagong
Photo courtesy of Bangladesh Parjatan Corporation, Dhākā

In the early fourteenth century the Chittagong district became part of Bengal under the governance of the Delhi Sultanate, and the Arakanese, now free of Burmese rule, returned to Chittagong in 1459. The Arakan leaders were still Buddhist, but they were quite comfortable with Muslim culture and found many ways to merge the two ways of life. Their interest in Chittagong, 150 miles up the coast from the Arakan capital of Mrohaung, was primarily centered on its magnificent harbor on the Indian Ocean. Like the Portuguese who were to follow shortly, the Arakans conducted slave-raids by sea, resettling their captives in the Arakan kingdom as farm laborers.

This was a time of prosperity, expanded trade and industry, and relative tolerance. Chittagong was the southeast terminus of a 2,000-mile trade route to the Khyber Pass, and the Bay of Bengal was well protected as ships left Chittagong laden with goods for distant ports in Asia, Africa, and the Mediterranean. Urban life did not extend beyond the last house in Chittagong, however; the outlying land remained densely forested and was populated by peoples who worshiped *walī,* or holy men, and grew crops by a nomadic system of slash-and-burn agriculture called *jhum.*

During two centuries of Arakanese rule, Chittagong experienced only brief interludes of outside aggression. Vasco da Gama scouted the area in 1498 and reported Bengal as "a country that abounds in silver." Less than half a century later the Portuguese had established a center of trade in Chittagong, which quickly became known as the place to establish businesses out of the sight of the Portuguese viceroy of India.

These piratical Portuguese merchants assimilated quickly into Bengali society; a visitor to Chittagong in 1607 observed that the Portuguese "do only traffic, without any fort, order, or police, and live like natives of the country." In the sixteenth century the city briefly fell under Afghan and Pathan rule, and several skirmishes with the empire-building Mughals were avoided through diplomacy. In 1586 the Mughals actually entered Chittagong Harbor, but they were graciously presented with elephants and withdrew after great shows of courtesy on all sides.

Nonetheless, the Arakan leaders were not pleased with the Portuguese presence, and in 1607 the Arakans stormed a pirate settlement on Dianga Island, off the coast of Chittagong, killing at least 600 Portuguese. The Portuguese viceroy at Goa retaliated in 1615, attacking the Arakan capital of Mrohaung. Five years later, however, the two sides realized they had common interests in Chittagong and became partners in the slave trade. The Portuguese pirate communities continued to be raided, but by the Mughals, not the Arakans.

The Portuguese were followed into Chittagong by the Dutch, British, and French, but it was the Mughals who finally captured Chittagong in 1666, arriving from the jungle with a 6,500-man army supported by 288 ships of war bound for Chittagong Harbor. After three days of battle, the Arakanese surrendered the city, which promptly became the capital of a new *sarkār,* or Mughal district. Chittagong's Mughal rulers consisted of a *faujdār,* or military commander, and an *āmil,* or tax collector, accompanied by numerous Hindu administrators and many of the original ground soldiers, who stayed to keep the peace and later settled the land in and around Chittagong.

Under Mughal rule, Chittagong immediately underwent dramatic economic and social changes. Among the first was the conversion of *jhum* farming to plowed-field cultivation. The responsibility for organizing labor to clear the land and for introducing animals, machinery, and rice-transplanting techniques into the roughly cleared jungle fell on local men, primarily Muslims, who worked for the *zamindars,* or absentee landlords, who were primarily Hindu. The conversion from jungle to rice-paddy was so swift and effective that record crops soon were being produced, with a corresponding surge in human population in the region.

Another change was the rise of a landed class, which was achieved through the issuance of *sanads,* or documents allowing the caretakers of religious sites tax-free rights to the land in perpetuity. Beginning in the 1720s, rural mosques sprang up at a startling rate, resulting from the issue of nearly 300 *sanads,* nearly all to Muslims—although the occasional Hindu temple and Brahman community were also recognized.

The struggle between the Mughals and the British for dominance in Bengal began at the end of the seventeenth century, and in 1688 William Heath of the British East India Company even attempted to seize Chittagong. Conflict continued for decades, involving French interests in the area as well, until finally in 1757 the British took Bengal at the Battle of Plassey.

Eager to establish a factory (trading settlement) in Chittagong, the British dispatched a representative of the Calcutta Council to Chittagong to negotiate in 1758. Agha Nizām, the local official meeting this envoy, rebuffed all advances, and a representative of the British East India Company ominously observed that soon would come a time "when we can command instead of requesting." The time came in 1766; having installed Mīr Qasīm and other local leaders who would favor its interests, the company was officially granted Chittagong, beginning a 200-year British presence in the city.

The initial effects of British rule were disastrous: as a possession of the British East India Company, Chittagong's fate was determined by purely commercial interests. The countryside was stripped of goods, the people were financially ruined, and anything that remained was destroyed in the famine in 1770. Under the governance of Warren Hastings (1772–85), British administration improved. Hastings pushed through numerous tax, military, and administrative reforms, separating the government from the commercial enterprise that had reigned during the first generation of British occupation.

The region improved economically, particularly for Hindu landowners, under Charles Cornwallis, who succeeded Hastings as governor-general in 1786 and enacted further reforms. Most of the people who had obtained property during Mughal rule were able to retain their land, since the British honored *sanads.* Still, Chittagong was far from a modern city; although it was the second-largest city in Bengal, one visitor in the 1790s described it as overrun with people but consisting of a cluster of villages of humble grass and bamboo huts. By the beginning of the nineteenth century, however, Chittagong was not only prosperous but had a minor reputation as a haven for intellectuals and artisans.

British rule in Chittagong was not uncontested. The Burmese, who had conquered Arakan in 1785, engaged in border disputes with the British intermittently from 1795 until 1811. During this time, the Arakanese fled their occupied land and sought refuge in Chittagong by the thousands, which further incensed the Burmese. The British administration was loath to become involved, either in refusing admittance to Arakanese refugees or by enforcing their return to their homeland, and managed to avoid outright conflict with the Burmese for several decades. However, the situation worsened in 1811 when a large party of Arakanese refugees from Chittagong stormed Arakan. In 1823 the Burmese laid siege to the island of Shāhpurī, a British East India Company holding near Chittagong, and the following year William Pitt Amherst declared war. The Bengal army marched through Chittagong and the dense jungle beyond to reach Arakan; the terrain made conditions worse, and the war lasted for two years before the Burmese withdrew.

In 1864 Chittagong became a municipality and continued to provide the British with exports from its district's rich resources and plentiful labor. Like the rest of Bengal, however, Chittagong did not always enjoy the prosperity it generated for others; its economic decline was hastened by the British practice of price-control and taxation, particularly of the lucrative cotton industry, which was perceived as a threat to England's mills. British administration also meant Indian acceptance of crop exports (even in times when Indians went hungry) and the imports of newly industrialized Britain, such as railroads, instead of other products that might have been more productive to the region.

By the end of the Victorian era, Bengal was ready for liberation. British attempts to derail the independence movement by pitting Muslims and Hindus against one another had largely failed, and the government's final tactic was to withdraw the British capital in India from Calcutta to New Delhi. This hastened a decline in Bengal prosperity that had begun with the opening of the Suez Canal in 1870. Trade shifted west, through Bombay, leaving Bengal a relatively poor part of the nation.

As the twentieth century dawned, Chittagong found itself under unpopular and ineffectual British rule. Bengal was partitioned in 1905, but the division was so controversial that it was revoked six years later, when the new province of Bengal was created. Muslims, the overwhelming majority in Chittagong, felt disadvantaged by the new balance of power and formed the Muslim League in 1906.

Chittagong was involved in some of the nonviolent nonparticipation events of the new era. In 1921 came the Chāndpur Affair, in which several thousand tea coolies left the plantations following unsuccessful strikes for higher wages, only to be stranded in midjourney by transportation strikes. Orchestrating the train stoppages from Chittagong was J. M. Sen Gupta, the president of the Railway Employees Union, who suspended service throughout the Chittagong region and beyond. Less than a decade later a daring raid was conducted on the police armories in Chittagong; frustrated by England's lack of response to Mohandas Karamchand (Mahatma) Gandhi's civil disobedience campaign against the salt laws, a group of renegades escaped to the hills with large quantities of weapons, which were not recovered for years.

The region Chittagong occupied seemed marked for crisis in the mid–twentieth century. The most devastating event occurred in 1943, when a famine killed 5 million in the region while the ruling British shipped food from India to the troops in World War II. In 1947 the British quit India, and Bengal was partitioned along religious lines, with Chittagong becoming part of the province of East Bengal in newly formed Muslim Pakistan. Bengalis immediately began rioting for rights equal to those of their Western Pakistani countrymen. Although the region was renamed East Pakistan in 1955, Bengalis continued disputes with the government until March 1971, when the Pakistani army finally clashed with the Bengali rebels. With India's intervention, the Bengalis won their war of independence in December 1971, and Bangladesh was made a nation.

The war took a dreadful toll on Chittagong and its environs. Communications among Chittagong and other cities were constantly interrupted, as bridges were destroyed and rail service suspended. Perhaps acting on a rumor that Chittagong had been proposed as the site for a Soviet naval base in return for Russian assistance to Bangladesh, the United States sent an aircraft carrier into the Bay of Bengal. In Chittagong Harbor, no ship was safe from rebel interference; the Indians attacked the harbor repeatedly to prevent the transportation of goods to the Pakistanis. Almost all work in the city ceased, leaving the city economically devastated. Many people took refuge in India during the fighting; they returned in the spring of 1972 to a ruined city. A year after the fighting, sunken ships still were being recovered from the bottom of Chittagong Harbor, with both Americans and Soviets assisting in the relief operations.

Aid poured into Bangladesh, and Chittagong received loans to upgrade its water management system, install effective safeguards against flooding, and improve roads. Internal power struggles still plagued the government, however, and in 1981 President Zia ur-Rahman was assassinated in Chittagong by dissidents believed to have been led by General M. A. Manzur, commanding officer of the Chittagong district. For two days Chittagong was held by the rebels, then retaken by the government, which subsequently court-martialed several dozen of Manzur's officers in Chittagong, sparking riots in Dhākā when death sentences were announced for twelve of the men.

Chittagong is now a primary industrial city. Its harbor, which for some years has handled much of the business formerly routed to Calcutta, is supplemented by two new ports that are closer to the source of Bangladesh's principal exports of jute, jute products, and textiles. Chittagong Harbor, however, has a much greater capacity to receive and ship goods than the rest of Chittagong's transportation systems. With nearly two dozen berths, the harbor is well equipped for large cargo.

In addition to the port area, Chittagong has several distinct districts: the Old City, the British City, and the Modern City. The oldest section of Chittagong is the Sadarghāt, on the banks of the Karnaphuli River. The old riverfront city area borders the Portuguese area, which is the small Christian outpost in this Muslim City. Among the historic sites in this area is the Church of our Lady of the Holy Rosary, established by the Portuguese in the mid–seventeenth century and rebuilt in the Gothic style. Near the Old City is the British City, now the business district of Chittagong. The colonial presence is still apparent in the numerous governmental buildings, including the Circuit House, Secretariat, and High Court. The Modern City contains contemporary buildings and most of Bangladesh's industry: a steel mill, oil refinery, and factories producing cigarettes and wood products.

Chittagong is home to numerous mosques, among which the most notable is Qadam Mubarak (Footprint), which, as its name suggests, features a block inset with Muḥammad's footprint; the structure dates from 1336. Shahl Jāma-e-Masjid, constructed in the late seventeenth century, is a fortress-like structure with a striking minaret. Finally, Chandanpura Mosque, although of negligible historical interest, is a particularly beautiful structure.

Other spiritual sites in Chittagong include the Mazhar of Sultan Bayazid Bostami, a shrine that hosts a *mela* (religious festival) during the Shab-e-Bharat festival and is home to a group of turtles famed for having been evil spirits sometime around the ninth century. The Chilla of Badar Shāh, named for a fourteenth-century Sufi, is a spot for meditation in the Old City. Just outside Chittagong is Shatpura, a village containing Buddhist and Hindu temples and meditation areas.

What is now the Islamic Intermediate College was constructed by the Portuguese in the eighteenth century as an arsenal, and local legend describes tunnels, secret compartments, and other trappings of intrigue; unfortunately, few visitors are admitted. Accessible to all is the Ethnological Museum in the Modern City, which contains relics and descriptions of the native peoples of Bangladesh.

Further Reading: A good early history of Chittagong is L. S. S. O'Malley's *Eastern Bengal District Gazetteers: Chittagong* (Calcutta: Bengal Secretariat Book Depot, 1908). Richard M. Eaton's *The Rise of Islam and the Bengal Frontier, 1204–1760* (Berkeley: University of California Press, 1993) provides a clear account of Chittagong as part of Bengal prior to the British occupation. James J. Novak's *Bangladesh: Reflections on the Water* (Bloomington: Indiana University Press, 1993), although not specific to Chittagong, contains an excellent, concise history of the country, as well as analyses of contemporary conditions. In *Bangladesh: Biography of a Muslim Nation* (Boulder, Colorado: Westview, 1984), Charles Peter O'Donnell describes modern Bangladesh, beginning with the British occupation and detailing twentieth-century history. The traveler to Chittagong will find useful information about historic sites and modern accommodations in Jon Murray's *Bangladesh: A Travel Survival Kit* (second edition, Hawthorn, Victoria, and Berkeley, California: Lonely Planet, 1991).

—Sappho Charney

Chittaurgarh (Rājasthān, India)

Location: In central Rājasthān, 71 miles northeast of Udaipur.

Description: A steep monolithic plateau of rock, 3 miles long, which rises 558 feet from the surrounding plain and is crowned with the remnants of Rājasthān's oldest and most historic fort.

Contact: Government of India Tourist Office
State Hotel, Khasa Kothi
Jaipur 302 001, Rājasthān
India
372200

Chittaurgarh (*garh* means fort) was the stronghold of the Mewār Rājputs from approximately 728 until 1568, when it fell to Akbar, the greatest of the Mughal emperors. Its name has evolved, via Chitrakut, from Chitrang, a Rājput leader. Although mostly uninhabited since the sixteenth century and partly ruinous in consequence, Chittaurgarh retains buildings of great importance, in particular the Jaya Stambh (Tower of Victory), one of India's most famous structures. As with so many of the country's monuments, precious little survives in the form of contemporary reports on which to base an accurate record of major historical events in Chittaurgarh's history. Most information has therefore depended on hearsay from varied sources, which are rarely in precise accord.

Allegedly, Chittaurgarh was founded by Bhīma, a heroic prince of the *Mahābhārata* epic, which would place the establishment of the fort at approximately 1500 B.C. Buddhism did not reach this part of India until the conversion of Mauryan King Aśoka in 261 B.C., and, because the religion lost converts quickly following that king's death, Buddhist artifacts discovered on the site, the oldest finds at Chittaurgarh, may be dated to the mid–third century B.C. It is known that Rājputs occupied the fort in approximately 730 (728 and 734 have both been suggested), when Bappa Rawal, leader of the Guhilla clan, married a daughter of their leader; in so doing it appears that he was presented with Chittaurgarh as part of her dowry, although some historians believe that armed conflict may have been involved in the transaction.

Guhil (the Cave-Born) had founded the Guhillas, ancestors of the Sīsōdia Dynasty, in the sixth century. His descendants lived in the state of Mewār in an area close to present-day Udaipur. First they settled at Ahar, and later at Nāgda, which still exists, although it is partly in ruins. Both locations were set in a plain and therefore not easily defensible; the transfer of the Guhillas to the great escarpment of Chittaurgarh was obviously to their advantage. An important difference between Chittaurgarh and the other forts of Rājasthān, with the exception of Jaisalmer, is that the walls of the fort enclosed and protected not only the accommodations of the clan's ruler but also the homes in which his subjects lived (their settlement was known as Chittor, or Chitor, the name still used for the town below the escarpment). After the Sīsōdias abandoned the fort in 1568, the town was reestablished, although this time at the foot of the escarpment, on the west side, where it remains to this day, and from where the road zigzags upward to the fort via a series of defensive gateways. The summit of the rock is ribbonlike, rarely exceeding half a mile in width. Virtually everything of importance is to be found in the central third of the three-mile-long enclosure, and apparently this has always been the case.

The oldest structure to survive at Chittaurgarh is part of a Sun temple within the Kalika Mata, which dates from the eighth century and may, therefore, have been constructed by Bappa Rawal out of gratitude for acquiring the fort. Until quite recently, it was believed that the oldest of Chittaurgarh's two great towers, the Kirti Stambh (Tower of Fame), had been erected in 895, even though it was known as the Tower of Allata, who ruled one century later. Because of its stylistic features, however, historians now generally agree that the structure must date from the twelfth century. The tower is the work of followers of the Jain religion, and the multiplicity of carved nudes representing *tīrthaṇkaras* (pathfinders) indicates that the builders belonged to the Dighambara sect, members of which practiced total nudity. It is believed that a Jain merchant erected the tower in praise of the first *tīrthaṇkara,* Ādinātha. Only one other structure appears to predate the 1303 siege of Chittaurgarh: the Nilkantha Madadeo Temple, dedicated to Siva and probably built in the thirteenth century.

In 1303, the great fort was attacked by Delhi sultan 'Alā'-ud-Dīn Khaljī, probably because he wished to extend his empire, although according to tradition he did so in order to possess the beautiful Princess Padmini, who lived within. Padmini certainly existed and was probably the favored wife of Bhīm Singh, the uncle and adviser of the young Rana Lakshman, although some dispute this. Apparently, Khaljī had glimpsed Padmini during a visit to Chittaurgarh and was smitten with desire. He abducted her husband, Bhīm Singh, but Bhīm Singh managed to trick his captors and was released. The first attack by Khaljī was repulsed with the help, so it is said, of a Trojan Horse ruse. Padmini visited Khaljī, accompanied by her serving maids; the maids were, in fact, Mewār troops in disguise, and together with the bearers of their *palanquins* (a type of sedan chair) they set about Khaljī's astonished force. After regrouping, the sultan's army mounted a second attack, which proved irresistible. During the siege, each of the eleven Sīsōdia princes was made Rāna for a day before being sacrificed. As defeat became certain,

The Tower of Victory, Chittaurgarh
Photo courtesy of Christopher Turner

the court ladies, dressed in their wedding finery, marched to their ritual death by immolation, known as a *johar*.

A cave near the Gaumakh Tank is reputedly where the *johar* took place; Padmini was the last to perish. It is said that Rājput ladies entered the flames without displaying fear, both when taking part in a *johar* or throwing themselves on the funeral pyres of their husbands (an act known as *satī*); there is little doubt that they would have been heavily drugged with opium on either occasion. Following the immolation of their womenfolk, the Rājput warriors, dressed in their saffron wedding robes, and similarly drugged, opened the gates and rushed at Khaljī's troops. Although 7,000 of them were slaughtered, the Sīsōdias, led by Rāna Hamir, returned ten years later to govern Chittaurgarh once more.

What is known as Padmini's Palace is a late-nineteenth-century reconstruction of a thirteenth-century pavilion, which undoubtedly stood within the male quarters of the Rāna's palace. It could not, therefore, have been a residence of the princess; more likely her husband lived there. The palace overlooks an island on which stands another nineteenth-century reconstruction of a thirteenth-century pavilion, believed to have been the summer quarters of Padmini. Allegedly, ʿAlā'-ud-Dīn Khaljī first had seen her reflection in its waters (although an alternative version states that Khaljī had seen her reflected in a mirror). The original bronze gates of the pavilion were taken by Mughal emperor Akbar to embellish his new palace at Āgra Fort, where they remain.

During their ten-year occupation of Chittaurgarh, the sultan's Islamic forces had done a great deal of damage to the fort's temples. This included the complete loss of an eighth-century Sūrya temple; it was replaced on the same site by Rāna Hamir with a temple to Kālī. Also dating from the fourteenth century is an exquisite Jain temple to Shantinath. An earlier temple was similarly replaced by Rāna Mokal, in 1428, with the Samideshwar Temple to Siva.

Maḥmud Shāh, the third Delhi sultan of the Sayyid Dynasty, fought the Sīsōdias in 1450 but appears to have lost a crucial battle to them, and a further siege of Chittaurgarh was avoided. The leader of the Sīsōdias from 1433 to 1468 was Rāna Kumbha, a charismatic man who inspired great love and respect from his subjects and never lost a battle. With the exception of the Tower of Fame, Chittaurgarh's most famous surviving buildings date from his period of rule and are grouped together close to the fort's entrance. Although in ruins, many elements within the Palace of Rāna Kumbha are still distinguishable, including the solid watchtowers, the women's area (zenana) with its *jali* screens, and the stables. The complex is a reconstruction of the early-fourteenth-century palace of Rāna Hamir. To the southwest is the heir apparent's palace, the Kanwar Pade-Ka Mahal. One of the largest temples in the complex, the Kumbha Shyam (or Vriji), dedicated to Vishnu, was rebuilt by Rāna Kumbha in 1448. It is easily recognized by the high *sikhara* tower. Rāna Kumbha is said to have married the poetess Mīrā Bāī (although this is disputed), and she reputedly built the nearby Jata Shankar Temple, dedicated to Siva.

Of far greater importance than any of Rāna Kumbha's other buildings, however, is the Jaya Stambh (Tower of Victory), possibly constructed between 1458 and 1468, and now the symbol of Chittaurgarh. It may possibly have been erected to celebrate a victory over Mohammad Khaljī of Maliva in 1440. An alternative suggestion is that the tower was constructed from 1440 to 1448 to mark the rebuilding of the Kumbha Shyam Temple. The fifteenth century saw a revival of Jain architecture at Chittaurgarh, and this tower marks its high point. All surfaces are deeply carved, and the nine stories are clearly delineated; the two upper and three lower stories are greater in area than those of the central four, giving an impression of an unbalanced pack of cards about to topple over. In 1468, Kumbha was assassinated by his son, who became Rāna Udai Singh I. Reviled by all for this patricide, Udai Singh became known as Hatyara (Murderer). Although it is said that he was killed by a flash of lightning in 1473, it seems more likely that Hatyara was struck down by a human hand.

Ratan Singh II (reigned 1528–31) built a rectangular palace for his occupancy shortly before his death. Much of the palace, including its six great watchtowers, has survived, although it was altered at the south end to accommodate women. Ratan Singh was succeeded by the precocious Vikramāditya, still in his teens. Within four years, however, the youth's brief rule was interrupted by the second great siege of Chittaurgarh.

Sīsōdian ruler Rāna Raimal had taken the town of Muzaffar hostage during a campaign on the Gujarāt border in the late fifteenth century, and Bahādur Shāh, sultan of Gujarāt, decided in 1535 that the time was now ripe to exact retribution from the Sīsōdias for this insult. Again, as defeat loomed for Chittaurgarh, a great *johar* was ordered. It is said that 13,000 women died in the flames; they were led to their immolation by Karnavati, mother of the infant prince, Udai Singh, whose escape she had organized. A thick layer of ash has been excavated at Maha Sati Chowk, a wooded terrace to the southwest of the Tower of Victory, where it is believed the *johar* took place. One who did not perish in the flames was the queen mother, Jawahir Bāī, who had died bravely fighting the enemy. Bagh Singh, the prince of Deolia, was crowned rāna before leading 32,000 Rājput warriors clad in saffron robes through the gates to their slaughter; not one was captured alive, and every clan lost its chief. A stone near the Padal Pol gate marks the spot where Bagh Singh fell.

The Mughal emperor Humāyūn was eventually prevailed upon to intervene, and his forces quickly removed Bahādur Shāh's troops from Chittaurgarh. However, Vikramāditya was disposed of and, in 1541, Udai Singh II became rāna. An unsuccessful ruler, he incurred the displeasure of Humāyūn's son, Akbar, for refusing to accept Mughal suzerainty. The seeds were sown for Chittaurgarh's third and final siege, which took place in 1567.

Akbar, as was customary at the time, personally led the attack on the fort, building a mound from which his troops were able to fire cannon balls over the defensive wall. The mound was called Mohar Magri, for Akbar paid his men one *mohar* (a gold coin) for every container of earth added to the mound (*magri*).

Two teenage Rājput princes, Jaimal and Phatta, lost their lives in the battle. Akbar himself apparently slew Jaimal; *chattris* (stone monuments) beside Bhairon Pol gate mark where they fell. It is said that both the mother and wife of Phatta died fighting at his side. Near the Gamukh tank are the two palaces within the fort allegedly occupied by the youthful heroes.

Although Chittaurgarh was held against impossible odds for four months, another *johar* was eventually ordered; nine rānis and five princesses were among those immolated. By tradition, this *johar* took place in the cellars to the Kumbha Palace. Approximately 8,000 Rājputs were slaughtered in the battle that followed, 1,700 of them Sīsōdias. In addition, Akbar ordered that the 4,000 peasants cowering within the walls of the fort be murdered, an act of viciousness uncharacteristic of the emperor. Meanwhile, Udai Singh II had decided to leave the fort before Akbar's arrival, in order to organize guerrilla raids on the approaching army. He survived the battle and, together with his small band of followers, founded the city of Udaipur, which bears his name.

In 1616, Jahāngīr, Akbar's son and successor, returned Chittaurgarh to the Sīsōdias, but they were by then happily settled at Udaipur and, in any case, Jahāngīr would not permit them to rebuild the fort's defenses, which made it extremely vulnerable. Chittaurgarh was abandoned.

In 1925 Rāna Fateh Singh decided to build a new residential palace at Chittaurgarh for his occupancy. It has since been converted to a museum of sculptures excavated at the fort. Facing the former palace is the modern Archaeological Museum. A small settlement has developed around what remains of the great fort. Many of its inhabitants offer their services as guides. Chittaurgarh, unlike most of the other important forts of Rājasthān, is undoubtedly a ruin, albeit a romantic and impressive one. Little more than the Tower of Victory and Tower of Fame appear to be subject to local preservation measures.

Further Reading: *The Trials and Triumphs of the Mewār Kingdom* by Hugh Davenport (Udaipur: Maharana of Mewar Charitable Foundation, 1975) is a difficult-to-obtain volume, only generally available in specialized libraries, but it relates in detail the history of the Sīsōdia Dynasty from Chittaurgarh to Udaipur. Chittaurgarh, among other Rājput forts, is described in *Rajput Palaces: The Development of an Architectural Style 1450–1750* by G. H. R. Tillotson (New Haven, Connecticut, and London: Yale University Press, 1987).

—Christopher Turner

Chŏnju (North Chŏlla, South Korea)

Location: Twenty-one miles east of the Yellow Sea coast and 120 miles south of Seoul.

Description: Former capital of the ancient province of Chŏlla, now capital of North Chŏlla province; capital of the kingdom of Later Paekche from 892 to 935; seized by peasant rebels in 1182 and 1894; ancestral home of the Yi Dynasty; an important center of the Korean independence movement in the late nineteenth and early twentieth centuries.

Contact: Korea National Tourism Corporation
10, Ta-dong
Chung-gu
Seoul 100-180
South Korea
(02) 7299 600

The name Chŏnju sometimes is written as Jeonju because of differences in the systems used to write Korean words in Roman letters. In either spelling, it is unfortunately all too easy for non-Koreans to confuse this city with either Chongju, another city in the same province, or Ch'ŏngju, the capital of North Ch'ungch'ŏng province. Chŏnju has been one of the main settlements on the Honam Plain since ancient times, benefiting from its position on the main route from northern Korea through the Nyorong Mountains, which lie south and east of the city, to the southern coast, but also sharing fully in Korea's complex history of dynastic change, peasant revolt, and intervention by neighboring empires.

Little reliable information exists about the history of Chŏnju in particular or of Korea in general before approximately A.D. 300. By that date, the peninsula was divided into three kingdoms, Koguryŏ in the north, Silla in the southeast, and Paekche in the southwestern region, which includes Chŏnju. Each of them paid tribute to the Chinese emperors and incorporated the Chinese writing system, Confucian principles of government, and Buddhist religion into their cultures. Chŏnju is believed to have been founded as a market town within Paekche about 57 B.C. It is one of many places in southwestern Korea from which artifacts of the Paekche Kingdom have been gathered for display at museums in Kongju and Puyŏ, both Paekche capitals at different periods, but other remnants of Paekche culture still can be seen inside Anhaengsa, Ch'ilsongsa, and the other Buddhist temples that stand in Wansan Park in Chŏnju.

The distinctive southwestern culture in which Chŏnju participated was disrupted when the kingdom of Silla, with the support of the Tang Dynasty of China, conquered Paekche in 660. Having absorbed Koguryŏ in 668, Silla proceeded to ward off the threat of Chinese domination in a series of campaigns that lasted until approximately 676. The region around Chŏnju now became part of a unified and largely independent Korea, also known as Unified Silla. In 685 Chŏnju became one of the nine *chu,* the provincial capitals of the kingdom, each the headquarters of a civilian governor appointed by the royal court (itself still located in Komsung, modern-day Kyŏngju, in the southeast of the country).

As in the Chinese Empire, on which the courtiers and Confucian-educated officials of Unified Silla consciously modeled their regime, peasant revolts against the burden of taxation repeatedly challenged the authorities. From 889 onward these revolts spread throughout the kingdom, and Chŏnju became the headquarters of one of the most powerful rebel leaders, Kyŏnhwŏn. In 892 (or, according to some sources, 900) he made the city, renamed Wansan, the capital of a new kingdom of Paekche, known to historians as Later Paekche. It also served as his main base for a series of campaigns against Silla, culminating in the destruction of Komsung and the assassination of King Kyŏngae in 927. Meanwhile in the north, Koguryŏ also had been revived, by Kungye, a former Silla prince and monk who had made himself its ruler in 901, but had been overthrown by his minister, Wang Kŏn, in 918.

With Silla disintegrating, the struggle for supremacy over the peninsula was waged by Wang Kŏn in the north and Kyŏnhwŏn in the southwest. If the latter had won, Wansan/Chŏnju might have become the capital of Korea, but Wang Kŏn's forces invaded Later Paekche in 934, and in the following year the defenders of Chŏnju submitted to Later Koguryŏ. Wang Kŏn's triumph was completed in 936 with the formal abdication of the last Silla monarch.

Under the Koryŏ monarchy established by Wang Kŏn (who also is known by his posthumously conferred honorific name, T'aejo), Chŏnju reverted to its earlier status as a provincial capital and enjoyed some decades of peaceful growth as a market town and a leading center for making paper from mulberry, bamboo, and other plants—a tradition that continues today. In 1182, however, the city was seized by peasant rebels once again. On this occasion they were assisted by government troops garrisoned in the city who resented being pressed into shipbuilding and other heavy labor alongside the slaves owned by the dynasty. The Koryŏ regime proved to be more powerful than Unified Silla had been; the uprising was suppressed brutally only forty days after it had begun.

However, those who fled from the city during or after these events may have included the ancestors of Yi Sŏng-gye, who was to be the victor in yet another civil war and to found a new dynasty, in 1392. Having been weakened for decades, first by a Mongol invasion and then by continual Japanese piracy, Koryŏ submitted to this prominent military

Koch'Ang-Upsong Fortress, near Chŏnju
Photo courtesy of Korea National Tourism Corporation, Chicago

commander, whose accession was partly engineered and generally welcomed by the officials of the Koryŏ government. The Yi Dynasty, which considered Chŏnju its ancestral home, was the longest-lived in Korean history, ruling until Japan annexed Korea in 1910. Yi Sŏng-gye was noted for his program of land reform, his encouragement of scholarship and the arts, and his promotion of neo-Confucian philosophy. Under the Yi Dynasty, which revived the ancient name Chosŏn (Land of Morning Calm) to denote its state, the center of power and culture shifted to the new city of Seoul, southeast of the older capital, Kaesŏng. Meanwhile, Chŏnju became the capital city of a reorganized Cholla, one of the eight provinces of the Yi Kingdom, and in 1413 it was given a special status as one of only four cities in which copies of the official chronicles, the *Chosŏn wangjo sillok* (Annals of the Chosŏn Dynasty), were preserved for posterity. The former Confucian academy in which they are preserved is still a prominent building in Chŏnju.

From the seventeenth century onward the province of Chŏlla become one of the main areas in Korea for missionary activity by the Catholic Church, spreading out from the Jesuit mission in Beijing into northwestern and southern Korea and gaining numerous converts until Christianity was formally banned by the national government in 1795. Christian worship continued nevertheless, at least among sections of the wealthy and educated classes, which perhaps helped to make the peasants of the province especially receptive to the religious movement known as Tonghak (Eastern Learning), founded by Ch'oe Che-u from Kyŏngsang province in 1860. His followers, protesting against both oppression by the government and the landowners and the influence of Christianity and other foreign ideas, led rebellions throughout southern Korea, which continued even after Ch'oe was executed in 1864 (because, ironically, his references to a supreme ruler in heaven had convinced officials that he was a Christian).

Ch'oe Che-u's successor Ch'oe Si-hyŏng compiled the scriptures of the movement, established a regular network of local and provincial leaders, and maintained a constant program of propaganda against the government. In 1892, when the movement was formally banned, thousands of members of its Southern Assembly gathered at Samnye, near Chŏnju, to demand the rehabilitation of their movement and its founder. During 1893, they organized demonstrations at many other sites in southern Korea and finally, in February 1894, the Southern Assembly commander Chon Pong-jun proclaimed a new rebellion. In May and June his forces advanced on and captured Chŏnju itself, after massing in the surrounding countryside and defeating the troops sent from the city to bar their way.

While Ch'oe Si-hyŏng and others in the Northern Assembly of the Tonghak movement denounced this resort to violence by the Southern Assembly, the government, unable to recapture the city with its own troops and resources, turned to China for assistance. By the time that the Southern Assembly forces, falsely promised tax and rent reductions and restrictions on foreign traders, agreed to leave Chŏnju and return to their villages, the Japanese also had begun to intervene. This led directly to the Sino-Japanese War of 1894–95, in which the ancient empire of China fought with the new power of Japan for decisive influence over the kingdom that lay between them. The outcome was the exclusion of China from further influence in the peninsula and the securing of Korea's formal independence from China, at the cost of great and growing Japanese control. As for the Tonghak, the southern armies moved northward from Chŏnju in a vain attempt to resist the Japanese, which ended with the execution of Chon Pong-jun and other leaders and the dispersal of the movement.

Korea became a Japanese protectorate in November 1905, after Japan's victory over Russia, which also had sought control of Korea; the peninsula then was annexed by Japan in August 1910. Over the next thirty-five years, as the Korean people were exploited and their culture suppressed, a variety of resistance movements appeared and disappeared, most of them taking inspiration from the Declaration of Korean Independence of March 1, 1919. This document, which was read aloud on that day to crowds totaling 2 million people all over the country, had been composed and signed by thirty-three activists, among whom were fifteen members of Ch'ondogyo (The Teaching of the Heavenly Way), the nationalistic religious organization that had been created in 1905 out of the remnants of Tonghak. In Chŏnju up to 50,000 people joined in the series of twenty-one demonstrations that followed the reading of the declaration. These demonstrations continued disrupting Japanese control of the city throughout the year, in support of what became known as the March First Movement and its slogan, "Tongnap manse" (Long live independence). Independence leaders sought international recognition, but Japan had been on the winning side in World War I, which had ended just four months earlier, and the Western powers were not interested in the problems of one of its colonies. A Korean delegation was turned away from the Versailles Peace Conference, and the March First Movement was suppressed. Its leaders created a provisional government-in-exile at Shanghai.

Chŏnju grew during the Japanese occupation, doubling its population between 1925 and 1949, when it reached 100,000, and spreading far beyond the line of the ancient city walls, destroyed on the orders of the Japanese military authorities. The P'ungnammun Gate is the only section left standing in Chŏnju today.

In 1945, following Japan's defeat in World War II, Korea was placed under the new and untried authority of the United Nations. Its officials supervised elections in most provinces in May 1948 but were unable either to enter the region that became North Korea or to prevent the division of the country into two mutually hostile states, each allied with one of the great powers of the Cold War; South Korea (which includes Chŏnju) aligned with the United States, and North Korea formed a close relationship with the Soviet Union. War broke out between them in July 1950, when North Korean forces launched a massive military campaign against South Korea. This included a landing at Kunsan on the Yellow Sea coast and the conquest of large areas in North and South Chŏlla provinces. In Chŏnju, which was not on the front line, some degree of normality was maintained—for example, Chŏnbuk National University was established there in 1951—even as the war became an international confrontation between UN forces under the leadership of the United States and Chinese troops sent to assist Kim Il-sung, the dictator of North Korea. By the time an armistice was signed in July 1953, about 2 million civilians had been killed throughout Korea; there also were about 300,000 military casualties. Chŏnju was just one among the many cities of South Korea damaged by bombardment and deprived of thousands of men injured or killed in the fighting.

After a decade of recovery and rebuilding, Chŏnju received its present city boundaries and local government system in 1963, at which time approximately one-fifth of the population within its official area was engaged in agriculture. With the decline of farming and the expansion of manufacturing as the main sector of employment, as well as the commencement of domestic air services between Chŏnju and other cities in 1969 and the completion of the Honam Highway in 1970, Chŏnju has been transformed greatly within a generation. It now is included in a region of mainly light industry, known as Chŏnju-Iri-Kunsan in reference to the three principal cities within it; Chŏnju functions as the region's primary site of service industries and, since 1968, of a large paper mill. The city's population now exceeds 400,000. Nevertheless, the region is less prosperous than the rest of the country.

Chŏnju also is popular as a starting point for visits to two provincial parks, areas of historic interest and natural beauty that are administered by the North Chŏlla provincial government. The Moaksan Provincial Park, about twenty miles southwest of the city, is noted both for the mountain, 2,604 feet high, for which it is named, and for the Kumsansa Temple, said to have been founded in 599, which contains two large gold-leafed statues of the Buddha and which is still a center of shamanism. In Korea the chief activity of this ancient tradition, which has affinities with the ancient religious practices of Siberia and with certain forms of Shintō in Japan, is the *kut,* a ritual in which the *mudang,* a spirit medium who is usually a woman, enters a trance state in which she is said to communicate between the living and the dead. The Maisan Provincial Park, about forty miles east of Chŏnju, is named for the twin-peaked "horse ears" mountain that dominates the landscape, rising to heights of 2,223 feet on its eastern, "male" summit, Sutmaisan, and 2,247 feet on its western, "female" summit, Ammaisan. Between the two stands the T'apsa, a Buddhist pagoda constructed from hundreds of rocks stacked one on another.

Further Reading: Several recent books offer detailed, scholarly accounts of Korean history. Among the most useful are *A New History of Korea* by Ki-baik Lee, translated by Edward W. Wagner with Edward J. Shultz (Cambridge, Massachusetts, and London: Harvard University Press; Seoul: Ilchokak, 1984); Wanne J. Joe's *Traditional Korea: A Cultural History* (Seoul: Chung'ang University Press, 1972); and *The History of Korea* by Han Woo-keun, translated by Lee Kyung-shik (Seoul: Eul-Yoo, 1970). David Rees's *Short History of Modern Korea* (Port Erin, Isle of Man: Ham, and New York: Hippocrene, 1988) also offers a good English-language account. Korean government publications provide an alternate source of information. A wealth of facts about the country can be found in *A Handbook of Korea* (ninth edition, Seoul: Korean Overseas Information Service, 1993). Such government publications should be used with caution, however, as they are often biased and nationalistic.

—Patrick Heenan

Colombo (Sri Lanka)

Location: On the west coast of Sri Lanka, on the Indian Ocean just south of the mouth of the Kalani River.

Description: Largest city and former administrative capital of Sri Lanka; an important seaport where colonial powers once vied for control of the spice trade.

Site Office: Ceylon Tourist Board
78 Steuart Place
P. O. Box 1504
Colombo 3
Sri Lanka
(43) 7059 or (43) 7060

Colombo, with a population of approximately 1 million, is ten times as large as any other city in Sri Lanka, but it did not begin to grow to any considerable extent until the sixteenth century. It had been a small seaport for centuries prior to that. The port first was mentioned by the Chinese Buddhist pilgrim Fa Xian, writing in the fifth century A.D., who called it Kao-lan-pu. The Sinhalese, an Indo-Aryan people who had settled in Sri Lanka in the sixth or fifth century B.C, referred to the town as Kolamba, which probably derives from a Sinhalese word meaning "port" or "ferry." Whatever the site's name, its role as a seaport became its defining feature.

Arab traders, drawn by the potential for commerce in spices, arrived in the eighth century. They called the settlement Kolambu and developed it further over the next few centuries. Arab settlers arranged the mission sent by Bhuvanaika Bāhu to the Egyptian court in 1238, and the settlement at Colombo is referred to as early as 1346 by Arab traveler Ibn Baṭṭūṭah as "the largest and finest in Senderib," as Sri Lanka was then called.

The first Europeans to visit Sri Lanka were the Portuguese. On November 15, 1505, Dom Lourenço de Almeida anchored his ship in the harbor at Colombo after being blown off course near southern India. De Almeida immediately ordered the Portuguese coat of arms to be carved into a rock near the front of the bay, thus presaging nearly 450 years of European domination of Sri Lanka. The rock bearing the Portuguese seal was rediscovered only in 1898, having been hidden for an indefinite period within a police headquarters demolished in that year.

The Portuguese took an immediate interest in Sri Lanka's valuable cinnamon and determined to establish a fortified presence in Colombo. They quickly formed an alliance with King Vijayabāhu, who headed Kotte, one of three kindgoms between which the island was divided at that time. Opposition from Arab traders in Kotte and Malabar initially thwarted the Portuguese ambition to fortify; a modest rampart completed in 1519 was demolished in 1524. The Portuguese forced Vijayabāhu to expel the Arab trading community in 1526, and they were able to rule Sri Lanka's cinnamon trade without considerable opposition for several decades thereafter. A fort gradually was constructed and modified throughout the rest of the century. Initially, a single rampart approximately four miles long surrounded the central town, which lay on a naturally protected swath of land; the fort was bordered by the sea on the north and west sides, and by a formidable lagoon inhabited by crocodiles on the south. Hence, only the eastern face was vulnerable, and it was protected by the outer town, in which both Portuguese and Sinhalese lived. Some 1400 Portuguese families lived within the fort itself.

The Portuguese found ways to exploit their strong position. When the kingdom of Kotte was partitioned among three rulers in 1521, they succeeded in forcing Bhuvanaika Bāhu, who retained the portion around Colombo and the city of Kotte, to accept a politically subordinate status in the hope that the Portuguese would protect what remained of his kingdom against the designs of his aggressive and ambitious brother, Māyādunnē, ruler of the neighboring rebel state of Sitavaka. The Portuguese position was strengthened again when, in the 1540s, the ruler of Kandy, a kingdom in central Sri Lanka, also turned to them for protection against Māyādunnē. Finally, the Portuguese tightened their hold on the northern Jaffna Kingdom during the same period in order to secure control of the maritime trade from the Indian Malabar Coast, as well as control of the pearl fishing. Jaffna was ruled by the Tamils, who were largely Hindu; the Sinhalese, who ruled Kotte, were primarily Buddhist.

Bhuvanaika Bāhu died in 1550, and the Portuguese intervened against Sitavaka in the fight for the succession, hoping to uphold the right of Bhuvanaika Bāhu's grandson Dharmapāla to the throne, and that of his son-in-law Vidiye Bandara to the regency. Dharmapāla became a Christian convert, thereby antagonizing a large section of his kingdom, increasing his dependence on the Portuguese, and positioning Māyādunnē and his son Rājasinha as defenders of Buddhism. Although Sitavaka forces heightened their attacks, they failed to annihilate the Portuguese because Sitavaka lacked artillery sufficient to destroy the fortifications of Kotte and Colombo. Nonetheless, the Portuguese decided to retire to Colombo, abandoning the city of Kotte in 1565. The kingdom of Kotte had been reduced to the Portuguese fort of Colombo.

When Māyādunnē died in 1581, his son and successor Rājasinha already had established for himself a great military reputation. The Portuguese harried the Sitavaka rulers, raided the coastal regions, made forays to destroy temples, and exploited their naval power to establish themselves in Jaffna and at Galle. Additionally, the Portuguese

Hindu temples in Colombo
Photo courtesy of The Chicago Public Library

exacted tribute from Trincomalee and Batticaloa in the east and from Puttalam in the northwest. Rājasinha failed in 1578 to conquer Kandy, but in 1579 he began a two-year siege of Colombo, which survived on reinforcements and supplies from Goa. Colombo failed to mount a counteroffensive, and Rājasinha established his military headquarters at Biyagama, scarcely more than nine miles from Colombo. The Portuguese were locked into the city and the immediately surrounding countryside.

On his second attempt, Rājasinha succeeded in annexing the kingdom of Kandy. The Portuguese rightly assumed that Rājasinha's victory was a prelude to another attempt on Colombo, which they refortified in 1582 and which underwent a renewed siege in 1587–88. Once again Colombo was saved by reinforcements from the sea, and within five years Sitavaka power was destroyed by internal unrest and the rebellion of Kandy in 1590. Rājasinha died of a septic wound in 1593, and almost the whole kingdom of Kotte was restored to its 1521 boundaries, although under Portuguese domination. Of the old Sinhalese kingdoms, only Kandy remained independent of direct Portuguese rule.

The first threat to the Portuguese was the appearance of Dutch ships in 1595–96. King Philip II of Spain had banned both the Dutch and the English from trading with Iberian ports in a vain effort to stem the rise of his two strongest maritime rivals. The Dutch, however, were sufficiently established in financial strength, seagoing experience, and administrative skills to make the long trip around the Cape of Good Hope to the Indian Ocean, where they amassed influence and territory during the sixteenth century. In 1602 the Dutch founded the United East India Company (or Vereenidge Ooost-Indische Campagnie, V.O.C.), and for a century it was the world's strongest commercial concern. Backed by a state monopoly, it set out to challenge the Portuguese for the spice trade with the East; it was later to be joined and then rivaled by the English.

Dharmapāla died on May 27, 1597, having bequeathed the kingdom of Kotte to the Portuguese crown. Revolts against the Portuguese intensified after his death, however: at least six revolts occurred by 1619. The Kandyans, under the leadership of the future Rājasinha II, began organizing incursions into Portuguese-held territory in 1628. A treaty was signed in 1633, but by 1638 the Kandyans had found in the Dutch the maritime allies they needed to expel the Portuguese (whose fort at Colombo the Portuguese had saved twice by maritime support from Goa) from the entire island of Sri Lanka. Between 1629 and 1636, Dutch cruisers had destroyed nearly 150 Portuguese ships, and between 1637 and 1644 they had blockaded the Portuguese enclave at Goa nine times. In return for military support against the Portuguese, the Kandyans in 1638 assigned monopoly rights over the spice trade to the V.O.C. and undertook to reimburse the military expenditure of the Dutch.

The Dutch took the east coast cities of Trincomalee and Batticaloa from the Portuguese in 1639 and returned them to the Kandyans. However, the Dutch retained Galle and Negombo, which controlled the cinnamon trade, on the grounds that they had not been reimbursed for the expenses of these expeditions. Meanwhile, the Portuguese rebellion of 1640 against Habsburg rule in Europe had produced a brief peace between the Portuguese and the Dutch until the resumption of war in 1652. The final phase in the expulsion of the Portuguese from Sri Lanka then began, and in May 1656 Colombo surrendered to the Dutch. The final defeat of the Portuguese occurred in June 1658 with the surrender of Jaffna. In 1663 the Dutch also conquered the Portuguese provinces in Malabar and drove the Portuguese out of southern India.

The Dutch seige of Colombo was a protracted and bloody affair. On October 19, 1655, the Hollanders began an attack on the fort's eastern front, having easily subdued the outer city beyond and entrenched in its remains. From there they conducted a two-week artillery assault on the fort's eastern bastions, reducing them to rubble. Despite his severely compromised position, the Portuguese captain general, Antonio de Sousa Coutinho, refused to surrender. The Dutch director general, Gerard Hulft, then determined to take Colombo by storm. The Dutch assault, which began on November 12, was a disaster; when Hulft's men attempted to scale the fort's eastern wall, they were cut down by bullets and scorched by burning gunpowder dropped on them by the city's resilient military and civilian populations. The Dutch withdrew after 300 of their troops were killed, another 340 wounded, and Hulft himself was shot in the leg. Thereafter, the Dutch altered their strategy; they literally starved the Portuguese citizens of Colombo into submission. Those Portuguese who attempted to flee were brutally shot or hanged by Dutch troops beyond the fort. Finally, on May 7, 1656, a combined Dutch and Sinhalese force, including several hundred Kandyans, scaled the battered walls of the fort and slaughtered the weary Portuguese who had survived eight months of siege.

Once in control of Colombo, the Dutch rebuilt the fort and the city within according to the Portuguese plan, although the new bulwarks were constructed to better withstand an attack from European artillery. No structures from the Dutch fort are still intact, but the business center of Colombo was built in 1869 using masonry taken from its obsolete remains, and the area is still called "Fort" today. The Oute Stad (outer town), now known as the Pettah, was arranged along a series of five streets, each a half-mile long, interestected by a second set of five streets running at right angles to the first. About 500 families of both Dutch and Portuguese descent lived in the Oute Stad, in houses with high roofs and thick, whitewashed walls. An area of the Oute Stad known as Wolvendhal (Vale of the Wolves) came to be occupied by both Dutch soldiers who had taken Sri Lankan wives and by Sinhalese locals who served Dutch interests and who converted in religion, dress, and manner to Dutch ways. The Dutch built a church on Wolvendhal Hill in 1749, on the site of an old Portuguese Catholic chapel. The church is one of relatively few Dutch structures in Colombo that survives in nearly its original state.

Just south of the fort lies Slave Island, so called because of events that took place during the time of Dutch rule. The Portuguese had brought slaves from East Africa to Colombo in the early seventeenth century, and the Dutch retained them as servants. Near the beginning of the eighteenth century, the Africans violently revolted, killing some of their Dutch caretakers. After the insurrection was suppressed, the Dutch removed the rebels to a peninsula accessible only via the fort, and it is that peninsula that ever since has been known as Slave Island. In the late seventeenth and early eighteenth centuries, Javanese and Malay mercenaries fighting for the Dutch lived there. Today, the area is easily accessible to the rest of the city, and it is a busy commercial and residential sector.

Cinnamon thrived in the Kalani Valley and on the coastal stretches of the Kotte Kingdom. The Portuguese had earlier introduced a variety of measures (including burning surplus stock to keep the price up) to engineer a dramatic increase in its price, a strategy in which the Dutch were to surpass them. Cinnamon rose from one and one-half guilders a pound in the 1660s to three guilders for the rest of the century. In the mid–eighteenth century, it reached six guilders, and in the 1780s topped out at eight or nine. Of the ten or so varieties of Sri Lanka cinnamon, three or four were considered among the best in the world. The European market for the finest grades could never be satisfied. Colombo was first given an export monopoly, and a fixed proportion of the crop had to be sold to the state. These measures proved ineffective in raising adequate revenue, however, and the trade was made a royal monopoly. The valuable areca nut crop also was subjected to forced sale to the Kotte government in Colombo.

Trouble erupted when the Dutch cynically claimed that the Kandyans had not paid their military expenses, in the process absurdly undervaluing the cinnamon, areca, elephants, and land revenue they had taken. They claimed to be owed an astronomical balance of 7,265,460 guilders, a sum that neither they nor the Kandyans took seriously. The Dutch took Jaffnapatam and approximately half of the remaining areas formerly controlled by the Portuguese. In charge of the Dutch operation as commissary and superintendent over Coromandel, Surat, Sri Lanka, and Malacca, was Admiral Ryklof van Goens, who was stationed at Colombo. Against his wishes, van Goens was instructed to pursue a non-expansionary policy and to achieve reconciliation with Kandy. His dream was to found a Dutch East Indies political empire, with Sri Lanka as its core and Colombo as its capital.

Beginning in the 1650s, the British and the Danes were using Sri Lanka's eastern ports for their small-boat trading with Bengal, but van Goens's hand was much strengthened when Rājasinha II, who had formed an alliance with the British, in 1665 called on Dutch aid to quell a rebellion. The Dutch doubled the amount of territory they controlled between 1665 and 1670. The V.O.C. declared a monopoly in the trade of almost all goods except rice. Vessels were licensed to sail only into Jaffna, Colombo, and Galle. The Kandyans now looked to the French, who were seeking trading posts to match the British East India Company, for support against the Dutch. Van Goens was succeeded briefly by his son in 1675 when he himself became governor general at Batavia (Jakarta), but his expansionary policy in Sri Lanka was reversed when his son was replaced in 1681, and in that year he himself retired.

The British East India Company sent its first exploratory mission from Madras to Sri Lanka in 1762, but its concern became critical when Dutch and French interests joined against the British in 1780, when France was preparing an invasion of India. Access to Trincomalee became vital since, in the days before steam, only a deep, natural port on the windward side of the Indian subcontinent could provide shelter from monsoons and other bad weather. The British captured the port in January 1782 and that year sent a second mission to Kandy. When they lost Trincomalee again to the French in August, and also lost Madras, their hold on the subcontinent suddenly became precarious. It became secure again only with the end of the war with France in 1783.

The British took aggressive measures to defend their interests in Sri Lanka following a series of threatening political events. The French occupation of several Dutch territories in January 1795, the establishment of the Batavian Republic, and the danger of revolutionary insurrection in various British colonies overseas made the British especially wary of losing ground to the French in Asia. The alliance between the French and a disloyal faction of the Dutch nobility forced Count de Meuron, the hereditary leader of the Netherlands, to flee to England. De Meuron was given asylum at Kew Palace in London, and there he was made to sign a letter as general and admiral of Holland enjoining governors and commanders to surrender colonies and forts immediately into British hands. The "Kew Letter" was used by the British as authorization to annex a dozen Dutch colonial territories.

Dutch officials in Sri Lanka sided with the new government seated in Holland rather than with the count, and so they resisted the British occupation of Sri Lanka. They massed their meager force of 1,617 soldiers in Colombo and hoped to receive reinforcements from Batavia and the Netherlands, but none arrived. In January 1796, the British sent 5,500 armed representatives of the British East India Company to capture Colombo and the rest of the island. By this time, the British controlled the seas around Sri Lanka, and they were easily able to land at Negombo, from where they marched toward the capital. By February 12, the British had captured Oute Stad. Realizing that resistance was futile, the Dutch surrendered three days later, and all of maritime Sri Lanka was in British control within weeks of the capitulation of Colombo.

The British at first regarded Sri Lanka, which they called Ceylon, as a military outpost, whose trade was incidental to its role in their political scheme. Permission was not granted until 1832 for Europeans to be allowed to own territory outside Colombo. Administration was centered on the capital. A road to Kandy was built, fully bridged and ready by 1832. Economic growth was accelerated further with the development of coffee plantations northeast of Colombo. When the opening of the Suez Canal increased the maritime traffic, Sir William Gregory had to choose between Galle and Colombo as the site for a new port; he chose Colombo. The port, bounded on the south by a slight promontory, is enclosed by breakwaters of which the longest, about one mile long, was built between 1875, when the prince of Wales laid the first stone, and 1884.

The appearance of Colombo changed dramatically under British occupation. The city's population more than doubled during the nineteenth century, and many of the new residents were Tamils who came from Jaffna seeking English educations and economic opportunity. The old Dutch fort was demolished between 1869 and 1871, and the swampy moat filled in. The streets were lighted with gas in 1872, and electricity was introduced in 1892. The first Buddhist temple in Colombo was begun in 1789, during the time of Dutch occupation, but it bears a British crown inscribed in the upper half of its altar, which was completed only in 1872. The British were somewhat more tolerant of Buddhism than were either the Portuguese or the Dutch, and numerous Buddhist buildings were erected in Colombo during their reign. Many Dutch structures were renovated by the British, and now show a confluence of syles. Temple Trees, for example, the splendid estate in which contemporary Sri Lankan prime ministers reside, was originally a Dutch brandy distillery. The distillery passed through a series of private owners after the British took control of Sri Lanka, and it was the Englishman John Philip Green who named and decorated the house, and who laid out the beautiful, English-style garden for which the estate is best known today.

In the early twentieth century, a movement for independence from Britain emerged. Colombo's industrial workers and their trade unions were particularly active in this effort, which gained strength between the two world wars. The outbreak of World War II meant that Sri Lanka's independence would have to wait. Colombo proved vital to the Allies' war effort, providing an important supply link with the Pacific theatre. Three years after the war, in 1948, Sri Lanka finally was granted its independence; the new nation's capital was Colombo.

Since then, political developments have been influenced chiefly by world rises in the price of rice, a staple of the Sri Lankan diet, and by conflict between a Sinhalese-speaking Buddhist population and an English-speaking Christian elite, with the Tamils, associated with the south Indian Hindus, caught in the middle. In 1956 Solomon Bandaranaike, leader of the MEP (Mahajana Eksath Peramuna) coalition, came to power with a large majority, and soon set out on a policy of mass nationalization of industry. He was assassinated by a Buddhist monk in 1959 and is now regarded as a martyr to democratic government.

Inflation and other economic difficulties, as well as interethnic tensions, have made Sri Lanka difficult to administer. The Tamils, who account for less than 20 percent of Sri Lanka's population, see themselves as severely oppressed and have agitated, sometimes violently, for a separate nation; the Sinhalese sometimes have engaged in equally violent reprisals. During anti-Tamil riots in 1983, Colombo's Pettah district, with a large Tamil population, was virtually leveled. Violence between the two groups continued, and there were several large-scale massacres, the worst in 1985. Tamil demands for a separate state nearly had been contained when a Sinhalese Marxist revolution broke out in 1988. It is estimated that up to 17,000 were killed in the three years it lasted. The 1990s have been marked by continued clashes between Tamil separatists and government troops, who are largely Sinhalese. On May 1, 1993, President Ranasinghe Premadasa was assassinated by a suicide bomber, believed to be a Tamil secessionist, as he watched a May Day parade in Colombo. His successors have attempted to negotiate an end to the fighting, but that latest round of peace talks collapsed in mid-1995.

In the 1990s, Colombo has lost its role as Sri Lanka's administrative capital to Kotte, the former capital of the kingdom of the same name, just seven miles from Colombo and renamed Sri Jayawardhanapura Kotte. However, Colombo is so much bigger than any other city on the island that it is difficult to imagine that it will not remain the island's most important center. All the embassies, museums, and international organizations have their headquarters there; it has the island's only international airport; and it is at the center of the road and rail networks. More significant still, Colombo remains Sri Lanka's most important harbor, handling more than 3 million tons of cargo passing between Europe and Asia each year.

Further Reading: *Glimpses of Colombo* by Ishvari Corea (Colombo: Municipal Council, 1988) provides an overview of the city's history. Most other works in English containing information about Colombo are devoted more generally to Sri Lanka, or to some period or aspect of the city's development and culture. The best of the general works is *A History of Sri Lanka* by K. M. De Silva (London: Hurst, and Berkeley and Los Angeles: University of California Press, 1981). Also very useful is *Sri Lanka: A Travel Survival Kit* by John Noble, Susan Forsyth, and Tony Wheeler (fifth edition, Hawthorn, Victoria, and Berkeley, California: Lonely Planet, 1993). Both books contain reliable surveys of other publications.

—Claudia Levi and Christopher A. Hoyt

Corregidor Island (Cavite, Philippines)

Location: In the entrance to Manila Bay; the bay is located on the eastern side of the island of Luzon, the northernmost large island of the Philippine Archipelago, opening onto the South China Sea. Corregidor lies about three and one-half miles off the southern edge of the Bataan Peninsula, about six miles southeast of the southern Bataan port of Mariveles, and about twenty-eight miles west southwest of Manila. It splits the entrance to Manila Bay into two channels: the two-mile-wide North Channel and the six-and-one-half-mile-wide South Channel.

Description: Small, rocky, tadpole-shaped island that has long been fortified as a defense position to protect Manila Bay; site of major World War II battles in 1941–42 and 1945. Today it is a shrine memorializing participants in that war.

Contact: Department of Tourism
Paskuhan Village, 2000
San Fernando, Pampanga
Philippines
961 2665 or 961 2612

Corregidor Island, destined to play an important role in World War II, served a strategic military purpose for four centuries prior to that conflict. It was not inhabited when the islands that came to be known as the Philippines were visited by Ferdinand Magellan, a Portuguese explorer sailing on behalf of Spain. He claimed the islands for the Spanish Crown. Ruy López de Villalobos, leader of a subsequent expedition, named one of the islands "Filipina" in honor of the Spanish crown prince, who was to become King Philip II; the name eventually applied to the entire island group.

Recognizing Corregidor's strategic position at the head of Manila Bay, the Spanish installed three cannon on the island to provide warnings in the event of approach by unfriendly vessels. Each cannon had its own ammunition bunker and crew quarters. Corregidor also served as a point for relaying semaphore messages between ships patrolling the South China Sea and the commander of Fort Santiago in Manila. In 1836 the Spanish added a lighthouse to Corregidor to assist the numerous commercial ships going to and from Manila.

United States involvement with the Philippines and Corregidor began with the Spanish-American War in 1898. The United States, long dissatisfied with Spain's governance in the Philippines, blamed Spain for the destruction of the battleship *Maine* in Havana Harbor, Cuba, on February 15, 1898, although the cause of the explosion was never conclusively determined. After the United States declared war on Spain in April, Commodore George Dewey was ordered to sail to the Philippines and attack the Spanish forces stationed there. On May 1, Dewey's Asiatic Squadron of six warships slipped into Manila Bay, passing by Corregidor without incident, just out of range of Corregidor's guns. After Dewey's famous order to his captain, "You may fire when you are ready, Gridley," the Americans sank all ten Spanish vessels in the bay. The war ended in August, and following the Treaty of Paris, signed December 10, 1898, Spain gave Cuba its freedom and ceded Guam, Puerto Rico, and the Philippines to the United States.

The United States constructed substantial forts on Corregidor and on its three tiny neighboring islands, Caballo, El Fraile, and Carabao. These works were completed by 1914. Defensive strategists compared Manila Bay to Gibraltar, since the forts were able to withstand attack from the sea by the largest warships then in use. Great improvements in military aviation during the 1920s, however, reduced the effectiveness of the Corregidor fortress complex. Because the Philippines were due to be given their independence in 1946, the U.S. Congress refused to spend a great deal on fortifying Corregidor against air attack, instead funding limited improvements such as short-range antiaircraft guns and concrete walls around some of the installations.

By 1941, despite its weakness against airborne assault, Corregidor remained an impressive fortress, known to the people stationed there as the Rock. Fifty-six coastal guns were emplaced on high elevations on the island. Two of the largest, capable of firing shells weighing 700 pounds seventeen miles with excellent accuracy, were on the western tip of Corregidor facing the South China Sea. Unfortunately, they were mounted out in the open rather than in armored turrets. A large network of tunnels was excavated out of volcanic rock under Malinta Hill. These would provide critical protection again Japanese air attacks when the war began. About 5,000 Filipino and American troops were assigned to Corregidor, most of them artillerists. Most Americans were housed in a large, three-story concrete building located on Topside. The world's longest barracks, it was known as Mile-long Barracks although, at 1,520 feet long, it was less than one-third of a mile. Remaining Americans lived in concrete barracks on Middleside, a lower elevation along the eastern slopes of Topside. Filipino units were housed in wooden barracks on the eastern end of the island called Bottomside next to the small airfield known as Kindley Landing Field. Roads, trails, and thirteen miles of electric trolley tracks provided access and transportation to various parts of the island. During 1941 the self-confidence of the Corregidor garrison remained strong.

For many years before the beginning of World War II, American military strategists knew that Japan would be the

Cannon on Corregidor Island
Photo courtesy of Philippine Consulate General

most likely enemy in the Pacific. Preparation for the possibility of a war with Japan, which would certainly include a Japanese assault on the Philippines, resulted in a top-secret document called War Plan Orange. The central assumption of the plan was that Japan would successfully invade the Philippines and that the weaker American and Filipino forces would retreat into the mountainous Bataan Peninsula. If forced out of Bataan, they would withdraw to the island of Corregidor and wage a defensive battle for six months. By this time a strong American relief force would arrive. The main weakness of War Plan Orange was seen clearly by then Lieutenant General Douglas MacArthur, the new commander of U.S. forces in the Far East. It would take far longer than six months, he believed, to recruit and send to the Philippines a relief force powerful enough to defeat an entrenched Japanese army. The Navy had already concluded that such a relief effort would take two to three years. The unrealistic War Plan Orange set the stage for an overwhelming American-Filipino disaster in the Philippines.

MacArthur's forces in 1941 were made up of approximately 19,000 U.S. Army personnel, 12,000 well-trained Philippine Scouts (military professionals), and approximately 100,000 soldiers of the Philippine Army, which had been assembled only recently and had not been thoroughly trained. Most of these forces were stationed on the island of Luzon, which was expected to be the Japanese invaders' primary objective. While this assessment was correct, Japan's Imperial General Staff had formulated a much more complex and ambitious plan involving all of Southeast Asia. The Japanese aimed to make surprise attacks on the Philippines and Hawaii, then planned to overrun Guam, Wake Island, British Malaya, Hong Kong, Siam, Burma, the Dutch East Indies, and French Indochina. The enormous oil and rubber sources of these areas would then be available to the resource-starved Japanese empire.

The Japanese air attack on Pearl Harbor on December 7, 1941, caught the U.S. Navy's Pacific Fleet and the nearby military airfields completely unprepared. The fleet was devastated, and more than half the aircraft on the island were eliminated. American forces on Luzon were equally unprepared, MacArthur having believed that a Japanese attack could not take place before April. Five hours after the Pearl Harbor raid, a massive Japanese aerial assault coming from Formosa struck military bases throughout the Philippines. Most of MacArthur's air force was destroyed. The surviving aircraft and the U.S. Asiatic Fleet were quickly ordered to flee south. On December 10 the first Japanese Army detachments came ashore in northern Luzon, and on December 23 approximately 43,000 troops of Japan's Fourteenth Army stormed the Lingayen Gulf beaches some ninety-five miles northwest of Manila.

The Japanese commander, Lieutenant General Masaharu Homma, had told his superiors that he would capture the Philippines in eight weeks, making Manila's port facilities available for use in other Japanese ventures. The Japanese easily defeated the American and Filipino forces, and MacArthur ordered a withdrawal to the Bataan Peninsula in keeping with War Plan Orange. He then abandoned his Manila headquarters, moved to Corregidor with his staff, and declared Manila an open city to prevent its destruction by the Japanese. On January 2, 1942, the Japanese Army occupied Manila without opposition. American and Filipino forces on Corregidor and on Bataan, however, continued to deny the Japanese the free use of Manila Bay.

Beginning on January 9, General Homma's army carried out a series of successful attacks against the American-Filipino lines on Bataan. A Filipino counterattack regained ground and stalled the Japanese offensive. His troops worn out, Homma had to end his assault and ask his superiors to send reinforcements from China. MacArthur contacted Washington asking for carrier-launched air strikes against the Japanese forces, together with supplies and reinforcements for his troops. MacArthur did not know the American and British Combined Chiefs of Staff had already decided to reinforce Europe first and deal with the Japanese later. Officials in Washington lied to MacArthur, telling him that relief was on the way, thus encouraging the Americans to keep defending their positions. MacArthur eventually realized that help was not forthcoming, but he was prepared to hold his ground at any cost. MacArthur was needed to command future operations, however, and in early March President Franklin D. Roosevelt ordered him to leave the Philippines. On March 11 MacArthur, his staff and family, and several Filipino political leaders left Corregidor aboard a PT boat on a hazardous journey by ship and plane to Australia. Command of the American-Filipino forces was assumed by General Jonathan Wainwright.

The American forces on Bataan and Corregidor were not completely abandoned. During the slightly more than four months until the surrender on May 6, the American command in Australia made desperate attempts to send medical supplies, ammunition, and food. Blockade-running ships were dispatched from Australia, Java, and Hawaii, but only three freighters reached their destination in the Philippines and not all of these supplies could be transshipped to Corregidor. United States submarines carried cargoes of food and ammunition from Java and Australia, delivering them to Corregidor at night. These deliveries were too small to affect the outcome of the military action. But the ships and submarines did provide escape for some government officials and technically trained military personnel whose services were desperately needed. Large amounts of gold and silver bullion were also rescued. During the final days before the surrender, two Navy PBY aircraft unloaded medical supplies at Corregidor and evacuated a group of army nurses; one plane was damaged in an accident and its passengers were captured. These attempts to break through the Japanese blockade, while involving heroic efforts, ultimately failed. Still, that the attempts had been made satisfied some sense of national honor.

On March 31 General Homma began a powerful assault on American-Filipino positions on Bataan, aided by substantial tank and infantry reinforcements. An intense battle developed during which the Japanese broke through the defenders' lines. Americans and Filipinos were in a state of collapse from malnutrition and exhaustion and nearly defenseless because of lack of ammunition. On April 9 the Bataan garrison surrendered to the Japanese and became their prisoners. The plan to evacuate them called for groups of 100 prisoners to be taken to camps about sixty miles from the battle zone; the prisoners would make part of the journey on foot and part via railroad. Many of the prisoners, however, were too sick and weak to walk even half a mile, and they were subjected to brutal punishment when they faltered on the journey, which became known as the Bataan Death March. Of the approximately 70,000 men who began the march, about 10,000 died on the way from sickness, beatings, and execution. After the war, General Homma was tried in Manila as a war criminal. Held responsible for the death march, he was executed by a firing squad in 1946.

The events on Bataan brought a flood of refugees to Corregidor, increasing the island's population from approximately 9,000 to more than 15,000, including members of the Army, Navy, and Marine Corps, and male and female civilians. This population increase compounded existing food shortages and sanitation problems. Since January 5, the Corregidor garrison had been on half rations, which were applied as well to the new refugees. Military personnel from Bataan were integrated into the Corregidor defense system, but the garrison as a whole remained weak. In early May Japanese artillery began a nonstop firing program against the island. To ensure accurate hits, Japanese artillery spotters were suspended in a gondola beneath a hot air balloon, a technique used in the U.S. Civil War and learned by the Japanese. The saturation bombardment destroyed American artillery positions, devastated beach defenses, detonated minefields, and cut telephone lines. During the night of May 5, Japanese amphibious forces landed on the eastern tail of the island near Kindley Field. American reserve forces counterattacked but were decimated by overwhelming artillery barrages from Bataan. When Japanese tanks came ashore, the American-Filipino situation became hopeless. To avoid further casualties, General Wainwright surrendered Corregidor and all forces in the Philippines on May 6, 1942. A Filipino resistance movement endured, however, and General MacArthur vowed to return to the islands.

He did so in 1944. In July of that year MacArthur's Southwest Pacific Forces had fought their way north from Australia to within 300 miles of Mindanao, the southernmost island of the Philippines. The decision was made to liberate the Philippines and transform Luzon into a massive troop and supply base to support the invasion of the Japanese home islands. United States troops landed on Leyte on October 20 and by January 1945 were attacking Manila and preparing to seize Corregidor in order to reopen Manila Bay to Allied shipping. The American Sixth Army, assigned to Corregidor, decided to combine an amphibious assault from Bataan with parachute landings on the island, the latter operation being exceptionally risky. On February 16 the combined operation took place with about 25 percent of the first wave of paratroopers becoming casualties. The air and sea forces fought a bloody battle with Japanese troops until February 28, when organized Japanese resistance came to a halt. More than 5,000 Japanese died defending Corregidor, with 20 prisoners taken. United States casualties totaled 1,005 men, with 455 of that number killed in action. On March 2 MacArthur and his staff returned to Corregidor as he had left it in 1942, aboard a quartet of PT boats. The invasion of the Japanese home islands never took place.

Corregidor was ceded by the United States to the Philippines government in 1946 and was later turned into a national shrine of the Pacific War. It is visited yearly by thousands of travelers, among them Americans, Filipinos, and Japanese. Gun positions, now nearly covered with vegetation, and ruins of the Mile-long Barracks can be viewed. The white marble Pacific War Memorial, on the summit of the island, contains a museum of wartime memorabilia.

Further Reading: *Corregidor: The End of the Line* by Eric Morris (New York: Stein and Day, 1981; London: Hutchinson, 1982) is a thorough, well-written wartime history of Bataan and Corregidor that includes many personal narratives by participants. Two excellent histories emphasizing Corregidor's recapture in 1945 are Gerard M. Devlin's *Back to Corregidor* (New York: St. Martin's, 1992) and Lieutenant General E. M. Flanagan Jr.'s *Corregidor, The Rock Force Assault, 1945* (Novato, California: Presidio, 1988).

—Bernard A. Block

Darwin (Northern Territory, Australia)

Location: Port town situated on a flat peninsula at the northeastern entrance of a large natural harbor known as Port Darwin in Beagle Gulf.

Description: Capital of the Northern Territory and northernmost city in Australia. Named for famed British naturalist Charles Darwin. Site of intensive Japanese aerial attacks in February 1942 and widespread devastation by a tropical cyclone in December 1974.

Site Office: Northern Territory Tourist Commission
33 Smith Street Mall
GPO Box 4392
Darwin, Northern Territory 0801
Australia
(89) 81 4300

Early British interest in establishing a northern Australian base for the protection of the Torres Strait sea route and the exploitation of eastern Indonesian trade led to the establishment of garrison settlements at Melville Island in 1824, Raffles Bay in 1826, and Port Essington in 1838. After the abandonment of Port Essington in 1849, northern Australia sparked little interest until the south-north crossing of the continent by the Scottish-born explorer John McDouall Stuart on his third attempt in 1862 led South Australians to believe that the area was promising for cattle and sheep grazing. This, together with A. C. Gregory's earlier exploration of the Victoria River area in 1855, prompted the colonial government of South Australia to obtain permission from the British government to extend its borders to the northern coasts of the continent in 1863. In keen competition with the other colonies for economic growth and population, the South Australian government believed that this expansion would open profitable trade with the islands to the north and boost the pastoral industry. The area annexed was subsequently known as South Australia's Northern Territory until its transfer to the Commonwealth government as a dependent territory in 1911.

In 1839 Captain J. C. Wickham of H.M.S. *Beagle* had discovered a natural harbor, which he named Port Darwin after the naturalist Charles Darwin, who had been on board during the ship's earlier voyage around the world. John Lort Stokes, a lieutenant on the *Beagle,* subsequently published a highly favorable account of the area in his *Discoveries in Australia* (1846). However, it was not initially considered by the South Australian government as a site for the capital of its new territorial acquisition. Instead, official attention was focused on Adam Bay in Van Diemen Gulf to the northeast, owing largely to the influential British publicist and cartographer George Windsor Earl, who had strongly recommended Adam Bay for its healthy climate and its access to the interior by means of the Adelaide River. B. T. Finniss, who led the first official expedition to the north coast in early 1864, accordingly chose Escape Cliffs at Adam Bay as the site for the capital. It was to be named after Britain's prime minister at the time, Viscount Palmerston. Meanwhile, Finniss's deputy, J. T. Manton, had investigated Port Darwin and strongly recommended it to the authorities in Adelaide as "scarcely inferior to Sydney Harbour."

When the Escape Cliffs location quickly proved to be totally unsatisfactory because of annual flooding, two further expeditions were dispatched to select an alternative capital, and a final decision was made on the Port Darwin site. South Australian surveyor-general G. W. Goyder surveyed the area between February and September 1869, laying out 700,000 acres for agricultural and pastoral leases, as well as the town of Palmerston and two other town sites nearby. Groyder's gridiron plan was directly derived from Colonel William Light's earlier plan for the city of Adelaide.

The completion of the overland telegraph line between Adelaide and Palmerston in 1872, providing Australia's direct link with Europe through the submarine cable from Java, symbolized South Australia's confidence in its new acquisition. Government House, built in 1883, and other substantial official buildings in the Fort Hill area at the southern end of the peninsula also reflected official commitment to the future. Although officials had high hopes for the settlement's future as an entrepôt for trade with the islands to the north—the second Singapore envisaged by Earl and other publicists of northern settlement—Palmerston remained a sleepy backwater largely forgotten by the rest of Australia. Restrictive immigration policies excluding Asians brought to an end the age-old Macassan (Indonesian) bêche-de-mer (sea cucumber) industry on nearby coasts, and difficulty of access to the interior meant that the port could not easily serve its pastoral hinterland.

For many years, the only stimuli to the economy of Palmerston were the development of a pearling industry after 1884 and the discovery of gold at Pine Creek, prompting the construction of a linking railway. The gold rush and the railway also brought about the first importation of Chinese coolie labor via Singapore, which subsequently changed the ethnic and cultural composition of Palmerston. Ruled by a resident appointed by the South Australian government, the settlement in many ways came to resemble Dutch and British colonial outposts in Indonesia and Malaya. Vulnerable to tropical cyclones, it was almost destroyed in 1878, 1882, and 1897, and at the turn of the century its population had barely reached 1,000.

The transfer of the Northern Territory to the Commonwealth in 1911 did not bring about significant change beyond

Aerial view of Darwin
Photo courtesy of National Trust, Darwin

the re-naming of Palmerston to Darwin. Indeed, it reflected the South Australian government's unwillingness to meet the territory's administrative bill and its utter pessimism about future economic prospects. The construction at Bullocky Point of a huge meat packing plant in 1917 by Vestey's, a British company with 30,000 square miles of pastoral leases in the Northern Territory, Queensland, and Western Australia, temporarily raised hopes of economic growth and drew workers from various parts of Australia. However, high wages and Vestey's ability to fulfill its contracts through its South American operation at two-thirds of the cost led to the closing of the works in 1920. Nor did the extension of the railway line from Pine Creek to Birdum and from Oodnadatta to Alice Springs in 1929 stimulate further economic development and settlement. Political action by Darwin workers during the early 1920s brought about the virtual expulsion of two successive government administrators and the gaining of a modest measure of representation in the Commonwealth Parliament.

During those decades, the territory's relatively unconstrained frontier lifestyle, which often involved heavy drinking and promiscuous behavior between white men and Aboriginal women, was vividly captured by the novelist Xavier Herbert in *Capricornia*, published in 1936. By that time most of the survivors of the Larrakia tribe of Aborigines that had originally inhabited the area had been gathered together in what was known as the Darwin Compound and in other government and missionary institutions, including a leprosarium at Mud Island.

The one development in the 1920s and 1930s that offered hope for Darwin's future was its use as the main place of entry and departure for commercial flights between Europe and Australia. Celebrated Australian aviators Keith and Ross McPherson Smith made the first flight from England to Australia in 1919. By 1934 regular passenger service linked Australia with the rest of the world. The advent of World War II and a new awareness of the strategic importance of Darwin for Australia's security brought about its first significant growth. The building of military, naval, and air force facilities and the stationing of a large garrison provided a major boost for the remote town. It also provided paid employment and social welfare entitlements for the first time to many Aboriginal workers.

However, the bombing of Darwin by the Japanese, commencing with two full-scale raids by 199 aircraft on February 19, 1942, destroyed many defense and shipping facilities. Almost 250 servicemen and civilians were killed, and many more were wounded. The ensuing military and civil panic resulted in a headlong exodus of the population to the south, and a Commonwealth government Royal Commission was appointed to examine the circumstances of the bombing. The vulnerability of Australia's "front door" had been revealed dramatically by the same Japanese naval task force that had attacked Pearl Harbor three months earlier. A further

World War II defense post, Darwin
Photo courtesy of National Trust, Darwin

fifty-eight air raids on defense installations were recorded between March 8, 1942, and November 12, 1943.

After the war, a new commitment to northern development by the Commonwealth government led to the rebuilding of Darwin as a planned modern city, necessitating the compulsory acquisition of all land held under freehold title. Although much of the plan was abandoned by 1950, government construction of housing and office buildings resulted in Darwin's rapid expansion and its achievement of city status in 1959. The development of the nearby Rum Jungle uranium mine and other mineral developments also fueled commercial growth at a rate that made Darwin the fastest-growing city in Australia during the 1960s and early 1970s. Population increased from 15,500 in 1961 to more than 35,000 in 1971. Although there was still no rail link between Alice Springs and Darwin, the wartime construction of a sealed north-south highway brought about better communications.

Darwin's second great crisis was Cyclone Tracy, Australia's largest natural disaster. The storm's 100 mile-an-hour winds ripped through the city for five hours on the early morning of December 25, 1974, destroying 90 percent of all houses and shops and killing at least 50 people. All communications, water, electricity, and sanitation were cut and the survivors left sheltering in the ruins. After the evacuation of most of the population by air and sea, reconstruction was begun by the Commonwealth government with an eye to greater security against cyclonic conditions. New regulations required that buildings be able to withstand winds up to 180 feet per second.

By the end of 1977, the Darwin Reconstruction Commission had supervised the building of 2,000 new houses and the rebuilding of 7,000 more. Rapid population growth exhausted available land to the north of the city and led to the development of the satellite town of Palmerston twelve miles to the south. Achievement of statehood in 1978 also ushered in a new era of relative political independence after a long history of government by remote control from Adelaide, Melbourne, and Canberra.

Although Darwin's economy continued to reflect its role as an administrative and services center, the establishment of Australia's first Free Trade Development Zone marked government determination to open trade with neighboring Southeast Asia and to employ contract Asian workers in manufacturing. In the meantime, the arrival of Vietnamese-Chinese boat people in the early 1970s and other refugees from East Timor after 1974 helped to make Darwin a cosmopolitan city with a population (including Palmerston) of more than 78,000 in 1994. Two of its lord mayors in recent times have been ethnic Chinese, and the city boasts a wealthy and powerful Greek community. The advent of Aboriginal land rights and the growing popularity of Aboriginal art also has aided Darwin's indigenous people after decades of social and economic marginalization.

In the mid–1980s, the University College of the Northern Territory was established on two campuses, the Darwin Institute of Technology and the Darwin Performing Arts Centre. In addition, the Northern Territory Museum of Arts and Sciences was extended. To the northeast the Holmes Jungle Nature Park preserves the natural rain-forest environment, but more adventurous visitors use the city as a starting point for expeditions to Kakadu National Park, Ayers Rock, and the Olgas. Direct air links with Singapore, Brunei, and Bali maintain Darwin's close access to island Southeast Asia.

Further Reading: The early history of Darwin is explored by Robert Reece in "Palmerston (Darwin): Four Expeditions in Search of a Capital," in *The Origins of Australia's Capital Cities* (Cambridge and New York: Cambridge University Press, 1989). Developments up to the late 1960s are described in detail by Douglas Lockwood in *Australia's Pearl Harbour: Darwin 1942* (Melbourne: Cassell Australia, 1966; revised edition, Adelaide: Rigby, 1984) and *The Front Door: Darwin 1869–1969* (Adelaide: Rigby, 1968). Darwin's historical relationship with its hinterland is discussed in *Far Country: A Short History of the Northern Territory* by A. Powell (Carlton, Victoria: Melbourne University Press, 1982; second edition, 1988).

—Bob Reece

Datong (Shanxi, China)

Location: In northeastern Shanxi province on the edge of the Mongolian steppe. Datong stands on a north-south tributary of the Sanggan River about 180 miles almost due west of Beijing and the same distance north of the provincial capital, Taiyuan. Close to the Inner Mongolian border, which here follows the line of the Ming Dynasty Great Wall.

Description: Strategic location for the control of northern China but difficult to defend from the north. Land poor for agriculture but has enormous mineral deposits, especially of iron and high-quality coal. Favored as a capital by the nomadic Tuoba Wei regime but later abandoned. Crucial sector of the Ming frontier defenses, seeing the heaviest concentration of wall building. In the twentieth century, Datong was the center for the warlord Yan Xishan. Mineral resources are its chief source of income, while the Yungang caves are nearby, and its old city is home to architectural and sculptural rarities.

Site Office: CITS
Yungang Hotel
Yingbin Xilu
Datong
China
23215

The first known settlement of the site of Datong was under the Zhou Dynasty (c. 1122–256 B.C.). In the Warring States period (403–221 B.C.) it became part of the Zhao Kingdom as Pingcheng county, said to have been founded by King Wuling (ruled 325–299 B.C.), who also built a series of fortresses past the town in 300–299 B.C. to protect lands taken from the nomadic Xiongnu. Under the Han (206 B.C.–A.D. 220) the site commonly was called Pingshun. Near here, in 200 B.C., Emperor Gaozu (ruled 206–195 B.C.) was surrounded and almost defeated by the Xiongnu at Mount Baideng. As a result, the Han made a treaty with the Xiongnu in 198 B.C. that defined the boundary between the two groups. Some Chinese scholars believe this line could correspond to a short line of ruined wall, possibly built by the Qin (221–206 B.C.), running east-west just south of Datong.

Pingcheng county remained inhabited under the kingdoms of Wei (220–265) and Jin (264–420) but first rose to prominence during the Northern Wei Dynasty (386–534); this dynasty was founded by the Tuoba, a subdivision of the nomadic Xianbei, centered since the third century on the Yinshan region (southeastern Inner Mongolia). In the early fourth century the weakening of the Eastern Jin (265–316) led to the Tuoba acquisition of lands in northern Shanxi. In 313 Chief Yilu established a northern capital in the traditional Tuoba heartland, while restoring the old city of Pingcheng (east of modern Datong) as the southern capital, so placed that it controlled the newly acquired lands. He also built a "New Pingcheng" thirty-three miles farther south on a hill on the north bank of the Lei River (flowing into the Sanggan) and garrisoned under his eldest son, Liuxiu, who governed the southern part of the Tuoba domains from there. In 315 the Jin emperor recognized Tuoba strength by making Yilu prince of Dai, but there followed seventy years of instability until the Tuoba recovered under Daowu Di (ruled 386–409), who came to control all the territory between the Ordos (within the great bend of the Yellow River) and the Yinshan.

Daowu Di called himself emperor from 396 and established his capital at Pingcheng two years later. Here he based the huge cavalry armies with which he controlled the Yinshan, northern Shanxi, central Hebei, and the Ordos and, according to William Jenner, "created a new capital by compulsion and violence." The Pingcheng area was populated by forced migration. For example, in 398 more than 460,000 officials, commoners, and artisans were moved to "fill out the capital," and in the next year 90,000 prisoners of war joined them. The new arrivals were given land and plowing oxen, but their function very definitely was to feed the capital.

Although there was some consideration of moving the capital farther south in 403 and 415, Emperor Mingyuan Di (ruled 409–424) settled there permanently. By 422 the outer walls of the city measured nearly ten miles around. The capital—organized into imperial areas, suburbs, streets, and wards—contained palaces, ancestral temples, and ceremonial altars. A deer park larger than the city, not far outside the walls, was linked to the palace by canals. A policy of sedentarization was well under way, and nomadism was forbidden. The official Cui Hao (381–450) oversaw the extensive adoption of Chinese institutions, including administrative methods, and a written penal code in place of unwritten, customary law. As defense against the nomadic Rouran became more important, the Wei came to think more like a sedentary than a steppe power, and as their sedentary population rose in numbers, so their reliance on agricultural taxes became greater. In addition, the Tuoba increasingly were attracted by the prestige of Chinese culture, Chinese crafts, luxurious living, and Buddhism.

As the Northern Wei expanded south during the fifth century, they used the conquered peoples to augment the population of the Pingcheng area, governing with strict regulations aimed at maintaining control and expanding agriculture in the dry, cold climate. Despite all efforts, the region never could produce enough food to supply the capital, necessitating difficult and expensive transportation from the fertile lands of Hebei to the south. Nevertheless, building works continued, with new

Shanhua Temple, Datong
Photo courtesy of Consulate General of China, Chicago

palaces constructed by Taiwu Di (ruled 423–452), in his last two years after much pressure from his court, and by Wencheng Di (ruled 452–465), who employed the earliest known Wei architect, Gao Shanming, to design his Taihua Palace (demolished in 492). Visitors from the southern states commented on the size of the palace complex, with buildings in brick and tamped earth, and observed palace slaves engaged in weaving, brewing, animal husbandry, horticulture, metalwork, and woodwork. A large proportion of the population appears to have comprised soldiers and their families, and despite firm laws, Pingcheng could be an unruly place; in 454, for example, there was a three-day roundup of "evildoers and desperadoes," and between 458 and 466 prohibition was enforced by the death penalty, in an effort to put a stop to drunken quarreling over affairs of state. Southerners also criticized the Xianbei's continued practice of animal sacrifices, the free and unveiled movement of the empress dowager, and the practice of sitting rather than kneeling.

In 476 the empress dowager Feng took power and instituted a drastic sinicization policy. She appointed Chinese officials rather than Xianbei, regularized official salaries and advancement, and acted against corruption. Her regime encouraged agriculture while ending the policy of forced migration, increased control over the agricultural population, replaced non-Chinese ceremonies, and created new law codes. Buddhism was actively promoted as the state religion, and the monasteries were granted dependent populations of semifree farmers or unfree, convicted criminals. Pingcheng at this time contained about 100 monasteries and convents, with approximately 2,000 monks and nuns. The most dramatic legacy of this patronage of Buddhism is the Yungang Caves west of Datong, where huge Buddha statues were created in the cliffs above the Wuzhou River. The first cave was carved in the 450s during the rule of Wencheng Di, who, as heir apparent, had mitigated the brief persecution of Buddhism by his father after 446; most work, however, was carried out in the period 489–523. The statues vary between 24 and 160 feet tall, and the five main images probably represented the preceding Wei emperors. The empress dowager Feng also commissioned ten more palace buildings in Pingcheng between 476 and 488, and in 492 she had some older palaces razed in order to build a new one; tree-lined, stone embankments channeled the river around the new palace complex. The designer Jiang Shaoyu played a major part in these works.

Meanwhile, the Rouran continued to raid nearly every year from 485 to 493, but now they were held off by border defenses built north of the capital and by the Wei's allowing profitable Rouran "tribute missions" to come to Pingcheng. While the city appears to have become less socially divided, its growth exacerbated the problems of food supply, and there also were signs of discontent in a conspiracy led by a Buddhist monk that was suppressed in 481. Also, although sinicization was official policy, a Datong tomb dating from 484 contains mostly objects in a non-Chinese style, such as camels, packhorses, and soldiers in Xianbei clothing.

In 492 Emperor Xiaowen Di, who was born in Pingcheng, remarked that Datong was "a place from which to wage war, not one from which civilized rule can come." This fact—combined with the difficulty of supplying Pingcheng from the northern China plain, the need for greater attention to the southern frontier than to the northern frontier, and probably the harshness of the weather—inspired Xiaowen Di in 494 to move his capital 600 miles due south to a newly rebuilt city at Luoyang; there Empress Feng's sinicization policies were continued and extended. Despite some resistance and much hardship, most of Luoyang's population and livestock were taken there from Pingcheng, although the old capital continued to exist, as evidenced by continued work at Yungang, where the last dated inscription is from 524.

Datong continued in fairly uneventful existence for the next four centuries. The Tang (618–907) called the place Yunzhou and added to the Yungang Caves. In 640 the Tang established Dingxiang county nearby, only to dissolve it in 682 as a result of banditry, moving the population to Shuozhou. In 742–758 the county was known as Yunzhong, before recovering its old name and moving to Yongjizha, on the site of the old city of Datong, where repairs were undertaken in 813. In the ninth and tenth centuries Yunzhou changed hands several times. In 843 it was one of four prefectures comprising Datong Circuit, which increased in status until it became an important frontier governorship. In 876 the Shatuo Turk Li Keyong briefly occupied Yunzhou, his own prefecture, because of a shortage of supplies, prompting an imperial expedition against him; two years later, however, he was back in favor as Datong's governor, defending the court against the rebel Huang Chao.

In 936 Yunzhou was one of the "Sixteen Prefectures" handed over to the Liao (907–1125) in return for their assistance in replacing the Later Tang (923–936) with the Later Jin (936–947) Dynasty. Yunzhou did not return to Chinese hands for another 440 years. In 1044 the prefectural capital of Liao Yunzhou became the new Western Capital (Xijing) and head of a circuit of the same name. The city saw much new building, of which the gems were the wooden Huayan temples. Named for one of the seven major scriptures of Buddhism, the temples originally housed stone and bronze statues of all preceding Liao emperors. The main hall of the Lower Huayan Temple, built in 1038, contains twenty-eight Liao statues. Behind this is the only wooden structure surviving from the Liao: a carved tower in which scriptures were stored. The Upper Temple was destroyed at the end of the Liao, but the Daxiong Hall was rebuilt in 1140 by the Jin Dynasty (1115–1234). This is the largest surviving Buddhist hall in China, measuring some 90 feet wide by more than 150 feet long; it was decorated with murals and ceiling patterns during various periods. The Jin, in 1128, also rebuilt the Shanhua Temple established in the Tang, and this survives in the south of the city.

The Huayan temple's collection of scriptures includes some from the Ming Dynasty (1368–1644), and Buddhas and ceiling paintings also survive from this period, along with many other old parts of the city. Datong was the home of the Ming founder's thirteenth son, Zhu Gui, outside whose residence was the "Nine Dragon Screen," more than 140 feet long and 25 feet high; the surviving city walls were built by the Ming general Xu Da (1332–85). After 1422, when the Ming emperor Yongle (ruled 1403–25) withdrew the last of the Ming's forward defense garrisons, Datong became the most important of the "nine border garrisons," while remaining vulnerable owing to its location south of a plain offering no natural barriers. Accordingly, it became the most heavily defended stretch of the Ming "Great Wall," and significant sections are still visible.

Probably by the early fifteenth century there were already a couple of east-west earth ramparts blocking the southward route along the Yu River on which Datong stands—a southern, "secondary border" about thirty miles north of the city, and a northern, "great border" thirty miles beyond that—but these works quickly fell into disrepair. In 1449 the Oirat Mongol leader Esen, feeling shortchanged by the gifts bestowed by the Ming on a Mongol "tribute" mission, led a retaliatory attack on Datong. Although this failed, Esen's forces captured the Ming emperor Zhengtong, paraded him before the city and received a ransom for him; but Datong did not open its gates. The Mongols continued to Beijing, but the Ming court selected a new emperor, and Esen returned to the steppe.

During the 1470s and 1480s, regular Mongol raids targeted the frontier between the Ordos and the Juyongguan Pass just north of Beijing, which was undefended save for the garrisons at Datong and Xuanfu. Some Ming advisers suggested an expedition to retake the whole Ordos region, but eventually a policy of wall building won out, and in 1484 Yu Zijun was given charge of military affairs in Datong and Xuanfu. He recommended the eastward extension of defenses he had built earlier, to create a line of fortifications 433 miles long, using 86,000 workers for a period of several months. Work was to have begun in spring 1485, but court politics cut the plan short. The scheme was revived by Yang Yiqing in 1506 as a first step toward a grander scheme of recovering control of the Ordos. This time work began, but again the project fell prey to court politics after only thirteen miles had been completed.

By this point the Mongols had occupied the territory where the earlier "great border" and "secondary border" had been built; the Ming troops stationed nearby were in dispersed locations; the frontier fortifications were much neglected; and the court sent central officials there only occasionally. However, changing strategy meant that from 1513 the region was placed under a single military official,

Hall of Guanyin, Datong
Photo courtesy of Consulate General of China, Chicago

who from the early 1520s became known as the "supreme commander." Discipline problems deriving from the poverty of the land, the extreme cold, and the fruitlessness of fighting the Mongols provoked two major mutinies at Datong, in 1524 and 1533. Ironically, these were in opposition to court plans to strengthen defenses in the area with five new forts, completion of which was delayed by the risings until 1539. At the same time, more Mongols were settling along the border, and their leader, the Altan Khan, founded the border city of Hohhot west of Beijing, effectively neutralizing Datong. Then, in 1544, Weng Wanda (1498–1552), chief architect of the Ming system of frontier defenses, was appointed supreme commander in the region, where he did much wall building; a recent archaeological survey has provided extensive information about this activity.

From 1546 to 1548 Weng oversaw the building of new fortifications north and south of Datong and Xuanfu, including forty-six miles in Datong Circuit, along with seven forts and 154 signal towers, all completed with less expenditure than estimated. For this Weng and a fellow official were promoted, and the emperor noted that 1545 had seen no raids on the area, although the Chinese "renegade" Wang San came close to winning a battle in the area in 1547. Previously, the primary line of defenses had been the southerly fortifications, allowing raiders to penetrate easily to the passes just north of Beijing. Apart from walls, there were forts, towers, and, crucially, signal beacons, with garrisons ranging from several dozen men to fewer than ten for the smaller towers and up to several thousand men and horses in the larger forts. Some of the towers also began to be equipped with firearms, which terrified the Mongols. Repair and extension was an almost continuous process, with major rebuilding of Weng Wanda's defenses directed by Yang Bo, minister of war and supreme commander of Datong and Xuanfu, from 1555. The defenses of Datong were strengthened from 1574 with strong towers—each garrisoned by 100 men—about every third of a mile along the inside of the borderline, some of them linked by walls. Earlier earth walls were faced with stone or rebuilt in solid brick or stone. By 1587 there were nearly 900 towers for signalling and possibly defense in the Datong region alone, along with 72 forts, many of which acquired brick or stone facings after 1572.

These works were enabled partly by the relationship established in 1571 with the Mongol leader Altan Khan in a meeting just beyond the Datong border defenses. Here the khan and his followers pledged allegiance to the Ming and promised to respect the frontier, in return for a princely title and seal for the khan and Ming military titles for his nobles. The peace brought by this deal reduced army expenses for the Xuanfu, Datong, and Shanxi regions such that in 1577 they were twenty to thirty percent of the pre-peace costs. The subsidies paid to the Mongols amounted to a tenth of defense expenditures, and farming returned to normal. As late as 1590 an official commented that no military action had been needed anywhere on the frontier between Xuanfu and Gansu.

The end of the Ming saw many rebellions, which by 1636 had spread to northern China under the leadership of Li Zicheng (1606–45). In 1643 Li moved his headquarters to the Wei valley in Shenxi and in February 1644 proclaimed his Dashun Dynasty in Xi'an, but it was when he took Datong that spring that resistance to him collapsed. From there he went on to take Beijing, only to be defeated by the Manchus and killed during his retreat.

Datong was of little note during the Qing (1644–1912), although the scriptures stored at the Huayan temple include a rare copy of the *Longcang*, one of the Qing imperial collections. After the fall of the Qing, however, the area of northern Shanxi around Datong became the stronghold of the warlord Yan Xishan (1883–1960). In 1917, after the collapse of Chinese president Yuan Shikai's power, Yan added the civil governorship of Shanxi to his military governorship and remained in control there until the end of World War II.

Yan tended to be weaker than his rivals, but in his early years he often held the balance of power such that his neighbors did not attack him, bringing a remarkable peace to Shanxi when other areas were in turmoil. Yan was keen to modernize Shanxi socially, morally, and economically, under a composite ideology of his own devising, and his reforms earned Shanxi the name of "Model Province." Shanxi contains more than half of China's coal reserves, including most of the high-quality seams, and Yan took all mineral deposits into state ownership when he became governor. The coal around Datong was to be extracted by the Tongbao Mining Company, for which Yan provided most of the investment capital, enabling the purchase of modern machinery; this allowed the drastic overhaul of outdated, inefficient practices, producing a near-doubling of production from 1920 to 1926. Yet the most productive mines in Shanxi remained those at Datong with a strong Japanese presence among the stockholders: Yan's investment was insufficient to compete with foreign-owned businesses. Even if output had been higher, exploiting Shanxi's mineral wealth by exporting it required better communications, for Datong was the only major town in Shanxi with access to a railway (the Beijing-Suiyuan line), and Yan refused to build new lines for himself, constructing roads instead.

Yan tried to keep out of the war between the Mukden (Shenyang) clique and Feng Yuxiang in 1926, but he felt compelled to try to stop Feng's withdrawal north along the Beijing-Suiyuan line through Datong, losing northern Shanxi to Feng for his pains. Subsequently, he sided against the Mukden clique's leader, Zhang Zuolin, making a significant contribution to the success of the Northern Expedition in 1928. But in 1930 Yan formed a temporary regime independent of the nationalist government and, along with Feng Yuxiang and Wang Jingwei, tried to remove Chiang Kai-shek from power.

The 1930s saw serious and worsening economic problems in Shanxi as elsewhere in China, particularly unemployment, leading Yan to institute a Ten-Year Plan for economic reform. The centerpiece of this was the narrow-gauge Tong-Bu Railway, named for its starting point of Datong and endpoint of Buzhou, built as cheaply as possible in 1932–37. Although this transformed Shanxi's export potential, it was still not enough to make the province's fortune.

By 1936 an anti-Japanese movement was growing all over China, and that summer the Manchurian warlord Zhang Xueliang held secret negotiations with Yan Xishan, who was feeling Japanese pressure on his borders. The Japanese Guandong Army had carried out acts of sabotage that included blowing up a large supply dump in Datong, convincing Yan that the Japanese were about to attack there, and leading him to disagree with Chiang Kai-shek's belief that the communists were the greatest threat to China. The Japanese sought to use growing Mongolian nationalism to expand their power into northern China, and in 1937 the northern Shanxi area around Datong was among territories given to the Federated Autonomous Government, a Japanese puppet state under a Mongol prince with a Japanese "supreme advisor." This new regime was to be linked by the Kalgan-Datong-Baotou railway line, and the Japanese aimed to exploit the area's iron and coal resources and develop electricity production. Although Yan had by now accepted from Chiang Kai-shek the command of a Second War Zone, including Shanxi and the neighboring provinces, the leadership of his forces was appallingly inept, and they offered almost no resistance to the Japanese invasion. A trusted commander surrendered Datong without a fight after his troops fled, abandoning or at best destroying their equipment. The Japanese occupied Shanxi until 1945, and nationalist Datong fell to the communists on May 1, 1949.

In recent years Datong was famous as the location of the last factory producing steam railway engines, which had opened in 1959 and finally closed in the 1980s. The city remains the leading coal producer of Shanxi province, with other major industries being iron and manufacturing cottons for export. Datong retains one of the largest and most intact "old cities" to be found anywhere in China.

Further Reading: Datong is not one of the better-known cities of China, and, accordingly, information is scattered, with much of it available only in Chinese. However, William Jenner's *Memories of Loyang: Yang Hsüan-chih and the Lost Capital (493–534)* (Oxford and New York: Oxford University Press, 1981) provides a good chapter on Northern Wei Pingcheng. Arthur Waldron's *The Great Wall of China: From History to Myth* (Cambridge and New York: Cambridge University Press, 1990) gives an extensive account of the building of the Ming fortifications in the Datong region. Donald G. Gillin's *Warlord: Yen Hsi-shan in Shansi*

Province 1911–1949 (Princeton: Princeton University Press, 1967) is a full biography of Yan Xishan, but this should be read alongside more recent, though general, works, such as Jonathan Spence's *The Search for Modern China* (New York and London: Norton, 1990).

—Naomi Standen

Delhi (Delhi, India)

Location: In Delhi territory, some 709 feet above sea level, between the Yamuna River to the east and the Arāvalli Hills to the southwest.

Description: Capital city of India, combining the remaining monuments of earlier cities with Old Delhi, former capital of the Mughal Empire, and New Delhi, former capital of the British Empire in India.

Site Office: Government of India Tourist Office
88 Janpath
New Delhi, Delhi 110001
India
3320005, 3320008, 3320109, 3320266, or 3320342

The Delhi of today, capital city of an independent federal republic and home to more than 8 million people, has developed on and around the sites of eight earlier cities. Of these the first was Hindu, the last British, but those between were all created by Muslim rulers, whose palaces and mosques not only form the main historic legacy of pre-modern Delhi but also inspired much of the design of the British buildings in New Delhi.

The location of the city attracted Indian rulers of all kinds from ancient times because of its strategic and commercial value: it has long dominated transport networks along the corridor between the Himalaya and the Thar Desert as well as the fertile zone between the Ganges and Yamuna Rivers. This was the area in which many of the events recounted in the *Mahābhārata,* the Hindu epic composed approximately 2,000 years ago, are said to have taken place, and Delhi is mentioned by name in some of the songs of the Hindu Bards, compiled around the same period. Archaeological excavations in 1955 and later, which uncovered ancient remains below the seventeenth-century citadel of Shergarh, provide some evidence to support these legendary references and, therefore, the claim that a city, perhaps called Indraprastha, was founded on or near the site of modern Delhi around the ninth century B.C. It was probably this settlement that was referred to as "Dilli" by the Greek geographer Ptolemy of Alexandria, writing in the first century A.D. However, the establishment of the first historically verifiable Delhi, by the Tomara Dynasty, one of the leading families among the Rājput people of northwestern India, is usually considered to have occurred between 736 and 850. This settlement appears to have been relatively unimportant until 1060, when the Tomara ruler Anangpal either established or enlarged a major fortress at Delhi, called Lal Kot.

During the twelfth century, sporadic raids by Turkish and Afghan Muslim armies gave way to sustained campaigns of conquest and settlement across northern India. This pattern of settlement created a patchwork of small states scattered among the existing Hindu monarchies. Among these, the Tomara state based in Delhi fell to the Muslims in 1192, when its ruler Prithviraj Chauhan was killed at the battle of Tarain. The Muslim general Mu'izz-ud-Dīn Muḥammad of Ghur ordered the building at Delhi of the Quwwat-ul-Islam Masjid, the Might of Islam Mosque, to commemorate the victory. This arcaded structure, completed approximately 1199, used materials taken from twenty-seven Hindu temples, including, as a freestanding monument in its grounds, the Iron Pillar, originally erected by a Gupta ruler in the third century A.D. to honor the god Vishnu, and now noted for the 98 percent purity of the iron from which it was made.

By about 1204 all the Hindu states had passed under the control of Muḥammad of Ghur, who also exercised power over much of what is now Afghanistan from his base at Lahore. In 1206 he was succeeded by a former slave, Quṭb-ud Dīn Aybak, who was to become known as the founder of the so-called Slave dynasty of Muslim rulers, and who ordered the construction next to the Quwwat-ul-Islam Masjid of the Quṭb Minar, the "axis tower," 238 feet high, which, according to the inscriptions on it, was intended to cast the shadow of Allah on East and West alike. It was the Slave dynasty who moved their seat to Delhi from Lahore after the Mongol invasions had disrupted their links with Afghanistan, and who established the Delhi Sultanate, the paramount state in northern India. The city's status as a center of Muslim culture was further enhanced after 1258, when Baghdad, the leading city of Islam at that period, was conquered and destroyed and refugee scholars and artists came to India. Among these new arrivals were Persian craftsmen and courtiers, whose tradition of absorbing pre-Islamic and non-Islamic forms of ceremony and architecture continued at Delhi, notably under the ruler Balban, between 1266 and 1287.

Only three years after Balban's death, however, his successor Shams-ud-Dīn was deposed and the dynasty replaced by Jalāl-ud-Dīn Firūz Khaljī and his family, who were Afghan Turks. By 1316 they had taken control of most of what are now India, Pakistan, and Bangladesh by conquering the various Rājput and other smaller states and keeping the Mongols at bay. Their triumphs, and the accompanying influx of yet another refugee group, this time of Seljuk Turks fleeing the Mongols, were both reflected in 'Alā'-ud-Dīn Muḥammad Khaljī's foundation of Siri, usually counted as the second citadel at Delhi, in 1304, and the construction in the following year of the Alai Darwaza, a magnificent red sandstone and white marble gateway for the Quṭb Minar.

The Khaljī Dynasty in turn was supplanted by another group of provincial upstarts. In 1320 the Sultanate passed into the hands of the Tughluq Dynasty, founded by Ghiyās-ud-Dīn Tughluq, who had been governor of the

The Quṭb Minar, Delhi
Photo courtesy of Christopher Turner

Dīwān-i-Khas (Hall of Private Audience), at Delhi's Red Fort
Photo courtesy of Christopher Turner

Punjab until that date. He then created the third city of Delhi, Tughluqābād, which now lies in ruins on an escarpment near the modern city. His son and successor, Muḥammad, who reigned from 1325 to 1351, tried to move the capital, first to Jahānpanāh, a new site between the old quarters of Lal Kot and Siri, and then away from the Delhi area altogether, to a location on the Deccan plateau far to the south. These decisions appear to have been resisted by the people of the city and they were never fully realized. Instead, in 1354 the next sultan, Fīrūz, created Firozābād, a new fortress city on the banks of the Yamuna River, four miles from Siri and eight miles from the Quṭb Minar.

The glory and prosperity of Firozābād at its height are now commemorated only by more ruins, surrounding a sandstone pillar, forty-six feet high, erected by the Buddhist ruler Aśoka during the third century B.C. and brought to the site by Fīrūz, for in 1398 the Tughluqs too were overthrown as the armies of the Mongol leader Timur (known to the West as Tamerlane) swept through India. After their destruction of the city, and the dispersal of much of its remaining population across northern India, Delhi took decades to recover its political prestige and economic status, under two more dynasties of sultans, the Sayyids (from 1414 to 1451) and the Lodīs (from 1451 to 1526), none of whom had the wealth or the power to match the building programs of their predecessors. They are best remembered today for the more than fifty tombs of members of their families that are still to be seen in and around Delhi, many of them within the public park in the south of the city known as the Lodī Gardens.

In April 1526 Bābur, an Afghan warlord from Kabul who claimed to be descended from both Timur and the other great Mongol commander Genghis Khan, led about 10,000 soldiers to victory over the 100,000 troops of the Sultan Ibrāhīm Lodī in the battle of Pānīpat. With Ibrāhīm dead on the battlefield, Bābur proceeded to establish what has become known as the Mughal Empire. Its most pervasive legacy is perhaps the Urdū language, developed from the centuries of communication between the Persian-speaking Mughal court and its local subjects, who used Hindi dialects, but the heritage of Mughal architecture and painting is also considerable.

Bābur and his first few successors alternated their residence between Delhi and Āgra, tending to favor the latter city up to 1638. Thus, for example, the only sign in Delhi of Bābur's four years as ruler is the mosque he commissioned at Sambhal, now a suburb of the city. However, during the

The Lakshmi Narayan Temple, Delhi
Photo courtesy of Christopher Turner

fifteen years, from 1540 to 1555, that Bābur's son Humāyūn was supplanted by his vassal Shēr Shāh of Sūr and then by the latter's son Salīm, these two usurpers, known as the Sūris, saw to the building of one of Delhi's most prominent monuments, the Purana Qila. Known to the British as the Old Fort, of which only two gateways and a mosque, the Qila-i-Kuhna Masjid, are still standing, it commemorates Shergarh, the sixth city at Delhi. (Some authorities attribute at least the beginning of work on the Old Fort to Humāyūn.) After Humāyūn's death in 1555, just a few months after his restoration, a tomb was commissioned for him by his widow Haji Begum, who had accompanied him into exile in Persia (now Iran). This octagonal, domed structure of sandstone and marble, completed in 1564 to a design by Mirak-Mirza Ghiyath that combines Persian and Indian styles, is now one of the most visited of the many rulers' tombs in the capital.

Akbar, the son of Humāyūn and Haji Begum, is often considered the greatest of the Mughals, for he consolidated the empire by bringing the Hindu leaders into his system of government, abandoning forced conversions to Islam, and reforming the sultanate's finances, thus providing the material basis for an ambitious building program. The masterpieces of his fifty-year reign (from 1555 to 1605) are generally agreed to be the reconstruction of the Lal Qila (Red Fort) at Āgra and the new city of Fatehpur Sīkri nearby, rather than any structures in Delhi. It was Akbar's grandson Shāh Jahān, ruler from 1628 to 1657, who decisively shifted the balance toward Delhi, moving the central bureaucracy there from Āgra in 1638, the year he began the seventh city of Delhi, Shāhjahānābād. Yet Shāh Jahān is probably still best known for the Tāj Mahal, the tomb he commissioned for his wife Mumtāz Mahal in Āgra.

The name "Old Delhi" conventionally refers only to Shāhjahānābād. Unlike its predecessors in the area, its main buildings survive in relatively robust condition and in larger numbers, and most of its city gates are still standing. Its original street plan is believed to underlie several of the main thoroughfares in the capital, including Chandni Chowk, the avenue between the two main buildings commissioned there by Shāh Jahān. These were the Jāmi Masjid, still the largest mosque in India, which is noted for the patterns of interspersed red sandstone and white marble on its exteriors; and the Lal Qila, or Red Fort, a complex of marble palace buildings completed in 1648. Neither should be confused with the structures of the same names in Āgra.

The Lal Qila in Old Delhi follows the general pattern of Muslim rulers' palaces, centering on two principal chambers, the Dīwān-i-Am (Hall of Public Audience) and the Dīwān-i-Khas (Hall of Private Audience), set among lesser buildings and extensive formal gardens. At Delhi these are known as the Hayat Baksh Bagh (Life-Bestowing Gardens). The whole octagonal compound is enclosed within a fortified outer wall, protected by the Yamuna River on one side and an artificial moat (empty of water since 1857) on the other. However, none of these defenses was sufficient to ward off the armies of Nāder Shāh, a Turkish adventurer who had already conquered Persia and who invaded Delhi in 1739, allowing his troops to massacre at least 30,000 people before departing with many of the treasures of the Red Fort, in particular Shāh Jahān's golden and bejeweled Peacock Throne. In 1739, as in several other years, the famous Persian inscription in the Dīwān-i-Khas must have seemed especially ironic: "If there is a paradise on Earth, it is here, it is here, it is here."

'Ālamgīr (Aurangzeb), the son of Shāh Jahān and Mumtāz Mahal, came to the throne in 1658 after killing his brothers and imprisoning his father (who remained a captive in Āgra, within sight of the Tāj Mahal, until his death in 1666, after which he too was buried inside it). During 'Ālamgīr's reign, which lasted until 1707, the Mughal Empire reached the peak of its geographical extent and material wealth, but campaigns against the local rulers of the Deccan, far to the south, led to his absence from Delhi throughout most of the years after 1681. His main monument in Delhi is a small mosque built for his private use inside the Red Fort, the white Moti Masjid (Pearl Mosque).

'Ālamgīr was the last Mughal ruler with the wealth and military strength to expand his territories. During the eighteenth century, the empire underwent a political and economic decline and Western European empires expanded from their footholds in the subcontinent. This process had already begun in 1612, when Akbar's son Jahāngir had first granted trading rights to the British East India Company. In 1712 the success of a company surgeon in curing the emperor Farruksiyar of venereal disease led to the granting of further concessions, and the steady shift in the balance of power between the company, then based in Calcutta, and the Mughals culminated in 1772 in the company's appointing the first of several Delhi Residents, representatives who were to exercise decisive influence over the Mughals, the company's nominal overlords.

By 1857 almost all of the territory now occupied by India, Pakistan, Bangladesh, Sri Lanka, and Burma was either directly controlled by the company or ruled under British supervision by local dynasties. Delhi itself and the region around it formed the kingdom of Bahādur Shāh II, who was descended from the Mughal emperors but who depended on a pension from the British. In spite of his record of collaboration, he was hailed as leader by many of the Muslims taking part in the Indian Mutiny, which broke out at several places under British rule in that year. The mutineers first attacked the British at Meerut, after several *sepoys* (Indian soldiers in the British army) refused to use the grease issued to them for their cartridges because they believed it contained pork (offensive to Muslims) or beef (offensive to Hindus). Hundreds then marched on Delhi, where they massacred British residents, many of them at the Lahore Gate of the Lal Qila, before moving on to Kānpur and Lucknow. After the rising had been suppressed, with vengeful brutality, the British first put the king on trial, in the Dīwān-i-Am of the Lal Qila, and then exiled him to Rangoon in Burma (modern-day Yangon, Myanmar); they also put up a Mutiny Memorial to the Europeans killed in Delhi, in a characteristically Victorian Gothic style, which can still be seen in Old Delhi today.

From 1858, when the Indian Empire passed from the East India Company into the hands of the British government, Calcutta remained the capital while Delhi was relatively neglected. In 1902, however, Marquess Curzon of Kedleston, the British viceroy and governor-general, chose Delhi as the location for a Durbar, an official celebration of King Edward VII's accession to the throne in the previous year, partly because of its greater accessibility by road and rail from other parts of the subcontinent, but perhaps also because of Curzon's desire to associate the British Raj with its Mughal predecessor. The Durbar events, which took place in December 1902 and January 1903, included a review of 34,000 soldiers, a state ball and reception, a procession of international representatives that drew crowds of more than 1 million spectators, and a salute of 101 guns. Only nine years later, in December 1911, King George V, visiting Delhi for his own Durbar on the banks of the Yamuna in front of the Lal Qila, announced that the imperial government would be transferred to Delhi as of April 1, 1912.

The transfer appears to have been intended both as a concession to nationalist feeling and as a reassertion of the British claim to be legitimate successors of the Mughals; certainly the architecture of what would be the eighth city at Delhi suggests both aesthetic concession to Indian models and political assertiveness. The site of what the British called New Delhi, covering ten square miles on and around Raisina Hill, between Old Delhi to the north and the Quṭb Minar to the south, was first divided by a hexagonal grid into five districts allotted to carefully designated and divided social groups, then entrusted to the architects Edwin Lutyens, already well known for designing homes for the wealthy in Britain during the late nineteenth and early twentieth centuries, and Herbert Baker, famous for his Union Buildings (1913) in Pretoria, South Africa. Pressure from the British officials in Calcutta and Delhi, a public campaign in Britain, led by the playwright George Bernard Shaw, the novelist Thomas Hardy and others, and perhaps the influence of George V himself all combined to persuade Lutyens and Baker to set aside their aversion to anything but European models in favor of buildings decorated with Indian motifs and constructed of red sandstone and white marble, in tribute to Mughal traditions.

Among these monuments of British rule in New Delhi, the largest is the Viceroy's House, designed by Lutyens, a vast domed palace, larger than Louis XIV's palace at Versailles, standing to the west of the Kingsway or Rajpath, the two-mile-long avenue that bisects the complex. This was not completed until 1931, by which time Lutyens and Baker had fallen out, each blaming the other for the design error that caused this centerpiece building to "vanish" behind Raisina Hill when approached along the Kingsway. When India gained independence in 1947, the Viceroy's House became Rashtrapati Bhavan, and since 1950 it has been the official residence of the presidents of India. Lutyens was also responsible for the overall layout of the district for the Imperial Record Office (now the National Archives), and for the palaces provided for the rulers of Hyderābād and Baroda, the leading Indian princes. These stand at the eastern end of the Rajpath on either side of Lutyens's other major work, the India Gate, a triumphal arch 140 feet high, which commemorates the more than 70,000 Indian soldiers who died during World War I and during the Afghan War of 1919, and which now also houses a memorial to soldiers killed in the war between India and Pakistan in 1971.

When not quarrelling with Lutyens, Herbert Baker concentrated on designing the two Secretariats, which now house the ministries of home affairs, finance, and foreign affairs, and the circular Council House, which was added to the plans only in 1919, with the creation of the first Legislative Council, and which now, as the Sansad Bhavan, houses the Indian parliament. Junior members of the architectural team took on other assignments. Thus Robert Tor Russell, who designed more of the buildings than any other single person, was responsible for the arcaded blocks around Connaught Place and Connaught Circus, now the commercial center of the city, the colonnaded Eastern and Western Courts nearby, which originated as hostels for legislators, and the building which, as Flagstaff House, was first the residence of the commander-in-chief of the imperial forces, then, from 1948, the home of Jawaharlal Nehru, the first prime minister of India. Today, as the Teen Murti Bhavan, it is a museum dedicated to Nehru's memory. Meanwhile, Henry Medd designed both the Anglican Cathedral of the Redemption, completed in 1935, and the Catholic Cathedral of the Sacred Heart, and Arthur Shoosmith designed the Garrison Church of St. Martin, opened in 1930, a monolithic structure built with more than 3 million bricks.

Yet New Delhi did not retain its exclusively British imperial character for long. As early as 1938, for example, the industrialist Raja Baldeo Birla sponsored the building of the Lakshmi Narayan Mandir, a Hindu temple honoring the goddess Lakshmi, to the west of Connaught Circus. Additionally, to its east and southeast there are now also memorials to prominent leaders in the struggle for independence, which was achieved in August 1947 at the cost of dividing the former empire into two states, India and Pakistan (then including what is now Bangladesh). The black marble Raj Ghat honors Mahatma Gandhi, who was assassinated in Delhi in January 1948, having come to the city to help restore calm after the murderous upheavals associated with the achievement of independence and the consequent transfers of millions of people between the two new states. A garden known as Shanti Vana, laid out in honor of Nehru after his death in 1964, is the place where Nehru, his daughter Indira Gandhi, and her sons Sanjay and Rajiv were each cremated. Indira and Rajiv Gandhi, namesakes but not relatives of the Mahatma, both became prime minister but were both also assassinated (by Sikh and Tamil dissidents respectively).

Over the decades of independence, which have been marked by individual and communal violence but also by huge social and economic advances, the capital of India has expanded across the Yamuna River with the construction of Ghaziābād and other residential suburbs. Squatter settlements also have continued to grow on all sides of New Delhi. These now house perhaps one-third of the total population of the city, and stand as a salutary reminder that a city does not consist of historic monuments alone, however magnificent such mosques, palaces, government buildings, churches, and temples may be. For Delhi, as for other cities endowed with a significant architectural heritage (much of it colonial in origin), Indian authorities face the difficult task of preserving such buildings at the same time as they address the pressing needs of the living population.

Further Reading: *The Penguin Guide to the Monuments of India,* volume two, *Islamic, Rajput, European* by Philip Davies (London and New York: Viking, 1989) includes both a comprehensive history of the eight cities of Delhi and detailed descriptions of its most important buildings, illustrated with photographs and plans. Philip Ward's *Rajasthan, Agra, Delhi: A Travel Guide* (Cambridge and New York: Oleander, 1989) provides a vivid account of contemporary Delhi, based on the author's own idiosyncratic impressions. New Delhi in particular is the subject of Robert Grant Irving's *Indian Summer: Lutyens, Baker and Imperial Delhi* (New Haven, Connecticut, and London: Yale University Press, 1981).

—Patrick Heenan

Dhākā (Dhākā, Bangladesh)

Location: In the Dhākā division in the center of Bangladesh, on a branch of the Dhaleśwarī River known as the Buriganga, near the confluence of the country's great waterways, the Maghna, the Ganges (known within Bangladesh as the Padma), and the Brahmaputra, known as the Jamuna.

Description: Capital and largest city of Bangladesh and the commercial and industrial center of the country; historically important as a provincial capital under the Mughal Empire and a center of Muslim nationalist movements.

Site Office: Bangladesh Parjatan Corporation
National Tourism Organization
233 Airport Road
Tejgaon, Dhākā 1215
Bangladesh
325155 9

Dhākā's long history has been somewhat overshadowed by its role as the modern capital of Bangladesh. Once the East Bengal province of India, later East Pakistan, Bangladesh was founded among much turbulence in 1971 and has continued to see upheaval ever since. Dhākā, however, has been a significant site since the seventeenth century.

Dhākā dates to the fourth century A.D., but it was a small and unimportant town until the Mughals made it the capital of their Bengal province in 1608. Bengal had been brought under Mughal control in 1576 after having been governed by a variety of Indian, Afghan, and independent rulers. Dhākā was to have been called Jahāngīrnagar, in honor of the reigning Mughal emperor, Jahāngīr, but one account claims that the Mughal viceroy gave the city the name of Dhākā after he heard drums being beaten to welcome him (*dhak* is the Bengali word for drum). Other stories concerning the city's name say it derives from the *dhak* tree, yet others from the Hindu goddess Dhākeśwarī. Although Dhākā today is largely Muslim, its religious history includes periods of Hindu and Buddhist dominance. Monuments from both these religions exist in the region, including a shrine to Dhākeśwāri in the western section of Dhākā.

Dhākā's access to waterways made it ripe for development as a commercial center. Because this access also made the city a target for piracy, the Mughals quickly erected forts to protect their river traffic from local Arakanese pirates and from their sometime allies, the Portuguese. The alliance between the Portuguese and the Arakanese pirates captured the city and held it for a brief period in 1626. The Mughals persevered, however, and Dhākā continued to develop commercially, even during the twenty-year period (1639–1659) when it relinquished its capital status to Rājmahāl across the Ganges. As many as 100 ships arrived annually in Dhākā, and many caravans came on the overland routes. Rice, sugar, oilseeds, and fine muslin (for which Dhaka weavers were particularly renowned) were among the goods exported from the city; goods imported included luxury items from Persia, Afghanistan, Turkey, and central Asia. Other European traders—French, Dutch, and English—followed the Portuguese and vied for favor with the Mughals.

The Mughal rulers built caravansaries to accommodate traders. One of these, the Barā Katrā, still stands near the Buriganga River, although it is in a ruined state. Dating from 1644, and thus one of the oldest Mughal constructions extant at Dhākā, the Barā Katrā was laid out in a quadrangular shape around a central courtyard, where cells were built to house travelers. The few remaining sections of the caravansary include an imposing arched southern gateway, with ornate plaster decoration, and octagonal corner towers on the east and west walls. Another, smaller, caravansary is the nearby Chota Katrā, dating from 1663.

The Mughals also built magnificent mosques at Dhākā: more than 700 of them stand throughout the city, some even predating the Mughals; the Bayt ul-Mukarram, for instance, is said to date from the fifteenth century. The oldest existing Mughal mosques date from the early eighteenth century, including Khān Muhammad Mirdha Mosque and Kartalab Khān Mosque. A Catholic church, the Church of Our Lady of the Rosary, is older; dating from 1687, it is the oldest church in Bangladesh. Much of the Mughal period was marked by religious tolerance, and Dhākā hosted foreign missionaries as well as foreign traders. A group of Augustinians, led by Bernard de Jesus, had arrived in Dhākā in 1599 and made the city the headquarters for its missionary work in 1616. The Mughals, however, did believe in containment of the European presence; Europeans were assigned to a section north of central Dhākā, and this is where they built their homes, churches, and offices.

Construction of a major fortress, the Lālbāgh Fort, began in Dhākā in 1678. The fort, however, never was finished. The favorite daughter of Shayesta Khān, the Mughal governor of Bengal, died while construction was underway, and he took her death as such a bad omen that the work was abandoned. Portions of the complex that were completed include the governor's residence and audience hall (now a museum of Mughal crafts). Also completed was a mausoleum for the governor's daughter, who was known as Bibi Pari, meaning "fairy" or "fair lady." The mausoleum is more than twenty yards square and has a dome that once was gilded but now is covered in copper. It is in good condition and can be viewed by visitors.

During the latter part of the seventeenth century, Dhākā served the Mughals not only as a political and com-

Ashan Manjil, Dhākā
Photo courtesy of Bangladesh Parjatan Corporation, Dhākā

mercial center, but as a staging post for the campaign of Emperor 'Ālamgīr (Aurangzeb) to expand his realm. In 1661 Mir Jumla, 'Ālamgīr's governor of Bengal, Bihār, and Orissa, set out from Dhākā with a force of 30,000 infantry, 12,000 cavalry, and several hundred vessels, including 10 floating batteries. His destination was the region of Assam, just north of Bengal. He succeeded in capturing Kathalbari, capital of the kingdom of Kuch Bihār, and he renamed Kuch Bihār 'Ālamgīrnar. The rāja of Kuch Bihār converted to Islam and became an ally of the Mughals. Twenty years later, however, the Mughals were driven out of Assam.

Toward the end of the century 'Ālamgīr, whose military campaigns had been costly, began to have problems maintaining the loyalty of Bengal and collecting tax revenue from the residents. A rebellion broke out in Bengal in 1696–97 that the Mughals quelled, and in 1701 'Ālamgīr sent a new imperial representative, Kartalab Khān, to Dhākā to make sure taxes were collected. He succeeded only after surviving an assassination attempt by Bengal's governor, Asim ud-Din, who happened to be 'Ālamgīr's grandson. Asim ud-Din was exiled and the provincial capital was moved in 1704 to Maksudābād, which Kartalab Khān soon renamed Murshidābād after the new name that had been conferred upon him, Murshid Qulī Khān.

The loss of capital status hastened Dhākā's decline, which had begun several years earlier when the new city of Calcutta began to take business away from Dhākā. After 'Ālamgīr's death in 1707, the Mughal Empire began to fragment and the British East India Company began to consolidate its control over India. The East India Company had established a branch in Dhākā as early as 1666, but its representatives did not maintain good relations with the Mughals. After 'Ālamgīr's death, however, the Mughal emperors were reduced to titular status, and power shifted to regional rulers called nabobs. In the middle of the eighteenth century, the death of Bengal nabob Aliverdi Khan and the incompetence of his successor, Sirāj-ud-Dawlah, gave the British an opening. East India Company troops defeated the Bengalis at the key battles of Plassey and Buxar and won control of the province. Dhākā officially passed to British control in 1765. The East India Company allowed native officials to remain in office, although in a subordinate position to the British, until 1824, when the British took over direct administration of the city.

The British made their homes and offices in the old European section of the city and pushed out other European powers; the Dutch, for instance, relinquished their property to the British in 1781. A few Greek and Armenian traders had come to the area in the eighteenth century (the Armenians had developed the region's jute trade and in 1781 constructed their Church of the Holy Resurrection, which still stands), but they, too, were forced out by the British. The British also made changes in the region's economy, developing huge plantations around Dhākā for the cultivation of indigo, sugar,

Seven-domed mosque, Dhākā
Photo courtesy of Bangladesh Parjatan Corporation, Dhākā

tea, tobacco, and jute. These crops have remained staples of the area.

Still, Dhākā continued to decline. It suffered through famines when floods destroyed the local rice crop in 1784 and 1787. Its muslin business suffered, outstripped by other manufacturing centers. In the seventeenth century Dhākā had been the most important city in Bengal; in the eighteenth and nineteenth centuries it lost that role to Calcutta, which surpassed Dhākā not only commercially but culturally as well. A university was established in Calcutta in 1857; none existed in Dhākā until 1921. Dhākā's population decreased and its poverty increased.

Dhākā regained some importance in the early twentieth century. In 1905, Lord Curzon, viceroy and governor-general of India, divided the large and unwieldy province of Bengal into eastern and western portions. Dhākā became the capital of East Bengal. This brought a new wave of building in Dhākā, as government offices, homes, churches, and schools went up. Bengali Hindus greatly resented the partition, partly because in East Bengal it created a Muslim-majority province, and partly because they saw it as a means of undermining the Indian nationalist movement, which was particularly strong in Bengal. For the Muslims of Dhākā and the rest of East Bengal, the partition provided welcome relief from the dominance exercised by Calcutta and planted the seeds of a national Muslim consciousness. The All-India Muslim League was founded in Dhākā in 1906. Originally, its primary role was to represent the interests of the Muslim economic elite to India's British rulers, and it emphatically stated its allegiance to the British. It developed, however, into an organization that advocated a fair share for Muslims in the governance of India and, eventually, a separate Muslim nation. Hindu unrest persuaded the British in 1911 to revoke the partition of Bengal, but the work of the Muslim League continued. Particularly strong and charismatic leadership came from Mohammed Ali Jinnah, who became the league's president in 1934.

After the end of World War II, Britain accepted the inevitability of Indian independence. Competing Hindu and Muslim interests were accommodated by partition, and in 1947 East Bengal became the easternmost province of the Muslim nation of Pakistan. (Informally recognized as East and West Pakistan, the two portions of the country were designated officially as such in 1956.) Dhākā received the status of a secondary national capital. The existence of a divided Pakistan was troublesome from the start, as the country's two sections had little in common other than religion and were separated by a distance of nearly 1,000 miles. East Pakistan had no desire to play a subordinate role in the administration of the country and resented the political dominance of West Pakistan. Few East Pakistanis were appointed to leading positions in the government. Additionally, economic development focused on West Pakistan. The most emotional issue, however, was that of language. Top officials

Lālbāgh Fort, Dhākā
Photo courtesy of Bangladesh Parjatan Corporation, Dhākā

of Pakistan's government declared that Urdū would be the national language, even though it was not native to any part of Pakistan, having originated in Delhi and Uttar Pradesh in India. A majority of East Pakistanis spoke Bengali, and they rose up against the language measure. Several student demonstrators were killed by police in Dhākā on February 21, 1952, still observed as Martyrs' Day in Bangladesh. In September 1954, the government finally backed away from the language issue, declaring Bengali an official language along with Urdū and any other languages the government might choose to recognize.

Other issues continued to divide East and West Pakistan, however. East Pakistan failed to achieve parity in government employment and economic development. Opposition to Pakistan's president, Mohammed Ayub Khan, increased in the mid-1960s owing to the further deterioration of East Pakistan's economy and to Pakistan's war with India over Kashmir; hostile relations with India and recurring military skirmishes between Pakistan and India left East Pakistanis feeling very insecure about the vast shared border between them in light of the lack of military concentration in East Pakistan. East Pakistani leaders were jailed or otherwise silenced. Ayub resigned in 1969 in favor of his chief general, Agha Muhammad Yahya Khan, who imposed martial law. Talks concerning a new constitution failed to provide a solution satisfactory to East Pakistan. Then in 1970 a cyclone and tidal wave devastated East Pakistan, which perceived the national government's relief efforts to be inadequate. Armed rebellion broke out in East Pakistan, and in March of the following year government troops were sent in to quell the uprising. The ensuing war was brief but brutal. Rape and other atrocities against civilians were widespread. By November 1971 government troops had captured Dhākā and other large cities, and 10 million refugees had fled to India. Tensions between India and Pakistan, however, led to Indian intervention on behalf of the rebels in December. Dhākā and the rest of East Pakistan were liberated quickly, and on December 16, 1971, the independent country of Bangladesh—"land of the Bengalis"—was born, with Dhākā as its capital.

The new nation had a high rate of poverty and illiteracy. Its educated class, perceived by Pakistan to be the force behind the independence movement, had been decimated, and its economic life and communications systems had been disrupted severely by the war. A famine in 1974–75 brought even more suffering. Mujibur Rahman, an independence leader who had become president, was murdered, along with his family, in a military coup in 1975. Martial law, a countercoup, and installation of a military triumvirate to govern the country followed. Constitutional government emerged under President Zia ur-Rahman in 1979. He proved a competent leader and attracted foreign aid to his troubled country, but he was assassinated during another military coup in 1981. Martial law was again imposed, and for the next decade empty promises came from the military leaders that

Star Mosque, Dhākā
Photo courtesy of Bangladesh Parjatan Corporation, Dhākā

elections would soon be held. They finally were held in 1991, and Zia ur-Rahman's widow, Khaleda Zia, became president. She encountered opposition from Islamic fundamentalists, a small but powerful minority in Bangladesh, and as of late 1995 had agreed to step down before her term ended the following year.

Bangladesh remains an impoverished country, heavily dependent on foreign aid. Dhākā remains its largest city; since independence, the population of Dhākā has risen from fewer than 2 million to more than 5 million. Many people have come to Dhākā from rural areas in search of greater economic opportunity. Dhākā has the country's greatest concentration of business and industry; modern commercial and residential sections have grown up around the older part of the city, with its narrow streets, historic buildings, and bazaars where European traders once set up shop. Textile manufacturing remains a staple of the Dhākā economy, and in the surrounding area the crops once raised on British plantations continue to be cultivated. Although densely populated, Dhākā is cleaner and more orderly than many South Asian cities—partly because many of its residents prefer rickshaws to automobiles—and offers more active social and cultural life than any other city in Bangladesh.

Further Reading: Because Bangladesh was for so long a part of India, much of the information about Dhākā is contained in general works of Indian history. Notable among these is *The New Cambridge History of India,* edited by Gordon Johnson, C. A. Bayly, and John F. Richards (29 vols., Cambridge and New York: Cambridge University Press, 1987–). Also helpful is R. E. M. Wheeler's *Five Thousand Years of Pakistan: An Archaeological Outline* (London: C. Johnson, 1958). A helpful travel guide is *Bangladesh: A Travel Survival Kit* by Jon Murray (Hawthorn, Victoria, and Berkeley, California: Lonely Planet, 1985; second edition, 1991).

—Claudia Levi and Trudy Ring

Dien Bien Phu (Vietnam)

Location: In a broad valley in far northwestern Vietnam, at an altitude of 1,000 feet, a few miles from the Laotian border and approximately 170 miles west-northwest of Hanoi. The valley is bounded by the jagged limestone mountains of the Pu Xam Xao range, which straddles the Laos-Vietnam border.

Description: A small and isolated village in the tribal territory of the T'ai, who form an ethnic minority in Vietnam. The T'ai name for Dien Bien Phu is Muong Thanh. Located in a major opium-producing area, Dien Bien Phu has long been one of the principal centers of the opium trade. The area fell to the French in 1887. Minor skirmishes took place around the village at the conclusion of World War II. The long and bloody Battle of Dien Bien Phu in 1954 resulted in a resounding defeat of the French colonial forces by the communist Viet Minh.

Contact: Vietnam Tourism
30A Ly Thuong Kiet Street
Hanoi
Vietnam
255552 or 264154

The mountainous area of Dien Bien Phu has long been inhabited by various tribal groups. The T'ai, who first arrived in the twelfth century, constitute the largest ethnic group, followed by the Hmong, who settled on the mountain slopes in the eighteenth century. The Hmong grew poppies, from which the T'ai processed opium and then traded it, principally to the Vietnamese and Chinese. To the T'ai, Dien Bien Phu is known as Muong Thanh (Heaven's Country). T'ai legend explains that Muong Thanh was in communication with the heavens and was the cradle of humanity.

Dien Bien Phu remained isolated from Vietnamese government control until the mid–nineteenth century. In 1841, the ruling emperor of the Nguyen Dynasty established the administrative district of Dien Bien Phu—which means "seat of the border county prefecture"—in order to consolidate his hold over the borderland and to suppress the activities of bandits preying on the opium trade. One of the last areas of Vietnam to submit to French colonial rule, the T'ai tribal territories became a French protectorate in 1887. The French installed at Dien Bien Phu a single administrator who was to ensure that locally-produced opium ended up in French hands. Despite a Hmong insurrection in 1918, the village remained under the nominal control of the French colonial administration until the Japanese occupied it during World War II.

The French collaborated with the Japanese until the latter attacked French troops in March 1945. Dien Bien Phu briefly became the headquarters of the desperate French attempts to counter the attack. Early in May of the same year, the Japanese marched into the village and laid plans to convert it into a massive military base. Before they could do more than enlarge its tiny airstrip, the Japanese were replaced by Chinese nationalist forces in August, who in turn had to make room for returning French troops.

The nationalist Viet Minh declared Vietnamese independence in September 1945. The proclamation was followed by insurrections concentrated in Hanoi, Hue, and Saigon (now Ho Chi Minh City), but the Viet Minh also found extensive support in the countryside. By 1946, the conflict between the Viet Minh and the French had escalated into the First Indochina War. Throughout much of the war, the French army stationed troops at Dien Bien Phu, but for years these troops did not see action. In October 1952, during the Black River offensive, the French-Laotian battalion at Dien Bien Phu was evacuated to be redeployed at the front. The Viet Minh immediately moved into the area. In the following year, the village became a staging post for a series of attacks on Laotian targets, recalling French attention to the Dien Bien Phu base.

The French High Command quickly formed plans to retake Dien Bien Phu and convert it into a major land-air base (or "airhead" in military parlance). The base was to be a sealed "hedgehog" position, supplied by air and invulnerable to Viet Minh artillery. Its purpose was to cut off the Viet Minh routes into Laos and to replace other strongholds in T'ai tribal territory, at Na San and Lai Chau, that were becoming increasingly untenable. The T'ai tribal government was to be transferred from Lai Chau to Dien Bien Phu to counteract the growing influence of the Viet Minh over the local population. Both the French and the Viet Minh were manoevering for position at the Geneva talks to be held in May 1954, each side hoping to pull off a major military victory to strengthen its hand in negotiations.

The information about climate, terrain, and supply lines provided by the intelligence service should have jettisoned French plans for Dien Bien Phu. European ground troops were no match for the Viet Minh in the jungle. Exceedingly heavy monsoon rains put tanks out of commission six months out of the year. The rains would also endanger air supply lines, which were tenuous at best. Virtually no materials with which to build fortifications were locally available, and French air capacity was simply insufficient to supply what was needed. In addition, a similar hedgehog position at Na San had proved only barely defensible in the short run and far too expensive to maintain in the long run. General Navarre, who was in charge of the planning for the Dien Bien

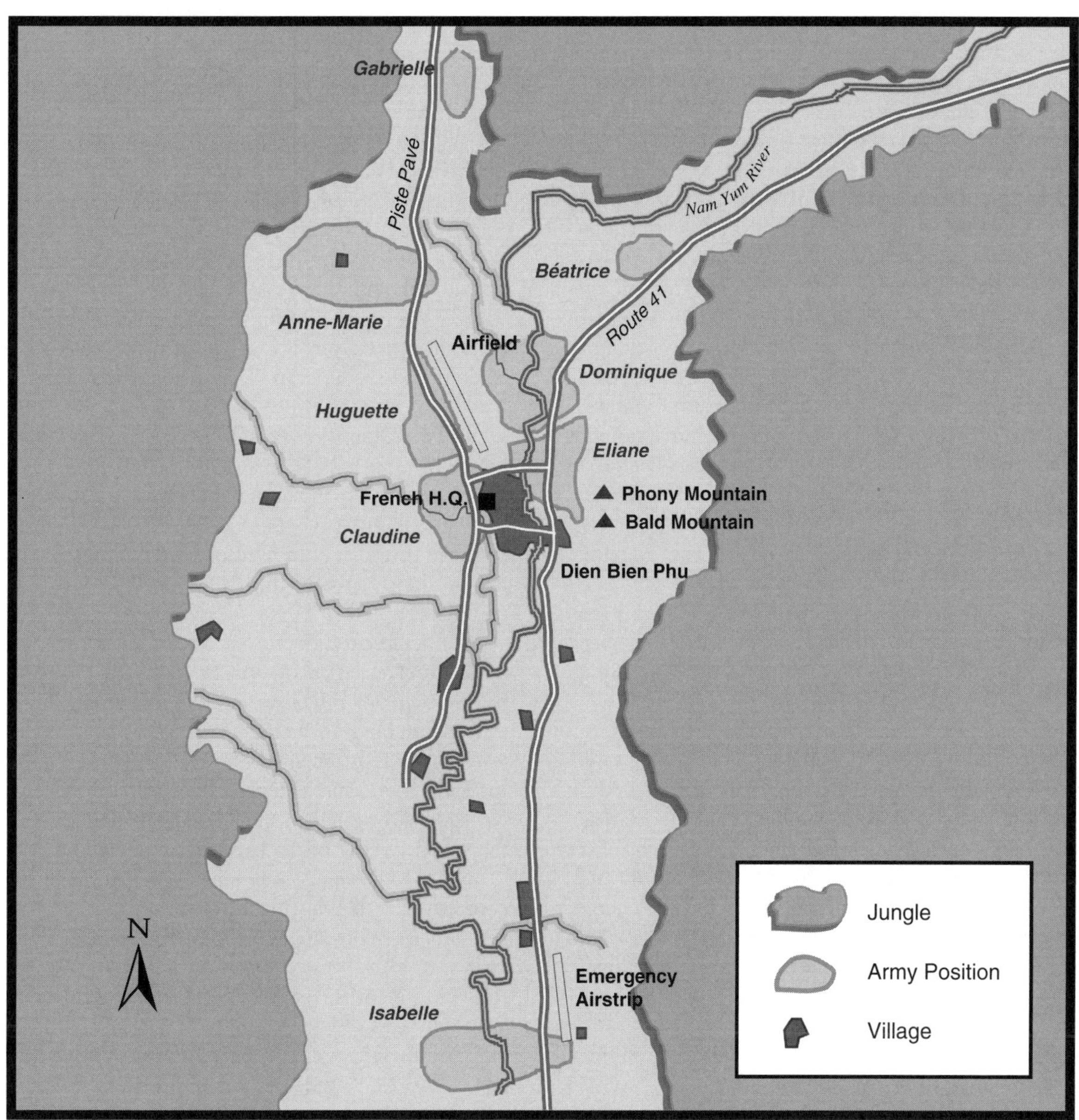

Map representing the battle at Dien Bien Phu
Illustration by Tom Willcockson

Phu operation, ignored this information and forged ahead despite misgivings among many of his staff. The French also fatally underestimated the Viet Minh's capacity to move troops and supplies through the mountainous jungles, at the same time overestimating their own technological superiority. Sharp criticism of the plan to dig in at Dien Bien Phu came from the French High Command in early November 1953. But the report, which pointed out that the strategy exposed French weaknesses and played to Viet Minh strengths, was put aside.

Over protestations from fellow officers, Navarre ordered an airdrop of elite paratroops at Dien Bien Phu on November 20, 1953. They retook the outpost with some difficulty, encountering only a few Viet Minh soldiers, who, however, put up fierce resistance. The nationalists, under General Vo Nguyen Giap, had withdrawn most of their troops into the surrounding mountains. Giap later explained that his operations at the base and his raids into Laos had all been designed to bait the French into committing a significant share of troops and resources to Dien Bien Phu, where he was confident he could defeat them in a major battle. As the French began to expand the base, Giap began to move thousands and thousands of Viet Minh troops to the area. Ho Chi Minh, the nationalist leader, declared in a newspaper interview that appeared on November 29 that he was prepared to negotiate an armistice. However, his apparent intentions were to start such negotiations only after the expected Viet Minh victory at Dien Bien Phu had become a fact.

In the days following the first airdrop, the French flew in supplies and additional troops, bringing the garrison to 4,560 men. The garrison immediately set about expanding the airstrip, digging light fortifications, opening up their fields of fire, and pushing patrols and outposts into the jungle of the surrounding mountains. Two airfields were constructed alongside the Nam Yum River, over which several bridges were built. The valley floor was cleared of all vegetation—which had the unfortunate result of leaving the French artillery emplacements without any kind of cover. All the villages throughout the valley were dismantled for building supplies and for cooking fuel, which was also in very short supply.

The French quickly realized that supplies for adequate defenses could neither be found in the valley nor brought in by air; and they certainly were not equipped to move supplies through the jungles. In the end, the fortifications at Dien Bien Phu were a mere shadow of what the original plans had called for. The hastily constructed field hospital also fell far short of the capacity that would be required in a major confrontation. Winter weather conditions, moreover, frequently prevented aircraft from landing, while perpetual fog and thick cloud cover also made it very difficult to perform airdrops with any precision. About 20 percent of arms, munitions, and other supplies dropped were never recovered.

On December 8 and 9, Lai Chau was evacuated, but the T'ai government chose to go into exile rather than re-establish itself at Dien Bien Phu. Support for the Viet Minh among local villagers therefore continued unabated. French and T'ai troops that had been stationed at Lai Chau were ordered to march to the new airhead, to serve as reinforcements of the garrison already established there. A major airborne operation was launched on December 11 to assist in the troop withdrawals, but the retreating column immediately came under attack and soon disintegrated, suffering heavy casualties. Throughout late December, survivors of the Lai Chau rearguard limped into the valley. Only one of three French officers, nine of thirty-four non-combatants and 175 of 2,000 troops were to reach the short-lived safety of Dien Bien Phu.

Around Christmas, the base at Dien Bien Phu had begun to take shape. Rather than build a solid defensive ring, the French engineers had opted to construct a classical pattern of interlocking and mutually supporting positions, each subdivided into compartments. The positions were given French women's first names in alphabetical sequence. (Rumor had it that they were named for the mistresses of the commanding officer, Colonel de Castries, whose military fame was far outstripped by his reputation as a womanizer.) The center of resistance consisted of five strongpoints—Huguette, Anne-Marie, Dominique, Claudine, and Eliane—built around Dien Bien Phu itself and designed to protect the central airstrip. Claudine contained the central command post. The northern approaches to the valley were guarded by Gabrielle and Béatrice. Three and one-half miles south of the main position lay Isabelle, which protected an auxiliary airstrip and the southern approaches to the valley. The Viet Minh had been observing the frantic construction activities from mid-December onward and were therefore very well informed with regard to the layout and the strengths and weaknesses of the airhead.

The nationalist army, meanwhile, was engaged in a massive and highly successful logistical operation that established a forward supply base at Tun Giao, thirty miles northeast of Dien Bien Phu. Some 40,000 logistical troops and 260,000 civilians moved supplies along three different jungle trails. Although the French expended half of their aerial capacity to cut Viet Minh supply lines, they rarely managed to interrupt supply efforts and troop movements for more than brief periods of time. In the end, some 50,000 well-supplied Viet Minh soldiers were stationed in a tightly-drawn circle around the Dien Bien Phu airhead. Although the French had not thought it possible, the Viet Minh troops had also dragged heavy artillery up the mountain slopes surrounding the base, to positions that gave them a clear line of fire to the French defenses. Masters at camouflage, the Vietnamese had hidden their artillery so well that not even the flash from gunfire could be spotted.

In preparation for the main battle, the nationalists carried out a series of attacks aimed at diverting French resources to other theaters. Attacks on Laotian targets and the central highlands of Vietnam on December 20 forced Navarre to redeploy reinforcements and supplies originally intended for Dien Bien Phu. The actual attack on the Dien Bien Phu airhead was originally scheduled for January 25, 1954, but on the very morning of the battle Giap decided that the risk of losing, though small, was unacceptable. He postponed the confrontation to allow his men to drag their howitzers further up the mountain slopes and to dig tunnels along the approaches to the French defensive positions. Throughout the following months, serious skirmishes took place in the surrounding area, however. On March 6 and 7 the Viet Minh attacked the airfields at Hanoi from which the French were being supplied, and many aircraft were damaged or destroyed.

Finally, on March 13, 1954, General Giap launched his first offensive strike, targeting the airstrip and destroying three of the six bearcat fighter planes the French had at their disposal. Béatrice and Gabrielle, the two northern defensive positions, came under fire next, while Viet Minh sappers and suicide troops with explosives opened passages through the wire entanglements. After about eight hours of fighting, the French gave up Béatrice. Gabrielle held in the first wave of attack, but in the evening of March 15 Gabrielle was abandoned after a devastating second assault. The loss of the northern positions was a disaster for the French. The northern hills were tactically vital to the defense of the base because their crests offered positions from which the enemy could direct fire into the center of the camp.

On March 15, the T'ai soldiers began to slip away from the French base, and by the following day T'ai desertions had reduced the garrison strength by one-fifth. Since many T'ai had been stationed at Anne-Marie (one of the central positions), this part of the central defenses fell on March 17. A few days later the airstrip was judged unsafe for landing, and supplies were airdropped from that point on. Dien Bien Phu was effectively cut off, except for radio transmissions. The wounded could no longer be evacuated, while the field hospital was woefully inadequate to meet the needs of the wounded. Morale in the French camp, never high, now suffered seriously. The first week of fighting had been a bloody calamity for the French, as its airhead was transformed into a besieged fortress, while for the Viet Minh it had been a costly but tremendous success.

The remainder of March saw a relative lull in the fighting. Through a series of counterattacks, the French managed to retake Isabelle. However, this position later proved to be of little use to the defense of the camp. A French aircraft attack on Viet Minh positions on March 28, although successful, was insufficient to turn the tide. The Viet Minh, meanwhile, continued to dig miles upon miles of trenches, almost totally encircling the French center. Some approach trenches led to within 150 yards of the French wire.

On March 30, the second phase of the confrontation began with a Viet Minh artillery bombardment followed by waves of infantry attacks. By nightfall, Dominique 1 and 2 were lost. The entire position would have fallen if not for the African colonial artillery regiment, who set their fuses to zero and fired at minimum elevation at the approaching waves of infantry, with devastating results. By midnight, Eliane 1 and 2 and Huguette 7 were given up, although they were temporarily recaptured in counterattacks before dawn. In the following weeks, different compartments of Huguette were repeatedly to change hands. Although the Viet Minh made little progress, the shortage of supplies on the French side meant that attrition weighed much more heavily on them.

The French position was now undeniably desperate, and the French Chief of Staff called on the United States for help. A Pentagon study group, sympathetic to the French cause, recommended the use of atomic weapons, and this idea was championed by several government officials. In the end, U.S. President Eisenhower decided to let direct aid to the French depend on NATO support. When such support was not forthcoming, the plans were dropped and the French were left to fend for themselves. Early in April, the French dispatched a relief force from Laos, whose primary goal was to cut Viet Minh supply lines, while its ultimate aim was to break through to the beleaguered garrison. Progress was slow and costly, and the expedition eventually came to a grinding halt some eighteen miles south of Dien Bien Phu.

At the same time, Giap, declining to push for a quick, decisive blow, opted for a gradual, attritional approach. He switched the emphasis of the Viet Minh attack to the traditional tactics of siegecraft and trench warfare. On April 1, Françoise was given up. The bitter contest over Huguette and Eliane still continued. Through the extension of the system of trenches, the Viet Minh could now reach the wire entanglements under complete cover in many places. French supplies were running critically low, because many planes had been lost to the Viet Minh's anti-aircraft guns, while the drop zone was now so small that it was almost impossible to target precisely.

On April 18, the Viet Minh launched another major strike, which led to the surrender of Huguette four days later. After another lull that lasted some ten days, the Viet Minh was set to deliver the finishing blow. A major bombardment and an all-out infantry attack on all central positions began on May 2. The French command began to prepare for a massive breakout as the only alternative to surrender. On May 6, Eliane was finally overrun. By mid-morning on May 7, the situation in the remainder of the French positions was hopeless. At a command conference, a breakout was discussed but dismissed as suicidal. Instead, the French decided to cease firing but to refrain from a formal capitulation. By the end of the day, the red Viet Minh flag went up over the French command bunker.

The following day, the nationalists rounded up the surviving French troops for an immediate march to prison camps in the Viet Bac, more than 300 miles to the east. The march lasted sixty days, and few men survived. Only 73 of the approximately 14,000 soldiers who fought for the French at Dien Bien Phu managed to escape capture. However, about 2,000 deserters began to emerge from their hiding places in the valley when the fighting stopped.

Almost as soon as the nationalists had declared victory, the Geneva talks began. The agreement ultimately reached at this summit fatefully divided Vietnam along the seventeenth parallel, giving the Viet Minh control over North Vietnam while South Vietnam remained in French hands. This solution was meant to be temporary: the country was to be reunified within two years, and a general election was to determine its government. The eventual refusal by the temporary South Vietnamese government to participate in the scheduled elections ultimately led to the Second Indochina War and to intense U.S. involvement in the conflict.

Further Reading: Many accounts of the Battle of Dien Bien Phu have been written. The best and most readable of these are *The Battle of Dien Bien Phu* by Jules Roy, a French soldier who resigned his commission in protest over French military policy in Vietnam (New York: Harper and Row, and London: Faber, 1965); *Hell in a Very Small Place: The Siege of Dien Bien Phu* by Bernard B. Fall (Philadelphia: Lippincott, 1966; London: Pall Mall, 1967); and *Dien Bien Phu: The Epic Battle America Forgot* by Howard R. Simpson, who visited the base just before the battle broke out (Washington: Brassey, 1994). A highly engaging history of both Indochina wars, enlivened by numerous eye-witness accounts, is available in Stanley Karnow's *Vietnam: A History* (New York: Viking, 1983; second edition, New York and London: Viking, 1991). An excellent account of the growth of Vietnamese nationalism and the emergence of the Viet Minh is included in *Anatomy of a War: Vietnam, the United States, and the Modern Historical Experience* by Gabriel Kolko (New York: Pantheon, 1985; as *Vietnam: Anatomy of a War, 1940–1975*, London: Allen and Unwin, 1986).

—Richard White and Marijke Rijsberman

Dunedin (South Island, New Zealand)

Location: On the east coast of South Island, 190 miles southwest of Christchurch on the shore of Otago Harbour.

Description: The southernmost major city in the world, Dunedin originated in 1848 as a planned religious community of Scots-Presbyterians. A gold rush in the 1860s greatly increased the area's population and urban growth. In the early twentieth century, the city became famous as the base of operations for several Antarctic expeditions. Today it is known for its wealth of Victorian architecture.

Site Office: Dunedin Visitor Centre
48, The Octagon
P.O. Box 5457
Dunedin, South Island
New Zealand
(03) 474 3300

Modern Dunedin retains much of its Victorian heritage, most clearly visible in its wealth of historic buildings: the churches, the elegant and solid commercial buildings, the schools and the university, and even many houses. Moreover, Dunedin's streets, parks and gardens, the water supply and drainage system, all date to the nineteenth century. Any attempt to change, whether by creating a mall in the inner city or establishing a one-way traffic system, has to confront this historical legacy.

The past pervades modern Dunedin to such a degree because virtually every aspect of the town's development was methodically planned in advance during the Victorian era. Dunedin was envisioned as a New Edinburgh, a genuine Scottish municipality transported intact to the South Pacific with the goal of creating there a religious utopia. The idea of a New Edinburgh was conceived in Scotland by men and women who had never visited New Zealand and had no idea of where their imagined home would be located. They dreamed, however, of establishing a more just and godly community based on the Free Church of Scotland and Edward Gibbon Wakefield's principles of systematic colonization.

The Free Church had been formed following an episode known as the Disruption, which occurred in Scotland in the early 1840s. The Disruptors asserted the claims of the City of God against English Erastianism (after the Swiss Protestant theologian Thomas Erastus, who promoted the dominance of state over church), which pervaded the established Presbyterian Church. Inspired by religious enthusiasm and a deep-seated intolerance for the sins of the world, the Disruptors believed that each congregation should choose its own minister. The Reverend Dr. Thomas Chalmers, leader of the Disruption, articulated the Free Church's vision of a national church that could, in the Calvinist tradition, impose godly order upon not only its members but the entire community. Chalmers believed that a revitalized parish could adapt Presbyterianism to the needs of an urban-industrial society.

A small minority of Disruptors, however, believed that it would be easier to start anew, in a new land. In 1845, led by Captain William Cargill and the Reverend Thomas Burns, they persuaded the General Assembly to give its blessing, and a poorly attended meeting established the Lay Association, charged with founding a theocratic community in the New World. They made contact with Wakefield, whose elaborate theory of systematic colonization had inspired the settlement of South Australia, Wellington, Nelson, and New Plymouth. However, Wakefield concluded that the absence of religious cohesion had brought failure to all these earlier efforts. Hence his interest in the idea of a Scots-Presbyterian colony. The leaders of the Lay Association, like Wakefield and his New Zealand Company, shared a dislike for the social consequences of the Industrial Revolution and dreamed of recreating an older agrarian community. Both groups also believed it possible to transplant civilization, which essentially meant church and school, into the wilderness, thus avoiding the worst consequences of unsystematic colonization.

While men and women dreamed of their godly city, Frederick Tuckett, the New Zealand Company's surveyor, selected the site. After walking down much of the South Island's east coast, Tuckett arrived at "the head of . . . [Otago's] inner or upper harbour." He wrote in his diary: "good timber is abundant; the soil, not withstanding that the surface is often rocky and stony, appears to be fertile. . . . There is certainly more available and eligible land on the shores of this vast inland sea than on any portion of Banks' Peninsula. . . ." Tuckett recognized that access would be "formidable," and hoped to find a still better site when he headed south. But he did not. On the basis of Tuckett's recommendation, the New Zealand Company bought the Otago Block from the local Ngai-tahu. In 1845 a young English surveyor, Charles Kettle, set sail for Otago. He had worked in Wellington for three years and then returned to Britain, where he became a publicist for the New Edinburgh settlement in Otago. In 1845 he was chosen to survey the city-to-be and arrived at Koputai (Port Chalmers) in February 1846. After surveying this site, he moved to the future capital of the future Otago province, then little more than a swampy wilderness.

Kettle created an imaginary New Edinburgh intended to reproduce what to him were the special features of the Scottish capital. The imaginary town had been given the Gaelic name for Edinburgh, Dunedin, nicely capturing the nostalgic belief that the past had once contained a more perfect community. Kettle divided the inner city into streets

View of Dunedin, c. 1888
Watercolor illustration by George O'Brien, courtesy of Otago Settlers Museum, Dunedin

whose very names evoked the settlement's origins. But since the dream of a godly utopia shaped by the finest Scottish traditions had to be situated on a complex landscape on the other side of the world, Kettle and his assistants had to make several allowances for the topography of the site. The rectangular grid Kettle adopted, inspired by Edinburgh's New Town (a brilliant triumph of eighteenth-century urban planning), had to be adapted to the new site's precipitous hills. Yet the vision of a planned and rational city shaped his survey of New Edinburgh. Kettle provided for ample public parks, a green belt around the town, public cemeteries, and wide main streets. He also located suitable areas for suburban sections at Anderson's Bay, North East Valley, and the Upper Kaikorai District. J. T. Thomson, the chief surveyor for Otago from 1857 until the province was abolished in 1876, added considerably to Kettle's work, but the basic plan remained: as Dunedin grew, it followed Kettle's survey lines. Kettle provided for the excavation of Bell Hill, the reclamation of much of the tidal mud flats, and for a drainage system.

The reality that greeted the first ships sent by the Otago Association bore little resemblance to Kettle's vision for the future, however. Swamps dotted with flax dominated the northern part of the site; mud flats spread across what was to be the inner city; and the hills were covered with thick bush and innumerable streams and springs. During the 1850s, although the streets surveyed by Kettle constituted an ironic commentary on the muddy reality, Princes Street nevertheless took shape, Bell Hill began to disappear, and as the brave took up residence toward the Octagon (or still farther north), they built their houses within the contours of the town plan. John Barr, the unofficial poet laureate of the new colony, nicely captured in his poems the tension between the idealism and the materialism of the new settlers, their desire to build a new society redeemed from the ills of that which they had chosen to leave, and their commitment to a more narrowly defined pursuit of individual wealth and comfort.

Then, around the turn of the decade, gold was discovered. Dunedin's population doubled in the last six months of 1861 and in another three years had reached nearly 16,000. Tents, jerry-built houses, and tenements crowded the streets. No provision existed for the disposal of sewage or garbage. Animals, hens, and humans competed for space, empty sections became rubbish dumps, and rats infested the area. Hawkers gutted fish in the streets, and by the end of the 1860s industrial refuse, especially from the breweries, compounded the problems. Some regarded these conditions as a yet stronger spur to pursue the founders' original vision. Others rejoiced in the frenzied growth and prosperity.

Dunedin was the last beneficiary of the gold rushes that swept around the Pacific rim. The influx of miners—mostly young men from Britain's working classes—upset the Scots-Presbyterians who wished to consolidate their dominance. Moreover, the miners were a boisterous and hard-drinking crew. Entrepreneurs like Shadrach Jones and a host of other merchants arrived. Jones developed the Vauxhall Gardens across the harbor. In the town center, pubs, dancing halls, theatres, and oyster bars proliferated. Charles Thatcher, the unofficial laureate of the miners, soon followed the horde, wittily inventing new and topical lyrics for the popular tunes of the day. He celebrated the democratic, egalitarian, and boisterous spirit of the "New Iniquity," as he named the miners.

> On the diggins we're all on a level you know;
> The poor man out here aint oppressed by the rich
> But, dressed in blue shirts, you can't tell which is which.

Thatcher mocked the original settlers—the "Old Identity"—and applauded the "noisy, dirty, drinking, smoking, cursing crowd."

By 1863 Dunedin had been transformed and greatly enlarged. The Presbyterians launched an architectural competition for a new church, and before long the elegant spire of a New First Church, designed by R. A. Lawson, dominated the inner city. Soon the Wesleyans, Anglicans, Catholics, and the town's small Jewish community were each erecting houses of worship. In 1867 Otago held the first of its great industrial exhibitions. While the religious expressed their faith in gothic forms, the merchants and bankers, to the amusement of several satirists, preferred the form of the classical temple.

The alluvial goldfields declined in 1864–65, and Dunedin became less boisterous. In the 1870s, however, Dunedin boomed again thanks to Julius Vogel's ambitious development policies. Growth placed pressure on the original vision of a New Edinburgh, and some suggested that various reserves, including the town belt, might be leased for grazing. The major political battles revolved around the council's campaign, led by the irascible Londoner, H. S. Fish, to take over the water and the gas companies. The prosperous 1870s saw a rapid growth in the number of large companies based in Dunedin, many of which built handsome head offices in either stone or brick. A great number of these buildings were designed by R. A. Lawson, whose structures soon came to dominate Dunedin's townscape.

Dunedin became the colony's industrial, commercial, and financial capital. Within the city, large clothing factories, engineering works, Sew Hoy's several factories, flour mills, and a whiskey distillery were established. Industrial growth also occurred on the cheaper land of South Dunedin, North East Valley, and the Kaikorai Valley. The Union Steam Ship Company, which would dominate the Pacific by World War I, was also established during this period. That company helped to ensure that the harbor—the southernmost in the world—was developed to cope with the growing fleet of ever-larger and more power ships.

Visitors in the 1870s, such as the English novelist Anthony Trollope, remarked on the stable and prosperous character of Dunedin, with its abundance of elegant stone buildings, its ample parks and reserves, and its cultural vitality. The university and the museum, although quite small, gave the city a significant intellectual and cultural life. The dominance of Scots and Presbyterians also imparted a distinctive tone to public life.

The Long Depression, which hit Otago in 1879 and lasted until 1896, hurt Dunedin. The city lost population, and the "exodus" from the promised land became a political issue. Yet manufacturing industry expanded. The cable cars introduced during this period to provide transport between the city and its hill suburbs eventually became a symbol of Dunedin, as familiar as the university's clocktower or the spire of First Church.

In the late 1880s, when the city's leaders decided to organize another great industrial exhibition, public concern mounted concerning the appearance of the inner city, where vacant sections still became rubbish dumps. Led by Alexander Bathgate, in 1888 concerned citizens formed a Reserves Conservation Society and took in hand the task of creating the Queen's Gardens. Charged with the spirit of the new times, this organization did not collapse after achieving the object for which it had been formed, but turned to new tasks, such as planting trees and lawns in the Octagon, previously a muddy waste. In 1903, the city council responded to the new concern over the environment by appointing David Tannock as superintendent of Dunedin's parks and reserves. A winter garden was opened in 1908, and in the next few years Tannock supervised the addition of a rhododendron dell, a band kiosk, a deer park, and a Shakespeare garden. Tannock also oversaw completion of the Oval, where subsiding areas had become rubbish dumps. Whatever its problems, however, Dunedin's towering hills and town belt did not fail to impress. When Mark Twain visited in 1895, he joked that a party of Scots had once set out to find paradise, and finding Dunedin had stopped.

In the nineteenth century Dunedin and Otago played an important and often decisive role in shaping New Zealand's response to the major political and social issues of the day. The women's movement gathered momentum locally, spearheaded first by the Women's Christian Temperance Union and then the Franchise League. The latter led the crusade for women's franchise, obtained in 1893. Nor were the men far behind. In 1889–90 the city's workers led the colony in forming trade unions and seeking to obtain for working men a stronger (and more reliable) political voice. They succeeded beyond their wildest dreams in the elections of 1890, returning three unionists and three radicals who played a key part in making the colony, in one observer's phrase, "the world's social laboratory." Locally, too, the unions became important institutions, their leaders prominent citizens.

Dunedin gained many cultural amenities between the end of the Long Depression and World War I. These included a free public library; two specialized libraries (one containing Robert McNab's collection of 4,000 volumes relating to the early history of New Zealand, and the other composed of Thomas Morland Hocken's remarkable collection of books, manuscripts, maps, and paintings); an art gallery; and a museum.

During the same period, Dunedin's architectural heritage was greatly enriched by a new generation of architects. Perhaps the most distinguished was Francis Petre, whose work includes St. Dominic's Priory, St. Joseph's Cathedral, a number of parish churches, a magnificent Italianate castle for Edward Cargill, two elegant commercial buildings, and a number of houses.

The Victorian heritage remained a guide into the Edwardian years, but several architects revolted against the classical and gothic styles previously in vogue. Ernest George, in his design for the Olveston mansion (now a major tourist attraction), used locally made brick with contrasting decoration, roughcasting, Marseilles tiles, and colored glass windows. Architect Basil Hooper was keen to create a regional style by using regional materials and craftsmen skilled in their use. He not only designed several fine houses for wealthy clients but won the competition for designing houses for workers (under the 1905 Workers' Dwelling Act) and supervised the construction of St. Paul's Anglican Cathedral, designed by Edmund Sedding.

Edmund Anscombe also contributed to the revolt against Victorian styles, successfully translating the monumental character of the Victorian public buildings into brick. His finest achievement was the Exhibition Buildings, erected on the reclaimed Lake Logan for the Dunedin and South Seas Exhibition of 1925. More than 3 million people visited this exhibition, the city's largest and most ambitious. Anscombe provided for the formal architectural splendor that people expected of the exhibition, but organized the space around the new ethos of consumerism. Where previous exhibitions permitted people only to come and stare, this one encouraged them to play and participate.

The 1925 Exhibition celebrated and advertised Dunedin's claim to be New Zealand's financial, industrial, and cultural capital. Ironically, the throng of visitors meant that the 1926 census incorrectly reported a growth in the city's population. The figures misled a generation. In reality, the decline first evident in the 1890s had been gathering momentum. Yet demographic decline did not immediately diminish Dunedin's importance, and in the long run it allowed much of the city's rich architectural legacy to survive. The dramatic expansion of the university and the medical school, and the creation of a permanent home for the art gallery boosted the city's pride and complacency. Some talked of Dunedin as New Zealand's educational and cultural capital.

In the 1920s Dunedin's geographic location as the southernmost port in a sizeable city also added to its sense of importance. Robert Scott based his second and ill-fated Antarctic expedition at Port Chalmers, the city's deep-water port. After learning that the great Norwegian explorer Roald Amundsen had beaten them to the South Pole, Scott's entire party perished. Their expedition focused worldwide attention on the city from which Scott and his party had sailed. In 1916 Ernest Shackleton also used Dunedin as a staging post before sailing south into the Antarctic's icy seas. When the great American commander Richard Byrd decided to explore further the Antarctic continent he, too, chose Dunedin as his staging post. Byrd arrived there in November 1928, but unlike previous explorers his visit was photographed and filmed by a battery of accompanying crews. His solo flight across the North Pole had already made him an international celebrity, and Dunedin basked in reflected glory. When Byrd's eighty dogs fell ill on Quarantine Island in Otago Harbour, Dr. John Malcolm of Dunedin's Otago University consolidated the city's reputation by quickly devising a new formula for dog biscuits. Richard Hudson's large confectionery and biscuit factory lent equipment and staff, who labored through the night to produce the new biscuits. At 6 A.M. on December 2, 1928, Byrd and his *City of New York*, together with twenty New Zealanders, left Victoria wharf, assisted by the tug *Dunedin*. A vast crowd cheered their departure. Despite a local salt's prophesy of disaster (he reminded Byrd of Coleridge's Ancient Mariner), no disaster befell the expedition, and the local solution saved the dogs.

The years following 1928 were difficult. Although the new town hall had opened and the city had acquired a new post office that towered over the graceful Stock Exchange, the Great Depression saddled the city and its council with expensive and bewildering obligations in the area of social welfare. Many of the government's responses, such as the municipal milk scheme, were innovative and effective.

After World War II, the approaching centennial for Otago quickened a sense of the past and of the need to plan for the future. Despite much protest, the city's tramways and cable cars were gradually scrapped and replaced with trolleybuses. The municipal government acted after the war to meet the shortage of housing by building virtually new suburbs in Corstorphine and Wakari. The council, to commemorate those who died in the war, decided to upgrade the facilities available for recreation at the Caledonian ground. The provincial centennial in 1948 was a spectacular event, and the city celebrated with enthusiasm. The triumph of Otago's rugby team in this its golden year further enhanced the sense of civic and provincial pride. In 1948, in fact, Otago teams won almost every national sporting honor available. The royal visit of 1953–54 only enhanced the mood of civic pride and euphoria.

The next thirty years saw more decline, however, with the inner city bearing the brunt of falling population and loss of revenue. In an effort to confront this decline, the city council hired experts to offer advice, imposed new zoning regulations, continued to reclaim areas in the harbor, and tried to encourage new industry with offers of cheaper services and lower rates. These policies did not succeed, for the economic problems of the city and the region were probably too complicated for a municipal solution. The major industries since the 1880s, engineering and clothing, were in decline. But since the traditions of Dunedin and Otago strongly emphasized the quality of the urban environment, the decrease in economic and industrial growth enhanced, to many people's minds, the overall quality of life there. Many Victorian buildings of distinction survived, as did much of the inner-city housing stock, and the citizens were now intensely protective of their parks, reserves, and the town belt. The greatest achievements of the postwar councils lay in adding to Dunedin's amenities. The Caledonian all-weather track, the Moana swimming pool, Momona Airport, the John Wilson Memorial Drive, and a new civic center and library were great achievements. As the university grew spectacularly in the late 1960s and early 1970s, the city cooperated in creating a traffic-free campus.

Modern Dunedin, while greatly enhanced by its handsome civic amenities, its splendid legacy of Victorian architecture, and the slower pace of life resulting from decline, remains as it always has been a mood as well as a place. Its citizens have shared much besides a handsome townscape and a beautiful landscape. Dunedin is also a network of communities. For some citizens, its pubs and sports teams have imparted much of the charm; for others, the city's magic lies in its theatres, especially perhaps the Globe, or even its beaches and its hills, the peninsula or the so-called Golden Coast. Tourists come to see the yellow-eyed penguins, the seal colonies, and the only colony of albatrosses in the world near a human settlement. In the 1970s and 1980s, as the city's industrial and commercial base shrank further, the university became the major and dramatic source of growth. But in the end, for its citizens and its exiles, Dunedin's character and identity are contained in its long main streets that run along the foot of towering hills and that, with their shops and offices and pubs, provide them with a measure of what a city ought to be.

Further Reading: A comprehensive history of the site may be found in *City of Dunedin: A Century of Civic Enterprise* by Kenneth Cornwall McDonald (Dunedin: Dunedin City Corporation, 1965) and in *A History of Otago* by Erik Olssen (Dunedin: J. McIndoe, 1984). Several fine studies of Dunedin's architecture are available, including *William Mason: The First New Zealand Architect* by John Stacpoole (Auckland: Auckland University Press, and London: Oxford University Press, 1971); *Colonial Architecture 1820-1970* by John Stacpoole and Peter Beaven (Wellington: Reed, 1972); *Buildings of Dunedin* by Hardwicke Knight and Niel Wales (Dunedin: J. McIndoe, 1988); and *Historic Buildings of New Zealand,* volume II: South Island, edited by Frances Porter (Auckland: Methuen, 1983).

—Erik Olssen

Dunhuang (Gansu, China): Dunhuang Town

Location: In northwest China, approximately 200 miles south of the Mongolian border and 500 miles northwest of Lanzhou, capital of Gansu province.

Description: Small desert town in Gansu province, formerly one of the most important settlements on the old trade route known as the Silk Road, which stretched from Xian in China to the Mediterranean Sea.

Site Office: Dunhuang Tourist Bureau
1 Dong Dajie, 736200
Dunhuang, Gansu
China

Today a small town with a population of 14,000, Dunhuang was an important oasis settlement in the days of the ancient Silk Road, when its population reached 76,000. Dunhuang was a source of provisions for caravans heading west across the desert beyond Lop Nor. The nearby Mogao Caves, which are responsible for attracting most of the visitors to the town today, owe their existence in some measure to the Silk Road merchants, many of whom financed paintings in this Buddhist cave complex either to secure religious blessings, and therefore safety, on the journey, or to express thanks for a trip already completed.

The Silk Road was actually a network of trade routes that stretched from China through Central Asia and finally to the Mediterranean Sea. It began in Xian (formerly known as Changan), capital of the Han and Tang Dynasties, and continued northwest in two branches before rejoining at Lanzhou. The single route then followed the curve of the Qilian Shan Mountains northwest to Anxi, where it divided into its two major branches. One branch, known as the Northern Silk Road, continued northwest to Hami, then turned southwest in two branches along either side of the Tian Shan Mountains and continued through a variety of networks to Central Asia, the Middle East, and East Europe. The other branch, known as the Southern Silk Road, led southwest from Anxi to Dunhuang, then followed the Altun Shan and Kunlun Shan Mountains before curving north along the Karakoram range and joining a branch of the Northern Road at Kashgar. From Kashgar, three different routes led farther west. The Southern Silk Road was the older of the two major paths and offered a more direct route to the West, but it was much more arduous, skirting as it did the northern foothills of the Kunlun Shan Mountains and the southern edge of the Taklamakan Desert.

On the southern route, Dunhuang was the end of the line for Chinese merchants carrying silk and other items from the East. Here they sold or bartered their goods to Central Asian middlemen, who in turn traded the merchandise to Persians, Syrians, and Greeks farther west. Greek and Jewish merchants then sold the goods throughout the Roman Empire. Each transaction was figured into the final cost of silk and other Eastern wares.

The trade route was inaugurated during the reign of Han emperor Wu Di. In 138 B.C. he sent an aide named Zhang Qian to seek an alliance with residents of Fergana against the Xiongnu people. Zhang Qian failed to negotiate an alliance during what turned into a thirteen-year journey, but upon his return to Xian, he bewitched the court with his tales of Central Asia. The emperor, sensing the potential to greatly extend Han influence, sent out a number of additional expeditions along what would become the Silk Road.

At this time, Dunhuang was the westernmost outpost of China. It had been settled and fortified by the Chinese in the late second century A.D. following a military campaign against the Xiongnu. Emperors of the Han Dynasty (206 B.C.–A.D. 220) built a series of fortified beacon towers connecting the oasis to Jiayuguan, the westernmost major fortification of the Great Wall. The towers were used for the exchange of signals among garrisons and eventually gave the town its name, which translates literally as Blazing Beacon. Most importantly, the towers gave protection to merchants traveling along the Silk Road and ensured Chinese control over this portion of the route. Some of the beacons may still be viewed on the road between Dunhuang and the railway station at Liuyan.

Central Asian merchants traveling to and from Dunhuang faced near-overwhelming physical conditions (still largely evident to travelers in the region) ranging from scorching, arid deserts to snow-covered mountains. During the hottest months they moved by night. Sandstorms could halt travelers for days. In addition to such natural dangers, merchants also faced the threat of bandits. Eventually, they safeguarded against such attacks by joining together in huge caravans—some with as many as 1,000 camels—protected by armed guards. Each of the two-humped (Bactrian) camels could carry up to 500 pounds.

Once they reached Dunhuang, these caravans traded for a variety of Eastern goods, but it was silk that drove commerce along the route. Well into the first millennium A.D., China was the Western world's only source of silk, and the Silk Road was for centuries the only way to import the commodity. By the fourth century two-thirds of the Byzantine (Eastern Roman) Empire's treasury was spent on luxury items, including silk, from the East. The resulting caravan traffic brought untold wealth to Dunhuang.

The Chinese merchants who carried the silk east to Dunhuang were, of course, seeking imports from the West in exchange. The earliest of these imports were alfalfa and grape-

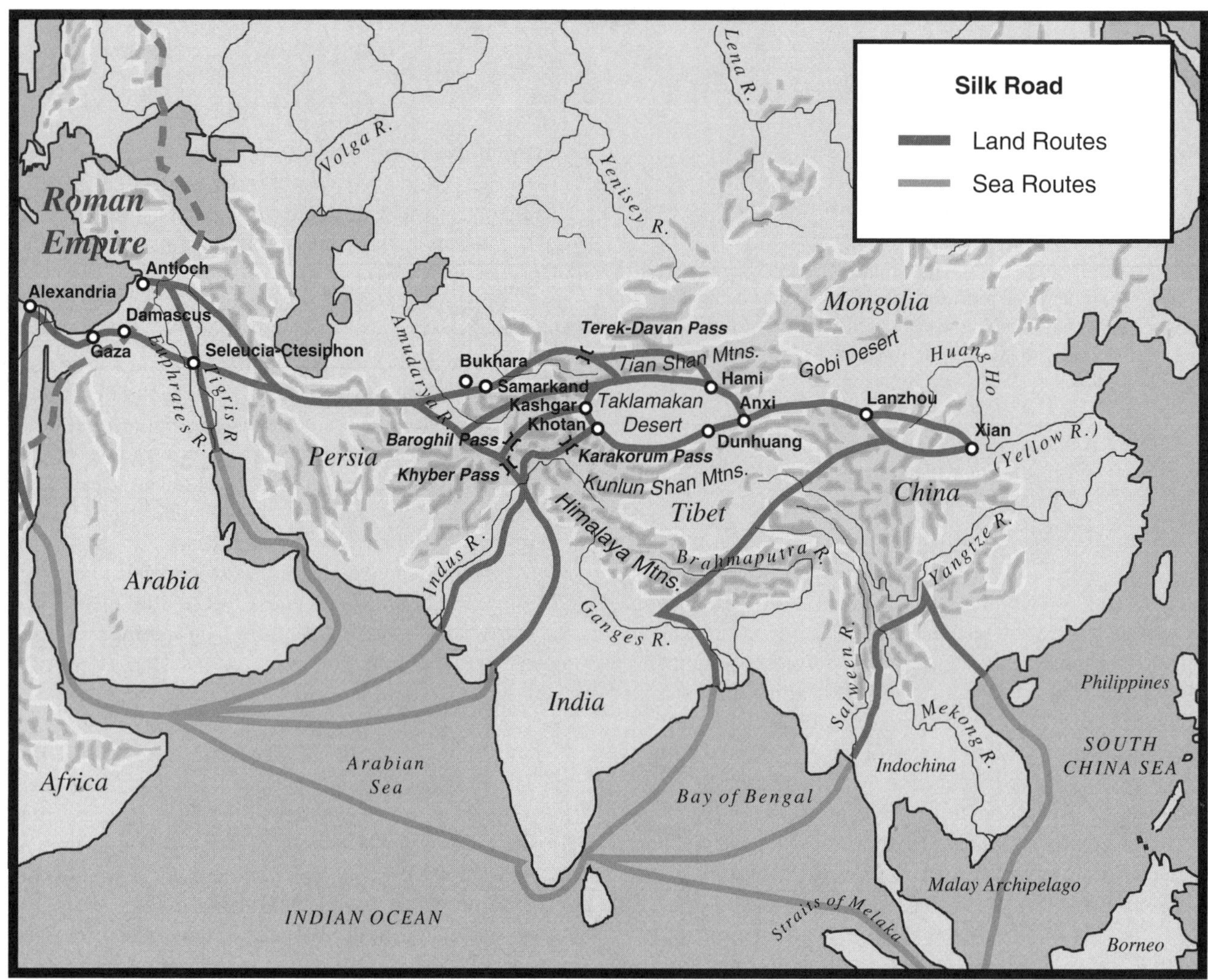

Map of the Silk Road
Illustration by Tom Willcockson

vines. Later, from Persia and elsewhere, came dates, pistachio nuts, peaches, pears, and walnuts, as well as dyes and oils of frankincense and myrrh. Central Asian products included almonds, jade, cucumbers, and onions. India yielded spinach, sandalwood, and pepper, but its most important product was cotton. The most crucial import for the Chinese traders, however, was horses. The Chinese considered horses from Fergana, Kucha, Mongolia, Bukhara, and Samarkand to be vastly superior to their own, and the emperors used these imported mounts as the foundation of the Chinese army's cavalry.

Dunhuang saw more than the exchange of mere commodities, however. Here, as at other border towns on the Silk Road, Eastern and Western cultures met for the first time. One of the most notable concepts to spread into China from the West was Buddhism, which arrived in the first century A.D. This ancient religion from northern India took such firm hold over the Chinese that, for a period in the sixth century, it was officially adopted by the royal court.

In time, Dunhuang developed a sizeable Buddhist community, and the oasis became a stopping point for Chinese Buddhist pilgrims on their way to India. By the fourth century, Buddhist monks had begun to carve grottoes in a cliff face fifteen miles from the town, where monks could meditate and pilgrims could rest before they embarked upon the arduous journey west. The breathtaking decorations at the resulting temple complex, the Mogao Caves, were partly funded by wealthy merchants passing through Dunhuang.

Dunhuang's prosperity was dealt a blow when the Han Dynasty fell in the third century A.D. and political instability beset the Tarim Basin, where the oasis lies. Many merchants turned to sea routes instead of the Silk Road. By the sixth century the new, less arduous Northern Silk Road was also taking business away from the Southern Road.

Tibetans conquered Dunhuang in the latter half of the seventh century. The conquerors were soon weakened by internal strife, however, and were driven from the area in 851 by a private army commanded by Zhang Yichao. For his pains Zhang was granted privileges and titles from the Tang court, including rule over Dunhuang. His family controlled the town until 911, when it came under the sway of Uighuristan. Through the period of Uighur rule, Dunhuang's leaders continued to be Chinese; numerous political marriages were arranged between Dunhuang's ruling Cao family and the daughters of the king of Khotan.

Traffic along the Silk Road had continued to decline during this period, and it vanished almost completely by the end of the Tang in the tenth century. Succeeding dynasties were less open to foreign ideas and goods, and eventually sea routes carried almost all of the East-West trade.

Furthermore, the Chinese had lost their carefully protected monopoly on silk production. According to legend, the secret of silk manufacture first spread west in A.D. 440, when a Chinese princess carried silkworm eggs in her headdress to Khotan following her marriage to the king. About 550 two Nestorian monks brought the silkworm to Constantinople, where both church and state established silk production facilities. By that time Persians had also acquired the secret.

In 1036 Dunhuang fell to the Xi Xia kingdom. It was probably in response to Xi Xia ascendancy that the monks at the Mogao Caves began to leave the region. In 1227 Dunhuang was invaded by the Mongol armies of Genghis Khan. Forty-eight years later, Marco Polo passed through the town on his way to visit the Mongol capital at Beijing. Dunhuang's population had declined significantly by the time it came under the influence of the Muslim Chagatai Khanate in the early sixteenth century. It did not become a major settlement again until 1760, when the Manchurian Qing Dynasty took control of the area.

In the late nineteenth century Dunhuang began to attract international attention as word spread about the survival of the Mogao Caves. With the discovery in 1900 of a treasure trove of manuscripts in one of the caves, archaeologists began descending on Dunhuang with ever-increasing frequency. So significant was this find that a field of study known as "Dunhuangology" developed.

Dunhuang continued to impress its foreign visitors. A description of the town in the 1930s is given by the missionaries Mildred Cable and Francesca French in *The Gobi Desert:*

> The people of Tunhwang [Dunhuang] viewed themselves as the elite of the Gobi land, and were abnormally proud of their oasis. They had plenty of money to spend and opened their markets freely to goods from other places, but prided themselves on being a self-supporting community. . . . The market-place was always busy with merchants coming and going, the professional story-teller took his stand each day to amuse the moving crowd, and gaily dressed women came in carts from the farms for a day's shopping and to see their friends. The granaries overflowed with wheat, and the town reckoned itself to be the safest and most prosperous place imaginable, priding itself on its trade-route nickname of "little Peking."

Today Dunhuang is a small town with one main street and two small hotels, although it does host a busy market every day. Carpets and agricultural produce are the area's mainstays. There is a small museum run by the Dunhuang Research Institute (founded in 1943) on the south side of the main road. Included in the collection are reproductions of manuscripts found in the Mogao Caves, reed torches that were used for the beacons, and bamboo slips used for record keeping during the Han Dynasty. The ruins of the old town walls and a 52-foot-high tower can be seen about 820 feet west of the current town center. Just south of the town is the Mingsha (Singing Sand) Hill, so called because an entire army was buried there during a sandstorm. It is said the soldiers' ghosts can still occasionally be heard playing military drums and horns.

Further Reading: *The Silk Road* by Judy Bonavia (London: Collins, and Lincolnwood, Illinois: Passport, 1988) provides much information on Dunhuang and general background on the Silk Road. *The Silk Road* by Luce Boulnois (London: Allen and Unwin, and New York: Dutton, 1966) is a valuable historical work, as is Irene Franck and David M. Brownstone's *The Silk Road: A History* (New York: Facts on File, 1986; Oxford: Facts on File, 1988). Interesting mid-twentieth-century descriptions of Dunhuang and other sites on the Silk Road can be found in *The Gobi Desert* by missionaries Mildred Cable and Francesca French (London: Hodder and Stoughton, 1942; reprint, London: Virago, 1984). For a discussion of the archaeological rediscovery of the area in the early twentieth century, Sir Aurel Stein's own *On Ancient Central Asian Tracks* (London: Macmillan, 1933; Chicago: University of Chicago Press, 1964) is still valuable, but Peter Hopkirk's *Foreign Devils on the Silk Road: The Search for the Lost Cities and Treasures of Chinese Central Asia* (London: Murray, 1980; Amherst: University of Massachusetts Press, 1984) provides a more contemporary view of the intense competition between foreign antiquarians, who took away with them to far-away museums many of the region's most precious artifacts.

—Tim Pepper

Dunhuang (Gansu, China): Mogao Caves

Location: Fifteen miles southeast of the city of Dunhuang in northwest China's Gansu province.

Description: A collection of caves carved out of a mile-long rock cliff and filled with Buddhist carvings, gilt and colored murals, and statues. The caves were also the repository of many of the earliest printed documents found in China, including the world's oldest surviving printed book, the Diamond Sutra.

Contact: Dunhuang Tourist Bureau
1 Dong Dajie, 736200
Dunhuang, Gansu
China

Best known in the West as the Mogao Caves (named after the site's administrative district during the Tang Dynasty), the temple complex southeast of Dunhuang is perhaps better referred to by the Chinese name Qianfodong (Thousand Buddha Caves). These caves house one of the world's great art treasures (now protected by the United Nations): the largest surviving collection of early Chinese Buddhist art, including 2,400 painted sculptures and 500,000 square feet of murals.

Buddhism came early to the area, for the Dunhuang oasis was a stopping point on the Silk Route, the path through which Buddhism entered China in the first century A.D. In 366 Buddhist monks began carving grottoes in a cliff alongside the River Da, some fifteen miles from town. The caves, excavated along the northern end of the cliff, served as domiciles and places of meditation, and soon they attracted a large community of monks and pilgrims. During the Tang Dynasty (618–907), Mogao was the last major stopping point in China for Buddhist pilgrims venturing west to India. It was here that they rested and prepared for the arduous journey along the Southern Silk Road.

The caves themselves are structurally unexceptional. Most are square-shape, often (especially in the earlier sites) with a central square stone pillar decorated with figures, around which the monks perambulated while meditating. What makes the caves so remarkable are their wealth of decorations. The monks apparently sponsored a small army of artists, many of whom were quite famous at the time; over the course of several hundred years, these artists covered every inch of wall and ceiling space with dazzling murals and filled the caves with stucco figures. When the monks exhausted all available space on the cliff face around the end of the Tang Dynasty and could no longer carve out new caves, they began to redecorate the old ones.

The caves' many murals consist mostly of icons, scenes from the Buddha's life, images of paradise, and portraits of patrons (many of whom were wealthy merchants passing through Dunhuang on the Silk Road). To create the murals, artists took the following steps, as described by Frances Wood, author of *Blue Guide China:*

> The surfaces were plastered with mud, then successive layers of plaster, dung, and animal hair or straw. The surface was then smoothed and dressed with white kaolin (china clay) to provide a smooth surface for painting. Pigments were mixed with water and painted onto the dry plaster surface; the major pigments were malachite green, azurite blue, orpiment yellow, iron oxide or earth red, cinnabar vermillion, red ochre, kaolin white, white lead, lampblack (using soot from oil lamps), and powdered and leaf gold and silver.

The pigments have proved remarkably durable, although the pink flesh tones have oxidized to dark grey, and dark outlines have formed around the figures over the centuries. The stucco statues in the caves were painted with the same pigments.

A paper stencil found in the Mogao Caves (and now in the British Museum's Stein Collection) provides insight into the techniques used to create mural designs. Evidently, figures were first drawn onto paper and then tiny holes punched around their outlines. By placing the paper against the wall and blowing or rubbing red chalk through the holes, artists could produce a dotted outline of the figure to serve as a guide during painting. More importantly, artists could repeat the process as often as they wished, creating multiple copies of the design. Eventually artists replaced paper stencils with clay or metal stamps. These techniques most likely relate to the development of printing in China at this time.

In fact, many of the earliest surviving specimens of Chinese printing were discovered in the Mogao Caves. Most notable among these is the Diamond Sutra, a Buddhist religious text. Produced on a twenty-six-foot paper scroll and dated 868, it is the world's oldest printed book. (Earlier printed materials survive in Japan, but they are far simpler and do not qualify as a book.) Wood-block printing, the technique used to produce the Diamond Sutra, required first a scribe to write the text on a piece of thin paper, which then would be laid on a block of wood upon which the text would be cut out. The sophistication of the Diamond Sutra suggests that this was not an early example of printing, but rather of a technique that had already been refined. Its quality is truly remarkable for a text that was produced 500 years before printing first began in Europe.

Also found at Mogao were a wealth of handwritten paper documents. Most of these are religious works, such as Buddhist sutras, but there were also secular items, such as

View of cliff facade at Mogao Caves
Photo courtesy of China National Tourist Office, Los Angeles

histories, medical and mathematical texts, census reports, and receipts. The earliest dated document is from A.D. 406, a remarkable 800 years before paper was common in Europe. Many of the documents were probably local municipal records stored at the temple complex.

All of these documents—a total of 45,000—were discovered in a single, sealed cave now known as the Cave of Scriptures. Evidently they had been placed there for safekeeping by the monks some time after 1004, the year indicated on the last dated document. The temple complex had been in decline since its heyday in the Tang Dynasty and had been threatened by a variety of invaders. Most likely, it was the invasion of the Xi Xia in the eleventh century that led to the sealing of the Cave of Scriptures and drove many of the monks from the cliff. Other monks remained, however. Based on decorative styles found in the caves, scholars believe that new artistic work was being done there well into the Yuan Dynasty (1234–1368); some experts hold that the monks did not completely desert Mogao until the sixteenth century.

Abandoned and undisturbed for centuries, the caves remained remarkably well preserved, a result, no doubt, of the region's dry desert conditions. The first Europeans to visit the caves in modern times were the Russian explorer Nikolai Prejewalsky and members of a Hungarian geological expedition; both came in 1879. The number of foreign visitors increased markedly after 1900, when a Taoist priest named Wang Yuanlu uncovered the Cave of the Scriptures. His discovery initiated what has been dubbed the Great Manuscript Race. The first foreign antiquarian to investigate the cave was Hungarian-born scholar Sir Aurel Stein, who was working at that time for the British government. When Stein arrived in 1907, Wang Yuanlu had appointed himself caretaker of the cave complex and was attempting to raise money for the restoration of its statuary. For £130, Stein purchased several painted silk banners and more than 10,000 scrolls and manuscript fragments. Ironically, Stein could not read Chinese and had no idea of the true value of his purchase. Only when he returned home did he discover that among the scrolls was a treasure trove of rare printed calendars and religious tracts, including the Diamond Sutra. Most of the manuscript documents were copies of major Buddhist sutras, but they were significant for their paper, ink, and calligraphy. The Stein Collection is now divided between the British Museum in London and the National Museum in New Delhi.

In 1908, Frenchman Paul Pelliot became the next Westerner to venture into the caves. As a sinologist, he was more selective about the materials he purchased. The Pelliot Collection of the Bibliothèque Nationale in Paris is smaller than the Stein collection but contains a greater number of precious items. All told, they cost Pelliot approximately £90.

In 1911 the caves were visited by Zuicho Tachibana, who collected documents for Count Kozui Otani, abbot of a major Buddhist temple in Kyōto. In 1914 further items were removed by Russian scholar Sergei Oldenburg. Today there are no original documents remaining in the Mogao caves; they reside in London, Paris, New Delhi, the Tōkyō National Museum, St. Petersburg's Academy of Sciences, and Beijing. Copies can be seen in the Dunhuang Museum.

In 1924 Langdon Warner, an American representing Harvard's Fogg Museum, visited the site and was appalled at its deterioration, particularly the damage caused by 400 White Russians who were detained in Dunhuang after fleeing Russia earlier that decade. He wrote, "My job is to break my neck to rescue and preserve anything and everything I can from this quick ruin. It has been stable enough for centuries, but the end is in sight now." Unfortunately, Warner's method of preservation involved actually removing murals from the walls. That was, after all, his original assignment for the Fogg Museum.

Today the caves are protected by the United Nations. Of the 1,000 or more caves originally carved into the cliff, roughly 500 remain; of these, 40 are open to the public, and only a portion of those are shown on any one tour. They stand in three or four rows along the mile-long cliff. Wind and sand erosion of the facade have made the upper caves difficult to reach. Wooden ladders and balconies once provided access here, but these have now been supplanted by concrete structures. Large metal doors, opened only by official tour guides, guard each cave.

Because the monks redecorated earlier caves once there was no room to carve new ones, modern scholars cannot date particular caves with great accuracy. Taking this difficulty into account, researchers provisionally date 23 of the surviving caves to the Wei period (comprising the Northern Wei Dynasty, 386–534, and the Western and Eastern Wei Dynasties, 534–557); 95 to the Sui period (581–618); 213 to the Tang period (618–907); 33 to the Five Dynasties period (907–959); 98 to the Song period (960–1276); 3 to Tangut or Xi Xia (early eleventh century); and 9 to the Yuan Dynasty (1234–1368).

The caves commonly open to visitors in recent years begin chronologically with Cave 246, carved during the Northern Wei period. Cave 257, another Northern Wei cave, is renowned for its wall paintings telling the story of the Deer King (a birth story about one of the Buddha's previous lives; a number of other such stories are depicted throughout the caves). Other paintings include Buddhist angels and a walled garden filled with flowers as well as a four-story tower. Both Caves 257 and 259 reveal Indian influences.

Other early cave paintings include a figure with four arms and four eyes (Cave 249), holding up the sun and the moon; a red deer drinks from the river in which this figure stands. Many of the caves feature representations of benefactors who, through their sponsorship of painters, hoped they would reach paradise more quickly. Some 4,000 such portraits are found in Cave 428, dating from the Later Zhou Dynasty (557–80). Buildings from various periods in various styles are also depicted (notably in Cave 420, from the Sui period), offering valuable insight into early wood structures.

From the Tang period come some of the Mogao Caves' finest wall paintings. Excellent early Tang landscapes—more realistic than earlier Wei landscapes—are

Statuary and wall painting inside Mogao Caves
Photo courtesy of China National Tourist Office, Los Angeles

found in Cave 209, for example, and in Cave 323 a landscape many consider the finest of any painted at Mogao depicts a group of Buddhists in a boat rowing past a mountain range.

In addition to wall paintings, statues of the Buddha constitute the objects of primary interest at Mogao. Statues of over 100 feet in height (Cave 96) down to a 55-foot "Sleeping Buddha" (Cave 148) date from the Tang period. The latter statue shows the dying Buddha ready to enter Nirvana, and the paintings in the cave relate to that theme. Many of the Buddhas on the walls of Cave 365 (Middle Tang) have had their faces scratched off by Muslims who objected to portrayals of the human form. This is a rare example of damage at the Mogao Caves, which, apart from the natural erosion of the exteriors, are generally well preserved. Most of the damage that has been done is attributable to Muslims or the White Russian visitors of the 1920s.

The Late Tang is represented by Caves 16 and 17. Cave 16 is notable mainly for its patterned tile floor; Cave 17, extremely small, is the Cave of Scriptures. Of the later caves, one from the Five Dynasties period (Cave 98) contains some of the finest tenth-century paintings in the entire Mogao collection. These include a group of portraits of the family of the king of Khotan, a hunting scene, and an elaborate painting of an all-female orchestra—done in a variety of styles. Cave 146 features some donor paintings that are significantly larger than those of the earlier periods. The later donor paintings also show these patrons in much richer garments than do the earlier ones.

Cave 55 from the Northern Song period (960–1127) features more major paintings, which are similar in style to those in an illustrated copy of the Lotus Sutra found in the caves and now held by the British Library. The ceiling paintings in Cave 256, also Northern Song, have come off, revealing the chisel marks of the monks who carved the cave. Cave 454, another from the Northern Song, served as a chapel for women.

Caves 354 and 367 date to the Tibetan Xi Xia period (882–1227) and show significant influence of Tantric Buddhism, an esoteric sect that gained many followers in Tibet. The caves dating from the Yuan Dynasty are rarely opened; they are decorated in Tibetan style.

Away from the caves there are a number of stupas, which are burial places for the ashes of some of the Dunhuang monks. The most impressive of these is the large and elaborate Stupa of Wang Yuanlu, discoverer of the Mogao manuscripts.

Further Reading: *Blue Guide to China* by Frances Wood (London: Black, and New York: Norton, 1992) is well researched and contains thorough descriptions of the Mogao Caves. Roderick Whitfield and Ann Farrer's *Caves of the Thousand Buddhas: Chinese Art from the Silk Route* (London: British Museum, and New York: Braziller, 1990) features the British Museum's collection of paintings and banners from Dunhuang. Similarly, for information on printing, see Frances Wood's *Chinese Illustration* (London and Dover, New Hampshire: British Library, 1985). Peter Hopkirk's *Foreign Devils on the Silk Road: The Search for the Lost Cities and Treasures of Chinese Central Asia* (London: Murray, 1980; Amherst: University of Massachusetts Press, 1984) provides a history of the Great Manuscript Race of the early twentieth century.

—Tim Pepper

Easter Island (Rapa Nui *or* Isla de Pascua; dependency of Chile)

Location: The easternmost Pacific Island in the Polynesian group, Easter Island lies in the eastern Pacific Ocean, approximately 1,200 miles east of Pitcairn Island and 2,300 miles west of the Chilean coast.

Description: An isolated island of sixty-four square miles, with a population of 2,000. Most inhabitants live in one town, Hanga Roa, which has a single paved street. The island boasts more than 17,000 archaeological sites: in addition to the 800 famous, giant statues, it contains ancient quarries, abandoned stone huts, tombs, and caves decorated with primitive artworks. Easter Island was annexed by Chile in 1888.

Site Office: Servicio Local de Turismo
Tuu Maheke and Apina Streets
Hanga Roa
Easter Island

Contact: Sernatur (Servicio Nacional de Turismo)
Avenida Providencia 1550
Santiago
Chile
(2) 361416

Three now extinct volcanoes thrust upward from the ocean floor to form Easter Island, tiny and isolated in the middle of the Pacific Ocean. It has no natural harbors and only one small beach. Fresh water is scarce, and only a few plant and animal species are now to be found in the largely desolate landscape. Although it seems improbable, a small number of Neolithic seafarers colonized this island sometime between A.D. 400 and 700, built a flourishing and complex society, and produced an astonishing array of art treasures.

Most likely, Easter Island's first human inhabitants had set out from the Marquesas, which lie more than 2,000 miles to the northwest. They made the journey in large double canoes loaded with men and women, chickens, plant cuttings and seeds, and stowaway rats. Besides their supplies, they brought the rich traditions of Polynesian culture, which formed the basis of Easter Island's extraordinary society.

According to local legend, the colonists, led by King Hotu Matua (*matua* means father), came from a homeland called Hiva. Some legends cite a rivalry between Hotu Matua and his brother as the reason for the king's voyage of exploration. Others contend that the king had been forewarned of Hiva's destruction by a tidal wave. Traveling in two large canoes, the Hivans made landfall at the Anakena beach, where two babies were born as soon as the new settlers landed. The island was called Te Pito-te-henua, or Navel of the World, to commemorate, legend suggests, the cutting of the umbilical cords of the first native-born inhabitants. The name is also translated as "Center of the World," which, given the island's extreme isolation, is perfectly understandable.

Easter Island's oral history recounts the arrival of a second landing party, consisting of men only. These men, who came from a different place, pierced and stretched their earlobes and were therefore called "Long-Ears." The earlier settlers, by contrast, became known as "Short-Ears." The "Long-Ears" intermarried with women from the "Short-Ear" community, and according to legend the two groups managed for the most part to live side by side peacefully. However, periodic hostilities between these two groups form an important theme in the local legends and serve to explain the tragic decline of the community throughout the sixteenth, seventeenth, and eighteenth centuries. No historical evidence has been found to support these indigenous claims that Easter Island was colonized by two different, culturally distinct groups.

Anthropologists speculate that the colonization of Easter Island was part of a wave of eastward migration of Polynesian islanders during the first few centuries A.D. Tribal warfare, perhaps as a result of overpopulation, is commonly thought to have been the immediate cause of these movements. The Polynesians had invented a canoe-and-outrigger setup that allowed them to navigate great distances across the stormy Pacific and so opened up the eastern reaches of Polynesia. Nevertheless, many of the parties that set out in search of new land must have perished at sea, either in storms or as a result of food and water shortages.

The legends say that these travelers found the island barren, much like it is today. However, there is now ample evidence to the contrary. At the time of the settlers' arrival, Easter Island presented a hospitable and fertile environment. The rich layer of topsoil, though shallow and easily eroded to expose the solid rock, was suitable for agriculture. The staple of the islanders' diet was apparently the yam, which they had brought with them and cultivated successfully in their new home. Moreover, pollen analyses of soil deposits indicate that the island was covered by lush and variegated tropical forests, which supplied the community's need for timber, fuel, fibers, and forest fruits. The ocean yielded plentiful fish, shellfish, porpoises, and seals, while various species of land- and seabirds also provided necessary proteins. Clearly, Easter Island once offered the resources to sustain a community of at least several thousand people.

Archaeological findings attest to a rapid population growth. The settler community flourished, growing into a society that bore many of the hallmarks of Polynesian culture. Easter Island had a highly stratified social organization that placed great emphasis on kinship ties, clan membership, and genealogy. Food surpluses sustained both a dominant priestly

Giant stone figures, Easter Island
Photo courtesy of National Tourism Board of Chile, Santiago

class, a warrior class, and a range of specialized craftsmen, particularly stonecutters. The twin concepts of *mana* (power, energy) and *tapu* (taboo) organized the islanders' religious life. *Mana,* which brought good luck and prosperity, was transmitted to the tribe through the person of the chief. *Tapu,* visited on the tribe or on individuals by evil spirits, was the result of disobeying any of an elaborate set of rules. As was the case elsewhere in Polynesia, social stability was threatened by persistent internecine warfare.

Although in its heyday the island community showed many similarities to other Polynesian societies, a number of significant differences gave Easter Island a unique position in the Polynesian group. Cut off from contact with the outside world, the islanders independently developed sophisticated agricultural and engineering techniques that took them far beyond the achievements of their Polynesian ancestors. They developed a written language for use in religious ceremonies and for legal record-keeping. Most impressively, they began to carve colossal statues from the soft lava rock using only stone tools. They quarried these monoliths in the interior of the island and then transported them to the shore by rolling them over logs.

Easter Island's justly famous sculptures represent different deities from the Polynesian pantheon as well as important ancestors. Belonging to a clan rather than the whole community, each sculpture, or *moai* as it is called in the native dialect, is a repository of that clan's *mana.* Photographs of these sculptures are by now universally familiar: squat bodies are topped by elongated, angular heads with severe eyebrows, long jutting noses, square jaws, and disdainful, pouting mouths. The eye sockets, now empty, were once filled with shells and coral. Some of these giants were supplied with "topknots," carved separately out of a different kind of rock. Miracles of engineering, the sculptures are also a tribute to human ingenuity and creativity. The statues vary in height, ranging from six to thirty-three feet (the islanders created taller statues as time progressed). The largest completed statue weighs eighty-two tons, excluding the topknot, which weighs another ten tons. Once completed, the statues were set on giant platforms, or *ahus,* invariably facing inland.

The islanders erected some 200 completed sculptures. Far more and far larger sculptures, abandoned at various stages of completion, lie in the quarries, surrounded by the stonecutters' tools. Apparently, the sculptors became more and more ambitious before abandoning their work altogether: the unfinished *moai* measure up to sixty-five feet in length. What caused the carvers to throw down their adzes remains one of the most tantalizing of Easter Island's many mysteries.

Giant stone figures, with topknots, Easter Island
Photo courtesy of National Tourism Board of Chile, Santiago

Over the years, a number of more or less fanciful explanations have been offered, but scientific research is beginning to provide some solid clues. Archaeologists and paleontologists are piecing together a story of catastrophic environmental decline caused, ironically, by the island community's spectacular successes.

Scientists have dated the first signs of deforestation on the island to the ninth century. As the population grew, islanders cut timber faster than it could be replenished. The forests gradually retreated until the very last tree was cut down around 1500. Soil erosion very slowly reduced the land available for agriculture, while different animal species became extinct one after another as a result of habitat destruction and because the islanders began to rely more and more heavily on the island's fauna for their food supply. While the environment deteriorated significantly, if slowly, the islanders apparently did nothing to modify their demands on the limited—and disappearing—resources. In fact, the community seems to have peaked, both in population and artistic activity, between 1200 and 1500. During these centuries, when resources were rapidly being exhausted, the population on Easter Island had expanded to at least 7,000 (some estimates give numbers almost three times as high).

The complete disappearance of trees meant that the islanders could no longer obtain the logs or manufacture the ropes they needed to transport the *moai*. More catastrophically, they could no longer build seaworthy canoes and thus could not fish for porpoises, a very important part of their diet. They were now marooned on their devastated island with an insufficient food supply and barely enough fuel to cook their meager meals. As food became scarce, the complex social order broke down quickly. The islanders had developed extremely effective weapons using obsidian points, and they fought each other in intense struggles between clans. Cannibalism appears to have become widespread, women and children forming the most obvious targets. In the course of these upheavals, workers dropped their tools and abandoned the *moai* in the quarries. Vandals "blinded" the completed statues by removing the coral and shells from their eyes; later they toppled and smashed many monuments.

Evidence suggests that a major battle was fought at the Poike Peninsula at the island's northwest corner, a battle still remembered in local legend. A defensive ditch, probably dug sometime during the sixteenth century, separated the peninsula from the rest of the island. It was filled with wood to form a barricade behind which the Long-Ears had entrenched themselves. One of their wives, herself a Short-Ear, tricked the Long-Ears into making an attack, and they were caught in front of their own defenses. The wood in the ditch was then set ablaze, and all but three of the Long-Ears were driven to their death in the fire. In fact, layers of ash found in the ditch indicate a major conflagration in the late seventeenth century.

During the island's most brutal period, following 1500, the warrior class gained the upper hand in the island's social organization. The warlike Birdman cult reinforced their dominance. According to the cult, the god Makemake chose the Birdman—a warlord who ruled the entire island for a year—in an annual test of skill and courage. Every spring a group of young athletes swam shark-infested waters between the Orongo coast and two small islets off the shore. There they waited for the sooty terns to nest and start breeding. The first athlete to retrieve an egg from the nests and swim back to Orongo became that year's Birdman, the top warrior of the island. Island priests sanctioned the practice and led the Birdman's installation ceremonies. After the ritual, the army of the new Birdman went on a rampage, destroying the crops of rival clans. Men, women, and children were taken prisoner. Many were viciously tortured, sometimes to death, and in secret ceremonies victims were sacrificed and eaten. Survivors were kept as slaves. After these annual outbreaks of violence, hostilities would diminish. However, the Birdman received tribute from other islanders throughout the year. The last Birdman ceremonies took place as late as 1867.

On Easter day 1722, the first Europeans set eyes on the island. Dutch explorer Jacob Roggeveen and his crew spent part of a day there and named it Paaseiland (which means Easter Island in Dutch). The explorer described the island as barren and the people as cold, hungry, and generally miserable. They welcomed the newcomers with open arms and were eager for all they had to offer. However, in a skirmish over the Dutchmen's weapons, a dozen islanders were killed or wounded. Roggeveen did not see a single tree, and his reconnaissance party did not find evidence of any animals besides humans, chickens, rats, and insects. He was also struck by the virtual absence of women, whom he surmised to be jealously guarded by the menfolk and hidden in the modest dwellings. In truth, few women may have been left alive. Puzzled but impressed by the *moai*, Roggeveen noted that a few of them were upright, a state of affairs that still held in 1770, when a Spanish ship docked at the island for three days. According to the ship's logs, islanders again welcomed the sailors warmly and willingly accepted Spanish sovereignty.

By the time British explorer Captain James Cook landed at Easter Island a mere four years later, not a single *moai* was left standing. By then, the population was greatly reduced: Cook put the number of islanders at about 700, two-thirds of whom were men. Nevertheless, resources had been so severely depleted that even these few hundred could barely sustain themselves. The islanders Cook saw were hungry and stole everything that wasn't nailed down. The same observation was made by Captain Jean-François de la Pérouse, who arrived in 1786 with two French frigates, the *Boussole* and the *Astrolabe*. La Pérouse, who admittedly stayed but one day, described a society organized along generally egalitarian lines. It was his understanding, for instance, that the island's yam plantations were held in common. Moreover, he added, "a man has but little temptation to make himself king of a people almost naked, and who live on potatoes and yams." He surmised that "these Indians not being able to go to war from the want of neighbors, have no need of a chief."

Sadly, nothing could be further from the truth. The Birdman cult still held sway, and, apart from the Birdman's depredations, the island's tiny fiefdoms warred on each other constantly. Given the size of the island, clan battles often pitted family members against one another. Vendettas dominated daily life. Meanwhile, plantations were tilled by slaves—people of enemy clans who had been taken in combat. They "belonged" to the local chiefs and suffered most direly in the conflicts.

The violence caused by visiting Europeans soon augmented this strife: islanders were sometimes shot "for fun," and women were kidnapped to serve as concubines. In 1862, Spanish slavers from Peru strewed the Anakena beach with gifts and then kidnapped 1,000 islanders who had been tempted by the bait. The captives were shipped off to work in the guano caves on Peru's Chincha Islands. Among them were almost all of the priests, the only ones who could read the so-called *rongo-rongo* script. This incident, therefore, dealt a serious blow to the community's cultural continuity. Bishop Jaussen of Tahiti protested the kidnapping through the French envoy to Peru, and Peruvian authorities ordered the captives' return. However, maltreatment, starvation, hard labor, and disease had already killed 900 of them. On the return voyage, most of the survivors died of smallpox, while the fifteen who made it back to Easter Island brought the disease with them, causing an epidemic that decimated the remaining population.

In 1864, the first missionary, Brother Eugène Eyraud, arrived on Easter Island and soon converted the few hundred surviving souls. The Birdman cult ceased, to the relief of all but the warriors. Christianity was not seen as an unmixed blessing, however, as the people felt cut off from the *mana* of the ancestors. In 1870 a French entrepreneur, Jean-Baptiste Dutroux-Bornier, made use of these mixed emotions to stir a rebellion against the missionaries. He planned to deport the native islanders to Tahitian plantations in order to raise sheep on the empty island. The missionaries were indeed driven away, and some islanders were taken to Tahiti. But the 100 who remained killed Dutroux-Bornier in 1877.

Chile annexed Easter Island in 1888. Chilean ranchers raised sheep there for a short time before a Scottish wool company leased the island from the Chilean government early in the twentieth century. During this time the islanders were virtually interned in Hanga Roa, the main village, which was surrounded by barbed wire. In 1914, a group of British research institutions, including the British Museum and Cambridge University, sponsored a private scientific exploration led by Katherine Scoresby Routledge, who published her observations in 1919. She was followed by Alfred Metraux, an ethnologist, who published detailed studies of the island's people and culture during the 1940s and 50s.

The mid–twentieth century saw a number of imaginative, although misguided, speculations about the origins of Easter Island culture. Thor Heyerdahl proposed that the first colonists had come from Pre-Inca civilizations in Peru, where archaeologists found fitted stone masonry and large carved statues somewhat like those at Easter Island. To prove his point, Heyerdahl built a Peruvian raft, called the *Kon-Tiki,* and sailed the more than 2,000 miles to the island from the coast of South America. His exploits brought him wealth and fame, but the many similarities between Easter Island and other Polynesian societies clearly prove his thesis wrong. Heyerdahl later copublished a scholarly catalog of archaeological sites on Easter Island that is still well respected. In the 1960s and 1970s, Swiss supernaturalist Erich Von Däniken sold popular books postulating that extra-terrestrials had carved Easter Island's statues before being whisked back into space.

European interest in Easter Island has brought some modest improvements in the twentieth century. A variety of research teams is now to be found on the island at virtually any time, and efforts have been made to restore a few of the toppled *moai*. In 1960, unfortunately, a tidal wave hit the island, and several *moai* that had been re-erected were sent sprawling 300 feet inland, dealing the piecemeal restorations a significant blow. Most of the islanders today live by tourism, which brings a slow but steady trickle of visitors to the remnants of Easter Island's extraordinary past.

Further Reading: Sebastian Englert collected local legends during his more than thirty years spent on the island and published them as *Island at the Center of the World* (New York: Scribner, 1970). Alfred Metraux's *Easter Island: A Stone-age Civilization of the Pacific* (New York: Oxford University Press, and London: Deutsch, 1957; originally published as *L'Ile de Pacques,* Paris: Gallimard, 1941) is still a solid source of information on the culture of Easter Island. Thor Heyerdahl's *Aku-Aku* (New York: Ballantine, and London: Allen and Unwin, 1958) and *Easter Island: The Mystery Solved* (New York: Random House, and London: Souvenir, 1989) make for entertaining reading, but they are anything but reliable, although the latter volume has magnificent photographs and vividly describes the most recent history of the island. *Easter Island: Island of Enigmas* by John Dos Passos (New York: Doubleday, 1971) includes the reports of early European explorers.

—Jean L. Lotus and Marijke Rijsberman

Elephanta Island (Mahārāshtra, India)

Location: An island in the Arabian Sea in Bombay Harbor, approximately five miles east of the city and about three miles west of the mainland.

Description: Called Ghārāpuri in Hindi, Elephanta Island varies in size with the tides, measuring between four and six square miles. Once an important port and the capital of the Koṅkaṇ Maurya Dynasty, the island is now known only for its rock-cut temples. The most famous of these is the Siva cave, of uncertain date, which holds a series of magnificent reliefs of that deity.

Contact: Government of India Tourist Office
123 Maharishi Karve Road
Bombay 400 200, Mahārāshtra
India
(20) 32932, (20) 33144, (20) 33145, or (20) 36054

If, as one local observer has quipped, Bombay is the "Big Mango," the New York of India, then Elephanta Island is the city's Liberty Island. A short boat ride from modern Bombay with its sprawling commercial and industrial developments, Elephanta gives expression to India's spiritual roots. The island's famous rock-cut temples, testimony to the greatness of ancient Hindu civilization, are of uncertain date and attribution. Art historians date their construction anywhere from the late fifth to the late eighth century, attributing the work variously to each of the ruling clans that held sway in the region during those centuries.

Although Elephanta's early history is shrouded in mystery, it is clear that the story properly starts with the rise of the Gupta Empire in northern India in the early fourth century. After several centuries during which Hinduism had declined, the Guptas fostered the religion in their empire. A flowering of Brahmanism, the forerunner of modern Hinduism, made itself felt both within Gupta territory and far beyond. Gupta rule was also characterized by an upsurge in Hindu art and architecture. Craftsmen experienced an unprecedented freedom of artistic expression, which is evident, for instance, in the influence of the initially much more developed Buddhist art on their work. The rock-cut temples constructed in the north under the Guptas are especially relevant to Elephanta, whose temples show marked similarities to several northern specimens.

If the Gupta rulers were responsible for creating the artistic climate that made the Elephanta temples possible, it is clear that they did not commission them. Although Gupta influence reached as far south as Mahārāshtra, the region's coastal area was under the immediate control of the Koṅkaṇ Maurya Dynasty by the late fifth century. Elephanta Island (the name the Portuguese gave the island) was then called Pūri (or Pūrikā) and functioned as the Koṅkaṇ Maurya capital. Records of frequent pirate attacks indicate that Pūri was an important port city. Some historians hold that the Koṅkaṇ Mauryas were responsible for the rock-cut temples, including the Siva cave. This attribution is paired with a construction date in the mid–sixth century.

However, because theirs was a small kingdom, few scholars think it possible that the Koṅkaṇ Mauryas were the planners and makers of the temple caves, which must have involved an almost superhuman excavation effort. Local tradition insists that the caves were not man-made, but in all likelihood they were hewn in their entirety from the solid rock by humans. Thousands of tons of rock must have been carved away with relatively simple tools. A small state is unlikely to have had the resources to sustain such a massive and labor-intensive project, even if it had the community of craftsmen capable of producing sculpture of such consistently high quality as is seen in the Siva temple.

Although most historians assume that the Koṅkaṇ Mauryas were independent, some—albeit highly inconclusive—evidence suggests that they stood in a feudal relationship to the Kalacuri Dynasty. The Kalacuris held sway in Mahārāshtra from the early sixth century, and some contemporary inscriptions allege that they subjugated Pūri around 540. The historical accuracy of these inscriptions is doubtful, however. Rulers of the time often boasted of conquests they had not in fact made. Nevertheless, the Siva cave on Elephanta is sometimes ascribed to the Kalacuris, with dates ranging from the late fifth to the early sixth century.

The Kalacuris are known to have controlled other areas in which notable cave temples were excavated, yet whether they were in fact responsible for any of these projects (which in any event do not show very close similarities to the Elephanta temples) remains unclear. Some elements of the iconography of the Siva reliefs derive from the Pashupata Siva cult of worship to which the Kalacuris subscribed. Although the sculptures on Elephanta were carved at a time when Brahmanism was still polytheistic, they demonstrate the monotheistic tendencies of Pashupata Saivism, which resolves all conflicting elements in the figure of Siva. The triple-headed Siva on Elephanta is a particularly striking case in point, but many of the reliefs in the Siva temple similarly represent a union of opposites. These iconographic characteristics are invoked as evidence in support of the hypothesis that the shrines were built under Kalacuri auspices. However, the force of this argument is considerably diminished by the fact that the Koṅkaṇ Mauryas also seem to have been Pashupata.

The Kalacuris were eventually vanquished by the Cāḷukyas, who made themselves master of Pūri in the seventh

Siva Trimurtī, Elephanta Island
Photo courtesy of Air India Library, New York

century. The island was first attacked by King Kīrtivarman, a Cāḷukyan ruler who undertook a major campaign of territorial expansion in the late sixth century. Although Kīrtivarman made some headway farther south along the coast, the Koṅkaṇ Mauryas (with or without the aid of their putative overlords, the Kalacuris) withstood this initial attack. Around 620, however, the island fell to an armada of hundreds of ships sent by Kīrtivarman's successor, Pulakeśin II. The Cāḷukyas appear to have held Pūri for some time, and consequently they too have been credited with the construction of the Siva temple sometime in the mid–seventh century.

Around the middle of the eighth century, the Cāḷukyas were swept aside by the Rāṣhṭrakūṭas, the last ruling house to whom the Elephanta temples have been attributed. Construction dates vary from the early seventh to the late eighth century. The Kailāsanātha temple at Ellora, which was built by the Rāṣhṭrakūṭas around 750 and has many similarities to the Elephanta temples, is adduced as additional evidence for this hypothesis.

Another dynasty calling itself Cāḷukyan ruled Pūri from around 972 to 1190. Subsequently, the island became the property of the rulers of Ahmadābād, who in turn ceded it to the Portuguese when they settled in the Bombay area. By then the island was called Ghārāpuri, a name it still retains in Hindi. The Portuguese, however, renamed it Elephanta Island, for the colossal statue of an elephant posted at one of the boat landings. (The elephant statue collapsed in the nineteenth century and was subsequently taken to Bombay's Jijā India Udyan, or Victoria Gardens, where it was reconstructed.) The temples lost their religious significance with the island's transfer to the Portuguese, and the Hindu population abandoned them as places of worship.

The Portuguese left Elephanta in 1661, having given the swamp that would become the city of Bombay to the English as part of a wedding dowry. But before they left, the Portuguese did considerable damage to the sanctuaries. It is said that their military used the various reliefs of Siva in the main temple for target practice. Only one Siva relief remained unscathed, and that was the giant Trimurtī. The Portuguese also removed a stone from the island with an inscription that may have indicated who built the temples and who worshiped there. The inscription has never been recovered. The Siva cave was restored in the 1970s after centuries of neglect, but the other caves on the island, three of which contain important sculpture, remain badly damaged.

The temples at Elephanta come at the end of an Indian tradition of carving temples out of solid rock, which began in the second century B.C. or even earlier. The Siva temple on

Elephanta, among the last to be cut in India, is regarded as one of the most impressive examples of the form. The temple, also referred to as the Great Cave, is located one-half mile up a steep hillside facing the water. Squat columns with simple cushion capitals flank its low, unassuming main entrance, giving no indication of the spacious hall and rich reliefs within. The Great Hall, a rough square with sides approximately 150 feet long, stretches deep into the hillside. The principal Siva relief is located centrally on the south wall opposite the main entrance. The north-south axis leading from the entrance to the central Siva relief gives the hall an unusual orientation for a Saivite temple, which was conventionally laid out on an east-west plan. In fact, the north-south axis is abated by a cross-cutting east-west axis along more conventional lines. Additional smaller sanctuaries were hewn out of the rock at the east and west ends of the temple, the eastern sanctuary functioning as a kind of ceremonial entrance. These elements of the layout create an axis focused on the freestanding Siva shrine toward the temple's west end. The north-south axis appears to be a reluctant compromise with the exigencies of the hillside location.

The freestanding shrine is a square cell reaching from floor to ceiling, with a doorway on each side. Each door is flanked by two huge, ornately carved figures called *dvarapalas,* which are counted among the finest examples of this kind of sculpture in India. Approximately fifteen feet tall, these heavily-muscled attendants guard the divine symbols inside, the *liṅgam* and the *yoni*. These stylized representations of the male and female genitalia symbolize the cosmic male and female principles in the Hindu religion. In the Pashupata Saiva faith they jointly function as the symbol of supreme unity.

Large pillars line the hall, spaced at generous intervals that counteract the potentially claustrophobic effect of a cave temple. The temple's principal glory is to be found on the wall spaces between the pillars: the reliefs that depict the god Siva in various poses, each representing a different incarnation. On one side of the doorway just inside the north entrance is a relief of Siva Yogishvara, the Great Ascetic. He is balanced on the other side of the entrance by Siva Natarāja, the Lord of the Dance, who is performing the *tandava,* the cosmic dance that shakes the world. Another relief depicts Siva with his wife Pārvatī, sitting enthroned in their home on Mount Kailāsha in the Himalayas. Another panel shows the marriage of Siva to Pārvatī. He is also represented with Ganesh, the playful elephant-headed deity who is worshiped as the patron god of Bombay today.

The union of male and female in a single form thematically links the three panels on the south wall. On the left is Siva Ardhanārīśvara, who is male on one side of the body and female on the other. The panel to the right represents Siva Gaṇgādharamurtī, showing the scene in which Gaṇgā, goddess of the Ganges River and one of Siva's many wives, becomes one with the god, entangled in his hair. In the center stands the bust of the great Siva Trimurtī, over twenty feet high. The three-headed Trimurtī, uniting all cosmic forces within himself, is the crowning glory of Elephanta and one of the most impressive and famous sculptures of India's ancient civilization to have survived the onslaughts of time.

One widely accepted interpretation of the Trimurtī identifies the heads with different incarnations of the deity. The head on the right, which wears an expression of rage, is Siva as Rudra, the Destroyer and the male principle. Details of the hair and jewelry indicate that the head on the left is female. Standing out for its remarkably serene expression, it has been identified as Siva in the form of Vishnu, the Preserver. The middle head is often seen as the reconciliation of Rudra and Vishnu—Siva as Brahmā, the Creator. As Joseph Campbell describes it in *The Way of the Animal Powers,* "the presence in the center is the mask of Eternity, the ever-creating mysterium, out of which all pairs of opposites proceed: female and male, love and war, creation and annihilation. Though beheld externally, this mystery is to be known internally, as the indwelling Source and End of all that has been or is to be."

Śaṅkara, the influential ninth-century Vedic philosopher who gave the Vedas a monotheistic basis, casts a different light on the sculpture. In his *Morning Meditations,* he describes the state of enlightenment pursued by adherents to the Hindu religion in terms that might well apply to the Trimurtī:

> I am neither male nor female, nor am I sexless.
> I am the Peaceful One, whose form is self-efful-
> gent, powerful radiance. I am neither a child, a
> young man, nor an ancient; nor am I of any
> caste. I do not belong to one of the four life-
> stages. I am the Blessed-Peaceful One, who is
> the only Cause of the origin and dissolution of
> the world.

The Trimurtī sculpture gives some indication that it once had, or was intended to have, five heads. Excrescences on the back and the top of the sculpture have tempted many scholars to consider that the Trimurtī was once in fact the Siva with five faces described by an ancient text. The symbolism of the three heads is so powerful and persuasive, however, that many interpreters sweep aside the suggestion that the Trimurtī is incomplete.

Western scholars have pointed to ancient Greece and its Dionysiac cult in their search for parallels to the Elephanta Siva. Although ascetic, Siva is also a living, dancing god with an intense appreciation for the pleasures of the body. Interestingly, the Greeks who invaded India under Alexander the Great drew the same comparison. They also found parallels between Krishna and Hercules and between Indra and Zeus. But although the Greeks may have had some influence on Indian temple architecture, they clearly did not have an impact on indigenous sculptural traditions.

The Siva temple on Elephanta is only one of more than 1,200 rock-cut temples that have been discovered in India. Fewer than 100 of these were built as Brahman sanctuaries; the greatest number were Buddhist. Moreover, since sculptural traditions in India began with a flowering of

Buddhist art, the face of the Buddha can be detected in much of the Elephanta sculpture, particularly in the serene incarnations of Siva.

Today, Elephanta Island stands apart from the nearby bustle, glitter, and overcrowding of Bombay. However, launches bring throngs of tourists to the island daily, and guides still offer to carry visitors up the steep hill to the caves in palanquins.

Further Reading: Karl Khandalavala's *Mahārāshtra* (Bombay: Marg, 1985) contains an in-depth look at the debate over the origins of the rock-cut temples on Elephanta. An informative description of the temples, as well as a balanced look at their influences and origins, is contained in *The Art of Ancient India: Buddhist, Hindu, Jain* by Susan L. Huntington (New York: Weatherhill, 1985). For more on the various meanings of the Trimurtī and other depictions of Siva, two books written by Heinrich Zimmer and edited by Joseph Campbell stand out: *Myths and Symbols in Indian Art and Civilization* (New York: Bollingen Foundation/Pantheon, 1946) and *Philosophies of India* (Princeton: Bollingen Foundation/Princeton University Press, 1951; London: Routledge and Kegan Paul, 1952). Both make for fascinating reading. Joseph Campbell's *Historical Atlas of World Mythology*, Vol. I, *The Way of the Animal Powers* (London: Summerfield, and New York: A. van der Marck, 1983) is also highly informative.

—Jeffrey Felshman and Marijke Rijsberman

Ellora (Mahārāshtra, India)

Location: In the Deccan hills of central India, approximately twenty miles northwest of Aurangābād.

Description: Ellora is a sacred site for three of India's native religions: Hinduism, Buddhism, and Jainism. It is highly unusual to Western eyes because the holy places at Ellora were not constructed from the bottom up, but quarried from the top down or sculpted from the outside in. In the years between approximately A.D. 600 and 1100, more than 100 caves were cut from the hills. The caves vary in the complexity of their excavation and their decoration, ranging from simple worship halls and living quarters to wonderfully ornate mountains of stone. Only thirty-four caves are considered principal holy sites, and of these the great Hindu temple dedicated to Siva, the Kailāsanātha Temple, is by far the largest and most impressive.

Contact: Government of India Tourist Office
Krishna Vilas
Station Road
Aurangābād 431 005, Mahārāshtra
India
31217

In September of 1810, John Seely, an officer in the Bombay Native Infantry, took time from his duties to travel in the rough interior of India in search of a place he had heard tales about. The site, called Ellora, was reported to contain magnificent temples dedicated to the Hindu god Siva. Seely had visited and was fascinated by the Hindu temple of Elephanta, on an island in Bombay Harbor, although he had found it in a somewhat damaged state: the Portuguese, deeply offended by the representations of the Hindu gods and goddesses, had smashed many of the temple's sculptures some years previous. Although troubled by rumors of bandits in the wild foothills of the Deccan and warned by British authorities not to go, Seely put together a party and set out to cover more than 300 miles to his goal: the largest and most unusual collection of sculpted temples in the world.

Seely was not the first European to visit Ellora. He was, however, the first to measure and describe in detail the treasures of the Ellora caves. Many of them had been deserted for years and were no longer used as places of worship. Some had been desecrated by zealous Muslims during their occupation of Mahārāshtra in the fifteenth, sixteenth, and seventeenth centuries. Nearby temples still in operation, however, gave Seely ideas about the function and meaning of many of the carvings at Ellora. He spent about two weeks measuring and studying the caves, and then returned to his duties.

Seely was forced to return to England in 1823, having contracted a tropical disease. He published his descriptions in *The Wonders of Ellora* (1825), which revealed the secrets of the caves to the European world and made them a major attraction for travelers in the British Raj. Although he recovered from his illness and returned to India with his family in 1826, he became ill again, died, and was buried in an English cemetery in Bombay. The site of his grave has been lost in the myriad building projects of the modern Indian government.

The Ellora caves probably were originally excavated for the use of itinerant monks seeking shelter during the rainy season. Ellora lies very near the place where two major trade roads meet—the routes between Pathan and Broach, and from the pilgrimage site of Ajanta to Ujjain—and monks probably made a living from the patronage of traders on these roads. The site was protected and patronized by the rulers of the Deccan and western India, including the Cālukya and Rāṣhṭrakūṭa Dynasties, after the decline of the Gupta Empire in the fourth century A.D. Unlike other sites dating from the same period—the Ajanta caves to the northeast, for example—Ellora never was "lost" or destroyed and was visited occasionally by Arabs or Europeans even before Seely made his expedition from Bombay in the early nineteenth century.

The caves at Ellora are divided among the Buddhists, the Jains, and the Hindus. Of these, the Buddhist caves are the oldest, dating from between approximately A.D. 600 and 800. They are associated with the Vajrayāna sect of the Mahāyāna, or Greater Vehicle, school of the religion. Mahāyāna Buddhism recognized Siddhārtha Gautama, the historical Buddha, as only one of many Buddhas who represent universal truth. It also drew heavily on the theology expressed in the ancient *Upanishads*—theological and philosophical works dating from around 800 B.C. Unlike the older and more traditional school of Buddhism, called the Hinayana, or Lesser Vehicle, Mahāyāna Buddhism did not concentrate on an individual's path toward enlightenment. For the Mahāyāna, the goal of a Buddhist was not to attain nirvana (escape from selfish desire) but to worship an enlightened bodhisattva. The bodhisattva, an almost-Buddha, chooses to put off his own nirvana in order to help others attain enlightenment. His self-sacrifice gains him such merit, or good karma, that he can pass some of it on to people who devote themselves to him.

The Buddhist caves at Ellora fall into two broad categories: the *viharas,* the cells where the individual monks lived and studied, and the *chaityas,* the shrines that house the stupas, where relics of the Buddhas and the bodhisattvas are kept. Both originally were made of wood and were constructed to shelter the monks through the monsoon season. The early *viharas* were generally plain and undecorated. However, as the Buddhists became more powerful and at-

Kailāsanātha Temple, Ellora
Photo courtesy of Air India Library, New York

tracted rich patrons, their cells became both more elaborate and more permanent, gaining in decoration and in substance. By the seventh century A.D., Buddhist monks were excavating permanent residences and places of worship and study from solid rock.

One *vihara* cave in the Buddhist group, which served as a study and dining hall, contains a shrine decorated with the images of the principal bodhisattvas of the Vajrayāna sect: Padmapāṇi, representing infinite compassion, and Vajrapāṇi, representing universal wisdom. Another cave in the group, mixing *vihara* and *chaitya* elements, honors the ancient original materials of the monks: its roof is decorated with beams carved to look like wood, which serve no structural purpose, and the pillars of the hall are similarly decorated. This cave also contains a stupa, a characteristic Buddhist monument symbolizing death and rebirth into the enlightened state of nirvana. A third cave, three stories high, is a typical *vihara* on the first two stories, but the topmost floor is lavishly decorated with images of Buddhas, sea dragons, and other symbols.

The Jain caves, on the north end of the site, are more recent than the Buddhist caves. They date from between approximately A.D. 800 and 1100. Many of the Jain caves at Ellora were dedicated to the Digambara, or "sky-clad," sect, who were famous for refusing to wear clothing and pursuing an ascetic way of life. An early patron of the Jains was the early ninth-century Rāṣhṭrakūṭa king Amoghavarsha, who himself embraced the faith and promoted it—perhaps at the expense of the Buddhists, whose decline in Ellora dates from about this period. Despite the Jains' reputation for austerity, their caves at Ellora are often lavishly decorated. The focus of worship in the primary Jain cave is the figure of the great teacher Mahāvīra, traditionally considered the founder of the Jain religion. However, the cave also contains images of Matanga, the god of wealth, and Sidhaika, a fertility goddess. In addition, many other carvings decorate the cave, including portrayals of demigods, animals, flying couples, and *nagarājas,* or serpent-kings.

The caves between the Jain and the Buddhist sites are dedicated to Hindu deities, especially the god Siva. The largest work of these is the Kailāsanātha Temple. Its name is derived from the legendary Mount Kailāsa, the home of Siva and the center of the universe. Like the Jain caves, Kailāsanātha was produced with support of members of the Rāṣhṭrakūṭa Dynasty, particularly King Krishna I. However, Kailāsanātha is earlier than the Jain works; it dates from about

Kailāsanātha Temple, Ellora
Photo courtesy of Air India Library, New York

A.D. 765. From a vantage point on the hills surrounding the temple, a traveler can appreciate the accomplishment of the artists who sculpted Kailāsanātha out of more than 200,000 tons of rock. The artists began by splitting away from the mountainside a single block of stone measuring 200 feet by 100 feet; they did this by digging small trenches and forcing the rock apart with tree trunks that expanded after being soaked in water. Over a period of about 100 years, the sculptors slowly carved the temple and the cliff walls surrounding it into one of the largest and most magnificent examples of architectural sculpture in the world.

Siva, the god to whom the temple is dedicated, is, with Vishnu and Brahmā, one of the three major gods of the Hindu pantheon. In many ways, Siva is the most distinctive of the three: he is the god of dynamism and change, who exemplifies the process of *saṃsāra,* the everlasting cycle of death and rebirth that permeates the Indian worldview. In his form of Natarāja, the master of the Great Dance, Siva brings the universe into being; as Maheshvara, the Great Lord, he creates the world and endows it with knowledge; and as Mahākāla, lord of Transcendent Time, he presides over the end of things. Siva is identified with extreme ascetic practices, and some of his followers mortify their bodies to show their contempt for worldly existence. He serves as the supreme yogi, demonstrating his mastery of *kuṇḍalinī* energy, from which all sexual and spiritual strength is derived. Siva's emblem is the *liṅgam*, a phallic stone that usually serves as the focal point in his temples. The *liṅgam* is sometimes represented in connection with its female counterpart, the yoni. Siva is sometimes also shown with his vehicle, the bull Nandi, representing strength and justice.

The temple area is separated from the rest of the Elloran caves by a carved entrance, in which images welcome the worshiper into the holy mountain Kailāsa, the abode of Siva. These include the goddesses Gaṇgā and Yamunā, representing the holy rivers of the same name. They are flanked by water serpents and serpent kings (*nagas*) and queens (*naginis*) who serve as guardians of the mysteries contained within. Just beyond the entrance, by the inner door leading to the temple courtyard, are other images representing the good fortune that awaits the faithful: representations of Kubera, the god of wealth; Ganesha, the elephant-headed son of Siva, the god of good beginnings and domestic happiness; Durgā, an avatar of Pārvatī, Siva's consort, who destroys evil, represented by the buffalo demon Mahisha; and Lakshmi, the consort of Vishnu, the goddess of fortune, prosperity, and beauty.

The walls surrounding the temple are divided into a number of individual shrines, each dedicated to a famous event in Hindu literature or mythology. Most of them represent scenes from the life and works of Siva—his marriage to his consort Pārvatī, and the origin of the *liṅgam* symbol, for instance—but some show other popular Hindu deities. In particular, there are panels telling stories about Krishna and Narasingha, both incarnations of Vishnu. The exterior of the temple itself, also profusely decorated, contains legends from the two great Indian epics, the *Mahābhārata* and the *Rāmāyaṇa*. The *Mahābhārata* panel shows scenes from the war between the Pāṇḍava family and the Kaurava family, which had usurped the Pāṇḍavas' throne. The poem includes a long scriptural passage narrated by Krishna, who appears as a character in the poem, and the bottom lines of the panel depict legends from Krishna's own life. The *Rāmāyaṇa* tells the story of the warrior Rāma's efforts to rescue his wife Sita from the demon-king Rāvana. Another panel shows Rāvana's futile effort to insure victory in the *Rāmāyaṇa* by stealing Siva's sacred Mount Kailāsa. This panel emphasizes Siva's power, showing him stabilizing the mountain with one foot.

The shrine itself also has a second floor raised above the level of the entrance. This floor consists of a long hallway leading to an inner sanctum that houses the *yoni-liṅgam*, representing the presence of the god. Although the walls of the hallway, like those of the exterior, are profusely decorated, the sanctum itself is unadorned and austere. There is a circular open space around the sanctum so that the worshipers can walk around it, completing the sacred circumnavigation. The liquid with which the *yoni-liṅgam* is anointed, or lustrated, collects in a small bowl, and devotees can drink it or wash in it, symbolically representing their spiritual rebirth in the god's presence. At the back of the sanctum are five shrines, each housing a miniature replica of the temple itself.

The Kailāsanātha Temple is one of the greatest—perhaps the greatest—accomplishments of the Rāṣhṭrakūṭa Dynasty. The Rāṣhṭrakūṭa kings, who had friendly links with the Arab powers to the west, were regarded with awe by the traders and merchants from the Middle East. One merchant, named Suleiman, ranked them as a power with China, Baghdad, and Constantinople. By the late tenth century, however, the Rāṣhṭrakūṭas had declined in influence. In 973, the Rāṣhṭrakūṭa territories passed to the control of the Cālukya dynasty. In the eleventh and twelfth centuries, Turkish invaders from Afghanistan conquered the territory around Ellora, and Muslims proved their zeal by smashing the idols of the Hindus. Temples that had been desecrated in this way—Kailāsanātha and the caves of Ellora among them—no longer were considered holy to the local Hindus, Jains, and Buddhists. By the time John Seely arrived at the site in 1810, the holy sites of the Rāṣhṭrakūṭas were used as housing for low-caste people, who hung their laundry on the carvings.

Further Reading: A good general introduction to India, including the role of religion in the history of the country, can be found in F. Watson's *A History of India* (New York and London: Thames and Hudson, 1979). R. Sen's *Hinduism* (London: Penguin, 1981) explains the diverse and seemingly contradictory nature of one of the world's foremost religions. Alistair Shearer's *The Traveler's Key to Northern India: A Guide to the Sacred Places of Northern India* (New York: Knopf, 1983) offers assessments of religious sites, including Ellora, and some introduction to the religions themselves.

—Kenneth R. Shepherd

Fatehpur Sīkri (Uttar Pradesh, India)

Location: In the southwest corner of Uttar Pradesh state, northern India, twenty-three miles west of Āgra.

Description: Constructed by Akbar, the greatest of the Mughal emperors, Fatehpur Sīkri is the most extensive example of the adoption of Hindu architectural forms by Muslims in India. It contains a great mosque and an abandoned palace, both more than four centuries old, which have survived in pristine structural condition.

Contact: Government of India Tourist Office
191, the Mall
Āgra 282 001
Uttar Pradesh
India
363377 or 363959

Prior to 1568, the site of Fatehpur Sīkri was little more than a secluded ridge southwest of Sīkri village. The ridge's most famous resident was Shaik Salīm Chishtī, a saint, or holy man, of the ascetic Chishti sect of Muslims. In 1568, Salīm Chishtī was host to a visitor even more famous than himself—Mughal emperor Akbar—and their meeting gave rise to the remarkable complex of red sandstone mosques, tombs, and palace halls of Akbar's new capital city.

Akbar, a great admirer of the Chishtī sect, made annual pilgrimages on foot from his capital at Āgra to the shrine of Saint Khwājah Muīn-ud-Dīn Chishtī in the city of Ajmer, more than 300 miles away. Small wonder, then, that the emperor chose to visit Salīm Chishtī, who lived a mere twenty-three miles from the capital. When Akbar arrived, the eighty-nine-year-old Salīm Chishtī prophesied that the emperor would at last father a son. Akbar was overjoyed at the news, for despite having 300 wives, the twenty-six-year-old emperor had yet to produce a male heir. Akbar's first Hindu wife, a daughter of the mahārāja of Amber, became pregnant almost immediately and spent the final months of her pregnancy close to Shaik Salīm to ensure that the prophecy of a male child materialized. It did, and the infant was named Salīm in honor of the saint (the prince would later adopt the name Jahāngīr shortly before becoming emperor in succession to his father).

Overcome with joy at the birth of his son, Akbar immediately commissioned a great mosque, known as Jāma Masjid, to be built on the ridge. Work began in 1569. According to an inscription, Fatehpur Sīkri's Jāma Masjid was completed in 1571. By far the largest mosque in India at the time, its courtyard measured 360 feet by 139 feet. The masons also built a small mosque to the west of it for Shaik Salīm, in which the saint spent the last years of his life (he died in 1572) in prayer and meditation. The Stonecutter's Mosque, as it is known, still stands, although it is not open to non-Muslims. Its serpentine brackets are echoed in the shrine of the saint, which was constructed between 1571 and 1580 in the courtyard of the great mosque. Jahāngīr added the marble facing and screen some years later, but the original red sandstone dome was not clad with marble until 1868. Barren women still make pilgrimages to the shrine, tying pieces of string to its screen and praying for a child. Exquisite mother-of-pearl inlay decorates the underside of the tomb's canopy.

All the roofs of the mosque, except that of Salīm's shrine, are surmounted by regularly spaced Hindu *chattris,* which resemble fringes; apart from these, the overall appearance of the courtyard, with its pointed arches, is Persian, in contrast to the adjacent palace, which is primarily Hindu. Within the prayer hall, however, the corbels and columns are certainly Hindu in style, although the latter are twice as high as Hindu examples. It has been suggested that the builders of the prayer hall came from Gujarāt state, where similar features appear in contemporaneous mosques. A tomb of sandstone, next to Salīm's shrine, accommodates several descendants of the saint, the most important being his grandson, Islam Khan, who governed Bengal for Jahāngīr.

Akbar celebrated his victory over the Gujarātīs by adding a monumental south gateway to the mosque in 1576, the Buland Darwāza (Lofty Gate). This gateway forms an imposing vertical feature: its apparent height is accentuated by the steep flight of steps that leads to it from the path to the village below. In spite of the gateway's rooftop *chattris,* this is the most Islamic architectural feature to be seen at Fatehpur Sīkri. Interestingly, the deeply recessed, pointed arches are fringed, harking back to the style of the Khaljī sultans, who ruled Delhi from 1290 to 1320. In the main arch an inscription records a quotation from Jesus, emphasizing Akbar's interest in all religions, and a reminder that Muslims also regard Christ as a prophet. The Buland Darwaza is completely out of scale with the rest of the mosque, eclipsing the royal entrance from the east, and appears to serve primarily as a statement emphasizing Akbar's great power.

Immediately following completion of the main mosque in 1571, work began on the royal palace. Akbar had fathered another son the previous year, again as prophesied by Salīm, and this may have convinced the emperor that transferring the court from Āgra to Sikrī would prove auspicious. Akbar's conquest of Gujarāt in 1572 is believed to have led to the addition of the prefix Fatehpur (Victory) to the name of his new city. After seven years, the palace, along with its adjacent residential accommodations erected primarily for courtiers, were sufficiently completed for Akbar to transfer his court there from Āgra. Work on the site, however, continued until 1585. Red sandstone, available locally, proved to be

The palace at Fatehpur Sīkri
Photo courtesy of Christopher Turner

an excellent building material for both the palace and the seven-mile-long wall that protected the city on three sides. The northwest side faced a deep, man-made lake, now dried up except after particularly heavy monsoons. In 1584, a messenger of England's Elizabeth I recorded that, like Āgra, Fatehpur Sīkri was much larger than London.

The palace of Fatehpur Sīkri is a unique Mughal development. It was not designed to form a section of a fort, as were the royal palaces of Āgra, Delhi and Johore. Additionally, it is the only major palace that dates entirely from the reign of one Mughal emperor; none of Akbar's successors (except Jahāngīr for a brief period) occupied it. Although most architecture surviving from Akbar's period is distinguished by the abundant use of Hindu features, the basic layout of the palace follows the Islamic preference for a series of separate pavilions rather than great ranges of buildings divided into separate rooms. As was usual in India, the palace is subdivided into a small public area, a *mardana* (male quarters), and a *zenana* (female quarters); the *zenana* occupies two-thirds of the palace's total area.

Pavilions are grouped around courtyards oriented along a north-south axis; owing to the configuration of the ridge on which the city is built, these are staggered diagonally northeast to southwest. No other Islamic leader gave preference to Hindu over Muslim architecture to such an extent as did Akbar at Fatehpur Sīkri, and it is probably no coincidence that, at the time, the emperor was experimenting with other religions, much to the disquiet of the mullahs. Whether Akbar instructed his builders to adopt Hindu styles or simply left them to apply their own local traditions to the architectural detailing remains unknown; regardless, his acceptance of Hindu features must have given much pleasure to the indigenous population and assisted the emperor's policy of unifying his subjects.

Most of what apparently were the original pavilions have survived. However, with few exceptions, no reliable records have survived that tell of their individual functions. In the nineteenth century, each pavilion was given a name for the sake of identification, but these designations are supported by little historical corroboration. One building that has been defined with certainty is the Dīwān-i-Am (Hall of Public Audience). Facing a sunken, cloistered courtyard, it is much smaller than the equivalent pavilions at Āgra and Delhi, possibly because Fatehpur Sīkri never matched these cities in

Sculptural detail of column, Fatehpur Sīkri
Photo courtesy of Air India Library, New York

size, and fewer members of the public therefore brought their pleas in person to the emperor. The central bay, reserved for the emperor, was screened with latticed *jalis,* but the pavilion is otherwise Hindu in style.

Behind the Dīwān-i-Am stands the *mardana* courtyard, the most important in the complex. Dominating it is the most mysterious of Fatehpur Sīkri's buildings, a pavilion usually referred to as the Dīwān-i-Khas (Hall of Private Audience). Completely Hindu in style, it appears from the outside to be a two-story structure, but is, in fact, a lofty hall, with a high central pedestal surmounted by a richly carved corbel fanning out to support a screened area. On this stands the emperor's throne, from which walkways lead directly to the four corners of the hall. All that is known with certainty about this hall is that it was completed in 1575. Some dispute that it could have served as the Dīwān-i-Khas, because it would have been impossible for the emperor to see or be seen by everyone in the hall. In spite of this apparent drawback, Akbar may have preferred the greater intimacy afforded by such an arrangement. Akbar's chronicler, Abu'l Fazl, records the emperor dispensing justice from the "throne of sovereignty in the lofty hall," which certainly describes this building.

During his stay at Fatehpur Sīkri, Akbar, although illiterate, devoted much time to the contemplation of the world's leading religions; he was the least bigoted of the great Mughals and permitted his subjects complete religious freedom. Eventually, Akbar came to the conclusion that the truth could be reached only by merging the basic precepts common to all religions: thus evolved Dīn-i Ilāhī (God's Religion). In 1575, Akbar established what appears to have been a debating society, which met in the Ibadat Khana (House of Worship), where not only religions, but also current scientific and philosophical theories were examined. It has been alleged that what is known as the Dīwān-i-Khas served as the Ibadat Khana, and that building's completion date of 1575 obviously supports this view. A contemporary writer describes the venue for the debating society as being divided into four separate halls, but it is conceivable that screens or curtains were fixed beneath the walkways of the Dīwān-i-Khas, thereby creating four separate areas.

Almost equally mysterious is the adjacent Ankh Michauli (Closed Eyes) Pavilion, so named, it is said, because Akbar played blindman's bluff in its three rooms with his concubines. An alternative, and more believable, suggestion is that the building was a treasury, "closed eyes" referring to the recesses behind stone doors, in which gold and silver were kept. Some support for this theory is given by the carved monsters forming struts in one of the rooms, which may have been intended to frighten would-be burglars.

Lines inscribed in the center of the courtyard appear to represent a pachisi board on which a game similar to ludo was played: it is said that Akbar used slave girls as pieces. At the southeast corner of the courtyard is the Rumi Sultana (Turkish Sultana's House). Akbar had a Turkish wife, but she would certainly not have been quartered here, in the male area of the palace. With its exquisite carving, it seems more likely that Akbar used this single-room building for his own occupation. It is important to bear in mind that in India the residential pavilions of royal palaces appear to have been designed with flexibility in mind, serving as areas in which to eat, sleep, or relax as required, with no furniture installed for specific uses. A feature of the decor of the Rumi Sultana is its sumptuous dado, carved to depict forest scenes; sadly, the heads of the animals have been chiseled out, presumably by a fundamentalist Muslim who objected to the representation of God's work by man.

Dominating the *zenana* sector is the highest building in the palace, the Panch Mahal (Five Palace) so named for its five superimposed stories, which resemble a pagoda. Originally, the Sunahra Makan (Golden House) was decorated internally and externally with gilded murals, hence its name. The building is alternatively referred to as Mariam's House, as it is believed that Jahāngīr's mother, Mariam-uz-Zamani (Mary of the Age) lived here. Mariam, born a Hindu, is said to have become a Christian convert, and part of a mural may depict the wings of an angel in an Annunciation scene. However, several Hindu gods are carved on the brackets, which would appear to contradict this theory. Mariam-uz-Zamani is known to have lived at Fatehpur Sīkri after her husband's death, and this pavilion may well have provided her accommodation.

Adjacent to the private garden of Mariam's House stands the Hawa Mahal (Wind Palace), where, according to Abu'l Fazl, Akbar frequently spent the night with his chosen partner. A covered walkway from this pavilion to the Hathi Pol (Elephant Gate) provided the women with concealed access to their quarters from outside the palace.

The largest courtyard in the *zenana* encloses Jodhā Bāī's Palace, a building that is designed, strangely, with a Hindu layout based on ranges of buildings rather than separate pavilions. Jodhā Bāī was Prince Salīm's first wife, whom he married when he was just sixteen, in 1585. As this was the year in which Akbar deserted Fatehpur Sīkri for good, she could have spent only a short time at the palace; there is little doubt that the buildings of Jodhā Bāī's Palace accommodated several of Akbar's many wives.

One of the earliest of the palace's buildings, the two-story Birbal's House, was completed in 1571. Rāja Birbal, a close friend and adviser of Akbar, was the only leading Hindu to follow the emperor's Dīn-i Ilāhī religion, but, as a male, he could not possibly have lived here, for the building is located within the *zenana*. Both internally and externally, the building is decorated with exceptional geometric carving in an Islamic style that contrasts sharply with much of the complex's Hindu features.

In 1585, Akbar left Fatehpur Sīkri for Lahore, which he used as a base in his campaign against the rebellious Punjabis. Surprisingly, instead of returning to Fatehpur Sīkri after his victory, he remained in Lahore, establishing his court in the city (now part of Pakistan). Almost certainly, Akbar found the cooler, less arid climate of Lahore more congenial than that of Fatehpur Sīkri, and he remained in Lahore until 1599, when he removed the capital again to Āgra. Akbar made a brief return visit to Fatehpur Sīkri in 1601, an event that is recorded by a Persian inscription within the arch of the Buland Darwāza. It is said that the emperor merely passed through the city on his way back to Āgra; he did not even spend the night in Fatehpur Sīkri. Akbar died in Āgra in 1605.

Some have alleged that Fatehpur Sīkri was abandoned by the court because its water supply had dried up, but there is no evidence for this. Jahāngīr's mother certainly continued to live there, and, to escape the Āgra plague of 1619, Jahāngīr resided in the palace of Fatehpur Sīkri, even though much of the city itself had been in ruins for at least ten years. Apart from this brief period, however, Jahāngīr, like his father, preferred to live either in Lahore or, during the summer, in Kashmir, with its much cooler climate. Owing to their enormous wealth, the Mughals often abandoned great projects merely on a whim: Fatehpur Sīkri is probably the most spectacular example of their profligacy.

Today, the great palace of Fatehpur Sīkri is an unoccupied museum, but the adjacent mosque still functions as such. Numerous pilgrims continue to visit its shrines of Shaik Salīm Chishtī. Few people inhabit the now barren site of the former city; the modern settlement lies below the escarpment, where public buses from Āgra terminate.

Further Reading: *The Great Moghuls* by Bamber Gascoigne (London: Cape, and New York: Harper and Row, 1971) is a well-illustrated book dealing with the history of the Mughals from Bābur to ʿĀlamgīr, and served as the basis for a BBC television series of the same name. *Fatehpur Sīkri* by V. J. Flynn (Bombay: n.p., 1975), while difficult to obtain, is the most comprehensive available source on the city. *Mughal India* by G. H. R. Tillotson (London: Viking, and San Francisco: Chronicle Books, 1990), part of the Architectural Guides for Travellers series, provides excellent plans and illustrations of leading Mughal buildings.

—Christopher Turner

Fiji

Location: Fiji consists of more than 300 islands (ninety-one of which are inhabited) and 540 islets situated in the southwest Pacific Ocean, some 1,300 miles north of New Zealand. Viti Levu and Vanua Levu in the northwest sector comprise 87 percent of Fiji's total land area (6,148 square miles). The Koro Sea separates the central Lomaiviti cluster from Lau (fifty-seven eastern islands, which include Lakemba) and the southern island Kandavu and Ono. Fiji also includes Rotuma, a small Polynesian dependency located 300 miles to the north.

Description: Fiji was settled in approximately 1300 B.C. The rise of the Bau state in the early 1800s coincided with the arrival of European traders, whalers, and missionaries; Cakobau, the preeminent Bauan leader, ceded Fiji to Britain in 1874. Rotuma was annexed by the colony in 1881. Between 1879 and 1916 more than 60,000 indentured Indian laborers arrived in the islands. Efforts to reform Fiji's constitution led to independence, which was achieved on October 10, 1970. In 1987 Colonel Sitiveni Rabuka led two military coups against the government, and declared Fiji a republic; civilian rule was restored in 1992.

Site Office: Fiji Visitors' Bureau
Scott Street
GPO Box 92
Suva
Fiji
(679) 302 433

Evidence of the earliest human settlement in Fiji, Lapita pottery with *pointellé* decoration dating to approximately 1300 B.C., comes from Yacuna Islet and Natunuku in northeast Viti Levu. Striking parallels between pottery from this initial Sigatoka phase (1290–1100 B.C.) and Lapita ware found in a continuous distribution from eastern Melanesia to western Polynesia led to the theory, now generally accepted, that Fiji was the staging point for initial voyages to western Polynesia and, together with Tonga and Samoa, the site where these early pioneers developed Polynesian culture. The later Fijian ceramic traditions, Navatu (100 B.C.–A.D. 1100), Vuda (1100–1600), and Ra (1600–present), suggest that after 1000 Fiji may have seen influxes of people from New Caledonia and Vanuatu.

Because Fiji is located at the border between Melanesia and Polynesia, designations that blur the complexity and internal variations of these two cultural areas, scholars have tended to portray it as a genetic and cultural melting pot. Broadly, ethnic Fijians exhibit both Melanesian and Polynesian physical characteristics. The Fijian and Polynesian languages diverged from a common ancestor, proto–Central Pacific, around 1500 B.C. Fijians, Tongans, and Samoans have been in regular contact for centuries; the Fale Fisi (Fijian House) established during the middle of the seventeenth century offers a prominent example: because the children of the highest Tongan chief would be outranked in ceremonial status by the children of his sister, the Tui Tonga Fefine, convention required that she marry a Fijian. Such external influences notwithstanding, the Fijians have developed distinct cultural traditions and identities.

Traditional Fijian society was hierarchical, with ruling chiefs *(turaga)* chosen on the basis of descent and leadership ability. *Turaga* possessed great ritual authority as embodiments of the ancestor god (the *vu*), and they wielded considerable political influence. Various Fijian ceremonies involved human sacrifice, as the ultimate expression of this power. Massive, double-hulled sailing canoes *(drua)* were launched over living persons. "Eat me!" was a commoner's deferential greeting to a chief; *turaga,* in turn, bestowed corpses (for eating) from outside the community to their people in exchange for the first fruits of the season. Nineteenth-century missionaries were astounded by the contrast between these practices and the Fijians' emphasis on decorum and ceremony.

The basic social unit of Fijian society was the *tokatoka* (extended family), whose members made up the *mataqali* (clan). Five or six *mataqali* formed the *yavusa,* a group claiming descent from a founding father, each with its own *tukutuku raraba,* or history. Some *yavusa* also incorporated with unrelated people and amalgamated into states known as *vanua.* On the eve of European contact, seven *vanua* dominated Fiji: Lakemba in the Lau islands; Rewa, Verata, and Bau in southeastern Viti Levu; and Cakaudrove, Macuata, and Bua on Vanua Levu. In the nineteenth century *vanua* consolidated into *matanitu,* or kingdoms, as rival chiefs vied for political supremacy.

Communities forged political and social linkages through *sala vakavanua* (paths of the land), which facilitated the exchange of critical resources such as seafood and fine mats and the contribution of household surpluses for their chiefdom's maintenance. Consequently, settlements were fluid and Fijians frequently were embroiled in wars over territory. An elaborate system of ring-ditch and ridge-top fortifications was developed in approximately A.D. 1200 to protect habitation areas.

Abel Janszoon Tasman became the first European to visit the Fiji Islands, while searching for a sea route from the Indian Ocean to Chile. On February 5, 1643, the Dutch explorer reached Nggele Levu in the archipelago's northeast sector, but foul weather and dangerous shoals prevented him

Government House, Suva, Fiji
Photo courtesy of The Chicago Public Library

from anchoring. After crossing Nanuku Reef, he came upon Taveuni and neighboring islands, then sailed between the eastern Ringgold Islands and eastern Vanua Levu, which he named Prins Willems Eijlanden, before spotting Thikombia and steering northwest for New Guinea.

On July 2, 1774, Captain James Cook charted a southern outlier, Vatoa, which he called Turtle Island. He had met Fijians in Tonga, where he learned of their home's existence, but he had chosen not to make it an object of his explorations, a decision that puzzled fellow officer George Gilbert. Cook may have been the first to call the archipelago "Fiji," a corruption of its indigenous name, "Viti."

William Bligh was the European who discovered the greatest number of Fiji islands, on his celebrated voyage from Tonga to Timor following the mutiny on the *Bounty,* and for a time they were known as Bligh's Islands. He reached Yagasa Levu and Moce on May 4, 1789, and accurately fixed the positions of twenty-three islands, despite constantly having to bail out his launch and, on one occasion, outrun two Fijian canoes that gave chase near Viti Levu. Passing between the latter and Vanua Levu, an area now called Bligh Water, he sighted the northwestern Yasawas.

On his return voyage to Fiji in 1792, Bligh noted the existence of Oneata, Lakemba, Yathata, and Kandavu. His journal, the earliest written account of the Fiji Islands, includes the following description of Ngau: "Nothing could exceed the beauty of the country at this time. It was cultivated far up into the mountains in a regular and pretty manner. Fine plantation walks and shades of cocoanut and other trees near were rendered more picturesque by the dwellings that were among them. . . . Everything seemed to show that [the Ngauans] were an industrial and social people."

More sustained contact between Europeans and Fijians had occurred in August 1791, when a petty officer named Mr. Oliver, in command of the schooner *Resolution,* became separated from Captain Edward Edwards on their search for *Bounty* mutineers. The residents of Matuku hosted Oliver and his weary crew for five weeks; Edwards, in the meantime, discovered Rotuma before reuniting with Oliver in Samarang, Java.

Subsequent surveys contributed more accurate maps and charts of Fiji, advances that accelerated the arrival of sandalwood traders, beachcombers, and whalers. The British and Ratu Tanoa of Bau negotiated a Port Regulation Treaty, which secured the protection and provisioning of foreign ships in return for payment of harbor dues and pilot services, as well as the sailors' pledge to comport themselves properly.

Sandalwood, prized by the Indians and Chinese for burning as incense, commanded staggering prices in the Chinese market and precipitated "rushes" akin to the scramble for gold; a booming trade in the islands peaked during the years 1808–1810. Fiji's sandal trees were depleted by 1816, but the trade in bêche-de-mer (an edible sea slug), pearl-shell, coconut oil, tortoiseshell, and whales' teeth quickened in the late 1830s. The bêche-de-mer trade brought Fijians and Europeans into greater contact, since large numbers of Fijians worked to harvest and dry the slugs. Fijian chiefs bargained shrewdly for the muskets, gunpowder, tobacco, and tools brought by the traders, and amply rewarded beachcombers who taught them how to use and repair the new weapons.

William Cary, sole survivor of the *Oeno,* a whaling ship wrecked off Vatoa Island in April 1825, became a favorite and adopted son of King Toka of Lakemba; he fought in Fijian wars with his childhood companion David Whippy, a whaler who had established his own "kingdom" on Ovalau and worked as an interpreter for ships collecting sandalwood and bêche-de-mer. Swedish castaway Charles Savage helped Naulivou of Bau and his brother Tanoa expand their power base, but Bau, an islet fringing southeastern Viti Levu, achieved preeminence independently of the beachcombers.

Through marriage alliances, diplomacy, and military prowess, Ratu Banuve and his son Ratu Naulivou brought Lomaiviti, northern Lau, and northern and eastern Viti Levu under Bauan control, and gained tributary rights to neighboring Viwa and central and southern Lau. Naulivou's grandson, Ratu Seru Cakobau, became one of Fiji's most powerful chiefs, proclaiming himself *Tui Viti* (King of Fiji). By 1850 Cakobau had subjugated his sometime ally Rewa and prevailed over much of coastal Viti Levu, Vanua Levu, Taveuni, and Lau.

The rise of Bau coincided with the arrival in 1830 of the first missionaries in Fiji: Hape and Tafeta, two Tahitian London Missionary Society teachers; failing to win the acceptance of chief Tui Nayau of Lakemba, they attracted a small following on Oneata. Five years later Wesleyan missionaries David Cargill and William Cross arrived at Lakemba, escorted by an envoy of Taufaahau (who made himself King George Tupou I of Tonga in the 1830s).

Many Lakembans and resident Tongans were eager to learn to read and write, using the Fijian orthography developed by Cargill, but feared arousing their chiefs' hostility by embracing Christianity; the latter, for their part, were loathe to abandon polygamy, warfare, and the capacity to exact tribute, their main avenues to power. The Wesleyans were more successful at Rewa, where they set up a printing press in 1839, until the conflicts with Bau forced them to abandon the mission there. Mission stations at Somosomo, Nadi, and Bua suffered a similar fate. Catholic Marists made small inroads at Bau and Cakaudrove after 1844.

Under the banner of Wesleyan Methodism, Enele Maafu, who had been appointed governor of Fiji's sizable Tongan population by his cousin King George Tupou I of Tonga, spread his influence from Lau to the Yasawa chain, posing a formidable threat to Cakobau. Cakobau's ceaseless attacks and intervention in dynastic disputes incited revolts, but Tupou assured him of Tongan support if he converted to Christianity. On April 28, 1854, the beleaguered Fijian chief declared himself Christian and *Na Lotu nei Ratu Cakobau,* "Cakobau's religion," the religion of Bau. In 1855 Tupou and Maafu combined forces with Cakobau to vanquish Bauan rebels at Kaba in Rewa, and many Fijians subsequently adopted Christianity.

When Fijians looted the home of U.S. commercial agent John B. Williams, which had been set ablaze by his own Fourth of July celebrations, Williams blamed Cakobau and demanded $5,000 compensation; further inquiries raised the claim to $43,531. Unable to pay the debt at the end of the two-year grace period, in 1858 Cakobau asked William T. Pritchard, the first British consul to be appointed to Fiji, to cede the islands to Great Britain; his conditions were that he retain the title and rank of Tui Viti and that Britain compensate the Americans, in exchange for 200,000 acres of land. The British Government refused the offer, discounting Pritchard's appraisal of Fiji's agricultural potential and usefulness as a station for naval forces and steamship lines, and dismissed him.

Eventually, the Melbourne-based Polynesian Company agreed to pay the balance of the American debt in return for 200,000 acres of land and other privileges. This was done in the hope of developing Fiji in the style of the East India Company. Short-lived experiments in centralized government followed, including Maafu's Lau Confederation, which leased land to Europeans, and the Kingdom of Bau, declared in 1867 with Cakobau as its king.

Soaring cotton prices sparked by the American Civil War, coupled with publicity generated by the Polynesian Company's investment, triggered the Great Fiji Rush of the late 1860s and early 1870s. Australians and New Zealanders established cotton plantations in Taveuni, Viti Levu, and Vanua Levu; when cotton prices declined, the settlers switched to copra (coconut meat) processing. To support this boom, approximately 2,000 laborers from Vanuatu, Kiribati, Tuvalu, and the Solomon Islands were recruited between 1864 and 1869. Levuka grew into a thriving commercial center with hotels, businesses, private homes, and a theatre; it was said that ships could navigate the reef passages into Levuka by following the gin bottles floating in the ebb tide.

Planters formed organizations such as the Fiji Planters' Protection Association to settle their frequent disputes with Fijians over land claims; by custom, Fijians sold the use of the land, not the land itself, which was communally owned by the *mataqali* or the *tokatoka.* The murder of Wesleyan missionary Thomas Baker in 1867 by the Navua people of Viti Levu further underscored the fragility of the Bau Kingdom. In 1871, Levuka's *Fiji Times* expressed the settlers' conviction that Europeans would rule the islands, perhaps with a Fijian king who would be "only a puppet, the strings of which [would be] pulled by a white man."

Indeed, when the European-dominated Cakobau Government (1871–74) was formed, with Cakobau as its nominal head and Maafu his viceroy, it strove mainly to preserve European interests. In 1873 Cakobau entreated his chief secretary, John B. Thurston, to ask the British government if it would consider an offer of cession if Fiji made such a proposal. The seeming impossibility of a workable Fijian government caused commissioners E. L. Layard and J. G. Goodenough to press for annexation; this time, however, Cakobau withdrew the offer of cession. Several months later, fearing that Fiji would become "like a piece of drift-wood on the sea, and be picked up by the first passer-by," Cakobau, along with Maafu and eleven other ruling chiefs, signed the unconditional Deed of Cession, which became official on October 10, 1874. Sir Hercules Robinson, the former governor of New South Wales, established a provisional administration, which moved from its cramped quarters in Levuka to Suva, Viti Levu, in 1882. The new government now also controlled the Polynesian island of Rotuma; rent by wars between Wesleyan and Marist factions, it had been annexed to the Crown Colony of Fiji in 1881.

Sir Arthur Hamilton Gordon's tenure as Fiji's first governor began inauspiciously. Cakobau and his younger sons returned from a visit to Sydney carrying measles, and the ensuing epidemic killed an estimated one-quarter of the Fijian population. In 1875 and 1876 Gordon needed Fijian aid in suppressing the Kai Colo, the fiercely independent mountaineers of Viti Levu. Gordon was, however, an experienced administrator who established the foundations of modern Fiji. With Thurston's assistance, Gordon hammered out a system of "indirect rule" that aimed not merely to adapt indigenous customs for expedience but to "seize the spirit in which native institutions had been framed, and develop to the utmost extent the capacities of the people for the management of their own affairs." The sale of Fijian land was forbidden, and only purchases made legally by Europeans before Cession were recognized.

To revitalize Fiji's economy, which was depressed by the boost in U.S. cotton production following the Civil War, Gordon approved the introduction of indentured Indian workers, whom he had observed in Trinidad and Mauritius. He strongly opposed the idea of Fijians working for Europeans in their own country, and in 1877 he became the western Pacific high commissioner responsible for policing the conduct of British subjects and British vessels in nearby unannexed islands. The 1872 Pacific Islanders Protection Act imposed greater restrictions on the labor traffic than previous legislation, and an 1883 ordinance limited Fijian labor contracts.

The 60,553 Indians who arrived in Fiji between 1879 and 1916 largely contributed to the growth of the colony's sugar industry. The majority were young men of the "middle agricultural castes" from Bihār, Uttar Pradesh, and Madras. Few families emigrated; the government of India had specified a proportion of 40 women to 100 men for emigration to Fiji, but this number proved difficult to reach. The laborers were free to return home at Fiji's expense after working a second five-year contract, but more than half decided to remain in the colony. For many, however, life "in the lines" was hellish; harsh living and working conditions contributed to high infant mortality rates and the breakdown of caste distinctions, among other problems.

In 1904 six European members were elected to the Legislative Council, but this failed to mollify disgruntled European settlers, who pressed unsuccessfully for federation with New Zealand. The council included two Fijians nominated by the Council of Chiefs, but no Indian representatives. Inspired by the upsurge of Indian nationalism and the example set by Mohandas Karamchand Gandhi (also known as Mahatma Gandhi), Indians led by attorney Manilal Maganlal Doctor and his Indian Imperial Association of Fiji petitioned the government for reforms and organized strikes of Indian workers. This led to the end of the indenture system, which was abolished on January 1, 1920.

The somewhat higher standing enjoyed by ethnic Fijians did not, however, extend to their rank outside Fiji. Britain rejected those who wished to fight during World War I and limited their service to cargo and boat handling. In this atmosphere, many Fijians supported Apolosi R. Nawai, whose underground Viti Company aimed to secure economic self-sufficiency for Fijians. The participation of Europeans living in Fiji swelled the number of "Fijians" who served during World War I to 788. In World War II, however, many ethnic Fijians were decorated for their exploits in Guadalcanal and Malaya. So skilled were they in jungle fighting, that the phrase "not yet arrived" was deemed more appropriate for them than "missing in action." Of the 11,000 Fijians who served during World War II, 264 were Indians; their awakening political consciousness at home and abroad led the British and ethnic Fijians alike to accuse them of disloyalty to the British Crown.

In the 1940s and 1950s advances in education, mass communication, transportation, and efforts to promote individual enterprise were counterbalanced by a reversion to the protective stance that was characterized by the Gordon administration. Under the direction of Ratu Sir Lala Sukuna, an Oxford-educated Speaker of the Legislative Council, the Great Council of Chiefs and Fijian Affairs Board reaffirmed conservative policies that perpetuated Fijians' ties to their communal villages. The Native Land Trust Board, created in 1940, reiterated the sovereignty of Fijian lands.

By the mid-1940s the Indian population exceeded that of the ethnic Fijians (130,000 versus 119,000 in 1946). Many Indians were subtenants of the Colonial Sugar Refining Company, which had dominated Fiji's sugar industry. These Indo-Fijians, who had been born in Fiji, were making great strides in business, agriculture, and education and demanding equal participation in the colony's political and economic life. In 1963 women and ethnic Fijians gained the right to vote for their representatives, and the Legislative Council was enlarged to include four ethnic Fijians, four Indians, and four Europeans among its elected Unofficial Members. Two years later their numbers were increased to fourteen, twelve, and ten, respectively, the latter including individuals from other ethnic groups.

Led by Ratu Sir Kamisese Mara, the Alliance Party (a coalition of Sukuna's Fijian Association; the General Electors' Association representing Europeans, part-Fijians, and Chinese; and the Fiji Indian Alliance) shepherded Fiji to independence. On October 10, 1970, Fiji became an independent dominion within the British Commonwealth. Ratu Sir George Cakobau, great-grandson of Ratu Seru Cakobau, was designated the nation's first Fijian governor general, and Ratu Mara was elected its prime minister.

In 1986 the Indian-dominated National Federation Party united with the Fiji Labor Party headed by Dr. Timoci Bavadra to defeat the Alliance Party and capture key cabinet posts, including Labor and Immigration, Fijian Affairs, and Land. The Coalition was committed to addressing the concerns of all races, but it confronted protests and firebombings by the pro–ethnic Fijian Taukei Movement.

On May 14, 1987, Colonel Sitiveni Rabuka entered the House of Representatives with ten armed guards and calmly announced a military takeover; Coalition members were removed at gunpoint to the military headquarters. Governor General Ratu Sir Penaia Ganilau declared a state of emergency. Rumors of American involvement in the coup circulated because Fiji had been receiving substantial funding from the United States since it lifted the ban on visits by U.S. nuclear warships, and an American amphibious assault ship was seen cruising the area; both Rabuka and U.S. officials adamantly denied this allegation. When the Coalition, Taukei, and the Great Council of Chiefs failed to reach a compromise on constitutional reform, Rabuka launched a second coup, on September 26, 1987, and declared Fiji a republic.

Rabuka installed Ratu Ganilau as president and Ratu Mara as prime minister. Fiji's new constitution, announced officially on July 25, 1990, assures ethnic Fijians a majority of seats in the Senate and House of Representatives and appointment to the posts of president, prime minister, and army chief. The Great Council of Chiefs formed *Soqosoqo ni Vakavulewa ni Taukei* (SVT), the Fijian Political Party, amid continued strikes by the trade unions, and elected Rabuka its president. Rabuka's concessions to the trade unions and pledge to reexamine the constitution and land leases won him the support of the Fiji Labour Party and election as prime minister in 1992.

Today, the vast majority of Fiji's population is divided nearly evenly between ethnic Fijians and Indians. Fijians gained the majority by a narrow margin when many Indians fled the islands in 1987. Intermarriage between Indians and indigenous Fijians still is rare. Small pockets of Chinese and Pacific Islanders (mainly from Rotuma, Banaba, Tuvalu, Kiribati, Tonga, and the Solomon Islands) also live in the archipelago. Although full- and part-Europeans comprise only 2.6 percent of the population, English is the country's official language. The Bauan dialect transcribed by Cargill and Cross is the predominant form of spoken and written Fijian, and Indians mostly speak Hindi. The majority of ethnic Fijians are Methodist, and the Indians are Hindu and Muslim.

Further Reading: *Fiji: A Short History* by Deryck Scarr (Sydney and London: Allen and Unwin, and Laie, Hawaii: Institute for Polynesian Studies, 1984) spans the period from initial settlement to 1982. Brij V. Lal's insightful study, *Broken Waves: A History of the Fiji Islands in the Twentieth Century* (Honolulu: University of Hawaii Press, 1992), details more recent events. Excellent sources covering Fiji's colonial history include *Adventurous Spirits: Australian Migrant Society in Pre-Cession Fiji* by John Young (St. Lucia, Queensland: University of Queensland Press, 1984); J. D. Legge's *Britain in Fiji, 1858–1880* (London: Macmillan, and New York: St. Martin's Press, 1958); and *Fiji's Indian Migrants: A History to the End of Indenture in 1920* by K. L. Gillion (Melbourne, London, Wellington, and New York: Oxford University Press, 1962).

—Maria Chiara

Fujinomiya (Shizuoka, Japan)

Location: On Honshū (the main island of Japan), ninety-one miles west of Tōkyō, seven miles northwest of the city of Fuji, and some nine miles southwest of Mount Fuji; now inside the Fuji-Hakone-Izu National Park.

Description: The site of the main shrine associated with Mount Fuji and the traditional starting point for pilgrimages up the sacred mountain.

Contact: Tourist Information Office
JR Atami StationView Plaza
11-1 Tawara-Honmachi
Atami, Shizuoka 413
Japan
(0557) 81 6002

The city of Fujinomiya (Shrine of Fuji) has grown up around the Sengen Jinja (Sengen Shrine), the most important of several Sengen shrines dedicated to the goddess Konohana Sakuyahime. Her name means "princess of the flowers blossoming on the tree," and she personifies Mount Fuji, the highest mountain in Japan, which stands some nine miles northeast of the city and which has long been revered by worshipers from across the country. Fujinomiya has been the starting point for their pilgrimages to its peaks for more than 1,000 years. The Sengen cult is part of Shintō, the indigenous religion of Japan.

The mountain appears to have originated in extensive volcanic activity some 600,000 years ago, but probably did not acquire a separate and distinctive shape until 300,000 years ago. Since then, there have been three volcanoes in the vicinity, known to geologists as Komitake, Ko Fuji (Old Fuji), and Shin Fuji (New Fuji). The last of these, which became active 10,000 years ago and gradually obliterated the earlier two with layers of lava and rock, rises dramatically out of the surrounding countryside and is visible, like a traditional Japanese fan held upside-down and half-opened, from the sea and from most places on the nearby Kanto Plain. Mount Fuji has a diameter of nearly twenty-five miles at the base, and is surrounded by lava fields covered with alpine vegetation; the tree cover on the lower slopes gives way to bare red and gray lava at approximately 8,000 to 9,000 feet above sea level. At the top there is a crater, 260 feet deep and around 1,800 feet in diameter, surrounded by eight peaks, of which the tallest, Kengamme, stands 12,388 feet above sea level. Although the mountain is isolated, in geological terms it forms part of the Fuji Volcanic Zone, a chain stretching from the Mariana Islands far in the Pacific, through the Izu Islands in Tōkyō Bay and the Izu Peninsula to their north, and into the Nagano and Niigata prefectures. Because the volcanic materials that cover the mountain's slopes and the land around it are extremely porous, there is very little surface water on or around Fuji, except in the form of the permanent snow on its upper slopes. The only bodies of water are Lakes Yamanaka, Kawaguchi, Sai, Shōji, and Motosu, the so-called Fuji Five Lakes (Fuji Goko), which lie on the north side of the mountain, and the streams and paddies of Gotemba, a town to the east of the mountain.

Gotemba was the first settlement to be founded in the area, at least 2,000 years ago. At that time the inhabitants of the area were not Japanese. The word "Fuji" is probably derived from "Fuchi," the goddess of fire and the hearth in the religion of the Ainu people, who resisted the advance of the Japanese from Kyūshū and western Honshū for centuries. The Ainu hunted and fished over large areas of eastern Honshū as late as the ninth century A.D., before being driven back into Hokkaido, the northern island where their descendants live today. It seems likely that they, too, worshiped the mountain, although there is no archaeological or documentary evidence that they did so (they had no writing system of their own). According to Japanese tradition (which may ultimately derive from the Ainu), Fuji appeared not 300,000 years ago but at some time during the summer of the year 286 B.C. It is difficult to imagine what real event lies behind this tradition, although it perhaps points to a major eruption in that year or even, given the unreliability of dates derived from ancient Japanese chronicles, a few centuries later. As for the shrine at what is now Fujinomiya, the assertion that it was founded in 806 is probably reliable, although it appears to have been preceded, by some 100 years, by the Murayama Sengen Shrine; only two small buildings belonging to this shrine, located in a village near Fujinomiya, remain today. By the time of this shrine's original construction, the Ainu had been conquered and dispersed northward by the incoming Japanese.

Seven miles north of Fujinomiya is the Shiraito no taki, "The Waterfall of White Threads," which is 85 feet high and 427 feet wide. This site is associated with the legend of the Soga brothers, Sukenari and Tokimune, who spent eighteen years planning vengeance on Kudō Suketsune, the man who had murdered their father. They killed Kudō during a hunting trip near the falls in 1193. In the same year Minamoto Yoritomo, the first of the *shōguns* (military commanders) who exercised power in the name of the emperors for almost 700 years, visited the shrine from his headquarters at Kamakura. He is said to have inaugurated the *yabusame* mounted archery contests, which are still held in Fujinomiya every May. A cherry tree that stands near the small shrine dedicated to the Soga brothers in the nearby village of Karijuku is supposed to be the very same tree to which Yoritomo tied his horse during this visit.

View of Mount Fuji
Photo courtesy of Japan National Tourist Organization

From an early date, pilgrimages to Fujinomiya were organized by local associations, mostly from the Kanto Plain; these associations, devoted to the worship of Mount Fuji, combined elements of Shintō with Buddhism, the official religion of Japan (it was imported from China and Korea in the sixth century). In particular, association members equated the deity Konohana Sakuyahime with Miroku (Maitreya in Sanskrit), the manifestation of the Buddha who is to be incarnated in the distant future and who is conventionally represented as a young man meditating. Over the centuries, the Fujinomiya shrine acquired a network of more than 1,300 branch shrines at locations throughout central Honshū, including one at the summit of the mountain itself. As a result, the Fujinomiya shrine is also known as Fujisan Hongu, the main shrine of Mount Fuji. Fujinomiya also has long been associated with the Nichiren-shū sect, founded by the priest Nichiren to promote his own version of Buddhism, characterized by the supremacy of the ancient text known as the *Myōhō Renge Kyō* (Lotus Sutra) and by Nichiren's claim to be an incarnation of the Bodhisattva Jogyo. Nichiren eventually gained more followers because of his claims to have predicted, or even caused, the storms that repelled the attempted invasion of Japan by the Mongols in 1274 and 1281 (the basis of the myth of the *kamikaze,* the "divine wind" that would protect Japan from its enemies). Taiseki-ji, one of the prominent temples of this sect, was established some five miles north of Fujinomiya by Nikkan, one of Nichiren's disciples, early in the fourteenth century.

However, the Fuji cult remained the dominant religious group in and around the city, which was becoming one of the most popular destinations for pilgrims in Japan. Its importance was officially recognized in 1604, when the present buildings of the Fujinomiya Sengen Shrine, including its enormous vermilion-painted wooden *torii* (gateway) and its unusual two-storied *honden* (worship hall), were constructed on the orders of Tokugawa Ieyasu, who had become *shōgun* the year before. His capital city was Edo (now Tōkyō), on the Kanto Plain, only ninety-one miles from Fujinomiya, and he may have had sincere religious motives for becoming involved in supporting the shrine. But since he was, above all else, a shrewd and very effective political operator, he was probably responding to the popularity of Hasegawa Kakugyō (who is said to have lived, somewhat implausibly, from 1541 to 1646), the most famous of the Fujinomiya shrine's many *oshi,* the wandering priests whose missionary activities spread the worship of the sacred mountain around the country.

As a result of the efforts of Hasegawa and his colleagues, the pilgrimage to the top of Fuji-san (Mount Fuji) became a highly organized event, managed by the increasingly numerous Fujikō, as the local associations of worshipers became known under the strict system that Tokugawa Ieyasu's grandson Iemitsu introduced for registering religious organizations. The final section of the pilgrimage began with a long walk from Fujinomiya to the base of the mountain and continued by way of ten recognized stages, each provided with resting points and lesser shrines, to the crater. Like many other sacred Shintō places, the holiest area, above the eighth of these stages, was forbidden to women. This ban probably may be explained by the hypothesis that the religion's taboos against anything connected with death, disease, or decay extended to menstrual blood. Even today only prepubescent girls are permitted to take part in ritual dances at most Shintō shrines.

The most recent eruption of Fuji-san occurred in 1707 and spewed ash over a radius of at least sixty miles, causing panic in Edo and altering the shape of Hōeizan, the cone on its southeastern slope. (The mountain is still regarded as an active volcano although little more than smoke has issued from it since then.) This dramatic event combined with declining economic and social conditions to give renewed vigor to the Fujikō movement, which was now explicitly centered on the worship of Miroku and on the expectation of his imminent arrival on Earth to preside over an era of peace and justice. Fujikō followers, in Fujinomiya and elsewhere, frequently took part in the extraordinary movement of the late eighteenth and early nineteenth centuries, known as *eejanaika* (isn't it good?), in which enormous crowds danced for days on end, attacked the homes of the rich and powerful, and proclaimed the Age of Miroku. As a result, the Tokugawa regime banned the Fujikō altogether in 1849.

While the traditional mass pilgrimages died out, at least for the moment, Fuji-san continued to be one of the most visited sites in Japan, usually by way of Fujinomiya, a route that was still carefully maintained. The opening of Japanese relations with Europe and the United States brought non-Japanese visitors for the first time. The first of these is believed to have been Sir Rutherford Alcock, the British ambassador, in 1860; in October 1867, Fanny Parkes, the wife of Alcock's successor Sir Harry Parkes, accompanied her husband on a climb to the summit and thus became the first woman, Japanese or other, ever to pass beyond the eighth stage onto the sacred upper slopes. She avoided causing a scandal among traditionalists (knowingly or not) in part by being non-Japanese and by ascending in the autumn, after the close of the conventional pilgrimage season.

Soon afterward, the Tokugawa *shōgunate*, which initially had fostered the Fuji cult and then had tried to stamp it out, was overthrown. The new government intervened in the religious sphere in order to remove the ban on Christianity, disestablish Buddhism, and raise the status of Shintō in general and the cult of the imperial family in particular. As a result of the upheavals that the regime initiated, the Sengen Shrine and its branches were purged of all images and practices associated with Buddhism. This now was derided as an alien religion, and the remaining Fujikō associations were reorganized as sects of Shintō, notably the Maruyama-kyō, Fusō-kyō, and Jikkō-kyō. These still exist, although they are significantly smaller and less well known in contemporary Japan, which is increasingly secularized.

Since 1930 Taiseki-ji, the Nichiren-shū sect's temple near Fujinomiya, has been the religious center for members of the Sōka Gakkai, a lay organization of Nichiren followers, which paid for the complete rebuilding of the temple, in reinforced concrete, in 1958. Today, Nichiren's ideas still play a part in Japanese society, notably through the Sōka Gakkai, which has acquired numerous followers in Europe and the Americas, and through the Kōmeitō, a political party with several members in the Japanese Diet, which started as an offshoot of the religious organization.

In modern times, Fujinomiya's importance has dwindled somewhat in comparison to other settlements in the region. Both the Fuji Five Lakes area and Hakone, the center of a volcanic area of hot spring resorts to the southeast of Mount Fuji, began to be developed as resort areas during the 1930s. The towns and villages of the Izu Peninsula and the coastal resort of Shimoda also have attracted increasing development, especially after the designation of the Fuji-Hakone-Izu National Park, which covers parts of Yamanashi, Kanagawa, and Shizuoka prefectures as well as the Izu Islands in Tōkyō Bay. Furthermore, there are now five alternative routes to the summit, from Fuji-Yoshida, Gotemba, Lake Kawaguchi, Lake Shōji, and Subashiri. The route from Fuji-Yoshida is probably the most used today because that city is the closest of the six to Tōkyō. The Fujinomiya path, however, remains the only one leading to the mountain from the southern, coastal side. The main industry of Fujinomiya, which has a population of over 100,000, is the production and processing of paper and pulp rather than the servicing of the Sengen Shrine and the pilgrims and tourists passing on their way to Mount Fuji. Even so, the shrine's annual festival on July 1, marking the start of the two-month official climbing season, is a major event in the city's calendar, and the shrine itself remains as a monument to what was once among the most popular religious movements in Japan.

Further Reading: Tsuya Hiromichi's book *Geology of Volcano Mount Fuji* (Tōkyō: Geological Survey of Japan, 1968) is the standard work on the origins and nature of the mountain itself. Standard histories such as Conrad Totman's *Early Modern Japan* (Berkeley, Los Angeles, and London: University of California Press, 1993) provide the wider context for understanding the development and suppression of the Fujikō movement.

—Patrick Heenan

Galle (Sri Lanka)

Location: On the southwestern coast of Sri Lanka, approximately sixty-five miles southeast of Colombo.

Description: An important trading port from the thirteenth century (possibly much earlier) until the nineteenth century, Galle is the site of a fort occupied by three successive colonial powers: the Portuguese, the Dutch, and the British.

Contact: Ceylon Tourist Board
78 Steuart Place
P. O. Box 1504
Colombo 3
Sri Lanka
(43) 7059 or (43) 7060

Few records exist that concern the site of the Sri Lankan port of Galle prior to A.D. 1267. Ancient Greek and Latin geographers might have known the place as the Cape of Birds; Galle may also have been the Odoka referred to by Ptolemy. Some historians have speculated that Galle was the biblical city of Tarshish, source of gold, silver and other precious commodities for Solomon and Jehosaphat. It certainly became an important commercial crossroads where Arab merchants traded with their Malay and Chinese counterparts more than 2,000 years ago. The famous Moroccan traveler Ibn Baṭṭūṭah visited Sri Lanka and Galle (which he called Qali) in 1342; he met there other Muslims who reported that Galle had been a port since ancient times.

Sinhalese fleeing Tamil armies in the north settled Galle and the surrounding lowlands during the twelfth and thirteenth centuries. Since the ecology of the region would not support the large annual rice crop on which the Sinhalese economy had been based in the north, they increased foreign trade to compensate. Merchants moved onto the peninsula that protects Galle's excellent natural harbor, and from there they exported cinnamon, areca nuts, elephants, and gems. The traders imported mostly cloth and dry fish.

When the first Europeans arrived in Sri Lanka in the early sixteenth century, Galle lay in the kingdom of Kotte, which encompassed the southwestern lowlands. Kotte contended with two rival states on the island then: the Tamil stronghold Jaffna in the far north, and the newly independent Sinhalese province of Kandy, which extended from the central highlands to portions of the southeastern coast. Don Lourenço de Almeida of Portugal landed in Galle in 1505 after he was blown off course near southern India. He took an immediate interest in Sri Lankan cinnamon, a valuable commodity in the European market. In turn, Kotte's King Vijayabāhu eagerly sought an alliance with the Portuguese to gain a military advantage over Jaffna and Kandy.

De Almeida and Vijayabāhu signed a treaty that rendered Kotte a client state of Portugal. Throughout the next century, the Portuguese gained influence over all the island's littorals, leaving only Kandy truly independent. Galle changed little during that period, although the Portuguese firmly controlled its economy. Surprisingly, the Portuguese even continued to recognize Galle as a sanctuary for criminals, in accordance with Sinhalese custom. In general, Portuguese administrators interfered relatively little in native affairs once the local rulers had submitted to the Europeans. Instead, the Portuguese stationed themselves in their fort at Colombo, using their unrivaled naval force to control Sri Lanka's maritime trade. The Portuguese named the city Galle and made the cock its symbol, having assumed that the Sinhalese *galla,* which means rock—an allusion to the city's rocky bay—derived from the Latin *gallus,* which means rooster.

The Portuguese transformed Galle into a military base during the seventeenth century to protect the valuable cinnamon harvest from other Europeans. The Dutch, in particular, had developed into a redoubtable sea power, and the Portuguese built several forts as defense against them. General Constantino de Sa de Noronha oversaw construction of the fort at Galle, completed in 1625. Massive bulwarks, modified several times throughout the years, have dominated Galle's landscape ever since.

The Portuguese took advantage of Galle's unique geography for defensive purposes. The peninsula that juts southward into the sea on the western side of the bay spirals modestly back toward land, forming a small inner harbor well protected both from storms and from enemy ships. The Portuguese erected a formidable rampart along the isthmus to protect against attack by land and relied mostly on the rough seas and rocky shores to prevent invasions from the south. Three large bastions—São Jago, Santo Antonio, and Conceição—divided the bulwark evenly, and water towers at its ends were designed to wash invading troops into a moat. The Portuguese built a battery large enough to house twenty guns on the rocky point of the peninsula; another battery, on the far side of the harbor, could attack ships sailing into the inner harbor.

The city of Galle was located on the peninsula itself, ensconced within its ring of defenses. In the short time the Portuguese governed there, they erected a factory, a monastery, a cathedral, police barracks, and several smaller structures. The building of the European town displaced the Sinhalese, who subsequently settled the perimeter of the greater harbor beyond the peninsula.

The Kandyans—isolated in the mountains and gradually impoverished by Portuguese policy—struck a military alliance with the Dutch in 1638. In exchange for expelling the

One of the fortifications at the harbor in Galle
Photo courtesy of Embassy of the Democratic Socialist Republic of Sri Lanka, Washington, D.C.

Portuguese, King Rājasinha II (ruled 1635–87) signed a treaty stating that Dutch forces would be "recouped in cinnamon, pepper, cardamom, indigo, wax, rice and other valuable products." In addition, the Kandyans were obligated to build warehouses and a powder magazine for Dutch use, to sell one elephant to the Dutch for each one sold to a third party, and to "resist to the utmost" any "enemies of the Dutch" who might try to gain power in Sri Lanka.

The Dutch wrested control of Trincomalee and Batticaloa from the Portuguese the following year and handed over these port cities to the Kandyans. However, ambiguous language in the treaty led to disagreement about the actual amount that the Kandyans had agreed to pay according to the terms of the treaty; in lieu of payments not received, the Dutch retained Negombo when they defeated the Portuguese there in 1639. This retaliation severely strained the Kandyan-Dutch alliance, yet Rājasinha continued to collaborate with the Dutch on plans for further attacks on the Portuguese.

The war for control of Sri Lanka highlighted Galle's strategic value. The city's well-protected harbor could berth a fleet large enough to attack Colombo, Jaffna, or Trincomalee. Command of the Dutch offensive against Galle fell to Admiral Willem Coster. He divided his troops into three task forces, which successively attacked the São Jago Bastion on March 12, 1640. After a six-week siege, the Dutch finally fought their way into the town, where they continued to meet fierce resistance. They defeated the Portuguese only after several days of hand-to-hand combat that left at least 100 troops from each colonial army dead. Sinhalese laborers had to spend three days removing corpses from the streets and burying them in mass graves.

Rājasinha angered the Dutch by having his troops descend on Galle only after the Portuguese had been defeated. Not surprisingly, the Dutch accused the Kandyans of hiding until all danger had passed before arriving to take away their half of the booty as prescribed by the treaty of 1638. Incensed, Coster traveled to Kandy to extract the high payments that the Dutch continued to demand of the kingdom. The Dutch deliberately may have asked for an impossibly large sum to justify remaining in Sri Lanka; they certainly stood to benefit economically by doing so. In any case, Coster's apparently rude behavior offended the Kandyan nobility. Unidentified bandits cut his throat on his return trip, almost certainly as punishment for his indiscretion, although Rājasinha denied any involvement.

The Dutch, even more distrustful of Rājasinha after Coster's murder, retained Galle under their immediate rule rather than entrust it to the Kandyans as originally agreed. Galle served as the Dutch capital of Sri Lanka until the Dutch conquered Colombo in 1656; it remained an important economic and military post thereafter.

The battle for Galle depleted the Dutch forces, and they could not retain Negombo when the Portuguese counterattacked. Soon after, the Dutch lost control of the countryside around Galle, too. The Kandyans offered their old allies little assistance, leaving the Dutch temporarily reduced to survival rations. Dutch reinforcements arrived in 1641, but they were not enough to manage any attacks on Portuguese-held cities. When a cease-fire signed three years earlier in Europe took effect in Asian waters in 1643, the Dutch were confined to the rocky peninsula of Galle, just a stone's throw from some of the island's finest cinnamon acreage, but were denied rights to any of the precious spice. The Dutch remained sequestered there until war resumed in 1652, whereupon they took Sri Lanka relatively quickly. They captured Colombo in 1656 and ousted the last of the Portuguese from the island with the conquest of Jaffna in 1658.

The Dutch moved their capital to Colombo as soon as they captured it, but they retained and rebuilt the fort and town of Galle. They followed the Portuguese design but strengthened the defenses on the peninsula. The Dutch began by replacing the main bulwark—which the Portuguese had constructed from earth reinforced with tree trunks—with a larger wall of lime-bound, solid stone. They enlarged the three bastions by 1663, later renaming them Sun, Moon, and Star, successively from east to west. After 1710 the Dutch doubled the size of the Moon bastion and added four new embrasures to it. Still the biggest gun battery in Sri Lanka, this large structure dominates the local landscape.

The Dutch divided Sri Lanka into three administrative centers, of which Galle was one, in which a single *commandeur* had authority over both soldiers and civilians. The *commandeur* at Galle governed the Sinhalese population according to a native scheme, although Hollanders held the positions of greatest authority. Most important, he installed a *mudaliyar* to control the local militia and a *korala* in charge of the rest of the population. The Dutch rewarded Sinhalese headmen in subservient administrative positions with land grants.

Governor Petrus Vuyst oversaw renovation of the fort during his tenure from 1726 until 1729. By the time he finished, the main rampart rose to a considerably greater height than that of most fortresses in the era of black-powder wars, protecting houses, hospital, church, administrative offices, and other buildings of the city from cannon fire. To compensate for its vulnerable height, the Dutch built the northern wall to an extraordinary depth. The rampart itself measures 100 feet thick at the base, and the Sun and Star bastions each 150 feet thick. The Moon bastion's incredible depth of 400 feet made it nearly impossible to breach. By the end of Vuyst's administration, the Dutch also had built a substantial wall around the perimeter of the entire peninsula, from the Star bastion to the battery on the northeastern spit; most of these Dutch fortifications remain standing.

Despite the monumental visibility of the fortifications, one of the most impressive projects the Dutch undertook was a waterborne-sewage system within the fort. Twice each day the incoming tide filled a network of brick-lined sewers six to ten feet below sea level, and waste was carried to sea on the outgoing current. The scheme of the drains subsequently was forgotten, only to be rediscovered in 1922, when an outbreak of bubonic plague required that rats in the sewers be exterminated. Exemplary of Dutch engineering prowess, the reactivated system still functions as planned.

In 1795 the Dutch ruler fled to England when Francophiles within his government arranged for French troops to occupy Holland. The British, eager to acquire Sri Lanka to gain strategic advantage over the French in the Indian Ocean, pressured the Dutch leader, Count de Meuron, to surrender the colony. On February 16, 1796, the Dutch ceded ownership of Galle to the British in a treaty drafted in Colombo. The Hollander reluctantly sent papers to his officers in Sri Lanka ordering them to capitulate, but they refused to comply.

In response to the Dutch insubordination, the British East India Company sent a sizable armed force from Madras, which easily captured Jaffna and Colombo. Officer Lachlan Macquarie then marched from Colombo to Galle with 30 artillery men and 700 Madras sepoys. When they arrived on February 23, Commandeur Fretsz, having decided against staging a futile resistance, tearfully handed over keys to the various gates in the garrison. The British troops marched in with "drums beating" and "colours flying" to the humble salutes of the Dutch.

Compared to their total rebuilding of Colombo, the British made only modest changes to the fort at Galle during their long colonial tenure. They drained the moat in front of the northern rampart and drove a new entrance between the Sun and Moon bastions. They built a road along the eastern wall and removed many of the parapets on the seaside bulwark. In 1869 the British honored Queen Victoria with a clock tower in a style conspicuously incongruous with the surrounding Dutch architecture.

Galle remained an important port city through the mid–nineteenth century. By the 1830s it featured several agency houses successfully trading in Europe. However, British policies that favored colonies elsewhere in Asia restricted local merchants' profits; Galle's economy suffered further when the Suez Canal opened in 1869. The British built a breakwater in Colombo to improve the harbor and thereby accommodate increased traffic in the Indian Ocean. Merchants in Galle continued to import cotton and export tea, but by 1890 shippers had transferred most commercial traffic to Colombo.

The old, fortified city on the peninsula hardly has changed since the late eighteenth century. The expanded commercial port, on the other hand, now extends beyond the isthmus in two directions: to the west lies the Kaluwalla District, and to the east the market and the Kerkhof (the old Dutch cemetery). The modern Sri Lankan government has developed the shores of the greater harbor with the intention of transforming Galle into a fishing port, but those changes have not affected the fort or those buildings within its walls.

Further Reading: Two books contain both a brief history of Galle and a good description of the fort: *Links between Sri Lanka and the Netherlands: A Book of Dutch Ceylon* by R. L. Brohier (Colombo: Netherlands Alumni Association of Sri Lanka, 1978) and *The Dutch Forts of Sri Lanka: The Military Monuments of Ceylon* by W. A. Nelson (Edinburgh: Canongate, 1984). *Nagel's Encyclopedia-Guide: Ceylon* (Geneva: Nagel, 1980) offers a short but informative history of Galle. *A Short History of Ceylon* by Humphrey W. Codrington (London: Macmillan, 1926; reprint, Freeport, New York: Books for Libraries, 1970) offers a more detailed political history.

—Christopher A. Hoyt

Gayā (Bihār, India)

Location: On the Phalgu River in the state of Bihār, approximately 60 miles south of Patna and 250 miles northwest of Calcutta.

Description: A major Hindu pilgrimage center, the city of Gayā is said to have been blessed by Vishnu, to whom the Vishnupad Temple is dedicated.

Contact: Bihār State Tourism Development Corporation
Information Centre
Fraser Road
Patna, Bihār 800001
India
225320

Gayā's historic significance derives entirely from its role as one of the most important Hindu shrines in India. Gayā and the surrounding area have come under a succession of rulers, but the city has not been the site of major political or military events. It is notable primarily because devout Hindus believe that Vishnu, one of the religion's trinity of deities—the others being Brahma and Siva—endowed the city with the power to cleanse Hindus of their earthly sins. Therefore, many pilgrims come to Gayā to hold funeral ceremonies and/or offer prayers for their dead loved ones. In particular, funeral rites held under the sacred banyan tree within the grounds of Gayā's Vishnupad Temple are believed to ensure the deceased's entry into heaven.

The legend from which the city derives its name and religious significance concerns a once-pagan monster named Gayā, who had spent many years atoning for his sins and as a result became holy. Thereafter, all who came in contact with him would ascend to heaven. As Gayā moved about at will, the population of the universe, including hell, began to diminish. Yama, the ruler of hell, and other minor deities asked the major gods to rectify this situation. Vishnu therefore asked Gayā to lie down so that a sacrifice could be performed upon his body. While Gayā was prone, Yama placed a large stone on him to keep him down. The monster would not stay still, however, and Vishnu struck him with a mace. Surprised, Gayā protested that he would have remained still if Vishnu had only asked him to do so. Grateful for Gayā's cooperation, Vishnu promised to grant him a wish. Gayā wished for the place where he lay to be named for him, and for pilgrims to come to the site to achieve salvation for themselves and their ancestors, without the need for reincarnation. Vishnu is said to have left his footprint in the vicinity. The spot became holy, and a temple was built on it in 1787. The supposed footprint, approximately fifteen inches long, is shown on a rock displayed in a silver basin inside the temple.

The legend of the Gayā monster may not have originated until sometime between the fifth and seventh centuries A.D., as it is not mentioned in the earliest Hindu works. The Hindu religion grew out of a marriage of the beliefs of the indigenous Indian peoples and those of the Aryans, who around 1500 B.C. came to the Indian subcontinent from the area between the Caspian and Black Seas, some of them settling in the area around Gayā. Gayā was a Hindu town at the time it was visted by Siddhārtha Gautama, the historic Buddha, in the fifth century B.C. He is said to have attained his enlightenment at Bodh Gayā, just south of Gayā, and he also is believed to have spent some time meditating on Brahmjūnī Hill, near the modern temple site. The town of Gayā apparently was receptive to his doctrines, and may have wholeheartedly embraced Buddhism for a time.

The spread of Buddhism undoubtedly was helped along by the ruler Aśoka, an emperor of the Maurya Dynasty in the third century B.C. During the preceding century, the Mauryas had supplanted the Maghada kings as rulers of Gayā and the surrounding area. Aśoka expanded the realm until the Mauryas controlled most of India. After his often-bloody conquests, however, he became a devout Buddhist and made Buddhism the state religion. Embracing a philosophy of peacefulness and tolerance, Aśoka promoted his beliefs by issuing edicts that were carved on rock pillars and in caves around the kingdom. Some of his inscriptions are in the Barābar Caves, about twenty miles north of Gayā. These caves, which were designed to provide a place of retreat for ascetics, were the basis for the "Marabar" caves in E. M. Forster's novel (and David Lean's film) *A Passage to India.*

Hinduism survived, however, by incorporating some Buddhist elements, such as addressing societal concerns in addition to the individual's spiritual salvation. As the Maurya realm broke up into smaller entities after Aśoka's death, Hinduism enjoyed renewed popularity. The Guptas, who ruled the region encompassing Gayā in the fourth and fifth centuries A.D., were especially strong supporters of Hindu religion and culture. The town of Gayā itself, however, was largely deserted when the Chinese Buddhist monk Fa Xian visited it in the fifth century. But about 200 years later, when another Chinese Buddhist pilgrim, Xuan Zang, came to the site, he found that although it was sparsely populated it was strongly fortified, and its residents were Hindu. Scholars have theorized that in the interim between these two visits the legend of the monster named Gayā developed, and that the legend attempted to demonstrate that Hinduism was superior to Buddhism: Gayā, the monster, symbolizing Buddhism, had made salvation too easy.

Whatever the merits of this theory, Gayā became well established as a Hindu place of pilgrimage by the tenth century. The Hindu religion continued to survive even as the

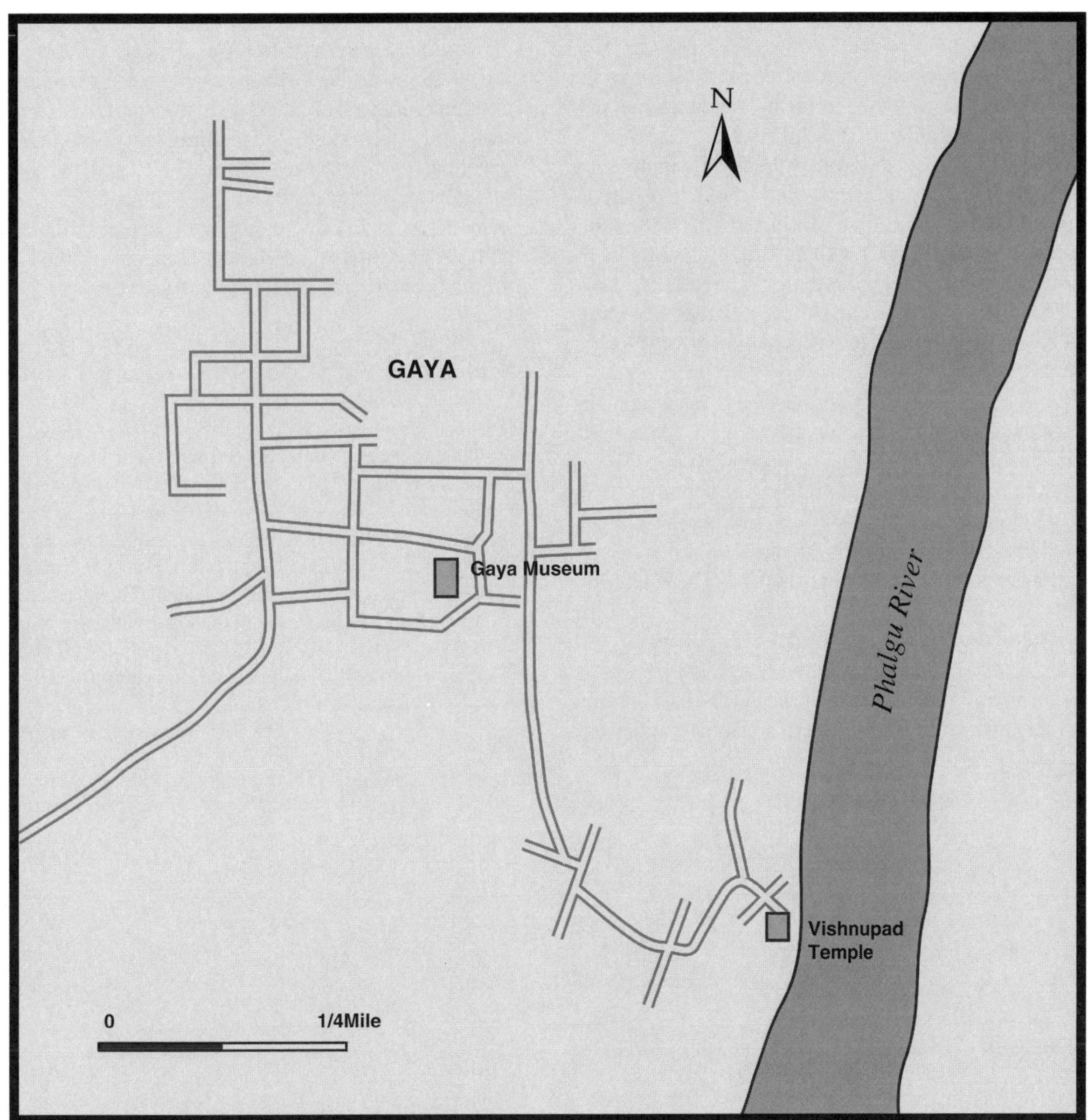

The position of the Vishnupad Temple along the Phalgu River, Gayā
Illustration by Tom Willcockson

region came under the rule of adherents of Islam, beginning in the twelfth century. Its Muslim rulers included a variety of independent monarchs, the Delhi sultanate, and the Mughal Empire.

The cult of Gayā was still strong in the eighteenth century, when the Mughals' power was waning and the British were showing great interest in India. About mid–century, drought and consequent crop failures were causing famine in the area, and the silting up of rivers around Gayā was causing further economic distress. Still, to the British Gayā appeared prosperous: military officers visiting the town in the 1760s found it "spacious with many good buildings" built of brick and stone. Gayā also possessed a "plentifully supplied bazaar," according to these chroniclers. The harsher realities of the economic situation that developed in the wake of the British, however, may well have led to a religious revival, encouraging pilgrimages to Gayā. Not only were the poor likely to seek solace in religion; the wealthier classes probably used religion to their own advantage since a strengthening of Hinduism meant a strengthening of the caste system, which helped preserve scarce resources for the elite. The British, whose East India Company took possession of Gayā in 1765, also favored the strengthening of the caste system as a means of controlling the native population.

The Vishnupad Temple of Gayā was constructed in 1787 under the auspices of the Rani Ahalyābāī of Indore, a British protectorate. Overlooking the Phalgu River, the temple rises to a height of nearly 100 feet and contains eight exquisitely carved pillars. Traditionally, only Hindus have been permitted to enter, but there have been reports of non-Hindus being allowed inside in recent years. Pilgrims to the site bring funeral cakes and other offerings, and many cremations take place along the banks of the Phalgu.

The British further developed the town, laying out a new section for European residents, and establishing schools and hospitals. During the Indian Mutiny of 1857–58, when Indian soldiers rebelled against their British commanders, many valuables were brought here from Calcutta for safekeeping. The railroad came to Gayā in the nineteenth century, making it easier for religious pilgrims and other travelers to go there.

Through the years of British rule, Gayā maintained its significance as a Hindu pilgrimage site, as it has since India became independent in 1947. Gayā's population today is about 250,000, but the number of pilgrims who journey there each year is approximately 300,000. While the Vishnupad Temple is the most important Hindu shrine in the area, numerous others exist, including Pret Sīla (The Hill of Ghosts) just northwest of town, where offerings may be made to placate Yama, and Rām Sīla, north of Gayā, where the evil spirits under Yama's control reside; worship of these spirits is said to keep them from harassing the dead. The Gayā region also has many places that are sacred in Jainism and Buddhism; Bodh Gayā, nine miles south of Gayā, is the holiest of all Buddhist sites. Within Gayā itself, additional sites of interest are the Gayā Museum, which houses archaeological exhibits, and the Brahmjūnī Hill, just southwest of the temple, which has 1,000 stone steps leading to its summit, offering an excellent view of Gayā, Bodh Gayā, and the surrounding region. In addition to its role as a pilgrimage site, Gayā is home to Magadha University, with several affiliated colleges and libraries, and is a commercial center for the agricultural products of the surrounding countryside.

Further Reading: Although not a recent publication, volume 6 of the *Encyclopaedia of Religion and Ethics,* edited by James Hastings (13 vols., Edinburgh: Clark, and New York: Scribner, 1908–27), provides an excellent introduction to the Gayā legend and the town's role in the Hindu religion. For the general Indian historical context, the best modern English source is *The New Cambridge History of India,* edited by Gordon Johnson, C. A. Bayly, and John F. Richards (29 vols., Cambridge and New York: Cambridge University Press, 1987–), especially volume 2, parts I and II. Highly recommended as a single-volume introduction to the history of India and Hinduism is Sinharaja Tammit-Delgoda's *A Traveller's History of India* (Moreton-in-Marsh, Gloucestershire: Windrush, and Brooklyn, New York: Interlink, 1994).

—Clarissa Levi and Trudy Ring

Ghaznī (Ghaznī, Afghanistan)

Location: Ghaznī, also the name of a province and a river, lies approximately ninety miles southwest of Kābul in eastern Afghanistan.

Description: A small, easily accessible commercial town with a long history, especially notable as the capital of the Ghaznavids, Afghanistan's first Muslim dynasty, in the eleventh century.

Contact: Embassy of the Republic of Afghanistan
2341 Wyoming Avenue N.W.
Washington, D.C. 20008
U.S.A.
(202) 234-3770

In the sixth or seventh century A.D. Ghaznī became probably the most westerly major center of Buddhism, other than Bāmiān, in the ancient world. It also became one of the most easterly settlements reached by the original Islamic expansion of the sixth and seventh centuries. Under one of its Muslim rulers, Maḥmūd I (971–1030), who made an estimated seventeen raids on Indian territory beyond the mountains of Afghanistan, Ghaznī became an extremely wealthy capital city. It also developed into a highly prosperous commercial center, partly because it was on the main trade route between the Amu Darya (Oxus) Valley, the towns at the western end of the Silk Road (Samarkand, Bukhara, Balkh, Mary), and the Indus Valley.

Ghaznī today is scattered over a collection of discrete sites at the base of the terminal spur of a ridge of hills, in a position commanding the plain to the south toward Kandahār. The town is clustered below the walls of the castle, erected on an elevated site to the north. The partly artificial mound on which the castle ruins and the old town walls enclosing it now stand is just under one mile in circumference. Slightly over a mile to the east is the site of the medieval palace of the Ghaznavid kings, enclosed between two triumphal minarets of decorated brick, and about two miles farther east is the village with the enshrined tomb of Maḥmūd and a museum. A Buddhist stupa and monastery, layers of which somehow survived the Islamic conquest, lie about a mile from the main road, due south from the palace. Shortly before the Soviet invasion of Afghanistan, the area between the fortress and the palace was, in spite of its deep archaeological significance, being used as a tank training area as well as for other military purposes.

Very little is known about Ghaznī before the tenth century, and the existence there of Buddhist ruins poses special questions. Ghaznī is the only known Buddhist settlement of considerable size to the west of the mountain range separating Afghanistan from modern Pakistan and to the south of passes, such as the Khyber, leading northwest from Pakistan to the Amu Darya Valley. It is commonly held that these passes provided a trade route via which Buddhism reached towns such as Bāmiān, to the west of the passes, and Balkh, in the Amu Darya Valley. Both cities contain extensive Buddhist remains, most likely dating from the sixth or seventh centuries. But Ghaznī lies south of the passes. Furthermore, the towns of Balkh, Bamian, and Ghaznī can be connected on a direct northwest-southeast line pointing toward the Gumal Pass in South Waziristan, well south of the Khyber Pass, and from there to the Indus Valley. If a line of Buddhist ruins does in fact run from Ghaznī north to Balkh along such a route, the history of Buddhism in Central Asia, and the relation of Buddhist monasteries to the trade routes, may well need reexamination.

Ghaznī was probably a Greek city. No one is certain, but it seems likely to have been the city recorded by Ptolemy as Gazaga or Gauzaga. It must have existed before Alexander the Great's time, after which it became yet another of the towns named Alexandria. It was in the satrapy of Arachosia, the fertile area to the south of Ghaznī around the Helmand River. This area, like Ghaznī, was ruled from the Greek town of Kābul (then known as Kophen and later in China as Ki-pin); the political relationship most likely gave rise to economic ties between the two cities, especially considering that the region's economic viability depended on trade. The coexistence of Buddhist and Greek cultures in Ghaznī is not at all astonishing, although it would be interesting to know the logistics of the dovetailing arrangements, which may have meant simply the mingling of a Greek system of civil administration with a Buddhist moral code. Little information exists on the subject, however. The only positive reference to Ghaznī before the Arab conquest is that of Xuan Zang in A.D. 644. He writes of Hosina (Ghaznī) as one of the capitals of the Tsaukuta or Arachosia, and as "a place of great strength."

The town's Buddhist site, now known as Tepe Sardar, consists of a stupa on a hilltop surrounded by a row of smaller stupas, some of them very richly decorated, and the monastery. The smaller stupas are multistoried and covered in Buddha images, arranged in an irregularly serrated row, some of them situated above the ground on a base in the form of a lotus leaf, with access by tall flights of terraced steps. Any dedicatory inscription on the main stupa was removed long ago, so that dating, however probable, must remain conjectural. The style of the decoration, involving Buddha on an elephant throne, indicates a relatively late date, but one still early enough to include Sāsānian motifs; these considerations point to the seventh century. In 1969 a large figure of an Indian goddess on an elephant modeled in reddish local clay on a core of gray clay was recovered below the site's destruc-

City walls, Ghaznī
Photo courtesy of Mr. Rashid Uddin, Park Travel Agency, Chicago

tion level, providing evidence that Buddhist practice at the site incorporated polytheistic elements.

The large stupa was built first, in two stages showing differences of structural techniques. Once the flanks and moldings had been completed and the cornices decorated in stucco, the terraces still remained incomplete. The destruction seems to have taken place when the site had already decayed, and the Buddhas were half buried. The wooden roof was destroyed by a fire that left most of the smaller clay figures unharmed, even preserving some by baking them. The gray clay core made the application of the rich final decorative modeling relatively easy and allowed for the ornamentation to be carved in greater depth and detail than would have been possible on the stone. Some of the small heads of soldiers are clearly taken from Mongol models, indicating that there were Mongol troops in the service of Ghaznī during the seventh century.

Throughout the first three centuries of Islam, the history of Ghaznī is obscure. The Arabs appear to have penetrated into Khorāsān and Zabulistan, of which Ghaznī had been the chief town, during the reign of ʿAbd al-Malik ibn Marwān in the late seventh century, fighting and defeating the local ruler. The Ṣaffārids, an Islamic dynasty ruling much of eastern Persia in the ninth century, penetrated to Ghaznī and Kābul. It was they who rebuilt Ghaznī, which probably had already fallen to the Islamic conquest of Yaʿqūb ebn Leys about 871, while the Hindu dynasty at Kābul held out. One Islamic historian, no doubt erroneously, ascribes the building of Ghaznī's fort and city to Amir ebn Leys, brother and successor of Yaʿqūb.

The Būyids, although Shi'ites, ruled the ʿAbbāsid caliphate from Baghdad from 945 to 1055, but it was the Sāmānids, the first native Persian dynasty after the Islamic conquest, who built up Buhkara and Samarkand and who controlled the great empire in the east during the ninth and most of the tenth centuries. It extended over Transoxiana, Khorāsān, and parts of Afghanistan, but lost power to enforce tribute from its outlying areas soon after the middle of the tenth century. It had become dependent on Turkish mercenaries, always difficult to control, and about 955 a Turkish officer called Alptigin was made governor of Khorāsān. In 962, after a change of ruler in Bukhara, he found it desirable to move eastward into Afghanistan and made himself governor of Ghaznī and of the surrounding region of Zabulistan. He and his successors were recognized and occasionally supported by the Sāmānids, but they resisted Sāmānid suzerainty whenever it became too demanding.

In 977 the Turkish troops in Ghaznī deposed their commander for misrule and chose in his place another Turkish officer, Abū Manṣūr Sebüktigin, Alptigin's son-in-law, who still regarded himself as owing allegiance to the Sāmānids. He made his son, Maḥmūd, governor of Khorāsān. When, in 997, a quarrel disrupted the Sāmānid Dynasty, Maḥmūd, who had become emir of Ghaznī upon

Minaret at the fort of Ghaznī
Photo courtesy of Mr. Rashid Uddin, Park Travel Agency, Chicago

his father's death and his brother's abdication, declared his independence from the Sāmānids, while another Turkish dynasty, the Karakhanids, took Transoxiana. Sebüktigin already had begun raiding the Punjab and had erected fortresses on the Indian border. His son, Maḥmūd, a Sunni, consolidated his hold on Khorāsān and had his governorship of the province ratified by the Baghdad caliphs. In exchange, he agreed to mention the caliphs in the Friday mosque prayers in Khorāsān. In 1008 Maḥmūd defeated the Karakhanids near Balkh. They made no further attempt to move south of the Amu Darya River.

Maḥmūd's systematic winter raids across northern India, which assumed something of the character of a holy war, led to his domination of the Punjab, the Ganges plain, and Gujarāt and to the acquisition of invaluable spoils. He also plundered the famously rich Hindu temple at Somnāth and controlled the Indus Valley, the whole of Afghanistan, and eastern Persia. Tens of thousands were massacred on these raids. Maḥmūd, the person chiefly responsible for the spread of Islam on the Indian subcontinent, had wanted his son Muhammad to succeed him, but upon Maḥmūd's death in 1030, Muhammad was rejected by the army in favor of another of Maḥmūd's sons, Ma'sūd I. Ma'sūd made Lahore a twin capital of his empire with Ghaznī. Neglecting the Seljuk threat from the west, Ma'sūd continued to raid India, but was forced to return to confront the Seljuks, who decisively defeated him in 1040 at Dandanqan, near Mary.

Ma'sūd was murdered by the army in 1041, but sporadic fighting with the Seljuks continued until 1059 under his successor Ibrāhīm, who ruled until 1099. He reached a settlement with the Seljuks, which lasted half a century, until the death of Ibrāhīm's son Ma'sūd III, who ruled from 1099 to 1115. Western Afghanistan went to the Seljuks, but the east to the Ghaznavids. There is a description of Ghaznī at this period, by the geographer Baihaqi, which mentions the absence of noxious insects, the healthy climate with snow in winter, and the terrible floods of 1031, which swept away roads, bridges, and houses.

Ghaznī was a large commercial center. The historian al-Mukaddasi describes Ghaznī under Sebüktigin as the center of a fertile crescent. The citadel contained the ruler's palace. The town or *madina* consisted mostly of markets. There was a wall with four gates. Several other markets and the community's houses were relegated to a suburb. Another chronicler, Ibn Hauqal, notes that in this era the somewhat less important city of Kābul handled 2 million dinars' worth of indigo a year. By the time that the Hindu Shahi rulers of Kābul finally were eliminated in 1019, Ghaznī's raids into India already had brought back huge riches.

Baihaqi writes that Maḥmūd built his palace on a site called Afghan-Shah and created the Sad-Hazara Garden as well as the Fruzi Palace and Garden, where his tomb now stands. The marble slab on Maḥmūd's tomb is of a later date than the tomb itself, and the wooden doors, also later than the tomb, are now in the fort at Āgra. It was Maḥmūd who made Ghaznī a cultural center, endowing it with a large library and an important *medrese* (school of theology). All palaces were surrounded by gardens, and some gardens were created independently of permanent buildings. At Ghaznī Maḥmūd installed desert parks watered by pipes with silver mouths. Maḥmūd brought back to Ghaznī the best craftsmen he could find on his Indian raids. His buildings and the associated decorative arts cultivated at Ghaznī during his reign were the product of Persian and Indian traditions with an altogether more refined standard of workmanship than previously available at Ghaznī, which had no important native artistic tradition. Ma'sūd I accelerated the import of foreign artisans. His palace was built to his own designs, and was both paid for and decorated with the spoils from India. He built a large mosque and stables for 1,000 elephants, while also instigating irrigation works. The importance of irrigation systems can be gauged from the fact that they were always the first things Genghis Khan sought to destroy before capturing and razing the cities in his path.

Ghaznī's weakness was its vulnerability to Turkish raids from the west. Maḥmūd's dynasty had been of Turkish origin, and when the Seljuks eventually were accommodated by the territorial division under Ibrāhīm, they already had conquered the remainder of Iran, taken Baghdad, and threatened Ghaznī. Ma'sūd III died in 1115, and Bahrām Shah succeeded to the throne in 1118 with only the support of the Seljuk sultan Sanjar, whose vassal he therefore became. Ghaznī itself was occupied by Sanjar in 1117 and 1135, and Sanjar's Seljuk throne in turn came under pressure from the rising power of Ghūr, which began to challenge the Ghaznavids from the mountainous region east of Herāt.

Bahrām put to death one of the princes of Ghūr who had sought refuge in Ghaznī, and the prince's brother then drove Bahrām out of Ghaznī. Bahrām retook the town, paraded the prince's brother ignominiously through it, and then hanged him with his vizier on the bridge. After a battle on the Helmand, Ghaznī was sacked in 1151 by a younger brother of the two brothers Bahrām had killed, the Ghūr ruler Ala-ud-Dīn Husain, who thereby earned himself the nickname Jahansuz (World-Burner). Ghaznī's position at this time was complicated by the fact that the area of Afghanistan was contested by three Central Asian powers: a declining Seljuk power, the northern Chinese Karakitai (also known as the Western Liao), and the Karakhanids, whom the Karakitai had made their vassals. Sanjar was defeated by the Karakitai in 1141. Bahrām died in 1157.

This political instability allowed the Ghūrids to make inroads into the region, leaving them in a dominant position when the situation again stabilized; members of the dynasty ruled in Firuzkoh and Bāmiān, and the principal Ghūrid line was able to recover Ghaznī in 1173 and Herāt in 1175. In 1186 the remains of the Ghaznavid principality in Lahore were eliminated. The Ghūr rulers then overextended themselves, however. Mu'izz ud-Dīn Muhammad of Ghūr invaded Transoxiana; he was defeated decisively in 1202 and assassinated in 1206, thus opening the way to the Khwarizm-shahs to occupy both Ghūr and Ghaznī in 1215–16. Within five years this vast empire, stretching from Hamadan to the Indus and from Transoxiana to Seistan, was to be swept away by Genghis Khan, who razed Ghaznī in 1221. Mu'izz ud-Dīn's lieutenants, meanwhile, continued to dominate parts of northern India, and it was from their number that Ẓahīr-ud-Dīn Muḥammad (better known as Bābur), founder of the Mughal Dynasty, finally emerged as king of Kābul and Ghaznī in 1504.

After its destruction by Genghis Khan, Ghaznī's role in the history of central Asia diminished. It remained subject to the Mongols, sometimes ruled from Persia and sometimes from Turkistan. It was devastated by the Mongols again in 1326, and about 1332 Ibn Baṭṭūṭah reported that the city was in ruins. In 1401 the Mongol conqueror Timur (Tamerlane) made his grandson, Pir Muhammad bin Djinhangir, governor of Ghaznī, along with Kābul and Kandahār. Bābur called Ghaznī "a mean place" and wondered why its princes ever had chosen it as a seat of government. Ghaznī, now ruled from Delhi and Āgra, remained in Mughal hands until the invasion of Nāder Shāh in 1738, having been defended successfully by 'Ālamgīr (Aurangzeb), the last great Mughal emperor, against the Persians. After Nāder Shāh's death, Ghaznī came into the hands of Aḥmad Shāh Durrāni, founder and first ruler of Afghanistan. In the Anglo-Afghan wars of the nineteenth century, the site, scarcely a town, was taken by the British in 1839 and again, after an uprising, in 1842. Between Nāder Shāh's conquest and the British occupation in 1839, only two western European travelers are known to have left any account of a visit to Ghaznī: George Forster, while posing as a Muslim in 1783, and Godfrey Thomas Vigne, who reached the town with a merchant caravan from Multan in 1836, traveling over the Gumal Pass.

Although the British withdrew their troops from Afghanistan in 1843, Britain continued to regard the area as a key buffer zone between India and Russia, and participated in establishing the borders of modern Afghanistan in the late nineteenth century. During this era Ghaznī regained some importance as the primary town on the road from Kābul to Kandahār. It has developed into a modern commercial town that provides a market for textiles, furs, livestock, and agricultural products. It is also noted for the manufacture of Afghan sheepskin coats and houses a museum rich in ancient artifacts.

The recent history of Ghaznī is violent. After the Soviet invasion of 1979, Soviet and Afghan government forces frequently fought with Afghan guerrillas around Ghaznī, and the guerrillas held the town briefly in 1981. The Soviets withdrew in 1989, and a new government was installed in 1992, but internal strife has continued to plague Afghanistan.

The Ghaznī Plain still awaits proper excavation. The town has large numbers of Ghaznavid tombstones and marble graves, and the lower portions of minarets of Ma'sūd III and Bahrām Shah, victory towers or religious monuments, are still standing. Ma'sūd's minaret led to the discovery of his palace, through an inscribed fragment of stone found in a field. Another inscription, dated 1112, allowed the whole complex to be dated. At the complex's heart is a large open rectangular court paved with marble and measuring 164 by 102 feet. Even the surrounding footpath is paved with marble. In the center of each of the four walls surrounding the courtyard was an *ivan,* or vaulted open-fronted hall, an early example of what was to become a standard architectural form for buildings of quite different sorts.

An Islamic *ivan* always has one side open and always is covered by a barrel vault. On the north wall of Ma'sūd's palace, the *ivan* had an imposing vestibule and served as a monumental entrance, and the southern *ivan* contained a throne room. On east and west walls small rooms flanked the *ivans,* and there was a pillared mosque in the northwest corner. The decoration of the courtyard was exquisite, with the upper portions bearing terra-cotta and stucco ornamentation in sculptured geometric patterns painted in yellow, red, and blue. Along with the formal patterns of the marble Islamic decoration are hunting scenes. The lower part of the wall has a Persian inscription 820 feet long, carved in stone.

Further Reading: Only formal works of history deal in detail with the history of Ghaznī, and then only with aspects or periods of it. The best modern evocation of historic Afghanistan is Peter Levi's *The Light Garden of the Angel King: Journeys in Afghanistan* (London: Collins, and Indianapolis: Bobbs-Merrill, 1972). For more technical material, *The Archaeology of Afghanistan from Earliest Times to the Timurid Period,* edited by F. R. Allchin and Norman Hammond (London and New York: Academic Press, 1978) is indispensable. There are some very useful pages in W. Montgomery Watt's *The Majesty That Was Islam: The Islamic World 661–1100* (London: Sidgwick and Jackson, and New York: Praeger, 1974). Also useful for historical background is a biography entitled *Sultan Maḥmūd of Ghaznī: A Study* by Muhammad Habib, (Bombay: D. B. Taraporevala, 1927; revised edition, Delhi: S. Chand, 1951).

—Anthony Levi

Goa (India)

Location: On the Koṅkaṇ coast of western India, 340 miles south of Bombay, in the coastal plain below the Western Ghāts Mountains.

Description: Former Portuguese colonial territory, now a state of India; has numerous important ports, although most of the population has traditionally depended on agriculture. The former colonial capital, Old Goa, contains numerous Christian churches dating from the sixteenth and seventeenth centuries, and there are important Hindu temples in nearby Ponda. Today the area is a focus for international and local tourism.

Site Office: Government of India Tourist Office
Communidade Building
Church Square
Panaji, Goa
India
(43) 412

The most splendid and famous period in Goa's history was in the sixteenth and early seventeenth centuries, when it was the center of a vast Portuguese maritime empire, but its history goes back much further. It became part of the India-wide empire of the Mauryas in the third century B.C. and subsequently passed through the hands of several regional Hindu empires. In the eleventh century, under the Kadamba Dynasty, it grew into a major commercial power, with the emphasis on sea trade. The region's coastal location and relatively good harbors have made it a center of maritime trade for much of its history.

In the thirteenth century the Yādava Dynasty took over the area, with the Kadambas ruling in name only. Ministers appointed by the Yādava kings carried out numerous public works, including the building of the temple of Sri Mahadeva. The Muslim sultanate of Delhi, however, conquered the area in the early fourteenth century, ending both Yādava and Kadamba power. Later in the century, Goa became part of the south Indian kingdom of Vijayanagar, and it continued to be a center for trade, especially for the importation of Arabian horses to serve the armies of central and southern India. A Hindu stronghold, Vijayanagar drew the opposition of the Muslim Bahmanī sultanate, which conquered the Goa region in 1469. Soon after this the Bahmanī sultanate dissolved, and Goa was ruled from the late fifteenth century by one of its Muslim successor states, Bijāpur, based in the western Deccan area over the Western Ghāts Mountains from Goa. Despite these political changes, Goa continued to be a major port, and its population remained overwhelmingly peasant and Hindu.

The Portuguese began their great period of exploration in the fifteenth century. Bartolomeu Dias rounded the Cape of Good Hope in 1488. In 1497 King Manuel I sent Vasco da Gama on his epoch-making voyage. Da Gama rounded the cape and proceeded up the east coast of Africa to Melinde, where the friendly local sultan provided him with a pilot. With his help da Gama crossed the Arabian Sea and reached Calicut, in southwest India, in May 1498, making him the first European to round Africa and reach the East. After investigating the trade possibilities of the area, he returned to Portugal, receiving a hero's welcome in August 1499.

Goa was acquired as the central element of a wide-ranging and grandiose Portuguese strategy. Portugal's main aim was to control trade in the Indian Ocean area. The Portuguese also had a history of antipathy to Muslims. These two considerations merged to the advantage of the Portuguese, for the most valuable trade was in spices, and this was largely controlled by Muslim merchants from many different areas. Thus if the Portuguese could take over this trade they not only would acquire a monopoly over a very valuable product, but would also be dispossessing their enemies. The Portuguese even claimed the right to control and tax all other trade in the Indian Ocean. Trade in spices was declared to be a monopoly of the Portuguese king, and no Asian ships were allowed to carry any. Further, all Asian traders had to carry a pass, or *cartaz*, from the Portuguese authorities. During the first half of the sixteenth century, the Portuguese came close to achieving their goals, primarily because their ships were stronger and had cannon on board, while most Asian ships did not.

During their first decade in India, the Portuguese concentrated on the Malabar (today Kerala) area in southwest India, as this was an important pepper-producing region. However, their second governor, the farsighted Afonso de Albuquerque, came to realize the advantageous location of Goa. The area had two good harbors in the estuaries of the Mandavi and Juari Rivers, and its location in the middle of the west coast of India made it well situated to dominate trade over the whole Arabian Sea. Pepper and other spices could come to Goa from the south, while cotton textiles and other products arrived from the great production area of Gujarāt to the north. In 1510 Albuquerque set out with an armada to conquer Goa.

The battle for Goa was a bloody one. At first the Portuguese succeeded in capturing the capital, also called Goa (now called Old Goa). The Bijāpur forces counterattacked, however, and the Portuguese were forced to withdraw to their ships and wait for reinforcements, which could only arrive after the southwest monsoon had ended. Once he had more troops, Albuquerque landed again and was able to

Basilica of Bom Jesus, Old Goa
Photo courtesy of Christopher Turner

Sé Cathedral, Old Goa
Photo courtesy of Christopher Turner

conquer the town and territory of Goa definitively on St. Catherine's Day, November 25, 1510. All Muslim defenders were put to the sword, and Portuguese soldiers were encouraged to marry Muslim women, whom the Portuguese found preferable to the local Hindu women because they were, as Albuquerque said, "white and virtuous." Goa remained a Portuguese possession from 1510 through 1961.

Goa's wider role was as capital of the far-flung Portuguese seaborne empire, which spread from China and Japan all around the Indian Ocean to East Africa. Two or three ships arrived from Portugal each year, and went back from Goa loaded with spices, textiles, and other goods. Small Portuguese fleets patrolled up and down the west Indian coast, assisting local merchant ships that were carrying goods to Goa, and attacking those that opposed the self-proclaimed Portuguese monopoly of sea trade. Goa was where the viceroy or governor and the archbishop lived, where the High Court and the inquisition functioned, and the place from which were issued orders to govern, at least in theory, the actions of Portuguese all over their vast maritime network.

Late in the sixteenth century, the capital city was at its opulent height. With a population of some 75,000 in 1600, and surrounded by three Portuguese-ruled districts with a total population of some 250,000, Goa had become rich from the profits of trade and plunder. Of the city's total population in 1600, some 1,500 were Portuguese or mixed Portuguese, 20,000 were native Hindus, and the rest local Christians and African slaves. The Muslims had been killed or driven out in 1510. This was a frontier city, with its inhabitants divided on racial, religious, and ethnic grounds. White males born in Portugal were at the top, local Hindus at the bottom, at least in theory. Most of the so-called Portuguese population were in fact *mestizos,* that is, the result of unions between Portuguese men and local women, for few Portuguese women could be persuaded to settle in Goa. Portuguese and *mestizos* dominated the military, political, and religious life of the town, but the economy was largely controlled by local and neighboring Hindus. The vital trade with the rich area of Gujarāt to the north was dominated by Gujarātī traders, and most sources of government revenue in Goa were collected in tax-farming arrangements by Goan Hindus. Although official Portuguese policies were often bigoted and racist, there was in fact considerable interaction among the various ethnic groups in practical areas. For example, the medicine practiced at the great Royal Hospital in Goa was a blend of European and Indian remedies, as the Portuguese authorities believed

Tower of the temple at Tambdi Surla, Goa's oldest building, dating from the thirteenth century
Photo courtesy of Christopher Turner

that some diseases were specific to India and so best treated by Indian methods.

The elite in Goa lived in considerable style, as is revealed by the accounts of several European visitors to the city around 1600. Military leaders swaggered through the streets accompanied by their own armed retinues, in effect private armies. Their wives were carried about in palanquins, with slaves attending to every whim: one to carry a parasol to keep off the sun, one to keep flies off the grande dame, four to carry the palanquin, and so on. Household slavery, with the slaves being mostly black Africans from Portuguese possessions in East Africa, was endemic in Goa. Many accounts describe the huge numbers of slaves kept by every Portuguese household and also by seminaries, monasteries, and nunneries. They were often brutally treated, and were frequently hired out by their owners to work as laborers or prostitutes. Human flesh was cheap: in an auction the top price for a fine Arabian horse could be 500 cruzados; for a much desired female slave who could sing, sew, and was certified to be a virgin, it was 30. In short, Goa in the sixteenth century was a lavish, profligate, scandalous city, the "Golden Goa" of legend.

In the Portuguese Empire, religion and politics went hand in hand. Goa had an archbishop and an inquisition from 1560. The inquisition was designed to control any backsliding from "pure" Roman Catholicism. It persecuted "new Christians," that is, Jews who had been forced to convert to Christianity, with some vigor. Sixteenth-century Goa's greatest savant, the botanist and doctor Garcia da Orta, was denounced in 1580, twelve years after his death, for secretly having been a Jew. His bones were dug up and ceremoniously burned. Partially converted Hindus also were subject to investigation and punishment.

The inquisition can be seen as part of the radical reform movement within Catholicism known as the Counter-Reformation. The new militant order of the Society of Jesus, or Jesuits, was part of the same movement. One of its founders, Francis Xavier, spent some time in Goa in the 1540s. After his death in 1552, his miraculously preserved body was brought back to Goa and became an object of veneration and worship. Even today in Goa his festival (death) date, December 3, is a major religious festival in which Goan Catholics and Hindus participate. Xavier, who was made a saint in 1622, undertook mass conversions of Hindus to Catholicism in Goa and elsewhere.

The state fostered this mid-century conversion drive. Hindu temples were destroyed, and lands that supported them were allocated to new Christian churches. The result was that by 1600 about 25 percent of the population of the territory of Goa was Christian. Hindu temple priests fled with the most sacred of their temple deities to neighboring areas ruled by the Muslim sultanate of Bijāpur. In consequence, Goa's most significant Hindu temples today are located just beyond the borders of the area ruled by the Portuguese in the sixteenth century. Many of the most famous are around the town of Ponda, easily accessible from Old Goa and Panaji, including the Shri Mangesh, Shri Mahalsa, and Shri Shantadurga temples.

The Portuguese built several large-scale churches in their capital of Goa. This area, now a ghost town in which only churches remain, is today called Old Goa, and is a main focus for tourism. Among the splendid sixteenth- and seventeenth-century religious buildings that have survived (virtually no secular buildings remain) is the Basilica of Bom Jesus, in which is to be found the preserved body of St. Francis Xavier. This impressive building, completed in 1605, measures 180 feet in length, 52 feet in width, and 59 feet in height. Even larger and more impressive is the Sé Cathedral, 114 feet high, 249 feet long, and 180 feet wide. Several other spectacular churches and convents are still to be seen in Old Goa today. Some years ago Old Goa had an ill-kept appearance, with huge churches rising out of a virtual jungle. Today the area is better tended, the churches better preserved.

Goa's prosperity was built on Portugal's control of sea trade. From late in the sixteenth century, this control was threatened by competition from other European powers. Most damaging were Dutch merchants organized in the efficient and well-focused Dutch East India Company. During the first half of the seventeenth century, they slowly whittled away Portuguese possessions. Melaka, Sri Lanka, and the Portuguese forts in Malabar were all lost, and Goa itself was blockaded by Dutch fleets from 1638 to 1644 and from 1656 to 1663. The Portuguese Empire declined into a moribund state. Goa also was threatened, beginning in the late seventeenth century, by the new and militant Hindu Marāṭhā power. In 1739 this group conquered the important area of Bassein, north of Bombay, and from then the Portuguese Empire in India consisted of only Goa along with Diu and Damān on the coast of Gujarāt. However, the area of Goa was enlarged in the second half of the eighteenth century by the acquisition of seven new provinces surrounding the old heartland area. Portuguese rule over these "New Conquests" was light, and the population remained overwhelmingly Hindu.

Goa, of course, suffered from this general decline. The population fell, so that while in 1630 the "Old Conquests," the heartland, had contained perhaps 250,000 people, by 1800 it was fewer than 180,000. The only wealthy people left were Hindu merchants and traders, and the remaining Portuguese found life there difficult. The capital of Old Goa declined, for it was an unhealthy place with polluted water and subject to numerous epidemics, especially cholera. After much procrastination and discussion, the capital of the reduced Portuguese Asian Empire was moved down the Mandavi River to Panaji, near the open sea and the bar. The new capital was built between 1827 and 1835, and the move was officially completed in 1843. Old Goa was left to decay, its population by then consisting mostly of clerics and nuns who did the best they could to maintain the more significant buildings.

From late in the eighteenth century, the British moved to conquer all of India; the process was virtually completed by 1818. As a by-product of the Napoleonic Wars, Goa itself was occupied by British forces from 1799 to 1815. Portuguese possessions in India now functioned in the gaps and interstices of the British raj. Most important was Portugal's role in the opium trade to China. The British made this a monopoly, but Indian ships flying Portuguese flags were for a time able to circumvent this, and in the early years of the nineteenth century they plied a very profitable trade, the proceeds of which funded the construction of most of the government buildings in the new capital of Panaji.

Goa in the late nineteenth and early twentieth centuries can only be described as a backwater. Agriculture had become stagnant, trade minimal, and consequently many young Goan men left to pursue work or education in British India and Portuguese areas in East Africa. By 1921 it was estimated that up to 200,000 Goans lived outside their native area; Goa's population at this time was 470,000. These Christian migrants often did very well indeed, for unlike Hindus they had no food restrictions, and their tastes in music and art were Western. Many cooks and stewards on board British ships, and dance bands all over India, were Goan. Remittances home from these migrants provided a major source of funds for the remaining population.

After World War II, a tide of decolonization swept Asia. British India became independent in 1947, and soon after the French agreed to surrender their coastal enclaves. Only Goa, Damān, and Diu remained as colonial vestiges in India. The Portuguese now claimed that these areas were not part of India at all, but of Portugal. In 1951, rather disingenuously, the Portuguese Colonial Ministry was renamed the Ministry for Overseas Provinces. Indian Prime Minister Jawaharlal Nehru pursued diplomatic means to try to reunite the Portuguese areas with India, but Portugal, under the dictator Antonio de Oliveira Salazar, refused to budge. His NATO allies, especially the United States, supported this stance, and finally India lost patience and sent in its army in December 1961, the event being variously described as the "liberation" or "occupation" of Goa.

Since 1961, Goa has been subjected to a much more intense range of external forces than ever before. It has been integrated into the Indian Union, and much progress has been made in matters such as electrification, education, and communications. Large iron ore deposits, more or less ignored under the Portuguese, have become a major export and source of income, and the port of Marmagao on the Juari River has increased greatly in size. The economy remains dominated by the same Hindu families who controlled it under the Portuguese, but there also has been an influx of Indians from outside Goa, so that today more than half the population is made up of persons not born in the area. After 1961, Goa was a Union Territory, but fears of the loss of Goa's distinctive identity, based especially on its language of Koṅkaṇī, led to increasing demands for full statehood, and this was achieved in 1987.

The vast rise in iron ore exports constitutes the major change in the Goan economy since 1961, but there have been other changes as well. For example, the traditional fishing industry has been undermined by modern deep-sea trawlers, many of them foreign. Most conspicuous of all has been the very large expansion in the tourist trade, which has had profound economic and social effects on Goa, especially on the coastal areas. In the late 1960s and 1970s many foreign visitors were so-called hippies, whose lifestyles the conservative Goan Catholics opposed. Over the past ten years or so, government policy has encouraged middle-class tourists. Middle-class Indians also have made Goa, with its touch of the exotic, a popular destination. The results for Goa have been mixed. Much of the capital to build the hotels and resorts comes from outside Goa, or indeed outside India. Water and electric power go first to the hotels, and much agricultural land has been taken over for development. Ironically, Goa's main appeal, as an "untouched" tropical paradise, is under threat from the influx of tourists seeking this very ambience. On the positive side, tourism provides employment for young Goans, and many historic buildings are now better preserved. These include the complex of religious buildings at Old Goa, and the forts at the estuaries of the Mandavi and Juari Rivers. The seventeenth-century Fort Aguada, on the left bank of the estuary of the Mandavi River, is today occupied by the lavish Fort Aguada Beach Resort.

Further Reading: The history of the Portuguese Empire in India, and of Goa in particular, is summed up in M. N. Pearson's *The Portuguese in India* (New York and London: Cambridge University Press, 1987). For wider coverage of the Portuguese Empire, including India, see C. R. Boxer's *The Portuguese Seaborne Empire, 1415–1825* (New York: Knopf, and London: Hutchinson, 1969). See also *Goa through the Ages,* volume II, *An Economic History,* edited by T. R. de Sousa (New Delhi: Concept, 1990), and *Goa: Cultural Trends,* edited by P. P. Shirodkar (Panaji, Goa: Directorate of Archives, 1988) for two examples of recent work from the wealth of revitalized Goan historiography. There are now many lavish books that describe and illustrate Goa's history and monuments. Among them are *Goa* (New Delhi: Vikas, 1984); *Golden Goa* (Bombay: Marg, 1980); and the distinguished Indian novelist Manohar Malgonkar's *Inside Goa* (Government of Goa, 1980), with illustrations by the famous Goan cartoonist and illustrator Mario de Miranda. Best of all is *Goa* (New Delhi: Lustre, 1986), which contains stunning photos by Jean-Louis Nou and a good text by Mario Cabral e Sa.

—M. N. Pearson

Golconda (Andhra Pradesh, India)

Location: Five miles west of Hyderābād in the north central portion of the state of Andhra Pradesh in southeastern India.

Description: A ruined city and fortress complex, Golconda was the capital of a kingdom of the same name ruled by the Quṭb Shāhi Dynasty from 1512 to 1687; it was one of the five Muslim kingdoms of southern India's Deccan region. The city and kingdom were conquered by the Mughal emperor 'Ālamgīr (Aurangzeb) in 1687–88 and annexed to the Mughal Empire.

Contact: Government of India Tourist Office
3-6-369/A-30, Sandozi Building, second floor
26 Himayat Nagar
Hyderābād, Andhra Pradesh 500 029
660037

Golconda, which was to have its greatest glory as the capital of the Quṭb Shāhi Kingdom in the sixteenth and seventeenth centuries, was founded as an outpost of the Kākatīya Empire in the twelfth century. The Kākatīyas, a Hindu dynasty whose capital was at Warangal, about ninety miles to the northeast, built a large mud fortress atop a nearly 400-foot granite hill at the site that was to become Golconda.

The Bahmanīs, a Muslim dynasty, conquered the Deccan region in the fourteenth century and reinforced the fort at Golconda. In 1512, Qulī Quṭb Shāh, an administrator in the Bahmanī government, declared himself independent and set up a kingdom with its capital at Golconda. Qulī Quṭb Shāh had been allied closely with Muḥammad Gawan, a minister to the Bahmanī sultan Muḥammad Shāh III. Muḥammad Shāh, his judgment impaired by alcoholism, had wrongly suspected Muḥammad Gawan of treason and had him executed; this action led Qulī Quṭb Shāh to leave the sultan's court and to set himself up as an independent ruler some years later.

Qulī Quṭb Shāh and his successors expanded the Golconda fortress into an impressive complex in the heart of their city. The citadel was surrounded by three walls, one around the fortress itself, another around the hill on which it stood, and another around the city below. The fortress wall had eighty-seven bastions with cannon and eight large gates. Each gate had inner and outer doors with a guardroom between them. One, the Victory Gate, was covered with iron spikes as a further defensive measure, especially against elephant attack. All the gateways are decorated with relief sculptures of birds and animals. The walls are all well preserved, and some of the cannon are still in place.

Within the fortress were built the royal palace and harem, mosques, temples, meeting halls, stables, military barracks, and an arsenal. The complex had an early air conditioning system, in which water to cool the rooms of the palace was pumped through clay pipes that rose the entire height of the citadel, about 200 feet. Water wheels known as "Persian wheels" and powered by bullocks provided the force to pump the water. The citadel also was praised for its acoustics; it was said that any sound made at the Victory Gate could be heard at the very top of the complex. Modern visitors are known to make a good deal of noise to test the acoustics. There is rumored to be an underground tunnel from the foot to the top of the hill, but visitors are not allowed to investigate this.

Members of the Quṭb Shāhi family were buried in a beautiful series of tombs on a low plateau north-northwest of the fortress. The tombs are built of either black granite or greenstone and adorned with onion domes, arches, sculptures, and inscriptions. The larger tombs have attached mosques. The rulers oversaw design and construction of their tombs during their lifetimes. The tombs have been restored since the late nineteenth century and may be visited today. Formal gardens surround the tombs, and nearby stands the structure where the kings' bodies were washed before burial.

The city of Golconda was the capital of a kingdom that occupied the area between the Godāvari and Krishna Rivers and stretched to the Bay of Bengal. Its economy was based on agriculture, trade, and, most important, diamond mining. Among the gems mined in the territory were the Koh-i-Noor and Hope diamonds, both once stored in the palace vault. The region had been famous for its diamonds even before the founding of the kingdom; the gems attracted Marco Polo to the area in the thirteenth century.

Although the Quṭb Shāhi rulers generally were capable administrators and skilled military adventurers, they had their share of internecine strife. Qulī Quṭb Shāh was deposed and murdered by his own son, Jamshid, in 1543, when Qulī was ninety years old. Jamshid's successor, Ibrāhīm, who came to the throne in 1550, joined an alliance with two other Deccan kingdoms, Ahmadnagar and Bijāpur, to make war on the neighboring Vijaynagar Kingdom. Religious differences—the Deccan kings were Muslim, the Vijaynagar rulers Hindu—and the dispute over possession of the fortified town of Rāichūr were the primary causes of the war. In the Battle of Tālikota in 1565, the Deccan states won a resounding victory that marked the end of the Vijaynagar Kingdom. Golconda and Bijāpur received a disproportionate share of the spoils.

The Quṭb Shāhi kings were interested in more peaceful pursuits as well; they were noted patrons of the arts and letters. Long narrative poems were the most popular form of literature in their language, Urdū, and this form flourished at the Quṭb Shāhi court. Muḥammad Qulī Quṭb Shāh, king from 1581 to 1611, was himself a highly regarded poet.

Golconda Fort, Golconda
Photo courtesy of Air India Library, New York

Muḥammad also was the founder of Hyderābād, which he built because he found the city of Golconda too congested. He developed Hyderābād in approximately 1590 and moved the royal court there, although Golconda continued to be an important military stronghold for the kingdom. Members of the royal family also continued to be buried there; Muḥammad's tomb, rather appropriately, is one of the most beautiful in the complex.

The Mughal Empire, founded in 1526 by Bābur, entered a period of expansion during the seventeenth century. The Mughals made a series of attacks on the Deccan in the early part of the century. The most successful was by Shāh Jahān, who conquered the area in 1636. The Quṭb Shāhis were able to hold on to Golconda, however, by accepting Mughal suzerainty. The terms of the agreement allowed Golconda and Bijāpur to invade areas to the south, while the Mughals could expand to the east and northwest. Shāh Jahān had an affection for Golconda based upon his having taken refuge there while in rebellion against his father, Jahāngīr, in 1622.

Golconda and Bijāpur together conquered much of the Coromandel Coast of southeastern India. This area was noted for its export of textiles, and its conquest made many of Golconda's leaders wealthy from the maritime trade. Treasures looted from Hindu temples were another source of riches. In particular, Muḥammad Said, chief minister of the kingdom of Golconda, became so ostentatiously wealthy that the king, Abdullah Quṭb Shāh, tried to have him assassinated. This failed attempt provoked Muḥammad Said into alliance with the Mughal emperor ʿĀlamgīr (Aurangzeb), who came to the throne in 1658, after having deposed his father, Shāh Jahān.

ʿĀlamgīr was to prove less indulgent toward Golconda than his father had been. He attacked the kingdom several times, and finally forced it to pay a huge tribute. In the meantime, another power, the Marāṭhās, had arisen in the region. The founder of the Māraṭhā Dynasty, Śivajī, was the son of a Bijāpur government official. He made war with Bijāpur and with the Mughals, set up an independent kingdom, and managed to weaken Mughal power significantly. After he died in 1680, his son, Sambhājī, proved a less formidable king, but the Marāṭhās continued to be the primary threat to the Mughals. Golconda, stinging from its treatment at the hands of ʿĀlamgīr, had entered into a defensive alliance with Śivajī in 1674 and continued to support the Marāṭhās strongly.

ʿĀlamgīr's attack on Golconda in 1687 was thus primarily an attack on the Marāṭhās. The Quṭb Shāhi family fled from Hyderābād to the Golconda fortress, where their army held out against 'Ālamgīr's forces for eight months before capitulating (a traitorous Golconda general assisted the Mughals). Golconda was annexed to the Mughal Empire. The last king of Golconda, Abul Hasan Quṭb Shāh, was imprisoned by by 'Ālamgīr in a fort at Daulatābād, where he died after thirteen years in captivity. The Quṭb Shāhi treasury, containing gold, silver, and gems, was shipped to Delhi.

The Mughals finally overran most of the Deccan Peninsula, but the war put a strain on the empire's economy, and the Marāṭhās continued to fight, even after the capture and execution of Sambhājī in 1689. 'Ālamgīr proved to be the last of the great Mughal rulers; the empire, weakened and factionalized after his death in 1707, was vulnerable to domination by western European colonial powers, with Great Britain eventually becoming the most powerful. In the area around Golconda, including Hyderābād, a succession of native rulers called nizāms maintained limited power while accepting British suzerainty from the end of the eighteenth century to the coming of Indian independence in 1947.

One of the Mughal rulers restored some of Golconda's structures in the eighteenth century, but by the early nineteenth century the town was largely abandoned and in ruins, with the citadel being used as a prison for the most hated enemies of the nizām of Hyderābād—enemies who included his sons and wives. At the end of the century, Salar Jang, prime minister to the nizām of Hyderābād, led efforts to renovate the Quṭb Shāhi tombs and replant the gardens surrounding them. Indian government archaeologists now manage the fortress complex and the tombs, and their restoration efforts are ongoing.

Remains of various buildings within the fortress walls, including the armory, several palaces, mosques, and temples, can be viewed by visitors. A former royal mint houses a museum of stone sculptures. The royal tombs are the most impressive structures of Golconda, however.

The historic fortress recently has received a modern addition: equipment for a sound and light show. The show is held year-round every day except Monday; it is presented in Hindi three nights a week, in English two nights, and in the Telegu language one night, making Golconda a site of contrast between the old and the new.

Further Reading: Information on Golconda must be pieced together from general histories of India and from travel guides with historical content. The most authoritative work on Indian history is *The New Cambridge History of India,* edited by Gordon Johnson, C. A. Bayly, and John F. Richards (29 vols., Cambridge and New York: Cambridge University Press, 1987–). Also useful is Vincent A. Smith's *The Oxford History of India: From the Earliest Times to the End of 1911* (Oxford: Clarendon Press, 1919; fourth edition, edited by Percival Spear, New York and Oxford: Oxford University Press, 1981). Among travel guides, some of the best are *India: A Travel Survival Kit* (Hawthorn, Victoria, and Berkeley, California: Lonely Planet, 1981; fifth edition, 1993) and *South Asian Handbook 1994,* edited by Robert Bradnock (Bath, Avon: Trade and Travel Publications, and Lincolnwood, Illinois: N. T. C., 1993).

—Clarissa Levi and Trudy Ring

The Great Wall (China)

Location: Discontinuous locations throughout northern China, from Inner Mongolia and the Bohai coast, west through Liaoning, Hebei, Shanxi, Shaanxi, Ningxia, and Gansu. The traditional start and end points are Shanhaiguan in the east and Jiayuguan in the west, but in fact there was never a single wall.

Description: Series of fortifications built in different places at different times, chiefly with the aim of defending the sedentary cultural region of China from the nomadic steppe people to the north.

Site Office: (for the main viewing spot at Badaling)
CITS
Chongwenmen Hotel
2 Qianmen Dongdajie
Beijing
China
(1) 755017

The modern Chinese phrase for what we call the Great Wall, *wanli changcheng,* translates as "10,000 *li* long wall" (a Chinese *li* is roughly one-third of a mile). However, defensive walls have a long history in China and have been referred to by many different names, including "long walls" *(changcheng),* "walls-and-ditches" *(qiangqian),* "strategic walls" *(saiyuan),* and "border walls" *(bianqiang).* The Great Wall we see today is not, as is often claimed, the remains of a single great project carried out by the "first emperor" Qin Shihuang and regularly updated through the ages. Rather, it is the result of monumental effort by the Ming Dynasty (1368–1644). The reality of Chinese frontier walls, however, is completely overshadowed by the myths that have grown up around an imagined "Great Wall" and by the historical importance of the wall as a symbol.

The first written records of Chinese walls refer to the Spring and Autumn period (722–481 B.C.), when what we now call China consisted of many competing kingdoms. Some scholars claim that the Qi state built walls during the reign of Duke Huan and his minister Guan Zhong between 685 and 645 B.C., but the earliest clearly dated mention is to a wall of the Chu state in what is now southern Henan, which had already been built in 656 B.C. Nearly a mile of this wall has been excavated. Walls of this period and of the following Warring States period (403–221 B.C.) were built as defenses against hostile neighbor states. The "square walls" *(fangcheng)* of Chu were originally erected against its neighbors Jin and Qi, and in 299 B.C. these fortifications were subject to a joint attack by the states of Qi, Wei, and Han. In the fifth century the Qin built a wall in two stages (461 and 409 B.C.) along the west bank of the River Luo following the Jin occupation of the Hexi region (modern Shaanxi.) By 404 B.C. the Qi state had a wall across which the Jin attacked, and in 351 B.C. the Qi built embankments as defenses. The Qi walls, located in Shandong, contain the most extensive remains of all the early walls. The last of them, more than 333 miles long, was built between 319 and 301 B.C. to defend against Chu. Marquis Su of Zhao built a wall against Wei sometime after 346 B.C., with further building recorded in 333–307 B.C. Remains of this wall can be seen in Hebei.

During the later Warring States period, walls were also built as defenses against nomads, at that time usually groups of Xiongnu tribes. The Xiongnu were not always self-sufficient, particularly in commodities such as grain, and when they could not trade for what they needed, they took to raiding the peripheral territories of their sedentary neighbors. The Zhao built two northern walls for this reason. The earlier wall was superseded when King Wuling (who ruled from 325 to 299 B.C.) took lands from the Xiongnu and built a new northern wall in 300–299 B.C. to protect his gains. Some sections of this wall have been located by archaeologists in Inner Mongolia. The state of Yan, in northeastern China, also built a northern wall against nomads, even though Yan maintained friendly relations with them. Estimates suggest this wall was begun in the period 311–279 B.C., and some sections have been found in Hebei and Inner Mongolia. King Zhaoxiang of Qin built a wall to defend against the Yiju nomads, perhaps in 272 B.C.

During the same period, walls were also built to defend against the rising power of Qin. Wei began a western wall against the Qin in the mid–fourth century B.C. This wall was also intended to consolidate Wei's control over several newly acquired Qin cities. Work continued on it until at least 351 B.C. and remains are visible in Shaanxi. In 356 B.C., Wei added an eastern wall against the Qin, running south of the Yellow River. Yan built a southern wall against Qin from 334 to 311 B.C. Remains can be seen in northern Hebei. Chu walls from earlier times were reused as defenses against Qin, and even non-Chinese peoples such as the Yiju built walls against possible Qin depredations.

These walls were not all on the east-west line we usually imagine for the "Great Wall," but frequently ran north-south. Significantly, most walls seem to have focused on reinforcing what the sources refer to as "strategic places" rather than creating continuous defenses in open terrain. Hence the Chu walls included a series of fortifications reinforcing natural strong points, while the wall built by Zhao against Wei secured strategic places along two rivers that formed the border between the two states. The Qin and Wei also built walls along rivers. The walls were simple ramparts of earth or other local materials, such as the layered twig and clay remains found in Gansu. The related fortifications, of which the most prevalent are beacon towers vitally important for military signaling, were also simple earth structures. None of these fortifications remained effective for very long: without regular maintenance they simply eroded.

The first emperor of the Qin Dynasty (221–206 B.C.), Shihuang (ruled from 246 to 210 B.C.), is credited with the building of the so-called Great Wall by ordering his general Meng Tian to link together several pre-existing walls. The Qin had just unified all the earlier Chinese states under one ruler, and the wall was intended to keep out the Xiongnu nomads. Although there would again be periods of competing states within "China Proper," the chief purpose of wall building from now on would be the protection of the sedentary world from the steppe peoples. The wall then became the symbol of everything that divided these different civilizations.

Chinese tradition, adopted by fascinated westerners, holds that the work involved in building the wall was phenomenal, causing great hardship, especially to conscript laborers. The legend of Meng Jiangnü gives expression to this myth. Meng Jiangnü's husband was conscripted to work on the wall, and when winter came she went to take him warm clothes against the bitter northern cold. Upon arriving, she heard he had already died. As she wept in grief a section of wall collapsed to reveal his bones, enabling her to give them proper burial. In fact, the earliest version of this story does not mention the wall, and, similarly, the historical sources for the building of the wall are surprisingly scanty and unclear about what exactly was involved. According to the texts, the wall followed natural features from Lintao (in modern Gansu) to Liaodong (modern Liaoning), covering a distance of 10,000 *li*. Sections of this wall are visible in Gansu, Ningxia, Shaanxi, Hebei, and Liaoning. Some scholars read the textual evidence as meaning that the wall ran north of the great loop of the Yellow River surrounding the Ordos desert, implying a great deal of new building by Shihuang. However, Arthur Waldron and other scholars, following an alternative reading of the same text, propose that walls built by the pre-imperial Qin state, particularly one built during the first half of the third century B.C. running through Gansu and Shaanxi, formed part of Qin Shihuang's Great Wall, along with the northern wall built by King Wuling of Zhao around 300 B.C., and the northern Yan wall from about the same period. This interpretation gives a more satisfactory explanation of the textual and archaeological evidence, even though it diminishes the achievement, and the cruelty, of Qin Shihuang.

It is widely but erroneously believed that once this Great Wall was built by Qin Shihuang, later dynasties did no more than maintain or restore a structure that already ran from Shanhaiguan (Hebei) to Jiayuguan (Gansu.) In fact, during the long period between the Qin and Ming Dynasties, the Han (206 B.C.–A.D. 220), Northern Wei (A.D. 386–534), Northern Qi (550–574), Sui (581–618) and Jin (1115–1234) carried out significant wall building, while some other dynasties carried out repairs on small sections of wall. As Waldron points out, while some dynasties built extensive fortifications, "contemporary sources suggest that they were not continuations of the Qin's Great Wall." However, the *idea* of a wall persisted from Han times onward, such that in relations between the Han and the nomadic Xiongnu an unspecified wall is cited as the boundary between the two, including places nowhere near the line of the Qin wall.

Waldron argues persuasively that post-Qin walls were independent attempts, built at various times and in various locations, to resolve particular defensive problems. By the beginning of the Han Dynasty in 206 B.C., the nomadic Xiongnu were perceived as a major threat. Nonviolent methods of dealing with them gave way to a period of defense by military conquest under Han Wudi (ruled from 141 to 87 B.C.), including fortifications to protect Han gains in the northwest. Following a major defeat of the Xiongnu in 121 B.C., fortresses were built across Gansu in order to protect the Hexi corridor. This line was extended further west in 111 and 110 and again from 104 to 101. Wudi's energetic policies were too costly to sustain, however, and by the later part of the Han Dynasty border security was provided by fortified settlements of farmer-soldiers and sections of wall that carefully utilized natural strong points in the same way that some of the Warring States walls had done.

The end of the Han in A.D. 220 was followed by 360 years of divided rule in China, with non-Chinese regimes frequently in control of the north. Chief among these was the Northern Wei (386–534), whose early rulers campaigned actively against their nomadic neighbors, the Rouran. The Northern Wei also built fortifications, including walls, against the Rouran in 423 (667 miles) and 446 (333 miles). These walls may have been intended to enable the Northern Wei to concentrate on fighting their southern neighbor, Liu Song. Another line of defense was provided by a series of six frontier military commands, established in 429. All these defenses lay in present-day Hebei and Inner Mongolia. In the later fifth century, Northern Wei rulers rejected their nomadic origins in favor of a thoroughgoing policy of sinicization. They halted their regular campaigns against the nomads, and instead an official named Gao Huan sought the building of a wall 333 miles in length as a permanent defensive measure. He claimed that his wall could be completed in a month, but, he added, "its benefit will be felt for one hundred generations." Gao built his wall in forty days in 543, under the Northern Wei successor state of Western Wei (534–550). The same dynasty also built forts at strategic places in 545. Other states also constructed various fortifications during this "Period of Disunion." The Northern Qi (550–574) built approximately 1,000 miles of walls altogether, some of which incorporated lookout towers and gateways in stone. The Later Zhou (557–580) repaired some of these fortifications in 579, following nomadic raids.

The Sui, the next unifier of China Proper, benefitted from a relatively peaceful northern frontier. Nevertheless, the Sui built or repaired sections of wall in 581, 585, 586, 587, 607, and 608. These projects could involve tens of thousands of conscripted laborers, but often took only about three weeks. Some scholars claim these walls had no real strategic

Great Wall of China
Photo courtesy of China National Tourist Office, New York

purpose, but rather served to demonstrate the military strength of the regime. The second Sui emperor also built a grand new capital, defended by a ditch running 667 miles across Shanxi, Henan, and Shaanxi. It is often claimed that the later walls of the Ming Dynasty were built on the foundations of the Northern Qi and Sui walls, but there is no written or archaeological evidence for this.

The Tang Dynasty (618–907), built no walls—only a handful of forts in the northwest. The significance of a division between steppe and sedentary worlds was lost on a dynasty whose founders successfully ruled both. The Song Dynasty (960–1276) also built virtually no walls, although for completely different reasons. Northern frontier defenses, including fortresses, preoccupied Song rulers during the early part of the dynasty, but in 1005 the treaty of Shanyuan established a stable frontier with the formidable nomadic empire of the Liao (907–1125), and peace was maintained by diplomatic means until 1115. The Liao, however, did build sections of wall, mostly in Liaoning, because the dynasty included a large sedentary population that was raided by the nomadic Jürchen Jin. After the Jin conquered the Liao, the Jin were themselves hard pressed by the Mongols and built several walls against them, including major works begun in 1138 and 1181 and others continuing until 1198. The most extensive of these are in Mongolia (Inner and Outer), running far to the north of the Ming wall. Remains show that in places there was a dual line of defenses. Liao and Jin walls feature technical improvements such as inner and outer walls with moats, semicircular towers, battlements, and parapets. These were not enough to stop the Mongol conquest, however, and once the Mongol "world empire" was complete walls once again became redundant. However, the development of the *idea* of a northern frontier wall can be seen in a thirteenth-century historical atlas. This shows the wall following the same single line on every map, even those maps for mythological periods long before any walls were built.

The Ming (1368–1644) were the greatest wall builders. Beginning with an open frontier, they created in three centuries what Waldron calls "the most carefully closed border in pre-modern Chinese history." For most of the first century of the dynasty, steppe campaigns rather than walls kept the postdynastic Mongol tribes in check along the Ming frontier. The Hongwu emperor in the later fourteenth century fortified strategic passes and established two lines of garrisons in an ill-defined frontier zone. An inner, defensive series was built from 1368 to 1376, while the "eight outer garrisons" in forward positions were built mostly during the late 1380s and early 1390s, by which time the Mongols had weakened. A military signaling system on a grand scale was also planned in 1397. The outer garrisons, intended to be self-sufficient, instead became such a drain on resources that the Ming Yongle (ruled from 1403 to 1425) and Xuande (1426 to 1436) emperors withdrew them. Simultaneously, they reinforced earthen ramparts and made new ones, built stone walls in selected strategic spots, and deployed more troops in defense of the frontier.

In 1449 the Mongols destroyed a major Ming army at Tumu and took the emperor captive. In the wake of this Ming defeat, fortifications were strengthened at about fifty major passes between Tumu and Beijing, including the most important pass, Juyongguan, which guards the immediate approach to the capital. Preexisting border embankments and ditches were raised and deepened. The Mongols had recovered some of their strength and established a continuing presence in the strategic Ordos region within the great bend of the Yellow River, thus threatening the traditional Chinese heartland of the Wei River valley and possibly even the capital. The Ming response was governed by political infighting at court, which revolved around the question of whether to attempt to reconquer the Ordos. For nearly a century there was no consistent policy, so that wall building, extensions, and repairs were carried out only sporadically. After the failure of renewed military campaigning in the 1460s and early 1470s, the first major wall was built by the official Yu Zijun in 1474 south of the Ordos desert, in the hope of containing the Mongols. An earthen rampart that took 40,000 people several months to build, this "great border" ran 567 miles from Qingshuiying (northeastern Shaanxi) to Huamachi (northwestern Ningxia) and included more than 800 strong points, sentry posts, beacon towers, and the like. Another wall built to the west in the same year stretched 129 miles from modern Lingwu county to Huamachi. In 1485 work began on 433 miles of wall, but this project was abandoned when the minister in charge fell from power. For fifty years no major construction on the "great border" took place. Nevertheless, a "secondary border" was built close to the "great border" during the reign of the Hongzhi emperor (1488–1505), and a "new border" was built throughout the first half of the sixteenth century. These works created a defense system in two lines, patrolled by permanently stationed troops, but in the meantime many of the earlier earthen walls eroded until they were of no defensive use.

The greatest phase of wall building began after the ultimate rejection in 1548 of another plan to reconquer the Ordos. By now the Ming refused to trade with the nomads, compelling them to raid for the goods they needed to sustain themselves, and the Ming then built more walls and installed further garrisons to contain the raiding. The "nine border garrisons," largely planned by the official Weng Wanda during the first half of the sixteenth century, formed the main defensive units of the Ming army. They were located at Liaodong (modern Manchuria), Jizhou (northeast of Beijing), Xuanfu (northwest of Beijing), Datong (northern Shanxi), Taiyuan (west of Datong), Yansui or Yulin (south of the Ordos), Guyuan (central Shaanxi), Ningxia (eastern end of the Gansu corridor), and Gansu (western end of the Gansu corridor). The walls built as part of this defensive scheme arose roughly in sequence from west to east. The westernmost fort on the line, Jiayuguan, standing alone at the end of the Gansu corridor since 1372, was reinforced with brick in 1539. In addition, from 1539 to 1541 a "western long wall" (ten miles) and an "eastern long wall" (twenty-four miles) were built to improve security, and a "northern long wall" (ten miles) was added in 1573. Walls built during the late fifteenth century west of the Yellow River's northward loop were repaired and extended in the sixteenth century. The Xiguanmen wall (twenty-seven miles) of 1531 may still be seen west of modern Yinchuan (Ningxia). From the east bank of the southward loop of the Yellow River, new northern and southern defense lines were built from 1546 onward to enclose the garrisons of Xuanfu and Datong, possibly converging northeast of Juyongguan. These walls running west from Beijing were the most important part of the Ming defenses and were continually added to. In their heyday there were about 528 miles of wall, with up to four parallel lines in some places.

These defenses could not be breached by the Mongols, but they were easy enough to circumvent. In 1550 a Mongol raid skirted the edge of the heavily fortified section of frontier and then dropped south to Beijing, with the Ming army incapable of stopping them. To counter the Mongol advance, earlier Ming defenses running from Beijing to the sea via the fort of Shanhaiguan were repaired and greatly extended with secondary forts and the like from 1551 onward. Between 1569 and 1579, some 1,200 watch towers with accompanying sections of wall were built to reinforce the chief strategic points along the entire line (800 miles) between a point northeast of Datong and Shanhaiguan. Work was still not complete by the end of the dynasty. Other fortification lines were also built, for instance in the Gansu corridor and at Liaodong. The reigns of Jiajing (from 1522 to 1567), Longqing (1567 to 1573) and Wanli (1573 to 1620) saw the greatest period of Ming wall building. Following earlier models, fortifications included numerous forts, watchtowers, and many beacon towers for signaling. All these were still built mostly of earth until around 1572, after which many forts were faced with brick or stone. The earthen walls themselves also acquired stone facings or were built wholly of brick or stone. This involved skilled, labor-intensive work. Conscripted labor was no longer adequate, and it took 100 people to do what had previously been done by one.

Under the early Qing, the Ming defenses were regarded by many Chinese as, in Waldron's words, "the embodiment of futility and failure." For their part, the Manchu rulers had little use for anything so closely associated with keeping out "barbarians" such as themselves. But where there had been no confusion of the Ming walls with earlier—particularly the Qin—walls, a process of conflation began, fueled in the west by seventeenth-century Jesuit misinterpretations of Chinese records. Europeans picked up on the myth of the

Great Wall. Their fascination with the idea of the wall fostered the unquestioning adoption of many "facts" about it, such as the suggestion that it can be seen from the moon, or even, as historian Joseph Needham maintains, from Mars.

In 1952 the communist government began to restore some sections of the wall, but this project was abandoned during the political campaigns of the late 1950s. During the Cultural Revolution (1966–75), several hundred miles of wall were demolished so that the stone could be used in construction works. Since Mao Zedong's death, however, the wall has been turned into a symbol of China as part of the effort to define modern China's national identity. Chinese scholars have claimed a virtually continuous history for a monolithic Great Wall, starting from the linking project undertaken by Qin Shihuang and carrying on even into the Qing. These interpretations tend to treat any kind of frontier fortification as part of a *changcheng,* even in the case of clearly discrete forts or beacon towers. The myth of the Great Wall lives on.

In 1984 Deng Xiaoping issued the slogan, "Let us love our China and restore our Great Wall!" and he is being taken literally. The remains we see today are from the last period of Ming wall building in the sixteenth century. Most people now visit the heavily restored Ming "Great Wall" at Badaling ridge, just to the north of the Juyongguan pass. Shanhaiguan and Jiayuguan are also popular places for viewing the wall, and restoration work is being conducted at other sites, including defenses predating the Ming.

Further Reading: As yet, no standard work on the wall exists in any language, mostly because it has until recently been treated as a given in Chinese history rather than a subject for investigation in its own right. *The Great Wall of China: From History to Myth* by Arthur Waldron (Cambridge and New York: Cambridge University Press, 1990) is the best, perhaps the only, work to address problems raised by a consideration of what the Great Wall actually was. Most of the other relevant works are in Chinese. Joseph Needham's *Science and Civilisation in China,* volume 4 (Cambridge and New York: Cambridge University Press, 1975) contains a chapter on the wall that provides helpful remarks on the techniques of wall building in general. However, Needham's comments on the Great Wall must be treated with caution, particularly his claim that it is the only man-made work to be visible from Mars. The best photographs of the remains of the wall along its entire length are by Daniel Schwartz and are to be found in his *The Great Wall of China* (London and New York: Thames and Hudson, 1990.) The accompanying essay entitled "The Great Wall in History" by Luo Zhewen is a fine example of the conventional modern Chinese view of the wall.

—Naomi Standen

Guadalcanal (Solomon Islands)

Location: In the eastern half of the Solomon Island Archipelago, which comprises seven large and hundreds of small islands, spread across 900 miles of the southwest Pacific Ocean; approximately 1,500 miles northeast of Sydney, Australia.

Description: A 2,000-square-mile volcanic island, Guadalcanal is the largest of the Solomons. It was first discovered by Spanish explorers in 1568 and became a British colony in 1893. Japan attacked and invaded the island in 1942; it was the site of tremendous air and sea battles between Japan and the United States and its allies from August 1942 to February 1943, resulting in the first major Japanese retreat in the war and the beginning of the U.S. "island hopping" campaign. Since the end of World War II, the capital of the Solomons has been the city of Honiara, situated on the north coast of Guadalcanal; its harbor is enclosed by the sides of a promontory jutting out dramatically into the Pacific Ocean. The Solomon Islands achieved full independence in 1978.

Site Office: Ministry of Culture, Sports, and Tourism
P.O. Box 620
Honiara, Guadalcanal
Solomon Islands
677 203479

Guadalcanal is most famous as the site of some of the fiercest fighting of World War II. The battles for Guadalcanal were crucial in turning the tide of the war to the Allies' favor and brought the island to the world's attention. The U.S. military who arrived there in the summer of 1942 knew little of Guadalcanal or its inhabitants, other than that the popular name of the archipelago was "Cannibal Islands."

The Solomons have been inhabited since at least 2000 B.C., and artifacts found on Guadalcanal have been radiocarbon dated to about 1000 B.C. Melanesians are the indigenous inhabitants of the Solomon Islands, as well as such islands as Papua New Guinea, Fiji, and Vanuatu. The Solomons are sufficiently distant from one another that they developed great differences in language and culture. British rule in the nineteenth century gave rise to a version of the English language known as Pidgin. It is today the official language of the Solomons, the first language ever to unite the Solomon Islanders.

A Spanish captain, Alvaro de Mendaña de Neyra, and his crew on the *Admiranto* and *Capitana,* were the first Europeans to visit the Solomons. They arrived in 1568, after embarking the year before on a long voyage of discovery from Peru. A detailed log of the journey, meticulously kept by the captain's navigator and the steward, recorded the seafarers' surprise at discovering a people who lived wholly naked; on the other hand, the natives had never seen white people, nor, for that matter, anyone clothed from head to foot. Melanesians gave vent to their astonishment by throwing stones at the Spaniards and brandishing their weapons, while the Spanish fired their far more effective guns at them and prepared for a fight. The seamen were desperate for the island's abundant food and obsessed with the possibility that there might be gold for the taking. In fact, Mendaña named the archipelago the Solomon Islands after the biblical King Solomon, whose gold was used in the building of the Temple in Jerusalem.

As the Spaniards explored the islands, they proceeded to name them: Guadalcanal (Great Island), San Cristobal, Santa Isabel, Santa Cruz, San Marcos, Florida. Most of the names have been retained to this day. Besides naming the islands and the archipelago to which they belonged, the Spanish introduced sweet potatoes and yams, marking a decisive change in the Melanesian diet. The Spanish found no treasure in the Solomons, however, and left after six months.

Other explorers, French and British, came and went; because the Melanesians were a warlike people who practiced cannibalism, most Europeans saw no value in the unfriendly islands of the Solomons until the late nineteenth century. The exceptions were missionaries and whalers. Missionaries from a great number of Christian denominations arrived on all the Solomon Islands beginning in the early nineteenth century, and whaling ships began coming in 1849. The Europeans had a tremendous impact on the Melanesians. The missionaries introduced a new religion and other Western customs, and frequently came into conflict with the Melanesians. Those who particularly offended the natives were killed and eaten. The Melanesians did not practice cannibalism because they had a taste for human flesh; rather, it was a means to insult their enemies. Horrified by the islanders' cannibalism, the Europeans came to frown upon all native customs, even arts and handicrafts. Of course, the newcomers brought their own peculiar institutions, most notably the slave trade, which began in earnest in the 1860s. As many as 60,000 natives from Guadalcanal and the rest of the Solomons were taken to work as slaves on plantations in Australia and on Fiji.

In the 1880s colonial powers began to take an interest in the Solomons. The new German Empire was particularly eager to gain overseas possessions and ignited a competition with Great Britain for control of the Solomons. Germany established a protectorate over the northern Solomons in 1884, and the British made the southern islands, including Guadalcanal, a protectorate in 1893. Eventually, cannibalism and the slave trade ceased, and the British established an

Original Henderson Field on Guadalcanal, November, 1942
Photo courtesy of National Archives, Washington, D.C.

administrative capital, Tulagi, on Tulagi Island, just off Guadalcanal. Missionaries continued their work on the islands and established schools, hospitals, and clinics.

In the early twentieth century, big business in the form of large agricultural plantations run by whites, mostly Australians, arrived in the Solomons. Copra (the flesh of coconuts that, when pressed, is used in a variety of consumer products) became a valuable cash crop. Tourism, the mainstay of the Solomons today, was unknown. Although tropical, the islands lacked the breathtaking beauty of Tahiti or Hawaii.

The Solomons were scarcely touched by World War I, in which the Japanese refrained from actively participating. Even with the rise of a newly belligerent Japan in the 1930s, the inhabitants of the Solomon Islands, including the population of nearly 700 Europeans, saw little cause for alarm, because the islands were so remote. The bombing of Pearl Harbor on December 7, 1941, and the conquest of nearby New Guinea in January 1942 changed complacency into fear. Many refugees from New Guinea poured into Tulagi.

Shortly after the conquest of New Guinea, most Europeans left the Solomons in panic. Many missionaries stayed, however, and some became part of the extensive Coastwatching network in the Solomons that performed vital anti-Japanese intelligence work for the Allies.

The Solomons were largely defenseless; none of the Allies had considered them of any strategic importance. By the spring of 1942, the Japanese military decided to seize the islands in order to build an airfield from which they could reach and conquer the New Hebrides, Fiji, and finally, New Zealand, in an effort to isolate Australia from the outside world. Thus, the Japanese would be masters of the Pacific.

When the Japanese swept into the Solomon Islands in the spring of 1942, they encountered a bewildered native population, accustomed to Europeans, not Asians, in positions of authority. Friendly at first, the Japanese established a civilian government in Tulagi and proceeded to introduce Japanese laws and currency and build their airfield on Guadalcanal's northern coast.

The Melanesians, who had been shocked and dismayed at the hasty departure of the Europeans from their islands and had not been entirely happy with British rule, might well have allied themselves with the Japanese had their conquerors treated them as partners. But the Japanese began behaving aggressively and ruling arbitrarily, and the Melanesians soon flocked to the Coastwatchers, aiding them as excellent scouts and rescuing downed pilots and shipwrecked sailors (among whom was the young and grateful John F. Kennedy).

The Japanese had ensconced themselves for barely three months on Guadalcanal when 11,000 U.S. Marines, along with their Australian, New Zealander, and Fijian allies, landed on the island (to be followed by tens of thousands more) on August 7. U.S. victories at Midway and in the Coral Sea had made the Guadalcanal campaign possible. The action was planned hastily, with the goal of capturing the airfield before the Japanese could put it to use, and the Allied forces knew little of the geography of the island or of Japanese military strategy. Thus, although the Allies occupied Guadalcanal and its poorly defended airfield with little resistance, the Japanese reacted by attacking an Allied screening force off nearby Savo Island two days later. The Japanese dealt the U.S. Navy one of its worst defeats ever; four cruisers and a destroyer were sunk, 1,270 men were killed, and another 709 men wounded. Buoyed by their victory, the Japanese launched an effort to retake Guadalcanal and the airfield.

A series of fierce battles ensued. Both the Allies and the Japanese received reinforcements. The Japanese, however, often put in their troops piecemeal—a strategy that placed them at a disadvantage, but one that they sometimes could not avoid, for their reinforcements arrived in small groups and at various intervals from all over East Asia.

Through August, the Allies held a small strip of land around the airfield, which they had named Henderson Field in honor of one of the heroes of Midway. Gradually, they spread out over a wider territory to resist the Japanese attacks. A major attack came in early September. The Japanese managed to come within 1,000 yards of the field but were turned back in what became known as the Battle of Bloody Ridge, so named for a ridge, south of the airfield, from which the Allies fought. The Japanese lost 1,200 men, the Allies far fewer.

Meanwhile, at sea, U.S. and Japanese forces had engaged northeast of the archipelago in late August. There was no clear winner in this action, known as the Battle of the Eastern Solomons. Early in October the naval forces met again at Cape Esperance on the northwestern tip of Guadalcanal. Neither side suffered great losses, but both received reinforcements. Thus replenished, the Japanese forces made another land attack on Henderson Field October 23, but their assault was coordinated poorly and failed.

On November 12 the campaign entered its most important phase. In a renewed effort to take Henderson Field, the Japanese attempted to land a surface force under naval escort. The ships came under heavy U.S. bombardment, and in an engagement that lasted just twenty-four minutes the Americans lost six ships and the Japanese three. The naval battle prevented further Japanese attacks on Henderson Field that night, but the next morning the Japanese again attempted to land reinforcements and bombard the airfield. U.S. air and sea forces, however, managed to shell the Japanese ships and inflict heavy damage. There was another clash at sea the following night. The Japanese finally managed to land only one-third of their reinforcing troops and a fraction of their supplies, and the three-day Naval Battle of Guadalcanal was a decisive U.S. victory. Along with Allied victories the same months at El Alamein and Stalingrad, the victory at Guadalcanal gave the Allies the upper hand in the war. The cost had been great, however; so many ships and planes on both sides had been sunk that the waters between Guadalcanal and the nearby Solomon Islands of Savo and Gela came to be known as Iron Bottom Bay.

The Japanese managed to cling to isolated positions on Guadalcanal, but by early February 1943, their troops, most of them starving and disease ridden, were picked up by their destroyers in the dead of night. By June, most of the western Solomons had been cleared of Japanese troops, but only after heavy casualties and bitter fighting. The United States gained control of the Pacific sea routes and went on to mount "island hopping" campaigns to capture the heart of the Japanese Empire.

Throughout the rest of the war, Guadalcanal remained a major U.S. base. During their stay, the Americans cleared jungle and built excellent roads leading to and from their base at Honiara on the northern coast of Guadalcanal. Because the capital, Tulagi, had been destroyed during the fighting, the colonial government moved its capital to Honiara on the north coast at war's end.

The thousands of Americans in the Solomon Islands exceeded the number of native Melanesians, whose population declined further because of the diseases introduced by Japanese and Allied troops and the dearth of medical help, which missionaries had previously provided them. Nonetheless, the Americans were extremely popular among the Melanesians, thousands of whom volunteered to work in the Solomon Islands Labor Corps to assist the U.S. forces on the island. Unlike the British, the Americans invited the natives to socialize with them and took a sympathetic interest in the Melanesians. Melanesians were deeply impressed by the sight of African-American soldiers and sailors interacting with white Americans at church services, little realizing that the U.S. military was completely segregated in other respects. The Americans also were critical of the British colonial regime. Dissatisfied before the war, Melanesians after the war hardly could tolerate the return of British rule.

British rule did return, but postwar policies were far different from prewar ones. The government actively assisted in the improvement in living conditions and in the general welfare of the Melanesian people, rather than leaving social services in the hands of the missionaries, who had meager resources. A teachers' training college and other institutions of higher education were established, as was a legislative council. The colonial government also inaugurated a major drive to eradicate diseases on the islands, such as leprosy, malaria, and tuberculosis, and to improve sanitation and hygiene. The government's objective was to prepare the islanders for self-rule and eventual independence. In 1978, independence for the Solomon Islands finally arrived, and they joined the British Commonwealth as equals.

Tourism has become a mainstay of the economy, along with agriculture. Thousands of World War II veterans, including many Japanese, have returned to visit the sites of the great battles. The Solomons also are increasingly popular with Australians, who constitute the majority of nonveterans visiting the islands. A steady outpouring of books and movies about Guadalcanal since World War II (among the most famous, the book and film version of *Guadalcanal Diary* and the film *Victory at Sea*) has kept the island in the public consciousness. Guadalcanal has many memorials to World War II, from sunken battleships just off the coast to tanks and gun embankments located throughout the island.

Further Reading: For treatment of the great battles on Guadalcanal during World War II, military historian Eric M. Hammel's engagingly written books are unsurpassed: *Guadalcanal: Starvation Island* (New York: Crown, 1987); *Guadalcanal: Decision at Sea* (New York: Crown, 1988); and *Guadalcanal: The Carrier Battles* (New York: Crown, 1987). For those seeking an illustrated one-volume account, Robert D. Ballard's excellent *The Lost Ships of Guadalcanal* (New York: Warner, and London: Weidenfeld and Nicholson, 1993) is valuable, offering not only a historical but a contemporary look at Guadalcanal. Also worth consulting is Richard Tregaskis' classic *Guadalcanal Diary* (New York: Random House, 1943). For historical background on the Solomon Islands, the best and most thorough work is Judith A. Bennett's *Wealth of the Solomons: A History of a Pacific Archipelago, 1800–1978* (Honolulu: University of Hawaii Press, 1987). Charles Elliot Fox's *The Story of the Solomons* (Taroaniara, Soloman Islands: D. O. M., 1967; revised edition, Sydney: Pacific Publications, 1975) presents the material from a Melanesian perspective; the author is himself a native missionary in the Solomons.

—Sina Dubovoy

Guangzhou (Guangdong, China)

Location: At the mouth of the Zhujiang (Pearl River), in southern Guangdong province, approximately ninety miles northwest of Hong Kong.

Description: Long known in the West as Canton, Guangzhou is the capital of Guangdong province and southern China's foremost industrial and commercial center.

Site Office: Guangdong Tourism Bureau
185 Huanshi W Road
510010 Guangzhou
Guangdong
China
(20) 6677410

Chinese writings trace the history of the Guangzhou region to almost 3000 B.C. It was referred to variously as Nanjiao, Nanhai, and Nanyueh. Some form of contact and even tributary relations seem to have existed with northern China during the Shang Dynasty (1766–1122 B.C.) or earlier. As the region is separated from the north by high mountain ranges, contact can only have been intermittent and infrequent, however. Many Chinese documents make reference to the region's periodic insubordination to northern authorities down to the Zhou period (1122–256 B.C.).

Historians speculate that the first walled settlement on the site of modern Guangzhou was built early in the first millenium B.C. Legend dates the building of the first walled city to the third century B.C., however. One legend tells us that in 334 B.C. the Yueh people built a pavilion on the north bank of the Pearl River. Five immortals, dressed in costumes of different colors and riding rams, appeared at this pavilion, prayed that there never be famine in the area, left an ear of rice, and then reascended to the heavens. The five sheep they left behind turned into rocks. Regarding these events as a good omen, the people built a walled town named Nanwu, which was later to grow into Guangzhou. "The City of Immortals" and the "Sheep or Sheep-Rock Town" have been used over the centuries as alternative names for modern Guangzhou. Another legend attributes the city's founding to refugees from the state of Wu in the lower Yangtze basin who had fled after their defeat by the state of Yueh in 473 B.C.

The historical record for the region starts with the Qin Dynasty (221–206 B.C.), which, after unifying northern China, extended its power southward. The first emperor of the Qin Dynasty apparently needed some of the region's special products, including rhinoceros horns, ivory, tortoise shells, and pearls. In 218 B.C., he sent a force of one-half million men to subjugate the Pearl River region and ensure a steady supply of the desired items. A canal was dug at this time to connect the Pearl River to the Yangtze River to facilitate the movement of troops and goods. Three years of continuous campaigning ended in disaster, but a second expedition, of 214 B.C., was more successful. The area submitted to Qin control and was then divided into three prefectures: Nanhai, Guilin, and Xiang. Half a million people were moved from northern China to live in the delta, undoubtedly for the purpose of facilitating control and assimilation. Nanhai, which included the later Guangzhou, was placed under the control of a military governor, Ren Xiao, and his lieutenant, Zhao To.

During the transition period from the Qin to the Han Dynasty (206–202 B.C.), Ren Xiao, on his deathbed, advised Zhao To to sever ties with the north so as to insulate the delta from the wars and chaos there. Zhao To took the advice and made himself king, changing the district's name to Nanwu. Zhao To established his capital at Panyu, modern Guangzhou. In 196 B.C., the founder of the Han Dynasty conferred on Zhao To the title of Wang or Lord of Nanyueh. In response to the unstable political situation of the early Han Dynasty, however, Zhao To and his successors alternately pursued policies of submission and insubordination to their (frequently nominal) rulers. In 183 B.C., Zhao To even assumed the title of emperor and attacked and occupied several prefectures in the neighboring province of Hunan.

By the time of Emperor Wu Di (140–86 B.C.), the Han Dynasty had consolidated its rule. In 112 B.C., it put a forceful end to Nanyueh's semi-independence, and the old name Nanhai prefecture was restored. Under Emperor Ling (A.D. 168–184), the prefecture became Jiaozhou, with its administrative headquarters at Panyu. According to a Chinese source, gifts of ivory, rhinoceros horns, and tortoise shells carried by Roman ambassadors arrived in the city by way of Vietnam in A.D. 166. This seems to have been the first European contact with Guangzhou. The same source also records a second visit by Roman merchants in A.D. 264.

By A.D. 210 the Han Dynasty was rapidly disintegrating, and Panyu came under the control of the state of Wu. It was during this period that the name Guangzhou first came into use. However, after the conquest of the state of Wu by the Jin Dynasty (265–420), Guangzhou was renamed Nanhai. Guangzhou became a major port during the Jin, and foreign cultural influences and technological innovations entered southern China through Guangzhou at this time. The arrival of a Buddhist monk from India in 281 marked the beginning of Buddhist influence in the region. The first Buddhist monastery in Guangzhou is said to be the Baoen Guangxiaosi (Temple of Filial Piety and Gratitude), which was founded late in the fourth century and became the main base of Buddhist missionaries to southern China. In 401 a monk from Kashmir erected the first Buddhist temple at the complex. In 502 a bodhi tree was planted in front of the temple, which

Huata (Flowery Pagoda) at the Temple of Six Banyan Trees, Guangzhou
Photo courtesy of China National Tourist Office, New York

Chen Clan Temple, Guangzhou
Photo courtesy of China National Tourist Office, New York

survived until 1800, when it was blown down by a typhoon. Fortunately, an off-shoot of the tree had been planted at Shaoguan, and in 1802 a small branch of that tree was successfully replanted at Guangxiao Temple.

In 404 Guangzhou was attacked and taken by the army of Lu Xun, the leader of a peasant rebellion that had started in 399 in Zhejiang. Lu Xun occupied and governed the Guangzhou region for five years, during which time he opened silver mines near the city to fill his treasury. He also built a fleet of 1,000 boats, some reportedly more than 100 feet high and containing 4 decks. In 410, he led his forces northward to attack the Jin Dynasty but was defeated and killed, while his followers were driven out to sea.

Zen Buddhism arrived in Guangzhou in the early sixth century, leaving an indelible mark on the city's culture. Bodhidharma, one of the earliest Zen Buddhists, visited the city in 527. His visit eventually led to the founding of the so-called Southern School of Enlightenment of Zen Buddhism, which flourished in Guangzhou under its founder, Huineng (638–713). According to Buddhist tradition, Huineng shaved his head under the bodhi tree, and the chief monk of the Guangxiao Temple buried his hair in front of the temple and built a pagoda on top of it. It is known as the Yifata (Sacred Hair Pagoda), one of only five extant brick pagodas in Guangdong dating to the Tang Dynasty.

Another famous Buddhist temple was built in Guangzhou in the sixth century, to house a Buddhist relic from Cambodia. The temple, known as the Temple of Six Banyan Trees, is noteworthy for its beautiful pagoda, popularly known as Huata (Flowery Pagoda). The Flowery Pagoda was burned down in the early Song period but rebuilt in 1086. Numerous images of the Buddha are carved on the inner side of the walls. In the fourteenth century, a copper pillar with a golden pearl, since lost, was added to the octagonal structure. From the outside, the building appears to have nine stories, but in fact it has seventeen.

Politically, Guangzhou was dominated in the second half of the sixth century by an indigenous Yueh woman, who came from a family of local chieftains. A gifted political and military leader, she managed to stabilize Guangzhou and suppress numerous rebellions during the transitions from the Liang to the Chen Dynasty in 557 and from the Chen to the Sui Dynasty in 589. In 590 the founder of the Sui Dynasty conferred on her the title of Lady Jiaoguo in recognition of her loyalty and ability and her contribution to the maintenance of peace and order in the region. She was made an official governor of Guangzhou, a distinction rarely granted a woman.

The first city-planning program was introduced to Guangzhou in the early eighth century. Song Jing, an able

Dr. Sun Yat-sen Memorial Hall, Guangzhou
Photo courtesy of China National Tourist Office, New York

Tang official who was banished from the imperial court and appointed governor of Guangzhou, encouraged planned constructions of shops and markets. In addition, he promoted the use of tiles for roofs. Although the art of making bricks and tiles had been known since the time of the Qin and the Han Dynasties, residents of Guangzhou had continued to use Chinese fan palm for the roofs of their houses, possibly for economic reasons. As a result, Guangzhou suffered frequent fires until Song Jing's civil improvements significantly reduced the risk of major conflagrations. The people of Guangzhou were so grateful to his administration that after his return to the north, they erected a hall, the Yi-ai-tang (The Hall of Love [He] Left Behind) to remember and honor him.

Guangzhou's foreign trade, meanwhile, increased to such an extent that Emperor Taizong (627–650) established the Office of Controller of Shipping. An increasing number of foreign merchants and their families, mostly Arabs who traded in rhinoceros horns, ivory, and spices, began to take up residence in Guangzhou. There also were sizable contingents of Persian and Indian merchants. A special school was established at this time to teach foreign children Chinese.

By the mid–eighth century, Guangzhou's Muslim community had grown into a city-within-the-city. Muslim priests ministered to the spiritual needs of the community, while Muslim judges arbitrated disputes. Available evidence points to 741 as the most probable date when the first mosque, the Huaisheng Mosque (Mosque in Memory of the Saint) was built in Guangzhou. The mosque's distinctive minar, or tower, is about 180 feet high and originally had a light at its top to guide ships by night and a golden weathercock to aid sailors navigating up and down the Pearl River by day. Two sets of spiral staircases, each of 153 steps, led to the top, and every May and June the faithful would climb these stairs and sing prayers for a favorable monsoon wind. In 1343 the mosque was burned down, but it was rebuilt in 1350. Repair was undertaken twice more under the Ming and the Qing Dynasties, but the minar retained its original shape and size. In 1955, a glass dome was placed over the top of the tower to prevent rainwater from being blown through the stair door.

The Muslim community at Guangzhou became so strong that Chinese officials began to worry about their influence. Foreign merchants even began to fill official positions. For instance, an Arab merchant was at one point in charge of Guangzhou's customs revenues as well as the province's salt and tea trade. Official worries about the presence of foreigners were not unfounded: in 758 a group of Persians and Arabs based on Hainan Island off the South China coast invaded Guangzhou, causing considerable damage to houses and stores. It was not the last time the city was invaded. A raid led by Huang Chao, a frustrated scholar turned salt-smuggler and rebel, led to more extensive damage in 879, and this time it was the foreign community that suffered most severely. One document claims that 120,000 foreigners perished in the sacking. Historians suggest that this number should be divided by ten to compensate for the customary exaggerations, but that still leaves a massacre of gruesome proportions. Nevertheless, foreign traders were not to be deterred, and the number of foreign families in Guangzhou late in the eleventh century has been estimated at 10,000.

From 907 to 959, China experienced a period of division, during which northern China witnessed a succession of five dynasties, while southern China was carved into nine kingdoms. Guangzhou came under the Southern Han Dynasty (917–971), whose rulers were known for their extravagance. In 934, its founder built a palace with a golden roof and silver floor. Timbers were decorated with silver ornaments, and even drains were studded with pearls. The last Southern Han ruler built an equally extravagant administrative hall, which was extensively decorated with silver and mica. These buildings have disappeared, but many of Guangzhou's historic surviving sites and monuments also date to the Southern Han period. The best known are two iron pagodas known as the East and West Pagodas. The East Pagoda, built in 967, is a seven-story square structure about twenty feet high and resting on a carved stone base. It contains 900 Buddhist shrines, each with a miniscule statue of the Buddha inside. The pagoda was moved to the Guangxiao Temple in the thirteenth century. The West Pagoda, built in 963 and now also at Guangxiao Temple, has been damaged and now only has three stories.

From the tenth until the thirteenth century, Guangzhou continued to grow, while foreign trade increased. In the mid–eleventh century the city walls were expanded, and in 1065 and 1071 an East Town and a West Town were added to the city. Two government schools made Guangzhou the cultural center of southern China. In 1107, it was given the status of *shuaifu,* the seat of the highest government office of the region. However, in the late thirteenth century, Quanzhou, because of its proximity to the Southern Song capital at Hangzhou, became the more favored destination of Arab and Persian traders. Until the arrival of European traders, Guangzhou's volume of trade fell behind that of Quanzhou.

Early in the fourteenth century, a water-clock was installed on the Qinghai Tower. This famous invention served the residents of Guangzhou until the mid–nineteenth century, although the tower was once destroyed by fire and rebuilt in 1375. Matteo Ricci, the famous Jesuit who was in China from 1580 to 1610, is said to have admired the clock so much that he attempted, unsuccessfully, to replicate its mechanism. Unfortunately, the Qinghai Tower was destroyed for good by the British when they invaded Guangzhou in 1857 during the Second Opium War.

Under the Ming Dynasty (1368–1644), Guangzhou became the seat of a greatly expanded prefectural government responsible for the administration of fifteen counties. In 1380, Guangzhou's three separate walled towns were combined and extended northward by almost two miles toward the Yuehsiu Range. After a short period of expansive and aggressive external diplomatic efforts, the Ming Dynasty began to turn inward and became conservative and introspective. It adopted a restrictive trade policy, and only tributary trade was permitted. As legal trading opportunities were limited, smuggling and piracy became rampant on the coast.

In the fifteenth century, Guangzhou experienced another influx of Muslims, as Muslim troops were transferred to the city from other parts of China. Three additional mosques were built to minister to the new residents. The Muslim cemetery on the outskirts of Guangzhou bears witness to the importance of Muslim soldiers in the imperial army. Three tombs, marked by a red stone tablet with the words "The Muslim's Loyal Trio," are the final resting places of three soldiers who died defending Guangzhou against the invading Manchus at the end of the Ming Dynasty. The tombs and the mosques, together with the burial ground of early Muslim imams, are now protected as national monuments.

The Portuguese were the first Europeans to arrive in Guangzhou waters in 1517. They received permission to trade but not to disembark, and their ships were not allowed to sail further upriver than Whampoa Harbor, some ten miles from Guangzhou. In 1563, however, the Portuguese gained permission to use Macau, then a deserted small peninsula at the mouth of the Pearl River. From then on, Portuguese trade with China bypassed Guangzhou. Jesuit missionaries, including Matteo Ricci, often visited the city from their base in Macau, and Christianity gained a permanent, if tenuous, foothold.

Dutch merchants attempted to open trade at Guangzhou in 1604 and 1607 but failed, possibly owing to Portuguese influence from Macau. They occupied Taiwan as a trading base in 1624. Imperial authorities finally licensed the Dutch East India Company to trade regularly at Guangzhou in 1729. British East India Company merchants, who first attempted to establish commercial relations in 1635, began trading annually at Guangzhou as early as 1699. Their main base of operations was at Macau, which they shared with the Portuguese.

The Mings' restrictive maritime trade policy was continued under the Qing Dynasty. Despite some promising and amicable beginnings in the early eighteenth century, the Qings made Guangzhou the only port for overseas trade in 1757, and strict rules limited the movements of foreigners in the city. For example, foreigners were confined to their depots on an island in the Pearl River. They were not allowed to go into the city freely, and they were allowed to visit only a few places for recreation three times per month on fixed days. They were not allowed to bring their families to Guangzhou with them. Predictably, the restrictive rules caused considerable discontent and eventually played a part in the outbreak of the Opium Wars, which pitted China against Britain in the mid–nineteenth century.

The First Opium War broke out in 1839, when Chinese authorities tried to suppress illegal British opium imports. Three years later it was clear that the faltering Qing Dynasty was no match for the Europeans. The war ended, and Guangzhou narrowly escaped becoming a British colony by paying the victors a huge ransom. The Second Opium War, which lasted from 1856 to 1858, took place when the country's government had already been weakened by the Taiping rebellion and had even more devastating results for the Chinese. At the end of the war, the British and the French built an exclusively western settlement on Shamien Island, facing the Guangzhou waterfront. In the wake of the second Sino-British conflict, China began to lose control over its own ports, and Shanghai came to overshadow Guangzhou as China's largest center for international trade.

One of Guangzhou's most curious monuments dates to the interbellum years. In the late 1840s a hall was built at the Hualin Temple to house 500 life-size *luohan* (statues of *arhat* or saints). The sculptures, many of them copied from statues at a Hangzhou temple, include a variety of figures of less than saintly stature. One figure, seated and dressed in imperial robes and headgear, is named the Achievement Buddha. It has been identified as the Qing emperor Qianlong (1736–1796). No doubt he was included for the purpose of pleasing the Qing court. The other figures sit on brick bases, and each has a porcelain incense pot in front of him. The 100th *arhat* has been identified as Marco Polo, the Venetian traveler who was in the service of the Chinese Mongol court late in the thirteenth century.

In the early twentieth century, Guangzhou became the revolutionary base of the Nationalist Party under Sun Yat-sen's leadership. An uprising at Guangzhou in 1911 was quickly and bloodily suppressed by the Qing authorities, but it formed the prelude to the defeat of the Qing by Sun Yat-sen's forces later in the year. In the 1920s, under the nationalist Republic of China, a massive modernization of the city was undertaken, and its present layout was determined at that time. City-planning activities were halted in 1926, when Jiang Jieshi (Chiang Kai-shek) launched his Northern Expedition against the warlords in 1926 and achieved a measure of unification of China under his Nationalist Government or Guomindang in 1928. The political situation in China was anything but stable, however, and in 1925 the communists established the National Peasant Movement Institute at Guangzhou. The institute, run by the Guangzhou Commune under Mao Zedong, trained revolutionary leaders, who were then sent to organize the peasantry across the country. The Guangzhou Commune was crushed in 1927 by the Guomindang.

Guangzhou suffered a series of air strikes in 1937, after the outbreak of the Sino-Japanese War, and the city fell to the Japanese in 1938. Liberated in 1945, the city again came under Guomindang control. After 1949, when the communist government took over, urban improvement projects were again carried out on a large scale. That Guangzhou is now a city of many parks and museums is the result primarily of communist initiative. In the current climate of economic reform, Guangzhou has begun to regain its former dominance. It is now a prosperous and bustling city of 3.5 million inhabitants, and the primary destination of overseas Chinese seeking to resettle in China.

Further Reading: Numerous guidebooks to China contain detailed descriptions of Guangzhou. John Summerfield's *Beijing, Guangzhou, Shanghai* (New York: Fodor, 1988) lists major historic sites and monuments. Peter W. Fay's *The Opium War 1840–1842: Barbarians in the Celestial Empire in the Early Part of the Nineteenth Century and the War by Which Means They Forced Her Gates Ajar* (Chapel Hill: University of North Carolina Press, 1975) gives an excellent account of Chinese relations with the West through Guangzhou in the eighteenth and nineteenth centuries. "Economic Reforms and Socialist City Structure: A Case Study of Guangzhou, China" by C. P. Lo (*Urban Geography* 15, no. 2 [1994], pp. 128-149) describes the changes the city underwent in the twentieth century.

—Kit S. Liew and Marijke Rijsberman

Guwāhāti (Assam, India)

Location: On the Brahmaputra River in Assam, a state in the extreme northeast of India, connected to the rest of the country only by the narrow Silīguri Corridor; nearly 125 miles east of the border with West Bengal and about 62 miles north of the border with Bangladesh.

Description: Guwāhāti, also known as Gauhāti, once the capital of the historic region of Assam, has a population of about 600,000 and is famous for its temples and for the access it offers to northeast India and wildlife reserves. Although not the capital of the modern state of Assam—Dispur has that position—Guwāhāti is the state's leading business center and the political seat of its Kāmrūp district.

Site Office: Government of India Tourist Office
B.K. Kakati Road, Ulubari
Guwāhāti 781 007, Assam
India
547407

Guwāhāti is the historic capital of the region of Assam and the primary commercial center of the modern Indian state of the same name. The historic region of Assam was larger than the present state; it covered the land occupied today by all seven of northeast India's states and territories, as well as a portion of modern-day Pakistan. It came under the rule of several different dynasties, reaching its peak under the Ahoms, a tribe from Burma who controlled the area from the thirteenth to the eighteenth centuries. They were the original builders of Guwāhāti's most famous site, a shrine to the goddess Satī, also known as Kālī, consort of Siva. The temple has been destroyed and rebuilt since its initial construction in the thirteenth century, but it remains a holy place to Hindus and a popular attraction for non-Hindus, who are not allowed to enter the main shrine but have permission to view other portions of the structure.

Only a few facts are known about Guwāhāti and Assam before the coming of the Ahoms. Assam was called Kāmarūpa in ancient times, and Guwāhāti, then known as Pragjyotishapura, was its capital until the middle of the seventh century A.D. The region was settled by a diverse group of tribes. Early legends arising in the region suggest a dynastic conflict mirrored in the rivalry of the devotees of Krishna, the eighth and peasant incarnation of Vishnu, and those of Siva, the god of creation and reproduction, represented with phallic imagery. The first historically documented rāja of the region dates from late in the first century A.D., but names of semilegendary rulers are known from as long ago as the first millennium B.C., including King Narakāsura, whose son Bhagadatta distinguished himself in the great war recounted in the epic poem the *Mahābhārata,* which is understood to have mythologized real events, chiefly concerning the absorption of the social and religious attitudes of invaders into indigenous Indian culture.

The region generally was able to retain its independence from various empires and invading forces, but by the fourth century A.D. the king of the ancient ruling Hindu dynasty in Assam was acknowledging the overlordship exercised by Samudra Gupta, the second of the Gupta emperors attempting to reestablish the perished glories of the old Mauryan Empire on the subcontinent. Assam was independent of the Guptas' successors, however, and also resisted outside cultural forces, such as the Buddhist religion. In spite of the failure of Buddhism to take root in Assam, the Chinese traveler Xuan Zang, who had left western China for India in search of early Buddhist writings and relics, visited the Assam court in 640. He reports that the king was Kumar Bhaskara Barman, and his description of the people as small and dark-complected suggests they were descended from East Asian stock. Although Xuan Zang found very few Buddhists in Assam, where Hinduism was the religion of the people, he was able to document the depth and fertility of the soil and describe the towns surrounded by moats filled with water from banked-up lakes.

Little more is known of Assam before the thirteenth century. There were Pāla rulers there, presumably from the Buddhist Pāla Dynasty in Bengal, and the region appears from time to time to have been united under a single monarch, although it was more often divided into petty fiefdoms. For some centuries control of the region was disputed between Koch, Ahom, and Chigitia powers. Only in the early thirteenth century did the Ahoms arrive from Burma and the Chinese frontier to found a dynasty that lasted for centuries. Originally Buddhist, the Ahoms absorbed the region's Hindu culture, although no Ahom king officially converted to Hinduism until 1655. Guwāhāti—which received this name sometime after the Ahom conquest—served for a time as the seat of a provincial governor, and in 1786 it became the dynastic capital.

Guwāhāti was an important city to the Ahoms, as indicated by the construction of the Kamakhya Temple, dedicated to Satī, in the thirteenth century. According to legend, Satī threw herself on a funeral pyre in mortification after her father's affront to Siva. Siva went around the world with her body and wreaked so much havoc that Vishnu, the Hindu god of creation, pursued him and eventually chopped Sati's body into pieces. Her *yoni,* or vagina, is said to have fallen on Guwāhāti's Nalachal Hill, representing Siva's *liṅgam* (a phallic symbol). The temple was built on the site of this symbolic union. Human sacrifices once were made at the temple; after they were prohibited, animal sacrifices took their place, and

Temple at Guwāhāti
Photo courtesy of Air India Library, New York

these continue today. The present temple was built in 1665 from the remains of earlier ones after destruction by Muslim invaders. It is shaped like a group of beehives and is a fine example of the Assamese style of architecture. It has been refurbished several times and remains a center for worship of Satī, with practices strongly influenced by the Tantric brand of Hinduism, with its strong sexual and occult overtones. Non-Hindus are allowed to view the sacrifices and purifications at the temple, but may not enter the main shrine, where the stone *yoni* lies under a gold canopy. Not even the people assigned to clean the temple are permitted to see the stone; they must carry out their work blindfolded.

The invasion that caused the temple's destruction was one of a series that menaced Guwāhāti and Assam from the thirteenth through the seventeenth centuries, although with no lasting success. The Assamese acquired the reputation of being warlike and predatory, accustomed to sailing down the Brahmaputra in fleets of canoes to raid the rich districts of the delta before retiring to the forests and swamps. In 1638 they pillaged the countryside around Dacca (Dhākā), and their territory was ravaged in return by the governor of Bengal. The king of Assam, Jayadhwaj Singh, renewed his raids on the delta during the civil wars between the sons of Mughal Emperor Shāh Jahān in the late 1650s. 'Ālamgīr (Aurangzeb), who emerged victorious in the civil wars and became Mughal emperor in 1658, was determined to avenge the repeated attacks. He sent an invading force of 12,000 cavalry, 30,000 foot soldiers, and several hundred armed vessels into Assam in 1661. His general, Mīr Jumla, to whom 'Ālamgīr owed much of his earlier success in defeating his brother Shujā, was incensed by a raid on Guwāhāti by the Ahoms, who captured twenty of his guns there; Guwāhāti had come under Mughal control in the 1630s and would change hands frequently thereafter. Mīr Jumla's army, considering the conflict with the Assamese a holy war (the Mughals were Muslims), retook Guwāhāti, as well as Garghaon, which yielded considerable military supplies and treasure, and Kathalbari, the capital of neighboring Kuch Bihār. Mīr Jumla defeated the rāja and obtained the submission of most of the tribal chieftains, but was driven back by the heavy rains and the Ahoms' interruption of his supply routes. Famine, disease, and desertions decimated his army.

Mīr Jumla's chronicler noted that the favorite Assamese tactic always had been to cut the supply lines of an invading force, a strategy clearly dictated by the topography. If that failed, the Assamese declined battlefield confrontation, burned the grain fields, and took the peasants into the mountains, where they awaited the rainy season. The chronicler writes,

> In this manner . . . numerous armies have been sunk in that whirlpool of destruction, and not a soul has escaped. . . . Assam is a wild and dreadful country abounding in danger. . . . Its

> roads are frightful, like the path leading to the nook of death. . . . The inhabitants resemble men in nothing beyond this, that they walk erect on two feet. . . . Every army that entered the limits of this country made its exit from the realm of life; every caravan that set foot on this land deposited its baggage of residence in the halting-place of death.

When the rains ended, the Mughal army was nonetheless still able to reengage the Ahoms, whose king sued for peace and agreed to become a Mughal vassal, to send a daughter with a dowry to the imperial court, to surrender large amounts of treasure and many elephants, and to give up tracts of territory in the west and north. On Mīr Jumla's death in 1663, owing to the hardships of the campaign, the Ahom king did none of these things; instead, he and the subsequent Ahom kings successfully confronted the Mughal commanders. Guwāhāti itself changed hands eight times in fifty years, but ended under Ahom control in the 1680s, when it was recovered by Ahom king Gadadhar Singh and became the residence of the Ahom governor of lower Assam.

Gadadhar Singh, a strong ruler, not only drove out the invaders but resolved internal disputes among Ahom nobles. He oversaw the building of many roads, bridges, and temples in Guwāhāti and the rest of Assam. He was succeeded in 1696 by Rudra Singh, another powerful monarch, who reigned until 1714. Shortly thereafter, however, a general decline in Assamese social order appears to have taken place, and the kingdom became unstable. Throughout northeast India land records were not properly maintained, so that it was impossible to impose reasonable fiscal assessments. The economy was agrarian, and everyone, from the individual peasant to the government itself, had an interest in agriculturally productive land. In 1786, the same year that Guwāhāti became capital of all Assam, Lord Charles Cornwallis became British governor general of India and attempted to reform the land situation; Assam was not technically under British rule at this time, but the British still were influential. Cornwallis established a system of outright ownership of land and therefore a hereditary landed aristocracy. The solution proved worse than the problem, as it upset the traditional balance by making landowners a class of absentee *rentiers*. Cornwallis's successor, Sir John Shore, reversed Cornwallis's policy, but Assam already was suffering internal dissension, which led to an invasion by Burma in 1817.

The result was the Burmese Wars of 1824–26, 1852, and 1885. Bodoahpra, the Burmese king, died after a thirty-seven-year reign in 1819, and was succeeded by his grandson Hpagyidoa. In 1821–22 Burma annexed Assam. The Burmese court at Ava, on the Ayeyarwady (formerly Irrawaddy) River near Mandalay, had announced its intention of taking Chittagong and Calcutta, and the British felt obliged to protect their interests. They drove the Burmese from Assam early in 1825, and in February 1826 confirmed its cession by the Treaty of Yandabo. The second and third wars did not affect Assam directly, but after the 1826 cession Guwāhāti was made the seat of the British administration of the state. The British developed tea plantations throughout Assam, with Guwāhāti serving as a center for the processing of this crop. The British also laid out a network of roads and, for their amusement, founded numerous golf clubs in the region. The tea industry, now in Indian hands, remains the core of Guwāhāti's economy. In 1874 the British headquarters moved to Shillong in the Khāsi Hills, now the capital of the state of Meghālaya. Guwāhāti, still an important city, suffered severely in the earthquake of June 12, 1897. Earthquakes continue to plague the area.

When India became independent in 1947, Assam had to give up some territory to the new nation of Pakistan. Reorganization of Indian states after independence reduced Assam to its present area, bordering Bhutan and the state of Arunachal Pradesh on the north, the states of Nāgāland and Manipur on the east, the states of Mizorām and Tripura to the south, and the states of Meghālaya and West Bengal—and the nation of Bangladesh—on the east. Since modern-day Bangladesh, formerly the Indian state of East Bengal, became part of Pakistan in 1947 and an independent country in 1971, Assam and the other eastern states have been isolated from the rest of India; only a narrow strip of land connects them to the remainder of the nation. An independence movement, marked by periodic outbreaks of violence, has threatened Assam's major industries: tea (the state produces 60 percent of India's tea) and oil (Assam produces 50 percent of India's output of this commodity). By the early 1990s, the Indian military had quelled most of the violence, but the atmosphere was still tense. Many Assam residents feel neglected by the Indian government and resentful of the many illegal immigrants who have come to their state from Bangladesh; many immigrants were killed during the 1980s.

The continuing tensions have led to travel restrictions, although Guwāhāti usually has been open to foreign tourists; visitors, however, are advised to check on the current situation before planning trips. Guwāhāti has much to attract visitors. In addition to the Kamakhya Temple, it is home to the Hindu Janardhan Temple, which contains an image of Buddha, indicating that while Buddhism won few adherents in Assam, the eclectic Assamese culture assimilated Buddhism into Hinduism to some degree. The Umananda Temple of Siva on Peacock Island in the Brahmaputra River, dating to the rule of Gadadhar Singh, is visited annually by thousands of Hindus during the Shivratri festival. The Nabagṛaha Shrine, or Shrine of the Nine Planets, is situated on Chitrashala Hill to the east of the central part of the city, and was once a center for astronomical and astrological study. The Hayagriba Madhab Temple at Hajo on the north bank of the Brahmaputra, about twelve miles from Guwāhāti, is an important place of pilgrimage for Hindus, who regard it as sacred to Vishnu, and for Buddhists, who believe that Buddha attained nirvana here, and that the temple contains his relics. Also in Hajo is the mosque of Pīr Giyasuddīn Aulia, known as the Pao Mecca, believed by

Muslims to be one-quarter as holy as Mecca's great mosque. Guwāhāti also has several museums and is a busy, vibrant city, with its prosperity fueled by tea processing, oil refining, shipping on the Brahmaputra, and higher education—the city has a university and a law school.

Visitors also are attracted by Guwāhāti's proximity to two wildlife parks. The larger, northeast of Guwāhāti on the banks of the Brahmaputra, is the Kaziranga Reserve, home to the world's largest population of the rare one-horned rhinoceros, about 1,000, although in 1908, when the reserve was established, the species was on the verge of extinction. The park also has buffalo, deer, elephants, tigers, bears, and many species of water birds. The Manas Wildlife Sanctuary on the edge of the Himalayas, northwest of Guwāhāti, has numerous streams and is among the most beautiful of India's wildlife parks. It was established as a tiger reserve in 1928, and it, too, is home to the one-horned rhinoceros and a great variety of water birds in addition to tiger and buffalo.

Further Reading: In addition to the relevant sections of *The New Cambridge History of India,* edited by Gordon Johnson, C. A. Bayly, and John F. Richards (29 vols., Cambridge and New York: Cambridge University Press, 1987–) and Vincent A. Smith's *The Oxford History of India: From the Earliest Times to the End of 1911* (Oxford: Clarendon Press, 1919; fourth edition, edited by Percival Spear, New York and Oxford: Oxford University Press, 1981), *A History of India* by Hermann Kulke and Dietmar Rothermund (London: Croom Helm, 1986) is valuable. Of the many guidebooks to the area, one of the best is *India: A Travel Survival Kit* (Hawthorn, Victoria, and Berkeley, California: Lonely Planet, 1981; fifth edition, 1993).

—Anthony Levi and Trudy Ring

Gwalior (Madhya Pradesh, India)

Location: North central India, 150 miles south-southeast of Delhi, in the state of Madhya Pradesh.

Description: Old fortress town that once was the capital of the princely state of the same name; passed through the hands of many conquerors; new city, Lashkar, built adjacent to it about 1800.

Site Office: Madhya Pradesh State Tourism Development Corporation
Hotel Tansen
6 Gandhi Road
Gwalior
Madhya Pradesh
India
(34) 0370 or (34) 0371

Gwalior's imposing fortress dominates the surrounding town and provides a clear indication of why this area was contested by so many different rulers for so many centuries. The fortress, atop a 300-foot sandstone hill, has the appearance of being impregnable; Bābur, founder of the Mughal Dynasty, called it "the pearl amongst fortresses of Hindi." The fort was not truly impregnable, as evidenced by the number of times it has changed hands, but it was a strategic site, as control of Gwalior was considered crucial to control of the central provinces of India.

According to legend, Gwalior was founded in A.D. 8. In that year a local chieftain, Sūraj Sen, was cured of leprosy by a drink of holy water (taken from a sacred pool that still can be seen within the Gwalior fortress) offered by a Hindu saint named Gwalipa, to whom a shrine still stands in Gwalior. The grateful Sūraj Sen set up a town and fort named for the holy man, who told Sūraj Sen to take the surname Pal; Gwalipa promised that as long as Sūraj's descendants kept this name, they would remain in power in the region. Eighty-three descendants did so, but the eighty-fourth called himself Tej Karan, and the family lost its realm.

A definite historical record of Gwalior, however, begins in the late fifth century, when the fort was held by Toromāṇa, a king of the Hūna tribe, who controlled a large realm that included the Mālwa tableland of central India and the western reaches of the Gupta Empire. Mihirakula, his son and successor, built a sun temple at Gwalior, according to an inscription in the fort. (The temple that stands at Gwalior today is a new construction, built to emulate the sun temple at Konārak.) Mihirakula, whose capital was at Siālkot (now in Pakistan), not Gwalior, was known as a despot, a conqueror (he extended his kingdom into Afghanistan), and a persecutor of Buddhists. He was driven from his throne in approximately 528 by the kings of Magadha and Mandasor. He then seized power in Kashmir, but died shortly thereafter.

Gwalior next appears in the historical record as a possession of the Gurjāra-Pratihāra clan of the Rājput people in the ninth century. The Rājputs had a reputation for courage and independence, but were split into so many clans that they seldom acted in concert for any extended period. They also were great promoters of Hindu religion and culture, and defended their faith against Muslim invaders. The Gurjāra-Pratihāras claimed to be descended from Lakṣmaṇa, younger brother of Rāma, the legendary hero who was believed to be an incarnation of the Hindu god Vishnu. They are credited with building Teli-kā Mandir Temple within the Gwalior fort, probably in the ninth century. Initially, the temple was dedicated to Vishnu, but later it may have been converted to the worship of Siva, another member of the Hindu trinity (the third major deity is Brahmā). The temple displays a mix of regional styles, including Dravidian and Indo-Aryan, and is extensively decorated with sculptures. Above the thirty-foot-high doorway is a figure of Garuḍa, a man-bird creature believed to convey Vishnu on his travels. Near Teli-kā Mandir are a pair of temples, the Sās Bahū (Mother-in-Law and Daughter-in-Law) Mandir, likely dating from the eleventh century and also a center for the worship of Vishnu.

The Rājputs controlled Gwalior for some time. They fought off a Muslim attack led by Maḥmūd of Ghaznī in 1021. Another Muslim conqueror, Quṭb-ud-Dīn Aybak, ruler of Delhi, succeeded in taking Gwalior from the Rājputs in 1196, but the Rājputs regained it in 1210. Quṭb-ud-Dīn Aybak's son-in-law and successor Iltutmish then retook Gwalior in 1232. Rather than submit to Iltutmish's forces, the Rājput women of Gwalior committed mass suicide by burning, an act known as *satī* or jauhar. The Jauhar Tank where their sacrifice took place still exists. The fortress town remained under Muslim control until 1398, when the Tomara (also spelled Tonwar) branch of the Rajputs took power.

The most distinguished of the Tomara kings was Mān Singh, who ruled from 1486 to 1516. He had the political and military skill to maintain his Hindu kingdom's independence despite the presence of powerful Muslim rulers nearby. He also was a patron of the arts who attracted many noted musicians to his court. His most enduring contribution to Gwalior, however, was architectural. The Mān Singh Palace, located within the fortress walls and still in excellent condition, is sometimes called the Chit Mandir (Painted Palace) because of the extensive pictorial decoration on its exterior. Both paint and tiles were used to represent ducks, peacocks, and elephants. The predominant blue tones mixed with touches of green and gold are striking against the palace's red sandstone background. The enormous palace has an eastern face about 300 feet long and 100 feet high. Of its four stories, two are below ground. The underground section, with its innovative ventilation system, could be used

Mān Singh Palace (Chit Mandir), Gwalior
Photo courtesy of Air India Library, New York

either as a prison or as a place of refuge when the fort was being besieged. (A later ruler of Gwalior, the Mughal emperor ʿĀlamgīr, had his brother Murad imprisoned and executed here.) Next to his palace, Mān Singh built the Gujri Mahal Palace for his favorite queen, Mrignayani. This palace now houses an archaeological museum noted for its collection of Hindu and Jain sculptures.

Mān Singh and his army were able to defend Gwalior against attack by Sikandar Lodī, the sultan of Delhi, in 1505. Sikandar's son, Ibrāhīm, made an assault on the fort in 1516. Mān Singh was killed early in the fighting, but his forces, passing to the control of his son, held out for a year before surrendering. Within about ten years, the Mughals rose to power; the dynasty's founder, Bābur, took Gwalior as part of his process of conquering the Delhi sultanate. The Mughals' hold on the city was contested by the Afghans, under Shēr Shāh, who captured it in 1542, but the Mughal emperor Akbar took it back from Shēr Shāh's successors in 1558.

The Mughals built palaces, named for Emperors Shāh Jahān and Jahāngīr, at Gwalior; these rubble-and-plaster constructions still stand, but they are of little architectural importance. The Mughals carried out acts of destruction as well as construction at Gwalior. Bābur's troops defaced a group of caves and sculptures that had been carved during the previous century on the rock faces flanking the road to the fort's southern entrance. These carvings, made by adherents of the Jain religion, of which Gwalior had long been an important center, were subsequently restored. Nearly 100 of them in all, the carvings range from tiny niches to caves large enough for human habitation to statues of important Jain teachers. They are divided into five principal groups.

The Mughal period also was marked by construction outside the fortress walls, in the old city of Gwalior, north and northeast of the fort. The Jāmi Masjid, dating from 1661, is a beautiful mosque built of sandstone quarried from the hill on which the fort stands. Nearby is the tomb of Muḥammad Ghaus, a Muslim saint who assisted Bābur with his conquest of Gwalior. It is a fine example of Mughal architecture, with domes, towers, and delicate ornamental carving. Another famous tomb in the vicinity is that of Tānsēn, a singer who was a favorite at Akbar's court. The tomb is simple, but Tānsēn's reputation makes it a popular pilgrimage site for musicians. There once was a tamarind tree near the tomb; according to legend, chewing the leaves of the tree would improve one's voice.

During the seventeenth and eighteenth centuries, a new power, the Marāṭhās, rose to challenge the Mughals. ʿĀlamgīr (Aurangzeb), who reigned from 1658 to 1707, was the last of the Mughal emperors to exercise any real authority. His actions, however, also paved the way for the empire's decline: his Islamic fundamentalism alienated many of his subjects, and his wars with the Marāṭhās and their allies strained the empire's economy. In approximately 1751 the Marāṭhās were able to take Gwalior from the weakened Mughals.

Under the Sindhia branch of the Marāṭhās (from 1745 to the 1840s), Gwalior played a key role in India's struggle with the British. The Sindhias had risen from poverty to a position of power through military and civil service to the Marāṭhā *peshwa* (leader). About 1770 they obtained a grant of much central Indian territory from the *peshwa,* and set up the state of Gwalior. The Sindhia capital originally was at Ujjain, but they eventually moved it to the city of Gwalior. The Sindhias engaged in many military expeditions to expand their territory. An alliance by other Marāṭhā leaders with the British resulted in the British capture of Gwalior in 1780, but Mahādāji Sindhia, the Gwalior ruler, managed through skillful negotiation to persuade the British to recognize his independence. He eventually wielded much power in India, and was able to avoid serious conflict with the British during the remainder of his reign, which ended with his death in 1794. His adopted son, Daulat Rāo Sindhia, succeeded him.

In the power struggle that followed the deaths of key Marāṭhā leaders at century's end, the Marāṭhā confederation's nominal head, Baji Rao II, asked for British protection, which would make the Marāṭhās subordinate to British officials in India. Several Marāṭhā clans, including the Sindhias, repudiated this agreement, bringing on the Marāṭhā War in 1803. Daulat Rāo Sindhia suffered a series of defeats by the British that year, and at year's end he was forced to sign a treaty that stripped him of much of his territory, including the city of Gwalior. The city was restored to him two years later, but tension with the British continued, as Daulat Rāo failed to follow through on promises to assist the British militarily.

After Daulat Rāo's death in 1827, Gwalior had a succession of ineffective rulers, mostly of minority age, under whom there ensued much internal strife and concentration of power in the hands of the military. The British governor-general of India, Edward Law, earl of Ellenborough, decided to intervene in 1843, sending troops led by Sir Hugh Gough. After two costly defeats, the Gwalior government signed a peace treaty ceding to the British territory that would produce enough revenue to finance a British garrison at the capital. This treaty also limited the size of Gwalior's own army and appointed a regency council that would run the government when rulers were not of age. The Sindhias thus remained nominal rulers of Gwalior, but the British actually controlled it.

Tension between native Indian soldiers and their British leaders eventually led to the Indian Mutiny of 1857–58. The Indian forces at Gwalior, numbering about 6,500, joined the uprising, although Jayaji Rāo, the Sindhia mahārāja, supported the British. Gwalior became the scene of some of the most intense fighting of this period. In June 1858, after the insurrectionary forces had been defeated at Jhānsi, about sixty miles away, they occupied the Gwalior fort. Among those fighting the British was a woman, Rani Lakshmi Bai of Jhānsi, who resented that the British had not allowed her to rule in her own right after her husband's death. She was killed in the fighting at Gwalior; her body, clad in men's clothing, was discovered when the British recaptured the fort. She

Teli-kā Mandir Temple, Gwalior
Photo courtesy of Air India Library, New York

became revered by the Indians in much the way Joan of Arc is revered by the French, and a monument to her was built in Gwalior.

After putting down the mutiny, the British rewarded Jayaji Rāo with grants of territory, but maintained possession of the Gwalior fort. They finally relinquished it to Jayaji Rāo's son, Mādhava Rāo Sindhia, in 1886, by which time it no longer held any strategic significance. Both Jayaji Rāo and Mādhava Rāo were considered efficient rulers and were co-operative with the British. Because of this they received appointments to various positions of influence within the British Empire. Jayaji Rāo also received British loans to finance the construction of his Jai Vilas Palace, built from 1872 to 1874 to a design by Sir Michael Filose. It stands south of the fortress, in the new town of Lashkar, which means "the camp," a name it acquired after Daulat Rāo Sindhia set up camp there in the early nineteenth century. The enormous palace was built in something of a rush, to be ready for a visit by the Prince of Wales. Resembling an Italian palazzo, it is elaborately decorated, containing what are claimed to be the two largest chandeliers in the world; elephants were brought in to test the strength of the ceiling from which they are suspended. The palace is still the residence of the local mahārāja (since Indian independence, a position of prestige but no power), but part of it is a museum. Tombs of the Sindhia rulers are located nearby, as is the Moti Mahal, another palace of the Sindhia mahārājas, now used as an office building.

The Sindhias continued to govern Gwalior until the city and state were integrated into independent India in 1947. Lashkar, the new town built adjacent to the Gwalior site in the early nineteenth century, has a popular bazaar and an economy based on manufacturing and commerce. Located in almost the exact center of northern India, it has excellent transportation facilities providing access to most of the subcontinent's major cities and historic sites. Gwalior itself remains one of the area's most interesting historic sites, displaying the influences of the succession of rulers who laid claim to the allegedly impregnable fortress.

Further Reading: As there is no comprehensive source on the history of Gwalior, it is best to consult general histories of India. The most authoritative is *The New Cambridge History of India,* edited by Gordon Johnson, C. A. Bayly, and John F. Richards (29 vols., Cambridge and New York: Cambridge University Press, 1987–). A much earlier work, Vincent A. Smith's *The Oxford History of India: From the Earliest Times to the End of 1911* (Oxford: Clarendon Press, 1919; fourth edition, edited by Percival Spear, New York and Oxford: Oxford University Press, 1981) is still of some value. Travel guides that feature useful sections on Gwalior include *India: A Travel Survival Kit* by Hugh Finlay, Geoff Crowther, Bryn Thomas, and Tony Wheeler (Hawthorn, Victoria, and Berkeley, California: Lonely Planet, 1981; fifth edition, 1993) and *South Asian Handbook 1994,* edited by Robert Bradnock (Bath, Avon: Trade and Travel Publications, and Lincolnwood, Illinois: N. T. C., 1993).

—Clarissa Levi and Trudy Ring

Hakodate (Hokkaidō, Japan)

Location: At the foot of Mount Hakodate, on the southeastern end of the Oshima Peninsula in the southwest portion of the island of Hokkaidō (formerly Ezo), in Hokkaidō prefecture.

Description: A port city, one of the first in Japan to be opened to international trade, and the site of the Goryōkaku fortress.

Site Office: Hakodate Tourist Information Center
12-14 Wakamatsu-cho
Hakodate, Hokkaidō
Japan
(138) 23 5440

Hakodate lies on the southwestern extremity of the island of Hokkaidō, on an isthmus below Hakodateyama (Mount Hakodate), 1,099 feet high, the upper part of a submerged extinct volcano. The city's development over the past 700 years or so has been conditioned by its reliance on the mountain for protection and on the sea for food and prosperity.

The city is appreciably older than any other Japanese settlement on the island, which was known as Ezo until 1886. Before the first Japanese settlers arrived, Ezo was the home of the Ainu people, who are ethnographically distinct from the Japanese. Scholars still dispute whether the Ainu entered the island directly from Siberia, with whose peoples their culture shares some features, or retreated to it from Honshū, the main island of Japan, where there were certainly Ainu as late as the ninth century A.D. (for example, Mount Fuji, the highest and best-known mountain in Japan, probably takes its name from an Ainu word). Their history in relation to the Japanese is all too similar to the history of native Americans and other indigenous peoples. After centuries of Japanese conquest and assimilation, the Ainu now number fewer than 20,000, and their culture, based on complex oral traditions but lacking either writing or centralized institutions, has been reduced to providing souvenirs for tourists.

It may well be the case that, like most place names in Hokkaidō, "Hakodate" derives from an Ainu word, since the Ainu inhabited the Oshima Peninsula on which the city stands as well as the rest of the island. An alternative and surely less plausible explanation of the name, which is written with characters meaning "box" and "building," is that it refers to the castle built there by the Kanō family in the fifteenth century, some 200 years after Japanese settlement began in the area. Hakodate, dependent on fishing and perhaps on sporadic trade with Siberia, appears to have developed quite rapidly into one of the main Japanese settlements, located in the island's southwestern corner, the area nearest to Honshū and farthest away from concentrations of Ainu. For several centuries this remained a frontier zone, remote from events in the area around Kyōto, which was the heartland of the Japanese polity, economy, and culture. In 1603, however, Tokugawa Ieyasu became the latest of several warlords to force a powerless emperor to appoint him *shōgun* and proceeded to allocate the 75 percent of Japanese territory that he did not rule directly to a number of *daimyō* (lords) subordinate to him. In 1606 he granted control of southwestern Ezo to the Matsumae family, who continued to govern it until 1869. Although they presumably took charge of the Kanō family's castle at Hakodate, they had their headquarters in another castle at Fukuyama, fifty-seven miles southwest of Hakodate. (The area they governed ceased to be named for them in 1869, but Fukuyama has been renamed Matsumae in their honor instead.)

Under the rule of the Matsumae, who effectively had a free hand in developing the fishing industry and suppressing the Ainu, the Oshima and Shakotan Peninsulas were opened up to further Japanese settlement, while the rest of Ezo was left largely untouched. In 1633 the Matsumae sponsored the foundation of Koryu-ji at Hakodate, which is believed to be the oldest Buddhist temple on the island; and in 1654 they permitted the opening of perhaps the first hot spring resort on the island, at Yunokawa, four and one-half miles from Hakodate.

By 1639 the Tokugawa Bakufu (tent-government) in Edo (now Tōkyō) had completed the imposition of a strict foreign policy that is often misleadingly, and Eurocentrically, referred to as "isolation," but which is better understood as a version of the mercantilist system of supervised trade, practiced at the time by most European countries as well as by China and Korea. As in those other cases, the aim was to maximize benefits for the rulers while minimizing contracts that might produce military threats to their power. Thus, although the British, Spanish, and Portuguese, who were suspected of having colonizing intentions, were forbidden to enter Japanese waters, the Dutch were given a trading post at Nagasaki, while Koreans and Chinese also traded through designated routes and ports. Ezo, remote both from the heartland of Japan and from the Eurasian landmass, probably remained unaffected either way by this policy until around 1741, when ships from Russia, a power unknown to the Japanese 100 years earlier, but now rapidly expanding to the east, began to put in at Hakodate in search of fuel and provisions. By then Hakodate was one of the leading fishing ports on Japanese territory, and the Matsumae lords appear to have turned a blind eye to collaboration between their subjects and the exotic foreigners, presumably preferring to exploit an additional source of trade and revenue rather than enforce a policy that no longer seemed to make sense.

The Bakufu was greatly alarmed by reports from Hakodate—probably exaggerated or distorted, since what-

A view of Hakodate, with Goryōkaku Fortress in the foreground
Photo courtesy of Japan National Tourist Organization

ever Russians had actually landed there were fishermen, not naval personnel—and took matters into its own hands. In 1799 the regime imposed direct rule on the Matsumae domain, appointing the first of a series of officials, the Ezo bugyō or Hakodate bugyō, to enforce the exclusion policy. In 1807 their powers were extended over the entire island. Fourteen years later, however, with the Russians turning their attention to eastern Siberia, Alaska (until 1867), northern Sakhalin, the Kamchatka Peninsula, and, just to the north of Ezo, the Kuril Islands, the Bakufu decided that the emergency was over and restored the Matsumae.

Little more than a generation passed before the Russians joined with the British and the Americans in pressing Japan to abandon the exclusion policy altogether. An American delegation, under Commodore Matthew Perry, first opened negotiations with the Tokugawa regime, having arrived at Edo in July 1853, one month before a Russian embassy led by Admiral Putyatin arrived at Nagasaki. Both embassies returned, to the same ports, in the following year, Putyatin's in January and Perry's in February. The outcome for Perry was the Treaty of Kanagawa, which he and a Bakufu delegation signed in March 1854 and which opened Shimoda and Hakodate, the first two "Treaty Ports," to American ships. Perry himself visited both cities soon afterward. In October the British Admiral Sterling secured similar rights for British ships at Nagasaki and Hakodate, and in February 1855 Putyatin at last signed a treaty that temporarily determined the boundary between Russia and Japan and opened all three ports to Russian vessels. Putyatin's was also the first of the many treaties that created "extraterritorial" status for foreigners residing at the ports, who were to be subject to their own countries' laws rather than to Japan's. Thus, within a matter of months Japan had been officially opened to contact with three of the most powerful trading nations in the world. A foreign quarter, now known as Motomachi, was established near Koryu-ji in 1854 and a coaling station was established in 1855 to supply both foreign vessels and the first Japanese steam ships, using coal from mines farther inland. Foreigners were not allowed to settle permanently in Motomachi until 1857, when the Americans once again led the way in negotiating with the Bakufu. Further treaties signed in 1859 removed all remaining restrictions on foreigners' activities in the city. Today a foreigners' cemetery and a number of European-style houses are all that remain of the quarter.

Russian Orthodox Church of the Resurrection, in the Motomachi area, Hakodate
Photo courtesy of Japan National Tourist Organization

The predominance of Russians among the foreign residents in these years is indicated by the establishment in 1862 of the Orthodox Church of the Resurrection—the Haristos-sei Kyōkai in Japanese—built in Byzantine style at the foot of the mountain, from which Father Ivan Nikolai Kasatkin introduced the Russian form of Christianity into Japan. After a fire in 1907, the church was rebuilt in 1916. Nevertheless, the Bakufu remained extremely suspicious of the Russians' intentions and ordered the building of the Goryōkaku, a fortress in the shape of a five-pointed star, on the side of Hakodateyama. It was constructed between 1855 and 1864. The first European-style fortress in Japan, it was designed by Takeda Ayasaburō, who had studied European traditions of military engineering while living in the Netherlands as one of the first Japanese permitted to study abroad.

The fortress, however, became the location not for international conflict but for the final confrontation between forces loyal to the last Tokugawa *shōgun*, brought there by sea from Edo by the admiral Enomoto Takeaki, and the new imperial army, commanded by Kuroda Kiyotaka, which had been raised by the group of modernizing officials that had overthrown the Bakufu. Enomoto's 2,000 soldiers sustained a provisional government for a "republic of Ezo" until the besieging imperial troops forced them to surrender in May 1869. (The final battle is reenacted at the fortress every May, and uniforms and weapons from the two sides are displayed in a small museum in its grounds.) Hakodate was then made the headquarters of a new body of officials, the Kaitakushi or Development Agency, which took over from the Matsumae and was charged with modernizing the island, later renamed Hokkaidō (literally, the Northern Sea Circuit).

In 1871, however, the Kaitakushi was moved inland to Sapporo, a planned city created as a purpose-built capital, and Hakodate reverted to a subordinate role as a "gateway" to Hokkaidō from Honshū and as a decreasingly important entrepôt for foreign trade, in competition with more centrally located rival Treaty Ports, such as Yokohama and Kōbe. During the remaining years of the Meiji period (1868–1912), the city underwent further modernization, which in practice meant further adoption of European and American manners and methods. In 1879, for example, the Hakodate Hakubutsukan (Museum) was established under the guidance of Horace Capron, an American working as an adviser to the Kaitakushi. Today it displays local archaeological finds, Ainu artifacts, and items relating to the life of the poet Ishikawa Takuboku in its main building and in the neighboring museums of archaeology and fisheries. The latter is housed in the original wooden building constructed in a European style in 1879, which is now one of the oldest structures in the city. Around the time the museum was opened, the British scientist Thomas Blakiston was in Hakodate, making the observations that have earned him a memorial on Mount Hakodate, indicating the importance of what has come to be called the "Blakiston Zoological Line." This refers to his discovery that Honshū and Hokkaidō contained mutually distinct species of birds and animals, and that the Tsugaru Strait marked the "line" between the two.

Perhaps the strangest imports from the West to arrive in the Hakodate area in these years are the Trappist monastery established about sixteen miles outside the city in 1895 and the Trappist convent established only about two miles from the city three years later. These institutions, the only Catholic religious houses in Japan, were founded by Okada Furie, a naturalized Japanese citizen originally from France. Both structures are now much better known for their butter and cheese production than for their Christian religion, which, in all its forms, has attracted barely 1 percent of the Japanese population.

More conventional types of modernization occurred in 1896, when Shibusawa Eiichi and Ōkura Kihachirō founded the Hakodate Dock Company, a shipbuilding enterprise, and in 1899, when the fortifications of the city were extended from the Goryōkaku to take in a large section of the mountain, which was closed to the public from then on. This further protection of Hokkaidō against the Russians was never tested, for the Russo-Japanese War, which broke out five years later, was won by Japan at Port Arthur and at Tsushima Strait, while in Hakodate quiet and steady development culminated in 1913 with the introduction of streetcars, which still run in the city today.

Although Sapporo was the capital of Hokkaidō, Hakodate remained the largest city on the island until 1934, when a major fire destroyed about two-thirds of its buildings, and a large number of its people moved away, never to return. Recovery from this disaster began immediately but was slowed down, and then reversed, as Japan carried on its disastrous campaign for military and naval supremacy in eastern Asia, which ended in total defeat in 1945. Hakodate, like other cities, had been heavily bombed from 1941 onward; now it was effectively demilitarized. The fortifications on the mountain were dismantled and a cable car was installed to help open up the slopes for recreation; the Goryōkaku was reopened as a public park.

Hakodate is now the third-largest city in Hokkaidō, with a population of approximately 320,000. Since 1952, when the Japanese fishing fleet was permitted to reenter the North Pacific, the city has once again become the main Japanese port for the ships that operate in the fishing season between July and December each year, and it is well known for the squid and other seafood sold at its fish market, which opens at daybreak. It is a sign of the centralizing times, however, that the Hakodate Dock Company, still a major employer in the city, has long since moved its headquarters to Tōkyō. For the people of Hokkaidō, most of whom are descended from settlers brought in after 1869, the few buildings remaining in Hakodate from before the 1934 fire and wartime bombing serve as valued relics of the Japanese pioneers—and their Russian and American advisers and collaborators—whose outlook, including their hardiness and their thirst for innovation, as well as their disdain for the Ainu, still influences life on the island.

Further Reading: The frontier island of Hokkaidō and its oldest city have both been largely disregarded by Japanese and non-Japanese writers alike. However, for fascinating accounts of what Hakodate was like when it was a Treaty Port see *Unbeaten Tracks in Japan* by Isabella Lucy (Bird) Bishop (2 vols., London: Murray, and New York: Putnam, 1880; reprint, Boston: Beacon, 1987) as well as Hugh Cortazzi's anthology *Victorians in Japan: In and Around the Treaty Ports* (London: Athlone, and Atlantic Heights, New Jersey: Humanities Press, 1987). Takiji Kobayashi's novella *The Factory Ship* (1929), translated by Frank Motofuji (in *The Factory Ship and the Absentee Landlord,* Tōkyō: University of Tōkyō Press, 1973) offers an unforgettable account of conditions on ships in the North Pacific fishing fleet, albeit from a revolutionary Marxist standpoint that most readers today will find variously sad, laughable, or mystifying.

—Patrick Heenan

Hami (Xinjiang Uighur Autonomous Region, China)

Location: Northeast of the Tarim Basin at the head of the Gansu corridor, south of the Tian Shan mountain range and west of the Gobi Desert. The Xinjiang region has been variously known in Western literature as Chinese Turkistan, Eastern Turkistan, and Chinese Tartary.

Description: A strategically important oasis city on the ancient silk route and one-time principal city of the city-state of Hami, or Komul as it is known in Turkic languages, Hami is today a busy commercial town.

Contact: Xinjiang Tourism Bureau
46 Jianguo Road
830002 Urumqi, Xinjiang
China
(991) 227912

For centuries Hami was the major hub of East-West communication. All caravans and envoys traveling along the Northern Silk Road from the West to the Chinese capital were obliged to pass through Hami. Here the two branches of the Northern Road, which skirted the southern and northern foothills of the Tian Shan Mountains, converged before passing into China. As an outpost of the Chinese Empire, lodged between two worlds, it was of considerable strategic importance. Not surprisingly, its history is that of a turbulent frontier city racked by frequent warfare.

Little is known about the early history of Hami, but there are written references to it as early as the second century B.C., and tombs that have been excavated there are estimated to be 3,000 years old. Known by various names throughout its history, it is commonly identified by scholars as the Yiwu, or Yiwulu, of the Eastern Han Dynasty (A.D. 25–220). The Chinese early recognized the value of the site's location but had to vie with nomadic tribes for control of it. In A.D. 73, in an effort to reassert imperial power over the troublesome Xiongnu people, the Chinese established a military colony there. By the end of the century, however, the Chinese had lost it to the Xiongnu, and it was not until 119 that a Chinese army of about 1,000 soldiers marched from the Chinese city of Dunhuang to reestablish the garrison. Once again neighboring rulers, including the king of Turfan, the city-state lying to the north, offered their submission to the Chinese emperor, but it was not long before nomadic tribes attacked and annihilated the Yiwu garrison. Yet again it was reestablished, only to be attacked and nearly destroyed by the Huyan Xiongnu tribe of Barkol in 151; the prodigious efforts of the Chinese soldiers were all that kept their force from being wiped out.

After the Xiongnu were neutralized by another tribe a few years later, there ensued a period of peace and prosperity. Buddhist religion, Indian literature, and Greek art came to Hami along the Silk Road in the early centuries A.D. Even when the Han Dynasty disintegrated into civil war, the various nomadic tribes were too busy fighting one another to try to conquer the oasis towns on the trade routes. In time, new powers arose and sought control of the strategic town of Hami. In 456 the Toba, the Turkic-Mongol rulers of northern China who founded the Northern Wei Dynasty (386–534), occupied the Hami oasis. From there, two years later, they launched a raid against the Juan-juan, a group of Mongols who previously had raided Toba territory. The Northern Wei kingdom became fragmented in the sixth century, and the region around Hami appears to have fallen to the khanate of the western Turks (T'u-chüeh), who had their winter quarters on the shores of the Issyk Kul or in the Talas Valley, but whose lands extended to the mountains east of Hami. Control of Hami subsequently passed back and forth between the western and eastern Turks.

Not until the Tang Dynasty (618–907) did the Chinese reassert control over the western trade routes. In the early seventh century the Chinese reoccupied Hami, known in the Chinese annals of this period as Yizhou. It was about this time that the Chinese Buddhist pilgrim Xuan Zang spent several weeks in Hami, resting in order to regain his strength after his arduous crossing of the Gobi Desert. Other visitors to Hami in this period included Muslim missionaries from the Middle East. Although the Chinese remained nominal protectors of Hami throughout the Tang period, it appears that from the late eighth to mid–ninth century, the Tibetans established their presence there, finally driving out the Chinese in 851.

The old nomadic Uighur Empire, founded in 744, did not extend to Hami, but after its collapse in 840 one group of Uighurs emigrated westward and settled on the eastern slopes of the Tian Shan range before moving into the area of Turfan and Hami. The indigenous non-Turkic people of the region gradually began to speak Uighur, and the area became known as Uighuristan. There appears to have been a large degree of religious tolerance in Uighuristan; from the tenth century Buddhists, Muslims, Manicheans, Nestorians, and pagans coexisted. Indeed, Buddhist communities remained in the region until the early fifteenth century, by which time Islam was the predominant religion in the region. The Uighurs also exerted considerable cultural influence in the area; for instance, after the Mongol conquest, the Mongolian language was written with the Uighur alphabet.

Hami in the Middle Ages came under the influence of a variety of nomadic Mongol tribes. The Mongol holdings were consolidated into an empire by Genghis Khan in the thirteenth century. Upon the division of the Mongol Empire at Genghis's death in 1227, Hami was passed to Chagatai, his second son. It remained the possession of Chagatai's descen-

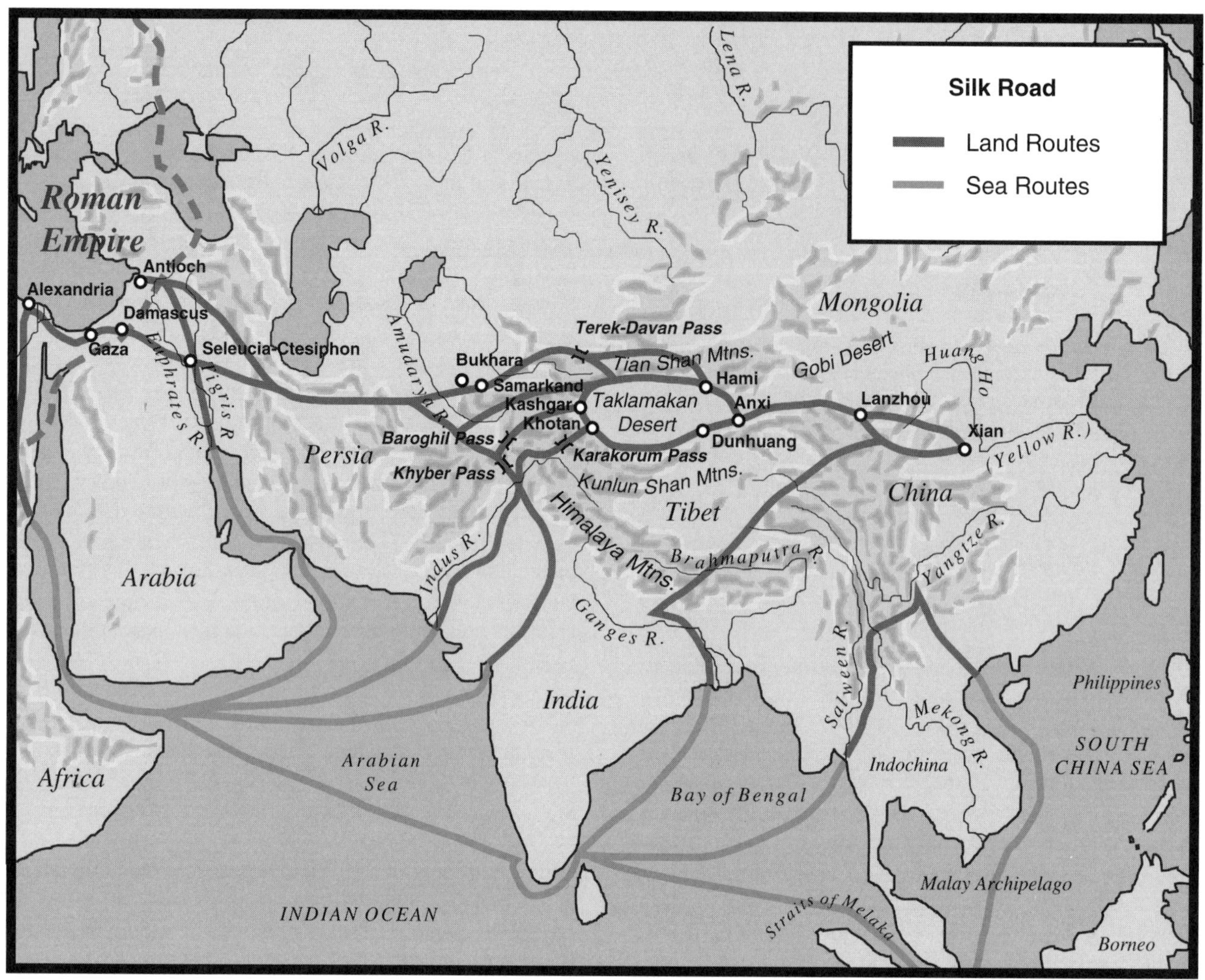

Map of the Silk Road
Illustration by Tom Willcockson

dants into the next century. Under the Mongol Empire, overland trade routes corresponding to the old silk routes saw renewed traffic to and from Europe; once again, Hami became an important stopping point for caravans.

In the 1270s Marco Polo visited Hami and came away with a description of a somewhat decadent city, with attractions including luxuriant gardens and delicious fruits, most notably its melons. Polo writes:

> The inhabitants are worshippers of idols and have their peculiar language. They subsist on the fruits of the earth, which they possess in abundance, and are enabled to supply the wants of travelers. The men are addicted to pleasure and attend to little else except playing upon instruments, singing, dancing, reading, writing, . . . and the pursuit, in short, of every kind of amusement.

Polo then describes the Mongol khan's vain attempts to force the inhabitants to relinquish their custom of abandoning "the females of their family to accidental guests" for the duration of their stay in the city.

In 1368 the Ming Dynasty came to power, supplanting the Mongol rulers of China. Initially, however, Hami was not under direct Ming control. In 1390 the Hami ruler, a Chagatai by the name of Unashiri, received an envoy from the Chinese Ming court and agreed to pay tribute in horses (the horse trade was very important in Hami). The following year relations between China and Hami became strained when Unashiri requested permission to hold a series of horse fairs, a demand that Ming emperor Hongwu for some reason considered inappropriate. Ming troops were dispatched against Hami and were victorious. After Emperor Yongle ascended the Chinese throne in 1403, the court encouraged better relations with Hami in order to secure a good supply of military horses. In 1406 a Chinese military colony was established at Hami, but the region continued to be administered by local rulers who sent tribute to the Ming court. The area was at peace and trade was thriving.

Hami once again drew the attention of Mongol nomads, however. By the mid–fifteenth century, the Oirats of northwestern Mongolia were consolidating their conquest of the steppes. Under their chieftain Ensen they moved to secure their frontier in the west. Attacking Hami in 1443, 1445, and 1448, they finally forced the Ming out of their strategic foothold.

There then followed one of the most turbulent periods of Hami's political history. After the death of Ensen in 1463, the region was invaded by a nomadic tribal group, and the local khan fled. The ruling family returned to power only with Chinese assistance three years later. Then in 1473 the ruler of Turfan, 'Ali (a descendant of the eastern branch of the Chagataites), seized the Hami oasis from the local ruler, Hanshan, who was regarded by the Ming as a vassal of China. The Chinese advanced, driving 'Ali back to Turfan, but as soon as the Chinese forces turned back, he reoccupied Hami. Nevertheless, 'Ali was obviously aware that his hold on Hami was tenuous, for in 1476 he sent an embassy with tribute to the Chinese court. In 1482 Hami was reconquered by Hanshan, but six years later Hanshan was killed in an ambush by 'Ali's son, Ahmed, who then took possession of the region. The following year, Hanshan's followers recovered Hami, but their victory was short-lived. In 1493 Ahmed captured the new ruler of Hami as well as the Chinese resident and held them hostage. In anger, the Chinese court closed the frontiers with Turfan, halted all trade and tribute missions, and expelled Uighur traders from the neighboring region of Gansu. This led to so much local resentment against Ahmed that he was finally compelled to leave. In 1513 the local ruler of Hami submitted to Khan Mansur, Ahmed's eldest son, and in 1517 Mansur settled in Hami, which he used as a base for raids into China.

The Oirat confederation broke up after Ensen's death in the mid–fifteenth century, but by the late seventeenth century the Dzungars, descendants of the Oirats, had formed a reconstituted western Mongol state and established themselves as a major Central Asian force. Under their leader Galdan, the Dzungars now took possession of Turfan and Hami from the eastern branch of the Chagataites. However, in China the Manchurian Qing had come to power; Emperor Kangxi was on the throne and was intent on reestablishing China's hold over eastern Turkistan. In 1690 and 1695 he sent his troops against Galdan and succeeded in destroying the Mongol forces. With the death of Galdan in 1697, the emperor did not attempt to consolidate Chinese rule over the Dzungar region, but he secured control of Hami by persuading the Muslim khan of Hami, 'Abd-Allah Tarkhan-beg, to recognize his suzerainty. A Chinese garrison was once more established at Hami, now the focal point of a new ring of defenses in the northwest. Nevertheless, during the early eighteenth century Hami endured several Dzungar attacks.

In 1755, during the reign of Emperor Qianlong, the Qing Dynasty finally resolved to conquer the Dzungar region north of the Tian Shan Mountains. Hami offered little resistance, and indeed the ruling family was instrumental in assisting the Qing in their subsequent conquest of the Tarim Basin. Thereafter Hami became a major supply center for the Chinese forces that throughout the nineteenth century were sent periodically to eastern Turkistan to quell revolts. In 1865 Hami fell briefly to the Kashgar rebel Yakub Bek, who conquered much of Xinjiang between 1862 and 1875. However, it was soon back under Chinese control and served as a strategic headquarters from which the Chinese general Zuo Zongtang directed the reconquest of eastern Turkistan from 1875 to 1877. In 1884 Eastern Turkistan was officially designated as a province of China, but Hami remained a semiautonomous principality and was allowed to retain its khan and local elite in recognition of the service provided by the local rulers during the campaigns of the eighteenth century. The population of Hami at this time was composed, as it is today, of Chinese Muslims (Hui), Han Chinese, and Turkish Muslims, the latter of whom were to reclaim the old name Uighur only in 1935.

With the collapse of the Qing Dynasty and the onset of the Republican period, Hami remained, at least nominally, under local rule. It was in fact the last remaining khanate in Eastern Turkistan. The indomitable British missionaries Mildred Cable and Francesca French were at Aratam, the khan of Hami's summer residence to the northeast of the city, to record his death there in March 1930. The Chinese provincial governor, Jin Shuren, decided that this was an opportune moment to terminate the Hami principality. The heir was summoned to Urumqi, the provincial capital, where it was resolved that Hami would be divided into three administrative districts; the new khan was given the nominal title of high advisor to the governor and compelled to reside in Urumqi. The former principality may have left much to be desired, but for the Turkic Muslims of Hami it held strong religious as well as temporal significance. Whether the new khan was, as has been alleged, an incompetent opium addict was of no consequence to his people; rumors of his confinement in Urumqi exacerbated grievances concerning corrupt magistrates and tax collectors. In 1931 the Turkic Muslims of Hami rose in an open revolt and besieged the provincial troops in the old fortified city. Government forces were rapidly dispatched, and the result was an uneasy stalemate. Realizing that their cause was all but lost, the Hami insurgents sent for assistance to Ma Chongying, a Chinese Muslim general based in Gansu. Ma made forty-three attacks on the besieged Chinese garrison in Hami before retreating to Gansu. Two years later he returned and briefly administered the little that was left of Hami before continuing on his mission to conquer the whole province. The city was largely in ruins; not even the khan's palace and gardens escaped destruction.

When the provincial government finally regained control of Hami it was with Soviet assistance. Governor Sheng Shizai, Jin Shuren's successor, enjoyed close relations with the Soviet Union. In yet another display of Hami's strategic importance, it was here that the Soviets chose to station the Red Army Eighth Regiment from 1937 to 1943.

After the end of World War II there was some agitation for an autonomous Uighur nation in Xinjiang, but the civil war between Nationalist and Communist forces soon pushed this issue aside. The victorious Communists continued to have trouble with the Uighurs, who had little in common with the Chinese ethnically, religiously, or linguistically. In 1955 Xinjiang was designated the Uighur Autonomous Region, although it remained part of China. Uighur resentment against the Chinese increased during Mao Zedong's Cultural Revolution (1966–75), when mosques were closed. After Mao's death in 1976, his successors allowed the mosques to reopen. Demands for Uighur independence have continued into the 1990s, but they have been tempered somewhat by the prosperity brought by the development of industry in the region. Mining, manufacturing, and agriculture form the basis of Hami's economy today; the city is still a fertile oasis and is still famous for its melons.

Today there is not a great deal of historical interest to see in Hami with the exception perhaps of an impressive Muslim tomb complex, known as the Tombs of the Hami Kings. Only a few of the Hami rulers and their families are buried here. The complex is said to have been built from 1820 to 1840, with financial support from the Qing government, but there is evidence it may date from an earlier period. A stone tablet at the site is dated 1706 and mentions that architects were invited from Beijing to design major buildings in the city.

Another site of interest in Hami is the Tomb of Gai Si, a Muslim missionary who came to the region in the seventh century. He died at Xingxingxia, near Hami, but his remains were dispersed during World War II. In 1945 he was reburied in Hami. Also worth visiting is the Hami Cultural Office Museum, which displays artifacts found in 3,000-year-old tombs about twelve miles from the city. The graves were excavated in 1978 and again in 1986.

Further Reading: While no major work has been written in a western language on Hami, scattered references to the city and its history can be found in René Grousset's *The Empire of the Steppes: A History of Central Asia,* translated from the French by Naomi Walford (New Brunswick, New Jersey: Rutgers University Press, 1970; originally published as *L'Empire des Steppes,* Paris: Payot, 1939); Mildred Cable and Francesca French's *The Gobi Desert* (London: Hodder and Stoughton, 1942; reprint, London: Virago, 1984), and Andrew Forbes's *Warlords and Muslims in Chinese Central Asia* (Cambridge and New York: Cambridge University Press, 1986).

—L. J. Newby

Hangzhou (Zhejiang, China)

Location: Eastern China, near the mouth of the Qian Tang River, approximately 100 miles southeast of Shanghai in the province of Zhejiang.

Description: Populated for thousands of years, the city of Hangzhou rose to greatness as the capital of the Southern Song Dynasty during the twelfth century. An immense cultural and economic center, Hangzhou amazed the celebrated Marco Polo upon his visit in the late thirteenth century. Polo declared Hangzhou to be the greatest city on earth. After the fall of the Song, Hangzhou and its scenic West Lake continued to attract both foreign and Chinese visitors, and today it remains a popular tourist destination.

Site Office: Zhejiang Tourism Bureau
1 Shihan Road
Hangzhou 310007
Zhejiang
China
(571) 5155597

Lying just north of the Qian Tang River in what is today the province of Zhejiang, the city of Hangzhou has fascinated both the Chinese and outsiders for centuries. A Chinese phrase from a Yuan Dynasty (1234–1368) poem by Yang Chaoying, "In heaven above there is paradise, on earth there are Suzhou and Hangzhou," serves to illustrate the place this city occupies in the hearts and minds of the Chinese people. The great thirteenth-century traveler Marco Polo held the city in similar regard, declaring Hangzhou to be "without doubt the finest and most splendid city in the world."

The city was formed some 2,000 years ago as silt from the river created a small bar near the estuary of the Gulf of Hangzhou. To reinforce the precarious sandbar, inhabitants of the area built a dike, in time creating the famous Xi Hu, or West Lake, referred to in countless stories, paintings, and poems throughout Chinese history. The settlement remained a small fishing village for centuries, until the time of the Sui Dynasty (581–618) and the Sui rulers' relentless construction of canals to link their territory.

The importance of the Sui canals is similar to that of the Great Wall built centuries earlier by the Qin emperors. Under Sui Yangdi, the Grand Canal was constructed, effectively linking northern and southern China culturally, politically, and economically. It was during this period of construction around 610 that the city of Hangzhou began to establish itself as a town of importance.

Situated on the crucial link between the two halves of the empire, Hangzhou quickly became a vital commercial center. The emphasis on trade expanded as agricultural development around Hangzhou made the region the empire's most important agrarian sector.

Hangzhou and its breathtaking West Lake became the subject of numerous poems during the Tang Dynasty (618–907), a period renowned for its development of the arts. Bai Juyi, one of China's most beloved poets, was made governor of Hangzhou in 822 and built a dam at West Lake that continues to bear his name. Another literary figure, the brilliant poet Li Qingzhao, fled south from advancing nomads, making Hangzhou her home in the early twelfth century.

Despite advances made during the Sui Dynasty, Hangzhou did not become a truly world-class city until invading barbarians—the Jürchens from Manchuria, who had established the Jin Dynasty in 1115—pushed the Song Dynasty south from its capital at Kaifeng (where the dynasty had been in place from 960 to 1276) to Hangzhou (thus the designation Southern Song, 1127–1276). The Tang Dynasty had been troubled with occasional advances by warring nomads from outside the empire's boundaries, and these invasions continued during the reign of the Song. The Xia and Kitan tribes harassed the Song to the point that one emperor in 1004 decided to pay tribute to them in hopes that they would leave his empire alone. The attempt did pacify the two tribes, but the dynasty's troubles started anew in 1125 when the formidable Jin tribe toppled the Kitan and advanced on Song territory.

By 1126, the Jin had conquered the Song capital of Kaifeng and taken all valuables and most of the royal family north to their newly founded capital at Beijing. One Song prince escaped capture and fled south, later setting up court at Hangzhou and establishing the Southern Song Dynasty in 1127.

The Jin did not let the new dynasty rest, however, and continued their push south. The Jin advanced—their cavalry slowed by the myriad lakes, streams, and rivers of central China—and for the first three years of the new Southern Song they effectively harassed the fledgling dynasty. At one point, the Jin actually captured Hangzhou. The turning point came for the Southern Song in 1130 at the battle of Huangtian Dang, near the Yangtze River, where for the first time the advancing Jin were defeated.

From their capital at Hangzhou, the Song gathered strength and numbers, and by 1137 they had turned back the advancing Jin and regained a small fraction of the territory lost by the fall of the Northern Song. General Yue Fei, a commander of the Song forces, waged particularly successful battles against the Jin. Yue Fei, however, was ultimately put to death in 1143 by a member of the Song court. Two decades later, the emperor Xiao Zong posthumously restored Yue Fei's good name and had the general buried in Hangzhou in a grand mausoleum, which still stands. Their southern kingdom at last free from attacks, the new Song leadership made

Lingyin Si (Temple of Inspired Seclusion), Hangzhou
Photo courtesy of China National Tourist Office, Los Angeles

peace with the Jin, abandoning the millions of ethnic Chinese in the northern part of the land to the "barbarian" Jin.

As the capital of the Southern Song, Hangzhou exploded with people and development. Just as the center of the empire had been pushed south, the center of Chinese culture shifted to Hangzhou as well. In a short period of time, Hangzhou went from an important commercial center to an imperial capital, its population reaching 1.75 million by 1275.

Cosmopolitan Hangzhou had not only the good fortune to be located on the Grand Canal, but it boasted as well paved streets and numerous smaller canals for easy transportation. Some 117 graceful arched bridges set off by weeping willows decorated a number of canals, adding to the beauty already lent Hangzhou by West Lake. The Song kept their lovely capital as safe and clean as possible, setting up both a public sanitation unit and a fire brigade of some 2,000 members.

Compared to those in the rest of the empire, inhabitants of Hangzhou were fantastically wealthy. Rich families owned large compounds boasting private baths, their houses filled with paintings that became highly developed and prized during the dynasty. Numerous shops were stocked with both daily necessities and costly luxuries. Citizens of Hangzhou had easy access to scarce and expensive traditional Chinese medicine, exotic fish to be raised by the elite at leisure, decorations for the home, and such decorations for the body as hairpieces and cosmetics.

The city boasted the best in entertainment as well. Countless tea shops offered refreshment in scenic pavilions along the lake. Fine restaurants served complex dishes and delicacies, among these being dog and "two-legged mutton" (i.e., human flesh). Elegant and lovely courtesans offered their singing and conversation skills—among others—for a price. And the picturesque West Lake framed by the lush hills and graceful willows was a veritable playground for the wealthy, who passed their time in leisure aboard colorful boats enjoying the good life the Song brought to Hangzhou.

The city's commercial sector also flourished during this dynasty. The sheer number of people occupying Hangzhou warranted a brisk trade with other regions. Hangzhou's prime location on the Grand Canal and its proximity to the ocean served as an advantage, too, as both trade on the waterways and shipbuilding industries grew strong and profitable.

The rule of the Song in Hangzhou was marked by a decided focus on the arts and the ideals of Confucianism. Military concerns, however, were given conspicuously little attention by Song rulers, who far preferred to devote themselves to more intellectual and esoteric pursuits. Although they did what they thought was best for their subjects, in the end the Song emperors' lack of military strength was their ruin.

As had happened before, fierce nomadic warriors swooped down on China; this time it was the Mongols laying waste to the Jin Dynasty in the north. Sensing their inability to withstand the Mongol onslaught, Jin rulers sought assistance from their Song neighbors to the south. Unfortunately for the Song, the rulers in Hangzhou were too short-sighted to see the impending danger the invaders represented to their own empire, and instead they took the opportunity to seek revenge on the Jin. The combined Song and Mongol forces under Genghis Khan crushed the Jin by 1233.

Their ancient foe in ruin, the Song rulers now turned their attention to the Mongols. Confident in their superiority, the Song foolishly ordered an attack on their former allies. The conflict lasted for decades. As the fierce Mongol cavalry swept south in pursuit of the Song, their way was slowed by the same lakes and rivers that generations before had slowed the Jin. Despite their inferior forces, the Song rulers fought bitterly. When the Mongols finally captured Hangzhou in 1276, court officials fled south. A mere three years later, Kublai Khan, grandson of Genghis Khan, defeated the last shreds of Song resistance and united China under the Beijing-based Yuan Dynasty.

Despite the defeat of the Southern Song, the city of Hangzhou was spared destruction and continued as an important cosmopolitan center under the Yuan. It was this Hangzhou that Marco Polo visited in the late thirteenth century. At the command of the Yuan ruler Kublai Khan, Marco Polo made several extensive journeys through China. One journey saw him in an official post at nearby Hangzhou, and from his position there Marco Polo made frequent visits to the still-great city of Hangzhou.

Hangzhou, with its latticework of canals and majestic West Lake, reminded the traveler of his boyhood home in Italy: Venice. Intoxicated with its beauty and cosmopolitan aura, Marco Polo described Hangzhou in painstaking detail, eager to paint a vivid picture of the city still devoted to the pursuit of Chinese intellectualism and arts. He declared that in its wealth and sophistication, Hangzhou surpassed any other city in the world. Polo wondered at its immense population—his Venice had only 50,000 inhabitants, compared to the more than 1 million citizens of Hangzhou—and he marveled at the town's layout and aesthetic wonders. Hangzhou possessed countless wide public squares, its wealthy lived in marvelous two-story houses, and water drawn from West Lake flowed through the canals, taking the city's refuse out to the estuary and eventually to sea.

Polo writes of 12,000 stone bridges spanning the town's wide waterways, of the pleasure craft taking advantage of West Lake's loveliness, and of the countless gardens, temples, palaces, and monasteries in Hangzhou. Although 12,000 bridges is likely an exaggeration on Polo's part, later travelers such as the Arab Ibn Baṭṭūṭah echo his other descriptions.

Of the city's inhabitants, Polo writes of their passion for the arts and study of philosophy, citing their pursuit of peace and general disregard for military matters. He is captivated by the beautiful women of Hangzhou, by the fabulous crafts and silks available in the marketplaces, and by the countless forms of entertainment available. The diet of Hangzhou's residents amazes Marco Polo; he marvels at the number of people eating both fish and meat—costly luxuries at the time—in the course of the same meal.

Some decades later, in the 1320s, the Italian friar Odoric visited Hangzhou and confirmed what Polo wrote, declaring "It's the greatest city in the whole world, so great that I should scarcely venture to tell of it." Odoric did tell of it, marveling like Polo at its sheer size, the circumference of which he estimated at 100 miles. The huge population of the city shocked Odoric as well, and he wondered "how such an infinite number of persons could inhabit and live together."

Eventually, the Yuan Dynasty (1234–1368) gave way to the Ming (1368–1644), which in turn fell to the Qing (1644–1912). Throughout these long periods, travelers and Chinese alike continued to tell of Hangzhou's marvels, and it remained both a popular resort area and successful commercial center. Two Qing emperors, Kangxi (reigned 1661–1722) and Qianlong (1736–96), made numerous visits to Hangzhou during their reigns.

Despite its position of cultural and commercial importance, Hangzhou could not thrive forever, and the once-fabulous capital of the Song was nearly destroyed in the mid–nineteenth century. The Taiping Revolt that began in the early 1850s soon swept southern China. As the ruling Qing Dynasty failed to quell the disturbance quickly, the Taipings gained momentum and moved north. In 1861, the rebellion reached Hangzhou and the city soon fell into rebel hands. The imperial army rallied and recaptured Hangzhou in 1863, but the severe battles waged during the city's initial capture and later liberation decimated its population and all but destroyed the city itself.

Once proud and glorious, Hangzhou now contained only a fraction of the bridges, temples, pavilions, and monasteries that had filled the city in the era of the Song. Those landmarks that survived the Taiping Rebellion were in turn eradicated or severely damaged by Mao Zedong's Red Guards during the Cultural Revolution of the 1960s and 1970s.

One historic monument that managed to survive the ravages of war and time is Lingyin Si (Temple of Inspired Seclusion). Built in the early fourth century, Lingyin Si has been rebuilt and restored numerous times. Some during the Cultural Revolution were in favor of destroying the temple and monastery complex, but others wanted it spared. The matter went as high as Chinese premier Zhou Enlai, who decreed that both the temple and the tenth-century carvings and inscriptions on the nearby rock were to be saved, although the monks would be turned out and forced to do hard labor. A number of elderly monks were allowed to return to the temple in the 1970s, and the temple remains one of the great tourist attractions of the city.

Today, Hangzhou is once again a capital city—the capital of Zhejiang province, one of China's most prosperous. The city has a population of approximately 1.2 million and covers some 165 square miles. The long-standing beauty of West Lake and the surrounding hills, bridges, and pavilions continue to make Hangzhou a popular destination for foreign tourists and the Chinese alike.

No longer approaching the economic stature it possessed under the Song, Hangzhou continues to be a commercial center, widely known for its silk and famous Dragon Well tea. A number of universities in Hangzhou draw students from around China and the world, and the town's pharmaceutical industry enjoys nationwide fame.

Although the zenith of Hangzhou is long past, its memory is still alive in the countless paintings, stories, and poems left from the Tang, Song, Yuan, Ming, and Qing Dynasties. Hangzhou and the lovely West Lake remain despite centuries of war and aggression, providing modern-day China with its proverbial "heaven on earth."

Further Reading: Dun J. Li's *The Ageless Chinese* (New York: Scribner, 1965; third edition, New York: Macmillan, 1978) provides a comprehensive look at China, from its beginning in the Neolithic period until the chaotic time of Mao's Cultural Revolution. *The Chinese Machiavelli* (New York: Farrar Straus, and London: Secker and Warburg, 1976) by Dennis and Ching Ping Bloodworth paints a similar picture of this 3,000-year culture, as does John King Fairbank in *China: A New History* (Cambridge, Massachusetts, and London: Belknap Press of Harvard University Press, 1992). Readers interested in the numerous travelers who reached China and Hangzhou in the days of the emperors will be especially interested in Nigel Cameron's *Barbarians and Mandarins* (New York and Tokyo: Weatherhill, 1970).

—Monica Cable

Hanoi (Vietnam)

Location: The capital of the Socialist Republic of Vietnam, situated in the delta of the Red River in the north of the country, eighty-five miles from the Gulf of Tonkin and the South China Sea.

Description: A city, now of more than 3 million people, that served as the capital for various Vietnamese dynasties and for colonial French Indochina. From 1954 to 1976 it was the capital of North Vietnam, and since 1976 it has been the capital of the reunified Vietnamese state. A city of lakes and temples, Hanoi was ravaged by war in the twentieth century; economic sanctions against the country, a result of Vietnam's occupation of Cambodia, delayed reconstruction until the 1990s.

Site Office: Vietnam Tourism
30 A Ly Thuong Kiet Street
Hanoi
Vietnam
255552 or 264154

Hanoi is a city far older than its name. A small lakeside village on the spot was known as Dai La. Ly Thai To chose it as the capital of his Vietnamese kingdom in 1010 and renamed it Thang Long. A later name was Dong Kinh, often used in colonial times in a Western transcription, Tonkin, to identify the whole of northern Vietnam. Whatever the name, the city has been the capital of the Vietnamese state for most of its history, and Hanoi's development and character are best understood in that context.

The site at the confluence of the To Lich and Red Rivers in the Red River delta has been inhabited since the Neolithic Age. The ancient tribes of the Viet people that emerged there were joined in a unified state in the third century B.C., with the creation of a kingdom initially known as Au Lac. In what are now Hanoi's western suburbs, the king An Duong founded his capital at Ke Chu, which became the site of the Co Loa citadel fortress in 257 B.C. The kingdom, later known as Nam Viet, was formed amid the danger of Chinese invasion. Nam Viet was conquered by the first of the great Chinese dynasties, the Han, in 111 B.C. For several centuries the area was part of China, and the people were much influenced by Chinese culture.

In A.D. 939 the Vietnamese state broke away and established its independence from China, although it was required to pay a regular tribute and remained under Confucian influences. The capital of the independent state, which was ruled in quick succession by the Ngo, Dinh, and Le Dynasties, was first located at Hoa Lu, a town some sixty miles from Hanoi. But when Ly Thai To came to power as the first ruler of the Ly Dynasty (the kingdom was known as Dai Viet), he chose to rule from the site of Hanoi, which he called Thang Long (Ascending Dragon). Supposedly, the king saw a golden dragon flying above the site, a sign that convinced him to create a new capital on the spot.

Thus, the village of Dai La was transformed from a modest settlement built on stilts over the To Lich River into a royal capital fortified by dikes and artificial hills. Already standing was a citadel built in A.D. 791, during Chinese rule. Between this structure and West Lake a city was built that housed the mandarins and troops of the king, as well as the general public. Within this city, a walled Royal City was created for the king's court. This, in turn, surrounded the Forbidden City, which was inhabited by the king, his queens, and royal concubines. Many palaces were built in Thang Long during the early eleventh century; the city's famous Temple of Literature and One Pillar Pagoda were also built at this time.

Hanoi was abandoned as the capital briefly during the rule of Ho Qui Ly, a regent who had deposed the last king of the Tran Dynasty. However, his new capital of Tay Kinh only survived until 1407. The weakness of the late-fourteenth-century Viet state enabled the Ming Dynasty to reassert China's control over its former province, resulting in twenty years of Ming occupation. The emergence of the Le Dynasty under the leadership of Le Thai To finally ended Chinese dominance and resulted in the reinstatement of Hanoi as the kingdom's capital in 1430. Le Thai To is associated with the Lake of the Restored Sword (Hoan Kiem Ho) in the heart of Hanoi. According to legend, the king received a magic sword from the Divine Tortoise of the lake, which enabled him to persevere in a ten-year resistance movement (1418–28) against the Chinese. Le Thai To renamed the city Dong Kinh (Eastern Capital), which later was changed to Tonquin and was known to Europeans as Tonkin.

In the sixteenth century, when the southern Vietnamese frontier had spread over much of the Cham territory, there were three effective governing families: the Mac, the Trinh, and the Nguyen. The Trinh and the Nguyen virtually divided the realm in the following century with a kind of frontier established between them at the Song Gianh. Overall, the Le Dynasty continued to reign but not rule, symbolizing a unity also expressed in elements of a common culture that the Vietnamese attempted to sustain even as they moved south. The city of Hanoi was now the capital of the Trinh. The capital of the Nguyen was at Hue, although by the early eighteenth century their domains had, at the expense of the Khmers, reached a new frontier in the remote south, and their territory included Saigon (since renamed Ho Chi Minh City).

The eighteenth century was a period of stress in both parts of the realm. Both the Trinh and the Nguyen regimes faced major problems and pressed heavily on those they

Ho Chi Minh Mausoleum, Hanoi
Photo courtesy of Permanent Mission of Vietnam to the United Nations, New York

ruled. In 1776 the great Tay Son Revolt began, named after the southern village that was home to the three brothers who led the rebellion, Nguyen Hue, Nguyen Lu, and Nguyen Nhac, known collectively as the Tay Son brothers. The brothers founded a new dynasty even as they faced a new Chinese invasion. The Tay Son army defeated the Chinese on Tet (New Year) 1789 at Dong Da, a suburb of Hanoi. Tay Son control, however, was short-lived. When the emperor died in 1792, a Nguyen prince, Nguyen Anh, established himself as king under the name Gia Long and, thus, another imperial dynasty emerged. Former rulers of the south, the Nguyen reunified the state and moved the capital from Hanoi to Hue. Hanoi became the capital of one viceroy, and Saigon the capital of another. This new kingdom was named Vietnam.

The Nguyen, like preceding dynasties, had difficulty holding the Vietnamese state together. Like earlier rulers, Gia Long's successor, Minh Mang, attempted to do so by borrowing from the Chinese model, including an elaborate civil service, although much of it was inappropriate in south Vietnam. It was also Minh Mang who, in 1820, ordered Hanoi's destruction as a response to the Chinese emperor, who would not recognize the capital at Hue. In 1831, he created the province of Ha Noi (Within the River), also giving this name to the former capital's citadel.

But the Nguyen Dynasty did not face challenges merely from within Asia; it also faced the Europeans. Traders and missionaries had made contact with Vietnam in the sixteenth and seventeenth centuries, and Europeans had supplied weapons to the Trinh and the Nguyen. Their missionaries had left behind Christian communities that survived despite persecution by Confucianist authorities. Now, pressed by their own rivalries, these foreigners were more assertive and better armed. The French had reached an understanding with the Nguyen before the Tay Son Rebellion and had offered help to the Nguyen prince who became Emperor Gia Long. However, in its subsequent attempts to maintain the hard-won unity of the state, the dynasty greatly reduced its European contacts.

The French, however, were unwilling to relinquish the commercial opportunities they saw in Vietnam. In 1858 a French expedition supported by Spanish auxiliaries moved on Da Nang and established it as a French military base. The following year the French seized Saigon under the pretext of responding to attacks on missionaries. These events tested Vietnam's ability to protect its territory; the result was a peace treaty in 1862 that ceded several southern provinces to France.

Just over ten years later, the French made less successful advances on northern Vietnam and Hanoi. Francis Garnier, a French naval officer and explorer, seized the Hanoi citadel and made himself master of the delta, only to be slain by a Chinese bandit. Soon after, the French agreed to leave the citadel and retreat to Haiphong. The resulting treaty of 1874, however, declared the Red River open to trade and permitted the appointment of consuls at Hanoi, Haiphong, and Qui Nhon.

In 1882 the French again attacked the citadel in Hanoi, sending 250 soldiers from Saigon. The death of their leader, Henri Rivière, led to reinforcements and occupation of the entire delta. The Vietnamese rulers now accepted a French protectorate over northern and central Vietnam and, in 1888, the court gave the French the "freehold" of Hanoi. It became a capital again, but now of French Indochina, a union of Cambodia, Laos, and the Vietnamese territories of Cochinchina, Annam, and Tonkin.

During the colonial period Hanoi changed greatly, but it managed to retain many of the characteristics given it by its long history as a capital since 939. At the time of the clash with the French, Hanoi was indeed an agglomeration of capital, commercial town, and juxtaposed villages. The first comprised the citadel, where the representatives of the Nguyen emperor resided. The commercial town lay between river and citadel, divided into a Chinese quarter, home to the richer merchants, and a Vietnamese quarter of artisans. To the south lay a number of enclaves, including the temple of Confucius, the examination compound, the mint, and the south fort (which would be ceded to the French). The villages were scattered amid the marshes and rice paddies of the delta.

The examination compound, where mandarin aspirants had competed, was the site of Garnier's first camp and was occupied by the French until 1876. Later a palace was built for the imperial representative, subsequently used by the Library and Archives. The site also was used by the Gendarmerie and the École des Arts Pratiques. The citadel, built under Gia Long, was a quadrilateral Vauban-style structure, the ramparts of which, largely destroyed under municipal orders in the late 1980s, were to become the outlines of main thoroughfares. Inside, the royal pagoda was on the site of a palace built by Ly Thai To. Its central pavilion, built on a sacred knoll, was razed in 1886. The citadel also contained warehouses, stables, a prison, a firing range, temples, and a great banyan tree. The French installed a race track and watched the races from a tower built by Gia Long.

The commercial town was bounded by the Lake of the Restored Sword, the Red River, and the citadel; it was a place of narrow and congested streets protected by numerous gates. Much of it was burned in 1883, but it was rebuilt quickly under French guidance. It remained a sector with narrow streets, virtually lanes, a densely populated part of a densely populated town, placed in one of the most densely populated zones of the world. Each commodity sold here was relegated to particular streets; the goods thereby gave their names to the different quarters, some of which still bear these names today.

The French city lay between the lake and the fort that had been designed to protect Hanoi against attacks from the river. Fortified at first, it became the site of the French residence-general, the university, and the École Française d'Extrême-Orient. The French quarter developed more to the west than to the south, effectively linking fort and citadel. In independent Vietnam, that too became densely populated.

The focus of French rule, Hanoi was also to be the focus of the struggle for independence from the French. Fearing an interruption of colonial rule during World War II, Vichy France compromised with the Japanese, who left the government in place. However, in March 1945 the Japanese displaced the colonial rulers, and the French troops in Hanoi were interned in the citadel. News of the surrender prompted the emperor's viceroy to set up a political direction committee. But a mass demonstration in front of the Municipal Theater on August 17 clearly showed where the state's political future lay: with the Communist-led Viet Nam Doc Lap Minh (League for the Independence of Vietnam, better known simply as the Viet Minh), which had been founded in 1941 by Ho Chi Minh. Late in August 1945, having journeyed across flooded fields, Ho Chi Minh arrived in Hanoi and settled in a flat at 48 Hang Ngang Street. On September 2, the day that U.S. general Douglas MacArthur formally accepted the Japanese surrender in Tokyo, Ho Chi Minh read a declaration of Vietnamese independence in Ba Dinh Square.

It soon become clear, however, that the French meant to return to Indochina. Open conflict with the new Democratic Republic of Vietnam began in Hanoi in December 1946, and bitter fighting ensued. Supported by China, the Viet Minh waged a guerrilla war against the U.S.-backed French, who, by 1949, had reasserted their right to all of Vietnam; the French renamed it the Associated State of Vietnam and declared the former emperor head of state. This conflict, which became known as the First Indochina War, ended with the defeat of the French at Dien Bien Phu in 1954, when Hanoi was occupied once more by the Democratic Republic of Vietnam.

The resulting peace agreements, known as the Geneva Accords, divided the country at the seventeenth parallel. But the peace did not last. The Viet Minh soon were pitted against a new regime in the south, the Republic of Vietnam, which was backed by the United States in the Second Indochina War, known in the U.S. simply as the Vietnam War. U.S. bombs hit Hanoi first on April 17, 1966, and several quarters were razed by the B52s. The conflict did not end until July 1976, after Hanoi had suffered thirty years of war.

The reconstruction of Hanoi would, however, be long in coming. The reunification of the country was followed by conflict with the Khmer Rouge regime in Cambodia, and, consequently, with the Chinese. This resulted in stiff economic sanctions from Western countries; Vietnam was politically and economically isolated, except for its alliance with the Soviet Union. Hanoi became a decrepit shadow of its elegant colonial image. Several years after the end of the war, returning tourists found peeling paint, antique plumbing, and rats scurrying through hotel lobbies. Only in the mid-1980s did the regime turn to *doi-moi* (renovation). Economic reform and the withdrawal of troops from Cambodia in 1989 promised to improve Vietnam's foreign relations and to encourage foreign investment.

Unfortunately, the city now faces the problem of inadequate regulation and planning. Reconstruction efforts have resulted in the indiscriminate demolition of old buildings. The French villas and old city are now under threat from the economic change that has been initiated. From the developers' perspective, the problems of bureaucracy and corruption are compounded by a conservationist movement that hopes to save Hanoi's architectural past. Ideally, the designation of business and residential centers will allow the development of much needed housing and commercial properties while saving the historical buildings that have survived bombs and decay.

The ancient center of the city, in fact, has few scars from the wars and has preserved its temples, lakes, and the narrow, commercial streets of Ba Muoi Sau Pho Phuong (Thirty-six Streets and Districts). The Temple of Literature, One Pillar Pagoda, and Lake of the Restored Sword are popular tourist spots in the old city. Modern attractions in Hanoi include several museums and the Ho Chi Minh Mausoleum, where the leader's embalmed body is displayed in a glass casket. City authorities hope that tourism will bolster the economy of Hanoi, which is already a center of agriculture, communications, and industry.

Further Reading: The best history of the Vietnamese is Tran Minh Cham's *Le Viet-nam: Histoire et Civilisation* (Paris: Alliance Vietnamiennes, 1955; revised edition, 1984). On early colonial Hanoi, readers should consult André Masson's *The Transformation of Hanoi, 1873–1888,* translated by Jack A. Yaeger and edited by Daniel F. Doeppers (Madison: Center for Southeast Asian Studies, University of Wisconsin, 1983). Also valuable is Neil Sheehan's *Two Cities: Hanoi and Saigon* (London: Cape, 1992). For a good tourist guide to Vietnam and Hanoi, turn to *Insight Guides: Vietnam* (Boston: APA, 1991), edited by Helen West.

—Nicholas Tarling and Paula Pyzik Scott

Herāt (Herāt, Afghanistan)

Location: In the middle valley of the Harī Rūd in the province of Herāt in northwestern Afghanistan.

Description: An ancient oasis city of Central Asia, Herāt's possession has been much disputed between Persians, Turks, and Afghans. Its period of greatest historical significance was under the Timurid Dynasty, when from 1405 to 1506 it was the capital of a powerful state and the center of a brilliant Islamic cultural flowering. Situated north of the main Afghan divide but at its lowest point, Herāt communicates easily with most of the traditional centers of culture in the region—Kandahār, Khorāsān, Balkh, Mary, Neyshābūr, and Transoxiana. In the nineteenth century, Herāt was often described as the key to India. Although its monuments have suffered considerably over time, Herāt remains a major historical site.

Contact: Embassy of the Republic of Afghanistan
2341 Wyoming Avenue N.W.
Washington, D.C. 20008
U.S.A.
(202) 234-3770

Herāt is in many ways a typical Central Asian oasis settlement. To create this fertile environment, the brown waters of the Harī Rūd, fed by the snows of the Paropamisus Mountains to the southeast, have been dammed and diverted before they evaporate in the deserts of the Kara Kum. From Neolithic times, diversion canals *(kariz),* wells, and springs have formed the bases of intensive, irrigated agriculture in the area. If the scholar Colin Renfrew's theory of Indo-European expansion is accepted, Herāt had become a Persian settlement by 5000 B.C. Initially only a group of fortified villages, these most likely coalesced into an urban center by the last millennium B.C. under the auspices of the still little known pre-Achaemenid Bactria. Herāt was probably an early seat of Zoroastrianism, which later became the official religion of the Achaemenid Dynasty. With the partial unification of Persia by the Achaemenids, Herāt became a communications center, the seat of a satrap, and a provider of troops for the massive parade expeditions by which the empire operated. The ancient fortified citadel to the north of Herāt was most likely constructed by the Achaemenids. The site has never been satisfactorily excavated, however, and its origins are therefore uncertain.

Alexander the Great captured Herāt in 330 B.C. at the start of what was to prove one of the most difficult of his campaigns. The difficulties, however, convinced him of the region's defensive value; Herāt, like Kandahār, was selected as one of his garrison foundations. To this day, the old walled city has an incongruously Western-style gridiron street plan. Following the death of Alexander, Herāt became part of the Seleucid Empire, then of the Greco-Bactrian Kingdom. Proper excavations of the site probably would reveal Hellenistic features similar to those found at Ay Khānom, to the northeast of Herāt. With the fall of the Greco-Bactrian Kingdom in the second century B.C., Herāt passed successively into the dominions of the nomadic Kushāns and the Sāsānians of Persia. In the fourth and fifth centuries A.D., it was subject to attacks by the White Huns from the north, which required the attention of the Sāsānian shah himself.

With the coming of Islam, Herāt became part of the eastern provinces of the universal caliphate. The spread of Islam exposed Herāt to wider influences, but it did not bring with it the imposition of Arabic, except as the language of religion. Persian remained both the vernacular and the language of choice for secular high culture. With the decline of the caliphate after 850, Herāt came successively under the rule of the Taharids, the Sāmānids of Bukhara, the Ghaznavids, the Seljuks, the Ghorids of central Afghanistan, and the Khwarazmshah of Khiva, the last four of whom were speakers of Turkish or Pashtun.

Around this time an invention first seen in Herāt began to spread to distant regions: the windmill had been developed in response to the 120-day wind, the local manifestation of the northeast monsoon. It went west via the crusaders to take its vertical form in Europe, and east via the caravan trade to take its horizontal form in the salt fields of Chang Lu in China.

Herāt fell to Genghis Khan's army of Khorāsān without serious fighting in 1220. When the city received news of the successes of its former governor Jalāl ad-Dīn Mingburnu farther south, the city revolted and was sacked by the returning Mongols in 1221. The writer Juvaini intended to compose a chapter on its destruction, but, if written, it has not survived, and we lack a contemporary account of one of the worst acts of Mongol ferocity. Marco Polo probably passed through in 1272 but did not describe Herāt, presumably because it was still in ruins. By this time, the territory was part of the Il-khanate of Persia, which ruled the city through its vassals, the Karts.

With the collapse of the Il-khanate in the mid–fourteenth century, the Karts became virtually independent, but they were increasingly drawn into the politics of the Chagatai Khanate. (Chagatai was Genghis Khan's son, who received Transoxiana and parts of China as vassal states when Genghis Khan died. His rule established a khanate.) In these matters, the Karts generally supported Timur (Tamerlane) against his various enemies, thus forging an alliance between Herāt and Timur's capital of Samarkand. In 1381, Timur, no

Jami Masjid, Herāt
Photo courtesy of Embassy of the Islamic State of Afghanistan, Washington, D.C.

longer needing the Karts, imposed direct rule. He sent trusted emirs to Herāt, garrisoned the city with *qa-uchin* units (a kind of professional provost corps), and appointed as titular governor, first his eldest son Jehāngīr, and then, in 1396, his youngest, Shāh Rokh. Herāt was treated as a second capital, no doubt because of its location on transcontinental trade routes, which it was an object of Tamerlane's policy to revive so as to unite nomads and sedentary dwellers. In this respect Herāt, on both north-south and east-west trade routes, occupied a more central position than Samarkand itself.

After Timur died in 1405 with no designated heir, a rivalry ensued among the three eligible princes. Pir Muhammed, son of King Jahāngīr of India, was based at Kandahār and might be said to represent legitimacy and primogeniture; Khalīl, son of another of Timur's sons Miran Shāh, was the choice of the Turkish army at Otrar; and Shāh Rokh at Herāt commanded the support of the Persian civil administration, good finance, and a certain number of *qa-uchin* units. Shāh Rokh was also married to Guhar-shad, daughter of one of Timur's most aristocratic marshals. The civil war lasted five years, but Shāh Rokh's mixed portfolio proved stronger than the single holdings of his rivals. By 1410, Herāt had changed places with Samarkand (to which Shāh Rokh sent his eldest son, Ulūgh Beg, as viceroy and partner) to become the capital of the Timurid Empire, a position it retained with interludes (notably under Abu Said, 1451–56) until 1507.

In the hands of Shāh Rokh and Ulūgh Beg, the Timurid Empire assumed a new character that reached its peak in Herāt during the reign of Sultan Husain Bāī-qarā, from 1469 to 1506. Diplomacy was substituted for force as a means of keeping open the trade routes. Conquest and looting were abandoned. Taxes raised on trade through the un-Islamic *tamgha,* or capital levy on guilds, were channeled into urban renewal, educational endowment, and poverty relief to stem the popular discontent mobilized by the Naqshbandī Dervish order, whose leaders allied with newly converted nomads to attack the half-secularized Timurid courts. Under Shāh Rokh and Husain Bāī-qarā, the administration of Herāt was altered to make the relationship between court, city, dervishes, and nomads mutually supportive. In the long run, the design could not be sustained, but the attempt to do so gave Herāt its unique moment in time.

We are fortunate to possess two accounts of Herāt in its golden age: one at its beginning, one at its end. The first is contained in the *Hsi-yü fan-kuo chih* (A Treatise on the Native States of the Western Regions), which is the report of Chen Cheng, ambassador of the Ming emperor Yongle to the court of Shāh Rokh in 1414. Chen Cheng wrote:

> Ha-lien, also called Hei-lu, is southwest of Samarkand. . . . It lies in a level plain . . . crossed by a westward-flowing river and surrounded by great mountains in all directions. . . . In the northeast corner of the city resides the ruler whose house is made of bricks. . . . The houses are all built of bricks. The houses of the powerful families and ministers are similar to that of the ruler of the state.

The ambassador's picture, drawn before the urban renewal program had gotten underway, was of a civilized but undistinguished city. But Chen Cheng, of course, was an outsider, and could not penetrate into an intellectual ferment that was not yet embodied in bricks and mortar.

Quite different is the second account: that of the Mughal emperor Ẓahīr-ud-Dīn Muḥammad (known as Bābur); born and bred in Central Asia, Bābur shared Timurid culture to the full. Herāt under Husain Bāī-qarā remained for him the ideal: "His was a wonderful age; in it Khorāsān, and Herī [Herāt] above all, was full of learned and matchless men. Whatever the work a man took up, he aimed and aspired at bringing that work to perfection." Explaining why he could not refuse an invitation to stay in the Timurid capital, Bābur concluded: "Besides this, the whole habitable world has not such a town as Herī had become under Sl. Husain Mīrzā [Sultan Husain Bāī-qarā], whose orders and efforts had increased its splendor and beauty as ten to one, rather, as twenty to one. As I greatly wanted to stay, I consented to do so."

Bābur spent the next weeks making merry and sightseeing: "Every day of the time [sic] I was in Herī I rode out to see a new sight; my guide in these excursions was Yūsuf-i-alī Kūkūldāsh; wherever we dismounted, he set food before me. Except Sultan Husain Mīrzā's Almshouse, not one famous spot maybe, was left unseen in those forty days." Among the buildings Bābur then lists are the shrine of Gāzurgāh; the tomb of sheik and poet Jāmī; the *medrese* (school); the tomb and Friday mosque of Guhār-shād, wife of Shāh Rokh; the covered market in the center of the old city; and the immense charitable foundation of Mīr Alī Shīr Nawa-ī, who was not only Husain Bāī-qarā's prime minister, but also a notable patron of the arts and the first poet in Chagatai Turkish, the language in which Bābur himself wrote.

The Timurid culture of Husain Bāī-qarā's Herāt had several layers. At its core was an Islamic modernism: the mysticism of Jāmī, which relativized both the *sharia* (religious law) and the letter of the Koran. Next, there was a Persian secularism, which used the medieval epic *Shāh-nāma* to inspire the lifestyle of a cultivated elite of knights, scholars, and aesthetes. Third, as the material embodiment of these values, there was a sustained connoisseurship in books, calligraphy, illustrations, custom-designed clothes, weapons, accoutrements, and carpets. Around these pursuits, buildings, mosques, *medrese,* dervish hostels, tombs, shrines, almshouses, covered markets, pavilions, and gardens arose throughout the city.

Of these buildings, the most famous was the so-called *musalla* of Guhār-shād. The word *musalla* denotes a space outside a city wall reserved for religious ceremonies. At the northwest corner of the walled city on a road going north, Guhār-shād built a mosque and farther north a *medrese* that contained her own tomb. Strictly speaking, only the mosque was a *musalla*. However, the term was applied not only to the *medrese* and tomb, but also to another *medrese* built yet farther north by Husain Bāī-qarā. Each building had four minarets, all exquisitely tiled, as was the dome of the tomb. In its heyday, the whole complex must have looked extraordinarily impressive.

Unfortunately, only hints of its splendor remain. Husain Bāī-qarā's *medrese,* the last built, was the first to go. By the early nineteenth century, it was largely in ruins, although its four minarets, denuded of their tiles, remained. In 1885, British officers, in Afghan service and expecting a Russian attack, ordered the destruction of Guhār-shād's mosque to clear the field of possible fire from the walls, although the four minarets were left standing. By 1887, Guhār-shād's *medrese* had lost one of its minarets and was much dilapidated, except for the tomb itself. Further losses followed. In 1915, the German agent Oskar von Niedermayer took a celebrated photograph that showed nine minarets: four at Husain Bāī-qarā's *medrese,* one at Guhār-shād's, and four at her mosque. The mosque lost two minarets in an earthquake in 1933, and another fell, apparently in 1951, although Ella Maillart's photo of 1939 already shows a total of only six. So on the eve of the Soviet invasion of 1979, only six minarets were in place. Author Radek Sikorski was able to observe the site in 1990, when he photographed the sad, last minaret of the mosque, now reduced to a pitiful stump. The last minaret of Guhār-shād's *medrese* was badly tilted, but the four minarets of Husain Bāī-qarā's still stood. Also surviving was Mīr Alī Shīr Nawa-ī's Friday mosque in the old city.

Herāt fell to the Uzbeks in 1507, but the new masters of Transoxiana did not long retain possession. In 1510 their leader Muḥammed Shibani was defeated and killed at the battle of Mary (Merv) by Shah Esmā'īl I, founder of the Shi'ite Ṣafavid Dynasty of Persia. Herāt fell into its dominions. The Uzbeks, orthodox Sunnis, made strenuous efforts to recover the city, but they never succeeded more than momentarily. The only effect of the bitter dynastic-religious war, which lasted for much of the sixteenth century, was the devastation of Khorāsān and the disruption of the trade routes on which prosperity depended. From an imperial capital, Herāt sank to a border citadel. Its population, possibly 300,000 in Husain Bāī-qarā's days, fell to 100,000 or fewer by the early nineteenth century.

Because the city remained in Persian hands until 1750, its population is still today predominantly Persian speaking: unlike Mary or the cities of Transoxiana, it was not Turkified, although Ṣafavid rule was insufficient to make it Shi'ite. With the dissolution of the Ṣafavid Empire in the early eighteenth century, Herāt came into the hands of the Persian conqueror Nāder Shāh, and then in 1750 it passed to Aḥmad Shāh Durrāni, the founder of the Afghan state. Under Aḥmad Shāh's successors, however, especially in the early nineteenth century, the Afghan state was shaken by disputes of succession, tribal interventions, localized rebellions, and personal feuds. The new Qājār Dynasty in Persia took advantage of these disturbances to launch a series of attacks to recover Herāt for Persia. As with the Uzbek attacks in the sixteenth century, none of them was more than momentarily successful. The British in India preferred that Herāt be held by a weak Afghanistan rather than a strong Persia, which might be manipulated by France. On more than one occasion, but notably in 1837–38, small-scale British assistance made a crucial difference in the Afghan retention of the city.

In 1885, Russia seized the Afghan oasis at Panjdeh, in what is today Turkmenistan. Because the Russians had already taken Mary, the British believed this new move foreshadowed further extension of power in the region, threatening British India. Herāt, its population down to 10,000, became a strategic preoccupation for the British and remained so until the Anglo-Russian agreement of 1907. British military planners considered constructing a railway linking Herāt to the Persian Gulf, but the Seistan line, as it was called, was never built. In the end it was not Russia but Germany that threatened the British in Afghanistan. During World War I, a German mission was dispatched to Kābul. One of the mission's members was Oskar von Niedermayer, and it was on this trip that he took the famous photographs of Herāt. King Amānollāh Khān of Afghanistan did eventually attack India, but only after the European war had come to a close.

Modernization came to Herāt during the reign of King Zahir (1933–73), when a new town was laid out to the east of the old walled city and improved hotel facilities were provided to attract tourists. These hopeful developments were ended by the republic of 1973, the first communist revolution of April 1978, and the second, with Soviet military backing, in December 1979. In March 1979 Herāt was the scene of the first major uprising against the communists. Herāt subsequently became a major Soviet base, but the region around the city, although subject to Soviet aerial incursions and home to semineutral local militias, became the territory of one of the most enlightened of the *mujahidin* (Islamic resistance) leaders, Esmā'īl Khan. Following the Soviet withdrawal in 1989, Esmā'īl generally took the side of *Jamiat-i Islami* (an inclusive, pro-Western alliance) against the exclusive, radically anti-Western *Hezb-i Islami,* the like-minded Shi'ite militias, and the militant student movement *Taliban.* Within the spectrum of Afghan politics, Herāt still stood, as in the days of the Timurids, for reason and moderation, and saw no disloyalty to Islam in assuming this stance.

Further Reading: For a general survey of the city's history, see *Historical and Political Gazetteer of Afghanistan,* volume 3, *Herāt and Northwestern Afghanistan,* edited by Ludwig W. Adamec (Graz: Akademische Druck-u Verlagsanstalt, 1975). For an examination of the entire Afghan region in antiquity, see Colin Renfrew's *Archaeology and Language: The Puzzle of Indo-European Origins* (London: Cape, 1987; New York: Cambridge University Press, 1988) and F. L. Holt's *Alexander the Great and Bactria: The Formation of a Greek Frontier in Central Asia* (Leiden: Brill, 1988). For the Timurid Empire and culture, see Beatrice Forbes Manz's *The Rise and Rule of Tamerlane* (Cambridge and New York: Cambridge University Press, 1989); Dietrich Brandenburg's *Herāt: Eine*

Timuridische Hauptstadt (Graz: Akademische Druck-u Verlagsanstalt, 1977); Bernard O'Kane's *Timurid Architecture in Khurāsān* (Costa Mesa, California: Mazda, 1987); Lisa Golombek's and Donald Wilbur's *The Timurid Architecture of Iran and Turan* (Princeton, New Jersey: Princeton University Press, 1988); and Thomas W. Lentz's and Glenn D. Lowry's *Timur and the Princely Vision: Persian Art and Culture in the Fifteenth Century* (Los Angeles, California: Los Angeles County Museum of Art, 1989). For Herāt's recent history, see *Danziger's Travels: Beyond Forbidden Frontiers* by Nick Danziger (London: Grafton, 1987; New York: Vintage, 1988) and Radek Sikorski's *Dust of the Saints: A Journey to Herāt in Time of War* (London: Chatto and Windus, 1989; New York: Paragon House, 1990).

—S. A. M. Adshead

Hikone (Shiga, Japan)

Location: In Shiga prefecture in the central region of Honshū (the main island of Japan), 258 miles west of Tōkyō and 40 miles northeast of Kyōto, on the northeastern shore of Lake Biwa.

Description: Hikone is best known as a castle town associated with the Ii family, who were prominent during the Edo period (1603–1868) as officials of the *shōgunate* and as patrons of the arts.

Site Office: Tourist Information Office
JR Hikone Station Side
40-7 Nanko, Furusawa-cho
Hikone, Shiga
Japan
(0749) 22 2954

Hikone, which today has a population of around 100,000, originated as what the Japanese call a *monzen-machi,* a market town in front of the gates of a Buddhist temple, but it is better known as a *jōka-machi,* a settlement below a castle. Since the completion of Hikone Castle in 1622, this former home of the Ii family has dominated the city, first as a seat of local government, and more recently as the main tourist attraction and landmark. The castle site was previously occupied by Hogon-ji, a temple that is said to have been founded in 1080. Over the centuries its main object of worship, a statue of the Buddhist goddess of mercy, Kannon (Avalokitesvara in Sanskrit), attracted many pilgrims, and the temple became well known as the thirtieth stage in the traditional pilgrims' circuit of the thirty-three Kannon temples in the Kinki region (the region around Kyōto, the capital city of Japan from 794 to 1868).

The market town that developed around the temple was by no means the first settlement on the shores of Biwa-ko (Lake Biwa), the largest lake in Japan. Because of its proximity to Kyōto, the area had been strategically important for centuries. Its location on the eastern shore, closer to the villages of central Honshū than to the capital itself, may well have placed Hikone at a disadvantage, especially in comparison to Ōtsu, which is located southwest of the lake, within easy reach of Kyōto, and which still outranks Hikone in size and status.

Hikone acquired a special role in 1600, however. The warlord Ii Naomasa (1561–1602), who, earlier that year, had chosen the winning side at the Battle of Sekigahara (the decisive conflict that ended thirteen decades of civil war), took control of an existing castle at Sawayama, a hill northeast of the modern city's location. Two years later, his son Ii Naokatsu succeeded him as lord of the area around this castle, but he was replaced just a year later, in 1603, by his own brother, Ii Naotaka (1590–1659), on the orders of the *shōgun* Tokugawa Hidetada (whose father Ieyasu had led the winning side at Sekigahara and made himself master of Japan). It is said that Naokatsu had refused to support Ieyasu and Hidetada in their plans to attack Ōsaka Castle and destroy their only serious rivals, the family of Toyotomi Hideyoshi, Ieyasu's predecessor as supreme warlord. It was Naotaka who, in 1622, completed the construction of a new castle at Hikone, having taken over the project from his brother in 1603, along with the domain. The builders reportedly used stones taken from demolished castles at Nagahama, Ando, and Sawayama to create its outer defenses; they also rebuilt the former temple's main gate, brought another gate to the site from Nagahama, and took the keep from yet another abandoned castle, at Ōtsu. The three-storied keep, which affords superb views over the lake and the countryside, is surrounded by labyrinthine passages among stout stone walls and ramparts, which themselves are spread across the hill, Konkizan. In addition, the castle was approached by heavily forested slopes. All of these defenses suggest that Naotaka still expected further conflict; in fact, the castle would never be attacked.

Ii Naotaka also is remembered for his other, more peaceable activities, which have assured his reputation as an outstanding cultural patron. He arranged for Hogon-ji, the temple that his castle had replaced, to be rebuilt on a larger scale on the island of Chikubushima in Lake Biwa and, in 1617, founded another temple, Ryōtan-ji, which contains a classic example of a Zen dry garden, composed of forty-eight stones arranged on a bed of white sand. In addition, he commissioned a set of screens from a member of the prominent Kanō family of painters; the screens are now displayed in the castle's museum next to its main gate. To the north of the castle keep, Ii Naotaka established two formal gardens, known as Rakurakuen (Garden of Pleasure upon Pleasure) and Hakkeien (Garden of Eight Views). The latter was designed by Kobori Enshū, a famous master of the tea ceremony and landscape gardener who was born in Hikone. His design is focused on miniature versions of the eight wonders of Ōmi province, which can be seen from the shores of Lake Biwa: the snow on Mount Hira, the flight of wild ducks at Katata, the night rain at Karasaki, the bells of Miidera Temple, the sun and breeze at Awazu, sunset at Seta, the autumn moon at Ishiyama, and the fishing boats returning to Yabase.

Hikone Castle remained the headquarters of the local Ii lords until 1868. They were counted among the *fudai daimyō* (the attached lords), generally descended from the winners at Sekigahara, who were entrusted with posts in the Tokugawa capital at Edo (present-day Tōkyō). The domains of the *fudai daimyō* often were located at points where they could help protect Tokugawa lands, and especially such cities as Kyōto and Ōsaka, from the *tozama daimyō* (the outside lords), who were allocated lands farther away from the main population centers. The most powerful of the *daimyō* of Hikone was Ii Naosuke, who inherited the castle and the town from his brother in 1845,

Hikone Castle, Hikone
Photo courtesy of The Chicago Public Library

when he was thirty years old and already active as an official in Edo. In 1858, he was appointed tairo, chief minister of the *shōgunate*, and in this capacity he arranged for the young and malleable Tokugawa Iemochi to be chosen as the next *shōgun* and for the regime to enact a series of treaties with the United States, France, and the United Kingdom.

Japan had opened relations with these and other Western countries only five years earlier. Prior to that time, the Netherlands had been Japan's sole European trading partner since the early seventeenth century. Relations with foreign powers were accordingly still extremely controversial, especially among those tozama daimyō and their advisers who wanted an opportunity to wrest power from the Tokugawas and their allies. It was probably as an expression of accord with these xenophobic views that, in 1860, a group of warriors murdered Ii Naosuke in Edo. He was thus the first victim of political assassination in Japan since the violent chaos of the sixteenth century; sadly, he was by no means the last. Only eight years later, the Tokugawa *shōgunate* was overthrown by a coalition of officials and warriors, some of whom had been among the harshest critics of Ii Naosuke. Unlike the Matsudaira family of Aizu-Wakamatsu, who resisted the new regime out of loyalty to the old order from which they had benefited, the Ii family joined with the majority of the *daimyō* in supplying troops for the new imperial army assembled to defeat the Matsudaira (blood relatives of the *shōgun*) and their allies. In 1870, all the *daimyō* surrendered their offices and lands to the government; like other castles in Japan, Hikone's was abandoned and partly demolished, only to be restored as a tourist attraction after World War II.

Meanwhile, Hikone, which received a charter as a city in 1937, developed into a mostly unremarkable small city of light industry and commerce, increasingly dependent on Kyōto (the regional metropolis forty miles away), to which it has been connected, since before World War I, by the Tōkaidō line of the Japan railway network. Today, Hikone's historic sites, apart from Hogon-ji on Chikubushima, are concentrated in and around its castle, which is once again recognized as the former home of an aristocratic family that faithfully served the Tokugawa *shōguns* for more than 250 years and that helped to sponsor the flourishing national culture of their era.

Further Reading: Hikone and the Ii family figure in several histories of early modern Japan, notably Conrad Totman's absorbing study, *The Collapse of the Tokugawa Bakufu 1862–68* (Honolulu: University of Hawaii Press, 1980).

—Patrick Heenan

Hirado (Nagasaki, Japan)

Location: At the northeastern end of the island of Hiradoshima, off the coast of Kyūshū Island, 791 miles southwest of Tōkyō and 70 miles north of Nagasaki; now inside Saikai National Park.

Description: A small seaport town, Hirado was a pirate base for centuries and then a center for trade with Europe and for Christian missionary activity between 1549 and 1641; it also was the base for Japanese invasions of Korea in 1593 and 1597.

Contact: Nagasaki Prefectural Tourist Federation
Nagasaki Kōtsu Sangyō Building
3-1 Daikoku-machi
Nagasaki City 850, Nagasaki
Japan
(0958) 26 9407

Many standard histories of Japan still assert that Hiradoshima, an island of some sixty-six square miles, was governed by the aristocratic Matsuura family from the eleventh century until 1871. Local tradition claims that the family was descended from a warrior who arrived on the island much earlier, as a member of the ill-fated expeditionary force sent by the semi-legendary empress Jingo to invade Korea in the second or third century. (A sword displayed in the museum inside Hirado Castle was once claimed to be his.) This legend may reflect the rise of a Matsuura family to local prominence sometime before the eleventh century.

Historical research, however, has shown that the Matsuura lords of later times were descended from a group of pirate families, the Matsuura-tō, who terrorized northwestern Kyūshū from the 1220s onward, preying on vessels passing between Japan and Korea from bases on Hiradoshima and other small islands off Kyūshū. Their activities were temporarily disrupted in 1227, when ninety of them were executed in the presence of a Korean ambassador on the orders of Mutō Sukeyori, the governor of Kyūshū. Mutō had been appointed by the *shōgunate*, the military regime that then governed Japan from Kamakura, far to the east on the main island on Honshū. But Mutō's successors were less effective in discouraging the pirates; the very remoteness of the region from centers of power and wealth, combined with the temptation offered by the international trade (even though such trade was fitful and uneven), resulted in the revival of pirate activity. By the sixteenth century, when Japan as a whole was plunged into decades of brutal civil war, the pirate groups on Hiradoshima, on neighboring islands, and on the Kyūshū coast included Chinese and Koreans as well as Japanese. They dealt not only in such luxury goods as silk, cotton, brocade, and other textiles, but also in slaves captured from settlements on the southern coast of China. One of the most powerful of these pirates, the Chinese sea captain Wang Zhi, had his headquarters on Hiradoshima, from where he directed both violent and peaceful trading activities in intriguingly close collaboration with Matsuura Takanobu. This leading member of the more respectable wing of the Matsuura family was recognized by his fellow-warlords and by the vestigial national government in Kyōto as the *daimyō* (lord) of northwestern Kyūshū.

Hiradoshima was thus one of the least promising areas for the opening of legitimate trade with Europe or for Christian missionary work; yet, by an accident of geography, it was one of the first and most prominent centers for both of these activities. Portuguese merchants arrived on the island in 1549, seven years after their first landfall on Japanese territory, at Tanegashima, another small island off the coast of southern Kyūshū. At that point Hirado itself was still a relatively unimportant settlement, dependent mainly on fishing in the coastal waters, but also conducting small-scale trade (not all of it piratical) with ports in southeastern Korea. During the following year, the Jesuit priest Francis Xavier came to Hirado after being expelled from Kagoshima (in southern Kyūshū), and then started his long journey on foot to Kyōto. After his departure Hiradoshima became the base for the missionary activities of his colleagues Cosme de Torres and Gaspar Vilela.

A campaign against pirates, conducted between 1556 and 1559 by the Chinese official Hu Zongxian and culminating in the execution of Wang Zhi, made life significantly easier for traders and missionaries alike. Those pirates who remained in the area lost much of their power in 1567, when the Ming Dynasty reopened official trade relations with Japan and Korea. By then, however, the Portuguese had turned their attention away from Hirado to other ports, notably Yokoseura, now part of the city of Nagasaki, on the Kyūshū mainland. The main reason for their departure was probably the hostility they perceived on the part of Matsuura Takanobu. In 1558 he had expelled the Jesuits from his domain, following the conversion to Christianity of his retainer Koteda Yasutsune, the governor of Hiradoshima, and he continually interfered in relations between the Portuguese merchants and their Japanese contacts in Kyūshū. Accordingly, in 1562 the merchants took their vessels out of the harbor at Hirado and sailed to Yokoseura. This city was governed by Ōmura Sumitada, an enemy of Matsuura Takanobu who was baptized in the following year. Matsuura reacted to this turn of events by sending ships into Yokoseura Harbor to attack the Portuguese. It was the expedition's abject defeat by Portuguese guns and cannon, then almost unknown to the Japanese, that convinced all the local lords to seek peace with the strange but powerful foreigners, if only to learn more about their weapons.

Hirado Castle, Hirado
Photo courtesy of Tourism division/Nagasaki prefectural government

Nagasaki grew rapidly as an international port and center of Christian conversions, while Hiradoshima largely reverted to fishing, local trade, and smaller-scale piracy until 1584. In that year a merchant ship out of Manila, capital of the Spanish colony of the Philippines, sought safety from bad weather in Hirado Harbor. Matsuura Shigenobu, Takanobu's son and successor, welcomed their offer of regular commercial dealings with the Philippines and thus brought about the collapse of the Portuguese monopoly on European contacts with Japan, which both he and his new Spanish partners had long resented. It is important to note, however, that at this time Spain and Portugal had been united for four years under one ruler, King Philip II, while retaining separate administrations.

As the Jesuits continued their missionary work in Hirado, Nagasaki, and elsewhere in Kyūshū, they attracted the attention of the powerful warlords of Honshū, where the civil wars were drawing to a close. National hegemony was established first by Oda Nobunaga, then by Toyotomi Hideyoshi, who reunified the country during the 1580s. Although Toyotomi was apparently intrigued by Christianity and had amicable dealings with many individual Jesuits and Japanese converts, in 1587 he suddenly and puzzlingly ordered the expulsion of all Christian missionaries from Japan. Most departed from Hirado, on a Portuguese ship, yet those who remained found, just as puzzlingly, that they could continue their work largely undisturbed. It seems likely that Toyotomi's inconsistent behavior was due to the tensions, both in his own mind and among his advisers, between seeking to increase trade and fearing its consequences for national unity and independence. These would continue to be major issues for his successors.

Toyotomi also had ambitions to make himself master of East Asia by conquering Korea, China, and even the Philippines. Accordingly, in 1593 and again in 1597 Hirado served as campaign headquarters for Toyotomi's two attempts to realize this dream, both of which collapsed in brutal but unsuccessful onslaughts on Korea, the second ending abruptly with his death in 1598. When Matsuura Shigenobu came home from Korea in 1599, he brought a number of prisoners of war, some of whom introduced the style of pottery still made at Mikawauchi on Hiradoshima, and others who were put to work on a new castle in the town of Hirado. (Many of their compatriots made similar forced contributions to Japanese cultures, as prisoners of other local lords.) In the same year, however, Shigenobu, mourning the death of his favorite son, killed himself by burning the castle down around him.

In April 1600 the Dutch vessel *Liefde* arrived at Hirado after a voyage from England, which had lasted nearly two years and had seen the loss of the four ships accompanying it. Captain Quaeckerneck and other members of the *Liefde* crew were detained in the city for five years. Some of them instructed the local *samurai* (warriors) in the use of guns and cannon, while the captain engaged in delicate and complicated negotiations with the regime of Tokugawa Ieyasu, Toyotomi's successor as ruler of Japan and the first of a new line of *shōguns*. In 1605 the captain was permitted to leave for the Netherlands, having secured trading rights for his country, and in July 1609 a trade mission headed by Abraham van den Broek and Nicolaes Puyck arrived at Hirado on board two vessels of the Vereenigde Oost-Indische Compagnie (V.O.C.), the United East India Company, which had been founded in Amsterdam in 1602. After visiting Tokugawa Ieyasu in his retirement at Sunpu (now part of Shizuoka City), the two Dutchmen returned to Hirado with official permission to establish a trading post, of which van den Broek became the first head. As part of their agreement with the Japanese government, the Dutch promised not to seek converts to Christianity.

Meanwhile, Will Adams, the English pilot of the *Liefde,* had entered Tokugawa Ieyasu's service, advising him on naval affairs and taking the Japanese name Miura Anjin. Perhaps the most significant advice he gave Ieyasu was to confirm the ruler's suspicion that the Spanish and Portuguese hoped to seize control of Japan, as they had of the Philippines and other territories in Asia. Adams, who died in 1620, received the unique honor for a non-Japanese of elevation to *samurai* status; centuries later he underwent the more peculiar honor of being fictionalized as the hero of James Clavell's novel *Shōgun* and of the television series based upon it. The people of Hiradoshima still claim that Adams's tomb is to be found in what is now Sakikata Park, on a hill above the city of Hirado, in defiance of the assertion by the authorities of Yokosuka, near Yokohama, that he was buried there. It is possible that both claims have some accuracy, for the ashes of the celebrated dead were sometimes divided between two sites associated with their lives.

Promises by the Dutch not to seek converts to Christianity, combined with Adams's inflammatory assertion that the Spanish and Portuguese had plans to incorporate Japan into their joint empire, made life very difficult for other European powers in Japan. All proselytizing on behalf of Christianity was forbidden in 1612, whether by the Portuguese Jesuits or by the Spanish Franciscans, who had started their mission in Hirado in 1593. The Tokugawa regime was not ready to break off commercial relations at this time; only one year later an English trading post was established at Hirado, headed by Richard Cocks. After Tokugawa Ieyasu's death in 1616, however, the merchants began to suffer restrictions similar to those already placed on the missionaries. When the Dutch sought a renewal of their permit from Tokugawa Ieyasu's son Hidetada, the *shōgunate* officials, apparently angered at the implicit suggestion that Hidetada could not be trusted to follow Ieyasu's decisions, responded by declaring that Hirado and Nagasaki were the only locations in which European merchants would be permitted to reside and trade. All missionaries were ordered to leave the country immediately, but (as in 1587) many remained, with the connivance of local lords and officials.

By this stage, Hirado was the busier of the two international ports; it contained trading posts from all four of the European maritime powers. But matters were not improved by tensions among these groups. In 1618, for example, friction between the Dutch and the English erupted into a pitched battle that had to be settled by Japanese officials. The departure of the English between 1621 and 1623 was also a blow. In this case the reasons for leaving were economic, not political: their trading post went bankrupt, and their employers, the British East India Company, decided that they could get copper more easily and cheaply from the domestic British copper industry than from Japan. As Cocks and his colleagues left Japan, the regime's hostility to Christians turned to active persecution. In 1622 fifty-one Japanese converts were executed at Nagasaki; in 1623, when Hidetada's son Iemitsu was installed as *shōgun*, fifty more were executed. Furthermore, all Japanese were ordered to register at Buddhist temples. Suspected Christians were tortured and then forced to show that they had repudiated the alien faith by treading on *fumie,* images of Jesus. Those who refused were executed. In 1624 all Spanish nationals were banished from Japan, and Japanese Christians were forbidden to leave the country; in 1625 Portuguese nationals, already effectively banished from Hirado the year before, were forbidden to remain in Nagasaki except to process the single annual trade shipment. These decisions meant further economic decline for Hirado; those local Japanese who had become Christians fled to Nagasaki, and the Dutch were the only Europeans left trading in the city.

In 1628 a Japanese vessel that called at another Dutch post, Fort Zeelandia on the island of Taiwan, was impounded and its crew imprisoned. They, in turn, managed to capture the commander of the fort, Pieter Nuyts, and took hostages with them back to Japan. The *shōgunate* immediately suspended all trade through Hirado, relenting only in 1632 when Nuyts, under pressure from the V.O.C. , surrendered himself to the Japanese; he was jailed until 1636. In 1633 Nicolaes Koeckebacker arrived to take command of the Hirado trading post and to cope with the increasingly harsh rules imposed by both the *daimyō* of Hirado and by the *shōgunate.* In 1935 Japanese ships were forbidden to travel beyond the country's coastal waters, and Japanese living abroad were forbidden to return. The Portuguese were confined to Dejima, an artificial island in Nagasaki Bay; the Dutch were confined to Hirado in 1637. It seemed only a matter of time before the Portuguese and Dutch followed the Spanish and were banished altogether.

In 1638, however, the outbreak of a rebellion by local farmers, led by Christian converts at Shimabara in northwest-

View of the harbor from Hirado Catholic church
Photo courtesy of Tourism division/Nagasaki prefectural government

ern Kyūshū, gave the Dutch an opportunity to prove themselves useful to the *shōgunate*. The lord of Hirado commandeered a Dutch gunship, which fired 426 rounds into the castle where the rebels were under siege and, thereby, helped to secure the defeat of the rebels. This action followed the final decrees, issued in 1639, against the Portuguese, who were blamed (probably falsely) for fomenting the rebellion, and helped to secure an exclusive role for the Dutch as commercial intermediaries between Japan and Europe.

It was also in 1639 that Koeckebacker, who had been reluctant to accede to the demand for aid against the rebels and yet was condemned throughout Europe as a traitor to Christianity, was replaced by François Caron. Arriving just as the anti-Christian faction inside the *shōgunate* was pressing for the expulsion of the Dutch as well as the Spanish and Portuguese, Caron's hopes of maintaining trade with Japan appeared to be seriously undermined by events in 1640. That year sixty-one members of the last Portuguese trading mission to Japan were executed, and the remaining fifteen deported; moreover, it was discovered that a new Dutch warehouse in Hirado was inscribed not only with the accepted and familiar symbol "VOC" but with the year of construction according to the Christian calendar. After this incident the *shōgunate* decided to allow the Dutch to continue trading, but also to punish them for this insensitivity by having all the Dutch buildings destroyed. In 1641 the Dutch trading post was transferred to Dejima, where it was to remain the only link with Europe until 1854.

After serving for several centuries as a base for pirates and for a few decades as an international port, Hirado and the island that it dominates ceased to play a part in the national history of Japan. The Matsuura family that governed the island from the castle in Hirado was now far removed from its pirate origins, and although the successive heads of the family were recognized by the Tokugawa *shōguns* as lords of the island, they were among the least wealthy or powerful of the 260 or so *daimyō* who governed the three-quarters of Japan not directly controlled by the *shōgunate*. They were not, of course, poor or powerless by comparison with their farming and fishing subjects. Indeed, in 1702, they were able to build the Miyukibashi, an impressive stone bridge that still stands to the south of modern Hirado, and, in 1707, they were given special permission by the *shōgunate* to rebuild Hirado Castle. In 1870 however, two years after the last *shōgun* resigned under pressure from the imperial court and its supporters, the castle was demolished and the last Matsuura lord, reckoned to be the thirty-eighth of his line, joined the other feudal lords in returning his lands and offices to the emperor. Finally, in 1906, fire swept through Hirado, destroying most of what little had remained of the European trading posts.

Even so, several European remnants and memorials can still be seen in and around Hirado. The stone wharf that lay below the Dutch post, a small lighthouse, and part of the wall around the post, approximately 100 feet long and 7 feet high, have been preserved and restored; along with a network of covered staircases and paths on the hills around the city, they are said to have been constructed by the Dutch. There are also many objects from China, the Netherlands, and elsewhere on display in three museums in the city. One is located inside Hirado Castle on Mount Kameoka, which, like most castles in Japan, is a twentieth-century reproduction; this castle was built in 1962. The Kankō Shiryōkan, the city's Tourist Museum, is somewhat larger, and the Imoto Collection Museum stands near an islet, Kurokojima, on which the palm trees are said to have been planted by the Dutch. Several monuments, all erected after 1868 in Sakikata Park, honor Will Adams and a number of other foreign merchants and priests. One memorial stone, erected in 1949, commemorates Francis Xavier; a church was built in his honor in 1931. In addition, the Tourist Museum displays objects made and used by the *kakure-kirishitan* (hidden Christians), a group of native Japanese who outwardly conformed to the Buddhist order imposed by the Tokugawa regime but secretly maintained a version of the Christian faith, which they had learned from the Jesuits. These relics include statues of Kannon (Avalokitesvara in Sanskrit), the Buddhist goddess of mercy, which are disguised images of the Virgin Mary; figures of the Buddha decorated with crosses; and Buddhist rosaries that were used as Catholic rosaries. Such remnants also can be found in museums and churches in other parts of Hirado and on neighboring islands, silent testimony to a marginal but enduring secret tradition that lasted until 1865, when Christianity was permitted once again in Japan. At that time, some 20,000 hidden Christians received communion from Catholic priests in Nagasaki.

Today there are over 30,000 people living in the city of Hirado, a larger number than at any time in the past. Tourism has helped to sustain a settlement that might otherwise resemble other small, outlying settlements that are losing population and resources to the enormous cities of Kyūshū and Honshū. It also has helped to keep alive the memory of the small groups of Portuguese, Spanish, Dutch, and English merchants, and the Jesuits and their Japanese followers, who were swept into Hirado, and eventually out again, by economic and political forces beyond their control.

Further Reading: *The Christian Century in Japan, 1549–1650* by C. R. Boxer (Berkeley: University of California Press, and Cambridge: Cambridge University Press, 1951) is one of several books in English that treat the brief era of Hirado's prominence as an international port. This strikingly racist text, which describes all Japanese as "bellicose," has been superseded to some extent by more recent and more thoughtful books, such as Grant K. Goodman's *The Dutch Impact on Japan* (Leiden: Brill, 1967; revised edition, as *Japan: The Dutch Experience* (London and Dover, New Hampshire: Athlone, 1967), George Elison's *Deus Destroyed: The Image of Christianity in Early Modern Japan* (Cambridge, Massachusetts: Harvard University Press, 1973), and *The Cambridge History of Japan*, volume 4, *Early Modern Japan*, edited by John Whitney Hall (Cambridge and New York: Cambridge University Press, 1991).

—Patrick Heenan

Hirosaki (Aomori, Japan)

Location: The city of Hirosaki is situated in the northern part of Japan's principal island, Honshū, in the Aomori prefecture and on the same latitude as New York, Rome, and Madrid.

Description: Hirosaki is the political, economic, and cultural center of the Tsugaru region of Aomori prefecture and is known chiefly for the remains of Hirosaki Castle, originally built in 1611. Its traditional Neputa Festival, a folk celebration, is the most famous of its kind in Japan and attracts thousands of visitors, as does the Cherry Blossom Festival each spring.

Site Office: Hirosaki City Tourist Bureau
2-1 Shimoshirogane-cho
Hirosaki, Aomori
Japan
(172) 37-5501

Although the modern Japanese city of Hirosaki is little more than one hour's flight from Tōkyō, it is not well known outside of Japan. Aomori prefecture, of which Hirosaki is one of the largest cities, has a long history of isolation, both geographical and climatic, and for this reason it has retained a cultural autonomy that has disappeared elsewhere in Japan. Its traditions and customs, arts and handicrafts are unique to the area. Human-shaped clay figures, called *Dogu,* dating as far back as 10,000 B.C. to the Jomon (10,000–300 B.C.) and Yayoi (300 B.C.–A.D. 300) periods, have been found in the prefecture. It is not known whether these are toys, jewelry, or religious artifacts.

An ancient capital of the Tsugaru clan and a castle town during the Edo (or Tokugawa) period of Japanese history (1603 to 1867), Hirosaki harks back to an earlier era; its older residents have retained the ancient Tsugaru-ben dialect. In 1900 Hirosaki adopted as its city emblem the Manji or reversed swastika that had been used during feudal times as the crest of the Tsugaru clan and is said to have symbolized the denial of self-interest and the devotion of the individual to the greater society.

Central to the city's development, Hirosaki Castle, in Hirosaki Park, was completed in 1611 as a stronghold of the feudal Tsugaru. For 260 years, under the control of twelve succeeding generations of Tsugaru lords, Hirosaki developed into the flourishing political, economic, and cultural center of the entire Tsugaru region. The castle was begun by the clan's founder, Tamenobu, and completed by his son, Nobuhira. Sited on top of a steep cliff overlooking the Iwaki River, the castle dominated the fan-shaped Tsugaru Plain. The first building on the site had a huge main keep with five stories, ten gates, and eight watchtowers, built amid a maze of narrow passageways designed to confuse invaders. However, in 1627 it was struck by lightning and burned to the ground. The castle's main keep was not rebuilt until 1810 (perhaps construction was delayed to avoid displeasing the shogun's government in Edo, modern Tōkyō), when it was replaced by the three-story structure that can be seen today, the only remaining castle in Japan with its walls intact.

Hirosaki Castle has an inner and outer citadel protected by three concentric square moats and breastworks. To the southwest of the capital are thirty-three Zen temples and shrines, built by Lord Nobuhira, which doubled as guardhouses in wartime and served to form strong ties between the political and religious authorities of the region—ties that still exist today. From north to south the castle covers about 3,200 feet; from east to west it measures about 2,000 feet. It covers an area of about 147 acres. The castle and its grounds were opened to the public in 1874. A museum situated in the tower contains a collection of old arms and armor.

The focal point of the group of southwestern temples is the Tsugaru family temple, Tainezan Chōshōjī, or "the temple of the great victory," possibly named after an ancestor of the Tsugaru family, Mitunobu Ōura, who was known as the Great Victor. Until the completion of the temple, the Tsugaru family had moved their temple whenever they moved, first from Tanesato (modern-day Ajigasawa) to Taira (Iwaki today), then to Horikoshi and finally to its present site near the castle. A noteworthy structure outside the southwestern complex is the Saishōin Temple with its five-story pagoda, Saishōin Gojū-no-tō, which was built as an offering to the spirits of warriors who had died during the fierce battle for the unification of Tsugaru. The northernmost pagoda in mainland Japan, it was built between 1656 and 1667. The pagoda is 100 feet high with a base 18 feet wide. The impetus for its building came from Kyōkai, a prominent local priest, who was encouraged by Nobumasa, fourth lord of Tsugaru.

In 1616 the founder of the Tsugaru *shōgunate*, Ieyasu, died, and shrines to him, known as Tōshōgu, were built in feudal capitals all over Japan. Lord Nobuhira was married to Ieyasu's stepdaughter Maten, and because of this the Hirosaki Tōshōgu was deemed the resting place of part of Ieyasu's soul. The roof of the shrine is Chinese in style and, unlike the other Tōshōgu shrines, which are painted in bright colors, this one is in plain wood. Guarding the weak northeastern quarter of the town is the Hachimangu shrine. Dedicated to Hachiman, god of war, it was begun in 1608 and completed in 1612.

The district surrounding the castle, Nakamachi, includes several traditional houses that were built for the *samurai,* the feudal military caste that was considered socially superior to merchants. *Samurai* were permitted to wear two swords and to cut down any member of another class who offended them.

Hirosaki Castle, Hirosaki
Photo courtesy of Japan National Tourist Organization

The nineteenth century, during which Japan ceased to be isolated from the rest of the world, saw many developments in Hirosaki. In July 1871, during the Meiji era, Hirosaki was declared a prefecture. Two months later, however, the prefecture was renamed Aomori prefecture, and the seat of local government moved from Hirosaki to the city of Aomori. Five years after railway service began in 1894 with the building of Hirosaki Station, Hirosaki was officially designated a city in April 1889. The city's reputation as a garrison town commenced with the arrival of the Eighth Division of the Japanese Army, which was based there from 1898.

During the Meiji era, when Japanese culture looked to the West and Japanese painting was influenced by Western art, notably Impressionism, Hirosaki was introduced to Western-style architecture. Buildings of Western design include the Renaissance-style 59th National Bank, close to the southeast gate of Hirosaki Park, now known as the Aomori Bank Memorial Hall, designed by Hirosaki master builder Sakichi Horie, who eschewed traditional Japanese architecture in favor of what he believed to be Western designs. In 1971 the building was designated an important cultural property. Western-style houses were also built for missionaries and other westerners who had been invited to teach in Hirosaki. As a consequence of their arrival, many Japanese converted to Christianity and several churches were built. These include the Gothic-style United Church of Christ in Japan, built in 1907; the Hirosaki Catholic Church, dating from 1910; and the Anglican Church of the Ascension, built in 1878.

Apples have been grown in the Hirosaki region since 1875, in orchards at the foot of Mount Iwaki, a dormant volcano known as the "Mount Fuji of Tsugaru." Today the Tsugaru area produces about 40 percent of Japan's total apple yield. Apples are said to have been introduced by John Inge, an American teacher at the Tōō Gijuku School in Hirosaki, who is said to have brought the first apple into the Aomori prefecture and given his pupils their first taste of Western apples. In 1974 Hirosaki marked the Centennial Celebration of Apples; descendants of John Inge were invited from the United States for the event. In 1877 a sericulturist from Hirosaki, Shigeki Yamano, planted a trial apple tree in his garden; the first harvest yielded three apples. Hirosaki University School of Medicine now stands on the site. In 1898, apple trees in the area were damaged by disease, making it necessary to introduce new methods of cultivation, which in time made apples a viable commercial crop. In 1990 sales of apples from the prefecture surpassed $1 billion for the first time. In September 1991 a typhoon ruined apple crops throughout Aomori prefecture, but with support from all over Japan and the efforts of local farmers and agricultural organizations, the industry was saved.

Thousands of cherry trees were planted as a gesture of goodwill to the citizens of Hirosaki after the Meiji Restoration of 1868. In spring the cherry blossom line moves northward across Japan, and during the Golden Week holiday in early May, Hirosaki celebrates its annual Cherry Blossom Festival, Hirosaki Sakura Matsuri, when thousands of visitors come to see the moats and terraces of Hirosaki Castle filled with the snow-like blossoms of the trees and illuminated at night.

After the Cherry Blossom Festival comes the ancient Neputa Festival, Neputa Matsuri, lasting from the first to the seventh of August, when the hot summer nights are alive with the haunting sounds of flutes and drums and the color of huge and brilliantly illuminated fan-shaped paper floats that are pulled through the streets, depicting fierce *samurai* in combat and beautiful maidens from Japanese and Chinese legends, each night following a different route through town. There are even small floats for children. The floats are later thrown in the river, reenacting an ancient purification rite in which paper images of people and crops were cast into the river to dispel bad luck. Leading the procession is the giant drum, *Go-Joppari-daiko,* about eleven and one-half feet in diameter and played by seven musicians. Hirosaki's Neputa Festival, the oldest and most famous of its kind in Japan, dates to 1713 during the rule of Nobuhisa, the fifth Tsugaru lord. Various explanations have been offered for its origin, including early folk festivals in which people paraded with lanterns to encourage a good harvest. It is also said to have its origins in the Bon Festivals, Buddhist celebrations honoring and welcoming back the spirits of dead ancestors; such festivals are called *Nemurinagashi* or "floating away sleep." Also known as Obon or Urabon, the festival is said to be a Chinese-Japanese version of the Sanskrit Ullambana, a ceremony that was supposed to rescue the souls of the dead from the sufferings of hell. The festival, already being celebrated in China by the early sixth century, was first recorded in Japan in 657.

October sees the Maple and Chrysanthemum Festival, when the sharply dropping temperatures of autumn transform the trees almost overnight into a mass of red and gold. The white walls of Hirosaki Castle stand out against a sea of scarlet maples and green pines, and visitors can admire beautiful life-size dolls depicting figures from legend, sculpted from chrysanthemum blooms. Despite the celebrations, the atmosphere is one of melancholy and nostalgia, expressing regret for the passing summer and approaching winter.

In addition to its festivals and historic structures, Hirosaki is also a center for the manufacture of numerous traditional local handicrafts. For many generations the Tsugaru people have considered kites, for example, both toys and artistic products. Kite-making originated in the homes of the feudal retainers. Traditional designs taken from legends include *samurai* in combat, echoing those used in the Neputa Festival. Tsugaru-yaki ceramics simulate the snow-covered appearance of Tsugaru in winter: they are of dark glazed enamel with a streak of white running through. The beautiful and highly detailed Kogin-zashi embroidery dates back to the feudal Tsugaru. The geometric stitches originated as the darning of weak spots in the *sashiko* or quilted coat, to be worn on special occasions. These embroideries are typically handed down from generation to generation. Simple, cylindrical wooden dolls, Tsugaru Kokeshi, are made on a lathe and intricately painted in bright colors while the Tsugaru-nuri lacquerware, made in the area for more than 300 years, has a smooth surface glaze that is achieved by no fewer than forty individual layers of lacquer, each one applied, scoured, and polished.

Hirosaki, which escaped serious damage during World War II and has since shared in Japan's postwar economic growth, has become renowned in the twentieth century as a center of learning. The National Higher School, predecessor of Hirosaki University, was established in 1921.

Further Reading: Since Hirosaki is practically unknown outside Japan, the best way to obtain information on the city is to write to the Hirosaki tourism and municipal authorities. Most travel guides to Japan provide brief mentions of the city. For general background on Japan, *The Kodansha Encyclopaedia of Japan* (Tōkyō and New York: Kodansha, 1983) is very comprehensive, and *Japan Before Buddhism* by J. E. Kidder Jr. (London: Thames and Hudson, and New York: Praeger, 1959) provides a perspective on Japanese prehistory. Additional information, particularly on the architecture of the Tokugawa shoguns, may be found in *The Art and Architecture of Japan* (Harmondsworth, Middlesex, and Baltimore, Maryland: Penguin, 1974).

—Jackie Griffin

Hiroshima (Hiroshima, Japan)

Location: On the southwestern coast of Honshū, the main island of Japan, facing Hiroshima Bay in the Inland Sea, 542 miles west-southwest of Tōkyō.

Description: Major port and population center of southwestern Honshū and capital of Hiroshima prefecture; the first city in the world to be attacked and destroyed with an atomic weapon.

Site Office: Hiroshima City Tourist Information Center
Peace Memorial Park
1-1 Nakajima-Cho
Naka-ku
Hiroshima, Hiroshima
Japan
(82) 247 6738

Hiroshima is probably better known around the world than almost any other Japanese city, apart from the capital, Tōkyō, and Nagasaki, the only city that shares with Hiroshima the distinction of having been almost completely destroyed, in a few seconds in 1945, by an atomic bomb. Inevitably, the bombing and its aftermath—as well as continuing controversies over whether it is ever right to use such weapons, and whether their use really accelerated Japan's surrender and the end of World War II—have dominated images of the city, inside Japan as elsewhere, and drawn attention away from the four centuries of development that preceded August 6, 1945.

Those centuries in turn had been preceded by an unknown number of years during which the settlement that was to become Hiroshima had been just one among many fishing villages lining the shores of what is now called Hiroshima Bay, long famous for its oysters. From the late twelfth century it shared in the prosperity that resulted from the opening of the bay to increased trade with the rest of Japan, under the patronage of the powerful Taira family, who rebuilt the main shrine on the nearby island of Miyajima. During this period the settlement was culturally and, to some extent, economically dominated by Mitaki-ji, a temple of the Zen sect that stands among forests and near three waterfalls, to the northwest of the present city center, and which includes among its many buildings the enormous and richly decorated Fudō-in Kondō, the Golden Hall of Fudō-myo-o (Acala in Sanskrit), one of the Guardian Kings venerated in Buddhism.

In 1582 the town was chosen as one of the gathering points for land and sea forces that were to invade Korea (unsuccessfully, as it turned out) under the leadership of Toyotomi Hideyoshi, the general who had just reunified Japan after more than a century of civil wars. Seven years later a local warlord, Mōri Terumoto, who had been prominent both in the civil wars and in the failed invasion, began the construction of a castle, Ri-jō (Carp Castle), on one of the many islands scattered among the six branches of the Ōta River, in the delta now known as the Hiroshima Plain. After the site had been reclaimed from a swamp and piles had been driven deep into the soil, the project was completed in 1593 with the digging of the castle's outer moats, which were raised above the level of the surrounding land so that they could be broken and used to flood the area if the castle ever was attacked. The settlement that grew in the shadow of the castle as more land was reclaimed became known as "Hiroshima," which means "broad island."

In 1600, two years after Hideyoshi's unexpected death had led to a renewal of civil conflict, Mōri Terumoto had the misfortune to choose the losing side in the battle of Sekigahara, a choice that cost him control of Hiroshima. The new *shōgun*, Tokugawa Ieyasu, ordered him to become a monk, transferred his son to another castle at Hagi, and gave the Ri-jō to Fukushima Masanori. Fukushima in his turn was transferred elsewhere in 1619, after trying to expand the castle without permission from the Tokugawa regime, and from that year until the *shōgunate* was abolished in 1868 Hiroshima was governed by *daimyō* (lords) who were members of the Asano family, starting with Asano Nagaakira, all of whom were to be buried at Mitaki-ji. Nagaakira in particular is also famous because of the formal garden, the Shukkei-en, which he had laid out in 1620 to a design by the tea-master Ueda Munetsutsu on ground to the east of the castle, along the banks of the Kyō River. Its pavilions and teahouses, used by Nagaakira and his court and by their successors, are arranged around an artificial lake, once again filled with colorful carp today, which was constructed to resemble the former Xi Hu, or West Lake, at Hangzhou, the capital of China during the Song Dynasty.

Under the Asano *daimyō*, Hiroshima gradually spread from the settlement around the castle to other islands in the Ōta River, but it was during the Meiji Period (1868–1912) that it underwent significant expansion and development. In 1871, when Hiroshima prefecture was created, the castle became the headquarters of the governor sent to the city by the new administration in Tōkyō, and in 1889, when Hiroshima was given the status of a municipality, a modern port was constructed on the island of Ujina to further the city's commercial development. Industrialization continued with the extension through the city of a railroad that formed part of the Sanyo Line, from Kōbe in central Honshū to Shimonoseki at the western end of the island, completed in 1894.

Hiroshima's connection with the Japanese armed forces, briefly made in 1582, was renewed and expanded in 1894, when the city was chosen as the headquarters for the forces engaged in the first Sino-Japanese War (1894–95). Mutsuhito, the ruler known posthumously as the Meiji em-

Cenotaph, Hiroshima Peace Memorial, Hiroshima
Photo courtesy of Japan National Tourist Organization

peror, resided in the city for the duration of the conflict, and the Diet (the Japanese parliament) also met there. Ten years later, during the Russo-Japanese War, Hiroshima was again crucial as an assembly point and supply depot. Its career as an important element in Japan's increasingly militarized economy had begun.

The Japanese victories in wars with China and Russia encouraged an expansion of the armed forces as the government sought to catch up with the Western imperial powers by adding more colonies to its empire. Korea, which had been the main focus of the war with China, was more and more dominated by Japanese "advisers" until 1910, when it joined Taiwan (which Japan had seized in 1876) as a Japanese possession. In 1915 Japan also took over several islands in the South Pacific that had been controlled by Germany. Then, throughout the 1920s and 1930s, the army used Japan's financial interests in Manchuria, established in 1905, as a springboard for gradually increasing its control of China. These imperial ventures, which involved the killing of thousands of civilians, the destruction and looting of several Korean and Chinese cities, and many other atrocities, were accompanied by a gradual militarization of political and social life in Japan.

Hiroshima benefited economically throughout these years, as steelmaking, shipbuilding, and other supply industries expanded. Although civilian industries were not entirely neglected (for example, Mazda began producing trucks in Hiroshima in 1931), the primary customers for Hiroshima's goods were the armed forces, whether the army, which had its regional headquarters for Chugoku (southwestern Honshū) in the city, or the navy, which had its largest base and arsenal at Kure, also on Hiroshima Bay. By 1940 the population of Hiroshima was approximately 344,000 and still growing, and it was the seventh largest city in the country.

The expansion of the Japanese Empire continued steadily, unchecked by the Western powers from whom the Japanese had learned many of their methods, until December 1941, when Japan's unprovoked attack on Pearl Harbor led the United States and its allies to declare war. Over the following three years, most Japanese cities were destroyed or damaged by heavy bombing, but Hiroshima was one of the few that was left untouched. Meanwhile, as the publication in 1995 of previously classified papers has confirmed, the U.S. government had decided as early as May 1943 that the atomic bomb being developed by the Manhattan Project would be used first, not against Nazi Germany, but against the Japanese Navy. (Part of the rationale for this decision was that the Germans, unlike, it was supposed, the Japanese, would be able to seize on any bomb that failed to explode and use it to further their own research, which was believed to be far advanced.) By 1945, however, the Japanese Navy was virtually defunct, and a new first target was needed. It appears that Hiroshima was chosen partly because it had not already been razed to the ground by conventional weapons; partly because, compactly laid out as it was between sea and hills, it offered a suitable testing ground to measure the effects of an atomic explosion on a populated area; and partly because, on the day that it was bombed, there was much less cloud cover over the city than over the alternative targets: Nagasaki (bombed three days later), Niigata, and Kokura.

The four-ton atomic bomb, codenamed "Little Boy," was dropped over the city by the U.S. Air Force bomber plane *Enola Gay* at 8:15 A.M. on August 6, 1945. It exploded approximately 1,870 feet above the ground, unleashing a fireball that is estimated to have reached a temperature of 2,000 degrees Celsius (3,632 degrees Fahrenheit), destroying 92 percent of the buildings within two miles of the epicenter of the explosion. Between 200,000 and 260,000 people were killed immediately and at least 150,000 others were injured. Out of a wartime maximum population of nearly 400,000, only about 135,000 people were left living in the ruins by November. The after-effects of the attack, which were barely understood or predicted in 1945 but which decisively set it apart from conventional bombing, have led to the deaths from radiation sickness of at least 100,000 more people, many born long after the bombing.

Despite the unprecedented scale of the destruction, and in defiance of the widespread belief that the city would remain a wasteland for many decades because of the effects of radiation, reconstruction began in earnest soon afterward, with the help of disaster relief funds from the United States and elsewhere. A hospital, laboratories, and other buildings of the Atomic Bomb Casualty Commission were established on Hijiyama, a hill to the east of the city, and their activities are still coordinated with those of the Prefectural Medical College, which in 1953 was absorbed into Hiroshima University (itself created by an amalgamation of older schools in 1949). The Shukkei-en was reopened in 1951 and the castle in 1958, as a museum of local history.

Many of the reconstruction projects were supervised by the eminent architect Kenzo Tange, who was given the responsibility of transforming the city into what is intended to be an international shrine of peace. The most prominent monument, the Heiwa Kinen Kōen (Peace Memorial Park), has been developed on the site of the prewar city center, to the southwest of the castle. It began with a Cenotaph, designed by Tange, a structure in the shape of an inverted U (resembling the upper part of a covered wagon), which stands over a stone chest carved with the names of some of the dead, and a Peace Flame, also designed by Tange and unveiled in 1952. Both are aligned with the ruin, standing across the river from the park, which has become known as the Genbaku Dōmu (Peace Dome), the former Industrial Promotion Hall of the city's Chamber of Industry and Commerce, which was the only building left even partially standing in the city center after the blast. The park also contains, among other memorials, a statue commemorating one of the many child victims of the bombing, who thought that if she could fold 1,000 *origami* (folded paper) cranes she would be saved; she managed to complete only 644 before her death. The paper crane has since become a symbol of the peace movement. Each year on August 6 a Peace Festival is held to commemorate the bombing and promote the end of nuclear proliferation.

The park stretches from the Cenotaph southwest to the Heiwa Kinen Shiryōkan, the Peace Memorial Museum, also designed by Tange. The museum contains a moving and thought-provoking display of the effects of the bomb on Hiroshima and its Japanese citizens, including such objects as the shadow of a man imprinted by the blast onto a stone wall, and the lunchbox, still containing rice, dropped by a young boy near the epicenter of the blast. It is striking that, in contrast to most modern museums, its exhibits and their captions make no attempt to place the event in any larger context, whether to justify Japanese expansionism before the war, as a vociferous minority in Japan would like, or to denounce it, as many in Hiroshima and elsewhere would prefer. (It is surely relevant, for example, that the boy who dropped the lunchbox was on his way not to school but to conscripted labor in a munitions plant.)

Another noticeable absence from the museum is anything more than passing references to the many non-Japanese victims of the bombing, including more than 20,000 Koreans brought to the city as forced laborers. Only in 1970 was a memorial to them unveiled, on a site across the river and away from the Peace Park. Another memorial structure located outside the park is the Memorial Cathedral of World Peace, first suggested by Hugo Lassalle, a missionary priest from Germany, and constructed near the Shukkei-en, to a design by Murano Tōgō, in 1954. This building, one of the largest Christian churches in Asia, is decorated with such gifts from overseas as an altar from Belgium, an organ from Cologne, a set of bells from Bochum, and bronze doors from Düsseldorf.

Hiroshima today, with a population of more than 1 million, has once again become a major port and a center for chemicals, textiles, metallurgy, and other industries, including the production of Mazda vehicles and Kirin beer. It is also noted, among the decreasing number of Japanese interested in such things, for its streetcar system (one of the few remaining in the country), which has a variety of streetcars acquired from other cities that have abandoned the system. But it is because of the bomb that the city has become known worldwide, and primarily to see its peace memorials that visitors are attracted to it.

Further Reading: John Hersey's *Hiroshima* (first published as a special edition of *The New Yorker,* August, 1946; New York: Knopf, 1946; expanded edition, Knopf, 1985; London: Penguin, 1986) is based on extensive interviews with six survivors of the atom bomb blast. Ibuse Masuji's novel *Black Rain* (Tōkyō and New York: Kodansha, and London: J. Martin, 1969), an account of one family living in the hills above the city in 1945, also is partly based on factual sources and has been adapted for the cinema. Notable recent books include Robert Jay Lifton and Greg Mitchell's *Hiroshima in America: Fifty Years of Denial* (New York: Putnam, 1995), a critical look at the bombing, and Stanley Weintraub's *The Last Great Victory: The End of World War II, July-August 1945* (New York: Dutton, 1995), an objective day-by-day chronicle.

—Patrick Heenan

Ho Chi Minh City (Vietnam)

Location: On the banks of the Song Gai Gon (Saigon River), fifty miles from the South China Sea.

Description: Originally the Khmer port of Prey Nakor, later the capital of the French colony of Cochinchina and of South Vietnam, and a focus of the Vietnam War; now the leading industrial and commercial center of Vietnam.

Site Office: Vietnam Tourism
69-71 Nguyen Hue Street
Ho Chi Minh City
Vietnam
291276, 290772, 290776, or 292442

Ho Chi Minh City is probably still better known, at least in English-speaking countries, as Saigon, the French colonial name by which it became famous when it was the capital of the U.S.-backed South Vietnamese regime. Since that regime was overthrown in 1975, however, Greater Saigon has been renamed in honor of the first leader of the Vietnamese Communist Party and national liberation movement. "Saigon" survives as the name of the central district of the conurbation and as the conventional transliteration of "Song Gai Gon," the river on which Ho Chi Minh City stands. But the city has had still other names in the course of its development over approximately 900 years.

The region between the Mekong River delta and the South China Sea that now includes the city has been subject to a series of different states and peoples. By the second century A.D. it was under the occupation of the kingdom of Funan, comprising most of what are now Cambodia and southern Vietnam. Funan was a small but significant sea power, benefiting from its geographical position on the trade routes between China and India, and its rulers are believed to be the ancestors of the Khmer Dynasty of Cambodia. During the sixth century Funan was superseded by another state, Chenla, which originated in a rebellion by the Kambuja people of the middle Mekong River region against the Funan rulers. Chenla in turn gave way to the rising power of Jayavarman II, the ruler who united the various Khmer states in 802. The empire he established proved to be long-lasting, controlling an even larger area than had Funan or Chenla and basing itself at Angkor (now in Cambodia) from 890.

Along the Khmer Empire's eastern border was the state of Champa, whose rulers, originally from the Malayan Archipelago, gradually extended their power over most of what is now south-central Vietnam. The region that is now northern Vietnam, ruled by the Chinese since the third century B.C., broke away in 939 to become the independent kingdom of Dai Viet. Neither of these smaller states was yet in a position to prevent the steady expansion of the Khmer Empire into what are now Laos and Thailand.

At the height of the Khmer Empire's economic and political strength, during the eleventh and twelfth centuries, its rulers established and fostered the growth of Prey Nokor, a port city on the banks of the Song Gai Gon, about fifty miles from the coast. It is possible that there already had been a settlement at this location in the Mekong marshes for some centuries, depending, as Prey Nokor did, on the handling of goods traded between the countries bordering the South China Sea and the interior provinces of the empire. Prey Nokor, however, generally is considered the precursor of Saigon. Such a trading center was bound to be one of the prizes in the struggle for power that developed in the thirteenth century between the declining Khmer Empire and the expanding kingdom of Champa, and by the end of that century the Cham people had seized control of the town.

Like their predecessors in the region, the rulers of Champa did not enjoy supremacy for long. Dai Viet, having fought off Chinese attempts at reconquest and come under the control of the Le Dynasty, was looking to expand in order to feed and accommodate its rapidly growing population. In 1471 forces led by Emperor Le Thanh Tong seized most of the territory of Champa, apart from Prey Nokor and some other areas in the Mekong Delta. Mass migration from the north brought the Confucian and Buddhist culture of the Viets into the countryside around Prey Nokor and into the city itself. There it met and mingled with the Khmer and Cham cultures, long influenced by elements of the Hindu, Muslim, Polynesian, and Southeast Asian cultures that intersected with one another in the ports of the South China Sea.

Christianity was added to this cosmopolitan mixture about 1550, when Portuguese missionaries first reached the Vietnamese coast. Economic links with Europe began to develop soon afterward, and by the end of the seventeenth century the dominant player was the French East India Company, representing the European monarchy from which most missionaries were being sent. In 1623 the Dai Viet imperial court succeeded in becoming the leading beneficiary on the Vietnamese side of the international trade by asserting its claim to customs dues on goods passing in and out of Prey Nokor, which was still a Cham city.

The imperial court welcomed the strangers from France and the other European maritime powers because they were willing to share some of their knowledge of medicine, astronomy, and weaponry, but distrusted them because of their potential for subversion. This turned out to be a shrewd judgment on their part. Rival factions among the Vietnamese aristocracy took advantage of the weakness of the emperors to carve out greater territories and powers for their families, often with the support of the Europeans. By 1674 the Trinh family, backed by the Dutch, who were then the main rivals of the French, controlled the northern part of the empire from what is now Hanoi, while the French and the Portuguese backed the Nguyen family, who controlled the south from the imperial capital, Hue, in central Vietnam. Both families had nominal allegiance to the Vietnamese emperor, who by now was largely a figurehead.

During the 1680s more Viet peasants settled east of the Mekong River, while a growing number of Chinese merchants settled in the district now known as the Cholon (Great Market). This section of Ho Chi Minh City is still home to the largest ethnic Chinese community in Vietnam. These population changes were the prelude to the final extinction of the small Cham states in the Mekong Delta. In 1691 the Vietnamese occupied Prey Nokor, renaming it Gia Dinh; in 1698 they annexed the remainder of the Mekong Delta and created two provinces, Tran Bien and Phien Tran (also known as Gia Dinh, for the city that dominated it). Gia Dinh's position as the economic and political center of the region was confirmed when the first Vietnamese viceroy took up residence there a year later, and its citadel gave it strategic preeminence as well.

The decades of stability that followed the conquest permitted work to begin on two Buddhist pagodas that still stand today. The Glac Lam Pagoda, completed about 1744 (but restored in 1900) is now the oldest pagoda in the city. It is famous for its two different statues representing manifestations of the Buddhist goddess of mercy, Quan The Am Bo Tat (Avalokitesvara in Sanskrit) and for the fourteen gilded images of Buddhist and Taoist deities in its worship hall, arranged to form a mandala (plan of the cosmos). The Glac Vien Pagoda, which contains a similar range of statues, was completed about fifty years later and is associated with the nineteenth-century emperor Gia Long, who frequently worshiped at the pagoda.

Between the completion dates of these two temples came still another round of political and military conflict. A rebellion led by three brothers from the village of Tay Son, near Hue, broke out in 1771. Five years later the Tay Son rebels captured Gia Dinh, and by 1783 they effectively controlled the entire country. But in 1788 the imperial official Nguyen Phuc Anh used French mercenaries recruited for him by Pierre-Joseph-Georges Pigneau de Béhaine, the Catholic bishop of Adran, to recapture the city. (The bishop's tomb in Ho Chi Minh City is decorated with a flying dragon bearing a sword on its back and holding a Bible.) Nguyen Anh then used Gia Dinh as the headquarters for his campaign to suppress the rebels, and in 1802 he made himself emperor, under the name Gia Long (from the cities Gia Dinh and Thang Long).

Although Gia Long returned to the imperial capital of Hue, Gia Dinh remained the military and political center of the southern region of his empire, while the Chinese district of Cholon became the economic center. Unfortunately, Gia Long unwittingly had opened the door to further French intervention. His successor, Minh Mang, feared that the French encouraged the rebellions that took place during his reign, and had French priests executed. In reprisal, France sent a military expedition into Vietnam. In 1858 the French captured Da Nang; in 1859 they took control of Gia Dinh, renaming it Saigon. The southern region of Vietnam became the French colony of Cochinchina, with Saigon as its capital, in 1867. At first the Vietnamese court did not accept this loss of territory, and the Chinese imperial court tried to reassert its ancient claim that Vietnam was merely one of its tributary states, but in 1874 officials from both courts reluctantly signed the Treaty of Saigon, recognizing the French presence. But French ambitions did not stop there: in 1883 Annam (central Vietnam) and Tonkin (northern Vietnam) were made into protectorates.

Under French occupation Saigon served as the port of exit for the rice, rubber, and coal extracted from the country through exploitation of the peasantry, who provided a cheap, unskilled labor force. The city underwent significant changes in its architecture and culture, becoming a European metropolis of wide boulevards lined with trees and majestic public buildings, including the red brick Notre Dame Cathedral, built in neo-Romanesque style between 1877 and 1883; the neo-Classical residence of the French governors of Cochinchina, known as the Gia Long Palace, built in 1886; and the richly decorated Hotel de Ville (City Hall), built between 1901 and 1908. There was even an opera house, built very much in the French style. It is not surprising that in his novel *The Gentleman in the Parlor*, written in 1926, the British writer W. Somerset Maugham described Saigon as having "the air of a little provincial town in the South of France."

However, there were other new buildings in colonial Saigon that were not European at all. The Mariamman Hindu Temple, built at the end of the nineteenth century, is today the last remaining among several built by residents from India, whose descendants, numbering around 400, still worship there today. Among the many Chinese temples of the city, the Taoist "Emperor of Jade" Pagoda (Phoc Hai Tu or Chua Ngoc Hoang), built in 1909, is the largest and its images the most ornate and numerous. Saigon also has a Central Mosque, built in 1935 for its thriving Indian Muslim population, of whom about 5,000 remain.

French rule was neither universally popular nor passively accepted. Frequent rebellions made the lives of colonial officials difficult and sometimes dangerous, although for many years the revolts did not seriously threaten the French power. Like the larger cities of other colonized nations, Saigon became something of a haven for anticolonial and revolutionary groups. These often included migrants from northern Vietnam because of a quirk of French administration. The politically minded tended to move southward because the relatively liberal Napoleonic law code had been introduced in Cochinchina; the protectorates continued to operate under an adapted form of the more repressive Vietnamese imperial laws. Some of the more radical groups came together in 1930 under the leadership of Ho Chi Minh to form the Communist Party of Indochina, which was banned immediately by the colonial authorities.

World War II was the turning point in the fortunes of the French in Indochina, as of the other colonial powers. The

Van Duyet Temple, Ho Chi Minh City
Photo courtesy of The Chicago Public Library

French Vichy regime, established after the German invasion of France in June 1940, allowed the Japanese to take control of Indochina, and in September Saigon became the headquarters of the Japanese Imperial Army for Southeast Asia, although civilian administration remained in the hands of French officials. In May 1941, in response to this dramatic turn of events, Ho Chi Minh, who had returned from exile in the Soviet Union, formed the Viet Nam Doc Lap Dong Minh, the League for the Independence of Vietnam, which has become known in English as the Viet Minh. This movement included not only communists but other nationalists who wished to oust all of their foreign oppressors, and its forces fought alongside American troops in guerrilla warfare against the Japanese and the French. Following the liberation of France in July 1944, the Japanese seized complete control of Indochina, only to relinquish their hold after their defeat and surrender in August 1945. The Viet Minh then captured Hanoi, and on September 2, 1945, the Democratic Republic of Vietnam, commonly called North Vietnam, was established with Ho Chi Minh as its president.

Meanwhile, in southern Vietnam, where the Viet Minh had captured Saigon, British troops arrived from Burma with the aim of returning the whole country to French colonial rule. They even rearmed captured Japanese soldiers and used them to drive the Viet Minh out of the city before handing southern Vietnam over to France. In 1950 a French-sponsored regime known as the Associated States of Vietnam was established in the south with the former emperor Bao Dai as its head of state and with economic and military aid from the United States. By 1953 the United States was paying 80 percent of the costs of the French military effort against Ho Chi Minh's republic. This struggle came to an end in 1954, when the French were defeated at Dien Bien Phu. In October 1955 Saigon became the capital of still another state, the Republic of Vietnam—usually referred to as South Vietnam—under the corrupt presidency of Ngo Dinh Diem, a fervent anti-communist.

In 1960 Diem's opponents joined together in the National Liberation Front (NLF) of South Vietnam. This movement was denounced by both Diem and his American allies as communist-inspired and was to become famous under the nickname they gave it, the Viet Cong (literally Vietnamese Communists). It certainly received financial support and some political direction from Ho's regime, but at first it included Buddhists and other nationalists as well as communists. As the NLF grew, the number of U.S. military advisers in South Vietnam rose as well, from 650 in 1960 to 11,000 in 1962, and the stage was set for the latest military conflict in Saigon's troubled history. During 1963 Diem's forces fired upon groups of Buddhist protesters in the city, a monk burned himself to death in public—the first of several to do so—and the government arrested hundreds of monks and nuns at pagodas throughout the south. Neither the removal of Diem from office in a coup d'etat assisted by the CIA (Central Intelligence Agency of the United States), nor his assassination soon afterward was sufficient to calm the situation. At the end of the year the United States began bombing North Vietnam, claiming that Ho's regime had stirred up the trouble in the south, and the first American combat troops arrived in 1965.

In response, some 14,000 soldiers of the North Vietnamese People's Army of Vietnam (PAVN) entered the south in 1965. By 1967 there were more than 500,000 American troops in Vietnam, fighting against both the PAVN and the NLF (or Viet Cong). Saigon became the focus of world attention as reporters and camera crews brought war into the living rooms of television viewers for the first time in history; it also became famous, or notorious, for the bars, nightclubs, and brothels that catered to the troops from the United States (and Australia) and to journalists from all over the planet.

Saigon came under direct attack by the NLF and the PAVN during the Tet Offensive in 1968. The U.S. Embassy was occupied by the guerrillas for one day and large areas of the city were destroyed or damaged. The offensive was a failure in military terms, but even so it has been seen as the moment when the U.S. decision-makers were forced to begin considering withdrawal from Vietnam. The secret intervention in Cambodia engineered by President Richard M. Nixon and Secretary of State Henry Kissinger from 1970 prolonged the war, but by the spring of 1975 the PAVN had captured most of what had been South Vietnam. Early on April 30, PAVN forces entered Saigon, where they met only token resistance. The South Vietnamese government surrendered within a few hours. More than 1,000 American officials and residents and 6,000 Vietnamese were evacuated by helicopter from Saigon as PAVN tanks rolled into the city.

The fall of Saigon, an event firmly imprinted on the memories of those who experienced it—and those who watched it on television—at last brought an end to the war of national liberation that had begun, ironically enough, with cooperation between the Viet Minh and the United States thirty-four years earlier. Vietnam was reunified, Saigon was renamed Ho Chi Minh City six years after Ho's death in Hanoi, and the Gia Long Palace became the Museum of War Crimes, featuring photographs of mutilated bodies and exhibits indicting the United States for its part in the war. While the United States had lost more than 58,000 soldiers between 1965 and 1975, the Vietnamese had suffered far greater losses. More than 3 million people had died, about 4 million people had been wounded, and much of the country had been devastated by bombing, which had included the use of toxic chemicals. In the south, which had become almost completely dependent on American aid and business, most of the infrastructure was obliterated and many areas were filled with land mines. Millions of refugees had flooded into Saigon and other cities; there were large numbers of orphans, amputees, and heroin addicts to be cared for and rehabilitated. Although the government in Hanoi sought international aid (including the reparations promised by Kissinger but never delivered), its invasion of Cambodia in 1978 was used as a pretext for denying all forms of aid, either from individual Western governments or from international organizations.

As the economic situation grew even worse, resentment toward the large ethnic Chinese commercial community in the Cholon district of Saigon increased, but the authorities turned a blind eye to anti-Chinese incidents, and some officials even encouraged them. Many ethnic Chinese from Cholon joined the thousands of "boat people" who left Vietnam during the early years of reunification. In spite of the country's isolation, poverty, and ethnic unrest, however, Vietnam's government, with assistance from the Soviet Union, engineered a gradual revival of Ho Chi Minh City. Many of its slums were cleared, thousands of former soldiers were given work, most refugees were returned to the countryside, and the health and education systems were overhauled. These were the successes in the government's efforts to build a socialist utopia; unfortunately, the government also developed large and inefficient industries based on the Soviet model, and much of Vietnam remained impoverished.

In 1989 the Vietnamese government opened the economy to outsiders, introducing nationwide market-oriented reforms, which often were first tried in the still lively commercial districts of Ho Chi Minh City, where some private enterprise had flourished even when most industry was owned by the state. In 1995 the United States ended its thirty-year embargo on trade, permitting American businesses to follow their European and Southeast Asian rivals in trying out a new market for products ranging from soft drinks to electrical goods and in using what is still one of Vietnam's chief attractions for such foreign investors, its pool of cheap and (especially in Ho Chi Minh City) skilled labor. With increasing economic growth, however, has come a revival of social problems that had seemed to be lessening. Some parts of Ho Chi Minh City are reverting to slum conditions, drug dealing and prostitution have reappeared, and some reporters have suggested that the city is beginning to resemble once again the Saigon of the 1960s. The city's economic activity is believed to compose between 40 and 60 percent of the national budget, thus, perhaps, accentuating the social and cultural differences between the north and the south, which unified Vietnam has never properly addressed. In addition, the city is still occasionally a focus of political unrest, which may increase as the economy develops further. In 1992, for example, several Buddhist monks from the An Quang Pagoda, one of many that have revived in recent years, were placed under house arrest after openly criticizing government officials.

Today, Ho Chi Minh City is one of the most densely populated conurbations in the world. The population of the metropolis as a whole, including Saigon, Cholon, and ten other districts, is thought to have reached 5 million in 1995, presenting problems, such as inadequate infrastructure, mass unemployment, and falling standards of health, that economic growth, even at Vietnam's present rapid rate, seems unlikely to be able to overcome. Having been at various times an important entrepot, a political capital, and a target for guerrilla fighting, Ho Chi Minh City is now entering upon a new career, as the engine of Vietnam's economic reconstruction. Whether it can fully safeguard its cosmopolitan heritage of Vietnamese, Khmer, Chinese, Indian, and French buildings and monuments in this new era is an open question.

Further Reading: Many books have been written about the Vietnam War. Among the most impressive of these are Neil Sheehan's *Two Cities: Hanoi and Saigon* (London: Cape, 1992), Gabriel Kolko's *Anatomy of a War: Vietnam, the United States, and the Modern Historical Experience* (New York: Pantheon, 1985; as *Vietnam: Anatomy of a War 1940–1975* (London: Allen and Unwin, 1985), and John Pilger's *Heroes* (London: Cape, 1986; revised edition, London: Pan, 1989). Works by two novelists, W. Somerset Maugham's *The Gentleman in the Parlour: Record of a Journey from Rangoon to Haiphong* (London: Heinemann, and New York: Doubleday, 1930) and Graham Greene's *The Quiet American* (London: Heinemann, and New York: Bantam, 1955), also bring Saigon's past to life.

—Monique Lamontagne

Hong Kong

Location: Situated at the mouth of the Zhujiang (Pearl River) on the southeastern coast of Guangdong Province, China. With a total area of 409 square miles, the territory of Hong Kong comprises Hong Kong Island, the Kowloon Peninsula, and the New Territories on the mainland together with 236 adjacent islands.

Description: Geographically and historically part of China, Hong Kong belonged to part of the Xinan district and the greater culture of southern China before the British acquisition. Its growth as a city began with the British occupation of the island in 1841, which then had only a population of about 5,000. Since then, the territory has grown into a metropolis with a population over six million. It is a leading commercial and financial center in Asia, and the world's eighth largest trading economy. On July 1, 1997, Hong Kong will revert to China.

Site Office: Citicorp Center
18 Whitfield Road, 11th floor
North Point
Hong Kong
2807 6543

Hong Kong is part of the Zhujiang Delta on the southeastern coast of the Guangdong province, which has been populated since prehistoric times. The region is rich in the archaeological remains of prehistoric settlements, mostly along the shores of the islands and near the Tuen Mun River. Excavations indicate three phases in the region's prehistory. Coarse, cord-marked artifacts indicate settlement during the Middle Neolithic period (around 3000 B.C.). The Late Neolithic period (2500–1500 B.C.) is represented in local finds by finer decorated pottery and polished stone tools. Pottery decorated with stamped geometric designs derives from the period beginning around 1500 B.C. Many scholars see a close link between the prehistoric culture of this region and the northern Stone Age culture of Longshan and the bronze motifs of the Shang Dynasty (1766–1122 B.C.) of ancient China.

Little is known of the early aboriginal inhabitants. Some studies suggest that they were related to sea-faring people of Malaysian-Oceanic origin. However, recent evidence from Chinese and local sources indicates that the early people of the region belonged to native tribes of South China, notably the Yue and the She. Analyses of archaeological sites support the belief that these people practiced the primitive type of slash-and-burn agriculture, occasionally supplemented with gathering, hunting, and fishing. These living patterns were also common among the ancient tribes of South China.

The Hong Kong region fell under Chinese overlordship as early as the third century B.C. Finds of pottery and coins of this period indicate the presence of the Chinese of the Qin Dynasty (221–206 B.C.). Artifacts associated with the Han Dynasty (206 B.C.–A.D. 220) are also well represented. The Han Tomb at Li Cheng Uk on the Kowloon Peninsula also provides notable evidence of a Han presence. According to Chinese documentary sources, present-day Castle Peak (Tuen Mun) at the western end of the New Territories was a port of call for ships engaged in China's external trade with Southeast Asia, India, and the Middle East during the Tang Dynasty (618–907). During these early periods, the region was also known for pearl collecting (at the Tolo Harbor of Taipo), salt production (at the Kowloon Bay), and incense-tree plantations (at Lek Yuen on Shatin and Sha Lo Wan on Lantau Island). However, these small-scale industries declined by the time of the Ming Dynasty (1368–1644).

Hong Kong's population fluctuated considerably beginning around A.D. 1000. At that time, the established settlers were the Tangs, Lius, Mans, Haus, and Pangs, forming the so-called five great clans of the region. Most of these early settlers spoke the Cantonese dialect, and they came to be known as Punti (Local People). Most subsequent settlers are called Hakka (Guest People). Large-scale Chinese migration to the region began during the Song Dynasty (960–1276), recurring periodically at later dates. The Hong Kong area suffered constant raids by bandits and pirates during the Late Ming Dynasty, which caused many inhabitants to flee. The area suffered more intense upheaval when, in 1662, the Qing government ordered a compulsory evacuation in response to attacks from Taiwan. As the people left the area, their settlements were wiped out, explaining the scarcity of ancient historical remains. When the evacuation order was finally lifted in 1669, some of the earlier communities returned and claimed land in the more fertile plains of Yuen Long, Kam Tin, and Shang Yue. Most of the newcomers were Hakka from the north, and they had to settle for the coastal and hilly parts of the region, while the Tanka (Boat People) resettled along the shores of the islands. When the British appropriated the territory in the nineteenth century, they found these three major ethnic groups—Punti, Hakka, and Tanka—and one minority, the Hoklo, who were sea-nomads from the northern shore of Guangdong and Fukien.

The British established control over the region through a series of unequal treaties imposed on China in the nineteenth century, the heyday of Western imperialism. British soldiers first landed on the island—which had been eyed by British traders at Guangzhou for its deep natural harbor and strategic location on the Far East trade routes—in the course of the First Opium War (1839–42). The war was sparked by the Chinese government's attempt to ban opium

View of Hong Kong and harbor
Photo courtesy of Hong Kong Tourist Association, New York

imports by the British, who used the occasion to launch a major military confrontation. The object was to force more favorable trading conditions from isolationist Qing China. The Qing authorities ceded the island to Britain by the Treaty of Nanking (Nanjing) in 1842. At the time of the transfer, the name of Hong Kong—which means "Fragrant Harbor"—probably was attached only to a small, walled village on the southern shore, but the British adopted the name for the entire island.

Conflict between the Qing authorities and western traders, this time both British and French, soon erupted again in what is commonly referred to as the Second Opium War. Conflicting interpretations regarding the operations of the treaty-port system gave the Europeans an excuse to mount an expedition to further liberalize trade. Again, China suffered a defeat, and this time the Qing were forced to grant the Kowloon Peninsula opposite Hong Kong Harbor to the British in 1860.

The British further extended colonial territories by a lease of the area north of Kowloon up to the Shenzhen River and including the adjacent 236 islands. The ninety-nine-year lease agreement, signed by Britain and China in June 1898, was a concession wrung from the Qing government in the wake of the Sino-Japanese War, which ended in 1895. The leased area, which came to be known as the New Territories, formed a part of the colony but was administered separately from the island of Hong Kong and the Kowloon Peninsula. Before the British arrival, the New Territories had been the more developed part of the region and had some fine examples of Chinese historical buildings, including ancestral halls, temples, and traditional houses. Unlike Hong Kong and Kowloon, it did not immediately undergo much urban development after being incorporated into the colony. Chinese traditional village culture, customs, and way of life remained almost unchanged for many years.

The development of Hong Kong as a city began in 1841, when the British first landed on the island. It had then only about 3,000 inhabitants on land and some 2,000 fishermen living afloat. Some construction was soon underway, attracting laborers from the Whampo area. Yet, development was initially slow not only because of the island's low population density, but also because fever, typhoons, piracy, and the unruly behavior of early immigrants created an inhospitable environment. Even many of the British merchants who had hoped to turn the settlement into an "emporium of China trade" lost their confidence by the late 1840s. Although firms like Jardine and Matheson, Dent and Company, and Gilman and Company continued their operations, no small number of other trading houses went bankrupt or moved to the newly opened treaty ports in China.

Conditions for development began to change when thousands of people flocked to Hong Kong during the disturbances in southern China caused by the Taiping Rebellion (1850–64). By the early 1860s, Hong Kong and the newly acquired Kowloon Peninsula together suddenly had a population close to 160,000. From that time on, the territory attracted repeated waves of immigrants, especially in times of political upheaval and economic hardship in China. But the population remained transient; many came only for temporary shelter or economic gain.

Initially, Hong Kong's trade was mainly between China, Britain, and India, with opium as the major commodity traded. But the further liberalization of trade in China and other parts of Asia and the growth of Chinese communities abroad in the late 1850s stimulated an expansion in the colony's trade. As ocean-going shipping entered the port more frequently, branches of financial banks, such as the Standard Chartered Bank and the Mercantile Bank, were created. The Hong Kong and Shanghai Banking Corporation was established in 1864. International shipping companies such as the Peninsula and Oriental and Butterfield and Swire were also established. Trade relations were opened with Japan, Korea, Southeast Asia, and the West Pacific. By 1890, Hong Kong handled about 40 percent of China's external trade and had established its position as an important entrepôt in the East.

Physical expansion of the urban area on Hong Kong was accomplished through reclamation projects and by cutting into the rocky landscape. The earliest reclamation produced the Bonham Strand (1851) and Bowrington (1859). Important projects begun in 1890 added Pedder Street, Chater Road, Des Voeux Road, and Connaught Road to the central district. These streets remain the heart of the city today.

The population was predominantly Chinese, accounting invariably for over 96 percent of the total figure. British, Indian, and Portuguese communities were among the larger non-Chinese groups. A blending of the cultures of East and West was evident from the earliest days, when Western-style buildings were erected alongside traditional Chinese houses. Various Western churches and Chinese temples coexisted to provide places of worship and community services. Traditional festivals such as the Dragon Boat, Mid-Autumn, and Tomb Visit Days were declared public holidays, as were Easter and Christmas. Newspapers and magazines were published in English and in Chinese. Chinese classics and history were taught in the various schools alongside subjects in Western culture, science, and technology. The triumph of this bicultural education system was the foundation of the University of Hong Kong in 1911.

Throughout the pre–World War II period, little change was made in Hong Kong's government structure. The typical British colonial administration was headed by a governor representing the British Crown. He was assisted by the Executive Council (Execo) and the Legislative Council (Legco), which each had a membership consisting for the most part of British officials. The small number of unofficial members was appointed from among leading British merchants and prominent professionals. The Chinese were underrepresented. The first Chinese member was appointed to the Legislative Council in 1884, and the Executive Council received its first Chinese member only in 1926. In 1941, there were still only three Chinese members in the Legco and one in the Execo.

The Japanese occupation of Hong Kong, lasting from 1941 to 1945, marked the darkest chapter in the history of the territory. The Japanese attacked on December 8, 1941. The small garrison stationed in Hong Kong consisted of only four battalions, which were reinforced by two Canadian battalions shortly before the December attack. The outnumbered garrison could not withstand the onslaught of two divisions of well-trained Japanese troops, and Hong Kong surrendered on Christmas Day after three weeks of resistance. For almost four years, Hong Kong suffered under Japanese oppression. British civilians and prisoners of war were interned for the duration of the conflict. Trade came to a wrenching halt, and residents were abruptly plunged into poverty. All public services and utilities were neglected or disrupted altogether. Food shortages, exacerbated by an Allied blockade and heavy Japanese losses toward the end of the war, caused widespread starvation. Large numbers of people fled to mainland China and Macau, at the same time that Japanese authorities organized mass deportations. By 1945, the population had dwindled from 1.6 million to 600,000.

During the war, the Allies officially considered the return of the New Territories to China upon a Japanese withdrawal. But talks apparently came to nothing, for a variety of reasons. Chiang Kai-Shek, the Chinese representative in the Allied leadership, did not have a strong position, given the political upheavals in mainland China. And Winston Churchill objected strongly to the revocation of the lease, possibly because of the Soviet Union's claim on the China border. Even before Japanese troops withdrew from the colony, the British prepared to return. News of the surrender of Japan was received in Hong Kong on August 14, 1945. Immediately, a provisional government was established by released British interns. On August 30, Rear Admiral Cecil Harcourt arrived with units of the British Pacific Fleet. After a short period of military government, civilian administration was restored on May 1, 1946, when the prewar governor, Sir Mark Young, resumed office.

Hong Kong made a speedy economic recovery. Many prewar residents returned to provide the labor for reconstruction and the re-establishment of the entrepôt trade. However, Hong Kong soon faced serious problems. The Korean War (1950–53) and a United Nations embargo nearly struck a death blow to Hong Kong's trade, the backbone of the territory's economy. Meanwhile, the swelling population had to be housed and fed. The communist takeover of China in 1949 led to an influx of immigrants unparalleled in the history of the territory. The population reached 3 million by 1960 and continued to rise in the following decades, putting ever more pressure on the government.

To solve these problems, Hong Kong turned to industrialization, and its success has been described as a miracle. Capitalizing on the influx of cheap labor, entrepreneurship, skill, and capital from China, Hong Kong's initial industry concentrated on textile and clothing, artificial flowers, toys, and inexpensive household utensils aimed at Asian markets. Hong Kong competed successfully with neighboring countries because of its relative stability, free trade, low taxation, and absence of exchange duties. Extensive banking, shipping, and insurance facilities, coupled with the government's commitment to improving the infrastructure, were also important factors.

In the 1970s, the city saw the construction of skyscrapers, new road links, multilane highways, overpasses, tunnels, and mass transit railways, which completely changed the face of urban Hong Kong. Hong Kong International Airport doubled its handling capacity between 1984 and 1988. The port of Hong Kong also underwent significant development, particularly in providing for container traffic. Meanwhile, Hong Kong's industrial base, in the face of rising production costs and a tight quota system, moved into more sophisticated production in fashion-design, electronics, and electrical appliances. Its markets were extended to include the United States, Canada, and Australia, while the older markets of Japan and China were expanded. As a consequence of China's reopening to free trade in the 1970s, Hong Kong resumed its dominant role in China's external trade, becoming the most important gateway for the import of capital, material, and technology into China.

Shortage of usable land led to large-scale reclamation projects and the leveling of hills, around Victoria Harbor, at New Kowloon, and in the New Territories. These urban developments finally transformed the rural landscapes of the New Territories into modern urban townships. One of the important features of Hong Kong's postwar development has been the increase in the provision of public housing and other social services. Close to 50 percent of Hong Kong residents now live in public housing. Various social services, which had long been the province of Christian missionaries and traditional Chinese organizations, were taken over by the government, beginning in the 1970s. Education is among the most important of these. Free primary education was introduced in 1971 and extended to secondary education in 1978. Technical and vocational training institutes were established as Hong Kong's industries increasingly required skilled workers. Six new universities offer Hong Kong residents unprecedented opportunities to pursue a higher education.

For the greater part of Hong Kong's British history, the people have had little say in its government. In the wake of a riot in 1967, however, the British authorities set up the so-called District Office—the first serious attempt to bridge the gap between the government and the people. Since then, the administration has undergone a process of gradual democratization. District boards, consisting of appointed as well as elected members, were organized in 1982 and provide a more effective forum for public participation in local government. Members of the Legislative Council have been elected rather than appointed since 1985.

In 1972, China declared in the United Nations General Meeting that Hong Kong was an integral part of China and indicated that it would resume jurisdiction over the territory at an "appropriate time." Talks between Britain and China began in early 1980 and resulted in the so-called Joint Declaration, signed on December 19, 1984, which provides for the restoration of Hong Kong to China on July 1, 1997. The territory will then become a Special Administration Zone (SAR) of the People's Republic of China. According to the declaration, the SAR will have a high degree of autonomy and will be able to maintain its capitalist economy and lifestyle for fifty years. A Basic Law Drafting Committee has designed a new set of basic laws to govern the area, and their work was ratified by China's National People's Congress in 1990. Details of the implementation of the Joint Declaration are left to the Sino-British Joint Liaison Group. Meanwhile, the people of Hong Kong await with anxiety the arrival of the historic moment when Britain withdraws from its last foothold in the East, and the territory becomes the Special Administration Region of the People's Republic of China.

Further Reading: *An Illustrated History of Hong Kong* by Nigel Cameron (Hong Kong, Oxford, and New York: Oxford University Press, 1991) is a masterful, concise history of the region that makes for delightful reading. Jan Morris's *Hong Kong: Epilogue to an Empire* (second edition, Harmondsworth, Middlesex: Penguin, 1993) gives a comprehensive account of the territory's development, noting in particular the cultural confrontation of East and West. *Hong Kong: The Last Prize of the Empire* by Trea Wiltshire (second edition, Hong Kong: FormAsia, 1993) contains many historical and contemporary photographs and vivid, informative text.

—Ng Lun Ngai-ha

Hue (Vietnam)

Location: On the eastern coast of central Vietnam, approximately five miles inland from the South China Sea, on the Huong Giang (Perfume River). Hue lies more than 400 miles south of Hanoi and almost 700 miles north of Ho Chi Minh City (formerly Saigon).

Description: A settlement since ancient times, Hue frequently passed from Vietnamese, to Cham, to Chinese hands in its early history. In more recent centuries, the city has been the cultural heart of traditional Vietnamese society. In the late seventeenth century, a citadel, called Phu Xuan, was built, and some fifty years later the city became the capital of southern Vietnam. In 1802, Hue became the imperial capital of a unified Vietnam under the founder of the Nguyen Dynasty. The citadel was entirely rebuilt during his reign. With the division of the country in 1954, Hue lost its function as capital and began a long, if slow, economic decline. Hue was the focus of the most prolonged battle in the Tet Offensive of 1968 and was very heavily damaged.

Site Office: Thua Thien-Hue Tourism
30 Le Loi Street
Hue
Vietnam
542369, 542288, or 542355

The origins of the ancient city of Hue lie buried beneath centuries of unrecorded history. The eastern region of Indochina frequently changed hands among the kingdom of Nam Viet (later Dai Viet, now Vietnam), the kingdom of Champa (a Hindu civilization that has since disappeared altogether), and the Chinese empire. The city makes its first recorded appearance in Chinese documents, where it is mentioned as the seat of Chinese military authority in Nam Viet around 200 B.C. However, the Chinese did not maintain a continuous presence in Nam Viet, which periodically regained its political autonomy. Nam Viet was also preyed upon by the Chams: around A.D. 200, for instance, Hue was incorporated into Champa. Despite their early presence, the Hindu Chams did not leave much of a mark on Vietnamese culture and no trace of them remains at Hue, which has been oriented to China for much of its history.

After centuries of intermittent Chinese overlordship, Hue was officially ceded in 1306 to the kingdom of Dai Viet, which had gained its nominal independence from China in 968. During the centuries following Chinese withdrawal from the region, a succession of Dai Viet dynasties maintained their capital at Hanoi in northern Vietnam. Hue was a quiet backwater. But after the later Le Dynasty crumbled in the early sixteenth century, the country came to be ruled by two competing families: the Trinh, who controlled northern Vietnam, and the Nguyen, who controlled central and southern Vietnam. Under Nguyen control, Hue began to gain in importance, and in 1635 the city was chosen as the Nguyen family seat.

In 1678, construction of the first Nguyen citadel of Phu Xuan was begun under the Nguyen ruler Hien Vuong. The fortifications on the north, or left, bank of the Huong Giang River may have been meant as a defense against the Trinh, since the two ruling families periodically attempted to dislodge each other. In the 1650s, for instance, Hien Vuong had fought a prolonged though fruitless war against the Trinh in the north. But the Phu Xuan ramparts were apparently never manned for any military conflict. Undoubtedly, the citadel's primary function was to symbolize the Nguyen's might. The original structure was entirely replaced during the nineteenth century by the later citadel.

The Buddhist Nguyen Dynasty began building monumental pagodas at Hue in the late seventeenth century. The two most important lie on the south, or right, bank of the Huong Giang River, a short distance away from each other. The Bao Quoc Pagoda, built in 1670, survives essentially unchanged. The Tu Dam Pagoda, founded in 1695, is one of the best known in Vietnam, but the original buildings have disappeared, to be replaced by an uninspired twentieth-century structure. The Chinese influence at Hue is evident in the origin of the pagodas, both of which were founded by Chinese monks. The other important pagodas at Hue were built in the mid–nineteenth century, during the reign of Thieu Tri. One of these, the Thien Mu Pagoda, lies on the left bank, west of the citadel. It has an octagonal tower over seventy feet high and is one of the most celebrated buildings in Vietnam. Another is the Dieu De National Pagoda, which became the center of Buddhist protest against the South Vietnamese government in the 1960s.

Until 1744, the Nguyen recognized the house of the later Le as the *de jure* rulers of the country, but in that year the pretense was finally abandoned. Hue officially became the capital of central and southern Vietnam. However, Nguyen reign was soon disrupted by the Tay Son rebellion, which broke out in 1771. The revolt was led by three brothers from a wealthy merchant family from Tay Son, a port on the central Vietnamese coast south of Hue. Sweeping through the country, the revolt enjoyed extensive support among the peasantry, who hoped for land reform. The Tay Son brothers dislodged the Nguyen from central Vietnam by 1773, and they occupied the Phu Xuan citadel for almost twenty years. In 1783 they captured Saigon and made themselves master of all of the Nguyen territory. Turning their attention to northern

Thien Mu Pagoda, Hue
Photo courtesy of The Chicago Public Library

Vietnam next, they routed the Trinh in 1786 and thus reunified the country.

In the meantime, the sole surviving member of the Nguyen Dynasty, Nguyen Anh, who had managed to flee to Thailand, had returned to southern Vietnam with a band of French mercenaries. In the mid–1780s, he began building an army, training Vietnamese troops and supplying them with the aid of French missionaries. Since the hoped-for land reforms were not forthcoming under the Tay Son brothers, the rebellion had lost its popular base by this time. Nguyen Anh made gradual advances against the Tay Son rebels, until he was able to defeat them decisively in 1792. He spent the next ten years consolidating his control over the country, including the northern regions, and eliminating the rebels' descendants. After winning major battles at Hue and Hanoi in 1802, Nguyen Anh proclaimed himself emperor, took the name of Gia Long, and established his imperial capital at Hue.

In 1804, Gia Long began a massive reconstruction of the citadel. Laid out roughly in a square and surrounded by a system of moats and canals, the citadel covers an area of about two and one-half square miles. It is surrounded by a high earthen wall that was later clad in a layer of brick more than six feet thick. Ten fortified gates give access to the walled city. The eleventh, the Ngo Mon Gate, defines the central axis of the citadel's river front and leads into the Imperial Palace. An array of imperial symbols legitimizing Gia Long's reign is stationed along this central axis. At one end, near the river, stands the flag tower, which, as the foremost symbol of sovereignty in Vietnam, has been much fought over, both in the uprisings against French colonial rule in 1945 and again during the Tet Offensive in 1968. The so-called Nine Holy Cannons are arranged on either side of the central axis just inside the citadel ramparts. These cannon were cast from bronze captured during the war on the Tay Son rebels. The four to the east represent the seasons, while the five to the west represent the elements of metal, wood, water, fire, and soil. Thus, they identify Gia Long's dynasty with the natural order of things.

On the other side of the Ngo Mon Gate lies the Trung Dao Bridge, which crosses into the front courtyard of the Imperial Palace and simultaneously emphasizes the separateness of the palace from the world of ordinary mortals. This bridge leads straight into the emperor's reception hall, the so-called Thai Hoa Palace. The front courtyard also contains the gigantic Nine Dynastic Urns, the first of which were cast in 1835 and 1836. Each massive urn is associated with a different Nguyen emperor and is decorated with ancient Chinese motifs.

The central axis continues into the heart of the Imperial Palace but is visually interrupted by a wall separating the front courtyard from the inner court, which once held the Forbidden Purple City, the private imperial residence. Access to the inner court is gained only through gates located at the far ends of the wall. Immediately beyond the wall on the central axis lie the Halls of the Mandarins, where court officials prepared for the imperial ceremonies that played such a conspicuous role in Gia Long's reign. The Forbidden Purple City itself was leveled during the fighting of the Tet Offensive and, with the exception of the library, has not been rebuilt. Most of the area of the imperial residence is now used for the cultivation of vegetables, as are other parts of the citadel.

Although Gia Long had wiped out the Tay Son rebellion, its support among the peasantry raised fears of renewed popular unrest. To consolidate his image as Vietnam's legitimate ruler and to guard against future uprisings, Gia Long focused much of his energy on reviving rigidly hierarchical social structures and traditional ceremonies. The minister of rites, the most important functionary in Gia Long's court, helped the emperor orchestrate a set of ritual cults that occupied the majority of the court's time and attention. The foremost of these was the cult of heaven, which centered on the Nam Giao (Temple of Heaven). This temple, built on the right bank of the Huong Giang River and based on a Chinese model, consists of series of terraces that represent the hierarchical universe of traditional Vietnamese culture. Every three years, the emperor, as intermediary between heaven and earth, presided over a series of elaborate ritual sacrifices associated with the heavenly cult. The Nam Giao temple survives, but the central altar has been replaced with a memorial to the North Vietnamese soldiers killed in the Second Indochina War (commonly referred to in the United States as the Vietnam War). The emperor also led the twice-yearly rituals of the cult of Confucius, the annual rites of the cult of agriculture (which were simultaneously carried out in every town and village of Vietnam by imperial representatives), and the secret rituals of the cult of the emperor's ancestors that took place in the Forbidden Purple City.

Another striking aspect of Gia Long's reign—still evident in Vietnamese culture—was his committed orientation to China. His court, his government organization, his architecture, and his religious convictions were closely modeled on the Chinese imperial example. His program of civil improvements, including irrigation and land reclamation schemes as well as roads, ports, and bridges, were also patterned after traditional Chinese practices, heavily favoring small-scale rice cultivation and rejecting technological innovation.

Gia Long died in 1820, and his body was interred in a tomb in the hills about ten miles south of Hue. The burial complex comprises, apart from the central sepulchre, a courtyard ringed with sculpture, a pavilion celebrating the emperor's glorious deeds, a temple for his worship, and a lotus pond. The area between Gia Long's tomb and the city has since become an extended imperial cemetery, the landscape dotted with pagodas and the tombs of many of the Nguyen emperors. They all follow, more or less faithfully, the layout and style of Gia Long's burial complex.

Gia Long was succeeded by Minh Mang, who persecuted the Catholic missionaries in his realm to guard against the pollution of the pure Confucianism he himself professed and wished his subjects to adopt. His successor, Thieu Tri, who ruled from 1841 to 1848, pursued this anti-Catholic policy even more assiduously, provoking the anger of the French, who maintained trading posts as well as missions on the central Vietnamese coast. What began on the part of the French as a retaliation against the expulsion and execution of missionaries in the late 1840s gradually became a concerted effort to colonize Vietnam and the rest of Indochina. In 1883, after a final skirmish involving a bombardment of Hue, all of Vietnam fell under French control, officially becoming a French protectorate. Although the French left the Hue citadel to the Vietnamese, they housed their colonial administration on the right bank of the Huong Giang. This area of the city was gradually transformed into a French quarter.

Immediately after Vietnam bowed to colonial rule, the Nguyen Dynasty experienced a prolonged struggle for the succession to the now virtually meaningless position of emperor. A series of palace coups took place at Hue, and emperors died under mysterious circumstances almost as soon as they were installed. In spite of these maneuverings, the Nguyen rulers were reduced to puppets, confined to their ceremonial functions at the Hue citadel, and replaced at will by the French if they associated themselves with gathering nationalist sentiment. This situation continued essentially unchanged until World War II, when the Japanese occupied Vietnam.

Even as the French colonial authorities collaborated with the Japanese occupiers, the Vietnamese nationalists settled their hopes of eventual liberation from colonial oppression on the Japanese and cooperated with them as well. When the French resumed control at war's end, the Viet Minh declared Vietnam's independence, and communist guerillas took up arms against colonial forces. Some minor skirmishes took place at Hue in 1945. The conflict escalated into the First Indochina War by the following year. To stem the communist tide and retain some popular support, the French removed the Nguyen emperor, who went into exile, and installed a provisional administrative committee of noncommunist Vietnamese at Hue in 1947. In 1949 this puppet government was moved to Saigon, and Hue lost its position as the country's main political focus. The city nevertheless maintained itself as the cultural and spiritual heart of Vietnam.

The First Indochina War came to an end in 1954, when the Geneva Accords negotiated a cease-fire and divided the country into French-controlled South Vietnam and communist-controlled North Vietnam. Hue found itself some fifty-five miles south of the so-called Demilitarized Zone, or DMZ, along the seventeenth parallel, which formed the boundary between north and south. Fighting in South Vietnam soon resumed, as the Viet Cong, which had broad support in the countryside, was unwilling to acquiesce in a permanent division. The South Vietnamese government, under Ngo Dinh Diem, enjoyed French and American protection.

However, Diem jeopardized this support with his persecution of South Vietnam's Buddhist community, which led to a series of protest actions concentrated principally at Hue. The protests, beginning in 1963, dramatically staged the self-immolation of monks and nuns and made the front-page news all over the world. French and U.S. support of Diem's government was compromised in the West, as horrified voters were confronted by the gruesome television and newspaper images of men and women setting themselves ablaze. Later in the year, Diem was deposed and assassinated in an army coup encouraged by the United States.

The Buddhist protest movement was led by the monk Tri Quang, whose organizational headquarters were in the Dieu De Pagoda at Hue. In 1966, he formed an alliance with a faction of the South Vietnamese army under general Nguyen Chanh Thi. Thi spearheaded a noncommunist rebellion that took over Hue and Da Nang in 1966 and held out against the South Vietnamese army until June 1967, when the alliance with the Buddhists dissolved. Half a year later, in January and February of 1968, Hue became the stage for the bloodiest engagement of the Tet Offensive. After twenty-five days of heavy artillery strikes and house-to-house fighting, Hue was largely reduced to rubble and the citadel lay in ruins. In the first days of the battle, communist forces had rounded up and killed an estimated 3,000 Hue inhabitants who had had some connection to the South Vietnamese authorities. During the fighting, 150 U.S. marines, 400 South Vietnamese troops, and approximately 5,000 North Vietnamese and Viet Cong soldiers lost their lives. An uncounted number of civilians fell victim to the shelling; estimates range from 2,500 to 4,500 dead.

Hue remained in South Vietnamese hands until March 25, 1975, when communist troops marched into the city. Shortly thereafter, North Vietnam subdued the South Vietnamese and reunified the country. Hue is now a modest provincial city, whose cultural treasures, partly rebuilt after the devastations of the Tet Offensive, still play an important role in the national identity of Vietnam.

Further Reading: *Indochina* by Bernard Philippe Groslier (Cleveland: World, and London: Muller, 1966) includes an overview of Vietnam's early history. *Vietnam: A Travel Survival Kit* by Daniel Robinson and Robert Storey (second edition, Hawthorn, Victoria, and Berkeley, California: Lonely Planet, 1993) is a practical guide to travel in Vietnam that gives a concise history of the country and a description of its notable cities. *Understanding Vietnam* by Neil L. Jamieson (Berkeley, Los Angeles, and London: University of California Press, 1993) is a study of the historic, religious, and philosophical foundations of Vietnamese society. Stanley Karnow's *Vietnam: A History* (New York: Viking, 1983; second edition, New York and London: Viking, 1991) is a detailed and highly readable chronicle of both Indochina wars, enlivened with many eyewitness accounts. *The Vietnam Wars: 1945–1990* by Marilyn B. Young (New York: HarperCollins, 1991) also presents the history of the struggle for a united, independent Vietnam after World War II. The work explores both foreign involvement and Vietnam's internal conflicts. Keith William Nolan's *Battle for Hue: Tet 1968* (Novato, California: Presidio Press, 1983) gives a somewhat breathless but solidly researched blow-by-blow account of the fighting at Hue in 1968.

—Rion Klawinski and Marijke Rijsberman

Hyderābād (Andhra Pradesh, India)

Location: Hyderābād lies in the state of Andhra Pradesh in the eastern part of the Deccan Plateau on the edge of south India. The city is located on the banks of the Mūsi River, a tributary of the Krishna River, and sits across the Mūsi from the former British garrison, which now has become the city of Secunderābād.

Description: Hyderābād is today the capital of Andhra Pradesh state. Before Andhra Pradesh came into being in 1956, this Deccan city was the capital of the Muslim state of Hyderābād. During British rule, the state covered a great part of the central and northern Deccan (over 80,000 square miles) and was ruled semi-independently by the nizām of Hyderābād. Prior to the rule of the nizām, Hyderābād was the capital of the Quṭb Shāhi Kingdom that was created in the early sixteenth century.

Site Office: Government of India Tourist Office
3-6-369/A-30, Sandozi Building, second floor
26 Himayat Nagar
Hyderābād Andhra Pradesh 500 029
India
660037

Since its founding in 1591, Hyderābād has been one of the most vibrant centers of Islamic culture and learning in all of India, no doubt the result of its status as capital for two of southern India's major Muslim powers: first, the Quṭb Shāhi Dynasty, and later, the independent state of Hyderābād. The Quṭb Shāhis rose to prominence following the fall of the Bahmanī Kingdom (1347–1490s), another Muslim power that ruled over a great part of the Deccan, including the area where the city of Hyderābād now lies. The collapsing Bahmanī Kingdom split into four separate kingdoms: Ahmadnagar, Berar, Bijāpur, and Bidar. Qulī Quṭb al-Mulk, founder of the Quṭb Shāhi Dynasty, began his career as governor of Tilaganga, a Bidar territory. As Qulī Quṭb al-Mulk extended his holdings, the territory he ruled became increasingly distant from the Bidar capital. From 1515 forward, he acted as ruler of an independent kingdom and fought with the kingdoms of Bijāpur and Bidar. By the time of his death in 1543, Qulī Quṭb al-Mulk had united a large part of the eastern Deccan under one kingdom. The kingdom reached its height of territorial and political power during the rule of Ibrahim Quṭb Shāh (1550–80), who defeated the Vijayanagaran Empire, conquered the southern part of Orissa, and annexed the kingdom of Berar in the northern part of the Deccan, extending Quṭb Shāhi rule almost to the boundaries of the former Bahmanī Kingdom.

Although Ibrahim Quṭb Shāh may have led the kingdom to its greatest political power, his successor, Muhammad Qulī Quṭb Shāh (reigned 1580–1612), fostered the kingdom's cultural growth. Instead of military conquest and empire, Muhammad focused on strengthening the kingdom internally. With this in mind, in 1591 he shifted the capital from the fort of Golconda to a site on the bank of the Mūsi River, thereby founding the city of Hyderābād. The construction of the city marked a new era of Quṭb Shāhi culture, for Hyderābād soon established an unrivaled tradition of patronage of Islamic art, literature, and learning in southern India.

Muhammad planned to surround and protect the old city of Hyderābād with bastioned walls, but these were not completed until the early eighteenth century. The city is connected to the outlying areas via four bridges, the oldest of which was erected in 1593. Muhammad Qulī Quṭb Shāh was responsible for the complex of royal and ceremonial structures that form the focal point of the city. The most important and celebrated structure in that complex is the Chārminār (Four Minarets), considered by many to be the most magnificent urban building constructed in India during the Middle Ages. The Chārminār is a large archway that stands at the crossroads of the city's four major streets. The archway occupies a surface area of more than 9,600 square feet and consists of four great arches. Above the arches, an arcaded balcony encircles the building, and on each corner stands a minaret approximately 180 feet high. Atop each of these minarets is a bulbous dome characteristic of Indo-Saracenic style. (Saracens were Arab Muslims who lived during the time of the Crusades.) At the western end of the roof, the architects placed a small mosque, with the rest of the roof serving as a court. Today, the Chārminār stands in the middle of the busy and heavily populated city. Although part of the charm of this monument lies in its having been integrated into the modern city, its beauty and durability fade daily under the strain of city pollution and traffic.

The next great architectural achievement of the Quṭb Shāhi Dynasty came during the rule of Muhammad Qulī Quṭb Shāh's successor, Muhammad Quṭb Shāh (1612–26). The Mecca Mosque (or Makkah Masjid), begun in 1617 but not completed until 1693, during the occupation of Hyderābād by the Mughal ruler 'Ālamgīr (Aurangzeb), ranks among the city's most magnificent monuments. This huge mosque can accommodate crowds numbering 10,000 people for the daily Islamic prayer. The peripheral bays of the great prayer hall are domed, and the central bay is capped with a pointed vault. In keeping with the Quṭb Shāhi style, the frontal facade is flanked by two short minarets, again with arcaded balconies and bulbous domes.

Apart from these considerable architectural achievements, some extant Quṭb Shāhi art has been discovered. They

Mecca Mosque, Hyderābād
Photo courtesy of Air India Library, New York

reveal a distinct Deccani aesthetic style. Unlike the Mughals of northern India, who were Sunni Muslims, the Quṭb Shāhis were followers of the Shi'ite branch of Islam. The very name of their capital city reflects this fact: Hyder is an alternate name for ʿĀlī, hero and martyr of the Shi'ite faith. As Shi'ites, the Quṭb Shāhis sought to establish cultural ties to Persia, not Delhi. Their conscious effort to remain separate from the northern Sunni tradition led to a distinct artistic culture. The south Indian taste for full shapes gave these imported Islamic forms a rich flavor alien to the conservative art of the Mughals. Where Mughal paintings often depicted war scenes, Deccani painting most often focused on relaxed settings such as courts and gardens. The first eight paintings of the Quṭb Shāhi Dynasty to be found were all dedicated to Muhammad Qulī Quṭb Shāh; in clear contrast to the Mughal tradition of visual arts, these paintings celebrate Muhammad Qulī Quṭb Shāh as the first known Urdū poet in India, rather than as a military or political leader.

Such associations with Islamic literature and scholarship, perhaps more than anything else, became the hallmark at Hyderābād. Although Hyderābādi rulers professed Shi'ite allegiance, they patronized and encouraged Islamic culture and learning irrespective of specific sects. From the first Quṭb Shāhi ruler to the last nizām of the independent state of Hyderābād, they consciously promoted Arabic, Persian, and Urdū literature, and encouraged Islamic theological education that transgressed Sunni and Shi'ite boundaries.

This period of cultural and political vibrancy came to an end when the Mughal Empire extended its rule over the Deccan. Beginning as early as the 1590s, the Mughals undertook military campaigns in the Deccan, cutting into the northern parts of the Quṭb Shāhi Kingdom. The Mughal forces did not forge deeply into the kingdom until approximately 1656. After a brief Mughal occupation in 1656, Abdullah Quṭb Shāh (1626–72) regained some of the lost territory and for a time eliminated the Mughal threat to Hyderābād. However, the Mughal concentration on the Quṭb Shāhi Kingdom and the city of Hyderābād created another threat to Quṭb Shāhi sovereignty. The major imperial rival to the Mughals during the late seventeenth century were the Marāṭhās. Any military target of the Mughals almost automatically became a target of the Marāṭhās as well. From 1656 to 1685, the Marāṭhās,

Chārminār, Hyderābād
Photo courtesy of Air India Library, New York

Mughals, and Quṭb Shāhis intermittently fought over the territory in the eastern part of the Deccan. Finally, in 1686, the Mughals under the command of 'Ālamgīr successfully seized the capital of Hyderābād, bringing about the end of the Quṭb Shāhi Dynasty.

The Mughals ruled in Hyderābād for thirty-eight years, but the latter half of this period saw the steady erosion of their real authority. After the death of 'Ālamgīr in 1707, the Mughal Empire all but collapsed. The few Mughal rulers who succeeded 'Ālamgīr exercised little power in a dwindling and bankrupt empire. 'Ālamgīr's financial irresponsibility had drained the Mughals' resources and hampered their ability to fund military campaigns or defense. Moreover, his religious fanaticism had alienated the Hindu subjects in his empire, who now gravitated toward such Hindu rulers as the Marāṭhās. During this period of political disarray, independent kingdoms broke away from Mughal rule. Such was the case in Hyderābād. Āsaf Jāh Nizām-ul-Mulk (reigned 1724–48), the Mughal viceroy in the region, declared the former Quṭb Shāhi Kingdom to be the independent state of Hyderābād in 1724. Once again, the city became the locus for Indo-Islamic art, architecture, literature, and scholarship.

The nizām of Hyderābād, as Āsaf Jāh came to be known, enjoyed true independence for only a short period of time. Starting in the middle of the eighteenth century, the entire Deccan was caught up in the struggle between the French and the British for control over the Indian subcontinent. By 1750, the state of Hyderābād had already lost its valuable sea access in Orissa to the British, who were advancing steadily down the Coromandel Coast from Bengal. At the same time, the French stepped up their effort at founding an empire in South Asia. To a great extent, this imperial contest focused on the Deccan. In 1749, the French, under the command of Joseph Francois Dupleix, made major gains against the British in the Carnatic and the Deccan. These victories gave the French considerable leverage in the political affairs of the area. When Āsaf Jāh Nizām-ul-Mulk died in 1748, the French seized this opportunity to place a hand-picked ruler on the throne of Hyderābād. At first, they supported Muzaffar Jang, grandnephew of the nizām, and marched with him toward the capital. Unfortunately for the French, Muzaffar Jang died en route, whereupon the French commander, Charles Marquis de Bussy, quickly picked a new puppet, Salābat Jang, one of the former nizām's sons. By placing him upon the throne, the French gained control over the state of Hyderābād. They would not enjoy their control for long, however. In 1751, Robert Clive, founder of the British Empire in India, began his assault on the French holdings. He drove the French out of Bengal and reestablished the British military and trading stronghold. This first victory led eventually to the further victories over the French in the Deccan and the south in 1760.

Having gained control of the Deccan and Hyderābād, the British installed their own leader on the throne, Nizām Ālī Khān. The state of Hyderābād, although officially an independent region, became a protected ally of the British East India Company. This imposed alliance proved quite valuable to the British during the last quarter of the eighteenth century, when they faced challenges from the Marāṭhās and the kingdom of Mysore, first led by Hyder Alī and later by Tippu Sultan. When the Marāṭhās and Hyder Alī joined forces to fight the British in 1780, the nizām of Hyderābād remained loyal to the British. Similarly, when Tippu Sultan resumed Mysore's fight against the growing empire of the British East India Company, the nizām refused to aid his fellow Muslim leader. In 1798, Hyderābād became the first state to be included in Lord Wellesley's subsidiary alliance system. This system, in essence, dictated that the company protect a state from external attack in return for the control of its foreign relations. For this purpose, it provided a subsidiary force of company troops commonly stationed in a cantonment near the capital, such as Secunderābād. The state itself paid for this protection force out of its revenues. In addition to this unbalanced political alliance, the nominally independent states in India were compelled to share an allocated amount of land revenues with the company, and later with the British crown. The nizāms of Hyderābād lived under this alliance system from 1798 until Indian independence in 1947. The alliance with Hyderābād and other states proved to be a critical aid to the British during the revolt of 1857. If many of the independent states had joined the rebellious forces, British supremacy in India may have been even more seriously threatened.

Although the political and financial constraints the British government imposed considerably undermined the local nizām's independence, Hyderābād still enjoyed greater freedom than the states under direct rule. This measure of freedom and the extra leverage given to the nizāms by their displays of loyalty allowed them to make the state of Hyderābād, and the capital city in particular, a symbol of Muslim culture and pride. Throughout the nineteenth and early twentieth centuries, the nizāms funded such central institutions as the medical college, the high courts, and the legislative council.

The true passions of the nizāms, however, focused on the institutions of Islamic learning. The great Indian Muslim educator, Sir Sayyed Ahmad Khan, after witnessing the damage done to the Muslim community in the aftermath of the revolt of 1857, encouraged Muslims to come to Hyderābād to be educated and to serve as the leaders for the rebuilding of Muslim society in India. In 1888, the Dairatul-Maarif-it Osmania was founded to collect rare and original Arabic manuscripts and translate them into Urdū. Translation and preservation of religious texts was a paramount project of this institution. The collection of the Salar Jang Museum of Hyderābād stands as testimony to the sheer quantity of Islamic texts and relics amassed by the nizāms over the years: there are 8,856 Urdū, 3,226 Persian, and 2,110 Arabic volumes in the museum. Furthermore, famous Urdū writers like Zafar Ālī Khān and Maulvi Abdul Haq came to work in Hyderābād during the nineteenth century.

Perhaps the greatest achievement of the nizāms in the area of Muslim education came when Nizām Mīr Usmān founded Osmania University in Hyderābād in 1918. Osmania University was the first in India to use a native language, Urdū, as a medium of instruction. A university college was started for women in 1926, long before other Muslim areas in India allowed women's education. Despite their ambiguous political control and the constant overlordship by the British, the tremendous wealth of the nizāms, which came mostly from their ownership of 10 percent of state lands, allowed them to patronize the Hyderābād culture lavishly.

During the end of the nineteenth and beginning of the twentieth centuries, the nationalist movement consumed the entire Indian political scene. The nizāms of Hyderābād, however, remained isolated from these mainstream political movements and struggled to maintain the state's insularity. An indication of their success came shortly after the independence of India, when sociologist S. C. Dube interviewed villagers just outside Hyderābād who said they had never heard of Mahatma Gandhi, Jawaharlal Nehru, or the Congress struggle against the British.

The intense patronage of Arabic and Persian learning and literature, the names of their monuments (i.e., Mecca Mosque, Medinah Market, etc.), and the Indo-Saracenic style of their architecture all made clear not only that the nizāms wished to remain culturally isolated from India, but that they believed, as had their predecessors, that their sources of cultural influence came from Persia and the Middle East. But culturally and religiously, the nizāms were quite out of step with the vast majority of their subjects, who were Hindu. Hindus always had been the majority in the city and state of Hyderābād. During the reign of the nizāms, Hindus accounted for approximately 85 percent of the population. Language differences also came into play. Although the vast majority of their Hindu subjects spoke Telugu, the nizāms patronized and used the language of the Muslim elite, Urdū. Quite consciously, the nizāms and the Muslim elite tried to keep the city of Hyderābād, as well as the region they controlled, a tiny remnant of the medieval Muslim rule and kingship in India. This situation would naturally seem to breed communal antagonism and a general animosity among the Hindu majority for the Muslim elite and rulership, but, surprisingly, no evidence exists of communal discord or a Hindu revolt against Muslim rule in the years before Indian independence.

The cultural walls that separated Hyderābād from the rest of India, however, came crashing down when India achieved independence from the British in 1947. At that time, the nizām declared somewhat naively that he wanted to maintain his independence. The newly founded Indian government previously had annexed all of the independent princely states except for Hyderābād, which stood out as a particularly embarrassing and insulting affront to its proclamations of unity and nationhood. After allowing the nizām one year to join voluntarily, the Indian government finally sent in troops in September 1948. After four relatively bloodless days of fighting, the nizām surrendered and the state of Hyderābād officially became part of the Indian nation. A military government ruled in Hyderābād for four years until popular elections were held in 1952. Although the nizām maintained his title, the position was divorced of any power, and the government appropriated his vast personal land holdings. As a result, the nizām no longer could serve as the cultural patron of Islamic arts and learning, a function that had been the hallmark of the Hyderābādi rulership for over two centuries. Moreover, many of the middle-class Muslim intellectuals, fearing the consequences of Hindu Indian rule, fled to Pakistan. The once-flourishing store of Muslim intellectual and artistic assets was seriously depleted.

In 1956, the state of Hyderābād was eliminated altogether. As part of the pan-Indian reordering of states according to language groups, the city of Hyderābād and some surrounding regions became part of the newly created state of Andhra Pradesh. Language differences now became a fierce and polarizing issue all over India, including Hyderābād, where Telugu speakers clashed with the Urdū-speaking members of the Muslim community. The language conflict also led naturally to a conflict of religious communities. Starting in the 1950s, the tide of Hindu nationalism has grown in Hyderābād, and the incidents of communal strife have increased steadily. The long isolation of Hyderābād from these realities of political and cultural life in India have made their intrusion even more shocking. Now, Hyderābād has to face the realities of Indian urban life, with all its difficulties as well as its promises of progress, particularly of greater political and economic equality. Yet amid the new composite Indian culture being developed, one can still see the vestiges of the Islamic culture of the nizāms and their dynastic predecessors.

Further Reading: A good illustrated and narrative history of the Deccan during the Middle Ages is *The Islamic Heritage of the Deccan,* edited by George Michell (Bombay: Marg, 1986), which includes outstanding photos of Quṭb Shāhi monuments and painting, as well as a valuable chronology of kingdoms in the Deccan and south India from the thirteenth to the sixteenth centuries. *Discovering Islam: Making Sense of Muslim History and Society* by Akbar S. Ahmed (London and New York: Routledge and Kegan Paul, 1988) does a wonderful job of analyzing the composition of Hyderābādi society, past and present. Two standard histories of India that discuss the history of Hyderābād in the context of larger political movements are *A History of India, Vol. I,* by Romila Thapar (Harmondsworth, Middlesex, and Baltimore, Maryland: Penguin, 1966) and *A New History of India* by Stanley Wolpert (New York: Oxford University Press, 1977; fourth edition, 1993). For a more detailed look into Indian history turn to *The New Cambridge History of India,* edited by Gordon Johnson, C. A. Bayly, and John F. Richards (29 vols., Cambridge and New York: Cambridge University Press, 1987–).

—Shome Chowdhury

Hyderābād (Sind, Pakistan)

Location: In the lower valley of the Indus River, about 125 miles from the river's mouth in the Arabian Sea and 112 miles east of Karāchi.

Description: Former capital of the emirs of Sind, with historic sites including remains of an eighteenth-century fort and royal tombs; one of the largest cities in Pakistan and an important commercial, industrial, and educational center.

Contact: Pakistan Tourism Development Corporation
Hotel Metropol
Club Road
Karāchi, Sind
Pakistan
(92) 21 516 252

Hyderābād as it exists today was founded only in the eighteenth century, but its location was historically significant prior to that time. The city stands on the site of the ancient city of Nīrūn-Kot, where in 711 the Hindu ruler Nīrūn surrendered to the Arab invasion led by Muhammad ibn Qasim, the conqueror of Sind. During its recorded history up to that time, Sind had gone through periods of Persian, Greek, Mauryan, and Kushān rule. Under the Kushāns in the early centuries A.D., the site of Hyderābād probably was one of the places from which goods were shipped to and from ports on the Red Sea and the Persian Gulf. The Kushān Empire fell apart in the third century, and Sind passed to a branch of the Rājputs, then briefly to the Persians again before a Hindu dynasty was founded by a Brahmin named Chach in 622. This dynasty remained in power until the Arabs arrived.

The precipitating factor behind the Arab invasion of Sind was the seizure of an Arab fleet by pirates off the coast of Sind in 709. The first two expeditions sent to avenge this act failed; Muhammad ibn Qasim succeeded with a force that included 6,000 Syrian horses, a camel corps, and an enormous catapult operated by 500 men. The Arab general is said to have built a mosque at Nīrūn-Kot.

Only scant records exist concerning the site of Hyderābād over the next several centuries, during which Sind came under a variety of Muslim rulers. In the sixteenth century Sind became part of the Mughal Empire, based in Delhi, but the Mughals did not maintain a particularly firm hold on the region. In 1701, with the Mughals facing major problems elsewhere in their empire, Emperor ʿĀlamgīr (Aurangzeb) recognized the independence of the Kalhōrā Dynasty of Sind, although the Mughals kept an administrator in Tatta, then the capital of Sind, until 1742. In 1742 the capital was moved to Khudābād, which had to be abandoned when the Indus River changed its course and moved away from the city twenty years later.

Several new sites for capital cities were considered, but one, Narsapur, was destroyed by a flood and another, Allahābād (not to be confused with the city of the same name in India), never got past the developmental stage. In 1768 Ghulām Shāh Kalhōrā, ruler of Sind, settled on the location of ancient Nīrūn-Kot and founded Hyderābād. The city was named for the prophet Muḥammad's son-in-law, ʿAlī, who also was known as Hyder. A slab of stone bearing his handprints and footprints sits in the center of Hyderābād.

Ghulām Shāh ordered the construction of the Pukka Qila (brick fort) on a plateau overlooking the city. The fort, by all accounts large and lavish, doubled as a royal residence. Its foundation stone bears an inscription that translates: "Oh God, bring peace to this city." In fact, the next few years in Hyderābād, up to Ghulām Shāh's death in 1772, were marked by peace and prosperity. Irrigation technology improved and the economy developed: indigo, sugar, and other products began to be cultivated in the countryside; fine buildings were erected in the city; and art and poetry flourished at the Kalhōrā court.

Few structures remain from this period, however. Of the Pukka Qila, the only sections that survive today are portions of the nearly fifty-foot-high outer wall, a tower, the main gate, and an interior room that was part of the harem quarters. The faded wall paintings and red lacquered ceiling in this room provide some idea of the original glory of the fort. The Pukka Qila also contains a small historical musuem. Near the Pukka Qila stands another ruined fort, the Kucca Qila (mud-built fort), also known as the Shāh Makkai Fort. Ghulām Shāh had it built in 1771 to protect the tomb of a Muslim saint, Sheikh Muhammad Makkai, who was said to have come to the area from Mecca 500 years earlier. He married a Hindu woman who converted to Islam; they are believed to have died and been buried together. Despite the fort's ruined state, the tomb remains an important pilgrimage site for Sindhis. Another significant building is Ghulām Shāh's tomb, the most outstanding of the twenty-one Kalhōrā tombs at Hyderābād. It once was capped with a dome, which collapsed and was replaced with a flat roof. It retains, however, some of its beautiful blue-and-white tile decoration and an inscription reading, "The emperor of the world, Ghulām Shāh: before him the firmament kissed the earth."

The Kalhōrā Dynasty fell apart after Ghulām Shāh's death. His successors—including his son, Safaraz, and brother, Ghulām Nabi, who murdered Safaraz and took over the throne in 1776—came into conflict with the rulers of the neighboring kingdom of Balūchistān. A Balūchi dynasty, the

Kalhōrā tombs, Hyderābād
Photo courtesy of Embassy of Pakistan, Washington, D.C.

Tālpurs, won control of Sind in 1782, and rule of the region was divided among three branches of the Tālpurs. Hyderābād remained the capital. The Tālpurs occupied the Pukka Qila and further developed the city, constructing their own royal tombs and other buildings.

Early into the period of Tālpur rule, Sind began to attract the attention of the British, whose interest there was sparked by French encroachment in that region. In 1809 Lord Minto, the British governor-general of India, negotiated a treaty with all three Tālpur branches providing for diplomatic relations between Britain and Sind and the exclusion of the French from the region. When the treaty was confirmed in 1820, it also provided for the exclusion of Americans. In 1832, another treaty between Britain and Sind stated that "the two contracting powers bind themselves never to look with the eye of covetousness on the possessions of the other." The treaty stipulated that the British would send no armed ships or persons bearing military supplies into Sind and that no British merchants would be allowed to settle there; they could conduct business in Sind, but had to return to India afterward.

British policy changed under the administration of Lord Auckland, who became governor-general in 1835. Driven partly by fears of Russian expansionism in the regions north of India, Auckland sent an army into Sind and announced the suspension of the 1832 treaty. Further measures taken by the British forced the emirs of Sind to finance a British military presence and accept the British East India Company's currency. A British resident, or administrator, also was installed in Hyderābād. The effect of all these moves was to deprive the emirs of their sovereignty.

After Afghanistan successfully challenged the British in the First Anglo-Afghan War of 1839–42, the emirs of Sind were inspired to try to reclaim their independence. Their effort was doomed, however, as the British had decided they needed control of Sind and its primary waterway, the Indus River, for military and commercial operations. Moreover, so some historians contend, the British may well have felt the need for a conquest to compensate for their failure in Afghanistan. Lord Ellenborough, Auckland's successor, sent Sir Charles Napier to Sind in September 1842 to take command of all British Indian troops there. Napier, an ambitious soldier who saw an opportunity to make a name for himself, wrote in his journal, "We have no right to seize Sind, yet we shall do so, and a very advantageous, useful, humane piece of rascality it will be." Napier provoked the Sindhis into attacking the British residency in Hyderābād, and war ensued. The British besieged the Pukka Qila, which the Tālpurs had made their headquarters. The most decisive action, however, was a British victory at Miani, a few miles outside Hyderābād, in February 1843. Sind was annexed by the British in June, and Napier was named governor. The emirs and their families were exiled to Bengal. In the next decade, thanks partly to the intervention of sympathetic Englishmen, they were given pensions and allowed to live in Sind again, albeit without power.

The British conquest left physical marks on Hyderābād. After the Pukka Qila was damaged by fighting, many sections of it were left to deteriorate further, although the British later constructed new barracks for their own troops within the fort. The British also laid out a mall and built administrative offices. The capital, however, was transferred to Karāchi. While Hyderābād's political importance declined, it remained a significant commercial center, noted for its local handcrafted leather, metal, and textile goods, along with modern manufactured products such as glass, paper, and plastics. Hyderābād and Sind became part of the Muslim nation of Pakistan when it was carved out from India upon independence from Britain in 1947.

In the twentieth century, modern residential and industrial developments have surrounded the old portion of Hyderābād, which is marked by narrow and winding streets and centered on the ruined forts and the Shāhi Bazaar. The bazaar, at one and one-half miles the longest in Pakistan, sells many local handcrafted items; it is noted especially for glass bangle bracelets. Hyderābād also has developed into an educational center. The University of Sind, which has thirty-two affiliated colleges, moved here in 1951 from Karāchi, where it had been founded in 1947. Additionally, Hyderābād has a medical college and several vocational schools. Local museums include the Institute of Sindhology at the university and the Sind Provincial Museum, one of the best in Pakistan, which has one section devoted to archaeology, another to Sindhi crafts, and a third designed for children.

Hyderābād's growth has been impeded in recent years by violent interethnic clashes, largely between native Sindhis and immigrants from India. As a result, travel in Pakistan has become hazardous; crimes from robbery to kidnapping are common. As of the mid–1990s, foreigners were advised not to make inessential visits.

Further Reading: Because the separation of India and Pakistan is relatively recent, much of the information on Hyderābād and its province, Sind, is to be found in general works of Indian history. A quick overview is available in Vincent A. Smith's *The Oxford History of India: From the Earliest Times to the End of 1911* (Oxford: Clarendon Press, 1919; fourth edition, edited by Percival Spear, New York and Oxford: Oxford University Press, 1981). A more recent and very useful one-volume study is *A New History of India* by Stanley Wolpert (New York: Oxford University Press, 1977; fourth edition, 1993). For more detail, see *The New Cambridge History of India*, edited by Gordon Johnson, C. A. Bayly, and John F. Richards (29 vols., Cambridge and New York: Cambridge University Press, 1987–). An interesting look at Sind and Hyderābād through nineteenth-century British eyes is available in *A Glance at Sind before Napier* (Karāchi, London, and New York: Oxford University Press, 1973; originally published as *Dry Leaves from Young Egypt*, 1849). This account was written by Edward Backhouse Eastwick, a British official in Sind who came to deplore his government's actions in seizing Sind and displacing its rulers. The 1973 reprint features a helpful introduction by H. T. Lambrick.

—Claudia Levi and Trudy Ring

Ise (Mie, Japan)

Location: In the central region of Honshū, the main island of Japan, eighty-seven miles southeast of Kyōto, ninety-nine miles southeast of Ōsaka, and inside the Ise-Shima National Park.

Description: A city that has grown around Ise Jingū, a religious complex consisting of the Gekū, the Naikū, and about 100 minor Shintō shrines, dedicated to the goddesses of the sun and of the harvest and other deities; closely associated with the Japanese imperial family.

Contact: Japan National Tourist Organization
1st floor, Kyōto Tower Building
Higashi-Shiokojichō
Shimogyō-ku
Kyōto, Kyōto
Japan
(75) 371 5649

Ise, a city in Mie prefecture with a population of about 106,000, is probably better known throughout Japan than any other city of its size because of Ise Jingū, a complex of more than 100 shrines of Shintō, the indigenous religion of Japan, which have dominated the area for at least 1,300 years. The two main shrines in particular, which are known as the Toyouke Daijingū or Gekū (the Outer Shrine) and the Kō Taijingū or Naikū (the Inner Shrine), are the location for important rituals associated, respectively, with the protection of the rice harvest and with the veneration of the sun goddess, the supposed ancestor of the Japanese imperial line. They are also now unique in Japan for being ceremonially destroyed and rebuilt every twenty years. Their central compounds, hidden from view behind fences and set in heavily forested parks, have a mysterious and awe-inspiring atmosphere even today, when few even among the thousands of Japanese visitors know much about their history and significance, and even fewer believe in the sun goddess, the harvest goddess, and the other deities they honor.

The Gekū, the Outer Shrine, is traditionally visited first. This is the shrine of Toyouke-hime no Ōmikami, the goddess of the harvest, who is said to have descended from heaven along with Ninigi no Mikoto, the grandson of the sun goddess Amaterasu no Ōmikami and grandfather of Jimmu Tennō, the mythical first emperor of Japan. The shrine compound is surrounded by a forest, which covers about 220 acres, and is entered by way of a wooden bridge. The avenue, running between still more trees, then continues under a wooden *torii* (the customary gateway of Shintō shrines, consisting of two columns joined at the top by two cross-beams); past the Anzaisho, a small rest house used by emperors when visiting Ise, and the Sanshujo, a rest house for other members of the imperial family; under another *torii;* and then past other buildings, such as the Kagura-den, a hall for performances of sacred dances by shrine maidens, to the Tomotamagaki Minami Gomon, a thatched gatehouse set into the southern section of a cedarwood fence, the first of four concentric fences surrounding the rectangular shrine compound.

There almost every visitor to the Gekū has had to stop, for even now only the emperor, his representatives, or priests of Ise Jingū are permitted to pass under the white curtain that hangs in the gateway at the second of these fences. Others must be content with glimpses of the inner courtyard of raked white gravel and three thatch-roofed buildings made from unvarnished *hinoki* (Japanese cypress) wood. Two small Hoden, treasure houses for ceremonial equipment and clothing, stand in the north of the compound; in front of them, and closely resembling a larger version of them, is the Shoden, or Main Hall. It is a rectangular wooden structure, approximately twenty feet high, thirty-three feet wide, and nineteen feet deep. It is divided into three bays and rests on a platform supported by columns, surrounded by a railed veranda, and fronted with an elongated covered porch. On top of its pitched roof are the *katsuogi,* a single log running the length of the building, from which the thatch descends; the *chigi,* a number of small beams that criss-cross the *katsuogi;* and the *mochikake,* rows of pegs at each end. All of these features can be seen from outside, above the tops of the four fences. Since there are no nails in the three buildings, which are held together by dowels, the only materials used apart from thatch and wood are the engraved gold and copper facings on the ends of the beams and on the doors.

Next to the compound is a rectangular open space, the *kodenchi,* equal in area to the compound itself, and also covered with white gravel. This marks the area where the next rebuilding of the shrine will take place. At its center is a very small wooden enclosure housing the top of a sacred wooden pillar, called the heart pillar, mostly buried in the earth. In addition, on a hill in the grounds of the Gekū are three lesser shrines, the Tsuchi no Miya, the Kaze no Miya, and the Taga no Miya, dedicated respectively to the earth, the wind, and the living spirit of Toyouke. Each of these, the most important among the numerous lesser shrines included in the Ise complex, also is accompanied by a *kodenchi* of white gravel.

The Naikū, which is about three miles to the southeast of the Gekū, is dedicated to Amaterasu, the sun goddess. Visitors enter its grounds, forested like those of the Gekū and covering about 165 acres, by way of the Ujibashi, the shrine bridge, made of *hinoki* and *zelkova* wood, which has a span of 335 feet over the Isuzu River. A path then leads from the bridge under a *torii* and then up the river bank to a set of steps that go down onto a stony beach, the Mitarashi, where visitors are expected to rinse their hands and mouths (many also feed

Gekū, or Outer Shrine, Ise
Photo courtesy of The Chicago Public Library

the ancient carp there). According to some accounts, this beach is where the primeval deity Izanagi purified himself after fleeing from the hellish dwelling of his estranged wife Izanami and produced Amaterasu in the act of wiping his eyes. Other accounts place her descent from heaven, long after her birth beside a river there, on the summit of Mount Kamiji, the holy mountain that overshadows the district of Ise.

From the sacred river, visitors proceed along the cedar-lined avenue under a second *torii,* then past one of two shrine stables housing sacred horses, the sacred cow shed, another Kagura-den, and a number of buildings used to store offerings and for purification rituals, to another set of stone steps, leading to another thatched and curtained gatehouse set in another one of four fences. Once again, only members of the imperial family and priests of Ise Jingū may go farther. In the graveled space beyond the gate, this one measuring about 413 feet by 174 feet, stands the Shoden of the Naikū. This closely resembles its counterpart at the Gekū and is similarly accompanied by two Hoden.

The greatest difference between the two Shoden, and the feature that lends the Naikū greater sanctity, is that the Kō Taijingū contains a sacred object, the Yata no Kagami, a circular bronze mirror of the type frequently found inside the *kofun,* the gigantic mound-tombs built for emperors between the third and sixth centuries. That such mirrors were imported from the Asian mainland before the Japanese began producing their own versions raises the intriguing possibility that this mirror, which has been one of the most revered symbols of Japanese nationhood, was made outside Japan, perhaps in Korea (where, some historians and archaeologists argue, the Japanese imperial family may have originated anyway). According to Ise tradition, the mirror is a reproduction of the one handed to Ninigi by his grandmother at the foundation of Japan. The mirror originally was kept in the emperors' palaces, then deposited at Kasanui in what is now Nara prefecture, before being brought to Ise. It is considered one of the three treasures without which no emperor can succeed to the throne; the others are the Murakumo no Tsurugi, a sword kept at the Atsuta shrine in Nagoya, and the Magatama, a set of jewels kept in the Imperial Palace in Tōkyō. As at the Gekū, the Naikū compound stands next to a *kodenchi,* a graveled area surrounding a buried wooden pillar, of which the top is protected by a wooden enclosure. Again as at the Gekū, the park around the Naikū contains a number of lesser shrines, among which the most important is the Aramatsuri, behind the compound, which honors the living spirit of Amaterasu.

The origins of these mysterious monuments of ancient Japanese religion are as obscure as those of the imperial line that has been closely associated with it. The architectural style of the Shoden and Hoden, which is known as Shimmei-zukuri, suggests that the association began at a very early date, for it resembles that of the treasure houses built for emperors during the Yayoi period (c. 300 B.C.–A.D. 300). Both types of building have wide entrances parallel to the roof ridge, supporting posts embedded in the earth, and straight-sided pitched roofs rather than the curved ones, derived from Chinese architecture, which most Shintō shrines have in common with Buddhist temples. Also, in early Japanese history imperial residences were surrounded by white gravel and protected by multiple fences, and were periodically rebuilt, or simply abandoned, to avoid pollution by decay or death.

Yet it does not necessarily follow that the Ise buildings, like the treasure houses, were first constructed before A.D. 300. The style continued to be used at imperial residences long after that date, which in any case is a convenient approximation. It is also quite possible that, as at other religious centers the world over, the shrines were first constructed in a style that was already archaic at the time. The fact that the *chigi,* the *katsuogi,* and the *muchikake* on the shrine buildings are entirely decorative may be an indication that their original construction took place at a later time than that of the treasure houses, in which these features were integral to the structure. It is also clear, from the presence of such Chinese features as the flaming jewel motifs on the railings of both Shoden, that Ise was not immune from the enormous influence of Buddhist styles introduced during the sixth century. On the other hand, all these decorative elements may have been added at a later stage to buildings that had indeed originated during the Yayoi period, but nobody can be certain, since the periodic destruction of the shrines prevents any claims about dates from being tested by archaeological methods.

If the stylistic connection between Ise Jingū and the imperial line is suggestive but inconclusive, the documentary evidence is not much more reliable. The oldest sources are the chronicles compiled at the imperial court beginning in 712, when the shrines already had been in existence for an unknown period. These chronicles, which combine myth, legend, and history to glorify the dynasty, variously claim that the Naikū was founded in the first century B.C., or in the fourth century A.D., or—according to the fullest account—that both main shrines were established in the third century A.D. by Himiko (Yamato-Hime-Mikoto), a female member of the imperial family, in response to a vision of Amaterasu no Ōmikami, the sun goddess. She is said to have been a daughter of a ruler named Suinin Tennō and to have acted on his behalf in order to ward off a plague that had devastated his predecessor's court.

Archaeologists and historians now agree that all of these dates are probably too early, and most would doubt whether Suinin Tennō ever existed (quite apart from the fact that this name, or title, is made up of Chinese elements probably unknown in Japan at the time). It is the word "Yamato Hime," meaning "princess of Yamato," which is most significant. "Yamatai," a variant form of the place name, is known from Chinese records of the third century, but it is still disputed whether it then referred to the center of Honshū, the main island of Japan, or to an area in the north of Kyūshū, the island to the southwest (and therefore nearer Korea and China). Until 1871, however, Yamato was the name of what is now Nara prefecture, to the northwest of Ise. From around the fifth or sixth century this province, the heartland of Japanese culture from some time in the Yayoi period onward, became the main base of the religious and political leaders who would later be called Tennō, Heavenly Kings, and who would later still become known to the West, somewhat misleadingly, as emperors. They were probably at first the heads—and perhaps only the high priests, not the supreme rulers—of one among several clans in central Honshū, each controlling its own territory and claiming descent from its own local guardian deity, but their clan gradually increased its political and religious power.

In this connection yet another legend about Ise may well represent part of the process of absorbing pre-existing cults into the Yamato religious system—and it may also help to explain why Ise, uniquely, has two main shrines instead of one. According to this tradition, the shrine of the harvest goddess, Toyouke-hime no Ōmikami, was located at Manai, in what is now Kyōto prefecture, until 478, when the ruler (or perhaps high priest) whom the chronicles call Yuryaku Tennō was instructed by Amaterasu to found the Gekū. But there is no reason to regard this legend as any more reliable (or, for that matter, any less) than the legends about the founding of the Naikū.

It seems reasonable to conclude that the historical truth about Ise Jingū, and about the early rulers of central Honshū, is now lost, or at best hidden and undiscoverable, somewhere within the chronicles. But it is at least certain that the shrines were well established, and highly regarded, by the early eighth century, and very probable that they were then already at least 200 years old. During those years the Yamato state entered a new phase of development, importing, absorbing, and adapting many features of Chinese and Korean culture. Thousands of new words—including, interestingly, "Tennō," "Jingū," "Gekū," and "Naikū"—were made from Chinese elements and written with Chinese characters; Taoist and Buddhist beliefs began to challenge the indigenous religion maintained at Ise and other shrines; and the Confucian ideal of monarchs blessed by heaven so long as they conducted rituals to safeguard the harvest probably reinforced the paramount role of the high priest (or perhaps ruler) of Yamato.

The creation in 646 of Ise province, with the city, then called Uji-Yamada, as its capital and much of its land owned by Ise Jingū, seems to confirm its importance. But the tradition that the ceremonial renewal of the shrines was first carried out in 690, under the empress Jito, is more difficult to interpret. If it represents simply the usual Shintō aversion to decay and death, it is unclear why it was not practiced earlier. It is also unclear whether Ise Jingū was the first shrine to undergo renewal, a custom once practiced at other leading shrines, such as the Kasuga Taisha in Nara and the Izumo

Taisha in Shimane prefecture; this custom was later abandoned—at Kasuga in the seventeenth century, at Izumo in the eighteenth, and elsewhere at other times. Whatever the reasons for its introduction, and whenever it really began, the paradoxical outcome is that these repeated dismantlings and replacements with nearly exact copies probably have preserved the general layout, structure, and appearance of the shrines, although it is known that some details have been changed.

The rituals conducted inside the compounds of the Gekū and the Naikū focus on the production of Japan's staple food and on the continuation of an imperial dynasty, which, even when it had little or no political power, retained a symbolic importance. It is not surprising that special provisions were made to set Ise Jingū, the location of such crucial events, apart from other Shintō shrines, as well as from the Buddhist traditions that had come to dominate the imperial court and, increasingly, the country. First, from some unknown date up to 1339, when two rival emperors contended for the throne, the shrines were placed under the control of a celibate high priestess who was usually a member of the imperial family. This custom, which presumably lies behind the legend of Himiko, may have been another example of the Yamato Dynasty's absorption of earlier cults, in this case local practices involving shamanesses, who played important roles in ancient Japanese religion. Secondly, and again beginning at some unknown date, Buddhist priests and nuns, and anyone else who was obviously not a worshiper of the Ise deities, were forbidden to enter the grounds of the Naikū and the Gekū. This prohibition may have been enforced at some other shrines but was by no means universal, for Shintō shrines and Buddhist temples usually were built together. Even at Ise the custom was abandoned after 1868, ironically at a time when the new modernizing government that had replaced the Tokugawa *shōgunate* that year was taking steps to separate Shintō and Buddhism. Thirdly, Ise Jingū is still the only Shintō site regularly visited by the emperors and other members of the imperial family. The ceremonies marking the accession of a new emperor, such as those held for Emperor Akihito, supposedly the 124th of his line, in 1989, still include a formal visit to Ise, during which secret rituals, probably connected with the harvest, are conducted at both of the main shrines.

These distinctive customs indicate that in some sense Ise Jingū was regarded as the private family shrine of the emperors, and therefore was visited only by the imperial family and court nobles. However, at some point during the fifteenth century, when the imperial court was in dire financial straits and the disintegration of the country culminated in the Ōnin War (1467–77), the first of several conflicts that lasted until 1600, the shrines also became a destination for pilgrimages by commoners. These were encouraged by *oshi,* traveling shrine priests who claimed that such visits would help to secure salvation, and organized by *kō,* associations of worshipers in many towns and villages. During the Edo period (1603–1868), when Japan under the Tokugawa *shōguns* enjoyed peace and prosperity following decades of civil wars, and the city was ruled by a *bugyō* (magistrate) appointed by the *shōguns,* the Ise pilgrimage, called the O-Ise Mairi, became even more popular. In each of the years 1650, 1705, 1771, and 1830, when religious fervor swept through the country, the number of pilgrims is said to have exceeded 2 million. This is about the same as the number of visitors who have come to Ise annually in the late twentieth century. It was also under the Tokugawas that the two Kaguraden and other subsidiary buildings at both main shrines were rebuilt with elaborately decorated curving gables of the Chinese style long familiar in the architecture of Buddhist temples. Even the buildings inside the compounds may have been altered during this period. The railed veranda around each of the halls, and the copper decorations on the ends of their roof beams, characteristic of Buddhist temples rather than of Shintō shrines, may have been added or enhanced, and their thatched roofs may have been remodeled to their present appearance, making them perceptibly curved rather than running in the straight lines typical of ancient farmsteads and storehouses.

If these and other details make the Gekū and the Naikū somewhat less "pure" sanctuaries of ancient Japanese religion than traditionalists would care to admit, it is their regular renewal that now makes them unique, both in Japan and in the world. Sixty-five buildings at the two shrines, and their contents, are taken apart and replaced by exact replicas assembled and built on the kodenchi, the open spaces next to each compound, in a series of ceremonies culminating in the Shikinen-sengu or Sengu-shiki, the celebration of the renewal. This procedure, normally carried out every twenty years, appears to have been abandoned during only two periods of crisis, first, for 123 years in the fifteenth and sixteenth centuries, when Japan was in a more or less continuous state of civil war, and then between 1929 and 1953, when Japan was engaged in, and then recovering from, its disastrous pursuit of military and economic supremacy in East and Southeast Asia.

The sixty-first Sengū-shiki, celebrated in October 1993, followed the established series of renewal activities, performed over the previous eight years at a total cost of more than 5 billion yen. First, in May 1985, there was the blessing of the *hinoki* grown specially for the shrines in the Kiso Mountains in Nagano prefecture. Numerous ceremonies linked the practical preparations that followed, including the dispersal of materials from the existing buildings to other Shintō shrines, the O-kihiki, the ritual log-pulling on sledges and floats, carried out by teams of Ise citizens from the Isuzu River to the two shrine sites in the summer of 1986 and 1987; and, during 1989, the ritual replacement of the Ujibashi. The result was that in 1994, when the Toyouke-Daijingū and the Kō Taijingū were inaugurated, they were, as Peter Popham puts it in his book *Wooden Temples of Japan,* "both the newest and the most ancient [buildings] in the country." They are also still the most puzzling and, for many visitors, Japanese and non-Japanese alike, the most impressive.

Further Reading: There are two interesting accounts of Ise Jingū, each combining architectural study with history and each illustrated with maps and plans: Kenzo Tange and Noboru Kawagoe's *Ise: Prototype of Japanese Architecture* (Cambridge, Massachusetts: MIT Press, 1965); and Watanabe Yasutada's *Shintō Art: Ise and Izumo Shrines,* translated by Robert Ricketts (Tōkyō: Heibonsha, and New York: Weatherhill, 1974).

—Patrick Heenan

Iwo Jima (Volcano Islands, Japan)

Location: One of a group of islands near Japan known as the Volcano Islands, which comprise the southern extension of an island chain known as the Nanpo Shoto. This chain extends 750 miles in a southerly direction from Tokyo Bay, ending roughly 300 miles north of the Mariana Islands. Iwo Jima is situated 660 nautical miles from Tokyo.

Description: A small island, obscure for most of its existence, Iwo Jima became famous in 1945 as the site of one of the largest battles fought during World War II. The battle was a dramatic but costly victory for the United States over Japan. Since half of the island is in the range of an active volcano and the other half is occupied by defense forces, no site office is established on the island.

Unlike Japan, the country to which Iwo Jima belongs, Iwo Jima does not have a long and intricate history. Although the Volcano Islands were discovered by the Japanese in the late sixteenth century (roughly fifty years after a Spanish sea captain named Bernard de Torres sighted them), the first recorded reference to Iwo Jima itself was not made until 1673. In that year an Englishman named Gore called it "Sulphur Island," referring, of course, to its volcanic composition.

In 1861, Japan made formal claim to the Bonins, the group of islands just north of the Volcano Islands along the Nanpo Shoto. From 1887 to 1891, the Japanese began systematically colonizing the Volcano Islands. Thus Iwo Jima became a remote and quiet territory of the Japanese Empire. The succeeding fifty years saw almost no change on the island. In 1943, the civilian population on Iwo Jima was still only 1,091. While most of the inhabitants were employed either in a small sugar mill or in a sulphur refinery on the island, some cultivated vegetables, sugar cane, and dry grains for local consumption. Fishing, too, played a significant role in the local economy. This serene and obscure little island, however, was about to act as the stage for one of the most dramatic battles of World War II. After 1945, the name "Iwo Jima," for Americans, would be identified almost invariably with bloody victory in the island-hopping war with Japan.

The capture of Iwo Jima was actually the penultimate step in the United States's military master plan for defeating the Japanese. The strategy called for the United States to begin the war effort with a westward thrust across the Pacific from Hawaii, moving from one island to the next; once its troops had penetrated into the heart of the Asian Pacific, the attack was to be turned northward, with an invasion of the Japanese mainland as the ultimate goal. Each captured island provided much-needed airfields for the planes that would then attack the next target farther west.

By 1944, when U.S. forces had reached as far west as the Mariana Islands, the time had come to turn the forces north and head for Japan itself. Lying roughly halfway between the Marianas and Japan, Iwo Jima provided the ideal base from which air strikes against the mainland could be directed and supported. "The conquest of Iwo Jima," writes military historian Richard Natkiel, "offered U.S. forces the prospect of a base near Japan that could provide fighter support and emergency-landing facilities for Marianas-based aircraft on bombing runs to Tokyo."

By August 10, 1944, U.S. troops had taken the southern Marianas. By September, amphibious troops were occupying positions in the Palau Islands and Ulithi, enabling them to take the Philippines if so desired. The next step was to advance past the Marianas through the Bonins to Japan, a move that required the capture of Iwo Jima. The Japanese soon perceived the U.S. strategy and reacted accordingly.

In 1941, the Japanese garrison in the Volcano Islands (which at that time was stationed on Chichi Jima, not Iwo Jima) comprised only 1,400 men. By 1943, this number had risen to 3,800, and the Chidori airfield was built on Iwo Jima to house 1,500 naval personnel and 20 planes stationed there. With the construction of Chidori, Iwo Jima became the center of Japanese military activity in the Volcano Islands. By the end of May 1944, Japanese army forces on Iwo Jima numbered 5,170 men, with 13 artillery pieces, more than 200 light and heavy machine guns, and 4,652 rifles. In addition, 56 artillery pieces were employed by the Iwo Naval Guard Forces. After Saipan fell in June 1944, the Japanese redirected resources initially intended for Saipan to Iwo Jima. Between June and August, 9,600 troops were added to the island's defenses. The number of Japanese troops on Iwo Jima eventually swelled to 23,000.

The Japanese knew that the United States would try to take Iwo Jima in order to make use of the airfields, and they were determined to defend the island at all costs. Lieutenant General Tadamichi Kuribayashi, in charge of the defense, devised an extremely effective plan. The Japanese literally dug themselves into the island. They made use of existing caves, dug others (sometimes making them up to thirty or forty feet deep), connected all the caves with an elaborate tunnel system, buried tanks so that only the muzzle of the cannon was above ground, built blockhouses and emplacements for weapons, and hid heavy artillery pieces in the rocky volcanic terrain.

The U.S. forces, meanwhile, were making their own preparations. Admiral Chester W. Nimitz, commander in chief of the Pacific Fleet, was put in charge of Operation Detachment, the code name used for the invasion of Iwo Jima. In the planning phase of the operation, 371 photo sorties were flown in order to obtain reliable aerial maps of the island. In

Flag raising on Iwo Jima
Photo courtesy of National Archives, Washington, D.C.

addition, the submarine *Spearfish* lay off the coast of Iwo Jima so that its crew could spy on troop activity through its periscope. From November 15 to 30, 1944, U.S. forces took part in training exercises in the Maalea Bay area of Maui, Hawaii.

Much of the preparation for Operation Detachment involved an extensive bombardment of the island. Iwo Jima suffered the longest preliminary bombardment in U.S. military history, beginning in June 1944 and continuing until the invasion on February 19, 1945. The workhorses of this bombardment were the B-24 aircraft of the Seventh Air Force stationed in the Marianas. They executed a seventy-four-day campaign of bombing that began on December 8. While the U.S. aircraft were bombing, the Navy and the Marines were amassing a lethal assault force.

On February 14, all forces, complete with naval and air cover, began heading toward Iwo Jima. On February 17, the *Nevada*, the *Idaho*, and the *Tennessee* moved to within 3,000 yards of shore. While these ships came under heavy and costly attack, four underwater demolition teams managed to gather intelligence on the conditions of the beaches and other information that was needed to proceed with a military landing. With all the pieces in place, the U.S. Marines were set to come ashore.

The signal to launch came at 7:25 A.M. on February 19. Twenty minutes later, 482 vehicles, carrying 8 battalions of Marines, were churning up the water. By 8:30 A.M., the first assault wave crossed the departure point and headed toward the beaches on the east side of the island. Thereafter, successive assault waves were dispatched as soon as the preceding wave had managed to advance 250 or 300 yards. Each assault wave had thirty minutes to traverse the 4,000 yards from the departure point to the shore. At 8:57 A.M., U.S. planes flew in low over beaches to fire on enemy positions. The first wave of Marines landed at 9:02, the second at 9:05. During the first few minutes, Japanese resistance was light. As Japanese soldiers emerged to man their defensive positions, however, their retaliation intensified.

As the Marines scrambled ashore, they faced the fire from 120 guns of over 75-mm, 300 antiaircraft guns of over 35-mm, 20,000 rifles and machine guns, 130 howitzers, 20 mortars, 70 rocket guns, and 60 antitank guns. It quickly became apparent, moreover, that the months of intense bombing had done very little to damage the Japanese defenses.

They had dug in too well for anything short of several consecutive direct hits to do any significant damage. The density of the Japanese entrenchment was also amazing. In one area of the central plateau that was roughly 1,000 yards by 200 yards, the Japanese had 800 separate "strong points," such as caves and blockhouses.

Despite the heavy fire, by 10:30 A.M. elements of all eight U.S. battalions had landed. By day's end, six infantry regiments, six artillery battalions, and two tank battalions had landed and were defending the narrow beachhead. In all, 30,000 American troops had stormed the beaches. Casualties were high, with 501 men killed, 1,755 wounded, and 18 missing. However, these figures were not as high as the United States had feared; some analysts had predicted that up to 5 percent of the entire landing force would die. All night the Marines waited in anticipation of a counterattack, but none was made. Instead, the Japanese remained hidden among the rocks and debris; their strategy was to continue using the subterranean tunnel system to retreat from one position to the next, at no point exposing themselves to U.S. forces. It was not until the eighth day of battle that the Marines could actually see the Japanese and close with them in hand to hand combat.

Once the landing force had secured the beachhead, three distinct sectors of activity were initiated. The Marines in the center seized the air base in the middle of the island, while the troops to their left began the assault on Mount Suribachi, and the forces to the right of center scaled the plateau beyond the beaches, beginning the bloody drive northward. On the first day following the invasion, ground in all three sectors was extremely difficult to gain. Penetration ranged from 200 yards at Mount Suribachi to 500 yards at the air base. Within five days the assault on Mount Suribachi had succeeded, and the Marines could then throw their main force into the northward thrust. The fighting would continue, however, for thirty more devastating days.

Taking Mount Suribachi was the first step in a very long and very bloody campaign. Despite the wet weather, which, combined with the presence of volcanic ash, caused automatic weapons to clog, the Twenty-eighth Marine regiment was able to surround the volcano by 4:30 P.M. on the fourth day of battle. The only route up Suribachi lay along the north face, and so on the fifth day of the battle, the Marines scaled the volcano on the northern side. By 10:15 A.M., advance patrols had reached the crater's rim, and by 10:20 the U.S. flag had been raised. Contrary to popular belief, this was not the flag seen in Joe Rosenthal's famous picture of five Marines struggling to plant the U.S. flag on Iwo Jima. It was, rather, a smaller flag (measuring fifty-four inches by twenty-eight inches). A second, larger, flag was brought up from one of the ships later that day, and it is this flag raising that was memorialized by that photograph. The photograph is also misleading in that the assault on Mount Suribachi marked the beginning of the struggle on Iwo Jima rather than its conclusion. Rosenthal's picture, which many take to be the symbol of U.S. victory in the Pacific, actually records one victorious moment in a battle that would continue to rage for another month.

In fact, even as Suribachi was being taken, the Fifth Amphibious Corps, under the command of General Harry Schmidt, was going up against the very heart of the Japanese defense. General Kuribayashi had concentrated his defense in the central and northern part of the island. In *Iwo Jima: Amphibious Epic,* Lieutenant Colonel Whitman S. Bartley writes, "From blockhouses, bunkers, pillboxes, caves, and camouflaged tanks, enemy guns jutted defiantly. Every possible approach to the north was contested by weapons with well-integrated fields of fire. The enemy had so deftly prepared this area that it had been impossible to neutralize or destroy an appreciable number of positions before ground troops landed."

The U.S. troops had superior numbers, but they were able to penetrate the strong Japanese defenses only through a slow but unrelenting effort. Nine days into the campaign, the exhausted Marines finally took the airfield in the center sector; two days later, U.S. forces landed sixteen light planes on the island. These planes helped both in evacuating the wounded and in supplying the front lines. Five days later, on March 4, the first B-29 landed on Iwo Jima, refueled, and proceeded; already, then, the assault was bearing fruit. Then, on March 5, after fourteen days of fierce battle, there was a break in the fighting while replacement troops were sent in.

Fighting resumed on March 6, with the Marines inching their way toward Kitano Point at the island's northern extremity. Bartley's description conveys how the Marines were forced to advance: "The infantry advanced until pinned down by fire. Then, when hostile positions were located, armored dozers, working ahead of the line under protection of tank and infantry fire, prepared a road over which the Shermans [tanks] could advance to engage the enemy. After flame tanks had neutralized the area, the infantrymen advanced while demolition teams dealt with bypassed caves and pillboxes." It was only in this painstakingly slow and precarious manner that U.S. forces could drive back the Japanese.

The Japanese troops, moreover, were utterly committed to fighting until death. Of the 23,000 Japanese garrisoned on the island, only 1,083 survived at the end of the battle, and many of these were Korean prisoners of war. General Kuribayashi never let his men forget their duty to the empire. As the battle raged, his rhetoric became steadily more impassioned. By March 18, twenty days into the battle, Kuribayashi, sensing the end of the battle, ordered all surviving officers and men to attack the enemy until the last. Kuribayashi's men were as steadfast as he desired.

Their determination notwithstanding, the Japanese were driven backward in a northeastern direction. By March 16, they had been forced into a rocky gorge on the western half of Kitano Point. Yet they refused to give up. Eight days later, on the thirty-fourth day of battle, the pocket of Japanese resistance had been reduced to an area of 50 by 50 yards. On March 23, Kuribayashi sent his last radio dispatch to Japanese intelligence on Chichi Jima: "To all officers and men of Chichi Jima. Good-bye." The Japanese held out in Kitano Point until March 26. It was on this date, at 8 A.M., that the capture and occupation of Iwo Jima was officially pronounced complete.

Although original projections by U.S. intelligence were that the battle would last less than a week, thirty-six days had passed before the island was secured. In the process, American casualties reached 26,000, including 6,800 killed or missing, making Iwo Jima the fourth costliest battle for Americans in the Pacific theatre. It was also the only battle in the war in which American casualties outnumbered Japanese. As costly as the battle was in terms of human life, however, it can be argued that the capture of Iwo Jima saved more American lives than it took. Estimates of how many crewmen of U.S. vessels were saved as a result of air-sea rescue missions from Iwo Jima are as high as 27,000. In addition, 2,250 B-29s returning from raids on Japan made emergency landings on Iwo Jima. How many of these planes would have survived without this air base remains a matter for speculation.

Finally, the battle of Iwo Jima is significant for what it taught the U.S. military high command. The Japanese determination to fight until the death caused the United States to rethink its strategy. The battle of Iwo Jima showed on a small scale just how devastatingly high casualties would be if any attempt were made to invade the Japanese mainland. According to some, it was at this point that the United States began seriously considering how the use of atomic weapons might actually *save* lives. In the words of military historian Richard Humble, "The casualties suffered on Iwo . . . made the Allied strategists wince at the prospect of what would happen when the time came to land on the Japanese mainland. Any alternative prospect of bringing the war to a speedy end seemed preferable. The fall of Iwo Jima pointed the first invisible finger at Hiroshima and Nagasaki."

Further Reading: *Iwo Jima: Amphibious Epic* by Lieutenant Colonel Whitman S. Bartley, USMC, (Washington, D.C.: U.S. Government Printing Office, 1954) is certainly the most exhaustive and informative account from the American perspective. For more concise, less technical, and eminently more readable accounts of the battle see the section devoted to Iwo Jima in Richard Natkiel's *Atlas of Battles: Strategy and Tactics, Civil War to Present* (Greenwich, Connecticut: Military Press, 1984). Other useful accounts include the chapter in Richard Humble's *Famous Land Battles: From Agincourt to the Six-Day War* (Boston and Toronto: Little Brown, 1979) and the chapter entitled "Climax in the Central Pacific" in D. Clayton James and Anne Sharp Wells's *From Pearl Harbor to V-J Day: The American Armed Forces in World War II* (Chicago: Dee, 1995). For a revealing discussion of the symbolic value of Joe Rosenthal's famous picture of the Marines planting the U.S. flag on Iwo Jima, see Parker Bishop Albee Jr.'s and Keller Cushing Freeman's *Shadow of Suribachi: Raising the Flags on Iwo Jima* (Westport, Connecticut: Praeger, 1995).

—Lawrence F. Goodman

Jaipur (Rājasthān, India)

Location: Center of Rājasthān State, in northwest India, approximately 150 miles southwest of New Delhi, 250 miles east of the Pakistan border.

Description: When mahārājas still rode elephants to do battle in the desert, Jaipur was protected by the defensive wall that nearly surrounded it. Now, much of the wall is gone, elephant riding is ceremonial, and the title of mahārāja has been abolished. But the old city of Jaipur, which has become the capital of the state of Rājasthān and is sometimes called the "Pink City" because of its pink buildings (pink symbolizing hospitality), remains much as it was when planned and laid out in 1727 by its founder, Mahārāja Sawai Jai Singh. Jai Singh's palace, after housing generations of mahārājas, has now been converted into a museum by his last descendant, who himself lives in only a small part of the building. The streets of spacious old Jaipur are boulevards broad enough to allow the passing of several elephants shoulder to shoulder. But Jaipur has experienced exponential growth in recent decades, and the old city is surrounded by sprawling modern neighborhoods.

Site Office: Government of India Tourist Office
State Hotel, Khasa Kothi
Jaipur 302 001, Rājasthān
India
372200

Jaipur was built in 1727 on a plain surrounded by hills. The new city came into being to replace an older city, Amber, which lay higher up in the hills. The warlike Rājputs had taken Amber from the Minas tribe in the eleventh century, and the city functioned as the central stronghold of a Rājput princely state until the arrival of the Mughals in the sixteenth century. The changes Amber went through during the period of Mughal dominance had a shaping influence on the development of Jaipur.

Beginning in the early sixteenth century, with Bābur, the first of the great Mughals, Muslims asserted control over the (mostly Hindu) northern regions of India. On his father's side, Bābur claimed descent from Timur (also known to English speakers as Tamerlane and Tamburlaine), who had headed one of the famed "Mongolian hordes" on a raid through India. On his mother's side, Bābur thought himself descended from another well-known Mongolian conqueror, Genghis Khan. In the early years of the sixteenth century, Bābur made many forays into what was then called Hindustan from his base in Kābul, north of India. By 1527 he had conquered most of north central Hindustan, an empire's worth of kingdoms. Amber was one of the smaller of these.

Bābur was a poet and artist as well as a military leader. Wherever he established his court, he constructed gardens. He wrote poetry that was transcribed onto elegant printed manuscripts, and he was a patron of the arts. Scores of brilliant miniature illustrations of court life were produced during his reign. While Bābur united diverse Indian territories and the arts flourished, not all was poetry and beauty. Differences in religion between the ruler and the ruled led to occasional violence and mass conversions, presumably not all voluntary. It has been theorized that the cross-breeding of Muslim dogma and Rājput custom led to the creation of *purdah,* the set of rules by which women are hidden from public view for life.

Bābur's grandson Akbar ascended to the throne of the Mughal Empire in 1556, when he was thirteen years old. Like his father before him (and his children after him), Akbar had to fight a series of battles to consolidate his rule. A year and one-half after his succession, however, he had eliminated all the competition and ruled one of the largest empires in the world. He changed the face of northern India, building some of its most famous monumental structures, but he also remade his empire socially. For these achievements he was called Akbar the Great.

Before Akbar's rise to power, India's Hindu population had suffered severely at the hands of the new Muslim rulers. With the Mughals in power, Hindus were often massacred, their religion was proscribed, and the laws discriminated against them in other ways as well. But all this began to change in 1562, when Akbar married the daughter of the Rāja Bihar Mal of Amber. Though Akbar's predecessors had also married Hindus, Akbar was the first to allow his Rājput wife to practice her religion. The marriage signaled a new era in northern India. The Rājputs became the Mughal emperor's closest indigenous allies. A combined army of Mughal soldiers and Rājput warriors (who were the most feared fighters in the region) solidified Akbar's military might. Religious tolerance ruled public life in the empire, unequal taxes were revoked, and constraints on the freedom of non-Muslims were lifted. The result was a flowering of social life barely known before.

Akbar invited divines of all religions to his court and listened to their debates. After many years of searching for answers to his religious questions, he attempted to establish a religion of his own devising. The so-called Divine Faith was an ecumenical construct Akbar decided upon after meeting with various Muslim sects, Hindus, Zoroastrians, Portuguese Jesuits, and Jews. A monotheistic religion, Akbar's faith was based on individual virtue and reason and required neither priests nor temples. Akbar still tolerated Hindu customs at his court, even after he introduced his own beliefs as a new religion. But despite its many admirable traits, the Divine

Hawā Mahal (Palace of the Winds), Jaipur
Photo courtesy of Christopher Turner

City Palace, Jaipur
Photo courtesy of Air India Library, New York

Faith did not survive Akbar's rule. The princely state of Amber remained predominantly Hindu.

Akbar's marriage to the Amber princess also raised the status of the Royal House of Amber. Bhagwan Das and Mān Singh of Amber became Akbar's first two Hindu counselors. To underline his loyalty, Mān Singh led a Mughal army in battle against an army of fellow Rājputs and won. Later, Akbar appointed him governor of Bengal. When Akbar died in 1605, Mān Singh was the most powerful noble in the country.

The prominence of the Amber Rājputs in Mughal times was further reinforced by the fact that Akbar's oldest son and heir descended from them through his mother. Though Akbar had a large harem and thousands of women roamed his court, for many years the emperor remained without a male heir until the birth of Jahāngīr, whose mother was Akbar's first Amber wife. Jahāngīr succeeded Akbar as emperor in 1605.

For the century following Akbar's rule, Amber's royal line was among the most powerful of Hindu royalty. Though a small fortified city in the barren hills of the Rājput desert, Amber itself was a center of political power, the capital of an important state. By the early eighteenth century, the Mughal Empire was beginning to crumble, however. The last of the Mughals to rule anything resembling an empire was 'Ālamgīr (Aurangzeb), who died in 1707. Before his death, the emperor had managed to undo most of the ties formed with indigenous princes through his religious fanaticism. He even had reinstated the *jizyah,* the hated tax imposed on "unbelievers." In this way, he undermined the foundations of Mughal control over northern India.

No strong central leader emerged after 'Ālamgīr's death, and the Rājput princes saw no reason to continue paying tribute to the empire. The ruling mahārāja of Amber at that time was Jai Singh II (also known as Sawai Jai Singh). Jai Singh abandoned Amber, leaving the fortress in the care of the few surviving Minas, and built Jaipur, the new capital of the state of Amber and center of the Rājput princely states, in 1727. Governing his state at a time of great upheaval, when there were many contestants for power in the vacuum created by the weakness and finally the death of 'Ālamgīr, Jai Singh was, by necessity, a crafty military ruler. And the city he planned and built needed strong defenses. Although not as remote as Amber, Jaipur was backed against a mountain range to make it more easily defensible. In addition, it was was ringed by an almost continuous wall.

Although the fort at Amber remained a shrine and a link to the Rājput ancestors, Jai Singh broke with the past, designing a city that incorporated the ideas of Europe's foremost city planners of the time. It is said that Jaipur's broad boulevards and rectangular blocks were inspired in part by plans from France and Italy that Singh studied. Nevertheless, the newly constructed city was traditionally Indian in several ways, being based in part on the principles of ancient Hindu architecture and city planning. The pink-washed sandstone of the older buildings symbolizes hospitality in traditional fashion. The boulevards and the defensive wall surrounding the old city conform to Hindu custom as well. Jai Singh's plans were so well executed that Jaipur is still referred to as a model of town planning.

Besides practicing statecraft and civic planning, Jai Singh was proficient in several other arts as well. Unlike the Mughals however, he was a scholar and a scientist with a particular interest in mathematics and astronomy. He commissioned Sanskrit translations of many European works on mathematics and astronomy, studied them, and occasionally made corrections. He also studied the best astronomical tables available in Europe and found that they were, on the whole, less exact than his own, in part because he had more powerful telescopes at his disposal. Jaipur still bears the traces of Jai Singh's interest in astronomy, in the form of the Jantar Mantar, one of the five observatories Jai Singh built in India. (The others were constructed at Delhi, Vārānasī, Ujjain, and Mathurā.) Construction of the Jaipur observatory was begun when the city was first laid out. Its scale is overwhelming. The sundial's gnomon, which has a stairway running to its tip, is over ninety feet tall. Other gigantic measuring devices look like abstract sculptures or even children's playground equipment, but each has a specific astronomical purpose, making it possible to track the movements of the heavenly bodies with great exactitude.

Jai Singh built his palace (now called the City Palace) in the center of Jaipur. The rose-colored complex is adjacent to the pink and orange observatory. The Chandra Mahal, or royal apartments, forms the center of a constellation of buildings, courtyards, and gardens. Today the palace has been converted into a museum, and the Chandra Mahal functions as the central exhibition halls. The museum's collection includes Rājasthānī, Mughal, and Persian-style art and textiles, as well as an extensive armory that exhibits the many ingenious devices that made the Rājput armies so effective in centuries past. Another palace, called the Hawā Mahal (Palace of the Winds), which functioned as a hot-weather retreat for the royal family for many years, was constructed later in the century. The building, notable for its stone screens over the window openings designed to let in the breezes during the stifling Jaipur summers, still forms one of the main tourist attractions in the city.

During Jai Singh's rule, which lasted until 1743, the Rājput princely states gradually regained their political autonomy. By the mid–eighteenth century, however, the British were already well established in northern India, even though few indigenous rulers considered them a threat to their independence. During the second half of the eighteenth century, the British gradually expanded the areas under their control. In 1799, the hired forces of the British East India Company defeated a confederate army led by the Marāṭhās at Mysore, and the British became the dominant power on the subcontinent.

The Rājput aristocracy in Jaipur, although nominally part of the Marāṭhā confederation, made their peace with the English following the Marāṭhā defeat. The political situation in the Rājput states was unstable at the end of the eighteenth century and seemed to be deteriorating. Ill winds were blowing across the desert: armies trooped through the region, and highway robbers followed. Death and misery came in their wake. The Rājputs were courageous fighters, but without unity they were easy targets for the better organized English. The colonial authorities amalgamated the Rājput princely states into one administrative unit called Rājputana, with its capital at Jaipur. Although they had lost their independence to the colonial rulers and had no say in British national policy in India, the Rājput princes, including the Jaipur mahārājas, retained a fair amount of power over affairs in their own states.

The Rājputs eventually became the best of allies to the British. Their military prowess was legendary, their battle pride extraordinary. By 1900, armies raised by Rājput princes and mahārājas were fighting alongside British troops in China. Some of the princes accumulated extraordinary wealth under the colonial system, at the expense of their common subjects, who were also pressed into service whenever the British required military assistance. During World War I, the city donated troops, supplies, airplanes, and cash. With the rendering of these services, Jaipur received increased importance and status within the empire, while fabulous wealth found its way into the coffers of the mahārāja.

The Jaipur mahārāja added the wealth acquired under British rule to a treasure that had been accumulating for centuries and was hoarded in the so-called Tiger Fort at old Amber. Guarded by custodians from the Minas tribe, the Amber treasury gave rise to a variety of legends. According to one of these, every mahārāja since Jai Singh's days was allowed, once during his reign, to view the trove and choose one object for himself from its fabled riches. Local tradition tells of the most astonishing gems and jeweled gold pieces that thus came into the hands of the Jaipur rulers. When India gained its independence in 1947, the ruling mahārāja, Mān Singh, is said to have confronted the Minas custodians and given them a choice of handing over the entire trove either to him or to the new Indian government. Allegedly, the Minas chose to keep the wealth in Rājput hands, and Mān Singh did in fact die one of the wealthiest men in the world. Mān Singh was also known throughout the colonial empire as an extraordinarily skilled and dedicated polo player. In fact, he died in the saddle in 1970 on a polo field in England.

After independence, the new government of India created the new state of Rājasthān out of Rājputana and appointed Mān Singh as *rājpramukh,* a kind of president. Although the Jaipur Rājputs were very wealthy, Rājasthān was among the poorest states in India and had one of the highest illiteracy rates in the country. Jaipur itself had virtually no industry, in part because the British had systematically destroyed industrial enterprise throughout the country to create markets for their own products. India had been allowed to supply raw materials to England, but not goods. Artisans and people working in small industries were thrown out of work, and India was forced to step backward into a more agricultural economy. One of the most important industries of Jaipur, the textile industry, had been completely wiped out in the process.

Jaipur's fortunes rose when its people no longer had to pay the price of colonialism and of the mahārāja's upkeep. Industry grew once again, and the city of Jaipur experienced a population explosion. Between the middle of the 1980s and the early 1990s, for instance, the population of Jaipur more than doubled. The open-air markets are still held daily, and they are the prime venue for the craft products for which Jaipur long has been famous. Merchants drive a thriving trade in delicate, brightly colored fabrics, finely cut precious gems, and brass- and enamelware in bazaars named after the old city gates. Amber's old forts are now museums, and the citizens are still renowned for the hospitality symbolized by the city's original pink buildings.

Further Reading: For more on the Great Mughals, the Rājput mahārājas, and their involvement with Jaipur and Rājputana, see *The Great Moghuls* by Bamber Gascoigne (London: Cape, and New York: Harper and Row, 1971) and *The Maharajahs* by John Lord (New York: Random House, and London: Hutchinson, 1971). *The Discovery of India* by Jawaharlal Nehru (Calcutta: Signet, New York: John Day, and London: Meridian, 1946) contains little information about Jaipur, and only part of a short chapter is devoted to Sawai Jai Singh. But Nehru's book, part history, part reportage, and part social analysis, gives a fascinating account of India's history.

—Jeffrey Felshman

Jaisalmer (Rājasthān, India)

Location: In extreme western Rājasthān, in the heart of the great Thar Desert, 183 miles northwest of Jodhpur.

Description: Jaisalmer was founded in 1156 by Prince Rāwal Jaisal; its economy was tied to the caravan routes linking India to Central Asia. The city's fortunes also were bound up with the clan rivalries among the warlike Rājput peoples of the region. In modern times, the decline of land trade routes led to the city's eclipse, although it has revived since the 1960s thanks to its strategic position on the border with Pakistan and the increase in the number of tourists drawn to its remote, fortified, and unspoiled location.

Site Office: Moomal Tourist Bungalow
Amar Sagal Road
Jaisalmer, Rājasthān
India
2406

Jaisalmer, "The Golden City" (so named because of the color the setting sun imbues to the Jurassic sandstone of the city's ramparts), is a remote desert stronghold that featured prominently in the colorful and heroic period of Rājput history from the twelfth to the fifteenth centuries. Jaisalmer served as the capital of the Bhatti Rājputs of the "lunar" dynasty. As well as the city itself, the name Jaisalmer applied to the surrounding state (now incorporated within Rājasthān). It was one of several states that often were at war with one another and with more distant authorities. The city entered a period of decline in the eighteenth century, which has been reversed only recently.

The foundation of Jaisalmer has origins in both myth and reality. Prince Jaisal had seized control of the previous Bhatti capital, Lodurva, from his nephew Bhojdeo, to whom he had been appointed regent. Unsure of his ability to retain the loyalty of vassal princes, Jaisal sought a more defensible location nearby as the seat of his power. According to the story passed on in the ballads and recorded in *Annals and Antiquities of Rājast'hān* by Lieutenant Colonel James Tod, a nineteenth-century British administrator and diplomat, he consulted a Brahman hermit, Eesul. The hermit told the story of the triple-peaked hill of Trikuta, which sat above his hermitage. To this hill, he said, the god Krishna had come in the "silver age" to attend a great sacrifice and had predicted that many years in the future a descendant of his lunar clan would build a castle there. The dual attractions of the prophecy and the naturally strong defensive position convinced Jaisal to locate his capital there, and he began laying the foundations of the city of Jaisalmer on "the day of the sun," the 12th of Sravan in the year 1156. With the hermit's recounting of the prophecy, however, came a warning that the intended castle would be attacked, sacked two and one-half times, and at least temporarily lost to the Bhattis.

The fort atop the 260-foot-high Trikuta Hill is the most imposing of the city's buildings, especially when seen on the approach to Jaisalmer through the desert. Expanded considerably since 1156, it is now distinguished by ninety-nine bastions, mostly built between 1633 and 1647, which follow the contours of the hill. Although smaller than the forts at Chittaurgarh and Kumbhalgarh, it is the second oldest in Rājasthān. Even today, around one-fourth of the old city's population lives within the fort; the area is densely packed with temples, houses, and palaces. The largest palace within the fort area is the seven-story edifice of the former mahārāja.

Prince Jaisal's rule over the city that bears his name lasted twelve years before he was succeeded by his second son, Salbahan, whose fame derived from his raids into neighboring territory. This contributed to the Bhatti Rājputs' reputation as the most feared of the desert clans. Salbahan ran afoul of court intrigues and was succeeded in 1200 by his elder brother Kailun, who earlier had been expelled from the city. Kailun ruled for nineteen years and was responsible for the defeat of an invading army of Balūchis (from what is now Balūchistān in modern Pakistan). His son, Chachick Deo, frequently waged war against neighboring states during his thirty-two-year rule, often for possession of nothing more significant than small forts or waterholes. Chachick Deo was succeeded by his grandson, Kurrun, who did likewise during a reign of twenty-eight years. His son, Lakhun, was, however, mentally unstable; among other eccentricities, he ordered clothing made and houses built for the jackals that howled when it was cold. He ruled for only four years before being succeeded by his son, Poonpal, whose fierce temper soon led to his overthrow. Kurrun's elder brother, Jaetsi, then came to the throne in 1276.

In the last decade of the thirteenth century, Jaetsi's sons brought the first great disaster on the city. Disguised as corn merchants, they took an army to attack a convoy bearing treasure to the then sultan of Delhi, 'Alā'-ud-Dīn Muḥammad Khaljī. After Jaetsi's sons had carried off the goods to Jaisalmer, the city was besieged by the sultan's army. This conflict is seen by some Indian writers as part of a wider struggle between the Hindu Rājputs and the Muslim rulers of Delhi during the thirteenth and fourteenth centuries—a struggle from which Jaisalmer, by virtue of its remote location, was largely spared. Only an act of gross provocation could bring the forces of the sultan against the city.

Deeds of valor conducted in the defense of Jaisalmer during the long siege became part of traditional folklore and are still recounted at festivals today. According to legend, by maintaining part of their forces outside the city's formidable

Jaisalmer Fort, Jaisalmer
Photo courtesy of Christopher Turner

walls, the defenders were able to harry the enemy and withstand the besiegers for eight years. Jaetsi died during the siege, and his son Moolrāj succeeded him as ruler. Moolrāj's brother Ruttunsi befriended the commander of the besieging forces, Nabob Mahboob Khan, with whom he would play chess between the lines of the two armies. The Jaisalmer troops fended off renewed attacks after Moolrāj's accession, but their provisions eventually were exhausted and they prepared themselves for a final gesture of sacrifice.

At that moment, the sultan's army withdrew, not knowing the defenders were about to surrender. Mahboob Khan's brother, however, gained access to the fortress and learned of its inhabitants' desperate situation. He escaped and informed his comrades, who resumed the siege. Ruttunsi counseled that there was only one honorable course of action: for the women of the city to commit ritual suicide *(jihar)* and the men to ride out to battle. By Tod's account, 24,000 females died by fire and sword and 3,800 warriors, clad in armor and saffron robes and intoxicated with opium, rode out to do battle with the sultan's forces. Moolrāj and Ruttunsi were killed, along with 700 of their men. The defeat and subsequent plunder fulfilled one of Eesul's prophecies. Ruttunsi's sons, however, were spared thanks to an understanding between him and his chess-playing friend. The Delhi forces occupied the castle for two years, then tore it down. It remained deserted for a considerable time, since the Bhattis lacked the means to rebuild it.

The second enactment of the rite of *jihar* and the resulting sack of the city came not long after the first, early in the fourteenth century. A rival chief had tried to settle in the ruins of Jaisalmer, but was repulsed by the Bhatti chiefs, Doodoo and Tiluksi. Doodoo then rebuilt the city, and Tiluksi did much to rebuild Bhatti power, but he overreached himself by stealing the Delhi sultan's prized stud horse. The retaliatory attack that followed led to another *jihar,* in which 16,000 women and girls died and Doodoo, Tiluksi, and 1,700 of their followers were killed in battle.

Ruttunsi's son, Prince Gursi, came of age about this time and did much to reestablish Jaisalmer. The Delhi sultan gave him permission to do so in gratitude for his assistance in defending Delhi against invasions. Gursi rebuilt and stabilized the city, but he was soon thereafter assassinated by the envious descendants of Doodoo and Tiluksi. His widow, Bimladevi, before committing suicide as required by custom, completed the construction of a reservoir, Gursi-sirr, which her husband had been building and which long re-

Torana arch, entrance to a Jain temple at Lodurva, near Jaisalmer
Photo courtesy of Christopher Turner

One of the carved sandstone havelis, *Jaisalmer*
Photo courtesy of Christopher Turner

mained the city's main supply of fresh water. Gursi's adopted son and successor, Kehur, and his sons kept up the Bhatti traditions of feuding with neighbors and extending the power of Jaisalmer. In one of their raids, a number of wealthy merchants were captured and were freed from bondage only on the condition that they settle within the state of Jaisalmer. A total of 365 agreed to do so and thus brought a great influx of wealth to the region.

Many of the city's merchants were of the Jain faith. From the twelfth to the fifteenth centuries, a group of Jain temples was constructed within the fort. The group's most noteworthy temples include the Parśvanatha, Sambhavanatha, Rishbhanatha, and Shantinatha. Within the temple complex is the Gyāna Bhandār library, which contains more than 1,000 manuscripts, some of them dating to the twelfth century and written on palm leaves in black ink and bound with painted wooden covers.

The wealth of Jaisalmer merchants came chiefly from the trade routes of the region. The city was a staging post on camel trade routes from Jodhpur (and deeper inside India) via Phalodi and Pokaran to Rohri (a commercial center in Sindh), from where caravans left for Kandahār in Afghanistan and beyond. Goods traded on these routes included opium, silk, indigo, sugar candy, iron, ivory, coconuts, scented wood, and dried fruits. A lively barter trade was conducted in the Manik Chowk, or main market square. For the rulers of the city, trade represented a key source of income. As late as 1835, when land trade routes were in decline, half the city's revenue still came from duties on goods in transit.

While the city's prosperity and influence grew, the petty feuding with neighbors continued, sometimes turning on an incident as small as the theft of a horse. The rulers of Jaisalmer were often ready to come to the assistance of those of their vassals who had been slighted or suffered material loss at the hands of clans in the surrounding area. Toward the end of the fifteenth century, however, the traditional ballads recording the doings of the Bhatti clan deviate from the lives of the rulers of Jaisalmer itself to deal with the deeds of another branch of the clan, so much so that there is little mention of the Bhattis beyond "the mere enumeration of their issue," as Tod puts it.

During the early sixteenth century, the hermit Eesul's prophecy of the "half-sack" of the city was fulfilled. An ostensibly friendly Pathan chief had persuaded Lunakaran, the ruler of the city, to allow the women of his harem to visit their counterparts in Jaisalmer. The palanquins that were supposed to transport the women, however, actually were filled with soldiers, who attacked the Jaisalmer palace guards. Lunakaran killed several of his family's princesses so they would not be captured, but the raiders were expelled without the city as a whole being sacked—hence the "half-sack."

This incident notwithstanding, part of the reason for the shift in emphasis in the ballads may be that Jaisalmer entered a peaceful period with the rise of the Mughal Empire, established in 1526. This tranquility meant that merchants from Gujarāt, Mālwa, Marwar, and Mewār made their way to Jaisalmer, bringing with them not only their wealth and business acumen but also skilled craftsmen and artists, who were employed in the construction and embellishment of houses, temples, and palaces.

It was during this period of prosperity that merchants began constructing the *havelis,* magnificent mansions that count among the architectural jewels of the city today. The greatest extant *havelis,* however, actually date from a period in which Jaisalmer in general had begun to decline, as the art of the *silavats* (stone carvers) who decorated the mansions with elaborate facades reached its height during the eighteenth and nineteenth centuries. The skill with which they carved Jaisalmer's yellow sandstone has been likened to that applied to the marble of the Tāj Mahal. The largest of the city's *havelis* is the Patwon-ki-haveli (House of the Brocade Merchants), built over a 50-year period beginning in 1800, by a merchant family who controlled 300 trading centers from China to Afghanistan. Constructed slightly later, the Nathmalji-ki-haveli (the mansion of Nathmalji), built in the late nineteenth century by the state's prime minister, is another noteworthy residence.

Jaisalmer's great period of peace and prosperity had its origins in the harmonious relationship between the Bhatti rulers and the Mughal emperors in Delhi. Emperor Akbar was the first to obtain the submission of Jaisalmer, in 1570. Har Rai not only submitted to the emperor, he gave his daughter in marriage to him as well. The good relations developed further as Bhatti forces served in the Mughal armies, with princes of the ruling Jaisalmer family obtaining positions of command. Another Bhatti princess was the mother of the eldest son of Emperor Jahāngīr. Under Kalyandas (reigned 1626–51), Sabal (or Subbul) Singh (reigned 1651–61) and Amar (or Umra) Singh (reigned 1661–1702), Jaisalmer became one of the foremost Rājput states, ruling over the southern Thar Desert from Phalodi and Bārmer to Bhawalpur.

The preservation and expansion of this realm still depended on the military prowess of the Jaisalmer rulers, who faced an important rival in the state of Bīkaner to the northeast. Amar (or Umra) Singh was succeeded by Jeswunt Singh, under whose rule the territory of the state began to be nibbled away by neighboring rivals, particularly the rulers of the new state of Bahwulpoor. Not only did Jaisalmer suffer military reverses; the city's economy began to be adversely affected by the rise of seaborne trade during the eighteenth century. Following the acquisition and development of Bombay by the British in the 1660s, sea routes gradually took business away from the hazardous overland routes. By the early nineteenth century, the transit duties that formerly were the leading source of state revenues had dwindled to virtually nothing because of the decrease in commerce and the corruption of some of the Bhatti chiefs.

The decay of trade coincided with a period of weak rule under Moolrāj II (reigned 1762–1820), who left much of the administration in the hands of his ministers, Swarup Singh and Salim Singh, the latter of whom became minister at the age of eleven. While maintaining his power over the royal

The Patwon-ki-haveli, Jaisalmer
Photo courtesy of Christopher Turner

family through a mixture of subtlety and ferocity, Salim Singh also manifested that power through the building of another of the city's great *havelis,* the Salim-Singh-ki-haveli, with its blue cupola roof and superb carved brackets in the form of peacocks.

The decline of Mughal power in the eighteenth century was accelerated by the growing rivalry between the British and French in India. The extension of colonial rule was most strongly opposed by the Marāṭhās in western and central India. Jaisalmer, located some distance from the heart of contention, was left largely unscathed during the rise of the Marāṭhās; British wars against the Marāṭhās in the late eighteenth century also had little impact on the city. However, by 1818, the British East India Company (then the agent of British rule in India) began to appreciate the commercial value of Jaisalmer, which occupied a strategically significant position on the border of Rājasthān (over which British control was being extended) and Sindh (which was conquered in 1843), as well as being in an ideal situation to block any invasion that might come through Persia. It was, in any case, the only Rājput state that had not accepted British protection at that stage. A treaty negotiated by Tod in 1818 extended British protection to the principality and drew the British into its affairs. In 1829, for instance, they intervened to help settle a dispute between Jaisalmer and Bīkaner. Whatever the political significance of British protection, it did nothing to arrest the commercial decline of the city, not least because the treaty also secured the power of minister Salim Singh, which, as Tod admitted, was "one of the many instances of the inefficacy of our system of alliances to secure prosperity."

Economic decline continued through the remainder of the nineteenth century even as a handful of merchants and political officials still were wealthy enough to build great mansions. Jaisalmer entered a period of obscurity. By the early twentieth century, commercial decline was reflected in population loss in the state, from 115,701 in 1891 to 88,311 in 1911 and 67,652 in 1931. The population of the city itself shrank to just 4,000 by 1931. At the time of independence in 1947, the leaders of Jaisalmer had meetings with Mohammed Ali Jinnah to discuss the state's incorporation into Pakistan. It did, however, join India and the city became the administrative headquarters of Jaisalmer district of the state of Rājasthān. The city, however, remained small; its population in 1961 was 8,362.

Wars with Pakistan in 1965 and 1971 brought a resurgence in Jaisalmer's fortunes, for its strategic position was realized once more. The continuing possibility of war between India and Pakistan and the likelihood of conflict in the Thar Desert have led to the establishment of important airbases in the vicinity. The Oil and Natural Gas Commission of India also has established a number of facilities in the area, and economic development also has been encouraged by construction of irrigation works.

The railway came to Jaisalmer in 1968, further stimulating the tourist industry, which has enjoyed government support since the 1960s. The annual desert festival, inaugurated in 1979, is held in January and February, chiefly as a means to attract more visitors to the city. Apart from the city's architecture and markets, one particular attraction for tourists is the opportunity to go on camel safaris into the surrounding desert. Economic growth has contributed to a rise in the city's population from 16,578 in 1971 to an estimated 38,813 in 1991.

Further Reading: Although difficult to obtain, James Tod's *Annals and Antiquities of Rājast'hān* (2 vols., London: Smith Elder, 1829–32; edited by William Crooke, 3 vols., London: Milford, and New York: Oxford University Press, 1920) is the best source for the chronicles of the city and state from 1156 to 1818. Later writers have mined Tod's material for their accounts of Jaisalmer up to the early nineteenth century. The politics of Jaisalmer's incorporation into British India are dealt with in Anil Chandra Banerjee's *The Rājput States and the East India Company* (Calcutta: Mukherjee, 1951; as *The Rājput States and British Paramountcy,* New Delhi: Rajesh, 1980). Jaisalmer's place in the history of Rājasthān as a whole is covered in Dharm Pal's *Rājasthān* (New Delhi: National Book Trust, 1968). Nand Kishore Sharma's *Jaisalmer: The Golden City* (third edition, Jaisalmer: Seemant Prakasham, 1982) is an enthusiastic account by a local author. Various guidebooks touch on the city's principal attractions, among which *Rājasthān,* edited by Samuel Israel and Toby Sinclair (Singapore and New York: APA Productions, 1988), is probably the most well-rounded account.

—Graham Field

Jakarta (Special Capital City Territory, Indonesia)

Location: On the north coast of western Java.

Description: Now the capital city of Indonesia, Jakarta stands on the sites of two precolonial towns (Sunda Kalapa and Jayakarta) and two colonial cities (Batavia and Weltevreden). Its cultures and structures reflect much of its complex history.

Site Office: Kanwil V Depparpostel DKI Jakarta
Jl. K. H. Abdurrohim 1
Kuningan Barat
Jakarta 12710
Indonesia
(21) 5202256 or (21) 5251316

The city of Jakarta (which has also been called Jacatra, Jayakarta, and Batavia), Indonesia's capital and most populous city, lies at the heart of West Java's northern coastal plain. To the north, the city touches the placid, muddy waters of the Java Sea, to the south it runs toward the foothills of the island's volcanic spine, and to the east and west it sprawls through new suburbs and industrial estates across fertile countryside that once was called the rice bowl of Java.

The area around Jakarta is one of the cradles of civilization in Indonesia. One of the oldest stone inscriptions in the Indonesian Archipelago, a record of the deeds of King Purnavarman of Tarumanegara dating from the fifth century A.D., was found near Jakarta, and archaeological excavation has shown evidence of much earlier, Stone Age inhabitants. The region did not develop, however, as an early center of political power. Great kingdoms rose and fell in the volcanic valleys of central and eastern Java and on the Sumatra shore of the Strait of Melaka, but western Java remained a backwater, perhaps because settlements on the coastal plain were too vulnerable to piratical attacks from neighboring regions.

Only in the twelfth century, when rising levels of commerce began to draw even the isolated coasts of Java and Sumatra into the complex trading world of Southeast Asia, did a significant settlement emerge on the site of modern Jakarta. This was the port of Sunda Kalapa, harbor for the Hindu-Javanese kingdom of Pajajaran. The capital of Pajajaran was in what is now the city of Bogor, strategically located at the foot of passes leading between the volcanoes, but the kingdom's existence is shadowy: very few contemporary records of Pajajaran have survived, and archaeological excavation has yet to reveal much of the kingdom's character.

Pajajaran's control of Sunda Kalapa was probably casual. We know from elsewhere in the archipelago that kingdoms based in the conservative agricultural interior generally recognized that the complex business of port management was best done on the spot rather than directed from some distant capital; these kingdoms often preferred to keep the more dynamic, entrepreneurial coastal regions at arm's length to avoid possible disruption to the stable hierarchical structures of the interior. Thus, the ruler of Sunda Kalapa, although subject to Pajajaran, was able to sign treaties with other powers, including the Portuguese, who visited the port in 1522 in search of pepper for the trade to Europe.

The Portuguese shared with Sunda Kalapa a political concern as well as trading interests. Alongside their commercial ambitions, the Portuguese saw their presence in Asia as part of a mission to fight Islam. Ironically, their military power helped to spread the religion of the Prophet, as rulers turned to their Muslim counterparts in search of allies against the technologically sophisticated Europeans. The Portuguese, nonetheless, sought to make alliances when they could with non-Muslim rulers who also felt threatened by Islam. Sunda Kalapa, for its part, was most certainly at risk. To the east, the Cheribon area had been captured by Javanese Muslims in the late fifteenth century, and Sunda Kalapa's ruler signed an agreement with the Portuguese allowing them to build a fort as part of the town's defenses. The agreement was in vain. Within two years, Muslim raiders from Central Java had taken both Sunda Kalapa and the port of Banten to the west. When the Portuguese returned in 1527 to build their fort, they found the Muslims in control, and the Europeans were beaten off by a Banten army under the command of General Fatahillah, who renamed the town Jayakarta (Victorious and Prosperous). Much later, the municipal government of Jakarta was to designate 1527 as the year of the founding of the city.

Jayakarta under Muslim rule remained a minor port, its ruler subordinate to nearby Banten. In the early seventeenth century, however, the town was transformed by the abrupt arrival of representatives of the Dutch East India Company, or V.O.C. Dutch merchants had begun to challenge Portuguese dominance in Asian waters from late in the sixteenth century, and in 1602 the various independent Dutch commercial operations were combined to form the V.O.C. The Dutch government chartered the new company, giving it quasi-sovereign powers in the entire region from the Cape of Good Hope eastward to Cape Horn. With the official backing of the Dutch state, the company could wage war, make treaties, seize territory, and issue its own laws throughout this vast domain.

At first, Jayakarta was only one of several ports where the Dutch set up trading posts, and their position there was weak. In 1618–19 the post only narrowly survived attacks from English traders, the sultan of Banten, and even the prince of Jayakarta himself. The defenders celebrated their survival by renaming the fort Batavia after the prehistoric inhabitants of the Netherlands.

Asia was too far from Europe for the company's day-to-day affairs to be administered effectively from Amsterdam, and V.O.C. authorities soon looked for a site they

Istiqlal Mosque, Jakarta
Photo courtesy of Indonesia Tourist Promotion Office, Los Angeles

could make their headquarters in Asia. Jayakarta attracted their attention for several reasons. The town was located strategically near the Sunda Strait, between Java and Sumatra, which was the main V.O.C. gateway to the Indonesian Archipelago. It also commanded the western end of the Java Sea, through which the spice trade from the Moluccas had to pass. The town possessed a fertile hinterland and could be made into a significant supply center. And it was remote from what were then the great powers of the archipelago: the kingdoms of Mataram in central and eastern Java, Aceh (Atjeh) in Sumatra, and Riau-Johore on the Malay Peninsula.

In 1619, therefore, as soon as the siege of the fort was over, the V.O.C.'s governor general, Jan Pieterszoon Coen, decided to establish his headquarters there. Bearing in mind the hostility of the prince of Jayakarta, Coen ruthlessly destroyed the Indonesian town, razing its buildings to the ground and driving the people away. At first nothing but the Dutch fort remained, but as the center of V.O.C. activities in Asia, Batavia soon attracted other settlers—European colonial officials, Malay, Chinese, Arab, and Indian traders, as well as large numbers of slaves from other parts of Asia brought in to work on the V.O.C.'s ambitious building programs or on the farms that sprang up in the surrounding countryside to supply the growing city.

For two centuries, Batavia was the capital of the Dutch enterprise in the East. During this long colonial summer, the physical character of the city changed dramatically. Seventeenth-century Batavia soon came to resemble a Dutch city. Sturdy, brick houses of two stories faced a grid of tree-lined canals that provided the main means of transporting goods. Conditions in the cramped rooms of these houses, with their low ceilings and small windows, must have been oppressive by modern standards, but most visitors to Batavia were full of praise for the city's amenities.

Early Batavia had something of the atmosphere of a frontier town. Everyone was an immigrant, and everyone was there with the idea of making money. The profits of the V.O.C. were vast, and wealth was readily available for those astute enough to collect it, whether by straightforward trading, by selling provisions to the company, by joining the booming construction industry, or by running one of the opium dens, grog shops, or brothels that sprang up in the port city. Even the slaves, if they survived the rigors of labor in the city, sometimes could buy their freedom and try their hands at other ventures.

The city became a racial and cultural melting pot. The administration was controlled by Europeans of many nationalities: the V.O.C., a little like the later French Foreign Legion, would take capable Europeans into its service wherever they came from, and Germans and Scandinavians became especially numerous in its lower ranks. The rest of the city, however, was Asian, from Turks and Persians to Japanese and

Ryukyuans, with Chinese the most numerous. The most successful Asians lived alongside the Europeans in the finest canal houses; the less prosperous lived in back streets or in temporary settlements outside the city limits.

Very few Europeans or Chinese brought wives with them. Instead, they married or, more often, established informal liaisons with indigenous women. The mixed-race children of such unions sometimes were recognized officially by their fathers and accepted into their paternal ethnic groups, sometimes left with their mothers and absorbed into indigenous society, but wherever they went, they carried a mixed cultural heritage. Before long, the European community in Batavia spoke Malay more often than Dutch, chewed betel, wore light tropical clothing such as sarongs, and bathed twice a day—all of which startled new arrivals from Europe. Indonesian migrants to Batavia, too, often lost their separate cultural identity within a few generations, merging gradually to become a new ethnic group, the Betawi (from the local pronunciation of Batavia).

A few physical traces of the seventeenth-century city survive today in what is still called the Kota (City) district of Jakarta: a few canals, an old V.O.C. warehouse, and—best preserved of all—the town hall, facing a cobbled square where parades were held and public executions took place. European colonial society has long since disappeared, but the greatest legacy of the seventeenth century is the Betawi community, which still retains many distinctive cultural elements in the vast ocean of contemporary Jakarta society.

The seventeenth century was the golden age of the V.O.C., and the wealth of the Indies extended the era of prosperity for the company and for Batavia a couple of decades into the eighteenth century. Then, however, the V.O.C. began to decline. Administration in the city became, in some respects, harsher and more erratic than before, and the company took terrible vengeance on those it saw as its enemies. In 1722, as punishment for suspected plotting to overthrow V.O.C. rule, a local Eurasian called Pieter Erbervelt was sentenced to be drawn and quartered. His fate still is commemorated in a warning monument topped by a skull impaled on a spike. In 1740 a revolt among Chinese peasants in the Batavia countryside led to the massacre of more than 1,000 Chinese in the city and a lasting alienation between the Chinese and their Dutch rulers. It was after these events that the Chinese first were required to live in a "Chinatown," just south of the city; the area, now known as Glodok, remains one of the main Chinese areas of Jakarta.

The company decreed not only where people would live but what they could wear in public. Different ranks were allowed different degrees of display, and one of the early mixed-race communities, the Mardijkers, prided themselves on being granted permission to wear hats, normally a European privilege.

Absolute company power, however, could not stop Batavia's decline. The city developed a growing reputation for unhealthfulness as the canals were choked slowly with the volume of sewage and other rubbish produced by the city's 35,000 people. Drinking water became scarce and unreliable. Flooding became more common as a result of siltation caused by erosion in the now-deforested hinterland, and the temporary swamps that developed became a breeding ground for malaria-carrying mosquitoes. When Captain James Cook visited Batavia in 1770 after sailing up the east coast of Australia, almost all his crew fell ill. "The unwholesome air of Batavia," he wrote in his journal, "is the death of more Europeans than any other place upon the Globe."

While the central city fell into decline, building began to spread to the south, to higher and healthier ground. The fine palace of Governor General Reinier de Klerk, now part of the national archives, was built during this era.

The V.O.C. had been established as a commercial trading venture with the formidable additional resources of an army, a navy, and a quasi-sovereign charter to lend weight to its operations. By the end of the eighteenth century, however, the company structure was obsolete. It controlled a substantial empire on land but was not structured to administer, and the V.O.C. remained devoted to monopoly in an era when free trade was increasingly the order of the day. The company was inefficient in its operations, and many of its employees were deeply corrupt. So weak was the V.O.C. that its abolition by the Dutch parliament in 1799 took place virtually without resistance.

Its reversion to direct Dutch government rule brought major transformation to Batavia. Under Governor General H. W. Daendels and his successors, the headquarters of the colonial administration was moved out of the city entirely and into a region called Weltevreden (Well-Content) around a vast parade ground called the Koningsplein (King's Square). Since renamed Medan Merdeka (Freedom Square), this park is now in the heart of Jakarta. In the early nineteenth century, however, it was considered to be a distant outlying area.

During the nineteenth century, Weltevreden was able to capture much of the allure of Batavia as a center of European civilization in Asia. Fine government buildings were put up, especially facing the Koningsplein, and comfortable new suburbs appeared behind them. With the opening in 1886 of deep-water port facilities at Tanjung Priok, on the coast a few miles northeast of old Batavia, the Batavia-Weltvreden conurbation confirmed its commercial importance. For the indigenous people of the Indonesian Archipelago, on the other hand, Batavia had no special significance. It was the capital of their alien rulers rather than a significant center of Indonesian culture. The structure of the city was determined by its European and Chinese residents; Indonesians occupied the interstices of the colonial city, living in crowded, makeshift *kampung*, or urban villages, clustered along the flood-prone riverbanks or behind the European buildings, away from the main roads.

Only in the early twentieth century did the place of Batavia in Indonesian society begin to change with the establishment of new, advanced educational institutions in the city. The fine building of the Law School (1926), facing the Koningsplein, which since has been taken over by the Department of Defense, is perhaps the most striking symbol of the way in which Batavia came to be Indonesia's main window on the Western world. Indonesians in Batavia became increasingly aware of the contradictions between Western philosophies of justice and democracy on the one hand and the practice of colonialism in the Indies on the other. To take charge of the fine buildings and institutions in Batavia and to turn them into a tool for the welfare of all Indonesians came to be one of the central aims of the nationalist movement.

In the end, Batavia fell not to an Indonesian revolution but to the Japanese, whose troops landed on Java at the beginning of March 1942. Reluctant to allow their capital to be destroyed in fighting, the Dutch declared Batavia an open city and, under the new name Jakarta, it became the headquarters of the Japanese military administration on Java for the duration of the war. The Dutch returned in 1945 to find that Indonesian nationalists had declared independence on August 17, and for the next four years the status of the city was contested. It was the capital of both the reinstated Netherlands Indies and of the new Republic of Indonesia, and the standoff was repeated at the municipal level, with two city halls attempting to manage the one city. By 1949, however, the Dutch were defeated, and Sukarno, as president of the Republic of Indonesia, moved into the white palace of the governor general, facing the Koningsplein (Medan Merdeka).

Independent Jakarta became a fascinating tangle of contradictions. It was a place of rough street politics and an urbane cosmopolitan culture. The slums that sprang up to house the rapidly growing population of migrants from other parts of Indonesia contrasted sharply with the ostentatious luxury of new elites grown wealthy from their privileged access to government. In a multiethnic state, Jakarta was the most Indonesian of cities, yet it was also a center of opposition politics and, increasingly, of fundamentalist Islam.

Under Sukarno, Jakarta was intended to be a showplace of Indonesian modernity. Wide boulevards and broad ring roads linked different parts of the city, and grandiose monuments and state buildings were constructed to show the world what Indonesia could achieve. The most spectacular was the Freedom Monument in the center of Medan Merdeka, clad in Italian marble and topped with a gold-plated flame. Sadly, Sukarno's rule was a time of economic decline, and the country could ill afford these extravagances.

Under President Suharto, who has ruled Indonesia since Sukarno was deposed in 1967, the emphasis has changed. Jakarta is much more a city of commerce, and the rows of skyscrapers that line the main roads contain shopping malls, apartments, universities, and the offices of private companies, rather than government agencies. Jakarta is still a place of great inequality, however, with impoverished slum dwellers clinging uneasily to the margins of a city that enjoys their cheap labor but regards them as unsightly and unmodern.

Further Reading: Susan Abeyasekere's *Jakarta: A History* (Singapore, Oxford, and New York: Oxford University Press, 1987) is the best general account of the city's history. Adolf Heuken's *Historical Sites of Jakarta* (Jakarta: Cipta Loka Caraka, 1982) is an excellent survey of surviving historic buildings, although a number of sites he discusses have become unrecognizable since the book was published. Bernard H. M. Vlekke's *Nusantara: A History of the East Indian Archipelago* (Cambridge, Massachusetts: Harvard University Press, 1943) is dated in its historical analysis but is full of gripping anecdotes of life in colonial Batavia.

—Robert Cribb

Jodhpur (Rājasthān, India)

Location: In extreme northwest India, on the edge of the Thar Desert, 112 miles west of Jaipur.

Description: City that once was the capital of a principality of the same name; the city dates to the fifteenth century, when the fort that dominates its landscape was built, and the state to the thirteenth. Both were founded by the Rathor clan of the Rājputs, who erected many of the historic buildings that still stand in the city of Jodhpur.

Contact: Government of India Tourist Office
State Hotel, Khasa Kothi
Jaipur 302 001, Rājasthān
India
372 200

Jodhpur today is part of the state of Rājasthān, which is sometimes called, appropriately, Rājputana—the country of the Rājputs. The Rājputs (an abbreviated form of Rāja-putra, or King's Sons) were a group of Indian rulers who played a key role in the development of the country in the Middle Ages and, in certain regions, in later centuries as well. They were divided into thirty-six clans, one of which was the Rathor clan, founders of Jodhpur.

The Rathors established the state of Jodhpur in 1211, a few years after they had lost their territory of Kanauj to Muslim invaders. The Rathors, like other Rājputs, were strong defenders of the Hindu religion. The many Rājput clans were so independent of one another, however, that they seldom united in a common cause, a factor that ultimately worked against them.

The Rathors first settled at Pāli, then made their capital at Mandor, known today for the beautiful gardens that surround the former cremation ground of the Rathor rulers. They found Mandor too vulnerable to attack, however, so in 1459, under their ruler Rāo Jodha, moved their capital about five miles south and founded the city of Jodhpur. The new site had a great defensive advantage in its 400-foot-high sandstone bluff, on which the Rathors erected the Meherangarh (Majestic Fort). The earliest portions of the fort date to 1459, but numerous additions were made to it over the years. Of the many fortresses in Rājasthān, the Meherangarh is possibly the most imposing of them all. Its walls are more than 100 feet high in places and pierced with multiple gateways. Particularly notable among them are the Fateh (Victory) Gate, built by Mahārāja Ajit Singh to commemorate his victory over the Mughals in the eighteenth century, and the Loha (Iron) Gate, which bears the handprints of many royal widows who committed *satī* (ritual suicide) on their husbands' funeral pyres.

Within the fort are numerous palaces, surrounded by courtyards. Work on the first palace began in 1499, but the oldest structure that survives today dates to 1640. The palaces were decorated lavishly; one can still see much of the ornamentation, including the wonderful stone latticework on the windows. The palaces today serve as a museum housing a fantastic collection of the Rathor Rājputs' treasures, including jewelry, clothing, paintings, palanquins, musical instruments, and weapons. The weapons were made at the nearby armory, which displays a further collection of arms. The craftsmen who made them lived at the fort and evidently were highly skilled. They made swords and daggers in a variety of shapes and decorated the handles intricately. They also made shields of a broad range of materials, including crocodile and rhino hides, wood, and steel, and created armor for both humans and animals, including a piece desiged to protect an elephant's trunk.

A large city developed around the fort; approximately 100 years after the fort was built, the city was encircled with walls comprising 101 bastions and 7 gates. The walls still stand, clearly separating the old city from the new. Jodhpur benefited from being on the trade route between Gujarāt and Delhi, and a prosperous business class known as Marwaris developed. Their name came from the popular name for the state, Marwar (Land of Death), perhaps a reference to the invaders who met death in Marwar or to the residents' willingness to die in battle. The Marwaris, however, conducted a living, thriving trade in such items as opium, copper, silk, sandalwood, dates, and coffee. The city also became known for and lent its name to the riding breeches called jodhpurs.

From this city the Rathor Rājputs exercised power that was based not only on military skill but on alliances forged through marriages with neighboring ruling families. Because of these alliances they had influence over many neighboring states. The Mughals, who rose to power in the early sixteenth century, were eager to recruit the Rājputs to fight under Mughal leadership, pay tribute to the Mughal emperors, and intermarry with Mughal nobility. Akbar, the third and possibly the greatest of the Mughal emperors, succeeded in imposing Mughal hegemony on the various Rājput clans after a series of military victories in the 1560s. Rathor ruler Rāna Udai Singh submitted to the Mughals and agreed that his sister Jodhbai would become one of Akbar's wives. In return he received the restoration of territories that Akbar had captured and the title of rāja. His son, Sawāi Rāja Sur Singh, became one of Akbar's leading military commanders, conquering Gujarāt and the Deccan for the Mughal Empire. The Rathors retained a measure of autonomy, and the whole arrangement was an example of Akbar's skill at forging partnerships with the Hindu Rājputs, traditional enemies of Muslims such as himself.

Jaswant Thanda, memorial to Jaswant Singh II, with Jodhpur Fort in the background
Photo courtesy of Christopher Turner

Akbar was noted for his tolerance of other religions, as was his son, Jahāngīr. Jahāngīr's son, Shāh Jahān, was more conservative, however, and his son, ʿĀlamgīr (Aurangzeb) was a Muslim zealot. ʿĀlamgīr's religious fundamentalism brought him into conflict with the Rathors of Jodhpur. In 1678 Jodhpur rāja Jaswant Singh died without heir, but one of his wives was pregnant. This led ʿĀlamgīr to assert his right to rule Jodhpur directly and to convert Jaswant Singh's posthumous son to Islam. He invaded the state the following year, sacked the capital and other major cities, and sought to force the conversion of all the Rathors. The leaders of Jodhpur joined forces with the rulers of the states of Jaipur and Udaipur against the Mughals. This culminated in the Rājput War, in which the Rathors and other Rājputs won some concessions from the Mughals.

When ʿĀlamgīr died in 1707, he left a Mughal Empire that had been weakened by his military ventures (which had been extremely costly) and his religious fervor (which had alienated many of his subjects). The succeeding Mughal emperors lacked the authority to enforce their demands for tribute payment, and they quickly became emperors in name only. Jodhpur took advantage of Mughal weakness to increase the territory under its control. Jaswant Singh's son, Ajit Singh, took revenge on the Mughals when he captured Ajmer from them. His successor, Abhai Singh, captured Allahābād.

Jodhpur was itself weakened, however, by the alliance it had made with Jaipur and Udaipur. The alliance involved a series of marriages and a number of complicated rules concerning succession within the three states. Disputes concerning succession arose frequently and led various rival aspirants to ally themselves with the Marāṭhās, the rising power in India during the eighteenth century. This eventually led to subjugation of the Rājput states by the Marāṭhās; the Sindhia Marāṭhā clan of Gwalior ruled Jodhpur for a time. Jodhpur finally won peace and security by accepting British protection in 1818.

The rulers of Jodhpur were on good terms with the British, who helped put down a people's uprising in 1839 but never took total control of the state. Jodhpur remained loyal to the British during the Indian Mutiny of 1857–58, and under British protection the city continued to develop and grow. Construction of a series of cenotaphs honoring Jodhpur's rulers began in 1899 near the fort. In 1929 construction began on the most noteworthy building in the new part of the city, the Umaid Bhawan Palace. This new residence for the Jodhpur mahārāja was a famine relief project, designed to provide employment in a period when the monsoons had failed for three consecutive years. It ultimately provided employment for more than 3,000 people by the time it was completed in 1944. The 347-room sandstone and marble palace was de-

Clocktower in the center of Sardar Market, Jodhpur
Photo courtesy of Christopher Turner

signed by H. V. Lanchester in a style called Indo-Deco, which, as the name implies, marries traditional Indian designs with Art Deco. Architectural critics consider it the best example of this style. Most of it is now used as a luxury hotel, but after India won its independence and the regional mahārājas lost their power, an agreement was negotiated that allowed the mahārāja, and subsequently his descendants, to continue to live there. The state of Jodhpur was absorbed into the state of Rājasthān in 1949.

The city of Jodhpur remains one of the most interesting in India. In addition to the monuments already noted, the old part of the city has many beautiful buildings of intricately carved sandstone, particularly along the Sadar Bazaar. An excellent view of the city is available from the fort. Jodhpur has many Hindu temples, and the various Hindu festivals are celebrated enthusiastically here. Several interesting historic sites lie just outside Jodhpur. Mandor, in addition to its gardens, contains a palace built by Ajit Singh in approximately 1724, the ruins of an eighth-century Hindu temple, and shrines to the Rathor heroes and their gods. About thirty miles from Jodhpur is an ancient desert town called Osiān, which was dominated by adherents to Jainism from the eighth to the twelfth century. It was a prosperous center of trade, which funded numerous exquisitely sculpted Jain and Hindu temples. The largest is dedicated to Mahāvīra, the founder of the Jain religion.

Further Reading: Information on Jodhpur is available in various general histories of India. The most important of these is *The New Cambridge History of India,* edited by Gordon Johnson, C. A. Bayly, and John F. Richards (29 vols., Cambridge and New York: Cambridge University Press, 1987–). Vincent A. Smith's *The Oxford History of India: From the Earliest Times to the End of 1911* (Oxford: Clarendon Press, 1919; fourth edition, edited by Percival Spear, New York and Oxford: Oxford University Press, 1981) also remains worthwhile. Travel guides with helpful sections on Jodhpur's history and landmarks include *India: A Travel Survival Kit* (Hawthorn, Victoria, and Berkeley, California: Lonely Planet, 1981; fifth edition, 1993) and *South Asian Handbook 1994,* edited by Robert Bradnock (Bath, Avon: Trade and Travel Publications, and Lincolnwood, Illinois: N. T. C., 1993).

—Claudia Levi and Trudy Ring

Jolo (Sulu, Philippines)

Location: City and island in the southern Philippines, in the Sulu Archipelago.

Description: Formerly the center of the Muslim sultanate of Sulu; currently part of the autonomous region of Muslim Mindanao. The island's and city's name has been rendered variously throughout its history. Early English accounts often used Sooloo, later Sulu. The Spaniards rendered the word as Xolo, later Jolo. In Mindanao it is rendered as Sulug; the Sulus themselves pronounce and write it Sug, which means a sea-current, and they call themselves Tausug.

Contact: Department of Tourism
T. M. Kalaw Street, 207
1000 Ermita
Manila
Philippines
599031

Jolo is now within the Republic of the Philippines, but its relationship with the rest of the Philippines is, and long has been, fraught with tension. The history of the town is bound up with a larger history of social, religious, and political struggle, the core of which is the firm establishment of Islam, from the fifteenth century A.D. in what is now the southern part of the Philippines.

Although the Sulu Archipelago and its neighboring islands are seen now as part of the southern Philippines, their geographic position has at times given them a larger role in Southeast Asia. In particular they acted as a focus for trade with China from the eastern parts of the Indonesian Archipelago. Pearls and tortoiseshell were among the goods taken to China in return for silk and other luxury items. The Sulu links with northern Borneo—a source of edible nests for the China market—persisted into the twentieth century and lie behind the still unresolved Philippine claim to the Malaysian state of Sabah.

There were Muslims in the Sulu Archipelago before the creation of an Islamic sultanate. A grave on the slope of Mount Dajo is dated A.H. 710 (the 710th year of the Hegira, or A.D 1310), and was well preserved until recent times; it later became the traditional site for the crowning of the sultans. The *makhdum* (Muslim missionaries) who speeded conversion during the late fourteenth century may have come from the Muslim colonies in the Chinese ports. But Sharif Abū Bakr, the man who established the sultanate of Sulu, is generally thought to have come from Johore in Malaysia, where the sultanate of Malacca (Melaka) had been founded at the beginning of the century. Abū Bakr soon established himself as a force in the archipelago, marrying the daughter of Raja Baguinda (who had invaded Sulu in 1390 and captured the ancient capital at Bansa) and founding the sultanate of Sulu around 1450. Islam spread rapidly under the sultanate, which was governed by *sharia* (Islamic law).

The sultanate of Sulu was, in scholar Thomas Kiefer's phrase, a segmentary state. Its ruler was no autocrat, but rather acted as the first among equals. The *datus* (chiefs) held power, and much of that, and of their prestige, derived from the extent of their following. The capital city came to reflect the structure of the realm, just as it also was to be a focus of its turbulent history and its resilient people. The early sultans ruled from Maymbung or Bwansa, but eventually the city of Jolo became the capital. After the Spanish conquest in 1876, the sultan moved to Maymbung. The sultanate existed well into the twentieth century, until the first president of the Commonwealth of the Philippines decided in 1936 not to recognize a successor to Sultan Jamal-ul-Kiram.

The Spanish conquest followed a long struggle, and it did not conclude it. The conversion to Islam of the peoples in this part of Southeast Asia, and the establishment of Islamic states, had been interrupted by the arrival in the sixteenth century of the Europeans: the Portuguese, the Spaniards, and the Dutch. The Spaniards make their main focus the islands they named after the future King Philip II. Islam was not yet established in Luzon and the Visayas, although there were Bruneis at Manila. In these parts of the archipelago, the Spaniards had an opportunity for their missionary zeal, and under their patronage Franciscans, Dominicans, Recollects, and Jesuits of the Counter Reformation took up the task. Together with the native elite, the missionaries became the essential basis of Spanish rule.

This desire to convert the natives to Christianity only made it more difficult to incorporate those parts of the islands that had become Muslim and where sultanates had been established. The Portuguese and, still more, the Dutch, found it easier to work with Muslim rulers, but the Spaniards found this impossible. Their relations with Sulu, as with Brunei and Mindanao, were marked by violence and hostility, and any treaties that they made with the rulers tended but to mark pauses in the struggle. The conflict, indeed, caused the people to identify more closely with Islam and undoubtedly helped to ensure their survival through the centuries as a virtually independent people.

The first major expeditions conducted by the Spaniards against Sulu was led by Esteban Rodríguez de Figueroa in 1578. Perhaps the most famous was that of Sebastian Hurtado de Corcuera in 1638, for some years after which Sulu was occupied. In retaliation for Spanish attacks upon Sulu, the peoples of the archipelago engaged in what was often called "piracy": raids upon the virtually defenseless shores of Luzon and the Visayas. These attacks had an economic motive as well. Coastal inhabitants were carried off and made slaves. Southeast Asia for most of its history has been sparsely populated. To maintain the independence of Sulu and take advantage of its position and its commercial potential, labor was essential. The raids were a way to acquire it; indeed, slaves made up the crews on the raids.

The subsequent pressures on Spain from the Dutch loosened the Spaniards' grip on Sulu, and in 1646 the Spaniards withdrew. In 1663 they even abandoned Zamboanga, which had been established as an outpost in the Moro (Filipino Muslim) lands at the request of the Jesuits. In the eighteenth century the Spaniards made a new attempt. They entered into a treaty with Sultan Alimuddin I in 1737, but his admission of the Jesuits encouraged opposition, headed by a rival, Bantilan. In 1750 he received baptism as Fernando, but the Spaniards feared treason and imprisoned him. In Jolo, meanwhile, Bantilan became sultan, and conflict with Spain reached a new height.

It was at this point that the British captured Manila in the Seven Years' War. They returned it at the peace table in 1764. Before the taking of Manila, Alexander Dalrymple urged the East India Company to intervene in the Sulu Archipelago, and he secured from Bantilan a grant of the island of Balambangan. Following the conquest of Manila, it was decided that Fernando should be freed to confirm the grant and return to Jolo. After Manila was returned to the Spanish in 1764, the company did indeed decide to occupy Balambangan, although the British government itself was far from enthusiastic. Jolo raiders—encouraged by Sultan Israel and the Spaniards—turned the British out.

The rivalries of the Europeans could stand an Asian state in good stead. In the subsequent decades, the sultanate sustained its independence of the Spaniards, who were fully occupied by their attempts to regain control over the rest of the Philippines following the British attack; they feared that the British attempt would be repeated during the French wars and that the Philippines would go the way of Mexico and most of their Latin American possessions. During this period Sulu flourished anew as a trading center, not merely as a piratical state. The Englishman Spenser St. John, who visited the region in the late 1840s, thought Jolo "by far the most beautiful island I have seen," the people "manly, and not too cunning."

At this time, the town of Jolo lay along the banks of a tidal stream, called Suba' Bawang, and at the head of the roadstead, even over the shoal and beach and into the roadstead itself. "That portion of the town which is not within the stockades is built in regular Malay fashion, on piles," Captain Henry Keppel wrote of Jolo in 1848–49. "The houses run in rows, or streets; and outside of them is a platform about 6 feet wide to walk upon. This is supported underneath by a light scaffolding of bamboo." A swamp to the south and west offered protection from assault from that direction, but the settlement was open to attack from the sea and from the east. On the high land to the east the strongest forts were erected. On the outskirts defending the approaches lay various *kuta* (strongholds) belonging to *datus*. The best stronghold was Datu Daniel's Fort. Others included Panglima Arabi's Kuta, defending the inland approach.

In 1836 the Manila government again attempted a diplomatic approach. José M. Halcon made a kind of alliance with Sultan Jamalul Kiram I. Still, no Spanish officers, civil or military, were established in the archipelago. On behalf of the British government, Sir James Brooke made a treaty (never ratified) with the sultan in 1849, following Brooke's treaty with Brunei in 1847. The consequences of the treaty, however, showed that European rivalry could indeed have disadvantages for the sultanate. The Brooke venture clearly spurred Spanish governor Urbiztondo to a new assertion of Spain's alleged rights over the sultanate in 1850–51; he attacked the island of Jolo, destroying the fortifications and much of the old town and securing a treaty of incorporation. Spenser St. John later wrote that he regretted the Spanish action. If the sultan and his nobles had been guided, and the pirate haunts dealt with, he believed "there would have been no occasion to destroy the pretty town of Sugh."

Despite their victory in 1851, the Spaniards established no officials there, and the British did not accept their sovereignty. Under Governor General José Malcampo the Spaniards mounted another major expedition in 1876 and finally established a garrison at Jolo. They had been influenced by the intensification of Islamic resistance and the expansion of European rivalry. The British, the Germans, and the Spaniards eventually reached a modus vivendi in 1877. In 1885 they agreed that, while Spain would not support Sulu's claims over North Borneo (where the British had established a chartered company to govern the territory), their own claims over Sulu would not be challenged. Sulu's involvement in piracy had not made it easy for the British to uphold its independence, although the British had protested at the violence of the Spaniards, partly because of the possible effect on their own Muslim subjects. Juramentados (Muslims under oath to kill the infidel) made life insecure in the town of Jolo itself, but in subsequent years Spanish settlements were made in other islands of the archipelago.

After the Spanish occupation, Jolo comprised the walled town of Tiyangi Sugh; San Remondo, to the south; Tulay, to the west; and Busbus to the east. The walled town was laid out with broad, clean, tree-lined streets, substantial houses for the officers, parks, and a market, church, theatre, hospital, and schoolhouse. Fort Alfonso XII was built on the site of Daniel's Fort, and Fort Asturias on Panglima Arabi's Kuta. In 1891 General Arolas erected a monument in Tulay to Corcuera, Urbiztondo, and Malcampo, the conquistadores of 1638, 1851, and 1876.

The treaty ending the Spanish American War ceded the Philippines to the United States, and Americans soon made their way to Jolo. Ada Pryer, who visited the city in 1898, found it attractive in appearance but boring: "It has a half continental half oriental air, a broad boulevard planted with trees stretching away before one with Chinese shops on either side." The general impression was "that everyone has

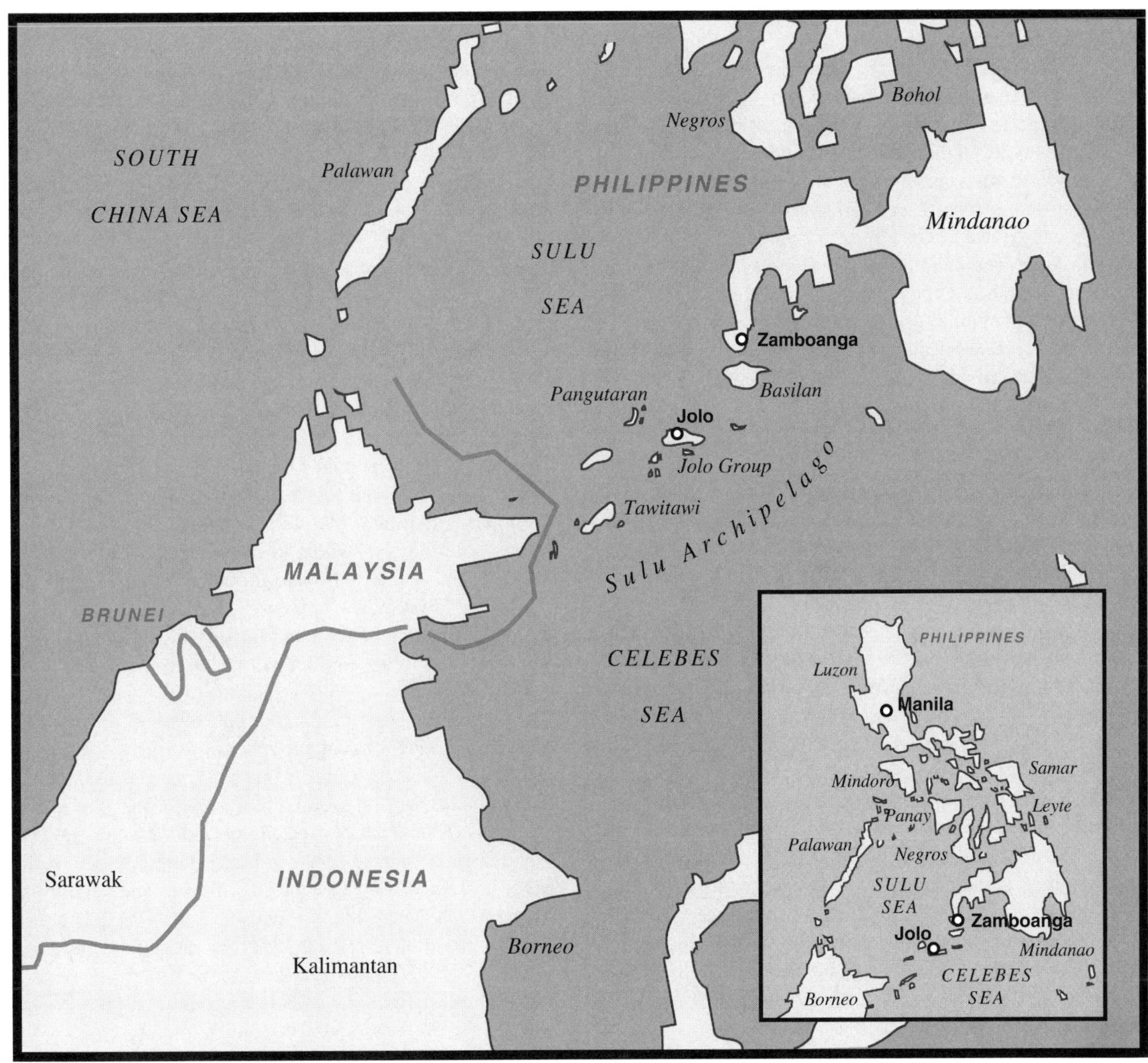

Map of the Sulu Archipelago, showing the position of Jolo; inset of the Philippines
Illustration by Tom Willcockson

just awakened from a lazy sleep and is proposing to take another nap as soon as possible." A long row of Chinese houses and shops began at the lower point of the Tulay Delta and stretched out to sea. There the Chinese had resided for many generations, and by the time the Americans arrived they controlled the trade of the archipelago.

When the Americans took over the Philippines, they found it desirable to enter into negotiations with the sultan of Sulu, resulting in the Bates Agreement of August 20, 1899. Only when the U.S. regime was firmly established in Luzon and the Visayas did they turn to the south and, abrogating the treaty in 1904, set about the reduction of opposition by military conquest. The climax was a major conflict on Mount Bagsak between General John J. Pershing's forces and the Moros in 1913. Afterward, civilian government was inaugurated by Frank W. Carpenter, and Americans proceeded to promote Filipinization and to develop self-government in the Philippines.

The American presence also left its mark on Jolo. In the 1920s Arolas's monument to the Spanish conquistadores was replaced by a statue of a uniformed nurse pointing the way to the hospital. Another new monument was unveiled in the main plaza, topped by a figure of the patriot, José Rizal, and below that figures of a Moro with a plough and a Christian Filipino as a blacksmith. Writing then, Sixto Y. Orosa thought the town "presented a most cheerful appearance, and there is much that suggests the romantic. The scene is enlivened by the Moro, passing lightly by in gay attire." The juramentados belonged to the past. The monuments testified to American purpose in the future.

Under American rule, the Moros enjoyed some measure of representation and acknowledgment of their unique status. Migration of Christian Filipinos from the north had been occurring throughout the early twentieth century, but it was curtailed somewhat by the American recognition that confrontation between Moros and Christian Filipinos would jeopardize the rich areas of Mindanao and the Sulu Archipelago. The American regime set up the Bureau of non-Christian and Tribal Groups as a body of popularly elected leaders from the minority communities as a voice for their needs and grievances. Because of these policies, and because of Moro distrust of the Christian Filipinos, many Moros had come to trust the Americans and rely upon them for the safeguarding of their rights. In 1934 the Americans announced a program that would bring independence in 1946. For Sulu natives, the prospect of being ruled by Christian Filipinos was no more welcome than being ruled by Americans, and for some it was less welcome. A delegation of natives sent to speak before the U.S. Congress in 1924 declared, "You have left us defenseless, and it is your duty to protect us or return to us the weapons you took from us."

From the outset, the Moro fears about the prospect of Christian Filipino rule came true. The Filipino government abolished the bureau that the Americans had established, effectively leaving the Muslims of Mindanao and the Sulu Archipelago without a political voice. In addition, the independent republic stepped up its efforts to colonize those regions by encouraging the mass migration of Christian Filipinos to the area. The independent government also saw the southern areas as ideal land to be appropriated for economic development, especially in the form of free trade zones for major multinational companies, regardless of Moro opinion. Those companies became the sole employers and governors of the regions they occupied, further reducing the voice of Moros in their own affairs. These deeply felt injustices began to manifest themselves in the activism of the late 1960s. As elsewhere around the world, the Philippines (and especially Manila) saw an increase in student political demonstration. Muslim acts of violent protest further strained the relations between Moros and Christians, already precarious as a result of President Ferdinand Marcos's domestic policies and the environment of anti-Muslim sentiment and prejudice stirred by propaganda.

This environment of tension erupted in 1968 when the Jabidah Massacre became headline news. Although the facts of the event remain uncertain, it appears that Christian military officers massacred a troop of Muslim army men for not following orders to attack their own homeland. To further enrage the Moro population, court-martial hearings fully acquitted all the officers. This incident and the increased violence between Muslim and Christian gangs in the southern Philippines encouraged Moros to band together in an organized fashion; ultimately, they formed the Moro National Liberation Front (MNLF) in 1969. Nur Misuari, a respected intellectual among campus radicals at the University of the Philippines in the mid-1960s, took up the mantle of Moro leadership, becoming the MNLF chairman. As Jolo was the home of Nur Misuari and several of his associates, the city became an MNLF stronghold—and a target for government reprisals.

The MNLF leadership, understanding their need for outside help against the larger, better-equipped and well-trained Philippine Army, sought links with Islamic nations such as Libya and Malaysia. Furthermore, they began to time their offensives, insurgencies, and major battles around strategic moments, such as the 1973 Cotabato Offensive on the eve of the Islamic Foreign Ministers Conference, and the Jolo War of 1974, which coincided with the Islamic Summit Meeting in Lahore, Pakistan. The conflict was at its peak between 1973 and 1975, during which time approximately 50,000 people were killed, both civilian and military. Jolo often bore the brunt of the violence. A bombardment in February 1974 gutted the city's commercial center and the district of Tulay. "A whole town was reduced to ashes, tens of thousands of people were uprooted, hundreds killed on both sides," writes T. J. S. George. The city's fate, as he said, helped to internationalize the Muslim cause.

By 1976 the conflict had begun to wane. The Philippine government, severely weakened by the costs of the war, began to seek out avenues of diplomacy, with offers of amnesty, land, and political concessions. At the same time, the MNLF was losing its aid from nations such as Malaysia, which had come under pressure for their support of terrorist guerillas. Talks between the Moros and the government led to a cease-fire and a promise of Moro autonomy in 1976. The truce broke down because the government failed to live up to its promises, but by then the Muslim leadership had become factionalized, the foreign aid for their movement had evaporated, and the Moro people themselves had grown weary of the continued fighting. Although sporadic clashes between Moros and the government continued, the war basically had come to an end.

After Corazon Aquino wrested control of the Philippines from Marcos on the wave of People Power, she embarked upon her plan for national reconciliation. Part of that plan was to award the Moros autonomy. The MNLF, acknowledged by the government as the main force in Moroland, agreed to autonomy and relinquished its goal of total independence. The Sulu Archipelago and parts of Mindanao finally achieved this status of autonomy in 1990. Since then, Jolo and the rest of the Moro areas have remained peaceful.

Further Reading: The best historical accounts of the Sulu sultanate are Najeeb Mitry Saleeby's *The History of Sulu* (Manila: Bureau of Printing, 1908) and Cesar Adib Majul *Muslims in the Philippines* (Quezon City: University of the Philippines Press, 1973). Volume 2 of Spenser St. John's *Life in the Forests of the Far East* (London: Smith Elder, 1863) gives an account of the town in the mid–nineteenth century. Another firsthand account of the Spanish settlement, written by a visitor in the 1890s, is contained in *Mrs Pryer in*

Sabah: Diaries and Papers from the Late Nineteenth Century, edited by Nicholas Tarling (Auckland: University of Auckland Press, 1989). P. G. Gowing's *Mandate in Moroland* (Quezon City: University of the Philippines Press, 1977) and T. J. S. George's *Revolt in Mindanao: The Rise of Islam in Philippine Politics* (Kuala Lumpur and New York: Oxford University Press, 1980) cover the Muslim population in more recent times.

—Nicholas Tarling and Shome Chowdhury

Junāgadh (Gujarāt, India)

Location: In the center of the Kāthiāwār Peninsula (now known as Saurāshtra) in the west-central Indian state of Gujarāt. Only thirty-one miles from the Arabian Sea coast, Junāgadh is one of the most westerly located towns in the country. It lies at the foot of Gīrnār Hill, one of the few areas of high ground on the peninsula.

Description: Despite its remoteness, Junāgadh remains popular with travelers owing to the temples on Gīrnār Hill, to the historical buildings in the town center, and to the Aśokan edicts, which have been preserved there for over 2,000 years.

Contact: Tourism Corporation of Gujarāt
H. K. House
Ashram Road
Ahmadābād, Gujarāt
India
(44) 9683

Those who make the long trip to Junāgadh, venturing out to the far western edge of India, usually come to see the most ancient of Junāgadh's historical monuments: the Aśokan Edicts. Little if anything is known about Junāgadh's pre-Aśokan history. The inscription of the Aśokan Edicts onto rocks in the Junāgadh area allowed this fairly isolated city to enter into the Indian historical record. Without these inscriptions, Junāgadh's recorded history may not have begun until long after, and certainly would not have carried the importance Aśoka's name lent it.

The Aśokan Edicts of Junāgadh, dating from about 250 B.C., are a series of moral laws and regulations carved onto a rounded granite boulder. They are now housed in a small building open to tourists on a road running east from the town center. The edicts were carved onto this and other stones and pillars in India at the behest of the Mauryan emperor Aśoka, who ruled from 272 to 235 B.C. over the most expansive Buddhist empire India has ever seen. The Mauryans came to power during uncertain times following the invasion (and then retreat) of Alexander the Great in 326 B.C. At its height, the Mauryan Empire extended over all of modern-day India with the exception of the southern tip of the subcontinent; it unified the diverse cultures of India for almost 140 years. The founder of the empire and grandfather of Aśoka, Candra Gupta Maurya (ruled c. 321–297 B.C.), built and expanded the empire from his base in Pāṭaliputra (modern-day Patna). Candra Gupta abdicated in 301 B.C. to become a Jain monk; while living in a monastery, he fasted until he died. Bindusāra (ruled c. 297–272 B.C.), Candra Gupta's son and successor, expanded greatly upon his father's already significant military successes. By the end of his reign, Bindusāra had extended the empire to include all of India as far west as the heart of modern-day Afghanistan (including Junāgadh), as far north as the Himalayas, as far east as the Ganges Delta and as far south as modern-day Mysore. Until the reign of Aśoka, one area in India remained hostile and unconquered: Kalinga, an independent state on the Bay of Bengal. In 261 B.C., Aśoka invaded Kalinga. He conquered this defiant state only after a savage and costly war, during which approximately 100,000 fell in battle and many tens of thousands more died of disease and malnutrition.

Disgusted by the devastation of the war, Aśoka embraced Buddhism, adopting the principles of *dharma* (righteousness or moral law) and *ahimsa* (nonviolence toward all living things). He preached tolerance of other religions and dedicated himself to building wells, hospitals, and other public works throughout the empire. However, no significant architectural legacies from his rule remain. Aśoka's primary monuments are the edicts that were carved onto rocks and pillars in various locations, mainly in southern, eastern, and northeastern areas of the empire; in western India, rock edicts have been discovered only in Junāgadh and Sopāra, north of Bombay. The carving of these edicts was part of Aśoka's campaign to spread messages of goodwill and tolerance to his subjects after the violence of the Kalinga campaign. The edicts preach nonviolence toward animals and humans, equal treatment for other religions, respect for all people—even one's enemies—regardless of social class or caste, and adherence to the principles of *dharma*. Definite confirmation of Aśoka's authorship of these edicts came only after further archaeological discoveries in 1915. The edicts were written in the Brāhmī alphabet (the source of the modern scripts of India, Sri Lanka, Java, Tibet, and Burma) using the Prākrit dialect.

Besides serving as a source for moral guidance and regulation, the Aśokan Edicts provide a valuable sketch of the complex political organization of the Mauryan Empire. The inscriptions, along with information from other sources, reveal that the emperor, who ruled from the imperial capital of Pāṭaliputra, appointed four viceroys, and beneath them, a number of provincial governors (*pradesikas*) to administer specific regions of the empire. According to inscriptions dated in the post-Aśokan period, Junāgadh had a provincial governor at least as early as the reign of Candra Gupta Maurya. A man named Pushyagupta held the office at this time; Yavanarāja Tushaspha held it under Emperor Aśoka. The existence of provincial governors stationed in Junāgadh indicates that the city was a significant location in the Mauryan Empire. The importance of Junāgadh to the Mauryans is further attested by their construction of Uparkot (Upper Fort) in a slightly raised area in what is now the eastern part of the city center. Nothing remains of the original

Part of the Jain temple complex on Gīrnār Hill, Junāgadh
Photo courtesy of Jonathan Drori

Mauryan construction, which was repeatedly rebuilt and extended over the centuries.

When Aśoka died in 235 B.C., the unifying force and moral center of this vast and multicultural empire was lost. As a result, the empire splintered into many fragments, giving way to the emergence of regional kingdoms and allowing foreign forces to make inroads into the South Asian subcontinent. These foreign incursions into India came mainly from the northwest by forces that came to be known as Indo-Greeks. The Indo-Greeks came from the fallen Achaemenid rule in Iran and from the fragments of Alexander the Great's army. The most notable Indo-Greek ruler who came to power in northwest India was Menander (ruled c. 155–130 B.C.), known as Milinda in Indian sources. Many historians consider that Menander likely ruled over the Kāthiāwār Peninsula, including the city of Junāgadh.

Upon the death of Mithridates II in 88 B.C., the Indo-Greeks were overrun by the Śakas (known also as Scythians), a nomadic power from Central Asia. Initially their rule did not extend as far south as the Kāthiāwār Peninsula, but the invasion of the Kushāns from Central Asia into northwestern India around A.D. 78 forced the Śakas southward. The Śakas soon took control of the Kāthiāwār Peninsula as well as parts of the Deccan and chose Junāgadh as their new capital. Gatamiputra Śātakarni of the Sātavāhanna Kingdom temporarily interrupted Śaka rule in the Kāthiāwār Peninsula (as well as in Junāgadh) for approximately twenty-five years, when his forces from the Deccan conquered the stronghold of Śaka power. The Śakas regained control of the peninsula when the most famous and successful Śaka ruler, Rudradāman I, took power. Around A.D. 150 Rudradāman I contributed inscriptions to the famous Aśokan Edicts at Junāgadh as a declaration of his sovereignty in the area. Aside from these inscriptions, all evidence of the Śaka Dynasty and any record of rulers from that period comes from numismatic sources (coin engravings). From these sources, we can gather that Śaka rule in Junāgadh came to an end with the rule of Rudra Simha III in 398.

Although no evidence exists to suggest that the Śakas adhered to the Buddhist faith, a considerable amount of Buddhist monastic construction and art at Junāgadh has been traced to that period. The Buddhist Caves, dug into rock at various locations throughout the city approximately 2,000 years ago, have come to be important Buddhist historical monuments. Most of the caves are in the area of the Uparkot, which was strengthened when the city served as the capital of the Śaka Dynasty. The oldest are the Khapara Khodia Caves. Unfortunately, the caves served as a quarry for builders in the medieval and later periods, resulting in the complete disappearance of the upper story. It is thought that the monks abandoned the hermitage here because continued excavations had made cracks appear in the rock and allowed rainwater to seep in. On the southern side of the fort are 150-foot-high caves that are later and better preserved (they date to sometime around the second century A.D. or earlier). Known as the Baba Pyara Caves, they served as a thirteen-cell Buddhist monastery and are decorated with Buddhist symbols, including the fish, the *triratna*, *swastika*, and *ankusa*. The third and latest group of caves, also three stories high, is located in the Uparkot near the Adi Chade Step-Well. Known simply as the Buddhist Caves, they include intricate pillar carvings from the second century A.D.; Śaka coins from the third and fourth centuries were discovered there as well.

The Śakas were succeeded in Junāgadh by the Gupta Empire, which pushed into western India in 398. The Guptas, in turn, lost control of the region to the Maitraka Dynasty following the death of Skanda Gupta in 467. Soon after, Junāgadh fell from prominence; the Maitrakas moved the capital of the peninsula from Junāgadh to Valabhī around 470. The move might have occurred because of the recurrent flooding of the town from the overflow of Lake Sudarshan; Skanda Gupta had carved records of such flooding on the Aśokan rocks as early as 450. After the demise of the Maitraka Dynasty, at the close of the sixth century, various dynastic factions attempted to claim parts of the Kāthiāwār Peninsula. During this period, the political scene in Junāgadh is somewhat hazy. Evidently it was ruled by the Pratihāra Kingdom based in Kanauj (or by a Pratihāra tributary) from the beginning of the seventh century until the end of the ninth. That this area receives scant attention in sources dealing with the history of the Pratihāra Kingdom suggests Junāgadh did not play a central role.

Beginning around the ninth century, northern Rājputs claiming their descent from the ruling warrior families found in the *itihasa* (history) and *purana* (stories and legends) literary traditions began asserting themselves militarily in the Kāthiāwār region. Because of the Islamic and nomadic Afghan invasions into northern India, Rājput clans were forced out of their traditional bases into areas like Junāgadh. By 875 one of these Rājput dynasties, the Chudasmas, had gained control over Junāgadh and eventually took control of the surrounding peninsula. The Chudasma Dynasty ruled in Junāgadh for over four centuries.

The Chudasma ruler Graharipu, who died in 982, hacked back much of the jungle surrounding the long-neglected Uparkot. In 1098, Navghan II transferred the Chudasma capital from Vamanasthali to the Uparkot, and the ancient fort enjoyed a resurgence. The current appearance of the Uparkot is mainly the result of rebuilding and reconstruction that took place during the Middle Ages, especially under Chudasma guidance. Through this reconstruction, the Uparkot was transformed into a virtually impregnable fortress. In places the walls are more than sixty-five feet high. An ornate triple gateway forms the entrance. There are two magnificent step-wells in the fort area. The Navghan Step-Well, named after Navghan I (c. 1060), consists of a 10-foot-wide passage winding down seven flights to a depth of 120 feet. The cistern, in conjunction with a large granary in the complex, would have allowed defenders to withstand extended sieges. The other step-well is known as the Adi Chadi, supposedly named after two water-carrying slave girls. Both

Darbar Hall, Junāgadh
Photo courtesy of Jonathan Drori

wells are Chudasma in origin and date from the eleventh century.

The Jain and Hindu temples on the summit of nearby Gīrnār Hill share little of the city's history, but all seem to have been built during the period of Chudasma rule. This coincidence suggests that Chudasma rulers acted indifferently, perhaps even favorably, toward the Hindus and Jains who constructed and worshiped at the temples. Some evidence even suggests that the Hindu Chudasma kings patronized the construction of the temples. For example, a genealogy of the Chudasma kings can be found on the wall at the left entrance of the Deva Kota temple complex. Gīrnār Hill is an extinct volcano that rises magnificently above the surrounding flat land of the peninsula. There is a legend about the creation of the hill itself, as there is about most religious sites in India: a giant traveling south, carrying rocks from the Himalayas, dropped fragments in the peninsula, thereby creating the hill.

Pilgrims and tourists reach the temples by persevering up a flight of 10,000 stone steps that climb to the summit of the hill, over 3,600 feet above. Most people start their walk from the end of the road just under 2 miles from the center of Junāgadh (the road takes one as far as step number 3,000). Gīrnār Hill is always busy with pilgrims and travelers, most of whom begin the climb at dusk to avoid climbing in the heat of the day.

The main Jain complex on Gīrnār Hill consists of a number of temples grouped together along a ledge, below the summit of the mountain. The Jain religion has many similarities to Buddhism and was founded at about the same time (c. 500 B.C.) by Mahāvīra, the twenty-fourth and last of the Jain prophets, who are known as *tīrthaṇkaras* (finders of the path). Apart from Pārshva, the twenty-third *tīrthaṇkara*, no historical documentation exists for any of the Jain prophets prior to Mahāvīra, who in effect systematized an existing body of ideas and deities under the name that refers to himself, *Jina* (the Conqueror). The largest temple on Gīrnār Hill is dedicated to Nemināth, the twenty-second Jain *tīrthaṇkara*. It was constructed between 1128 and 1159 and consists of a great courtyard with images of *tīrthaṇkaras* around the colonnade. In the central shrine is a large black image of Nemināth with depictions of his emblem, a conch shell. There are many smaller images around the temple. Close by is the Temple of Mallināth (1231), the ninth *tīrthaṇkara*, erected by two brothers, Vastupala and Tejapala. They invested the great wealth of their family in temples here and on Mount Ābu in Rājasthān. The temple is in the form of a court with shrines on three sides and an entrance on the fourth. In the main shrine is an image of Mallināth, whose color is blue and whose emblem is an urn. The two other shrines are dedicated to the Jain pilgrimage temple at Pārshvanātha in Bihār (the birthplace of the twenty-third *tīrthaṇkara*), and to a monument called Sumeru, which in Hindu myth represents the center of the earth. On the ceilings are carved representations of flying figures and images of women. The temple is a gathering place for *sadhus* (holy men), and a great fair is held there during the Kartika Purnima festival in November or December. Other temples in the complex include those dedicated to the first *tīrthaṇkara*, Rishabhadeva (Rīshabhanāth), on whose throne are figures of all twenty-four *tīrthaṇkaras*. Kumārapāla's temple is one of the oldest, named after a local king (1145–1172) who founded many Jain and Hindu temples throughout Gujarāt.

Beyond the Jain temples, on the pinnacles of Gīrnār Hill, are much smaller Hindu temples. On top of the peak is the Temple of Amba Mata, where newlyweds come to worship at the shrine of the goddess in order to ensure a happy marriage. This temple is believed to date from 1159, around the same time as the Nemināth Temple, which mentions the Hindu structure in an inscription. This Hindu temple, decidedly less somber than the Jain temple, is dedicated to the consort of Siva, Parvati.

In the fifteenth century Muslim forces conquered the Junāgadh area and the Uparkot Fort after centuries of intermittent battle. Sultan Mahmud Beghada of Gujarāt defeated the last independent ruler of the Chudasma clan in 1472, bringing an end to Hindu supremacy in Junāgadh and, with it, the era of Jain and Hindu temple building. A period of Muslim architectural construction now began in the city. Among the most impressive of the new Muslim structures is the Jāmi Masjid (Friday Mosque), built at the Uparkot complex from a former Chudasma royal palace. Its construction dates from the start of Muslim rule of Junāgadh. The Mosque looks like a fortress, rising from a brick platform, with solid walls and a slim column—more turret than minaret—rising from each corner. The mosque has never been completed, and parts of it remain open to the sky. This unfinished mosque stands as the most significant architectural contribution to Junāgadh during its rule by the sultans of Gujarāt, who also built most of the surviving fortifications of the lower city. Outside the mosque, overlooking the walls, is a sixteen-foot-long cannon called Nilam. It was cast in Egypt in 1531 and was left behind by Ottoman admiral Süleyman Pasha, who was assisting the Sultan of Gujarāt in his struggle against the Portuguese at Diu in the same year. In another part of the Uparkot there is a second cannon, much smaller, which was also left by Süleyman Pasha during the defense of Diu. When Diu was lost, both cannon were brought here.

The sultans of Gujarāt ruled Junāgadh for approximately 100 years, during which time they changed the city's name to Mustafabad (the name did not stick). In 1573 the great Mughal emperor Akbar defeated the sultan's forces and officially annexed the Kāthiāwār Peninsula to the Mughal Empire. Between 1573 and 1707, the Mughals ruled Junāgadh through the hands of appointed nabobs, as was their custom all over India. In 1707, when Emperor 'Ālamgīr (Aurangzeb) died, the Mughal hold over the peninsula loosened. An independent nabob, Bahadur Khan, took power in Junāgadh and initiated a weak dynasty that lasted until its final defeat at the hands of the British East India Company in 1806. The British East India Company held this territory until all the British Indian possessions came under the rule of the Crown in 1857.

From 1806 to 1947, Muslim nabobs served as political figureheads in Junāgadh, which for all intents and purposes fell under the yoke of the British Empire. Although without political power, the nabobs received generous stipends from the British Empire, which allowed them to keep up the appearance of nobility. During the nineteenth and twentieth centuries, they constructed a series of tombs in an ornate complex of buildings in the center of town. These replaced the humbler tombs 550 yards to the south at Chittakhana Chowk, built in the eighteenth century by the independent nabobs. The nineteenth-century mausolea of the nabobs is an extraordinarily ornate complex of buildings, constructed between 1878 and 1892. Buried here are Mahabat Khanji II along with two of his successors, Bahadur Khanji III and Rasul Khanji. The most ornate mausoleum is that of Rasul Khanji's chief minister Bahauddin, founder of the Bahauddin College and known also by his Hindu title Vazir-e-Azm (Great Minister). His tomb features a complex design of arches, domes, and carvings, with inscriptions written in silver plate.

Much of the present-day appearance of the town also dates from the latter half of the nineteenth century. This was when Nawab Mahabat Khanji II (ruled 1851–82) rebuilt the city with the help of the British Political Agency. Together they built public institutions such as bazaars, a clock tower, gateways, schools, hospitals, and district courts. One of the largest buildings dating from this time is the Bahauddin College, built in Venetian Gothic style, with a great hall measuring 100 feet by 60 feet. The palace of the nabobs was the Darbar Hall, now a museum furnished as it had been in the late nineteenth century, during the height of the nabobs' affluence; visitors to the building can see fine carpets, an armory, thrones, and a gallery of royal portraits. In 1863 a zoo was established at Sakkar Baug, approximately two miles from the center of town on the road to Rajkot. It was designed to breed Gir lions, which were in danger of becoming extinct in the wild. Tigers and leopards can be seen here now. In the Gir Lion Sanctuary, thirty-seven miles south of Junāgadh, Gir lions roam free—one of the very few places in India where they still do. The nabobs used to hunt lions here, but since 1900 the area has been a strictly guarded reserve.

At the partition of India in 1947, the nabob of Junāgadh, Mahabat Khanji III, wanted his tiny state to become part of Pakistan. However, the inhabitants, who are predominantly Hindu, voted overwhelmingly (190,870 to 911) to remain part of India. Even in an independent India, the nabob held no power or influence. Realizing this, he went into exile in Pakistan.

Further Reading: A very good travel guide that covers the monuments of Junāgadh and Gīrnār Hill in detail is *Gujarāt Damān Diu: A Travel Guide* by Philip Ward (Cambridge: Oleander, 1994). The book is both a personal travelogue and a practical guide book. A more practical book on the whole of India is *India: A Travel Survival Kit* by Geoff Crowther et al. (fifth edition, Hawthorn, Victoria, and London: Lonely Planet, 1993). A couple of good general histories of India are *A History of India, Vol. I*, by Romila Thapar (Harmondsworth, Middlesex, and Baltimore, Maryland: Penguin, 1966) and *A New History of India* by Stanley Wolpert (New York: Oxford University Press, 1977; fourth edition, 1993). Two books specifically on the monuments and history of Junāgadh are *Junāgadh* by K. V. Soundara Rajan (New Delhi, India: Archaeological Survey of India, 1985) and *Junāgadh and Gīrnār* by Shambuprasad Harprasad Desai (Junāgadh: Sorath Research Society, 1972).

—Andrew Beattie and Shome Chowdhury

Kābul (Kābul, Afghanistan)

Location: On the Kābul River, six miles upstream from its junction with the Logar River, in a fertile triangular-shaped valley in the Kābul province of east-central Afghanistan; south of the Hindu Kush and at a crossroads of ancient trade routes.

Description: Capital of Afghanistan and of the Kābul province; an important communications center since ancient times, it rose to prominence in the mid–sixteenth century as the capital of a principality ruled by Bābur, founder of the Mughal Empire; the site of many major events in Afghan history, it has suffered greatly in the civil conflict of the late twentieth century.

Contact: Embassy of the Republic of Afghanistan
2341 Wyoming Avenue N.W.
Washington, D.C. 20008
U.S.A.
(202) 234-3770

Kābul has been occupied since antiquity; it has been identified with the towns of Kubha, mentioned in the *Rigveda* about 1500 B.C., and Kabhura, noted by Ptolemy in the second century A.D. Because of its location in a valley encircled by mountains, with easy access to mountain passes, at the point where ancient north-south and east-west trades routes met, it has been invaded and conquered many times throughout its history.

Aryan tribes from Iran settled in the area about the sixth century B.C. Cyrus II of Persia conquered the Kābul Valley later that century, about 540, and incorporated the region into the Achaemenid Empire. Darius the Great consolidated Cyrus's conquests. Alexander the Great drove out the Persians about 330 B.C.; after his death seven years later, the area passed to the Seleucid Empire (founded by one of Alexander's generals), then to the Mauryans, the Greco-Bactrians, the Śaka-Parthians, the Kushāns (who introduced and promoted Buddhism in the region), the Hepthalites, and the Sāsānians.

Around this time Chinese Buddhist pilgrims made extensive travels across the region. The most famous of these pilgrims was Xuan Zang, who passed through the area in A.D. 657 Kābul was known to the Chinese as Kao-Fu, and in 659 the Chinese Tang Dynasty crushed the Western Turks. Until 751, sixteen kingdoms north and south of the Hindu Kush nominally recognized the authority of the Chinese emperor.

Muslim traders from the Middle East brought their religion to the Kābul Valley in the seventh century. Military invasions by adherents of Islam followed. The Muslims were successful in capturing the valley a few times, but were able to hold it only for brief periods. The inhabitants always would rise in revolt, and those who had converted to Islam would go back to their former religious practices. Local rulers were able to prevail until they began to fight among themselves, making possible the first substantial Muslim occupation when the Ṣaffārids captured the valley in 871 and began forced conversions to Islam.

The Islamization of the Kābul Valley proceeded further under the Ghaznavids, who occupied the area in the tenth century. The Ghaznavid Empire enlarged the small town of Kābul, establishing a military base and a commercial bazaar there. Goods from China, India, Central Asia, and the Middle East passed through Kābul.The town had a prosperous business quarter and was walled and fortified. The walls, or at least portions of them, predated this era; sections still standing in the twentieth century were believed to date to the fifth century A.D. The fortress, known as the Bālā Ḥissār, was destroyed by the British in the nineteenth century; the date of the original structure remains unknown. Kābul continued to prosper under the Ghūrids, who brought the Ghaznavid Empire to an end in the mid–twelfth century. It still was not a center of power, however, and was overshadowed by Ghaznī and Firuzkuh.

The Khwarezm-Shahs drove out the Ghūrids in 1206. In their turn they were conquered by the Mongols, under Genghis Khan, in 1219. His immediate successors, sons Ögödei and Tuluy, expanded the Mongol Empire to include most of what is now Afghanistan, but after their deaths the empire became fragmented and a native dynasty arose—the Karts, who were to be the last native dynasty to rule Afghanistan until the eighteenth century. Kābul declined during this period. In 1333 the traveler-writer Ibn Baṭṭūṭah described it as a mere village with few points of interest beyond a hermitage.

In 1383 a new wave of Mongol invaders, under Timur (Tamerlane), overthrew the Karts and captured most of Afghanistan, including Kābul. Moving east to further conquests, Timur put his grandson, Pir Muhammad, in charge of Kābul, Kandahār, and Ghaznī. After Timur's death in 1404, Kābul became the center of a principality ruled by members of the dynasty he established, the Timurids. The Timurids frequently fought with one another for control of the town, but nonetheless Kābul and the rest of Afghanistan prospered under their rule.

Kābul was still a relatively small town in 1504, when Bābur, a descendant of both Timur and Genghis Khan, displaced its ruler, Mukim Arghun, and made it the capital of an independent princely state. Bābur developed Kābul's role as a trade center where caravans exchanged goods from Persia, India, China, and Central Asia. He also established a mint there, which continued to produce coins until the time of the last great Mughal emperor, ʿĀlamgīr (Aurangzeb). Bābur was

View of Kābul
Photo courtesy of Mr. Rashid Uddin, Park Travel Agency, Chicago

extremely fond of Kābul and in his memoirs wrote favorably of its climate, commerce, natural beauty, and amenities. He had a particular appreciation of plant life and other natural features; he is said to have identified sixteen different kinds of wild tulips growing on the hills around Kābul. In keeping with this interest, he developed many formal gardens in the town.

Bābur described one of these gardens at length in his *Bāburnama:*

> Opposite to the fort of Adinahpur, to the south, on rising ground, I formed a char-bagh [elevated garden] in the year 1508. It is called Bagh-i-Vafa [the Garden of Fidelity]. It overlooks the river, which flows between the fort and the palace. In the year in which I defeated Behar Khan and conquered Lahore and Dibalpur [1526], I brought plantains and planted them here. They grew and thrived. The year before I had also planted sugar-cane in it, which throve remarkably well. . . . It is on an elevated site, and enjoys running water, and the climate in the winter season is temperate. In the garden there is a small hillock, from which a stream of water, sufficient to drive a mill, incessantly flows in the garden below. The four-fold field-plot of the garden is situated on this eminence. On the south-west part of this garden is a reservoir of water twenty feet square, which is wholly planted round with orange trees; there are likewise pomegranates. All around the piece of water the ground is quite covered with clover. This spot is the very eye of the beauty of the garden.

Additionally, Bābur used Kābul as a base for his military expeditions against Kandahār, Central Asia, and neighboring Afghan tribes in the Kābul Valley. By 1523 he had managed to quell dissent in Afghanistan sufficiently to allow him to launch an invasion of India. Within three years he had defeated Ibrāhīm, the last Lodī Afghan ruler of India, and was able to establish the Mughal Empire, which eventually came to control a large portion of the Indian subcontinent. Kābul was the capital of a province within the empire.

Bābur died in Āgra in 1530. Nine years later his body was brought to Kābul and buried in a garden that he had laid out on the slopes of the Shir Dawaza mountain. He asked to have no monument, but his successors built them anyway. Mughal emperor Shāh Jahān built a gray marble mosque over his grave about 1640, and a tomb of black, pink, and green marble and alabaster was constructed by Afghan ruler ʿAbdorraḥmān Khān about 1880. An inscription was placed over the main entrance of the mosque: "Only this mosque of beauty, this temple of nobility, constructed for the prayer of

Bagh-i-Vafa Palace, Kābul
Photo courtesy of Mr. Rashid Uddin, Park Travel Agency, Chicago

saints and the epiphany of cherubs, was fit to stand in so venerable a sanctuary as this highway of archangels, this theatre of heaven, the light garden of the Godforgiven angel king whose rest is in the garden of heaven, Ẓahīr-ud-Dīn Muḥammad Bābur the Conqueror." Writer Peter Levi found the tomb and mosque in good condition when he visited Kābul in the late 1960s, but still concluded that no memorial would be adequate for the great Bābur.

Kābul remained under Mughal control during the struggle for Afghanistan between the Mughals and the Persian Ṣafavids that began after Bābur's death and continued for 200 years. The Ṣafavids intermittently controlled Kandahār, from which they could exert pressure on Kābul, but they never brought the city within their sphere of influence for long.

Bābur was succeeded in Kābul by his son Kamran, who was dispossessed by his brother Humāyūn in 1545. During a war between the brothers Kamran twice regained possession of the city but could hold it only briefly. In 1553 Kamran finally surrendered to Humāyūn, who had his brother blinded. Humāyūn died in 1556 and was succeeded by his son Akbar, who expanded and strengthened the Mughal Empire. His son and successor, Jahāngīr, lost Kābul to the Persians in 1611 but recaptured it four years later. The empire peaked under Jahāngīr's successor, Shāh Jahān. A list of Shāh Jahān's victories accompanied the memorial inscription at Bābur's tomb.

At the height of the empire many improvements were made to Kābul, most notably the construction of an arcaded and roofed bazaar, the Char Chato, in the seventeenth century. The bazaar was 600 feet long and 30 feet wide and was lighted at night. It displayed a huge selection of goods, providing evidence of Kābul's continued importance as a place of trade.

Also during the period of Mughal rule, however, Kābul had to contend with frequent raids by the tribes who inhabited the surrounding mountains. These tribes remained virtually independent of Mughal governance and often invaded the Kābul Valley in search of plunder. Mughal attempts to subdue the tribes were unsuccessful. During the reign of ʿĀlamgīr, an imperial army was destroyed when trying to pass from Khost to Kābul, and the mountain tribes had to be bribed to allow travelers to go between Kābul and Peshāwar.

The Mughal Empire began to fragment after ʿĀlamgīr's death in 1707; his successors were emperors in name only. Persian military leader Nāder Shāh put an end to Mughal control of Kābul when he captured the city in 1739. He then invaded India, defeated Mughal emperor Muhammad Shāh, and annexed all Mughal territories west of the Indus River, including the city and province of Kābul.

Nāder Shāh's reign was short-lived, however. He was assassinated in 1747 and Aḥmad Khān Abdālī, the commander of his 4,000-man corps of Afghan bodyguards, was elected king. He took the title Durr-i Durrān (Pearl of Pearls) and became known as Aḥmad Shāh Durrāni. He conquered

Kābul and other cities, eventually coming to rule over a realm that included most of Afghanistan and northern India. It was the second largest Muslim empire in the eighteenth century; only the Ottoman Empire encompassed more territory. Aḥmad Shāh, who made his capital at Kandahār, was a respected ruler. Undoubtedly, his popularity was due in part to the fact that he relied on the fruits of conquest rather than heavy taxation to support his government.

Aḥmad Shāh died in 1773. His son and successor, Timur Shāh, did not enjoy the firm support of tribal chieftains that had allowed his father to govern effectively, and he had to put down frequent rebellions. Because most of the opposition was centered in Kandahār, he moved his capital to Kābul. He managed to remain in power, although sometimes tenuously, until he died in 1793. He was buried in Kābul.

He was succeeded by his fifth son, Zaman Shāh, who was obsessed with becoming as successful a conqueror as his grandfather had been. Toward this end, he repeatedly invaded India, weakening the Durrāni monarchy and threatening the British who held power there. The British persuaded Fatḥ ʿAlī Shāh of Persia to mount a campaign against Zaman to draw his attention away from India. Fatḥ ʿAlī expanded on the British plan by providing Zaman's brother Maḥmūd, governor of Herāt, with money and troops and urging him to invade Kandahār and Kābul. He took both cities, had Zaman blinded and imprisoned, and ascended the throne in 1800.

The Durrāni Empire already had begun to weaken, however, and there were numerous revolts in Kābul. Forces opposed to Maḥmūd invited another brother, Shāh Shojāʿ, to intervene, and he captured Kābul in 1803. This was a difficult period for the Afghan rulers; tribal chiefs had become difficult to control, provinces in the hinterlands were declaring their independence, the Sikhs of the Punjab posed a military threat in the east, and the Persians constituted a similar threat in the west. Also at this time, the British learned that Napoléon had proposed a joint French-Russian invasion of India, and turned to Afghanistan to set up a combined defense should the invasion occur (it never did). But while Shāh Shojāʿ was meeting with British diplomat Mountstuart Elphinstone at Peshāwar in 1809, forces loyal to Maḥmūd and his vizier, Fatḥ Khān Barakzāi, captured Kābul and put Maḥmūd back on the throne. They defeated Shāh Shojā's troops, and he fled Afghanistan, receiving protection from the British in India.

Maḥmūd put great power in the hands of Fatḥ Khān and his tribe, the Barakzāi. Maḥmūd's son Kamran, jealous of Fatḥ Khān's position, had him blinded and, later, killed. Kamran also made an enemy of Fatḥ Khān's brother, Dōst Moḥammad, who raised an army in 1818 and conquered Kābul and other major Afghan cities. In 1826 he received the title of emir in Kābul, thus founding the Barakzāi Dynasty.

The British, again fearful of Russian influence, met with Dōst Moḥammad in Kābul in 1837 to discuss a possible alliance. Dōst Moḥammad, for his part, hoped the British would help him recover Peshāwar, which had fallen to the Sikhs some years earlier. The British would not agree to this and left Kābul after noticing a Russian agent there. The governor general of India, Lord Auckland, then ordered an invasion of Afghanistan with the goal of restoring the friendly Shāh Shojāʿ to the throne. The invasion, which developed into the First Anglo-Afghan War, began in 1839. The British captured Kandahār and Ghaznī in short order and installed Shāh Shojāʿ at Kābul in August of that year. Dōst Moḥammed fled, was captured at Bukhara, escaped, was forced to surrender to the British at Kābul, and was exiled to India. The Afghans, resentful of having a ruler forced on them by an outside power, mounted frequent insurrections against the British. An outbreak of violence in Kābul in September 1841 forced the British to evacuate the Bālā Ḥissār for a base north of the city, where they were besieged almost immediately. Sir William Hay Macnaghten, who had come to discuss peace terms with the Afghan rebels, was murdered, and the British finally concluded they had to leave Afghanistan. On January 5, 1842, 4,500 British and Indian troops, accompanied by 12,000 civilians, left Kābul, having been given a promise of safe passage by Akbar Khān, Dōst Moḥammad's son and the rebel leader. He went back on his promise, however, and the column was slaughtered during its retreat. Shāh Shojāʿ was murdered following the British withdrawal, and his son Fatḥ Jang was placed on the throne.

The British recaptured Kābul in September and took revenge by burning the Char Chato bazaar. Shortly thereafter, however, the new governor general, Lord Ellenborough, decided to pull the troops from Afghanistan. When they left Kābul they took Fatḥ Jang with them, as he considered his position untenable without British support. Shāhpur, another of Shāh Shojā's sons, was declared emir but was soon deposed by Akbar Khān, who held the city for his father. Dōst Moḥammad returned from India in 1843 and took his place on the throne of Kābul. He expanded his territories and reigned until his death in 1863.

His third son, Shīr ʿAlī, succeeded him. Shīr ʿAlī was deposed by his two brothers in 1866 but returned to power in 1868, ruling from a city that by now had a population of 140,000. During Shīr ʿAlī's reign, the rivalry between Britain and Russia over Afghanistan surfaced again. Because of various disputes with the British, he refused to receive a British diplomatic party, but did receive a Russian one. Outraged, the British launched the Second Anglo-Afghan War in November 1878. British troops advanced on Kābul and captured it in December; Shīr ʿAlī fled to Mazār-i Sharīf, where he died in February, and his son Yaʿqūb Khān became emir of Afghanistan. Yaʿqūb Khān agreed that the British could station a permanent embassy in Kābul, which they did in July. In September, however, members of the British diplomatic corps were murdered in Kābul, leading to renewed fighting. British forces captured Kābul in October, were besieged there by an Afghan army, but eventually emerged victorious.

The British forces were led by Frederick Roberts, whose first impressions of Kābul he recorded in his memoir *Forty-One Years in India* (1897):

> At last I was at Kābul, the place I had heard so much of from my boyhood, and had so often wished to see! The city lay beneath me, with its mud-coloured buildings and its 50,000 inhabitants, covering a considerable extent of ground. To the south-east corner of the city appeared the Bal Hissar, picturesquely perched on a saddle just beneath the Shahr-i-Darwaza heights, along the top of which ran a fortified wall, enclosing the upper portion of the citadel and extending to the Deh-i-Mazang gorge.

Following their victory, the British exiled Ya'qūb Khān to India, and the British offered the Kābul throne to 'Abdorraḥmān Khān, a cousin of Shīr 'Alī. 'Abdorraḥmān managed to resolve Afghanistan's external and internal conflicts. During his reign, the boundaries of the country were settled to the satisfaction of both the British and the Russians. He also fought numerous small internal wars to assert his central authority. 'Abdorraḥmān made many physical changes in the capital city as well. The Bālā Ḥissār had been destroyed by the British and was not rebuilt (its ruins, however, remained visible well into the twentieth century). But he did build a new royal palace, surrounded by beautiful gardens, on the outskirts of the city. His other constructions included hospitals, arsenals, and bazaars. They were not architecturally remarkable, but they were serviceable. 'Abdorraḥmān also modernized Kābul's roads and communications.

His son and successor, Ḥabībollāh Khān, continued the program of modernization and maintained good relations with the British. The latter factor kept Afghanistan from entering World War I on the side of the Central Powers but also led to Ḥabībollāh's assassination by anti-British activists in 1919. His successor, Amānollāh, declaring "death or freedom" to a crowd in Kābul, launched the Third Anglo-Afghan War, but sued for peace after a month of indecisive battles. The treaty with the British affirmed Afghanistan's independence and its right to manage its own relations with other countries; the Column of Independence to commemorate this treaty was erected in Kābul. Also at this time, Afghanistan negotiated a treaty of friendship with the recently established Soviet Union, becoming one of the first countries to recognize the Soviet regime.

Amānollāh built his own capital at Dar-ul-Aman, about six miles from Kābul. It contained an impressive house of parliament, several other government buildings, and residences for the royal court and other high-ranking officials. After he lost power, the capital was moved back to Kābul. His fall was hastened by his liberal reforms, such as removing the veil from women and instituting coeducational schools, which outraged religious conservatives, and his plans to transform Kābul into a European-style city. Civil war began in 1928 and Amānollāh abdicated in 1929.

His successor, Muhammed Nāder Khān, introduced a more conservative constitution to pacify Islamic fundamentalists and oversaw a bloody purge of his political opponents. His brief reign also saw the founding of a medical school that eventually became Kābul University, with the addition of other academic departments. He was assassinated, however, in 1933, and was succeeded by his nineteen-year-old son, Mohammad Ẓahīr Shāh.

Ẓahīr carried out programs of economic development and social reform, including major construction in Kābul, a process that slowed during World War II (in which Afghanistan was neutral) but accelerated afterward. Whole new neighborhoods were built in Kābul, streets were paved, and modern high-rise buildings replaced many old structures. Hydroelectric power stations were built to supply the city in the 1950s and 1960s.

Under Ẓahīr Afghanistan became a constitutional monarchy. Internal power struggles, however, resulted in Ẓahīr's overthrow by his former prime minister, Mohammad Daud Khān, in 1973. Daud Khān initially embraced socialistic policies, but he gradually moved to a more centrist stance. Two major leftist parties united against him and took over the government in 1978; Daud Khān and most of his family were killed.

The new government, under President and Prime Minister Nur Mohammed Taraki, announced far-reaching reforms, including land redistribution and equality for women. Many Afghans perceived these reforms as pro-Soviet and believed they would undermine the country's traditional culture. It did not help that the Taraki government tolerated no dissent. Violent revolts began in the summer of 1978, bringing destruction to Kābul and other cities, and early in 1979 U.S. ambassador Adolph Dubs was killed, putting U.S. assistance beyond Afghanistan's reach. Taraki relinquished his post of prime minister to Hafizullah Amin in March 1979, while remaining president, but factional fighting soon broke out between supporters of each. Taraki was killed in one such clash in September, and Amin appealed to the United States and Pakistan for aid. Two months later, however, the Soviet Union invaded Afghanistan, killed Amin and many of his allies, and installed their own prime minister.

Resistance to the Soviet occupation began almost immediately, and the war brought great suffering to all of Afghanistan. Kābul initially was safer than outlying areas and so received a flood of refugees that swelled its population to nearly 2 million. In the early years of the war the Soviets had the advantage, but outside military aid, particularly from the United States, Britain, and China, internal alliances among resistance groups, and pressure from the United Nations helped the Afghans gain the upper hand. Soviet leader Mikhail Gorbachev agreed to withdraw troops from Afghanistan, and the last Soviet soldier left in February 1989. The withdrawal did not bring peace, however. President Mohammad Najibullah, who had been installed during the Soviet occupation, remained in power despite predictions his government would collapse when the Soviets left, and Muslim rebels continued to fight government forces fiercely. Najibullah's government finally disintegrated in 1992, but new president Burhanuddin Rabbani drew opposition from Islamic fundmentalists, and the conflict has continued unabated despite occasional attempts at peacemaking. Kābul, once a haven from the war, has become the scene of much fighting. Many of its residents have been killed or have fled the city; its population had been reduced to an estimated 600,000 by mid-1995. Much of the city is in ruins, and no end to the devastation is in sight.

Further Reading: Entries on Kābul and Afghanistan in *The Encyclopedia of Islam* (Leiden: Brill, 1913; revised edition, 1987) provide much information on various aspects of the city's history. Excerpts from Bābur's *Bāburnama* describing the gardens of Kabul can be found in C. M. Villiers-Stuart's *Gardens of the Great Moghuls* (London: Black, 1913). Louis Dupree's *Afghanistan* (Princeton, New Jersey: Princeton University Press, 1973) provides an extensive account of national history, with numerous references to Kābul. Peter Hopkirk's *The Great Game: On Secret Service in High Asia* (London: Murray, 1990; with subtitle *The Struggle for Empire in Central Asia,* New York: Kodansha, 1992) examines Anglo-British rivalry throughout Afghanistan. Ludwig Adamec's *Kabul and Southeastern Afghanistan* (Graz: Akademische Druck-u Verlagsanstalt, 1985) contains a series of accounts of Kābul in the early twentieth century. Frederick Roberts's experiences at Kābul are recorded in *Forty-One Years in India* (London: Bentley, 1897). Peter Levi's *The Light Garden of the Angel King: Journeys in Afghanistan* (London: Collins, and Indianapolis: Bobbs-Merrill, 1972) contains excellent descriptions of Kābul before the recent destruction. The 1980s and 1990s have brought a spate of books, too numerous to mention, on the Afghan-Soviet conflict and the continued fighting between Islamic fundamentalists and moderates.

—Richard White and Trudy Ring

Kaifeng (Henan, China)

Location: In an area crossed by several major rivers in northern Henan Province, which forms part of the North China Plain. Kaifeng lies on the Bien River, which flows southeast into the Huai River. Today, after several major changes in its course, the Yellow River passes the city a few miles to the north.

Description: An ancient imperial capital for seven dynasties between the fourth century B.C. and the thirteenth century A.D. It was the last Chinese capital situated in the Yellow River valley. Lying at the head of the Grand Canal, the chief artery between north and south China, Kaifeng also became a commercial metropolis. The city declined when the focus of the Chinese empire shifted to Beijing. Changes in the course of the Yellow River and frequent flooding contributed to this decline. Recently, Kaifeng, with its ancient treasures, has been singled out in government plans to promote tourism.

Contact: Henan Tourism Bureau
16 Jinshui Avenue
450003 Zhengzhou, Henan
China
(86) 371 5952707

The Yellow River valley formed the heart of ancient China, and the 120-mile stretch of the valley between Kaifeng and Luoyang, another ancient Chinese capital, is truly an archaeologist's delight. In many places excavations reveal six layers studded with significant finds dating as early as the second millennium B.C. In Kaifeng itself, digging to any depth is likely to uncover some ancient treasure. In 1986, for instance, municipal workers digging trenches for water mains came upon the famous Bridge of Zhou, a work of great art and engineering skill, dating to the time of the Northern Song Dynasty in the eleventh century A.D.

Kaifeng's exact beginnings are unclear. Lord Zhuang of the State of Zheng (774–500 B.C.) has been credited with the foundation of the first walled settlement of Kaifeng, which means a newly founded frontier. However, a more likely date for the city's foundation is 362 B.C. In April of that year, Wei Hui Wang (Prince Hui of the State of Wei) moved his capital eastward from Anyi in modern Shaanxi to Kaifeng, which he called Daliang. The move eastward was motivated by Hui's desire to put some distance between himself and a strong western neighbor, the rising state of Qin.

In some ways, the site was not advantageous for a capital. Lying on a wide open plain without physical barriers, the city was difficult to defend. Moreover, the site was at risk of frequent flooding by the unpredictable Yellow River, even though at the time it ran some twenty-five miles north of the city. A system of dikes formed only a precarious defense against the river's massive flood waters. Yet the fertile flood plains were a tremendous source of wealth, while the city's position in the vicinity of the Yellow River, the Ji River, and the Huai River, all major waterways flowing northeast or east to the Pacific Ocean, gave Kaifeng a strategic commercial advantage.

Hui began building a system of canals to join the many rivers and form a regional communication network with Daliang at its heart. Over the following century, the city grew into a major trading center as well as a seat of political power. But its growth was cut short in 255 B.C., when Wei's longtime enemy, the state of Qin, attacked the city. When Daliang refused to surrender, the Qin army breached a section of dike along the Yellow River. The resulting flood nearly wiped the city from the map. For the next six centuries, as the seat of an administrative district, it was of no more than provincial importance.

Under the Han Dynasty (206 B.C.–A.D. 220), the city underwent some reconstruction, however. In 168 B.C., Emperor Wen conferred the title Liang Xiao Wang (Prince Xiao of Liang) on his son, Liu Wu. Kaifeng became his capital. Liu Wu restored the city walls and undertook some further construction. Finding the city too damp for comfort, he moved his own residence to higher ground at Huayang. Although Kaifeng's political importance at this time was minimal, it became celebrated as a center of the arts, mostly music and poetry. Liu Wu built the Chuitai (Music Platform), in memory of the famous musician Shi Kuang from the state of Jin of the Spring and Autumn period (770–476 B.C.). The Chuitai lay southeast of the city proper, at Huayang, on a spot where Shi Kuang was said to have performed long ago. Here Liu Wu and his musician friends gathered to give private musical performances. The magnificent Liang Garden laid out around the Chuitai became legendary in Chinese literature. Three famous eighth-century Tang poets, Li Bo, Du Fu, and Gao Shi, visited Kaifeng and sang the praises of the garden. Ever since, the Liang Garden has become synonymous with Kaifeng and has spurred the imagination of generations of Chinese poets and literati.

The collapse of the Han Dynasty led to a long period of civil war and disorder, during which Kaifeng was a constant battlefield for contending forces. In 534 A.D. the city recovered somewhat, being made into the seat of the regional prefecture, but it was demoted later to a district seat again. However, by that time work had started on the Grand Canal, which initially joined the Yellow River to the Huai and later extended to the Yangzi as far south as Hangzhou, a major port on the southern coast. The first stretch, by itself, was more

The Iron Pagoda, Kaifeng
Photo courtesy of China National Tourist Office, Los Angeles

than 300 miles long. In 605, all males in the region between the age of fifteen and fifty—more than a million—were conscripted to dredge and widen the Bien River and build roads on both banks. Driven mercilessly by authorities trying to meet a deadline set by the emperor, thousands died of exhaustion and drowning.

When the Grand Canal was finished, the empire had connected Hangzhou with Beijing in the north and with Luoyang in the northwest, both cities almost 2,000 miles away from the port. As a consequence, it became possible to transport the products of southeast China more cheaply and efficiently to the north, to meet the needs of cities in the interior. Emperor Yang of the Sui Dynasty (581–618), who had ordered the building of the canal, traveled by boat from Kaifeng to Yangzhou three times. On the first trip, his retinue, including palace women, officials, and monks, numbered more than 100,000. About 80,000 of them were employed to pull his convoy of boats, which was more than sixty miles long, through the canal.

Under the Tang Dynasty (618–907), Kaifeng, then known as Bienjing, was made a prefecture again. Moreover, after the An-Shih Rebellion (755–763), the Tang government stationed a strong military force there to defend it. In 781, the military commander rebuilt the city wall to a length of more than six miles. Because of its position at a nodal point in the system of rivers and canals that interconnected the distant parts of the huge Chinese empire, Kaifeng's volume of trade increased. The city also recovered some of its former cultural significance; poets, artists, and scholars visited Bienjing and left favorable reports of its amenities. However, the latter days of the Tang were marked by wars and disorder that brought serious hardship to Kaifeng. It is estimated that its population declined from about 600,000 to about 83,000 in that period.

The founder of the Later Liang (907–923), the first dynasty of the Five Dynasties period, made Kaifeng his capital and also elevated the Bien prefecture to a commandery with jurisdiction over both the Junyi and the Kaifeng counties. To house the offices of the commandery, a new walled section was created inside the city, but otherwise few changes took place. Altogether, four dynasties of the Five Dynasties period made Kaifeng their capital, but these reigns were too unstable to bring much benefit to the city. It was not until the end of the period, when Kaifeng became the capital of the Later Zhou Dynasty (951–960), that its political importance began to translate into real advantages.

In 955, Emperor Zhou Shizhong created a plan for Kaifeng's outer city. An outer wall was built by more than 100,000 laborers conscripted for the project. The resulting structure was more than fifteen miles long, and it was said to be as strong as any wall in existence. The new streets were straight and wide enough for large vehicles. Army barracks and storage buildings were constructed in carefully selected sites. The city's burial grounds were moved more than two miles outside the city. The emperor also restored the network of waterways, with Kaifeng once again the focal point. This construction program prepared Kaifeng for its role as the national capital of a unified China.

Zhou Shizhong died before he could consolidate his dynasty. He left a seven-year-old boy on the throne, which gave his popular commander in chief, Zhao Kuangyin, the opportunity to stage a coup d'état. In 960, Zhao left Kaifeng, leading his army north to fight an alleged advancing Khitan force. His brother and military officers staged a riot at the Chen Bridge about twelve miles north of Kaifeng, and Zhao was called to quell the disturbance. When he arrived, his co-conspirators forcibly placed the imperial robes on his shoulders. Zhao then returned to Kaifeng and tearfully asked the imperial widow and her son to make way for him. Since Zhao was supported by the army, the young emperor had little choice but to submit to the new regime, and thus the founding of the Northern Song Dynasty was accomplished. It took Zhao and his brother, who later succeeded him, twenty years to unify and consolidate their empire, which lasted until 1127. Kaifeng, then named Dongjing, prospered under the Song and became the foremost industrial and commercial center of China. At the time of the city's greatest prosperity, annual revenues collected by the government amounted to 550 million coins. Only two other cities in China had annual revenues exceeding 400 million coins.

The Song government stimulated production on an unprecedented scale. Eventually, state-owned craft industries alone employed as many as 80,000 craftsmen, technicians, and administrators. The armament industry was the single biggest employer, putting to work 3,700 armament specialists and 5,000 technicians. Iron foundries, arms factories, shipyards, weaving plants, pottery factories, tea plantations and processing plants, wineries, and printing presses formed the backbone of Kaifeng's industrial economy. Production was diversified and characterized by a high degree of division of labor. The weaving industry, for instance, at one time operated 400 looms and produced many types of textiles. Silk weavers, for instance, created more than forty different brocades and design patterns.

The merchant economy flourished also. Traders were organized into 160 different trade guilds; government records indicate that 6,400 major business houses and 20,000 business households were engaged in Kaifeng's trade. In addition to bringing local products to market across China, Kaifeng traders handled a major share of China's tributary trade with border states and trading centers in Southeast Asia, West Asia, and Africa. The city also supported a large foreign community, including Koreans, Japanese, Indonesians, Malays, Thai, Vietnamese, Indians, Arabs, Persians, and East Africans. Merchants were the most numerous, but missionaries and envoys to the Song court also played a significant role.

During these years, the city underwent many physical changes. One of the first of these involved the creation of an imperial city. The new rulers chose for their imperial quarters the old walled commandery area dating to the Tang period. In 962, they expanded the complex and extended the walls by more than a mile to create a city within the city. Both govern-

Dragon Hall, Kaifeng
Photo courtesy of China National Tourist Office, Los Angeles

ment offices and the imperial residence lay inside the walls, which were pierced by seven gates. The outer wall was redesigned and strengthened to a thickness of more than sixty-five feet and a height of more than forty feet. To enhance its defensive capabilities, it was laid out in curves. The wall was surrounded by a wide moat fed by four different rivers, three of which flowed through the city itself. The Bien River passed through the heart of the trading center and remained the most important waterway, both for military and commercial purposes. Later in the Song period the outer wall was straightened, apparently for aesthetic reasons.

The city was divided into a commercial and a residential area, according to ancient Chinese city-planning principles. Over time, however, growing commercial prosperity had the effect of blurring the boundaries, and the separation was no longer enforced. In 965, shopping hours were deregulated, with the result that business came to be conducted not only in the usual daytime business hours but also in the so-called Devils' Market, which operated until midnight.

According to one estimate, by the twelfth century the urban population had grown to 1.7 million. A city of Kaifeng's size naturally required an advanced system of government, and early in the eleventh century its administrative systems were revised. The city was divided into eight divisions and 120 subdivisions to meet administrative needs. An extensive police force attended to public order and security, with patrol offices—each staffed by five soldiers—reportedly spaced a mere 100 feet apart along all of Kaifeng's streets. Because the use of wood and straw in construction created a significant fire hazard, every subdivision was equipped with fire watchtowers and heavily manned fire stations. To improve sanitation, sewage drains were installed to channel waste into the river.

Kaifeng supported a large and creative scientific community, and many inventions originated there, most notably the compass, movable type, and an armillary sphere that became the prototype of the modern astronomical clock. The city's large armament industry spurred the development of military technology, leading to an array of innovative designs for rockets, canons, and guns.

Neither its impressive fortifications nor its advances in weapons technology, however, were able to defend Kaifeng against the Jürchen invaders from Manchuria, who began to press into Song territories early in the twelfth century. In 1126, the Jürchen laid a long siege to Kaifeng, which soon suffered shortages of food and supplies so severe that an impoverished mob plundered the imperial garden for firewood. The following year, Kaifeng was starved into submission by the Jürchen. A remnant of the Song government fled south to Nanjing and later to Hangzhou, where the dynasty, under the name of the Southern Song, continued its reign for another 150 years. Meanwhile, the Jürchen Jin Dynasty, which now ruled much of northern China, established itself at Kaifeng. The city was renamed Bienjing and became one of the five capital cities of the Jin.

In 1153, the Jin ruler moved his capital from Manchuria to Beijing and at the same time undertook reconstructions at Kaifeng with the idea of making it his capital. He actually moved there in 1161, but he was soon murdered, and Beijing was restored as the capital. A prosperous Jewish community of traders and craftsmen, several hundred strong, sprang up during this time. Historians trace the arrival of the Jews to Kaifeng to the early twelfth century, although a tablet dated 1512 claims they entered China during the first centuries of the Common (Christian) Era. The oldest known synagogue in Kaifeng was built in 1163. The community declined in the seventeenth century, and disappeared altogether in the eighteenth.

Early in the thirteenth century, the Jin began to feel the pressures of the expanding Mongol Empire and moved their capital to Kaifeng once again. Both the outer and inner city walls were rebuilt, and an extra length of wall was added to the outer city. The imperial domain and palaces were extended and restored to their former glory. The move to Kaifeng was in vain, however. The Mongols destroyed the Jin Dynasty in 1234, and the victors, under the rule of the Yuan Dynasty, chose Beijing as their capital.

Kaifeng began to lose its political and economic eminence. The first blow to its commercial centrality was delivered by the construction of a new canal connecting Tianjin, Beijing, and the Yangzi basin, bypassing Kaifeng. The city was captured in the mid–fourteenth century by the Red Turban rebels, who held it as their capital for ten years, until they were crushed by the Ming Dynasty (1368–1644). Because of its history, the founder of the Ming Dynasty considered making Kaifeng his capital, but political and economic reality favored first Nanjing and later Beijing. Kaifeng's central political role in China had come to an end. The city became the capital of Henan province and was governed by the emperor's son Zhou Wang, who built a huge princely residence on the palace site of the former Song and Jin Dynasties and reconstructed the walls.

The steady decline of Kaifeng since the Song Dynasty also was a result of the mercurial behavior of the Yellow River, which changed its course many times in this period. The first of these changes occurred in 1194 and took the river to a distance of approximately thirteen miles from the city. A new change of course in 1391 brought the river so close that Kaifeng virtually sat on its south bank. In 1448 it again broke through the dike, and Kaifeng found itself on the river's north bank. Thirteen years later the Yellow River again swung north of the city. Since 1493, the Yellow River has followed its present course, passing Kaifeng to the north by about six miles. Major floods accompanied these changes in course.

During the peasant rebellions of the late Ming period, Kaifeng again suffered a flood disaster, this one caused by human interference. In 1642 the city was surrounded by peasant rebels who, when they failed to take Kaifeng by force, decided to starve the defenders to their knees with a siege that lasted from April to September. In desperation, the defenders breached the dike at two places northwest of Kaifeng. The rebels abandoned the siege, but the whole city was submerged. Only about 30,000 of the 370,000 inhabitants survived. Two years later, when it came under the control of the Qing Dynasty (1644–1912), Kaifeng and its vicinity were still covered with yellow water and sand. Reconstruction was slow. In 1662 the city was rebuilt on the Ming foundations, and in 1718 a new inner city was built northeast of the former Ming palace to house a garrison. After another disastrous flood in 1841, Kaifeng was again rebuilt, essentially in the shape the city retains today. Only traces of the great Song city remain.

Flooding was not over yet, however. Statistics reveal that, on average, the Yellow River overflowed its banks twice every three years. Between 1855 and 1938, its lower reaches were flooded no less than fifty-seven times. Kaifeng itself was flooded six times, while the surrounding area was submerged more than forty times. As a result, all the rivers and lakes that gave Kaifeng its economic prosperity were buried or choked by mud and became unusable. The soil became alkaline, and the forests and other vegetation were all destroyed. Kaifeng itself lay in a basin 130 feet below the Yellow River dike.

In the early twentieth century, Kaifeng's economy suffered another blow when it was bypassed by the Beijing-Guangzhou railway. The city saw some new industrial development, but the traditions of city planning were long forgotten. Unplanned, sprawling outgrowths were the result. By 1954, Kaifeng had declined so much that it lost its status as the provincial capital to Zhengzhou. Today, Kaifeng is an autonomous municipality and a regional administrative center. Modern technology has succeeded in containing the destructive power of the Yellow River. The city has undergone some beautification, and the countryside is productive again. With an eye to Kaifeng's rich history, provincial authorities have floated an ambitious plan to recreate an entire Song city in the middle of modern Kaifeng. The plan would involve rebuilding Song temples, pagodas, and government buildings. The descendants of Song traders would be invited to return and set up shop once more. Artists and artisans practicing their crafts with ancient methods and equipment would operate along the canals and in the temples and shrines. The scheme is perhaps too grand to be realized, but Kaifeng's Song past is certainly worth a great deal of attention.

Further Reading: *The Yellow River: A 5,000 Year Journey through China* by Kevin Sinclair (London: Weidenfeld and Nicholson, 1987), based on the BBC television documentary of the same name, gives a fascinating account of the civilizations, ancient and modern, along the Yellow River and touches on Kaifeng's history at various points. *Cambridge Encyclopedia of China*, edited by Brian Hook and Denis Crispin Twitchett (Cambridge and New York: Cambridge University Press, 1982; second edition, 1991), is also a mine of information.

—Kit S. Liew and Marijke Rijsberman

Kamakura (Kanagawa, Japan)

Location: On the Pacific coast of the island of Honshū in Kanagawa prefecture, twenty-eight miles southwest of Tōkyō and ten miles south of Yokohama.

Description: Seat of the first Japanese *shōgunate* (military government) from 1185 to 1333, a center of Japanese Buddhism, and now also a holiday resort.

Site Office: Kamakura City Tourist Information Service
JR Kamakura Station
Komachi
Kamakura, Kanagawa
Japan
(467) 22 3350

By contemporary Japanese standards, Kamakura is a relatively small city, its population only around 140,000, its main streets and buildings crammed between the Pacific Ocean to the south and deeply wooded mountains to the east and west. Yet this seaside resort, close enough to both Tōkyō and Yokohama to be a bedroom community for thousands who work in those giant cities, was once the center of political power in Japan. Like Nara, another former capital, it continues to hold a special place in Japanese cultures; also like Nara, it has an entire period of Japanese history named for it.

Kamakura was founded in the eighth century, or perhaps earlier, in a region remote from the centers of population in the Kinki (the Home Provinces, around modern Ōsaka, Nara, and Kyōto). For many years it was an obscure fishing village, spread around two Buddhist temples, both dedicated to Kannon (Avalokitesvara in Sanskirt), the goddess of mercy. The temple known variously as Sugimoto-dera, Sampon-ji, or Okura no Kannon is said to have been established by a priest called Gyoki in 734, although its present buildings were completed in 1678. They contain three statues of Kannon in her eleven-headed form, one of which is said to have been sculpted by Gyoki himself. By contrast, the Hasedera Temple, founded in 736, contains just one image of her, a gilded wooden figure nearly thirty feet tall. According to legend, this statue was brought ashore at Kamakura after having been carved hundreds of miles away at the original Hasedera, in the town of Hase (now in Nara prefecture), and then set adrift as an offering.

The Kamakura period, which saw the transformation of this village, is conventionally said to have begun in 1191, when the warlord Yoritomo, whose father had lived there, chose it as the location for his new military regime, known as the Bakufu (tent government). Yoritomo had come to prominence about twenty-five years before as the head of the Minamoto family, also known as the Genji, which had long been powerful in the eastern provinces of Japan. They led the opposition to the Taira family, also known as the Heike, whose head, Kiyomori, had seized power in the capital, Heian-kyo (now Kyōto), in 1156. Following Kiyomori's death, Yoritomo's younger half-brother, Yoshitsune, had won two significant victories over the disunited Taira, at Yashima, on the island of Shikoku, in 1181 and then at Dan-no-Ura, at the western end of the island of Honshū, in 1185; and since the infant emperor Antoku had drowned with many of the Taira at Dan-no-Ura, there was a vacuum of power that Yoritomo hastened to fill. The Minamoto took the place of the Taira as guardians of the imperial line and therefore as the political and military masters of the country. What happened next has provided the basis for numerous legends embodied in verse, drama, and painting ever since: Yoritomo turned against Yoshitsune, drove him out into the wilderness, and then had him killed; according to one version of the story, however, Yoshitsune escaped and reappeared later as Genghis Khan.

Kamakura now began to be more than just a village and the site of one of Yoritomo's military camps. In 1188 the *samurai* (warrior) Ashikaga Yoshikane, an ally of Yoritomo's, founded the temple Jomyo-ji on his family estate in Kamakura. Most of the complex has been destroyed over the centuries, and only one building remains, completed as recently as 1756. In 1911 Yoritomo had himself appointed *Sei-i-tai shōgun* (Barbarian-suppressing Great General) by the emperor Toba II, whom he had raised to the throne in 1183, even before Antoku's death, and who remained in Heian-kyo. Thus began the first of the *shōgunates*, the *samurai*-based regimes that, at least formally, would govern Japan in the name of the powerless emperors for all but a few of the next 677 years.

Yoritomo commemorated his achievement of this supreme effective power over Japan by having his family's Shintō shrine, founded by his ancestor Yoriyoshi in 1063, moved to his new city. The contemporary version of this shrine, appropriately dedicated to Hachiman, the god of war, was completed in 1828 after—as usual with wooden buildings in Japan—centuries of building, destruction by fire, and rebuilding. It stands above a pond known as Genpei no Ike, the pool of the Minamoto and Taira, which contains white lotuses for the former, red for the latter, on Tsurugaoka (Crane Hill), at the head of Wakamiya-oji, a straight avenue running through Kamakura down to the seashore. It also houses the city museum, a gallery of modern art, and a training center for martial arts. Nearby are a smaller shrine dedicated to Inari, the fox-god who protects rice harvests, marked by numerous small wooden *torii* (shrine gates), and the Wakamiya (junior shrine) for which the avenue is named, a group of black-lacquered buildings first constructed in 1624.

Great Buddha, Kamakura
Photo courtesy of Japan National Tourist Organization

Yoritomo is also said to have founded still another shrine, dedicated to Benten (in Sanskrit Bishamonten, the only female among the seven Gods of Fortune), which stands in a heavily wooded gorge to the west of Tsurugaoka. This shrine, one of the most popular places in the city, is famous as Zeniarai (money-washing) Benten. It is said that those who dip their money into the shrine's spring, one of its many streams and pools, or even the smoke of one of its incense-burners, will receive the same amount again. The buildings that housed Yoritomo's Bakufu were destroyed long ago, and their site to the east of Tsurugaoka is now occupied by the education and fine arts faculties of Yokohama University.

Kamakura was favored by Yoritomo and his successors not only for its defensible site and its historic connection with their hereditary estates, but probably also for its sheer distance from the old capital, which the samurai may well have regarded as decadent and corrupting. By the time Yoritomo died in 1199, Kamakura, with a new harbor built on the ocean shore, had begun to be integrated into the network of coastal shipping that already connected the underpopulated eastern region in which it stands with the centers of population and economic activity around Kyōto. The warlord who had brought the town its new status and prosperity lies beneath a simple cairn of stones near Yokohama University.

Yoritomo's widow, Masako, the daughter of the warlord Hōjō Tokimasa, who had allied himself to Yoritomo in spite of his own Taira ancestry, was a powerful figure in her own right, even after she entered a convent at her husband's death—hence her nickname, Ama-Shōgun (the nun-*shōgun*). In 1203 she and her father led the conspirators who replaced her elder son Yoriie with her younger and more favored son Sanetomo as *shōgun*; two years later she did not hesitate to have her father exiled when he turned against her. Then in 1219, after Sanetomo was assassinated by his nephew, Yoriie's son Kugyo, the priest in charge of the Hachiman shrine, she arranged for him to be deified along with his father at another Shintō shrine near Tsurugaoka, known as Shirahata-gu (white banner shrine) in reference to the flag of the Minamoto family, and had an infant from the noble Fujiwara family in Kyōto appointed as *shōgun* in his place. The *shōguns*, regents for the emperors, would now be superseded by regents in their turn, since the Minamoto line, extinct with Kugyo's execution, was effectively replaced by Masako's Hōjō relatives.

In 1221 the Hōjō easily defeated an uprising by supporters of Toba II, now technically in retirement but still influential in Kyōto, and still resentful of the *samurai's* power over Japan. After Masako's death in 1225, her relatives followed her lead by arranging for nonentities from the imperial and Fujiwara families to fill the post of *shōgun* while they acted as *shikken* (regents). Under the terms of their laws, proclaimed at Kamakura and imposed on the old nobility at Kyōto—notably the *Joei Shikimoku* of 1232—Japan was ruled by *jito* (stewards) on Bakufu lands and by *shugo* (constables) elsewhere, offices that were filled by *samurai* rather than courtiers.

Masako also initiated the Hōjō custom of patronizing the popular new Buddhist sects—often collectively referred to as Kamakura Buddhism—then developing in Japan in response to the decline of the Kyōto court and its patronage of the older sects, the arrival of another wave of ideas from China, and the growing insecurity of life in uncertain conditions that many Buddhists regarded as signs of *Mappo,* the predicted last stage of the Buddha's teachings before the end of the world. Masako seems to have been attracted (it is not known how sincerely) both to the worship of Amida (in Sanskrit Amitabha, Buddha of the western paradise known as Jodo, or Pure Land), and to the Zen practice of meditation. In 1200 she founded the temple of Jufuku-ji, near where Yoritomo's father had lived, and gave it to Eisai, founder of the Rinzai sect of Zen Buddhism; she is said to have been buried in its grounds.

Masako also founded Kotokuin-Josen-ji, an Amidist temple that no longer exists. In its place is the most visited structure in the city, the Kotokuin Daibutsu (Great Buddha). This hollow statue of Amida seated in meditation, made of bronze plates laid over a frame, more than 37 feet high and weighing 120 tons, was installed in 1252, to replace a wooden statue of Amida donated to the temple by Masako. At that time it was the main image inside the temple's worship hall, but ever since the destruction of the building by a tidal wave in 1495 the Great Buddha has been exposed to the open air. It is now situated inside a garden, in which the trees have been laid out in such a pattern that the statue suddenly appears to visitors as they turn a corner on the path from the street; and it is especially popular among children because a door in its back provides access to its cool, dark interior.

The Hōjō regents also sponsored the building of several temples in the city during their 116 years in power. Among those which remain today are Komyo-ji, founded by Hōjō Tsunetoki in 1243, which is famous for its *emakimono,* horizontal paintings on silk; Jokomyo-ji, founded by Hōjō Nagatoki in 1251; Gokuraku-ji, founded by Hōjō Shigetoki in 1259, which houses a standing image, dating from the twelfth century, of the historical Buddha, Siddhārtha Gautama; and Tokei-ji, founded by Hōjō Kakusan, widow of the regent Tokimune, in 1285, which is better known as the Enkiri-dera, the temple of cutting the ties, because of its traditional role as a refuge for women escaping from unhappy marriages.

However, the largest and best known of the Hōjō foundations are the Zen temples, most of them in the hills to the north of the old city. Zen Buddhism, the form of the religion that places most emphasis on meditation—*dhyana* in Sanskrit, *zen* in Japanese—had existed within the older sects for hundreds of years but became a separate movement after the arrival in Kamakura and elsewhere of Chinese priests who practiced what they called *ch'an* and who were fleeing from the Mongol invasion of their homeland. Zen was never to become more than a minority movement in Japan and, in spite of its popular image outside the country, is in many ways atypical of Japanese religion and culture. But the minority it first appealed to was the most important one, the samurai elite headed by the Hōjō family.

Masako's Jufuku-ji seems to have been the first Zen temple in Kamakura, but the leading Zen temple in the city has long been Kencho-ji, which was established by Hōjō Tokiyori in 1253 as a residence for the Chinese priest Tao-Lung, known in Japan as Rankei Doryu. Its characteristically austere buildings, laid out on a single axis among paulownias and juniper trees said to have been grown from seeds brought from China, were destroyed by fire in 1415 and replaced during the seventeenth century by the priest Takuan, under another family of shoguns, the Tokugawa; but he is believed to have retained the original layout and external appearance of the complex. The treasures displayed in the temple's Hondo (Main Hall) include a number of *emakimono* and a statue of the founder. Today it is surrounded by a forest of Japanese cedars and other trees. It stands opposite Enno-ji, a much smaller temple, founded in 1250, which houses statues of Enma, the king of the dead, the nine other kings of Hell, and Datsueba, the aged woman who removes the clothing of the dead after they have crossed over from the world of the living.

Three other Zen temples stand out either for the treasures they contain or for their locations. Jochi-ji, established in 1281, houses a famous group statue, the Sanzebutsu (Buddhas of Three Worlds), representing Siddhārtha Gautama, the Buddha who lived and died in India (called Shaka in Japan), Amida, and Miroku (Maitreya in Sanskrit), the Buddha who is to be incarnated in the distant future. Engaku-ji, founded in 1283 by Hōjō Tokiyori's son and successor Tokimune, has since spread over its steep hillside and now includes seventeen sub-temples, among which one, the Shozoku-in, contains the thatch-roofed Shariden (Relic Hall), in which is kept a tooth said to be one of the Gautama's. The Engaku-ji complex was badly damaged in the Great Kanto Earthquake of 1923, and a railroad now bisects its grounds. Finally, Zuisen-ji, on the eastern outskirts of the city, was founded in 1327 by the priest Soseki and is famous for its orchards of plum trees and Japanese maples.

In contrast to their patronage of Zen and their tolerance of the Pure Land sects, the Hōjō regents were consistently hostile to the third form of Kamakura Buddhism, initiated by the thirteenth-century priest Nichiren when he founded yet another sect, named for himself. Soon after beginning to preach the supremacy of the ancient Buddhist text known in Japan as the *Myoho Renge Kyo* (the Lotus Sutra), along with his unique right as an incarnation of the Bodhisattva Jogyo to interpret that text's meaning, Nichiren left Kyōto for Kamakura to challenge what he saw as the political and religious errors of the Hōjō regime, including their inexplicable reluctance to submit to his authority and join him in denouncing all the existing Buddhist sects as heretical. The regent Tokiyori responded by sentencing him to two periods of exile and, according to legend, later ordering his execution. (Nichiren's sect's temple of Ryūkō-ji, to the west along the coast from Kamakura, is said to mark the spot where, in 1271, a lightning bolt struck the sword from the executioner's hand.)

In spite of such setbacks, Nichiren eventually gained more followers through his claims to have predicted, or even caused, the storms that repelled the attempted invasions of Japan by the Mongols in 1274 and 1281 (the basis of the myth of the *kamikaze,* the "divine wind" that would protect Japan from its enemies). There are three major temples of Nichiren's sect in Kamakura: Myōhon-ji, founded by his disciple Hiki Daigakusaburo in 1274; Hongaku-ji, established in 1436 on the site of one of Nichiren's residences to house a portion of his ashes, brought from his tomb in Yamanashi prefecture; and Ankokuroni-ji, established during the eighteenth century and named for Nichiren's memorandum to Hōjō Tokiyori, *Rissho Ankokuron.* He is said to have written it in 1260 in a cave that can be seen on the temple's grounds. Today Nichiren's ideas still play a part in Japanese society, notably through the Soka Gakkai, an organization of laypeople loyal to his teachings, which sponsors the Komeito, a political party with several members in the Japanese Diet, and which has attracted disciples in Europe and the Americas.

Kamakura's temples, whether affiliated with Pure Land, Zen, Nichiren or other sects, contain numerous statues made during the revival of religious sculpture, which took place during the thirteenth century. This movement is often called Kamakura sculpture, although Kyōto and Nara were also centers of the new technique of *yosegi-zukuri,* the making of statues from several pieces of wood fitted and glued together, which came to replace the older *ichiboku-zukuri* technique of carving a single block, exemplified by the Kannon at Hasedera. Among those statues now displayed in the city's Municipal Museum of Fine Art, the most outstanding are generally held to be the figures of Kannon from the Tokei-ji temple; Jizo, the Bodhisattva who protects travelers and children, from the Jochi-ji; and Shoko-o, one of the Buddhist kings of Hell from the Enno-ji. Other statues from the period exist elsewhere in the city, such as the jade-eyed statue of Jizo in Jufuku-ji; the triad of Yakushi Nyorai, the Buddha associated with healing, and his two attendant Bodhisattvas in Kakuon-ji, a temple founded in 1218 by the Hōjō family; and the memorial statue of Hōjō Tokiyori in Kencho-ji. Something of this tradition continues in the lacquered woodcarvings, known as Kamakura-bori, which still feature among the products of the city, although most contemporary examples of it are machine-made items for the tourist trade.

The Kemmu Restoration, the brief seizure of power in and around Kyōto by Emperor Daigo II in 1331, was the catalyst for the collapse of the Hōjō regime. Ashikaga Takauji, the general sent west by Hōjō Takatori to crush the imperial forces, eventually decided to take power himself. In 1333 Takauji's ally Nitta Yoshisada seized control of Kamakura and forced Takatori and about 870 of his advisers and samurai to commit *seppuku,* the stomach-piercing form of suicide also known as *hara-kiri.* The cave in which they gathered to die, still pointed out today, was in the grounds of the Hōjō family's temple, Tōshō-ji, which has long since disappeared but is believed to have stood near the family residence, itself later replaced by another temple, Hokai-ji. Meanwhile, Takauji first worked with Daigo and then, when he proved reluctant to reward him, pushed him and his followers out of the capital into the mountains of Yoshino. By 1338 Takauji had installed another branch of the imperial family on the throne and made himself *shōgun.* The Kamakura period had come to its end.

The new *shōgun* had ensured that no resistance would be mounted from Kamakura by installing his own troops there in 1335. One of their duties was to keep guard on Daigo's son Prince Morinaga, who had been taken hostage and eventually died in captivity in Kamakura in 1335. In 1349, having established himself in Kyōto, Takauji made his nine-year-old son Motouji *kanryo* (governor) of Kamakura and therefore nominal ruler of the eastern provinces, although effective power rested in the hands of the Uesugi family. The Uesugi commemorated their triumph, in the time-honored fashion of Japanese victors, by endowing yet another temple, Meigetsu-in, but they were not left to enjoy it in peace for long. For more than 100 years the city was the location for repeated conflicts between Motouji's branch of the Ashikaga family and the Uesugi, culminating in 1454 with the murder of Uesugi Noritada, the destruction of much of the city by his enraged followers, and the hurried departure of his rival Ashikaga Shigeuji. The Hōjō family, still nursing their historic grievance against both the Ashikaga and their Uesugi allies, took advantage of this crisis to begin working against both families. During the civil wars that spread throughout Japan in the sixteenth century, the Japanese made themselves rulers of the Kanto plain from their castle at Odawara, so that by 1519 Kamakura had lost even the vestiges of its former political status.

Even so, Kamakura remained important as a religious center throughout the following centuries, during which the Ashikaga *shōgunate* declined and collapsed (in 1573) and the Tokugawa *shōguns* controlled Japan from their castle at Edo (now Tōkyō), between 1603 and their downfall in 1868. In 1869 the new Japanese government installed in Tōkyō sponsored the establishment of the Kamakura-gu (Kamakura shrine) in memory of Daigo's son Morinaga, as one of many expressions of their policy of downgrading the various families of *shōguns* in Japanese history and building up the prestige of the imperial family. The shrine stands near the cave in which Morinaga was held captive. Continuing the pattern of combining modernization with selective revival of the past, the city's Municipal Museum of Fine Art was opened in 1928 in a concrete building known as the Kokuho-kan (National Treasures Building), designed to resemble an *azekura,* a wooden storehouse of the Nara period (710–784), in which to display selections from among approximately 2,000 statues, paintings, scrolls, and other objects saved from the destruction of an older museum by the Great Kanto Earthquake of 1923.

Like other historic capitals such as Nara and Kyōto, Kamakura was deliberately exempted form bombing by American planes during World War II. Since the defeat of Japan in 1945, Kamakura has taken up once more its most enduring role, not as a place of political intrigue and military adventure, but as a destination both for Buddhist pilgrims and secular sight-seers. It has added to its historic attractions a Museum of Modern Art, opened in 1951 in a Modernist building set on metal columns on the shore of the Genpei no Ike.

Further Reading: Michael Cooper's *Exploring Kamakura* (Tōkyō and New York: Weatherhill, 1979) is perhaps the most interesting of the small number of books about the city obtainable outside Japan. The varieties of Kamakura Buddhism are usefully explored in books by H. Byron Earhart, notably *Japanese Religion: Unity and Diversity* (Belmont, California: Wadsworth, 1969; third edition, 1982). The Taira and the Minamoto are described in two medieval works that deserve to be better known, *The Tale of the Heike,* translated by Hiroshi Kitagawa and Bruce T. Tsuchida (Tōkyō: University of Tōkyō Press, 1975), and *Yoshitsune,* translated by Helen Craig McCullough (Tōkyō: University of Tōkyō Press, and Stanford, California: Stanford University Press, 1966).

—Patrick Heenan

Kanazawa (Ishikawa, Japan)

Location: Along the northwest side of Honshū, Japan's main island, facing the Sea of Japan, 180 miles west-northwest of Tōkyō.

Description: Once a castle town, now the capital of Ishikawa prefecture, with a population of more than 450,000; seat of the lordly Maeda family during the period of the Tokugawa *shōgunate.*

Site Office: Kanazawa Tourist Office
3-1, Hirookamachi
Kanazawa, Ishikawa
Japan
(762) 31 6311

Kanazawa, currently the capital of the Ishikawa prefecture, once was a wealthy castle town run by the Maeda, one of Japan's most powerful clans during the Tokugawa period. Although most of the family's original castle has been destroyed by fire, a garden of the early lords has been well preserved: Kenrokuen Park, designated a national "famous spot" in 1922. The Edo-period garden is one of the most magnificent parks in Japan. It and other historic sites in Kanazawa give the city the atmosphere of "old Japan."

The origins of Kanazawa are buried in legend. As the story goes, 1,200 years ago a peasant farmer and a wealthy young woman named Wako came together because of a vision. Both the farmer, Imohori Tōgorō, and Wako's father dreamed of a visitation from the goddess of mercy, Kannon. The goddess prophesied that the two should marry; however, Wako would have to give up luxuries in order to be with the farmer. They lived happily for many years until one day Wako's father sent bundles of gold to her. Not aware of the value of gold, Tōgorō innocently fed the gold to ducks. Wako was upset, but Tōgorō grabbed a sack of potatoes and led her to a nearby well. He scrubbed the potatoes in the water and gold appeared. The couple distributed the gold to neighbors and commissioned a statue of Kannon to be built. The well and the statue of Kannon are now located in Kanazawa's Kenrokuen Park. The legend gave Kanazawa its name, which means "marsh of gold." It can be deduced from the legend that the area was not only a source of agricultural products, but of gold deposits as well. In fact, Kanazawan handicrafts, such as Kutani pottery and lacquered tea ware, often are adorned with gold lace.

Thus, the area saw mostly peaceful agrarian activity through the twelfth century. During this period, however, certain farming families became increasingly prosperous, some achieving status of lord. One such family was the Togashi, who built a fortress at nearby Takao. Their survival depended on rice taxes, border traffic, and their own vast accumulation of wealth.

In the late fifteenth century, the period of the warring states began. The Ashikaga *shōgunate* had difficulty maintaining military control outside its Kyōto capital. Its limited authority led to many power struggles, such as the Ōnin War (1467–77) and the peasant uprisings in 1485, and resulted in the emergence of a number of *daimyō* (lords), whose families consolidated and controlled great portions of land. Farmers all over Japan were forced both to supply sustenance to and serve as soldiers in the continuous battles. Concurrently, Buddhism, imported to Japan by the king of Paekche in Korea as early as A.D. 552, had spread considerably. One branch of Buddhism that won particularly strong support from the long-suffering peasants was the Ikkō sect, which chose the future site of Kanazawa as its headquarters. Located on a rise of land between the Sai and Asano Rivers, the area was then called Oyama Gobō, a choice location for the Ikkō priests. One of the most influential leaders of Ikkō, Rennyo, the eighth head priest of the sect, taught that the peasants would find a happy afterlife with the Amida Buddha. A charismatic and successful leader, he encouraged the local peasant uprising of 1485, which led to three years of fighting and ended with the Ikkō priests in firm control of Oyama Gobō and the surrounding province of Kaga. This "peasants' kingdom" endured for nearly 100 years. The Ikkō sect was aided by an alliance with the Ishiyama Honganji priests of Ōsaka, who established a branch at Oyama Gobō.

Still, other leaders had designs on the region. A warrior named Oda Nobunaga had conquered much of Japan in the late sixteenth century, and in 1580 he sent his forces into Oyama Gobō, which they captured. The peasants' kingdom came to an end.

In 1582, the powerful Oda Nobunaga, just short of attaining national control, was assassinated in Kyōto. In the fight to succeed him, the two leading contenders were Toyotomi Hideyoshi and Shibata Katsuie. To settle the dispute, Katsuie marched his armies into Ōmi early in 1583 and engaged Hideyoshi's armies in battle. Hideyoshi was victorious, pushing Katsuie back into a castle at Kita-no-shō (now Fukui): Katsuie committed suicide when the castle fell after a three-day siege. A powerful warrior by the name of Maeda Toshiie initially had supported Katsuie, but after Hideyoshi gained the advantage in 1583, Toshiie reassessed the situation and shrewdly backed Hideyoshi instead. Hideyoshi, aware of the Maeda family's power, accepted Toshiie into his army. After Katsuie's death, Toshiie led an attack against Katsuie's remaining troops at Oyama Gobō. Toshiie's army took the town easily. Soon afterward, Hideyoshi triumphantly marched through the city and assigned Toshiie two more districts to head in Kaga, which doubled his already impressive realm. He also was instructed to move his headquarters to Oyama Gobō, which was thereafter referred to as Kanazawa.

Kanazawa Castle
Photo courtesy of Japan National Tourist Organization

Maeda quickly converted Kanazawa from a small religious center to a powerful castle town. The castle was located where the Honganji headquarters formerly stood, on ground between the Sai and Asano Rivers. Construction was an enormous project. For security, massive castle walls were built, measuring approximately 738 yards east to west and 733 yards north to south with a height of 197 feet and a thickness of 6.5 feet. Rocks were carted from a quarry approximately 50 miles to the east; they were cut in the desired shapes before being lifted into place. Dozens of workers were killed during construction, as sections of the walls collapsed twice. Using water from the Sai and Asano Rivers, the laborers also created a labyrinth of moats and canals around the castle walls. Although the Honganji officials had dug some moats prior to 1583, the Maeda expanded the system considerably.

In the next decade, the Maeda family arranged the dwellings of the town's inhabitants for strategic purposes. The castle had nine enclosures, with the most secure of these assigned to the royal family. The *samurai* warriors and important administrators occupied the other enclosures. Later, some royal aides were moved outside the castle to guard approaches from the northwest and southeast. Houses were constructed with secret rooms and escape routes; some houses appeared to be four stories yet were actually seven. Temples that had been associated with the Honganji alliance were transported to new sites, most within a mile of the castle. One reason for this was to allow officials to keep a close watch over the monks; another was to make the temples available for use as temporary garrisons. The Maeda family also endowed a new group of temples and shrines that conducted official ceremonies for the family and had the right to collect taxes from surrounding villages.

In the spring of 1599, prior to the completion of these massive construction projects, Maeda Toshiie died. There soon arose rumors that his successor, his son Maeda Toshinaga, was plotting a campaign against Tokugawa Ieyasu, who was to establish the Tokugawa *shōgunate*. Toshinaga may have considered an attack, but in the end he pursued the diplomatic strategy characteristic of his father;

he allied himself with the dominant power. To quell the rumors, Toshinaga sent his mother to the capital city of Edo (Tōkyō) in order to become a hostage at the Tokugawa stronghold there. It was customary for many of the powerful *daimyō* to send wives or other relatives to be hostages to show their allegiance to central authority.

In 1616, numerous temples were moved southwest of the castle across the Sai River to form a new urban center. Other temples were moved to the base of Mount Utatsu, across the Asano River. There were two principal reasons for this reorganization: first, to improve defenses by connecting the temples with new *samurai* residences on the town's perimeter, and second, to provide more living space for the expanding commoner population, composed of merchants and artisans and known as *chōnin*. The *chōnin* were in great demand during this period; all castle towns required them to produce and distribute military equipment. The Maeda *daimyō* had to lure the *chōnin* to the city, therefore, by providing grants of land for shops and residences.

Another project of this decade was the diversion of a secondary branch of the Sai River into the main channel. This undertaking, the construction and transfer of temples, and the expansion of the castle encouraged a great deal of economic growth. The government invested substantial sums in these efforts, which drew carpenters, stone artisans, and the like to the burgeoning city. Other business activities developed, such as horse trading and the sale of fish and vegetables. One group of marketplaces for these activities was built just north of the castle near a bridge across the Asano River; a second group was built near the Sai River bridge. Roads were also constructed as early as 1610, one stretching from the port of Miyonokoshi to the northwestern entrance of the castle town. Additionally, during this period the government dug a canal between the Asano River and the Shimoyasuechō ward northeast of the castle to provide more docking and storage facilities for barges coming upriver.

The early Maeda lords—Toshiie, Toshinaga, and Toshitsune, who came to power in 1614—laid the foundations of Kanazawa's system of government. The municipal laws did not treat all citizens equally; the *samurai* enjoyed certain privileges the *chōnin* did not. At the same time, however, many members of the *chōnin* class played important roles in city administration. Although the Maeda held the ultimate power, they recognized that all the classes of the city shared common interests.

Street crime was a major problem in the early seventeenth century, and many of Kanazawa's laws dealt with acts of violence. Punishment often was severe. In some cases, theft was punished by boiling the perpetrator to death in a barrel. Crucifixion was another common means of execution. The government applied penalties equally across all class levels and viewed the severity of punishment as a deterrent to further crime. In the cases of thievery, even children were put to death.

The third Maeda lord, Toshitsune, was a great patron of the arts. From 1610 to 1620, Kanazawa saw the development of Kabuki drama, popularized by traveling troupes of players. Kanazawa residents received the performances enthusiastically. There was a seamier side to Kabuki, however: troupe members, both male and female, often doubled as prostitutes, and their entourages included members of criminal gangs, who frequently got into fights with locals. After outbreaks of violence in 1611 and 1612, Kabuki performances were banned in Kanazawa. The prohibition, however, was unpopular and short-lived. In 1614, Toshiie's widow, Hōshun'in, who had been sent to Edo in 1599 as a political gesture, returned to Kanazawa, and Toshitsune sponsored a series of Kabuki performances for her. Other forms of entertainment also flourished, such as *jōruri* musical drama, *ayatsuri* puppet theatre, and *noh* drama. These forms of entertainment helped the various social classes mix. The Maeda lords also developed the rituals of the tea ceremony; this elite activity eventually filtered down to the common people. Not all of Kanazawa's social life was so exalted; houses of prostitution did a brisk business.

By 1630, Kanazawa had grown from a community of a few thousand individuals to a major urban center of 50,000. With the period of the warring states over and the Tokugawa *shōgunate* in firm control at Edo, the importance of the *samurai* class diminished while that of the *chōnin* increased. The *daimyō* were forced to reside half of the year in Edo, leaving Kanazawa to govern itself and therefore enlarging the power of the local authorities.

Two fires, in 1631 and 1635, caused great damage to the castle town. The government had to reorganize the city and relocate the merchants and many of the *samurai*. Other changes occurred at this time; with the realm at peace and the role of the *samurai* growing smaller, many artisans who had specialized in weapons turned to making household utensils.

At midcentury the local government became increasingly bureaucratic. It enacted a number of laws aimed at maintaining class distinctions, but other legislation was reformatory and egalitarian in nature, such as a system of uniform tax rates that freed peasants from the whims of their landlords. (It must be noted that the new tax system, while standardized, increased the overall tax burden and put a strain on the more marginal tenant farmers.)

During the remainder of the seventeenth century, Kanazawa became a rather more staid community. There were new regulations on prostitution and theatrical performances and voluntary limits on urban growth. The *chōnin* continued to dominate the city's economy, and Kanazawa continued to prosper through the remaining years of the Tokugawa *shōgunate*. The Maeda were on especially good terms with the Tokugawa, and several marriages took place between members of the two families. As a result, the Maeda, unlike some *daimyō* families, never had their lands reduced. This loyalty to the *shōgun* worked against the Maeda when the Tokugawa regime was overthrown in the middle of the nineteenth century. The Maeda had little power under the new Meiji rulers, and Kanazawa declined both in economic and political importance. The *samurai*, most of whom lost their jobs, began to leave

Kanazawa, and the remaining residents adapted by developing a textile industry and producing and selling traditional crafts, such as lacquer and pottery. Kanazawa never became a major industrial center, however, and this factor helped spare it from destruction in World War II.

The Maeda castle has been damaged by several fires, but its remains are still impressive. They consist of a number of buildings as well as the outer protective walls, replete with watchtowers. At the corner of the castle walls is Kenrokuen Park, one of the largest and most beautiful parks in Japan. Work on the park began in the 1670s, was interrupted by fires and financial problems, and finally was completed in the early nineteenth century. A reminder of the wealth and power of the early Maeda lords, the park contains acres of gardens, carp-filled lotus ponds, thatched-roof tea houses, and finely trimmed pine trees.

Kanazawa suffered somewhat during Japan's economic downturn in the early 1990s, but the economy on the whole remains sound and diversified, with retailing, government facilities, and a number of schools, including a national university, several private colleges, and a municipal arts college. Also, local handicrafts, such as Kutani pottery and lacquered tea ware, are profitable. Traditional culture, including Kabuki theatre and the tea ceremony, still flourishes in Kanazawa, but must compete with such modern amusements as baseball, golf, cinema, and trips to Tōkyō's Disneyland.

Further Reading: Most of the books written on Kanazawa have not been translated, but there are some informative works in English. *Kanazawa: A Seventeenth-Century Japanese Castle Town* by James L. McClain (New Haven, Connecticut, and London: Yale University Press, 1982) is the most comprehensive, scholarly account of Kanazawa available in English, covering the years of urban growth from 1583 to 1700. *Kanazawa, the Other Side of Japan* by Ruth Stevens (Kanazawa: Society to Introduce Kanazawa to the World, 1979) provides only a brief historical outline and is designed primarily to draw tourists, but does give one a taste of modern Kanazawan culture, including detailed descriptions of traditional local crafts. It also features a plethora of color photos and maps. *Japan: Its History and Culture* by W. Scott Morton (New York: Crowell, 1970; third edition, New York and London: McGraw-Hill, 1994) does not cover Kanazawa in particular, but provides good background on Japan's history from 3000 B.C. to the present.

—David Flood

Kānchipuram (Tamil Nādu, India)

Location: On the banks of the Vegavathi River, thirty-one miles southwest of the city of Madras, in the Madras District of the state of Tamil Nādu in southeastern India.

Description: Kānchipuram is one of the seven sacred cities of Hinduism. It was founded by the Pallava Dynasty and then became the capital of their kingdom; in A.D. 897 it fell under the rule of the Coḷa Dynasty. A spectacular temple city and place of pilgrimage and worship, Kānchipuram contains a fantastic collection of architectural monuments that span more than 1,000 years of Indian history.

Contact: Government of India Tourist Office
154 Anna Salai
Madras 600 002, Tamil Nādu
India
(82) 69685

The ancient city of Kānchipuram, also known as Siva Vishnu Kānchi or simply as Kānchi, is one of the seven cities in India held sacred by Hindus. With its structures documenting more than 1,000 years of Indian history, it remains a vibrant religious and cultural center. Associated most closely today with Hinduism, Kānchipuram also has been host to Buddhist and Jain sects through the ages. The city's temples are distributed among three zones: the Vishnu shrines are in the east, the Siva sanctuaries are found on the northern outskirts, and the Jain shrines are located to the south, across the Vegavathi River. Kānchipuram also is famous in Indian history for serving as the capital of the great Pallava Kingdom, which covered much of the eastern portion of what is now Tamil Nādu between the third and ninth centuries A.D. Kānchipuram remained an important city, although no longer a capital, during the successive Coḷa, Vijayanagar, and Nayaka periods.

For the era preceding the Pallavas, the history of Kānchipuram is unclear. Some scholars believe that Kānchipuram may have fallen within the boundaries of the Mauryan Empire at its height during the reign of Aśoka in the third century B.C. Aśoka promoted Buddhism throughout India and constructed many stupas in honor of the Buddha. The Chinese pilgrim Xuan Zang, who visited the court of the Pallavas in A.D. 642, recorded seeing a 100-foot-high stupa that had been erected by Aśoka. The stupa no longer exists. Xuan Zang also claimed the Buddha himself had visited the region in the fifth century B.C. and won adherents to his faith. The city subsequently became part of the first Coḷa Kingdom (mid–third century B.C. to fourth century A.D.). Coḷa princes are said to have built Buddhist temples in the city before the rise of the Pallavas.

The first recorded Pallava king to have ruled his kingdom from Kānchipuram was Sivaskandavarman, who is believed to have reigned in the mid–third century A.D. It has been difficult to ascertain which of the Pallava kings in the early dynastic succession were actually in occupation of the throne or Kānchipuram itself. Scholars are not even certain that Sivaskandavarman was the first Pallava king, as there is an inscription that challenges this theory. The inscription records a myth in which a man named Virakurcha married the daughter of the *naga* king—*nagas* are mythological serpents— and thereby acquired the throne of the Pallava Kingdom. Although obviously steeped in mythology, the story offers the possibility that Virakurcha was a real man and the first Pallava king of Kānchipuram. An association with *nagas* was a common means by which Hindu rulers asserted a divine right to govern.

The first Pallava king of Kānchipuram whose reign can be dated precisely is Siṃhavishnu, who ruled from A.D. 575 to 600, but little more than this is known about him. It is not until the reign of his successor Mahendravarman I, also known as Chitrasena, that any details are recorded. Mahendravarman I was a patron of the arts and began excavating temples out of monolithic rocks during his reign from 600 to 630. This marked a transition point in southern Indian temple building, with permanent materials replacing wood. A sculptural relief of Mahendravarman I and his queens is found in one such cave temple in the Pallava port of Mahābalipuram. This period of temple excavation correlates with Mahendravarman I's conversion from Jainism to Hinduism, specifically the worship of Siva, by the saint Appar. Warfare with the rival Cāḷukya Kingdom was prevalent in this period. The defeat of Mahendravarman I by his Cāḷukya adversary was recorded in an inscription at Aihole: "he caused the splendor of the Lord of the Pallavas . . . to be obscured by the dust of his army and to vanish behind the walls of Kānchipuram."

In 630 Mahendravarman I was succeeded by Narasiṃhavarman I Mahāmalla on the Pallava throne. Narasiṃhavarman I was an aggressive ruler who added vast amounts of territory to his kingdom. He marched against the rival Cāḷukyas and conquered the city of Vātāpi, where a pillar was erected with an inscription describing the event. He also helped an exiled prince of Sri Lanka, Mahāvamsa, regain his kingdom. The first attempt to do so failed; the second, for which Narasiṃhavarman supplied a larger army than he had previously and accompanied it from Kānchipuram to the port of Mahābalipuram, where it set sail for Sri Lanka, was a success. The invasion was compared with the Hindu legend of Rāma's conquest of Lanka. Narasiṃhavarman, whose surname Mahāmalla means "great wrestler," raised the Pallava power to unprecedented levels.

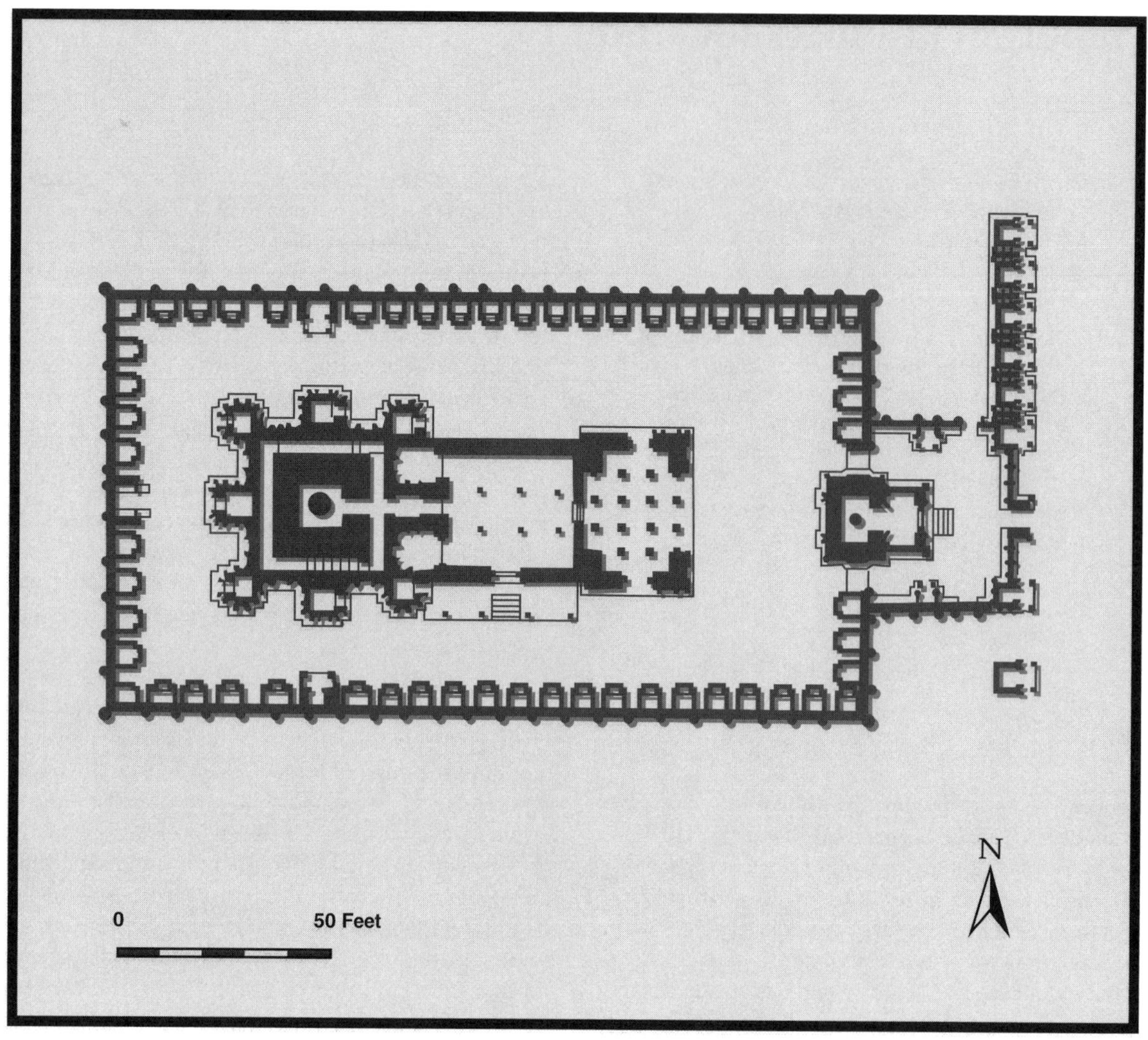

Plan of the Kailāsanātha Temple, Kānchipuram
Illustration by Tom Willcockson

Invaluable accounts of Kānchipuram during Narasiṃhavarman I's reign have been provided by the Chinese pilgrim Xuan Zang, who came to the court in Kānchipuram about 642 and stayed for an extended period. As a Buddhist pilgrim, Xuan Zang was interested primarily in the religious activities of Kānchipuram, and thus kept records of the temples of the Buddhists, Jains, and Hindus. None of the temples from this era have survived. Xuan Zang also described the climate as hot, the soil as fertile, and the people as brave in battle and dedicated to learning. Literature, music, and dance had been encouraged by the Pallava kings since the early years of their dynasty. Bodhidharma, founder of the Zen Buddhist sect, studied here in the sixth century A.D., and the Hindu philosopher Śankara lived and worked here in the eighth century.

Kānchipuram and the Pallava Kingdom remained at peace for several years, then came into a period of renewed conflict with the Cāḷukyas during the reign of Paramesvaraman I. The two dynasties made many raids and counter-raids into one another's territory. On April 25, 674, the Pallavas suffered a humiliating defeat at the hands of the Cāḷukyas, and Kānchipuram fell to the Cāḷukya king Vikramaditya I. Contemporary accounts of the Pallava-Cāḷukya battles refer to horrific fighting "in which tall horses looked like billows; in which elephants caused distress in their path, just as sea-monsters produce whirlpools; . . . in which javelins, pikes, darts, clubs, lances, spears, and discuses were flying about; . . . in which both large armies had lost and dropped arms, necks, shanks, thigh bones, and teeth." It is not clear how long the Cāḷukyas held Kānchipuram, but the Pallavas eventually reclaimed their capital. The Pallavas continued to develop Kānchipuram, constructing more magnificent temples, even though the dynasty's power had diminished.

The oldest surviving monument in Kānchipuram is the great Kailāsanātha Temple, erected by Rājasiṃha (sometimes known as Narasiṃhavarman II) at the beginning of the eighth century. It is one of the oldest extant structural stone temples built in southern India, along with the Shore Temple at Mahābalipuram. Before this, temples were constructed of wood or were carved from solid rock. Kailāsanātha Temple, dedicated to Siva, rises into a pyramidal tower at the center and is capped with a small dome-like roof. The main sanctuary houses a *liṅgam*, or phallic symbol. The temple also contains numerous smaller shrines featuring Siva images. The temple's design is simple and tasteful, making it an excellent example of early Dravidian architecture. It is the only temple at Kānchipuram that is free of the later, somewhat gaudy decoration favored by the Coḷa and Vijayanagar kings. Beautiful sculptures are still visible within the temple, as are the remains of eighth-century murals.

One of the finest Pallava monuments at Kānchipuram is the Vaikuntha Perumal Temple. Built by Nandivarman II in the late eighth century, it is effectively the architectural successor of the Kailāsanātha Temple. Dedicated to Vishnu, the Vaikuntha Perumal Temple has three vertically stacked sanctuaries. In each sanctuary is an image of Vishnu in a different posture—the first standing, the second seated, and the third lying. The logical and complex plan of the temple provided a prototype for the much larger shrines to be constructed all over Tamil Nādu. The external cloisters, for instance, with their lion pillars, are predecessors of the grand thousand-pillared halls of later temples.

The Cāḷukyas again invaded and occupied Kānchipuram in the middle of the eighth century. The Pallavas once more were able to recapture their capital, only to see it attacked by another power, the Rāshtrakūtas of the Deccan. The Pallavas tried to strengthen their hold on their kingdom by forging an alliance, through a royal marriage, with the Rāshtrakūtas, but even this measure could not protect the Pallavas from the increasing power of the Coḷas. The Coḷas allied themselves with the Pāṇḍyas, and together the two groups attacked and conquered the Pallava realm in 897. Thus ended the rule of one of the greatest dynasties in Indian history. The Coḷas added the Pallava territory to their kingdom and occupied Kānchipuram. Kānchipuram was no longer a dynastic capital, however, for the Coḷa maintained their capital at Thānjavūr. The Coḷas' extensive military campaigns, under their great king Rājarāja I (reigned 985–1014), led to the subjugation of most of the southern subcontinent as well as the island of Sri Lanka.

Like their predecessors the Pallavas, the Coḷas also built temples at Kānchipuram. The only temple of pure Coḷa architectural style to survive is the Jvarahareshvara Temple, built in the twelfth century. All other Coḷa temples had additions made to them in later centuries, especially during the period of Vijayanagar rule. The Jvarahareshvara Temple has a distinctive elliptical sanctuary connected to a rectangular antechamber.

Part of the huge Vardarāja Temple complex, on the north bank of the Vegavathi, dates from late in the Coḷa period (twelfth and thirteenth centuries). It is the principal Vishnu temple at Kānchipuram and incorporates four enclosures, with many shrines. The temple was built on the site where Brahmā is said to have made a fire sacrifice to invoke Vishnu. The design of the innermost enclosure was based upon the altar described in the legend. The temple has two towering *gopuras* (gateways). The smaller of the two, on the west side, dates from the Coḷa period, while the steeper, pyramidal eastern *gopura* is typical of the later Vijayanagar style of architecture. It most likely was added in the sixteenth century. A Jain temple, called Vardhamāna, lies south of the river and also was built in the late Coḷa period, with subsequent additions.

In the late fifteenth century, the Coḷas were usurped by the expanding Vijayanagar Empire, centered at Vijayanagara (often referred to as Hampi), to the west of Kānchipuram. Despite being subjugated, the city maintained its importance as a religious center, and many temples were erected or altered. The largest of the temples at Kānchipuram was constructed, for the most part, by the Vijayanagar king Krishna Devarāja in 1509. This structure, the Ekāmbareshwara Temple, incorporated portions built by the Pallavas and Coḷas, but the greater part of the construction of the twenty-two-acre complex was completed under Krishna Devarāja. As the principal Siva sanctuary at Kānchipuram, it is adorned with massive *gopuras;* the main one is 192 feet high. The temple has a thousand-pillared hall and five enclosures with many different shrines. The main sanctuary has an earth *liṅgam* said to bear the fingerprints of Siva's consort, Pārvatī.

As well as being the main Siva shrine, the Ekāmbareshwara Temple is important for a sacred mango tree in one of its courtyards. The name of the temple is in fact a modification of Ekā Amra Nathar, which means "Lord of the Mango Tree." The tree is said to be 3,500 years old. Its four branches represent the four Vedas, the oldest Hindu religious texts. It is said that the fruit from each branch has a completely different taste. Although the tree is revered as a manifestation of god, it is the only shrine at Kānchipuram where non-Hindus may move about freely.

Another interesting temple built by the Vijayanagar kings is the Varadarājaperumal Temple, which is similar to the Ekāmbareshwara in many respects. It, too, has huge outer walls and a thousand-pillared hall, but its most notable feature is a huge chain carved from a single block of stone.

Today one of the most important religious structures at Kānchipuram is the Kamakshiamman Temple, dedicated to Pārvatī. Every February and March, the temple is the site of the famous cart festival, for which representations of other deities are brought here in wooden chariots. The gateways, like most of the rest of the temple, date from the late Vijayanagar period (sixteenth and seventeenth centuries), but the pyramidal towers capping them are modern additions.

Kānchipuram declined somewhat after the Vijayanagar Empire collapsed in the seventeenth century. It was attacked later in that century by Muslims, who plundered the temples, and by the Hindu Marāṭhās. In the eighteenth century the region drew the attention of colonial powers. Robert Clive used the Ekāmbareshwara Temple as a military base in the British campaign to capture Arcot in 1751, and

Kānchipuram subsequently was sacked twice by the French. Through it all, however, Kānchipuram has remained an important pilgrimage center. It also has become famous for its high-quality, handwoven silk, produced here since the sixteenth century. The silk is noted for its vivid colors and intricate patterns. Production of cotton is another important local industry. Kānchipuram also continues to be an educational center, with several colleges affiliated with the University of Madras.

Further Reading: *The History of the Pallavas of Kanchi* by R. Goplan (Madras: University of Madras Press, 1928) is the most thorough analysis and description of Pallava history at Kānchipuram. Although some of its information is dated, this work remains valuable as the only book devoted solely to the subject. *Studies in Indian Temple Architecture* (New Delhi: American Institute of Indian Studies, 1975) contains an excellent chapter on late Pallava architecture. The rest of the book is recommended for a wider perspective on Indian temple architecture. *Early Chola Temples: Parantaka I to Rajaraja I* by S. R. Balasubrahmanyam (Bombay: Orient Longman, 1971) covers the early Coḷa period of history at Kānchipuram. *The Penguin Guide to the Monuments of India,* volume 1, by George Michell (London and New York: Viking, 1990) contains a section on Kānchipuram that covers most of the important temples. The work, written by one of the foremost authorities on Indian architecture, does not contain much historical information. *The Art and Architecture of the Indian Subcontinent* by J. C. Harle (Harmondsworth, Middlesex, and New York: Penguin, 1986) covers all aspects of art and architecture in the subcontinent. The chapters on the Pallavas and the Coḷas are recommended. Although this work, too, focuses primarily on the monuments, it includes some of the history of Kānchipuram. *The Life of Hiuen-Tsiang*, translated by Samuel Beal (London: Kegan Paul, 1911), is an autobiography detailing the life and travels of the pilgrim Hiuen-Tsiang (Xuan Zang). One section describes the pilgrim's visit to Kānchipuram.

—Lulu Wilkinson

Kandahār (Kandahār, Afghanistan)

Location: Southeast Afghanistan, about 300 miles southwest of Kābul, on a level, fertile plain between the Tanrk and Arghandab Rivers, in the Kandahār province.

Description: City occupying a strategic position on the trade and invasion routes into Afghanistan; the southern point of the Kābul-Kandahār-Herāt triangle, control of which has been deemed necessary for military dominance of the country. Once the capital of Afghanistan, it is, after Kābul, the nation's second-largest city.

Contact: Embassy of the Republic of Afghanistan
2341 Wyoming Avenue N.W.
Washington, D.C. 20008
U.S.A.
(202) 234-3770

Kandahār's origins can be traced to the sixth century B.C., when the region was settled by Aryan tribes from Persia. In 540 B.C. Persian king Cyrus II incorporated it within the Achaemenid Empire after subduing some small Afghan tribal kingdoms. Darius the Great (ruled 522–486 B.C.) strengthened the Achaemenid control of the region, and in his time Kandahār—possibly known then as Kandarash—most likely was part of the satrapy of Harahuvat.

Alexander the Great captured the region from the Persians in 330 B.C. He had a new town, called Alexandria of Arachosia, built on the site of Kandahār; it was one of seven cities he developed in the interior of Asia. The name Kandahār probably was adopted some time later, despite theories that it derives from Iskander, the Asian name for Alexander. The town was largely an agricultural center; the surrounding area, then known as Arachosia, was famed for its grapes and pomegranates, which still are grown in the region and which undoubtedly were among the goods traded on the caravan routes that passed through the city. Artifacts excavated from this period include stone hoes, awls, terra-cotta bull figurines, and sun-dried brick building materials.

After Alexander's death in 323 B.C., the city passed to the Seleucid Empire, founded by Alexander's military commander Seleucus I Nicator, and in 305 Seleucus ceded it to the Mauryan Empire of northern India. Mauryan emperor Aśoka, a devout Buddhist, may have introduced that religion to the area in the third century B.C. Aśoka disseminated his beliefs through rock inscriptions executed in various parts of his empire, and several such inscriptions were discovered at Kandahār in the 1950s and 1960s. Scholars know with certainty that Buddhism reached the area by the fourth century A.D., when a Buddhist monastery and stupa were contructed in Kandahār. After the Mauryan Empire collapsed about 185 B.C., Kandahār was ruled by the Greco-Bactrians, followed by the Śaka-Parthians, the Kushāns, the Persian Sāsānians, and the Zabulites, a branch of the Chionite people of the Central Asian steppes. Another branch of the Chionites conquered the ancient Buddhist kingdom of Gandhāra, in the upper Indus River valley, in A.D. 520. An alternate name for that kingdom was Kandahār, and refugees from Gandhāra may have provided the name for the modern city and province of Kandahār. The refugees also brought with them a holy relic, Buddha's begging bowl, which was placed in a shrine in Kandahār.

In the seventh century Muslim armies began invading the region, and on some occasions they succeeded in capturing Kandahār, but they did not hold it for any extended period until the tenth century. The inhabitants who had converted during these occupations always retained their old belief systems after the invaders had left. Kandahār at this time was still a rather small town and was overshadowed by other settlements.

The Muslim invaders who succeeded in firmly establishing their religion in Kandahār were the Ghaznavids, under their powerful leader Maḥmūd of Ghaznī, who came in the tenth century. Descriptions of Kandahār from this period indicate that it developed into a typical eastern Islamic town with a citadel, walls around the town proper, and suburbs outside the walls. After the Ghaznavid Empire fell in 1150, Kandahār passed through the hands of local chiefs, then the Seljuk Turks, then the Turkomans in quick succession until the Ghūrids established themselves there in 1153. Despite the waves of invasion, the town grew and flourished.

Genghis Khan and his Mongol forces stormed and captured Kandahār in 1222 and made it part of the Mongol Empire. The empire began to weaken later in the century and in 1278 Kandahār fell to a native Afghan dynasty, the Karts, who ruled first as vassals of the Mongols and later became independent. In 1389 the town was recaptured by the Mongols under Timur (Tamerlane), who bequeathed it to his grandson Pir Muhammad, and for the next century Kandahār remained under Timurid rule. As Timurid control of Kandahār weakened in the late fifteenth century, the town fell to the sultanate of Husayn Baiqara of Herāt. He used Kandahār as a mint town and put it under the control of a governor named Dhu'l-Nun Beg, a member of the Arghūnid tribe (and the grandson of Timur), who eventually declared himself independent and made Kandahār his capital. In 1498 he invaded Herāt, having recruited an army from Kandahār and other towns within his dominion.

Dhu'l-Nun Beg's efforts at territorial expansion, however, brought him into conflict with a conqueror who would prove much more powerful: the Timurid descendant Ẓahīr-

Mausoleum of Aḥmad Shāh, Kandahār
Photo courtesy of Embassy of the Islamic State of Afghanistan, Washington, D.C.

ud-Dīn Muḥammad (better known as Bābur), who was developing an empire along the Indo-Afghan frontier and would later found the Mughal Dynasty. In 1505 Bābur drove Dhu'l-Nun Beg's son Mukim Arghun from Kābul to Kandahār. Then in 1507 Dhu'l-Nun Beg was killed by the Uzbeks, who subsequently captured Herāt. Mukim and his brother Shāh Beg were trapped in Kandahār between Bābur and the Uzbeks, under their leader Shaybānī. Bābur reached Kandahār first, capturing it in 1507. Bābur made his son Nasir Mirzā governor of the town, but the Arghunids retook it in 1512, having allied themselves with Shaybānī. In 1510 Shaybānī was killed and Shāh Beg took over Kandahār. Bābur continued to try to reclaim the city, however, and after two unsuccessful attempts finally won it in 1522, following a long siege. The next year Bābur invaded India. By 1526 he had overthrown the Lodī Afghan rulers of India and established the Mughal Empire.

After Bābur died in 1530, Kandahar became the object of nearly constant warfare between his descendants and the Ṣafavids of Persia. The Ṣafavids regarded Kandahār as an appanage of Khōrasan, which was among their possessions, and saw the Mughals as usurpers. Kamran Mirzā, another of Bābur's sons, successfully defended Kandahār against Ṣafavid attacks from 1534 through 1536. Then a rivalry between Kamran and his half-brother, Mughal emperor Humāyūn, resulted in Humāyūn making an alliance with the Persians, who supplied an army with which he attacked Kandahār in 1545. Humāyūn was victorious, and in keeping with an agreement he had made, he handed Kandahār over to the Persians. A month later, however, he went back on his promise and seized the city for himself. Civil war raged between Humāyūn and Kamran until 1553, when the latter surrendered and was blinded.

After Humāyūn's death in 1556, the absence of his son and successor Akbar on a military campaign in India gave the Ṣafavids an opportunity to march on Kandahār. The Ṣafavid leader Shah Tasmasp captured the city in 1558 and annexed it to the Ṣafavid Empire. Akbar retook the city in 1594. His successor Jahāngīr lost it again to the Ṣafavids in 1609, but recovered it soon afterward. The Persians captured the town again in 1621, but the Mughals regained it about 1638 with some unintentional help from the Uzbeks. The Uzbeks had unsuccessfully invaded Khōrasan and retreated to Kandahār, which they captured after the Ṣafavid governor of Kandahār, Ali Mardan, defected to the Uzbek side. Then, fearing the Ṣafavid ruler would execute him for his treachery, Ali Mardan evacuated the city, went to the Mughal court to pay homage, and turned Kandahār over to Mughal emperor Shāh Jahān. Shāh Jahān, like Jahāngīr and Humāyūn before him, had coins minted in Kandahār.

The Mughals also left a mark on Kandahār in the form of the Chel Zina, consisting of forty-nine steps cut into a rocky hillside and leading to a platform surrounded by an arched niche in which lists of the victories of Bābur and Akbar were inscribed. The somewhat crude carving of the steps suggests that they may date from an earlier era and that perhaps the Mughals adapted the site, which may have housed a shrine to previous rulers.

Mughal control of Kandahār lasted only until 1648, however, when the young Ṣafavid Shāh ʿAbbās II captured it. The Mughals never were able to recover it, despite attempts by both Shāh Jahān and his successor ʿĀlamgīr (Aurangzeb). Kandahār, by now an important city with impressive walls, became the capital of a Ṣafavid province. Its governors included, from time to time, the princes of the Ṣafavid royal family.

Ṣafavid rule of Kandahār lasted until 1709, when a local Afghan tribe, the Ghilzays, rebelled. The Ghilzays initially had allied themselves with the Ṣafavids and supported them against the Mughals. They eventually came to desire control of the region, however. Mīr Veys Khān, a Ghilzay leader, clashed with the Ṣafavids, was imprisoned, gained their confidence, and was released. Once free, he invited Gorgīn Khān, the Persian governor of Kandahār, to a banquet. At the gathering, however, Mīr Veys killed Gorgīn Khān and his small army and declared himself independent. The Ṣafavids attempted to recapture the city, but Mīr Veys held it until his death in 1715. He was entombed in Kandahār.

His son Maḥmūd strengthened the Ghilzay hold on Kandahār by driving out a rebellious tribe, the Abdālīs (a branch of the Pashtuns), and by capturing Eṣfahān from the Ṣafavids. He finally drove the Ṣafavids from the Persian throne and became shah briefly, from 1722 until his death in 1725. The Ghilzay hold on Persia weakened after his death, however, and Nāder Qolī Beg, later to become Nāder Shāh, drove them out in 1729. He then captured Kandahār in 1738, after a siege that lasted a year and a half. He destroyed the city and built a new one, called Nāderabad after himself, two miles to the southeast. He had coins minted bearing both the names of Kandahār and Nāderabad. Nāder Shāh expelled most of the Ghilzay people from the Kandahār region and repopulated it with the Abdalis, who had assisted him in his conquest.

Following Nāder Shāh's assassination in 1747, Aḥmad Khān Abdālī, the commander of his force of bodyguards, was elected king of the Afghan people. He took the title Durr-i Durrān (Pearl of Pearls) and became known as Aḥmad Shāh Durrāni. His people, the Abdālīs, became known as the Durrānis. He destroyed Nāderabad and built a new city of Kandahār slightly east of the old city. He called the new city Ahmadshāhi, after himself, adding to the name the epithet Ashraf al-Bilad (Most Illustrious of Cities), a term that appears on Durrāni coins struck at the time. Ahmadshāhi became his capital, and among his constructions in the new city was a mosque to house a cloak supposedly worn by the prophet Muhammad. The mosque was still standing in the twentieth century.

Aḥmad Shāh went on many military campaigns to extend the Afghan-controlled realm, which became the second largest Muslim empire in the world in the latter half of the eighteenth century, surpassed in size only by the Ottoman holdings. He died in 1773 and was entombed in Kandahār; his tomb—octagonal in shape, decorated with colorful porcelain bricks, and surmounted by a dome and minarets—has remained one of the outstanding architectural features of the city and an important pilgrimage site.

After Aḥmad Shāh's death, possession of Kandahār was contested among his descendants, leading his son and successor, Timur Shāh, to move his capital to Kābul. He was able to keep Kandahār within his realm despite the frequent rebellions there. He was succeeded in 1793 by his fifth son, Zaman Shāh, who in 1800 was deposed by his brother Maḥmūd, who seized Kandahār, Kābul, and the rest of the Durrāni realm. Another brother, Shāh Shojāʿ, overthrew Maḥmūd in 1803 but had difficulty holding onto Kandahār, which changed hands several times between the forces of Maḥmūd and Shāh Shojāʿ until Maḥmūd returned to the throne in 1809.

The Durrāni Dynasty came to an end with the rise to power of Dōst Moḥammad, brother of Shāh Shojā's vizier, Fatḥ Khān. He won control of Afghanistan in 1826 and made another of his brothers, Kuhandil Khān, governor of Kandahār. In 1834 Shāh Shojāʿ, with the help of Sikh leader Ranjit Singh, attempted unsuccessfully to recover Kandahār, in a siege that lasted fifty-four days and left 16,000 dead.

More turmoil was ahead for Kandahār. The British rulers of India at this time feared Russian influence in Afghanistan, so a mission under Sir Alexander Burnes met with Dōst Muḥammad in 1837 in an attempt to forge an alliance. Negotiations broke down, however, and in 1839 the British invaded Afghanistan, starting the First Anglo-Afghan War. The British captured Kandahār with little difficulty in April of that year and installed Shāh Shojā', who had become their ally, as emir of Kandahār and Kābul.

Shāh Shojā's sons and British forces kept the peace in Kandahār in 1839 and 1840, but by 1841 the British garrison there was coming under periodic attack from rebellious Afghans, who were not about to accept a foreign occupation or a ruler installed by the occupiers. The attacks continued into the next year, when the British finally evacuated the city. In 1843 the new governor general of India decided to end the war altogether, and Dōst Moḥammad, who had been exiled to India in 1840, returned to claim his throne. His brother Kuhandil once again became governor of Kandahār. Kuhandil ruled in dictatorial fashion until his death in 1851.

When Kuhandil died, his son Muhammad Sadik seized power in Kandahār, leading Dōst Moḥammad to intervene and install a governor of his choice, Ghulam Haidar Khān. After Dōst Muḥammad died in 1863, he was succeeded by his third son, Shīr 'Alī, who became embroiled in civil war with his brothers. There were frequent battles for Kandahār in the 1860s, with Shīr 'Alī's forces emerging as the final victors in 1868.

Shīr 'Alī had poor relations with the British, leading to the Second Anglo-Afghan War in 1878. After the British deposed Shīr 'Alī's successor, Ya'qūb Khān, in 1879, the rule of most of Afghanistan passed to 'Abdorraḥmān Khān, but a separate state was created around Kandahār. Rebel Afghan forces dealt the British one of their severest defeats of the war near Kandahār on July 27, 1880, at the Battle of Maiwand, and then besieged Kandahār itself. The British won back the city in September and withdrew from it in 1881, having abandoned the idea of a separate Kandahār state and granted rule of the entire country to 'Abdorraḥmān Khān.

There were some internal disturbances in Kandahār over the succeeding years, but on the whole the city flourished in the late nineteenth and early twentieth centuries. Residential sections and busy bazaars displaying goods from England, Russia, the Middle East, India, and Central Asia sat in the shadow of the citadel and walls that had been built by Timur Shāh. Vineyards and orchards surrounded the city, as they still do today. As the twentieth century proceeded, Kandahār became an important modern transportation and communications center, with major highways and an international airport. The city is positioned along the main routes to Iran and Pakistan. Its population reached about 178,000 in the late 1970s.

In the twentieth century Kandahār also has become a center of the Pashtun nationalist movement, since it is populated primarily by people of Pashtun heritage. After India and Pakistan were partitioned in 1947, the Afghan government and Pashtun activists urged that Pashtuns living in Pakistan be given the option of voting on the formation of an independent Pashtun state, or possibly for union with Afghanistan. This has led to ill feelings between Pakistan and Afghanistan, with Afghanistan casting the only vote against Pakistan's admission to the United Nations and Pakistan closing its border on occasions. The issue has faded to the background in recent years due to more pressing concerns, but it may well surface again.

During the Afghan-Soviet war of 1979–89 and the civil conflict that followed the Soviet withdrawal, Kandahār has been besieged frequently, with much attendant suffering by the populace and destruction of property. By the middle of 1995, however, the city was enjoying some degree of peace and stability under the control of the Taliban, an Islamic fundamentalist group opposed to the more moderate Islamic national government. The situation in Afghanistan remains volatile, however, and Kandahār, occupying a position that has been militarily important for so many centuries, is likely to be affected by events in the country as a whole.

Further Reading: Entries on Kandahār and Afghanistan in *The Encyclopedia of Islam* (Leiden: Brill, 1913; revised edition, 1987) are comprehensive and informative. Ludwig W. Adamec's *Kandahār and South-Central Afghanistan* (Graz: Akademische Druck-u Verlagsanstalt, 1980) is an excellent collection of late-nineteenth- and early-twentieth-century European accounts of Kandahār and its environs. Peter Hopkirk's *The Great Game: On Secret Service in High Asia* (London: Murray, 1990; with subtitle *The Struggle for Empire in Central Asia*, New York: Kodansha, 1992) examines Anglo-Russian rivalry throughout Afghanistan's history. Peter Levi's *The Light Garden of the Angel King: Journeys in Afghanistan* (London: Collins, and Indianapolis: Bobbs-Merrill, 1972) contains a view of Kandahār through the eyes of a traveler with an appreciation of history.

—Richard White and Trudy Ring

Kandy (Sri Lanka)

Location: Sixty miles east-northeast of Colombo, on the Kandy Plateau in central Sri Lanka.

Description: Kandy once was the name for both a Sinhalese kingdom (1474–1815) and its capital; the kingdom resisted colonial conquest for nearly 350 years, and during its last two centuries Kandy was the only remaining independent territory in Sri Lanka. The city is known for its elaborate architecture, an artificial lake constructed by Sri Wickrama Rājasinha in 1806, and the Temple of the Tooth, which houses a tooth supposed to have belonged to the Buddha.

Contact: Ceylon Tourist Board
78 Steuart Place
P. O. Box 1504
Colombo 3
Sri Lanka
(43) 7059 or (43) 7060

The city of Kandy lies in the forests at the mountainous core of Sri Lanka, a region first populated by Sinhalese seeking refuge from Tamil armies attacking from the north. The site was home only to a Buddhist monastery until 1474, when the Sinhalese general Vikramābāhu declared independence from his king in Kotte and established the seat of an autonomous state called Kande-uda-rata (the country on the mountains). His people knew the city as Senkadagala.

Three successive colonial forces determined Kandy's history. The Portuguese were the first to appear, and the first to use the present name for both the kingdom and its capital. In 1505 Don Lourenço de Almeida was blown off course near southern India and landed at Colombo, which lay in the kingdom of Kotte. He took an immediate interest in Sri Lankan cinnamon, which was quite costly in Europe. In turn, Kotte's King Vijayabāhu was eager to ally himself with the Portuguese in order to gain a military advantage over the two rival kingdoms in Sri Lanka at that time: the renegade Kandy to the east and Tamil-ruled Jaffna in the north.

Once the Portuguese were permitted by treaty to build a fort at Colombo, they began trading. However, Portuguese demands for cheap cinnamon and taxes soon ended their friendly relations with Kotte. The Sinhalese fought an unsuccessful war with the Portuguese from 1520 to 1521, and thereafter Kotte became a client state of the victors. In the turmoil that followed, another secession occurred, and the powerful new state of Sitavaka emerged.

Despite the poor outcome of Kotte's alliance with the colonialists, King Viravikrama (ruled 1542–57) of Kandy signed a treaty with the Portuguese in 1546. Worried that Sitavaka would overrun his domain, Viravikrama willingly made his state a satellite of Portugal. The Portuguese installed a small military force and several Roman Catholic priests in the capital to remind the Kandyans of their subservience.

Viravikrama's gambit resulted in thirty-six years of relative peace, a period during which he built up Kandy in the grand style for which it is famed. The incorporation into Sinhalese Buddhism of Hindu ideas regarding nobility resulted in a tradition of honoring Kandyan god-kings by erecting palaces, shrines, and elaborate waterworks. According to the American geographer James Duncan, "These landscapes were modeled upon descriptions of the cities of the gods in heaven on the top of Mount Meru." Viravikrama's greatest architectural achievement was the first in a series of temples to house Kandy's most precious relic: a tooth supposed to have belonged to the Buddha, which made its way to Sri Lanka from India in the fourth century A.D.

In the meantime, Sitavaka had grown strong enough to attack Kandy in 1581, having already taken back most of Sri Lanka from the Portuguese. The Sitavakans won the war handily, forcing King Karaliyadde Bandara (1557–81) of Kandy to flee to the Portuguese. An unfaithful Kandyan chief, coupled with a diminished Portuguese presence owing to its soldiers having to participate in other Asian conflicts, aided the Sitavakans in their victory. For almost ten years, King Rājasinha of Sitavaka maintained control over all parts of Sri Lanka except Jaffna, the fort at Colombo, and two renegade provinces. However, he depleted his kingdom with continued failed attacks on Colombo that the Portuguese were able to subdue using their superior sea power. In 1590 a large population of Kandyans revolted against Rājasinha, and by 1593 they had succeeded in expelling Sitavakan forces.

After liberation from Sitavaka, the Kandyans' relations with Portugal reversed. Their new king, Vimaladharmasuriya (ruled 1592/94–1604), was determined to return Kandy to Buddhism and independence, and he expelled the Portuguese missionaries and soldiers from the kingdom. At the same time, the Portuguese were running an aggressive and largely successful campaign to dominate Sri Lanka through both military might and surreptitious influence. By the early 1590s they had control of a good portion of the littorals (coastal regions), including Sitavaka and Jaffna. Intent on solidifying their position, the Portuguese then attempted to conquer Kandy.

A garrison led by General Pero Lopez de Souza attacked the city of Kandy in 1594, whereupon the Portuguese installed the daughter of Karaliyadde Bandara, the former king who had ruled Kandy prior to the Sitavakan takeover. Queen Dona Catherina was clearly a puppet of the Portuguese and consequently lacked the allegiance of her people. The deposed Vimaladharma easily arranged the defection of those Sinhalese forces acting in conjunction with

The Dalada Maligawa complex, containing the Tooth Relic Temple, Kandy
Photo courtesy of Mr. Herath Navaratne, Information Officer, Embassy of Sri Lanka, Washington, D.C.

Tooth Relic Temple, Kandy
Photo courtesy of Air India Library, New York

the Portuguese, enabling his own troops to slaughter the colonial soldiers and capture the queen. Vimaladharma took Dona Catherina as his bride, thus further legitimizing his own claim to the throne.

During the next few years, Vimaladharma fought off many smaller Portuguese attacks, thus providing him time to erect many elaborate constructions in Kandy. He surrounded the city with a massive wall punctuated by eighteen towers; he also commissioned a new two-story temple for the Tooth Relic, a new Buddhist monastery, and a superb palace built by Portuguese slaves. By the beginning of the seventeenth century, Kandy was the majestic capital of the last autonomous territory in Sri Lanka.

King Senerath came to the throne upon his brother Vimaladharma's death in 1604, continuing to rule until 1635. In 1617, after thirteen years of fighting the Portuguese, Senerath signed a new treaty with them. Sitavaka had recouped its strength, and Senerath was worried that Kandy would be conquered for a second time. This treaty led to a period of detente with the Europeans, but it did little to improve the Kandyans' status: the Portuguese merely recognized the sovereignty of King Senerath. In exchange, the Kandyans acknowledged Portuguese hegemony over conquered coastal regions and their power to levy taxes, and promised not to admit enemies of Portugal into the Kandyan state.

The Dutch East India Company began negotiating with the Kandyans as early as 1602 with the hope of gaining leverage in the cinnamon trade, but Portugal, a stronger sea power, remained dominant in Sri Lanka well into the 1620s. In fact, by the middle of the 1610s, the Portuguese had won back control of nearly all of Sri Lanka except Kandy. As Dutch power waxed, however, the Portuguese thought it necessary to defend their territory more aggressively. Contrary to the guidelines of the 1617 treaty, the Portuguese built new forts in Kandyan port cities. This led to open war in 1628. The Kandyans' guerrilla tactics forced the Portuguese to retreat to their maritime strongholds.

The Portuguese, however, were set on controlling the entire island of Sri Lanka, and troops led by General De Mello attacked Kandy in 1638. A good deal of the city burned again, although there are conflicting reports of who set the fires this time. The conflagration destroyed a monastery, the temple of the god Ganesh, and the Temple of the Tooth. The Kandyans later surrounded and slaughtered their enemies in a battle at Gannoruwa, near Kandy, and a new period of rebuilding began.

Kandy's Rājasinha II (ruled 1635–87) finalized a treaty with the Dutch in 1638. In exchange for expelling the Portuguese, the Dutch were to receive a monopoly on Sri Lanka's cinnamon and reimbursement for the cost of their battles. The following year, the Dutch captured two Sri Lankan provinces from the Portuguese and handed them over to Kandy. In 1640, however, the Dutch kept several ports they had captured, ostensibly in lieu of payments owed them by Kandy according to the 1638 treaty. In fact, this self-serving interpretation of the agreement allowed the Dutch to retain properties providing convenient access to cinnamon.

In the mid–seventeenth century the governments of Portugal and the Netherlands agreed to the transfer of all Sri Lankan bases and plantations to the Dutch, but Portuguese officials on the island refused to comply. A war resulted in 1652 in which the Kandyans helped fight against the Portuguese. The Dutch captured Colombo in May 1655, securing the rest of maritime Sri Lanka by 1658.

After the Dutch came to power, Governor Ryklof Van Goens imposed a policy to reduce the area of Kandyan control and to establish Sri Lanka as the headquarters of Dutch operations in the Far East. In the latter half of the seventeenth century, that policy was interpreted in ways that forbade the Kandyans the use of the island's ports for shipping. Thus Kandyan noblemen were denied the lucrative trade of spices and textiles with southern Indians. Kandyans fought back by closing off the central forests to Dutch commerce and by running their own ships through Dutch blockades. However, these actions had little benefit for Kandy.

Despite the financial difficulties caused by Dutch control of the coasts, Kandy was relatively peaceful during the century of Dutch rule. Having discovered that cinnamon could be cultivated in the lowlands, the Dutch saw no need to conquer the mountains. For their part, the Kandyans did not do all that they might have to upset Dutch control of the lowland plantations. Apparently, they were reluctant to jeopardize the modest amount of foreign trade they still managed through bribery and smuggling.

During the period of Dutch rule, the Sinhalese peacefully relinquished power in Kandy to the Tamils, their traditional enemy. King Narendrasinha (ruled 1707–39) died in 1739 without a legitimate Sinhalese heir, and the throne passed to the queen's brother, Sri Vijaya Rājasinha (ruled 1739–47), from southern India. The transition, although not altogether welcome, went smoothly for two reasons: first, the strict Sinhalese caste system demanded a nobleman of rank not available within Kandy; second, members of the Kandyan elite were loath to render power to their rivals within the state.

The Tamil-led Nayakkar Dynasty remained in power until Kandy finally was subjugated by the British in 1815. Yet there is no doubt that the Tamils weakened Kandy politically. Nayakkar kings were shrewd in their management of power struggles among Kandy's elite, but their lack of interest in the peripheral provinces had deleterious effects. Local chiefs became both disaffected and too powerful, and so eventually the kingdom lost cohesion. In addition, Nayakkar kings surrounded themselves with Tamil relatives, causing further tensions between royalty and the Sinhalese nobility of Kandy.

In the 1750s events transpired in the southwestern lowlands that led to a break in the Kandyan-Dutch peace. Governor Schreuder's land policy severely restricted deforestation to protect wild cinnamon. When cinnamon prices suddenly doubled in Europe, he began taking over private Sinhalese plantations where local farmers could not prove ownership. His unpleasant dealings led to a popular uprising in 1760. The Kandyans came to the aid of the rebels, and the Dutch responded with military attacks. The first assault, in 1762, was a miserable failure for the Dutch. In 1765 they attacked again, under the command of General Van Eck, and this time they captured the city of Kandy.

Van Eck's report reveals just how much the city had developed under Nayakkar rule. Among the constructions he found were a temple to Vishnu containing an imported statue, an elaborate royal garden, and another containing the sacred Bo tree. There were two houses of relics, and to the west of these stood another temple that still exists. The palace had been expanded and filled with sundry valuables. One eyewitness reported the Dutch pilfering of "much treasure, consisting of gold, silver, precious stones, gold and silver cloths, velvets, silk stuffs, [and] fine linen of all sorts in abundance." Three days of pillaging by Dutch soldiers destroyed the palace, the Temple of the Tooth, and much of the audience hall.

Soundly defeated, with their capital in ruins, the Kandyans had little choice but to sign a disadvantageous treaty in 1766 that served to isolate and thereby impoverish them even further. The Dutch took control over an area from the lowlands inward four Sinhalese "miles" along the entire coast. For the first time, the Kandyans had to depend on the Europeans for such basic necessities as salt and fish.

The third, and final, colonial force to control Sri Lanka was England. Shortly before the Dutch raid on Kandy, the English East India Company contacted the Kandyans to discuss forming an alliance against the Dutch. However, political events in Europe prevented any significant action before 1796. In that year Holland ceded rights to its holdings in Sri Lanka to the British, but Dutch officials on the island refused to relinquish control. Another war ensued. A massive armed force of the English East India Company took Jaffna easily and then marched on Colombo, where they met little opposition.

After the British conquered the maritime provinces, they were keen to take control of Kandy. To defend their territory against other Europeans, they needed land access between their fort at Colombo in the southwest and their naval base at Trincomalee in the northeast. A power struggle within Kandy following the death of King Rajadhi Rājasinha (ruled 1782–98) offered the British an opportunity to take over. They sided with a Sinhalese claimant to the throne, but when they marched into Kandy to install him, the British, finding he had little support, were forced to withdraw.

The British staged an armed invasion of Kandy in 1803, but General MacDowall and his soldiers arrived to find that Sri Wickrama Rājasinha (ruled 1798–1815) and his people had fled into the forest with the Tooth Relic and other treasures. In addition, the Kandyans had set fire to their own capital once again in order to prevent its desecration. The British gratuitously added to the destruction by burning the royal gardens. They occupied Kandy for several months afterward, until the Kandyans returned to the city and executed them.

The British were reluctant to fight another war against the Kandyans following this bloody defeat, and a period of uneasy peace began. King Sri Wickrama took this time to build up Kandy more magnificently than ever before. Many of the impressive works for which Kandy is famous today originated during this era. Sri Wickrama installed a single huge gate to replace the two that opened before the Temple of the Tooth and the palace. He dug a moat around the entire complex and put in drawbridges. Shops and homes were erected in the western part of the city. Finally, he oversaw the construction of an artificial lake on what was originally a marsh. From 1806 until 1812 he employed up to 3,000 men to build a dam that trapped waters from a passing stream. The fruit of this massive effort was Lake Bogambara, more than two miles in circumference and forty-six feet deep.

Thanks to divisions within the kingdom, the British finally were able to take control of Kandy in 1815. The king had alienated himself from the Sinhalese population by committing offensive acts toward Kandy's Buddhist monks. Several of the disaffected chiefs invited the British to march on Kandy without opposition. The king fled, and the disloyal chiefs signed the Kandyan Convention on March 2, 1815. The treaty may be summarized as having put a Briton in place of the Kandyan king. Unlike the case in other Sri Lankan provinces, this treaty permitted chiefs to retain authority over local affairs and for Buddhist traditions and laws to continue in Kandy. Nevertheless, Kandy was now a subservient part of the royal crown colony of Ceylon.

The Kandyans quickly grew tired of their new caretakers. In violation of the treaty, the British did not support Buddhist life, and the authority and status of the chiefs were being undermined. More important, the loss of the kingship upset the Kandyan social structure. The king had been the hub of the caste-based community, and without a royal headman, chiefs and commoners alike became unsettled by their loss of defined roles and rank.

In July 1817 a popular rebellion began with the objective of installing a new Kandyan king. At first, the war went well for the rebels, but in the summer of 1818 the British brought in reinforcements from India and began brutally to suppress the guerrillas. It was not long before the British had captured both the Tooth Relic and the rebel leaders. The Kandyans grew disheartened after these losses, and the war ended in September 1818.

When the rebellion was over, the British began to institute a series of policies that depleted and later dissolved the kingdom of Kandy. A proclamation in 1818 reduced the authority of the chiefs and imposed a tax structure that sapped rebellious provinces. The British also eliminated the possibility of another Kandyan war by crisscrossing the island with roads and, later, trains. Roads made Kandy's mountains easy for British soldiers to traverse and its forests difficult for guerrilla rebels to hide in. The key to Kandy's survival through two centuries of powerful enemy attacks had been eliminated.

In 1832 the Colebrooke-Cameron reforms united Kandy and the littorals under a single administration, and within smaller offices it grouped all but the centermost Kandyan province with lowland neighbors. The Kandyan sense of national identity survived, contrary to the express purpose of the new administrative structure. Even today the Sinhalese distinguish between lowlanders and highlanders. However, the Kandyans seldom have acted as a political unity since the Great Rebellion. The Kandyan riots in 1848 protesting British labor practices and religious policies were an exception that had some positive effect. Then, in the 1920s Kandyans united against economic and social reforms pushed by Colombo's working class. Nevertheless, the Kandyan kingdom essentially dissolved into greater Sri Lanka in the nineteenth century.

The city of Kandy evolved into a central way station for coffee and, later, tea being transported from mountain plantations to ports. Kandy also is an important destination for Buddhist pilgrims visiting the Temple of the Tooth and for the Buddhist festival Kandy Perahera.

Further Reading: *The City as Text: The Politics of Landscape Interpretation in the Kandyan Kingdom* by James S. Duncan (Cambridge and New York: Cambridge University Press, 1990) is probably the only monograph devoted to a discussion of Kandy; it is an excellent book, but it is an abstruse work in interpretive geography written for academicians. Two well-documented histories of Sri Lanka that have abundant material on Kandy are *Sri Lanka: A History* by Chandra Richard De Silva (New York: Advent Books, 1987) and *A History of Sri Lanka* by K. M. De Silva (London: Hurst, and Berkeley and Los Angeles: University of California Press, 1981). The former has a bit more information on economic and legal changes under colonial rule, the latter on religious and social changes. For an amazingly detailed look at how British administrators devised and instituted policies in Sri Lanka, and at how specific events within Kandy determined the impact of those policies, see the multivolume *Ceylon under British Occupation* by Colvin R. De Silva (Colombo, Ceylon: Colombo Apothecaries, 1953).

—Christopher A. Hoyt

Karāchi (Sind, Pakistan)

Location: Major port on the Arabian Sea, northwest of the Indus River delta, in southern Pakistan.

Description: Largest city and industrial center in Pakistan, third-largest city on the subcontinent, and capital of Pakistan until 1959; fishing hamlet in mid–eighteenth century, turned into major seaport when British took control after 1839; provincial capital during British rule, and capital of West and East Pakistan after independence and partition in 1947.

Site Office: Pakistan Tourism Development Corporation
Hotel Metropol
Club Road
Karāchi, Sind
Pakistan
(92) 21 516 252

The history of Karāchi is barely 250 years old. In the early eighteenth century Karāchi, then known as Kalachi-Jo-goth after the most prominent fisherman in the hamlet, was a new settlement situated in an unhealthy swamp, surrounded by many miles of uninhabited desert. Not even water was available; it had to be brought from the Indus River, miles away. The area was conquered in 1795 by the Muslim Mīrs of Tālpur, who proceeded to build a mud fortress at Manora Head, a hill overlooking the village of Karāchi.

By the early nineteenth century, however, the British already were in control of most of India and were bent on conquering the ancient province of Sind. In 1839 the British ship HMS *Wellesley*, under the command of Rear Admiral Maitland, anchored nearby to attack the newly built fort. The Mīrs had allied themselves earlier with the Catholic French, both being anti-British. However, no one inside the fort fired a shot at the British, who calmly took possession. This was the beginning of British rule in present-day Pakistan, one of the last areas of the Indian subcontinent to come under their control. Karāchi would become the gateway into the interior of the subcontinent; the British built a railway network that radiated from Karāchi to the Khyber Pass on the border of Afghanistan, one that is still the pride of Pakistan.

For the century in which the British governed the area, vast changes came to Karāchi. In 1843 Karāchi became the administrative capital of Sind province, with Sir Charles Napier as its governor. As a result of developing and modernizing the port and introducing the railway, thousands of immigrants streamed into Karāchi, from as far away as the Ottoman Empire and China. By 1848 there were 50,000 inhabitants. Economic opportunity was evidenced by the many banks that sprang up and by the huge homes of merchants. Added to the polyglot population was distinctly British architecture; the Victorian railway station, Mereweather Tower, Frere Hall, the baroque Sind Club, the Masonic Hall, and the Victoria Museum all were built before the turn of the century. Churches also were constructed: St. Andrew's Church, built in English medieval style, became the tallest structure in the city with its 147-foot spire. Roman Catholics soon built an imposing church, convent, bishop's residence, and school; subsequently, generations of Muslim Indians were educated in St. Patrick's school. On the outskirts of Karāchi, the British built Clifton, resembling a typical English coastal resort town (now a tourist attraction). The streets in the five-square-mile downtown area bore English names, and the British-controlled city council was not long in introducing street paving and cleaning. Toward the end of the century, the council also took measures to eradicate or contain long-standing illnesses such as malaria. All this time, the British rigidly segregated themselves from the non-European population, which was treated as inferior and subordinate.

Karāchi was released from British rule when it became part of the newly created country of Pakistan in 1947. In that year, the British gave the Indian subcontinent its bitterly fought independence. The leader of the Muslim League in India, Mohammed Ali Jinnah, a British-educated lawyer, led the movement for partitioning the subcontinent into ethnically homogeneous, discrete countries, without regard, as it proved later, to the economic viability of the new Muslim state. Mohandas Karamchand Gandhi (also known as Mahatma Gandhi), the Hindu independence leader, also a British-educated lawyer but in every way Jinnah's opposite, was appalled at the prospect of Hindu and Muslim Indians separating themselves after both had fought as one for independence. Nonetheless, he acquiesced when he realized that religious antagonisms had been stoked up to such a degree that a unified India was no longer viable and that the British had approved the partition.

As a result, Pakistan arose as an independent Muslim state led by Jinnah, although West Pakistan and East Pakistan (present-day Bangladesh), were separated from each other by a thousand miles of Indian land. For hundreds of years, Hindus and Muslims had lived side by side in these areas, along with many other ethnic minorities such as Afghans, Chinese, Burmese, and even Armenians, Jews, and Lebanese. The partition seemed to bring the worst out of both major ethnic groups. Hindus rushed into India, along with many other minorities, as Muslims fled; along the way, people were massacred as each side tried to grab as much territory as possible. The human cost of partition was incredible: in a few months in 1947, at least 250,000 people were killed, and 12 million Hindus and Muslims had fled their homelands. Moreover, the differences between East and West Pakistan were so pronounced that war erupted between the two in 1971, with

View of Karāchi
Photo courtesy of The Chicago Public Library

India taking the side of East Pakistan, which achieved its independence and proclaimed itself the Muslim state of Bangladesh.

At the onset of independence from the British, there was no doubt that Karāchi, West Pakistan's largest city, would become the capital of the new Pakistan (West and East). At that time the city's population hovered at 250,000; over the span of the next fifty years, it would swell to 5 million. For a century the British had developed and modernized the port, maximizing its economic potential. Unfortunately, Jinnah (who died in 1948) and his disciples were bent on introducing heavy industry—such as steel mills—to Karāchi; Gandhi always had adamantly opposed such plans for India, preferring small, homegrown industries that could sustain the vast numbers of poor. The introduction of large-scale industrialization to a country where the business elite (in the hands of minorities) had fled or been killed, and where illiteracy reigned, proved unwise.

Moreover, Pakistan had no identity except in its religion. The official language, Urdū, is spoken only by a small minority, a fact that has led to much tension and resentment. Pakistan's second official language is English, which still is widely spoken in Karāchi. Therefore, to emphasize Islam was to emphasize Pakistan. Karāchi, for so long associated with the old India and with British, and therefore Christian, culture, was unsuitable as the capital of the new Muslim state. Consequently, the government lavished millions of dollars on the building of a new capital with the appropriate name of Islamābād, situated safely in the interior, far from the corrupting influences of a cosmopolitan seaport such as Karāchi. In 1959 Islamābād officially became the new capital of West and East Pakistan, and it remained so until East Pakistan seceded in 1971. Meanwhile, Karāchi is still a city where women participate openly in public life, unlike some places in Pakistan's interior. This is perhaps less a British legacy than the result of two centuries of trade and communication with the outside world.

Today, Karāchi is beset with so many problems that its own mayor has referred to the city as a madhouse. Sectarian, communal, ethnic tensions have exploded to ferocious levels, in large part because of the huge chasm that exists between the rich and the poor and the tremendous overcrowding of a city where slums stretch for many miles. In 1981 the city government officially doubled the geographic area of Karāchi, from 285 to 730 square miles, discovering in the process that only 1.6 square miles of the city were devoted to municipal parks. While this fact appalls many visitors from developed nations, Karāchi has many miles of sea coast and beaches that offer relief to the city's inhabitants. Overcrowding, however, is another matter. Since independence, Karāchi has become the recipient of seemingly all of South Asia's refugees, from the millions of Afghans fleeing their war-torn country, to Urdū-speaking Muslims from Bangladesh, to Kashmirīs from India. All have received a safe haven in the bulging city, adding to the internal tensions and strife resulting from poverty, congestion, and political instability.

Political and sectarian conflicts, never far beneath the surface in Pakistan, have become extremely violent in recent years. Islamic terrorists, numbering in the thousands, hold Karāchi's citizens in a deadly grip. In 1994 the result of such turmoil was a death toll approaching 1,000, a figure shocking to Europeans, but about average—or even below average—for the murder rate of a major American city. Four hundred of these victims were praying in mosques, Sunni Muslims killed by Shi'ite Muslim extremists. The next year, three of the city's victims were American diplomats. Coupled with a huge trade in heroin exiting Karāchi, these events have eroded further the promise of the great city.

Nonetheless, as recently as the late 1980s, Karāchi was modernizing, the infrastructure improving, and the World Bank was quite satisfied with the government's stringent fiscal policies. Since then, some intrepid western tourists have returned to the seaport, a gateway to historic wonders in the surrounding region. The determined tourist will find a city that seems to have escaped the homogenization prevalent in the rest of the world. The city boasts hundreds of fascinating old bazaars, many of them specializing in a particular product such as carpets, jewelry, and the like, as in medieval times. There are thousands of mosques, in contrast to the relative handful of churches that stand like isolated beacons of an alien belief. Because of their minority status, the churches are wary and carry on a precarious existence; nonetheless, they always are filled on Sundays. For a century St. Andrew's spire was the highest point in the city. Since independence, it has been supplanted by the Habib Bank, a skyscraper.

Besides churches, many other monuments of British rule are still standing. One of the most interesting is the ramshackle headquarters of the Sind Wildlife Management Board, located in the former Masonic Hall (built 1845). Among the organization's tasks is protecting the sanctuary for giant marine turtles located on Sandspit, the sandbank that separates Karāchi from the open sea; it is one of only nine turtle sanctuaries in the world that is financed by the World Wildlife Fund. Another famous wildlife refuge is Hāleji Lake, fifty miles outside of Karāchi, where migratory birds settle in for the winter, providing an excellent place for bird watching. Karāchi's most famous monument is of relatively recent origin: the mausoleum and last resting place of Mohammed Ali Jinnah. An arresting, domed building situated within the city limits of Karāchi, the space-age looking tomb contains not only the founder's grave but the tombs of his family members as well; it is approached by a pathway lined by fifteen pools.

Karāchi is also the starting point for trips outside the city. Clifton, the beautiful nineteenth-century British seaside resort, is now home to many wealthy Pakistanis. Along the country's crumbling superhighway lies the Makli Hills, the largest cemetery or necropolis in the world; the last resting place of one million dead, its tombs date back to the fourteenth century. Bhanbore, the most famous archaeological site near Karāchi, has revealed extremely ancient remains, spanning the many civilizations that took root in the area before Islam. Also close by is Thatta, the ancient capital of Sind, which boasts the centuries-old Shāh Jahān Mosque. Filled with breathtakingly beautiful Islamic art, it is constructed entirely from local materials. All of these historic places lie within a radius of fifty miles of Karāchi.

Further Reading: The only relatively recent book on Karāchi in English is the brief, illustrated *Karachi* by Mohammed Amin, Duncan Willetts, and Brian Tetley (Karāchi: Pak American Commercial, 1986). Many guidebooks provide chapters on this great seaport city; among the best are *Spectrum Guide to Pakistan* (revised edition, Edison, New Jersey: Hunter, 1993) and *Insight Guides: Pakistan*, edited by Tony Halliday (Singapore: APA, and New York: Prentice Hall, 1990). A comprehensive treatment of Pakistan for the general reader is *Pakistan: A Country Study* (sixth edition, Washington, D.C.: U.S. Government Publications, 1995).

—Sina Dubovoy

Karakorum (Uburkhangai, Mongolia)

Location: About 200 miles west-southwest of Ulaanbaatar, the capital of Mongolia, on the east bank of the Orhon River.

Description: Karakorum, once the capital of Genghis Khan's Mongol Empire, lies in ruins scattered in the vicinity of the present-day town of Harhorin. Many of the stones used to build the original city of Karakorum were carried away to build the nearby Buddhist monastery at Erdenzu Hiid.

Site Office: Juulchin Foreign Tourism Corporation
Chingis Khan Avenue, 5B
Ulaanbaatar 210543
Mongolia
328428 or 322884

In the thirteenth century, the city of Karakorum was chosen by Genghis Khan to be the capital of the Mongol Empire. As the center of an empire extending from the China Sea in the east to the Ukraine in the west, and from the far reaches of Siberia in the north to India in the south, Karakorum was one of the most important cities of its time. Ironically, Genghis Khan rarely visited his capital city; he spent most of his time journeying from one camp to another or on the numerous battlefields of his ever-expanding empire. Still, the city was for some fifty years the focal point of one of the world's largest empires and, until its destruction by the Chinese, Karakorum was the seat from which the great Mongol khans ruled much of the world.

The history of Karakorum begins in the late twelfth century, when a Mongol chieftain named Temüjin began to acquire power over the Mongol tribes through an ongoing series of struggles, sometimes in alliance with his neighbors and sometimes on his own. In time, Temüjin became one of the principal leaders among a group of related Mongol clans. By the end of the twelfth century, he had established his capital in the city of Karakorum, located in the center of Greater Mongolia and thus a convenient gathering spot for the Mongol tribes. In 1206, when a Mongol *kuriltai,* or council, declared Temüjin to be khan of the Mongols and gave him the honorific title Chinggis Khan—usually romanized as Genghis Khan—Karakorum emerged as one of the most important cities in East Asia.

As part of his plans for further conquest, Genghis Khan centralized control of Mongol society in a manner never before seen. He oversaw the distribution of food supplies, horses, and sheep. He set up an intelligence system, took a census, and established a more efficient system of military recruitment. He also assembled a group of Chinese and Muslim military experts to provide advice and planning for the army. In a short time Genghis Khan had established an impressive system of military and political control, which organized all aspects of Mongol society to support his expansionist policies. In addition to making administrative changes in Mongolian society, Genghis Khan ordered that all important events during his reign be recorded. Because of his vanity Mongolian history—a matter of fragmentary and unreliable accounts before this time—was written down for later generations.

Following Genghis Khan's death in 1227, his son Ögödei became khan. Ögödei is said to have built many of Karakorum's first permanent structures (his father had relied primarily on caravan wagons to house his followers). About 1254 Friar Willem van Ruysbroeck, an envoy of King Louis IX of France, made a 5,000-mile journey to the Far East to meet with Asian leaders on behalf of his monarch. Inspired at first to meet Sartach, a leader of Tartar troops in Russia who had converted to Christianity, Ruysbroeck went on to visit Ögödei Khan at his court in Karakorum as well. His account of the visit, written upon his return to France in 1255 as a report to King Louis, predates that of Marco Polo by almost fifty years.

Ruysbroeck describes the khan's palace at Karakorum as being surrounded by three high walls, in an arrangement similar to that at a monks' priory, and set upon a raised mound so as to dominate the grounds. Outside the palace was a walled compound containing barns in which the khan's many gifts of tribute and various provisions were stored. The palace itself was designed much like a church, with a central nave, two side aisles, and two rows of pillars. The building was laid out so that the top of the nave was to the north and the aisles due west and east. The khan's throne was at the far north end of the nave and was set above the rest of the palace. The khan sat upon a panther skin when holding court. Two sets of steps led to the throne: one was used for going up to see the khan, the other was used to come down after seeing him. The nave was an open expanse where visitors to the court stood, with men on the khan's right and women to his left. Along either side of the nave was a raised amphitheatre of benches where the royal family members sat. At the south end of the nave, across from the khan's throne, were three doors. Visitors who entered here were greeted with an impressive view down the full length of the palace.

At the central door on the south end of the palace was a remarkable silver fountain in the shape of a tree surrounded by four lions. Four spouts issued from the mouths of gilded serpents whose tails wrapped around the trunk of the tree. From the first spout flowed wine, from the next, mare's milk, from the third, a honey drink, and from the last spout came rice mead. On top of the tree was a silver angel holding a trumpet. Whenever drinks were needed for those in the pal-

The main temple at the Erdenzu Hiid Monastery, Karakorum
Photo courtesy of Juulchin Foreign Tourism Corporation, Ulaanbaatar

ace, the head cup-bearer would call out to the angel to produce drinks. A man hidden within the silver tree would blow into a tube, making the angel appear to blow its trumpet. Servants in a nearby cavern then would pour beverages into pipes connected to the statue so that, suddenly and as if in response to the angel's signal, the liquids would pour out of the four spouts into vases from which the cup-bearers would serve. The entire show, designed, Ruysbroeck explains, by a smith named William of Paris, must have astounded the superstitious who saw it.

Russian excavations, the results of which were first published in 1965, revealed that the palace at Karakorum measured 165 by 135 feet. Its floor was covered with glazed tiles of pale green, and its wooden pillars rested on granite bases lacquered in bright colors. Despite the size of the palace and the relative opulence of its decoration, the khan maintained his nomadic lifestyle, perhaps as a form of defense against his enemies, and used his great palace at Karakorum only twice a year, when he passed through the area on his trips to and from the various grazing lands his people used for their cattle.

The city had numerous brick buildings and religious shrines. It also was noted for its sculpture, particularly giant stone tortoises that marked the city's boundaries. A center for trade in the area, Karakorum also was surrounded by rich farmland irrigated with waters from the Orhon River.

Ruysbroeck found Karakorum a surprisingly cosmopolitan city, filled with a wide variety of peoples from the far corners of the Mongol Empire, including Turks, Arabs, Tibetans, and Russians. Some were there as slaves, others were engaged in trade, while still others served as mercenaries or interpreters for the Mongol armies. Some visitors from western Europe ultimately settled there as well. When it came time for Ruysbroeck to return to Europe, his traveling companion, one Bartholomew of Cremona, was reluctant to make the long and arduous journey home and chose to remain in Karakorum instead.

When Ruysbroeck returned, his writings about Karakorum gave Europe its first description of Buddhism. The monk learned about the religion by talking to local lamas (monks) in Karakorum. His account of their rituals and everyday activities emphasized the similarities between Buddhist worship and Roman Catholic worship, particularly the common use of prayer beads and the singing of devotional hymns by choirs.

In 1271 Marco Polo left his native Venice with his father and uncle on a trading journey to Asia that saw him spend some twenty-four years away from home. For much of that time Polo served as an emissary to the Mongol ruler Kublai Khan (who had succeeded Ögödei in 1260), acting as his agent in foreign missions. During his travels in the East, Polo visited Karakorum, at that time a less important city than in the time of Willem van Ruysbroeck, primarily because

Stupa at Erdenzu Hiid Monastery, Karakorum
Photo courtesy of Juulchin Foreign Tourism Corporation, Ulaanbaatar

Kublai Khan had moved the Mongolian capital to the Chinese city of Beijing. Polo records that Karakorum was some three miles in circumference and surrounded by an earthen wall. Although no longer the political capital, Karakorum continued to hold great sentimental significance to Mongol tribesmen. Also, in Polo's time the palace remained in use as the seat of a local administrator.

The Mongols' Yuan Dynasty ruled China until 1368, when it was overthrown by the Ming Dynasty. Bilikt Khan, son of the last Mongol emperor, Togon Timur, settled in Karakorum that year and began some building projects. Hostilities between the Chinese and the Mongols persisted; although the Mongols had been expelled from China, their power had not been broken completely. In 1388, a Chinese army invaded Mongolia, took 70,000 prisoners, and destroyed much of Karakorum. The Mongols subsequently rebuilt portions of the city.

In the mid–sixteenth century the last of the great khans was driven from the Mongol homelands and the area became a battleground for warring tribal factions. Karakorum was destroyed by invading Chinese led by Altan Khan of the Tumet, who subjugated much of the region and forced Mongolian princes to pay tribute. The ruins of the original city were used in 1586 to construct the nearby monastery of Erdenzu Hiid. Karakorum was reduced to a small village and lost much of its former prestige.

Under Chinese rule, Mongolia was neglected in the belief that lack of development would keep the Mongols backward and weak. Another by-product of Chinese rule was the growth in power of Buddhist religious institutions. Thousands of Mongols became Buddhist lamas, partly to avoid the excessive taxes imposed on ordinary Mongols by their Chinese masters. Gifts of land and regular tithes brought great wealth to religious leaders. Along with the wealth and resulting influence in society came corruption. Effectively immune to Chinese laws, the chief lamas ruled their monasteries with an iron hand. Harsh punishments, including death by beating, were common.

Erdenzu Hiid was Mongolia's first monastery. Its location at Karakorum was appropriate, given the political and historic significance of the area. Erdenzu Hiid was an impressive complex housing at one time some 10,000 Buddhist lamas and containing more than sixty temples. The first Khutukhtu, a lama who ruled Mongolia as both spiritual and political leader, was a sculptor who reportedly fashioned the many sacred statues still on display at the site. This lama was criticized for having a wife; according to legend, the critics were mollified when they saw her sculpt a statue of Buddha from a mass of molten bronze with her bare hands. He was not the only member of the religious community to flout the rules concerning celibacy; many of the monks had either male or female lovers. Life in the monastery brought a certain amount of privilege and luxury.

Stone Tortoise, Karakorum
Photo courtesy of Juulchin Foreign Tourism Corporation, Ulaanbaatar

Today the monastery is surrounded by a wall nearly 500 yards square. Much of the enclosed area is empty grassland, the many temples long since torn down by communist officials. Only three Buddhist temples remain; these are open to the public and house a collection of artifacts, including seventeenth- and eighteenth-century figurines and religious statues made of stone. One of the temples, known as Ögödei's Temple, also contains fragments of thirteenth-century wall paintings of Buddhas.

From the seventeenth century onward a split developed between the northern, or outer, Mongols, whose territory included Erdenzu Hiid, and the southern, or inner, Mongols. The split became official in 1911, when the northern Mongols, taking advantage of the fall of the Qing Dynasty in China, declared their independence and established the nation of Outer Mongolia. The new nation became allied with Russia (and, subsequently, the Soviet Union) as a defense against the Chinese. In 1924 it became the Mongolian People's Republic, the world's second communist country.

Under communist rule, Buddhist institutions were attacked mercilessly. Buddhist lands and wealth were confiscated and lamas were forced out of their monasteries, often in mid-winter, to make their way in the bitter cold. Although some lamas were murdered by communist troops, most were sent to prison camps or work brigades. The monastery of Erdenzu Hiid was closed.

During the years of communist rule, Karakorum, now known as Harhorin, was the site of one of the country's most important state farms. The communist government arranged for a Chinese construction program to dig a sluice to divert water from the river to a hydroelectric plant. The water also was used to irrigate nearby fields. The present town of Harhorin is arranged around a central square where drab office buildings common to many former communist nations can be found. An electrical power station, several hundred houses, and a fuel dump make up the rest of the small community.

The collapse of the Soviet Union brought with it changes in Mongolia as well. Free elections were held in which a much moderated Communist Party won control of a democratic government. The monastery at Erdenzu was reopened and a handful of lamas returned to live there once again, having quietly survived the era of communist oppression by working in the country as farmhands or herdsmen. They have refurbished what remains of the monastery, which has become a tourist attraction, and restored the daily rituals of the Buddhist faith. Each day they call the locals to prayer with a blast on a conch shell. Two of the original four large stone tortoise sculptures that marked the boundaries of the ancient city can still be seen near the walls of Erdenzu Hiid. Also near the monastery is a small hill upon which is a large phallic stone marked with ancient engravings.

Further Reading: *Contemporaries of Marco Polo*, edited by Manuel Komroff (New York: Boni and Liveright, and London: Cape, 1928), contains the writings of four early Western travelers into the farthest reaches of Asia, including the account written by Willem van Ruysbroeck of his journey to visit the khan. *The Travels* by Marco Polo, translated by R. E. Latham (Harmondsworth, Middlesex, and Baltimore, Maryland: Penguin, 1958), contains an account of Polo's brief visit to Karakorum as well as a description of Mongol customs and culture of the time. Victor P. Petrov's *Mongolia: A Profile* (New York: Praeger, and London: Pall Mall, 1970) provides a detailed overview of Mongolian history since the earliest times, as well as information about the country's history as a communist republic. A similar approach is found in *The Modern History of Mongolia* by C. R. Bawden (New York: Praeger, and London: Weidenfeld and Nicolson, 1968; second edition, London and New York: Kegan Paul, 1989). An informative U.S. government publication, including an account of Mongolian history along with detailed information on recent economic and political trends, is *Mongolia: A Country Study*, edited by Robert L. Worden and Andrea Matles Savada (second edition, Washington, D.C.: Federal Research Division, Library of Congress, 1991). The best travel guide to Mongolia is Robert Storey's *Mongolia: A Travel Survival Kit* (Hawthorn, Victoria, and Berkeley, California: Lonely Planet, 1993), which provides recent information on accommodations, transportation, and historic sites. Tim Severin's *In Search of Genghis Khan* (London: Hutchinson, 1991; New York: Atheneum, 1992) is an account of the author's travels in Mongolia, visiting sites associated with the great Mongol leader.

—Thomas Wiloch

Kashgar (Xinjiang Uighur Autonomous Region, China)

Location: In the southwest of the Xinjiang Uighur Autonomous Region of China on the Kizil Su, a tributary of the Tarim River. The Xinjiang region has been known variously in Western literature as Chinese Turkistan, Eastern Turkistan, and Chinese Tartary.

Description: An important political, religious, and economic center on the ancient Silk Road; also known in modern times as Kashi.

Contact: Xinjiang Tourism Bureau
46 Jianguo Road
830002 Urumqi, Xinjiang
China
(991) 227912

The oasis city of Kashgar lies to the east of the Pamirs at an intersection of the ancient Silk Road. Here the trade routes that skirted the northern and southern fringes of the Takla Makan Desert converged, and from Kashgar travelers crossed the Pamirs to Fergana before heading west through Sogdiana or Bactria to Merv (now Mary).

Like Yarkend, Khotan, Kucha, and the other small city-states of the Tarim Basin, Kashgar is thought to have been populated by Śakas (Indo-Europeans) from before the end of the second century B.C. For much of the second century the area was under the sway of the Xiongnu. Early attempts by the Western Han Dynasty (206 B.C.–A.D. 9) to check the advance of its northern neighbors met with little success, but from 115 to 60 B.C. the struggle for supremacy in the region intensified. When the Chinese conquered Fergana in 101 B.C., the city-states of the Tarim Basin were cowered into sending tribute to the Han. However, Han power in the region remained tenuous and was eroded by the end of the Western Han Dynasty.

The earliest specific references to the city-state of Kashgar (Shule) appear in the Chinese dynastic histories. The *History of the Later Han* records that Kashgar was brought under Chinese control at the end of the first century A.D. by General Ban Chao. At the time of Ban Chao's arrival in the Tarim Basin, Kashgar had been subjugated by the ruler of the city-state of Kucha. Ban Chao restored a Kashgarian king to the throne, thereby securing a new vassal for the Eastern Han (A.D. 25–220), and then proceeded westward, gaining the submission of some fifteen more states. Despite Ban Chao's impressive conquests, however, the Chinese failed to consolidate their position, and by the mid–second century their hold on the region was lost. According to the Chinese records, Ban Chao himself retired to the Eastern Han capital of Luoyang, where he died in A.D. 102. However, in the 1930s there was still a temple at Kashgar purported to hold his tomb.

Our knowledge of the political and cultural history of Kashgar from the third through sixth centuries is decidedly fragmentary, but it appears that, like other cities of the Tarim Basin, Kashgar fell under the rule of the Juan-juan (possibly related to the Xiongnu), the Hephthalites (Persians), and, in the mid–sixth century, the Turks. During the Tang Dynasty (618–907), the Chinese once again turned their attention to Central Asia and control of the trade routes to the West. In the early 690s Chinese garrisons were established at Kucha, Karashahr, Khotan, and Kashgar, but their position was challenged repeatedly by Turk and Tibetan forces. In the latter half of the seventh century the region was occupied briefly by the Tibetans, but by the early eighth century the Chinese had reestablished a military presence in Kashgar.

The establishment of Buddhism in the Tarim Basin probably began in the third or fourth century. When the Chinese Buddhist monk Fa Xian traveled through the region on his way to India in the late fourth or early fifth century, Buddhism already was established in several of the city-states. Two centuries later, when the Buddhist pilgrim Xuan Zang passed that way, he encountered flourishing centers of Hinayana Buddhism. Thus, despite the political vicissitudes and the arrival of other religions—including Zoroastrianism, Nestorianism, Manichaeanism, and, of course, Islam—Buddhism was entrenched so well that it retained a significant foothold in the area until at least the twelfth century. Over the course of centuries, however, Buddhist temples gradually were erased as Islam encroached on the holy Buddhist sites. Thus, by the early twentieth century the physical evidence of Kashgar's rich Buddhist heritage had all but vanished, reduced—according to the sister of the British consul—to the ruins of two stupas to the north and south of the British consulate.

Although the Chinese maintained a garrison in Kashgar into the eighth century, the city-state continued to enjoy local autonomy. The Arab invasion of Kashgar in 711 has been the subject of much academic debate; recent scholarship argues that although the Arabs did not hold Kashgar for any length of time, evidence clearly shows that they conducted a lightning raid on the city. A more persistent threat, however, were the Tibetans. By the end of the eighth century, both the Tibetans and the Karluks (a tribe of the Western Turks) were extending their influence throughout Eastern Turkistan. The Karluks established a hold over the north and west of the region and are thought to have assumed control of Kashgar sometime between 766 and 775; however, the Sino-Tibetan treaty of 783 afforded the Tibetans dominion throughout Eastern Turkistan. Only in the late ninth century, after the collapse of the Tibetan Empire, did the Turkic tribes reassert their authority in the form of the Turkic Karakhanids.

Tomb of Apak Khoja, Kashgar
Photo courtesy of The Chicago Public Library

Kashgar probably became the capital of the Karakhanids sometime after 893. According to tradition, the first Turkic ruler to accept Islam was Satok Bughra Khan of the Karakhanid Dynasty in 966. From Kashgar, the Muslim Khan started his campaign against the Buddhist city-states to the east, notably Khotan. Local legends abound concerning Satok Bughra Khan and his descendants. Ali Arslan, Satok Bughra Khan's grandson (also recorded as his nephew), is said to have been killed in battle against the Buddhists. According to popular belief, his body was buried on the battle site at Ordam Padshah, fifty miles southeast of Kashgar, but his head was taken back to Kashgar, where it was enshrined north of the city at Daulatbagh. Also during this period, in approximately 1069, the poet and scholar Yusuf Has Hajip lived in Kashgar, where he wrote the *Kutadghu bilik*, a didactic poem intended to serve as a moral guide to kings. Yusuf Has Hajip is revered as one of the region's preeminent literary figures, and his tomb still can be seen in Kashgar.

Under two centuries of Karakhanid rule, the Kashgar region saw Islam gain considerable ground at the expense of Buddhism. Yet neither Buddhism nor Nestorianism (a Christian doctrine whose founder, Nestorius, was condemned in 431, after which his followers broke from the Byzantine Church) was eradicated. Indeed, in the twelfth century under the Kara-khitai, who replaced the Karakhanids, Nestorianism flourished, and Kashgar became a center of the Nestorian Church. In the early thirteenth century, Kashgar was overrun by the forces of Genghis Khan, and upon the division of the empire, the region passed into the hands of his son Chagatai. The Mongols also seem to have adopted a policy of religious tolerance, and, as evidenced by Marco Polo when he passed through Kashgar at the end of the century, Nestorianism and Islam continued to coexist. The people of Kashgar, Polo wrote,

> subsist by commerce and manufacture, particularly works of cotton. They have handsome gardens, orchards, and vineyards. Abundance of cotton is produced there as well as flax and hemp. . . . Besides the Mahometans [Muslims] there are amongst the inhabitants several Nestorian Christians, who are permitted to live under their own laws and to have their churches.

The Chagatai khans enjoyed nominal sovereignty in the Tarim Basin until the seventeenth century, but in Kashgar from the mid–fourteenth to the early sixteenth century, power lay in the hands of the Dughlat khans, another Mongol clan. In 1514, however, the Dughlat khan Abū Bakr was overthrown by the warrior Sa'īd Khan, and the Chagatai khanate was temporarily reestablished. In the early sixteenth century Hazrat Makhdum-i A'zam, an Islamic miracle-worker from Bukhara, visited Kashgar and received the patronage of the ruling khan.

In the seventeenth century the religious and political influence of Apak Khoja (Khoja Hidayetullah), the great-grandson of Makhdum-i A'zam, was such that he posed a threat to the ruler, Isma'il Khan, and was banished from the city. Assisted by the Dzungars (Western Mongols), who held sway in the area north of the Tianshan range, Apak Khoja returned to Kashgar, from where he ruled the area of Yarkend, Khotan, Aksu, Kucha, and Turfan as a nominal Dzungarian protectorate.

When Apak Khoja died in 1693, he was entombed in the mausoleum where he had buried his father. Situated two miles southeast of the city, Apak Khoja's tomb, as it became known—with its large dome and decorative facade of green, blue, and white tiles—is still one of Kashgar's most impressive buildings; the site, which includes a large mosque, has become a center of Muslim veneration. To the Chinese, the mausoleum also is known as the tomb of Xiang Fei, a Kashgarian concubine of the Qing emperor Qianlong in the eighteenth century. Legend has it that her body was returned to her beloved homeland for burial. No historical evidence confirms this legend, however.

By the time of Apak Khoja's death, and possibly earlier, the descendants of Makhdum-i A'zam clearly had become divided into two rival sects. The Ak-taghliq and the Kara-taghliq, the White and Black Mountaineers, derived their names from their respective Kirghiz supporters; a particularly bloody power struggle now developed between them. Once again, the Dzungars intervened, and the Kashgarian throne finally was awarded to the Black Mountaineers. In the 1750s, when the Dzungars themselves were hard pressed by the Chinese, renewed disturbances arose in the Tarim Basin, and this time the Dzungars gave their support to the White Mountaineers. By 1757, however, the Manchu forces of the Chinese Qing Dynasty had all but eliminated the Dzungars; the White Khojas, refusing to accept Chinese supremacy, revolted in 1758. Chinese troops marched on the Tarim Basin, the Turkic forces were defeated swiftly, and the ruling Khojas fled across the Pamirs.

A citadel was built at Kashgar for the Manchu garrison, and for the next 100 years the city remained an important administrative and military center of Qing authority in the Tarim Basin. This was the first time that the Chinese had consolidated their rule over the entire region of Eastern Turkistan. Nevertheless, the Manchus interfered little in the traditional way of life of their Muslim subjects and left the civil administration of the Tarim Basin largely in local hands. Kashgar continued to prosper as a religious and commercial center, yet Qing rule did not go unchallenged. From the 1820s, the city was attacked periodically by descendants of Apak Khoja who still were living in exile in neighboring khanates. The Khojas were supported variously by the khans of Kokand, by Kirghiz tribes, or by the Kashgarians themselves; nevertheless, between 1820 and 1840, the Khojas' repeated attempts to dislodge the Manchu forces were largely unsuccessful; at their most successful, the Khojas secured a few months' control of Kashgar and the surrounding region. However, by the 1850s the Qing Dynasty clearly was in crisis, and its hold on its distant western dominion was weakening.

In 1868 Buzurg Khan of Kokand took advantage of the Chinese Muslim revolts that had spread to Eastern Turkistan from the Kansu region of China and invaded Kashgaria. Victory was swift, but hardly had he established his seat of government in Kashgar when one of his generals, a certain Yakub Beg, usurped the throne. Thereafter, Yakub Beg held the region for twelve years.

These events coincided with the rise of the Anglo-Russian rivalry in Central Asia, the so-called "Great Game." Consequently, for at least the next sixty years, the Tarim Basin attracted much attention from Western diplomats, soldiers, explorers, and scholars. As a result, an extensive body of Western literature exists on the region dating from this period.

Many of those who traveled to Kashgaria in the 1870s commented on the reassertion of Islam under Yakub Beg's rule. Islamic law was enforced strictly, and numerous religious sites were restored. It was under Yakub Beg's rule, for example, that Kashgar's largest and most famous mosque, the Id Kah mosque, was enlarged and renovated.

In 1877 the Chinese general Zuo Zongtang reconquered the region, and in 1884 it finally became a province of China. By the early twentieth century, both the British and Russians had established consulates in Kashgar. Under George Macartney, the first British consul, Chini Bagh, as the consulate was known, gained a reputation for the hospitality it afforded Western travelers. This was emulated by his successors, and visitors to Chini Bagh included the explorers and archaeologists Sven Hedin, Aurel Stein, Albert von Le Coq, and many more. In addition to the British and Russian consulates, the other notable foreign presence in Kashgar at the turn of the century was the Swedish mission, which was known not only for the medical services it offered the local community but for possessing the only printing press in Kashgar.

During the republican, or nationalist, period (1911–49), when Kashgar again was caught up in rebellion against Chinese rule, it was on this press that the newly formed Islamic Republic of Eastern Turkistan published its literature. The new republic was short-lived; founded in November 1933, by February 1934 it had been torn asunder by a combination of internal strife and the onslaught of the Chinese Muslims (Tungans). In mid–1945, soon after the republican government had established an armistice with the insurgents in the Ili area of northern Xinjiang, another rebellion broke out in Kashgar, but by autumn 1946 the Chinese nationalist government had reasserted its authority.

After 1949 the province of Xinjiang was brought increasingly into the Chinese political and cultural sphere.

While the population of Kashgar remained primarily Turkic, Uighur, Kazakh, and Kirghiz, Han Chinese were encouraged to immigrate to the region in large numbers. Islamic practices were restricted severely, and with the onset of the Cultural Revolution, mosques were closed and frequently damaged or destroyed.

For ten years the cultural and economic life of the city stagnated, but since Beijing initiated its program of economic reform in 1978, and particularly after the opening of the Karakoram Pass in 1986, Kashgar again has become a vital center of trade. Tourism has had a significant impact on the economy, and both the former British and Russian consulates have acquired a new function as hotels. Islam also is recovering from the blow it was dealt during the Cultural Revolution, and Kashgar once again is establishing itself as a center of Islamic learning.

Further Reading: *The Cambridge History of Early Inner Asia*, edited by Denis Sinor (Cambridge and New York: Cambridge University Press, 1990), contains essays covering a wide range of topics, with much valuable information relating to Kashgar. An earlier, less scholarly account of Kashgar may be found in *Through Deserts and Oases of Central Asia* by Ella Constance Sykes and Percy Molesworth Sykes (London: Macmillan, 1920). For a limited look at the multi-national influences on Kashgar during three decades prior to World War I, see *Macartney at Kashgar: New Light on British, Chinese, and Russian Activities in Sinkiang 1890-1918* by C. P. Skrine and Pamela Nightingale (London: Methuen, 1973; Hong Kong and Oxford: Oxford University Press, 1987). Another useful source on Central Asia is *Foreign Devils on the Silk Road: The Search for the Lost Cities and Treasures of Chinese Central Asia* by P. Hopkirk (London: J. Murray, 1980; Amherst: University of Massachusetts Press, 1984).

—L. J. Newby

Kashihara (Nara, Japan)

Location: In Nara Prefecture on Honshū (the main island of Japan), thirteen miles south of Nara City and twenty-four miles southeast of Ōsaka.

Description: The site of the supposed residence of Jimmu Tennō, the legendary first emperor of Japan, Kashihara is noted today for its nineteenth-century Shintō shrine and its historic museum; it is close to the ancient capital, Asuka, and numerous burial mounds.

Contact: Nara City Tourist Center
23-4 Kami-Sanjo-cho
Nara 630, Nara
Japan
(0742) 22 3900

Kashihara, a city in Nara Prefecture, should not be confused with another ancient settlement, variously known as Kashiwara or Kashihara, in Ōsaka prefecture. The first city is the better known of the two because of its association with the creation of the Japanese state and with the lives of some of its earliest emperors, both legendary and historical. According to the earliest chronicles of Japan, the *Kojiki* and the *Nihongi* (or *Nihon Shoki*), compiled after A.D. 712, it was at Kashihara (Oaktree Plain) that the legendary figure Jimmu Tennō, a descendant of the sun goddess Amaterasu no Omikami, founded the first Japanese imperial court. He is supposed to have arrived at the site in 660 B.C., after a sea journey from the southwestern island of Kyūshū, and to have ruled over what became Yamato province (modern-day Nara prefecture) until his death in 585 B.C. According to these dates, however, Jimmu would have lived to the obviously impossible age of 120, after a reign of 75 years. Since 1945, when the official prohibition on questioning the content of the ancient chronicles was lifted, archaeological research in Japan, coupled with documentary research in China, has tended to undermine much of the detail in both the *Nihongi* and the *Kojiki*, although some scholars suggest that there was a real person behind the legend of Jimmu. He may have been a local ruler who conquered much of the area around Kashihara some time after 62 B.C. or, perhaps, as late as the third or fourth century A.D. If he existed, he could not have taken the title tennō (emperor), an honorific that was composed in the seventh century from Chinese loanwords that were unknown in Japan during any of his possible lifetimes; however, he may have used all or part of the name Kamu-Yamato-Iware Hiko-no-mikoto, an alternative given in the chronicles.

In accordance with the taboos against death and decay that still characterize Shintō, the indigenous religion of Japan, Jimmu's capital at Kashihara was abandoned by his successor. Kashihara is said to have remained uninhabited until 92 B.C., when the emperor Sujin, another legendary ruler, chose it as the site for a shrine in which he deposited the sacred mirror, supposedly given to the emperors by Amaterasu herself, which is one of the three symbols of the imperial line (along with the sword and jewels). At that date the place appears to have been known as Kasanui. Sujin's shrine eventually was abandoned when the mirror was transferred to Ise, perhaps as early as the third century A.D. but almost certainly no later than the sixth century A.D. The city was abandoned despite the fact that it lies only two and one-half miles northwest of Asuka, the site of one of the imperial residences for which there is some reliable historical evidence. The most important structure located there is the Buddhist temple Asuka-dera (also known as Ango-in), which, like all other ancient wooden buildings in Japan, has been destroyed and rebuilt several times over the centuries. If it indeed was founded in 588, as tradition asserts, it may have been the first temple built expressly for Buddhist worship in the country. Its founder is said to have been Soga Umako, then the head of the Soga family, which, from 552 onward, actively propagated Buddhism. Asuka-dera also is famous for its bronze statue of the historic Buddha Siddhārtha Gautama (known in Japan as Shaka Nyorai), said to have been made in 606.

The Soga clan eventually defeated the opponents to their new religion and, in so doing, were able to take control of the Japanese throne. Asuka became the residence of the empress Suiko, who was Soga Umako's sister, from her accession in 593 to her death in 628, and of her nephew and chief minister Shōtoku Taishi (Prince Shōtoku), who is said to have been born in Kashihara in 574 and to have died in Asuka in 622. Shōtoku presided over the final adoption of Buddhism as the state religion of Japan, founding Shitennō-ji, the great temple of Ōsaka, and writing (or at least endorsing) the Seventeen-Article Code, a mixture of Confucian and Buddhist moral precepts that is sometimes referred to as the first Japanese constitution. Shōtoku also is said to have founded Tachibana-ji, a temple that supposedly marks the site of his birthplace, although it is nearer to Asuka than to Kashihara. Still another temple, Okadera (or Ryūgai-ji), was founded in Asuka in 663, after the town had been abandoned by Suiko's successor. This contains a sixteen-foot-high statue of Kannon (Avalokitesvara in Sanskrit), the Buddhist goddess of mercy, said to have been made of clay gathered from China and Korea as well as from the countryside nearby.

The area between and around Kashihara and Asuka is also unusually rich in *kofun*, the round, square, or keyhole-shaped burial mounds, often within moats, that were constructed between the third and sixth centuries A.D., probably for emperors and powerful nobles. These also are to be found elsewhere in Nara prefecture, in Ōsaka prefecture, in parts of

Mausoleum of the emperor Jimmu, Kashihara
Photo courtesy of Japan National Tourist Organization

Kyūshū, and elsewhere in Japan; there are thought to be at least 10,000 altogether, which vary greatly in size, style, and probable importance. The most-visited mound in the Kashihara district is also the one least likely to have any connection with the person who is traditionally supposed to be buried in it. This is supposedly the tomb of Jimmu, at the foot of Unebiyama, a hill to the north of the city. The mound has been sanctified with a *torii,* the simple gateway of two columns joined by two cross-bars that signifies a Shintō shrine; it is visited by worshipers to this day.

A mound near Asuka, Takamatsu-zuka, was excavated as recently as 1972. It is notable for its elaborate mural paintings of courtiers, dressed in Chinese-style robes, dating from the seventh or eighth century. The stylistic resemblance to murals in ancient Korean tombs and the arrangement alongside paintings of a dragon, a tiger, a snake, and a turtle (which represent four of the twelve signs of the Chinese zodiac) are striking evidence of the impact made by the culture of the East Asian mainland on Japan during the sixth and seventh centuries. Much to the horror of Japanese nationalists in modern times, perhaps one in three of the nobles surrounding the early emperors, as well as many of the craftsmen and artists who created the mounds and temples, were themselves, or were descended from, Korean and Chinese immigrants. Since the discovery of these murals, the tomb has been resealed and an underground chamber has been built next to it to display full-scale photographs of the works.

Perhaps the single most striking tomb in the area is the one known as the Ishi-butai (Stone Stage) near Tachibana-ji, simply because it is incomplete and open to the air. It includes the remains of a corridor with walls six feet high, and a square chamber with walls rising to around sixteen feet, constructed of enormous rocks and boulders; this almost certainly typifies the structures that elsewhere are out of sight, deep inside the mounds of earth. It is also possible that this was the tomb of Soga Umako himself; so, it may have been the last such burial in Yamato before the court adopted the Buddhist practice of cremation. Other *kofun* within walking distance of Kashihara include two large examples, believed to be those of the emperors Kinmei, who died in 571, and Mommu, who died in 707. If these ascriptions are accurate, they confirm the scholarly consensus that Kashihara, Asuka, and the fertile valley in which they stand continued to be used for religious purposes, perhaps also for the shifting imperial residences, until 687. In that year Fujiwara, the first planned urban settlement in Japan, was laid out on a grid pattern based on that of the Chinese capital city of that era, Chang'an (modern-day Xian). The southern edge of its rectangular grid probably lay along what is now the road between Asuka and Kashihara. Fujiwara was occupied by two emperors in succession, thus breaking the ancient cycle; it, too, was abandoned in 710 for a new grid-based city, the site of which can be seen on the outskirts of Nara City.

Kashihara Jingū Shrine, Kashihara
Photo courtesy of Japan National Tourist Organization

Kashihara Jingū, the Shintō shrine that honors Jimmu and his wife Himetatara Isuzuhime, was established in 1889, twenty-six years after scholars of the imperial court (aided by legends rather than by scientific research) decided that the site was once occupied by Jimmu's palace (or house, or encampment). The site is on the other side of Unebiyama (Mount Unebi) from the *kofun* that is purported to be the tomb of Jimmu. The shrine buildings, set in a dense forest and approached along a broad graveled avenue, were originally made from timber taken from the former imperial palace in Kyōto, but they were reconstructed in 1939 and have been restored since, in 1963 and 1983. The style of the buildings, which has been maintained faithfully, was intended to recall the original simplicity of imperial palace architecture before it was influenced by Chinese styles. But even less was known of ancient Japan in 1889 than is known now, so the buildings actually follow a standard Shintō pattern with curved overhanging Chinese-style roofs. Annual celebrations at the shrine, the hill, and the tomb still take place on February 11, a date designated as National Foundation Day since 1966; until 1945 it was regarded as the date of Jimmu's accession. This festival attracts enthusiastic support from extreme nationalist groups, who park their large black armored buses nearby and switch off their famously loud public address systems before entering the shrine grounds to mingle with the crowds of ordinary Japanese visitors enjoying the national holiday.

Near the shrine stands a museum devoted to the ancient history of Yamato province, which is officially called the Nara Kenritsu Kashihara Kokogaku-kenkyusho Fuzoku Hakubutsukan (The Museum Attached to the Nara Prefecture Archeological Research Institute of Kashihara). Fortunately, it is generally known as the Yamato Rekishikan, literally the Yamato History Hall. Its exhibits include fossil remains of animals from up to 30,000 years ago and fragments of pottery ranging from that created around 10,000 years ago to that created during the Yayoi Period, approximately 300 B.C. to A.D. 300. Many of these latter items were uncovered at Tawaramoto three miles north of Kashihara. The most impressive objects in the museum were discovered inside burial mounds. These include *haniwa,* the small terra-cotta figures of human beings and animals found in or near *kofun,* which are thought to represent the ruler's courtiers and servants. The name *haniwa,* which means "ring of clay," refers to their positioning around the middle or top of a typical burial mound, where they strengthened the structure both literally and symbolically. (At some earlier time actual courtiers and servants may have been buried with the ruler, although in Japan, unlike in mainland Asia, there has been no archaeological confirmation of such a practice.) There are also examples of gray pottery, clearly based on Korean models or perhaps even imported from that country, which was more culturally sophisticated at the time; pieces of armor and weapons found with human remains, almost all of which appear to have been male; *magatama,* comma-shaped jewels that form part of the imperial regalia of Japan; and bronze mirrors, of the type first imported from China and Korea and then made in Japan, which were often representations of the sacred mirror of Amaterasu, another imperial symbol.

Kashihara today has a population of over 100,000 and is largely a bedroom community for nearby Nara City. Yet, like other small cities in Nara prefecture, it has taken part in the postwar economic transformation of Japan while preserving much of its semirural beauty and ancient tranquility.

Further Reading: *Japan Inside Out,* a massive, idiosyncratic, and impressive guidebook by Jay, Sumi, and Garet Gluck (second edition, Ashiya, Japan: Personally Oriented Limited, 1992), provides both details and context on Kashihara, Asuka, and other places important to the ancient history of Japan. Two ancient official histories that are the only documentary sources for the story of Jimmu are the *Kojiki, or, Records of Ancient Matters,* translated by Basil Hall Chamberlain (Yokohama: R. Meiklejon, and Rutland, Vermont: Tuttle, 1982) and *Nihongi: Chronicles of Japan from the Earliest Times to* A.D. *697,* translated by W. G. Aston (2 vols., London: Kegan Paul, 1896; Rutland, Vermont: Tuttle, 1972).

—Patrick Heenan

Kāthmāndu (Nepal)

Location: Nepal lies in a 54,000-square-mile area between Tibet and India, bordered by the Himalaya Mountain range to the north and the Terai Plains to the south. Kāthmāndu lends its name to both the valley region in the center of the kingdom and the capital city in the center of the valley, the latter situated at the confluence of the Bāghmati and Vishnumati Rivers. Twelve miles by seventeen miles in area, the Kāthmāndu Valley rises 4,500 feet above sea level.

Description: Kāthmāndu and its neighboring towns Lalitpur and Bhaktapūr are medieval communities only recently accessible to Western travelers. Governed by oligarchies for centuries, Nepal's capital city remains economically depressed and mired in a long-standing caste system. Religiously, however, Kāthmāndu is one of the chief centers of Eastern thought, providing a common ground for Hindus and Buddhists, and its vibrant spiritual and artistic community has made the area a favorite destination of foreign travelers since the 1950s. Kāthmāndu's population is approximately 300,000, although Lalitpur practically has merged with the capital.

Site Office: Ministry of Tourism and Civil Aviation
Singh Durbar
Kāthmāndu
Nepal
(1) 225 579

The Kāthmāndu Valley has a spiritual heritage matched by few other parts of the globe. Its 200 square miles feature approximately 2,700 shrines, Hindu and Buddhist alike. According to Buddhist legend, the valley is located on the site of a vast, ancient lake, drained long ago by the bodhisattva Manjushrī. Manjushrī had come to worship Lord Swayambhu, the Supreme Being emanating in the form of a bright flame from a lotus blossom tossed into the center of the lake by the first Buddha, Vipasuri. Wishing to improve worshipers' access to the deity, Manjushrī sliced through a hill to the lake's south, creating a gorge that carried the waters away and left a natural site for settlement. Hindu legends credit the god Vishnu with a similar alteration of the course of nature in the Kāthmāndu Valley. This is just one of the myriad ways in which the tales of Buddhists and Hindus intertwine in Nepal.

Although the kingdom is predominantly Hindu, for centuries Buddhists have enjoyed respect for, and even assimilation of, their own beliefs here. As a result, the Kāthmāndu Valley is rife with stupas, the concentric shrines favored by both religions. Just to the west of Kāthmāndu, across the Vishnumati River, is the best known of these monuments, the Swayambhunath Stupa. One of Buddhism's more important shrines, this stupa was built in honor of Lord Swayambhu on the spot of the long-vanished, thousand-petal lotus blossom. At Swayambhunath, huge painted symbols of the Buddha's eyes overlook the stupa's 365 steps and its panoramic view of the city. Swayambhunath is surrounded by shrines celebrating other gods and goddesses, such as those of Earth, Wind, and Boundless Light. Known for its simian patrons, Swayambhunath often is called the "Monkey Temple."

The stupas of the Kāthmāndu Valley share several elements. These include the aforementioned eyelike ornamentation; prayer wheels that surround a domed base symbolizing the womb of the Buddha's mother; a series of rings representing the "thirteen steps of becoming pure"; and a crown that signifies the achievement of nirvana. Hindu temples in Kāthmāndu provide the odd sight of worshipers honoring their gods—who recognize all manner of human behavior—by going about their daily routines (doing laundry, playing games, and napping) on the grounds.

To the east of Kāthmāndu, near its airport, is Pashupatinath, the only Hindu temple of the valley that does not admit the faithful of other beliefs to its inner sanctum. This stupa celebrates Siva as Lord of the Animals; inscriptions discovered on the site trace back to A.D. 477, and the stupa may date as far back as 1,000 years before that. Also to the east are the Āryaghat—the cremation platform of the royal families of Kāthmāndu—and the Temple of Guhyeshwari, where Sati, wife of Siva and originator of the self-immolation ritual, is enshrined.

Until the eighteenth century, the kingdom of Nepal was restricted to the immediate surroundings of the Kāthmāndu Valley. With the Himalayas to the north and the Terai swamp region along Nepal's southern border with India, the area was difficult to traverse. A seventh-century Chinese traveler is attributed with naming the country, after he heard in India of the neighboring land called "Ni-Po-La." Others claim that "Nepal" is derived from "Newar," the indigenous people of the valley. "Nepal" was the word the hill-dwelling Gurkhas used to describe the valley, and only recently has "Nepal" become accepted as the name of the entire country.

The Newars, claimants to the lineage of Manjushrī, are thought to be the original inhabitants of Kāthmāndu Valley, although they are less well known to the outside world than are either of their Nepali neighbors, the Himalayan porters called Sherpas, or the Gurkhas, mercenary warriors from the hills to the north of the valley. The Newari language is more closely related to the Tibeto-Burman derivation of the Himalayas than it is to the official Nepali language, which is spoken by slightly fewer than half of the valley inhabitants.

Kāthmāndu Valley
Photo courtesy of Air India Library, New York

The Kāthmāndu Valley has been a refuge for political and religious outcasts for centuries. Some historians believe the Kirāti Dynasty—whose rule from the eighth century B.C. marked the beginning of recorded history in Nepal—came from east of the valley, although other experts consider the Kirātis an indigenous people. Under Kirāti rule, around the late sixth century B.C., the valley was exposed to Buddhism; during the reign of the seventh of twenty-eight Kirāti kings, Siddhārtha Gautama is said to have visited the Kāthmāndu Valley and rested at Lalitpur (Pātan), one of three sister cities (along with Bhaktapūr and the capital, Kāthmāndu) that comprise the hub of activity in the valley. In A.D. 300 the last of the Kirātis, Gasti, was defeated and replaced by the first of the Lichhavi (also spelled Licchavi) Dynasty.

The Lichhavis, who ruled for 550 years, inherited a prosperous land from the Kirātis, whose 1,000-year rule had been made possible by the lucrative trade route shuttling woven and metal handicrafts and animal products between Tibet and India. The Lichhavis, descended from the Rājputs of northern India, introduced the Hindu religion and its caste system to Nepal. As well, their patronage of the Buddhist art still on view at ancient *chaityas* (chapels) helped establish the first Golden Age of Nepalese art.

In the seventh century, the Chinese traveler Wang Xuan Zhe remarked on the impressive architecture and culture he saw on a sojourn through the Kāthmāndu Valley; he wrote of a seven-story palace, lavishly adorned, with dragon-shaped fountains and a bejeweled king ruling from a throne resembling a lion. The introduction during the seventh century of Buddhism to neighboring Tibet greatly enhanced trade between the two countries; a Newari princess had married a Tibetan king, and her ambassadorship led to a healthy demand in Tibet for bronze iconic sculpture made in her homeland. The ensuing trade fostered its own set of legends: each year on the Nepali holiday of Chakandeo Jātrā, the ancient Newari trader Singha Saratha Bāhu is celebrated. On a traders' expedition to Tibet, he supposedly was the only Newari to escape the clutches of Tibet's mesmerizing women, returning home to the valley riding a winged, white horse.

A political and social "Dark Age" lay in waiting, however, brightened only by the founding of the city of Kāthmāndu (at first called Kantipur) in the tenth century by King Gunakamadeva. The king claimed he had a vision of Lakshmi, the goddess of wealth, who advised him to build a city at the convergence of the Bāghmati and Vishnumati Rivers, where he would oversee 18,000 houses and an economy trading 100,000 rupees daily. According to legend, the king threw a series of religious festivals attended by a deity in disguise who, upon his discovery, was detained by an overzealous group of Tantrists. The king promised to release the god in exchange for a celestial tree, which he ordered made into a sacred building called a *kasthamandap*—an early form of the name Kāthmāndu. The current *kasthamandap* is thought to be the oldest existing wood building in the world.

By the beginning of the thirteenth century, the three main towns of Kāthmāndu Valley had entered complex relations with one another that revolved around the commerce developed on the Tibet-India trade route. At this time, the Malla epoch began, so named because its first king, Arideva, received notice of his son's birth while he was engaged in his favorite pastime—wrestling, or *malla*. The Malla kings were said to be incarnations of the Hindu god Vishnu, but they were receptive and generous to Buddhists, many of whom held positions in the royal court.

Throughout their long tenure, the Mallas—attentive to culture and the arts—sponsored a number of new buildings and monuments in Kāthmāndu Valley. To the west of the *kasthamandap* is Basantapur Square, site of the nine-story Basantapur Tower at the Royal Palace. The seventeenth-century palace sometimes is called Hanumān Dokha Palace, because a red-clay-smeared statue of Hanumān the monkey-god stands watch at the Durbar Square entrance. Kāthmāndu's Durbar Square alone boasts more than fifty monuments, including the three-tiered Maju Deval Temple; a large bas-relief of Kal Bhairav, a six-armed god wearing a garland of human heads, said to have been a lie detector for its confessors, who would expire at its foot if they did not tell the truth; and a statue of King Pratap Malla, financier of many of the square's sites, including the Hanumān Dokha Palace.

Across Basantapur Square from the tower stands the Kumāri Bahal, residence of the Royal Kumāri, the most important of Nepal's twelve living goddesses chosen from eligible virgin Newari girls to symbolize the incarnation of the Hindu goddess Durgā. The Kumāri keeps her position until she reaches puberty, appearing only rarely in public at festivals such as the Indra Jātrā, the annual event signifying the end of monsoon season. The Kumāri Dasain ceremony takes place at the Taleju Temple, a late-sixteenth-century structure that stands behind the Royal Palace; nearby, a stone inscription, translated into fifteen languages, is said to spill milk if a visitor succeeds in reading all the entries.

Despite the Mallas' flourishing culture, they were vulnerable to internal machinations and to the hostility of religious opponents such as the sultan of Bengal, a Muslim who invaded Nepal and leveled many important stupas. By the end of the fourteenth century, King Jayasthiti Malla was obliged to forge an uneasy union of the three centers of Kāthmāndu Valley activity.

During the rule of Jayasthiti's grandson, Yaksha Malla, Nepal extended its domain north to the Tibetan border and south to the Ganges River. After Yaksha's death, chaos reigned in the valley; royal Rājput refugees from the south who had taken up residence in the hills to the north of Kāthmāndu prepared the Gurkhas, their standing army, for a conquest of the entire region. As Yaksha's three kingdoms—Kāthmāndu, Lalitpur (Pātan), and Bhaktapur (formerly Bhādgāon)—vied for each other's respect with increasingly elaborate palaces, mostly centered on each town's Durbar Square, the Gurkhas' Shāh Dynasty plotted the valley's takeover. Feuding among the towns heightened when the king of Bhaktapur detained visitors from Kāthmāndu for wearing "big-city clothes"; when Kāthmāndu retaliated, the king of Bhaktapur invited the Gurkhas to invade the valley. The Shāhs' ninth king, Prithvi Nārāyan Shāh, culminated twenty-six years of battle with the residents of the valley when he took up residence in the Royal Palace in Kāthmāndu in 1768.

A commercial treaty between the Shāhs and the British, signed during the early part of the nineteenth century, soon became strained, as disputes arose on the Terai plains between Nepalese natives and British associates from India. When the Gurkhas were put down in 1816, they were obliged to sign a treaty of friendship and accept a British resident. That resident, however, never realized much responsibility in Nepal (other than an annual meeting with the king), and the country remained uncolonized. (Prior visitations by Westerners included the missionary efforts of Jesuit priests, who had settled in the valley during the time of the tolerant Mallas but were expelled by the Shāhs.) The Gurkhas would later come to Great Britain's aid on several occasions—during the Sepoy Mutiny in India in 1857, for instance, and as the Gurkha Brigade of the British army during both world wars.

As governmental power gradually passed from the king to the post of prime minister, various executives attempted power plays in Nepal. The most successful and gruesome of these actions occurred in 1846, as the Army General Jung Bahadur led a mass murder of noblemen and officials at the Kot Courtyard in Kāthmāndu, a bloody event that came to be known as the Kot Massacre. As many as 500 victims have been claimed in that raid. Taking the title of Mahārāja, the first of the so-called Rana Dynasty made the prime minister's position hereditary, stripping the Shāh kings of their lawmaking privileges while leaving their figurehead status intact to appease constituents who believed the Shāhs had divine bloodlines.

Despite the violent nature of their rise to power, the members of the "Ranocracy" espoused some reformist ideals, attempting to restrict capital punishment and slavery and to abolish the tradition of *sati,* the ritual suicide of widows on their husbands' funeral pyres. Although they sought this sort of progress, the Ranas continued to live opulently at the expense of Kāthmāndu Valley's commoners.

The Ranas eventually came undone at the hands of their own antiquated power structure and the infighting it fostered. In 1881 fringe members of the aristocracy plotted to overthrow the Rana family at a state dinner; when they bungled the plan, forty-five nobles were executed. In 1885 the nephews of the prime minister schemed to kill their uncle. When they succeeded, the eldest brother, Bir Shumsher, assumed the throne. Bir's death in 1901 made room for the "Good Rana," his brother Deva Shumsher, who set in motion more reforms, including improved education. For his efforts,

Deva was bound and removed from Kāthmāndu, just five months into his residency. His successor, Chandra Shumsher, ruled for twenty-eight years, completing the abolition of both slavery and *sati*.

During their reign, the Ranas oversaw the design of many elaborate palaces, the most impressive of which was Chandra Shumsher's Singha Durbar (Lion Palace), a 1,700-room estate influenced by the Roman, Greek, English, and Indian styles the Ranas had grown to love as they traveled abroad. This lavish residence was decorated with chandeliers, marble, and mirrors that had to be carried over Nepal's mountains by porters. It was sold to the state by the Ranas, who used the proceeds to build still more estates for themselves. The Singha Durbar—used for several years in the 1950s as the meetinghouse for the new Nepali government—was in large part destroyed by fire, possibly arson, in 1974. General Kaiser S. J. B. Rana's palace, featuring a library of 35,000 rare books and manuscripts, still exists in its original state; nearby stands the Nārāyānhiti Palace, official living quarters of King Birendra (and of the Shāhs since 1896).

Faced with Tibet's imminent conversion to communism at the hands of China, the government of newly independent India was strongly committed to stabilizing Nepal, its buffer zone to the north. The Nepali Congress Party was formed in India, and the mild-mannered Shāh king Tribhuvan, dressed as a peasant, met in secret with India's ambassador to Nepal.

In 1950, after 104 years of oppressive Rana rule, Tribhuvan's family aborted a planned leopard-hunting trip and escaped into the sanctuary of the Indian embassy, where the king was granted asylum. By some accounts, Tribhuvan was a victim of the Ranas' traditional ploy to control the Shāhs by introducing them to substance abuse and debauchery at a young age; by other accounts, he was a clean-living athlete and a good husband to his two wives (one of them a Rana princess). In either case, Tribhuvan was an unlikely candidate to lead the nation out from under the rule of the Ranas. Yet when Jawaharlal Nehru's sympathetic Indian government offered a comfortable exile to the Ranas in exchange for their abdication, they accepted. In 1951 Tribhuvan opened Nepal's doors to the outside world, ending the nation's mysterious, centuries-long insularity.

After Tribhuvan's death in 1955, his son Mahendra was coronated in 1956. To the delight of the Western media, Mahendra wore sunglasses and a $2-million crown. Yet the world also saw, in stark contrast to the image he presented, a small nation of peasants who had scarcely changed their customs for hundreds of years. In the previous century, while the Ranas were spending tax revenues on themselves, Nepal did not see its first public hospitals or schools built until 1890; by 1949 there were still only ten high schools nationwide. Newspapers did not exist in the largely illiterate country, and radio broadcasts were not instituted until 1946. But newly arriving visitors were charmed by the medieval streets, marketplaces, and houses of worship that dominated Kāthmāndu and its sister cities. The bazaars in Kāthmāndu at Asan Tol and Indra Chowk—with their stalls offering grains, firewood, and terra-cotta wares—continue the age-old traditions of the Newars, who still make up nearly half of the population. The Western backpacking revolution of the late 1960s made Kāthmāndu's "Freak Street" bazaar a mandatory stop on the globetrotting circuit.

On Mahendra's death in 1972, the king's son Birendra ascended to the throne; following the advice of astrological forecasters, he was not crowned officially until February 1975. During the 1970s, UNESCO restored much of the five-acre Hanumān Dokha Palace, which had been largely destroyed in an earthquake in 1934. Twelve of the palace's original fifty courtyards remain, including the Nassal Chowk, traditional coronation site for the Shāh kings.

Further Reading: *The Kāthmāndu Valley Towns: A Record of Life and Change in Nepal* by Fran P. Hosken (New York: Weatherhill, 1974) has one of the most concise and well-written histories of the region available. The section on Kāthmāndu in *Cadogan Guides: India–Kāthmāndu–Nepal* by Frank Kusy (third edition, London: Cadogan, and Old Saybrook, Connecticut: Globe Pequot, 1993) is up-to-date and much more extensive in its presentation of history than many other guidebooks. *Kātmāndu* by Colin Simpson (Sydney: Angus and Robertson, 1967; New York: Taplinger, 1968) is something of a travelogue that includes a fair share of useful background information. *Kāthmāndu: The Forbidden Valley* by R. Ian Lloyd and Wendy Moore (New York: St. Martin's, 1990) is a handsome book of photos with helpful text. Finally, *Kāthmāndu and the Kingdom of Nepal* by Prakash A. Raj (fifth edition, Berkeley: Lonely Planet, 1985), although a slender traveler's volume, contains some indispensable information not found elsewhere.

—James Sullivan

Khajurāho (Madhya Pradesh, India)

Location: In the Chhatarpur district of Madhya Pradesh in the heart of Central India; thirty-four miles south of Mahobā, twenty-nine miles east of the city of Chhatarpur, and twenty-seven miles northwest of Pannā.

Description: Capital of a principality ruled by the Chandela Rājputs from the ninth to the eleventh century; site of magnificent Hindu and Jain temples, built by the Chandela rulers and notable for their architectural style and the sexual imagery of their sculptural decoration.

Site Office: Government of India Tourist Office
Near Western Group of Temples
Khajurāho 471 606, Madhya Pradesh
India
2047 or 2048

Khajurāho had a brief period of prominence from the ninth to the eleventh century, when it was the seat of a principality ruled by the Chandela clan of the Rājputs. Their primary accomplishment was the building of eighty-five magnificent temples, of which twenty remain. The temples, dedicated to Siva, Vishnu, Sūrya, Śakti, and the Jain *tīrthaṇkaras* (prophets), are stylistically much alike, differing only in their cult images, but are among the greatest monuments of India. They represent the pinnacle of central Indian architecture and are particularly noteworthy for their beautiful sculptural decoration, filled with erotic images indicating the important role that sex, as a life-giving force, played in many Indian belief systems, especially in the Tantric doctrines that influenced Hinduism, Buddhism, and Jainism during the Chandelas' era. Although the sculptures feature many nonsexual scenes, the sexual portrayals are the most famous and the most memorable.

Before the Chandelas established their principality, the region around Khajurāho had been part of many other kingdoms and empires. It was part of the kingdom of Vatsa until about the fourth century B.C., and of the Mauryan Empire until the second century B.C., when the region passed into the possession of the Śungas. A number of dynasties, such as the Kushāns, Bhāraśiva-Nāgas, Vākāṭakas, Guptas, Vardhanas, and the Pratihāras, ruled over the region in the centuries that followed. The epics and the *Purāṇas* refer to the sacred hills of the region; and the *Visnudharmottara* describes it as a country of warlike traditions. The inhabitants of the region were known for their military skills.

The area became culturally important in the second century B.C., when the wonderful stupa of Bhārhut with its beautifully carved balustrade was constructed. Art and architecture flourished under the Guptas, and the tradition continued under their successors, such as the Pratihāras, who built a number of temples in the region during the ninth century.

The Chandela Rājputs established themselves in the region in the ninth century. Descended from the indigenous tribes of the Bhārs and the Gonds, they sought to raise their status by propagating myths that connected them with the lunar dynasty of ancient Kshatriyas. The first Chandela ruler, Nannuka, had his seat of authority at Khajurāho. He was followed by Vākpati, under whose sons Jayaśakti and Vijayaśakti the family rose to prominence. The Chandelas seem to have initially accepted the suzerainty of the Pratihāras. Harśadeva (c. 900–25) added greatly to the status of the family. His son Lakśavarman, also known as Yaśovarman (c. 925–50), was a powerful ruler who built the great Lakśmaṇa Temple at Khajurāho.

His son Dhaṅga ruled for fifty-two years (c. 950–1002). He threw off the suzerainty of the Pratihāras and made the Chandelas the most powerful dynasty in northern India. He was a devout worshiper of Siva and a patron of art and culture. Two of Khajurāho's greatest temples—Viśvanāth, dedicated to Siva, and Pārśvanāth, dedicated to the Jain *tīrthaṇkaras*—were built during his reign. The first was built by the king himself and the second by a man called Pahila. Dhaṅga's son and successor, Gaṇḍa, had a relatively short reign (c. 1002–17), but the Jagadambī (or Devi Jagadamba) Temple dedicated to Vishnu and the Citragupta Temple dedicated to Sūrya were built under his patronage.

His son and successor Vidyādhara (c. 1017–29), called Bida by the Muslim historian Ibn-al-Athir, is described by him as the most powerful ruler of his time. He spearheaded the resistance to Maḥmūd of Ghaznī and led a huge army against him in 1019. The battle proved inconclusive, and Maḥmūd returned to Ghaznī, only to come back in 1022 and challenge Vidyādhara again. Maḥmūd, however, failed to conquer the fort of Kalinjar, and the unsuccessful siege ended with an exchange of gifts between the two rulers.

Khajurāho's greatest temple, Kaṇḍarya Mahādeva, almost certainly was built by Vidyādhara as a supreme statement of his success against his enemies, including Maḥmūd, and as an architectural tribute to his god, Siva. Epigraphs describe Vidyādhara as a devotee of Siva, and King Virimda, mentioned in a short inscription on a *maṇḍapa* pilaster of the great temple, might be Vidyādhara himself, with Virimda serving as his pseudonym.

Persistent incursions by the Kalacuris and the Muslims accounted for the decline of the Chandelas. After Vidyādhara, the only ruler of note was Kīrtivarman (c. 1070–98), who defeated the Kalacuris and built many monuments. He was a great connoisseur of the arts and letters, and there is a possibility that the temples of Javari and Caturbhuja were

Temples at Khajurāho
Photo courtesy of Air India Library, New York

built under his patronage. His grandson Paramardin Parmal (c. 1156–1202) was defeated by Prthvī Rāja Cāhamāna of Delhi in 1182 and by Quṭb-ud-Din Aybak in 1202. The latter defeat was a blow from which the Chandelas could never recover.

Khajurāho was reduced to a small village as the Chandelas transferred most of their activities to the hill forts of Mahoba, Ajayagarh, and Kalinjar. Ibn Baṭṭūṭah visited Khajurāho in 1335 and noted the existence of temples, as well as the presence of resident ascetics. The temples suffered some damage and desecration at the hands of Sikandar Lodī in 1495. By the sixteenth century, however, Khajurāho was forgotten by the rest of the world, its isolation helping to save it from extensive desecration by Muslims.

Still, the temples decayed over the next few centuries. They drew the outside world's attention again when they were spotted by C. J. Franklin, a military surveyor, about 1819. He described them as "ruins," but his scarcely legible writing led to the misreading of "ruins" as "mines." Real credit for rediscovering the temples belongs to Captain T.S. Burt, who visited Khajurāho in 1838. He noted the "superior height and age" of "seven Hindoo temples, most beautifully and exquisitely carved as to workmanship, but the sculptor had at times allowed his subject to grow a little warmer than there was any absolute necessity for his doing. . . ."

Alexander Cunningham was next to survey the antiquities of Khajurāho, between 1852 and 1855. Although he described the sculptures as "highly indecent and most of them disgustingly obscene," he still studied them closely, counting and measuring 872 sculptures on the Kaṇḍarya Mahādeva Temple, most of them two and one-half to three feet high. He found "the general effect of this luxury of embellishment . . . extremely pleasing although the eye is often distracted by the multiplicity of detail." After studying the inscriptions, he concluded that most of the temples dated from the tenth and eleventh centuries. Since 1904, the Archaeological Survey of India has taken care of these temples with the cooperation of the Chandela princes of the Chhatarpur state, which became a district of Madhya Pradesh in independent India.

The temples may be divided into three primary groups. The largest and most important is the Western Group, which includes the Caunsatha Yogini, the Lalguan Mahādeva, Lakṣmaṇa, the Mātangeśvara, the Varāha, the Viśvanātha, the Nandi, the Citragupta, the Jagadambī, and the Kaṇḍārya Mahādeva Temples standing in two more or less parallel rows. The Eastern Group, near the village of Khajurāho, comprises three Brahmanical temples, the Brahmā, Vāmana, and Javari, and three Jain temples, the Ghantai, Ādinātha, and Pārśvanātha. The Southern Group consists of the Duladeo and Caturbhuja Temples.

The Caunsatha Yogini (c. A.D. 900) is the oldest of the Khajurāho temples. Standing on a rocky promontory, it consists of an open-air quadrangular structure built around a courtyard, 102 by 60 feet, which originally was enclosed by sixty-seven chapels dedicated to various aspects of Śakti or the Mother Goddess. The surviving chapels are crowned with simple curvilinear spires, and the central shrine houses an image of Durgā killing the buffalo demon. As Yogini Temple is related to Hindu Tantrism, the shrine is a clear indication of the significance of Tantric practices in Khajurāho.

The Caunsatha Yogini, Brahmā, and Lalguan Mahādeva Temples are built wholly or largely of granite, but all the other temples at Khajurāho are built of fine sandstone, buff, pink, or pale yellow in color. Except for these three temples and the temples of Varāha and Mātangeśvara, all the other temples have a distinct architectural character, distinguishable from what is found in other parts of India, and mark the high point of the central Indian building style.

Temples in this style are built on a high masonry platform (*jagati*), as if to elevate them above their mundane surroundings. They have no enclosure walls, but a broad terrace serves as an open ambulatory around each temple. The temples are constructed on an east-west axis, with a basic plan consisting of a *mukhamaṇḍapa* (portico), *maṇḍapa* (assembly hall), and *antarala* (vestibule) leading to the *garbhagṛha* (inner sanctum). The larger temples also have lateral transepts with balconied windows, which turn the *maṇḍapa* into a *mahāmaṇḍapa* (great assembly hall), and an inner processional passage around the sanctum, with this passage illuminated by the balconied windows on the sides as well as in the rear. The inner ambulatory is in fact an extension of the *mahāmaṇḍapa*, from where it is approached. Some of the temples also have a subsidiary shrine at the four corners of their terrace. Each temple has a *vedibandha* (basement) of pronounced height supporting the *jangha* (walls) and openings of the inner compartments, and above them a cluster of roofs culminating in a soaring *śikhara* (spire). A number of vertical projections provide a pattern of light and shade. A massive plinth is adorned with a series of mouldings, and the intermediate parts of the solid structure are relieved by the open balconied windows, which admit light and air into the interior and add to the play of light and shadow throughout the building.

Each compartment of the temple has a separate roof. The portico has the smallest and the lowest, followed by the higher roof of the central hall, the two rising up to converge on the main spire like mountain spurs leading to a higher peak. The Indo-Aryan style of temple tower is developed most fully at Khajurāho, where the central *śikhara* is buttressed at different levels on its sides by many lesser additions of itself, known as *urusringas*.

The lone entrance to the temple is always in the east, reached by a flight of steps leading to the plinth. The doorway and the ceilings of the portico and the main hall are exquisitely carved, as are the capitals of the pillars and the architraves in the main hall. The vestibule leads to the threshold of the sanctum, where the main deity is enthroned.

Kaṇḍarya Mahādeva, dedicated to Siva, is the greatest temple of Khajurāho. The central tower, buttressed by eighty-four subordinate ones, rises to a height of 102 feet. The body of the temple is adorned by sculptural friezes of great variety and beauty. Only the Jain temple dedicated to Pārśvanātha, although smaller, approaches the Kaṇḍarya Mahādeva Temple in terms of aesthetics and workmanship. The Jain temple was perhaps the earlier of the two, having been built about 950–70, and may have served as an inspiration for the larger temple.

The most celebrated features of the Khajurāho temples are the bands of two or three parallel friezes running around the entire structure, adorned with exquisite sculptures depicting the gods commingling with humanity in the pursuit of *kāma*—the libido, or life-force. These sculptures cover every available inch of space and dazzle the viewer with their vitality. The Kaṇḍarya Mahādeva Temple alone boasts almost 900 figures of gods, men, and women, each a masterpiece.

The sculptures of Khajurāho include depictions of gods and goddesses, some of which exhibit a touch of freedom from the prescribed style; *surasundaris*, or celestial beauties and dancers, carved in the round or high relief; and demigods, such as cherubs and celestial musicians. The secular sculptures include domestic scenes, teachers and disciples, dancers and musicians, and erotic couples and groups. Fantastic creatures and heraldic beasts such as the *vyala* also appear frequently.

These sculptures are products of spiritual devotion, combined with a lively imagination, refined aesthetic sensibility, great artistic ingenuity, and technical competence. They are notable particularly for their depiction of shapely, youthful female figures. These alluring women often appear as attendants to the gods, but they also are shown on a human plane in activities such as disrobing, yawning, scratching their backs, looking into mirrors, touching their breasts, rinsing water from their hair, plucking thorns from their feet, fondling babies, playing with parrots and monkeys, writing letters, making music, making themselves beautiful, and making love. The sculptured figures form part of the temple walls, yet have an almost three-dimensional appearance. The legs are often elongated; the poses are often deliberately exaggerated.

The Pārśvanātha and Viśvanātha Temples contain some of the finest sculptures of Khajurāho. The Lakṣmana Temple has some of the most erotic, and the Kaṇḍarya Mahādeva Temple displays a maturity of style in its depiction of tall and slender figures, their faces charged with emotion, moving in every conceivable direction. In the erotic sculptures, called *mithunas*, gods, kings, priests, ascetics, and common men and women alike savor the joys of sex. Al-

Temple reliefs, Khajurāho
Photo courtesy of Air India Library, New York

though the early British explorers were scandalized by them, these sculptures are far removed from pornography; they are compelling expressions of great art and bold exclamations of the beauty and rapture of love. They recall prehistoric fertility cults, in which representations of genitalia were objects of worship. The *liṅgam* (phallic image) and *yoni* (stylized vagina) symbolize the act of creation, the union of opposites, and the very antithesis of death. Thus, they were worshiped in their stylized forms as early as the third millennium B.C., in the Indus Valley Harappan civilization. Classic Indian literature frequently celebrated the libido and used a great deal of sexual symbolism. Over time, folk and tribal magico-religious beliefs and rituals associated with sex were incorporated into common Indian religious rites, and the Tantric doctrines that developed in India about the fifth century A.D. were particularly celebrative of the sensual. Also, sexual images came to symbolize peace and prosperity. The Rājput patrons of medieval art and architecture brought with them the sexual rituals associated with their tribal heritage and integrated them with more orthodox modes of worship. The Brāhmas were happy to incorporate the new elements, not only to please their new masters, but also because they found them attractive.

In medieval India, sex became an aristocratic preoccupation, as evidenced by temple prostitution and the rise in status accorded feudal lords who had many courtesans or concubines; the erotic portrayals at Khajurāho may also derive, in part, from these preoccupations. Lighter explanations also exist for the temples' decoration. Erotic sculptures are believed to protect the temples from lightning. The goddess of thunder cannot touch representations offensive to her chastity, and Indra, the Lord of the Thunderbolt, does not damage what is but a replica of his own paradise and its activities.

Further Reading: Alexander Cunningham published the accounts of his survey of Khajurāho in the *Archaeological Survey Report,* volumes 2, 7, 10, and 21, between 1871 and 1885. Those interested in detailed study may consult H. Zimmer's *The Art of Indian Asia: Its Mythology and Transformations* (New York: Pantheon, 1955); E. Zannas and J. Auboyer's *Khajuraho,* (The Hague: Mouton, 1960); Stella Kramrisch's *The Hindu Temple* (Calcutta: University of Calcutta Press, 1946; reprint, Delhi: Motilal Banarsidass, 1976); and Krishna Deva's *Khajuraho* (New Delhi: Brijbasi, 1986).

—Sarva Daman Singh

Khyber Pass (North-West Frontier, Pakistan; Kābul, Afghanistan)

Location: On the border between Afghanistan and northern Pakistan; approximately ten miles west of Peshāwar, in the Hindu Kush Mountains.

Description: One of the most famous mountain passes in the world, the Khyber Pass offers a route through the rugged mountains that divide the Indian subcontinent from Afghanistan and Central Asia. Some thirty-three miles long and only a few feet wide at its narrowest (before modern improvements), the pass possessed enormous strategic importance as the most direct route between India and the West. Consequently, local tribes and foreign military forces battled over control of the pass for centuries.

Contact: Pakistan Tourism Development Corporation
House No. 2, St 61, F-7/4
Islamābād 44000
Pakistan
(51) 811001

The Khyber Pass is one of the world's most strategically important routes. For thirty-three miles it follows a jagged mountain gorge that winds between modern-day Afghanistan and Pakistan. Before airplane travel, the Khyber Pass provided the shortest and most direct route from the arid plains of Central Asia to rich India. Armies of many nations have fought countless battles to control passage through this narrow ravine.

A natural fortress comprised of the world's highest mountains guards the Indian subcontinent, long a desirable destination for merchants and would-be conquerors. To the north lie the Himalayas, walling off China and the Far East. On India's northwest flank are the peaks of the Hindu Kush. Those who wished to tap India's treasures had to thread their way through stone and snow, powerful winds and blazing sun. The mountain paths were, write authors Larry Collins and Dominique Lapierre, "desolate, forbidding terrain, serrated ridges, rocky slopes, barren valleys with hardly a bush for cover, scorched by the sun in summer, swept by wild, freezing rains in winter."

From the Hindu Kush (or Hindu killer mountains, so named because slaves captured on India's tropical plains often died when new masters tried to bring them through these snowy hills), a range of mountains extends south toward the Sulaiman Range. Five passes traverse this stretch, with two having borne the most traffic. One was the Bolan Pass, eighty miles long and the easier track into India. The second route, while more difficult, was shorter and more direct. This was the Khyber Pass.

The Khyber Pass's position on India's northwest corner placed it close to the main trade routes from China and Central Asia. Caravans from Tashkent, Bukhara, Samarkand, Herāt, Mashhad, and Kashgar used the pass to travel from Kābul to Peshāwar. From Peshāwar, travelers could push into central India or float down the Indus River to the Arabian Sea.

Commerce may have discovered the Khyber Pass, but military adventure gave it fame. Persian, Greek, Mughal, and Afghan generals all reputedly used it to invade India. "Ground into the dust of the pass," writes historian James W. Spain, "is Persian gold, Greek iron, Tatar leather, Mogul gems, Afghan silver and British steel." Another historian remarks that "it has been said without too much exaggeration that every stone in the Khyber has been soaked with the blood of battle; the name has become synonymous with treachery, feuds and barbaric guerilla warfare." Just as often as it provided an entrance, the pass gave would-be emperors an exit when India proved too difficult to subdue.

In modern times, England deemed the Khyber Pass and surrounding region essential to its colony's defense. Winston Churchill climbed the Khyber Pass when he served with the army in India. Native tribesmen fired on Rudyard Kipling when he visited Fort Jamrud as a journalist from the *Civil and Military Gazette* in Lahore. Kipling later popularized and romanticized the Khyber region in his "Ballad of the King's Jest," "Ballad of East and West," and "Lament of the Border Cattle Thief."

The Khyber Pass is a river gorge formed by two streams. It cuts between ocher-colored walls of shale and limestone soaring 600 to 1,000 feet in places. Parts of the pass are wide enough to form a small valley, dotted with houses and cultivated fields. In other stretches, however, the pass was—prior to modern improvements—so narrow that travelers could nearly touch opposing walls with outstretched hands as they threaded through switchbacks and hairpin turns.

To travel the pass from west to east, as many caravans and most conquerors did, required entering the pass at Torkham in Afghanistan (elevation 1,404 feet). After passing through a small valley, the pass narrowed and climbed steeply. A few miles in was Landi Kotal—at 3,500 feet, the highest point in the pass. Here was the Mess of the Indian Army's famous Khyber Rifles regiment, and other fortifications built by both native and foreign armies. After Landi Kotal, the pass descended to the Ali Masjid fortress, and then to its eastern mouth (elevation 1,670 feet). Four miles beyond is Fort Jamrud, built by the Sikhs during their wars against the local Pathan tribesmen. About ten miles farther on is the ancient city of Peshāwar.

View of Khyber Pass
Photo courtesy of Embassy of Pakistan, Washington, D.C.

The inroads of civilization have changed the appearance and atmosphere of the route. Since 1925, a railroad has operated through the pass. Today visitors can drive the pass in under an hour and face no greater hardship than a traffic jam. Before the days of roads and rails, however, traversing the Khyber Pass could take three days, always under the eyes of hostile Pathan tribesmen.

Since the days of Herodotus, the Pathans have been famous for their warlike, independent nature. An ethnic group native to western Afghanistan, the Pathan nation consists of dozens of tribes. Each tribe is in turn divided into clans called *khels.* Pathans speak Pushtu, an Iranian dialect, and regard themselves as Muslims. Technically, they are citizens of Afghanistan, yet the only code they reputedly recognize is Pukhtunwali (Way of the Pathan), a body of tribal law.

Revenge is fundamental to this code of conduct, just as raiding has been fundamental to the economic life of the Pathans. Traditionally, tribes in the region made their living by robbing travelers. Because well-protected sniper positions or Pathan-built stone fortifications called sangars protected nearly every foot of the Khyber Pass, shooting one's way through was nearly impossible, even for a larger and better-armed force. Their fondness for revenge kept the Pathans in a state of nearly chronic warfare. Every male belonged to a tribal army (or *lashkar*) and carried one or more knives and a variety of gun called the *jezail.* In capable hands the *jezail* was highly accurate, and the Khyber tribesmen were exceptional shots.

Of the many Pathan tribes living throughout India's northwest frontier, one of the best-known was the Afridi. The Afridi claimed the area surrounding the Khyber Pass as homeland and guarded it rigorously. Caravans seeking to use the pass had to bargain with the Afridi for safe passage. The usual fee was a toll determined by the Afridi. Even after collecting their toll, however, the Afridi would sometimes murder the travelers and plunder the caravan.

All the difficulties the Khyber Pass presented did not prevent foreign armies from using it during a period stretching twenty-five centuries. Sources disagree on whether certain generals actually followed the Khyber Pass or neighboring routes, such as the Qipchak, Bolan, or Khawak Passes. Several historians, however, associate the Khyber Pass with Darius I of Persia's campaign to conquer India in the fifth century B.C., and with Alexander the Great's invasion in 327 B.C. Neither Darius nor Alexander reached far into the subcontinent, nor did either have any lasting influence there.

Beginning around A.D. 1000, however, a new warrior began raiding India with more significant effect: Maḥmūd of Ghazna (now Ghaznī). Leader of Afghanistan's Islamic nation, which the Mamluk Turks had established, Maḥmūd of Ghazna was both attracted by India's wealth and repulsed by its Hindu religion. With these incentives, he attacked India seventeen times from 1001 to 1026, employing the Khyber Pass for at least one of these missions. Maḥmūd never really controlled the regions he conquered; he saw himself more as a purger of Islam's rival religions in the East. His legacy was as the "Idol Smasher," the conqueror who razed Hindu temples and religious sites with stunning thoroughness.

Two hundred years later, in 1221, Ghengis Khan may have used the Khyber Pass to lead his Mongol army down the

Khyber Pass entrance
Photo courtesy of Mr. Rashid Uddin, Park Travel Agency, Chicago

Peshāwar Valley into India. This type of foray was to become something of a family tradition. In the waning years of the fourteenth century, a descendent of Ghengis Khan, Timur the Lame (Tamerlane), repeated his ancestor's campaign. Sources disagree on whether Timur used the Khyber Pass or the Khawak Pass, but it is certain that he invaded India and warred with the Pathans.

In the early sixteenth century, another descendent of both Genghis Khan and Timur, Ẕahīr-ud-Dīn Muḥammad (known as Bābur), the founder of the Mughal Dynasty, led his army through either the Khyber Pass or the Qipchak Pass to assault India. Bābur, the first invader actually to conquer India, was also the only foreign leader ever reputed to control the area around the Khyber Pass for any length of time. Yet even he never completely subjugated the Pathans. In the late sixteenth century, Bābur's grandson, Akbar, built a road through the Khyber Pass. For his temerity, the Pathans cut Akbar's army of 8,000 men to shreds.

After two centuries of rule, the Mughal Empire weakened. In 1739, Nāder Shāh of Persia plunged through the Khyber Pass to challenge Mughal power. Nāder Shāh used a unique approach: he hired an army of Pathans, led by a native general named Aḥmad Khān Abdālī, to lead the thrust into India. When a usurper murdered Nāder Shāh in Persia in 1747, Aḥmad Khān (who became Aḥmad Shāh Durrāni) kept the lands he had helped conquer around the Indus River, as well as much of what comprises present-day Afghanistan, in effect becoming the founder and first ruler of that country. Every ruler of Afghanistan from Aḥmad Shāh Durrāni's time until the mid–twentieth century was a descendent of this family.

British influence in the Khyber region began about a century later, in the early 1800s. The foreign nation that probably did most to publicize the Khyber Pass was the only one that never used it to conquer India, but to defend it.

The British adventure in India began on September 24, 1599, with the creation of the East India Trading Company. Although England's oft-stated objective in maintaining its colony was trade, not territory, protecting its business interests inevitably involved it in local politics. Calcutta, in the east, was the base of British operations. By the beginning of the nineteenth century, however, England's interests had spread west toward the uneasy mountain border with Afghanistan. Further spurring British activity in the area were signs of expansion by Czarist Russia. England deeply feared that Moscow had designs on its colony.

The British initially demonstrated their stake in the Khyber region by building roads, then forts. They called the area the North-West Frontier, or simply the Frontier. Eventually, they stationed troops there permanently. England's strategy along the frontier recognized that the natural flow of people (or armies) through the mountain passes moved from west to east. Therefore, defending the region meant moving troops quickly north and south, parallel to the mountains, either to close the passes or to intercept an enemy coming through them.

Once established in the Khyber region, England quickly found itself involved in its constantly shifting alliances and wars. A bitter lesson came during the First Afghan War, when the British invaded Afghanistan in 1839 and set up a puppet regime in Kābul. Their intent was to establish a strong presence in the region to counter Russian influence. Instead, their occupation provoked intense resentment on the part of the Afghans. On November 2, 1841, a mob murdered the British second-in-command and initiated a siege against British soldiers and their families. Eventually, British forces and followers in Kābul—some 17,000 men, women, children, and staff—were ordered to leave. Most never reached safety. Nearly all 17,000 died of cold, starvation, or at the hands of native tribesmen.

A few months later, the British Army of Retribution marched through the Khyber Pass to seize the handful of prisoners still held. This force was the first foreign army to make it through the Khyber Pass on sheer fighting power since Bābur's. The Army of Retribution reached Kābul, retrieved the hostages, and returned to India. Yet the experience of the First Afghan War was so bitter that, for a while at least, the British treated areas west of the Indus as hands-off.

They could not keep their distance for long. In 1843 and 1849, Britain annexed first Sind province and then the Punjab as essential to their strategic interests. Doing so gave the British direct control over the North-West Frontier, an area covering about 40,000 square miles. But how to manage it was yet another problem. Traditional warfare techniques were useless in fighting the guerrilla skirmishes or ferocious tribal onslaughts of the Frontier. Of the two armies that served in India—British and Indian—it was the Indian Army that learned to fight and win in the Khyber region.

Unlike the British army, which was manned entirely by Englishmen, the Indian army consisted of native soldiers (or *sepoys*) led by British officers. A few corps of the Indian army gained special fame fighting in and around the Khyber Pass region. One was the Punjab Frontier Force, or "Piffers of Punjab," a specialized combat team. The heart of the Piffers was the Queen's Own Corps of Guides, a force made up mostly of Pathan natives. The Guides became the Frontier's *corps d'élite,* declaring their unique status partly by originating uniforms of a then-obscure local fabric called "khaki." Another famous regiment comprised of natives was the Khyber Rifles, who bunked in Landi Kotal fortress at the summit of the Khyber Pass.

Fighting along the Frontier was nearly continual. Between 1858 and 1902, Britain sent armed forces, ranging from a few hundred men to 40,000, into the mountains more than forty times to wage battle against the natives. Interspersed with these large assaults were countless minor skirmishes. As a result, nearly every bend in the Khyber Pass has its plaque to mark where soldiers of the Indian Army died fighting.

As control of the Frontier shifted between British and Pathan forces, so did opinion in England on the wisdom of trying to hold such a difficult territory. Treaties and policies were made and unmade often as England, Russia, and Afghanistan vied for influence in the area throughout the nineteenth century. In 1857, Britain and Afghanistan signed a treaty of support and noninterference. That treaty proved crucial a few months later when the Sepoy Revolt threatened to overthrow British control over its colony. By not taking advantage of Britain's weakness and sending hostile forces down the Khyber Pass, Afghanistan played a crucial role in helping Britain hold the Frontier and ultimately quash the rebellion. Such cooperation was the exception rather than the rule, however. From 1848 to 1878, tensions were so high that Afghans and British rarely used the Khyber Pass.

In the mid–nineteenth century, Russia advanced into Turkistan and Samarkand, destabilizing the fragile peace in that region. Russia's inroads into Central Asia deeply alarmed England, which again sought a treaty with Afghanistan to counter the threat. When Afghanistan's *amir* dismissed the British, the latter decided they had no choice but to take Kābul by arms. The resulting Second Afghan War (1878–80) threatened to become an exact replay of the first.

In 1878, Britain sent two large forces into Afghanistan through the Khyber and Bolan Passes under Major Louis Cavagneri. Cavagneri took Kābul and briefly established a garrison there. On September 3, 1879, the Afghans slaughtered Cavagneri and his entire staff. Within a month, Britain retaliated by sending in a new army led by General Frederick Roberts. Roberts took Kābul and repulsed subsequent onslaughts by enormous Afghan forces. The war ended with Britain withdrawing its forces to India and dictating the 1879 Treaty of Gandamak, which ceded control of the Khyber Pass to Britain.

Under the Treaty of Gandamak, the Khyber Pass again became the chief route between Central Asia and India. Security of the route rested largely with the Khyber Rifles, a crack regiment of 350 Afridi tribesmen led by their part-Afghan commander, Colonel Sir Robert Warburton. Under Warburton, parts of the pass were widened and forts at Landi Kotal and Ali Masjid reinforced. Warburton also set up a traffic system that sent caravans through the pass twice a week, escorted by units of the Afghan army and the Khyber Rifles.

This relative quiet ended with a great Afridi uprising in August 1897. In a matter of days, Afridi forces seized the Khyber Pass and temporarily destroyed Britain's entire control of the North-West Frontier. Britain's response was the Tirah Expedition, so named for its scorched-earth policy of destroying the Afridi-Orakzai homeland in the Tirah Valley region. Britain retook the Khyber Pass in the winter of 1897–98. However, the process was seen as too costly for Afridis and British alike.

The Third Afghan War began in May 1919 when Afghans seized the western end of Khyber Pass. A few days later, Britain declared war on Afghanistan. When Afridi *sepoys* in the Khyber Rifles began deserting, the unit was ordered disbanded (although it was later reinstated). The Indian army quickly retook the pass.

On the night of August 14, 1947, the Union Jack was lowered over Landi Kotal for the last time, and India was born as a nation. Pathan tribesmen near the fort roasted whole sheep over fires to celebrate the event. They invited the men of the Khyber Rifles to join them, and enemies of many years feasted together.

Further Reading: *The People of the Khyber: The Pathans of Pakistan* by James W. Spain (London: Hale, 1962; New York: Praeger, 1963) offers a personal account of this diplomat's travels among and fascination with the Pathan tribes of the Khyber region, with some historical background. For a riveting, lurid, and extraordinarily detailed description of the people and events surrounding Britain's involvement with the Frontier, see *Khyber: British India's North-West Frontier: The Story of an Imperial Migraine* by Charles Miller (New York: Macmillan, and London: Macdonald and Jane's, 1977). Witty and sardonic, Miller skewers everyone caught up in Britain's obsession with the distant, barren region that it was convinced held the key to the defense of its prized colony, India. In Arthur Swinson's *North-West Frontier: People and Events 1839–1947* (London: Hutchinson, and New York: Praeger, 1967), the author tells the same story a little more briefly and in only slightly less entertaining fashion. Other sources containing useful information about the history of Khyber Pass include *A New History of India* by Stanley Wolpert (New York: Oxford University Press, 1977; fourth edition, 1993) and *Freedom at Midnight* by Larry Collins and Dominique Lapierre (New York: Simon and Schuster, and London: Collins, 1975).

—Karen Terry

Konārak (Orissa, India)

Location: On a virtually deserted coastal plain by the Bay of Bengal, twenty miles southeast of Puri and some thirty-five miles southeast of Bhubaneswar, capital of Orissa. Konārak stands so near the shore that it was used as a navigation aid by sailors for many centuries.

Description: Konārak is the site of an extraordinary thirteenth-century temple complex known as the Sun Temple. Originally consisting of twenty-eight temples, the complex was apparently never finished and fell out of use in the seventeenth century. By the mid-nineteenth century, much of the temple had collapsed. Restoration efforts in the twentieth century have preserved only sections of the original complex.

Contact: Government of India Tourist Office
B-20, Kalpana Area
Bhubaneswar, Orissa 751014
India
54203

The origins of the Sun Temple, or Sūrya Deula, at Konārak are obscure. Where history is silent, local traditions have supplied numerous legends to explain Konārak's origins. One of the most common of these states that Sāmba, son of Krishna (an avatar of Vishnu) built the temple as an offering of gratitude to Sūrya after the god cured him of leprosy. Sāmba, who was extremely handsome, had made fun of Nārada, a wise man very proud of his looks. In revenge, Nārada tricked Sāmba into watching his father's wives while they were bathing. When Krishna learned of Sāmba's spying, he cursed him with leprosy. Although Krishna regretted the curse when he learned that Sāmba had been tricked, he was unable to effect a cure and could only suggest that his son pray to Sūrya who, in addition to being the sun god, was also a healer. After twelve years, Sūrya gave Sāmba his blessing and told him to bathe in the sea at Konārak to be cured.

Despite the popularity and appeal of the Sāmba legend, historians date the beginning of construction to the reign of the Gaṅga king Narasiṃha I (reigned 1238–64). The elaborate and extraordinary sculpture at Konārak contains several likely references to Narasiṃha. For instance, guardian figures at the main gate to the temple complex, consisting of an elephant, a rearing lion, and a man, are thought to represent the power of the Gaṅga kings. Art historians take the image of the man and lion together to be a specific representation of Narasiṃha himself, since Narasiṃha is the name of Vishnu's fourth incarnation, in which the god took the form of a man-lion to kill an evil demon. Such possible representations of Narasiṃha make it likely that construction of the temple was in fact financed by the king's treasury.

Analysis of the abundant sculpture suggests that the temple complex was built in commemoration of Narasiṃha's victories over the invading Muslims, who had been pressing into Orissa from the west. Although the temple is dedicated to the Vedic sun god Sūrya, military motifs are everywhere present in the elaborate decorative program. Specific evidence to support this theory is found in a monolithic statue consisting of a set of royal horses, now badly weathered, as is most of the sculpture at Konārak. Art historians have interpreted the horses, which are trampling two men under their hooves, as a representation of Gaṅga military might. More tentatively, they have identified the trampled men as the Muslim sultans of Bengal, Tughar Khān and Iktiyar Yazbak, who were among the foes Narasiṃha defeated in the years immediately before construction at Konārak began. However, Orissa in general, and the Gaṅga kings in particular, had a long tradition of independence and military honor, and their soldiers had a widespread reputation as fierce warriors. Even without a military feat to motivate the construction of the temple, the martial images would most likely have made their way into its remarkable sculpture.

Another, more fanciful, theory does not draw from any architectural evidence but takes its cue instead from Narasiṃha's nickname, lāngulia, meaning "the tailed one." This theory holds that Narasiṃha built the temple to Sūrya the healer in the hope that the deity would remove an appendage from the base of his spine. However, it is not known how Narasiṃha acquired his nickname. Whether he actually had an unusually large tailbone the historical record does not reveal.

Whatever motivated its construction, it is clear that the complex originally stood only yards from the sea. Silt from the Bay of Bengal gradually moved the shoreline east, and by now the remains of Konārak are fully two miles inland. The oldest buildings at Konārak appear to be two smaller temples in the southwest corner of the compound, the Vaishnava Temple and the Māyādevī Temple. Both are much better preserved than the main temple because, centuries ago, the silting action accelerated by monsoons covered them entirely, partially protecting them.

The Māyādevī Temple, dedicated to Sūrya, was uncovered in the early decades of the twentieth century. It originally housed a famous statue of Sūrya. This image, according to local lore, moved out of its shrine of its own accord after it overheard two priests talking about the advances of the Muslim army. It found another shelter more to its liking in a shrine about eight miles away. The Vaishnava Temple, which was not uncovered until 1956, is thought to be the oldest of the temples, although scholars do not know by

The Sun Temple, Konārak
Photo courtesy of Air India Library, New York

how many years it predates construction of the main temple. It is dedicated to Vishnu, like Sūrya a solar deity.

The main temple itself is without parallel in Indian temple architecture. It consists of three distinct parts: the *jagamohana* and the *deul,* both of which were once crowned with corbeled domes, and the *natamandira,* which was set a short distance apart. The *jagamohana* and the *deul* are shaped like a giant chariot, with twenty-four wheels carved into the base of their walls. At one time, seven colossal sculptured horses strained to pull the chariot along. Only one of these has been well enough preserved to give an impression of the original effect. The main temple buildings resemble the famous chariot (or juggernaut) of Vishnu that is carried through the streets of Puri in the annual Jagannātha Temple festival. The chariot at Konārak, however, does not belong to Vishnu but to Sūrya and represents the celestial vehicle in which the sun god was daily pulled across the sky. The buildings lie on an east-west axis, paralleling the course of the sun through the heavens.

Three images of Sūrya are carved into the walls and placed in such a way that they catch the sun at sunrise, noon, and sunset. On the southern side, the god, catching the noon sun, is surrounded by images of the king and the high priest submitting themselves to the worship of the god. Sūrya is attended by two servants named Dandi and Pingala, as well as the warriors Ushā and Pratyushā, who drive away darkness with their arrows. Also in attendance is Aruna, the charioteer of the dawn, who drives the great chariot of the sun god across the sky. Vishnu and Brahmā also appear, not as attendants but as symbols of the creating and sustaining forces of life.

The giant wheels carved into the walls represent not only the sun god's means of transportation, but also the passage of time. The great wheel of karma represents the cycle of cause and effect that determines the Hindu universe. It also carried the spirit from one incarnation to the next. The wheels of the temple are intricately carved with images of divine maidens, couples embracing, and, on the hub of one wheel, Narasiṃha riding an elephant and crushing his enemies.

In front of the temple stands a small pavilion known as the Hall of Dance, or *natamandira.* In the Jagannātha Temple procession, ecstatic dancers precede the chariot of the god. The *natamandira* served the same purpose for the main temple at Konārak. It was the center for ritual dancing, as well as a place to offer dramas, music, and banquets in honor of Sūrya. Many Hindu temples had both a Hall of Dance and a Hall of Celebration, or *bhogamaṇḍapa,* another separate building commonly used for banquets. At Konārak the *bhogamaṇḍapa* seems to have been incorporated into the *natamandira.* The exterior walls of the *natamandira* are covered with carvings of the heavenly nymphs. Some of these are shown performing the sacred dances of the sun god, but just as many are engaged in simple everyday tasks, such as bathing or tending children. The carvings of the nymphs are marked by an extraordinary sensuality, reflecting the joy of life within the sun god's domain.

The carvings also represent the daily business of the temple itself. The temple dancing girls, or *devadāsīs,* were considered to be the earthly incarnations of the heavenly nymphs, and they performed dances from the great myths and stories depicted in some of the *natamandira* wall carvings. The office of the *devadāsīs* served several purposes. In addition to its religious function, it also provided employment for unwanted daughters. Hindu dowry practices make having daughters an extremely expensive proposition, and in many families the birth of a girl occasions more concern than rejoicing. The office of the temple dancers, therefore, represented an attractive alternative to more ruthless methods of disposing of unwanted female children. For this reason, perhaps, the dancers continued to be recruited long after the temple had been abandoned.

Technically married to the god Sūrya, the dancers were commonly taken as concubines by the kings and upper ranks of Orissan society. By the eighteenth century, the reputation of the *devadāsīs* had sunk so low that the king of Orissa himself had occasion to scold them for the scandals in which they were involved, including, most offensively, consorting with lower castes. Despite their unsavory reputation, some of the girls maintained their ancient dancing art. As late as the early twentieth century, one young *devadāsī* danced before the holy image in the Jagannātha Temple at Puri, so entrancing her audience that they threw themselves at her feet at the end of her performance.

The most celebrated feature of the Konārak temple is its sculpture, remarkable both for its expressiveness and sensuality and for the delightful humor that marks many of the figures. (One carving, for example, shows a monk being entertained in a very worldly manner by three women at once, whom he teases by dangling his money pouch just out of reach.) Even though time has erased much of the decorative sculpture, the carvings still display a stunning variety of forms. Apart from those already mentioned, there are many male and female figures engaged in all the activities of everyday life. Some of the most captivating among these represent couples joyfully making love. The overall effect is of an exuberant celebration of creaturely existence.

As befits a temple, supernatural beings are also depicted in great profusion. The walls of the temple are crowded with divine nymphs, fantastic animals, and serpent kings and queens. Each of these symbols has a different meaning to the Hindu faithful. In addition to their role as ecstatic celebrants at Sūrya's court, the nymphs also represent the natural sensuousness that pilgrims to the holy site must strive for. The serpent kings and queens are keepers of secret wisdom, while the fantastic animal figures are both heraldic devices and images to awaken unconscious feelings in the worshiper's mind. In addition, there are many representations of sacrificial fire, one of Sūrya's most important manifestations.

A small hut still stands just outside the temple compound, at the northeast corner. It contains representations of the nine planets and the gods associated with them, as well as two deities who originally graced the main temple building. These were moved to the shrine of the nine planets for safekeeping during restorations in the early twentieth century. Unlike the Sun Temple itself, the astrological shrine is still in use. Ceremonies to propitiate the astrological deities take place every Saturday, and occasionally ancient Vedic fire sacrifices are performed.

The main temple at Konārak fell into disuse in the early seventeenth century. Because of the threat of invading Muslim forces, a local ruler removed the holy image of Sūrya from its sanctuary inside the main temple and sent it to Puri. Soon afterward, Muslims entered the temple and removed the finial, or kalasha, from the top of the jagamohana tower. They apparently believed the kalasha to be of solid gold, although it was more likely made of gilded copper. The temple essentially ceased to be a sacred space once Sūrya's image and the *kalasha* were gone, and worshipers abandoned the complex to the elements.

After the *kalasha* was removed, the iron dowels that held the dome in place were exposed to weathering. Eventually the dowels either gave way or were removed for scrap metal, and the dome collapsed. As late as 1848, parts of the *jagamohana*'s great tower still stood to a height of about 100 feet. In that year, however, a gale wind brought it down. By 1870 the sanctuary itself was buried in a mass of broken stone and rubble. Because of its exposed location on the shore, the stone carvings also sustained extensive damage from the monsoon winds, while the encroaching sands drifted higher and higher, eventually submerging the entire first story of the main temple.

The British government had long been aware of the condition of the site before any restoration was undertaken. As early as 1806, the Marine Board requested funds to repair the temple, not because it recognized Konārak as an architectural treasure, but because the Marine Board needed a navigational aid along the Bengal coast. The British governor claimed that the expense involved would outweigh any benefits and refused to fund the project. Although the subject was reconsidered on several occasions, the temple had to wait until 1915 for funds to cover even the most elementary restorations.

Between 1915 and 1953, the site was renovated and repaired in piecemeal fashion: the porch of the temple was filled with sand to prevent its collapse, and the exterior was stripped of its coat of moss, lichens, and salt particles. In addition, trees were planted between the temple and the sea in order to slow the damage caused by monsoons. Even though only half of the main temple survives, Konārak is considered by many to be one of the most impressive Hindu sites in India.

Further Reading: Two fine volumes of Indian history are W. H. Moreland and Atul Chandra Chatterjee's *A Short History of India* (London and New York: Longmans, 1936; fourth edition, New York: McKay, 1966) and A. L. Basham's *The Wonder That Was India: A Survey of the Culture of the Indian Sub-continent before the Coming of the Muslims* (New York: Grove, and London: Sidgwick and Jackson, 1954). For a close examination of Konārak itself, the best source is Alistair Shearer's *The Traveler's Key to Northern India: A Guide to the Sacred Places of Northern India* (New York: Knopf, 1983). Shearer's guide also gives background information about Orissa and the local traditions of sun-god worship.

—Kenneth R. Shepherd and Marijke Rijsberman

Kongju and Puyŏ (South Ch'ungch'ŏng, South Korea)

Location: Kongju lies eighty miles south of Seoul; Puyŏ is twenty miles southwest of Kongju on the Kŭm River.

Description: Kongju served as the second capital of ancient Paekche, one of Korea's Three Kingdoms, from 475 to 538. The capital then moved to the more accessible Puyŏ until 660, when Paekche was defeated by another of the Three Kingdoms, Silla, and its Chinese allies. Kongju later became a site of political opposition to oppressive governments and a base of support for Korean nationalism.

Contact: Korea National Tourism Corporation
10, Ta-dong
Chung-gu
Seoul 100-180
South Korea
(02) 7299 600

Today's provincial towns of Kongju and Puyŏ are yesterday's royal cities, capitals of Korea's ancient Paekche Kingdom. Kongju, then called Ungjin, was Paekche's second capital from 475 to 538, while Puyŏ, then called Sabi, served as the third and final Paekche capital from 538 to 660. Although political power shifted away from these cities centuries ago, Kongju and Puyŏ continue to celebrate the historical and cultural legacy of the Paekche Kingdom.

Paekche emerged as a kingdom in the Korean Peninsula's southwestern region during the early centuries A.D. Two other kingdoms formed at the same time: Koguryŏ, encompassing the northern Korean Peninsula and part of Manchuria, and Silla, comprising the southeastern region of the peninsula. Territorial struggles between these three kingdoms dominated Korean history for seven centuries.

Paekche's origins are not entirely clear. Korean legend dates its establishment to 18 B.C. and names the leader Onjo as its founder. Onjo is said to have been the second son of the founder of the northern kingdom of Koguryŏ. When his elder brother came to power in Koguryŏ, the legend explains, Onjo traveled south to the Han River region and established a kingdom of his own, with its capital south of modern Seoul. Scholars have concluded that Paekche's founders did in fact migrate to the Han River region from the north, but that they came from northern or central Manchuria, beyond Koguryŏ. These settlers were members of the Puyŏ tribes, a powerful group engaged in constant struggle with the Koguryŏ Kingdom. The tribe that left the Puyŏ league to migrate south, called Paekche, may have settled at Inch'on, on the west coast, before acquiring territory in the region around modern Seoul.

From the Han River valley, the Paekche tribe began to expand southward, into a region populated by the Ma-han tribes. The Ma-han league, strongest of the three Han tribal groups inhabiting the southern Korean Peninsula, held territory south from the Han River along the west coast. Culturally and technologically at an advantage, the Paekche eventually conquered the Ma-han tribes, gradually conquering all their territories in southwestern Korea.

Paekche's evolution from a migrant tribe to a formidable kingdom occurred during the third and fourth centuries. A clue to Paekche's early power can be found in an attack on the Han River region in 246 by forces from two Chinese commanderies based in Korea. Clearly, the Chinese organized the strike because they perceived Paekche as a threat to their control over the area. Unexpectedly, Paekche, under King Koi, defeated the Chinese and killed their commander. Koi, who ruled from 234 to 285, proved himself a leader of strength and vision. He incorporated tribes across the Han River region into his growing kingdom and devised a highly structured, centralized government to supervise its administration.

In 260 Koi appointed officials to six distinct ministries to oversee affairs of court and state. The organization of Koi's ministries of the Imperial Household, Finance, Rituals, the Royal Guard, Justice, and Defense followed the Chinese custom of separating military and civil responsibilities. Koi also established order in his aristocratic government by designating sixteen ranks within the bureaucracy, each rank distinguished by official dress of a specified color. To curb government corruption, he decreed laws of ethical behavior and prescribed punishments for the crimes of bribery, theft, and extortion. Another example of a Chinese influence in the kingdom was the political organization of Paekche and its capital city, sometimes referred to as Hansan or Hansŏng, just south of Seoul. Both kingdom and capital were divided into five administrative districts according to the five traditional Chinese directions: north, south, east, west, and center. By the end of King Koi's reign, in 286, Paekche had emerged as a strong, stable kingdom rivaling Koguryŏ.

King Kŭnch'ogo, who reigned from 346 to 375, sought to strengthen Paekche's relationships with China and Japan, Korea's neighbors to the west and east. Although separated from China by the Yellow Sea, Paekche had never been completely isolated from Chinese influence. Drawing on cultural commonalities, King Kŭnch'ogo worked to fortify Paekche's economy, security, and reputation as a kingdom by establishing trade relations with South China's Eastern Jin Dynasty. He also maintained commercial ties with Japan. These relationships proved vital in the transmission of Chinese culture to Korea and, subsequently, of Chinese and Korean culture to Japan.

Religion may have been China's most significant cultural export to Korea and Japan. During the fourth century,

King Muryŏng's Tomb, Kongju
Photo courtesy of Korea National Tourism Corporation, Chicago

two major Chinese religious movements—Confucianism and Buddhism—gained acceptance in Paekche. Confucianism, strictly speaking less a religion than a framework of morals and ethical behavior, was closely associated with the imperial administration in China, and it became influential with the Paekche government as well. Chinese texts imported into Paekche served as the earliest Confucian primers. But before long the kingdom had its own Confucian scholars, as several Confucian universities were founded in Paekche in the fourth century. A Paekche scholar of this period, Wang In, played an important role in transmitting Confucianism to Japan by teaching the Confucian *Analects* and the *Thousand Character Classic* to members of Japan's Yamato court.

An Indian Buddhist missionary, the monk Marananda, arrived in Paekche from China in 384. His teachings found many willing converts in the kingdom, including members of the royal court. Buddhism soon became a major religion in Paekche and remains so in Korea today. During the fifth century, Buddhist priests from Paekche and Koguryŏ traveled to Japan, introducing the religion and its architecture, sculpture, and painting to a receptive Japanese population. From the fourth to the seventh centuries, Japan relied on such cultural exchanges with Paekche to enrich its own developing culture. Paekche trends in architecture and art heavily influenced Japanese styles, a fact substantiated by recent findings at Japanese archaeological sites.

During King Kŭnch'ogo's reign, however, cultural exchanges between China, Paekche, and Japan were frequently a matter of secondary importance. Territorial conflict often was a more pressing concern on the Korean Peninsula, as the king sought to establish Paekche as a preeminent political power and to expand on King Koi's territorial gains. By 369, he had won control of all remaining Ma-han lands in the peninsula's southwestern region and incorporated them into the Paekche Kingdom. He then targeted Kaya, a small Han tribal region on the southern coast between Paekche and Silla (which also had an eye on the area). Eliciting military support from his new Japanese allies, Kŭnch'ogo ordered a series of raids in 369 that discouraged Silla's plans for Kaya, which subsequently fell to Paekche.

During the same year, Paekche's northern border came under attack. Koguryŏ, the warlike kingdom on the northern Korean Peninsula, invaded Paekche lands in the Han River valley, a strategically desirable and often disputed territory. Paekche's army forced Koguryŏ to retreat. Two years later, in 371, perhaps in retribution for the earlier action, Paekche invaded Koguryŏ with 30,000 troops. Koguryŏ's king, Kogugwon, died in the battle that ensued, and King Kŭnch'ogo led his victorious troops as far north as modern P'yŏngyang. The territorial gain was only temporary, however.

The military campaigns of King Kŭnch'ogo's reign foreshadowed the rivalries, clashes, and shifting allegiances between Koguryŏ, Paekche, and Silla that characterized the

Chŏngnimsa, Five-Story Pagoda, Puyŏ
Photo courtesy of Korea National Tourism Corporation, Chicago

Three Kingdoms period of Korean history. During the fifth century, Koguryŏ revived its powerful army and embarked on a campaign of massive territorial expansion. In 427, in preparation for the campaign, Koguryŏ's ambitious King Changsu transfered his capital from a mountainous northern city to P'yŏngyang, on the plains around the Taedong River. Fully aware of Koguryŏ's threat, Paekche and Silla forged an alliance against their common northern neighbor in 433. The alliance held, but when a Koguryŏ attack loomed in 472, Paekche's King Kaero sought additional support from the Wei state of northern China. His plea went unheard. The dreaded invasion came in 475, when Koguryŏ's army of 30,000 attacked Paekche's capital and seized the vulnerable city and the surrounding Han River valley with apparent ease. Koguryŏ soldiers captured Kaero, and King Changsu triumphantly ordered his execution to avenge the death of his ancestor Kogugwon more than a century earlier.

Faced with this threat to its very existence, Paekche moved its capital to the mountains eighty miles south, beyond Koguryŏ's immediate grasp. The inaccessible, mountainous location of the new capital city of Ungjin (now called Kongju) provided natural protection to a kingdom nearly decimated by Koguryŏ's attack. In this remote city, Paekche began to rebuild. King Tongsong, who assumed the throne in 479, reaffirmed Paekche's alliance with Silla through marriage. He also ordered a campaign of construction, building military outposts and fortresses along Paekche's borders, including the border with ally Silla. At Ungjin itself, the royal palace, built on a hill, was enclosed by the walls of the Kongsan Fortress. Only ruins of these structures survive today.

During the sixty-three years that Ungjin functioned as the kingdom's capital, Paekche was relatively peaceful and experienced considerable prosperity. The agricultural economy flourished, and artisans developed a distinctive Paekche style, evident in the artifacts buried in Ungjin's royal tombs. The Paekche royal tombs stand together on a wooded hill called Sangsan-ri just outside modern Kongju. Their distinctive mound shapes reflect a Chinese influence, particularly from the Southern Liang Dynasty (502–557). A horizontal entrance corridor leads to the tomb chamber, which is covered with a sloping mound of earth. Although the tombs' form is derived from Chinese models, the interior murals in the burial chambers reflect Koguryŏ's influence. Koguryŏ artisans had adapted Chinese traditions of tomb painting, portraying the deceased engaged in a variety of activities such as hunting and fishing. The Chinese motif of the Directional Deities (north, south, east, west) was also adopted. Unlike the Chinese, the Koguryŏ craftsmen painted the murals directly onto the stone walls. Paekche's Tomb Six at Sangsan-ri features murals very similar to the Koguryŏ models, including one of the four Directional Deities. However, these and other Paekche paintings of the same time are distinguished from the Koguryŏ murals by a more delicate, refined style, which also characterized Paekche sculpture.

Koransa Temple, Puyŏ
Photo courtesy of Korea National Tourism Corporation, Chicago

The Paekche royal tombs proved easy targets for looters throughout the centuries. But when archaeologists began excavations to repair some of the decaying Paekche tombs in 1971, they discovered a previously unknown tomb with a remarkable cache of artifacts. This unusual brick tomb proved to be the burial place of Paekche king Muryŏng, who ruled from Ungjin between 501 and 523, and his queen. The thousands of objects found in Muryŏng's tomb evince the outstanding craftsmanship of Paekche artisans. The finely worked jewelry, toiletries, and tableware testify particularly to the sophistication of the metal workers' art. Together, these artifacts comprise one of the most significant archaeological discoveries in modern Korean history. The grave has now been sealed, but the collection is on view at Kongju's museum.

By 538, Paekche had regained enough stability and confidence to seek a new capital in a more accessible location. King Sŏng, who succeeded Muryŏng, ruling from 523 to 553, chose Sabi, now known as Puyŏ, as Paekche's third capital. Although located only twenty miles southwest of Ungjin, Sabi's location offered two major advantages over its mountain-bound predecessor. Situated on the Korean Peninsula's broad southwestern plain, Sabi allowed easy access to the surrounding agricultural region that served as the basis of Paekche's economy. Its location on the Kŭm River also made it possible to travel directly to China via the Yellow Sea. Once established in his new capital, King Sŏng reorganized Paekche's government structure, instituting a system of twenty-two separate central government offices. He also redrew the boundaries of the five administrative districts of Paekche, ostensibly for more effective government.

The city of Sabi, divided into five districts in the traditional manner, was located in a bend of the Kŭm River, at the base of a steep hill called Mount Puso-san. The Paekche royal palace and protective fortress were built high above the city proper, atop Mount Puso-san. Within the castle compound stood a number of pavilions, including Songwoldae (Moon-gazing Pavilion), which faces west, and Yongilru (Sun-greeting Pavilion), which faces east. Both pavilions have been reconstructed. A few surviving foundation stones on the slopes of Mount Puso-san mark the location of the Paekche army's arsenal and foodstores, where carbonized beans, rice, and barley can still be found.

Paekche monuments at modern Puyŏ are not confined to Mount Puso-san, however. Another royal pavilion, designed as a garden retreat for the ladies of the court, stood near Kungnamji Pond on the south side of Sabi. Today it lies in ruins amid the rice paddies. Most structures of the Paekche period have long since decayed or been destroyed, but one significant monument of ancient Sabi remains intact: a stone pagoda that stands on the grounds of Chŏngnimsa Temple in Puyŏ and was probably built to house religious relics and other sacred objects in the seventh century. The pagoda has five stories, which, demarcated by softly curving eaves, taper to the top in a graceful progression. As one of only three stone pagodas surviving from the entire Paekche period, the Chŏngnimsa Pagoda has become highly significant in the study of Paekche architecture. Scholars interpret its fluidity of line, stability, and simplicity as an architectural expression of Paekche's refined artistic sensibility.

Royal Paekche tombs, dating from 538 to 660, stand on the outskirts of modern Puyŏ. Excavations of these mound tombs have unearthed no burial treasures to rival those of King Muryŏng's tomb at Kongju, although one tomb does contain a ceiling mural of artistic significance. The mural depicts a lotus flower and flying clouds, painted in the typical Paekche style. The tombs are open to visitors, but most of the contents have been removed for preservation.

The removal of the Paekche capital from Ungjin to Sabi was, initially at least, highly beneficial. Paekche's economy further improved, and the kingdom rebuilt its military under the direction of King Sŏng. With a renewed confidence in Paekche's military capabilities, Sŏng initiated a plan to win back Han River valley lands lost in 475. He made a pact with Silla's King Chinhung to stage a joint attack against their common enemy Koguryŏ, which had been weakened by internal conflict. Together, the two kingdoms successfully invaded the Han River region in 551. Dividing the reconquered territories, Paekche occupied the lower Han (western) lands, and Silla occupied the upper Han region. Paekche thus achieved its goal but also laid the foundation for its ultimate destruction. Silla's appetite for land had been whetted. Just two years later, in 553, Silla betrayed its ally, driving Paekche out of the lower Han valley and claiming the land for itself.

Infuriated by these treacherous actions, King Sŏng retaliated by leading an invasion force into battle against Silla at Kwansan Fortress, just over Paekche's border. Silla's army shattered the Paekche forces, and the king was killed. The outcome of Paekche's ill-starred vengeance signaled a profound shift in power among the three kingdoms. Silla's power continued to increase during the late sixth and early seventh centuries. Aware of the threat posed by his eastern neighbor, Paekche's King Mu carried out occasional strikes on Silla's border in the early seventh century. Although these strikes posed a serious challenge to Silla's army, they did not result in any significant territorial gains for Paekche; rather, they merely expended significant military and economic resources. King Mu's successor, King Ŭija (641–60), initiated another series of raids that proved more successful strategically. In 642 the Paekche army captured Taeya-sŏng and forty other strongholds in the Paekche-Silla border zone.

Alarmed by these events, Silla's Prince Kim Ch'unch'u traveled to China to secure the Tang Dynasty's support against Paekche and Koguryŏ. Silla's proposal proved attractive to the Tang. Their recent efforts to subdue the Koguryŏ Kingdom had met with staunch resistance, and an alliance with Silla opened up the possibility of attacking Koguryŏ on two fronts. Paekche, too, understood the advantage of alliance. About the same time that Silla made a pact with Tang China, Paekche and Koguryŏ formed their own alliance to foil Silla's obvious territorial designs. In 655, their joint forces staged another attack against Silla, winning thirty border forts. Silla's call on the Tang Dynasty for military support resulted in another failed Chinese attack on Koguryŏ's stalwart defenses. Kim Ch'unch'u, now king of Silla, suggested that the combined forces of China and Silla take the entire Korean Peninsula by eliminating Paekche, the weaker kingdom, and then attacking Koguryŏ.

Silla had correctly perceived Paekche's weakness. After the success of Paekche's border attacks, King Ŭija had neglected his defenses to a dangerous degree. Serious dissent within Paekche's government further weakened the kingdom. Silla and Tang China seized their opportunity in 660 with a two-pronged attack on Sabi. Silla's troops crossed the border and attacked Sabi from the east, while the Tang army sailed across the Yellow Sea, landed at the mouth of the Kŭm River, and marched upstream to the Paekche capital. This strategy could not have been more effective. Silla general Kim Yu Sin led his forces across the hills of Tanhyon to the Hwangsan Plain, where they destroyed a small Paekche force sent to stop their advance. Victorious, the Silla army then successfully besieged Sabi-song, a fortress built to protect the capital. After the fall of Sabi-song, the combined strength of Tang and Silla marched on the capital city.

Paekche's royal court erupted in chaos at the enemy's approach. King Ŭija fled the city to take refuge at Ungjin, the remote former capital. For other members of the court, however, escape was not possible. Rather than surrender their honor to the invading armies, 3,000 ladies of Paekche's royal court gathered on a cliff at Mount Puso-san, high above a bend in the Kŭm River. From there they leapt to their deaths in a mass suicide. Today the cliff is called Nakhwaam, or "Rock of the Falling Flowers," in their memory. Their suicide, seen as a heroic self-sacrifice, is annually reenacted in the Festival for Three Thousand Maidens, which figures prominently in a recent novel by the American Richard Wiley. Abandoned by its king and under siege, Sabi surrendered quickly. King Ŭija also admitted defeat, effectively ending the Paekche Kingdom.

Although it fought in concert with Silla, Tang China aspired to rule the Korean Peninsula alone. In the aftermath of Paekche's defeat, the Tang asserted their authority, creating an administrative office staffed by Chinese at Ungjin and governing Paekche under its own plan. Yet Paekche did not submit to Tang rule immediately. A rebel force, organized by a member of the Paekche royal family and his supporters, clashed with the occupying army and regained more than 200 strongholds. The return of Paekche prince Pung from Japan served as a catalyst for the rebels. Embracing Pung as Paekche's new king, they attacked occupied Ungjin and Sabi and even defeated Silla and Tang forces in occasional conflicts. The movement collapsed, however, when a fierce struggle erupted among its three leaders, two of whom were eventually murdered. Silla and Tang struck at the demoralized Paekche rebels, who finally surrendered in 663.

By 668, Silla and Tang China had together defeated Koguryŏ. The entire peninsula was then united under the Unified Silla Kingdom, which ruled Korea for almost 300 years. Paekche became a province of Silla, which established a military administration in Sabi in 671. Although Sabi declined in importance, Ungjin gained new significance as a site of political opposition to oppressive Korean governments as well as foreign intervention. During the late period of Unified Silla, for instance, internal power struggles erupted among the aristocracy. In this volatile atmosphere, a large-scale revolt with a base at Ungjin seriously threatened Silla's stability in 822. The leader of the rebels was Kim Hŏn-ch'ang, who was a descendant of the Silla king Muyol and put himself forward as the true heir to Silla's throne. Kim Hŏn-ch'ang's father had been denied his right to the throne in 785 by a usurper. Seeking vengeance for this misdeed, Kim Hŏn-ch'ang garnered wide support in several provinces, but the Silla aristocracy eventually smothered the rebellion.

The line of Silla kings gradually lost power and abdicated to an army general, who founded the Koryŏ Kingdom in 936. More than 200 years later, the spark of rebellion was struck again in Kongju. Koryŏ king Uijong and the central aristocracy maintained an extravagant court, supported chiefly by extortionate taxes on peasant farmers and by the labor of government-owned slaves (called *chonmin*). A village of government slaves adjacent to Kongju rose in rebellion in January 1176. Led by two men named Mangi and Mangsoi, the *chonmin* wrested control of the Kongju garrison from government soldiers and widened their protest into Ch'ungch'ŏng province, even threatening Koryŏ's capital. Burdened by extreme taxation, the local peasantry joined the uprising. The rebellion was quelled one year later, after Mangi was captured. This spontaneous revolt was to be followed by more organized rebellions centuries later.

The so-called Tonghak Struggle of 1894 stirred up the anger of the peasants with an organized doctrine. Tonghak (Eastern Learning) espoused the equality of all people. Korean peasants also interpreted the doctrine as a call to nationalism and independence from Japan and the West. Peasant farmers in Ch'ungch'ŏng province (including Kongju and Puyŏ) began protesting peacefully in 1893. Their calls for national independence drew no response from the Korean government, but when the peasants resorted to violence, Korean king Kojong requested support from China. The rebels agreed to a cease-fire, but Chinese troops had already arrived. The Chinese took Kongju, a center of Tonghak revolt, in June 1894.

The rebels dispersed, but the crisis did not end. The Japanese government, which saw the rebellion as an opportunity for military intervention in Korean affairs, sent forces to Korea. The soldiers entered Seoul and expelled the Chinese army. Tonghak nationalists rallied against the Japanese in Ch'ungch'ŏng province and stormed Kongju. The renewed rebellion was quickly defeated by well-armed Japanese troops, who massacred Tonghak supporters and local peasant farmers. Although the Tonghak Struggle was defeated, it had sown seeds of political awareness among the peasantry, particularly in Ch'ungch'ŏng province.

Another political movement, the Seoul-based Independence Club, was founded in 1896 by Koreans educated in Western liberal ideas. The club, whose membership was open to all citizens, demanded Korean independence, basic human rights, a democratic constitutional government, and a new system of education and industrialization. Its progressive program garnered support far beyond Seoul, particularly in Ch'ungch'ŏng province. The first club branch was organized in Kongju. Although the club was officially suppressed several years later, its political ideals lived on among Koreans.

The Japanese invaded Korea in 1910, occupying it until 1945. After World War I, sporadic protests for Korean independence grew into a national movement. Inspired by Woodrow Wilson's doctrine of national self-determination, representatives from many Korean religions gathered in Seoul in 1919 and declared Korean independence. Students took to the streets of Seoul in peaceful demonstrations in support of the declaration. The movement spread rapidly across Korea, sparking peaceful protests in virtually every province. In Kongju, some 14,000 citizens participated in twelve demonstrations. But the Korean people's protests against oppression did not find an international audience, and Korea's Japanese government crushed the nationalist movement in a campaign of terror.

Today, both Kongju and Puyŏ are small provincial towns that bear few visible reminders of their past as Paekche capitals. Surviving monuments such as King Muryŏng's Tomb at Kongju and the Chŏngnimsa Pagoda at Puyŏ are regarded as national treasures. Artifacts that embody the magnificence of Paekche craft—gold crowns and jewelry, jade, bronze mirrors, funeral urns, and a range of sacred Buddhist art—are preserved and on display in the Kongju National Museum and Puyŏ National Museum. Annual festivals celebrating the Paekche heritage, including the Puyŏ Festival for Three Thousand Maidens (which conveniently leaves out Silla's role in the attack on Sabi), play an important role in Korea's sense of national identity.

Further Reading: Several recent books offer detailed, scholarly accounts of Korean history. Among the most useful are *A New History of Korea* by Ki-baik Lee, translated by Edward W. Wagner with Edward J. Shultz (Cambridge, Massachusetts, and London: Harvard University Press; Seoul: Ilchokak, 1984); Wanne J. Joe's *Traditional Korea: A Cultural History* (Seoul: Chung'ang University Press, 1972); and *The History of Korea* by Han Woo-keun, translated by Lee Kyung-shik (Seoul: Eul-Yoo, 1970). David Rees's *Short History of Modern Korea* (Port Erin, Isle of Man: Ham, and New York: Hippocrene, 1988) also offers a good English-language account. Korean government publications offer an alternate source of information. A wealth of facts about the country can be found in

A Handbook of Korea (ninth edition, Seoul: Korean Overseas Information Service, 1993). Such government publications should be used with caution, however, as they are often biased and nationalistic. Richard Wiley's *Festival for Three Thousand Maidens* (New York: Dutton, 1991; Harmondsworth, Middlesex: Penguin, 1992) sets its denouement against the backdrop of the Puyŏ festival, which is stirringly described.

—Elizabeth E. Broadrup

Kot Diji (Sind, Pakistan)

Location: In the Sind province of southeastern Pakistan, 22 miles south of Rohri and approximately 175 miles northeast of Karāchi.

Description: Pre-Harappan village that flourished on the Indus River from approximately 2800 to 2400 B.C. A small, rural settlement, Kot Diji predated the urban Harappan cities that dominated the Indus River valley during the next millennium (2500–1700 B.C.). Excavations have revealed advances in agriculture, pottery making, and building techniques achieved by Kot Diji's pre-Harappan settlers. Kot Diji also was inhabited during the Harappan age. The combined archaeological evidence from Kot Diji's pre-Harappan and Harappan periods provides insight into the development of one of the world's earliest civilizations. In modern times, Kot Diji became the site of a Tālpur fortress. British forces occupied the fort in 1843 during their campaign to annex Sind to India. Today, little of pre-Harappan Kot Diji remains, although the Tālpur fort survives intact.

Site Office: Pakistan Tourism Development Corporation
Hotel Metropol
Club Road
Karāchi, Sind
Pakistan
(92) 21 516 252

Kot Diji, a small farming village during the Bronze Age, has emerged as an important archaeological site in the modern age. Located in southeastern Pakistan's Sind province, Kot Diji lay buried beneath the Indus River plain until its discovery in the mid–twentieth century. Artifacts found at the site, including pottery, metal fragments, and mud bricks, document the development of one of the world's earliest civilizations—the Indus River valley civilization, which culminated in the great Harappan cities. Kot Diji's significance is best understood within the larger context of the mature Harappan civilization.

Now considered the first urban culture of the Indian subcontinent, the Harappan civilization was unknown to scholars until the twentieth century. Intrigued by large, earth-covered mounds at Harappa, on the Ravi River in the Punjab province of present-day Pakistan, archaeologists began exploring the site in 1921. Excavations soon revealed an immense, walled city, dating from 2300–1750 B.C., below the site. One year later, a contemporaneous city sharing Harappa's size and civic plan was unearthed 400 miles south at Mohenjo-daro, on the Indus River in Sind province. Together, these two highly organized Bronze Age cities suggested the existence of a heretofore unknown, and technologically advanced, culture in the prehistoric Indus Valley.

In the decades following the discovery of these sites, scholars expanded their investigations of the Harappan civilization (named for the site of the first discovery). Smaller Harappan-era settlements soon came to light throughout the Indus River valley, including Kot Diji, twenty-five miles east of Mohenjo-daro. Harappa and Mohenjo-daro apparently functioned as large political or administrative centers for a civilization that encompassed more than 100 villages and towns, spread over thousands of square miles within and beyond the Indus River valley.

Harappan settlements often developed near the Indus River and its tributaries, which offered access to water and navigable trading routes. The Indus, however, was prone to extensive and destructive flooding. Following the Mesopotamian example, the early Harappans devised ways of channeling and redirecting floodwaters into arid land. These irrigation techniques allowed the Harappans to control flooding while feeding growing urban populations from newly cultivated land.

The Harappans' desire to control and order their natural environment clearly extended to their urban environment as well. Excavations of Harappa, Mohenjo-daro, and many smaller towns and villages (including Kot Diji) reveal uniform characteristics of architecture and civic planning, suggesting a highly organized central authority at work. Many Harappan cities and towns, for example, featured dual settlement areas: a raised citadel, fortified by brick ramparts, and a less grand, low-lying town, also protected by a wall. Archaeologists speculate that the citadels contained important civic buildings and homes of prominent citizens, while the lower towns housed craftsmen and laborers. The Harappan zeal for urban planning, however, is evident in both areas. Streets and blocks, arranged on north-south and east-west axes, conformed to a standard grid. Bricks used to build homes and walls were created in sizes standard throughout the Harappan region. The Harappans also controlled living conditions in their cities by constructing sanitation systems that were cleaner and more effective than some used in India today. Covered brick drains removed sewage from public streets and individual homes. In some larger towns, water was pumped into homes through terra-cotta pipes with faucets.

Cities such as Harappa (whose population has been estimated at 35,000) could not have prospered without the ample food supply made possible through irrigation. Archaeological evidence suggests that wheat, barley, melons, peas, sesame, dates, and other crops were grown locally. The remains of multiple granaries have been unearthed at several Harappan cities. Although these may have been used simply

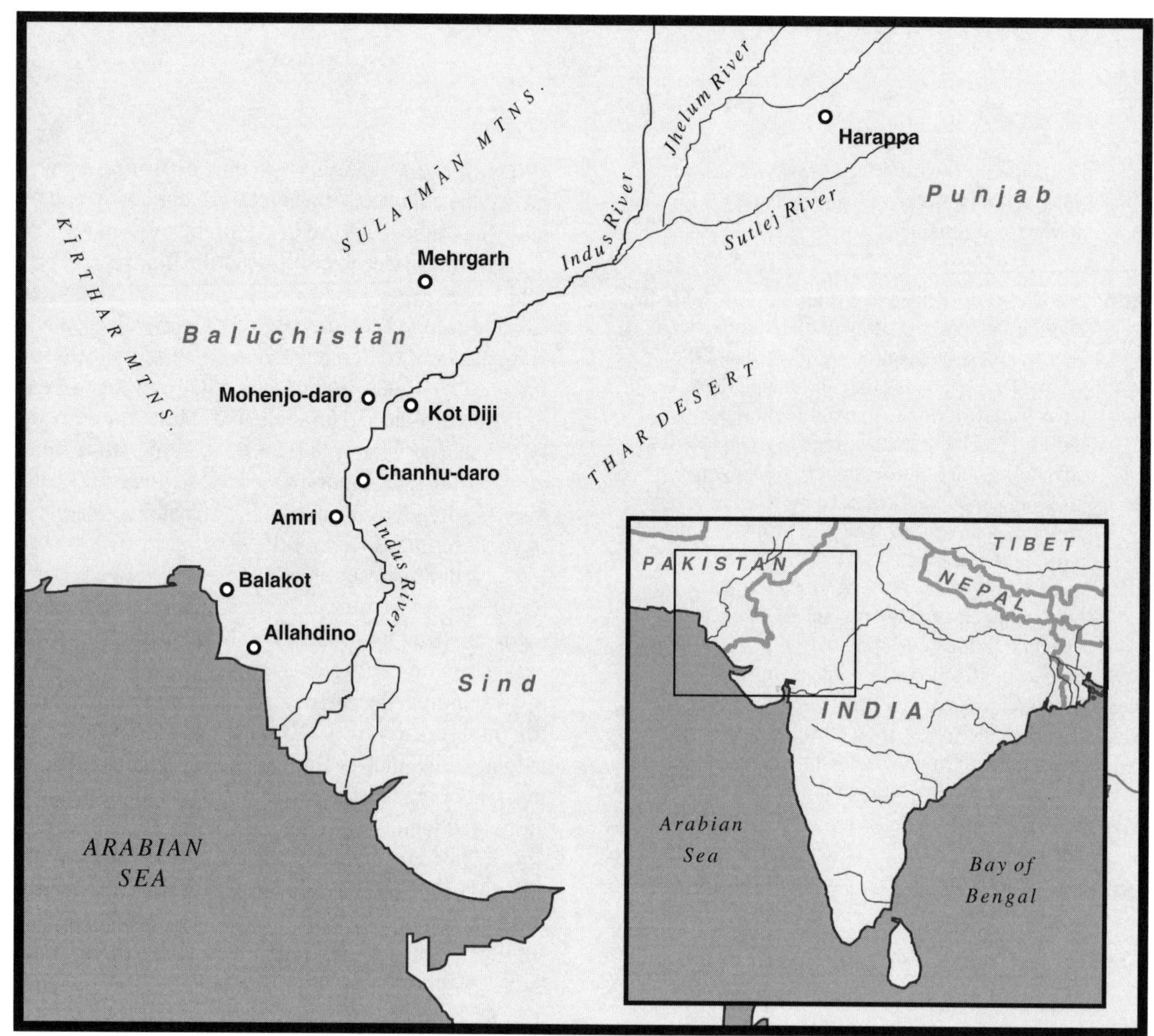

Map of Indus River valley civilizations
Illustration by Tom Willcockson

as storage for wheat and barley, they also may have played a role in Harappan trade, storing products for export or supplies from imports.

The Harappans utilized the network of waterways in the Indus Valley to become accomplished traders. Distinctive Harappan pottery and inscribed seals found in Iran, Mesopotamia, and western Asia indicate extensive trade contacts. Harappan traders probably exchanged materials such as stone, wood, and ivory for more luxurious goods, including gold from southern India, turquoise from Iran, and copper, silver, and lapis lazuli from Afghanistan. The Harappans also apparently pioneered the cultivation of cotton, which they spun, dyed, and traded to other lands.

In order to conduct their trade most effectively, the Harappans devised a uniform system of weights and measurements. This system, used throughout the Harappan civilization, incorporated graduated weights ranging from small handheld weights to larger ones lifted by pulleys. Seals inscribed with pictographs have been excavated within the Harappan region and beyond. These artifacts confirm that the Harappans were literate, although the meaning of the known characters has only partially been decoded.

The excavations conducted in the Indus Valley in 1921–22 revealed an urban civilization of technological and cultural sophistication. This discovery shattered long-held academic notions about the "backwardness" of ancient India. Scholars who had credited the beginning of civilization in India to the Aryan invasions were forced to agree that organized civilization evolved 1,000 years earlier, at the hands of India's pre-Aryan peoples. Scholarly inquiry then turned to the roots of this Indus civilization to find out how it developed and from what cultures or models it may have originated.

Kot Diji offers a wealth of insight into the development of civilization in the Indus Valley, from its earliest period to the mature Harappan culture. Scholars have identified approximately sixteen levels of occupation at the site. The lowest ten levels date from pre-Harappan settlement, beginning before 2700 B.C. The top three levels, which date from after 2400 B.C., represent occupation by the Harappan culture. The intermediate levels reveal a mix of pre-Harappan and Harappan artifacts, as well as evidence of a destructive fire. Archaeologists studying these layers have concluded that the roots of Indus Valley culture lie to the west, in the older agricultural communities of Balūchistān (the hilly province of southwestern Pakistan) and Iran.

Clues to the connection between Indus and Balūchi cultures emerged in Bronze Age artifacts discovered in both regions. Similarities in these artifacts (particularly pottery) and agricultural techniques led scholars to postulate a migration of tribal peoples from the Balūchistān hills eastward to the Indus River. Farming communities existed in Balūchistān during the fourth and third millennia B.C. Farming in this mountainous region was difficult; hunting provided food to supplement often low crop yields. Although their culture was relatively unsophisticated, these early farmers were not completely isolated. Many of these tribes had come to Balūchistān from neighboring Iran. Scholars speculate that they may have had contact with the advanced Mesopotamian civilization, which developed in the valleys of the Tigris and Euphrates Rivers west of the Iranian plateau. Mesopotamia provided an example of what the mature Harappan society eventually became: a literate, urban civilization thriving in an irrigated, flood-controlled river valley.

Motivated by difficult, mountainous conditions and guided perhaps by the Mesopotamian model, the farming peoples of Balūchistān began to migrate eastward toward the fertile Indus River valley in approximately 3000 B.C. The subsequent development of agriculture in Sind supports the migration theory. The Balūchi peoples eventually transformed the Indus Valley into a rich agricultural region by applying their own farming techniques and adopting Mesopotamian flood-control and irrigation methods. Within five centuries, the unique Indus civilization (first pre-Harappan, then mature Harappan culture) evolved throughout the Indus Valley.

The early settlement at Kot Diji spanned the period between the arrival of Balūchi peoples in Sind and the beginning of urban Harappan culture. Scholars generally date this pre-Harappan village culture to approximately 2700–2200 B.C. Kot Diji, one of the first such villages to be excavated, lent its name to a distinctive pre-Harappan culture now known as the "Kot Diji culture."

During Kot Diji's earliest period, its people were predominantly farmers. Clues left in the earth reveal that these settlers had mastered the technique of plowing still used by Rājasthānīs and other Indians today. These Bronze Age farmers depended largely on stone, especially agate and chalcedony, as a material for buildings and tools. Dwellings had stone foundations, and stone was carved to make beads and leaf-shaped arrowheads. Similar arrowheads found at contemporaneous village sites in Mesopotamia, Afghanistan, and Iran reinforce the cultural connections between Sind and its western neighbors. Pottery unearthed at Kot Diji also suggests cultural ties to Balūchistān. During Kot Diji's early period of settlement, potters created distinctive redware by hand. Storage jars painted with black bands at the neck and globe-shaped vessels with flanged rims frequently have been excavated in Kot Diji's oldest layers. Scholars speculate that both types of pottery derived from styles created in the Zhob valley of northern Balūchistān.

As the centuries passed, the Kot Dijian settlement grew beyond its Balūchi origins and began to evolve toward the mature Harappan culture. The Kot Dijians began to use the potter's wheel to produce more refined redware vessels, which were decorated with black-painted figures and patterns. The humped Indian bull (*zebu*) appears on many vessels, suggesting that it may have held religious significance. More characteristic, however, are vessels painted with distinctive geometric patterns. These designs feature straight and wavy lines, triangles, and intersecting circles. The pattern of intersecting circles appears very rarely in Mesopotamia and Iran, leading scholars to credit its development to the pre-Harappan Indus Valley. This pattern and others recur in vessels of the later Harappan period, providing a cultural link between the pre-Harappan and mature Harappan civilizations.

Other characteristics of the early settlement at Kot Diji suggest the villagers' influence on the Harappans. During the latter part of Kot Diji's pre-Harappan period, a citadel was constructed, probably as a means to survive the Indus's flooding. Homes constructed of unburnt mud bricks were aligned in regular blocks in a way that prefigured Harappan city planning. At some point, a defensive wall apparently was built around the village. Kot Diji's farmers began to use metals, as indicated by copper and bronze fragments found in later levels of excavation. Semiprecious stones found at Kot Diji, including lapis lazuli from Afghanistan, prove that the pre-Harappan Indus peoples retained contact with the western lands from which their culture had evolved. The presence of such stones probably signifies early efforts at trade, which became more important in the larger Harappan cities.

Kot Diji's pre-Harappan settlement survived until the middle of the third millennium B.C. Archaeological evidence shows that a different, though related, culture (referred to as mature Harappan) occupied the site thereafter. Signs of a destructive fire occur in the excavated layers dating from about 2400 B.C. Scholars have theorized that the Harappans, who had developed settlements elsewhere in the Indus Valley, seized Kot Diji, burned it, and rebuilt it as a Harappan town. Kot Diji's new inhabitants clearly were influenced by the site's pre-Harappan plan, for the rebuilt town had similar, but larger, mud-brick homes, aligned streets, and a defensive wall.

This Harappan phase of occupation began in approximately 2300 B.C. and lasted until 1750 B.C. This end date coincides with the gradual decline of the Harappan civilization, an event that has sparked debate among scholars. A theory maintaining that Aryan invaders destroyed the mature Harappan civilization has been discredited. Some scholars argue that a series of devastating floods triggered by earthquakes overwhelmed the Harappans in approximately 1700 B.C. Others, pointing to the vastness of the Harappan civilization, dismiss this theory in favor of one according to which unspecified ecological, political, and economic forces caused the decline and desertion of the great Harappan cities.

Whatever the cause, Kot Diji became uninhabited in approximately 1750 B.C. Although no settlement has existed there in modern times, Kot Diji did become the site of a monumental Tālpur fortress. The Tālpurs, a Balūchi tribe, gained control of Sind by 1802. They constructed an immense brick fortress on the crest of a hill at Kot Diji soon thereafter. Invading British forces occupied the fort in 1843, during their successful campaign to squelch the Tālpurs and annex Sind to India. The fortress survives in excellent condition.

Further Reading: Several books provide a general introduction to the prehistoric Indus Valley, including Stanley A. Wolpert's *A New History of India* (New York and Oxford: Oxford University Press, 1977; fourth edition, 1993) and *A History of India* by K. Antonova, G. Bongard-Levin, and G. Kotovsky, translated by Katharine Judelson (Moscow: Progress Publishers, 1979). More in-depth and scholarly, yet highly readable works devoted exclusively to India's ancient history are Shashi Asthana's *History and Archaeology of India's Contacts with Other Countries from Earliest Times to 300 B.C.* (Delhi: B. R. Publishing, and Columbia, Missouri: South Asia Books, 1976), H. D. Sankalia's *Prehistory of India* (New Delhi: Munshiram Manoharlat, 1977) and N. N. Bhattacharyya's *Ancient Indian History and Civilization: Trends and Perspectives* (New Delhi: Manohar, and Columbia, Missouri: South Asia Books, 1988).

—Elizabeth E. Broadrup

Krakatau (Indonesia)

Location: Krakatau, also spelled Krakatoa, is an uninhabited volcanic island in the Sunda Strait, which connects the South China Sea and the Indian Ocean. Krakatau lies approximately halfway between Java and Sumatra; the island is about twenty-five miles from Java's west coast.

Description: Krakatau was, before 1883, a roughly oblong-shaped island approximately five and one-half miles from north to south and two and one-half miles across. The well-forested island had several volcanic cones. The southern cone, called Rakata, was about 2,600 feet high. At the northern end was a lower cone of some 300 feet called Perbuwatan. Two small islands named Verlaten and Lang lie a few miles from Krakatau's north end. The circular arrangement of the islands indicates that this was the site of an enormous volcanic explosion thousands of years ago. The area remains a locus of volcanic activity because the Indian Ocean crustal plate is being subducted, or forced under the southeastern edge of the Eurasian plate. The intense heat generated by this process is the cause of the destructive eruptions that have plagued the Sunda Strait throughout the years, most spectacularly in August 1883. This eruption sank much of the island's previous landmass and led to the deaths of an estimated 36,000 inhabitants along the surrounding coastal areas.

Contact: Kanwil V Depparpostel DKI Jakarta
Jl. K. H. Abdurrohim 1
Kuningan Barat
Jakarta 12710
Indonesia
(21) 5202256 or (21) 5251316

The Sunda Strait between the South China Sea and the Indian Ocean is one of the world's most important and heavily used sea lanes. In the late nineteenth century, hundreds of ships of the British Empire and other seagoing European nations passed through the strait every year on their way to and from Asian ports of trade. The strait is fifteen miles wide at its narrowest point. About thirty miles west of this area is the volcanic island Krakatau, with its small companion islands Verlaten, Lang, and the oddly named Polish Hat, the last little more than a group of rocks showing above the ocean surface. Little was known about these islands in the late nineteenth century, although they appeared on British Admiralty charts as an aid to navigation through the strait. Seamen used Krakatau as a landmark on their voyages, often citing the island in detailed logs that typically related a ship's progress, events aboard, and unusual sights. Much of what is known about dramatic occurrences at Krakatau—including the catastrophic events of 1883—can be attributed to the logs of various ships.

Located on the edge of a crustal plate, the islands of Indonesia and the Sunda Strait always have been areas of intense volcanic activity. The theory of plate tectonics was unknown to scientists of the nineteenth and early twentieth centuries, and volcanoes were seen simply as outlets or vents for the tremendously hot subterranean materials of the planet. Modern geologists know that a volcano at Krakatau nearly two miles high erupted and exploded thousands of years ago; its pulverized summit collapsed into a large, circular, flooded area called a caldera. The shattered rim of the ancient volcano became the volcanic islands known later as Krakatau. Magma seeping up from underground throughout the centuries created a new volcano known as Rakata to the Javanese, Krakatau to the Dutch, and Krakatoa to the English.

Krakatau and its neighboring islands were uninhabited and seldom visited except by woodcutters from Java and Sumatra, who came periodically to cut timber from the flourishing forests. Fishermen also came to the waters around Krakatau, and British naval survey parties may have landed briefly. Otherwise, very little is known about Krakatau prior to 1883. There are reports from ships' logs of an eruption that apparently took place between May 1680 and November 1681. This eruption is said to have destroyed Krakatau's vegetation and covered the surrounding sea with large quantities of pumice, a volcanic rock made of glassy froth filled with bubbles, which is light enough to float on water. This volcanic activity may have been centered at the cone called Perbuwatan at the north end of Krakatau Island. In any case, the vegetation grew back, and in the late nineteenth century Krakatau was considered a beautiful sight by the passengers of steamships passing through the strait.

After the eruption of 1680–81, Krakatau remained quiet for two centuries. On September 1, 1880, a series of earthquakes occurred in the vicinity of Krakatau, one of them strong enough to damage a nearby lighthouse and to be felt 1,000 miles away in Australia. After this, a few years of quiet ensued. Then, on the morning of May 20, 1883, sounds like the booming of large cannon were heard in the Javanese city of Batavia (now Jakarta), about 100 miles from Krakatau. The source of the noise was revealed the next day when Krakatau began to expel jets of steam and ash that drifted to the Java coast. A passing ship saw vapor emerging from the base of the volcano, an indication that Krakatau's main chimney might be plugged, forcing gases to build up inside the mountain. Bright flashes of light, loud explosions, and clouds of smoke and ash were observed. Chunks of pumice fell on the

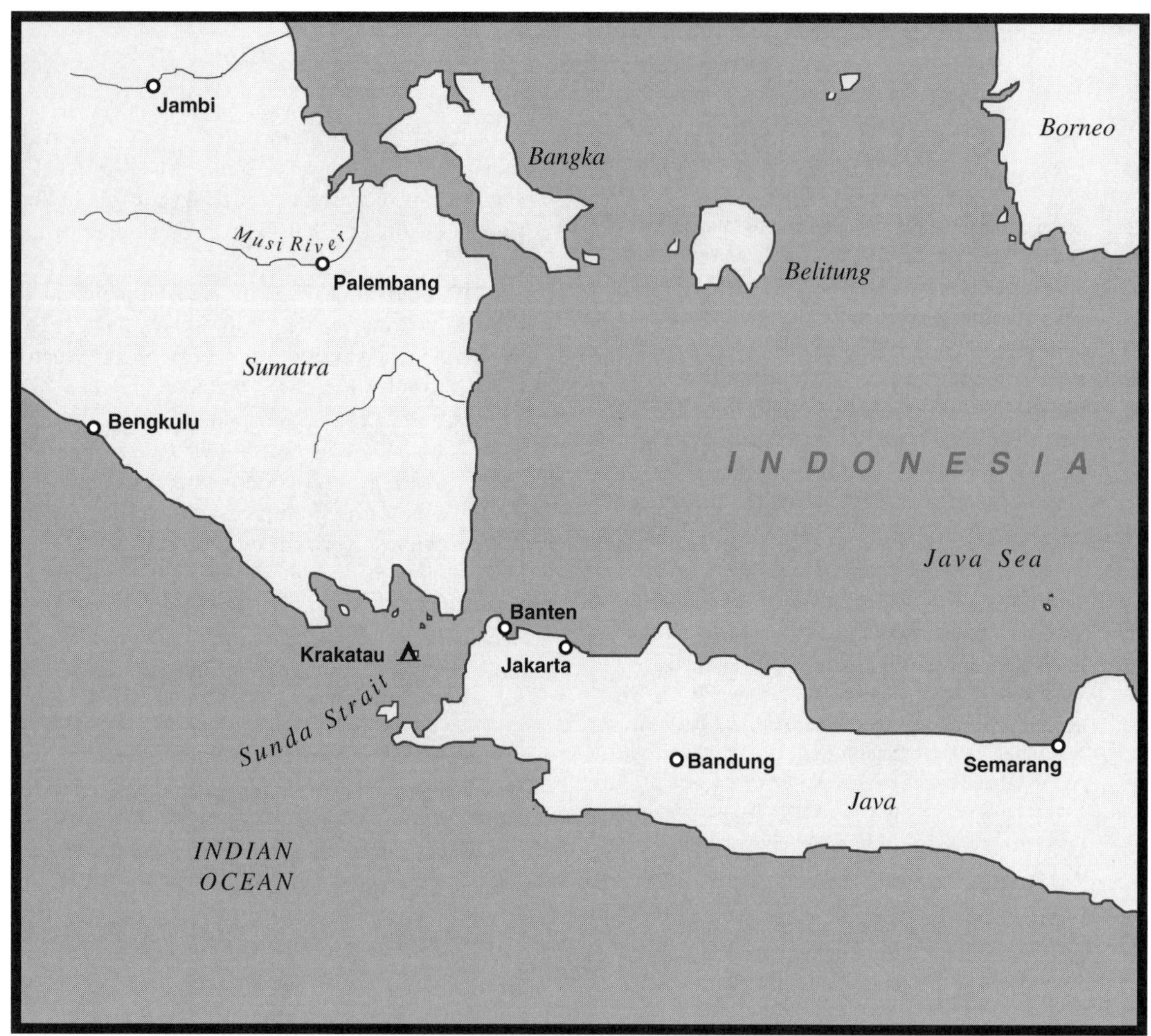

Map showing the volcanic island of Krakatau in the Sunda Strait between Sumatra and Java
Illustration by Tom Willcockson

land and on the decks of passing ships, some as far as 300 miles away.

Krakatau soon settled into a quiet state, and on May 26 a ship left Batavia with an exploration party. Despite more explosions, the steamer arrived at Krakatau on the morning of Sunday, May 27. The island was covered with finely ground volcanic glass that looked like snow. Trees had been destroyed by a rain of pumice. Some vegetation had survived on the tallest volcanic cone, Rakata, showing that the major volcano on the island had not yet erupted. The smaller cone at the north end of the island, Perbuwatan, was erupting fiercely, with loud explosions shaking the ground about every ten minutes. Several courageous explorers actually climbed the erupting cone and looked down into the volcano's mouth. They saw a shield of rock covering molten lava with a large hole in the center noisily throwing out steam. Deafened and driven back by the heat, the party climbed back down the slope while observers on the ship photographed a dark mushroom cloud rising above the island. The visitors left without casualties. They were the last people to set foot on Krakatau before the final eruption and live to tell about it.

The eruption continued during June, July, and most of August. Earthshaking explosions and tremors rocked the strait. Residents along the shores of Java and Sumatra became accustomed to the noise, the falling dust, and the masses of pumice floating on the sea for hundreds of miles. Very few people became alarmed enough to evacuate the area; the decision to stay cost thousands of coastal inhabitants their lives when Krakatau finally exploded. Since the beginning of volcanic activity on May 20, Krakatau essentially had been turning itself into an enormous bomb: gases blocked by the clogged chimney of the volcano created intense pressure inside and beneath the island. Cool sea water infiltrated the covering rocks and came into contact with the magma at the volcano's center, further diminishing the ability of the increasing gas pressure to escape. Finally, on August 26–27, Krakatau exploded in a chain of immense detonations.

Early on the afternoon of Sunday, August 26, loud explosions were heard in Batavia and in other communities along the Java shore. A ship approximately 120 miles east-northeast of Krakatau reported a 15-mile-high column of smoke and vapor rising above the Sunda Strait. Another British vessel about 10 miles south of Krakatau saw the volcano covered with turbulent black smoke, and hot chunks of pumice began to batter the ship. Other ships reported dense masses of black clouds around the island, with fire shooting up from the volcano and floods of burning lava rolling down the flanks of the volcanic cones. Early on August 27 the blasts became one continuous explosion. The moist tropical air combined with volcanic dust to cause a rain of mud, which fell on ships and made several so top-heavy that they nearly capsized. In Batavia and other coastal towns on both sides of the strait, mud and dust rained down, and sunlight was blocked out as far as 150 miles from Krakatau. The explosions were heard in Timor, nearly 1,350 miles from the strait, and rumbling sounds reached Indian Ocean locations up to 3,000 miles away. Krakatau's explosions reverberated farther than any other sounds in recorded history without the aid of modern electronic technology.

On Wednesday, August 29, two days after the climactic eruption, a passing ship was able to move through the thick masses of pumice floating on the sea and obtain a view of the remains of Krakatau. Most of the northern half of the island had vanished. The largest cone, Rakata, was sliced in half vertically, leaving a 2,600-foot-high cliff. The two smaller cones on the island had vanished; where they had been, now only water stood. Part of the 2,600-foot-high peak of the largest cone, together with the smaller volcanic cones, had collapsed nearly 1,000 feet beneath the sea. Since Krakatau was known to be uninhabited, the first observers were not overly concerned about casualties. But unknown to the ships in the strait, a disaster of vast proportions had occurred along the nearby coasts of Java and Sumatra. Although the eruptions on August 27 caused some casualties from falling superheated ash, dust, and pumice (mostly along the coast of Sumatra, which was closer than Java to the site of Krakatau), the greatest devastation was caused by seismic sea waves, called tsunamis, created by the explosion. These waves, estimated to have been 100 to 115 feet tall, spread out from the volcano with enormous force, rolling over the heavily populated towns along the Javanese and Sumatran coasts of the Sunda Strait. More than 3,500 people were killed by the waves at the Javanese towns of Anger, Batavia, and Banten. Many small islands and villages were obliterated, their populations vanishing as if they had never existed. Thousands of bodies were found floating on the sea or washed inland. So many victims vanished in the waves that the exact number of people who died will never be known. It is estimated that more than 36,000 people perished in the aftermath of Krakatau's eruption.

One of the most striking aspects of Krakatau's deadly eruption was its effect on the earth's atmosphere and climate, which measurably changed for several years. Huge clouds of volcanic dust, ashes, and finely ground pumice were jettisoned into the atmosphere and carried around the world by the jet streams. The clouds blocked sunlight, causing temperatures to fall worldwide during the ensuing months. The growing season in Britain was shortened by a week during the year. The world's mean annual temperature fell as much as one degree Fahrenheit in 1884, and the planet cooled perceptibly throughout the rest of the 1880s. Modern scientists studying records of the Krakatau phenomena and those of other eruptions have determined that the veil of volcanic particles typically survives one to two years in the atmosphere. Cooling is concentrated in the first one or two years after a major eruption, and slight cooling persists for several more years, since the oceans are slow to recover from the cooling effect.

The massive explosions that destroyed much of Krakatau left the surface of the surviving part of the island and that of its close neighbors Verlaten and Lang Islands covered by tens of yards of hot ash and pumice. Because the plant, animal, and insect populations had been totally destroyed, scientists infer that the subsequent biological renewal at Krakatau must have consisted entirely of imported organisms carried by winds, birds, or the sea. There has been some controversy about whether plant life actually was eradicated, but the weight of evidence suggests that this was the case. One scientist visiting Krakatau in October 1883 found not a single plant and a year later found only a few blades of grass. Twenty-six plant species were counted in 1886, 61 species in 1897, 108 species in 1906, and 276 species by 1928. Thus, as Krakatau's environment has improved slowly over the years, a variety of trees, bushes, and plants—including many orchids—have found suitable conditions for growth.

Similarly, biologists believe that all of Krakatau's fauna was destroyed in 1883, although several experts have made a case for the survival of some earthworms and larval insects buried deep in the ground. Animals probably repopulated Krakatau gradually, with plant-eating species establishing themselves first, followed by carnivores and parasites. Newly arrived species multiplied rapidly at first but in the long run established normal proportions within the animal population. Fauna could reach the island by air, either flying or transported by the wind, or by sea, swimming or carried by driftwood or other flotsam. Ninety percent of the island's fauna probably arrived by air from Java or Sumatra.

Krakatau remained quiet for forty-four years, until in 1927 explosive submarine eruptions began near the north rim of the caldera that had formed after the 1883 eruption. Within a year, a cinder cone had formed above sea level and was named Anak Krakatau (Child of Krakatau). This new incarnation of the Krakatau volcano has grown fitfully over the years through small periodic eruptions. Waves from the Indian Ocean eroded some of the new volcanic cone, but since 1960 lava flows have formed a protective cap on the volcano. Anak Krakatau, with a cone nearly 500 feet high, will continue to grow without the diminishing effect of erosion. The volcano still rumbles and smokes occasionally, ensuring that

Krakatau itself will remain uninhabited. Nevertheless, the new volcano, like its predecessors, is near the coast of Java, now one of the most densely populated areas in the world. According to geologists, however, it will be many thousands of years before the magma accumulating slowly beneath Krakatau explodes with the violence witnessed in 1883.

Further Reading: *Krakatau 1883* by Tom Simkin and Richard S. Fiske (Washington: Smithsonian, 1983) is a large compilation of reports—originally published between 1885 and the early 1980s—on the eruption and its aftermath, including descriptions, monographs, technical reports, and scientific accounts, all translated into English. With numerous rare photographs, this book is an essential and widely available source for the study of Krakatau. David Ritchie's *The Ring of Fire* (New York: Atheneum, 1981) is a well-written and well-illustrated discussion of volcanism that includes a long, informative section about Krakatau. Robert and Barbara Decker's Volcanoes (New York: Freeman, 1981) includes a concise, illustrated chapter on Krakatau. Peter Francis's Volcanoes: A Planetary Perspective (Oxford and New York: Oxford University Press, 1993) provides a discussion of the eruption of Krakatau and its aftermath with excellent maps, charts, and photographs. Bill Dalton's *Indonesia Handbook* (Chico, California: Moon, 1992) is an informative guide for those considering a visit to Krakatau.

—Bernard A. Block

Kuching (Sarawak, Malaysia)

Location: The capital of Sarawak, Kuching is situated on the Sarawak River on the island of Borneo.

Description: A settlement since the 1820s, Kuching was further developed under the auspices of James Brooke, the rāja of Sarawak. During the nineteenth century, the town became an important trading capital. Today it is the largest town in east Malaysia and the eighth-largest urban center in Malaysia. Kuching remains a pleasant city to visit; it retains some interesting architecture despite heavy bombing by the Japanese during World War II.

Site Office: Tourism Malaysia, Sarawak Regional Office
Ground Floor, Aurora Hotel
Jalan Tun Abang Haji Openg
93000 Kuching
Sarawak
Malaysia
(82) 246 575

The origin of the word *Kuching* is the subject of considerable debate. The first rāja of Sarawak, James Brooke, made reference to the settlement *Kuchin'* in 1839. It is thought that the word is derived from the Malay word for cat, *kuching*, or from a corruption of *Cochin*, both the name of an Indian trading port on the Malabar Coast and a generic term in China and British India for a trading harbor. Mrs. Dougall, a British woman, writing to her son in the nineteenth century, said that Kuching derived its name from a stream of the same name. As far as can be ascertained, the name Kuching was already in use by the time Brooke arrived in the late 1830s.

The village of Kuching dates to the 1820s, when it was a small colony, probably populated by pirates. The sultan of Brunei had nominal control over Sarawak, but he was interested only in exacting a minor tax from the region. However, his interest grew when antimony (an element used in alloys and medicines) was discovered in the area in approximately 1824. Pengeran Makota, a Brunei prince, moved to Sarawak in the early nineteenth century and developed Kuching between 1824 and 1830. He chose the site because it was south of the coastal swamps and was conveniently located between the river mouth, twenty-one miles away, and the antimony mines, twenty-five miles upriver. It was also an easy site to defend.

Following the discovery of antimony ore, Chinese migrants began to move into the area in substantial numbers, working predominantly in the ore industry, but also setting up trading posts. As antimony mining increased, the Brunei sultanate demanded higher taxes from Sarawak. This highly unpopular move led to civil unrest, which culminated in a revolt. The sultan of Brunei sent his uncle Muda Hasim to deal with the crisis. Following Hasim's arrival, the population of Kuching increased from a few hundred people to approximately 1,500 in 1839. A visitor to Kuching that same year described the village as consisting of

> a collection of mud huts erected in piles. . . . The residences of the Rāja [Hasim] and his 14 brothers occupy the greater part, and their followers are the great majority of the population. When they depart for Borneo [Brunei], the remainder must be a very small population, and apparently poor.

Hasim, however, proved unequal to the task of quelling the rebellion and asked the visiting Briton James Brooke to help him. Brooke succeeded in this task and was rewarded with a large amount of antimony, a house in Kuching, and the title of Rāja and Governor of Sarawak. The city was in fact little more than a village. Excluding Hasim's court, the population numbered between 600 and 800 and was composed mostly of Malay nobles from Brunei and some Chinese traders. The houses were made of nipah palm and mud, and were built on piles on the river bank. Following Brooke's arrival, however, Kuching underwent great change. Brooke built his house on the right bank of the river, near Hasim's palace. It was designed to resemble a Swiss cottage. Migration to the city increased rapidly from 1841, and Kuching expanded accordingly.

After the murder of Hasim and his brothers by the indigenous Dyak peoples, who were opposed to the oppression by and supremacy of the Brunei nobles, the sultan of Brunei was forced to grant Brooke tenure over Sarawak in perpetuity, persuaded in part by the fact that the guns of the British Royal Navy were trained on the sultan's palace. Brooke's new status was partially recognized by Queen Victoria in 1847. He was appointed governor of Labuan (the island that Brunei had ceded to Britain), and consul-general of Brunei. However, his most important triumph, his title of Rāja of Sarawak, went unrecognized. The British government also refused to accept Sarawak as a protectorate; the region would not gain this status until 1888.

Brooke returned to Sarawak and invested most of his personal fortune in developing the region. He created a paternal government and worked to increase the size of his holdings—at the expense of Brunei. As Sarawak increased its land mass, Brunei shrank. By 1853, Sarawak had doubled its size, moving its border east to Kabong. Eight years later its border had moved to Bintulu.

Under the guidance of James Brooke's nephew Charles, who succeeded him as rāja in 1868, Sarawak ex-

Fort Margherita, Kuching
Photo courtesy of Malaysia Tourism Promotion Board, New York

panded further, reaching its present borders. Sarawak and Kuching developed considerably during Charles Brooke's era. One of his main priorities was to stabilize the region's economy, as Sarawak's expenditures exceeded its revenues. Most of Sarawak's income in the mid–nineteenth century derived from antimony, arrack (rice rum), opium, and prawn farms. By 1875, the region was exporting vast quantities of sago (starch), and this became the main export and backbone for the country's economy. Charles Brooke also encouraged the migration of Chinese settlers from Malaysia to plant pepper. With this in mind, he kept the price of opium down and, consequently, immigration increased. Moreover, Sarawak was solvent by 1877.

Brooke's improvements included the introduction of an effective sanitation system. The population was particularly afflicted by outbreaks of cholera; the first recorded case was in 1858, and the most serious outbreak occurred thirty years later, in 1888, when approximately 1,000 people died. Dysentery was also a common cause of death in the region. Despite such challenges, the city developed quickly, and by 1874 a prison, hospital, Fort Margherita, and many other impressive buildings were erected. Traders began to build brick shops, and started what is today known as Gambier Street. Another lasting change instituted by Brooke was the official adoption of the name Kuching in 1872.

Margaret Brooke (born Margaret de Windt), the wife of Charles Brooke, provides an interesting look at Kuching during this period in her autobiography *My Life in Sarawak:*

> The little town looked so neat and fresh and prosperous under the careful jurisdiction of the Rāja and his officers, that it reminded me of a box of painted toys kept scrupulously clean by a child. The Bazaar runs for some distance along the banks of the river, and this quarter of the town is inhabited almost entirely by Chinese traders, with the exception of one or two Hindoo shops. . . . Groceries of exotic kinds are laid out on tables near the pavement, from which purchasers make their choice. At the Hindoo shops you can buy silks from India, sarongs from Java, tea from China, and tiles and porcelain from all parts of the world, laid out in picturesque confusion, and overflowing into the street.

A fire effectively destroyed the city in January 1884. A witness recorded that wealthy people and traders alike tried to save merchandise in the main bazaar, while less scrupulous people stole the goods, benefiting from the confusion. The fire raged through Carpenter Street, China Street, and Bishopsgate Street and destroyed many lovely buildings, making hundreds of people homeless. It took many years to rebuild, but development and reconstruction resumed between 1890 and 1917.

By 1900 street lights had been introduced, and the city had a telephone service. A medical headquarters was built in 1909. The city benefited most from the opening of a railway between 1912 and 1916, when the terminus was constructed close to the Islamic mosque in the city. In the first quarter of the twentieth century Sarawak's economy was most stimulated by the success of the rubber industry. First introduced into the region in 1908, when experimental estates were opened, rubber became an extremely successful crop. Kuching, subsequently, experienced boom periods from the 1910s to 1920s and again during the late 1930s. As the rubber trade flourished, the population of the city also increased.

Following Charles Brooke's death in 1917, Kuching and its environs came under the control of Brooke's extravagant sons Vyner and Bertram. The years that followed, until the Japanese occupation of Kuching in 1941, are remembered as frivolous ones. The writer Somerset Maugham visited Sarawak in 1921 and based a series of stories on the flamboyant society he found there. For the most part it was a small European elite who enjoyed the luxury of Sarawak's society during this period. Although many Europeans fled to their homelands following the outbreak of World War II, a surprising number stayed, only to be interned by the Japanese. Bombers attacked Kuching on December 18 and 19, 1941, and the city surrendered to Japan days later, on Christmas Eve.

Initially between thirty and sixty prisoners of war were interned in Kuching's Zaida building; they were kept in humiliating conditions. By May 1942 the prisoners had been taken to Padingan, to a newly constructed camp. They were then moved to a larger camp, near Batu Lintang Road, in July 1942, where the majority of them spent the rest of the war. These prisoners of war were mainly European civilians, Dutch military personnel, Indonesian prisoners, and Punjābī officers. By October 1942 a large British and Australian military contingent was interned in the camp as well. Most of the prisoners initially believed that the war would be over shortly and that Britain would rescue them. As part of a treaty signed in 1888, Britain had agreed to defend Sarawak in the event of a hostile attack. However, Britain's forces were occupied in Europe fighting Nazi Germany; a Punjābī regiment was eventually sent to Sarawak to defend the region. Conditions in the camps gradually deteriorated, especially after 1943, when young, more hostile guards replaced the original ones. By March 1945 the camps had become forced labor areas, and most were producing *ubi kayu*, a vegetable. When the internees finally were liberated in August 1945, the Allies found 2,500 people in the camps.

When Kuching began to recover from the suffering and destruction inflicted on it during the war, it tried to revitalize its flagging economy. Agricultural production was reduced drastically during the war, in part because of the lack of labor, but also because of the decline of Sarawak's export markets. There were schemes to increase rice production and thereby make Kuching self-sufficient; however, the rising prices of rubber and pepper, two of the area's most successful crops, prevented any serious investment in rice. The outbreak of the Korean War in 1950 served to further increase the price of these commodities.

Post-war Kuching experienced great change, both politically and structurally. On July 1, 1946, Sarawak became a British Crown colony. The following month the rāja of Sarawak retired, and on October 29, 1946, Sir Charles Noble Arden Clarke became the first governor and commander in chief of the region. The cession of Kuching to Britain was an unpopular move, a fact evidenced by the fatal stabbing of governor Duncan Stewart in December 1949.

During the 1950s, an internal secessionist movement gained impetus, especially after neighboring Brunei became self-governing in 1959. In 1962 the prime minister of Malay, Tengku Abdul Rahman, invited Singapore, Sarawak, Sabah (northern Borneo), and Brunei to join the Federation of Malaysia. At the same time, the People's Party in Brunei suggested that Sabah, Sarawak, and Brunei unite. An uprising by the People's Party in December 1962 in Brunei was quelled with the aid of British troops, but unrest resurfaced in 1963. Indonesia, incredulous that Sabah and Sarawak would consider such a union, also became involved in the dissent. Kuching swarmed with troops, but the conflict did not last long. Finally on September 16, 1963, Sarawak and Sabah became part of the Federation of Malaysia, and the European representative was replaced by the Kuching Malay leader Datu Abang Openg.

Kuching is now the largest town in east Malaysia, with a population of some 300,000. This number is striking when compared to the city's size in 1947, when 34,500 people lived and worked in Kuching. The city has turned into a bustling state capital, a place with only moderate tourist appeal. The city does, however, boast a fascinating bazaar and the impressive Sarawak Museum, which houses ethnographic and natural history exhibits, including the Borneo collection begun 100 years ago by Charles Brooke. Many visitors use the location as a starting point for trips to nearby Bako National Park. Furthermore, the city has maintained much of the character of its colonial past; few of Kuching's buildings were destroyed during Japanese occupation in the 1940s. The city's religious and British administration buildings remain, giving the town a lovely architectural mix.

The varied religious buildings of Kuching are testimony to the region's diverse ethnic mix. Tua Pek Kong, the main Chinese temple, can be found at the east end of the town, on the bank opposite to Fort Margherita. The building is thought to be in an auspicious position at the meeting point of two rivers, overlooking many lovely hills. Although the temple is an important place of pilgrimage today, it has suffered from neglect in the past. The temple, which is possibly the oldest building in Kuching, underwent substantial renovations in 1876. One of the walls was damaged in 1941 during a bombing.

Other notable Chinese temples include one on Ewe Hai Street and another on Tabuan Street. The former is dedicated to the god Kuek Seng Ong and is a favorite place of worship among the Hokkien people. Every year, on the evening of the twenty-second day of the second moon, a figure of the god is carried in a sedan chair through the main roads of Kuching. The Tabuan Road Temple escapes the notice of many travelers coming to Kuching. As well as housing a Buddhist shrine, the temple has a fine collection of Buddhas, left in care by their owners for a variety of reasons. There are also shrines to the gods of the Moon, Sun, and War; situated behind the main temple is a nunnery where only women are allowed to pray.

At the west end of Kuching lies the Indian Mosque, which, like Tua Pek Kong, was renovated in 1876. Wooden walls and a new shingled roof were added to the earlier, more delicate structure. Initially only South Indian Muslims were allowed to use the mosque, although this restriction later was rescinded.

The oldest Christian building is St. Thomas Cathedral, which is situated on a small hill. Although the cathedral compound is open to the public, Kuching's oldest confirmed building, the Bishop's House, is not. Built in 1849 for the first bishop, Thomas Francis McDougall, the structure has changed much since its earliest days; it now encompasses a garage, bathrooms, living rooms, and an office.

A short boat ride across the river takes the visitor to the Astana (Palace), the old Brooke residence, which now serves as the home of the governor of Sarawak. Constructed in 1870 to house Charles and Margaret Brooke, the building was originally three individual structures. The upper floor of the west section houses the governor's residence and is closed to the public; in the central, upper area are the official entertaining rooms: dining room, drawing room, and a fine terrace; the upper floor of the east wing is kept for guests. The lower floor, which runs the length of all three upper sections, was the scene of some extravagant suppers and balls; it was also briefly the first prison of internees in 1941. On the grounds behind the house are monuments to the children of Margaret and Charles Brooke, who died at sea in October 1873.

The official Brooke cemetery can be found near Fort Margherita. A tiny area, it includes three documented graves belonging to Annie Brooke (the first wife of Captain Brooke), her small son Francis, and Julia Brooke (the captain's second wife). Another grave may be found in the cemetery, that of the unbaptized stillborn baby of Margaret Brooke, who was buried here secretly following the refusal of the bishop to bury the child in consecrated ground.

Margaret Brooke's husband was a keen advocate of construction, and many fine buildings were erected during his time as rāja of Sarawak. In 1874, the Court House was built. This building has a very lovely ceiling, worked by the Baram people. In 1878 work was begun on Fort Margherita, to be finished the following year in time for Brooke's birthday. The impregnability of the fort was important, for it guarded the most important way into Kuching. Today the fort is worth visiting for its collection of arms and weapons. The Round Tower, built in 1886 after the great fire that destroyed much of the city, looks much like a fortress and occupies a strategic position, overlooking the town. Today, however, it is used as the offices of the Labour Department.

Although Kuching contains many fine buildings, just walking through the streets is an experience in itself. The oldest street in Kuching is the Main Bazaar, which runs alongside the river near the central market. The markets along Gambier Road, filled with every taste, smell, and color imaginable, offer further evidence of Kuching's ethnically diverse population.

Further Reading: A well-written history of the region during the administration of the Brooke family is provided by *The White Rajas: A History of Sarawak 1841–1946* by Steven Runciman (Cambridge: Cambridge University Press, 1960). For a good travel guide, turn to *Malaysia* (Singapore: Travelbugs, 1992), which features historical information as well as useful tips for the traveler. *My Life in Sarawak* by Lady Margaret Brooke (London: Methuen, 1913) is an affectionate autobiographical account of life in Sarawak by the wife of Charles Brooke. M. G. Dickinson's *Sarawak and Its People* (Kuching: Borneo Literature Bureau, 1962) gives a general but detailed introduction to Sarawak, suited to history or social anthropology students. For a more thorough social history exploring 150 years of this city's development, turn to *From Kampung to City: A Social History of Kuching, Malaysia, 1820–1970* by Craig Alan Lockard (Athens: Ohio University Press, 1987). *Let's Visit Brunei* by S. and P. J. Hassall (London: Macmillan, 1988) is a comprehensive guide to Brunei, full of facts and statistics.

—A. Vasudevan

Kumbakonam (Tamil Nādu, India)

Location: On the southeast coast of India, along the Cauvery River and near the Bay of Bengal, approximately 190 miles south of Madras.

Description: Kumbakonam is a center of Brahmanism, a destination for Brahman pilgrims, and a showcase for historic Indian architecture, much of it built by the Cōḷa kings. Among its numerous Hindu temples are two major temples dedicated to Brahmā (Brahmā and Chakkarapani Temples) and three dedicated to Siva (Nageśvara, Sarangapani, and Kumbeshwara Temples). Every twelve years, pilgrims flock to the city to participate in the bathing festival held in the sacred Mahāmagham Tank.

Contact: Government of India Tourist Office
154 Anna Salai
Madras 600 002, Tamil Nādu
India
826985 or 869695

According to ancient Purāṇic tradition, Kumbakonam originated at the very epicenter of the creation cycle following the Great Deluge. Brahmā, the creator, had feared that he would lose the seeds of creation during the flood and prayed to Siva for a plan to preserve them until after the waters receded. Siva instructed him to seal the seeds inside a clay pitcher filled with nectar and water and place the pitcher on the peak of Mount Meru; the rising waters would then carry the pitcher to a holy spot in the south where the new cycle of creation could begin. All went according to plan, but when Brahmā tried to retrieve the seeds following the flood, fire sprang from the pitcher and he was unable to approach it. Once more he prayed for assistance from Siva. The god appeared as a hunter and shattered the pitcher with an arrow, allowing Brahmā to gather the seeds and begin the process of creation. Although shards from the pitcher had scattered in all directions, the nose-like piece and the base remained there; the town that developed on that site was therefore known as Kumbhaghonam (Nose of the Pitcher), which eventually changed into Kumbakonam.

This tradition also gave rise to the Mahāmagham Bathing Festival for which Kumbakonam is best known today. According to the story, the nectar that spilled from Brahmā's broken pitcher gathered in two pools, each of which gave rise to a sacred tank at its site. The Potramarai Tank is located near the Adi Kumbeshvara Temple; the Mahāmagham Tank, about 1,000 feet to the southeast, is the more famous of the two and is the site of the bathing festival held every twelve years. The attendance of dignitaries and holy men at these festivals raised the status of the town as an important destination for leaders and common worshipers alike.

Historically, Kumbakonam first rose to prominence as a center of the Cōḷa Kingdom. The Cōḷas had been a force in the Cauvery Delta since the third century B.C., but they were eclipsed by the Pāṇḍyas and Pallavas after the fourth century A.D. They again rose to prominence in the ninth century, and reached their peak under the kings Rājarāja I (ruled 985–1012 or 1014) and his son Rājendra I (ruled 1012 or 1014–44). It was Rājendra I who greatly expanded the small village of Kumbakonam, to celebrate his victory over the king of Bengal and his march to the Ganges River in 1023. According to official inscriptions, Rājendra had spent part of his youth in the palaces of Solanmaligai (Pazhayarai), only three miles west of Kumbakonam.

At their peak, the Cōḷas controlled an area from the Krishna-Godāvari Delta in the north to Sri Lanka in the south, and from the Arabian Sea in the west to the Bay of Bengal in the east, where they kept a sizeable fleet. The Cōḷas are renowned for their construction of irrigation projects, which allowed large-scale rice cultivation along the Cauvery. With their sizeable maritime presence, they interacted regularly with Asians and the Chinese from the tenth to thirteenth centuries. Their artwork, however, as exemplified by Kumbakonam's temples, gates, and tanks, does not always suggest this contact. As strict Hindus, the Cōḷas actively worked to eliminate the influence of Buddhism and Jainism, which they saw as heretical sects. The Cōḷa kings gave extensive land grants around Kumbakonam to the Brahman religious aristocracy, and they allowed these local rulers a great deal of autonomy. Kumbakonam became a major center of religious study and worship.

The Cōḷas oversaw the construction of numerous Hindu temples in Kumbakonam. These temples typically consisted of an upright ground story, a tapering body of many receding levels, and a dome. They are covered almost entirely with sculpture and decorative molding. Each temple has a gateway, or *gopuram*, which leads to the main enclosure. This gateway derives its name from the "cow gate" of the village, which later became the village gate, and finally the entrance to the temple. The *gopurams* at Kumbakonam are said to be especially massive and grand. Most of the Cōḷa temples feature successive enclosures, long courts with subsidiary temples and buildings, halls complete with thousands of pillars, and covered colonnades.

Nageśvara, one of the oldest surviving temples in Kumbakonam, expresses the splendor of the Cōḷa Kingdom. Fine stone sculpture rests on a lotus base. The absence of certain types of friezes typical of later Cōḷa temples is evidence that Nageśvara was built during the formative stages of Cōḷa architecture, sometime around the tenth century, most likely during the reign of King Parantaka I (A.D. 907–940). The early Cōḷa temples show a noticeable simplification of

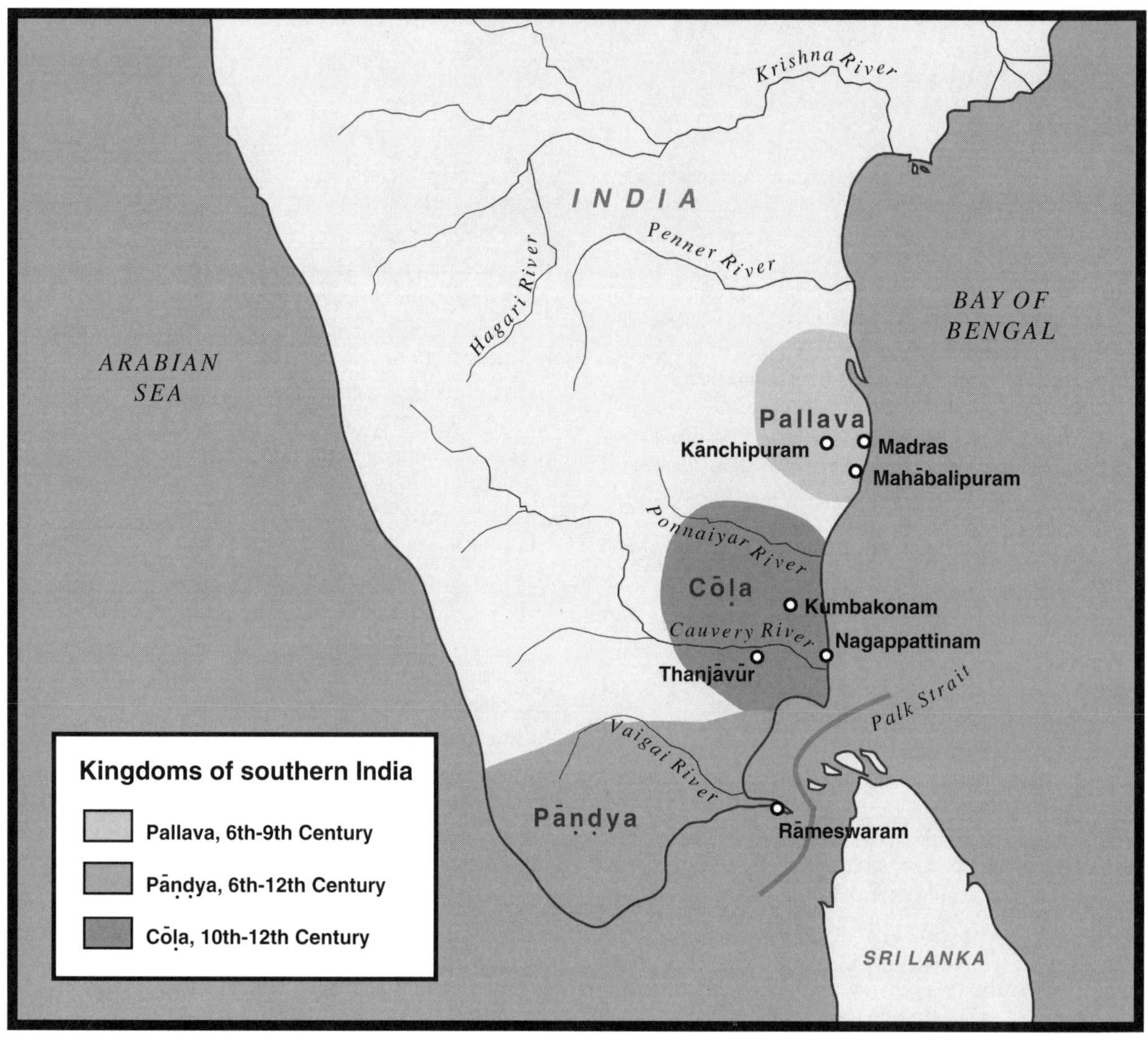

Map showing Kumbakonam in relation to the Cōḷa, Pāṇḍya, and Pallava kingdoms
Illustration by Tom Willcockson

features present in temples of previous periods, including that of the Pallavas. Simpler moldings replaced the lion motif on pillars. Different animal images did appear, however, often in a repeated pattern. Full-length figures rest in recesses along the wall, rendered in a manner similar to the images of saints in Gothic cathedrals. Unlike most other Cōḷa temples, Nageśvara houses a series of secular portraits, rather than exclusively religious depictions.

Sarangapani, situated in the center of the city, has a main gate decorated with relief carvings of dancers. The significance of these relief panels remains a question for scholars of temple art and Indian religion. Certain panels point to an affiliation with Vishnu and not Siva, whom the Cōḷa kings worshiped. Evidently, the reliefs were not created with the rest of the temple or did not originally belong to it at all. According to recent analyses of the site, the relief panels were carved as part of a different temple in the twelfth century and only later transferred to the Sarangapani *gopuram,* which was most likely built in the fourteenth century. The interior of the temple also contains intricate dance sculpture.

After the reign of the Cōḷa rulers, Kumbakonam, along with other cities in the Thanjāvūr district, became part of the Pāṇḍya kingdom of Madurai in 1290 before falling to the Vijayanagar Empire around 1340. A Vijayanagar emperor, Krishna Devaraya, visited Kumbakonam in 1524 and bathed in the Mahāmagham Tank on Mahāmagham day.

In 1535 the area came under the rule of the Nayaks, whose second king, Achyutappa, was supposedly crowned at Kumbakonam. The Nayaks left a lasting legacy in the city with their additions to the Mahāmagham Tank. Mahārāja Govinda Dikshita, a minister for three successive Nayak rulers, oversaw construction of stone steps on all four sides of the tank and sixteen *maṇḍapas* (prayer halls where images of the deity rest) along the sides. In each of the *maṇḍapas* he consecrated a Siva *liṅgam* (phallic symbol).

Marāṭhā armies conquered the Nayaks in 1673, and Muslim Mughals invaded in 1691. The growing presence of Europeans in the area marked the following decades. By the time the British formally annexed the Thanjāvūr district during the last half of the eighteenth century, Kumbakonam and the surrounding area had declined. The British first invaded in 1771, aided by forces under the nabob of Arcot. Two years later they conquered the area and imposed a crippling system of revenue collection that skimmed 59 percent of the area's gross produce. Kumbakonam's citizens fell into poverty. The British restored the region's rulers to power, but only as puppets.

The economic situation in Kumbakonam deteriorated even further in 1781–85, when Hyder Alī, a Muslim governor and general of Mysore, enabled by the French and Dutch, tried to rid southern India of the British. His advancing armies plundered villages, massacred tens of thousands of townspeople, forced thousand more into exile, and destroyed irrigation channels that had facilitated agriculture since the time of the Cōḷas. The district was plunged into famine, and its population declined drastically. Even then, however, Hyder Alī's occupying government seized a large percentage of what minimal crops were produced.

The British reconquered the region in 1785, but their demand for revenue was no less draconian than Hyder Alī's had been. For almost a century the region also was a major source of forced labor for the plantations in Ceylon, Burma, Malaya, Mauritius, and the West Indies. The British restored the export of textiles that had been hindered during the war, but on the whole, conditions continued to deteriorate.

The British East India Company governed Kumbakonam as part of a district of Madras Presidency from 1799 to 1858, after which the British government assumed direct control of India. The Kumbakonam municipality was officially constituted in 1866. In 1869, the city benefited from the opening of the Suez Canal; Kumbakonam could receive British goods and export its brass and silk more easily. Traffic in the city increased as workers built and repaired roads and bridges, allowing passage of oxcarts and grain exports to other districts. The railroad reached the area between 1873 and 1877, linking Kumbakonam with the ports of Madras, Tuticorin, and Nāgappattinam.

The quality of life continued to improve for residents of Kumbakonam throughout the twentieth century. Epidemics declined after 1921 and literacy increased. Further growth took place in the agricultural sphere in 1934, when laborers completed construction on the Mettur Dam up the Cauvery River from Kumbakonam, intensifying wet paddy production. Bus and truck transport developed, as well as factories producing industrial parts and processing food. In more recent years, Kumbakonam has become a major center for the fertilizer industry and a leading producer of silk and brass. The population of Kumbakonam reached an estimated 91,643 in 1951 and had risen to 141,639 by 1981.

During the 1950s, Kumbakonam became involved in the Communist Party's efforts to renew declining interest in their organization. In 1957–58, a group of communist tenants and laborers exercised considerable power, but the spirit of communist militancy gradually declined, most likely because of improving economic conditions.

Throughout the economic growth and political changes of the last century, the city has continued to develop its traditional role as a center of Brahmanical worship and study. By 1950, most of the city's large community of Tamil Brahmans belonged to sects who followed the teachings of the eighteenth-century philosopher Śaṅkarāchārya.

First and foremost, however, Kumbakonam is renowned among Hindus for its Mahāmagham Bathing Festival, held every twelve years when the stars and planets achieve a rare configuration, usually at the end of February or the beginning of March. Unlike other bathing festivals in India, the Mahāmagham Festival lasts only one day, greatly increasing the concentration of participants at the tank. During the most recent festival, in 1992, the number of pilgrims reached into the millions.

The Mahāmagham tank lies just south of the city's clock tower and railway station and southeast of the principal ancient Siva shrine, Kumbeshwara. This temple centers on a *liṅgam* purported to have been made by Siva himself from the broken pieces of the pot *(kumbh)* Brahmā had asked him to shatter. The temple's east entrance is approached via a covered market selling an assortment of cooking pots (a local industry) as well as the usual bazaar items. At the entrance one passes the temple elephant, with a painted forehead and necklace of bells. Beyond the flagstaff, a hallway whose columns feature painted brackets representing *yali* (a mythical beast) leads to the *gopuram* entranceway. A figure of Siva's bull, Nandi, faces the main sanctuary housing the *liṅgam*.

The Mahāmagham Tank itself is trapezoidal, covering an area of five and one-half acres and reaching a depth of ten feet. Nineteen small spring wells in the tank feed it with holy waters. Some of the wells carry the names of the lords of the quarters, and others are named after holy rivers. During the festival, people come to the tank carrying deities from all the temples in Kumbakonam. At noon, they bathe in the tank surrounded by the deities. They believe that the tank purifies the sacred rivers, like the Ganges, of the sins left by humans that bathe in them. Further, the pilgrims believe that those purified waters will cleanse away their own sins. Throughout the day, the faithful offer oblations and give charitable gifts in the hope of being rewarded in this life and the life hereafter.

Further Reading: Two books by Kathleen Gough trace the social and economic changes occurring in the Thanjāvūr district in recent years and also offer a brief history of Kumbakonam from Cōḷa times to the present day: *Rural Society in Southeast India* (Cambridge and New York: Cambridge University Press, 1981) and *Rural Change in Southeast India: 1950s to 1980s* (Oxford and New York: Oxford University Press, 1989). A. Kuppuswami's *The Crest Jewel of Divine Dravidian Culture* (Kumbakonam: Sri Venkateswar, 1980) presents the legend of Kumbakonam's origin and describes rituals performed during the Mahāmagham Tank Festival. *Dance Sculpture* *in Sarangapani* by Kapila Vatsyayan (Madras: Society for Archaeological, Historical, and Epigraphical Research, 1982) discusses in great detail the sculpture decorating Kumbakonam's Sarangapani Temple and includes more general information on other temples in the city. Suresh Pillarti's *Introduction to the Study of Temple Art* (Thanjāvūr: Equator and Meridian, 1976) provides a helpful overview that frequently uses Kumbakonam's temples as examples.

—Christine Ann Longcore

Kurukshetra (Haryāna, India)

Location: In northern India, about twenty-five miles north of Karnāl and about 100 miles north of Delhi.

Description: Together with the sacred fields of the Kurukshetra Plain, the city of Kurukshetra is an ancient holy site and pilgrimage center to Hindus. Kurukshetra was the battlefield of the Bhārata War, recounted in the central narrative of the *Mahābhārata*. In more recent centuries, the city also has become sacred to Sikhs and Muslims.

Contact: Government of India Tourist Office
88 Janpath
New Delhi, Delhi 110001
India
3320005, 3320008, 3320109, 3320266, or 3320342

The history of Kurukshetra extends to remote antiquity, to a time only dimly perceived through archaeology and the creative flourishes of ancient Indian literature. The area was settled before the migration of the Aryans into northern India in the first half of the second millennium B.C. Archaeological excavations have uncovered stone and copper tools and primitive pottery dating from the period between 2000 and 1500 B.C. The societies that produced these artifacts are thought to have lived by agriculture, and some of the tools indicated that they occasionally supplemented their diet with game and fish.

The Aryan peoples are thought to have supplanted the established tribes by degrees, generally in less than peaceful ways. The arrival of the Aryans marks the beginning of the Vedic Age, which is captured—although not necessarily with great fidelity to actual circumstance—in the Vedas and other early Indian texts. Unfortunately, their testimony can rarely be corroborated by external evidence. According to the ancient *Atharvaveda* and the *Brāhmaṇas*, the first clan to hold sway in the area of Kurukshetra was that of the Bhāratas, who are said to have endowed the region with religious significance. The Tristu, another clan, supplanted them and reportedly expanded the area under their control, particularly in the course of the many wars waged by Kings Divodaśa and Śudasa. When the Tristu clan declined, the Purus temporarily reinvigorated them but could not prevent the ultimate accession of Kuru, an Aryan chieftain from the northwest.

Under Kuru, who gave his name to the settlement and plain of Kurukshetra (which means "field of Kuru"), the region experienced a tremendous upsurge in prosperity and political significance. The ancient texts even give Kuru credit for establishing agriculture and imposing moral order. Kuru is deified in the ancient literature, and the religious significance of the Kurukshetra Plain is explained by a story in which Kuru plowed parts of his own body into the soil, thereby giving fertility to the land. The settlement of Kurukshetra became the spiritual capital of Kuru's kingdom, but his political capital was established at Hastināpur, a city that has not survived.

Kuru was succeeded peacefully by his sons and their sons for several generations until a dispute over the succession broke out between two half-brothers and their sons. On one side ranged Paṇḍu and his five sons, who are collectively known as the Paṇḍavas. They were led by Yudhishthra. Paṇḍu's half-brother Dhritarāshtra and his sons, one hundred strong, known as the Kauravas and led by Duryodhana, comprised the other side of the conflict. Hostilities eventually led to a devastating war, into which nearly all of the settled kingdoms of India came to participate and which forms the epic centerpiece of the *Mahābhārata,* one of the most venerated of ancient Indian texts. According to the epic, a bloody battle was fought on the Kurukshetra Plain, at a place called Thānēsar on the outskirts of Kurukshetra. After eighteen days of hand-to-hand combat, stratagems, and outright murder, the Paṇḍavas emerged as the victors. Together with Dhritarāshtra, they were the only surviving members of the Kuru clan. In the wake of the mayhem, the survivors gathered all the bodies of the ranking chiefs and gave them proper burial, while the corpses of the thousands upon thousands of foot soldiers were burned in one gigantic funeral pyre. Their bones littered the plains and long served as a vivid reminder of the bloodshed to succeeding generations. The epic battle also redoubled the sanctity of the fields and holy pools of the Kurukshetra Plain.

Some historians have doubted that the Bhārata War ever took place, but most scholars certify the battle as a historical event and generally give it an approximate date of 1400 B.C. Corroborating references to the battle may be found in many other ancient texts; moreover, Kurukshetra was of great strategic value, lying at the gateway between the Himalayas and the Ganges Plain. The Ganges Valley area became the center of Indian civilization late in the second millennium B.C., and its defense against invaders from the north was crucially dependent on control over Kurukshetra. In fact, it is thought likely that Kurukshetra saw more than one battle in its early history. That the present version of the *Mahābhārata* gives us a true picture of the magnitude, the circumstances, or the details of the conflict is much less probable.

The text of the *Mahābhārata* is anything but an eyewitness account, having grown out of an oral tradition that was not greatly interested in the factual accuracy of the stories it transmitted. It is thought that the story of the Bhārata War may not have been versified until the ninth or eighth century B.C., well after the battle took place. The original verse

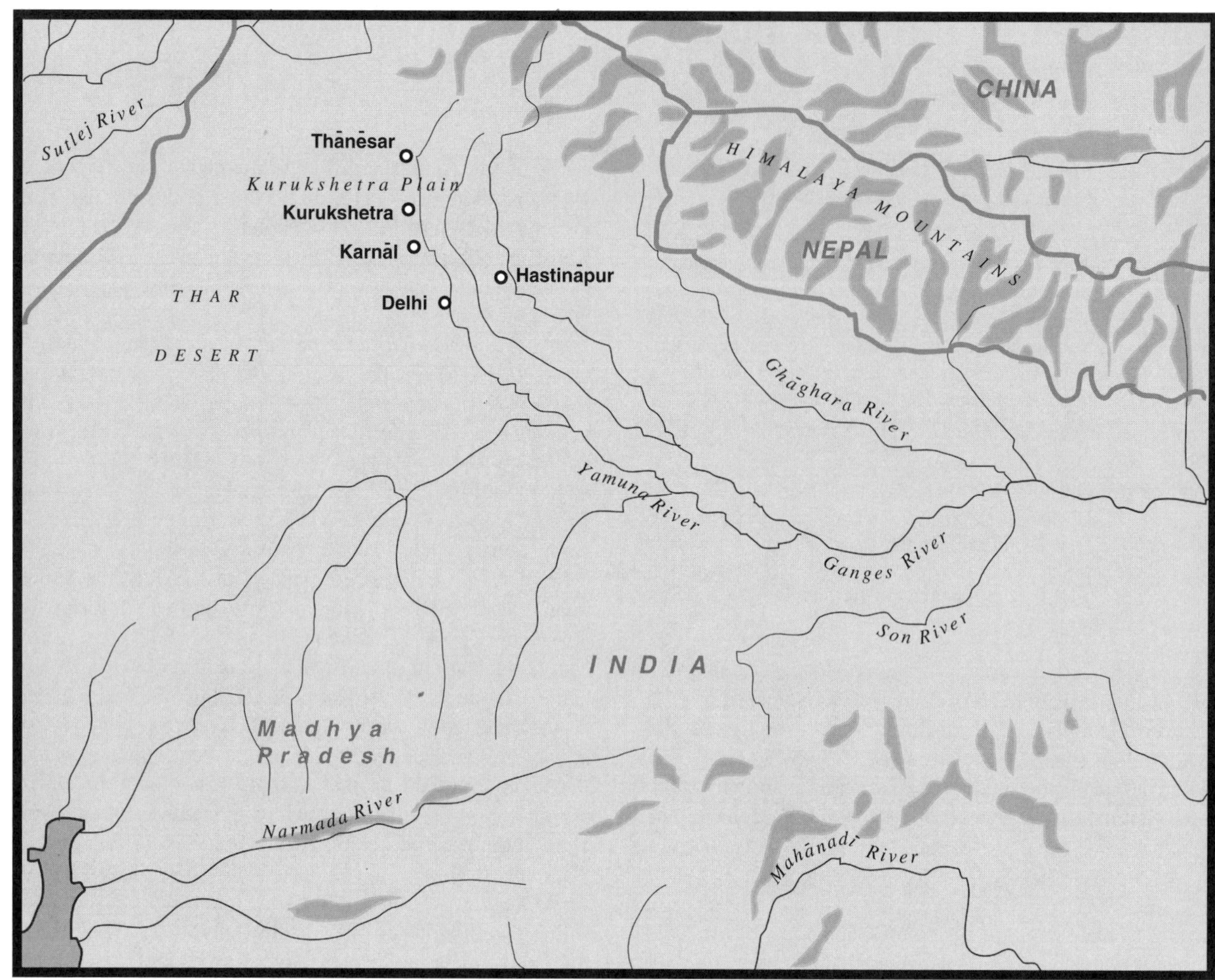

Regional map of the Kurukshetra Plain at the time of the Bhārata War
Illustration by Tom Willcockson

account of the battle was some 8,800 couplets long, while in numerous retellings it eventually grew to 20,000 couplets. Not only was the story of the battle itself greatly elaborated in the bardic tradition, but interpolations and additions of all kinds take up another 80,000 couplets in the version that survives for the modern reader. The earliest written version of the story is tentatively dated to 400 B.C., and further additions and changes were made to the written text as late as A.D. 400. The *Mahābhārata* was created, then, by generations of storytellers, the earliest of whom was centuries removed from the events recounted.

According to the ancient texts, Yudhishtra, the leader of the Paṇḍavas, became king of Kurukshetra and maintained his seat at Hastināpur. Yudhishtra's successors moved the capital to Asandivat, nearer Karnāl. Another period of prosperity is thought to have followed the war, and during these centuries Kurukshetra is thought to have gained in religious stature. The *Mahābhārata* makes clear that a visit to Kurukshetra absolves the faithful of all sin, while those lucky enough to die there go directly to heaven. Eventually, the Kuru clan became disunited again, and this time the kingdom was divided into three parts. The division weakened Kurukshetra, which started to decline in fortunes and importance. Many near-eastern tribes, including the Abhiras, the Jāts, and the Yautiyas, moved into the region, and over time they were assimilated into the population.

With the cultural contribution of these newcomers, Kurukshetra acquired a different character in the fourth century B.C. The area continued to depend primarily on agriculture, but it came to be ruled by local oligarchies. A new warlike spirit is commonly attributed to the Yautiyas, who had long enjoyed a reputation as fierce warriors. Kurukshetra became known for its invincible armies and redoubtable elephants. In this era, the invading army of Alexander the Great refused to follow their leader into Kurukshetra, and ancient historians ascribed this refusal to Kurukshetra's fearsome reputation, although, of course, it is always possible that Alexander's soldiers simply decided they had gone far enough from home.

But not even the heritage of the Yautiyas prevented the conquering armies of the Mauryas from incorporating Kurukshetra into their empire in the late fourth century B.C. The Mauryas reestablished a measure of peace and prosperity, and Kurukshetra became a center of Buddhist as well as Hindu religion. There is also evidence that art and literature flourished under this dynasty. Following the disintegration of the Mauryan Empire, Kurukshetra disappeared into the general chaos of invasions that befell much of northern India. Whatever the circumstances of life in Kurukshetra during the first centuries of the Common (Christian) Era, changes of overlordship were a constant. Towards the end of the first century, the Kushāns established dominion in much of northern India, including Kurukshetra, but their control began to weaken approximately 100 years later. Kurukshetra recovered its independence until it fell to the Gupta Empire early in the fourth century. The Guptas were Hindu, and because of their patronage Kurukshetra experienced something of a renaissance as a religious center.

When the Gupta Empire, in turn, began to disintegrate in the second half of the fifth century, Pushpabhuti, once a feudatory and possibly a distant relation of the Guptas, made himself king of the Kurukshetra region and again endowed it with some political significance. The new king chose Thānēsar, the ancient battlefield of the Bhārata War, for his capital. Under Pushpabhuti's descendants, the kingdom rose to greatness, becoming the foremost power in Hindustan by the beginning of the seventh century. The most important ruler of the dynasty was its last one, Harsha, who ascended the throne in 606. Harsha set out to conquer all of India and recapture the glory of the Gupta Empire. He brought all of northern India under his control in a matter of six years, including Nepal and perhaps even Kashmir.

Possessed of a great deal of political wisdom, he secured the allegiance of local rulers in many of the conquered territories and left them to rule in his name. The Chinese Buddhist traveler-pilgrim Xuan Zang visited Harsha's court and wrote a very favorable account of him, praising his justice and generosity as well as his activities as a patron of the arts and a playwright. No doubt Xuan Zang's admiration was in part a result of the fact that Harsha encouraged Buddhism during his reign. The peace and prosperity that prevailed after Harsha's conquests made his court a center of cosmopolitanism, attracting scholars, artists, and religious visitors from far and wide.

Harsha unfortunately had no successors, and on his death in 647 civil war broke out over the succession to the throne. Historical records give little insight into this undoubtedly turbulent period, however. Kurukshetra was certainly still esteemed as a holy place, but political upheaval must have deterred a good number of the faithful from undertaking a pilgrimage there. In 733, an army from Kashmir took Kurukshetra by force but did not have the resources to establish permanent overlordship. Three years later a local dynasty, the Tomaras, founded by Anangpala I, took the area and managed to maintain control over their realm until the early ninth century, when Kurukshetra lost its independence to Bengal. Kurukshetra continued in this state, much reduced since the glorious days of Harsha, until the invasions of the Muslims in the eleventh century.

In 1014, Maḥmūd of Ghaznī swept through the area and sacked Thānēsar, which had been called Jaipala under the Tomaras. Twenty years later another band of Muslim marauders repeated the disaster. Although the local Hindu states formed a confederacy to repel any further Muslim advances, they were powerless to stop the repeated waves of Muslim forces sweeping into India. At first the invaders came merely to rob and plunder, but later they established themselves on a permanent basis. In 1206, Kurukshetra was annexed to the Delhi Sultanate under Quṭb-ud-Dīn Aybak. Primarily a Hindu center of worship, Kurukshetra was neglected by the new rulers, but it was never forgotten by the Hindu populace. Religious persecution was at times intense, and Buddhism disappeared from India altogether under these stresses. Hinduism managed to adjust to the new circumstances, however, and the holy pool at Kurukshetra was quietly maintained and visited.

In 1240 a rebellion broke out on the plains, and the Muslim regent was killed, resulting in a short-lived independence. After Muslim rule was reimposed, the region remained firmly under the control of Delhi until 1388, when the sultanate was beginning to crumble. Kurukshetra regained its independence until the raids of Timur (known in the West as Tamerlane) into northern India created an opportunity for the Sayyids to take power. Because the Sayyids generally were ineffective rulers, Kurukshetra is thought to have enjoyed a degree of autonomy, but certainly it must have been impossible for this Hindu religious center to recapture its former glory in the context of Muslim dominance. The subsequent rulers, the Lodis, came to power in 1450, and they seem to have been determined to subdue Kurukshetra and destroy its importance as a Hindu sacred place. Although they were not successful in destroying Kurukshetra altogether, they inflicted a great deal of physical destruction on the site, which explains why Kurukshetra has virtually no ancient architecture to show for its glorious past.

In 1526, Bābur, the founder of the Mughals, swept through India to establish an empire that eventually comprised almost the entire subcontinent. He occupied Kurukshetra, but the local population rose in rebellion, which was bloodily suppressed. Under the Mughal emperor Akbar, who ruled from 1556 to 1605, a standard system of administration was imposed on the region as part of the effort to improve the workings of the highly centralized empire. Akbar also insisted on religious tolerance, and Kurukshetra underwent another renaissance as a spiritual focus for Hindus. It also developed at this time as a holy place for Muslims and Sikhs. The Sikhs in particular held Kurukshetra in high regard because it was patronized by some of their most charismatic gurus. Gurū Nanak (c. 1469–1539), the founder of Sikhism, visited Kurukshetra in 1504 during a solar eclipse, a particularly holy time. He was followed by nine other gurus who visited and taught at Kurukshetra. Nirmala, a Sikh sect, made Kurukshetra its permanent home. In addition, Kurukshetra became an important center for Sufi saints, thus continuing its tradition for holiness throughout the period of Mughal rule.

As Mughal power waned in India in the late seventeenth and early eighteenth centuries, Kurukshetra repeatedly changed hands between the Mughals and the Sikhs. When the British took Delhi in 1803, the Sikhs then controlling Kurukshetra rose in rebellion but could not defeat the superior power of the British. In 1805 Kurukshetra passed into the British Raj, and although there were various revolts against British rule in the area throughout the nineteenth century, the colonial rulers remained in control until Indian independence in 1947.

Following independence, Kurukshetra came into its own again. A refugee camp for Hindu Pakistanis was established in the city after the partition, and the thousands of refugees eventually resettled in the area, reinvigorating its culture and economy. In 1956 a university was established at Kurukshetra to confirm its cultural importance. In 1968, a government organization was formed to oversee historical restoration and the overall development of the city. Sadly, Kurukshetra has very few remains to be restored. That, however, does not deter the thousands of pilgrims who flock to the city during solar eclipses, when the cleansing power of all of India's sacred waters is thought to be concentrated in Kurukshetra's holy pool. This pool, or tank, almost 4,000 feet long and almost 2,000 feet wide, is still lined with bathing *ghāts,* or steps, on the northern or western banks. Two islands in the center of the pool contain small temples as well as the ruin of what is said to have been a castle built by the Mughal emperor 'Ālamgīr (Aurangzeb) to house the tax collectors who levied a religious tax on non-Muslims. Besides the Kurukshetra tank, hundreds of other holy sites in the area also continue to attract large numbers of religious visitors.

Further Reading: A general history of Kurukshetra is available in Bal Krishna Muztar's *Kurukshetra: Political and Cultural History* (Delhi: B. R. Publishing, 1978). Although detailed and thorough, it is aimed primarily at readers already well familiar with Indian history. Vincent A. Smith's *The Oxford History of India: From the Earliest Times to the End of 1911* (Oxford: Clarendon Press, 1919; fourth edition, edited by Percival Spear, New York and Oxford: Oxford University Press, 1981) is a highly readable source for the background information missing from Muztar's study. The best English translation of the *Mahābhārata* is that of J. A. B. van Buitenen (3 vols., Chicago: University of Chicago Press, 1973–80). Chakravarthi V. Narasimhan's graceful prose translation of excerpts of the *Mahābhārata* (New York: Columbia University Press, 1965) also includes a useful introduction and genealogical tables.

—Robert Kellerman and Marijke Rijsberman

Kyŏngju (North Kyŏngsang, South Korea)

Location: In southeastern Korea, 34 miles east of Taegu, the provincial capital, and 223 miles southeast of Seoul.

Description: Kyŏngju, a modern country town with approximately 122,000 inhabitants, is Korea's "culture city." Called first Sorabol and later Komsung, the city was the political and cultural capital of the great Silla Kingdom (57 B.C.-A.D. 935), which unified the Korean Peninsula in the seventh century. Kyŏngju and its environs are still dotted with a wealth of ancient Silla monuments. After Silla fell, the city became a regional capital of the Koryŏ Dynasty and was sacked during the Mongol invasions of the mid–thirteenth century and the Imjin War of 1592 to 1598. UNESCO has designated Kyŏngju one of the world's ten most significant ancient cultural cities.

Contact: Korea National Tourism Corporation
10, Ta-dong
Chung-gu
Seoul 100-180
South Korea
(02) 7299 600

Ancient Korea was a mosaic of tribes and tribal leagues that gradually amalgamated into the Koguryŏ, Paekche, and Silla Kingdoms. Koguryŏ, which occupied the mountainous region of the upper Yalu River in the north, was the first kingdom to emerge. It was strongly influenced by Chinese culture. Paekche, occupying southwestern Korea, was the next kingdom to form. It maintained trade relations with both China and Japan from a very early date and was a conduit for the transmission of Chinese culture eastward. The history of Koguryŏ and Paekche was dominated by territorial conflict.

Silla, the third kingdom, was, initially at least, much more peaceful than the neighboring kingdoms but also less open to foreign influence. Historical evidence indicates that Silla arose out of an alliance of the more powerful of the Chin-han tribes in southeastern Korea. These tribes were concentrated in and around Saro, or Sorabol, a walled city-state near present-day Kyŏngju. Sorabol gradually evolved into the capital of a highly organized tribal league. Its leaders—referred to as kings in local tradition, though hardly that at first—came from the Pak, Kim, and Sok families. It was not until 356 that kingship became hereditary (in the Kim clan), with the accession of King Naemul. The name Silla did not gain currency until the fifth century. Historians generally agree that it was not until the early sixth century that Silla emerged as a true kingdom on a par with Paekche and Koguryŏ.

Nevertheless, Silla's foundation is conventionally dated to 57 B.C., the year in which, Korean tradition says, the first king ascended Silla's throne. According to the legends, six village chiefs had decided to merge their domains into the kingdom of Sorabol (which means "capital"). Shortly afterward, a shining white horse appeared and deposited an egg-shaped gourd from which a radiant young boy emerged. Local elders named the boy Pak. In 57 B.C., at the age of thirteen, he became Hyok-ko-se (Bright Ruler), the first king of Silla. His queen was a woman reputedly born from the rib of a female dragon. Their burial mounds at O-nung in south Kyŏngju attest to their existence, even if we doubt their supernatural origins.

Eggs figure in many of the kingdom's legends, which is why outsiders sometimes referred to the Chin-han irreverently as the Chicken People. The first member of the Sok clan to rule Silla, or Saro, as it was still called, was T'al-hae, who claimed to have been hatched from an egg heralded by a magpie. According to the story, he tricked the reigning king into relinquishing Panwol-song, the crescent-shaped fortress that once stood in central Kyŏngju and was Silla's royal palace until the end of the dynasty period. When asked to prove his assertion that his grandfather, a blacksmith, had once lived there, he directed the king's servants to dig up the yard. The iron filings and charcoal he had surreptitiously buried there convinced King Nam-hae of his claim to ownership. T'al-hae was installed as king around A.D. 57.

The third royal family of ancient Saro was also said to have supernatural origins. One morning King T'al-hae was awakened by the raucous crowing of a rooster. Servants sent to investigate the cause of the uproar found a white rooster perching before a gold box containing a baby boy. The king named the infant Al-chi, adopting him as his son and giving him the family name of Kim (Gold). It was not until 262, however, that the Kim family contributed a king to Saro, with the installation of Mi'ch'u. The kingdom became known as Kyerim (Chicken Forest) under the Kim family.

Eventually Saro forged a tenuous alliance with Koguryŏ, as insurance against possible depradations by Paekche and the unconquered Kaya tribes in the southwest. In 400 Saro and Koguryŏ combined their military forces to drive out Japanese invaders. The next 150 years were a time of great prosperity for Saro, which gradually became the equal of Paekche and Koguryŏ. The territory of the Kaya Federation was annexed. The kingdom also became more oriented toward China as it grew in importance. During the reign of Chijung-wang (500–13), it began calling itself Silla, a name of Chinese origin, and the city of Sorabol became Komsung. The king himself assumed the Chinese title for king, *wang*. Silla's territories were expanded to the north during these years, while its administration became more formalized.

Ch'omsong-dae Observatory, Kyŏngju
Photo courtesy of Korea National Tourism Corporation, Chicago

Silla's government plotted Chinese bureaucratic structures onto traditional Korean aristocratic relationships. A rigidly hierarchical status system, referred to as *kolp'um* (literally, "bone ranks"), dictated a person's position in social life, occupation, and government office. The top five ranks of officialdom were reserved for *songgol* (sacred bone) and *chin'gol* (true bone). Men of the third rank could aspire to the sixth office grade, while fourth- and fifth-rank males could advance only to the tenth and twelfth office grades, respectively. The oligarchic *Hwabaek*, a meeting of clan leaders traditionally convened at four hallowed places on the outskirts of Sorabol, was replaced by a system of thirteen specialized offices, including an Executive Office, a Department of Justice, a Board of Censors, and a Foreign Relations Department.

Another element of Chinese influence on Silla was Buddhism, which was officially recognized as the state religion by King Pop-hung in the early sixth century. It did not gain widespread adherence until the martyrdom in 528 of Ich'adon, a monk who had prophesied that his blood would run white to prove the veracity of the new religion. When Ich'adon's prophecy was fulfilled, King Pop-hung renounced the throne to become a Buddhist priest, and his queen became a nun. Buddhist pagodas were built in many parts of the kingdom, particularly in the Komsung area. Korean monks studied Buddhism in China and India and introduced Confucian literature and a variety of Buddhist sects into Korea.

Although Silla women wielded considerable political influence as royal consorts, secondary wives, regents, and courtiers, few occupied posts comparable to those of men. However, Silla did have a number of powerful queens. Queen Son-dok, who ruled from 632 to 647, was noted for cultivating in Korea the Chinese culture of the Tang Dynasty. She promoted Confucianism at her court and in the government, and sent students to Chinese schools and introduced Chinese court dress, technology, and other elements of Chinese culture. The military school she established came to form the backbone of the officer corps of the Silla army, and it was this cadre of officers that effected the unification of Korea a generation later.

Science, religion, literature, and the arts flourished under Queen Son-dok's sponsorship. The Punhwang-Sa Pagoda, constructed in 634 at Komsung under Son-dok's auspices, is the oldest surviving pagoda in Korea. Originally seven or nine stories high, it still holds the 1,300-year-old gilt statue of the Buddha. The queen, who was passionately interested in astronomy, also commissioned the building of the Ch'omsong-dae (Nearer the Stars Place), near the center of Komsung. Built in 647, it is the oldest existing astronomical observatory in East Asia and Korea's oldest secular structure. Its bottle shape most likely drew inspiration both from Korean aesthetics and Chinese cosmology, which posited a round heaven rotating around a square earth. The top platform, which indicated the eight cardinal points, may have

Overhead view of Pulguk-Sa Temple, Kyŏngju
Photo courtesy of Korea National Tourism Corporation, Chicago

supported an armillary sphere for observation of unusual celestial phenomena, such as comets and solar eclipses. Alternatively, the thirty-foot-high structure could have functioned as an open-domed observatory for charting the positions of constellations and for the calculation of the solstitial and equinoctial points. (Korean court astronomers strove to enhance their rulers' prestige by accurately predicting solar and lunar eclipses. In addition, the movements of the larger planets were thought to augur the rise and fall of rulers and states, while solar halos were taken to portend disaster.)

While Silla had been gaining strength, Koguryŏ was weakening by the mid–sixth century, after having made significant inroads into Paekche territory. In response, Silla and Paekche entered into an alliance to reconquer former Paekche lands along the Han River. Their joint armies defeated Koguryŏ in 551, and Silla became master of the upper Han region. King Chin-hung of Silla, emboldened by this success, then turned on his ally in 553, dealing a crushing blow to King Sŏng of Paekche at Kwansan-song (modern Okeh'on), taking control of the entire Han River region. He also made further advances on Koguryŏ territory. By the late sixth century Silla controlled the key Han and Naktong River basins and was in direct contact with Tang China.

After more than a century of border skirmishes with Paekche, Silla secured military aid from the Tang government and launched a campaign to conquer all of Paekche. Under the brilliant military leadership of General Kim Yu-sin and Prince Kim Ch'un-ch'u (later King T'aejong Muyol), Silla forces took Paekche's capital in 660, putting the entire court to rout. Paekche ceased to exist, and its territories were incorporated into Silla. Koguryŏ fell in 668, bringing most of the Korean Peninsula under Silla's control. The kingdom's next concern was to deal with its Tang ally, which had aided Silla in the hopes of incorporating the entire Korean Peninsula into the Chinese Empire.

The Chinese established an administrative district system after the fall of Koguryŏ, supporting its administrative authority with a massive military presence. Silla managed to maintain its independence only by inciting rebellions in the new districts and expelling the Chinese from their base at P'yongyang in 671. It was not until 735, however, that Tang China signed a treaty recognizing Silla's sovereignty over the land south of the Taedong River.

Unencumbered by military conflict or local rivals and stimulated by the culturally advanced Tang Dynasty, Silla entered a period of great prosperity and cultural advances. Royal authority was strengthened and the kingdom's administration even further centralized. Komsung, the political and economic heart of a kingdom strong enough to withstand the Tang, became the hub of a remarkable cultural renaissance. The city expanded, and its center was reconstructed on a grander scale, following the layout of the Chinese city of Xian. Komsung's population soon surpassed 1 million. An

Burial Mounds at Tumuli Park, Kyŏngju
Photo courtesy of Korea National Tourism Corporation, Chicago

indication of the population's prosperity may be found in an ancient source that claims the city's houses all had tile roofs, an expensive proposition.

A proposal to transfer the capital to the more centrally located Taegu was dismissed because of the aristocracy's close ties with Komsung. To make government more efficient, five subcapitals were designated, at modern Namwon, Ch'ŏngju, Wonju, Ch'ungju, and Kimhae. Officials from Komsung were dispatched to administer the district thus created.

Some of the most famous Buddhist shrines of Komsung, indeed in Korea, were built during the reign of Kim Tae-song in the mid–eighth century. The Pulguk-Sa, standing on the slopes of Mount Toham, ten miles southeast of Komsung, actually dates to the early years of the sixth century, having been built by the convert-king Pop-hung. This Buddhist temple was redesigned in 751 by Kim Tae-song. Its symmetric stone staircases, the three-tiered Sokka-t'ap Pagoda, and the more elaborate Tabo-t'ap Pagoda attest to the versatility of Silla architects. Hidden in the base of the Sokka-t'ap was a woodblock print of the Dharani Sutra, the oldest known woodblock print in the world.

Nearby Sokkuram Grotto, another of Kim Tae-song's creations, is considered to be one of the world's most classically beautiful Buddhist shrines. The artificial grotto, rediscovered accidentally in 1909 by a postman seeking shelter from a sudden downpour, was so skillfully constructed that it appears to be part of the landscape. Although it had stood for centuries without maintenance, no moisture had seeped into the chamber, leaving its stone reliefs in a state of perfect preservation. In the reliefs the four Deva kings, bodhisattvas and arhats (disciples of Buddha), and the goddess of mercy surround the central figure of a massive yet graceful white granite Buddha.

International trade flourished in Silla. By the eighth century, four government-sponsored markets were operating in Komsung. Books were among the prized imports from Tang China, to which Silla exported silk, ginseng, gold and silver ornaments, and fine paper. Dubbed the "gold-glittering nation" in a ninth-century Arabic text, Silla pioneered advances in shipbuilding and navigation that facilitated its trade with Chinese, Japanese, Indian, and other foreign merchants.

Silla became known for its paper manufacture and its bronze bell casting. The latter craft reached its pinnacle in the eighth century. Komsung's most famous bell, the flawless, eleven-foot-high Emillie Bell of the Pongdok-sa Pagoda, was completed in 770 to honor King Song-dok and is connected with a tragic tale. According to legend, the chief priest of Pongdok-sa was visited in a dream by a spirit who argued that the temple bell would ring only after the sacrifice of a child who had been born in the year, month, day, and hour of the dragon. Such a child was located, and the monk persuaded the child's mother, a poor widow, to sacrifice her child for Buddha. The already finished bell was melted down for

Punhwang-Sa Pagoda, Kyŏngju
Photo courtesy of Korea National Tourism Corporation, Chicago

recasting, and the three-year-old girl was thrown into the molten metal. The recast bell was named for the sound of its peal, which was likened to a child's cries for its mother, "Emi! Emi!"

During the reign of King Hye-gong (765–80), Silla went into a slow decline from which it never recovered. *Chin'gol* (true bone) noblemen vied for the throne, while lesser aristocrats sought to replace the bone ranks with the more meritocratic Chinese system of organizing the bureaucracy. Merchants appropriated trade formerly monopolized by the government. Wealthy landowners and monks amassed what amounted to small independent states at the expense of peasants and the Silla treasury. Peasant insurrections were common, although they did not gather enough force to threaten the government in a serious way. As the power of the central government crumbled, Silla's territory shrank, and warlords emerged to take advantage of the weakened monarchy. Hye-gong himself was assassinated by a usurper, Kim Yangsang. In spite of these internal difficulties, the kingdom survived for another 150 years.

Silla ultimately fell at the hands of rebel general Kyŏnhwŏn, who in 892 (or 900) proclaimed the state of Later Paekche. In 927 Kyŏnhwŏn attacked Komsung, where King Kyŏngae, ignoring all warnings of an impending invasion, was enjoying himself at his summer retreat, the Posok-jong Bower. Kyŏnhwŏn killed the king, sacked Komsung, and appointed to the throne Kyŏng-sun, a descendant of Munsong, the forty-sixth Silla king. In 936 Kyŏng-sun was forced to abdicate the throne, turning it over to Wang Kŏn, who did not belong to the Kim family and had not been in line for the succession. Komsung's Anap-ji, the famed botanical gardens constructed in 674 by King Mun-mu to celebrate Silla's unification of the peninsula, ironically became the setting of the formal surrender.

Wang Kŏn made a radical break with the Silla past, founding the state of Koryŏ in its stead and moving his capital to Songdo. Wang Kŏn treated his former enemy as an honored guest in Songdo, offering Kyŏng-sun his daughter in marriage and presenting him with territories around the former Silla capital, which from that date became known as Kyŏngju. In 1018, Kyŏngju became the eastern regional capital of the Koryŏ Dynasty and slowly became something of a backwater.

Between 1231 and 1273 Koryŏ was engulfed in a series of Mongol invasions. Kyŏngju was sacked, and numerous cultural treasures perished in the devastation. Further damage was done late in the sixteenth century during the Imjin War with Japan. Kyŏngsang province, where Kyŏngju is situated, was especially hard hit by the invasions of General Toyotomi Hideyoshi, launched between 1592 and 1598 with the objective of conquering China. The Japanese army destroyed or carried off many of Kyŏngju's finest works of art.

Kyŏngju lay largely forgotten until early in the twentieth century. Excavations sponsored by the Korean and Japanese governments focused on Kyŏngju's more than 200 royal tombs. A wealth of priceless jewelry and works of art have been recovered from many of the tombs. For example, the early sixth-century Ch'ongma-ch'ong (Heavenly Horse Tomb) yielded a delicately fashioned gold crown with curved jade pendants dangling from high peaks resembling trees and antlers, symbols of shamanistic power. However, the tomb is named for the most historically significant object it contained, a painting of a white galloping horse on a birch-bark saddle guard, the first Silla painting from the pre-unification period to be discovered. The fifth-century Kumgwan-ch'ong (Gold Crown Tomb) contained a dazzling array of gold objects, including an intricate crown and a belt from which a gold fish and other ornaments were suspended. It also yielded Roman glass vessels, evidence of ancient Saro's international trading activities. The national museums of Kyŏngju and Seoul house the 11,526 relics recovered from the tombs.

In 1971 the Republic of Korea, with the assistance of the International Bank for Reconstruction and Development, initiated a comprehensive tourist development plan aimed at restoring Kyŏngju's historic sites and developing buildings and roads in the Kyŏngju area. Eight years later UNESCO designated Kyŏngju as one of the world's ten most significant ancient cultural cities, for its role in the development of the Korean nation and East Asia as a whole. Agriculture, education, and small-scale industry contribute to Kyŏngju's economy, but tourism sustains it. Every year, more than 1 million visitors converge on Korea's "museum without walls."

Further Reading: Edward B. Adams' exhaustive *Kyongju Guide: Cultural Spirit of Silla in Korea* (Seoul: Seoul International Tourist Publishing, 1979) recounts the history and legends of Kyŏngju's attractions; it is filled with color photographs and maps. *South Korea Handbook* by Robert Nilsen (Chico, California: Moon, 1988) summarizes Kyŏngju's history and describes its principal monuments. For a broader treatment of Kyŏngju's historical significance, see Han Woo-keun's *The History of Korea,* translated by Lee Kyung-shik (Seoul: Eul-Yoo, 1970). *Women of Korea: A History from Ancient Times to 1945*, edited by Yung-Chung Kim (Seoul: Ewha Woman's University Press, 1977) illuminates the contributions and daily lives of women in ancient Korea, while *Science and Technology in Korea: Traditional Instruments and Techniques* by Sang-woon Jeon (Cambridge, Massachusetts, and London: M.I.T. Press, 1974) discusses Silla advances in science.

—Maria Chiara and Marijke Rijsberman

Kyōto (Kyōto, Japan)

Location: On the island of Honshū, in Kyōto prefecture, 27 miles north of Nara, 26 miles northeast of Ōsaka, and 304 miles west of Tōkyō.

Description: Capital of Japan from 794 to 1868 (but not always the country's political center), famous for its Buddhist temples and gardens, its Shintō shrines, and other cultural treasures.

Site Office: Japan National Tourist Organization
Kyōto Tower Building, first floor
Higashi-Shiokojicho, Shimogyo-ku
Kyōto, Kyōto
Japan
(75) 371 5649

The city of Kyōto recently celebrated the 1,200th anniversary of its foundation in 794, with special events based around the Buddhist temples, Shintō shrines, and residences of past rulers, which, in spite of modern development, still dominate the skyline and layout of the city, from its central districts around the Kamo River to the mountains on its outskirts. The history of Kyōto is inextricably bound to the traditional political and religious institutions of Japan: the hereditary *tennō,* usually known as emperors, who have almost always functioned much more as popes than secular monarchs; the nobles and warlords who were usually the real powers in the land; and the various sects of Japanese Buddhism, most of which originated in the city.

However, there were emperors, nobles, and Buddhists in Japan long before Kyōto was founded. Around the middle of the sixth century, Buddhism was accepted by the ruling families who gathered around the emperors in a succession of temporary capitals. These families went on to dominate everyday life both in Nara, the first permanent capital city, founded in 710, and in its successor, Nagaoka, founded in 784. Only ten years later Emperor Kammu and his advisers abandoned Nagaoka, partly because it was feared that the evil spirit of a murdered imperial prince had entered the court, and more pragmatically, to remove his court from the influence of the Buddhist priests, who were major landowners and political players. A new site was found five miles away, on which the city that is now Kyōto was begun.

Its original name was Heian-kyō (Peace-tranquility-capital) and, like its two predecessors, it was laid out on a grid-plan based on that of Chang'an (modern Xian), the capital of China during the Tang Dynasty. A vast main avenue, Suzaku-Ōji (now reduced to a standard city street, Senbon-dōri), ran from north to south, and nine numbered streets, still the basis of the Kyōto city plan, ran from east to west across it. The Gosho, the palace compound that occupied as much as 20 percent of the city's original area, was laid out at the northern end of Suzaku-Ōji; at the southern end stood the Rashō-mon, the city gate, which is long gone but still famous as the title both of a novella by Akutagawa Ryūnosuke and of Akira Kurosawa's film inspired by the novella. The modern city center is somewhat to the east of Heian-kyō as originally planned, since the marshiness of the land on the western side and the presence of the Kamo River as the main means of long-distance transport in the east had encouraged a shift in that direction ever since Kammu's arrival.

Even prior to the arrival of the court in 794, at least three significant Shintō shrines and three major Buddhist temples existed in the vicinity. Two of the Shintō shrines, Shimogamo Jinja and Kamigamo Jinja (the Lower and Upper Kamo Shrines), are said to have been founded by Emperor Kimmei sometime between 540 and 570 to honor the god of the nearby mountains, his wife, the goddess of the river, and their son, the god of thunder. The third shrine, Fushimi Inari, founded in 711 for the worship of the deities connected with the rice harvest, consists of several buildings spread over a mountainside and linked by hundreds of *torii,* orange-painted shrine gates guarded by statues of foxes.

One of the Buddhist temples, Chobo-ji, is said to have been founded as early as 587. Today it is better known as the Rokkakudō, the six-sided hall, in reference to its hexagonal main building, the present version of which dates only from 1876. Another of the temples, associated with the powerful Fujiwara family, was built in Kyōto in the seventh century but was moved to Nara between 710 and 730; it is still there today. The third, known as Kiyomizu-dera in Higashiyama (the Eastern Hills), is noted for its *hon-do* (main hall), which, with its shingled roof, resembles a gigantic farmhouse rather than a temple. It is built on a platform supported by elaborate scaffolding and overlooking the wooded valleys below. The present Kiyomizu-dera was completed in 1633, following the sixth fire to damage or destroy it.

Inside Heian-kyō itself only two Buddhist temples were permitted at first, Sai-ji and Tō-ji (the Western Temple and the Eastern Temple), both at the southern end of Suzaku-Ōji. Although the former no longer exists, Tō-ji has remained on the same site since its foundation in 796. Its pagoda, 184 feet high, is the tallest in Japan, and its kōdo (lecture hall) houses a display of ancient statues representing the Buddha Dainichi (Vairocana in Sanskrit), his four attendant Buddhas of the Diamond World, five Bodhisattvas, the five Angry Gods, and the four Heavenly Kings. These images, arranged to form a *mandala* (pattern of the universe), were installed some time after 823, when Tō-ji was given to the new Shingon sect of Buddhism by Kammu's successor, Saga. Tō-ji also has a statue of the sect's founder, the priest Kūkai, which, how-

Daigo-ji Temple, Kyōto
Photo courtesy of Japan National Tourist Organization

Kinkaku-ji, or Temple of the Golden Pavilion, Kyōto
Photo courtesy of Japan National Tourist Organization

ever, dates from 1233, more than 400 years after the visit to China that inspired his religious innovations.

Saichō, a contemporary of Kūkai's who had also been to China, founded another sect, Tendai-shū, in 805, building its chief temple, Enryaku-ji, on Hiei-zan (Mount Hiei), about twelve miles northeast of the capital, in order to protect the city from the demons that were believed to come from that direction. In choosing the temple's location he was true to the esoteric tradition that he and Kūkai shared, for their followers, whether in China or in Japan, usually lived among mountains, away from the distractions of city life.

From about 858 Heian-kyō, which may have had a population of roughly 100,000 during its first century, was dominated by the Fujiwara family through their monopoly of the posts of *kanpaku* (chancellor or chief minister) and *sesshō* (regent for infant emperors) and through arranging marriages with members of the imperial family. The latter practice culminated in the eleventh century with the accomplishments of Fujiwara Michinaga, eight of whose sons-in-law and grandsons became emperors. The Fujiwara family's supremacy was briefly interrupted by the rise to power of Sugawara Michizane in the late ninth century, but they soon arranged his downfall and exile to Kyūshū. Michizane, deified after his death in 903, is honored as a patron of learning at Kitano Tenman-gū, a Shintō shrine founded in 974, and its branch shrines throughout Japan.

The Fujiwara and other noble families sponsored the establishment of many more Buddhist temples on and around Hiei-zan, Higashiyama, and elsewhere. Among these the outstanding example is the Byōdō-in, built about 1053 on a Fujiwara estate at Uji, around twelve miles southeast of the capital city. Since a fire in 1483 its only remaining building has been the Hō'o-dō (Phoenix Hall), which has long side-aisles to represent the bird's wings and a chamber at the back to represent its tail, and which stands by a pool in a garden representing the western paradise of the Buddha Amida (Amitabha). It is now known to almost everyone in Japan, if only because its facade appears on the ten-yen coin. The legacy of the Fujiwara years also includes two extraordinary prose works by women at the imperial court, the realistic novel Genji Monogatari (The Tale of Genji) and Sei Shonagon's journal, the *Makura No Zōshi* (The Pillow Book).

Eventually the Fujiwara found themselves facing stronger challenges than Michizane's, from two directions. From the late eleventh century Sanjō II and other emperors exerted considerable influence as "cloistered emperors," that is, by abdicating and becoming priests but manipulating their successors, who were usually minors. During the same period the Taira (or Heike), the Minamoto (or Genji), and other families of *samurai* (warriors) increased their influence on events, both as courtiers in Kyōto and as rulers of outlying provinces, until in 1156 Tairi Kiyomori supplanted the Fujiwara.

New temples continued to be founded during these turbulent years. For example, in 1164 Emperor Shirakawa II established the Sanjūsangendō (rebuilt around 100 years later), a long, low building containing 1,001 gold-covered wooden statues of Kannon (Avalokitesvara), the goddess of mercy, as well as figures of other protective deities. But Heian-kyō now became the focus of a nationwide civil war, as the Minamoto, headed by Yoritomo, rebelled against the Taira. After Kiyomori's death in 1181, a military campaign commanded by Yoritomo's half-brother Yoshitsune ended at Dan-no-Ura in western Honshū with the victory of the Minamoto and the drowning of the infant emperor Antoku, who was Kiyomori's grandson.

Heian-kyō survives in three festivals still held every year in the city. The Aoi Matsuri (Hollyhock Festival) in May, which probably began during the fifteenth century, includes a procession of people in historic costumes between Kamigamo and Shimogamo; the Gion Matsuri (Gion Festival) in July, which features a similar but larger procession, began in 869 as a strategy of the Shintō shrine of Yasaka against an epidemic; and the Jidai Matsuri (Festival of the Ages) in October, which began in the 1890s, consists of yet another procession, of people representing every century of Kyōto's history, moving between the Gosho and the Heian shrine. Otherwise even the name Heian-kyō has long since given way, first, to the popular term Miyako (capital city), in use from its beginnings, and, predominating since 1868, the more formal, literary name Kyōto, also meaning capital city.

The center of political and military power now moved away from Kyōto to Kamakura, in the distant eastern provinces, where Minamoto Yoritomo established a new regime after having the emperor Toba II, whom he had raised to the throne two years before Antoku's death, appoint him Sei-i-tai-Shōgun (Barbarian-suppressing Great General) in 1191. Kyōto's wealth and prestige declined while Japan was ruled from Kamakura by the Minamoto, and then, from 1219, by the Hōjō family, relatives of Yoritomo's wife. In 1221 a rising on behalf of Toba, now a cloistered emperor, was put down by the Hōjō, whose only use for members of the old Kyōto families was to make them into figurehead *shōguns*.

The thirteenth century, which seemed to the nobles to be governed by very different ideals from those associated with the name Heian-kyō, also saw the beginning of intellectual and cultural movements in favor of returning to the simplicities, even austerities, of earlier times, alongside a renewal of Chinese influence. A new school of *sumi-e* (charcoal ink pictures) began to rival the ancient *yamato-e* (Japanese painting) tradition, and new *kara-yō* (Chinese style) temples were constructed, especially for the Zen sect brought from China at this time. These include Nanzen-ji, a complex of temples, meditation halls, and gardens laid out from 1293 onward behind an enormous triple gate in Higashiyama; Daitoku-ji, another complex, started in 1319, which is now noted for the gravel and stone gardens laid out in its grounds, perhaps designed by Kobori Enshū (1579–1647); and Ryoan-ji, founded approximately 100 years later, which has another and even better known garden, interpreted by some as depicting the heads of a female tiger and her cubs (stones) appearing above the waves of the sea (raked gravel).

These and other Zen temples, following the trend set 400 years earlier, were located away from the city center. However, the more populist Jōdo-shū (Pure Land Sect), founded by Hōnen (1133–1212), and the Jōdo Shin-shū (Pure Land Truth Sect), founded by his disciple Shinran (1173–1262), built their temples inside Kyōto and other cities, thereby maintaining closer contact with the masses, to whom they brought the message of salvation through the mercy of Amida. Hōnen's sect still has its headquarters at the temple of Chion-in in Kyōto, founded in 1234; Shinran's sect initially built its Hongan-ji (Temple of the Original Vow) in 1271 at the site of his tomb, which is now inside the grounds of Chion-in.

In 1331 Emperor Daigo II defied the Hōjō by seizing power in and around Kyōto. The general Ashikaga Takauji was ordered to suppress this rising but instead arranged for the Hōjō leadership to be forced to commit suicide and tried to work with Daigo. When the emperor refused to reward his efforts, however, he expelled the imperial court from Kyōto, put a rival emperor on the throne, and, in 1338, made himself *shōgun*. Daigo's southern dynasty continued at Yoshino (now in Nara prefecture) while the rival northern emperors in Kyōto took their orders from the Ashikaga, whose main residence was built by Yoshimitsu (1358–1408), the third Ashikaga *shōgun* in the Muromachi district, significantly to the north of the Gosho and therefore symbolically superior to it.

Yoshimitsu was probably the greatest of the Ashikaga line. He reunited the imperial lines in 1392 and sent an emissary to China, reestablishing trade relations that had been disrupted since the Mongol rulers of China had tried to invade Japan in 1274 and 1281. At the cost of accepting formal Chinese suzerainty over Japan, he thus contributed to a revival of Kyōto's economy, its merchants and craftsmen prospering through catering to the demands of the *shōguns*, their *samurai* followers, and their equivalents in China and Korea. In 1394 Yoshimitsu founded a Zen temple inside a formal garden, now known as Kinkaku-ji (the Temple of the Golden Pavilion), a square three-story building of thatched roofs and gold-painted walls and verandas. Its destruction by an arsonist in 1950, which inspired Yukio Mishima's novel named for the temple, was followed by an exact reconstruction, completed in 1955. Yoshimitsu was also the patron, and perhaps the lover, of Zeami, the actor and playwright who, with his father Kan-ami, formulated the basic rules that still govern the masked dramas of Noh, the oldest surviving theatrical tradition in Japan.

Ashikaga authority was generally much weaker than that of Hōjō, as the local *shugo* (constables) and *jito* (stew-

Heian Jingū, Shintō shrine, Kyōto
Photo courtesy of Japan National Tourist Organization

ards) increasingly asserted autonomy by converting what had been public lands into private, hereditary possessions, much as analogous officeholders did in the feudal systems of western Europe, Ottoman Turkey, and Mughal India. The *shōguns* preferred to concentrate on aesthetics rather than politics. Thus Yoshimasa, the eighth Ashikaga *shōgun*, began his Ginkaku-ji (the Temple of the Silver Pavilion) in Higashiyama in 1473 and completed it in 1480. Its name refers back to Yoshimitsu's pavilion, and its garden rivals his in extent and beauty, but in fact it was never painted silver, being instead a small thatched building with *shōji* (paper and wood shutters) around its two floors. Yoshimasa continued with this project and with his patronage of the tea ceremony and of the Kanō school of painting (both of which would become major traditions in Japanese culture), even as the Ōnin War (1467–77) broke out between *samurai* factions disputing the succession between Yoshimasa's brother and his infant son. The capital outside Yoshimasa's garden retreat was almost completely destroyed and abandoned during these ten years.

During the nationwide conflicts initiated by the Ōnin War, which were to last for about 100 years, Kyōto became the battleground for two militant Buddhist movements, the Ikko-shū (single mind), based around the Jōdo Shin-shū, and the Nichiren-shū sect, which had also been founded in the thirteenth century. In 1532 the latter effectively conquered most of the city, but only four years later it was driven out by an army hired by the Ikko-shū, which then ransacked and burned many of the temples and palaces. In 1568 what was left of Kyōto came under the control of the warlord Oda Nobunaga. His first major act was to suppress the warrior-monks of the Tendai sect, who controlled enormous amounts of land and other wealth from their 3,000 or more temple buildings on and around Hiei-zan. In 1571 most of the monks were slaughtered and Enryaku-ji and their other bases were destroyed, leaving only one building, the small Shaka-dō (Buddha Hall), untouched. Two years later Nobunaga deposed Yoshiaki, the last and least powerful of the Ashikaga *shōguns*.

After Nobunaga was assassinated in 1582, his successor as ruler of most of Japan, Toyotomi Hideyoshi, permitted the Tendai monks to return to Hiei-zan and begin the rebuilding of their headquarters, which today consists of about 125 buildings spread among the mountain forests. Having completed the reunification of the country from his headquarters at Ōsaka, Hideyoshi returned to Kyōto in 1593 to build a new residence, Momoyama Castle, near the Fushimi Inari shrine. The only parts of this castle remaining after its demolition in 1632 were transferred to sites elsewhere in the city—its ornate roofed gateway to Nijō Castle and a set of elaborately painted rooms to Nishi Hongan-ji temple; a rather unconvincing and decidedly smaller replica of the castle was built on the site in the early twentieth century and rebuilt in 1964.

Hideyoshi died in 1598. Five years later his lieutenant Tokugawa Ieyasu, chosen as one of the regents for Hideyoshi's infant son, had himself made *shōgun* and moved the political capital once again, this time to Edo (later renamed Tōkyō), a city even farther east than Kamakura. Ieyasu's imposition of what has been called the Pax Tokugawa, the repressive but stable regime that lasted more than 250 years and fostered peaceful economic and cultural development after centuries of civil wars, is commemorated in Kyōto by four major buildings. One of these, Nijō Castle, was built between 1603 and 1626 on the probable site of Kammu's original Gosho as the Kyōto residence of the *shōguns*, who hardly ever visited, and of the governors whom they appointed to supervise the imperial family and the old nobility. It is richly decorated with wood carvings, paintings, and furniture of the period, but its most striking feature is the series of "nightingale floors" in the corridors, designed to creak when stepped on to alert the occupants that visitors, including potential assassins, were approaching. The castle has been open to the public since it was given to the city in 1893. Another of the structures commemorating the Pax Tokugawa is Katsura Rikyū (or Katsura Detached Palace), built between 1620 and 1642 for the imperial prince Hachijo no Toshihito and his family and decorated with paintings by Kanō School artists. It has come to be regarded as a model of classic Japanese style, inspiring Frank Lloyd Wright and other modern architects, but it is better known inside the country for its three teahouses, grouped around a pool in its equally classic and influential formal garden designed, like those at Daitoku-ji, by Kobori Enshu.

The other two great Kyōto monuments of Ieyasu's time are the gigantic head temples of the two divisions of the Jōdo Sin-shū: Nishi Hongan-ji and Higashi Hongan-ji (Western and Eastern Hongan-ji), each consisting of a Taishidō (Founder's Hall) and an Amida-dō (Amida Hall) connected by a roofed corridor. Shinran's sect had been driven out of the city by the monks of Hiei-zan in 1465 and had regrouped around a new headquarters in Ōsaka as a militant movement of peasants and craftsworkers, often also called Ikko-shū (One Mind), against warlords, nobles, and mainstream sects alike. Having attacked Kyōto in 1536, it governed several provinces until its savage suppression by Oda Nobunaga between 1574 and 1580. Its remnants, still considered dangerous by Nobunaga's successors, were permitted to build a new Hongan-ji in Kyōto in 1591; this is Nishi Hongan-ji, which still claims seniority and is somewhat better known, partly because of its flamboyantly decorated main gate and its statue of Shinran, allegedly carved by Shinran himself and later covered with a mixture of lacquer and his ashes. Higashi Hongan-ji, the biggest of all the wooden buildings in Kyōto, was established in 1602 after Tokugawa Ieyasu took advantage of a split in the hereditary leadership of the sect to divide its assets and congregations. It also has a presumed self-portrait of Shinran and is famous for its massive rope, plaited from the hair of female worshippers and given to the temple in 1895.

Kyōto in the Tokugawa period was a political backwater but by no means an economic one. With a population of more than 400,000 it remained Japan's second-largest city, outstripping Ōsaka, and was regarded, along with Ōsaka and Edo, as one of the Sankyō, the "three capitals" of Japan. Its main industries were textiles, which, with new Chinese and Korean techniques introduced during the seventeenth century, expanded from a tradition of silk production that probably began soon after the city was founded, and has long been associated with the Nishijin district; the production of Kiyomizu, Awata, and other local types of porcelain; and printing and publishing. Its most powerful citizens were the merchant families who had made fortunes by supplying and funding the armies during the civil wars that Ieyasu had brought to a close.

After the Great Fire of Kyōto in 1788, which destroyed many of the city's temples, the Gosho was finally moved to the site it occupies today, although the present buildings were erected in 1854 after yet another, fortunately localized, fire had destroyed the eighteenth-century structures. Its austere, low-lying buildings, surrounded by white gravel and an extensive park, offer a striking contrast to the magnificence of Nijō Castle nearby and are a visible reminder of the religious, rather than political, role of the emperors throughout Japanese history. They are still used for the enthronement of emperors (as in 1989 for Emperor Akihito), and the ornate thrones used in the ceremony can be seen on the limited occasions that the palace is open to visitors.

From 1865 onward Kyōto became the center of intrigues by leaders of the outlying provinces of Satsuma, Chōshū, Tosa, and Hizen against the Tokugawa *shōgunate*, encouraged by Emperor Kōmei, who objected to the opening of Japan to trade with the United States and western Europe. Following their triumph over the *shōgun*'s forces in 1868, Kōmei's son and successor, Mutsuhito, now known as the Meiji emperor, inaugurated the Meiji period (1868–1912) and moved to the new capital, Tōkyō. Kyōto, in spite of its name, was now no longer the capital city even for symbolic purposes.

In 1894 the 1,100th anniversary of the founding of Heian-kyō was marked by the opening of by far the largest Shintō shrine in Kyōto, the Heian Jingū, an orange, green, and white structure based on what was known of the Daigoku-den (Hall of State), the main building in Kammu's palace. The structure was intended to assert the revival of a state-sponsored Shintōism in opposition to Buddhism, which was then distrusted by the ruling groups as excessively universalist and therefore not sufficiently patriotic. Similar motives inspired the founding of the Kyōto National Museum in 1897. The museum has since been expanded to hold and display one of the largest and most varied collections of Japanese art—prehistoric, Shintō, Buddhist, and other—in the country.

The anti-Buddhist aspect of government policy was soon abandoned, but the nationalist ideology that had inspired it, centered on the symbolic figure of the emperor, continued to gather strength. Its advocates eventually led Japan to conquer Taiwan and Korea, invade China with great brutality, and challenge the United States and the European colonial powers. These actions culminated in World War II, but Kyōto, like Nara and Kamakura, was spared destruction in the conflict.

Kyōto today has some 1,600 Buddhist temples, more than 250 Shintō shrines, and numerous other historically important institutions. The city overshadows its predecessor Nara in sheer wealth of heritage, although not in tranquility or greenery; it surpasses its successor Tōkyō in heritage, tranquility, and greenery alike. Clearly a city of more than 1.5 million people is much more than an open-air museum, and the Kyōto authorities have often run into controversy in fulfilling their dual responsibilities of protecting historic sites and servicing a modern community. But, if only because tourism is a major source of city revenues and private profits, it is very likely that compromises will continue being made and that the ancient capital, founded in an effort to escape the political domination of Buddhist priests, will continue being physically dominated by Buddhist temples.

Further Reading: Herbert E. Plutschow's *Historical Kyōto* (Tōkyō: Japan Times, 1983) is one of the best of the many guides to the city. The imperial court of Heian-kyō is brought to life in the pages of *The Pillow Book* of Sei Shōnagon, translated by Ivan Morris (Harmondsworth, Middlesex, and Baltimore, Maryland: Penguin, 1970), and *The Tale of Genji* by Murasaki Shikibu, translated by Edward Seidensticker (New York: Knopf, 1978).

—Patrick Heenan

Lahore (Punjab, Pakistan)

Location: In eastern Pakistan, on the upper plains of the Indus Valley, on the Rāvi River, a tributary of the Indus.

Description: The capital of the Punjab province and second largest city of Pakistan, Lahore served as a capital for many foreign rulers—Muslim, Mongol, and British—before becoming part of independent Pakistan. Its old city boasts beautiful buildings and gardens.

Contact: Pakistan Tourism Development Corporation
House No. 2, St 61, F-7/4
Islamābād 44000
Pakistan
(51) 811001

According to Hindu legend, the god Loh, son of Rāma, founded Lahore, or Loh-awar, meaning Loh's Fort. This account may not satisfy modern scholars, but it is all we have, for any other knowledge of the city's origins disappeared from human memory long ago. Lahore may have been the city referred to by Ptolemy of Alexandria when, in A.D. 150, he wrote of a city called Labokla. Five hundred years later a Chinese writer, Xuan Zang, visited a city near the Rāvi River that contained many Brahman families—those of the highest Hindu caste. Was this also Lahore? It is safe to state that Lahore has been inhabited since the beginning of the second century, when a series of Hindu dynasties controlled the Punjab. Subject to the vagaries of war, politics, and commerce, it was destined to prosper and suffer alternately. The Rāvi River, one of the major tributaries of the Indus, provided the site with fertile land, while its position between the kingdoms of Afghanistan, Persia, and India ensured that it would play a significant role in the great political and commercial events of the region.

Lahore's proper history began during the great Muslim expansion of the seventh century. The Hindu city was first attacked by Afghans spreading the Prophet Muḥammad's word in 682 and was finally disabled by Sabaktin, the governor of Khorāsān, 300 years later. Sabaktin's son Mahmūd of Ghaznī completed the task by driving the Hindu ruling family from the city in 1022. He then handed the city to his favorite, Malik Ayaz, who dazzled the city with his extraordinary rebuilding program. Lahore became the capital of the Ghaznavid province and rose to such prominence that it became known as Little Ghazna. It became a cultural center as well and was home to some important early Persian poets. The first reliable reference to Lahore dates from this period: it is contained in the *Tārīkhul Hind,* compiled by al-Biruni sometime near 1030. After the fall of the Ghaznavid rulers in 1186, control of Lahore passed among a number of tribes and kingdoms that capitalized on the political instability in the region.

An even greater threat loomed beyond the squabbling petty kingdoms of Persia and Afghanistan: beginning in the fourteenth century, the Mongols began sweeping through the Punjab from Sind, devastating the areas around Lahore. Then in 1524 the founder of the Mughal Dynasty, Bābur (Ẓahīr-ud-Dīn Muḥammad), captured Lahore; his son Mirza Kamran would later take the city for himself and build its first garden, a portion of which still exists. Under the Mughals, Lahore blossomed as a cultural and political center.

The Mughal ruler Akbar intensified building activities when he moved his capital to Lahore in 1584. He would bring the city to the height of its glory during his relatively brief residence, which lasted until 1598. (During the 1580s and 1590s, Akbar was also actively expanding the Mughal Empire and creating administrative policies that would greatly benefit his successors, making his attention to Lahore all the more remarkable.) Akbar built a wall around the city and refurbished its fort. His palace included lavish private apartments and grand audience halls as well as offices for his bureaucracy. A contemporary account, the *Ain-e-Akbari*, noted:

> His Majesty plans splendid edifices, and dresses the work of his mind and heart in the garment of stone and clay. Thus mighty fortresses have been raised, which protect the timid, frighten the rebellious, and please the obedient. They afford excellent protection against cold and rain, provide for the comforts of the princesses of the Harem, and are conducive to that dignity which is necessary for worldly power.

Akbar's court attracted a community of poets, painters, and artisans of all types. A school developed of painters who were masters of the miniature, and the city grew famous for its expert weavers. The seventeenth-century historian ʻAbdul-Hamid wrote of Lahore carpets: "So soft and delicate are [they] that compared with them, the carpets made at Kirmān in the manufactory of the kings of Iran look like coarse canvas."

Nor was the court devoid of romance. Legend relates how the king observed the growing affection between his heir, Prince Salim Jahāngīr, and a beautiful courtier called Anarkali. Akbar was so outraged at this betrayal that he had the girl buried alive within a wall. After his succession, Jahāngīr built a lavish tomb in her memory. The tomb, if not the legend, stands up to historical scrutiny.

View of Shālīmār Gardens, Lahore
Photo courtesy of Embassy of Pakistan, Washington, D.C.

Jahāngīr succeeded his father in 1605, and although the court was no longer at Lahore, he returned a year later when his own son Khusraw initiated a rebellion against him. Khusraw did so with the support of the Sikh Gurū Arjun, who thereby set a precedent in Sikh-Muslim relations; until this time, the Sikhs living in Lahore had cultivated a peaceful community. In putting down the rebellion, Jahāngīr executed Arjun, along with many of his followers. This action outraged members of the Hindu sect and sparked the militant anti-Muslim sentiment that escalated during the following centuries and remains strong to this day.

Although not the site of his court, Lahore was the city in which Jahāngīr had grown up and remained the ruler's favorite city. The sponsor of many ambitious building projects, he was especially interested in enlarging and restoring the Lahore Fort. In 1611 a British traveler named William Finch was stunned to find it decorated with paintings that included Christian subject matter, the result of the influence of Jesuit missionaries and European art; he described Lahore as "one of the greatest cities of the East." A great mural in cut, glazed tile was commissioned to decorate the exterior of the fort, depicting scenes filled with people and animals in brilliant colors. Jahāngīr also renovated his father's audience hall, the Dīwān-i-Am.

Unlike Akbar, Jahāngīr was little interested in politics and government, preferring to study art and nature. Fortunately for his political fortunes, he married well. In 1611 he wed Nūr Jahān, a brilliant Persian widow, who assumed the responsibilities of government for some fifteen years. After Jahāngīr's death, his heir Shāh Jahān built for him a great tomb across the River Rāvi in Shāhdara. The emperor had stipulated that his tomb be plain and open to the sky. Nonetheless, Shāh Jahān ordered the construction of a great mausoleum that, while simpler in design than some royal monuments, required ten years to complete. The building was composed of two walled quadrangles. Once inside the inner quadrangle, one passed through a garden to reach the mausoleum itself, a red sandstone structure seated on a raised platform with each corner topped by a tall slender minaret. The sarcophagus lay within a small vaulted chamber inside, open to the skies as Jahāngīr had wished.

Jahāngīr's successor was for a time in doubt as Shāh Jahān and his brother Shāhryar fought for the title outside the city, with Shāh Jahān emerging as the victor. Although he moved his court to Āgra after the first year of his reign, his affection for Lahore, where he had been born and raised, remained steadfast. He was keenly interested in the Lahore Fort, and he lost little time in making his own mark there. He built the octagonal tower called the Saman Burj and the Elephants' Staircase, which allowed the courtiers to ride up to their apartments on their elephants. He built the palace called *naulakha*, the word referring to its great price. The decorations of these apartments were great wonders, with their marble walls, mosaics of semi-precious stones, and rich paintings. Most wonderful of all was the Shish Mahal, or Mirror Palace, with its walls and ceilings encrusted with hundreds of small mirrors. Shāh Jahān also built the Pearl Mosque, a beautiful, small mosque used by the royal family. The emperor's continued interest in the city lent it a certain cachet, and resident nobles were encouraged to contribute to its improvements. The result was a flurry of architectural activity. Among the finer buildings was the Wazīr Khān Mosque; built in 1634, it is covered with lavish floral tiles, making it a rare survivor from the era of the great Punjab tilemakers. The architect Ali Mardan Khān constructed the luxuriant Shālīmār Gardens for Shāh Jahān in 1642. Gardens were also built by ladies of the Mughal court for their refreshment and amusement. Although few of these gardens now remain, in the late nineteenth century a British observer could still describe Lahore as "a city of trees and flowers."

Unfortunately, this era of peace and prosperity did not last. Lahore's status declined after Shāh Jahān was overthrown by 'Ālamgīr (Aurangzeb), his third son. 'Ālamgīr's major contribution to Lahore was the construction of the Bādshāhī Mosque, completed in 1674. Its design was taken from a mosque in the holy city of Mecca. The faithful, called to prayer from four graceful minarets, entered by the grand stairway into a large paved courtyard fronting the prayer hall. A massive, simple structure surmounted by three enormous onion domes of white marble with gold spires, the Bādshāhī Mosque is one of the largest mosques in the world. Yet Lahore did not hold 'Ālamgīr's interest, which lay in military conquest; thus while prospering commercially, Lahore lost its position as imperial favorite.

After 'Ālamgīr's death in 1707, the Muslim Mughals faced the first serious threat to their Indian empire. Although he had increased the size of his empire, he weakened it through his strict adherence to Islamic law to justify his government; the policy of religious tolerance introduced by Akbar had been discarded and the Muhgal alliance with Hindus destroyed. The region was invaded by would-be conquerors, first Muslims such as Nāder Shāh of Persia, and then by the Sikhs. An old injury, Jahāngīr's massacre of the Sikhs at Lahore, was to be repaid in kind: in 1767 the Sikhs seized the Punjab. Over the next few decades, they destroyed much of the Mughal legacy of gardens and architecture, and forbade the use of the city's mosques. During the reign of Mahārāja Ranjit Singh (which officially began in 1801), a British visitor described Lahore as "a melancholy picture of fallen splendor . . . all was silence, solitude and gloom."

Even so, Ranjit Singh did much to restore the city. Although he had no interest in rebuilding the city's lost splendor, he brought political power back to Lahore by establishing it as the capital of his realm. He took control of a significant territory around the city, and this seizure drew the attention of the British colonial forces in nearby India. In 1809 both parties agreed to a mutual border along the Sutlej River, signing a treaty that would, however, last only as long as the rulers of Lahore were strong enough to defend it. Ranjit Singh celebrated this event by increasing the city's fortifications.

The contention for Ranjit Singh's throne after his death (in 1839) eventually led to the first Sikh War with the British in 1845. When the British defeated the Sikhs the following year, they placed troops at Lahore; originally quartered there on a temporary basis to stabilize the government, they soon found reason to stay. In 1849 Britain annexed the Punjab, and the Union Jack flew over the Lahore Fort. All of India (including the Punjab) was effectively ruled by the British East India Company until 1858; at that point Parliament transferred governance to the British Crown. The move was largely a response to the Sepoy Mutiny of 1857, an attempt by Indians to regain their independence that was initiated at Lahore. The strategic value of the city, with its fort and arsenal, loomed large in their quest to command the Punjab. The British, however, were able to put down the revolt and retain the garrison.

The British instituted an energetic program of reforms, including the building of roads and bridges, the improvement of sanitation, and the rationalization of street plans. A judicial system was established, and land and tax laws were systematized. The garrison was removed to barracks outside the city, reducing the military aspect of the community. In essence, the new regime westernized Lahore, introducing such British necessities as newspapers, an agricultural society, and cricket. The British also showed some interest in the city's past; they restored the Bādshāhī Mosque, which had been used by Ranjit Singh as a powder magazine, to the Muslim population. Lahore seemed to prosper under British rule. In 1854 the first census recorded the population of Lahore at 94,000, and by the end of the nineteenth century this figure had nearly doubled.

The British constructed a number of buildings, many of which are still in use today; the Railway Station (1859) to accommodate this new means of transportation, the Punjab Exhibition Building (1864), the Mayo Hospital (1871), and the Lahore Cathedral (1880) are a few of these. The University of the Punjab was chartered in 1882, making it the oldest university in modern Pakistan. Indeed, much of the social structure of modern Lahore dates to the British reinvention of the city in the second half of the nineteenth century.

In 1940 the Muslim League, a Muslim nationalist group, formally advanced the idea of dividing India into Hindu and Muslim nations. The name "Pakistan" had already been created by Choudhry Rahmat Ali, from an acronym for the Muslim provinces which would form the new nation: *P*unjab, *A*fghan province, *K*ashmir, *S*ind, and Balūchi*stān*. When the British agreed to withdraw from India in 1947, violence broke out between Sikh and Muslim activists. Rioting in Lahore devastated the city, as it soon devastated the nation. Even after the state of Pakistan was created, the Punjab saw a horrifying escalation of bloodshed. Refugees, both Hindu and Muslim, streamed across the country, and more than 1 million people died. For a time the fate of Lahore itself was in doubt, but it was finally assigned to Pakistan.

Today the city serves as the capital of the Punjab province. Sprawling over thirty square miles, it has a population of approximately 3 million. The fortifications that once surrounded the old city have largely been replaced by gardens. A road encircling the remaining rampart gives access, via thirteen gates, to the old city, some of which has managed to survive the upheaval of the centuries. The mosque of Wazīr Khān and the tilework on the north wall of the Lahore Fort give a flavor of the Mughal capital. Also still extant are the Bādshāhī Mosque, Ranjit Singh's mausoleum, the tomb of Jahāngīr, and the Shālīmār Gardens. Newer commercial, industrial, and residential areas have expanded to the south of the old city. Lahore is now an important center of commerce and banking. One-fifth of Pakistan's industries are based there, including its most important, the textile factories. Furthermore, the city is an educational center; in addition to the University of the Punjab, it is home to the Faisal Shaheed University of Engineering and Technology and many other colleges and schools.

Further Reading: *Lahore: Illustrated Views of the 19th Century* by F. S. Aijazuddin (Ahmedabad: Mapin, and Middletown, New Jersey: Grantha, 1991) provides a good historical overview along with a series of annotated color portraits of the city, its structures, and monuments, made throughout the centuries by various artists. Also well illustrated is *Lahore: The City Within* by Samina Quraeshi (Singapore: Concept Media, 1988), which gives more attention to Lahore's cultural heritage and includes color photographs of the modern city and its people.

—Elizabeth Brice

Lhasa (Tibet, Xizang Autonomous Region, China)

Location: In southern Tibet, at the eastern end of the Tibetan Himalayas, elevation 11,975 feet; near the Lhasa River (a tributary of the Brahmaputra, here known as the Tsangpo).

Description: Lhasa is the capital of Tibet, which since 1950 has been occupied by the People's Republic of China. Lhasa first became the capital of Tibet in the seventh century and gained lasting religious importance during the seventeenth century.

Site Office: Tibet Tourism Bureau
Yuanlin Road
Lhasa 850001
Tibet
China
(891) 63 34330

Among the more striking and important features of Lhasa is its inaccessibility . Much of its history has been shaped by the geography of Tibet, which often is called the "roof of the world." Except for a small part of the country in the south at an elevation of 2,000 feet, Tibet is on a plateau that ranges from an elevation at Lhasa of approximately 12,000 feet to high mountain regions of 16,000 to 18,000 feet. Tibet is surrounded on three sides by mountains: some of them, the Himalayas, are the tallest on earth. Vast stretches of this territory are inhospitable, with temperatures that vary greatly, ranging in Lhasa from eighty-five degrees Fahrenheit during the day to minus two degrees Fahrenheit at night. There is hardly any rain or vegetation in these high plateau expanses, and strong winds sweep uninterrupted across the terrain. The region is also sparsely populated, offering little in the way of accommodation to the traveler. Only in the twentieth century were any roads built in Tibet; before that, no wheeled vehicles were used, and travel was undertaken on horseback or mule on narrow paths across huge distances. Owing to these geographical characteristics, most of Tibet's population has been centered in the fertile southern valley of the Brahmaputra River (here called the Tsangpo). In this valley stand Tibet's major monasteries and cities, including Lhasa.

Recorded Tibetan history began in the seventh century with a young king called Songtsen Gampo (c.608–650), who still is hailed as one of Tibet's national heroes. He reigned from 629 to 650, gaining supremacy over the various Tibetan tribes, uniting and establishing Tibet as a force to be reckoned with in Central Asia, even occupying Nepal in 640. His successful demand at the Chinese court in 641 for a Chinese princess to be his wife gives an indication of his stature and the regard in which Tibet was held during his reign. The princess granted to him was Wen Cheng, the daughter of the Tang Dynasty emperor Tai Zong. Songtsen Gampo also took a Nepalese wife named Tritsun, and together these two wives converted him to Buddhism. He is remembered as a religious king who sought to establish Buddhism as the religion of Tibet, supplanting the older Bön religion. He sent a young scholar called Sambhota to India to study Buddhist teachings and to learn Sanskrit, so that on his return he would be able to devise a Tibetan script for the transcription of Buddhist writings. Within only twenty years this new script found widespread application in the writing of laws and reports, as well as in the ever-growing collection of transcribed Buddhist texts.

Songtsen Gampo first made Lhasa the Tibetan capital. On Lhasa's Red Hill, Songtsen Gampo built the first Potala fortress for his two wives. This original Potala later was destroyed to make room for the larger Potala Palace, which still tops the hill. Songtsen Gampo also built the Jokhang Temple and the Ramoche Temple to house the sacred Buddha statues his wives had brought with them. To the pilgrims coming to Lhasa, the Jokhang Temple is the most important building, as it is the spiritual center of Tibet. This temple houses the Sakyamuni Buddha, brought to Tibet by Songtsen Gampo's Chinese wife and revered as Tibet's holiest of holies. The oldest parts of the temple were built by craftsmen from Tibet, Nepal, China, and Kashmir. It is constructed concentrically, with an open cloister featuring a row of prayer wheels all around it. From this cloister a dark, narrow passage leads into the main hall, which is surrounded by numerous smaller chapels. At the back of the main hall, behind statues to Padmasambhava, Sakyamuni, and Chenrezi, is the shrine containing the Sakyamuni Buddha. Pilgrims coming to Lhasa would circumambulate along the Lingkor, the outer pilgrim road encircling the entire old city. An inner pilgrimage route directly in front of the Jokhang is called the Barkhor.

The first form of Buddhism introduced to Tibet drew from two differing strands, represented by Songtsen Gampo's two wives. The first was the Indian tradition and the second the Chinese Chan Buddhist faith (which became known in Japan as Zen). Early Tibetan Buddhism also incorporated elements of the much older Bön religion, with its more demonic and magical overtones, and embraced aspects of Indian Tantrism. During the reign of Songtsen Gampo's descendant Trisong Detsen (ruled 755–797), the two principal strands of Tibetan Buddhism were seen to conflict with one another. Trisong Detsen ordered a debate to be held at Tibet's first monastery, Samye, which he had founded in 779. The debate was attended by Chinese and Indian Buddhist scholars—among them the great Indian tantric mystic Padmasambhava—who were each made to defend the validity of their beliefs. In the end, the Indian version prevailed,

Panorama of Potala Palace, Lhasa
Photo courtesy of Consulate General of China, Chicago

and Chinese Buddhism was banned from Tibet; even so, some elements of Chan Buddhism remained in the uniquely Tibetan mix of Buddhism that had evolved by then. A mural inside the Potala Palace commemorates Trisong Detsen's debate.

A noted military commander, Trisong Detsen further strengthened the Tibetan presence in Central Asia, sending his armies as far away as Samarkand and Chang'an (modern Xian), then the capital of China. His great enthusiasm for Buddhism, however, paved the way for more and more authority in secular affairs to be granted to the ever-increasing numbers of monks. When Trisong Detsen's grandson Ralpachen came to power in 815, he relinquished all statesmanship to a monk. This move cost Ralpachen his life: his brother Lang Darma murdered him in 836, became king himself, ousted the monk who had assumed all secular authority from Ralpachen and, as a strong supporter of the old Bön religion, caused the Buddhist monasteries to be closed and the monks and scholars to be persecuted. This radical reversal of the work of both Songtsen Gampo and Trisong Detsen led to the collapse not only of the Buddhist faith in Tibet but of the strong, united country these men had forged through their military expertise. Following Lang Darma's own murder in 842, Tibet disintegrated into a region of warring factions, ushering in an extended period of lawlessness and disunity.

Tibet's political disarray continued for several centuries, and, accordingly, Lhasa's importance languished. Nonetheless, Buddhist missionaries and scholars began to return to Tibet in 978. In 1042 Atisha, a great Indian teacher of Mahayana Buddhism, arrived in Tibet and began his missionary activities. In his wake, Buddhist monasteries were founded in western and central Tibet, notably Reting Monastery (1057) and Sakya Monastery (1071). The renewed interest in Buddhism took the form of several sects, each of which supported slightly different interpretations of the doctrine. The most important of these sects during this period were the Red Hats and the Black Hats. Sakya Monastery became the most powerful of the new monasteries: when Tibet was forced to pay tribute to the Mongols under Genghis Khan in 1207, the abbot of Sakya converted the Mongols to Buddhism, paving the way for the later influence of Tibetan lamas at the Mongolian court.

Tibet's fortunes took a turn for the better with the birth of Tsong-khapa (1357–1419). Another of Tibet's national heroes, whose image can be seen in many monasteries all over Tibet, this scholar founded a Buddhist sect that came to be known as the Gelugspa, or Yellow Hats; in time, the Yellow Hats became the dominant sect in Tibetan Buddhism. In 1409 Tsong-khapa founded the first Yellow Hat establishment, Ganden Monastery just outside Lhasa. Tsong-khapa's disciples founded the huge monasteries of Drepung (1416) and Sera (1419), thereby completing in the immediate vicinity of Lhasa a triumvirate of Tibet's great seats of learning. The power and appeal of the Yellow Hat sect lay in the reformist spirit of its founder, who felt that the rivalries among the sects—especially the resentment toward special privileges accorded Sakya Monastery under Mongol domination—were detracting in large part from the fundamental teachings of Buddhism. Thus, for the monks at Ganden and the later Yellow Hat monasteries, Tsong-khapa insisted on celibacy, strict morality, and dedication to a purified doctrine following the teachings of Atisha.

The Yellow Hat sect provided a line of abbots who later became known as the Dalai Lamas. A lama is simply a very scholarly and learned monk, but the title *Talé* (Dalai), meaning "ocean," as in "ocean of wisdom," was bestowed upon the Tibetan spiritual leader by the Mongols. The First Dalai Lama, a disciple of Tsong-khapa named Gedün Truppa (1391–1474), founded Tashilhunpo Monastery in Shigatse in 1447, acting as its first abbot. He and his successor, Gedün Gyatso (1475–1542), received the "Dalai" designation posthumously, because it was not until 1578 that the Mongol prince Altan Khan conferred the title on Tashilhunpo's third abbot, Sonam Gyatso (1543–88). Sonam Gyatso was considered to be the reincarnation of his predecessor, who, in turn, had been chosen as the reincarnation of the first abbot. Owing to this lineage, the first lama actually to use the honorific title is known as the Third Dalai Lama.

It was not until the seventeenth century that religion and the administration of the country became uniquely and inseparably mixed. One of the most important leaders was the great Fifth Dalai Lama, Ngawang Lozang Gyatso (1617–82). The Fifth pronounced himself, his four predecessors, and all future Dalai Lamas—as well as the revered king Songtsen Gampo—to be reincarnations of Chenrezi, the bodhisattva of compassion, giving the rulers of Tibet, as the Dalai Lamas had by then become, the status of god-kings. The reign of the Fifth Dalai Lama saw the resurgence of Lhasa's fortunes, as well as the reunification of Tibet and the flowering of Buddhism once more.

Politically, Tibet developed a special relationship with China beginning with the installation of the Qing Dynasty in 1644. From then on, it was important to the Chinese to maintain good relations with the Tibetans, owing to the prestige of the Dalai Lama among the Mongols, who posed a constant threat to the Chinese Empire.

Many of Lhasa's surviving monuments were built during the rule of the Fifth Dalai Lama. Most important is the landmark of Lhasa, the Potala Palace, built between 1645 and 1693. This vast structure—with more than 1,000 rooms, thirteen stories high (330 feet), 1,310 feet east to west, and 1,150 feet north to south—rises more than 1,000 feet atop the Red Hill, above the valley floor and the rest of the city. The sheer bulk of the Potala is awe-inspiring. The sloping stone walls are an average of ten feet thick, although they are even thicker at the base, with copper added, to protect against earthquakes. The lake behind the hill formed in the pit left after great quantities of earth were removed to be used for mortar in the construction of the palace. The Potala consists of a Red Palace and a White Palace, separated by a small yellow portion, where the huge religious banners called *thankas* were stored when they were not rolled over the vast external walls of the palace on ceremonial occasions. The Red Palace is the sacred part of the Potala, in which the large burial tombs, or stupas, of eight of the Dalai Lamas are kept. These wooden stupas of some twenty feet in height are thickly covered with gold into which precious stones and large amounts of turquoise have been mounted. The largest of these stupas, in the West Chapel, is that of the Fifth Dalai Lama. Rising to forty-eight feet, this monument is coated with 8,200 pounds of thickly laid gold studded with gems. An extensive library of ancient Buddhist scriptures houses texts on long, thin pieces of paper that have been wrapped in yellow silk and placed between two boards for storage. The White Palace is the secular administrative center, containing the governmental offices and living quarters of the officers, a printing house, and a seminary.

The upper stories of the Potala are built of wood, and the upper exterior walls are made from fine twigs wedged into the walls so that only the ends are visible from the outside. These are then painted a dark rust-red, the same particularly holy color used for the Red Palace. This same twig technique and the color also can be seen on the Jokhang Temple. The wood-framed windows of the Potala are the typical trapezoid shape found in traditional buildings, whether holy or secular, all over Tibet.

Chokpori (Iron) Hill, one of central Tibet's four sacred mountains, became the site of a famous seventeenth-century monastic medical school. As well, the Jokhang Temple, enlarged seven times since its construction a millenium earlier, received its final embellishments in 1660 under the patronage of the Fifth Dalai Lama. Not far from Lhasa is the Norbulingka, or Summer Palace, which was built by the Seventh Dalai Lama in 1755; each successive Dalai Lama added more rooms or buildings to this complex.

In the eighteenth century the Chinese Empire was able to strengthen its influence over Tibetan affairs, especially when Chinese troops were called upon by Lhasa to help quell a civil war in 1728 and further civil disturbances in 1750; the Tibetans also relied on the Chinese to repel a Gurkha invasion from Nepal in 1792. These incidents caused the Chinese emperor to send two Ambans, or representatives, to Lhasa, who were to speak for Chinese interests in Tibet: they were not, however, given any administrative powers and simply were to be consulted by the Tibetan government on matters that might have an impact on the Chinese Empire.

An important effect of Qing involvement in Tibet was the closing of the country's borders to foreigners in

1792. This effectively sealed off the country from normal trade or missionary contact with individuals, and politically Tibet tried hard throughout the nineteenth century to avoid the pressures of its neighbors to enter into treaties and trade agreements. By the mid–nineteenth century, however, Manchu power in China had declined, and the Chinese Army was unable to assist Tibet in its wars against Ladakh (1842) or Nepal (1858).

The Thirteenth Dalai Lama, Thupten Gyatso (1876–1933), was a great statesman who valiantly tried to open up Tibet to the curious outside world; complicating this effort was the need for the Dalai Lama to withstand the pressures of international politics, which at the beginning of the twentieth century saw in Tibet a buffer between the rival powers of British India, Russia, and China. By 1904 Tibet's isolation was disrupted by a British expedition into the region under Colonel Francis E. Younghusband, who reached Lhasa and forced the Tibetans to sign a trade treaty. By 1906 the Chinese and the British signed a treaty concerning Tibet without involving the Tibetans; this treaty, which effectively recognized Chinese suzerainty over Tibet, encouraged the Chinese to send troops to Lhasa to assert their control over the country, and in 1910 the Dalai Lama fled to India. However, Chinese occupation was short-lived, as the Chinese revolution in 1911–12 allowed the Tibetans to repel the Chinese occupying force and reestablish their independence, which they maintained until 1951.

In 1951 the Chinese communists reached Lhasa, declared Tibet "liberated" from its feudal past, and announced the country's new status as an autonomous region of the People's Republic of China. The Potala Palace remained the seat of Tibetan government (although the fourteenth Dalai Lama moved to the Norbulingka, which he found far more comfortable and convenient than the dark, damp Potala) until the Chinese occupation forces reacted to an uprising among the Tibetans in 1959 with fierce reprisals, forcing the present Dalai Lama to escape to Dharmsala in India. (In the mid–1990s he lived there with other Tibetan refugees, heading a Tibetan government in exile.) During the retaliation of 1959, the Chinese destroyed the seventeenth-century medical school that occupied Chokpori Hill. The Chinese since have crowned the sacred mountain with a tall antenna.

During the Cultural Revolution of 1966–75, the Chinese destroyed many more of Tibet's sacred buildings and monuments. But even the ruthless Chinese Red Guards did not dare to touch the golden, jewel-encrusted Sakyamuni Buddha in the Jokhang Temple. However, the Jokhang's outer pilgrim route, the Lingkor, has been largely destroyed by the Chinese in order to make way for New Lhasa, a city springing up around the ancient capital consisting of administrative buildings, department stores, schools, hospitals, and housing for Chinese officials.

Since the early 1980s, when Chinese authorities allowed a religious revival in Tibet, pilgrims once again can be seen slowly circumambulating the Jokhang along the inner circle, the Barkhor, in a clockwise direction as decreed by the Buddhist faith, often prostrating themselves at every step. The Barkhor also is packed with traders selling their wares, from daggers and traditional pieces of jewelry to prayer wheels, prayer flags, and sutras. The Barkhor remains largely intact, although in 1985 part of this inner circle was destroyed in order to open up a plaza in front of the temple, from which a wide avenue leads toward New Lhasa.

Each of the three great monasteries surrounding Lhasa—Ganden, Drepung, and Sera—is once more a working monastery, although at a far-reduced capacity than before the Chinese invasion of 1951, when typically 12,000 monks lived and worked in each. At the Potala Palace—now a state museum—feeble electric bulbs and a multitude of yak butter candles illuminate the rich red, vibrant blue, bright yellow, and gold of the decorated woodwork and the intricate ornamentation of the shrines and stupas. Many of the walls are decorated with murals displaying in great detail the important events of Tibetan history. Even with the sprawl of New Lhasa, the Potala Palace can be seen for miles around: on the approaches to Lhasa, pilgrims on their way to the Jokhang Temple can be seen prostrating themselves on the ground in the knowledge that their pilgrimage has nearly reached its zenith.

Further Reading: Hugh Edward Richardson's *A Short History of Tibet* (New York: Dutton, 1962; revised as *Tibet and Its History,* Boston: Shambhala, 1984) gives an excellent introduction to Tibetan history from its beginnings until the Chinese invasion and subsequent Tibetan uprising in 1959. David Snellgrove and Hugh Richardson's *Cultural History of Tibet* (New York: Praeger, and London: Weidenfeld and Nicholson, 1968; revised edition, Boulder, Colorado: Prajna, and London: Routledge, 1980) is another standard work on Tibet's cultural evolution. John Snelling has written a comprehensive introduction to Buddhism entitled *The Buddhist Handbook: A Complete Guide to Buddhist Schools, Teaching, Practice, and History* (London: Century, 1987; Rochester, Vermont: Inner Traditions, 1991). Tibet has fascinated travelers for centuries, and some of the most evocative books on Lhasa and Tibet have been written by such visitors. These include Alexandra David-Neel, a nineteenth-century Parisian, who wrote *My Journey to Lhasa* (London: Heinemann, and New York: Harper, 1927) and *Magic and Mystery in Tibet* (London: Lane, 1931; New York: Kendall, 1932); Heinrich Harrer, a German soldier in World War II, wrote *Seven Years in Tibet* (London: Hart-Davis, 1953; New York: Dutton, 1954); and Giuseppe Tucci contributed *To Lhasa and Beyond* (Oxford: Oxford University Press, 1956). For the more recent history of Tibet, the autobiography of the fourteenth Dalai Lama (Bstan-dzin-rgya-mtsho), *Freedom in Exile* (New York: Harper Collins, and London: Hodder and Stoughton, 1990), gives fascinating insight into the dramatic impact of the twentieth century on the Tibetan people. *Tibet: The Facts*, a report compiled by the nonpolitical Scientific Buddhist Association in London for the United Nations Subcommission on Human Rights in 1984 (second revised edition, Dharmsala, India: Tibetan Young Buddhist Association, 1990), is essential, though horrifying, reading for anyone interested in the fate of Tibet today.

—Hilary Collier Sy-Quia

Luang Prabang (Luang Prabang, Laos)

Location: In northern Laos on the banks of the Mekong River, at the confluence of its tributary the Nam Khan. The city is the capital of the province of the same name.

Description: Formerly the capital of the Lao kingdom of Lan Xang, from the mid–fourteenth to the mid–sixteenth centuries; later the royal capital of independent Laos. This quiet and graceful city still preserves the finest examples of northern Lao Buddhist architecture.

Contact: Lao National Tourism (Lanatour)
8/2 Lane Xang Avenue
P.O. Box 5211
Vientiane
Laos
216671 or 212013

The ancient city of Luang Prabang has been known by three different names in the course of its history. The earliest, Meuang Sua, dated probably from the eleventh century. The site was renamed Xieng Dong Xieng Thong after becoming the center of the first localized Lao kingdom on the upper Mekong in the thirteenth century; it retained that name during the two centuries it was capital of the extensive Lao Kingdom of Lan Xang. When the capital was moved to Vientiane, Xieng Dong Xieng Thong was renamed Luang Prabang, meaning "City of the Lord (Buddha) of Fine Gold," in honor of the famous Phra Bang Buddha image that was the palladium of both the kingdom and the city, and is still the most revered Buddha image in Laos today.

The original inhabitants of the region of Luang Prabang were the Khamu, a people speaking an Austroasiatic language related to Cambodian (Khmer). They may have formed a small principality, although the evidence is inconclusive. If so, it was probably under the influence of the Mon kingdom of Haripunjaya to the west, centered on what is now the northern Thai city of Lamphun. The Mon, who also spoke an Austroasiatic language, were ardent Theravada Buddhists, and Mon monks were instrumental in spreading their beliefs throughout mainland Southeast Asia.

In the Lao chronicles, the formation of the earliest principality in the region of Luang Prabang is shrouded in myth. The territories presided over by fifteen "snake kings" are said to have been consolidated into a small kingdom by two brother hermits. It was this kingdom of Meuang Sua that was eventually seized by Lao warriors who began moving into the area from the northeast, probably as early as the tenth century. Their leader, according to the Lao chronicles, was Khun Lo, eldest son of Khun Borom, the mythical common ancestor of all the Tai peoples (including the Lao, the Thai of Thailand, and the Shan of Burma).

An alternative account inserts two other dynasties before Khun Lo, one founded by a sandalwood merchant (possibly Mon) from Vientiane, the other by a shadowy figure known as Khun Sua (Lord of Sua), who may have been Khamu. All we can be sure of is that Khamu, Mon, and Lao all contributed in some way to establishing the early kingdom of Meuang Sua. The name itself is a combination of the Lao term *meuang,* referring to a political-administrative entity of variable size, and *Sua,* an Indian word cognate with Java, which indicates Buddhist or Hindu influence.

By the thirteenth century we are on firmer historical ground, for by then a Lao dynasty claiming descent from Khun Lo was ruling a kingdom the name of which had been changed to Xieng Dong Xieng Thong. This is a purely Lao name probably referring to dual towns *(xieng)* or palaces presided over by the king and his viceroy *(uparat).*

Luang Prabang was probably chosen as the administrative center of a northern Lao kingdom because of its topography. Theravada Buddhists traditionally believed that a parallelism existed between the divine macrocosm, the abode of gods such as Indra and Brahma, and the earthly microcosm. Thus just as the holy Mount Meru stood at the center of the divine realm, so a sacred mountain should stand at the center of any earthly kingdom. At Luang Prabang, Mount (Phu) Si rises in the angle between the River Khan and the Mekong, with the city built around its base. Its steep summit is crowned by a stupa, and on the slope of the hill a depression in the rock is revered as a footprint of the Buddha, both indications of its holy status.

Early in the fourteenth century, a young prince (and probably also his father) were expelled from Xieng Dong Xieng Thong, either because the father had seduced one of the king's wives, or because he posed a threat to the throne. The young prince, Fa Ngum, was brought up at the court of Angkor, capital of the Kingdom of Cambodia. When he came of age, Fa Ngum married a Khmer princess and at the head of a Khmer army set out to reconquer his patrimony. His victorious march north succeeded in unifying the petty Lao principalities of the central Mekong, and by the time he seized Xieng Dong Xieng Thong from his uncle in 1354, he had cobbled together the first extensive Lao kingdom.

Fa Ngum named his kingdom Lan Xang Hom Khao (the Kingdom of a Million Elephants and the White Parasol). In so doing he was making a statement about his military might, for elephants were the engines of war in Southeast Asian armies. A white parasol was the traditional symbol of kingship. Until the Lao monarchy was abolished in 1975, the king was always shaded in public by a multitiered white umbrella. For the next three and one-half centuries, the King-

Temple of Xieng Thong, Luang Prabang
Photo courtesy of Martin Stuart-Fox

dom of Lan Xang was a powerful state in mainland Southeast Asia, capable of holding its own against its neighbors: the northern Tai Kingdom of Lan Na (A Million Ricefields), and the Siamese Kingdom of Ayutthaya, Cambodia, and Vietnam.

Fa Ngum and his successors adorned their capital with fine palaces and imposing Buddhist temples. According to the Lao chronicles, Fa Ngum's Cambodian queen was responsible for bringing the Phra Bang Buddha image from Cambodia to Laos. Fa Ngum, however, preferred to worship the powerful spirits *(phi)* of his ancestors. Initially, the Phra Bang got no farther than Vientiane; not until 1513, 160 years later, was it finally installed in a newly constructed temple in Xieng Dong Xieng Thong.

The Phra Bang is a fine example of northern Tai sculpture, although the popular Story of the Phra Bang claims it was cast in Sri Lanka and miraculously transported to Cambodia before being brought to Laos. Cast in bronze and then gilded, the standing image is 32 inches high and weighs 95.7 pounds. For the Lao it has always been the most sacred and powerful in its protective properties of all Buddha images.

Magical potency and the symbolism of power were of great significance among the kingdoms of Southeast Asia. Lan Xang was held together by royal patronage, feudal oaths of allegiance, and payment of tribute. Rulers of constituent principalities *(meuang)* had to make the arduous journey every three years to Xieng Dong Xieng Thong to present their tribute in person and renew their oaths of loyalty to the king. In time, princely rulers came to reside at the capital, where they were appointed to administrative or ceremonial office at court, while their *meuang* were administered by the *uparat,* or second ruler.

Among the most important symbols of kingship and power was possession of a white elephant. Any white elephant captured was royal property, although the capturer would be handsomely rewarded. It was a white elephant "the color of taro" (an edible white root) that provoked a devastating war between Lan Xang and Vietnam in 1469. According to the Lao chronicles, Emperor Le Thanh Tong of Vietnam, hearing of this wondrous animal, asked to be sent a sample of its hair to verify its color for himself. To insult the emperor, however, the Lao prince of Xieng Khuang on the Plain of Jars replaced the hair with a morsel of dung, which so incensed the emperor that he declared war.

Five columns of troops, elephants, and horses invaded Lan Xang. Taken unawares and outnumbered, Lao armies fought valiantly but were unable to prevent the fall of Xieng Dong Xieng Thong to the invaders. The elderly Lao king fled down the Mekong while his capital was looted and destroyed. Only the efforts of his son succeeded in rallying the shattered Lao forces, calling up reinforcements, and driving out the Vietnamese. Monks and citizens together, we are told, then set about the task of rebuilding the city and restoring the five most important monasteries.

The reign of King Visulrat (1501–20) marked a high point in the history of Luang Prabang. The king ordered the transfer of the Phra Bang from Vientiane and built a magnificent new temple, Vat Visun, to receive it. The great image hall *(bot)* stood until 1887, and the uniquely shaped stupa, known to local inhabitants as the "watermelon stupa," remained standing until 1914. Both have since been reconstructed. King Visulrat extended his royal patronage to other monasteries, and learned monks from throughout the Tai world were invited to take up residence at Xieng Dong Xieng Thong. Patronage of the Sangha (the Buddhist monastic order) was beneficial to the king as well; the teachings of the monks legitimated the kingship. According to their doctrines, the king had the right to rule because of his superior *karma* (moral merit) acquired in previous lifetimes.

Two developments, both evident by the mid–sixteenth century, had a profound impact on the fortunes of Luang Prabang. The first was the steady shift in power and population toward the south. Lao settlers had been moving south down the Mekong Valley to the vicinity of Champasak, and also onto the Khorat plateau (now northeastern Thailand), cutting the jungle and establishing new villages. Xieng Dong Xieng Thong was no longer the center of the Lao world: Vientiane was in a better position to extract tribute and recruit troops from these newer settlements.

The second development was the advent of the Burmese. In 1548 the great Burmese conqueror Tabinshwehti demanded that the Siamese king of Ayutthaya hand over his three white elephants. This was no less than a declaration of war, for to have agreed would have been to accept Burmese hegemony. The Burmese invaded but were forced to withdraw. Ten years later they succeeded in reducing the northern Tai principalities to tributary status. The threat to the Lao kingdom was obvious.

In 1560 King Xetthathirat of Lan Xang transferred his capital from Xieng Dong Xieng Thong to Vientiane, farther from the Burmese, more defensible, and better positioned for the recruitment of armies. Xetthathirat took with him two sacred images—the Phra Kaeo (Emerald Buddha, now in Bangkok) and the Phra Saek Kham—but left the Phra Bang in the city he renamed Luang Prabang in its honor. In order partly to assuage local pride, partly to retain local loyalty, the king also ordered construction of what is to this day the most beautiful of the temples of Luang Prabang, the royal Vat Xieng Thong, whose graceful curving multiple roofs make its image hall the finest example of sixteenth-century northern Lao architecture.

Transfer of the capital reduced Luang Prabang to the status of a regional *meuang*. Within less than a century, its population had shrunk to as few as 10,000, less than a quarter that of Vientiane. In its heyday during the first half of the sixteenth century, it probably counted at least three times as many people, not including the nearby villages where inhabitants wove silk and other fabrics, worked silver, and made paper, pottery, and other products for the court.

The Kingdom of Lan Xang was at its apogee during the long reign of King Surinyavongsa (1637–95). After his death, succession disputes led within two decades to division into three weakened kingdoms of Vientiane, Luang Prabang, and Champasak, each claiming the mantle of Lan Xang. During the struggle for power, the Phra Bang was carried off to Vientiane, and the kings of Luang Prabang were unable to secure its return.

Within less than a century, all three Lao kingdoms had been forced to accept the suzerainty of Siam (Thailand). In part this resulted from the division of the Lao world, but it was also caused by the changing balance of power that had been occurring throughout much of the sixteenth and seventeenth centuries between the maritime and inland states of mainland Southeast Asia. Greatly increased trade with several European powers and the purchase of new military technology gave the Siamese and Burmese an advantage that the landlocked Lao kingdoms lacked. During all this time Luang Prabang was so remote that, so far as we know, no European merchant ever reached it.

The early nineteenth century marked the last attempt by the Lao king Anuvong of Vientiane to throw off Siamese suzerainty. But the Lao world remained divided, and the king of Luang Prabang failed to lend his assistance. In 1827–28 the Siamese sacked and destroyed Vientiane, a fate Luang Prabang escaped. In 1839, in recognition of its loyalty, the Siamese returned the Phra Bang to Luang Prabang.

The city by then retained but a shadow of its former greatness. As its tax base diminished, its monasteries began to fall into disrepair, and by 1861 when the French naturalist Henri Mouhot became the first known European to visit the city, its population had shrunk to a mere 7,000 or 8,000.

Mouhot was charmed by Luang Prabang, however. "The Lake of Geneva does not present scenes more beautiful than many here on the river," he wrote home in one of his last letters. Tragically, Mouhot died of malaria soon after setting out again on his explorations. His grave, not far from the city, was located by the French Mekong Expedition a few years later, and a commemorative stone has since been erected.

By the 1880s the French were eager to extend their Indochinese empire west of Vietnam. Seizing on the relative weakness of Siam, they secured the posting of Auguste Pavie as consul in Luang Prabang. Within months, a bandit force of disgruntled upland Tai and Yunnanese descended on the city and sacked it. The royal palace and several monasteries were destroyed, including the ancient image hall of Vat Visun. Pavie was instrumental in helping King Unkham flee his burning capital.

This gave the French the opportunity they had been looking for. Six years later, after a bit of gunboat diplomacy, the French established a protectorate over most of the territories of present-day Laos. Although Vientiane became the administrative capital of French Laos, Luang Prabang was the seat of the only remaining recognized Lao monarch. A new palace was built in semi-European style. The Phra Bang, which had been saved from the sack of the city, was installed in Vat Mai Temple while Vat Visun and other monasteries were reconstructed.

The French graced the city with several colonial ochre-colored brick-and-stucco villas and offices, a couple of schools, and a hospital. Chinese merchants were encouraged to establish a commercial center. But during fifty years of French rule, Luang Prabang remained a remote backwater, frozen in time. Not until the 1930s was a road constructed from Vientiane, along which a few hardy tourists managed to make their way.

After World War II, which had little impact on the city, the king of Luang Prabang was declared the King of Laos. Among his first acts was to remove the Phra Bang to the palace for safekeeping. The intention was to build a new royal *vat* to house it, as the Emerald Buddha is in the precincts of the royal palace in Bangkok, but the project was never carried through.

During the First Indochina War between the French and the Vietnamese communist movement and their Lao and Cambodian allies, Luang Prabang was twice threatened when communist forces drove to within a few miles of the city. On both occasions, however, the citizens were unperturbed: a highly respected blind monk had already prophesied that no harm would come to the city, and he was right.

After the Kingdom of Laos obtained full independence from France in 1953, Luang Prabang remained the royal capital, for the king preferred his more intimate palace there to the much larger palace constructed for official occasions in the administrative capital of Vientiane.

During the Vietnam (Second Indochina) War that followed the breakdown of the second Lao coalition government and devasted much of the country between 1963 and 1973, Luang Prabang again escaped damage. Because it was the royal capital, communist forces spared it attack, although they did twice destroy fighter planes at the airport. Several new government and commercial buildings were erected, some with American funding, but the charm of the old parts of the city was preserved.

With the seizure of power by the communist Pathet Lao and declaration of the Lao People's Democratic Republic in December 1975, the 600-year-old Lao monarchy was abolished. The last Lao king, Savangvatthana, initially remained in Luang Prabang, but in May 1977 he was arrested and banished to remote Vieng Xai, near the northeastern frontier with Vietnam, where he subsequently died. The palace became a national museum, with the Phra Bang as its most prized exhibit.

Luang Prabang thus escaped the destruction of three wars between 1940 and 1975. The monasteries rebuilt after the sack of 1887, or restored during the French period, have been lovingly preserved. While some religious architecture is more modern (notably offices and accommodation for monks), the many monasteries of Luang Prabang have preserved not only their original architectural styles but also their peaceful ambience. Nowhere do the traditional northern Lao styles of both religious and secular architecture blend so perfectly for the strolling tourist. Luang Prabang has a charm and tranquility that are uniquely Lao.

Further Reading: No history either of the city or province of Luang Prabang exists in English, nor does any satisfactory general history of Laos. For the history of Lan Xang see the rather dated *History of Laos* by Sila Viravong (New York: Paragon, 1964) or the brief overview in *Laos: Keystone of Indochina* by Arthur Dommen (Boulder: Westview, 1985). A brief historical introduction is provided in Thao Boun Souk's *Louang Phrabang: 600 ans d'art bouddhique lao* (Vientiane: Vithagna, 1974).

—Martin Stuart-Fox

Lucknow (Uttar Pradesh, India)

Location: In northern India, in the state of Uttar Pradesh (of which it is capital), about 105 miles from the Nepalese border and 46 miles northeast of Cawnpore (Kānpur).

Description: Capital of the nabobs of the province of Oudh in the eighteenth and nineteenth centuries, and as such a center of late Mughal culture, with many buildings from that era; besieged at length in 1857, during the Indian Mutiny; in 1916, site of the signing of the Lucknow Pact between Hindu and Muslim supporters of Indian self-government.

Site Office: Directorate of Uttar Pradesh Tourism
Chitrahar Building
3 Naval Kishore Road
Lucknow, Uttar Pradesh
India
(22) 8349, (22) 5165, (22) 1776, or (22) 5555

Lucknow today is not a particularly attractive city, although it is a busy commercial and political center as the capital of Uttar Pradesh. It enjoyed its grandest period as the residence of the nabobs of the province of Oudh, Muslim rulers who controlled this section of India after the Mughal Empire began to decline and fragment in the early eighteenth century. The nabobs moved their capital here from Faizābād in 1775, during the reign of Asuf-'ud-Dawlah. Although he developed Lucknow as it stands today, the site was not totally uninhabited before 1775. Some ancient pottery fragments have been discovered in the vicinity, and a noble family built a fortress here in the late thirteenth century. 'Ālamgīr (Aurangzeb), the last of the great Mughal emperors, who ruled from 1658 to 1707, built a mosque here on the right bank of the Gomati River.

The province of Oudh has a long history. The region was once the ancient kingdom of Kośala, which had its capital at Saketa (Ayodhyā). The area later came under a succession of rulers, including the Guptas, the Delhi sultans, and the Mughals. In 1724 Saadat Khan, who governed Oudh for the Mughal Empire, asserted his independence and founded the line of the nabobs of Oudh. Oudh lost much of its power after the British defeated Nabob Shujā-'ud-Dawlah at the Battle of Buxar in 1764, but ten years later Oudh, with British assistance, conquered new territories and regained prestige. The British supported the nabobs of Oudh because they saw the territory as an important buffer against the Marāṭhās, who posed one of the greatest threats to British control of India at this time. Against this background Asuf-'ud-Dawlah, who became nabob in 1775, moved his capital to Lucknow, which he intended to make a city of great architecture and gracious living.

Some of the buildings of Lucknow are impressive indeed, while others are simply garish, and in any case the nabobs' building program drained their treasury. Probably the greatest structure built by Asuf-'ud-Dawlah is a mausoleum called the Bara Imambara (Great Imambara), built in 1784 a few hundred yards south of 'Ālamgīr's mosque. The nabob conceived the mausoleum as a means to create work for the people, who had been devastated by a great famine that year. It is built of clay and brick, with wood used for ornamentation, and has no beams or pillars; it is supported by weight distribution alone. Its central hall is one of the largest vaulted galleries anywhere. The ground floor has three chambers; Asuf-'ud-Dawlah and the building's architect are entombed in one of them. The upper floor, reached by an external stairway, is laid out as a labyrinth. In the building's courtyard is a mosque with two towering minarets; the mosque is off limits to non-Muslims. Nearby is another great architectural monument, the Rumi Darwaza (Turkish Gate), a copy of one in İstanbul. It also was built in 1784 and complements the mausoleum well. A British journalist once wrote that the gate "recalls Kublai Khan's Xanadu."

Another project, planned by Asuf-'ud-Dawlah but completed by his successor Saadat Ali Khan, was a pleasure palace, completed in 1800 and taken over by the British in 1856 for use as the residency, or headquarters, of the British administrators of the area. Later to play an important role in the Indian Mutiny, the building originally was notable for its design, including a network of underground chambers that provided escape from the summer heat. Nearby are the stone tombs of Saadat Ali Khan and his wife, Begum Mursheedzadi.

Saadat Ali Khan died in 1814; he proved to be the last of the Oudh nabobs with any great ability for governing. He had given up some of his autonomy to the British East India Company, ceding territories to the British in exchange for promises of military aid, thus making Oudh essentially a British protectorate. He was a reasonably capable administrator, however, in contrast to his successors, who were lazy and self-indulgent. Despite these shortcomings, the nabobs continued to erect many lavish buildings in Lucknow, among them the Chattar Manzil (Umbrella Palaces), royal pavilions built in the 1820s; the Moti Mahal (Pearl Palace), originally built by Saadat Ali Khan but expanded by his son Ghāzī-'ud-Dīn Haidar; Ghāzī's tomb, the Shāh Najaf Imambara, noted for its extensive interior ornamentation; the Hussainabad Imambara, built in 1837 by Nabob Muhammad Alī Shāh as a mausoleum for himself and his family (like the Bara Imambara, it also was a famine relief project); and the Kaisarbargh Palace, built between 1848 and 1850 for Nabob Wajid Alī Shāh.

All this construction led the British writer Rudyard Kipling to write in his novel *Kim* that "no city— except for Bombay, the queen of all—was more beautiful in her garish style than Lucknow." In *Kim,* Kipling's eponymous hero

The Bara Imambara, Lucknow
Photo courtesy of Air India Library, New York

attended La Martiniere's School, which exists in fact just outside Lucknow. The school originally was an estate called Constantia, built for a Frenchman named Claude Martin, who served as an intermediary between the British and the nabobs of Oudh. It was unfinished at the time of his death in 1800, but his will stipulated that it be completed and turned into a private school. He is entombed in the basement of the school, which is still in operation.

Lucknow at this time gained renown as a cultural center, for the nabobs of Oudh also were noted for their patronage of the arts. Lucknow developed distinctive forms of dance, music, poetry, and calligraphy. The particular eating habits of the nabobs also led to the evolution of a regional cuisine, still noted for rich desserts and such dishes as meat and vegetables baked in sealed clay pots. Additionally, the city was famed for its silks, perfumes, and jewelry.

Still, the nabobs' poor governance of their territories continued, leading the British to annex Oudh in 1856. Lord Dalhousie, the British governor general, found semiautonomous Indian regions troublesome and believed centralized administration to be the key to British financial and military security in India. He formulated a policy by which Britain could annex any territory upon the ruler's death if there was no direct male heir, or any territory that had been subject to continual mismanagement. The British used the latter reason to justify their takeover of Oudh and deposition of Wajid Alī Shāh. They sent him to a palace in Calcutta and provided him with a generous annual pension—£120,000. The nabob is said to have been so engrossed in a game of chess that he failed to attend to his duties even as British soldiers marched into Lucknow. This story formed the basis of Prem Chand's novel, *The Chess Players,* which was made into a film by the great

Indian director Satyajit Ray in 1977. Prem Chand attributed Lucknow's fall to its frivolity: "small and big, rich and poor, were alike dedicated to sensual joys. One would be devoted to song and dance; another would be enjoying the fumes of opium."

Dalhousie's takeover of Oudh and other territories, along with the general British insenstivity to Hindu and Muslim religious practices and reluctance to treat Indians as social equals, led to discontent that culminated in the uprising known as the Indian Mutiny of 1857–58. The mutiny, a rebellion of Indian troops serving under British commanders, was to have particularly tragic consquences for Lucknow. The immediate pretext for the mutiny was the issuing of rifle cartridges that the Indians believed to be greased with the fat of cows, sacred to Hindus, or pigs, forbidden to Muslims. Troops across India refused to use the cartridges (which needed to be bitten off before firing) and also took stronger actions, such as killing their officers and those officers' wives and children. On May 1, 1857, an Indian regiment at Lucknow refused to use the offending cartridges. Sir Henry Lawrence, the chief British commissioner at Lucknow, quickly ordered the troops disarmed and the residency fortified. As outbreaks of rebellion continued around Oudh in May and June, Lawrence gathered all members of the Lucknow British community, along with the Indians who supported them, into the residency compound. There were a total of 3,000 people within the compound when it was attacked by the mutineers on the night of June 30.

A long and miserable siege ensued. Lawrence was mortally wounded within the first few days. Food and medical supplies were scarce; surgeons had to perform amputations without chloroform. Disease was rampant; there were outbreaks of cholera, smallpox, scurvy, and typhoid. Julia Inglis, whose husband, Sir John Eardley Wilmot Inglis, took command after Lawrence fell, kept a diary of the events. Part of her harrowing account, published as *The Siege of Lucknow,* reads as follows:

> July 1st—Poor Miss Palmer had her leg taken off by a round shot to-day, she, with some other ladies, having remained in the second storey of the Residency house, though warned it was not safe . . . . July 4th—Poor Sir Henry [Lawrence] died to-day, after suffering fearful pain . . . . July 8—Mr. Polehampton, one of our chaplains, was shot through the body to-day whilst shaving . . . . October 1st—I was with Mrs. Couper nearly all day, watching her baby dying . . . . My baby was ill to-day. Sharp musketry firing at 10 A.M.

Relief forces commanded by Generals Sir Henry Havelock and Sir James Outram arrived in late September and got past the mutineers into the residency compound. This gave the British community false hope that the siege was over, but the fighting only grew more intense. Mutineers dug tunnels in which to plant explosives to blow up the residency. A soldier named Henry Kavanagh managed to infiltrate the tunnels and shoot mutineers as they attempted to lay mines, however. Starvation and sickness continued within the residency walls; Havelock himself was sufferering greatly from dysentery. Finally Kavanagh volunteered for another daring action: he would try to make it through the rebels' lines to contact another relief force commanded by Sir Colin Campbell. After swimming the Gomati River, he finally reached Campbell, whose forces arrived November 17. The residency was evacuated five days later; of the 3,000 British and Indians who had taken refuge there, fewer than 1,000 had survived.

Although the civilians had been moved to safety, the fighting continued, and the British would not regain control of Lucknow until March 1858. The rebel forces in other cities held on for several months, but the revolt eventually was broken. The consequences were far-reaching. Most important, the British Crown took control of India from the British East India Company.

The residency has been left much as it was when the siege ended, with its walls still bearing the marks of shells. A small museum has been installed within the compound. At a ruined church nearby is a cemetery with the graves of 2,000 people who died in the besieged residency; Lawrence's grave is among them. After India gained independence, an obelisk honoring the rebels was erected in the vicinity.

The British constructed numerous buildings and bridges in Lucknow and also developed many parks. Lucknow played one more key historic role in 1916. That year both the Indian National Congress, a Hindu-dominated Indian independence organization, and the All India Muslim League met at Lucknow, where they agreed on a constitutional reform plan concerning such matters as the proportion of seats to be allotted to Hindus and Muslims in provincial legislatures. Most of the provisions of the so-called Lucknow Pact were put into force by India's British rulers in the Montagu-Chelmsford Reforms of 1919. The pact represented a significant coming-together of Hindus and Muslims, but it eventually led to discord as Muslims became discontented with their quota of representative positions. Hindu-Muslim differences culminated in the establishment of the separate Muslim nation of Pakistan when India became independent in 1947.

Lucknow today is a busy state capital and commercial center. Its historic buildings, their style described as "debased Mughal," stand amid modern ones. The arts and culture are important to modern Lucknow residents, as they were to the nabobs; the city has several museums, the most notable being the State Museum, the largest in Uttar Pradesh. It has a significant collection of ancient sculptures and other artifacts; pieces associated with the British Raj, however, have been relegated to the back yard. Major Hindu and Muslim religious festivals are celebrated in Lucknow, and each February the Lucknow Festival, ten days of music, dance, theatre, and processions, provides an idea of what the city must have been like in the days of the nabobs.

Further Reading: Information about Lucknow, especially its role in the Indian Mutiny, is available from a variety of sources. Christopher Hibbert's *The Great Mutiny: India 1857* (London: Lane, and New York: Viking, 1978) is particularly helpful, as are the relevant volumes of *The New Cambridge History of India,* edited by Gordon Johnson, C. A. Bayly, and John F. Richards (29 vols., Cambridge and New York: Cambridge University Press, 1987–), especially John F. Richards's *The Mughal Empire* (1993) and C. A. Bayly's *Indian Society and the Making of the British Empire* (1988). For a quick overview, Vincent Smith's *The Oxford History of India: From the Earliest Times to the End of 1911* (Oxford: Clarendon Press, 1919; fourth edition, edited by Percival Spear, New York and Oxford: Oxford University Press, 1981) is still useful.

—Claudia Levi and Trudy Ring

Luoyang (Henan, China)

Location: On the north bank of the Luo River, west Henan, south of the Huang Ho (Yellow River).

Description: Ranked with Xian, Beijing, and Nanjing as the four ancient capitals of imperial China; especially famous for having been the "Capital of Nine Dynasties," with the Eastern Zhou Dynasty (770–256 B.C.) being the first and the Later Tang Dynasty (A.D. 923–35) the last; renowned for its ancient Buddhist grottoes and monasteries.

Site Office: Henan Tourism Bureau
16 Jinshui Avenue
450003 Zhengzhou
China
(371) 5952707

The modern city of Luoyang occupies an area where ancient Chinese peoples of the Neolithic Age congregated. Archaeological relics unearthed there include colored pottery of the Yangshao culture and the black pottery of the Lungshan culture. In 1960, an ancient palace site covering more than 107,600 square feet was discovered on the eastern outskirt of Luoyang; it is believed to be the capital, Xihao, of the early Shang Dynasty (traditional dates given as 1766–1122 B.C.).

The earliest name of Luoyang was Luoyi. Its history dates back more than 3,000 years to the time of King Cheng (Cheng Wang, 1063–1025 B.C.), the second king of the newly founded Western Zhou Dynasty (1122–771 B.C.). On the advice of his regent, Zhou Gong (the Duke of Zhou), he decided to build a new capital east of his capital, Gao (near modern Xian). The reasons for building it were twofold. First, the new site was in the center of the Zhou Empire and well defended by trusted vassals on all sides. Second, the king needed to consolidate his control of the middle reaches of the Yellow River basin inhabited by the remnants and subjects of the former Shang Dynasty, who were referred to as "obstinate people."

Under the guidance of the duke of Zhou, work on Luoyi commenced in 1059 B.C. A city of considerable scale, at the time it was referred to as a metropolis. Archaeologists working on this site have found sufficient evidence to estimate the city's area at seven and three-quarters square miles. Records show that it had a total of twelve gates, three on each side. The existence of the southern, northern, and eastern gates have been confirmed. The east gate was also called the Ding (Caldron) Gate, since it was believed that the Nine Caldrons, symbols of imperial power, were moved into the city through it. Each gateway had three lanes; vehicles used the center lane, which led directly to the Imperial Palace. To date, however, the main highway and the main city gate have not yet been discovered. All the remnants of the former Shang nobility, the "obstinate people," were relocated to this city and guarded by an army of 20,000 men. King Cheng spent much time in this city, further enhancing its importance. Not until 770 B.C., however, when the Zhou capital in modern Xian was sacked by barbarians, did the Zhou Dynasty move its capital permanently to Luoyi. This marked the beginning of the Eastern Zhou Dynasty, which was to last until 256 B.C. (although some sources indicate it lasted through the Warring States period down to the establishment of the Qin Dynasty in 221).

Although most cities in ancient China were primarily political and administrative rather than commercial centers, Luoyang during this period was frequently referred to as an industrial and commercial center. Its inhabitants, mostly subjects of the former Shang Dynasty, perpetuated their legacy of wealth by concentrating their energies on trade and industry. They were described disapprovingly by Han Confucians as "cunning, false, and profit-loving," emphasizing money and belittling morality. Pottery, bonework, and stonework sites of considerable scale have been excavated in the northwestern part of Luoyang.

The permanent move of the capital to Luoyang stabilized the Zhou Dynasty. Its close vassals rallied to enhance the grandeur of the imperial capital by extending Luoyang and adding two new palaces, the North and the South Palace. For the next 500 years Luoyang flourished while the country degenerated into a state of disorder and civil war that did not end until the rise of the Qin (221–206 B.C.) and the Western Han (206 B.C.–A.D. 9) Dynasties.

Both the Qin and the Western Han Dynasties located their capitals in or near modern Xian. The first emperor of the Qin Dynasty gave Luoyang to his chief minister, Lu Buwei, who was made a marquess of 100,000 households. Lu was a wealthy businessman before entering the Qin's service. Some suspected that he was the first emperor's real father. He launched a building program to further develop and beautify Luoyang. It has been said that Liu Bang, founder of the Han Dynasty, visited the South Palace in Luoyang in 202 B.C. and was so impressed that he contemplated making Luoyang his capital. He changed his mind only after being counseled by his ministers on the strategic importance of Xian to the security of his newly founded empire. Two centuries later, however, one of his descendants, Liu Xiu, who regained the empire from the usurper Wang Mang and reestablished the Han Dynasty as the Eastern (or Later) Han Dynasty, had no such scruples: he made his capital at Luoyang, where it remained for the next two centuries.

During this period, Luoyang became a busy, prosperous trading and cultural center where a great variety of consumer goods was made, bought, and sold. There were

White Horse Monastery, Luoyang
Photo courtesy of China National Tourist Office, Los Angeles

even book marts where poor scholars could browse and read. Wang Chong (A.D. 27–c. 100), a philosopher renowned for his broad learning, was credited with having derived his knowledge in this way. Luoyang became China's highest seat of learning. It was here that the famous Han historian Ban Gu, who died in A.D. 92, wrote his innovative *History of the Former Han Dynasty*. It was also here that the world's first seismograph and armillary sphere (an astronomical device) were invented. Luoyang was especially famed for being a literary center where famous scholars, poets, and writers gathered. The invention of paper in the first century A.D. greatly facilitated the spread of learning. Life in Luoyang was so extravagant, and so many people were engaged in trade and secondary industries, that it became the object of considerable attention and criticism from Confucians who frowned on what they felt were nonessential pursuits.

During the end of the second and the beginning of the third centuries, the Eastern Han Dynasty disintegrated. Luoyang sustained great damages. In A.D. 190 the Han emperor, Xian Di, was forced by a powerful minister, Dong Zhuo, to move his capital to Chang'an (modern Xian). Luoyang's population, said to be several millions, was also forced to move to Chang'an. Dong Zhuo then set fire to the palaces, government offices, and houses, practically razing Luoyang and everything within sixty miles to the ground. Although Dong Zhuo's rebellion was put down within a short time, Luoyang did not recover its former glory until several decades later, under both the kingdom of Wei (220–65) and the Western Jin Dynasty (265–316).

From 318, China entered a period of division and disorder sometimes referred to as the North-South Dynasties, which lasted until 581 when the Sui Dynasty was established. During the early phase of this period, Luoyang suffered repeated destruction until the rise of the Northern Wei (386–534), whose sixth emperor, Xiaowen Di (471–99), wishing to sinicize his dynasty rapidly, moved his captial from modern Datong southward to Luoyang in 493. From that time, Luoyang regained its former importance as the political and commercial center of north China, to which large numbers of foreign merchants from West Asia came.

This was also the age of Buddhism in China, and Luoyang became one of its major centers. The extent of Buddhist influence in this period was most visible in the architectural landscape of Luoyang. The earliest surviving landmark of Buddhist influence in China is the White Horse Monastery, built in A.D. 68 to house two Indian monks and

The Longmen Grottoes, Luoyang
Photo courtesy of China National Tourist Office, Los Angeles

the scriptures brought back from India by Emperor Ming Di's two emissaries. By the reign of Yongjia (307–12) of the Western Jin Dynasty, the number of Buddhist temples had increased to forty-two. Under the Northen Wei, this number reached 1,367, marking the peak of temple building in Luoyang. Some of these temples were immense. The Yongning Monastery (constructed in 516), as described by Yang Xuanzhi in *A Record of Buddhist Monasteries in Lo-yang,* had a nine-storied wooden stupa that extended 900 Chinese feet above ground and was capped by a 100-foot mast. On top of this mast was a bejeweled golden jar sitting on thirty tiers of golden plates, and under each plate hung a golden bell. Hung from the corner of each of the nine roofs were other golden bells, totaling 120 in all. "On long nights when there was a strong wind," wrote Yang Hsuan-chih, "the harmonious jingling of the bejeweled bells could be heard more than five kilometers [3.1 miles] away."

About seven and one-half miles south of modern Luoyang lies another of the area's major surviving Buddhist legacies: the Longmen Grottoes. In these grottoes are thousands of Buddhist shrines carved on its hard marble surfaces over the ages. About 30 percent of them were completed in the North-South Dynastic period. The earliest dates to 495. Together with Dunhuang and Yungang, they rank as the greatest monuments of Chinese art.

With the rapid dynastic transition from Northern Wei to the Western Wei in 534, and then to the Eastern Wei in 550, Luoyang's former accomplishments soon diminished in importance, and many of its buildings were demolished. When China was reunifed under the Sui Dynasty (581–618) Luoyang was destroyed so extensively by wars that a new site, five and one-half miles west, was chosen for the new capital. Partly in recognition of Luoyang's growing economic and strategic importance, and partly to satisfy his personal ego, Emperor Yang Di (ruled 604–18) launched an enormous building program. Its scale could be imagined from the recorded employment: 2 million men were on the job each month for an entire year.

Yang Di, one of the most vainglorious, extravagant rulers in history, spared nothing to give his capital the magnificence and security he thought he deserved and needed. An extensive system of moats was dug for the defense of Luoyang. A vast canal-building program was also undertaken to connect Luoyang with Chang'an in the west, the city of Cho near modern Beijing in the north, and with the sea in the east. The famous Grand Canal that connects China's two major river systems, the Yellow (Huang Ho) and the Yangtze River basins, was completed during this period. For building Yang Di's palaces in Luoyang, huge logs had to be transported from Jiangxi in south China. It is recorded that each log required 3,000 men to move. The iron hubs under each log had to be changed every couple of miles, and the process yielded a top speed of only six to nine miles per day. Yang Di, however, did not live to enjoy his beautiful capital for very long. After a life of indulgence and excess, he was killed by his own officers, and his empire fell to an official who established the Tang Dynasty (618–907).

The Tang Dynasty made Chang'an (Xian) its capital, but Luoyang, as the starting point of the famous ancient Silk Road across Central Asia, remained important enough to the empire, economically and politically, that it continued to be acknowledged officially as the eastern capital. Tang rulers spent a great deal of their time there.

Empress Wu (684–705) changed the name of the dynasty from Tang to Zhou in 690. She was probably the last ruler noted for spending lavishly on Buddhist constructions in Luoyang. Several enormous building projects were undertaken. The first was a three-story building, the Ming Tang (Hall of Enlightenment), built in 988. Its base measured 352.5 square feet, it stood more than 345 feet in height, and it had a 12-foot-tall iron peacock on the top. The second was a 5-tiered structure, the Tian Tang (Heavenly Hall). Towering above the Ming Tang, the Tian Tang was used to house huge Buddhist statues. Unfortunately, both buildings were destroyed by fire in 695, although a new Ming Tang was built in 696.

To symbolize the universal nature of her empire, Empress Wu built the Axis of the Heavens in 694. Of bronze and iron, it was 14.1 feet in diameter and stood 123.4 feet high. Its base was an iron mount with a circumference of nearly 200 feet. Around the mount were dragons and unicorns made of bronze. On top of the axis was a bronze dew plate exceeding 35 feet in diameter. On the plate were 4 vertical dragons nearly 12 feet high, each holding a glass bead.

To express her imperial authority in the traditional way, Empress Wu cast 9 huge tripods (caldrons) to be placed in 9 major urban centers of her empire. The largest was in Luoyang, her "Divine Capital." It was over 21 feet tall, with a capacity for holding nearly 109 metric tons of rice. The rest were slightly smaller. All together about 374 tons of bronze was used.

All these extravagant constructions did not survive long after the death of Empress Wu. Her successor immediately restored the dynastic name of Tang and proceeded to destroy all monuments built during her reign. Five decades later, Luoyang itself was all but wiped out during the An Lushan Rebellion (755–63). An Lushan was a boisterous young general who gained the trust of the Tang emperor Xuanzong and his favorite concubine, Yang Guifei (the latter adopted him as her legal son and was rumored to have made him her lover). An Lushan was made the head of three regional commanderies along the northeastern frontiers with more than 200,000 troops under his control. In 755, he headed a rebellion that was only put down after eight years of war. Neither Luoyang nor the Tang Dynasty ever recovered from this event.

The demise of the Tang Dynasty was slow but certain. It ended in 907 and was succeeded by a rapid succession of five short-lived dynasties. Thus this period is known as the Five Dynasties period (907–59). The first three made Luoyang their capital, but China's economic center had shifted away from Luoyang, which had already lost its former political and economic importance. Years of incessant warfare had devastated the region's economy, and China's economic center had shifted southward to the fast-developing regions in the Yangtze and Pearl River basins. In recognition of this fact, the Later Jin Dynasty (936–47), hardly two years after making Luoyang its capital, abandoned it for Kaifeng. Thereafter, Luoyang never again regained its former national political and economic preeminence.

The Song Dynasty (960–1276), which ended the period of the Five Dynasties, also made Kaifeng its capital. In 1034, a new Luoyang was built. It became a prestigious center of learning and was home to Neo-Confucian doyens such as Cheng Hao and Cheng Yi; Sima Guang wrote most of his famous historical work, *History as a Mirror,* there. Luoyang had always been known for its beautiful gardens. It retained this fame during the Song period, as shown in *A Record of Luoyang's Famous Gardens* by a Song contemporary, Li Gefei.

Luoyang was destroyed and rebuilt twice more under the Yuan (1234–1368) and the Ming (1368–1644) Dynasties. The Qing Dynasty (1644–1912) rebuilt the city walls, which had been demolished by peasant rebels during the late Ming period. But this measure was not enough to restore the glamour and importance the city once knew. In the first half of the twentieth century, it was further diminished by civil wars and the Japanese invasion, until it became a run-down city of only about 100,000 inhabitants.

Since the restoration of peace in recent decades, Luoyang has been rapidly modernized, industrialized, and extended. It now has a population of about 1 million. More significantly from the historical point of view, however, is the recognition and emphasis given to Luoyang as a national historical and cultural heritage worthy of treasuring and protecting. This means that Luoyang's two major historical legacies, the White Horse Monastery and the Longmen Grottoes, will receive the care and preservation they deserve.

Further Reading: Yang Hsuan-chih's *A Record of Buddhist Monasteries in Lo-yang,* translated from Chinese by Yi-t'ung Wang (Princeton, New Jersey: Princeton University Press, 1984) provides an interesting account of Luoyang during the North-South Dynasties period. *Zhongguo liu ta gudu,* edited by Chen Qiaoyi (Beijing: Zhongguo Qingnian, 1983) gives a short comprehensive historical account in Chinese.

—Kit S. Liew

Macau

Location: A Portuguese territory on a peninsula of the estuary of the Pearl River in southern China, forty miles west of Hong Kong and ninety miles south of Guangzhou (Canton). The territory also comprises the islands of Taipa and Coloane.

Description: Important from the sixteenth century onward as the most significant focus for European contact with China and, at times, with Japan.

Site Office: Macau Government Tourist Office (MSTO)
Direccão dos Servicos de Turismo
Largo do Senado 9, Edif Ritz
CP3006
Macau
57 29 17

After the conquest of Melaka (Malacca) by Alfonso de Albuquerque in July 1511, the Portuguese made a determined effort to open up trade with China. These attempts met with little success at first, but the discovery of Japan by the Portuguese in 1542 improved that situation. Since the Chinese had forbidden direct trade with Japan from about 1480, the Portuguese saw the opportunity of acting as middlemen between the two countries. From about 1550 a series of annual fairs for the exchange of goods was held on the island of Sanchuan (St. John) fifty miles southwest of Macau, and it was here that the celebrated missionary St. Francis Xavier died in 1552. The fair was moved to another island to the east, Lampacao, in 1554 or 1555. It was then that the Portuguese discovered Macau. A letter dated there in 1555 bears witness to the Portuguese presence, even though the date usually given for the foundation of the town is 1557.

Macau was at that time probably a fishing village, and the Portuguese would have been unauthorized squatters between trading seasons. One of its original Chinese names was Amao, the bay of Ama, goddess of sailors, which was turned by the Portuguese into Amacao (Amacon to English visitors of the sixteenth century), and ultimately into Macau. The temple of A-Ma-Miu, which lies close to the southern extremity of the peninsula, is the oldest building there, dating from the early sixteenth century, before the arrival of the Portuguese.

The permanent Portuguese settlement at Macau was at first unofficial and no doubt the result of some unwritten agreement (involving bribery) between the captain-major of the Japan Voyage and the local Guangdong authorities. There was no formal treaty with the Chinese about Macau and no cession of territory until the Treaty of Tianjin in 1862, which granted sovereignty to Portugal. It is said that the emperor of China did not get to hear of its existence for twenty years or so. The informal nature of the Portuguese colony always created a degree of ambiguity about its status, and the history of Macau is filled with incidents in which Chinese authorities exerted their ultimate control over the place by interfering in its administration. During times of tension they also cut off food supplies through the Barrier Gate, which they had constructed across the neck of the peninsula in 1573. (The present Barrier Gate dates from 1870.) The viceroy of Guangdong and Guangxi regarded the magistrate of the Heungshan district, with its present capital at Shekki, as having jurisdiction over the numerous Chinese inhabitants of Macau, and from 1688 to 1849 a Chinese custom house levied dues on all goods exported in Portuguese ships.

Macau grew rapidly. In 1578 a Jesuit visitor reported the population at 10,000. In 1576 a diocese of Macau had been established, with jurisdiction over China, Japan, Korea, and Cochin-China (Vietnam). Bishop Dom Leonardo de Sa in 1582 brought about the creation of a municipal council, or Senado da Camara, with elected aldermen and magistrates. The place assumed as its official name the City of the Name of God. This collective decision was ratified by the Viceroy of Portuguese India at Goa, Don Duarte Menezes, who signed a decree on April 10, 1586, granting the City of the Name of God of Macau in China the same privileges as those of Evora in Portugal. The decree is the first known recognition of the place by Portuguese authorities. Whether, as many suppose, the Portuguese national poet Luis de Camôes visited Macau in 1557 remains uncertain.

Macau succeeded so quickly because of its key position in the Portuguese monopoly trade between China and Japan. Already by 1550, before Macau had been founded, a trading system had been established whereby a carrack, or "Great Ship," sailed from Goa for Melaka with Indian fabrics and such European luxury products as wine; at Melaka spices and sandalwood (used for burning as incense) were obtained; thence it sailed for Macau and traded for Chinese gold and for silk, which was brought downstream from Guangzhou. The following year, the carrack voyaged to Japan and traded its silk for silver, along with smaller quantities of distinctively Japanese products such as lacquer cabinets and other items of furniture. The silver was used at Macau to buy next year's silk, and the carrack returned to Goa with gold, silk, pearls, ivory, and porcelain, some of which ultimately found its way to Europe. The whole process lasted two or three years and in 1571 resulted in the foundation of the port of Nagasaki in Japan. The extraordinarily profitable Japan Voyage, as it was called, was granted by the Portuguese Crown to a captain-major of the Voyage of China and Japan, usually a *fidalgo,* or gentleman, on an annual basis. For his term of office, he was regarded as the representative of the Portuguese Crown in relation to foreign

Facade of St. Paul's Church, Macau
Photo courtesy of Macau Tourist Information Bureau

powers and essentially acted as governor of Macau for the duration of his stay. Macau thus became the sole point of contact between Europe and the closed empire of China. As long as the Japan Voyage lasted, Macau was one of the wealthiest places in the world. Macau for a time also had an important gun foundry, established in 1629 by Manoel Tavares Bocarro to supply Portuguese forts in the east. The gun foundry depended on copper imported from Japan, however, and did not long outlast the interruption of the Japan trade.

In 1640 the Japan trade was stopped as a consequence of the policy of the Tokugawa *shōgun* to extirpate Christianity in his dominions. The size of the Christian community in Japan, some 300,000, owed much to Macau's having become the center for Catholic missionary activity in the Far East, expanding upon the work of St. Francis Xavier and others. It was on the "Great Ship" that Jesuit missionaries made their way to Japan, and the trade, particularly bullion brokerage, was vital to the survival of the Christian mission there. Macau also was the place of entry for Jesuit missionaries to China. These men were not necessarily Portuguese (the founder of the mission at Beijing, Matteo Ricci, was Italian), but all came out in Portuguese ships to Macau under the terms of the Padroado Real (royal patronage of the church overseas). Under this papal arrangement, the Portuguese Crown acted as patron of the Catholic missions in India, by which was meant the huge area extending from the Cape of Good Hope to Japan. At Macau the Jesuit college of Madre de Deus (also known as St. Paul's) was the headquarters of missionary activity in the Far East, particularly under the vigorous and able Alessandro Valignano, another Italian, who was vicar-general and Visitor of the Orient from 1574 to 1606. The Church of the Jesuit college exhibited a fusion of oriental and occidental influences in its decorative detail. It was designed by yet another Italian Jesuit, Carlo Spinola, and built in the early seventeenth century by Chinese and Japanese Christian craftsmen. It was burned down in 1835, but the striking facade—Macau's most celebrated early monument—remains.

In addition to the Jesuit college and the cathedral, Macau had monasteries belonging to the Augustinian, Dominican, and Franciscan friars, along with three parish churches. Disputes among the various religious orders were commonplace, sometimes resulting in violence. A more positive aspect of religious life in Macau was the Santa Casa da Misericordia, or Holy House of Mercy, a charitable institution founded in 1569 as a branch of the mother house in Lisbon. It looked after the sick and indigent, mainly Christian, and had a leper hospital attached to it. The buildings survive today.

The Dutch arrived in Chinese and Japanese waters in 1600 and soon became a serious menace to the Portuguese trade monopoly. A group of Dutchmen attempting to reconnoitre Macau in 1601 were executed as pirates, but soon the Dutch were effectively disrupting the Japan Voyage. In 1603 the Dutch captured the carrack returning to Melaka in the Straits of Singapore. In July of the same year, they took the carrack due to sail for Japan, laden with gold and silk, at its anchorage in Macau. Apparently, no one was on board at the time. The Portuguese responded by sending out more ships and by issuing instructions to the captain-general to build fortifications. From 1618 the annual "Great Ship" to Nagasaki was given up in favor of fleets of smaller ships, galliots of 300 to 400 tons. A carefully planned Dutch attack was made on Macau in 1622 as part of a grand design entertained by the Dutch East India Company to take over Portuguese-controlled territories. A miscellaneous assemblage of Portuguese soldiers, citizens, African slaves, friars, and Jesuits managed to withstand the attack. Following this defeat, the Dutch made no further attempts to take Macau, although they continued to harass the Portuguese fleet.

In the wake of the Dutch attack on the city, serious attention was paid to its fortifications. In the early 1620s, Governor Francisco Mascarenhas had orders to attend to these matters. In addition to strengthening existing forts, he built a wall of *chunam* (a very tough local material consisting of a mixture of earth, straw, lime, and oyster shells) across the peninsula, to prevent assault from the landward side. The *chunam* wall provoked a response from the Guangdong authorities, who ordered the cessation of the work. In the end the Portuguese tore down a part of the wall as an act of formal compliance in March 1624, but after payment of a suitable bribe they went on to complete the project in 1629. The entire episode illustrates the nature of the relationship between the Portuguese and the imperial authorities. Antonio Bocarro's 1635 book on Portuguese overseas possessions lists six forts in Macau with a total of seventy-three guns. Of these the old Jesuit fort, the Monte, and the Bom Parto, Barra, and Guia forts survive.

A Dutch fleet of four ships appeared off Macau in 1627 and prevented the sailing of the annual Nagasaki fleet. The Dutch were driven off, and their flagship was destroyed, but the Portuguese were unable to safeguard their ships in the Straits of Melaka. Many valuable Portuguese ships were lost during the third decade of the seventeenth century. In 1641 the Dutch captured Melaka and so cut the trade link between Macau and Goa. However, this disaster and the loss of the Japan trade in 1640 did not mean the end of Macau. Despite an official prohibition of trade between Spanish and Portuguese colonies, Macau had maintained a thriving trade with Manila in the Philippines, trading Chinese silk for South American gold. Thus in 1640 Macau was still prosperous, with a population of 600 married Portuguese and some 26,000 others, mostly Chinese. But the late seventeenth century was a difficult time: the separation of Portugal and Spain caused a break in the Manila trade; the Manchu conquest of China dislocated the trade with Guangzhou; and in 1662 the Manchus forcibly depopulated the maritime provinces. Dealing another blow to Macau, Emperor Kang Xi opened the ports of China to foreign trade in 1685. In 1699 an English East India Company ship visited Guangzhou, and from that date the company sent ships to Chinese ports annually, bypassing Macau.

Macau's trade steadily declined throughout the early eighteenth century, and the main resource became the commerce with Timor and Solor for sandalwood, gold, beeswax, and slaves. During one short-lived period of prosperity, from 1717 to 1723, an imperial edict forbade Chinese junks to voyage anywhere save Japan, so handing over the tea trade with Batavia (now Jakarta) to the Portuguese. But the Chinese suggestion in 1719, repeated in 1733, that all Chinese-European trade should be carried out exclusively through Macau, was rejected, first by Macau's senate, which feared the increased power the move would give the Chinese customs commissioner, and then by the bishop, who objected to the presence of an excessive number of Protestants. Apart from the brief boom, Macau's population declined in the eighteenth century. By 1747 there were only 90 European Portuguese men and 13,000 others, about half what it had been a century earlier. Visitors to Macau, including Alexander Hamilton in 1718–19 and William Hickey in 1769, all commented on its air of decay, in sharp contrast with the highly favorable impression given by Peter Mundy in 1637. In 1762 the Jesuits, who had played such a significant role in Macau's history, were expelled and deported to Europe following numerous complaints of corruption.

Macau was not entirely moribund, however. Since Portugal and Holland had become allies in the war against France, a modest country trade was conducted, involving the import of spices, cotton, and opium from India and the export of silk, tea, and porcelain. The development of Guangzhou as the major port for the trade between China and Europe also brought certain benefits to Macau. European traders, who were not allowed to spend the entire year at Guangzhou, became accustomed to living at Macau during the summer months, at first officially as lodgers, then, when Guangzhou became the only port open to foreign trade in 1757, permanently. From this time the various national East India companies were able to trade under their own names from Macau. In 1761 the French and Dutch companies rented accommodations there, followed by the Danish and Swedish. In 1770 the English East India Company established a permanent base at Macau, eventually taking over four large houses on the waterfront of the Praia Grande, next to the Governor's Palace. The president of the Select Committee of Supercargoes, the body set up to control British traders in China, had a large house in the northwest corner of the walled area. Its famous garden, the Casa Garden, contained the Rocks or Grotto of Camões, named for the poet Luíz Vaz de Camoes, who in the mid–sixteenth century spent several years in military service in the Far East. In 1821 a Protestant cemetery was established. In due course, the British presence in Macau clearly overshadowed that of other European nations. Notable residents included the portrait and landscape painter George Chinnery, and Robert Morrison, who translated the Bible into Chinese.

Difficulties with the Chinese authorities over trade conditions led the British to consider obtaining a trading station on the China coast with extra-territorial jurisdiction. At various times from the late eighteenth century onward, the Chinese considered acquiring Macau from Portugal for this purpose. In 1802 the British sent a force to Macau to prevent a feared invasion from the French, who were at war with Portugal; but because hostilities ended in Europe, the troops did not land. However, in 1808 the process was repeated, and this time Macau was occupied by a British force under Admiral William Drury. The Portuguese, worried that the British occupation might turn out to be permanent, acquiesced reluctantly. In the end the Chinese authorities stopped all foreign trade at Guangzhou and forced a British withdrawal before any fighting took place.

Macau participated for some time in the trade in opium with China, particularly in the early nineteenth century, when Malwa opium from central India reached the city in Portuguese ships from Goa and Daman. High customs dues charged at Macau later drove the trade away to the island of Lintin in the Pearl River estuary. In addition, Chinese inspection of trade goods at Macau could be so strict that what was technically an illegal trade could no longer be conducted from there. In 1839, under pressure from the Chinese, the British left Macau *en masse*, and the emperor's commissioner, Lin Ze, charged with the suppression of the opium trade, entered Macau in triumph. In 1842, during their successful war with China, the British transferred their superintendency of trade from Macau to Hong Kong, and Macau's importance declined still further.

The British victory encouraged the Portuguese to take a bolder line with the Chinese, and in 1845 Macau was declared a free port. A unilateral declaration that Macau was Portuguese territory was recognized by China in 1887 (but repudiated again by the nationalist government in 1928). However, the growth of Hong Kong, the opening of other Chinese ports to foreign trade, and the silting of Macau's harbor meant that in the late nineteenth and twentieth centuries its trade was exclusively local. Its reputation for gambling, gold smuggling, drugs, and triad gangs developed at this time. Its population in 1900 was approximately 75,000.

During World War II, Japan did not occupy Macau, but the Japanese demanded and obtained the right to house-to-house searches. Refugees from the mainland swelled its population temporarily to 600,000. In 1951 Macau was declared an overseas province of Portugal. However, the period of the Cultural Revolution, when China renewed its claim to Macau, showed the basic weakness of the Portuguese position. The Portuguese effectively backed down in the face of rioting and intimated that they would pull out. After the fall of the Salazar dictatorship in 1974, this view was reiterated, and in 1979 a new agreement formally recognized Macau as Chinese territory under Portuguese administration.

In 1991 Macau contained 355,693 people, which gives it one of the highest population densities in the world. Since it has participated in the Pacific region's economic expansion, Macau's economy has grown to embrace textiles, the production of toys and electronic goods, and tourism, as well as gambling, which is highly organized there. Two bridges now connect the peninsula with the island of Taipa, a new airport is under construction, and there is a new deep-water port on the second island, Coloane. Much land reclamation is under way, some of which will be undertaken in conjunction with the Zhuhai (a town designated as a special economic zone) of the People's Republic of China, to which Macau will revert on December 20, 1999, two years after Hong Kong.

Further Reading: The standard history of Macau in English is by Carlos Augusto Montalto de Jesus, *Historic Macao* (Hong Kong: Kelly and Walsh, 1902; reprint, Hong Kong: Oxford University Press, 1984). A shorter, more popular history is *A Macau Narrative* by Austin Coates (Hong Kong: Oxford University Press, 1987). The same author's *Prelude to Hong Kong* (London: Routledge and Kegan Paul, 1960) deals with Macau's role in the eighteenth and nineteenth centuries. Also to be recommended is C. R. Boxer's *Fidalgos in the Far East: 1550–1770* (The Hague: Nijhoff, 1948; second edition, Hong Kong: Oxford University Press, 1968), a readable account of the Portuguese personalities associated with the place and their social and economic milieu. Shann Davies's *Chronicles in Stone* (Macau: Department of Tourism, 1985) is an account of Macau's historic buildings.

—A. E. Brown

Madras (Tamil Nādu, India)

Location: On the southeast coast of India, facing the Bay of Bengal. Madras is the capital of the state of Tamil Nādu and the fourth-largest city in India.

Description: Madras has been the site of important events in the history of modern India and contains buildings dating from the late seventeenth century onward that are closely associated with British rule in India.

Site Office: Government of India Tourist Office
154 Anna Salai
Madras 600 002
Tamil Nādu
India
(82) 69685

The city of Madras dates to the early years of the English East India Company, which was founded in 1600. European traders were attracted to the southeastern (or Coromandel) coast of India because of its skilled weavers and the fine textiles—calicoes, muslins, and chintzes—that were produced in the area. These were much sought after for export to Southeast Asia and Europe. The English East India Company first tried to establish itself at Machilīpatnam (Masulipatam), but was hindered by rival Dutch traders and the exactions of Indian officials. A base at Armagon also proved unsatisfactory, and in August 1639 Francis Day, chief agent factor there, found a more suitable site, on a sandy spit of land facing the Bay of Bengal and protected to the west and north by the brackish Cooum River. Day concluded a treaty with the local ruler, the raja of Chandragiri, a subordinate of the decaying Hindu empire of Vijayanagara, which granted the company half the revenues of "Madrasapatam" and permission to build a fort.

Although the English had been trading with India since 1611, this small patch of low-lying and almost uninhabited land was the first territory acquired by the English in India. Construction on a fort, named after St. George, patron saint of England, was begun in March 1640, and the following year it became the company's headquarters on the Coromandel Coast. Entirely rebuilt in the eighteenth century, Fort St. George has remained the geographical and political heart of the city: it still houses the secretariat of the state government of Tamil Nādu.

Like Bombay (1661) and Calcutta (1690), Madras was founded by the British on land free of existing settlement and away from established Indian trading and administrative centers. As a consequence, the British factory enjoyed a large measure of political and commercial independence. Nonetheless, the Coromandel Coast had a long history of trade and urban settlement, as witnessed by the Pallava port of Mahābalipuram further south and the Portuguese settlement of St. Thomé, named after the apostle St. Thomas, who reputedly landed there and died at nearby St. Thomas's Mount. St. Thomé has long since been swallowed up by the growth of Madras, though evidence of the early Portuguese presence remains in the Luz Church, said to have been founded in 1516, and St. Thomé Cathedral, originating in the mid–sixteenth century but rebuilt in the 1890s.

Fort St. George soon attracted a sizable population of Portuguese traders from St. Thomé, as well as Tamil, Telugu, and Armenian merchants. It also acquired 300 or 400 families of Indian weavers, dyers, and other artisans and laborers, who settled around the fort. From an early date, a distinction existed between the fortified White Town, with its warehouses, barracks, and houses for European residents, and the Black Town (renamed George Town in 1906) immediately to the north, where Indians lived. The old division is still evident in the layout of the city, with Fort St. George separated by open spaces from the bustling commercial streets to the north.

By the end of the seventeenth century, Madras had emerged as the main British settlement in India (though it was shortly to be overtaken by Calcutta) and a major port, despite the absence of a natural harbor. Goods and passengers had to be ferried by boat through the surf to and from ships waiting offshore. The initial settlement in White Town was elegant and spacious, the houses interspersed with fruit trees and gardens, and was enclosed by an outer defensive wall. The principal building surviving from this period, and the most eloquent evocation of the early history of Madras, is St. Mary's Church. Built between 1678 and 1680 as a place of worship for the company's servants, St. Mary's is reputed to be the oldest British building in India and its oldest Protestant church. Its walls are over four feet thick, and it has a "bombproof" roof, massive enough to withstand bombardment as well as the cyclones that periodically batter this coast. A spire was added in 1692 and rebuilt following the French siege of 1759. The church was not only the center of the religious life of the European community in White Town but also a place of refuge during times of war and the focus of early medical, educational, and charitable activities for the European and Eurasian poor.

Outside, on the north side of the church, are tombstones commemorating some of the earliest inhabitants of Madras. Inside, St. Mary's contains monuments to the governors of Madras and commanders-in-chief of the Madras Army. Among them are the graves of Sir Thomas Munro, one of the most celebrated governors of Madras, who died of cholera in 1827, and Lord Pigot, who defended Madras against the French in 1759 but was impeached in 1776 and imprisoned by members of his own council. Also in the church is a large monument to the Lutheran missionary and emissary Frederick Swartz, who died in 1798. The tombstone of David Yale, who died in 1688, aged four, lies in the old burial ground nearby. He was the son of Elihu Yale, governor of Madras (1687–92) and the benefactor after whom Yale University was named. It was also in this church that Robert Clive, one of the principal architects of British rule in India, was married to Margaret Maskelyne, the sister of one of his comrades-in-arms, in February 1753. St. Mary's served as the fort's garrison church from the early nineteenth century until August 1947, when the last British troops left in recognition of Indian independence. The nearby Fort Museum, located in an old exchange building, contains further relics of the company in Madras.

For most of the first century of its existence, Madras lay relatively undisturbed and free to develop peacefully. The power of the Mughals barely reached this far south, though their forces briefly besieged the city in 1702 and a *subah* (province) was established at Arcot, inland from Madras, which later became the seat of the nabobs of the Carnatic. While the number of Europeans remained small (in the 1720s there were probably few more than 400 Europeans in Madras, most of them soldiers), the Indian town grew rapidly. Early estimates claim that as many as 40,000 Indians lived in Madras by 1670, and 100,000 by 1700, but such estimates (before the first proper census of 1871) are notoriously unreliable.

A great change in the fortunes of Fort St. George came with the outbreak of the War of the Austrian Succession in Europe in 1740, when conflict between England and France spread to their Indian possessions. The English had been competing with the Dutch, stationed at Pulicat, twenty-five miles north of Madras, for a long time. They were also threatened by the rise of the French East India Company with its headquarters at Pondicherry, eighty-five miles to the south. The first French attack came in September 1746, when a fleet from Mauritius under the Comte Mahé de la Bourdonnais appeared off Madras. After a brief bombardment, Governor Morse capitulated. For the next three years, until August 1749, the city remained in French hands, and the English were obliged to transfer their affairs to Fort St. David at Cuddalore. However, Madras was restored to the English under the Treaty of Aix-la-Chapelle in exchange for Cape Breton Island. The city regained its former position as company headquarters on the Coromandel Coast in April 1752.

During the French occupation, the old Black Town, nestling close to the walls of the fort and including the houses of Armenian as well as Indian merchants, was demolished and moved further north to provide a clear line of fire around the fort and so improve its defensive strength. With the return of the British, the fortifications were further rebuilt and strengthened with an elaborate series of ramparts and ditches, the remains of which are still in evidence.

Conflict between the English and French continued intermittently after 1749, as the competing companies supported rival claimants to the titles of nabob of the Carnatic and his overlord, the nizām of Hyderābād. They also began to recruit Indian troops (sepoys) and armed and disciplined them in Western style in order to augment their limited European manpower. It was seapower that proved most decisive in the ensuing conflict, however. The Anglo-French struggle openly resumed with the outbreak of the Seven Years War in Europe in 1756. The French again had the initial advantage, and under their commander, the Irish-born Thomas Arthur Lally, they captured Fort St. David and advanced on Madras. They laid siege to the city from December 1758 until mid-February 1759, occupying Black Town and bombarding Fort St. George from the north. Due to the increased strength of the defenses and the timely arrival of an English fleet, the French failed to subdue Madras this time. The lifting of the siege marked a turning point in the protracted Anglo-French struggle for supremacy in south India. Lally was defeated by Eyre Coote at the battle of Wandiwash in January 1760, and Coote went on to attack the French at Pondicherry, which fell after a lengthy siege in January 1761. The French threat to British power in India was effectively over.

But Madras was not yet free of danger. The aggressive policies and military strength of the Muslim rulers of Mysore, Hyder Ali and his son Tippu Sahib, continued to threaten the English position. Hyder ravaged the countryside close to the city in 1769 and again in 1780. Only with the storming of Srirangapatnam (Seringapatam) and the death of Tippu in May 1799 was the power of Mysore finally crushed.

The struggle against the French and Mysore transformed Madras from a small, essentially commercial enclave on the edge of the Bay of Bengal into the administrative and military capital of a vast province, extending over a large part of southern India. Between 1760 and 1800, Fort St. George became a major military base, the headquarters of a Madras Army of four regiments of European soldiers and twenty or more battalions of Indian sepoys. As a result of the seizure of territory during the Mysore wars and the annexation of the possessions of the nabob of Arcot in 1801, Madras consolidated its position as the capital of southern India, eclipsing all of its European and Indian rivals. The Madras Presidency, with its headquarters at Fort St. George, now stretched from the southern boundaries of the Tamil country north to the borders of Orissa and from the Bay of Bengal to the Malabar district on the west coast.

As its commercial, military, and administrative importance increased, the city itself acquired neighboring villages and settlements, partly for defensive purposes, but also to accommodate its growing population. Once separated from Fort St. George by paddy fields, groves, and gardens, places like Egmore, Tondiarpet, Mylapore, and St. Thomé (annexed in 1749 to forestall a French occupation) gradually became absorbed into the city itself. By the late eighteenth century, the area in and to the north of Fort St. George was marked by elegant buildings that impressed visitors arriving by ship for the first time. The artist William Hodges observed in 1781: "The English town, rising from within Fort St George has

St. Thomé Cathedral, Madras
Photo courtesy of Milton Mann

from the sea a rich and beautiful appearance. The stile of the buildings is in general handsome. They consist of long colonades, with open porticoes, and flat roofs and offer to the eye an appearance similar to that what we may conceive of a Grecian city in the age of Alexander." The brilliant appearance of the buildings was enhanced by the use of *chunam,* a polished plaster made from lime extracted from seashells.

By the 1830s few English residents still lived in Madras proper. Until the end of the French wars, there had been little European settlement beyond the walls of Fort St. George, but, especially after the end of the Mysore wars, stylish European country houses, set in spacious compounds, were built across the plain to the southwest of the old city, along the line of Mount Road (now Anna Salai) and towards the Adyar River to the south. With its wide, tree-lined roads and scattered houses, interspersed with fields and Indian villages, Madras, until very recently, possessed a far more relaxed, spacious, and semirural atmosphere than its more congested rivals, Calcutta and Bombay.

But a spate of building and civic improvement followed the city's surge in prosperity. Its newfound role as the capital of a huge province and the spirit of military pride engendered by the successful struggle against the French and Mysore also contributed to an increase in building and beautification. In 1800 the governor of Madras moved his residence out of the congested fort to a new and more spacious building in nearby Triplicane. In 1802 the Banqueting Hall (now called Rajaji Hall) was constructed next to the governor's residence to celebrate the triumph of British arms at Srirangapatnam three years earlier. Scarcely less imposing a monument was the Memorial Hall, erected in 1860. As the city expanded, the number of churches outside the confines of Fort St. George increased. In the 1770s, following the Anglo-French wars, a Roman Catholic cathedral and an Armenian church were built in George Town. They were followed in 1815 by St. George's Cathedral on Mount Road and St. Andrew's Church in Egmore in 1821. Both of the latter, designed by the architect Thomas de Havilland, drew heavily on familiar church designs in Britain (conspicuously, in the case of St. Andrew's, from St. Martin-in-the-Fields in Trafalgar Square), but they included features appropriate both to the imperial spirit of the age and Madras's tropical climate. As with the Banqueting and Memorial Halls, these Protestant churches were visible symbols of the British determination to be permanent rulers of India. And yet, as was not atypical in colonial port cities in Asia, these new imperial palaces and places of worship coexisted in the townscape of Madras with the Portuguese churches of St. Thomé, with the Hindu Kapaleeshwara temple in Mylapore, and several mosques, the principal of which was the Walajah mosque in Triplicane, built by the nabobs of Arcot in the late eighteenth century. Madras boasted fewer Indian grand residences than Calcutta, but when the nabob of Arcot fled to Madras in the 1760s and became a pensioner of the British, a palace was built for him at Chepauk close to the shore and Fort St. George. With the death of the last nabob, Ghulam Muhammad, in 1855, the palace was taken over by the government of Madras and used to accommodate the Board of Revenue.

The spaciousness of the city was preserved by the creation of public parks (the People's Park, on the western edge of George Town, was opened in 1859), and by a broad esplanade, known as the Marina, which was laid out along the seafront from the fort to St. Thomé and was completed in 1885. Many of the earlier public buildings, like Government House and the Memorial Hall, had announced the rulers' confident spirit and imperial purpose through the use of solid and imposing classical architecture. Following the demise of the company and the takeover of India by the British Crown in 1858, a new spate of building in the Indo-Saracenic style began. This style sought to combine selected aspects of Hindu and Muslim architecture—domes, minarets, pointed arches, and canopied balconies—with the functional requirements of modern buildings. Recalling the architecture of the imperial Mughals and local nabobs, the Indo-Saracenic style also emphasized the grandeur and the "Indianness" of the British Empire in India. Although the style was developed elsewhere in India as well, some of its finest examples were produced in Madras between the 1860s and early 1900s in the work of two government architects, R. F. Chisholm and H. C. Irwin. Together they gave Madras a new and alluringly oriental appearance, notably with the Senate House (1874–79), the Madras High Court (1889–92), and the Law College (1894), which are near the Marina. Egmore Railway Station (1905–8), further inland, is another signal example of the newer style. Chisholm also drew upon the Hindu architecture of Travancore for his Post and Telegraph Office (1875–84). These buildings still dominate the Madras skyline.

The population of Madras grew more slowly during the nineteenth century than those of Bombay and Calcutta. Kipling called Madras "a withered beldame . . . brooding on ancient fame," but the city was not as inert and backward-looking as his description suggests. Madras remained India's third-largest city throughout the colonial period. In the first complete census of 1871, its population was 367,552; by 1901 this had risen to 509,346. By the 1930s the city sprawled along the Bay of Bengal over a ten-mile stretch, its municipal boundaries extending over thirty square miles. Its continuing growth was stimulated by expanding commercial activity, based in George Town, and by the construction of railways linking the city with the rest of India (the line to Bombay was completed in 1871). The rail link made Madras a major outlet for a wide variety of goods, including cotton, food grains, and leather. Construction of the harbor was completed in 1896, which helped to consolidate the commercial importance of the growing metropolis, as did the emergence of a modern textile industry. (The old export trade to which Madras owed its origins had died out early in the nineteenth century.) The city's Buckingham and Carnatic mills employed 7,000 workers by 1908 and 9,000 thirty years later. Together with the railway workshops at the neighboring city of Perambur, they helped tranform the area to the west of the fort into an industrial environment.

By the outbreak of World War I, Madras, with its great array of commercial, administrative, educational, and cultural institutions, had taken on many of the classic forms and functions of a colonial port city. But it was always more than a British town. It was also a major cultural and political center for the Tamil and Telugu populations of the presidency and a magnet to professional and working-class migrants from as far away as Malabar and Mysore. The city has continued to grow since 1947, but it was spared the large influx of refugees that rapidly swelled the populations of Calcutta, Delhi, and Karāchi after the partition of India. By 1991 Madras had 5.4 million inhabitants, thus retaining its position as the fourth largest city in post-Independence India.

Following the breakup of the old Madras province in 1956, Madras city became the capital of the new state of Tamil Nādu. As such it has been at the center of the struggle to assert a distinctive Tamil identity in politics and cultural life. This struggle was led by the Drāviḍa Munnetra Kazhagham, which first came to power under C. N. Annadurai in 1967. Following his death the next year, Annadurai was buried on the Marina, opposite Senate House, in a shrine that has become a place of political pilgrimage. Madras (known as Chennai in Tamil) is also a center for Carnatic music, dance, and the thriving Tamil film industry. Despite attempts to turn it into a truly Tamil capital and despite the effects of recent urban expansion and development, Madras nevertheless retains a remarkable number of its colonial sites and monuments.

Further Reading: The early history of Madras is recounted in detail in several works, including Henry Davison Love's three-volume *Vestiges of Old Madras, 1640–1800* (London: J. Murray, 1913), J. Talboys Wheeler's *Madras in the Olden Times* (Madras: Higginbotham, 1882), and Mrs. Frank Penny's, *Fort St George: A Short History of Our First Possession in India* (London: Swan Sonnenschein, 1900). There is a useful summary article on Madras City in the *Imperial Gazetteer of India Provincial Series: Madras*, vol. I (Calcutta: Superintendent of Government Printing, 1908), pp. 497–521. An informative discussion of the growth and character of the colonial city may be found in Susan M. Neild's "Colonial Urbanism: The Development of Madras City in the Eighteenth and Nineteenth Centuries," in *Modern Asian Studies*, 13, no. 2 (1979): 217–46. The later history of the city is discussed in C. S. Srinivasachari's *History of the City of Madras* (Madras: Varadachary, 1939). The city's colonial architecture is discussed and extensively illustrated in two recent works, Sten Nilsson's *European Architecture in India, 1750–1850* (London: Faber, and New York: Taplinger, 1968) and Thomas R. Metcalf's *An Imperial Vision: Indian Architecture and Britain's Raj* (London and Boston: Faber, 1989).

—David Arnold

Mahābalipuram (Tamil Nādu, India)

Location: Twenty-four miles south of Madras, on the Bay of Bengal near the mouth of the Kāverī (Cauvery) River.

Description: The seaport and second capital of the Pallava Dynasty; an important historical site because of the numerous temples located there, including some of the earliest stone temples, both monolithic and structural, in southern India.

Contact: Government of India Tourist Office
154 Anna Salai
Madras 600 002
Tamil Nādu
India
(82) 69685

The ancient site of Mahābalipuram, also known as Māmallapuram, is important in Indian history as the second capital and seaport of the Pallava Dynasty, whose kingdom was centered at Kānchipuram, about thirty miles to the northwest. The Pallavas succeeded the Andhra, or Sātavāhana, Dynasty as rulers of southeast India and are known to have existed since the first century B.C. They were to become rulers of the Tondaimandalam, the area around Madras and Kānchipuram, from the third century A.D. The Pallava kings are best known for their rivalry with the Cāḷukyas, with whom they were frequently at war. The height of the power of the Pallava Dynasty was between the fifth and eighth centuries.

Our understanding of Mahābalipuram's early history has changed greatly in recent years. Several early scholars believed there was no occupation of Mahābalipuram prior to its development by the Pallavas in the sixth and seventh centuries. Recent archaeological discoveries, however, suggest that this analysis is incorrect. Coins of the Romans, Bactrians, and Andhras have been discovered in the sands of the city's ancient port, indicating that the site was in use as an international trading center from a much earlier date than was previously supposed. Details concerning this period, however, will remain unknown until further archaeological research is undertaken.

The historical name for Mahābalipuram is Māmallapuram, by which it is often known today. This older name translates as Town of Mahāmalla, in reference to the city's greatest patron, Narasiṃhavarman I Mahāmalla. Mahāmalla itself means Great Wrestler. Mahābalipuram, the corrupted modern form, has a completely different translation: Town of the Great Demon King Bali, a reference to the god Vishnu's vanquishing of the demon.

The Pallava kings patronized many religions during their period of rule. Many references indicate that the Pallavas were originally Buddhists, but some scholars stipulate that they were followers of Jainism. Certainly adherents of both religions lived in the kingdom, but which faith the kings themselves practiced remains unclear. One exception is King Mahendravarman I (reigned 600–30), whose conversion to Hinduism from Jainism by the saint Appar is recorded. His reign correlates to an era of prolific temple building at Mahābalipuram.

The earliest Pallava king to be associated with temple building at Mahābalipuram was his predecessor, Simhavishnu, who reigned from 575 to 600. A shallow sculptural relief in the Adivaraha Maṇḍapa (sometimes referred to as the Adivarahasvami Maṇḍapa), depicts Simhavishnu standing with his queens, who are represented in a pose of adoration. The *maṇḍapas* are shallow, open-sided, excavated cave temples. An inscription below clearly identifies the relief to be Simhavishnu. But the identification of Simhavishnu with the excavation of the temple is thrown into question by the adjacent relief, which depicts his successor Mahendravarman I. It is most likely that the work was begun during the reign of Simhavishnu and completed by Mahendravarman I.

An author and patron of the arts, Mahendravarman I was responsible for the excavation of many temples dedicated to Siva. The early temples of Mahābalipuram are essentially cave temples, excavated into the sides of the low-lying granite hills. This was the traditional style of temple construction throughout the subcontinent, as can be seen in the famous Buddhist cave temples of Ellora and Ajanta. The cave temples of Mahābalipuram are not on the same scale as these earlier shrines, and they are composed usually of single cells, and never more than two cells. The small size of the caves most likely owes to the extreme hardness of the granite rock, which required a laborious excavation process. The temples often have openings ornamented with distinctive columns, square at the top and bottom with an octagonal section in the middle. The columns are purely decorative, as they are not needed to support the monolithic rock structure above.

Scholars face great difficulty assigning a precise date to most of the temples at Mahābalipuram because of their prolonged period of construction. It has been estimated that the excavation of the caves took as long as a century, so those temples begun under one monarch's reign would have been completed during that of his successor or even later. Therefore the kings represented in the relief carvings may or may not be the monarchs responsible for their initial construction. It is clear, however, that Mahendravarman I's successor Narasiṃhavarman I (reigned 630–60) was responsible for a larger proportion of the temples at Mahābalipuram than any other monarch. Narasiṃhavarman I encouraged artistic activity and underwrote the building of many temples. He also was a successful military commander, as he expanded the Pallavas'

One of the rathas *at Mahābalipuram*
Photo courtesy of Air India Library, New York

Arjuna's Penance, Mahābalipuram
Photo courtesy of Air India Library, New York

territory and helped a Sri Lankan prince regain control of the island. This naval expedition set sail from the port of Mahābalipuram, after having been escorted from Kānchipuram by the king himself.

Descriptions of Mahābalipuram during the reign of Narasiṃhavarman I are provided by the writings of the Chinese pilgrim Xuan Zang, who visited the kingdom in 642. Xuan Zang, a guest at the court for an extended period, recorded his observations of the kingdom's temples and monasteries. Another chronicler, Tirumangai Ālvār, records that in the port of Mahābalipuram were "vessels bent to the point of breaking, laden as they are with wealth, big trunked elephants, and nine gems in heaps." This is certainly an indication of the prosperity of Mahābalipuram as a trading port under the rule of Narasiṃhavarman I.

The cave temples excavated during Narasiṃhavarman's reign are similar in form to the earlier ones but are more sophisticated in their decoration. The Varaha Maṇḍapa, for instance, has slender fluted columns dividing the opening, showing a definite influence of Greco-Roman classical architecture. The capitals of the columns have a striking resemblance to Roman capitals, and many of the regal figures in the sculpted panels are depicted in the European style of sitting, rather than the Indian cross-legged pose. As the style created at Mahābalipuram became the basis of the classic Dravidian style of southern India, this European influence spread throughout the region.

Among the most fascinating features of Mahābalipuram are the so-called *rathas*, which stand in a line slightly closer to the coast than the *maṇḍapas*. The *rathas* are small monolithic buildings entirely carved from a single elongated mound of solid granite. Many observers have speculated about the origin and function of the *rathas*. With the exception of the Durgā Ratha, the *rathas* are in an unfinished state, with some interiors only partially hollowed out. The most immediate perception of the *rathas* is that they are temples, but not even the Durgā Ratha, which was completed, has any remnants of a shrine inside. So if the *rathas* were not temples, what was their purpose? Some scholars have proposed that they were a type of experiment in which stone masons attempted to reproduce wooden structural temples in stone. This theory is supported by the fact that each *ratha* is different. It may be that the experiment was abandoned in favor of the quicker process of structural building in stone. Owing to their unfinished state, the *rathas* may always remain a mystery.

Another monument that has been the subject of much debate is the carving known to scholars as Arjuna's Penance. This remarkable work, thought to have been created during the reign of Narasiṃhavarman I, has become one of the most celebrated of early Indian sculptures. It was carved in relief on the faces of two huge boulders and depicts numerous gods, people, and animals gathered in an attitude of reverence and facing the cleft between the two rocks. Two large elephants with an infant elephant between their legs dominate the composition on the right boulder. Scholarly debate has focused on the subject of the animals' reverence. Initially it was assumed that the gathering was in honor of Arjuna (the hero to whom Krishna delivered the *Bhagavad Gītā*), who is depicted standing on the left. But because the figures are all facing toward two *nagas* (serpent deities) in the cleft between the rocks, it would appear that they are, in fact, the subject of homage. The sculpture apparently represents a story from Indian mythology, the descent of the Ganges. This theory is supported by the presence of a cistern above the rocks, from which water was released down the cleft. The sculpture is artistically noteworthy for the extraordinary naturalism and delicate carving of the figures.

Narasiṃhavarman's son Rājasiṃha, also known as Narasiṃhavarman II, who reigned at the end of the seventh century, was responsible for the building of the famous Shore Temple on the seafront of Mahābalipuram. Originally the temple was inland, but owing to the erosion of the coastline it now stands on the shore. The Shore Temple is one of the earliest structural temples to have survived in southern India. The pyramidal, towered temple contains three shrines and honors both Siva and Vishnu. Unfortunately, much of the exterior sculpture has been weathered by the sea; a protective wall built around it in recent years is expected to prevent further deterioration, although it has made the experience of viewing the temple somewhat less dramatic by fencing it off from the crashing waves. The beautifully carved interior has escaped the forces of nature. Within the inner sanctum, the incorporation of the bedrock, carved with an image of Vishnu, indicates that this part of the shrine dates from an earlier period than the rest of the structure. Around the perimeter of the temple, hundreds of sitting Nandis (Siva's bull) are carved. The Shore Temple is of a similar date and style to the Kailāsanātha Temple in the Pallava capital of Kānchipuram. It has been designated a UNESCO World Heritage site.

Mahābalipuram faded from history when the great Coḷa Dynasty conquered the Pallava realm in A.D. 897. Mahābalipuram probably remained a trading port but was no longer a place of importance, and eventually it was deserted altogether. Antiquarians rediscovered it in the nineteenth century, and today it has been resurrected as a tourist site. It is essentially a small town with two primary streets. An archaeological museum has been established to preserve sculptures and architectural fragments found in the vicinity. In addition to businesses catering to travelers, Mahābalipuram has an art school that teaches stone carving and the history of temple sculpture. The many great examples of such sculpture here serve both to inspire students and draw many visitors.

Further Reading: *History of the Pallavas of Kanchi* by R. Gopalan (Madras: University of Madras Press, 1928) is essential reading for the history of the Pallava Dynasty. Although it focuses on Kānchipuram, it contains many references to Mahābalipuram. Somewhat out of date and incorrect in a few of its conclusions, it is nonetheless the only book devoted solely to the history of the Pallavas. *Art and Architecture of the Indian Subcontinent* by J. C. Harle (Harmondsworth, Middlesex, and New York: Penguin, 1986) contains an interesting and comprehensive chapter that focuses on Mahābalipuram from an art historical perspective. *Mahābalipuram* by C. Sivaramamurti (fourth edition, New Dehli: Archaeological Survey of India, 1978) concentrates on the site itself.

—Charles Savile

Mandalay (Myanmar)

Location: On the Ayeyarwady (formerly Irrawaddy) River in northern Myanmar (formerly Burma), approximately 365 miles north of Yangon.

Description: The last capital of the Konbaung Dynasty, Mandalay was built as a sacred Buddhist center by King Mindon Min in 1857. It was annexed by the British in 1886 and occupied by the Japanese during World War II. The city is graced with numerous elaborate shrines despite its diminished grandeur. When the government returned to the use of native Burmese place-names throughout the country in 1989, Mandalay's name went unchanged.

Contact: Ministry of Hotels and Tourism
77-91 Sule Pagoda Street
Kyauktada Township
Yangon
Myanmar
(1) 77966 or (1) 75328

Once the romantic subject of Rudyard Kipling's verse and Hollywood movies, Mandalay survives as a dusty river port whose residents struggle daily with poverty and political repression. Yet the city remains the cultural center of Myanmar, its role as protector of Buddhism demonstrated amply by the many prominent pagodas and monasteries that house 20,000 monks.

Pagodas on the site predate the establishment of the city. In 1847, a decade before Mandalay's founding, the Myanmarese king Pagan Min built the Eindawya Pagoda, a gilded shrine that houses a Buddha image made of chalcedony. The shrine marks the site near the Ayeyarwady River where Pagan had been living when he acceded to the Lion Throne of the Konbaung Dynasty at Amarapura. His defeat in the Second Anglo-Burmese War (1852–53) cost him the much-contended throne, however, when his brother Mindon Min deposed him in 1853. Whereas the much-feared Pagan had executed thousands of people during his brief reign, the new king approached his duties in a relatively progressive manner.

A devoutly religious man, Mindon decided to move his court from Amarapura to a site several miles north on the banks of the Ayeyarwady River, in accordance with the Buddha's prophecy from the top of Mandalay Hill that a sacred center would be built there on the 2,400th anniversary of Buddhism. Mindon chose the base of the 775-foot Mandalay Hill, not far from the Eindawya Pagoda, as the site for the founding in 1857 of a monastery, the Atumashi Kyaung (Incomparable Monastery). As was customary when relocating royal courts, he had the palace compound at Amarapura dismantled and rebuilt as the Shwe Myo Taw (Royal Golden City) at the foot of Mandalay Hill just west of the monastery; the complex was protected by a wall and moat.

Apparently, Mindon was not too progressive to forgo the Myanmarese custom of burying people alive when building new cities: he reportedly had fifty-two poor souls sealed into the four corners of Mandalay's foundations, in the hope that their spirits would guard the city. The gridded city, approximately a walled square, represents Tavatimsa, an important Buddhist heaven for the Myanmarese. Mindon finally relocated his court and government to Mandalay in 1861, along with some 150,000 subjects from the former capital. Mindon encouraged the development of artisans' guilds, many of which still serve the trades responsible for carving alabaster, marble, and wood, casting bronze, and producing gold leaf.

Pagodas dominate the landscape of Mandalay, with a great many clustered on the south side of Mandalay Hill; three covered stairways wind up the hill past the festively decorated shrines. The Kuthodaw Pagoda, begun in 1857, represented Mindon's efforts to fulfill the Buddha's prophecy. Five thousand masons spent eight years copying the entire Tripitaka, or canon of Buddhism, from palm leaf manuscripts to 729 marble slabs, each housed in its own miniature white pagoda on the temple grounds. When Mindon convened the Fifth Buddhist Synod in Mandalay in 1879, he ordered a complete reading of the Tripitaka, a feat that took 2,400 monks six months to accomplish. In 1866 at the Sandamuni Pagoda, near the south stairway leading up the hill, two of Mindon's sons murdered Prince Kanaung, the king's brother and chosen heir. The murder sparked a palace rebellion, and to avoid further strife Mindon never named a new successor.

In 1878 Mindon completed the Kyauktawgyi Pagoda, which he intended to model after the Ananda Pagoda—paragon of the Myanmarese classical style—in Bagon (Pagan). The turmoil in the wake of Kanaung's assassination prevented the king from proceeding with his grand plans. Even so, a Buddha carved from a single block of pale green marble from the nearby Sagyin quarry distinguishes the pagoda. In order to bring the 800-ton piece to Mandalay, 10,000 Myanmarese workmen spent two weeks dragging it through a specially constructed canal. Away from Mandalay Hill, the Mahamuni (Arakan) Pagoda in the city's southern section houses the twelve-foot Mahamuni (Great Sage) statue that the Arakanese tribe discovered and restored in the western Myanmarese jungle. Completely covered with gold leaf by pilgrims, the image is ascribed special powers, and only men may touch the statue.

According to Brahmin-Buddhist cosmology, the royal palace also had sacred connotations: its Great Audience Hall stood at the center of the universe. A seven-tiered golden spire

Stupas at the Kuthodaw Pagoda, Mandalay
Photo courtesy of The Chicago Public Library

atop the hall—which also housed 133 apartments for the king's many wives and concubines—soared above the multi-ton, ruby-studded Lion Throne; the tower symbolized Mount Meru, mythological home of the gods. The Duck, Elephant, Deer, and Lily Throne Halls once clustered about the central structure.

Unlike his predecessor, Mindon agreed to work with the British, and he even instituted European business and engineering practices to improve the state structure, build roads, and establish a telegraph system. During Mindon's reign, Europeans often managed factories equipped with European machinery. Mindon died in 1880; his dreams for Mandalay survived him by only six years.

The British had coveted the region for many years and wanted to make it part of their Indian empire. They also wanted to thwart France's plans to build a railway between Mandalay and Haiphong in Annam (Vietnam). Upon Mindon's death, one of his wives and her daughter, Supayalat, had conspired to have a lesser son of Mindon, Prince Thibaw, crowned king, with Supayalat as his chief queen. The British soon used Thibaw as a scapegoat to justify an invasion of northern Myanmar. In keeping with Myanmarese custom—which stipulated only that no blood be spilled on Myanmarese soil—Thibaw had set about eliminating all potential rivals to his throne. He had his victims tied into red velvet sacks and beaten to death; their blood remained in the sacks, technically leaving the ground spotless. A raucous festival under way in Mandalay drowned out the victims' cries for mercy. When the British heard of the massacre, they announced the news to the world, depicting Thibaw as a barbarian. They raided Mandalay in 1885, formally annexing northern Myanmar on January 1, 1886; the British exiled Thibaw and Supayalat to India and rapidly imposed colonial rule in Mandalay. With complete disregard for Myanmarese sensibilities, the foreigners appropriated the Shwe Myo Taw for a barracks and renamed it Fort Dufferin. British officers used the Lily Throne Room as a clubhouse. The Lion Throne disappeared during the raid, only to surface in London some years later.

Mindon's private residence, the Golden Palace, was spared the ignominious fate of the rest of the royal palace. The Golden Palace had been moved after his death in 1880 to the vicinity of sacred structures at the base of Mandalay Hill. A masterpiece of carved teak highlighted with lacquer, glass mosaics, and gold leaf, the palace immediately became the Shwe Nandaw Monastery.

The British imported Indian citizens to run the government offices, and the latter soon dominated the country's economy. The Myanmarese, subjected to the most virulent racism, soon were outnumbered in their own land. An underground movement to create an independent Myanmar was born at Rangoon University during the 1920s. The Japanese provided the group's leaders, including Aung San and Ne Win, with schooling in guerrilla warfare. Called the Thakin movement after the Myanmarese phrase for "my owner"—an appropriation of a title reserved for the ruling Europeans—the well-trained group evolved into the Burma Independence Army (BIA) and, subsequently, into the Burma National Army (BNA). Originally numbering thirty members, the BIA/BNA grew to 23,000 and aided Japan when that country invaded Myanmar in 1942.

Japan wanted Myanmar for several reasons. First, the country boasted rich oil reserves and other natural resources. Second, and more pressing, Japan needed to control the strategic Burma Road, built between 1937 and 1939 to connect Lashio, northeast of Mandalay, with Kunming in the Chinese province of Yunnan. From Lashio, the Japanese easily could reach Mandalay and sail down the Ayeyarwady to the sea. When the United States government extended the Lend-Lease program to Nationalist China in 1942, the potential flow of military equipment on the Burma Road prompted the Japanese to act. The advance of the Fifteenth Army, led by Lieutenant General S. Iida, took the British by surprise. They abandoned Yangon on March 7, 1942, and retreated from Mandalay by the end of April. The British forces and their commander, Field Marshal Harold Alexander, employed a scorched-earth policy during their retreat to India, burning much of Myanmar to the ground. The Japanese established their high command headquarters for northern Burma at Fort Dufferin, making the former royal compound a primary target for Allied bombers. Over the next two years, the Allies made two unsuccessful attempts to retake Myanmar and the Burma Road, but in neither case did the fighting reach Mandalay. The war in Myanmar had its own peculiar rhythm, set by monsoons in the south and the unreliable flow of supplies.

In 1945, after the Japanese had suffered heavy losses in a battle at Imphal-Kohima in India, the British Fourteenth Army thought the time right to retake Myanmar. The United States was content to keep the Japanese out of northern Myanmar and perhaps to gain control of Mandalay. The British, however, led by Lord Mountbatten, Allied supreme commander for Southeast Asia, and Lieutenant General William Slim, determined to reach Yangon at the southern tip of Myanmar. After capturing numerous bridgeheads across the Chindwin River in western Myanmar, Slim planned to draw the Japanese into battle on the dry Shwebo Plain, northwest of Mandalay between the Chindwin and Ayeyarwady Rivers. The Japanese commander, General Hyotaro Kimura, had no intention of fighting on the Shwebo Plain and planned instead to pull his men east of the Ayeyarwady and annihilate the Allies when they crossed the river. Meantime, Aung San, suspicious of Japan's commitment to Myanmarese independence, had brought his Burmese National Army troops over to the Allies.

Even in the dry season, the Ayeyarwady measured 500 yards across at its narrowest point and a harrowing 4,000 yards at its widest. In the early morning hours of February 14, the Fourteenth Army crossed at the narrowest point, Nyaungu, and slipped between two Japanese regiments. By the first week of March, the Allied Nineteenth Indian Division was advancing on Fort Dufferin. The Japanese and their few remaining Myanmarese sympathizers held out until March 20 before escaping through drains in the moat. Most of the escapees seem to have been captured and executed within a few days.

Soon after the war, in the spring of 1947, the British Labour government granted Myanmar independence, and Aung San set up a transitional government run by his Anti-Fascist People's Freedom League. Barely three months later, on July 19, Aung San and six other members of the executive council were assassinated. U Nu, another member of the Thakin movement, continued their work, and on January 4, 1948, at 4:20 A.M., Myanmar declared itself an independent nation. The delayed date and unusual hour of the official ceremony stemmed from the ancient Myanmarese belief in astrological influences. In a symbolic acknowledgment of Myanmar's restored sovereignty, Lord Mountbatten arranged for the return to Mandalay of the Lion Throne. (It now is housed in the National Museum at Yangon, with a replica on display in Mandalay.)

The war left Myanmar's economy a shambles, and the new country struggled with independence as numerous factions jockeyed for power. Allied bombing had destroyed much of Mandalay, including the heavily targeted royal palace sector. Among the exquisite teak structures that once had housed the royal administration, only the Golden Palace survived; it had been removed from the targeted area and installed as a monastery among the temples and monasteries on Mandalay Hill. The Golden Palace is Myanmar's sole surviving example of royal wood construction.

In 1962 General Ne Win, one of Aung San's compatriots in the Thakin movement, orchestrated a military coup in Yangon and installed himself as the country's dictator. Ne Win imposed a strict isolationist policy, and for the next twenty-five years, the world had little contact with Myanmar. The military government dealt swiftly and severely with insurrections mounted by students, Karen tribesmen, and others.

The volatile situation peaked in the summer of 1988, when a people's movement emerged from meetings between students and Buddhist monks. The movement grew to include government workers. A march of nearly 100,000 protesters in September in Yangon resulted in a massacre as soldiers turned their guns on the crowd. A full-fledged rebellion ensued.

Mandalay escaped the worst of the violence, in large part because of the power of the monks. Demonstrators surrounded Fort Dufferin, where the army and police force were ensconced. The monks agreed to keep the demonstrators from storming the fort if the army and police agreed not to interfere in the uprising. The monks formed a local militia

Marble statue of the Buddha in Kyauktawgyi Pagoda
Phtot courtesy of Embassy of the Union of Myanmar, Washington, D.C.

named the Red Eagle Brigade for the abbot who led the force. The Red Eagles fostered an atmosphere of cooperation, enabling them to control the prices of goods and services in the area. Mandalay's pagodas, monasteries, and university buildings accommodated meetings, while kiosks displayed current information throughout the city. Underground newspapers ran pictures of suspected government informants.

An unexpected leader of the democracy movement emerged in the form of Aung San Suu Kyi, the expatriate daughter of the Myanmarese national hero, Aung San. She had returned to Yangon in April 1988 to care for her dying mother, only months before the first major demonstrations throughout the country. Drawn into the political activities that were sweeping the nation, Suu Kyi traveled the country holding pro-democracy rallies and publicly criticizing the government of Ne Win. In July 1989 the government placed her under house arrest. Her influence continued to grow despite her absence from the streets; the regime freed Suu Kyi on July 10, 1995, an event that suggests the possibility of compromise on the part of the government.

Despite these recent troubles, the city of pagodas remains the thriving religious center that Mindon Min intended it to be 150 years ago. Yet given Mandalay's poverty, the government has been hard pressed to justify its expensive concrete reconstruction of the royal palace at Fort Mandalay, where Myanmar houses military troops for the region.

While the rest of Myanmar continues to deteriorate, Mandalay may prosper yet from its prominent position on the Burma Road. Inexpensive goods from China have passed through Mandalay along this route since a bilateral agreement in 1988; as well, the traffic in illicit drugs also has burgeoned recently along the Burma Road. Indeed, Myanmar holds the dubious distinction of being the world's largest producer of raw opium, and the government has made only token gestures to stop the lucrative heroin industry.

Further Reading: *A History of Modern Burma* by J. F. Cady (Ithaca, New York: Cornell University Press, 1958), although dated, remains useful. Also out of date, but with much specific material relating to Mandalay, is *Mandalay and Other Cities of the Past in Burma* (London: Hutchinson, 1907). A good recent source for Myanmarese history is *Historical Dictionary of Myanmar* by Jan Becka (Metuchen, New Jersey, and London: Scarecrow Press, 1995). In spite of the fact that it is essentially a travel guide, *1994 Thailand, Indochina and Burma Handbook* (Bath, England: Trade and Travel Publications, and Lincolnwood, Illinois: Passport Books, 1994) offers an in-depth look at the history of Myanmar and its various leaders. For a realistic description of the battle over Myanmar in World War II, see *The Great Battles of World War II* (London: Hamlyn, and Chicago: Regnery, 1972) by Henry Maule, a former British correspondent for the *New York Daily News*. A notable book on the democracy movement is *The Lands of Charm and Cruelty: Travels in Southeast Asia* by Stan Sesser (New York: Knopf, 1993; London: Picador, 1994), best known for his reports on Myanmar in *The New Yorker*.

—Mary F. McNulty

Māndu (Madhya Pradesh, India)

Location: In central India, approximately sixty miles southwest of Indore.

Description: Capital of the independent kingdom of Mālwa from 1401 to 1561. After it was incorporated into the Mughal Empire, Māndu was maintained as a rather marginal military outpost. The site still was put to military use by the Hindu Marāṭhās in the eighteenth and nineteenth centuries. Today Māndu lies deserted and its significance resides chiefly in its impressive Muslim architectural remains.

Contact: Government of India Tourist Office
Near Western Group of Temples
Khajurāho 471 606, Madhya Pradesh
India
2047, 2048

Although today Māndu is nothing but a deserted hill fort in central India, at the height of its glory it was the seat of Mālwa, a prosperous independent Muslim kingdom. Between 1401 and 1526, many impressive buildings, including palaces, mosques, and royal tombs, were erected there. The buildings combine Hindu elements with a basically Islamic architectural style. It is for its generally well-preserved and unique architectural heritage that Māndu still commands our attention today.

Māndu stands out because—together with Dhār a short distance to the north—it developed a style that largely forgoes the elaborate sculptural ornamentation characteristic of so much of India's architectural tradition. Māndu's monumental buildings rely on simplicity of line and, above all, mass to give expression to the worldly power of its Muslim rulers and to the nature of their religious convictions. The heavy masonry, the buttressed walls, and the closed facades convey an aura of austerity and fierce independence. Once, however, these were softened by a brilliant use of color, the only decorative feature that the builders permitted themselves. Although Muslim prohibitions on the creation of images forbade the builders from adopting Hindu sculptural traditions, the tiling, colored glazes, and inlay work bore witness to a local Hindu influence in the wealth of their detail and the brilliance of the color. Unfortunately, in many of the buildings only traces remain of this most perishable element, and the radiant color that once enriched Māndu's architecture can in many instances only be guessed at.

Situated on a lone rock outcropping in the Vindhyas, Māndu is nearly encircled by a deep ravine. A natural causeway leads to the main gate on the northern side. The crown of this highly defensible hill was first fortified in the sixth century, but it was not until the tenth century that Māndu began to play a role in the politics of central India. The area was then part of the vast territories of Rāja Bhoj of the Paramara Dynasty, which maintained a capital first at Ujjain and later at nearby Dhār. Rāja Bhoj expanded the fortifications, enclosing the entire hilltop plateau of more than eight square miles with a massive wall. He also built a royal residence and a series of Hindu temples. His reign was largely peaceful, and Māndu functioned primarily as a royal retreat.

The disintegration of the Paramara Dynasty was followed by an extended period of conflict among many independent kingdoms that sought to expand their influence in the region. A measure of stability finally returned to Māndu when it was conquered by the Muslim rulers of Delhi in 1304. The Hindu kingdom of Mālwa, of which Māndu was part, was absorbed into the Delhi Sultanate and governed by the Khaljī and Tughluq dynasties through the fourteenth century. The invasion of Timur (better known to the English-speaking world as Tamerlane) into northern and central India in 1398 spelled the end of the Delhi Sultanate. As power relations shifted, the governor of Mālwa carved out the area under his control as an independent kingdom in 1401.

The Afghan Shihāb-ud-Dīn Ghūri, the erstwhile governor and then king of Mālwa, took the title of Dilawar Khān and became the founder of the Ghūri Dynasty under which Māndu came to greatness. Although Dilawar Khān kept his capital at Dhār, he built a mosque at Māndu in 1405. The building is designed around a central court enclosed by a colonnade. The richly detailed decoration in the entrance and the courtyard bears witness to a Hindu inspiration. Dilawar Khān also reinforced Māndu's fortifications. Most of the work undertaken mined the older Hindu structures for building materials, and as a consequence none of the Hindu buildings have survived intact. However, their elements can still be traced in the surviving walls, gates, mosques, tombs, and royal residences.

The new king of Mālwa enjoyed his rule for only four years and died (possibly by poisoning) shortly after building the Māndu Mosque. His son assumed the title of Hoshang Shāh and moved his capital from Dhār to Māndu, which was renamed Shadiābād, or City of Joy. Hoshang's reign was extremely warlike, and he was not always very successful in his military campaigns. His rule was interrupted when he was defeated in a war with the neighboring kingdom of Gujarāt and held prisoner for a year. Ultimately, he was restored to his sultanate and reigned until 1432. Despite his warlike tendencies, Hoshang ushered in the golden age of Māndu's monumental architecture.

One of the first of Hoshang's construction projects was the Delhi Gate, which guards the main entrance to Māndu at the northern causeway. This battle-scarred gate stands on

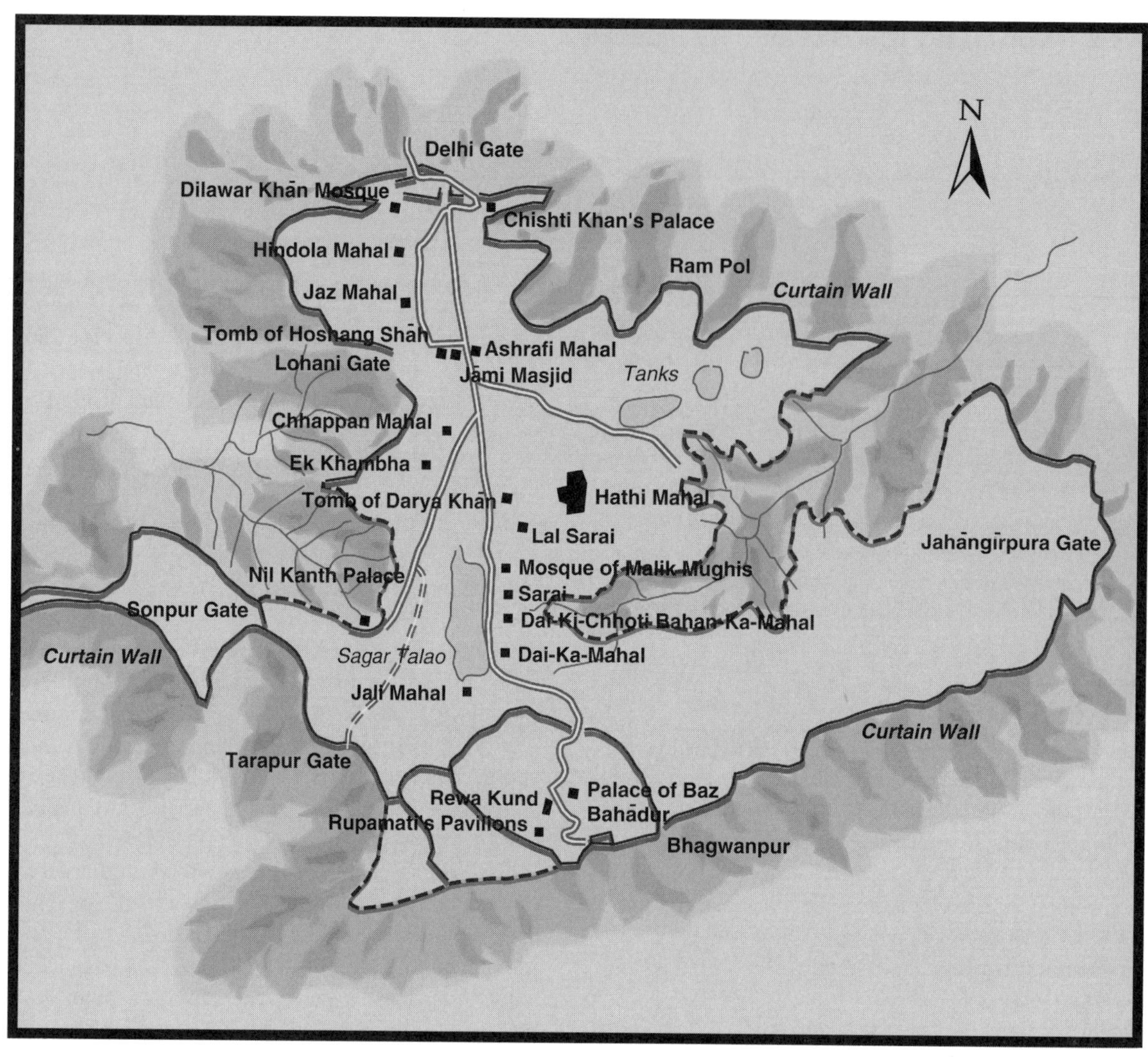

Map of Māndu
Illustration by Tom Willcockson

the upper reaches of the steep hillside, and its long and narrow stepped passageway was designed to accommodate elephants. Hoshang also began construction on Māndu's chief mosque, the Jāmi Masjid, later in his reign. It was finished in 1454 by Mahmūd I. This huge structure is thought to have been patterned after the great mosque in Damascus, Syria. Its square courtyard measures 260 feet on each side, and its prayer wall has no fewer than fifty-eight small domes and three large ones. Reportedly, the Mughal emperor Shāh Jahān sent his architects to Māndu to study this mosque before they created a design for his own masterpiece, the Tāj Mahal. Hoshang Shāh's tomb lies immediately behind the mosque, and it is built in a mixture of native Hindu and imported Islamic styles. Its interior is lit by stone *jali* screens that bear the stamp of Hindu refinement in their design. The long, narrow hall behind the tomb enclosure has a typically Islamic barrel-vaulted ceiling. The exterior decoration combines both the Hindu and Islamic traditions in its rosettes in relief and its lotus flowers with blue enameled stars.

Hoshang's son Mohammed Shāh, the last king of the Ghūri Dynasty, ruled for only one year before he was poisoned by his minister, Mahmūd Khān. The usurper ascended the throne under the name Mahmūd Shāh I Khaljī, creating a new dynasty, and ruled for thirty-three turbulent years. His reign was marked by constant conflict with neighboring states, which frequently resulted in territorial expansions for Mālwa. Mahmūd Shāh was an exceptionally able warrior, and he took the kingdom to its greatest size. He also developed a reputation on the Indian subcontinent for his depredations against Hindu adversaries, building an impressive record of temple destruction and enslavement of the Hindu population.

Few monuments from Mahmūd Shāh's reign have survived intact, as they were, for the most part, poorly designed and built. One of his more notable architectural achievements was the Tower of Victory, which originally had seven stories. Only the base still stands. The building was erected to celebrate a victory in battle over the kingdom of Chitor, but the outcome of the battle must have been dubious, since Chitor built a similar structure to proclaim its victory over Māndu. Another important ruin is the Ashrafi Mahal, built in the early years of Mahmūd's reign. Originally a *medrese,* or religious college, Mahmūd extended it to house his own tomb. The remains of the tomb suggest that it once may have been among the architectural glories of Māndu, a huge building with a brilliantly colored dome.

In 1469, Mahmūd Shāh's son Ghiyās-ud-Dīn ascended the throne and reigned until 1501. An inefficient ruler, he devoted himself primarily to women: he reputedly had 15,000 women in his seraglio, a thousand of them as personal guards. Palaces built in Māndu during his reign attest to his love of pleasure. They include an audience hall, the Hindola Mahal (Swinging Palace), so named because its sloping side walls convey the impression of a swinging motion. Its windows are filled with screens of delicate tracery. The Jaz Mahal (Ship's Palace), perhaps Māndu's most famous building, also dates to the late fifteenth century. The building resembles a ship, as it is much longer than it is wide and is situated between two lakes. From a distance the palace appears to float on the water. Once entirely staffed by women, the Jaz Mahal served as Ghiyās's harem. Its architecture is elegant and graceful, and the arcaded ground floor, the steps to the roof terrace, and the three large halls and bath were all enlivened by colored glazes.

Rebellion brewed at the end of Ghiyās's long and peaceful reign, but the most dangerous of Ghiyās's adversaries turned out to be his own son, Nasir-ud-Dīn. Nasir, apparently weary of waiting for his father to make room for him in the natural way, poisoned Ghiyās in 1500. As might be expected in a man who murdered his father, Nasir was a brutal ruler, but not therefore any more effective than Ghiyās had been. He is said to have died of remorse, in 1512, leaving Mālwa in a state of decline, with royal authority under siege. His son, Mahmūd II, was dominated by his advisers. Power relations at the Mālwa court are adequately illustrated by the fact that the only notable construction activity from the reign of Mahmūd II was built not for the king, but for one of his advisers, Darya Khān. The Hathi Mahal, or Elephant Palace, originally a pleasure palace that gained its name because the short and massive pillars supporting the building resemble elephants' legs, was converted into Darya Khān's tomb. Built of red masonry and decorated with elaborate mosaics, it has a central dome and four corner domes.

Dominant as the advisers may have been, they did not prevent Mālwa's defeat at the hands of Bahādur Shāh of Gujarāt in 1526. Mahmūd II was executed when Māndu fell to the invaders, and in 1531 all of Mālwa was annexed by Gujarāt. In 1534 the Mughal emperor Humāyūn defeated Bahādur, but control of Mālwa reverted to its former rulers when Humāyūn became occupied with matters elsewhere in his empire. Baz Bahādur, the final independent ruler of Māndu, took power in 1554, but his interest lay in music rather than in architecture. Unlike his predecessors, he occupied an existing palace at the southern end of the citadel. This building lies near the Rewa Kund, a sacred tank that supplies the palace with water, and it is characterized by a mixture of Hindu and Muslim building elements. The palace has as its focus an open court with a cistern and an octagonal pavilion projecting off its north side and overlooking an old garden. Another part of the Rewa Kund complex of buildings consists of Rupamati's Pavilions, named for Baz Bahādur's mistress. Legend claims that Rupamati was a beautiful Hindu singer from the plains, for whom Baz Bahādur built the pavilions to persuade her to leave home and join him. The pavilions are square in design and covered with hemispherical domes, from where, according to legend, Rupamati could see the Narmada River and her homeland on the plains below.

The Mughal Empire did not leave Mālwa in peace for long. Rather than face the advancing troops of the Mughal conqueror Akbar in 1561, Baz Bahādur fled the city. With Akbar's conquest, Māndu's independence ended, and the capital of Mālwa was moved back to Dhār. Construction at the city did not come to a halt, but no additional monumental buildings were undertaken. The Mughals maintained the fort and added a few minor buildings. One of these is the Nil Kanth Palace, built between 1574 and 1575 by Budagh Khān, the officer in charge of Māndu under Akbar. Typical of Mughal architecture, this palace takes advantage of the landscape, incorporating a pool in its open courtyard, to which water is channeled through the palace itself. Inscriptions on the walls record Akbar's victories in the Deccan in 1600–01, when Māndu was used as a camp for his campaigns. Māndu again served as a military encampment in 1615, when Jahāngīr used the place as a headquarters to oversee a renewed campaign in the Deccan. Two years later, Jahāngīr returned and began restorations on many of Māndu's old buildings.

Even after the kingdom of Mālwa was subsumed into the expanding Mughal Empire by Akbar, it still retained a degree of autonomy. But Mālwa's self-determination came to an end when the Mughals themselves fell to the invading Marāṭhās in 1732. The new overlords also used Māndu's fortifications, and some traces of their construction activities remain. Nevertheless, Māndu had lost its political importance and major building campaigns were definitively over. Eventually, the hilltop site was deserted altogether.

Further Reading: Volume 2 of the *The Penguin Guide to the Monuments of India* by Philip Davies (London and New York: Viking, 1989), devoted to Islamic, Rājput, and European sites, contains detailed descriptions of many of Māndu's buildings. *Architecture of Mughal India* by Catherine B. Asher (Cambridge and New York: Cambridge University Press, 1992), a volume in *The New Cambridge History of India,* edited by Gordon Johnson, C. A. Bayly, and John F. Richards (29 vols., Cambridge and New York: Cambridge University Press, 1987–) focuses on the historical and cultural development of Muslim architecture in India rather than specific sites. A good and concise general history of India is available in Vincent A. Smith's *The Oxford History of India: From the Earliest Times to the End of 1911* (Oxford: Clarendon Press, 1919; fourth edition, edited by Percival Spear, New York and Oxford: Oxford

University Press, 1981). Finally, travel information may be found in many guidebooks to India. One of the better of these is Geoff Crowther's *India: a Travel Survival Kit* (Hawthorn, Victoria, and Berkeley, California: Lonely Planet, 1981; fifth edition, 1993), which contains a good historical overview.

—Robert Kellerman

Manila (Manila, Philippines)

Location: Manila lies on Manila Bay, a natural harbor on the Philippine island of Luzon, about 700 miles south of Hong Kong in the South China Sea.

Description: The capital city of the Republic of the Philippines, Manila was founded in 1571 by the Spaniard Miguel López de Legazpi and claimed as a colony for the Spanish king Philip II, who gave his name to the islands. It has served as the nation's capital ever since and is now a busy metropolis of some 9 million inhabitants.

Site Office: Department of Tourism
T. M. Kalaw Street, 207
1000 Ermita
Manila
Philippines
599031

The city of Manila lies on the eastern shore of Manila Bay, a large natural harbor into which the Pasig River flows from the southeast. The city derives its name from the *nilad* plant that once grew in a flowering profusion along the banks of the river. Manila proper covers only fifteen square miles, encompassing the historic district of Intramuros and a few surrounding neighborhoods. However, the greater metropolitan area covers more than 246 square miles, encompassing the cities of Manila, Caloocan City, Quezon City, and Pasay City and is home to 9 million people (1990 census), 13 percent of the total population of the Philippines. With a national annual growth rate of 2.3 percent and a population density of 32,000 persons per square mile in the metropolitan area, Manila's congestion, sanitation, transportation, and housing are the key challenges faced by the municipal government today.

Most histories of Manila begin with the Spanish conquest in the sixteenth century, mainly owing to the lack of historical records or physical evidence about the indigenous population before then. However, some of the Spanish conquerors wrote accounts of what they found, and from these records we can gain an impression of pre-Hispanic Manila. All across the Philippines, people who had migrated from the Malay Peninsula and Indonesia (not far to the west of the Philippine Archipelago) established settlements. The boats used by these peoples were called *barangays,* a term that later came to denote a village inhabited by one clan and survives today to describe a municipality. Each clan was under the jurisdiction of a *datu,* the patriarchal head. When several *barangays* merged into larger units, they came to be ruled by *rajas,* who collected taxes and levies to fund their courts, much as in feudal Europe. There were about forty such Malay settlements around the Manila Bay when the Spanish first arrived there. The kingdom of Namayan, inland from the mouth of the Pasig River, encompassed a large area that later became the suburbs of Spanish Manila.

Although the Spanish eventually conquered the islands, they were certainly not the first foreigners to arrive in the Philippines. Chinese traders settled there from A.D. 1000 onward, contributing significantly to the eventual shaping of the Philippine nation. South Asia provided another strong cultural influence, manifested principally in a writing system based on Sanskrit, brought to the Philippines by the Indonesian settlers from the Srivijaya and Majapahit empires. In the mid-fifteenth century, the Islamic religion arrived in the southern archipelago from Brunei and by the mid-sixteenth century had spread as far north as Manila, although the arrival of Spanish missionaries reversed this trend. Other traders frequented Manila Bay, notably the Japanese and mainland Chinese.

Miguel López de Legazpi and his fleet left the Mexican port of Puerto Navidad in 1564 with instructions to colonize the Philippines. He had made his base farther south than Manila on the island of Panay, whence he dispatched Martin de Goiti and Captain Juan de Salcedo in 1570 to capture Manila. Goiti and Salcedo failed in their first attempt, owing precisely to the strategic advantages of the city's location, which they could surmise and admire when they first cast anchor in the bay, with its outlet only twelve miles wide. They found the *kuta* of Raja Sulayman—a fort built of palm logs, defended by a narrow mound and protruding bronze and iron artillery, which they later discovered was cast in a foundry within the fort. Goiti left Manila, having engaged in battle with the Malays and burned the *kuta,* and it was not until the following year that Legazpi himself returned and took the settlement peacefully. In 1595 the Spanish celebrated the founding of Manila as the capital of the archipelago of disunited tribal groups and clans.

In 1571, however, the Spaniards were faced with an urgent need to defend their new conquest from various threats. In their competition for the Oriental spice trade, the Spanish faced the rivalries of the Portuguese and the Dutch, as well as of the English. The Japanese and Chinese each had their own designs on controlling the region's commercial activity, and in addition attacks could be expected from the Muslim inhabitants of the southern Philippines, notably of Mindanao. Unrest from within the ranks of the newly subjugated indigenous Malays closer to Manila also had to be accounted for. One Chinese pirate named Limahong in particular staged two attacks on Manila in 1574 with a fleet of 4,000 soldiers and sailors on 62 heavily armed junks, laden with many supplies as well as with an additional 2,000 civilians with which to found a colony of his own. Although he was defeated on both occasions, his efforts, combined with

Church of San Agustin, Manila
Photo courtesy of The Chicago Public Library

the devastation caused by fires in 1577, 1579, and 1583, left Manila in ruins.

Under the Jesuit priest Antonio Sedeño, who became Manila's first architect, the city took on its famous appearance of a medieval walled city, which was to remain a distinctive feature in Southeast Asia until the destruction of Intramuros during World War II. Although Manila Bay provided the city with a site sheltered from the worst of tropical weather, earthquakes remained a constant threat to any construction. To defend against fire, Sedeño chose stone and wood construction, using stone, adobe, and clay for bricks and roof tiles, combined with lime made from the abundance of sea shells, as well as granite imported from China. Sedeño designed a central square, or *plaza mayor,* similar to many found in Spain and in Spanish colonial towns, around which the most important buildings and streets were arranged concentrically. He also designed the city's defenses, giving it stone bulwarks, walls, and other fortifications. Then he designed the residences of important individuals such as Bishop Salazar, and other religious and governmental buildings. Sedeño was able to oversee the construction of Intramuros, as the fortified Spanish core of Manila came to be called, employing native labor as well as that of Chinese settlers, whom he taught to hew and cut stone and to fire bricks and tiles in a kiln. His work was completed under the next governor general, Gomez Perez Dasmariñas (in office from 1590 to 1593), who recruited the forced labor of many native Filipinos and Chinese settlers and who raised taxes from the population with which to pay for the completion of Intramuros. These fortifications were augmented in the eighteenth century, under renewed threats (this time from the British), with the addition among other things of ten new bulwarks and eight gates.

Within these fortifications, a distinctive architecture arose to provide elegant and earthquake resistant government buildings and private residences. This architectural style was an ingenious modification of the Spanish colonial style of Mexico, combined with the taste of the Spanish Peninsula, and carried out by local Filipino and Chinese labor, giving the final result a curious cultural blend. Typically, the ground floor of a residential building was constructed of stone or adobe brick, the walls having independent wooden posts to withstand seismic movements. The floor consisted of granite slabs brought from China. The first floor was then constructed of wood and constituted the main living area of the house. The signature feature of this style was the use of large win-

Aerial view of Manila
Photo courtesy of Philippine Consulate General

dows on horizontal hinges at the top, consisting of many tiny panes of thin, translucent capiz shells, such as can still be seen in some old Manila and provincial Philippine buildings today. The city building ordinance imposed construction of an *azotea,* a utility terrace made entirely of stone, on which all washing was done and where dried goods such as rice were stored. This kind of house, once widespread in Manila and called *bahay-na-bato,* is almost non-existent now, as is the nineteenth-century adaptation of this design, called the Antilles house after the Spanish designs in Cuba and Puerto Rico, which was built entirely of wood and had beautifully hand-painted interiors.

Even the thick buttress walls of some buildings, known as "earthquake baroque," could not withstand the terrible earthquake of 1886, after which modern measures such as the widespread use of corrugated iron sheets imported from Britain for roofing were introduced, with an altogether less picturesque effect. Since then the destruction caused by World War II, combined with the demands of an ever burgeoning population, have further compromised the architectural beauty of the city.

Sadly, the splendor of Intramuros under Spanish rule is difficult to imagine today, since very little of the old walled city survived the Japanese occupation and American retaking of Manila during World War II. An early seventeenth-century Spanish chronicler, Antonio de Morga, described the government buildings as elegant and spacious, their many windows looking out over the sea and their courtyards and colonnades providing the backdrop to the promenades of luxuriously dressed Spanish officials. Much of this luxury came from Manila's traditional role in the trade routes of Southeast Asia, and specifically from the Spanish controlled Acapulco-to-Manila galleon trade.

This famous trade route formed the linchpin of the Spanish conquest of the Philippine Islands. Driven by strictly mercantilist economics, the wealth of a nation was measured solely in terms of its accumulated gold and silver. A tightly regulated economy was to ensure a favorable balance of trade with other nations. Thus under the Spanish, Philippine trade was limited to the route to Acapulco in Mexico, another Spanish colony. Trade with other European nations was forbidden, although the Japanese and Chinese traders were still granted access to Manila under stringent regulations. As stated in a series of laws governing the Manila-Acapulco trade, a 250,000 peso limit was placed on the amount of merchandise the Philippines could export; this merchandise was permitted to leave Manila for Mexico (Nueva España) in only two vessels per annum with a maximum load of 300 tons each. However, these ships could return to Manila with 500,000 pesos worth of merchandise from Acapulco. Space on the galleons was allocated to individuals and institutions, and an entire subsidiary trade grew up around the allocation of space in the hold. The galleons would leave Manila in July in order to take advantage of favorable weather on the perilous journey. They would return early the following year, laden with silver and bullion, exposing themselves to the danger of piracy in the treacherous San Bernadino Strait between Samar and Leyte.

Initially the galleon trade was a mere concession to the Spanish inhabitants of the Philippines, giving them a modest livelihood; it later provided the Philippine government with a taxable revenue. The Spanish clearly wanted to maintain firm control over commerce in the New World. The rule stipulating that Chinese goods not be shipped from Manila to Acapulco was invariably ignored, resulting in a net outflow of silver to Chinese traders—precisely what the Spanish wanted to avoid. This trade, albeit lucrative only to a privileged few, could not fail to invite the jealousy of other powers in the region. The Dutch in particular made sustained efforts to cripple the galleon trade. They tried twice to blockade Manila, but, failing that, resorted to sporadic attacks on the Spanish galleons at sea, thus jeopardizing Manila's lifeline. Then the Dutch set up a naval base on the island of Formosa (present day Taiwan) in order to intercept the vital Chinese vessels. These brought silks, spices, indigo, fine porcelain, precious jewelry and gemstones, ivory and jade, lacquered furniture and other wood carvings to Manila, then at the center of an international trade embracing indirectly many nations of Southeast Asia, including Japan, China, Siam, Cambodia, Malaya, Borneo, and India.

In retaliation to the Dutch move, the Spanish authorities in Manila established their own outpost on Formosa in 1626. During the following decade, Dutch attacks decreased as the Dutch East India Company concentrated its efforts on consolidating its hold over Java, yet they recommenced strikes against Spanish trade vessels in 1645, trying to intercept the sea-weary galleons on their homeward stretch into the port of Manila. Miraculously, the galleons were able to defend themselves against the superior force of the Dutch fleet and avert a capture of their precious cargo of American silver. By 1648, far away in Europe, the Spanish and Dutch signed the peace treaty of Westphalia, after which Dutch attacks on Spanish trade in the Far East ceased. The galleon trade itself fell into decline in the late eighteenth and early nineteenth centuries, owing to Napoléon's invasion of Spain, coupled with the Mexican Wars of Independence, making Spain's monopoly on trade an impossibility. In 1815 the last great galleon set sail for Acapulco, after which the exotic trade between the Orient and the New World came to an end.

Manila itself was still subjected to sporadic raids by the Muslims based in the south, and in the eighteenth century the city, honored by Philip II as *Insigne y siempre leal ciudad* (distinguished and ever loyal city), actually fell to the sea-faring British and was occupied by them for two and a half years (1762–1764). However, the Spanish regained control and ruled over the Philippines until the late nineteenth century, when they were faced with a new threat to their authority: a nascent Filipino sense of nationhood and a call for independence.

Rousing the indigenous population to question Spanish rule required the active involvement of the Chinese mestizo community. Chinese settlers had been arriving in the Philippines since as early as A.D. 1000, and by the time of the Spanish conquest a recognized Chinese settlement had arisen in Manila called the Chinese Parian. These Chinese settlers, mostly from Fujian Province, married local Filipinos and thereby established a distinct class of mestizo, quite separate from the Chinese traders who arrived in Manila to sell their merchandise. The *Mestizo de Sangley,* as the Spanish referred to them, formed the basis of the emerging middle class, providing many invaluable services for the Spanish ruling class, initially acting as traders, artisans, or servants, and later controlling construction, trade, agricultural production, and banking. By the end of the nineteenth century, the half million Chinese mestizos far outnumbered the Spanish mestizos and in some provinces made up a third of the population: 46,000 lived in Manila. From the beginning, this power was a constant irritation to the Spanish, who considered the Chinese mestizo the lowest social class, lower even than the *indio* or native Filipino. Consequently, several massacres of Chinese mestizos occurred, particularly in 1603, thus causing many of them to flee to the provinces and to other cities in the Philippines. This movement extended the Chinese mestizos' trade network and furthered their integration with the native Filipinos all over the archipelago, thus precluding their identification with the Spanish ruling class.

By the late nineteenth century, wealthy Filipino and mestizo families were sending their sons to be educated in Spain, where a more liberal atmosphere prevailed than in Manila. Many young men returned to the Philippines with new ideas of liberty and national identity. Among them was the Philippine national hero, Dr. José Rizal, who returned to the Philippines from Spain in 1892 and founded the *Liga Filipina,* aimed at creating a sense of national unity among the diverse peoples of the entire Philippine Archipelago. While Rizal did not call for independence, remaining loyal to Spain and the Spanish to the end, he aroused the suspicions of the Spanish authorities, who executed him on December 30, 1896.

Genuine cause for Spanish concern, however, could be found among the less privileged classes, where activists calling for independence from the colonial power had formed a revolutionary organization called Katipunan under the leadership of Andres Bonifacio, a self-educated warehouseman. Plans for a revolt were uncovered by the Spanish in August 1896, forcing the hand of Katipunan to act early. Although revolts broke out around Manila, the movement was defeated after several months of fighting and Spanish promises of reform. Coinciding with the uneasy truce were hostilities between Spain and the United States, who secured a naval

Street scene, Chinese section of Manila
Photo courtesy of The Chicago Public Library

victory in Manila Bay in May 1898. The rebels, under the leadership of Emilio Aguinaldo, aligned themselves with the Americans led by Admiral George Dewey, only to be bitterly disappointed when the victorious Americans decided to keep control over the Philippines: one colonial power had been exchanged for another. The Philippine nationalist movement simply concentrated its efforts against the U.S. command over the islands and forced the Americans to view their period of rule as one of educating the Filipinos toward self rule, a process that took up the first decade of the twentieth century.

President William McKinley sent out two Philippine Commissions in 1899 and 1900, the second of which established civil government in Manila in 1901, acting both as legislature and the governor general's cabinet. In 1907 the Philippine Commission was transformed into the upper house of a bicameral body and a new Philippine Assembly was directly elected by a restricted, but Filipino, electorate. By 1913 there was a Filipino majority in the commission, although defense and foreign affairs remained under U.S. control.

In preparation for full independence, a ten-year Commonwealth was inaugurated on November 15, 1935 under the presidency of Manuel Quezon and the Nacionalista Party. This transitional arrangement was to give advantages to Filipino traders seeking to export goods to the United States, freeing them of tariffs. The most significant export to the U.S. was Philippine sugar. When the Depression hit hard in the United States in the 1930s, Filipino nationalists found an unexpected ally in the agricultural producers of America, who feared the preferential treatment given to Philippine products.

Any American plans to help the establishment of democratic institutions in the Philippines during the Commonwealth period fell by the wayside in 1941 at the height of World War II, when the Japanese invaded the Philippines on December 8. Manila was declared an "open city" before Christmas, and the American general Douglas MacArthur, in the Philippines to help shore up the defense, had to evacuate his headquarters to Corregidor. Filipino and American forces were forced to surrender to the Japanese in May 1942, and thereafter the country was governed by an executive commission consisting of members of an old Filipino elite, who had been collaborating with the Japanese since their invasion and who were directly appointed by the invaders. This executive commission was replaced in September 1943 by a puppet state under the Japanese-appointed president José Laurel. The Philippines were liberated under the leadership of General MacArthur in October 1944, when civil government was returned to the commonwealth. In April 1946, Manuel A.

Roxas, leader of the newly founded Liberal Party, was elected as the first president of the Republic of the Philippines, which was proclaimed on July 4, 1946.

At the end of World War II, Manila lay in shambles. Intramuros, once the best fortified city in the Orient, was in ruins. The country faced grave economic problems and lacked the resources to rebuild its infrastructure and economy. Only American aid made any recovery possible, and this was bought at the price of allowing U.S. military naval bases to be established in various parts of the Philippines, which proved to be invaluable to the Americans during the Vietnam War. American companies also had to be granted preferential rights in the extraction of natural resources in the Philippines, providing a potent reminder of the economic colonialism to which the islands had been subjected for the previous four centuries. Only in 1991, when the renewal of some of the U.S. naval base leases became due, did the Philippine government decide to forfeit the income derived from bases such as Subic Bay to the north of Manila and vote against an extension of the lease.

Tragically, the economic problems of the country were greatly exacerbated by the twenty-year dictatorship of Ferdinand Marcos and his wife Imelda, who together plundered an untold fortune from the country's economy before they were ousted from power during a peaceful revolution in February 1986. A tiny fraction of that theft can be seen on display in the Malacañang Palace in Manila, the official residence of the last eighteen Spanish governors general, the American civil governors, and the Philippine presidents.

Manila attracted the world's attention in February 1986 with a remarkable display of what has come to be known as "people power," foreshadowing the dramatic events of 1989 in Eastern Europe. Under pressure from the Reagan Administration in Washington to prove continuing support for his rule under martial law, Ferdinand Marcos called a snap election for early February. In 1983, the principal opponent to the Marcos regime, Benigno "Ninoy" Aquino, was assassinated at Manila Airport as he returned to the Philippines from the United States. The Marcoses were generally believed to be responsible for his murder.

Aquino's widow, Corazon Aquino, refused to take on the role of politician and never wavered from referring to herself as a housewife and mother. When the snap election was announced, the opposition to Marcos rallied around her, although she refused to stand for election until nominated to do so by 1 million Filipinos. A concerted campaign soon raised those votes and she agreed to stand. Ferdinand Marcos did not consider her a serious threat, and his government refused to believe that the country would elect a totally inexperienced woman as president. Nevertheless, the Marcos government reportedly arranged to pay voters to tour the country and cast votes in multiple locations, thus swelling the results in favor of the incumbent regime. This blatant corruption was met with defiance as Filipinos around the country guarded their ballot boxes, in some places paying with their lives to defend their right to a fair election. Reports of the falsification of the election results reached the international media, exposing Marcos to further scrutiny from the West.

The breakthrough in what came to be known as the "snap revolution" came with the defection from the Marcos camp of two prominent military leaders, Fidel Ramos and Ponce Enrile. They managed to make their defection known to the public, which rallied to support and protect them from undoubted retaliation. That civilians should take to the streets to defend members of the military was unprecedented. During the next couple of days, nuns and civilians faced armed tanks on EDSA, one of the main streets of Manila, and Cardinal Jaime Sin gave vital support to the revolution by encouraging members of the armed forces to desert the Marcos regime and join the people instead. Eventually, the state-controlled media channel was captured and Cory Aquino was inaugurated as president, the news of which was broadcast throughout the country even while the Marcoses were airlifted out of the Philippines, first to Guam and then to Hawaii.

The euphoria of ousting Ferdinand and Imelda Marcos was relatively short-lived, as Corazon Aquino's political inexperience became quickly apparent as she faced the complexities of Philippine politics after martial law. One of her campaign promises had been to negotiate a peace settlement with the communist guerillas, but these negotiations collapsed following the brutal shooting of unarmed demonstrators on Mendiola Bridge near the Malacañang Palace. The unlikely alliance of two former Marcos men and an unwilling and inexperienced Corazon Aquino also quickly revealed its weak points, as Enrile set about to undermine Aquino's authority by suggesting that her government was infiltrated by left-leaning politicians who had a disproportionate and dangerous influence on the impressionable president. Aquino was given no choice but to dismiss Enrile from her government, after which he rallied those disappointed with the slow progress made by the Aquino government into an opposition movement. Despite Enrile's aspirations, Fidel Ramos, the other former Marcos adviser who supported Aquino in 1986, succeeded Corazon Aquino at the end of her first term in 1992.

Further Reading: Books on the city of Manila and its history include *Old Manila* by Ramon Ma. Zaragoza (Oxford: Oxford University Press, 1990), *Focus on Old Manila*, edited by Mauro Garcia and C. O. Resurreccion (Manila: Philippine Historical Association, 1971), and *The Colonization of the Philippines and the Beginnings of the Spanish City of Manila* by Nicholas Zafra (Manila: National Historical Commission, 1974). See also "Spanish Philippines in the 17th Century: A Beleaguered Outpost of the Empire" by Domingo Abella (paper presented at the Sixth International Conference on Asian History, International Association of Historians of Asia, Yogyakarta, August 26–30, 1974). For a more general introduction to the Philippines, consult some of the following: *The Philippines: A Singular and a Plural Place* by David Joel Steinberg (Boulder, Colorado: Westview, 1982), *The Filipino Nation: The Philippines: Lands and Peoples, A Cultural Geography* by Eric S. Casiño (Manila: Grolier International Philippines, 1982), and *The Filipino Nation: A Concise History of the Philippines* by Helen R.

Tubangui, Lesie E. Bauzon, Marcelino A. Foronda, Jr., and Luz U. Ausejo (Manila: Grolier International Philippines, 1982). For specific information regarding recent Philippine history, including the overthrow of the Marcos regime and the considerable problems now faced by the country, see *Impossible Dream* by Sandra Burton (New York: Warner Books, 1989); *Imelda Marcos* by Carmen Navarro Pedrosa (London: Weidenfeld and Nicholson, and New York: St. Martin's, 1987); and "The Snap Revolution" by James Fenton in *Granta* (Cambridge), volume 18, Spring 1986.

—Hilary Collier Sy-Quia

Mathurā (Uttar Pradesh, India)

Location: On the right bank of the Yamunā (Jumnā) River, about thirty-five miles northwest of Āgra and about ninety miles southeast of Delhi. The city of Mathurā lies in the district of the same name. Both are also referred to as Mathurā-maṇḍala and Braja-bhūmi.

Description: Mathurā's history extends to remote antiquity, when the city occupied a nodal position on a number of transregional land routes joining north and south, east and west. Mathurā has been called an epicenter of Indian culture. To Buddhists and Jains it became a center of religious and artistic activity as early as the third or second century B.C. To Hindus, Mathurā is the birthplace of Krishna, and it remains a great center of Krishna worship and pilgrimage today. The Hindu, Buddhist, and Jain art of Mathurā had a profound influence on the development of religious art in India.

Site Office: The Department of Archaeology
Mathurā Museum,
Mathurā
Uttar Pradesh
India

Contact: Government of India Tourist Office
191, the Mall
Āgra 282 001
Uttar Pradesh
India
363377 or 363959

Mathurā lies within the range of the Ganges River valley area, which saw the rise of an urban civilization in the first millenium B.C. But the region around Mathurā had been inhabited long before by various seminomadic Neolithic cultures. Around 1200 B.C., these Stone Age people gave way to a more settled culture that is known primarily by its characteristic pottery, Painted Gray Ware, which continued to be produced until the fifth century B.C. Copper tools, including celts and harpoons, are associated with this culture from its beginning, and iron was introduced in the first millenium B.C. Historians speculate that a caste system based on kinship groups formed the basis of its social organization. The people were ruled by kings, whose position became more central over time.

Before the Painted Gray Ware disappeared from the region, a rising urban culture built the first true city of Mathurā. The Buddhist text *Aṅguttara Nikāya* refers to sixteen great states that flourished in northern India around 600 B.C. Śūrasena, with its capital at Mathurā, was one of these. Greek writers corroborate the Buddhist evidence by referring to the Sourasenoi and their city Methora. Little is known about the Śūrasenas except what can be gleaned from the ancient literature of India. The *Rigveda* mentions the Yadus as participants in the so-called battle of the ten kings, and some believe the Śūrasenas to be their descendants. The Śūrasenas are linked with the Yādava clan in the *Vishnu Purāṇa*. The *Purāṇas* also refer to the foundation of Mathurā by Śatrughna, the younger brother of Rāma, hero of the *Rāmāyaṇa*. Other works refer to the people of Mathurā as Andhaka and Vṛṣṇi. The latter reportedly were organized along the lines of a republican corporation, which had Vāsudeva Krishna as its chief. (Krishna is also referred to as a Yādava prince born at Mathurā.) Interestingly, the epic *Mahābhārata* refers to these same people as *vrātyas,* or deviators from orthodoxy. Whatever the exact nature of relationships between dominant clans, it is clear that Mathurā had considerable regional importance by the sixth and fifth centuries B.C.

Late in the fourth century B.C., Mathurā was incorporated into the Mauryan Empire, which, for a brief time, controlled the entire subcontinent, with the exception of the southern Tamil regions. Excavations in several quarters of Mathurā, notably Kaṭrā and Dhūlkoṭ, show a transition from mud-wall houses to brick buildings in the Mauryan layer. Extensive mud fortifications also are thought to date to the period of Mauryan rule, although they may have been built earlier. A different kind of pottery, the more sophisticated Northern Black Polished Ware, as well as significant numbers of coins, are also associated with the Mauryan period. The archaeological remains indicate that Mathurā enjoyed considerable prosperity, becoming an important entrepôt on several trade routes. Fine cottons and other luxury goods seem to have been the most important local products traded to different parts of India. There are indications that the city had guilds of merchants and craftsmen. Although it was visited every few years by imperial auditors, Mathurā actually was governed by a bureaucracy whose ranks were supplied locally to a great extent.

As a trading center with far-flung connections to other regions, Mathurā played a particularly important role in the dissemination of new ideas. One of the most significant aspects of Mathurā's history during the third and second centuries B.C. was its role in the spread of Buddhism and Jainism. Starting as cults, both movements began to develop into major religions by the time of the Mauryans. Buddhism was personally favored by the Mauryan emperor Aśoka, who reigned in the middle of the third century B.C. Buddhist monasteries and temples, as well as a variety of Jain monuments, were built in many parts of the empire. Religious communities could rely on imperial patronage, the largesse

Standing Buddha, Mathurā
Photo courtesy of Sarva Daman Singh

of local guilds, and donations made by traveling merchants at their accustomed stops. It is for this reason that Mathurā could support extensive religious communities and came to be particularly rich in religious architecture. Although the different structures and their furnishings have suffered heavy damage over the centuries, many important sculptures and inscriptions survive from Mathurā's Mauryan era.

The development of a distinctive style of figurative sculpture is another of the signal contributions made by Mathurā to India's ancient culture. Hinduism and Jainism were among the first Indian religions to produce images of deities, leading eventually to the victory of divine anthropomorphism over the amorphous abstractions of older Hindu, Jain, and Buddhist philosophy. Easy access to a mottled red sandstone quarried locally aided the transition from wood and clay to stone in iconic and decorative sculpture in the third or second century B.C. The older images made of perishable material have been lost with time, but the iconographic tradition has survived in the later stone monuments. With its massive size, rigid frontality, and elemental vigor, Mathurā's ancient sculpture still has the power to inspire awe in the modern viewer.

One of the earliest works to have been discovered is a colossal standing statue of a *yakṣā*, or guardian spirit. On the basis of its inscription—as yet undeciphered—and its stylistic characteristics, archaeologists have dated the sculpture to the third or second century B.C. Other monumental images representing *yakṣās* and *yakṣīs* (the *yakṣās*' female counterparts) found in the region symbolize the celebration of prosperity and abundance. Together, they indicate the growing popularity of anthropomorphic images at Mathurā. An image of Balarāma from Mathurā is one of the earliest of a Hindu god in Indian art and shows him with a canopy of seven serpent hoods over his head, holding a club in his right hand and a plough in his left. An even earlier representation of the same deity has been found on a punch-marked coin of the third century B.C. The earliest image of a Jain *tīrthaṇkara*, or prophet, at Mathurā probably dates to the second century B.C.; it depicts the prophet seated in meditation.

Interestingly, some of the early sculptures record the names of both the artists and their teachers. Sculptures unearthed elsewhere also bear the names of these same sculptors, supporting the notion that sculpture came to be one of Mathurā's export products. Although the extent of the trade in sculpture is difficult to assess, it is clear that the city had a significant impact on the development of figurative sculpture elsewhere in the country. Mathurā's influence on the art of southern India eventually reached beyond the country's borders into parts of Southeast Asia.

Following Aśoka's reign, the Mauryan Empire began to decline, losing its dominant position in northern India to the Śunga Dynasty in the course of the second century B.C. The center of the Śungas' domain lay in Magadha, farther east in the Ganges River valley area, and whether Mathurā formed part of their territories at any time is not known. Raids by Indo-Greek rulers later in the same century certainly would have weakened or destroyed Śunga control, if it ever existed. A period marked by the rise of local rulers and dynasties may be inferred from the discovery, in and around Mathurā, of coins inscribed with the names ending in -mitra and -datta. Historians surmise that the city emerged as an autonomous center governed by local kings during the first century B.C. Commercial activity is thought to have intensified, bringing added prosperity. As corroborated by inscriptions and religious art, Mathurā was exposed to the crossing currents of both indigenous and immigrant ideologies that contributed to the growth of a truly cosmopolitan culture.

Before the end of the first century B.C., then, the city had become one of the most important centers of commerce, religion, and culture in the region. However, that period saw major movements of population groups in northern and central India. Mathurā's prosperity attracted one of these groups, the Śakas, who eventually conquered extensive territories in western India. Thought to have been of Scytho-Parthian origin, these people established their authority over Mathurā just before the start of the Common (Christian) Era, leaving a wealth of inscriptions and coins to testify to their presence. Their rulers took the titles Kṣatrapa (which has been westernized as "satrap") and Mahākṣatrapa ("grand satrap"). The so-called Lion Capital inscriptions found at Mathurā record the enshrinement of the Buddha's relic by Mahākṣatrapa Rājula, a female ruler, for the sake of universal happiness. According to the epigraphic record, she also was responsible for the construction of a stupa and a *vihāra* (Buddhist monastery) for Sarvāstivādin monks. Expressing a wish for shared deliverance through common merit, the inscriptions evoke the kind of collective compassion that later was to characterize Buddhism everywhere in India.

The Śakas did not support only Buddhism at Mathurā. Inscriptions dating to the time of Mahākṣatrapa Śodāsa (c. A.D. 10–25) record the ruler's munificence toward Jains and Hindus as well. One of these inscriptions begins with a salutation to Vardhamāna or Mahāvīra, a Jain *tīrthaṇkara*, and records the installation of an *āyāgapaṭṭa*, a stone tablet for the worship of the enlightened. Another inscription celebrates the installation of images of five Hindu deities. Four of these deities are of local significance, but the fifth is Vāsudeva Krishna. A shrine to Vāsudeva Krishna also was constructed at this time, which provides evidence of the rise of Krishna worship at Mathurā early in the first century A.D. The *bhakti* Hindu cult of Vishnu also had been gaining increased currency in central and northwest India since the second century B.C. and found adherents in Mathurā. *Bhakti* cults emphasized a life of devotion rather similar to the meditative aspects of Buddhism and Jainism.

One critically important development in Buddhist sculpture evidenced at Mathurā was the depiction of the Buddha himself. Growing out of the tradition of *yakṣā* images, sculptures of the Buddha first were created more or less simultaneously at Mathurā and Gandhāra in a parallel but probably independent process of development. Buddha images were definitely produced at Mathurā during the Śaka

Statue of a yaksī, *Mathurā*
Photo courtesy of Sarva Daman Singh

period. The quintessential Buddha image is a direct stylistic descendant of the earlier *yakṣā* in his unyielding solidity and earth-bound serenity. The image also is inspired by the yogī tradition, as the Buddha is seated in the lotus position, in deep meditation, with half-closed eyes focused on the tip of his nose to facilitate the inward gaze. One of the earliest known representations of the Buddha, dated to the first century B.C., is a somewhat flattened relief from Mathurā, which shows the Buddha seated on an inverted, five-stepped platform supported by two recumbent lions beneath the base. The platform is thought to symbolize Mount Meru, which is at the center of Buddhist cosmology. The Buddha's station atop Mount Meru would thus convey both his universality and the stability he imparts to the cosmos.

The standing Buddhas of Mathurā are most often portrayals of bodhisattvas (enlightened beings who delay entering nirvana so that they may aid others). The emphasis is again on the frontal aspect, and the clinging drapery and typical *dhotī* (loincloth) establish a connection with the *yakṣā* images. A parasol held aloft by a massive post symbolized the sovereignty of the Universal Teacher. A heavy, round face and shaven head are typical of the early images at Mathurā. Later images have curly hair tied in a knot or forming a tuft. A halo behind the head appeared in figures by the end of the first century A.D. The representation of bodhisattvas at this time also indicates the currency of aspects of Mahāyāna Buddhist philosophy as early as the first century A.D.; Mahāyāna (Greater Vehicle) Buddhism emphasizes the role of *bodhisattvas* in aiding the spiritual development and salvation of others, while Hinayana Buddhism focuses solely on the attainment of nirvana.

Before the end of the first century, the Śakas lost their dominion over Mathurā to the kingdom of Kushān. The Kushāns, originally of southern Chinese origin, presided over the greatest flowering of religious art in the city, and their patronage undoubtedly contributed to this golden age. Buddhas and *bodhisattvas* are freely portrayed. Also surviving from this period are a plethora of Jain sculpture, including more than 100 standing and seated representations of Jina (Mahāvīra, the first Jain *tīrthaṇkara*), many *āyāgapaṭṭas*, and a vast quantity of architectural fragments. The images of Jina, lost in meditation, share many of the characteristics of the Buddha statues and have the same solidity. Hindu deities, including Vishnu, Sūrya, Siva, Kārtikeya, and Devī, also figure in the sculpture of the Kushān period. Common features in the iconography of the three religions continued to occur.

A new element in the decorative programs of this time is the depiction of ordinary human figures in religious contexts. These illustrate not only the search for bliss in life despite its transience but also the beauty of creation. Among the most refined of these images are carvings of young women. A series of voluptuous seminudes carved on the railing pillars of a Buddhist stupa at Bhūteśvara indicate a wholehearted embrace of human sexuality alongside the cultivation of ascetic ideals. The juxtaposition of the sacred and secular in the Kushān art at Mathurā shows a frank appreciation of all that life—which was not seen as an impediment to striving for the ultimate goal—has to offer. This integration also meant that individual householders, as well as the ruling aristocracy, patronized the arts and supported the communities of ascetics.

Another important development of the Kushān period was the establishment of a *devakula* at Māṭ, some nine miles from Mathurā. The purpose of the *devakula* has been much debated. Devoted to the practice either of ancestor worship or the worship of a family deity, the Kushāns installed the statues of at least three kings in this shrine. The shrine was destroyed just before or after the end of the Kushān period in the third century A.D.

Mathurā's commercial prosperity began to wane after the third century, with the decline of the Kushāns. They were eclipsed by the Yaudheyas and Nāgas, who in turn were defeated by Samudra Gupta, the Gupta emperor who ruled from 330 to 380. The Buddhist pilgrim Fa Xian, who visited the city around 400, describes a flourishing Buddhist community. While Mathurā's volume of trade diminished during the Gupta period, its artistic production was enriched by the exquisite aesthetic impulse of the Gupta age. Both the seated and standing Buddhas were refined and came to embody supreme statements of death-defying tranquillity and redeeming love. Their simplified contours have been interpreted as expressing the connection between form and idea and between the limited and the limitless. The same inspiration suffuses the Hindu images of the period, which proclaim a progress towards the realization of the divine.

With the crumbling of the Gupta empire over the fifth and sixth centuries, Mathura entered a period of great turbulence and commercial decline. The city was sacked and laid waste early in the sixth century by the Hūnas, whose repeated invasions finally undermined the Guptas. Another Chinese visitor, Xuan Zang, records that the city was governed by the Maukharīs of Kanauj in the seventh century. By this time, the glorious days of Mathurā's art were over, but the city had blossomed into a great center of Krishna worship. It remained so in the eleventh century, when Maḥmūd of Ghaznī sacked Mathurā again. He torched the temples, carrying off many religious treasures, including statues of solid gold and silver.

Less than 100 years later the city passed into the Delhi Sultanate under Quṭb-ud-Dīn Aybak, who ruled from 1193 to 1210. Later the city became part of the Mughal Empire. The years of Muslim domination were marked by periods of intense religious oppression alternating with times of religious tolerance. Buddhism disappeared from Mathurā and from India altogether as a consequence of persecution. Hinduism adapted to the changing circumstances and continued to flourish in spite of restrictions, discrimination, and sometimes mortal danger. However, many temples were razed or converted to mosques. In 1669, for instance, the emperor 'Ālamgīr (Aurangzeb) demolished the splendid Keśava Deva Temple and built a mosque in its place. Incensed by the desecration of this shrine, the local Jāt peasantry under the leadership of Gokula rose in revolt against Mughal authorities. Although the movement soon was crushed by the imperial army, the people rose again in 1685 under Rāja Rām. For six years, they defied imperial rule and plundered Muslim monuments in the region. Although this rebellion was put down in 1691, the spirit of revolt lived on. Early in the eighteenth century, a new leader, Chūrāman, led the people in an uprising following 'Ālamgīr's death. His nephew Badan Singh founded the kingdom of Bharatpur, and the family continued to wield great influence in and around Mathurā.

A power vacuum created by the disintegration of the Mughal Empire in 1748 produced significant upheavals at Mathurā, which was sacked yet again in 1757. The repeated episodes of plunder and destruction explain the absence of intact ancient architecture and the mutilation of many surviving statues at Mathurā. For a brief time the Marāṭhā Empire made itself master of the city, but before long it had to cede many of its territories, including Mathurā, to the British. Although the local peasantry rose in rebellion in 1857 during what was dubbed the Mutiny by British authorities, the colonial rulers generally were successful in channeling the energies of their Mathurā subjects into the soothing rhythms of Krishna worship.

In the second half of the nineteenth century, the British archaeologist Alexander Cunningham explored and excavated a number of sites at Mathurā, collected sculptures, deciphered inscriptions, and published accounts of his research in his *Survey Reports*. Another notable scholar who helped preserve the legacy of Mathurā was F. S. Growse. He was instrumental in the establishment of the famous Mathurā Museum in 1874. Slowly, Mathurā's historical record was pieced together and its importance in the development of Indian culture clarified. However, many unresolved questions about Mathurā's past remain, and the city continues to be an object of study for archaeologists around the world.

Apart from its archaeological interest and its attractions to devotees of Krishna, the modern city is of very modest significance. It is a major rail junction, but it has not seen any industrial development to speak of. As a consequence, the city has changed very little in the last centuries. A boat ride on the Yamunā reveals a skyline still marked by myriad Hindu shrines and the towering minarets of 'Ālamgīr's mosque.

Further Reading: *Mathura: The Cultural Heritage* by Doris Meth Srinivasan (New Delhi: Manohar, and Columbia, Missouri: South Asia Books, 1989) contains a wealth of essays addressing various aspects of Mathurā's ancient past. The city's Buddhist art has been most widely studied, and R. C. Sharma's *Buddhist Art of Mathura* (Delhi: Agam, 1984; as *Buddhist Art: Mathura School*, New Delhi: Wiley Eastern, New Age International, 1995) gives a readable overview of findings in this area. More general studies of ancient Buddhist art in India that throw light on Mathurā's sculpture are A. K. Coomaraswamy's *The Origin of the Buddha Image* (second edition, New Delhi: Munshiram Manoharlal, 1972) and *The Image of the Buddha*, edited by David L. Snellgrove (Paris: Unesco; Tokyo: Kodansha; and London: Serinda, 1978). *A New History of India* by Stanley Wolpert (New York: Oxford University Press, 1977; fourth edition, 1993) is a concise general history of India that will serve to place developments at Mathurā in a broader context.

—Sarva Daman Singh and Marijke Rijsberman

Mazār-i-Sharīf (Balkh, Afghanistan)

Location: Twenty-eight miles south of the Amu Darya (Oxus) River in a quasi-desert region in the Balkh province of northern Afghanistan; about 9 miles east of the town of Balkh, 217 miles south of Samarkand, and 186 miles northwest of Kābul.

Description: Mazār-i-Sharīf (Tomb of the Saint) is famed chiefly for its religious significance as the supposed burial place of the fourth caliph, ʿAlī ibn Abī Ṭālib, son-in-law of the prophet Muḥammad and husband of his daughter Fāṭima, to whose line the Shi'ite Muslims are still faithful. Mazār-i-Sharīf replaced Balkh as the principal town of northern Afghanistan partly because of its religious importance and partly because of the military cantonments it incorporated. It has become the center of Afghanistan's rug and carpet industry and is also a major market for silk and cotton.

Contact: Embassy of the Republic of Afghanistan
2341 Wyoming Avenue N.W.
Washington, D.C. 20008
U.S.A.
(202) 234-3770

Travel writer Peter Levi has described Mazār-i-Sharīf as "an unattractive town with a restored mosque something like a poor relation of Brighton Pavilion built in porcelain under Queen Victoria." This accurate if unkind comment correctly suggests that the town's historic importance is not linked to its attractiveness to tourists. Rather, it is important as the holiest place in Islamic Afghanistan. It holds this status because it is presumed to be the burial site of Muḥammad's adopted son, later his son-in-law, ʿAlī. Before the rise of Islam, however, northern Afghanistan, including the region of Mazār-i-Sharīf, undoubtedly was occupied by the Greeks, and the area was even earlier a center, if not the actual birthplace, of Zoroastrianism. The Mazār-i-Sharīf region eventually was brought within the Bactrian-Sogdian satrapy of Alexander the Great's empire, and Mazār-i-Sharīf probably numbered among the ten or twelve unnamed cities, or military colonies, he founded there.

Although the geographical term Bactria designates a general region without precise borders, and there is some dispute about exactly what it includes, it is normally thought acceptable to regard it as more or less coterminous with the Amu Darya (Oxus) Valley. Under the satrap Diodotus, that valley loosened its association with the Seleucid Empire, and Bactria became permeated by Buddhism in the third century B.C. under Mauryan emperor Aśoka. Unfortunately, the region is largely unexcavated. Archaeologists investigating Balkh, where ruin mounds apparently stretch for fifteen miles, so far have confined research to one mound, believed to cover the ruins of the citadel of the town of Bactra (Balkh), and have reached only the fifteenth-century stratum. It took an entire generation of archaeologists to uncover the first Greek coins at Shūsh (Susa) in Iran, and one might expect a similar rate of progress in Afghanistan.

There is much evidence that, under the Greeks of the third and second centuries B.C., Bactria was a vast garden complex sustained by an extensive system of irrigation canals (destroyed by the Mongol invaders of the thirteenth and fifteenth centuries A.D.). The deserts, bigger now than those recorded by Ptolemy could have been, have reclaimed the watercourses that once made agriculture possible in the region. The irrigation system almost certainly derived from the area's earliest historically known inhabitants, the Achaemenids, an ancient Persian dynasty descended, according to tradition, from Achaemenes (seventh century B.C.). Their leader, Cyrus II the Great (died 529 B.C.), originally a vassal of the Mede king Astyages, rebelled, took the Mede capital of Ecbatana (Hamadan), brought together the Medes and the Persians, and colonized the whole area from the eastern Mediterranean to the Indus Valley, reaching nearly as far north as the Aral Sea.

Under the Achaemenian Dynasty, Mazār-i-Sharīf was at the center of a heavily irrigated and fertile stretch of Central Asia. Its population and religion originated in Persia. One notable Persian import was Zoroastrianism, a religion originating in the sixth century B.C. Like Buddhism and Confucianism, Zoroastrianism is more an ethical code than a system of formal beliefs; it is of great importance as one of the earliest patterns of ritual behavior to postulate one omnipotent, invisible God. Fire was the apt symbol of God. There is a clear transmission of Zoroastrianism to the early Greek Christian theology of Origen, as also to such Greek thinkers as Plato and Plotinus. The magi said to have journeyed to Bethlehem to pay homage to the infant Jesus were Zoroastrian wise men. Mazār-i-Sharīf was an early principal center of the preaching of Zoroastrianism, and even claims to be the birthplace of the prophet Zoroaster (founder of the religion), although most of the evidence suggests that he was born farther west.

The Achaemenian Dynasty endured until Alexander the Great defeated Darius III in 330 B.C. Alexander left the indigenous religious practices and beliefs of his vassal empire undisturbed. In the late fourth century B.C., after Alexander's death, Mazār-i-Sharīf became part of the Seleucid Empire, founded by one of Alexander's generals. This empire gradually broke up, leaving Mazār-i-Sharīf as part of the Greco-Bactrian kingdom during the second century B.C. In 246 B.C. Ptolemy III of Egypt invaded Syria and claimed sovereignty as far east

Shrine of ʿAli Mazār-i-Sharīf
Photo courtesy of Mr. Rashid Uddin, Park Travel Agency, Chicago

as Bactria. The Greek-speaking world was rapidly losing power, and about 130 B.C. the Greco-Bactrian kingdom fell to the Scythians, who were being pushed back toward the Punjab by the Yüeh-Chi nomads (Tocharians). It was the Yüeh-Chi who occupied Mazār-i-Sharīf, sweeping away traces of Greek culture before founding their own mighty Kushān Empire, which finally extended through Central Asia and most of India, as far east as Vārānasī and as far south as Sanchi. The Kushān Empire fell in turn to the Sāsānian Dynasty, which controlled Central Asia from A.D. 224 until the Islamic conquest, which reached Mazār-i-Sharīf in 651.

Mazār-i-Sharīf's connection to events in the early years of Islam have brought the town its lasting fame. After Muḥammad died in 632, conflict over succession began immediately, fueled by the ambiguity inherent in the dual functions of military commander and religious leader that the new Islamic leader would have to fill. There was also the unresolved question of the extent to which Muḥammad's was a specifically Arab movement. It was only when the ʿAbbāsid Dynasty (750–1258) came to power with a non-Arab majority that Islamic subjects were subjected to pressure to convert to Islamic religious belief and practice. The first three of Muḥammad's successors, the caliphs, did not attach great importance to ritual observance. They were Abū Bakr (c. 573–634), Muḥammad's father-in-law who inaugurated Islam's expansionary policy; ʿUmar ibn al-Khaṭṭāb, another of Muḥammad's fathers-in-law, who continued the expansion and was assassinated in 644; and the Umayyad ʿUthmān ibn ʿAffān, who promulgated the Koran, continued the policy of conquest, and was murdered in 656.

The next caliph was ʿAlī, Muhammad's cousin and adopted son, who married the prophet's daughter Fāṭima. By submitting the succession to arbitration, ʿAlī conceded that the religious leadership of Islam was not necessarily hereditary. He was murdered in 661 on the orders of his rival and successor, Mu'āwiyah I, Islamic governor of Syria, who moved the Islamic capital from Medina to Damascus and founded the Umayyad Dynasty. Islam's vast majority today, the Sunni Muslims, accept the line of spiritual leadership originating with Mu'āwiyah. Only in Iran are the Shi'ites, who venerate ʿAlī and regard his descendants as *imams* (religious leaders), in a majority. Mazār-i-Sharīf remains an exception in Afghanistan, which is 80 percent Sunnite, but where the holiest of Muslim shrines is the Shi'ite Blue Mosque at Mazār-i-Sharīf.

ʿAlī is thought to have been buried in Iraq, and there is no explanation for the appearance of his remains in Mazār-i-Sarīf. The resting place was revealed to a *mullah* (religious teacher) in a dream in the early twelfth century, and a shrine was built on the site in 1136 at the behest of Seljuk sultan Sanjar. The Turkish Seljuks had begun to settle in the lands of the ʿAbbāsid caliphate in the tenth century. From 1055 they ruled from Baghdad, capital of the caliphate, under ʿAbbāsid suzerainty, with the title of sultan.

Shrine of ʿAlī, Mazār-i-Sharīf
Photo courtesy of Mr. Rashid Uddin, Park Travel Agency, Chicago

The twelfth-century shrine was destroyed by Genghis Khan in his initial sweep through Central Asia between 1216 and 1223 after conquering China. He had heard that there was a great treasure hidden in ʿAlī's Mazār-i-Sharīf shrine and, in an apparently unsuccessful attempt to find it, simply razed the building, so that the site of ʿAlī's grave was once more lost. The location was again revealed during the reign of the Timurid sultan Husain Baiqara, who in 1481 ordered another elaborate shrine to be erected there. It formed the basis for today's Blue Mosque, although the building has been modified substantially. Only the two main domes are original, and none of the fifteenth-century decoration remains. It is nonetheless one of the more colorful buildings in Afghanistan, and its outer court is still a gathering place for sacred singers and reciters. Near the east corner of the Blue Mosque is a ruined mausoleum with a vaulting system typical of the early Timurid architecture of Herāt and elsewhere. The dome is erected on a system of concentric arches (squinches) joining walls at an angle to one another. The squinches extended into the supports, allowing a circular dome to be constructed on a polygonal base.

With the rediscovery of the burial site in the fifteenth century, Mazār-i-Sharīf began to grow in size and importance. It came under a succession of ruling bodies, none of which held it for very long. In the sixteenth century, control of Mazār-i-Sharīf passed briefly to the Ṣafavids and later to the Mughals in the mid–seventeenth century. In the nineteenth century the weak Afghan kingdoms, which by then included Mazār-i-Sharīf, found themselves squeezed between the Russians, who wanted access to the Arabian Sea and the Indian Ocean, and the English, who wanted to contain czarist power to the north. The British and the Afghans were at war from 1878 to 1880. Finally, toward the end of the century, the British and Russians drew the borders of modern Afghanistan.

After World War II, it became clear that Afghanistan's allegiance leaned heavily toward the Soviet Union. Now the United States rather than Britain worried about the extension of Russian influence; to counter Soviet influence in the country, the United States gave financial aid to Afghanistan, helping build the long circular road that runs southwest from Kābul, turns northwest at Kandahār, northeast at Herāt, and passes through Balkh and Mazār-i-Sharīf before returning to Kābul.

In 1979 the Soviets invaded Afghanistan and installed a government in Kābul. The Soviets set up a military base in Mazār-i-Sharīf and began building a new road and rail bridge in the region. The Soviets withdrew in 1989, and a new president was elected in 1992. However, factional fighting continued in the region throughout the 1990s, and as the 21st century approached, Afghanistan remained unsafe for visitors.

Further Reading: Of general interest is Peter Levi's stylish *The Light Garden of the Angel King: Travels in Afghanistan* (London: Collins, and Indianapolis: Bobbs Merrill, 1972). Specialized materials include A. V. Williams Jackson's *Zoroaster: The Prophet of Ancient Iran* (London: Macmillan, 1898; New York: Macmillan, 1899); Grégoire Frumkin's *Archaeology in Soviet Central Asia* (Leiden and Köln: Brill, 1970); *The Archaeology of Afghanistan from Earliest Times to the Timurid Period,* edited by F. Raymond Allchin and Norman Hammond (London and New York: Academic Press, 1978); and W. W. Tarn's *The Greeks in Bactria and India* (Cambridge: Cambridge University Press, 1938; third edition, Chicago: Ares, 1985).

—Anthony Levi

Melaka (Melaka, Malaysia)

Location: On the west coast of the southern Malay Peninsula, approximately 120 miles up the coast from Singapore.

Description: The main trading city and empire of maritime Southeast Asia during the fifteenth century.

Site Office: Melaka Tourist Information Center
Jalon Kota
7500 Melaka, Melaka
Malaysia
(6) 236 538

The settlement of Melaka was founded approximately 600 years ago, on the site of a grove of emblic (*melaka*) trees near the mouth of a river feeding into the narrow, strategic strait between Sumatra and the Malay Peninsula. The town grew quickly, and for a little less than a century it was the premiere metropolis in maritime Southeast Asia, a powerful center of trade and culture. After 1511, however, it fell into the hands of a series of conquerors and declined dramatically in power and influence. Today, Melaka (also spelled Malacca) is a relatively minor state capital in the Federation of Malaysia, with virtually no remains surviving from its period of greatest glory.

Like Rome, Melaka was founded by exiles who underwent many adventures in the long journey from their original home. Like Virgil's account of the founding of Rome, the stories of Melaka's origins also have a legendary quality in which historical fact is difficult to untangle from myth. The legends trace Melaka's origins to an exiled prince from the once-great empire of Srivijaya, whose capital lay upstream on the Musi River in southern Sumatra on the site of the modern city of Palembang. Srivijaya enjoyed its great age of prosperity from the seventh to the eleventh centuries, when it controlled the lucrative trade passing through what was later called the Strait of Melaka. Srivijaya, however, fell into decline during the eleventh century owing to warfare with enemies from India and Java, as well as to new Chinese trading policies. During the following centuries, Palembang suffered the ignominy of being subject sometimes to Java, sometimes to its northern neighbor and rival, Jambi. Even in the brief intervening periods of relative independence, Palembang was no more than a minor regional center.

The descendants of Srivijaya's great rulers chafed under this minor status, and in approximately 1377, after another destructive attack from Java, a prince of Palembang who is normally called Paramesvara (although this may have been a title rather than a proper name) abandoned the stricken city to seek a site where the fortunes of his dynasty might be reconstructed with less interference. The options available to him in the Southeast Asia of the late fourteenth century were limited. To the east, the great Javanese empire of Majapahit, which had been the cause of Paramesvara's flight, dominated, while to the west and north the rising Siamese state of Ayutthaya had begun to seek hegemony over the northern regions of the Malay Peninsula. Between these two powers lay a no-man's land on either side of the Strait of Melaka, and it was to this region that Paramesvara headed.

The strait between Sumatra and the Malay Peninsula was of immense strategic significance. Through those narrow waters passed most of the commerce between China and the Spice Islands on the one hand and India and the West on the other. Srivijaya had built an empire of power and wealth based on tapping and servicing this trade, but its capital was a considerable distance from the strait itself. The narrowest point of the strait saw little development because it appeared to offer few advantages to human settlement. Low, muddy islands and malarial mangrove swamps dominated the Sumatra coast, while the peninsular coast presented only a narrow strip of arable land between sea and mountains. In an age when population was the most important measure of a kingdom's wealth, the narrows seemed to be unable to sustain a state on a scale that could challenge the resources of Srivijaya.

For Paramesvara and his small band of exiles, however, security was the most important consideration. To obtain it, they settled first on the island of Singapore at the very mouth of the strait before moving to Muar and then to Bertam; they finally settled on the site they called Melaka in approximately 1400. Their adventures during these twenty-odd years of wandering have been recorded both in an indigenous chronicle, the *Sejarah Melayu,* or "Malay Annals," and in a Western account, the *Suma Oriental,* or *Complete Treatise of the Orient,* by the Portuguese apothecary Tomé Pires. The *Sejarah Melayu* is the more dramatic account, tracing Paramesvara's dynasty back to Alexander the Great and including episodes such as an attack by swordfish on Singapore and a battle with monitor lizards in Muar. The annals also describe in considerable detail a form of social contract between rulers and their subjects in which cruelty and injustice by rulers is punished by divine intervention.

Within a few decades, Melaka grew from a settlement of exiles to the most powerful state in maritime Southeast Asia. Several factors contributed to this dramatic transformation. First, the decline of Majapahit removed a major rival; Ayutthaya and its vassals continued to be a threat, but the Siamese lacked the naval power that had made Java so formidable. The northern Sumatra state of Samudra-Pasai, from which the island of Sumatra derived its name, was a rival for much of the fifteenth century, but it was an up-and-coming power, not an established empire with the resources to nip

St. Peter's Church, Melaka
Photo courtesy of Malaysia Tourism Promotion Board

Melaka's ambitions in the bud. Second, the trade route between India, China, and the Spice Islands was now so lucrative that a major port could survive by servicing it without relying on any significant hinterland of its own. Palembang had become the heart of the Srivijayan Empire partly because its position on the Musi River made it a major outlet for products from the Sumatran interior. Melaka had privileged access to a gold-mining area in the interior, but its command of interregional trade was its great strength. A deep-water harbor, abundant fresh water, an army and navy, and a government sympathetic to trade were all that Melaka needed to be a success.

Melaka's willingness to provide the facilities that traders needed was, perhaps, its greatest strength. Some of these facilities were physical, such as underground warehouses where traders could store goods while they waited for the winds to change. Melaka's rulers, moreover, inherited from Srivijaya a special relationship with the semipiratical *orang laut,* or people of the sea, preventing them from preying unduly on the commercial traffic that was Melaka's lifeline. The administrative system, too, was geared to the interests of traders. The ruler of Melaka appointed four *syahbandar* (literally, "lords of the harbor"), whose tasks included the allocation of warehouses, the policing of weights and measures, and the settlement of disputes. Each *syahbandar* was responsible for traders of a designated ethnic group: one controlled the Gujaratis from northwestern India, who were the largest foreign contingent in the harbor; another had charge of the other traders from countries to the west of Melaka, from Arabia to Pasai; the third governed traders from the rest of maritime Southeast Asia, while the fourth was responsible for Chinese and other traders from East Asia. Melaka was famous for its cosmopolitanism, and Tomé Pires reported that he heard eighty-four languages spoken there in a single day. A simple harbor tax of 6 percent on the value of goods meant that merchants could plan their commercial strategies without the uncertainty and irregularity that often plagued other ports.

Two more factors, however, clinched commercial preeminence for Melaka. First, its rulers enjoyed a special relationship with China at an unusual time in Chinese history. The Ming Dynasty's Yongle emperor, who came to power in 1403, abandoned the customary official Chinese hostility to trade and established a bureau of maritime trade as a kind of state trading corporation. The Chinese commercial strategy involved seeking out reliable allies in what they called the "South Seas," where their vessels would receive protection as well as the use of various facilities. Melaka was quick to offer tribute to China, and owing to the city's position and its sympathetic policies, China chose Melaka early on as a major ally: the emperor declared Paramesvara to be a king and presented him with a formal inscription containing the moral and political philosophy of the Ming Dynasty.

Throughout most of the history of maritime Southeast Asia, ambitious rulers had periodically sent tribute to the Chinese Empire. Although the Chinese invariably interpreted these missions as offering political and cultural submission to China, the tributes generally did not lead to significant political or cultural links. Indigenous rulers derived prestige at home from having a relationship with distant empires but had no intention of being subordinate to China; indeed, rulers often sent tribute to two or more rival powers. Tribute was also the price that Southeast Asian states had to pay to be allowed to trade in China, and in fact tribute missions often were thinly disguised trading expeditions. In Melaka's case, however, tribute led to a period of close cooperation with China. Paramesvara himself visited the Chinese court at least once, and his successors followed suit. The Ming emperor Yongle sent a series of naval expeditions to Southeast Asia under the command of the eunuch admiral Zheng He, who used Melaka as his principal base in the region from approximately 1405 to the 1430s.

Melaka's other major source of success was its conversion to Islam. Paramesvara had followed the Hindu-Buddhist religious practices that had become established in much of Southeast Asia in the period after A.D.100. He appears, however, to have become Muslim close to the end of his life in approximately 1414. This adoption of Islam probably was a tactical measure to increase the attractiveness of the port to Muslim traders rather than an act of faith, but it led to a gradual growth in Muslim influence in the court. Only in 1446 did a ruler of Melaka take the title *sultan* and proclaim his rule to be based on Islamic principles.

Muslims certainly had been present among the foreign traders at Melaka right from the foundation of the kingdom: by the beginning of the fifteenth century, Islam already was widespread among the traders of the Indian Ocean. Islam was a missionary religion whose followers often enthusiastically sought to convert those they saw as heathen, but the faith of the Prophet also had philosophical attractions for traders. The traditional religions of South and Southeast Asia—even including Hinduism and Buddhism—tended to be associated with spirits of place. Those who traveled for trade or other reasons left behind not only their familiar social environment but their accustomed spiritual environment, venturing into worlds where the spiritual terrain was unknown and dangerous. The God of Islam, who is the same everywhere and at all times, was inherently appealing to those who wanted a firm spiritual footing wherever they went. Islam also attracted traders through its emphasis on individual faith and on the fundamental equality of all believers. Equality fit the spirit of the marketplace, where all met on equal terms, while the emphasis on individual faith partly freed traders from sometimes onerous community obligations—such as the distribution of wealth to relatives—that could make commercial planning difficult.

At the height of its power, Muslim Melaka was one of the great port cities of the world and the largest city in Southeast Asia. It is said that at any one time as many as 2,000 vessels could be found in its harbor (many of them must have been bringing food to the city's 200,000 or so inhabitants) and that its merchants kept their accounts in terms of gold bars weighing 170 kilograms. Melaka never became the center of a large empire because territorial expansion offered no prospect of increasing the wealth it derived from trade: its tributaries were limited to a few nearby regions that needed to be controlled for security reasons. Melaka's cultural influence, however, spread much more widely, and its literature, art, music, titles, and style of government all became the model for new Muslim states throughout maritime Southeast Asia. Melaka's prestige was also a major factor in the emergence of Malay as the region's lingua franca.

Melaka's era of greatness was short-lived. Vasco da Gama's rounding of the Cape of Good Hope in 1497 marked the beginning of a sudden and catastrophic Portuguese intrusion into the Indian Ocean. Portugal's second viceroy in Asia, Afonso de Albuquerque, captured a series of key ports around the ocean's rim and in 1511 launched an attack on Melaka, capturing it after a siege of only a month. The city fell partly because of Portugal's superior military technology: with cannon and better ships, the Portuguese were able to command the maritime approaches to Melaka with little difficulty. The Melaka court itself also was divided at the time by factional rivalries, which hampered effective action against the Portuguese. The blow to Melaka, however, came not so much from military defeat as from the fact that the Portuguese remained in occupation. In traditional Southeast Asian warfare, rival powers tried to destroy each other's capital cities and to capture their people, but the permanent occupation of a city was relatively unknown. Sultan Mahmud Syah, therefore, who had retreated into the interior when the power of the Portuguese became apparent, fully expected to recover his capital when the Portuguese departed. De Albuquerque's decision to garrison and fortify Melaka left the sultan without a capital to return to, and his dynasty was forced to roam the region in search of a new base until it finally succumbed to factional struggles in 1699.

The Portuguese gained relatively little from their conquest. Melaka had been wealthy because of the people who came there rather than for any inherent value. Now that Christian Portuguese held the city, with a new stone fort on the site of the former Grand Mosque (built using stones from the mosque itself and from the graves of deceased sultans), many Muslim traders went to other ports. Muslim Aceh (Atjeh), on the northern tip of Sumatra, rose to prominence, while refugees from Melaka established a new, rival center in nearby Johore. Neither of these ports approached the onetime power of Melaka, but they drew trade from the Portuguese, swiftly reducing the city to a shadow of its former self. Raids

Porta de Santiago, Melaka
Photo courtesy of Malaysia Tourism Promotion Board

from Aceh, Java, and elsewhere made Melaka an even less attractive entrepôt for traders, and the Portuguese also came to realize the disadvantages of a location that depended on imports of food.

Melaka did not die, however: the city became a significant Portuguese naval base, and Portuguese forces defeated an Acehnese attack in 1629 so resoundingly that the power of Aceh was crippled for a generation. Portuguese settlement also began to create new cultural forms in the Malay Archipelago: Portuguese words entered Malay to describe such new concepts as *kemeja* (shirt) and *bendera* (flag), and Portuguese musical styles blended with indigenous forms to create new rhythms. Another lasting legacy was the mixed-race Indo-Portuguese and Malayo-Portuguese families whose surnames are still a prominent part of Melaka's social geography. Catholicism remains a major religion in Melaka, although the main Portuguese church, built during the sixteenth century, now lies in ruins. Even as a beachhead for Western influence, however, Melaka soon was eclipsed.

Early in the seventeenth century, the Dutch East India Company began operations in the archipelago. The company established its headquarters at Batavia, near the Sunda Strait between Java and Sumatra, which became an increasingly important alternative route from the Indies to the West. The Dutch immediately challenged Portuguese power farther east in the Moluccas and soon turned their attention to Melaka, which fell to a combined Dutch-Johore force after a five-month siege in 1641. Although the Dutch at first had great hopes of transforming Melaka into a major center for their own trade, they soon adopted a policy of favoring Batavia; Melaka became a pleasant but relatively minor regional post for the company. As in other Dutch colonial towns, the Chinese played a prominent role in local trade and commerce, and Melaka came to be known as a center of the so-called Baba Chinese culture, a hybrid culture of the descendants of Chinese migrants that incorporated many local and Western elements, especially in cuisine and language. By the early eighteenth century, Melaka had become so marginal to Dutch interests that the company seriously considered abandoning it. Inertia prevailed, however, and the Melaka administration spent most of the rest of the century engaged in quiet smuggling and governing a territory that seldom stretched more than a few miles from the fort, while around it rival indigenous states fought for dominance.

Melaka's status as a picturesque backwater was reinforced in 1786 with the founding of a British settlement on the island of Penang 250 miles to the north. The new port soon attracted trade away from Melaka, partly because it was better run and catered more to English-speaking traders, partly because its rulers used the sale of opium to defray administrative costs, allowing Penang to operate with lower fees than Melaka. The founding of Penang marked the passing of the Malay Peninsula into a British sphere of influence in which Dutch Melaka increasingly became an anomaly. In 1795 the British occupied the city to prevent it from falling into French hands during the Napoleonic Wars. Unfortunately, during the occupation the British demolished the fort that had been the symbol of European power in Melaka, although a single gate was left standing, and the Dutch city hall also survives. The British restored the city to the Dutch in 1818 as part of the postwar settlement but in 1825 resumed control as part of a general tidying up of colonial borders in the region.

Melaka's history since British annexation has been unremarkable. Initially a minor outpost of the Penang Presidency of the British East India Company, in 1867 Melaka joined Penang and the British settlement of Singapore in the Crown Colony of the Straits Settlements. Japan occupied the city along with the rest of the peninsula from 1942 to 1945. In 1957 Melaka became a state in the independent Federation of Malaya, which was expanded in 1963 and renamed the Federation of Malaysia. Whereas Penang and Singapore remained oriented to trade through the Strait of Melaka, Melaka itself largely lost its external orientation, becoming a local center for tin production, plantation rubber, and general agriculture, as well as a minor financial center. Melaka today has little to show for its glorious past.

Further Reading: The most important work on Melaka is the magisterial *Melaka: The Transformation of a Malay Capital, c. 1400–1980*, edited by Kernial Singh Sandhu and Paul Wheatley (2 vols., New York and London: Oxford University Press, 1983), although its historical value is marred by the absence of a proper discussion of 140 years of Portuguese rule. *The Suma Oriental of Tomé Pires*, edited and translated from the Portuguese by Armando Cortesão (2 vols., London: Hakluyt Society, 1944; reprint, Columbia, Missouri: South Asia Books, 1990), contains a fascinating description of Melaka in its heyday. Barbara Watson Andaya and Leonard Y. Andaya's *A History of Malaysia* (London: Macmillan, 1982; New York: St. Martin's, 1984) includes a sound scholarly analysis of the historical significance of the Malay sultanate.

—Robert Cribb

Miyajima (Hiroshima, Japan)

Location: A small island off the southwestern coast of the main Japanese island of Honshū, nine miles southwest of Hiroshima; now incorporated into the city of Hiroshima.

Description: A small island dominated by the wooden buildings of the Itsukushima Shrine, including its famous gate built in the sea, and those of other religious institutions.

Contact: Hiroshima City Tourist Information Center
Peace Memorial Park
1-1 Nakajima-Cho
Naka-ku
Hiroshima, Hiroshima
Japan
(82) 247 6738

Miyajima, "shrine island," has been regarded as one of the holiest places of Shintō, the indigenous religion of Japan, for at least 800 years, and the shrine that gives the island its popular name probably was founded approximately 1,400 years ago. Like other great shrines in Japan, such as those at Ise and Nikkō, it has attracted numerous pilgrims ever since its foundation and figures prominently in literature and painting. Like them, too, it has been affected by the changing fortunes of the governing families of the country, as well as by the complex processes of the assimilation, and later separation, of Shintō and Buddhism, the other major Japanese religion.

The island, an outcrop of granite that has an area of approximately eleven and one-half square miles, lies in Hiroshima Bay, part of the Seto Naikai, the Inland Sea, which is surrounded by the large islands of Honshū, Kyūshū, and Shikoku. At some unknown date, but probably well before the sixth century A.D., a local cult of the sea goddesses developed among the fishing villages on the nearby Honshū coast and on the islands in the bay, just as elsewhere in Japan other natural objects and phenomena became the basis of other cults, most notably the worship of the sun goddess at Ise. At this time Miyajima appears to have been known as Aki, which was also the name of the ancient province it occupied until Hiroshima was created in the 1870s.

During the sixth century, various local cults were first reinterpreted as components of a single religion, which was given the name Shintō, the Way of the Gods. The introduction of this word, which is made up of Chinese elements, was one result of the major transformation of Japanese culture that took place during this period, as many features of Chinese and Korean culture were imported into Japan. These included not only thousands of linguistic elements but also the doctrines of Buddhism, which became the official religion of the imperial court, then centered in what are now Nara, Ōsaka, Kyōto, and Mie prefectures at the other, eastern end of the Inland Sea.

The sixth century was also the period when the main shrine of Miyajima is said to have been established, around the year 593. This suggests, not that worship suddenly began there with the building of the shrine, but that the pre-existing cult was absorbed into the Shintō system then being developed alongside Buddhism but increasingly under its influence. These religious developments in turn indicate that this was the period when the imperial court gained sufficient power and prestige to be able to impose its will far beyond the region of central Honshū, where it had been founded sometime during the Yayoi period (c. 300 B.C.–A.D. 300).

Thus, probably from the formal foundation onward, the local sea goddesses were identified as Tagori-hime, Takitsu-hime and Itsukushima-hime (or Ichikishima-hime). "Hime" means "princess," an appropriate title for deities who were the daughters of a powerful Shintō deity associated with the imperial court. According to some sources, this was the sun goddess Amaterasu no Ōmikami, the supposed ancestor of the imperial line who is worshiped at Ise; according to other sources, it was her violent brother Susa-O no Mikoto, the god of winds and storms. Among the three goddesses, Itsukushima-hime came to be considered the most important and to be worshiped at Itsukushima Dai-Myōjin, the Great Illuminating Deity of the island.

The name Itsukushima historically has been applied to island, shrine, and deity alike, but because it means "strict island," its use as a place name presumably came first. Today, however, it is the shrine that is usually called Itsukushima, while the standard name for the island, used by the Japan Railways system, the local tourist office, and other bodies, is Miyajima. The island's reputation for strictness was based on the rules that governed access to it; these may well have been introduced when the shrine was founded. For many years the only people permitted to live on the island were the priests and priestesses of the shrine. Later, when pilgrims were permitted to enter the sacred precincts, the ancient prohibition on births and deaths on the island continued, a reflection of the traditional Shintō fear of ritual pollution by blood, death, or decay. This rule was abolished in 1868, but even now burials and cremations are not allowed on the island. Another ancient ban, on dogs, is also still maintained.

In spite of its relative remoteness from the center of political and religious activity and the unusual (but not unique) strictness of its rules, Miyajima cannot have remained isolated for long from the increasingly Buddhist mainstream of Japanese culture. In 749, for example, the emperor Shōmu ordered that a *kokubunji,* a national Buddhist

Itsukushima Shrine, Miyajima
Photo courtesy of Japan National Tourist Organization

temple with a monastery and a convent attached to it, be built in every province. The absorption of Buddhism into the life of the residents of Miyajima and the surrounding area was enhanced further early in the ninth century, when Kōbo Daishi, the founder of the esoteric Shingon-shū sect of Buddhism, established the Gumonji-dō. Like other Shingon temples, it occupies a site on a mountainside, near the top of Misen, which, at 1,739 feet above sea level, is the highest point on Miyajima. It was probably around this time or soon afterward that the goddess of Miyajima was reinterpreted as an incarnated form of one of the numerous manifestations of the Buddha, as were other Shintō deities throughout the country. Itsukushima Dai-Myōjin was equated with the Goddess of the Sea Palace, a daughter of the Dragon King of Shakatsura (Sagara in Sanskrit), one of the eight Dragon Kings, living in the depths of the sea, who had been brought into Japanese folklore from Hindu mythology by way of Chinese Buddhism. She had been just eight years old when she attained enlightenment while listening to a sermon by the Buddha, and had become Taizokai, a goddess venerated by the Shingon-shū sect who appears to have represented fertility (her name means "womb-store-world").

By the twelfth century Miyajima appears to have entered a period of neglect, and the buildings of the shrine fell into disrepair. Its revival, and its elevation to a role of national importance, dates from 1168, when the entire island was declared officially to be a sacred site by Taira Kiyomori, the "Priest-Premier," who had become the most powerful official at the imperial court the preceding year. According to *Heike Monogatari* (*The Tale of the Heike*), the anonymous thirteenth-century chronicle that describes the rise and fall of Kiyomori and his family, the Taira or Heike, he had become a devotee of the goddess of Miyajima at the beginning of his official career, when he was living near the shrine as governor of Aki province. On a pilgrimage to Kōya-san, the holy mountain (in what is now Wakayama prefecture) on which stands the head temple of the Shingon-shū sect, he had a vision of Kobo Daishi, who instructed him to repair the shrine in recognition of the fact that Miyajima was one of only two places in Japan where the Buddha manifested himself to worshipers. This appears to mean that the island already was considered sacred, not only to the ancient sea goddess (or goddesses), but also to Amaterasu no Ōmikami, who is still worshiped there now. She was identified with the Buddha of

Dancer performing bugaku, *ancient court dance, at the Itsukushima Shrine, Miyajima*
Photo courtesy of Japan National Tourist Organization

the Universe, called Vairocana in Sanskrit and Dainichi Nyorai in Japanese, who is the main object of worship in the Shingon-shū sect (which now has about 12 million members).

While still a provincial governor, Kiyomori had begun to fulfill his vow to Kobo Daishi by arranging for the imperial court to sponsor and partly fund a major reconstruction of the shrine. His devotion to the project continued while he and many of his relatives secured the leading offices in the imperial court, and his daughter Kenreimon-in was married to one emperor and became the mother of another. In addition, the Taira donated a number of treasures to the shrine of their guardian goddess, including thirty-three scrolls they had inscribed with the Lotus Sutra, one of the most important Buddhist (not Shintō) scriptures. These scrolls, officially designated a National Treasure, are now kept in the Hōmotsukan, the Treasure Hall of the shrine.

The chronicle claims that the family's attainment of supreme political power had resulted from Kiyomori's possession of a magic sword that had been given to him by a mysterious youth—a messenger of Itsukushima Dai-Myojin—and that their decline and fall in turn were due to her punishment of their misdeeds, by appearing to Kiyomori in the form of a young woman and taking back the sword. It was then given to Yoritomo, the head of the Minamoto or Genji family, which would overthrow and destroy the Taira four years after Kiyomori's death. Yoritomo went on to become, in 1192, the first of the *shōguns* who were to rule Japan, in the name of the emperors, for nearly every one of the ensuing 676 years. Perhaps Itsukushima Dai-Myojin was even more powerful than the writer of the *Heike Monogatari* gave her credit for being.

The main shrine of Miyajima is, then, a monument to the power of the Taira family and its intimate links with the imperial line. Its wooden buildings, painted white within vermilion frameworks and roofed with the sweeping tiled gables that Buddhist craftsmen had introduced from China, stand on a number of wooden platforms placed on stilts, so that at high tide they give the impression of floating on the waves. The effect is heightened at night, especially during the Kangen-sai festival, traditionally held in the sixth month of the old lunar calendar and now in August, when the light of lanterns on numerous boats, launched out to sea to guide the returning spirits of the dead, augments the candlelight from the stone lanterns around the buildings.

In addition to such standard shrine buildings as the Honden (Main Hall), the Heiden (Offerings Hall), the Haiden (Prayer Hall), and the Haraiden (Purification Hall) the complex includes a Takabutai, an open-air stage on which sacred dances are performed every January. Male dancers in orange robes, wearing masks based on those donated to the shrine by the Taira, participate in *bugaku,* the ancient court dances brought from Tang Dynasty China; female shrine attendants dressed in white and red perform *kagura,* literally, "god's music," a recreation of the songs and dances performed by the goddess Ame-no-Uzume no Mikoto to entice Amaterasu out of the cave in which she hid from the other deities.

These buildings, connected by covered boardwalks, lie on a single axis, which passes from the summit of Misen, through the halls and beyond them, out into the sheltered bay, on the northwestern shore of the island. It terminates 525 feet from the shore, at a vermilion-painted wooden *torii,* the traditional Shintō gateway of two columns joined at the top by two cross-beams. It may be that it was placed in the sea, rather than on the landward side where most visitors enter the shrine, to provide a ceremonial entrance for the Taira and other favored pilgrims arriving by boat, or even perhaps for the sea goddess herself. It is believed that another reason for its location was to evoke the Buddhist doctrine of the Pure Land ruled by the Buddha Amida (Amitabha in Sanskrit), which was said to lie far to the west. The *torii,* which is buttressed by additional, somewhat lower supporting columns attached to each of the main columns by extra beams, and covered by a gently curved narrow roof over the upper cross-beam, is the largest in Japan and has become one of the country's best-known landmarks.

Kiyomori's basic structures and layout have been preserved faithfully through rebuildings and extensions over the centuries, but there have been some significant additions. Two minor shrines, which may have been founded before Kiyomori's time but which have been rebuilt to fit in with the main shrine, stand together at the end of the arched Sori-bashi, a vermilion-painted bridge jutting out from the shore. One is dedicated to Ōkuninushi no Ōmikami, one of the gods who helped Amaterasu create Japan, the other to Tenjin, the divine form of the court official Sugawara Michizane (845–903), who is regarded as the patron of calligraphy and learning. The grounds of the main shrine also contain Daigan-ji, a Shingon Buddhist temple founded in 1201 and dedicated to Benzaiten or Benten (Sarasvati in Sanskrit), a goddess of fortune and music, as well as a five-story pagoda built in 1407. The presence of these Buddhist structures within an area supposedly reserved for Shintō deities confirms that the two religions had become as closely intermingled on the "strict island" as elsewhere in Japan. Indeed, once Daigan-ji had been established, the deity of Miyajima became identified primarily with Benzaiten, who grew to be widely known throughout Japan and was worshiped at some 6,000 branch shrines.

Contributions from thousands of devotees went toward the construction of two more sacred buildings in the late sixteenth century. In 1568 an open-air theatre was built on another platform jutting out over the bay from the western shore, away from the main shrine axis but connected to the other buildings by more boardwalks. It is now the oldest of its type remaining in Japan. Every April it is the venue for performances of highly stylized *noh* dramas, in which masked actors depict ghosts or deities. Twenty-one years after the theatre was built, Toyotomi Hideyoshi, the general who finally reunited Japan after decades of civil wars, ordered the construction of the Senjokaku, the Thousand Mats Hall, on a hill northeast of the main shrine. In spite of its name, it contains fewer than half that number of the fitted *tatami* mats that are the traditional flooring of Japanese buildings. In 1872 it became one of a number of Hokoku Jinja, "shrines for the protection of the nation," designated throughout Japan in honor of Hideyoshi.

By that date the modernizing regime that had seized power in 1868 was imposing a policy of complete separation between Shintō and Buddhism, casting aside thirteen centuries of coexistence in favor of creating an ahistorical, "pure" State Shintō focused on the symbolic figure of the emperor. On Miyajima the two Shingon temples were disaffiliated from the main shrine, but when the *torii* was rebuilt in 1874–75, the new policy, which would have meant removing its Chinese-style roof, was disregarded.

The main shrine and its *torii,* viewed from the sea with Misen looming behind them, traditionally have been considered to form one of the Nihon Sankei, the three best views in Japan (along with the sandbar at Amanohashidate and the islands of Matsushima). Although the 3,300 residents of

Miyajima understandably see no reason not to share in the conspicuous prosperity of contemporary Japan, the island of the sea goddess, by whatever name she is known, is still largely unspoiled, a fragment of the Middle Ages surviving into the present.

Further Reading: *Heike Monogatari* is available in English as *The Tale of the Heike*, translated by Hiroshi Kitagawa and Bruce T. Tsuchida (2 vols., Tōkyō: University of Tōkyō Press, 1975; New York: Columbia University Press, 1977), and in a more recent edition, translated by Helen C. McCullough (Stanford, California: Stanford University Press, 1988). Lively descriptions of contemporary Miyajima may be found in two thought-provoking accounts of travels in *Japan, The Inland Sea* by Donald Richie (New York and Tōkyō: Weatherhill, 1971; London: Century, 1986) and *The Roads to Sata: A 2,000-Mile Walk through Japan* by Alan Booth (New York and London: Penguin, 1985).

—Patrick Heenan

Miyazaki (Miyazaki, Japan)

Location: Near the mouth of the Oyodo River on the southeastern coast of Kyūshū (the southwestern island of Japan), 924 miles southwest of Tōkyō and 79 miles east of Kagoshima.

Description: Capital city of Miyazaki prefecture; supposed first headquarters of Jimmu Tennō, the mythical first emperor of Japan.

Site Office: Tourist Information Center
1-8 Nishiki-cho
Miyazaki City 880, Miyazaki
Japan
(0985) 22 6469

Miyazaki City is not so much a historic place as a legendary one. Until quite recently it was regarded by almost all Japanese as the cradle of their civilization, although it probably was not. It has played no significant role in the development of Japanese culture since the mysterious events recounted in legends attached to the city. Furthermore, almost all of the historic buildings and artifacts that once existed in Miyazaki were destroyed by heavy bombing during World War II. Since the war the city has been rebuilt completely and has acquired an air of spaciousness and modernity very different from most long-established cities. Yet, even taking these points into account, Miyazaki retains its special status, and archaeological research since 1945 has tended to support rather than undermine its claims to have once been a center of political power and cultural influence.

Miyazaki stands on the shore of the Pacific Ocean, near the mouth of the Oyodo River; it dominates a fertile alluvial plain that lies inside the subtropical belt. This combination of climate and soil conditions has made it possible since ancient times to harvest two rice crops per year, rather than just one. Farmers also grow wheat, barley, soybeans, and vegetables on terraces farther inland. These crops have supported a relatively dense population for centuries, albeit at a low level of commercial and industrial development. Like other cities in southern Kyūshū, Miyazaki has been isolated from mainstream Japanese society because of geographical factors; the mountains surrounding the Miyazaki plain effectively hampered communications with northern Kyūshū, and with other islands, until recently.

The principal historic site remaining in the city is Miyazaki Jingū, a large Shintō shrine. Surrounded by a forest and approached along an avenue lined with cedars, it honors Jimmu Tennō, the first Japanese emperor. According to the oldest Japanese chronicles, the *Kojiki* and the *Nihongi* (or *Nihon Shoki*), neither of which dates from earlier than A.D. 712, Jimmu's great-grandfather, the god Ninigi no Mikoto, was a grandson of the sun goddess Amaterasu no Ōmikami. Legend says that Ninigi descended from the High Plain of Heaven to a mountain in Kyūshū (which has since been identified as Takachiho, to the north of modern Miyazaki). Some time before 660 B.C., Jimmu supposedly set out from what is now Miyazaki on a voyage of conquest through the Inland Sea (lying between Kyūshū and Honshū), which eventually brought him to a new headquarters at Kashihara, in what is now Nara prefecture. It is impossible to know what historical events lie behind this foundation myth, which was taught as history in all Japanese schools until 1945. One clue may be that both Amaterasu's name and Jimmu's voyage call to mind the fact that in the traditional religion of Okinawa, and in Hong Kong, the sea goddess was called Ama. This seems to support the current scholarly consensus that the Yamato emperors were descended from invaders who had entered Japan, perhaps via Okinawa, from Korea or elsewhere on the East Asian mainland. If Jimmu existed, and if he ever visited Miyazaki, the belief among some scholars is that he must have done so during the first century B.C., while others place his exploits as late as the third or fourth century A.D. The shrine itself may date from as early as the eighth century, although its present buildings were completely reconstructed in 1907.

Regardless of the origins of the Jimmu legend, the probability is strong that there was a powerful local dynasty in the vicinity of Miyazaki, whether it developed indigenously or as a result of an invasion from the mainland. It probably shared its culture, and perhaps also some political structure, with the dynasty that eventually became the Japanese imperial family. The main evidence for this connection consists of the more than 300 *kofun* (burial mounds) that stand in and around Saitobaru, some eighteen miles north of the modern city. These were constructed during the Kofun Period (approximately A.D. 300 to 700), named by Japanese historians in recognition of the importance of the 10,000 or so mounds that have been identified, in central Honshū and northern Kyūshū. Whether some or all of the local mounds were constructed for members of what became the Japanese imperial family is the subject of scholarly debate. They may belong to a powerful group of allies, or even a number of different landowners. Following archaeological excavation, the area has been laid out as a park, and two of the mounds have been opened to the public.

In view of the sheer number and importance of these ancient monuments, there is a certain poignancy in the fact that Miyazaki has been historically insignificant in the centuries since they were built. Beginning in the seventh century it was the capital city of Hyūga province, which had virtually the same boundaries as the modern Miyazaki prefecture. During the twelfth century, however, with the disintegration

Aoshima Shrine, Miyazaki
Photo courtesy of Japan National Tourist Organization

of the administrative system under which provincial governors were appointed, real local power passed to the warrior bands that supplanted such officials in most parts of Japan. The Shimazu family, which had its base in what is now Kagoshima prefecture, absorbed most of Hyuga, including Miyazaki, into its vast domain. In 1587, Toyotomi Hideyoshi, the warlord who was to reunify Japan after decades of civil war and social upheaval, invaded Kyūshū and drove the Shimazu forces back into their original base in the southwest. After Hideyoshi's death in 1598, Japan was reorganized as a federation of feudal domains under the military regime of the Tokugawa *shōgunate*, which ruled from 1603 to 1868. During this period Miyazaki became a castle town, the center of a feudal domain, and a stopping point in the nationwide trading network. By way of the Inland Sea, Miyazaki now came into regular contact with Kyōto, the cultural and spiritual center of the country.

The Tokugawa *shōgunate* was replaced by a new regime in 1868, and the feudal system was abolished. In 1870 Hyuga became Miyazaki Prefecture, with Miyazaki serving as the seat of a governor appointed by the Home Ministry. Following the completion of the national railroad system, which reached Miyazaki City at the time of the World War I, the city and its environs attracted many new settlers. Given the national government's hostility toward archaeological investigations prior to 1945, as well as the constant pressure of local population growth, the urbanization of Miyazaki has been accompanied by the inadvertent destruction and loss of priceless evidence about the city's past.

One mile to the northwest of Miyazaki Jingū stands the Heiwadai Kōen (Peace Tower Park), an expanse of woodland originally planted during World War II. It surrounds a curious monument, the Heiwadai or Peace Tower, erected in 1940 to celebrate "peace" between Japan and Burma. The park also contains a flower garden decorated with 400 figures based on *haniwa,* the statues of human beings and animals that are often found in or near burial mounds of the type constructed in and around Saitobaru. The revival of Miyazaki after Japan's defeat in 1945 culminated in the use of the hall that stands in the center of the *haniwa* garden as the starting point for the transportation of the Olympic flame to Tōkyō for the 1964 Games. Since that symbolic event the city has continued growing; its population is now near 290,000. It has also become the main entry point for the Nichinan Kaigan Quasi-National Park, a coastal area of scenic beauty that runs for sixty-two miles south of the city. But it remains a matter of regret that Miyazaki unavoidably retains so little of its ancient and intriguing history.

Further Reading: The ancient official histories that are the only documentary sources for the story of Jimmu are the *Kojiki, or, Records of Ancient Matters,* translated by Basil Hall Chamberlain (Yokohama: R. Meiklejon, and Rutland, Vermont: Tuttle, 1982) and *Nihongi: Chronicles of Japan from the Earliest Times to A.D. 697,* translated by W. G. Aston (2 vols., London: Kegan Paul, 1896; Rutland, Vermont: Tuttle, 1972).

—Patrick Heenan

Mohenjo-daro (Sind, Pakistan)

Location: In the Sind province of southern Pakistan, on the Indus River, 140 miles northeast of Karāchi; 400 miles southwest of Harappa.

Description: Mounds mark the site of the largest city of the Indus Valley civilization, which flourished during the third and second millennia B.C.; excavations begun in 1922 have revealed an extensive, sophisticated, and wealthy culture.

Contact: Pakistan Tourism Development Corporation
Hotel Metropol
Club Road
Karāchi, Sind
Pakistan
(92) 21 516 252

Three thousand years ago, one of the world's earliest urban cultures flourished in the fertile flood plains of the Indus River, on the western side of the Indian subcontinent. Its two great cities fell and decayed until they were no more than mounds of rubble, and the existence of the people who had built them was forgotten. The mounds themselves were known, however; the northern mound, in the Punjab, was known as Harappa, and the one in the south was called Mohenjo-daro (Mound of the Dead).

Sir Alexander Cunningham first visited Harappa in 1853 and undertook small-scale excavations there in 1872. Unfortunately, the site soon was raided to provide ballast for the Lahore and Multān Railway. The large building and the flights of steps that Cunningham had seen were gone. Indeed, much of the ruins at Harappa were gone, transformed into 100 miles of railway bed. Despite this devastation to the area, archaeologists discovered hints of a remarkable past when they began serious excavations there in 1921. The following year Rakhal Das Banerji undertook the first excavations at Mohenjo-daro; between the two sites—but especially at Mohenjo-daro—archaeologists excavated clues that allowed them to reconstruct a detailed picture of the once-thriving Harappan (or Indus) civilization.

Until archaeologists uncovered artifacts of considerable age at Mohenjo-daro and Harappa, they had not suspected the existence of any ancient civilization on the Indian subcontinent: no evidence of any such culture had ever surfaced. Suddenly they found evidence not only in India (the sites now lie in Pakistan) but also corroborating evidence in the Middle East. In particular, stone seals that archaeologists had discovered at ancient Mesopotamian sites also appeared in great numbers at the two Harappan sites. Archaeologists concluded that the Harappans had traded with people at such places as Susa in modern Iran. Sir John Marshall, director general of the Archaeological Survey of India, supervised further excavations at Mohenjo-daro, beginning in earnest the recovery of one of the most remarkable cities of antiquity; the archaeologist Ernest J. H. Mackay conducted subsequent expeditions, which later were augmented by the brief studies of Sir Mortimer Wheeler and George Dales.

The civilization revealed by the excavations at Mohenjo-daro and at Harappa reached its peak between 2500 and 1700 B.C.: it ranks as the third oldest after Mesopotamia and Egypt. The Harappans inhabited an area twice as large as Mesopotamia, extending from the upper reaches of the Indus River in the Punjab to the river's delta in the Arabian Sea 300 miles west of Karāchi, and 800 miles southeast to the Gulf of Cambay. In addition to the two major cities, approximately 100 other Harappan villages and towns have been located, indicating a very robust, prosperous, and far-ranging population.

The origins of the Harappan civilization remain unclear, although some evidence suggests its evolution from earlier cultures in the area. Mesopotamian urban culture may also have influenced the pre-Harappans; using techniques similar to those of the Mesopotamians, the Harappans farmed the Indus River valley by irrigating the surrounding land and by building earthworks to control the river's annual flooding. They raised a variety of crops, including wheat, barley, peas, melons, mustard, and sesame, and were the first people known to have cultivated cotton for the production of cloth. Apparently adept at animal husbandry, they kept domesticated dogs, cats, both humped and shorthorn cattle, buffalo, fowl, and possibly pigs and sheep; horses, camels, donkeys, and possibly elephants provided transportation. The Harappans supplemented their diet with fish from the Indus River and wild animals from the surrounding countryside.

The evidence at Mohenjo-daro shows that the Harappans possessed skills in metallurgy and the creation of jewelry, textiles, and pottery; they likely were adept at woodworking as well, although evidence of that craft has long since disappeared. The Harappans traded with Mesopotamia, southern India, Afghanistan, and Persia to acquire gold, silver, copper, lapis lazuli, and turquoise to supplement their local materials. Harappan artifacts, including the mysterious stone seals dating from approximately 2400 to 1900 B.C., have been found in Mesopotamia, but scholars infer from the surprising dearth of Mesopotamian artifacts at Mohenjo-daro and other Harappan sites that trade with Mesopotamia occurred by some indirect route.

Several art objects found at Mohenjo-daro reveal not only the artistry of the people who created them but something about Harappan customs as well. Stone sculptures, carved variously in steatite, limestone, or alabaster, predominate. These often depict a conventional, seated male figure

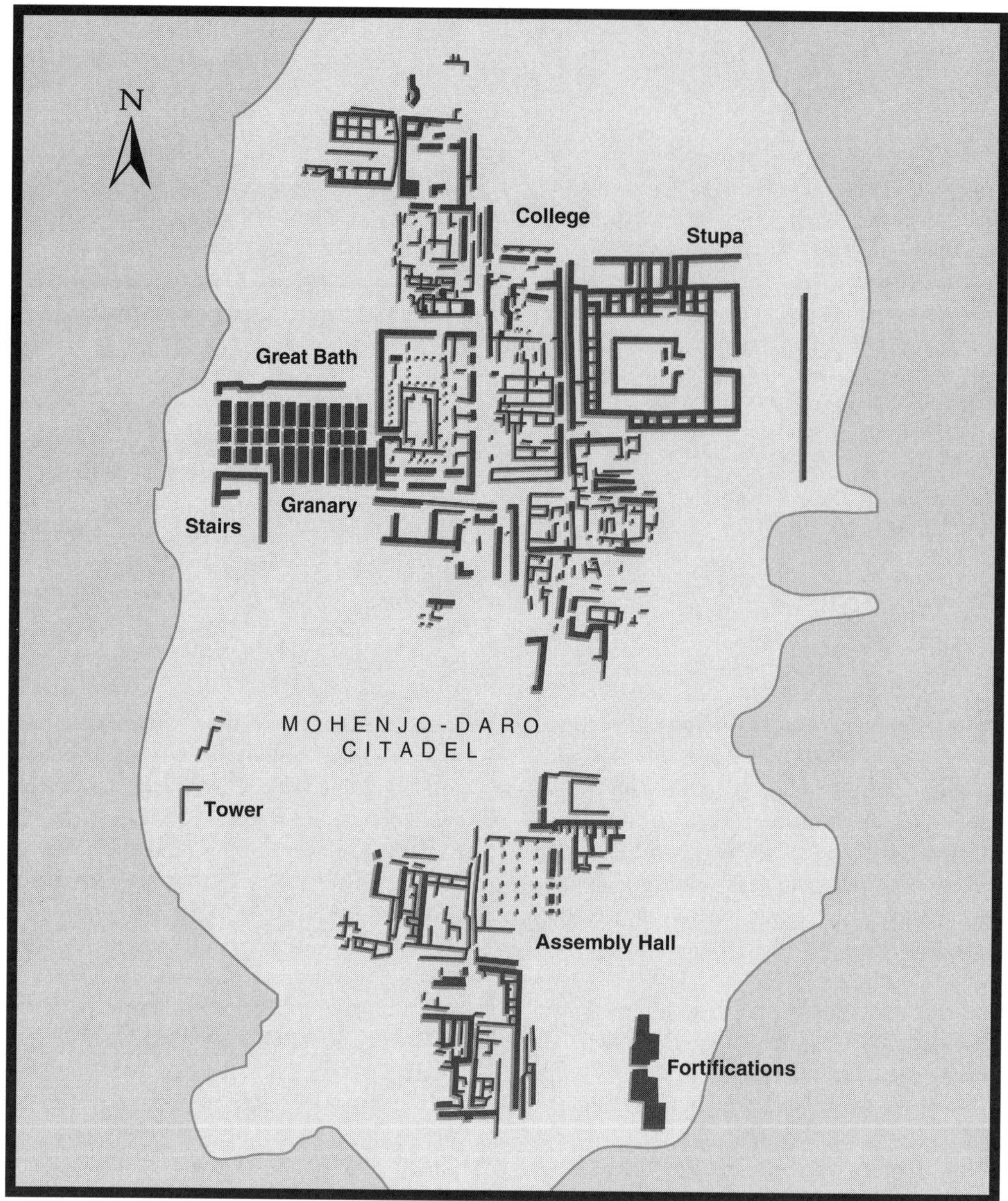

Excavation plan of Mohenjo-daro
Illustration by Tom Willcockson

that may represent a god. Bearded but without mustaches, these males have their hair pulled back in a bun and wear robes draped over one shoulder. The few bronze figures that have been recovered include the most famous Harappan artifact, a diminutive statue of a dancing girl that measures only four and one-half inches high; its relaxed, lively pose contrasts with the formal posture of the stone statues.

Many terra-cotta figurines have surfaced at Mohenjo-daro; depicting both humans and animals, some of these objects may represent divinities, and some are deliberately grotesque. The human figures comprise mostly crudely modeled females and may have been related to fertility rituals. Fully three-fourths of the terra-cotta figures depict cattle—bulls, in particular—of the humped, shorthorn, or buffalo variety. An occasional human-animal combination appears among these figures as well.

We know little of the Harappans' political relations with their neighbors. Fortifications in the cities imply the need for defense, but against whom? Copper and bronze weapons have been found, including knives, spears, short swords, arrowheads, and axes. A curious type of baked clay pellet, possibly for use with slings, has been found in two weights. But these artifacts are so general as to be equally useful against the animals of the jungle as against other humans. There is as yet no hard evidence for actual military activity on the part of the Harappans. Among the purely domestic tools found were cleavers, razors, stone implements of various types, and mace-heads.

Steatite seals found at Mohenjo-daro
Photo courtesy of Embassy of Pakistan, Washington, D.C.

The relationship between Mohenjo-daro in the Sind and Harappa in the Punjab also remains obscure. Both cities may have served simultaneously as capitals of their provinces, or one location may have succeeded the other as a center of political power. Although both cities covered significantly larger areas than did the other Harappan towns and were identical in plan, Mohenjo-daro's circumference of approximately three miles made it the larger of the two. Mohenjo-daro's remarkable regularity of design represents the earliest known example of urban planning. Two mounds comprise the city's profile. The higher one to the west, known as the citadel, features brick fortifications on a man-made platform of mud brick varying from twenty feet high on the south to forty feet on the north. Apparently the administrative and political center for Mohenjo-daro, this site later accommodated a Buddhist stupa and monastery built in the second century A.D. The lower city occupied the larger, lower mound to the east. Today, the Indus River flows three miles away, but a branch or canal of the river once ran between the citadel and the lower city. Flooding from the Indus undoubtedly posed a critical threat to the city in ancient times, and the high water table in the area still proves a continual difficulty for excavators.

Upon the citadel mound, archaeologists uncovered remains that seem to represent the major public buildings of Mohenjo-daro: the so-called Great Bath, Granary, College, and Assembly Hall. The large tank known as the Great Bath, presumably for ritual bathing, measures thirty-nine feet by twenty-three feet with a depth of eight feet. A courtyard edged with a corridor once surrounded the bath, with brick steps leading into the water at the north and south ends. The floor and sides of the bath represent substantial masonry construction employing baked bricks set in gypsum mortar, with a bitumen layer for waterproofing. At the southwest corner, an outlet led to a large drain that carried water down the west side of the citadel.

Small chambers beyond the corridors on three sides of the bath included one with a large well that probably supplied the water for the bath. Another building across the street from the Great Bath housed eight private bathrooms, each nine and one-half by six feet, drained via a central passage. Each room contained its own staircase leading to the second story, now gone. Although we know nothing of Harappan religion, this complex likely served a religious function; Hinduism and other modern religions still feature ritual bathing.

The Granary adjoined the Great Bath's western wall. The barter-based Harappan economy evidently relied on the agricultural produce of the Indus Valley as the basis for trade. The Granary, then, served not merely as a storehouse for food but as the equivalent of a state treasury. The original timber construction, which has long since disappeared, rested on twenty-seven solid-brick piles five feet high that were separated by narrow open passages; these passageways permitted air to circulate beneath the grain. The entire foundation of 150 feet by 75 feet later was enlarged on the south side. A loading platform served the Granary on the north side. The Granary was built at the same time as the citadel itself. The Great Bath, on the other hand, was constructed later, at the same time the additions were made to the Granary. Just south of the Granary, the remains of a great staircase approximately twenty-two feet wide rises from the plain to the top of the citadel. The presence of a well at the foot of the stair and a small bathroom at the top indicate that some sort of ritual bathing may have been required of visitors to the citadel.

Although Marshall suggested that the building known as the College, to the northeast of the Great Bath, might have housed the city's priests, evidence of its precise function has eluded archaeologists. This large building contained a number of rooms and a courtyard thirty-three feet square. Archaeologists are more certain about the structure known as the

Stupa mound, Mohenjo-daro
Photo courtesy of Embassy of Pakistan, Washington, D.C.

Assembly Hall, located in the southern part of the citadel. A large hall ninety feet square, it has four rows of brick piers divided it into five aisles. This much-remodeled building clearly was designed for some type of assemblage.

The plan for the lower portion of Mohenjo-daro follows a grid of north-south and east-west streets around rectangular blocks, each roughly 1,200 feet by 800 feet and subdivided by smaller streets and lanes. Excavators have uncovered six or seven of these blocks along with an intersection where two major avenues meet at a right angle. Extrapolating from the explored area and assuming continued regularity, Mohenjo-daro would have been a city one mile across with twelve major blocks in three rows of four, with the central western block being the citadel. The major thoroughfares were as wide as thirty feet, with smaller side lanes or alleys measuring from five to ten feet wide. Although unpaved, these streets contained brick-lined drains and featured manholes for regular cleaning. Earthenware pipes carried waste and water from the houses into the street drains. Small, single-room structures occasionally found on street corners probably sheltered night watchmen.

The presence of a large number of comfortable houses in the lower town indicates the existence of a prosperous middle class. External doors opening onto the side lanes allowed access to these dwellings, most of them two stories with central courtyards. These houses usually possessed bathrooms and well rooms, and some even featured latrines with seats. The brick walls originally were plastered with mud; timber ornament and woodwork probably adorned the buildings at one time.

In addition to what were obviously dwellings, archaeologists have excavated other structures that have raised more questions than answers; some of these may have been commercial or public sites, but scholars understand only vaguely the implications of these additional discoveries. Still other buildings apparently housed barracks, perhaps for slaves or subsistence workers.

The outer walls of Mohenjo-daro's buildings were constructed of baked brick laid in an English bond pattern, with alternating courses of headers and stretchers. Mud brick occasionally appears in interior construction, but the interiors routinely were plastered with mud. In rare instances, external brickwork seems to have served a decorative function, so it is difficult to determine whether the exterior walls were customarily plastered as well. The Harappans undoubtedly used timber in construction and possibly for architectural decoration, but no examples survive.

What sort of people built this remarkable city? That the city was carefully planned indicates some sort of unified authority, but what form this authority took remains unknown. Little archaeological evidence suggests the existence of a priesthood and even less that of a king or aristocratic ruler. While most scholars have considered the Harappan cities themselves evidence of some type of centralized authority, Pakistani scholar Syed A. Naqvi has suggested that the Harappan civilization may in fact have been the first democracy.

Among the evidence for a civil authority is the uniform system of weights commonly unearthed at Harappan sites. Made of various types of stone, they range from extremely large weights raised by ropes or other lifting devices to tiny weights possibly used by jewelers. Their uniform accuracy seems to argue for some central regulation. The system, unique to Harappan culture, uses a binary base for the smaller weights and a decimal base for the larger ones.

Excavation of the Mohenjo-daro ruins has proved two facts beyond doubt: first, the city repeatedly suffered devastation by flooding from the Indus, after which rebuilding occurred; and second, the more recent layers clearly show a deterioration in construction standards.

Unfortunately, scholars have been left with more questions than answers about the Harappans. Among the first and most intriguing objects unearthed in the two cities were the small stone seals, inscribed with elegant portrayals of animals, both real and imagined, and marked with the writing known as the Indus script. Sir Mortimer Wheeler called these seals "the outstanding contribution of the [Harappan] civilization to ancient craftsmanship." Usually made of steatite, each seal featured a square face approximately one inch across and had a perforated boss on the back through which a cord might be strung. The stone was cut with a saw and then finished by knife and abrasive; after the design was inscribed with chisel and drill, the seal was coated with an alkali and baked to a white finish.

Animals predominate the designs, but humans and hybrid human-animal figures also occur. Where the artisan intended realism, the animals are extremely well observed. Some of the seals evoke a clear symbolic or religious intent. A one-horned ox ranks as the most frequently depicted animal; it is shown standing next to a device known as a standard, which probably had some religious significance. Images of real animals include short-horned and humped cattle, rhinoceroses, tigers, elephants, antelopes, and crocodiles.

The Indus script may pose the greatest mystery of all. The inscriptions found at Mohenjo-daro are notably brief, the longest containing only seventeen characters. Inscriptions appear on stone seals, on seal impressions in baked clay tablets, on small copper tablets, on pottery stamps, and as graffiti on potsherds. The brevity of the inscriptions makes deciphering more difficult, and it may be that they simply indicate proper names. Despite tentative efforts to decipher the script, the puzzle of this language continues to fascinate scholars. Some experts have concluded that the Indus script belongs to the proto-Dravidian linguistic family; others believe it could be an offshoot of ancient Sumerian. Until more lengthy examples are found or until linguists resolve the matter, many of the puzzles of Mohenjo-daro will remain unsolved.

The reasons for the demise of the Harappan civilization remain a mystery as well. Early on, scholars concluded that Mohenjo-daro had fallen to a violent assault related to the Aryan invasion of the Indian subcontinent. This theory followed the discovery of five groups of skeletons in the ruins that appear to have been victims of murder. However, experts since then have become less convinced by that theory: not only is dating of the approximately thirty skeletons uncertain, but no other evidence suggests an assault on Mohenjo-daro. Further, all of the skeletons were found in the lower town rather than in the citadel. It now seems likely that a more formidable foe, nature, destroyed Mohenjo-daro and, eventually, the entire Harappan culture. Indeed, a combination of environmental and agricultural factors may have brought about the decline and fall of Mohenjo-daro and the Harappan civilization.

Life in Mohenjo-daro depended on the Indus River and its tributaries. This great river, running 1,800 miles from southwestern Tibet to the Arabian Sea, served as an important source of water for the Harappan farmers tilling the hot plains. But it also floods periodically, especially during the monsoon season from July to September; this flooding clearly posed a problem for Mohenjo-daro. Moreover, intensive agriculture may have overworked and overgrazed the land. Finally, geological evidence shows that an uplift in the earth's crust raised the coastline of the Arabian Sea near the delta of the Indus; this would have forced much of the river inland, perhaps causing a more permanent state of flooding than the Harappans could manage. The increase in soil salinity would have lowered food production. Mohenjo-daro may have declined first, leaving Harappa, higher and with a lusher landscape, to assume political leadership. In the end, the Harappans may have migrated to more fertile areas, to the southeast around the Gulf of Cambay, abandoning their great inland cities and integrating with other established cultures.

Further Reading: *The Indus Civilization: Supplementary Volume to the Cambridge History of India* by Sir Mortimer Wheeler (third edition, Cambridge and New York: Cambridge University Press, 1968), while outdated, is still the standard source of material on the Harappan culture. More recent investigations and findings can be found in *Ancient Cities of the Indus* (Durham, North Carolina: Carolina Academic Press, and New Dehli: Vikas, 1979) and in *Harappan Civilization: A Contemporary Perspective* (New Delhi: Oxford and IBH, in collaboration with the American Institute of Indian Studies, 1982; second edition, with subtitle *A Recent Perspective,* 1993), both edited by Gregory L. Possehl. Ruth Whitehouse places the Harappan culture in the context of other ancient urban cultures in *The First Cities* (Oxford: Phaidon, and New York: Dutton, 1977).

—Elizabeth Brice

Mount Ābu (Rājasthān, India)

Location: In the southwestern corner of the state of Rājasthān, near its border with the state of Gujarāt, at the southern end of the Arāvalli Mountains.

Description: The highest mountain between the Himalayas in the north and the Nīlgiri Hills in the south of the subcontinent, with a hill-station town of the same name; the town itself is a popular tourist resort, but it is surrounded by religious sites, including the most sacred temple complex of the Jain religion.

Contact: Government of India Tourist Office
State Hotel
Khasa Kothi
Jaipur 302 001, Rājasthān
India
372200

Mount Ābu is important to many native Indian religions and sects. According to Hindu legend, the sage Vasishtha lived there long ago with his magic cow Nandini, who was able to grant wishes. One day she fell into a nearby lake while grazing, and Vasishtha, fearing that she might drown, appealed to the gods for help. The gods responded by sending the cobra Arbuda, carrying a large rock on its hood, to the rescue. Arbuda dropped the rock into the lake, splashing the water out and saving Nandini. The rock became Mount Ābu, a derivation of a phrase meaning "Arbuda's hill." Another legend tells how the gods sought the sage's help after Parashu Rāma, an incarnation of the god Vishnu, killed all the members of the *kshatriya,* or warrior caste, to avenge his father, a Brahman of the priestly caste. Vasishtha performed a special fire ceremony and from the flames created four new *kshatriyas,* from which were descended important clans of the Rājput people, including the royal families of Udaipur and Jaipur. What are alleged to be Vasishtha's home and the firepit he used in the ceremony can still be seen at Gamukh, a Hindu temple complex located six miles from the town of Mount Ābu.

Many sects and religions have shrines and teaching ashrams on Mount Ābu. For the Jains, however, Mount Ābu houses the most sacred of their holy places. Most histories trace the founding of Jainism to Mahāvīra, "the Great Hero," who lived in the sixth century B.C. Jain tradition, however, holds that Mahāvīra was only the latest in a line of *tīrthaṇkaras,* great teachers who have achieved enlightenment. The word "jain" itself comes from a term meaning "conqueror," and believers are followers of "the Conqueror," Ādinātha, the first *tīrthaṇkara. Tīrthaṇkaras* are considered superior to the gods because of their moral state, and pious Jains worship them as examples to be followed.

Jainism, derived partly from prehistoric religions, has much in common with Hinduism as well. The Jains base their view of life on an ancient belief in a dualistic universe—divided between good and evil forces—and the idea that each individual houses an immortal spirit, which they call *jiva.* The goal of a Jain's existence is to separate the *jiva* from its fleshly house by transcending the material world. The Jains also worship many Hindu gods and recognize the validity of the worldview expressed in the ancient *Upanishads,* the great books of Hindu philosophy dating from the first millennium B.C. From this perspective, the major purpose of life is self-discovery: to understand and come to know one's own soul and how it relates to the world. Jains also believe in *saṃsāra,* the cycle of alterations between death and rebirth, and in karma, the rule of cause and effect that dominates the universe. Karma, signifying "action" or "work," means that the actions people take in their lives have consequences. Positive actions or thoughts will return positive results to the doer or thinker, and negative actions or thoughts will likewise produce a negative outcome. Negative thoughts in particular lead the individual farther away from truly understanding and appreciating the *jiva.* The Jains believe that the only way to escape the cycle of *saṃsāra* and achieve enlightenment is by accumulating enough positive karma. They do this through *ahimsa*—nonviolence toward all living things. All Jains are vegetarians, and they have as little as possible to do with occupations such as butchering, soldiering, hunting, and farming. Many in fact are merchants or, in modern times, stockbrokers. A Jain monk takes the doctrine of *ahimsa* to extremes, wearing a veil to keep from accidentally swallowing insects, and using a small broom to shoo small animals out of his path. Some monks adhere so strictly to this practice that they actually starve themselves to death in pursuit of enlightenment. Some further show their disdain for worldly things by refusing to wear clothes. Because the monastic life is so demanding, there are only a few Jain monks today, primarily in the larger cities of India.

The most important Jain holy site is the complex at Dilwāra, about one and one-half miles from the hill station of Mount Ābu. It consists of five separate temples: the Vimala Shāh temple, built for the chief minister of the medieval ruler of Gujarāt; the Unfinished Temple, commissioned by Brahmā Shāh, minister of the mahārana of Udaipur, who stopped construction on the building so that the funds earmarked for it could be spent instead on one of Udaipur's wars; the Tejapāla Temple, built in 1230 by two wealthy merchant brothers; the Digambara Temple, the only building on the site dedicated to the traditional "sky-clad," or nudist, sect; and the Chaumukha Temple, traditionally thought to have been built in their spare time by the masons working on the other buildings. Although the temple's exteriors are rather plain,

Dilwāra Temple, Mount Ābu
Photo courtesy of Air India Library, New York

their interiors contain some of the best architectural sculpture in all India.

The Vimala Shāh Temple was commissioned by Mahāsethji Vimala Shāh, the prime minister of Bhīm Deva, king of the state of Gujarāt about 1031. Like many Hindu temples in the west of India, the Vimala Shāh Temple consists of a large outer building enclosing a smaller inner sanctum, housing the image of the dedicatee, in this case the *tīrthaṇkara* Ādinātha. However, the function of the Jains' temple is not to worship the *tīrthaṇkara*, but to help worshipers reenact the holy event that the temple commemorates. Because the *tīrthaṇkara* achieved enlightenment, believers who repeat the events of his life can also escape the cycle of *saṃsāra*.

Despite the famous asceticism of the Jains, the outer portion of the Vimala Shāh Temple is lavishly decorated with scenes featuring gods and goddesses from Hindu mythology. In addition to representations of Ādinātha and the sacred mountain Shatrunajaya (carved with channels to carry holy water), there are images of the deities Chakrasuri with her attendant man-bird Garuḍa; legends concerning the incarnations of Krishna; Shitalā, the goddess of smallpox; Durgā, the family deity of the founder of the Temple; Sarasvatī, goddess of wisdom and wife of Brahmā, the creator; Padmāvatī, who teaches worshipers yoga and esoteric practices; and Narasingha, the man-lion, fourth incarnation of the god Vishnu. The sanctum itself is rather plain, and houses only the holy image of Ādinātha.

Brahmā Shāh's Unfinished Temple also is dedicated to Ādinātha. Dating from the late thirteenth century, it was intended originally to be the greatest of all the buildings in the complex. Like some of the images from the Vimala Shāh Temple, it shows influences from the northeast of the country: Himalayan motifs and images drawn from the Tantric Buddhist traditions of that area. Because the temple was left incomplete, the only item of real interest is the image of Ādinātha, made of a mixture of gold, silver, copper, brass, and zinc, and believed to weigh more than four and one-half tons.

The Tejapala Temple was built by the brothers Tejapala and Vastupala about 1230 to honor Neminātha, the twenty-second *tīrthaṇkara*. The *tīrthaṇkara* is represented in a standing position, as are the carvings of the founders and their wives. The dominant element of the temple is the image of the Cosmic Man. It divides the human form into three sections, each representing a part of the universe. The section below the waist represents the underworld; the torso represents the heavens, where the gods dwell; and the head represents the place where the *tīrthaṇkara* dwells.

The Digambara Temple reflects the austerity of the "sky-clad" sect that established it. The only symbols decorating the temple are flags adorned with *svastikas,* which—despite their twentieth-century connection with the German Nazi party—are in fact an ancient Indian symbol, predating the Aryan invasion of the first millennium B.C. In fact, the symbols have been found in association with the Harappan civilization in the Indus valley, dating from about 2500–2000 B.C. As it is used in India, the *svastika* shows the many forms the material world can assume, all coming from a single point, representing the spirit. The *svastika* can face either to the right or to the left, representing the two paths to enlightenment: through ritual and worship (the right-hand path) or through asceticism and esoteric practices (the left-hand path). In some cases, the *svastika* has a semicircle and a dot over it, representing the lotus blossom, which signifies the great cycle of death and rebirth.

The Chaumukha Temple, supposedly built as an act of piety by stonemasons involved in the construction of the other temples, dates from the thirteenth and fourteenth centuries. Its sanctum contains an image of the *tīrthaṇkara* Pārshvanātha, the immediate predecessor of Mahāvīra, which has four faces to represent the spreading of enlightenment to the four cardinal directions. The hall itself is structured to represent the halls of learning where the *tīrthaṇkaras* sit and explain their perceptions of the Universal Truth to the gods. One of the temple's exterior walls houses a small image of Ganesha, the elephant-headed god of business success and domestic happiness, demonstrating that the practice of Jainism is not incompatible with the worship of the popular Hindu gods.

The temples at Dilwāra are contemporary with or in some cases predate the great European Gothic cathedrals. Unlike many Buddhist and Hindu temples, the Jain holy sites escaped destruction during the period of Islamic domination of India. In part, this was because the Muslim rulers of the land were largely tolerant toward their subjects, allowing them relative freedom of worship as long as they acknowledged their Islamic overlords. The Jains, perhaps because of their practice of *ahimsa,* may not have been perceived as a political threat. Intolerance toward Hindus and other non-Islamic people did not become a great problem until the late seventeenth century, when the fanatical Muslim 'Ālamgīr (Aurangzeb) began a new round of Hindu persecution. By that time, most of western India, including Mount Ābu, was under the control of Hindu princes of the Marāṭhā nation, who largely respected the Jains' religious freedom. In addition, western India prospered through trade with Europe during this period, and the Jains, made up largely of the merchant and banking classes, grew wealthy. Their religious communities, shut off from the rest of the world by walls, supported by public taxes as well as private contributions, flourished. Jains continue to wield great influence in India today, although they number only about 1.5 million.

The hill-station town of Mount Ābu has been a popular retreat for centuries. Many rulers of neighboring princely states had summer residences there, taking advantage of the cooler climate afforded by the site's altitude, more than a mile above the surrounding plain. During the British Raj, the town was the headquarters of the resident, or administrator, of the surrounding area, and housed a sanatorium for British soldiers. The town is centered on Nakki Lake; a fourteenth-century temple stands on the lakeshore. Of the many religious sites surrounding the town, the Dilwāra temples are the most significant, but others include the Gaumukh complex, which features a huge marble cow as well as a marble figure of the Hindu god Siva's bull, Nandi; the Achaleshwar Temple at Achalgarh, dedicated to Siva, and with an enormous hole said to stretch to the underworld; the Durgā Temple at Adhar Devi; and the Atri Rishi Temple at Guru Shikhar.

Further Reading: For a general introduction to the differences in religious structures and decoration, see Benjamin Rowland's *The Art and Architecture of India: Buddhist, Hindu, Jain* (third edition, Harmondsworth, Middlesex, and Baltimore, Maryland: Penguin, 1971). *The Wonder That Was India: A Survey of the Culture of the Indian Subcontinent before the Coming of the Muslims* by A. L. Basham (New York: Grove, and London: Sidgwick and Jackson, 1954) offers a comprehensive overview of the period during which many of these sacred shrines and places were dedicated. Finally, Alistair Shearer's *The Traveler's Key to Northern India: A Guide to the Sacred Places of Northern India* (New York: Knopf, 1983) not only provides a handy overview of major religious sites in guidebook format, but also offers background information on the religions themselves.

—Kenneth R. Shepherd

Mount Everest

Location: The Chomolungma massif, the crown jewel of the Himalayan mountain range capped by the summit of Mount Everest, straddles the border of Nepal and Tibet in southern Asia.

Description: At 29,028 feet, Mount Everest is the highest point on earth. Since it was designated as such in the nineteenth century, numerous climbers have attempted to reach its peak; the first to succeed were Sir Edmund Hillary and Tenzing Norkey in 1953. Several other parties have followed them to the top of Mount Everest.

Contact: Ministry of Tourism and Civil Aviation
Singh Durbar
Kāthmāndu
Nepal
(1) 225 579

Long before British explorers became aware of the immense peak that they would christen Mount Everest, the native peoples of Tibet and Nepal were referring to the awesome mountain as "Chomolungma"—"Goddess Mother of the World." In the mid-nineteenth century, England's recognition of the mountain as the highest point on earth raised to fever pitch the public's excitement over the sport of mountain climbing. For decades, the geographic and diplomatic obstacles of the region surrounding Everest made climbers' reconnaissance difficult and their hunger to conquer the mountain acute. In 1924, George Mallory and Andrew Irvine were lost as they neared the summit (it was Mallory, when asked his reason for attempting to scale the mountain, who had answered, "Because it is there"). In 1953, Tenzing Norkey and Sir Edmund Hillary became the first to reach Everest's summit. Since their ascent, several nations have sponsored successful assaults on the mountain.

The formation now known as Mount Everest began to take shape below sea level some 450 million years ago, in the early Paleozoic era. About 30 million years ago, that formation began its inexorable rise from the ocean floor; although erosion offsets the mountain's growth, it continues to rise to this day. Temperatures on the upper portions of Mount Everest never rise above the freezing point, and yet the proximity of the sun gives climbers the strange sensation of being hot on one side, cold on the other. June to September is monsoon season on Everest, during which severe winds and rainstorms originating on the Indian Ocean sweep over the region.

Everest rises 29,028 feet above sea level. At approximately 9,800 feet above sea level, lack of oxygen causes human beings to experience such problems as labored breathing and quickened blood circulation. Headaches, loss of appetite, and an excess of lactic and acetone acids in the muscles, causing great fatigue, are all symptoms of the collective ailment known as "mountain sickness." A height of approximately 23,000 feet is known as the "dangerous altitude," at which oxygen is at the minimum needed for survival; and 26,250 feet, at which oxygen supplies are reduced to one-third that of sea level, is known as "the death line." However, experienced climbers can survive at these heights by "acclimatizing" themselves to the extreme conditions. In recent years, climbers of Everest have debated the merits of using oxygen tanks to complete the ascent; in 1978, climbers Reinhold Messner and Peter Habeler conducted the first successful assault on the mountain without the use of supplemental oxygen supplies.

The Himalayan mountain range stretches across 1,500 miles of land along the north border of India. Its 100-mile width encompasses the humid plains of India, the foothills and forest region at the base of the range, the Lesser and then Greater Himalaya, and, finally to the north, the barren uplands of Tibet. More than 1,000 peaks in the range rise above 20,000 feet. (To put that figure in context, Tanzania's Mount Kilimanjaro stands 19,565 feet tall.) The greatest concentration of tall peaks occurs in the eastern Himalaya, at the juncture of Tibet and Nepal.

From the north, climbers approach Everest through Tibet's Rongbuk Valley, a remote and uncompromising area marked by glacial flows that provide distinct routes to the base of the mountain. Since World War II, climbers have been obliged to approach Everest from the south, as Nepal's embracing of foreigners has coincided with Tibet's tighter border restrictions. From Kāthmāndu, the two-week trek to Everest leads through miles of jungle that gradually give way to steadily inclining ridges. The indigenous Sherpas, a people who traditionally have provided porters for foreign expeditions, maintain a community at Namche Bazaar, a day's hike from the Tyangboche Monastery, a Buddhist encampment set high in the Himalayas. The monastery is the last vestige of civilization trekkers encounter before reaching the Khumbu Glacier and the area now known as Base Camp. There is now an Everest View Hotel, complete with airstrip, nestled between Namche and Tyangboche; however, most climbing parties prefer to march from Kāthmāndu, as the rising altitude of the journey helps acclimatize them to the rigors ahead. Also in the region is the Sagarmatha National Park, named for the Nepali term for the mountain. This was established by Sir Edmund Hillary, with the help of the government of New Zealand, to conserve the forested area around the mountain.

Until the mid–nineteenth century, another Himalayan mountain, Kangchenjunga, was thought to be the world's largest at more than 28,000 feet. But workers conducting the Great Trigonometrical Survey of India in 1849 took note of a higher summit they called "Peak XV." After measurements were taken from each of six observation towers an average of 111 miles away, a height of 29,002 feet was determined for the new discovery. That height was the officially accepted figure until 1955, when it was revised to 29,028 feet.

By 1865, Peak XV had yet to be given an English name. That year, India's surveyor general, Sir Andrew Waugh, suggested naming the mountain after his immediate predecessor, Sir George Everest, who had been an integral part of the Great Trigonometrical Survey. "No man has done as much for the geography of Asia," claimed Waugh. But Everest himself was not flattered: he pointed out that speakers of the local Persian and Hindi dialects would have trouble with his British surname, which was untranslatable into their languages. Although geographers and cartographers generally follow the policy of rendering a mountain's name in the native tongue, Waugh countered that the Nepali government's refusal to accommodate visitors made it impossible for Westerners to learn the mountain's local name.

Reports from the region held variously that the mountain was known as "Devadhunga" (The Abode of Deity) or "Gaurisankar" (which later was proven to be another peak some thirty-six miles from Everest) in Nepal, and as "Chingopomari" in Tibet. The latter was adopted provisionally by England's Royal Geographical Society in 1862, but influential members of the society and the Alpine Club bickered over the jumble of names. It would appear that Waugh deliberately ignored all evidence regarding another local term, "Chomolungma," a name recognized by foreigners as early as 1733, when the Parisian Jean Baptiste d'Anville mapped a certain "Tschoumou-Lancma" in the Tibetan Himalaya. Officially, Waugh won out when, in 1865, "Mount Everest" was made the name of record for the imposing figure looming to the east. Now, the challenge was to climb it.

In 1905, two officers of the Royal Geographical Society, C. G. Rawling and C. H. D. Ryder, observed the Everest pyramid from a distance of sixty miles, concluding that the North Ridge would be the most appropriate route up the mountain. In 1909, an Italian explorer, the duke of Abruzzi, expressed interest in mounting an assault on Everest; rebuffed by the impossible restrictions on travel in both Tibet and Nepal, he settled for K2, the world's second highest mountain, located in the Karakoram region of northern Kashmir. As it turned out, Italian climbers would retain K2 as their destination of choice, while the French came to favor Annapurna, the Germans Nanga Parbat, and the English Everest.

In 1920, after years of protracted negotiations, British mountaineers finally were granted their request to mount an assault on Everest. With the blessing of India's viceroy, Lord Curzon, the British resident at Lhasa, Sir Charles Bell, obtained the Dalai Lama's permission for passports to the Himalaya through Tibet. On the resultant paperwork, Everest was referred to as "Chha-mo-lung-ma," providing documentation of the local term; in recent years, Chomolungma has become the universally recognized name for the entire Everest massif.

Despite strained relations in the region, the British enjoyed special privileges in Tibet. Believing Tibet to be plotting with Russia, the British had sent Colonel Francis Edward Younghusband there in 1903, with the stated purpose of negotiating border and trade agreements. The Tibetans resisted, but ironically, Younghusband's restraint in leading his troops against the Tibetan forces won the colonel their favor. A treaty was concluded in 1904. The British supplied arms to Tibet during its defense against a Chinese invasion, and in 1910 British-ruled India provided a refuge for the exiled Dalai Lama. With political strife occurring in China, the Chinese army retreated from Tibet in 1913. Tibet would remain autonomous until 1950, when it came under Chinese sovereignty.

With Nepal's borders closed to foreigners, the route to Everest through Tibet was the only option for early attempts. World War I took its toll on Everest plans, as key figures went down in battle: Geographical Society officer Rawling was killed, and Charles Granville Bruce, an expert in dealing with native porters, was badly wounded. As a result of the loss of these young men, the first serious assaults on Everest were manned largely by members of mountaineering's Old Guard. Further obstacles awaited: although Russian and Chinese threats in Tibet waned, India saw Japan as a new impediment to relations with Tibet. At one point, India denied permission for an approach through Kamet, an area that was accessible through India itself. To make matters more complicated, the Alpine Club and the Royal Geographical Society were at odds over which climbers would make up the initial expedition.

With Bruce physically unfit to lead the delegation, Lieutenant Colonel Charles Kenneth Howard-Bury was chosen, in part because he pledged to support the trip with personal funds. Of a proposed £10,000 in financial backing, between £3,000 and £4,000 actually was raised, including £100 from King George V and £50 from the Prince of Wales. The average age of the crew was forty-four; such experienced men as fifty-six-year-old Harold Raeburn, the team doctor A. F. R. Wollaston, and the physiology expert Dr. A. M. Kellas made up the core group. Joining the climbing party were the surveyors Henry Morshead and Oliver Wheeler; George Mallory, an initially reluctant participant; and G. H. Bullock, a last-minute replacement. Their plan was to reconnoiter the area and then return one year later to mount an assault on Everest.

Problems beset the entourage from the outset. The grizzled Scotsman Raeburn proved too old for the grueling march toward Everest. Not long into the approach, both he and Wheeler were stricken with stomach ailments. Meanwhile, the fifty-three-year-old Kellas contracted dysentery and grew so weak that he had to be carried on a stretcher. He died of heart failure and was buried at the point along the approach where the party first glimpsed the summit.

Raeburn's illness was serious enough to force his retirement, and the doctor Wollaston took him to Sikkim for treatment, leaving the remainder of the party with none of its

Mount Everest (on the left)
Photo courtesy of The Chicago Public Library

three physicians (Raeburn, coincidentally, also was a doctor). The party went on, however, and amid the fly-infested sand dunes and mud flats of the long Everest approach, an excited Mallory reported, "We're just about to walk off the map." Forty miles north of Everest, the group pitched its first base camp at Tingri Dzong, where Wollaston, who had returned, set up a darkroom, and the surveyors Morshead, Wheeler, and A. M. Heron took to their tasks. The young climbers Mallory and Bullock set out for Everest.

They camped at the Rongbuk Monastery, sixteen miles from Everest, where they regained their confidence with the blessing of the head lama. From there, the approach (the Rongbuk Glacier) is not unlike a highway, albeit a severely pockmarked one. At the peak called Ri-ring, roughly a mile above their party's next base camp at 17,500 feet, Mallory and Bullock confirmed that the North Face was the appropriate route to the top of Everest. Between their vantage point and the North Face lay a steep hollow the group named the Western Cwm. Setting out to find whether the Cwm connected to the west portion of the split Rongbuk Glacier, their surveillance photos were ruined when Mallory inserted the plates backwards, and they spent two days reshooting the lost photos. After discovering that the Cwm and the West Rongbuk Glacier were separated by a nearly sheer frontier ridge, the pair and their porters rejoined their leader Howard-Bury at his camp to the east. Later, after exhaustive searches from the east, Mallory and Bullock concluded that the approach they were seeking lay back at the first, northern route they had unsuccessfully explored, where, unbeknownst to them, the Rongbuk Glacier apparently turned back on itself.

At the same time, Wheeler found a way to the East Rongbuk Glacier, an approach more attractive than the desolate northern region in that it provided a good base, at the town of Kharta. Although Mallory was disappointed with his own miscalculations and his ineptitude with the camera, he was invigorated by the reconnaissance's discoveries. A hasty late-summer assault was mounted, but Mallory's men were only able to reach the North Col, or pass, before the monsoon winds turned them back. Mallory, by now smitten with the mountain, knew that the weary party was lucky that poor weather ended their efforts: "Thank God it was like that," he was quoted, "with no temptation to go on."

The next year, members of the follow-up British expedition, including Mallory, T. H. Somervell, and E. F. Norton, nearly reached the northeast ridge above the North Col, climbing to a height of 27,000 feet. En route, an avalanche below the North Col took the lives of seven porters, offsetting the party's success. Two years later a third British expedition took place, seeking to fulfill the great hopes following the first two fact-finding missions. Indeed, on this try Norton and Somervell topped 28,000 feet—without the aid of oxygen or down-padded garments. At that point, however, Somervell succumbed to a savage cough, and Norton was forced to give in when he was able to progress only another 80 feet in one hour. Norton was so shaken that he requested rope to navigate a relatively easy descent to rejoin Somervell; he was thereafter disabled for several days by snow blindness.

A few days later, Mallory and the young climber Andrew Irvine mounted the first serious assault on the summit. When last glimpsed by fellow climber Noel Odell, they were going strong for the top. But clouds obscured their colleague's view after they had reached 28,000 feet, and the pair never were seen again. Odell signaled the terrible news to Norton by arranging their sleeping bags in the shape of a cross. Mallory—robust, increasingly determined, and ultimately tragic—became synonymous with Great Britain's burning desire to scale Everest. His reason for attempting the climb—"Because it is there"—is by now legendary.

By the close of the third British expedition, a total of twelve climbers had perished; despite Mallory and Irvine's near-miss, a fourth effort was not launched until 1933. On that attempt, climbers P. Wyn Harris, F. S. Smythe, and L. R. Wager almost reached Norton's high point. At Mallory's Camp VI, they came upon the lost climbers' tent, still in remarkably good condition, as well as a candle-lantern and a lever-torch that worked on first try. Below the summit, they also found an ice-axe thought to belong to Mallory and Irvine—the only recognized relic of the climbers discovered to date. Subsequent efforts at Everest, while no closer to reaching the summit, greatly increased knowledge of the mountain's conditions. Leader E. E. Shipton's 1935 reconnaissance, for instance, ascertained for the first time that prudent attempts should be made between the end of the bitter cold season and the beginning of monsoon season. Among his porters was the Sherpa Tenzing Norkey, who would become one of Everest's first two conquerors on his seventh excursion, in 1953. In 1936, Shipton and Wyn Harris scouted the North Col from the west, along the West Rongbuk Glacier. But war in 1939 put Everest attempts on hold; soon the Tibetan borders would be closed to travelers.

In 1950 and 1951 the British became the first to attempt an Everest assault from the newly accessible Nepali side to the south. The latter try was jointly sponsored by the Royal Geographical Society and the Alpine Club in their new "Himalayan Committee" (which supplanted the earlier Everest Committee). On it, the seasoned leader Shipton, accompanied by Edmund Hillary, Tom Bourdillon, and Dr. Michael Ward, navigated for the first time the Khumbu Icefall, a treacherous but negotiable glacial formation that since has become the route of choice to the coveted peak. At the top of the icefall, they were prevented from reaching the Western Cwm by an immense crevasse, but the stage was set for future approaches from the south.

In 1952, an expedition from Switzerland succeeded in placing the Sherpa Tenzing and the Swiss climber Raymond Lambert just 1,142 feet from the summit on the Southeast Ridge before they were forced to retreat. Their route involved ascending the Lhotse Face of Everest toward the South Col, since known as the "Geneva Spur." Three months later the Swiss tried again, with less success, but they had established the route by which most subsequent teams would attempt the mountain.

In 1953 the seemingly insurmountable mountain was finally scaled. A sturdy and well-equipped crew led by Colonel John Hunt and Dr. Charles Evans saw nine climbers of eleven reach the South Col, accompanied by nineteen of twenty-seven Sherpas. On May 26, Evans and Tom Bourdillon reached the south summit—28,700 feet— before being forced to return as they ran out of oxygen. Three days later, Edmund Hillary and the porter Tenzing set out for the top, having spent a night at 27,900 feet. By 9:00 A.M., they reached the south summit, gathering two bottles of oxygen that Evans and Bourdillon had left. In good conditions, with firm snow and agreeable weather, they achieved the very peak of Everest about 11:30, staying long enough to unfurl their flags and snap a few photos. They also buried an offering to the Buddhist gods and a crucifix before retreating to the South Col where George Lowe congratulated them with a bowl of soup.

In subsequent years, the mountain has been approached and conquered by members of several teams from around the globe. Swiss climbers were the second to the summit—four men made it on a 1956 expedition. In 1960 a huge entourage of more than 200 Chinese and Tibetan men and women is said to have placed three climbers atop Everest, but this claim was disputed for years, as Westerners were unable to obtain verification. In 1963, an American team was the first to traverse Everest, ascending from the west and descending to the southeast. Beforehand, they had not announced their intentions; rather, they posited a planned West Ridge foray as a simple reconnaissance mission. But while two men (Barry Bishop and Luther Jerstad) were reaching the summit from the South Col, another part of the team approaching from Everest's west side weathered a storm fierce enough to rip their tents from their moorings and forged on. Two men, Willi Unsoeld and Tom Hornbein, crossed over the peak and joined the two others who had gotten there hours before—the ninth, tenth, eleventh, and twelfth climbers to do so. A difficult night spent trying to navigate the descent resulted in two of the Americans losing all their toes to frostbite, but another record had been set.

Other notable occurrences on Everest in recent years include the first person to ski the mountain: Japan's Yuichiro Miura skied the Lhotse Face in 1970, reaching an estimated speed of almost 100 miles per hour and using parachutes to slow himself; a film crew recorded his feat. In 1973, another Japanese team accomplished the first post-monsoon ascent; two years later, the first woman to reach the summit, Japan's Junko Tabei, avenged injuries she had sustained in an earlier avalanche by conquering the Everest peak. In 1978, Messner and Habeler conducted the aforementioned first ascent without oxygen.

In 1975, a large Chinese expedition placed nine scientists atop the summit. They remained there for seventy minutes, performing a battery of tests on climate conditions at the highest point on earth. There have been persistent reports, denied by the Chinese government, that this expedition discovered a frozen body just below the point at which Mallory and Irvine were last seen, some fifty years earlier. In 1979, the Sherpa Ang Phu—the first person to climb Everest twice using two separate routes—was killed in a fall. Considering the recent proliferation of successes at Everest, Ang's death and the unending questions about Mallory and Irvine serve as reminders of Everest's relentless nature. Although the mountain has been rendered less threatening by scientific progress, its allure continues to take its toll on even the most adept of the men and women who accept its challenge.

Further Reading: *Everest: A Mountaineering History* by Walt Unsworth (Boston: Houghton Mifflin, and London: Lane, 1981) is an extensive, almost encyclopedic look at the mountain and its suitors. Another important resource, *A History of British Mountaineering,* by Robert Lock Graham Irving (London: Batsford, 1955), contextualizes Everest's role in fostering global interest in mountain climbing. *The Roof of the World: Exploring the Mysteries of the Qinghai-Tibet Plateau* by Zhang Mingtao and Members of the Chinese Academy of Sciences (New York: Abrams, 1982) contains a useful section on the geologic makeup of the mountain, and *Everest: Expedition to the Ultimate* by Reinhold Messner (London: Kaye and Ward, and New York: Oxford University Press, 1979) includes a detailed appendix entitled "Twenty-Five Years of Everest History." Finally, *Mountains of the Gods: The Himalaya and the Mountains of Central Asia* by Ian Cameron (Oxford and New York: Facts on File, 1984) and *Soldiers and Sherpas: A Taste for Adventure* by Brummie Stokes (London and New York: M. Joseph, 1988) provide some useful, anecdotal information.

—James Sullivan

Multān (Punjab, Pakistan)

Location: Situated in the lower Punjab, four miles from the left bank of the Chenāb River.

Description: An important ancient city and place of pilgrimage, Multān is famous for a sun temple and its bejeweled statue, destroyed in the tenth century A.D. Today Multān is a thriving industrial city.

Contact: Pakistan Tourism Development Corporation
Hotel Metropol
Club Road
Karāchi, Sind
Pakistan
(92) 21 516 252

Multān has been an important city for several thousand years and was once the most influential city in the area. Its location at the original confluence of the Rāvi and Chenāb Rivers (they now meet some twenty-four miles to the north) and at the apex of the main trade routes through northwestern India helped it to become a wealthy, fortified city, and to remain so for almost 2,000 years.

According to legend, Multān is the place where Satan landed after being thrown out of the Garden of Eden. Other sources assert that the *Rigveda,* one of the earliest Hindu texts, was conceived there. Another ancient myth suggests that Osiris, King of Egypt, invaded Asia and occupied Multān. Literary sources suggest that the city existed in the sixth century B.C., when Gandhāra and Kāmboja controlled most of modern-day Pakistan. Multān is believed to have fallen under the administration of Kāmboja, which controlled it until the Achaemenian Empire emerged in the sixth century B.C.

The city remained under Achaemenian control for almost 200 years, until Alexander the Great invaded the Indian subcontinent in 326 B.C. As Macedonian forces attacked the ramparts of the city, Alexander the Great received a chest wound. According to Robin Lane Fox in his book *Alexander the Great,* a three-foot arrow struck the great leader, penetrating his corset; however, he managed to kill his attacker before collapsing from his injury. Consequently, his forces invaded the city and all of the inhabitants were massacred.

Multān, like Taxila and other strongholds in India, never came under the full influence of the Macedonian Empire. Following Alexander the Great's death in 323 B.C. and the subsequent disintegration of his massive empire, Multān fell into other hands. Candra Gupta Maurya began to expand his empire in India and other parts of Asia after his victory over Seleucus I, a general in Alexander the Great's army, in 305 B.C. Afghanistan, Gandhāra, the Punjab, Balūchistān, the lower Himalayas, Nepal, and the valley of Kashmir became part of the Mauryan Empire; Multān was annexed by the Mauryans as part of this campaign. At the end of the third century B.C., the Mauryan Empire began to disintegrate, as the Bactrians (Indo-Greeks) began to gain importance in the northern plains of India. After asserting their independence from the Mauryan Empire, they took control of Multān. Meanwhile, the Śakas, who were entrenched in northwestern India, began to expand their territories, causing the Indo-Greeks to fortify their cities against possible attack. This process of fortification was to little avail, for the Śakas eventually drove them west to the plains of Punjab. The Śakas were in turn deposed in the first century B.C. by the Parthians, who would control northwestern India until the first century A.D. They were replaced by the Kushāns, who ruled the region until around the fourth century A.D. and were responsible for the construction of stupas, temples, and monuments all over Asia.

For most of the Kushān period, Multān's history is vague. Multān was pillaged by the White Huns (Hepthalites) in A.D. 470, and much of the city was destroyed during this period. However, the city was liberated from the White Huns by a Hindu king who claimed the title Vikramāditya (Sun of Valor) in A.D. 544. Subsequently, Multān developed and expanded into a cultivated city; it became one of the four main cities of the Hindu Raī Empire, along with Iskanda/Iskalanda, Siwistan, and Brahmanābād. During the era of the Hindu kings, Multān became a center of trade and commerce and developed a cosmopolitan society and culture. There were no established caste or arranged marriage systems, and the inhabitants were predominantly vegetarian. Excavations have shown that the city had a good drainage and sewage system and had houses built of burnt brick. It also had been fortified and was surrounded by a moat.

The Chinese pilgrim Xuan Zang visited the city in A.D. 641. He described the visit in his diaries, referring to the city as Mulasthanapura. The city had a large, wealthy population and was famous for its magnificent Temple of the Sun, dedicated to the sun god Āditya. The bejeweled human image housed in the temple drew pilgrims from all over Asia. It is reported to have had a golden crown and jeweled eyes. Unfortunately, the statue was destroyed by the Qarmaṭian leader in A.D. 950, who also murdered all of the temple priests. The statue was later restored in the twelfth century, and the seventeenth-century writer Thévenot described the sun god as having pearl-drop eyes and a body clothed in red leather. The idol was, however, destroyed again during the reign of 'Ālamgīr (Aurangzeb), the seventeenth-century Mughal emperor.

Although the Temple of the Sun and its statue survived invasion by the Muslims under Muhammed bin Qāsim in A.D. 712, the Arabs benefited greatly from booty taken from the building. Muhammad bin Qāsim was a twenty-two-year-old

Tomb of Rukn-e ʿAlam, Multān
Photo courtesy of Embassy of Pakistan, Washington, D.C.

commander who had already taken most of the Sindh, and Multān, with its famous temple, was an inevitable conquest. The city subsequently became the easternmost outpost of the Islamic empire. For the duration of their occupancy in Multān, the Arabs collected the vast sums donated by pilgrims to the temple. Thousands of people visited the temple each year, giving the Arabs a means of controlling the citizens of Multān. When trouble arose, the Islamic leaders simply threatened to break the Āditya statue.

Overall, the Arab rule of Multān was relatively peaceful. The Hindu citizens were left to practice their own religion. Over time, however, people began to convert to Islam, and Arabic became the predominant language of the city. Islamic influence also extended to education, although during the reigns of 'Abbāsid-al-Manṣūr (A.D. 753–774) and Hārūn-al-Rashīd (A.D. 780–808), of the 'Abbāsid Empire based in Baghdad, Sindhi and Multāni learning began to influence Islamic education, particularly in the fields of mathematics, medicine, alchemy, astronomy, and astrology.

Multān remained under Islamic rule until 1818, although its rulers changed many times during this period. In 1005 Maḥmūd of Ghaznī invaded Multān, taking it from the Qarmaṭian army (a heretical Islamic sect). In the battle the famous idol of Āditya was destroyed, much to the anguish of the city's people. The temple would be replaced by a mosque. The Ghaznavids ruled the city for over 150 years.

Mu'izz-ud-Dīn Muḥammad ibn Sām of Ghūr (Afghanistan) invaded Multān in 1176 and defeated the Ghaznavid ruler stationed there, thus beginning a new era in the town's history. The Sufi Sheik Baha-ud-Dīn Zakaria (1182–1264) was an extremely cultured and educated man who fought for the education and equality of his people. He promoted agriculture and trade in the city. He is honored by the Tomb of Baha-ud-Dīn Zakaria (The Ornament of the Faith), which was built from 1262 to 1264. Raised on a square base, with an octagonal second stratum and a dome, this building features some of the earliest examples of blue-tile work in India and Pakistan. Unfortunately, it was damaged in the nineteenth century by the British, but was repaired and expanded in the late nineteenth and twentieth centuries.

Sheik Baha-ud-Dīn Zakaria's grandson Shah Rukn-e 'Alam also is buried in a tomb, one that dominates the fort mound in the city. The graceful structure features blue and turquoise tiles surmounted by a large white dome; its restoration was recently awarded the Aga Khan Architectural Award. The octagonal red brick structure was built by Tughluq Shah but was dedicated by his own son to Rukn-e 'Alam (Pillar of the People) in memory of his selflessness. Sheik Rukn-e 'Alam was a politically active leader who used to travel to Delhi to present the plights of his people. He offended other Sufis, who considered him to be unclean, a thought with which he agreed, as he believed that only his "master" was unpolluted by the world.

Timur (Tamerlane), the Mongol, ruled the city beginning in 1398. The Langah Dynasty, however, would rule the region during most of the fifteenth century; it established a university in the city, near the Tomb of Baha-ud-Dīn Zakaria. The city now attracted scholars, philosophers, and artists from all over Asia. Multān became part of the Mughal Empire in the sixteenth century, by which time it had a centrally organized administration and was a religious and cultural center. In 1739 Nāder Shāh of Persia took control of the city, although his reign did not last long; Aḥmad Shāh Durrāni conquered Multān in 1752. Durrāni's reign lasted just over twenty-five years; he was succeeded by Muzaffar Khān. During Khān's rule, Multān suffered numerous Sikh invasions. The Sikhs (Sanskrit for "learner" or "disciple") attempted six invasions of the city between 1803 and 1817 before Sikh leader Ranjit Singh finally took it in 1818. Muzaffar Khān and his five sons were massacred along with most of Multān's citizens; looting of the city's buildings was so extensive that even the floor of the palace was dug up and taken away.

In the following years Sikh rule of the city proved eventful. Relations between the Sikhs and the British, who were firmly entrenched in India by the nineteenth century, brought disaster to Multān. The Sikh governor, Sawan Mal, was shot in 1844 and was succeeded by his son Mulrāj. After the first British-Sikh war, the British had imposed a revenue tax on the Sikhs, which Mulrāj refused to pay. Two British men, Lieutenant William Anderson and Alexander vans Agnew, arrived in the city just as rumors were spreading that the British were going to invade Multān and kill all of its inhabitants. The two men were murdered, bringing immediate retaliation from the British. Herbert Edwards, the future political agent of Bannu, stormed Multān and drove Mulrāj to the city's citadel. The siege was prolonged as Sikh forces sent from Lahore arrived to join in the fray. The fighting lasted until January 1849, when the city walls were stormed by British general Whish, almost nine months after the two British officers had died. The city had suffered much through the battle, and many of the fine buildings and monuments had been burned to the ground. When the British finally gained control of Multān, little of its finery remained.

Multān did not prosper greatly under British rule; its golden age was over and many of its art and architectural treasures had been destroyed, including the famous Temple of the Sun and its idol. The town became a municipality in 1857 but would not change much until it benefited from rail and air transportation. Since the partition of India and Pakistan, it has become an industrial center famous for its hand-knotted carpets. In addition to wool, silk, and cotton mills, the area supports manufacturing facilities for soap, glass, and fertilizer. The traditional handicrafts of ceramics and camel-skin products are thriving.

Indeed, some things in Multān are very slow to change; an ancient Persian phrase says that "Dust, heat, beggars, and tombs are the four specialties of Multān." Travel guides report that although far fewer beggars now reside in the city, the heat and dust are as oppressive as ever. More importantly, many of the city's famous tombs also remain. In addition to the Tomb of Baha-ud-Dīn Zakaria and the Tomb of Rukn-e ʻAlam at the fort mound, a number of Hindu and Muslim tombs, as well as temples and mosques, remain standing.

Also on the fort mound is the tomb of the Sufi martyr Shams-e-Tabriz. Reportedly born in A.D. 1165 in Afghanistan, Shāh Shams came to Multān at the beginning of the thirteenth century. He is one of the most popular saints in Multān and was supposed to have been the master of the Sufi saint Maulana Jala-ud-dīn Rumi, who founded Sufi dervishes in Quinia. Murdered at the age of 111, Shāh Shams is supposed to have been flayed alive and to have walked the streets of Multān holding his own skin in his arms. His tomb, built in 1787 by his descendants, is a square-based building topped with a bright green dome. The original building was destroyed by fire in 1780. The restored tomb is packed with pilgrims every June 1, the martyr's day.

About one-half mile southwest of the fort mound lies the Gardezi compound, which includes the Tomb of Syed Yūsuf Gardezi. Yūsuf Gardezi is reputed to have arrived in Multān riding a lion and carrying a staff in 1080, on a journey from Afghanistan. He believed greatly in offspring and is described as having as many children as there are pigeons. His tomb is a square windowless building erected in the mid–sixteenth century by Salim Shāh Suri. It is completely decorated with lapis lazuli tiles. His snake and lion are reputedly buried in the enclosure. Visitors are reported to have heard the saint speak to them and to have seen him extend his hand to them. The Gardezi compound contains several other buildings: the Tomb of Abdul Jalil, which stands in the southeast corner; a sixteenth-century mosque; and an assembly hall built in 1878, which is still used for religious occasions.

Some two miles away stands the Tomb of Alī Akbar (the grandson of Shāh Shams-e-Tabriz), which, after the Tomb of Rukn-e ʻAlam, is the most beautiful building in Multān. Originally constructed in the sixteenth century, this building is similar in design to Rukn-e ʻAlam's tomb and is decorated with white-on-blue tiles.

The city of Multān is rich in history and culture, with its remaining treasures preserved amid the trappings of a modern, industrialized city. Although most of its historic buildings have been destroyed and reconstructed at some time, Multān still bears witness to the prominent role it played for thousands of years in political and religious developments in lower Punjab.

Further Reading: *South Asian Handbook 1993: Indian Subcontinent* (second edition, London: Trade, and New York: Prentice Hall, 1992) contains a concise entry on Multān and provides a historical and cultural survey; it is a good starting point for research. Isobel Shaw's *Pakistan Handbook* (London: Murray, 1989; Chico, California, 1990) is a good balanced guide to Pakistan. The entry on Multān provides well-researched historical background and fairly detailed information on the site today. For general historical information on Multān, *Pakistan* (Singapore: APA, 1990) is suitable for the traveler if not for the student or reader with a deeper interest in the site. *Imperial Gazetteer Punjab,* volume 2 (Calcutta: Superintendent of Government, 1908), provides precise information on the history of specific regions in Asia. This volume, although dated and heavily British-biased, gives a fairly detailed historical survey of Multān. *Multān: History and Architecture* by A. Nabi Khan (Islamābād: Institute of Islamic History, 1983) presents a detailed but rambling survey of the history and main buildings of Multān. It is definitely aimed at the academic or student of history, art history, or architecture.

—A. Vasudevan

Nagasaki (Nagasaki, Japan)

Location: Nagasaki, the capital city of Nagasaki prefecture, lies on the northwestern shore of Kyūshū in Japan, on the East China Sea and at the mouth of the Urakami River, approximately 590 miles southeast of Tōkyō.

Description: The industrial city of Nagasaki is one of Japan's oldest—and, formerly, most important—trading posts. From 1639 to 1854, it was the only Japanese city allowed to trade with the outside world during the isolationist period of the Tokugawa *shōgunate*. On August 9, 1945, during World War II, the city was destroyed by an atomic bomb, leading to the Japanese surrender to the Allies.

Site Office: Nagasaki City Tourist Information
1–88, Onoecho
Nagasaki, Nagasaki
Japan
(958) 23 3631

Nagasaki is situated on the extreme west coast of Kyūshū, on one of the steeply sloped inlets of Nagasaki Bay. Until the late twelfth century A.D., the area was a fishing village, Fukae-no-ura, ruled over by a *daimyō* (feudal lord) Nagasaki Kotaro, who gave his name to the city. The city has been an important trading port since 1571, when the local *daimyō* Ōmura Sumitada opened it up to European vessels involved in the East Indian trade. Spanish, Dutch, and Portuguese trading posts were set up, and Nagasaki harbor became Japan's first gateway to the Western world, a role that was to prove significant during the following centuries.

The first Europeans to reach Kyūshū and Japan were Portuguese traders. In 1543 three Portuguese were shipwrecked from a Chinese junk on an island off Kyūshū. They carried muskets and were thus responsible for introducing firearms to Japan. St. Francis Xavier arrived with a group of Portuguese Jesuits in 1549 and before long virtually controlled Nagasaki. The Jesuits brought Western scholarship to Japan; they learned the language and compiled the first Japanese cross-linguistic dictionary. This initial period in Euro-Japanese relations is evident in the art of the period, namban—most famous for painted screens that show Portuguese ships in Nagasaki harbor. The Portuguese also left their mark on the Japanese language and in their cooking, some traces of which can still be found today.

The Christian *daimyō*, Ōmura Sumitada, ceded Nagasaki and its hinterland to the Portuguese Jesuits in 1580. The Christians won the respect of the Japanese and, consequently, many converts, including some members of the ruling classes. Overseas trade continued to flourish as well. Some Japanese leaders feared that Christianity was becoming a powerful political force, however, and in 1587 Toyotomi Hideyoshi, taking control of Nagasaki, banned the religion. The ban was prompted by the arrival in Nagasaki of four Spanish Franciscan monks from Manila, on a diplomatic mission. They were given permission to proceed to Kyōto on condition that they not proselytize—a promise they failed to keep.

More problems arose when a Spanish galleon, the *San Felipe,* was stranded on the coast near Nagasaki and its cargo confiscated. When the ship's pilot boasted to the Japanese authorities about Spain's territorial conquests and the success of Spanish missionaries, Hideyoshi became convinced that Christianity was a political threat and issued his Anti-Christian Edict. As a result of this policy, on February 5, 1597, twenty Japanese and six foreign Christians were crucified on Nagasaki's Nishizaka Hill for refusing to recant their beliefs. A monument and small museum stands on the site today.

On April 19, 1600, Will Adams, an English navigator on the Dutch ship *Liefde,* landed near Nagasaki and became the first Englishman to settle in Japan. Impressed with Adams's knowledge, the *daimyō* Tokugawa Ieyasu, who succeeded Hideyoshi in 1600 and founded his *shōgunate* in Edo (now Tōkyō) in 1603, thus becoming the virtual ruler of Japan, made Adams his official shipbuilder. Adams also became Ieyasu's adviser on foreign trade and, although he still had a wife at home, married a Japanese woman. When after five years he sought to leave Japan, he was forbidden to do so. Because trade with the Portuguese had to be carried out through the Jesuit missionaries, Adams encouraged the *daimyō* to trade with the Dutch, for whom there were no such restrictions.

Initially Ieyasu was more tolerant of the Portuguese and other foreign Christians than his predecessor, as he recognized their importance in trade. He put no restrictions on the missionaries, and even allowed the Spanish to open a mission in Edo. However, the arrival of Dutch traders in 1609 and the English in 1613 gave him cause for concern, introducing as it did an element of Catholic-Protestant rivalry. In addition, Ieyasu's chief political rival enjoyed his strongest support in western Japan, where Christianity was particularly influential. In 1614 the Tokugawa government, in a change of tactics, banned Christianity and expelled its missionaries. The Christian underground that developed in the wake of this action was particularly strong in Nagasaki. Today Nagasaki's Urakami Catholic Church stands on the site where Christians once worshiped secretly in defiance of the *shōgunate's* ban.

Foreign trade continued to be a source of conflict. In 1628 a Portuguese ship was detained at Nagasaki in retaliation for a Spanish attack on a shuinsen (a ship bearing the *shōguns'* vermilion seal, *shuin*) in Siam. These seals, issued

Ōura Cathedral, with a view of Nagasaki Harbor, Nagasaki
Photo courtesy of Japan National Tourist Organization

to individuals for a specified voyage, were not transferable. From 1635, the Japanese were forbidden to make any foreign voyages, apart from specially licensed voyages to the Ryukyu Islands and to Korea. For most of their overseas trade, the Japanese had to rely on European or Chinese traders arriving at the port of Kyūshū. Ships permitted to trade were to carry the *shuin*. More than taking its part in a drive toward national unity, this move was aimed at ensuring the safety of Japanese shipping by controlling the activities of Japanese pirates, *wakō*. A commissioner was appointed in Nagasaki to oversee the Vermilion Seal Ship Trade (*Shuinsen bōeki*). The scene was set for Japan's withdrawal from the outside world, a period that lasted more than 200 years and was to halt Japan's progress in science and technology. From 1639 to 1854, Japan was virtually closed to the outside world by the National Seclusion Policy (*sakoku* or "closed country") of the Tokugawa *shōgunate*. Before the Tokugawas appeared on the scene, Japan had been fragmented. Now their aim was to consolidate the unity they had achieved, to strengthen their authority at home and in East Asia, and to prevent Western powers from having any political influence in Japan. Christianity was proscribed, and overseas travel by Japanese people was forbidden.

Most foreigners, including the Portuguese and Spanish, were expelled. Only the Dutch (who were more trusted than other Europeans because they had never sought religious converts), some Chinese living in Nagasaki, and an occasional visiting envoy from Korea were allowed to remain, albeit under the strictest supervision. Their trading rights out of Nagasaki, the only Japanese port open to the West, were severely limited: the Dutch were restricted to a small post on Deshima, a tiny, fan-shaped, artificial island in the harbor, connected to the mainland by a bridge. A three-acre area constructed in 1636 by building a canal across a narrow peninsula, Deshima supported warehouses, the offices of the Dutch East India Company, and homes for its officials. Some ten to fifteen Dutch officials were in residence, supervised by their chief merchant, called by the Dutch *Opperhoofd* and by the Japanese *Kapitan* from the Portuguese *capitao*. The only Japanese with whom foreigners were allowed to have contact were those involved in official business, as well as prostitutes in licensed Nagasaki brothels.

From the late seventeenth century, Deshima provided Japan's only contact with the outside world, and through the Deshima traders a small amount of new scientific and medical knowledge filtered through from Europe. A few scientists and scholars were posted to Deshima and were able to bring back to Europe information about Japan. Western scholars there included the Dutch doctor and scientist Philipp Franz von Siebold (1796–1866), who landed on Deshima in August 1823. Three years later he went to Edo to pay respects to the *shōgun* and was befriended by the *shōgun's* astronomer Takahashi, who made him a gift of maps. Unfortunately, to give maps of Japan to a foreigner was a treasonable offense and the astronomer was thrown in jail, where he died. Siebold's servant was arrested and tortured and Siebold himself made to grovel on his knees in front of the governor of Nagasaki to beg forgiveness. Siebold was turned away from Japan, but he was still able to bring back to Holland more than 1,000 Japanese trees and plants for use in research. Other Western scholars also returned with Japanese artifacts. A German doctor, Engelbert Kämpfer (1651–1716), pretending to be Dutch, traveled throughout Japan, recording his experiences in a diary. Swedish botanist Carl Peter Thunberg (1743–1822) returned with what were perhaps the first Japanese prints to be brought to Europe. Kämpfer's collection went to the British Museum, while Thunberg's is now in Stockholm.

The Japanese, intrigued by their Dutch visitors, developed a number of myths about them. It was said that when a Dutchman had a relationship with a prostitute in Nagasaki, on his return to the Netherlands his wife would know by his expression and his relatives would kill him. Japanese scholar Hirata Atsutane, writing in the early nineteenth century, ascribed the shorter lifespan of the Dutch to drink and sexual excess, and he described them in very unflattering terms: "They have eyes like animals and no heels. To urinate they lift up one leg like a dog."

The Dutch were rarely permitted to leave Deshima, apart from an annual journey to Edo to pay homage to the *shōgun*. Only a chosen few made the long journey, which took place in late January or early February at the beginning of the Japanese lunar year, and they were expected to offer gifts as a form of taxation. For the journey the Dutch chief merchant temporarily acquired the status of a *daimyō,* traveling with a few fellow Dutchmen and many Japanese. The benefits were entirely to the advantage of the Japanese and heavily taxed the Dutch resources.

The Dutch were not wholly unwelcome in Nagasaki as they were not only a contact with the outside world but brought in European manufactured goods, some minerals, and spices. Despite their isolation, many Japanese desired knowledge of Western culture, technology, medicine, and other sciences, and these entered Japan at Nagasaki through the Dutch. A few students were even able to obtain Dutch books. In the late nineteenth century, a Dutch naval medical officer, J. L. C. Pompe van Meerdevoort, was invited to Nagasaki to teach medicine. He was to found Japan's first Western-style hospital and medical school. This period was known as *Rangaku,* "Dutch learning," and during it the Japanese, through Nagasaki, assimilated Western knowledge. Eventually this was to contribute to the decline of Japan's feudal system and to its new role in the second half of the nineteenth century as one of the world's leading powers. In 1855 Japan's first modern shipbuilding yard was built in Nagasaki harbor by the Tokugawa *shōgunate* with help from the Dutch. The Dutch also supervised the construction of arsenals at Nagasaki.

In the mid–nineteenth century the Japanese were forced to change their isolationist stance, both by the realization that other countries were making industrial progress and by visits from foreigners bent on opening the country to trade. The American Matthew Perry arrived in 1854 and shrewdly bypassed Nagasaki, where foreigners usually were waylaid, landing instead in Uraga, in Tōkyō Bay. The United States and Japan joined in the Treaty of Kanagawa that year, effectively opening Japan to overseas trade. England and Russia soon negotiated trade agreements with Japan as well. With the expansion of commerce, Nagasaki lost its status as Japan's only foreign trading port. During the Meiji Restoration of 1868–1912, however, Nagasaki continued to be an important center of commerce, even though it was no longer the preeminent one. Trade with China and Southeast Asia was conducted in Nagasaki, and until 1903 it was the winter port of the Russian Fleet. It also developed a large shipbuilding industry. Under a privatization program, what had been a government shipyard was leased in 1884 to entrepreneur Iwasaki Yatarō and sold in 1887 to his company, Mitsubishi. Renamed Mitsubishi Nagasaki Zosensho in 1893, it was the largest privately owned shipyard in Japan until the end of World War II.

During World War II, the second atomic bomb to be dropped on Japan by the United States fell on Nagasaki on August 9, 1945, three days after the first one was dropped on Hiroshima. Because Nagasaki was a smaller city than Hiroshima, it suffered smaller losses of life and property, but the destruction was still massive. At least one-third of the city was destroyed. While the number of deaths remains a matter of some debate, it has been estimated as high as 75,000, including persons killed outright in the blast and those who died of radiation sickness later. Only 3 percent of those affected were military personnel.

Nagasaki had not been the first choice as the second bomb's target. The first choice was the town of Kokura (now part of the city of Kitaykyūshū), where there was an arsenal. The bombers encountered dense clouds over Kokura, however, and proceeded to Nagasaki, which had been designated as the alternate target because of the Mitsubishi shipyard and other industries important to the war effort. As it was, the bomb, known as Fat Man (in honor of British prime minister Winston Churchill), landed three miles away from the shipyard, the most important military target in Nagasaki, but only half a mile from the next most important site, the Mitsubishi Arms Manufacturing Plant. It made a direct hit on the Urakami neighborhood, where a prisoner of war camp was located.

The use of atomic bombs in Japan has remained controversial to this day; moreover, the bombing of Nagasaki has proven perhaps even more troubling than that of Hiroshima. The decision to use atomic weapons in general has been seen variously as a means to end the war without an invasion of Japan, which may have cost even more lives; as an act of revenge (justified or not, depending on one's point of view) for the Japanese attack on Pearl Harbor in 1941; as an atrocity visited upon a nation that was ready to surrender; or—in a decidedly minority opinion—as a show of U.S. strength in anticipation of a third world war. As to the bombing of Nagasaki specifically, historians and others have questioned why the United States did not allow Japan more time to consider surrender before deploying the second bomb. Telford Taylor, who had been chief prosecutor at the Nürnberg war crimes trials, has called the Nagasaki bombing a war crime in itself: "The rights and wrongs of Hiroshima are debatable, but I have never heard a plausible justification of Nagasaki."

The justification made by U.S. Army General Leslie Groves, in charge of the Manhattan Project, which developed the bombs, was that two bombings in quick succession were needed to bring Japan to its knees. There was no specific directive from U.S. President Harry Truman for the Nagasaki bombing, just a general order that all atomic bombs in the U.S. arsenal were to be used as soon as they were ready. Some historians have criticized Truman for not maintaining stricter control of the process. After Nagasaki, he did order that no more bombs were to be dropped without his express permission.

For Japan's part, Emperor Hirohito had decided as early as June that his country must seek peace, but Japan's military leaders opposed him. The Hiroshima bombing gave greater impetus to the peace effort, and on the same day Nagasaki was bombed, Hirohito's prime minister, Suzuki Kantarō, had been meeting with the military to try to persuade them of the necessity of surrender, but they remained determined to fight. After the second bombing, Hirohito decided to go over the heads of the military and surrender unconditionally. Several top officers attempted a coup to prevent him from doing so, but they were unsuccessful, and some generals and admirals committed ritual suicide rather than face the surrender. Hirohito announced his surrender to the United States on April 14.

Postwar Nagasaki has been rebuilt into a major industrial city, and has become a focal point of the antinuclear movement. Despite industrialization, it has a relaxed atmosphere, a blend of East and West. Amid the modern structures built after the bombing, some nineteenth-century buildings still remain. These include the Glover Mansion, built in 1863 by a British merchant, Thomas Glover, who formed a trading house in Nagasaki in 1859 and introduced the first steam locomotive and the first mint to Japan. Married to a Japanese woman, he settled in Nagasaki and built himself a fine house with views of the harbor. It remains frozen in time, his possessions and furniture just as they were when he lived there. Glover Mansion is reputed to have inspired the setting for Puccini's opera, *Madame Butterfly,* although this is by no means confirmed.

Another striking building is Jūrokuban Mansion, built in 1860 to provide accommodation for the staff of the American consulate. Today it is a museum celebrating the early trade between the Japanese and the Dutch and Portuguese. The Ōura Cathedral, built by French missionaries in 1865 to commemorate the twenty-six Christian martyrs, is the oldest Gothic-style building in Japan and has beautiful stained-glass windows. Built in 1893 by Chinese residents of Nagasaki, Tōjin-kan Chinese Mansion is a gallery of Chinese arts and crafts. Nagasaki also has some wooden houses built in the nineteenth century by the Dutch.

A small garden, a reconstructed warehouse, and a museum are all that is left of Deshima, the island in Nagasaki harbor that once housed the Dutch trading community. The island was rejoined to the mainland, with the filled-in site providing quays and port facilities. Perhaps Nagasaki's most noteworthy site, however, is a somber black pillar in the Peace Park, marking the exact hypocenter of the atomic blast, then the Urakami branch of Nagasaki prison, where 134 prisoners and warders were completely vaporized. Nagasaki has become a place of pilgrimage and a monument to the folly of atomic war.

Further Reading: *Cultural Atlas of Japan* by Martin Collcutt, Marius Jansen, and Isao Kumakura (Oxford: Equinox, and New York: Facts on File, 1988) includes a wealth of information on Japan for the non-specialist, covering literature, society, and Japanese culture. *Into Japan* by John Lowe (London: John Murray, and Salem, New Hampshire: Salem House, 1985) is a comprehensive history. *The Modern History of Japan* by W. G. Beasley (London: Weidenfeld and Nicolson, and New York: Praeger, 1963; third edition, London: Weidenfeld and Nicolson, and New York: St. Martin's, 1981) illustrates the transition from feudal nation into modern industrial giant, including Nagasaki's role as port and industrial center. Janet Hunter's *The Emergence of Modern Japan* (London and New York: Longman, 1989) covers general Japanese history since 1853. Also of interest is *Japan* by E. W. F. Tomlin (London: Thames and Hudson, and New York: Walker, 1973). For specific information on the bombings of Hiroshima and Nagasaki, the fiftieth anniversary of the event has been the occasion for the publication of numerous books on this subject. Robert Jay Lifton and Greg Mitchell's *Hiroshima in America: Fifty Years of Denial* (New York: Putnam, 1995) questions both the deployment of the bomb on Nagasaki and the United States's justification of the use of atomic weapons. Stanley Weintraub's *The Last Great Victory: The End of World War II, July/August 1945* (New York: Dutton, 1995) is a straightforward day-by-day account of the events leading to the end of the war. *Hiroshima: Why America Dropped the Atomic Bomb* by Ronald Tataki (Boston: Little Brown, 1995) puts forth the theory that the bombings of Hiroshima and Nagasaki were preparation for a possible third world war. *Children of the Atomic Bomb: An American Physician's Memoir of Nagasaki, Hiroshima, and the Marshall Islands* by James N. Yamazaki with Louis B. Fleming (Durham, North Carolina: Duke University Press, 1995) is a moving account of a Japanese-American doctor's relief efforts in the bomb-ravaged areas.

—Jackie Griffin

Nanjing (Jiangsu, China)

Location: In the southwest part of Jiangsu province on the Yangtze River, 186 miles northwest of Shanghai.

Description: Capital of the Jiangsu province and one of China's major urban centers. Has evidence of settlements dating to approximately 7000 B.C.; used as a capital by many different dynasties. Served as the first capital of the Republic of China. Site of the "Rape of Nanking" (sic.) in the World War II era.

Site Office: Jiangsu Tourism Bureau
255 Zhongshan Road North
21003 Nanjing, Jiangsu
China
(25) 3327144

Nanjing (also spelled Nanking) has been a major urban center for the past 2,000 years. Presently the capital of the Jiangsu province, it previously has served as the capital of the southern kingdom of Wu (222–80), the Eastern Jin (317–420), the Southern States of the Nan Bei Chao era (420–589), the early part (until 1420) of the Ming Dynasty (1368–1644), the Heavenly Kingdom of Great Peace (also called the Taipings; 1851–64), and the Republic of China (1912–49). Although the city has suffered extensive damage over the centuries from the numerous wars fought in and around it, Nanjing nevertheless retains many ancient structures, including large parts of the town walls. The first settlements in this area date to about 7000 B.C. and belong to the Beiyinyang Neolithic culture. Pottery, stone tools, and woven cloth have been dated to this period. In 1955 several Beiyinyang burial sites were found near the Drum Tower in the center of Nanjing. Later Bronze Age settlements have been discovered on either side of the Yangtze.

During the so-called Warring States period (403–221 B.C.), a site for the production of swords was situated near the present-day Chaotian Gong Temple Museum. It supplied three neighboring states. In 333 B.C. a walled town was constructed to the west of Nanjing. It was known initially as Jinling (Golden Hill), a name still popular throughout the city today (most notably the Jinling Hotel, which towers above the city's central intersection). Jinling later changed its name to Shitou Cheng (Stone City). Its focal point, Qingliang Hill, is today a park.

According to legend, Qin Shihuang Di, emperor of Qin and otherwise known as the "Great Unifier," upon his arrival at Nanjing in 210 B.C. was told by a seer that a new emperor would arise there. Fearing a potential threat to his power, Qin took the seer's warning as the cue to order earthworks to be dug, in the belief that construction of buildings in a certain place or facing in a certain direction could influence natural forces and the outcome of events. In spite of his efforts, Qin Shihuang Di did see the emergence of many future rulers in Nanjing, although none challenged Qin's authority directly. In A.D. 229 Sun Quan moved the capital of the kingdom of Wu here. He built a new walled city on the site of Shitou Cheng. Part of Sun Quan's sandstone wall stands today in the western part of Nanjing, integrated with a Ming city wall dating to the fourteenth century. Also during Sun Quan's reign a temple was constructed for a Buddha relic brought to Nanjing by Kang Sanghui (Samghavarman in Sanskrit), a Buddhist missionary known for translating Sanskrit sutras into Chinese. In 280 the ruler of Wu was overthrown by the Western Jin Dynasty, which had been based to the north in Luoyang.

The following centuries saw numerous local dynasties rise and fall in the Nanjing area. After the Western Jin were conquered by barbarians, a member of the house established the Eastern Jin, with Nanjing as its capital. Nanjing became a significant cultural center. Painter Gu Kaizhi (c. 344–406) stayed here, as did the poet Xie Lingyun and the calligrapher Wang Xizhe. The renowned translator Fa Xian promoted Buddhism from Nanjing.

In 420 Liu Yu, a military leader under the Eastern Jin, took power and established a dynasty known as the Earlier Song (420–79). Most of this dynasty's history was violent; it waged numerous wars with the Northern Wei, which ruled the area north of the Yangtze. The dynasty was overthrown in 479 by a general who established the equally warlike Southern Qi Dynasty, which lasted until 502. At Danyang, forty-three miles east of Nanjing, can be found a series of beautiful tombs dating from this period; their delicate stone carving contrasts with the plainer stone sculptures of the later Ming tombs around Nanjing. Other monuments surviving from this period include a series of Buddhist caves filled with stone figures and carved walls twelve miles east of Nanjing at Qixia Shan. These caves were founded in the fifth century by a hermit named Ming Sangshao, who was inspired by a vision of a Buddha. When this monk died shortly after receiving his vision, his son began to carve out the caves, a task that continued up to the Ming period, 1,000 years later. Unfortunately, much damage was done to the figures during the Taiping rebellion, and late nineteenth-century attempts at restoration did more harm than good.

After the Southern Qi Dynasty was overthrown by a general who set up the Southern Liang Dynasty (502–57), Nanjing remained the capital. The enlightened first Liang emperor, Wu Di, established state-supported colleges, promoted commerce, and built palaces and other public works in the city. He eventually became a devout Buddhist and retired to one of his temples to pursue a monastic existence, only to be persuaded later, with some difficulty, to resume his rule.

Ancient town walls of Nanjing
Photo courtesy of China National Tourist Office, Los Angeles

The Drum Tower, Nanjing
Photo courtesy of China National Tourist Office, Los Angeles

He financed the first publication of a full compilation of the Buddhist scriptures (the Tripitaka) and wrote on Buddhist ritual. According to legend, when during the reign of Wu Di a monk preached on the hill named Yuhua Tai ("Terrace of the Rain of Flowers," just beyond the Zhonghua Gate), flowers rained from the sky and fell upon his audience. The flowers were said to have turned into little colored pebbles, which today are offered for sale under saucers of water. Also on this site is a monument to the estimated 100,000 communists who were executed on Yuhua Tai by the nationalists between 1927 and 1949.

A number of tombs dating from the Liang Dynasty survive today only a few miles from the city. They are marked by tall columns and solidly carved winged lions. The tombs belong to Xiao Jing, a cousin to the emperor Wu Di who served in his administration, and three of Wu Di's brothers.

In the later years of the Liang Dynasty, a revolt headed by a general named Hou Jing caused much destruction and led to a great famine in which half the population of the area died. In 557 another military leader rebelled and the Liang Dynasty fell to the Southern Chen Dynasty. The Chen Dynasty won some territory from the Northern Qi, but attempts to capitalize on this success led to their defeat at the hands of the Northern Zhou (557–81). (The Southern Chen, though defeated, managed to continue in name at least until 589.) The Northern Zhou were soon overturned by the Sui Dynasty (581–618), which united China after years of bloody conflict.

Under the Sui, Nanjing lost its status as capital but remained an important urban settlement and center of culture. At the end of the Tang period (618–907), when China again became divided, it became the capital of several southern dynasties, until the Song Dynasty (960–1276) again united China. It was during the Song period that the Xuanwu Lake to the north of the town center was given its name. Xuanwu means "dark warrior," and the lake derives this title from a black monster that was reported to emerge from the waters. Today the lake is used for recreation and fish farming.

Nanjing remained out of the historic spotlight until the establishment of the Ming Dynasty (1368–1644). The first Ming emperor, Hongwu, first established his capital at Fengyang in his native Anhui. Six years later he moved his capital to Nanjing, where he built a palace consisting of three major courtyards and some more town walls, several sections of which still stand. Because of the hilly terrain and the river, the city wall of Nanjing is not in the form of a perfect rectangle, the usual shape for Chinese town walls. The

Chaotian Gong Temple Museum, Nanjing
Photo courtesy of China National Tourist Office, Los Angeles

Nanjing wall took twenty years to build and was approximately twenty miles long—the longest city wall in the world. It is an average thirty-nine feet in height and once had 13,616 cannon positioned on top of it. The city walls originally had thirteen gates; another eleven were added later. At that section surviving today in the south of the city stands an imposing gate known as the Zhonghua, which has been restored. The name Zhonghua (one of the words for China) was first used for the gate in 1912. Previously it was known as the Jubao (Massed Treasure). The stone and brick structure has three inner gates and enough room to garrison 3,000 soldiers. It covers an area of more than 160,000 square feet; one can walk along the top of it today. All of the bricks are inscribed with the name of the superintendent and the brick-master plus the date that they were made; the bricks come from five different provinces.

Also dating from the period of the first Ming emperor is the still-standing Drum Tower, originally built in 1382 and frequently restored since. The tower is so named because it once housed several sets of drums, which were used to mark the watches of the night, to welcome important visitors, or to sound alarms. The top of the tower offers an excellent point from which to view the city. Nearby, dating from 1388 and contained in a bell tower, is a huge bronze bell weighing more than a ton, one of the largest bells in China.

Hongwu was the only Ming emperor to be buried in the vicinity of Nanjing (all the others rest near Beijing). The remains of his tomb may still be visited today. The area it covers is approximately equal to that of the Forbidden City in Beijing, which is essentially a copy. Construction of the tomb began in 1381, while the emperor was still living, and was completed in 1383. In 1382 Hongwu's wife, the empress Ma, was buried in the tomb, which was thereafter known as Xiao Ling (the Filial Tomb). Hongwu joined her there in 1399. The tomb was originally encircled by a wall some fourteen miles long, but the wall no longer exists. Along the approach to the tomb remains a stone gateway known as the Xiamafang (Place Where Officials Dismount from their Horses). About one-half mile beyond this is the three-arched Dajin Men (Great Golden Gate) next to which is the Sifang Cheng (Square City), a brick monument featuring an inscription detailing Hongwu's achievements. The path leading to the tomb is lined first with stone animal figures, then with sculptures of four generals and four ministers, and finally, nearest the tombs, with trees. Originally there was a large hall here with an enclosed walk behind it leading to a tower and a huge mound. The complex is much reduced today. The hall was destroyed in 1853 and replaced by a smaller structure twelve years later. Although portions of the floor of the original building remain visible, the tower's wooden superstructure is gone.

Several other tombs dating from the Ming period lie scattered around Nanjing. One of the more famous is that belonging to Xu Da (1332–85), a distinguished general who fought alongside Emperor Hongwu. Like other non-imperial tombs of the era, the tomb of Xu Da consists of a sepulchral mound known as a tumulus, fronted by a stone identifying who is buried there and a series of carved stone figures. Another military leader of the time, Li Wenzhong, is memorialized by a funerary stele inscribed by the first Ming emperor.

After Hongwu's death, power was seized by one of his sons, the prince of Yan, although the kingdom had actually been bequeathed to a grandson. The usurper moved the capital to Beijing in 1420. Much of Nanjing, including the imperial palace, was left in ruins. What remained of the palace was used in the construction of the Taiping palaces during the nineteenth century.

Nanjing's status as a capital was reinvoked when the Ming Dynasty fell to the Manchus and the Ming gradually moved south after 1664. The fragmented Ming lasted only a few years. Nanjing became historically important again in 1853, when it was chosen as the headquarters for the anti-Qing Taiping leaders (giving rise to what became known as the Taiping Rebellion from 1850 to 1864). A museum located in the home of one of the leaders, Yang Xiuqing, provides an introduction to the movement. The museum contains maps illustrating how the Taiping armies at one stage threatened Beijing itself, in addition to texts explaining Taiping ideology, which advocated land redistribution, equality in marriage, and education reform.

The Taiping Rebellion was put down in 1864 with the help of foreign aid. In its aftermath in 1865, a Confucian temple, the Chaotian Gong (Heaven-facing Palace) was built in Nanjing. The elaborate temple is now a museum displaying many vestiges of Nanjing's past. Among its possessions are the remains of the "porcelain pagoda," an early symbol of Nanjing commented upon by Longfellow in his poem "Keramos." The pagoda, actually made of glazed brick, was built in the early fifteenth century by the Ming emperor Yongle in honor of his mother and was destroyed during the Taiping period.

Nanjing was proclaimed capital of the Republic of China on January 1, 1912, the constitutional monarchy retaining power in Beijing until 1928, at which point Nanjing became the capital of all China. Nanjing contains the tomb of the provisional first president of the republic, Sun Yat-sen, who held power only for a few months beginning in 1911; he stepped down in 1912 because he believed the country would not accept him, a southerner, as president, and therefore feared his presidency would impede the unification of China. His tomb, which took three years to construct, sits on a twenty-acre site with a mausoleum designed to be more impressive than those of the old emperors. Sun was interred here in 1929, four years after his death. His final resting place is reached via a series of walks, steps, and archways and finally an enormous white marble stairway.

Sun, originally from the Guangdong province, spent most of his life outside China. He attended schools in Hawaii and Hong Kong, practiced as a medical doctor in Macau, lived for a time in Japan, and traveled widely while plotting against the Qing and developing his vision for China. He opposed the Qing because he believed they were ineffective against foreign imperialism. After leaving the presidency, he became director of railways for China.

During the period of the Chinese Republic, the government had little actual power, as the Japanese posed a threat from without and the Communist Party from within. Still, much of present-day Nanjing dates to this period, which introduced broad tree-lined avenues (an estimated 240,000 sycamore trees grow in the city) and Western-style architecture.

Nanjing's population suffered heavily during both the Sino-Japanese War and World War II. The Japanese captured Nanjing on December 12, 1937. Chiang Kai-shek's nationalist government escaped to Chogqing, and a figurehead government was installed by the Japanese. In what became known as the "Rape of Nanking," some 400,000 of the city's citizens were killed between 1938 and 1945, many in particularly brutal fashion. The city suffered little structural damage, however. When Japan was defeated in 1945, Nanjing again became China's capital, but civil war broke out between the nationalists and the communists. The communists took Nanjing on April 23, 1949, and the new government made Beijing its capital.

In the postwar period, Nanjing has remained a provincial capital and a major industrial city. Today some 2,000 factories operate in Nanjing, producing metallurgical and chemical equipment, ships, telecommunications instruments, synthetic fibers, silk, and wood and ivory items. In addition to its ancient monuments, Nanjing's attractions include a recently opened museum to the martyrs of the Japanese invasion.

Further Reading: For very good background, see Barry Till's *In Search of Old Nanjing* (Hong Kong: Joint, 1982). *Blue Guide to China* by Frances Wood (London: Black, and New York: Norton, 1992) is typically impressive and informative. Brian Catchpole's *A Map History of Modern China* (London and Exeter, New Hampshire: Heinemann, 1977) provides very useful introductory coverage of China's history. Also to be recommended are Jacques Gernet's *A History of Chinese Civilisation,* translated by J. R. Foster (Cambridge and New York: Cambridge University Press, 1982; as *Le Monde chinois,* Paris: Armand Colin, 1980), or Witold Rodzinski's *The Walled Kingdom: A History of China from 2000 B.C. to the Present* (London: Fontana, and New York: Free Press, 1984).

—Tim Pepper

Nara (Nara, Japan)

Location: Twenty-five miles south of Kyōto in the Kinki region of the island of Honshū in Japan.

Description: Chief town of Nara prefecture and cradle of Japanese culture; imperial capital from A.D. 710 to 784; site of numerous monasteries and other religious shrines.

Site Office: Nara City Tourist Center
23–4 Kami-Sanjo-Cho
Nara, Nara
Japan
(742) 22 3900

Nara was not founded until 710, but the surrounding area began to develop as a cultural and religious center a century earlier. Between A.D. 601 and 607, Empress Suiko's nephew and regent, Prince Shōtoku-Taishi, founded a monastic complex, Hōryū-ji, in the village of Ikaruga, on the western edge of the Nara plain. It remains standing today, one of the best surviving examples of T'ang period architecture, and its western temple's five-story pagoda is one of the oldest wooden buildings extant in the world. Built largely on Chinese principles, "Hōryū-ji" means "Temple of the Prosperity of the Buddhist Law." It was inaugurated in 616. To commemorate the death of Shōtoku in 621, the court ladies embroidered the *Land of Heavenly Longevity* (*Tenjukoku*), a piece modeled after Chinese examples, in which Shōtoku is shown enjoying paradise after death. The embroidery depicts tortoises, which symbolize longevity, as well as lotuses and bodhisattvas, enlightened beings who remain voluntarily on earth in order to save others. The oldest known piece of Japanese embroidery, a fragment of it is preserved at the nunnery of Chūgūji, located at the eastern end of Hōryū-ji.

In 710 Empress Gemmei, who reigned from 708 to 714, transferred her capital from Fujiwara to Heijō, later called Nara, which may have been attractive in large part because of the proximity of Hōryū-ji and the favorable climate. In Japan the capital was wherever the emperor chose to live. At one time *miyako*, now "capital," meant honorable dwelling. Since the emperor's dwelling was the most honorable dwelling of them all, *miyako* eventually signified the imperial residence. It was the custom to abandon a royal palace upon the death of an emperor in order to avoid contamination associated with death. Since 646 the Japanese had borrowed from the Chinese the concept of a capital with its administrative and military connotations, while still maintaining along with it the idea of *miyako*. When they moved, they dismantled the buildings, mansions, and temples, and by use of a grid system they reassembled their structures in an equivalent position in the new site. As the imperial government grew, it became more expensive and disruptive to move, and Nara became the first official or semipermanent capital of Japan. "Nara" means "level land," good for rice fields and for building. Nara, and Japan's succeeding capitals, Nagaoka and Kyōto, are all in a fertile plain, unlike most of Japan, which is mountainous.

The Japanese modeled the grid pattern of their new capital at Nara upon the Tang metropolis of Chang'an (Xian) in China. Yet Nara, at three by two and two-thirds miles, was much smaller than its Chinese model, which measured six by five miles. The Japanese plan proved too ambitious, however, and the proposed western half of the new city was not built. Nara may have had a population of 200,000 by the middle of the eighth century. It had no defensive walls or moat, an indication that the country was generally at peace during that time.

Nara remained the religious and imperial capital from 710 to 784, now known as the "Nara period." During this time, Japan first began building roads, bridges, and public baths. As the influence of Buddhism grew, the practice of cremation began to replace burial, and banishment began to replace execution. The era was characterized by rivalry between the imperial state and the Buddhist Church, the state making efforts to control the whole country, while Buddhism was working toward expanding its own sphere of power. Land ownership and taxation became important issues. There were about 6 million people living in Japan at the time, most of them commoners doomed to short lives marked by hardship, while the flourishing court and priesthood were economically unproductive. It was difficult to collect sufficient revenue to support the ruling class. On the other hand, the arts, especially sculpture and architecture, flourished during the Nara period. The Tempyō period (725–94) of artistic development, in which Buddhist sculpture reached its apex, coincided with much of the Nara period. It was Empress Gemmei who minted the first Japanese copper coinage, indicating that the court was becoming increasingly cultivated.

In the same year in which Nara was designated the capital city, the Kōfuku-ji, the family temple of the powerful Fujiwara clan, was founded in Nara. It had 175 buildings; 6 survive, 4 of them designated National Treasures. At mid-century, the Fujiwara family founded the neighboring shrine of Kasuga Taisha, one of the three leading Shintō shrines of Japan. Still in existence today, the complex has been rebuilt more than fifty times.

Chinese cultural influence on Japan reached its peak in the century following the foundation of Nara. By the fifth and sixth centuries, the Japanese had already adopted a version of the Chinese system of writing, although the two languages belong to entirely different language groups. At the time writing first came into Japan, most likely through Korean scribes, the Japanese ruling class regarded writing as

Temple, Nara
Photo courtesy of Japan National Tourist Organization

something for which they could pay specialists. Writing, used for routine administrative duties, the keeping of accounts, and diplomatic correspondence, was a task for clerks—a mechanical activity carrying no more prestige than weaving or painting. During the Nara period, however, writing became important to members of the Japanese elite as they began to perceive its possibilities in the dissemination of religion and political philosophy. Histories were written to glorify rulers, and the knowledge of poetry became a mark of breeding. The Empress Gemmei ordered the compilation of the *Kojiki,* a historical record, and the *Fūdoki,* a topographical survey of the provinces listing their products, in 712 and 713. The *Kojiki* (*Record of Ancient Matters*) was one of the most important literary works of the Nara period.

Nihon Shoki (*The History of Japan*) appeared in 720. This chronicle and *Kojiki* both mixed myths and traditions to create a "history" intended to compare favorably with China's. The writing of the *Kojiki* and *Nihon Shoki* shows the ruling dynasty's efforts to preserve and reconcile Shintō, Japan's earlier religion, with the recently imported Buddhism. Shintō deities were integrated with Buddhist ones and placed into a single hierarchy. Another great literary achievement of the Nara period was the *Manyō-shū* poetry anthology, which was published in 760.

In 724 Emperor Shōmu began his reign. A strong supporter of Buddhism, he established a monastery and a nunnery in every province of his realm. By 740, having failed to unite his country against Hirotsugu, leader of the powerful Fujiwara family, Shōmu was exiled to Kuni, Shigaraki, and Naniwa. He was back in Nara in 745. As a symbolic attempt to unite the country behind Buddhism, he ordered the casting of a large bronze Buddha (Daibutsu) at Tōdai-ji Temple in Nara. Hundreds of tons of copper and tin were cast. The resulting figure was more than 50 feet high, weighed 550 tons, and was covered in gold leaf. The pedestal was made up of 56 bronze lotus petals, each about 10 feet high. Shōmu, who had given up his throne in 749 to become a monk, came out of retirement in 752 to dedicate the statue. A hall built around the Daibutsu was 282 feet long, 164 feet wide and 150 feet high. The hall was destroyed by fire in the twelfth century; the present hall is two-thirds the size of the original. The statue has been damaged and rebuilt several times; the only remains of the original are portions of the lotus-petal throne. Still, the rebuilt statue is impressive, the largest bronze sculpture in the world.

Great Buddha, Tōdai-ji Temple, Nara
Photo courtesy of Japan National Tourist Organization

During the early Nara period, Buddhism was embraced mainly in the capital and by the ruling class. Later, inspired teachers spread Buddhism to the provinces and the common people. An early teacher was Gyōki (668–749), who raised funds for the construction of the Tōdai-ji Temple and encouraged charitable works, such as the building of bridges, dikes, roads, and village clinics. Regarded as a saint by the population, Gyōki has been called Japan's first civil engineer and is credited with producing the first map of Japan.

Another teacher was Ganjin (Chien Chen), a Chinese priest invited to Japan to promote Buddhist doctrines and to train priests. He made five attempts over a twelve-year period to cross the sea to Japan, but became blind before he reached his destination. In 755 Shōmu granted Ganjin the land in Nara on which to build a monastery. After Shōmu's death, construction was suspended for a time, but Empress Kōken, Shōmu's unmarried daughter, ordered that the monastery be completed, and it was finished in 759. The empress gave a gift, a framed plate inscribed with the designation Tōshōdai-jī, "Tang Buddhist Monastery."

Empress Kōken was a fervent Buddhist who fell under the sway of the politically ambitious priest Dōkyō. She gave him housing in the imperial palace, offices of state, and the title *hōō,* "King of the Buddhist Law," a title that had been reserved for emperors abdicating to join the priesthood. Kōken's support of Dōkyō brought her into conflict with the aristocracy, and in 758 two of the Fujiwara family persuaded her to abdicate in favor of Prince Ōi (Junnin), a puppet under Fujiwara Nakamaro. In 764 a battle ensued between the followers of Dōkyō and those of Fujiwara Nakamaro. Dōkyō was victorious and persuaded Kōken to take back her throne, this time under a new name, Empress Shōtoku, and exile Ōi to an island, where he soon died. In 764–65 Empress Shōtoku built Saidai-ji (Great Western Temple) and ordered the casting of the bronze images of the Four Heavenly Guardians trampling on demons, symbolizing the reign of Buddhist peace over the forces of evil and strife.

When Empress Shōtoku died without an heir in 770, the now all-powerful Dōkyō, with his ambitions for the throne, was exiled by the Fujiwaras. The Japanese thenceforth prevented females from taking the throne until nearly 1,000 years later, when the imperial office no longer held much power.

Because of the inordinate influence of the Buddhist hierarchy at Nara, including the experience with Empress Shōtoku, the Emperor Kammu decided to move his capital in 784. A favored member of Kammu's court, Fujiwara no Tanetsugu, located a site at Nagaoka, but the area was troubled by natural disasters. Additionally, one year after construction began, the emperor's younger brother, Prince Sawara, ambitious for the throne, murdered Fujiwara. Kammu, who considered these events bad omens, abandoned the Nagaoka site in favor of a new location. Kyōto, the new site, was completed in 794 and remained the capital until 1868, when Tōkyō displaced it.

Nara declined in size and political significance after the capital was moved, but it remained an important religious center and place of pilgrimage. The various religious complexes were restored and rebuilt in the succeeding centuries. The population outside of the monasteries eventually dwindled to practically nothing, but new waves of settlement gave rise to the modern city, which by the twentieth century was home to 325,000 people.

Most of Japan's main cities were devastated during World War II, but Nara and its successor capital Kyōto were spared. The Hōryū-ji pagoda was dismantled during the war for safekeeping. Many original timbers were used in its reassembly. Nishioka Tsunekazu, a master carpenter, worked on the restoration of Hōryū-ji for twenty years. He found that its original builders had adapted foreign techniques to local geography and climate. They gave the buildings deeper eaves because of Japan's rainy weather, and they sank key pillars deep into the ground to strengthen them against typhoons and earthquakes. The work shows that the seventh-century builders had a thorough understanding of their materials. Tsunekazu found that the builders had used trees grown on northern slopes of mountains for the north side of the building, southern-slope trees for the south side of the building and so on for the four directions. Trees grown on a southern slope have more branches, hence knots, which make them strong. The timbers on the southern side of the main hall of Hōryū-ji are knotty while the northern-side timbers are not. The builders had combined the various qualities of timber to create the strongest buildings, which explains, according to Tsunekazu, why such a wood building could last 1,300 years.

In an imperial wooden storehouse, the Shōsōin, are the personal belongings of the Emperor Shōmu, some 9,000 items from as far away as Persia. Some of these items were used in the ceremonies dedicating the Daibutsu. A selection of items from the Shōsōin treasury is made each year for display at Nara National Museum from late October to early November. The collection includes books, masks used in religious ceremonies, folding screens, bamboo flower baskets, arrows, plates, trays, collections of beads, mirrors, furniture, table utensils, musical instruments, armor, games, medicines, herbs, carpets, silver, and glass items. Emperor Shōmu's widow gave these items to Tōdai-ji after he died in 756.

Today Nara's many religious shrines, and annual festivals associated with them, draw numerous visitors to the city. Nara has almost no heavy industry, its economy dependent instead on tourism and craft products such as wooden dolls, lacquerware, and ceramics. Modern buildings have surrounded the ancient ones, but the city has retained much of its historic charm and small-town atmosphere.

Further Reading: The scrupulously researched *Japanese Achievement* by Hugh Cortazzi (London: Sidgwick and Jackson, and New York: St. Martin's, 1990) presents a thorough overview of Japanese historical, societal, and cultural achievements, with due emphasis on artistic, literary, and religious developments. *A History of Japan to 1334* by George Sansom (Stanford, California: Stanford University Press, 1958; London: Cresset, 1959), the first of a three-volume history, and considered something of a classic, is more concerned with political and social aspects of Japan. Both give considerable attention to the Nara period. *Japanese Capitals* by Philip Ward (Cambridge: Oleander, 1985; New York: Hippocrene, 1987) provides an excellent guide to the religious complexes of Nara.

—L. R. Naslund

Nāsik (Mahārāshtra, India)

Location: In western India, approximately 110 miles northeast of Bombay, on the banks of the holy Godāvari River, which flows through the Deccan Plateau to the Bay of Bengal.

Description: One of the cities of the Kumbh Mela, Nāsik is a major Hindu pilgrimage site. The city has a history of continuous settlement that dates at least to the second century B.C. It now incorporates the ancient village of Pañcavaṭī, where Rāma, protagonist of the *Rāmāyaṇa,* is said to have lived for a time. A group of ancient Buddhist and Jain rock-cut monasteries and temples lies a few miles from Nāsik.

Contact: Government of India Tourist Office
123 Maharishi Karve Road
Bombay 400 200, Mahārāshtra
India
(20) 32932, (20) 33144, (20) 33145, or (20) 36054

Archaeological research shows that humans have lived in the vicinity of Nāsik since the Stone Age. However, the earliest reliable historical records referring to the city date to the second century B.C. They indicate that Nāsik was by then a well-established settlement at a ford in the Godāvari River. The town probably owed its existence to its location along one of the principal trade routes into the interior from Sopāra, a port on India's west coast. An indication of Nāsik's prosperity is to be found in the fact that the city already had organized guilds of artisans and merchants.

An indirect, even earlier, reference to Nāsik is to be found in the *Rāmāyaṇa*. Historians think that the bulk of this ancient Hindu epic was written between the eighth and the fifth centuries B.C., although additions were made as late as the third century A.D. Events recounted are of a much earlier date, taking place around 1600 B.C. or before. The poem alleges that the legendary hero Rāma spent a period of exile at Pañcavaṭī, on the left bank of the Godāvari River at Nāsik, with his wife Sītā and his brother Lakṣmaṇa. It was from a cave near Pañcavaṭī that Sītā was abducted and carried off to southern India, motivating Rāma's heroic and ultimately successful quest for Sītā that takes up the greater part of the narrative. Although the *Rāmāyaṇa* does not refer to Nāsik itself, some commentators think the city's name derives from an episode in which Lakṣmaṇa cuts off the nose (*nasika* in Sanskrit) of the ogress Sūrpanakha, who had attempted to murder Sītā so as to gain Rāma's affections for herself. The etymology seems fanciful, and whether Nāsik or even Pañcavaṭī existed long before the second century B.C. cannot be confirmed by independent evidence.

More information about Nāsik is available from about 120 B.C. onward, in records left in the Pāṇḍu Lēṇa, the row of mostly Buddhist monasteries and temples hewn out of the nearby Triraśmi Hills. Inscriptions indicate that, in the latter days of the Maurya Dynasty, the Sātavāhannas carved out an independent kingdom in the western region of the Deccan Plateau. Historians disagree about the date King Simuka Sātavāhanna first established the kingdom, but the best evidence seems to point to a date close to 120 B.C. Nāsik seems to have functioned as the Sātavāhanna capital, and archaeological excavations have uncovered the remains of mud-wall houses and a wealth of coins, weapons, and pottery. Through the port of Sopāra, the city maintained frequent contact with Arab traders, who were interested in the region's minerals and carried semiprecious stones like agate and carnelian to the Mediterranean region from Nāsik.

The Sātavāhannas were Hindu, but that apparently formed no obstacle to their financial support of the rock-cut Buddhist monasteries in the Triraśmi Hills. Mendicant Buddhist monks, mostly from India's east coast, roamed the western Deccan as part of a major missionary undertaking. Possibly in search of resting places for the rainy season, they were able to persuade the local population, Buddhist or not, to create small monasteries in the tradition of the rock-cut sanctuaries of northern India. Hundreds of Buddhist, and eventually Jain and Hindu, temples were thus created in western India between about 200 B.C. and A.D. 700. While many of these temples are not particularly noteworthy, others are showcases of the best sculpture produced in India during those centuries.

The first monastery, or *vihara*, to be cut into the rock face at Nāsik was excavated some time between 90 and 70 B.C. In comparison with other *viharas* at Pāṇḍu Lēṇa and elsewhere in India, this first *vihara* is small and undistinguished, its sculpture and reliefs of small artistic value. A carved doorway with a veranda immediately behind it leads into a small chamber, which in turn leads to a set of cells. The *vihara* contains a *dagoba*, a miniature funerary mound that functions as an indirect representation of the Buddha. Like the later Buddhist caves at Pāṇḍu Lēṇa, the Hinayana Buddhist monastery does not contain any images of the Buddha himself; these were considered idolatrous and are associated only with Mahāyāna Buddhism. The cave's importance resides chiefly in its inscriptions honoring the various donors, including merchants, monks and nuns, and officials from Nāsik and other trading centers along the western Ghāts. The Sātavāhannas, as the principal donors, took occasion to record the early history of the dynasty on the *vihara* walls.

Decades after the excavation of the first *vihara*, the Sātavāhanna Kingdom fragmented among the different branches of the family, and Nāsik itself came under the control of the Kṣaharāta Kṣatrapas, a Śaka dynasty. The origin of the Śaka people cannot be definitively ascertained; the term *Śaka* in ancient Sanskrit was applied to any person of foreign descent. It is likely, however, that the Śakas were either Turkish or Mongol in origin. The principal Kṣaharāta king to rule over Nāsik was Nahapāna, who ruled from about A.D. 50 to 100 and was the principal contributor to the most impressive *vihara* carved at Pāṇḍu Lēṇa.

Known as Cave 8 in the Pāṇḍu Lēṇa row, the monastery has an elaborately carved facade with a veranda. The facade itself is organized by a design of beautifully patterned bands, a common decorative feature in Buddhist architecture in India. Three doorways give access to the interior of the cave, while two windows provide a modicum of natural light. The central chamber, nearly square, measures approximately forty-three by forty-five feet and was once focused on a relief of the *dagoba*. Now the relief depicts a Hindu deity, having been recarved at a much later date to suit the requirements of Hindu worship. (Other caves have undergone a similar fate, and some were later embellished with images of the Buddha by Mahāyāna Buddhist patrons.) Sixteen cells ring the Nahapāna cave chamber along the side and back walls. The principal architectural attraction of the *vihara* is the design of the highly sculptured pillars that support the verandah. Set on a bell-shaped base, each rounded pillar has an elegant inverted bell-shaped capital, and the connection with the architrave is embellished with carvings of animals. A simple frieze that repeats the patterns of the facade bands runs above. Although the Nahapāna *vihara* is by no means the last cave to be excavated at Nāsik, it is commonly considered the highest expression of the form found there.

Around A.D. 100, the Sātavāhannas returned to power, retaking Nāsik under King Gautamīputra Śātakarṇi, who has left the second most celebrated *vihara* in the Pāṇḍu Lēṇa row. Known as Cave 3, it is a fairly close copy of the Nahapāna cave, but the style of its sculpture is less balanced and refined. After going through a turbulent period around the middle of the second century A.D., the Sātavāhannas temporarily recovered their equilibrium under Yajñaśri Śātakarṇi, who ruled from about 152 to 181. Some time in the third century, however, the Sātavāhannas relinquished control to the Abhiras, about whom little is known beyond their mention in the cave inscriptions.

With the passing of Sātavāhanna control, Nāsik entered a long period of political instability. Although the city seems to have continued to prosper as a center of trade, its rulers did not stay in place long enough to leave a lasting cultural legacy. The Abhiras soon gave way to the Vakataka Dynasty, under which Nāsik enjoyed the status of being the royal capital for a brief time. Before long, parts of the Deccan were incorporated into the Gupta Empire, and Nāsik became one of the principal centers on the Guptas' western frontier. The empire eventually collapsed under pressure from a series of Ephthalite invasions, and Nāsik passed into the hands first of the Traikūṭakas and then of the Kaṭacurris, before finally being conquered around 640 by the Cāḷukyas, who after some 200 years in turn gave way to the Rāṣhṭrakūṭas, whose rule ended about 1100. Through all these changes, the city retained its importance in the region, functioning as the northern capital of the Cāḷukya Dynasty and as district headquarters under the Rāṣhṭrakūṭas.

It is obvious that the continuous power struggles eventually weakened the Mahārāshtra region, as well as other parts of western and northern India. Thus vulnerable, the country fell prey to Muslim invaders, who initially made only sustained forays but eventually established permanent control over much of northern India. By the mid–twelfth century, Mahārāshtra fell under the control of various Muslim rulers. In 1312, Nāsik was incorporated into the territories of the Delhi Sultanate, then passed to the Bahmanīs in 1347, before becoming a possession of Nizām Shāhi of Ahmadnagar in 1487. In 1637, the city finally became a part of the Mughal Empire, which maintained its control until 1717.

During the years of Muslim control, Nāsik was renamed Gulshanābād, which means "City of Roses." A new section of the city sprang up on the left bank of the Godvari, just south of Pañcavaṭī. The new Muslim settlement was heavily fortified by a surrounding wall with gates, some of which survive, most notably the Delhi Darwaji, Kazipura Darwaji, and Bhagur Darwaji. The Muslims predictably also built a series of mosques, the largest of which is the Jāma Mosque. The Muslim quarter is now known as Junī Gadhī. Extensive damage was done to the Buddhist caves of Pāṇḍu Lēṇa, particularly at the beginning and end of the Muslim era, when religious intolerance on the part of the rulers led to extensive persecution of Buddhists and Hindus. In fact, Buddhism disappeared from India altogether at this time, the Muslim persecutions serving as a death blow to a religion that had increasingly withdrawn to its monasteries and other institutions of learning and kept itself apart from the common people.

When Nāsik passed into the Mughal Empire, the emperor Shāh Jahān combined the four Deccan provinces, including Mahārāshtra, under a common administrative structure headed by a viceroy. Each of the provinces had a governor who was accountable to the Deccan viceroy. The governor of Ahmadābād, the western Deccan province, held court at his capital city of Nāsik. This arrangement did not work very well, owing to internal struggles between the imperial court and the viceroy, which occasioned frequent changes in leadership. As a consequence, the Deccan suffered an economic decline—in which Nāsik shared—and the governors experienced considerable difficulty collecting revenues. The situation was exacerbated by a legacy of military conflict and famines associated with the Mughal conquest. A renewal of religious persecution under Shāh Jahān and his successor 'Ālamgīr (Aurangzeb) further alienated the local populace and, perhaps more importantly, the indigenous Hindu rulers of the Deccan.

As imperial control weakened, the Marāṭhā Dynasty, a warlike family of Hindu princes native to the Deccan, began

Hindu temples at Nāsik
Photo courtesy of A.P. / Wide World Photos, New York

to make inroads on Mughal territory. Under the leadership of Śivājī, the Marāṭhā army captured several strategic Mughal fortresses in the course of the 1660s. In 1674 Śivājī took the title of *chatrapati* (emperor) of Mahārāshtra, and the Mughals were powerless to dislodge him. This fact was officially recognized in a 1717 treaty, in which the Mughals confirmed Marāṭhā control of the Mahārāshtra region, including Nāsik.

When the Marāṭhās made themselves masters of Nāsik, the city regained its ancient name and entered upon a new period of prosperity. Nāsik became a fashionable retreat for the Marāṭhā nobility living in Pune, some seventy miles to the south. The most important Marāṭhā families built houses at Nāsik, both in the ancient city center on the right bank and in a newly developed quarter on the left bank of the Godāvari, just north of Pañcavaṭī. The new rulers rebuilt the Hindu temples destroyed under the rule of ʿĀlamgīr and constructed new ones. The two most important surviving Hindu temples are the temple of Siva as Skull Lord and the temple of the Black Rāma. Both temples are furnished in the style described for Hindu temples in the *Rāmāyaṇa*.

The Marāṭhās also built the *ghāts*, or steps, along the banks of the Godāvari, which for centuries now have formed the center of religious life in the city, as Hindu pilgrims from all over the country come to bathe in the holy river. Nāsik is one of the four cities of the Kumbh Mela, where, according to Hindu myth, drops of the nectar of immortality fell to earth. Every three years, one of the cities celebrates the special Kumbh Mela festival, making for a twelve-year cycle. During the year Nāsik celebrates the Kumbh Mela, the Godāvari is thought to concentrate within itself the purifying powers of all of India's holy rivers, attracting throngs of bathers to the riverbank *ghāts*.

The Marāṭhās enjoyed about a century of independent rule over the Deccan; they effectively lost control to the British by 1818. Marāṭhā attacks on the crumbling Mughal Empire in the late seventeenth and early eighteenth century had given the British East India Company an opportunity for expansion—an opportunity they zealously pursued. Internal dissension between ruling Marāṭhā families played into the hands of the British conquerors. By the early nineteenth century, the British had so far consolidated their position that they were able to challenge the Marāṭhās directly and inflicted a major defeat on Marāṭhā forces at Mysore in 1799. In the next two decades, British troops gradually tightened the noose around the dwindling Marāṭhā army, until this last independent dynasty of indigenous rulers was forced into a formal surrender of its autonomy in 1818.

Although many Marāṭhā government policies were in direct opposition to Western ideas, the British resident stationed at Pune, Mountstuart Elphinstone, believed that Marāṭhā rule had considerable merit and did not wish to make radical changes in the government system to which the people were accustomed. In consequence, few changes immediately made themselves felt at Nāsik after the British takeover. Many of the Marāṭhā nobles kept their positions in the regional government; the one difference was that they had to answer to the British East India Company rather than to the Marāṭhā Peshwa. In time, however, Nāsik underwent extensive expansion under British rule. As the colonial administration became more elaborate, a new district with government buildings and official residences sprang up to the west of the ancient city.

The Pāṇḍu Lēṇa, meanwhile, suffered more serious damage. Heavy rains and flooding ravaged a significant portion of the art of the Buddhist cave temples. More seriously yet, some of the caves were turned into quarries and were entirely obliterated by the use of dynamite. When these devastations took place and who was responsible for them is uncertain. Since dynamite was introduced to India by Europeans, we can assign a relatively recent date to the damage and be fairly certain that it was done under British auspices. Despite the fact that some of the ancient temples lie in ruins, Pāṇḍu Lēṇa remains Nāsik's principal attraction to non-Hindu visitors.

For Hindu visitors, the sacred Godāvari River remains the city's principal attraction. The *ghāt*-lined banks of the river, besides serving the practical purposes of cleaning and bathing for local residents, attract many Hindu travelers and pilgrims year-round. Every twelve years, Nāsik is home to the Kumbh Mela, India's largest religious pilgrimage festival and gathering. According to legend, Vishnu was carrying a pot *(kumbh)* of nectar *(amrita)* when a fight broke out among the gods, causing Vishnu to spill four drops. Drops fell at Prayag, Hardwār, Ujjain, and Nāsik—all cities that sit on the banks of major Indian rivers—and as a result, each place has become a major *tīrtha* ("ford of a river" that serves as a pilgrimage site from where the devout may cross from the finite world into the celestial kingdom). The Kumbh Mela is held every three years at each successive holy *tīrtha,* creating a twelve-year cycle. Thus every twelve years religious ascetics at various levels of mendicancy, millions of religiously devout Hindu pilgrims, Indian and non-Indian tourists, as well as the local population converge on the banks of the Godāvari in Nāsik, setting up a city of tents administered and controlled by army and police forces. Here the pilgrims perform holy rites purifying themselves in the river and praying to Vishnu. The next Kumbh Mela in Nāsik will take place in 2003, whereupon the city will once again be transformed into a huge fair of religious celebration and rejoicing.

Further Reading: Vidya Dehejia's *Early Buddhist Rock Temples: A Chronology* (Ithaca, New York: Cornell University Press, 1972; with subtitle *A Chronological Study,* London: Thames and Hudson, 1972) includes a scholarly account of the rock-cut temples of Pāṇḍu Lēṇa and the earliest history of the city. *The Cave Temples of India* by James Fergusson and James Burgess (London: Allen, 1880; second edition, New Delhi: Munshiram Manoharlal, 1988) gives excellent and highly readable descriptions of Nāsik's caves. Noble Ross Reat's *Buddhism: A History* (Berkeley: Asian Humanities, 1994) presents a comprehensive history of the Buddhist religion. Among concise histories of India, Vincent A. Smith's *The Oxford History of India: From the Earliest Times to the End of 1911* (Oxford: Clarendon Press, 1919; fourth edition, edited by Percival Spear, New York and Oxford: Oxford University Press, 1981) remains without compare. *India in the Ramayana Age: A Study of the Social and Cultural Conditions in Ancient India as Described in Valmiki's Ramayana* by Shantikumar Nanooram Vyas (Delhi: Atma Ram, 1967) is a thoroughly enjoyable study of the social and cultural habits of the Indian people during the age of the *Rāmāyaṇa.*

—Denise Coté and Marijke Rijsberman

Niah Caves (Sarawak, Malaysia)

Location: On the north coast of the island of Borneo, ten miles inland on the Niah River, in a 1,300-foot pile of limestone known as Gunong Subis (Sobis Mountain).

Description: A twenty-six-acre cave complex with archaeological evidence of 40,000 years of continuous human habitation.

Contact: Tourism Malaysia, Sarawak Regional Office
Ground Floor, Aurora Hotel
Jalan Tun Abang Haji Openg
93000 Kuching
Sarawak
Malaysia
(82) 246 575

One of the most extensive Miocene limestone cave formations in the world, the Niah Caves contain evidence of the longest known continuous human habitation (approximately 40,000 years) in Southeast Asia. Although they had long been one of the main sources of the glutinous swiftlets' nests used in Chinese cuisine, the caves did not come to European knowledge until Alfred Russel Wallace's 1856 visit to Sarawak. Although Wallace did not actually see the caves himself, he was certainly given information about them by someone who had, and he was aware of the existence of bone remains there. His letter on the subject to that other great evolutionary theorist, T. H. Huxley, in 1864, produced the suggestion that Niah and the other limestone caves at Bau in West Borneo should be made the object of a special expedition to search for evolutionary evidence of early man. Huxley, at that time expounding his theories about Neanderthal Man, was anxious to find evidence of further links in the chain of human evolution from the higher apes.

Nothing came of this suggestion, however, and it was not until 1873 that the naturalist and explorer A. H. Everett visited Niah and recorded the first detailed description for the *Sarawak Gazette:*

> We were soon repaid for our climb by the sight which met our gaze; we found ourselves standing at a mouth of a large arched cavern, several hundred feet broad, and over two hundred feet high, huge stalactites were pending from the ceiling, and a fringe of vegetation drooping from its outer edge. . . . We commenced our exploration of the cave by walking up a gentle incline, a soft flooring of dry scentless guano under foot. We were met by thousands of bats and swallows, the latter are the manufacturers of the edible nests. . . . Now descending a gentle declivity, we found ourselves in an immense amphitheatre; the roof of the cave assuming a circular shape, high in the centre resembling the interior of a dome. . . . Thousands of nests were to be seen clinging to the pillar. . . . The most flimsy stages of bamboo tied together by rattans shewed us the simple means employed by the native in collecting them from their seemingly uncomfortable position.
>
> Through rifts in the mountain side stole many coloured rays of light, throwing a dim religious light over the scene. Through this ghostly dimness, the black mouth of branch caverns could be seen.

To the consternation of his native guides, Everett took away a human head from the main cave, causing guides to obstruct entry to some of the other caves containing removable relics.

With funds from the Royal Society, the British Association for the Advancement of Science, and the Zoological Society of London, Everett returned to Sarawak in 1878 to make a more thorough exploration of the West Borneo caves for fossil remains of the forerunners of the anthropoid apes. On this occasion he was described *in situ* at Bau by the American naturalist, William Hornaday:

> Here was an evolutionist, with his war-paint all on, and his weapons in his hand—pick, shovel and sieve. Imagine the sensation of a Darwinian actually looking for and finding the link between man and the great apes!

It is not clear whether Everett revisited Niah during this expedition, but the animal remains taken back to Britain afterward were pronounced "wholly without interest except to local naturalists." Everett himself concluded that the humans with whom the remains were associated had reached an advanced stage of civilization. He theorized that the northwest coast of the island of Borneo had emerged too recently from the sea for there to be cave deposits of great antiquity. Another theory held that in the tropics, early humans had no need of caves as shelter. Consequently, there was little interest in investigating Niah and other cave complexes in the tropics until the 1950s. Nor did any of the descriptions made by visiting scientists to Niah after Everett's time suggest that there were signs of human activity in the caves complex.

The first systematic archaeological excavations at Niah were undertaken by the then-curator of the Sarawak Museum, the now legendary Tom Harrisson, in 1954.

Niah Caves
Photo courtesy of Malaysia Tourism Promotion Board, New York

Through carbon dating, subsequent discoveries of human bone material were determined to be approximately 50,000 years old, making Niah one of the oldest inhabited sites in the world. Harrisson had first gone to Niah in 1947 in his capacity as custodian of the birds' nest industry, then monopolized by the hunter-gatherer Punan people who claimed, as the earliest inhabitants of Borneo, to have discovered the caves. Guano digging had also been carried on there since about 1928, with no regard for the safety of archaeological deposits.

Discovering some human bone remains and pottery near the caves site, Harrisson decided to make a systematic investigation. Trial pits excavated in the Main (West) Mouth in 1954 brought to light Neolithic polished stone tools, Mesolithic edge-ground tools, and worked stone flakes. Further excavations in 1957 revealed a number of other stone-tool sequences. The results made possible the financing of much more ambitious expeditions in 1958 and 1959, which succeeded in locating the earliest Paleolithic layer associated with human habitation.

Among the other new discoveries in 1958 was a rock ledge "beach" of carved wooden funeral boats containing human remains and more than 100 wall paintings of insect-like and human figures, executed in red hematite and ranging in size from a few inches to three feet. This evidence suggested extensive funerary and other rituals in the caves and burials from the Neolithic to the early Iron Age. These included the so-called deep skull of Niah, which Harrisson originally estimated to be about 40,000 years old. Bones of larger animals such as rhinoceros, orangutan, tapir, bear, and giant (bearded) pig suggested that these formed part of the cave dwellers' diet. Fish bones and shells were also discovered. In addition, in the more remote parts of the cave complex, quantities of Chinese Tang (A.D. 618–907) and Song (A.D. 960–1276) Dynasty ceramic ware indicated early trade activity associated with the birds' nests. Neolithic pottery remains revealed that the cave dwellers were themselves skilled craftsmen.

Criticism of Harrisson's techniques and methodology (he had received no formal archaeological training), together with the accusation that his massive excavations had ruined the entire site for other archaeologists, raised doubts about the validity of his findings. One of his closest associates asserted that "he could not and would not take direct criticism" and that his attitude to the Niah site was proprietary in the extreme. Harrisson's untimely death in January 1976 meant that his long-awaited final report on the Niah excavations was never completed. Subsequent work by the Malaysian archaeologist Zuraina Majid challenged Harrisson's basic findings, notably the stone-tool sequence that he identified. However, there is little doubt that Niah offers evidence of an evolving stone-tool technology and of cultural progress in early Southeast Asia since earliest human habitation.

For the visitor, one of the great experiences at Niah is to witness the early evening exodus of the huge bat population from the mouth of the Great Cave at the time when the swiftlets return to their nests.

Further Reading: The best sources for the successive archaeological projects at Niah are "The Caves of Niah: A History of Prehistory" by Tom Harrisson, in *Sarawak Museum Journal* (Kuching) volume 8, number 12, 1958; "The Niah Research Program" by Wilhelm G. Solheim II, in *Journal of the Malaysian Branch of the Royal Asiatic Society* (Singapore) volume 50, 1977; and *The West Mouth, Niah, in the Prehistory of Southeast Asia,* by Zuraina Majid (Kuching: Sarawak Museum Journal Special Monograph No. 3, December 1982).

—Bob Reece

Nikkō (Tochigi, Japan)

Location: Seventy-five miles north of Tōkyō, inside Nikkō National Park in Tochigi prefecture.

Description: A small mountain town that is the site of the Tōshōgū, the mausoleum and shrine of Shōgun Tokugawa Ieyasu; the Daiyūinbyō, the mausoleum and shrine of his grandson Shōgun Iemitsu; and other religious institutions.

Site Office: Nikkō City Tourist Information Center
Tobu Nikkō Station
4 Matsubara-cho
Nikkō, Tochigi
Japan
(288) 53 4511

Nikkō, a town of approximately 24,000 inhabitants, is spread over the heavily forested lower slopes of Futara-san (Mount Futara), also known as Nantai-san. Like Fujisan (Mount Fuji) and a number of other mountains throughout Japan, Futara-san has been venerated as a sacred site for hundreds of years. Its history reflects the development of both of the main religions of Japan: Shintō, an accumulation of local naturalistic cults, and Buddhism, the more sophisticated and systematized faith imported from China and Korea in the sixth century. The high point of Nikkō's history came in the early seventeenth century, with the construction of the Tōshōgū, the enormous and magnificent complex that commemorates Tokugawa Ieyasu, the greatest of all the Japanese *shōguns*, and which, as both a Shintō shrine and a Buddhist mausoleum, represents the most complete synthesis of the two religions.

It is not known how or when Futara-san first acquired its religious significance. Since it stands on the northern edge of the Kantō Plain, in the east of Honshū, the main island of Japan, the mountain was remote from the more heavily populated region in the center of the island, where a recognizable Japanese culture first developed during the Yayoi period (c. 300 B.C.–A.D. 300), in and around what is now Nara prefecture. Eastern Honshū, which the ancient Japanese called Azuma and which seemed to them to be a mysterious and wild frontier province, was then sparsely inhabited, not by Japanese but by the ethnographically distinct Ainu people. They maintained their neolithic culture there against incursions by the Japanese until the ninth century A.D., when they finally were driven out (to take refuge in the northern island of Hokkaidō, where fewer than 20,000 of their descendants remain today). Some traces of their presence in eastern Honshū remain even now. Fuji-san, which stands on the western edge of the Kantō Plain, probably takes its name from an Ainu word, and it is possible that Futara-san also was first venerated by the Ainu.

In this context the tradition that the Buddhist monk Shodo came to the mountain, perhaps around 784, and founded both a Buddhist temple, Shihonryū-ji, and a Shintō shrine, the Futara-san (or Futara-yama) Jinja, may well represent an assimilation of an older cult into Japanese tradition, just as pagan sites and rituals were often absorbed into Christianity in Europe. The shrine is dedicated to the spirit of the mountain and to Ōkuninushi no Ōmikami, his wife Tagorihime no Ōmikami, and their son Ajisukitakahikone no Ōmikami, three of the several deities who took part, according to legend, in the construction of the Japanese Archipelago. It occupies three separate sites, having its Hongu, or Main Shrine, in the grounds of the Tōshōgū in Nikkō itself; its Chūgūsha, or Middle Shrine, on the shores of Lake Chūzenji nearby; and its Oku-miya, its Deep (or Far) Shrine, which is the holiest of the three, on the summit of the mountain.

By the time Shodo arrived, however, Japanese culture itself already was being modified by a larger process of assimilation between Shintō and Buddhism, which had been introduced from the Asian mainland only about 200 years earlier. The indigenous deities, ranging from Amaterasu no Ōmikami, the sun goddess and supposed ancestor of the imperial line, to the local spirits of trees, rivers, and mountains all were being reinterpreted as manifestations of the Buddha, and it is quite likely that Shihonryū-ji and the Futara-san Hongu, which are now in separate but neighboring compounds, originally were closely connected. Over the centuries, however, Shihonryū-ji became the headquarters of a network of about 300 Buddhist foundations in the area around Nikkō. Among these was Rinnō-ji, a temple of the Tendai-shū sect of Buddhism, founded in 848. This eventually became the most important of the group. In its compound today, which lies some distance from its original two halls, stands the Sambutsudō, the Three Buddhas Hall, the largest single building in the town. It was built in 1648 to house three gilded wooden statues, each twenty-six feet high, which represent Amida (Amitabha in Sanskrit), the Buddha of the Western Paradise, and two forms of Kannon (or Avalokitesvara), the goddess of mercy, one with a horse's head attached to her forehead to signify compassion for animals and the other with multiple limbs, known, with some exaggeration, as the Thousand-Handed Kannon.

However, these older foundations were and are much less visited, and were historically much less patronized by the wealthy and powerful, than the Tōshōgū, one of the masterpieces of what is now called the Edo or Tokugawa period (1603–1868). Edo was the name for the city that is now Tōkyō; Tokugawa was the family name of the *shōguns* who governed Japan from Edo during these 265 years; and the first of them was Tokugawa Ieyasu, who is both buried and enshrined at the Tōshōgū. Ieyasu, born in 1542, first came to national promi-

Lake Chūzenji and Kegon Falls, Nikkō
Photo courtesy of Japan National Tourist Organization

Tōshōgū Shrine, Nikkō
Photo courtesy of Japan National Tourist Organization

nence as a lieutenant to Toyotomi Hideyoshi, the military leader who had completed the work of his own master, Oda Nobunaga, by reunifying Japan after about 120 years of civil war and disintegration. Neither Nobunaga nor Hideyoshi had taken the title of *shōgun*, awarded to the effective rulers of Japan by the powerless imperial court between 1192 and 1573, but after Hideyoshi's death and his own victory at the battle of Sekigahara in 1600, Ieyasu had the title revived in 1603. He then allocated domains around Japan to some 260 *daimyō* (the lords who were to govern the 75 percent of the country not ruled directly by the Tokugawa Dynasty) and imposed new rules on the imperial court, the Shintō shrines, and the Buddhist temples. Although he formally retired in 1605, handing over the *shōgunate* to his son Hidetada, he continued to exercise power from his castle at Sumpu (now part of the city of Shizuoka) until his death in 1616. He then was interred temporarily at a smaller shrine, on Kunō-zan (Mount Kuno) near Sumpu; today this shrine also is called the Tōshōgū.

Yomeimon Gate, Nikkō
Photo courtesy of Japan National Tourist Organization

The names "Tōshōgū," which means "eastern shining shrine," and "Nikkō," which means "sunlight," both derive from Tōshō Dai-Gongen, the posthumous name that was bestowed on Ieyasu by the imperial court. The granting of such names is a Buddhist tradition, not a Shintō one, and Ieyasu's posthumous name, which means "Great Avatar Illuminating the East," refers to the belief that Ieyasu had been an avatar, an earthly manifestation, of Yakushi (Bhaishaja-guru in Sanskrit), the Buddha of Healing who rules the Eastern Emerald World. At the same time, the reference to the sun, and the fact that the "shō" in "Tōshō" is written with the same character as the "terasu" in "Amaterasu," probably were meant to indicate that Ieyasu was held to have a special connection with the Shintō sun goddess, and the imperial line supposedly descended from her. It is therefore fitting that the memorial complex at Nikkō is distinctive in its intermingling of Shintō and Buddhist structures and motifs. Just as the human being Ieyasu had completed the military and political unification of the country, so the divine being Tōshō Dai-Gongen was to symbolize its religious unification.

Soon after the interment on Kunō-zan, Tokugawa Hidetada ordered the preparation of his father's permanent resting place on Futara-san, which stood on Tokugawa family land and was accessible from the Tokugawa headquarters in Edo (now Tōkyō) yet also suitably remote. The funds for the project were raised by exacting contributions from the *daimyō,* who would continue to pay for its upkeep until their offices were abolished in the 1870s. The first stage, carried out in 1617, consisted of relocating the main shrine of the Futara-san Jinja within the enormous compound that was to be dominated by the Tōshōgū. Work began on the main complex in 1623, the same year that Hidetada formally surrendered the *shōgunate* to his son Iemitsu, who then took charge of the project. He ensured that the last and greatest phase, the building of the inner compound, which began in 1634, would be completed within two years, in time for the installation of Ieyasu's remains and the inauguration of the shrine on the twentieth anniversary of his death.

The craftsmen brought to the site under Iemitsu's orders may have numbered around 15,000. They included master carpenters from Edo, Kyōto, and Nara, who either had worked on, or had been trained by those who worked on, Hideyoshi's Momoyama Castle and the Tokugawas' Nijō Castle, both in Kyōto, developing the somewhat baroque building style known as Momoyama, characterized by the generous use of gold leaf and intricate carvings of natural objects. They were joined by numerous Korean temple builders, who had been taken as prisoners during Hideyoshi's fruitless invasions of their country in the 1590s and who had helped to introduce the latest building techniques from Korea and China. Presumably in order to make the shrine as distinctive as possible, they and their co-workers took the Momoyama style to its extreme at Nikkō, using roughly 25 million sheets of gold leaf and enormous amounts of black lacquer and white paint to cover exteriors and interiors alike, and applying naturalistic but brilliant blue, red, green, and brown pigments to the 5,147 carvings that decorate the 29 main buildings of the complex. The result is that these and the lesser buildings generally have much more in common with Chinese and Korean styles of architecture and sculpture than with earlier indigenous Japanese styles. For example, the carvings include several images of the mandarin orange, then a rare and expensive delicacy in Japan.

The project also involved adding to the forests that already covered much of Futara-san. It is said that between 25,000 and 40,000 Japanese cedars and other indigenous evergreens were planted between approximately 1631 and 1651, under the direction of Matsudaira Masatsuna, *dyaimyō* of Kawagoe and a distant relative of the Tokugawas; he was one of two officials appointed by Iemitsu to oversee work on the Tōshōgū. Of these trees at least 13,000 remain in place today, lining the avenues and paths that connect the Tōshōgū with the three Futara-san shrine sites, with Rinnō-ji, and with Shihonryū-ji, all of which were completely rebuilt during the late seventeenth century.

The Omote-sandō, the widest and longest of the avenues, starts at the point on the Daiya River where the monk Shodo is said to have crossed with help from two giant serpents. In their place today are two bridges, placed next to each other. One, the Shinkyō, the Sacred Bridge opened only for festivals, is a modern copy of the 1636 original that was washed away by floods in 1902; the other is for everyday use. From their western ends a path takes visitors to the Futara-san Hongū and Shihonryū-ji, while the avenue leads on to Rinno-ji and then, past a series of stone figures, now weathered and moss-covered, of *daimyō* and other Tokugawa retainers sitting crosslegged, to the entrance of the Tōshōgū.

The entrance itself, at the top of a stone stairway, is one of the few uniquely Japanese structures in the complex; it is an example of a *torii,* the gateway characteristic of Shintō shrines, consisting of two pillars joined at the top by two cross-bars. Although these usually are made of wood, the *torii* at Nikkō is granite. The twenty-eight-foot-high structure is decorated with a gigantic *shimenawa,* the sacred rope often seen at Shintō shrines, but bears on its cross-bars a placard with the Buddhist title "Tōshō Dai-Gongen."

Beyond the *torii,* and to one side of the series of steps and platforms that connect the shrine structures, stands a five-story pagoda, equally characteristic of Buddhist temples. Completely rebuilt in 1818, it stands 131 feet high. At the end of another stone stairway stands the Omotemon, the Front Gate, the first of the three ceremonial gatehouses, which again are characteristic of Buddhist temples, set at points along the mountain slope, a practice more usually associated with Shintō. The Omotemon, which is thirty feet high, is also known as the Nio-Mon, the Two Kings Gate, because it is flanked by figures of the Deva Kings, Buddhist guardians who now seem incongruous at the entrance to a Shintō shrine but, like so much else that is Buddhist in the Tōshōgū, did not appear so when they were made and installed. The courtyard beyond the Omotemon, lined with lanterns donated by *daimyō,* contains a number of interesting buildings, among which two stand out because of their distinctive decorations. The Yakushidō or Honchidō, a hall dedicated to the worship of Yakushi, the Buddha of Healing, is noted for the charcoal ink drawing of a dragon on its ceiling, a masterpiece of Kanō Yasunobu, who was a member of the leading family of artists patronized by the Tokugawa Dynasty. The drawing is still known as the Naku Ryū, "the dragon which cries out," because of the legend that the picture originally cried out to worshipers, even though it is a copy of the original installed after the hall was burned down in 1961. The stables for the shrine's sacred horses, the only structure in the Tōshōgū that has plain, unlacquered wood surfaces, is famous for the carving, just beneath its roof, of the three wise monkeys, the originals of all the figures known as "Hear No Evil, See No Evil, Speak No Evil."

The courtyard also contains gifts from two of the countries with which the Tokugawa regime had commercial and diplomatic relations (giving the lie to the often-repeated claim that it maintained a policy of complete seclusion from the outside world). The gigantic bell, sounded from outside by a log rather than, in European style, from inside by a clapper, was donated by the royal family of Korea, while a candelabrum and two lanterns, all made of bronze, were gifts from the government of the Netherlands, which inadvertently committed lèse majesté by decorating them with the Tokugawa family crest (the hollyhock in a circle) upside down.

During the Tokugawa period only members of the ruling family, *daimyō,* and higher-ranking *samurai* (warriors) were permitted to go beyond the outer courtyard and up yet another stone stairway to the next terrace, having laid aside any weapons they were carrying. At the top of the stairs stands the second gatehouse, which is formally known as the Yomeimon, the Solar Brilliance Gate. It has been nicknamed the Higurashimon, the Twilight Gate, in reference both to the claim that visitors would need to stay until twilight to take in all the details of its design, and to the similarly magnificent gatehouse of that name at the Nishi Hongan-ji, a temple in Kyōto also built in the Momoyama style. The Yomeimon has twelve columns, all painted white to make them appear larger than they are, supporting a massive superstructure elaborately decorated with images of dragons, both carved and (on the inner ceiling) painted; lions, tigers, and elephants, non-native animals represented formally rather than naturalistically by artists who probably never had seen them; turtles, rabbits, and various waterfowl; and such symbolic plants as bamboo and pine.

The next courtyard contains the Mikoshigura, the warehouse for the *mikoshi,* the portable shrines carried in festival processions every year; the Kaguraden, the hall used for performances of the *kagura,* sacred Shintō dances; and the administrative offices. Next comes the Karamon, the Chinese Gate, which stands immediately before the Haiden (Oratory) and the Honden (Main Hall) of the shrine, in the middle of a roofed wall, its stone lower half supporting a wooden upper half covered with gilded grilles. Like the Yomeimon, this inner gatehouse is also elaborately carved with both mythical and real animals and plants. On top of its main roof ridge is a particularly striking figure, in bronze rather than wood, of a *tsutsuga,* another mythical creature associated with religious and political power.

The sanctity of the two central structures of the complex, where the spirit of Ieyasu was believed to reside, is indicated, as at other religious sites in Japan, by the requirement to remove one's shoes, as if one were entering a private home. The Honden, which is fifty-two feet long, thirty-three feet wide, and forty-six feet high, contains the focus of worship, a gilded box-like object called the Misorandono or Gokuden, which is said to hold Ieyasu's spirit. Since 1873 it also has been considered to enshrine the spirits of his predecessor Toyotomi Hideyoshi and of Minamoto Yoritomo, the twelfth-century *shōgun* whom Ieyasu claimed as an ancestor.

The Honden is the holiest spot within the Tōshōgū, but originally it was not the most exclusive. On the right-hand side of the inner compound stands yet another richly decorated gatehouse, the Sakashitamon, which was reserved for the use of members of the Tokugawa family and shrine officials alone. This gives on to a flight of about 200 stone steps, protected by a corridor of red-lacquered wood, leading up a steep slope to the Oku no In, the Deep (or Far) Precinct. This enclosed terrace contains Ieyasu's tomb, the Hōtō, which is inside a second Buddhist pagoda—appropriately, since Shintō traditionally has shunned death and decay, leaving Buddhism to take care of funerals and memorials.

To the west of the Tōshōgū and the Futara-san main shrine, and often overlooked by visitors today, is the Daiyūin-byō, the mausoleum of Tokugawa Iemitsu, who was buried there in 1653, two years after his death. This group of smaller and less elaborate buildings in the style of the Tōshōgū includes a series of six gates, the other three guarded by images of Buddhist deities, a Honden containing a notably realistic seated statue of Iemitsu, and his bronze tomb. Most of his successors in the *shōgunate* are buried, not at Nikkō, but either at Kan-ei-ji, a Buddhist temple in Tōkyō, or at Zōjō-ji, another temple in Shiba. Both were linked to branch shrines of the Tōshōgū, the earlier of the two having been built near Kan-ei-ji in 1627 and rebuilt in the same style as the Nikkō shrine in 1651.

As a further indication of its importance, the Tōshōgū was placed under the supervision of a succession of imperial princes, who were required to reside in Edo and to visit Nikkō three times a year. All the *shōguns* also made regular pilgrimages to their ancestor's mausoleum. For religious purposes, however, both the Tōshōgū and the Futara-san shrine were affiliated with Rinnō-ji until the fall of the Tokugawa *shōgunate* in 1867 and the establishment of a new, modernizing regime, acting in the name of the teen-aged Meiji emperor, in 1868.

Among the many measures the new rulers took to abolish the customs of the Tokugawa era, the separation of Shintō from Buddhism figured prominently—at least to the extent that it was possible to separate them after centuries of intermingling. Many Buddhist images were removed from the Tōshōgū during the 1870s, and have been preserved inside the two ancient halls of Rinnō-ji ever since; Ieyasu was joined in his inner shrine by Hideyoshi and Yoritomo; and the Tōshōgū and its more than 100 branch shrines around the country were absorbed, along with most other identifiable Shintō shrines, into the system known as State Shintō. This government-controlled religion was to dominate the intellectual and cultural life of Japan, with some disastrous effects, until it was abolished under the new constitution introduced in 1946, during the U.S. occupation following World War II.

Since then, like all other religious institutions in Japan, the Tōshōgū has had to rely on private donations, which have increased markedly since World War II as tourism has developed and interest in the Tokugawa period revived. Today Nikkō is accessible by train or car, and its remoteness and tranquility have been considerably reduced, although they are not completely lost even now. The main events in the town, which have attracted both reverent pilgrims and indifferent tourists for centuries, remain the Spring and Autumn

Festivals at the Tōshōgū, held on May 17 and 18 and on October 17 respectively, which both include processions of men dressed as *samurai*. Nikkō is also a base for visits to other sites within the National Park named for the town, such as Lake Chūzenji, the Kegon Waterfalls, which are 325 feet deep, the *onsen* (hot springs) on the Kinu River, and the theme park, the Edo-Mura, which commemorates everyday life under the Tokugawas. But Nikkō literally would not be Nikkō without the Tōshōgū, a monument that still divides opinion in Japan just as, for example, baroque and rococo buildings in Europe please some visitors but repel others. Those who enjoy the magnificent display at such other buildings of the Edo period as the Nishi Hongan-ji, the Higashi Hongan-ji or Nijo Castle (all in Kyōto) can appreciate the Tōshōgū as the quintessence of Tokugawa glory, a superb synthesis of Shintō forest, mountain, and *torii* with the polychrome celebration characteristic of East Asian Buddhism; but those who admire the relatively simple, barely decorated ancient shrine halls of Ise tend to find the buildings of Ieyasu's memorial gaudy or even absurd.

Further Reading: Among the ever-increasing number of books in English intended to describe and explain the Edo period culture that produced the monuments at Nikkō, none has surpassed in vividness or thoughtfulness Sir George Sansom's *Japan: A Short Cultural History* (London: Cresset, and New York: Century: 1931). A more specialized text, Naomi Okawa's *Edo Architecture: Katsura and Nikkō,* translated by Alan Woodhull and Akito Miyamoto (Tōkyō: Heibonsha, and New York: Weatherhill, 1975), usefully compares and contrasts the Tōshōgū with another Edo period masterpiece, the Katsura Detached Palace in Kyōto.

—Patrick Heenan

Norfolk Island (Australian External Territory, Australia)

Location: In the South Pacific Ocean, situated 1,041 miles east-northeast of Sydney, 660 miles northwest of Auckland, and 479 miles south-southeast of Noumea.

Description: The second British settlement in the South Pacific and the oldest Australian external territory, its significance derives from three historical phases: the first penal settlement from 1788 to 1814, the second penal settlement from 1825 to 1854, and as a settlement from 1856 for the descendants of the HMS *Bounty* mutineers, transferred from Pitcairn Island.

Site Office: Norfolk Island Government Tourist Bureau
P.O. Box 211
Norfolk Island 2899, Australian External Territory
Australia
(67) 232 2147

In 1774, during his second voyage, Captain James Cook discovered (and, in the name of Britain, claimed) an island five miles long and three miles wide with a total area of 8,527 acres and a coastline of about nineteen miles. It was named after the Howard family, dukes of Norfolk. At this time, the island was uninhabited, but evidence, such as stone tools, has been found of earlier human occupation; the few artifacts found to date, however, have allowed investigators to determine little about these early inhabitants. The island is mostly surrounded by steep cliffs with an average elevation of 350 feet, although two peaks, Mount Pitt and Mount Bates, reach more than 900 feet. At the time of Cook's landing, the island was densely vegetated with trees reaching down to the shoreline. Norfolk and two smaller islands to the south, Nepean and Phillip, form a part of the volcanic Norfolk Ridge that extends from New Caledonia to New Zealand.

In the same year (1788) that he founded the New South Wales colony in Sydney Cove, British naval officer and colonial administrator Arthur Phillip sent Lieutenant Philip Gidley King with three naval men, two marines, two other free men, and nine male and six female convicts, to establish a penal settlement at Norfolk Island. Three factors informed the decision to settle the island. The first derived from Britain's desire to secure the region against other colonizing interests. The French scientific naval expedition under Jean-François de Galaup, comte de La Pérouse, had anchored off Norfolk Island in the very same month Phillip and the First Fleet arrived at Botany Bay. On the day Phillip began to transfer the First Fleet to Port Jackson (Sydney Cove), Pérouse's fleet sailed into Botany Bay to the surprise of the first British settlers in the South Pacific. The second motivation for settling the island was also related to the appearance of European naval vessels. The Norfolk Island pine, of which there was a great abundance, was useful in the construction of masts and spars for the British navy. The third motivation was found in the exploitation of the flax plant, which also grew abundantly on the island, for the production of clothing, cords, and ropes.

The first penal settlement at Norfolk Island was under the command of Lieutenant King until 1790, when he was replaced by Major Robert Ross. King returned to the command of the settlement in 1791, now in the position of lieutenant governor, and remained until 1796. King became governor of New South Wales in 1800. A succession of commandants followed until the penal settlement was abandoned in 1814.

Upon arriving at Norfolk Island on board HMS *Supply*, King had difficulty finding a natural harbor in which to safely land his party. King's party finally landed and established the settlement at Kingstown (Kingston) on the south of the island. Toward the end of the first year King's convict paramour, Ann Innet, bore him a son named Norfolk. A second son, Sydney, was also born to the couple before the end of King's first period at Norfolk Island. King spent an interim period in England before returning to Norfolk with a wife, Anna Josepha Coombe. Three children were born from this union while King was on Norfolk Island, including Philip Parker King, who became a noted Australian explorer and the first Australian Fellow of the Royal Society.

The settlement at Norfolk Island, while continuing to grow in size, faced the constant problem of drawing provisions to what was an out-station of an already isolated outpost. The difficulties were demonstrated when a supply ship, HMS *Sirius*, was wrecked in 1790, although, in this case, crew and stores were saved. The *Sirius* had arrived with HMS *Supply* with more convicts, which lifted the island population from 149 to 498 persons. The *Sirius* was to go to India to bring back more supplies when it was swept onto the shore reef in Sydney Bay. One of *Sirius*'s anchors and a number of its cannon have been preserved and are displayed on the island. The problem of supplies became a point of contention among the island settlers, who formed a fraternal society in 1798 in an attempt to address their grievances. New South Wales governor John Hunter saw the society as seditious and banned it. The settlers were able to supplement their food supplies by hunting petrel, seabirds that nested on Mount Pitt.

Challenge to authority marked the island's early history. In 1789 a convict plot to seize command of the island and escape to Tahiti was revealed to King, who was able to thwart the plan. In 1794 King foiled a mutiny led by members of the New South Wales Corps recently stationed at Norfolk Island. The mutiny arose from the arrest of a soldier following a brawl between the soldiers and the settlers. King caught the

Interior of St. Barnabas Chapel, Norfolk Island
Photo courtesy of Norfolk Island Government Tourist Bureau

mutineers by seizing their arms, left in the barracks when sixty-five soldiers were sent away on various assignments, and by forming a militia of forty-four marines and seamen settlers. When the soldiers returned, the militia arrested twenty of them as mutineers. King himself was reprimanded when he took an unauthorized leave of absence from the island in 1793. He was escorting back to New Zealand two Maoris who had been taken to Norfolk Island to demonstrate flax weaving. In his absence, he left Captain Nicholas Nepean in charge.

Among the noted visitors to Norfolk Island during this period of settlement were D'Arcy Wentworth, the colonial surgeon, and George Raper, the accomplished artist. Norfolk also was home to several religious leaders. Reverend Richard Johnson and Reverend Samuel Marsden represented the Church of England. Reverend Henry Fulton, an Irish Protestant minister, had been imprisoned in New South Wales in 1798 for his participation in revolutionary activities in Ireland; freed in 1801, he came to Norfolk as chaplain. Two Irish Catholic priests, Father Peter O'Neil and Father James Harold, were political prisoners on the island. O'Neil returned to Ireland after his pardon in 1803; after Harold was freed, he established a school on Norfolk.

Each of the commandants left a mark on Norfolk Island. The development of the island progressed under King. In 1789 the first road on the island was completed, traveling from Sydney Bay to Anson Bay via Mount Pitt on the west side of the island. In the same year settlers were placed at Cascade on the east side, which became the center of the flax industry. An agricultural center called Queenborough (Longridge) was later established to the west of Kingstown.

Major Robert Ross, in charge of the island in 1790 and 1791, proved to be a difficult leader, not only treating convicts harshly, but causing discontent among the marines and free settlers. His first act in command was to establish martial law, an act motivated by the wreck of the *Sirius* and intended to prevent the theft of food supplies. He also attempted unsuccessfully to introduce a system of putting prisoners into small self-sufficient groups, with the expectation that they would support themselves by farming and hunting, and reducing their allotments from the public stores of food. The prisoners proved incapable of cultivating a sufficient amount of food, however, and became opposed to Ross's scheme, which was abandoned when King returned to the island.

In an attempt to improve communications with Sydney, Captain John Townson, commandant of Norfolk from 1796 to 1799, arranged the construction in 1798 of the twenty-five-ton sloop *Norfolk*, the largest boat built on the island to that time. The boat's purpose originally was to take messages to Governor Hunter in Sydney. When Hunter saw the boat, however, he was impressed with its potential for use in exploration. It was accordingly fitted out for an exploratory voyage, and in 1799 it was used by Matthew Flinders and George Bass to circumnavigate Van Diemen's Land (Tasmania).

Captain Thomas Rowley, who had charge of Norfolk for eight months in 1799 and 1800, ordered the seizure and destruction of stills when it was found that people were suffering from health problems caused by drinking spirits hot from the stills. While this action brought protest, Rowley enjoyed much support from the Norfolk community during his brief tenure. His successor, Joseph Foveaux, who served from 1800 to 1804, aborted a convict plot to seize the island. He blamed the plot on Irish political prisoners and ordered the hanging—without a trial—of two Irish convicts whom he believed to be the ringleaders. Foveaux's contemporaries describe him as cruel and obsessed with the punishment of convicts. One account accuses Foveaux of imprisoning one of his sergeants on a fabricated charge so that he could take the sergeant's wife as a lover; Foveaux married the woman, Ann Sherwin, several years later in England.

There are conflicting accounts of the next commandant, Captain John Piper, who served from 1804 to 1810. Some describe him as moderate and gentlemanly, others as ruthless and inhumane. Piper found a lover in Mary Ann Shiers (or Shears), the daughter of a convict. She bore him two sons while on Norfolk Island, and he married her some years after they had left the island. It was Piper who was ordered to begin the evacuation of the island. The British had decided to abandon Norfolk because it was costly to maintain, was so far from Sydney, and did not possess a safe anchorage. In 1792 the population of the island had reached 1,115; by 1810 it was reduced to 177.

The evacuation continued under Lieutenant Tankerville Alexander Crane, whose tenure lasted from 1810 to 1813. William Hutchinson, a civilian, was left in 1813 with a party of thirty-four persons to prepare for the final abandonment. New South Wales governor Lachlan Macquarie saw that the Norfolk Island settlers were transferred to Port Dalrymple, Van Diemen's Land, and given grants of land in a place Macquarie called Norfolk Plains.

In 1825 a second penal settlement was established at Norfolk Island, this time as a place of secondary punishment, that is, for convicts who committed further crimes while serving sentences. In the words of New South Wales governor Ralph Darling, the government policy was to make Norfolk Island "a place of the extremest punishment, short of Death." In 1844 the island was annexed to Tasmania. The Tasmanian historian, Reverend John West, in 1852 stated:

> Always a place of banishment, even as a colony, Norfolk Island seemed destined to exhibit the extremes of natural beauty and moral deformity. The language of Holt, the Irish rebel, who spent several months there, might be better suited to a latter period, but expressed the intensity of his abhorrence, not wholly unfounded—"That barbarous island, the dwelling place of devils in human shape; the refuse of Botany Bay—the doubly damned!".

The command of the second penal settlement was given first to Major Robert Turton, who arrived with six women and six children (who were all withdrawn in 1827), thirty-four soldiers, and fifty-seven convicts. The second penal settlement continued Norfolk Island's reputation of convict and military revolts. In September 1826, convicts attempted to make a surprise attack on the garrison and take control of the island. During the fray, fifty convicts were able to seize a boat and sail for Phillip Island. The convicts were later recaptured after some resistance. In December of that year convicts being brought to Norfolk on the HMS *Wellington* seized the ship just before it reached the island. The convicts then steered the ship to the Bay of Islands, New Zealand, where it was later recaptured. In both incidents ringleaders were tried and hanged in Sydney.

In 1834 another aborted convict revolt took place. Convicts in the island hospital overpowered their guards. They were joined by prisoners from other parts of the island before the revolt was suppressed. Nine convicts died in the fray and thirteen were hanged. In 1839 the second mutiny in the history of the island took place. Soldiers went into a rage when the commandant, Major Thomas Bunbury, ordered their storage huts demolished. The soldiers ostensibly used the huts to store tools and produce, but Bunbury discovered they also kept stolen goods there. The mutinous regiment and Bunbury were replaced by troops under the command of Major Thomas Ryan. In 1842 convicts attempted to seize the brig HMS *Governor Phillip* anchored off Cascade. The affair ended in bloodshed with the crew overpowering the convicts. In 1846 another convict uprising left four officials dead; thirteen convicts were executed, including the bushranger William Westwood, also known as Jacky-Jacky.

The commandants of the second penal colony left marks on the island in a variety of ways. Major Joseph Anderson, who served from 1834 to 1839, was responsible for two buildings that still stand: the Commissariat Store (now All Saints' Church) and the Military Barracks (now the Administration Building). Bunbury, commandant in 1839 and 1840, promoted agriculture on the island as a way to make the community self-supporting. Captain Alexander Maconochie, who served from 1840 to 1844, presented a more humane administration. He introduced a system of allowing prisoners to earn marks for good behavior; enough marks could gain their freedom. Misconduct led to the loss of marks. Criticism of Maconochie's reforms led to his dismissal. Major Joseph Childs, commandant from 1844 to 1846, reversed Maconochie's policies. After reports of cruelty to prisoners under Childs were investigated, Childs was also removed.

The regime of John Price, from 1846 to 1853, was considered the most stern and harsh, however. He encouraged prisoners to inform on one another, and he subjected transgressors to a variety of brutal physical punishments. His severity was such that he met a violent death at the hands of vengeful convicts at Williamstown, near Melbourne, in 1857.

Clergy played a prominent role in the reports on the second penal settlement and the evaluation of its future. The Roman Catholic vicar-general William Ullathorne, the Quaker missionary James Backhouse, and the chaplain Thomas Beagley Naylor were among those who reported conditions on the island. The clergymen were often appalled at what they saw. The Roman Catholic bishop of Hobart, Robert Willson, visited the island in 1846, 1849, and 1852, and it was he who, after observing the distressing conditions existing under Price's administration, recommended that the penal settlement be closed. A decision to evacuate Norfolk Island had been made in 1846, but it was revoked in 1848. In 1852 Willson's recommendation was accepted and the convicts were gradually evacuated, the last leaving for Hobart in 1856.

With Norfolk becoming vacant, it was suggested that the island would make a suitable home for the inhabitants of Pitcairn Island, which had become overcrowded and had limited natural resources. The islanders were descended from the crew that had mutinied on the HMS *Bounty* in 1789. Reverend George Hunn Nobbs, a Pitcairn Island leader and husband of Sarah Christian (the granddaughter of Fletcher Christian, the instigator of the *Bounty* mutiny), helped negotiate the Pitcairners' removal to Norfolk Island. In 1856, 194 of these descendants were taken aboard the *Morayshire* and shipped to Norfolk Island. The island was administratively separated from Tasmania and reestablished as a distinct settlement of the British Crown administered by the governor of New South Wales.

Another religious leader who influenced the development of Norfolk Island was the Anglican bishop of New Zealand, Reverend George Augustus Selwyn, who had been seeking to move the Melanesian Mission College there from Auckland since 1853. He visited the island with Reverend John Patteson in 1856. In 1861 Reverend Patteson became the first missionary bishop of Melanesia. In 1866 the headquarters of Church of England Melanesian Mission was established on Norfolk Island with a training school, St. Barnabas College, situated below Mount Pitt.

There were difficulties in these early years of the post-convict era. The islanders were discontent with Hobbs's leadership and with what was seen as interference by the New South Wales governor. Two groups of settlers went back to Pitcairn Island, one in 1858, the other in 1863. An epidemic of enteric fever broke out in 1867. Nevertheless, the settlers on Norfolk Island developed their community, which was prohibitionist and sabbatarian.

In 1875 the islanders were given the old Commissariat Store as All Saints' Church after the earlier church building was destroyed by a cyclone. In 1880 the missionaries completed St. Barnabas Chapel as a memorial to Bishop Patteson, who was killed by natives in the Solomons. In 1885, after the visit of Methodist missionaries Mr. and Mrs. A. H. Phelps, a Methodist congregation met in the old Military Barracks, which they repaired. A Methodist church was later built in Middlegate. In the 1890s the son of George Hunn Nobbs, Alfred Nobbs, converted to the Seventh-Day Adventist faith and led some of the islanders into that church. The congregation met in the old prison chapel until a church was built at

Middlegate. Catholics were few in the early years of the settlement; a Catholic church was not built on the island until 1957, also in Middlegate.

The other major area of activity on Norfolk Island in the early period of the post-convict era was whaling. Shortly after arriving on Norfolk Island, several Pitcairners joined the crews of U.S. whaling ships, where they gained expertise that allowed them to develop their own whaling industry. Whaling remained a major activity on Norfolk until the 1960s, when a dearth of whales in area waters led to the industry's demise.

With the turn of the century, there were new developments on the island. In 1902 the Pacific Cable Station was built at Anson Bay. The cable extended from Canada through Fiji and Fanning Island to Norfolk, where the cable split into two parts, one going to Southport, Queensland (Australia) and the other to Auckland, North Island (New Zealand). The cable helped link Norfolk to the rest of the world, and also provided employment for numerous islanders.

In 1897 the British government turned administration of Norfolk Island over to the governor of New South Wales. Then in 1914, the Australian federal goverment took over the island as a territory of Australia. Since then the island has been governed through a resident administrator.

For a short time in the 1920s, banana production became a leading industry when demand in New Zealand and Australia increased. In the early 1930s, the Norfolk Islanders began considering tourist trade as a possible source of revenue. The development of commercial air service to the island in the 1940s was the key to the tourist industry. The economy of the island has since relied on tourism; approximately 20,000 visitors arrive per year. The attraction is two-fold. First, the Norfolk Island National Park occupies the higher-northern sections of the island. It contains subtropical rainforest with Norfolk Island pines. Second, the remaining structures of convict buildings, dating from the second penal settlement, have been preserved as an excellent example of convict life.

In the 1960s, immigration and tax avoidance became contentious issues. The islanders were concerned that the large influx of "mainlanders" (new settlers) would disturb their traditional lifestyle. The Immigration Ordinance of 1968 regulated movement onto the island. Norfolk Island's tax-free status began to be exploited in the 1960s, making Norfolk Island a haven for Australian companies that wished to avoid paying taxes. From 1964 through 1971 approximately 1,754 new companies were registered on the island and only 190 companies were deregistered. The Income Tax Assessment Act of 1973 curtailed this activity.

In 1976 a Royal Commission headed by Sir John Nimmo made recommendations on the future of Norfolk Island, which led to the Norfolk Island Act of 1979. Under this act, the island was granted a Legislative Assembly and Executive Council to run its own affairs, but the island was retained as a territory of the Australian Commonwealth. There still remain, however, some questions in the minds of the Norfolk Islanders concerning their status in the Commonwealth of Australia.

Further Reading: The overall historical survey of Norfolk Island is found in Merval Hoare's *Norfolk Island: An Outline of Its History 1774–1987* (St. Lucia, London, and New York: University of Queensland Press, 1969; fourth edition, 1988). Hoare has also produced a text that discusses the recent history of the island, *The Winds of Change: Norfolk Island 1950–1982* (Suva, Fiji: Institute of Pacific Studies of the University of the South Pacific, 1983). A history of the two penal settlements on Norfolk Island is found in Margaret Hazzard's *Punishment Short of Death: A History of the Penal Settlement at Norfolk Island* (Melbourne: Hyland, 1984). A collection of essays on the penal settlements has been edited by Raymond Nobbs in two volumes, *Norfolk Island and Its First Settlement 1788–1814* (Sydney: Library of Australian History, 1988) and *Norfolk Island and Its Second Settlement 1825–1855* (Sydney: Library of Australian History, 1991). Peter Clarke's *Hell and Paradise: The Norfolk-Bounty-Pitcairn Saga* (Ringwood: Viking Penguin, 1986; London and New York: Viking, 1987) is a well-illustrated coffee table book that focuses on Norfolk Island's connection with the *Bounty* mutiny and Pitcairn Island.

—Neville Buch

Nouméa (South Province, New Caledonia)

Location: Southwestern coast of New Caledonia, the largest island of the archipelago of the same name in the South Pacific Ocean, approximately 950 miles east of Australia.

Description: The only major city in the French island territory of New Caledonia, thought to have been settled by Southeast Asian peoples about 1500 B.C. The island people lived in relative isolation until Britain's Captain James Cook came upon the island in 1774. The islands were annexed by the French in 1853, and Nouméa was founded in 1854 as a port. The city served as a base for Allied operations during World War II and is today the seat of territorial government and the focal point of tourism in New Caledonia.

Site Office: Office du Tourisme de la Province Sud et Nouméa
24, Rue Anatole France
BP 2828
Nouméa, South Province
New Caledonia
(687) 28 75 80

New Caledonia, an archipelago consisting of the large island of the same name and several smaller islands, is a tropical paradise in the South Pacific Ocean. It is a place of breathtaking beauty, surrounded by azure waters and adorned with lush vegetation. However, its history is the familiar tale of European imperialism and the native population's quest for independence. After existing in relative isolation for several centuries, it was "discovered" in 1774 when the English explorer James Cook stumbled upon it on one of his voyages. It is widely believed that Southeast Asian people crossed the Pacific to Australia and various Pacific Islands, including New Caledonia, about 1500 B.C. This was no mean feat; the melting of the polar ice caps created a vast ocean and the seafarers apparently crossed some 6,000 miles of open sea in primitive vessels, probably little more than rafts. Although Melanesians, ancestors of Australian aborigines and Papua New Guinea highlanders, were on New Guinea during the same period, it is generally thought that they did not follow the Southeast Asians to the South Pacific for several generations. However, some geneticists theorize that a few Melanesian women were likely on the first boats to the Pacific Islands. Ultimately, the inhabitants of New Caledonia became known as Melanesians or Kanaks.

Tumuli found on the archipelago's small Isle of Pines and at Païta on the main island, and megaliths found in various locations suggest that the island chain was inhabited even before the arrival of the Southeast Asian canoes. In addition, rock engravings have been found near mountain peaks. The origin of these crosses, circles, spirals, and other geometric forms has not been determined; these symbols do not seem to have developed into a written language. In any event, the Southeast Asian inhabitants adapted to their oceanic environment. Within 1,000 years of their arrival, they had replaced the primitive rafts with double-hulled vessels used to explore the inner reaches of the Pacific Islands. These vessels held up to 100 people, as well as the plants and domestic animals that were transported to establish new settlements. The Melanesians also developed a highly complex and diversified system of community that was able to deal effectively with the hardships of a seafaring culture. Families often were separated by long sea trips and suffered tragedies in shipwrecks, yet the islanders managed to carry on.

By the eighteenth century, Europeans had explored and colonized much of the world, with the exception of the South Pacific Ocean. In 1768, the British Royal Society and the British Admiralty commissioned the first scientific expedition to the Pacific; a forty-year-old naval captain named James Cook was appointed as its head. On that first trip, Cook discovered and charted New Zealand and the Great Barrier Reef of Australia. Four years later Cook embarked on another exploration from July 1772 to July 1775 that has been called one of history's greatest sailing ship adventures. In September 1774, Cook, the son of a Scottish migrant farmer, landed on New Caledonia quite by accident and named it after an ancient word for Scotland.

Cook's journal entry described the inhabitants as pleasant and friendly. Encouraged by Cook's glowing reports, French navigator Antoine-Raymond-Joseph de Bruni, Chevalier d'Entrecastraux, sailed to New Caledonia in 1793. His reception was not as pleasant; he found the island's residents surly and prone to engaging in cannibalism. Given the island's meteorological pattern of monsoon followed by a long dry period, it is possible that Cook was lucky enough to land during the wet, growing season, when food was plentiful. Despite the island's potential for colonization, neither England nor France was particularly interested at the time. By the 1830s, however, the burgeoning tea trade between China and Europe found a profitable commodity in the sandalwood of New Caledonia. Adventurous beachcombers collected the sandalwood and traded it to China for tea that was then traded to Europeans living in Australia for iron, tools, glass, and tobacco. Business was brisk, and after the island's sandalwood supply was depleted within twenty-five years, the beachcombers offered slaves and copra, the latter a dried coconut meat yielding coconut oil.

Christian missionaries arrived in the 1840s, initially with disastrous results. Converting the island's inhabitants proved difficult and many of the missionaries were killed. The island's remote location and the chronic shortages of food and

Amédée Lighthouse, off the coast of Nouméa
Photo courtesy of Destination Nouvelle-Calédonie, Nouméa

supplies only served to exacerbate the Europeans' misfortunes. The situation eased slightly by the 1850s as Caledonians grew more accepting of the Europeans' presence; the riches that they brought with them were particularly appealing. During this period, an estimated 50,000 native people and 100 Europeans were living in New Caledonia.

Napoléon III (Louis-Napoléon) of France, believing that rehabilitation of criminals was best accomplished by removing them from the supposedly corrupting influences of society, began relocating convicts to New Caledonia (despite reports from the South Pacific that New Caledonia itself was not uncorrupted). Settlement of convicts there also provided a way to develop the land with free labor. Some years earlier, on January 1, 1844, a French captain had negotiated a treaty with the native population granting the French right to claim sovereignty at any future date. Louis-Napoléon decided to exercise that right in 1853 by annexing the island. He then instructed his navigators to find a suitable harbor for the landing of prisoners. A year later, the city of Port-de-France was founded on the southwestern coast; the name was changed to Nouméa in 1866. Once again the remoteness of the island and rebellion on the part of the native population hampered development, and it was not until September 1863 that France declared New Caledonia a penal colony.

The first group of deportees, 250 in all, arrived in 1864. They immediately were set to work erecting prison structures and administrative buildings in Nouméa, Yahoué, and Bourail. Forestry projects also provided work for the prison population, which over the next fifteen years would swell to 6,000 men and women as a result of political events at home. France's ignoble defeat at the hands of the Germans in the Franco-Prussian War and the treaty signed by the conservative-dominated National Assembly angered France's socialists and other left-wing elements, who feared the assembly would reinstate the monarchy. Rebel Parisians formed their own government, the Paris Commune, and staged a series of mob actions that culminated in bloody street fighting during the week of May 21 to 28, 1871. Twenty thousand members of the Commune were killed and thousands more were sent to France's penal colonies. Five thousand political prisoners landed in New Caledonia. Although most of the prisoners returned home after the French government granted them a general immunity in 1880, they left their mark on the island. One of the most famous prisoners was Louise Michel, a Parisian teacher and anarchist, who remained in Nouméa for several years to teach in a girls' school and to provide instruction for the Kanaks. Another was journalist Henri de Rochefort, who eventually deserted his left-wing views and came to support far-right political causes after the amnesty. Labrulle, an architect, drew the original plans for the Nouméa Cathedral. During the same decade, Kabyle rebels in the French-owned territory of Algeria also were deported to New Caledonia. Many of these prisoners remained on the island after their sentences were commuted in 1894; they established a Muslim settlement near Bourail.

New Caledonia suffered a severe drought in 1878 with wide-ranging consequences. In true imperial fashion, the French, in search of grazing land for their cattle, encroached on Kanak tribal farmland in the west. When the Kanaks protested, a government commission responded by eliminating a substantial portion of native land rights. A rebellion by native landholders ensued, but it was quelled quickly by the better-equipped European army. In the aftermath, Melanesian villages and crops were destroyed, rebels were deported or executed, and the percentage of Melanesian-owned land continued to decrease.

French-Melanesian relations worsened as the imperial government imposed forced labor, curfews, and travel restrictions. Particularly devastating was the 1899 head tax on male Melanesians that required them to work for European settlers and the government. In 1917, after eighteen years of laboring under these regulations, the Melanesians again rose in rebellion, only to be defeated once more.

During the 1870s, a rich supply of copper ore, cobalt, and nickel was found in the soil of New Caledonia. The discovery of these natural resources, particularly nickel, was a prodigious boost for the island's economy. Chinese, Southeast Asian, Japanese, and Javanese workers were recruited by the Société Le Nickel company to work in its factories. The influx of money allowed the island and its chief city to make some progress, albeit slow and subject to delay from the lack of supplies. A shipping line was established between Marseilles and Nouméa via the Suez Canal in 1882; an undersea cable brought telegraphic services to the island from Australia in 1893. In 1905 a postal service was launched between France and Nouméa. Medical facilities and schools were opened around this time. The European settlers built attractive and spacious houses adorned with verandas and surrounded by gardens.

By the turn of the century, civilian governors had replaced military leadership but not necessarily repression. Governor Feillet, who arrived in 1894, was notoriously lacking in sympathy for the native population. He ordered a decrease in each Melanesian's land reserve, to slightly more than seven acres, and refused to allow tribes to select their own chiefs. In spite of this mistreatment at the hands of the French, several hundred Melanesian men volunteered to fight in World War I.

When the war ended, New Caledonia suffered a short economic downturn that was changed by a nickel boom in 1925. In addition, the new French governor, Guyon, encouraged the Kanak tribes to plant and sell coffee. He also pushed for further development of Nouméa, which was still a pastoral town of only about 10,000 people. However, before this new surge of activity could take hold, the world was plunged into economic depression after the 1929 stock market crash. Nevertheless, just prior to the outbreak of World War II, New Caledonia was able to celebrate the establishment of a private radio transmitter and airmail service, and Nouméa saw major public works projects, including the construction of new roads and the installation of electric street lights. Another nickel boom just prior to the war brought renewed prosperity to the capital.

Although the war cut off communications with France, New Caledonia was able to receive news and supplies from Australia. Nickel was sent through Australia to be sold in the United States. The governor at this time, Henri Sautot, was a DeGaulle supporter, and his influence convinced many islanders to become involved in the Free France movement. Once again, Melanesians volunteered for military service, enlisting in the Pacific Battalion. In May 1941, a hydroplane base was built at Nouméa and an airfield was installed at Tontouta several miles up the coast.

After the Japanese attacked Pearl Harbor, New Caledonia became the general headquarters for the Allies' South Pacific operations. On March 12, 1942, an American expeditionary corps of about 20,000 men arrived in Nouméa, and the town's population more than doubled overnight. By the end of the year, American civilians arrived to begin the construction of a runway on the Gäiacs Plain. For the remainder of the war, 100,000 to 130,000 troops were stationed on the island, which also served as a medical post for soldiers injured in the fighting at Guadalcanal. It is estimated that between 1942 and 1943, 1 million American soldiers passed through New Caledonia.

A few shrewd Caledonians were able to save some of the money that American soldiers seem to dispense endlessly, but for the most part the island's inhabitants struggled with an impoverished economy after the war. The push for self-government continued, particularly in the rural areas outside Nouméa, and the movement was bolstered by a decree from the Trustees Council of the United Nations that all colonial mandates be eliminated. Regulations governing native laborers were repealed in 1946, French citizenship was granted to all island residents in 1953, and by 1956 New Caledonia's locally elected officials had achieved a significant level of autonomy. However, economic realities convinced many people that the island should remain a territory of France.

A coalition formed between Melanesians and a small number of Europeans resulted in the creation of the Caledonian Union party, which campaigned on a platform of full local self-government. The party was instrumental in establishing a Territorial Assembly in 1957 that had the power to elect a territorial administrator. By the 1970s, most of the Europeans had left the Caledonian Union as it moved toward support for complete independence. The Independence Front, made up of the Caledonian Union and other similar groups, coalesced into the Kanak Social National Liberation Front (Front de Libération Nationale Kanake et Socialist, or FLNKS). FLNKS' growing influence led the French government to offer complete self-government in territorial affairs in an effort to head off the drive for independence. The self-government ruling, called the Lemoine Statute, was rejected by FLNKS, which boycotted the November 1984 elections and set up roadblocks outside Nouméa.

France responded to the boycott with a counter-offer that would grant independence but allow French residents to retain their French citizenship and residential rights. The European and non-Melanesian community (also known as "settlers"), centered in Nouméa, rejected this proposal. In the 1985 elections, FLNKS achieved a majority throughout New Caledonia except in Nouméa, where the settler-based party, Rally for Caledonia in the Republic (Rassemblement pour la Calédonie dans la République, or RPCR) held onto its power.

In 1988, an uprising by Kanak separatists led French prime minister Michel Rocard to negotiate peace between the pro-independence and anti-independence forces. The resulting agreement, known as the Mantignon Accord, provided for a referendum to be held in 1998 on New Caledonia's independence. Violence erupted again the following year, with the assassination of FLNKS leader Jean-Marie Tjibaou and his second-in-command, Yeiwene Yeiwene, by pro-independence militants who believed FLNKS had bowed to French interests. Racial polarization and controversy over the issue of independence continue to plague New Caledonia.

Today Nouméa is the center of New Caledonia's primary industry: tourism. In particular, the city is known for its restaurants, ranging in cuisine from classic French to Melanesian to Indonesian to Tahitian. Examples of nineteenth-century French colonial architecture can be seen in such neighborhoods as the Baie de l'Orphelinat, the Vallée des Colons, and the Latin Quarter. In the center of the city is the Place des Cocotiers, which features brilliantly planted gardens, a replica of a nineteenth-century bandstand, and a statue sculpted by Paul Mahoux. Another historic site is the 1887 stone cathedral built by convicts from the penal colony.

Just off the coast of Nouméa and visible from the city is the Amédée Lighthouse and Island. The lighthouse was constructed in France during the reign of Napoléon III. French naval officers returning to Paris after service in New Caledonia expressed the island's need for a lighthouse. Constructed of curved cast iron plates, the tower weighed more than 400 tons after its completion. It was then shipped piece by piece to New Caledonia in 1865. Viewed from below, the 247 interior steps are said to resemble a nautilus.

Further Reading: Apart from the standard travel guidebooks, little information has been published about Nouméa. *New Caledonia Today* by Arlette Eyraud, translated by Melissa Thackway (Paris: Les Editions du Jaguar, 1993), is notable for its discussion of the island's history, people, flora, and fauna. It includes dozens of stunning photographs.

—Mary F. McNulty

Ōsaka (Ōsaka, Japan)

Location: On the southern coast of the island of Honshū in Ōsaka prefecture, facing Ōsaka Bay in the Inland Sea, 320 miles west of Tōkyō and 26 miles southwest of Kyōto.

Description: One of Japan's largest cities, a major port and business center, and one of its "three capitals" between 1603 and 1868.

Site Office: Ōsaka Tourist Information Office
JR Ōsaka Station
3-1 Umeda, Kita-ku
Ōsaka, Ōsaka
Japan
(6) 345 2189

Ōsaka occupies an area of low-lying fertile land at the mouth of the navigable Yodo River and at the foot of the Ikoma Mountains to the east and north. It has therefore historically been relatively easy to connect the site both with the interior of the island of Honshu and with the islands of Kyūshū and Shikoku, which also have coasts on the Seto-naikai (the Inland Sea); and it has understandably attracted human settlement since prehistoric times. Indeed, according to legend, it attracted Jimmu Tennō, the supposed first emperor of Japan, who is said to have landed at the Yodo estuary, perhaps during the seventh century B.C., and to have given the place its original name, Naniwa (rapid waves). This name survives both as Naniwa-ku (Naniwa Ward), a southwestern section of modern Ōsaka, and as Namba, a district in the south of the city.

The development of ancient Naniwa is as mysterious as Jimmu himself, who may well never have existed. Archaeological excavations, which were discouraged in Japan until after 1945 precisely because they might have led some to question official histories, have recently shown that there had been settlement in and around Naniwa from thousands of years earlier. However, the site's history does not become plausible until around the fourth century A.D. Probably about this time, the empress Jingō, who is said to have been the first of several Japanese rulers to attack Korea, founded the great shrine of the sea gods at Sumiyoshi, approximately five miles south of modern Ōsaka. This shrine was rebuilt in 1818, preserving the archaic style of thatched wooden buildings. Perhaps a generation or two later, the emperor Nintoku made Naniwa his capital, draining the marshes around the river and beginning the network of canals that still characterize parts of the modern city. But again, the evidence for Nintoku's existence is meager. It is even uncertain that the mound-tomb said to contain his remains, seven miles south of Ōsaka, has any connection with him, since the Imperial Household Agency, which manages the site, does not permit excavations. Clearly, however, a wealthy and powerful ruler, whatever his name was, lies buried here: the tomb is the largest in the world, a heavily forested artificial hill, appearing keyhole-shaped from the air, surrounded by three moats.

After Jimmu, Jingō, Nintoku, and several other semi-legendary rulers had come and gone, Naniwa entered the records, both Japanese and Korean, for the first time early in the sixth century. It is believed that Buddhism was brought to Japan sometime between 538 and 553, when the ruler of Paekche, a kingdom in southwestern Korea, sent a number of Buddhist images and scriptures to the Japanese emperor Kimmei, on a ship that put in at Naniwa. (Kimmei himself was probably at least partly Korean, and a large Korean community likely existed in ancient Naniwa just as it does in Ōsaka today.)

Within approximately fifty years of this turning point in Japanese history, and after a period of confusion and uncertainty during which factions of the nobility fought over the question of accepting the new and alien religion, Naniwa became the first of many Japanese *monzenmachi,* "towns in front of gates," that is, the gates of Buddhist temples. In 588 the regent Shōtoku Taishi (now probably best known in Japan as the face on the 10,000-yen bill) founded Shitenno-ji, the Temple of the Four Heavenly Kings, the oldest surviving Buddhist temple in the country and one of the few ancient monuments left in Ōsaka today. Its buildings, placed on a straight axis from its Nandaimon (Southern Great Gate) to its Kōdō (Lecture Hall) in the north, with its five-story pagoda by far the dominant structure in the group, have been damaged and repaired repeatedly during their more than 1,400 years, but they still preserve an archaic style and layout, in contrast with most later temples, which have the pagoda placed to the side of, or even some distance from, the other buildings. Today the temple is the venue for annual performances of *bugaku,* the ancient court dances preserving Chinese forms long lost in China itself. These take place on April 22, believed to be the date of Shōtoku's death.

Just as, for centuries, many European cathedrals served multiple functions (as expressions of religious belief, assertions of political power, and centers of trade and urban development as well as of artistic achievement), so, too, in Japan the major temples, founded by rulers or nobles, became conduits for ideas and arts from China and Korea, sponsors of distinctive Japanese art forms, and the focal points of political and commercial networks. Naniwa's growing importance as a center of trade and communications was reinforced when the imperial court was again located in the city, under the emperors Kōtoku (who reigned from 645 to 654), Temmu (672–686) and Shōmu (724–749). It may well have declined, however, after 794, when the emperor Kammu (781–806) established a permanent capital

Ōsaka Castle, Ōsaka
Photo courtesy of Japan National Tourist Organization

city at what became Kyōto, twenty-six miles inland. The vestiges of one of the imperial palaces have been uncovered at a site near Ōsaka Castle.

Beginning in 894, Japan was isolated from China for approximately 100 years following a deliberate policy initiated by the imperial minister Sugawara Michizane. After his fall from power and his death in exile in Kyūshū in 903, Michizane was rehabilitated and proclaimed one of the gods of Japan's other main religion, Shintō. He is still honored today as a patron of learning at the Tenma-gu, a shrine in northern Ōsaka, as well as in Kyōto and many other places. The Ōsaka Tenma-gu, founded in 949 and last rebuilt in 1901, is now an island of calm in Umeda, the central business district of the city, although it becomes very crowded for two days every July when a huge festival known as the Tenjin Matsuri takes place, beginning with a parade of boats along the Yodo River.

During the succeeding centuries, Naniwa was gradually overshadowed by the port city of Sakai, seven miles to the south. After Sakai achieved autonomy from the landowning nobles around 1400, it increasingly offered refuge to skilled workers and merchants fleeing from the factional conflicts that nearly destroyed Kyōto during the Ōnin War (1467–77). Sakai also benefited from the diversion of trade with China away from its rival, Hyōgo (now Kōbe), which then had its trade frequently disrupted by pirates. Meanwhile, Ōsaka, as it had become known by this period, began its long career as a *jōkamachi,* a "town below a castle," by becoming the headquarters of the militant Buddhist movement known as Ikkō-shū (single mind), created by Rennyō and other leaders of the Jōdo Shin-shū (Pure Land Truth) sect when they fled from Kyōto in 1465, after monks from the rival Tendai sect destroyed their main temple in the city, the Hongan-ji (Temple of the Original Vow). After a second Hongan-ji at Yamashina, near Kyōto, was burned down by a local warlord in 1532, yet another Hongan-ji, which had been built on a hill called Ishiyama in Ōsaka in 1496, became the fortified base from which priests directed their armies of peasants and townspeople in their struggles against warlords, court nobles, and rival sects alike; these priests and their followers seized control of several provinces during the chaotic *Sengoku Jidai,* the period of warring states (1467–1573).

From 1574, however, the warlord Oda Nobunaga, who had fought his way to control over most of Honshū and taken over Kyōto in 1568, turned to deal with both Sakai and Ōsaka. He savagely suppressed the Ikkō movement throughout the country, imposed his own rule on Sakai in 1577, and had the Ishiyama Hongan-ji destroyed in 1580. Following Nobunaga's assassination in 1582, his successor as hegemon, Toyotomi Hideyoshi, left Kyōto in 1583 to direct the building of his own castle on the site of the Ishiyama Hongan-ji, but permitted the remnants of the Jōdo Shin-shū sect to build a new Hongan-ji at Tenma, in Ōsaka, in 1585, before they moved back to Kyōto in 1591.

Two years later Hideyoshi himself moved on from the city (to another new castle, Momoyama, in the Kyōto suburb of Fushimi), but Ōsaka Castle remained one of the chief fortresses of his government, the first to control the whole of Japan in more than 120 years. After his death in 1598, his widow Yodo and his son Hideyori, born in 1593, remained inside the castle with their retainers and warriors, trying to assert Hideyori's claim to power, until 1615. In that year they committed suicide in the castle's ruins after a lengthy siege by the forces of Tokugawa Ieyasu, who had been chosen by Hideyoshi as one of his son's guardians; Tokugawa Ieyasu had seized power in 1600 and had himself appointed *shōgun* (military ruler) by the powerless emperor in 1603. It is said that Ieyasu's own death in 1616 was hastened by the injuries he sustained in the battle for Ōsaka Castle.

Ieyasu's son and successor Hidetada, who had commanded the Tokugawa army during the siege, had a castle rebuilt and appointed the first of several *jōdai* (governors) to govern the city from it in 1619. Throughout the 265 years of the Tokugawa *shōgunate* (1603–1868) Ōsaka was regarded, along with the emperor's residence of Kyōto and the *shōgun's* capital of Edo (now Tōkyō), as one of the *Sankyō,* the "three capitals" of Japan, and the merchants of Sakai, Fushimi, and other former rivals were required to settle there. Ōsaka's population probably reached more than 400,000 by 1750, but it was still the smallest of the capital cities. Like Edo and Kyōto, it formed part of the Tokugawa family's domain, about one-fourth of the territory of Japan. Almost all trade among the 260 or so *han,* the domains of the *daimyō,* the nobles who governed the remainder of the country under Tokugawa hegemony, now passed through Ōsaka, where such materials as metals, cotton, sake, soya, and charcoal were processed. Above all, Ōsaka was where the *daimyō* could sell the rice surrendered to them as taxes by the farmers, or obtain long-term credit on the strength of it, and so maintain their expensive and increasingly indebted ways of living. The leading merchants, their social inferiors, soon came to rival the *daimyō* in wealth by developing bills of exchange, certificates of deposit, and other sophisticated financial instruments.

Thus it was in Ōsaka, nicknamed *Tenka Daidokoro,* "the great kitchen of the nation," that a new *chōnin* (townspeople's) culture emerged, which has contributed at least as much to the complexity of Japanese culture as have the imperial Buddhism of Kyōto or the cosmopolitanism of modern Tōkyō. Ōsaka patriots insist, for example, that *sushi* (raw fish or meat on vinegared riceballs) was invented in the city, that the engineering tradition that gave Japan its pre-modern ships, canals, bridges, and major buildings began here, and that the woodblock prints known as *ukiyo-e* (floating world pictures) were first made here, too. Although historians still debate these claims, which are challenged by the natives of Tōkyō, there is no doubt that Ōsaka was the first home of a truly popular culture, urban and literate, to some extent cutting across the rigid divisions among warriors, townspeople, and farmers and centered on the district called Dōtonbori, along the banks of a new canal cut in 1615 to plans by the engineer Dōton. This has been the entertainment district of Ōsaka ever since.

The most enduring representatives of this culture are the novelist Ihara Saikaku (1642–93) and the playwright Chikamatsu Monzaemon (1653–1724). Saikaku was a poet who spent the last eleven years of his life writing some of Japan's first realistic prose fiction, describing life among the merchant class and perhaps disguising satire and social criticism behind the Buddhist and Confucian moral messages approved by the government (although scholars argue about this). Chikamatsu, sometimes called the Shakespeare of Japan, wrote classic plays, often about the dilemmas posed by *giri* (duty) and *ninjō* (human feeling), for the *bunraku* puppet theatres of the city; these plays have since entered the Kabuki repertoire. The works of both writers continue to be adapted for the cinema and television, perhaps most notably in two films directed by Mizoguchi Kenji, *Saikaku Ichidai Onna* (*The Life of Oharu,* 1952) and *Chikamatsu Monogatari* (*The Love Suicides at Sonezaki,* 1954).

However, the Ōsaka merchants' virtual monopoly on trade, the material basis for this cultural flowering as well as for the fortunes of such contemporary commercial empires as Sumitomo, Sanwa, Daiwa, and Marubeni, did not last much beyond Chikamatsu's lifetime. It was steadily undercut by the rise of independent merchants, in Omiya, Ise, and other areas, by the development of rival cities under several of the *daimyō,* and especially by the growth of Edo, which by the middle of the eighteenth century was the largest city in the world. The leading *daimyō,* forced to leave their families in Edo as hostages and to serve at the *shōgun's* court, naturally preferred to do business there. Ironically, many of the merchants of Ōsaka encouraged them to do so, partly by investing in improved coastal shipping between the two cities and partly by flouting the Tokugawa laws by moving their residences and businesses to Edo. The consequent shift in the national center of gravity is indicated by the career of another great Ōsaka-born artist of the Tokugawa period, Nakajima Tetsujirō (1760–1849), who had to go to Edo to find patrons for his wood-block prints and eventual fame under the name of Hokusai.

The city that Hokusai and many others left behind them underwent a relative decline during the last decades of the Tokugawa period, following years of failed rice harvests in 1733, 1787, and again in the 1830s, and therefore famine in the countryside and economic upheaval in the cities, while many *daimyō* defaulted on their debts, ruining some of the leading merchant houses. The growing numbers of landless laborers moving to Ōsaka in an often fruitless search for work briefly found a champion in Ōshio Heihachirō, a minor official of the city government who organized a spectacular but hopeless uprising in 1837. After the executions of Ōshio, his family, and many of his followers, Ōsaka appears to have submitted to fate, and its citizens played relatively little part in the events that followed the arrival of the American mission commanded by Commodore Matthew C. Perry in 1853 and the collapse of the Tokugawa policy of isolation.

Just as a siege of Ōsaka Castle had marked the triumph of the Tokugawa Dynasty over its last remaining opponents, so another siege of the same castle was one of the events in the dynasty's fall from power in 1868. This time the castle was reduced to ruins, which were then left untouched while a regional headquarters was built on the grounds for the new modern army created by the government established in Edo (by then renamed Tōkyō and made the residence of the emperor). Ōsaka joined in the rapid modernization that characterized the Meiji period (1868–1912), opening its port to international trade in 1868 and becoming the first headquarters of Japan's two leading newspapers, the *Asahi Shimbun* and the *Mainichi Shimbun,* both of which, however, soon moved to Tōkyō. Since 1871, Ōsaka has also been the headquarters of the national mint, which manufactures all Japanese coins and many medals. The mint's head offices are still inside the brick building constructed for it at Sakuranomiya on the bank of the Yodo, now a rare historic monument in itself. The national mint's garden is perhaps even better known, since its cherry trees attract large crowds when they blossom in the spring.

The imperial government did not permit modernization to get out of control or to threaten its own position. Even as telegraphs, railroads, and other wonders of the age were introduced to the country, the government used its control of religious and educational institutions to revise the standard versions of Japanese history. In 1880, for example, a Shintō shrine with the title Hōkoku (Protection of the Nation) was established on the grounds of Ōsaka Castle to honor the spirits of the Toyotomi family, who were rehabilitated in order to be presentable as defenders of the emperors against the ambitions of the Tokugawa Dynasty. It was to this shrine that the soldiers garrisoned nearby were brought on annual parades and to celebrate Japanese victories against the Chinese in 1894 and the Russians in 1905.

Even so, the transformation of the merchant city of Ōsaka into a modern metropolis continued, and the face of the city was significantly altered, with, for example, the creation of a number of public parks. Nakanoshima Park, opened in 1891 and incorporating the Tenma-gu shrine, lies next to the City Hall at the eastern end of the island for which the park is named, between the Dōjima River and the Tosabori (Tosa Canal). In 1926 the Sumitomo family gave the city their formal garden, the Keitaku-en, which lies next to Tennōji Park, the largest open space in the city and the location of its Fine Art Museum, which displays, among many other treasures, twelfth-century illustrations of the eleventh-century novel *Genji Monogatari* (*The Tale of Genji*) and several paintings by Ogata Kōrin (1661–1716). In 1931 a replica of the main buildings of Ōsaka Castle was put up, the remaining four towers of the original twenty were cleaned and repaired, and part of the grounds was cleared to make yet another park. The only basis for the reconstruction was a single large screen depicting the battle of 1615, painted by an unknown artist of the seventeenth century; representing more than 5,000 warriors fighting around the castle, this screen is now displayed inside the keep.

The Japanese Western Army, controlled from the headquarters in the grounds of Ōsaka Castle, played a part in the brutal and disastrous campaigns that led to the annexation of Korea in 1910, the conquest of large parts of China in the 1930s, and, eventually, the defeat of Japan itself in World War II. Like other major cities, Ōsaka was almost completely destroyed by Allied bombing, but it has since been rebuilt largely to serve its business community and to develop further its role as the center of the network of transport and communications throughout the Kansai, the region that also contains Kyōto, Kōbe, and Nara. The city remains crucial to the Japanese economy. It is home to about 2.7 million people and the capital of Ōsaka prefecture, which has a population of approximately 7.5 million; about half of Japan's exports are sent through its harbors, and its 30,000 or so factories produce about one-fourth of the country's output.

Ōsaka today is characterized by broad avenues and elevated expressways, the stations and lines of several different railroad companies, and the office blocks of the many corporations that still have either their national or their regional headquarters here. By 1964 the central business district, Umeda, was already so heavily used that the Tōkaidō *Shinkansen* (the New Trunk Line, carrying high-speed "bullet trains"), which opened that year, was given a separate station some miles away from the center. Similarly, Expo 70, the first international exposition to be held in Asia, was located on a suburban site twelve miles to the north, which has since been developed, as Senri New Town, around the National Ethnological Museum, opened with the funds left over from the exposition. The reclamation of land from the sea, which has been going on since long before Dōton's day, and the extension of underground shopping arcades throughout the central districts of the city, also suggest the enormous cost of real estate in the city.

A few prewar buildings survive, either as historic monuments or as housing for the poor and marginal, who still include many of the Korean residents of Ōsaka and perhaps most of the city's *burakumin* (outcasts who still suffer discreet and unofficial discrimination). Shitennō-ji was rebuilt by 1960, and the castle park became the location for two museums. Inside the castle itself, rebuilt yet again but now using reinforced concrete, portraits and possessions of the Toyotomi family may be viewed. Inside the former military headquarters is the city's historical museum, displaying, in rotating exhibits, an increasing number of finds from the archaeological excavations it helps to fund; a somewhat fanciful model of the ancient emperors' palace at Naniwa; several screens painted in the days of Hideyoshi and Ieyasu, some showing Dutch and Portuguese traders; and an important collection of puppets and sets from the *bunraku* theatre.

Much of the spirit of Saikaku's pleasure-seeking merchants also survives in Ōsaka, chiefly in the district of Namba and Dōtonbori, which are as renowned for their stores, bars, Korean and other restaurants, gaudy neon signs, and sheer noisiness as for the gambling, prostitution, and drug dealing that sustain the *yakuza,* the criminal syndicates that are more powerful in the Kansai than anywhere else in Japan. Among the varied attractions of these districts stand two postwar establishments dedicated to the traditional arts, the Shin-Kabuki-za (New Kabuki Theatre) and the Bunraku-za (Bunraku Theatre), the latter sponsored by the national government and opened in 1984 in an effort to preserve the puppet theatre, the one traditional art that originated in Ōsaka.

The building of the Bunraku-za, the recent remodeling and extension of Tennōji Park, and the gradual conversion of the former freight yards around Ōsaka's main railroad station into an area of new homes, hotels, offices, and open spaces, are all signs of the continuing vitality of the city and, perhaps, of a new concern for improving its public facilities. Ōsaka fortunately sustained relatively little damage in the unexpected earthquake of January 1995 (the first major quake in the Kansai in 400 years) and may even benefit from the economic growth that is expected to result from the rebuilding of the devastated parts of Kōbe and Nishinomiya nearby. While it would take a great deal more than economic growth alone to make Ōsaka as beautiful or evocative as Kyōto or Nara, it still retains its own charms, its own distinctive atmosphere enthusiastically defended by its citizens, mainly against Tōkyō, and, amid the expressways and the office blocks, its own important historic monuments.

Further Reading: Ōsaka naturally figures largely in general histories of Japan, among which Sir George Sansom's *Japan: A Short Cultural History* (London: Crescent, and New York: Century, 1931) is still the best written and the most intelligent. It is largely free of the obsession with "unique" national character that disfigures most academic texts, in English as in Japanese. Ōsaka has not attracted as much attention from writers in English as have Kyōto or Tōkyō; instead, the best way to get to know the city in its "golden age" is to read any of the several available translations of works by Chikamatsu or Saikaku.

—Patrick Heenan

Pagan (Myanmar)

Location: In central Myanmar (formerly Burma), on the Ayeyarwady (formerly Irrawaddy) River, approximately ninety miles southwest of Mandalay.

Description: An ancient ruined city founded in A.D. 847–49, Pagan served as the capital city of the Pagan Dynasty from the eleventh to the thirteenth centuries; it has been damaged by pillaging, the environment, and an earthquake in 1975.

Contact: Ministry of Hotels and Tourism
77-91 Sule Pagoda Street
Kyauktada Township
Yangon
Myanmar
(1) 77966 or (1) 75328

Pagan is one of the most important ancient cities in Myanmar, the country that until 1989 was called Burma. Revered for its stunning architecture and several thousand pagodas, the city was capital of the Pagan Dynasty for nearly 200 years. A much-visited tourist site, Pagan is famous today for its beautiful temples and statues that have survived earthquake, invasion, and pillaging. It is thought to have been settled by the Pyu king Thamuddarit in the second century A.D. Almost 600 years later (around 847–49), the Burmese king Pyinbia fortified the city by erecting walls. Pagan did not achieve much status or power until the eleventh century, however, when the forty-second ruler of the Pagan Dynasty became king.

Despite its location in the arid, desert-like region of north Myanmar, approximately ninety miles southwest of Mandalay, the site for Pagan was well chosen. It lies on the Ayeyarwady—formerly Irrawaddy—River, halfway between Minbu (downriver) and Kyaukse (upriver); both of these sites were significant rice-producing regions in early times. It is thought that Pagan's role in uniting diverse political groups along the river was dependent on this inland position, which made it easier for the dynasty to amass wealth and support from Kyaukse and Minbu (unlike far-off coastal towns such as Arakan and Tenasserim, which were successful trade areas). This region surrounding the Irrawaddy River was originally populated by the Pyu and Mon. The Burmese predecessors of the Pagan Dynasty came to the basin in the ninth century and, during the next 100 years or so, transformed Pagan into the power base of northern Burma, while the Mon kingdom controlled southern Burma from Thaton.

The military strength of the Pagan Dynasty reached new heights in 1044 when King Anawrahta became its ruler. Anawrahta pursued a policy of territorial expansion, and his most celebrated victory was over Thaton in 1057. Some historians argue that the pursuit of Thaton resulted from Anawrahta's conversion to the Theravāda strain of Buddhism (a fundamentalist form, also known as Hinayana) by a Thaton monk named Shin Arahan. According to this version of the story, Anawrahta asked the king of Thaton for copies of the scriptures (Tripiṭaka). However, the Thaton king, considering the people of Pagan to be barbarians, refused to provide the sacred texts. As a consequence of this refusal, Anawrahta invaded Lower Burma, sacking Thaton, and amassing all the cultural and material wealth in the city. A more probable explanation may be that Anawrahta's invasion of Thaton was linked to a general territorial expansion, which naturally threatened Lower Burma and the Mon people.

The capture of Thaton and Lower Burma not only brought cultural wealth to Pagan, it also opened up trade relations between the dynasty and Ceylon (Sri Lanka) and with merchants along the coast of the Bay of Bengal. Following the conquest of Thaton, most of the city's scholars and artisans, as well as the cultured Mon royal family, were moved to Pagan. The city benefited considerably from this influx of talent, becoming famous for its art; it also developed into a center of Buddhist learning, drawing pilgrims from all over Asia.

Anawrahta began the construction of Pagan's several thousand pagodas. Prior to the Mongol invasion in the thirteenth century, Pagan is thought to have had some 13,000 temples; today this number is closer to 4,000. The construction of these pagodas was financed by the large wealth amassed by the royal family during its conquests, and labor was supplied mostly by slaves. Historians and archaeologists believe that a central enclave within the city walls housed the aristocracy (primarily Mon) and important administrative buildings. The rest of Pagan's citizens probably lived outside the fortifications in lightly constructed buildings similar to those that the Pagan people live in today.

Most of the city's buildings were constructed with wood and have subsequently disintegrated. Religious structures were built for the most part of brick, carved brick, and terra-cotta; although many have been destroyed by the natural elements or by a devastating earthquake in 1975, many remain standing today. An important survivor from this era is in fact a Hindu temple, the Shwe Sandaw Pagoda. Built in 1057, it once housed several images of the Hindu god Ganesh (also known as Gaṇeśa, Gaṇapati), the elephant-headed son of the gods Pāravatī and Siva. Statues of the Hindu god once stood on each corner of the five walkways. The *hti* (spire) was damaged during the 1975 earthquake and can be seen lying near the temple. A sixty-foot dormant Buddha can be found inside a long thin building in the temple enclave; this was built during the eleventh century. The existence of the pagoda and

Buphaya Pagoda, Pagan
Photo courtesy of Embassy of the Union of Myanmar, Washington, D.C.

the Nat Hlaung Temple (a Hindu temple built in A.D. 931) testify to the religious tolerance practiced by Pagan's citizens.

Anawrahta was killed in an accident in 1077 and was succeeded by his eldest son Sawlu, whose first challenge was dealing with a Mon uprising. Sawlu asked his half-brother Kyanzittha to help him but ignored the latter's defense strategy when the crisis arose. Sawlu was taken prisoner by the Mon. He mistrusted his half-brother so much that when Kyanzittha came to rescue him, Sawlu thought he was going to be murdered and alerted his captors. Unfortunately, his action led to his execution by the Mon (to prevent any similar attempt at rescue).

Kyanzittha succeeded Sawlu in 1084. He successfully suppressed the Mon revolt, and Pagan experienced a period of growth, prosperity, and unity under his rule. Kyanzittha harbored great respect for Mon culture, and much of the art produced during his rule is Mon influenced. During this period, the leaders of intellectual and cultural life were predominantly Mon. The Mon dialect was spoken among the ruling class, and the Burmans (Pagans) wrote their own dialect in Mon script. Under Kyanzittha, a recognizable Burmese culture emerged out of various indigenous strains, including Mon, Burman, Pali, and Pyu customs.

Many of Pagan's famous pagodas were built during Kyanzittha's reign and reflect the importance of Theravāda Buddhism. This can be seen in the Shwe Zigon Stupa and the Ananda temple, both erected during Kyanzittha's twenty-eight-year rule. The large, Mon-influenced Shwe Zigon Stupa is square at the base and has a bell-shaped main body. Its decorative staircases, spires, and jewel-encrusted gold finial were much admired before the building suffered considerable damage in 1975.

The Ananda Temple is one of the most impressive buildings in old Pagan. Although it also was damaged in the 1975 earthquake, the temple has been renovated extensively. Built in 1091, it was supposedly inspired by the vision of a group of Indian monks who visited Kyanzittha's kingdom. They had lived in the legendary Nandamula Temple and through meditation made this temple appear to the king, who tried to recreate the Himalayan cave-structure in Pagan. Shaped like a Greek cross, the Ananda Temple contains four anterooms, which surround a central structure; inside are four recesses housing large teak Buddhas, each approximately thirty feet high. The south-facing Kasapa and north-facing Kakusandha are the original statues; the east-facing Konagamana and west-facing Gautama were stolen and have been replaced by copies. The temple is topped with a golden stupa and flanked by four smaller pagodas. Now used as a center for meditation and learning, the Ananda Temple hosts a festival each January, drawing large crowds of local residents and tourists.

Following Kyanzittha's death in 1112, he was succeeded by his grandson Alaungsithu (1112–67). During Alaungsithu's reign, the influence of Mon culture began to

Gawdawpalin Temple, Pagan
Photo courtesy of Embassy of the Union of Myanmar, Washington, D.C.

wane as Pagan developed a clear sense of its own style, although examples of both Mon and Burmese architecture date from this period. Alaungsithu traveled across his extensive empire endowing monasteries with land and building temples to spread the word of Buddha. Two such temples still stand in Pagan, the That Byinnyu (1150s) and the Shwe Gugyi (1131). The largest building inside the city, the That Byinnyu is similar in style to the Ananda Temple; it houses an east-facing Buddha. The Shwe Gugyi is the oldest example of the two-tiered style of Burman temple and is unusual in that it is north-facing, as opposed to the usual east-facing alignment. This temple is remembered for being the place in which Alaungsithu was murdered by his son Narathu.

To absolve himself of the crime of murdering his father, Narathu built the city's largest shrine, the Dhammayangyi Temple, approximately one-half mile southeast of the city walls. The building also resembles the Ananda Temple, but was never completed owing to Narathu's untimely demise at the hands of his former father-in-law, Pateikkaya. Overall, the reigns of Narathu (1167–70) and his successor Naratheinhka (1170–73) were largely unremarkable apart from being periods of intrigue and violence. Naratheinhka was succeeded by his brother Narapatisithu, who ruled from 1173 to 1210/11, and was possibly the last of the great kings of Pagan.

During Narapatisithu's reign, the wealthy and corrupt monkhood, which had benefited from the Pagan kings' policy of allowing temples and monasteries to exist in tax-free lands, was brought under the king's control. A shortage of land and money led Narapatisithu to "cleanse" the monkhood by announcing that its behavior was reprehensible and, consequently, reclaiming its possessions. The king sent the monks to Ceylon to be retrained; they returned to ordain new, pure monks in Pagan. Thus, Narapatisithu managed to reform his corrupted monasteries while increasing the crown's treasury and lands. Narapatisithu used part of his newly gained wealth to erect new temples, further examples of the emerging Burmese style. The exoneration of the monkhood was, however, short-lived, as Narapatisithu's successors began to give large tracts of land to the monasteries, eventually to the king's own detriment. The power of the monasteries grew as that of the monarch began to decline. Gradually, the Pagan powerbase dwindled, and rival political factions arose within the once unified empire. (The Mon were one of the groups that benefited from the disintegration of the empire; an independent Mon state emerged in 1281 at Pegu.)

Narapatisithu was succeeded by Nantaungmya (1210–34), who was followed by Narathihapate, the king who is linked with the downfall of the Pagan Empire. Faced with the advances of the Shan as well as the armies of Kublai Khan, Narathihapate was also a victim of his own vanity. An inscribed tablet at the Minlazedi Pagoda (1284) boasts of the strength of King Narathihapate's army, of his 3,000 concubines, and of his enormous appetite. Legend states that during the construction of this temple a rumor began to circulate that the fall of the Pagan Empire would follow its completion. Accordingly, the king stopped the work, only allowing it to resume when an advisor reminded him that one of the main Buddhist tenets is that all life is evanescent. Shortly after the building was completed (sometime between 1283 and 1301), the heralds of Kublai Khan arrived to negotiate the payment of a tribute to the Khan. Narathihapate refused to allow Kublai Khan's men into the city. When a second delegation was sent to Pagan, the king had them beheaded, finally drawing the Khan's wrath upon himself and the city.

Although some sources claim that Kublai Khan's armies destroyed most of the 13,000 pagodas and shrines in Pagan, most historians deem this unlikely since the Khan was himself a Buddhist. Weather and flooding must have destroyed many of the city's wooden monuments; other damage was done by the Pagan king himself. When Narathihapate heard that the Mongols had invaded Burma, he reportedly had several thousand pagodas destroyed in an attempt to fortify the city. Later he fled from Pagan, earning the name Tarokpyemin (the king who ran away from the Chinese). The Mongols, however, would not take Pagan until 1287, after Narathihapate's death, and they would ultimately be driven out of the city and the lowlands by the Shan, a group of people from the eastern part of what is today Myanmar, in the valleys of the Ayeyarwady Basin.

After the fourteenth century, Pagan's political significance was limited to its immediate locality in the Ayeyarwady Basin, and even this dwindled as Ava and Toungoo were established as political centers by the Burmanized Shans and refugee Burmans, respectively. Subsequently, Pagan's once great empire was divided among various factions. Not until the sixteenth century did Myanmar once again unite as one empire under the Toungoo Dynasty. In 1752 the Mon Empire reasserted itself under Alaungpaya, who pursued a policy of territorial expansion. His policy alarmed Myanmar's neighbors, especially British-controlled India, which engaged in two wars with Myanmar, first from 1824 to 1826, and later in 1852. Myanmar controlled Assam briefly, but ceded this and other territories to the British, eventually losing its independence to Britain in a third war in 1885.

Under British rule Myanmar became Burma, a province of India. It lost many of its religious rights and economic wealth during this period. Britain declared Burma independent of India in 1937, and the country gained total independence in 1948. Following a military coup in 1962, Burma became a socialist country, and gradually, through mismanagement and corruption, its economic wealth was depleted. Civil rioting erupted in 1987 and 1988 and was suppressed violently by the government, and even though opposition parties won the election in 1990, the army still maintained control in the mid-1990s. The name Myanmar was officially adopted in 1989.

Myanmar's recent turbulent history has not left Pagan's people unscathed. Following the civil riots of the late 1980s, thousands of working-class people were relocated from towns such as Mandalay and Yangon into malaria-infested rural areas and villages unsuited to mass migration. It is estimated that in 1989 and 1990 more than 500,000 people were forcibly relocated, and thousands of elderly people and children died in transit.

Pagan, a relatively small town, was cleared of its 5,200 inhabitants in April and May of 1990 to prevent contact between tourists and local people. This action has not, however, discouraged thousands of tourists from visiting the site. Tourism has been encouraged by the restoration of many buildings; with several thousand of its original 13,000 pagodas still existing, the ancient city of Pagan remains a spectacular example of eleventh- through thirteenth-century Buddhist architecture.

Further Reading: For a photographic guide to Pagan, with minimal text, turn to the *Pictorial Guide to Pagan* (second edition, Rangoon: Ministry of Union Culture, 1963). *Burma: Insurgency and the Politics of Ethnicity* by Martin Smith (London and Atlantic Heights, New Jersey: Zed Books, 1991) is a densely-detailed analysis of the origins and problems of modern Burma. Paul Strachan's *Pagan: Art and Architecture of Old Burma* (Whiting Bay, Aran, Scotland: Kiscadale, 1989; as *Imperial Pagan: Art and Architecture of Burma,* Honolulu: University of Hawaii Press, 1990) covers Pagan's wonderful art, sculptures, and architecture, and is complete with plans. The travel-oriented *Insight Guide to Burma* (Singapore: APA, 1988) is a detailed, illustrated guide with more than the usual analysis of individual sites. For historical information, volume one of *The Cambridge History of South East Asia,* edited by Nicholas Tarling (2 vols., Cambridge, New York, and Victoria, Australia: Cambridge University Press, 1992) is a good starting point for the student or general reader interested in gaining more information. Finally, the *Historical and Cultural Dictionary of Burma* by Joel M. and E. G. Maring (Metuchen, New Jersey: Scarecrow, 1973) provides brief entries on cultural, historical, political and social figures, places, movements, and words.

—A. Vasudevan

Paharpur (Rājshāhi, Bangladesh)

Location: Approximately three miles west of the Jamālganj Railway Station, twenty-nine miles northwest of Mahāsthān (the ancient city of Puṇḍravarddhana), and some thirty miles southeast of Bangarh (the former city of Kotivarsha); in the Rājshāhi district in northern Bangladesh.

Description: Paharpur contains the ruins of the largest Buddhist monastery found south of the Himalaya Mountains, believed to have been founded by Dharmapāla I, of the Pāla Dynasty in the late eighth century A.D. Formerly known as Somapura Vihara, this site was a major educational and religious center for almost 500 years, until its decline in the thirteenth century A.D.

Contact: Bangladesh Parjatan Corporation
National Tourism Organization
233 Airport Road
Tejgaon, Dhākā 1215
Bangladesh
325155 9

The ruins of the Buddhist monastery at Paharpur are the largest of any yet discovered south of the Himalaya Mountains. The archaeological site covers more than twenty-seven acres of land, and the central building is so large that it is referred to as the *pahar,* meaning "hill," hence the local name of the site: Paharpur. The original name of the complex is thought to have been Somapura Vihara.

The ruins were discovered by Dr. Buchanan Hamilton, who visited the site between 1807 and 1812 while surveying for the British East India Company. He noted in his journals that he found a huge pile of bricks, between 100 and 150 feet high, which was covered in trees and bushes. Hamilton surmised that Paharpur was the most significant archaeological site in the Dinājpur Division; he believed that the ruins were those of a Buddhist stupa. The site was then visited by a Mr. Westmacott in 1875, who agreed with Hamilton's theory about the original function of the *pahar.* Finally, Sir Alexander Cunningham (known as the father of excavation in India) visited Paharpur in 1879. Cunningham found that the perpendicular height of the erection was some eighty feet above ground level, far smaller than his colleague Hamilton had estimated. Cunningham believed that the central hill had originally been a Brahmanical temple, because he found a terra-cotta plaque representing Kālī. Archaeologists and social anthropologists would later realize that the art and architecture of the site was an amalgamation of different religious and cultural influences. Cunningham's conclusion about the mound was proven wrong and Hamilton's ideas were confirmed when subsequent excavation revealed that the mound was indeed a Buddhist stupa. Hamilton dated the ruins to the Pāla Dynasty (eighth to twelfth centuries), a supposition that also has been authenticated.

The history of northern Bengal is sketchy. Unfortunately, the often extreme weather conditions of Bengal (virulent monsoons, flooding, and heat), the use of impermanent construction materials, and war have destroyed much historical evidence. It is thought that the region at one time formed part of the Mauryan Empire in the third century B.C. However, more information is known about the Gupta Empire, which began in the mid–fourth century A.D. The Guptas expanded their empire to control the whole of northern Bengal, but the empire began to wane in the middle of the sixth century. It is believed that at the beginning of the seventh century western and possibly northern Bengal were controlled by the Gauḍa king Śaśānka, a vehement opponent of Buddhism.

During the Gupta period, in approximately A.D. 478 (Gupta year 159), a copper-plate grant was given to Nāthasarmma, a Brahman, to buy some land. It is reported that the money earned from the land was used to buy goods for worship of the *arhats* (those who had reached nirvana) and to build a hostel for a Jain teacher living in Vatagohali. Puṇḍravarddhana and Vatagohali (modern Mahāsthan and Goalbhita, near to Paharpur) also were mentioned in this grant. Hence, it is probable that a Jain *vihara* (monastery) was located near Paharpur from the late fifth century A.D. onward. The Chinese Buddhist pilgrim Xuan Zang, who visited southern Asia in the seventh century A.D., went to Puṇḍravarddhana and commented that most of the monks there belonged to the Jain monastic community, and that some 100 Brahmanical temples and 20 monasteries existed there. Since he made no reference to Somapura Vihara (Paharpur), it is likely that no Buddhist religious center operated there at this time.

The Pāla Dynasty emerged in the eighth century A.D. under the ruler Gopāla and became a dominant power in eastern India, uniting the different factions that existed prior to their ascent to power under one centralized administration. At the height of their dominance, the Pālas controlled Bengal, Bihār, and Assam. Buddhism was promoted vigorously during the Pāla era, and many stupas and *viharas* were built throughout their territory, especially in the late eighth and early ninth centuries under the rulers Dharmapāla and Devapāla.

It is believed that Somapura Vihara was a special center of Buddhist activity built during Pāla rule. The remote location of the site is thought to have provided a retreat for Buddhist monks and pilgrims far away from the noise of the city; the tranquility and remoteness of the *vihara* were two of the site's attractions. The development of a large rural settle-

Buddhist monastery, Paharpur
Photo courtesy of Bangladesh Parjatan Corporation, Dhākā

ment of monks suggests that the *vihara* received donations from a wealthy patron, most probably the royal family. Some terra-cotta seals found during the excavation of Paharpur record that the "illustrious Somapura" was founded by Dharmapāla (c. 770–810), which indicates that the religious community was founded sometime in the late eighth century A.D. The reputation of the Buddhist center quickly spread through Asia.

In the late ninth century A.D. the power of the Pālas was temporarily weakened as the Gurjara-Pratihāra Empire encroached on Pāla territory. An inscription found on a pillar in Paharpur tells of a Gurjara invasion. By the late tenth century, however, the Pāla Dynasty was reinvigorated under the rule of Mahipāla I. During this time, parts of the complex at Somapura Vihara were rebuilt, reflecting an injection of money from the Pāla ruler. According to the Tibetan *Pag Sam Zon Zang,* Mahipāla I paid tribute at the *vihara* at Somapura.

Following the death of Mahipāla I and his successor Nayapāla, the Pāla Kingdom was invaded by the Chedi ruler Karṇa, then by Rājendra I, the Cōḷa king, and finally by the Kaivarta Kivya. By the late eleventh century A.D. the Pāla fortunes were once again reviving, this time under Rāmapāla. During this period Somapura again received attention and tributes from the Pāla rulers. The twelfth century A.D., however, marked the beginning of the end for the complex. The rise of the Sena Dynasty brought an end to the influence of the Pāla Dynasty (the Senas were great patrons of orthodox Hinduism), although a pillar inscription, reportedly donated to Somapura by Daśabalagarbha, dating from the twelfth century A.D. intimates that the complex was still well known during this period. By the thirteenth century the prosperity of Somapura had ended. The Muslim invasion of India during this period effectively brought an end to large-scale Buddhist worship, and many of the stupas and buildings at Somapura were destroyed. The site was abandoned until Buchanan Hamilton brought it to public attention in the early nineteenth century.

Although Cunningham wanted to excavate extensively at Paharpur later in the nineteenth century, the zamindar (landowner), the rāja of Balihar, prevented him from doing so. Cunningham was allowed only to clear some of the jungle area around the mound and to perform some superficial digging. It was left to the national Archaeological Department to begin the first extensive excavations of the site. In 1919 they declared Paharpur to be a protected site under the Ancient Monuments Protection Act. Following the acquisition of a huge subsidy from the Varendra Research Society, excavation began in 1923. A team composed of students and academics from the University of Calcutta was sent to the region; however, digging was confined to the southwest corner of the monastery when financial problems arose. The Archaeological Department resumed excavation in 1925–26 and continued work until 1934. During this period the main staircase, the north side of the central ruin, the northern *maṇḍapa* (pillared hall) and surrounding passageway, the monks' cells, and the Satyapir Bhīta mound were among the areas excavated.

The ruins that were excavated by the Indian Archaeological Department early in this century reveal a unique complex, stylistically removed from any other religious buildings found in India. The cruciform main temple of Paharpur is one of the most unusual architectural constructions of ancient India. It is thought that a Jain temple or stupa dating from the late fifth century A.D. was situated close to the temple, thereby requiring the main temple to expand vertically rather than horizontally. The temple was a terraced, three-story building, topped by a shrine, and decorated with carved brick cornices and numerous terra-cotta reliefs. It was multiroomed, with a continuous link of antechambers and passages and a surrounding veranda on each level. The style of the temple is believed to have been influenced by temple architecture in Java, Cambodia, and Burma; in fact, the architecture of the temple most closely resembles religious buildings found in central Java. A close relationship existed between east India and the Malay Archipelago in the first part of the Pāla era, as is evident in the design of the early Pāla buildings at Paharpur. The principle of using a central area from which a series of outer projecting planes were mounted one on top of the other can also be seen in temple architecture in Burma. It is believed that the idea of square, decorated terra-cotta panels, which are commonly found in Burma, originated at Paharpur.

Visitors to the main temple entered from the north via a monastery gateway, eventually emerging in a huge courtyard flanked by stupas and images of gods, goddesses, animals, and nymphs depicted on two raised terra-cotta plaques. By way of the main staircase these visitors would ascend to the first level of the temple and enter the veranda, which was decorated by two rows of carved plaques. The antechambers were the earliest part of the second terrace to be excavated.

The Sangharama (sleeping quarters) of Paharpur is thought to be the largest building of its kind ever constructed in India. In its earliest form the building was made of wood on a stylobate of stone or brick; however, as the monastery expanded it was transformed into a brick structure. Each of the four structures projecting from the main cave measured 922 by 919 feet and consisted of four rows of cells that flanked the four sides of the inner courtyard. Each cell was approximately thirteen and one-half by fourteen feet and opened onto a terrace. In the center of three of the sides, archaeologists found a separate block of three cells surrounded by a passageway. In total there were 186 cells. A large hall was situated in the remaining wall, on the north side, and this formed the main entrance. An outer wall, which is thought to have been the same thickness as the one surrounding the main temple, enclosed the building. Originally conceived as simple living quarters, the monastery became an important center of learning as a residential university.

The Satyapir Bhīta mound is situated approximately 300 yards to the east of the monastery and was at most six to seven feet high. A main temple was the most important building in this area. Divided into two parts, it contained a shrine and a pillared hall, surrounded by a veranda. Five terra-cotta plaques inscribed with the creed of Buddha were found in the courtyard, dating from the eleventh century A.D. This entire structure has been revealed by the archaeological projects.

The excavations at Paharpur unearthed a wealth of Bengali art and architecture, bridging a gap in Indian art history. Many beautiful sculptures and plaques have been found, although some are in a poor state of repair. Others illustrate the diversity of religious and cultural influences on the architecture of the complex. Terra-cotta plaques found in the main temple have images of Siva, Vishnu, Brahmā, and Buddha. Images of the elephant-headed Hindu god Ganesh and stories from the *Rāmāyaṇa* and *Mahābhārata* carved into terra-cotta plaques or stone pillars have been retrieved. A gray sandstone Ganesh, shorter than two feet high and slightly wider, was discovered at the site. An image of Siva depicting the legend in which the deity is offered a cup of poison also was recovered, as well as statues of Agni, Yamuna, and Krishna. Various inscribed pillars and images of Buddha confirm historic events in the site's history, such as the Gurjara invasion.

Although relatively little literature exists on Paharpur, and the site receives only brief mention in guide books to Bangladesh, it remains one of the most important archaeological finds in Asia. Paharpur is one of the few ancient religious settlements found in this region, which is subject to extreme climatic conditions, and excavations there have yielded a wealth of historical and artistic knowledge about this area of Asia.

Further Reading: *Excavations at Paharpur, Bengal* by Kashinath Narayan Dikshit (Delhi: Memoirs of the Archaeological Survey of India, number 55, 1938) is an illustrated analysis of the archaeological activity at Paharpur, with historical and geographical background. C. Chandra Das Gupta's *Paharpur and Its Monuments* (Calcutta: Mukhopadhyay, 1961) is a small pamphlet that details the history and main sites of Paharpur. It includes a concise bibliography of archaeological-based sources. For an historical overview of the site, readers should consult *Guide to Paharpur* by M. A. A. Qadir (Bangladesh: Department of Archaeology, 1980); this work is aimed at the reader with a deeper interest in Paharpur or Indian archaeology in general.

—A. Vasudevan

Palembang (South Sumatra, Indonesia)

Location: On the lower Musi River in South Sumatra.

Description: Port city, former site of the maritime empire of Srivijaya.

Site Office: Kanwil III Depparpostel Sumsel and Jambi
Jl. Demang Lebar Daun Kapling IX
Palembang, South Sumatra 30137
Indonesia
(711) 310025 or (711) 356661

The Strait of Melaka (Malacca), between Sumatra and the Malay Peninsula, has been a major channel of international trade for 2,000 years. It offered the most direct maritime route between India and China when trade between the two civilizations began to develop in approximately 100 B.C., and it was located at the critical geographical point where sailors wanting to catch the annual monsoons in the Bay of Bengal and the South China Sea often had to wait for a change of wind. It was also a logical meeting point for traders delivering goods from the Indonesian Archipelago into the India-China trade route. For most of the past two millennia, therefore, the strait has been the site of a major, powerful trading city. At the close of the twentieth century, the city-state of Singapore occupies this role; its predecessor was the glittering Sultanate of Melaka. The most enduring of these maritime powers, however, was the kingdom of Srivijaya (Glorious Victory), which flourished from the seventh century to the eleventh century, with its capital at or close to the site of the modern city of Palembang.

Palembang's location, fifty miles upstream on the Musi River, which reaches the sea well south of the mouth of the Strait of Melaka, does not initially appear to be especially suited for controlling trade in the strait. Palembang's advantage, however, lay in its hinterland. The middle reaches of the Musi drain a fertile countryside that could produce much of the food needed to sustain a large city, while the river and its tributaries also gave access to the products of the mountainous interior of southern Sumatra. Local chiefs in what was to become Srivijaya had their first taste of wealth as purveyors of camphor, gold, pine resin, and other local products, rather than as gatekeepers. For more than a millennium, moreover, the trade between India and China was dominated by merchants and shippers from the Indonesian Archipelago itself. A secure economic base within the region was more important than a central location on the main trade route.

At the time of the earliest commercial expansion, the peoples of the Malay world were divided into numerous small communities of farmers, hunters, and fisherfolk. Their chiefs shared authority with the community as a whole, and there was a strong sense of communal obligation. The flow of new wealth into these communities upset the political order, allowing an unprecedented accumulation of wealth in the hands of those who controlled trade. To bolster their new preeminence against the demands of communal obligation, many chiefs turned to Indian political ideas, which exalted the ruler to the status of a god-king and provided an ideological format for much larger political institutions. Throughout the western part of the archipelago, ambitious local rulers employed Indian priests to instruct them in the cosmology of Indian kingship and to develop courts appropriate to the glory of a god-king.

Although this process of absorbing Indian political and cultural ideas is well understood for the Malay world as a whole, few details are known of the earliest history of Srivijaya. The earliest extensive record of the kingdom comes from a Chinese Buddhist pilgrim, Yijing, who stayed in Srivijaya in the late seventh century for many years to study Buddhism. He describes a city where more than 1,000 monks studied Buddhist doctrine under the patronage of the king and which was engaged in a series of energetic campaigns of conquest, possibly reaching as far as parts of Java. Chinese official records also show that the rulers of Srivijaya regularly sent missions to China. The Chinese court interpreted these envoys as tribute-bearers acknowledging their subordination to China, but evidence from the Malay world suggests that they were probably trading operations carried out by Srivijayan diplomats who enjoyed privileged access to the Chinese capital.

Legends describe the ruler of Srivijaya as fabulously wealthy and powerful—so rich, it was said, that he threw a bar of gold into the water every day, and at low tide the city was dazzled by the glare from the accumulated gold. In reality, the ruler's authority came from the careful management of three powerful groups: the chiefs and warlords of the interior, who controlled the supply of forest products; the merchants and courtiers of the city itself; and the leaders of the semipiratical *orang laut* (people of the sea), who formed the backbone of the Srivijayan navy. The *orang laut* were especially important to the power of Srivijaya, for they forced all ships passing through the Strait of Melaka to call at a port designated by the Srivijaya ruler and so were able to concentrate commerce on Palembang. The city itself was the main center of culture in the region, a place of fine crafts such as woodworking and of literature. There was widespread literacy—probably higher than that in Europe during the same period—in the local *ka-ga-nga* alphabets, which were derived ultimately from Sanskrit script, and there was a vibrant literary culture. Unfortunately, because much of this literature was written on perishable strips of palm leaf, only fragments of it have survived.

In time, Srivijaya's position came under threat from powerful rivals. Javanese kings were strong enough to launch

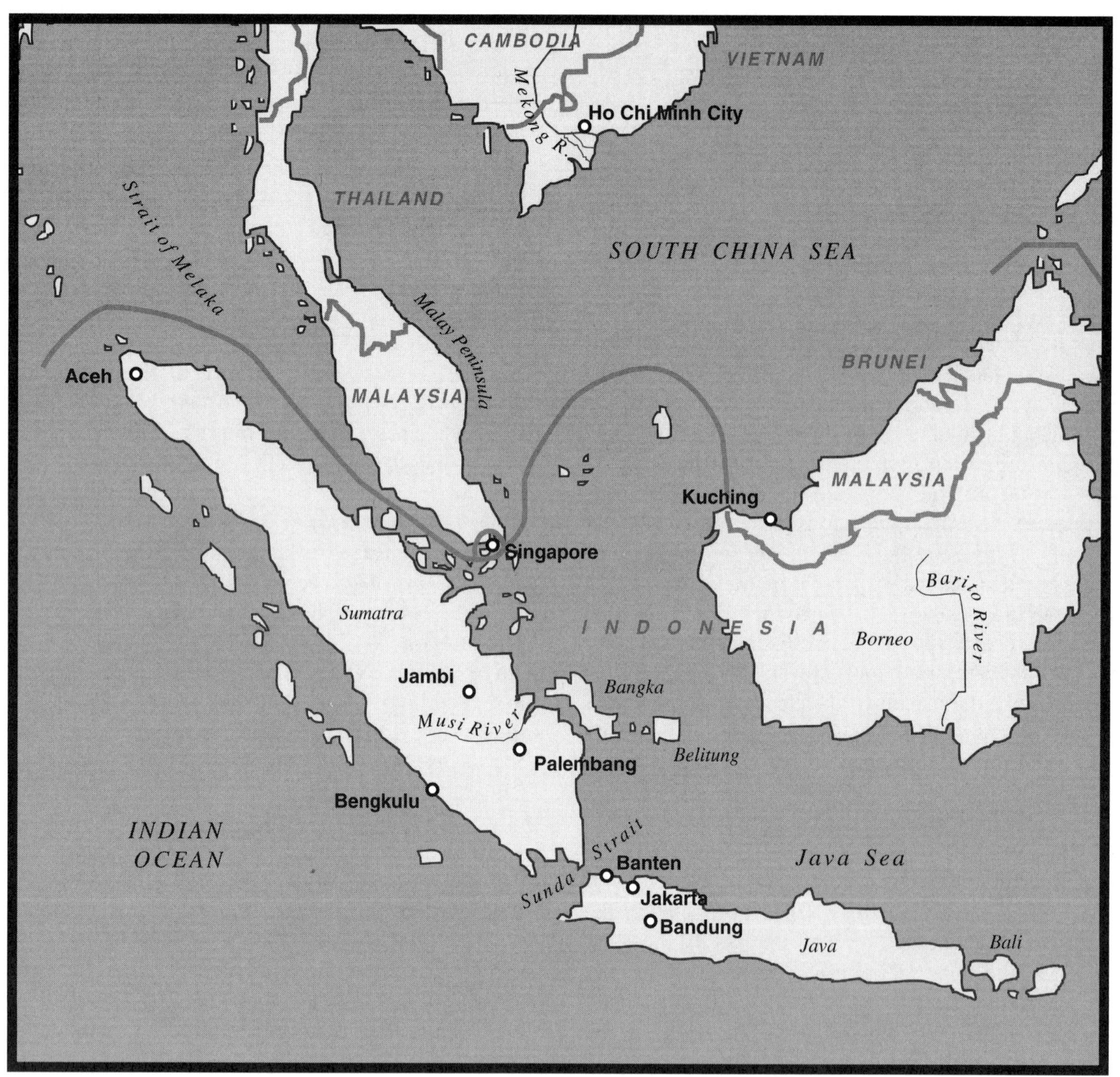

Map of western Indonesia, showing the position of Palembang
Illustration by Tom Willcockson

a raid on the kingdom in the late tenth century, although Srivijaya was able to respond in kind shortly afterward. Then in 1025 an expedition from the kingdom in southern India sacked the Srivijaya capital. This blow was followed by a major change in the structure of Southeast Asian trade from about the twelfth century, with the arrival for the first time of Chinese traders in significant numbers. With the backing of the Chinese Empire, these traders sought to diminish Srivijaya's stranglehold on the commerce of the Strait of Melaka, and they deliberately patronized and encouraged the development of other ports. As external trade became more important, too, Palembang's position away from the mouth of the strait became an increasing disadvantage. By the twelfth century the capital of Srivijaya had shifted north to the port of Jambi, sometimes called Malayu.

Palembang remained a significant regional port, first under the suzerainty of Jambi and, in the thirteenth century, under the distant domination of the great Javanese empire of

Singosari. Aware that China was unhappy with Singosari's power, local leaders in Palembang sent envoys to China seeking recognition and protection, but Singosari intervened, kidnapping and murdering the Chinese return mission. A few years later, Prince Paramesvara of Palembang again tried to assert the city's independence, but his efforts were crushed by a Javanese naval expedition; he was forced to flee and eventually founded the city of Melaka. Remaining in Palembang were several thousand Chinese traders and settlers, who fell under the control of a Chinese pirate, Liang Danming. Liang's depredations of the region's trade were so serious that a Chinese naval expedition was sent to destroy him in 1405; Liang himself was captured and sent to Beijing for execution.

For more than a century after the downfall of Liang, unfortunately, no record of any kind survives concerning the history of Palembang. The fifteenth century saw the Melaka sultanate's greatest power, and whatever commercial life continued in Palembang was eclipsed thoroughly by Srivijaya's new successor on the opposite shore of the Strait of Melaka. In 1511, however, Melaka fell to the Portuguese, at about the same time as the great Javanese empire of Majapahit finally disintegrated. In the ensuing interregnum, a Javanese nobleman, Geding Sura, fled to Palembang with his followers and established a new dynasty.

Palembang was now Muslim. Islam had spread widely in the Indonesian Archipelago from the fifteenth century, partly because its omnipresent God and its insistence on the equality of believers suited the ethos of mobile trading communities, partly because direct trading contact with the Middle East brought a new missionary drive in Southeast Asia. Although Palembang never became a center of Indonesian Islamic thought to the extent that the cities of northern Sumatra did, its royal mosque, built in 1740 and still standing, is an outstanding piece of Muslim architecture. Then, as now, however, the Musi River was the heart of the city. More than one-third of a mile wide, with numerous creeks on either side, the river was main street and marketplace. Settlement ran for several miles along its banks, and few houses were located more than a couple hundred yards from the water. Many houses, in fact, were built on rafts so that they rose and fell with the tides and with the annual floods.

The new rulers of Palembang led a far-from-secure existence. At the end of the sixteenth century, they were under attack from the newly emerged West Java state of Banten, which already had established a firm foothold in the southernmost Sumatra region of Lampung. A few years later, Palembang was threatened by the aggressive policies of the sultan of Aceh (Atjeh) in the far north of Sumatra and joined an alliance of states against him, although its distance from Aceh spared Palembang direct attack. Then Palembang fell under the domination of another Javanese power, the Muslim kingdom of Mataram, seeing it as a less dangerous foe than its immediate neighbors Jambi and Banten, both of which had designs on Palembang's territory.

Palembang's wealth in this era was based on pepper, which had displaced cloves and nutmeg as the most lucrative spice of the Indies. Cultivation of pepper led to the extensive clearing of rainforest in areas around Palembang, creating desolate zones of unproductive *alang-alang* grass once farmers had moved on. Pepper also attracted the attention of the Dutch East India Company, or V.O.C., which established a trading post in Palembang in 1619; in 1642 the company obtained a treaty giving it monopoly rights over pepper trading in the port. Tension mounted between the Dutch and the local authorities as the V.O.C. sought to enforce its monopoly, and in 1657 there was an attack on Dutch ships at Palembang. The company responded in its usual ruthless fashion with an attack in 1659 in which Palembang was burned to the ground.

By the early eighteenth century, pepper had lost much of its bite in international trade, and the Dutch largely lost interest in Palembang. In approximately 1710, however, alluvial tin deposits on the nearby island of Bangka, which belonged to Palembang, began to be developed on a large scale, mainly as a result of the arrival of independent Chinese miners. The Dutch at once sought a share of the profits and forced the sultan to sign a series of treaties giving them a monopoly on trade in the ore. The monopoly was seldom tightly enforced, because the V.O.C. was in a state of administrative decline in the eighteenth century; when the company finally collapsed at the end of the century, the ruling sultan launched an attack on the remaining Dutch posts in his territory, killing nearly all those who defended them.

With tin an increasingly valuable resource, the sultan, Mahmud Badaruddin, now made a bid for full independence. He repudiated British claims to suzerainty made during the British occupation of Java at the time of the Napoleonic Wars; the British responded by attacking him, sacking the court, and installing the sultan's more cooperative younger brother, Najamuddin, in his place. The Dutch attempted to recover their influence at court after 1816, but Najamuddin was uncooperative, keeping his contacts with the British and continuing to work for independence. When the exasperated Dutch sent an expedition in 1818, which captured Najamuddin and exiled him to Batavia, they found themselves facing even more implacable opposition under Badaruddin. A Dutch garrison finally was established in Palembang in 1821, but it faced attacks and an attempted mass poisoning before the Dutch intervened again to exile the sultan and establish direct colonial rule.

Colonial rule reordered the economy of Palembang. Bangka and the neighboring tin island of Belitung were separated administratively from Palembang and ceased to have significance for the local economy. New crops appeared, however, to serve the international market, including cotton, coffee, tobacco, and rubber. Western-owned plantations were allowed to develop, but they never came to dominate the local economy in the way they did in some other regions of the archipelago. The discovery of oil and coal encouraged the colonial government to provide a good communications infrastructure, including a railway.

Modernity thoroughly transformed Palembang. Repeated conquest and periods of decay meant that little of the older cities remained. In fact, virtually all memory of Srivijaya had disappeared. Only in 1918 did a French archaeologist, George Coedès, publish research, based mainly on Chinese texts, that showed the existence of Srivijaya. Even then, considerable doubt remained about where the capital of the kingdom had been located. Only in recent decades have further archaeological discoveries in the Palembang region indicated with certainty that Srivijaya's center was there.

Palembang is Sumatra's second-largest city, and southern Sumatra is a generally prosperous region, but throughout the twentieth century the city has been something of a cultural and political backwater. It was not a major center of nationalist agitation against colonialism, although many nationalist organizations maintained branches there, and few figures from Palembang were prominent in the national movement. The only exception was the charismatic medical doctor A. K. Gani, who starred in a prewar film entitled *Asmara Murni* (Pure Passion). Oil wells made Palembang a major target when the Japanese invaded the Netherlands Indies in early 1942, but the region did not suffer disproportionately from the Japanese occupation. In October 1945, following the Japanese surrender, Palembang was occupied by British Indian troops with the task of accepting the Japanese surrender and arranging for the restoration of colonial rule. As elsewhere in Indonesia, these troops encountered unexpectedly strong resistance from local nationalists. The British Indian and, later, Dutch troops were unable to penetrate far beyond the city, and the nationalist government of the new Republic of Indonesia governed the surrounding countryside.

For two years, the economy of urban Palembang depended on regular shipments of supplies sent up the Musi under Dutch naval guard. Outside the city, the story was different. The rubber and coffee plantations of the hinterland became a major economic resource for the republicans on Sumatra. Using pack animals and small boats, they transported vast quantities of produce to Singapore, avoiding Dutch patrols who sought to put an economic blockade around the republic. This trade supported not only the republic's government and army in southern Sumatra, but a wide range of independent armed organizations pledged to fight to defend independence. All of these organizations were patriotic, but their ideologies varied from Islam to communism to naive patriotism, and they were seldom amenable to control by the official organizations. The relative calm that repeated Dutch pacification campaigns had created in the countryside was now lost. Gani, who as local republican strongman was involved heavily in the trade to Singapore, once described himself as "the biggest smuggler in Southeast Asia"; his unparalleled access to funds earned him the post of minister of economic affairs in one of the republican cabinets.

In July 1947 the Dutch felt strong enough to break out of their narrow perimeters in Palembang in a military action designed to seize the main coal and oil fields of the region and to establish a broader base for political planning. Dutch intentions became clear in August 1948, when they created a "State of South Sumatra," with its capital in Palembang, to be part of a federal Indonesia they were building as a rival to the nationalist republic. It was a futile action, for the state never enjoyed popular support, and it was one of the first of the federal states to dissolve itself after the Dutch finally recognized Indonesia's independence at the end of 1949.

The habits of autonomy the national revolution created, however, did not disappear with independence. Throughout the 1950s, South Sumatra was a wealthy province oriented toward export; it especially resented central government tariff and exchange rate policies that made the province's exports less competitive. This resentment exploded in December 1956 into a mutiny in which military and civilian authorities refused to accept the authority of the central government until major political changes were made, although there was no talk of secession. Political concessions and limited military action persuaded the mutineers to back down, but Palembang won at least one monument from the conflict. President Sukarno included the construction of a bridge over the Musi in his country's war-reparations package from the Japanese. Although the river itself remains the heart of Palembang, the Ampera Bridge, opened in 1964, has come to be the main symbol of a thriving port and industrial center with a cosmopolitan population.

Further Reading: No single work covers the entire history of Palembang. The history of Srivijaya has been better recorded, despite the fragmentary nature of the evidence. The first volume of *The Cambridge History of South East Asia,* edited by Nicholas Tarling (2 vols., Cambridge, New York, and Victoria, Australia: Cambridge University Press, 1992), contains the most accessible accounts. For the period from the fall of Srivijaya to the Japanese invasion, the most useful source is *A History of Modern Indonesia: 1300 to the Present* by M. C. Ricklefs (Bloomington: Indiana University Press, and London: Macmillan, 1981; second edition, London: Macmillan, and Stanford, California: Stanford University Press, 1993). There is no recommended work for the period since 1942.

—Robert Cribb

Penang (Penang, Malaysia)

Location: Island situated off the northwest coast of mainland Malaysia, from which it is split by a channel. Approximately 113 square miles in area, and roughly oval in shape, its largest city is Georgetown, Malaysia's main seaport.

Description: Also known as Penang Island and Pulau Pinang, the island was a possession of the sultans of Kedah until Captain Francis Light founded a British colony there in 1786. Penang was once the major British trading center in the region. It joined the independent Federation of Malaya in 1957 and became a state of Malaysia in 1963. Penang contains a number of historic buildings, but has recently suffered overdevelopment resulting from tourism.

Site Office: Malaysia Tourism Promotion Board
Number 10, Jalan Tun Syed Sheh
Barakbah
10200 Penang
Malaysia
(4) 2620066

Renowned for its lovely beaches, hospitality, delicious cuisine, and interesting environment, Penang has drawn tourists since its settlement as a British colony in the eighteenth century. Known locally as Pulau Pinang, Penang was once one of the busiest ports in Asia. In modern times tourism has surpassed trade as the mainstay of the economy, although the island's rural population remains dependent on subsistence farming.

According to legend, a trader named Ragam discovered and settled Penang while on a journey from Sumatra; the date of this event remains unknown. Ragam named the island Pulau Bersatu (Single Island). After the Portuguese discovered the island during their exploration of Asia in the fifteenth century, the island became known as Pulo Pinaom or Pulau Pinang (Betel Nut Island), after the betel nut palms that grow there.

Until the eighteenth century, the island came under the jurisdiction of the sultans of Kedah. In the 1780s war broke out between Siam and Burma, both of which pressed Sultan Abdullah Mukarram Shāh of Kedah to side with them. Instead, the sultan played the countries against each other while seeking outside protection from a European power. He approached an Englishman, Captain Francis Light, who had been befriended by Sultan Muhammad J'wa Mu'assam Shāh II, Sultan Abdullah's predecessor, and invited to stay in the fort at Kuala Kedah. Earlier, in 1771, Light had been engaged by both the trading company Jourdain, Sulivan, and de Souza, and by the British East India Company to find a local trading base. When Abdullah approached him he immediately saw the possibilities of his new position and contacted the East India Company, suggesting Penang Island as a possible new settlement. The company sent an envoy to discuss the matter with the sultan, but nothing came of the talks. It was only in 1784 that negotiations began again, this time directly between Abdullah and Light.

There is considerable debate over the reasons for British interest in Penang. One school of thought emphasizes the island's strategic importance as the site of a potential British naval base; a second school emphasizes the commercial importance of Penang for British merchants as a much-needed settlement on the China-India trade route. Both motives involved combating Dutch competition in the area, and, most likely, a combination of both factors led to the decision to colonize Penang.

The negotiations between Light and the sultan led to a preliminary agreement in 1786, by which the company would lease the island in exchange for the British protection of Kedah and the sum of £30,000 per annum. Although the new governor general of the British East India Company refused to get involved in local politics, Light kept this secret from Abdullah, and the British occupied the island on August 11, 1786. Light quickly renamed the site Prince of Wales Island and established Georgetown port, in honor of the British king, George III.

The sultan repeatedly confronted Light about finalizing the agreement and granting him the stipulated military aid, but the latter managed to conceal the truth for almost five years. When Sultan Abdullah finally began to suspect the deception, he amassed an army. He was given support by the sultans of Selangor and Trengganu, and in 1791 pirates from Sulu, Borneo, and Illanun offered help by attacking the port from the Prai River. Realizing the danger of his position, Light requested additional forces and attacked the sultan's coalition army. Ultimately, Light defeated Sultan Abdullah's 10,000 men, a fact owing more to internal dissension in the latter's forces than to any strategic superiority of the British army. The sultan was forced to accept a less-than-satisfactory treaty, which stipulated the payment of 6,000 Spanish dollars per annum—far less than the sum originally discussed—and revoked his right to intervene in island politics. Four years later a further treaty was signed by which Kedah relinquished control over Province Wellesley, a tract of land on the peninsula opposite Penang, and the sultan's fee rose to 10,000 Spanish dollars. The sultan still receives this sum annually.

The island that Abdullah ceded to the British in 1786 had a small population, mostly of Malay fishermen; it was for the most part uncleared jungle. In order to encourage clearance of this vegetation, Light is said to have fired silver coins into the dense undergrowth and offered immigrants the right

Kek Lok Si Temple, Penang
Photo courtesy of The Chicago Public Library

to any land that they cleared. In direct contrast to the policies of the Dutch and Portuguese, he declared the port duty free and opened it to ships of any nation. As a result, Malays, Indians, Chinese, and Sumatrans, among others, flooded into the port. By 1796 the population had expanded to 7,000 people; by 1801 it was more than 10,000.

Light further encouraged the growth of pepper and other spices, importing clove and nutmeg plants from the Molucca Islands. Unfortunately, the expense of growing these more exotic spices meant that only European planters were willing to experiment with them. The Asian immigrants tended to plant only pepper. As the colony grew, more merchants moved to the island. Penang drew trade from Kedah and became the center of commerce in pepper from north Sumatra and contraband Malay tin (the Dutch held the legal monopoly).

In 1800, six years after Light's death, a lieutenant governor was sent to Penang, marking the introduction of a European-based administration on the island. By 1810 Penang had become a presidency government, like Bombay, Madras, and Bengal, and followed the British system of law and justice. For a short time, Penang became the core of British territorial expansion. In 1826, Penang's importance grew when it became the capital of the Straits Settlements, which included Penang Island, Melaka, and Singapore.

Ultimately, however, Penang proved to be a disappointing trading center for the British East India Company. Food shortages, competition from traders in north Sumatra, southern Burma, southwest Thailand, and northwest Malaya, as well as the expense involved in running a heavily bureaucratic European system, all worked against the success of the colony. Penang suffered in 1829 when the British founded a new colony at Singapore, which quickly developed a successful trading economy—the kind that the East India Company had originally hoped to create in Penang.

Over the next 100 years Penang experienced boom periods, once when tin was discovered on the nearby peninsula in the 1850s, and again at the beginning of the twentieth century, when demand for rubber (a commodity produced in abundance on the island) increased. Despite its occupation by the Japanese during World War II, Penang suffered little. After 1945, the independence movement grew on the island, influenced by political activity in neighboring countries. The end of British control of Asia was coming to an end. Malaya became an independent country in 1957, and on August 31 of the same year Penang entered the newly formed Federation of Malaya. It became a state of Malaysia in 1963.

Today Penang Island remains quite cosmopolitan, a legacy left by the mixture of races that have lived there in comparative harmony since the eighteenth century. Georgetown, Penang's historic center and port, is a beautiful city that effectively blends old and new, East and West. The old part of the city is full of winding, narrow streets and tiny shops selling spices, pepper, and craft goods. The city's architecture is a testament to the diversity of cultures that exist on the island. Georgetown has its own Chinatown and Little India, and English, Thai, Burmese, and Chinese-influenced buildings can be seen throughout. Georgetown remains a pleasant place to visit, although the high-rise hotels have also taken their place on the skyline since the 1970s. Today it suffers slightly from overdevelopment, the result of the growth in tourism during the twentieth century.

One particularly fascinating historic building in the city center is Fort Cornwallis. Of the many stories explaining the location of the fort, the most popular reports that it was erected on the spot where Captain Francis Light first set foot on the island. Another claims that Light fired silver coins into the jungle from the location. The original wooden fort was replaced by the present stone structure in 1804–05. The fort walls are flanked by impressive cannon, including the famous Sri (or Seri) Rambai Cannon, made of brass in the sixteenth century and supposedly a gift from the Dutch to the sultan of Johor. It eventually came via Aceh and Selangor to Penang in 1871, after the British claimed it as booty. According to local tradition, the cannon has special powers to bless infertile women with children. It is most often seen draped with flowers of tribute.

The diversity of Penang's religious beliefs can be seen in the temples, churches, and mosques found throughout Georgetown. St. George's Church is Southeast Asia's oldest Christian place of worship. Near this lies the Kuan Yin (Goddess of Mercy) Temple, built in 1800. Part of the original roof, decorated with porcelain figurines, can still be seen. It is thought to be the oldest Buddhist shrine on the island.

Nearby lies Sri Mariamman Temple, which was built in 1883. Inside the temple are dedications to the Nava Grahas, the planets of Indian astrology. The Sri Mariamman contains reliefs from the Hindu pantheon and houses the celebrated bejeweled statue of Lord Subramaniam.

The current structure of the Kapitan Kling Mosque was built in the early twentieth century to replace the original 1801 construction. A group of southern Indian Muslims came to the island at the beginning of the nineteenth century and erected the mosque, which stands in a street of the same name. The mosque is named after the title given to the leader of the Muslim community. The Acheen Street Mosque, also known as the Masjid Melayu Mosque, was built in 1808, just after the Kapitan Kling. It is notable for its minaret.

The Chinese influence on Penang is unmistakable. When Light opened the island to new immigrants, large numbers of Chinese traders, fishermen, and shopkeepers were among the first to settle on Penang. Inevitably, the centuries-old custom of clan houses also came to the island. These houses, also known as *kongsi,* arose from the need to provide support and friendship to newly arrived clan members. Membership to the clan houses was quite restricted, and members often shared the same surname. The Khoo clan, who came from the Hokkien province of China, became one of the most influential clans in Penang. The Khoos joined the Lims, Yeohs, Cheahs, and Tans to form the Goh Tai Seng (Five Big Surnames), who controlled Hokkien clan life in Penang for most of the nineteenth century. When gang warfare erupted in August 1867 between the Hokkien-dominated Khian Tek Triad and the Cantonese-dominated Ghee Hin Triad, it was complicated by the involvement of the predominantly Indian and mutually antagonistic Red and White Flag Societies. British forces on the island put down the riots after a few days, and Khoo Thean Teik of the Khoo clan was arrested for planning and instigating the uprising. Such was his power that British authorities reduced his death sentence to a short jail term. Subsequently, Khoo became involved in philanthropic acts.

Although the clans still exist, relations between them are today much friendlier. One of the most notable surviving clan houses is the Khoo Kongsi, known as the Dragon Mountain Hall. Erected in 1894, the original temple complex was built in honor of Tua Sai Yeah, a general of the Qin Dynasty during the third century B.C. The temple, extraordinarily lavish in scale and design, mysteriously burned to the ground soon after its completion in the early twentieth century. Because some felt that the gods had been offended by the expense lavished on the clan house, this building was replaced by a smaller and much less costly temple. The Khoo Kongsi is nevertheless quite ornate. Blue dragons decorate the roof, and the interior is carved with depictions of Chinese legends.

Some of the island's most impressive temples are situated outside Georgetown. Wat Chayamangkalaram Thai Temple can be found at Lorong Burmah. It houses the third-largest reclining Buddha in the world; the figure is 108 feet long. The temple is flanked by gargantuan multiheaded dragons. Opposite this temple is the Dhammikarama Burmese Buddhist Temple. A much less elaborate building, the temple houses a large Buddha, guarded by two huge stone elephants.

In the hills at Air Itam (also spelled Ayer Hitam) is the Kek Lok Si Temple, thought to be the largest Buddhist complex in Southeast Asia. Initial construction began in 1890, but the complex has had several additions since then. Probably the most notable building in the temple complex is the ninety-eight-foot pagoda, built over seven stories. It combines Chinese, Thai, and Burmese architectural traditions.

The Snake Temple can be found at Sungai Kluang, near the island's industrial region. Erected in 1850, the temple is decorated with several live vicious-looking pit vipers who lie around the altar. It was built in memory of a Buddhist priest, Chor Soo Kong, and each year on his birthday the number of snakes mysteriously increases.

Penang is also famous for its long stretches of relatively unspoiled beaches, such as Tanjung Bunga and Batu Feringghi (Foreigner's Rock). Unfortunately, the sea has become very polluted—the price of heavy tourism on the island.

Further Reading: *Malaysia, Singapore and Brunei: The Rough Guide* by Charles de Ledesma (London and New York: Rough Guide, 1994) is a well-researched travel guide that supplies basic historical and cultural information. *Malaysia* (London: New Holland, 1995) provides concise, detailed information in an easy-to-use format, and is a good starting point for anyone with a general interest in Malaysian culture. It also has a bibliography. *West Malaysia and Singapore* (Singapore: Periplus, and Lincolnwood, Illinois: Passport, 1993) contains quite detailed information on the historic sites in these regions. *A Short History of Malaysia, Singapore, and Brunei* by C. Mary Turnbull (Stanmore, New South Wales: Cassell, 1979) presents a well-written historical survey. *Malaysia, Singapore, and Brunei, 1400–1965* by Joginder Singh Jessy (revised edition, Penang: Darulaman, 1972) is a textbook history of these regions aimed at the serious student or the general reader with a serious interest.

—A. Vasudevan

Peshāwar (North-West Frontier, Pakistan)

Location: Just south of the Hindu Kush mountain range, at the western edge of the Vale of Peshāwar, approximately ten miles east of the Khyber Pass.

Description: Capital and largest city of the North-West Frontier province; historically important as the capital of the ancient kingdom of Gandhāra and as a trade center on the caravan routes through Central Asia; noted for many grand buildings that show the influence of the variety of peoples who have passed through Peshāwar; in the late twentieth century, the destination for many war refugees from Afghanistan.

Contact: Pakistan Tourism Development Corporation
House No. 2, St. 61, F-7/4
Islāmābād 44000
Pakistan
(51) 811001

Peshāwar's diverse character derives from its location along the principal trade and transportation routes from the Mediterranean to China. As a market town, it was a destination for merchants from Bukhara, Kabul, and Samarkand. Additionally, all armies invading India from Central Asia, North Africa, Anatolia (Asia Minor), and Eastern Europe had to pass through it. Peshāwar therefore displays a variety of cultural and religious influences, all of which have contributed to the vitality of the city.

Primitive stone tools, perhaps half a million years old, have been discovered near Peshāwar, but it is unclear whether the site has been inhabited continuously since then. It is clear that the Buddhist kingdom of Gandhāra developed in the fifth century B.C. and incorporated the Vale of Peshāwar, a fertile region that extends eastward from the city. It is not certain whether the city was established at that time; there is no written reference to it earlier than the second century A.D. Many Gandhāran relics have been found in Peshāwar and in the surrounding area; some of them were removed from the country, but the Peshāwar Museum today has one of the best collections of Gandhāran artifacts remaining in Pakistan.

Gandhāra existed until the eleventh century A.D., but it never was independent for long. It came under the influence of a variety of invaders, including Persians under Darius the Great, Macedonians under Alexander the Great, the Mauryan Empire, and the Bactrian Greeks. The Mauryans, under their great emperor Aśoka in the third century B.C., were particularly influential. Aśoka had become a Buddhist and embraced a policy of pacifism and tolerance after a period of bloody warfare. He expressed his philosophies in edicts that were carved on rocks throughout his empire; several of these are in the region around Peshāwar. The Mauryan Empire declined shortly after Aśoka's death in 235 B.C., and the Bactrians and other waves of invaders contributed to the instability of the region until the Kushān Empire brought peace in the second century A.D. The most prominent Kushān king, Kaniṣka, made his winter capital at Peshāwar—or Poshapura (City of Flowers), as it was dubbed in a rock inscription from this period, the first written reference to the city. Peshāwar has been known by a variety of names; its current name, which means Frontier Town, is attributed to Akbar, the sixteenth-century Mughal emperor.

Kaniṣka was a great patron of Buddhism and made the city a pilgrimage center. Stupas, temples, and monasteries were built throughout Gandhāra. The largest Buddhist stupa known to exist on the Indian subcontinent dates from the Peshāwar of this period; its ruins were discovered in the Shahji-ki Dheri mounds just east of the city. The Chinese pilgrim Xuan Zang recorded that in 630 A.D. the stupa, now only a pile of rubble, had five stories, nearly 660 feet high, with a superstructure of twenty-five gilded copper discs.

Commerce as well as religion flourished under the Kushāns. About this time, the Khyber Pass became an important portion of the Silk Road, the primary caravan route across Asia. A section of the route split at Peshāwar; travelers could either cross the Khyber Pass to Bactria, Persia, and the eastern Mediterranean, or travel down the Indus River and then take land and sea routes to the Persian Gulf. Some of the goods that went westward through Peshāwar were turquoise, lapis lazuli, cotton, silk, and indigo. Items that went eastward included linen, topaz, coral, frankincense, glass vessels, gold and silver goods, and wine. Cultural influences came along the trade routes as well; the Kushāns adopted Roman standards of weight and placed the images of some western mythological characters on their coins.

Renewed invasions brought this golden era to an end. The Sāsānian Empire made the Kushān territories into vassal states in the third century. Then, after the Sāsānian Empire was weakened by overexpansion, the White Huns invaded from Central Asia, plundering Peshāwar in the fifth century. The city remained an important Buddhist center, as observed by a famous Chinese Buddhist pilgrim of that era, Fa Xian. In the seventh century, another pilgrim, Xuan Zang, found Buddhism in decline but still noted several impressive features of Peshāwar, including a large fortress, almost certainly on the site where later forts were built. About this time the Hindu religion started winning an increasing number of adherents, and by the ninth century it outstripped Buddhism in Peshāwar. From the tenth through the twelfth century the region was invaded periodically by Muslim armies, who promoted conversion to Islam and eventually founded the Delhi Sultanate. By this period the term Gandhāra had disappeared from use. Then in 1221 Genghis Khan and his

View of Chowk Yadgar-Qissa Khawani bazaar, Peshāwar
Photo courtesy of Embassy of Pakistan, Washington, D.C.

Mongols stormed Peshāwar and destroyed what few buildings the previous invaders had left standing. The Mongols, who generally promoted Islam in the west and Buddhism in the east, rebuilt the city in an architectural style that blended Muslim and Hindu influences—after all, they had to use a native, largely Hindu, work force.

Peshāwar remained obscure for a period, then rose to prominence again under the Mughal Empire, founded by Ẓahīr-ud-Dīn Muḥammad (better known as Bābur), a descendant of both Genghis Khan and Timur (Tamerlane), in the sixteenth century. The Mughals recognized the city's important position on the trade route and set about making improvements. Bābur renovated and occupied Peshāwar's fortress, known as the Bālā Hisār, and developed the beautiful Shālīmār Gardens nearby. Imperial quarters within the fortress were outfitted with rich furnishings, and the gardens were noted for their variety of trees and plants. The third Mughal emperor, Akbar, conducted military campaigns to protect the region's trade and, so the story goes, gave Peshāwar its name. The volume of trade that went through the area is evident from the fact that an accidental fire in the fort in 1546 destroyed 1,000 camel-loads of goods belonging to merchants who had taken shelter there when fighting temporarily obstructed the route. By this time the merchandise along the route included horses from Central Asia, fruit, silk, and porcelain from China, and textiles and spices from India.

In the middle of the seventeenth century Jahanara Begum, daughter of the fifth Mughal emperor, Shāh Jahān, developed a caravansary and a mosque on a site called Gor Khatri at the end of Sethi Street. In earlier times Gor Khatri was the location of the Tower of Buddha's Bowl, where the sacred alms bowl was kept. After that it became sacred to Hindus; it may have been either a site for funeral sacrifices or for the training of practitioners of the yoga philosophy. The Mughals, however, gave the area an Islamic character. The caravansary and mosque have been destroyed, but an imposing gateway to the caravansary still stands. The street takes its name from the Sethi family, wealthy merchants involved in much of the trade that went through Peshāwar. Many of their descendants still live on the street in impressive houses that feature elaborate balconies and intricately carved wooden doors.

Another Mughal construction in Peshāwar is the Mahābat Khān Mosque, constructed by and named for Mahābat Khān, governor or Peshāwar during the reigns of Shāh Jahān and his successor, ʿĀlamgīr (Aurangzeb). The white mosque is similar in design to the Bādshāhī Masjid at Lahore, although it is smaller. With excellent proportions, twin minarets, and an ornate prayer hall, it is a great example of Mughal architecture. It was damaged severely in a fire in 1898 but was rebuilt faithfully.

Despite the Mughals' best efforts to maintain their hold on Peshāwar, its remoteness from their centers of power made this difficult at best. The empire as a whole also was beginning to weaken during the reign of ʿĀlamgīr, the last great Mughal, in the late seventeenth century. He lost Peshāwar to a popular uprising inspired by the poet-warrior Khushal Khān Khattak. Then after ʿĀlamgīr's death in 1707, the Afghans won control of the area. In 1799 the Afghan ruler Zamat Shāh made a young Sikh named Ranjit Singh governor of Lahore. Ranjit Singh, who became known as the Lion of the Punjab, went on to win control of numerous other cities, capturing Peshāwar in 1823. He destroyed Bābur's fort and the Shālīmār Gardens, later building a mud fort on the site. He also demolished the mosque at Gor Khatri and replaced it with Sikh temples, which still exist. His administrators found another use for the Mahābat Khān Mosque; they are said to have hanged condemned men from the minarets.

The Sikh hold on the region was extremely tenuous, and after Ranjit Singh's death in 1839 a period of anarchy ensued. The Sikh army invaded nearby British-held territory in 1846, in the First Sikh War, but was driven back. The Second Sikh War broke out in 1849, with the British victorious once more, and they annexed Peshāwar and the surrounding area. The British had been eager to use the region as a buffer against possible invasion by Russia and had sent emissaries to Peshāwar as early as 1809. The British set up their cantonment in an area where their troops had camped in 1848–49, just west of the walled old city of Peshāwar. The cantonment was a self-contained community of government buildings, schools, homes, churches, and clubs along wide, tree-shaded streets. Notable buildings that still stand include St. John's Church, the oldest in Peshāwar, constructed between 1851 and 1860; Edwardes College, dating to 1855; and All Saints Church, built in 1883. A rail line and train station were built between the cantonment and the old city. Within the old city, the British rebuilt the Bālā Hisār fort in brick.

In 1893 the establishment of the Durand Line, dividing British India from Afghanistan, created serious problems between the British and the area's Pathan tribes because the line cut through Pathan lands. Seeing the British as a threat to their independence, the Pathans engaged in a series of revolts beginning in 1897. As a result, Lord Curzon, the British governor general, set up a separate North-West Frontier province, administered from Peshāwar, in 1901. The British administrators gave the Pathans and other area tribes a measure of autonomy, but tribal uprisings continued as late as 1937.

Another development of the early twentieth century was the establishment of Islamia College and Collegiate School, predecessor to the University of Peshāwar, a few miles west of the old city in 1913. Today this area, known as the university town, has a large residential section surrounding the university and its affiliated institutions.

In 1947 British India was divided into the two independent nations of India and Pakistan, with Peshāwar becoming part of Pakistan. In the 1950s and 1960s the North-West Frontier province continued to be the site of skirmishes with the Pathans, who desired a nation of their own. Since then the government of Pakistan has courted the Pathans with educational and agricultural assistance and has attempted to encourage them to abandon their nomadic existence for a more settled life.

The Soviet Union's invasion of Afghanistan in 1979 led to a flood of 3.5 million Afghan refugees into Pakistan. The North-West Frontier province, especially Peshāwar, absorbed the majority of the refugees. Many of them have taken service jobs and settled more or less permanently in Peshāwar. Peshāwar also became a center for war relief agencies, operated mainly by Westerners; by 1988 there were seventy-nine such agencies in the city. Even more refugees arrived from Afghanistan after earthquakes in 1991 and 1992. Only a few of the Afghans have returned to their country since the Soviet military withdrawal in 1989 and the installation of a new government in 1992.

Peshāwar today is a bustling city with a diversified economy. The manufacture of textiles, leather goods, carpets, and other products is important, as is, of course, the state government. Foreign merchants continue to be a presence in Peshāwar, selling their goods at the city's many lively bazaars. Little remains of the city walls, but the Bālā Hisār fortress still stands. Unlike some historic forts in this part of the world, it is not a museum; it is a base for the Pakistani army and is not open to the public. Many other reminders of Peshāwar's past are open to public view, however. The mix of Buddhist, Hindu, Muslim, and Sikh religious monuments, the bazaars, the British colonial buildings, and the modern structures of the university area provide evidence of the many and varied influences that have been at work during Peshāwar's long history.

Further Reading: R. E. M. Wheeler's *Five Thousand Years of Pakistan: An Archaeological Outline* (London: C. Johnson, 1950) is particularly useful. Also, as Pakistan once was part of India, Vincent A. Smith's *The Oxford History of India: From the Earliest Times to the End of 1911* (Oxford: Clarendon Press, 1919; fourth edition, edited by Percival Spear, New York and Oxford: Oxford University Press, 1981) contains most of the basic information on Pakistan's history. One of the better travel guides is *Pakistan: A Travel Survival Kit* by John King and David St. Vincent (fourth edition, Hawthorn, Victoria, and London: Lonely Planet, 1993).

—Claudia Levi and Trudy Ring

Pitcairn Island (Pitcairn Islands)

Location: A small volcanic island in the South Pacific Ocean, approximately 1,350 miles east-southeast of Tahiti and 3,300 miles east-northeast of Auckland, just off the most direct sea route between New Zealand and the Panama Canal, which lies 4,100 miles to the northeast.

Description: Discovered and named by Commander Philip Carteret of the British navy in 1767. First settled as a hideout by Fletcher Christian and the *Bounty* mutineers in 1790. A unique Anglo-Polynesian community arose from the mutineers' intermarriage with the Tahitian women who accompanied them. For almost twenty years, the Pitcairn community remained unknown to the outside world. Thereafter it enjoyed considerable romantic acclaim because of its origins and the admirable nature of the community that had emerged after a macabre beginning. Pitcairn, along with the other islands in the Pitcairn group, has been a British colony since 1838 and is still populated by descendants of the *Bounty* mutineers. The population reached around 200 just before World War II, but there has been a rapid decline in population since then.

Contact: The Secretary, Island Council, Pitcairn
c/o The Commissioner for Pitcairn
British Consulate General
Auckland
New Zealand

Pitcairn's discovery was the direct result of a British policy "to make discovery of countries hitherto unknown," initiated by the Admiralty in 1763. In 1767 Commander Philip Carteret, cruising the South Seas in pursuit of this policy, sighted an uncharted island that, as he noted in his *Account of a Voyage Round the World,*

> appeared like a great rock rising out of the sea; it was not more than 5 miles in circumference and seemed to be uninhabited; it was however covered with trees and we saw a small stream of fresh water running down one side. . . . I would have landed but the surf rendered it impossible. . . . It is so high that we saw it at a distance of more than 15 leagues and it having been discovered by a young gentleman, son to Major Pitcairn, we called it Pitcairn's Island.

Carteret was the first navigator to put Pitcairn on the charts, but because of the prevailing "dark and hazy weather" and a faulty chronometer, his navigational fix was some degrees off. This error effectively assured Pitcairn of a further period of inviolability. A remote and tiny island with no safe access did not arouse Admiralty interest. These factors made Pitcairn the ideal hideaway for Fletcher Christian and his accomplices after their seizure of the *Bounty* in 1789.

The reasons for the mutiny have been endlessly dissected, although the proceedings of the court martial at Portsmouth in 1792 probably provide a more accurate account of the event than anything published later. In particular the two MGM films on the mutiny, which probably reached a wider audience than all the books combined, have firmly displaced fact with mythology, depicting Captain William Bligh as a savage tyrant and Master's Mate Fletcher Christian's mutineers as men driven beyond endurance. Little of this accords with the truth. Bligh was an inflexible commander and superb seaman, who was unusually sparing of punishment but had a sailor's command of invective. Christian and his followers were enraptured by their long idyll ashore in Tahiti and were tempted to desert duty in favor of an easy tropical life with the pleasures offered by Polynesian women. When the mutineers set Bligh adrift with eighteen loyal seamen in an open twenty-three-foot launch, he managed to navigate them 3,618 miles to Timor and safety in forty-one days. Despite starvation rations, only one man died—killed by natives at Tofua. Christian's mutineers made for themselves a very different fate: over the next decade all but one died in internecine savagery on Pitcairn. The island's early history was tragic. Pitcairn only became fashionably romantic later, after the emergence of a unique Anglo-Polynesian community.

In the immediate aftermath of the mutiny, Christian had no firm plan other than to escape the navy's retribution. He was the undisputed leader because he alone was capable of navigation and command at sea. Many of those who remained aboard the *Bounty* after the mutiny were in fact opposed to it, and according to the bosun's mate, Morrison, a plot to retake the ship was suspected. All arms were kept in the custody of active mutineers, while Christian began the search for a refuge. First they tried Tubuaï, within a week's sailing of Tahiti. They met with a fierce reception from the indigenous population, a dozen of whom died in the battle of "Bloody Bay." The attempt at settlement was abandoned after four months, when increasing native hostility and the collapse of discipline among the seamen led to a final return to Tahiti. Determined to quit the *Bounty*, the majority of the crew disembarked, leaving only nine mutineers out of an original twenty-five.

On September 23, 1789, five months after the mutiny, the *Bounty* left Tahiti for the last time. It was sound and well provisioned. In addition to Christian and his men, there were six volunteer Polynesian men, nine Polynesian women, and one baby on board. Christian renewed the search for an

Landing jetty, Pitcairn Island
Photo courtesy of the Office of the Governor of Pitcairn, Henderson, Ducie, and Oeno Island

isolated and preferably uncharted and uninhabited island capable of supporting a small community. Initially they headed west, touching on Raratonga (where, tradition holds, the *Bounty* introduced the orange). This visit was cut short when a mutineer shot a friendly native. Continuing west, the *Bounty* touched on the Friendly Islands (Tonga) and the Fijian group, but after eight weeks of fruitless cruising Christian turned about. He had presumably found Carteret's report of Pitcairn's Island, which was mentioned in *Hawkesworth's Voyages*. Two more months passed before the mutineers sighted Pitcairn on January 12, 1790. Their first impressions accorded with Carteret's report. The sea was so rough that no landing could be attempted until three days later, when Christian led a reconnaissance party ashore.

According to mutineer John Adams (as recorded by Captain F. W. Beechey in 1825), Christian returned after two days "with a joyful expression . . . the Island exceeded his most sanguine hopes." It was fertile, temperate, rich in wild fruits and coconuts, but uninhabited and demonstrably barely accessible. In short, it was ideal for fugitives.

Disembarkation took place on the north side (as it still does), where the *Bounty* was run in close enough to make it fast to a tree near the shoreline. Everything movable was carried ashore and the sails were used as tents for a temporary camp above the landing place. Then the mutineers debated the ship's fate. It would be visible from far out at sea: should it be destroyed or run aground and then stripped down? Mutineer Quintal recklessly set the *Bounty* on fire during the debate, and the ship was soon burned to the waterline. The die was now cast, and the date of the *Bounty's* burning, January 23, 1790, rather than that of landing, has since been kept as Pitcairn's major anniversary.

Initially the tiny settlement prospered. The tented encampment was replaced by a village of huts hidden by trees. The dogs the settlers had brought were killed, lest their barking should be heard at sea. Hogs, goats, and fowl were released to forage for themselves, and communal and individual cultivation areas were laid out. Not the least of the Pitcairners' luck was their inheritance of wild fruits and trees from unknown earlier settlers. As the island was explored, stone hatchets, roughly hewn images, and ancient burial places were discovered, but nothing to indicate any recent occupation or visit.

During the voyage from Tahiti, there were no reports of racial friction between the seamen and the six Polynesian men. The fact that every mutineer had his own woman, while

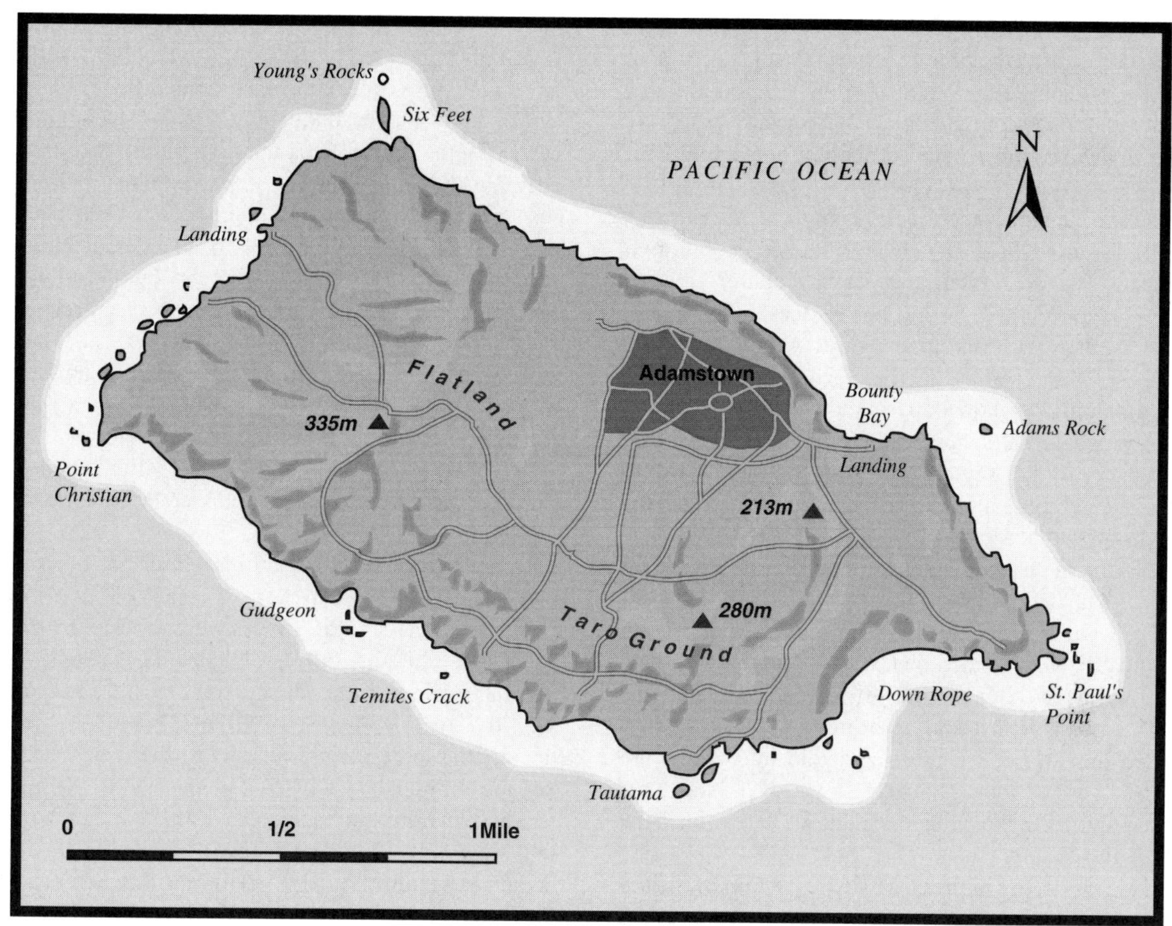

Pitcairn Island
Illustration by Tom Willcockson

six Polynesians shared three seems to have caused no jealousy—the arrangement accorded with Polynesian custom. But very soon the Polynesian men began to be treated as servants rather than equals, and when Christian divided up the land into permanent holdings he gave them none. Major trouble arose when the wife of mutineer Williams died and he demanded the wife of a Polynesian, Tararo. She was apparently willing and moved in with Williams, changing her name to Nancy. Outraged, Tararo and his fellows plotted to kill the whites. Their plot was betrayed by the women, and four of the six were rounded up. Tararo and another had fled. The four captives were offered pardon if they killed the fugitives. They accepted, and according to legend Nancy betrayed Tararo's hiding place. So the first blood was shed, Polynesian killing Polynesian, in 1791.

Meantime, the first "born Pitcairners" were arriving. Thursday October Christian was born in 1790, and soon several others followed. No children were born to the women living with the Polynesian men, who were increasingly maltreated. By 1793 the four Polynesians had had enough, but they kept their plans secret. Securing muskets, they shot Williams, Christian, and three others, leaving only four mutineers alive. Midshipmen Young and Adams were taken prisoner, while Quintal and McCoy hid in the bush. Then the Polynesian men fought over their choice of women among the new widows. Two were killed before the women took a hand and successfully conspired with Young and Adams to kill the other two. Within four years, eleven of the fifteen men who had landed from the *Bounty* had been killed. The four white seamen then divided the community among their households.

An underlying tension continued for years. Several women wanted to leave the island, so the seamen built them a boat, but (in Young's phrase) "according to expectation, she upset" when launched. Subsequently, a conspiracy against the men was thwarted, but apart from dire threats no retribution was taken. Now there was a respite until McCoy and Quintal began distilling spirits in 1797. Both became addicted and violent, McCoy throwing himself off a cliff. Quintal continued unrestrained, and after his wife died he demanded Arabella, Christian's widow. Young, her protector, refused, and when threatened by Quintal decided to strike first, helped by Adams. They axed Quintal to death while he was drunk.

By the turn of the century the Pitcairn population consisted of two white men, nine Polynesian women, and twenty children. Young was in bad health and spent some time before his death in 1800 helping Adams to improve his reading skills. He used the *Bounty* Bible and a prayer book as texts. It was probably the combination of religion and raw spirits (for Adams continued to drink) that caused him to have a "vision" of the Archangel Michael about to attack him. This fright wrought a fundamental change in Adams: he became devoutly Christian and tried, as best he knew, to lead his tiny community toward virtue. The children looked upon him as their father. As the island patriarch, he held church services on Sundays and decreed fasting on Wednesdays and Fridays—the Wednesday fasts arising from Adams' confused recollection of Ash Wednesday. For the first time Pitcairn achieved tranquillity, still in total isolation. Though ships had been sighted occasionally, none had tried to land. The subsequent discovery of the Anglo-Polynesian community would astonish—and delight—a world that had almost forgotten the *Bounty's* disappearance.

The first to discover and admire what now existed on Pitcairn was Mayhew Folger, an American skipper, on February 6, 1808. On sighting the island, he deduced that it could only be Pitcairn, as described by Carteret. He was surprised to see a Tahitian-style canoe put off toward him from the supposedly uninhabited island, even more so when the natives hailed him in good English and told him they were Englishmen. Their leader, Thursday October Christian, explained enough to make Folger realize he had solved the mystery of the *Bounty*. Ashore, he met "our father" (John Adams) and was deeply impressed by what he found. His log relates, "to do them justice, I think them a very humane and hospitable people, and whatever may have been the errors or crimes of the mutineer [Adams] in times back, he is at present in my opinion a worthy man."

Folger reported his discovery to the British navy within the year and again in 1813 but apparently evoked no interest. Nothing more happened until late in 1814, when two British frigates hove to off Pitcairn and were puzzled, according to Captain Pipon, "as in all the charts in our possession there was no land laid down in or near this longitude." Folger's reports had clearly not been circulated to the fleet. Like Folger, the British captains were soon enlightened by the appearance of Thursday October, "a tall fine young man about six feet high with dark black hair and a countenance extremely open and interesting." When they went ashore, the island community was apprehensive, fearing the warships had come to remove their "father." They were entirely mistaken; the captains had no such intention. Pipon recorded, "it would have been an act of great cruelty and inhumanity to have taken him from his family," while Captain Staines referred to Adams's "exemplary conduct and fatherly care of the whole of the little colony." The charts now being corrected and Pitcairn properly located, ships' visits increased. Jenny, a Polynesian woman who had originally been mate to Adams on Tahiti, traveled there in 1817, and it was from her, as well as from Adams, that the oral record of the aftermath of the mutiny and the first decade of bloodshed on Pitcairn was derived.

Visitors to the island in these early decades were favorably impressed by the rising generation, describing them as of good physique, copper-colored but with European features. Almost everybody remarked on their courtesy and piety. By the early 1820s the community had grown above fifty, and Adams began to worry about outstripping Pitcairn's resources. In 1825, when Captain F. W. Beechey arrived and recorded Adams's full statement of all that had occurred, Adams confided his fears of overpopulation and sought British assistance in moving the Pitcairners to a place where their future would be secure. Beechey's report stimulated a flurry of activity in London. Enquiries were made among colonial authorities and overseas missionaries to find a suitable spot for relocation. In 1829 arrangements were made to resettle the community on Tahiti, and in 1831, after Adams's death, a British transport arrived to transfer those Pitcairners who wished to go to Tahiti.

The migration to Tahiti in March 1831 proved a complete disaster. From the very moment of their arrival, the young and innocent Pitcairners were shocked by the amorality of the Tahitians. In R. B. Nicolson's account, "About 50 Tahitian women came aboard [on arrival] and their actions with the men . . . both on deck and below, were enough to decide [the Pitcairners] future there and then." They landed, and the Tahitian queen offered them a handsome tract of land and help in building houses. Nevertheless, they were acutely unhappy, and when they began to fall ill with fever they decided to return. Pitcairn's purer air did not cure the fever, however. Between March and November, sixteen of the eighty-seven Pitcairners who had gone to Tahiti died of the fever, including Thursday October Christian and Edward Young, son of Midshipman Young, who had succeeded Adams as Pitcairn's leader.

The experience of Tahiti left a lasting mark on the Pitcairners: a degree of confidence was lost, and without a proper leader the community fell for a while under the spell of a confidence trickster, Joshua Hill. He arrived on Pitcairn in October 1832, well aware of the migration disaster and purported to hold a commission from Britain "to adjust the internal affairs" of Pitcairn. This was a lie, but both the Pitcairners and the three resident Englishmen were initially deceived. In a short time, Hill gained the backing of the Quintal family, quarreled with and displaced the Englishmen, and assumed total authority as "President of the Commonwealth." Dissenters from his orders were given summary physical punishment, but his "reign of tyranny and oppression" eventually turned most islanders against him. British suspicions were aroused by the pretentious tenor of communications he sent them, and in 1837 Lord Edward Russell arrived to investigate. At a meeting of all the islanders, Hill was exposed as a charlatan and ordered to leave. Subsequently he addressed yet another memorandum to Britain demanding payment for his services.

The next year, 1838, Captain Russell Elliott reported that, to prevent future abuses, the Pitcairners wished to establish some form of authority with legal status on the island.

Visiting ships' crews sometimes badly misbehaved on Pitcairn, denying that it was under British protection, "as they had neither colours nor written authority." Hill had amply demonstrated the damage that even one individual could do when there was no acknowledged authority. Elliott therefore decided to confer "the stamp of authority on their election of a magistrate or elder, to be periodically chosen from among themselves . . . and answering to Her Majesty's Government." On November 28, 1838, an election was held, and the choice for chief magistrate was Edward Quintal, recently Hill's lieutenant. The vote was given to all island-born Pitcairners of eighteen years or older, male and female, putting Pitcairn in the forefront in recognizing women's rights. The date of the election has since been regarded as that on which Pitcairn became a British colony. Ten "Laws and Regulations" reflecting unique island needs were promulgated. This generally progressive legislation made school attendance mandatory.

Elliott also recommended regular annual visits by British warships. The first such, in 1839, brought a Lieutenant Lowry, who recorded his impressions. He noted "some of the girls were very pretty and would be considered beauties in England"; that the islanders had barred distillation, "since when drunkenness has not been known"; and finally that "they seem aware that they are far better off and happier than the generality of mankind." He opined also that they were unlikely ever to migrate again. He was wrong. From the mid–1840s it was clear that the population would eventually rise beyond Pitcairn's capacity to sustain it, and there was widespread discussion of the options. Bitter memories of the Tahitian fiasco formed the undertone of the debate. One thing was certain: the Pitcairners wanted to stay under the British flag.

Matters came to a head in 1853. Population was approaching 200, and a drought had demonstrated the community's vulnerability to famine and disease. "In one week there were not more than ten persons capable of attending to their own wants—it was for some weeks actual starvation," reported Nobbs, the English island pastor. It became known that Norfolk Island was being vacated as a convict settlement, and in 1854 the British government indicated that it would facilitate transfer there, if the Pitcairners so wished. They were consulted in 1855, and a majority opted to migrate. When a naval transport arrived in 1856, all chose to leave. Conditions on Norfolk were promising: plenty of resources and facilities were available. But, predictably, many Pitcairners soon began to yearn nostalgically for home. Some professed dissatisfaction at not having sole rights over Norfolk, after finding that they came under the jurisdiction of New South Wales. They maintained that Norfolk had been "given to them alone" by Queen Victoria. But this was special pleading; they had asked to be relocated and had been given their own island under British protection. On Norfolk they had all they could reasonably ask. The great majority settled on Norfolk, where they have since prospered, but forty-two islanders eventually returned to repopulate Pitcairn. However, it proved difficult to rekindle the old Pitcairn spirit. Outside interest was waning, and few ships called. Those that did reported a deteriorating, disunited, and even lawless community.

A halt was called to this deterioration after the conversion of the whole Pitcairn community to Seventh Day Adventism in 1884. The virtues of religion, unity, and sobriety were regained, and slowly the population increased again, reaching its maximum (200) in 1936. Since World War II, however, there has been a constant decline. There are now far more Pitcairners in New Zealand than on Pitcairn.

In a census taken on December 20, 1994, the population stood at forty-four. That is no bigger a population than after the return from Norfolk, and it is noteworthy that eleven of the forty-four are older than sixty-five. Despite the Adventist ban on liquor and stimulants, Pitcairn harbors a convivial and cheerful society with a great sense of community. The international sale of Pitcairn stamps organized through the Crown Agents provides financial stability. Revenue has also been obtained from the leasing of fishing rights within Pitcairn's 200-mile fisheries zone. These funds pay for the maintenance of the radio station and other public facilities. There is no taxation, and Pitcairners are paid, very modestly, for public work (to which all adult males are liable) and for elective public offices such as that of magistrate. Medical treatment has always been a problem for the islanders, and the Adventist pastor's wife is customarily a trained nurse. In recent years the governor's staff have tried to arrange for a succession of short-term medical officers, but the occasional tragedy still occurs when no one on the island is qualified to give treatment. All island families still possess and work on their inherited land holdings and participate in fishing from the two public diesel launches or their own boats. As seamen, the Pitcairners retain all the small boat skills of their ancestors.

In material terms, life on Pitcairn has much improved from the past. But the future of Pitcairn is not a matter of financial viability or of goodwill and generosity on the part of Britain. It depends entirely on the willingness of a sufficient number of able-bodied Pitcairners to stay on their island as residents, operating the boats and keeping vital public services functioning. The margin of safety in these respects is now very narrow indeed.

Permission to visit and reside temporarily on the island is granted only after approval by the island council and the commissioner. Settlement by non-Pitcairners is not permitted. Passengers from passing ships are sometimes allowed brief access to the island if weather and sea conditions permit. There is no other access than by sea.

Further Reading: *The Pitcairners* by R. B. Nicolson (Sydney: Angus and Robertson, 1965; London: Angus and Robertson, and New York: Tri-Ocean, 1966) gives an authoritative and comprehensive account from the mutiny up to the early 1960s. Largely derived from original sources, it carefully distinguishes fact from myth. *Pitcairn: Children of the Bounty* by Ian Ball (London: Gollancz, 1973; as *Pitcairn: Children of Mutiny*, Boston: Little Brown, 1973) provides a lively investigative account of the history of Pitcairn and vivid impressions of life on the island a generation ago. *Pitcairn's Island* by Charles Nordhoff and James Hall (Boston: Little Brown, 1934; London: Chapman and Hall, 1935) provides an engaging account of the first twenty years of settlement. *Fragile Paradise: The Discovery of Fletcher Christian, Bounty Mutineer* by Glynn Christian (Boston and Toronto: Little Brown, and London: Hamilton, 1982) is a pious work by a remote but direct descendent of Fletcher Christian with more imagination than verification in the history, but it also has useful recent information and excellent island photographs. *Mutiny on the Bounty: 1789-1989,* published in 1989 as a commentary by the British National Maritime Museum for its bicentenary exhibition, is sumptuously illustrated and has an admirable and scholarly text. Finally, *Hell and Paradise: The Norfolk-Bounty-Pitcairn Saga* by Peter Clarke (New York: Viking, 1986; London: Viking, 1987) gives a melodramatic account of both Pitcairn and Norfolk Islands. The illustrations are better than the text.

—Terence Daniel O'Leary

Plassey (West Bengal, India)

Location: Eighty-five miles north of Calcutta, east of the Bhagirathi River.

Description: Plassey was the site of the decisive victory of the British East India Company troops, headed by Robert Clive, over the army of the nabob of Bengal, Sirāj-ud-Dawlah, on June 23, 1757, which signaled the beginning of British dominance in Bengal.

Contact: Government of India Tourist Office
4 Shakespeare Sarani
Calcutta, West Bengal 700 001
India
(24) 21402, (24) 21475, or (24) 25813

Plassey, once known only as a favored hunting site of the eighteenth-century nabobs of Bengal, gained a place in history on June 23, 1757, as the site of the famous battle between the British forces and the army of the nabob of Bengal. The nabobs' loss at Plassey changed the face of India, marking both the beginning of British control in Bengal and the collapse of the Muslim Mughal Empire.

Mughal rule in India began in 1526 as the result of a successful military campaign by Bābur against the Delhi sultanate. Bābur was a descendant of both the Mongol invader Genghis Khan and the Turkic conqueror Timur (Tamerlane). The Mughals were skilled at war and politics; they also were great patrons of the arts and architecture. Their most famous construction is the Tāj Mahal at Āgra. The Mughal realm eventually covered almost all of northern and central India, and parts of the peninsular area in the south.

Mughal authority in India relied upon the peaceful coexistence of the Muslim and Hindu populations. The sixth and last great emperor of the Mughals, ʿĀlamgīr (Aurangzeb), who came to the throne in 1658, reversed this policy of tolerance and attempted to force Islam upon his Hindu subjects. By first forbidding the construction of new Hindu temples and eventually launching a campaign to destroy all Hindu places of worship and schools, ʿĀlamgīr incensed various Hindu nationalist groups, most notably the Marāṭhās, who ruled an independent kingdom centered on Mahārāshtra in southwestern India. The Marāṭhās, tiring of ʿĀlamgīr's proselytizing crusades, were finally pushed to the edge by his reinstatement in 1679 of the *jizya,* a poll-tax levied on all non-Muslim subjects, which had been banned for obvious political reasons by Emperor Akbar in 1564. Under the guidance of Śivājī, the founder of the Marāṭhā Kingdom, this group became the most powerful opponent to the Mughal Empire and also paved the way for European domination of India.

Weakened by the constant Marāṭhā invasions, the Mughals' realm became fragmented. The Mughal Empire, separated into provinces governed by a *subadār* or nabob, had now begun to rely upon each individual nabob as a ruler unto himself with his own army and taxation policies. These nabobs relied little upon support from Delhi, and the empire became weak as a result of division. The adage "divide and conquer" eventually became the battle cry of the European traders who set up shop in India, and the splintering of the Mughal Empire was their most deadly weapon.

By 1740, the Bengal region of India had come into the hands of Aliverdi Khan. Aliverdi, noted for his alleged usurpation of the Bengal nabobship from its patrilineal successor, controlled Bengal relatively without incident for sixteen years from his capital at Murshidābād. Indian and European historians alike portray Aliverdi as a competent and peace-loving ruler under whose aegis the British, French, and Dutch trading companies prospered for many years.

Initially, the British, unlike their competitors in European trade, deliberately removed themselves from native affairs and did not attempt to colonize the areas in which they conducted their business. However, when the constant invasions of Madras in southern India by the Marāṭhās began to threaten English commerce in that region, the British were compelled to intervene on behalf of the nabob of the Carnatic region. This interference in civil matters resulted in the British being plunged headlong into Indian affairs in other areas of the country, namely Bengal.

The British East India Company in Bengal was centered at Fort William in Calcutta. Since this settlement was closest to the mouth of the Hooghly River, the English at Calcutta clearly dominated the French settlements at Chandernagore and the small Dutch station at Chinsura. During the rule of the nabob Aliverdi, the Europeans were forbidden to fortify their settlements except to protect against the occasional Marāṭhā invasions. Despite the ongoing conflict between the French and the English in southern India—which was the result of the War of the Austrian Succession (1740–48)—the company's operations in Bengal remained undisturbed, under the strict guidance of the nabob.

The nabob Aliverdi Khan died in 1756. He left his young, obstinate grandson, Sirāj-ud-Dawlah, as heir to the position of nabob of Bengal. Sirāj-ud-Dawlah, threatened not only by the growing power of the English in Bengal but by conspiracy against him within his own court, had a disastrous reign that ended with his defeat at Plassey in 1757.

Sirāj-ud-Dawlah's estranged aunt, Ghasita Begum, began a conspiracy to keep her nephew from the throne. Ghasita involved some British military deserters and a leading noble, Mīr Jaʿfar, in her plan to oust Sirāj-ud-Dawlah. Her co-conspirators, however, all mistrusted one another, and the plot fell apart before it fairly began. Sirāj-ud-Dawlah sent emissaries to persuade Ghasita to surrender, which she did, beginning a series of events that led to Sirāj-ud-Dawlah's defeat at the Battle of Plassey. Ja'far, whose later actions played an important part in the British victory, was replaced as commander in chief, and the son of a co-conspirator, Krishna Das, fled to the protection of the English at Calcutta. (Krishna Das allegedly paid the exorbitant sum of 50,000 rupees for British protection.) When Sirāj-ud-Dawlah's demand for the return of the fugitive Das went unanswered, his abhorrence of the British was all but set in stone.

The English general of Calcutta, Roger Drake, also provoked the nabob's fury by ignoring his repeated demands to discontinue fortifications of Fort William. The nabob, wary of all Europeans, felt that could he be rid of the British in Bengal, the deposing of the French and Dutch would be a simple task. Sirāj-ud-Dawlah marched on Calcutta with 50,000 men on June 16, 1756. When Drake heard of the nabob's advance, he pleaded with the French at Chandernagore for help, arguing that to stand with the British against the nabob could also work to French advantage. The French, however, already having refused the nabob's request for assistance, remained neutral spectators.

The British at Fort William in Calcutta, despite their supposed re-fortifications, were miserably unprepared for battle. The fort was in a state of disrepair and their weaponry was outdated. Drake and other English leaders refused to believe that the nabob would dare to attack Calcutta; consequently, the British garrison was no match for the nabob's troops, which captured the fort and imprisoned a number of the surviving defenders in a small cell that became known as "The Black Hole of Calcutta." The number of British actually imprisoned has been a matter of dispute ever since, as has the number of those who died. Indian historians contend that Sirāj-ud-Dawlah had no knowledge of the decision to lock up the prisoners, but the British held him responsible nonetheless.

Sirāj-ud-Dawlah held Calcutta for nearly a year before the British retaliated. Although the "Black Hole" incident and the loss of the Calcutta factory were foremost in their minds, the British at Madras were dubious about taking revenge for this act owing to their ongoing conflict with France in Europe during the Seven Years War (1756–63). The retaking of Calcutta would require the British to remove ships from the Coromandel Coast of India, an area of the southern region off the Bay of Bengal that had seen much fighting between the French and British in recent years. Fortunately for the British, Robert Clive had recently returned to India from London where he had received accolades for his skill and leadership in the battles against the French in the Coromandel region. Clive's victory at Arcot turned the tide of war in favor of the British, and he soon set his sights on the situation in Bengal.

Robert Clive was the primary player in this drama involving the British and the Mughals in India. Clive's military skill and manipulative abilities sent the French governor of Pondicherry, Joseph-François Dupleix, back to France in ruins. Prior to the loss at Arcot, Dupleix had controlled the nabob of the Carnatic to the point where Dupleix himself actually ruled, with the nabob as his personal puppet. After the Battle of Plassey, Clive found himself in the same position, with one important difference: his "rule" of Bengal resulted in British dominance of India for the next century.

Sirāj-ud-Dawlah was incapable of holding Calcutta and controlling the rest of his domain simultaneously. The further weakening of Mughal rule in India, coupled with his incompetence as a leader, left him vulnerable to manipulation and blind to the treasonous activities of those who surrounded him. His former aide, Mīr Ja'far, covetous of the nabob's position, was laying the foundation of his usurpation of the throne by dealing in secret with both British and French delegates and recruiting powerful men in Calcutta to his cause by promises of money and position. These dealings did not escape Clive, who later would use Mīr Ja'far and his cohorts to take complete control of Bengal.

Clive and his army, consisting of 900 European soldiers and 1,500 sepoys, sailed toward Calcutta from Madras on October 16, 1757. The sepoys, native Indians trained in European military tactics, proved to be as useful to Clive in Bengal as they had been to the French in Madras. Clive and his army easily took Calcutta from the nabob on January 2, sending Sirāj-ud-Dawlah back to his capital at Murshidābād.

With the loss at Calcutta, the nabob restored to the British all company rights they had enjoyed under Aliverdi Khan. In addition, the nabob also agreed to pay for their losses at Calcutta and gave permission to the British to mint their own coins in Bengal, a privilege that even Aliverdi had not granted. These concessions to the British were not unalloyed, however, for Sirāj-ud-Dawlah had entered into a scheme with the wealthy merchant Omichand, who had once been a favorite of Aliverdi. The nabob had arranged for Clive's emissaries to meet with Bengali delegates in Omichand's orchard. Rightfully suspecting that the nabob had no intention of signing the treaty, the British left the orchard and reported to Clive. Clive, believing that the nabob's ruse was intended to relax the British military stance by persuading them that peace was imminent, immediately ordered an attack on the nabob's camp, situated twenty miles upriver from Calcutta; Sirāj-ud-Dawlah, beaten once again, signed the treaty on February 9, 1757.

Sirāj-ud-Dawlah immediately began to court the French at Chandernagore. Since war between Britain and France had been openly declared at home, the French and British were now enemies in the previously neutral Bengal region. The French had a capable force stationed less than 200 miles from Calcutta in the Northern Cicars, and the French station at Chandernagore was well fortified. Sirāj-ud-Dawlah, unsure of whose alliance he should cultivate, tried to position himself on good ground with both the French and British, all the while plotting revenge for his humiliation at Calcutta.

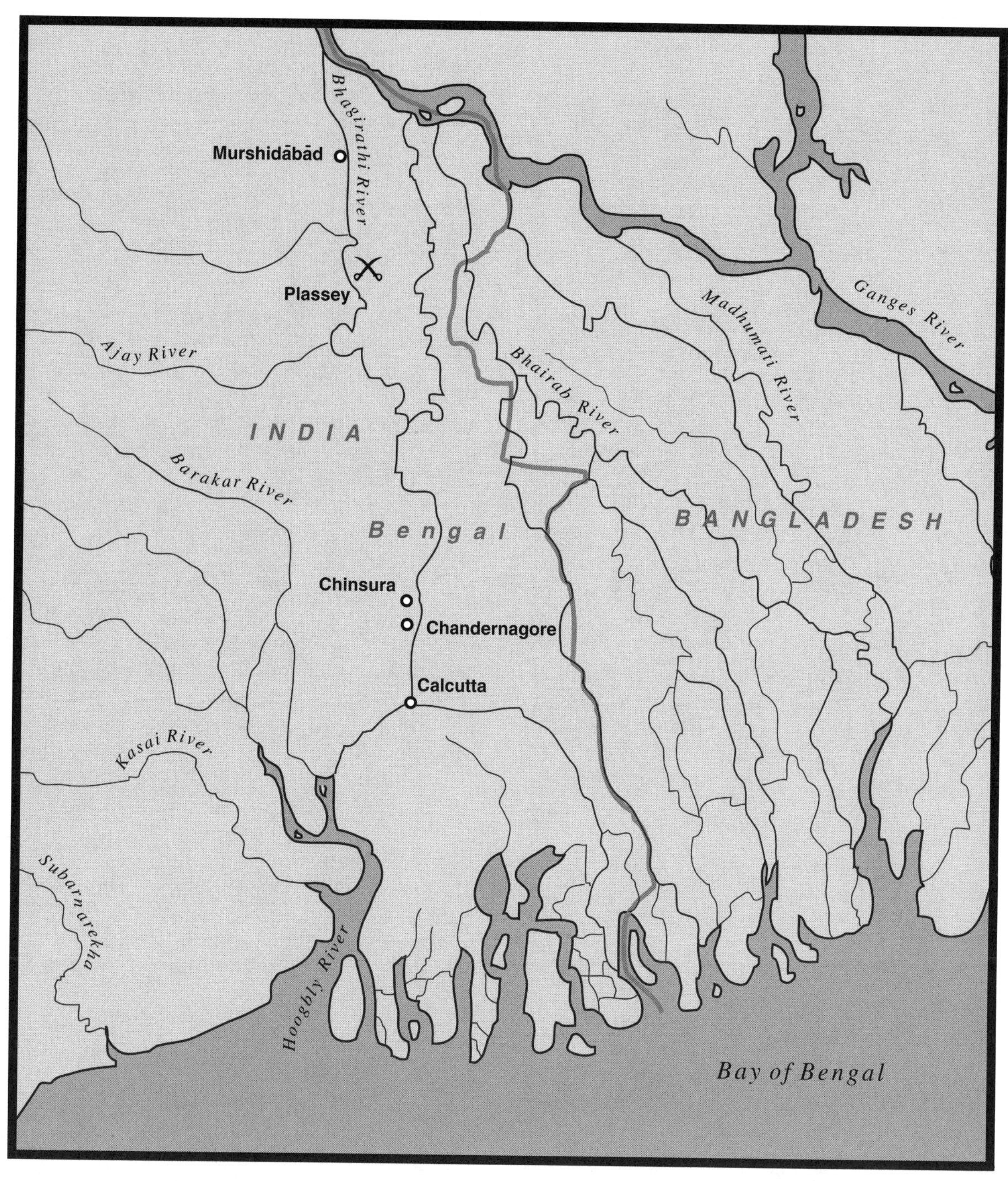

Regional map of Bengal, showing Plassey's position along the Bhagirathi River
Illustration by Tom Willcockson

These machinations by the nabob did not prove to be to his advantage, however. The Afghans had recently sacked the Mughal capital at Delhi, leaving Sirāj-ud-Dawlah without any protection. Forced to seek British aid, the nabob was easily manipulated by Clive, who asked his permission to attack the French stronghold at Chandernagore. Clive extracted an ambiguous answer from the nabob, which Clive then construed as acquiescence. The nabob's reluctance to intervene at this time worked to the advantage of the British. Not only was the attack on Chandernagore a success, but the nabob found himself completely without allies and therefore vulnerable to Clive's exploitation.

Ongoing intrigue at the court of Sirāj-ud-Dawlah further weakened the nabob's position. Omichand had entered into a scheme with the estranged nobles in Murshidābād. In exchange for a percentage of the large treasure rumored to be held at the capital of the nabob, Omichand would conduct the negotiations between the British and the conspirators. When the British committed themselves to take part in the conspiracy against the nabob, Omichand raised his stakes. He demanded from them an even larger commission, without which he would divulge the whole plot to Sirāj-ud-Dawlah. Mīr Ja'far, who would become nabob of Bengal after Sirāj-ud-Dawlah's ousting, agreed to this manipulation since he felt his position at this stage of the contest to be vulnerable.

Not allowing himself to be at anyone's mercy, Clive drafted two copies of the treaty with Mīr Ja'far. One copy, called the "red treaty," included the commission that Omichand demanded; the "real" document did not. Clive's actions in securing the appropriate signatures on these two treaties raised questions about his character for many years to come. Admiral Charles Watson of Calcutta, without whose signature the treaties would be invalid, refused to sign the fictitious document and thereby participate in duping Omichand. Unwilling to let the game stop there, Clive forged Watson's signature to the treaties.

The treaty with Mīr Ja'far included continuance of all privileges granted previously by Sirāj-ud-Dawlah in the treaty of February 9, 1757. In addition to these demands, Mīr Ja'far agreed never to take up an offensive alliance against the British, to exclude the French from Bengal, to pay 500,000 rupees to the European inhabitants of Calcutta, to reimburse the company for its losses in that city in the sum of 1,000,000 rupees, and to make other monetary and military compensations that left the new nabob virtually powerless.

With the two signed treaties in hand, Clive then wrote to Sirāj-ud-Dawlah on June 13, accusing him of breaking the treaty of February 9 by maintaining alliance with the French. Receiving no reply, Clive marched to the village of Plassey, where it was believed the nabob's army was stationed, on June 14. Mīr Ja'far, serving as military spy, had to this point informed the British of the nabob's army's movements. Yet now, for reasons unknown, Mīr Ja'far was suddenly silent; perhaps he had decided to betray Clive as he had the nabob. Unsure of how to proceed, Clive halted his army some fifteen miles outside of Plassey to await word from Mīr Ja'far.

The last correspondence from Mīr Ja'far arrived on June 22 telling Clive that the nabob's army had positioned itself in Muncarra, a village outside Plassey. Upon his arrival at Plassey, Clive learned that the nabob's troops had in fact advanced and were only three miles outside of the groves that bordered Plassey. Clive's army entered the village and took the nabob of Bengal's hunting lodge, "Plassey House," as his headquarters. The nabob had positioned his army about one mile from the British location, and both sides waited until daybreak of June 23.

Although quite out of character, Clive's anxiety over Mīr Ja'far's silence was understandable. Unaccustomed to relying upon the actions of other men to govern his own, Clive began to plan his battle strategy with fewer men than he had previously thought available to him. Mīr Ja'far, as an officer of Sirāj-ud-Dawlah's army, had led his troops to Plassey along with those of other conspirators in the army. He and Clive had planned to turn the nabob's own army against him at the crucial point of the battle, thus guaranteeing victory. Mīr Ja'far, however, was in a situation that did not allow him freedom of correspondence, so Clive became fully aware that the British could very well lose this battle.

Sirāj-ud-Dawlah's army numbered 50,000 men. Although these troops were for the most part inexperienced, the nabob was armed with heavy artillery. A battalion of French forces also stood ready to battle the British. Clive's forces, unaccompanied by those of the Mughal dissenters, numbered only about 3,000 with little artillery. Clive had at one point consulted his officers and decided to delay the battle, but he soon changed his mind and marched on the nabob's forces without the aid of Mīr Ja'far.

Mir Ja'far, in the end, was unable to come to their aid. He attempted to advance his men to the side of the British, but the British, thinking Mīr Ja'far was attacking, opened fire, so Mīr Ja'far withdrew. The army of the nabob, although strong in number, was no match for the more sophisticated army of the British. The battle was little more than a skirmish, and the nabob's disorganized troops were defeated easily, having been demoralized by the quick retreat of Sirāj-ud-Dawlah, who fled to the palace at Murshidābād.

Clive's victory at the battle of Plassey marked the beginning of British dominance in Bengal. Mīr Ja'far—now holding the position of nabob—found himself beholden to Clive, not only for his failure on the battlefield at Plassey but for the inability to honor the treaty he had signed. Mīr Ja'far's son, Miran Beg, executed Sirāj-ud-Dawlah and paraded his corpse through the streets of Murshidābād to solidify the dominance of his father as the newly appointed nabob.

After the death of Sirāj-ud-Dawlah, the palace treasury was opened, much to the disappointment of Mīr Ja'far. The fortune held at Murshidābād was not nearly as large as had been claimed, and the new nabob began his reign deeply in debt to the British. The British, under Clive, were fully aware of the power they held in Bengal and fought to preserve it over the succeeding decades.

Robert Clive was appointed "Baron of Plassey" and became one of the richest and most highly regarded men in London, despite the "red treaty" scandal. Omichand, victim of the falsified treaty, is said to have gone mad from the shock; he died shortly thereafter. Omichand bequeathed most of his wealth, surprisingly, to charities in England. Mīr Ja'far continued to be the English puppet and nominal figurehead of the Bengal province until his death in 1765. He is known primarily in Indian history as a principal player in the collapse of the Mughal Dynasty in India.

The British East India Company continued to dominate the Bengal province, including the village of Plassey, until the British Crown assumed control over India in 1858. India finally became independent of England in 1947. Plassey faded into the relatively peaceful oblivion that it enjoyed prior to the events that had, for a short and disastrous time, thrust the little village into the spotlight of world history. Today the battlefield is marked by monuments, but the Bhagirati River has eroded much of the site.

Further Reading: Tapanmohan Chatterji's *The Road to Plassey* (Calcutta: Orient Longmans, 1960; London, Longmans Green, 1961) provides a descriptive narrative of the events leading to and immediately following the Battle of Plassey from an Indian point of view. Michael Edwardes's *Plassey: The Founding of an Empire* (New York: Taplinger, and London: Hamilton, 1969) gives an objective account of the rise of British dominance in India. Percival Spear's *The Oxford History of Modern India: 1740–1975* (Delhi and New York: Oxford University Press, 1978) is a well-written history of India. Patrick Turnbull's *Clive of India* (Folkestone: Bailey and Swinfen, 1975) is a thorough biography of Robert Clive.

—Denise Coté

Polonnaruwa (Sri Lanka)

Location: North Central Province, approximately eighty miles north-northeast of Colombo, on the southern edge of Sri Lanka's arid northern plains.

Description: The capital of Sri Lanka from approximately 993 until 1255, the last period in which the Sinhalese governed the entire island. Home to some of Sri Lanka's finest sculpture and architecture and modern-day site of some of its most impressive ruins. First city of the extraordinary twelfth-century king Parākramabāhu the Great.

Contact: Ceylon Tourist Board
78 Steuart Place
P. O. Box 1504
Colombo 3
Sri Lanka
(43) 7059 or (43) 7060

For several centuries prior to its establishment as the Sri Lankan capital in 993, Polonnaruwa was an important economic and political center. The city lies on the southern edge of the island's arid northern plains, a region settled and developed by Sinhalese from northern India beginning in the sixth or fifth century B.C. Theirs was an hydraulic culture; the ancient Sinhalese economy centered on an annual harvest of wet rice in a region that suffered unpredictable and sometimes severe droughts. Polonnaruwa became agriculturally viable in the late third century A.D., when King Mahāsena built the Minnēriya Reservoir just outside the city. Three hundred years later, King Aggabodhi I and his successor, Aggabodhi II, significantly expanded the irrigation network and, in turn, increased Polonnaruwa's agricultural importance.

Polonnaruwa became a political center in the late seventh century owing to its location. The capital city, Anuradhapura, lay approximately thirty-three miles to the northwest, inconveniently distant from the emerging agricultural market in Ruhuṇa, the southeastern province of ancient Sri Lanka. Polonnaruwa became an administrative midway, and a series of four kings ruled from there beginning in approximately 680. During the same period, increased trade with Arab and East Asian merchants who landed in port cities east of Polonnaruwa made the city an ideal site for markets and revenue collection.

At least two accounts exist concerning why and when the capital was transferred from Anuradhapura to Polonnaruwa. Each begins with Sinhalese involvement in the power struggle between three bellicose Hindu powers in southern India: the Pallava, the Pāṇḍya, and the Cōḷa. In the late seventh century, the Sinhalese king Mānavamma sided with the Pallavas against the Pāṇḍyas, for only with the aid of the former had he been able to assume the disputed Sri Lankan throne. The Pāṇḍyas proved the stronger force by the mid–ninth century, however, and soon turned their might against the Sinhalese. Aided by the Tamil population of Sri Lanka, they sacked Anuradhapura during the reign of King Sena I (ruled 833–853). The Pāṇḍyas soon withdrew, but only after extracting large war payments from the Sinhalese. According to one account, Sena I moved his capital to Polonnaruwa after the Pāṇḍyas exited the devastated Anuradhapura, and Polonnaruwa remained the capital from that time. A more common history dates the move to more than 100 years later, when the rival southern Indian kingdoms drew the Sinhalese into yet another round of battles.

During the tenth century, the Cōḷas overran Pallava and prepared to absorb Pāṇḍya, too. The Sinhalese, distraught at the prospect of Cōḷan hegemony over southern India and their own inevitable domination by such an aggressive power, allied with their old enemy, the Pāṇḍyas. Sinhalese forces fought against the Cōḷas on the mainland but were defeated soundly. The Pāṇḍyan king fled to Sri Lanka, and the Cōḷas pursued. For years, the Cōḷas' tactic was to disrupt any troop movements in Sri Lanka before opponents could become well organized, which they accomplished through sporadic but destructive forays onto the island.

In 993 the Cōḷa king Rājarāja (ruled 985–1014) changed policy and attacked the island with the intention of ruling. He succeeded in capturing the northern plains, making the Sinhalese heartland of Rājarata (King's Country) a province of Cōḷa under the direct authority of his monarchy. The second history of Polonnaruwa contends that Rājarāja moved the capital to Polonnaruwa for military reasons. Anuradhapura was vulnerable to attack from the north by Pāṇḍyas from the mainland and from the south by rebel Sinhalese. Polonnaruwa, however, was protected by distance from the northern coast, where foreign troops would land, and by a river against Sinhalese armies approaching from Ruhuṇa.

The Cōḷas have been credited with introducing Hindu influences to Sri Lankan culture and architecture. Most obviously, stone was used increasingly to build religious structures. The Siva Devale No. 2, the oldest surviving monument in Polonnaruwa, in fact is built entirely of stone, a small version of the grander Cōḷan constructions on the mainland. The walls of the Temple of the Tooth Relic at Polonnaruwa feature a similarly monumental use of stone. On the other hand, the only sizable group of paintings to have survived from the same period, those in the Tivanka image house, were executed in the older Ajanta tradition of India; the Cōḷans seem to have had little stylistic influence on Sri Lankan art of the Polonnaruwa Period.

Rājarāja's son Rājendra (ruled 1014–44) assumed the Cōḷan monarchy in 1014 and soon began a military campaign

The Gal Vihara, Polonnaruwa
Photo courtesy of Mr. Herath Navaratne, Information Officer, Embassy of Sri Lanka, Washington, D.C.

to control all of Sri Lanka. His forces ventured into Ruhuṇa and captured the Sinhalese royal family and treasure in 1017. The Sinhalese king, Mahinda V, remained a prisoner in southern India until his death twelve years later. Ruhuṇa quickly won back its independence, but the Sinhalese kingdom was thrown into another period of political strife during which a host of noblemen disputed rights to the throne. Cōḷan raiders exacerbated the situation by killing at least two Sinhalese headmen who had amassed considerable support in their respective bids for the monarchy.

Prince Kitti, who was born in Ruhuṇa in 1039, managed to defeat numerous rivals and pretenders by the age of fifteen, and at sixteen he was crowned sub-king and renamed Vijayabāhu. Developing into a strong military leader, Vijayabāhu fought a lengthy but effective war of attrition against the Cōḷas. He stood little chance of liberating his people, however, until political and military events on the Indian mainland worked in his favor.

In the 1060s the Cōḷan Kingdom suffered both from internal disputes and from losses to Pāṇḍya. Cōḷa's King Kulottuṅga, more interested in retaining power at home than in exerting control over Sri Lanka, committed few troops to the battle against Vijayabāhu's persistent rebels. In 1066 Vijayabāhu launched a two-pronged attack on the Cōḷas and managed to recapture Polonnaruwa. His depleted army was insufficient to defend against a counterattack, however, and Vijayabāhu cautiously retreated. He recouped his strength in coming years, while Kulottuṅga denied reinforcements to his own battalions in Sri Lanka. In 1070 Vijayabāhu won a second great battle and finally expelled the southern Indian interlopers.

Following two years spent suppressing a rebellion, Vijayabāhu was crowned king of all Sri Lanka in 1072 or 1073. He immediately began a long, prosperous period of rebuilding the kingdom, for it had disintegrated badly under Cōḷan rule. He resolved political rivalries, repaired waterworks, and restored the Buddhist order. Unfortunately, few specifics are known about Vijayabāhu's building projects in Polonnaruwa. He definitely repaired a section of the Alahara Canal, a conduit for water from the Minnēriya Reservoir, and he built a temple for the esteemed Tooth Relic, a tooth supposed to have belonged to the Buddha, which made its way to Sri Lanka from India in the fourth century A.D.

Vijayabāhu left no obvious heir upon his death after forty years as king of the unified Sri Lanka, and the country again lapsed into a period of infighting and degradation. The island was divided among four powers: despite the nominal regency of Vijayabāhu's brother Jayabāhu over the so-called

King's Country in the northern plains, the real power there resided with the Kaliṅgan prince Vikramābāhu, who ruled from Polonnaruwa; the Southern Country was controlled by Vijayabāhu's nephew Manabharana, and Ruhuṇa was split between Manabharana's brothers, Siri Vallabha and Kitti Sirimegha.

After approximately twenty-two years of such an arrangement, the young Prince Parākramabāhu of the Southern Country befriended Gajabāhu II, the son of Vikramābāhu who now ruled the King's Country. Parākramabāhu managed to make himself an invited guest in the Polonnaruwa palace, but he had expansionist ambitions and surreptitiously intrigued with Gajabāhu's subjects. Once Parākramabāhu had succeeded his own father as ruler of the Southern Country, he stormed Polonnaruwa and captured Gajabāhu.

Manabharana of Ruhuṇa—Siri Vallabha's son and Parākramabāhu's cousin—defended Gajabāhu in order to prevent Parākramabāhu from becoming too powerful and succeeded in staving off the latter. However, the young Manabharana imposed his authority so severely on those he had liberated that Gajabāhu actually asked Parākramabāhu for aid against him. Parākramabāhu survived the open warfare that followed, while his two rivals fell from power.

In 1153 Parākramabāhu was crowned king of all Sri Lanka, and he declared Polonnaruwa his capital. Parākramabāhu retained the throne for thirty-three years, but his authority often was challenged, especially by rebellious factions in Ruhuṇa. To maintain power, he centralized and magnified the authority of the monarchy. This change, in conflict with a long tradition of permitting Sri Lankan chiefs considerable autonomy, eventually proved destructive to the country.

Despite the fact that Parākramabāhu's totalitarian governance eventually harmed his people, he is remembered for the astounding number and quality of building projects he oversaw in Sri Lanka, as well as for rebuilding the social, political, and religious structures of the community. He accomplished so much under such difficult conditions that the historian E. Ludowyk compares Parākramabāhu's genius of leadership with that of Russia's Peter the Great. Parākramabāhu's great insight was to act on the fact that in the hydraulic culture of the Sinhalese, political and economic strength derived from the waterworks. His wisdom is noted in the *Cūlavaṃsa*, a chronicle kept by Buddhist monks in which Parākramabāhu shines as the greatest hero. There the king is quoted: "Truly in such a country not even a little water that comes from the rain must flow into the ocean without being made useful to man." During his reign, Parākramabāhu oversaw the renovation or construction of 165 dams, 3,910 canals, and 2,539 reservoirs.

Parākramabāhu's projects in Polonnaruwa rank among the most ambitious and impressive in Sri Lanka's history. The king modeled his earthly city according to his vision of the heavenly city ruled by Śakra, king of the gods. The capital was enclosed by a rectangular wall with fourteen gates, each named for a mythical Buddhist figure. Inside the wall was a rectilinear latticework of streets running north-south and east-west. At the southern end of the city stood the king's enclosure and his island park, which he named Nandana after Śakra's own divine garden. To the north and west lay a pleasure garden and various temples.

Parākramabāhu built for himself a seven-story palace with 1,000 rooms, of which three stories of brick wall survive. Hundreds of ornate pillars and golden bells decorated the palace; according to Parākramabāhu's monks, the clusters of pearls suspended in the king's sleeping quarters reflected the moonlight like the river Ganges. Artisans trained in the same Indian tradition that produced the famous cave paintings of Ajanta and Bāgh painted the palace colorfully, along with many of the religious buildings in Polonnaruwa. A smattering of their work—depicting deities, kings, and noblemen in elaborately detailed costumes—still adorns the ruins of Polonnaruwa; the walls of the Tivanka image house preserve the style better than any other site on the island.

The Gal Vihara may have been Parākramabāhu's finest artistic venture. Four images of the Buddha—carved from a single, massive slab of granite—represent his three main positions: seated (two variations), standing, and reclining. Originally, each statue occupied its own enclosure, but today they form an outdoor ensemble. The forty-six-foot-long reclining figure is the most famous of the images; its exceptional quality led the eminent Sri Lankan historian K. M. De Silva to note: "The consummate skill with which the peace of the enlightenment has been depicted, in an extraordinarily successful blend of serenity and strength, has seldom been equaled by any other Buddha image in Sri Lanka."

The Parākrama Samudra (Sea of Parākrama), the largest reservoir ever built in ancient Sri Lanka, undoubtedly rates as Parākramabāhu's greatest construction. The reservoir's embankment, averaging forty feet in height and more than eight miles long, incorporated stone blocks weighing more than ten tons apiece. The Aṅgamadilla Canal filled the reservoir from the south, and the Alahara irrigation system continued to the north. In addition to its practical function, the reservoir complex carries cosmological significance as an evocation of the mythical Ocean of Milk at the foot of Mount Meru, home of the gods.

Unfortunately, while Parākramabāhu's great feats produced a beautiful city, his excessive spending on irrigation networks, temples, and a variety of overseas ventures financially drained the kingdom. When he died in 1186, the kingdom began a decline from which it never recovered. Just one year after assuming power, Parākramabāhu's successor was killed by a rival. Then Parākramabāhu's son-in-law, Nissaṅka Malla, defeated that rival and took tenuous control of the kingdom. The new king was linked ancestrally to the Kaliṅga, a Hindu enemy of the Sinhalese from the mainland.

During his nine-year reign (1187–96), Nissaṅka Malla continued Parākramabāhu's tradition of building, although he accomplished far less. He oversaw the construction of the largest *dagaba* (the Sri Lankan form of the Indian Buddhist stupa) to be erected in Sri Lanka since the third century. He created the Great Quadrangle, an ensemble of temples that the art historian Benjamin Rowland has described as one of the "most beautiful and satisfyingly proportioned buildings in the entire Indian world." The Nissaṅka-lata-maṇḍapa pavilion features granite columns sinuously carved to resemble lotus stems capped with unfolding buds.

Nissaṅka Malla apparently modified the *vatadage* (Circular Relic House), an elaborate and important temple used for rituals involving the Tooth Relic, which was protected by brick walls fifteen feet high. In his time, the base of the *vatadage* comprised layered platforms, the lowest and largest of which was approximately 120 feet in diameter. Following tradition, a moonstone slab graced the foot of the entrance, and from it rose an elaborate staircase leading past two sets of pillars to the *dagaba* itself. Inside, images of the seated Buddha faced each of four doorways at the cardinal points of the circular space.

After Nissaṅka Malla died of unknown causes, Sri Lanka fell into a state of political disarray far worse than any that had come before. The throne passed to the infant king Dharmasoka, but he was killed by his own father, Anikanga, who arrived with an invading force from Cōḷa. Anikanga ruled for only seventeen days before a local general installed Parākramabāhu's widow on the throne. After she was ousted and then returned to power, Parākramapāṇḍya, a Pāṇḍyan with enough legitimate claim to the Sinhalese throne to stay in power for three years, permanently deposed her.

The last king to rule at Polonnaruwa was Māgha, a south Indian of Kaliṅgan lineage who had familial ties to Nissaṅka Malla. Māgha's rule destroyed Polonnaruwa. An intolerant Hindu, he allowed the capital's Buddhist temples and monasteries to fall into disrepair, and soon Polonnaruwa's monks dispersed to other sites in southern Sri Lanka and abroad. In short order, Māgha essentially liquidated the kingdom, distributing its wealth among favored Kaliṅgans. After Māgha's death in 1255, raiders from southern India pillaged the city ever more frequently. King Vijayabāhu IV made some effort to restore the city during his rule from 1271 to 1273 but without lasting effect. Gradually, the Sinhalese abandoned Polonnaruwa as they began their historic migration into the forested hills to the southwest and to the far coast beyond. The fall of Polonnaruwa brought to an end more than 1,500 years of Sinhalese control of Sri Lanka.

The death of Nissaṅka Malla, the disastrous policies of Māgha, as well as the intrusion of south Indian political figures onto the Sri Lankan scene, thrust the kingdom of Polonnaruwa into political uncertainty. Kaliṅgan and Pāṇḍyan rulers with political ties to the south Indian kingdoms preyed upon this instability to assume power in Rājarata (northern Sri Lanka), the area previously held by the Sinhalese dominated Polonnaruwa Kingdom. The imposition of non-Sinhalese rule on this area by various dynastic factions compelled members of the traditional Sinhalese ruling class to abandon Polonnaruwa and move toward centers of Sinhalese power in the southwestern part of the island. This division of the island, with Tamil forces to the north and Sinhalese to the south, continues to be a part of contemporary Sri Lanka's volatile ethnic geography. Even though south Indian forces had firmly established themselves in the area previously belonging to the Polonnaruwa Kingdom, various Sinhalese rulers made efforts to regain their historical territory, including Polonnaruwa itself. However, the Sinhalese never again regained that area and never again gained total control of the island.

The rule of Kaliṅgan and Pāṇḍyan forces over various parts of northern Sri Lanka did not last long. They soon faced competition of their own from the Indian mainland. By the fourteenth century, a south Indian dynasty of Tamil origin called the Ārya Chakravartis seized power in the northern part of the island, establishing a capital at Nallūr in the Jaffna Peninsula at the very northern tip of the island. After the migration of Sinhalese and the ethnic division of the island between Tamil and Sinhalese, Polonnaruwa never again became a political center. Rather, because it was cut off from its traditional Sinhalese rulers and did not serve any strategic or symbolic importance in the new Tamil part of Sri Lanka, it quickly turned into a sleepy village filled with ancient ruins.

Throughout Sri Lanka's colonial period, first with the Portuguese (1593–1653), then Dutch (1658–1796), and finally the British (1796–1948), Polonnaruwa served no political or economic role. Only recently, with the renovation of Polonnaruwa's ancient reservoirs, has agricultural production of tobacco and rice revived. This increased production has led to the repopulation and revitalization of the area. Moreover, the Sri Lankan government, recognizing the historical value of these sites, has begun to revive them as major tourist destinations. Still, the continued fighting between Sinhalese Buddhists and Tamil Hindus over separatist issues has left the entire island in disarray and placed all sites of religious and historical significance in jeapordy.

Further Reading: The history of Polonnaruwa appears to be available only within histories of all Sri Lanka and usually is recounted in surprisingly little detail. *A Short History of Ceylon* by Humphrey W. Codrington (London: Macmillan, 1926; revised edition, 1939; reprint, New York: Books for Libraries, 1970) contains more specific information than most. It is a well-researched academic work, but the dates and sequence of events can be difficult to piece together from the text. Two very well-written histories with shorter but more cogent accounts of Polonnaruwa are *Sri Lanka: A History* by Chandra Richard De Silva (New York: Advent Books, 1987) and *A History of Sri Lanka*, by K. M. De Silva (London: Hurst, and Berkeley and Los Angeles: University of California Press, 1981).

—Christopher A. Hoyt and Shome Chowdhury

Port Arthur (Tasmania, Australia)

Location: On the Tasman Peninsula in southeastern Tasmania, about sixty miles southeast of Hobart.

Description: As a result of the British convict transportation system in the early to mid–nineteenth century, Port Arthur became the jail for an empire. Beginning in 1830 as a secondary penal settlement, it became a prison town that received about 12,700 convicts during the fifty years of its active service. This isolated penal establishment symbolizes the image in Australia of the transportation of convicts and is often referred to as "hell on earth."

Contact: Tasmanian Travel Centre
80 Elizabeth Street
Hobart, Tasmania
Australia
(2) 30 0250

In 1827 the crew of the colonial brig *Opossum* reported to Colonel George Arthur, lieutenant governor of Van Diemen's Land (Tasmania), the discovery of a deep, sheltered inlet on the peninsula in which they had taken refuge during a storm. This isolated site, they reported, boasted imposing natural barriers while also being rich in natural resources, including sought-after quality timber. After surveying the area, Arthur concluded that this site had the appropriate resources to create an ideal penal settlement. The isolation and inaccessibility of the Tasman Peninsula was its most attractive feature. Joined to the mainland only by a fifty-yard stretch of land, known as Eaglehawk Neck, the site would be secure and require minimum supervision of the convicts. "Geology," author Robert Hughes has remarked, "had conspired with Lieutenant Governor Arthur to give the prisoners of the crown a moral fright as their ships hauled in." Port Arthur reflected a significant aspect of Australia's convict and colonial heritage. It was an impressive monument to its founder. Yet the fact that Port Arthur bears his name similarly suggests that he shares the notoriety surrounding the penal settlement.

Port Arthur represented the most significant period of Tasmania's history as far as European settlement is concerned. It was established in 1830 primarily as a secondary penal settlement, a jail for habitual criminals. Offenses included assault, sheep and cattle theft, absconding from road parties, and attempted escape. For convicts sent to Port Arthur from other Australian colonies or other British colonies throughout the world (including Canada, South Africa, and India), it must have appeared as one vast prison without walls, an image fostered by Arthur. While several out-stations were established on the eastern colonies of Australia, Port Arthur was considered the largest and the most notorious. It provided convicts with employment in the dangerous and hard labor of timber-felling and milling, mining, boat building, and government projects. By 1832 plans were under way to close neighboring Maria Island and Macquarie Harbour and establish Port Arthur as the only penal settlement in Tasmania. It is estimated that 12,700 convicts served time at Port Arthur—one out of every six inmates taken to Van Diemen's Land. The vast population of convicts, compared to the limited number of prison personnel, called for a highly efficient governor, a description befitting George Arthur.

Arthur assumed office as lieutenant governor of Van Diemen's Land in May 1824. Before doing so he had Van Diemen's Land declared a separate colony, giving him full power and greater independence from New South Wales. Arthur took a very public and disciplined attitude toward both the role of transportation and his penal settlement. His aim was to degrade convicts and make transportation a painful and feared punishment. This is reflected in his dispatches *Observations upon Secondary Punishment* (Hobart, 1833) and *Defence of Transportation* (Hobart and London, 1835). Arthur instructed his staff that "The most unceasing labour is to be exacted from the convicts and the most harassing vigilance over them is to be observed." In 1827 he asserted that the convicts "should be kept rigidly at the spade and pick-axe and wheel barrow . . . from morning till night, although the immediate toil of the convicts be the only beneficial result of the labour." Brutal punishment acted as a deterrent, which encouraged prisoner reform, according to Arthur's logic. He adhered to this philosophy before a select committee of the House of Commons in Britain. When asked "Do you think [the convicts] felt deeply degraded by being there?" he replied "Very much." Yet this attitude apparently had the endorsement of other Port Arthur officials, including Thomas Lemprière (a commissioned officer), who stated that "a penal settlement is, and ought to be, an abode of misery to those whose crimes have sequestered them from the society of their fellow creatures."

Upon taking command of the settlement, Arthur controlled the development of the colony as chief executive, chief jailer, and guardian of morality, remaining accountable only to the Colonial Office. During his twelve-year commission, Arthur tightened convict discipline by increasing work hours, ending the payment of wages, creating chain gangs, and establishing a convict contract scheme whereby prisoners were assigned to work for free settlers as cheap labor on urban or rural work. This system was based on mutual good behavior as supervised by an ever-strengthening police force. Screening was thorough for convicts and settlers alike, particularly those settlers applying for female domestic servants. Governor Arthur's humorless character was not alone unpopular among the convicts. Many free settlers also had forged

Historic site of Port Arthur
Photo courtesy of Visitor Services, Port Arthur Historic Site

anti-Arthur factions designed to counter his autocratic mastery over all aspects of administration. Among their grievances were his attempts to control the press by the introduction of a licensing system. He argued that so long as the colony was designed to receive convicts, freedom of the press would be a dangerous challenge to authority. Free settlers also criticized the monopoly he held over the economy and the sale of land. Thus, accounts depicting Port Arthur as a "modern Gomorrah" and Arthur himself as a tyrant were largely attempts by free settlers to discredit both.

While there may have been a tendency to homogenize Port Arthur prisoners, evidence shows that the prisoners themselves were as diverse as all other Australia-bound transportees. Yet records do indicate that many Port Arthur prisoners were likely to be single, serving a longer sentence of transportation for offenses against property, and to have been formerly laborers or agricultural workers. The average age of a Port Arthur convict was about twenty-three, slightly lower than that of other transportees. Most were men reconvicted of minor offenses; some were brought straight from England. Good behavior could be rewarded with tickets-of-leave as well as conditional or free pardons. Despite the limited nature of their original offense, convicts released with tickets-of-leave were a constant source of alarm and committed much of the colony's violent crime.

Adjacent to the adult convict prison was Point Puer, a reformatory prison for transported boys. Forming part of the Port Arthur penal establishment, Point Puer was located across Opossum Bay on the tip of land next to the main settlement. Male children aged between nine and eighteen were transported there for offenses mostly related to theft. Like Port Arthur, Point Puer was well isolated with barracks separating it from the main settlement and huge cliffs along the shoreline. The adolescents were segregated from the adult prisoners to avoid "contamination." The juvenile population at Port Arthur climbed rapidly, and in all more then 2,000 of what Arthur described as the "little depraved felons" served time at the reformatory prison. These prisoners were educated and given religious instruction (although not very successfully), and some were taught a trade. By 1837 trades included baking, shoemaking, carpentry, tailoring, gardening, nail making, and blacksmithery. Considered an enlightened experiment for its time, the trade education program was as good as that available in England in the 1830s. If a boy were able to find a middle path between the overwhelming authority and the pressures of his peers, he had a reasonably promising future; if not, he remained caught up in the system, where, as Lord Stanley suggested, "every hardship and degradation awaits him and where his sufferings will be severe."

At both the Point Puer and the main settlement, the brutal forms of punishment have been the most enduring and infamous legacy of Port Arthur. Yet while the punishment there was horrendous, it was in fact more lenient than in other British colonies. As opposed to the indiscriminate whims of other Australian governors, Arthur attempted to enforce punishment according to the severity of the crime. Punishment ranged from chastisement to execution. The penal settlement provided Governor Arthur with a large workforce, which he could employ at various dangerous and unremitting forms of work. Working in the coal mines, for example, was considered a dreadful form of punishment with extremely hard labor, darkness, confinement, and the constant fear of cave-ins.

Although Arthur claimed to despise such brutal methods, in the 1820s and well into the 1830s floggings and public hangings were a cheap and efficient form of punishment. Later he introduced chain gangs and leg irons (weighing from thirteen to twenty-seven pounds), which were also used extensively for punishment. Women convicts were flogged on the back or had their scalps shaved. During the 1840s, in tune with Britain's "enlightened" methods of penal discipline, some of the more brutal forms of punishment were discontinued. These included stonebreaking while chained in a tiny stall, dragging logs of wood chained to leg irons, and the infamous treadmill. Solitary confinement replaced these more oppressive forms of punishment.

The Model Prison, built between 1848 and 1852, aimed to achieve instruction and probation of the prisoners. Based on England's Pentonville Prison, it featured the ability to silence and separate prisoners. Numerous surviving prison records give historians an insight into punishment at Port Arthur. Records of a Scottish horse thief named Robert Williamson indicate that among countless other punishments, he received thirty-six lashes for tampering with his leg-iron in 1835, one month on a chain gang for having vegetables in his possession in 1836, and ten days in solitary confinement in 1837 for grossly indecent expression and malicious conduct toward a fellow prisoner.

Not surprisingly, escape was a constant focus for many prisoners. However, the natural boundaries made escape virtually impossible. To flee over the cliffs and into the sea was unthinkable for an unequipped convict. Thus would-be escapees turned their attention to Eaglehawk Neck, the fifty-yard stretch of land that was the only way to leave the Tasman Peninsula and reach the mainland on foot. However, with the arrival of Charles Booth in February 1833, escape became impossible. As Port Arthur's commandant for eleven years, Booth achieved Arthur's hopes of taking "the vengeance of the Law to the utmost limits of human endurance." Booth's first major achievement was to introduce a security system at Eaglehawk Neck designed to foil the most sophisticated escape attempts. Booth increased the number of guards, added a row of oil lamps, and introduced eighteen tethered guard dogs (a breed of kangaroo and sheep dog) across the Neck. These dogs formed an impassable line. Arthur reported to a select committee of the House of Commons in England that the "line of very fierce dogs stationed from shore to shore . . . [had been] so successful that it has not been known that more than two prisoners have ever escaped from Port Arthur."

Among Commandant Booth's less infamous reforms were the semaphore system, a long-range communication system able to contact Hobart, and the first Australian railway, powered by convicts rather than engines. The semaphore system was a chain of signal stations, the first of its kind in Australia. It operated using semaphores, tall polls each having three sets of double arms, similar to railway signals. Messages were then translated according to the angle of the arms. By 1844, twenty-two stations had been established with some 11,300 signals that were able to communicate news swiftly of escaped convicts or other crises in Port Arthur.

Booth's ingenuity also added a small chapter in the history of Australian transportation with the introduction of his railway. Booth engineered a four-and-one-half-mile railroad between Norfolk Island and Port Arthur. Transporting both people and supplies, it provided a fast and simple alternative to the arduous detour by sea. Without an engine, the four-passenger carts were motored by convicts pushing crossbars at the front and the rear. While the speed of the cart reflected the terrain, it could hurtle down a hill at up to thirty miles per hour, no doubt a frightening experience for the nineteenth-century settlers. Many shared Lieutenant Governor William Denison's apprehension when he commented in 1851 that seeing himself "seated, and pushed along by these miserable convicts, [was] not very pleasant." But Booth's railroad provided the only viable means of travel from Hobart to Norfolk Island. The security, communication, and transportation systems Booth developed, despite their being somewhat primitive, allowed Port Arthur to shed its shanty-like appearance and to resemble a substantial town. Timber buildings and stone and brick structures, including an imposing freestone church, gave the town a look of permanence beyond its convict origins.

Long after transportation from Britain ceased, Port Arthur continued to receive reconvicted transportees and colonial-born criminals. However, by 1869 the convict settlement became difficult to maintain. During the 1870s, a Select Committee found that the cost of running the prison was too great for the small number of convicts it housed. Inadequate staffing and the desperate need of repair to most of the buildings made the operation of Port Arthur even more difficult. In 1877 most prisoners were transferred to jails in Hobart. Until 1890 the crumbling prison housed pauper invalids, the mentally ill, and the criminally insane. After the Port Arthur prison was officially closed, citizens attempted to cast off the convict legacy that had made the settlement famous. Embarrassed by its shameful past, the local community shunned the prison. With the first sale of crown land in 1877, Port Arthur began to grow as an independent town. In the same year it was renamed Carnarvon by those who wanted to deny the existence of the penal settlement. The *Tasmanian Mail* reported in September 1877 that with the removal of Port Arthur from the map "the last stain which remained upon Tasmania had passed away." Their wish was nearly completely granted after bushfires raced through the settlement in 1897–98, destroying many of the buildings.

As the historical value of Port Arthur became evident and citizens began to recognize the tourist potential, its original name was returned and attempts were made to restore the fire-damaged buildings. In more recent years, extensive work has been undertaken at Port Arthur. As a result, all the major ruins have been opened to visitors, and many significant buildings have been restored. The Government Gardens, created in the 1840s and tended until 1877, have also been fully restored. Port Arthur is one of the few major Australian ruins to be restored solely for historical appreciation. Notable original buildings that may be viewed today include the Penitentiary, the Model Prison (the showpiece of the remains), the Asylum, the Commandant's House, the Guard Tower, the Hospital, and the Isle of the Dead, the cemetery where more than 1,760 convicts were buried in communal graves. Recently, a major computerized convict database was introduced, enhancing the accessibility of Port Arthur's history by complementing existing information with a comprehensive record of the people who passed through Port Arthur. This system enables visitors to trace details of their convict ancestry. Today Port Arthur attracts some quarter of a million visitors annually and is under the care of the National Parks and Wildlife Service. It is sixty miles by road from Hobart, Tasmania's capital, and its natural landscape, once frightening to the convicts, is now considered by visitors to be both beautiful and tranquil.

The existence of such impressive ruins adds to the infamy and notoriety that already surrounded the penal colony of Port Arthur. While it is still considered a "hell on earth" and the "scene of unceasing suffering," historians and official records have since indicated that while it may have been a place of untold misery, it was not as severe as its counterparts on Norfolk Island or Macquarie Harbour. The myth began after newspaper editors in the 1830s condemned it as "a place worse than death" (written most likely as an attempt to discredit Arthur's governorship). This description was widely circulated and believed after the publication of Marcus Clarke's famous novel *For the Term of His Natural Life: The Grim and Tragic Story of Life in an Australian Penal Colony* (1886), which was made into a motion picture filmed on location in Port Arthur in the 1920s. The novel, which condemned the brutality of the penal system and raised sympathy for the convicts, gave its historical allegiance not to events in Port Arthur where the novel was set, but to a combination of fictitious events and actual incidents from Norfolk Island, Macquarie Harbour, and Port Arthur. Yet the myth has remained largely unchallenged for 160 years, and, like all myths, dies hard.

Further Reading: Many available texts treat the topic of Australian convict and transportation history. The most recent and notable of these are *The Fatal Shore: A History of the Transportation of Convicts to Australia, 1787–1868* by Robert Hughes (New York: Knopf, 1986; London: Collins Harvill, 1987) and *The Convict Settlers of Australia* by Leslie L. Robson (Carlton, Victoria: Melbourne University Press, 1994). For texts dedicated to the Port Arthur settlement, see *Port Arthur: A Place of Misery* by Maggie Weidenhofer (Melbourne and New York: Oxford University Press, 1981). Ian Brand has published four texts on Port Arthur, including *Port Arthur and Its Outstations, 1827–1898* (Tasmania: Jason Publications, 1978). For an eyewitness account from the editor of *The Colonial Times*, see *The History of Van Diemen's Land, 1824–1835* by Henry Melville, edited by George Mackaness (Sydney: Horwitz Publications and the Grahame Book Company, 1965).

—Joseph M. Siracusa

Prambanan (Central Java, Indonesia)

Location: Near the boundary of Yogyakarta Special District and Central Java provinces; approximately ten miles east-northeast of Yogyakarta and twenty-five miles west of Solo (Surakarta).

Description: Major temple complex, site of a ninth-century Hindu temple dedicated to the god Siva. The largest Hindu temple complex in Java, it is considered an outstanding example of Hindu art. The complex stands on three levels of man-made terraces and at one time had well over 200 small temples on the two lower levels. Only two have been repaired. The focus of restoration has been on the top level (main courtyard), where eight major and eight minor temples stand. Particular attention has been paid to the three largest temples, dedicated to Siva, Brahmā, and Vishnu.

Contact: Diparda D. I. Yogyakarta
Jl. Malioboro 14
Yogyakarta 55213
Indonesia
(274) 562811, ext. 218

The Prambanan Plain in Central Java has the greatest concentration of ancient Buddhist temples in Indonesia. The great Buddhist temple Borobudur is a mere twenty-five miles away. Yet amid these many Buddhist temples, the Prambanan complex, with its largest structure, a Hindu *candi* (temple) dedicated to the god Siva, rises above the plain in a wealth of sculptural beauty and detail.

Although some very sketchy historical records suggest that Indian culture began to move into Java as early as the first century B.C., the first verifiable Indian traces there are dated several centuries later. An early Sanskrit Pallava inscription dated 654 Saka (the equivalent of A.D. 732) indicates that the first Siva temple in Java was Brahman and modeled after one in southern India. There is no doubt that a strong link prevailed between Java and India: Javanese princes were sent to India to be educated, and some immigration occurred from southern India to Java, although not on a large scale. India's religions may have been brought by traders, or perhaps from Buddhist Brahman missionaries. Another theory holds that Indonesian royalty may have imported Buddhism into their courts. Whatever the reason, Buddhism probably did not become prevalent until the Sailendra Dynasty, based in nearby Sumatra and ruling a large portion of the Malay Peninsula, Java, and the Sunda Islands, became instrumental in spreading Indian culture throughout the Indonesian Archipelago beginning in the eighth century.

The few existing records are obscure regarding the Buddhist and Hindu dynasties in central Java from the eighth through the tenth centuries A.D., when the Prambanan temples were constructed. In the middle of the eighth century, two dynastic and cultural influences appear to have been strong: the Buddhist Sailendras of the south and the Hindu Sanjayas of Old Mataram in the north. It is thought the Sailendra kings began to control central Java around 750. This occurred when, for reasons unknown, the local Javanese king moved east. But early in the ninth century the king returned to central Java, and Hindu Saivism (the worship of Siva) again became the region's official religion.

To celebrate the restoration of Hinduism, the construction of Prambanan was begun around 835. It rivaled the great Buddhist monument of Borobudur and was built near the Buddhist temple Candi Sewu, the largest in the region. A series of smaller Hindu temples was also built in an area previously separating the two religious domains. This building activity appears to have paralleled a unification of the two religious groups. Certainly, the now-dominant Hindus were tolerant of the Sailendra Buddhists. It is possible that Rakai Pikatan, a Hindu of Old Mataram, married Pramodhavardhani, a Buddhist Sailendra princess, thus uniting the two great powers. If so, this would explain why Candi Sewu was allowed to remain standing when Prambanan was built nearby. The marriage would also explain why Prambanan, as well as other smaller Hindu temples in the area, show both Saivite and Buddhist influences in their sculpture and architecture.

Temple reliefs found at Prambanan, Borobudur, and in East Java indicate that earlier Javanese temples had been wooden. By the beginning of the ninth century, when Prambanan was built, workers used bricks made of lime, sand, and water that, while generally of good quality, yet varied in size and were often insufficiently dried. The resulting rough exterior of the bricks was smoothed by rubbing the surfaces of one against another. This procedure improved the adherence of the bricks, which workers then bound together using an agent made of plant sap.

An inscription on Prambanan's main Siva temple dated 856, the year of the structure's completion, states that it was built under the auspices of the king. According to some sources, this king was Dhaksa (or Daska); according to others, it was Rakai Pikatan. Temples in Prambanan's second precinct were evidently built by important people in the kingdom rather than by the king himself; the smaller temples in the countryside were built by less wealthy individuals.

Prambanan was an ambitious plan, built on three walled man-made terraces corresponding to the three precincts. Little has survived of the outer precinct, but the inscription dated 856 states that the Opak River was diverted during its construction, thus creating a major irrigation system upstream. Unlike the two inner walls, the outer wall was not aligned along the primary axis.

Hindu temple at Prambanan
Photo courtesy of Indonesia Tourist Promotion Office, Los Angeles

Inside another wall lies the second precinct, a square area that itself rises in three stepped terraces. Each terrace was lined with shrines of identical size and shape, although the decoration varied. The temples on the four corners of each level had two entrances, one on each outermost wall; all other temples had one entrance facing away from the complex's center. It is estimated that 224 temples once stood inside this middle precinct.

The final precinct is known as Lara Jonggrang (often this name is applied to the entire temple complex). Inside its enclosing wall lies the central courtyard, containing the three major temples devoted to the Hindu Trinity. The temple to Siva, the largest, towers 154 feet in the center. Smaller than the Siva temple, but equal in size to each other, are temples to Vishnu to the north and Brahmā to the south. All three structures face east, and opposite each is a smaller temple dedicated to the gods' mounts. The central temple contains a spectacular statue of Nandi, Siva's bull; most likely, the others once contained statues of Garuḍa, the sun-bird for Vishnu, and Hamsa, the sacred goose for Brahmā. Two even smaller temples, one on the north wall and one on the south, stand between the row of main temples and the row of temples dedicated to the animal mounts. Referred to as Candi Apit, these temples bear the same features as the main temples but are much narrower, hence the name Apit, which means squashed or pinched. Nine smaller shrines line the courtyard walls: one in each corner, one in the middle of each wall (just inside the courtyard's four entrances), and a central shrine located just to the left of the eastern entrance to the Siva temple. These shrines housed market stones used to gauge alignments during construction. The whole complex is off-center; the row of three main temples is aligned just west of the courtyard's main north-south axis. Tiers of elongated and gadrooned stupas, more Buddhist than Hindu, decorate the high-terraced shrine roofs, giving the temples a pyramidal appearance.

Prambanan is filled with rich sculpture marked by symmetry and symbolism. Carvings are free flowing and less formal than those on Borobudur. Ringing the base of the Siva temple is a menagerie of hares, geese, birds, deer, and other creatures; carved niches hold small lions flanked by trees of life. The outer balustrade of the terrace is decorated with those objects the ancient Javanese expect to see in heaven: stylized half-human, half-bird celestial beings in niches with dancers and singers scattered between the heavenly groups. The dancers signify Natarāja, the Lord of Dance, who is believed to dance at the end of each era, destroying the world so it can be recreated. The Hindu symbolism of the stars moving around Mount Meru, central mountain of the universe, is not clear. The Siva temple may be interpreted as the central mountain, with the smaller temples representing the stars around it.

There are four entrances to the Siva temple, one facing each of the cardinal directions. Each entrance is approached via a separate staircase. The main, eastern staircase begins with a wide (seven and one-half-foot) flight of eighteen steps to a landing. From here one may either proceed up a much narrower flight of ten steps to the temple entrance or down one of two staircases located on either side of the landing and running parallel to the face of the building. These side staircases lead to a walkway around the temple. As each of the other three entrances has a similar arrangement of platforms and stairways, in order to circle the temple along the walkway one must continually climb up and down the side staircases. Each of the four entrances leads to a separate, small *cella* (interior space, usually housing a statue). The eastern *cella,* approximately ten feet square, is particularly ornate, with carved spiral- and rosette-patterned walls. Unlike the other three *cellas,* it connects via a corridor to the large, inner sanctum in the center of the temple.

The inner sanctum *(garvagriha)* houses the statue of Siva. Nine feet tall and with four arms, he stands on a lotus petal (actually a Buddhist symbol) atop an elaborately carved pedestal supported by a snake. Siva is wearing a prayer cord, a flywisk, and a snake as a caste cord. The wall behind the statue is covered with delicate rectangular tracery. The entrance to the sanctum is guarded on either side by carved figures.

Whereas the eastern *cella* functions as an antechamber for the sanctum and is therefore empty, the other three *cellas* contain statues. On Siva's right, in the south *cella,* stands the pot-bellied, bearded Agastya, the divine teacher. Agastya's elephant-headed son, Ganesha, stands in the west chamber. Durgā, Siva's consort, is on his left in the north *cella.*

This statue of Durgā figures in the local legend that gave the courtyard complex the name Lara Jonggrang, which means Slender Maiden. According to the story, a princess of this name was being courted against her wishes by Bandung Bondowoso, son of King Ratu Boko. Hoping to be rid of her unwanted suitor, she gave Bondowoso the impossible task of building a thousand temples in one night. With the help of gnomes, Bondowoso was close to accomplishing his charge when Lara, seeing this remarkable feat, quickly ordered her servants to begin pounding rice, which they normally did only at dawn. The roosters, hearing the pounding, thought it was daylight and began to crow. The gnomes heard the roosters and assumed daylight was approaching. Not wanting to be discovered, they fled, leaving the last temple unfinished. Incensed at the trick, Bondowoso turned the princess into a statue, presumably the statue of Durgā in the Siva temple. Here the goddess is depicted with eight hands in the process of killing the demon buffalo, Mahiśa.

Along the temple's walkway, on the inside of a high balustrade, is an elaborately carved frieze illustrating the great Hindu epic, the *Rāmāyaṇa.* The reliefs are possibly a reaction to the Buddhist frieze of Borobudur. The *Rāmāyaṇa* is a moral, mythical, and symbolic story of Prince Rāma, a reincarnation of Vishnu, the Preserver. The story embodies the ethics of human relationships and the fight between good and evil. The main characters are Rāma, a devotee of truth; his wife, Sītā, a model of womanliness and wifely devotion; Rāma's brother, Lakṣmaṇa, personifying brotherly love and

Hindu temple at Prambanan
Photo courtesy of Indonesia Tourist Promotion Office, Los Angeles

courage; and Rāvaṇa, the antagonist filled with deceit, lust, and hatred.

The twenty-four lively reliefs begin to the south of the east stairs and run clockwise. The first relief shows the awakening of the god Vishnu, reclining on a cushion in the heart of the sea with various aquatic life around. A serpent is behind Vishnu. The mount Garuḍa, on Vishnu's right, gracefully offers him a lotus. A group of good spirits on Vishnu's left pray for him to descend into the world as an incarnation so he can punish the demon-king Rāvaṇa.

The epic proceeds, showing Rāma's father, Rāma's victory over demons, his marriage to Sītā, and preparations for Rāma's coronation, which is thwarted by the trickery of his stepmother, who wishes to place her own son on the throne. Rāma, Sītā, and Lakṣmaṇa go into exile, where they have various adventures. The kidnap of Sītā by Rāvaṇa is shown dramatically. He is carrying her away in an air chariot with a flying demon at his shoulder. Rāma then tries to free Sītā with the help of his ally Hanumān and an army of monkeys running wildly through jungles, fighting the demons. A distinctive rendering in a later panel shows Rāma killing Valin, an enemy, in order to win Surgriva as an ally. This unity is depicted by a remarkable sculpture of trees weaving the scene together. The last panel on the Siva temple (although not the end of the story) shows a monkey army building a bridge to Lanka where Rāvaṇa lives.

The *Rāmāyaṇa* representations conclude on the balustrade of the Brahmā temple to the south. These panels show Rāma and Rāvaṇa in battle, and Rāma and Sītā united. The balustrade of the Vishnu temple, to the north, depicts scenes from the life of Krishna, another incarnation of Vishnu.

Unlike the Siva temple, the Brahmā and Vishnu temples each have only one internal chamber. The temple of Brahmā, god of creation, contains a central statue of Brahmā with four heads and four arms. Three other images of Brahmā are on the back wall, one with four arms, one with six, and the third with eight. The various hands all represent different attributes of Brahmā. The Vishnu temple houses a four-armed statue of that god, along with a dwarf, a man-lion, and a two-armed figure holding a four-armed figure of Lakshmi in its hand.

For reasons unknown, the king of Central Java left the Prambanan Plain around 930 and moved the government to East Java. Earthquakes and volcanic eruptions in the sixteenth century toppled or buried the abandoned temples. Candi Prambanan lay in decay. Over the centuries it deteriorated further at the hands of thieves who despoiled the temples in search of treasures and local people collecting building materials from the forgotten site.

It was in this dilapidated state, fragments strewn over the Prambanan Plain, that the temple complex remained until 1911, when the Dutch government, which then controlled Indonesia, prepared to restore the Siva temple. Several factors, notably the movement for Indonesian independence in the early years of the twentieth century, delayed the project until 1930, however. The restoration was completed and the Siva temple officially dedicated on December 20, 1953, by Sukarno, who had been proclaimed the first president of the Indonesian Republic in 1945. Renovation of the Brahmā temple was begun in 1977 and completed ten years later. Vishnu was dedicated by President Suharto on April 27, 1991, after nine years of renovation.

At the close of the twentieth century, stones still lie scatterd about the Prambanan complex. Restoration continues, but because of missing fragments, some parts cannot be restored. The outer wall is almost completely gone, although the south gate can still be seen. No buildings from this outer precinct remain. On the top level, in the three small temples once containing the gods' mounts, only Nandi the bull, one of Prambanan's finest sculptures, remains. Of the 224 small shrines in the outer courtyard, only two have been restored.

Today the Prambanan complex is under the jurisdiction of the Department of Antiquities. In order to keep the complex free from modern-day vandals and looters, the government has built a park around it. It includes a museum housing archaeological finds and restoration information. On certain nights of the year, performances of the *Rāmāyaṇa* ballet and traditional trance dances are held in an outdoor theatre in the park.

Further Reading: *Ancient Indian Colonies in The Far East,* volume 2, *Suvarnadvipa* by Ramesh Chandra Majumdar (Dacca: Asoke Kumar Majumdar, 1937) is a very good account of the culture, civilization, and art of Indonesia. It contains detailed descriptions of the temple complex as it existed during the early stages of restoration, and includes several plates showing the *Rāmāyaṇa* reliefs and the temple's general plan. *The Temples of Java* by Jacques Dumarcay, translated and edited by Michael Smithies (Oxford and New York: Oxford University Press, 1986), is devoted to the evolution of Javanese temples, with information regarding their construction, architecture, and religious symbolism, as well as historical information of the Hindu Renaissance in Java and Prambanan.

—Sue Montgomery

Puri (Orissa, India)

Location: On the Bay of Bengal, 260 miles southwest of Calcutta.

Description: A seaside resort and major Hindu center where pilgrims come to worship at the twelfth-century A.D. shrine of Jagannātha, a god who combines the attributes of Krishna and Vishnu, two powerful gods of the Hindu pantheon.

Contact: Government of India Tourist Office
B-20, Kalpana Area
Bhubaneswar, Orissa 751014
India
54203

As a seaside town with a long, wide, and sandy beach where waves break in from the Bay of Bengal, Puri attracts numerous tourists throughout the year, primarily from Calcutta. The center of life in Puri, however, is not its lovely beach, certainly the best on the eastern Indian seaboard; life here is focused on the temple of Jagannātha (or Jagannāth)—the lord of the universe—located in a plaza in the central part of the town. The temple is set inside a high-walled enclosure, which only Hindus may enter. The temple tower dominates the landscape for miles around, and the first sight of it is always exciting to the Hindu pilgrims who come to worship at this shrine. In the days of the sailing ships, this tower provided a landmark to the sailors who in the seventeenth century and later used to refer to this as the "White Pagoda," as opposed to the "Black Pagoda" of the thirteenth-century Sun Temple of Konārak farther east along the coast. Before a road was built along the shore, Konārak was only a night's bullock-cart journey from Puri.

For the people of the modern Indian state of Orissa where Puri is located, Jagannātha is a very special god. The various nuances of Jagannātha worship and the folk and Sanskritic traditions that have been built around it have permeated all aspects of life here. The Orissan countryside is dotted with shrines dedicated to this god. The devotional literature of the regional Oriya language deals mostly with Jagannātha, who has played a major symbolic role in forging a "national" identity among the Oriya-speaking people in modern times. They believe he looks after their welfare, and they go through life with his name on their lips. When the lower part of the copingstone of the temple tower or Amalaka Sila fell down on June 14, 1990, questions arose concerning the welfare of the state. Some took the fall of the stone as a sign that the lord had decided to withhold his blessings from the people. When the stone was replaced by another of the same size and weight (seven tons) on February 28, 1991, the final lifting work could not be done at night when the lord was asleep; it had to wait until 5:30 A.M., when he was believed to be awake.

Jagannātha worship is not limited to Orissa; the Puri shrine is important to Indian Hindus as a whole. Apart from Orissa, however, reverence for Jagannātha historically has been strongest in Bengal, especially before its partition in 1947. Caitanya, a Bengali and the founder of one of the most powerful and persistent devotional or *Bhakti* movements of India in the early sixteenth century (which survives today in the form of the Hare Krishna movement), spent many years of his life as a devotee of Jagannātha and finally, as the devout prefer to believe, had his corporeal body merged into the idol form of the deity himself. The Jagannātha temple in Puri continues to play a very large part in the religious and cultural life of Orissa and of eastern India generally.

Jagannātha is worshiped in his temple along with Balabhadra and Subhadrā, the brother and sister respectively of Vāsudeva-Krishna, one of the chief gods of the Hindu pantheon. Their presence indicates that Jagannātha is visualized as a form of Krishna. At the same time, he also is believed to be related to the man-lion or Narasingha form of Vishnu, another major deity of Hinduism. Thus Jagannātha combines the forms of both Krishna and Vishnu.

The idols contained in the temple depicting Jagannātha, Balabhadra, and Subhadrā are fashioned of wood and appear unfinished. Two stumps suggestive of human arms protrude from the sides of the thick, massive heads (except in the case of the Subhadrā image). All three deities have bodies made of uncarved, painted wooden blocks. Large, circular eyes dominate the faces. This seemingly primitive iconography of the Jagannātha idol may have been derived from such tribal groups as the Sabaras of northern Orissa. The images are periodically renewed in a strictly controlled ritual involving a traditionally sanctioned group of carpenters.

From the time the deity wakes up in the morning to the time he is put to bed at night, a detailed round of worship proceeds under a special class of temple priests. In June and July of each year, he and his two associates are taken out in their respective chariots, each fashioned according to prescribed measurements and color, to the Gundicha temple about one-fifth of a mile away, from where they return, again in chariots, at the end of the appointed period of about nine days. This is the *Rathayātrā* or the chariot/car festival in which the pilgrims and others who pull the chariots by ropes are supposed to accumulate great religious merit. People often are crushed under the wheels, sometimes accidentally, sometimes willfully as acts of self-immolation under the divine chariots.

The construction of the Jagannātha temple began in A.D. 1136 and was completed around the end of the twelfth century; the specific history of the town of Puri is essentially the history of that temple. Since its "general history," accord-

Jagannātha temple, Puri
Photo courtesy of Dilip K. Chakrabarti

ing to the *Imperial Gazetteer of India* (1908) "is that of Orissa," and since no specific historical record of Puri exists until the twelfth century, a brief history of the state of Orissa will fill in some of the gaps.

The uplands of Orissa show evidence of prehistoric habitation beginning with the lower Paleolithic stage. The link between this area and the settlement of the delta region of Orissa is unclear, but it is possible that toward the end of the second millennium B.C. or somewhat later, people began to settle the delta. By the time Orissa became a part of the pan-Indian Mauryan state in the third century B.C., it must have been transformed into a rich agricultural land of narrow alluvial valleys interspersed with uplands. The uplands were also rich in raw materials such as timber and minerals. Two major urban sites are known from the Mauryan period: ancient Tosala (modern Sisupalgarh, near Bhubaneswar) and ancient Samapa (modern Jaugada, in the Ganjam area).

The post-Mauryan period, beginning in the early second century B.C., was dominated by a political leader named Khāravela, who apparently established the basis of a regional state covering all of modern Orissa. Because of its location, Orissa at this time had been at the mercy of a wide range of political forces; much of this instability remains vague owing to a general lack of documented evidence. Khāravela belonged to the Cheti Dynasty, and although he is known to have had a successor, the dynasty soon faded into oblivion.

Scholars have debated whether Orissa during the early centuries A.D. was under the rule of the Kushāns, who had their capital in Mathura in northern India, or of the semi-mythical Murundas. A record from the early fourth century mentions a king Guhasiva. Later in the century, however, Samudra Gupta of the Gupta Dynasty of northern India passed through Orissa on his way to southern India on a military campaign. Gupta recorded that Orissa was ruled by several political units, each with its own king.

The region continued to change hands among a number of dynasties until the eleventh century, when the Gaṅga line, which had figured in the region several centuries earlier, reemerged. Under the Imperial Gaṅgas, as this later line is now known, a pan-Orissan kingdom was formed, possibly for the first time since Khāravela of the Cheti Dynasty. The king most important to the history of Orissa and Puri is Anantavarmana Chōḍagaṅga, who in 1077 succeeded his father, Rājarāja, the first powerful monarch of the Imperial Gaṅgas. Anantavarmana Chōḍagaṅga began construction of the Puri temple. After a long reign during which he considered himself the lord of the whole of Orissa, he abdicated in 1146. Anantavarmana Chōḍagaṅga made his influence felt in Andhra and Bengal as well.

From 1205 onward Orissa suffered periodic incursions by the Muslims, who had annexed Bengal. At first these invasions were mostly unsuccessful. Narasiṃha I, reputedly the greatest ruler of the Imperial Gaṅgas (and builder of the most famous temple in Orissa, the Sun Temple of Konārak), repulsed the Muslim invaders twice, in 1235 and 1247. However, the Muslims invaded successfully in 1361, destroying a large number of temples as far as Cuttack. The Imperial Gaṅga line continued until 1435, when the throne was occupied by the Gajapati Dynasty of the Sūryavaṃśis. Mukundadeva, the last Gajapati king, died fighting against the Muslims in 1568, and Orissa passed into the hands of the Afghan power of Bengal.

Afghan control of Orissa was short lived. In 1584 the Afghans acknowledged the sovereignty of the Mughal rulers of Delhi over the entire region. However, the Mughals came directly to Orissa in 1592 and placed it under the governorship of Manasimha, a famous general of the Mughal king Akbar. Orissa was declared a separate *subah* or province of the Mughal Empire, but when ʿĀlamgīr (Aurangzeb), the last of the Great Mughals, died in 1707, Orissa passed into the hands of the semi-independent Muslim governor of Bengal, Murshid Qulī Khān. Under his fanatical and intolerant representative Muḥammad Taqi Khan, between 1727 and 1734, Orissa had a difficult time, as he desecrated many Hindu religious images. Even the Puri temple was not free from his sacrilege.

The Marāṭhās from the Deccan took possession of Orissa around the middle of the eighteenth century, but by this time British influence had begun to spread in Bengal. After occupying Madras and Mysore, the British needed control over the east coast for safe passage from Bengal to the south. Orissa featured on this route; its conquest was achieved in 1803 with the capture of Cuttack. The British seriously interfered with the economy and tax system of Orissa, contributing to a disastrous famine in Orissa from 1865 to 1867. However, the British recognized the importance of Jagannātha of Puri and initially appointed a separate official to look after the administration of his legacy. Puri was eventually converted into the headquarters of a district of the same name.

Scholars have long debated the origin and evolution of the Jagannātha cult. Whether the cult had already existed in 1136, when the imperial Gaṅga king Anantavarmana Chōḍagaṅga began the construction of the Puri temple, remains uncertain. Initially, it appears, only Purushottama-Krishna and his consort Lakshmi were worshiped in the temple. Jagannātha worship in its present form gained ground approximately a century later, when in 1230 the imperial Gaṅga king Anaṅgabhīma dedicated his kingdom to the god Purushottama-Jagannātha of Puri and declared that from then on he and his successors would rule under divine order as Jagannātha's sons and vassals. This gave Jagannātha worship in Orissa a tremendous boost and, more important, led to an inextricable relationship between the Puri temple and the ideal and acceptance of kingship in Orissa. Even now, although kingship has ceased to operate, the present heir of the Gajapati line of kings at Khurda performs ritual duties in and around the temple. For instance, when the chariot festival or *Rathayātrā* begins, he has to sweep the street in front of the chariots with a broom.

The temple itself is set inside two walled enclosures. The outer enclosure measures 670 feet by 640 feet and is encircled by a 20- to 30-foot-high wall with four gateways. The inner enclosure measures 420 feet by 315 feet and also has four openings. The main temple is 55 feet long on an east-west axis. The temple tower rises up to 192 feet from the level of the surrounding courtyard. Including its porch, which is commonly known as *jagamohana,* the temple measures 155 feet across the center. A dancing pavilion *(natamandira)* and a pavilion where food offerings to the deities could be placed *(bhogamandira)* were added later, making the temple complex 300 feet long. Both the inner and outer enclosures contain numerous other smaller shrines where the devotees can pay homage to a wide range of divinities of the Hindu pantheon. The temple tower and the body are decorated with a great variety of sculptures, including some of couples making love.

The religious service at the temple comprises daily rounds of offerings and worship. Some twenty-four major festivals are held there each year, the most important of which is the chariot festival. The daily offerings of cooked food are subsequently shared among the temple functionaries and sold to the pilgrims who, while in Puri, are supposed to partake of the food sanctified by Jagannātha. The temple gates are closed and the temple enclosures cleared of pilgrims when food is offered to the deities.

Further Reading: The best detailed introduction to the Jagannātha cult is *The Cult of Jagannath and the Regional Tradition of Orissa*, edited by Anncharlot Eschmann, Hermann Kulke, and Gaya Charan Tripathi (Delhi: Manohar, 1986). The two-volume *A History of Orissa,* edited by N. K. Sahu (Calcutta: Sushil Gupta, 1956), contains chapters from some nineteenth-century administrators, with an additional historical chapter by the editor.

—Dilip K. Chakrabarti

Qin Tomb (Shaanxi, China)

Location: The Qin Tomb is located just over three miles east of present-day Lintong county, in Shaanxi province; less than a mile to the south is the Li Mountain, and in the north is the Wei River.

Description: Burial compounds of Qin Shihuang Di, who first unified the Chinese empire. Since 1974, chambers and pits of the compound have been successfully excavated, revealing more than 10,000 burial items, including an entire life-size terra-cotta army, with chariots, cavalry, infantry, and accompanying items such as horse-reins and various weapons. These artifacts are of immense archaeological, historical, and artistic value.

Contact: Shaanxi Tourism Bureau
15 Chang'an Avenue
710061 Xian
China
751051

Qin Tomb complex is the burial site of Qin Shihuang Di (reigned 221–210 B.C.), the first emperor of the Qin Dynasty in China (221–206 B.C.) and the first ruler to unify China. Using superior military strategy, he was able to defeat his six arch rivals (each of whom ruled a portion of what is today China), ending the period of feudalistic rule and placing the multiracial China under his rule. He was not only a good military commander but also a good administrator: his concern was to centralize power in his hands. To this end he replaced the former autonomous feudal principalities with districts and prefectures ruled by officials sent directly from the central authorities. He codified the legal system of the time, ordered that weights and measures be made uniform, prescribed uniform standards for all markets in China, and ordered that a common written language be adopted for the empire. Shihuang Di was also notorious for his harsh suppression of the Confucian scholars and their teachings. By his command many Confucian scholars were buried alive, and all their writings burned. At the same time, he gave full support to legalist scholars who helped him build and expand his administration with a pragmatic approach.

Shihuang Di continued to maintain a gigantic army after he had unified China, as military threats from the Hsungzars and other nomadic tribes still loomed in the north. As a means of further protecting his empire, he began constructing the Great Wall, the completion of which cost vast financial resources and cut short countless human lives. Shihuang Di's cruelty and exorbitant spending caused widespread resentment of his rule. At least three attempts were made to assassinate him, but each failed. In his final years, his primary concern was how to prolong his life; it is said that he sent a mission to as far away as present-day Japan to look for pills for an everlasting life.

Since he did not find everlasting life in Japan or anywhere else, Shihuang Di set out to ensure that he would enjoy the same lifestyle in death as he had during his life. During China's feudal period, slaves, women, and soldiers were commonly buried alive in the same tomb with their departed master, so that the latter could be served in his afterlife in the manner to which he had become accustomed. Many people had feared that Shihuang Di would order the burial of all his soldiers with him on the occasion of his death. Fortunately, Shihuang Di lived at the end of the feudal period, by which time this custom had died out. Instead of burying his army alive, he ordered an army of life-size terra-cotta soldiers and horses to be erected alongside his gigantic grave, which was cut out of a mountain and built in accordance with the symbolic patterns of the cosmos.

Possibly because of the dry weather of north China, the tomb has remained remarkably well preserved. Exploratory excavation was begun as early as 1961, when the Chinese government declared that the tomb was to be permanently preserved as one of the country's important cultural and historical relics. Since this date, some walls, doors, water tunnels, tiles, clay figures, remains of houses, and the burying ground itself (covered on the surface by trees) have either been excavated or identified. The first major excavation was undertaken in 1974 and 1975. The excavated structure is trough shaped, 689 feet long (discounting doors and tunnels), 197 feet wide, and 14.8 to 21.3 feet deep. Totaling 135,630 square feet in surface area, the structure is supported by large, uniform, criss-crossing hardwood pillars erected horizontally and vertically. On the eastern side of the complex stands a wall of stone bricks, the first of its kind built by the Chinese. The floor, also constructed of stone bricks, was laid out in a convex shape to facilitate the flow of dripping water and maintain the dryness of the central parts of the pit. The tomb is a masterpiece of architecture in view of its early date of construction; graves in the succeeding Han Dynasty were usually built in the same manner.

In the section of the tomb complex known as the Number One Pit were found approximately 6,000 terra-cotta life-size figures, together with thousands of weapons, pieces of ornaments, and numerous other architectural remains. These figures, dressed as warriors, appear ready for battle. They are organized as a full-scale, disciplined army, with a main central force surrounded by vanguard and reserve units and other soldiers protecting the flanks. Each warrior wears a uniform of either green or red, with brown or black armor. The buttons, too, are uniformly colored.

Uniformity of costume aside, the human figures show immense variation of pose and facial expression. One, for

Terra-cotta soldiers at Qin Tomb
Photo courtesy of China National Tourist Office, New York

example, has a square face and appears quite mature; his lips are tightly closed, and his eyes, wide open and gazing forward, suggest experience and confidence in battles. The face of another figure is long and younger looking; his head bends thoughtfully toward the floor. Yet another figure's face is round and smiling; he appears as if returning from a victorious battle. Similarly, the terra-cotta horses strike a variety of poses; some are galloping, some neighing, some shaking their heads, others wagging their tails. The standard of craftsmanship throughout is outstanding.

The first excavation in 1974–75 was followed in May 1976 by the excavation of a second tomb complex, known as the Number Two Pit. It has an area of 64,600 square feet and contains more than 1,000 artifacts. Number Two Pit reveals many similarities to Number One Pit. Each was constructed using similar methods and materials, and the depth of the pits is nearly identical. The sizes of the terra-cotta warriors and horses are also similar, as are the soldiers' uniforms and shoes. Many of the same weapons found in Number One Pit were also excavated at Number Two Pit.

Unlike Number One Pit, however, which is an oblong shape, Number Two Pit resembles a carpenter's square (two perpendicular oblongs). Moreover, while the first tomb contains mostly foot-soldiers, the second contains a greater number of cavalrymen and war chariots, providing evidence that warfare during this early period of Chinese history was relatively complex and involved long-distance attacks. Further evidence for this theory comes from the excavation of heavy crossbow shots. Two or three warriors stand atop each chariot; one of them is a crossbowman, and the others carry spears. Each chariot is drawn by four horses with reins and bridles but without stirrups (which came into use only much later).

A greater variety of costume and pose features among the figures of Number Two Pit as well. Here, uniquely, generals hold their swords with both arms, warriors hold the reins of horses in the cavalry section, and warriors hold out their arms as if shooting crossbows. The second pit demonstrates a greater variety of costume because it contains not only infantry but a complete combat force with generals, chariots, and cavalry. The total number of figures is not as great as those found in Number One Pit, however.

Around 1980 a third major excavation was made. Number Three Pit, much smaller than the previous two, contained only one chariot, six warriors, and a few weapons. Judging from the figures' uniforms, archaeologists speculate that this is the chamber of the commanders.

Between 1974 and 1980, archaeologists also excavated several chambers adjacent to the three sites. One of these chambers was presumably reserved for storing copper chariots, each of which is drawn by four terra-cotta horses. In another chamber, weapons made of alloy were found. Although many of the excavated artifacts were ruined by time or by fire, the weapons remained intact and still shone when excavated. In 1980, somewhat outside these chambers, archaeologists excavated a lesser known site containing figures dressed as underlings and laborers.

As recently as July 1995, another major discovery at the Qin Tomb site was announced. Archaeologists there uncovered sacrificial temples covering 50,000 square feet. The temples were used to offer food to the dead emperor. Historical records indicate that ritual offerings were made four times daily, and once a month a large sacrifice was held.

The Qin Tomb itself, where the emperor was buried, has not yet been excavated, although, gauging from the condition of the excavated areas, archaeologists consider it to be intact. Historical records of the emperor's tomb indicate that it was spectacular. According to Chinese historian Sima Qian, who lived during the Han Dynasty (206 B.C.–A.D. 220), the interior, divided into two compartments, was a gigantic subterranean palace built over the course of 36 years by 700,000 forced laborers. Inside the precincts were individual palace chambers, pavilions, and offices that were filled with exquisite wares and precious jewelry. It was defended by mechanically triggered crossbows that were set to shoot unwelcome visitors. It even featured elements meant to resemble the outside world, such as man-made rivers, heavenly constellations, and the so-called immortal fire, said to be sustained by whale oil. How much of this treasure remains intact is unknown.

Further Reading: *Eastern Zhou and Qin Civilizations* by Li Xeuqin, translated by K. C. Chang (New Haven, Connecticut, and London: Yale University Press, 1985), provides valuable background information for the period of the Qin Tomb's construction. *Records of the Grand Historian* by Ssu-ma Chien (Sima Qian), translated by Burton Watson (Hong Kong: Chinese University of Hong Kong, and New York: Columbia University Press, 1993), contains the Han historian's firsthand descriptions of the tombs. *The First Emperor of China*, edited by Li Yu-ning (White Plains, New York: International Arts and Sciences, 1975), represents a twentieth-century reevaluation of the role of the first emperor in Chinese history. *China's First Unifier: A Study of the Ch'in Dynasty as Seen in the Life of Li Ssu* by Derk Bodde (Leiden: Brill, 1938; reprint, Hong Kong: Hong Kong University Press, 1967), while dated, is still useful. The best visual treatments of the tomb and its artifacts are *Son of Heaven: Imperial Arts of China* by Robert L. Thorp (Seattle, Washington: Son of Heaven Press, 1988); *The First Emperor of China: The Greatest Archeological Find of Our Time* by Arthur Cotterell (London: Macmillan, and New York: Holt Rinehart, 1981); and *Underground Terracotta Army of Emperor Qin Shi Huang* (Beijing: New World Press, 1985; revised edition, as *Wonders from the Earth: The First Emperor's Underground Army*, San Francisco: China Books and Periodicals, 1989).

—Adam Yuen-chung Lui

Quanzhou (Fujian, China)

Location: In southeastern Fujian province, close to the northern shore of the estuary of the Jin River; 122 miles southwest of Fuzhou and 66 miles northeast of Xiamen.

Description: Port and city, one of the centers of ancient Chinese culture; site of commercial and trading activities in traditional China, with many relics showing contacts with foreign countries; regarded as the starting point of the so-called Sea Silk Route in medieval China; one of the principal homes for Chinese living in Taiwan and working overseas.

Contact: Fujian Tourism Bureau
24, Dong Da Lu
Fuzhou 350001, Fujian
China
(591) 7553794

Quanzhou, for centuries a well-known port of call, has been known by many names during its long history, among them Qingyuan, Wenling, Citong, Ruitong, Zaiton, Licheng, Quannan, and Hulu Cheng. As early as the sixth century, Quanzhou received a steady stream of traders and missionaries from other parts of Asia and from Africa. In 558 and 565, for instance, Paramartha, the famous Indian monk from the Malay Peninsula, visited Quanzhou, where he translated some Buddhist texts into Chinese before setting sail for Guangzhou. By the later part of the Tang Dynasty (618–907), Quanzhou had developed overseas trade to such an extent that it ranked with Guangzhou and Yangzhou as one of the largest ports in China. During the Five Dynasties period (907–959), the area of Quanzhou city was extended. To beautify the environment, Governor Liu Congxiao oversaw the planting of numerous pricked Chinese parasol trees *(citong shu),* giving rise to one of the city's numerous names: Citong Cheng (City with Pricked Chinese Parasol Trees).

The history of the area around today's Quanzhou city dates back over 1,000 years. Founded in 700 under the name of Wurong Zhou, the city changed its name to Quanzhou in 711 during the Tang Dynasty. According to the Quanzhou gazetteer, the name Quan was derived from the clear spring that flowed out of the Qingyuan Mountain.

By the Song Dynasty (960–1279), Quanzhou reached another peak of foreign trade and had become one of the world's most famous seaports. In 1087, customs services were established to collect taxes from ships arriving from Arabia, Persia, Japan, and Southeast Asia, and also to manage their operations within the port city. Archaeological evidence bears witness to both the extent of this trade and its importance to the city. On Nine-day Mountain, one can still find rocks inscribed during the Southern Song Dynasty (1127–1276) to commemorate the banquets city officials customarily gave to departing foreign merchants. The banquets were held at the mountain's famous Tongyuanwang Temple and were accompanied by the ceremony of paying for a good monsoon. Elsewhere in the city, archaeologists in 1966 uncovered a tombstone inscribed with four lines of Arabic and some poorly rendered Chinese, evidently the work of foreign visitors. More than 100 such tablets with Arabic inscriptions have since been unearthed, indicating the great extent of the Middle Eastern and North African presence in Quanzhou.

Under the Yuan Dynasty (1234–1368), Quanzhou became China's greatest port and was renowned throughout the world. Ships set sail from Quanzhou with silk, tea, copper, iron, and porcelain for ports in more than half the known world, reaching as far as Japan to the east, Persia and Arabia to the west, and islands in the distant South Pacific. When the Venetian traveler Marco Polo visited Quanzhou in the thirteenth century, he was attracted by its scenery and people. He wrote:

> The amount of traffic in gems and other merchandise entering and leaving this port is a marvel to behold. . . . I assure you that for one spice ship that goes to Alexandria or elsewhere to pick up pepper for export to Christendom, Zaiton [Quanzhou] is visited by a hundred. For you must know that it is one of the two ports in the world with the biggest flow of merchandise.

Polo called the city Zaiton (also seen as Zaitun and Zayton), an Arabic name from which we derive the English word "satin," one of the exotic fabrics exported from the city. The name Zaiton might itself have originated from a corruption of Citong or Ruitong, another early name for the city.

During this period, Quanzhou was visited by a great number of Islamic traders and merchants. The city is mentioned in the writings of Khaja Rashid E-din from Persia, Abdul Fedha from Syria, and Ibn Baṭṭūṭah from Morocco. Over the course of the Song and Yuan Dynasties, a sizeable Muslim community developed in Quanzhou. Several of these immigrants worked their way into the city bureaucracy and were given posts of importance overseeing various aspects of trade and commerce. The Muslims built several mosques in the city, many of which still stand. Thousands of Muslims lie buried in the ten communal graves north of the city. The earliest stone marker there is dated 1171.

Officials of the early Ming Dynasty (1368–1644) encouraged continued trade and foreign contacts. As a result, Quanzhou remained one of the busiest ports along the China coast. The Mings, like their Song predecessors, established

Kaiyuan Temple, Quanzhou
Photo courtesy of The Chicago Public Library

special officers to look after customs and to manage affairs with foreigners. Quanzhou continued to attract its share of famous visitors. The famous Chinese eunuch envoy, Zheng He, stayed in Quanzhou for some time during the fifth of his seven expeditions to the Western Ocean.

Just as the world came to Quanzhou's doorstep, so the Chinese used Quanzhou as the point of departure for distant ports. According to an inscription found in the Putian Xiangying Temple in Fujian province, Quanzhou natives had set sail to Sumatra during the Northern Song period (960–1127). In 1953, a stone tablet was excavated in Nanjiao Chang, an old training field within Quanzhou, recording the visit to Persia of a Chinese envoy from the Yuan Dynasty (1234–1368). Other records indicated that a Ming official, Zhang Qian, departed from Quanzhou for an official visit to Borneo in 1451.

Quanzhou's commercial activities and the broadening of its cultural contacts suffered a series of blows during the latter part of the fifteenth century. Owing to widespread piracy by, among others, the Wokou (Japanese pirates with Chinese collaboraters) along the southeast China coast, the Ming government banned all seafaring activities. The problems of Japanese pirates was particularly acute for Quanzhou: at one point, the pirates actually occupied the city. The decline of Quanzhou as a center of foreign trade in south China did not truly come about until the 1560s, however, when Yue Kang (Moon Harbor), a major smuggling port close to Xiamen, emerged and replaced it as a center of maritime activities.

The ban on overseas trade was tightened in the seventeenth century by the Qing emperors (1644–1912), who wished to cut the financial resources of their arch enemy, Zheng Chenggong, better known in the West as Koxinga. Koxinga led the remaining forces loyal to the Mings, whom the Qings had overthrown, and financed his operations though piracy. To deny him this economic support, the Qings not only banned overseas trade but in the early 1660s ordered that the coastal population move inland.

The increased European presence in the area further eroded the city's economic position. As the Europeans established colonies in Southeast Asia, they dominated what were once among Quanzhou's most important overseas markets. The Treaty of Nanjing in 1842 brought European competition even closer to home; the terms of the treaty included the opening of Fuzhou and Xiamen to foreign trade. Quanzhou's economy could take no more assaults; unemployment forced many of the city's inhabitants to migrate as laborers to Southeast Asia.

Quanzhou's economy remained bleak until the unification of China in the twentieth century by the communists, who transformed Quanzhou from a cultural center and port of call to an industrial city. Atop the former graveyards now stand high-rise factories processing such goods as sugar, flour, and honey. The site where criminals were once executed is now an automobile assembly plant. Other plants are devoted to such industries as mechanical engineering, electronics, shipbuilding, plastics, textiles, shoes and leather manufacturing, pottery, and pharmaceuticals. According to 1991 statistics, in addition to several hundred state-owned factories, the city has 1,418 private enterprises, owned either by foreign investors or by joint-venture companies.

Alongside modern industries, traditional handicraft industries such as bamboo weaving, wood carving, enamelware making, and embroidery flourish in Quanzhou. Many of these traditional products find welcome markets abroad. In addition, Quanzhou exports such agricultural products as rice, sugar cane, fresh seafood, and honey to other parts of China and abroad. Quanzhou also has become a cultural, educational, and scientific center, with more than a dozen cinemas and theatres, at least six major medical centers, and five universities.

Local government has conducted an aggressive campaign to modernize and improve the city's infrastructure. Whereas old Quanzhou city contained only a single paved street, decorated by two pagodas, now 6,300 miles of roadway run within the city and connect it with the immediate suburbs. Three main roads, known as Dongda Road, Round-the-city Road, and the Nine-one Road, are paved with marble stones. High-rise buildings line these roads, and trees shade the many pedestrian paths. Two bridges—the Floating Bridge of the Western Gate and the newly built Quanzhou Bridge—span the Jin River, and a twenty-mile-long embankment protects the city against floods.

The government has also taken pains to preserve Quanzhou's historic heritage. The city contains one of China's most famous monasteries, Kaiyuan Temple. The temple supposedly was built on the spot where lotuses sprouted miraculously from a mulberry tree (the structure was initially known as White Lotus Temple). Kaiyuan is well preserved, with a great hall in the Ming style and carefully tended topiary surrounding it. To the west of the hall is a mulberry tree, reputedly that of the legend. On either side of the hall stands a pagoda, and behind lies the Sweet Dew Vineyard Hall. All four structures are ornately decorated, frequently with carvings depicting scenes from the life of the Buddha. In addition to the Kaiyuan Temple, the city boasts the historic Twin Stone Pagodas; Wen Miao Temple, one of the country's oldest Confucian temples; and Luoyang and Anping, two well-preserved stone bridges.

Much of historic Quanzhou bears witness to its seafaring past and its many foreign visitors. The city contains several surviving mosques, most of which resemble modified Chinese pagodas, but the largest and most famous of them, Qingzheng Temple, invokes Islamic architecture with its pointed gate and scooped vaulting. The mosque was constructed in 1009 and later restored in 1309, 1350, and 1609. A short distance east of the city lies the Muslim graveyard, which includes a tomb said to contain the remains of two Islamic missionaries who visited the city during the Tang Dynasty. The Chinese envoy Zheng He is said to have visited the tomb during his stay in the city; it is now a pilgrimage site open only to Muslims.

The Museum of Overseas Trade located within the Kaiyuan Temple enclosure houses many other relics of the city's past. The museum's main attraction is a wooden trade ship from the thirteenth or fourteenth century, unearthed in the 1970s during the dredging of Houzhu, the city's ancient port. The ship evidently sunk on its return from a foreign harbor, and thus it contains none of the pottery or other precious cargo exported from Quanzhou. Preserved aboard, however, were many of the items imported into the city, including tortoise-shell, herbs, and containers of frankincense and mercury. In addition to these items, the museum houses a wealth of other archaeological remains, including headstones inscribed in Arabic, stone crosses that once marked the graves of the city's Nestorian Christian residents, and relics from the city's Manichean community. Such attractions have turned the city into an increasingly popular destination for tourists, both from China and abroad.

Further Reading: Many of the best sources of information about Quanzhou are in Chinese. For a discussion of the city's history, see *Gu Citong Gang* (Ancient Zaytun Port) by Zhuan Weiji (Xiamen: Xiamen University Press, 1989), *Quanzhou Yu Woguo Zhonggu de Haishang Jiaotong* (Quanzhou and Chinese Medieval Maritime Activities) by Li Donghua (Taiwan: n.p., 1986), and *Tangsong Shidai Minnan Quanzhou Shidi Lungao* (On Historical Geography of Quanzhou, South Fujian, in the Tang and Song Dynasties) by So Kee Long (Taiwan: n.p., 1991). For information on contemporary Quanzhou, see *Fujian,* edited by Lu Xiang (Hong Kong: Zhonghua Shuju, 1977); *Quanzhou Youji* (Travels in Quanzhou), edited by Quanzhou Duiwai Wenhua Jiaoliu Xiehui (Xiamen: Lujiang, 1985); and *Zhongguo Kouan Gailan* (Survey of Ports in China), edited by Tang Xiaoguang and Zhao Yiren (Beijing: n.p., 1992). An excellent English-language source on historical Quanzhou is *Community, Trade, and Networks: Southern Fujian Province from the Third to the Thirteenth Century* by Hugh Roberts Clark (Cambridge and New York: Cambridge University Press, 1991). Useful general histories of China include John Kong Fairbank's *China: A New History* (Cambridge, Massachusetts: Belknap Press of Harvard University Press, 1992) and Jonathan D. Spence's *The Search for Modern China* (New York and London: Norton, 1990).

—Adam Yuen-chung Lui

Qufu (Shandong, China)

Location: Situated in China's northern coastal province of Shandong, approximately 100 miles south of the provincial capital of Jinan.

Description: Qufu is famous as the childhood home and place of death of the philosopher Confucius. With its expansive Confucian temple complex, the town is a modern-day mecca for both scholars and tourists.

Contact: Marketing Department of Shandong Tourism Bureau
88 Jingshi Road
Jinan 250014, Shandong
China
86 531 2965858 6109

Once the capital of an ancient dukedom, Qufu is renowned for its most famous citizen, a man whose thoughts and philosophy have greatly affected not only China, but most other East Asian nations as well: Kong Fuzi, more commonly known as Confucius.

During the Spring and Autumn period of Chinese history, from 722 to 481 B.C., Qufu was the capital of the small and insignificant state of Lu. According to tradition, Confucius was born in 551 B.C., the illegitimate son of an old retired soldier (distantly related to the illustrious Kong family of a neighboring state) and a very young peasant girl. Little is known about Confucius's parents, or about his first years in a remote village called Zou, or about the early days after his father's death, when the family moved closer to the state capital at Qufu.

Although accurate accounts of the birth and childhood of Confucius are lost to time, his teachings were well documented by his students and later scholars and are preserved in the Chinese classic *Lunyu,* or *The Analects.* Regarded as a great teacher and philosopher equal in importance to Gautama Buddha, Socrates, and Jesus Christ, he is known in Asia as Kong Fuzi or simply Kongzi (Master Kong); Jesuits in the seventeenth century romanized the teacher's name to Confucius, and it is by this name that he is known in the West.

Despite his family's low social standing and lack of wealth, Confucius managed to receive the traditional education of the day, a systematic study of the ancient classics. Fully educated in these texts, Confucius was retained by the Duke of Lu in a series of low administrative posts starting when he was nineteen years old. By age fifty, Confucius had risen to the post of prime minister of Lu and was a trusted adviser to the duke.

Confucius's philosophy urged propriety and good manners; each citizen was obligated to perform the duties accorded by rank, thereby forming a solid society, albeit one firmly entrenched in a complex hierarchy. One of the cornerstones of Confucianism is the idea of *li,* which can be translated roughly as "attitude" or "ritual". In order to have a stable society, laws and regulations are not enough. Instead, the citizens must govern themselves by strict adherence to codes of etiquette, of *li. Li* entails a host of prescribed actions to be followed in particular social situations such as dealing with a socially inferior person or taking a wife. In addition, it is through the observance of *li* that religious rituals are performed to honor ancestors.

A second concept held dear by Confucius was that of *ren,* or "humanity". The character *ren* itself consists of two adjacent pictographs—that of "man" and that of "two"—indicating that *ren* represents how two persons should interact. Later scholars equate the Confucian ideal of *ren* with that of goodness, or the Judeo-Christian golden rule urging men to "do unto others as you would have them do unto you." Other ideas important to Confucianism are *yi,* often translated as "uprightness" or "honesty"; *zhi,* or "knowledge"; *xin,* meaning "faithfulness" or "integrity"; and one of the most crucial ideals of all, *xiao* or "filial piety".

The man who paid attention to all that Confucius held dear and who adhered to the ideas of *li* and *ren* was referred to as the *junzi,* commonly translated as "gentleman" or "superior man"; the Chinese character indicates the son of a prince or other nobility. Confucian scholars claim that if people would only emulate the ideal *junzi* and pay strict attention to *li,* society would be free from disorder. According to these beliefs, the government needs to form a framework of laws only to control the common people.

None of Confucius's ideas was revolutionary, or even new, for that matter. All were grounded in the classics. As he moved from state to state, he urged the contemporary rulers of the Zhou Dynasty (1122–256 B.C.) to return to the policies of the early—and possibly legendary—Zhou kings Wen and Wu, whose reigns were said to have been a golden age. Perhaps not surprisingly, Confucius encountered great resistance when attempting to instill his doctrine in China's ruling class, which was preoccupied with riches and worldly pleasures. Time after time he became a trusted adviser to a local ruler only to fall out of favor when the ruler grew tired of the discipline Confucius advocated.

A failure in his own eyes, Confucius ultimately returned to his childhood home of Qufu to continue his teaching and writing. He died in 479 B.C. and was buried in Qufu, close to the riverbank north of the city, on lands that today remain part of the Kong Family compound. The grave mound lies in the center of a small cemetery, and the fifteenth-century gravestone bears the inscription "Grave of the Sacred King of Culture, who achieved Absolute Perfection."

Dacheng Dian in the Confucian Temple Complex, Qufu
Photo courtesy of China National Tourist Office, Los Angeles

Although Confucius never realized his goal of attaining an important government post or of capturing a sympathetic and loyal royal ear, he passed his philosophy and knowledge to a large number of disciples. It has been through the work of these students, both those who studied with Confucius himself and those who immersed themselves in his words after his death, that Confucianism has made such a lasting impact on the Eastern world.

After Confucius's death, his disciples moved into small huts built around his grave. From the time of their construction in the fifth century B.C., these huts have remained occupied, gradually becoming part of the Confucian temple built by the Kong lineage. The first temple on the present-day site was built one year after Confucius died and was commissioned by the duke of Lu, Lu Aigong. The temple complex was built on the spot where the house of Confucius once stood and has survived over 2,000 years of damage, repairs, and additions. Although Confucius and his ideas were never warmly embraced by ruling powers during his life, his philosophy of moderation and balance has been adopted and adapted by scores of Chinese rulers since his death. The longevity of his ideals has made Qufu a mecca for pilgrims for thousands of years. The same rulers who governed by his rules also contributed greatly to the upkeep and additions at the Confucian complex at Qufu.

The Confucian temple complex is quite large, covering some fifty-four acres, and contains several pavilions, courtyards, halls, and ceremonial gates. The complex was constructed in a style similar to the Forbidden City in Beijing and the Summer Palace outside the capital's city limits; it remains one of the best examples of ancient Chinese architecture.

The complex is laid out along a north-south grid, with accompanying buildings branching out to the east and west. The entire grouping is protected by a traditional red wall with four defense towers overlooking the perimeter. The first two of the nine courtyards are entered through gates dating to the Ming (A.D. 1368–1644), with the second guarded by a pair of Han Dynasty (206 B.C.–A.D. 220) stone warriors, each standing over seven feet tall.

In the inner regions of the complex lies the Pavilion of the Literary Star, first built in 1018 and then rebuilt and enlarged in 1191 and again in 1500. This pavilion once housed a collection of calligraphy by a series of Chinese emperors and remains one of the classic Chinese buildings on the temple grounds. Another nearby pavilion houses over fifty stelae (carved stone slabs) bearing inscriptions from various emperors, evidence of Confucius's long-standing impact on Chinese government.

One of the most important halls, built in 1569, is called the Apricot Altar and is located on the site where Confucius himself taught his students. The altar bears a stone tablet from the twelfth century, and an impressive stone censer (ornate cauldron used for burning incense) from the time of the Song (960–1276) is located just outside of the structure.

The heart of the complex is the Dacheng Dian, or Hall of Great Achievements. First built in the eleventh century, this hall stands over 100 feet tall and is 111 feet long and 177 feet wide. Since its construction, the Hall of Great Achievements has been the site of countless ceremonies in honor of Confucius. The present structure dates to 1724 and holds not only statues of Confucius, but those of his sixteen students as well.

The temple complex also contains a pavilion built in honor of Confucius's wife, about whom very little is known. The Hall of Sleep was first built in 1019 and then was completely reconstructed and enlarged in 1730. Further insight into Confucius's personal life also may be seen in the Hall of the Signs of the Wise Man, where some 120 stone engravings portray stages of the teacher's life. The carvings, dating from the eighth to the thirteenth centuries, are further testament to the longevity and importance of Confucius and his philosophy.

While Confucius and his ideas have endured, both his philosophy and his monuments have been assailed from numerous sides. One of the most brutal attacks came during the Qin Dynasty (221–206 B.C.) from Qin Shihuang Di, the famous emperor credited with building the Qin Tomb near Xian as well as some of the initial sections of the Great Wall. Not known for his tolerance of opposing viewpoints, Qin Shihuang Di—an avowed Legalist—ordered Confucian scholars executed and the teacher's works burned.

Confucianism played a large part in China's political and social arenas throughout the dynasties, occasionally sharing the spotlight with both Taoism and Buddhism. Confucianism's emphases on citizens conforming with the duties accorded to their position in life, respecting those above them in status, and working together for the good of society as a whole all benefited the emperor.

The Communist revolution of 1949 also promoted many of these values, but since the communists battled all things associated with ancient society and tradition, Confucianism became one of the communists' main targets. The ancestor worship and feudal hierarchy promoted by Confucius were antithetical to the communists' ideals and turned them against everything associated with the ancient philosophy. In 1948, the seventy-seventh generation direct descendant of Confucius finally fled Qufu for Taiwan, ending the 2,500-year Kong family residence in that town.

The assault against Confucius continued during the 1960s, when the tumultuous Cultural Revolution saw countless statues of Confucius smashed or otherwise damaged. Qufu itself was the site of a Red Guard rampage and suffered at the hands of the young people as they burned, defaced, and looted the otherwise quiet town. Fortunately, the Kong family archives, a priceless collection of historically important works, escaped unscathed.

By 1979 the Red Guards were silenced and Confucius returned to popularity, with millions of yuan allocated for repairs to the Confucian complex in Qufu. The fabulous architecture of the entire Confucian complex remains an excellent example of Chinese imperial architecture, second only to the Imperial Palace of Beijing. Once graced by the sage himself and later by numerous emperors and nobles coming to pay their respects, Qufu and its Confucian temple complex remain a cultural mecca for scholars and tourists, both Chinese and foreign.

Further Reading: Betty Kelen's *Confucius in Life and Legend* (New York: T. Nelson, 1971; London: Sheldon, 1974) is a very readable depiction of the life and teachings of Confucius. Leonard Cottrell's *The Tiger of Ch'in: The Dramatic Emergence of China as a Nation* (New York: Holt Rinehart, 1962; with subtitle *How China Became a Nation*, London: Evans, 1962) provides an excellent account of the persons, places, and events important in China's early imperial history. A similar approach is taken in *The Great Wall of China* by Robert Silverberg (Philadelphia: Chilton, 1965) in reconstructing China's thousands-year-old history detail by detail, highlighting such important figures as Confucius. Readers interested in the lasting impact of Confucianism on China will enjoy Scott Morton's *China: Its History and Culture* (New York: Lippincott and Crowell, 1980; third edition, New York: McGraw-Hill, 1995) and the concise historical account given by Charles Hucker in *China to 1850* (Stanford: Stanford University Press, 1978). Two travel books provide excellent descriptions of the Confucian temple complex at Qufu: *China* (Stuttgart: Baedeker, 1994) and *China: A Travel Survival Kit* by Alan Samagalski, Robert Strauss, and Michael Buckley (second edition, South Yarra, Victoria, and Berkeley, California: Lonely Planet, 1988) offer historical and architectural details of the complex at Qufu and other related sights in the town itself.

—Monica Cable

Quilon (Kerala, India)

Location: Situated on the Malabar Coast of southwestern India, near Asthamudi Lake.

Description: Port town also called Collam, Kollam, Coulon, and Coilon. Known from early times as an important commercial town, it now serves as the administrative headquarters for the Quilon district.

Site Office: Government of India Tourist Office
Willingdon Island
Cochin 682 009, Kerala
India
6683521

A southern Indian myth tells that Paraśurāma, a god known for his belligerent temperament, threw his battle axe far out into the sea in a fit of rage. The waters parted and the land of Kerala emerged. Modern Kerala is a long thin state that stretches along the Malabar Coast. Renowned for its beauty, Kerala is composed of what used to be the kingdoms of Travancore and Cochin. Quilon, a harbor town situated in southern Kerala, was once one of the most important trading ports in India. From an early time traders journeyed there from Arabia, China, and Africa to buy spices and silks.

Quilon (pronounced Koy-lon) is the Anglicized version of the Malayālam word *Kollam.* The city is mentioned in several historic texts under many different names. Sulaman called it *Male* in A.D. 851; Benjamin of Tudela used the name *Chulam* in 1166; Pauthier in his edition of Marco Polo referred to it as *Kiulan;* in 1273 Abulfeda called it *Coilon* or *Coilun;* Father Odoric referred to it as *Polumbum;* and in the sixteenth century Barbosa called it *Coulam.* Some historians argue that the town was named Kollam after a great (unknown) event that took place, giving rise to the Kollam era. It is possible that the word *Kollam/Kolam* is derivative of *kulam,* the Malayālam word for "tank," or is a mixture of two words *ko* and *illam,* literally meaning "king's palace."

Little is known of the area's prehistory; few ancient sites have been found in the region. Quilon district is, however, known for its inscriptions: the ninth-century A.D. Tariśapalli Copper Plates, the tenth-century A.D. Mampalli Plate, and the Rameśwarathukoil Inscription, which dates from A.D. 1102. The last-named is written in Tamil, the predominant language of south India in this period, and records donations to the temple in Quilon.

Pliny (A.D. 23–79) gave an accurate description of the trade route to the Malabar Coast at a time when the main articles exchanged were cotton and pepper. Certainly, the prosperity of the region owed much to Quilon's success and popularity as a trading port. By the ninth century A.D. Quilon was established as the trade and political center of the Kulaśekhara Dynasty of the Venāḍ Empire (A.D. 800–1102). Both the Chinese and Arabs were now trading extensively with Quilon. Many historians argue that the name Kollam dates from this period, when the Kollam Era (an alternative date system) was established in A.D. 825. The reason for the establishment of this new era is subject to debate.

The town's early associations with Europe and Christendom date between A.D. 52 and A.D. 774–95, the time period when Thomas of Kana is thought to have built a church in Quilon (one of seven founded in Kerala). Christian churches were established in the area by at least the sixth century, as verified by the Byzantine monk Cosmos Indicopleustus, who traveled to the Malabar Coast in A.D. 522. Cosmos mentioned that Christian places of worship existed in Taprobane (Sri Lanka) and in Mali (Quilon).

Jewish merchants also were important traders on the Malabar Coast, visiting the area frequently and establishing centers at Koḍungallar (Tiruvanchikkulam), Quilon, and Cochin, where there remains a small Jewish colony to this day. Although Arab merchants did not make their presence known in the area until the eleventh or twelfth century, the Arab merchant Sulaman visited the coast around A.D. 851, when he spoke of the large number of Chinese ships stopping in Quilon on their return from Persia. Sulaman stated that Quilon was the most important port in India at this time.

In the eleventh century a hundred-year war broke out between the Kulaśekharas of Mahodayapuram and the Imperial Cōḷas. During the war, the Keralans, led by the Venāḍ chief Ramar Tiruvadi Koyiladhikari Kulaśekhari Chakkravarti, made their capital at Quilon, the most vulnerable town in their southern territories. Ramar was driven out of Quilon by the Cōḷa general Naralokavira in 1096. Subsequently, Quilon was burned in the hope that it would break Venāḍ resistance, and the Cōḷa general became known as *Kollam Azhivu Kanan*: "he who destroyed Kollam." In 1099 the Venāḍ leader attacked and regained Quilon, and consequently a new, independent Venāḍ Empire was born. Quilon developed and expanded during this period, and trade links with other countries and empires were strengthened. Throughout the twelfth century, Quilon and the Venāḍ Empire repeatedly fell into Cōḷa hands only to be retaken by the indigenous Keralan rulers.

Rabbi Benjamin of Tudela visited Quilon between 1159 and 1173. He noted that the extreme heat prevented trade during the day. When evening fell, traders came out to deal in pepper, fruit, spices, cinnamon, and ginger, among other things. The traveler and diplomat Marco Polo visited Quilon in the thirteenth century as a representative of the court of Kublai Khan. He estimated that the pepper trade between Quilon and China's largest city amounted to forty-three loads of pepper per day. However, the competition

River scene near Quilon
Photo courtesy of Jonathan Drori

from Arab traders was fierce; at the end of the thirteenth century, the first Roman Catholic missionary in India, John of Monte Corrino, reported that the Chinese, Christian, and Jewish traders had been ousted from the Quilon market by Muslims, who had begun to settle in the town in great numbers.

As the spice trade increased, Quilon prospered, and European interest in India, almost inevitably, became more intense. The Portuguese explorer Vasco da Gama discovered a sea route to India via the Cape of Good Hope in 1498. Landing at Calicut (Kozhikode) on the Malabar Coast, da Gama ordered his men to buy every spice the natives could offer. Despite buying overpriced goods that were often of poor quality, da Gama returned to Portugal and sold his goods at a 3,000 percent profit, thereby covering the cost of his two-year expedition by more than sixty times. News of da Gama's success brought other expeditions to India, and the Portuguese began trade negotiations with local leaders.

In the fifteenth and sixteenth centuries, the area now known as Kerala was not ruled by any large empire or kingdom. Rather, during this period of initial European contact, Kerala was a conglomeration of sometimes warring chiefdoms. For a brief period in the sixteenth century, the Vijayanagar Empire held sway in this region but failed to maintain their control.

The rani (queen) of Quilon first invited the Portuguese to the city in 1501 to discuss the pepper trade. The Portuguese refused because da Gama had close relations with the rāja of Cochin, their chief supplier of pepper. Unperturbed, the rani negotiated with the rāja of Cochin to allow her some of the European trade. Two Portuguese ships would be permitted to visit Quilon and buy pepper; this gesture marked the beginning of trade relations between Quilon and Portugal. Gradually, relations between Portugal and Quilon improved, but were temporarily set back by a misunderstanding that led to a revolt in 1505. The uprising occurred after a captain in the Portuguese fleet arrived in Quilon to find Arab ships loading with pepper. He confiscated the pepper, and fighting erupted. Rumors began to circulate that the Arabs had seized all of Portugal's possessions and murdered all the Portuguese in Quilon.

Duarte Pacheco was sent to the port to investigate and found that only one man had been killed, but all of the Portuguese ships lay empty while the Arab vessels were loaded with pepper and spices. He unloaded the ships, an act that once again led to fighting; this time the Arabs caught and murdered thirteen Portuguese men and burned down the Church of St. Thomas. In retribution the Portuguese viceroy Francisco de Almeida sent his son Lorenzo to burn all the ships in Quilon port. To prevent further destruction, the rani negotiated with the Portuguese. Finally in 1516 a treaty was signed in which the Quilon royal family agreed to rebuild the church and give a large quantity of pepper to the Portuguese crown as compensation. The Portuguese also were made exempt from custom tax and given the monopoly over the spice and pepper trade with Quilon.

The terms of the treaty proved difficult to meet, and the rani was unable to deliver all of the promised pepper. She agreed to allow the Portuguese factor, also a naval captain, to build a house in Quilon. Instead, he erected a fort and stole 5,000 bullock loads of pepper from local traders. This uncharitable move led to rioting during which the fort was besieged and damaged. The Portuguese, stranded in Quilon, were rescued from the sea by ships sent from Cochin. Despite the Portuguese duplicity, the rani again signed a less-than-favorable treaty, in which she agreed to pay for damages and to sell all of the pepper held in her own stores to the Portuguese. The latter continued to make themselves unpopular by hijacking local ships, pursuing Christian conversions with zeal, and finally plundering the Hindu temple at Teralakhara, in the Quilon district.

As Portugal continued to antagonize its host country, the Dutch and English began to take a serious interest in India, and competed to find a northern route to the subcontinent. Although England remained largely unsuccessful until the seventeenth century, the Dutch began to expand their empire to the East, reaching Java in 1595. In 1602 the Dutch East India Company was founded to pursue interests in the East; it made contact with Quilon in 1658 and signed a peace treaty the following year. Quilon officially became a Dutch protectorate, with the Dutch agreeing to rid India of the unpopular Portuguese.

The Dutch officer in charge, Van Goens, stationed a garrison in the city to protect it from possible invasion. The Portuguese had amassed a combined army of 3,000 of their own men and a few thousand Nairs (the warrior caste). As soon as Van Goens left Quilon to pursue other territories, the force attacked the garrison and drove the Dutch out of the city. The Dutch would not recapture Quilon until two years later, in 1661.

After the founding of the English East India Company in 1600, England successfully began to infiltrate Indian trade. English merchants followed the Dutch method of "triangular trade"; they invested gold in south Indian weaving, sold the goods in Bantam (Banten) in exchange for pepper and cloves, and finally sold the spices for a 400 percent return on their original investment of gold specie. Thus, English interest was directed to the south, and by 1642 the English had fortified an area that was to become known as Madras (Tamil Nādu).

The 1654 treaty between Portugal and Oliver Cromwell's English Commonwealth further damaged the Portuguese monopoly over trade in India. It gave English traders the right to trade in any Portuguese holding in Asia. Later, this treaty was recognized by Charles II as well. Hence, as Portugal's presence in India began to fade, the Dutch and English worked together, even as they competed for trade and territory there.

The mid–eighteenth century marked a period of great political change in the region. A leader named Mārtāṇḍa Varma attempted to consolidate the various autonomous kingdoms into a single state, which would become known as Travancore; obviously, his plans met stiff resistance from the rulers of these smaller states—Quilon, Kayamkulam, and Kottarakara. The conflict was complicated by the presence of the Dutch, who fortified their base city of Quilon against an invasion by Travancore forces. The Travancore army, led by Mārtāṇḍa Varma, attacked Dutch forts and defeated Dutch forces in July 1741 at the Battle of Colachel. The 6,000-strong Travancore army then marched to Quilon and attacked the city. A subsequent battle ended in a Travancore defeat, but the involved parties sued for peace, resulting in the Treaty of Mannas in 1742. As part of this agreement, many territories belonging to the Quilon royal family were ceded to the emerging kingdom of Travancore.

Dutch power in southern India, however, was waning. In October of 1795, the British gained control of Dutch Quilon, which eventually became part of British Madras. A treaty negotiated in the same year between Britain and Travancore agreed that an English infantry and artillery force would be stationed in Quilon.

Between 1798 and 1811, Balarma Varma ruled Quilon as a vassal of the British Empire. During this period, the city experienced rapid growth and development. The Anandavalleeswaram Temple and palace were built during this time, and merchants began to move to Quilon from Madurai and Tirunelveli. As British power increased, local resentment of the heavy presence of British troops grew, culminating in a rebellion in 1809. Led by Velu Tampi, this rebellion is famous for the proclamation issued by Tampi that declared the British were treacherous and would soon sit in the palaces and places of power in India. Tampi stated that the British would suppress the Brahman communities and any native traditional or religious customs. Tampi called on his fellow men to rise up against this tyranny. His army is estimated to have been between 20,000 to 30,000 men. Although Tampi's forces fought valiantly, they were defeated by the British, and Velu Tampi subsequently committed suicide.

The nineteenth century brought an end to Quilon's importance as a port and center of public office and administration. During the reign of Swati Tiruna (1829–47), Trivandrum, the present capital of Kerala, became the political center. Quilon managed to retain some of its importance as the head office of the school district during the British era.

In 1885, when Sri Mulam Tirunal came to power, still under the rule of the British Empire, he further increased Quilon's facilities by opening a women's hospital and irrigation works, developing the road network between Quilon and Shencottah, and developing a railway link in 1904; the rail link was extended to Trivandrum in 1918, and Ernakulam (Cochin) in 1957. Quilon opened its first Agriculture Demonstration Farm in 1907.

Quilon was involved in the early activities of the Indian National Congress. Through men such as C. Kesaran and T. W. Varghese, both from Quilon, the city became involved in the Abstention, or Nivarthana, Movement of the 1930s. This movement emerged from the demand for proportional representation on the legislative council of Travancore, which had been created in 1888; votes previously had been limited to people with property, normally of the upper castes. The Joint Political Congress, or All Travancore Samyukta Rashtreeya Samiti, demanded both proportional representation and responsible government at the state level. The Congress demanded a boycott of the elections until their demands were met. Consequently, C. Kesaran was arrested and charged with sedition on June 7, 1935. As a result of the Nivarthana Movement, a public service commissioner was appointed to ensure that all communities were fairly represented. The movement also had a religious dimension; the lower caste and untouchable communities threatened to convert to Christianity if the temple restrictions limiting entry to lower castes were not rescinded. As a result, the Temple Entry Proclamation was passed in November 1936, opening temple doors to all castes.

The Joint Political Congress became the Travancore State Congress in 1938 and continued to demand responsible government. Again C. Kesaran was among the leaders. Following a public meeting that erupted into a riot in which several local people were killed, all of the leaders of the congress were arrested. Mohandas Karamchand Gandhi (also called Mahatma Gandhi) subsequently asked the congress to suspend its policy of civil disobedience, and this practice was abandoned. The political destiny of Quilon and Kerala would be linked with that of independent India. R. Sankar and Kumbalathu Sanku Pillai, both originally from Quilon, were important members of the Indian National Congress; Sankar was especially decisive in shaping state policy.

In the twentieth century Quilon has declined in importance. Once the most important port in India, Quilon now exports goods on a much smaller scale. The town is the site of several manufacturing and processing industries, including cashew refinement and packaging. Although it has five colleges, it is primarily known as a railway town and as the gateway to the "backwater trip," a popular boat trip along the remote rivers and villages between Quilon and Alleppey. This excursion draws many tourists to the town, but apart from the boat trip, there is little else to tempt the tourist to stay in Quilon. The ruins of the ancient Portuguese fort at Thangasseri is less than two miles from Quilon but is not a great tourist attraction. Thus, one of the most important and prosperous ports in ancient India is today a small, little-visited town of winding streets and wooden houses.

Further Reading: Among the many general histories and gazetteers, the *Gazetteer of India, Kerala: Quilon,* edited by A. S. Menon (Trivandrum, Kerala: Superintendent of Government Press, 1964), is an essential but out-of-date source that gives insight into every aspect of cultural, historical, social, and environmental life in Quilon from the earliest times to the 1960s. *Kerala: The Land and the People* by Krishna Chaitanya (Delhi: National Book Trust, 1972; second edition, 1979) is a good, concise book, especially regarding the city's history up to the fifteenth century. K. V. Eapen's *A Short History of Kerala* (Kottayam: Kollett, 1983) is a concise book that focuses mostly on the European colonization of India. A fascinating although obscure book, *Native Life in Travancore* by the Reverend Samuel Mateer (London: Allen, 1883), reveals the finer details of life in Travancore by a representative of the London Missionary Society who lived and worked there for more than fifty years. *A New History of India* by Stanley Wolpert (New York: Oxford University Press, 1977; fourth edition, 1993) is a detailed treatment exploring the history of India from 2500 B.C. to the time of Indira Gandhi.

—A. Vasudevan

Rāmeswaram (Tamil Nādu, India)

Location: A small island (thirty-four square miles), located along a narrow stretch of coral reef between the southern tip of India and Sri Lanka (formerly Ceylon) in the Palk Bay, where the Indian Ocean and the Bay of Bengal meet.

Description: Also known as Iameccaram, Rāmeswaram is a major Hindu pilgrimage center because of its connections with the *Rāmāyaṇa*. The principal village is also called Rāmeswaram and is the site of the Rāmanathaswami, one of the largest and most beautiful temples in southern India. The island also holds a large number of holy baths.

Contact: Government of India Tourist Office
154 Anna Salai
Madras 600 002, Tamil Nādu
India
(82) 69685

The history of Rāmeswaram is not well known. This small island of sand dunes, umbrella trees, and pilgrimage sites was always an outpost of the Tamil kingdoms that dominated southern India at various times. Rāmeswaram does make an occasional appearance in local chronicles, but these have received little attention—and, consequently, little confirmation—from modern historians. Dates, usually given in regnal years of local rulers, bear an uncertain relationship to dates of the Common (Christian) Era.

What is clear is that, since time immemorial, Rāmeswaram was a possession of the rājas of Rāmnād until, in the wake of Indian independence, it became a part of the state of Tamil Nādu. The Rāmnād family had its origins in the ancient Maravar tribe, which maintained a capital at Rāmanāthapuram on the mainland. As tributaries of the first Pāṇḍya Kingdom (third century B.C.–fourth century A.D.), they had some control over the southeastern coast of India opposite from Rāmeswaram. The Rāmnād rājas made themselves extremely useful to their Pāṇḍya overlords, on several occasions beating back attacks by the Cōḷas, a rival dynasty to the north of Pāṇḍya. As a consequence, the Rāmnād rājas enjoyed a favored position in the Pāṇḍya Kingdom, being allowed, among other honors, to use the title of *setupathi*, meaning guardian of the *setu*—the coral reefs that extend from Rāmeswaram's southeastern tip to Sri Lanka. When the Pāṇḍya Dynasty crumbled in the fourth century, the Maravars seem to have become independent and expanded their territories. How long this independence lasted is unclear, but by the seventh century they were once again tributaries of the reinvigorated Pāṇḍya Dynasty.

In the middle of the twelfth century, the king of Lanka (now Sri Lanka) made war on the Pāṇḍyas. Although he seems to have made little headway on the whole, he did conquer the island of Rāmeswaram and built a temple there. The location of this temple is not known, and whether anything of it survives therefore cannot be confirmed. It is unlikely that Lanka held Rāmeswaram for long, because no trace of a Lanka presence is in evidence today.

In the thirteenth century, the Pāṇḍya Empire was divided into six administrative provinces. The province of Rāmnād was one of these, and Rāmeswaram must have been retaken by then, because it was included in the district. The Setupathi was appointed the provincial governor. According to the local chronicles, Rāmnād flourished until the Muslim expansions into southern India.

A number of Muslim dynasties had held large parts of northern India since the late twelfth century and began to expand into the southern reaches of the subcontinent early in the fourteenth century. Before long the Pāṇḍya Kingdom succumbed to the Muslims' superior military organization, although it subsisted as a tributary to the Muslim overlords until the sixteenth century. The Rāmnād rājas seem to have made use of the new power relations in the region to gain their independence from Pāṇḍya. Rāmnād is thought to have split from Pāṇḍya around 1380, but unfortunately the details of the separation are not well understood. The Setupathis continued to reign independently until about a decade after 1762, the year they granted permission to traders of the Dutch East India Company to build a fortress at Rāmeswaram. The British, battling with the Dutch and Portuguese for control over trade with India, attacked the Dutch Rāmeswaram outpost in 1773. Chasing the Dutch off the island, the victorious British also took the occasion to subjugate Rāmnād. The Setupathis once again lapsed into a familiar tributary role and continued thus until 1947, when their title was officially abolished by the new government and their territories became a part of the state of Tamil Nādu.

What Rāmeswaram lacks in well-attested history it makes up in lore and legend. Some of the most important events of the *Rāmāyaṇa*, the ancient epic that has become scripture in the Hindu religion, take place on Rāmeswaram. The greater part of the *Rāmāyaṇa* deals with Rāma's quest for Sītā, his wife, who had been abducted by the demon king Ravāna and taken to Lanka. The quest nears its end when Rāma finally finds his way to Rāmeswaram and prepares for his battle with the demon king on Lanka. To locate Sītā, Rāma's faithful companion, the monkey king Hanumān, jumps across the ocean from Mount Gandamadhana to Lanka, an impressive hundred-mile leap.

The location of Mount Gandamadhana is highly contested; several places on the mainland claim to be this sacred site. Local tradition has identified Rāmeswaram's one modest hill as Mount Gandamadhana, even though the *Rāmāyaṇa*

Corridor in the Rāmanathaswami Temple, Rāmeswaram
Photo courtesy of National Geographic Image Collection, Washington, D.C.

leaves no doubt that Hanumān leapt to Lanka all the way from the mainland. Rāmeswaram's Mount Gandamadhana is located a few miles north of Rāmeswaram village and is the site of a rather dilapidated temple, the Ekanta-Rāmeswaram, as well as the ruins of an ancient Rāmnād palace and fortress. According to the *Rāmāyaṇa,* Rāma held his council of war in the Ekanta-Rāmeswaram while awaiting Hanumān's return. It is clear, nevertheless, that the present temple is not nearly old enough to have sheltered the epic hero. The ruined fort holds a representation of Rāma's footprints, in the place where he is thought to have addressed his troops prior to their invasion of Lanka.

Another very important site on Rāmeswaram is Dhanushkodi, close to the Rāma Setu (Rāma's Bridge). These coral reefs, which stretch almost uninterrupted to Sri Lanka and lie just below the surface of the ocean, are also known as Adam's Bridge in western cartography. Muslim tradition holds that Cain, after slaying Abel, carried his brother's corpse over the bridge to Rāmeswaram to bury him there. Two strange rectangular, tomb-like structures standing near the eastern shore of the island are said to house the bones of the biblical brothers. Of course, the Hindu population has little use for this legend and prefers the *Rāmāyaṇa*'s account of the building of the bridge.

Without boats and lacking Hanumān's leaping ability but desperate to cross the waters, Rāma asks the ocean to recede so he and his armies can walk the dry ocean floor to Lanka. After three days of waiting, Rāma loses his patience and begins to shoot arrows into the waves. The wounded ocean, begging Rāma's mercy, suggests that the monkey Nala and his army construct a bridge. Nala, who is also known as the divine architect, is ready to oblige and builds a causeway with the aid of an army of bears, squirrels, and monkeys. Rāma and his huge army cross to Lanka, defeat Ravāna's army, kill the demon king, and liberate Sītā.

Although no mention is made of it in the *Rāmāyaṇa,* local legend maintains that Rāma destroyed the bridge after his return from Lanka to Rāmeswaram. The story goes that

Vibhishana, Ravāna's successor as ruler of Lanka, requested that Rāma break up the bridge to protect Lanka from future invasions. Rāma acceded to the request and used his bow to reduce the bridge to rubble. This is the reason that the modern visitor, standing at the tip of the island at Dhanushkodi, can make out no more than the remnants of the once-glorious bridge under the surface of the water.

Since Ravāna had been a Brahman before his deterioration into evil, Rāma committed a sin when he killed the demon. Returning to Rāmeswaram to ask Siva for absolution, Rāma is instructed to install a *liṅgam* (a monolithic phallic symbol representing the male principle in the universe and one of Hinduism's most important objects of worship) on the island at the hour of the Muhurtha. Rāma immediately orders Hanumān to fetch a suitable stone from the banks of the Narmada River, but the monkey king does not return in time. Concerned that the Muhurtha not be missed, Rāma and Sītā fashion a liṅgam of sand, calling it Rāmaliṅgam. Rāma sanctifies the makeshift construction and pays it proper homage in obedience to Siva's instructions. Upon his return, Hanumān, disappointed and enraged that his expedition has been for nought, wraps his tail around the sand *liṅgam* in an attempt to uproot it. Rāmaliṅgam, however, is not to be moved, even though Hanumān applied such wrenching force to the *liṅgam* that—believers say—his tail left an imprint at its base. Acknowledging his debt to Hanumān, Rāma then installs the stone *liṅgam* also, calls it Visvaliṅgam, and gives it precedence to Rāmaliṅgam in all worship.

Local tradition holds that the two *liṅgams* survive undisturbed to this day. Rāmanāthaswami Temple, at the center of Rāmeswaram village, is said to have been built around them. In truth, there is very little clarity about the dates of this temple's construction. Some sources date the first buildings to the twelfth century, but most likely the outer walls, parts of the towers (or *gopuras*), and most of the shrines at the center of the complex were not built until the fifteenth century. The inner walls may have been added late in the sixteenth or early in the seventeenth century. It is fairly certain that the principal glory of the temple, the elaborately carved inner *prakaram*, or corridor, was not erected until the eighteenth century. Two of the four entrance towers are still not finished, while the largest tower, over the east entrance, was completed only at the turn of the century.

Rāmanāthaswami is one of the most famous of India's Dravidian temples, both for its size and for the refinement of its ornamental sculpture. The temple is laid out in a rectangle, its east-to-west sides 865 feet long and its north-to-south sides 657 feet long. The main entrance on the east side of the building faces the ocean. Three sets of corridors are built one inside the other, while the central space within the inner corridor holds the most important shrines and holy bathing places. Most of the area between the outer wall and middle corridor is occupied by gardens. A portico on the east side of the outer wall gives access to the main tower, which is 186 feet high and consists of nine stories. The temple's massive corridors are of a length unequaled anywhere in India, measuring a total of 4,000 feet. The longest unbroken stretch of corridor is 700 feet long. Although the corridors open into transverse galleries leading to the various shrines, these openings are obscured by the heavily ornamented pillars lining the sides. The overall, tunnel-like effect is visually disorienting with its wealth of repeating sculptural detail.

The Rāmanāthaswami is sacred to Vaisnavites and Saivites alike and is visited every year by thousands of pilgrims belonging to both sects. Inside the temple, in addition to the Rāmaliṅgam and the Visvaliṅgam, are over twenty *tīrthas*, or holy baths, and numerous shrines that the pilgrim is expected to visit. The most important of the holy pools and wells is the Koti Tīrtha, which reportedly was formed by Rāma himself. Finding an insufficient supply of water for the ritual bathing of the Rāmaliṅgam, he pressed the ground with the point of his bow. A pool formed immediately. Other holy baths in the temple include the Chakra Tīrtha, whose waters are believed to restore broken or amputated limbs, and the Sankha Tīrtha, where the bather can hope to be freed of the sin of ingratitude.

Pilgrims who wish to be freed of all sins must first bathe in all the other *tīrthas* at Rāmeswaram, both inside and outside the temple, prior to bathing in the Koti Tīrtha. The holiest of these other sites are the Lakṣmaṇa Gunda and Dhanushkodi. The Lakṣmaṇa Gunda is the first stop on a pilgrimage to the island, and the pilgrim is to follow there an elaborate ritual including two ablutions and a haircut. The faithful then proceed to Dhanushkodi, where a bath in a lagoon is to be followed by thirty-five baths in the holy pool. Ideally, the pilgrim takes an extended period of time, as long as nine months, to complete the Dhanushkodi rituals, but those in a hurry have been known to make all the requisite stops on the island within the space of a few hours. Many of the holy sites scattered across the island are, in fact, routinely skipped by all but the most devout.

Until Indian independence, the Setupathi assumed responsibility for the upkeep and restoration of Rāmanāthaswami Temple and its grounds and for the maintenance of hostels for pilgrims who visit the island. The Setupathi claimed descent from the boatman, Guha, who ferried Rāma across the Ganges, although the *Rāmāyaṇa* neither mentions that Guha traveled to Rāmeswaram with the hero nor that he was appointed keeper of the bridge, as the Setupathis insist. Pilgrims believed that the purifying powers of the *tīrthas* would not take effect until the pilgrim had paid respects to the Setupathi in Rāmanāthapuram on the mainland on the return journey.

The 11,000 islanders who make a permanent home on Rāmeswaram find a major source of income in the never-ending stream of pilgrims. Fisheries account for another portion of their livelihood, while agriculture is practiced on a very modest scale and without the benefit of plows. Residents say this is in answer to a religious prohibition, the land being too sacred to be defaced by the plowshare. However, religious scruple ceded before the need to sanitize the island's numerous pools of standing water after malaria reached epidemic proportions early in the twentieth century. Around the same time, Rāmeswaram began purifying its own drinking water supply, which has also led to significant public health improvements. Nevertheless most guides to pilgrims still advise caution in the performance of the ritual baths.

Further Reading: A highly readable prose translation of the *Rāmāyaṇa* is available in William Buck's *The Ramayana: King Rama's Way* (Berkeley: University of California Press, 1976; London: New English Library, 1978). R. K. Narayan's *Gods, Demons and Others* (New York: Viking, 1964; London: Heinemann, 1965) recounts the most loved Indian legends and myths in easily readable short-story format and provides detailed commentaries. *Tamil Temple Myths: Sacrifice and Divine Marriage in the South Indian Saiva Tradition,* by David Dean Shulman (Princeton: Princeton University Press, 1980), is an exploration of Tamil myths, the Saivite cult, and their relationship to the whole of Hinduism. G. Jouveau-Dubreuil provides a concise overview of Dravidian temple architecture in *Dravidian Architecture,* translated by Sakkottai Krishnaswami Aiyangar (Madras: S.P.C.K., 1917; reprint, New Delhi, Asian Educational Services, and Columbia, Missouri: South Asia Books, 1987).

—Denise Coté and Marijke Rijsberman

Samarkand (Samarkand, Uzbekistan)

Location: Samarkand is the capital city of the oblast of the same name and is approximately 161 miles north of the border with Afghanistan, 217 miles by rail southwest of Tashkent, and 155 miles east of Bukhara, although the direct distances are considerably shorter. At a height of 2,461 feet above sea level and within sight of two mountain ranges, Samarkand is directly east of the Kyzylkum Desert.

Description: Central Asia's principal tourist attraction, an important cotton-growing center, and a city of 600,000, Samarkand is famous chiefly because of its status as the capital city of the fourteenth-century Mongol conqueror Timur (Tamerlane). He and his successors ordered the construction of numerous extraordinary buildings; many of these still stand, having undergone restoration while Samarkand was part of the Soviet Union. Since the Soviet breakup, Samarkand has been one of the leading cities of the Republic of Uzbekistan.

Site Office: Intourist Service Bureau
Hotel Samarkand
University Boulevard
Samarkand
Uzbekistan
(35) 8812 or (35) 1880

Samarkand, "the home of all the romance and poetry in the east," once was the opulent capital of Timur, the self-proclaimed conqueror of the world, and even today observers are challenged to find appropriate words to describe its beauty and vivid colors. As was the case in St. Petersburg, parts of Samarkand benefited from the meticulous and energetic restoration efforts of the Soviet regime. Its skyline still features the soaring minarets and domes of cobalt blue, glistening turquoise, deepest sapphire, and reflected amethyst atop its mosques, mausoleums, and other noteworthy buildings. Samarkand also still contains what George Nathaniel Curzon, sometime viceroy and governor general of India, called "the noblest public square in the world" when he visited it in 1888 on the newly opened Trans-Caspian Railway.

It was in an oasis on the Zarafshan River, which now runs three miles to the north, that the fourteenth-century Mongol conqueror Timur chose to develop Samarkand, which translates as Strewer of Gold. In the time of Timur the site already was known as Mirror of the World, Garden of the Blessed, and The Fourth Paradise. The area already had a long history before the physically debilitated Timur—lame from a wound in one leg, with one eye lost to tuberculosis, and with the use of only one arm—created of it a city with beauty both prodigal and prodigious, the product of a conquest that may well have left some 17 million dead, some of them slaughtered with unbelievable brutality.

An official 2,500th anniversary was celebrated at Samarkand in 1970, but the site is known to have been inhabited for some 40,000 years. It first came into prominence as Afrasiab (called Maracanda by Westerners), capital of the Sogdian Empire, but human remains from the Paleolithic era (35,000–10,000 B.C.) were discovered in 1937, and relics of Neolithic populations dating from 6,000 to 4,000 B.C. were discovered between 1966 and 1972. The remains of an outer city wall dating to about 1,500 B.C. have been found along the eastern edge of the ancient site, but convention demands the dating of Afrasiab proper to about 500 B.C.

Afrasiab may have been the name of the first king of Sogdiana—the land between the Oxus (Amu Darya) and the Jaxartes (Syr Darya), known from the epic poem *Shāhnāma*—or it may have been only the name of the place, a few hundred yards east of the center of modern Samarkand. It once covered almost 2,000 acres and virtually none of the ancient site, now covering 741 acres, has been touched since the city was razed by Genghis Khan in 1220. By the fourth century B.C. Afrasiab was a major settlement, known for its magnificence and surrounded by an 8.5-mile wall, of which one surviving section is 42.5 feet high. The city was at the perimeter of the Persian Achaemenid Empire, which arose in the sixth century B.C. and imposed tribute, but promoted trade and prosperity through a huge area as far west as Turkey, Egypt, and Mesopotamia, as far north as the Caspian and Aral Seas, and as far east as the Hindu Kush Mountains, including the whole of Persia.

In the late fourth century B.C. the Achaemenids were overthrown by Alexander the Great, who took Afrasiab without a struggle when he crossed the Hindu Kush in 329 B.C. A later rebellion, although it engaged the Greeks for eighteen months, was crushed when its leader was assassinated by his own army. The city was subsequently raided by horsemen from the steppes, drawn from the Aryan tribes that already had invaded northern India, but the walls always were rebuilt, the warehouses restocked, and trading revived.

By the middle of the second century B.C., the Chinese had arrived with bales of silk, a priceless commodity in the West, and the Afrasiab oasis became a major stopping point on the network of trade routes known as the Silk Road. The oasis lay on the Northern Silk Road, which divided into two routes along either side of the Tian Shan Mountain range. Merchants departing the oasis could travel in three possible directions. Moving north from Afrasiab they reached Tashkent. Traveling east from Afrasiab they reached Kashgar, a nexus point for a variety of routes, including those leading

Gūr-e-Amīr (tomb of Timur), Samarkand
Photo courtesy of A.P. / Wide World Photos, New York

west to the Hindu Kush. Traveling west from Afrasiab they reached Bukhara and a path to the Middle East.

Caravans seldom made the entire journey from the West to China. It was usual for Greek, Arab, Roman, Iranian, and Indian traders to sell their goods to Central Asian nomads, who took them across mountains, passes, and steppes to trade with the Chinese. About 100 B.C., however, the Greeks discovered the practicability of exploiting annual monsoons for sea transport. The overland routes suffered further during the middle years of the first millennium A.D., as the secret of silk production spread outside China. Many towns along the overland silk routes suffered.

Maracanda became renowned for its fine paper and its glass, but little is known about the city's history for the following 1,000 years. The dominant religion in the oasis at this time appears to have been some form of fire-worship, no doubt related to Persia's Zoroastrianism. Over the centuries, the town fell under the rule of a succession of invaders including Yüeh-Chi nomads, founders of the mighty Kusham Empire; the White Huns, who were on the move to the Hindu Kush; and the Turks.

During the seventh century the Buddhist pilgrim Xuan Zang visited the oasis on his way to India. He reported that the town, which he referred to as Sa-mo-kien, contained a flourishing and respected community, with about half of the population employed in trade, and the other half in agriculture. Another Chinese traveler remarked on the cultivation there of the commercial arts.

With the conquest of the city by Muslim invaders in 710, Islam came to Samarkand, as it now was called. The first mosque was built in the western corner of the Afrasiab site, and the city was governed from Mary as part of Khorāsān (northeastern Iran and western Afghanistan), then belonging to the Islamic Umayyad Empire. In the late ninth century Samarkand, still the largest and richest city in Transoxiana, became part of the Sāmānid Empire based in Bukhara. It was noted for its use of canals and artificial ponds to nourish fruit orchards and green vegetation. From the eleventh to the thirteenth centuries, Samarkand passed through the hands of the Seljuk Turks, the kingdom of Khwārezm from the Amu Darya Delta, and a tribe of pagan nomads, the Karakitai. The civilization of Samarkand flourished under Islamic domination, although religious control tightened. Then in 1220 came the Mongol conqueror Genghis Khan, who already had conquered the whole of northern China with the support of tribes from southern Siberia and Mongolia. He then turned westward toward the Islamic lands, taking all of Central Asia (including Russia as far north as Kiev), Afghanistan, and Khorāsān. Bukhara yielded after a short siege, and Balkh put up no resistance.

There are varying accounts of what happened at Samarkand, where about 110,000 men are said to have put up a valiant defense. Genghis Khan appears to have blocked the canals supplying the town with water. One chronicler, Ibn-ak-Asir, says the conqueror's troops cut open pregnant women and killed the fetuses they were carrying. About 300,000 or 400,000 inhabitants of Samarkand are said to have been killed or forced to flee when the town was razed, and the original site of Afrasiab was abandoned for a patch of wasteland immediately to the south, a site that is the present "old town" of Samarkand. Nonetheless, when Marco Polo visited Samarkand fifty years later, he found on its new site "a very large and splendid city," and some accounts say that much of the original city was saved. There is agreement that the population fell by about three-quarters, to some 100,000, all that the wrecked irrigation system could support. Still, Arab traveler and writer Ibn Baṭṭūṭah described Samarkand in 1333 as "one of the largest and most perfectly beautiful cities in the world."

Undoubtedly, it was the city's size and splendor that led Genghis Khan's descendant Timur to choose Samarkand as his capital. Timur was born in 1336 in Shakhrisabz, then called Kesh, about sixty miles over the Kerafshan Mountains. He ruled the Mongol realm from 1370 until his death in 1405. The barbarism of his campaigns, which left towers of skulls and walls of bodies, is truly gruesome; between 1372 and 1402 Timur sacked and butchered his way to Delhi and Baghdad across Persia, up to the Caucasus, across eastern Anatolia into Syria, and then eastward across Iraq and back to Persia. A further campaign took him to the Aegean coast before he returned again through Persia to Samarkand.

Timur wanted to rule the world, but he also wanted to secure the fortune of his dynasty and his capital, disadvantaged by changing patterns of trade, new markets, the abandonment of the silk roads, and the destruction of the oases by Genghis Khan. He also had an unwavering compulsion to create great monuments, in Samarkand and elsewhere, to himself and his wives. Most were imposing, and some extraordinarily beautiful. Timur always used the finest materials, jewels, artists, and craftsmen. He had armies of enslaved workers and ninety-five Indian elephants to carry the loads that slaves could not, and he recruited a flood of tile-makers, glaziers, and mosaic-workers from Baghdad, Damascus, Isfahan, Shīrāz, Delhi, and China. He murdered architects whose work displeased him, and called his square the Rīgestān, or place of sand, after the sand strewn to absorb the blood of the executed.

The opulence of Timur's capital was documented by Ruy González de Clavijo, a diplomat sent by King Henry III of Castile to Samarkand to negotiate a treaty with the Mongol ruler. He failed, but recorded the feasting, the piles of precious stones, the silk tents, and the extravagant use of invaluable materials. In 1404, reported Clavijo, the city was larger than Seville, with extensive suburbs, orchards, and vineyards. There were pleasure gardens, palaces, fine houses, and many foodstuffs for sale.

Among the early building projects was the Shakh-i-Zindeh complex, a now much decayed mosque and series of mausoleums in the northeast quarter of the present town. One enters the complex through the 1434–35 portal commissioned by Timur's grandson, Ulūgh Beg, a noted poet, mathematician, theologian, and astronomer, murdered by his son for the heresy associated with inquiring into the workings of the universe. The complex contains the finest glazed decoration in Central Asia. The full range of blues in the mosaics of the court blends with the browns and golds of the earthen walls——"sea and sand with sunshine caught between them," as historian Rosita Forbes wrote in the 1930s. Of all the mausoleums, the most spectacular is that of Shadi Mulk Aka, built in 1372, combining with skill and refinement the whole spectrum of decorative techniques, with stylized flowers, calligraphy, and abstract designs using every shade of blue and every visual motif available to the craftsmen, probably from Azerbaijan. It is still in nearly perfect condition.

To the west of the mausoleums, but still east of the Rīgestān, are the remains of the vast Bībī Khānom Mosque, never finished and now largely destroyed. A Russian shell hit the dome in 1868, but it remained more or less intact until it was damaged by earthquakes in 1897 and 1907. The mosque is now being restored according to plans discovered in St. Petersburg in 1974. In the meantime, the courtyard has become a cotton market, its walls used as a quarry for other constructions, and its great gates melted down. The mosque was built between 1399 and 1404, to a huge scale, with a portal alone nearly 100 feet high, and an even higher dome. Both were decorated with majolica mosaics, carved marble, and painted and gilded papier mâché. They stood at the west end of a vast colonnade of 427 by 335 feet, paved with marble and with a minaret at each corner. The main gates opposite were made of seven different metals and were flanked by ceramic columns 164 feet high. A huge marble lectern for an enormous Koran once stood under the dome, but is now in the courtyard. The Koran for which it was constructed was brought to Samarkand from Damascus by Timur. Since 1989 it has been in the hands of the Islamic authorities in Tashkent.

One notable feature of Samarkand architecture is the fluted dome, of which the finest example is the Gūr-e-Amīr, or ruler's tomb, where Timur is buried. He died on his way to China at the head of an invading army of 200,000 and was buried in the mausoleum he had built for his grandson, Muḥammad Sultan, who had died fighting in Turkey in 1403. Timur had had the ribbed cantaloupe dome rebuilt on the scale of the Bībī Khānom Mosque. The outer dome is now 105 feet high, and the inner dome is 59 feet, with supporting struts between them. Beneath the outer dome, a 33-foot-high inscription on the drum reads: "There is no God but Allah, and Muḥammad is his prophet." Beneath lies an octagonal hall with six cenotaphs of marble and one of jade—apparently the biggest slab of jade in the world—for Timur himself. It broke in two when Nāder Shāh tried to remove it in 1740. The walls of the hall have hexagonal green alabaster tiles up to head height, where there is a band of once-gilded marble. Higher up, bands of calligraphy surround clusters of stalactites and blue and gold geometric patterns.

The Rīgestān was primarily a marketplace, with caravansaries for itinerant merchants. Timur used it for pronouncements, executions, and the exhibition of the heads of his victims on spikes. Between 1417 and 1420 Ulūgh Beg built his *medrese* or academy on the west side, decorated with a mosaic of stars over the immense portico. The exterior is totally covered with mosaic, using every variety of motif known to Islam: floral, spiral, calligraphic, and geometric. Behind the facade is a courtyard and a mosque, with two stories of lecture halls and students' rooms.

By the time the Shirdar Medrese facing and mimicking that of Ulūgh Beg was built two centuries later, between 1619 and 1635, the street level had risen about ten feet. In spite of its ribbed cupolas, this building is considered inferior to that which it faces. It became a Russian hotel and now contains gift shops. The northern side of the square is occupied by the Tilakari Medrese, built from 1646 to 1659, for which a caravansary was torn down. The facade is 394 feet, and next to the *medrese* is a mosque, restored in 1979, with 4.5 pounds of gold leaf used on the one-quarter-acre *trompe l'oeil* ceiling alone. The effect it has on the visitor can be gauged by the words of Geoffrey Moorhouse, who observed it in 1979:

> Here was a richness of colour greater than I had ever seen anywhere before, a splendour of red beyond the opulence of rubies and a royal blue of such intensity that it would have hurt the eyes if it had been unrelieved. It was made perfect not only by the alliance with red, but by flashes of orange and dull gleamings of gold which punctuated it. . . .

Unfortunately, the restored decoration is threatened by dampness.

Other important buildings were constructed in and near Samarkand, notably the Ulūgh Beg Observatory, where Timur's grandson plotted the position of sun, moon, planets, and 1,018 other stars, and calculated the length of the year to within less than a minute. What remains of his sextant was found in 1908, a perfect arc of marble-clad brick calibrated in degrees and minutes, decorated with signs of the zodiac, and aligned with one of the earth's meridians. The observatory, torn down for religious reasons after Ulūgh Beg's murder, must have been at least 100 feet high and have had three stories.

The other building that must be mentioned is Timur's Ak-Saray Palace at his birthplace, Shakhrisabz, which took a quarter of a century to build. Only a ruin remains, but the main entrance arch was 164 feet high with a span of 72 feet. The scale was larger even than that of Bībī Khānom. Over the palace is the sad inscription of a ruler remembered as much for his atrocities as his patronage: "Let he who doubts our power and munificence look upon our buildings."

Even before Timur's time, Samarkand had a number of prominent citizens, including the poet and astronomer Omar Khayyām (1048–1131) and one of the greatest of the Arab philosophers, Ibn Sīnā, known in the West as Avicenna (980–1037). The city declined quickly after Timur's era, however. By 1505 Samarkand had been invaded by the Uzbek

Turks and the capital had moved to Bukhara, after which few visitors arrived before the Russian conquest of 1868 and the building of the Trans-Caspian Railway two decades later. Bābur (Zahīr-ud-Dīn Muḥammad), a descendant on his father's side of Timur's third son and on his mother's of Genghis Khan, spent much of his life trying unsuccessfully to recover Samarkand. He did succeed in establishing the Mughal Dynasty of India, but Samarkand collapsed into anarchy.

In 1841 Samarkand still had the appearance of a typical Central Asian town, with a citadel, high mud-brick walls, lookout posts, and gates that were locked at sunset. In 1868 the city was invaded and conquered by General Konstantin Petrovich Kaufmann of Russia. The city walls were demolished and a new fortress was built where the citadel had been. The Russians built a commercial and industrial district to the west of the old portion of Samarkand. Shortly after the rise of the Soviet Union, the city served briefly as the capital of the Uzbek Soviet Socialist Republic, a status it relinquished to Tashkent in 1930. It is only recently, after World War II, that the Soviet authorities seriously turned their attention to more than sporadic restoration work, and that Samarkand has begun to take on again the extraordinary aspect it once had.

Further Reading: Much information on Samarkand is available in Kathleen Hopkirk's *A Traveller's Companion to Central Asia* (London: John Murray, 1993); Dominic Streatfield-James's *Silk Route by Rail* (Hindhead: Trailblazer, 1993); and Giles Whittell's *Central Asia: The Practical Handbook* (Old Saybrook, Connecticut: Globe Pequot, and London: Cadogan, 1993). For the Timurid Empire and culture, see Beatrice Forbes Manz's *The Rise and Rule of Tamerlane* (Cambridge and New York: Cambridge University Press, 1989).

—Claudia Levi

Samoa (Western Samoa and American Samoa)

Location: The Samoan islands have a total land area of 1,170 square miles. Located in the southwest Pacific Ocean, some 1,800 miles northeast of New Zealand, Western Samoa consists of Savaii and Upolu and the much smaller Apolima, Manono, Fanuatapu, Namua, Nuutele, Nuulua, and Nuusafee. American Samoa comprises six islands located east of Western Samoa—Tutuila, Aunuu, Muliavu (Rose Island), the Manua group (Tau, Olosega, and Ofu)—and Swains Island, a coral atoll situated 280 miles northwest of Tutuila.

Description: The Samoan islands, first settled in approximately 1000 B.C., were the staging point for pioneering voyages to the Marquesas and other Pacific island groups. The whalers, beachcombers, and missionaries who arrived in the early nineteenth century generated American, British, and German interest in the islands. An 1899 treaty partitioned Samoa between Germany and the United States. New Zealand seized German Samoa in 1914. Swains Island, part of Tokelau, was incorporated into American Samoa in 1925. On January 1, 1962, Malo Sa'oloto Tuto'atasi o Samoa i Sisifo, the Independent State of Western Samoa, became the first independent Pacific island nation. American Samoa remains an unincorporated territory of the United States; its residents are U.S. nationals who may apply for full citizenship after six months' residence in the United States. The Samoans, who are predominantly Polynesian, speak both Samoan and English and live mainly on Upolu and Tutuila, where Apia and Pago Pago, the respective capitals of Western and American Samoa, are located.

Site Offices: Western Samoa Visitors' Bureau
P.O. Box 2272
Apia
Western Samoa
685 20180

American Samoa Office of Tourism
P.O. Box 1147
Pago Pago
American Samoa 96799
684 633 1091

The submerged site of Ferry Berth at Mulifanua, Upolu, has yielded the earliest evidence of human habitation in Samoa: Lapita potsherds dating between 1020 and 860 B.C. Within the triangle of Samoa, Tonga, and Fiji, Lapita settlers developed the characteristic Polynesian culture in the first millennium B.C. Using their intimate knowledge of winds, currents, and the relative positions of celestial objects, settlers from Samoa reached the Marquesas by A.D. 300; from the Marquesas and Society Islands, Polynesian navigators discovered and colonized Easter Island, Hawaii, New Zealand, and other island groups of the central and eastern Pacific by A.D 1300.

When the renowned Maori historian Te Rangi Hiroa (Sir Peter Buck) informed a group of Samoans that their ancestors had crossed the Pacific from Asia, one audience member replied, "The rest of the Polynesians may have come from Asia, but the Samoans—No. The Samoans originated in Samoa." That is to say, Samoan oral history does not confirm these archaeological discoveries. According to an early-nineteenth-century account, the god Tagaloa produced from a rock the Earth and Sea; Tui-tee-lagi, who held up the Sky, Immensity, Space, and Clouds; and humans imbued with Spirit, Heart, Will, and Thought. He also created Fatu, the first man, and Ele-ele, the first woman. Tagaloa the Messenger (a god created by Tagaloa the Creator) caused the Fiji and Tongan islands to emerge from the sea, but their distance from Manua (the first of the Samoan islands to be created) was so great that he could not walk between them comfortably, so he made Savaii, Tutuila, and Upolu surface. The Messenger then placed Fue, a creeping vine, in the sun, where it rotted and attracted swarms of maggots. Tagaloa the Creator molded them into humans, placed them on the Samoan islands, and charged them with respecting Manua. He further decreed that Manua-tele and Sa-tia-i-le-moa, sons of Night and Day, would rule the offspring of Fatu and Ele-ele, hence the names Manua and Samoa.

These traditions led to the development of a highly localized political organization from which many characteristics survive in modern Samoa. *Matai* (heads of families and villages) were comprised of *alii* (chiefs who traced their ancestry back to the gods) and *tulafale* (orators with executive power). *Matai* deliberated important political and legal decisions in the village *fono* (council) and allocated the land and titles of their *aiga*, the extended families who elected them. Groups of ten to thirty *aiga* formed *nuu*, politically autonomous villages, each with its own history, traditions, and political organization, which at times coalesced into fluid districts and territorial divisions.

Samoan oral history commemorates long-standing ties with the people of Tonga, Fiji, Tokelau, Uvea, and Futuna through trade, intermarriage, and warfare. In the late thirteenth century the Samoans drove out Talakaifaiki, the fifteenth Tui Tonga, who had occupied Upolu and Savaii. The departing Tongan congratulated Tuna and Fata, the Samoan men who had engineered his expulsion, saying, "Malie toe, malie tau" (Well fought, brave warriors); thus, their brother, Savea, became the first of the Malietoa line of rulers.

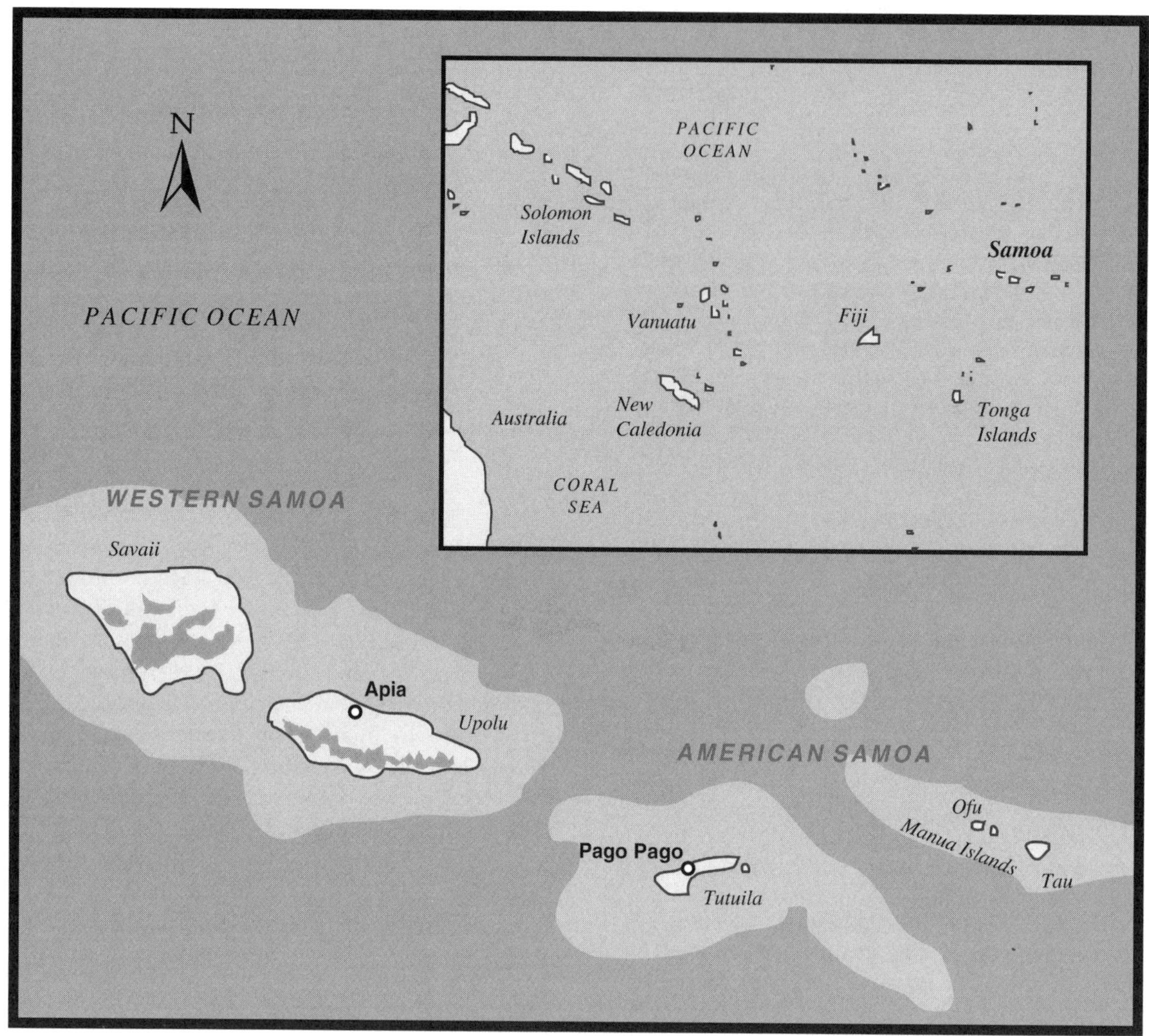

Map of Samoa, with inset of South Pacific Islands
Illustration by Tom Willcockson

The first European to visit Samoa was Jacob Roggeveen, who revived his father's proposal to the West India Company to probe the southern Pacific Ocean for its supposed vast storehouse of wealth. On June 13, 1722, he came upon Muliavu and the Manua group, naming them Vuyle Eyland (Foul Island, because of its forbidding reef) and Boumans Eylanden, after Captain Cornelis Bouman. Roggeveen conjectured that the "Indians" were indigenous—he could recall no records of Spaniards planting colonies of native Peruvians and Chileans in the Pacific—yet the possibility that their ancestors had crossed the ocean in lightweight canoes seemed, to him, "mockery rather than serious thought." The Europeans observed Tutuila and Upolu, which they called Thienhoven and Groeningen, before passing Savaii in the night without noticing it.

Roggeveen was followed by the French explorer Louis Antoine de Bougainville, who sighted Tutuila, Upolu, and the Manua Islands in May 1768; witnessing the inhabitants' navigational talents, he christened the archipelago the Navigator Islands. Charged with mapping and surveying "all the lands which had escaped the vigilance of [Captain James] Cook," Jean-François Galaup de La Pérouse landed at Tutuila on December 6, 1787. Following days of friendly trading, a scuffle between the islanders and Europeans provoked the Samoans into attacking and killing twelve of his crew, including his second-in-command and the ship's physician. The anguished La Pérouse skirted Upolu and Savaii, writing later, "I am a hundred times more angry against the philosophers who praise them [the Noble Savages] than against the savages themselves. Lamanon whom they massacred was saying the day before that these men are worth more than us." The Samoans' reputation for ferocity dissuaded Captain Edward Edwards, on the prowl for *Bounty* mutineers, from landing there to replenish his provisions, but it failed to stem the tide of whalers and beachcombers who arrived in the 1820s.

Having learned about Wesleyan Methodism from Tongans and Tahitians, Samoan chiefs actively recruited and even kidnapped shipwrecked sailors who would preach Christianity, baptize, and administer the sacraments in their own fashion. This arrangement brought coveted European goods, enlarged European political influence, and eased the reception of John Williams and his London Missionary Society colleagues. The Siovili cult, a blend of Christian and Samoan tenets introduced by a charismatic Samoan visionary, reinforced the belief that adopting Christianity would bring the Samoans the wealth and power of these *papalagi* (literally "sky-breakers," because they seemed to have come from another world).

Williams arrived at Savaii in August 1830, introduced by Fauea, a Samoan chief he had met on his travels. The London-born ironmonger secured the backing of Malietoa Vainuupo, while the Samoans debated the merits of the new *lotu* (religion).

At Fauea's suggestion, the Tahitian and Rarotongan teachers Williams left on the islands refrained from immediately prohibiting the people's canoe races and other pastimes, and concentrated on building chapels and imparting the Gospel. By 1841 the majority of Samoans professed Protestant Christianity, numerous churches and schools had been established, and a printing press on Upolu was issuing hymn books and scriptures translated into Samoan.

Rapid conversion not only fulfilled the war goddess Nafanua's prophesy that a new religion would supplant the old one, it also satisfied the Samoans' love for oratory and European goods. Samoans worked to ensure that Wesleyan Methodism, Roman Catholicism, Mormonism, and Seventh Day Adventism gained smaller but lasting footholds in the islands. This success, however, belied the developing *lotu*'s uniquely Samoan flavor. By contrast with Tonga and other states where a monarch enforced mass conversion to Christianity, Samoan factionalism kept religious decisions firmly within the province of the *nuu* (village) and *fono* (council). Samoan pastors trained at Upolu's newly built Malua Institution acquired the sacred power of village chiefs; they approved nominations for church fellowship and met regularly to discuss church affairs. The women continued to dress in the traditional Samoan manner and urged the mission teachers' wives to do the same. And no amount of preaching or "blue laws" could repress the Samoans' enjoyment of dancing and sports, particularly cricket.

Meanwhile, whalers sparked American and European interest in Pago Pago's outstanding harbor. In 1838 Samoan chiefs and British Captain Drinkwater-Bethune negotiated regulations stipulating the payment of harbor dues and the conduct of foreign sailors. Lieutenant Charles Wilkes of the United States Exploring Expedition concluded a similar treaty with Malietoa Vainuupo in 1839 and appointed a provisional American consul, John Chauner Williams, the son of Reverend John Williams; George Pritchard of the London Missionary Society represented British interests. The German consul was Theodor Weber, who pioneered copra processing in Samoa.

Malietoa Vainuupo died in 1841, and the various titles that made him *tafaifa* (paramount ruler) scattered. For some forty years the Samoans fought over these titles and over territories, even as the Americans and Europeans strengthened their interests in the islands. Planters and settlers appropriated lands vacated by Samoans during these wars; the American-based Central Polynesian Land and Commercial Company, for example, is alleged to have purchased half the territory of the Samoan islands. When the conflict subsided in 1873, the Samoans set up a new government comprising joint kings Malietoa Laupepa and Tupua Pulepule, a *fono* of Taimua (council of seven chiefs from the main districts), a *fono* of Faipule (council of thirty-six members representing subdistricts), a chief judge, a registrar, and secretaries of treasury, state, interior, war, and land.

U. S. President Ulysses S. Grant authorized Colonel Albert B. Steinberger to investigate burgeoning American activity in Samoa, following an 1872 agreement between High Chief Mauga and U.S. Commander Richard W. Meade that permitted the installing of a coaling station at Pago Pago Harbor. Steinberger secretly promised Germany that he would uphold its interests in Samoa in return for German support of his political ambitions. Meanwhile, he conveyed the impression that the United States planned to declare a protectorate over the islands that would safeguard Samoan lands from foreign intervention. Acting on Steinberger's advice, the Samoans restructured the government and installed Steinberger as premier in 1875. American consul S. S. Foster suspected Steinberger of colluding with Germany and arranged to have him deported.

Hostilities between the United States, Britain, and Germany intensified, and the three powers dispatched warships to Apia to protect their nationals. On March 15–16, 1889, a great hurricane destroyed all but one of the ships and killed 155 sailors. Attempts to reach a compromise failed, and the foreigners continued to capitalize on Samoan contests for supremacy. The 1889 Berlin Act, for instance, divided authority among the three foreign states, designated Malietoa Laupepa as "king," and appointed a foreign chief justice. Negotiations culminated in a tripartite convention signed by the three powers on December 2, 1899, that partitioned the Samoan islands between the United States and Germany. The United States received the islands east of longitude 171 degrees: Tutuila, Aunuu, Muliavu, and the Manua group; Germany accepted Upolu, Savaii, and their satellites. By the convention's terms, Britain renounced claims in Samoa in return for the cession of German rights in Tonga, Niue, West Africa, Zanzibar, and the Solomon Islands.

Cession of American Samoa (except Manua) became official on April 17, 1900, when Commander B. F. Tilley raised the U.S. flag in Tutuila. Tuimanua Eliasara reluctantly ceded his domain in 1904, and in his will decreed that the title of Tuimanua would die with him so that its holder would not suffer the indignity of being governed by a foreign state. A 1925 Congressional resolution incorporated Swains Island, a coral atoll geographically and culturally part of Tokelau, into

American Samoa. An American, Eli Hutchinson Jennings, had established a profitable copra plantation on the atoll, and his descendants desired American protection of their holdings. Tokelauans have repeatedly challenged the 1983 Treaty of Tokehega, which transferred sovereignty over the island to the United States.

Governor Wilhelm Solf's administration (1900–1910) brought economic prosperity to the German islands, but he antagonized Samoans by dismantling time-honored institutions including the right of the elite Tumua and Pule orator groups to confer the titles that constituted the *tafaifa*. Namulauulu Lauaki Mamoe, a renowned *tulafale* (orator) led the Mau a Pule movement, which asserted Samoan rights to self-determination, until his exile to Saipan in the Mariana Islands.

To oblige Britain, New Zealand seized German Samoa in 1914 and obtained a League of Nations mandate over the islands in 1920. The New Zealand Administration's handling of an influenza outbreak resulted in the deaths of one-fifth of the population of Western Samoa, as the islands were named after World War I. Resentment peaked when the administration usurped the prerogative of the council of *matais* (heads of families and villages) to banish troublemakers from the village and punished dissidents by revoking their *matai* titles. Brigadier General George Richardson, who became administrator in 1923, enlarged the advisory capacity of the *fono* of Faipule with the intention of putting it in charge of a district council that would replace the district and village *fono*.

This attempt to break with tradition only served to further alienate the Samoan people. Olaf Frederick Nelson, a part-Samoan business leader, founded an opposition newspaper, the *Samoa Guardian*, and a political organization called O le Mau (the Samoan League) that employed nonviolent resistance tactics such as the abandonment of government-sponsored copra projects and the demand for Samoan representatives in the Legislative Council. A Royal Commission upheld the administration's stance and deported Nelson, who continued to galvanize the Mau to pressing for self-government.

On December 28, 1929, Mau patriots clashed with military police, and eleven Samoans were killed, including Tupua Tamasese Lealofi III, who exhorted his followers, "My blood has been spilt for Samoa. I am proud to give it. Do not dream of avenging it, as it was spilt in maintaining peace. If I die, peace must be maintained at any price." The government declared the organization seditious, and Mau men fled to the hills to regroup; the Women's Mau, led by Tamasese's widow, Alaisala, continued the struggle. After the more receptive New Zealand Labour Government took office in 1936, the Mau won thirty-three of the thirty-nine seats in the new *fono* of Faipule and an increase in the number of Samoan legislators, victories that renewed their objective to form an autonomous government.

Although the Mau of American Samoa pressed for civilian administration, most of the Samoan witnesses who testified before the Presidential Commission that visited the islands in 1930 favored the continuation of the U.S. Naval Administration. Congress defeated bills recommending the creation of an organic act for American Samoa and the bestowal of U.S. citizenship upon its inhabitants.

Pago Pago was shelled by Japanese forces on January 11, 1942, and many Samoans found employment opportunities at the U.S. military stations in Upolu and Tutuila; young Samoan men joined the U.S. Navy and Marine Corps Reserve. American Samoans argued that their military service entitled them to U.S. citizenship.

Western Samoa became a New Zealand Trust Territory in 1946. In a plebiscite held in 1961 Western Samoans demonstrated their almost unanimous desire for independence. On January 1, 1962, Western Samoa became the first independent Pacific island nation.

On July 1, 1951, the U.S. Department of the Interior assumed jurisdiction over American Samoa, ending fifty-one years of naval administration. A Future Political Status Study Commission, created in 1969, ruled out independence, unification with Western Samoa, commonwealth status, and change in American Samoa's relationship with the United States.

Today American and Western Samoa share an economic dependence on traditional crops, including coconuts, taro, and bananas. Whereas Western Samoa has developed an export market for these and other products in Australia and New Zealand, American Samoa's agricultural production mostly satisfies domestic consumption. This country's export income is primarily derived from its American-owned fish canneries; the largest employer is the U.S. Department of the Interior. In Western Samoa investments in airport facilities and luxury hotels have finally increased tourism, which has been limited by the high cost of travel to the islands.

Further Reading: *Lagaga: A Short History of Western Samoa,* edited by Malama Meleisea and Penelope Schoeffel Meleisea (Suva, Fiji: University of the South Pacific, 1987), written from a Samoan perspective, is an excellent source on Western Samoa, as is *Samoa Mo Samoa: The Emergence of the Independent State of Western Samoa* by J. W. Davidson (Melbourne and New York: Oxford University Press, 1967). For a treatment of American Samoa, turn to *Amerika Samoa: A History of American Samoa and Its United States Naval Administration* by J. A. C. Gray (Annapolis: U.S. Naval Institute, 1960). K. R. Howe's *Where the Waves Fall: A New South Sea Islands History from First Settlement to Colonial Rule* (Sydney: Allen and Unwin, and Honolulu: University of Hawaii Press, 1984) also highlights the perspectives of Pacific islanders. Striking illustrations enhance *Myths and Legends of Samoa,* compiled by C. Stuebel and Brother Herman (Wellington, New Zealand: Reed, 1976; revised as *Tala o le Vavau: The Myths, Legends and Customs of Old Samoa,* Auckland: Polynesian Press, 1987).

—Maria Chiara

Sānchi (Madhya Pradesh, India)

Location: In central India, approximately forty-five miles northeast of Bhopāl.

Description: Near the village of Sānchi, on a hill some 300 feet high, stand some of the best preserved Buddhist monuments of India. They include stupas, balustrades and superbly carved gateways, prayer halls, temples and monasteries, a pillar inscribed with an edict of the Mauryan emperor Aśoka, and countless inscriptions and sculptures. The Great Stupa dates to the third century B.C.; artistic activity was nourished at Sānchi by a Buddhist presence down to the twelfth century A.D. After centuries of oblivion, the monuments were rediscovered in 1818.

Site Office: Archaeological Survey of India
The Archaeological Museum
Sānchi, Madhya Pradesh
India

Contact: Government of India Tourist Office
Near Western Group of Temples
Khajurāho 471 606, Madhya Pradesh
India
2047 or 2048

Situated almost at the center of India, Sānchi was a great center of Buddhist activity from the third century B.C., if not earlier still, until the twelfth century A.D. Then it disappeared from memory, despite its physical visibility on top of a hill, to be discovered by General Taylor in 1818. He found the hemispherical dome of the Great Stupa and three of its magnificent gateways still intact. The southern gateway lay where it had fallen. Part of the railing on top was still in place. Taylor did not know what to make of his find, although he recognized that his discovery was of great significance: the monuments conveyed an unmistakable impression of great antiquity and civilization, and the sculptures spoke of a world that was no more.

And indeed, it is a mystery that Sānchi survived while the neighboring city of Vidiśā, only five miles away, was sacked repeatedly, its shrines obliterated by waves of Muslim iconoclasm. The explanation of the monument's survival lies perhaps in the extinction of Buddhism at Sānchi just prior to the Muslim conquest of the region. Without life or religious activity on the hill, the complex, located in a desolate area, was apparently soon forgotten even by its closest neighbors.

Taylor's mystifying discovery was initially linked to the monuments of ancient Egypt. Reports stirred the imagination of another British soldier, Captain E. Fell, who paid Sānchi a visit and published an account of his findings in the *Calcutta Journal* in 1819. A few years later, a Captain Johnson conducted disastrous excavations at Sānchi, succeeding only in damaging the monuments. He left a gaping hole in one side of the Great Stupa, a heap of rubble, and another collapsed gateway, which had stood intact for two millenia. Stupas 2 and 3 had survived in near-perfect condition until Johnson's misbegotten expedition.

The well-known archaeologist Alexander Cunningham was the first to realize that the Sānchi complex was of Buddhist origin. He made copies of the short Brāhmī inscriptions, which allowed cryptographers to decipher the Aśokan Brāhmī script and subsequently made it possible to read the Sānchi inscriptions themselves. Cunningham went back to Sānchi in 1851. During that visit, he drove shafts down the stupas and cut into their sides in search of relics. He discovered the bone relics of Sāriputa and Mahāmogalāna, two of the Buddha's closest disciples, in Stupa 3, and those of ten other saints and teachers in Stupa 2. As soon as these momentous identifications had been made, the Buddhist world awoke to reclaim an ancient place of pilgrimage. Cunningham published his *Bhilsa Topes* in 1854 and suggested the removal of the two fallen gateways to the British Museum, "where they would form the most striking objects in the Hall of Indian Antiquities." The gateways remained where they belonged only because the government was deterred by the costs of transportation and the likelihood of damage in transit. Another British archaeologist, C. F. Maisey, also led early excavations at Sānchi, publishing his findings in *Sānchi and Its Remains* (1892).

Although the work of Cunningham and Maisey resulted in several useful publications, Sir John Marshall later accused them of "general spoliation of the site by hasty excavations." It was only after 1869, when Napoléon III asked the begum of Bhopāl to let him have one of the fallen gateways of the Great Stupa to adorn the boulevards of Paris, that the British suddenly became aware of the need to preserve these great monuments. In 1881, the government appointed a Major Cole to carry out the requisite repairs. He filled the breach made in the Great Stupa by Johnson in 1822 and re-erected the fallen southern and western gateways, as well as the gateway in front of Stupa 3.

Systematic excavation of the site and preservation of the monuments were first undertaken by Sir John Marshall and Albert Foucher between the years 1912 and 1919. Marshall discovered more buildings, undertook further repairs, and cleared and landscaped the site. He also established a museum to display or store movable antiquities and fragments recovered from the area. As a result of his labors, Sānchi was established firmly as one of the most important Buddhist antiquities in India and an invaluable archaeological site.

The monuments at Sānchi date at least to the days of the Mauryan emperor Aśoka, who ruled most of India in the

Archway leading to the Great Stupa, Sānchi
Photo courtesy of Air India Library, New York

The Great Stupa, Sānchi
Photo courtesy of Sarva Daman Singh

third century B.C. Aśoka, a Buddhist of considerable conviction, constructed stupas and temples in many parts of his empire, but Sānchi surely must rank as one of the most imposing. Aśoka had married Devī, the daughter of a banker at Vidiśā, when he was still the viceroy of Ujjayinī. His son Mahendra later was sent to Sri Lanka to propagate Buddhism. Before he left, ancient records say, Mahendra visited his mother in Vidiśā, who took him to a lovely monastery with a stupa and a pillar, located at a place identified as Cetiyagirī. This must have been Sānchi, which is the only place in the vicinity that fits the description.

Sānchi has no direct association with the life of the Buddha, so it is not immediately obvious why Aśoka singled it out as the site for one of his most magnificent monuments. The emperor may have been influenced in his decision to build a stupa and monastery and to erect a pillar on top of the hill by the existence of a Buddhist community at the site. The proximity of Vidiśā, one of the most prosperous cities of the region, to which the emperor was also linked by marriage, must have been the decisive factor.

The Great Stupa, descended from the ancient funeral mounds of Vedic times, commemorates the life and teachings of the Buddha and of the other distinguished teachers of Buddhism. After the Buddha's death at Kuśinārā, his relics were divided among eight claimants, who each raised a stupa over the bodily remains. Because the sacred relics were the only tangible links between the earthly life of the Buddha and the transcendent reality of nirvana, the stupa came to be understood as an indirect representation of the great teacher. Legend has it that Aśoka opened the eight original stupas and redistributed the Buddha's relics over 84,000 stupas across his realm to honor the 84,000 sections of the holy *Tripiṭaka* (Buddhist scriptures). Exaggeration aside, it is clear that Aśoka played an important role in making the stupa the prime symbol both of the Buddha and of Buddhism, the principal cult object of faithful worship. Following Aśoka's reign, the stupa came to be seen simultaneously as the body of the Buddha, as the architectural expression of his teachings, and as the symbol of the *parinirvana*, the bridge between the seen and the unseen.

Aśoka's original stupa at Sānchi was made of bricks embedded in mud. Nearly hemispherical in shape, it was about sixty feet in diameter at the base. It had a *harmikā* railing at the top, with an umbrella in the middle. A raised terrace surrounded the structure. An ambulatory passage at the ground level was fitted with a circular wooden balustrade, while a second balustrade was set at the edge of the terrace. No relics were found in the Great Stupa, but Marshall speculated that it once contained remains of the Buddha himself and that these had been destroyed by the Śunga king Puṣyamitra. This king has gone down in history as a great hater of Buddhism and destroyer of its monuments, so that he presents himself as an obvious candidate for the putative desecration of the Great Stupa.We do not know, however, whether his reputation was deserved. Since the other stupas at Sānchi contained the relics of the Buddha's associates and other important Buddhist missionaries, Marshall's assumption seems reasonable enough, although it is probably beyond proof.

Besides representing the Buddha himself, the Great Stupa is an image of the "world mountain." Its hemispherical dome touches eternity at every point, and the umbrella's shaft represents the link between the fertility of the earth and the transcendent reality above. The (putative) relic within was the seed, the fire element, that triggered the aspiration and ascent of the faithful. The complex cosmological symbolism of the stupa juxtaposes the circle and the swastika to contrast the cyclic nature of finite existence with the linearity of the progress toward illumination. The ambulatory passages are figurative representations of the lower and higher levels of spiritual awareness. The heart of the complex represents the Great Void or the Ground of Infinity.

Aśoka's pillar has succumbed to the ravages of time, although its stump may still be seen near the South Gateway to the Great Stupa. Broken lengths of the shaft are now shielded from the elements by a canopy, and the capital and the four crowning lions have been removed to the local museum. Forty-two feet high, round, and gently tapered, the highly polished pillar was once a majestic monolith carved out of Chunār sandstone and inscribed with Aśoka's Schism Edict. This edict was meant to preserve harmony in the polity by encouraging religious tolerance. The lions that perched atop the monument symbolize not only the Buddha known as Śākya Simha but also Aśoka's imperial authority. Transport of the massive column from the quarry at Chunār, 500 miles away, to the top of the hill at Sānchi must have involved considerable engineering skill.

The fortunes of Sānchi, which had no independent economic base, were intertwined with the fate of nearby Vidiśā. Support of the community of monks at Sānchi after Aśoka's reign came primarily from the neighboring city, and when Vidiśā prospered or suffered so did the hilltop monks. Fortunately, when the Śungas appropriated large parts of India from the Mauryas in the second century B.C., Vidiśā became the main city of central India and the seat of a provincial Śunga government. It grew in importance, and the construction begun by Aśoka at Sānchi was continued. Subsequent centuries saw many dynasties come and go at the city, but it retained its commercial importance until the twelfth century, when it fell on hard times under Muslim domination.

Around the middle of the second century B.C., probably at the initiative of Vidiśā, the Great Stupa was enlarged to a diameter of more than 120 feet. It also was heightened to fifty-four feet and encased in stone. The wooden railing set along the ambulatory was replaced with a massive stone balustrade rising to a height of more than ten feet. Its ponderous proportions are highlighted by the plainness of the design. Most of the uprights, crossbars, and coping stones bear votive inscriptions recording the names of donors, including monks, nuns, and laymen. The layout of the original terrace also was altered, being raised to a height of sixteen feet above the base of the stupa. A double stairway on the south side gave access to the ambulatory laid out on the terrace. A second stone balustrade was erected alongside the terrace ambulatory. A new *harmikā* railing around a three-tiered umbrella came to replace the original railing. The design of the new railing was probably derived from wooden originals, copying characteristics of wood carving in the detail.

Stupa 3, which once held the relics of Sāriputa and Mahāmogalāna, was built at about the same time that the Great Stupa was altered. It has a slightly more hemispherical dome, rising to a height of more than thirty-five feet, including the *harmikā* and umbrella. The stupa's total diameter, including its raised terrace, is almost fifty feet. A sculptured gateway sets the structure off from the rest of the complex. Stupa 2, similar in size and design to Stupa 3, has been dated to the last quarter of the second century B.C. Unlike the others, it was built on the slope of the hill and stands on a constructed terrace. The sculptures on its railing were added much later. These carvings are not primarily concerned with the close imitation of nature, seeking instead to communicate aspects of the Buddha's teachings through established symbols, such as the lotus, the *pipal* tree, the wheel, and the stupa itself.

The famous four gateways were constructed around the Great Stupa, facing the cardinal directions, in the final years of the first century B.C. Like the *harmikā* railing surmounting the stupa, the gateways are thought to derive from wooden prototypes, and in their profusion of decorative sculpture they stand in sharp contrast to the unadorned austerity of the balustrade. Two square columns with elaborate capitals are connected by three massive architraves separated by rows of decorative balusters and free-standing sculpture. The composition is decidedly massed at the top. About thirty-four feet high and twenty feet wide, unsupported by struts or buttresses, the gates seem to defy gravity, hiding their structural elements beneath a wealth of sculptural reliefs.

Very little carved stone sculpture predates the Sānchi gateways, and the sophistication of their carvings is astonishing in an art form so young. Apparently, a mature wood- and ivory-carving tradition was translated to the new medium without appreciable loss. An inscription actually informs us that the South Gateway was carved by Vidiśā's ivory workers. The gateways portray many events of the Buddha's life, including his birth, his great renunciation, his enlightenment, and his first sermon. The image of the Buddha himself is actually still missing from these scenes; his pervasive presence is indicated only by symbols. The elephant symbolizes his conception through mother Māyā's dream. An image of the lotus signifies his birth. His great departure is represented by means of a horse. The tree serves as a symbol of his enlightenment, the wheel of his first sermon, and the stupa of the *parinirvana*. Empty thrones, footprints, and umbrellas everywhere announce his presence. In addition to scenes from the Buddha's life, there are depictions of stories associated with the Buddha's previous lives, such as those of Viśvantara and Saddanta. The War of the Relics is also represented, as is Aśoka's visit to the stupa at Rāmagrāma.

But the gateway carvings also represent the varied world of nature and humanity, crowding every aspect of Buddhist philosophy into the sculpture in a highly concrete form. Only a few examples can be mentioned here. Prosperity, ensured by the Buddha's triumph, is conveyed by nymphs kicking dormant trees into abounding blossom. A *yakṣī*, a female guardian spirit, personifies life arising out of water and earth in the majestic form of a tree, while her seductive sexuality gives an intimation of the power of nature. The Buddha's mother is portrayed as Gajalakshmi, the mother of all existence, seated on the lotus she herself personifies. Her right hand holds a lotus; her left foot rests on another, so as to expose her sex, also identified with the lotus. Two elephants, symbolizing rain clouds and standing on lotuses, pour heavenly water over her from pitchers held in their uplifted trunks. Such concrete representations of Buddhist abstractions stand closer to the more concrete forms of popular worship, and one function of the elaborate sculpture on the gateways may have been to help ordinary people relate more easily to the abstractions of Buddhist philosophy.

The principal architectural elements of the Sānchi complex were complete by the start of the Common (Christian) Era. But building on a more modest scale continued for the next eleven centuries. Stupas, prayer halls, monasteries, and temples were added in daunting numbers; only a few of the more notable later additions can be mentioned here. In A.D. 450 and 451, four images of the meditating Buddha were installed in canopied shrines in the ambulatory passage of the Great Stupa, against the terrace wall. At about the same time, Temple 17 was built. It consists of a single square chamber entered through a portico supported on pillars, and it is notable for the elegant simplicity of its design. Temple 18, built in the seventh century, is one of the rare examples of a constructed prayer hall, or *caitya,* in early India. (They were more commonly hewn out of the rock face of hills and mountains.) Temple 18 lies in ruins, however, with only the plinth, some of the great columns, and parts of the architrave still standing. Temple 45 dates to the tenth or eleventh century and is a good example of the use of a curvilinear spire. Temples 46 and 47 were built in the eleventh century, part of the last construction efforts at Sānchi.

Historians speculate that early in the twelfth century, Sānchi was deserted, for reasons unknown. As a consequence, the complex escaped the ravages of Muslim iconoclasm and survives for the modern visitor in a rare state of perfection. In addition to a steady stream of tourists, Sānchi now draws many students of history, art, and religion as well as Buddhist pilgrims from every part of the world.

Further Reading: The standard reference work on Sānchi is still Sir John Marshall's *The Monuments of Sānchi* (3 vols., London: Probsthain, 1940; reprint, Delhi: Swati, 1982), written with A. Foucher and N. G. Majumdar. Marshall also wrote an introduction for the general public in *A Guide to Sānchi* (Calcutta: Superintendent of Government Printing, 1918; third edition, Delhi: Manager of Publications, 1955), which is still very readable and informative. Debala Mitra's *Sānchi* (New Delhi: Director General of Archaeology, 1957; fourth edition, New Delhi, Archaeological Survey of India, 1978) includes an account of more recent archaeological findings.

—Sarva Daman Singh

Shanghai (China)

Location: Situated just south of the mouth of the Yangtze River on the East China Sea.

Description: The site of a fishing village as early as the eighth century A.D., Shanghai grew into a thriving commercial and industrial center during the late nineteenth century, when it was dominated by foreign interests. The city was the site of the Chinese Communist Party's first meeting and later became a showcase of the success of communism. Benefiting from the economic reforms of the late twentieth century, Shanghai today is China's most important commercial and industrial center. Like Beijing and Tianjin, it is a special administrative unit of China that does not properly belong to any province.

Site Office: CITS
66 Nanjing Road East
Shanghai
China

The great city of Shanghai, called the Pearl of the Orient and the Paris of the East during its heyday of the late nineteenth and early twentieth centuries, came from humble beginnings. It started as a small fishing village established on the site in approximately A.D. 750, making it a relative newcomer among great Chinese cities. Strategically located south of the mouth of the Yangtze River on the East China Sea, Shanghai grew and prospered in part because of its proximity to these waterways, as well as the smaller Huangpu River that runs through town.

Over the course of three centuries, the small village grew into a town. The bewildering maze of narrow cobblestone alleys lined with tiny cottages located near today's busy downtown area is the remains of the Chinese City or Old Town, thought to be the oldest surviving part of Shanghai, dating to the early eleventh century. The walls surrounding this fascinating section of Shanghai were torn down around 1912. In 1292 the region was incorporated by the ruling Mongols of the Yuan Dynasty into Shanghai County.

Despite its prime location near two major waterways and the ocean—the name Shanghai itself means "up from the sea"—the potential for development in Shanghai was overlooked for centuries in favor of its well-known neighbor Hangzhou. Famous for its beautiful scenery and worldly pleasures as recorded by Marco Polo, Hangzhou was the capital of China under the Southern Song and remained an important city even after the Mongols established the Yuan Dynasty.

Although Shanghai remained in the shadow of the glorious Hangzhou, it was developed by the Yuan rulers as part of their program of sweeping improvement to China's transportation infrastructure. With their capital at the northern city of Beijing, the Yuan found it necessary to revamp existing transportation routes—both on land and on water—to move foodstuffs grown in the south to the growing population in the north. In addition to digging two new canals to bring goods north of the Yangtze, the Yuan also developed Shanghai as a port, loading ships in the city's harbor along the Huangpu and sailing them north along the coast. By the seventeenth and eighteenth centuries, Shanghai had grown into an important trading center, boasting a large cotton-processing industry and a population of more than 200,000.

It was not, however, until the mid–nineteenth century that Shanghai became an important and well-known city, both for the Chinese and for foreign powers seeking to gain a foothold in the country. England had been trading heavily in China for quite some time, and by the late eighteenth century the balance of trade was greatly in China's favor. Trade was restricted primarily to southern China and the city of Canton (known today as Guangzhou), where England's East India Company bought significant amounts of tea, silk, and other commodities, paying largely in gold and silver. The Chinese purchased few goods in return, for they felt the West had nothing to offer. Speaking of China's self-sufficience, the Qing emperor Qianlong remarked, "We possess all things."

This one-sided trade, while good for China, was frustrating for foreign powers seeking to profit from the country's huge consumer market. After decades of British gold and silver had flooded into China, the 1820s saw trade between the two countries begin to balance, and in 1826 it finally turned in favor of the British. The commodity ultimately responsible for this change was brought from the British colony in India: highly addictive opium.

Chinese rulers had long recognized opium to be a dangerous substance. The Qing emperor Yongzheng outlawed the sale and usage of the drug in 1729, and the later emperor Jiaqing banned its cultivation and importation into China in 1796. Profits reaped by firms such as the East India Company and Jardine, Matheson and Company compelled other traders to enter the illicit industry, however, and the opium trade grew despite prohibition. With its strategic waterfront location, Shanghai played an important role in this growing trade. Opium was brought into the port of Hong Kong from India and then smuggled up the coast to Shanghai, from where it was transported farther inland along the Yangtze River.

In 1836, the Qing court at Beijing was in a quandary over how to resolve both the social and economic problems caused by the increasing opium trade. Daoguang, the Qing emperor, decided in 1838 that the trade was too harmful to China, and ordered the cultivation, importation, sale, and use

The Yu Yuan garden pavilion complex, Shanghai
Photo courtesy of China National Tourist Office, New York

Pagoda at Long Hua Temple, Shanghai
Photo courtesy of China National Tourist Office, New York

of opium halted. He appointed the official Lin Zexu to carry out this order. Lin's subsequent efforts urging foreigners to concentrate instead on the tea and silk trade went unheeded. In the spring of 1839, angered at the continued opium traffic, Lin ordered all foreign trade in Canton stopped. Under his proclamation, all Chinese workers were to leave their positions in foreign companies or households and all non-Chinese to be held under house arrest. The crackdown lasted six weeks until the foreigners finally surrendered some 20,000 chests of opium stocked in Canton.

Outraged by the treatment of British subjects and determined to protect the incredibly lucrative opium trade, the British Parliament sent 16 warships and 4,000 troops to China, thus starting the Opium War of 1839–1842. Britain's gunboats fought their way up the coastline, invading and occupying Shanghai on June 19, 1842, and gaining access to inland areas via the Yangtze. To save their country from destruction, the Chinese sued for peace, and on August 29, 1842, the Treaty of Nanking (Nanjing) was signed aboard the British ship *Cornwallis*, anchored in the Yangzte.

The Treaty of Nanking contained five major points, among these the opening of five previously closed ports to British trade: Canton (Guangzhou), Amoy (Xiamen), Fuzhou, Ningbo, and Shanghai. Furthermore, Article 2 of the treaty clearly stated that these cities were to be open as residences for British traders and their families, and that foreign commerce was not to be restricted by Chinese "molestation or restraint." Other powers, such as France and the United States, quickly signed similar treaties with China, giving themselves nearly identical privileges in Shanghai and other coastal towns.

The development of trade in four of the five treaty cities moved disappointingly slowly for the British, French, and American merchants. In Shanghai, however, the new settlement in the foreign concession area grew quickly. Once a marshy area along the Huangpu River, the concession at Shanghai soon had more than 100 merchants, 5 doctors, 17 missionaries, and the staffs of the newly formed consulates allowed by the Treaty of Nanking. In 1855, 437 foreign ships entered the port, up from 44 in 1844. The silk trade was worth more than $20 million by the mid-1850s, and more than 20,000 chests of opium were arriving annually.

Under the treaty, the concessions in Shanghai and other towns were supposed to be exclusively for foreigners and would be governed by representatives of each foreign country in residence. As far as Chinese law was concerned, the concessions were tiny sovereign states possessing their own legal system and were not subject to imperial rule or taxation. The foreign concession in Shanghai had numerous Chinese living within its boundaries, so many that they eventually outnumbered the foreigners. Because they lived within the concession's boundaries, however, they were subject to foreign rule and foreign discrimination. The British Public Park in Shanghai did not allow these Chinese to enter; a sign at the park's entrance stated "Dogs and Chinese Not Allowed."

The booming concession at Shanghai was threatened during the Taiping Rebellion. The region around the lower Yangtze saw bitter fighting from 1860 to 1864, and the riches of Shanghai together with its port made the city a prize sought by both the Taipings and the Qing. Concerned what would happen if their center of commerce fell into the hands of the radical Taipings, the foreign powers in Shanghai sponsored their own armed forces, called the Ever Victorious Army. Commanded first by an American and later by an Englishman, the Ever Victorious Army captured many cities along the lower Yangtze and played a significant role in the ultimate defeat of the Taiping rebels.

With peace restored to Shanghai, trade and development continued. The Chinese bourgeoisie in Shanghai, consisting primarily of native merchants working in foreign trade, began to grow. Called *compradors* from the Portuguese word for buyer, these merchants were contracted by foreigners to handle the Chinese end of the business. While most of the profit went to concession merchants, the *compradors* made a handsome living from commissions, interest, handling fees, and their own personal investments. The first *compradors* in Shanghai came with the trade as it moved north from Canton. In 1854, this class numbered only about 250; it grew to 700 by 1870 and mushroomed to some 20,000 by the turn of the century.

As trade made the foreign concessions in Shanghai wealthier and more powerful, the Chinese government began to worry that the foreigners might become so powerful that they could take over the entire country. Determined to maintain control over China, Qing rulers initiated the Self-Strengthening Movement in the latter half of the nineteenth century. The movement was begun not to profit from the new and innovative ideas of the Western powers, but "to learn the superior techniques of the barbarians to control the barbarians," as the scholar Wei Yuan (1794–1856) put it in his fifty-volume work, *An Illustrated Gazetteer of the Maritime Countries (Haiguo Tuzhi)*.

One of the most important products of this movement was the establishment of three munitions factories in Shanghai in 1862. Grateful for foreign aid in defeating the Taiping rebels, the Qing also feared the superior firepower of the Western forces, especially having suffered defeat during the Opium War and later skirmishes with the British in Beijing. Prince Gong, having seen firsthand the superiority of Western military technology, was delighted and amazed to discover that the former enemies had no qualms about training Chinese troops in military maneuvers and helping develop armaments factories. Jiangsu governor Li Hongzhang set up the factories in Shanghai in 1862 and subsequently ordered his men to learn about cannon from the British and about rifles from the Germans.

Convinced that China must learn from the West, Li established a foreign language school in Shanghai in 1863. Complacent about their cultural and military supremacy throughout their long history, the Chinese now were faced with clearly superior technology and techniques. If they did not learn diplomatic, shipbuilding, and military secrets from the West, it was, according to Li, quite probable that their age-old enemy Japan would seize the opportunity to assume an advantage over China.

Building on his belief that the Chinese military must be strengthened, Li and the governor of Liang-Jiang (an old administrative area including the modern provinces of Jiangsu, Anhui, and Jiangxi), Zeng Guofan, established the Jiangnan Arsenal in Shanghai in 1865. The first operation of its kind in China, the arsenal utilized U.S.-made machines to manufacture guns, cannon, and modern ships. In addition, the arsenal boasted a translation bureau that translated nearly 100 important Western titles into Chinese, including works on natural science and modern technology.

The second period of the Self-Strengthening Movement, from 1872 to 1885, saw improvements in China's industrial and communications base. Convinced that China's bolstered defenses could not singlehandedly eradicate poverty, Li urged Qing officials to pay more attention to the development of native-owned trade. In accordance with Li's suggestions, the Shanghai Cotton Cloth Mill was established in 1878. Although the mill initially received financial aid from the government, the responsibility for its success or failure lay solely with the merchants and appointed officials who ran the factory. To improve communications, the newly formed Imperial Telegraph Administration authorized and instituted China's first telegraph line, running from Shanghai to the northern port city of Tianjin.

Shanghai saw little development during the third phase of the movement (1885 to 1895), designed to increase China's light industry. Continuing to oversee most of the improvements made during this period, Li did establish the Longzhang Paper Mill in Shanghai in 1891.

Although the Self-Strengthening Movement encountered problems obtaining capital and adapting foreign technology, it served to introduce China to modern industrialization and capitalism. Shanghai profited greatly from the movement, with the establishment of the arsenal and a number of factories. The population in Shanghai and other coastal cities targeted by the movement exploded as nearby farmers migrated to the urban areas seeking work in the new factories.

Whatever the success of the Self-Strengthening Movement, the foreign entities in their insulated concessions also were becoming richer and more powerful. By the end of the nineteenth century, foreigners in Shanghai controlled most of the city's commerce, dominating banking, shipping, customs, and industry. As demonstrated by the Self-Strengthening Movement, the Chinese were wary of their wealthy guests—and some groups were more concerned than others. One radical group, the Yi He Quan, or Boxers, grew in numbers in Shandong, Henan, Jiangsu, and Anhui provinces. The group originated from an anti-Qing secret society, but by the 1890s it had become antiforeign and intent on freeing China from the Western powers and the Christian faith recently accepted by a number of Chinese.

As the Boxers gained power, they attacked settlements in Beijing and Tianjin, burning foreign residences and killing both foreigners and Chinese Christians. The Qing court, eager to free their country from what some members saw as budding imperialism by the Japanese, British, Americans, French, and Germans, encouraged the Boxers. Provincial authorities in southeast China, however, ignored Beijing's commands and entered into an agreement with several foreign consuls in Shanghai. Under the agreement, the officials in Guangzhou, Wuhan, Nanjing, and Shandong would suppress Boxer assaults on their own territories and protect foreign possessions and lives, while the consular officials promised to leave the defense of Chinese territory in the southeast to the Chinese. This agreement served the dual purpose of protecting foreign investment and alleviating Chinese fears of foreign interference.

The rest of China, however, was subjected to foreign invasion in response to the Boxer Rebellion. In the summer of 1900, an international force of some 18,000 troops (consisting of Japanese, Russians, British, Americans, French, and a small number of Austrians and Italians) left Tianjin for the capital at Beijing. When peace was finally declared later that year, the foreign forces claimed victory. Shanghai escaped the ravages wrought by the Boxers, but the British wanted to take no further chances with their investments; in 1900, shortly after the rebellion ended, they brought in Sikh forces from India to police their concession.

After the fall of the Qing Dynasty in the early twentieth century, the concessions in Shanghai continued to prosper. By the 1920s, both the numerous concessions and the waterfront (the Bund) in Shanghai contained fabulous mansions and elegant Art Deco buildings. Luxurious and exclusive clubs catered to the wealthy foreign businessmen and generally did not permit Chinese to enter. It is estimated that by 1926, foreign investment in Shanghai and the surrounding area reached $1 billion—and the profits went almost exclusively to foreign-held firms. The riches amassed by Western and Japanese merchants stood in stark contrast to the poverty of the masses of Chinese who lived outside the concession limits.

As the gap between the wealthy foreigners and starving Chinese continued to grow, conflict seemed inevitable. Dissatisfied with the inequitable distribution of wealth and resources in China, the Chinese Communist Party (CCP) formed in the early twentieth century, holding its first official meeting in Shanghai in July 1921. National dissent and the growing mistrust of foreigners escalated with the disastrous events in Shanghai in the spring of 1925.

In May, striking Chinese workers were locked out of their Japanese-run factory. The angered crowd of workers rushed the factory, breaking in and damaging equipment. The Japanese forces guarding the facility fired on the crowd, killing one of the striking employees. On May 30, the tense situation in Shanghai worsened as thousands of Chinese students and workers demonstrated outside the foreign police station, protesting foreign imperialism and calling for the release of six Chinese students who had been arrested. Although the protest began peacefully, the crowd grew, and eventually shouts of "Kill the foreigners!" were heard. The British officer in charge ordered the protesters to leave, but only ten seconds later commanded his combined Sikh and Chinese forces to open fire. In the chaos that followed, eleven protesters were killed and twenty more injured. Later known as the "May Thirtieth Atrocious Incident," the action heightened the country's distrust of foreigners and was a clear indication of the rift soon to develop between Chiang Kai-shek's nationalist forces and those of Mao Zedong's communist party.

Early in 1927, a series of labor strikes and communist uprisings in Shanghai led to retaliation by the local business community and the more conservative factions within the nationalists. In what became known as the Shanghai Coup, nationalist troops marched into the city on April 12, attacked headquarters of labor unions, and captured union and communist leaders, including Zhou Enlai, future premier of the People's Republic of China. Zhou managed to escape, but many other union and communist activists were executed.

While struggles between the nationalists and communists grew, Shanghai and its foreign concessions continued to prosper. As Asia's largest manufacturing center, Shanghai employed some 200,000 workers and boasted countless dance halls, opulent hotels, opium dens, restaurants, and brothels, the latter employing some 30,000 prostitutes. The heady days were not destined to last, however, as the threat of Japanese aggression began to grow.

The Japanese had annexed Korea in 1910 and viewed China's northern region of Manchuria as the next logical conquest. Japanese forces finally took the main city of Mukden (modern-day Shenyang) on September 16, 1931, and added several other northern cities to their territory within a week. In January of the next year, Japanese forces turned their attentions southward to Shanghai.

A local warlord's Nineteenth Route Army was stationed at Shanghai and fought bitterly against the January 28 invasion. Faced with nearly impossible odds, the army defended the city for more than two months but at last admitted defeat. International powers, already critical of previous Japanese aggression and concerned about the invasion's effect on business interests in Shanghai, loudly criticized the Japanese attack and pressed for a negotiated peace. Through mediation, an agreement was reached on May 2, 1932, and the Japanese evacuated the occupied area of Shanghai.

Hostilities between Japan and China continued, however, In July 1937 shots were fired by an unknown source at Japanese troops near the Marco Polo Bridge just outside Beijing. Japan had been entitled to station soldiers there, to help secure the area between Beijing and the coast, by an agreement negotiated at the end of the Boxer Rebellion. In the 1930s the Japanese army was deploying troops in greater numbers and over a greater area than permitted by the agreement, and skirmishes with the Chinese were frequent, although terms of peace usually were worked out soon afterward. After the so-called Marco Polo Bridge incident, however, both the Chinese and Japanese took a tougher stance, leading to a full-scale war that neither side quite expected. On August 14, Chinese forces attacked Japanese warships in the Huangpu River at Shanghai. The Japanese retaliated at once, and the Second Sino-Japanese War began with a bloody three-month battle for Shanghai. Shanghai's defenders fought valiantly, but the city suffered great loss of life and destruction of property before it fell to the Japanese in November. International efforts at a negotiated peace failed, and soon the Sino-Japanese conflict became part of the worldwide one.

With the defeat of the Japanese at the end of World War II, the nationalist and communist forces at last came head to head in China's civil war. Although supported by a number of international powers, Chiang Kai-shek's nationalist government was riddled with corruption and ultimately lost to the more popular Chinese Communist Party. Gaining ground since the war began in 1945, the communists captured Shanghai after the city put up a token defense in May 1949. On October 1 of the same year, Mao Zedong established the People's Republic of China at the northern capital of Beijing.

As Mao's CCP set to turn Shanghai into a communist showcase, the few foreigners who had remained in the city departed. Former foreign concessions and international hotels were seized as the country underwent land reform and nationalization of property. Shanghai's existing industries were expanded and modernized. A comparison of per capita food consumption figures from 1930 to those of 1956 demonstrates that the communists did succeed in improving the quality of life in the city. According to statistics, Shanghai residents consumed 65.7 percent more pork, 379.5 percent more eggs, and 12.5 percent more rice in 1956 while enjoying a 48.5 percent increase in living space.

Shanghai's prosperity and growth came to a halt, however, during the chaotic days of the Cultural Revolution. Officially started by Mao in 1966 to banish old customs and ideas and bring China into the modern era, the Cultural Revolution led to the seizure of Shanghai later that year by a radical Red Guard group, the Scarlet Red Guards. Shanghai and its commercial areas were nearly paralyzed as thousands of Red Guards descended on the city, severing railway connections and causing severe food shortages as various guard factions fought among themselves for control of the region. The Scarlets' demands for better wages and conditions for workers were criticized as materialistic by Cultural Revolution leaders.

With help from the military, order was restored to Shanghai in January 1967. On February 5 of the same year, radical leaders in Shanghai, including two future members of the Gang of Four, declared the formation of the Shanghai People's Commune, an administrative organization run by the common people and based on the Paris Commune of 1871. Under the precepts of the commune, government regulation in China would be completely decentralized, putting power into the hands of the people. Mao initially supported the concept but soon backed away from it. Within seventeen days the commune and all its principles were rejected by the Communist Party and the bureaucratic Revolutionary Committee took control.

The Cultural Revolution ended in 1970, and China at last began to look for a place in the international arena. Mao Zedong, nearly eighty years old, was in poor health and grooming Zhou Enlai as his successor. Seeking membership in the United Nations and recognition by the U.S. government, the Chinese government offered an invitation to President Richard Nixon to visit the country. During his stay in early 1972, Nixon met with numerous leaders, including Mao. Before the visit ended, they issued the Shanghai Communique from the city on February 28, detailing the newly formed relationship between the United States and China.

The Shanghai Communique is known primarily for its stance on Taiwan: according to the agreement, the United States recognizes the People's Republic as the "true" China. Other important strides indicated by the document include an agreement to share science and technology, cooperation between the two powers to combat Soviet interference in Asia and the Pacific, and a promise to continue to normalize relations between the United States and China. As Nixon left Shanghai—previously a city nearly ruled by foreign powers—he remarked that "never again shall foreign domination . . . be visited upon this city. . . ." Zhou, who died in 1976, is remembered by both countries as an important and skillful statesman.

Mao Zedong also died in 1976, after which a brief power struggle ensued between the Gang of Four (Mao's wife Jiang Qing, Wang Hongwen, Zhang Chunqiao, and Yao Wenyuan) and Mao's new heir apparent Hua Guofeng. Hua acted swiftly and within a month had jailed the four (also known as the Shanghai Gang for their previous associations with the city) for the excesses of the Cultural Revolution.

With the Gang of Four toppled, Shanghai began to turn its attention back to its roots: commerce. In 1984 the Chinese government granted Shanghai and certain other cities the right to deal directly with foreign companies, and today Shanghai rivals the southern city of Guangzhou (Canton) as China's most consumer-oriented, capitalistic city. As China continues to open up and Westernize, Shanghai continues to lead the way. The city's port facilities rank in the world's top ten, and the long-standing industrial and commercial base still makes Shanghai China's center of trade. On the cutting edge of capitalism, Shanghai established a stock exchange in 1986.

During the pro-democracy demonstrations of 1989, the citizens of Shanghai, like those of numerous other cities around China, took part. Students and workers alike thronged Shanghai's wide boulevards and paraded along the historic waterfront, paralyzing the already crowded city transportation systems. After the army gunned down students in Beijing's Tiananmen Square on June 4, the Chinese government enforced a news blackout; it is not known for certain if protesters in Shanghai also met with military reprisals.

Shanghai continues to develop today, as evidenced by the near-constant construction throughout the city. Foreigners flock to Shanghai in droves, seeking a foothold in the city they once ruled. Development and trade are the undisputed rulers of modern-day Shanghai as this city seeks to regain its former title, the Pearl of the Orient. Shanghai's historic sites are interspersed with modern buildings. The Bund, a popular gathering place where one often can encounter street performers and peddlers, still is lined with elegant Western-style buildings from the 1920s, including the 1927 Customs House, which still serves this function, and the former Hong Kong and Shanghai Bank building, now housing the municipal government. The latter structure has a striking dome. The park that once excluded dogs and Chinese is at the northwest end of the Bund. Other noteworthy architecture can be seen in what was the French concession area, with its impressive townhouses and apartment complexes. This area also includes the building that hosted the first Chinese Communist Party meeting; it is now a museum. Among the other landmarks of Shanghai are the Yu Yuan, a garden-pavilion complex developed by a Ming administrator in the sixteenth century, and the Long Hua Temple, which has the only pagoda in Shanghai. The first pagoda on the site was built in the third century, long before there was a town here; there have been numerous rebuildings since.

Further Reading: Dun Li's *The Agless Chinese: A History* (New York: Scribner, 1965; London: Dent, 1968) takes a comprehensive look at Shanghai throughout its history. *The Rise of Modern China* by Immanuel C. Y. Hsu (Oxford and New York: Oxford University Press, 1970; fifth edition, 1995) provides an exhaustive account of the events leading up to the founding of the People's Republic in 1949. Two other general histories with valuable references to Shanghai are Jonathan Spence's *The Search for Modern China* (New York and London: Norton, 1990) and John King Fairbank's *China: A New History* (Cambridge, Massachusetts, and London: Belknap Press of Harvard University Press, 1992). Readers particularly interested in the events following Mao Zedong's death will find value in Roger Garside's *Coming Alive: China After Mao* (New York: McGraw-Hill, and London: Deutsch, 1981).

—Monica Cable

Shanhaiguan (Hebei, China)

Location: Two hundred sixty miles east of Beijing near the Bohai Coast, at the border between present-day Hebei and Liaoning provinces. Shanhaiguan stands on the Yu River about three miles west of the sea at the narrowing of the coastal plain, with mountains enclosing it on the inland side.

Description: A strategic site used either as a defense against invasion from peoples "north of the Wall" or as a corridor for communications between northern China and Manchuria. Not noted as a major site of settlement in earlier times, Shanhaiguan became a crucial location when the Ming made it the easternmost end of their Great Wall and fortified it heavily. Much of the Ming building has been restored, and the town is now a popular tourist destination.

Contact: Hebei Tourism Bureau
22 Yucai Avenue
Shijiazhuang 050021
China
(311) 614319

The present Shanhaiguan is close to the site of the ancient pass of Yuguan. Despite frequent claims, there is no evidence that either place was the easternmost end of the Great Wall built under Qin Shihuang (ruled 246–210 B.C.). His wall probably followed the line of older fortifications built during the period of the Warring States (403–221 B.C.) under the kingdom of Yan, which ran far to the north of Shanhaiguan, through present-day Liaoning province. Under the Han (206 B.C.–A.D. 220), the name Yu was attached only to a river, although the Han District of Yangle covered the area in which Shanhaiguan now stands.

The present site of Shanhaiguan probably was fortified first by the Northern Qi (550–574), but the first definite record of fortification in the area is from the Sui Dynasty (581–618). The Sui walled a place called Linyuguan, some twenty-two miles to the west of modern Shanhaiguan and further inland, in the third lunar month of 583. Five years later Emperor Wen Di (ruled 589–605) ordered the prince of Han to lead troops through this pass to subdue the Koguryo state in the Korean peninsula. The Tang (618–907) continued this venture, with the second emperor, Tang Taizong, going in person to fight the Koreans in early 645, returning at the end of the year through the same pass, now called Yuguan, at the head of 3,000 of his best cavalry. By 785 a garrison was based at Yuguan, and eight more were established northward from there to Jinniukou. During the eighth century, the territory in this area came under the control of virtually autonomous governors, so that by the period of the Five Dynasties (907–959) no garrison appears to have remained; only a narrow route surrounded by farmland permitted carts through to the northeast.

The area of the Liao River valley to the north of the pass provided nomadic peoples with a strong base, offering fertile land for grazing and grain production and giving on to one of the main invasion routes into northern China: the coastal corridor beside the Bohai Sea. This stretch of land narrows at the point where Shanhaiguan now stands, making it a natural defensive point, but it was not fully utilized as such until the territories "north of the Wall" became integral parts of regimes that also ruled parts of China Proper. The Liao Dynasty (907–1125), established by the non-Chinese Kitan people, acquired the area including the passes in the early tenth century. Yuguan continued to exist, but under Emperor Shengzong (982–1031) the Liao founded Qianmin county farther east, on the site of modern Shanhaiguan. However, the town did not become important until the Jin Dynasty (1115–1234), founded by the Jürchens, established a capital at Beijing. The Jin promoted the county of Qianmin to garrison status, and from 1328 the Mongol dynasty of the Yuan (1234–1368) garrisoned it as well.

The most striking feature of Shanhaiguan today is the section of the Great Wall that can still be seen there. Built under the Ming (1368–1644), this wall illustrates how the beginnings of serious defensive building in the area were not the "long walls" *(changcheng)* we usually associate with the Great Wall, but fortifications reinforcing strategic spots. General Xu Da (1332–85) took troops to repair the passes in the vicinity of Shanhaiguan early in 1381, and when a new Shanhai Guard was established in the autumn, he began building a wall around the town. The first fort was begun at the end of 1382 and had a forty-foot-high wall. At this time the pass was moved from its old location at Yuguan to the new garrison, which thus acquired the name Shanhaiguan: *guan* means pass, while *Shanhai* means mountains (*shan*) and sea (*hai*). Yuguan became no more than a stop along the road. During the reign of the Ming emperor Hongwu (1368–98), much building occurred around the garrison, including the Beishuiguan (northern water gate) less than a mile north of the town, which provided a route through the border wall for the Yu River, and a fort three miles to the south at the southern sea pass, commonly called Laolongtou (Old Dragon Head) and sometimes Ninghaicheng (Sea-calming Fort). One Chinese scholar argues that "long walls" also were begun at this time, but these appear to have been limited in scale. While defenses were strengthened all along the Ming frontier under Emperor Yongle (ruled 1403–25), the phrase *changcheng* is not found in the Ming court records until 1429, when it was reported that the *changcheng* beyond the passes in Shanhaiguan and other places collapsed owing to heavy rain.

Gate leading into Shanhaiguan
Photo courtesy of A.P. / Wide World Photos

We are fortunate to have a firsthand account of Shanhaiguan completed in 1488. A Korean official called Ch'oe Pu (1454–1504) was shipwrecked off the Chinese coast, arrested, and escorted back to Korea via Shanhaiguan. He reported that the pass itself stood on the top of Mount Jue, north of the garrison wall. Ch'oe Pu's party stopped at numerous wayside stations that provided food and other necessities to travelers. Between Shanhaiguan and the Yalu River (which marked the Korean border), these walled stations stood between ten and twenty miles apart. Within Shanhaiguan, beacon towers stood about every three miles, while outside the pass these were replaced with distance markers every couple of miles. Cho'e Pu recorded that road conditions outside of Shanhaiguan were deteriorated, and the population became increasingly sparse, poor, and uncivilized the further he journeyed from the garrison.

Regardless of the real extent of the "long walls" in the Shanhaiguan area, by the time of Ch'oe Pu's journey legends about the Great Wall already had taken hold. He was told that portions of the defenses he saw had been built by the Qin (even though their border had run well to the north) and was shown the "husband-lookout tower" where Meng Jiangnü had stood. The legend of Meng Jiangnü related that her husband had been conscripted to build Qin Shihuang's Wall. When Meng Jiangnü brought winter clothes to him and found he had died, the Wall collapsed to reveal his bones. Some versions hold that this enabled Meng Jiangnü to take the bones home for proper burial, others that she threw herself into the sea upon viewing her husband's remains. A tomb, claimed to be that of Meng Jiangnü and dating from the Qin, is in Linyu county, within which Shanhaiguan is now located. The story was popular enough to give rise to two temples bearing Meng Jiangnü's name. One, the Zhennü (Devoted Woman) Temple just outside Shanhaiguan, has been dated to the Song Dynasty (960–1276) by a couplet-hanging it contained. The other, called the Lienü (Woman Killing Herself after Her Husband's Death) Temple, stands four miles east of the town. Although it has often been dated to the Song, it appears to have been constructed or reconstructed during the Ming, in 1594. Under the last Ming emperor Chongzhen (ruled 1628–44), nineteen chaste-widow suicides were buried there. This suggests that the version of the legend according to which Meng Jiangnü drowns herself had gained wider popular currency than the version whereby she removes her husband's bones for proper burial; the wider currency of the former version can in turn, perhaps, be explained by the increasing frequency of widow suicide during the Ming period. Stone tablets in the temple include one commemorating its renovation during the Qing Dynasty (1644–1912); the temple was restored again in 1928.

Shanhaiguan was one of the three most important passes along the wall, along with Jiayuguan (Gansu) and Juyongguan (just north of Beijing). After the initial wave of fourteenth-century fort building, walls were built at 170 strategic places between Shanhaiguan and Juyongguan in the period 1488–1505. The actual fortress of Shanhaiguan stands about six miles from the sea and is part of a complex including a large arched gate, now restored, bearing a sign announcing it as the "First Pass Under Heaven" *(tianxia di yi guan)*. The original calligraphy on this sign was by Xiao Xian, a native of Shanhaiguan who in the late fifteenth century earned notice for his virtue by retiring to an eremitic life on Mount Weichun near his hometown in preference to taking an official post in the capital. Noted as one of the thirty-two great calligraphers of the Ming, Xiao Xian also wrote fine poetry.

Most of the earlier fortifications around Shanhaiguan were superseded during the sixteenth century, when the Ming carried out their most impressive wall building. In 1550 the Mongol chief Altan Khan penetrated China as far as the walls of Beijing. The Ming, no longer able to muster the resources to fight off such raids, built walls instead. Since the Altan Khan's raid revealed the particular weakness of the northeast, work began on the defenses at Shanhaiguan and in the Jizhou region (east of the capital) in 1551. In 1565 secondary forts and other defensive works were built, and these efforts continued throughout a court debate—which lasted from 1567 to 1573 and eventually resolved nothing—on how to handle the northern border defenses. Most of this work was directed by Tan Lun (1520–77), who was appointed senior vice minister of war and supreme commander of the defense areas of Ji (which included Shanhaiguan) and Liao in 1568. By this time the fortifications had decayed so much that in the spring of 1569 Tan chose the most important points along the border from Shanhaiguan inland to a point near Datong (an 800-mile stretch that had proven difficult to defend) to reinforce against emergencies. His ambitious proposals were scaled down to build 1,200 signal towers—each manned by thirty to fifty soldiers—during a ten-year period.

As Ming policy embraced wall building ever more firmly, Shanhaiguan grew in importance; in 1571 it was separated from Jizhou commandery and became an independent command. The section of wall now extending from the fortress to the sea was built by Qi Jiguang, commander of Jizhou from 1569 to 1583. In 1575 Shanhaiguan was placed under a Xieshou battalion in the Eastern Circuit and renamed Shanhai Route. In 1584 more fortifications were added, and defensive building continued at Shanhaiguan throughout the last years of the Ming Dynasty.

During this period the Jürchen (later known as Manchus) took control of the territory of Liaodong, east of the pass, and although some Ming officials clamored for its recovery, most saw a sound defense against any similar raids as the only option. In 1622 the Ming established the Longwu battalion at Old Dragon Head Fort, adding three further battalions there in 1633. Other defenses extended the wall northeastward from Shanhaiguan to Jilin. A series of ditches and embankments (already observed by Ch'oe Pu in the previous century) were planted with willow trees. This barrier, intended to halt cavalry troops, was not enough to prevent the Jürchen from driving south through the pass in 1644.

The rise of the Jürchen in Liaodong saw their leader, Nurhaci, planning as early as 1622 to attack China through the Shanhaiguan Pass. Rebellions from his Chinese subjects in Liaodong in 1623 and 1625 postponed Nurhaci's plan. Although the Ming had some military successes against the Jürchen during 1626, growing numbers of Chinese shifted their allegiances to Nurhaci's successor, Hong Taiji, including the generals commanding the defenses at the mouth of the Yalu River. In 1638 the Jürchen, now calling themselves Manchus, conquered Korea and repeatedly raided the area near the Ming capital, despite the Ming's frontier defenses. After the strategic city of Jinzhou fell to the Manchus in 1642 following a ten-year siege, two of the last Ming generals of any ability surrendered to the victors. Shanhaiguan was the last frontier defense post left to the Ming, guarded by the great general Wu Sangui. As the Manchus rose in power, rebels against the Ming regime had taken control of large parts of northern China. In the spring of 1644, one of these, Li Zicheng, seized the capital, Beijing, and toppled the dynasty. Considering that Wu Sangui was the last defender of the Ming, Li then marched on Shanhaiguan, while Wu headed west to meet him. Wu's march left Shanhaiguan open for the new Manchu regent, Dorgon, to pass unhindered down the coast and through the pass, thus trapping Wu into a choice between the rebel on the one hand and the invader on the other. Doubtful of Li's effectiveness, Wu chose to surrender to the Manchus, who in turn promised him safe treatment.

Wu's defection to the Manchus ensured the defeat of Li Zicheng outside Shanhaiguan and the subsequent establishment of the Qing Dynasty as rulers of China. Although the northern limit of the Qing empire lay well beyond that of the Ming, the Manchus recognized the strategic importance of Shanhaiguan and early in the dynasty established a garrison there, with an army under a senior general. This garrison initially retained the late-Ming name of Shanhai Route but later was changed to Youji. The area came under the jurisdiction of Zhili province.

In 1708 the Jesuits began a ten-year survey of the Qing domains, including the Great Wall starting at Shanhaiguan, for the Kangxi emperor. The cartographic expedition led by Father Jean-Baptiste Regis produced a fifteen-foot-long map of the wall. Armies continued to be stationed at Shanhaiguan throughout the dynasty, with occasional administrative reorganizations. In 1848 the collection of customs revenues was begun under the superintendency of the ministry of population. These early signs of the impact of the outside world on China's coastal regions accelerated during the late nineteenth century as railways came to northeast China. A line connecting towns in the Tangshan and Tianjin regions, begun in 1880, was extended in 1894 by a spur into Manchuria that ran through the pass at Shanhaiguan. Popular opposition to the lines was expressed in 1900 when the joint foreign force opposing the Boxer Rebellion attacked Old Dragon Head in Shanhaiguan. The Boxer forces counterattacked and tore up the nearby railway. After the Boxer Rebellion, the foreign powers' hold on their concessions increased, and Shanhaiguan became a resort for European troops on leave, with Catholic and Methodist missions and a Chinese population of 1,000 families. According to the traveler William Edgar Geil, in 1908 the Great Wall had upon it "a white lighthouse, a searchlight, and a temple to literature." Two Qing temples survive to this day: the Chongxing Temple, just northwest of Shanhaiguan, and the Wenquan (Hot Spring) Temple, named for a local phenomenon, twelve miles to the west.

Although the defensive role of the pass was of lesser consequence in an enlarged China, Shanhaiguan continued to be a significant route of communications and frequently found itself involved in wider events. In 1922 Wang Jinmei, one of the founders of the Chinese Communist Party (CCP), was sent to Shanhaiguan by Li Dazhao to lead the workers' movement there, while at approximately the same time the locally born general Tian Zhongyu (1869–1935) established a middle school and several primary schools in Shanhaiguan.

In October 1924 the northeastern warlord Zhang Zuolin took advantage of a coup in Beijing against his main rival, Wu Peifu, and sent troops south through Shanhaiguan. Zhang's troops penetrated to the Yangzi region, enabling Zhang to develop a power base in Beijing; this worried the nationalists so much that they launched the Northern Expedition against Zhang and his allies. In 1928 the government moved to Nanjing, and Zhili province was renamed Hebei. Two years later a trio of northern leaders tried to remove Chiang Kai-shek from power. This gave Zhang Zuolin's son, Zhang Xueliang, the opportunity to send troops through Shanhaiguan to occupy northern Hebei, giving him control of the northern sections of the Beijing-Wuhan and Tianjin-Pukou railways, as well as of the large Tianjin customs revenues.

In 1931–32 the Japanese established the puppet state of Manchukuo in Manchuria. A League of Nations commission reported in January 1933 that China should retain sovereignty, and in response Japan ordered troops into Rehe province. Meanwhile, the Japanese Army also attacked Shanhaiguan, occupying it despite the desperate counterattacks of the Chinese under General He Zhuguo. This seizure consolidated the Japanese hold on Rehe, which effectively was conquered by April. By the end of May the Japanese had extended their control into Hebei and forced the Chinese to agree to the Tanggu Truce, which demilitarized northeastern Hebei and, even though the Japanese formally withdrew to the Great Wall, turned Shanhaiguan into a gateway for invasion rather than a barrier against it. By the end of October 1938, the nationalist government had lost control of China's east coast from Shanhaiguan southward.

The Japanese continued to occupy Shanhaiguan until the end of World War II, when, on August 30, 1945, the People's Liberation Army (PLA) entered Shanhaiguan and instituted a temporary government. Meanwhile, American-brokered talks tried to prevent a communist-nationalist civil war, but fighting continued as American supplies arrived to aid the nationalists. In October, American and nationalist troops disembarked at the port of Qinhuangdao, occupied it, and advanced toward Shanhaiguan. The PLA fought a twenty-day holding action there before withdrawing. Having secured the communication route, many of the best nationalist forces struck through Shanhaiguan at the communists, hoping to loosen their hold on the northeast. Ongoing talks and fighting resolved nothing, and the nationalists attacked Manchuria again in July 1946. These assaults pushed the communists north across the Sungari River and out of the coastal area north of Shanhaiguan, through Jinzhou to Mukden (Shenyang) and Changchun. During the spring of 1947, this route was one of four major corridors through northern China still being kept open by the nationalists, but the communists held most of the countryside. Under the leadership of Lin Biao, the PLA by May 1948 was besieging effectively the major cities of Manchuria, forcing the nationalists to abandon them. The nationalist retreat from Shanhaiguan and Qinhuangdao began in November 1948, and in December Shanhaiguan was placed under the jurisdiction of the newly liberated Qinhuangdao.

In March 1949 Shanhaiguan became part of Liaoxi province, and the town was promoted briefly to city status until it was placed again under Qinhuangdao's administration in November 1952. In this early part of the People's Republic, restoration work was carried out on, among other things, the First Pass Under Heaven, by Liu Xiangzhai (1883–1963). Liu had been a palace painter at the Qing court, specializing in painted figures, temple wall paintings, and ancient technology. He restored the traditional eaves and roof-ridge creatures on the gate tower and painted the roof supports, rafters, and patterned decoration as they would have been originally.

During 1971 Mao Zedong turned against Lin Biao, Mao's designated successor and the hero of the anti-Soviet skirmishes in the far north. When Mao began undermining Lin Biao's position within the leadership, Lin, according to unverifiable CCP documents, responded by trying to plan Mao's assassination; when this failed, he took a car from Beidaihe to Shanhaiguan airfield and fled with his family aboard a Trident airplane, which crashed on September 13 in Mongolia, killing all aboard.

In the late 1970s a huge dry dock was constructed at Shanhaiguan, one of several projects requiring an impressive amount of technological skill. Shanhaiguan remains under the jurisdiction of Qinhuangdao city, which since 1984 has been designated one of fourteen open coastal cities. The main industry of Shanhaiguan itself is tourism, most of which focuses upon the restored remains of the Great Wall defense system, including the city walls, the First Pass Under Heaven, and Old Dragon Head, as well as the connecting wall itself.

Further Reading: Information on Shanhaiguan is extremely scattered, even in Chinese. As to Western languages, Jonathan Fryer's *The Great Wall of China* (London: New English Library, 1975) contains numerous references to Shanhaiguan and is readily accessible, but the book tends to confuse fact and legend. Arthur Waldron's *The Great Wall of China: From History to Myth* (Cambridge and New York: Cambridge University Press, 1990) attempts to correct many misconceptions about the wall and along the way includes much information on Shanhaiguan. An account of Ch'oe Pu's travels can be found in John Meskill's complete translation *Ch'oe Pu's Diary: A Record of Drifting Across the Sea* (Ann Arbor, Michigan: University Microfilms, 1959), which includes much else besides the description of Shanhaiguan.

—Naomi Standen

Shenyang (Liaoning, China)

Location: In the plain of the Liao River valley, in northeastern China, almost 400 miles from Beijing and some 120 miles from the Korean border. Capital city of Liaoning province, southernmost of the provinces forming Manchuria.

Description: Site of settlement from earliest times, Shenyang first rose to prominence as the capital of the predynastic Qing regime. The city has been called variously Shenjing and, from 1634, Mukden. During the early twentieth-century Japanese expansion in Manchuria, Shenyang was a Japanese stronghold. The city retains an imperial palace but is mostly noted for an industrial output in China second only to Shanghai.

Site Office: Liaoning Tourism Bureau
113 Huanghe South Avenue
Shenyang 110031
Liaoning
China
(24) 6807316

The earliest known inhabitants of the Shenyang area established a culture known as the Xinle more than 7,000 years ago. They lived by farming, fishing, and hunting in a land of dense forests, marshes, and rivers. The Liao River basin was highly fertile, and by about the first millennium B.C. several groups appear to have been living in this area, including the Huimo, Sushen, ethnic Chinese, and Donghu. The last-named group is best known as a seminomadic people who relocated their animals to new pastures in accordance with the seasons. In later written records about the Spring and Autumn period (722–481 B.C.), the Donghu are said to have been a fierce people who excelled at mounted archery and held slaves acquired through war or raiding. However, archaeological evidence shows that by the Warring States period (403–221 B.C.) agriculture also flourished. Excavations have revealed extensive and sophisticated use of iron implements, including hoes, shovels, sickles, and pickaxes. Archaeologists have found other objects dating to this period as well: bronze plaques with animal decoration and bronze Donghu swords found at Zhengjiawazi. These swords, which are usually associated with nomadic cultures, have turned up alongside less sophisticated agricultural implements of stone, including pickaxes and adzes, as well as bone spades. These findings suggest that separate communities with different lifestyles coexisted in the same general area.

States controlling northern China were keen to incorporate this area into their territories because of the easy maritime links between it and the Shandong Peninsula. According to the *Shiji (Records of the Grand Historian)*, future Shenyang was part of the territory taken from the Donghu by the state of Yan in 300 B.C. Yan had sent a general Qin Kai to Liaodong, as the area was known, and he took somewhere between 1,000 and 3,000 square *li* (a Chinese *li* is about one-third of a mile) of land, building a wall from Zaoyang (modern Huailai Xian, Hebei) to Xiangping (modern Liaoyang) to prevent any Donghu retaliation and dividing up the territory into five administrative districts or prefectures. The early Former (or Western) Han (206 B.C.–A.D. 9) also had designs on the region and established commanderies there after defeating the Donghu in 128 B.C. One of the county towns in the Shenyang region, Houcheng, became the seat of the Defender of the Central Region and had a major army stationed there, thus forming an important military base. Several theories have been offered concerning the location of Houcheng, but excavations in 1971 suggest that the ruins of an ancient city found near the imperial palace in Shenyang are those of the garrison town.

In A.D. 107 the area covered by modern Shenyang was divided between the two prefectures of Liaodong and Xuantu. In the second century A.D. the two prefectures came under separate governments, Liaodong being appropriated by a Han governor in 189. After the kingdom of Wei (220–265) replaced the Han, the two areas were reunited under Wei control. Wei was followed by the Western Jin Dynasty (265–316), which reorganized the administrative structure of the Liaodong region. The fourth century brought civil war, drought, and locusts, and in the ensuing chaos massive southward migrations from northern China took place. In 404, toward the end of the Eastern Jin Dynasty (317–420), the Korean state of Koguryo occupied the Liaodong and Xuantu prefectures, establishing the cities of Xuantucheng and Gaimoucheng within the present boundaries of Shenyang. The remains of Gaimoucheng lie beneath the southeastern suburbs of the modern city.

Following the unification of China by the Sui (581–618), the emperor Yangdi led an army to defeat Koguryo in 612 and, having retaken the Liaodong-Xuantu area, set up a new Liaodong prefecture, unrelated to the previous districts of that name, in what is now Shenyang. Koguryo remained a threat, however. In 645 the Tang (618–907) emperor Taizong sent an expeditionary force to fight Koguryo again. On this occasion both the Korean cities were taken, but it was another twenty years before the Koguryo state was altogether destroyed. Liaodong, along with the rest of the Tang empire, was then divided into governor-generalships, prefectures, and counties. Almost 250 years of peaceful development followed the Tang reorganization.

In 916 the Shenyang area came under the control of the nomadic Kitan people, who established the Liao Dynasty (907–1125). In 921 the founding emperor, Abaoji, established

Imperial Palace, Shenyang
Photo courtesy of Liaoning Tourism Bureau

Shenzhou on the present site of Shenyang. In the period to 1074, the Liao gradually established another five prefectures and six counties in the surrounding districts, under the overall jurisdiction of Dongjing circuit. This administrative expansion suggests an increasingly dense population, as Chinese farming communities under Liao rule took advantage of the peace prevailing in this area after the defeat of Liao's neighbors in the Liaodong Peninsula in 926. The numerous surviving Buddhist temples and stupas, many of which contain reliquaries and documents, reflect Liao's position as the leading Buddhist state of the time.

The nomadic northeastern neighbors of the Liao, the Jürchen, who established their Jin Dynasty (1115–1234), took Shenzhou from the Liao in 1116. In 1143 the region under Shenzhou's direct control was expanded when three of the prefectures set up by the Liao were demoted, making Shenzhou the prefectural seat for five dependent counties. At the end of the dynasty, the earthen walls were destroyed as the Jin were overthrown by the advancing Mongols. The Mongols established the Yuan Dynasty (1234–1368), which eventually ruled all of China.

Shenzhou was reestablished as an administrative district in 1262, and in 1296 it was brought under a new circuit named Shenyang. The name is derived from the town's location north of the River Shen. (Traditional Chinese concepts of positioning say "that which is north of mountains is *yin*,

Pazheng Hall, Imperial Palace, Shenyang
Photo courtesy of Liaoning Tourism Bureau

that which is north of water is *yang,"* so that the town to the north of the River Shen becomes Shenyang.) The earthen walls around the city were rebuilt when it became the circuit seat. Shenyang administered a large area, including five route commands and fourteen prefectures. It also functioned as a military headquarters whenever an eastward expansion was attempted, most notably in 1299, when the target was Japan.

Shenyang remained under the Yuan until 1368, when the Ming Dynasty took control over the area. Five guard garrisons were established in Shenyang late in the fourteenth century, and the whole set was placed under the office of the Liaodong chief guard commander. Subsequently, four of these garrisons were either placed under other districts or abolished, dividing the territory of modern Shenyang under several authorities and leaving the city in control of only Fushun and Puhe Battalions. The earthen wall was rebuilt in 1388 as a brick wall, part of a trend in the Ming to make fortifications of more durable materials. The new wall was about three miles around and over twenty-two feet high, with double walls, moats, and city gates built with four arches. Within the city, the two main streets formed a cross.

The city again changed hands in 1621, passing once more to the Jürchen, who, still living in the north, had united under the Great or Later Jin Dynasty. The new Jin capital was first established at Liaoyang and then, in 1625, at Shenyang, which was briefly known as Shenjing (*jing* meaning capital). At Shenyang the Jin emperor began work on a great palace, which eventually incorporated Manchu, Chinese, and Tibetan elements. He was succeeded by Hong Taiji, who completed the palace and made many changes in Shenyang. The Ming brick walls were essentially rebuilt and raised by eleven feet in approximately 1631. Corner towers were added, and the gates were strengthened with additional towers and arches. An extra main street was added in each direction, to divide the city into nine main districts. In 1634 its name was changed to Mukden, meaning "flourishing" in Manchu. It was usually known in Chinese by an abbreviated translation of the Manchu name Shenjing. In addition, Taiji established institutions following Ming models, most notably a bureaucracy comprising six ministries, headed by Jürchen ministers who were frequently absent, but staffed with Chinese officials chosen by competitive examination.

Zhang Zuolin's "Marshal Mansion," Shenyang
Photo courtesy of Liaoning Tourism Bureau

Hong Taiji changed the dynastic name from Great Jin to Qing in 1636 and declared that the Jürchen were henceforth to be known as Manchus. The Manchu armies and the Mongols who had joined them were each organized into eight "banners" for military purposes and to facilitate population registration. This system was extended to Chinese subjects of the Qing for the first time with the establishment of two Chinese banners in 1637. These two were increased to a full eight by 1642. In the area around Mukden a dual system operated, with banner organization continuing alongside the preexisting Chinese civilian administration, but in Mukden itself none of the population was registered under the banner system. From his capital, Taiji directed raiding parties against northern China, exacerbating and taking advantage of a situation already producing peasant revolts among the Ming population.

In 1644, the year after Taiji's death, one of these revolts overthrew the Ming and occupied the capital. The Qing prince regent, Dorgon, marched south and took Beijing from the rebels. Beijing immediately became the Qing capital, while Mukden was maintained as a secondary capital. Although matters concerning the Ministry of Personnel were controlled from the Qing court in Beijing, Mukden maintained its own establishments for the other five government ministries, including those responsible for justice and war, until 1905. Once all of China was under Qing control, a new administrative district called Fengtian prefecture was established within Mukden city, with the aim of improving household registration for taxation purposes. During the Kangxi (1661–1722) and Qianlong (1736–96) reign eras, more building on the imperial palace was carried out, and a copy of the great compilation ordered by the Qianlong emperor, the *Siku quanshu,* was deposited there.

Successive waves of immigration to Liaodong and areas farther north, with or without government sponsorship, intensified during the nineteenth century and brought commercial development to Mukden and its nearest port, Yingkou. In 1895 Liaodong was handed over to Japan at the end of the Sino-Japanese War, only to be returned at the insistence of Russia. In an effort to protect the northeast against Japanese expansionism, the Qing government signed a secret treaty with Russia in 1896, granting the Russians permission to build the Chinese Eastern Railway across Siberia to Vladivostok. In 1898 the Russians acquired a twenty-five-year lease on the peninsula they had rescued from Japanese occupation, along with the right to build the South Manchurian Railway connecting Dalian and Lüshun (Port Arthur) with their Chinese Eastern Railway. The line ran past Mukden, and a station was built in the western suburbs of the old city. Although there was no formal arrangement, the Russians ran the railway territory as if it were a concession, with separate municipal, police, judicial, and military administrations. From there they occupied the whole of Manchuria after the Boxer Rebellion of 1900 on the pretext of restoring order, and they sought new privileges from China before reluctantly withdrawing.

In 1905 the Qing established the administration for Fengtian province in Mukden, and later that year the Japanese defeated the Russians in a battle there, but they were unable to follow up, owing to a lack of ammunition. When the Russo-Japanese war ended with Russia's surrender, the lease on the peninsula, the South Manchurian Railway territory, and all associated privileges were handed over to Japan. A further treaty gave Japan the right to extra "settlements" at Mukden among other places, under the administration of the new government-general of the peninsula. Japan had by now also acquired control of the enormous coal deposits around Mukden, along with other natural resources in Manchuria. The South Manchurian Railway Company, despite repeated Chinese protests, exercised what were in effect colonial powers in the towns along the line, including Mukden. The company, modeled upon the East India Company, had the Japanese government as its majority shareholder and was overseen by the governor-general. As if to reflect the passing of the old order, the banner organization based in Mukden was abolished in 1907, ending the separate administration of banner families and requiring major bureaucratic reorganization. In the same year the British completed a rail link between Mukden and Beijing.

When the Qing ended in 1912, Mukden became the base for the locally born warlord Zhang Zuolin. He first allied himself with the provisional president of the new republic, Yuan Shikai, but he was soon the *de facto* leader of an autonomous Fengtian province, under which Mukden, now called Fengtian city, gained a separate government for the first time. In 1915 Zhang Zuolin's authority was recognized, after he made life impossible for the Beijing appointee who briefly replaced the outgoing governor. In that same year, however, Yuan Shikai granted Japan's Twenty-One Demands, which included extending the leases of the peninsula and the South Manchurian Railway concession to ninety-nine years, giving full economic rights to Japanese subjects in Manchuria, and allowing the Japanese their own police and economic advisers. The young leaders of the Japanese Guandong army stationed in this region had ambitions both for themselves and for a greater Japan that were not necessarily approved by the Tōkyō government. For the next quarter of a century they took every opportunity to expand their control and influence in Guandong and beyond. The Japanese consolidated their influence as much through economic as political means, and the fourfold rise in soybean production between 1907 and 1927 was the direct result of Japanese intervention. By 1929 Fengtian province was responsible for one-third of China's total coal and iron production, yet it contained only 3 percent of the total population.

Although Zhang Zuolin received sound fiscal advice, he could not match Japan's resources. He trod a careful line, which often involved seeking help from and accommodation with the Japanese, but also included efforts to diminish their hold on Manchuria. Zhang developed what is known as the Mukden Clique (or Fengtian Clique) by building personal loyalties with a diverse group of civil and military people. By 1920 he had effective control of all three Manchurian provinces (Fengtian, Jilin, and Heilongjiang), and his clique was strong enough to challenge its neighbors. Despite its Japanese backing, the Mukden Clique was defeated by Zhili (modern Hebei province) during a brief war in 1922. When the nationalist government formally dismissed Zhang, his power base remained intact and he simply declared Manchuria independent. In 1924 Zhang won a second war with Zhili, not least because a large payment to the Zhili general Feng Yuxiang encouraged him to assist the Fengtian side.

By 1925 Zhang's effective authority covered much of eastern China as well as most of the north, and he had become the main opponent of Chiang Kai-shek's nationalist (Guomindang or GMD; in Pinyin, Kuomintang or KMT) government in Nanjing, prompting the Northern Expedition. At the same time, Zhang's military projects resulted in savage taxation and runaway inflation, which impoverished the majority of Zhang's population and led to workers' strikes and peasant rebellions. The Nanjing forces closed in on Zhang in Beijing during the spring of 1928, and the Japanese, seeking to avoid damage to their interests south of Manchuria, persuaded Zhang to withdraw north from Beijing, promising that they would prevent a KMT advance. Just outside Mukden, however, Zhang's train was blown up by associates of the Guandong army. Zhang's assassination pushed his son, Zhang Xueliang, into the arms of the Nanjing government and strengthened Chinese nationalism in the northeast. In 1929 the province was renamed Liaoning and the city Shenyang.

The Shenyang Incident of September 18, 1931, probably engineered by the Japanese-controlled Guandong army, brought further upheaval to the region. The Japanese accused Chinese soldiers of detonating two explosions on the South Manchurian Railway and attacking Japanese railway guards. The Japanese attacked the main Chinese barracks and forcibly occupied the city (again renamed to Fengtian). The Guandong army extended its occupation to areas throughout

Manchuria, a development the Japanese government seemed powerless to prevent. The Nanjing government, while requesting the League of Nations to end the fighting, ordered Zhang Xueliang to withdraw his forces from Manchuria. The occupation was complete by the end of the year, and in March 1932 the puppet state of Manchukuo was established with its seat at Lüshun under the nominal leadership of the former emperor of the Qing, Puyi. When the League of Nations refused to recognize Manchukuo as an independent state, Japan left the organization permanently, and in 1934 Puyi formally acceded as emperor in Changchun, with an administration dominated by Japanese officials and "advisers." Manchuria's major industries now fell mostly under Japanese control, and the infrastructure benefited considerably from extensive Japanese investment and technological advances.

Despite local, communist-led resistance, Fengtian remained under Japanese occupation throughout the war. At Yalta in February 1945, Joseph Stalin demanded, and was promised, all of Russia's former rights in Manchuria as his price for joining the Pacific war. China was not consulted, and despite a Sino-Soviet agreement before the Russian invasion of Manchuria, the Soviet army plundered the region before it departed. The Chinese communist army, with Soviet backing against the KMT, entered and garrisoned Fengtian after the victory over Japan, and it briefly became Shenyang again, under a United Democratic government, which introduced land reform. At the end of the year the government and army both withdrew, allowing KMT troops to reoccupy it in March 1946. The KMT placed Shenyang first under Liaoning province and then in 1947 under direct central control. While the KMT was still being aided by the United States, the communists now had no external help. Nevertheless, by May 1948 the Red Army surrounded Shenyang, which held 200,000 well-trained KMT troops, complete with armor and artillery support. The city fell to Lin Biao's eighth Manchurian offensive in the autumn.

Since then, numerous administrative changes have placed Shenyang variously under city governments, people's governments, and under direct central control. Friendly relations were maintained with the Soviet Union by allowing the retention, until no later than 1952, of privileges granted by the KMT. In 1949 land was redistributed to the peasants, and much of China's industrial investment under the first Five-Year Plan (1953–57) went to rebuilding the Manchurian industrial base. Present-day Shenyang has a strong city administration under the jurisdiction of Liaoning province. It remains a powerhouse of Chinese industry, boasting extensive overseas business contacts. It was a testing ground for the experiments of the mid–1980s in local responsibility for factory productivity and management. It also retains one of the last surviving statues of Mao Zedong, built in 1969 in Red Flag Square.

Further Reading: Information specifically on Shenyang in Western languages is not readily available, and this essay has made considerable use of Chinese materials. However, for the twentieth century, Gavan McCormack's *Chang Tso-lin in Northeastern China, 1911–1928: China, Japan and the Manchurian Idea* (Folkestone: Dawson, and Stanford, California: Stanford University Press, 1977) tells a good deal of the modern story of Shenyang. Further information pertaining to the city may be gleaned from the fifteen-volume *Cambridge History of China,* edited by Denis C. Twitchett and John K. Fairbank (Cambridge and New York: Cambridge University Press, 1978–) and Jonathan Spence's *The Search for Modern China* (New York and London: Norton, 1990).

—Naomi Standen

Shigatse (Tibet, Xizang Autonomous Region, China)

Location: In south-central Tibet, close to the border with Nepal, in the foothills of the Himalayas; approximately 140 miles west of Lhasa.

Description: Shigatse is the site of the second-most-important religious center in Tibet, Tashilhunpo Monastery, founded in 1447. The town around the monastery, with an estimated population of 40,000, is Tibet's second-largest city. The old city now is surrounded by a modern, undistinguished Chinese city almost equal to the old settlement in size.

Contact: Tibet Tourism Bureau
Yuanlin Road
Lhasa 850001
Tibet
China
(891) 63 34330

Shigatse, nestled in the brown hills that rise up sharply behind the town, was once a fortified stronghold as well as the site of a vast, extremely powerful monastery, which once controlled an area called Tsang—the surrounding region of western Tibet to the Nepalese border. At the confluence of two major rivers, the Tsangpo (Brahmaputra) and the Nyanchu (Liancuo), the town lies in a fertile, sixty-mile-long valley stretching from Shigatse to Gyantse, where barley and wheat, staples of the traditionally austere Tibetan diet, long have been cultivated.

Lang Darma (reigned 836–842) was the last Tibetan ruler to hold sway over a united Tibet. When he was murdered in 842, Tibet disintegrated into warring factions. Various clans, tribes, and, later, different Buddhist sects—notably the Black Hats and the Red Hats—vied for power and control over large areas of Tibet, including the region around Shigatse. The importance of the valley for food and the trade with the Nepalese who passed through Shigatse enabled first the ruling family and, later, the monastery to derive tithes and tributes from the local population and taxes on all commerce; the resulting wealth made Shigatse a rival to Lhasa in power and influence.

The Tsang region first was controlled by various noble families who—during the revival of Buddhism after the arrival in 1042 of the Indian Mahayana teacher Atisha in western and central Tibet—supported the establishment of the Red Hat sect and of powerful monasteries, notably those at Shalu and Sakya; the latter at one stage controlled all of Tsang with the assistance of its Mongolian sponsor, who in 1254 granted the monastery the theoretical right to rule all of Tibet. The ruling families ensured that their own relatives became monks and abbots at these monasteries, thus guaranteeing uninterrupted control of the region.

The dominance of Buddhist monks in the secular administration of the country took hold only in the early fifteenth century, under the guidance and inspiration of Tibet's great Buddhist reformer, Tsong-khapa (1357–1419). Tsong-khapa founded a sect, called the Gelugspa or Yellow Hats, based on celibacy, rigorous morality, and a strict interpretation of the teachings of Atisha. He and his disciples founded the three great monasteries around Lhasa: Ganden (1409), Drepung (1416), and Sera (1419); in 1447 his nephew Gedün Truppa founded the fourth great Yellow Hat monastery—Tashilhunpo—in the heart of Red Hat–dominated Tsang. This new monastery comprised four tantric colleges, each with its own abbot. Tashilhunpo's enormous *thanka* wall—nine stories tall and clearly visible from Shigatse—rivaled that of the Potala in Lhasa. On three feast days a year, vast painted banners *(thankas)* depicting a Buddha or other religious motif were unfurled over this wall.

Gedün Truppa served as first abbot of Tashilhunpo and died in that office in 1475. Soon afterward, a young monk named Gedün Gyatso was recognized as the reincarnation of the first abbot, and his successor, Sonam Gyatso, in turn was considered a reincarnation. A notable scholar, Sonam Gyatso was also a zealous missionary intent on promoting the fledgling Yellow Hat sect. In this endeavor he went to the Mongolian court and in 1578 succeeded in converting the Tümed prince Altan Khan and his followers. This act had several important repercussions. First, it introduced a powerful patronage for the Yellow Hat sect, ensuring its supremacy over all Tibet to the exclusion and banishment of all other sects, including the Red Hat sect, which until then had been so powerful in the region around Shigatse that it had defied the establishment of a Yellow Hat monastery in its territory. Second, it was the khan of Mongolia who conferred on Sonam Gyatso the title *Talé* (Dalai), meaning "Ocean." Even though Sonam Gyatso was thereby the first Dalai Lama to be given the title, he was considered the third incarnation of Gedün Truppa; thus both his predecessors were named Dalai Lamas posthumously. It was the first abbot of Tashilhunpo, therefore, who also was acknowledged as the First Dalai Lama.

Although the religious and secular administrations of the kingdom of Tibet had traditionally been intertwined, the figure of the Dalai Lama—at once spiritual leader and secular head of state—presented the most obvious manifestation of this union. It was not until the seventeenth century, under the rule of the great Fifth Dalai Lama (1617–82), that Tibet finally was reunified. The Fifth Dalai Lama initiated a significant change within the Yellow Hat sect. Ruling from Lhasa, with the help of his powerful Mongolian patrons he was able to suppress all rivals to the Yellow Hat sect, establishing this form of Lamaism (Tibetan Buddhism) as the state religion for

View of Shigatse from the ruins of an ancient fort
Photo courtesy of J. Ackerly / International Campaign for Tibet

a reunited Tibet. Furthermore, the Fifth Dalai Lama declared himself, his four predecessors, and all future Dalai Lamas to be reincarnations of Chenrezi, the bodhisattva of compassion and patron saint of Tibet. This elevated the Dalai Lamas to the status of god-kings in the eyes of the Tibetan population.

Recognizing Tashilhunpo's importance as a stronghold for the Yellow Hats in the important Tsang region, the Fifth Dalai Lama appointed his revered and respected tutor as the monastery's abbot, giving him the title of Panchen Lama (*panchen* means "great scholar"), the spiritual right hand to the Dalai Lama for all of Tibet. Once this appointment had been established, claims were made that the Panchen Lama too was a reincarnation, in this case of Amitabha, the Buddha of Infinite Light. Furthermore, this reincarnation was traced back several centuries to include other abbots of Tashilhunpo, retroactively making the new abbot the fourth, not the first, Panchen Lama. As has been the case with the Dalai Lamas and other high-ranking lamas (a lama is a very learned monk), each successor Panchen Lama has been found by searching for the reincarnation of the previous one.

Although the relationship between the Dalai Lama and the Panchen Lama was meant to be purely spiritual, leading some Tibetans to consider the Panchen Lama as even holier than the Dalai Lama owing to the former's freedom from any worldly responsibilities, several Panchen Lamas did get very involved in Tibetan politics. Thus occasional rivalry flared between Lhasa and Shigatse—between the authority of the Dalai Lama and that of the Panchen Lama—that mirrored the ancient power struggles between the warlords and noble families of western Tibet and their counterparts in Lhasa.

The Sixth Panchen Lama (1738–80) was a notable example of a charismatic man who sought contact with the outside world, very much independently of the wishes or plans of the Dalai Lama in Lhasa. In the late eighteenth century, military disturbances along Tibet's Himalayan border began to trouble the Panchen Lama, who tried to intervene when British forces under Warren Hastings repelled the Bhutanese at Cooch Behar in Bengal and penetrated into Bhutan itself. The Panchen Lama's letter aroused the curiosity of Hastings, the governor general of Bengal since 1772, who already had explored—with officers of the British East India Company—the possibility of approaching Tibet as a source of silver and gold; as well, Hastings saw Tibet as a possible alternative route to China, with which Britain already had lively trade relations.

Encouraged by the Panchen Lama's letter about Bhutan, Hastings chose to send the young George Bogle as a British envoy to Shigatse. Bogle's account provides a personal record of early contact between Tibet and the Western world: he was befriended and entertained by the Sixth Panchen Lama for several years before returning to British India with a Tibetan wife. Originally, Bogle was instructed to ascertain the trading possibilities between Tibet and British India, as well as to convey the friendly feelings of the British toward the Tibetans. As a sign of the Panchen Lama's independence in entertaining Bogle, who arrived at Tashilhunpo Monastery in 1775, Bogle never reached Lhasa. Although the Panchen Lama appeared unable to secure an invitation for Bogle at the capital, in fact he had become a more prominent and powerful figure than was the current Dalai Lama. The Seventh Dalai Lama had died when the Panchen Lama was a young man, and the Eighth Dalai Lama was young and undistinguished, lacking any initiative for making contact with the outside world. This left the Sixth Panchen Lama as the effective regent. In addition, the Panchen Lama in Tashilhunpo did not have to endure the intervention of Chinese emissaries, or Ambans, who were posted to Lhasa, although these operatives may have played their part in thwarting any attempts by the Panchen Lama to get Bogle a welcome in the capital itself.

Despite failing to reach Lhasa, Bogle's mission was considered highly successful: he stayed in Shigatse as the Panchen Lama's guest long enough to gain the latter's friendship and respect, as well as that of the Panchen Lama's family. Bogle became fluent in the Tibetan language and very knowledgeable about Tibetan society, eventually marrying the Panchen Lama's sister. A second mission was planned in 1779, during which Bogle was to try to negotiate a direct communication with China via the Ambans in Lhasa. However, the Panchen Lama was about to travel to China, where he then died of smallpox, and a year later Bogle himself died in India. However, the memory of the friendship between the charismatic Sixth Panchen Lama and the young Scotsman lived on in Shigatse among the relatives of the Panchen Lama and the monks of Tashilhunpo, making the area more open to foreign contact than were other parts of Tibet, especially Lhasa.

This openmindedness was betrayed a decade later when the aggressive Hindu Gurkhas stirred up border disputes and in 1788 invaded Tibet, well aware of the riches of Tashilhunpo, which lay within relatively easy reach of an invading army. Before they reached Shigatse, however, the Gurkhas were bought off with the promise of an annual tribute, negotiated by Chinese imperial representatives. This tribute was paid once, after which the Dalai Lama refused further payments, as he had not been consulted in the original tribute agreement. The Gurkhas were quick to retaliate and soon advanced on the rich spoils of Tashilhunpo Monastery. It took the force of a Chinese army to repel them and recapture the loot.

After 1792 and the expulsion of the Gurkha invaders, Tibet closed its doors to foreigners, blocking the steady stream of Western missionaries and traders who had crossed the border into Tibet since the days of Marco Polo. (Jesuits based in Goa on the Indian subcontinent had tried to set up missions in western Tibet as early as the 1620s.) Even subsequent contact with the British had little in common with the friendly relations that had been established by Bogle and the Sixth Panchen Lama in the 1770s.

The fortunes of the Panchen Lamas declined after the heyday of the eminent Sixth Panchen Lama. Rivalries between Tashilhunpo and Lhasa were exacerbated by the Chinese and, to a lesser extent, by the British, who played the two against each other in order to obtain trading privileges. In 1904 a British expeditionary force under Colonel Francis E. Younghusband impelled the authorities in Lhasa to sign a trade agreement with British India. This aggressive behavior took place against the background of an international power struggle among the British, Russian, and Chinese empires, each of which suspected the others' intentions in Tibet, which lay as a buffer between them.

The most severe conflicts between a Panchen Lama and a Dalai Lama arose in the early twentieth century. The Ninth Panchen Lama (1883–1937) harbored constant disagreements with the Thirteenth Dalai Lama (1876–1933) and gave in to the attentions of both the British and the Chinese, who by wooing him sought to undermine the Dalai Lama's authority in Lhasa. Eventually, the Panchen Lama fled the anger of the Dalai Lama and died in exile in China. The Ninth Panchen Lama's successor became even more controversial. The Tenth Panchen Lama (1938–89) was not confirmed as a true reincarnation until he was eleven years old. Even then, some doubt remained in the minds of many Tibetans, especially as his loyalties toward his country seemed uncertain: he was employed by the new Chinese administration of Tibet, working for many years in Beijing. He returned to Tibet regularly, promoting cultural and development programs there, as well as attending the annual prayer festival of *Monlam* in Lhasa.

Tashilhunpo Monastery suffered less damage during the Cultural Revolution than did other sites in Tibet. Since the early 1980s the complex has been under extensive restoration. The monastery is once more a working religious institution with 600 Buddhist monks, and the striking ensemble of reddish-brown buildings with black-and-white trim is again as glorious (Tashilhunpo means "Mound of Glory") as the large monuments in Lhasa. Among Tashilhunpo's treasures are an eighty-six-foot-tall statue of the Maitreya Buddha that contains 614 pounds of gold and 330,000 pounds of copper and brass, housed in the Maitreya Hall built in 1914 by the Ninth Panchen Lama; a single finger of the Buddha is almost four feet long. Inside the Panchen Lama's palace is the stupa, or tomb, of the Fourth Panchen Lama; covered in silver and gold and studded with precious jewels, the tomb rivals those of the Dalai Lamas in the Potala Palace in Lhasa. The monastery's great courtyard features 1,000 representations of the Sakyamuni Buddha along its walls, as well as a garden for debates where young novices hone their rhetorical skills

Tashilhunpo Monastery, Shigatse
Photo courtesy of Consulate General of China, Chicago

as they complete their education in Buddhist philosophy and religion.

At Tashilhunpo, while on a visit to Shigatse in 1989, the Tenth Panchen Lama died of a heart attack; he was buried at the monastery. No reincarnation has yet been found for him.

Further Reading: Hugh Edward Richardson's *A Short History of Tibet* (New York: Dutton, 1962; revised as *Tibet and Its History,* Boston: Shambhala, 1984) gives an excellent introduction to Tibetan history from its beginnings until the Chinese invasion and subsequent Tibetan uprising in 1959. David Snellgrove and Hugh Richardson's *Cultural History of Tibet* (New York: Praeger, and London: Weidenfeld and Nicholson, 1968; revised edition, Boulder, Colorado: Prajna, and London: Routledge, 1980) is another standard work on Tibet's cultural evolution. John Snelling has written a comprehensive introduction to Buddhism entitled *The Buddhist Handbook: A Complete Guide to Buddhist Schools, Teaching, Practice, and History* (London: Century, 1987; Rochester, Vermont: Inner Traditions, 1991). Tibet has fascinated travelers for centuries, and some of the most evocative books on the country have been written by such visitors. These include Alexandra David-Neel, a nineteenth-century Parisian, who wrote *My Journey to Lhasa* (London: Heinemann, and New York: Harper, 1927) and *Magic and Mystery in Tibet* (London: Lane, 1931; New York: Kendall, 1932); Heinrich Harrer, a German soldier in World War II, wrote *Seven Years in Tibet* (London: Hart-Davis, 1953; New York: Dutton, 1954); and Giuseppe Tucci contributed *To Lhasa and Beyond* (Oxford: Oxford University Press, 1956). For the more recent history of Tibet, the autobiography of the fourteenth Dalai Lama (Bstan-dzin-rgya-mtsho), *Freedom in Exile* (New York: Harper Collins, and London: Hodder and Stoughton, 1990), gives fascinating insight into the dramatic impact of the twentieth century on the Tibetan people. *Tibet: The Facts*, a report compiled by the nonpolitical Scientific Buddhist Association in London for the United Nations Subcommission on Human Rights in 1984 (second revised edition, Dharmsala, India: Tibetan Young Buddhist Association, 1990), is essential, though horrifying, reading for anyone interested in the fate of Tibet today.

—Hilary Collier Sy-Quia

Sīgiriya (Sri Lanka)

Location: Near the center of Sri Lanka, about forty miles south-southwest of Trincomalee.

Description: The ruins of a city constructed under the direction of King Kāśyapa I in the late fifth century A.D. It is most famous for the palace he built on the summit of a sheer-faced rock approximately 600 feet tall.

Contact: Ceylon Tourist Board
78 Steuart Place
P. O. Box 1504
Colombo 3
Sri Lanka
(43) 7059 or (43) 7060

Sīgiriya is an ancient, abandoned city near the lush, mountainous heart of Sri Lanka. The town was built in a wide, flat valley, but at its center rises a peculiar formation of red gneiss rock approximately 600 feet tall. This rock tower is shaped like a squat mushroom set upon the verdant plain, and is exceptionally beautiful. In the fifth century A.D., when King Kāśyapa I built his royal city there, large portions of the western face of the rock were covered with lime plaster upon which murals were painted. Most of the images have since faded, but the western face remains unnaturally shiny and is known today as the "mirror wall." Visitors say that the cliff glows magnificently in the evening sun, an effect complemented by swirling black streaks of minerals washed down from the summit by Sri Lanka's tropical rains.

Beginning in the second or third century B.C., Buddhist monks occupied the caves at the foot of the rock, very soon after Buddhism was introduced to the island in the middle or late third century B.C. by Mahendra, a missionary generally believed to have been the son of the Mauryan emperor Aśoka. The monks decorated and inscribed at least twenty caves, but archaeologists have not yet sufficiently analyzed these works or the other few artifacts left by these earliest residents to confidently date or understand their activities. It appears they were religious recluses who shunned life in the more active and lucrative settlements to the north, most notably Anuradhapura, the prosperous Sinhalese capital, which lay approximately thirty miles northwest.

The best evidence to date suggests that the caves at Sīgiriya were abandoned between the first and fifth centuries A.D., following the period of early monastic settlement. Scant fragments of pottery and masonry have been found that may derive from this period, but they have not yet been properly dated. When King Kāśyapa gained the throne in Sri Lanka in A.D. 477, he began the construction of his magnificent and unique city at Sīgiriya, a project that occupied his builders for eighteen years.

The gruesome history of Kāśyapa's rise to power and of his subsequent interest in Sīgiriya was recorded by his great-uncle, Mahanamo. Kāśyapa's father, Datu Sen, was the Sinhalese heir to the Sri Lankan throne during a period in which the Tamils had seized control of the kingdom. In 459, Datu Sen succeeded in expelling the interlopers from his territory and thus also revived the Sinhalese order. Datu Sen then embarked upon a period of rebuilding to reverse the damages done by the Tamil occupiers. He is reported to have spent much of his royal treasure to construct hospitals, reservoirs (the Sri Lankan economy at that time was centered on the irrigation of arid lands), and monasteries, and to repair statues and religious edifices. In the *Mahavamsa,* a record of Sri Lankan history kept by Buddhist monks, one reads of Datu Sen: "Who can describe in detail all the good deeds that he has done?"

Datu Sen had a taste for revenge, however, which led to his undoing. His only daughter was reportedly flogged by her husband, the commander of the royal army. Datu Sen was so outraged by this abuse that he had the commander's mother stripped and cruelly executed as revenge. The son-in-law then turned against his king and managed to gain the aid of Kāśyapa, then a young prince. Datu Sen was soon imprisoned, and Kāśyapa acquired the kingship. The commander then convinced the young king that Datu Sen kept a hidden treasure intended for Kāśyapa's brother, Moggallana, who had fled to India. The claim was false, but Kāśyapa believed it and demanded that his father lead him to the riches. Datu Sen supposedly recognized the plot against him, and resigned himself to death. He led his captors to the artificial lake known as Kalawewa, the creation of which he himself had funded, and there he happily took his last bath. After this, he is reported to have pointed to the waters and to his friend Mahanoma, the recorder of this tale, and to have said, "These are all the treasures that I possess," whereupon he was returned to jail. Kāśyapa was so angered that he had his father stripped and the door to his cell permanently bricked-up.

Fearing that his terrible deeds would draw the wrath of his exiled brother and the disloyalty of his own people, Kāśyapa left Anuradhapura and built a fortified palace atop the rock at Sīgiriya. Its sheer sides could not be climbed, but Kāśyapa had a staircase carved into it that spirals from the base to the summit. He surrounded the city beneath the butte with a pair of exceptionally sturdy ramparts, within which he built gardens, ponds, a monastery, and other constructions, many of which have not yet been excavated. During his reign, Kāśyapa is said to have regretted his crimes and sought to atone for them by building monasteries and granting lands to Buddhist clerics throughout Sri Lanka.

Kāśyapa's brother, Moggallana, did indeed return from India with an army in 495, whereupon he exacted his

Sīgiriya
Photo courtesy of Mr. Herath Navaratne, Information Officer, Embassy of Sri Lanka, Washington, D.C.

revenge. Kāśyapa supposedly was advancing upon the site where the rival armies were locked in battle when he came upon a marsh too deep for his elephant to pass. He turned back in order to find another route, but his soldiers mistook his action for withdrawal. They then retreated themselves, and Kāśyapa was left defenseless. Rather than be killed, he committed suicide on the battlefield.

After only eighteen years of rule, Kāśyapa's architectural achievements at Sīgiriya were astounding. Tons of brick and timber were carried up the cliff on the precarious stairs and used to construct his fortified palace. The summit has an area of approximately three acres, and the fortress more than covered its entirety. The base of the palace walls was built at a point some distance down the sloping top of the butte. Thus, the palace walls appeared to be a continuation of the rock itself, and denied invaders any station from which to mount an attack. There are several layers of building upon the summit, and flights of stairs leading between various levels have been excavated. In the southeastern section lay a pond partly tiled with limestone, and there were several cisterns; keeping the palace supplied with water was a formidable task. The functions of most of the summit buildings, however, have not been determined.

On the northern face of the rock was a modest plateau, roughly seventy-two by thirty-six yards, bordered by a stone-and-brick wall. Upon it Kāśyapa's sculptors erected an enormous lion made of brick and stucco. Zigzagging stairs leading from the plateau to the summit passed through the lion's mouth, which probably served as an imposing main entrance to the palace. It is for this threatening sculpture that Sīgiriya, the lion rock, is named.

At ground level, an outer rampart approximately 600 yards in front of the rock's western face housed the main entrance to the royal city. Today, there is a museum where the main gate once opened. Kāśyapa appears to have expected trouble, for within this outer rampart lay two moats and an inner rampart. The inner rampart continued around all sides of the lion rock and enclosed an area of approximately 300 by 500 yards on the eastern side, as well as a still larger area to the west. A gap between the eastern and western ramparts on the southern side of the rock marks the northern extreme of a reservoir that is nearly two miles long. Smaller gaps on both the northern and southern sides were probably lesser entrances to the Sīgiriya complex. The eastern area has not yet been excavated, but the layout of the western enclosure is fairly well documented.

The western enclosure appears to have been an extensive park occupying approximately 100 square acres. Guardhouses made with brick walls seven feet deep stood on either side of the causeway leading into the complex through the main gate. The causeway, lined by brick walls on either side, continued straight toward the rock, passing first through a walled-in garden evenly divided into four sections, and then between a pair of moated miniature islands. Two additional islands bordered the north and south ramparts, respectively. The path passed between an octagonal pond and a rock garden before finally entering the terraced land ascending to the foot of the rock. Throughout this area, naturally situated boulders have been gracefully integrated with the manicured landscape.

The terraced area at the western foot of the lion rock is mottled with boulders and caves, several of which have been cleverly modified with brick so as to create secret chambers. Some of the chambers provide access to a number of ponds that may have been used for royal baths. Boulders in this area are scarred with carvings that indicate buildings were once in place here, but the style and purpose of such constructions is unknown. Still, archaeologists have taken to calling this section of Sīgiriya the "inner city." In one of the caves a Buddhist *vihara* (shrine) still houses the remains of a sculpture of Buddha. Still other Buddha figures found in this area clearly date from the time of ancient occupation. Along the seam of a massive boulder split down the middle, there was carved a throne and two benches. The setting may have served as Sri Lanka's first council hall.

The terraces climb partly up the western side of the rock, which above this point is sheer. This is where the spiral staircase to the summit begins; in the galleries above the stairs plaster was applied to the rock face and painted upon, creating the mirror wall. Murals survive only in one sheltered pocket of the wall; they were first conserved in 1897 by Muhandiram Perera. The paintings are similar to those at Ajanta, except that they depict only women, drawn from the waist up. At first sight the women appear to be naked, but they actually wear diaphanous veils and are decorated with jewels, ribbons, flowers, and tiaras. The principal figures, ladies of Kāśyapa's court, have flesh tones of orange and yellow, while their servants are painted in a darker greenish-blue. The ladies are shown carrying offerings of flowers to Piduragala, a *vihara* north of Sīgiriya.

The mirror wall also is decorated with graffiti, concerning various subjects and providing some historical record of events in Sri Lanka, from the time of the galleries' construction through the thirteenth century. Half of the graffiti was drafted by Sri Lanka's elite, who have indicated their rank in their work. The remainder is anonymous and may be assumed to have been painted by citizens of no special standing, for the literacy rate in Sri Lanka has been high since the time of Kāśyapa's rule.

The history of Sīgiriya after the time of Kāśyapa remains to be revealed by modern analysis. Archaeological research conducted in the 1980s indicates that there was some monastic life at the site in the sixth and seventh centuries accompanied by modest construction, but apparently the city was largely disused. The monks appear to have left by the eighth century, and between their departure and the thirteenth century there was some further building in brick and gneiss. However, the city seems to have been mostly abandoned during this period and then fully abandoned until the seventeenth century, when Sīgiriya became an outpost of the Kandyan Kingdom. From this time until the area's conquest by the British in 1815, it remained the only Sinhalese domain in Sri Lanka not under colonial control. The first substantial archaeological work at Sīgiriya was conducted in the late nineteenth century, and a second phase has continued from the 1950s through the present day.

Further Reading: *Sīgiriya* by W. B. Marcus Fernando (Colombo: Archaeological Department, 1967), although difficult to obtain, is an excellent, detailed booklet on the remains at Sīgiriya. Two books from the early twentieth century contain excellent firsthand descriptions of Sīgiriya from that time, as well as detailed histories of Kāśyapa's rise to power and his building projects: *The Lost Cities of Ceylon* by G. E. Mitton (London: Murray, 1916; New York: Stokes, 1917) and *The Ruined Cities of Ceylon* by Henry W. Cave (London: Low Marston, 1897; fourth edition, London: Hutchinson, 1907).

—Christopher A. Hoyt

Singapore

Location: The Republic of Singapore is an island that lies about seventy-five miles north of the equator, at a narrow point of the Strait of Melaka (Malacca), at the tip of the Malay Peninsula. It includes one main island and several offshore islets.

Description: The island nation of Singapore has served historically as a trade entrepôt. It became a British settlement in 1819 and grew steadily after that date. Since World War II, Singapore has undergone rapid industrialization, becoming one of the most important centers of industrial manufacturing, financial services, technology, and tourism in Southeast Asia.

Site Office: Singapore Tourist Promotion Board
Raffles City Tower 36-04
250 North Bridge Road
Singapore 0617
(65) 339 6622

Among the so-called Newly Industrialized Economies of Southeast Asia, known colorfully as the Little Dragons, Singapore stands out as the most striking success story. Once merely a quaint colonial outpost, Singapore has developed into one of the busiest ports in the world, with the highest per capita income in Asia after Japan. Economic figures detailing Singapore's success go on and on, in many instances equaling the economies of the West. This success derives from two primary sources: Singapore's central position in the Southeast Asian market, and the energies of the diverse peoples drawn to it by its free market opportunities.

The interest of Singaporeans in their island's historical legacy is negligible. To put it simply, the Singaporean historical memory extends only a short way into the island's past. The date most often given for the birth of Singapore is 1819, when Stamford Raffles first stepped ashore and established a British East India Company settlement there. In a part of the world where histories tend to be ancient and rich, where modern cultures enthusiastically celebrate their ancient cultural heritage, Singapore is an anomaly. Nevertheless, the island does have an interesting precolonial history worth accounting.

Located near the midway point in the sea route between China and India, the Malay Archipelago and the Strait of Melaka served as an entrepôt and rendezvous point for traders from the kingdoms and empires of the Asian mainland and the Indian subcontinent since at least the first centuries A.D. The centrality of the Strait of Melaka in the ancient sea routes eventually led to the rise of powerful maritime empires in the region, beginning with Srivijaya, which was based in Palembang on Sumatra.

According to an account written in the seventh century A.D. by the Chinese traveler-pilgrim I-Ching, the island of Singapore, known then as Temasek, was a possession of the Srivijaya Empire. (The name Temasek means "Sea Town" in Malay.) Srivijaya's strength and durability depended primarily upon its ability to control and profit from traffic in the Strait of Melaka. The empire effected its control by providing easily accessible ports along the strait and by suppressing piracy. Employing a powerful fleet, Srivijaya compelled all ships to visit its ports and pay taxes and duties. Sitting at the mouth of the Strait of Melaka, Temasek functioned as a strategic outpost in Srivijaya's control of the Sino-Indian trade route.

By the thirteenth century, Srivijaya's might declined and two new empires vied for control of the region and its flourishing trade economy. The Thai Ayutthaya Empire, which had holdings in Malaya further north along the strait, emerged as the dominant power in mainland Southeast Asia in the thirteenth and fourteenth centuries. The Majapahit Empire, based on Java, emerged as the major power in insular Southeast Asia. Both empires cast a desirous eye on strategic Singapore. A seventeenth-century Malay chronicle, the *Sejarah Melanyu (Malay Annals),* states that in the fourteenth century the island of "Singapura" suffered raids by the Javanese from the south and the Thai from the north; both at various times claimed the island as a vassal state. The same chronicle also recounts a legend that explains the origin of the name Singapura: a great trading city was founded on the island in 1299 by a ruler from Palembang, Sri Tri Buana, who named the city Singapura (Lion City) after he sighted a strange beast there, which he decided could only be a lion. As the chronicle points out, whoever gained control over the Strait of Melaka and the Sino-Indian trade would acquire the means to dominate all of Southeast Asia. Ayutthaya and Majapahit fought over Singapura and other sites in the strait for precisely this reason.

Both the chronicle and several Portuguese accounts note the arrival in 1388 of King Paramesvara to the Malay Peninsula. He had left Palembang following a disagreement with Majapahit authorities. Paramesvara initially took control of southern Malaya, including Singapore. However, Majapahit forces drove him further north, and he settled at Melaka, which he turned into a major port and the seat of the powerful new kingdom of Melaka. In 1414, he converted to Islam and established the Melaka sultanate. The Hindu Majapahit Empire, meanwhile, was withering away. Its decline has been connected with the rising influence of Islam in the region. When the Islamic state of Melaka emerged on the Malay Peninsula, many rulers of small kingdoms dependent on trade cut their ties with Majapahit and converted to Islam in the hopes of promoting their trading prospects. The Melaka sul-

Chinese temple in Singapore
Photo courtesy of Aaron D. Cushman and Associates, New York

tanate came to control most of the Malay Peninsula, eastern Sumatra, and Singapore.

A Chinese traveler, Wang Ta Yuan, described the island in the early fifteenth century, providing the earliest surviving first-hand account. He called the island Long Ya Men (Dragon Teeth Gate), a possible reference to the treacherous western entrance of Keppel Harbor. Although some trading did take place on the island, most of the inhabitants lived by piracy. Singapore apparently afforded shelter to several hundred pirate ships. However, a small settlement of Malay and Chinese traders was situated on the terraced hill now known as Bukit Larangam.

The Portuguese attacked the Melaka sultanate in 1511, taking the city, in the attempt to take control of the strait. The reigning sultan fled south to the tip of the Malay Peninsula, eventually establishing the Johore sultanate, which controlled Singapore. Being incorporated into Johore does not seem to have resulted in an increase in trade on the island. In fact, after the Portuguese attacked it in 1613, Singapore's legitimate trade diminished further. The Portuguese destruction of Singapore and Dutch control over the trade routes for the next few centuries effectively undercut any role that Singapore could play in political or economic developments in Southeast Asia. As opportunities for piracy declined, the community dwindled. By the early nineteenth century, it had perhaps only 1,000 inhabitants.

At this time, the emergent industry in pepper and gambier (a natural astringent used in tanning and dying) gave Singapore's fortunes a modest boost. Both crops came to be cultivated on Singapore, and Chinese laborers, often indentured servants, were brought from mainland China to work the fields. Even though these industries helped repopulate the island, the emergence of Singapore as a major force in Southeast Asia was due to the British.

In the late eighteenth and early nineteenth century, the British began to focus their efforts to break Dutch control in the region on the Strait of Melaka. They could not allow Dutch holdings in Southeast Asia to break contact between their Indian empire and Guangzhou (Canton), where they drove a profitable trade in tea and opium. From his remote base at Bengkulu, on Sumatra's west coast, the only remaining British settlement in the Indonesian archipelago, Sir Stamford Raffles sought to edge out the Dutch. In 1818, he persuaded the governor general in Bengal that British security in the strait was threatened by Dutch interests on Sumatra. He received permission in 1819 to acquire a settlement on Sin-

Sultan Mosque, Singapore
Photo courtesy of Aaron D. Cushman and Associates, New York

gapore, which was retained despite Dutch protest. The Anglo-Dutch treaty of 1824 led to the withdrawal of the British from Sumatra and the Dutch from the Malay Peninsula. The division revived the importance of Singapore, establishing it, along with Penang, as the major British East India Company outpost in Southeast Asia.

Raffles envisioned Singapore as "a great commercial emporium and a fulcrum, whence we may extend our influence." In fact, as the treaty indicated, the British did not intend to contest Dutch political dominion in the Indonesian Archipelago. Instead the positional advantages of Singapore were to be turned to commercial account. Raffles made the Singapore settlements into a free-trade zone, exempt from taxes and duties. As a result, it attracted Malayan, Chinese, Indian, and Indonesian traders, all of whom already had been participating in the region's commerce. The island became a stop for traders from India and China and an entrepôt for Southeast Asian trade in general. In addition, along with Penang, Singapore was transformed into a hub of British East India Company affairs in the region. Related construction activities for administrative buildings and housing for British officials created an influx of workers. Although the traders arrived voluntarily, the British East India Company imported Indian convicts and indentured servants from mainland China to build Singapore's public works.

Visitors marveled at the growth of Singapore's trade and the diversity of its traders. Not long after the British settlement came into being, Singapore became the base of numerous merchant houses from all over the world. In 1846, there were six Jewish, five Chinese, five Arab, and two Armenian trading companies, as well as one American and one Indian company and numerous European houses. The British relied on the Chinese as middlemen between European and Asian merchants, a role they had traditionally played.

Many of the Chinese came from other ports in the area, but increasingly they also came from the mainland. The Malay community also grew, as large numbers of Malays came from the peninsula and the trade cities looking for economic opportunity. Owing to Chinese dominance in the trading business, however, the Malays worked mostly as fishermen, woodcutters, and boatmen, playing a role no less important to the developing city. Until about 1860, the Malays were the second largest group in Singapore, behind the Chinese. Indians, many of them traders and laborers from India and the British settlement in Bengkulu, eventually overtook the Malay population. Most of the immigrants in the early period came to make a quick fortune and return to their home communities. But their intentions to leave most often went unrealized. In the beginning, the communities were composed mostly of men. In 1860, Chinese men outnumbered women fifteen to one, for example.

In relative terms, Singapore remained a small town with 52,000 inhabitants in 1845. It had an enclave for the temenggong, the indigenous governor, at Telok Blangah and another for the sultan of Johore at Kampong Gelam—both east of the Singapore River that bisects the city center. Government buildings were concentrated to the east of the river, Chinatown to the west. A mudflat became Commercial Square (later Raffles Place), the commercial heart of the city. Like colonial cities in India and Australia, Singapore was a beneficiary of the architectural efflorescence of the early nineteenth century that produced a kind of tropical Palladian style in many parts of the British Empire. Some examples of this classically inspired architecture still survive among Singapore's modern high-rises.

In 1867 Singapore broke its connection with the East India Company and became part of the new Crown Colony of the Straits Settlements. The following decade brought a host of changes. In general, the 1870s saw a shift toward a new economic relationship between Europe and Asia. Increasingly, Europe became a manufacturer, while Asia became a supplier of raw materials. As a consequence, intra-Asian trade diminished in significance. Singapore acquired new responsibilities as the British colonial government made treaties with Perak and Selangor that placed these Malay states under British control. As the peninsula was thus opened, new trading opportunities arose. By the 1870s, Singapore was the major entrepôt for rubber, tin, and gambier, and in the early years of the new century it became a distributor, and later a refiner, of oil from the Malay Peninsula and the Indonesian Archipelago.

Late in the nineteenth century, the American naturalist W. T. Hornaday called Singapore "the handiest city I ever saw. . . . It is like a big desk, full of drawers and pigeon-holes, where everything has its place, and can always be found in it." A contemporary British visitor added that it was "a perfect paradise, full of shady avenues of flowering trees." By the turn of the century, the city was no longer content with such praise and began to pursue a grander style to match its growing commercial importance. The luxurious Raffles Hotel was opened by the Sarkies brothers in 1886. (A major renovation in recent years has recreated the elegant building.) The Raffles Museum and Library was built in 1887. The Town Hall was renovated and reopened as the Victoria Memorial Hall in 1905. Chinatown became the focus of the Improvement Trust, created in 1920. The Post Office (1928) and City Hall (1929) helped create "the image of a showcase city," in the words of James Warren.

Singapore's commercial boom necessitated improvements in infrastructure and in financial and communications services. In the early twentieth century, the banking industry of Singapore began to prosper. Initially the industry was owned predominantly by the British, but many other communities also entered the business, including the Chinese, Americans, Australians, and French. The telegraph modernized Singapore's international communications. The port facilities were greatly improved with the building of dry docks, the installation of machinery for loading and unloading, and the replacements of ox carts by trucks and trains. By 1909, it was possible to travel from Singapore to Penang by train and railroad ferry. The Johore Causeway linked road and trail transportation between Singapore and the peninsula in 1923.

After World War I, Singapore was chosen as the site of the British eastern naval base, to be used only when the navy was to be deployed in the east in response to a local crisis. It was built, slowly and reluctantly, at Sewabang on the northern shore of Singapore Island. During World War II, British forces at the base were significantly understrength, and Singapore surrendered to the Japanese on February 15, 1942. The Japanese occupied the city until 1945, renaming it Shohan (Light of the South). They interned all Europeans and Australians at Changi, at the eastern end of the island, and they executed many of the Indian soldiers that had been stationed in Singapore. Around 20,000 Indian troops joined the Japanese Army under pressure, while yet others joined because the Indian leader Subhas Chandra Bose had allied himself with Japan with the aim of achieving independence for India. Singapore's Chinese population bore the brunt of the occupation. Some were imprisoned, but according to some estimates as many 25,000 were executed. The Japanese also appropriated the capital of Singapore merchants. The economy crumbled as the port lay idle. Blockades led to shortages of food and essential materials. Physically, the city suffered little damage, but the attitudes of rulers and ruled underwent a significant change.

The British emerged from the war determined to put their empire on a new footing. The Malay states, Penang and Melaka, were to be formed into a Malayan Union, which, it was thought, would be better able to provide for the economic, social, and political development of its people. Singapore, however, was to remain a crown colony and a base for the power that the British still wished to deploy east of Suez. It became a garrison town as well as a commercial and political center. Singapore was too small to survive as an independent state, it was thought—both by the British and by the People's Action Party (PAP). PAP, under the leadership of Lee Kuan Yew, hoped for independence through a merger with Malaya, which would create an economic base sufficient for the development of socialism.

In 1958, Britain granted Singapore internal self-government, while maintaining control over the island's defense and foreign affairs. In the first general elections of 1959, Lee Kuan Yew was elected prime minister. In 1963, the British finally gave up the colony, allowing Singapore to join the newly independent Federation of Malaysia. However, the merger with Malaysia was short-lived. Malaysia was suspicious of Singapore's rich Chinese majority and accused Lee

Kuan Yew of siding with the communist Indonesians in the struggle over Sabah and Sarawak on Borneo. The Singaporeans, for their part, feared that the government of Kuala Lumpur would pursue Malay interests at the expense of the island's diverse population and would try to diminish the influence of PAP. These conflicts led to civil unrest in 1963 and 1964, when Malays and Chinese in Singapore fought in the streets. Finally, after two years of political infighting, the Malaysian Federation voted to allow Singapore to become an independent state.

Lee Kuan Yew now turned his attention to building an independent nation, seeking to take advantage of the island's ideal geographic location. Although devoid of natural resources, Singapore has managed over the past twenty-five years to become a major Southeast Asian industrial, commercial, and financial power. The city-state turned its attention to the technology market and has jumped to the forefront of this cutting-edge field. However, Singapore's exceptional cleanliness, efficiency, wealth, and safety did not come without costs. Reclamation, a feature since the 1820s, proceeded on an unprecedented scale in the new industrial center of Jurong in the 1960s and between Collyer Quay and Changi in the 1970s and 1980s. As the skyline changed, so did the inhabitants' way of life. In thirty years, 87 percent of the population has been relocated, as the skyscrapers of the central city and the housing blocks of the suburbs almost obliterated Chinatown and literally overshadowed the old European bungalows. Some of colonial Singapore remains, but not much. The drive to make Singapore a city-state of global importance has wiped out all but traces of the island's past. The derisive nickname "Singapore, Inc.," reflects the state's priorities fairly well. Some observers conclude that Lee's government has created a clinically clean, puritanical, patriarchal, and controlled Orwellian society, where spiritual and cultural values fall far behind the prerogatives of wealth. Many Singaporeans argue, however, that the benefits far outweigh the costs. Boasting the highest living standard in Asia behind Japan, a life expectancy over 70, and a virtual absence of slums, beggars, homeless, and unemployed, Singapore has achieved and surpassed the standards of many first-world economies. On the whole, most Singaporeans prefer this to a more traditional or permissive but impoverished society.

Further Reading: C. M. Turnbull's *A History of Singapore 1819–1975* (Kuala Lumpur, Oxford, and New York: Oxford University Press, 1977; second edition, with subtitle *1819–1988,* 1989) offers a highly readable account of Singapore's history beginning with the colonial period. *A History of Singapore,* edited by Ernest Chew and Edwin Lee (Singapore, Oxford, and New York: Oxford University Press, 1991), consists of essays by various writers. J. W. Warren's *Rickshaw Coolie: A People's History of Singapore 1880–1940* (Singapore and New York: Oxford University Press, 1986) is part of a trilogy on the "underside" of the city's history. *Singapore* by Sally Backhouse (Newton Abbot: David and Charles, 1972) is a good general guide. Norman Edwards's *The Singapore House and Residential Life 1819–1939* (Singapore, Oxford, and New York: Oxford University Press, 1990) and T. H. H. Hancock's *Coleman's Singapore* (Kuala Lumpur: MBRAS/Pelanduk, 1986) both examine the city's architectural past. *Singapore and Singaporeans,* edited by Nicholas Tarling (Auckland: University of Auckland Press, 1992), includes excerpts from the writings of nineteenth- and twentieth-century visitors. An excellent look at modern Singapore is provided in *Singapore: The Legacy of Lee Kuan Yew* by R. S. Milne (Boulder, Colorado: Westview, 1990).

—Nicholas Tarling and Shome Chowdhury

Somnāth (Gujarāt, India)

Location: Somnāth sits on the shores of the Arabian Sea on the southern tip of the Kāthiāwār Peninsula in the western Indian state of Gujarāt. Located in the Junāgadh district, Somnāth is only about fifty miles from the district capital, Junāgadh.

Description: Sacred to both Vaisnavite and Saivite worshipers, Somnāth (known also as Prabhās, Prabhās-Pātan, and Somanātha) has become one of the major religious cities of western India. Destroyed numerous times by Muslim invaders in the medieval era, the town, which houses Krishna temples and the Temple of Somanātha, has nevertheless survived. The town's resiliency, as much as anything else, has attracted the praise and devotion of Hindu Indians.

Contact: Government of India Tourist Office
123 Maharishi Karve Road
Bombay 400 200, Mahārāshtra
India
(20) 32932, (20) 33144, (20) 33145, or (20) 36054

As a pilgrimage site (*tīrtha*) of both historical and contemporary significance, Somnāth ranks among the most sacred in all of India. It serves simultaneously as a sacred site for the two main religious followings of Hinduism—worshipers of Krishna (an avatar of Vishnu) and of Siva—and its fortunes have been linked inextricably with the state of religious worship in the area. When the religious life of Somnāth declined as a result of external political forces, the vibrancy of the town itself declined; when political circumstances allowed for the open worship of the Hindu gods, the town flourished.

The religious significance of Somnāth to worshipers of Krishna stems from the *Mahābhārata,* one of the two major Sanskrit epics (the other being the *Rāmāyaṇa*). The diverse didactic and legendary materials of the *Mahābhārata* surround a central narrative of the dynastic struggle between two related families, the Kauravas and Pāṇḍavas, and of the divine intervention by Krishna. Krishna belonged to the Yādava clan, which hailed from Mathurā (north of modern Delhi). Exiled at an early age by the wicked King Kaṃsa, he returned in his teenage years to slay the tyrant. Assuming the leadership of the clan, Krishna led the Yādavas to the western coast of the Kāthiāwār Peninsula and established the clan at Dvāraka in the Prabhās region, where Somnāth later developed. In the meantime, the struggle between the Kauravas and Pāṇḍavas had escalated to the point of war. The Pāṇḍavas had spent a sentence of exile in Prabhās performing austerities with Krishna. Given a choice between having the military support of Krishna's vast army or merely having Krishna as a charioteer, the Pāṇḍavas chose Krishna. The Pāṇḍavas, although bound to noncombatancy, were inspired by Krishna's divine promptings. The eighteen-day battle between these clans represented a universal battle between divine and demonic forces, with the Pāṇḍavas being incarnations of the divine. Krishna and the Pāṇḍavas annihilated the vast Kaurava clan and army. Having achieved his purpose, Krishna returned to Dvāraka as a true avatar. Not long after his return, a battle between Yādava chiefs led to the death of Krishna's brother and son as well as most of the Yādava clan. Lamenting his loss in the nearby forest, Krishna was killed by a hunter who mistook him for a deer. The hunter shot Krishna in the heel, his one mortal spot.

Thus, Somnāth became a holy place of Hinduism not only because it served as the home of Krishna and the entire Yādava clan, but more importantly because it marked the spot where Krishna died. Temples and monuments were erected on the spots where Krishna meditated (Dehotsarga), where he died (Bhalka Tīrth), and where he was cremated (Trivenī Ghāt). The dates of the *Mahābhārata*'s composition range from between 400 B.C. and A.D. 400, and most scholars agree that it must have been composed over a period of time by several different authors. The time period of the events related in the *Mahābhārata* ranges between 1500 and 1000 B.C. With such indefinite datings, the beginnings of Krishna worship in Somnāth cannot be accurately determined.

The origins of Saivism in Somnāth can be found in another religious text. A portion of the Skanda Purāṇa relates the origins of Siva worship at the temple of Somanātha. According to this narrative, King Daksha Prajapati had twenty-seven daughters whom he gave in marriage to the moon god, Soma (Chandra). Soma, although obligated to all his wives, fell in love with one in particular, Rohinī. Because of her exquisite beauty, Soma paid Rohinī exclusive attention at the expense of the twenty-six other women, who complained to Daksha about their inattentive husband. Daksha warned him, but Soma seemed oblivious. Consequently, Daksha cursed him, saying "thou shalt wane." Because of this curse, Soma began to shrink, and as a result the vegetation stopped growing. The gods became concerned and asked Daksha to rescind his curse. Daksha agreed on the condition that Soma act equally among his wives and that he take a bath in the sea at Prabhasa. Soma did this and regained his strength. To show his gratitude, Soma erected a golden temple of Siva and named it Somanātha (Lord of Soma). The Skanda Purāṇa also describes the Siva *liṅgam* (phallic symbol) of Somanātha, which further indicates that the temple of Somanātha existed in the pre-Purāṇic period. As with the *Mahābhārata*, however, the dating of the Purāṇas has remained largely undetermined. The Skanda Purāṇa is grouped with a later set of Purāṇas dating perhaps as late as the eighth

Somanātha Temple
Line drawing by Tom Willcockson

century A.D. The Purāṇic reference states that the temple of Somanātha was established in the sixth century B.C., but no concrete archaeological evidence exists to verify this date. Rather, archaeological excavations done in 1950 found that the first temple, made of brick, was constructed around the first century A.D.

Archaeological excavations also have revealed that Somnāth was part of the Harrapan civilization (c. 2500 B.C.–1700 B.C.), one of the oldest in the world; Somnāth, known then as Minoor, was its westernmost town. Somnāth does not reappear centrally in the historical record until the eleventh century A.D., when it fell to the Islamic Afghan invader Maḥmūd of Ghaznī. In the intervening years, the Kāthiāwār Peninsula fell within the realm of many rulers, none of whom can be definitively established in Somnāth. Among the most notable of these rulers were the Mauryans, the Indo-Greeks led by Menander, the Sakas of Central Asia, the Guptas, the Maitrakas, and the Cāḷukyas.

Local tradition claims that descendants of the Cāḷukyas came from the Somnāth region. Mūlarāja Solankī (reigned A.D. 979–996), of the Cāḷukyas, seems to have been a great patron of the cult of Somanātha. In fact, it has been postulated that Mūlarāja Solankī built the grand temple of Somanātha at the spot where an ancient temple had existed. The tremendous wealth of the Somanātha Temple, which later became booty for Muslim invaders, was provided in great part by the Solankī Dynasty. It was also during the Solankī period that the temple of Somanātha assumed a more than local reputation and following. Epigraphic evidence shows that several major rulers during this period undertook pilgrimages to the site and made endowments to the temple. The great-grandson of Mūlarāja, Bhīmadeva I, came to rule in Gujarāt in 1022, four years before Maḥmūd of Ghaznī's invasion.

Maḥmūd began his plunder of northwest India in 997 and ultimately undertook approximately seventeen raids of northwest Hindu Indian cities. Inspired by iconoclasm and greed, he usually chose temple sites that were depositories of vast wealth in cash, golden images, and jewelry—most likely donations of worshipers. Hearing of Somanātha's great wealth, Maḥmūd set his sights on Somnāth in 1025. Maḥmūd sacked the town, looting and destroying the sacred temple. A description from a thirteenth-century Arab historian tells of the temple's great wealth and Maḥmūd's unbridled ferocity:

> Somnat—a celebrated city of India situated on the shore of the sea and washed by its waves. Among the wonders of that place was the temple in which was placed the idol called Somnat . . . . Everything of the most precious was brought there as offerings, and the temple was endowed with more than ten thousand villages . . . . A thousand brahmans were employed in worshipping the idol and attending on the visitors, and five hundred damsels sung and danced at the door—all these were maintained upon the endowments of the temple. The edifice was built upon fifty-six pillars of teak covered with lead. The shrine of the idol was dark but was lighted by jewelled chandeliers of great value. Near it was a chain of gold weighing two hundred mans. . . . When the Sultan went to wage religious war against India, he made great efforts to capture and destroy Somnat, in the hope that Hindus would become Muhammadans. He arrived there in the middle of. . . . December A.D. 1025. The Indians made a desperate resistance. They would go weeping and crying for help into the temple and then issue forth to battle and fight til all were killed. The number of slain exceeded 50,000. The king looked upon the idol with wonder and gave orders for the seizing of the spoil and the appropriation of the treasures. There were many idols of gold and silver and vessels set with jewels, all of which had been sent there by the greatest personages in India.

Completely ravaged by Maḥmūd's raid, the temple of Somanātha would be resurrected later, only to be destroyed again by other Muslim marauders. The introduction of Muslim forces to the Indian political scene, initiated by the raids of Maḥmūd, placed Hindu sacred sites such as Somanātha in constant peril.

Immediately following Maḥmūd's departure, Bhīmadeva I restored the temple with the help of other Kāthiāwār leaders, such as Ra Navghan of Junāgadh. Siddharāja Jayasimha (reigned 1094–1143), grandson of Bhīmadeva I, commissioned a learned Saivite brahman whom he brought from Vārānasī to develop the region as a center for religious learning. Siddharāja's successor, Kumārapāla (reigned 1144–72), built a new temple, furthering the status of Somnāth as a sacred place of religious learning and knowledge. The new temple and atmosphere of religious learning inspired other kings and officers to build small temples at Somnāth, to both Krishna and Siva, truly creating a Hindu temple town.

Another cycle of destruction and restoration followed the ascendancy of 'Alā-ud-Dīn Khaljī to the throne of Islamic Delhi in 1296 and the spread of his rule over Gujarāt. After his forces destroyed and looted the whole of Somnāth, Ra Navghana IV of the Chudasma clan ruling in Junāgadh once again reconstructed the temple, mainly by restoring the broken *liṅgam* to its place. Muḥammad Tughluq of the Tughluq Dynasty took Gujarāt in 1345, once again razing the temple at Somnāth. Ra Muktasimha, one of the last of the Chudasma clan, reclaimed Somnāth and tried to restore the temple of Somanatha after the Tughluq Dynasty in Delhi declined. When Muzaffar Khān, the former Tughluq governor of Gujarāt, asserted his independent rule he immediately set upon Somnāth as a military target. Thus, Somanātha was destroyed for a fourth time. Without completely rebuilding the temple, a local rāja of Somnāth resumed worship in the structure, which prompted Muzaffar Khān to invade again in 1402.

As Western colonial rulers proved, zealous and avaricious plundering of religious sites was not a trait exclusive to Muslim invaders. When the Portuguese admiral D'Castro invaded the Prabhas region in 1546, he, too, destroyed and plundered the holy city. After the Portuguese departed and Mughal rule in Gujarāt commenced, religious worship at the temple of Somanātha revived for a short period during the tolerant rule of Akbar (1556–1605) but fell once again when the zealous Aurangzeb (who reigned as Mughal emperor 'Ālamgīr from 1658 to 1707) ordered the temple destroyed by pulling down its dome and breaking its *liṅgam* to pieces.

From the time of its destruction by 'Ālamgīr until its resurrection in 1951, the temple and town lay essentially dormant and lifeless. Clearly, Siva worship and other religious devotion continued to be practiced; nevertheless, without an active and endowed temple, the vibrant religious culture of Somanātha died, as did the pilgrimage tradition it spawned. Because the temple went through so many destructions and restorations, leaving a jumble of ruins, excavations cannot definitively recount when the temple was razed and by whom. In fact, the temple may have been invaded fewer times than the accepted history relates. Undoubtedly, the tale of its recurrent destruction adds to the allure and importance of the site. Furthermore, it seems unlikely that each raid destroyed the entire temple complex. Rather, the marauders probably dismantled and looted strategic parts, such as the *liṅgam* and the treasures, while leaving the basic structure intact. Thus, each rebuilding process may not have been from the ground up, and the resumption of worship might not have taken long.

In 1950 preparation began for the latest reconstruction of the temple of Somanātha, this time at the behest of the Indian government, which created the Somnāth Trust for the site's reconstruction and maintenance. A great deal of archaeological excavation and study needed to be done before construction could begin; remains from the older sites can still be found in the complex. Actual construction on the new temple began in 1951 and was completed in 1962. Built at a cost of 25 million rupees, the new temple is 125 feet long and 114 feet wide. The roof-tower *(śikhara)* stands at approximately 125 feet. A 51-foot-high gate entrance was added to the complex in 1970, between the temple and the shore of the Arabian Sea. In 1975, a local patron proposed the construction of an additional prayer hall *(maṇḍapa)* to the front of the temple.

All of these restorations and additions were designed with great care to recall the medieval Hindu temples of northern India. The *maṇḍapa* that forms Somanātha's base structure is made of the traditional sandstone and is decorated with elaborately carved pillars and sculptures of gods and goddesses, of both Saivite and Vaisnavite orientation. In keeping with the medieval northern Indian style, the *maṇḍapa* can be divided into horizontal sections. The bottom section, known as the *pītha,* rests on a high platform and is devoid of sculptural figures. Some carvings appear on the next section, known as the *maṇḍovara,* but it is on the cornice that the sculptures are the most numerous and elaborate. The *śikhara* consists of many small superstructures, replicating the design of the main structure. The first floor of the temple now houses a museum hall with artifacts and exhibits that detail the structure's history.

In addition to Somanātha, there are several other notable Saivite temples in Somnāth; many are in ruins, but a few have been renovated. The Rudreśvara Temple, dated to the tenth century, may have been destroyed along with Somanātha by Maḥmūd of Ghaznī. It most likely was rebuilt after this raid, only to fall into ruin again, the result of another raid or of simple neglect. As part of the recent renovations, this temple has been completely restored. It measures fifty-one feet long and twenty-nine feet wide. Its porch is supported by four pillars, each of which is divided into horizontal sections decorated with carvings of human figures dancing and coupling. The Venesvara Temple sits on the outskirts of the town. Its only surviving feature is its *śikhara*, which dates to the tenth century. Another important Saivite site is the Somanātha Temple of the Marāṭhā queen Ahalyābāi Holkar, built in 1783, after the queen visited Somnāth and saw its great temple in ruins. Ahalyābāi Holkar's temple, located approximately 100 yards from the original (and restored) Somanātha Temple, does not reflect the medieval northern architecture of its predecessor; its walls are undecorated and its *śikhara* is lotus shaped. Its shrine is underground, perhaps to protect it from marauders.

Generally, Saivite pilgrims visit Somnāth to perform *pujas* at the temples and to perform *shradh* in the nearby sea. *Pujas* consist of giving offerings to the god—usually in the form of food, although sometimes more valuable possessions are included—along with meditative prayer. The brahmans who preside over Somanātha Temple conduct these ceremonies. The other major form of worship, *shradh*, entails bathing in holy waters. Pilgrims perform *shradh* in the Arabian Sea across from Somanātha Temple to commemorate both Siva and Soma, the moon god, who is said to have built the first Somanātha Temple. There are, of course, specific days on which the performance of these rituals takes on special meaning. The completely moonless night in a month, if it falls on Monday, which is sacred to Siva, is considered appropriate for worshiping him; any religious acts done on that day are believed to be of great religious merit. Ultimately, the pilgrimage itself, the act of traveling to the sacred site, serves the purpose of religious worship and proves one's devotion.

Somnāth is sacred to worshipers of Krishna, as well, and is known for several Vaisnavite temples and monuments. The Somnāth Trust erected a temple at Bhalka Tīrth, the place were the hunter Jara shot Krishna; inside lies a marble image of Krishna. At the confluence of the Hiranya, Saraswati, and Kapila Rivers, upon a *ghāt* (a set of steps leading to the river) lies Trivenī Ghāt, the site where Krishna was cremated and finally laid to rest. A memorial chapel, known as Gītā Mandīr, was constructed nearby in 1963. All eighteen chapters of the *Bhagavad Gītā* have been inscribed on marble slabs and fixed on the pillars of this monument. Krishna worshipers come to Trivenī Ghāt to pray at the temple and to bathe in the holy waters in which Krishna immersed himself. Many Vaisnavites come to these spots on the twelfth day of the lunar month, the day Krishna achieved eternal divinity.

Hindus are drawn to Somnāth not only by its religious significance, but also by its history as the site of devastating and repeated persecution of Hindus in the bygone days of Muslim India. Thus, its survival and rebirth represents to many Hindus the resiliency and destiny of their faith and culture. The endurance of both the Krishna and Siva traditions of Somnāth is testimony to the devotion of their followers throughout the town's history.

Further Reading: *Prabhās and Somnāth* by Shambuprasad Harprasad Desai (second edition, Junāgadh: Sorath Research Society, 1975) contains the most comprehensive account of Somnāth's recorded history, beginning with Mauryan rule and focusing on the Muslim raids of the medieval period. A source that focuses more specifically on the archaeological findings of the past fifty years and what those findings tell us about ancient Somnāth is *Saivite Temples and Sculptures at Somanātha* by Shiv Narayan Pandey (Delhi: Ramanand Vidya Bhawan, 1987). *A Guide to Somnāth* by P. H. Premani (Jamnagar: Somnāth Trust, 1977) serves basically as a tourist guide to the important sites of Somnāth, providing very little beyond travel information. Two comprehensive surveys of Indian history, which discuss the history of Gujarāt in the context of larger political movements, are *A History of India, Vol. I*, by Romila Thapar (Harmondsworth, Middlesex, and Baltimore, Maryland: Penguin, 1966) and *A New History of India* by Stanley Wolpert (New York: Oxford University Press, 1977; fourth edition, 1993).

—Shome Chowdhury

Srīnagar (Jammu and Kashmir, India)

Location: Situated in the foothills of the Himalaya Mountains, 5,200 feet above sea level in the vale of Kashmir. Part of the disputed territory between India and Pakistan, it still is officially considered Indian.

Description: Srīnagar is the summer capital of the Jammu and Kashmir state. Although it was once a popular honeymoon destination, tourism has declined there in the last twenty years owing to the rise of political terrorism in the region.

Contact: Government of India Tourist Office
88 Janpath
New Delhi, Delhi 110001
India
3320005, 3320008, 3320109, 3320266, or 3320342

Srīnagar lies in the shadow of two hills, Hari Parbat and Shankaracharya Hill, the latter of which was once known as Takht-i-Sulaiman (Solomon's Throne). Owing to its proximity to the mountains and its beautiful location between Dal Lake and Nagīn Lake, Srīnagar had long been a popular destination for foreign visitors. However, recent terrorist activity has reduced the number of tourists visiting the area. The kidnapping of a group of trekkers in 1995 aroused so much indignation among the Srīnagar population that the whole city went on strike to show that it did not support this kind of political violence.

The city has always had a reputation for art and culture; indeed, Srīnagar roughly translates as the "city of knowledge and education" (*srī* means "the beauty of knowledge" and *nagar* equates to "city"). Home to the University of Kashmir since 1948, it has been a center of learning for hundreds of years (particularly Sanskrit studies). The original town, Srīnagari, was founded in the third century B.C. by the emperor Aśoka on the site that is now occupied by the village of Pandrethan. Rāja Pravarasena settled the area currently known as Srīnagar in the sixth century A.D. The new city, initially named Praparapura, was established close to Srīnagari, along the banks of the Jhelum River. According to legend, Pravarasena chose the site of Srīnagar because of a chance encounter with a devil. While walking one night Pravarasena saw a demon on the opposite bank of the Mahāsarit River. Extending his bent leg across the river, the incubus dared the king to cross to the other side. Pravarasena drew his sword and cut the leg off with one mighty swipe. The devil was delighted by the king's impudence; he told Pravarasena that he should return the next morning and construct his city wherever he found a sign. When Pravarasena returned he found city plans drawn out at the foot of Hari Parbat. The fact that Dal Lake is divided from the Tsont-i-kul canal by a leg-shaped earthen dike is supposedly explained by this legend.

Soon after Srīnagar's inception, the ancient Brahman scribe Kalhaṇa wrote in his historical chronicle of early India called *Rājata raṇgiṇī* that the city had some 3,600,000 houses, some of which reached the clouds. In more reliable accounts, Mirza Haidar and Abul Fazl wrote that many of the houses in Srīnagar were at least five stories high and were constructed completely of wood. Each house was multi-terraced and had several apartments and galleries. Many such houses still exist in old Srīnagar.

Srīnagar has long been popular with foreign visitors. During the era of the British Raj, the city was a common destination for British men and women seeking to escape the heat of Delhi. One such British traveler, Mrs. Hervey, who visited the city on her way from Tartary, Tibet, and China in 1853, left a record of her impressions. Traveling mostly by horse and yak, she reached the city to find that waterways formed its streets and that one was required to travel by boat. Hervey was disappointed and disgusted by the state of inner Srīnagar, concluding that it was "filthy and impassable (for a lady at least)." The rivers and canals were topped by crudely constructed wooden bridges, which supported shops. The rāja lived in a fortified palace perched on the banks about the Jhelum River, next to a bazaar. Mrs. Hervey noted, however, that even the poorest habitation was covered with flowers, vines, or fruit trees, and that poplars could be found on all the streets.

Mrs. Hervey commented in her journal that the rāja had outlawed "dissolute activity" (freeliving) in 1849. The large numbers of English people traveling and living in Srīnagar apparently had brought about a lapse in moral standards within the city. At the same time Srīnagar experienced a population decline. From 1822 to 1823, the province of Kashmir had an estimated population of 800,000, of which 240,000 lived in Srīnagar. Less than thirteen years later Baron Hugel estimated that Kashmir's population had dropped to 600,000 and that Srīnagar's numbers had been cut in half, to some 120,000. Mrs. Hervey blamed this decline on the tyranny of Sikh rule, famine, and pestilence. Indeed, Srīnagar was plagued by cholera and typhoid. Kashmir already had experienced nine separate outbreaks of cholera prior to the particularly harsh epidemics of 1888, 1892, 1902, 1906, and 1910. In 1892, the death toll rose to some 5,781 people, and it is said that the mortality rate rose to 600 people per day. The only traders doing business were those selling white cotton to wrap the dead. After this event a more sanitary water and drainage system was introduced. However, even today all drainage flows into the lakes, and many Jhelum-Kashmiris

Floating Market, Srīnagar
Photo courtesy of Air India Library, New York

still are forced to use these waters as their primary source for bathing, drinking, washing, and funerary rites.

The city also was plagued by fire, flooding, and earthquakes. The predominantly wooden houses made the city especially vulnerable to these perils. Before the nineteenth century, Srīnagar had been destroyed and rebuilt five or six times. Two major fires in 1892 and 1899 devastated large portions of the city. Similarly, the city's proximity to both water and snow has made it susceptible to flooding, which caused disasters in 1893 and 1903. In warm winters melting snow descends to flood the city. The entire Kashmir Valley is subject to earthquakes; eleven earthquakes have occurred there since the fifteenth century. A major earthquake in 1828 killed hundreds of people and destroyed most of the housing in the city. In 1885 the city was plagued by tremors that lasted from May 30 to August 16.

Although the area surrounding Srīnagar is verdant and fertile, the city's population was radically reduced during the year 1877 to 1879 by a great famine. Within two years the population declined from 127,400 to 60,000 people. However, by the end of the nineteenth century the population had risen again to some 122,000 people.

During the nineteenth century, the city's trade was dramatically affected by these frequent visitations of plague, fire, and natural disasters, we well as by war in Europe. The Kashmiri shawl-making industry employed approximately 25,000 to 28,000 people at its height in the mid- to late 1860s, and it generated some 2.5 to 2.8 million rupees annually from exports. Napoléon Bonaparte first had popularized the Kashmir shawl by presenting one to his empress Josephine. The removal of Kashmir's key export markets following the outbreak of fighting between Germany and France in 1870 decimated Kashmir's shawl industry. The famine further destroyed this trade, as large numbers of traders died from starvation. The survivors switched to the carpet industry to try to retain some income.

Modern Srīnagar runs for nearly two miles along the Jhelum River, which effectively divides the city into two parts. Originally the inhabitants were allowed to build only on the right-hand side of the river bank. It is thought that Ananta (1028–63) moved his palace to the left bank, thus beginning the spread of the city. Srīnagar is now a mass of bridges and canals that traverse the whole city. The Jhelum, a fast, muddy river, runs through the city and eventually joins Dal Lake and the Anchar lakes. The Jhelum is famous for its quaint wooden bridges, which have numbered up to ten; many, however, are being replaced. The oldest remaining bridge, actually the second one to be built in Srīnagar, is the Amira Kadal. Many of the finest and oldest buildings line the banks of the Jhelum in the northern part of the city. It is here that many of the original tall wooden houses can be found.

The city features many historic sites, even if they are often overshadowed by the natural beauty of the lakes and mountains. The imposing Hari Parbat Fort is worth visiting, if only for the panoramic view it offers. The fort itself was constructed during the eighteenth century by Atta Mohammed Khān; its outer walls, built by Akbar, are believed to date from 1592 to 1598. This wall has two gates and is approximately 100 feet high and 3 miles long. Inside the fort enclosure is a temple dedicated to the goddess Sarikā (which may be visited only with special permission, as the fort is used as an arsenal).

The Shāh Hamdan Mosque is one of the oldest Islamic religious buildings in the city. Constructed in 1395, it was destroyed twice by the violent fires that raged through Srīnagar in the fifteenth and early eighteenth centuries. The mosque rises above the Jhelum and is square shaped, mounted by a triangular spire-topped roof. The Shāh Hamdan Mosque is celebrated for the intricate papier-mâché work found in its interior. The Jāmi Masjid, however, is the city's most prestigious mosque (it may be the largest in Kashmir). Like the Shāh Hamdan Mosque, the Jāmi Masjid has repeatedly burned down. After the last fire in 1674, the emperor 'Ālamgīr (Aurangzeb) had the structure rebuilt according to the original specifications of 1385. The Jāmi Masjid is a wooden building, supported by some 300 pillars, each constructed from a single fifty-foot deodar tree.

The son of Sultan Sikander, the builder of the original Jāmi Masjid, is entombed in the Zain-ul-Abidin Tomb, found on the east bank of the river. The tomb is in need of repair, but is interesting because of its Persian-influenced architecture and what are thought to be the oldest Pāli inscriptions in Kashmir. Hazratbāl Mosque has perhaps the most impressive location of all the religious buildings in the city. It was erected on the banks of Dal Lake, where it is framed by the mountains behind it. Recently reconstructed in white marble, the mosque houses a hair of the prophet Muḥammad, which was apparently brought to India in the seventeenth century.

Srīnagar is known as a city of gardens. Grounds landscaped by the Mughals can be found all over Asia, but in the beautiful environs of Srīnagar, between the mountains and Dal Lake, they find their most striking setting. Designed on a grid-like terrace and divided by a stone waterway, the gardens were introduced during Akbar's reign. One of the finest and indeed smallest of the gardens is the Chasma Shai, which was landscaped in 1632 by Ali Mardan Khān. It is located near the Sufi Pari Mahal college, which has recently been restored. The former school was built by Emperor 'Ālamgīr's brother, who was interested in philosophy and Sufism (an ascetic, mystical Muslim sect). The largest of the Mughal gardens is the Nishāt Bagh. It contains ten terraces and is some 600 by 370 yards; despite its size the gardens are almost always crowded. The lovely Shālīmār Bagh (Garden of Love) is set back from the lake. Emperor Jahāngīr built these gardens for his beloved wife Nūr Jahān in 1616; they were originally known as Farah Bakhsh (Delightful Garden). In the Mughal era the top terraces were reserved solely for the use of the royal party. They were extremely impressive and housed a black stone and marble pavilion. Sound and light shows are now performed there during the summer season.

Approximately three miles from the Shālīmār gardens is the Shādharwan, the supposed location of the Fourth International Council of Buddhism held in A.D. 300. The original monastery is said to have contained stupas and other religious constructions and artifacts. In addition to Hindu, Muslim, and Buddhist sites, Srīnagar is the location of the Prophet's Tomb or Rauzabal, believed by some to be Christ's final resting place. It is said that after the resurrection, Christ, accompanied by Thomas and Mary, made his way east through Damascus to northwest India (modern Pakistan). Mary, according to this version of events, died near Rāwalpindi, but Thomas and Christ journeyed to Kashmir, from where Thomas continued to south India and founded several churches. Christ is alleged to have settled in Kashmir, married a local girl, and lived to the age of eighty-five. After his death he was supposedly buried in old Srīnagar. Many texts exist referring to Christ's life in Kashmir. (According to local tradition, Moses is also buried somewhere in Kashmir.)

Most visitors come to the city either to begin trekking or to stay on one of the many houseboats moored on Dal and Nagīn Lakes (to the east and north of the main city). Dal Lake is actually composed of three separate lakes: Gagribal, Bod Dal, and Lokut Dal. Vast areas of the lake are completely covered by giant lilies and colorful flora and fauna. Other sections are populated by hundreds of closely built houseboats and resemble parts of the mainland. A causeway links Dal Lake to Nagīn Lake (the Jewel in the Ring). This lake is far more beautiful and serene than Dal Lake; the water is much less polluted, and the atmosphere is more relaxed. It is possible there to escape the harassment of traders selling from large *shakiras* (boats). Although recent terrorism has brought a decline in tourism, the city's economic well-being also is supported by the manufacture and sale of traditional products such as shawls, jewelry, silk, and papier-mâché. Moreover, the city's attractions have proven to be long-lasting and promise to survive the tides of politics.

Further Reading: *Diary of a Journey from Srinagar to Kashgar* by H. I. Harding (Kashgar: Swedish Mission Press, 1922) is a lovely anecdotal account of the journey of a British diplomat from Srīnagar to Kashgar, and includes some delightful details about the city and Kashmir. *The Adventures of a Lady in Tartary, Thibet, China and Kashmir,* by Mrs. Hervey (3 vols., London: Hope, 1853) is an interesting account of genteel travel by boat during the late nineteenth century. Mrs. Hervey provides some detailed sketches of old Srīnagar and its society. Another dated yet informative book is the *Imperial Gazetteer of India,* volume 23 (Oxford: Clarendon, 1908); this volume includes a small section on Srīnagar that provides information on the history, population, geography, and educational institutions of the city. A more contemporary work, written for tourists, is *A Handbook for Travellers in India, Nepal, Kashmir, Bangladesh and Sri Lanka* (twenty-second edition, edited by L. F. Rushbrook Williams, London: Murray, 1975).

—A. Vasudevan

Sukhothai (Thailand)

Location: In the central part of upper Thailand, about 280 miles north of the capital at Bangkok.

Description: A city of ruins that is now visited by half a million tourists each year. Dating to the height of its prominence during the thirteenth and fourteenth centuries, the former capital city's wealth of architectural jewels includes impressive Buddhist stupas and ancient Tai palaces. After years of neglect, these buildings are in the process of being fully restored, under the direction of UNESCO and the Thailand Fine Arts Department.

Contact: Tourist Authority of Thailand (TAT)
372 Bamrung Nuang Road
Bangkok 10100
Thailand
(2) 226 0060, (2) 226 0072, (2) 226 0085, or (2) 226 0098

In 1978 the ruins of the ancient Tai capital city called Sukhothai were designated a Historical Park. Until the decree, the deserted, overgrown city had been inhabited only by a handful of farmers and Buddhist monks. Today, the ruins of Sukhothai are one of Thailand's most popular national attractions, and the streets of the onetime seat of government are crowded with vendors catering to its visitors.

The best-known king of Sukhothai, Ramkhamhaeng (Rama the Bold), took the throne during the latter part of the thirteenth century. He built Sukhothai into the wellspring of Siamese civilization, as well as an important center of Buddhist thought. As the author of the first of Sukhothai's official records (the Inscriptions), Ramkhamhaeng is considered the father of his country. Ramkhamhaeng's city featured three concentric walls divided by manmade moats; the city's landmarks, such as its Buddhist temples, reliquary mounds, and statuesque icons of the Buddha, can still be seen in and around the ramparts in varying stages of decay.

In 1833, the Siamese prince and future king Mongkut (Rama IV) came to study Buddhism at Sukhothai. While there, his party discovered the first of Ramkhamhaeng's Inscriptions. Prince Mongkut appointed a commission to decipher the strange language that promised to reveal so many important aspects of ancestral Siamese culture. The commission's work was not finished until the early part of the twentieth century.

Before Sukhothai emerged as the medieval home of the Tai kings, it apparently had been a traders' town, with activity focused around a road that ran from the southwest to the northeast, paralleling the line of hills to the west of the city. Researchers are uncertain of the identity of the earliest settlers at Sukhothai. From the fifth century, the region that would come to be known as Siam had been ruled by the Mon, who were superseded by Angkor's Khmer Empire sometime in the eleventh century. The Tai people, the most direct ancestors of the modern-day Thai, arrived in Sukhothai shortly after the Khmer takeover, although it is unclear whether they took advantage of a temporary lapse in the Khmer rule or if they fought for the right to inhabit Sukhothai.

The Khmers' reign in Sukhothai was brief but significant. During a portion of their century-long occupancy, they were ruled by Jayavarman VII (reigned 1181–1215 or 1219), who is still considered the most important Khmer leader. Jayavarman, a Buddhist successor to the Angkorean Hindu tradition, ordered throughout his jurisdiction the erection of statues that depicted himself as an incarnation of the Buddha. A partially preserved statue of this type has been discovered at Sukhothai, one indication of the Angkorean legacy. Jayavarman's domain at Sukhothai lay just to the north of the walled center of the future Tai city.

The most impressive of the Khmers' constructions at Sukhothai was a three-towered building that became part of the Wat Phra Phai Luang Monastery. Like many of the structures at Sukhothai, the towers were built of stone and covered with stucco, a pliant manmade material that allowed for intricate detailing. Several buildings were added to the monastery after the Khmer era, and only one of Wat Phra Phai Luang's three towers remains. During their reign, the Tais redesigned its facade, but a few of the Khmers' original etchings can still be seen.

During the Khmers' reign in ancient Siam, Buddhism and Hinduism existed peaceably, side by side. The Mon's advocation of Hinayana Buddhism, bound to the orthodoxies of the historic Buddha, gradually spread among the Khmers. Then, the Mon's close ties with the island kingdom of Sri Lanka brought a still more orthodox interpretation of the Buddha's teachings, Theravada Buddhism, to the Khmers' attention. Although the Tai have long been credited with introducing Theravada Buddhism to the Khmers, recent scholarship indicates the opposite is true: the Khmers introduced the religion to the Tai after learning it from the Mon.

With the arrival of the Tai in Sukhothai, the city's architecture began to reflect their influence. Apart from portions of Wat Phra Phai Luang, only one edifice still in existence may definitively be labeled a Khmer creation: the San Ta Pha Daeng, a shrine that may once have stood at least three or four stories high, located along a main roadway to the south of the Khmers' inner city. Until recently, this shrine was misleadingly represented as a remnant of Brahman Hindu philosophy. In fact, the shrine has been more accurately identified as both Hindu and Buddhist, as well as a tribute to the Phi Sua, one of the greatest deities of Southeast Asia prior to the region's exposure to the religions of India. This guard-

Temple ruins, Sukhothai Historical Park
Photo courtesy of Tourism Authority of Thailand, Chicago

ian spirit was most likely invoked at Ta Pha Daeng by the Tai, after they wrested control of the city from the Khmers, to ensure their immunity from counterattack. The folkloric deity apparently was not troubled by the presence of Angkorean icons at Ta Pha Daeng, which had, after all, not protected the city from the Tai invasion.

That invasion, according to Inscription 2, occurred in the mid–thirteenth century, as two Tai chieftains led their people into Sukhothai, establishing the earliest Tai stronghold in Southeast Asia and leading some modern historians to claim that the event was the birth of Thailand. One of the two chieftains, Si Indradit, was the first Tai king at Sukhothai; for centuries, he was equated with the legendary Tai king Phra Ruang, until Si Indradit's son and successor, Ramkhamhaeng, was identified as such in the early twentieth century.

Historians believe the Tai people originated in a region near what is now Dien Bien Phu, near the border of China and northern Vietnam. When, about A.D. 1000, they left this area in search of other land in Southeast Asia, the Tai became divided into several different groups, with distinct dialects and religious beliefs. Although the Tai who settled in Laos are now known as the Lao, those who went to Sukhothai are considered the modern Thai (or Siamese).

Newly settled at Sukhothai, the Tai built a Theravada Buddhist monastic complex called Wat Aranyik. Their most important early contribution to the city, however, was their shrine to Phi Muang, the ancient Southeast Asian god of the land, a deity with absolute power, greater still than that of the Phi Sua, the deity that served the regional ruler. The Phi Muang at Sukhothai was described in Inscription 1 as living on Phra Khaphung (the Honored Lofty Place), an unidentified site just south of the city that may either have been a mountain or may be the pyramid known as Kon Laeng (Blocks of Laterite). Whichever the site, most likely the Tai people used it for making sacrificial offerings of buffalo, pigs, and poultry to the god who watched over their livelihood. By the time Ramkhamhaeng wrote Inscription 1, Phi Muang was being referred to in its Buddhist incarnation as Phi Devata. By the fourteenth century, the Phi Muang's benevolence was viewed as a karmic barometer of the Tai king's piety. Buddhist thought was gradually replacing the forces of nature as the Tais' almighty arbiter.

With the ascension of Ramkhamhaeng, the city of Sukhothai began to lend its name to the Muang Sukhothai, a loose federation of neighboring areas united under the aegis of the Sukhothai king. Formed as a response to the regional

Temple ruins, Sukhothai Historical Park
Photo courtesy of Tourism Authority of Thailand, Chicago

power of the Mongols, Ramkhamhaeng's 1287 alliance with the leaders of the Lanna and Phayao Kingdoms paved the road for his eventual dominance over the region. The Chinese called his kingdom "Sien"; the Khmers, "Syam." In 1283 Ramkhamhaeng began work on his Inscription 1, a three-foot-tall stone pillar engraved in a new, vernacular script devised by the king himself in an effort to be understood by all of his subjects—Tai, Mon, and Khmer.

Inscription 1 told of a thriving city nestled among the fertile farmlands and orchards of the region. The land yielded mango, coconut, and rice in abundance; trade was prosperous and unfettered; and on festival days the people of the countryside filled Sukhothai to its bursting point, paying homage to the strength of Ramkhamhaeng. The king encouraged Theravadan worship by appointing the monks' leader, the Sangharaja (the monks were known as Sangha). For that position Ramkhamhaeng selected a well-schooled clergyman from peninsular Thailand and presented him with a *wihan,* or monastery, now known as Wat Saphan Hin (Stone Bridge Monastery), located on a hilltop to the west of the city walls. At the time of the appointment the monastery was known, like the earlier Tai monastery, as Aranyik (Monastery of Forest-Dwelling Monks). The *wihan* was dominated by a 40-foot statue of Buddha. Historians note that the Tai had not yet developed their talent for sculpture to an advanced stage, but that the Buddha at Aranyik (called "Phra Attharat" in Inscription 1) compensated in size for what it lacked in artistry. After undergoing various restoration processes, the statue remains standing today.

Supplementing his Buddhist beliefs, Ramkhamhaeng professed his faith in ancient Southeast Asian custom by planting a sacred sugar-palm grove in the center of his walled compound. By the 1290s, Ramkhamhaeng's kingdom was spreading, and he ordered a huge rock wall built to surround his Buddhist stupa at Si Satchanalai, thirty-four miles north of Sukhothai. The wall's completion signaled the birth of a new entity: Muang Satchanalai-Sukhothai. Si Satchanalai, also known as Sawankhalok, became an important religious center and maintained a close relationship with Sukhothai. Sukhothai itself was still marked less by Buddhism than by elements based on folk customs—its walls, its sugar-palm grove, and its four impressive gates indicating the city's territorial rights in four directions.

On most days, Ramkhamhaeng held court from his perch atop a stack of granite slabs located in the center of his sugar-palm grove. The structure was known as Manangsilabat, after a mythical rock formation from which Himalayan lions were said to have roared out Buddhist teachings. When Mongkut discovered the Inscriptions in 1833, his entourage also unearthed a piece of stone that has been accepted as a remnant of Ramkhamhaeng's throne. That slab is now ensconced in the royal palace in Bangkok, but some historians have argued that the stone was not large enough to accommodate the cabinet members and religious leaders who joined the king for his daily meetings. Those researchers are now convinced that his throne was really a step pyramid that still stands in the center of Sukhothai. That pyramid anchored a complex of structures that included several *wihan* and two *sala* (image houses), one for the Buddha and one for another deity, Phra Masa.

Manangsilabat seems to have been the last major architectural accomplishment for Ramkhamhaeng. The next set of Inscriptions, dating to the 1330s and 1340s, indicates that Sukhothai underwent drastic changes shortly after the king's death—not many of them for the better. Speculation has it that Ramkhamhaeng did not die of natural causes; one legend suggests that he drowned in a river at Si Satchanalai. His son, Loethai, does not appear to have been prepared for the responsibility of administering a growing kingdom with multiple ethnicities and religious beliefs. Sukhothai lost many vassal states, such as Pegu and Tak to the west, during his reign. By the time Inscription 2 was engraved, Sukhothai no longer maintained the delicate balance of power between ancient Southeast Asian customs and Buddhism; the Theravada Buddhists now exercised an authority that superseded even that of Sukhothai royalty.

Inscription 2 refers to Loethai as "Dharma Raja" (the king who rules according to Buddhist doctrine), calling him a well-educated man of conviction. Despite the praise, however, Loethai's legacy was dispatched in a mere two lines of the text. The author of Inscription 2 was a distinguished Tai from neighboring Muang Rat, Si Satha—grandson of Pha Muang, the chieftain of legend who paired with Si Indradit to wrest Sukhothai from the Khmers. At age thirty-one, Si Satha became a devout Buddhist, and he abandoned his wife and family to devote himself to the religion. He roamed through the Tai realm, spreading the word of the Buddha by building stupas and statues, before arriving in Sukothai to help lead the city's embrace of Buddhism.

About 1330, Ramkhamhaeng's "throne" was transformed into a Theravadan shrine when a tower was erected atop the step pyramid to create a home for a Buddhist relic. During the 1340s, Si Satha further embellished the site, bestowing upon it two more Buddhist relics he had received on an excursion to the Theravadan holy land on the island of Sri Lanka. The pyramid then became the focal point of Sukhothai's most important center of Buddhist worship. Wat Mahathat (Monastery of the Great Relics) was constructed around it, and a total of 200 buildings were erected in the area. This revision of the centerpiece of the great city was the primary event that Si Satha wished to record when he wrote Inscription 2, a situation that may explain the record's dearth of words about Dharma Raja and its exhaustive description of Si Satha's pilgrimage to Sri Lanka.

The stupa built for the Buddhist relics presaged a new style of Sukhothai architecture. The step pyramid was surrounded by eight secondary towers connected to the pyramid by ramparts, and the primary tower rose above the *raun that* (relic house), first in an ovoid bulb and then a spire (added later). The base of the stupa featured carvings illustrating the *Five Hundred Jataka,* the tale of the Buddha's various incarnations prior to his final earthly manifestation during the sixth century B.C.

Si Satha recounted the tale of his acquisition of the two tiny relics in Inscription 2: while he was helping restore the Mahiyangana Stupa in Sri Lanka, the relics there flew through the air mischievously until they were coaxed down by the visiting Tai aristocrat. Two relics landed on Si Satha's forehead, and the astonished Sri Lankans bowed at his feet and declared him a future Buddha. As most purported relics of the historical Buddha were very small and nondescript in shape, tales such as this provided evidence of their authenticity.

After such good fortune, Si Satha was dismayed to find the home he had left a decade earlier in a state of disrepair. Wat Mahathat was overgrown with vegetation, and the engravings of the *Five Hundred Jataka* had not been completed. Undaunted, Si Satha set about restoring Wat Mahathat. In the process, he changed its appearance dramatically, incorporating imagery and architectural details that he had seen in Sri Lanka. Feeling that some of the scenes of the *Jataka* were too mundane and therefore unworthy of the Buddha, Si Satha had the plaques removed, to be used as ceiling tiles in an indoor stairway of a Sukhothai image house. Despite this inconspicuous placement, however, scholars have determined that the work done on the *Jataka* plaques was quite influential on later artworks in Sukhothai and was of higher quality than the art of the next Thai capital, Ayutthaya.

Sukhothai's next ruler, Loethai's son Luthai, began his ascendancy to the throne by serving as viceroy at Si Satchanalai. While there, he immersed himself in Buddhist texts and wrote *Trai Phum (The Three Worlds),* still considered one of Thailand's greatest literary achievements. *Trai Phum* describes thirty-one layers of existence: the four highest are abstract, together labeled as the "world without form"; the sixteen aspects of the "world with partial form" are reserved for the leading gods; the lowest levels, the "world of desire," are the realm of mere mortals. Despite his Buddhist indoctrination, Luthai chose to secure his succession to the throne by force, marching with an army into Sukhothai in 1347 to become Mahadharma Raja I, the great Dharma King; the reason for his taking the city in this manner remains unknown. Indicative of his desire to shift the ruling power at Sukhothai away from the theologians, Luthai's coronation was performed by the leaders of the neighboring regions, rather than the officials of the city itself. Luthai next attempted to offset the concentration of religious power when he built a palace a mere 175 yards from the Mahathat stupa. The palace has not survived, but its foundation suggests it was quite impressive. The king also built his own royal monastery outside the city walls, at a new city center, located in a grove of mango trees, midway between Ramkhamhaeng's sugar-palm grove and the Aranyik Monastery. Additionally, Luthai instituted the practice of building *mondop* (cubicle-shaped image houses) in Sukhothai; the ruins of two, dedicated to Buddha and to Siva and Vishnu, can be seen in his Mango Grove Monastery. Reportedly, two statues of Siva and Vishnu now enshrined in Bangkok's National Museum are the original statues from Luthai's image house. The statues provide an artistic link between the Sri Lanka-influenced *Jataka* engravings and the bronze Buddhist statuary that was forthcoming in Sukhothai.

At least half of Luthai's fourteen-year reign was spent outside of Sukhothai, at Phitsanulok, thirty-seven miles to the southeast, and in other territories of the federation led by Sukhothai. Because of his frequent movement, Luthai required a palladium, a sacred image that could travel with him. His Phra Buddha Sihing (The Sinhalese Buddha) was purportedly the handiwork of a Sri Lankan king, completed in A.D. 156. Legend asserts that Ramkhamhaeng sent for the image; when its ship sank, it was miraculously buoyed to the Tai city of Nakhon Si Thammarat.

During Luthai's reign, the Inscriptions were updated at a rapid pace. Dating to the mid–fourteenth century, Inscriptions 8 through 11 chronicle events such as the festivities of the Footprint on Khao Phra Bat Yai (The Greater Footprint Hill) and Luthai's construction of a giant canal that stretched from Sukhothai to Phitsanulok. Although these were joyous occasions, the Inscriptions from this period indicate a certain instability confronting Luthai, as the *muang,* or city-state, ruled by Sukhothai grew beyond his control. Not long after the death of the Sangharaja, Luthai used the ceremonial Kathin festival to resign his throne. He then became a monk at the Mango Grove Monastery. He claimed that he would become a bodhisattva, an enlightened being who helps others find salvation. A solemn parade marched down Royal Avenue to commemorate Luthai's decision; the Inscriptions claim that the earth moved during the ceremony. The new monk made his first and only contribution to the collection at Wat Mahathat: a twenty-seven-foot-high bronze Buddha statue, the largest ever fashioned in Thailand.

In the wake of Luthai's abdication, Sukhothai fell into a steady decline, weakened by the relentless advances of neighboring powers in Lanna, Nan, and Ayutthaya. The Inscriptions from the late fourteenth century describe the unrest and bickering in the city under the reigns of Luthai's successors, the Mahadharma Rajas II, III, and IV, rather than these rulers' accomplishments. Among those accomplishments were Mahadharma Raja III's seizure of the city of Nakhon Sawan from his antagonists at Ayutthaya, in 1400. In 1384 Luthai's ashes had been interred in a four-sided stupa located just south of Wat Mahathat; the Sangharaja who ordered Luthai's temple built was one of the leaders who would bring the Sangha renewed prominence in Sukhothai. By 1404, the Sangha had assumed the power of lawmaking from Sukhothai royalty—only to be challenged by the Ayutthayans, who were making increasingly frequent overtures in the once-strong city to the north. For twenty years, Mahadharma Raja IV reigned the *muang* not from Sukhothai but from Phitsanulok, until in 1438 his crumbling constituency was finally and decisively engulfed by that of Ayutthaya.

After its subordination, Sukhothai was best known for its burgeoning pottery export. Although Thai legend suggests that Ramkhamhaeng brought 500 potters from Mongolia to launch the industry, it is more likely that potters from Si Satchanalai and Vietnam influenced the Sukhothai artisans. Excavation awaits a series of fifty or so kilns recently uncovered near Wat Phra Phai Luang, the results of which may help document differences between the Sukhothai style and that of Si Satchanalai. The two styles, frequently confused, are often catalogued under the blanket term of Sawankhalok ceramics. Sukhothai's pottery trade continued to flourish into the sixteenth century, and examples of it are exhibited today in museums around the globe.

Upon Bangkok's establishment as the new Thai capital in 1782, the Chakkri Dynasty began to appropriate the many treasures, Buddhist and otherwise, of Sukhothai. In 1808, Phra Buddha Si Sakyamuni, the huge statue Luthai had placed at Wat Mahathat, was taken to Bangkok, where it remains on display at Wat Suthat.

Little is known of the gradual emigration that rendered the city of Sukhothai barren, but the Thai government's 1978 designation of the long-dormant ancient city as a Historical Park has revived its activity. Nearly 500,000 visitors now arrive yearly to explore its ruins, restoration of which is being directed by Thailand's Fine Arts Department in conjunction with UNESCO. The park at Sukhothai was officially dedicated during the sixtieth birthday festivities of the current Thai king, Rama IX. In keeping with the city's great tradition of Buddhist monasticism, 2,500 monks joined the celebration, and 60 new monks were ordained.

Further Reading: The best English-language source for information on this ancient city is Betty Gosling's *Sukhothai: Its History, Culture, and Art* (Singapore, Oxford, and New York: Oxford University Press, 1991), a slim but comprehensive volume that takes into account most of what is known about Sukhothai. Helpful sources for background material include D. G. E. Hall's *A History of South-East Asia* (London: Macmillan, and New York: St. Martin's Press, 1955; fourth edition, 1981); David K. Wyatt's *Thailand: A Short History* (New Haven, Connecticut, and London: Yale University Press, 1984); and *Buddhism: A History* by Noble Ross Reat (Berkeley, California: Asian Humanities Press, 1994).

—James Sullivan

Suzhou (Jiangsu, China)

Location: In China's Yangtze River basin, in Jiangsu province, approximately fifty miles west of Shanghai and twelve miles east of Lake Tai, on the old Imperial Canal.

Description: One of China's oldest cities, Suzhou is famed for its elaborate gardens, silk, historic architecture, and canals, the last of which have caused many observers to compare the city to Venice. Founded in the sixth century B.C., Suzhou was a major commercial center of China until the twelfth century A.D. Because of its strategic location along major waterways, the city also was a heavily garrisoned stronghold that was frequently contested in wars between China's dynastic rulers and their foes. Today, Suzhou is considered one of the loveliest towns in China, and its scenic beauty and many historic landmarks attract millions of tourists each year. An old Chinese proverb says: "Above are the Halls of Heaven; here below, Suzhou and Hangzhou."

Contact: Jiangsu Tourism Bureau
255 Zhongshan N Road
210003 Nanjing, Jiangsu
China
(25) 3327144

Little is known about the settlement of Suzhou until 514 B.C., when He Lu, the king of Wu, made it his capital. The inhabitants at that time already were well advanced in the skills of iron smelting. The king reportedly is buried on nearby Tiger Hill, a major landmark of the area today. The name Suzhou was not conferred on the site until A.D. 589, under the Sui Dynasty (581–618). The city experienced considerable development under the subsequent dynasties of Tang (618–907) and Northern Song (960–1127). During the latter period, walls were built around the city and the earliest of its celebrated gardens were established. By this time, Suzhou had become renowned for its silk weaving.

Suzhou was favored with many canals, which connected into a regional network of waterways that joined China's Grand Canal, first built in the early seventh century and later improved under China's technologically advanced Mongol rulers. Suzhou thus became an important center for waterway transportation. During the Tang Dynasty, the city also became a military stronghold, with a large imperial garrison in place to protect the water route from rebels in the provinces. In the tenth century, Suzhou's strategic location made it the target of bitter struggles between China's northern dynasties and the independent regions in the south.

Late in the twelfth century, China's great Huang Ho (Yellow River) deviated from its course north of the Shandong Peninsula and began to flow through a valley at Suzhou. Now positioned at a vital junction between the great river and the Grand Canal, Suzhou became a major commercial and transportation hub. Suzhou was one of the most important cities in China when it was visited in the 1280s by the Venetian explorer Marco Polo. He called the city "Sin-gui" and later dictated his recollections, taking the viewpoint of the Mongol rulers who had conquered all of China by 1279:

> Sin-gui is a large and magnificent city, the circumference of which is twenty miles. The people have vast quantities of raw silk, and manufacture it, not only for their own consumption, all of them being clothed in dresses of silk, but also for other markets. There are amongst them some very rich merchants, and the number of inhabitants is so great as to be a subject of astonishment. . . .
>
> They have amongst them many physicians of eminent skill, . . . [as well as] persons distinguished as professors of learning, or, as we should term them, philosophers, and others who may be called magicians or enchanters. On the mountains near the city, rhubarb grows in the highest perfection, and is from thence distributed throughout the province. Ginger is likewise produced in large quantities. . . . Under the jurisdiction of Sin-gui there are sixteen respectable and wealthy cities and towns, where trade and arts flourish. By the name of Sin-gui is to be understood "The City of the Earth."

During the Ming era (1368–1644), the nation's rulers undertook civil reform by abolishing slavery, improving the lot of the poor, and breaking up the estates of the rich. As part of the movement, the Ming regime imposed outrageously high taxes in such wealthy areas as Suzhou and forced thousands of the city's privileged residents to relocate. Nevertheless, Suzhou continued to prosper. The beauty and splendor of its gardens, pagodas, and temples were sources of considerable pride among the Chinese.

The magnificence of Suzhou inspired both artistic genius and cultural trends. The city was home to Shen Chou, the foremost painter of the Ming era, and to his most gifted follower, the painter-calligrapher Wen Zhengming. Another famous native of the city was the sixteenth-century writer Gui Yuguang, known for his evocative essays and stories. During the seventeenth century, the musicians of Suzhou's Kunshan district popularized a gentle, melodious style of musical

Tiger Hill Pagoda, Suzhou
Photo courtesy of China National Tourist Office, Los Angeles

drama that was to spread through much of China and remain popular for 300 years. Another Suzhou resident, Feng Menglong, compiled a series of short-story anthologies, collectively known as *The Three Sayings,* that went on to become best-sellers in the early seventeenth century.

During the first half of the nineteenth century, Suzhou's importance as a water transportation center diminished as competing towns emerged along the Grand Canal and the Yellow River returned to its former course. However, the town's commercial fortunes revived with the construction of railway links, both east-west and north-south. At mid-century, Suzhou was captured by supporters of the Taiping Rebellion, a civil uprising directed against the nation's unpopular Manchu (Qing) rulers. The Taiping rebels sought a more egalitarian society, including equality for women (a revolutionary idea in those times). By 1865, the rebellion had been suppressed by Manchu forces with the aid of British and French troops. Suzhou suffered both physical and economic damage during the Taiping occupation. Suzhou rebuilt, but it still lost business to Shanghai and other cities. Another effect of the rebellion was that the British and French intervention gave the Western world a stronger foothold in China and, in 1896, Suzhou was opened to foreign trade based almost exclusively on its silk enterprises.

Suzhou was the site of a major battle during the Second Sino-Japanese War, which preceded World War II. It was largely untouched, however, by the subsequent Japanese occupation. Then in the Communist Revolution of 1945–49, Suzhou was the scene of a sixty-five-day battle that proved to be one of the most important in the conflict between nationalist and communist armies. The two sides, with about 600,000 soldiers each, fought for control of the city from November 1948 to January 1949. The nationalist side already was in low spirits because of several major defeats, and its commanders made several poor decisions in the battle for Suzhou. When the battle finally ended on January 10, the nationalists had lost 500,000 men. The communists' victory gave them control of key rail lines and opened the way to further attacks on northeastern China. By the autumn of 1949, the communists controlled most of mainland China. The nationalist government withdrew to Taiwan, and shortly thereafter Mao Zedong proclaimed the People's Republic of China.

Today, Suzhou shows few of the scars of war. Its numerous canals and narrow lanes have prevented the kind of modernization that has taken place in other Chinese cities. Consequently, Suzhou retains its picturesque appearance, and its classical gardens, pagodas, and temples remain largely intact. The population of Suzhou totals nearly 700,000. The old part of the city, which has remnants of entrance gates dating back to 514 B.C., is under government protection as a cultural and historic treasure.

Among Suzhou's historic sites is Tiger Hill, or Huqiu, located just northwest of the town and reputed to be the burial place of Suzhou's founder, the king of Wu. The entrance gate resembles a tiger's mouth, hence the hill's name. Additionally, a tiger was said to have appeared on top of the hill when the king was buried. Tiger Hill has several attractions popular with tourists. One is Shi Jian Shi (the Stone Where Swords are Tried), a thick bisected stone said to be severed by the king of Wu's sword. Nearby is the Pillow Stone, upon which, according to local legend, the monk Shengong slept. The Zheng Naing Mu (Tomb of the Good Wife) was built in tribute to a noblewoman who killed herself rather than submit to the life of a courtesan upon the death of her husband. Qian Ren Shi (Thousand Stone Men) is a pool surrounded by rocks representing those of the Wu king's followers who were killed as part of his burial rites. Another reputed burial place of the king is a pool known as Jian Chi (Sword Pond), where the historic monarch supposedly was laid to rest with some 3,000 of his favorite swords.

The 150-foot-high Tiger Hill Pagoda, built in 961, is one of the oldest pagodas in China. It is distinctly tipped to one side, a trait it shares with the Leaning Tower of Pisa, constructed many centuries later. The pagoda was the scene of exciting discoveries made in 1956 when workers carrying out routine repairs uncovered a stone casket containing Buddhist scrolls, coins, pottery, prayer beads, and tools, all dating back more than 1,000 years. These findings revealed the year of the pagoda's construction, which previously had been undetermined. Other historic pagodas in Suzhou include Shuang Ta Si (Two Pagoda Temple), renowned for its bonzai gardens, and Bei Si Pagoda, an eight-roofed structure believed to date to the twelfth century.

Among Suzhou's historic temples is the Xuanmiao Guan Taoist Temple, or Temple of Mystery, presumed to have been founded around the third century, but damaged and rebuilt several times. Its temple hall is among the oldest in China and includes three gilded statues of Taoist saints. The entrance pavilion houses statues of the four Celestial Guardians. Within the courtyard is a large, double-roofed building with upturned roof-corners housing statues of Taoist gods. Xiyuan Si (West Garden Temple) was founded during the Ming era, destroyed during the Taiping Rebellion, and rebuilt in the early twentieth century. Its central pavilion has a splendidly decorated ceiling and contains statues of Buddha, his disciples, and the Celestial Guardians.

Suzhou's Hanshan Si (Cold Mountain Temple) is located along a small canal on the edge of town. It is named for the Buddhist poet Hanshan, who lived there during the Tang period. The structure was founded in the sixth century, burned down during the Taiping Rebellion, and reconstructed under the Qing Dynasty (1644–1912). When a breeze blows through the traditional gingko tree outside the temple's entrance pavilion, the leaves of the tree are said to be fanning Buddha. Among other features inside the temple are a courtyard and a tower containing the replica of a bell stolen by Japanese pirates. Donated by Japanese philanthropists, the replacement bell rings in the Chinese New Year. The temple was memorialized in the poem "Mooring by Fengqiao at Night," by the famed Zhang Ji. Inside the various buildings within the temple are poems inscribed by Yue Fei, Wen Zhengming, Tang Yin, and other masters.

West Garden Temple, Suzhou
Photo courtesy of China National Tourist Office, Los Angeles

Suzhou is especially renowned for its splendid gardens. Most were laid out during the last several centuries by wealthy merchants, landowners, and administrators, several of whom had chosen Suzhou as the ideal location to spend their retirement years. At one time, the city claimed some 200 elaborate gardens. Those remaining today include not only trees, shrubs, and flowers, but also ponds, mountains, pavilions, terraces, halls, and towers. The designers of these gardens worked to create many different landscapes within a limited amount of space. They also strove to create a poetic mood. Fish and birds are found in many of the gardens. Another common sight in Suzhou's gardens is a decoration made of Taihu stones, which are oddly shaped, porous rocks from China's Lake Tai, where limestone exposed to water over a period of years develops in unusual formations and is filled with holes.

Of the four most famous gardens in all of China, two are located in Suzhou. One is the Liu, or Remaining, Garden, named for its first owner, whose name, Liu, is pronounced the same as the Chinese word for "remaining." First designed in the Ming era, the garden features small lakes, bridges, and many buildings including the Hall of the Mandarin Ducks, which are love symbols in China. A section of the garden is devoted to the cultivation of miniature trees, one of which dates back more than 200 years. The other of China's four renowned gardens is the ten-acre Zhuo Zheng Yuan, or the Humble Administrator's Garden, the largest in the city. The land on which the garden is located once held the home of the poet Lu Guimeng. Early in the sixteenth century, it became the residence and garden of the imperial censor, Wang Xianchen. His son inherited the garden but lost it gambling. Ownership then passed through many hands until the garden was made public property in 1952. Built on marshy lands, the garden features many large ponds and presents the illusion of floating on water. The garden's name comes from the Chinese adage: "To cultivate the garden for a living is really the politics of a humble man."

The city of Suzhou is also famous for its embroidery. Excavations near the city have uncovered embroidered handiwork dating back 1,000 years, to a period when most residents raised their own silkworms. Suzhou embroidery falls into three categories: the popular, officials', and palace styles. Double-sided embroidery, with both sides of the work identical, is the most valued. Another historic legacy of Suzhou is a form of storytelling known as *pingtan,* which dates back many centuries. As the *pingtan* artist weaves his tale, he accompanies himself with a musical instrument and a few small props such as fans or wooden percussion instruments. *Pingtan* eventually became popular throughout China.

While silk-weaving remains the prime industry of Suzhou today, the city also has such diverse industries as chemicals, metal, ceramics, boat-building, watchmaking, electronics, and the manufacture of televisions. Additionally, many Suzhou inhabitants specialize in producing tapestries, velvets, embroideries, sandalwood fans, and other crafts. Surrounding villages raise silkworms, shrimp, tangerines, and jasmine flowers for tea. Strategically positioned near rich coal fields, Suzhou also has become the hub of a major mining district developed under communist rule.

Further Reading: Information on Suzhou is not very extensive. Interesting discussions about Chinese civilization, with occasional references to Suzhou, can be found in *China's Imperial Past: An Introduction to Chinese History and Culture* by Charles O. Hucker (Stanford, California: Stanford University Press, and London: Duckworth, 1975). *The Cambridge Encyclopedia of China,* edited by Brian Hook (Cambridge and New York: Cambridge University Press, 1982; second edition, 1990), is a good source of concise information on specific subjects. Among the better travel guides are *Fodor's China* by John Summerfield (fourteenth edition, New York: Fodor, 1994); *Magnificent China: A Guide to its Cultural Treasures* by Petra Haring-Kuan (Hong Kong: Joint Publishing, 1987); and *China Guide* by Ruth Lor Malloy (eighth edition, Washington, D.C.: Open Road, 1994).

—Pam Hollister

Sydney (New South Wales, Australia)

Location: In the state of New South Wales, on Australia's east coast, between the Blue Mountains on the west and the Pacific Ocean on the east, surrounding Port Jackson, an inlet of the Pacific Ocean.

Description: Home for 40,000 years to Aboriginal Australian peoples, and in the late eighteenth and early nineteenth centuries the site of a British penal colony, Sydney has grown into an energetic and cosmopolitan city, one of the largest areas of urban habitation in the world, measuring approximately 45 miles from east to west, 28 miles from north to south, and situated around a beautiful harbor.

Site Office: Sydney Convention and Visitors Bureau
80 William Street
Sydney NSW 2011
Australia
(2) 331 4045

The first people to live in Australia were Asians who sailed to the continent in canoes or rafts. Ancestors of the Australian Aborigines, these nomadic people eventually colonized the entire continent, including the area around Sydney Harbor, which was created by a rise in sea level at the end of the last ice age. Their agrarian society endured for many thousands of years before the arrival of European colonizers. Dutch and Spanish explorers came to Australia during the seventeenth century (and there is evidence that Indians, Chinese, and Malays preceded them), but for years the western Australian coast remained the only part of the continent known to the outside world.

In 1769 Englishman Captain James Cook, sailing to Tahiti in a refitted coal ship, *HMS Endeavour,* to chart the transit of Venus during an eclipse, was commanded by the British Admiralty to search for "the unknown Southland" and to claim it for Britain. With him were botanists Joseph Banks and Carl Solander and astronomer Charles Green. Cook came to the east coast of Australia after rounding New Zealand. His second in command, Lieutenant Zachary Hicks, was first to spot land, what is now Point Hicks, on April 19, 1770. Sailing north up the coast, Cook and his crew landed in Botany Bay at Kurnell, ten miles south of Sydney Harbor. Cook originally named the site Stingray Harbor because of the huge stingrays he saw, but later renamed it Botany Bay after the fine botanical specimens found there. Cook stayed a week, then sailed north, striking a reef but beaching beside a river mouth, now the Endeavour River, where his crew met friendly Aborigines. He claimed the east coast of Australia for the British Crown and called the area New South Wales. *Endeavour* arrived back in England on July 12, 1771, with fewer than two-thirds of the men having survived the journey.

Seventeen years later, eleven British ships of the First Fleet sailed into Botany Bay with more than 700 male and female convicts. Requiring somewhere to send them now that the United States had become independent, the British government had decided that the east coast of Australia was to be its new penal colony. Crime in England was at an all-time high, owing chiefly to deprivation; this was a time when a man, woman, or child could be hanged for stealing a piece of bread. Prison space was scarce; even the old prison hulks—old ships deemed no longer seaworthy—on the Thames River were overcrowded. By sending the convicts to Australia, the government could use their labor to establish a strategic new military base and to exploit the area's natural resources.

West Africa had been suggested for the penal colony but was declared unsuitable because conditions there were considered too harsh, even for convicts. Sir Joseph Banks suggested Botany Bay. The convicts, he claimed, would be able to grow crops, build houses, and catch fish. He said the natives were friendly and would offer no resistance. Furthermore, he contended, because they were nomadic, it would not be necessary to compensate them for use of the land, which obviously belonged to no one in particular. Occupation by the convicts also would help Britain consolidate its claim to the region and fend off incursions by rival European powers.

In charge of the convoy was Captain Arthur Phillip, who was to be governor of the colony. An experienced naval man, he also had knowledge of farming. Arriving in Botany Bay on January 18, 1788, he found conditions very different from those described by Cook and Banks, who had arrived in April, during the autumn. Now it was high summer, the land was arid, and the rivers had dried up. Furthermore, Botany Bay lacked a protected deep-water anchorage basin, which Phillip considered a necessity. He was forced to move on.

Governor Phillip, along with forty male convicts and marines, sailed up the coast and discovered a suitable small cove, which he named Sydney Cove after the British home secretary. Arriving on January 26, 1788, later celebrated as Australia Day, he landed at Manly Beach (which he named after the physique of the Aborigines he found there), erected a flagpole, and claimed the land for Britain. Six days later two French ships landed, under Captain Jean-François de la Pérouse, but left after a few days. Today a memorial stands at La Pérouse to the north of the bay.

Women were not let off the ships for several days, but there were drunken scenes on the men's first night ashore. The wildness of the new land was a shock for convicts who came chiefly from overcrowded London hovels. Those who tried to escape into the bush very quickly returned, voluntarily.

Before long, male and female convicts were cohabiting and Governor Phillip had to send to England for more women.

Living conditions were difficult. Scurvy, dysentery, and other illnesses were rife. Food was scarce and the punishment for stealing was hanging. The convicts built themselves huts from mud and twigs or lived in caves as winter approached. The Aborigines, who had lived in the area for more than 40,000 years, were adept at foraging for plant roots, hunting, and fishing, but the convicts took much of the fish, firing over the heads of Aborigines if they approached their boats. The Aborigines suffered in other ways from the arrival of the Europeans; their numbers declined rapidly as they contracted new diseases to which they had no resistance, such as smallpox. On Phillip's arrival he estimated that there were about 1,500 Aborigines in the area. Two years later half of them had died. Phillip brought three Aborigine men to live at Government House, but it was hardly to their benefit. One managed to escape, another died of smallpox, and the other, Bennelong, became a favorite and a small house was built for him on a promontory, Bennelong Point, where the Opera House stands today. Phillip even took him to England and presented him to King George III, but eventually Bennelong came to feel he belonged in neither the Aboriginal world nor the European. He died under mysterious circumstances, possibly a victim of a tribal battle in 1813.

The land immediately around Sydney proved unsuitable for growing vegetables and crops. Much of the livestock that had survived the arduous sea journey with the First Fleet soon died. Nine months after the party's arrival Governor Phillip sent a warship to South Africa to buy food, effectively marooning those who were left, including convicts, soldiers, and officials. At the end of the second year there was a further shortage of food. People were reduced to eating rats, dingoes, and snakes while desperately awaiting the arrival of supply ships from England. Two and one-half years later, after a voyage taking a year, the *Lady Juliana* arrived with female convicts, followed by four more ships with convicts and soldiers. In 1789 a supply ship, *The Guardian,* went down after hitting an iceberg near the Cape of Good Hope.

The arrival of additional convicts stretched the food supply even thinner, at a time when the colony was threatened by famine. The grain harvest was decimated by disease, and what was left was consumed by rats. At Government House dinners, guests had to bring their own bread. The arrival of the Third Fleet in 1791 brought a further 2,000 mouths to feed, raising the total population to 7,000, but fortunately, three supply ships arrived just in time from England.

Before long the streets of Sydney resembled the less salubrious areas of London in filth and debauchery. The convicts more or less looked after themselves. They lived in hovels in an area marked by sandstone rocks at the entrance to the harbor, now a popular tourist spot known as the Rocks. In the early nineteenth century, however, it was a slum populated by drunks, deserters, prostitutes, thieves, and rats. Raw sewage ran in the streets, and hovels became grog shops and brothels. Jan Morris, in her book *Sydney*, paints a grim picture of this period, with wallabies, chickens, and pigs in the streets and goats in the cemetery; gangs of convicts in leg irons; drunken sailors searching for brothels; ragged children; naked Aborigines, sometimes dressed incongruously in cast-off Western clothes; and an occasional body on a gibbet. The soldiers were often little better off than their captives, and the officers assigned duty there were frequently those with little chance of successful army careers.

Convicts' sentences varied; some were as short as seven years, others were for life. Good behavior could mean a shortened sentence or a grant of a small piece of land to work in Australia, even a total pardon, in which case the prisoner would have to buy a passage home. Free settlers lived to the east of what was to become the Tank Stream; convicts to the west. Even today there is de facto segregation, with the more affluent living in Sydney's eastern suburbs.

By the time Phillip returned home in 1792, there had been some improvement, at least in the food supply. The land around Sydney was supporting farm animals and growing vegetables and other crops, including imported orange trees and grapevines. Some brick buildings and roads had been constructed. Phillip's first few successors were less competent than he, although they carried on some development.

The town of Paramatta to the west of the city had been founded in 1788 by Phillip, who needed farmland to feed his Sydney Cove settlement. A number of buildings from this period exist today, including the oldest known house in Australia, Elizabeth Farm House, built in 1793 by John Macarthur, Phillip's successor as governor. A road was built from Sydney, a second Government House constructed, and an area of forest cleared for farming by Irishmen brought here after the Irish rebellion of 1798.

The Rum Rebellion of 1808 led to the deposition by the New South Wales garrison, the so-called Rum Corps, of Governor William Bligh (of *Bounty* fame) for trying to curb their monopoly on goods arriving in Sydney. Following as governor of New South Wales in 1809 was an army man, Lachlan Macquarie, who was responsible for Sydney's transformation from a penal settlement into a city. During his time in office New South Wales grew four-fold, as he encouraged free settlers and emancipated convicts to make their homes in the region. Concerned about the colony's morality, Macquarie enacted stricter liquor laws and made church-going compulsory for convicts. Among his other actions were banning pigs from Sydney's streets and forbidding naked bathing. Macquarie returned to Scotland in 1822, leaving a legacy of fine streets, roads, bridges, and public buildings, including new barracks, and he did much to improve the lot of the convicts as well as the free settlers. Some soldiers and officials already had taken every advantage to make money out of their situation, building prosperous homes and farms outside the city.

Macquarie's tenure saw the first crossing of the Blue Mountains (named for the blue haze emanating from the eucalyptus trees), which lay outside Sydney like an impenetrable barrier. Attempts to cross them failed until May 1813,

Sydney Opera House and Harbour Bridge, Sydney
Photo courtesy of Tourism New South Wales

when three men set out from Sydney to discover what lay on the other side, not by following valleys, as previous parties had done, but by tracking along a ridge. The three, Gregory Blaxland and William Lawson, both farmers, and William Wentworth, son of a woman convict and a naval surgeon, showed that it was possible not only to cross the mountains but to do so with sheep and cattle. The raising of merino sheep, imported from Spain, eventually became a prosperous pursuit in this area. The discovery of a pass through the mountains also proved useful during the drought of 1813, when Macquarie sent surveyor George Evans even farther over the mountains to discover fertile land and a river. Macquarie also encouraged development of farms along the Hawkesbury River north of Sydney.

One of Sydney's most important citizens arrived the following year. Francis Howard Greenway came as a convict from Bristol to serve time for forging a signature. He was also a trained architect, a follower of Beau Nash. Pardoned by Macquarie for producing a successful design for the South Head lighthouse, Greenway became his civil architect, for a fee of three shillings a day. He was responsible for some of Sydney's most distinguished buildings, including St. James's Church, the Supreme Court of New South Wales, and Macquarie Street Barracks. Trading ships began to arrive, and a small river, which now enters the harbor at Circular Quay, became the Tank Stream, a source of fresh water. A bridge joined the east and west. The governor's white house with its superb garden and tame wallabies overlooked the harbor.

By 1838 convicts were no longer being transported to Australia's east coast, although the west coast continued to receive them for an additional thirty years. Altogether more than 80,000 convicts arrived in New South Wales. For many years Sydney was answerable only to London, and until 1851 it had control over Melbourne. In 1856 Sydney became the capital of the colony of New South Wales; now genteel and somewhat claustrophobic in the Victorian manner, it had come a long way from the original penal settlement. The railroad came in the 1850s, and gold and copper deposits were discovered around Australia about this time as well. The city boomed: during the second half of the nineteenth century the population increased by about 10,000 each decade.

The British influence continued to be strong. As in London, Sydney's major park was named Hyde Park, and the Botanical Gardens were inspired by London's Kew Gardens. Sydney University on the Paramatta Road began as an Oxbridge-style place of learning, and shops, such as the upmarket David Jones, founded in 1828, were based on London's genteel counterparts. The Customs House overlooking Sydney Cove displayed a statue of Queen Victoria; government buildings vied with London's Whitehall. Architectural styles were derived from those popular in England; in the late nineteenth century Victorian buildings with much ornamental ironwork became very fashionable, and they still are prized today.

Despite the progress, public health was still bad, and there was great social inequality. At the turn of century trade unions began to develop, aiming at equality and a good standard of living for all. The most important event of this era, however, was the birth of the Commonwealth of Australia, independent of England, in 1901. Now a fully Australian city, Sydney continued to develop. The suburbs now extended toward the Blue Mountains, down to Botany Bay. Going to the beach became a popular way of relaxing. Even buildings acquired a relaxed air, with verandas, arcades, and canopies over sidewalks.

An outbreak of bubonic plague in 1900 resulted in the destruction of much of the Rocks, site of the colony's first convicts' huts, fort, observatory, and windmill. The Rocks were saved in the 1960s and 1970s by the Builders Labourer Federation (BLF); when the state government had plans for redevelopment, members of the powerful BLF withdrew their labor, thus preserving many of the historic buildings and parks. In the 1970s the Rocks were taken over by Sydney Cove Redevelopment Authority. Today the cobbled lanes, shops, pubs, and restaurants make up a fashionable and expensive piece of real estate and a popular spot for tourists.

As did other cities around the world, Sydney suffered during the Great Depression of the 1930s. Soup kitchens and homeless people were common sights. By now the population had risen to more than 1 million. Unemployment was relieved by a major public works project, the Sydney Harbour Bridge. Opened in March 1932 at the low point of the Depression, the bridge was a symbol of the New Australia and the decline of the British Empire. This era also was marked by the arrival of immigrants from continental Europe and Asia. Although the majority of the population continues to be of British or Irish ancestry, today Sydney is quite multicultural.

Sydney's superb location and beautiful harbor make tourism a major industry, but the city is primarily commercial, relying on its port. Iron and steel industries grew up on the outskirts of the city as a result of deposits of high-grade black coal discovered in the Hunter Valley in the north, along the Illawarra Coast to the south, and in the Blue Mountains.

Central Sydney runs from Central Station to Circular Quay, where ferries leave for all parts of the harbor and the neighboring beaches. One of these, Manly, was a fishing village until in 1857 a wealthy English immigrant developed a resort along the lines of those he remembered back home. At the time there were strict rules governing swimming, which was considered slightly indecorous. At Manly in 1902 a man named William Gocher was arrested for violating the Police Offences Act, which prohibited public bathing between 9 A.M and 8 P.M. Today there is no such problem. Of the area's thirty beaches, the most famous is probably Bondi Beach. Posters in 1930s called it "The Playground of the Pacific." A pavilion for changing opened first in 1911, to be replaced in 1928 by an Art Deco edifice that included a Turkish bath, massage room, ballroom, cafe, and theatre. Today it is preserved as a historic building under the National Trust.

In today's cosmopolitan Sydney, old and new blend amicably, and sympathetic use has been made of the city's heritage. The Power House Museum was part of Sydney's first working power station and tram depot of 1902. The magnificent copper-domed Queen Victoria Building has been restored to provide a sophisticated shopping mall.

George Street, one of modern Sydney's main thoroughfares, was once known as Sergeant Major's Row, part of Governor Phillip's grand plan for the city. Another major artery is Macquarie Street, named for Sydney's most famous colonial governor and the site of many historic buildings, including the Parliament House, dating from 1829 and still the seat of New South Wales government, and the Conservatorium of Music, once part of the governor's quarters.

Dominating the harbor at Bennelong Point, once Cattle Point, where settlers landed their cattle, is the amazing, shell-like structure of the Opera House, opened by Queen Elizabeth II in 1973. Designed by a Dane, Joern Utzon, who was chosen by international competition, the building was based on Mayan temples. Despite its cost of 102 million Australian dollars, raised by a national lottery, the building has had problems. The design of the interior had to be changed as work proceeded, and the small size of the stage and lack of parking have sparked criticism. Still, the Sydney Opera is arguably one of the most dramatic buildings in the world, vying for attention with the spinnakers of yachts on the harbor.

Further Reading: Jan Morris's *Sydney* (London: Viking, and New York: Random House, 1992) provides a vivid portrait of the city. *History of Australia* by Australians C. M. H. Clark, Meredith Hooper, and Susanne Ferrier (Cambridge: Lutterworth, 1988), ostensibly written for young people, is nevertheless fascinating for its contemporary descriptions, personalities, and social background. Ronald W. Laidlaw's *Mastering Australian History* (South Melbourne: Macmillan, 1988) brings the social and political history of Australia up to modern times. *Australia, Beyond the Dreamtime* by Thomas Keneally, Patsy Adam-Smith, and Robyn Davidson (London: BBC Books, and New York: Facts on File, 1987) provides descriptions of three significant periods in Australian history by three modern Australian writers, covering Sydney from its role as a penal colony to the contemporary fight to preserve the city's heritage in the face of property developers.

—Jackie Griffin

Tahiti (Society Islands, French Polynesia)

Location: In the central South Pacific, 3,500 miles east of Australia and 2,381 miles due south of Oahu; largest and most populous of the Society Islands, themselves among the 130 islands of French Polynesia; the Society Islands are, in turn, divided into the Leeward and Windward Islands, the latter of which contains Tahiti.

Description: A rugged, mountainous island 402 square miles in area, Tahiti was settled by Polynesians from other Pacific islands in two waves, in approximately A.D. 400 and 650–775. Europeans first discovered Tahiti in 1767, and the French explorer Louis-Antoine de Bougainville claimed the island for the French in 1768. The advent of English Protestant missionaries in 1797 brought rapid Europeanization to the island; in its wake came diseases and depopulation, commercial exploitation, and increased settlement by Europeans, Americans, and Chinese migrant laborers. English Protestant missionaries were followed in the 1830s and 1840s by French Roman Catholic missionaries, and by renewed French claims on the islands. In 1838, the French established a protectorate over Tahiti, and in 1888 annexed it as a colony. It remains today under French authority.

Site Office: Fare Manihini
Boulevard Pomare
B. P. 65 Papeete
Tahiti
French Polynesia
(689) 50 57 00

The beauty and tropical abundance of Tahiti have been its blessing as well as its curse throughout the island's history. Its first human settlers, Polynesians who migrated to Tahiti in the 400s, found fertile land for their few subsistence crops, a superabundant supply of breadfruit (their mainstay), and deep, pure running streams at every turn. These inhabitants multiplied quickly, and word of the island's abundance and easy living attracted a second, greater wave of immigrants from other islands several hundred years later, from approximately 650 to 775. Captain James Cook, sailing around Tahiti in the late eighteenth century with his small staff of scholars and experts, marveled at the populousness of the island, which he (or perhaps one of his staff) gauged at approximately 70,000. The Spanish, who tried and failed to establish a colony on Tahiti in 1772, revised this figure to a mere 16,000, but a later estimate bore out Cook's original guess.

Europeans who arrived on the island invariably saw its native inhabitants as radiantly care-free, happy, and unfettered. Nude young girls swam to greet incoming ships, middle-aged women went about unselfconsciously bare breasted, and men of all ages were unashamed of their languid lifestyle and ignorance of the European work ethic. Even the most sophisticated and well-traveled Europeans had difficulty moving beyond this idyllic impression to see that the Tahitians were, of course, far from unfettered by social convention. Some Europeans soon realized that the class chasms in Tahitian society were in many ways deeper than those at home. All visitors eventually became aware of the many rigid taboos (from the Tahitian word *tapu*) governing the lives of Tahitians, the violation of any one of which could result in a swift death sentence. Elaborate rules dictated the preparation and consumption of many foods; women could not eat with men, a taboo so strict that not even the most highborn woman could escape it. The supposed uninhibited behavior of native Tahitian girls applied only to those girls from the lowest classes; wellborn Tahitian females were virtual prisoners in their homes. Certain Tahitian customs positively horrified the Europeans: these included infanticide, human sacrifice, polygamy, and incest (marriage among closely related members of the same family was believed necessary to preserve the racial purity of the wellborn).

Historians do not know for certain who was the first European to visit Tahiti, but it may have been Pedro Fernández de Quiros, a Spaniard who recorded coming upon an island he named Isla de Amat in 1606. The island was officially "discovered" in 1767 by Captain Samuel Wallis, who named it King George III's Island. Wallis was so taken by the island's loveliness and the exotic natives that he was sure he had found paradise on earth. He had stumbled upon Tahiti during a commercial voyage from England, one purpose of which was to find the legendary South Land, or Terra Australis. Although he and his crew never found this South Land, they put Tahiti on the map. From that time forward, a steady stream of foreign ships docked at the island, which soon gained a reputation as a refuge for Europe's detritus—mutineers, beachcombers, and escaped convicts en route to Botany Bay in Australia.

French captain and explorer Louis-Antoine de Bougainville arrived in Tahiti in 1768 and proceeded to claim the island, which he named New Cytheria, for France. In the Treaty of Paris of 1763, France had forfeited almost all of its colonial possessions to England. Soon afterward, French seamen like Bougainville (an army officer with no formal naval training) were encouraged by King Louis XV to explore vast stretches of the Pacific, claiming island after island for France. These claims meant little to England and other European powers—or to France itself—at the time. From a commercial standpoint, the Pacific islands were considered valueless in the eighteenth century. This assessment would change in the nineteenth century.

Point Venus Lighthouse
Photo courtesy of Tahiti Tourisme, El Segundo, California

In 1769, a year after Bougainville had claimed Tahiti for France, the island was visited by it most famous European explorer: Captain James Cook. Both Cook's and Bougainville's voyages to the Pacific involved a great deal more than a hunt for the fabled South Land. They brought with them linguists, cartographers, naturalists (the learned naturalist Joseph Banks sailed with Cook), and artists to study and record the flora, fauna, and social customs of the inhabitants. Among the important pieces of information Cook recorded was the natives' name for the island—Tahiti—which eventually supplanted the more unwieldy King George III's Island. Cook's men undertook their first voyage to the South Pacific in 1767 on behalf of the Royal Society in London. Perhaps for this reason Cook named the island chain to which Tahiti belongs the Society Islands, although other records indicate he did this because of the close proximity of the various islands within the chain.

In the eighteenth century apparently only religious organizations saw any real value in Tahiti. In fact, the first venture undertaken by the newly established London Missionary Society was to Christianize the island. About thirty missionaries set sail on the *Duff* for Tahiti in the summer of 1796. Most of these missionaries were married, a few had children, and the majority were without theological training. By and large they came from the lowest classes and sought missionary work in part to escape poverty in England. Their choice was certainly not an easy one; the journey to Tahiti took six months, first bringing them to Rio in Brazil, then another 13,820 miles around Africa's Cape of Good Hope (not around South America, as one would assume), then south of Australia, north of New Zealand, and finally to the Society Islands. Their arrival in Matavai Bay, Tahiti, in March 1797 is commemorated as an official Tahitian holiday.

The missionaries were totally unprepared for what they would encounter. Although Tahitian sexual mores and nudity indeed shocked them, these were less offensive than the widespread practice of infanticide and human sacrifice, which the missionaries tried in vain to stop. They brought with them a printing press and endeavored to learn the natives' language. They did not force conversions; in fact, the missionaries had so little success that the majority wished to return, and most of them did, after a year. More than one of them, according to reports sent regularly to headquarters in London, "apostatized" or "went native," especially after falling in love with a Tahitian woman.

The chief of the Tahitians, Pomare II, came to see in the missionaries a chance to acquire firearms for use against his enemies. He elated the few remaining missionaries by announcing in 1812 that he wished to be baptized. Predictably, this calculated act did not result in Pomare II's hoped-for alliance with the English king; instead, the missionaries found themselves becoming arms dealers to the Tahitian king, whom they desired to see triumph over his pagan enemies. Pomare II, armed and satisfied, returned immediately to his native lifestyle, but his example led to mass conversions of his Tahitian followers, who were accustomed to following the lead of their authoritarian rulers.

In 1825, the Evangelical Congregation in Rome declared that "the South Sea Islands now appear as the bastion of heresy and not of paganism," an unwitting compliment to the efforts of the London Missionary Society, which did not consider Roman Catholics to be Christians. The Apostolic Prefecture of the South Sea Islands, established in 1830, duly proceeded to send Catholic missionaries to Tahiti, some of them Irish, others French. Catholicism appealed to the natives because it condemned neither dancing nor moderate drinking. Although the Protestant-controlled government expelled Catholic missionaries and in 1838 enacted a law prohibiting Catholics from proselytizing, they failed to put a stop to the practice.

Tahiti had changed vastly by that time. Gone was most of the native population, ravaged by the onslaught of western diseases, cheap rum, and the bloody warfare that ensued as modern armaments replaced native bows and arrows. The number of native inhabitants now hovered very near 16,000, the same figure the Spaniards had wrongly estimated for Tahiti in the time of Captain Cook. Land was plentiful, and by the late 1830s fruit, sugar cane, copra (dried coconut meat used in coconut oil processing), and coffee were grown for export, and pearl fishing became increasingly important. Tahiti clearly had market value, but the market was heavily labor intensive, and the population declining.

Aware of the island's unrealized commercial value, France now chose to make good on the claims that Captain Bougainville had staked for France decades earlier on Tahiti and more than 100 other South Pacific islands. With the end of the Napoleonic wars and the humbling Congress of Vienna in 1814–15, the French government became increasingly interested in commercial enterprises overseas as a possible prelude to establishing an empire to rival that of its arch nemesis, Great Britain. Their interest in the Society Islands was spurred by the Roman Catholic Church, itself frustrated over the slow pace of its proselytizing efforts there. France made its move in 1838, declaring a protectorate over the islands. When the British consul in Papeete, George Pritchard, protested, the French forcibly expelled him. In London the British government, preoccupied with its other, more lucrative colonial possessions, barely responded to the French usurpation in tiny, far-off Tahiti.

When Catholic missionaries began arriving in the islands once again in the early 1840s, they found a native rebellion taking place against French rule, a rebellion fully supported by Queen Pomare IV, whose government the French recognized only nominally. The French did not quell the rebels until 1847. (The timing was fortunate for France: a year later, that country became embroiled in the Revolution of 1848.) Although the French did not defeat the Tahitians, they did threaten the queen with annexation of her island if she did not return to Papeete from her place of exile. Reluctantly, Pomare returned and reigned as a puppet monarch. Her son and heir, Pomare V, handed over his right to rule in 1880. Eight years later, France formally annexed Tahiti and the other Society Islands. Sporadic native rebellions against French rule continued into the twentieth century.

Papeete, a town of about 3,000 inhabitants in the 1840s, remained the capital of Tahiti. Some 100 French officials, at the helm of which were the "commissaires," ruled the islands. The French expelled neither Protestants nor Americans, the other large foreign presence on the islands. Even after World War I and the shuffling of control of many South Pacific islands to the League of Nations, the French held on tenaciously to their Pacific island empire.

To compensate for the diminished native workforce, French and American businessmen in Tahiti started importing workers from Asia, a move that decisively changed the ethnographic makeup of the island. A boatload of 1,200 Chinese immigrants landed in Papeete in 1864 to work at jobs disdained by whites. Although some of the immigrants became small shop owners and opium dealers, they were a segregated and despised minority. Agriculture was the mainstay of the islands, with tourism a distant, hardly conceptualized possibility.

Nonetheless, Tahiti's beauty and remoteness lured to its shores a few eccentric Europeans and Americans, some of whom left their indelible mark on the island. The naturalist Charles Darwin, en route to other destinations, stopped to admire Tahiti's superabundant flora and fauna in 1835. In 1842, the unruly young sailor Herman Melville was jailed in Papeete (as recounted in his novel *Omoo*); his jail is now a tourist shrine. Decades later, Scottish writer Robert Louis Stevenson wove Tahiti into many of his stories and into at least one novel, *Treasure Island,* while he struggled to recover on the island from tuberculosis. In 1891 Henry Adams, the American intellectual and descendant of two presidents, visited Tahiti.

That year also marked the arrival of French artist Paul Gauguin, the nineteenth-century European visitor most closely associated with the island. He had journeyed to Tahiti to create, in his words, "simple art." "In order to achieve this," Gaugin wrote,

> it is necessary for me to steep myself in virgin nature, to see no one but savages, to share their life and have as my sole occupation to render, just as children would do, the images of my own brain, using exclusively the means offered by primitive art, which are the only true and valid ones.

Gauguin's debarkation in Papeete proved a disappointment. He was dismayed to find Papeete a European town in miniature, denuded of all authentic Polynesian culture and dominated by a snobbish French officialdom that he came to loathe (the feeling would soon prove mutual). Even when he settled in a distant village to live with the Tahitian natives, he was surprised at how little remained of the "virgin nature" he had expected. Gauguin lived in Tahiti from 1891 to 1893 and again from 1895 to 1901. In his paintings he immortalized the Tahitians (including his Tahitian common-law wives) and their ancient way of life, and he sympathized with their loss of identity and culture. Perhaps for these reasons they liked the eccentric genius and eventually erected a museum to him. Today the Paul Gauguin Museum is a popular stopping place and an important cultural monument in French Polynesia.

Tahiti escaped largely unscathed from the traumas of the twentieth century. During World War II, the American naval presence on neighboring Bora Bora brought no large-scale attacks from the Axis powers, only one minor shelling of Papeete by a German U-Boat in search of target practice. Similarly, the anticolonial revolts that broke out across the globe following the war bypassed Tahiti. In 1958, in fact, when the French were conceding defeat in their colonial wars in Indochina and Algeria, they allowed the Tahitians to vote for or against independence, and the majority voted *non.* Somewhat incongruously (perhaps just to be safe), the French colonial government sent a leading Tahitian nationalist, Pouvanaa a Oopa, into a twelve-year exile.

An American invasion of Tahiti followed World War II—not a military operation, however, and the invasion's directors lived not in Washington, but Hollywood. In the 1950s and 1960s such box office hits as *Kon Tiki* and *Mutiny on the Bounty* were filmed on location there. The latter starred Marlon Brando, who soon after completing the film built himself a house in Tahiti; he was one of numerous members of the jet set to do so. Since then, Tahiti has become a major stop for island-hopping Americans, its economy linked to American markets and the vast bulk of its 166,000 tourists (still a drop in the bucket compared to Oahu's annual invasion of 800,000) coming from the United States. Not only Hollywood movies, but the novels written by James Norman Hall in the 1950s—the *Bounty* trilogy, *Hurricane,* and *The Dark River*—did much to publicize Tahiti. The literary tourist can enjoy a visit to the house where Hall lived, now a museum.

Papeete has evolved into the "Paris of the Pacific," a beautiful, cafe-studded colonial city. With more than 25,000 inhabitants, it is the only city of its size in French Polynesia and the center of French Polynesian government. (It was also the headquarters of France's underground nuclear testing program.) The city, whose name in Tahitian means Water in a Basket, a place where natives fetched water, recovered rapidly from a devastating fire in 1884, which obliterated half of the small town, and from a huge cyclone in 1906.

Papeete Museum preserves a record of Tahiti's archaeological and ethnographic history. Beyond the city limits, in the lush countryside surrounding the capital, one can visit the tomb of the last reigning king of Tahiti, Pomare V. Nearby lies Matavai Bay, where Captains James Cook and William Bligh (the latter of the notorious *Bounty*) landed in the late eighteenth century. In the tiny hamlet of Papeari stands the Gauguin Museum. English novelist Somerset Maugham lived nearby, where he wrote *The Moon and Sixpence,* his biographical novel about Gauguin. The museum contains no original paintings by Gauguin, but it does contain many items that once belonged to him. Although Gauguin's various houses have not survived, one can visit the site of his last home, which lies adjacent to a very old Polynesian pagan shrine.

Further Reading: Tahiti's past is especially well treated in *Early Tahiti as the Explorers Saw It, 1767–97* by Edwin N. Ferdon (Tucson: University of Arizona Press, 1981). Another excellent source is Petra-Angelika Rohde's *Paul Gauguin auf Tahiti* (Rheinfelden: Schäuble Verlag, 1988). Alhough focusing on the famous French artist, the first few chapters overview Tahitian history, from its earliest days to the advent of the Europeans. The best guidebook in English is *Tahiti and French Polynesia: A Travel Survival Kit* by Robert F. Kay (Hawthorn, Victoria, and Berkeley, California: Lonely Planet, 1992). Although not a travel guide per se, David Stanley's *Tahiti-Polynesia Handbook* (Chico, California: Moon, 1989) offers invaluable information on all aspects of Tahiti.

—Sina Dubovoy

Tainan (Taiwan, China)

Location: In southwestern Taiwan, on the coast of the Strait of Taiwan opposite mainland China.

Description: Once a small settlement of aboriginal tribes and a few Chinese and Japanese merchants, Tainan was invaded by the Dutch in 1624. The Dutch promptly built Fort Zeelandia (also called Anping Fort) and made Tainan their headquarters on the island. The pirate leader and Ming loyalist Koxinga defeated the Dutch in 1661 and established his own government on the island. Taiwan and its capital of Tainan remained a stronghold for the deposed Ming Empire until it was ultimately captured by the Qing in 1682. Under Japanese occupation in the late nineteenth and early twentieth centuries, Tainan was an important military base for the Japanese until they surrendered the island in 1945. Today, Tainan is the fourth-largest city on Taiwan and remains the historical and cultural capital of the island.

Site Office: Tourism Bureau
Second Floor
90 Chungshan 4th Road
Tainan, Taiwan
China
(06) 226 5681

The oldest city on the island of Taiwan, Tainan's rich history is evident in the numerous temples and monuments dating from the last several centuries spread throughout the city's narrow alleys and wide thoroughfares. Once populated only by aboriginal peoples and a small settlement of Chinese émigrés and Japanese traders, Tainan today has a population of over 650,000 and is the island's fourth-largest city.

Modern settlement at Tainan can be traced to the early seventeenth century, a time when various European powers sought to establish trade empires in Asia. As trade in the region increased, bands of pirates became rich by raiding ships passing through the Strait of Taiwan. One man, Li Han, better known to Europeans as Captain China, thought to organize the numerous feuding bands. Around 1623, he called a meeting of the pirate captains on Taiwan Island, at a site occupied by a small settlement of Taiwanese natives along with Japanese and Chinese traders; this settlement would later become the city of Tainan. Eventually, some 500 pirate ships were united under the leadership of Li Han and his flag.

Under Captain China, the pirates flourished. Passing merchant ships (with the exception of those belonging to Japan and China) were robbed, the loot taken to pirate storehouses on Taiwan, sorted, and ultimately sold in markets opened by Li Han himself. Captain China vanished at the height of his career (he is believed to have died of natural causes), and his lieutenant, Zheng Zhilong, replaced him as chief and continued to increase Captain China's empire in northern Taiwan.

A more formidable empire—that of the Dutch—soon became established on the island. The Portuguese had put Taiwan (or Formosa, as they called it) on European maps a century before, but the island had been largely ignored by European countries. And although the Dutch ultimately used the island as a center of trade in Asia, it was not their first choice. For some time the Dutch had sought in vain to gain a stronghold in China, but the Chinese refused to compromise the trade monopoly of the Portuguese, who operated out of their colony at Macau. Exasperated, the Dutch began building fortifications and a trading settlement in the Pescadores, or Penghu Islands, in the Strait of Taiwan. The proximity of the Dutch to their own borders alarmed the Chinese, however, and the emperor suggested that the Dutch occupy Taiwan instead. Under the agreement that the two countries would at last enter into a trade relationship, the Dutch moved to Taiwan and in 1624 began constructing Fort Zeelandia near modern-day Tainan.

In their early years on the island, the Dutch concentrated largely on converting the native peoples to Christianity and fighting the Spanish, who began establishing settlements in the north. After a local uprising in 1653, the Dutch built another fort in Tainan to strengthen their hold on the island. Constructed of a strange mixture of sugar-water, rice paste, and crushed clam shells (the local Chinese called the mortar "red hair's clay" in reference to the Dutch settlers' coloring), the new Fort Provintia (also called Fort Providentia) became the central office for officials of the Dutch East India Company. Fort Zeelandia remained the seat of the political administration.

Meanwhile, important events on the mainland were shaping Taiwan's destiny as well. After three centuries on China's dragon throne, the Ming Dynasty began to falter. The weakened imperial court relied increasingly on the protection of Captain China's former lieutenant, Zheng Zhilong. Additionally, as Zheng's band of pirates grew steadily more powerful (records indicate he had more than 1,000 ships at his disposal), the emperor gave him control of the weak imperial navy in 1628. It was under this combined group of ships that the Ming court was protected when it fled from Beijing (Peking) to its capital in exile at Fuzhou in 1644, driven out by the invading Manchus.

Following the suicide of their emperor, the Ming court was weaker than ever. The new emperor, Long Wu, realized the importance of Zheng Zhilong's loyalty; he therefore honored Zheng by granting his twenty-year-old son use of the imperial family name and an important position in the new court. This son, formerly named Zheng Zhenggong, became

Fort Zeelandia (Anping Fort), Tainan
Photo courtesy of Taiwan Tourism Bureau

known throughout the region as Guo Xing Ye (Lord with the Imperial Surname). This nickname among Europeans became Koxinga, and it is by this name that the man credited with freeing Taiwan from foreigners and establishing a Ming stronghold dedicated to overthrowing the Qing is known today.

In 1646, Long Wu devised a two-pronged attack on Manchu-held regions to the north. According to the plan, Ming soldiers would attack by land while Zheng Zhilong's pirate navy would attack by sea. Koxinga, commander of the Ming forces in southern China, would remain in Fuzhou in case the Dutch attacked from their capital at Tainan. Zheng disagreed with the proposal, but the emperor initiated the attack. As Zheng feared, the invasion failed, and Zheng Zhilong was captured and held by the Manchus. When Koxinga refused to surrender his Ming forces to the Manchu army, the latter executed his father.

With the Chinese mainland now under control of the Manchus, Koxinga moved his base to a small island off the coast of Amoy (Xiamen). From this new headquarters, Koxinga redoubled his efforts. He retook the province of Fujian and for the next twelve years launched successful invasions of Manchu lands to the north. Eventually, however, Koxinga was forced to retreat to Amoy. The Manchus then worked to starve Koxinga's forces out of their stronghold by removing the towns in the region that his pirates raided for supplies. Unable to withstand the Manchurian tactics, Koxinga and his band left Amoy for the island of Taiwan.

From their capital at Tainan, the Dutch, under Governor Coyett, were concerned. Owing to the pirates' activities, the island was already populated by Ming loyalists, and the Dutch feared that Koxinga would attack Forts Zeelandia and Provintia. Their concerns were well founded; in 1661, shortly after landing in Taiwan, Koxinga and his army of 30,000 attacked. Fort Provintia, despite its strong walls and tall watchtowers, fell quickly, and the remaining Dutch forces fled to Fort Zeelandia to regroup. Abandoned by the Dutch, Fort Provintia became Koxinga's headquarters as he continued his assault on Zeelandia. The Dutch fought hard despite their dwindling numbers. After a six-month siege, Dutch forces had dropped to a mere 500, and with defeat imminent, they surrendered. Koxinga allowed the Dutch to leave Taiwan with their possessions, forcing them to abandon only their weapons. With Taiwan free of Dutch control, Koxinga changed Fort Provintia's name to Cheng Tien-fu and established his own government.

With his capital at Tainan, Koxinga set about ridding Taiwan of all remnants of Dutch rule. He tried to eradicate

Confucian temple, Tainan
Photo courtesy of Taiwan Tourism Bureau

the Dutch Reform Church and establish instead a Confucian order to spread ideals by which Chinese emperors had ruled for centuries. After the government was in place, Koxinga toured his new territory.

During this tour, Koxinga paid great attention not only to his Ming loyalist subjects, but to the Hakka, Hoklos, and aboriginal tribes as well. Previously excluded and maltreated by Chinese rulers, these groups were impressed with Koxinga's fairness. Koxinga himself was amazed at the amount of vacant land on Taiwan, and upon his return to Tainan set about developing the agrarian sector. He proclaimed that when not actively training or fighting, all soldiers would be required to farm, and he subsequently gave each member of his force a plot of land. More refugees were recruited from the mainland by Koxinga's offer of land to farm and protection from taxes for three years.

After establishing an able and just government on Taiwan, Koxinga turned his attentions back to deposing the Manchus. From his base at Tainan, Koxinga considered adding Ming bases in the Philippines and sent an emissary there to meet with the Spanish, who controlled the islands. The Spanish governor warmly received Koxinga's ambassador, but Spanish military officers were dismayed at the ecstatic reception the ambassador received from the 13,000 Chinese living in Manila. Remembering the fate of the Dutch, the Spanish were fearful of Koxinga's attentions, and discovering (or perhaps fabricating) that a Chinese in Manila had killed a Spaniard, the Spanish military impounded the Taiwanese ships and retaliated by killing some 6,500 Chinese in Manila.

Koxinga's ambassador returned to Tainan and reported the massacre. Confident that his ships and troops could defeat the Philippines and secure the islands as another Ming stronghold, Koxinga prepared to attack Manila. Before the invasion could be launched, however, Koxinga fell ill; he died on May 1, 1663.

Koxinga's son Cheng Ching then assumed the throne and, although wooed by the Manchus, Cheng Ching remained loyal to his father's cause of patriotism. Cheng Ching continued to attract Chinese to the island, increasing the Chinese population to some 400,000. Cheng Ching is also credited with erecting the first Confucian temple on the island in 1665. Originally consisting only of an offering hall, the temple in Tainan was enlarged during the eighteenth century. During their occupation of the island, the Japanese used the temple as a military base, and it was subsequently damaged in Allied bombing attacks in World War II. The temple was restored in the late 1980s and today remains a credit to Koxinga's pious son.

Cheng Ching died at an early age in 1681, and the throne was left to his fifteen-year-old illegitimate son. Angry

Chihkan Tower, on the site of Fort Provintia, Tainan
Photo courtesy of Taiwan Tourism Bureau

that the throne of Koxinga was now held by an illegitimate child, Koxinga's first wife had the child strangled and put forward a younger son of Cheng Ching's to rule.

The internal dissension in Tainan did not go unnoticed by the Manchurian Qing Dynasty in Beijing. The Manchus attacked, and in 1682 the island fell. Convinced that the security of the southern mainland was at risk while Taiwan remained an independent territory, the Qing placed the island under the jurisdiction of Fujian in 1683 and established a county government in Tainan, which remained the island's capital for another two decades.

When Taiwan officially became a Chinese province in the 1880s, Liu Ming-ch'uan, the first governor, officially moved the capital north. Until this time, Tainan was simply called Taiwan. As this was also the name of the island, the city's name was changed to Tainan, or South Taiwan, while the capital became Taipei, or North Taiwan.

Taiwan changed hands again after Chinese and Japanese forces met in Korea in 1894 during the Tong Hake Rebellion. Japan overwhelmed the Qing, and China had no alternative but to agree to the Treaty of Shimonoseki, which ceded Taiwan to the Japanese. The people of Taiwan refused to accept Japanese rule, however, and on May 25, 1895, Taiwan proclaimed itself Taiwan Min-chu Kuo, or the Republic of Taiwan. As an independent republic, Taiwan ignored the Chinese treaty with Japan and prepared to treat any Japanese interference as a declaration of war. On May 29, Japan invaded.

Geographically close to Japan, the new capital at Taipei fell quickly. Although Taipei was the island's official capital, the most important city in the hearts and minds of the people remained Tainan. Insulted and afraid that their city might fall into enemy hands, the loyalists of Tainan thronged in front of the Temple of Cheng, invoking the spirit of their long-dead hero Koxinga to return and defeat the advancing invaders. Despite the near-constant supplications to Koxinga, Tainan fell to General Nogi and his Japanese forces on October 21.

Under the Japanese, Taiwan experienced severe social unrest, evidenced by the nineteen major revolts during the fifty years of occupation. In addition to the organized uprisings, the Japanese were subjected to near-constant harassment by Chinese and aboriginal bandits who attacked at night only to disappear by morning.

Despite the unpopular occupation, Taiwan and Tainan prospered. The island and Tainan especially was an important military base for the Japanese, both in their war against China and later during World War II, and the inhabitants of Taiwan were considered Japanese citizens, if only second-class. Under the Japanese, the people of Taiwan enjoyed their first educational system, a highly developed public health program (initiated solely because countless Japanese died on the island during the first few years of its annexation), and the development and expansion of both industry and agriculture. The Taiwanese had food to eat and proper shelter—more than may be said for their mainland Chinese cousins—but any profit made from Taiwan's success went directly back to Japan.

As Japan's harassment of the Chinese mainland increased, factories on Taiwan began to build stockpiles of equipment and munitions, and the island's military bases were modernized and expanded. The mainland Chinese feared the Japanese were preparing to launch another assault, but intelligence reports seemed to indicate the developments were unrelated to the war with China.

On December 8, 1941 (December 7 in the United States, owing to the international dateline), the reason for the expansions on Taiwan became clear. Japanese Zeros from Tainan Air Base were scheduled to depart at 4:00 A.M. to conduct an attack on U.S. forces in conjunction with the naval air force located near the Hawaiian Islands. As the pilots in Tainan were being briefed on their mission—an attack on the American bases in the Philippines—an unseasonable thick fog rolled in and blanketed Tainan. At 4:00 A.M., the scheduled departure time, the fog was too thick for takeoff, and the Japanese fighter pilots were forced to wait.

While the pilots in Tainan waited, their naval counterparts commenced the attack on Pearl Harbor. The news was announced over the Tainan Air Base loudspeakers that the attack in Hawaii had been successful and a surprise blow had been dealt to the Americans. Later announcements indicated that U.S. forces in the Philippines had learned of the Japanese attack, and the Japanese base at Tainan was put on alert for possible retaliatory strikes. But the strikes never came, and at 10:00 A.M. the fog had cleared sufficiently for the planes to depart for the Philippines, where the Japanese again surprised American forces and nearly destroyed U.S. air power in the region.

The near destruction of the U.S. forces in the Philippines quite possibly saved Tainan from absolute destruction during the war, and it was only toward the end of World War II that the island suffered any bombing attacks. Prior to that point, Taiwan continued its role as the storehouse and staging point for the Japanese military. The first Allied air strike occurred in 1943. Taiwan was bombed by Allied forces, but the attack was on a single airfield and most of the island remained untouched. This changed a year later when more than 1,000 Allied aircraft began to bomb the island in earnest, destroying the northern port of Keelung. Subsequent attacks destroyed Japanese airfields, and since Tainan was the site of an important Japanese base, the city suffered with the rest of Taiwan. Fortunately, the Allies were careful to restrict their attacks to military targets, and aside from the damage sustained by the Confucian temple, the historical sites in Tainan were largely spared from destruction.

With Japan's unconditional surrender after the war, Tainan and the rest of the island were free. The Taiwanese were eager to join the Republic of China, and Chiang Kai-shek announced that his government would assume control of the island as soon as possible. In October 1945, Chiang named General Chen Yi as governor of Taiwan, much to the despair of the Taiwanese. As former governor of neighboring Fujian province, Chen Yi had a reputation for severe rule and outright corruption.

Tainan and the rest of the island suffered under Chen Yi; the dictator seized all factories and property that had been held by the Japanese, and the 30,000 nationalist troops that accompanied Chen to the island looted the countryside. Taiwan for the first time in its history experienced a rice shortage.

In 1947, Chen Yi left Taiwan and was later beheaded at the order of Chiang Kai-shek for his misrule of Taiwan and subsequent dealings with Mao's Communist Party. In 1949, Chiang Kai-shek and a number of his officers abandoned the Chinese mainland and set up the nationalist government in Taipei. Although Tainan had been the island's capital several centuries before when Koxinga's forces fled from the advancing Qing, Taipei had been used to govern the island since the 1880s, and Tainan was left alone to modernize at its own pace. No longer the political center, Tainan remains the historical and cultural center of the island nation, and its municipal government is careful to keep its centuries-old heritage alive, encouraging industry to locate outside the bounds of the town's historical center.

With the damage suffered from Allied attacks repaired, the Tainan Air Base remains an important part of Taiwan's defense against attacks from the mainland. The base, the port at nearby Anping, and the fishing industry are the main sources of employment for the city's 650,000 inhabitants. Despite its large population and busy port, Tainan today remains best known for—apart from its most famous citizen, Koxinga—its historic temples, memorials, and forts. Fort Zeelandia may still be toured, and on the site of Fort Provintia stands the Chihkan Tower, erected in 1879, which contains some portions of the original fort and important artifacts dating from Tainan's early history.

Further Reading: *Formosa: A Study in Chinese History* by W. G. Goddard (Ann Arbor: University of Michigan Press, and London: Macmillan, 1966) paints a fascinating picture of the early history of Tainan, including the rise and ultimate fall of Koxinga and his House of Cheng. *Taiwan: The Other China* by I. G. Edmonds (Indianapolis, Indiana: Bobbs-Merrill, 1971) is also a detailed account of the powers that struggled over Tainan and the rest of the island, from the days of Koxinga and the Dutch through the Japanese occupation.

—Monica Cable

Takayama (Gifu, Japan)

Location: Approximately 210 miles northwest of Tōkyō in the central part of Honshū island, at the heart of the Takayama Basin, adjacent to the Japanese Alps National Park.

Description: A mountain town noted for its historic temples, houses, and stores, often nicknamed "Little Kyōto."

Site Office: Hida Tourist Information Office
1, Showa-cho
Takayama, Gifu
Japan
(577) 32 5328

Takayama, which means "high mountain," is a relatively small town, with a population of only about 65,000. It lies along both banks of the Miya River in the sparsely populated, mountainous northern half of Gifu prefecture. Its very remoteness from the crowded and fast-changing metropolitan centers of modern Japan has helped to preserve Takayama's historic streets and buildings, which now attract visitors from all over the country.

For more than 1,100 years, until the system of prefectures was introduced in 1871, the area around Takayama was the province of Hida (even now the town is better known in Japan as Hida-Takayama). Takayama's status as the capital of the province was officially confirmed as early as the year 746, when it became the location of the *kokubunji,* one of the network of Buddhist temples, with monasteries and convents attached, that were ordered to be set up in each province by the emperor Shōmu. Hida Kokubunji, as it is still known, is now the oldest temple in Takayama, although nothing of it survives that dates from before the sixteenth century, except, perhaps, a gingko tree in its grounds, which may have been planted when the temple was founded. Its buildings now include a Honden, or Main Hall, built in 1615 to contain its two objects of worship, statues of Yakushi, the Buddha of Healing, and of Kannon, the bodhisattva of mercy; and a three-story pagoda, last rebuilt in 1821.

The word "Hida" still is used frequently by the town's tourist office, because it recalls the traditions of the *Hida no takumi,* the master carpenters from this province whose nationwide reputation initially was established in the twelfth century. The secrets of their craft were either passed on to members of their extended families or transmitted to apprentices. Many of these master carpenters, who were exempt from taxes or forced labor, left Takayama and the other, smaller towns of Hida to work on the palaces, shrines, and temples of Kyōto and Edo (now Tōkyō). Others journeyed around the country, applying their skills to temples and the residences of nobles as members of guilds, known as *za* or *nakama.* Still others, however, must have remained in Takayama to construct and maintain the buildings of its historic quarters, which stand as monuments to their traditions, even though those traditions began to be superseded by modern construction methods more than a century ago.

From about the middle of the fifteenth century the carpenters would have found new patrons in members of the Anenokōji family of *samurai* (warriors), who during that period had achieved a dominant position in the town and throughout the province. However, no complete buildings remain from their decades of power, which coincided with what the Japanese call the Sengoku Jidai, the Period of Warring States, during which central authority collapsed and the fortunes of such warrior dynasties rose and fell in repeated and very destructive civil wars. In 1587, soon after the warlord Toyotomi Hideyoshi had succeeded in imposing his own dictatorship on almost all of Japan, the Anenokōji were displaced by Hideyoshi's ally Kanamori Nagachika, who built a castle on a hill to the south of the town. After Hideyoshi's death, his former lieutenant Tokugawa Ieyasu founded the dynasty of *shōguns* that was to complete the work of reunification and rule Japan, in collaboration with provincial *daimyō* (lords), throughout the Edo period (1603–1868). Ieyasu confirmed the Kanamori in their possession of supreme power in Hida, but in 1692 Takayama and much of its hinterland became part of the directly ruled domains of the Takayama family.

Most of the town's historic buildings date from the Edo period. In the town center the area around the main street, known as San-machi-suji, the Avenue of the Three Lanes, has received official recognition as a conservation zone. The three lanes that lie parallel to the street and give it its name—known as Ichinomachi, Ninomachi, and Sannomachi, or First, Second, and Third Lanes—are lined with wooden houses and stores built during the Edo period. Among them are several small sake breweries, distinguished from the other buildings by the traditional symbol of a hanging basket filled with cedar branches; the town's Kyōdokan, or museum of local history, which contains exhibits of traditional crafts as well as several wooden statues carved by Enshū, a seventeenth-century Buddhist priest; an archaeological museum that still contains secret corridors and hidden openings in the exterior walls, presumably installed by the wealthy sake-brewing family who originally lived in it; and small museums of local *shibukusa-yaki* pottery and *shunkei-nuri* lacquerware.

Another historic area consists of a single steep hillside avenue to the east of the town center, which is about two miles long and is known as the Higashiyama Teramachi (Temple District on the Eastern Mountain). It is lined with five Shintō shrines, thirteen Buddhist temples, two merchant houses from the Edo period, and the Takayama Jinya, a complex of homes

Takayama Jinya, Takayama
Photo courtesy of Japan National Tourist Organization

and storehouses, built in 1615 and rebuilt in 1816, which formed the headquarters of the local administration. In 1974 the Jinya buildings, which had become dilapidated, were carefully restored, the small formal garden behind the main building of the group was replanted, and the interiors of the storehouses were converted into exhibition spaces, one of which offers details of the various tortures that were applied to felons under the extremely strict laws of the Tokugawa regime.

Takayama's architectural treasures also include two buildings from around 1880, constructed after European traditions had begun to influence Japanese builders. One of these, a house built for the prominent merchant family, the Kusakabe, is now the Mingeikan, a museum of folk crafts; the other, the former home of the Yoshijima family, also is preserved as a historic monument. Both stand outside the town center, on the far side of the Miya River.

Since 1960 Takayama also has included still more historic buildings, which were moved piece by piece to locations in the town from the district of Shirakawagō, about fifty-five miles northwest of Takayama, when the Mihoro dam was constructed across the Shō River. Several farmhouses, built to three or four stories and with steeply pitched and thatched roofs (in the style known as *gasshō-zukuri,* the Japanese designation suggesting their resemblance to hands joined in prayer) were grouped together to form the nucleus of the Hida Minzoku-Mura (Folklore Village), which now contains thirty traditional buildings that are fitted out with appropriate furnishings and implements. In addition, a large Buddhist temple, Shōren-ji, founded in Shirakawagō in the thirteenth century and extensively rebuilt during the sixteenth century, was transferred to a site overlooking Takayama on an area of higher ground called Shiroyama, near the ruins of the Kanamori family's castle. Its Honden (Main Hall), which is said to date from 1504, was allegedly constructed of wood from a single massive cedar tree. The Honden is also famous for its collection of paintings by Kanō Tanyū and Maruyama Ōkyo, leading artists of the seventeenth century.

In 1984 another building was opened in Takayama that cannot (yet) be called historic but still attracts almost as many visitors as the older sights. The new religion known as Shukyō Mahikari, founded by Okada Kotama in 1959 and famous for its faith-healing rituals and organic farming projects, chose Takayama as the location for its Main World

Interior of the Yoshijima Heritage House, Takayama
Photo courtesy of Japan National Tourist Organization

Shrine, built on an enormous terrace among the mountains. It includes, along with its worship hall, a large aquarium, a pipe organ imported from Denmark, and curious tall structures called Towers of Light.

The annual high point in the preservation and celebration of Takayama's history is the Sannō Festival at the Hachiman Shrine, held every April 14 and 15, and derived from the Gion Festival in Kyōto. Like its model, its main event is a procession of twenty-four traditional floats decorated with traditional textile designs, but in Takayama many of these floats carry large mechanical figures of acrobats, some dating from the Edo period, which are operated on up to thirty-six strings by as many as eight puppet masters. When they are not in use for the festival, the floats and their puppets are displayed in the Takayama Yatai Kaikan, a museum dedicated to their preservation and repair. The festival attracts about 500,000 visitors to Takayama every year and provides a focus for their exploration of a town of museums and traditional buildings that retains something of the atmosphere of traditional Japan.

Further Reading: The Hida Tourist Information Office in Takayama has published several booklets in English about aspects of the town's history. The best account in English of traditional Japanese carpentry and architecture is still Edward S. Morse's fascinating and beautifully illustrated *Japanese Homes and Their Surroundings* (New York: Harper, 1885; London: Low Marston, 1886; reprint, New York: Dover, 1961).

—Patrick Heenan

Takht-i-Bahi (North West Frontier, Pakistan)

Location: In the North West Frontier province, approximately fifty miles from Peshāwar, ten miles northeast of Mardān, and three miles northeast of the village of Shahr-i-Bahlol.

Description: The site of a ruined Buddhist monastery built around the first century A.D., one of the masterpieces of the Gandhāran culture.

Contact: Pakistan Tourism Development Corporation
House No. 2, St 61, F-7/4
Islamābād 44000
Pakistan
(51) 811001

The Buddhist *vihara* (monastery) at Takht-i-Bahi was abandoned at least 1,300 years ago and has fallen into ruin. Its principal statues and reliefs have been removed for display elsewhere, in nearby Peshāwar but also far away in Berlin. Only roofless walls and tumbled stones remain at the site to recall the once-magnificent culture of the Buddhist kingdom of Gandhāra, a crossroads of Asian and European traditions within which Takht-i-Bahi was an important religious center.

Gandhāra, which had its capital at Peshāwar but also included Swāt, Buner, Dir, and Bajaur, was originally a province of the Persian Empire, into which it was incorporated during the sixth century B.C. After the temporary collapse of that empire and the brief incursion into the region by its conqueror, Alexander the Great, Gandhāra became part of the Mauryan Empire around 320 B.C., then passed in succession into the hands of Bactrian Greeks around 200 B.C., the Scytho-Parthians or Śakas about 100 years later, and, from around A.D. 65 to 78, the Kushāns, who made it the center of an empire that was to stretch from the Aral Sea to China and incorporate Bengal and other parts of northern India. It was the Kushāns, coming into a region that was already undergoing cultural hybridization, who presided over the Buddhist kingdom of Gandhāra and (probably) the building of Takht-i-Bahi and other monasteries, until they were overthrown during still another invasion, led by Shāpur I of Iran, in 241. The political and cultural framework in which Takht-i-Bahi almost certainly was created thus lasted for only about 200 years and reached the heights of its geographical extent and its power and wealth during the reign of its greatest king, Kanishka, in the second century A.D. Kanishka and his successors derived their wealth from their conquests of the Oxus, Indus, and Ganges-Yamuna river networks and their control of the trading route on which silk, gold, and spices were carried from India and China to Iran and the Roman Empire. They derived their legitimacy from their patronage of the Buddhist religion. By the time that they took control of Gandhāra, Buddhism had been established in the region for approximately 300 years and already had begun the transition from a non-theistic ideology, based on the repudiation of desire and the attainment of Nirvana, to the complex faith, centered on salvation by a variety of Buddhas (those who have attained perfect enlightenment) and Bodhisattvas (enlightened beings who renounce Nirvana in order to save others), that was to spread from Gandhāra across Asia in subsequent centuries. This development entailed the incorporation of elements from the other cultures the early Buddhists encountered in Gandhāra and neighboring regions, ranging from the numerous Iranian and Hindu deities who were venerated as Bodhisattvas to such motifs as the lotus pedestal, taken from ancient Egyptian religion by way of Hellenistic cults.

Against this background of imperialism combined with cosmopolitanism, Takht-i-Bahi may be seen as one of several monasteries founded by the rules of Gandhāra both to express their own personal faith (assuming that they had any) and to make their rule acceptable to their subjects, for whom religion had greater potential as a factor for unity and stability than language or ethnicity could have had. Unfortunately, it is now impossible to be sure which ruler founded Takht-i-Bahi in particular, or even to which dynasty he belonged. A minority of scholars have attributed the city's creation to the Scytho-Parthian ruler known by the Greek name Gondophernes, whose capital city is said to have been near the site of the monastery; one of the site's inscriptions, dated by some scholars to the year A.D. 45, refers to him. This theory, however, is only marginally more reliable than the legend that Gondophernes once played host to St. Thomas (the disciple of Jesus who is believed to have brought the Christian gospel to India); the dating system used in the inscription has not been definitively deciphered. Most scholars have preferred the conclusion, on grounds of artistic style, that the monastery probably was completed under Kanishka, although it may well have been started before his time. Yet, this, too, is problematic, since the fragmentary evidence for his reign has led different scholars to assign his accession to a range of years between A.D. 78 and 225, and this mystery in turn has given rise to the suggestion that there may have been a Kanishka II and even a Kanishka III. In short, the only safe assertion is that the monastery was built sometime between the first century B.C. and the third century A.D.

The monastery's location on a ridge in a relatively isolated corner of the Peshāwar Valley, about 490 feet above the valley floor, is not much easier to explain. It is known that early Buddhism, like early Christianity, normally required its monks to live and worship in places physically remote from centers of population; yet it is not clear whether Takht-i-Bahi was in fact as remote then as it is now. In addition, the priests and scholars of Gandhāra, who probably were well aware that the Buddha never visited the region, nevertheless equated

Remains of Buddhist monastery, Takht-i-Bahi
Photo courtesy of Embassy of Pakistan, Washington, D.C.

locations in the Peshāwar Valley with places he had visited, and the site of Takht-i-Bahi may have been chosen to represent such a place, perhaps even the plain on which the Buddha sat under a bodhi tree and attained enlightenment.

The plan of the site is a simple one, conforming to the needs of the monastic community and influencing, directly or indirectly, the layout of Buddhist temples and monasteries across southern and eastern Asia. The main hall, used for communal worship, stands on the western side of a large courtyard, which measures about 120 feet by 50 feet and is surrounded by 28-foot-high walls, into which are set individual cells for the monks and covered shrines with niches for statues, reliefs, and stupas. The tower-like stupas had originated as grave markers, but they developed in Gandhāra into drum-shaped columns, often placed on pedestals and sometimes containing sacred relics. Beyond these to the south is another larger courtyard surrounding the platform on which once stood a single enormous stupa, probably containing supposed relics of the Buddha himself. All the buildings at the site, now stripped of the glass, stucco, and gold leaf that gave color and variety to the walls, ceilings, and courtyard pavements, are made of a variety of stone blocks, with the shrine niches and other openings topped by overhanging cornices reminiscent of thatched roofs.

The artifacts for which Gandhāra is best known are the sculptures and reliefs, sometimes carved in blue schist or green phyllite but usually in the more pliable medium of stucco, which once adorned Takht-i-Bahi and other monasteries. These sculptures sometimes are referred to as "Greco-Buddhist," but this label has fallen into disuse because it can be misleading. Neither the Scytho-Parthians (Śakas) nor the Kushāns, who appear to have entered the region from original homelands in Central Asia, had any direct connection with Greece or Greek traditions. Greek and Roman styles had found their way into the Gandhāra artists' and craftsmen's cultural milieu through earlier invasions and continuing trade, however, and these styles clearly influenced the artists' output. But for the same reasons of historical development and commercial interchange, their works also include elements derived from Iranian and Scythian models, and all these features were combined in the service of a religion that was then (far more than now) still very much an offshoot of Hindu tradition; truly, Indian motifs and images were dominant in Gandhāran art.

Within this hybrid culture, the creating of statues of the Buddha and reliefs depicting events in his life was the single most distinctive activity, for it is believed that these were the first Buddhist works in which human figures rather than abstract symbols were used as objects of veneration, a reflection of the transformation of Buddhist religious ideas and practices. The Buddha, the Bodhisattvas, and their followers are depicted in apparently Roman clothing and with European features; furthermore, the figures maintain the classical proportions between body height and head height of five to one, just as in Greek and Roman sculpture. Yet these are clearly not Greek or Roman figures, since they also display the elongated earlobes, the third eye on the forehead, and the cranial bump on top of the head that are the *lakshana* (sacred marks) of Buddhahood, and the robes they wear, although depicted with the curved folds typical of the Hellenistic style, are those of Buddhist monks.

It is regrettable that most of the statues and reliefs have vanished from Takht-i-Bahi over the centuries. It is not known for certain what happened to the monastery after the collapse of the Kushān Kingdom with the overthrow of its last ruler, Vāsudeva, in 241. Early in the fifth century the Chinese traveler Fa Xian reported that the monasteries of the Peshāwar Valley were still active and prosperous, but his account does not specifically refer to Takht-i-Bahi. The White Huns, led by Mihīrakula, who overran the valley during the 520s, are believed to have destroyed many Buddhist buildings and massacred the monks and their lay supporters. By the seventh century, when another Chinese traveler, Xuan Zang, passed through Gandhāra, he found the monasteries in ruins and many of the cities and villages deserted.

Takht-i-Bahi was first excavated by professional archaeologists between 1907 and 1913, when the Archaeological Survey of India, a branch of the British imperial administration, sent first D. B. Spooner and then H. Hargreaves to the site. Since 1947 it has been preserved and partially restored by the authorities of independent Pakistan. As at other Gandhāran sites, the relatively few sculptures and reliefs remaining after the devastation caused by earthquakes, climate, wars, and thieves have almost all been removed from their original positions for safekeeping. Some of them, including fragments of Buddhas that once were twenty feet high, may now be seen in and beside a small courtyard, protected by a modern roof, at the southwestern corner of the monastery; others are displayed in the Peshāwar Museum, about fifty miles away, along with a scale model of the monastery as it first appeared. But perhaps the single most magnificent artifact from the monastery is now in the Staatliche Museum in Berlin. This statue of a young Buddha seated crosslegged on a cloth-covered platform, his head surrounded by a halo, has lost both forearms over the centuries but is still an impressive object. Like other Gandhāran statues, it has a flat and unworked back, suggesting that it originally was placed against a wall, probably inside a niche, as the object of worship in one of the shrines of the monastery. Thousands of miles from the place where it was made and hundreds of years after the disintegration of the Gandhāran culture that gave it meaning, it retains an evocative power that the ruins of Takht-i-Bahi itself can no longer match.

Further Reading: Several books about the culture of the Buddhist kingdom of Gandhāra have appeared in recent years, but Madeline Hallade's *Gandhāran Art of North India and the Graeco-Buddhist Tradition in India, Persia, and Central Asia,* translated by Diana Imber (New York: Abrams, 1968), is still perhaps the most interesting; certainly, with its photographs by Hans Hinz, it is one of the most beautiful.

—Patrick Heenan

Tatta (Sind, Pakistan)

Location: In Sind province, fifty-five miles east of Karāchi, fifty miles southwest of Hyderābād and three miles west of the Indus River.

Description: Also known as Thatta, Tatha, and Thato; formerly a major port on the Indus River and the capital city of Sind until 1742; now noted for its historic mosques and the numerous tombs on the nearby Makli Hills, perhaps the largest Muslim cemetery in the world.

Contact: Pakistan Tourism Development Corporation
Hotel Metropol
Club Road
Karāchi, Sind
Pakistan
(92) 21 516 252

The history of Tatta, formerly the capital city of Sind but now a town of only about 30,000 people, has been shaped largely by the nature of the Indus River delta in which it stands. Tatta reached the peak of its wealth, power, and population between the sixteenth and eighteenth centuries, when it was a prosperous port city on the banks of the river's main channel, with a population of perhaps 100,000 largely dependent on the produce of the alluvial Indus plain and the trade passing up and down the river and into the Arabian Sea. In those years it was a valuable prize, governed and fought over by a succession of local rulers interacting with the great Mughal Empire based at Delhi. Its gradual decline since those days has been due mainly to the constant silting and rechanneling of the delta, which eventually deprived the city of access to the trade and led the older districts of the city and the surrounding countryside to turn into desert.

As a result of this process—in conjunction with the effects of occasional earthquakes, frequent military struggles, and repeated damage and theft by later generations—Tatta's development has been spasmodic and uneven; furthermore, as with other historic sites on and around the Indus, the historical record itself has been rendered incomplete and unreliable by the disappearance of numerous buildings and documents and the movement of populations. What remains are some historic mosques within the city itself and, dominating the city's skyline, the Makli Hills above Tatta, on which a flattened area of approximately six square miles is covered by an enormous number of tombs and graves constructed under the Sammā, Arghūn, Tarkhan, and Kalhora Dynasties.

What happened in Tatta before the rise of the first of these dynasties during the fourteenth century is, on the whole, more a matter of legend than of ascertainable fact. For example, Tatta often is cited as the place where Alexander the Great gathered his troops for embarkation on the ships that were to transport them down the Indus to the sea after their campaigns in the subcontinent. But the most significant events are the best documented, beginning with the Muslim Arab invasion of Sind, under the command of Muḥammad ibn-Qāsīm, in A.D. 711. Acting on behalf of Caliph al-Walīd I, the invaders incorporated the trading center of Debal, or Daybul, near the coast, into an embattled Arab state. It generally is agreed that modern Tatta stands on or near the site of Debal and that the later city is a refoundation of the earlier, probably in response to changes in the course of the Indus. Under the Arabs, Debal frequently was threatened by the rebellions and incursions of the traditional local Hindu rulers, but it benefited from the destruction of several nearby rival cities by earthquake in 787. By about 874 it was recognized as the capital city of Lār, a region roughly corresponding to lower (southern) Sind, and it already may have been the headquarters of the Sūmṛah clan, a branch of the Rājput people whose members converted to Islam and who were to become the most powerful family in the region during and after the period of Arab rule.

The Arabs were expelled from Sind by the forces of Maḥmūd, sultan of Ghaznī, led by his vizier (chief minister) Abdur Razzāq, in approximately 1025, but their presence in the province had a lasting impact; the transformation of Sind into a mainly Muslim region was assured as a number of dynasties, from various other Muslim centers, came and went, each in turn further subjugating the traditional cultural and social structures of the Hindu population. As for Debal, it seems to have gone into decline around this time, perhaps because the river changed course yet again and silted its harbor, or possibly because the departure of the Arabs led to depopulation.

It is not clear what power the Sūmṛah Dynasty actually wielded in the aftermath of this decline, or indeed whether they remained at Debal or moved their capital to some other part of the Indus Valley, but it is believed that they maintained much of their supremacy by submitting to the sultans of faraway Delhi, for whom they acted as governors of southern Sind. The Delhi sultanate was created in the late twelfth century, when the slave general Quṭb-ud-Dīn Aybak, who had conquered Sind in 1187 on behalf of his master Muḥammad of Ghūr, made himself paramount ruler of the Muslim states and founded what is known as the Slave Dynasty, centered first at Lahore and later at Delhi.

Over the centuries of Sūmṛah rule Sind acquired its enduring pattern of Muslim clan networks in the countryside and mixed populations of Muslims and Hindus in the cities, and developed the syncretism of Muslim and Hindu beliefs that continues to make Sindi religious practices unique in the Indian subcontinent. The tomb of the mystic Pīr Patho, located to the south of modern Tatta, provides a striking example. Pīr Patho, who died in approximately 1300, was a member of the Suhrawardī branch of Sufism, the mystical sect of Islam, yet his tomb also is venerated by Hindus, who know him as Rāja Gopīchand.

Within a few years of Pīr Patho's death the city of Tatta figures in the historic record as an important settlement and port, control of which would secure power over most or all of lower Sind. Its evidently high status reinforces the supposition that it was in some sense a continuation of Debal, the former capital, and that at some point during the twelfth or thirteenth century it had taken over Debal's role as the Indus Delta's main port of call for seagoing ships. At any rate, it was from their base at Tatta that, about 1320, the Sūmṛah rose against Ghiyās-ud-Dīn Tughluq, who became sultan of Delhi in that year. However, in 1333 or, according to other sources, 1351, the Sammā, another Rājput clan, seized Tatta, overthrew the Sūmṛah, and conquered the Indus Delta and the rest of lower Sind.

Unar, the first of the Sammā to take the kingly title of Jām, died in Tatta in 1354 in the midst of rebellions against his rule. His son Jām Junah then successfully defended lower Sind against an attempted invasion by the Mongols and consolidated the kingdom, even mounting attacks on the Punjab and Gujarāt and attracting the vengeful attention of a later sultan, Fīrūz Shāh Tughluq (who reigned at Delhi from 1351 to 1388). The local legend that the Suhrawardī sage Makhdum Jahaniyan (also known as Jahangasht) traveled to Tatta and succeeded in preventing war between the sultan and the Sammā may or may not have a basis in fact, but in either case it reflects the influence that such mystics came to have in the affairs of Sind.

Under Junah's successors Tatta flourished in the role once played by Debal, both as the major entrepôt for trade between the interior of Sind and the Arabian Sea and as the seat of government for lower Sind and, at least when local chieftains were not rebelling, for most of upper (northern) Sind, too. The fifteenth century seems to have been a golden age for Tatta, as the refined and scholarly Qadiri branch of Sufism came to be the leading religious group in the city, which began to attract more and more immigrants from Baluchistan. The greatest of the Sammā rulers was Jām Nizam-ud-Dīn, also known as Jām Nindo, a scholar rather than a warrior, who ruled at Tatta between 1463 and his death in 1509. He is sometimes credited with founding the city, which suggests that he may well have been responsible either for an important building program or for moving its center to a more advantageous site on the banks of the Indus, or possibly both. He is buried on the Makli Hills, beneath an ochre-colored stone cube decorated with bands of daisies, palms, and diamonds alternating with bare surfaces and fronted by a profusion of columns and arches around a false window and balcony.

The Sammā Dynasty did not long survive Jām Nindo. In 1520 Tatta was conquered by Shāh Beg, the head of the Arghūn Dynasty, which governed Kandahār. After forcing Nindo's son Jām Fīrūz into exile in Gujarāt, the new ruler was met with resistance organized by the Suhrawardī teacher Makhdum Bilawal. This resistance soon was suppressed and Bilawal was executed, but the Arghūn Dynasty lasted for only thirty-four years. Shāh Beg's son Mīrzā Shāh Ḥasan, who preferred sailing on the Indus to governing the kingdom, died in 1554 and Tatta fell to an alliance of rebellious Arghūn warriors with Tarkhan clansmen from upper Sind, led by Mīrzā 'Isā Khān, founder of the Tarkhan Dynasty.

One year later Mīrzā 'Isā Khān asked the Portuguese, based at Bassein, to help him in his war against the sultan of Bakhar. When they reached Tatta the governor of the city told them that they were not needed and refused to pay the costs of their journey. In retaliation the Portuguese attacked Tatta itself, killing more than 8,000 people, burning most of its buildings, and looting as much treasure as they could find (including, for example, the blue and white tiles later used to decorate the Jesuit church at Bassein). Following the departure of the Portuguese raiders, Mīrzā 'Isā Khān brought lower Sind back into submission to the Delhi Sultanate, now in the hands of the Mughal Dynasty; in practice, however, control of the region continued to be exercised by Mīrzā 'Isā Khān and his Tarkhan successors.

In 1592 the Mughal emperor Akbar, as distrustful of the Tarkhans as he was of other local rulers beyond his direct supervision, launched the first of a series of campaigns to reconquer lower Sind, and in 1601 the Tarkhan ruler Mīrzā Jānī Beg surrendered Tatta to his forces. Mīrzā's tomb—an octagonal block, decorated with bands of bare and glazed brickwork and inscriptions in Arabic, standing on a sandstone pedestal within an airy courtyard—is one of the most impressive on Makli Hills, as befits the last ruler of Sind able to mount any effective resistance to the centralizing tendencies of the Mughals.

In 1626 Shāh Jahān, the second son of Emperor Jahāngīr, launched the second of his two rebellions against his father and marched his forces, numbering only about 500 men, to Tatta in the hope of using the city as his headquarters. Sharif-ul-Mulk, Jahāngīr's governor of Tatta, brought nearly 14,000 troops to Tatta to resist the prince. They were unable to prevent a brief but destructive siege, which Shāh Jahān called off when he realized that it was futile, and later that year the death of Shāh Jahān's elder brother Parvīz assured his succession to the imperial throne.

Reigning as emperor from 1628 to 1658, Shāh Jahān is best known for ordering the building of the Tāj Mahal at Āgra, but he also gave attention to the city that had spurned his advances in 1626. Its economic and political importance to the Mughal state is evidenced indirectly by the magnificence of the tombs built on the Makli Hills for the governors and other officials appointed by Shāh Jahān to oversee the city's activities. These include the square red-brick monument, embellished with a Persian dome and four towers, built for the minister Dīwān Shurfa Khān in 1639, and the elaborately decorated Mughal-style tomb, set within a high-walled courtyard, that was commissioned by 'Isā Khān the Younger (Mīrzā 'Isā Khān's grandson) for his father and himself ('Isā Khān died in Tatta in 1644).

Mosque of Shāh Jahān, Tatta
Photo courtesy of A.P. / Wide World Photos, New York

Although Shāh Jahān probably never visited Tatta again after becoming emperor, his patronage also is commemorated by the Jāmi Masjid, a mosque in the city that bears the same name as mosques he founded in Delhi and Āgra. The construction of the mosque at Tatta began in 1647, but it was not completed until after his death and the accession of his son 'Ālamgīr (Aurangzeb). It has ninety-three domes and is decorated with mosaics in glazed faience and painted stucco arabesques. Stucco also was used on the frontages of the wood and mud houses that still stand around the mosque, although many of these buildings, which have up to seven stories structured around bamboo frames, have lost the stucco over the centuries.

The last notable mausoleum to be completed on Makli Hills is that of Mīrzā Tungril Beg, who died in 1679. The absence from the cemetery of memorials to later Tarkhan rulers may reflect a decline in their power and wealth, perhaps because the Indus River once again was beginning to change its course, but possibly also because of the impact of frequent rebellions, especially in upper Sind, and wars with neighboring states. As for the Mughal Empire, to which Sind was still subject, it reached the peak of its geographical extent and material wealth under the rule of 'Ālamgīr (1658–1707), and declined thereafter as the British and other western European imperial powers expanded from their various footholds on the coasts. Nevertheless the empire retained great influence for some decades to come, and in Sind it was chiefly responsible for the rise to power of the Kalhora clan, whose leaders it chose as *subadars* (governors) of upper Sind, from 1700, and then, from 1719, of lower Sind as well, thus displacing the Tarkhans.

Nūr Muḥammad Kalhora was governor of Sind in 1739 when Nāder Shāh, the emperor of Persia and Afghanistan, launched the massive invasion of the Mughal Empire that dealt the decisive blow to that dynasty's supremacy in the subcontinent. In 1742 his forces arrived outside Tatta: Nūr Muḥammad fled, and the city was plundered and largely destroyed. After attacking Delhi itself, Nāder Shāh forced Emperor Muḥammad Shāh to surrender all his lands west of the Indus, including Tatta and lower Sind. In 1747, however, Nāder Shāh was murdered by a group of courtiers, and the province was seized by the Afghan ruler Aḥmad Shāh Durrāni. Throughout these changes the Kalhoras, originally loyal to Delhi but content to accept their new masters, retained control of the province, but, having abandoned Tatta, they governed it first from Khudabad and then from Hyderābād, a new city founded by Ghulam Shāh Kalhora in 1768 (not to be confused with Hyderābād, the capital of Andhra Pradesh state in India).

Another factor in the abandonment of Tatta was a change in the course of the Indus River. Beginning in the mid–eighteenth century, the main channel shifted away from the city, causing major changes in the microclimate around Tatta. In effect, the city was cut off from the fertile and humid Indus plain and became an outlying district of Kohistan, the drier, mountainous region to the west that borders on Balūchistān.

Meanwhile, the Kalhoras were superseded in 1782 by the Mīrs or Amirs (rulers) drawn from a Balūchi clan, the Tālpurs. After the death of Fatḥ ʿAlī, the first of the line, Sind was divided among three branches of the dynasty. They cooperated with the British East India Company, which had replaced the Mughals as the paramount power, during the First Anglo-Afghan War (1839–42), accepting the temporary imposition of British garrisons at Tatta, Karāchi, and other strategic sites. The Amirs rebelled, however, when they discovered that Lord Ellenborough (Edward Law), the newly appointed governor general of the company's territories, wanted to make the occupation permanent. On the pretext that the Amirs were disregarding the existing commercial treaties with the company, Ellenborough chose Major General Sir Charles Napier to lead new forces into Sind and Balūchistān. In January 1843 the Amirs, understandably alarmed at Napier's advance, began gathering their own forces in Hyderābād; in February Napier's troops easily conquered the entire province. The Amirs were exiled and Ellenborough appointed Napier governor of Sind—without, at any point in the venture, consulting the British East India Company or the British government—and thus Tatta became part of the British Empire in India, being designated a municipality in 1854.

Over the decades since the British conquest, Tatta has receded into the background of Sindi affairs as Karāchi has grown to become the capital of the province, which was reestablished by the British in 1937 and joined the independent Muslim state of Pakistan ten years later. Today Tatta is the trading center for such regional enterprises as textile manufacturing, sugarcane cultivation, and camel breeding. The dead buried on the Makli Hills, including thousands of ordinary Muslims as well as rulers and officials, now far outnumber those living in the city below.

Further Reading: A great deal of interesting material on Tatta and Debal is included in Henry Cousens's *The Antiquities of Sind, with Historical Outline* (Calcutta: Government of India Central Publication Branch, 1929; reprint, Karāchi and London: Oxford University Press, 1975). *Sind Revisited* by Sir Richard Burton (2 vols., London: Bentley, 1877) records the impressions Tatta and other Sindi cities left on a Victorian mind. Sarah F. D. Ansari's *Sufi Saints and State Power: The Pirs of Sind 1843–1947* (Cambridge and New York: Cambridge University Press, 1992) includes a useful survey of the role of Islam, particularly Sufism, in the history of the province.

—Patrick Heenan

Taxila (Punjab, Pakistan)

Location: About twenty-two miles from both Islamābād and Rāwalpindi, at the axis of ancient trade routes from China, Central and West Asia, and India.

Description: One of the greatest archaeological treasures in Asia. The former site of an important university in the Kingdom of Gandhāra, it flourished from the sixth century B.C. to the sixth century A.D. First discovered in 1852, Taxila's ruins extend some twenty-five square miles and are divided into three cities.

Contact: Pakistan Tourism Development Corporation
House No. 2, St 61, F-7/4
Islamābād 44000
Pakistan
(51) 811001

Taxila's name (Takṣaśilā in Sanskrit) literally means "The City of Cut Stone" and is thought to have been derived from Takṣa, son of Bharata, an incarnation of the Hindu god Vishnu. According to the epic *Rāmāyaṇa,* Bharata settled Taxila and named it after his son, its first king. The epic *Mahābhārata* is said to have been recited for the first time at Taxila. The city also appears in Buddhist legends, including the Jātaka stories, collected in approximately the fourth century B.C., and later in the works of Chinese writers Fa Xian and Xuan Zang.

Sir John Marshall's excavations in the early part of the twentieth century found evidence of four different periods of settlement in Taxila. The first, a site east of the Tamra Nala (Tamra River), could not be dated by Marshall but is believed to have been settled before 1000 B.C. It was followed by three consecutive settlements at Taxila, the Bhīr Mound, Sirkap, and Sirsukh, each of which was abandoned in favor of the newer city. By the seventh century A.D., all of Taxila was in ruins.

Taxila became widely known as a cultural and intellectual center in the sixth century B.C. The city housed the main university in the Kingdom of Gandhāra and was renowned for scholarship in mathematics, medicine, and astronomy. When Alexander the Great invaded India in 326 B.C., following his successful colonization of Bactria and the area that is today Afghanistan, he was met by Āmbhi (Omphis), the ruler of Taxila. A friendly alliance was created between the two leaders, and Alexander the Great and his army camped in Taxila (most probably at the Bhīr Mound settlement), where they rested and enjoyed the hospitality of their benevolent host. Although Taxila possessed abundant resources and had a benevolent administration, subsequent excavations of the area around the Bhīr Mound suggest that Alexander's army probably would have entered an unimpressive town, at least in its physical appearance; the Bhīr Mound most likely resembled a typical Indian village, with small plastered houses lining the winding narrow streets. Nevertheless, the culture and society of Taxila is described with admiration by various members of Alexander the Great's entourage. The guests apparently took part in discussions with philosophers and holy men living in the city. Onesicritus, a former student of Diogenes and Socrates, was ordered to talk with the various religious leaders in the city and note their customs and practices. Although Alexander left a military installation in the city, his influence there was limited by his early demise and the disintegration of his empire.

Over the next two to three hundred years, the city became part of various empires. Following Alexander the Great's death, Taxila became a provincial capital under Mauryan rule. Aśoka, son of the Mauryan king Bindusāra, was viceroy to the city during his father's reign. Aśoka ascended the throne in approximately 272 B.C. A devout convert to Buddhism, Aśoka promoted the religion throughout his kingdom, with the result that many stupas (Buddhist mounds or monuments) were built. It was during this period that the central core of the Dharmarājika Stupa, near the Bhīr Mound, was constructed.

Following Aśoka's death in 235 B.C., the Mauryan Empire began to disintegrate. When the Bactrians (under Demetrios) became sufficiently independent to break away from the Mauryan Empire, Taxila fell into Indo-Greek hands, effectively bridging the gap between East and West. In approximately 170 B.C., the Bhīr Mound was deserted for a new city, Sirkap, which was built by the Bactrians at Taxila. The new settlement was situated to the northeast of the Bhīr Mound, on the opposite side of Tamra Nala. The new city was fortified against the possible invasion of the Śakas, who were then entrenched in northwestern India. Taxila remained part of the Bactrian Empire until the first century B.C., when the Śakas took control of the city and made it their northern capital, to function in congress with their southern capital at Muttra (Mathurā). The Śakas, in turn, were ousted by the Parthians, who ruled the city until the first century A.D., when the Kushāns led by Kujūla Kadphises invaded and captured Taxila.

From the beginning of Kushān rule in A.D. 60 until the city's demise at the hands of invading Huns in the fifth century A.D., Taxila experienced a golden period. The Kushāns constructed the new fortified city of Sirsukh, on a plain to the northwest of Sirkap. The Kushāns were strong advocates of Buddhism and patronized the religion throughout their empire. Several thousand stupas, temples, and monuments were built, drawing pilgrims from across Asia. Images of Buddha were constructed throughout the Kushān Empire, and for 500 years Taxila reigned as the center of Gandhāran Buddhist art. This form combined traditional elements of Indian art with late Hellenistic influences. The area around the Dharmarājika Stupa became the focal point of this artistic activity. Taxila's location at the crossroads of the main trade routes to China, India, and Central and West Asia helped it to flourish as both an intellectual and spiritual meeting ground.

This thriving city would suffer a violent and untimely end. The existence of Sāsānian copper coins in the city suggests that Taxila was invaded by the Sāsānians early in the fourth century A.D., although little else has been found to verify this. The city seems to have been unchanged by such an event. The Chinese traveler Fa Xian visited Taxila in the early fifth century A.D. and commented on the strength of Buddhism and the abundance of stupas and religious architecture there. Taxila's demise came approximately between A.D. 450 and 455, when the Huns invaded and desecrated the city. Thousands of beautiful temples, sculptures, and carvings were destroyed during the invasion. When Xuan Zang visited the city in the seventh century, Taxila was in ruins and had become a protectorate of Kashmir. The importance of Taxila was forgotten, and only rubble remained.

It was left to the archaeologist Sir Alexander Cunningham, the pioneer of excavation on the Indian subcontinent, to bring the city back into public knowledge. Beginning in 1863, he carried out two main excavations and identified the spot known locally as Saraikela to be the site of ancient Taxila. Sir John Marshall continued and expanded on Cunningham's original work, rediscovering the city, its stupas, and temples. Marshall excavated the area around the Bhīr Mound and found evidence of four settlements built one on top of the other. Although he found it difficult to date the earliest ruins, he estimated that the last settlement dated to the second or third century B.C.

One set of ruins Marshall found could possibly date to the reign of the Mauryan king Aśoka; some of the articles found were burnished black objects similar to those discovered in other Mauryan settlements in Muttra (Mathurā) and Sānchi. The unorganized nature of the Bhīr Mound suggests that it was not a planned city like Sirkap and Sirsukh, but a settlement that arose to accommodate surplus population. The east part of the mound appears to have been the housing sector, evolving around a system of squares, possibly differentiated by various professions. Most houses would have had stone foundations and wooden structures supporting the roof. Residents were served by an effective sewage system using both private and public pits. The western part of the mound seems to have had an official, possibly religious function. The Pillared Hall or Temple, decorated with terra-cotta images of gods and goddesses, suggests a religious connection. It is possible that the temple was once a Hindu shrine; if so, this building would be one of the earliest such shrines ever found.

The Dharmarājika Stupa, or Chir Tope, one of Taxila's most celebrated sites, lies east of the Bhīr Mound and Sirkap. The central stupa is thought to date to Aśoka's reign in the third century B.C.; however, the forty-six-foot-high Great Stupa probably was built and expanded in subsequent centuries. The Great Stupa is surrounded by sixteen reinforcing walls that radiate outward, hence its name Dharmarājika, which is derived from the words *dharma-cakra,* meaning "wheel of law." The main structure has four sets of stairs at its principal points, which lead to the top of the stupa base. Surrounding the Great Stupa are many other smaller buildings, stupas, and temples of varying architectural styles; they are thought to have been donated by visiting pilgrims. Of special interest is a chapel in the northeast corner that houses the feet of a huge Buddha, believed originally to have been thirty-five feet high.

The subsequent settlement at Taxila, Sirkap (the name literally means "severed head"), dates from approximately 170 B.C., and was occupied until approximately A.D. 80. Its ruins can be found northeast of the Bhīr Mound, on the Hathial Spur and plains of the valley, to the west of the Tamra Nala. Unlike the Bhīr Mound, it was designed on a uniform grid-like plan. The central street runs north-south and has a series of smaller roads running off it. The whole area was surrounded by a long thick wall, approximately twenty feet thick, thirty feet high, and three miles long. It is estimated that there were seven different phases of construction in Sirkap, of which the earliest dates from the same era as the Bhīr Mound. Most, however, originated during the Parthian occupation of the city, predating an enormous earthquake that destroyed many fine buildings constructed prior to A.D. 50. On either side of the half-mile-long main street were shops, backed by private dwellings. Most of the houses in Sirkap were two to three stories high and had an average of twenty rooms on each floor. The houses also contained an unusual feature, *taikhanas,* underground rooms in which many pieces of sculpture, art, and jewelry have been found.

Almost every street in Sirkap had a stupa or temple. The lovely Apsidal Temple stands east of the main street. It is possibly the most interesting building in the city. Of Buddhist construction, it is roughly rectangular in shape and occupies nearly an entire block. Built on the rubble of a building destroyed in the earthquake of the first century A.D., the temple is approximately seventy-seven yards by forty-four yards and is elevated fifty feet above the street. It can be reached from the main road by a double staircase, which is lined with small monk cells. The stupa has deteriorated beyond recognition, but it is believed to have stood in the apse.

Across the street lies the Shrine of the Double-Headed Eagle, constructed in the first century A.D. The architecture of this building mixes Greek and traditional Indian styles. A double-headed eagle towers over the top of a central niche, between a row of Corinthian pilasters. The eagle was an emblem favored by the Scythians, and later by Russia, Germany, and Ceylon (Sri Lanka). An inscription on a marble pillar (now found in the Taxila Museum) explains that the pillar was erected in 275 B.C., when Aśoka was viceroy of Taxila. It is thought that this pillar was moved from an original site in the Bhīr Mound. Sirkap is full of such interesting buildings, although most of its treasures have been moved to

Excavated ruins at Taxila
Photo courtesy of Embassy of Pakistan, Washington, D.C.

the Taxila Museum. Objects that still can be found in this shrine include toys, jewelry, statues, and domestic items such as utensils, tools, and surgical instruments.

On a hill overlooking Sirkap is the Kunala Stupa and monastery; only a small part of this area has been excavated. According to legend, Kunala was the son of the Emperor Aśoka. His stepmother fell in love with him but was rejected. Embittered, she persuaded her husband to send his son to Taxila as envoy of the city, and then forged a letter with Aśoka's seal accusing Kunala of treacherous actions. The town's leaders were ordered to put out Kunala's eyes, an action that they were loath to perform because of his popularity. Kunala himself ordered that the leader carry out his father's request, and he was blinded. Consequently, the stepmother was executed for her deception. The Kunala Monastery is supposed to have been erected on the site where Kunala lost his eyes. Because of this legend, it has been a popular place for blind pilgrims to visit.

The last of Taxila's cities is Sirsukh, founded by the Kushāns to the northeast of Sirkap after A.D. 80. However, little of this rectangular town has been excavated. It is thought that Sirsukh was developed because a plague devastated the city of Sirkap just after the Kushān invasion. Other factors contributing to the decision might have included the belief that conquerors should honor their success with a new city, and the difficulty that the Kushāns envisioned in defending a hilly city such as Sirkap.

Following the construction of the new city, the Kushāns erected several thousand stupas and temples. The most impressive of these are at Jaulian, Pippala, and Mohra Moradu, to the southeast of Sirsukh. The buildings excavated at Jaulian are perhaps the best examples of Gandhāran architecture in Taxila. The monastery and stupa at this site are celebrated internationally; they are not only the best preserved buildings in Taxila, but the stupa is the only one in Pakistan that indicates the original splendor of its decoration. Today both a guard and a modern roof protect the stupa. Jaulian consists of three complexes: the courts of the main and lower stupas and the monastery. In the main court the spherical base of the stupa is decorated with images of large meditating Buddhas, which date to the fifth century A.D. Another image of Buddha may be found to the east of the steps leading to the main stupa. This figure, known as the Healing Buddha, is believed to aid pilgrims after they place their fingers in his navel. The lower stupa court is surrounded by chapels. Part of this court is sectioned off to protect the reliefs of five stupa bases, which are decorated with Buddhas attended by lions, elephants, and naked gyrating figures, all carved out of plaster. The monastery lies to the west of the lower court and once was surrounded by statues of Buddha. It lies in the middle of twenty-eight monk cells, which originally were plastered and painted.

The older sites at Mohra Maradu and Pippala also feature the remains of Buddhist monasteries and stupas. Mohra Maradu dates to the beginning of the third century A.D. The votive stupa at this complex is in extremely good condition and is complete apart from the original paint and gilt work; it has been protected behind wooden doors in one of the monk cells. The base of the main stupa is decorated with delicate reliefs of Buddha, although their heads have been removed for safety (they may be seen at the Taxila Museum). The structures at Pippala originated during the first century A.D. but were rebuilt in the fifth century. A well-preserved plaster stupa is located in a monk's cell.

Excavations at Taxila have uncovered a wealth of historical, artistic, and architectural treasures in its three main cities. Although only a fraction of the ruins have been excavated, some of the oldest and best preserved examples of Gandhāran architecture may be found there. Some fifty separate archaeological sites and the Taxila Museum are now open to tourists and scholars, revealing the city's fascinating past.

Further Reading: The three-volume work by John Marshall entitled *Taxila: An Illustrated Account of Archaeological Investigations* (London: Cambridge University Press, 1951) is a most comprehensive investigation of the city and its monuments and details Marshall's own excavations of the city. *Some Ancient Cities of India* by Stuart Piggott (London, New York, and Bombay: Oxford University Press, 1945) contains an exhaustive chapter on Taxila, detailing the history and monuments of the site (it is, however, somewhat dated). For a brief history and basic information, turn to the *Collins Illustrated Guide to Pakistan* by Isobel Shaw (London: Collins, 1989). A concise description of the archaeological remains at Taxila is provided by *A Handbook for Travellers in India, Pakistan, Nepal, Bangladesh, and Sri Lanka*, edited by L. F. Rushbrook Williams (London: Murray, 1975), although this work lacks much in the way of historical detail. *Pakistan* (Singapore: APA, 1990), one of the better travel guides to Pakistan, includes an excellent entry on Taxila. Informative, clear, and easy to use, it covers the three main sites and includes a discussion of the main stupas and temples.

—A. Vasudevan

Thanjāvūr (Tamil Nādu, India)

Location: Two hundred eighteen miles south of Madras, the principal city of the state of Tamil Nādu in southern India.

Description: The headquarters of a district of the same name, Thanjāvūr (also known as Tanjore and Tanjāvūr) is renowned for its Rājarājeśvara (or Bṛhadīśvara) Temple (a UNESCO World Heritage Monument), a temple to Siva built by King Rājarāja I of the Cōḷa Dynasty in the early eleventh century.

Contact: Government of India Tourist Office
154 Anna Salai
Madras 600 002
Tamil Nādu
India

Thanjāvūr's history until the thirteenth century is inextricably associated with the history of the Cōḷa Dynasty of southern India, and it is famous almost exclusively because it contains one of the greatest temples built by the Cōḷa kings in the early years of the eleventh century. The original name of this temple, as recorded in royal inscriptions of the period, is Rājarājeśvara, which means "the temple of the god of Rājarāja," the king who built it. However, since the seventeenth century it has been known by its Sanskrit name, Bṛhadīśvara, which literally means "great god."

The Cōḷas are known as Cōdas in the third-century B.C. inscriptions of the king Aśoka of the Mauryan Dynasty, which in its heyday ruled a vast tract of country from the southern flank of the Hindu Kush range in Afghanistan to at least the southern state of Karnātaka in India. The Cōdas are included in these inscriptions among the "borderers" of the empire. Usually this has been taken to mean that the Cōda territory lay outside the limits of the Mauryan Empire, constituting a region immediately beyond the Aśokan frontier. But the meaning of the inscriptions is ambiguous: "border" or "limits" could also denote territory just inside the frontier of the Aśokan Empire, designating the ancient Cōdas as subjects of the Aśokan realm.

Such finer points aside, the Cōḷa heartland was the Cauvery Delta, at the head of which Thanjāvūr is located, and which is one of the most important foci of political power in southern India. As the Aśokan inscriptions suggest, the Cōdas had some kind of state organization in the third century B.C. Although no archaeological evidence supports this hypothesis, a third-century B.C. brick-built wharf, equipped with sturdy wooden poles for anchoring boats at the site of Kāverīpattinam in the Cauvery Delta, suggests that the Cōdas had organized to the point of establishing transportation, and possibly trade routes, with other regions.

The modern Tamil Nādu coast, on which the city of Madras is located, is known as the Coromandel Coast, a name derived from a Tamil word designating the land of the Cōḷa people. In the early centuries A.D., this seaboard witnessed extensive maritime activities stretching in one direction to the Mediterranean via the Indian Ocean and in the other to southeast Asia, even as far as China. Coins from Rome, China, and other countries, along with pottery and glassware, have been found throughout this region.

That the Cōḷas were present in the Cauvery Delta during this period is well attested by the evidence furnished by a distinct genre of Tamil documents known as the Śangam literature. Its dating, although uncertain, probably falls within the first three or four centuries A.D. From the miscellaneous descriptions in this literature, a composite picture emerges of life in the ancient Cōḷa land—a picture fleshed out by anecdotal material all too often missing in other historical treatments of India. The scholar K. A. Nilakanta Sastri, paraphrasing the Śangam literature, clearly conveys the impression of rural prosperity. In the numberless small villages of the Cōḷa country, he wrote,

> bright-faced maidens, wearing tasteful jewels and innocent looks, keeping watch over the paddy drying in the open, flung their curved ear-ornaments of gold at the fowl that came to eat the grain. Little children, with anklets on their feet, played about on the thresholds of houses, with their toycarts with three wheels and no horses, and shouted out to people to get out of their way.

Karikāla, the first major Cōḷa king, reputedly raised the flood-banks of the Cauvery River, "along whose banks the sweet cane's white flowers wave like pennoned spears uprising from the plain." Thus the association between the Cōḷa kings and the construction of irrigation devices along the Cauvery is fairly old, and this tradition matured significantly during the reigns of the later and more famous Cōḷa kings. The fertility of the Cauvery Delta depends on the silt brought by the Cauvery River, which is so rich that manure was largely unnecessary in premodern agriculture there. This is a classic rice-growing area of the subcontinent, depending mostly on the region's two monsoon seasons.

For the period between the end of the Śangam Age around the fourth century and the revival of Cōḷa power in the Cauvery Delta in the ninth century, little is known of the Cōḷa kings except that they were eclipsed in the south by the power of the Pāṇḍya Dynasty of Madurai and in the north by the Pallava kings of Kānchipuram in the hinterland of modern Madras. The Cōḷa revival took place under King Vijayālaya,

Stairway leading to a Brahmā temple, Thanjāvūr
Photo courtesy of National Geographic Image Collection, Washington, D.C.

who reputedly captured the city of Thanjāvūr and built a temple there in honor of the goddess Durgā. Thus Thanjāvūr obviously existed as a city before the mid–ninth century A.D., but for how long we cannot say. The first Cōḷa capital was at Urayūr (near modern Tiruchchirāppalli, upstream along the Cauvery), but it appears that the Cōḷa capital was shifted from Urayūr to Thanjāvūr during this period. Thanjāvūr has been mentioned as the place where Vijayālaya's successor, Āditya I, was crowned. He reigned between A.D. 871 and 907. His successor, Parāntaka I, died in 93, and for almost thirty years the Cōḷa Kingdom was politically weak. But with the accession of Rājarāja I in 985, the dynasty came to overshadow all others in the region from Sri Lanka in the south to the Krishna-Godāvari Delta in the north and the Mysore Plateau in the west. The Cōḷa Dynasty endured until at least the middle of the thirteenth century.

The zenith of this dynasty was reached under Rājarāja I (ruled 985–1012 or 1014) and his son Rājendra I (ruled 1012 or 1014–44); as the Cōḷa capital, Thanjāvūr, likewise, enjoyed its greatest prosperity during their reigns. Rājendra I is considered the greatest Cōḷa monarch because he directed an expedition as far east as the Bengal Delta, and under him the naval force of the Cōḷas went unhindered to southeast Asia as far as Borneo and Sabah. The entire southern region including Sri Lanka was, of course, within the orbit of his direct power. But for Thanjāvūr, it was Rājendra's father, Rājarāja I, who had the greatest impact; it was under his rule that the Rājarājeśvara Temple of the god Siva was constructed.

Although the exact date that construction began on the temple is unknown, scholars have surmised that the project might have been initiated in the nineteenth year of the king's reign (1003–04), when the written record first mentions the title Rājarāja. The date of the temple's completion and consecration has been recorded in an inscription on the structure's wall: on the 275th day of the 25th year of his reign, Rājarāja I dedicated the gold-plated copper finial of the temple tower.

Many other inscriptions are engraved throughout the temple walls, most of them detailing the various precious objects donated by the king, his queens, and various members of the royal family. The inscriptions also mention a large number of villages, the revenues derived from which were supposed to have been spent on the upkeep of the temple. Extensive lands were donated to the temple from all over the Cōḷa Kingdom. The revenue had to be paid in both paddy (threshed, unmilled rice) and gold, although in the case of the villages in the Cōḷa heartland, the emphasis was on paddy. The details of this revenue as they are inscribed in the temple suggests that the Cōḷa kings conducted precise land revenue surveys throughout their kingdom.

About 160 lamps and torches were needed to light the temple complex, and for the supply of *ghee,* or clarified butter (plain vegetable oil is not appropriate in a temple), the king made extensive grants to shepherds and cowherds in different parts of his kingdom. Each lamp was allocated a particular number of milk buffalo and cows. In inscription after inscription, such details are set down, to be effective "as long as the sun and the moon endure." Even now, this great temple is a living entity where thousands of devout Hindus worship every day. The focus of life in Thanjāvūr remains the Rājarājeśvara Temple.

The temples of this and later periods in southern India served a variety of economic functions: landlord, employer, consumer of goods and services, and even bank. The temples had their own treasuries and were intricately linked to the economy of their geographical areas in various ways. Temple functionaries were divided into three major groups: treasurers (recruited only from among the Brahmans, or priestly class), general functionaries or "servants" of the temple, and accountants. The temple servants included, among others, security guards and women versed in various fine arts, including singing and dancing.

The temple complex measures 790 feet east to west and 400 feet north to south. One enters the complex from the east, passing through three separate entrances. The outer entrance marks a fortification wall with bastions, located on the inner side of a moat. The second entrance, called a *gopuram* (Tamil for temple gateway), is located in an inner enclosing wall and leads to the *gopuram* of the large courtyard. The courtyard measures roughly 500 feet by 250 feet, and in its center stands the main shrine, which covers an area of roughly 180 by 100 feet. The shrine itself, called the *vimana,* is topped by a tower that rises more than 200 feet from the floor of the courtyard. The *garbhagriha* (sanctum sanctorum, or the chamber in which the deity is located) measures 325 square feet. The cella has two stories, each topped by an overhanging cornice. The tower rises 13 stories above this and is topped by an 85-square-foot granite block estimated to weigh 80 tons. Holy bulls, or Nandis, adorn the four corners of this granite block. The gilded copper finial, which is 12.5 feet high and contains 253 pounds of copper and 35 pounds of gold, rises with this slab as its base.

The plinth of the *garbhagriha* is approximately 16 feet high, rising in two moldings. The deity in the center is a huge, monolithic *liṅgam* (phallic stone, emblem of Siva), which rises two stories above the *garbhagriha* floor. A corridor extends between the outer and the inner walls of the sanctum, thus forming a circumambulatory path around the deity. All the walls on the lower story, except the eastern wall, through which is the central opening to the sanctum, are decorated with murals depicting scenes from mythology and religion. The original murals were painted over in the seventeenth century with new images. The walls of the second story are decorated with bas-relief stone panels depicting 81 of the 108 *karaṇas* (dance positions) of Bharatonatyam.

In front of the *garbhagriha* is a hall, or *ardhamaṇḍapa,* which served as the bathing hall of the deity. A bathing platform stands in the center of the hall. The large pavilion, or *mahāmaṇḍapa,* in front of the bathing hall contains six pillars arranged along both axes. Another pavilion, the *mukhamaṇḍapa,* in front of this arrangement, marks the mouth of the central shrine complex, which is entered by a sweeping flight of broad steps. Finally, in the same axis but at a little distance from the *mukhamaṇḍapa* stands the pavilion of Nandi, or the holy bull, which gazes at the image of his lord, Siva. The figure of this bull is a huge monolithic sculpture, measuring 12 feet high, 20 feet long, and 9 feet broad, and weighing an estimated 25 tons. Away from this complex, along the inner line of the enclosing wall on all four sides, is a multipillared, raised platform giving access to a large number of cellas used for different votive purposes.

No description can adequately convey the sheer beauty of the innumerable large sculptures of different gods, goddesses, and semidivine beings set in various parts of the shrine walls. Records show that, in addition to stone sculptures, as many as sixty-six metal images were donated by the king and members of the royal family. Of this number, eleven images were of gold and silver, but perhaps the true glory of the Cōḷa sculptures in the temple are the masterly bronze figures.

The Cōḷas moved out of the political focus in the middle of the thirteenth century. The Cauvery Delta, including the city of Thanjāvūr, then became a bone of contention between the Pāṇḍya kings of Madurai and the Hoyasala kings of the Mysore Plateau, or south Deccan. The grip of the Pāṇḍya kings was perhaps more secure; in the temple precinct there are two Pāṇḍya inscriptions, one recording the construction of the temple to Amman and the gift of a village to go with it, and the other recording donations of land in several villages for this particular temple. Perhaps as the result of an invasion from Delhi in the fourteenth century, the Muslims exerted some influence on this area, but they were soon overshadowed in the region by the emerging power of the Vijayanagar kings of south Deccan. Again, inscriptions in the temple precinct record gifts from two Vijayanagar kings. In the sixteenth century a general of the Vijayanagar Kingdom declared himself independent in this area, and one of his successors in the early seventeenth century established a separate Nayaka Dynasty in Thanjāvūr. They have left behind some architectural remains both in the town and elsewhere in the area. The palace in Thanjāvūr, architecturally unedifying but important for its library (containing a large collection of Tamil and Sanskrit manuscripts and old bronze images), dates from the Nayaka period.

In the late seventeenth century, the Marāṭhās in the service of sultans of the kingdom of Bijāpur in the Deccan usurped power in the Thanjāvūr area. The Marāṭhās made gifts of jewels to the temple and undertook some works of renovation in the temple compound.

The British first appeared on the scene in 1749, grabbing a small part of the territory of these Marāṭhās. With their base in Madras, the British could not ignore the Cauvery Delta. They sought help from the Thanjāvūr Marāṭhās in their struggle for power in southern India against the French on the one hand and Hyder Alī of Mysore on the other. Christian missionaries entered the area as early as the first half of the seventeenth century, with their principal base at Nāgapattinam in the delta. In Thanjāvūr itself a large church—Schwartz's Church—was established in the late eighteenth century.

The British soon fell out of sympathy with the Thanjāvūr Marāṭhās, and Thanjāvūr became a "protected state" under the British in 1776. Soon afterward, the Marāṭhās exercised sovereign authority only within their fort in Thanjāvūr and its immediate vicinity, subject to the control of the British government. On the death without heirs of the Marāṭhā chief in 1855, even their titular dignity dissolved, and Thanjāvūr became a full-fledged British territory.

Since the middle of the nineteenth century, Thanjāvūr has remained fairly quiet. The British shifted the seat of power in the Coromandel Coast to Madras, and Thanjāvūr's importance became restricted to its great temple. The Rājarājeśvara Temple came under the protection of the central Archaeological Survey of India, which has its headquarters in Delhi and a regional office in Madras, which maintains a regular conservation staff in the temple. Thanjāvūr derives substantial economic benefits from the pilgrim and tourist trade associated with the temple. The only major change in the nonreligious sector of the city's life in recent years has been the establishment of a university, which focuses mainly on the historical and archaeological heritage of the Cauvery Delta.

Further Reading: *The Imperial Gazetteer of India,* volume 23 (Oxford: Clarendon, 1908), offers under "Tanjore" a still useful and concise historical and geographical introduction to the site. For the Cōḷas, the best introduction is K. A. Nilakanta Sastri's *The Cōḷas,* volume 1 (Madras: Madras University, 1935; second edition, 1975). For information on the temple, see S. R. Balasubrahmanyam's *Middle Chola Temples: Rajaraja I to Kulottunga I (A.D. 985–1070)* (Faridabad, Haryana: Thompson, 1975).

—Dilip K. Chakrabarti

Tianjin (China)

Location: Just inland from the Yellow Sea's Bohai Bay in northern China, approximately sixty-five miles southeast of Beijing.

Description: Tianjin was the site of an important grain storage area as far back as the Yuan Dynasty (1234–1368). Owing to its strategic location on both inland waterways and ocean shipping lanes, Tianjin grew rapidly to become an important commercial center. In the mid–nineteenth century, Tianjin was frequented by numerous foreign powers seeking a foothold in the growing China market. Today Tianjin is China's third largest city; like Beijing and Shanghai, it has been designated a municipality and is centrally governed from Beijing.

Contact: Beijing Tourism Bureau
28 Jianguo Menwai Avenue
100022 Beijing
China
(1) 5158252

Located some sixty-five miles southeast of Beijing on the North China Plain, the city of Tianjin has long been one of China's most important commercial centers. First mentioned in records of the Song Dynasty (960–1276), Tianjin gained importance under the Mongolian Yuan Dynasty (1234–1368) and became a garrison town and shipping station during the Ming Dynasty (1368–1644). Treaties with foreign powers in the nineteenth century opened the city up to the British, German, Japanese, and other powers seeking a trading foothold in China. During these events and subsequent periods of political turmoil, the city's location near the Yellow Sea on the Bei River and Grand Canal often involved Tianjin in military conflict. But its location also proved to be the city's saving, for it became extremely valuable to both foreign and domestic governments.

Construction of the Grand Canal, a man-made link to the rice paddies of the Lower Yangtze, was critical to the development of Tianjin. Created and expanded under the Sui Dynasty (581–618), the Grand Canal's extension to the north was primarily the work of Sui Yang Di. By 609 the canal ran from the southern city of Hangzhou to as far north as the Tianjin and Beijing region. This enormous undertaking effectively facilitated the transportation of grains grown in southern China to the northern capital and expanding frontier regions. Although the Grand Canal remained in use during subsequent dynasties, not until the Yuan Dynasty did Tianjin began to develop, primarily as a place to store grain. As Emperor Kublai Khan extended the canal to the newly chosen capital at Beijing, the Mongols needed a place to store grain and other goods shipped from the south, and Tianjin—situated near the coast—became that place. When Khan's extensions were complete, Tianjin found its geographical location even more advantageous: now the city was situated strategically on both established inland and ocean trade routes.

To protect the important and growing city of Tianjin, fortifications were built during the fifteenth century, turning the town into a walled garrison. The trade that had started centuries before flourished; the town's river and canal were crowded with small boats and junks, and sailors who had docked in the nearby ocean port visited Tianjin's well-stocked shops. A Dutch envoy visiting Tianjin in the seventeenth century marveled at the city's bustling atmosphere. The envoy reported Tianjin to be a heavily populated city with numerous temples and shops. He also noted the volume of trade, remarking "it would be hard to find another town as busy as this in China—because all the boats which go to Beijing, whatever their port of origin, call here, and traffic is astonishingly heavy."

During the nineteenth century, however, the conflicting desires of foreign traders and the Chinese government would bring trouble to Tianjin during the Second Opium War (or Arrow War). The balance of trade had begun to shift during the 1820s, when Chinese exports of silk and tea were surpassed by the large-scale British import of opium (from India); this proved devastating to the Chinese economy. China's efforts to combat this problem resulted in the Opium War of 1839–42, and in their defeat by the British. The Treaty of Nanjing ended the war and gave the victors increased access to China through the cities of Canton (Guangzhou), Amoy (Xiamen), Foochow (Fuzhou), Ningbo, and Shanghai.

Events would soon prove that this agreement did not satisfy either side. The British proceeded to push north to the forts of Dagu, which guarded the mouth of the Bei River and the gate of Tianjin. Under the command of Lord Elgin and Baron Gros, the British and French forces found the local governor lacking "full powers" to negotiate trade, and in 1858 the British seized control of both the outlying forts and the city of Tianjin. Horrified at the loss of this important and strategic city, the Qing rulers gave officials full power to negotiate with the British on behalf of the court and sent them off to Tianjin in June of that same year.

Negotiations were conducted between the British and Chinese envoys led by Guiliang, an aging grand secretary. The British sought several concessions from the Chinese, including the opening of additional ports to foreign trade and a resident minister in the Chinese capital at Beijing. The Chinese resisted the idea of a diplomatic residence in the capital, but Elgin and his assistant Horatio Lay held firm. Continuing to protest, Guiliang signed the Treaty of Tianjin (Tientsin) on June 26, 1858. The treaty also included the opening of ten new ports for trade; allowed unrestricted travel for foreign missionaries throughout China; granted foreigners the right to travel throughout China with a passport issued by their consul and signed by Chinese authorities; and allowed unrestricted foreign travel within thirty-three miles of the open ports.

Not forewarned of the final contents of the treaty, the Qing emperor Xianfeng was furious at this outcome. The greatest outrage was the concession to allow foreign diplomatic representation within China, a privilege that seemed to shatter the Qing notion that China was the universal ruler of all countries. To have foreign diplomats living within the imperial capital signaled the end of the tributary system the Chinese had adopted with their subject countries for thousands of years. Eager to reassure the emperor of his sovereignty (and frantic to save his own life), Guiliang tried to show the court that the treaty was the only way to preserve peace. Besides, Guiliang reasoned, the treaty should not be regarded as a sacred contract. If in the future the terms of the treaty should become unbearable, the emperor need only renounce the agreement as mismanaged politicking undertaken by lowly courtiers, after which the treaties would become "waste paper." At another time, Guiliang remarked to the ruler that the foreigners probably would not even like Beijing, particularly if made to pay their own keep during the dusty and bitterly cold winter months.

The Chinese and British envoys were scheduled to meet the following year, 1859, to exchange their ratified treaties. Guiliang and Elgin, however, first met at the Shanghai Tariff Conference in October. More at ease now that negotiations were farther away from the imperial capital, Guiliang attempted to regain lost ground and persuade Elgin to reconsider establishing residences in Beijing. Swayed by Guiliang's charm and skill, Elgin made a gentleman's agreement that if the treaty ratifications were properly exchanged in Beijing, the diplomatic residence could be set up in another area of China.

The following year, Frederick Bruce was named British Envoy Extraordinary and Minister Plenipotentiary to China; he was instructed to go to Beijing for the treaty exchange and then to set up residence in Shanghai. When Bruce arrived in China in May, Chinese authorities attempted to change the treaty ratification venue to Shanghai, which enraged Bruce. Determined to reach the capital, Bruce set sail north to the mouth of the Bei River near Tianjin, where the Chinese had set up a river blockade and reinforced the Dagu forts. Trying to avoid violence, the Chinese agreed that Bruce could go on to Beijing, but that he should take the less visible route north of the forts. Bruce refused, indicating that the importance of the treaty and his diplomatic position required that he be allowed to proceed honorably to Beijing through Tianjin instead of skulking through the back route. With this goal, Bruce ordered his forces to clear the river blockade. On June 25, 1859, some 600 British marines and engineers entered the mouth of the river, where they promptly got stuck in the thick mud of low tide. Their vulnerable position spelled disaster when the two Chinese forts suddenly erupted with gunfire, killing more than 400 of the British troops and seriously wounding their admiral.

Embarrassed and overpowered, the British retreated to Shanghai, where Bruce was criticized by the Crown for his aggression. Still determined to finalize the Treaty of Tianjin, the Crown sent Lord Elgin back to China with an accompanying force of some 41 warships, 143 transports, and more than 11,000 British and French troops. The huge envoy arrived at the mouth of the Bei River in August of 1860. Horrified at the proximity of the forces to the imperial capital, Guiliang once again was sent by the court to Tianjin. As before, the British insisted on being received in Beijing, and Elgin set off to the capital accompanied by some 500 soldiers.

On the road to the capital, Elgin sent a group led by Harry Parkes to ensure the reception would be properly arranged. Parkes, however, was met and subsequently taken captive by the Imperial Commissioner, Prince Yi. Livid at such continued insults, Elgin and his forces descended on Beijing, forcing the emperor to flee to Manchuria. Nearly alone in the imperial capital, Elgin, seeking revenge for the insult to the Crown and the execution of several of the British captives, burned the fantastic Summer Palace of the Qing. With the emperor hiding in Manchuria and his younger brother Prince Gong left to negotiate with the barbarians, the Treaty of Tianjin was ultimately finalized on October 18, 1860, the very day the Yuan Ming Yuan (Summer Palace) was destroyed. Gong also signed the Conventions of Beijing, which made even further concessions to the foreign powers; this included increased indemnity, British control of Kowloon Peninsula (including Hong Kong), and, for French Catholic missionaries, the right to own property inside China. Furthermore, Tianjin was secured as a port open to foreign trade.

Eager to protect their newly gained territory, the British forces now readied their arms in support of the Qing. During the treaty negotiations, the growing Taiping forces in southern China had been steadily gaining ground and converts in their quest to overthrow the Qing and establish their own Heavenly Kingdom. The Taipings' avowed dedication to Christianity had originally piqued the interest of foreigners, who found the Manchurian Qing leaders unfathomable and unreachable. As the Taiping leader Hong Xiuquan's religious zeal grew uncontrollable and began to border on the insane, however, foreigners lost interest in the Taiping cause and became more concerned about keeping territories gained under treaty with the Qing. Ultimately, the Ever-Victorious Army (equipped and led by foreign mercenaries) marched alongside Qing forces and led to the defeat of the rebellion.

With the threat of invasion eradicated, foreign powers began building their concession areas in Tianjin. Before the end of the nineteenth century, the British had been joined by a number of other foreign traders from countries that also had gained concession rights from China, including the Japanese, Germans, Austro-Hungarians, Italians, and Belgians. Similar to the concessions in Shanghai, each country's territory was a self-governed enclave complete with its own schools, medical facilities, and churches.

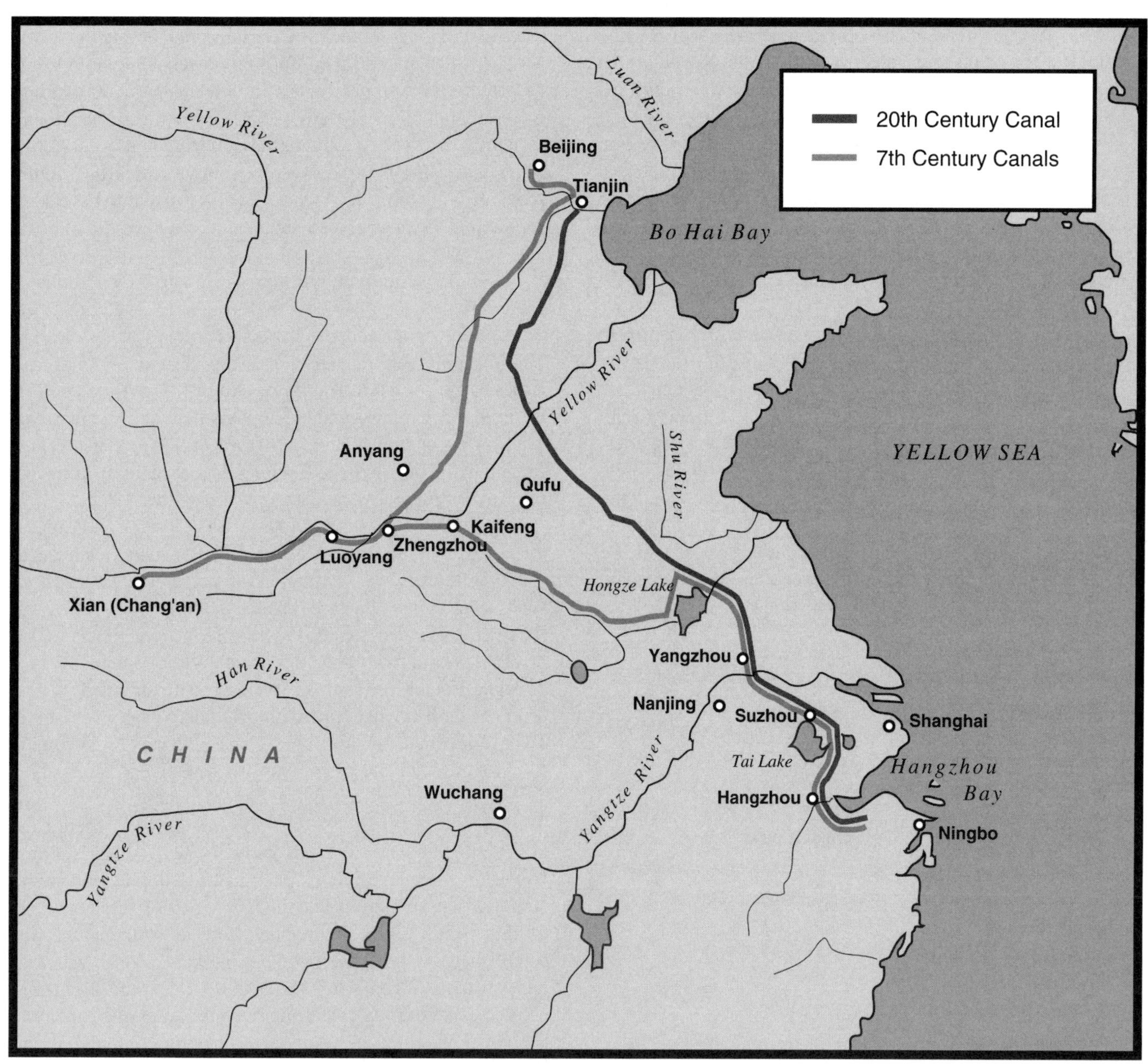

Map illustrating the course of the Grand Canal in the seventh and twentieth centuries, showing the position of Tianjin
Illustration by Tom Willcockson

The growing presence of Christianity, and the Catholic Church in particular, touched off a violent uprising in the city in 1870. Catholics in Tianjin had recently built an impressive new church on what previously had been the site of an imperial park and Buddhist temple. Tianjin's citizens objected to the location of Notre Dame des Victoires, and rumors began to spread throughout the city that the church and its French-run orphanage were secretly kidnapping local children and subjecting them to hideous torture and sexual abuse. When many Chinese grew reluctant to hand children over to foreigners, orphanage nuns began to offer a premium for each child brought to the facility. The premium, combined with an inherent distrust of foreigners, only served to reinforce the rumors.

As Chinese crowds began to harass foreigners in Tianjin, the French consul complained to Chinese authorities and demanded that the hecklers be silenced. Local officials did nothing, however, allowing Chinese agitation to grow.

Frustrated by the lack of response, the French consul Henri Fontanier rushed into the magistrate's quarters and, drawing a pistol, shot and killed a Chinese bystander. The Chinese who had gathered outside erupted in fury at the death of the bystander. In the violence that followed, Fontanier and his assistant were killed, as were several French traders and their wives. The church and orphanage were burned, and the two priests and ten nuns running the orphanage were slaughtered. In the melee, three Russians were mistaken for French and killed, and a number of British and American churches also were burned. Frantic to calm the city, foreign gunboats rushed to the nearby port, where they anchored, demanding punishment for those responsible for the massacre.

The anti-foreign sentiments expressed in Tianjin in 1870 proved to be an indication of problems to come. In the late nineteenth century, the Boxer Rebellion was cause for serious concern among foreigners living in or trading with China. Stemming from a variety of Chinese secret societies, the Boxers' original goal in 1899 was "Overthrow the Qing, wipe out the foreigners." Later that same year, the motto had changed significantly to "Support the Qing, wipe out the foreigners." The Boxers were particularly opposed to the Christian religion promoted by the foreigners, as indicated by the following phrases penned by the rebels:

> There are many Christian converts
> Who have lost their senses,
> They deceive our Emperor,
> Destroy the gods we worship,
> Pull down our temples and altars,
> Permit neither joss-sticks nor candles,
> Cast away tracts on ethics,
> And ignore reason.
> Don't you realize that
> Their aim is to engulf the country?

And the catchy jingle:

> Their men are all immoral;
> Their women truly vile.
> For the Devils it's mother-son sex
> That serves as the breeding style.
>
> No rain comes from Heaven,
> The earth is parched and dry.
> And all because the churches
> Have bottled up the sky.
>
> When at last all the Foreign Devils
> Are expelled to the very last man,
> The Great Qing, united, together,
> Will bring peace to this our land.

By 1900 the Boxers had expanded in numbers and were viewed as a threat to the peace in foreign-held regions. That spring, foreign forces shot randomly at bands of Boxers, attempting to frighten them into submission. That tactic backfired in mid-June, when Boxers attacked both Beijing and Tianjin, killing a number of Christians and looting the towns. As the violence continued, foreign powers sent more troops to protect their interests, but in June 1900, 2,000 foreign troops marching from Tianjin to Beijing were attacked by the Boxers and forced to retreat after suffering heavy casualties. Later that same month, Western troops successfully routed the Qing from the Dagu forts at Tianjin in order to have some protection for their forces should the violence turn into an all-out war.

Fully supported by Empress Dowager Cixi, the Boxers continued their attacks on foreign- and religious-held areas. Seeking to end the battles, a foreign army of some 20,000 combined Japanese, Russian, British, French, and American troops left Tianjin on August 4 and marched on Beijing. The Empress and her nephew fled the city and set up a temporary capital at Xian, where they ruled until the foreign forces finally defeated the Boxers. The peace treaty known as the Boxer Protocol was enacted in September 1901.

After the fall of the Qings in 1912, foreign and Chinese trade continued to prosper in Tianjin. The marshy lands surrounding the city were exploited for salt, and other industries such as glass manufacture, chemical production, and textile factories expanded rapidly. When the accumulation of silt forced a new harbor to be built some thirty-one miles away at Tanggu, Tianjin lost some of its bustle but continued its high level of involvement in international trade. Some years later in 1919, Nankai University was established in the city, becoming a very successful and prestigious private Chinese university.

With the advent of the Sino-Japanese war in 1937, Tianjin was occupied by the Japanese but was spared the destruction the latter wrought on other cities such as Nanjing. Under the Boxer Protocol signed in 1901, Japan was free to station troops in Tianjin, and the Japanese took full advantage of this right. When the puppet state of Manchukuo was established in 1932, the last Qing emperor, Puyi, was kidnapped from Tianjin and taken north to "rule" the newly created Japanese state. Despite occupation by the Japanese, Tianjin maintained its status as a thriving commercial and industrial area.

Industrialization of the city continued after the founding of the People's Republic of China (PRC) in 1949. The communists concentrated on expanding the existing production of chemicals and textiles, while encouraging new industries such as rubber, metallurgical, and consumer products including cigarettes, bicycles, electronics, cameras, and watches. In China, Tianjin-made Flying Pigeon bicycles and Seagull watches are still prized as high-quality products. Tianjin would, however, along with the rest of China, suffer in the chaos that marked the early years of the PRC. The Suppression of Counterrevolutionaries Campaign, begun in 1950, threw Tianjin into a period of violence as some 492 people (mostly former nationalists or secret society members) were executed, many of them publicly. During the same campaign, government authorities used the terror wrought by these proceedings to attack a growing religious group, the Yiguan Dao (Way of Basic Unity Society). Using mass meetings to accuse suspected members, the communists coerced some 15,000 people per day into ending their religious affiliations; this occurred at the height of the terror in April 1951. In 1967, violence broke out again as the fanatical Red Guards of Mao's wife Jiang Qing fought among themselves in Tianjin. Gathered together to demonstrate against the treatment of ethnic Chinese in Indonesia, factions of the Guards rioted for several hours. By the time army troops and local workers finally calmed the groups, some 200 youths had been injured. As soon as the riot had ended, the factions began fighting again, and local officials were forced to ask for outside help.

Today, Tianjin continues to be an important port and industrial center. The city suffered a large earthquake in 1976 that all but destroyed the nearby town of Tangshan; after being closed to international visitors for a number of years, Tianjin rebuilt its industrial base and resumed production. In 1984, factories in the city became incorporated into a nationwide experiment, which took control away from the central government and made factory leaders responsible for the administration of the plants. A second university, Tianjin University, has been built, and agricultural production in the city's outlying areas has been encouraged. Throughout the centuries, Tianjin has maintained its importance in China's transportation and industrial sectors, helping it to become the country's third largest city. As such, Tianjin has been designated a municipality; along with Beijing and Shanghai, it falls under the direct rule of the national government.

Further Reading: John King Fairbank has written two excellent historical accounts of China, including the city of Tianjin. The first, *China: A New History* (Cambridge, Massachusetts, and London: Belknap Press of Harvard University Press, 1992), offers a detailed and extensive look at the several thousand years of Chinese history. The second book, *The Great Chinese Revolution 1800–1985* (New York: Harper and Row, 1986; London: Chatto and Windus, 1987), concentrates primarily on events that shaped modern China. Jonathan Spence's *The Search for Modern China* (New York and London: Norton, 1990) provides another in-depth and readable account of the last four centuries, detailing how people, powers, and events have shaped the People's Republic of China. Readers wanting more information on Mao Zedong and his influence on post-1949 China will enjoy Stanley Karnow's *Mao and China* (New York: Viking, and London: Macmillan, 1972). Two excellent tourist guides with detailed information on Tianjin are *Fodor's China* by John Summerfield (New York: Fodor, 1994) and *China: A Travel Survival Kit* by Alan Samagalski, Robert Strauss, and Michael Buckley (second edition, Victoria, Australia, and Berkeley, California: Lonely Planet, 1988).

—Monica Cable

Tokelau (Territory of New Zealand)

Location: The three coral atolls of Tokelau—Atafu, Nukunonu, and Fakaofo—together comprise a total land area of 3.9 square miles. Situated between latitudes 8 degrees and 10 degrees south and longitudes 171 degrees and 173 degrees west, Tokelau lies 300 miles north of Apia, Western Samoa.

Description: Tokelauans traditionally have attributed their origins to: 1) immigrants from Samoa, Rarotonga, or Nanumanga in Tuvalu, or 2) supernatural creation on Tokelau. Contact with Europeans was sporadic until the mid–nineteenth century, when missionaries and traders arrived and Peruvian slave raids and dysentery epidemics decimated the population. The Union Group, as Tokelau was then known, became a British protectorate in 1889, part of the Gilbert and Ellice Islands Colony in 1916, and a New Zealand territory in 1948. Its inhabitants, who speak both the official Tokelauan language and English, are British subjects and New Zealand citizens, and many Tokelauans have emigrated to New Zealand for employment. Fakaofo, which maintained sovereignty over the other atolls until 1918, accommodates most of Tokelau's population of approximately 1,600 persons. Nukunonu, with the fewest inhabitants, remains entirely Roman Catholic, Atafu is Protestant, and members of both churches live on Fakaofo.

Contact: Official Secretary
Office for Tokelau Affairs
P.O. Box 865
Apia
Western Samoa

Tokelau consists of three low-lying coral atolls extending from northwest to southeast, between Tuvalu (formerly the Ellice Islands) and Samoa. Each atoll lies on top of a reef and out of view of the others, with its village located on the sheltered, western side. Atafu, the northernmost atoll, has the smallest area (0.8 square mile) and the highest elevation (15 feet). Nukunonu, the largest atoll (2.1 square miles), lies about sixty miles northwest of Fakaofo, whose sixty islets form a triangle of one square mile. Tokelau is also the name of an islet in the northeast corner of Nukunonu. Situated 110 miles south of Fakaofo is Olosega, now politically associated with American Samoa, whose history is intimately bound with that of Tokelau.

Tokelauans are predominantly Polynesian, but the date of the atolls' initial settlement remains unknown. However, narrative, genealogical, and historical evidence suggests that Fakaofo was colonized in the mid–sixteenth century, possibly by drift voyages of people from Samoa; the two island groups share linguistic and cultural affinities. Tokelau's oral traditions, recounted in songs and stories at lively gatherings, preserve these events and other *mea mai anamua*, "things from the past."

Legends relate that the first humans on the atolls, Kava and Pio, came from Samoa. Significantly, the word *tokelau,* the indigenous name of the island group, means "north" in Tokelauan, and one of its variants, *to'elau*, denotes "northeast" in Samoan. Several *tala* (tales) attribute the Tokelauans' origins to immigrants from Rarotonga or Nanumanga in Tuvalu, others to a maggot that grew inside a beached fish pecked open by a bird. Yet other stories, echoing themes in Polynesian cosmogony, tell that the first humans, Kava and Singano, both men, were "hatched" from stones. The god Tiki-tiki (Maui) and the woman Talanga emerged from the stones next, and became the ancestors of the human race. According to another Fakaofo creation story, the Tokelau islands were submerged beneath the ocean until Tiki-tiki and Talanga dredged them up with a fishing line; a different version recalls that Lu, the son of Tiki-Tiki and Talanga, pulled up Nukunonu and Atafu by grabbing them by the roots of coconut trees.

Te Vaka, the son of Kava Vasefanua, the first historical chief of Fakaofo, figures prominently in Tokelau *tala* chronicling Fakaofo's ascendance over the other atolls, a supremacy that lasted until 1918. In the Fakaofo account of the campaign, the war leader launched a swift attack on Nukunonu and massacred its villagers, laying claim to all the land his warriors were marching over, until they reached a spot where a woman had hung her skirt as a *tapu* sign forbidding them to proceed further. The women of Fakaofo, in turn, tried to frighten off Atafu raiders by starving them out, then by assembling a mock battle fleet of canoes; the raiders left, towing the daughter of the Fakaofo chief behind them, until she was eaten by sharks. Te Vaka retaliated in kind and pursued the Atafu people as they fled to other islands; generations later, Tonuia of Fakaofo planted a colony on Atafu.

Tokelau *tala* also commemorate Fakaofo's sovereignty over Olosega, formerly called Swain's Island after a whaling captain who purportedly "discovered" it in the 1820s. The Olosegans resented paying annual tribute to the god *Tui Tokelau,* and the high chief of Fakaofo warned the tribute-bearers that they would be punished for harboring hostile intentions. Their canoe was wrecked in a storm, with only one survivor; a drought struck Olosega, and famine depopulated the island, leaving it open for Fakaofoans to colonize.

The first European to visit Tokelau was British Commodore John Byron, who had been commissioned to survey

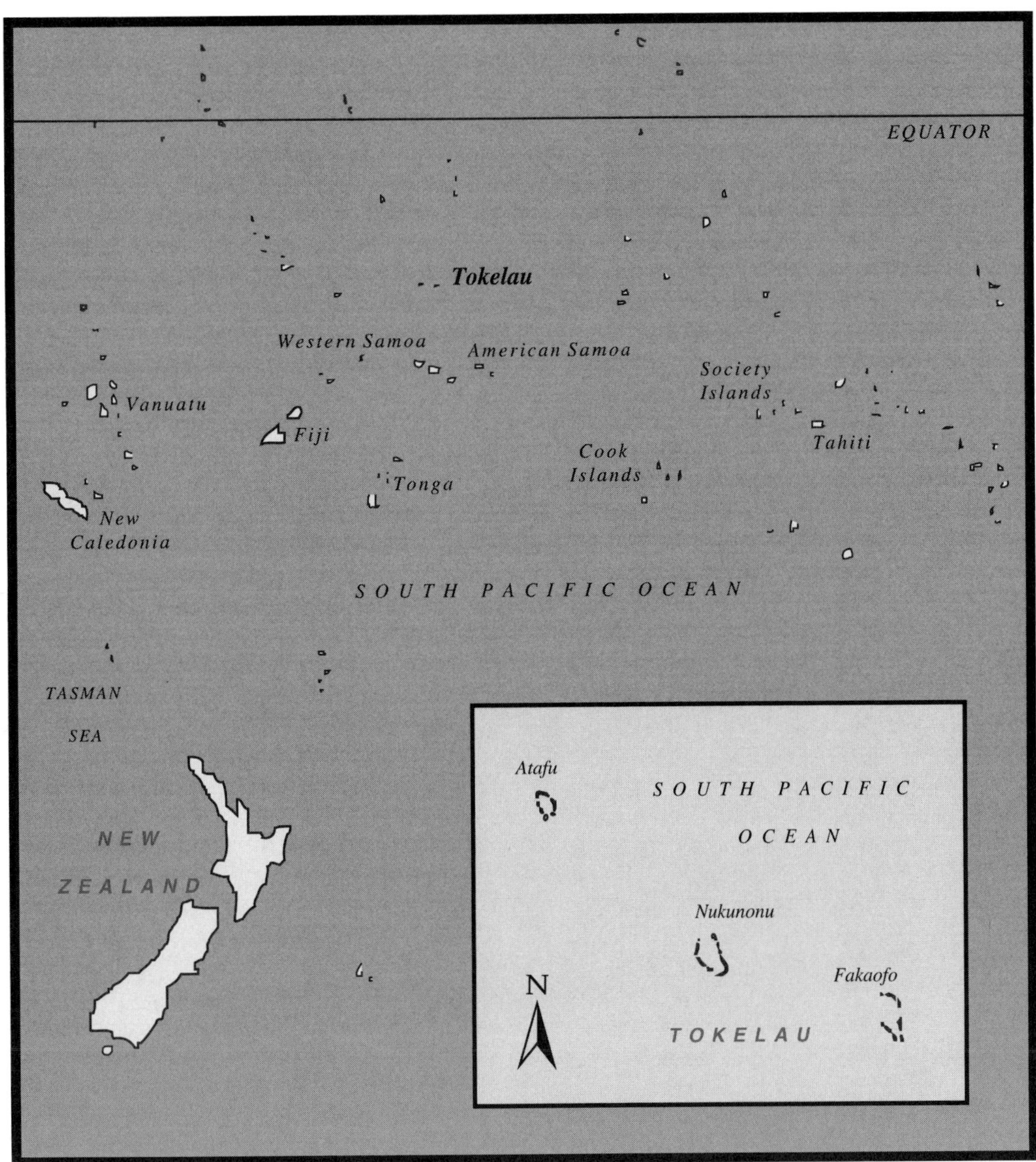

Map of Tokelau, showing its position relative to New Zealand
Illustration by Tom Willcockson

the South Atlantic (especially the Falkland Islands, believed to be the gateway to the Pacific Ocean and its commercial riches), to explore the west coast of North America, and to search for a northwest passage to Hudson's Bay. Sailing the *Dolphin,* Byron made landfall on the Falklands but then, ignoring his secret instructions, headed for the southwestern Pacific, intending to locate the mythical Isles of Solomon and their troves of gold and silver. On June 24, 1765, he reached Atafu, which appeared devoid of life except for lush vegetation and hordes of seabirds, its population having been driven off by Te Vaka; Byron renamed it Duke of York Island in honor of his royal patron. The crew replenished the ship's store of coconuts, which they had found an effective remedy for scurvy, before setting their course for the Ladrones Islands (the Marianas), anxious to conclude "the longest, hotest, and most dangerous Run that was ever made by Ships before."

On June 6, 1791, Captain Edward Edwards stopped at Atafu while searching for the *Bounty* mutineers; he had learned from Henry Hillbrandt, a mutineer captured on Tahiti, that Fletcher Christian had proposed to settle on Atafu. Edwards left the uninhabited island and sighted Nukunonu six days later, naming it Duke of Clarence Island; the people assembled on the shore fled before he could question them about Christian's activities.

Whalers called at Tokelau from the 1820s. In 1835 Captain Smith of the American whaler *General Jackson* identified Fakaofo as D'Wolf's Island, after his ship's owner, becoming the first Westerner to note the existence of a third atoll. Tokelau remained largely unexplored by Westerners until 1841, when the United States Exploring Expedition, formed in part to improve navigation in the Pacific Ocean, extensively surveyed the atolls, along with 278 other Pacific islands. Unaware of Smith's finding, the expedition, under the command of Lieutenant Charles Wilkes, designated Fakaofo as Bowditch Island after Nathaniel Bowditch, author of the classic navigation text *The New American Practical Navigator.*

When the expedition reached Atafu on January 25, 1841, the inhabitants unrolled mats and other wares, indicating their desire to trade, and invited the foreigners to stroll through their village. Horatio Hale, the expedition's ethnologist, conducted a detailed study of the islanders' customs and language. From the presence of double-hulled sailing vessels and the islanders' reports that their high chief lived on Fakaofo, Hale surmised that the people were living only temporarily on Atafu.

Fakaofo's residents—Hale estimated a population of 500 to 600 persons—received the expedition members cordially but showed great reluctance when the strangers inspected the enclosure that housed the Tui Tokelau. The expedition found no inhabitants on the nearby island of Olosega, rumored to have been visited in 1606 by the Portuguese navigator Pedro Fernández de Quiros.

During the 1840s, Samoan missionaries, assisted by a young convert from Nukunonu named Takua, converted that atoll's population to Roman Catholicism. In 1846 a famine in the wake of a devastating hurricane drove people from Fakaofo to seek relief on a nearby island, but a storm disrupted their voyage; the castaways landed on Uvea (Wallis Island), where they too were converted to Roman Catholicism by Marist missionaries. Six years later, a French priest named Father Padel arrived at Fakaofo to transport its population, devastated by another hurricane, to Uvea; the people demurred, until a French sailor accompanying the priest burned the god house of the Tui Tokelau. The majority of the 490 islanders who moved to Uvea became Catholics; only 90 of their compatriots remained on Fakaofo.

Delegates of the London Missionary Society arrived at Fakaofo in 1858, but the chief and his main counselors opposed a Samoan teacher's plan to settle on the atoll, arguing that he would starve. In 1861 the society dispatched two Samoan teachers, Maka and Mafala, to Atafu; their success on that atoll encouraged them to resume their campaign on Fakaofo. The chief there remained obdurate but allowed individuals who wished to adopt Christianity to move to Atafu; seventy-nine residents who opted for exile were blown off course and landed in Samoa. Several returning castaways died of dysentery, which quickly raged through the population, killing 64 of Fakaofo's 261 inhabitants. This calamity presaged an even greater disaster.

From September 1862 to April 1863, Peruvian slave raiders swept through Polynesia, snaring people from thirty-four islands. The Peruvian government had abolished slavery and the annual tribute of the Andean Indians in 1854; those rulings, coupled with an increase in cotton and rice cultivation fueled by the American Civil War, forced hacienda owners to look for alternative sources of cheap agricultural and domestic labor. An 1861 law authorizing the introduction of "Asiatic colonists"—ostensibly Chinese workers—paved the way for the "recruitment" of Polynesian laborers. At the forefront of the movement was Joseph Charles Byrne, a self-styled emigration expert whose enthusiastic appeal to Peruvian President Ramon Castilla to import New Hebrideans for agricultural and domestic work seemed, partly for geographical reasons, more practicable than the recruitment of Chinese workers. This system of indentured servitude frequently devolved into legally sanctioned slavery.

In February 1863 the Peruvian ship *Rosa Patricia* stopped at Olosega and signed on an American who had set up a copra plantation there, as recruiter for the island group, in all probability enticing him with an offer of "$10 a head or $1,000 for 'a goodly number.'" The "blackbirders," as the raiders were called, selected sixteen of Fakaofo's strongest men. A second "recruiting vessel," the *Rosa y Carmen,* arrived at Fakaofo and obtained forty-four men; its captain sent another boat to pick up four more men and seventy-six women and children. Slave ships carried off seventy-six of Nukunonu's residents and thirty-seven men from Atafu.

In a letter to one of his London Missionary Society colleagues, Maka, the Samoan pastor of Atafu, provided an arresting, eyewitness account of the raiders' methods:

> The captain . . . placed some things into the hold of the vessel—the best of the cloth, red cloth, and shirts, and trousers, and white and blue calicoes; and some things he kept on deck. Then the captain said to the men, "Look to the cloth on deck and that in the hold, and see which to choose." . . . But some of the crew were hidden in the hold, armed with cutlasses. . . . The chief was standing over the hatchway, when some of the crew seized him and threw him down into the hold. . . . Then the hatchway was immediately closed down upon them all.

Maka, whose own family was spared, refused to procure "recruits," despite the promise of payment in cash and clothing. All told, Tokelau lost 253 people— 47 percent of the estimated population at the time of the slavers' arrival.

Islanders who survived the harrowing journey to Callao, Peru, quickly succumbed to the endemic diseases, to the strange diet and routine, and to the often brutal living conditions awaiting them, as well as to severe depression. Humanitarian individuals and groups finally pressured the Peruvian Government in April 1863 to prohibit the disembarkation of Polynesian islanders who had been procured against their will. Further, in 1864 the Peruvian Government gave France 125,000 francs as reimbursement and indemnity for the harm suffered by French nationals and protected subjects. Of the thirty-seven persons who were repatriated to Polynesian islands (barely 1 percent of those taken to Peru from the region), none returned to Tokelau; the sole Tokelauan who managed to escape from Peru died of tuberculosis soon after returning home.

The depopulated Tokelau islands attracted traders and beachcombers of Polynesian, French, Portuguese, German, Scottish, and American nationality who married local women. One of these individuals, Jules Tirel, established a copra plantation on Olosega in the 1840s or 1850s. By the turn of the century, the populations of Fakaofo, Atafu, and Nukunonu had rebounded or even exceeded their pre-1862 figures.

In 1877 the British high commissioner of the western Pacific in Fiji declared jurisdiction over British nationals in the Tokelaus and other islands that previously had not been annexed or protected by treaties, in anticipation that these locations might prove useful as stations for a trans-Pacific cable. This ruling excluded the native inhabitants. The protectorate became official on June 22, 1889, when Commander C. F. Oldham raised the British flag in the Tokelau islands.

In 1916 Great Britain annexed the Tokelaus, by then known as the Union Group, as part of the Gilbert and Ellice Islands colony, abolishing the Tokelau office of *aliki* (high chief). Tokelauan institutions continued to provide leadership at the local level, however, with the participation of the *taupulega* (council of elders), *faipule* (village representative and commissioner of the court), *pulenuku* (village mayor), and *failautuhi* (village clerk). Whereas the *taupulega* on Atafu comprises the heads of each family, elders and heads of extended families form the Nukunonu council, and only the elders participate in Fakaofo's council.

Governance from distant Banaba (Ocean Island), where Tokelauans went to work in the phosphate mines, engendered improvements in medical services on Tokelau but complicated the island group's administration, so in 1925 New Zealand assumed authority over the four atolls, controlling the group from Western Samoa. The Tokelau Islands Act of 1948 formally made Tokelau a territory of New Zealand. Designated the Tokelau Islands under the Tokelau Nomenclature Ordinance of 1946, the group of atolls became known officially as Tokelau in 1976.

Overcrowding, compounded by the shortage of natural resources, has led to emigration, primarily to Western Samoa before 1962; after Western Samoa became an independent state that year, more people moved to New Zealand to take advantage of the Tokelau Resettlement Scheme instituted by that country during the 1960s to ease overcrowding and bolster Tokelauans' earning power. In addition to New Zealand's annual subsidies to the islands, the more than 2,000 Tokelauans living in New Zealand make substantial contributions to their native economy as well.

Since September 25, 1980, the New Zealand minister of foreign affairs has appointed the administrator of Tokelau, with the actual powers of administration delegated to the official secretary for Tokelau affairs in Apia, Western Samoa. A 1983 treaty between New Zealand and the United States demarcated Fakaofo from Olosega, recognizing U.S. claims to Olosega as part of American Samoa. The declaration derived, in part, from Eli Jennings' claim that he had been given the land by an Englishman, Captain Turnbull, in the 1850s. Tokelauans, on the other hand, assert that the *tala Vale O Pou*, which retells the deeds of Pou, the last high chief of Olosega, validates their ownership of the island.

The forty-five-member General *Fono* (Assembly) of Tokelau, with equal representation from the three atolls, handles financial matters and makes recommendations to the New Zealand Parliament. Villagers elect their local *faipule* and *pulenuku* through universal adult suffrage. The village women's committees, working with Tokelau health care personnel, have improved significantly village sanitation, maternal and child health, and nutrition.

During the 1980s, the South Pacific Commission instituted a fisheries training program in Tokelau to generate employment for the islanders, and a tuna cannery opened in 1990 to follow up on this effort. Further, during the 1980s New Zealand appropriated a 200-mile exclusive economic zone around the island group, another measure designed to improve catches.

Trouble beset the atolls in February 1990, however, when the cyclone Ofa ravaged the coconut crop, one of Tokelau's economic mainstays. As well, rising sea levels precipitated by global warming threaten to submerge the atolls. Yet a favorite skit performed on Tokelau—based on the decimating slave raids of the 1860s—attests to the islanders' resilience in the face of calamity: women *faluma* (clowns) dress as foreign sailors from a slave ship, brandishing weapons as they drag unwilling "captives" from among the audience.

Further Reading: *Historical Dictionary of Polynesia* by Robert D. Craig (Metuchen, New Jersey, and London: Scarecrow, 1993), and *Pacific Islands Year Book,* edited by John Carter (fifteenth edition, Sydney and New York: Pacific, 1984) contain sections that describe Tokelau's history, government structure, and economy. Gordon MacGregor's *Ethnology of Tokelau Islands* (Honolulu: Bernice P. Bishop Museum, 1937; reprint, New York: Kraus, 1971) highlights Tokelau's material culture, social organization, and history. *Slavers in Paradise: The Peruvian Slave Trade in Polynesia, 1862–1864* by H. E. Maude (Stanford: Stanford University Press, 1981) details the scope and impact of the slave raids on Tokelau and other Polynesian societies. An essential complement to these studies is *Songs and Stories of Tokelau: An Introduction to the Cultural Heritage,* edited by Allan Thomas, Ineleo Tuia, and Judith Huntsman (Wellington, New Zealand: Victoria University Press, 1990). Written from Tokelauan perspectives, the book shows how storytellers weave traditional and contemporary themes into their compositions.

—Maria Chiara

Tōkyō (Tōkyō, Japan)

Location: Pacific coast of Honshū, Japan's main island; located on the Kantō Plain, bordered by hills to the west and Tōkyō Bay to the east.

Description: Tōkyō is the largest and most densely populated urban region in the world, consisting of more than 25 million people living in 23 metropolitan wards (*ku*) and a vast number of satellite suburbs that have grown to keep pace with a rapidly expanding population. The site of repeated fires and earthquakes, Tōkyō has been built and rebuilt, often literally out of the ashes. With a history going back only about 400 years, Tōkyō is a relatively young city. In spite of its youth, Tōkyō has emerged as the political, financial, industrial, and cultural nexus of Japan.

Site Office: Japan National Tourist Organization
6-6,Yurakucho 1-chome
Chiyoda-ku, Tōkyō
Japan
(3) 3502 1461

Japan's diverse topography is reflected in the makeup of Tōkyō, much of which lies in the Kantō Plain, the largest tract of low-lying terrain in the country. The heart of metropolitan Tōkyō is located at the mouth of the Sumida River, which flows into Tōkyō Bay in the east. To the west and north of the plain lie volcanic mountain ranges, including Japan's highest mountain, Mount Fuji. Several broad rivers flow south and east through the Kantō Plain. However, with Tōkyō located near a fracture in the earth's crust, earthquakes are a constant threat.

On the surface it is a typical modern city, brash and dynamic, seemingly indistinguishable from other metropolises. In fact, many of Tōkyō's modern public landmarks are imitations of famous landmarks found in the West. Yet the Japanese make an important distinction between *omote* (front, exterior, public facade) and *ura* (back, interior, private space). Tōkyō has a modern facade that covers an older, often hidden interior. Elevated highways crisscross streets that have retained the same pattern for hundreds of years. Behind the broad avenues that contain chic department stores one finds a maze of ancient, winding passageways so narrow one can barely squeeze through them to find the tiny shops within. Corporate obelisks of glass and steel, and chunky, graceless concrete apartment complexes overlook diminutive gardens with precisely spaced bushes, flowers, and carefully cultivated miniature *bonsai* (dwarf trees). The old and the new, the gargantuan and the delicate, the refined and the shabby are frequently juxtaposed in Tōkyō.

Archaeological remains show evidence that the Kantō Plain was inhabited as early as 3000 B.C. Yet until the sixteenth century, it was made up of little more than fishing hamlets and farming villages. Its story, however, really begins in the tenth century, with a legend of thwarted ambition and uncanny events.

Although the Kantō Plain possessed a natural port to its east and defensive hills to the west and north, and although it held considerable space in which to expand, the center of Japanese politics, commerce, and culture lay to the west, in such cities as Kyōto, the ancient capital and home of the emperor, and Ōsaka, with its lively commercial trade. The Kantō Plain was seen as a remote, underpopulated, lawless region. Yet it was to this site that a minor nobleman of the Taira clan, Masakado, came when he turned his back on the imperial court of Kyōto.

The reasons for his leaving Kyōto are unclear and range from the lofty (unjust treatment) to the pragmatic (unfulfilled political aspirations). Building himself a power base on the Kantō Plain, Masakado set himself up as an independent ruler in defiance of the emperor in 935. The emperor sent forces to vanquish him. Masakado's last battle took place in the province of Shimōsa. According to legend, he was beheaded in Shimōsa, but his head flew on "wings of wrath" to the village of Shibaski on the Hibiya Inlet.

To those in west Japan, Masakado was a petty and insolent rebel; to the impoverished farmers and fishermen in the east who were resentful of the haughtiness and arrogance of those in west Japan, Masakado became a hero. A mound was built over the place where the head of Masakado was buried and a pillar erected over the mound. According to folklore, the spring where his head was cleaned for burial became charged with magic. This spring later became especially important as it flowed into what is now Tōkyō's business district.

For centuries, the stone pillar stood at the site where Masakado's head was buried. But in the rebuilding that took place after the 1923 earthquake, the pillar was moved to a part of Tōkyō where land was less valuable. Bad luck befell those in the area where the pillar had stood. Businessmen died suddenly or committed suicide. Companies failed. Accidents occurred. Once the headstone was restored with an elaborate commemorative inscription, the problems ceased. To this day, Masakado is remembered with small offerings of fruit, twigs, splashes of sake, and flowers left by neighborhood office workers at the base of the monument.

It was not until the fifteenth century that the Kantō Plain again rose to prominence in Japanese history. In 1457, a minor feudal lord, Ōta Dōkan, built a castle on a cliff not far from the sea, in the place where the Imperial Palace now stands. According to legend, the goddess Benten guided Dōkan up the bay toward the spot. In the form of a fish known locally as a *konoshiro*, she jumped from the waters of the bay in front of a certain hill. Clearly, she wished a castle to be built

A view of the Ginza, Tōkyō
Photo courtesy of Japan National Tourist Organization

there: *kono shiro,* although written with different characters, means "this castle." Located near the mouth of the Sumida River, the land became known as Edo, which means "Mouth of the River."

Famed as an excellent military strategist, able administrator, and gifted poet, Dōkan was slain in 1486 at the command of his own lord, who appears to have been jealous of his vassal (or perhaps simply suspicious of his loyalties). The castle and the town surrounding it soon fell into neglect and were essentially forgotten. Considered the founder of Tōkyō, Ōta Dōkan is today remembered with a bronze statue that stands outside the Tōkyō Metropolitan Government headquarters.

In 1590, Edo and seven other eastern provinces were given by Toyotomi Hideyoshi to his ally Tokugawa Ieyasu in exchange for territory along the East Sea Road (Tōkaidō). Ieyasu's senior retainers protested, claiming that the land Hideyoshi offered stood between the infertile hills to the west and swampland to the east, and that ultimately this was a ploy to push Ieyasu aside, as he was now Hideyoshi's most powerful rival. Ieyasu, however, accepted the eastern provinces.

When Hideyoshi died in 1598, he left his five-year-old son in the care of a regency council headed by Ieyasu. Within two years, Ieyasu maneuvered his opponents into armed insurrection and destroyed them in 1600 at the Battle of Sekigahara. In 1603 the title of *shōgun* (hereditary military governor) was granted to him by the emperor. Kyōto, the city of the emperor, still retained its official, if empty, status as the capital of Japan. Edo, Ieyasu's city in the east, surrounded by defensive hills and an easily fortified port, became the unofficial capital.

In 1590, the rudimentary castle built by Ōta Dōkan was in an advanced state of decay, surrounded by an impoverished village of fewer than 100 thatched hovels. By 1616, it was a city of more than 150,000 residents, with a palace of gilded pavilions surrounded by an extensive system of moats and bridges. The form of governmental and social organization Ieyasu devised in his thirteen-year rule survived two and one-half centuries through a line of fourteen descendants. Whether Ieyasu is regarded as a self-serving tyrant whose political repression held Japan back from progress, or as a hero who established a period of unbroken peace that enabled arts, crafts, and commerce to flourish, his shadow still looms over Japan and his spell still holds sway in the city he made famous as the administrative center of Japan.

The castle Dōkan built at the top of the bay was rebuilt by skilled surveyors and engineers who devised an ingenious form of defense. The castle was surrounded by a long spiral of moats that wound outward to the boundaries of the surrounding land. A supporting pattern of strategically placed bridges, gates, high stone walls, and thirty-six lookout towers stood where roads into and out of the castle crossed the moat, which made use of existing waterways. The castle lay in the innermost ring of the spiral and was itself made up of several fortresses surrounding the keep and principal fortress.

In order to maintain control over the feudal lords, the third Tokugawa *shōgun*, Iemitsu (Ieyasu's grandson), implemented a policy in 1634 in which all feudal lords were required to spend alternate years in Edo, away from their own fiefs. Wives and children of the feudal lords lived permanently in Edo as virtual hostages. Because of the concentration of aristocracy in Edo, thousands of craftsmen, merchants, and others came to the city to set up shops, banking houses, and other commercial enterprises. By 1720, Edo was the largest city in the world, with 1.3 million people.

Edo was divided into two main areas. The *shitamachi* (low city) to the east of the castle, lying in the flatlands around the bay and river deltas, was occupied by the common class and contained merchants, artisans, and laborers. The *yamanote* (high city) to the west of the castle, situated in the mountainous region, was occupied by the aristocracy and their retainers.

Within the *shitamachi* area was a prosperous commercial district known as Nihombashi (Bridge of Japan), bisected by the Nihombashi River. Starting out as a fish market that supplied the castle's needs and sold the excess catch to the public, the district grew to encompass different kinds of foods and eventually nonfood products.

Kanda, north of Nihombashi, and Kyōbashi, south of Nihombashi, were districts belonging to craftsmen such as plasterers, lacquerers, carpenters, swordsmiths, and dyers. The Ginza district, southeast of the castle, was well known for its silversmithing and minting of silver coinage.

As the town grew and prospered, commercial areas spread, especially along highways leading in and out of the city. Because of the biennial residency policy imposed on feudal lords, there were always large numbers of people moving to and from the city. Thus such places as Shinagawa on the Tōkaidō Road to the south, Shinjuku on the Kōshūkaidō Highway to the west, and Senju on the Nikkokaidō Road to the north thrived as towns of inns and entertainment districts at the outskirts of the city.

One of the most famous of these areas was Yoshiwara, established in 1617 as a specially zoned district for prostitution and entertainment. Originally located close to the Nihombashi district, after a fire in 1657 it was relocated to Asakusa in the northeast, where it virtually became a city unto itself. A moat was dug around it, both to keep nonpaying customers from entering or leaving undetected and to keep prostitutes from escaping. Most of the prostitutes were young girls from the countryside, sold without their consent to brothel owners by impoverished parents. However, as elsewhere in Japan, a strict hierarchy existed here, creating an aristocracy and lower class within what was called the "floating world"—a marginal world of prostitutes, gamblers, and entertainers within the larger social world of respectability and order. A top courtesan (*tayū*) in this "floating world" was an accomplished woman, although of humble birth, skilled in the arts of poetry, flower arranging, the tea ceremony, various musical instruments, card games, and sensory arts. A provincial stood little chance of attaining the status of *tayū*. The lowest rank was occupied by the *jōro* or *yuna*.

The *yamanote* districts to the west and southwest of the castle, where the aristocracy had their lavish homes, were marked by large, spacious tracts of land that were thinly populated. While the *shitamachi* district covered only 16 percent of Edo's surface, it supported about 179,000 people per square mile. The *yamanote* district, however, covered 69 percent of Edo's surface but supported only 36,000 people per square mile. In times of fires and earthquakes (all too frequent occurrences in Edo), the densely populated *shitamachi* area tended to sustain more damage and loss of life than the spacious *yamanote* section.

Many religious, cultural, and intellectual institutions can be found clustered north of the castle today because, according to ancient tradition, the northeast was an unlucky direction, known as a *kimon* (demon gate), a passage through which malevolent forces could enter. It was common practice for a settlement or village to protect itself spiritually by erecting a shrine or temple on its northeast side. In 1626, on the hills of Ueno northeast of Edo Castle, the third Tokugawa *shōgun,* Iemitsu, had the impressive Kanei-ji Buddhist temple built. Soon other temples and shrines followed to form a defensive spiritual shield. Along with the temples grew libraries, which in turn attracted scholars, paving the way for the many schools, research centers, museums, and parks one finds today in the districts of Ueno, Hongō, and Kanda.

Iemitsu was also responsible for Japan's becoming isolated from other countries. The move came after a century of uneasiness and outright violence in response to the spread of Christianity. Catholic missionaries, brought to the shores of Japan in 1549 by St. Francis Xavier, had made hundreds of thousands of converts, prompting the ruling class to question whether Japanese Christians could be entirely loyal to the emperor and his *shōgun*. Persecution began gradually in the late sixteenth century and grew in the seventeenth, culminating in the suppression of a 1637 Christian-led revolt in which 37,000 people were massacred at Shimabara on the island of Kyūshū. By 1639 Christianity was virtually eradicated and the country was officially closed to foreigners.

By the nineteenth century, the power of the *shōgun* was in decline. A series of famines from 1833 to 1836 led to unrest in the countryside among rural peasants. There were also problems in the urban region. Over the many years of unbroken peace, the samurai aristocracy had essentially become an unproductive consumer class, leading to the rise of a significantly wealthy merchant-commercial class. The hierarchical line separating the samurai aristocracy from the *nouveau riche* blurred as the ruling government itself became increasingly in debt to a commercial class that was beginning to resent its second-class status.

In addition, Japan felt pressures from Western nations wanting it to open its ports to foreign trade. By 1854, when Commodore Matthew Calbraith Perry of the U.S. Navy forced Japan to open some ports to international trade, the *shōgunate* was already buckling. By the 1860s, social and economic uncertainty had led thousands of people to leave once-flourishing Edo. The population, once 1.4 million, dropped to 600,000.

It was in this climate that interest in the emperor was awakened. For 1,000 years, the status of the emperor was as a quasi-mythical symbol in Kyōto from which the *shōgun* officially derived his right to rule. This legal technicality was now used against the *shōgunate;* if the emperor could give power, he could also take it away. In the winter of 1866–67, supreme governing power was returned to the seat of the emperor; a sixteen-year-old named Mutsuhito of the Meiji line ushered in the Imperial Meiji Restoration (1868–1912).

One of the first decisions of the new government was to move the imperial court from Kyōto, the ancient capital of the emperor, to Edo, the place where the *shōguns* had exercized their power. In order to offer solace to Kyōto, Edo's name was changed to Tōkyō (Eastern Capital) and Kyōto's name was changed to Saikyō (Western Capital), thus suggesting that the two were equivalent in importance. However, in time this formality was dropped; Tōkyō became the exclusive seat of power, and Kyōto maintained its old name and new status as the abandoned seat of government. With this turn in events, Tōkyō's population began to rise again and land value increased.

The Meiji era is known for its powerful, activist reforms in attempting to modernize Japan, which had not changed in more than 250 years. Such reforms included the abolition of the distinction between aristocratic and common persons, the establishment of prefectures with appointed governors instead of feudal domains, universal schooling, and various land and tax reforms as well as a constitutional government.

Tōkyō itself became a showcase to prove Japan's eagerness to enter into the modern era. The change was remarkably rapid. The city was physically converted along Western lines. Low wooden buildings and boat canal transportation were replaced almost overnight with gas illumination, multistoried brick-faced buildings, and steam trains.

When the Meiji government abolished the system of mandatory biennial aristocratic residence, many feudal lords returned permanently to their homes outside of Tōkyō, thus leaving extensive tracts of vacant land. Eventually most of the districts south of the castle (now the Imperial Palace) were given over to governmental ministries. In 1890, the first Diet Building was erected in Kasumigaseki. Districts such as Marunouchi, today headquarters for many of Japan's major banks and business firms, and Kasumigaseki, a site of major government offices, reflect the strong political-economic relationship found in the southern districts.

In 1912, Emperor Meiji was succeeded by his thirty-three-year-old son, Yoshihito, who reigned under the name Taishō. The Taishō era (which lasted until 1926) was liberal and prosperous; literature and aesthetics flowered, while social and political participation broadened. Tōkyō's rapid progress just as abruptly halted on September 1, 1923. At one minute past noon, one of the most devastating earthquakes in Japanese history shook Tōkyō. Measuring 7.9 on the Richter scale, the initial impact was followed by hundreds of aftershocks. Fires broke out. The air above the city became so intensely hot and unstable that firestorms were created, swept by fifty-mile-an-hour winds. By the end, 104,619 people were dead and 52,074 severely injured.

In 1926, Taishō's son, Hirohito, succeeded him, bringing about the Shōwa era. Still in the process of rebuilding Tokyo after the earthquake, Japan was hit hard by the economic depression that beset the world after 1929. In this climate, nationalism, conservatism, and militarism flourished. In 1941 Japan entered World War II by attacking possessions of Great Britain and the United States.

On the night of March 9–10, 1945, Tōkyō experienced one of its most devastating disasters. Air raids destroyed most of Tōkyō. Firestorms consumed the city's closely placed wooden buildings. Many people suffocated from the lack of oxygen that resulted from the consuming flames. Some died horribly in concrete buildings that became ovens. Others were trampled or drowned in the race to the Sumida River. By morning, broken bricks, melted glass, some concrete buildings, and a few twisted, charcoaled trees were all that remained in a vast and empty landscape. More than 100,000 people were dead.

As the recovery process advanced after the war, a distinct westward shift occurred in Tōkyō, with new commercial districts at the western periphery of Tōkyō emerging as powerful places of commerce. The crossroads at Shinjuku, Shibuya, and Ikeburkuro west of the Imperial Palace were transformed from small, local areas of commerce into major subcenters of Tōkyō known as *fukutoshin* (second heart of the city). Today, for many Japanese, Tōkyō's western districts, such as Shinjuku and Shibuya, represent the new material wealth achieved since the war, as well as new youth, vigor, and sophistication. Imposing corporate skyscrapers and elegant restaurants can be found in the western region, along with a vast array of dazzling entertainments and garish nightlife. In addition, the western region, once home of the *yamanote* aristocracy, is now the home of a rapidly expanding collection of suburbs, desperately attempting to keep pace with the growing city population. Small farms are increasingly being crowded out by *dachi* (cheap apartment complexes).

To the east lies what is left of the old *shitamachi* area, which still plays a vital role in the commercial life of Tōkyō. Nihombashi, once the center of Edo's commercial district, now contains securities firms and the Tōkyō Stock Exchange. Ginza, once famous for its silversmithing, is now famous for its department stores, specialty shops, and plush restaurants, as well as for being one of the first districts to be fully modernized during the Meiji era. Many of the most traditional aspects of the city are still visible in eastern Tōkyō; lavish modern hotels overshadow simple religious shrines, and traditional wooden tenement structures stand beside concrete multistory apartment developments.

Covering only 0.5 percent of Japan's land surface, Tōkyō today contains 10 percent of Japan's population and generates 40 percent of its commerce. Despite the city's westward expansion, it still provides too little space for the great numbers of people living there. Eye-searing air pollution, traffic congestion, housing and waste-management problems, inadequate social services, and poor land-use planning have all contributed to the creating of a city apparently on the edge of implosion, struggling to keep pace with a rapidly growing population shoved increasingly into smaller and smaller spaces. Tōkyō city planners are currently in the process of addressing these issues.

In spite of the problems modern Tōkyō faces, people still continue to come, attracted for the same reasons that drew people to Edo during the medieval period under the *shōgunate:* it is the most likely place in Japan to achieve success and find excitement. Unlike Kyōto, the ancient capital of the emperor, with its traditional, class-embedded, ritual conventions, Tokugawa Ieyasu's Edo was a place of ambitious, aggressive, even reckless spirit, rich in opportunity for the daring, industrious, imaginative, and lucky. This energetic spirit remains the hallmark of modern Tōkyō.

Further Reading: For a detailed examination of Tōkyō's urban geography, emphasizing the function and structure of the city's growth from historical times to the present, see Roman Cybriwsky's *Tōkyō* (Boston: G.K. Hall, and Chichester, Sussex: Belhaven, 1991). Fosco Maraini's *Tōkyō* (Alexandria, Virginia, and London: Time-Life, 1976) offers a highly readable account of Tōkyō historically and culturally, from a very personal perspective. *Tōkyō Now and Then* by Paul Waley (New York: Weatherhill, 1984) is a comprehensive book aptly subtitled *An Explorer's Guide.* Covering mythology and history and offering useful, detailed knowledge of important sites and how to reach them, Waley provides a thorough, engaging tour through Tōkyō past and present that can be used by both the careful researcher and the adventurous tourist. Ian Buruma's *Behind the Mask* (New York: Meridian, 1984; as *Japanese Mirror: Heroes and Villains of Japanese Culture*, London: Cape, 1984) gives an excellent look at Japan's historical and contemporary popular culture.

—Lynn Gelfand

Tonga

Location: A western Polynesian archipelago located between 15 degrees and 23 degrees south latitude and 173 degrees and 175 degrees west longitude. Consists of 172 volcanic and coral islands (of which 36 are inhabitated) covering 289 square miles. Encompasses three main island groups: the southern Tongatapu group, where the capital, Nukualofa, is located on Tongatapu Island; the central Haapai cluster; and the northern Vavau group, with outlying islands Niuafoo, Niuatobutabu, and Ata.

Description: Puleanga Fakatui o Tonga, the Kingdom of Tonga, was colonized in approximately 1200 B.C. by the ancestors of the Polynesian peoples. By A.D. 1200 Tongan society was highly stratified and headed by a paramount ruler, the Tui Tonga. In approximately 1470 a new royal line, the Tui Haatakalaua, assumed the administrative office of the Tui Tonga; the latter retained the religious duties of the title. The Tui Kanokupolu Dynasty, founded in 1610, later became the principal administrative power in Tonga. In 1852 King George Tupou I, the Tui Kanokupolu, united all of Tonga under his rule and negotiated treaties with Western powers that secured Tonga's sovereignty. His successors, especially the beloved Queen Salote and the present monarch, Taufaahau Tupou IV, inaugurated many economic, social, and political improvements, while encouraging Tongans to preserve their rich cultural heritage.

Site Office: Tonga Visitors Bureau
PO Box 37
Vuna Road
Nukualofa
Kingdom of Tonga
(676) 21733

Tonga is unique among Pacific societies in that it has retained its political independence throughout its history. During the nineteenth century, a period of considerable colonial expansion in the Pacific, Tonga held onto its sovereignty even as Fiji, Samoa, Hawaii, and other island groups were being annexed by foreign governments. In 1900 the Kingdom of Tonga became a British protectorate, a change that reduced but did not extinguish its independence. After resuming full independence in 1970, Tonga joined the Commonwealth of Nations.

Tonga was the first of the Polynesian islands to be colonized, by people who spoke pre-Polynesian, an East Oceanic branch of the Austronesian language family. These early settlers shared a cultural tradition called "Lapita," whose distinctive pottery has been found on islands extending from New Guinea in the west to Tonga and Samoa in the east. Sailing in double-hulled or outrigger canoes, Lapita peoples spread to New Caledonia and Vanuatu, continued eastward to Fiji, and reached the Tongan and Samoan Islands in approximately 1200 B.C. Together, Fiji, Tonga, and Samoa may in fact have been the "cradle" where the Polynesian way of life evolved and the point of embarkation for the Polynesians' initial voyages to the Marquesas Islands, Hawaii, and other archipelagos in the eastern Pacific Ocean.

On Tonga, Lapita craftsmen produced highly decorated vessels; later they manufactured plain ware before finally abandoning the ceramic craft at the beginning of the early Christian era. Little else is known of Tongan history before A.D. 1000, when massive earthworks were constructed on Tongatapu Island. The large, rectangular mounds, faced with coral, were the resting places of the chiefs and paramount rulers of the emerging Tui Tonga Dynasty, and the plainer, round structures most likely were the house platforms or burial mounds of commoners. By A.D. 1200, Tongan society was stratified and complex, with a centralized government.

According to Tongan oral history, the ancestors of the Tongans did not come from other islands but were created on Ata when Tangaloa Atulongolongo, grandson of the sky god Tangaloa, descended to earth in the form of a plover and dropped a seed containing a worm from which Kohai, Koau, and Momo, the first humans on Tonga, emerged. In approximately A.D. 950, Ahoeitu—the son of a Tongan woman, Ilaheva, and the sky god Tangaloa Eitumatupua—was murdered by his jealous half-brothers, then restored to life by his father. Ahoeitu descended to earth to govern Tongans as their sacred king, the Tui Tonga, displacing the Tui Tonga who was the offspring of a worm, and his half-brothers and their heirs became the Tui Tonga's attendants.

The Tui Tonga's person was sacred. Any house he entered became *tapu* (sacred, forbidden) and could not be occupied again. He owned all of the land in Tonga, and each new harvest was *tapu* until he, the earthly representative of the god Hikuleo, had received the *polopolo* (first fruits) at the *Inasi* ceremony. The Tui Tonga commanded the labor of his people and the sexual services of his female subjects. Ordinary persons deferred to him by performing the *moemoe*—kneeling before him and placing his feet on their heads or hands.

In approximately 1200 the eleventh Tui Tonga, Tuiatui, commissioned the building of the Haamonga-a-Maui (The Burden of Maui Carried on a Carrying Stick) at Hahake. This massive coral trilithon may have served as a calendrical instrument, as a symbol of dynastic unity, or as an assertion of Tuiatui's status, for he felt compelled to keep his attendants literally at arm's length by striking anyone who came within range of his club.

In the mid–thirteenth century the Tongans extended their influence, establishing sovereignty over Uvéa, Rotuma, Futuna, Samoa, Niue, Fiji, and distant Easter Island, mainly in order to collect tributes. The Samoans waged a long, bitter struggle before finally expelling the Tongans under Talakaifaiki; as the fifteenth Tui Tonga quit the island, he congratulated the Samoan leader on the latter's stalwart defense, and the Samoan adopted his compliment as a title, Malietoa (Well done, brave man).

In spite of, or perhaps because of, the tremendous power and privilege invested in his office, the Tui Tonga's existence was precarious: Havea I, Havea II, and Takalaua—the nineteenth, twenty-second, and twenty-third Tui Tongas, respectively—were assassinated. Following Takalaua's murder by his own subjects in approximately 1470, his heir, Kauulufonua Fekai, restructured the political framework to reduce the likelihood of his own assassination. He appointed governors to regulate affairs on Eua, Haapai, Vavau, the Niuas, and Uvéa, bestowed upon his brother Moungamotua a new office, the Tui Haatakalaua, which encompassed the administrative power of the Tui Tonga, and retained for himself the religious duties of the title. The Tui Haatakalaua came to rival the Tui Tonga in importance, but the position waned and died out in 1799.

By 1616 the sixth Tui Haatakalaua, Moungatonga, inaugurated a new hereditary line by conferring upon his son Ngata the title of Tui Kanokupolu. Initially inferior in rank, the office later eclipsed the Tui Haatakalaua, perhaps because the officeholder controlled Hihifo, the most contentious province in Tonga. In time, the Tui Tonga came to select the daughter of the Tui Kanokupolu to be the Moheofo, his principal wife and the mother of his heir.

Against this backdrop, Tonga hosted its first European visitors, Dutch merchants seeking to locate *Terra Australis Incognita*, the fabled, rich "New South Land." After sailing past Cape Horn and skirting the Tuamotu Islands, Jakob Le Maire and Willem Corneliszoon Schouten approached Tafahi in the northern Tonga group on May 9, 1616, where, Schouten recorded, they encountered "red folk who smeared themselves with oil." On Niuatobutabu and Niuafoo, which the foreigners dubbed Verraders Eylandt (Traitor's Island) and Goede Hope, Dutch and Tongans punctuated brisk trade with feasting and skirmishes brought on by Le Maire's refusal to drink the proffered *kava* and Tongan attempts to commandeer the Dutch ship. Following more serious altercations on nearby Futuna, during which six islanders were killed, Le Maire and Schouten sailed west until they reached the Moluccas and the East Indies trade.

Abel Janszoon Tasman, dispatched by the Dutch East India Company to investigate "the remaining unknown part of the terrestrial globe," sighted the island that now bears his name, sailed through the strait dividing New Zealand and reached Ata, the southernmost of the Tongan islands, on January 19, 1643. Friendly trading commenced on Ata, Eua, Tongatapu, and Nomuka, which the Dutch renamed Pylstaeres Eylandt, Middleburg, Amsterdam, and Rotterdam, respectively. In exchange for nails and knives, the Tui Tonga lavishly entertained and amply provisioned his guests. The Dutch, in turn, were impressed by the neatly fenced, plantation-style layout of the Tongans' gardens and the apparent absence of weapons, which led Tasman to conclude that "all was peace and friendship."

During the next 150 years, the Tongans received many English, French, and Spanish visitors, including Alejandro Malaspina, who claimed Vavau for the Spanish Crown in 1793, and Lieutenant William Bligh, commander of the H.M.S. *Bounty*. Bligh had just left Nomuka, in the central Tongan cluster, when the famous mutiny broke out on April 28, 1789, and he and eighteen others were cast adrift. They made their way to Tofua and traded with the Tongans, but departed hastily after being attacked. The *Bounty*, under Fletcher Christian, later stopped at Tongatapu on its journey in search of a settlement.

Captain James Cook, who disproved the existence of *Terra Australis*, visited Tonga in 1773, 1774, and 1777, and, like Tasman, assumed that the islanders enjoyed a tranquil, bounteous existence. "I thought I was transported into one of the most fertile plains in Europe," he wrote. "[H]ere was not an inch of waste ground, the roads occupied no more space than was absolutely necessary. . . . Nature, assisted by a little art, no where appears in a more flourishing state than at this isle."

Oblivious to a fruitless Tongan plot to assassinate him at Lifuka and seize his ship, Cook christened the archipelago the "Friendly Islands" because lasting, amicable relations seemed to prevail among its inhabitants, who had received him with much hospitality. The Europeans bartered for *tapa* (bark cloth) and other "curiosities," presented the chiefs with seeds and domesticated animals, and recorded the many aspects of Tongan life they witnessed, from fishing methods to *kava* drinking to the *Inasi* ceremony. Cook was an astute observer, but the intricacies of the Tongan ranking system eluded him, particularly the tripartite form of government and the *fahu* relationship, whereby a man's elder sister and her children were superior to him and to his descendants in ceremonial rank, a principle that applied to the Tui Tonga himself.

Cook's journals attracted whalers, traders, and other foreigners to the Pacific; in the late eighteenth and early nineteenth centuries, Tonga hosted upward of 100 of these strangers, most of them missionaries and beachcombers from Britain and various Pacific islands. Some of them successfully integrated themselves into their host society by making themselves useful as traders, interpreters, and laborers. William Mariner, a young survivor of the 1806 *Port au Prince* massacre, lived four years in Tonga as the adopted son of Chief Finau Ulukalala II and wrote a stirring account of his experiences. He interpreted for his hosts Christian doctrine and other European ideas recently introduced to them, and they educated him in the Tongan way of life.

Representatives of the London Missionary Society arrived in Tonga in 1797, only to face continual harassment

Port of Refuge Harbour, Vavau Islands, Tonga
Photo courtesy of Tonga Visitors Bureau, San Francisco

from beachcombers resentful of these new, rival suppliers of European goods. The missionaries also had to contend with the embarrassing defection of one of their members, George Vason, who adopted native dress and married into the Tui Haatakalaua's family. Even more distressing were the murders of three missionaries who had become caught up in a contest of power among claimants to the Tui Kanokupolu office. The British mission was abandoned in 1800.

When the Tui Kanokupolu vacated his position, Tupoumoheofo, the principal wife of the Tui Tonga Paulaho, declared herself the new Tui Kanokupolu. The rightful heir, Tukuaho, returned to Tongatapu, quickly deposed her, and installed his father, Mumui, in her place; Tukuaho later assumed the office. Tupoumoheofo and her husband fled the capital, and the title of Tui Tonga declined in power and prestige until it died out in 1865. Following Tukuaho's murder in 1799, civil war erupted on Tonga and raged intermittently until 1852.

Walter Lawry laid the groundwork for the first Wesleyan mission in Tonga, established in 1826. However, Lawry's successors faced formidable opposition from Tongan leaders who, while they valued European medicine, firearms, and other *papalangi* commodities, valued more highly their own traditions: Tongans countered the missionaries' ethnocentric attitudes and attempts to convert them with, "Your religion is very good for you, and ours is very good for us." Moreover, Christian doctrine, holding that all individuals were equal and entitled to go to heaven, regardless of social rank, and that no one had the right to appropriate the property of others, subverted the traditional Tongan social structure and undermined the authority of chiefs and the traditional priesthood.

Christianity gained a firm foothold in Tonga with the conversion in 1831 of Taufaahau, the brilliant military leader and ruler of Haapai. He had become skeptical of the Tongan gods, and viewed the adoption of Christianity as a means for consolidating his political supremacy and acquiring the wealth and power of the Europeans. After becoming Tui Kanokupolu, he promoted literacy and the mass acceptance of Christianity, defeated his rivals and, in 1852, united all of the Tonga islands under his rule as King Siaosi (George) Tupou I.

The king, known to his subjects as Tupou, concluded that Westernizing Tonga would preserve its sovereignty, and his monarchy, by securing international recognition of its political independence and economic viability, rightly earned him the appellation "The Maker of Modern Tonga." Influential in this process was the controversial Wesleyan missionary, the Reverend Shirley Waldemar Baker. The erstwhile stowaway, apothecary's assistant, and teacher became

Tupou's confidant and adviser; later, as his prime minister, Baker helped put into concrete form their joint vision of "Tonga for the Tongans."

To secure Tongan lands, the Law Code of 1862, a revised version of Tupou's earlier rulings, forbade the sale of land to foreigners and entitled every adult male to lease a parcel of land from his chief. Its Emancipation Edict abolished the obligation of lower-ranked persons to provide free food and labor to their social superiors; a poll tax levied on Tongans over sixteen years of age provided the revenues to pay compensatory pensions to chiefs and salaries to government officials. To prevent the new constitutional monarchy from being annexed by Western powers, the king inaugurated a constitution, which took effect on November 4, 1875, and negotiated treaties of friendship with France (1855), Germany (1876), Great Britain (1879), and the United States (1888).

These sweeping changes stimulated economic prosperity and a concomitant growth in public works as well as in the number of churches and schools. Change also brought dissension, particularly from traders, chiefs, and minor titleholders whose positions were undercut by the land reforms, from the Wesleyan Missionary Society in Australia, which condemned the Free Church of Tonga (recently seceded from its "parent" body), and from Tongan and British officials who feared that Baker's intervention in Tongan politics would compromise their own interests. Sir John Thurston, British High Commissioner for the Western Pacific, engineered Baker's deportation to New Zealand in 1890. King George Tupou I died three years later. The former premier returned to Tonga in 1898, but his influence in the kingdom's affairs was limited and short-lived; after suffering a series of personal tragedies, he died on November 16, 1903.

Germany's increasing involvement in helping Tonga resolve its financial difficulties led the British to seek greater control over the islands. Basil Thomson, sent by John Thurston to rectify the situation, pressured the new monarch, King George Tupou II, to sign a Treaty of Friendship (1900), which gave the British consul in Tonga control over Tonga's external affairs and proclaimed that Tonga was henceforth a British protectorate. A 1905 treaty authorized the British consul to dispense advice on Tonga's financial matters and to appoint or dismiss government officials.

When King George Tupou II died, his daughter, Salote Mafileo Pilolevu, became queen of Tonga on April 5, 1918. Queen Salote Tupou III initiated many progressive measures during her forty-seven-year reign. The Education Act of 1927 and 1929 made education compulsory; the Central Medical School in Suva, Fiji, established in 1929, served Tongan medical practitioners; a Teacher Training College opened in 1944; and government scholarships enabled students to undertake their secondary education abroad. The queen encouraged the cultivation for export of other crops besides copra (dried coconut meat from which oil is extracted) and launched many improvements, including the department of health, a land court, and a state savings bank. She also introduced telephones to Tonga.

Queen Salote was revered by her subjects and renowned for her piety, nationalism, intimate knowledge of Tongan traditions and family histories, and poetical and oratorical gifts. She attempted to heal the rift between the Free Church of Tonga and the Wesleyan Church, and in 1924 the two churches merged (they later split into the Free Church of Tonga and the Church of Tonga). Convinced that "the customs of a people are its heritage," she set up the Tongan Traditions Committee in 1952 and charged it with preserving Tongan myths, legends, and genealogies. As president of "Langa Fonua," she worked unstintingly to improve women's living conditions and encouraged them to produce and sell traditional handicrafts. Tongan women attained the right to vote in 1960.

During World War II, her tiny kingdom contributed armed forces, money, and land for airstrips to the Allied cause. Queen Salote attended the coronation of Queen Elizabeth II in London in 1953, endearing herself to the English people and the world. When Queen Elizabeth asked Salote why she did not raise the hood of her carriage to shelter herself from the downpour pelting the procession, the latter replied that in Tonga, one should not cover oneself in the presence of a higher chief (her royal hostess). The Tongan monarch prepared a warm welcome for Queen Elizabeth and the duke of Edinburgh when they visited Tonga later that year.

Queen Salote's insightful administration paved the way for the relaxation of British control over Tonga and the dissolution of its protectorate status in 1970. (Today, Tonga is an independent member of the Commonwealth of Nations.) Queen Salote died on December 23, 1965, and 50,000 people attended her funeral; Tongans still refer to her as "Our Beloved Queen." Prince Tungi, Queen Salote's son, became King Taufaahau Tupou IV. Building on his predecessors' accomplishments, he inaugurated improvements in education, health care, transportation, shipping, and air services.

Agriculture continues to be the mainstay of Tonga's economy; coconuts, bananas, vanilla, and pumpkins are principal export items. During the 1970s, job shortages forced many skilled tradespersons to seek employment overseas. A new core of "commoner elites," whose members have attained prominence through education and their positions in government and the church, have taken up permanent residence abroad, mostly in New Zealand, Australia, Fiji, and the United States. These international links have helped Tongan families to obtain jobs, property, and influence with local authorities.

Tourism offers considerable growth potential throughout Tonga. Principal attractions on Tongatapu are the white Victorian Royal Palace at Nukualofa, the ancient and modern Royal Tombs, located respectively at Mua and Malaekula, the Haamonga-a-Maui, the Centenary Chapel, the Heilala festival, held in July, and Talamahu Market.

In recent decades, Tonga has established diplomatic relations with the Soviet Union (1976), signed an agreement with the United States that permitted the latter's tuna fleet to fish in Tongan waters (1986), and concluded a friendship treaty with the United States that granted the safe passage of U.S. nuclear-capable ships within that zone (1988).

The government structure, consisting of a sovereign, assisted by a privy council, and a legislative assembly, has changed little since 1875. Since 1989, the Tongan Pro-Democracy Movement has sought to increase its representation in Parliament and has advocated a constitutional monarchy patterned after the British model; the Tongan king, however, has vigorously opposed such moves. More recently, the outspoken TPDM member Akilisi Pohiva organized protests against the government sale of passports and granting of citizenship privileges to foreigners.

Further Reading: *Friendly Islands: A History of Tonga*, edited by Noel Rutherford (Melbourne, Oxford, and New York: Oxford University Press, 1977), the first comprehensive study of Tongan history, contains articles written by an interdisciplinary panel of experts. *Shirley Baker and the King of Tonga* by Noel Rutherford (Melbourne, London, and New York: Oxford University Press, 1971) meticulously details the controversial partnership of the two men. Sione Latukefu's excellent study *Church and State in Tonga: The Wesleyan Methodist Missionaries and Political Development, 1822–1875* (Honolulu: University Press of Hawaii, 1974) expands on an important chapter of Tonga's history. *Tonga Islands: William Mariner's Account* by John Martin (Tonga: Vavau Press, 1991) and *The Journals of Captain James Cook on His Voyages of Discovery*, 4 volumes, edited by J. C. Beaglehole (Cambridge: Hakluyt Society of Cambridge University Press, 1955–74) reproduce two of the most important early accounts of Tongan society written by Europeans. Maria Chiara wishes to thank Dr. Noel Rutherford and Ms. Mary Fonua for their assistance in the writing of this essay.

—Maria Chiara

Tongariro (North Island, New Zealand)

Location: Central North Island, New Zealand, approximately 180 miles north of Wellington.

Description: Opened in 1907, Tongariro National Park became New Zealand's first national park and the second national park established in the world after Yellowstone. It was the gift of Maori Chief Horonuku to the government of New Zealand in 1887; it contains two active volcanoes, Mount Ruapehu and Mount Ngauruhoe, and comprises 185,943 acres.

Contact: Turangi Information Centre
Taupo District Council
Ngawaka Place
P.O. Box 34
Turangi, North Island
New Zealand
(7) 386 8999

When a group of Polynesians, who became known as Maoris, left their ancestral tropical home in the central Pacific and arrived in what is now New Zealand more than 1,000 years ago, they invested the area's majestic mountains with profound religious significance. One of the highest mountain peaks on New Zealand's North Island is Tongariro, at 6,457 feet. It and two higher peaks nearby—Mount Ruapehu (9,176 feet) and Mount Ngauruhoe (7,516 feet)—became the subject of many Maori legends.

The name *Tongariro* derives from a prayer said to have been uttered by the high priest Ngatoro-i-rangi, considered semi-divine by the Maoris. Newly arrived from his tropical homeland, he had never seen such awe-inspiring mountains or experienced such cold. He climbed up a high mountain, where he encountered fierce winds and heavy snow. In danger of dying from the cold, he prayed to his priestess sisters in the lowlands: *"Ka riro au; te tonga"*—*tonga* meaning south wind, and *riro,* "to be seized or be borne away." He prayed for a warming fire, which his sisters sent him in the form of a volcanic eruption. Ngatoro-i-rangi's life was saved, and henceforth the mountain range bore the name Tongariro. The legend goes on to describe how the great priest, surveying the lands below from his mountain height, claimed them all for his tribe, which would be called Maoris.

Yet another legend explains how the mountains became situated where they are. When the tall male mountains fell in love with the female mountain Pihanga, she rejected all but one, Tongariro. The rest wandered away disconsolately, and settled down elsewhere on the North Island. But the mountain Tauhara kept looking back at the beautiful Pihanga. To this day, Tauhara faces the beautiful mountain Pihanga across a lake. The others form peaks in Tongariro National Park.

Captain James Cook and his crew had never laid eyes on such majestic peaks when they arrived in New Zealand on their first Pacific voyage in 1769. Cook proceeded to claim the beautiful land for England and King George III, although his claim meant little. Only 120 years earlier, Dutch explorer Abel Tasman had been the first European to sight the two islands, which he named after his homeland, Zeeland. He claimed New Zealand for the Netherlands, but an attack by the Maoris discouraged Dutch colonization. Despite Cook's claim, the British Crown was not in the least interested in New Zealand until wave upon wave of Europeans began settling in this remote region of the Pacific in the early nineteenth century, mistreating the Maori natives as they did so, according to missionary reports. To provide greater law and order, and nominal protection for the Maoris, the British government decided to establish a formal presence in New Zealand, first through the appointment of a colonial administrator, then through the Treaty of Waitangi in 1840. Under the treaty, Maoris were asked to surrender their sovereignty in exchange for protection as British subjects and settlers were warned that Maori lands had to be purchased fairly. Nonetheless, tension escalated rapidly between the Europeans and Maoris, to the point where Maoris began to fear for their sacred mountains. The population of whites, hovering at 2,000 in 1840, exploded to 20,000 a decade later.

Many generations after Ngatoro-i-rangi's scaling of Tongariro, his direct descendants, the tribe Tuwharetoa, chose a supreme chieftain, Mananui. Unlike the majority of northern Maori chiefs, he refused to sign the Treaty of Waitangi in 1840. When a landslide killed him in 1846, his brother Iwikau held a tribal meeting that sought to draw the government's attention to the preservation of Tongariro, to no avail. New Zealand's infamous Land Wars were in full swing, with Maori tribes attacking white settlers and whites retaliating with the help of government troops. Defeated tribes forfeited their lands. Iwikau died in 1862; his brother and successor, Horonuku, continued to lead the Maoris in their struggle against hopeless odds. Years later, surveying the snow-capped peaks of Tongariro and adjacent Ruapehu and Ngauruhoe, Chief Horonuku began considering how he might save these sacred mountains from white encroachments.

By then, the mid-1880s, it was not just settlers, but commercial and industrial development that had arrived in New Zealand. The railroad in particular gobbled up huge amounts of timber and brought settlers to areas that had been inaccessible. At the same time, there were many farsighted New Zealanders who were alarmed at the rate at which native forests, plants, and birds were disappearing, because of development and the destructive effects of European plant and

Mount Ruapehu in Tongariro National Park
Photo courtesy of Tongariro / Taupo Conservancy

animal species. New Zealand's remoteness and isolation did not signify backwardness: two years after the world's first national park was established at Yellowstone in 1872, New Zealand's parliament passed the Forests Bill. This law granted the provinces the right to create state forest reserves, earmarked the sum of 10,000 pounds a year for forest conservation, and approved the appointment of a conservator of forests. Eleven years later, the Forests Act of 1885 made further provisions for forest conservation. In 1893, New Zealand women were the first in the world to win suffrage; thereafter they, too, would have a say in the conservation debate.

The time actually was ripe for Chief Horonuku's eventual plan to preserve the Maoris' sacred mountains, which whites coveted for their sheep-grazing potential. It was said that Chief Horonuku, upon overhearing an acrimonious argument in the local government Land Court (set up after the Waitangi Treaty to settle disputes over property issues) regarding Tongariro's ownership, decided to take the matter into his own hands. Pondering how the mountains could be spared white control, the chief turned to his European son-in-law, Lawrence Grace, who suggested offering the mountains as a gift to the nation, for the purpose of a recreational park. In that way, the mountains would be protected forever. The government already had set aside the Hooker Valley (future Mount Cook National Park) as a recreational area in 1885 and was expanding it the same year that the chief decided to offer the sacred mountains. Consequently, in September 1887, the government immediately accepted Chief Horonuku's formal donation of 6,000 acres including the summits of Tongariro, Ruapehu, and Ngauruhoe, which would become the nucleus of the future Tongariro National Park. This ended the debate, not always on civilized terms, as to who really owned the mountains.

Chief Horonuku's gift was a timely and priceless one. By the late 1880s, a lumber mill had been erected next to the park; others followed soon afterward. Taken together, the mills—serviced by a railroad—might have doomed what was to become Tongariro National Park. One after another, however, the owners closed down the mills as soon as sections of the forests were depleted.

The park did not open formally until 1907, because the amount of land donated, although generous, was not sufficient for a recreational park. At the same time, the government was zealous but haphazard in its acquisition of further land for parks: the most scenic areas were the most likely to be conserved, rather than less scenic but valuable wetlands and marshes.

Some well-meaning New Zealanders understood a "park" to mean recreation rather than conservation. Hence Tongariro's first park ranger, John Cullen, dismayed many of his better informed compatriots when he introduced foreign animal species, especially grouse, into Tongariro, from 1912 to 1920. His aim was to provide the same gentlemen's hunting opportunities at Tongariro as on the best and grandest English manors. A forest also was unimaginable to him without Scottish heather, a plant he introduced in great quantities, along with other British plants.

Eventually, the grouse all died out, but the heather survived. It was not lethal to native plants as were many other foreign plant species, but in order to plant such large areas with heather, Cullen burned native tussock grasses, causing considerable damage to the soil. The heather grew rapidly on the rich volcanic earth, fortunately providing a habitat in which native plants throve, making possible the growth of the kind of beech forests that originally covered most of New Zealand's North Island.

The expansion of the railroads did bring about a positive benefit: it increased the numbers of visitors to the parklands. As early as 1879, even before Chief Horonuku donated Tongariro, two Englishmen became the first Europeans to climb to the summit of Mount Ruapehu and catch a glimpse of Crater Lake. Fishing, hiking, and mountaineering became the most popular recreational activities at Tongariro, necessitating the construction of overnight huts (in the days before camping gear). In 1913, skiing finally became a popular pastime with the establishment of the first ski run, and the sport has grown in popularity ever since. In 1928, a modern hotel, Chateau Tongariro, was built in the park. Much renovated, it still operates and is considered to rank in the luxury class.

A constant menace at Tongariro National Park always has been the active volcanoes of Mount Ruapehu and Mount Ngauruhoe. Both mountains, as others on New Zealand's North Island, were formed from wave after wave of volcanic lava and ash. Periodically they erupt, spewing forth tons of rock debris, sizzling lava, and ash; some ash ejections have reached as high as four miles. In one of the worst volcanic eruptions in modern New Zealand's history, in late 1953 Mount Ngauruhoe belched forth 6.5 million cubic yards of lava. This tremendous downflow caused other physical problems, including a great flood of Crater Lake, whose natural outlet was dammed up by the lava; the flood suddenly crashed down into the valley below, causing a monumental train wreck that resulted in the deaths of nearly 200 people. Mount Ruapehu also has erupted numerous times in the last twenty-five years, including quite recently. In 1975, in an unusual occurrence, both volcanoes erupted simultaneously. Mount Tongariro's volcano is dormant, although not extinct, perhaps because, at 2 million years of age, it is the oldest of the three major peaks.

Tongariro is New Zealand's most important national park, distinguished for its great natural diversity, its active volcanoes, and its beautiful lakes. A great diversity of vegetation characterizes the park as well, from desert and alpine plants to tropical rainforest and beech forests, as well as wetlands vegetation and the native tussock, or grass, on the mountainsides.

On the northernmost edge of the park are interesting excavations of an ancient Maori village, which border Lake Rotoaira; in the same northern part of the park lie the popular Ketetahi Hot Springs, and at the easternmost part lies the Rangiro Desert. Although not a true desert, the cold, dry, windswept landscape gave rise to that appellation. In winter, the park lies buried under deep snow, and the two ski resorts, National Park and Ohakune, come alive with visitors. In December and January, New Zealand's summer months, the mountainsides burst with alpine blossoms.

Further Reading: The single most comprehensive survey of New Zealand's first national park is *The Restless Land: The Story of Tongariro National Park* (second edition, Wellington: Department of Lands and Survey, 1982). Richly illustrated, it is especially strong on the history and acquisition of the park. Another survey of Tongariro, also well illustrated, is Craig Potton's *Tongariro, A Sacred Gift: A Centennial Celebration of Tongariro National Park* (Auckland: Lansdowne Press, 1987). Guidebooks on New Zealand give excellent coverage to Tongariro, New Zealand's most important park.

—Sina Dubovoy

Ujjain (Madhya Pradesh, India)

Location: Western Madyha Pradesh, approximately 200 miles east of Ahmadābād and 115 miles west of Bhopāl.

Description: An ancient city dating to about 600 B.C. and with evidence of prehistoric and protohistoric occupation in the neighboring area. Capital of western Mālwa up to the eleventh century A.D., when the capital was shifted to Dhār. Mentioned in classical sources as an inland entrepôt with links to the coastal port of Barygaza (modern Broach) at the Narmada estuary in modern Gujarāt. One of the holiest cities of the Hindu religion.

Contact: Government of India Tourist Office
88 Janpath
New Delhi 110001
India
(33) 20005 or (33) 20008

Among Hindus, Ujjain derives its greatest significance from its role as one of the holiest cities of their religion. Several Hindu legends are associated with the city. According to one, when gods and demons were fighting over a container holding the nectar of immortality, drops of nectar fell on Ujjain and three other cities, thereby sanctifying them. Another says that Siva, one of the three most important Hindu gods, commemorated his victory over a demon by naming his capital Ujjayini, meaning "one who conquers with pride." Siva worship has been important in Ujjain since ancient times and continues to be so today. The Mahākāla Siva temple, which contains a *liṅgam*, or phallic symbol representing Siva, is one of the city's main religious institutions, and Hindu pilgrims also come here to bathe in the Sipra River. Beyond its religious role, however, Ujjain has a long history, dating to about 600 B.C., as the political, commercial, and cultural center of the Mālwa plateau of central India.

The Mālwa plateau is a rich agricultural plain at the foot of the east-west spread of the Vindhya range and is drained by the Chambal and the Narmada River systems. The plateau also provides the most important lines of communication between Gangetic India on the one hand and the Deccan and the west Indian coast on the other.

The human story of the Mālwa plateau extends well beyond the beginning of settlements at the site of Ujjain. The region, a vast stretch of undulating plains interspersed with flat-topped hills and covered by loamy soil, is singularly rich in prehistoric remains from the lower Paleolithic stage onward. River sections containing tools and fossils (including a human skull fragment, the only one from the lower Paleolithic period discovered in India), upper Paleolithic campsites with fragments of ostrich egg shells, and rock shelters with paintings dating at least from the Mesolithic period dot the countryside. From about the middle of the third millennium B.C., the number of human settlements began to increase considerably.

Excavators have observed a steady archaeological sequence in the development of villages in this region; the site of Kayatha near Ujjain provides a good example. Huts, typically rectangular or round, were made of wattle-and-daub or mud and had thatched roofs and lime-plastered walls and floors. Wheat, rice, and a variety of legumes were cultivated. Technology included a wide range of microlithic tools, a few polished stone implements, and a limited use of copper. (Iron began to be used locally sometime in the second half of the second millennium B.C.) Cattle were the most important domesticated animals. Villagers produced beads from semi-precious stones and steatite, as well as painted and plain wheelmade pottery and terra-cotta cattle figurines. A large number of such villages, averaging 200 inhabitants, lined the river banks.

The historic period in the region began about 600 B.C., when most of the subcontinent was divided, according to literary sources, into sixteen great principalities. The Mālwa region was included in one of these under the names of Akara and Avanti, corresponding respectively to eastern and western Mālwa. Ujjain figures in the historical record as the capital of Avanti or western Mālwa.

The archaeological site of ancient Ujjain stands on the east bank of the Sipra, a tributary of the Chambal. The site is divided into four main cultural periods. Period I, dated between 750 and 500 B.C., is marked by the use of wheelmade black-and-red pottery. Period II falls between 500 and 200 B.C. and yields pottery typical of a large part of northern India, Northern Black Polished Ware. Period III is placed between 200 B.C. and the ninth and tenth centuries A.D. Period IV comprises part of the medieval period. The Ujjain excavations were conducted mostly between 1955 and 1958 when the technique of radiocarbon dating was unknown in India, and thus the dates that have been suggested for the excavated periods are based on historical comparisons.

The plan of the site shows an irregular oblong measuring one mile by three-quarters of a mile. This space is surrounded by a rampart with eight openings, presumably gateways into and out of the ancient city. The river flows by the site immediately on its east and more distantly on the northern side. On the eastern and western sides, moats were dug. The rampart wall, made of heaped-up clay, was 245 feet wide at the base and 132 feet wide at the top. It was built during Period I and lasted up to the end of Period III. A couple of bamboo baskets and a few iron implements, including a spade, have been found inside the body of the rampart. The rampart wall was strengthened against the river's erosion

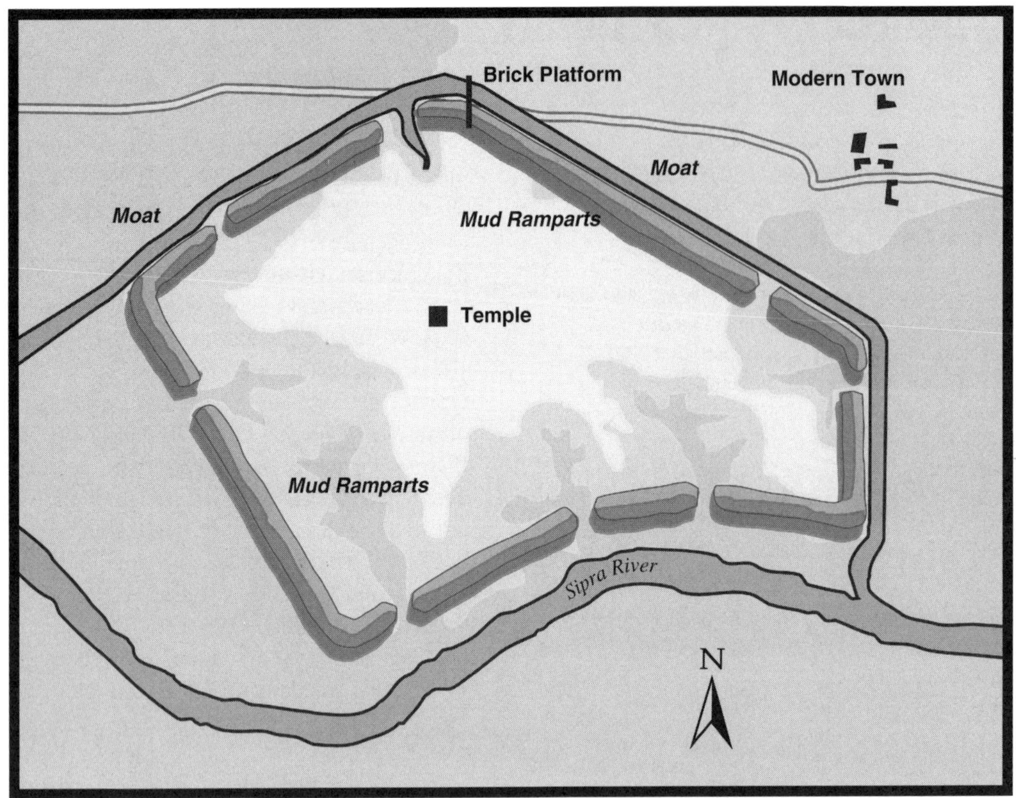

Archaeological site plan of the ramparts at Ujjain
Illustration by Tom Willcockson

through a connected series of well-cut wooden beams or sleepers stretching 350 feet, corresponding in length to an inward bend of the river. Sometime during Period II the outer edge of the rampart was reinforced with a brick wall three feet, nine inches wide. By Period III, the moat had been dug to the width of 129 feet.

No living quarters dating from Period I have been found inside the fortified habitation area. Attributable to that period, however, are traces of a wide, gravel-topped road that runs through a gateway in the northeastern corner of the eastern rampart wall. During Period II, houses were built of mud, mud-bricks, stone fragments, or burned bricks. These houses usually stood on plinths of rubble and clay. Flooring was typically constructed on a bed of rubble and then given a coat of clay. A large enclosure (thirty-four feet by twenty-six feet) with a low parapet wall made of burned bricks was found in the Period II area. This possibly was a water reservoir. Numerous iron objects have been found along with the evidence of ore-smelting at the site, while terra-cotta pits, wells, and drain pipes found among the building remains suggest that an elementary sanitation system was used. By Period III a stone-bead industry flourished at the site. The terra-cotta mold of a second-century A.D. Roman coin was found dating to this period. Period IV yielded mostly debris dating to A.D. 1600 at the latest and including some Mughal and later coins. The modern settlement of Ujjain is a short distance from the ancient site.

The archaeological picture of ancient Ujjain, however, does not tell the full story of the site. The kingdom of Avanti or western Mālwa, of which Ujjain was the capital, enjoyed a great reputation in Indian traditional literature. The *Purāṇas,* the principal body of this literature, treat a wide variety of themes including creation myths and ancient Indian ideas of cosmogony and cosmography. The *Purāṇas* include some political history as well. Two kings of Avanti, always mentioned jointly as Vinda and Anuvinda, are said to have fought on the side of the Kauravas in the Mahābhārata war. According to the *Matsya Purāṇa,* the king Karttaviryarjuna of the Haihaya Dynasty was the progenitor of the royal line of Avanti.

Avanti and its capital Ujjain emerge in the historical record as one of the major kingdoms during the time of the Buddha, who probably lived from the late sixth to the early fifth centuries B.C. Avanti's king during that period was Pradyota, who had extensive dealings with other contemporary kings from Gandhāra in the northwest to Magadha in southern Bihār. Pradyota fought with the king of the Vatsa Kingdom (roughly the modern Allahābād-Kausambi area), Udayana. In one of the famous love stories of ancient India, Udayana, while a prisoner in Ujjain, fell in love with Pradyota's daughter Vasavadatta and escaped to his own kingdom with her. During this time Avanti was a major center of Buddhism. A number of early Buddhist preceptors were born here, the most famous of them being Mahakachchayana, who was born in Ujjain to the family of a priest under Pradyota. According to tradition, Mahāvīra (Vardhamāna), the founder of Jainism in the sixth century B.C., also visited Ujjain.

In the third century B.C., or perhaps earlier, Ujjain was a major administrative center of the Mauryan Empire, which was based in Pāṭaliputra (modern Patna). In the first separate rock edict of Aśoka at Dhauli in Orissa, Ujjain is mentioned as the administrative seat of a Mauryan prince, underscoring the town's importance. Aśoka himself was stationed there as governor during his grandfather Chandragupta's reign; one of Aśoka's sons, Mahendra, was born at Ujjain. After Aśoka embraced Buddhism, his sons set out from the town to spread Buddhist teachings. The famous Sanskrit grammarian Pāṇini of the fifth century B.C. mentions Ujjain in one of his grammatical rules, as does Pāṇini's commentator Patānjali of the second century B.C.

The post-Mauryan situation in Ujjain is somewhat unclear. It appears that in the wake of the fall of the Mauryan Empire, Ujjain became the center of a local kingdom that issued its own copper coins. Most scholars date these coins—of which a wide variety have been found—to the period after the fall of the Mauryas but before the rise of the Guptas; some maintain they were issued during the time of the Mauryas themselves. On the obverse are found from two to seven distinct symbols, including a tree in a railing, fishes, or swastikas. A particularly intriguing figure on the obverse of some coins is that of a man carrying a long stick. Occasionally shown with three heads, this figure has been interpreted as the Hindu god Siva or Karttikeya, Siva's son and the god of war. On still others, a female figure is shown seated on a lotus; she has been identified with Lakshmi, the Hindu goddess of wealth. The reverse usually carries a symbol known as the "Ujjain symbol," a cross with arms ending in circles. Occasionally, the Ujjain symbol is replaced by the figure of a frog. Some coins from the Deccan region found at Ujjain suggest that the town during this period may have fallen under the influence of the Sātavāhana kings from that region.

In the early centuries A.D., especially from the second to the fifth centuries, Ujjain was associated with a dynasty known as the Western Kshatrapas. Some famous Kshatrapa rulers of the period were Chaṣtana, Rudrādaman, and Rudrasimha I. Originally Scythians or Saka chieftains, they were by this time completely Indianized and had developed matrimonial relationships with their royal contemporaries. A third-century A.D. king from the Krishna-Godāvari delta is known from his inscriptions to have married the daughter of a king of Ujjain.

During this period Ujjain was mentioned in Western sources as a major commercial center. According to the first-century A.D. nautical almanac *Periplus of the Erythraean Sea,* semi-precious stones, fine cotton, and other products went out from Ujjain to Barygaza (modern Broach) on the Gujarāt coast for export. The second-century Alexandrian geographer Ptolemy mentions the place as Ozene, the capital of Tiastenes (the Kshatrapa king Chaṣtana).

In the early fifth century A.D. Ujjain came under the rule of Candra Gupta II of the Gupta Dynasty of Magadha. He is identified with the king Vikramāditya of the Indian legends. The famous Sanskrit poet and dramatist Kālidāsa described Ujjain, where he wrote several of his works. The most important references are in the *Purvamegha* section of his *Meghadutam* (Cloud Messenger), which describes the city's palaces, the Sipra River, and the temple of Mahākāla Siva where drums were beaten during the time of the evening worship of the deity. (Ujjain had by this time become a major center of Siva worship.) The Mahākāla Siva temple, rebuilt after a thirteenth-century sacking, is still in use.

The Mahākāla temple also was mentioned in Bāṇabhaṭṭa's Sanskrit drama *Kādambarī,* written in the seventh century A.D. Ujjain was likely included in the kingdom of Bāṇabhaṭṭa's royal patron, King Harṣa, whose capital was at Kanauj near modern Kānpur in the upper Ganges valley. The Chinese pilgrim Xuan Zang visited India during the reign of Harṣa and left behind a description of the Ujjain region as Wu-She-Yen-Na. It had a rich and flourishing population, with a number of Buddhist monasteries, although most of the earlier monasteries were in ruins. There were some Hindu temples as well, and the king himself was a Hindu.

After the death of Harṣa in A.D. 648, Ujjain along with the rest of Mālwa became politically unstable, with all the contemporary powers of northern India and the Deccan region trying to control Mālwa because of its economic and geographical importance. For a time Mālwa shifted between the influences of the kings of Kanauj and the kings of the Deccan. The latter kings belonged to the Rāṣhṭrakūṭa Dynasty and had their capital at Malkhed. According to an early ninth-century inscription, the Rāṣhṭrakūṭa king Dhruva defeated a king of Mālwa. The Mahākāla Siva temple of Ujjain was mentioned not merely in an inscription of this period but also in a Rāṣhṭrakūṭa record of the early part of the tenth century. After the Rāṣhṭrakūṭa power declined, a new dynasty arose in Mālwa itself under the name of Paramara. The Paramaras shifted their capital to Dhār in the eleventh century. The most famous Paramara king was Bhoja, who was well known for his patronage of learning. After the decline of the Paramara power, Mālwa became subject to various local chiefs who possibly owed some allegiance to the Chāḷukyan Dynasty of Gujarāt.

Mālwa and with it Ujjain were sacked by the Muslim power of Delhi in 1235. Sultan Iltutmish plundered Ujjain and destroyed its temples, including the Mahākāla temple. It is said that he took the old Siva *liṅgam* of this temple with him to Delhi. In 1310 Mālwa became a province under the Delhi sultanate. It was brought under control by an officer of ʽAlā'-ud-Dīn Muḥammad Khaljī and thereafter ruled by the Muslim governors until the breakup of the Delhi sultanate. Shortly after the invasion of Delhi by Timur (Tamerlane) in 1398, the governor Shihāb-ud-Dīn Ghūri set up a kingdom in his own name in 1401. The Ghūri Dynasty's control of Mālwa and Ujjain ended later that century when the sultans of the Khilji Dynasty took power.

These independent Muslim kings generally had their capital at Māndu. Mahmud Khan was the most important Muslin sultan of Mālwa. In 1531 Mālwa was annexed by the Muslim power of Gujarāt but soon it came under the control of the Mughals, under whom Ujjain became the capital of a *subah* or province and the station of a Mughal mint. Mālwa was formally annexed by Akbar, the great Mughal who reigned through the second half of the sixteenth century.

After the overthrow of Akbar's grandson Shāh Jahān in 1658, a battle occurred near Ujjain between the contenders for Mughal power. The forces of Shāh Jahān's son 'Ālamgīr (Aurangzeb), who had overthrown Shāh Jahān, remained in power despite facing many struggles. Although the Mughals' hold weakened significantly after 'Ālamgīr's death in 1707, they continued to exercise power until midcentury, making some improvements in Ujjain. In 1733, during the reign of the Mughal Muḥammad Shāh of Delhi, Sawai Jai Singh of Jaipur in Rājasthān was appointed the governor of Mālwa. He chose Ujjain as the site for a new astronomical observatory because according to Hindu astronomy Ujjain is the first meridian of longitude. The observatory, Vedha Shala, still stands.

In 1750 the Sindhia branch of the Marāṭhās of the Deccan took control of Mālwa and thus Ujjain. The Sindhias' most notable work was the rebuilding of the Mahākāla temple. Ujjain's status declined, however, after the Sindhias moved their capital to the city of Gwalior in 1810. During British rule, Ujjain continued to be a part of the Sindhia Kingdom of Gwalior, subordinate, of course, to the British.

Ujjain has remained largely out of the historical spotlight during the nineteenth and twentieth centuries. It remains notable, however, for its many Hindu temples, especially the Mahākāla Siva temple, and for its status as one of the seven holy cities of India. The Kumbh Mela, the most sacred festival in the Hindu calendar, is held there every twelve years, most recently in 1992.

Further Reading: Little material is available specifically on Ujjain. *An Encyclopaedia of Indian Archaeology,* volume 2, edited by A. Ghosh (Delhi: Munshiram Manoharlal, 1989), contains some useful information on the ancient site. B. C. Law's *Ujjayini in Ancient Indian Literature* (Gwalior: Gwalior Archaeological Department, 1944) provides a literary perspective. Most of the geographical dictionaries of ancient India, especially B. C. Law's *Historical Geography of Ancient India* (Paris: Asiatic Society, 1954) contain brief entries.

—Dilip K. Chakrabarti

Ujung Pandang (South Sulawesi, Indonesia)

Location: On the Makassar Strait toward the southern tip of the southwestern peninsula of Sulawesi (formerly Celebes).

Description: Known as Makassar during the time of European intervention in Southeast Asian trade, Ujung Pandang was for centuries an important port of call for ships trading in Southeast Asia. It was also the main port of the maritime kingdom of Gowa, which at one time controlled not only much of Sulawesi, but also parts of Maluku, Kalimantan (Borneo), and Sumatra. Despite the presence of Portuguese, British, Danish, and Dutch trading posts in the city since the early sixteenth century, Gowa remained independent until 1667. The Makassarese continued to rebel against Dutch overlordship for the following 250 years.

Site Office: Diparda Tk.I Sulawesi Selatan
Jl. Jend. Urip Sumoharjo No. 269
Ujung Pandang 90222
Indonesia
(411) 320616

The name Ujung Pandang, which originally may have been Jumpandang, is variously translated as "Pandan Point," "the farthest point of the pandan tree" (the screw pine) or "the farthest point of sight." In the early seventeenth century, the Dutch renamed the city Makassar, after the people who were then dominant in the area, the Makassarese. The city is best known to Europeans as Makassar, but the original name was still used in 1824 by the indigenous people of the area, and it appears in a treaty between the Dutch and the states of South Sulawesi of that date. Only in the 1970s was the name changed back to Ujung Pandang.

The natural harbor of low-lying Ujung Pandang, strategically located on the Makassar Strait, was the home base of indigenous traders as early as the fourth century A.D. Prahus (a distinctive type of local boat) carrying palm oil, copra, and fish sailed to China, Indochina, Australia, Polynesia, and even to places as far away as Madagascar. Ships from Ujung Pandang were also responsible for a large share of the spice trade out of Maluku (the Moluccas, or Spice Islands). The Makassarese and Buginese, the two peoples native to the area around Ujung Pandang, renowned as shipbuilders, also were feared as pirates. By the fourteenth century, South Sulawesi had become a formidable naval power, operating principally from Ujung Pandang.

Politically, South Sulawesi was organized into three principal kingdoms, Luwu, Gowa, and Bone. Historians have unearthed the most information about Makassarese Gowa and Buginese Bone, in part because these kingdoms left behind extensive chronicles. The kingdom of Gowa began expanding at the expense of its neighbors early in the sixteenth century. Shortly afterward, in the 1540s, the Portuguese arrived at Ujung Pandang, receiving permission from the local kings to establish a trading post. The Portuguese already had a factory, or settlement, at Ambon in Maluku, and their base at Ujung Pandang was an attempt to consolidate their presence in the eastern Indonesian Archipelago. They had the dual aim of gaining control of the trade in spices and slaves and of converting the indigenous peoples of the area to Christianity. In both endeavors they met with a singular lack of success, as became clear by the beginning of the next century.

The king of Gowa converted to Islam in 1605, a religion even more odious to the Portuguese than his earlier animism. Moreover, the Gowa ruler set out to convert the neighboring states and was not intimidated by resistance. When the Buginese of Bone declined to join the new faith, Gowa went to war with them. By 1611 Bone was defeated and converted, and Gowa emerged as the unassailable power in South Sulawesi. The Makassarese fanned out over the Indonesian Archipelago and beyond, establishing a powerful trading empire that included control over territories from Maluku to Sumatra.

The main seat of the kingdom of Gowa was at Sungguminasa, seven miles south of Ujung Pandang. A wooden palace still stands and is now a museum, displaying historical artifacts, weapons, and royal costumes and regalia. A little more than a mile north of the Sunggaminasa palace compound lies the royal cemetery, which holds not only the tombs of many of the Gowa kings and sultans, but also the coronation stone, or *tomanurung,* where during coronation ceremonies a divine ancestor was thought to descend upon the newly installed ruler from the heavens.

The Portuguese fared no better in monopolizing the spice trade than they had in spreading their religion. They firmly ensconced themselves at Ujung Pandang by occupying the fortifications along the Ujung Pandang harbor, which they reconstructed in 1545. However, the indigenous traders were not inclined to give up their share of the spice trade to the newcomers. Moreover, before long British, Spanish, and even Danish traders joined the Portuguese at Ujung Pandang. The European competitor that was finally to push the Portuguese out of the area altogether, the Dutch V.O.C. (Vereenigde Oostindische Compagnie, or United East India Company), arrived in 1608. After capturing the fort from the Portuguese, the Dutch established a factory at Ujung Pandang in 1609. The Dutch again reconstructed and expanded the harbor fortifications, which they called Fort Rotterdam. The V.O.C. and later the Dutch government molded the history of the city and of South Sulawesi in general for the next 350 years.

Fort Rotterdam, Ujung Pandang
Photo courtesy of Indonesia Tourist Promotion Office, Los Angeles

The Dutch, like the Portuguese and British, envisioned monopolizing the spice trade. When, in 1615, the sultan of Gowa refused to surrender his trading rights, the Dutch withdrew their factory from Ujung Pandang and began a military campaign against Gowa that was to last for more than fifty years. The Makassarese were defeated in several confrontations with V.O.C. forces, and in 1637, 1655, and 1660 peace treaties were concluded that granted the Dutch the desired monopolies. However, the Makassarese simply continued to trade in spices, treaty or no. In the late 1630s, for instance, the sultan of Gowa entered into an alliance with several Malukan rulers in defiance of the 1637 treaty, and the "illegal" spice trade continued unabated. In 1641 open hostilities broke out again. Although by 1646 the Dutch had crushed this challenge to their military dominance, the Makassarese continued their trading activities. Meanwhile, the Dutch position in South Sulawesi had become even more tenuous. The Portuguese concentrated all their trading on Ujung Pandang after the Dutch had managed to capture Melaka (Malacca) from them in 1641. The British also maintained a significant presence in the city.

The wars between the Dutch and Makassarese were renewed in 1652. Three years later, the Dutch were able to force the second peace treaty. The Makassarese ignored the treaty and continued to wage war until, in 1658, they laid down arms, promising to obey the terms of the 1655 treaty. Again the promise was not kept, and again the Dutch lacked the clout to enforce its terms. A break in the conflict came with a Bone Buginese rebellion against Sultan Ḥasan-ad-Dīn of Gowa in 1660. The Buginese, under the leadership of

Arung Palakka, were crushed and had to flee Sulawesi, but the two-front war caused the Gowans to suffer another defeat by the Dutch. A third peace treaty, which turned out to be as meaningless as the previous ones, was signed. One positive result of the victory for the Dutch, however, was the permanent expulsion of the Portuguese from Ujung Pandang.

The defeated Buginese rebels made for Batavia (Jakarta) and there enlisted in the V.O.C. army. By 1663, Arung Palakka had entered into an agreement with the Dutch against Gowa. Three years later, Sultan Ḥasan-ad-Dīn's soldiers plundered two Dutch ships that had been stranded just off Ujung Pandang, killing the sailors. In response, the Dutch fitted out a fleet of twenty-one ships, carrying an army of Dutch, Malukan, and Buginese soldiers. After a futile attempt to take back their own stronghold at Ujung Pandang from Gowa, the Dutch fleet engaged the Gowan navy and defeated it, while Arung Palakka landed an army of his warriors just south of the city and was victorious in an overland campaign against Ḥasan-ad-Dīn. Ḥasan-ad-Dīn then had no choice but to sign the Treaty of Bungaya, which granted a monopoly on the spice trade to the Dutch, decreed the expulsion of the British from Ujung Pandang, and transferred the fortifications of Ujung Pandang to the Dutch once more. Although the treaty again turned out to be a meaningless piece of paper, the British were forced to depart the city. Shortly afterward, Gowa resumed the war. A second major campaign led by the Dutch and supported by the Buginese under Arung Palakka was waged in 1668 and 1669. This campaign finally led to the conclusive defeat of Gowa. Ḥasan-ad-Dīn renounced his claim to the sultanate, while Bone became the leading state in South Sulawesi under the kingship of Arung Palakka.

The Dutch were now, nominally at least, the undisputed masters of the entire island of Sulawesi. Fort Rotterdam at Ujung Pandang was their primary base, but they had other fortified settlements on the other peninsulas. In actuality, they had little control over Sulawesi except for the territories immediately surrounding the cities of Ujung Pandang and Manado in the north. Ironically, by the time the Dutch had subdued Gowa, spices were becoming less central to East Indian trade, bringing in diminishing profits. Textiles, coffee, and sugar were taking over as the major cash crops, and these were not to be had in significant quantities in the northeastern part of the archipelago. With Maluku no longer a goldmine, Ujung Pandang was of questionable value to the Europeans. In fact, by the late seventeenth and early eighteenth centuries, the factory at Ujung Pandang registered annual net losses. These losses owed partly to the inability of the Dutch to prevent continued uprisings by the Buginese and Makassarese until the early twentieth century.

The first major confrontation with the warlike Sulawesi tribes came on Java, however. Many Makassarese and Buginese had fled the devastation wrought by war and had begun pirating throughout the Indonesian Archipelago. They also hired themselves out as mercenaries to any kingdom contemplating war. Having allied themselves with Trunajaya, a contender to the throne of Mataram in Central Java, the Makassarese attacked and captured several ports in East Java in 1675. The V.O.C., which entered the conflict against the Makassarese, did not manage to dislodge the mercenaries from their coastal strongholds until four years later. In 1704, however, during the first Javanese War of Succession, the Makassarese fought alongside the V.O.C.

On Sulawesi itself open warfare once again broke out when Arung Sinkang, a Buginese nobleman from the Wajo Kingdom, tried to dislodge Bone from its dominant position. To this end, he began to make alliances with various factions on South Sulawesi in 1735. In 1739 Arung Sinkang attacked the court of Bone, burning the palace compound, and then marched on Ujung Pandang. The garrison stationed at Fort Rotterdam withstood the attack and forced the Wajo Buginese to retreat to their kingdom in the interior. The Dutch then sent a punitive expedition of Dutch and Bone troops into the interior in 1741. In spite of great expense and loss of life, this expedition failed to subdue the Wajorese. In pitched battle the Dutch were victorious every time, but, taking advantage of the difficult terrain and unusually heavy rains, the Wajorese were able to regroup after every defeat.

Dutch attempts to negotiate a treaty also came to nothing, for they could not persuade their Bone allies and Wajo enemies to agree to the same terms. When the expedition was about to give up and return to Ujung Pandang without having achieved its aim, the king of Tanette, another indigenous state, offered his support and inflicted serious losses on Lagusi, one of the principal Wajo towns. Negotiations were reopened, and for a moment it appeared that the Dutch could force the Wajorese to recognize the V.O.C.'s sovereignty. At the last moment, however, a dispute over the wording of the treaty arose, and finally the Dutch left for Ujung Pandang with no more than a promise from the Wajorese that they would sign the treaty. They never did. It was obvious by then that the Dutch simply had no authority in the interior of Sulawesi.

New difficulties arose later in the eighteenth century. One of the kings of Gowa, Batara Gowa II, had been found guilty of piracy and was exiled to Ceylon (now Sri Lanka) in the 1760s. In 1777 a man named Sankilang impersonated the exiled ruler and challenged Batara Gowa's successor. He gained a tremendous following and actually managed to depose the rightful ruler of Gowa, installing himself at Sunggaminasa. Disquieted by the unrest so close to Ujung Pandang, the V.O.C. involved itself in the conflict, defeating Sankilang in 1779. The impostor fled to the mountains with much of his following and most of the sacred regalia of Gowa. After his death, the regalia passed into the hands of the king of Bone, who then was recognized as king of Gowa by Sankilang's remaining followers.

By the late eighteenth century, posting losses every year and failing to control the indigenous states, the V.O.C. presence at Ujung Pandang was no more than a hollow show of military superiority. In 1799 the V.O.C. went bankrupt, and the Dutch government took over its holdings. In 1811, while the Netherlands were occupied with Napoléon Bonaparte, Ujung Pandang fell to the British, together with all the other Dutch possessions in the Indonesian Archipelago. In both 1814 and 1816, Bone and several other kingdoms in South Sulawesi attacked Ujung Pandang, but they were unsuccessful in their attempts to drive out the new colonists. After the Dutch resumed possession of Ujung Pandang, a large number of South Sulawesi states declared the Treaty of Bungaya void and refused to obey its terms. A Dutch diplomatic mission persuaded the states to renew the treaty, with the exception of Bone, which mounted an ultimately unsuccessful attack on Ujung Pandang in 1819. Before the Dutch could drive back the Bone forces, however, two garrisons had been completely annihilated.

The military conflict dragged on undecided until 1823, when Arung Datu, the queen of Bone, indicated that she was willing to renegotiate the treaty. A renewed diplomatic effort in 1824, however, failed to garner the queen's signature. Following a significant defeat of the Bone forces in 1825, inflicted by joint Dutch and Makassarese forces, the Dutch nevertheless had to abandon their attempts to subdue Bone, because a revolt in Java more urgently required the presence of available troops. Bone formally renewed the Treaty of Bungaya in 1838, but it did not give up its rebellious stance. Another very bloody war broke out in 1858. This time the open conflict did not last long, but the Dutch did not succeed in conclusively breaking Makassarese and Buginese resistance until 1906.

During the Japanese occupation of Indonesia in World War II, Ujung Pandang was transformed into an important military base for the Japanese. Consequently, it was heavily bombed by the United States, and much of the fragile old city was destroyed. Fort Rotterdam, one of the few stone buildings at Ujung Pandang, was damaged, but it has since been restored in the interest of tourism and now houses a museum. One section of the museum is devoted to Sulawesi history, while another contains ethnological exhibits.

Following the Japanese withdrawal from Indonesia and the declaration of independence by Republican nationalist forces at Jakarta, the king of Bone at Ujung Pandang was among the first of the indigenous rulers outside of Java to come out in support of the revolution. When Jakarta appointed a Republican governor to Ujung Pandang, most of the Makassarese and Buginese followed Bone's example and recognized his authority. Nevertheless, besieged first by the British and then, more fiercely, by the Dutch, the Republicans soon had to abandon Ujung Pandang. The governor was arrested, together with the kings of Bone and Luwu, and so the revolution came to a halt on Sulawesi.

Unable to crush the revolution on Java, the Dutch sought to contain it, and in 1946 they created a number of states with limited autonomy that were to be federated with the Netherlands. One of these states was East Indonesia, consisting of Sulawesi and Maluku. Ujung Pandang was made its capital. The people of Sulawesi, unlike its rulers, were not content with this arrangement. Revolutionary agitation continued in South Sulawesi, which occasioned one of the more horrendous episodes in the war for independence. Raymond "Turk" Westerling, a Dutch army officer, slaughtered some 3,000 mostly civilian Indonesians on South Sulawesi during a period of approximately three months in his attempt to root out the revolution from the island.

When the Netherlands finally gave up its claims to Indonesia and recognized its independence in 1949, the states created in 1946 were organized for a brief period into a federation with the Java Republic. However, an armed confrontation at Ujung Pandang in 1950 between Republicans and Ambonese soldiers (who had remained loyal to the colonial government throughout the war for independence) precipitated the demise of federalism. The unitary Republic of Indonesia was proclaimed several months later. Ujung Pandang has not always been a willing partner in the republic, however. The unsuccessful Permesta rebellion of 1957 began in Ujung Pandang, and the 1965 attempt to overthrow the government also found many supporters in the city. Not nearly all of these supporters were Chinese, as the official myth would have it.

Since 1965, Ujung Pandang has been quiet. The city, which has nearly 1 million inhabitants, is beginning to industrialize, albeit slowly. Special funding from Jakarta has bolstered efforts to attract tourists to this city rich in history and surrounded by a magnificent, virtually untouched landscape.

Further Reading: Most sources specifically devoted to Ujung Pandang and the Makassarese and Buginese are in Dutch or Bahasa Indonesian. The best general history of Indonesia is *A History of Modern Indonesia: 1300 to the Present* by M. C. Ricklefs (Bloomington: Indiana University Press, and London: Macmillan, 1981; second edition, London: Macmillan, and Stanford, California: Stanford University Press, 1993), which also pays more attention to developments in South Sulawesi than do most histories of Indonesia. Ailsa Zainu'ddin's *A Short History of Indonesia* (London: Cassell, 1969; New York and Washington, D.C.: Praeger, 1970) is also worth consulting and more easily accessible.

—Marijke Rijsberman

Vanuatu

Location: In the southern Pacific Ocean, 500 miles west of Fiji and 1,100 miles east of Australia.

Description: An archipelago of 13 major islands (as well as many smaller islands and islets) forming a rough Y-shape spanning 400 miles. More than 100 distinct languages and dialects are spoken, including English, French, and Bislama. Although much of the land remains jungle, some small cities, such as Vila and Luganville, have been developed. Live volcanoes dot some islands, such as Mount Yasur on Tanna. Most ni-Vanuatu (indigenous people) are Melanesian, although some islands were settled by Polynesians.

Site Office: Vanuatu National Tourist Office
Box 209
Port Vila, Efate
Republic of Vanuatu
(678) 22685, (678) 22515, or (678) 22813

The islands of Vanuatu were formed by volcanic upheaval approximately twenty million years ago. Coral reefs grew up around the islands as millennia passed. Active volcanoes still dot the islands today. Archaeological evidence shows that the islands were first inhabited around 3000 B.C. The first colonists were part of a proto-Melanesian wave of immigration that originated in Indonesia and eventually populated the Pacific Islands. The oldest human settlement in Vanuatu has been found on Malo Island. The so-called Lapita people, named after a site in Lapita, New Caledonia, date from 1400 B.C. They were known for their distinctive pottery, decorated with pinpricks. By 500 B.C., more Lapita people colonized the islands, intermarrying with the preexisting Melanesian inhabitants. The pottery was exported between A.D. 100 and 700, reaching all of the Vanuatu Islands as well as the Solomons.

Between A.D. 1000 and 1400, Polynesian explorers in fifty-man outrigger canoes colonized some of the Vanuatu Islands. These Polynesians were driven from their native lands by overpopulation and a rigid social hierarchy that exiled vanquished kings to the ocean. By 1200, all ceramic trading had ceased. In fact, the art of pottery-making was lost among the islanders. Historians speculate that a new governing group took power at this time. This is when Roymata, the first historical king of Vanuatu, is said to have governed northern Efate and southern islands until 1265. Vanuatu legend also records that in approximately 1475, a large island called Kuwae suddenly exploded into fragments, leaving only the small islands that now are called the Shepherds group. Scientific evidence confirms this legend.

Before European contact, Melanesians lived in tightly-knit clans that had little contact with one another. The clans feuded, and the flesh of select prisoners was eaten in cannibal ceremonies. In contrast to Polynesian societies, where kings were predetermined by birth in a rigid caste system, Melanesian social order was more democratic. Social standing was gained by working one's way through a graded system (*ni-mangki*). To advance to a higher level, island men (women were not included in the system) participated in pig-killing ceremonies; the larger the number of pigs slaughtered, the higher the islander advanced.

Islanders wore little clothing. Men wore only a penis sheath, called a *namba*, and women wore grass skirts. Men painted their skin and were fond of body ornaments, feathers, and necklaces. Women dressed less extravagantly and were consigned to most of the menial labor. Islanders subsisted on farming plantations of taro, sweet potatoes, bananas, and coconuts.

Spirits and ghosts of ancestors dominated island life in most locations. Sorcery and magic were used to placate evil spirits and to please benign ones, and suspected sorcery provided an excuse to make war on neighboring clans. For this reason, when European explorers appeared offshore in their ships during the seventeenth century, islanders believed they were ghosts of their own ancestors. The first Europeans to visit the islands in 1606 may have indeed looked ghostly after four months at sea. Explorer Pedro Fernández de Quirós led three ships on an expedition from Callao, Peru, to search for the fabled southern continent, *Terra Australis Incognita*.

Fervid with the spirit of the Counter-Reformation, Quirós was equally driven by the desire to claim new land for Spain as he was to conquer it for the Catholic Church. To that effect, several clerics joined the 200 soldiers on the trip. Quirós forbade swearing and gambling on board, and there were nightly religious services. The crew was short of supplies and near mutiny when they landed at Gaua on April 25, 1606.

First encounters between island residents and Spaniards were positive. Islanders swarmed to the boats, bringing gifts of bananas, and even carrying children on board. However, the Melanesians soon figured out that the Spaniards were merely men, not spirits, and they were not awed by European boats or equipment. They urged the Spaniards to depart immediately and refused to provision the ships.

When Quirós landed on Espíritu Santo, islanders and soldiers clashed. Hails of arrows answered shots from arquebuses. After the soldiers killed a few natives on the beach, they advanced inland, taking property, vegetables, and pigs abandoned by the fleeing islanders. Quirós decided that Espíritu Santo was the fabled southern continent. He orchestrated an elaborate mass of thanksgiving in which most crew members were "knighted" in a Templar-like ceremony. Afterward, Quirós became detached from reality, a condition his men readily perceived. He managed to start an ill-fated settlement meant to spread Christianity to islanders, but soon became ill and possibly suffered a nervous breakdown. Following a month of disorganized exploration, Quirós' ship returned to Mexico City, and the other two vessels, which had become separated from their leader, eventually reached Manila.

Records of these voyages were kept secret for 100 years. Governments of Spain and Portugal were busy tackling domestic problems but wanted to discourage European trade routes through the Pacific. However, 150 years later, English and French explorers dug up records of Quirós' expeditions in Madras. By this time, the search for *Terra Australis* had become a scientific quest rather than a religious or colonial one. However, control of sea trade routes remained an important issue. The Dutch had already begun colonies on some Pacific trade routes.

A race began between the English and French to chart the unknown Pacific, a race that would later develop into a co-government of the Vanuatu Islands. Representing the French was Louis-Antoine de Bougainville, a veteran of the French and Indian War. Bougainville set off for a round-the-world trip, reaching the Vanuatu Archipelago in 1768. The crew stayed only seven days, long enough to realize the islands were too small to be the austral continent. Bougainville named the island chain "Les Grandes Cyclades" after the famous Greek islands.

English Captain James Cook rediscovered the islands in 1774. He renamed the group "New Hebrides" because their terrain reminded him of Scotland. That name stuck until Vanuatu regained independence in 1980. Cook explored extensively for more than a month and recorded his own interpretations of island names including Erromango, Tanna, and Ambryn, which have been used to this day. The English sailors were astonished by the dark-skinned, relatively short Melanesians, since they had previously encountered only Polynesians. They noted the contrast between the islanders' stone-age living conditions and their highly developed civility, neat plantations, and beautiful singing and flute-playing.

Again, islanders had no use for the materials offered by Europeans. Cloth, which Polynesians were always eager to trade for, was of no use to Melanesians, whose only garments were *nambas*. Metal, nails, scissors, and other trinkets had no appeal, except as adornments. Islanders offered a single small pig when the British first landed, and when they received unsatisfactory gifts in exchange, they refused to part with any more livestock or chickens. As before in their dealings with Quirós, the islanders rejected most elements of Western society, and what they accepted they adapted to their own purposes.

After Cook's voyage, European contact with the island chain was infrequent. William Bligh passed with his crew from the HMS *Bounty* in 1789, after the famous mutiny. Otherwise, the islands were known only to whaling vessels, but crews remained quiet about geographical details. The area's reputation for ferocious natives kept Western explorers and colonists away from the islands until 1815, when sandalwood and bêche-de-mer were discovered on the archipelago. Australian and European traders sought these goods for sale in China, where bêche-de-mer, a sea slug, was used medicinally and sandalwood was burned in ancestor-worshipping ceremonies. In particular, sandalwood was seen as a means to offset the trade imbalance caused by the import of tea to Australia. However, European traders encountered great difficulties establishing the sandalwood trade. Clashes erupted between traders and Vanuatu natives, and massacres of natives occurred on Erromango and Efate Islands. Dishonest traders were assassinated by islanders they had cheated, and other traders were killed by islanders in revenge for the misdeeds of their predecessors. At the same time, European diseases attacked new-world immune systems, causing epidemics among the islanders.

The Europeans desperately needed a way to smooth the troubled trade relations. Natives were now finding uses for western metal objects they had previously dismissed; axes, shovels, saws, scissors, and fishhooks were absorbed into the islanders' everyday life. For example, Pentecost Islanders used axes and hand tools to build bigger platforms from which they practiced "land diving," a harvest-time ceremony similar to modern bungee jumping, using vines instead of rubber cords. Guns were also popular. Cloth and blankets were obtained purely for their garish colors and were used for adornment and decoration. One product, however, took the islands by storm: by 1848 islanders were hooked on tobacco. Not surprisingly, the traders were delighted, as the dried leaves were easy to transport in large quantities. A lucrative trade triangle of luxury goods had developed: traders brought tobacco to the islanders in return for sandalwood, which in turn would be traded to the Chinese for tea, which went to Australia. This success would be short-lived, however, for resources held out only until 1868, when the islands were completely stripped of sandalwood.

During this period, along with traders, a different kind of European stranger appeared to Vanuatu's inhabitants: the Christian missionary. Quirós' seventeenth-century Catholic fervor had begun a tradition of missionary journeys to the islands. To nineteenth-century Presbyterians, Melanesians appeared the most intractable, and therefore most challenging, of heathens. "Rumors of cannibalism are like catnip to missionaries, who are never happier than when bringing the Bible to savages," Paul Theroux wryly writes in his description of a Vanuatu visit, commenting on the islands' continued appeal to missionaries.

The first missionary on the islands was John Williams, sent by the London Missionary Society in 1839. He had established missionary colonies all over the Pacific Islands and had translated the New Testament into the Rarotongan language (spoken in the Cook Islands). Natives killed Williams on Erromango in November of that year. Other mission-

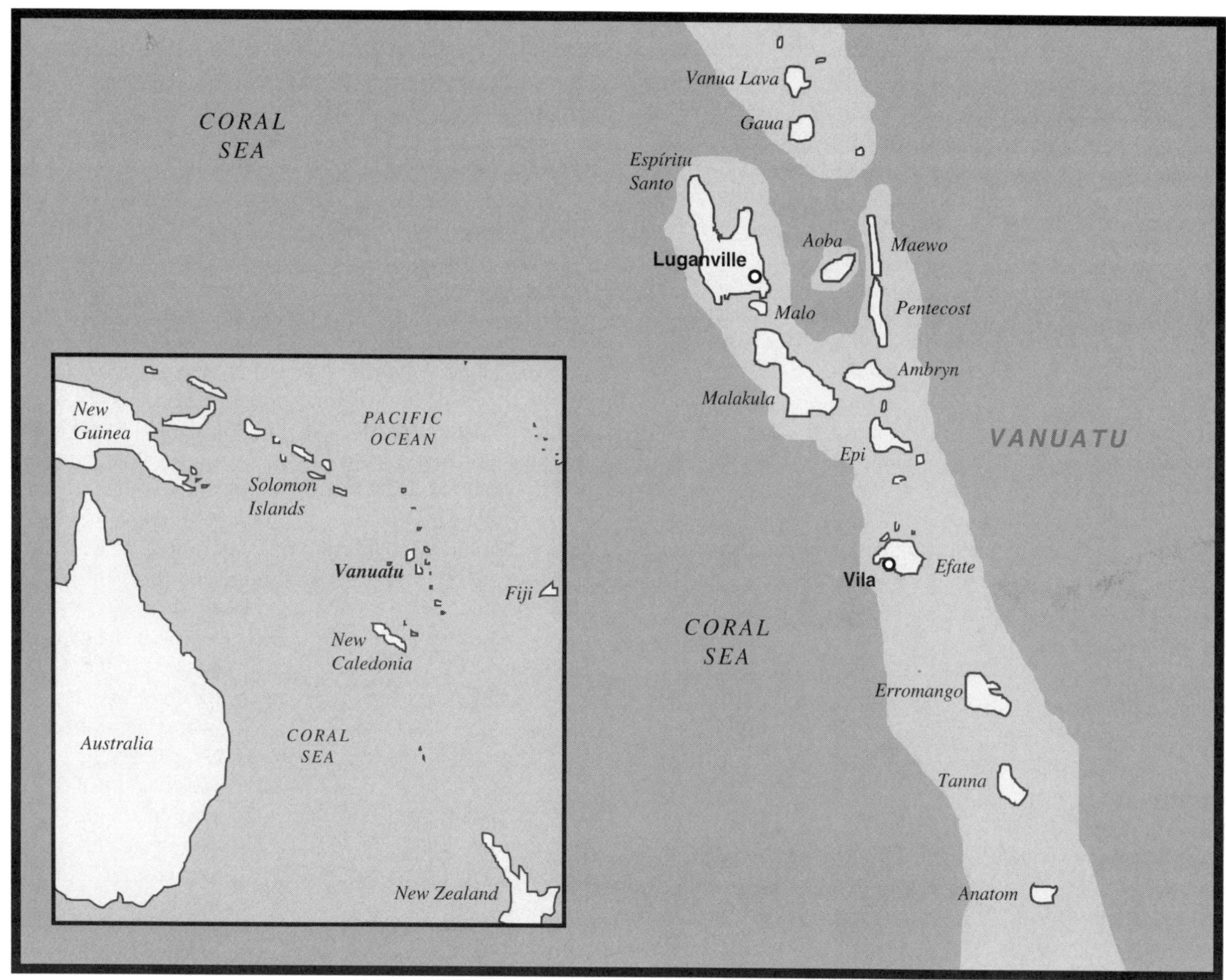

Map of Vanuatu, with inset showing its position relative to Australia
Illustration by Tom Willcockson

aries soon followed. The most successful of these was the Presbyterian John Geddie, who set up a mission colony on Anatom in 1848. Geddie, a Scottish immigrant by way of Canada, learned the local language and taught the islanders to read and write. He translated hymns and the New Testament into the local dialect. Geddie also converted 100 islanders, who were instructed to disseminate Christianity throughout the islands.

Islanders gave missionaries a mixed reception. In some cases, rivalries among Christian sects sprung up and pitted island followers against one another and against local traders, some of whom encouraged "pagan" groups. Clashes caused bloodshed between clans. In 1860, a measles epidemic wiped out huge portions of the island populations, showing natives that Christian "magic" was unable to save them. Pagan groups gained strength and expelled missionaries, including the Presbyterian minister John Paton, who was booted from Tanna. Paton caused an international scandal when he returned in 1865 with a British Navy ship that shelled his former mission town. Armed British soldiers landed and set fire to Tannese property. Island chiefs were forced to sign an apology for their earlier misdeeds. The Australian newspaper *The Empire* branded Paton a "sacerdotal hypocrite."

Meanwhile, another group of white men was taking advantage of the islanders. Beginning in 1863, Australian kidnappers or Blackbirders were luring islanders onto ships and transporting them to work on plantations in Fiji, Samoa, New Caledonia, and Queensland. Blackbirding severely diminished local populations. Sometimes entire villages would be enticed on board a ship to trade and then be kidnapped en masse. In 1872 labor traders on the *Carl*, a blackbirding ship, kidnapped and massacred a boatload of Epi islanders. The crew whitewashed the ship to avoid detection, but members of the HMS *Rosario* boarded and discovered the murders. Presbyterian missionaries raised an international outcry about this and other blackbirding incidents, which put an unflattering spotlight on the practice. Continued complaints finally ended the extremely lucrative trade in the early 1900s.

Europeans settled the islands during the 1860s, when they established cotton plantations in the hope of profiting on cotton shortages caused by the American Civil War. Settlers also grew cocoa, coffee, bananas, and vanilla. The French began efforts to gain control of the islands during the 1880s, when French trader John Higginson established the Compagnie Calédonienne des Nouvelles-Hébrides. The company purchased land to be given to French settlers, who soon outnumbered British settlers in Vanuatu. While the British would not give up their claim to the islands, both groups could agree that they needed protection against the local natives. In 1887, a Joint Naval Commission was established to protect French and British settlers. In 1906 the dual French-English government known as the Condominium began. Critics, however, labeled it the "Pandemonium," since the two governments' conflicts resulted in inefficiency. Meanwhile, the ni-Vanuatu population was left without any representation. Law enforcement was weak, allowing opium smuggling to thrive in Santo during the 1940s and cannibalism to survive in Malakula into the 1960s.

During World War II, more than one-half million American soldiers passed through a temporary military base constructed on Santo. The soldiers brought the trappings of American life, including movie theaters, automobiles, refrigerators, and millions of bottles of Coca-Cola. Many islanders were hired at a generous wage to build airstrips and staff the bases. Melanesians were impressed by the apparent equality between black and white military personnel. When the Americans left Santo, they offered to sell equipment to the local French government, but the French refused to pay even eight cents on the dollar for the equipment, insisting that the Americans give it to them. Instead, the Americans pushed much of the contents of their base into the ocean at Million Dollar Point and exploded it underwater. Today, after fifty years, the Pacific Ocean is spitting it back again. Beachcombers find a weirdly fascinating jetsam of recognizable objects, such as car doors, covered by slime, barnacles, seaweed, and mud.

Ni-Vanuatu natives were very impressed by what they saw at the U.S. military bases on Efate and Santo. "Cargo cults" recreated the seemingly magical objects they witnessed. Exposed to the mechanical wonders of the twentieth century, some indigenous groups, who hitherto lived in primitive isolation, built airplane-like sculptures from wood and cleared a jungle airstrip. Wooden radios were constructed with vines emerging from the back for antennas.

A new religion, the Jon Frum movement (also known as John Prum), had quietly emerged on Tanna Island during the 1930s. Jon Frum, a supernatural figure, appeared to islanders with instructions to expel the white man from the islands. On April 16, 1941, the Jon Frum movement came into the open. Tannese believers stopped working, boycotted church services, and spent all of their money in one afternoon. British and French authorities responded by arresting top Jon Frum leaders. For sixteen years, the religion went underground. Islanders were forbidden to even say the words "Jon Frum." However, the religion survives today, although it has changed through the years. A red cross is its symbol, after the American Red Cross symbol islanders saw on U.S. military vehicles. In religious ceremonies, islanders march with faux bamboo bayonets and paint "USA" in red on their bare chests.

The Vanuatu independence movement began in earnest during the 1960s. The archipelago's economy had dwindled after World War II, and the ni-Vanuatu population protested when Western landowners, who legally owned nearly all of the land, cleared inland spaces for livestock ranches. The ni-Vanuatu sought to protect the bush land and to assert their traditional posession of these areas. Two independence parties sprang up: the Nagriamel Party led by Jimmy Stevens rose from among French-speaking islanders, and the Vanauaaku Party led by Reverend Walter Lini rose from among Anglophones. Stevens petitioned the United Nations for independence in 1971, but Lini won an archipelago-wide election in 1979. Independence came on July 30, 1980, despite a secessionist movement led by a French-led group known as the Modérés. With the assistance of troops from Papua New Guinea, the new government restored order. Islanders adopted the name Vanuatu, which means in different languages: "our land," "the land which came from the sea," or "the place of ever-lasting land."

As always, reinterpretation typifies Vanuatu's contact with the world. Like the barnacle-covered debris on Million Dollar Point, recognizable elements of Western culture surface in Vanuatu, transformed by native *kastom* (custom). While tourism and banking have become important parts of the republic's economy, most of its people still work on plantations or practice subsistence farming. There is no direct taxation in Vanuatu. Modern resort cities share the flag with villages where cannibalism was still practiced into the 1960s. The islands' natives have mimicked and redefined European civilization since their first exposure to it, choosing some elements and rejecting others. The result is an amazing amalgamation of old and new.

Further Reading: For a recent, exhaustive study of Vanuatu's history with a focus on Tanna Island, see French anthropologist Joel Bonnemaison's *The Tree and the Canoe: History and Ethnogeography of Tanna* (Honolulu: University of Hawaii Press, 1994). For an academic treatment of the archipelago with a Post-Structuralist slant, see Lamont Lindstrom's *Knowledge and Power in a South Pacific Society* (Washington, DC: Smithsonian Institute Press, 1990). Also, David Harcombe's *Vanuatu: A Lonely Planet Travel Survival Kit* (Hawthorn, Victoria, and Oakland, California: Lonely Planet, 1995) provides a good overview of the archipelago's history subdivided by major island or island group. Paul Theroux's *The Happy Isles of Oceania: Paddling the Pacific* (London: Hamilton, and New York: Putnam, 1992) provides a wry, descriptive, first-person snapshot of Vanuatu during the early 1990s.

—Jean L. Lotus

Vārānasī (Uttar Pradesh, India)

Location: In northern India, 400 miles west-northwest of Calcutta; on the plains of Uttar Pradesh, along the banks of the Ganges River. Vārānasī sits between the Varanā (Averter) and Asi (Sword) Rivers, both rivers perpendicular to the Ganges, the Varanā running into the Ganges on the north, and the Asi joining it to the south.

Description: Also known as Bārānasi, Banāras, Benares, and Kāshī (Luminous, or City of Light), Vārānasī claims to be the oldest continuously inhabited city in the world. India's holiest Hindu pilgrimage site, it is home of some famous *ghāts* (stepped embankments) along the Ganges where pilgrims bathe. To the Hindus, dying in Vārānasī insures release from the endless cycle of death and rebirth. The Buddha is said to have preached his first sermon in a park on the city's outskirts. The city is also holy to Sikhs and Jains.

Site Office: The Mall, 15B
Vārānasī 221002
Uttar Pradesh
India
43744

Vārānasī has attracted pilgrims for over 2,500 years. One of the oldest living cities in the world, Vārānasī is regarded by Hindus as the place of creation and the permanent home of Siva, who, although omnipresent, is particularly visible and luminous in certain geographical places. Vārānasī, or Kāshī (City of Light), is the most luminous of all. The city is located where an old trade route through northern India intersects the Ganges River. This earthly geography is reflected in Vārānasī's spiritual role as a sacred *tīrthas* (ford or crossing place), at which one crosses the river of Saṃsāra (the repeated cycle of death and rebirth) into liberation. People come to Vārānasī to die, for to die there is to cross, finally, to the "far shore" beyond the cycle of life and death.

Vārānasī consists of four concentric circles of sacred zones. The largest, Kāshī, has a radius of about ten miles and a pilgrimage route requiring five days to complete. The zone extends into the countryside far beyond the city limits. The second zone, Vārānasī, is roughly equivalent to the area of the modern city; the third zone, Avimukta, is smaller, but both zones have pilgrimage routes taking one day. Inside Avimukta is the smallest of the zones, Antargriha (Inner Sanctum), an area immediately surrounding the central temple of Siva Vishvanatha.

The most ancient name of the area is Kāshī. Used 3,000 years ago to designate a kingdom of which this city may have been the capital, this name appears along with the city's other names in the Sanskrit writings praising the city. The name Kāshī possibly derives from the name of an ancient king, or from *kāsha,* a tall grass with silver flowers growing along the river. However, it is generally believed to have derived from the Sanskrit *kāsh,* meaning to look brilliant, shine, or be beautiful.

Found in both the Jātaka tales (fables recounting former lives of the Buddha) and in the *Mahābhārata* (a classical Sanskrit epic), the name Vārānasī is now the official name of the city, although in the past the name has taken the Pali form Bārānasi, which has been corrupted to Banāras and thence, in Muslim and British India, to Benares. Some speculate that the name Vārānasī may have come not from the combination of Varanā and Asi, its modern boundary rivers to the north and south, but from the name of the northern river alone, known in ancient times as Vārānasī. Archaeological records show that the city once lay on the Rājghāt Plateau in the north, possibly along the Varanā River where it met the Ganges, and did not continue south to the Asi as it does today.

In the second and early first millennia B.C. Vārānasī may have been the home of the Kāshīs, an Aryan tribe from northwestern India, and the base from which their kings engaged in a war later described in the *Mahābhārata.* Writings from later periods suggest that, at least according to popular tradition, Vārānasī had been the Kāshī capital. These writings relate that Kāshī was one of sixteen kingdoms where Aryan culture took hold in the eighth to sixth centuries B.C. To the north was the kingdom of Koshala and to the east lay the kingdom of Magadha. At the beginning Kāshī was the most powerful of the three kingdoms, but by the seventh century B.C. Koshala had gained ascendancy. (The king of Koshala was called Bārānasiggaho, Conqueror of Vārānasī.) Buddhist literature, especially the Jātaka tales, refer to the Vārānasī of this period as a magnificent capital, a trade and commercial center surrounded by twelve leagues of walls.

The Kāshī kingdom and its wealthy city Vārānasī became political puppets in the hands of the rival Magadha and Koshala kings during the sixth century B.C. When the daughter of Koshala's king married the king of Magadha, the bride's father presented Kāshī to the groom as a dowry, with the stipulation that Vārānasī's revenues went to pay for the new queen's bathing and perfume expenses. Later the king of Magadha's son, Ajātashatru, killed his father for the throne, and the widowed queen, it is said, died of grief. Koshala reclaimed Kāshī, but Koshala's king gave it away a second time, to Ajātashatru, again as a dowry for a second alliance. Eventually Magadha completely dominated both Kāshī and Koshala.

Throughout this period, Vārānasī's fame spread as a Hindu pilgrimage destination. The city also figures prominently in other religious traditions of the era. Following his

Boats on the Ganges, Vārānasī
Photo courtesy of Air India Library, New York

enlightenment, the Buddha is said to have traveled to the city to teach his companions what he had found, walking 200 miles from Gayā, where he had been meditating, and ferrying across the Ganges. Finding his companions in a park (now called Sārnāth) just north of Vārānasī, he preached to them the Four Noble Truths and the Eightfold Noble Path. At the park he also taught the son of a wealthy Vārānasī merchant; the son became a monk, and his parents became Buddhism's first lay followers. Buddha returned to the park occasionally during his travels. A monastic center grew up at Sārnāth and endured for 1,500 years.

Vārānasī also appears in the traditions of the Jain faith. Pārśvanātha, a *jina* (Jain spiritual leader), is said to have been born there in the eighth century B.C. Mahāvīra, another *jina*, spent time teaching in Vārānasī around the same time as the Buddha. Mahāvīra taught that one could achieve *moksha*, or release from the death-rebirth cycle, by nonaction, that is, by harming no one and abstaining from sinful thoughts and desires.

Vārānasī subsequently fell under various Hindu and Buddhist dynasties. In the third century B.C. Emperor Aśoka of the Buddhist Mauryan Dynasty constructed a stupa, a domed monument, at Sārnāth. Part of an Aśokan pillar, at one time over sixty-five feet high, still exists today. Its capitol, decorated with four lions, the symbol of the modern Indian state, now rests in the Sārnāth Archaeological Museum. During the second and first centuries B.C., the region was ruled by the Hindu Shunga kings. Records indicate that these kings performed the rare Vedic *ashvamedha* rites in Vārānasī on two separate occasions. The Shungas were followed by the Buddhist Kushāna Dynasty. In the fourth to sixth centuries A.D., during the Gupta Dynasty, Sārnāth became a great center of Buddhist art, known for its sandstone Buddha images. From the fall of the Guptas until the coming of the Muslim sultanate in the thirteenth century, Vārānasī was under the rule of Hindu kings and became a major, if not preeminent, center of Hindu pilgrimage, theology, art, and architecture.

In the seventh century A.D. the Chinese traveler Xuan Zang toured Vārānasī, noting 30 monasteries and 3,000 monks there. He described the city as three miles long, one mile wide, with clusters of villages, leafy trees, temples, and shrines. Streams of clear water flowed throughout the city. Contemporary Sanskrit writings note that during the high flood years, the plateau city of Vārānasī became an island, and such conditions were praised as auspicious.

The height of Vārānasī's prestige came in the eleventh and twelfth centuries, during the reign of the Gāhaḍavālas, Hindu rulers who considered themselves the protectors of the *tīrthas* (spiritual fords) of which Kāshī was one of the most important. Govindachandra, the most famous of these kings, made scores of donations to temples in the city and commissioned one of the earliest collections of Hindu literature. One volume of this work catalogues more than 350 shrines in the

Ghāts, *Vārānasī*
Photo courtesy of Air India Library, New York

city. The city soon became a major administrative center as well, and eventually the Rājghāt Plateau section of Vārānasī (today a rural area) became the capital of the Gāhaḍavāla Kingdom. Vārānasī was sacked and looted.

This golden age ended suddenly and violently in 1193 with the invasion of Muslim general Quṭb-ud-Dīn Aybak. According to one Muslim historian, the invaders destroyed 1,000 temples in Vārānasī, raising mosques in their places. Fourteen hundred camels hauled away the plunder. The city was rebuilt atop the rubble, although the Rājghāt of Vārānasī did not recapture its former splendor. Despite the end of the Gāhaḍavāla leadership, the Hindu elements of Vārānasī recovered; the Buddhist monasteries did not.

Muslim sultanates ruled the Ganges valley, including Vārānasī, for 500 years. Six times during these years the Hindu temples of the city were destroyed. The first occurred in the fourteenth century under Fīrūz Shāh Tughluq. A century later, under the Sharqī kings, the temples again were destroyed and their stones used in construction of a mosque in Jaunpur, sixty miles east of Allahābād. Under Sikandar Lodī (ruled 1489–1517), the Lodīs seized power from the Sharqīs, and parts of Vārānasī were again laid waste.

During this period lived Kabīr (1440–1518), one of India's great poets, who was born in Vārānasī to a family of weavers. Whether he was born a Muslim or a Hindu is unknown, although adherents of both religions claimed his remains upon his death. As author Diana L. Eck relates the legend, when "the cloth covering his body was lifted, there was nothing but a spray of flowers . . . [capturing] the essence of Kabīr's own message: he would not be classified by any religion." In fact, he ridiculed both Islam and Hinduism. To spite Hindu tradition, Kabīr refused to die in Kāshī, the sacred place where one could achieve a liberating death. His followers initiated a sectarian movement, the Kabīr Panth, after whose center in Vārānasī a section of the city, Kabīr Chaurā, is named.

One of Vārānasī's resident artists during the sixteenth century was the Hindu poet Tulsīdās, who, like Kabīr, wrote in the vernacular Hindi rather than the traditional literary language of Sanskrit. Tulsīdās rendered sacred Hindu literature into Hindi. The *Rāmcharitmānas,* his version of the *Rāmāyaṇa,* the epic celebrating Rāma, a king, hero, and avatar of Vishnu, was at first attacked by the orthodox; however, it remains Hindi's most popular classic.

In the sixteenth century began the liberal reign of the Mughal emperor Akbar (ruled 1556–1605), who allowed and even funded the rebuilding of Hindu temples in Vārānasī. Some of the city's *ghāts,* or stepped landing places for bathing along the Ganges, were built during this tolerant period, during which India's arts and literature flourished. A portrait of the city at this time has been recorded by the Englishman Ralph Fitch, who in 1584 traveled with letters of introduction from Elizabeth I to monarchs of India and China. Fitch arrived in Vārānasī by boat and noted bathers in the Ganges and old men praying, the "old men" being *ghātiās* or *pandās* who attend to the pilgrims.

The respite for Hinduism was short-lived, however. Emperor Akbar's grandson Shāh Jahān (ruled 1628–58) ordered that the seventy-six Hindu temples under construction in Vārānasī be destroyed. As late as 1668, at least some of the city's existing temples remained standing, as evidenced by the accounts of French traveler Jean Baptiste Tavernier, a jewel dealer who visited Vārānasī that year on the last of his six trips to India and described Bindu Mādhava, a great riverside temple. But Shāh Jahān's son, 'Ālamgīr (ruled 1658–1707), a fervent Muslim, would not suffer these to remain. He ordered that Vārānasī's greatest temples, including the Vishveshvara in 1669 and the Bindu Mādhava, be torn down and replaced with mosques on their sites. He even tried unsuccessfully to rename the city "Muhammadabād." Not a single prominent Hindu structure built before 'Ālamgīr's reign has survived.

Despite the calamaties to its temples, Vārānasī remained a center of learning and religious thought. The French scholar and doctor François Bernier visited the city in the latter part of the seventeenth century and pronounced it the "Athens of India."

After the Mughal Empire fell in the late seventeenth century, Vārānasī came under the rule of the Kāshīrāj, a family of Hindu kings, the first Hindu rulers of the city in 500 years. By the end of the eighteenth century, the Kāshīrāj were tributary vassals of the British. In 1781 Chet Singh, a Kāshīrāj king, resisted additional British tax demands, despite the arrival in Vārānasī of Warren Hastings (governor general of India from 1773 to 1785), who came to confront its ruler. Chet Singh was imprisoned in his palace but escaped on a rope made of unwound turbans. He then called up a local rebellion, and Hastings had to escape the city to save his life. Hastings returned with an English army, however, which quickly defeated the rebels. Chet Singh fled to Bundelkhand, and Hastings installed the former king's nephew on the throne.

Although Vārānasī was under British administration by 1794, the Marāṭhās continued to lead in cultural and religious matters. The city became the recipient of much Marāṭhā largess as a result of its having harbored the famous Marāṭhā hero Śivājī during his battles with the Mughal Empire. Vārānasī was greatly rebuilt in the eighteenth century, with a host of new temples and *ghāts* funded by the Marāṭhās.

The British also left their mark, constructing broad roads where there had been lanes, and draining and filling some of the lakes, ponds, and pools. In 1791 Warren Hastings approved a Sanskrit college in Vārānasī, a place for Sanskrit texts to be collected and studied. Western religious influences also came to Vārānasī through British initiatives: the Baptist Missionary Society in 1819 began the first of many nineteenth-century efforts to bring Christianity to the city.

In 1822 the British scholar James Prinsep made a map of Vārānasī that showed its network of pools and lakes. Urban growth blocked drainage of these waters, and as a result they became polluted. In the 1820s two of the larger lakes, Mandākinī and the Matsyodarī, were drained to a fraction of their former size and incorporated into municipal parks.

In 1823 and 1824 the Anglican bishop of Calcutta, Bishop Reginald Heber, visited Vārānasī and called the city "more entirely and characteristically Eastern than any I have yet seen." He wrote about the crowded, winding alleys lined with buildings mostly of three stories; he described houses with verandas, oriel windows, overhanging eaves, and galleries. Heber also noted a great number of small temples, many in the angles of the streets. There were, he added, no Europeans living in Vārānasī.

In 1853 the present buildings for the Sanskrit college were constructed (in an incongruous Gothic style), and the school was named Queen's College. Today it is called Vārānaseya Sanskrit Vishvavidyālaya (Vārānasī Sanskrit Ocean of All Learning). In the late nineteenth century the Zenana Bible and Medical Mission began a women's hospital, which is still in existence today.

Annie Besant, the English head of the Theosophical Society, along with the pandit and reformer Madan Mohan Mālavīya, began in 1905 making plans and raising funds for a new Hindu university that would teach modern sciences along with the more traditional religious and philosophical fare of the sort offered at Queen's College. The mahārāja of Vārānasī donated land. By 1916 Lord Hardinge, viceroy of India, laid the foundation stone of Banāras Hindu University. Its curriculum includes Sanskrit, commerce, engineering, agriculture, and medicine; the university is situated beyond the southern border of Kāshī.

In 1940 railroad contractors digging for landfill exposed part of the Rājghāt Plateau settlement, parts of the ninth-century B.C. city wall, and a wealth of pottery and artifacts. Excavations were carried out in the early 1940s and mid–1960s at Rājghāt, but the dig was quite limited compared to the size and importance of the site. The full archaeological record of the city is as yet incomplete.

In 1964 a white marble temple, the largest temple in the city, was raised in honor of Tulsīdās. Its walls are engraved with verses and scenes from the poet's great work, the *Rāmcharitmānas*.

Today Vārānasī, with more than 1 million inhabitants, is a labyrinth of narrow lanes. Although few of the city's buildings predate the sixteenth century, Vārānasī's riverfront has an ancient, ageless aspect, where ritual bathers still come to its two and one-half miles of *ghāts*.

Further Reading: The best source on Vārānasī in English is *Banaras: City of Light* by Diana L. Eck (New York: Knopf, 1982; London: Routledge and Kegan Paul, 1983), which details the city's rich religious heritage, particularly in the Hindu tradition. *India: A Modern History* by Percival Spear (Ann Arbor: University of Michigan Press, 1972) covers the political history of Vārānasī and India from its inception in ancient times to the first few years of the 1970s.

—L. R. Naslund

Vientiane (Vientiane, Laos)

Location: In central Laos on the banks of the Mekong River, opposite and a little upstream from the Thai town of Nong Khai.

Description: From the mid–sixteenth century Vientiane (or Vieng Chan) was the capital of the Lao Kingdom of Lan Xang, but was almost entirely destroyed during the Lao-Thai war of 1827–28. Chosen as the administrative capital of French Laos, it was rebuilt in graceful French colonial style and its ancient Buddhist monuments were reconstructed. Subsequently it became the capital of independent Laos. Now the capital of the Lao People's Democratic Republic, the city constitutes an administratively autonomous municipality within the province of Vientiane.

Site Office: Lao National Tourism (Lanatour)
8/2 Lane Xang Avenue
P.O. Box 5221
Vientiane
Laos
216671 or 212013

Archaeological discoveries on the plain of Vientiane have revealed Buddha images in the Mon style and inscriptions in old Mon dating from as early as the ninth century. At that time the Mon, a people speaking an Austroasiatic language related to Cambodian, ruled a powerful kingdom known as Dvaravati in central Thailand. They were ardent Theravada Buddhists; Mon monks were active in spreading their faith not only to what today is northeastern and northern Thailand, but also to Cambodia and Laos.

Whether the people of the Vientiane were themselves Mon is more doubtful. They probably did speak an Austroasiatic language, as do most of the ethnic minorities still living in Laos today. All we know is that the earliest local principality in the Vientiane area was called Chandapuri, an Indian name meaning "City of Sandalwood." That Mon influence continued into the eleventh century is evident from the rock-carved Buddhas at Vang Sang, some forty miles north of Vientiane, which bear an inscription dated 1006.

By the end of the twelfth century, the Vientiane region had been absorbed into the expanding Cambodian Empire. The garrison town of Xai Fong, near Vientiane, was the Cambodian administrative center for the central Mekong basin. From there the Khmer ruled a mixed population that by then included a new component, a people who for some centuries had been moving down the river valleys of northern Laos and Thailand. These were the speakers of Tai languages, ancestors of the modern Thai of Thailand, the Shan of Burma, and the Lao of Laos.

Cambodian control over the region of Vientiane was short-lived. By the mid–thirteenth century, Khmer power was in retreat as Tai princes carved out a number of independent *meuang,* the Tai term for a political/administrative entity of variable extent. The Lao of the Vientiane plain established their own *meuang* of Vieng Chan Vieng Kham, whose dual centers probably reflected the Tai institution of joint rule by a king and viceroy *(uparat).*

By the end of the thirteenth century, Vieng Chan Vieng Kham was tributary to the Tai kingdom of Sukhothai to the west (centered on the modern Thai city of the same name). The region was incorporated into the first extensive Lao kingdom founded by Fa Ngum in 1354, but only after a struggle. Fa Ngum was at first unable to capture Vieng Kham because of its protective "wall" of living bamboo. So he resorted to a ruse. Before pretending to withdraw his forces, he instructed his archers to fire golden-tipped arrows into the bamboo thickets. When the defenders cut down the bamboo in their eagerness to retrieve the arrows, Fa Ngum returned and took the town.

We may doubt the accuracy of this story from the Lao chronicles, but from this time on Vientiane was the most important of the regional *meuang* making up the Lao kingdom of Lan Xang Hom Khao (A Million Elephants and the White Parasol, a title signifying both military might and royal kingship). Its capital was Luang Prabang, then known as Xieng Dong Xieng Thong, 130 miles north of Vientiane upstream on the Mekong.

Over the next two centuries the Lao population steadily expanded, settling the fertile river plains of the central Mekong basin as far south as Champasak and parts of the Khorat plateau comprising what is now northeastern Thailand. Thus the center of the Lao world gradually shifted south too, from Luang Prabang to Vientiane, which was better positioned to collect taxes in the form of tribute and recruit troops from the newer settlements.

In 1560 the decision was made by King Xetthathirat of Lan Xang to move his capital from Luang Prabang to Vientiane. What precipitated the move at this time was not only the shift of Lao population, but also the rise of a new, powerful, and aggressive dynasty in Burma. Already Burmese armies had invaded the Siamese kingdom of Ayutthaya and reduced the northern Tai kingdom of Lan Na, with its capital at Chiang Mai, to tributary status. Luang Prabang was too vulnerable. Vientiane, by contrast, was more defensible and better able to raise an army in a hurry.

Xetthathirat set about embellishing his new capital with both a lavish palace complex and Buddhist monuments. Royal patronage of the Sangha, the monastic order, not only gained for the king great religious merit, but also thereby reinforced his royal legitimation, for Buddhism taught that reincarnation was determined by karma (accumulated moral merit). The king had the right to rule because of the good karma built up through previous lifetimes. Sangha and court thus enjoyed a mutually supportive relationship.

Xetthathirat brought with him from Luang Prabang two sacred Buddha images, leaving another image, the Phra Bang, in the city named after it. For the Phra Kaeo, the Emerald Buddha, Xatthathirat constructed the magnificent Vat Phra Kaeo, the columned image hall *(bot)* of which rests on a high plinth approached by elaborate stairways. The temple fell into ruin after a Siamese army carried off the Emerald Buddha in 1827, but was restored to its original form in the 1930s. It now serves as a museum of Lao religious art, principally some fine Buddhist sculpture dating from the eighth to the eighteenth centuries.

The other great Buddhist monument constructed by Xettathirat, the That Luang, or Great Stupa, has become the primary symbol of the modern Lao state. Originally situated less than a mile outside the city walls, it has since come to occupy a central position in the modern city that has extended beyond it.

The form of the stupa is uniquely Lao, and quite different from either Thai or Burmese stupas. The rectangular base is forty-five yards square, with offering pavilions at the center of each side, the whole being enclosed by surrounding cloisters. On the second of two upper terraces in the form of lotus petals rise thirty elongated smaller replicas of the central spire, thereby creating a harmoniously proportioned whole.

The That Luang escaped destruction in the Thai-Lao war of 1827–28, but in 1873 it was badly damaged by Chinese marauders seeking the gold treasure they believed it held. Reconstruction was carried out under the direction of the French School of the Far East, and today it is the venue for the largest annual festival held in Laos (each November, following the rainy season).

The seventeenth century saw the apogee of the kingdom of Lan Xang, coinciding with the long reign of King Surinyavongsa (1637–95). It was during this period that the first European merchants and missionaries penetrated the remote Lao kingdom. From their accounts it is evident that Vientiane was one of the richest and most magnificent cities of Southeast Asia, with its moated walls, its temples and palaces, its processions and religious festivities.

The first European to arrive, just four years after Surinyavongsa's accession, was Gerritt van Wuysthoff, a merchant employed by the Dutch East India Company, who took more than three months to work his way upstream from the Cambodian capital of Lovek to Vientiane. An alternative route was overland from Ayutthaya by elephant or oxcart, an almost equally long and arduous journey that was discouraged by the Siamese. Vientiane's remoteness thwarted van Wuysthoff's hopes of opening up trading relations with Lan Xang.

One year after van Wuysthoff's arrival, Italian Jesuit missionary Giovanni-Maria Leria arrived in Vientiane. While van Wuysthoff stayed only a few months, Leria remained for five years, without ever obtaining permission to proselytize. His account, though it comes to us secondhand (it was published by a certain G. F. de Marini in Rome in 1660), rings true. Here is how Leria described the king's palace:

> The royal palace, of which the structure and symmetry are admirable, can be seen from afar. Truly it is of a prodigious extent, and so large that one would take it for a town, both with respect to its situation and the infinite number of people who live there. The apartment of the king, which is adorned with a superb and magnificent gateway, and a quantity of fine rooms together with a great hall, are all made of incorruptible timber and adorned outside and in with excellent bas-reliefs so delicately gilded that they seem to be plated with gold rather than covered with gold leaf.

Unfortunately, what remained of the palace almost two centuries later was destroyed by the Siamese.

These European visitors tell us much about the region's form of government, its relations with neighboring kingdoms, its economy and trade, culture and religion. Neither of the men penetrated the inner workings of the court, but both were impressed by the evident power and wealth of the Sangha. Monks in Vientiane, van Wuysthoff notes in his journal, were "more numerous than the soldiers of the Emperor of Germany" and came from as far away as Cambodia and Siam to study at the great Lao monasteries.

The end of the reign of Surinyavongsa brought catastrophe to Lan Xang. The succession dispute that followed his death divided the kingdom into three weakened parts—Vientiane, Luang Prabang, and Champasak—all of which within less than a century had fallen under the suzerainty of Siam. But what weakened the Lao kingdoms was not just internal division. Increased trade during the sixteenth and seventeenth centuries had favored the maritime over the inland kingdoms, both in the accumulation of wealth and purchase of new military technology. By the late eighteenth century the Lao kingdoms were no match for the Siamese. In 1778 a Siamese army carried off the two most sacred Lao Buddha images, the Phra Bang and the Phra Kaeo.

In 1827 Anuvong, the last king of Vientiane, made a desperate attempt to free himself of Siamese suzerainty. The war that followed was a disaster for the Lao. A Siamese army forced Anuvong to flee Vientiane, then burned and looted his palace. When Anuvong returned to take up the fight, he was captured and taken in chains to Bangkok, where he died a miserable death. This time Vientiane was almost totally destroyed. The only structures spared were the That Luang and Vat Sisaket, an architectural gem built by Anuvong himself close to where his palace once stood.

For the next seventy years, after its population had been forcibly resettled by the Siamese on the Khorat plateau, the site of Vientiane was a wilderness. When members of the

That Luang Stupa, Vientiane
Photo courtesy of Martin Stuart-Fox

French Mekong Expedition reached Vientiane in March 1867, they found the place a desolate ruin, inhabited only by a few villagers and monks in decaying monasteries. The That Luang was still standing, if overgrown (it would be partially destroyed a few years later). Yet the site of Vientiane was so strategically located and geographically central that once the French had wrested the territories making up present-day Laos from Siam, it was the natural choice as the capital of French Laos. It was their occupation that led to the transcription of the city's name as "Vientiane," which, in English, results in a less correct pronunciation than "Vieng Chan."

Vientiane as it exists today is thus a construction, like Saigon, of French colonialism. The French laid out tree-lined avenues, built offices and barracks, and erected several fine villas for their senior officials. New monasteries were raised on the sites of ancient temples, such as Vat Ong Teu and Vat Chan on the Mekong, and Vat Simeuang with its altar to the tutelary deity of the city. Major restorations of the That Luang and Vat Phra Kaeowas were carried out. Chinese merchants were encouraged to set up shops in the commercial center, and the population was swelled by Vietnamese civil servants and artisans. In fact, Vientiane under the French was as much a Vietnamese city as it was Lao or French.

Vientiane suffered little from six months of Japanese occupation at the end of World War II. Following the Japanese surrender, the city was the scene of a struggle for power between Lao nationalists led by Prince Phetsarat and those who, like the king in Luang Prabang, looked forward to the return of the French. Despite the best efforts of the nationalist forces, however, the French reoccupied Vientiane in April 1946, and the Kingdom of Laos became a member state of the French Union.

Over the next few years Laos moved steadily toward full independence, which was achieved in October 1953. In addition to new political institutions, the infrastructure of a modern state had to be constructed. New buildings included a royal palace for official occasions, government offices, a National Assembly building, and a high school.

The end of the First Indochina War in 1954 did not usher in an era of either peace or prosperity. Despite the formation of a coalition government including all political factions, by 1958 Laos was caught up in the Cold War. A coup d'état in 1960 in the name of neutrality only led in December of that year to a pitched battle for control of the city. After three days of fighting that caused more civilian than military deaths, rightist forces retook Vientiane from its neutralist defenders.

International agreement backing the formation of a second coalition government was not enough to prevent Laos from being drawn into the Vietnam (Second Indochina) War. For a decade the country was subjected to the heaviest per capita bombardment in the history of warfare. Vientiane and other Mekong towns, however, were spared the worst impact of war. In fact, an artificial war economy flourished (and along with it corruption), thanks to the greatly increased flow of American aid.

The war years brought important changes to Vientiane. The population greatly increased, thanks both to the influx of refugees escaping the fighting and to migration from surrounding villages as people took advantage of increased opportunities for employment in the civil service, army, and police. Wealthy families built new villas as the city expanded to engulf nearby villages. The Hotel Lan Xang was constructed on the banks of the Mekong. American aid went into building a vast USAID complex and housing compound for American personnel; it now provides accommodation for the country's communist leaders.

The major changes to the city were brought about, however, by the projects of military strongman General Phumi Nosavan. The Avenue Lan Xang running from the palace to the National Assembly building was greatly widened, to the point where it encroached on Vat Sisaket, leaving the elegant little library perched on the new wall. A vast and still unfinished victory monument called Anusari, a sort of modern Lao version of the Arc de Triomphe in Paris, was erected at the upper end of the Avenue Lan Xang. New markets were built, as well as a casino to tap into the new wealth generated through trafficking in drugs and gold.

In 1973 a ceasefire was at last signed between government forces and the communist Pathet Lao, leading to the formation of a third coalition government. Two years later, following communist victories in both Cambodia and Vietnam, the Pathet Lao dispensed with the coalition and seized power. On December 2, 1975, the six-century-old Lao monarchy was replaced by the Lao People's Democratic Republic. Vientiane was declared the capital of the new state, thus ending the anomalous situation of having both a royal capital (Luang Prabang) and an administrative capital (Vientiane) under the Royal Lao regime.

Initially, the change of government led to a mass exodus from Vientiane of most of the Chinese and Vietnamese business community, who fled to Thailand. Soviet aid went more to cover the budget deficit and supply the army than into projects of urban improvement—just as American aid had done. The new regime undertook some construction, however. Overlooking the vast parade ground before the That Luang stands a new National Assembly building, while at the end of the parade ground is the memorial to communist soldiers who died in the Vietnam War. This takes the form of a traditional Lao stupa topped by a red star, a fitting if incongruous symbol of communist-Buddhist Laos.

With the economic reforms of the late 1980s came an influx of foreign investment. Thai investment went into building a new morning market, while Japanese aid financed a transport terminus just off the Avenue Lan Xang. As the number of tourists increased, new hotels and shopping complexes were built, a trend set to continue with the opening in 1994 of the first bridge across the Mekong. As the economic integration of mainland Southeast Asia gains pace, even greater changes can be expected in Vientiane.

Further Reading: No history exists of either the region or city of Vientiane. Indeed, there currently is no satisfactory general history of Laos in English. On the history of Lan Xang, there is only the rather outdated *History of Laos* by Sila Viravong (New York: Paragon, 1964), and a briefer treatment in Arthur Dommen's *Laos: Keystone to Indochina* (Boulder: Westview, 1985). A brief introduction to the history of the city can be found in *Guide pratique de Vientiane* (Vientiane: Vithagna, 1974).

—Martin Stuart-Fox

Vijayanagara (Karnātaka, India)

Location: On the banks of the Tungabhadra River, near the small town of Hospet in the state of Karnātaka, in the south central region of India, which is often referred to as the Deccan.

Description: Capital of the most powerful Hindu kingdom in the Deccan between the fourteenth and sixteenth centuries; set in a dramatic landscape of granite boulders; abandoned in the early seventeenth century, the ancient city, adjacent to the modern town of Hampi, has since undergone extensive excavation and restoration, which continue to this day.

Site Office: The Archaeological Museum
Kamalapuram
Vijayanagara, Karnātaka
India

Contact: Superintending Archaeologist
Archaeological Survey of India
Mid-Southern Circle
Bangalore 560011, Karnātaka
India

The city of Vijayanagara was founded on the banks of the Tungabhadra River by the five Saṅgama brothers in the early fourteenth century, near the sacred site of Hampi. Often the city itself is referred to as Hampi, which may cause confusion since Hampi is in fact the sacred religious center of the ancient city. Hampi itself was traditionally known as the Pampā-kshetra, Kishkindhā-kshetra, or Bhāskara-kshetra. The name Hampi is derived from the traditional name of the Tungabhadra River, Pampa. The site is endowed with natural beauty and strategic strength as well as strong religious associations, all of which ensured the successful establishment of the city of Vijayanagara and its extensive empire.

The earliest known habitation of Vijayanagara was during the Neolithic era. Excavations near the Viṭṭhala Temple have uncovered pottery and other artifacts dating to this period. Several inscriptions found on rock faces proclaim that Hampi was part of the realm of Aśoka, the great Mauryan emperor. Settlement at the site has been continuous since the Neolithic era because of its numerous associations with the Hindu epic, the *Rāmāyaṇa*. Hindu belief considers the river and surrounding hills as Kishkindhā, the home of the "monkey chiefs" of that epic, Vāli and Sugrīva. Among the numerous sites in the Deccan associated with the *Rāmāyaṇa,* two of the most venerated are the Malyavanta Hill, on which Rāma is said to have stayed, and a huge mound of ash in the nearby village of Nimbapuram, believed to be the cremated remains of Vāli. Thus Hampi has long been a center of pilgrimage for Hindu worshipers and a site of prolific temple building. With many of the temples still in use, Hampi remains an important pilgrimage destination.

The site's religious associations, together with its naturally defensive aspects, drew the Saṅgama brothers to found Vijayanagara, "the City of Victory," on the southern banks of the Tungabhadra River in approximately 1336. The natural defenses were provided by the river, which is almost unfordable, and the massive granite boulders that are strewn across the hilly landscape. The layout of fortifications built there incorporated the huge boulders and line of the hills into the defensive scheme. Construction of the new city, which stood opposite the older fortress of Anegondi on the northern bank of the river, was complete by 1343. Records indicate that the Saṅgama brothers were directed to the site by their guru Vidyāraṇya (some believe the city was named for the latter personage). The meteoric rise of their dynasty can to some extent be attributed to the Muslim invasions that had left the older Hindu kingdoms in disarray. Vijayanagara was to become the setting for a wealthy, cultured, and cosmopolitan society, where a variety of peoples were welcome, and the center of an empire that encompassed most of the southern half of the subcontinent.

This was a period of considerable political unrest with incessant warfare in the subcontinent. The Saṅgama Dynasty subdued frequent uprisings by rival Hindu and Muslim kingdoms, and engaged in nearly continuous conflict with the Muslim Bahmanī kingdom to the north. As a result, the city was heavily fortified, with seven concentric fortifications arranged in an elliptical shape around the heart of the city. Each line of characteristically tapering stone walls was intersected by fortified gateways and barbicans through which access was gained to the center. At the heart of the capital was the royal center, referred to in an inscription as the "city of Bukkaraya," that is, Bukka I, who ruled from 1354/55 to 1377; this area was guarded heavily. Several watchtowers were set within the city at points overlooking the main internal arterial routes. Defense of the city was also ensured by a huge standing army supported by "war elephants" and cavalry (Vijayanagara held exclusive control over the import of Arabian horses, bringing in 13,000 of them a year by the sixteenth century). The city was laid out in accordance with an urban plan, which incorporated specific zones such as the royal center and the religious center (Hampi), with suburbs and a complex irrigation system.

Although much of the city has since been destroyed, detailed descriptions of Vijayanagara written by foreign visitors have survived. Among the visitors to the Saṅgama court was the Italian Nicolo di Conti, who went there in approximately 1420. Di Conti describes Vijayanagara as a huge fortified citadel in a setting of mountains and valleys. Perhaps the most important account of the city is that of Abdul Razzaq, a diplomat from Herāt who visited in 1443, during the reign of Devarāya II. Razzaq describes many of the important buildings such as the halls of justice, the palace, and the fortifications, observing that Vijayanagara's "inhabitants have no equals in the world." He includes descriptions of the magnificent elephant stable, the largest structure within the royal center, with eleven arched chambers surmounted by alternating domes and vaults (each royal elephant was assigned its own chamber). The building has survived relatively intact, although it no longer houses elephants.

Like Nicolo di Conti, Razzaq was invited to attend the splendid Mahanavami Festival, at which he was presented to King Devarāya II, who was seated on a golden throne studded with precious gems. It is thought that the king presided over the festival processions from the multistory platform standing in the northeast corner of the largest enclosure within the royal center. Relief sculptures dating from this period depict processional elephants, horses, and people carved around the base. Additions were made to the structure during the succeeding centuries, but nothing remains of the wooden structure that once stood on top of the huge platform.

Although the Saṅgama Dynasty carried out major construction in the capital, only a few of the extant monuments can be dated with any certainty to the period of their rule. The Rāmachandra Temple complex, standing within the royal center, is dated by an inscription to the reign of Devarāya I, who ruled from 1406 to 1422. The central shrine of the temple, as indicated by the name, is dedicated to the god Rāma, while subsidiary shrines are dedicated to the many incarnations of Vishnu and Krishna. A Jain temple standing in the eastern corner of the royal center bears an inscription referring to Devarāya II, as does a mosque within the Muslim section, reflecting the liberal religious attitudes of this kingdom. Many other structures, both in the royal and religious centers of the city, are stylistically similar to these monuments, indicating that they are from the Saṅgama Dynasty, but because of successive rebuilding and insufficient data, precise dating of these structures has not been possible.

The end of the fifteenth century was a period of political instability for the Vijayanagaran Empire, with disruptive attacks from other kingdoms and political murders within the capital itself. The Saṅgama Dynasty was overthrown by the Sāluva Dynasty in approximately 1485. The Sāluvas then were overthrown by the Tuluva Dynasty in 1492, when the Tuluva general Narasa Nāyaka imprisoned the boy-king Immadi Narasiṃha and firmly gained control of the empire. Nāyaka's son was to reign briefly until he was succeeded by his stepbrother Krishnadeva Rāya, who ruled from 1509 to 1529. Under the rule of Krishnadeva Rāya, the empire flourished, conducting successful campaigns against the rival Bahmanī Kingdom as well as conquering vast amounts of new territory, expanding the empire as far north as Orissa.

The Tuluva Dynasty's reign is considered to be the golden age of Vijayanagara, marked by an increase in artistic and cultural activities, encouraged by the Tuluva kings. Artists and poets were supported by the royal court. Moreover, under the patronage of King Krishnadeva Rāya and his brother Achyutadeva Rāya, who reigned from 1529 to 1542, a substantial building program was undertaken. The sacred center of Hampi was enlarged greatly; the Virūpāksha Shrine there was expanded into a complex of temples. Its huge multistory gateways, called *gopura,* rise more than 150 feet above the landscape, dwarfing the main shrine. Southern Indian architecture during this period typically placed greater emphasis on the gateways than on the central shrine.

The Virūpāksha Temple is the main center of worship in Hampi today. The Tuluva Dynasty founded the new Krishna, Tiruvengalanatha, and Viṭṭhala temple complexes. The intricately carved Viṭṭhala Temple, dedicated to the god Vishnu, also has towering gateways, although not as high as those on the Virūpāksha Temple. In the courtyard stands a beautifully carved open *maṇḍapa* (covered hallway), with piers composed of columns and rearing horses (dated 1554). Adjacent to this is a small shrine housing an image of Garuḍa Vishnu's transport; the shrine is carved in the shape of a ceremonial temple chariot. Each of the four wheels is carved from separate stone blocks, allowing them to rotate freely on their axles.

Under the Tuluva Dynasty, the king's residence was moved outside of the city. Records indicate that a new city was built in one of the suburban areas of the old Vijayanagara. The old royal center was never abandoned; although little new building was carried out there during this period, some of the older structures were remodeled. A detailed record of the city under the Tuluva Dynasty is provided by the Portuguese visitor Domingo Paes, who came to Vijayanagara during the reign of Krishnadeva Rāya in 1520. Like the Saṅgamas, the Tuluvas were eager to establish diplomatic relations with the Portuguese, who were trading from their colonial port of Goa. Domingo Paes was overwhelmed by Vijayanagara:

> The people in the city are countless in number, so much so that I do not wish to write it down for fear it should be thought fabulous. What I saw . . . seemed as large as Rome, and very beautiful to the sight; there are many groves of tree within it, many orchards and gardens of fruit trees and many conduits of water which flow in the midst of it, and in places there are lakes.

Paes further declared that Vijayanagara was "the best provided city in the world."

Domingo Paes's description of the new royal center is invaluable to historians because, unlike the old royal center, almost nothing survives of this part of the city. Paes describes the ornate interior of the palace, mentioning a room completely paneled in ivory, a treasury, a bedchamber, and a room with a cot that hung from the ceiling by gold chains. Like Abdul Razzaq, Paes was invited to the Mahanavami Festival,

Entrance to the Viṭṭhala Temple, Vijayanagara
Photo courtesy of National Geographic Image Collection, Washington, D.C.

which he describes in great detail, along with the day-to-day life of the king.

The success of the empire was to continue under the rule of Sadāśiva, who ascended the throne in 1542. Sadāśiva founded several large temples in the suburban area of the city and expanded existing shrines in Hampi. But Sadāśiva progressively lost control of the empire to the military commander Rāma Rāya, Krishnadeva Rāya's son-in-law, who imprisoned the king and made himself ruler. Under the arrogant rule of Rāma Rāya, the empire became increasingly unstable, and relations with the Muslim sultans to the north worsened. Rāma Rāya treated the sultans with disrespect because no single Muslim ruler could possibly challenge the far superior military strength of Vijayanagara.

In 1565 the sultan of Bijāpur formed an alliance of all the Muslim armies and prepared for war against Vijayanagara. The armies of Vijayanagara were prepared for the assault and went to meet the rival armies at Talikota, about sixty miles northwest of the capital. The ensuing battle on January 26, 1565, proved disastrous for Vijayanagara. Rāma Rāya was killed at the outset; his head was cut off and put on a stake. Upon seeing the head of their commander held high on the stake, the Vijayanagara forces fled in panic and retreated to the capital. There they collected the imperial treasury and then fled to the fortress of Penukonda, about 120 miles southeast of the capital. Vijayanagara was left undefended at the mercy of the Muslim forces, who plundered the city.

Many uncertainties remain concerning the Muslim's sack of Vijayanagara. While no firsthand accounts of the sacking of the city are available, archaeological research has revealed the remnants of many charred wooden structures. Many buildings and temples were destroyed or severely vandalized, and valuable objects were smashed or stolen. It should be noted that subsequent looting by treasure seekers over the following centuries also has been responsible for the deterioration of the site. Not all of the city was destroyed by the Muslims. Most of the temples dedicated to Siva were left untouched, as was the Virūpāksha Temple in Hampi. It is believed that these temples escaped destruction through negotiations between the Vijayanagara leaders and the Muslim commanders. Many of the courtly buildings were left standing as well, which may have occurred because the Muslim commanders intended to occupy the city themselves. The dilapidated state of many buildings is the result of the ravages of time and the removal of certain architectural pieces by the government in an attempt to preserve them.

Rāma Rāya's brother Tirumala returned to Vijayanagara in an attempt to rejuvenate the capital. The Italian visitor Cesare Federici, who arrived in 1567, described Tirumala's palace and the heavily guarded gates. Scholars believe that there was some rebuilding and repairing of the damaged buildings around this time. It appears that Tirumala was unsuccessful in his attempt to repopulate the city, however, for the Muslims are known to have returned periodically and occupied the site. This is substantiated by the accounts of another Italian traveler, Filippo Sassetti, who met the governor of Bijāpur at Vijayanagara in 1585. By the beginning of the seventeenth century, Vijayanagara was abandoned. Tirumala established a new capital for a time at Penukonda, but internal strife and the opposition of the neighboring Muslim kingdoms caused the Vijayanagara Empire's final collapse around the year 1614.

In its abandoned state, the city of Vijayanagara was pillaged by treasure seekers and effectively disappeared from the map. The first foreign visitor to come to the abandoned site was the enthusiastic antiquarian Colonel Colin Mackenzie, in December 1799. He made plans of the site and described the layout of Vijayanagara, which are now in the India Office Library and Records in London. Although his account was not published, the first description of the site with translations of inscriptions was published in 1836. The first photographs of Vijayanagara were published in 1866, in *Architecture in Dharwar and Mysore,* accompanied by a text written by the respected architectural historian James Fergusson. In the 1880s the newly formed Archaeological Survey of India began a program of conservation in an attempt to prevent further deterioration of the monuments. Collapsing walls and door lintels were reinforced and guards posted to prevent theft.

Not until the 1970s was a comprehensive archaeological survey of Vijayanagara undertaken. Several teams of archaeologists under the direction of the Archaeological Survey of India and the Department of Archaeology of the Karnātaka Government began excavating Vijayanagara's old royal center. Further impetus to the excavations and research was provided by an international team headed by George Michell in 1980. Their extensive work has led to a greater understanding of Vijayanagara. Owing to the sheer size of the site, excavation and restoration have continued to the present day. Because the ruins of the greater Vijayanagara area encompass ninety-six and one-half square miles, much remains to be done.

Conservation of the monuments of Vijayanagara has become a problem in more recent years. The damming of the Tungabhadra River to produce hydroelectric power has rejuvenated and industrialized the nearby town of Hospet. As a result, the population in the surrounding region has increased significantly, as has that of Vijayanagara itself. Another reason for this repopulation is the increased popularity of Hampi as a site of pilgrimage, a trend that has had mixed results for the temples. Although the temples are now being looked after by local priests, the unauthorized occupation of the ancient structures is causing them considerable damage. Little has been done to control the influx of visitors and residents, who have begun erecting modern concrete structures within the site itself. Some new residents have been using blocks of masonry from collapsed structures as building materials. Irrigation within the site has also created problems, as the tilling of soil is destroying important archaeological material.

Clearly the threat to the preservation of Vijayanagara is considerable, but efforts to deal with this problem are underway. Several important sculptures have been removed and placed in the site museum, which was established in 1970, and replaced with plaster copies. In 1982 the government of Karnātaka created the Hampi Authority to oversee preservation and restoration of the site. For future programs of conservation and development, the Hampi Authority now has the support of UNESCO, which has added Vijayanagara to its World Heritage List, in recognition of the global importance of the site.

Further Reading: *The City of Victory, Vijayanagara: Medieval Hindu Capital of Southern India* by John M. Fritz and George Michell (New York: Aperture, 1991) combines excellent black-and-white photographs taken by John Gollings with text by the highly respected architectural historians J. M. Fritz and George Michell. This book covers all areas of potential interest. *The Vijayanagara Courtly Style* by George Michell (New Delhi: Manohar, 1992) provides historical insight as well as description of the monuments associated with court life. George Michell is perhaps the world's leading authority on Vijayanagara, and his writings are the most comprehensive and thoroughly researched. Michell's *The Penguin Guide to Monuments of India*, volume 1 (London and New York: Viking, 1989) covers the entire historical spectrum of Buddhist, Jain, and Hindu architecture in India. It has an excellent brief section on Vijayanagara. *Hampi Ruins, Described and Illustrated* by A. H. Longhurst (Madras: Government Press, 1917) is an early description of the site and includes illustrations. It provides an interesting comparison with contemporary literature on the subject as well as insight into the progress of restoration and dilapidation.

—Charles Savile

Waitangi (North Island, New Zealand)

Location: On the Bay of Islands, northeast coast of North Island, approximately 150 miles north of Auckland.

Description: Site of the signing of the Treaty of Waitangi between the British Crown representative and fifty Maori tribal chiefs in 1840; the Treaty of Waitangi marked the birth of New Zealand as a full-fledged British colony and modern nation; its Treaty House, along with more than 2,000 acres of land, were turned into an historic site and nature park in 1932–33 by acts of the New Zealand parliament.

Site Office: Waitangi National Trust
P.O. Box 48
Paihia, Bay of Islands
North Island
New Zealand
(9) 4027437

Every February 6, New Zealanders gather at Waitangi to commemorate the birth of their country. Waitangi connotes the Treaty House, built in 1834, with a few more structures added in more recent times. For some years Waitangi served as the official abode of the British Crown's first representative to New Zealand, James Busby, who was an enterprising and energetic lay missionary. He purchased 230 acres from the local Maoris in 1832 and subsequently added nearly 9,000 acres more, along the Waitangi River, in order to establish the planned town of Victoria. The town developed fully and succeeding owners sold most of the land. Across the bay from Waitangi lies the town of Russell, or Kororareka in Busby's day.

The Treaty House, a simple Georgian colonial home, overlooks a broad expanse of lawn that winds down to the beautiful Bay of Islands. The earliest depiction of Waitangi—a woodcut illustration published in a British book—prominently displays a flagpole behind the house, waving the Union Jack. Since 1947, the flag of an independent New Zealand has waved from the same spot. Behind the house lies a newer structure, a Maori meetinghouse, which native Maoris took the initiative to build soon after the Treaty House opened as a museum in 1932. Separate but sharing the same site, the meetinghouse was meant to symbolize unity between Maoris and *pakehas* (whites). Today, Maoris make up 9 percent of New Zealand's population of 3.4 million.

James Busby was the first European to make a permanent home at Waitangi, but others had shown interest in it earlier. One of them was William Hall, a lay missionary who had bought about fifty acres there from the Maoris in 1815. The transaction was not taken particularly seriously by the Maoris, however; military strength meant more to them than sales agreements, and in a few months they attacked Hall, burned his home and drove him out. Other missionaries later considered using Waitangi as a base, but in the end they chose other locations.

Busby's appointment as the British resident, or administrator, followed a period of informal British colonization of New Zealand. The British government had shown little interest in these islands, even though Captain James Cook had visited them in 1769 and asserted that Britain had the right to colonize them before any other nation. The British people, however, were far more enthusiastic than were their rulers, and by 1830 there was substantial British settlement in New Zealand. Some of these pioneers were missionaries, come to convert the Maoris to Christianity; others included whalers and seal hunters, both of whom developed a lucrative trade in the products derived from these animals.

The number of British who had settled in New Zealand finally convinced the Crown to establish a formal governmental presence there. In 1832 Busby, an Australian colonist who had shown great interest in New Zealand, was appointed "His Majesty's British Resident in New Zealand." He lived with local missionaries for a while, then, after protracted negotiations, convinced the Crown to finance the construction of what became the Treaty House.

The Crown never invested Busby with a great deal of power, largely because of opposition to the cost of maintaining a resident there. The opposition came both from within England and from the Australian colony of New South Wales, which had jurisdiction over New Zealand and rather resented Busby's presence. Within the limits of his authority, though, Busby generally proved a capable administrator from his base at Waitangi.

By the end of the 1830s, commercial interest in New Zealand had increased to the point that the Crown saw a need to strengthen its presence there. Therefore, the Crown sent Captain William Hobson of the Royal Navy to Waitangi to negotiate a treaty with the Maoris. On February 6, 1840, in a large tent in front of Busby's house, fifty northern Maori chiefs gathered to discuss terms with the British government. For the benefit of the Maoris, the resulting treaty was translated, albeit rather roughly, into their language. Its meaning was ambiguous; on the one hand, it promised to extend to them the protection of the Crown if they ceded complete sovereignty over their tribal lands; on the other hand, the Crown guaranteed that, in return, no one could take their land without their consent. Maoris could sell their land only to the Crown, not to private parties, who often had dealt unfairly with the natives. With the Treaty of Waitangi, the British government was going on record that New Zealand would not be annexed without the consent of the majority of the Maori people. Also, under the terms of the treaty, Hobson became lieutenant governor of New Zealand, a position that

Maori war canoe, Waitangi
Photo courtesy of The Chicago Public Library

superseded Busby's. Later the same year, Auckland was established as New Zealand's capital. Busby continued to live at Waitangi and lay out plans for his town. His son, William, succeeded him as owner of the property; Waitangi deteriorated after he left in the 1880s.

Relations between the British and the Maoris deteriorated even soooner. On paper, the treaty promised enlightened treatment of the native population. Maoris would never suffer the humiliating fate of American Indians, forced onto reservations. Moreover, to ensure fair treatment, the government set up a tribunal to adjudicate disputes between Maoris and white settlers. In the end, however, the Maoris poorly understood the treaty, partly because the translation was inexact, and partly because of their unfamiliarity with Western legal customs and procedures. The government was unable to stop private land sales immediately or to buy a great deal of land; what it did buy, it quickly resold to private interests and reaped huge profits. Private sales were legalized in 1862, providing further potential for exploitation of the Maoris. Land agents were often unscrupulous, and whites had no patience with the Maori custom of collective land ownership, entailing the consent of all before any land could be bought and sold; tribes refused outright to sell sacred areas, as well as those reserved for hunting and fishing, to the exasperation of whites. As a result, violence erupted between whites and Maoris on North Island. These have gone down in New Zealand history as the Land Wars, lasting from 1843 to 1847 and again from 1860 to the mid-1880s. Government troops often intervened on the part of the whites, and defeated Maoris had their land confiscated.

Not until the early twentieth century did the Maori population show signs of recovering from the ravages of warfare, exacerbated by disease, of the previous century. They finally were granted representation in parliament, in which a percentage of seats was set aside for them. Also, Maori chieftains were appointed to the Waitangi National Trust Board in 1932.

What happened at the Treaty House in 1840 reverberates to the present day. In the late twentieth century, many Maoris began to claim large tracts of land on the basis of the Treaty of Waitangi. The 1975 Treaty of Waitangi Act established a tribunal to deal with these claims. Land disputes have continued, with the Maoris winning some rounds and more conservative white New Zealanders opposing Maori claims and pressuring the government to turn productive fishing areas and other natural resources over to commercial interests.

Because the effects of the treaty continue to be felt, no historic place in New Zealand is more important than Waitangi National Reserve. Its preservation as a historic site in the 1930s would never have happened without the persistent efforts of one man, Vernon H. Reed, a wealthy white New Zealander and member of parliament. His main motive in preserving Waitangi was to allow future generations to appreciate how New Zealand became a colony of the greatest empire on earth, Great Britain; he considered the treaty signing "the greatest event in the country's history."

Waitangi in the 1930s was a shambles. "The Treaty House was dilapidated and the grounds neglected.... Fences were broken and of no use," Reed wrote in his memoirs. Few New Zealanders could even remember where Waitangi was, or what it was about. Nor could Reed interest the government in its preservation, although he had been trying since the turn of the century.

Matters took a new twist in late 1931, when the Treaty House and property once again were up for sale. New Zealand's governor general, Lord Bledisloe, and his wife happened to be vacationing in the nearby town of Paihia, in Reed's electoral district. Reed recounted, "I suggested that Their Excellencies should visit Waitangi," on which they had never laid eyes. They were so taken by the beauty and history of Waitangi that his Lordship "told me in strictest secrecy that he and Lady Bledisloe ... had decided to purchase the property and present it to the nation." It was Reed's finest hour; from then on, Waitangi has been in the spotlight.

Two acts of parliament had to be passed, in 1932 and 1933 respectively, before the "gift" could be accepted by the nation. The New Zealand government, owner of the "Waitangi National Reserve," had no intention of spending a single penny of tax revenue to maintain it. The property would have to be self-sufficient from the start. By then, the "gift" had become Lord and Lady Bledisloe's pet project, and they added sizably to it, determined to establish a native nature preserve of more than 1,000 acres alongside the restored house. The 1932 National Trust Board Act established the board that would administer the Treaty House and the 1,000 acres purchased along with it; a year later, the "Waitangi Endowment Act" provided for a further 1,300 acres. All of this would be most costly for the Waitangi National Trust Board to support.

Reed became Waitangi's first director, an able and zealous administrator. The first item on the agenda was the full restoration of the Treaty House, a challenging project amid New Zealand's, and the world's, greatest financial depression. The Treaty House, Reed writes, was in a sad state: "the front rooms of the house had been used as a shearing shed and a shelter for sheep at night. The roof and ceilings were falling down, and sacks replaced glass in the windows. The northern wing of the house had gone." Since William Busby had left, it had been sold and resold often, during which time it had deteriorated. However, a good deal of the house still was salvageable.

Originally, in 1832, James Busby had engaged Australian architect J. Verge to design the home. After considerable written haggling with the governor of New South Wales (whose approval was necessary) over the scope, price, and design of the house, it arrived from Sydney ready made, according to plan. Its most distinctive, eye-catching feature was the graceful veranda that ran the length of the house facing the bay. The house otherwise was quite small and ordinary, consisting of two front rooms (living room and bedroom), a few small rooms in back, and a hallway that extended from the front door to the backyard.

It seemed only fitting to Reed and the other members of the National Trust Board to engage two Australian architects to renovate and restore the house exactly as it looked in 1840, after Busby had added wings to the original structure. Replacement materials had to resemble as closely as possible the materials of the original house.

Maoris took an immediate interest in the restoration project. Some of them petitioned the National Trust Board for permission to erect a Whare-runanga, or great meetinghouse, on the same grounds as the Treaty House. Each Maori tribe represented at the original signing of the Waitangi treaty was to contribute some emblem of its tribal history or art. The Whare-runanga was completed at the same time as the Treaty House restoration, with only some trees separating the two buildings.

At the centennial of the treaty, Waitangi became the focus of a national commemoration. A contingent of eighty Maoris rowed the largest canoe in the world to Waitangi's shore, where they carried it to the Whare-runanga. The 117-foot intricately carved canoe, named the "Ngatokimatawhaorua," was a masterpiece of native art. It was their gift to the Waitangi National Reserve, and has become one of its most notable exhibits.

At this time New Zealand, as a British dominion, had entered World War II. Little could be done during the war years beyond maintaining the properties. Some attention was paid, however, to the reforestation of the surrounding acreage. Before the arrival of white settlers, the area where the Treaty House stands was densely covered by native kauri trees. More than 100 years later, the forest was gone and the native birds had lost their habitat and all but disappeared. The introduction of foreign plants, trees, weeds, and animals—including the Norwegian rat—had completely altered the original landscape; slashing and burning to clear nearby land for crops completed the damage. Sheep grazing destroyed what little remained of the wild vegetation.

Hence from the outset, the Waitangi National Trust Board appointed a Forestry Committee that planned the reforestation of the reserve and the introduction of a native bird and plant sanctuary. In time, an artificial freshwater lake was built, which attracted much bird life; New Zealanders were solicited for donations of live native plant, bird, and animal species. Someone even caught a native kiwi bird and brought it, in a box, to Reed's office, where the bird was fed worms; it subsequently was released into the sanctuary. Waitangi became a laboratory for the study of biodiversity, long before the concept was popular, and the project acquainted visitors with what New Zealand looked like before the arrival of Europeans.

Fundraising was a major preoccupation during the first decade of Waitangi's existence. Lord Bledisloe had made a monetary endowment for the upkeep of the museum properties, but this was seed money only; as the National Trust's projects multiplied, means had to be found to make Waitangi financially self-sufficient. Some ideas were ingenious, such as establishing a golf course and charging fees to the users, then renting out the golf links to local farmers for sheep grazing; everything was tried except charging admission fees to the two historic houses, because of the National Trust Board's zealous, missionary-like commitment to an open door policy for all visitors. This did, in fact, encourage visitors to come to the properties, and by the time admission fees finally were initiated after World War II, visitors were increasing in numbers. By then, a campground had opened; the bungalows built to commemorate the centennial were rented out as "vacation cottages"; the gift shop's souvenirs were selling, and prudent investments were yielding dividends. In 1947, Reed was proud of the fact that Waitangi's "hardship" years were over: after fifteen years, the properties finally were self-sufficient. At that point, the New Zealand government completely reversed itself and began providing an annual subsidy. Reed had given up on this prospect until an Australian official visited Waitangi and was dumbfounded that the government could "ignore" such a national treasure. Reed then decided to petition parliament for a subsidy, and no one was more surprised than he when it quickly materialized.

Every year, Waitangi Day (a national holiday) draws thousands of visitors, along with government officials, to the Treaty House, while Maori tribesmen launch the beautiful long canoe into the bay to commemorate the fifty northern Maori tribesmen who sailed into Waitangi on that day in 1840. Today, the Maori canoe is housed in a separate exhibit building, beside the Whare-runanga. There are numerous hiking trails throughout the beautiful reserve and bird sanctuary. The trails are extensive—the boardwalk leading to Haruru Falls is a three-hour round-trip walk. A road leads up to Mount Bledisloe, which offers a spectacular view of the surroundings, including the ocean. The Treaty House is home to a permanent exhibit on the history of Waitangi, as well as rotating exhibits on various aspects of New Zealand's history. The Visitor's Centre offers a film on Waitangi's history and restoration.

Further Reading: Although every guidebook to New Zealand devotes adequate attention to Waitangi, no full-length historical treatment of this distinctive site has yet appeared. Vernon Reed, the first director of Waitangi, who took the initiative to draw the government's attention to preserving Waitangi as an historical monument, left a detailed, highly readable account, *The Gift of Waitangi, A History of the Bledisloe Gift* (Wellington: Reed, 1957), which covers the park up to the mid-1950s. Lindsay Buick's *Waitangi, Ninety-Four Years After* (New Plymouth, New Zealand: Avery, 1934) contains a valuable, fifteen-page introduction that provides a detailed account of the early history of Waitangi, leading up to the signing of the treaty.

—Sina Dubovoy

Windsor (New South Wales, Australia)

Location: A town on the Hawkesbury River on the northwestern outskirts of Sydney, situated mostly in Hawkesbury Shire and partly in the city of Penrith.

Description: One of the five towns Governor Lachlan Macquarie founded in the Hawkesbury district as an important part of the early settlement of New South Wales. It is noted for historic buildings constructed under Macquarie's administration, a few designed by the convict architect Francis Greenway.

Site Office: Hawkesbury Visitor Center
P.O. Box s534
Winsdor, New South Wales 2756
Australia
(45) 88 5895

The existence of the New South Wales township of Windsor is tied to agricultural demands of the first European colonizers in Australia. In 1789, when the sandy soil of Sydney town—the first British penal settlement in the South Pacific—was found to be unsuitable for large-scale agriculture, Captain Arthur Phillip, first governor of New South Wales, led a small exploratory party north into Broken Bay in search of good farming land. What Phillip found was a river formed by the junction of two other streams (the Nepean and Groce Rivers), flowing eighty-seven miles north-northeast across a fertile coastal plain and parallel to the coast. Phillip named the river after Baron Hawkesbury, president of the Council of Trade and Plantations in England. In 1794, Phillip's successor, Lieutenant Governor Francis Groce, sent twenty-two settlers to land that Phillip had located on the Hawkesbury and recommended for farming. This settlement was called Green Hills and became the granary of the colony, producing barley, wheat, and maize.

In these early years, conflict arose between Hawkesbury settlers and the local Aboriginal community. In response, members of the New South Corps were sent to the Green Hills area to provide protection to the settlers. One of the first buildings in the area was the Government House, a long, low weatherboard cottage, to lodge the local commanding officer. (The building was demolished in 1919.) Conflict between the Aborigines and settlers led to intermittent warfare and massacres of the indigenous population. The Aborigines felt that farming practices in the district were depleting their access to natural food sources. In time, British troops were able to push Aboriginal defenders out of their own tribal land into the less fertile and outlying territory.

With river transportation on the Hawkesbury as the best means of traveling between the Green Hills settlement and Sydney, a boat-building industry became another attraction for the district. Andrew Thompson and John Grono, the area's first important boat-builders, built the largest vessels to be constructed in New South Wales at that time, including the 270-ton *Australian* and 100-ton *Governor Bligh.* River traffic remained important to the area until the 1880s, when successive floods silted up the channel, making the river unnavigable to large vessels. Until 1864, when the railway line from Sydney was completed, the river was the only viable means of transporting goods. Although early roads to the area were poor, road construction meant the district provided the first northern route to outlying settlements. In 1815, the Hawkesbury magistrate, William Cox, oversaw the construction of the first road over the Blue Mountain. European settlement could then spread over the other side of the coastal mountains into grazing land for cattle. This marked the end of the colony's dependence on the Hawkesbury district's agricultural output. In the first decade of the colony, poor farming production resulting from farmers' unfamiliarity with the Australian environment, from floods, and from lack of supplies shipped from England, had led to food shortages and famine.

It was in this period that farming communities in the Hawkesbury district formed the embryonic stages of Windsor and other townships. The farmers in the district were a political force who opposed the economic power of the emerging squatter aristocracy led by Captain John Macarthur, a former officer in the New South Wales Corps, and the leading colonial entrepreneur. The monopolistic trading practices of the squatters, along with the flooding of the Hawkesbury River, kept the district in poverty. An attempt by Governor William Bligh (better known today for his earlier role as captain of the mutinous *Bounty*) to stamp out monopoly trading was greatly supported by the Hawkesbury settlers. When Macarthur and his supporters deposed Bligh in a military coup d'état (1808), the Hawkesbury settlers rejected Macarthur's appointment to the colonial administration and continued to express loyalty to Bligh until his departure to England.

Political and economic stability was restored under the new governor, Lachlan Macquarie. In 1810, Macquarie toured the Hawkesbury district and founded five towns, in the process changing the name of Green Hills to Windsor, after the English town in Berkshire. In founding the towns (Windsor, Richmond, Castlereagh, Pitt Town, and Wilberforce), Macquarie was responding to concerns about periodic river flooding; hence, the site of Windsor (fifty-two feet above sea level) was placed as a refuge above known flood levels of the Hawkesbury. The town was nevertheless submerged in the great flood of 1867.

Under Macquarie's administration, three Georgian buildings that have survived to this day were constructed in

First Fleet graves at St. Matthew's Church, Windsor
Photo courtesy of Tourism New South Wales

Windsor: the Macquarie Arms Inn, St. Matthew's Church, and the Windsor Court House. The last two were designed by the convict architect Francis Greenway. The Macquarie Arms Inn, built by prominent emancipationist Richard Fitzgerald at the request of Macquarie, opened in 1815. In 1835 the inn was leased for five years as a mess for officers of the Fiftieth West Kent Regiment. It then became a private residence until 1874, when it became known as the Royal Hotel. The name of the hotel reverted to Macquarie Arms in 1961. The Windsor Court House, built by William Cox in 1822, houses the historic portrait of Macquarie that was commissioned at the request of the Hawkesbury residents. The courthouse was the last feature to be constructed in the period of the Macquarie-Greenway supervised building program, and is said to be the purest Greenway design to have survived. The Windsor-Richmond area also contains a number of stately Georgian and Victorian homes.

The oldest church building in Australia, the Presbyterian chapel in Ebenezer, north of Windsor, was built in 1809. The first Methodist Church in the Southern hemisphere was constructed in another Hawkesbury town, Castlereagh. Windsor had its own important historic church building, St. Matthew's (Anglican) Church, the foundation stone of which was laid by Macquarie in 1817. Considered to be Greenway's masterpiece, the church was completed in 1820. The first pipe organ built in Australia was placed in St. Matthew's Church in 1840.

The churches in Windsor and surrounding area are important not only as examples of early colonial architecture, but for their association with the leading clergy of the period. Reverend Samuel Marsden had consecrated and officially opened St. Matthew's Church in 1822. Two years later, according to some accounts, Reverend Dr. John Dunmore Lang conducted the first Australian Presbyterian communion service in Ebenezer Church. The Catholic Church community in Windsor was ministered by the first official Catholic clergy in Australia, including Reverends J. J. Therry and William Ullathorne, during the 1820s and 1830s. St. Peter's Anglican Church in Richmond was consecrated by the first Anglican bishop of Australia, Reverend William Broughton, in 1841.

Windsor and neighboring Richmond also made important contributions to Australian literature, science, culture, and industry through four of their noted citizens. The poet Charles Harpur was born in Windsor in 1813. Astronomer John Tebbutt, who discovered two comets that bear his name, constructed two observatories at the peninsula on the eastern side of Windsor. In 1873 Tebbutt was elected a fellow of the Royal Astronomical Society and later became the first president of the Australian branch. In 1876 Dr. Thomas Fiaschi became the first medical resident of the twin terrace buildings in Windsor's Thompson Square, known as the Doctor's House. Fiaschi was also the president of the Dante Alighieri Society and, as a local viniculturist, the president of the New South Wales Wine Association. Philip Charley, who bought the Belmont mansion on Richmond Hill, was one of the original investors in the Broken Hill lead mine in New South Wales, and a director of the Great Fitzroy copper mine in Queensland. Charley, a pioneering Australian motorist, in 1908 brought the first Rolls Royce to Australia.

In 1949, the council of Richmond merged with the council of Windsor, forming the Windsor Municipal Council. Richmond has the oldest and largest Royal Australian Air Force (RAAF) establishment. The RAAF acquired the Richmond airfield in 1927, at the time when the RAAF was the second most senior Air Force in the British Empire. The other noted institution in Richmond is the Hawkesbury Agricultural College, established in 1891. In the 1950s and 1960s, severe flooding destroyed surrounding farms (orange orchards and vegetable gardens). The town of Windsor has since supported small industries. It has also found another function as an important tourist site, illustrating the contribution of the Hawkesbury district to Australian colonial history.

Further Reading: An out-of-date and out-of-print text—but an important archival source—is James Steele's *Early Days of Windsor* (Sydney: Tyrrell's, 1916). It is a detailed list of the physical and organizational development of Windsor until 1915, making it an important primary source for the historian. In 1967 the State Planning Authority of New South Wales produced a booklet called *Historic Buildings: Windsor and Richmond* (Sydney: State Planning Authority of New South Wales, 1967), an important document for those interested in the area's architectural history. Three other major sources treat the township of Windsor in the examination of early history of the Hawkesbury district. D. G. Bowd's *Macquarie Country: A History of the Hawkesbury* (Sydney: Library of Australian History, 1982) provides substantial coverage of all aspects of the district's history. Bobbie Hardy's *Early Hawkesbury Settlers* (Kenthurst: Kangaroo, 1985) describes in more detail the first European members of the Hawkesbury community, and pays more attention than most texts to Aboriginal-settler conflicts. *Macquarie's Five Towns* (Sydney and London: Horwitz, 1970) features Bruce Adams's brilliant photographs of historic sites and Olaf Ruhen's concise and descriptive text.

—Neville Buch

Wuchang (Hubei, China)

Location: Part of the modern city of Wuhan, which is now capital of Hubei province; located at the confluence of the the Yangtze and Han Rivers, approximately 600 miles south of Beijing and 500 miles north of Guangzhou.

Description: A one-time dynastic and provincial capital that won its greatest fame as the site of Sun Yat-sen's republican forces' first victory in the revolution of 1911 that overthrew the Manchurian Qing Dynasty.

Site Office: Hubei Tourism Bureau
Qingshiqiao, Hanyang District
Wuhan 430050, Hubei
China
(27) 4822514

Wuchang is the oldest and most historically important of the three cities that amalgamated to form the city of Wuhan in 1950. Wuchang lies on the south bank of the Yangtze River. The former cities of Hanyang and Hankou, which joined with Wuchang to form Wuhan, lie on the north bank and are divided by the Han River. Although Wuchang is roughly 2,000 years old, little of its past survives in Wuhan, which is best known today as an industrial and university city and as the capital of the province of Hubei.

The region was inhabited even before Wuchang was founded. A Shang Dynasty settlement, about 3,000 years old, was excavated northeast of Wuhan in the 1950s and was explored further in the 1970s. The settlement, called Panlong Cheng, included a palace and a city, protected by walls and a moat, and several tombs, one with a human sacrifice. Like many other Shang sites, this included bronze artifacts. The bronze was produced locally, not imported from larger Shang centers.

The first written historical reference to Wuchang came about 2,000 years ago. The city initially rose to prominence as the capital of the state of Wu for a brief period in the 220s, during the Three Kingdoms period, before the capital was moved to Nanjing in 229. The ruler of Wu, Huang Wu, built a castle on Wuchang's She Shan (Snake Hill) on the banks of the Yangtze in 223. The castle's famous lookout tower, known as the Yellow Crane Tower, has been the subject of many legends concerning the tower's name. Several involve a man flying in on a yellow crane; another tells the story of a Taoist priest who drew a picture of a yellow crane on the wall of a wine shop to show his gratitude for the free wine he had received there. The crane came to life, danced for the customers, and made the wine shop's owner wealthy. The tower has been destroyed and rebuilt many times; the present one on the site stands 167 feet high and is based primarily on the tower as it appeared between 1868 and 1884, when it was destroyed by fire. The design incorporates some elements of earlier Yellow Crane Towers; pictures of them are on display inside the tower. The Wuchang city wall, which stood until the 1930s, also was built during the Three Kingdoms period. It is easy to discern the location of the wall from the layout of the town.

Wuchang again became a capital city during the Yuan Dynasty (1234–1368), which was established by the Mongols. It was the headquarters of a huge province that included what are now the provinces of Hubei, Hunan, Guangdong, and Guangxi. Mongol rule weakened after Kublai Khan's death in 1294, and during this period of instability a man named Chen Youjing established an independent kingdom around Wuchang. In doing so he incurred the wrath of Zhu Yuanzhang (founder of the Ming Dynasty under the imperial name Hongwu), who conquered the area and in 1363 killed Chen Youjing, who is now entombed on the southern slopes of Snake Hill. Within five years, the Ming Dynasty controlled all of China. Wuchang remained the capital of a greatly reduced province, incorporating only Hubei and Hunan. Throughout the political changes of the thirteenth and fourteenth centuries, much construction took place in Wuchang, including several noteworthy pagodas.

The Ming Dynasty lasted until 1644, when it was overthrown by the Manchus, who established the Qing Dynasty. The Qing maintained Wuchang as a provincial capital, with the province still encompassing the territory of Hubei and Hunan. One of the more noteworthy provincial officials of this period was Zhang Zhidong, a railroad promoter who was named governor general of the province in 1889. His enthusiasm led to the development of the area into a major railway and industrial center; in the 1890s China's first modern steel mill began operations in Hanyang. Zhang Zhidong's support for local control and financing of railroads, and his fear that foreign financing would threaten China's autonomy, resulted in the formation of the Railway Protection Movement, which was to contribute to the downfall of the Manchus in 1911, two years after Zhang's death.

Owing to mismanagement and lack of capital, local control of the railroads had proven generally unsuccessful. This concern led Sheng Xuanhui, the national minister of communications, to announce a plan to nationalize the railroad trunk lines (those covering long distances) and leave the branch lines to local interests. The national government then would be able to turn to foreign sources for financing and expertise. This move resulted in a revolt by provincial businessmen, who first refused to pay taxes, then took up arms. Their discontent combined with that of numerous other anti-Manchu groups, including railway workers, to produce the Republican Revolution of 1911. Wuchang was left vulnerable to the revolt when some of the imperial troops stationed there

Statue of Sun Yat-sen in front of the former Hubei Military Government Building
Photo courtesy of Consulate General of China, Chicago

were called away to quell the unrest in Sichuan (Szechwan) province. The revolutionaries were able to seize control of Wuchang easily on October 10, with the help of some of the remaining members of the imperial garrison who had come over to the side of the rebels. This was the first victory for the republican forces, and the revolution spread from Wuchang to other cities. Fighting continued for several weeks in the adjacent city of Hankou, which suffered great damage. The rebels were largely successful, and within two months representatives from seventeen provinces met to establish a provisional republican government under Sun Yat-sen and Li Yuanhong, a military officer from Wuchang.

The new government was a coalition of diverse political forces, and the coalition quickly weakened when it became dominated by the more conservative elements. To persuade the Manchus to abdicate the throne, Sun Yat-sen was forced to resign in favor of Yuan Shikai, who actually had aided the Manchus during the uprising. Under Yuan Shikai and regional warlords, China became a republic in name only. The events of October 10 in Wuchang retained symbolic meaning for the nation, however, and planted the seeds for the communist revolution of the late 1940s. The 1911 revolution is commemorated in Wuchang by a statue of Sun Yat-sen in front of the former Hubei Military Government Building, which the revolutionaries used as their headquarters. Renamed the 1911 Revolution Memorial Hall, it now contains a museum relating to the rebellion. Nearby is a tower called the Nine Women's Grave, memorializing nine women involved in an earlier uprising, the Boxer Rebellion of 1900.

Wuchang and its adjacent cities continued as centers of opposition to the status quo. The Chinese Communist Party was active in organizing industrial workers, and numerous strikes broke out in the Wuchang-Hanyang-Hankou region in the 1920s. Local warlords responded by brutally suppressing labor unions. In 1926–27 the area was the headquarters of the leftist faction of the Guomindang (GMD; also transliterated as Kuomintang, KMT), the revolutionary political party. This faction, which was opposed to KMT leader Chiang Kai-shek, was led by Wang Jingwei, who for a time allied himself with the Communist Party. Wang Jingwei eventually turned against his allies and ordered the deaths of 100,000 communist supporters in Wuchang and the surrounding area. Another of his former allies, Sun Yat-sen's widow Song Qingling, narrowly escaped execution. Chiang Kai-shek, facing threats from warlords as well as communists, was able to consolidate his hold on the party and the nation through his military campaign, the Northern Expedition, which captured the three-city area in 1926. Leftist political activism continued, however, as Mao Zedong recruited peasants in the region to the communist cause in the late 1920s.

Beginning in 1938, the cities were occupied by the Japanese, who held the area until 1945. The Communist Party won control of China in 1949, and the following year Wuchang, Hankou, and Hanyang were joined into one city, Wuhan, which then was targeted for a new wave of industrial development by Mao's first Five-Year Plan. The region's industrial base had suffered a blow in 1938, when the national government moved Hanyang's steel mill to Chongging (Chungking). The Five-Year Plan revived the area's steel industry and its manufacturing base in general: in addition to steel, products made in Wuhan today include trucks, railroad cars, farm equipment, glass, chemicals, machine tools, and electronic instruments.

Another development under communist rule was the construction of the Wuhan Bridge across the Yangtze in 1957. With one level for cars and trucks and another for trains, the Wuhan Bridge for the first time connected northern and southern China by rail. The Yangtze, which can accommodate ocean-going vessels as far as Wuhan, makes the city an important inland port. The city's other claims to fame include the University of Wuhan, one of China's leading educational institutions, and the Museum of Hubei Province, which has an exceptional archaeological collection, primarily from a tomb excavated at Sui Xian in 1978. The tomb belonged to a fifth century B.C. prince named Yi of the state of Zeng. The pride of the collection of artifacts from the tomb is a set of sixty-four bronze bells.

The other component cities of Wuhan, while not as significant as Wuchang, are yet of some historic interest. Hanyang was founded during the Sui Dynasty (581–618). Like Wuchang, it formerly was encircled by walls. Its most historic area is Gui Shan (Tortoise Hill), which stands across the Yangtze from Wuchang's Snake Hill. The hill is important in Chinese mythology as the spot where the god Yu is said to have stopped the local floods, with the help of a magic turtle who used its body to hold back the waters. A rock formation resembling a turtle projects from the top of the hill. Another rock, shaped like a zither, gives rise to the legend of a musician, Bo Ya, who felt that no one truly appreciated his zither playing except a hermit named Zhong Ziqi. Upon Zhong Ziqi's death, Bo Ya broke his instrument and vowed never to play again. Numerous temples and pavilions have been constructed on Tortoise Hill over the centuries; by 1949 they all had been destroyed, but some have been rebuilt, including the Guqin Terrace, where Bo Ya is said to have played. Two important tombs also stand on the mountain. One is that of Lu Su, a general in the state of Wu during the third century. The other belongs to He Jingyu, one of the first women to rise to leadership in the communist movement; she was killed during Wang Jingwei's purge in the late 1920s.

Another historic site of Hanyang is the Guiyan Si (Temple of the Return to the Fundamental Principle), a Buddhist temple originally built in the mid–seventeenth century but reconstructed in the nineteenth and twentieth centuries. Its most outstanding feature is the Hall of the 500 Luohan, featuring sculptures of 500 devout Buddhists who have become similar to patron saints; different prayers are addressed to different images. The temple also contains a beautiful jade Buddha sculpture presented to China by Burma in 1935. Other displays include bronzes from the Ming period and stucco figures on wood frames.

Hankou was a major commercial city during the Song Dynasty (960–1276) but later declined into a small fishing

Library Building for Buddhist Scriptures at Guiyan Si in Hanyang, near Wuchang
Photo courtesy of Consulate General of China, Chicago

village. Its commercial importance resumed after it became a treaty port, open to foreign trade, in the 1860s. Numerous foreign companies opened offices in Hankou in the late nineteenth century, and the city still has much attractive European-influenced architecture from this period. Because of twentieth-century industrial development, Hankou is now larger in area than either Wuchang or Hanyang.

Further Reading: A highly readable history of China is Jacques Gernet's *A History of Chinese Civilization,* translated by J. R. Foster (Cambridge and New York: Cambridge University Press, 1982; second edition, 1995; as *Le monde chinois,* Paris: A. Colin: 1972). *The Cambridge Encyclopedia of China,* edited by Brian Hook (Cambridge: Cambridge University Press, 1982) offers useful background on the overall history of the country and events in Wuchang, including the 1911 revolution. *Blue Guide: China* by Frances Wood (London: Black, and New York: Norton, 1992) offers more detail than most travel guides. An interesting portrait of Hankou in 1897, during its treaty-port era, is contained in Isabella Lucy Bird's *The Yangtze Valley and Beyond: An Account of Journeys in China* (2 vols., London: Murray, 1899; New York: Putnam, 1900; reprint, London: Virago, 1985; Boston: Beacon, 1987).

—Tim Pepper and Trudy Ring

Xian (Shaanxi, China)

Location: Along the banks of the Wei River in China's central Shaanxi province.

Description: Inhabited since the Neolithic Age, Xian has been the capital of several Chinese dynasties over the centuries. Under the Tang (618–907), the city, then known as Chang'an, was the greatest metropolitan center in the world and housed more than 1 million citizens inside its city walls. Although Xian is no longer the nation's capital, it remains a very rich cultural and historical center and possesses some of China's most important archaeological sites.

Site Office: Shaanxi Tourism Bureau
15 Chang'an Avenue
710061 Xian
China
751051

Throughout the thousands of years of Chinese history, the city of Xian and its surrounding area have played a vital role in the cultural, religious, and political developments of the country. Located in central China's modern Shaanxi province, Xian is the present capital of the province, and within its city limits, or very close by, have stood the capitals of a number of previous empires. Archaeological excavations in the Yellow River basin have unearthed remains of Neolithic communities, findings that have led to the region's claim to be the cradle of Chinese civilization. From the area's Neolithic beginnings through the modern era, Xian has remained one of Asia's richest historical centers.

The area around Xian has been inhabited continuously since at least 6000 B.C., as indicated by the Neolithic Banpo Village, lying six miles east of the modern city. This settlement was discovered in 1953 and was excavated from 1954 to 1957. From the discoveries at the site, archaeologists and historians have pieced together details on four Neolithic societies that inhabited the area from 6080 to 5600 B.C. The site of the village is on high ground for protection from the area's frequent flooding and is surrounded by a deep, protective moat. Banpo's 500 inhabitants lived in shelters that were partially underground, with low brick walls completing the structure.

Artifacts found at the site include hunting tools such as arrowheads and spears, as well as fishhooks and bolas, a weapon made from several stones connected by hemp rope and used to entangle the legs of wild animals. Pottery found in and around the village has helped identify the community as part of the Neolithic Yang Shao culture, known for earthenware painted with black geometric designs.

Xian first became an imperial capital during the time of the Western Zhou (1122–771 B.C.), when an emperor took up residence at Feng, an ancient site situated just outside the modern city. Four burial mounds stand across the Wei River to the northwest of modern Xian. These mounds are reported to be the tombs of the four Zhou kings, but the historical record is shrouded in both myth and contradictions, leaving the origin of the mounds uncertain.

Some centuries later, the nearby town of Xian Yang was developed by Qin rulers as their capital city. After Qin Shihuang Di, the first emperor of united China, came to power in 221 B.C., he expanded Xian Yang. He ultimately moved his court some miles south and west when the town became too large and crowded. At this new site on the southern banks of the Wei River some nine miles outside Xian, Qin Shihuang Di began construction of a fabulous palace complex, known today as A Fang. According to legend, every time the ferocious Qin armies defeated another enemy, Qin Shihuang Di would order a new building erected on the palace grounds; each new commemorative building was constructed in the architectural style of the defeated army's country. At the time that the complex was burned in 206 B.C. after Qin Shihuang Di's death, A Fang is believed to have consisted of 270 buildings. The ruins visible today are most likely palace foundations.

Qin Shihuang Di's mausoleum lies nearly twenty miles outside present-day Xian. The tomb itself is covered by a small hill; excavation has been initiated only recently, and in the mid-1990s it was still in the preliminary stages. According to historical accounts, 700,000 men were involved in the construction of the necropolis. The mausoleum is said to be a brilliant model of all of China, complete with jewels in the ceiling to depict the stars, and rivers of flowing mercury. The necropolis is spread over nineteen square miles, and the exact location of the tomb entrance remains hidden. Some doubt has existed throughout the centuries as to whether or not the emperor's body is actually buried on the site. Qin Shihuang Di was known to be paranoid; rumors have persisted since the time of the Qin that the necropolis was built to deceive his enemies and that his actual tomb is located elsewhere.

One superb Qin site that has been excavated is the army of terra-cotta soldiers belonging to Qin Shihuang Di, which lies less than a mile from his presumed burial place. Discovered in 1974 by local peasants digging a well, the terra-cotta army is one of the world's greatest archaeological finds. Three underground vaults have been excavated, containing more than 7,000 pieces combined. Each of the soldiers is life-size, and no two are identical. The army is set in battle formation, complete with chariots, horses, and weapons. The museum established at the site contains yet another remarkable display: a model Qin chariot in bronze complete with

The Museum of Ruins at the Imperial Huaqingchi-Huaqing Hot Springs, Xian
Photo courtesy of China National Tourist Office, New York

coachman and horses, discovered near the tomb in 1980. The model is a realistic copy of the chariots used by the emperor when inspecting his lands. The chariots and the army hint at what treasures still may lie sealed in the emperor's tomb.

When the Western Han (206 B.C.–A.D. 9) overthrew the Qin, the new emperor, Liu Bang, kept his capital in the area, establishing it several miles north of the present site of Xian and naming it Chang'an, or Long-Lasting Peace. A number of Han burial mounds remain in the hills surrounding Xian. The largest of the Han mounds belongs to Emperor Wu Di. According to historical accounts, Wu was interred in 87 B.C., clothed in a jade suit sewn with golden thread and accompanied in the tomb by his slaves and horses. Another impressive Han burial site is the tomb complex of Emperor Jing Di, who reigned in the mid–second century B.C. The complex was discovered in 1990 during a road construction project. Like Qin Shihuang Di's tomb, it contains numerous terra-cotta soldier figures; 700 of them had been found by the mid-1990s in eight of the complex's twenty-four graves. A total of 70,000 workers are said to have worked on the complex over a period of thirty-seven years. A cemetery in the vicinity contains about 10,000 graves, including those of numerous workers who died during the imperial mausoleum's construction.

During the Han period, Chang'an became the starting point of the famous Silk Road, a highly important trading network between China and points west. This important highway connected imperial China with other highly developed ancient civilizations, including those of Persia, Egypt, Turkey, Greece, and Italy. Although the city lost its capital status and declined in importance for several centuries after the fall of the Western Han, the Silk Road remained vital to China for centuries to come.

The area came into the spotlight again several hundred years later during the Sui Dynasty (A.D. 581–618), when Emperor Wen Di established his imperial capital southeast of the former Chang'an and renamed the city Daxing, or Great Prosperity. The Sui were the first rulers since the fall of the Han centuries earlier to purge China of foreign influences and unite feuding kingdoms under a centralized government. Under Wen Di, the Sui strengthened Daxing and the rest of northern China through implementation of conservative fiscal policies, an emphasis on crucial infrastructure improvements, and toleration of various religions and philosophies including Buddhism, Taoism, and Confucianism. A temple was founded in Daxing by the Sui, but was destroyed by the time of the Tang (618–907). The site of the Sui temple was later occupied by the Great Wild Goose

Pagoda (Da Yan Ta) and the Temple of Great Good Will (Ci En Si), both constructed by Tang Dynasty rulers.

Remembered for his fair-minded rule that laid the groundwork for a strong, unified China, Emperor Wen was replaced by his son Yang in 604. It was alleged that Yang had murdered his father, and in any case Yang's rule led to the demise of the Sui. A despotic ruler intent on self-glorification, Yang began construction on a fabulous imperial palace at Luoyang and soon moved the Sui capital out of the Xian area. Yang's one shining triumph, however, was the completion of his father's most ambitious project: the Grand Canal linking southern and northern China.

From the ashes of the Sui Dynasty rose the brilliant Tang Dynasty (618–907), remembered today for patronage of the arts and the importance its capital played in international trade. The dynastic capital was established on the site that is now Xian and took the name of an earlier capital, Chang'an. Under the Tang, Chang'an flourished, becoming the world's largest and most important city by the mid–eighth century. At its zenith under Emperor Xuanzong (reigned 712–756), Chang'an held some 1 million citizens within its city walls.

Under the Tang, Chang'an was an extraordinary metropolitan center, laid out as a neat grid of wide streets surrounded by pounded earth walls fortified with sun-baked brick. Completely surrounding the city, the walls of Chang'an stood about seventeen feet high and varied from seventeen to thirty feet thick at the base. Traffic flowed in and out of the Tang capital through the wall's eleven guarded gates.

As the canal and road system linking Chang'an with the rest of China—and indeed with the rest of the world—continued to expand, so did the imperial city. China's improved infrastructure fueled the growth of the country's international trade, and Chang'an quickly became not only the empire's commercial hub, but its religious and cultural one as well. Its important role in international trade drew numerous foreign merchants to the metropolis, and the city quickly adopted an international flavor as Muslims, Persian Zoroastrians, and Nestorian Christians from Syria set up small communities inside the city walls. Fueled by the need for personnel in the booming foreign trade sector and the imperial administration, the population of Chang'an topped 2 million by the eighth century.

Although the city's original Tang wall has been replaced by a later dynasty's ramparts, a number of monuments to the greatness of the Tang still remain today, most notably the Great Wild Goose Pagoda, the adjoining Temple of Great Good Will, and the Small Wild Goose Pagoda. Now situated outside Xian's Ming-Dynasty walls, the Great Wild Goose Pagoda and the Temple of Great Good Will once stood at the center of the Tang-era Chang'an. The temple was constructed in the seventh century by Tang prince Li Zhi—commonly known by his imperial name, the Gao Zong Emperor—to honor his mother, Empress Wen De. Completed in 652, the original temple complex consisted of 13 courtyards and more than 300 rooms. A fire consumed most of the temple in 1227, and the present structures date from Ming and Qing times.

The Great Wild Goose Pagoda was added at the request of the seventh-century Buddhist monk and pilgrim Xuan Zang. Xuan Zang spent several years studying Buddhism in India and collecting religious texts. Upon his return to China, Xuan Zang spent nearly twenty years translating these Buddhist works into Chinese. The pagoda was built by the emperor to house the more than 650 books and texts Xuan Zang had collected and translated. Originally, the pagoda had five stories, and it cracked shortly after its completion. During restoration in the early eighth century, another two levels were added, with three more stories constructed shortly thereafter. Later military assaults on Chang'an damaged the pagoda, and only seven levels remain today. Because of its solid construction and maintenance throughout the ages, the pagoda remains in relatively good shape, having withstood the region's frequent earthquakes. The base was rebuilt after the communist takeover in China in 1949, but fine Tang engravings remain on the pagoda's arched interior doorways. From the top of this structure, the burial mound of Qin Shihuang Di can be seen in the distance.

The other major remaining Tang site, the Little Goose Pagoda (Xiao Yan Ta) stands on the grounds of the former Jianfu Temple. Constructed in 684 by Tang empress Wu Ze Tian, the Jianfu Temple was a site for prayers for the deceased emperor Gao Zong. Hundreds of monks inhabited the temple complex, including the pilgrim Yi Jing, who, like Xuan Zang, visited India and returned to Xian in 705 to study and translate the Buddhist texts he had collected. The pagoda was constructed upon Yi Jing's return as a library for his collection. It is a tribute to Tang construction that the delicate pagoda still stands, considering the seventy earthquakes that have rocked the structure, resulting in a loss of two of the fifteen original stories.

Just outside of Xian are the Huaqingchi-Huaqing Hot Springs. Frequented by Chinese nobility for nearly 3,000 years, the hot springs were used during the Tang Dynasty by one of China's great beauties, the concubine Yang Guifei. Tang Emperor Xuanzong became so enamored of Lady Yang that he gave all of his attention to her and spent little or no time on national affairs. At this time, the Tang were having problems controlling border areas, and the emperor's lack of interest in his imperial duties enraged the military. One of Xuanzong's army officers, An Lushan, mounted a rebellion in 755 against the emperor and his lady, who were forced to flee Chang'an for their lives. The couple was captured by imperial forces, who in turn strangled the concubine in the name of national security. Humiliated and heartbroken, Xuanzong abdicated in favor of his son; the Tang Dynasty, however, was permanently weakened. The Tang limped into the early tenth century, when China entered a period of political disunion. Chang'an, once the largest metropolitan and trading center in the world, fell to rebels during a revolt brought on by a drought in 881. In the fierce fighting around the city, many of the Tang buildings were leveled.

Although it would never again be the site of an imperial capital, the city rose in stature again centuries later at the hands of the Ming (1368–1644). It was during this dynasty that Xian received its present name, meaning Westerly Peace. The Ming-period settlement at Xian commanded only one-fifth the territory occupied by the Tang Dynasty's Chang'an, but construction did take place to restore some of the city's former glory.

The city walls that stand in Xian to this day were built in the 1370s under the direction of Ming emperor Hong Wu on the Tang foundations. During this construction, the Ming added main gates, protected by watchtowers, at each of the four corners. A number of gates have been added in recent times to allow for modern traffic flow. The Ming era also saw reconstruction of the bell tower that had stood in the center of the Tang capital. Commonly used as Xian's city symbol, the impressive structure stands nearly 120 feet tall and houses a huge, two-and-one-half-ton iron bell.

As the Ming Dynasty began to crumble in the early seventeenth century, armed rebellions broke out frequently around the country. One rebel from famine-ravaged Shaanxi province, Li Cizhong, gained control of a faction wreaking havoc in the Yellow River basin. As his troops became more organized and more powerful, he began to consider taking the Ming throne as his own. In 1643, Li set up his own government at Xian in the Ming style. The Ming Dynasty fell the next year, and Li's regime was absorbed by the next imperial dynasty, the Qing.

Under the Qing, Xian prospered, but never to the extent that it had under the Tang. The most significant event in Xian during the Qing Dynasty was the removal of the imperial court there from Beijing from 1900 to 1902, as a result of the Boxer Rebellion.The city came to the political forefront again with the fall of the Qing. After the end of imperial rule, two factions—the nationalists under Chiang Kai-shek and the communists under Mao Zedong—struggled for control of China. While the two Chinese forces fought between each other in the 1930s, Japan invaded China. Fearing for their country's future—and concerned about their own apparent inferiority to the nationalist forces—the Chinese Communist Party began promoting cooperation between Chinese factions in a united front against the Japanese. Chiang, however, felt that the communists should be defeated before Japanese aggression could be dealt with—although some of his subordinates disagreed—and so on December 3, 1936, he flew to Xian to rally his troops to continue the effort against Mao's forces.

While in Xian, Chiang was arrested by his own officers at Huaqing Pool, fed by the same hot springs favored by Chinese rulers and beautiful courtesans for thousands of years. According to rumor, Chiang fled his rooms in the middle of the night and ran up Li Shan Hill, clad only in his robe and slippers. Nationalist leaders in their capital at Nanjing came to Chiang's rescue, and the entire Xian incident was over by Christmas Day, when Chiang was freed and his captors punished. He subsequently did establish a united front with the communists against the Japanese.

After the communists established the People's Republic of China in 1949, they carried out a program of industrial development in several inland cities, including Xian. Today Xian is the capital of Shaanxi province and a bustling industrial center with a diversified economy including manufacturing of steel, textiles, electrical products, and chemicals. Although it remains a large Chinese city—its population exceeds 1 million—its status pales in comparison to the brilliance it possessed under the Tang Dynasty. But the fabulous Qin-age terra-cotta warriors, ancient imperial tombs, and the still-standing Great and Small Wild Goose Pagodas make Xian one of China's richest historical centers.

Further Reading: Dun J. Li's *The Ageless Chinese* (New York: Scribner, 1965; third edition, New York: Macmillan, 1978) offers a very readable discussion of the rich history and culture of China, from the Neolithic communities of ancient times up to recent developments. *China to 1850: A Short History* by Charles Hucker (Stanford, California: Stanford University Press, 1978) presents a detailed but concise look at China's imperial past—including insight into the numerous dynasties that made their imperial capital in Xian and the surrounding area. Readers considering visiting the historically fascinating city of Xian will find practical information in a number of guidebooks. Insight Guides' *China,* edited by Manfred Morgenstern (Singapore: APA, 1990) includes travel information and enlightening essays on the political, historical, and cultural traditions of China. John Summerfield's *Fodor's China* (New York: Fodor, 1994) provides a look at the Xian of both the past and the present, as does *Baedeker's China* (Stuttgart: Baedeker, 1994). Travelers on a strict budget will find invaluable advice offered by Alan Samagalski, Robert Strauss, and Michael Buckley in *China: A Travel Survival Kit* (second edition, South Yarra, Victoria, and Berkeley, California: Lonely Planet, 1988).

—Monica Cable

Yanan (Shaanxi, China)

Location: Ringed by mountains, Yanan is a remote town on the Yan River, in the far northern part of central China's Shaanxi province.

Description: A small and isolated town, Yanan (also written as Yenan) became the Chinese Communist headquarters from 1936 to 1947. During this time, known later as the Yanan Period, the party gained much support; Mao Zedong developed there his particular brand of Marxism, commonly called Maoism. The Chinese Communist Party (CCP) left Yanan in 1947 during the civil war with Chiang Kai-shek's nationalists, who promptly captured the city. Since the foundation of the People's Republic of China in 1949, Yanan has been revered as the former CCP headquarters and is a popular pilgrimage destination for today's Chinese.

Contact: Shaanxi Tourism Bureau
15 Changan Avenue
710061 Xian, Shaanxi
China
(29) 751483

Populated at least as long ago as the Sui Dynasty (518–618), the town of Yanan has gained fame only recently. Yanan is best known as the headquarters of the Chinese Communist Party (CCP) after the Long March of 1934. Home to the CCP for more than a decade, Yanan was a communist sanctuary surrounded by nationalist-held territory, and was attacked frequently by Chiang Kai-shek's nationalist KMT (Kuomintang; also transliterated as GMD, Guomindang) forces. Yanan was where Mao Zedong developed his version of Marxism, known as Maoism, that would provide the governing principles of the future People's Republic of China.

Situated in a basin surrounded by mountains and at a road junction between a fertile area and an arid one, Yanan was a site of strategic importance long before it became famous. The Sui established a military base there, and Yanan became an important frontier defensive outpost during the Tang Dynasty (618–907). Successive dynasties maintained a military presence at Yanan, and invaders made the area a target. In the Middle Ages the most successful of these invaders were the Mongols, who in 1221 won a key victory at Yanan over the Jürchens, a Manchurian people who had established the Jin Dynasty that ruled northern China at the time. The Mongols went on to conquer all of China and set up the Yuan Dynasty.

Yanan subsequently entered a period of decline and remained obscure until the time of the Nian Rebellion, which erupted in 1851. The rebel Nian fought Qing forces in an area covering parts of Anhui, Jiangsu, Shandong, and Henan provinces. The Nian have been linked with several religious and political secret societies, but it is widely held that they were simply a roving band of poor peasants struggling to survive in China's strict class-based society.

In 1851, floods in northern Jiangsu province devastated numerous villages, and the Nian movement increased dramatically in size as villagers banded together for support. Similar floods along the Huang Ho (Yellow River) four years later had the same effect, and soon the Nian forces numbered nearly 50,000 and were finally perceived by the Qing court at Beijing to be a serious threat to local stability.

The Qing, already struggling with the Taiping Rebellion at Nanjing, sent forces to destroy the Nian and restore order to the region. Unfortunately for the imperial forces, the Nian were firmly entrenched in walled or moated villages and possessed well-armed troops and an effective cavalry. Nian troops frequently would attack neighboring villages, and despite orders from the group's leaders, many bands raped local women and looted villages before returning to their bases.

Although the Nian themselves came from the same humble background as most of the villagers they harassed, they showed little mercy. Qing forces tried to ease the misery caused by the marauding bands, but the imperial armies were highly ineffective against the elusive Nian. By the mid-1860s, the Nian had spread as far west as Shaanxi and had taken both Xian and Yanan. The Qing pursued, complaining that the Nian forces flowed across the countryside as "freely as mercury."

The Qing's constant pursuit of the rebels finally paid off in 1868. The Nian, originally grouped into five main bands, had become divided, and united imperial forces finally cornered the remaining rebels in Shandong and executed them, restoring peace to Yanan and other areas formerly raided by the Nian.

After the Nian Rebellion, however, Yanan was the scene of uprisings by Muslims through the remainder of the 1860s and into the 1870s. In the latter decade it was devastated further by droughts, which caused widespread starvation and depopulation. Droughts in the 1920s and 1930s were almost as bad and reduced Yanan's population even more.

By the mid–1930s Yanan was a small and isolated town deep in the valley of the Yan River, ringed by mountains, in which are innumerable caves. Yanan's remoteness and the many caves made the town a perfect site for the regrouping of Mao Zedong's battered Red Army after a year-long retreat from Chiang's nationalist forces.

Mao arrived in Yanan after having been driven out of his previous stronghold in southern Jiangzi province by the fifth of Chiang's "bandit extermination campaigns." The

Cave houses of the revolutionary leaders, Yanan
Photo courtesy of A.P. / Wide World Photos, New York

campaign proved disastrous for the countryside surrounding the communist soviet, as well; at least 2 million peasants are believed to have starved to death or been killed during the Kuomintang assault. Mao's 100,000-man army fought hard against the KMT but by October 1934 realized the futility of the struggles and opted to retreat from Jiangxi to the other communist stronghold near Yanan in Shaanxi province.

At their departure from Jiangxi, the communist forces numbered 90,000. In what became known as the Long March, the communists retreated through rivers and over snowy mountain ranges, all the while defending themselves from the pursuing KMT. One year and some 6,000 miles later, approximately 20,000 communist troops arrived in Shaanxi and set up their headquarters at Baoan. The base at Baoan proved to be temporary, and in December 1936, the communists moved to Yanan and established a permanent base, taking advantage of the surrounding mountains and caves for defense and shelter.

Also in December 1936, Chiang's nationalist and Mao's communist forces agreed that driving out the Japanese was of primary importance to China. Although the two men could not reconcile their political differences, they tentatively agreed not to send China into a civil war and instead to concentrate their military efforts on ridding China of the Japanese invaders. This spirit of cooperation was born out of what is now called the Xian Incident. Chiang had flown into Xian, near the CCP headquarters in Yanan, to encourage the grumbling KMT troops to finish off the communists once and for all. Mao's party, however, had been promoting cooperation among all Chinese factions in order to defeat the Japanese, urging all groups to set aside their differences with such slogans as "Chinese must not fight Chinese." In truth, a united struggle to defend China would give the CCP much-needed time to regroup after years of KMT assaults.

Weary of civil strife, the KMT soldiers in Xian began to agree with the CCP's United Front campaign. Rather than take inspiration from the presence of their leader, the nationalists rebelled. The Northeastern 105th division and members of Chiang's personal guard staged a mutiny on December 12. Chang Xueliang, former commander of the forces at Xian, took Chiang hostage and issued a series of demands, including government recognition of all political parties and an end to China's civil conflict.

Realizing that the mutineers were more interested in defeating Chiang Kai-shek than the Japanese, the CCP sent Zhou Enlai to help mediate. By Christmas, the nationalists agreed to cease the anti-communist campaigns and join with the CCP to fight the Japanese. Despite their promise to end their assaults on Mao's troops, the KMT continued to surround and blockade the communist-held regions around Yanan. While on paper the CCP and KMT were fighting the same enemy, in truth both groups fought two wars at once, battling both the Japanese invaders and each other, with the KMT centered in Sichuan and the CCP commanding territory in Shaanxi.

Even though it was officially subsidized by Chiang's nationalists, the CCP's Eighth Route Army operated independent of KMT control and refused to allow any nationalist officers in the region. The KMT relied on conscription and heavy taxation to support its military efforts, whereas the CCP expanded its power base by improving the lives of the native peasants, maintaining order in the area, and encouraging sustainable economic production and growth. By earning the support of peasants in the growing CCP-controlled region, Mao's Communist Party grew to an estimated 1.2 million members by 1945.

The so-called Yanan Period from 1937 to 1945 proved to be an era that profoundly influenced the nation that Mao would later found: the People's Republic of China. Historians compare the communists at Yanan to the characters in one of Mao's favorite books, the Chinese classic *All Men Are Brothers,* also known as *Water Margin.* Similar to the rebels in the story, the communists fought for survival, banding together in cooperation without a rigid social structure or formal command system. Based in Yanan's existing caves and new ones they had carved from the surrounding hills for shelter, the communists grew their own food, manufactured arms and ammunition, and disseminated their political and social ideas among the local peasants to assure their security and recruit others to join their cause.

More important, the Yanan Period saw the development of the two concepts that would form the basis of Maoism: the mass line and revolutionary nationalism. Throughout Chinese history, peasants had worked land owned by others and had little say in political or economic matters. This changed under Mao's mass line philosophy. He not only initiated a sweeping land reform program that gave the land to the tiller, but also brought the peasants of CCP-controlled Shaanxi a significant role in the region's political, economic, and military activities. The core of the doctrine was the belief that the ruling party should learn firsthand the masses' problems and priorities, and then taking that knowledge into account create a form of government that ruled in the best interests of the people.

While the mass line approach helped win support for the CCP, revolutionary nationalism helped the party gain real power. Once the CCP gained peasants' support through political and economic reforms, it could strengthen peasant loyalty to the party by rallying them to fight a national foe: the invading Japanese. Whether this loyalty stemmed from political alignment with the CCP or simple nationalism can be debated, but it served Mao's purpose of solidifying the CCP's position in impoverished Yanan and Shaanxi.

During the Yanan period, Mao Zedong dedicated much time to reading and writing, occasionally disappearing for days to read a new book or complete an essay. His essays written during this time can be divided into two categories: military and political concerns. Mao's military writings reinforced some of his previous comments on guerrilla warfare, discussing how soldiers must be brave in the face of danger but sensible enough to realize when they have encountered a superior adversary. The political essays sought to shape an ideology capable of bringing China into the modern era. Mao borrowed some of his ideas from Lenin, writing that China must first practice a "new democracy" before evolving further into socialism.

Mao was careful not to preach an absolute adoption of Marxism and was concerned about party members whose grasp of the political philosophy allowed them only to "repeat quotes from Marx, Engels, Lenin, and Stalin from memory," but not to apply the ideology to everyday life. Instead, Mao called for the "Sinification of Marxism," and his accompanying Mao Zedong Thought (commonly referred to as Maoism in the West) translated Marxism into philosophies familiar and comforting to the average Chinese peasant. He made peasants—rather than industrial workers, of which China had few—the key participants in the movement, and appealed to their historical and cultural pride. Mao also was wary of intellectuals.

Mao's development of Maoism and desire for CCP solidarity prompted the Rectification Campaign in February 1942. A forerunner of the Cultural Revolution that would sweep China two decades later, the Rectification Campaign sought to strengthen the CCP, which, through its recent rapid growth, had lost the unity and discipline it had gained during the Long March.

The rectification movement sought to eradicate three factors that Mao saw as evils: subjectivism, sectarianism, and party formalism. Subjectivism was the inability to put theory into practice. The war on sectarianism attempted to repair splits within the party and to bridge the gaps that divided civilians and soldiers, new and old party members, and other disparate groups. Party formalism was the use of meaningless words rather than practical measures. Mao accomplished his rectification partly through decentralizing party administration so that officials would have close contact with the common people. There also were several party meetings, in Yanan and elsewhere, at which members read the works of Mao and others and discussed party philosophies. Through his influential work Mao became a new national hero, the center of a cult of personality that would grow to fantastic proportions in the years to come.

The growing CCP in Yanan attracted not only the attention of the Chinese, but of numerous foreigners. One of the most famous visitors to and supporters of Yanan was American writer Edgar Snow, who helped break the Western-held notion that Mao's party was not an independent nationalistic force but a Soviet puppet. Snow's book *Red Star Over China* (1937) had a profound effect on the American image of Mao's China and depicted the communists as hardworking and patriotic while portraying Chiang's nationalist regime as fraught with corruption. Other Western journalists such as Gunther Stein of the Associated Press and Theodore White of Time-Life corroborated Snow's claims, adding their own criticisms of the "feudal China" that continued to exist under nationalist rule.

Intrigued by the glowing reports of Yanan, U.S. Marine Corps captain Evans F. Carlson received permission from Chiang Kai-shek to enter the communist-controlled area around Yanan in July 1937. Like previous visitors, Carlson was impressed, comparing the growing communist forces to the Minutemen of America's own revolution. In his reports, Carlson praised the Chinese soldiers for their conduct, camaraderie, and excellent relations with the surrounding peasants. He summed up his findings saying, "the Eighth Route Army is like the fish and the people like the water."

In July 1994, U.S. president Franklin D. Roosevelt secured Chiang Kai-shek's approval to send an official military observer to Yanan, and on July 22 what was known as the Dixie Mission arrived in the communist capital under command of Colonel David D. Barrett. Under the agreement with the nationalists, the purpose of the Dixie Mission was to examine the communist forces and determine how much they could contribute to the war against the Japanese if they were aided by the Americans. Barrett's reports indicated that the communists were well trained, but only as guerrillas; left alone, he felt, they would probably be little help against a strong Japanese enemy. If equipped and trained by the Americans, however, Mao's troops could make a significant contribution to the war effort.

In August 1944, Foreign Service officer John S. Service met with Mao in Yanan concerning communist-nationalist relations. Mao stressed that the communists did not want a civil war with the nationalists, but said he believed only American intervention would persuade Chiang to work with the communists. Furthermore, only the efforts of the American forces would free China of the Japanese—and that in liberating China the united assistance of both Mao's and Chiang's forces would be crucial. Both Service and political adviser John P. Davies urged Washington to consider aiding the communists; the future of China, Davies asserted, "is not Chiang's but theirs." Davies cautioned against altogether dropping support for the nationalists, however, because the cost of such a policy reversal would be great.

The reports coming out of Yanan were so glowing that the U.S. government considered covert association with the communists and began to explore possibilities for military cooperation. This was all kept secret to avoid embarrassing Chiang and his nationalists; still, when compared to the communists, the KMT came up quite short. Foreign journalists called the nationalist capital at Chongqing (Chungking) a "nightmare" and a "pathetic city," while CCP-held areas around Yanan were deemed "democratic China." In 1944, a plan was drawn up that would train and arm some 25,000 of Mao's troops; American military reports reflected the official belief that Yanan, as "the most modern place in China," would lead the rest of the country after the defeat of the Japanese.

The American plan, however, was revealed to Chiang Kai-shek by the conservative U.S. Naval Intelligence. As feared, Chiang was angered, and U.S. officials feigned ignorance and ultimately called a halt to the project. Mao's Yanan never received the international support it sought, but it had nonetheless achieved quite an impressive list of successes. While at Yanan, Mao had created and publicized a new political theory that would end feudalism in China and bring the country's millions of long-ignored peasants into the process of governing. The CCP at Yanan had also come to dictate orders to 18 other regional headquarters covering an area of nearly 400,000 square miles and including 100 million people—more than one-fifth of China's entire population. The party's rise to power during the years at Yanan made the CCP a serious competitor with Chiang's nationalists for the ultimate rule of China.

When World War II ended in 1945, the long-suppressed civil war between the Chinese nationalists and communists resumed. One of the CCP's first actions was to reinstate land reform, which had not been a priority for a few years, in numerous villages in northern China in an attempt to gain support of the countless poor peasants. While strengthening their control of the villages, the communists were willing to let key cities—including their former capital of Yanan—fall into KMT hands.

The CCP took the offensive in 1947, gaining control of the key area between the Huang Ho (Yellow River) and the Yangtze. The oppressive taxes imposed by the nationalists on areas they controlled, in addition to their harsh treatment of locals, caused many villages to turn to the communist side. A number of captured nationalist soldiers themselves criticized Chiang's regime and joined the ranks of Mao's communist army.

The United States, which had trained and equipped the nationalists, was disgusted with the behavior of Chiang and his forces, but could do little about their impending defeat. As CCP forces continued to overpower KMT regiments, more and more American-donated weapons fell into the hands of the communists. Former general George C. Marshall, appointed U.S. Secretary of State in 1947, succeeded in keeping the United States from intervening directly in the war, which most likely would have proved even more disastrous than later American involvement in Vietnam.

The communists emerged victorious, and on October 1, 1949, the People's Republic of China was declared, with its capital at Beijing. The formative years spent by the Chinese Communist Party at Yanan would never be forgotten. As Yanan had been when the CCP entered in 1936, the nation of China was poor and nearly broken, lacking unity, capital, technology, or fertile land. However, also like Yanan, China had one very rich resource: people. Mao, determined to transform China along the lines of the model of Yanan that had so impressed Edgar Snow and other visitors to the former CCP headquarters, set about to encourage the spirit of unselfishness and unity that had been so prevalent at Yanan.

After the departure of Mao and the Chinese Communist Party in the late 1940s, Yanan returned to its former status as a small town isolated in the mountains of Shaanxi. Today, with a population of only about 30,000, the city shares the spotlight with Mao's hometown of Shaoshan as the premier pilgrimage spot for patriotic Chinese. Visitors to Yanan can see the caves where the early communists lived and worked to create a new China. Four of Mao's residences at Yanan are maintained as museums, as is the Yanan Revolutionary Memorial Hall. Other historic landmarks at Yanan include the Baota (Precious Pagoda), a nine-story structure that dates to the Tang Dynasty, and the Wangto Dong (Cave of 10,000 Buddhas), which contains numerous tiny Buddha sculptures and which was used to house the Communist Party's printing press during the Yanan Period. Although Yanan is no longer the wellspring of new and revolutionary developments in political thought, its legacy continues to be revered as an example of communist success.

Further Reading: John King Fairbank's *China: A New History* (Cambridge, Massachusetts, and London: Belknap Press of Harvard University Press, 1992) offers an easy-to-read summary of China's ancient past, more recent dynasties, and the sweeping changes made during the twentieth century. *The Search for Modern China* by Jonathan D. Spence (New York and London: Norton, 1990) details more recent history, concentrating on the changes in China's political and social situations since the Ming Dynasty. *The Rise of Modern China* by Immanuel C. Y. Hsu (Oxford and New York: Oxford University Press, 1970; fifth edition, 1995) examines the country's history since the days of the Qing. Readers particularly interested in Mao Zedong will find much of value in Stanley Karnow's *Mao and China* (New York: Viking, and London: Macmillan, 1972).

—Monica Cable

Yangon (Myanmar)

Location: At the southern tip of Lower Myanmar (formerly Burma) on the Yangon River, a tributary of the Ayeyarwady (formerly Irrawaddy) River, where it empties into the Gulf of Martaban.

Description: Capital and largest city of Myanmar, Yangon was once a center of Buddhism and was a thriving administrative and commercial center under British colonial rule. It was invaded by the Japanese during World War II. In recent years, Yangon became the center for the movement to replace Myanmar's repressive military government with a democracy; a violent crackdown on the democratic movement took place there in 1988. In 1989, the government ordered the discontinuation of British-controlled place-names and the return to the country's indigenous names: Burma became known as Myanmar, and Rangoon became Yangon.

Site Office: Ministry of Hotels and Tourism
77-91 Sule Pagoda Street
Kyauktada Township
Yangon
Myanmar
(1) 77966 or (1) 75328

As the modern capital of Myanmar, Yangon has figured prominently in the country's tumultuous, often bloody history. Originally called Dagon, the site once featured little more than a river settlement occupied by the Mon, who probably migrated to the lower river basin nearly 2,000 years ago. The Mon brought the Theravada form of Buddhism—based on a canon of scriptures written in the ancient Pali language—to Myanmar from eastern India.

The village grew around the Shwe Dagon Pagoda, built as a reliquary for eight hairs of the Buddha. According to legend, two Myanmarese merchants traveling in India met the Buddha under the sacred Bo-tree. They offered him honey and cakes, for which he rewarded them with eight of his hairs. The merchants distributed four hairs among various kings they encountered on their journey home; the remaining four they presented to King Ukkalapa of Dagon, who built a shrine for them on Singuttara Hill. When the shrine later was reopened, the story goes, it contained all eight hairs.

In 1057 Anawrahta, king of the Pyus, a Tibeto-Burmese people who had settled in northern Myanmar, invaded Dagon and stole the sacred Pali canon. Prior to that time, the people of northern Myanmar had practiced the Mahayana and Tantric forms of Buddhism. After Anawrahta's conversion to Theravada Buddhism by a southern monk, he reformed Myanmarese Buddhism.

Dagon remained a quiet village for the next several centuries, although its annual market had earned some renown by the fifteenth century. The opening of a nearby port allowed European travelers to visit the region beginning in the late sixteenth century, and they occasionally included Dagon in their journals. The Shwe Dagon Pagoda, the continual embellishments of which provided the otherwise unremarkable village with an elegant focal point, no doubt left the greatest impression on foreigners.

Each monarch's desire to leave his or her imprint on the Shwe Dagon Pagoda resulted in the frequent changes that altered the shrine's size and shape throughout the centuries. In 1362 King Byinnyu of Bago (Pegu) raised the pagoda's height to seventy-two feet. Queen Shin Saw Bu of Bago, who topped the monument with a Mon-style pagoda during the late fifteenth century, donated her weight in gold for its gilding. Not to be outdone, her successor, King Dhammazedi, offered four times his own and his wife's weight in gold, which was pounded into gold leaf and layered on the stupa. The bells of the Shwe Dagon Pagoda have figured prominently in the shrine's colorful history. Dhammazedi installed a thirty-two-ton bell, but a seventeenth-century Portuguese adventurer named Philip de Brito Nicote absconded with it, planning to recast the bell into a cannon. The boat ferrying the bell across the Yangon River sank, however, and the bell was lost.

In his southward drive to conquer the Ayeyarwady River basin, Alaungpaya, the ruler of northern Myanmar who founded the Konbaung Dynasty in the mid–eighteenth century, seized control of the tiny Mon settlement in 1755. He renamed the village Yangon, meaning "The End of War"—a sadly ironic name, considering the strife that the place has experienced since that time—and made it the center of administration for southern Myanmar. Nonetheless, Yangon remained a quiet village behind its wooden stockade, home to a limited number of military personnel, government officials, Buddhist monks, and merchants.

During the nineteenth century, the threat to Yangon came from outside Myanmar's borders. The British were anxious to expand their empire beyond India; in fact, they referred to Myanmar as Further India. Not surprisingly, the Myanmarese wanted little to do with the British, and relations between the two groups were strained at best. A Myanmarese incursion into British India to avenge a tribal insult prompted the First Anglo-Burmese War, with the result that the British gained control of Yangon in 1824. Conquering armies in Myanmar customarily would confiscate a city's bells, and the British did just that when they removed the twenty-three-ton Maha Ganda Bell from the Shwe Dagon Pagoda. This time, the bell fell off the boat and landed in the riverbed. Using nothing more than bamboo floats and their fervent faith in

Buddha, the Myanmarese raised the bell to the surface and returned it to the shrine's northwest terrace. The Treaty of Yandabo, signed on February 24, 1826, temporarily returned control of Yangon to the Myanmarese king, but relations between the British and the Myanmarese continued to deteriorate. Yangon suffered a devastating fire during this period, but King Tharrawaddy rebuilt the village in 1841. He also donated the Shwe Dagon Pagoda's largest bell, which tips the scales at forty-two tons and still occupies its original pavilion.

The Second Anglo-Burmese War began in 1852, but the British military moved quickly to quell the hostilities, again taking control of Yangon as well as trade on the Ayeyarwady River. Yangon, still a village of thatched-roofed huts, suffered greatly from the protracted fighting, and the British set about re-creating the place to accommodate their colonial administrative and commercial operations. British engineers laid out the new city, which they called Rangoon, on a grid system designed to diminish the punishing effects of the monsoon season, which can dump up to 250 inches of rain from May to October. Shorter streets running northeast to southwest absorbed the impact of the prevailing winds. Stately homes for British officials and merchants looked out upon the wide, tree-lined boulevards.

King Mindon Min, based in the new royal capital at Mandalay, presented the Shwe Dagon Pagoda in 1871 with a gilded and gem-studded *hti*—an umbrella-like ornament—hung with bells of gold and silver. More than 1,000 diamonds cover the gold and silver weather vane, on top of which sits a diamond-encrusted orb that itself is topped by a seventy-six-carat diamond. After several centuries of monarchs trying to top previous renovations, the pagoda ended up covered with sixty tons of gold leaf; the Department of Archaeology has forbidden further changes without its permission.

The colonial city soon was bustling with foreigners—Europeans, Indians, Chinese, Malays, and Thais—who came to make their fortunes in oil, rice, and teak. The Myanmarese came to despise the Indians, who obtained positions of power in the local government. (Just before the outbreak of World War II, there were 250,000 Indians in Yangon, compared with 160,000 Myanmarese.) The natives especially reviled the Chettiars, a class of Indian money-lenders. By charging lower interest rates to Myanmarese rice paddy farmers in the Ayeyarwady Delta, the Chettiars built a prosperous business and grew quite influential. The encroaching foreign influences inspired the formation in 1906 of the Young Men's Buddhist Association (YMBA), an organization to preserve the country's cultural identity. For years the British colonists had offended the Myanmarese by refusing to observe centuries-old traditions of conduct such as removing their shoes when entering a pagoda. Now the YMBA could secure an abbot's authority to set dress restrictions for monastery visitors.

Relations between the Myanmarese and the British, always tenuous at best, continued to worsen. In 1920 the British opened Rangoon University in an effort to substitute European educational practices for Asian ones. Ironically, the university fostered the factions that ultimately drove the British from Myanmar. During the university's first year, Myanmarese students and monks organized strikes and demonstrations to push for independence, and the YMBA bolstered this movement.

Yangon continued to thrive during the 1920s, despite the nascent political opposition. The city's population, only a few thousand residents during the nineteenth century, had soared to hundreds of thousands during the early twentieth century. By the 1930s Yangon served as a busy hub for air travel throughout Southeast Asia. A major earthquake and subsequent tidal wave substantially damaged the city in 1930, but it was the worldwide economic depression that had begun in 1929 that brought the most turmoil to Yangon. The Chettiars forced thousands of farmers into foreclosure and soon controlled one-fourth of Myanmar's prime farmland. In May 1930 hostilities between the two groups erupted into riots in Yangon.

Unrest persisted throughout the 1930s. Encouraged by India's fight for autonomy and influenced by rising socialism, the Myanmarese staged strike after strike. A two-year rebellion begun in 1930 by a monk named Saya San provided the independence movement with its first martyr: the British hanged him on November 28, 1937, long after suppressing the original revolt. British troops reportedly slaughtered 3,000 Myanmarese during the Saya San Rebellion.

On the campus of Rangoon University, a student movement called Dobama Asiayon (We Burmans Association) was gaining support. The members called each other *thakin* (my owner), appropriating the title the Myanmarese long had been required to use in addressing the British. Led by Aung San and Ne Win, the group trained secretly with the Japanese, who had promised independence in exchange for the movement's support. In 1935 the British government granted Myanmar autonomy and, after another strike the following year, formally separated Myanmar from British India, although the colonialists remained in the country.

During World War II, with the aid of the Dobama Asiayon–founded Burmese National Army, the Japanese moved into Myanmar in 1942. Japan wanted control of Myanmar's rich natural resources and the strategic Burma Road, built by the Chinese between 1937 and 1939. The British were unprepared for Japan's invasion and abandoned Yangon on March 7, burning much of it to the ground as they retreated. Determined to retake Myanmar, the British made two unsuccessful attempts to reestablish sovereignty over the next two years. When the Japanese suffered heavy losses at Imphal-Kohima in India in 1945, the Allies decided to make another drive into Myanmar. Although the United States saw the proposed invasion simply as a way to keep the Japanese out of northern Myanmar, Lord Mountbatten, Allied supreme commander for Southeast Asia, and Lieutenant General William Slim planned to push the drive all the way to Yangon.

In addition to the British Fourteenth Army, the Allied forces in southeast Asia included Indian, Chinese, and American regiments. By 1945, the Burmese National Army, now known as the Patriotic Burmese Forces, had joined the Allied

Shwe Dagon Pagoda, Yangon
Photo courtesy of Embassy of the Union of Myanmar, Washington, D.C.

efforts after Aung San began to doubt the Japanese commitment to Myanmarese independence. Some of Aung San's detractors called the switch the work of an opportunist who saw the tide of the war turning and threw in his lot with the likely victors. Aung San's political party, the Anti-Fascist People's Freedom League (AFPFL), also lent its support.

By March 20 the Allies had taken Mandalay, and the armies rushed south to reach Yangon before the monsoon season hit in mid-May. The stiff winds and torrential rains would make land and sea attacks virtually impossible, and any delay would allow the Japanese time to recover their strength. Soldiers from both sides raced toward Toungoo, the site of Japanese General Honda's headquarters, and five airfields within striking range of Yangon. The impending battle created an atmosphere of desperation. Japanese forces had been ordered to fight to the death and save southern

Myanmar at all costs. Karen hill tribesmen, who had been trained secretly by the British, were called upon to burn bridges, block roads, and ambush Japanese troops.

The Allies arrived in Toungoo on April 22 and sent Honda fleeing. Six days later they stormed into Bago in a fierce siege that included house-to-house searches for Japanese soldiers and sympathizers. The monsoons started two weeks early, but Japanese forces already had been sorely depleted, and in May the Allies marched into Yangon virtually unchallenged. Nevertheless, 20,000 Japanese troops remained in hiding in Yangon. Allied regiments searched them out and annihilated them, leaving the corpses to rot in the streets.

After the war, the newly elected British Labour government granted Myanmar its independence. Aung San and other members of the AFPFL triumphantly began the process of creating a new Myanmarese government, but their euphoria was short-lived. On July 19, 1947, as the AFPFL executive council met in Yangon, assassins burst into the room, killing Aung San and several others. However, the work for independence continued, and on January 4, 1948, at 4:20 A.M. Myanmar celebrated its official independence. (The time was chosen for its astrological significance, an age-old Myanmarese custom.) Aung San's colleague U Nu became prime minister.

Establishing an independent nation in the wake of a devastating world war was no easy feat. The economy was a shambles and various factions jockeyed for power. Although Aung San had forged a pact among the various minority groups before his death, Karen tribesmen and several Communist organizations attempted to overthrow the government in 1949. Nine years later, the Freedom League split into two factions, and chaos reigned anew. U Nu charged Ne Win, by then a general, with restoring order so that elections could be held. The 1960 elections restored U Nu to power, but his willingness to cooperate with the ethnic minorities did not sit well with military leaders, who had become accustomed to their powerful position. In March 1962, General Ne Win and his officers staged a coup, imprisoning U Nu for four years before forcing him into exile.

The xenophobic Ne Win instituted a policy of strict isolationism, cutting off Myanmar and its capital from the rest of the world for twenty-five years. Only on exceptional occasions did Myanmar garner international attention, such as when a bombing staged by North Korean terrorists killed several members of the South Korean cabinet near the Shwe Dagon Pagoda in 1983. The once-rich country that had led the world in rice exportation now suffered from food shortages. Ironically, when Myanmar petitioned the United Nations in 1987 for "least-developed country" status in order to receive financial aid, the petition was nearly turned down because the Myanmarese literacy rate far exceeded the limits normally found in underdeveloped nations.

Worldwide attention again turned to Myanmar in 1988 as a loosely organized coalition of students and Buddhist monks began to hold rallies for reform. In late July, Ne Win's appointment of the reactionary general Sein Lwin to head the ruling Myanmar Socialist Program Party led to public demonstrations. On August 12 Sein Lwin was replaced by Maung Maung, who appeared to strike a conciliatory pose when he ordered the army off the streets. However, he also emptied the prisons of hundreds of criminals, allowing them to roam the streets of Yangon, robbing and looting. Many observers believed the government intentionally was inducing chaos to enable an apparently valid military crackdown. Further, the empty prisons now could accommodate hundreds of political prisoners.

On September 18–19, tens of thousands of Myanmarese gathered in Yangon to demand democratic elections. True to form, the government acted swiftly and violently, gunning down a great many civilians. The government closed schools and imposed curfews in Yangon. A military-run State Law and Order Restoration Council (SLORC) replaced the scant civilian control that had existed in the government.

Although Ne Win publicly resigned, he probably still controls the military apparatus that governs Myanmar. An eccentric recluse, the general lives in a compound in northern Yangon with a military contingent, fences, and land mines protecting him. In an apparent effort to establish his own legacy in the tradition of his royal predecessors, Ne Win built the Maha Wizaya Pagoda—in his own honor—near the Shwe Dagon Pagoda during the 1980s; the name means "Great Conqueror."

A different voice in Myanmarese politics emanates from Aung San Suu Kyi, the daughter of the martyred Aung San. Educated in London and India, she and her English husband were working and raising a family in London when her mother suffered a stroke in the spring of 1988. Suu Kyi returned to Yangon for the first time in many years, just as the government began its notorious massacre of demonstrators. She quickly became involved in the democracy movement.

Suu Kyi made her first public appearance on August 26, 1988. With the Shwe Dagon Pagoda as a backdrop, she introduced the Myanmarese people to the notion of basic human rights, giving the loosely organized democracy movement a focus. After cofounding the National League for Democracy (NLD) in September, she traveled throughout Myanmar organizing rallies and soon became a national symbol of freedom. Suu Kyi's bravery in defying a group of soldiers who had been ordered to shoot her greatly enhanced her fame.

After publicly criticizing Ne Win at a rally in 1989, Suu Kyi was placed under house arrest in Yangon. In spite of her imprisonment, her influence was powerful enough to contribute to a landslide defeat of the SLORC by the NLD in 1990 elections. However, the military government refused to relinquish its power. A Nobel Peace Prize in 1991 acknowledged international acclaim for her work toward democracy in Myanmar. The military junta agreed to let Suu Kyi accept the prize in person if she agreed to leave Myanmar forever. She refused, enduring another four years of seclusion before her release in July 1995. She likely will continue her campaign for a democratic government in Myanmar.

In recent years, the government has made some attempt to attract visitors to Myanmar. In 1991 the government agreed to a joint venture with a private developer for the extensive renovation of Yangon's Strand Hotel, an elegant structure built at the turn of the century that is notable for the dignitaries who have stayed there. But it is the golden Shwe Dagon Pagoda, rising 326 feet over Yangon, that remains the inviolable source of pride for the Myanmarese.

Further Reading: Two general histories of Yangon and Myanmar, although dated, are still frequently cited and may prove useful: *A History of Burma from the Earliest Times* by G. E. Harvey (London and New York: Longmans, 1925; reprint, New York: Octagon, 1983) and *A History of Modern Burma* by J. F. Cady (Ithaca, New York: Cornell University Press, 1958). A more recent source for information on the various personalities, events, and locales in the country is *Historical Dictionary of Myanmar* by Jan Becka (Metuchen, New Jersey, and London: Scarecrow Press, 1995). *Burmese Administrative Cycles: Anarchy and Conquest, c. 1580–1760* by Victor B. Lieberman (Princeton, New Jersey: Princeton University Press, 1984) provides background for the establishment of Yangon as a capital in 1755. For a look at Anglo-Myanmarese relations, consult *Empires in Collision: Anglo-Burmese Relations in the Mid–Nineteenth Century* by Oliver B. Pollak (Westport, Connecticut: Greenwood, 1979). Although essentially a travel guide, *1994 Thailand, Indochina and Burma Handbook* (Bath, England: Trade and Travel Publications, and Lincolnwood, Illinois: Passport Books, 1994) includes a fairly comprehensive section on Myanmar's and Yangon's history with numerous sidebars on the nation's leaders. *The Great Battles of World War II* (London: Hamlyn, and Chicago: Regnery, 1972) by Henry Maule, a former British correspondent for the *New York Daily News*, provides a thorough description of the assault on Yangon, albeit from the Allied point of view. There are numerous accounts of the struggle for democracy based in Myanmar. Notable among them are *The Lands of Charm and Cruelty: Travels in Southeast Asia* by Stan Sesser (New York: Knopf, 1993; London: Picador, 1994), best known for his pieces published in *The New Yorker,* and *Outrage: Burma's Struggle for Democracy* by Bertil Lintner (Hong Kong: Review, 1981; second edition, London: White Lotus, 1990), a Swiss journalist considered an expert on Myanmarese affairs. The February 1992 issue of *Current Biography* (New York) profiled Aung San Suu Kyi in its cover story.

—Mary F. McNulty

Yangzhou (Jiangsu, China)

Location: Yangzhou lies on the Grand Canal in Jiangsu province of eastern China, about twelve miles north of the Yangtze River and forty-five miles northeast of Nanjing.

Description: Nearly 2,500 years old, the city is famed today for its gardens and pavilions. Following the building of the Grand Canal by the Sui Dynasty in the early seventh century A.D., Yangzhou became the headquarters of a nationwide water-transport system and an important port in its own right. Attracting considerable foreign trade, the city once had thousands of foreign inhabitants, one of whom was Marco Polo, who worked there briefly as a local administrator. Yangzhou has a protected status under the Chinese government because of its historical and cultural significance. It is one of the most picturesque locales in China, featuring an abundance of traditional Chinese architecture and a pleasant atmosphere.

Contact: Jiangsu Tourism Bureau
255 Zhongshan N Road
210003 Nanjing, Jiangsu
China
(25) 3327144

Yangzhou was first settled sometime around the fifth century B.C. In its early years, the town served as a fief called Guangling in the state of Chu. After the unification of the Chinese Empire by the Qin Dynasty in 221 B.C., the city became an administrative center and was variously known as Guangling or Nan Yan. The name Yangzhou, once applied to all of southeast China, became associated exclusively with the city about the time of the Sui Dynasty's construction of the Grand Canal in the early seventh century A.D. Yangzhou was the southern terminus of the canal's interconnected system of waterways and its link to the Yangtze River. As the center of transportation between northern and southern China, Yangzhou was to become one of China's leading commercial and cultural centers, a role it held for many centuries. The town also served as the Sui Dynasty's southern capital.

Under the Tang Dynasty (618–907), China became more cosmopolitan and open to foreign trade than at any other time in its history. Yangzhou was among the port cities that attracted traders from such locales as the Russian steppes and as far away as the Middle East. Originally, traders came mostly by caravan. After 760, they began to arrive by sea from India and the Persian Gulf to Guangzhou and Yangzhou. Eventually, many Arabs, Jews, and Persians were to settle in Yangzhou, bringing their own religions and cultural traditions. They lived in their own communities, under their own ethnic leaders and laws, thus establishing small pockets of Islam, Judaism, Christianity, and Zoroastrianism in Yangzhou. These foreign influences were to leave their mark on Chinese music, dance, poetry, art, fashions, and cuisine. By the ninth century, Yangzhou reportedly counted more than 100,000 foreigners among its residents.

Yangzhou offered many attractions to outsiders. Whereas medieval Europe confined its few books and manuscripts mostly to monasteries and the private collections of the wealthy, Yangzhou had book markets as early as the ninth century. The Chinese had invented paper, most likely as early as the first century A.D., improved papermaking techniques over the centuries, and were pioneering printing technologies by the eighth century. With Yangzhou's book markets and other cosmopolitan features, it is not surprising that Arab visitors were to write words of praise regarding the glories of this picturesque town.

But Yangzhou also suffered its share of struggle during the internal rebellions and wars that marred the Chinese landscape throughout much of the city's history. Late in the seventh century, Empress Wu usurped the throne of the Tang Dynasty, ruling first through her weakling husband and sons, then abolishing the dynasty and ruling on her own. In one of several plots hatched against her, members of the Tang imperial family and their followers in the Yangtze Valley occupied Yangzhou and issued a proclamation against the empress claiming, in part, that "with a heart like a serpent and a nature like that of a wolf, she favored evil sycophants. . . . She has killed her own children. . . . She is hated by the gods and by men alike. . .". The empress was more impressed by the style of writing in the proclamation than dismayed by its contents. She was reported to have expressed regret that its talented writer had not achieved high office. Meanwhile, the rebels assembled a large army in Yangzhou and marched south toward what is now Nanjing. Their rebellion was crushed within a few months by the empress's forces.

Early in the thirteenth century, during the Song Dynasty, Genghis Khan and his Mongol army invaded China. Under his successor, Kublai Khan, Yangzhou was besieged by the Khan's trusted General Bayan en route to the conquest of Hangzhou. The Song forces were fully defeated by 1279, and all of China came under Mongol rule. Despite the ravages of war, Yangzhou remained a prosperous commercial center when the Venetian explorer Marco Polo visited the city around 1280. Polo knew the city as "Yan-gui" and later described it in a remarkable travel memoir he dictated while imprisoned in Genoa in 1298. Polo spoke from what he perceived to be the viewpoint of China's Mongol conquerors, under whose patronage he had come, referring to himself in

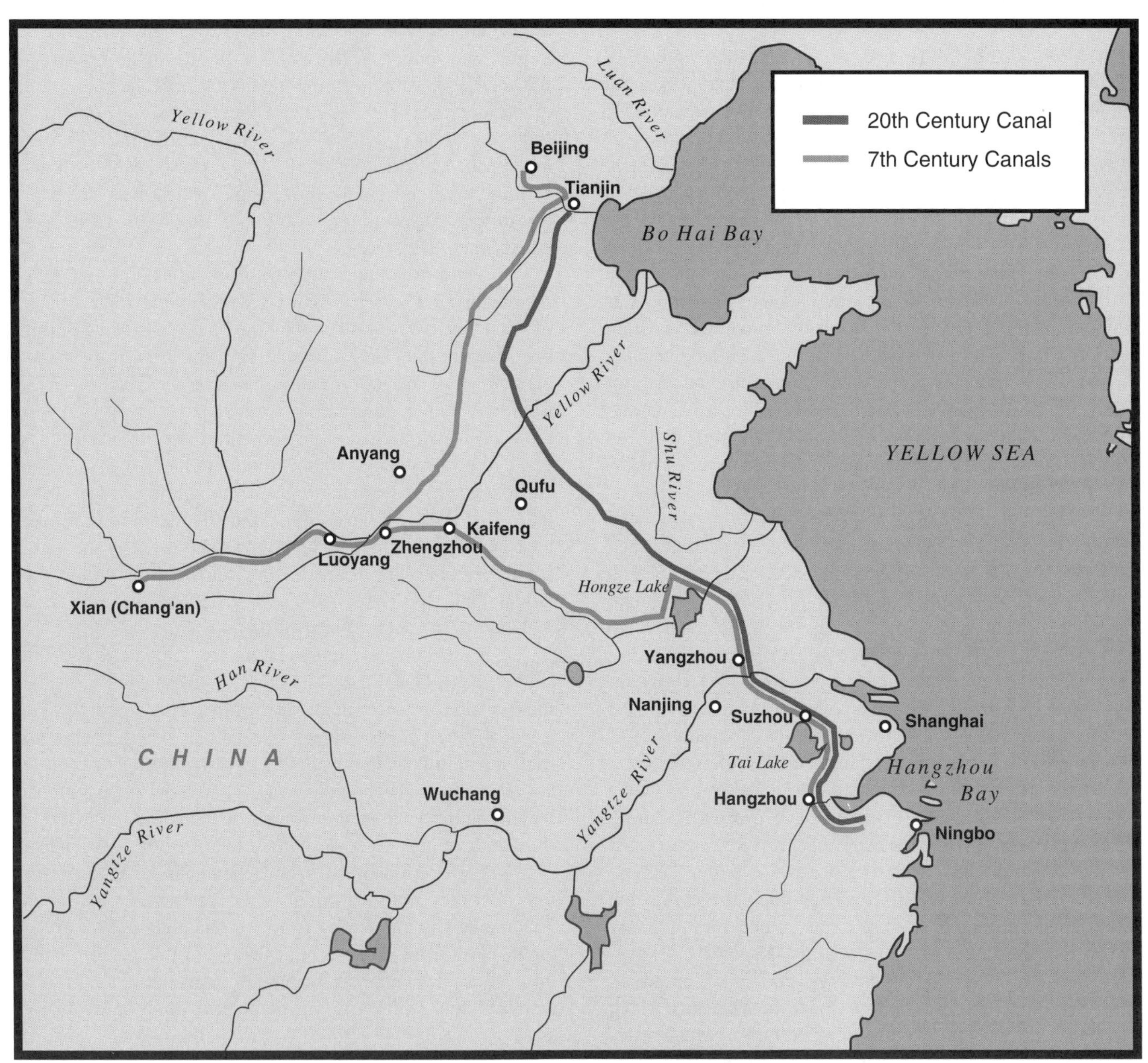

Map illustrating the course of the Grand Canal in the seventh and the twentieth centuries, showing the position of Yangzhou
Illustration by Tom Willcockson

the third person and reflecting the Mongol disdain for other cultures. Of Yangzhou he wrote:

> Proceeding in a southeasterly direction from Chin-gui, you come to the important city of Yan-gui [Yangzhou], which having twenty-four towns under its jurisdiction, must be considered as a place of great consequence. It belongs to the dominion of the Great Khan. The people are idolaters, and subsist by trade and manual arts. They manufacture arms and all sorts of warlike accoutrements; in consequence of which many troops are stationed in this part of the country. The city is the place of residence of one of the twelve nobles before spoken of, who are appointed by his Majesty to the government of the provinces; and in the place of one of these, Marco Polo, by special

order of the Great Khan, acted as governor of this city during the space of three years.

Polo's claim to have served as Yangzhou's governor is disputed by most historians, who believe that, at best, he may have served in some minor administrative capacity. He wrote of Yangzhou and other cities in China with such wonder and admiration that most Westerners, considering his descriptions wildly exaggerated, refused to believe him. According to tradition, Marco Polo was asked on his deathbed in 1324 to confess his lies; instead he replied that he had described only half the wonders he had seen.

Another foreign visitor to write about Yangzhou was the fourteenth-century friar Odoric of Pordenone, a small district in Italy not far from the border of what later became Yugoslavia. A member of the Franciscan brotherhood, Friar Odoric retraced much of Marco Polo's route in China and confirmed many of Polo's descriptions. In Yangzhou, he visited a Franciscan house and later described the citizenry as hospitable and the restaurants well patronized.

During the Ming Dynasty (1368–1644), the decline of the Grand Canal, and maritime trade in general, diminished Yangzhou's value as a port. Then, in 1645, during the Manchu invasion of China, Yangzhou became the scene of a brutal massacre. When forces loyal to the Ming rulers tried to establish a stronghold at Yangzhou, the Manchu invaders slaughtered the resisters over a ten-day period in a frenzy of killing that spread fear throughout other settlements along the Grand Canal. The Manchus were to rule China until 1911 under the name of the Qing Dynasty (the last Qing emperor, Puyi, was officially forced to abdicate in 1912), and China experienced considerable expansion and prosperity during the first century or two of Manchu rule.

Yangzhou, in particular, became a major Chinese cultural center from the sixteenth through the eighteenth centuries, despite its decline as a port. Since 1600, the city had been the headquarters of the wealthy and powerful Lianghuai Salt Administration. The city's government-licensed salt merchants grew enormously rich under the Manchus. Much of their wealth was lavished on opulent living, but a considerable amount also went to patronize the arts and education of Yangzhou, greatly increasing the city's glory. With its cultural advantages and scenic beauty, Yangzhou became a popular retreat for members of the Manchu royal family.

Yangzhou again suffered during the Taiping Rebellion (1850–64), when rebel forces seized the city in 1853 and crushed the imperial troops in a major battle there two years later. Ultimately, the rebellion was put down, but many of Yangzhou's temples and administrative buildings were destroyed during the fighting. Then massive flooding from the Grand Canal, beginning in 1855, destroyed grain production in areas surrounding the city, ending Yangzhou's role as a center for grain shipments. Changes in the salt administration contributed to further decline in Yangzhou's importance. In the early twentieth century, however, it retained some prosperity as a regional market town and producer of traditional handicrafts.

Since 1949, improvements in China's canal system have given new life to the city. Today, Yangzhou is an important center for food processing and textile industries, and its population numbers nearly 300,000. Its artisans are renowned for their expertise in crafts involving silk, lacquer ware, embroidery, and jade carving. Yangzhou's lacquered works today represent a tradition that extends back some 2,000 years and reached its peak during the Han Dynasty. Moreover, the Chinese often refer to the citizens of Yangzhou as "the masters of three knives," in recognition of their skills as barbers, cooks, and pedicurists.

The city contains many historic and scenic attractions. Among the best known is Shouxi (Slender West) Lake, a place of great beauty written about by the poet Wang Hang during the Manchu era. Here one can find the beautiful Xiyuan Garden, designed in 1751, and the Dahong Qiao, or Great Rainbow Bridge. Originally a wooden structure, it later was replaced by an arched stone structure, and its beauty was extolled by many poets. In the middle of the lake is the Xiao Jinshan island-hill, containing several buildings. Also at the lake is the Diaoyu Tai pavilion, reputedly the favorite fishing spot of the Qing emperor Qianlong, who ruled in the eighteenth century. Also at this historic lake is the Wuting Qiao Bridge built by Yangzhou's salt merchants in 1757 as a welcoming site for the emperor on his visits to the city.

Yangzhou is especially famed for its elaborately beautiful gardens. One, located in the southern part of the city, is the Heyuan Garden, built late in the nineteenth century by He Zangdao, the Chinese delegate to France. The garden contains a lengthy covered walkway twisting through the entire complex and connecting the various buildings and pavilions. Nearby is the Islamic-style Tomb of Puhaddin, built in the thirteenth century to contain the remains of this descendant of the Prophet Muḥammad who came to China as a missionary. Another noted garden is the classically designed Xiaopangu Garden, dating from the Qianlong period in the eighteenth century. The central feature of this garden is the Nine Lions Mountain, a manmade eminence that, from a distance, looks like a group of playful lions, individually standing, leaping, or sitting. A third is the Geyuan Garden, once owned by the painter Shi Tao, who lived from 1652 to 1718. Here, stones and flowers of many different colors are used to depict landscapes representing the four seasons.

One of the oldest institutions in the area is the Daming Si Temple, about two and one-half miles northwest of the city. The temple was founded in the fifth century; its present structure was constructed between 1860 and 1870. The temple contains eighteen carved wood statues of important figures in Buddhism, each standing about ten feet tall. The temple also contains a Memorial Hall dedicated to the monk Jian Zhen, who was born in the seventh century and grew up in Yangzhou. According to legend, Jian Zhen decided to become a monk when he was fourteen. He left the city for twelve years of study, returning to become the superior of Daming Si. Jian Zhen became known as a great teacher of Buddhism and, in 753, despite being blind, he left the city to teach in Japan, reportedly at the request of the Japanese emperor. Jian Zhen remained in Japan until his death in 763. His followers from Yangzhou, meanwhile, passed onto the Japanese their knowledge of literature, medicine, architecture, painting, handicrafts, woodcarving, and embroidery. The Monk Jian Zhen Memorial Hall, as it is officially called, is quite new. Plans to construct the hall grew out of a joint Chinese-Japanese festival held in 1963 in observance of the 1,200th anniversary of the monk's death. The memorial hall was completed in 1973 and is a reproduction of the famed Golden Hall of Japan's Toshodai-ji Temple in Nara. Near the Daming Si Temple is Pingshan Tang Hall, built in 1048 by a local civic official named Ouyang Xiu, who also was a famed writer and historian. He used the hall as a retreat in which he could relax and write poems. A memorial temple in his honor stands north of the Pingshan Tang Hall.

Outside the southern gate of Yangzhou is the Wenfeng Ta Pagoda, a magnificent seven-story structure built in 1582 overlooking the Grand Canal. It was from this site that centuries earlier, Jian Zhen embarked on his journey to Japan. North of the city, the Tianning Si Temple stands on what was once the home of Xie Ao, a third-century city official. Still remaining from that time are the main gate, the Hall of Celestial Guardians, and the Daxiong Baodian Hall. The Yangzhou City Museum, outside the Guanshu Men Gate in the northern part of the city, displays lacquered works, jewelry, jade pieces, and embroidery. A recent addition to the museum is the Marco Polo Hall, to which Italy contributed a bronze lion, the symbol of Venice. Also worth seeing in Yangzhou is the Xianhe (Crane) Mosque, built in the thirteenth century and one of the four best-known mosques in China.

Further Reading: Information specific to Yangzhou in English is scarce. Interesting discussions about Chinese civilization, with occasional references to Yangzhou, can be found in *China: A New History* by John King Fairbank (Cambridge, Massachusetts: Harvard University Press, 1992) and *China's Imperial Past: An Introduction to Chinese History and Culture* by Charles O. Hucker (Stanford, California: Stanford University Press, and London: Duckworth: 1975). *The Cambridge Encyclopedia of China,* edited by Brian Hook (Cambridge and New York: Cambridge University Press, 1982; second edition, 1990), is a good source of concise information on specific subjects. Three helpful travel guides are *Fodor's China* by John Summerfield (fourteenth edition, New York: Fodor, 1994); *Magnificent China: A Guide to its Cultural Treasures* by Petra Haring-Kuan (Hong Kong: Joint Publishing, 1987); and *China Guide* by Ruth Lor Malloy (eighth edition, Washington, D.C.: Open Road, 1994).

—Pam Hollister

Yogyakarta (Yogyakarta Special Territory, Indonesia)

Location: At the foot of the volcano Gunung Merapi, in Central Java, twenty miles from the southern coast.

Description: Officially founded as a city in 1755, Yogyakarta (commonly shortened to Yogya) is intimately bound up with the history of the sultanate of Mataram, which emerged as a major power in Central and East Java in the second half of the sixteenth century. In 1755 Mataram was split into the two kingdoms of Surakarta and Yogyakarta, and the city was established as the seat of the Yogyakarta sultan. It was the center of a revolt against the Dutch colonial government in the nineteenth century and was, for a time, the principal base of the Indonesian revolution in the twentieth. It is now the capital of the semi-autonomous district of Yogyakarta and the seat of the highest court of Indonesia.

Site Office: Diparda D.I. Yogyakarta
Jl. Malioboro 14
Yogyakarta 55213
Indonesia
(274) 562811

Yogyakarta, whose history as a city began relatively recently, lies at the heart of the area that formed the wellspring of ethnic Javanese culture. Not far from several sites where prehistoric prehominid and hominid skeletal remains have been found, the district of Yogyakarta consists of highly fertile wet-rice growing land that formed the economic base of a succession of Buddhist, Hindu, and, later, Islamic states. The first state to arise in the vicinity of Yogyakarta was the eighth-century kingdom of Mataram, which was subsumed later in the same century under the maritime empire of Shailendra. The Shailendra state produced the Buddhist monument of Borobudur, which lies approximately twenty-five miles northwest of present Yogya, as the city has come to be called. Less than half that distance from the city lies the ancient Prambanan Hindu temple complex, which was built in the late ninth century.

From the tenth to the sixteenth century, power on Java shifted to the coastal areas and to the empires that rose to greatness as a result of their trading activities all over Southeast Asia. Then, in the second half of the sixteenth century, a new kingdom known as Pajang arose in the interior of Central Java, in the area of present-day Surakarta. By this time most of Java had converted to Islam, and Pajang was no exception. Before long another kingdom split off from Pajang, taking the ancient Mataram territories around Yogya, under a Muslim ruler called Pamanahan. This latest kingdom, like its ancient predecessor called Mataram, had its seat at Kota Gede, now a suburb of Yogya, where the city's famous silversmiths have their workshops. Today, nothing reminds the visitor of the sixteenth-century court but the royal cemetery, where some of the earliest rulers of the second Mataram are buried.

The only information about the early years of Mataram comes from court chronicles whose reliability has been the subject of protracted debate. Pamanahan was apparently succeeded in 1584 by his son Senopati, who shortly afterward conquered Pajang. Around the turn of the century, Senopati also began a campaign against Surabaya, then the most powerful city-state on the East Java coast. The conquest of Surabaya and its allies and vassals was not completed until well into the reign of Senopati's grandson, Sultan Agung, who ruled from 1613 to 1646. (Although he acquired the title of sultan in 1641, this ruler is invariably referred to as sultan for the entire period of his reign.) One of Sultan Agung's first acts, apart from continuing the war on Surabaya and other smaller states, was to move the Mataram court to Karta, which lies some three miles south of Kota Gede.

Surabaya, stubbornly resisting the Mataram conqueror, survived many sieges as well as famines brought on by Agung's destruction of the rice crops in the coastal areas. However, Surabaya's allies fell one by one. When Agung's forces finally cut off its water supply in 1625, Surabaya had to bow to the inevitable. By this time, Mataram was essentially master of all of Central and East Java. It also had acquired several dependencies on the islands of Kalimantan (Borneo) and Sumatra. Agung then turned his attention to the Dutch V.O.C. (Vereenigde Oostindische Compagnie, or United East Inda Company), which had established its principal headquarters at Jacatra in West Java (renamed Batavia by the Dutch, now Jakarta). Initial hostilities between Mataram and the V.O.C. had taken place in 1618 and 1619, but these had been of limited scope and impact. In 1628, however, Sultan Agung beleaguered the V.O.C.'s fortifications at Batavia, ultimately to no effect. Another siege was carried out the following year—with disastrous results. The V.O.C. had managed to intercept and destroy the Mataram army's food supplies, so that the starving troops had to lift the siege after a month. Mataram did not again undertake a confrontation with the Dutch during Agung's reign, but Agung did not altogether abandon thoughts of expelling the Europeans and conquering West Java.

In 1645, after a relatively peaceful conclusion of a turbulent reign, Agung ordered the construction of a new royal burial complex at Imogiri, some seven miles south of the court at Karta (about eleven miles south of Yogya). Despite the partition of the Mataram sultanate in 1755, the rulers of both resulting Mataram kingdoms are buried here, in separate sections, as are rulers of the earlier, unified Mataram. Sultan Agung's tomb, installed shortly after construction began, forms

Gate at Imogiri Burial Complex, Yogyakarta
Photo courtesy of Indonesia Tourist Promotion Office, Los Angeles

the spiritual focus of the complex. The Hindu past of the Mataram Dynasty, never entirely effaced by its Muslim convictions, is apparent in the architecture of the complex, which is predominantly in the Hindu-Javanese style.

Agung's death in 1646 led to the succession of Amangkurat I, who inherited Agung's kingdom but not his ability to rule it. Amangkurat again moved the court, this time to Plered, northeast of Karta, in 1647. Construction of this magnificent court, little of which survives, appears to have continued until at least 1666. Besides the creation of the Plered court, the new king was not able to accomplish much, although his ambitions were limitless. He hoped to conquer Banten in West Java, the one remaining major Javanese power not under the control of Mataram. In 1657 an attack on Banten came to nothing, however. By then, the Mataram empire was crumbling.

Amangkurat was in the habit of murdering those who disagreed with his rule or otherwise offended him. In so doing, he created more enemies than he eliminated. He was in the end unable to field an army, because he trusted no one to command it and himself dared not leave the palace compound for fear that someone might avenge one murder or another. Allies and vassal states, no longer impressed with the might of Mataram, began to renounce their allegiance. To thwart the V.O.C., Amangkurat repeatedly ordered the closure of several important ports, thus destroying both their livelihood and the economic base of his own extended kingdom. Mataram lost overseas possessions and much of East Java in the 1650s. Meanwhile, rebellion was brewing in several other parts of the kingdom.

Amangkurat also fell into serious disagreement with his son, the crown prince, who was later to rule as Amangkurat II. Amangkurat's repeated attempts to murder his son in the 1660s, far from having the desired result, encouraged the crown prince in his plans to depose his father. Apparently at the instigation of the crown prince and under the leadership of his associate, Trunajaya, a revolt broke out on the north coast in 1675. Their ranks swelled by dissatisfied subjects, the rebels pushed inland, and in 1677 they took Plered. Amangkurat fled but, already in bad health, did not survive long on his ignominious journey. The crown prince, meanwhile, had been able to conceal his involvement with Trunajaya. The following year, the V.O.C., lured into the conflict by promises of trading rights in Mataram-controlled territory, suppressed the rebellion. In 1681, order was restored to Mataram, and the crown prince assumed the throne as Amangkurat II. The court was then moved to Kartasura and from there to Surakarta (in 1746), and thus the connection of the kingdom of Mataram with Yogyakarta was temporarily severed.

Mataram continued to experience upheaval during the early eighteenth century. In 1740 the Chinese population of the coastal cities staged a rebellion against the V.O.C., and many Javanese joined the revolt. Mataram briefly sided with the rebels but extricated itself again when it became clear that the V.O.C. would be victorious. A Mataram courtier, Mangkubumi, had been part of the rebellion, but in 1745 he agreed to crush the remnants of the rebel army for a reward to be given him by the Mataram king, Pakubuwono II. When Mangkubumi returned from his campaign having accomplished what he set out to do, the reward was not forthcoming, however. The following year Mangkubumi began another rebellion, this one specifically aimed at deposing Pakubuwono. He established his headquarters at a stronghold called Ngayogya, which was later to become the city of Yogyakarta. In 1749, Pakubuwono II died, and both the crown prince (who had the support of the V.O.C.) and Mangkubumi proclaimed themselves king. Although Pakubuwono officially had its support, the V.O.C. was not loath to see Mataram divided. In 1755, the company helped broker the Treaty of Giyanti, which partitioned Mataram into the kingdom of Surakarta, with Pakubuwono III as its *susuhunan* (king), and the sultanate of Yogyakarta, ruled by Mangkubumi, who now assumed the title of Sultan Hamengkubuwono.

The year following the conclusion of the treaty saw the transformation of the Ngayogya stronghold into the city of Yogyakarta, which means "prosperity without war." Hamengkubuwono's *kraton* (palace compound), which survives in somewhat altered form, was built at that time. Defensive walls, of more symbolic than practical value, were added later. These walls around the court city were a mere show, because in 1755 the Dutch built Fort Vreedenburg on a low hill commanding the *kraton*. Although its ostensible purpose was the protection of Yogyakarta from Javanese invaders, the V.O.C. needed only to train its heavy artillery on the *kraton* to crush any local challenges to its authority. The Dutch East India Company's overlordship of Yogyakarta was further spelled out by Hamengkubuwono's having to finance the permanent garrison at Fort Vreedenburg. The *kraton*, still at the heart of the city, is open to the public today, as is Fort Vreedenburg, now a museum with extensive exhibits on Yogya's role in the revolution following World War II.

Although Hamengkubuwono had acquired a kingdom, he was not yet secure in his position as ruler of it. In fact, Yogya came under attack the year after its official founding. Mas Said, a former comrade-in-arms and Hamengkubuwono's son-in-law, also wanted a piece of the pie and turned on the new sultan. He attacked the city in 1756, and nearly burned down the *kraton*. Although his attack on Yogya was unsuccessful, Mas Said continued to be a power to be reckoned with. The V.O.C. finally solved the problem by granting Mas Said considerable territories in Surakarta's realm and the title of Pangeran Adipati Mangkunegoro. Initially this arrangement was to be temporary, but later the title and the dependencies became hereditary.

The second half of the eighteenth century was peaceful. Contrary to initial Javanese expectation, treaties were arranged that permanently solidified the partition of Mataram into Surakarta and Yogyakarta. A new census was taken, new law codes were devised, and arbitration procedures to solve potential territorial disputes were developed. Hamengkubuwono I died in 1792 and was succeeded by his son,

Dieng Plateau in Central Java, near Yogyakarta
Photo courtesy of Sascha Feinstein

Hamengkubuwono II, who was, however, a much less able ruler. In 1799 the V.O.C. was declared bankrupt by the Dutch government, which took over its holdings but did not significantly change V.O.C. policies. Serious problems materialized in Yogya in 1810 when the V.O.C. marched on the city under the leadership of a governor-general who wished to eradicate feudalism on Java and demanded unconditional vassalage from the indigenous rulers. Thus coerced, Hamengkubuwono II had to abdicate, and his son was made prince regent. Parts of the Yogyakarta territories were annexed by the Dutch in 1811, just before Java and the other Dutch possessions in the Indonesian Archipelago fell into British hands.

In the confusion of the British takeover, Hamengkubuwono briefly regained his throne but lost it again in an ensuing conflict with the new colonial rulers, who continued the "reforms" initiated by the Dutch. The British attacked the city and took the *kraton* in 1812. Yogyakarta was again reduced in size by further land annexations, while the authority of the sultan was diminished by the installation of his brother as a second ruler, Pangeran Pakualam I. Pakualam, endowed with 4,000 Yogyakarta households, built his court, the Pakualaman, just outside the walled court city of the sultan. When the Dutch regained their Javanese possessions in 1816, they kept the new subdivision of Yogyakarta in force. To this day the descendants of Pakualam, who have all taken the same name, are still second-in-command in Yogyakarta, functioning as vice-governors to the sultan, who is governor of the semi-autonomous district.

Peace did not prevail for long in Yogyakarta following the Dutch repossession. What initially started as another conflict over the Yogyakarta succession in the early 1820s in the end became a full-scale revolt against Dutch colonial rule by 1825. This rebellion is known as the Java War. Diponegoro, one of the elder princes at the court, was passed over in the succession and withdrew to an estate in the countryside at Tegalrejo, a little more than two miles west of Yogya. There, in 1825, Dutch work crews desecrated a sacred shrine during construction of a new road, and Diponegoro's men clashed with the Dutch. In response to this minor incident, the Dutch sent troops to arrest Diponegoro, who fled and began a rebellion. He quickly gained a formidable following of Javanese peasants, who hoped he would lighten the dual yoke of oppression by the Dutch and the sultan. Many of the sultan's soldiers also went over to Diponegoro's side.

During the first three years of the war, the Dutch, unable to respond effectively to Diponegoro's guerilla tactics, lost much ground. They then implemented the so-called *benteng* system, building small forts all over the countryside, from which they could send out mobile units that made it impossible for the guerillas to hide out and regroup for their next attack. Soon the tide turned in favor of the Dutch, and by 1829 most of Diponegoro's allies had deserted him, leaving him virtually unsupported and with few troops at his disposal. The same year, his lieutenants surrendered, at which point he had little choice but to accept Dutch offers to open negotiations. In March of 1830, the parties met at Magelang, northwest of Yogya. When Diponegoro showed himself unwilling to meet Dutch terms, he was arrested and subsequently exiled to Sulawesi, where he died in 1855.

As the Java War thus came to an end, the Dutch punished Yogyakarta by annexing parts of its territories. Although the Java War broke Yogyakarta's back as a semi-independent district under colonial rule, Diponegoro is still hailed as a national hero. His memory has been a rallying point for the nationalist movement in Indonesia since the early twentieth century. His estate at Tegalrejo, destroyed by Dutch soldiers in 1825, has been reconstructed and is now a national monument and museum.

For the remainder of the nineteenth century, Yogyakarta was quiet. Rather than a center of military might, it became the center of ethnic Javanese culture, renowned for its literature, theatre (including the traditional *wayang* shadow plays), batik, silver, and other traditional arts. Ancient Hindu-Buddhist elements are mixed with the primarily Islamic outlook of Yogya culture. The city's strong sense of its heritage has also made it one of the principal centers of Indonesian nationalism in the twentieth century. As a consequence, the nationalist movement has been strongly oriented toward ethnic Javanese culture, which has repeatedly led to difficulties in other parts of the archipelago under the independent republic.

Following the Japanese occupation of the Indonesian Archipelago, which came to an end in 1945, Sultan Hamengkubuwono assumed the throne and began a series of drastic reforms of Yogya's government, making it one of the most progressive districts in the archipelago. In January of 1946, when Republican troops were driven out of Jakarta, Yogya became the seat of the Republican government. Almost three years later, the city was taken by Dutch forces and the government was arrested. Hamengkubuwono resigned in protest and locked himself up in the *kraton*. There are stories, possibly romanticized, about visits to the *kraton* by Sukarno (a leader in the independence movement), disguised in peasant dress, to confer with Hamengkubuwono. On March 1, 1949, Republican forces retook Yogya for one day under the leadership of Colonel Suharto, who was also to save the day for the republic in 1965 by suppressing a communist revolt. Later in 1949 Dutch troops evacuated Yogya under orders from the Dutch government, which was finally ready to abandon its claim on the archipelago. Yogyakarta retained a semi-autonomous status after independence in recognition of the city's loyalty during the revolution.

Further Reading: M. C. Ricklefs provides the best and most readable general history of Indonesia in *A History of Modern Indonesia: 1300 to the Present* (Bloomington: Indiana University Press, and London: Macmillan, 1981). *State and Statecraft in Old Java: A Study of the Later Mataram Period, 16th to 19th Century* by Soemarsaid Moertono (Ithaca: Cornell University Press, 1968) is a helpful study of the earlier developments in the Mataram kingdom, while George McTurnan Kahin's *Nationalism and Revolution in Indonesia* (Ithaca: Cornell University Press, 1952; London: Oxford University Press, 1953) discusses Yogyakarta's role in the nationalist movement in the twentieth century. Claire Holt's *Art in Indonesia: Continuities and Change* (Ithaca: Cornell University Press, and London: Oxford University Press, 1967) contains extensive discussions of ethnic Javanese art as it has developed at Yogyakarta.

—Marijke Rijsberman

Yungang Caves (Shanxi, China)

Location: The Yungang Cave complex lies ten miles from the modern Chinese city of Datong in Shanxi province.

Description: Dug into the side of a high cliff, the Yungang Buddhist Caves are China's earliest known example of cave rock carvings. Most of the immense stone statues and delicate wall carvings were completed during the Northern Wei Dynasty (A.D. 386–534); some cosmetic additions were made during the following centuries. Fortunately, damage inflicted by time and weather has not ruined the still-impressive Buddhist scenes that decorate the complex and make the caves one of the best examples of Chinese religious art.

Contact: CITS
Yungang Hotel
Yingbin Xilu
Datong
China
23215

Some ten miles outside the city of Datong in northern Shanxi province lie the Yungang Caves. Dug out of a high cliff face, this complex of 53 caves stretches some 3,280 feet up the hillside and contains more than 50,000 statues. Construction of the caves began during the Northern Wei Dynasty (A.D. 386–534), making the spectacular religious figures at Yungang the oldest examples of cave sculpture in China.

After the fall of the Han Dynasty in A.D. 220, China entered what is commonly referred to as the Period of Disunity, during which the country was parceled into small states and kingdoms and ruled by numerous barbarian dynasties. One group of people to arrive in China during this period were the Toba (commonly written as T'o-pa), a nomadic tribe that gathered in Shanxi province and gradually adopted the Chinese way of life. By 385, the Toba had united into a powerful political group and began challenging the local government. After the fall of the local ruling group, the Toba leader Toba Gui proclaimed the founding of the Northern Wei Dynasty (a completely separate entity from the earlier Kingdom of Wei that existed during the Three Kingdoms period from A.D. 220 to 265).

As foreign rulers, the Toba were faced with the challenge of securing the loyalty of their Chinese subjects. One tool the Toba found useful was Buddhism, with its emphasis on humility and pacificism. The first two Toba emperors warmly embraced Buddhism, partially in hopes that it might keep their subjects docile and partially in an attempt to eradicate the indigenous Confucian philosophy—a philosophy the barbarian rulers associated with Chinese uprisings.

The third Toba emperor, Toba Dao—also called Emperor Wu—disliked Buddhist teachings, so he converted to Taoism and subsequently proclaimed it the official religion of the realm. Thus began a period of terrible persecution of Chinese Buddhists, as shown by the following imperial decree issued in 446: "Let those in charge issue proclamations to the generals, the armies, and the governors that all stupas, paintings, and foreign sutras are to be beaten down and burned utterly; the *śramanas* (monks) without distinction of age are to be executed."

Emperor Wu died in 454, and his successor, Wen Cheng Di, promptly issued another imperial proclamation—this time one that allowed Buddhist activities to begin again in China. To keep close watch over the country's Buddhist population, the emperor appointed an official to the position of chief of monks. In the mid–fifth century, this official was a man named Tan Yao, and it became his particular mission to encourage the spread of Buddhism. The undertaking at Yungang—chiseling out a fabulous network of grottoes depicting the life of the Buddha and images of numerous other Buddhist figures—also has been credited to Tan Yao. Tan Yao believed that the Yungang Caves would serve both as penance for the terrible crimes against Buddhism during the days of Emperor Wu, and as a concrete example of the Wei Dynasty's wealth, power, and prestige, an example to be seen and copied by Buddhists all over the world.

The rock face at Yungang provided a permanent medium in which the Wei artisans could work; the earlier persecution already had shown how easily wooden and metal Buddhist artifacts could be destroyed. Although cave carvings had not been done previously in China, Buddhists from countries as far away as Sri Lanka had visited the Toba court at Datong and presented stone images of the Buddha. Undoubtedly, these foreign pieces of art served as models when Wei artisans began their work at Yungang.

The first caves to be carved are today assigned the numbers 16 through 20. These caves are primarily elliptical in shape and are occupied by gigantic carved figures of the Buddha, the tallest reaching some seventy feet in height. The first in this series of caves, occasionally referred to as the Caves of Tan Yao, is Cave 16. The center room of this oval-shaped cave is occupied by a huge Buddha standing on a lotus-shaped throne. The rest of the cave, really a niche to protect the main statue, is lined with 1,000 Buddhas and small niches.

The next cave, number 17, is also oval in shape and houses a giant Buddha, seated cross-legged on a throne. On the east wall of the cave is a seated Buddha carved into a niche, and a standing Buddha is carved into the west wall. These three primary statues in the cave are carved in a style distinct from the rest of the grotto complex and impart a

Exterior of Yungang Caves
Photo courtesy of Consulate General of China, Chicago

feeling of strength and firmness. Cave 17 is also unusual in that the cave floor lies below the outside ground level. An inscription inside the cave dates this work to 480.

Similarly oval in shape, Cave 18 houses a fifty-foot Buddha in the center of its floor. This statue is clothed in a garment depicting another 1,000 tiny Buddhas and leaving the figure's right arm bare. The east wall contains a very detailed carving of a bodhisattva (one who has attained enlightenment but chooses to remain mortal to help others become enlightened) bearing a vase of holy water. This carving is deemed a masterpiece of Chinese Buddhist art.

Cave 19 is marked by one of Yungang's largest statues of Buddha, standing some fifty-five feet high. This cave has two adjacent, smaller caves to the east and to the west. The carvings found inside Cave 19 and on the right-hand wall are noticeably plainer than the rest of the work done at Yungang. The exception to this is the sculptures on the left-hand wall, the style of which is continued at the Longmen Caves, constructed some years later when the Wei court moved from Datong to Luoyang.

The Buddha found in Cave 20 is the most recognizable figure of the entire complex. The front wall of Cave 20 has crumbled away, leaving the thirty-five-foot seated Buddha open to the elements. The figure's face is round and energetic in appearance; as with other examples of Buddhist art, the ears of this statue are huge and exaggerated.

These five early caves all contain immense statues of the Buddha, statues that are believed to represent five Northern Wei Dynasty emperors: Taizi, Taizong, Shizi, Gongzong, and Gaozong. Their portrayal as Buddhas comes from an idea propagated by the fourth-century monk Faguo, who proclaimed the Wei emperors to be *Tathagatas,* a name given to the Buddha that translates as "He who has thus gone." The immense size of these early statues indicates the first objective in constructing the Yungang grottoes: to create large, sturdy images of the Buddha that would survive both time and persecutions and remain as religious symbols for future generations.

The next series of caves constructed under Tan Yao are numbers 5 through 10. Artistically, these caves vary greatly from the original five. Instead of housing immense images of the Buddha, they are marked by the many carved portrayals of Buddha and his life, bodhisattvas, lesser deities, and musicians that line the cave walls. Of these five caves, numbers 5 and 6 are the most significant examples of Wei-era art.

Giant Buddha in the Yungang Caves
Photo courtesy of Monica Cable

The larger of these two is Cave 5, measuring more than seventy feet from east to west and nearly sixty feet north to south. The front of the cave is protected by a four-story wooden structure, built in the time of the Qing (1644–1912). In the center of this cave sits a fifty-six-foot-high sculpture of the Buddha, and on the walls are numerous niches and Buddhist images. The door to the cave is flanked by another two seated Buddhas under the bodhi tree (where Siddhārtha Gautama, the historic Buddha, was enlightened).

Cave 6 is perhaps even more spectacular. Also protected by the wooden structure, Cave 6 houses an impressive two-story pagoda some fifty feet high. The pagoda is extensively decorated with carvings of the Buddha. At the very top of the pagoda stand four smaller nine-story pagodas, each atop a carved elephant. The cave is enhanced by beautiful carvings on all four walls and the ceiling. In addition to the usual Buddhas, bodhisattvas, and other religious figures, the walls of Cave 6 depict scenes from the *Jataka,* stories of the former lives of the Buddha. This superb collection of carvings portrays scenes of his birth and his early years as a prince, his later life as an ascetic, and his ultimate enlightenment.

At the eastern end of the cave complex lie Caves 1 and 2. The caves are similar, both being square with carved pillars stretching from floor to ceiling. Both caves' walls are covered with carved Buddhas, although there is evidence of weather and time damage to the reliefs; the carvings in Cave 1 are the better preserved of the two.

Cave 3 clearly was built later than most of the caves at Yungang. Carved into a cliff face some eighty feet high, Cave 3 is the largest of all the caves in the complex. Twelve holes can be seen nearby on the cliff face, holes that, according to legend, held support beams for the Monastery of the Enchanted Cliff. The monastery no longer remains, but the cave continues to hold a large Buddha and two bodhisattvas in the back of its rear chamber. The style of these statues indicates that they were carved later than the complex's other figures—sometime during the Sui (581–618) or Tang Dynasties (618–907).

A particularly important cave in the Yungang complex is Cave 11. This cave houses a square pagoda-pillar covered with carved Buddha images. The original carvings are nearly obscured by an assortment of painted clay figures, added after the cave was completed. An inscription carved into the east wall dates the painted statues to the seventh year of the reign of Emperor Ta Ho, or 483.

The inscription provides insight into life and religion during the time of the Wei. According to the writing on the cave wall, this particular undertaking was funded by fifty-four people who had formed an organization to promote rock sculpture. According to the inscription, these people had not acquired enough merit in their past lives to escape from the cycle of rebirth. In this life, however, they had come to study the teachings of the Buddha and were committing their own money to the carving of the figures in his honor.

This group of people prayed that three things might come to pass: that there be peace in the land, that their deceased ancestors achieve salvation, and that the group's members act like bodhisattvas and lead others in the way of the Buddha. According to the inscription, the group's prayers for peace also included prayers for the prosperity and stability of the ruling house, an indication of the relationship between Buddhism and a strong and benevolent monarch.

Most of the work done at Yungang was completed during the Northern Wei Dynasty. The earliest written account of the cave complex appears in the writings of Li Taoyuan, an author who died in 527. In his commentary on the complex, Li writes, "The people have chiseled rocks and opened the mountains, and on the rock cliffs they have fashioned true images of such gigantic sizes and grandeur as to be rarely seen in this world."

Fortunately, the caves at Yungang largely have escaped the widespread devastation of Chinese culture and art that took place during the Cultural Revolution of the 1960s. While the forces of time and weather have caused several cave walls to collapse and have dulled the paint that once graced the stone carvings, the twenty-one caves at Yungang continue to be excellent examples of Buddhist art in China. The large-scale undertaking completed some 1,500 years ago shows not only the great skill of artisans during the Northern Wei, but also provides insight into the important role Buddhism played in the lives of the rulers and ordinary citizens who sponsored some of the caves' construction. Now protected and undergoing restoration as part of China's National Ancient Monuments, the twenty-one caves, 51,000 statues, and countless carvings remain true masterpieces of Chinese religious art.

Further Reading: Robert Silverberg's *The Great Wall of China* (Philadelphia: Chilton, 1965) offers a detailed look at ancient Chinese history and includes the era of the Northern Wei, during which the Yungang Caves were carved. A comprehensive account of Buddhism's introduction into China and the political and religious atmosphere at the time of the caves' origin is found in Kenneth Ch'en's very readable *Buddhism in China* (Princeton, New Jersey: Princeton University Press, 1964). Readers interested in visiting the cave complex will appreciate the descriptions and practical information contained in John Summerfield's *Fodor's China* (New York and London: Fodor, 1994) and Manfred Morgenstern's *China* (Singapore: APA, 1990).

—Monica Cable

Zamboanga (Zamboanga del Sur, Philippines)

Location: Zamboanga City lies on the Basilan Strait on the southernmost tip of Zamboanga Peninsula in western Mindanao. Mindanao is the large island in the southern Philippines, facing the Pacific to the east and the Sulu Sea and Borneo to the west.

Description: Zamboanga is a busy port, serving interisland and international trade. Local exports include hardwoods, copra, pearls, and rubber, as well as fish and fruit. Unlike the rest of the Philippines, which are Roman Catholic, Mindanao has a predominantly Muslim heritage, which predates by several centuries the Spanish colonization of the Philippines. Evidence of the Muslim faith can be seen in Zamboanga today alongside the remnants of the Spanish settlement.

Site office: Department of Tourism
Zamboanga Lantaka Hotel
Valderosa Street, 7000
Zamboanga City
Philippines
(62) 991 0217 or 991 0218

There is a charming folktale among the Bajau, a nomadic sea people, about how Zamboanga came by its name. It is said that many years ago the sultan of Johore wanted to marry, but that the only woman he considered beautiful enough was his own sister. He summoned the imam, or Muslim leader, who refused to bless this union, saying it was against the will of Allah. The second imam Johore asked responded likewise. Finally, the third imam, threatened with death if he did not perform the ceremony, agreed to marry brother and sister, but only if the wedding could take place many miles out to sea. The sultan agreed and ordered his subjects to align their boats so that they reached far out to sea, forming a temporary bridge over which the sultan, his bride, and the imam walked to the furthermost boat in the middle of the ocean. Just as the imam began to chant the marriage rites, a great storm rose and scattered all the boats far and wide. The sultan, his sister, and the imam were all drowned; the other boats were swept eastward until they finally reached the Sulu Islands. Among the Bajau, *zamboang* is the word to denote the post to which a boat can be tied at shore.

The more common, though less inspiring, explanation for Zamboanga's name is that it derives from the Malay word *jambangan*, meaning "place of flowers," referring to the many tropical flowers such as orchids and bougainvillea so predominant in the city. The Bajau can still be seen around Zamboanga today, serving as a reminder of Zamboanga's sea-faring history and its colorful independence from political developments elsewhere in the Philippine Archipelago.

Islam reached the Philippines in the thirteenth century, when a colony of Muslim traders settled in the Sulu Archipelago, southwest of Zamboanga. Since the ninth century, Sulu had been on a recognized trade route for Arab merchants; many of these, coming from Bengal, Persia, Hindustan, and Gujarat, made new settlements on Java, Sumatra, the Moluccas, and Borneo. The traders traveled via Sulu and Palawan to Luzon (Manila) and on to Formosa and southern Japan, where they were able to pick up substitute goods for those now denied them on the Chinese mainland. The Arab traders, ousted from China in the ninth century as a powerful threat, were once more welcomed to Chinese ports during the Sung Dynasty, but even then they did not abandon their trade route through the Philippines to Borneo. Chinese Muslim traders retraced the Arab route, and they, along with Muslim Mongols of the Yuan Dynasty (1270–1638), traded as far south as Sulu.

Written genealogies or *tarsilas* date Muslim ancestry of the sultans of Sulu and Mindanao to the mid–fifteenth century, documenting two Arabs who came to the Philippines from Molucca or Johore. The first was the Arab Malay Sharif Muhammed Kabungsuwan, who settled in Mindanao; the second was Sharif Abū Bakr, who founded his sultanate in Sulu. In subduing the native population, the Arabs used firearms, and when the Spaniards arrived in the region they discovered that their own firepower was matched by the native firearms, including muskets and small bronze canon *(lantaka)*.

Unlike the traders before them, these men set out to bring Islam to the new lands and to convert the indigenous population to their creed. The Islamic religion was not unfamiliar to the Filipinos, who had come into contact with its fundamental principles through the wise men and Muslim teachers who came to the islands in the wake of traders during the thirteenth and fourteenth centuries. Sulu especially had seen several earlier attempts to establish Islamic rule, ranging from the arrival of makhdum (Islamic missionaries) in Sulu in 1380 to the invasion in 1390 of Raja Baguinda and the subsequent capture of Sulu's ancient capital, Bansa. When Sharif Abū Bakr arrived from Johore, he established Arabic laws and introduced Arabic script, married Raja Baguinda's daughter, and founded the Sultanate of Sulu. Sharif Kabungsuwan settled in Cotabato in 1475 and from there undertook the conversion of the island, including the Zamboanga Peninsula, to Islam. By the time Spanish expeditions took seriously the project of colonizing the Philippines, the Muslim faith had spread north as far as Luzon, where Manila, as well as several other settlements, were ruled by an Islamic aristocracy. Although the arrival of the Spanish, with the concerted efforts of their missionary friars, turned the tide against Islam in the Philippines, its influence is still strong in the southern islands and cities, including Zamboanga. Today,

Walls of Fort Pilar, Zamboanga
Photo courtesy of Philippine Consulate General

Muslim Mosque, Zamboanga
Photo courtesy of Philippine Consulate General

the Muslim population (over 2 million of a total Philippine population of 60 million) is found on the islands of Mindanao, the Sulu Archipelago, Basilan, and in parts of Palawan.

As elsewhere in the Philippines, the indigenous population was arranged in villages or *barangays,* so named after the Malay boats that brought so many of the original inhabitants to the Philippines. Each *barangay* had a chieftain or leader called a *datu,* again a Malay word. Some villages grouped themselves together under the jurisdiction of a single *datu,* who then built himself a fort, or *kuta.* Not even these larger kingdoms had much real power, as they covered such relatively small areas inhabited by few people and with scant natural resources. The Spaniard Miguel López de Legazpi, on his expedition to Cebu in 1564, found that the land could not feed both the native population and his men.

With the arrival and establishment of the Muslims in the south, the indigenous, highly localized social order changed. In the Islamic parts of the Philippines, three codes of law existed: local law, administered by a village chieftain; Islamic law; and religious law. The highest social class was that of the *sharifs* and *datus,* after which came free men, and finally a slave class. The sultan and his council of *datus* administered the legislative body, collected taxes, and regulated trade. They were able to bond together in some form of unity, which enabled them to ward off the Spanish, who arrived in the region in the sixteenth century. The Muslims of the south never accepted Spanish rule, and even today the region retains a degree of independence from Manila and the rest of the Philippines.

Mindanao, the Zamboanga Peninsula, and the Sulu Archipelago are all home to some of the more colorful descendants of Moorish traders and settlers. Among them are the Bajau, whose brightly colored sailboats can sometimes be seen around the port of Zamboanga, although most of them live farther southwest in Sulu and coastal Borneo. Antonio Pigafetta, the chronicler for Ferdinand Magellan's first exploratory trip to the Philippines in 1521, noted communities of boat-dwellers off the coasts of both Cebu and Zamboanga. Traditionally, they gathered the pearls, coral, and shells needed by the mainland inhabitants for their China trade, but they also let themselves be hired as mercenaries. In this capacity their sea-faring and boat-building skills were highly prized. Another notable group is the Samal, also known for their boat-building expertise. They are marginally more sedentary today than the Bajau, living in a water village in Rio Hondo in Zamboanga City. Their settlement there consists of houses built on stilts over the water surface, reached by footbridge or boat.

Traditionally, the population of Zamboanga sustained itself on the island's rich resources, particularly fish and fruit. Rice, however—now one of the dietary staples—was imported from farther north in the archipelago to supplement the local production in the flood plains of Zamboanga del Sur. Such lowlands are limited on the Zamboanga Peninsula, for the range of hills, the Zamboanga Corderilla, runs very close to the coast. Today, the fishing industry is still important: commercial vessels based only on Zamboanga City and Naga have hauled as much as 26.5 million pounds a year. Other key crops are coconuts, which are exported from Zamboanga, and rubber: most of the rubber produced in the Philippines comes from plantations in Zamboanga and Basilan. Such crops benefit from Zamboanga's and Sulu's location beyond the typhoon belt.

In order to protect their share in the China trade, the Spanish came to Zamboanga in 1635. Their first act was to construct a fort, named after the Virgin of Del Pilar, revered by Christians and Muslims alike (the Muslims call her Miriam), so that they could monitor the movement of vessels between Sulu and Cotabato, on the main part of Mindanao. The fort also provided the Spanish with a possible military base for action in Mindanao, Sulu, and the Moluccas. The latter formed the basis of a contract between the Portuguese and the Spanish known as the Treaty of Zaragoza, which had been signed in 1530, in which the Spanish ceded all claims to the Moluccas and all territory west of "a line drawn pole to pole . . . 296 1/2 leagues east" of those islands in exchange for 350,000 ducats. This meant the Spanish claim on the Philippines themselves was disputable, and that the Spaniards' new proximity to the Moluccas, with the establishment of a fort at Zamboanga, was something of a provocation. In fact, the maintenance of such a fort so far from the rest of the Spanish colonial activity proved untenable. In 1663 Manila, the Spanish capital, was under threat from a Chinese attack, and all Spanish resources in Zamboanga were withdrawn to Luzon. However, the short-lived Spanish presence did produce a distinct language, still used in Zamboanga today, called *Chavacano,* a mixture of Spanish and Visayan, which is spoken in the Visayan Islands north of Mindanao. The fort played a role once more nearly 200 years later during the Philippine Revolution, when Zamboanguenos captured it, defying the Spanish colonialists and eloquently asserting their independence.

With the American arrival in the Philippines in 1898, many aspects of life in Zamboanga and its neighboring regions changed. The old systems of local rule were replaced by western ideas of municipal and provincial government. Elected mayors, governors, congressmen, and senators took the place of the traditional hierarchy under the sultanate. The American commitment to universal education opened up this defiantly separatist part of the Philippines to new and more radical ideas. Perhaps most importantly, Muslims began to be outnumbered by Christian immigrants; today the Muslim population of Mindanao and Sulu accounts for only 23 percent of the region's total.

Today, Zamboanga is a tourist destination for the more adventurous seeking to get away from the humid metropolis of Manila. The city was largely rebuilt after World War II, but remnants of Spanish-style architecture, domed mosques, and houses on stilts, as well as Fort Pilar, can still be seen. The busy port still boasts an air of Southeast Asian sea-faring exoticism. The northern side of the peninsula has spectacular beaches at Dakak. Other historic sites in the vicinity include Dapitan City and Talisay, notorious as the places of exile of the Philippine national hero José Rizal, who lived there from 1893 to 1896, when he returned to Manila and was executed. His house and clinic are still standing and can be visited by tourists.

Further Reading: For a general introduction to the Philippines, consult some of the following: *The Philippines: A Singular and a Plural Place* by David Joel Steinberg (Boulder, Colorado: Westview Press, 1982); *The Filipino Nation: The Philippines: Lands and Peoples, A Cultural Geography* by Eric S. Casiño (Manila: Grolier International Philippines, 1982); and *The Filipino Nation: A Concise History of the Philippines* by Helen R. Tubangui, Lesie E. Bauzon, Marcelino A. Foronda Jr., and Luz U. Ausejo (Manila: Grolier International Philippines, 1982). The history of the Philippines in the context of Southeast Asia, that is, sharing traits with Thailand, Laos, Cambodia, Malaysia and Indonesia, Burma, China, and Annam, is given a fascinating account in *The Philippines in the World of Southeast Asia* by E. P. Patañne (n.p.: Enterprise Publications, Philippines, 1972). *The Roots of the Filipino Nation* by O. D. Corpuz (Quezon City, Philippines: AKLAHI Foundation, 1989) gives more specific information about the Islamic history of the Philippines. For specific information regarding recent Philippine history, including the overthrow of the Marcos regime and the considerable problems now faced by the country, see *Impossible Dream* by Sandra Burton (New York: Warner Books, 1989); *Imelda Marcos* by Carmen Navarro Pedrosa (London: Weidenfeld and Nicholson, and New York: St. Martin's, 1987); and "The Snap Revolution" by James Fenton in *Granta* (Cambridge), volume 18, Spring 1986.

—Hilary Collier Sy-Quia

Zhengzhou (Henan, China)

Location: In the Henan province of China, forty miles west of Kaifeng, approximately fifteen miles south of the Huang Ho (Yellow River). Zhengzhou is located at the intersection of two major railroad systems, the Beijing-Guangzhou line and the Longhai line.

Description: The provincial capital of modern Henan, Zhengzhou is historically important for its archaeological finds dating back to Neolithic times. One of China's oldest cities, Zhengzhou was once a cultural center and capital of the Shang Dynasty, which ruled the area of Henan province from the eighteenth to the twelfth centuries B.C. (at some point during that period the dynasty changed its name to Yin) and gave to China such advances as horse-drawn chariots, a sophisticated bronze technology, and the first complete writing system. Excavations at Zhengzhou since 1950 have uncovered pottery kilns, bronze workshops, structural foundations, tombs, and other remains that reveal much about China's Bronze Age culture, especially regarding the characteristic worship of ancestors, ritual burial customs, and human sacrifices.

Site Office: Henan Tourism Bureau
16 Jinshui Avenue
450003 Zhengzhou, Henan
China
(371) 5952707

Located in the Henan province, the cradle of Chinese civilization, Zhengzhou was settled in times unknown, perhaps more than thirty centuries before the birth of Christ. The city is associated with the mythical emperor Fu Xi, who, according to legend, developed the basis of the *Book of Changes* or *Yi Jing* (also transliterated, more familiarly, as *I Ching*), during the thirty-fourth century B.C. He also was said to have taught early societies how to hunt and fish. Historical sources do not specifically mention any rulers of China until the Shang Dynasty, which began, according to tradition, in the Henan region in 1766 B.C. The dynasty, which numbered some thirty monarchs, changed its capital six times (the seventeenth Shang king, moreover, changed the dynastic title to Yin); one of these capitals was Ao, on the site of which Zhengzhou is believed to have developed. Ao also was the seat of the dynasty until about 1400 B.C., when the capital was moved northward to Anyang. At one time, the Shang kingship passed from brother to brother; later it passed from father to son. The kingdom encompassed a relatively small region around the Huang Ho, or Yellow River, in northern China. Information about this civilization is derived largely from the excavations made at Zhengzhou and nearby Anyang.

The Shang era is distinguished from earlier periods by its royalty's intense fascination with religious ritual, the earliest verifiable use of Chinese script, the production of bronze vessels, and the employment of horse-drawn chariots and carriages. Evidence from those times indicates that China underwent a relatively smooth transition from the numerous Neolithic villages of early times to the Bronze Age of the Shang period. The civilization of the Shang period was marked by sedentary, inland farming; there was little waterborne commerce or interaction with other societies.

During the Shang era, the society of Zhengzhou and other settlements in the area of modern Henan province was divided along the lines of rank, status, and occupation. The ruling class lived in the center of the city in an area that contained many large public buildings and altars, for religion played a large part in the society's daily life. The buildings in this area were of post-and-beam construction on pounded-earth platforms, designed in an architectural style much like that in Beijing's Forbidden City. Underground quarters were built for servants and storage. The foundations of these aristocratic homes were inlaid with patterns of large stones and bronze castings. Surrounding these buildings were the workshops of bronzesmiths, stonecarvers, potters, and other artisans. Beyond them lay the small, partly underground homes of farmers and, on the outskirts of the city, the burial grounds. Remains of all these types of structures have been uncovered, along with molds and furnaces for bronze and a considerable amount of pottery.

Excavations at Zhengzhou have uncovered a rectangular pounded-earth wall of considerable size that evidently surrounded the city's central section. By stamping or pounding layers of earth within a movable wood frame, early Chinese workers created a fortification as strong as cement. More than four miles in length, the wall found at Zhengzhou measured 30 feet high and 65 feet wide, thickening to almost 100 feet at its base. Its construction obviously required considerable labor and provides evidence of the Shang Dynasty's power over its subjects. In terms of workmanship and governmental ability to harness manpower, the ancient wall also represents a forerunner of the sophisticated dams, dikes, and irrigation ditches that were to be built in the twentieth century during China's "Great Leap Forward" under Mao Zedong.

Aside from its class system, Zhengzhou society was patriarchal in nature, although women of the aristocracy were allowed considerable freedom and equality with men. Evidence indicates that the people were robust and apparently consumed large quantities of alcohol. Human sacrifice was a common practice, conducted without regret, and documented in detailed inscriptions on animal bones. The people were also

Fourteen-story clock tower in February 7th Square, Zhengzhou
Photo courtesy of Consulate General of China, Chicago

Railway bridge across the Yellow River, near Zhengzhou
Photo courtesy of Consulate General of China, Chicago

warlike, and were well prepared to send an army of thousands on months-long expeditions. In fact, warfare may well have been the chief pursuit of the ruling class, which regularly recruited soldiers armed with spears and bows to attack non-Chinese "barbarians" or simply to fight for booty. Other evidence suggests that the people of Zhengzhou and other Henan settlements of the Shang period were accomplished in both agriculture and the raising of livestock. The chief domestic animal was the water buffalo, of which large herds were maintained not only to supply the inhabitants with meat but, more importantly, to provide a steady supply of animals for sacrifice and bones for use in divination. Hunting was another specialty of early Zhengzhou society.

Evidence uncovered in the twentieth century suggests that funeral ceremonies for Shang rulers were elaborate and involved widespread human sacrifice. The burial pits of Shang kings contained the bodies of servants, guards, and prisoners of war, armed with weapons and arranged in formation. Also found were the remains of chariots, horses, pet animals, and, in one case, an elephant. The deceased rulers were outfitted in splendid garb and surrounded by valuable jewels, pottery, and paintings. Although horrifying for their evidence of massive human sacrifices, the royal tombs are impressive. In particular, the bronze objects in the tombs provide evidence of their makers' artistry. The bronze vessels were covered with elaborate designs, which frequently included a stylized mask, apparently intended as some sort of charm to ward off evil or invoke a blessing from the gods. Bronze pieces also were decorated with highly stylized drawings and outlines of animals, arranged symmetrically.

Zhengzhou and other Shang sites in northern China have yielded the earliest bronze artifacts found in the country. During the Shang era, bronze was used more for ceremonial purposes and weaponry than for everyday functions. Excavations have uncovered evidence of bronze armor, harness fittings, and chariot riggings but, more often, splendid goblets and cauldrons, some weighing as much as 1,500 pounds. These were cast in clay molds in sections that later were put together so expertly as to appear to be the product of a single casting. Many early weapons were cast with small hollows to allow for the later insertion of turquoise or malachite. Later, ornamental vessels were inlaid with gold, silver, and copper as well. Inscriptions sometimes were added inside the bottoms of the vessels. Some of the bronze cauldrons were used for the libations consumed during religious rituals; more often they were buried in tombs to contain food and wine for the spirits of the deceased.

The bronze pieces and earlier pottery unearthed at Zhengzhou provide many answers about ancient Chinese civilization, but they also have raised one important question: how did advanced bronze metallurgy develop so suddenly from Neolithic pottery? In the Western world a transitional period, in which copper was forged and hammered, intervened between pottery making and bronze crafting. But the ancient Chinese seem to have moved directly from pottery to casting bronze without any such transitional period. Additionally, excavations at Shang sites such as Zhengzhou reveal an inexplicably high level of expertise in the use of bronze molds and the skill with which linear designs were carved into the finished pieces.

The greatest accomplishment of these early peoples, however, was the development of a writing system, as found on "oracle bones" used for divination. The discovery of these bones was a fairly recent one, beginning as late as 1899 when archaeologists found that Chinese pharmacists were selling what they called "dragon bones" carrying inscriptions in an ancient form of writing. The origin of these bones was eventually traced to an area near the Yellow River in modern Henan province. Initially, archaeologists of the National Government's Academia Sinica began excavations at the last Shang capital of Anyang. Later, after 1950, they found the earlier Shang capital of Ao, at Zhengzhou.

Since these discoveries, nearly 3,000 different pictographic characters have been found on turtleshells, shoulderblades of cattle, and bones of other animals unearthed at Zhengzhou and other ancient Henan cities. In early times, prophetic messages would be sought by applying a red-hot stylus to the bones to create cracks, which diviners then would interpret as ancestral advice. Later, the diviner inscribed specific questions to the gods, such as meteorological inquiries, whether a forthcoming royal child would be a son, or whether a king's illness was a sign that he had offended some ancestor. Such inscriptions on oracle bones represent the oldest known form of Chinese writing. The bones also were inscribed with records of ritual sacrifices and other services for the gods that were performed frequently, often accompanied by dance and music. Further inscriptions present a picture of agricultural work, which occupied the majority of the population, and the domestication of animals as well as the fashioning of vessels and utensils of stone and bone. Inscriptions frequently record the city rulers' hunting forays and plans for war.

Even after the Shang Dynasty moved its capital from Ao, the site remained well populated. In 1122 B.C., the Shangs were overthrown by the Western Zhou, another Chinese-speaking people who had migrated from the Wei River valley of western China and were considered barbarians by the Shang aristocracy. The Western Zhou, which ruled until 771 B.C., established one of their two capitals at what became Zhengzhou; Zhou tombs were among the finds later excavated at the city. During the Zhou period, Zhengzhou reportedly became the fief of the Guan family and was known as Guan Cheng, or City of Guan. In A.D. 587, it became the seat of a prefectural administration and was known as Guanzhou. Not until 605 did the city become known by its present name.

Zhengzhou maintained considerable importance during the subsequent dynasties of Sui (581–618), Tang (618–907), and Northern Song (960–1127). In the tenth century, it became the terminus of the New Bien Canal, which linked the city with the Yellow River to the north. The city of Zhengzhou and this water route played a significant role in supplying grain to the Song capitals of Luoyang and Xian (also referred to as Chang'an). Later in the Song period, when the dynasty moved its capital eastward to Kaifeng, Zhengzhou declined in importance; it remained obscure for several centuries. Early in the twentieth century, Zhengzhou achieved renewed importance as a major rail junction of the Beijing-Guangzhou line and the Longhai line, the latter giving Zhengzhou an eastward link to the cities of Kaifeng and Luoyang and a westward connection to the Shaanxi province. These advances in transportation made Zhengzhou a regional center for trade in such agricultural produce as grain, cotton, and peanuts.

On February 7, 1923, Zhengzhou became the starting point for a general strike of railway workers seeking improvements in wages and working conditions. More than 100 workers were killed or injured as the warlord Wu Peifu put down the strike. The event is commemorated by a fourteen-story clock tower, resembling a pagoda, built in 1971 in Zhengzhou's February 7th Square in the center of the city.

Late in the 1930s, the war with Japan exacted a heavy price from Zhengzhou. Forced into retreat from the area in 1938, the Chinese Nationalist Army blew up the retaining dikes of the Yellow River about twenty miles northeast of the town. The resultant flooding inundated a huge area, severely damaging the region's agricultural capabilities. Zhengzhou additionally lost much of its industry as the government moved many factories farther west, away from the path of the Japanese.

The fortunes of Zhengzhou took an upturn, however, when the communist government came into power in China in 1949. Since the new government redeveloped Zhengzhou's industry, the city now has textile plants, flour mills, cigarette factories, and food-processing plants, as well as locomotive and tractor-assembly plants. Coal mining just outside the city is an additional source of industrial employment. Zhengzhou's diverse economic base has attracted many workers from the north, and the city's population has swelled to nearly 1.5 million.

Modern, industrial Zhengzhou features only a few historic sites. The foremost is the Henan Provincial Museum, one of the best in China, because it contains the famed oracle bones, along with treasures and artifacts from all of Henan, the wellspring of Chinese civilization. Near the museum are the ruins of a Shang palace and remnants of the ancient city walls. Scattered around Zhengzhou are a few ancient pottery kilns, bronze foundries, and bone workshops. Not far outside the city is Dahe Village, a 5,000-year-old site with Neolithic remains and Shang ruins.

For devotees of kung fu, Zhengzhou is the nearest major city to the famed Shaolin Monastery, important in the development of Chinese martial arts and the site of filming for several kung fu movies. Shaolin was built around A.D. 500 and became known for the thirteen fighting monks who supported the first emperor of the Tang Dynasty. Depressions have been worn in the floor by generations of monks training in the martial arts. At one time, the monastery housed as many as 3,000 monks.

Further Reading: Information specifically on Zhengzhou is very limited, even in guidebooks about China. However, information on Chinese civilization, with some references to Zhengzhou, can be found in the following books: *China: A New History* by John King Fairbank (Cambridge, Massachusetts: Harvard University Press, 1992); *The Early Civilization of China* by Yong Yap and Arthur Cotterell (New York: Putnam, and London: Weidenfeld and Nicolson, 1975); *Early Chinese Civilization: Anthropological Perspectives* by K. C. Chang (Cambridge, Massachusetts: Harvard University Press, 1976); *A History of Chinese Civilization* by Jacques Gernet (Cambridge and New York: Cambridge University Press, 1982); and *China's Imperial Past: An Introduction to Chinese History and Culture* by Charles O. Hucker (Stanford, California: Stanford University Press, and London: Duckworth, 1975). *The Cambridge Encyclopedia of China*, edited by Brian Hook (Cambridge and New York: Cambridge University Press, 1982; second edition, 1990), is a good source of concise information on specific subjects.

—Pam Hollister

INDEX

Listings are arranged in alphabetical order. Entries in bold type have historical essays on the page numbers appearing in **bold** type.

A Fang Palace, Xian, China, 870
A-Ma-Miu Temple, Macau, 542
Abaoji (Liao emperor of China), 744-745
Abbai Singh (mahārāja of Jodhpur), 400
'Abbās II (shah of Persia), 441
'Abbāsid-al-Manṡūr (Arab ruler of Multān), 610
'Abbāsid Dynasty, 71, 163, 280, 579, 610
'Abd al-Malik ibn Marwān (fifth Ummayad caliph), 280
Abd Allah ibn Iskandar (ruler of Uzbekistan), 165
'Abd-Allah Tarkhan-beg (khan of Hami), 323
Abdālīs. *See* Durrāni Dynasty
'Abdorraḥmān Khān (ruler of Afghanistan), 415, 418, 442
Abdul-Aziz, Bukhara, Uzbekistan, 166
Abdul Fedha (Syrian writer), 704
Abdul Mumin (sultan of Brunei), 160
'Abdul-Hamid (historian), 522
Abdullah I (prince of Uzbekistan), 166
Abdullah Mukarram Shāh (sultan of Ketah), 665
Abdullah Quṭb Shāh (ruler of Hyderābād), 367
Abdur Razzāq (vizier of Ghaznī), 801
Abel (biblical), 715
Abhayagiri Dagaba, Anuradhapura, Sri Lanka, 38
Abhira (people), 506, 626
Aboriginies (Australian), 44-46, 153, 154, 156, 157, 209, 210, 644, 781, 782, 863
Abruzzi, duke of, 604
Abū Bakr (Dughlat khan), 457
Abū Bakr (first Muslim caliph), 579
Abū Bakr, Sharif (sultan of Sulu), 403
Abū Manṣūr Sebüktigin (governor of Ghaznī), 280-281
Abu Sa'id (Timurud ruler of Afghanistan), 165, 335
Abu'l Fazl (chronicler of Akbar), 262, 263, 767
Abul Hasan Quṭb Shāh (king of Golconda), 292
Abulfeda (Arab historian), 710
Academia Sinica, China, 904
Academy of Sciences, St. Petersburg, Russia, 244
Acapulco, Mexico, 180, 567-568
Aceh, Sumatra, Indonesia, 113, 114, 396, 584, 585, 663
Aceh War, 116
Achaemenes (Persian governor of Egypt), 578
Achaemenid Dynasty, 71, 72, 333, 410, 414, 439, 578, 608, 718
Achaleshwar Temple, Achalgarh, India, 602
Achalgarh, India, 602
Acheen Street Mosque. *See* Masjid Melayu Mosque, Penang, Malaysia
Achyutadeva Rāya (king of Vijayanagara), 856
Achyutappa (king of Kumbakonam), 502
Adam Bay, 208
Adamantine Throne. *See* Vajrāsana (Buddha's seat), Bodh Gayā, India
Adams, Henry, 788
Adams, John (*Bounty* mutineer), 674, 675, 676
Adams, Will (Miura Anjin), 342, 344, 612
Adam's Bridge. *See* Dhanushkodi, Rāmeswaram, India
Adelaide, Australia, 75, 208, 210
Adhar Devi, India, 602
Adi Chadi Step-Well, Junāgadh, India, 410, 412
Adi Kumbeshvara Temple, Kumbakonam, India, 501
Adi Malla (Indian ruler), 134
Ādil Moḥammad Khān (Bhopāl rebel), 120
'Ādil Shāh II (ruler of Bijāpur), 127
'Ādil Shāhi Dynasty, 125, 127, 128
Adināth Temple, Bīkaner, India, 129
Ādinātha (Jainian prophet), 191, 601
Ādinātha Temple, Khajurāho, India, 470
Āditya (god), 608
Āditya I (king of Cōḷas), 811
Āditya statue, Multān, Pakistan, 608, 610
Adivaraha Maṇḍapa, Mahābalipuram, India, 552
Administration Building, Norfolk Island, Australia, 642
Adyar River, 550
Aesop, 150
Afaqi Makhdumzadas Dynasty, 165
Afghan Church. *See* St. John's Church, Bombay, India
Afghan-Shah, Ghaznī, Afghanistan, 281
Afghan-Soviet War (1979-1989), 442
Afghan Turks, 218
Afghan War of 1848, 29
Afghan War of 1919, 223
Afghanistan, 1, 20, 26, 28-29, 50, 71-74, 79-81, 136, 166, 186, 218, 223, 225, 259, 279-283, 333-337, 372, 392, 408, 414-419, 439-442, 448, 473-477, 491, 522, 525, 578-581, 595, 669, 671, 672, 681, 699, 720, 803, 805
Afrasiab. *See* Samarkand, Samarkand, Uzbekistan
Afridi (people), 474, 476, 477
Agastya (god), 694
Ageng (sultan of Banten), 103
Aggabodhi I (king of Polonnaruwa), 684
Aggabodhi II (king of Polonnaruwa), 684
Agni (god), 660
Āgra, Uttar Pradesh, India, 1-5, 22, 24, 220, 222, 260, 261, 263, 282, 415, 524, 802
Āgra Fort, India, 193
Aguinaldo, Emilio, 569
Agung (sultan of Mataram), 888, 890
Ahalyābāī, Rani, 277
Ahalyābāi Holkar (Marāṭhā queen), 765
Ahar, India, 191
Ahdai-din-ka-jhonpra Mosque, Ajmer, India, 21-22
Ahmad Khān, Sir Sayyed, 369
Aḥmad Khān Abdālī. *See* Aḥmad Shāh Durrāni
Aḥmad Shāh I (Mughal emperor of India), 6, 7
Aḥmad Shāh Durrāni (founder and first ruler of Afghanistan), 73, 282, 336, 416-417, 441, 475, 610, 803
Aḥmad Sirhindī (Naqshbandī skeikh), 165
Ahmadābād, Gujarāt, India, 6-9, 253, 626
Ahmadnagar, kingdom of, 125, 290, 366, 626
Ahmadshāhi, Afghanistan, 441
Ahmed (ruler of Hami), 323
Ahoeitu (mythic king), 827
Ahom Dynasty, 308, 309, 310
Ahura Mazdā (god), 142
Ai, Banda Islands, Indonesia, 88, 89
Ai Fa (royal agent), 182
Aihole, India, 435
Ainu (people), 269, 317, 319-320, 632
Air Itam, Penang, Indonesia, 668
Airlangga (king of Kaḍiri), 68
Aizu Basin, 10
Aizu Shuzō Hakubutsukan, Aizu-Wakamatsu, Japan, 12
Aizu Shuzō Rekishikan, Aizu-Wakamatsu, Japan, 12
Aizu-Wakamatsu, Fukushima, Japan, 10-13, 339
Ajai Pal (Chauhān rāja of Ajmer), 20
Ajanta, Mahārāshtra, India, 14-19, 552, 684, 686
Ajātashatru (king of Magadha), 847
Ajavarman (king of Ayodhyā), 49
Ajisukitakahikone no Ōmikami (god), 632
Ajit Singh (mahārāja of Jodhpur), 399, 400, 402
Ajmer, Rājasthān, India, 20-23, 24, 260, 400
Ak-Saray Palace, Shakhrisabz, Uzbekistan, 721
Ak-taghliq (sect), 458
Akāl Takht (Immortal Throne), Amritsar, India, 27
Akara, kingdom of, 835
Akbar (the Great; Mughal emperor of India), 1-2, 3, 4, 5, 8, 20, 22, 24, 26, 27, 50, 123, 127, 129, 191, 193-194, 222, 260, 262, 263, 314, 383, 385, 392, 399-400, 412, 416, 417, 441, 475, 507, 522, 523, 524, 563, 611, 669, 671, 679, 764, 769, 802, 837, 849
Aki. *See* Miyajima, Hiroshima, Japan
Akihito (emperor of Japan), 377, 520
Aksu, China, 458
Ālī Khān, Alī, 369
Al-chi (legendary prince of Korea), 509
Ala-ud-Dīn Husain (ruler of Ghūr), 282
'Alā'-ud-Dīn Muḥammad Khaljī (sultan of Delhi), 191, 193, 218, 388, 764, 837
Alahara Canal, Sri Lanka, 685, 686
Alai Darwaza, Delhi, India, 218
Alaisala (Mau patriot), 726
'Ālamgīr (Mughal emperor of India), 5, 8, 22, 26, 27-28, 92, 117, 123, 127, 128, 222, 226, 282, 290, 291, 292, 309, 314, 366, 369, 371, 385, 400, 412, 414, 416, 441, 508, 524, 534, 576, 577, 602, 608, 626, 627, 671, 679, 699, 764, 769, 803, 838, 850
'Ālamgīr's Mosque, Mathurā, India, 577
Alaska, United States of America, 318
Alaungpaya (king of Burma), 62-63, 656, 879
Alaungsithu (king of Burma), 654-655
Albert Hall, Jaipur, India, 132
Albuquerque, Afonso de, 284, 286, 542
Alcock, Sir Rutherford, 271
Alexander III (the Great; King of Macedon), 71, 72, 73, 186, 254, 279, 333, 408, 410, 414, 439, 474, 506-507, 578, 582, 608, 669, 718, 798, 801, 805
Alexander, Harold, 558
Alexander, James, 14
Alexandria, Afghanistan. *See* Ghaznī, Ghaznī, Afghanistan
Alexandria of Arachosia. *See* Kandahār, Kandahār, Afghanistan
Alfonso XII (king of Spain), 404
Algeria, 646, 788
'Alī (Ali ibn Abī Ṭālib; fourth caliph), 73, 371, 578, 579
'Ali (Chagataite ruler of Hami), 323
Alī 'Ādil Shāh (ruler of Bijāpur), 125, 127
Ali 'Ādil Shāh II (ruler of Bijāpur), 127
Ali Arslan, 457
Ali Jinnah, Mohammad Ali, 175
Ali Mardan (Ṣafavid governor of Kandahār), 441, 769
Ali Mardan Khān (architect for Shāh Jahān), 524
Ali Masjid, Khyber Pass, North-West Frontier, Pakistan; Kābul, Afghanistan, 473, 476
Alice Springs, Australia, 45, 209, 210
Alimuddin I (sultan), 404
Aliverdi Khan (nabob) of Bengal, 136, 226, 679, 680
All-India Muslim League. *See* Muslim League
All Saints' Church, Norfolk Island, Australia, 642
All Saints Church, Peshāwar, Pakistan, 671
All Travancore Samyukta Rashtreeya Samiti. *See* Travancore State Congress
Allahābād, India, 168, 371, 400, 836
Allata (ruler of Chittaurgarh), 191
Alleppey, India, 713
Almeida, Francisco de, 712
Almeida, Lourenço (Lorenzo) de, 199, 272, 443, 712
Alpine Club, 604, 606
Alptigin (governor of Ghaznī), 280
Altan Khan (Mongol chief), 215-216, 453, 528, 741, 750
Altun Shan Mountains, 239
Alungpaya (king of Burma), 58, 62-63
Ama (goddess), 542, 592
Ama-Shōgun. *See* Masako
Amacao. *See* Macau
Amacon. *See* Macau

Amalaka Sila, Puri, India, 697
Amangkurat I (king of Yogyakarta), 890
Amangkurat II (king of Yogyakarta), 890
Amanohashidate, Japan, 590
Amānollāh Khān (ruler of Afghanistan), 336, 418
Amao. *See* Macau
Amar Singh, 392
Amara Deva, 140
Amara Simha, 140
Amarapura, Myanmar, 556
Amaterasu no Ōmikami (goddess), 374, 375, 376, 460, 587, 588-589, 590, 592, 632, 635
Amba Mata (god). *See* Pārvati
Ambarisha (king of Ayodhyā), 24
Amber, Rājasthān, India, 24-26, 383, 385
Ambhi (ruler of Taxila), 805
Ambikashwara (god). *See* Siva
Amboina Massacre, 89
Ambon, Moluccas, Indonesia, 87, 88, 89, 839, 842
Ambryn Island, Vanuatu, 844
Ame-no-Uzume no Mikoto (goddess), 590
Amédée Lighthouse, Nouméa, New Caledonia, 645, 647
American Samoa. *See* Samoa, Western Samoa and American Samoa
American Trading Company, 160
Amherst, William Pitt, 188
Amida Buddha. *See* Buddha Amida
Amin, Hafizullah, 418
Amira Kadal, Srīnagar, India, 769
Amitabha. *See* Buddha Amida
Ammaisan Mountain, 198
Amoghavarsha (king of Rāṣhṭrakūṭa), 257
Amoy. *See* Xiamen, China
Ampera Bridge, Palembang, Indonesia, 664
Amrita Saras pool, Amritsar, India, 27
Amritsar, Punjab, India, 27-30
Amsterdam, Netherlands, 90, 342, 395
Amsterdam, Tonga. *See* Tongatapu, Tonga
Amu Darya River, 71, 163, 281, 578, 798
Amu Darya Valley, 71, 73, 79, 80-81, 279, 578, 720
Amundsen, Roald, 237
An Duong (king of Au Lac), 329
An Lushan (Chinese rebel), 541, 872
An Lushan Rebellion, 541
An Quang Pagoda, Ho Chi Minh City, Vietnam, 356
An-Shih Rebellion, 422
Anāhitā, 72
Anak Krakatau, Krakatau, Indonesia, 495
Anakena beach, Easter Island, Chile, 247, 251
Anand Mahal (Palace of Delight), Bijāpur, India, 127
Ananda Pagoda, Bagon, Myanmar, 556
Ananda Temple, Pagan, Myanmar, 654, 655
Anandavalleeswaram Temple, Quilon, India, 712
Ānandpur, India, 28
Anaṅgabhīma (king of Gaṅga), 699
Anangpala I (Tomara ruler), 218, 507
Anangu (people), 45
Ananta (king of Srīnagar), 768
Anantavarmana Chōḍagaṅga (Gaṅga king of Puri), 699
Anap-ji, Kyŏngju, South Korea, 513
Anarkali (courtier), 522
Anatolia, Turkey, 720
Anatom Island, Vanuatu, 845
Anaukpetlun (king of Burma), 62
Anawrahta (king of Burma), 60, 653, 654, 879
Anchar lakes, 768
Andean Indians, 820
Anderson, Joseph, 642
Anderson, William, 610
Anderson's Bay, New Zealand, 235
Andhaka (people), 572
Andhra Dynasty. *See* Sātavāhana Dynasty
Andhra Pradesh, India, 290-292, 366-370, 803
Ando, Japan, 338
Andrew (saint), 448, 450
Anegondi fortress, India, 855
Anenokōji family, 795
Ang Phu (Sherpa mountaineer), 607
Aṅgamadilla Canal, Sri Lanka, 686
Anger, Indonesia, 495
Angkor, Siem Reap, Cambodia, 31-34, 52, 54, 353, 530, 771, 772
Angkor Thom, Cambodia, 33
Angkor Wat, Angkor, Cambodia, 33, 34
Anglicanism, 5, 223, 236, 237, 347, 641, 642, 864, 865
Anglo-Afghan Wars, 372, 417-418, 441-442, 476-477
Anglo-Burmese War, 63, 556, 880
Anglo-Dutch treaty, 759
Ango-in. *See* Asuka-dera, Asuka, Japan
Anhaengsa Temple, Chŏnju, South Korea, 195
Anhui, China, 111, 618, 736, 874
Anikanga (king of Sri Lanka), 687
Ankh Michauli (Closed Eyes) Pavilion, Fatehpur Sīkri, India, 262-263
Ankokuroni-ji Temple, Kamakura, Japan, 429
Anna Salai Road, Madras, India, 550
Annadurai, C.N., 551
Annam, Vietnam, 331, 354
Annapurna (mountain), 604
Anping, Quanzhou, China, 706
Anping Fort. *See* Fort Zeelandia, Tainan, Taiwan, China
Anscombe, Edmund, 237
Anson Bay, 641, 643
Antarctica, 234, 237
Antargriha (Inner Sanctum) zone, Vārānasī, India, 847
Anti-Christian Edict (Japan), 612
Anti-Fascist People's Freedom League (Myanmar), 558, 881, 882
Antoku (infant emperor of Japan), 426, 518
Anula (queen of Sri Lanka), 38
Anup Mahal, Junāgarh Fort, Bīkaner, India, 132
Anup Singh (ruler of Bīkaner), 132
Anuradhapura, Sri Lanka, 35-39, 140, 684, 754
Anusari, Vientiane, Laos, 854
Anuvinda (king of Avanti), 836
Anuvong (king of Laos), 532, 852
Anville, Jean Baptiste d', 604
Anxi, China, 239
Anyang, Henan, China, 40-43, 901, 904
Anzaisho, Ise, Japan, 374
Ao, China, 40, 901, 904
Aoi Matsuri (Hollyhock Festival), Kyōto, Japan, 518
Aomori, Japan, 345-348
Aomori Bank Memorial Hall, Hirosaki, Japan, 347
Aoshima Shrine, Miyazaki, Japan, 593
Apak Khoja (religious sage), 458
Apia, Western Samoa, 723, 821
Apolima Island, Western Samoa, 723
Appar (saint), 435, 552
Apricot Alter, Qufu, China, 709
Apsidal Temple, Taxila, Pakistan, 806
Aquino, Benigno (Ninoy), 570
Aquino, Corazon, 406, 570
Arabian Peninsula, 103, 172, 177, 704, 710
Arabian Sea, 142, 252, 284, 371, 448, 501, 580, 595, 599, 762, 765, 801, 802
Arabs, 73, 79, 80, 87, 186, 199, 256, 259, 272, 279, 280, 305, 306, 366, 371, 396, 422, 448, 452, 456, 608, 610, 625, 684, 711, 720, 759, 801, 884, 897
Arachosia. *See* Kandahār, Kandahār, Afghanistan
Arakan, Myanmar, 653
Arakanese Dynasty, 62, 186, 187, 188, 225, 556
Aral Sea, 578, 718, 798
Aram Bāgh, Āgra, India, 1, 4
Aramatsuri, Ise, Japan, 375
Aravālli (Arāvalli) Mountains, 20, 22, 218, 600
Arbuda (legendary cobra), 600
Archaeological Museum, Chittaurgarh, India, 194
Archaeological Survey of Ceylon, 35, 39
Archaeological Survey of India, 19, 595, 800, 812, 858
Arcot, India, 437, 503, 548, 550, 680
Arghandab River, 439
Arghūn Dynasty, 801, 802
Arghūnid (tribe), 439, 440
Arjun (Sikh gurū), 27, 523
Arjuna (Hindu hero), 555
Arjuna's Penance, Mahābalipuram, India, 555
Armagon, India, 547
Armenia, 168, 226, 547, 548, 550, 759
Arolas (Spanish general in Philippines), 404, 405
Arrow War. *See* Opium Wars
Artaxerxes (king of Persia), 72
Arthur, George, 688, 689, 690
Arūjmand Bānū Baygam. *See* Mumtāz Mahal
Aruna (charioteer), 479
Arunachal Pradesh, India, 310
Arung Datu (queen of Bone), 842
Arung Palakka (Buginese leader), 840-841
Arung Sinkang (Buginese nobleman), 841
Aruvi Aru River, 35
Ārya Chakravartis Dynasty, 687
Āryaghat, Kāthmāndu, Nepal, 464
Aryamitra (king of Ayodhyā), 49
Aryans (people), 134, 186, 276, 414, 439, 490-491, 505, 599, 602, 718, 847
Asaf Khān (administrator of āgra), 3
Asakusa, Japan, 824
Asan Tol, Kāthmāndu, Nepal, 467
Asandivat, India, 506
Asanga (Buddhist teacher), 50
Asano Dynasty, 349
Asano Nagaakira (*daimyō* of Hiroshima), 349
Asano River, 431, 432, 433
Ashikaga family, 426, 429-431, 518-519
Ashina family, 10, 12
Ashina Morinori, 10
Ashina Morishige, 10
Ashina Moritaka, 10
Ashrafi Mahal, Māndu, India, 563
Asi (Sword) River, 847
Asim ud-Din (governor of Bengal), 226
Aśoka (Mauryan emperor), 35, 37, 50, 121, 124, 136, 140, 142, 186, 191, 220, 276, 408, 410, 435, 439, 572, 578, 669, 727, 729, 730, 731, 754, 767, 805, 806, 807, 809, 837, 848, 855
Aśokan Edicts, Junāgadh, India, 408, 410
Assam, India, 174, 226, 308-311, 656, 657
Astana palace, Kuching, Malaysia, 500
Astyages (king of the Medes), 71, 578
Asuf-'ud-Dawlah, 534
Asuka, Japan, 460, 461
Asuka-dera, Asuka, Japan, 460
Asylum, Port Arthur, Australia, 691
Asylum of Faith (Dinapanah), Delhi, India, 1
Ata, Tonga, 827, 828
Atafu. *See* Tokelau, Territory of New Zealand
Atisha (Buddhist teacher), 527, 528, 750
Atjeh. *See* Aceh, Sumatra, Indonesia
Atri Rishi Temple, Guru Shikhar, India, 602
Atsuta shrine, Nagoya, Japan, 375
Atta Mohammed Khān, 769
Atumashi Kyaung (Incomparable Monastery), Mandalay, Myanmar, 556
Au Duong (king of Au Lac), 329
Au Lac, kingdom of. *See* Nam Viet, kingdom of
Auckland, Lord. *See* Eden, George
Auckland, North Island, New Zealand, 642, 643, 860
Augustinian order, 180, 181, 225, 544
Aung San, 558, 560, 880, 881, 882
Aung San Suu Kyi, 560, 882
Aungier, Gerald, 142

Aunuu Island, American Samoa, 723, 725
Aurangābād, India, 14
Aurangzeb. *See* 'Alamgīr
Australia, 44-46, 65, 75-78, 153-157, 206, 208-211, 298, 299, 300, 301, 356, 361, 493, 499, 639-643, 644, 646, 647, 688-691, 726, 760, 781-784, 830, 839, 844, 845-846, 859, 861, 863-865
Australian Aircraft and Engineering Company, Limited, 156
Australian External Territory, Australia, 639-643
Austria, 736
Austria-Hungary, 814
Autumn Festival, Nikkō, Japan, 637-638
Ava, Myanmar, 61, 62, 310, 656
Avalokiteśvara. *See* Kannon
Avalokiteśvara Bodhisattva, 18
Avanti, kingdom of, 835, 836
Avenue Lan Xang, Vientiane, Laos, 854
Avenue of the Three Laes (San-machi-suji), Takayama, Japan, 795
Averter River. *See* Varanā River
Avicenna (Islamic philosopher), 163, 721
Avimukta zone, Vārānasī, India, 847
Awang Alak Be Takar (ruler of Brunei), 158
Awazu, Japan, 338
Axis of the Heavens, Luoyang, China, 541
Ay Khānom, Afghanistan, 333
Aybak, Quṭb-ud-Dīn- (sultan of Delhi), 21
Ayer Hitam. *See* Air Itam, Penang
Ayers, Sir Henry, 45
Ayers Rock, Northern Territory, Australia, 44-46, 211
Ayeyarwady (Irrawaddy) River, 310, 556, 558, 653, 656, 879, 880
Ayodhyā, Uttar Pradesh, India, 47-51, 143, 534
Ayub Khan, Mohammed, 228
Ayutthaya, Ayutthaya, Thailand, 52-59, 96, 97, 757, 774, 775
Ayutthaya, kingdom of, 60, 62, 96, 97, 184, 531, 532, 582, 851, 852
Azerbaijan, Iran, 721
Azuma. *See* Honshū, Japan

Ba Dinh Square, Hanoi, Vietnam, 331
Baba Pyara Caves, Junāgadh, India, 410
Bābur (Ẓahīr-ud-Dīn Muḥammad; Mughal emperor of India), 1, 3, 4, 22, 50, 73, 165, 220, 282, 291, 312, 314, 335, 383, 414-416, 440, 441, 475, 507, 522, 671, 679, 722
Backhouse, James, 642
Bactra. *See* Balkh, Balkh, Afghanistan
Bactria, 165, 333, 414, 439, 552, 578, 578-579, 608, 798, 805
Badakhshān, Afghanistan, 71
Badal Mahal (Weather Palace), Junāgarh Fort, Bīkaner, India, 132
Badan Singh (founder of Bharatpur kingdom), 577
Badaruddin, Mahmud (sultan), 663
Bādshāhī Mosque, Lahore, Pakistan, 524, 525, 671
Badung, Indonesia, 70
Bāgh, India, 686
Bagh-i-Vafa (Garden of Fidelity), Kābul, Afghanistan, 415
Bagh Singh (prince of Deolia), 193
Baghdad, Iraq, 164, 218, 280, 281, 282, 579, 610, 720
Bāghmati River, 464, 465
Bago, Myanmar, 60-64, 774, 879, 882
Bago River, 60, 62
Bagon, Myanmar. *See* Pagan, Myanmar
Baguinda (rāja of Sulu), 403
Bahā' ad-Dīn Naqshband (religious leader), 165, 166
Bahā' ad-Dīn tomb complex, Bukhara, Uzbekistan, 166
Baha-ud-Dīn Zakaria (Sufi sheik), 610
Bahādur, Ganga Singh. *See* Ganga Singh Bahādur
Bahadur, Raja Rajendra Mullick, 174
Bahadur Khan (ruler of Junāgadh), 412
Bahadur Khanji III (ruler of Junāgadh), 413
Bahādur Shāh (sultan of Gujarāt), 142, 193, 563
Bahādur Shāh I (Mughal emperor of India), 26
Bahādur Shāh II (Mughal emperor of India), 222
Bahauddin (chief minister of Junāgadh), 413
Bahauddin College, Junāgadh, India, 413
Bahmanī Dynasty, 125, 284, 290, 366, 626, 855, 856
Bahrām Shah (ruler of Khorāsān), 282
Bahwulpoor, India, 392
Bai Juyi (poet), 325
Baie de l'Orphelinat, Nouméa, New Caledonia, 647
Baihaqi (geographer), 281
Baird, David, 94
Bajau (people), 897, 899
Bajaur, Pakistan, 798
Baji Rao II (Marāṭhā *peshwa*), 314, 628
Baker, Herbert, 223
Baker, Shirley Waldemar, 829-830
Baker, Thomas, 266
Bakery Hill, Ballarat, Australia, 77, 78
Bakhar, sultan of, 802
Bako National Park, Sarawak, Malaysia, 499
Bālā Ḥisār, Peshāwar, Pakistan, 671, 672
Bālā Ḥissār (fortress), Kābul, Afghanistan, 414, 417, 418
Balabhadra (god), 697
Balambangan Island, 68, 404
Balarāma (god), 574
Balarma Varma (ruler of Quilon), 712
Balban (sultan of Delhi), 218
Bali, Bali, Indonesia, 65-70, 211
Bali Strait, 68
Balkh, Balkh, Afghanistan, 71-74, 163, 279, 333, 578, 580, 581
Balkh River, 71
Ballarat, Victoria, Australia, 75-78
Ballarat Art Gallery, Australia, 78
Ballarat Reform League, Australia, 77
Balūchi (clan), 804
Balūchistān, Pakistan, 371-372, 388, 491, 492, 525, 608, 802, 804
Bāmiān, Bāmiān, Afghanistan, 79-81, 279, 282
Bāmiān Pass, 79
Bāmiān River, 79, 81
Bāmiān Valley, 79, 81
Ban Chao (conqueror of Kashgar), 456
Ban Chiang, Udon Thani, Thailand, 82-86
Ban Gu (Han historian), 539
Banaba, Kirabati, 821
Bāṇabhaṭṭa, kingdom of, 837
Banāras. *See* Vārānasī, Uttar Pradesh, India
Banāras Hindu University, Vārānasī, India, 850
Banda, Maluku, Indonesia, 87-91
Banda Sea, 87
Bandanaira, Banda Islands, Indonesia, 88, 89
Bandar Seri Begawan, Brunei Darussalam, 158, 160, 161-162
Bandaranaike, Solomon, 203
Bandjermasir, Brunei Darussalam, 160
Bandung Bondowoso, 694
Banerji, Rakhal Das, 595
Bangalore, Karnātaka, India, 92-95
Bangalore Palace, India, 95
Bangalore University, India, 95
Bangka Island, Indonesia, 663
Bangkok, Thailand, 52, 58, **96-100,** 182, 184, 532, 533, 774, 775, 852
Bangladesh, 168, 176, 186-190, 218, 222, 223, 225-229, 310, 448, 449, 657-660
Banks, Sir Joseph, 153, 154, 781, 787
Banksmeadow, Australia, 154, 156
Bānkura, India, 134-137
Banpo, China, 870
Banqueting Hall. *See* Rajaji Hall, Madras, India
Bansa, Sulu, Philippines, 897
Banteay Srei, Angkor, Cambodia, 33
Banten, West Java, Indonesia, 101-104, 113, 114, 395, 495, 663, 712, 890
Banten Girang, West Java, Indonesia, 101
Banten River, 101
Bantilan (sultan of Sulu), 404
Bao Dai (emperor of Vietnam), 355
Bao Quoc Pagoda, Hue, Vietnam, 362
Baoan, China, 875
Baoen Guangxiaosi, Guangzhou, China, 302
Baohedian (Hall of Preserving Harmony), Forbidden City, Beijing, China, 107
Baota (Precious Pagoda), Yanan, China, 878
Baphuon, Angkor, Cambodia, 33
Bappa Rawal (Guhilla leader), 191
Baptist Missionary Society, 850
Bara Imambara (Great Imambara), Lucknow, India, 534, 535
Barā Katrā, Dhākā, Bangladesh, 225
Barābar Caves, India, 276
Barakzāi Dynasty, 417
Baram Basin, 161
Bāranasi. *See* Vārānasī, Uttar Pradesh, India
Bārānasiggaho (king of Koshala), 847
Barbosa (academic), 710
Bare Island, 154
Barkhor road, Lhasa, Tibet, China, 526, 529
Barkol, China, 321
Bārmer, India, 392
Baroda, India, 223
Barr, John, 235
Barra Fort, Macau, 544
Barrett, David D., 877
Barrier Gate, Macau, 542
Bartholomew of Cremona, 452
Bartley, Whitman S., 381
Barygaza. *See* Broach, India
Basantapur Square, Kāthmāndu, Nepal, 466
Basantapur Tower, Kāthmāndu, Nepal, 466
Basilan, Philippines, 899, 900
Basilan Strait, 897
Basilica Minore del Santo Niño, Cebu City, Philippines, 181
Basilica of Bom Jesus, Goa, India, 288
Basmachi revolt, 166
Bass, George, 641
Bassein, India, 142, 288
Bassein, Myanmar, 802
Basu, Jyoti, 176
Bataan Death March, 207
Bataan Peninsula, Philippines, 206-207
Batara Gowa II (king of Gowa), 841
Batavia. *See* Jakarta, Special Capital City Territory, Indonesia
Bates Agreement, 405
Bathgate, Alexander, 236
Batticaloa, Sri Lanka, 200, 201, 273
Battle of Arcot, 680
Battle of Bataan, 206
Battle of Bloody Bay, 673
Battle of Bloody Ridge, 300
Battle of Buxar, 168, 226, 534
Battle of Chilianwālla, 29
Battle of Colachel, 712
Battle of Deorai, 22
Battle of Dien Bien Phu, 230, 331, 355
Battle of Gaugamela, 71
Battle of Gujarāt, 29
Battle of Huangtian Dang, 325
Battle of Imphal-Kohima, 558

Battle of Kābul, 29
Battle of Lahore, 1
Battle of Maiwand, 442
Battle of Mary, 336
Battle of Nong Sarai, 52, 56
Battle of Pānīpat, 1, 220
Battle of Peshāwar, 20
Battle of Plassey, 168, 171, 172, 188, 226, 680, 682
Battle of Sekigahara, 10, 338, 349, 634, 823
Battle of Tālikota, 125
Battle of Tarain, 218
Battle of the Eastern Solomons, 300
Battle of Toba-Fushimi, 12
Battle of Tonokuchihara, 12
Battle of Ueno, 12
Battle of Wandiwash, 548
Battles of Tarāin, 20-21
Batu Feringghi (Foreigner's Rock), Penang, Malaysia, 668
Batu Renggong (Dewa Agung of Bali), 68
Bau, Viti Levu, Fiji, 264, 265, 266
Bau, West Borneo, 629
Bavadra, Timoci, 268
Bay of Banten, 102
Bay of Bengal, 55, 56, 57, 58, 121, 186, 187, 189, 290, 408, 478, 501, 547, 548, 550, 552, 625, 653, 661, 680, 697, 714
Bay of Islands, 642, 859
Bayadari Palace, Sikandra, India, 1
Bayan (Mongol general), 884
Bayinnaung (king of Bago), 56, 62
Bayon Temple, Angkor, Cambodia, 33
Bayram Khān (Mughal regent of India), 1
Bayt ul-Mukarram, Dhākā, Bangladesh, 225
Baz Bahādur (ruler of Mālwa), 563
Beagle Gulf, 208
Beās River, 186
Beda Ula (king of Bali), 68
Beechey, F.W., 674, 676
Béhaine, Pierre-Joseph-Georges Pigneau de, 354
Bei River, 813, 814
Bei Si Pagoda, Suzhou, China, 778
Beidaihe, China, 743
Beijing, China, 196, 214, 215, 216, 241, 244, 296, 324, 325, 327, 420, 422, 424, 453, 459, 538, 544, 619, 620, 663, 708, 732, 736, 737, 738, 739, 742, 747, 748, 752, 790, 813, 814, 816, 817, 873, 874, 877, 901
  Forbidden City, 105-108
  Tiananmen Square, 109-112
Beijing-Guangzhou railway, 901, 904
Beijing-Suiyuan railway, 216
Beishuiguan, Shanhaiguan, China, 739
Bekung (rāja of Bali), 68
Belait, Brunei Darussalam, 161
Belgium, 174, 351, 814
Belitung Island, Indonesia, 663
Bell, Charles, 604
Bell, H.C.P., 39
Bell Harry Tower, Canterbury Cathedral, England, 174
Bell Hill, Dunedin, New Zealand, 235
Bells, Yangon, Myanmar, 879-880
Belmont mansion, Windsor, Australia, 865
Benares. *See* Vārānasī, Uttar Pradesh, India
Bencoolen. *See* Bengkulu, Bengkulu, Indonesia
Bengal, 1, 8, 35, 121, 123, 135, 136, 141, 168, 169, 170, 171, 172-176, 186, 187, 188, 189, 202, 226, 227, 260, 290, 308, 309, 310, 369, 373, 385, 466, 478, 480, 501, 507, 657, 679, 680, 682, 699, 751, 798, 897
Bengal Club, Calcutta, India, 174
Bengal Delta, 811
Bengali Renaissance, 173-174
Bengkulu, Bengkulu, Indonesia, 101, **113-116,** 758, 759
Benjamin of Tudela (rabbi), 710
Bennelong Point, Sydney, Australia, 782, 784
Benten. *See* Benzaiten
Bentinck, William, 174
Bentley, James, 77, 78
Benzaiten (goddess), 427, 590, 601, 822-823
Berar, kingdom of, 366
Berlin, Germany, 175, 798, 800
Bernier, François, 850
Bertolucci, Bernardo, 108
Besant, Annie, 850
Betawi (people), 397
Betwa River, 117
Bhādgāon. *See* Bhaktapūr, Nepal
Bhadra fort, Ahmadābād, India, 6
Bhagadatta (prince of Guwāhāti), 308
Bhagirati River, 682
Bhagur Darwaji, Nāsik, India, 626
Bhagwan Das (mahārāja of Jaipur), 24, 385
Bhāhjā, 17
Bhairon Pol gate, Chittaurgarh, India, 194
Bhaishaja-guru. *See* Yakushi
Bhaktapūr, Nepal, 464, 465, 466
Bhakti (Hindu cult), 574
Bhalka Tīrth, Somnāth, India, 762, 765
Bhanbore, Karāchi, Pakistan, 450
Bhandasar Temple, Bīkaner, India, 129
Bhār (tribe), 468
Bhāraśiva-Nāga Dynasty, 468
Bharata (incarnation of Vishnu), 805
Bhārata War, 505
Bharatonatyam (legendary), 811
Bharatpur, kingdom of, 577
Bhārhut, 17
Bhāskara-kshetra. *See* Vijayanagara, Karnātaka, India
Bhatti (people), 388-389, 392
Bhauma-Kara Dynasty, 123, 124
Bhawalpur, India, 392
Bhīm Deva (Gujarāt king), 601
Bhīma (legendary prince), 191
Bhīma River, 125
Bhīmadeva I (ruler of Gujarāt), 764
Bhīmbetka, India, 117
Bhindranwale, Jarnail Singh, 30
Bhīr Mound, Pakistan, 805, 806
Bhoj (Bhoja; Paramāra rāja of India), 117, 837
Bhojapal, India, 117
Bhojdeo (ruler of Lodurva), 388
Bhojpūr, India, 117
Bhopāl, Madhya Pradesh, India, 117-120
Bhubaneswar, Orissa, India, 121-124
Bhutan, kingdom of, 310, 751-752
Bhūteśvara, Mathurā, India, 576
Bhuvanaika Bāhu (ruler of Sri Lanka), 199
Bībī Khānom Mosque, Samarkand, Uzbekistan, 721
Bibi Pari (daughter of Shayesta Khān), 225
Bibliothèque Nationale, Paris, France, 244
Bida. *See* Vidyādhara
Bīdar, kingdom of, 125, 366
Bien River, 420, 422, 423
Bienjing. *See* Kaifeng, Henan, China
Bight of Bangkok, 96
Bihār, India, 1, 136, 138-141, 168-171, 175, 186, 226, 267, 276-278, 412, 657, 836
Bihar Mal (mahārāja of India), 24, 383
Bijāpur, Karnātaka, India, 92, **125-128**
Bijāpur, kingdom of, 284, 288, 290, 291, 366, 812, 857, 858
Bijāpur Plateau, 125
Bīka, Rao (founder of Bīkaner, India), 129
Bīkaner, Rājasthān, India, 129-133, 392, 394
Bilikt Khan (son of last Mongol emperor), 453
Bimladevi (wife of Gursi), 389
Bindu Mādhava, Vārānasī, India, 850
Bindusāra (Mauryan king of Magadha), 408, 805
Binnya U (Mon ruler of Bago), 60
Binnyadammayaza (Mon ruler of Bago), 60-61
Binnyaran I (Mon ruler of Bago), 60-61
Binnyaran II (Mon ruler of Bago), 61
Bintulu, Malaysia, 160, 497
Bīr Hambīr (king of Mallabhūm), 134
Bīr Singh II (ruler of Bishnupur), 136
Birbal (rāja of Fatehpur Sīkri), 263
Birdum, Australia, 209
Birendra (king of Nepal), 467
Birla, Raja Baldeo, 223
Bisayas. *See* Visayan Islands, Philippines
Bishnupur, West Bengal, India, 134-137
Bishop, Barry, 606
Bishop's House, Kuching, Malaysia, 500
Bishopsgate Street, Kuching, Malaysia, 499
Biyagama, Sri Lanka, 200
Bjīm Singh (advisor of Rana Lakshman), 191
Black Hats (Buddhist sect), 527, 750
Black Hole of Calcutta, India, 172, 680
Black Mountaineers. *See* Kara-taghliq (sect)
Black River (Kurokawa), Fukushima, Japan, 10
Black Sea, 276
Black Town, Calcutta, India, 172.
Blackbirders, 845-846
Blakiston, Thomas, 320
Blaxland, Gregory, 783
Bledisloe, Lord and Lady, 861, 862
Bligh, William, 265, 673, 782, 788, 828, 844, 863
Bligh Water, 265
Blocks of Laterite. *See* Kon Laeng, Sukhothai, Thailand
Blue Mosque, Mazār-i-Sharīf, Afghanistan, 579, 580
Blue Mountains, 782-783, 784, 863
Bo Ya (legendary musician), 868
Bo-tree, Anuradhapura, Sri Lanka, 35, 39
Bo-tree, Bodh Gayā, India, 138, 140
Bocarro, Antonio, 544
Bocarro, Manoel Tavares, 544
Bochum, Germany, 351
Bodh Gayā, Bihār, India, 17, **138-141,** 276, 278
Bodhi-druma. See Bo-tree
Bodhidharma (founder of Zen Buddhism), 304, 436
Bodhimanda, India, 138
Bodhisattvas, 17, 18, 33, 576, 798, 894
Bodoahpra (king of Burma), 310
Boghar. *See* Bukhara, Bukhara, Uzbekistan
Bogle, George, 752
Bogor, Indonesia, 395
Bohai coast, China, 293
Bohai Sea, 739, 813
Bohar Niwas, Bīkaner, India, 129
Bolan Pass, 473, 474, 476
Bom Parto Fort, Macau, 544
Bombay, Mahārāshtra, India, 6, 9, 117, **142-146,** 189, 252, 253, 255, 256, 392, 534, 547, 550
Bombay Harbor, 252, 256
Bombay Island, India, 142
Bombay School of Art, India, 14
Bon Festivals (Japan), 347
Bön religion, 526, 527
Bondi Beach, Sydney, Australia, 784
Bone, kingdom of, 839, 840-841, 842
Bonifacio, Andres, 568
Bonin Islands, 379
Booth, Charles, 690
Bora Bora, French Polynesia, 788
Borneo, 103, 158, 158-162, 403, 404, 497, 499, 568, 629, 665, 705, 761, 811, 839, 888, 897, 899
Borobudur, Central Java, Indonesia, 147-152
Borobudur (temple), Java, Indonesia, 692, 694

Borobudur Monument, Yogyakarta, Indonesia, 888
Boromaraja I (king of Thailand), 184
Borommaracha I (king of Ayutthaya), 54
Borommaracha II (king of Ayutthaya), 54, 59
Borommatrailokanat (king of Ayutthaya). *See* Trailok
Bose, Subhas Chandra, 175, 176, 760
Boshin Civil War, 12
Bosnia, 167
Botanical Gardens, Calcutta, India, 174
Botanical Gardens, Sydney, Australia, 783
Botany Bay, New South Wales, Australia, 153-157, 639, 781, 785
Botany Bay National Park, Australia, 154, 156
Bottomside, Corregidor Island, Philippines, 204
Bougainville, Louis-Antoine de, 724, 785, 787, 844
Bouman, Cornelius, 724
Bounty mutiny, 642, 673-676, 788, 828, 844
Bourail, New Caledonia, 646
Bourdannais, Mahé de la, 548
Bourdillon, Tom, 606
Bowditch, Nathaniel, 820
Bowditch Island. *See* Tokelau, Territory of New Zealand
Boxer Protocol, 816
Boxer Rebellion, 107, 109, 736, 737, 742, 816, 868, 873
Brahmā (god), 47, 135, 252, 254, 258, 276, 312, 437, 530, 601, 660, 692, 694
Brahmā Shāh (Udaipur mahārana minister), 600, 601
Brahmā Temple, Khajurāho, India, 470
Brahmā Temple, Kumbakonam, India, 501
Brahmā Temple, Prambanan, Indonesia, 695, 696
Brahmanism, 134, 188, 252, 254, 388, 472, 501, 503, 657, 716, 771
Brahmaputra River, 225, 308, 309, 310, 311, 526, 750
Brahmjūnī. *See* Gayaśīrṣa Hill, Bodh Gayā, India
Braja-bhūmi. *See* Mathurā, Uttar Pradesh, India
Brando, Marlon, 788
Brazen Palace, Anuradhapura, Sri Lanka, 38, 39
Brazil, 787
Brhadīśvara (Rājarājeśvara) Temple, Thanjāvūr, India, 809, 811-812
Bridge, Vientiane, Laos, 854
Bridge, Zhengzhou, China, 903
Bridge of the Imperial Way. *See* Yuluqiao, Forbidden City, Beijing, China
Bridge of Zhou, Kaifeng, China, 420
Bridges, Yangzhou, China, 886
Brighton-le-Sands, Australia, 156
Brighton Pavilion, England, 578
British Association for the Advanvcement of Science, 629
British City, Chittagong, Bangladesh, 189
British East India Company, 5, 62, 88, 89, 90, 119, 136, 137, 142, 143, 158, 160, 166, 168, 169, 171, 172, 173, 174, 188, 202, 222, 223, 226, 274, 277, 306, 342, 369, 372, 386, 394, 404, 412, 446, 503, 524, 534, 536, 544-545, 547, 586, 627, 628, 657, 665, 667, 679, 682, 712, 732, 748, 751, 757, 759, 760, 804
British Empire. *See* Great Britain
British Museum, London, England, 40, 242, 244, 251, 614, 727
British North Borneo Company, 160-161
British Royal Society, 629, 639, 644, 787
Brito Nicote, Philip de, 62, 879
Broach, India, 6, 835, 837
Broek, Abraham van den, 342
Broken Bay, 863
Brooke, Annie, 500
Brooke, Bertram, 499
Brooke, Charles, 160, 161, 497-499, 500
Brooke, Francis, 500
Brooke, James, 160, 404, 497
Brooke, Julia, 500
Brooke, Margaret, 498, 500
Brooke, Vyner, 499
Brooke family, 161
Broughton, William, 865
Bruce, Charles Granville, 604
Bruce, Frederick, 814
Bruce, James. *See* Elgin, Lord
Brune. *See* Borneo
Brunei Bay, 158
Brunei Darussalam, 158-162, 211, 403, 404, 497, 499, 565
Brunei National Democratic Party, 161
Brunei River, 162
Brunei Town. *See* Bandar Seri Begawan, Brunei Darussalam
Bruni, Antoine-Raymond-Joseph de (chevalier d'Entrecastraux), 644
Bua, Vanua Levu, Fiji, 264, 266
Buck, Sir Peter. *See* Te Rangi Hiroa
Buckingham Mill, Madras, India, 550
Budagh Khān (Māndu officer), 563
Buddh Gayā. *See* Bodh Gayā, Bihār, India
Buddha, 17, 18, 35, 37, 47, 50, 58, 59, 60, 63, 73, 81, 97, 98, 138, 140, 141, 147-150, 184, 185, 197, 213, 214, 242, 244, 246, 256, 276, 428, 429, 443, 460, 465, 512, 526-528, 529, 530, 531, 532, 533, 556, 559, 573, 574, 576, 588-589, 590, 616, 622, 623, 624, 625, 626, 632, 635, 636, 655, 660, 685, 707, 729, 730, 774, 795, 798, 800, 805, 806, 808, 836, 847, 848, 851, 852, 868, 878, 879, 893-896
Buddha Amida, 428, 429, 431, 517, 518, 590, 632, 751
Buddha Archaeological Museum, Bihār, India, 141
Buddha Gayā. *See* Bodh Gayā, Bihār, India
Buddha Hall. *See* Shaka-dō, Kyōto, Japan
Buddha of Healing. *See* Yakushi
Buddha of the Universe. *See* Vairocana
Buddha's Seat, Bodh Gayā, India, 138
Buddhism, 12, 13, 14, 15, 17-18, 33, 35, 37, 38, 39, 47, 48-50, 58, 59, 60, 61, 62, 63, 65, 73, 79, 96, 97, 98, 101, 113, 122, 124, 136, 138, 140, 141, 142, 147-152, 158, 163, 182, 184, 186, 187, 189, 191, 195, 198, 199, 202-203, 212, 213, 214, 225, 239, 240, 242, 244, 246, 254-255, 256, 270, 271, 276, 278, 279, 280, 302, 304, 306, 307, 308, 310, 312, 317, 321, 338, 342, 344, 345, 347, 349, 353, 354, 355-356, 362, 365, 376, 377, 408, 410, 412, 414, 426, 428, 429, 431, 435, 436, 439, 443, 447, 451, 452, 453, 454, 455, 456, 457, 460, 461, 464, 465, 466, 468, 483, 487, 500, 501, 507, 510, 512, 515, 519, 520, 521, 526-528, 529, 530, 538, 539-540, 541, 552, 556, 558, 560, 572, 574, 576, 578, 584, 587-589, 590, 597, 616, 618, 621, 622, 623, 624, 625, 626, 632, 635, 636, 637, 638, 648, 650, 651, 653, 656, 657, 659, 660, 661, 667, 668, 669, 671, 672, 685, 687, 692, 694, 709, 727, 729, 731, 745, 750, 752-753, 754, 756, 769, 771, 773, 774, 775, 778, 795, 798, 800, 805-806, 815, 836-837, 847, 848, 849, 851-852, 868, 871, 872, 879, 886, 888, 892, 893-896
Buddhist Caves, Junāgadh, India, 410
Buginese (people), 115, 839, 840-841, 842
Buhkara, Afghanistan, 280, 333
Builders Labourer Federation, 784
Buke-Yashiki (Warrior Museum), Aizu-Wakamatsu, Japan, 12
Bukhara, Bukhara, Uzbekistan, 74, **163-167,** 240, 417, 458, 473, 720, 722
Bukhara, Uzbekistan, 163-167
Bukit Larangam, Singapore, 758
Bukka I, king of Vijayanagara, 855
Buland Darwāza (Lofty Gate), Fatehpur Sīkri, India, 260, 263
Buleleng, Bali, Indonesia, 69
Bull Temple, Bangalore, India, 92, 95
Bullock, G.H., 604, 605
Bullocky Point, Australia, 208
Bunbury, Thomas, 642
Bund, Shanghai, China, 736, 738
Bundelkhand, India, 120, 850
Buner, Pakistan, 798
Bunnerong, Botany Bay, Australia, 156
Bunninyong, Victoria, Australia, 75
Bunraku-za (Bunraku Theatre), Ōsaka, Japan, 652
Burdwān, India, 136, 137, 168
Burial mounds, Kashihara, Japan, 460-461, 462-463
Buriganga River, 225
Burma. *See* Myanmar
Burma Independence Army, 558
Burma National Army, 558
Burma Road, Myanmar, 558, 560, 880
Burmese Wars, 310
Burnes, Sir Alexander, 166, 441
Burns, Thomas, 234
Burt, T.S., 469
Busbus, Jolo, Philippines, 404
Busby, James, 859, 860, 861
Busby, William, 860, 861
Bussy, Charles (marquis de), 369
Buxar, Bihār, India, 168-171
Būyid Dynasty, 280
Buzhou, China, 216
Buzurg Khan of Kokand, 458
Bwansa, Philippines, 403
Byakkotai (White Tiger Brigade), Japan, 12, 13
Byinnyu (king of Bago), 879
Byōdō-in Temple, Uji, Japan, 517
Byrd, Richard, 237
Byrne, John Charles, 820
Byron, John, 818-819
Byron, Robert, 71
Byzantine Empire, 239

Caballo Island, Philippines, 204
Cable, Mildred, 241, 323
Cain (biblical), 715
Caitanya (Bengali religious leader), 697
Cakaudrove, Vanua Levu, Fiji, 264, 266
Cakobau, Seru, 264, 266, 267, 268
Cakobau, Sir George, 268
Calcutta, West Bengal, India, 9, 121, 137, 140, 142, 143, 168, 169, 170, 171, **172-176,** 188, 189, 222, 223, 226, 227, 278, 310, 475, 535, 547, 550, 551, 659, 679, 680, 682, 697
Caldron (Ding) Gate, Luoyang, China, 538
Caldrons, Luoyang, China, 541
Caledonian Park, Dunedin, New Zealand, 237, 238
Caledonian Union (New Caledonia), 647
Calicut, India, 284, 711
Callao, Peru, 820, 843
Caloocan City, Philippines, 565
Cāḷukya Dynasty, 142, 252-253, 256, 259, 435, 436-437, 552, 626, 763-764
Cambay, India, 6
Cambodia, 31-34, 52, 53-54, 56, 59, 98, 99, 158, 304, 329, 331, 332, 353, 356, 530, 531, 533, 568, 659, 771, 772, 773, 851, 852, 854
Cambridge University, England, 251
Camões, Luis Vaz de, 542, 545
Campbell, Colin, 536
Campbell, Joseph, 254
Canberra, Australia, 210
Candi Apit, Prambanan, Indonesia, 694
Candi Sewu, Prambanan, Indonesia, 692
Candra Gupta II (emperor of India), 837
Candra Gupta Maurya (emperor of India), 186, 408, 608

Canning (viscount), 174
Canterbury Cathedral, England, 174
Canton. *See* Guangzhou, Guangdong, China
Cao family, 241
Cape Banks, Australia, 153
Cape Breton Island, Nova Scotia, Canada, 548
Cape Esperance, Guadalcanal, 300
Cape Horn, 395, 828
Cape Malay, 103
Cape of Birds. *See* Galle, Sri Lanka
Cape of Good Hope, 103, 144, 201, 395, 544, 584, 711, 782, 787
Cape Solander, Australia, 153
Cape Sutherland, Australia, 153
Capron, Horace, 319
Captain China. *See* Li Han
Captain Cook's Landing Place, Australia, 156
Carabao Island, Philippines, 204
Carboni, Raffaello, 77
Cargill, David, 266, 268
Cargill, Edward, 237
Cargill, William, 234
Carlson, Evans F., 877
Carnarvon. *See* Port Arthur, Tasmania, Australia
Carnatic mill, Madras, India, 550
Carnatic region, India, 548, 551, 679, 680
Caron, François, 343
Carp Castle (Ri-jō), Hiroshima, Japan, 349
Carpenter, Frank W., 405
Carpenter Street, Kuching, Malaysia, 499
Carteret, Philip, 673, 674
Cary, William, 266
Casa Garden, Macau, 545
Cascade, Norfolk Island, Australia, 641, 642
Caspian Sea, 276, 718
Castilla, Ramon, 820
Castle, Hikone, Japan, 338, 339
Castle, Hirado, Japan, 340, 343, 344
Castle, Hirosaki, Japan, 345, 347
Castle, Kanazawa, Japan, 434
Castle of Ōta Dōkan, Tōkyō, Japan, 822-824
Castle of the Crane (Tsuruga-jō), Aizu-Wakamatsu, Japan), 10, 11, 12-13
Castle, Ōsaka, Japan, 338, 650, 651
Castle Peak, Hong Kong, 358
Castle, Wuchang, China, 866
Castlereagh, Australia, 863, 865
Castles, Kyōto, Japan, 636, 638
Castries, de (French colonel in Indochina), 232
Cathay. *See* China
Cathedral, Lahore, Pakistan, 525
Cathedral, Nagasaki, Japan, 615
Cathedral, Nouméa, New Caledonia, 646, 647
Cathedral of Notre Dame, Ho Chi Minh City, Vietnam, 354
Cathedral of St. Thomas, Bombay, India, 143
Cathedral of the Redemption, Delhi, India, 223
Cathedral of the Sacred Heart, Delhi, India, 223
Catherine (saint), 286
Catherine of Braganza, 142
Catholicism. *See* Roman Catholicism
Cattle Point. *See* Bennelong Point, Sydney, Australia
Caturbhuja Temple, Khajurāho, India, 470
Caucasus Mountains, 720
Caucasus, Soviet Union, 167
Caunsatha Yogini, Kajurāho, India, 469, 470
Cauvery Delta, India, 125, 809, 812
Cauvery River, 501, 503, 552, 809
Cavagneri, Louis, 476
Cave houses, Yanan, China, 874, 875, 876, 878
Cave of Scriptures, Dunhuang, China, 244, 246
Cave of 10,000 Buddhas, Yanan, China, 878
Cave temples, Ajanta, India, 552
Cave temples, Elephanta Island, India, 252, 253-254
Cave temples, Ellora, India, 552
Cave temples, Mahābalipuram, India, 552, 554
Cave temples, Nāsik, India, 625, 626, 628
Caves, Ajanta, India, 14, 15-19, 21-26
Caves, Barābar, India, 276
Caves, Dunhuang, China, 239, 240, 241, 242-246
Caves, Elephanta Island, India, 252, 253-255
Caves, Ellora, India, 256-257, 259
Caves, Junāgadh, India, 410
Caves of Baba Pyara, Junāgadh, India, 410
Caves, Qixia Shan, China, 616
Caves, Sarawak, Malaysia, 629-631
Caves of Tan Yao, Datong, China, 212, 213, 214, 540, 893-896
Cavite, Philippines, 204-207
Cawnpore. *See* Kānpur, India
Cebu City, Cebu, Philippines, 177-181, 899
Cebuanos (people), 177, 181
Cedi Dynasty. *See* Cheti Dynasty
Celebes. *See* Sulawesi, Indonesia
Cemeteries, Āgra, India, 5
Centenary Chapel, Tongatapu Island, Tonga, 830
Central Intelligence Agency (United States), 356
Central Java, Indonesia, 147-152, 692-696
Central Medical School, Suva, Fiji, 830
Central Mosque, Ho Chi Minh City, Vietnam, 354
Central Polynesian Land and Commercial Company, 725
Ceremony of the Sword (Sikh rite), 28
Cetiyagirī. *See* Sānchi, Madhya Pradesh, India
Ceylon. *See* Sri Lanka
Chach (founder of Hindu dynasty), 371
Chachick Deo (ruler of Jaisalmer), 388
Chaḍdanta Jātaka painting, Ajanta, India, 17
Chagatai (son of Genghis Khan; ruler of Hami), 321, 333, 457
Chagatai khanate, 164-165, 241, 333, 457-458
Chaitanya Singh (rāja of Bishnupur), 136, 137
Chakkarapani Temple, Kumbakonam, India, 501
Chakkraphat (king of Ayutthaya), 56
Chakkri Dynasty, 96, 775
Chakkri Maha Prasad, Bangkok, Thailand, 97
Chakra Tīrtha, Rāmeswaram, India, 716
Chakrasuri (god), 601
Chalmers, Thomas, 234
Chāḷukyan Dynasty, 125, 837
Cham Dynasty, 31, 33, 54, 353, 354, 362
Chama Devi (queen of the Mons), 182
Chambal River, 835
Chamberlain, Azaria, 46
Chamberlain, Lindy and Michael, 46
Champa, kingdom of, 353, 362
Champasak, kingdom of, 532, 851, 852
Chan Buddhism, 526, 527
Chand, Prem. *See* Prem Chand
Chand Bardāī (Indian poet), 20
Chandannagar, India, 172
Chandanpura Mosque, Chittagong, Bangladesh, 189
Chandapuri, Laos, 851
Chandela Dynasty, 468-469
Chandelās (Indian ruler), 117
Chandernagore, India, 679, 680, 681
Chandīgarh, Haryāna, India, 30
Chāndpur Affair, 189
Chandra (god). *See* Soma
Chandra Mahal, Jaipur, India, 386
Chandra Mahal, Junāgarh Fort, Bīkaner, India, 132
Chandradeva (Gāhaḍavāla king of India), 50
Chandragiri, raja of, 547
Chandragupta (Mauryan king of India), 837
Chandrakasem Palace, Ayutthaya, Thailand, 59
Chang Kien (Chinese envoy), 72
Chang Lu, China, 333
Chang Xueliang (Chinese general), 875
Chang'an. *See* Xian, Shaanxi, China
Changchun, China, 743, 749
Changi, Singapore, 761
Changsu (king of Koguryŏ), 484
Chankramana (Holy Walk), Bodh Gayā, India, 140
Chao Phraya Delta, 96
Chao Phraya River, 52, 53, 58, 96, 99, 182, 184
Chao Phraya Valley, 52, 53-54
Chao Sam Phraya Museum, Ayutthaya, Thailand, 59
Chaotian Gong (Heaven-facing Palace) Temple Museum, Nanjing, China, 616, 619, 620
Char Chato, Kābul, Afghanistan, 416, 417
Charles II (king of Great Britain), 142, 712
Charley, Philip, 865
Chārminār (Four Minarets), Hyderābād, India, 366
Charnock, Job, 172, 173
Chasma Shai, Srīnagar, India, 769
Chaṣtana (Kshatrapa ruler of Ujjain), 837
Chateau Tongariro, Tongariro, New Zealand, 834
Chattar Manzil (Umbrella Palaces), Lucknow, India, 534
Chattar Niwas, Junāgarh Fort, Bīkaner, India, 132
Chatwin, Bruce, 71
Chauhān Dynasty, 20-21
Chaul, India, 142
Chaumukha Temple, Mount Ābu, India, 600, 602
Cheah (clan), 667
chedis. *See* Pagoda(s)
Chel Zina, Kandahār, Afghanistan, 441
Chen Bridge, Henan, China, 422
Chen Cheng (ambassador of Yongle), 335
Chen Dynasty, 304
Chen Yi (governor of Taiwan), 794
Chen Youjing (founder of Wuchang kingdom), 866
Chenāb River, 608
Cheng Ching (king of Taiwan), 792-793
Cheng Hao (Confucian doyen), 541
Cheng Tien-fu. *See* Fort Provintia, Tainan, Taiwan, China
Cheng Wang (Chinese king), 538
Cheng Yi (Confucian doyen), 541
Chenla, Cambodia, 31, 353
Chennai. *See* Madras, Tamil Nādu, India
Chenrezi (Buddhist god), 528
Chenrezi Statue, Lhasa, Tibet, China, 526
Cheribon, Indonesia, 395
Cherry Blossom Festival, Hirosaki, Japan, 345, 347
Chesda (king of Thailand), 98, 99
Chet Singh (Kāshīrāj king of Vārānasī), 850
Cheti Dynasty, 122, 699
Chettiars (money-lenders), 880
Chhatarpur, Madhya Pradesh, India, 468, 469
Chiang Kai-shek, 216, 307, 360, 620, 737, 742, 748, 794, 868, 873, 874, 875-876, 877
Chiang Mai, Chiang Mai, Thailand, 54, 56, **182-185,** 851
Chiang Saen, Thailand, 182
Chichi Jima, Japan, 379, 382
Chidori airfield, Iwo Jima, Japan, 379
Chien Chen. *See* Ganjin
Chieng Kwang, Laos, 86
Chiengtianmen. *See* Gate of Heavenly Peace, Forbidden City, Beijing, China
Chigitia (people), 308
Chihkan Tower, Tainan, Taiwan, China, 793, 794
Chijung-wang (king of Silla), 509
Chikamatsu Monzaemon (playwright), 651
Chikubushima Island, Japan, 338
Child of Krakatau. *See* Anak Krakatau, Krakatau, Indonesia
Childs, Joseph, 642
Chile, 247-251, 264
Chilianwālla, India, 29
Chilla of Badar Shāh, Chittagong, Bangladesh, 189

Ch'ilsongsa Temple, Chŏnju, South Korea, 195
Chin-han (tribe), 509
Chin-hung (king of Silla), 486, 511
China, 13, 40-43, 52-53, 57, 58, 60, 70, 71, 73, 79, 80, 82, 84, 87, 96, 99, 101, 103, 105-112, 113, 140, 147, 150, 156, 160, 161, 163, 164, 166, 172, 177, 180, 181, 182, 195, 197, 206, 208, 210, 212-217, 230, 239-241, 242-246, 266, 268, 270, 272, 276, 286, 289, 293-297, 302-307, 317, 321-324, 325-328, 329, 330, 331, 332, 340, 341, 344, 347, 349, 350, 353-354, 356, 358-361, 364, 376, 377, 386, 392, 396, 397, 403, 405, 414, 418, 420-425, 451, 453, 454, 456-459, 460, 461, 462, 463, 467, 473, 482, 483, 484, 485, 486, 487, 497, 498, 509, 510, 511, 512, 513, 515, 517, 518, 520, 521, 526-529, 533, 538-541, 542, 544-545, 546, 560, 565, 566, 567, 568, 580, 582, 583-584, 585, 587, 590, 604, 606, 607, 613, 616-620, 621, 632, 636, 644, 646, 648, 650, 651, 652, 661, 662, 663, 667, 668, 671, 701-703, 704-706, 707-709, 710, 711, 718, 720, 732-738, 739-743, 744-749, 750-753, 758, 759, 760, 773, 776-780, 781, 785, 788, 790-794, 798, 806, 809, 813-817, 820, 839, 844, 852, 853, 866-869, 870-873, 874-878, 880, 884-887, 890, 893-896, 897, 900, 901-905
China Sea, 451, 732
China Street, Kuching, Malaysia, 499
Chinamosta (god), 135
Chinatown, Georgetown, Malaysia, 667
Chinatown, Jakarta, Indonesia, 397
Chinatown, Singapore, 760, 761
Chincha Islands, Peru, 251
Chindwin River, 558
Chinese City, Shanghai, China, 732
Chinese Communist Party, 732, 736, 737, 738, 742, 743, 868, 873, 874-878, 904
Chinese mestizos. *See* Mestizo de Sangley
Chinese Parian, Manila, Philippines, 568
Chingopomari. *See* Mount Everest
Chini Ka Rauza, Āgra, India, 4
Chinnery, George, 545
Chinsura, India, 172, 679
Chintamani Temple, Bīkaner, India, 129
Chionite (people), 439
Chir Tope. *See* Dharmarājika Stupa, Taxila, Pakistan
Chisholm, R.F., 550
Chishti (sect), 260
Chit Mandir. *See* Mān Singh Palace, Gwalior, India
Chitor, India. *See* Chittaurgarh, Rājasthān, India
Chitrang (Rājput leader), 191
Chitrasena. *See* Mahendravarman I
Chitrashala Hill, Guwāhāti, India, 310
Chittagong, Chittagong, Bangladesh, 168, **186-190,** 310
Chittagong Harbor, Bangladesh, 187, 188, 189
Chittakhana Chowk, Junāgadh, India, 413
Chittaurgarh, Rājasthān, India, 22, **191-194,** 388, 562-563
Cho, China, 540
Chobo-ji. *See* Rokkakudō, Kyōto, Japan
Ch'oe Che-u (religious leader), 196
Ch'oe Pu, 741
Ch'oe Si-hyŏng (religious leader), 196, 197
Chogqing, China, 620
Chokpori Hill, Lhasa, Tibet, China, 528, 529
Chŏlla. *See* North Chŏlla, South Korea
Cholon (Great Market), Ho Chi Minh City, Vietnam, 354, 356, 357
Chomolungma. *See* Mount Everest
Ch'omsong-dae, Kyŏngju, South Korea, 510
Chon Pong-jun (Korean rebellion leader), 197
Chŏnbuk National University, Chŏnju, South Korea, 197
Ch'ondogyo (sect), 197
Chongging, China, 868, 877
Ch'ongma-ch'ong (Heavenly Horse Tomb), Kyŏngju, South Korea, 514
Chŏngnimsa Pagoda, Puyŏ, South Korea, 486, 487
Chongxing Temple, Shanhaiguan, China, 742
Chongzhen (Ming emperor of China), 741
Chŏnju, North Chŏlla, South Korea, 195-198, 512
Chŏnju-Iri-Kunsan, South Korea, 197
Chor Bakr, Bukhara, Uzbekistan, 166
Chor Minor, Bukhara, Uzbekistan, 166
Chor Soo Kong (Buddhist priest), 668
Choranaga (Sinhalese robber-king of Sri Lanka), 38
Chōshū, Japan, 12, 520
Chosŏn, South Korea, 196
Chota Katrā, Dhākā, Bangladesh, 225
Chota Nāgpur Plateau, 134
Christian, Arabella, 675
Christian, Fletcher, 642, 673, 674, 675, 819, 828
Christian, Sarah, 642
Christian, Thursday October, 675, 676
Christianity 24, 57, 58, 62, 73, 94, 107, 113, 163, 173, 174, 176, 177, 184, 189, 196, 203, 251, 263, 266, 271, 284, 286, 288, 289, 298, 306, 319, 320, 321, 330, 340, 341, 342, 343, 344, 347, 353, 354, 361, 403, 405, 406, 448, 449, 451, 452, 456, 457, 466, 500, 523, 544, 612, 613, 644, 646, 667, 676, 706, 710, 711, 712, 713, 725, 736, 752, 787, 790, 798, 812, 814, 815-816, 820, 824, 828-829, 839, 844-845, 850, 859, 872, 884, 900. *See also specific denominations*
Chu, China, 293, 884
Chua Ngoc Hoang. *See* Emperor of Jade Pagoda, Ho Chi Minh City, Vietnam
Chudasma Dynasty, 410, 764
Chugoku, Japan, 350
Chūgūji nunnery, Ikaruga, Japan, 621
Chuitai, Kaifeng, China, 420
Chulalongkorn (Rama V; king of Thailand), 97, 99, 150
Chunār, India, 730
Ch'ungch'ŏng, South Korea, 487
Ch'ungju, South Korea, 512
Chungking. *See* Chongging, China
Chūrāman (Indian rebel leader), 577
Church, Bassein, Myanmar, 802
Church of England Melanesian Mission, Norfolk Island, Australia, 642
Church of Our Lady of the Holy Rosary, Chittagong, Bangladesh, 189
Church of Our Lady of the Rosary, Dhākā, Bangladesh, 225
Church of St. Andrew, Karāchi, Pakistan, 448, 450
Church of St. George, Āgra, India, 5
Church of St. George, Penang, Malaysia, 667
Church of St. James, Sydney, Australia, 783
Church of St. John, Bombay, India, 143-144
Church of St. John, Calcutta, India, 173
Church of St. John, Peshāwar, Pakistan, 671
Church of St. Thomas, Quilon, India, 712
Church of San Agustin, Manila, Philippines, 566
Church of the Holy Resurrection, Dhākā, Bangladesh, 226
Church of Tonga, 830
Churches, Colombo, Sri Lanka, 201
Churches, Delhi, India, 223
Churches, Dunedin, New Zealand, 236, 237
Churches, Macau, 543, 544
Churches, Madras, India, 547, 549, 550
Churches, Melaka, Malaysia, 583
Churches, Nagasaki, Japan, 612, 613, 615
Churches, Norfolk Island, Australia, 640, 642
Churches, Thanjāvūr, India, 812
Churches, Tianjin, China, 815, 816
Churches, Tongatapu Island, Tonga, 830
Churches, Windsor, Australia, 864, 865
Churchgate Station, Bombay, India, 144
Churchill, Winston, 360, 473, 614
Churning of the Sea of Milk (mythology), 33
Ci En Si (Temple of Great Good Will), Xian, China, 872
Circassia, 166
Circuit House, Chittagong, Bangladesh, 189
Circular Quay, Australia, 783, 784
Citadel, Ahmadābād, India, 6
Citadel, Delhi, India, 1, 218, 220
Citadel, Hanoi, Vietnam, 331
Citadel, Hue, Vietnam, 362, 364
Citong Cheng. *See* Quanzhou, Fujian, China
Citragupta Temple, Khajurāho, India, 468, 469
City Hall, Melaka, Malaysia, 586
City of Angels. *See* Bangkok, Thailand
City of God (sect), 234
City of Khan. *See* Beijing, China
City of Roses. *See* Nāsik, Mahārāshtra, India
City of the Name of God. *See* Macau
City of Victory. *See* Bijāpur, Karnātaka, India
City Palace, Jaipur, India, 383, 386
Civic Center, Dunedin, New Zealand, 238
Civil War, American, 144, 207, 266, 820, 846
Cixi (empress dowager of China), 107, 108, 816
Clarke, Sir Charles Noble Arden, 499
Clarke, Marcus, 691
Clavell, James, 342
Clavijo, Ruy González de, 720
Clay, Bertie, 174
Clifton, Karāchi, Pakistan, 448, 450
Clive, Robert, 123, 168, 171, 172, 369, 437, 548, 679, 680, 681, 682
Clock Tower, Zhengzhou, China, 902, 904
Closed Eyes Pavilion. *See* Ankh Michauli Pavilion, Fatehpur Sīkri, India
Co Loa Fortress, Ke Chu, Vietnam, 329
Cochin, kingdom of, 710, 711, 713
Cochin-China. *See* Vietnam
Cocks, Richard, 342
Cōdas. *See* Cōḷa Dynasty
Coedès, George, 664
Coen, Jan Pieterszoon, 89, 396
Coilon. *See* Quilon, Kerala, India
Cōḷa Dynasty, 37, 39, 435, 501-502, 555, 684-685, 710, 714, 809, 811, 812
Colaba Peninsula, 144
Cold Mountain Temple. *See* Hanshan Si, Suzhou, China
Collam. *See* Quilon, Kerala, India
College, Vārānasī, India, 850
College at Tonga, 830
College, Fort William, Calcutta, India, 173
College (Hindu), Calcutta, India, 174
College (Islamic Intermediate), Chittagong, Bangladesh, 189
College, Mohenjo-daro, Pakistan, 597
College, Norfolk Island, Australia, 642
College, Richmond, Australia, 865
Collet, Joseph, 115
Collins, Larry, 473
Collyer Quay, Singapore, 761
Coloane Island, Macau, 542, 546
Cologne, Germany, 351
Colombo, Sri Lanka, 199-203, 272, 273, 274, 443, 446
Colon Street, Cebu City, Philippines, 180
Columbus, Christopher, 87
Commandant's House, Port Arthur, Australia, 691
Commercial Square. *See* Raffles Place, Singapore
Commissariat Store. *See* All Saints' Church, Norfolk Island, Australia
Communist Party of China. *See* Chinese Communist Party
Communist Party of India, 176

Compagnie Calédonienne des Nouvelles-Hébrides, 846
Conceiçao bastion, Galle, Sri Lanka, 272
Conch Shell Hall (Sazae-dō), Aizu-Wakamatsu, Japan, 12
Confucian Academy, Chŏnju, South Korea, 196
Confucian Temple, Tainan, Taiwan, China, 792, 794
Confucianism, 195, 327, 329, 330, 331, 353, 364, 376, 460, 483, 510, 538, 539, 578, 651, 701, 707-709, 792, 871, 893
Confucius, 707-709
Congress of Vienna, 787
Connaught Circus, Delhi, India, 223
Connaught Place, Delhi, India, 223
Conolly, Arthur, 166
Conservatorium of Music, Sydney, Australia, 784
Constantia. *See* La Martiniere's School, Lucknow, India
Constantinople. *See* İstanbul, Turkey
Conti, Nicolo di, 855-856
Convent of Nau Bahar (New Convent), Balkh, Afghanistan, 73
Conventions of Beijing, 814
Convents, Datong, China, 213
Cooch Behar, Bengal, 751
Cook, James, 153-154, 156, 250, 265, 397, 639, 644, 724, 781, 785, 787, 788, 828, 832, 844, 859
Cook Islands, 844
Cooks River, 153, 154, 156
Coomaraswamy, Ananda K., 15, 18
Coombe, Anna Josepha, 639
Coote, Eyre, 548
Cooum River, 547
Coral Sea, 300
Corcuera (Spanish conquistador), 404
Cordillera Central mountains, 177
Cornwallis, Charles, 94, 188, 310
Coromandel Coast, India, 202, 547, 548, 680, 809, 812
Corregidor Island, Cavite, Philippines, 204-207, 569
Corstorphine, New Zealand, 237
Cosmos Indicopleustus (monk), 710
Coster, Willem, 273
Cotabato, Philippines, 406, 897, 900
Coulon. *See* Quilon, Kerala, India
Council Hall, Bombay, India, 144
Council House, Delhi, India, 223
Counter-Reformation, 288, 403, 843
Court House, Kuching, Malaysia, 500
Courthope, Nathaniel, 89
Coutinho, Antonio de Sousa, 201
Covent Garden, London, England, 14
Cox, William, 863, 865
Coyett (Dutch governer in Taiwan), 791
Crane, Tankerville Alexander, 641
Crane Hill. *See* Tsurugaoka, Kamakura, Japan
Crane Mosque, Yangzhou, China, 887
Crater Lake, 834
Crimea, 166
Crimean War, 174
Cromwell, Oliver, 90, 712
Cross, William, 266, 268
Crown Colony of the Straits Settlements, 667, 760
Crusades, 366
Crystal Palace, London, England, 14, 92
Cuba, 204, 567
Cubbon (viceroy of India), 94
Cubbon Park, Bangalore, India, 94, 95
Cuddalore, India, 548
Cui Hao (Chinese official), 212
Cullen, John, 833-834
Cultural Office Museum, Hami, China, 324
Cultural Revolution (China), 297, 324, 328, 459, 529, 545, 709, 737-738, 752, 876, 896
Cunningham, Sir Alexander, 140, 141, 469, 577, 595, 657, 659, 727, 806
Curzon, George (Lord Curzon), 5, 175, 223, 227, 604, 671, 718
Customs House, Sydney, Australia, 783-784
Cuttack, India, 121
Cwm, Himalaya Mountains, 605, 606
Cyrus II (the Great: king of Persia), 71, 414, 439, 578

Da Nang, Vietnam, 331, 354, 365
Da River, 242
Da Yan Ta (Great Wild Goose Pagoda), Xian, China, 871-872, 873
Dacca, India. *See* Dhākā, Bangladesh
Daceyville, Australia, 156
Dacheng Dian (Hall of Great Achievements), Qufu, China, 709
Dadu. *See* Beijing, China
Daendels, H.W., 103, 397
dagabas (Buddhist shrines), Anuradhapura, Sri Lanka, 35, 37, 38, 39
Dagestan, 166
Dagon. *See* Yangon, Myanmar
Dagu forts, Tianjin, China, 813, 814, 816
Dahe Village, China, 904
Dahong Qiao (Great Rainbow Bridge), Yangzhou, China, 886
Dai La. *See* Hanoi, Vietnam
Dai Viet, kingdom of, 329, 353, 362
Daibutsu. *See* Buddha
Daigan-ji, Miyajima, Japan, 590
Daigo II (emperor of Japan), 429, 518
Daigoku-den (Hall of State), Kyōto, Japan, 520
Dainichi. *See* Vairocana
Dairatul-Maarif-it Osmania, Hyderābād, India, 369
Daitoku-ji, Kyōto, Japan, 518, 520
Daiya River, 632
Daiyūninbyō, Nikkō, Japan, 632, 637
Dajin Men (Great Golden Gate), Nanjing, China, 619
Dakak, Zamboanga, Philippines, 900
Daksha Prajapati (legendary king), 762
Dalai Lama, 528, 529, 604, 750, 751, 752
Dales, George, 595
Dalhousie, Lord (British governor general of India), 535, 536
Dalian, China, 748
Daliang. *See* Kaifeng, Henan, China
Dalmardan, Bishnupur, India, 136
Dalrymple, Alexander, 404
Damān, India, 8, 288, 289, 545
Damascus, Syria, 165, 562, 579, 720, 721, 769
Daming Si Temple, Yangzhou, China, 886
Damodar Singh (Bishnupur rebel), 136
Dan-no-Ura, Japan, 426, 518
Dandanqan, Turkmenistan, 281
Dandi (legendary), 479
Dandi salt march (India), 9
Danei Palace, Forbidden City, Beijing, China, 105
Daniel's Fort, Jolo, Philippines, 404
Danish East India Company, 57
Dante Alighieri Society, 865
Danyang, China, 616
Daoguang (Qing emperor of China), 732
Daowu Di (Tuoba emperor of China), 212
Dapitan City, Philippines, 900
Dar-ul-Aman, Afghanistan, 418
Dārā Shukōh (Mughal prince), 5, 22
Dargah, Ajmer, India, 20, 22, 23
Darius I (the Great; king of Persia), 414, 439, 474, 669
Darius III (king of Persia), 578
Darjeeling, India, 174
Darling, Ralph, 641
Darwin, Charles, 208, 788
Darwin, Northern Territory, Australia, 208-211
Darwin Compound, Australia, 209
Darwin Institute of Technology, Australia, 211
Darwin Performing Arts Centre, Australia, 211
Darwin Reconstruction Commission, Australia, 210
Darya Khān (adviser to Mahmūd II), 563
Das, Gopabandhu, 124
Das, Krishna, 680
Das, Madhusudhan, 124
Daśabalagarbha, 659
Daśaratha, 47
Dashun Dynasty, 216
Daska. *See* Dhaksa
Date Masamune (Japanese warrior), 10
Datong, Shanxi, China, 212-217, 296, 539, 893
Datong Circuit, 214, 215
Datsueba (goddess), 429
Datu Abang Openg (Malay leader), 499
Datu Sen (king of Sri Lanka), 754
Daud Khān, Mohammad, 418
Daulat Prole, Bīkaner, India, 132
Daulat Rāo Sindhia (ruler of Gwalior), 314, 316
Daulatābād, India, 142, 292
Daulatbagh, China, 457
Davies, Frederick, 156
Davies, John P., 877
Daxing. *See* Xian, Shaanxi, China
Daxiong Baodian Hall, Yangzhou, China, 887
Daxiong Hall, Datong, China, 214
Day, Francis, 547
Daybul. *See* Debal, Pakistan
de Gaulle, Charles, 647
de Havilland, Thomas, 550
de Jesus, Bernard, 225
de Klerk, Reinier, 397
De Mello (Portuguese general), 445
de Meuron (Dutch nobleman), 202
De Silva, K.M., 686
Debal, Pakistan, 801, 802
Deccan region, India, 8, 47, 125, 128, 220, 222, 256, 290-292, 366, 399, 410, 437, 563, 625, 626, 627, 699, 812, 835, 837, 855
Deep Singh, Bāba (saint), 29
Deer Throne Hall, Mandalay, Myanmar, 557
Deh-i-Mazang gorge, Afghanistan, 418
Dehotsarga, Somnāth, India, 762
Dejima Island, 342, 343
Dekker, Eduard Douwes, 104
Delhi, Delhi, India, 1, 5, 6, 9, 20, 21, 73, 117, 120, 125, 129, 136, 142, 172, 174, 175, 176, 187, 188, **218-224,** 228, 261, 277, 282, 284, 292, 367, 371, 386, 388, 389, 399, 507, 508, 551, 669, 679, 681, 699, 720, 764, 767, 801, 803, 812, 837
Delhi Darwaji, Nāsik, India, 626
Delhi Gate, Āgra, India, 2
Delhi Gate, Māndu, India, 561-562
Delhi Sultanate, 218, 534, 561, 576, 626, 801, 802, 803, 812, 837, 848
Delightful Garden. *See* Shālīmār Bagh, Srīnagar, India
Demak, Central Java, Indonesia, 101, 102
Demetrios (Bactrian leader), 805
Demilitarized Zone (Vietnam), 365
Democracy Wall, Tiananmen Square, Beijing, China, 111
Den Chai, Thailand, 184
Deng Xiaoping, 108, 111, 297
Denison, William, 690
Denmark, 57, 172, 202, 545, 839
Denpasar, Bali, Indonesia, 70
Dent, Alfred, 160, 161
Dent and Company, 360
Deogiri. *See* Daulatābād, India
Dervishism, 165, 166
Deshima Island, Nagasaki, Japan, 613-614, 615

Deshnok, India, 133
Deva Kota Temple, Junāgadh, India, 412
Devadhunga. *See* Mount Everest
Devamitra (king of Ayodhyā), 49
Devānampiyatissa (Sinhalese king of Sri Lanka), 35, 37
Devapāla (Pāla king of eastern India), 657
Devarāya I (king of Vijayanagara), 856
Devarāya II (king of Vijayangara), 856
Devī (god), 576
Devī (wife of Aśoka), 729
Devi Jagadamba. *See* Jagadambī, Khajurāho, India
Devil's Market, Kaifeng, China, 423
Devoted Woman Temple. *See* Zhennü Temple, Shanhaiguan, China
Dewa Agung (Divine Ruler of Bali), 68, 69, 70
D'Ewes, John, 77
Dewey, George, 204, 569
Dhākā, Dhākā, Bangladesh, 225-229
Dhākeśwarī (goddess), 225
Dhaksa (king of Prambanan), 692
Dhaleśwarī River, 225
Dhalkisor River, 134
Dhammayangyi Temple, Pagan, Myanmar, 655
Dhammazedi (king of Bago), 61, 879
Dhammikarama Temple, Lorong Burmah, Penang, 668
Dhanadeva (king of Ayodhyā), 49
Dhaṅga (king of Chandela), 468
Dhanushkodi, Rāmeswaram, India, 715, 716
Dhār, India, 117, 561, 563, 835, 837
Dharmapāla (Pāla ruler of eastern India), 657, 659
Dharmapāla (ruler of Kotte Kingdom), 199, 201
Dharmarājika Stupa, Taxila, Pakistan, 805, 806
Dharmasoka (infant king of Sri Lanka), 687
Dharmsala, India, 529
Dhātusena (Sinhalese king of Sri Lanka), 38
Dhauli, India, 121, 837
Dhritarāshtra (Paṇḍavas leader), 505
Dhruva (Rāṣhṭrakūṭa king of the Deccan), 837
Dhu'l-Nun Beg (governor of Kandahār), 439-440
Dhūlkoṭ, Mathurā, India, 572
Di Made (Dewa Agung of Bali), 68, 69
Dianga Island, 187
Diaoyu Tai, Yangzhou, China, 886
Dias, Bartolomeu, 284
Dibalpur, India, 415
Diem, Ngo Dinh. *See* Ngo Dinh Diem
Dien Bien Phu, Vietnam, 230-233, 331, 355, 772
Dieng Plateau, Indonesia, 891
Diet Building, Tōkyō, Japan, 825
Dieu De National Pagoda, Hue, Vietnam, 362, 365
Digambara (Jainian sect), 191, 257
Digambara Temple, Mount Ābu, India, 600, 602
Dilawar Khān (Shihāb-ud-Dīn Ghūri; Afghan king of Mālwa), 561, 837
Dilwāra Temple, Mount Ābu, India, 600-602
Dīn-i Ilāhī (God's Religion), 262, 263, 383, 385
Dinapanah (Asylum of Faith), Delhi, India, 1
Ding (Caldron) Gate, Luoyang, China, 538
Dingxiang, China, 214
Dinh Dynasty, 329
Diodotus II (Seleucid satrap), 71, 578
Diogenes, 805
Dionysian cult, 254
Diponegoro (Javanese prince), 891-892
Dir, Pakistan, 798
Disneyland, Tōkyō, Japan, 434
Dispur, India, 308
Diu, India, 6, 8, 288, 289, 412
Divine Faith. *See* Dīn-i Ilāhī
Divodaśa (Tristu king), 505
Dīwān-i-Am (Hall of Public Audience), Amber, India, 24, 26
Dīwān-i-Am (Hall of Public Audience), Delhi, India, 222
Dīwān-i-Am (Hall of Public Audience), Fatehpur Sīkri, India, 261-262
Dīwān-i-Am (Hall of Public Audience), Junāgarh Fort, Bīkaner, India, 132
Dīwān-i-Am (Hall of Public Audience), Lahore, Pakistan, 523
Dīwān-i-Khas (Hall of Private Audience), Āgra, India, 4
Dīwān-i-Khas (Hall of Private Audience), Amber, India, 26
Dīwān-i-Khas (Hall of Private Audience), Delhi, India, 220, 222
Dīwān-i-Khas (Hall of Private Audience), Fatehpur Sīkri, India, 262
Dīwān Shurfa Khān (Mughal minister), 802
Dobama Asiayon (Burma), 880
Doctor's House, Windsor, Australia, 865
Dōkan, Ōta (feudal lord), 822-823
Dōkyō (Buddhist priest), 624
Dominican order, 403, 544
Dona Catherina (queen of Kandy), 443, 445
Dong Da, Hanoi, Vietnam, 330
Dong Kinh. *See* Hanoi, Vietnam
Dong Zhuo (Chinese rebellion leader), 539
Dongda Road, Quanzhou, China, 706
Donghu (people), 744
Dongjing. *See* Kaifeng, Henan, China
Donwun, Myanmar, 60
Doodoo (Bhatti chief), 389
Dorgon (Qing prince regent), 742, 747
Dōst Moḥammad Khān (ruler of Afghanistan), 81, 117, 118, 417, 441-442
Dōton (Japanese engineer), 650
Dōtonbori, Ōsaka, Japan, 650, 652
Dragon Mountain Hall. *See* Khoo Kongsi, Penang, Malaysia
Drake, Roger, 680
Drake, Sir Francis, 158
Drāviḍa Munnetra Kazhagham (India), 551
Dravidians, 37, 165, 599
Dreaming (Aboriginal creation mythology), 44
Drepung Monastery, Lhasa, Tibet, China, 528, 529, 750
Drinkwater-Bethune (British captain in Samoa), 725
Drum Tower, Nanjing, China, 616, 619
Drury, William, 545
Du Fu (poet), 420
Duanmen (Gate of Correct Demeanor), Forbidden City, Beijing, China, 106
Dube, S.C., 370
Dublin, Ireland, 173
Dubs, Adolph, 418
Duck Throne Hall, Mandalay, Myanmar, 557
Dughlat Khanate, 457
Duke of Clarence Island. *See* Tokelau, Territory of New Zealand
Duke of York Island. *See* Tokelau, Territory of New Zealand
Duladeo, Khajurāho, India, 470
Duncan, James, 443
Dunedin, South Island, New Zealand, 234-238
Dunedin and South Seas Exhibition of 1925 (New Zealand), 237
Dungar Singh (ruler of Bīkaner), 132
Dunhuang, Gansu, China, 321
  Dunhuang Town, 239-241, 540
  Mogao Caves, 239, 240, 241, **242-246**
Dunhuang Museum, China, 244
Dunhuang Research Institute, China, 241
Dupleix, Joseph François (governor of Pondicherry), 369, 680
Durand Line, 671
Durbar Square, Kāthmāndu, Nepal, 466
Durgā (goddess), 24, 133, 134, 135, 258, 466, 470, 601, 694, 811
Durgā Ratha, Mahābalipuram, India, 554
Durgā Temple, Adhar Devi, India, 602
Durrāni, Aḥmad Shāh (Afghan warrior), 28-29, 610
Durrāni Dynasty, 73-74, 417, 441
Duryodhana (Kaurava leader), 505
Dusit Palace, Bangkok, Thailand, 99
Dusun (people), 158
Dutch East India Company, 62, 68, 69, 88, 89, 90, 102, 103, 113, 114, 115, 201, 202, 288, 306, 342, 395-397, 445, 544, 568, 585, 613, 663, 712, 714, 790, 828, 839, 840, 841, 852, 888, 890, 891
Dutch East Indies. *See* Indonesia
Dutch Reform Church, 792
Dutroux-Bornier, Jean-Baptiste, 251
Duṭugümuṇu (Sinhalese king of Sri Lanka), 38
Dvāraka, India, 762
Dvaravati, kingdom of, 851
D'Wolf's Island. *See* Tokelau, Territory of New Zealand
Dyak (people), 158, 497
Dyer, Reginald, 29
Dzungar (people), 323, 458

Eaglehawk Neck, Australia, 688, 690
Earl, George Windsor, 208
Earlier Song Dynasty, 616
Earp, Thomas, 144
East Bengal. *See* Bangladesh
East Brunei. *See* Brunei Darussalam
East China Sea, 612
East India Company. *See* British East India Company; Danish East India Company; Dutch East India Company; French East India Company
East Indies. *See* Indonesia
East Java. *See* Java, Indonesia
East Mebon, Angkor, Cambodia, 31
East Pagoda, Guangzhou, China, 306
East Pakistan. *See* Bangladesh
East Rongbuk Glacier, 605
East Sea Road (Tōkaidō), Japan, 823, 824
East Timor, 210
East Town, Guangzhou, China, 306
Easter Island, Chile, 247-251, 723, 828
Eastern Baray, Angkor, Cambodia, 31
Eastern Court, Delhi, India, 223
Eastern (Later) Han Dynasty, 538, 539
Eastern Hills. *See* Higashiyama, Japan
Eastern Jin Dynasty, 212, 616, 744
Eastern Learning (religious movement), 196-197
Eastern Orthodoxy, 319
Eastern Turkistan. *See* Xinjiang Uighur Autonomous Region, China
Eastern Wei Dynasty, 244, 540
Eastern Zhou Dynasty, 538
Ebenezer, Australia, 865
Ebenezer Church, Australia, 865
Ecbatana, 71, 578
Echigo Mountains, 10
Eck, Diana L., 849
École des Arts Pratiques, Hanoi, Vietnam, 331
École Française d'Extrème-Orient, Hanoi, Vietnam, 331
Eden, George (earl of Auckland and governor general of India), 372, 417
Edinburgh, duke of. *See* Philip (prince consort of Great Britain)
Edo. *See* Tōkyō, Tōkyō, Japan
Edo-Mura (theme park), Nikkō, Japan, 638
Edo period. *See* Tokugawa Shōgunate
Edward VII (king of Great Britain), 223
Edwardes College, Peshāwar, Pakistan, 671
Edwards, Edward, 265, 724, 819
Edwards, Herbert, 610

Eesul (hermit), 388, 389, 392
Efate Island, Vanuatu, 843, 844, 846
Egmore, India, 548, 550
Egmore Railway Station, India, 550
Egypt, 142, 165, 186, 199, 412, 578-579, 595, 608, 718, 727, 871
Eindawya Pagoda, Mandalay, Myanmar, 556
Eisai (founder of Rinzai sect), 428
Eisenhower, Dwight, 233
Ekāmbareshwara Temple, Kānchipuram, India, 437
Ekanta Rāmeswaram, Mount Gandamadhana, India, 715
Ekathotsarot (king of Ayutthaya), 56, 57
El Alamein, Egypt, 300
Ele-ele (mythic first woman), 723
El Fraile Island, Philippines, 204
Elara (Tamil king of Sri Lanka), 37-38
Elephant Cave (Hathigumpha), India, 122
Elephant Gate (Ganesh Pol), Amber, Italy, 24, 26
Elephant Gate (Hathi Pol), Fatehpur Sīkri, India, 263
Elephant Palace (Hathi Mahal), Māndu, India, 563
Elephant stable, Vijayanagara, India, 856
Elephant Terrace, Angkor, Cambodia, 33
Elephant Throne Hall, Mandalay, Myanmar, 557
Elephanta Island, Mahārāshtra, India, 142, **252-255**
Elephant's Staircase, Lahore, Pakistan, 524
Elgin, Lord (James Bruce), 813, 814
Eliasara (tuimanua of Samoa), 725
Elizabeth I (queen of England), 158, 261, 849
Elizabeth II (queen of Great Britain), 784, 830
Elizabeth Farm House, Sydney, Australia, 782
Ellenborough, Lord (Edward Law), 314, 372, 417, 804
Ellice Islands. *See* Tuvalu
Elliott, Gilbert John. *See* Minto, earl of
Elliott, Russell, 676-677
Ellora, Mahārāshtra, India, 253, **256-259,** 552
Elphinstone, Mountstuart, 417, 628
Elphinstone College, Bombay, India, 144
Emancipation Edict (Tonga), 830
Emerald Buddha. *See* Phra Kaeo
Emillie Bell, Kyŏngju, South Korea, 512-513
Emperor of Jade Pagoda, Ho Chi Minh City, Vietnam, 354
Empress of India. *See* Victoria (queen of Great Britain)
Enele Maafu, 266
Engaku-ji, Kamakura, Japan, 429
Engels, Friedrich, 876
England. *See* Great Britain
English East India Company. *See* British East India Company
Enkiri-dera, Kamakura, Japan, 428, 429
Enma (god), 429
Enno-ji, Kamakura, Japan, 429
Enomoto Takeaki (Japanese admiral), 319
Enrile, Ponce, 570
Enryaku-ji, Hiei-zan, Japan, 517, 519
Ensen (chieftain), 323
Enshū (Buddhist priest), 795
Entsu-ji, Aizu-Wakamatsu, Japan, 12
Eora (people), 153
Ephthalites, 626
Epi Island, Vanuatu, 845
Erastianism, 234
Erastus, Thomas, 234
Erbervelt, Pieter, 397
Erdenzu Hiid, Karakorum, Mongolia, 451, 453, 454, 455
Ernakulam, India, 713
Erp, Thadeus van, 150
Erromango Island, Vanuatu, 844
Escape Cliffs, Australia, 208
Esen (Oirat Mongol leader), 214
Esfahān, Iran, 441
Esmā'īl Khan, 336
Espíritu Santo Island, Vanuatu, 843-844
Estaing, Jean-Baptiste-Charle-Henri-Hector d', 115
Ethnological Museum, Chittagong, Bangladesh, 189
Eua, Tonga, 828
Euphrates River, 491
Eureka Hill, Ballarat, Australia, 78
Eureka Hotel, Ballarat, Australia, 77, 78
Eureka Stockade, Ballarat, Australia, 75, 78
Euthydemus, 71
Evans, Charles, 606
Evans, George, 783
Everest, George, 604
Everett, A.H., 629
Evora, Portugal, 542
Ewe Hai Street, Kuching, Malaysia, 500
Exhibition Buildings, Dunedin, New Zealand, 237
Eyraud, Eugène, 251
Ezo. *See* Hokkaidō, Japan

Fa Ngum (ruler of Laos), 530, 531, 851
Fa Xian (Buddhist monk), 49, 80, 140, 199, 276, 456, 576, 616, 669, 800, 805, 806
Faguo (Buddhist monk), 894
Faisal Shaheed University of Engineering and Technology, Lahore, Pakistan, 525
Faiz Moḥammad Khān (ruler of Bhopāl), 119
Faizābād, India, 534
Faizābād-Ayodhyā, India, 47
Fakaofo. *See* Tokelau, Territory of New Zealand
Fale Fisi (Fijian House), Fiji, 264
Falkland Islands, 819
Fang Lizhi, 111, 112
Fang river valley, Thailand, 182
Fanning Island, 643
Fanuatapu Island, Western Samoa, 723
Farah Bakhsh. *See* Shālīmār Bagh, Srīnagar, India
Farruksiyar (emperor of India), 172, 222
Fata (Samoan rebel), 723
Fatahillah (Javanese general), 395
Fateh Bi Begum (wife of Dōst Moḥammad Kāhn), 117
Fateh (Victory) Gate, Jodhpur, India, 399
Fateh Singh (rāna of Chittaurgarh), 194
Fatehgarh. *See* Old Fort, Bhopāl, India
Fatehpur Sīkri, Uttar Pradesh, India, 2-3, 5, 24, 26, 222, **260-263**
Fatḥ 'Alī (Tālpur ruler of Sind), 804
Fatḥ 'Alī Shāh (ruler of Persia), 417
Fatḥ Jang (king of Kābul), 417
Fatḥ Khān Barakzāi (vizier of Kābul), 417
Fāṭima (daughter of prophet Muḥammad), 578, 579
Fatu (mythic first man), 723
Fauea (Samoan chief), 725
Faujdar Moḥammad Khān (ruler of Bhopāl), 119
Fazil Moḥammad Khān (Bhopāl rebel), 120
February 7th Square, Zhengzhou, China, 902, 904
Federation of Malaysia. *See* Malaysia
Federici, Cesare, 858
Feillet (governor of New Caledonia), 646
Fell, E. (British captain in Sānchi), 727
Feng. *See* Xian, Shaanxi, China
Feng (dowager empress of China), 213, 214
Feng Menglong (Chinese writer), 778
Feng Yuxiang (Chinese general), 216, 748
Fengtian, China, 747, 748, 749
Fengyang, China, 618
Fergana, China, 239, 240, 456
Ferganaborn Khoja Ahmad Kasani. *See* Makhdum-i Azam
Fergusson, James, 14, 858
Ferrell, John, 77
Ferry Berth, Mulifanua, Upolu Island, 723
Festival for Three Thousand Maidens, Kongo and Puyŏ, South Korea, 486, 487
Festival of the Ages (Jidai Matsuri), Kyōto, Japan, 518
Fetepore. *See* Fatehpur Sīkri, India
Fiaschi, Thomas, 865
Fiji, 264-268, 298, 299, 300, 643, 674, 723, 821, 827, 828, 830, 845
Fijian House (Fale Fisi), Fiji, 264
Filipina. *See* Philippines
Filipinos. *See* Philippines
Filose, Sir Michael, 316
Finau Ulukalala II (Tongan chief), 828
Finch, William, 523
Fine Art Museum, Ōsaka, Japan, 651
Finniss, B.T., 208
Firdawsi (poet), 163
Fire Mountain (Gunung Api), Banda Islands, Indonesia, 88, 89, 90
Firozābād, India, 220
First Anglo-Afghan War, 81, 144, 372, 417, 441-442, 476, 804
First Anglo-Burmese War, 63, 879
First Indochina War, 230-233, 331, 365, 533, 853
First Opium War, 306-307, 358-359, 735
First Pass Under Heaven, Shanhaiguan, China, 743
First Sikh War, 671
Fīrūz Shāh Tughluq (Indian sultan), 220, 802, 849
Firuzkuh, Afghanistan, 282, 414
Fish, H.S., 236
Fitch, Ralph, 5, 849-850
Fitzgerald, Richard, 865
FitzRoy (governor of Australia), 75
Five Big Surnames. *See* Goh Tai Seng
Five Dynasties period (China), 244, 246, 422, 541, 704, 739
Five Lakes, Fiji, 269, 271
Five Palace. *See* Panch Mahal, Fatehpur Sīkri, India
Five Phoenix Tower. *See* Wumen, Forbidden City, Beijing, China
Flagstaff House. *See* Teen Murti Bhavan, Delhi, India
Flinders, Matthew, 641
Floating Bridge, Quanzhou, China, 706
Flora Fountain. *See* Hutatma Chowk, Bombay, India
Flores Sea, 87
Florida Island, Solomon Islands, 298
Flowery Pagoda. *See* Huata, Guangzhou, China
Fogg Museum, Cambridge, Massachusetts, United States of America, 244
Folger, Mayhew, 676
Folklore Village, Takayama, Japan, 795
Fontanier, Henri, 816
Foochow. *See* Fuzhou, China
Forbes, Rosita, 721
Forbidden City, Beijing, China, 105-108, 109, 619, 708, 901
Forbidden City, Hanoi, Vietnam, 329
Forbidden Purple City, Hue, Vietnam, 364
Foreigner's Rock (Batu Feringghi), Penang, Malaysia, 668
Formosa. *See* Taiwan, China
Forster, E.M., 276
Forster, George, 282
Fort. *See also headings beginning with* Citadel
Fort, Āgra, Utter Pradesh, India, 1-2, 4, 5, 22, 193
Fort, Amber, India, 24, *25*, 26
Fort, Bhopāl, India, 117
Fort, Chittaurgarh, India, 191-194
Fort, Colombo, Sri Lanka, 199, 201, 202
Fort, Golconda, India, 290, 292, 366
Fort, Gwalior, India, 26, 312
Fort, Jaisalmer, India, 191
Fort, Kuala Kedah, Malaysia, 665
Fort Aguada, Goa, India, 289
Fort Ajayagarh, Khajurāho, India, 469
Fort Alfonso XII, Jolo, Philippines, 404
Fort Asturias, Jolo, Philippines, 404

Fort Belgica, Banda Islands, Indonesia, 88, 89
Fort Concordia, Great Banda, Banda Islands, Indonesia, 89
Fort Cornwallis, Penang, Malaysia, 667
Fort Dufferin, Mandalay, Myanmar, 556, 557, 558
Fort Guia, Macau, 544
Fort Hill, Darwin, Australia, 208
Fort Hollandia, Great Banda, Banda Islands, Indonesia, 89
Fort Jamrud, Khyber Pass, North-West Frontier, Pakistan; Kābul, Afghanistan, 473
Fort Jamrud, Lahore, India, 473
Fort Junāgarh, Bīkaner, India, 129, 132, 133
Fort Kalinjar, Khajurāho, India, 468, 469
Fort Lahore, Pakistan, 523, 524, 525
Fort Mahoba, Khajurāho, India, 469
Fort Mandalay, Myanmar, 560
Fort Margherita, Kuching, Malaysia, 498, 500
Fort Marlborough, Bengkulu, Indonesia, 115, 116
Fort Museum, Madras, India, 548
Fort Nassau, Banda Islands, Indonesia, 88
Fort of Datu Daniel, Jolo, Philippines, 404
Fort of Jagaraga, Bali, Indonesia, 69
Fort of Junāgarh, Bīkaner, India, 129, 132, 133
Fort of Kempe Gowda, Bangalore, India, 95
Fort of Paknam, Bangkok, Thailand, 99
Fort Pilar, Zamboanga, Philippines, 898, 900
Fort Provintia, Tainan, Taiwan, China, 790, 791, 793, 794
Fort Revenge, Ai, Banda Islands, Indonesia, 89
Fort Rotterdam, Ujung Pandang, Indonesia, 839, 840, 841, 842
Fort St. David, Madras, India, 548
Fort St. George, Madras, India, 547, 548, 550
Fort San Pedro, Cebu City, Philippines, 181
Fort Santiago, Corregidor Island, Philippines, 204
Fort Speelwijk, Banten, West Java, Indonesia, 103
Fort Victoria, Ambon, Banda Islands, Indonesia, 89
Fort Vreedenburg, Yogyakarta, Indonesia, 890
Fort William, Calcutta, India, 172, 173, 174, 679, 680
Fort William College, Calcutta, India, 173
Fort Zeelandia, Tainan, Taiwan, China, 342, 790, 791, 794
Forts, Datong, China, 215
Forts, Delhi, India, 218, 220
Forts, Dhākā, Bangladesh, 225, 228
Forts, Lahore, Pakistan, 523, 524, 525
Forts, Lhasa, Tibet, China, 526
Forts, Macau, 544
Forts, Madras, India, 547, 548, 550
Forts, Melaka, Malaysia, 586
Forts, Tainan, Taiwan, China, 790, 791, 794
Forts of Dagu, Tianjin, China, 813, 814, 816
Foster, S.S., 725
Foucher, Albert, 727
Four Minarets. *See* Chārminār, Hyderābād, India
Foveaux, Joseph, 641
Fox, Robin Lane, 608
France, 34, 58, 90, 92, 94, 96, 97, 98, 99, 107, 115, 154, 172, 188, 202, 225, 230-233, 244, 274, 289, 298, 307, 316, 329, 330-331, 339, 353-355, 359, 364, 365, 369, 372, 385, 394, 438, 448, 503, 532-533, 545, 547, 548, 550, 557, 586, 604, 615, 639, 644, 646-647, 679, 680, 681, 682, 735, 736, 778, 785-789, 812, 813, 814, 815-816, 820, 821, 828, 830, 844, 846, 851, 853
Franchise League (New Zealand), 236
Francis Xavier. *See* Xavier, Francis (saint)
Franciscan order, 342, 403, 544, 612, 886
Franco-Prussian War, 646
Franklin, C.J., 469
Frederick, Caesar, 61
Free Church of Scotland, 234
Free Church of Tonga, 830
Free Trade Development Zone, Darwin, Australia, 210
Freedom Monument, Jakarta, Indonesia, 398
Freedom Square. *See* Medan Merdeka, Jakarta, Indonesia
French, Francesca, 241, 323
French East India Company, 353, 548
French Foreign Legion, 396
French Indochina, 206, 331, 354-355, 788
French Mekong Expedition, 532, 853
French Polynesia. *See* Polynesia
French quarter, Hue, Vietnam, 365
French School of the Far East, Vientiane, Laos, 852
Frere, Sir Bartle, 144
Frere Hall, Karāchi, Pakistan, 448
Fretsz (commandeur in Galle), 274
Friday Mosque. *See* Jāmi Masjid
Friendly Islands. *See* Tonga
Frum, Jon, 846
Fruzi Garden, Ghaznī, Afghanistan, 281
Fruzi Palace, Ghaznī, Afghanistan, 281
Fu Xi (mythic Chinese forefather), 40, 901
Fuchi (goddess), 269
Fudō-in Kondō, Hiroshima, Japan, 349
Fuji Five Lakes (Fuji Goko), Fujinomiya, Japan, 269
Fuji-Hakone-Izu National Park, Japan, 269, 271
Fuji-san. *See* Mount Fuji
Fuji Volcanic Zone, 269
Fuji-Yoshida, Japan, 271
Fujian, China, 568, 704-706, 791, 793, 794
Fujinomiya, Shizuoka, Japan, 269-271
Fujisan Hongu, Fujinomiya, Japan, 270
Fujiwara, Japan, 461, 621
Fujiwara family, 428, 515, 517, 518, 621, 622, 624
Fujiwara Michinaga (Japanese patriarch), 517
Fujiwara Nakamaro (Japanese regent), 624
Fujiwara no Tanetsugu (Kammu court member), 624
Fukae-no-ura. *See* Nagasaki, Nagasaki, Japan
Fukien, China, 358
Fukui, Japan, 431
Fukushima, Japan, 10-13
Fukushima Masanori, 349
Fukuyama, Japan, 317
Fulton, Henry, 641
Funan, Cambodia, 31, 353
Fushimi Inari, Kyōto, Japan, 515
Fusō-kyō (sect), 271
Futara-san, Nikkō, Japan, 632, 636
Futara-san Hongu, Nikkō, Japan, 632, 636
Futara-san Jinja, Nikkō, Japan, 632, 636, 637
Futuna Islands, 723, 828
Fuzhou, China, 705, 735, 790, 791, 813

Gadadhar Singh (Ahom king), 310
Gagan Mahal (Heavenly Palace), Bijāpur, India, 125
Gāhaḍavāla Dynasty, 50, 848-849
Gai Si (Muslim missionary), 324
Gäiacs Plain, New Caledonia, 647
Gaimoucheng, China, 744
Gaj Mandīr, Junāgarh Fort, Bīkaner, India, 132
Gaj Singh (ruler of Bīkaner), 132
Gajabāhu II (ruler of Sri Lanka), 686
Gajalakshmi (goddess), 731
Gajapati Dynasty, 699
Gajner Palace, Bīkaner, India, 132
Gal Vihara, Polonnaruwa, Sri Lanka, 686
Galaup, Jean-François de (comte de La Pérouse), 154, 250, 639, 724, 781
Galdan (Dzungar leader), 323
Galle, Sri Lanka, 199, 201, 202, **272-275**
Gama, Vasco da, 87, 187, 284, 584, 711
Gambier Street, Kuching, Malaysia, 498, 500
Gamō Ujisato (Japanese warrior), 10
Gamukh Temple, Mount Ābu, India, 600, 602
Gaṇapati. *See* Ganesh
Gaṇḍa (Chandela ruler), 468
Ganden Monastery, Lhasa, Tibet, China, 528, 529, 750
Gandhāra, kingdom of, 439, 574, 608, 669, 798, 800, 805, 806, 807-808, 836
Gandhi, Indira, 30, 176, 223
Gandhi, Mohandas Karamchand (Mahatma), 9, 124, 137, 146, 175, 189, 223, 267, 448, 449, 713
Gandhi, Rajiv, 223
Gandhi, Sanjay, 223
Gāndhīnagar, India, 6, 9
Gaṇeśa. *See* Ganesh
Ganesh (god), 26, 135, 254, 258, 445, 602, 660, 694
Ganesh Pol (Elephant Gate), Amber, Italy, 24, 26
Gang of Four (China), 737, 738
Gaṅgā (goddess), 258
Gaṅgā Canal, Bīkaner, India, 133
Gaṅga Dynasty, 478, 699
Ganga Niwas, Junāgarh Fort, Bīkaner, India, 132
Ganga Singh Bahādur (ruler of Bīkaner), 132, 133
Gangadhareshwara Cave Temple, Bangalore, India, 95
Ganges Plain, 281, 505
Ganges River, 47, 134, 168, 169, 170, 176, 186, 218, 225, 254, 501, 503, 555, 572, 574, 716, 798, 835, 847, 848, 849
Ganges Valley, 47-48
Gani, A.K., 664
Ganilau, Sir Penaia, 268
Ganjin (Buddhist teacher), 623
Gannoruwa, Sri Lanka, 446
Gansu, China, 216, 239-241, 242-246, 293, 294, 296, 297, 321, 323, 741
Gao, China, 538
Gao Huan (Wei official), 294
Gao Shanming (Wei architect), 213
Gao Shi (poet), 420
Gao Zong (Tang emperor of China), 872
Gaozong (Northern Wei emperor of China), 894
Gaozu (Han emperor of China), 212
Garcia da Orta (Goan botanist), 288
Gardabad. *See* Ahmadābād, Gujarāt, India
Garden, Miyazaki, Japan, 594
Garden of Eight Views, Hikone, Japan, 338
Garden of Fidelity (Bagh-i-Vafa), Kābul, Afghanistan, 415
Garden of Love. *See* Shālīmār Bagh, Srīnagar, India
Garden of Pleasure upon Pleasure, Hikone, Japan, 338
Garden of Repose (Aram Bāgh), Āgra, India, 1, 4
Garden of the Night, Bangkok, Thailand, 98
Gardens, Ahmadābād, India, 8
Gardens, Aizu-Wakamutsu, Japan, 11
Gardens, Delhi, India, 220, 222, 223
Gardens, Dunedin, New Zealand, 236
Gardens, Lahore, Pakistan, 522, 523, 524, 525
Gardens, Luoyang, China, 541
Gardens, Macau, 545
Gardens, Yangzhou, China, 886
Gardezi compound, Multān, Pakistan, 611
Garghaon, India, 309
Garnier, Francis, 331
Garrison Church of St. Martin, Delhi, India, 223
Garuḍa (mythic creature), 312, 601, 694, 695
Gasti (ruler of Kirāti), 465
Gatamiputra Śātakarni, 410
Gate, Miyajima, Japan, 587, 590
Gate of Correct Demeanor, Forbidden City, Beijing, China, 106
Gate of Heavenly Peace, Forbidden City, Beijing, China, 106, 107, 109, 110-111
Gate of Supreme Harmony. *See* Taihemen, Forbidden City, Beijing, China
Gates, Nanjing, China, 616, 619
Gates, Nāsik, India, 626
Gates, Nikkō, Japan, 636, 637

Gateway, Delhi, India, 218
Gateway of India arch, Bombay, India, 144, 146
Gateways, Sānchi, India, 730-731
Gaua, Vanuatu, 843
Gauguin, Paul, 788
Gauhāti. *See* Guwāhāti, Assam, India
Gaukushan complex, Bukhara, Uzbekistan, 166
Gaumakh Tank cave, Chittaurgarh, India, 193, 194
Gautama, Siddhārtha. *See* Buddha
Gautamīputra Śātakarṇi (Sātavāhanna king), 626
Gawalior (mahārāja), 1
Gayā, Bihār, India, 138, 141, **276-278,** 848
Gayaśīrṣa Hill, Bodh Gayā, India, 138, 276, 278
Gazaga. *See* Ghaznī, Ghaznī, Afghanistan
Geddie, John, 845
Geding Sura (dynasty founder in Palembang), 663
Gedün Gyatso (Dalai Lama), 528, 750
Gedün Truppa (Dalai Lama), 528, 750
Geil, William Edgar, 742
Gekū, Ise, Japan, 374, 375, 376, 377
Gela Island, 300
Gelgel, Bali, Indonesia, 68, 69, 70
Gelugspa. *See* Yellow Hat (sect)
Gemmei (empress of Japan), 621, 622
Genbaku Dōmu, Hiroshima, Japan, 351
Geneva Accords (Vietnam), 230, 233, 331, 365
Geneva Spur, Himalayan Mountains, 606
Genghis Khan (Mongol conqueror), 22, 71, 73, 79, 80, 81, 105, 164, 220, 241, 282, 321, 327, 333, 383, 414, 426, 439, 451, 457, 474-475, 527, 580, 669, 671, 679, 718, 720, 722, 884
Genji. *See* Minamoto family
Genpei no Ike, Kamakura, Japan, 426, 430
George (saint), 547, 667
George III (king of Great Britain), 665, 782, 832
George V (king of Great Britain), 132, 144, 175, 223, 604
George, Ernest, 237
George, T.J.S., 406
George Street, Sydney, Australia, 784
George Town, Madras, India, 547, 548, 550
George Tupou I (king of Tonga), 266, 827, 828, 829
George Tupou II (king of Tonga), 830
Georges River, 153
Georgetown, Malaysia, 665, 667
Germany, 13, 100, 110, 161, 174, 175, 298, 336, 350, 351, 355, 396, 404, 499, 602, 604, 646, 723, 725, 736, 788, 798, 800, 806, 813, 814, 821, 830
Geyuan Garden, Yangzhou, China, 886
Ghāghara River, 47
Ghantai, Khajurāho, India, 470
Ghārāpuri. See Elephanta Island, Mahārāshtra, India
Ghasita Begum (Bengalese noblewoman), 679-680
Gghāts at Vārānasī, India, 847, 849, 850
Ghāzī-'ud-Dīn-Haidar (son of Saadat Ali Kahn), 534
Ghaziābād, India, 224
Ghaznavid Dynasty, 73, 279, 281, 282, 333, 414, 439, 522, 610
Ghaznī, Ghaznī, Afghanistan, 79, **279-283,** 312, 414, 417
Ghee Hin Triad, 668
Ghilzay (tribe), 441
Ghiyās-ud-Dīn (king of Mālwa), 563
Ghiyās-ud-Dīn Tughluq (sultan of Delhi), 218, 220, 802
Ghulam Muhammad (Indian nabob), 550
Ghulam-Muḥammad Mosque, Calcutta, India, 174
Ghulam Shāh Kalhora, 803
Ghūr, kingdom of, 79, 282, 414
Ghūri Dynasty, 80, 561, 562, 837
Gia Dinh, Vietnam. *See* Ho Chi Minh City, Vietnam
Gia Long (emperor of Vietnam), 330, 331, 354, 364
Gia Long Palace, Ho Chi Minh City, Vietnam, 354, 356
Giant's Canal, Anuradhapura, Sri Lanka, 38
Gianyar, Bali, Indonesia, 69
Giap, Vo Nguyen. *See* Vo Nguyen Giap
Gibraltar, 204
Gifu, Japan, 795-797
Gilbert, George, 265
Gilbert and Ellice Islands. *See* Tuvalu
Giles, Earnest, 45
Gill, Robert, 14
Gilman and Company, 360
Ginkaku-ji, Higashiyama, Japan, 519
Ginza, Tōkyō, Japan, 823, 824, 825-826
Gion Matsuri, Kyōto, Japan, 518, 797
Gir Lion Sanctuary, Gujarāt, India, 413
Gīrnār Hill, India, 408, 412
Gītā Mandīr, Somnāth, India, 765
Glac Lam Pagoda, Ho Chi Minh City, Vietnam, 354
Glac Vien Pagoda, Ho Chi Minh City, Vietnam, 354
Glass House, Lāl Bagh Gardens, Bangalore, India, 92
Globe Theatre, Dunedin, New Zealand, 238
Glodok, Jakarta, Indonesia, 397
Glover, Thomas, 615
Glover Mansion, Nagasaki, Japan, 615
Goa, India, 8, 127, 188, 200, 201, **284-289,** 542, 544, 545, 752, 856
Goalbhita, Bangladesh, 657
Gobi Desert, 321
Gobind Singh (last Sikh gurū), 27, 28
Gocher, William, 784
Godāvari Basin, 125
Godāvari River, 290, 625, 626, 627, 628, 811
Goddess of Mercy Temple. *See* Kuan Yin Temple, Penang, Malaysia
Goede Hope. *See* Niuafoo, Tonga
Goens, Ryklof van, 202, 446, 712
Goh Tai Seng (Five Big Surnames), 667
Gohar Begum. *See* Qudsia III
Goiti, Martín de, 180, 565
Gokuden (Misorandano), Nikkō, Japan, 637
Gokula (Jāt leader), 577
Gokuraku-ji, Kamakura, Japan, 428
Gōl Gumbaz, Bijāpur, India, 127
Golconda, Andhra Pradesh, India, 125, **290-292**
Gold Crown Tomb. *See* Kumgwan-ch'ong, Kyŏngju, South Korea
Gold Museum, Ballarat, Australia, 78
Gold Rush, 208, 234, 235, 236
Golden Coast, Dunedin, New Zealand, 238
Golden Hall, Nara, Japan, 887
Golden Hall of Fudō-myo-o, Hiroshima, Japan, 349
Golden Hill. *See* Nanjing, Jiangsu, China
Golden Horn inlet, Turkey, 165
Golden House. *See* Sunahra Makan, Fatehpur Sīkri, India
Golden Palace, Mandalay, Myanmar, 557, 558
Golden Temple (Harimandir), Amritsar, India, 27, 28, 29, 30
Golden tower, Angkor, Cambodia, 32, 33
Gomati River, 534, 536
Gond (people), 468
Gondophemes (Śaka ruler), 798
Gong (Chinese prince), 735, 814
Gongzong (Northern Wei emperor of China), 894
Goodenough, J.G., 267
Gopal Singh (ruler of Bishnupur), 136
Gopāla (Pāla ruler of eastern India), 657
Gor Khatri, Peshāwar, Pakistan, 671
Gorbachev, Mikhail, 418
Gordon, Sir Arthur Hamilton, 267
Gorgīn Khān (governor of Kandahār), 441
Gorordo, Juan, 181
Goryōkaku fortress, Hakodate, Japan, 317, 319, 320
Gosho, Kyōto, Japan, 515, 520
Gosse, William, 45
Gotemba, Japan, 269, 271
Gough, Sir Hugh, 314
Government Gardens, Port Arthur, Australia, 691
Government House, Calcutta, India, 173, 175
Government House, Darwin, Australia, 208
Government House, Madras, India, 550
Government House, Sydney, Australia, 782
Government House, Windsor, Australia, 863
Government Museum, Bangalore, India, 95
Governor's Palace, Macau, 545
Govinda Dikshita (mahārāja), 502
Govindachandra (Gāhaḍavāla king of Vārānasī), 848
Govindarāja (governor of Ajmer), 21
Gowa, kingdom of, 839, 840-841
Goyder, G.W., 208
Grace, Lawrence, 833
Graharipu (Chudasma ruler of Junāgadh), 410
Granary, Mohenjo-daro, Pakistan, 597
Grand Canal, China, 325, 327, 420, 422, 540-541, 776, 778, 813, 872, 884, 886, 887
Grand Master. *See* Makhdum-i Azam
Grand Mosque, Melaka, Malaysia, 584
Grand Palace, Bangkok, Thailand, *97*
Grand Stupa. *See* Ruwanvelisaya Dagaba, Anuradhapura, Sri Lanka
Grand Trunk Road, Calcutta, India, 174
Grant, Ulysses S., 725
Great Audience Hall, Mandalay, Myanmar, 556-557
Great Banda, Banda Islands, Indonesia, 88, 89
Great Barrier Reef, 644
Great Bath, Mohenjo-daro, Pakistan, 597
Great Britain, 1, 5, 6, 8-9, 13, 14, 20, 23, 24, 29, 35, 39, 40, 44, 45, 50, 57, 58, 60, 62, 63, 68, 69, 78, 81, 87, 88, 89, 90, 92, 94, 95, 98, 99, 103, 107, 113, 114-116, 119, 120, 123-124, 128, 132, 136-137, 140, 142, 143, 144, 146, 154, 158, 160, 161, 162, 165, 166, 168-171, 172-175, 176, 186, 188-189, 201, 202, 203, 206, 208, 209, 218, 222-223, 225, 226-227, 244, 251, 253, 256, 261, 264, 265-266, 267, 272, 274, 277, 278, 282, 288-289, 292, 298-301, 306-307, 314, 316, 317, 318, 323, 336, 339, 344, 355, 358-361, 366, 369, 370, 372-373, 386, 392, 394, 400, 404, 412-413, 414, 417-418, 441-442, 446-447, 448, 449, 458, 459, 466, 472, 473, 475, 476, 477, 480, 489, 492, 493, 495, 497, 499, 503, 508, 522, 524-525, 529, 534, 535, 536, 544-545, 547, 548, 550, 556, 557, 558, 565, 566, 568, 577, 580, 602, 603-606, 610, 612, 614, 627-628, 629, 639-643, 644, 656, 663, 665, 668, 671, 673, 676, 677, 679, 680, 681, 682, 687, 689, 690, 699, 712, 714, 723, 725, 726, 727, 732, 735, 736, 737, 748, 751-752, 757, 758, 759, 760, 767, 778, 781, 782, 784, 785, 787, 803, 804, 812, 813-814, 816, 818-819, 820, 821, 825, 827, 828-829, 830, 831, 832, 838, 839, 840, 841, 842, 844, 845, 846, 850, 859-860, 863, 879-880, 882, 891
Great Buddha. *See* Kotokuin Daibutsu, Kamakura, Japan
Great Capital. *See* Beijing, China
Great Cave. *See* Siva cave temple, Elephanta Island, India
Great Dynasty (Sri Lanka), 35, 38
Great Fiji Rush, 266
Great Fire, Kyōto, Japan, 520
Great Golden Gate (Dajin Men), Nanjing, China, 619
Great Hall of the People, Beijing, China, 111, 112
Great Imambara (Bara Imambara), Lucknow, India, 534, 535
Great Kanto Earthquake (Japan), 429, 430
Great Leap Forward (China), 901
Great Mosque, Banten, West Java, Indonesia, 103
Great Quadrangle, Polonnaruwa, Sri Lanka, 686-687
Great Rainbow Bridge (Dahong Qiao), Yangzhou, China, 886
Great Stupa, Sānchi, India, 727, 729, 730

Great Stupa, Taxila, Pakistan, 805, 806
Great Stupa, Vientiane, Laos, 852, 853
Great Trigonometrical Survey of India (1849), 603-604
Great Vehicle. *See* Mahāyāna Buddhism
Great Wall, China, 105, 214, 239, **293-297,** 585-586, 701, 709, 739, 741, 742, 743
Great Western Temple (Saidai-ji), Nara, Japan, 624
Great Wild Goose Pagoda (Da Yan Ta), Xian, China, 871-872, 873
Great Within. *See* Danei Palace, Forbidden City, Beijing, China
Greater Footprint Hill, Sukhothai, Thailand, 775
Greco-Bactrian kingdom. *See* Bactria
Greece, 79, 226, 239, 254, 272, 279, 321, 333, 371, 473, 578, 669, 718, 720, 800, 871
Green, Charles, 781
Green, John Philip, 203
Green Hills. *See* Windsor, New South Wales, Australia
Green Mosque, Balkh, Afghanistan, 71, 73
Greenway, Francis Howard, 783, 863, 865
Gregory, A.C., 208
Gregory, William, 202
Griffiths, John, 14
Groce, Francis, 863
Groce River, 863
Groeningen. *See* Upolu Island, Western Samoa
Grono, John, 863
Gros, Antoine-Jean (baron), 813
Grotto of Camões, Macau, 545
Grottoes, Luoyang, China, 538, 540, 541
Groves, Leslie, 615
Growse, F.S., 577
Gu Kaizhi (painter), 616
Guadalcanal, Solomon Islands, 267, **298-301,** 647
Guam, 204, 206
Guan Cheng. *See* Zhengzhou, Henan, China
Guan Zhong (Qi functionary), 293
Guangdong, China, 302-307, 358, 542, 544, 620, 748, 866
Guangling. *See* Yangzhou, Jiangsu, China
Guangxi, China, 542, 866
Guangxiao Temple, Guangzhou, China, 304, 306
Guangzhou, Guangdong, China, 302-307, 542, 544, 545, 704, 705, 732, 735, 736, 738, 758, 813, 884
Guanshu Men Gate, Yangzhou, China, 887
Guanzhou. *See* Zhengzhou, Henan, China
Guard Tower, Port Arthur, Australia, 691
Guarisankr (mountain), Nepal, 604
Gugong, the Ancient Palace. *See* Forbidden City, Beijing, China
Guha (boatman), 716
Guhar-shad (wife of Shāh Rokh), 335
Guhasiva (king of Orissa), 699
Guhil (Indian clan founder), 191
Guhillas (clan), 191
Gui Shan (Tortoise Hill), Hanyang, China, 868
Gui Yuguang (writer), 776
Guiliang (Chinese grand secretary), 813, 814
Guilin, China, 302
Guiyan Si (Temple of the Return to the Fundamental Principle), Hanyang, China, 868
Gujarāt, India, 6-9, 29, 129, 142, 193, 260, 281, 284, 286, 288, 392, 399, 408-412, 561, 563, 583, 600, 601, 762-766, 802, 835, 837, 838, 897
Gujri Mahal Palace, Gwalior, India, 314
Gulbarga, India, 125
Gulf of Cambay, 6, 8, 595, 599
Gulf of Hangzhou, 325
Gulf of Lingayen, 206
Gulf of Martaban, 879
Gulf of Siam, 32, 53
Gulf of Thailand, 82, 96
Gulf of Tonkin, 329
Gulshanābād. *See* Nāsik, Mahārāshtra, India
Gumal Pass, Afghanistan, 279, 282
Gumonji-dō (temple), Miyajima, Japan, 588
Gunakamadeva (king of Kāthmāndu), 465
Gundicha temple, Puri, India, 697
Gunong Subis (Sobis Mountain), 629
Gunung Api (Fire Mountain), Banda Islands, Indonesia, 88, 89, 90
Gunung Jāti, Sunan (missionary), 101
Gunung Merapi (volcano), Yogyakarta, Indonesia, 888
Guo Xing Ye. *See* Koxinga
Guomindang. *See* Kuomintang
Gupta, J.M. Sen, 189
Gupta Dynasty, 14, 17, 18, 49-50, 122, 136, 218, 252, 256, 276, 312, 410, 468, 507, 534, 576, 626, 657, 699, 763, 837, 848
Guqin Terrace, Hanyang, China, 868
Gūr-e-Amīr, Samarkand, Uzbekistan, 73, 721
Gurjāra-Pratihāra Empire, 312, 659
Gurkha (people), 464, 466, 528, 752
Gursi (prince of Jaisalmer), 389, 392
Gursi-sirr (reservoir), Jaisalmer, India, 389, 392
Guru Shikhar, India, 602
Gusti Ngurai Rai (Bali rebel), 70
Gusti Sideman (Dewa Agung of Bali), 69
Guttika (Tamil ruler of Sri Lanka), 37
Guwāhāti, Assam, India, 308-311
Guyon (governor of New Caledonian), 646
Guyuan, China, 296
Gwalior, Madhya Pradesh, India, 312-316, 400, 838
Gwalipa (saint), 312
Gyāna Bhandār library, Jaisalmer, India, 392
Gyantse, China, 750
Gyōki (Buddhist priest), 426, 623

Haamonga-a-Maui, Hahake, Tonga, 827-828, 830
Haapai Islands, Tonga, 827, 828
Haatakalaua family, 827, 829
Habeler, Peter, 603, 607
Habib Bank, Karāchi, Pakistan, 450
Ḥabībollāh Khān (ruler of Afghanistan), 418
Habsburg Empire, 201
Hachijo no Toshihito (prince of Japan), 520
Hachiman (god), 345, 426
Hachiman Shrine, Takayama, Japan, 797
Hachimangu Shrine, Hirosaki, Japan, 345
Hadji Piardeh Shrine. *See* Hajji Piyade Shrine
Hagi, Japan, 349
Hahake, Tonga, 827-828, 830
Haidar, Ghulam (governor of Kandahār), 442
Haiden, Miyajima, Japan, 590
Haiden, Nikkō, Japan, 637
Haihaya Dynasty, 836
Hainan Island, 305
Haiphong, Vietnam, 331, 557
Haji (sultan of Banten), 103
Haji Begum (widow of Humāyūn), 222
Hajji Piyade Shrine, Balkh, Afghanistan, 71, 73
Hajjigak River, 79
Hajo, India, 310-311
Hakka (people), 358, 792
Hakkeien, Hikone, Japan, 338
Hakodate, Hokkaidō, Japan, 317-320
Hakodateyama. *See* Mount Hakodate
Hakone, Japan, 271
Halcon, José M., 404
Hale, Horatio, 820
Hall, James Norman, 788
Hall, William, 859
Hall of Celestial Guardians, Yangzhou, China, 887
Hall of Complete Harmony. *See* Zhonghedian, Forbidden City, Beijing, China
Hall of Dance, Konārak, India, 479
Hall of Enlightenment (Ming Tang), Luoyang, China, 541
Hall of Glory (Jas Mandir), Amber, India, 26
Hall of Great Achievements (Dacheng Dian), Qufu, China, 709
Hall of Heavenly and Earthly Union. *See* Jiaotaidian, Forbidden City, Beijing, China
Hall of Indian Antiquities, British Museum, London, England, 727
Hall of Love Left Behind (Yi-ai-Tang), Guangzhou, China, 305
Hall of Preserving Harmony (Baohedian), Beijing, China, 107
Hall of Private Audience (Dīwān-i-Khas), Āgra, India, 4
Hall of Private Audience (Dīwān-i-Khas), Amber, India, 26
Hall of Private Audience (Dīwān-i-Khas), Delhi, India, 220, 222
Hall of Private Audience (Dīwān-i-Khas), Fatehpur Sīkri, India, 262
Hall of Public Audience (Dīwān-i-Am), Delhi, India, 222
Hall of Public Audience (Dīwān-i-Am), Fatehpur Sīkri, India, 261-262
Hall of Public Audience (Dīwān-i-Am), Junāgarh Fort, Bīkaner, India, 132
Hall of Sleep, Qufu, China, 709
Hall of State. *See* Daigoku-den, Kyōto, Japan
Hall of Supreme Harmony. *See* Taihedian, Forbidden City, Beijing, China
Hall of the 500 Luohan, Hanyang, China, 868
Hall of the Mandarin Ducks, Suzhou, China, 779
Hall of the Signs of the Wise Man, Qufu, China, 709
Hall of Victory (Jai Mandir), Amber, India, 26
Halls of the Mandarins, Hue, Vietnam, 364
Hamadan. *See* Ecbatana
Hamburg, Germany, 174
Hamengkubuwono (sultan of Yogyakarta post-1945), 892
Hamengkubuwono I (Mangkubumi; eighteenth-century sultan of Yogyakarta), 890
Hamengkubuwono II (eighteenth-century sultan of Yogyakarta), 891
Hami, Xinjiang Uighur Autonomous Region, China, 239, **321-324**
Hamilton, Alexander, 545
Hamilton, Buchanan, 657, 659
Hamir (rāna of Chittaurgarh), 193
Hampi. *See* Vijayanagara, Karnātaka, India
Hampi Authority, Vijayanagara, India, 858
Hamsa (sacred goose), 694
Han Confucians, 538
Han Dynasty, 212, 239, 240, 241, 293, 294, 302, 305, 321, 323, 329, 358, 420, 456, 459, 701, 708, 739, 744, 886, 893
Han River, 482, 483, 484, 486, 511, 866
Han Tomb, Li Cheng Uk, Hong Kong, 358
Han Wudi (ruler of China), 294
Hanga Roa, Easter Island, Chile, 247, 251
Hanging Gardens, Bombay, India, 144
Hangzhou, Zhejiang, China, 306, **325-328,** 349, 420, 422, 424, 732, 776, 813, 884
Hankou, China, 866, 868-869
Hanna, William A., 88, 89
Hanoi, Vietnam, 230, 232, **329-332,** 354, 355, 356, 362, 364
Hansan, South Korea, 482
Hanshan (poet), 778
Hanshan (ruler of Hami), 323
Hanshan Si (Cold Mountain Temple), Suzhou, China, 778
Hansŏng, South Korea, 482
Hanthawaddy. *See* Bago, Myanmar

Hanumān (monkey deity), 47, 466, 695, 714, 715, 716
Hanumān Dokha Palace, Kāthmāndu, Nepal, 466, 467
Hanyang, China, 866, 868, 869
Haora, India, 174
Hape (missionary), 266
Haq, Maulvi Abdul, 369
Har Mandīr (temple), Bīkaner, India, 132
Haraiden (Purification Hall), Miyajima, Japan, 590
Harappa, Pakistan, 71, 472, 489-492, 595, 595-599, 597, 602, 763
Harcourt, Cecil, 361
Hardinge, Henry (viscount; viceroy of India), 175, 850
Hardwār, India, 628
Hardy, Thomas, 223
Hare Krishna (sect), 697
Hargobind (sixth Sikh gurū), 27
Hargreaves, H., 800
Harhorin. *See* Karakorum, Uburkhangai, Mongolia
Hari Parbat, Srīnagar, India, 769
Hari Parbat Fort, Srīnagar, India, 767
Harī Rūd, Afghanistan, 333
Harimandir (Golden Temple), Amritsar, India, 27, 28, 29, 30
Haripunchai. *See* Lamphun, Thailand
Haripunjaya (Mon kingdom center), 530
Harold, James, 641
Harpur, Charles, 865
Harrisson, Tom, 629-631
Harṣa (patron of Bāṇabhaṭṭa), 837
Harśadeva (Chandela ruler of Khajurāho), 468
Harsha (king of India), 507
Harshavardhaharna (king of Kanaju), 123
Hārūn-al-Rashīd (fifth caliph), 610
Haruru Falls, Waitangi, New Zealand, 862
Haryāna, India, 30, 505-508
Ḥasan-ad-Dīn (sultan of Gowa), 840, 841
Hasanudīn (king of Banten), 101-102
Hase, Japan, 426
Hasedera Temple, Kamakura, Japan, 426, 429
Hasegawa Kakugyō, 270-271
Hashim (sultan of Brunei), 160
Hasim, Raja Muda, 160, 497
Hashim ibn Hakim. *See* Muqanna', al-
Hastināpur, India, 505, 506
Hastings, Warren, 23, 173, 188, 751, 752, 850
Hathi Mahal (Elephant Palace), Māndu, India, 563
Hathi Pol (Elephant Gate), Fatehpur Sīkri, India, 263
Hathigumpha (Elephant Cave), India, 122
Hatta, Mohammad, 90
Hatyara. *See* Udai Singh I
Hau (people), 358
Havana Harbor, Cuba, 204
Havea I (Tui Tonga), 828
Havea II (Tui Tonga), 828
Havelock, Henry, 536
Hawā Mahal (Palace of the Winds), Fatehpur Sīkri, India, 263
Hawā Mahal (Palace of the Winds), Jaipur, India, 386
Hawaii, United States of America, 206, 209, 299, 620, 723, 794, 827
Hawkesbury, Baron (Charles Jenkinson), 863
Hawkesbury Agricultural College, Richmond, Australia, 865
Hawkesbury River, 783, 863
Hawkesbury Shire, Australia, 863
Hayagriba Madhab Temple, Hajo, India, 310
Hayat Baksh Bagh (Life-Bestowing Gardens), Delhi, India, 222
Hayat Moḥammad Khān (ruler of Bhopāl), 119
Hazrat Makhdum-i A'zam, 458
Hazratbāl Mosque, Srīnagar, India, 769
He Jingyu, 868
He Lu (king of Wu), 776
He Zangdao, 886
He Zhuguo, 742
Heath, William, 188
Heavenly Horse Tomb (Ch'ongma-ch'ong), Kyŏngju, South Korea, 514
Heavenly Kingdom of Great Peace. *See* Taipings
Heavenly Palace (Gagan Mahal), Bijāpur, India, 125
Hebei, China, 212, 293, 294, 739-743, 748
Heber, Reginald, 850
Hedin, Sven, 458
Heemskerck, Jacob van, 68, 69, 87
Hefei, China, 111
Heian Jingū shrine, Kyōto, Japan, 520
Heian-kyō. *See* Kyōto, Kyōto, Japan
Heiden (Offerings Hall), Miyajima, Japan, 590
Heijō. *See* Nara, Nara, Japan
Heike. *See* Taira Dynasty
Heilala festival, Tongatapu Island, Tonga, 830
Heilongjiang, China, 748
Heiwa Kinen Kōen (Peace Memorial Park), Hiroshima, Japan, 351
Heiwa Kinen Shiryōkan (Peace Memorial Museum), Hiroshima, Japan, 351
Heiwadai (Peace Tower), Miyazaki, Japan, 594
Heiwadai Kōen (Peace Tower Park), Miyazaki, Japan, 594
Helmand River, 279, 282
Henan, China, 40-43, 293, 295, 420-425, 538-541, 736, 874, 901-905
Henan Provincial Museum, Zhengzhou, China, 904
Henderson Field, Guadalcanal, Solomon Islands, 300
Henry III (king of Castile), 720
Hepthalites. *See* White Huns
Herāt, Herāt, Afghanistan, 73, 79, 163, 165, 282, **333-337,** 440, 473, 580
Herbert, Xavier, 209
Hercules (god), 254
Herī. *See* Herāt, Herāt, Afghanistan
Herodotus (Greek historian), 71
Heron, A.M., 605
Herringham, Lady (British artist), 14
Hexi. *See* Shaanxi, China
Heyerdahl, Thor, 251
Heyuan Garden, Yangzhou, China, 886
Hibiya Inlet, Japan, 822
Hickey, William, 545
Hicks, Zachary, 781
Hida. *See* Takayama, Gifu, Japan
Hida Kokubunji (temple), Takayama, Japan, 795
Hida Minzoku-Mura, Takayama, Japan, 796
Hida-Takayama. *See* Takayama, Gifu, Japan
Hiei-zan. *See* Mount Hiei
Hien Vuong (Nguyen ruler of southern Vietnam), 362
Higashi Hongan-ji (temple), Kyōto, Japan, 520, 638
Higashiyama, Japan, 515, 517, 518, 519
Higashiyama Teramachi, Takayama, Japan, 795-796
Higginson, John, 846
High Court, Bangalore, India, 94
High Court, Calcutta, India, 174
High Court, Chittagong, Bangladesh, 189
Higurashi-mon. *See* Yomeimon Gate, Nikkō, Japan
Hihifo, Tonga, 828
Hijiyama hill, Hiroshima, Japan, 351
Hiki Daigakusaburo (disciple of Nichiren), 429
Hikone, Shiga, Japan, 338-339
Hikuleo (god), 827
Hill, Joshua, 676, 677
Hill of Ghosts (Pret Sīla), Gayā, India, 278
Hillary, Sir Edmund, 603, 606
Hillbrandt, Henry, 819
Hillsdale, Australia, 156
Himalaya Mountains, 71, 218, 254, 311, 464, 473, 505, 526, 600, 603-607, 608, 750, 767
Himetatara Isuzuhime (wife of Jimmu Tennō), 462
Himiko (legendary daughter of Japanese ruler), 376, 377
Hinayana Buddhism. *See* Theravada Buddhism
Hindola Mahal, Māndu, India, 563
Hindu College, Calcutta, India, 174
Hindu Kush Mountains, 71, 79, 473, 669, 718, 720, 809
Hindu Sena Dynasty, 186
Hinduism, 1, 2, 3, 5, 6, 8, 9, 20, 21, 22, 24, 26, 27, 28, 29-30, 31, 33, 37, 47, 49, 50, 65, 68, 92, 94, 95, 96, 97, 98, 101, 113, 117, 119, 120, 121, 122, 123, 124, 125, 129, 132, 134, 136, 137, 140, 141, 142, 143, 147, 172, 174, 175, 176, 186, 188, 189, 199, 203, 218, 222, 223, 225, 227, 252, 253, 254, 256, 260, 261, 262, 263, 268, 276, 277, 278, 281, 284, 286, 288, 289, 290, 291, 308, 309, 310, 312, 314, 353, 354, 362, 370, 371, 383, 385, 386, 388, 399, 402, 412, 413, 435, 436, 437, 443, 448, 464, 465, 466, 468, 469, 470, 474, 479, 480-481, 501, 503, 505, 507, 508, 522, 523, 524, 525, 534, 536, 547, 550, 552, 561, 562, 572, 574, 576, 584, 588, 597, 600, 601, 602, 608, 610, 625, 626-627, 628, 653, 659, 667, 669, 671, 672, 679, 684, 687, 692, 694, 697, 700, 714, 715, 716, 762, 764, 765, 769, 771, 798, 800, 801, 802, 805, 806, 811, 835, 837, 838, 847, 848-849, 850, 855, 888, 890, 892
Hindustan. *See* India
Hirado, Nagasaki, Japan, 340-344
Hirado Harbor, Nagasaki, Japan, 341
Hiradoshima Island, Japan, 340, 341
Hiranya River, 765
Hirata Atsutane (Japanese scholar), 614
Hirohito (emperor of Japan), 615, 825
Hirosaki, Aomori, Japan, 345-348
Hirosaki Park, Japan, 345
Hiroshima, Hiroshima, Japan, 349-352, 382, 587-591, 614, 615
Hiroshima Bay, 349, 350, 587
Hirotsugu (Fujiwara leader), 622
Hiva (legendary kingdom), 247
Hizen, Japan, 520
Hmong (people), 230
Ho Chi Minh, 231, 331, 354-355, 356
Ho Chi Minh City, Vietnam, 230, 329, 330, 331, **353-357,** 365
Ho Chi Minh Mausoleum, Hanoi, Vietnam, 332
Ho Qui Ly (regent of Dai Vietnam), 329
Hoa Lu, Vietnam, 329
Hoan Kiem Ho, Hanoi, Vietnam, 329, 331, 332
Hobart, Australia, 642, 690, 691
Hobson, William, 859
Hocken, Thomas Morland, 237
Hodges, William, 548, 550
Hōeizan (volcanic cone), Fujinomiya, Japan, 271
Hogon-ji (temple), Hikone, Japan, 338
Hohhot, China, 215
Hōjō family, 428-429, 518
Hokai-ji (temple), Kamakura, Japan, 429
Hokkaidō, Japan, 269, 317-320, 632
Hokkien (people), 500, 667
Hoklo (people), 358, 792
Hokoku Jinja shrines (Japan), 590
Hokusai (artist), 651
Hollyhock Festival (Aoi Matsuri), Kyōto, Japan, 518
Holmes Jungle National Park, Darwin, Australia, 211
Holt, Thomas, 156
Holy Walk (Chankramana), Bodh Gayā, India, 140
Homma, Masaharu, 206, 207
Hōmotsukan (Treasure Hall), Miyajima, Japan, 589
Honam Highway, South Korea, 197
Honam Plain, South Korea, 195
Honchidō. *See* Yakushidō, Nikkō, Japan
Honda (Japanese general), 881, 882
Honden (Main Hall), Miyajima, Japan, 590
Honden (Main Hall), Nikkō, Japan, 637

Honden (Main Hall), Takayama, Japan, 795, 796
Hōnen (founder of Pure Land Sect), 518
Hong Kong, 206, **358-361,** 545, 546, 592, 620, 732, 814
Hong Kong Harbor, 359
Hong Taiji (Jürchen leader), 742, 746-747
Hong Xiuquan (Taiping leader), 814
Hongaku-ji (temple), Kamakura, Japan, 429
Hongan-ji (temple), Ishiyama hill, Ōsaka, 431, 432, 650
Hongan-ji (temple), Kyōto, Japan, 518, 520, 650
Hongan-ji (temple), Tenma-gu (shrine), Ōsaka, 650
Hongan-ji (temple), Yamashina, Japan, 650
Hongō, Tōkyō, Japan, 824
Hongwu (Ming emperor of China), 105, 295, 322, 618, 619, 620, 739, 866, 873
Hongzhi (Ming emperor of China), 296
Honiara, Guadalcanal, 298, 300
Honored Lofty Place. *See* Phra Khaphung, Sukhothai, Thailand
Honshū, Japan, 10, 269, 270, 317, 319, 320, 338, 340, 341, 344, 345, 349, 374, 376, 426, 431, 460, 515, 518, 587, 592, 621, 632, 648, 795, 822
Hō'o-dō (Phoenix Hall), Uji, Japan, 517
Hooghly-Chinsura, India, 172
Hooghly River, 172, 174, 176, 679
Hooker Valley, New Zealand, 833
Hooper, Basil, 237
Hoorn Islands. *See* Futuna Islands
Horikoshi, Japan, 345
Hornaday, William, 629, 760
Hornbein, Tom, 606
Horonuku (Maori chief), 832, 833, 834
Hōryū-ji, Ikaruga, Japan, 621, 624
Hoshang Shāh (king of Mālwa), 561-562
Hoshina Masayuki (Masanobu; *shōgun* of Japan), 10
Hosina. *See* Ghaznī, Ghaznī, Afghanistan
Hospet, India, 858
Hot Spring Temple, Shanhaiguan, China, 742
Hotel de Ville, Ho Chi Minh City, Vietnam, 354
Hotel Lan Xang, Vientiane, Laos, 854
Hotham, Charles, 75, 77
Hōtō (Ieyasu's tomb), Nikkō, Japan, 637
Hotu Matua (king of Hiva), 247
Hou Jing (Liang rebel), 618
Houcheng, China, 744
House of Birbal, Fatehpur Sīkri, India, 263
House of the Brocade Merchants, Patwon-ki-haveli, Jaisalmer, India, 392
Houtman, Cornelis de, 68
Houzhu, Quanzhou, China, 706
Howard family, 639
Howard-Bury, Charles Kenneth, 604, 605
Howrah. *See* Haora, India
Hoyasala Dynasty, 125, 812
Hpagyidoa (king of Burma), 310
Hsuan Tsung (emperor of China), 163
Hsungzar (tribe), 701
Hu Shi, 110
Hu Yaobang, 112
Hu Zongxian, 340
Hua Guofeng, 738
Huai River, 420
Huailai Xian, China, 744
Huaisheng Mosque, Guangzhou, China, 305
Hualin Temple, Guangzhou, China, 307
Huamachi, China, 296
Huan (ruler of Qi), 293
Huang Chao, 214, 305-306
Huang Di (Yellow Emperor of China), 40
Huang Ho. *See* Yellow River
Huang Wu (Wu ruler), 866
Huangpu River, 732, 735, 737
Huaqing Pool, Xian, China, 873
Huaqingchi-Huaqing Hot Springs, Xian, China, 872
Huata (Flowery Pagoda), Guangzhou, China, 304
Huayan temples, Datong, China, 214, 216
Huayang, China, 420
Hubei, China, 866-869
Hudson, Richard, 237
Hudson's Bay Company, 819
Hue, Vietnam, 230, 329, 330, 354, **362-365**
Hugel (baron), 767
Hughes, Robert, 688
Hūgli, India, 172
Hūgli River. *See* Hooghly River
Hui (prince). *See* Wei Hui Wang
Huimo (people), 744
Hulft, Gerard, 201
Hulu Cheng. *See* Quanzhou, Fujian, China
Humabon (Cebu chieftain), 177-178, 181
Humāyūn (Mughal emperor of India), 1, 3, 22, 165, 193, 222, 416, 440-441, 563
Humble, Richard, 382
Humble Administrator's Garden. *See* Zhuo Zheng Yuan, Suzhou, China
Hūna (people), 312, 576
Hunan, China, 302, 866
Hungary, 244
Huns (people), 333, 414, 456, 608, 669, 720, 800, 805, 806
Hunt, John, 606
Hunter, John, 639, 641
Huong Giang (Perfume River), 362, 364, 365
Huqiu. *See* Tiger Hill, Suzhou, China
Hurtado de Corcuera, Sebastian, 403
Husain Mīrzā. *See* Husain Bāī-qarā
Husain Bāī-qarā (sultan), 335, 336, 439, 580
Hussainabad Imambara, Lucknow, India, 534
Hutatma Chowk, Bombay, India, 144
Hutchinson, William, 641
Huxley, Aldous, 144
Huxley, T.H., 629
Huyan Xiongnu (people), 321
Hwangsan Plain, 486
Hyde Park, Sydney, Australia, 783
Hyder Ali (ruler of Mysore), 92, 94, 95, 369, 503, 548, 812
Hyder Ali-Tippu Sultan Palace, Bangalore, India, 95
Hyderābād, Andhra Pradesh, India, 223, 291, 292, **366-370,** 548, 803
Hyderābād, Sind, Pakistan, 371-373, 803, 804
Hye-gong (king of Silla), 513
Hyōgo. *See* Kōbe, Japan
Hyok-ko-se (king of Silla), 509
Hyotaro Kimura, 558
Hyūga, Japan, 592, 594

Iameccaram. *See* Rāmeswaram, Tamil Nādu, India
Ibadat Khana, Fatehpur Sīkri, India, 262
Iban (people), 158
Ibn-ak-Asir (chronicler), 720
Ibn-al-Athir (Muslim historian), 468
Ibn Baṭṭūṭah (Arab traveler), 199, 272, 282, 327, 414, 469, 704, 720
Ibn Hauqal (Arab historian), 281
Ibn Khurrdāhbih (Arab geographer), 60
Ibn Sīnā. *See* Avicenna
Ibrāhīm (ruler of Khorāsān), 281, 282
Ibrāhīm 'Ādil Shāh (ruler of Bijāpur), 125
Ibrāhīm 'Ādil Shāh II (ruler of Bijāpur), 127
Ibrāhīm Lodī (sultan of Delhi), 1, 220, 314, 415
Ibrāhīm Quṭb Shāh (Deccan king), 290, 366
Ibrāhīm Rawza (buildings), India, 127
Ichikishima-hime. *See* Itsukushima-hime
Ichinomachi (First Lane), Takayama, Japan, 795
Id Kah Mosque, Kashgar, China, 458
Ieyasu. *See* Tokugawa Ieyasu
Ihara Saikaku (poet), 651
Ii family, 338-339
Iida, S. (Japanese general), 558
Iimoriyama (hill), Aizu-Wakamatsu, Japan, 12, 13
Ikaruga, Japan, 621
Ikeburkuro district, Tōkyō, Japan, 825
Ikkō (sect), 431, 519, 520, 650
Ikoma Mountains, 648
Ikshvaku Dynasty (mythical), 47
Iktiyar Yazbak, 478
Ilaheva (mythic Tongan), 827
Illanun, 665
Illawarra Coast, 784
Iltutmish (sultan of Delhi), 21, 312, 837
Imjin War, 509, 513
Immadi Narasiṃha (Indian boy-king), 856
Immigration Ordinance of 1968 (Norfolk Island, Australia), 643
Immortal Throne (Akāl Takht), Amritsar, India, 27
Imogiri burial complex, Yogyakarta, Indonesia, 888-890
Imohori Tōgorō (mythic farmer), 431
Imoto Collection Museum, Hirado, Japan, 344
Imperial Canal, China, 776
Imperial City (Inner City), Beijing, China, 105
Imperial City Wall, Beijing, China, 109
Imperial Palace, Beijing, China, 709
Imperial Palace, Hue, Vietnam, 364
Imperial Palace, Luoyang, China, 538
Imperial Palace, Tōkyō, Japan, 375, 822, 825
Imperial Record Office. *See* National Archives, Delhi, India
Imperial Way, Forbidden City, Beijing, China, 107
Imphal, India, 880
Inari (god), 426
India, 1-5, 6-9, 14-19, 20-23, 24-26, 27-30, 35, 38, 39, 47-51, 52, 57, 63, 65, 73, 79, 82, 87, 89, 92-95, 101, 103, 113, 117-120, 121-124, 125-128, 129-133, 134-137, 138-141, 142-146, 147, 150, 158, 165, 166, 168-171, 172-176, 179, 186, 188, 189, 191-194, 199, 200, 201, 202, 218-224, 225, 226, 227, 240, 242, 244, 252-255, 256-259, 260-263, 264, 266, 267, 276-278, 282, 284-289, 290-292, 302, 305, 308-311, 312-316, 321, 353, 354, 360, 366-370, 373, 383-387, 388-394, 396, 399-402, 408-413, 414, 415, 416, 417, 435-438, 439, 440, 441, 442, 443, 451, 466, 468-472, 473, 475, 478-481, 489, 490, 497, 501-504, 505-508, 510, 512, 519, 522, 524, 525, 526, 529, 534-537, 540, 544, 545, 547-551, 552-555, 557-558, 561-564, 568, 572-577, 579, 582, 583, 595, 600-602, 603, 604, 608, 625-628, 656, 659, 661, 668, 669, 671, 679-683, 684, 685, 686, 687, 688, 692, 697-700, 710-713, 714-717, 718, 720, 722, 727-731, 732, 736, 752, 759, 760, 762-766, 767-770, 771, 781, 798, 800, 803, 804, 805, 806, 809-812, 813, 835-838, 847-850, 855-858, 872, 879, 880, 884, 897
India Gate, Delhi, India, 223
India Office Library and Records, London, England, 858
India-Pakistan War, 223
Indian Army, 173, 175
Indian Institute of Science, Bangalore, India, 95
Indian Mosque, Kuching, Malaysia, 500
Indian Museum, Calcutta, India, 174
Indian Mutiny (1857-1858), 5, 50, 144, 174, 222, 278, 314, 400, 466, 476, 524, 534, 536, 577
Indian National Congress, 146, 175, 536
Indian Ocean, 8, 39, 55, 65, 87, 186, 187, 199, 201, 264, 274, 284, 286, 493, 495, 580, 584, 603, 714, 809
Indochina. *See* Cambodia; French Indochina; Laos; Vietnam
Indochina Wars, 230-233, 331-332, 353, 355-356, 364, 365, 533, 570, 853-854

Indonesia, 65-70, 87-91, 101-104, 113-116, 115, 116, 147-152, 158, 161, 166, 186, 202, 206, 208, 395-398, 403, 493-496, 499, 565, 661-664, 692-696, 759, 760, 761, 817, 839-842, 843, 888-892
Indore, India, 277
Indra (god), 18, 254, 472, 530
Indra Chowk, Kāthmāndu, Nepal, 467
Indraprastha. *See* Delhi, Delhi, India
Indravarman I (Khmer king of Cambodia), 31
Indus River, 21, 371, 372, 439, 448, 475, 489, 522, 595, 597, 599, 669, 798, 801, 802, 803, 804
Indus Valley, 6, 71, 79, 82, 84, 279, 281, 371, 439, 472, 489-491, 522, 578, 595, 597, 801
Inge, John, 347
Inglis, John Eardley Wilmot, 536
Inglis, Julia, 536
Inland Sea. *See* Seto Naikai
Inner Court, Forbidden City, Beijing, China, 107, 108
Inner Golden Water Bridges, Forbidden City, Beijing, China, 107
Inner Mongolia, China, 212, 293
Innet, Ann, 639
Institute of Sindhology, Hyderābād, Pakistan, 373
Intharacha I (king of Ayutthaya), 54
Intharacha II (king of Ayutthaya), 55, 59
Intramuros district, Manila, Philippines, 565, 566, 567, 570
Iran, 4, 58, 71, 72, 73, 125, 132, 142, 163, 164, 166, 167, 218, 222, 225, 239, 240, 241, 280, 281, 282, 305, 306, 333, 335, 336, 367, 371, 386, 394, 396, 414, 416, 417, 439, 440, 441, 442, 473, 474, 490, 491, 522, 578, 579, 595, 669, 704, 705, 718, 720, 769, 798, 800, 871, 884, 897
Iraq, 84, 164, 218, 489, 490, 491, 579, 595, 610, 718, 720
Ireland, 78, 641, 787
Iron Bottom Bay, 300
Iron Gate. *See* Loha Gate, Jodhpur, India
Iron Pillar (monument), Delhi, India, 218
Irrawaddy River. *See* Ayeyarwady River
Irrigation project, Angkor, Cambodia, 31, 32-33
Irrigation project, Anuradhapura, Sri Lanka, 35, 37, 38
Irrigation project, Bactria region, Afghanistan, 578
Irvine, Andrew, 603, 606, 607
Irwin, H.C., 550
'Isā Khān the Younger (ruler of Tatta), 802
Isarasuntorn (king of Thailand), 98
Ise Jingū, Ise, Japan, 374, 375, 376, 377
Ise, Mie, Japan, 12, **374-378,** 460, 517, 651
Ise-Shima National Park, Japan, 374
Isfahan, Iran, 720
Ishakiyah Dynasty, 165
Ishaniyah Dynasty, 165
Ishi-butai (Stone Stage), Asuka, Japan, 461
Ishikawa, Japan, 431-434
Ishikawa Takuboku (poet), 320
Ishiyama hill, Ōsaka, Japan, 338, 650
Isla de Amat. *See* Tahiti, Society Islands, French Polynesia
Isla de Pascua. *See* Easter Island, Chile
Islam, 2-3, 5, 6-7, 9, 20, 21-22, 23, 24, 26, 27, 28, 29-30, 47, 48, 50, 58, 65, 68, 70, 71, 73, 79, 80, 87, 92, 94, 101, 103, 104, 113, 117, 120, 121, 122, 123, 125, 128, 129, 136, 137, 140, 142, 147, 153, 158, 161, 163, 165, 166, 174, 175, 186, 187, 188, 189, 218, 222, 225, 226, 227, 229, 241, 246, 256, 259, 260, 261, 263, 268, 272, 277, 279, 280, 281, 284, 286, 290, 305, 306, 309, 312, 314, 321, 323, 333, 335, 336, 353, 354, 366, 367, 369, 370, 371, 383, 388, 395, 399, 400, 403, 404, 406, 410, 412, 413, 414, 417, 418, 419, 437, 439, 442, 448, 449, 450, 451, 456, 457, 458, 459, 466, 469, 474, 478, 480, 500, 503, 505, 507, 522-524, 525, 534, 536, 548, 550, 561, 565, 568, 576-577, 578, 579, 584, 602, 608, 610, 626, 646, 659, 663, 667, 669, 671, 672, 679, 699, 704, 706, 711, 715, 720, 721, 727, 730, 731, 762, 764, 769, 801, 802, 812, 837, 838, 839, 849, 850, 855, 856, 857, 858, 872, 874, 884, 888, 890, 892, 897, 899, 900
Islam Khan (governor of Bengal), 260
Islamābād, Pakistan, 449
Islamia College and Collegiate School, Peshāwar, Pakistan, 671
Islamic Intermediate College, Chittagong, Bangladesh, 189
Islamnagarh, India, 118
Islas del Poniente. *See* Philippines
Isle of Pines, New Caledonia, 644
Isle of the Dead, Port Arthur, Australia, 691
Isles of Solomon (mythical islands), 819
Isma'il Khan (ruler of Kashgar), 458
Isma'il Samani (mausoleum), Bukara, Uzbekistan, 163
Israel (sultan of Jolo), 404
Istana Nurul Iman (palace), Bandar Seri Begawan, Brunei Darussalam, 162
İstanbul, Turkey, 165, 166, 241, 534
Isuzu River, 374
Italy, 13, 127, 132, 327, 385, 604, 736, 814, 871, 886, 887
Itimad-ud-Dawlah (father-in-law of Jahāngīr), 3
Itsukushima Dai-Myōjin, Miyajima, Japan, 587, 588, 590
Itsukushima-hime (goddess), 587
Itsukushima shrine, Miyajima, Japan, 587, 588, 589, 590
Iwaki, Japan, 345
Iwaki River, 345
Iwikau (Maori chieftain), 832
Iwo Jima, Volcano Islands, Japan, 379-382
Izanagi (god), 375
Izanami (goddess), 375
Izu Islands, 269, 271
Izu Peninsula, 269, 271
Izumo Taisha (shrine), Shimane, Japan, 376-377

Jabidah Massacre, 406
Jacatra. *See* Jakarta, Special Capital City Territory, Indonesia
Jacob, Samuel Swinton, 132, 133
Jadids (Muslim modernists), 166
Jaetsi (ruler of Jaisalmer), 388, 389
Jaffna, Sri Lanka, 199, 201, 202, 272, 273, 274, 443, 446, 687
Jaffnapatam, Sri Lanka, 202
Jagadambī (temple), Khajurāho, India, 468, 469
Jagannātha (god), 121, 479, 480, 697, 699, 700
Jagannātha Temple, Puri, India, 479, 480, 697, 699-700
Jagaraga, Bali, Indonesia, 69
Jagat (Jay) Malla (king of the Mallabhūm Dynasty), 134
Jahān (Mughal emperor of India), 120, 291, 309, 314, 400, 415, 416, 441, 671
Jahanara (First Lady of the Mughal Empire), 5, 671
Jahangasht. *See* Makhdum Jahaniyan
Jahāngīr (Mughal emperor of India), 1, 2-3, 8, 22, 26, 27, 165, 194, 222, 225, 260, 263, 291, 314, 335, 385, 392, 400, 416, 441, 522-523, 524, 525, 563, 769, 802
Jahāngīr Art Gallery, Bombay, India, 144
Jahāngīr Moḥammad Khān (ruler of Bhopāl), 119
Jahāngīr Palace, Gwalior, India, 314
Jahangiri Mahal, Āgra, India, 2-3, 4
Jahāngīrnagar. *See* Dhākā, Dhākā, Bangladesh
Jahānpanāh, India, 220
Jai Mandir (Hall of Victory), Amber, India, 26
Jai Pol (Victory Gate), Amber, India, 24
Jai Singh I (mahārāja of Jaipur), 24, 26
Jai Singh II (mahārāja of Jaipur), 26, 383, 385-386
Jai Vilas Palace, Gwalior, India, 316
Jaichand of Benares (Indian prince), 20
Jaigarh Fort, Amber, India, 26
Jaimal (Rājput prince), 194
Jainism, 6, 8, 9, 20, 23, 47, 48, 121, 122, 124, 129, 134, 191, 193, 256, 257, 278, 314, 392, 402, 408, 412, 435, 436, 437, 468, 501, 552, 572, 574, 576, 600-602, 625, 657, 837, 847, 848, 856
Jaipal of Bathindah (rāja), 20
Jaipur, Rājasthān, India, 24, 26, 132, **383-387,** 400, 600
Jaisal (prince regent of Lodurva), 388
Jaisalmer, Rājasthān, India, 129, 133, **388-394**
Jaisalmer Fort, India, 191
Jaivan (cannon), Amber, India, 26
Jakarta, Special Capital City Territory, Indonesia, 69, 102, 103, 104, 114, 115, 202, **395-398,** 493, 494, 495, 545, 585, 663, 841, 842, 888, 892
Jalāl ad-Dīn Mingburnu (governor of Herāt), 333
Jalāl-ud-Dīn Firūz Khaljī (Afghan Turk ruler), 218
Jaleb Chowk, Amber, India, 24
Jalliānwālla Bāgh Massarce, Amritsar, India, 27, 29
Jāma Masjid, Āgra, India, 5
Jāma Masjid, Delhi, India, 119, 120
Jāma Masjid, Fatehpur Sīkri, India, 260
Jāma Mosque, Nāsik, India, 626
Jamal-ul-Kiram I (sultan), 403, 404
Jambi, Indonesia, 582, 662, 663
James (saint), 783
James I (king of Great Britain), 88, 90
Jāmī (poet), 165, 335
Jāmi Masjid, Āgra, India, 222, 803
Jāmi Masjid, Ahmadābād, India, 6
Jāmi Masjid, Bijāpur, India, 127
Jāmi Masjid, Delhi, India, 222, 803
Jāmi Masjid, Gwalior, India, 314
Jāmi Masjid, Junāgadh, India, 412
Jāmi Masjid, Māndu, India, 562
Jāmi Masjid, Srīnagar, India, 769
Jāmi Masjid, Tatta, Pakistan, 803
Jammu and Kashmir, India, 3, 29, 228, 263, 302, 312, 507, 525, 526, 604, 608, 767-770, 806
Jamshetji Nusserwanji Tata, 144
Jamshid (Deccan king), 290
Jamuna River. *See* Brahmaputra River
Janardhan Temple, Guwāhāti, India, 310
Jang, Muzaffar, 369
Jang, Salābat, 369
Jang, Salar, 292
Jantar Mantar, Jaipur, India, 386
Japan, 10-13, 57, 63, 70, 89, 100, 103, 104, 107, 108, 110, 116, 141, 161, 175, 195, 196, 197, 204, 206-207, 208, 209, 216, 230, 242, 244, 269-271, 286, 298, 301, 307, 317-320, 331, 338-339, 340-344, 345-348, 349-352, 355, 360, 361, 365, 374-378, 379-382, 396, 398, 426-430, 431-434, 460-463, 482, 487, 497, 499, 512, 513, 515-521, 541, 542, 544, 545, 556, 558, 565, 567, 568, 569, 586, 587-591, 592-594, 604, 606, 612-615, 620, 621-624, 632-638, 646, 647, 648-652, 664, 667, 701, 704, 726, 736, 737, 742, 744, 748, 749, 757, 760, 761, 778, 790, 792, 793-794, 795-797, 813, 814, 816, 822-826, 842, 853, 854, 868, 873, 875, 876, 877, 879, 880, 881-882, 886, 887, 892, 897, 904
Japanese Alps National Park, Takayama, Japan, 795
Jara (hunter), 765
Jas Mandir (Hall of Glory), Amber, India, 26
Jaswant Singh (rāja of Jodhpur), 400
Jāt (people), 5, 506, 576-577
Jata Shankar Temple, Chittaurgarh, India, 193
Jāts, 5, 576-577
Jaugada, India, 699
Jauhar Tank, Gwalior, India, 312

Jaulian, Pakistan, 807-808
Jaunpur, India, 50, 849
Jaussen (bishop of Tahiti), 251
Java, Indonesia, 31, 65, 68, 69, 70, 87, 89, 101-104, 113, 114, 147-152, 158, 201, 206, 208, 395-398, 494, 495, 496, 568, 582, 585, 646, 659, 661, 662-663, 692-696, 712, 757, 841, 842, 888-892, 897
Java Sea, 87, 101, 395, 396
Java War, 891-892
Javanese War of Succession, 841
Javari (temple), Khajurāho, India, 470
Jawajir Bāī (queen mother of Chittaurgarh), 193
Jaya Stambh (Tower of Victory), Chittaurgarh, India, 191, 192, 193, 194
Jayabāhu (ruler of Sri Lanka), 685-686
Jayadhwaj Singh (king of Assam), 309
Jayaji Rāo (Sindhia mahārāja), 314, 316
Jayakarta. *See* Jakarta, Special Capital City Territory, Indonesia
Jayaśakti (Chandela ruler of Khajurāho), 468
Jayasthiti Malla (king of Kāthmāndu), 466
Jayavarman II (Khmer king of Cambodia), 31, 353
Jayavarman V (Khmer king of Cambodia), 32
Jayavarman VII (Khmer king of Cambodia), 33, 771
Jaz Mahal (Ship's Palace), Māndu, India, 563
Jeanneret, Charles-Édouard. *See* Le Courbusier
Jehosaphat (king of Judah), 272
Jelanktik, Gusti Ktut, 69
Jembrana, Bali, Indonesia, 69
Jenkinson, Anthony, 165-166
Jenkinson, Charles. *See* Hawkesbury, Baron
Jenner, William, 212
Jennings, Eli (American developer), 726, 820, 821
Jeonju. *See* Chŏnju, North Chŏlla, South Korea
Jerstad, Luther, 606
Jerudong, Brunei Darussalam, 161
Jessore, East Bengal, 24
Jesuits, 58, 196, 288, 296, 306, 340, 341, 342, 344, 383, 403, 404, 466, 523, 544, 545, 612, 742, 752
Jesus of Nazareth, 179, 181, 260, 342, 578, 707, 769
Jewel Walk. *See* Chankramana, Bodh Gayā, India
Jhanjiri Mosque, Bijāpur, India, 127
Jhānsi, India, 314
Jhelum River, 767, 768, 769
Ji. *See* Beijing, China
Ji River, 420, 741
Jiajing (Ming emperor of China), 296
Jian Chi (pool), Suzhou, China, 778
Jian Zhen (Buddhist monk), 886, 887
Jianfu Temple, Xian, China, 872
Jiang Jieshi. *See* Chiang Kai-shek
Jiang Qing (Gang of Four member), 738, 817
Jiang Shaoyu (Chinese designer), 213
Jiangsu, China, 109, 616-620, 736, 776-780, 874, 884-887
Jiangxi, China, 541, 736, 874-875
Jiaoguo, Lady (governor of Guangzhou), 304
Jiaotaidian (Hall of Heavenly and Earthly Union), Forbidden City, Beijing, China, 107
Jiaozhou, China, 302
Jiaqing (Qing emperor of China), 732
Jiayuguan. *See* Gansu, China
Jidai Matsuri (Festival of the Ages), Kyōto, Japan, 518
Jijā India Udyan (Victoria Gardens), Bombay, India, 253
Jikkō-kyō (sect), 271
Jilin, China, 741, 748
Jimmu Tennō (mythic first emperor of Japan), 374, 460, 461, 462, 592, 648
Jin Dynasty, 105, 109, 212, 214, 293, 294, 295, 302, 304, 325, 327, 424, 482, 541, 739, 744, 745, 746, 874, 420
Jin River, 704, 706
Jin Shuren, 323
Jina. *See* Mahāvīra
Jing Di (Han emperor of China), 871
Jingō (empress of Japan), 340, 648
Jinling. *See* Nanjing, Jiangsu, China
Jinling Hotel, Nanjing, China, 616
Jinnah, Mohammed Ali, 227, 394, 448, 449, 450
Jinniukou, China, 739
Jinzhou, China, 296, 741, 742, 743
Jito (empress of Japan), 376
Jizo (bodhisattva), 429
Joan of Arc (saint), 316
Jochi-ji (temple), Kamakura, Japan, 429
Jodhā Bāī (wife of Prince Salīm), 263
Jodhbai (wife of Akbar), 399
Jodhpur, Rājasthān, India, 129, 392, **399-402**
Jōdo Shin-shū (sect), 518, 519, 520, 650
Jogyo (bodhisattva), 270, 429
John (saint), 671
John of Monte Corrino (missionary), 711
John Wilson Memorial Drive, Dunedin, New Zealand, 238
Johnson, Richard, 641
Johnston, Reginald, 108
Johore, Malaysia, 158, 261, 403, 584, 585, 758, 760, 897
Jokhang Temple, Lhasa, Tibet, China, 526, 528, 529
Jokomyo-ji (temple), Kamakura, Japan, 428
Jolo, Sulu, Philippines, 403-407
Jolo War, 406
Jomon period (Japan), 345
Jomyo-ji (temple), Kamakura, Japan, 426
Jon Frum (John Prum) movement, 846
Jones, Shadrach, 235-236
Jourdain, Sullivan, and de Souza (trading company), 665
Juan-juan (people), 456
Juari River, 284, 289
Jubao. *See* Zhonghua Gate, Nanjing, China
Judaism, 73, 143, 166, 236, 239, 288, 383, 424, 448, 710, 711, 759, 884
Jufuku-ji (temple), Kamakura, Japan, 428, 429
Jumnā River. *See* Yamunā River
Jumpandang. *See* Ujung Pandang, South Sulawesi, Indonesia
Junāgadh, Gujarāt, India, 408-413, 762, 764
Junāgarh Fort, Bīkaner, India, 129, 132, 133
Junah (Sammā king), 802
Jung Bahadur (Nepalese general), 466
Junī Gadhī, Nāsik, India, 626
Junko Tabei, 606-607
Junnin. *See* Oi
Junyi, China, 422
Juramentados, Philippines, 404
Jürchen (people), 109, 325, 423, 424, 739, 741, 742, 745, 746, 747, 874
Jūrokuban mansion, Nagasaki, Japan, 615
Jurong, Singapore, 761
Juvaini (historian), 163-164, 333
Juyongguan, China, 296, 297, 741
Juyongguan Pass, China, 214
Jvarahareshvara Temple, Kānchipuram, India, 437
K2 (mountain), 604
Kabhura. *See* Kābul, Kābul, Afghanistan
Kabīr (Indian poet), 849
Kabīr Chaurā district, Vārānasī, India, 849
Kabir Panth (sectarian movement), 849
Kabong, Malaysia, 160, 497
Kābul, Kābul, Afghanistan, 1, 29, 165, 220, 279, 280, 281, 282, 336, 383, **414-419,** 439, 440, 441, 473, 476, 580
Kābul River, 414
Kābul Valley, 414, 415, 416
Kabyles (people), 646
Kadamba Dynasty, 284
Kaḍiri, kingdom of, 68
Kadmi Palace, Amber, India, 24
Kaero (king of Paekche), 484
Kaesŏng, Korea, 196
Kaga, Japan, 431
Kagoshima, Japan, 340, 594
Kagura-dens, Ise, Japan, 374, 375, 377
Kaguraden, Nikkō, Japan, 637
Kai Colo (people), 267
Kaifeng, Henan, China, 325, **420-425,** 541, 904
Kaikorai Valley, New Zealand, 236
Kailāsanātha Temple, Ellora, India, 256, 257-259
Kailāsanātha Temple, Kānchipuram, India, 436-437, 555
Kailāsha. *See* Mount Kailāsha
Kailun (ruler of Jaisalmer), 388
Kaisar-i-Hind (empress of India). *See* Victoria (queen of Great Britain)
Kaisarbargh Palace, Lucknow, India, 534
Kaivarta Kivya, 659
Kaiyuan Temple, Quanzhou, China, 706
Kakadu National Park, Australia, 211
Kākatīya Dynasty, 290
Kakrak, Afghanistan, 79
Kakrak River, 81
Kakrak Valley, 81
Kakuon-ji (temple), Kamakura, Japan, 429
Kālī (goddess), 24, 135, 172, 174
Kālī Temple, Amber, India, 24
Kālī Temple, Chittaurgarh, India, 193
Kal Bhairav (god), 466
Kalachi-Jo-goth. *See* Karāchi, Sind, Pakistan
Kalacuri Dynasty, 252, 253, 468
Kalani River, 199
Kalani Valley, 201
Kalgan-Datong-Baotou railway, 216
Kalhaṇa (Brahman scribe), 767
Kalhōrā, Ghulām Nabi (ruler of Sind), 371
Kalhōrā, Ghulām Shāh (ruler of Sind), 371
Kalhōrā, Safaraz (ruler of Sind), 371
Kalhōrā Dynasty, 371, 801, 803, 804
Kalhōrā tombs, Hyderābād, Pakistan, 371
Kālī. *See* Satī
Kālidāsa (Sanskrit poet and dramatist), 837
Kālīghāt (temple), Kalikshetra, India, 172, 174
Kalika Mata, Chittaurgarh, India, 191
Kalikshetra, India, 172
Kalimantan. *See* Borneo
Kalinga, kingdom of, 121, 122, 123, 124
Kaliṅga (people), 408, 686
Kalkatar. *See* Calcutta, West Bengal, India
Kaluwalla district, Galle, Sri Lanka, 274
Kalyan complex, Bukhara, Uzbekistan, 166
Kalyandas (ruler of Jaisalmer), 392
Kalyani Sima, Bago, Myanmar, 61, 62, 63
Kam Tin, Hong Kong, 358
Kamakhya Temple, Guwāhāti, India, 308
Kamakshiamman Temple, Kānchipuram, India, 437
Kamakura, Kanagawa, Japan, 269, 340, **426-430,** 518, 521
Kamakura-gu (shrine), Kamakura, Japan, 430
Kāmarūpa. *See* Assam, India
Kāmboja, India, 608
Kambuja (people), 353
Kamchatka Peninsula, 318
Kamet, India, 604
Kamigamo Jinja (shrine), Kyōto, Japan, 515, 518
Kammu (emperor of Japan), 515, 520, 624, 648
Kamo River, 515
Kämpfer, Engelbert, 614
Kampong Gelam, Singapore, 760
Kampung Ayer/Air, Brunei Darussalam, 162
Kamran (Mughal ruler), 416, 417, 440-441
Kaṃsa (king), 762

Kamu-Yamato-Iware Hikono-mikoto. *See* Jimmu Tennō
Kan-ami (actor), 518
Kan-ei-ji, Tōkyō, Japan, 637
Kanagawa, Japan, 271, 426-430
Kanak Social National Liberation Front (New Caledonian), 647
Kanaks. *See* Melanesians
Kanamori family, 795, 796
Kanamori Nagachika, 795
Kanauj, India, 50, 123, 222, 399, 410, 576, 837
Kanaung (prince of Burma), 556
Kanazawa, Ishikawa, Japan, 431-434
Kānchi. *See* Kānchipuram, Tamil Nādu, India
Kānchipuram, Tamil Nādu, India, 435-438, 552, 554, 555, 809
Kanda district, Tōkyō, Japan, 824
Kandahār, Afghanistan, 439-442
Kandahār, Kandahār, Afghanistan, 282, 333, 335, 392, 414, 415, 416, 417, **439-442,** 580, 802
Kandarash. *See* Kandahār, Kandahār, Afghanistan
Kaṇḍarya Mahādeva (temple), Khajurāho, India, 468, 469, 470
Kandavu Island, Fiji, 264, 265
Kandy, kingdom of, 199, 200, 201, 202
Kandy, Sri Lanka, 272-274, **443-447,** 756
Kandy Plateau, 443
Kanei-ji (temple), Tōkyō, Japan, 824
Kang Sanghui (Samghavarman; Buddhist missionary), 616
Kang Xi (emperor of China), 544
Kangchenjunga (mountain), 603
Kangen-sai festival, Miyajima, Japan, 590
Kangxi (Qing emperor of China), 323, 328, 742, 747
Kāṇheri, India, 142
Kanishka (Kushān king), 669, 798
Kankō Shiryōkan, Hirado, Japan, 344
Kannada, kingdom of, 125
Kannon (goddess), 12, 18, 338, 344, 354, 426, 431, 460, 518, 632, 795
Kanō family, 317, 338
Kanō Tanyū (artist), 796
Kanō Yasunobu (artist), 636
Kānpur. *See* Kanauj, India
Kantipur. *See* Kāthmāndu, Nepal
Kantō Plain, Honshū, Japan, 269, 270, 430, 632, 822
Kanwar Pade-Ka Mahal, Chittaurgarh, India, 193
Kao-Fu. *See* Kābul, Kābul, Afghanistan
Kao Hsien-chih (Tang viceroy), 163
Kao-lan-pu. *See* Colombo, Sri Lanka
Kapaleeshwara Temple, Mylapore, India, 550
Kapila River, 765
Kapilavastu, India, 138
Kapileśwar Temple, Bhubaneswar, India, 123
Kapitan Kling Mosque, Penang, Malaysia, 667
Kara Kum Desert, 333
Kara-taghliq (sect), 458
Karāchi, Sind, Pakistan, 142, 373, **448-450,** 551, 595, 804
Karakhanid Dynasty, 163, 282, 456-457
Karakitai Dynasty, 163, 282, 457, 720
Karakoram, Kashmir, India, 604
Karakoram Mountains, 239
Karakoram Pass, 459
Karakorum, Uburkhangai, Mongolia, 451-455
Karaliyadde Bandara (king of Kandy), 443
Karamnasa River, 168, 169, 170
Karamon (Chinese Gate), Nikkō, Japan, 637
Karan Mahal, Bīkaner, India, 132
Karan Prole (gate), Bīkaner, India, 132
Karan Singh (ruler of Bīkaner), 132
Karangasem, Bali, Indonesia, 68, 69
Karasaki, Japan, 338
Karashahr, China, 456
Karen (people), 63, 558, 882
Karijuku, Japan, 269
Karikāla (Cōḷa king), 809
Karluk (people), 456
Karṇa (Chedi ruler), 659
Karnāl, India, 20, 506
Karnaphuli River, 186, 189
Karnātaka, India, 92-95, 125-128, 809, 855-858
Karnavati (mother of Udai Singh II), 193
Karni Matra Temple, Deshnok, India, 133
Kart Dynasty, 333, 335, 414, 439
Karta, Indonesia, 888
Kartalab Khān. *See* Murshid Qulī Khān
Kartalab Khān Mosque, Dhākā, Bangladesh, 225
Kartasura, Indonesia, 890
Kārtikeya (god), 576, 837
Karttaviryarjuna (Haihaya king of Ujjain), 836
Kasanui. *See* Kashihara, Nara, Japan
Kasatkin, Ivan Nikolai, 319
Kāshī, kingdom of, 847
Kashgar, Xinjiang Uighur Autonomous Region, China, 239, **456-459,** 473, 718
Kashgar Dynasty, 163, 165
Kashi. *See* Kashgar, Xinjiang Uighur, China
Kāshī. *See* Vārānasī, Uttar Pradesh, India
Kashihara, Nara, Japan, 460-463, 592
Kashihara Jingū (shrine), Kashihara, Japan, 462
Kāshīrāj Dynasty, 847, 850
Kāshīs (people), 847
Kashiwara, Japan, 460
Kashmir. *See* Jammu and Kashmir, India
Kashmir Valley, 768
Kaśi. *See* Vārānasī, India
Kasim Khan (Mughal general), 92
Kasuga Taisha, Nara, Japan, 376, 377, 621
Kasumigaseki district, Tōkyō, Japan, 825
Kāśyapa I (king of Sri Lanka), 38, 754, 755, 756
Kaṭacurris (people), 626
Katamori, Matsudira. *See* Matsudira Katamori
Katata, Japan, 338
Kathalbari, India, 226, 309
Kāthiāwār Peninsula. *See* Saurāshtra, India
Kāthmāndu, Nepal, 464-467, 603
Kāthmāndu Valley, 464, 465, 466
Katipunan (Philippines), 568
Kaṭrā, Mathurā, India, 572
Katsura Rikyū, Kyōto, Japan, 520
Kaufmann, Konstantin Petrovich, 722
Kaurava (clan), 259, 505, 762, 836
Kausambi, India, 836
Kauulufonua Fekai (ruler of Tonga), 828
Kava (mythic human ancestor in Tokelau), 818
Kava Dynasty, 49
Kava Vasefanua (first chief of Fakaofo), 818
Kavanagh, Henry, 536
Kāverī River. *See* Cauvery River
Kavila (governor prince of Chiang Mai), 184
Kawagoe, Japan, 636
Kaya region, South Korea, 483, 509
Kayamkulam, India, 712
Kayatha, India, 835
Kazan, Russia, 166
Kaze no Miya (shrine), Ise, Japan, 374
Kazipura Darwaji, Nāsik, India, 626
Ke Chu, Vietnam, 329
Kedah, Malaysia, 665, 667
Kedleston Hall, England, 173
Kedu Plain, Central Java, Indonesia, 147, 148
Keelung, Taiwan, China, 794
Kegon Waterfalls, Nikkō, Japan, 638
Kehur (ruler of Jaisalmer), 392
Keitaku-en (garden), Ōsaka, Japan, 651
Kek Lok Si Temple, Air Itam, Penang, 668
Kellas, A.M., 604
Kelly, William, 77
Kemmu Restoration, 429
Kempe Gowda (Indian chieftain), 92, 95
Kencho-ji (temple), Kamakura, Japan, 428, 429
Kengamme (mountain peak), 269
Kennedy, John F., 300
Kenreimon-in (daughter of Taira Kiyomori), 589
Kenrokuen Park, Kanazawa, Japan, 431, 434
Keppel, Henry, 404
Keppel Harbor, Singapore, 758
Kerafshan Mountains, 720
Kerala, India, 199, 201, 284, 288, 548, 551, 710-713
Kerkhof cemetery, Galle, Sri Lanka, 274
Kesaran, C., 713
Kesari kings. *See* Soma Dynasty
Keśava Deva Temple, Mathurā, India, 576-577
Kesh. *See* Shakhrisabz, Uzbekistan
Keshta Raya (temple), Bishnupur, India, 134, 135-136
Ketetahi Hot Springs, Tongariro, New Zealand, 834
Kettle, Charles, 234-235
Kew Gardens, London, England, 783
Kew Palace, London, England, 202
Khachchawa (clan), 24, 26
Khaja Rashid E-din (Persian writer), 704
Khajurāho, Madhya Pradesh, India, 468-472
Khalīl (son of Miran Shāh), 335
Khaljī Dynasty, 125, 142, 218, 561
Khālsā Sikhs, 28
Khamu (people), 530
Khan Mansur (ruler of Hami), 323
Khān Muhammad Mirdha Mosque, Dhākā, Bangladesh, 225
Khan River, 530
Khanbaliq. *See* Beijing, China
Khapara Khodia Caves, Junāgadh, India, 410
Khāravela (Cheti ruler of Orissa), 122, 699
Khas Mahal (House Palace), Āgra, India, 4
Khāsi Hills, India, 310
Khawak Pass, 474, 475
Khian Tek Triad, 668
Khilji Dynasty, 837-838
Khitan (people), 109
Khiva, Uzbekistan, 163, 166, 333
Khmer (people), 329, 353, 530, 851
Khmer Empire. *See* Cambodia
Khmer Rouge (Cambodia), 34, 332
Khoja Ahmad Kasani. *See* Makhdum-i Azam
Khoja Ahrar (religious leader), 165
Khoja Islam (Bukharan leader), 165
Khoja Kalon (Juybari sheikh), 166
Khoo (clan), 667, 668
Khoo Kongsi, Penang, Malaysia, 668
Khoo Thean Teik (Penang rebel), 668
Khorāsān, Iran, 164, 165, 280, 281, 333, 336, 440, 441, 522, 720
Khorat Plateau, Thailand, 82, 84, 86, 532, 851, 852
Khost, Afghanistan, 416
Khotan, China, 241, 246, 456, 457, 458
Khudābād, Pakistan, 371, 803
Khumbu Glacier, Mount Everest, 603, 606
Khun Borom (Tai mythical ancestor), 530
Khun Lo (Lao leader), 530
Khun Sua (Lao leader), 530
Khurda, India, 699
Khurram (prince of India). *See* Shāh Jahān
Khushal Khān Khattak (poet-warrior), 671
Khusraw (son of Jahāngīr), 523
Khutukhtu (ruler of Mongolia), 453
Khvājeh Abū Naṣr Pārṣā (theologian), 73
Khwājah Muīn-ud-Dīn Chishtī (saint), 24, 260
Khwārezm, kingdom of, 333, 414, 720
Khwārezm-Shah Dynasty, 333, 414
Khyber Pass, North-West Frontier, Pakistan; Kābul, Afghanistan, 187, 279, 448, **473-477,** 669

Ki-pin. *See* Kābul, Afghanistan
Kiefer, Thomas, 403
Kim Ch'unch'u. *See* T'aejong Muyol
Kim Hŏn-ch'ang, 487
Kim Il-sung, 197
Kim Tae-song, 512
Kim Yu-sin, 486, 511
Kimanis, Brunei Darussalam, 160
Kimhae, South Korea, 512
Kimmei (emperor of Japan), 461, 515, 648
Kindley Landing Field, Corregidor Island, Philippines, 204, 207
King, Anna Josephs, 639
King, Norfolk, 639
King, Philip Gidley, 639, 641
King, Philip Parker, 639
King, Sydney, 639
King George III's Island. *See* Tahiti, Society Islands, French Polynesia
King's Square. *See* Medan Merdeka, Jakarta, Indonesia
Kingsford Smith, Sydney, 156
Kingstown (Kingston), Norfolk Island, Australia, 639
Kingsway, Delhi, India, 223
Kinkaku-ji (temple), Kyōto, Japan, 518
Kinki, Japan, 12, 426, 621
Kinu River, 638
Kipling, Rudyard, 473, 534, 550, 556
Kirāti Dynasty, 465
Kirghiz (people), 458
Kiribati, 266
Kirmān, Iran, 522
Kirti Stambh (Tower of Fame), Chittaurgarh, India, 191, 193, 194
Kīrtivarman (6th-century Cāḷukyan king of Pūri), 253
Kīrtivarman (11th-century Chandela king of Khajurāho), 468-469
Kishkindhā-kshetra. *See* Vijayanagara, Karnātaka, India
Kiso Mountains, 377
Kissinger, Henry, 356
Kita-no-shō. *See* Fukui, Japan
Kitan (people), 325, 739, 744
Kitano Point, Iwo Jima, Japan, 381-382
Kitano Tenman-gū (shrine), Kyōto, Japan, 517
Kitaykyūshū, Japan, 614
Kitti. *See* Vijayabāhu
Kitti Sirimegha (ruler of Ruhuṇa), 686
Kiyomizu-dera (temple), Kyōto, Japan, 515
Kizil Su, 456
Klungkung, Bali, Indonesia, 69, 70
Ko Fuji (volcano), Fujinomiya, Japan, 269
Ko Ratanakosin, Bangkok, Thailand, 96
Kō Taijingū. *See* Naikū, Ise, Japan
Koau (mythic human ancestor on Tonga), 827
Kob el Akhbar shrine. *See* Hajji Piyade shrine, Balkh, Afghanistan
Kōbe, Japan, 319, 349, 650, 652
Kōbo Daishi (Shingon-shū sect founder), 588, 589
Kobori Enshū (landscape gardener), 338, 518, 520
Koch (people), 308
Koch'Ang-Upsong Fortress, Chŏnju, South Korea, 196
Kōdō (Lecture Hall), Ōsaka, Japan, 648
Koḍungallar. *See* Tiruvanchikkulam, India
Koeckebacker, Nicolaes, 342, 343
Koenigsberger (architect), 124
Koestler, Arthur, 146
Kōfuku-ji (temple), Nara, Japan, 621
Kogugwon (king of Koguryŏ), 483, 484
Koguryŏ, kingdom of, 195, 482, 483-484, 486, 487, 509, 511, 739, 744
Koh-i-Noor diamond, 1
Kohai (mythic human ancestor on Tonga), 827
Kohima, India, 880
Koi (king of Paekche), 482, 483
Kojong (king of Korea), 487
Kokand, Uzbekistan, 163, 166, 458
Kōken (Shōtoku; empress of Japan), 623-624
Kokuho-kan, Kamakura, Japan, 430
Kokura, Japan, 351, 614
Kolamba. *See* Colombo, Sri Lanka
Kolambu. *See* Colombo, Sri Lanka
Kolambu (Samar chieftain), 177
Kolis (people), 142
Kollam. *See* Quilon, Kerala, India
Kōmei (emperor of Japan), 520
Kōmeitō (Japanese political party), 271
Komitake (volcano), Fujinomiya, Japan, 269
Komsung. *See* Kyŏngju, North Kyŏngsang, South Korea
Komul. *See* Hami, Xinjiang Uighur, China
Komyo-ji (temple), Kamakura, Japan, 428
Kon Laeng (pyramid), Sukhothai, Thailand, 772
Konārak, Orissa, India, 312, **478-481**
Konbaung Dynasty, 63, 556, 879
Kong family, 707, 708, 709
Kong Fuzi. *See* Confucius
Kongju and Puyŏ, South Ch'ungch'ŏng, South Korea, 482-488
Kongju Museum, Chŏnju, South Korea, 195
Kongsan Fortress, Kongju, South Korea, 484
Kongzi. *See* Confucius
Koningsplein (King's Square). *See* Medan Merdeka, Jakarta, Indonesia
Koṅkan, India, 284
Koṅkaṇ Maurya Dynasty, 252, 253
Konkizan hill, Japan, 338
Kōno family, 12
Konohana Sakuyahime (goddess), 269, 270
Kophen. *See* Kābul, Afghanistan
Koputai. *See* Port Chalmers, Dunedin, New Zealand
Korea, 195-198, 270, 317, 340, 341, 349, 350, 351, 360, 361, 375, 376, 381, 460, 461, 462, 463, 482-488, 499, 509-514, 520, 521, 542, 587, 592, 613, 621, 632, 636, 637, 648, 652, 737, 739, 741, 742, 793, 882
Korean War, 361, 499
Koro Sea, 264
Kororareka. *See* Russell, New Zealand
Koryŏ Dynasty, 195-196, 487, 509, 513
Koryu-ji Temple, Hakodate, Japan, 317, 318
Kośala, kingdom of, 47, 534, 847
Kōshūkaidō Highway, Japan, 824
Kot Courtyard, Kāthmāndu, Nepal, 466
Kot Diji, Sind, Pakistan, 489-492
Kot Massacre, 466
Kota Gede, Indonesia, 888
Koteda Yasutsune (governor of Hiradoshima), 340
Kothari Havelis, Bīkaner, India, 129
Koti Tīrtha, Rāmeswaram, India, 716
Kōtoku (emperor of Japan), 648
Kotokuin Daibutsu (Great Buddha), Kamakura, Japan, 428
Kotokuin-Josen-ji (temple), Kamakura, Japan, 428
Kottarakara, India, 712
Kotte, kingdom of, 199, 200-201, 202, 272, 443
Kotte, Sri Lanka. *See* Sri Jayawardhanapura Kotte, Sri Lanka
Kowloon Bay, 358
Kowloon Peninsula, 358, 359, 360, 814
Koxinga (ruler of Taiwan), 705, 790-792, 793, 794
Kōya-san (holy mountain), Wakayama, Japan, 588
Kozui Otani (Buddhist abbot), 244
Krakatau, Indonesia, 493-496
Krakatoa. *See* Krakatau, Indonesia
Krishna (god), 134, 135, 137, 259, 308, 388, 478, 555, 572, 574, 576, 577, 601, 660, 695, 697, 699, 762, 764, 765, 856
Krishna I (Rāshṭrakūṭa king of Kailāsanātha), 257
Krishna Devarāja (Vijayanagar king of Kānchipuram), 437, 502
Krishna-Godāvari Delta, 501
Krishna River, 125, 290, 366, 811
Krishna Temple, Vijayanagara, India, 856
Krishnadeva Rāya (Tuluva king of Vijayanagara), 856, 857
Krishnarāja Wodeyar (rāja of Mysore), 94
Krung Thep. *See* Bangkok, Thailand
Kṣaharāta Kṣatrapas (Śaka dynasty), 626
Kshatriyas, 468
Ku Na (king of Lan Na), 182, 184
Kuala Lumpur, Malaysia, 761
Kuan Yin Temple, Penang, Malaysia, 667
Kuber Parbat, Ayodhyā, India, 48
Kubera (god), 258
Kubha. *See* Kābul, Kābul, Afghanistan
Kublai Khan, 105, 182, 327, 452-453, 534, 655, 656, 813, 866, 884
Kucca Qila, Hyderābād, Pakistan, 371
Kuch Bihār, India, 309
Kucha, China, 240, 456, 458
Kuching, Sarawak, Malaysia, 497-500
Kudatissa (Sinhalese king of Sri Lanka), 38
Kudō Suketsune, 269
Kuek Seng Ong (god), 500
Kugyo (Buddhist priest), 428
Kuhandil Khān (governor of Kandahār), 441, 442
Kujūla Kadphises (Kushān leader), 805
Kūkai (founder of Shingon sect), 515
Kukeldush (religious school), Bukhara, Uzbekistan, 166
Kulaśekhara Dynasty, 710
Kulikitjeri (mythic Lira leader), 44
Kulottuṅga (Cōḷa king of Sri Lanka), 685
Kum Kam, Thailand, 182
Kŭm River, 482, 485, 486
Kumar Bhaskara Barman (king of Assam), 308
Kumārapāla (king of Junāgadh), 412, 764
Kumāri (goddess), 466
Kumāri Bahal, Kāthmāndu, Nepal, 466
Kumbakonam, Tamil Nādu, India, 501-504
Kumbeshwara Temple, Kumbakonam, India, 501, 503
Kumbh Mela festival, Nāsik, India, 625, 627, 628, 838
Kumbha (rāna of Chittaurgarh), 193
Kumbha Palace. *See* Palace of Rāna Kumbha, Chittaurgarh, India
Kumbha Shyam Temple, Chittaurgarh, India, 193
Kumbhalgarh, India, 388
Kumgwan-ch'ong, Kyŏngju, South Korea, 514
Kumsansa Temple, Chŏnju, South Korea, 197
Kumudasena (king of Ayodhyā), 49
Kunala (son of Aśoka), 807
Kunala Monastery, Taxila, Pakistan, 807
Kunala Stupa, Taxila, Pakistan, 807
Kŭnch'ogo (king of Paekche), 482, 483
Kundūz River, 79
Kungnamji Pond, Puyŏ, South Korea, 485
Kungye (ruler of Koguryŏ), 195
Kuni, Japan, 622
Kunio (mythic people), 44
Kunlun Shan Mountains, 239
Kunming, China, 558
Kunninggong, Forbidden City, Beijing, China, 107
Kunō-zan, Shizuoka, Japan, 634, 636
Kunsan, South Korea, 197
Kunshan, Suzhou, China, 776
Kuomintang, 868, 874, 875-876, 877
Kure, Japan, 350
Kuril Islands, 318
Kurnell, Australia, 781
Kurnell Peninsula, Australia, 153, 156
Kuroda Kiyotaka (Japanese general), 319
Kurokawa (Black River), Fukushima, Japan, 10

Kurrun (ruler of Jaisalmer), 388
Kuru (Aryan chieftan), 505
Kurukshetra, Haryāna, India, 505-508
Kurukshetra Plain, 505
Kusakabe family, 796
Kushān Empire, 49, 72, 333, 371, 410, 414, 439, 468, 576, 579, 608, 669, 699, 720, 798, 800, 805-806, 807-808, 848
Kusinārā, India, 138
Kuthodaw Pagoda, Mandalay, Myanmar, 556, 557
Kuwae, Vanuatu, 843
Kwansan-song. *See* Okeh'on, South Korea
Kyanzittha (king of Pagan), 654
Kyaukse, Myanmar, 653
Kyauktawgyi Pagoda, Mandalay, Myanmar, 556, 559
Kyerim, kingdom of, 509
Kyō River, 349
Kyōbashi district, Tōkyō, Japan, 824
Kyōdokan (museum), Takayama, Japan, 795
Kyōkai (priest), 345
Kyŏngae (king of Silla), 195, 513
Kyŏngju, North Kyŏngsang, South Korea, 195, **509-514**
Kyŏngsang, South Korea, 196, 513
Kyŏnhwŏn (Korean military leader), 195, 513
Kyōto, Kyōto, Japan, 12, 317, 338, 339, 340, 426, 428, 429, 430, 431, 462, **515-521,** 587, 594, 612, 621, 624, 636, 637, 638, 650, 795, 797, 822, 823, 825, 826
Kyū Aizu-han Gohonjin, Aizu-Wakamatsu, Japan, 11, 12-13
Kyūshū, Japan, 12, 269, 340, 341, 343, 344, 376, 461, 517, 587, 592, 594, 612, 613, 648, 650, 824
Kyzyl Kum desert, 164

La Martiniere's School, Lucknow, India, 535
La Na Kingdom, Thailand, 182, 184
La Pérouse. *See* Galaup, Jean-François de (comte de La Pérouse)
La Pérouse, Australia, 156, 157, 781
Labi, Brunei Darussalam, 161
Labokla. *See* Lahore, Punjab, Pakistan
Labrulle (architect), 646
Labuan Island, 160, 497
Ladakh, Jammu and Kashmir, India, 529
Ladrones Islands. *See* Mariana Islands
Lady Lansdowne Hospital, Bhopāl, India, 120
Lady Robinson's Beach, Botany Bay, Australia, 156
Lagusi, Indonesia, 841
Lahore and Multān Railway, 595
Lahore Cathedral, Lahore, Pakistan, 525
Lahore Fort, Pakistan, 523, 524, 525
Lahore Gate, Delhi, India, 222
Lahore, Punjab, Pakistan, 1, 2, 3, 4, 29, 218, 263, 281, 282, 406, 415, 473, **522-525,** 610, 801
Lai Chau, Vietnam, 230, 232
Lake Anā Sāgar, 20, 22
Lake Asthamudi, 710
Lake Bindu Sagara, 121
Lake Biwa, 338
Lake Bod Dal, 769
Lake Bogambara, 443, 447
Lake Chūzenji, 632, 638
Lake Dal, 767, 768, 769
Lake Gagribal, 769
Lake Hāleji, 450
Lake Inawashiro, 10, 12
Lake Issyk Kul, 321
Lake Kalawewa, 38, 754
Lake Kawaguchi, 269, 271
Lake Logan, 237
Lake Lokut Dal, 769
Lake Mandākinī, 850
Lake Maota, 26
Lake Matsyodarī, 850
Lake Motosu, 269
Lake Nagīn, 767, 769
Lake Nakki, 602
Lake of the Restored Sword, 329, 331, 332
Lake Rotoaira, 834
Lake Sai, 269
Lake Shōji, 269, 271
Lake Shouxi, 886
Lake Sudarshan, 410
Lake Tai, 779
Lake Xuanwu, 618
Lake Yamanaka, 269
Lakemba Island, Fiji, 264, 265, 266
Lakhun (ruler of Jaisalmer), 388
Lakśavarman (Chandela ruler of Khajurāho), 468
Lakshman (rāna of Chittaurgarh), 191
Lakshmi (goddess), 223, 259, 465, 695, 699, 837
Lakshmi Narayan Temple, Delhi, India, 221, 223
Lakṣmaṇa (legendary stepbrother of Rāma), 47, 312, 625, 694-695
Lakṣmaṇa Gunda, Rāmeswaram, India, 716
Lakśmaṇa Temple, Khajurāho, India, 468, 469, 470
Laksmināth Temple, Bīkaner, India, 129
Lāl Bagh Gardens, Bangalore, India, 92, 94
Lal Kot (fortress), Delhi, India, 218, 220
Lal Qila (Red Fort), Āgra, India, 222
Lal Qila (Red Fort), Delhi, India, 5, 220, 222, 223
Lal Singh, 133
Lālbāgh Fort, Dhākā, Bangladesh, 225, 228
Lalgarh Palace, Bīkaner, India, 132
Lalgarh Palace Hotel, Bīkaner, India, 133
Lalguan Mahādeva (temple), Khajurāho, India, 469, 470
Lalitpur, Nepal, 6, 464, 465, 466
Lally, Thomas Arthur, 548
Lalor, Peter, 77-78
Lamaism, 750
Lamanon (victim of Samoan massacre), 724
Lambert, Raymond, 606
Lampacao Island, 542
Lampang, Thailand, 184
Lamphun, Thailand, 182, 184, 530
Lampung, Sumatra, 101, 663
Lan Na, kingdom of, 54, 55, 56, 182, 184, 531
Lan Xang, kingdom of, 530-531, 532, 851, 852
Lanchester, H.V., 402
Land Wars (New Zealand), 832, 860
Landak, Borneo, 103
Landi Kotal, Khyber Pass, North-West Frontier, Pakistan; Kābul, Afghanistan, 473, 476
Lang, John Dunmore, 865
Lang Darma (ruler of Tibet), 527, 750
Lang Island, Indonesia, 493, 495
Langah Dynasty, 610
Lanka. *See* Sri Lanka
Lanka, India, 143
Lanna, kingdom of, 773, 775
Lantau Island, Hong Kong, 358
Lanzhou, China, 239
Lao Kingdom. *See* Laos
Lao Meng (king of Chiang Saen), 182
Lao-Thai War of 1827-1828, 851, 852
Laolongtou, Shanhaiguan, China, 739, 741, 742, 743
Laos, 84, 86, 97, 98, 99, 182, 230, 231, 232, 233, 331, 353, 530-533, 772, 851-854
Lapierre, Dominique, 473
Lapita (people), 723, 827, 843
Lapita, New Caledonia, 843
Lapu-lapu (chieftain), 179
Lār, Pakistan, 801
Lara Jonggrang, Prambanan, Indonesia, 694
Larrakia (people), 209
Lashio, Myanmar, 558
Lashkar, India, 312, 316
Lassalle, Hugo, 351
Lasseter, Harold, 45
Late Tang Dynasty, 246
Later Han Dynasty. *See* Eastern Han Dynasty
Later Jin Dynasty, 214, 541, 746
Later Koguryŏ Kingdom, 195
Later Liang Dynasty, 422
Later Paekche Kingdom, 195, 513
Later Tang Dynasty, 214, 538
Later Zhou Dynasty, 244, 422
Latin Quarter, Nouméa, New Caledonia, 647
LaTrobe, Joseph, 75, 78
Lau Islands, Fiji, 264, 266
Laugram, India, 134
Laurel, José, 569
Law, Edward. *See* Ellenborough, Lord
Law Code of 1862 (Tonga), 830
Law College, Madras, India, 550
Lawrence, Henry, 536
Lawry, Walter, 829
Lawson, R.A., 236
Lawson, William, 783
Lay, Horatio, 813
Layard, E.L., 267
Le Coq, Albert von, 458
Le Courbusier (Charles-Édouard Jeanneret), 9
Le Dynasty, 353
Le Maire, Jakob, 828
Le Receveur (naturalist and priest), 154
Le Thai To (king of Dai Viet), 329
Le Thanh Tong (emperor of Vietnam), 531
League for the Independence of Vietnam. *See* Viet Minh
League of Nations, 726, 742, 749, 788
Lean, David, 276
Lear, Edward, 144
Lee Kuan Yew, 760-761
Leeward Islands. *See* Society Islands
Legazpi, Miguel López de, 177, 179, 180, 181, 565, 899
Lei River, 212
Lek Yuen, Hong Kong, 358
Lemoine Statute (New Caledonia), 647
Lemprière, Thomas, 688
Lenin, Vladimir, 176, 876
Leonowens, Anna, 99
Leria, Giovanni-Maria, 852
Les Grandes Cyclades. *See* Vanuatu
Lesser Dynasty (Sri Lanka), 38
Lesser Sunda Islands, 65
Levi, Peter, 81, 416, 578
Levuka, Ovalau Island, Fiji, 266, 267
Leyte Island, Philippines, 207, 568
Lhasa River, 526
Lhasa, Tibet, Xizang Autonomous Region, China, 526-529, 750, 751, 752
Lhoste Face, Mount Everest, 606
Li Bo (poet), 420
Li Cheng Uk, Hong Kong, 358
Li Cizhong (Chinese rebel leader), 873
Li Dazhao, 742
Li Gefei (Chinese author), 541
Li Han (pirate), 790
Li Hongzhang (governor of Jiangsu), 735-736
Li Keyong (Shatuo Turk), 214
Li Mountain, 701
Li Qingzhao (poet), 325
Li Shan Hill, Xian, China, 873
Li Si, 42
Li Taoyuan, 896
Li Wenzhong (Ming military leader), 620
Li Yuanhong (republican military leader), 868
Li Zhi. *See* Gao Zong

Li Zicheng, 107, 216, 742
Liancuo River, 750
Liang Danming (pirate), 663
Liang Dynasty, 304, 422, 484, 618
Liang Garden, Kaifeng, China, 420
Liang-Jiang, China, 736
Liang Xiao Wang, 420
Lianghuai Salt Administration, Yangzhou, China, 886
Liao Dynasty, 109, 163, 214, 295, 739, 744-745
Liao River, 739, 741, 744
Liao Yunzhou. *See* Xijing, China
Liaodong, China, 744, 745, 746, 747, 748
Liaoning, China, 293, 294, 295, 296, 739, 742, 744-749
Liaoxi, China, 743
Liaoyang, China, 744, 746
Libya, 406
Licchavi. *See* Lichhavi Dynasty
Licheng. *See* Quanzhou, Fujian, China
Lichhavi Dynasty, 465
Lienü Temple, Shanhaiguan, China, 741
Lifuka, Tonga, 828
Light, Francis, 665, 667
Light, William, 208
Light of the World. *See* Nūr Jahān
Lighthouse, Nouméa, New Caledonia, 645, 647
Lighthouse, Tahiti, French Polynesia, 786
Lily Throne Hall, Mandalay, Myanmar, 557
Lim (clan), 667
Limahong (Chinese pirate), 565-566
Limbang River, 161
Lin Biao, 743, 749
Lin Ze, 545
Lin Zexu, 732, 735
Ling (Han emperor of China), 302
Lingarāja Temple, Old Town, Bhubaneswar, India, 121, 123
Lingkor road, Lhasa, Tibet, China, 526, 529
Lingwu, China, 296
Lingyin Si (Temple of Inspired Seclusion), Hangzhou, China, 328
Lini, Walter, 846
Lintao, China, 294
Lintin Island, 545
Linyu, China, 741
Lion Capital inscriptions, Mathurā, India, 574
Lion Gate (Sing Pol), Amber, India, 26
Lion Palace. *See* Singha Durbar, Kāthmāndu, Nepal
Lion Throne of Myanmar, 556, 557, 558
Liru (mythic people), 44
Lisbon, Portugal, 544
Little Bay, Australia, 156
Little Ghazna. *See* Lahore, Punjab, Pakistan
Little Goose Pagoda. *See* Xiao Yan Ta, Xian, China
Little India, Georgetown, Malaysia, 667
Little Kyōto. *See* Takayama, Gifu, Japan
Liu (people), 358
Liu Bang (founder of Han Dynasty), 538, 871
Liu Congxiao (governor of Quanzhou), 704
Liu Garden, Suzhou, China, 779
Liu Ming-ch'uan (governor of Taiwan), 793
Liu Song, 294
Liu Wu. *See* Liang Xiao Wang
Liu Xiangzhai, 743
Liu Xiu (Han emperor of China), 538
Liu Yu (Earlier Song Dynasty founder), 616
Liuxiu (Tuoba leader), 212
Liuyan, China, 239
Loang Spean, Cambodia, 31
Lodī Dynasty, 1, 220, 415, 440, 507, 849
Lodī Gardens, Delhi, India, 220
Lodurva, India, 388
Loethai (king of Sukhothai), 774
Lofty Gate (Buland Darwāza), Fatehpur Sīkri, India, 260, 263
Loh (god), 522
Loha (Iron) Gate, Jodhpur, India, 399
Loh-awar (Loh's Fort). *See* Lahore, Punjab, Pakistan
Lohapasada Monastery, Anuradhapura, Sri Lanka, 38, 39
Lomaiviti Islands, Fiji, 264, 266
Lombok, Lesser Sundas, Indonesia, 68, 69, 70
Lon Nol, 34
London, England, 8, 14, 140, 143, 261, 266, 676, 680, 725, 781, 782, 783
London Missionary Society, 266, 725, 787, 820, 828-829, 844
London Zoological Society, 116
Long Bay, Australia, 156
Long Hua Temple, Shanghai, China, 738
Long March of 1934 (China), 874, 875
Long Wu (Ming emperor of China), 790, 791
Long Ya Men. *See* Singapore
Longfellow, Henry Wadsworth, 620
Longhai railway, 901, 904
Longmen Grottoes, Luoyang, China, 540, 541, 894
Longqing (Ming emperor of China), 296
Longridge. *See* Queensborough, Norfolk Island, Australia
Longzhang Paper Mill, Shanghai, China, 736
Lonthor. *See* Great Banda, Banda Islands, Indonesia
Lop Nor, China, 239
Lopburi, kingdom of, 52, 53, 54
Lopburi River, 52
Lõpez de Villalobos, Ruy, 204
Lord, Simeon, 154
Lorong Burmah, Penang, 668
Lothal, India, 6
Loti, Pierre, 33
Louis IX (king of France), 451
Louis XIV (king of France), 223
Louis XV (king of France), 785
Love, Nigel B., 156
Lovek, Cambodia, 56, 852
Lowe, George, 606
Lower Huayan Temple, Datong, China, 214
Lower Myanmar. *See* Myanmar
Lowry (British naval officer), 677
Lu, China, 707
Lu (son of Tiki-tiki), 818
Lu Aigong (duke of Lu), 708
Lu Buwei (Qin chief minister), 538
Lu Guimeng (poet), 779
Lu Su (Wu general), 868
Lu Xun (ruler of Guangzhou), 304
Lua (people), 182
Luang Prabang, Luang Prabang, Laos, 52, **530-533,** 851, 852, 853, 854
Lucknow, Uttar Pradesh, India, 50, 222, **534-537**
Lucknow Festival, Lucknow, India, 536
Lucknow Pact, 534, 536
Ludowyk, E. (historian), 686
Luganville, Vanuatu, 843
Lunakaran (ruler of Jaisalmer), 392
Luo River, 293, 538
Luoyang bridge, Quanzhou, China, 706
Luoyang, Henan, China, 40, 214, 420, 422, 456, **538-541,** 616, 872, 894, 904
Luoyi. *See* Luoyang, Henan, China
Lüshun, China, 748, 749
Luthai. *See* Mahadharma Raja I
Lutyens, Edwin, 223
Luwu, kingdom of, 839, 842
Luz Church, Madras, India, 547
Luzon, Philippines, 177, 204, 206, 207, 403, 405, 565, 897, 900
Ly Dynasty, 329
Ly Thai To (king of Dai Viet), 329, 331
Ma (Ming empress of China), 619
Ma Chongying (Chinese Muslim general), 323
Ma-han (people), 482
Maafu (viceroy of Chief Cakobau), 266, 267
Maalea Bay, 380
Mac family, 329
MacArthur, Douglas, 206, 207, 331, 569
Macarthur, John, 782, 863
Macartney, George, 458
Macassar, Indonesia, 208
Macau, 306, 360, **542-546,** 620, 790
MacDowall (British general), 447
Macedonia, 608, 669
Machilīpatnam, India, 547
Mackay, Ernest J.H., 595
Mackenzie, Colin, 858
Macnaghten, Sir William Hay, 417
Maconochie, Alexander, 642
Macquarie, Lachlan, 274, 641, 782, 783, 784, 863, 865
Macquarie Arms Inn, Windsor, Australia, 865
Macquarie Harbour, 688, 691
Macquarie Street, Sydney, Australia, 783, 784
Mactan, Philippines, 177, 179
Macuata, Vanua Levu, Fiji, 264
Madagascar, 90, 115, 839
Madanmohan (god), 136
Mādhava Rāo Sindhia (ruler of Gwalior), 316
Madhya Pradesh, India, 117-120, 312-316, 468-472, 561-564, 727-731, 835-838
Madras, Tamil Nādu, India, 35, 168, 172, 202, **547-551,** 552, 680, 809, 812
Madras army (Great Britain), 14
Madras High Court, India, 550
Madre de Deus College, Macau, 544
Madura, Indonesia, 69
Madurai, India, 502, 712, 809, 812
Mae Hong Son, Thailand, 184
Maeda Castle, Kanazawa, Japan, 434
Maeda family, 431-434
Maeda Hōshun'in, 433
Maeda Toshiie, 431-432, 433
Maeda Toshinaga, 432-433
Maeda Toshitsune, 433
Mafala (Samoan teacher), 820
Magadha, India, 312, 574, 836, 837, 847
Magadha University, Gayā, India, 278
Maganlal, Manilal, 267
Magelang, Indonesia, 147, 892
Magellan, Ferdinand, 87, 158, 177, 179, 180, 181, 204, 899
Magellan's Cross, Cebu City, Philippines, 181
Māgha (king of Sri Lanka), 687
Maghada Dynasty, 276
Maghna River, 225
Maha Ganda Bell, Yangon, Myanmar, 879-880
Maha Sati Chowk, Chittaurgarh, India, 193
Maha Thammaracha (vassal ruler of Ayutthaya), 56, 59
Maha That Temple, Ayutthaya, Thailand, 59
Maha Wizaya Pagoda, Yangon, Myanmar, 882
Mahābalipuram, Tamil Nādu, India, 435, 547, **552-555**
Mahābat Khān (governor of Peshāwar), 671
Mahābat Khān Mosque, Peshāwar, Pakistan, 671
Mahabat Khanji II (ruler of Junāgadh), 413
Mahabat Khanji III (ruler of Junāgadh), 413
Mahābhārata War, 836
Mahābodhi Temple (Temple of the Great Enlightenment), Bodh Gayā, India, 138, 140-141
Mahādāji Sindhia (ruler of Gwalior), 314
Mahadharma Raja I (Dharma king of Thailand), 774-775
Mahadharma Raja II (Dharma king of Thailand), 775
Mahadharma Raja III (Dharma king of Thailand), 775
Mahadharma Raja IV (Dharma king of Thailand), 775

Mahajana Eksath Peramuna (Sri Lanka), 203
Mahājanaka Jātaka (Indian prince), 18
Mahakachachayana (Buddhist teacher), 836-837
Mahākāla (god), 258
Mahākāla Siva Temple, Ujjain, India, 835, 837, 838
Mahākṣatrapa Rājula (Śaka ruler), 574
Mahākṣatrapa Śodāsa (Śaka ruler), 574
Mahāmagham Bathing Festival, Kumbakonam, India, 501, 503
Mahāmagham Tank, Kumbakonam, India, 501, 502, 503
Mahāmogalāna (disciple of the Buddha), 727
Mahamuni Pagoda, Mandalay, Myanmar, 556
Mahamuni statue, Mandalay, Myanmar, 556
Mahanamo (historian), 754
Mahanavami Festival, Vijayanagara, India, 856-857
Mahāpadmā Nanda (Nanda ruler of Kalinga), 121
Mahārāja, H.H. *See* Ganga Singh Bahādur
Mahārāshtra, India, 6, 9, 14-19, 125, 142-146, 252-255, 256-259, 625-628, 679
Mahāsarit River, 767
Mahāsena (king of Sri Lanka), 38, 684
Mahāsethji Vimala Shāh (Gujarāt prime minister), 601
Mahāsthan, Bangladesh, 657
Mahathammaracha III (king of Sukhothai), 54
Mahāthupa. *See* Ruwanvelisaya Dagaba, Anuradhapura, Sri Lanka
Mahāvamsa (prince of Sri Lanka), 435
Mahavihara monastery, Sri Lanka, 61
Mahāvīra (founder of Jainism), 257, 402, 412, 574, 576, 600, 602, 837, 848
Mahāyāna Buddhism, 17-18, 33, 60, 148, 150, 256, 527, 576, 625, 626, 879
Mahazedi Pagoda, Bago, Myanmar, 62
Mahboob Khan (Indian military leader), 389
Mahendra (king of Nepal), 467
Mahendra (son of Mauryan emperor Aśoka), 140, 754, 837
Mahendravarman I (Pallavan king of Kānchipuram), 435, 552
Maheshvara (god), 258
Mahikavati, Bombay Island, India, 142
Māhīm. *See* Mahikavati, Bombay Island, India
Mahinda (Buddhist emissary to Sri Lanka), 35
Mahinda V (Sinhalese king), 685
Mahipāla (Pāla ruler), 659
Mahisha (mythic buffalo demon), 259, 694
Mahiyangana Stupa, Sri Lanka, 774
Maḥmūd (Durrāni ruler of Afghanistan), 417
Mahmūd I (king of Mālwa), 562
Maḥmūd I (king of Khorāsān), 279, 280-282
Mahmūd II (king of Mālwa), 563
Mahmud Beghada (sultan of Gujarat), 7, 412
Mahmūd Khān. *See* Mahmūd Shāh I Khaljī
Maḥmūd of Ghaznī (sultan), 20, 79, 439, 468, 474, 507, 522, 610, 763, 764, 765, 801
Maḥmūd Shāh (Ghilzay ruler of Kandahār), 441
Maḥmūd Shāh (sultan of Delhi), 193, 441
Mahmūd Shāh I Khaljī (king of Mālwa), 562, 838
Mahmud Syah (Malaysian sultan), 584
Mahmud Tarabi (Bukharan sieve maker), 164
Mahoba fortress, India, 20
Mahoux, Paul, 647
Maidan, Calcutta, India, 173, 175, 176
Maillart, Ella, 336
Main Bazaar, Kuching, Malaysia, 500
Main World Shrine, Takayama, Japan, 796-797
Maisan Provincial Park, Chŏnju, South Korea, 198
Maisey, C.F., 727
Maitland (British admiral), 448
Maitraka Dynasty, 410, 763
Maitreya Buddha, 150, 752
Maitreya Hall, Shigatse, China, 752
Majapahit Empire, 68, 101, 113, 565, 582, 663, 757
Majestic Fort. *See* Meherangarh, Jodhpur, India
Majid, Zuraina, 631
Maju Deval Temple, Kāthmāndu, Nepal, 466
Maka (Samoan pastor and teacher), 820
Makassar. *See* Ujung Pandang, South Sulawesi, Indonesia
Makassar Strait, 839
Makassarese (people), 839, 840, 841, 842
Makemake (god), 250
Makhdum Bilawal (Suhrawardī teacher), 802
Makhdum Jahaniyan (Suhrawardī sage), 802
Makhdum-i Azam (Naqshbandīyah leader), 165, 458
Makli Hills, Sind, Pakistan, 450, 801, 802, 803, 804
Makrāna quarries, Rājasthān, India, 3
Maksudābād. *See* Murshidābād, Bangladesh
Mala (mythic people), 44
Malabar. *See* Kerala, India
Malabar Hill, Bombay, India, 142, 144, 146
Malabar Point, India, 143
Malacanang Palace, Manila, Philippines, 570
Malacca. *See* Melaka, Malayasia
Malaekula, Tongatapu Island, Tonga, 830
Malakula, Vanuatu, 846
Malaspina, Alejandro, 828
Mālavīya, Madan Mohan, 850
Malay (people), 158, 565, 880, 899
Malay Archipelago, 101, 103
Malay Peninsula. *See* Malaya, Malaysia
Malaya, Malaysia, 52, 54, 56, 58, 65, 90, 98, 113, 201, 206, 208, 267, 272, 353, 396, 503, 565, 568, 582, 586, 665, 667, 692, 704, 757, 758, 759, 760
Malayadeśa, Sri Lanka, 35
Malaysia, 87, 158, 161, 358, 403, 406, 497-500, 582-586, 629-631, 659, 661, 665-668, 757, 760-761, 781
Malayu. *See* Jambi, Indonesia
Malcampo, José, 404
Malcolm, John, 237
Malietoa Laupepam (joint ruler of Samoa), 725
Malietoa Vainuupo (ruler of Samoa), 725
Malik Ayaz (ruler of Lahore), 522
Malinta Hill, Corregidor Island, Philippines, 204
Malkhed, India, 837
Malla Dynasty, 466
Mallabhūm Dynasty, 134, 136, 137
Mallas (people), 136
Malleson, G.B., 169
Mallināth (god), 412
Mallory, George, 603, 604, 605, 606, 607
Malo Island, Vanuatu, 843
Malo Sa'oloto Tuto'atasi o Samoa i Sisifo (Western Samoa), 723
Malua Institution, Upolu, Western Samoa, 725
Maluku. *See* Moluccas, Indonesia
Mālwa, kingdom of, 6, 117, 118, 119, 312, 392, 561, 562, 563, 835, 837-838
Mālwa Plateau, India, 117, 835
Malyavanta Hill, Karnātaka, India, 855
Māmallapuram. *See* Mahābalipuram, Tamil Nādu, India
Mamluk Turks, 474
Man (people), 358
Mān Singh (Tomara king of Gwalior), 312, 314
Mān Singh I (mahārāja of Jaipur), 24, 385
Mān Singh II (last mahārāja of Jaipur), 24, 386
Mān Singh Palace, Gwalior, India, 312, 314
Manabharana (ruler of Southern Country, Sri Lanka), 686
Manado, Indonesia, 841
Manai, Japan, 376
Manangsilabat, Sukhothai, Thailand, 773-774
Mananui (Maori chieftain), 832
Manas Wildlife Sanctuary, India, 311
Manasimha (governor of Orissa), 699
Mānavamma (king of Sri Lanka), 684
Manchu (people), 107, 216, 529, 544, 620, 741, 742, 746, 747, 778, 790, 791, 792, 793, 866, 868, 874, 886
Manchukuo. *See* Manchuria, China
Manchuria, China, 107, 108, 109, 241, 325, 350, 423, 424, 482, 737, 739, 742, 743, 744, 748, 749, 814, 816
Mandalay, Myanmar, 63, **556-560,** 656, 880, 881
Mandalay Hill, Myanmar, 556, 557, 558
Mandasor, kingdom of, 312
Mandavi River, 284, 288, 289
Mandor, India, 399, 402
Māndu, Madhya Pradesh, India, 561-564, 838
Māndu Mosque, Māndu, India, 561
Manghit emirs, 166
Mangi (rebel slave), 487
Mangkubumi. *See* Hamengkubuwono I
Mango Grove Monastery, Sukhothai, Thailand, 775
Mangrai (king of Chiang Saen), 182
Mangrai Dynasty, 184
Mangsoi (rebel slave), 487
Manhattan Project (United States), 615
Mani Parbat, Ayodhyā, India, 48
Manicheanism, 321, 456, 706
Manik Chowk, Jaisalmer, India, 392
Manila, Manila, Philippines, 103, 166, 177, 180, 181, 206, 207, 342, 403, 404, 544, **565-571,** 792, 844, 897, 899, 900
Manila Airport, Manila, Philippines, 570
Manila Bay, 204, 206, 207, 565, 569
Manipur, India, 310
Manjushrī (bodhisattva), 464
Manly Beach, Sydney, Australia, 781, 784
Manono Island, Western Samoa, 723
Manora Head, Karāchi, Pakistan, 448
Mantignon Accord (New Caledonia), 647
Manton, J.T., 208
Manua Islands, American Samoa, 723, 724, 725
Manua-tele (god), 723
Manzur, M.A., 189
Mao Zedong, 108, 110, 111, 297, 307, 324, 328, 737, 738, 743, 749, 778, 794, 868, 873, 874-878, 901
Mao Zedong Memorial Hall, Beijing, China, 111
Maori (people), 832, 859-860, 861, 862
Maple and Chrysanthemum Festival, Hirosaki, Japan, 347
Māra (demon), 138, 149
Mara, Sir Kamisese, 268
Maracanda. *See* Samarkand, Samarkand, Uzbekistan
Marananda (monk), 483
Marāṭhā Dynasty, 6, 8, 20, 22-23, 92, 118, 119, 123-124, 127, 128, 136, 142, 143, 288, 291, 292, 314, 367, 369, 386, 394, 400, 437, 503, 534, 561, 563, 577, 602, 626-628, 679, 699, 812, 838, 850
Marāṭhā War, 314
Maravar (tribe), 714
Marble Bridges, Forbidden City, Beijing, China, 106
Marble Palace, Calcutta, India, 174
March First Movement (Korea), 197
Marco Polo. *See* Polo, Marco
Marco Polo Bridge, Beijing, China, 737
Marco Polo Hall, Yangzhou, China, 887
Marcos, Ferdinand, 406, 570
Marcos, Imelda, 570
Mardijker (people), 397
Maria Island, 688
Mariam-ur-Zamani (Mary of the Age; wife of Emperor Akbar), 1, 24, 263
Mariamman Hindu Temple, Ho Chi Minh City, Vietnam, 354
Mariam's House. *See* Panch Mahal, Fatehpur Sīkri, India
Mariana Islands, 269, 379, 380, 819

Marina Esplanade, Madras, India, 550, 551
Mariner, William, 828
Marini, G.F., de, 852
Marist order, 266, 267, 820
Markham, Clements, 14
Marmagao, India, 289
Marquesas Islands, 247, 723, 827
Marsden, Samuel, 641, 865
Marseilles, France, 646
Marshall, George C., 877
Marshall, Sir John, 14, 595, 597, 727, 730, 805, 806
Martaban, Myanmar, 56, 58, 60, 61, 62
Mārtāṇḍa Varma (Indian unification leader), 712
Martin, Claude, 535
Martyrs' Day (Bangladesh), 228
Marunouchi district, Tōkyō, Japan, 825
Maruyama-kyō (sect), 271
Maruyama Ōkyo (artist), 796
Marwar, India, 392, 399
Marwari (people), 129, 133
Marx, Karl, 876
Mary (mother of Jesus), 344, 769
Mary (queen consort of Great Britian), 144
Mary, Turkmenistan, 71, 163, 333, 456, 720
Mary of the Age. *See* Mariam-uz-Zamani
Mas Said (Pangeran Adipati Mangkunegoro; Indonesian rebel leader), 890
Mas'ad III (sultan of India), 1
Masakado (Taira nobleman), 822
Masako (Ama-Shōgnun; widow of Yoritomo), 428
Masanobu. *See* Hoshina Masayuki
Masayuki. *See* Hoshina Masayuki
Mascarenhas, Francisco, 544
Mascot, Australia, 156
Mashhad, Iran, 473
Masjid Melayu Mosque, Penang, Malaysia, 667
Maskelyne, Margaret, 548
Masonic Hall, Karāchi, Pakistan, 448, 450
Ma'sūd I (ruler of Khorāsān), 281, 282
Ma'sūd III (ruler of Khorāsān), 281, 282-283
Masulipatam, India. *See* Machilīpatnam, India
Māṭ, India, 576
Matanga (god), 257
Mātangeśvara (temple), Khajurāho, India, 469, 470
Mataram, kingdom of (Java), 68, 102, 103, 396, 663, 692, 841, 888, 890
Matavai Bay, Tahiti, 787, 788
Maten (wife of Nobuhira), 345
Mathara Dynasty, 122
Mathurā, Uttar Pradesh, India, 386, **572-577,** 699, 762, 805, 806
Mathurā images (India), 18
Mathurā-maṇḍala. *See* Mathurā, Uttar Pradesh, India
Mathurā Museum, Mathurā, India, 577
Matraville, Australia, 156
Matsudaira family, 10-12, 339
Matsudaira Katamori (last daimyō of Aizu), 12
Matsudaira Masatsuna (daimyō of Kawagoe), 636
Matsumae family, 317, 318
Matsushima Islands, Japan, 590
Matsuura family (daimyō of Hirado), 340-341, 343
Matsuura Shigenobu (daimyō of Hirado), 340-341
Matsuura Takanobu (daimyō of Kyūshū), 340, 341
Matsuura-tō (Japanese pirate families), 340
Matuku Island, Fiji, 265
Mau a Pule movement (Samoa), 726
Mauga (high chief of Samoa), 725
Maugham, W. Somerset, 354, 499, 788
Maui (god), 818
Maui, Hawaii, 380
Maukharī (people), 576
Maulana Jala-ud-dīn Rumi (saint), 611
Maung Maung (Myanmar military leader), 882
Mauritius, 267, 503, 548
Mauryan Empire, 35, 37, 50, 121, 142, 186, 276, 284, 308, 371, 408, 410, 414, 435, 439, 468, 507, 572, 574, 608, 625, 657, 669, 699, 730, 763, 798, 805, 806, 809, 837, 848
Mausoleum of Isma'il Samani, Bukara, Uzbekistan, 163
Mausoleum of Itimad-ud Dawlah, Āgra, India, 3
Mausoleum of Job Charnock, Calcutta, India, 172, 173
Mausoleum of Mumtāz Mahal. *See* Tāj Mahal, Āgra, India
Mausoleum of Qin Shihuang Di, Xian, China, 870, 871, 872
Mausoleum of Shadi Mulk Aka, Samarkand, Uzbekistan, 721
Mausoleums, Āgra, Utter Pradesh, India, 1, 2, 3, 4-5
Mausoleums, Dhākā, Bangladesh, 225
Mausoleums, Lahore, Pakistan, 525
Mausoleums, Lucknow, India, 534
Mausoleums, Nikkō, Japan, 632, 637
Mawlana Khwajagi Amgangi (missionary), 165
Mawlawīyah (Whirling Dervishes), 165
May Fourth Movement (1919; China), 109-110, 112
May Thirtieth Atrocious Incident (1925; China), 736-737
Māyā (goddess), 140, 730
Māyādevī Temple, Konārak, India, 478
Māyādunnē (ruler of Sitavaka), 199
Maymbung, Philippines, 403
Mayo Hospital, Lahore, Pakistan, 525
Mayo Rajkumar College, Ajmer, India, 20, 23
Mazār-i-Sharīf, Balkh, Afghanistan, 71, 73, 417, **578-581**
Mazhar of Sultan Bayazid Bostami, Chittagong, Bangladesh, 189
McCormick Hospital, Chiang Mai, Thailand, 184
McCoy (*Bounty* mutineer), 675
McDougall, Thomas Francis, 500
McKean Rehabilitation Institute, Chiang Mai, Thailand, 184
McKinley, William, 569
McNab, Robert, 236-237
Meade, Richard W., 725
Mecca, Saudi Arabia, 165, 311, 371, 524
Mecca Mosque, Hyderābād, India, 366
Medan Merdeka, Jakarta, Indonesia, 397, 398
Medd, Henry, 223
Medina, Saudi Arabia, 579
Mediterranean Sea, 239, 809
Meerdevoort, J. L. C. Pompe van, 614
Meerut, India, 222
Meghālaya, India, 310
Meherangarh, Jodhpur, India, 399
Mehron-Nesā. *See* Nūr Jahān
Meigetsu-in (temple), Kamakura, Japan, 430
Meiji Restoration (Japan), 12, 319, 347, 349, 433, 520, 614, 637, 651, 825, 826
Mekong Delta, 353, 354
Mekong River, 52, 84, 99, 182, 353, 354, 530, 531, 851, 853, 854
Mekong Valley, 32, 532
Melaka, Melaka, Malaysia, 87, 102, 158, 202, 288, 403, 542, 544, **582-586,** 663, 667, 757, 758, 760, 840
Melanesia, 264, 298, 300, 644
Melanesian Mission College, Norfolk Island, Australia, 642
Melanesians (people), 644, 646, 647, 843, 844, 846
Melbourne, Australia, 78, 210, 266, 783
Melinde, Africa, 284
Melville, Herman, 788
Melville Island, Australia, 208
Memorial Cathedral of World Peace, Hiroshima, Japan, 351
Memorial Hall, Madras, India, 550
Memorial Hall, Yangzhou, China, 886-887
Menam River. *See* Chao Phraya River
Menander (Greek king in India), 410, 763
Mendaña de Neyra, Alvaro de, 298
Mendiola Bridge, Manila, Philippines, 570
Mendut (temple), Java, Indonesia, 147, 152
Menezes, Don Duarte (Portuguese viceroy of Goa), 542
Meng Jiangnü, 294, 741
Meng Tian, 294
Mereweather Tower, Karāchi, Pakistan, 448
Meridian Gate. *See* Wumen, Forbidden City, Beijing, China
Meru. *See* Mount Sumeru
Merv. *See* Mary, Turkmenistan
Mesopotamia. *See* Iraq
Messner, Reinhold, 603, 607
Mestizo de Sangley (people), 180, 181
Methodism, 236, 266, 267, 268, 642, 725, 742, 829, 830
Methodist Church, Castlereagh, Australia, 865
Methora. *See* Mathurā, Uttar Pradesh, India
Metraux, Alfred, 251
Mettur Dam, India, 503
Meuang Sua. *See* Luang Prabang, Luang Prabang, Laos
Meuron, de (Dutch leader in Sri Lanka), 274
Mewār, India, 191, 193, 194, 392
Mexico, 180, 565, 567-568, 568, 844
Miani, Pakistan, 372
Michael (archangel), 676
Michel, Louise, 646
Michell, George, 858
Mi'ch'u (king of Silla), 509
Middle Capital. *See* Beijing, China
Middle Tang period (China), 246
Middleburg. *See* Eua, Tonga
Middlegate, Norfolk Island, Australia, 643
Middleside, Corregidor Island, Philippines, 204
Midnapur district, Bengal, India, 136, 168
Midway Islands, 300
Mie, Japan, 374-378, 587
Migadippa (sculptor), 60
Migara (Sri Lankan military commander), 38
Might of Islam Mosque (Quwwat-ul-Islam Masjid), Delhi, India, 218
Mihīrakula (Hūna ruler in India), 312, 800
Mihoro Dam, Japan, 796
Miidera Temple, Japan, 338
Mikawauchi, Japan, 341
Mikoshigura, Nikkō, Japan, 637
Mildenhall, John, 5
Mile-long Barracks, Corregidor Island, Philippines, 204, 207
Milinda. *See* Menander
Million Dollar Point, Vanuatu, 846
Minamoto family (Genji), 269, 426, 428, 518, 590
Minamoto Yoritomo, 10, 269, 426-428, 518, 590, 637
Minamoto Yoshitsune, 426, 518
Minangkabau, Sumatra, Indonesia, 115
Minas (clan), 24, 383, 385, 386
Minbu, Myanmar, 653
Mindanao, Philippines, 177, 180, 207, 403, 406, 565, 897, 899, 900
Mindon Min (king of Burma), 556, 557, 560, 880
Ming Di (emperor of China), 540
Ming Dynasty, 105, 106, 107, 109, 212, 214-216, 293, 294, 295-296, 305, 306, 321-323, 328, 329, 340, 358, 424, 453, 541, 583-584, 616, 618, 619, 620, 704, 708, 739, 741, 742, 746, 747, 776, 790-792, 813, 866, 868, 872-873, 886
Ming Sangshao (hermit), 616
Ming Tang (Hall of Enlightenment), Luoyang, China, 541
Mingeikan (museum), Takayama, Japan, 796
Mingsha Hill, Dunhuang, China, 241

Mingyuan Di (emperor of China), 212
Minh Mang (emperor of Vietnam), 330, 354, 364
Minlazedi Pagoda, Pagan, Myanmar, 655
Minnēriya Reservoir, Anuradhapura, Sri Lanka, 38, 685
Minoor. *See* Somnāth, Gujarāt, India
Minto, earl of (Gilbert John Elliott), 175, 372
Mīr Alī Shīr Nawa-ī (poet), 335, 336
Mir-i Arab, Kalyan complex, Bukhara, Uzbekistan, 166
Mīr Ja'far (Indian general and ruler), 168, 169, 170, 171, 172, 173, 679-680, 682
Mīr Jumla (Indian general), 226, 309
Mīr Qāsim (Indian ruler of Bengal), 168-169, 170, 188
Mīr Veys Khān (Ghilzay leader), 441
Mīrā Bāī (poet), 193
Mirak-Mirza Ghiyath (tomb designer), 222
Miran Beg (son of Mīr Ja'far), 682
Miran Shāh (son of Timur), 335
Miri, Sarawak, Malaysia, 161
Mirisavati Dagaba, Anuradhapura, Sri Lanka, 38
Miroku (Buddha manifestation), 270, 271, 429
Mirror Hall (Sheesh Mahal), Amber, India, 26
Mirror Palace (Shish Mahal), Junāgarh Fort, Bīkaner, India, 132
Mirror Palace (Shish Mahal), Lahore, Pakistan, 524
Mirza Haidar (chronicler), 767
Mīrzā 'Isā Khān (Tarkhan ruler), 802
Mīrzā Jānī Beg (Tarkhan ruler), 802
Mirza Kamran (son of Bābur), 522
Mīrzā Shāh Ḥasan (son of Shāh Beg), 802
Mīrzā Tungril Beg (Tarkhan ruler), 803
Misen (mountain), Miyajima, Japan, 588, 590
Misorandano (Gokuden), Nikkō, Japan, 637
Missionaries of Charity order, 176
Misuari, Nur, 406
Mitaki-ji (temple), Hiroshima, Japan, 349
Mitarashi (beach), Ise, Japan, 374-375
Mithridates II (the Great; king of Parthia), 410
Mitra, Rājendralāla, 141
Mitsubishi Arms Manufacturing Plant, Nagasaki, Japan, 614
Mitsubishi Nagasaki Zosensho (shipyard), Nagasaki, Japan, 614
Mitunobu ōura (Great Victor; Tsugaru family ancestor), 345
Miura Anjin (Will Adams), 342, 344, 612
Miura family, 10
Miya River, 795, 796
Miyajima, Hiroshima, Japan, 349, **587-591**
Miyako. *See* Kyōto, Kyōto, Japan
Miyazaki, Japan, 592-594
Miyazaki, Miyazaki, Japan, 592-594
Miyazaki Jingū, Miyazaki, Japan, 592
Miyonokoshi, Japan, 433
Miyukibashi bridge, Hirado, Japan, 343
Mizoguchi Kenji (filmmaker), 651
Mizorām, India, 310
Moaksan Provincial Park, Chŏnju, South Korea, 197
Moana swimming pool, Dunedin, New Zealand, 238
Moce, Fiji, 265
Model Prison, Port Arthur, Australia, 690, 691
Modérés (Vanuatu), 846
Modem City, Chittagong, Bangladesh, 189
Mogalla (king of Sri Lanka), 38-39
Mogao Caves, Dunhuang, Gansu, China, 239, 240, 241, 242-246
Moggallana (brother of Kāśyapa I), 754-755
Mogul Empire. *See* Mughal Empire
Mohammad Khaljī (king of Maliva), 193
Moḥammad Khān (ruler of Bhopāl), 118, 119
Mohammed Shāh (Ghurī king of Māndu)), 562
Mohar Magri mound, Chittaurgarh, India, 194
Mohenjo-daro, Sind, Pakistan, 71, 95, 489, **595-599**
Moheofo (wife of Tongan Tui Tonga), 828
Mohra Maradu, Pakistan, 807, 808
Mokal (rāna of Chittaurgarh), 193
Moluccas, Indonesia, 87-91, 103, 158, 177, 179, 180, 396, 582, 583, 585, 667, 828, 839, 840, 841, 842, 897, 900
Mommu (emperor of Japan), 461
Momo (mythic human ancestor on Tonga), 827
Momona Airport, Dunedin, New Zealand, 238
Momoyama Castle, Kyōto, Japan, 519, 636, 650
Mon (people), 60-63, 182, 530, 653, 654, 655, 656, 771, 773, 851, 879
Mon-Khmer (people), 52, 53
Monasteries, Datong, China, 213
Monasteries, Luang Prabang, Laos, 531, 532, 533
Monasteries, Luoyang, China, 538, 539, 540, 541
Monasteries, Macau, 544
Monasteries, Mandalay, Myanmar, 556, 557, 558
Monasteries, Mathurā, India, 574
Monasteries, Mohenjo-daro, Pakistan, 597
Monasteries, Nara, Japan, 621, 623-624
Monasteries, Nāsik, India, 625, 626
Monasteries, Nepal, 603
Monasteries, Takht-i-Bahi, Pakistan, 798-800
Monasteries, Taxila, Pakistan, 807, 808
Monasteries, Tibet, China, 526, 527, 528, 529
Monasteries, Vārānasī, India, 848, 849
Monasteries, Vientiane, Laos, 853
Monastery, Ayodhyā, India, 50
Monastery, Ayutthaya, Thailand, 59
Monastery, Paharpur, Bangladesh, 657-659
Monastery, Zhengzhou, China, 905
Monastery of Forest Dwelling Monks, Wat Aranyik, Sukhothai, 773
Monastery of the Enchanted Cliff, Datong, China, 896
Monastery of the Great Relics, Sukhothai, Thailand, 774, 775
Monghyr, India, 168
Mongkut. *See* Rama IV
Mongol Empire, 22, 60, 71, 79, 81, 105, 109, 163, 164, 182, 186, 195, 214-216, 218, 220, 241, 270, 280, 282, 295-296, 307, 321-323, 327, 333, 383, 414, 424, 428, 439, 451-454, 457, 458, 474-475, 509, 513, 518, 522, 527, 528, 578, 626, 656, 671, 679, 718, 720, 732, 739, 741, 745, 773, 776, 802, 813, 866, 874, 884-885, 897
Mongolia, 240, 293, 294, 295, 383, 451-455, 720, 743, 775
Monk Jian Zhen Memorial Hall, Yangzhou, China, 886-887
Monkey Temple. *See* Swayambhunath Stupa, Kāthmāndu, Nepal
Monte Fort, Macau, 544
Monument to the People's Heroes, Beijing, China, 111
Moolrāj I (ruler of Jaisalmer), 389
Moolrāj II (ruler of Jaisalmer), 392
Moon bastion, Sri Lanka, 274
Moon Harbor, Xiamen, China, 705
Moon Palace. *See* Chandra Mahal
Moon-gazing Pavilion (Songwoldae), Puyŏ, South Korea, 485
Moorhouse, Geoffrey, 721
Morga, Antonio de, 567
Mōri Terumoto (*shōgun* of Hiroshima), 349
Morinaga (prince of Kamakura), 429-430
Mormonism, 725
Moro (people), 404, 405, 406
Moro National Liberation Front (Philippines), 406
Morris, Jan, 782
Morrison (*Bounty* mutineer), 673
Morrison, Robert (British translator), 545
Morse, (British governor of Madras), 548
Morshead, Henry, 604, 605
Moscow, Russia, 166, 475
Moses (biblical patriarch), 769
Moses, Charles Lee, 160
Mosque, Āgra, India, 1, 5, 222
Mosque, Ayodhyā, India, 48, 50
Mosque, Balkh, Afghanistan, 71, 73
Mosque, Banten, West Java, Indonesia, 103
Mosque, Bijāpur, India, 127
Mosque, Chandanpura, Chittagong, Bangladesh, 189
Mosque, Damsacus, Syria, 562
Mosque, Delhi, India, 119, 120, 218, 220, 222
Mosque, Dhākā, Bangladesh, 225, 229
Mosque, Jaunpur, India, 849
Mosque, Lahore, Pakistan, 524, 525
Mosque, Lucknow, India, 534
Mosque, Māndu, India, 561, 562
Mosque, Mazār-i-Sharīf, Afghanistan, 578, 579, 580
Mosque, Melaka, Malaysia, 584
Mosque, Nāsik, India, 626
Mosque, Penang, Malaysia, 667
Mosque, Tatta, Pakistan, 801, 803
Mosque, Triplicane, India, 550
Mosque, Vārānasī, India, 849, 850
Mosque, Vijayanagara, India, 856
Mosque, Yangzhou, China, 887
Mosque, Zamboanga, Philippines, 899
Mosque in Memory of the Saint, Guangzhou, China, 305
Mosque of Ahdai-din-ka-jhonpra, Ajmer, India, 21-22
Mosque of Aḥmad Shāh, Ahmadābād, India, 6
Mosque of Ahmadābād, India, 6
Mosque of Akbar, Ajmer, India, 22
Mosque of 'Ālamgīr, Mathurā, India, 577
Mosque of Bābur, Kābul, Afghanistan, 415-416
Mosque of Ghulam-Muḥammad, Calcutta, India, 174
Mosque of Guhār-shād, Herāt, Afghanistan, 335-336
Mosque of Ho Chi Minh City, Vietnam, 354
Mosque of Jhanjiri, Bijāpur, India, 127
Mosque of Mīr Alī Shīr Nawa-ī, Herāt, Afghanistan, 336
Mosque of Moti Masjid, Bhopāl, India, 120
Mosque of Omar Ali Saifuddien, Bandar Seri Begawan, Brunei Darussalam, 162
Mosque of Pīr Giyasuddīn Aulia. *See* Pao Mecca, Hajo, India
Mosque of Qadam Mubarak (Footprint), Chittagong, Bangladesh, 189
Mosque of Sardar Khan, Ahmadābād, India, 8
Mosque of Shāh Hamdan, Srīnagar, India, 769
Mosque of Shāh Jahān, Ajmer, India, 22
Mosque of Shāh Jahān, Tatta, Pakistan, 450, 803
Mosque of Shahbani Begum, Calcutta, India, 174
Mosque of Shuja'at Khan, Ahmadābād, India, 8
Mosque of Tāj-ul-Masajid, Bhopāl, India, 120
Mosque of Tipu Sultan, Calcutta, India, 174
Moti Mahal Palace, Gwalior, India, 316
Moti Mahal Palace, Lucknow, India, 534
Moti Masjid, Āgra, India, 5
Moti Masjid, Bhopāl, India, 120
Moti Masjid, Delhi, India, 222
Motomachi, Hakodate, Japan, 318
Mouhot, Henri, 33, 532
Mound of the Dead. *See* Mohenjo-daro, Sind, Pakistan
Mounds of Yin, Ayang, China, 40
Moungamotua (Tongan Tui Haatakalaua), 828
Mount Ābu, Rājasthān, India, 117, 412, **600-602**
Mount Bagsak, 405
Mount Baideng, 212
Mount Bates, 639
Mount Bledisloe, 862
Mount Cook National Park, New Zealand, 833
Mount Dajo, 403
Mount Everest, 603-607
Mount Fuji, 269, 270, 271, 317, 532, 822
Mount Futara. *See* Futara-san
Mount Gandamadhana, 714-715
Mount Hakodate, 317, 319, 320

Mount Hiei, 517, 519, 520
Mount Hira, 338
Mount Iwaki, 347
Mount Jue, 741
Mount Kailāsha, 254, 257, 258, 259
Mount Kameoka, 344
Mount Kamiji, 375
Mount Kilimanjaro, 603
Mount Kuno, Shizuoka, Japan, 634, 636
Mount Mahendrapura, Cambodia, 31
Mount Meru, 31, 33, 443, 501, 530, 557, 576, 686, 694
Mount Ngauruhoe, 832, 833, 834
Mount Pitt, 639, 641, 642
Mount Puso-san, 485, 486
Mount Road. *See* Anna Salai Road, Madras, India
Mount Ruapehu, 832, 833, 834
Mount Si, 530
Mount Sumeru, 148
Mount Suribachi, 381
Mount Suthep, 184, 185
Mount Unebi, 462
Mount Utatsu, 433
Mount Weichun, 741
Mount Yasur, 843
Mountbatten, Lord (Louis Mountbatten), 558, 880
Mrignayani (queen of Gwalior), 314
Mrohaung, Bangladesh, 187, 188
Mu (king of Paekche), 486
Mua, Tongatapu Island, Tonga, 830
Muang Rat, Thailand, 774
Muang Satchanalai-Sukhothai (Thailand), 773
Muang Sukhothai (Thailand), 772-773
Mu'āwiyah I (Umayyad caliph), 579
Mud Island, Australia, 209
Mughal Empire, 1-5, 6, 7-8, 20, 22-23, 24, 26, 27, 28, 50, 73, 117, 123, 127, 128, 129, 132, 136, 165, 168, 170, 171, 172, 175, 186, 187, 188, 193, 218, 220, 222, 223, 225-226, 260-261, 263, 277, 282, 290, 291-292, 309-310, 312, 367, 369, 371, 383, 385, 386, 392, 394, 399, 400, 412, 414, 415, 416, 440-441, 473, 475, 503, 507, 508, 519, 522-524, 534, 548, 550, 561, 562, 563, 576-577, 580, 608, 610, 626-627, 669, 671, 679-682, 699, 722, 764, 769, 801, 802, 803, 804, 838, 849, 850
Muḥammad (prophet), 73, 189, 441, 522, 578, 579, 769, 886
Muhammad (son of Maḥmūd I), 281
Muḥammad 'Ādil Shāh II (ruler of Bijāpur), 127, 534
Muḥammad Ghaus (saint), 314
Muḥammad ibn Qāsīm (Arab conqueror of Sind), 371, 608, 610, 801
Muhammad J'wa Mu'assam Shāh II (sultan), 665
Muhammad Makkai (saint), 371
Muḥammad of Ghūr, 20, 21, 801
Muḥammad Qulī Quṭb Shāh (Deccan king), 290-291, 366, 367
Muḥammad Said (chief minister of Golconda), 291
Muḥammad Shāh (Mughal emperor of India), 416, 803, 838
Muḥammad Shāh III (Bahmanī sultan), 290
Muḥammad Shaybānī (Uzbek ruler in Bukhara), 165
Muḥammad Sultan (grandson of Timur), 721
Muḥammad Taqi Khan, 699
Muḥammad Tughluq (ruler of Delhi), 220, 764
Muḥammed Shibani (Uzbek leader), 336
Mu'izz-ud-Dīn Muḥammad ibn Sām of Ghūr (Indian ruler), 218, 282, 610
Mukaddasi, al- (historian), 281
Mukden. *See* Shenyang, Liaoning, China
Mukim Arghun (ruler of Kābul), 414, 440
Mukteśvara Temple, Bhubaneswar, India, 123
Mukundadeva (Gajapati king of Orissa), 699
Mūladeva (king of Ayodhyā), 49
Mūlarāja Solankī (Cāḷukya ruler of Somnāth), 764
Mulasthanapura. *See* Multān, Punjab, Pakistan
Mulga (mythic people), 44
Muliavu Island, American Samoa, 723, 724, 725
Mulrāj (Sikh governor), 610
Multān, Punjab, Pakistan, 608-611
Multatuli. *See* Dekker, Eduard Douwes
Mumba (goddess), 142
Mumba Devi. *See* Bombay, Mahārāshtra, India
Mumtāz Mahal (Greatest Ornament of the Palace; empress of India), 4-5, 222
Mumtāzābād, Āgra, India, 4
Mumui (ruler of Tonga), 829
Mun-mu (king of Silla), 513
Muncarra, India, 682
Mundy, Peter, 545
Municipal Theater, Hanoi, Vietnam, 331
Munro, Hector, 168, 170
Munro, Thomas, 547
Munsong (king of Silla), 513
Muong Thanh. *See* Dien Bien Phu, Vietnam
Muqanna', al- (prophet), 163
Murād II (sultan of Turkey), 125
Murad (brother of Mughal emperor 'Ālamgīr), 314
Muromachi district, Kyōto, Japan, 518
Mursheedzadi (wife of Saadat Ali Khan), 534
Murshid Qulī Khān, 123, 226, 699
Murshidābād, India, 168, 226, 679, 680, 681, 682
Murunda (people), 122, 699
Muryŏng (king of Paekche), 485, 486
Muscovy Company, 165
Museum of Chinese History, Beijing, China, 111
Museum of Fine Art, Kamakura, Japan, 429, 430
Museum of Hubei Province, Wuhan, China, 868
Museum of Modern Art, Kamakura, Japan, 430
Museum of Overseas Trade, Quanzhou, China, 706
Museum of the Chinese Revolution, Beijing, China, 111
Museum of War Crimes, Ho Chi Minh City, Vietnam, 356
Mūsi River (India), 366
Musi River (Indonesia), 582, 583, 661, 663, 664
Musician's Gateway (Naubat Khana), Āgra, India, 5
Muslim League (India), 175, 189, 227, 525, 536
Muslims. *See* Islam
Mustafabad. *See* Junāgadh, Gujarāt, India
Mutijilda Gorge, Ayers Rock, Australia, 44
Mutiny Memorial, Delhi, India, 222-223
Mutō Sukeyori (governor of Kyūshū), 340
Mutsuhito (Meiji emperor of Japan), 349-350, 520, 825
Muttra. *See* Mathurā, Uttar Pradesh, India
Muyol (king of Silla), 487
Muzaffar Khān (ruler of Multān), 610
Muzaffar Shāh (sultan of Gujarāt), 6, 764
Muzzaffar, India, 193
Myanmar, 13, 52, 56, 58, 59, 60-64, 96, 98, 99, 138, 141, 174, 175, 182, 184, 187, 188, 206, 222, 308, 310, 503, 530, 532, 556-560, 594, 653-656, 659, 665, 667, 851, 868, 879-883
Myanmar Socialist Program Party, 882
Mylapore, India, 548, 550
Myōhon-ji (temple), Kamakura, Japan, 429
Mysore, India, 92, 94, 95, 369, 386, 503, 548, 550, 551, 628, 699, 812
Mysore Plateau, 811, 812
Mysore University, India, 95
Mysore Wars, 92

Na San, Vietnam, 230
Nabagraha Shrine, Guwāhāti, India, 310
Nacionalista Party (Philippines), 569
Nāder Khān, Muḥammed (king of Afghanistan), 418
Nāder Qolī Beg. *See* Nāder Shāh
Nāder Shāh (king of Persia), 73, 166, 222, 282, 336, 416, 441, 475, 524, 610, 721, 803
Nāderabad, Afghanistan, 441
Naemul (king of Saro), 509
Nafanua (goddess), 725
Naga, Philippines, 900
Nagahama, Japan, 338
Nāgāland, India, 310
Nagano, Japan, 269, 377
Nagaoka, Japan, 515, 621, 624
Nāgappattinam, India, 503, 812
Nāgas (people), 576
Nagasaki Bay, 342, 612
Nagasaki, Japan, 317, 318, 340-344, 349, 351, 382, 612-615
Nagasaki Kotaro (daimyō of Nagasaki), 612
Nagasaki, Nagasaki, Japan, 542, 544, **612-615**
Nāgda, India, 191
Nageśvara Temple, Kumbakonam, India, 501-502
Nagoya, Japan, 375
Nagriamel Party (Vanuatu), 846
Nahapāna (Kṣaharāta king of Nāsik), 626
Nahapāna cave temple, Nāsik, India, 625, 626, 628
Naikū, Ise, Japan, 374, 375, 376, 377
Naipul, Shiva, 146
Naipul, V.S., 146
Najamuddin (sultan), 663
Najibullah, Mohammad, 418
Nakajima Tetsujirō. *See* Hokusai
Nakamachi, Hirosaki, Japan, 345
Nakanoshima Park, Ōsaka, Japan, 651
Nakhon In. *See* Intharacha
Nakhon Sawan, Thailand, 54, 775
Nakhon Si Thammarat, Thailand, 52, 775
Nakhwaam (Rock of the Falling Flowers), Mount Puso-san, South Korea, 486
Naktong River, 511
Naku Ryū (drawing), Nikkō, Japan, 636
Nala (mythic monkey), 715
Nalachal Hill, Guwāhāti, India, 308
Nallūr, Sri Lanka, 687
Nam Giao (Temple of Heaven), Hue, Vietnam, 364
Nam Khan River, 530
Nam Viet, kingdom of, 329, 362, 565
Nam Yum River, 232
Nam-hae (king of Silla), 509
Namaśūdras (people), 186
Namba, Ōsaka, Japan, 648, 652
Namche Bazaar, Nepal, 603
Namua Island, Western Samoa, 723
Namulauulu Lauaki Mamoe (Samoan rebel), 726
Namwon, South Korea, 512
Nan, Thailand, 184, 775
Nan Yan. *See* Yangzhou, Jiangsu, China
Nanak (gurū), 508
Nanda Dynasty, 121, 186
Nandabayin (Toungoo king of Bago), 62
Nandaimon (Southern Great Gate), Ōsaka, Japan, 648
Nandana, Polonnaruwa, Sri Lanka, 686
Nandi (mythic bull), 258, 555, 602, 694, 696, 812
Nandi Hills, Karnātaka, India, 94
Nandi temple, Khajurāho, India, 469
Nandini (mythic cow), 600
Nandivarman II (Pallava king of Kānchipuram), 437
Nanga Parbat (mountain), 604
Nanhai. *See* Guangzhou, Guangdong, China
Naniwa. *See* Ōsaka, Ōsaka, Japan
Naniwa-ku, Ōsaka, Japan, 648
Nanjiao. *See* Guangzhou, Guangdong, China
Nanjing, Jiangsu, China, 105, 108, 109, 424, 538, **616-620,** 736, 742, 748, 749, 816, 866, 873, 884
Nankai University, Tianjin, China, 816
Nanking. *See* Nanjing, Jiangsu, China
Nannuka (Chandela ruler of Khajurāho), 468

Nanpo Shoto Islands, Japan, 379
Nantai-san. *See* Futara-san, Nikkō, Japan
Nantaungmya (king of Pagan), 655
Nanuku Reef, 265
Nanumanga, Tuvalu, 818
Nanwu, China, 302
Nanyueh. *See* Guangzhou, Guangdong, China
Nanzen-ji temples, Higashiyama, Japan, 518
Napier, Sir Charles, 372, 448, 804
Napoléon I (emperor of France), 115, 417, 568, 768, 841
Napoléon III (emperor of France), 646, 647, 727
Napoleonic Wars, 288, 586, 787
Naqsbandīyah (Muslim dervish order), 163, 165, 166
Naqshbandī hostel, Eyub, Turkey, 165
Naqvi, Syed A., 599
Nara, Japan, 460-463, 621-624
Nara Kenritsu Kashihara Kokogaku-kenkyusho Fuzoku Hakubutsukan, Kashihara, Japan, 462
Nara, Nara, Japan, 375, 376, 426, 429, 430, 461, 463, 515, 518, 521, 587, 592, **621-624,** 632, 636, 887
Nara National Museum, Japan, 624
Nara period (Japan), 430, 621-624
Naradatta (king of Ayodhyā), 49
Narai (king of Ayutthaya), 57, 58
Narakāsura (semi-legendary king of Assam), 308
Naralokavira (Cōḷa general), 710
Narapatisithu (king of Pagan), 655
Narasa Nāyaka (Tuluva general), 856
Narasiṃha I (Gaṅga king of Orissa), 135, 478, 699
Narasiṃhavarman I Mahāmalla (Pallava king of Kānchipuram), 435-436, 552, 554, 555
Narasiṃhavarman II. *See* Rājasiṃha
Narasingha (incarnation of Vishnu), 259, 601, 697
Naratheinhka (king of Pagan), 655
Narathihapate (king of Pagan), 655, 656
Narathu (king of Pagan), 655
Nārāyānhiti Palace, Kāthmāndu, Nepal, 467
Narendrasinha (king of Kandy), 446
Naresuan (king of Ayutthaya), 56-57, 59
Narmada River, 563, 716, 835
Narsapur, Pakistan, 371
Narshakhi (historian), 163
Narsinghgarh, India, 119
Nash, Beau, 783
Nāsik, Mahārāshtra, India, 625-628
Nasir Mirzā (governor of Kandahār), 440
Nasir-ud-Dīn (king of Mālwa), 563
Nasiyan (Red Temple), Ajmer, India, 23
Nassal Chowk, Kāthmāndu, Nepal, 467
Nat Hlaung Temple, Pagan, Myanmar, 654
Natal, Sumatra, Indonesia, 115
Natarāja (god), 258, 694
Nāthasarmma (Gupta Brahmin), 657
Nathmalji-ki-haveli, Jaisalmer, India, 392
National Aeronautical Research Laboratory, Bangalore, India, 95
National Ancient Monuments (China), 896
National Archives (Imperial Record Office), Delhi, India, 223
National Assembly building, Vientiane, Laos, 854
National Higher School, Hirosaki, Japan, 348
National League for Democracy (Myanmar), 882
National Liberation Front. *See* Viet Cong
National Museum, Bangkok, Thailand, 775
National Museum, Delhi, India, 244
National Museum, Kongju, South Korea, 487
National Museum, Kyōto, Japan, 520
National Museum, Puyŏ, South Korea, 487
National Museum, Yangon, Myanmar, 558
National Park, Tongariro, New Zealand, 834
National Parks and Wildlife Service (Australia), 691
National Peasant Movement Institute, Guangzhou, China, 307
National Power Research Institute, Bangalore, India, 95
National Seclusion Policy (Japan), 613
National Treasures Building, Kamakura, Japan, 430
Nationalist China. *See* Taiwan
Natkiel, Richard, 379
Natunuku, Viti Levu, Fiji, 264
Nau Bahar (New Convent), Balkh, Afghanistan, 73
Naubat Khana (Musician's Gateway) Āgra, India, 5
Naulakha Palace, Lahore, Pakistan, 524
Naulivou (Fiji islander), 266
Navarre (French general in Indochina), 230-231, 232
Navghan II (Chudasma ruler in India), 410
Navghan Step-Well, Junāgadh, India, 410, 412
Navidad, Mexico, 180
Navigators Islands. *See* Samoa, Western Samoa and American Samoa
Navua (people), 266
Nawai, Apolosi R., 267
Naxalbari, India, 176
Naxalite Movement, 137, 176
Nayaka Dynasty (India), 435, 502-503, 812
Nayakkar Dynasty (Sri Lanka), 446
Nayapāla (Pāla ruler of Paharpur), 659
Naylor, Thomas Beagley, 642
Nazar Moḥammad Khān (ruler of Bhopāl), 119
Ne Win, 558, 560, 880, 882
Nearer the Stars Place. *See* Ch'omsong-dae, Kyŏngju, South Korea
Needham, Joseph, 297
Negombo, Sri Lanka, 201, 202, 273, 274
Nehru, Jawaharlal, 223, 289, 467
Nelson, New Zealand, 234
Nelson, Olaf Frederick, 726
Nemināth (Neminatha; Jain prophet), 412, 601
Nemināth Temple, Bīkaner, India, 129
Nepal, 464-467, 507, 526, 528, 529, 603, 604, 606, 608, 750
Nepean, Nicholas, 641
Nepean Island, Australian External Territory, Australia, 639
Nepean River, 156, 863
Neputa Festival, Hirosaki, Japan, 345, 347
Nestorianism, 73, 321, 456, 457, 706, 872
Nestorius, 457
Netherlands, 8, 39, 57, 62, 65, 68, 69, 70, 87, 88, 89, 90, 101, 102, 103, 104, 113, 114, 115, 116, 142, 150, 160, 172, 187, 201, 202, 203, 225, 226, 272-274, 288, 306, 317, 319, 339, 342, 343, 344, 354, 395-398, 403, 404, 446, 499, 503, 544, 545, 547, 548, 565, 568, 585, 586, 612, 613, 614, 615, 637, 652, 663, 664, 667, 679, 687, 696, 712, 714, 758, 759, 781, 790, 791-792, 813, 828, 832, 839-842, 844, 888, 890, 891-892
Netherlands Indies. *See* Indonesia
New Amsterdam. *See* New York, United States of America
New Bien Canal, Henan, China, 904
New Brighton Hotel, Botany Bay, Australia, 156
New Caledonia, 264, 639, 644-647, 827, 843, 845
New Capital, India, 124
New Cytheria. *See* Tahiti, Society Islands, French Polynesia
New Delhi. *See* Delhi, Delhi, India
New Edinburgh. *See* Dunedin, South Island, New Zealand
New First Church, Dunedin, New Zealand, 236
New Fuji. *See* Shin Fuji (volcano), Fujinomiya, Japan
New Guinea, 265, 299, 644, 827
New Hebrides. *See* Vanuatu
New Kabuki Theatre, Ōsaka, Japan, 652
New Kowloon, Hong Kong, 361
New Lhasa. *See* Lhasa, Xizang Autonomous Region, Tibet, China
New Plymouth, New Zealand, 234
New South Wales, Australia, 75, 153-157, 267, 639, 641, 642, 643, 677, 688, 781-784, 859, 861, 863-865
New South Wales Corps, 863
New South Wales Wine Association, 865
New Territories, Hong Kong, 358, 359, 360, 361
New Town, Edinburgh, Scotland, 235
New York, United States of America, 90, 173
New Zealand, 234-238, 266, 267, 299, 300, 603, 639, 641, 642, 643, 644, 677, 723, 726, 818-821, 828, 830, 832-834, 859-862
New Zealand Company, 234
Newar (people), 464, 467
Neyshābūr, Iran, 163, 333
Ngai-tahu (people), 234
Ngarāja (sculpture), 18
Ngata (Tongan Tui Kanokupolu), 828
Ngatoro-i-rangi (Maori high priest), 832
Ngau, Fiji, 265
Ngawang Lozang Gyatso (Dalai Lama), 528
Ngayogya. *See* Yogyakarta, Yogyakarta Special Territory, Indonesia
Nggele Levu, Fiji, 264
Ngo Dinh Diem, 355-356, 365
Ngo Dynasty, 329
Ngo Mon Gate, Hue, Vietnam, 364
Nguyen Anh. *See* Gia Long
Nguyen Chanh Thi, 365
Nguyen Dynasty, 230, 329-330, 354, 362, 364, 365
Nguyen Hue, 330
Nguyen Lu, 330
Nguyen Nhac, 330
Nguyen Phuc Anh. *See* Gia Long
Nguyen That Thanh. *See* Ho Chi Minh
Niah Caves, Sarawak, Malaysia, 629-631
Niah River, 629
Nian Rebellion, 874
Nichinan Kaigan Quasi-National Park, Miyazaki, Japan, 594
Nichiren (Buddhist priest), 270, 429
Nichiren-shū (sect), 270, 271, 519
Nicholson (British admiral), 172
Nicoll, Robert, 158
Nicolson, R.B., 676
Niedermayer, Oskar von, 336
Nihombashi River, 824
Nihombashi, Tōkyō, Japan, 824, 825
Niigata, Japan, 269, 351
Nijō Castle, Kyōto, Japan, 520, 636, 638
Nikkan (disciple of Nichiren), 270
Nikkō National Park, Japan, 632, 638
Nikkō, Tochigi, Japan, 632-638
Nikkokaidō Road, Japan, 824
Nil Kanth Palace, Māndu, India, 563
Nīlgiri Hills, 600
Nilkantha Madadeo Temple, Chittaurgarh, India, 191
Nimbapuram, India, 855
Nimitz, Chester W., 379
Nimmo, John, 643
Nindo. *See* Nizam-ud-Dīn
1911 Revolution Memorial Hall, Wuchang, China, 867, 868
Nine Dragon Screen, Datong, China, 214
Nine Dynastic Urns, Hue, Vietnam, 364
Nine Holy Canons, Hue, Vietnam, 364
Nine Lions Mountain, Yangzhou, China, 886
Nine Women's Grave, Wuchang, China, 868
Nine-day Mountain, Quanzhou, China, 704
Nine-one Road, Quanzhou, China, 706
Nineveh, Iraq, 71
Ningbo, China, 735, 813
Ninghaicheng. *See* Laolongtou, Shanhaiguan, China
Ningxia, China, 293, 294, 296
Ninigi no Mikoto (god), 374, 375, 592

Ninomachi, Takayama, Japan, 795
Nintoku (emperor of Japan), 648
Nio-Mon. *See* Omotemon, Nikkō, Japan
Nirmala (sect), 508
Nīrūn (Hindu ruler of Sind), 371
Nīrūn-Kot. *See* Hyderābād, Sind, Pakistan
Nishāt Bagh, Srīnagar, India, 769
Nishi Hongan-ji, Kyōto, Japan, 520, 637, 638
Nishijin district, Kyōto, Japan, 520
Nishinomiya, Japan, 652
Nishizaka Hill, Nagasaki, Japan, 612
Nissaṅka Malla (king of Sri Lanka), 686-687
Nissaṅka-lata-maṇḍapa Pavilion, Polonnaruwa, Sri Lanka, 687
Nitta Yoshisada, 429
Niua Islands, Tonga, 828
Niuafoo, Tonga, 827, 828
Niuatobutabu, Tonga, 827, 828
Niue Island, Samoa, 725
Nivarthana Movement (India), 713
Nixon, Richard M., 356, 738
Nizām, Agha (Chittagong official), 188
Nizām ālī Khān (king of Hyderābād), 369
Nizām Shāhi (ruler of Ahmadnagar), 626
Nizām-al-Mulk (Persian politican), 118
Nizam-ud-Dīn (Nindo; Sammā ruler), 802
Nizām-ul-Mulk, Āsaf Jāh (Mughal viceroy), 369
Nobbs, Alfred, 642
Nobbs, George Hunn, 642, 677
Nobuhira (lord of Tsugaru), 345, 347
Nobumasa (lord of Tsugaru), 345
Nogi, (Japanese general), 793
Nomuka, Tonga, 828
Nong Khai, Thailand, 84
Nong Sarai, Thailand, 56
Nopphaburi Si Nakhonping Chiangmai. *See* Chiang Mai, Chiang Mai, Thailand
Norbulingka (Summer Palace), Lhasa, Tibet, China, 528, 529
Norfolk Island, Australian External Territory, Australia, 639-643, 677, 690, 691
Norfolk Island National Park, Australia, 643
Norfolk Plains, Tasmania, 641
Norfolk Ridge, 639
North Atlantic Treaty Organization (NATO), 233, 289
North Borneo. *See* Borneo
North China Plain, 105, 420, 813
North Chŏlla, South Korea, 195-198
North Col (Himalayan mountain pass), 605, 606
North East Valley, New Zealand, 235, 236
North Island, New Zealand, 642, 643, 832-834, 859-862
North Korea, 197, 882
North Kyŏngsang, South Korea, 509-514
North Palace, Luoyang, China, 538
North Pole, 237
North Vietnam. *See* Vietnam
North West Frontier, Pakistan, 669-672, 798-800
North-South Dynasties period (China), 539, 540
Northern Assembly (Tonghak religious movement), 197
Northern Black Polished Ware, 572, 835
Northern Circars, India, 680
Northern Expedition (China), 868
Northern Peace (Beiping). *See* Beijing, China
Northern Qi Dynasty, 295, 618, 739
Northern Silk Road, 239, 240
Northern Song Dynasty, 246, 422, 705, 776, 904
Northern Territory, Australia, 44-46, 208-211
Northern Territory Museum of Arts and Science, Australia, 211
Northern Wei Dynasty, 212-213, 244, 294, 321, 539, 540, 616, 893, 894, 896
Northern Zhou Dynasty, 618
Norton, E.F., 605, 606
Nosavan, Phumi, 854
Notre Dame Cathedral, Ho Chi Minh City, Vietnam, 354
Notre Dame des Victoires, Tianjin, China, 815, 816
Nouh Gumbad shrine. *See* Hajji Piyade shrine, Balke, Afghanistan
Nouméa Cathedral, Nouméa, New Caledonia, 646
Nouméa, South Province, New Caledonia, 644-647
Nu, U, 558, 882
Nubunaga, Oda, 634
Nukualofa, Tongatapu Island, Tonga, 827, 830
Nukunonu. *See* Tokelau, Territory of New Zealand
Number One Pit, Qin Tomb, China, 701-702
Nūr Jahān (Nūr Mahal; empress of India), 2, 3, 523, 769
Nūr Muḥammad Kalhora (governor of Sind), 803
Nurhaci (Jürchen leader), 741-742
Nuulua Island, Western Samoa, 723
Nuusafee Island, Western Samoa, 723
Nuutele Island, Western Samoa, 723
Nuyts, Pieter, 342
Nyanchu River. *See* Liancuo River
Nyaungu, Myanmar, 558
Nyorong Mountains, 195

Oahu, Hawaii, United States of America, 788
Obon. *See* Bon Festivals
O'Brien, Bob, 77
Ocean Island, Kiribati, 821
Ocean of Milk (mythical), 686
Octagon, Dunedin, New Zealand, 235, 236
Oda Nobunaga (Japanese warlord), 341, 431, 519, 520, 650
Odawara, Japan, 430
Odell, Noel, 606
Odoka. *See* Galle, Sri Lanka
Odoric of Pordenone (Franciscan friar), 328, 710, 886
Ofu Island, American Samoa, 723
Ogata Kōrin (artist), 651
Ögödei Khan (Mongol ruler), 414, 451, 454
Ohakune, Tongariro, New Zealand, 834
Ohiko (legendary general), 10
Ōi (Junnin; Japanese prince), 624
Oirat (people), 323
Okada Furie, 320
Okada Kotama, 796
Okadera, Asuka, Japan, 460
Okeh'on, South Korea, 486, 511
Okinawa, Japan, 592
Oku no In, Nikkō, Japan, 637
Ōkuninushi no Ōmikami (god), 590, 632
Ōkura Kihachirō, 320
Okura no Kannon, Kamakura, Japan, 426
Old City, Chittagong, Bangladesh, 189
Old Delhi. *See* Delhi, Delhi, India
Old Dragon Head. *See* Laolongtou, Shanhaiguan, China
Old Fort, Bhopāl, India, 117
Old Fort, Delhi, India, 222
Old Fuji. *See* Ko Fuji
Old Goa, Goa, India, 284, 288, 289
Old Town, Bhubaneswar, India, 121, 124
Old Town. *See* Chinese City, Shanghai, China
Oldenburg, Sergei, 244
Oldham, C.F., 821
Olgas, Australia, 211
Olosega Island, American Samoa, 723
Olveston Mansion, Dunedin, New Zealand, 237
Omar Ali Saifuddien (sultan of Brunei Darussalam), 161, 162
Omar Ali Saifuddien Mosque, Bandar Seri Begawan, Brunei Darussalam, 162
Omar Khayyām, 721
Ōmi, Japan, 338, 431
Omichand (wealthy merchant in India), 680, 681-682
Omiya, Japan, 651
Omote-sandō, Nikkō, Japan, 636
Omotemon, Nikkō, Japan, 636
Omphis. *See* Ambhi
Ōmura Sumitada, 340, 612
One Pillar Pagoda, Hanoi, Vietnam, 329, 332
Oneata Island, Fiji, 265, 266
O'Neil, Peter, 641
Onescritus (philosopher), 805
Ōnin War, 377, 431, 519, 650
Onjo (founder of Paekche kingdom), 482
Ono Island, Fiji, 264
O-nung, Kyŏngju, South Korea, 509
Onyaku-en, Aizu-Wakamutsu, Japan, 11
Oonadatta, Australia, 209
Opak River, 692
Opera House, Bennelong Point, Sydney, Australia, 782, 784
Opium Wars, 107, 306-307, 358-359, 735, 813
Opossum Bay,.Australia, 689
Ordam Padshah, China, 457
Ordos desert, 212, 214, 294, 296
Orhon River, 451, 452
Origen, 578
Orissa, India, 121-124, 136, 168, 170, 171, 175, 226, 366, 369, 478-481, 548, 697-700, 837, 856
Oriyans (people), 123, 124
Orosa, Sixto Y., 405
Orsini, Count (Italian art specialist), 14
Orthodox Church of the Resurrection, Hakodate, Japan, 319
Ōsaka, Ōsaka, Japan, 12, 338, 426, 431, 460, 519, 520, 587, 622, **648-652,** 822
Ōsaka Bay, 648
Ōsaka, Japan, 648-652
Oshima Peninsula, 317
Ōshio Heihachirō, 651
Osiān, India, 402
Osiris (god), 608
Osmania University, Hyderābād, India, 370
Ōta River, 349
Otago. *See* Dunedin, New Zealand
Otago Association, 235
Otago Harbour, 234, 237
Otago University, Dunedin, New Zealand, 236, 237, 238
Otrar, Afghanistan, 335
Ōtsu, Japan, 338
Ottoman Empire, 165, 417, 441, 519. *See also* Turkey
Oudh, India, 50, 534-536
Ōura Cathedral, Nagasaki, Japan, 615
Outback, Australian, 44
Oute Stad. *See* Pettah, Colombo, Sri Lanka
Outer Court, Forbidden City, Beijing, China, 108
Outer Gate. *See* Qianmen Gate, Beijing, China
Outer Gold Water Bridges, Forbidden City, Beijing, China, 106
Outram, James, 536
Ouyang Xiu, 887
Oval, Dunedin, New Zealand, 236
Ovalau Island, Fiji, 266
Overbeck, von (Austrian counsel in Sabah), 160
Oxford University, England, 267
Oxus River. *See* Amu Darya River
Oxus Valley. *See* Amu Darya Valley
Oyama Gobō. *See* Kanazawa, Ishikawa, Japan
Oyodo River, 592
Ozene. *See* Ujjain, Madhya Pradesh, India

Pa Sak River, 52, 59
Paaseiland. *See* Easter Island, Chile

Pacheco, Duarte, 711
Pacific Cable Station, Norfolk Island, Australia, 643
Pacific Islanders Protection Act, 267
Pacific Ocean, 247, 264, 298, 420, 592, 639, 644, 673, 704, 723, 724, 781, 785, 819, 820, 827, 843, 844
Pacific War Memorial, Corregidor Island, Philippines, 207
Padal Polgate, Chittaurgarh, India, 193
Padel (French missionary), 820
Padingan, Malaysia, 499
Padma River. *See* Ganges River
Padmasambhava (mystic), 526
Padmasambhava statue, Lhasa, Tibet, China, 526
Padmāvatī (yogi), 601
Padmini (princess of Chittaurgarh), 191, 193
Padmini's Palace, Chittaurgarh, India, 193
Paduka Seri Baginda Sultan Haji Hassanal Bolkiah Muizzadin Waddaulah (sultan of Brunei), 161
Paekche, kingdom of, 195, 431, 482-487, 509, 511, 513, 648
Paes, Domingo, 856
Pagan, Myanmar, 556, **653-656**
Pagan Dynasty, 60, 653-656
Pagan Min (king of Burma), 556
Pagewood, Botany Bay, Australia, 156
Pago Pago, American Samoa, 723, 725, 726
Pago Pago Harbor, American Samoa, 725
Pagoda, Hanoi, Vietnam, 331
Pagoda, Ho Chi Minh City, Vietnam, 354
Pagoda of the Great Golden God (Shwe Mawdaw), Bago, Myanmar, 60, 63
Pagodas, Ayutthaya, Thailand, 59
Pagodas, Bagon, Myanmar, 556
Pagodas, Chŏnju, South Korea, 198
Pagodas, Datong, China, 896
Pagodas, Ho Chi Minh City, Vietnam, 354
Pagodas, Hue, Vietnam, 362
Pagodas, Ikaruga, Japan, 621, 624
Pagodas, Mandalay, Myanmar, 556, 557, 559
Pagodas, Miyajima, Japan, 590
Pagodas, Nanjing, China, 620
Pagodas, Takayama, Japan, 795
Pagodas, Wuchang, China, 866
Pagodas, Xian, China, 871-872, 873
Pagodas, Yanan, China, 878
Pagodas, Yangon, Myanmar, 879-880, 881, 882, 883
Pagodas, Yangzhou, China, 887
Paharpur, Rājshāhi, Bangladesh, 657-660
Pahila (builder of Khajurāho temple), 468
Paihia, New Zealand, 861
Painted Gray Ware, Mathurā, India, 572
Païta, New Caledonia, 644
Pajajaran, kingdom of, 101, 395
Pajang, kingdom of, 888
Pak family, 509
Pakistan, 6, 29-30, 95, 142, 175, 186, 189, 218, 222, 223, 227-228, 263, 279, 308, 310, 312, 370, 371-373, 388, 394, 413, 418, 442, 448, 448-450, 473-477, 489-492, 508, 522-525, 536, 595-599, 608-611, 669-672, 767, 769, 798-800, 801-804, 805-808
Pakistan Civil War, 176
Paknam Fort, Thailand, 99
Pakualam I (ruler of Yogyakarta), 891
Pakualaman, Indonesia, 891
Pakuan, Pajajaran, West Java, Indonesia, 101
Pakubuwono II (Mataram king), 890
Pakubuwono III (Mataram king), 890
Pāla Dynasty, 308, 657, 659
Palace, Bangalore, India, 95
Palace, Beijing, China, 813
Palace, Bijāpur, India, 125
Palace, Bīkaner, India, 132
Palace, Calcutta, India, 174
Palace, Chepauk, Madras, India, 550
Palace, Chittaurgarh, India, 193, 194
Palace, Datong, China, 213
Palace, Delhi, India, 218, 223
Palace, Dusit, Bangkok, Thailand, 99
Palace, Fatehpur Sīkri, India, 261, 263
Palace, Hua, Vietnam, 364
Palace, Karakorum, Mongolia, 451-452
Palace, Lahore, Pakistan, 524
Palace, Lhasa, Tibet, China, 526, 527, 528, 529
Palace, Luang Prabang, Laos, 533
Palace, Lucknow, India, 534
Palace, Luoyang, China, 538, 541, 872
Palace, Mandalay, Myanmar, 556-557, 558, 560
Palace, Māndu, India, 563
Palace, Manila, Philippines, 570
Palace, Nanjing, China, 618, 620
Palace, Nukualofa, Tongatapu Island, Tonga, 830
Palace, Sīgiriya, Sri Lanka, 754, 755-756
Palace, Sunggaminasa, Indonesia, 839
Palace, Tōkyō, Japan, 822, 825
Palace, Vientiane, Laos, 852
Palace, Xian, China, 870
Palace, Yogyakarta, Indonesia, 890, 891, 892
Palace of Akbar, Ajmer, India, 20, 22
Palace of Akbar, Fatehpur Sīkri, India, 24, 26
Palace of Angkor Thom, Angkor, Cambodia, 32
Palace of Danei, Forbidden City, Beijing, China, 105
Palace of Delight, Bijāpur, India, 127
Palace of Earthly Peace, Forbidden City, Beijing, China, 10
Palace of Heavenly Purity, Forbidden City, Beijing, China, 107
Palace of Hyder Ali-Tippu Sultan, Bangalore, India, 95
Palace of Istana Nurul Iman, Bandar Seri Begawan, Brunei Darussalam, 162
Palace of Jodhā Bāī, Fatehpur Sīkri, India, 263
Palace of Mān Singh I, Amber, India, 24, 26
Palace of Ma'sūd III, Ghaznī, Afghanistan, 283
Palace of Rāna Kumbha, Chittaurgarh, India, 193, 194
Palace of the Winds, Fatehpur Sīkri, India, 263
Palace of the Winds, Jaipur, India, 386
Palas (people), 134
Palau, 379
Palawan, Philippines, 897, 899
Palembang, South Sumatra, Indonesia, 101, 102, 113, 115, 582, 583, **661-664,** 757
Pāli, India, 399, 654
Palk Bay, 714
Pallava Dynasty, 435-437, 501, 502, 547, 552, 554, 555, 684, 809
Palmerston, Australia, 210
Palmerston, Viscount (Henry John Temple), 208
Pamanahan (Muslim Indonesian ruler), 888
Pampa River. *See* Tungabhadra River
Pampā-kshetra. *See* Vijayanagara, Karnātaka, India
Pampanpalana (mythic bell bird), 44
Pan Geng (Shang ruler), 42
Panaji, India, 288, 289
Panamara Dynasty, 837
Panay, Philippines, 565
Pañcavaṭī. *See* Nāsik, Mahārāshtra, India
Panch Mahal, Fatehpur Sīkri, India, 263
Panchen Lama, 751, 753, 6752
Paṇḍava (clan), 505, 762
Pandit Vihara, Bangladesh, 186
Pandrethan, India, 767
Paṇḍu (descendant of Kuru), 505
Pāṇḍu Lēṇa, Nāsik, India, 625, 626, 628
Pāṇḍukhābhaya (Sinhalese king of Sri Lanka), 35
Pāṇḍya Dynasty, 259, 437, 501, 502, 684, 685, 714, 809, 812
Pang (people), 358
Pangeran Adipati Mangkunegoro. *See* Mas Said
Panglima Arabi's Kuta, Jolo, Philippines, 404
Pāṇini (Sanskrit grammarian), 837
Pānīpat, India, 1
Panjdeh, Turkmenistan, 336
Panlong Cheng, Wuchang, China, 866
Panwol-song, Kyŏngju, South Korea, 509
Panyu. *See* Guangzhou, Guangdong, China
Pao Mecca, Hajo, India, 310-311
Papeari, Tahiti, French Polynesia, 788
Papeete, Tahiti, French Polynesia, 787, 788
Papeete Museum, Tahiti, French Polynesia, 788
Papua New Guinea, 298, 644, 846
Parākrama Samudra reservoir, Polonnaruwa, Sri Linka, 686
Parākramabāhu (the Great; king of Sri Lanka), 39, 684, 686
Parākramapāṇḍya (Pāṇḍyan king of Sri Lanka), 687
Paramāra Dynasty, 117, 561
Paramartha (monk), 704
Paramatta, Australia, 782
Paramatta Road, Sydney, Australia, 783
Paramesvara (Palembang prince and founder of Meleka sultanate), 582, 584, 663, 757
Paramesvaraman I (Cāḷukya king), 436
Parāntaka I (Cōḷa king), 501, 811
Parashu Rāma (Vishnu incarnation), 600
Paraśurāma (god), 710
Parasurameśvara Temple, Bhubaneswar, India, 123
Pari Mahal college, Srīnagar, India, 769
Parian district, Cebu City, Philippines, 181
Paris, France, 727
Park, Waitangi, New Zealand, 859, 861-862
Parkes, Fanny, 271
Parkes, Sir Harry, 271, 814
Parkinson, Sydney, 153
Parks, Dunedin, New Zealand, 237, 238
Parks, Madras, India, 550
Parks, Miyazaki, Japan, 594
Parks, Nagasaki, Japan, 615
Parks, Nikkō, Japan, 632, 638
Parks, Norfolk Island, Australia, 643
Parks, Sārnāth, India, 848
Parks, Takayama, Japan, 795
Parks, Tongariro, New Zealand, 832, 833-834
Parks, Vārānasī, India, 850
Parliament House, Sydney, Australia, 784
Parmāb (Chandēl rāja), 20
Paropamisus Mountains, 333
Parr (British governor), 115, 116
Parsees. *See* Parsis
Pārśhvanātha (Jain prophet), 412, 468, 602, 848
Parsis, 142-143, 144
Pārśvanāth temple, Jaisalmer, India, 392
Pārśvanāth temple, Khajurāho, India, 468, 470
Parthians, 608, 805, 806
Party Rakyat Brunei, 161
Pārvatī (goddess), 24, 121, 133, 142, 254, 258-259, 412, 437, 653
Parvīz (Shāh Jahān's older brother), 802
Pasay City, Philippines, 565
Pashtun (people), 441, 442
Pashupata Saivism, 252, 253-254
Pashupatinath temple, Kāthmāndu, Nepal, 464
Pasig River, 565
Pāṭaliputra. *See* Patna, India
Pātan. *See* Lalitpur, Nepal
Patānjali (Pāṇini's commentator), 837
Pateikkaya (father-in-law of Narathu), 655
Pathan (people), 136, 187, 392, 473, 474, 475, 476, 671
Pathet Lao, 533, 854
Patiala, India, 20
Patna, India, 49, 168, 169-170, 408, 837
Paton, John, 845
Patrick (saint), 448

Patteson, John, 642
Patwon-ki-haveli (House of the Brocade Merchants), Jaisalmer, India, 392
Paul Gauguin Museum, Tahiti, French Polynesia, 788
Pavie, Auguste, 532
Pavilion, Yangzhou, China, 886
Pavilion of the Literary Star, Qufu, China, 708
Pavolova, Anna Pavlovna, 14
Pawon (temple), Java, Indonesia, 147
Pazhayarai, India, 501
Peace Dome. *See* Genbaku Dōmu, Hiroshima, Japan
Peace Festival Heiwa Kinen Shiryōkan, Hiroshima, Japan, 351
Peace Memorial Museum, Heiwa Kinen Shiryōkan, Hiroshima, Japan, 351
Peace Memorial Park, Heiwa Kinen Kōen, Hiroshima, Japan, 351
Peace Park and Tower, Miyazaki, Japan, 594
Peace Park, Nagasaki, Japan, 615
Peacock Island, Guwāhāti, India, 310
Peacock Throne, Delhi, India, 222
Pearl Harbor, Hawaii, United States of America, 206, 209, 299, 351, 615, 647, 794
Pearl Mosque, Āgra, India, 5
Pearl Mosque, Bhopāl, India, 120
Pearl Mosque, Delhi, India, 222
Pearl Mosque, Lahore, Pakistan, 524
Pearl Palace, Gwalior, India, 316
Pearl Palace, Lucknow, India, 534
Pearl River. *See* Zhujiang River
Pegu. *See* Bago, Myanmar
Peking. *See* Beijing, China
Peking Man, 109
Pelliot, Paul, 244
Penang, Penang, Malaysia, 586, **665-668,** 759, 760
Pengeran Makota (Brunei prince), 497
Penghu Islands, 790
Penitentiary, Port Arthur, Australia, 691
Penrith, Australia, 863
Pentecost Island, Vanuatu, 844
Pentonville Prison, England, 690
Penukonda fortress, India, 857, 858
People's Action Party (Singapore), 760, 761
People's Army of Vietnam, 356
People's Liberation Army (China), 112, 742-743
People's Park, Madras, India, 550
People's Party (Thailand), 99
Pepys, Samuel, 142
Perak, Malaysia, 760
Perambur, India, 550
Perbuwatan (volcanic cone), Krakatau, Indonesia, 493, 494
Perera, Muhandiram, 756
Perez Dasmariñas, Gomez, 566
Perfume River. *See* Huong Giang
Permesta rebellion (1957), 842
Pérouse. *See* Galaup, Jean François de (conte de La Pérouse)
Perry, Matthew Calbraith, 318, 614, 651, 825
Pershing, John J., 405
Persia. *See* Iran
Persian Gulf, 174, 336, 371, 669, 884
Peru, 251, 298, 818, 820-821
Pescadores, 790
Peshāwar Museum, Peshāwar, Pakistan, 800
Peshāwar, North-West Frontier, Pakistan, 416, 417, 473, 475, **669-672,** 798
Peshāwar Valley, 798, 800
Peter I (the Great; emperor of Russia), 686
Peter II (king of Portugal), 142
Petermann Mountains, 44
Petre, Francis, 237
Pettah, Colombo, Sri Lanka, 201, 202, 203
Phalgu River, 276, 277-278
Phalgudēva (lord of Kośala), 49
Phalodi, India, 392
Phatta (Rājput prince), 194
Phaulkon, Constantine, 58
Phayao, kingdom of, 182, 184, 773
Phayre, Arthur Purvis, 63
Phelps, Mr. and Mrs. A. H., 642
Phetsarat (prince of Laos), 853
Phi Devata. *See* Phi Muang
Phi Muang (god), 772
Phi Sua (god), 771, 772
Phien Tran, Vietnam, 354
Philip (prince consort of Great Britain), 830
Philip II (king of Spain), 180, 201, 204, 341, 403, 565, 568
Philippine Revolution, 900
Philippine Scouts, 206
Philippines, 158, 160, 161, 177-181, 204-207, 341, 342, 379, 403-407, 544, 565-571, 792, 794, 897-900
Phillip, Arthur, 154, 639, 781, 782, 784, 863
Phillip Island, 639, 642
Phimai, Thailand, 32
Phimeanakas Temple, Angkor, Cambodia, 32, 33
Phitsanulok, Thailand, 54, 56, 775
Phnom Bakheng Temple, Angkor, Cambodia, 31
Phnom Kulen. *See* Mount Mahendrapura, Cambodia
Phnom Penh, Cambodia, 33, 54
Pho Hai Tu. *See* Emperor of Jade Pagoda, Ho Chi Minh City, Vietnam
Phoenix Hall. *See* Hō'o-dō, Uji, Japan
Phra Bang Buddha, Luang Prabang, Laos, 530, 531, 532, 533, 852
Phra Buddha Sihing, Sukhothai, Thailand, 775
Phra Kaeo (Emerald Buddha), Bangkok, Thailand, 532, 533, 852
Phra Khaphung (Honored Lofty Place), Sukhothai, Thailand, 772
Phra Masa (god), 774
Phra Nakhon Si Ayutthaya. *See* Ayutthaya, Ayutthaya, Thailand
Phra Phetracha (king of Ayutthaya), 58
Phra Ram Temple, Ayutthaya, Thailand, 59
Phra Ruang (Thai king), 772
Phra Saek Kham (sacred image), 532
Phra Si Sanphet Temple, Ayutthaya, Thailand, 58-59
Phrae, Thailand, 184
Phraya Taksin. *See* Taksin
Phu Xuan, Hue, Vietnam, 362, 364
Phuc Anh. *See* Gia Long
Pibul Songgram, 100
Piduragala shrine, Sīgiriya, Sri Lanka, 756
Pigafetta, Antonio, 158, 177, 179, 899
Pigot, Lord (George Pigot), 547
Pihanga (legendary mountain), 832
Pillai, Kumbalathu Sanku, 713
Pillar of Aśoka, Sānchi, India, 730
Pillared Hall, Taxila, Pakistan, 806
Pillow Stone, Suzhou, China, 778
Pine Creek, Australia, 208, 209
Ping River, 182, 184, 185
Pingala (legendary), 479
Pingcheng. *See* Datong, Shanxi, China
Pingshan Tang Hall, Yangzhou, China, 887
Pingshun. *See* Datong, Shanxi, China
Pink City. *See* Jaipur, Rājasthān, India
Pio (mythic creature), 818
Pipal tree. *See* Bo-tree
Piper, John, 641
Pipon (British naval officer), 676
Pippala, Pakistan, 807, 808
Pīr Badr (saint), 186
Pīr Giyasuddīn Aulia Mosque, Hajo, India, 310-311
Pir Muhammad bin Djinhangir (governor of Ghaznī), 282, 335, 414, 439
Pīr Patho (Sufi mystic), 801-802
Pires, Tomé, 582, 583
Pitcairn, John, 673
Pitcairn Island, Pitcairn Islands, 639, 642, **673-678**
Pitt Town, Australia, 863
Place des Cocotiers, Nouméa, New Caledonia, 647
Plain of Jars, 531
Plassey, West Bengal, India, 679-683
Plato (Greek philosopher), 578
Pleasure Hall (Sukh Niwas), Amber, India, 26
Plered, Indonesia, 890
Pliny (the Elder), 710
Plotinus (Greek philosopher), 578
Pohiva, Akilisi, 831
Poike Peninsula, Easter Island, Chile, 250
Point Hicks, Australia, 781
Point Puer, Port Arthur, Australia, 689
Point Venus Lighthouse, Tahiti, French Polynesia, 786
Poivre, Pierre, 90
Pokaran, India, 392
Polish Hat Island, Indonesia, 493
Polo, Marco, 73, 105, 109, 164, 186, 241, 290, 307, 322, 325, 327, 333, 452, 457, 704, 710, 720, 732, 776, 884-886
Polonnaruwa, Sri Lanka, 39, **684-687**
Polynesia, 65, 247, 264, 353, 673, 674-675, 723, 785-789, 820-821, 839
Polynesians, 247, 785, 818, 820, 821, 827, 832, 843, 844
Pomare II (Tahitian chief), 787
Pomare IV (Tahitian queen), 787
Pomare V (Tahitian chief), 787, 788
Ponda, India, 284, 288
Pondicherry, India, 548, 680
Pongdok-sa Pagoda, Kyŏngju, South Korea, 512
Poonpal (ruler of Jaisalmer), 388
Pop-hung (king of Silla), 510
Popham, Peter, 377
Port Arthur, Tasmania, Australia, 320, **688-691**
Port Botany, Australia, 156
Port Chalmers, Dunedin, New Zealand, 234, 237
Port Dalrymple, Tasmania, 641
Port Darwin, Australia, 208
Port Essington, Australia, 208
Port Jackson. *See* Sydney, New South Wales, Australia
Port-de-France. *See* Nouméa, South Province, New Caledonia
Porta de Santiago, Melaka, Malaysia, 585
Portsmouth, England, 154, 673
Portugal, 7-8, 39, 57, 61, 62, 68, 87, 88, 101, 102, 113, 142, 158, 172, 177, 179, 186, 187-188, 189, 199-202, 203, 225, 252, 253, 256, 272-274, 284, 286, 288, 289, 306, 317, 340, 341, 342, 343, 344, 353-354, 360, 395, 403, 412, 443, 445-446, 542, 544, 545, 547, 550, 565, 584-585, 612, 613, 615, 652, 663, 667, 687, 711, 712, 714, 758, 764, 790, 802, 821, 839, 840, 841, 844, 856, 900
Poshapura. *See* Peshāwar, North-West Frontier, Pakistan
Posok-jong Bower, Kyŏngju, South Korea, 513
Post and Telegraph Office, Madras, India, 550
Potala Palace, Lhasa, Tibet, China, 526, 527, 528, 529, 752
Potramarai Tank, Kumbakonam, India, 501
Pou (Olosega high chief), 821
Pouvanaa a Oopa (Tahitian nationalist), 788
Power House Museum, Sydney, Australia, 784
Prabhās. *See* Somnāth, Gujarāt, India
Pradyota (king of Avanti), 836, 837
Pragjyotishapura. *See* Guwāhāti, Assam, India
Prah Khan, Angkor, Cambodia, 33
Prai River, 665

Praia Grande, Macau, 545
Prajadkipok (king of Thailand), 99
Prambanan, Central Java, Indonesia, 692-696
Prambanan Plain, Java, Indonesia, 147, 692, 695, 696
Prambanan Temple, Yogyakarta, Indonesia, 888
Pramodhavardhani (Sailendra princess), 692
Praparapura. *See* Srīnagar, Jammu and Kashmir, India
Prasat Thong (king of Ayutthaya), 57
Pratap Malla (king of Nepal), 466
Pratihāra, kingdom of, 134, 410, 468
Pratyushā (legendary warrior), 479
Pravarasena (rāja), 767
Prayag, India, 628
Pre Rup, Angkor, Cambodia, 31
Precious Pagoda (Baota), Yanan, China, 878
Prefectural Medical College, Hiroshima, Japan, 351
Prejewalsky, Nikolai, 244
Prem Chand, 535-536
Premadasa, Ranasinghe, 203
Presbyterianism, 234, 235, 236, 844, 845, 865
Presidency College. *See* Hindu College, Calcutta, India
Presidency General Hospital, Calcutta, India, 174
Pret Sīla (Hill of Ghosts), Gayā, India, 278
Pretoria, South Africa, 223
Prey Nokor. *See* Ho Chi Minh City, Vietnam
Priangan region, West Java, Indonesia, 103, 104
Price, John, 642
Prince of Wales Island. *See* Penang, Penang, Malaysia
Prince of Wales Museum of Western India, Bombay, India, 144
Princes Street, Dunedin, New Zealand, 235
Prins Willems Eijlanden, Fiji, 265
Prinsep, James, 14, 850
Pritchard, George, 725, 787
Pritchard, William T., 266
Prithvi Nārāyan Shāh (king of Nepal), 466
Prithviraj Chuahan (Tomara ruler), 218
Prithvīrāja (Chauhān rāja of Ajmer), 20-21
Prophet's Tomb, Srīnagar, India, 769
Proto-Malays (people), 65
Province Wellesley, Malaysia, 665
Pryer, Ada, 404-405
Ptolemy III (king of Egypt), 578-579
Ptolemy of Alexandria, 49, 163, 186, 218, 272, 279, 522, 578, 837
Pu Xam Xao Mountains, 230
Puccini, Giacomo, 615
Puerto Navidad, Mexico, 565
Puerto Rico, United States of America, 204, 567
Pugachenkova, G. A., 71, 73
Puhaddin (Muslim missionary), 886
Pukka Qila, Hyderābād, Pakistan, 371, 372, 373
Pulakeśin II (Cāḷukyan king of Pūri), 253
Pulau Pinang. *See* Penang, Penang, Malaysia
Puleanga Fakatui o Tonga. *See* Tonga
Pulicat, India, 548
Punan (people), 158, 630
Puṇḍravarddhana. *See* Mahāsthan, Bangladesh
Pune, India, 627, 628
Pung (Paekche prince of Japan), 486
P'ungnammun Gate, Chŏnju, South Korea, 197
Punhwang-Sa Pagoda, Kyŏngju, South Korea, 510
Punjab Exhibition Building, Lahore, Pakistan, 525
Punjab, India, 27-30, 73, 220, 263, 281, 417, 476, 489, 499
Punjab, Pakistan, 522-525, 595, 597, 608-611, 802, 805-808
Punti (people), 358
Purana Qila, Delhi, India, 222
Pure Land Sect. *See* Jōdo-shū
Pūri. *See* Elephanta Island, Mahārāshtra, India
Puri, Orissa, India, 121, 134, 479, 480, **697-700**
Purification Hall (Haraiden), Miyajima, Japan, 590
Pūrikā. *See* Elephanta Island, Mahārāshtra, India
Pūrṇavarmā (legandary king of India), 140
Purnavarman (king of Tarumanegara), 395
Puru (clan), 505
Purushottama-Jagannātha (god), 699
Pushpabhuti (king of Kurukshetra), 507
Pushyagupta (governor of Junāgadh), 408
Pushyamitra (Suṇga king of Ayodhyā), 49, 730
Putian Xiangying Temple, Fujian, China, 705
Puttalam, Sri Lanka, 200
Putyatin (Russian admiral), 318
Puyck, Nicolaes, 342
Puyi (Qing emperor of China), 107, 108, 749, 816, 886
Puyŏ Museum, Chŏnju, South Korea, 195
Puyŏ, South Korea. *See* Kongju and Puyŏ, South Ch'ungch'ŏng, South Korea
Pyinbia (king of Burma), 653
Pylstaeres Eylandt. *See* Ata, Tonga
P'yŏngyang, North Korea, 483, 484, 511
Pyramid temples, Angkor, Cambodia, 31, 32
Pyu (people), 653, 654, 879

Qadam Mubarak mosque, Chittagong, Bangladesh, 189
Qadiri (sect), 802
Qājār Dynasty, 336
Qali. *See* Galle, Sri Lanka
Qarmaṭians (sect), 608, 610
Qāsim Ali Khan. *See* Mīr Qāsim
Qi, China, 293, 294, 739
Qi Jiguang (commander of Jizhou), 741
Qian Ren Shi (pool), Suzhou, China, 778
Qian Tang River, 325
Qianfodong. *See* Mogao Caves, Dunhuang, Gansu, China
Qianlong (Qing emperor of China), 307, 323, 328, 458, 732, 747, 886
Qianmen Gate, Beijing, China, 109
Qianmin, China, 739
Qianqinggong, Forbidden City, Beijing, China, 107
Qila-i-Kuhna Masjid, Delhi, India, 222
Qilian Shan Mountains, 239
Qin Dynasty, 42, 109, 212, 293, 294, 296, 302, 305, 358, 420, 538, 668, 709, 741, 870-871, 884
Qin Kai (Chinese general), 744
Qin Tomb, Shaanxi, China, 701-703, 709
Qing Dynasty, 40, 106-107, 109, 165, 166, 216, 241, 296, 297, 305, 306, 323, 324, 328, 358, 359, 424, 454, 458, 528-529, 541, 620, 705, 732, 735, 736, 741, 742, 744, 747, 748, 778, 790, 791, 793, 794, 813-814, 816, 866, 872, 873, 874, 886, 896
Qinghai Tower, Guangzhou, China, 306
Qingliang Hill, Nanjing, China, 616
Qingshuiying, China, 296
Qingyuan. *See* Quanzhou, Fujian, China
Qingyuan Mountain, 704
Qingzheng Temple, Quanzhou, China, 706
Qinhuangdao, China, 743
Qipchak Pass, 474, 475
Qixia Shan, China, 616
Quaeckerneck (Dutch voyager to Japan), 342
Quakerism, 642
Quannan. *See* Quanzhou, Fujian, China
Quanzhou Bridge, Quanzhou, China, 706
Quanzhou, Fujian, China, 306, **704-706**
Quarantine Island, Dunedin, New Zealand, 237
Qudsia III (Gohar Begum; ruler of Bhopāl), 119
Queen Victoria Building, Sydney, Australia, 784
Queen's Gardens, Dunedin, New Zealand, 236
Queensborough, Norfolk Island, Australia, 641
Queensland, Australia, 209, 643, 845, 865
Quezon, Manuel, 569
Quezon City, Philippines, 565
Qufu, Shandong, China, 707-709
Qui Nhon, Vietnam, 331
Quilon, Kerala, India, 710-713
Quintal (*Bounty* mutineer), 674, 675
Quintal, Edward, 677
Quintal family, 676
Quiros, Pedro Fernández de, 785, 820, 843-844
Qulī Quṭb Shāh (Deccan king), 290
Qutaybah ibn Muslim (caliph of Bukhara), 163
Quṭb al-Mulk, Qulī (founder of Quṭb Shāhi Dynasty), 366
Quṭb Minar, Delhi, India, 218, 219, 220, 223
Quṭb Shāhi Dynasty, 290, 291-292, 366-367, 369
Quṭb-ud-Dīn Aybak (Muslim ruler in India), 50, 218, 312, 507, 576, 801, 849
Quwwat-ul-Islam Masjid, Delhi, India, 218

Raī Empire, 608
Ra Muktasimha (Chudasma ruler), 764
Ra Navghan of Junāgadh (Kāmthīāwār leader), 764
a Navghana IV (Chudasma ruler), 764
Rabbani, Burhanuddin (president of Afghanistan), 419
Rabindra Bharati University, Calcutta, India, 175
Rabuka, Sitiveni, 264, 268
Rādhā (goddess), 135
Raeburn, Harold, 604, 605
Raffles, Sir Thomas Stamford, 115-116, 150, 757, 758-759
Raffles Bay, 208
Raffles Hotel, Singapore, 144, 760
Ragam (trader), 665
Raghunath Singh I (rāja of Bishnupur), 134, 135
Raghunath Singh II (rāja of Bishnupur), 136
Rahatgarh, India, 120
Rahman, Mujibur, 228
Rahman, Tengku Abdul, 499
Rahman, Zia ur-, 189, 228, 229
Rahmat Ali, Choudhry, 525
Rāhula (son of Buddha), 18
Railway Station, Lahore, Pakistan, 524-525
Raimal (Sīsōdian rāna), 193
Rainbow Snak (mythic intermediary), 44
Raisina Hill, Delhi, India, 223
Raj Bhavan, Calcutta, India, 173, 175
Raj Ghat, Delhi, India, 223
Raja Baguinda (Islamic invader of Sulu), 897
Rāja Bekung (ruler of Bali), 68
Rāja Bhoj (Paramara ruler of Mālwa), 561
Rāja Gopīchand. *See* Pīr Patho
Rāja Rām (Indian rebel leader), 577
Raja Sulayman, 565
Rajabai Tower, University of Bombay, India, 143, 144
Rajadhi Rajasinha (king of Kandy), 446
Rajaji Hall, Madras, India, 550
Rājarāja I (Cōḷa king of India), 437, 501, 684, 699, 809, 811
Rājarājeśvara Temple. *See* Brhadīśvara Temple, Thanjāvūr, India
Rājarata, Sri Lanka, 35, 687
Rājasiṃha (Narasiṃhavarman II; Pallava king of Mahābalipuram), 436, 555
Rājasinha (king of Sitavaka), 199, 200, 443
Rajasinha II (king of Kandy), 201, 202, 273, 446
Rājasthān, India, 1, 3, 6, 20-23, 24-26, 129-133, 191-194, 383-387, 388-394, 399-402, 412, 491, 600-602
Rājendra I (Cōḷa king), 501, 659, 684-685, 811
Rajendravarman (Khmer king of Cambodia), 31
Rājgarh, India, 119
Rājghāt Plateau, 847, 849, 850
Rājmahāl, India, 225
Rajpath (Kingsway), Delhi, India, 223
Rājput Dynasty, 1, 20-21, 22, 23, 24, 132, 133, 218, 312, 371, 383, 385, 386, 388, 392, 399-402, 410, 465, 468, 472, 600, 801, 802

Rājput War, 400
Rājputana, India, 129, 386, 399
Rājshāhi, Bangladesh, 657-660
Rajwarra. *See* Rājasthān, India
Rakai Pikatan, 692
Rakurakuen, Hikone, Japan, 338
Ralpachen (Tibetan ruler), 527
Rām Dās (fourth Sikh gurū), 27
Rām Bāgh. *See* Aram Bāgh, Āgra, India
Rām Sīla (god), 278
Rāma (god), 47, 50, 143, 259, 312, 435, 522, 572, 625, 694, 695, 714, 715, 716, 849, 855, 856
Rama I (king of Thailand), 184
Rama IV (Mongkut; king of Thailand), 59, 99, 771, 774
Rama V (king of Thailand). *See* Chulalongkorn
Rama IX (king of Thailand), 775
Rāma Rāya (Krishnadeva Rāya's son-in-law), 857
Rama the Bold. *See* Ramkhamhaeng
Rāmachandra Temple, Vijayanagara, India, 856
Rāmagrāma, India, 731
Raman Research Institute, Bangalore, India, 95
Rāmanāthapuram, India, 714
Rāmanathaswami, Rāmeswaram, India, 714, 716
Ramaññadesa. *See* Bago, Myanmar
Rāmapāla (Pāla ruler), 659
Ramar Tiruvadi Koyiladhikari Kulaśekhari Chakkravarti (Venād chief), 710
Ramaracha (king of Thailand), 54
Ramathibodi I (king of Thailand), 52, 53-54, 59, 96, 97, 98
Ramathibodi II (king of Thailand), 55, 59
Ramesuan (king of Thailand), 54
Rāmeswaram, Tamil Nādu, India, 714-717
Ramkhamhaeng (king of Sukhothai), 52, 53, 771, 772, 773, 774, 775
Ramkot mound, Ayodhyā, India, 48, 49
Rāmnād, India, 714, 715
Ramoche Temple, Lhasa, Tibet, China, 526
Ramos, Fidel, 570
Rampuria, Bīkaner, India, 129
Ramsgate, Australia, 156
Rana, S.J.B., 467
Rana Dynasty, 466
Rāna Udai Singh (Rathor ruler), 399
Rangaku period (Japan), 614
Rangiro Desert, 834
Rangoon. *See* Yangon, Myanmar
Rangoon University, Yangon, Myanmar, 558, 880
Rani Lakshmi Bai, 314, 316
Ranjit Singh (Lion of the Punjab; founder of Sikh kingdom), 29, 441, 524, 525, 610, 671
Rankei Doryu. *See* Tao-Lung
Ranthambor, India, 22
Rāo Bīka (mahārāja of Bīkaner), 133
Rāo Jodha (mahārāja of Jodhpur), 129, 399
Rāo Kalyan (cenotaph), Bīkaner, India, 133
Rāo Singh (mahārāja of Bīkaner), 129
Rapa Nui. *See* Easter Island, Chile
Raper, George, 641
Rarotonga Island, 674, 818
Rāsa Mancha, Bishnupur, India, 134, 135
Rashō-mon, Kyōto, Japan, 515
Rāshṭrakūṭa Dynasty, 253, 256, 257, 259, 437, 626, 837
Rashtrapati Bhavan (Viceroy's House), Delhi, India, 223
Rasul Khanji (ruler of Junāgadh), 413
Ratan Singh II (ruler of Chittaurgarh), 193
Ratburana Temple, Ayutthaya, Thailand, 59
Rathor Rājputs, 129, 399-402
Ratu Banuve, 266
Ratu Boko, 694
Ratu Johar, 158
Ratu Naulivou, 266
Ratu Seru Cakobau, 266
Ratu Tanoa, 265
Rauzabal. *See* Prophet's Tomb, Srīnagar, India
Rāvaṇa (demon-king), 259, 695, 714, 715, 716
Ravanna (mythic king), 143
Rāvi River, 489, 522, 523, 608
Rāwal Jaisal (prince), 388
Rāwalpindi, Pakistan, 769
Rawling, C.G., 604
Ray, Satyajit, 536
Razadarit (Mon ruler of Bago), 60, 61
Razi (physician-philosopher), 163
Razzaq, Abdul, 856
Rectification Campaign (China), 876
Red City, Bāmiān, Afghanistan, 79
Red Eagle Brigade (Mandalay), 560
Red Flag Society (Malaysia), 668
Red Flag Square, Shenyang, China, 749
Red Fort. *See* Lal Qila
Red Guard (China), 111, 529, 709, 737, 817
Red Hats (Buddhist sect), 527, 750
Red Hill, Lhasa, Tibet, China, 526, 528
Red Palace. *See* Potala Palace, Lhasa, Tibet, China
Red River, 329, 331
Red Sea, 371
Red Temple (Nasiyan), Ajmer, India, 23
Red Turban rebels (China), 424
Reed, Vernon H., 861, 862
Regis, Jean-Baptiste, 742
Rehe, China, 742
Ren Xiao, 302
Renfrew, Colin, 333
Rennyō (Ikkō priest), 431, 650
Republican nationalists (Indonesia), 842
Republican period (China), 323
Republican Revolution of 1911 (China), 866, 868
Reserves Conservation Society (New Zealand), 236
Reservoirs, Anuradhapura, Sri Lanka, 35, 37, 38
Reting Monastery, Tibet, China, 527
Réunion, 90
Revolutions of 1848, 787
Rewa Kund, Māndu, India, 563
Rewa, Viti Levu, Fiji, 264, 266
Reza Khan, Muhammad, 171
Rhazes. *See* Razi
Ri-jō (Carp Castle), Hiroshima, Japan, 349
Ri-ring (mountain peak), 605
Riau-Johore, Malaya, 396
Ricci, Matteo, 306, 544
Richardson, George, 726
Richmond, Australia, 863, 865
Richmond Hill, Windsor, Australia, 865
Rīgestān (square), Samarkand, Uzbekistan, 720, 721
Ringgold Islands, 265
Rinnō-ji, Nikkō, Japan, 632, 636, 637
Rinzai (sect), 428
Rio Hondo, Zamboanga, Philippines, 899
Rishabhadeva (Jain prophet), 412
Rishbhanatha (temple), Jaisalmer, India, 392
Rivière, Henri, 331
Rizal, José, 405, 568, 900
Rmen. *See* Bago, Myanmar
Roberts, Frederick, 417-418, 476
Robinson, Sir Hercules, 267
Rocard, Michel, 647
Rochefort, Henri de, 646
Rock of the Falling Flowers. *See* Nakhwaam, South Korea
Rock-cut architecture, Ajanta, India, 14-19
Rock-cut temples, Elephanta Island, India, 252, 253-255
Rocks, Sydney, Australia, 784
Rodráiguez de Figueroa, Esteban, 403
Roggeveen, Jacob, 250, 724
Rohinī (goddess), 762
Rohri, India, 392
Rokh (governor of Herāt), 335
Rokkakudō, Kyōto, Japan, 515
Roluos, Cambodia, 31
Roman Catholicism, 58, 176, 180, 181, 196, 223, 225, 236, 266, 267, 288, 289, 296, 306, 320, 340, 341, 342, 344, 347, 354, 364-365, 383, 403, 404, 443, 448, 452, 466, 544, 550, 585, 612, 615, 641, 642, 643, 711, 725, 742, 752, 785, 787, 814, 815, 818, 820, 824, 843, 844, 865, 886, 900
Roman Empire, 49, 80, 239, 302, 514, 552, 669, 720, 798, 800, 809
Rome, Italy, 127
Rongbuk Glacier, Tibet, China, 605, 606
Rongbuk Monastery, Tibet, China, 605
Rongbuk Valley, Tibet, China, 603
Roosevelt, Franklin D., 206, 877
Rose, Hugh, 120
Rose Island. *See* Muliavu Island, American Samoa
Rosenthal, Joe, 381
Ross, Robert, 639, 641
Ross, Ronald, 174
Rotterdam, Tonga. *See* Nomuka, Tonga
Rotuma Island, Fiji, 264, 265, 267, 828
Rouletted Ware, Ayodhyā, India, 49
Round-the-city Road, Quanzhou, China, 706
Round Tower, Kuching, Malaysia, 500
Roura.. (people), 212, 213-214, 294
Routledge, Katherine Scoresby, 251
Rowland, Benjamin, 14, 17, 687
Rowley, Thomas, 641
Roxas, Manuel A., 570
Roy, Rammohan, 174
Royal Asiatic Society, 14
Royal Astronomical Society, 865
Royal Avenue, Sukhothai, Thailand, 775
Royal Geographical Society, 604, 606
Royal Hospital, Goa, India, 286
Royal Palace, Kāthmāndu, Nepal, 466
Royal Tombs, Tongatapu Island, Tonga, 830
Roymata (king of Vanuatu), 843
Rudra (god), 254
Rudra Simha III (Śaka ruler), 410
Rudra Singh (king of Assam), 310
Rudradāman (Kshatrapa ruler of Ujjain), 837
Rudradāman I (Śaka ruler), 410
Rudrasimha I (Kshatrapa ruler of Ujjain), 837
Rudreśvara Temple, Somnāth, India, 765
Ruhuṇa, Sri Lanka, 35, 38, 684, 685, 686
Ruitong. *See* Quanzhou, Fujian, China
Rukn-e 'Alam (Sufī sheik), 610
Rum Jungle, Australia, 210
Rum Rebellion (1808), 782
Rumi Darwaza (Turkish Gate), Lucknow, India, 534
Rumi Sultana (Turkish Sultana's House), Fatehpur Sīkri, India, 263
Run, Banda Islands, Indonesia, 88, 89, 90
Rupamati's Pavilions, Māndu, India, 563
Russell, Lord (Edward Russell), 676
Russell, New Zealand, 859
Russell, Robert Tor, 223
Russia, 161, 174, 189, 197, 244, 246, 317-318, 319, 320, 336, 350, 372, 417, 441, 451, 452, 454, 458, 459, 475, 476, 529, 580, 604, 614, 651, 671, 686, 720, 721, 722, 736, 748, 752, 806, 816, 884. *See also* Soviet Union
Russian Orthodoxy, 319
Russian Revolution, 166
Russo-Japanese War, 320, 350
Ruttunsi (brother of Moolrāj), 389
Ruwanvelisaya Dagaba, Anuradhapura, Sri Lanka, 38, 39
Ruysbroeck, Willem van, 451, 452
Ryan, Thomas, 642

Ryder, C.H.D., 604
Ryoan-ji (temple), Kyōto, Japan, 518
Ryōtan-ji (temple), Hikone, Japan, 338
Ryūgai-ji. *See* Okadera, Asuka, Japan
Ryūkō-ji (temple), Japan, 429
Ryukyu Islands, 613
Ryūnosuke, Akutagawa, 515

Sa, Dom Leonardo de, 542
Sa de Noronha, Constantino de, 272
Sa-tia-i-le-moa (god), 723
Saadat Ali Khan (Mughal ruler of Oudh), 534
Sabah, Malaysia, 158, 161, 403, 499, 761, 811
Sabaktin (governor of Khorāsān), 522
Sabal Singh (ruler of Jaisalmer), 392
Sabara (tribe), 697
Sābarmati Ashram, Ahmadābād, India, 9
Sābarmati River, 6, 9
Sabi. *See* Puyŏ, South Ch'ungch'ŏng, South Korea
Sabi-song (fortress), South Korea, 486
Sacred Hair Pagoda, Guangzhou, China, 304
Sad-Hazara Garden, Ghaznī, Afghanistan, 281
Sadal Singh, 133
Sadar Bazaar, Jodhpur, India, 402
Sadarghāt, Chittagong, Bangladesh, 189
Sadāśiva (Vijayanagara ruler), 857
Saddanta (previous incarnation of Buddha), 731
Sadik, Muhammad (ruler of Kandahār), 442
Ṣafavid Dynasty, 73, 280, 336, 414, 416, 440, 441
Safdar Jang (ruler of Oudh), 50
Ṣaffārid Dynasty, 79
Ṣafavids (people), 580
Saga (emperor of Japan), 515
Sāgar. *See* Saugor, India
Sagara. *See* Shakatsura
Sagarmatha National Park, Nepal, 603
Sagoda. *See* Ayodhyā, Uttar Pradesh, India
Sagyin quarry, Myanmar, 556
Sahajdhārīs Sikhs, 28
Saheth-Maheth, India, 47
Sai River, 431, 432, 433
Sai-ji (temple), Kyōto, Japan, 515
Saichō (founder of Tendai-shu sect), 517
Sa'īd Khan, 457
Saidai-ji (Great Western Temple), Nara, Japan, 624
Saigō Tanomo (Japanese warrior), 12
Saigon. *See* Ho Chi Minh City, Vietnam
Saigon River. *See* Song Gai Gon
Saikai National Park, Japan, 340
Saikyo. *See* Kyōto, Japan
Sailendra Dynasty, 31, 147, 692
St. Andrew's Church, Karāchi, Pakistan, 448, 450
St. Andrew's Church, Madras, India, 550
St. Barnabas Chapel, Norfolk Island, Australia, 642
St. Barnabas College, Norfolk Island, Australia, 642
St. Dominic's Priory, Dunedin, New Zealand, 237
St. George's Cathedral, Madras, India, 550
St. George's Church, Penang, Malaysia, 667
St. Helena Island, 90
St. James's Church, Sydney, Australia, 783
St. John, Spenser, 404
St. John Island. *See* Sanchuan Island
St. John's Church, Bombay, India, 143-144
St. John's Church, Calcutta, India, 173
St. John's Church, Peshāwar, Pakistan, 671
St. Joseph's Cathedral, Dunedin, New Zealand, 237
St. Martin-in-the-Fields Church, London, England, 550
St. Mary's Church, Madras, India, 547-548
St. Matthew's Church, Windsor, Australia, 864, 865
St. Patrick's School, Karāchi, Pakistan, 448
St. Paul's Anglican Cathedral, Dunedin, New Zealand, 237
St. Paul's Cathedral, Calcutta, India, 174
St. Paul's Cathedral, London, England, 143
St. Paul's Church, Macau, 543, 544
St. Paul's College, Macau. *See* Madre de Deus College, Macau
St. Peter's Anglican Church, Richmond, Australia, 865
St. Peter's Basilica, Rome, Italy, 127
St. Peter's Church, Melaka, Malaysia, 583
St. Petersburg, Russia, 718, 721
St. Thomas Cathedral, Kuching, Malaysia, 500
St. Thomé Cathedral, Madras, India, 547, 550
St. Thomé, India, 547, 548, 550
Saipan Island, 379
Saishōin Gojū-no-tō, Hirosaki, Japan, 345
Saitobaru, Japan, 592, 594
Saivism, 121, 122, 123, 124, 692, 716, 762, 764, 765
Śaka Dynasty, 14, 410, 414, 439, 456, 763
Sakai, Japan, 650
Śakas (people), 574, 576, 608, 626, 798, 800, 805, 837
Sakashitamon, Nikkō, Japan, 637
Sake-Brewing Museum, Aizu-Wakamatsu, Japan, 12
Sāketa. *See* Ayodhyā, Uttar Pradesh, India
Sakhalin Island, 318
Sakichi Horie (architect), 347
Sakikata Park, Hirado, Japan, 342, 344
Śakra (god), 686
Śakti (goddess), 468, 470
Sakya, China, 750
Sakya Monastery, Tibet, China, 527, 528
Śākya Simha Buddha, Sānchi, India, 730
Sakyamuni Buddha, Ajanta, India, 18
Sakyamuni Buddha, Lhasa, Tibet, China, 526, 529
Sakyamuni Buddha, Shigatse, Tibet, China, 752
Salar Jang Museum, Hyderābād, India, 369
Salazar (bishop of Philippines), 566
Salazar, Antonio de Oliveira, 289, 545
Salbahan (ruler of Jaisalmer), 388
Salcedo, Juan de, 565
Salīm (prince of India). *See* Jahāngīr
Salīm (saint), 2
Salīm (sūri ruler of Delhi), 222
Salīm Chishtī (saint), 260, 263
Salim Shāh Suri, 611
Salim Singh (minister of Moolrāj II), 392, 394
Salim Singh ki Haveli, Jaisalmer, India, 394
Salimgarh Kiosk, Āgra, India, 1
Salote Tupou III (Salote Mafileo Pilolevu; queen of Tonga), 827, 830
Sāluva Dynasty, 856
Samal (people), 899
Saman Burj, Lahore, Pakistan, 524
Sāmānid Dynasty, 163, 280, 333, 720
Samapa. *See* Jaugada, India
Samar, Philippines, 177, 180, 568
Samarang, Java, 265
Samarkand, Samarkand, Uzbekistan, 71, 73, 163, 164, 165, 240, 280, 333, 335, 473, 476, 527, **718-722**
Samatata, kingdom of, 186
Sāmba (god), 478
Sambhājī (Marāṭhā king), 291, 292
Sambhal Mosque, Delhi, India, 220
Sāmbhar, India, 20
Sambhavanatha Temple, Jaisalmer, India, 392
Sambhota (Tibetan scholar), 526
Sambutsudō (Three Buddhas Hall), Nikkō, Japan, 632
Samghamitra (king of Ayodhyā), 49
Samghavarman. *See* Kang Sanghui
Samideshwar Temple, Chittaurgarh, India, 193
Sammā Dynasty, 801, 802
Samnye, Korea, 196
Samoa (Western Samoa and American Samoa), 264, **723-726,** 818, 820, 827, 828, 845
Sampon-ji (temple), Kamakura, Japan, 426
Samudra Gupta (emperor of India), 122, 308, 576, 699
Samudra-Pasai, Sumatra, Indonesia, 582-583
Samunda harbor, Bangladesh, 186
Samye Monastery, Lhasa, Tibet, China, 526
San Agustin Church, Manila, Philippines, 566
San Bernadino Strait, 568
San Cristobal Island, Solomon Islands, 298
San-machi-suji (Avenue of the Three Lanes), Takayama, Japan, 795
San Marcos Island, Solomon Islands, 298
San Remondo, Jolo, Philippines, 404
San Ta Pha Daeng (shrine), Sukhothai, Thailand, 771, 772
Sānchi, Madhya Pradesh, India, 17, 579, **727-731,** 806
Sanchuan Island, 542
Sandamuni Pagoda, Mandalay, Myanmar, 556
Sandbar at Amanohashidate, Japan, 590
Sandringham, Australia, 156
Sandspit, Karāchi, Pakistan, 450
Sanetomo (shōgun of Kamakura), 428
Saṅgama Dynasty, 855, 856
Sanggan River, 212
Sangha order, 35, 61, 532, 851-852
Saṅghamitthā (Saṅghamitrā; daughter of Aśoka), 35, 140
Sangharama, Paharpur, Bangladesh, 659
Sangsan-ri, Kongju, South Korea, 484
Sanjar (Seljuk sultan), 163, 282, 579
Sanjaya Dynasty, 147, 692
Sanjō II (emperor of Japan), 517
Sanjūsangendō (temple), Kyōto, Japan, 518
Sankar, R., 713
Śaṅkara (philosopher), 254, 436
Śaṅkarāchārya (philosopher), 503
Sankha Tīrtha, Rāmeswaram, India, 716
Sankilang (Gowan rebel), 841
Sannō Festival, Takayama, Japan, 797
Sannomachi (Third Lane), Takayama, Japan, 795
Sans Souci, Australia, 156
Sansad Bhavan, Delhi, India, 223
Sanshujo, Ise, Japan, 374
Santa Casa da Misericordia, Macau, 544
Santa Cruz Island, Solomon Islands, 298
Santa Isabel Island, Solomon Islands, 298
Santo Antonio bastion, Galle, Sri Lanka, 272
Santo Island, Vanuatu, 846
São Jago bastion, Galle, Sri Lanka, 272, 273
Sapporo, Japan, 319, 320
Saracens, 366
Saraikela. *See* Taxila, Punjab, Pakistan
Sarajevo, Yugoslavia, 165
Sarangapani Temple, Kumbakonam, India, 501, 502
Sarasvati (goddess). *See* Benzaiten
Saraswati River, 765
Sarawak, Malaysia, 158, 160, 161, 497, 498, 499-500, 629-631, 761
Sarawak Museum, Kuching, Malaysia, 499, 629
Sarawak River, 160, 497
Sardar Khan (Mughal grandee), 8
Sarikā (goddess), 769
Sāriputa (Buddha disciple), 727
Sarkhej, India, 6
Sarkies brothers, 760
Sārnāth Archaeological Museum, Sārnāth, India, 848
Sārnāth, India, 138, 848
Saro, kingdom of, 509
Sartach (Tartar leader), 451
Sarvāstivādins (sect), 574
Sās Bahū Mandir (temples), Gwalior, India, 312
Sāsānian Dynasty, 72, 73, 79, 333, 414, 439, 579, 669, 806
Śaśānka (Gauḍa king of India), 122-123, 140, 657
Sasawat Minas (clan), 24
Sassetti, Filippo, 858

Sastri, K.A. Nilakanta, 809
Satī (goddess), 308, 309, 464, 657
Satake family, 10
Satan, 608
Sātavāhanna Dynasty, 122, 410, 552, 625, 626, 837
Satok Bughra Khan, 457
Śatrughna (Rāma's younger brother)), 572
Satsuma, Japan, 12, 520
Satyamitra (king of Ayodhyā), 49
Satyapir Bhīta mound, Paharpur, Bangladesh, 659
Saudi Arabia, 524, 579, 583
Saugor, India, 120
Saurāshtra, India, 408, 410, 412, 762, 763
Savage, Charles, 266
Savage Island. *See* Niue Island, Samoa
Savaii Island, Western Samoa, 723, 725
Savangvatthana (king of Laos), 533
Savea (Malietoa ruler), 723
Savo Island, Solomon Islands, 300
Sawai Jai Singh (governor of Mālwa), 838
Sawāi Rāja Sur Singh (Mughal military commander), 399
Sawan Mal (Sikh governor), 610
Sawankhalok. *See* Si Satchanalai, Thailand
Sawara (prince of Japan), 624
Sawayama, Japan, 338
Sawlu (king of Pagan), 654
Saya San Rebellion, 880
Sayid Subhān Kūlī Khān, 73
Saywell, Thomas, 156
Sayyid Dynasty, 193, 220, 507
Sazae-dō (Conch Shell Hall), Aizu-Wakamatsu, Japan, 12
Scarlet Red Guard (China), 737
Schmidt, Harry, 381
Schouten, Willem Corneliszoon, 828
Schreuder (Dutch governor of Sri Lanka), 446
Schwartz's Church, Thanjāvūr, India, 812
Scobie, James, 77
Scotland, 40, 88, 174, 234, 235, 236, 821
Scott, Robert, 237
Scythians, 186, 410, 579, 800, 806, 837
Sé Cathedral, Goa, India, 288
Sea of Flagstone, Forbidden City, Beijing, China, 107
Sea of Japan, 431
Sea of Parākrama. *See* Parākrama Samudra
Sea Silk Route, 704
Sea-Calming Fort. *See* Laolongtou, Shanhaiguan, China
Sebüktigin (founder of Ghaznavid Empire), 73
Second Indochina War. *See* Vietnam War
Second Opium War. *See* Opium Wars
Secretariat, Bombay, India, 144
Secretariat, Chittagong, Bangladesh, 189
Secretariats, Delhi, India, 223
Secunderābād, India, 366, 369
Sedding, Edmund, 237
Sedeño, Antonio, 566
Seely, John, 256
Sehore, India, 120
Sein Lwin, 882
Selangor, Malaysia, 665, 760
Seleucid Empire, 71, 163, 333, 414, 439, 578
Seleucus I (Nicator; founder of Seleucid empire), 71, 439, 608
Self-Strengthening Movement (China), 735, 736
Seljuk Turks, 163, 218, 281, 282, 333, 439, 579, 720
Selwyn, George Augustus, 642
Sena I (king of Sri Lanka), 37, 684
Sena Dynasty, 134, 186, 659
Senate House, Madras, India, 550, 551
Senbondōri, Kyōto, Japan, 515
Senderib. *See* Sri Lanka
Senerath (king of Kandy), 445
Sengen (cult), 269
Sengen Shrine, Fujinomiya, Japan, 269, 270, 271
Sengoku Jidai (Period of Warring States; Japan), 795
Sengū-shiki celebration, Ise, Japan, 377
Senjokaku (Thousand Mats Hall), Miyajima, Japan, 590
Senju district, Tōkyō, Japan, 824
Senkadagala. *See* Kandy, Sri Lanka
Senopati (Indonesian ruler), 888
Senri New Town, Ōsaka, Japan, 652
Seoul, South Korea, 196, 487, 514
Sephardic Jews, 143
Sepoy Mutiny. *See* Indian Mutiny
Sera Monastery, Lhasa, Tibet, China, 528, 529, 750
Serampore, India, 172
Serang, West Java, Indonesia, 103
Sergeant Major's Row. *See* George Street, Sydney, Australia
Seri Begawan. *See* Omar Ali Saifuddien
Seri Rambai Cannon. *See* Sri Rambai Cannon, Fort Cornwallis, Penang
Seria, Brunei Darussalam, 161
Seringapatam, India. *See* Srirangapatnam, India
Service, John S., 877
Serving, George V., 132
Seta, Japan, 338
Sethi family, 671
Sethi Street, Peshāwar, Pakistan, 671
Seto Naikai (Inland Sea), Japan, 349, 368, 587, 592, 594
Setupathis, 714, 716
Seven Mile Beach. *See* Lady Robinson's Beach, Botany Bay, Australia
Seven Years' War, 404, 548, 680
Seventh-Day Adventists, 642-643, 677, 725
Seville, Spain, 177, 720
Sha Lo Wan, Hong Kong, 358
Shaanxi, China, 293, 294, 295, 420, 701-703, 870-873, 874-878, 904
Shab-e-Bharat festival, Chittagong, Bangladesh, 189
Sha-Chi. *See* Ayodhyā, Uttar Pradesh, India
Shackleton, Ernest, 237
Shādharwan, Srīnagar, India, 769
Shadi Mulk Aka Mausoleum, Samarkand, Uzbekistan, 721
Shadiābād. *See* Māndu, Madhya Pradesh, India
Shāh 'Alam II (Mughal emperor of India), 136, 168, 169, 170, 172
Shāh Beg (Arghūn conqueror of Tatta), 802
Shāh Dynasty, 466
Shāh Hamdan Mosque, Srīnagar, India, 769
Shāh Ismaīl, 73
Shāh Jahān Begum (ruler of Bhopāl), 119, 120
Shāh Jahān Mosque, Tatta, Pakistan, 450, 803
Shāh Jahān (Mughal emperor of India), 2, 3-5, 22, 127, 222, 523-524, 562, 626, 802, 803, 838, 850
Shāh Jahān Palace, Gwalior, India, 314
Shāh Makkai Fort. *See* Kucca Qila, Hyderābād, Pakistan
Shah Murad (dervish emir), 166
Shah Murah of Kundūz, 74
Shāh Najaf Imambara, Lucknow, India, 534
Shāhābād, India, 168
Shahbani Begum Mosque, Calcutta, India, 174
Shāhdara, Pakistan, 3, 523
Shāhi Bāgh, Ahmadābād, India, 7
Shāhi Bazaar, Hyderābād, Pakistan, 373
Shahi Dynasty, 281
Shāhjahānābād, Delhi, India, 5, 222
Shāhji (Bijāpur administrator), 92
Shahji-ki Dheri mounds, Peshāwar, Pakistan, 669
Shahl Jāma-e-Masjid, Chittagong, Bangladesh, 189
Shāhpur (emir), 417
Shāhpurī, Chittagong, India, 188
Shahr-i-Darwaza heights, Afghanistan, 418
Shahr-I-Gholghola, Bāmiān, Afghanistan, 79, 81
Shahr-I-Zhohak, Bāmiān, Afghanistan, 79, 81
Shāhryar (brother of Shāh Jahān), 524
Shailendra, kingdom of, 113, 888
Shaka. *See* Buddha
Shaka-dō (Buddha Hall), Kyōto, Japan, 519
Shakatsura (Sagara; mythic Dragon King), 588
Shakh-i-Zindeh complex, Samarkand, Uzbekistan, 720-721
Shakhrisabz, Uzbekistan, 720, 721
Shālīmār Bagh (Garden of Love), Srīnagar, India, 769
Shālīmār Gardens, Lahore, Pakistan, 523, 524, 525
Shālīmār Gardens, Peshāwar, Pakistan, 671
Shalu, China, 750
Shamanism, 197
Shamien Island, China, 307
Shams-e-Tabriz (Sufi martyr), 611
Shams-ud-Dīn (ruler of Delphi), 218
Shan (people), 62, 530, 655, 656, 851
Shandong, China, 110, 293, 707-709, 736, 744, 776, 874
Shang Dynasty, 40-43, 302, 538, 866, 901, 903-904
Shang Yue, Hong Kong, 358
Shanghai, China, 111, 197, 307, **732-738,** 744, 778, 813, 814, 817
Shanghai Gang. *See* Gang of Four
Shanghai Tariff Conference, 814
Shanhaiguan, Hebei, China, 293, 294, 296, 297, **739-743**
Shanhua Temple, Datong, China, 213, 214
Shankaracharya Hill, Srīnagar, India, 767
Shanti Vana (garden), Delhi, India, 223
Shantinath Temple, Chittaurgarh, India, 193
Shantinatha Temple, Jaisalmer, India, 392
Shanxi, China, 212-217, 293, 295, 893-896
Shaoguan, China, 304
Shaolin Monastery, China, 905
Shaoshan, China, 878
Shāpur I (king of Persia), 798
Sharif Abū Bakr (Philippine sultan), 897
Sharif Muhammed Kabungsuwan (Philippine sultan), 897
Sharif-ul Mulk (governor of Tatta), 802
Sharqī, kingdom of, 849
Shatin Island, Hong Kong, 358
Shatpura, Bangladesh, 189
Shatrunajaya (sacred mountain), 601
Shaw, George Bernard, 223
Shaybānī (Uzbek leader), 440
Shayesta Khān (Mughal governor of Bengal), 225
She (tribe), 358
She Shan (Snake Hill), Wuchang, China, 866, 868
Sheesh Mahal (Mirror Hall), Amber, India, 26
Shekki, China, 542
Shen Chou (painter), 776
Shen Nong (mythic Chinese forefather), 40
Shen River, 745, 746
Shencottah, India, 712
Sheng Shizai, 323
Sheng Xuanhui, 866
Shengong (monk), 778
Shengzong (Song emperor of China), 739
Shenjing. *See* Shenyang, Liaoning, China
Shenxi, China, 216
Shenyang, Liaoning, China, 216, 737, 743, **744-749**
Shenzhen River, 359
Shenzhou. *See* Shenyang, Liaoning, China
Shepherd Islands, Vanuatu, 843
Shēr Shāh of Sūr (Afghan ruler of North India), 1, 222, 314
Shērgarh, India, 1, 218
Sherpa (people), 464, 603, 606
Sherwin, Ann, 641

Shi Jian Shi (Stone Where Swords are Tried), Suzhou, China, 778
Shi Kuang (musician), 420
Shi Tao (painter), 886
Shiba, Japan, 637
Shibaski, Japan, 822
Shibata Katsuie, 431
Shibusawa Eiichi, 320
Shibuya district, Tōkyō, Japan, 825
Shiers (Shears), Mary Ann, 641
Shiga, Japan, 338-339
Shigaraki, Japan, 622
Shigatse, Tibet, Xizang Autonomous Region, China, 528, **750-753**
Shigeki Yamano, 347
Shihāb-ud-Dīn Ghūri. *See* Dilawar Khān
Shihonryū-ji, Nikkō, Japan, 632, 636
Shihuang Di (Qin emperor of China), 293, 294, 297, 616, 701, 709, 739, 741, 870-871, 872
Shi'ite Muslims, 125, 280, 336, 367, 450, 578, 579
Shikinen-sengu. *See* Sengū-shiki
Shikoku, Japan, 426, 587, 648
Shila Devi (Kālī) Temple, Amber, India, 24
Shillong, India, 310
Shimabara, Japan, 342, 824
Shimazu family, 594
Shimoda, Japan, 271, 318
Shimogamo Jinja (shrine), Kyōto, Japan, 515, 518
Shimonoseki, Japan, 349
Shimōsa, Japan, 822
Shin Arahan (monk), 653
Shin Fuji (volcano), Fujinomiya, Japan, 269
Shin Saw Bu (Mon queen of Bago), 61, 879
Shin-Kabuki-za (New Kabuki Theatre), Ōsaka, Japan, 652
Shinagawa district, Tōkyō, Japan, 824
Shingon-shū (sect), 515, 588-589, 590
Shinjuku district, Tōkyō, Japan, 824, 825
Shinkyō (Sacred Bridge), Nikkō, Japan, 636
Shinran (founder of Pure Land Truth Sect), 518, 520
Shintōism, 197, 269, 270, 271, 374, 376, 377, 460, 461, 515, 517, 520, 521, 587, 588, 590, 592, 621, 622, 632, 635, 636, 637, 638, 650, 795
Shipton, E.E., 606
Shīr 'Alī (ruler of Kābul), 417, 442
Shir Dawaza mountain, Kābul, Afghanistan, 415
Shirahata-gu (White Banner Shrine), Kamakura, Japan, 428
Shiraito no taki (Waterfall of White Threads), Fujinomiya, Japan, 269
Shirakawa II (emperor of Japan), 518
Shirakawagō, Japan, 796
Shīrāz, Iran, 142, 720
Shīrāzi, Alami Afzal Khan, 4
Shirdar Medrese, Samarkand, Uzbekistan, 721
Shiroyama, Takayama, Japan, 796
Shish Mahal, Junāgarh Fort, Bīkaner, India, 132
Shish Mahal, Lahore, Pakistan, 524
Shitalā (goddess), 601
Shitennō-ji (temple), Ōsaka, Japan, 460, 648, 652
Shitou Cheng. *See* Nanjing, Jiangsu, China
Shizi (Northern Wei emperor of China), 894
Shizuoka, Japan, 269-271, 634
Shō River, 796
Shodo (Buddhist monk), 632, 636
Shohan, Singapore, 760
Shojā (emir of Kandahār and Kābul), 417, 441, 442
Shoko-o (god), 429
Shōmu (emperor of Japan), 587-588, 622, 623, 624, 648, 795
Shoosmith, Arthur, 223
Shore, Sir John, 310
Shore Temple, Mahābalipuram, India, 437, 555
Shōren-ji (temple), Takayama, Japan, 796
Shōsōin treasury, Ikaruga, Japan, 624
Shōtoku (empress of Japan). *See* Kōken
Shōtoku Taishi (regent of Japan), 460, 621, 648
Shōwa era, 825
Shozoku-in (sub-temple), Kamakura, Japan, 429
Shravanabelagola, India, 93
Shri Krishnan Das Haveli, Bīkaner, India, 129
Shri Mahalsa (temple), Ponda, India, 288
Shri Mangesh (temple), Ponda, India, 288
Shri Sadul Museum, Bīkaner, India, 133
Shri Shantadurga (temple), Ponda, India, 288
Shrine at Ise, Japan, 587
Shrine of 'Alī Mazār-i-Sharīf, Afghanistan, 580
Shrine of Dhākeśwarī, Dhākā, Bangladesh, 225
Shrine of Gāzurgāh, Herāt, Afghanistan, 335
Shrine of Hajji Piyade, Balkh, Afghanistan, 71, 73
Shrine of Ōkuninushi no Ōmikami, Miyajima, Japan, 590
Shrine of Saint Khwājah Muīn-ud-Dīn Chishtī, Ajmer, India, 260
Shrine of Siva, Elephanta Island, India, 254
Shrine of Tenjin, Miyajima, Japan, 590
Shrine of the Double-Headed Eagle, Taxila, Pakistan, 806
Shrine of the Nine Planets. *See* Nabagraha Shrine, Guwāhāti, India
Shrines, Anuradhapura, Sri Lanka, 35, 37, 38, 39
Shrines, Mandalay, Myanmar, 556
Shrines, Miyajima, Japan, 587, 588, 589, 590
Shrines, Miyazaki, Japan, 592, 593
Shrines, Nara, Japan, 621, 624
Shrines, Nikkō, Japan, 587, 632, 634-637, 638
Shrines, Takayama, Japan, 796-797
Shrines, Taxila, Pakistan, 806
Shuang Ta Si (Two Pagoda Temple), Suzhou, China, 778
Shujā (brother of 'Ālamgīr), 309
Shujā-'ud-Dawlah (ruler of Oudh), 50, 168-169, 170, 534
Shuja'at Khan (Mughal grandee), 8
Shukkeien (garden), Hiroshima, Japan, 349, 351
Shukyō Mahikari (religion), 796-797
Shumsher, Bir (Rana ruler), 466
Shumsher, Chandra (Rana ruler), 467
Shumsher, Deva (Rana ruler), 466-467
Shunga kingdom, 848
Shuozhou, China, 214
Shūsh. *See* Susa, Iran
Shwe Dagon Pagoda, Yangon, Myanmar, 62, 879-880, 881, 882, 883
Shwe Gugyi (temple), Pagan, Myanmar, 655
Shwe Mawdaw Pagoda (Pagoda of the Great Golden God), Bago, Myanmar, 60, 63
Shwe Myo Taw, Mandalay, Myanmar, 556, 557, 558
Shwe Nandaw Monastery, Mandalay, Myanmar, 557
Shwe Sandaw Pagoda, Pagan, Myanmar, 653
Shwe Zigon Stupa, Pagan, Myanmar, 654
Shwebo Plain, 62, 558
Shwethalyaung Buddha, Bago, Myanmar, 60, 63
Shyam Rai (temple), Bengal, India, 135
Si Indradit (Tai king of Sukhothai), 772, 774
Si Satchanalai, Thailand, 773, 774, 775
Si Satha (Buddhist sage), 774
Siālkot, Pakistan, 312
Siam. *See* Thailand
Siaosi. *See* George Tupou I
Siaui (brother of Samar chieftain), 177
Siberia, 166, 197, 317, 318, 451, 720, 748
Sichuan, China, 868, 876
Siddharāja Jayasimha, 764
Siddhārtha Gautama. *See* Buddha
Sidhaika (goddess), 257
Siebold, Philipp Franz von, 614
Siem Reap, Cambodia, 31-34
Sien, kingdom of, 773
Sifang Cheng, Nanjing, China, 619
Sīgiriya, Sri Lanka, 38, **754-756**
Sihanouk (prince of Cambodia), 34
Sikandar Jahān Begum (daughter of Qudsia III), 119-120
Sikandar Lodī (sultan of Delhi), 1, 128, 314, 469, 769, 849
Sikandarābād. *See* Āgra, Uttar Pradesh, India
Sikandra, India, 1, 2
Sikh Wars, 524, 671
Sikhs, 5, 27-29, 30, 168, 223, 417, 473, 505, 507-508, 523, 524, 525, 604, 610, 671, 672, 736, 737, 767, 847
Siking. *See* Xian, Shaanxi, China
Sikorski, Radek, 336
Silīguri Corridor, India, 308
Silk Road, 71, 73, 79, 80, 239-240, 241, 242, 279, 321, 456, 541, 669, 704, 718, 871
Silla, kingdom of, 195, 482, 483, 484, 487, 509-514
Sima Guang (writer), 541
Sima Qian (historian), 703
Siṃhavishnu (Pallava king of Kānchipuram), 435, 552
Simuka Sātavāhanna (king of Nāsik region), 625
Sin, Jaime (Philippine Cardinal), 570
Sīnā, Ibn. *See* Avicenna
Sind, Pakistan, 6, 371-373, 394, 448-450, 476, 489-492, 522, 525, 595-599, 801-804
Sind Provincial Museum, Hyderābād, Pakistan, 373
Sindhias (Marāṭhā branch), 314, 316, 400, 838
Sindia (Marāṭhā prince of India), 23
Sing Pol (Lion Gate), Amber, India, 26
Singano (legendary), 818
Singapore, 69, 144, 158, 160, 161, 208, 211, 499, 582, 586, 661, 664, 667, **757-761**
Singapore River, 760
Singarāja, Bali, Indonesia, 69
Singh, Ranjit. *See* Ranjit Singh
Singha Durbar (Lion Palace), Kāthmāndu, Nepal, 467
Singha Saratha Bāhu (ancient Newari trader), 465
Singhalese Buddhism, 182
Singhasari. *See* Singosari, Java
Single Mind sect. *See* Ikkō-shū
Singosari, Java, 113, 663
Singui. *See* Suzhou, Jiangsu, China
Singuttara Hill, 879
Sinhalese (people), 35, 37-39, 199, 201, 203
Sino-Japanese Wars, 13, 197, 307, 349, 359, 620, 737, 778, 816, 868
Sino-Tibetan treaty, 456
Siovili (cult), 725
Sipra River, 835, 837
Sir Joseph Banks Hotel, Botany Bay, Australia, 154
Sirāj-ud-Dawlah (nabob of Bengal), 123, 172, 226, 679, 680, 681, 682
Siri citadel, Delhi, India, 218, 220
Siri Vallabha (ruler of Ruhuṇa), 686
Sirkap. *See* Taxila, Punjab, Pakistan
Sirsukh. *See* Taxila, Punjab, Pakistan
Sīsōdia Dynasty, 3, 191, 193, 194
Sisupalgarh, India, 699
Sītā (legendary wife of Rāma), 47, 143, 259, 625, 694, 695, 714, 715, 716
Sitavaka, Sri Lanka, 199-200, 443, 445
Siva (god), 24, 31, 47, 65, 92, 97, 117, 121, 123, 133, 135, 141, 142, 172, 174, 191, 193, 252, 253-254, 255, 256, 257, 258, 276, 308, 310, 312, 435, 437, 464, 468, 501, 502, 503, 552, 555, 576, 602, 653, 660, 692, 694, 695, 716, 762, 764, 765, 775, 809, 811, 812, 835, 837, 847, 857
Siva Ardhanārīśvara (god), 254
Siva cave temple, Elephanta Island, India, 252, 253-254
Siva Devale No. 2, Polonnaruwa, Sri Lanka, 684
Siva Gaṇgādharamurtī (goddess), 254

Siva Natarāja (Lord of the Dance), 254
Siva Temple, Prambanan, Indonesia, 694, 695, 696
Siva Trimurtī (cave sculpture), 254
Siva Vishnu Kānchi. *See* Kānchipuram, Tamil Nādu, India
Siva Yogishvara (Great Ascetic), 254
Śivadatta (king of Ayodhyā), 49
Śivājī (founder of Marāṭhā dynasty in India), 8, 92, 127, 627, 679, 850
Sivaskandavarman (Pallava king), 435
Skanda Gupta (king of India), 49, 410
Sky Heroes (mythic), 44
Slave Dynasty (India), 20, 21, 218, 801
Slave Island, Sri Lanka, 201
slave trade, 69, 818, 820-821, 845-846
slavery, 90, 99, 195, 201, 251, 288, 298, 404, 467, 487
Slayer of the Invading Hordes. *See* Dalmardan, Bishnupur, India
Sleepy Lizard Women (mythic), 44
Slim, William, 63, 558, 880
Small Wild Goose Pagoda, Xian, China, 872, 873
Smim Htaw (Mon king of Bago), 62
Smim Sawhtut (Mon king of Bago), 62
Smith (American whaling captain), 819-820
Smith, Keith McPherson, 209
Smith, Ross McPherson, 209
Smythe, F.S., 606
Snake Hill (She Shan), Wuchang, China, 866, 868
Snake Temple, Sungai Kluang, Penang, 668
Snow, Edgar, 876-877, 878
Sobis Mountain (Gunong Subis), 629
Society Islands, French Polynesia, 723, 785-789
Society of Friends. *See* Quakerism
Society of Jesus. *See* Jesuits
Socrates (philosopher), 707, 805
Soekmono, R., 150
Soga family, 269, 460, 461
Soga Sukenari, 269
Soga Tokimune, 269
Soga Umako, 460, 461
Sogdian Empire, 718
Sohag Mandir, Amber, India, 26
Sok family, 509
Sōka Gakkai, 271, 429
Sokka-t'ap Pagoda, Kyŏngju, South Korea, 512
Sokkuram Grotto, Kyŏngju, South Korea, 512
Solander, Carl, 781
Solander, Daniel, 153
Solankī Dynasty, 764
Solanmaligai, India, 501
Solar Brilliance Gate, Nikkō, Japan, 637
Solar Race (mythical), 47
Solf, Wilhelm, 726
Solomon (biblical king of Israel), 272, 298
Solomon Islands, 266, 298-301, 642, 725, 843
Solomon's Throne. *See* Shankaracharya Hill, Srīnagar, India
Soma (god), 762, 765
Soma Dynasty, 123, 124
Somanātha Temple, Somnāth, India, 764, 765
Somapura Vihara. *See* Paharpur, Rājshāhi, Bangladesh
Somas (people), 123
Somervell, T.H., 605, 606
Somnāth, Gujarāt, India, 281, **762-766,** 763
Son River, 170
Son-dok (queen of Silla), 510
Sonam Gyatso (Dalai Lama), 528, 750
Song Dynasty, 158, 244, 295, 304, 325, 327, 328, 349, 358, 422-424, 541, 618, 630, 704, 709, 732, 741, 776, 831, 868, 884
Song Gai Gon (Saigon River), 353
Song Gianh, Vietnam, 329
Song Jing, 304-305
Sŏng (king of Paekche), 485, 486, 511
Song Qingling, 868
Song-dok (king of Silla), 512
Songkhla, Thailand, 57, 58
Songtsen Gampo (king of Tibet), 526, 527, 528
Songwoldae (Moon-gazing Pavilion), Puyŏ, South Korea, 485
Sooloo. *See* Sulu, Philippines
Sopāra, India, 408, 625
Sorabol. *See* Kyŏngju, North Kyŏngsang, South Korea
Sori-bashi (bridge), Miyajima, Japan, 590
Soseki (priest), 429
Sourasenoi. *See* Śūrasenas
South Africa, 688, 782
South Australia, Australia, 208, 209, 234
South China Sea, 65, 158, 204, 329, 353, 362, 493, 565, 661
South Ch'ungch'ŏng, South Korea, 482-488
South Dunedin, New Zealand, 236
South Gateway, Sānchi, India, 730
South Island, New Zealand, 234-238
South Kensington Natural History Museum, London, England, 144
South Korea, 195-198, 482-488, 509-514, 882
South Pacific Commission, 821
South Palace, Luoyang, China, 538
South Pole, 237
South Province, New Caledonia, 644-647
South Sulawesi, Indonesia, 839-842
South Sumatra, Indonesia, 661-664
South Vietnam. *See* Vietnam
Southern Assembly (religious movement), 196-197
Southern Capital. *See* Nanjing, China
Southern Chen Dynasty, 618
Southern Great Gate. *See* Nandaimon, Ōsaka, Japan
Southern Han Dynasty, 306
Southern Liang Dynasty, 484, 616, 618
Southern Qi Dynasty, 616
Southern School of Enlightenment of Zen Buddhism, Guangzhou, China, 304
Southern Silk Road, 239, 240, 242
Southern Song Dynasty, 325, 327, 424, 704, 732
Southport, Queensland, Australia, 643
Souza, Pero Lopez de, 443
Sovereign Hill Historical Park, Ballarat, Australia, 78
Sovereign Hill Quartz Mining Co., Ballarat, Australia, 78
Soviet Union 74, 112, 166, 167, 175, 189, 197, 279, 282, 323-324, 332, 336, 355, 356, 360-361, 418, 442, 454, 455, 580, 672, 718, 722, 738, 749, 830, 854, 877. *See also* Russia
Spain, 87, 103, 158, 160, 161, 177, 179-181, 201, 204, 251, 298, 317, 331, 341, 342, 343, 344, 403, 404, 405, 544, 565-568, 612, 613, 720, 781, 785, 790, 792, 828, 839, 843-844, 897, 899, 900
Spain, James W., 473
Spanish-American War, 204, 404
Spencer, Baldwin, 45
Spice Islands. *See* Moluccas, Indonesia
Spink, Walter, 15
Spinola, Carlo, 544
Spooner, D.B., 800
Spring Festival, Nikkō, Japan, 637-638
Square of Heavenly Peace. *See* Tiananmen Square, Beijing, China
Srah Srang, Angkor, Cambodia, 33
Sravasti. *See* Saheth-Maheth, India
Sri Jayawardhanapura Kotte, Sri Lanka, 203
Sri Lanka, 35-39, 47, 59, 61, 87, 138, 140, 199-203, 222, 272-275, 288, 435, 437, 443-447, 501, 503, 531, 554, 653, 655, 684-687, 710, 714, 715, 716, 754-756, 806, 811, 841, 893
Sri Mahadeva, 284
Sri Mariamman Temple, Penang, Malaysia, 667
Sri Rambai Cannon, Fort Cornwallis, Penang, 667
Sri Tri Buana (Palembang ruler), 757
Sri Vijaya Rajasinha (king of Kandy), 446
Sri Wickrama Rajasinha (king of Kandy), 443, 447
Sribuza, Brunei Bay, Brunei Darussalam, 158
Srīnagar, Jammu and Kashmir, India, 3, **767-770**
Srirangapatnam, India, 94, 174, 548, 550
Srivijaya Empire, 87, 113, 565, 582, 583, 661, 662, 663, 664, 757
Staatliche Museum, Berlin, Germany, 800
Staines (British sea captain), 676
Stalin, Joseph, 749, 876
Stalingrad. *See* Volgograd, Russia
Standing Buddha, Mathurā, India, 573
Stanley, Lord, 689
Star bastion, Sri Lanka, 274
Star Mosque, Dhākā, Bangladesh, 229
State Central Library, Bangalore, India, 94-95
State Law and Order Restoration Council (Myanmar), 882
State Museum, Lucknow, India, 536
Stein, Aurel, 244, 458
Stein, Gunther, 877
Steinberger, Albert B., 725
Sterling (British admiral), 318
Stevens, Jimmy, 846
Stevenson, Robert Louis, 788
Stewart, Duncan, 499
Sting-Rays Harbour. *See* Botany Bay, New South Wales, Australia
Stock Exchange, Dunedin, New Zealand, 237
Stockholm, Sweden, 614
Stoddart, Charles, 166
Stokes, John Lort, 208
Stone Bridge Monastery, Sukhothai, Thailand, 773
Stone City. *See* Nanjing, Jiangsu, China
Stone Stage. *See* Ishi-butai, Asuka, Japan
Stone Where Swords are Tried. *See* Shi Jian Shi, Suzhou, China
Stonecutter's Mosque, Fatehpur Sīkri, India, 260
Strait of Melaka (Malacca), 113, 395, 544, 582, 586, 661, 662, 757, 758
Strait of Taiwan, 790
Straits of Singapore, 544
Straits Settlements, 667, 760
Strand Hotel, Yangon, Myanmar, 883
Stuart, John McDouall, 208
Stupa, Anuradhapura, Sri Lanka, 37
Stupa, Bhārhut, Khajurāho, India, 468
Stupa, Bhūteśvara, Mathurā, India, 576
Stupa, Kuthodaw Pagoda, Mandalay, Myanmar, 557
Stupa, Mathurā, India, 574
Stupa, Mohenjo-daro, Pakistan, 597, 598
Stupa, Sānchi, India, 727, 730
Stupa, Sārnāth, India, 848
Stupa, Si Satchanalai, Thailand, 773
Stupa, Taxila, Pakistan, 805, 806, 807-808
Stupa, Wang Yuanlu, Dunhuang, China, 246
Su (ruler of Zhao), 293
Suatot, Henri, 647
Suba' Bawang, 404
Subashiri, Japan, 271
Subbul Singh. *See* Sabal Singh
Subhadra (goddess), 697
Subic Bay, Philippines, 570
Subramaniam, Lord, 667
Śudasa (Tristu king), 505
Śūdra caste, 65
Suez Canal, Egypt, 144, 188, 202, 274, 503, 646
Sufīsm, 20, 22, 125, 189, 508, 610, 769, 802
Sug. *See* Jolo, Sulu, Philippines
Sugawara Michizane, 517, 590, 650
Sugimoto-dera (temple), Kamakura, Japan, 426
Sugrib Parbat, Ayodhyā, India, 48
Sugrīva (legendary "monkey chief"), 855

Suharto, 398, 696, 892
Suhrawardī (sect), 802
Sui Dynasty, 244, 294, 295, 304, 325, 539, 540, 618, 739, 744, 776, 813, 868, 871, 872, 874, 884, 896, 904
Sui Xian, China, 868
Sui Yang Di (Sui emperor of China), 813
Suiko (empress of Japan), 460, 621
Suinin Tennō, 376
Sujin (legendary emperor of Japan), 10, 460
Sukarno, 70, 113, 116, 398, 664, 696, 892
Sukh Niwas (Pleasure Hall), Amber, India, 26
Sukhothai, kingdom of, 52, 54, 184, 851
Sukhothai, Thailand, 32, 52, 54, 182, 184, **771-775**
Sukuna, Sir Lala, 267
Sulaiman Range, 473
Sulawesi, Indonesia, 115, 839, 841, 842, 892
Suleiman (merchant), 259
Suleiman Kurrani (sultan of Bengal), 123
Süleyman Pasha, 412
Sulu, Philippines, 160, 403-407, 665, 897, 899, 900
Sulu Sea, 897
Sulug. *See* Jolo, Sulu, Philippines
Sumana (monk), 182
Sumatra, Indonesia, 87, 90, 101, 103, 104, 113-116, 150, 158, 395, 396, 494, 495, 582, 661-664, 663, 664, 667, 692, 705, 757, 758, 759, 839, 888, 897
Sumbawa, Indonesia, 68
Sumeria, 599
Sumida River, 822, 823, 825
Sumitomo family, 651
Sumiyoshi, Japan, 648
Summer Palace, Beijing, China, 708, 813
Summer Palace, Norbulingka, Lhasa, Tibet, China, 528, 529
Sumpu, Japan, 634
Sūmrah Dynasty, 801, 802
Sun bastion, Sri Lanka, 274
Sun Quan (Wu emperor of China), 616
Sun Temple, Chittaurgarh, India, 191
Sun Temple, Gwalior, India, 312
Sun Temple, Konārak, India, 478, 480, 697, 699
Sun Yat-sen, 108, 307, 620, 866, 867, 868
Sun Yat-sen statue, Wuchang, China, 867, 868
Sun-greeting Pavilion. *See* Yongilru, Puyō, South Korea
Sunahra Makan (Golden House), Fatehpur Sīkri, India, 263
Sunda Islands, Indonesia, 692
Sunda Kalapa, Indonesia, 395
Sunda Straits, 101, 113, 396, 493, 495, 585
Sung Dynasty, 897
Śunga Dynasty, 49, 140, 468, 574, 730
Sungai Kluang, Penang, 668
Sungari River, 743
Sunggaminasa, Indonesia, 839, 841
Sunni Muslims, 125, 165, 186, 281, 336, 367, 450, 579
Sunpu, Japan, 342
Supayalat (queen of Burma), 557
Suphanburi, kingdom of, 53, 54, 56
Supreme Court of New South Wales, Sydney, Australia, 783
Sūr. *See* Afghanistan
Surabaya, Indonesia, 888
Suraj Prole (Sun Gate), Bīkaner, India, 132
Sūraj Sen (legendary Gwalior chieftain), 312
Surakarta, Indonesia, 888, 890
Śūrasenas (people), 572
Surat, India, 6, 8, 142, 202
Surat Singh (ruler of Bīkaner), 132, 133
Surinyavongsa (king of Laos), 532, 852
Suriyamarin (king of Ayutthaya), 58
Sūrpanakha (mythic), 625
Sūrya (god), 468, 478, 479, 480, 576
Sūrya Deula. *See* Sun Temple, Konārak, India
Sūrya Dynasty, 123
Surya Pol (Sun Gate), Amber, India, 24
Sūrya Temple, Chittaurgarh, India, 193
Suryavarman I (Khmer king of Cambodia), 31-32
Suryavarman II (Khmer king of Cambodia), 33
Susa, Iran, 578, 595
Susa-O no Mikoto (god), 587
Sushen (people), 744
Sutan Sjahrir, 90
Sutherland, Forby, 153
Sutherland Shire, Botany Bay, Australia, 153
Sutlej River, 30, 524
Sutmaisan Mountain, 198
Suva, Fiji, 267, 830
Suwara Yoshitsura (Japanese samurai), 10
Suzaku-ōji. *See* Senbondōri, Kyōto, Japan
Suzhou, Jiangsu, China, 776-780
Suzuki Kantarō, 615
Swains Island, American Samoa, 723, 725-726, 818, 820, 821
Swartz, Frederick, 548
Swarup Singh, 392
Swāt, Pakistan, 798
Swayambhu (god), 464
Swayambhunath Stupa, Kāthmāndu, Nepal, 464
Sweden, 545, 614
Sweet Dew Vineyard Hall, Quanzhou, China, 706
Swinging Palace. *See* Hindola Mahal, Māndu, India
Switzerland, 606
Sword Pond. *See* Jian Chi, Suzhou, China
Sword River. *See* Asi River
Syam, kingdom of, 773
Śyāma Jātaka painting, Ajanta, India, 17
Sydney Bay, Australia, 639, 641
Sydney Cove, Australia, 639, 781, 782
Sydney Harbour, Australia, 208, 781, 784
Sydney Harbour Bridge, Australia, 784
Sydney Kingsford Smith Airport, Botany Bay, Australia, 153, 156
Sydney, New South Wales, Australia, 75, 153, 156, 267, 641, 642, **781-784,** 863
Sydney Opera House, Australia, 782, 784
Syria, 165, 239, 562, 578, 579, 720, 872
Syriam, Myanmar, 62
Szechwan. *See* Sichuan, China

Ta Ho (emperor of China), 896
Ta Keo, Angkor, Cambodia, 32
Ta Prohm, Angkor, Cambodia, 33
Tabanan, Bali, 70
Tabinshwehti (king of Burma), 61-62, 532
Tabo-t'ap Pagoda, Kyŏngju, South Korea, 512
Tabuan Road Temple, Kuching, Malaysia, 500
Tabuan Street, Kuching, Malaysia, 500
Tachibana-ji (temple), Asuka, Japan, 460
Tadamichi Kuribayashi, 379, 381
Taedong River, 484, 511
Taegu, South Korea, 512
T'aejo. *See* Wang Kōn
T'aejong Muyol (king of Silla), 486
Tafahi, Tonga, 828
Tafeta (missionary), 266
Taga no Miya (shrine), Ise, Japan, 374
Tagaloa (god), 723
Tagore, Rabindranath, 175, 176
Tagori-hime (goddess), 587
Tagorihime no Ōmikami (god), 632
Ṭāhirid Dynasty, 163, 333
Tahiti, Society Islands, French Polynesia, 251, 299, 639, 673, 676, 725, **785-789**
Tai (people), 182, 230, 232, 530, 531, 532, 851
Tai Zong (Tang emperor of China), 526
Taihedian (Hall of Supreme Harmony), Forbidden City, Beijing, China, 107
Taihemen (Gate of Supreme Harmony), Forbidden City, Beijing, China, 107
Taihua Palace, Datong, China, 213
Tainan Air Base, Taiwan, China, 794
Tainan, Taiwan, China, 790-794
Tainezan Chōshōjī, Hirosaki, Japan, 345
Taipa Island, Macau, 542, 546
Taipei, Taiwan, China, 793
Taiping Rebellion, 307, 328, 620, 735, 778, 814, 874, 886
Taipings, 616, 620, 814
Taipo, Hong Kong, 358
Taira. *See* Iwaki, Japan
Taira Dynasty, 349, 426, 428, 518, 588, 589-590, 822
Taira Kiyomori (samurai), 426, 518, 588, 589-590
Taiseki-ji (temple), Japan, 270, 271
Taishō (Meiji emperor of Japan), 825
Taiwan, China, 175, 206, 306, 342, 350, 358, 521, 558, 568, 704, 709, 738, 778, 790-794, 897
Taiwu Di (Northern Wei emperor of China), 213
Taiyuan, China, 296
Taizi (Northern Wei emperor of China), 894
Taizokai (goddess), 588
Taizong (Northern Wei emperor of China), 894
Taizong (Tang emperor of China), 305, 739, 744
Tāj Bauri, Bijāpur, India, 128
Tāj Mahal Hotel, Bombay, India, 144
Tāj Mahal, Āgra, India, 1, 2, 4-5, 22, 222, 392, 562, 679, 802
Tāj-ul-Masajid, Bhopāl, India, 120
Tak, Thailand, 774
Takabutai, Miyajima, Japan, 590
Takachiho (mountain), Miyazaki, Japan, 592
Takahashi (astronomer), 614
Takalaua (twenty-third Tui Tonga), 828
Takamatsu-zuka (burial mound), Asuka, Japan, 461
Takao, Japan, 431
Takayama Basin, 795
Takayama, Gifu, Japan, 795-797
Takayama Jinya, Takayama, Japan, 795-796
Takayama Yatai Kaikan, Takayama, Japan, 797
Takayutpi (Mon king of Bago), 61
Takeda Ayasaburō, 319
Takenukawa-wake (legendary general), 10
Takht-i-Bahi, North West Frontier, Pakistan, 798-800
Takht-i-Sulaiman. *See* Shankaracharya Hill
Takitsu-hime (goddess), 587
Takizawa Honjin. *See* Kyū Aizu-han Gohonjin, Aizu-Wakamatsu, Japan
Takla Makan (Taklamakan) Desert, 71, 239, 456
Takṣa (legendary), 805
Takṣaśilā. *See* Taxila, Punjab, Pakistan
Taksin (king of Siam), 96, 184
Takua (Samoan Catholic convert), 820
Takuan (Japanese priest), 428-429
T'al-hae (king of Silla), 509
Talaing (people). *See* Mon
Talakaifaiki (fifteenth Tui Tonga), 723, 828
Talamahu Market, Tongatapu Island, Tonga, 830
Talanga (legendary), 818
Talas River, 163
Talas Valley, 321
Taliban (Islamic fundamentalist group), 442
Talikota, India, 125, 857
Talisay, Philippines, 900
Tālpur Dynasty, 372, 448, 492, 804
Tālpur fortress, Kot Diji, Pakistan, 489, 492
Tamenobu (founder of Tsugaru clan), 345
Tamerlane. *See* Timur

Tamil (people), 37, 38, 39, 199, 202, 203, 223, 272, 443, 446, 503, 547, 548, 551, 572, 684, 687, 714, 754, 809, 812
Tamil Nādu, India, 267, 274, 435-438, 501-504, 547-551, 552-555, 679, 680, 699, 712, 714-717, 809-812
Tampi, Velu (Indian rebel), 712
Tamra River, 805, 806
Tan (clan), 667
Tan Lun, 741
Tan Yao (Buddhist missionary), 893, 894
Tanegashima, Japan, 340
Tanesato. *See* Ajigasawa, Japan
Tanette, Indonesia, 841
Tang Dynasty, 109, 158, 163, 195, 214, 239, 240, 242, 244, 246, 295, 304, 305, 321, 325, 358, 414, 420, 422, 456, 486, 487, 510, 511, 512, 515, 538, 541, 590, 618, 621, 630, 704, 739, 744, 776, 870, 871, 872, 873, 874, 878, 884, 896, 904, 905
Tang Yin (poet), 778
Tangaloa (god), 827
Tangaloa Atulongolongo (god), 827
Tangaloa Eitumatupua (god), 827
Tange, Kenzo, 351
Tanggu, China, 816
Tanggu Truce, 742
Tangshan, China, 742, 817
Tanhyon, South Korea, 486
Tanjāvūr. *See* Thanjāvūr, Tamil Nādu, India
Tanjore. *See* Thanjāvūr, Tamil Nādu, India
Tanjung Bunga, Penang, Malaysia, 668
Tanjung Priok, Indonesia, 397
Tank Stream, Sydney, Australia, 782, 783
Tanka (people), 358
Tanna Island, Vanuatu, 843, 844, 845, 846
Tannock, David, 236
Tanoa (Fiji islander), 266
Tanrk River, 439
Tānsēn, Gwalior, India, 314
Tantric Buddhism, 246, 309, 468, 470, 472, 526, 601, 879
Tanzania, 603
Tao-Lung (priest), 428
Taoism, 354, 376, 709, 778, 871, 893
Tapanoeli, Sumatra, Indonesia, 115
T'apsa Pagoda, Chŏnju, South Korea, 198
Tārāgarh Hill, Ajmer, India, 20
Tarāin. *See* Tarōrī, India
Taraki, Nur Mohammed, 418
Tarim Basin, 240, 323, 457, 458
Tarim River, 456
Tarkhan Dynasty, 801, 802
Tarokpyemin. *See* Narathihapate
Tarōrī, India, 20-21
Tarshish (biblical city), 272
Tartary, Chinese. *See* Xinjiang Uighur Autonomous Region, China
Tashilhunpo Monastery, Shigatse, Tibet, China, 528, 750, 751, 752, 753
Tashkent, Uzbekistan, 165, 166, 473, 718, 721, 722
Tasman, Abel Janszoon, 264, 828, 832
Tasman Peninsula, Australia, 688, 690
Tasmania, Australia, 641, 642, 688-691
Tasmasp (Ṣafavid leader), 441
Tatta, Sind, Pakistan, 450, **801-804**
Tau Island, American Samoa, 723
Taufaahau. *See* George Tupou I
Taufaahau Tupou IV (king of Tonga), 827, 830
Tauhara (legendary Maori mountain), 832
Tavatimsa (Buddhist heaven), 556
Tavernier, Jean Baptiste, 850
Taveuni Island, Fiji, 265, 266
Tavoy, Thailand, 55, 56, 58
Tawaramoto, Japan, 462
Taxila, Punjab, Pakistan, 608, **805-808**
Taxila Museum, Taxila, Pakistan, 806, 807, 808
Tay Kinh, Vietnam, 329
Tay Son, Vietnam, 354, 362
Tay Son brothers, 330, 354, 362, 364
Tay Son Rebellion, 330, 354, 362, 364
Taylor (British general in India), 727
Taylor, Telford, 615
Te Pito-te-henua. *See* Easter Island, Chile
Te Rangi Hiroa (Maori historian), 723
Te Vaka (son of Kava Vasefanua), 818, 819
Teacher Training College, Tonga, 830
Tebbutt, John, 865
Teen Murti Bhavan, Delhi, India, 223
Tegalrejo, Indonesia, 891, 892
Tegh Bahādur (seventh Sikh gurū), 27, 28
Tej Karan (legendary Gwalior ruler), 312
Tejapāla (Indian temple builder), 412, 601
Tejapāla Temple, Mount Ābu, India, 600, 601-602
Teli-kā Mandir Temple, Gwalior, India, 312
Telok Blangah, Singapore, 760
Telugu (people), 547, 551
Temasek. *See* Singapore
Temmu (emperor of Japan), 648
Temple. *See also headings beginning with* Pagoda
Temple, Ajmer, India, 20, 23
Temple, Amritsar, India, 27, 28, 29, 30
Temple, Angkor Wat, Cambodia, 33, 34
Temple, Ayutthaya, Thailand, 58-59
Temple, Bīkaner, India, 132
Temple, Bull, Bangalore, India, 92, 95
Temple, Ellora, India, 253, 256, 257-259
Temple, Gangadhareshwara Cave, India, 95
Temple, Hikone, Japan, 338
Temple, Kamakura, Japan, 426, 429
Temple, Kyōto, Japan, 520, 638
Temple, Miyajima, Japan, 588
Temple, Phnom Bakheng, Angkor, Cambodia, 31
Temple, Puri, India, 697
Temple, Takayama, Japan, 795
Temple City of India. *See* Bhubaneswar, Orissa, India
Temple Mountains, Angkor, Cambodia, 31
Temple of A-Ma-Miu, Macau, 542
Temple of Adināth, Bīkaner, India, 129
Temple of Amba Mata, Junāgadh, India, 412
Temple of Amman, Thanjāvūr, India, 812
Temple of Baphuon, Angkor, Cambodia, 33
Temple of Bhandasar, Bīkaner, India, 129
Temple of Borobudur, Central Java, Indonesia, 147-152
Temple of Brahmā, Prambanan, Indonesia, 695, 696
Temple of Caturbhuja, Khajurāho, India, 468
Temple of Cheng, Tainan, Taiwan, China, 793
Temple of Chintamani, Bīkaner, India, 129
Temple of Chion-in, Kyōto, Japan, 518
Temple of Confucius, Hanoi, Vietnam, 331
Temple of Filial Piety and Gratitude, Guangzhou, China, 302
Temple of Great Good Will, Xian, China, 872
Temple of Guhyeshwari, Kāthmāndu, Nepal, 464
Temple of Heaven, Hue, Vietnam, 364
Temple of Inspired Seclusion, Hangzhou, China, 328
Temple of Jagannātha, Puri, India, 479, 480, 697, 699-700
Temple of Javari, Khajurāho, India, 468
Temple of Jufuku-ji, Kamakura, Japan, 428
Temple of Kālīghāt, Kalikshetra, India, 172
Temple of Kapileśwar, Bhubaneswar, India, 123
Temple of Karni Matra, Deshnok, India, 133
Temple of Kumārapāla, Junāgadh, India, 412
Temple of Laksmināth, Bīkaner, India, 129
Temple of Literature, Hanoi, Vietnam, 329, 332
Temple of Mahābodhi (Temple of the Great Enlightenment), Bodh Gayā, India, 138, 140-141
Temple of Mariamman, Ho Chi Minh City, Vietnam, 354
Temple of Mendut, Java, Indonesia, 147, 153
Temple of Mukteśvara, Bhubaneswar, India, 123
Temple of Mystery, Suzhou, China, 778
Temple of Nemināth, Bīkaner, India, 129
Temple of Nemināth, Junāgadh, India, 412
Temple of Ögödei, Karakorum, Mongolia, 454
Temple of Parasurameśvara, Bhubaneswar, India, 123
Temple of Pawon, Java, Indonesia, 147
Temple of Philmeanakas, Angkor, Cambodia, 32, 33
Temple of Rishabhadeva, Junāgadh, India, 412
Temple of Shila Devi (Kālī), Amber, India, 24
Temple of Siva, Nāsik, India, 627
Temple of Siva, Prambanan, Indonesia, 694, 695, 696
Temple of Siva Vishvanatha, Vārānasī, India, 847
Temple of Six Banyan Trees, Guangzhou, China, 304
Temple of Somanātha, Somnāth, India, 762, 763
Temple of the Black Rāma, Nāsik, India, 627
Temple of the Four Heavenly Kings. *See* Shitenno-ji, Ōsaka, Japan
Temple of the Golden Pavilion. *See* Kinkaku-ji, Kyōto, Japan
Temple of the Great Enlightenment, Bodh Gayā, India, 138, 140-141
Temple of the Original Vow. *See* Hongan-ji, Kyōto, Japan
Temple of the Prosperity of the Buddhist Law, Ikaruga, Japan, 621, 624
Temple of the Reclining Buddha, Bangkok, Thailand, 98
Temple of the Return to the Fundamental Principles, Hanyang, China, 868
Temple of the Silver Pavilion, Higashiyama, Japan, 519
Temple of the Sun, Multān, Pakistan, 608, 610
Temple of the Tooth, Kandy, Sri Lanka, 443, 445, 446, 447
Temple of the Tooth Relic, Polonnaruwa, Sri Lanka, 684
Temple of Tribhuvanesvara, Bhubaneswar, India
Temple of Tulsīdās, Vārānasī, India, 850
Temple of Vajrāsana Mulagandhakuti Vihāra, Bodh Gayā, India, 140
Temple of Vishnu, Ayodhyā, India, 50
Temple of Vishnu, Prambanan, Indonesia, 695, 696
Temple of Walkeshwar, Bombay, India, 143
Temple of Wat Arun, Bangkok, Thailand, 98
Temple of Wat Chiang Man, Chiang Mai, Thailand, 182
Temple of Wat Phra Sing, Chiang Mai, Thailand, 185
Temple of Wat Phra That, Chiang Mai, Thailand, 184, 185
Temple of Wat Po, Bangkok, Thailand, 98
Temple of Wat Suan Dork, Chiang Mai, Thailand, 182
Temple of Xieng Thong, Luang Prabang, Laos, 531, 532
Temple Ta Keo, Angkor, Cambodia, 32
Temple Trees, Colombo, Sri Lanka, 203
Temples, Achalgarh, India, 602
Temples, Adhar Devi, India, 602
Temples, Aizu-Wakamatsu, Japan, 12
Temples, Angkor, Cambodia, 31, 32, 33, 34
Temples, Chittaurgarh, India, 191, 193
Temples, Chŏnju, South Korea, 195, 197
Temples, Colombo, Sri Lanka, 200, 202-203
Temples, Datong, China, 213, 214, 216
Temples, Delhi, India, 218, 221, 223
Temples, Elephanta Island, India, 252, 253-255
Temples, Guru Shikhar, India, 602
Temples, Hanyang, China, 868, 869
Temples, Ho Chi Minh City, Vietnam, 354
Temples, Ikaruga, Japan, 621
Temples, Kānchipuram, India, 555
Temples, Kyōto, Japan, 518, 520, 637
Temples, Lhasa, Tibet, China, 526, 528, 529

Temples, Luang Prabang, Laos, 531, 532
Temples, Luoyang, China, 540
Temples, Macau, 542
Temples, Mahābalipuram, India, 552, 554, 555
Temples, Māndu, India, 561
Temples, Mathurā, India, 576-577
Temples, Miyajima, Japan, 588, 590
Temples, Mount Ābu, India, 600-602
Temples, Multān, Pakistan, 608, 610
Temples, Mylapore, India, 550
Temples, Nanjing, China, 616, 619, 620
Temples, Nara, Japan, 621, 622, 623, 624, 887
Temples, Nāsik, India, 625, 626, 627, 628
Temples, Nikkō, Japan, 632
Temples, Sānchi, India, 731
Temples, Tainan, Taiwan, China, 792, 793, 794
Temples, Takayama, Japan, 795, 796
Temples, Taxila, Pakistan, 806, 807-808
Temples, Thanjāvūr, India, 809, 811-812
Temples, Tianjin, China, 815
Temples, Tōkyō, Japan, 824
Temples, Ujjain, India, 835, 837, 838
Temples, Vārānasī, India, 848, 849, 850
Temples, Vientiane, Laos, 852, 853
Temples, Vijayanagara, India, 855, 856, 857, 858
Temples, Xian, China, 871-872
Temples, Yangzhou, China, 886, 887
Temples, Yogyakarta, Indonesia, 888
Tempyō period, 621
Temüjin. *See* Genghis Khan
Tenasserim, Myanmar, 55, 56, 58, 653
Tendai-shū (sect), 517, 519, 632, 650
Tenjin (god), 590
Tenjin Matsuri festival, Ōsaka, Japan, 650
Tenma-gu (shrine), Ōsaka, Japan, 650, 651
Tennōji Park, Ōsaka, Japan, 651, 652
Tenzing, Norkey, 603, 606
Tepe Sardar, Ghaznī, Afghanistan, 279
Terai Plains, Nepal, 464
Teralakhara, Quilon, India, 712
Ternate, Moluccas, Indonesia, 87
Terra Australis, 785, 787, 828, 843, 844
Terrace of the Rain of Flowers, Nanjing, China, 618
Tet Offensive (Vietnam), 356, 362, 364, 365
Thai (people), 530, 851, 880
Thai Hoa Palace, Hue, Vietnam, 364
Thai Puan (people), 86
Thai To (Ly ruler of Dai Viet), 329, 331
Thai-Lao War, 851, 852
Thailand, 32, 33, 34, 52-59, 60, 62, 82-86, 96-100, 141, 150, 161, 177, 182-185, 206, 353, 364, 530, 531, 532, 568, 582, 665, 667, 771-775, 851, 852, 853, 854, 880
Thakin (Myanmar), 558
Thamala (Mon noble), 60
Thames River, 781
Thammik Rat Temple, Ayutthaya, Thailand, 59
Thamuddarit (Pyu king of Pagan), 653
Thānēsar, Kurukshetra, India, 505, 507
Thang Long. *See* Hanoi, Vietnam
Thangasseri, India, 713
Thanh Tong (Le emperor), 353
Thanjāvūr, Tamil Nādu, India, 437, 502, 503, **809-812**
Thar Desert, 129, 218, 388, 392, 394, 399
Tharrawaddy (king of Myanmar), 880
That Byinnyu (temple), Pagan, Myanmar, 655
That Luang, Vientiane, Laos, 852, 853
That Thanh. *See* Ho Chi Minh
Thatcher, Charles, 236
Thato. *See* Tatta, Sind, Pakistan
Thaton, Myanmar, 60, 653
Thatta. *See* Tatta, Sind, Pakistan
Theravāda Buddhism, 17, 34, 60, 61, 256, 456, 530, 576, 625, 653, 654, 771, 772, 773, 774, 851, 879
Theroux, Paul, 844
Therry, J.J., 865
Thévenot (17th-century writer), 608
Thibaw (king of Burma), 557
Thienhoven. *See* Tutuila Island, American Samoa
Thieu Mu Pagoda, Hue, Vietnam, 362
Thieu Tri (emperor of Vietnam), 362, 364-365
Thikombia, Fiji, 265
Thomas (saint), 547, 550, 712, 769, 798
Thomas Aquinas (saint), 500
Thomas of Kana, 710
Thompson, Andrew, 863
Thomson, Basil, 830
Thomson, J.T., 235
Thompson Square, Windsor, Australia, 865
Thon Buri, Thailand, 96, 98, 184
Thong Chan (prince of Ayutthaya), 54
Thong Duang. *See* Ramathibodi I
Thong, U (founder of Ayutthaya), 53
Thousand Buddha Caves, Dunhuang, Gansu, China, 239, 240, 241, 242-246
Thousand-Handed Kannon, Nikkō, Japan, 632
Thousand Mats Hall, Miyajima, Japan, 590
Thousand Stone Men. *See* Qian Ren Shi, Suzhou, China
Three August Ones (China), 40
Three Buddhas Hall, Nikkō, Japan, 632
Three Kingdoms period (220-265; China), 866, 893
Three Kingdoms period (475-538; Korea), 482-484
Three Pagodas Pass (Burma), 56
Thugs (sect), 174
Thunberg, Carl Peter, 614
Thūpārāmā, Anuradhapura, Sri Lanka, 37, 39
Thupten Gyatso (Dalai Lama), 529
Thurston, John B., 267, 830
Tian Shan Mountains, 239, 321, 323, 458, 718
Tian Tang (Heavenly Hall), Luoyang, China, 541
Tian Zhongyu, 742
Tiananmen Guangchang. *See* Tiananmen Square, Beijing, China
Tiananmen Incident (1976), 111
Tiananmen Square, Beijing, China, 105-108, 109, 110-111, 738
Tianjin, China, 111, 424, 736, 742, **813-817**
Tianjin University, China, 817
Tianning Si Temple, Yangzhou, China, 887
Tiastenes, India, 837
Tibet, China, 71, 141, 240-241, 246, 321, 452, 456, 465, 466, 467, 526-529, 603, 604-606, 746, 750-753
Tibetan Buddhism. *See* Lamaism
Tidore, Moluccas, Indonesia, 87
Tiger Fort, Amber, India, 386
Tiger Hill, Suzhou, China, 776, 778
Tiger Hill Pagoda, Suzhou, China, 778
Tigris River, 491
Tiki-tiki (god), 818
Tilaganga, India, 366
Tilakari Medrese, Samarkand, Uzbekistan, 721
Tilley, B.F., 725
Tilodaki stream, Ayodhyā, India, 48
Tilokaraja (king of Siam), 184
Tiluksi (Bhatti chief), 389
Timor, Indonesia, 265, 495, 545, 673
Timur (Tamerlane; Mongol conqueror), 6, 73, 165, 220, 282, 333, 335, 383, 414, 439, 475, 507, 561, 610, 671, 679, 718, 720, 721, 837
Timur Shāh (Durrāni ruler of Afghanistan), 417, 441, 442
Timurid Empire, 165, 333, 335, 414, 580
Tingri Dzong, Tibet, 605
Tippu (ruler of Mysore), 92, 94, 95, 369, 548
Tipu Sultan Mosque, Calcutta, India, 174
Tirah Valley, 476
Tirel, Jules, 821
Tiruchchirāppalli, India, 811
Tirumala (brother of Rāma Rāya), 858
Tirumangai Ālvār (writer), 554
Tiruna, Swati, 712
Tirunal, Sri Mulam, 712
Tirunelveli, India, 712
Tiruvanchikkulam, India, 710
Tiruvengalanatha Temple, Vijayanagara, India, 856
Tissawewa Reservoir, Anuradhapura, Sri Lanka, 35, 37
Tiyangi Sugh, Jolo, Philippines, 404
Tjibaou, Jean-Marie, 647
Tō-ji (temple), Kyōto, Japan, 515
To Lich River, 329
Toba (people), 321, 893
Toba II (emperor of Japan), 426, 428, 518
Toba Dao. *See* Wu (Toba emperor of China)
Toba Gui (founder of Northern Wei Dynasty in China), 893
Tocharians. *See* Yüeh-Chi
Tochigi, Japan, 632-638
Tod, James, 388, 389, 392, 394
Tōdai-ji Temple, Nara, Japan, 622, 623-624, 887
Tofua, Tonga, 673, 828
Tōgō, Murano (architect), 351
Togon Timur (Mongol emperor), 453
Tōjin-kan Chinese Mansion, Nagasaki, Japan, 615
Toka (king of Lakemba), 266
Tōkaidō (East Sea Road), Japan, 823, 824
Tokei-ji. *See* Enkiri-dera, Kamakura, Japan
Tokelau, Territory of New Zealand, 723, 725-726, **818-821**
Tokugawa Hidetada (*shōgun* of Japan), 338, 342, 634, 636, 650
Tokugawa Iemitsu (*shōgun* of Japan), 271, 342, 632, 636, 637, 824
Tokugawa Iemochi (*shōgun* of Japan), 339
Tokugawa Ieyasu (*shōgun* of Japan), 10, 270, 271, 317, 318, 338, 342, 345, 349, 432, 520, 612, 632, 634, 635-636, 637, 638, 650, 795, 823, 826
Tokugawa *shōgunate*, 10-12, 13, 270-271, 317-318, 338, 339, 342, 345, 349, 377, 429, 430, 431, 432-433, 520, 594, 612, 613, 614, 632, 634-637, 638, 650, 651, 795, 796, 823-824
Tokugawa Yoshinobu (*shōgun* of Japan), 12
Tōkyō, Tōkyō, Japan, 10, 11, 12, 269, 270, 271, 317, 318, 319, 320, 338, 339, 345, 349, 375, 379, 426, 430, 433, 434, 520, 521, 594, 612, 614, 624, 632, 636, 637, 650, 651, 652, 748, 795, **822-826**
Tōkyō Bay, 269, 271, 614, 822
Tōkyō National Museum, Japan, 244
Tōkyō Stock Exchange, Japan, 825
Tollygunge Club, Calcutta, India, 174
Tolo Harbor, Taipo, Hong Kong, 358
Tomara Dynasty, 218, 312, 507
Tomb (*See also headings beginning with* Mausoleum; Stupa)
Tomb, Datong, China, 214
Tomb, Sui Xian, China, 868
Tomb of Dīwān Shurfa Khān, Tatta, Pakistan, 802
Tomb of Mīrzā Jānī Beg, Tatta, Pakistan, 802
Tomb of Mirza Tungril Beg, Tatta, Pakistan, 803
Tomb of Abdul Jalil, Multān, Pakistan, 611
Tomb of Alī Akbar, Multān, Pakistan, 611
Tomb of Apak Khoja, Kashgar, China, 458
Tomb of Bābur, Kābul, Afghanistan, 415-416
Tomb of Baha-ud-Dīn Zakaria (The Ornament of the Faith), Multān, Pakistan, 610, 611
Tomb of Begum Mursheedzadi, Lucknow, India, 534
Tomb of Bishop Béhaine, Ho Chi Minh City, Vietnam, 354
Tomb of Gai Si, Hami, China, 324
Tomb of Ghāzī-'ud-Dīn-Haidar, Lucknow, India, 534
Tomb of Ghulām Shāh, Hyderābād, Pakistan, 371

Tomb of Gia Long, Hue, Vietnam, 364
Tomb of He Jingyu, Hanyang, China, 868
Tomb of Hongwu (Xiao Ling; the Filial Tomb), Nanjing, China, 619-620
Tomb of Hoshang Shāh, Māndu, India, 562
Tomb of 'Isā Khān the Younger, Tatta, Pakistan, 802
Tomb of Jāmī, Herāt, Afghanistan, 335
Tomb of Jing Di, Xian, China, 871
Tomb of King Muryŏng, Kongju, South Korea, 486, 487
Tomb of Li Wenzhong, Nanjing, China, 620
Tomb of Lu Su, Hanyang, China, 868
Tomb of Maḥmūd, Ghaznī, Afghanistan, 281
Tomb of Mariam, Sikandra, India, 1, 2
Tomb of Muḥammad Ghaus, Gwalior, India, 314
Tomb of Pīr Patho, Tatta, Pakistan, 801-802
Tomb of Pomare V, Tahiti, French Polynesia, 788
Tomb of Puhaddin, Yangzhou, China, 886
Tomb of Rukn-e 'Alam, Multān, Pakistan, 610, 611
Tomb of Saadat Ali Khan, Lucknow, India, 534
Tomb of Sardar Khan, Ahmadābād, India, 8
Tomb of Shams-e-Tabriz, Multān, Pakistan, 611
Tomb of Shuja'at Khan, Ahmadābād, India, 8
Tomb of Sultan Agung, Yogyakarta, Indonesia, 888, 890
Tomb of Sun Yat-sen, Nanjing, China, 620
Tomb of Syed Yūsuf Gardezi, Multān, Pakistan, 611
Tomb of Tānsēn, Gwalior, India, 314
Tomb of the Good Wife, Suzhou, China, 778
Tomb of the Saint, Balkh, Afghanistan, 417
Tomb of Wu Di, Xian, China, 871
Tomb of Xiang Fei, Kashgar, China, 458
Tomb of Xiao Jing, Nanjing, China, 618
Tomb of Xu Da, Nanjing, China, 620
Tombs, Anyang, China, 40-41, 42
Tombs, Danyang, China, 616
Tombs, Delhi, India, 220, 222
Tombs, Golconda, India, 290
Tombs, Junāgadh, India, 413
Tombs, Kongju, South Korea, 484-485
Tombs, Kyŏngju, South Korea, 513-514
Tombs, Lahore, Pakistan, 522, 523-524, 525
Tombs, Lhasa, Tibet, China, 528, 529
Tombs, Māndu, India, 562, 563
Tombs, Multān, Pakistan, 610-611
Tombs, Nanjing, China, 618, 619-620
Tombs, Sunggaminasa, Indonesia, 839
Tombs, Tatta, Pakistan, 801-802, 803
Tombs, Tongatapu Island, Tonga, 830
Tombs, Xian, China, 870, 871
Tombs, Zhengzhou, China, 903, 904
Tombs of the Hami Kings, Hami, China, 324
Tomotamagaki Minami Gomon, Ise, Japan, 374
Tondaimandalam, India, 552
Tondiarpet, India, 548
Tong-Bu Railway, 216
Tong Hake rebellion, 793
Tonga, 264, 265, 266, 674, 723, 725, **827-831**
Tongan Pro-Democracy Movement, 831
Tongariro, North Island, New Zealand, 832-834
Tongariro (legendary male mountain), 832
Tongariro National Park, New Zealand, 832, 833-834
Tongatapu, Tonga, 827, 828, 829, 830
Tongbao Mining Company, 216
Tonghak (religious movement), 196-197
Tonghak Struggle (1894), 487
Tongsong (king of Paekche), 484
Tongyuanwang Temple, Nine-day Mountain, China, 704
Tonie Sap, Angor, Cambodia, 31
Tonkin. *See* Hanoi, Vietnam
Tonquin. *See* Hanoi, Vietnam
Tontouta, New Caledonia, 647
Tonuia (legendary), 818
Tonwar. *See* Tomara Dynasty
Topside, Corregidor Island, Philippines, 204
Torii (gate) at Miyajima, Japan, 587, 590
Torii (gate) at Nikkō, Japan, 636
Torkham, Afghanistan, 473
Toromāṇa (Hūna king), 312
Torres, Bernard de, 379
Torres, Cosme de, 340
Torres Strait, 208
Tortoise Hill (Gui Shan), Hanyang, China, 868
Tosa, Japan, 520
Tosala. *See* Sisupalgarh, India
Toshali. *See* Bhubaneswar, Orissa, India
Tōshō Dai-Gongen. *See* Tokugawa Ieyasu
Tōshō-ji Temple, Kamakura, Japan, 429
Tōshōdai-ji Temple, Nara, Japan, 622, 623-624, 887
Tōshōgu (shrines to Tokugawa Ieyasu), Japan, 345
Tōshōgū (mausoleum and shrine), Nikkō, Japan, 632, 634-635, 636-638
Toungoo, Myanmar, 656, 881, 882
Toungoo Dynasty, 61, 62, 656
Tower of Allata. *See* Kirti Stambh, Chittaurgarh, India
Tower of Buddha's Bowl, Peshāwar, Pakistan, 671
Tower of Fame, Chittaurgarh, India, 191, 193, 194
Tower of Silence, Bombay, India, 142-143
Tower of Victory, Māndu, India, 562-563
Tower of Victory, Chittaurgarh, India, 191, 192, 193, 194
Towers of Light, Takayama, Japan, 797
Town Hall, Ballarat, Australia, 76
Town Walls, Nanjing, China, 618-619
Townson, John, 641
Toyotomi family, 338, 341, 349, 431, 513, 519, 520, 650, 651, 652
Toyotomi Hideyoshi (Japanese warrior and statesman), 10, 338, 341, 349, 431, 513, 519, 520, 590, 594, 612, 634, 636, 637, 650, 795, 823
Toyotomi Yodo, 650
Toyouke Daijingū. *See* Gekū, Ise, Japan
Toyouke-hime no Ōmikami (goddess), 374, 376
Trafalgar Square, London, England, 550
Traikūṭakas (people), 626
Trailok (king of Ayutthaya), 54-55, 56, 57, 59
Traitor's Island, Tonga, 827, 828
Tran Bien, Vietnam, 354
Tran Dynasty, 329
Trans-Caspian Railway, 718, 722
Transoxiana, Uzbekistan, 163, 165, 166, 280, 281, 282, 333, 336, 720
Trappist order, 320
Travancore, kingdom of, 550, 710, 712, 713
Travancore State Congress (India), 713
Treasure Hill, Miyajima, Japan, 589
Treaty House, Waitangi, New Zealand, 859, 860, 861, 862
Treaty of Aix-la-Chapelle, 548
Treaty of Allahābād, 171
Treaty of Amritsar, 29
Treaty of Bassein, 142
Treaty of Breda Charles II, 90
Treaty of Bungaya, 841, 842
Treaty of Friendship, 830
Treaty of Gandamak, 476
Treaty of Giyanti, 890
Treaty of Kanagawa, 318, 614
Treaty of Mannas, 712
Treaty of Nanjing, 359, 705, 735, 813
Treaty of Paris (1763), 785
Treaty of Paris (1898), 204
Treaty of Raisen, 119
Treaty of Saigon, 354
Treaty of Seringapatam, 94
Treaty of Shanyuan, 295
Treaty of Shimonoseki, 793
Treaty of Tianjin, 542, 813-814
Treaty of Tokehega, 726
Treaty of Waitangi (1840), 832, 833, 859-860, 861
Treaty of Waitangi Act (1975), 860, 861
Treaty of Westphalia, 568
Treaty of Yandabo, 310, 880
Treaty of Zaragoza, 179, 180, 900
Tree of Enlightenment. *See* Bo-tree
Trengganu, Malaysia, 665
Tri Quang (monk), 365
Tribhuvan (Shāh king), 467
Tribhuvanesvara Temple, Bhubaneswar, India, 123
Trikuta hill, 388
Trimurtī (mythic giant), 253
Trimurtī sculpture, Elephanta Island, India, 254
Trincomalee, Sri Lanka, 200, 201, 202, 273, 446
Trinh Dynasty, 329-330, 353-354, 362, 364
Trinidad, 267
Triplicane, India, 550
Tripolia Prole (gate), Bīkaner, India, 132
Tripura, India, 310
Triraśmi Hills, 625
Trisong Detsen (ruler of Tibet), 526, 527
Tristu Dynasty, 505
Tritsun (wife of Songtsen Gampo), 526
Trivandrum, India, 712, 713
Trivenī Ghāt, Somnāth, India, 762, 765
Trollope, Anthony, 236
Truman, Harry, 615
Trunajaya (contender for Mataram throne in Central Java), 841, 890
Trung Dao Bridge, Hue, Vietnam, 364
Tsangpo River. *See* Brahmaputra River
Tsaukuta. *See* Kandahār, Kandahār, Afghanistan
Tschoumou-Lancma. *See* Mount Everest
Tsong-khapa (Tibetan scholar), 527-528, 750
Tsont-i-kul canal, Srīnagar, India, 767
Tsuchi no Miya (shrine), Ise, Japan, 374
Tsugaru Dynasty, 345
Tsugaru Plain, Japan, 345
Tsugaru Strait, 320
Tsunekazu, Nishioka, 624
Tsuruga-jō, Aizu-Wakamatsu, Japan, 10, 11, 12-13
Tsurugaoka, Kamakura, Japan, 426
Tsushima Strait, 320
Tsutsuga (mythical creature), 637
Tu Dam Pagoda, Hue, Vietnam, 362
Tua Pek Kong (temple), Kuching, Malaysia, 499-500
Tua Sai Yeah, 668
Tuamotu Islands, 828
Tubuaï Islands, 673
Tuckett, Frederick, 234
Tuen Mun. *See* Castle Peak, Hong Kong
Tuen Mun River, 358
Tughar Khān, 478
Tughluq Dynasty, 218, 220, 561, 764
Tughluq Shah, 610
Tughluqābād. *See* Delhi, Delhi, India
Tui Haatakalaua (Tongan administrative leaders), 827, 828
Tui Kanokupolu Dynasty, 827, 829
Tui Nayau (chief of Lakemba), 266
Tui Tokelau (god), 818, 820
Tui-tee-lagi (god), 723
Tui Tonga Dynasty, 827, 829
Tuiatui (eleventh Tui Tonga), 827-828
Tukuaho (Tongan ruler), 829
Tulagi Island, 299, 300
Tulay, Jolo, Philippines, 404
Tulsīdās (Hindu poet), 849, 850
Tuluva Dynasty, 856
Tuluy (Mongol ruler), 414
Tumu, China, 296
Tun Giao, Vietnam, 232

Tuna (Samoan rebel), 723
Tungabhadra River, 855, 858
Tungans (people), 166, 458
Tuoba Wei (Chinese regime), 212
Tupa (chieftain of Cebu), 180
Tupia, 154
Tupou I. *See* George Tupou I (king of Tonga)
Tupoumoheofo (wife of Tui Tonga Paulaho), 829
Tupua Pulepule (joint ruler of Samoa), 725
Tupua Tamasese Lealofi III (king of Samoa), 726
Turfan, China, 321, 323, 458
Turkey 125, 163, 167, 218, 225, 626, 718, 721, 871. *See also* Ottoman Empire; Seljuk Turks
Turkish Gate (Rumi Darwaza), Lucknow, India, 534
Turkish Sultana's House (Rumi Sultana), Fatehpur Sīkri, India, 263
Turkistan, 71, 165, 166, 282, 323, 476
Turkistan, Chinese. *See* Xinjiang Uighur Autonomous Region
Turkmenistan, 336
Turks, 22, 163, 218, 259, 263, 280, 281, 282, 321, 323, 333, 396, 414, 439, 452, 456, 474, 579, 679, 720, 721-722
Turnbull (British landholder in Tokelau), 821
Turtle Island. *See* Vatoa Island, Fiji
Turton, Robert, 641-642
Tuscan Valley, Brunei Darussalam, 161
Tuticorin, India, 503
Tutong, Brunei Darussalam, 161
Tutuila Island, American Samoa, 723, 724, 725, 726
Tuvalu, 266, 818, 821
Tuwharetoa (Maori tribe), 832
Twain, Mark, 236
Twilight Gate. *See* Yomeimon Gate, Nikkō, Japan
Twin Stone Pagodas, Quanzhou, China, 706
Two Kings Gate, Nikkō, Japan, 636
Two Pagoda Temple, Suzhou, China, 778
Tyangboche Monastery, Nepal, 603

Uburkhangai, Mongolia, 451-455
Udai Singh I (Hatyara; rāna of Chittaurgarh), 193
Udai Singh II (rāna of Chittaurgarh), 193, 194
Udaipur, India, 3, 191, 194, 400, 600
Udayadityavarman I (Khmer king of Cambodia), 32
Udayadityavarman II (Khmer king of Cambodia), 32-33
Udayana (king of Vatsa), 836
Udon Thani, Thailand, 82-86
Ueda Munetsutsu (tea-master), 349
Ueno district, Tōkyō, Japan, 824
Uesugi family, 430
Uesugi Kagekatsu (regent of Japan), 10
Uesugi Noritada, 430
Uighuristan, 241, 321, 323, 324
Uija (king of Paekche), 486
Uijong (king of Koryŏ), 487
Uji-Yamada. *See* Ise, Mie, Japan
Ujina Island, Japan, 349
Ujjain, Madhya Pradesh, India, 314, 386, 561, 628, **835-838**
Ujung Pandang, South Sulawesi, Indonesia, 839-842
Ukkalapa (king of Dagon), 879
Ukraine, 451
Ulithi Islands, 379
Ullathorne, William, 642, 865
Ulūgh Beg (viceroy), 335, 720, 721
Ulūgh Beg Observatory, Samarkand, Uzbekistan, 721
Uluru. *See* Ayers Rock, Northern Territory, Australia
Uluru National Park, Northern Territory, Australia, 44
Umaid Bhawan Palace, Jodhpur, India, 400
Umananda Temple, Peacock Island, India, 310
'Umar I (Umar ibn al-Khaṭṭāb; second caliph), 579
Umayyad Dynasty, 579, 720
Umbrella Palaces (Chattar Manzil), Lucknow, India, 534
Umeda, Ōsaka, Japan, 650, 652
Umra Singh. *See* Amar Singh
Unar (Sammā king), 802
Unashiri (Chagatai ruler of Hami), 322
Unebiyama. *See* Mount Unebi
UNESCO. *See* United Nations Educational, Scientific, and Cultural Organization
Unfinished Temple, Mount Ābu, India, 600, 601
Ungata (mythic Kunia leader), 44
Ungjin. *See* Kongju, South Ch'ungch'ŏng, South Korea
Unified Silla, kingdom of, 195
Union Buildings, Pretoria, South Africa, 223
Union Carbide industrial accident, Bhopāl, India, 117, 120
Union Group. *See* Tokelau, Territory of New Zealand
United Church of Christ, 347
United East India Company. *See* Dutch East India Company
United Nations, 34, 197, 242, 244, 361, 418, 442, 647, 738, 846, 882
United Nations Educational, Scientific, and Cultural Organization (UNESCO), 34, 467, 509, 514, 555, 771, 775, 809, 858
United States Exploring Expedition, 820
United States of America, 40, 107, 144, 154, 160, 173, 177, 189, 197, 204, 206-207, 233, 244, 266, 289, 298, 300, 318, 319, 320, 331-332, 339, 351, 353, 355-356, 361, 364, 365, 372, 379-382, 404-406, 430, 450, 520, 521, 533, 558, 567, 568-569, 570, 580, 588, 606, 614-615, 643, 647, 723, 725, 726, 735, 736, 738, 742, 749, 781, 785, 788, 794, 816, 819-820, 821, 825, 830-831, 832, 833, 842, 846, 854, 877, 880, 900
University, Bangalore, India, 95
University, Dunedin, New Zealand, 236, 237, 238
University, Kurukshetra, India, 508
University, Multān, Pakistan, 610
University, Mysore, India, 95
University, Taxila, Pakistan, 805
University, Thanjāvūr, India, 812
University, Yangon, Myanmar, 558, 880
University College of the Northwest Territory, Australia, 211
University of Agricultural Sciences, Bangalaore, India, 95
University of Bombay, India, 144
University of Calcutta, India, 174, 175, 227, 659
University of Hirosaki, Japan, 347, 348
University of Hiroshima, Japan, 351
University of Hong Kong, 360
University of Kābul, Afghanistan, 418
University of Kashmir, Srīnagar, India, 767
University of Madras, India, 438
University of Peshāwar, Pakistan, 671
University of Punjab, Pakistan, 525
University of Rabindra Bharati, Calcutta, India, 175
University of Sind, Hyderābād, Pakistan, 373
University of Sydney, Australia, 783
University of Wuhan, China, 868
University of Yokohama, Japan, 427, 428
Unkham (king of Laos), 532
Unsoeld, Willi, 606
Uparkot, Junāgadh, India, 408, 410, 412
Uparkot Fort, Junāgadh, India, 412
Upolu Island, Western Samoa, 723, 724, 725, 726
Upper Kaikori District, New Zealand, 235
Upper Myanmar. *See* Myanmar
Upper Temple, Datong, China, 214
Urabon. *See* Bon Festivals
Uraga, Japan, 614
Urakami Catholic Church, Nagasaki, Japan, 612
Urakami district, Nagasaki, Japan, 614, 615
Urakami River, 612
Urayūr, India, 811
Urbiztondo (Spanish governor in Philippines), 404
Urdaneta, Andrés (Augustinian friar), 180
Urumqi, China, 323
Uruvelā, India, 138
Ushā (legendary warrior), 479
Usmān, Nizām Mīr, 369-370
'Uthmān ibn 'Affān (Muslim caliph), 579
Uttar Pradesh, India, 1-5, 47-51, 228, 260-263, 267, 534-537, 572-577, 847-850
Utzon, Joern, 784
Uvéa Island, 723, 820, 828
Uzbekistan, 163-167, 718-722
Uzbeks (people), 73, 165, 336, 440, 441, 721-722

Vaikuntha Perumal Temple, Kānchipuram, India, 437
Vairocana (Buddha of the Universe), 515, 588-589
Vaishnava Temple, Konārak, India, 478
Vaishnavism, 121, 123, 124, 134, 716, 762, 765
Vajrāsana (Buddha's seat), Bodh Gayā, India, 138
Vajrāsana Mulagandhakuti Vihāra Temple, Bodh Gayā, India, 140
Vajrayāna (sect), 256, 257
Vākāṭaka Dynasty, 14, 18, 468, 626
Vākpati (Chandela ruler of Khajurāho), 468
Valabhī, India, 410
Vale of the Wolves, Colombo, Sri Lanka, 201
Vāli (legendary monkey chief), 855
Valignano, Alessandro, 544
Valin (legendary), 695
Vallée des Colons, Nouméa, New Caledonia, 647
Vāmana Temple, Khajurāho, India, 470
Vamanasthali, India, 410
Vámbéry, Arminius, 166
Van Diemen Gulf, 208
Van Diemen's Land. *See* Tasmania, Australia
Van Eck (Dutch general in Kandy), 446
Vang Sang, Laos, 851
Vans Agnew, Alexander, 610
Vanua Levu Island, Fiji, 264, 265, 266
Vanuatu, 264, 266, 298, 299, 820, 827, **843-846**
Varadarājaperumal Temple, Kānchipuram, India, 437
Varāha (temple), Khajurāho, India, 469, 470
Varaha Maṇḍapa (cave temple), Mahābalipuram, India, 554
Varanā River, 847
Vārānaseya Sanskrit Vishvavidyālaya, Vārānasī, India, 850
Vārānasī, Uttar Pradesh, India, 47, 121, 138, 168, 169, 386, 579, 764, **847-850**
Vardhamāna. *See* Mahāvīra
Vardhamāna temple, Kānchipuram, India, 437
Vardhana Dynasty, 468
Varendra Research Society, 659
Varghese, T.W., 713
Vasabha (king of Sri Lanka), 38
Vasavadatta (princess of Ujain), 836
Vasco da Gama. *See* Gama, Vasco da
Vasishtha (Hindu sage), 600
Vason, George, 829
Vastupala (Indian temple builder), 412, 601
Vasubandhu (Buddhist teacher), 50
Vāsudeva (Kushān ruler), 800
Vāsudeva Krishna (god), 572, 574, 697
Vat Chan, Vientiane, Laos, 853
Vat Mai Temple, Luang Prabang, Laos, 532
Vat Ong Teu, Vientiane, Laos, 853
Vat Phra Kaeo, Vientiane, Laos, 852, 853
Vat Simeuang, Vientiane, Laos, 853
Vat Sisaket, Vientiane, Laos, 852, 854
Vat Visun (temple), Luang Prabang, Laos, 532

Vat Xieng Thong (temple), Luang Prabang, Laos, 531, 532
Vatadages, Anuradhapura, Sri Lanka, 37
Vatadages, Polonnaruwa, Sri Lanka, 687
Vatagohali. *See* Goalbhita, Bangladesh
Vātāpi, India, 435
Vatoa Island, Fiji, 265, 266
Vatsa, kingdom of, 468, 836
Vauxhall Gardens, Dunedin, New Zealand, 236
Vavau Islands, Tonga, 827, 828, 829
Vāyudeva (king of Ayodhyā), 49
Vaz, Julius, 124
Vedha Shala (observatory), Ujjain, India, 838
Vedic Hinduism, 186, 254
Vegavathi River, 435
Velasco, Don Luis de, 180
Venāḍ Empire, 710
Venesvara Temple, Somnāth, India, 765
Venice, Italy, 327, 452, 776
Venkaji (ruler of Bangalore), 92
Venkatappa Art Gallery, Bangalore, India, 95
Verata, Viti Levu, 264
Vereenigde Oost-Indische Compagnie. *See* Dutch East India Company
Verge, J., 861
Verlaten Island, Indonesia, 493, 495
Vermilion Seal Ship Trade, 613
Verraders Eylandt. *See* Niuatobutabu, Tonga
Versailles Palace, France, 223
Versailles Peace Conference, 132, 197
Vestey's (British company), 209
Vibhishana (ruler of Lanka), 716
Viceroy's House. *See* Rashtrapati Bhavan, Delhi, India
Victoria (queen of Great Britain), 78, 144, 174, 176, 274, 497, 578, 677, 784
Victoria, Australia, 75-78
Victoria, New Zealand, 859, 859-862
Victoria and Albert Museum, London, England, 14
Victoria Gardens, Bombay, India, 253
Victoria Harbor, Hong Kong, 361
Victoria Memorial, Calcutta, India, 175
Victoria Memorial Hall, Singapore, 760
Victoria Museum, Karāchi, Pakistan, 448
Victoria River, 208
Victoria Terminus, Bombay, India, 144
Victoria Wharf, Dunedin, New Zealand, 237
Victorian Royal Palace, Nukualofa, Tongatapu Island, Tonga, 830
Victory Gate, Amber, India, 24
Victory Gate, Golconda, India, 290
Victory Gate, Jodhpur, India, 399
Vidhana Soudha, Bangalore, India, 95
Vidiśā, India, 727, 729, 730
Vidiye Bandara (Sri Lankan regent), 199
Vidyādhara (Chandela ruler of India), 468
Vidyāraṇya (Saṅgama guru), 855
Vieng Chan. *See* Vientiane, Vientiane, Laos
Vieng Xai, Laos, 533
Vientiane, Vientiane, Laos, 97, 99, 530, 531, 532, 533, **851-854**
Viet (people), 329
Viet Bac, Vietnam, 233
Viet Cong, 355-356, 365
Viet Minh, 230-233, 331, 355, 356, 365
Viet Nam Doc Lap Dong Minh. *See* Viet Minh
Vietnam, 31, 33, 34, 82, 158, 210, 230-233, 302, 329-332, 353-357, 362-365, 531, 533, 542, 557, 775, 853, 854
Vietnam War, 233, 331-332, 353, 356, 364, 533, 570, 853-854
Vigne, Godfrey Thomas, 282
Vigraharāja IV (Chauhān rāja of Ajmer), 20
Vijaya (founder of Great Dynasty of Sri Lanka), 35
Vijayabāhu (king of Kotte), 199, 272, 443, 685
Vijayabāhu IV (king of Sri Lanka), 687
Vijayālaya (Cōḷa king of India), 809, 811
Vijayamitra (king of Ayodhyā), 49
Vijayanagar, kingdom of, 92, 95, 284, 290, 366, 435, 437, 502, 711, 812
Vijayanagara, Karnātaka, India, 547, **855-858**
Vijayapura. *See* Bijāpur, Karnātaka, India
Vijayaśakti (Chandela ruler of Khajurāho), 468
Vijitapura fortress, Anuradhapura, Sri Lanka, 38
Vikramābāhu (Kaliṅgan prince), 443, 686
Vikramaditya I (Cāḷukya king of India), 140, 436
Vikramāditya (ruler of Chittaurgarh), 193
Vikramāditya (legendary Indian king), 837
Vikramāditya (Hindu king of Multān), 608
Vila, Vanuatu, 843
Vilela, Gaspar, 340
Village of the Kok. *See* Bangkok, Thailand
Vimala Shāh Temple, Mount Ābu, India, 600, 601
Vimaladharma (king of Kandy), 443, 445
Vinda (king of Avanti), 836
Vindhya Mountains, 561, 835
Virakurcha (Pallava king of Kānchipuram), 435
Viravikrama (king of Kandy), 443
Virgil (poet), 582
Virgin of Del Pilar Fort, Zamboanga, Philippines, 898, 900
Virimda. *See* Vidyādhara
Virūpāksha Temple, Vijayanagara, India, 856, 857
Viśākhadeva (king of Ayodhyā), 49
Visala-Deva (Chauhān rāja of Ajmer), 20
Visayan Islands, Philippines, 177, 180, 403, 405, 900
Vishnu (god), 33, 47, 50, 123, 134, 135, 140, 141, 172, 193, 218, 254, 258, 259, 276, 308, 312, 435, 437, 466, 468, 478, 479, 502, 552, 555, 574, 576, 600, 601, 628, 660, 692, 694, 695, 697, 762, 775, 805, 849, 856
Vishnu Temple, Prambanan, Indonesia, 695, 696
Vishnumati River, 464, 465
Vishnupad Temple, Gayā, India, 276, 277-278
Vishnupur. *See* Bishnupur, West Bengal, India
Vishveshvara (temple), Vārānasī, India, 850
Visulrat (king of Laos), 532
Viśvanātha (temple), Khajurāho, India, 468, 469, 470
Viśvantara (previous incarnation of Buddha), 731
Viśvantara Jātaka (legendary prince), 18
Visvesvaraya Industrial and Technologial Museum, Bangalore, India, 95
Viti Levu Island, Fiji, 264, 265, 266, 267
Viṭṭhala Temple, Vijayanagara, India, 855, 856
Viwa Island, Fiji, 266
Vladivostok, Russia, 748
Vo Nguyen Giap, 231, 232, 233
V.O.C. *See* Dutch East India Company
Vogel, Julius, 236
Volcano Islands, Japan, 379-382
Volgograd, Russia, 300
Von Däniken, Erich, 251
Vriji Temple. *See* Kumbha Shyam Temple, Chittaurgarh, India
Vrṣṇī (people), 572
Vuyst, Petrus, 274

Wager, L.R., 606
Waghorā River, 14
Wainwright, Jonathan, 206, 207
Waitangi, North Island, New Zealand, 859-862
Waitangi National Reserve, New Zealand, 859, 861-862
Waitangi National Trust Board, New Zealand, 860, 861, 862
Waitangi River, 859
Wajid Alī Shāh (Indian nabob), 534, 535
Wajo, kingdom of, 841
Wakamatsu, Aizu-Wakamatsu, Japan, 10
Wakamatsu, Fukushima, Japan, 10
Wakamiya, Kamakura, Japan, 426
Wakamiya-oji, Kamakura, Japan, 426
Wakari, New Zealand, 237
Wake Island, 206
Wakefield, Edward Gibbon, 234
Wako (mythic woman), 431
Walajah Mosque, Triplicane, India, 550
Waldron, Arthur, 294, 295, 296
Walīd I (Islamic caliph), 801
Wallace, Alfred Russel, 629
Wallis, Samuel, 785
Wallis Island. *See* Uvéa Island
Wang Chong (Chinese philosopher), 539
Wang Hang (Chinese poet), 886
Wang Hongwen (Gang of Four member), 738
Wang Jingwei (Chinese opposition leader), 216, 868
Wang Kōn (Korean ruler), 195, 513
Wang Mang (Chinese usurper), 538
Wang San (Chinese renegade), 215
Wang Ta Yuan (Chinese traveler), 758
Wang Xianchen (Chinese imperial censor), 779
Wang Xizhe (calligrapher), 616
Wang Xuan Zhe (Chinese traveler), 465
Wang Yuanlu (discoverer of Mogao manuscripts), 244, 246
Wang Zhi (Chinese pirate), 340
Wangto Dong (Cave of 10,000 Buddhas), Yanan, China, 878
Wanli (Ming emperor of China), 107, 296
Wansan, Korea. *See* Ch'ŏngju, North Ch'ungch'ŏng, South Korea
Wansan Park, Chŏnju, South Korea, 195
War Cemetery, Htaukkyan, Myanmar, 63
War memorial, Corregidor Island, Philippines, 204, 207
War memorial, Delhi, India, 222-223
War memorial, Lucknow, India, 536
War memorial, Vientiane, Laos, 854
War of Succession (India; 1657), 22
War of the Austrian Succession, 548, 679
War of the Relics, 731
Warangal, India, 290
Warburton, Sir Robert, 476
Ward, Michael, 606
Warner, Langdon, 244
Warren, James, 760
Warring States Period (China; 403-221 B.C.), 109, 212, 293, 294, 538, 616, 739, 744
Warring States Period (Japan; 1467-1573 A.D.), 650
Warrior Museum, Aizu-Wakamatsu, Japan, 12
Wāśistha Dynasty, 122
Wat Aranyik, Sukhothai, Thailand, 772
Wat Arun, Bangkok, Thailand, 98
Wat Chayamangkalaram Thai Temple, Lorong Burmah, Penang, 668
Wat Chiang Man (temple), Chiang Mai, Thailand, 182
Wat Maha That, Ayutthaya, Thailand, 59
Wat Mahathat (Monastery of the Great Relics), Sukhothai, Thailand, 774, 775
Wat Phra Kaew, Bangkok, Thailand, 97
Wat Phra Phai Luang Monastery, Sukhothai, Thailand, 771, 775
Wat Phra Ram, Ayutthaya, Thailand, 59
Wat Phra Si Sanphet, Ayutthaya, Thailand, 58-59
Wat Phra Sing (temple), Chiang Mai, Thailand, 185
Wat Phra That (temple), Chiang Mai, Thailand, 184, 185
Wat Po (Temple of the Reclining Buddha), Bangkok, Thailand, 98
Wat Ratburana, Ayutthaya, Thailand, 59
Wat Saphan Hin (Stone Bridge Monastery), Sukhothai, Thailand, 773
Wat Suan Dork (temple), Chiang Mai, Thailand, 182

Wat Suthat, Bangkok, Thailand, 775
Wat Thammik Rat, Ayutthaya, Thailand, 59
Wat Yai Chai Mongkon, Ayutthaya, Thailand, 59
Waterfall of White Threads, Fujinomiya, Japan, 269
Watson, Charles, 682
Watson's Hotel, Bombay, India, 144
Waugh, Andrew, 604
Wavell, Archibald (first earl), 175
Way of Basic Unity Society (China), 817
Wazīr Khān Mosque, Lahore, Pakistan, 524, 525
Wazīr Moḥammad Khān (ruler of Bhopāl), 119
Wazirābād. *See* Balkh, Balkh, Afghanistan
Waziristan, Afghanistan, 279
Weather Palace, Junāgarh Fort, Bīkaner, India, 132
Weber, Theodor, 725
Wei, China, 293, 294, 321, 420, 484, 744
Wei Dynasty, 212, 214, 244, 539, 893
Wei Hui Wang (Prince Hui of the State of Wei), 420
Wei River, 296, 870, 904
Wei Valley, 216
Wei Yuan (scholar), 735
Weiner, Sheila L., 15
Wellesley, Arthur (Lord Wellesley), 369
Wellesley Province. *See* Province Wellesley, Malaysia
Wellington, New Zealand, 234
Weltevreden, Indonesia, 395, 397
Wen (Zhou emperor of China), 420
Wen Cheng (Tang princess of China and wife of Songtsen Gampo), 526
Wen Cheng Di (Toba emperor of China), 893
Wen De (Tang empress of China), 872
Wen Di (Sui emperor of China), 739, 871, 872
Wen Miao Temple, Quanzhou, China, 706
Wen Zhengming (Chinese painter-calligrapher), 776, 778
Wencheng Di (Northern Wei ruler of China), 213
Wenfeng Ta Pagoda, Yangzhou, China, 887
Weng Wanda (Ming supreme commander), 215, 296
Wenling. *See* Quanzhou, Fujian, China
Wenquan (Hot Spring) Temple, Shanhaiguan, China, 742
Wentworth, D'Arcy, 641
Wentworth, William, 783
Wesleyan Missionary Society (Australia), 830
Wesleyans. *See* Methodism
West, John, 641
West Bengal, India, 134-137, 172-176, 679-683
West Borneo, 629
West Brunei. *See* Brunei Darussalam
West Chapel. *See* Potala Palace, Lhasa, Tibet, China
West Garden Temple, Suzhou, China, 778
West India Company, 724
West Indies, 503
West Java, Indonesia, 101-104, 396
West Kalimantan. *See* Borneo
West Lake, Hangzhou, China, 325, 327, 328, 349
West Pagoda, Guangzhou, China, 306
West Pakistan. *See* Pakistan
West Rongbuk Glacier, 605, 606
West Town, Guangzhou, China, 306
Westerling, Raymond, 842
Western Baray reservoir, Angkor, Cambodia, 32-33
Western Court, Delhi, India, 223
Western Cwm, Himalaya Mountains, 605, 606
Western Ghāts (mountains), 143, 284, 625
Western Han Dynasty, 456, 538, 871
Western Isles. *See* Philippines
Western Jin Dynasty, 539, 540, 616, 744
Western Kshatrapa Dynasty, 837
Western Liao. *See* Karakitai Dynasty
Western Ocean, 705
Western Samoa. *See* Samoa, Western Samoa and American Samoa
Western Wei Dynasty, 244, 294, 540
Western Zhou Dynasty, 40, 538, 870, 904
Westmacott (archaeologist in Paharpur), 657
Westwood, William, 642
Whampoa, China, 306, 360
Whare-runanga, Waitangi, New Zealand, 861, 862
Wheeler, Mortimer, 595, 599
Wheeler, Oliver, 604, 605
Whippy, David, 266
Whirling Dervishes, 165
White, Theodore, 877
White Banner Shrine, Kamakura, Japan, 428
White Flag Society (Malaysia), 668
White Horse Monastery, Luoyang, China, 539-540, 541
White Huns (people), 333, 414, 456, 608, 669, 720, 800
White Lotus Temple. *See* Kaiyuan Temple, Quanzhou, China
White Mountaineers. *See* Ak-taghliq (sect)
White Palace. *See* Potala Palace, Lhasa, Tibet, China
White Tiger Brigade, Aizu-Wakamatsu, Japan, 12, 13
White Town, Madras, India, 547
Wickham, J.C., 208
Wihan Phra Mongkon Bopit, Ayutthaya, Thailand, 59
Wilberforce, Australia, 863
Wiley, Richard, 486
Wilkes, Charles, 725, 820
William III (king of Great Britain), 172
William of Paris, 452
Williams, John (British missionary), 725, 844
Williams, John B. (American commercial agent in Fiji), 266
Williams, John Chauner (American consul in Samoa), 725
Williamson, Robert, 690
Williamstown, Australia, 642
Willson, Robert, 642
Wilson, Woodrow, 487
Wimala (Mon noble), 60
Wind Palace. *See* Hawa Mahal, Fatehpur Sīkri, India
Windsor, New South Wales, Australia, 863-865
Windsor Castle, England, 95
Windsor Court House, Windsor, Australia, 865
Windt, Margaret de. *See* Brooke, Margaret
Windward Islands, 785
Withington, Nicholas, 8
Wokou (Japanese pirates), 705
Wollaston, A.F.R., 604, 605
Wolvendhal, Colombo, Sri Lanka, 201
Wolvendhal Hill, Colombo, Sri Lanka, 201
Woman Killing Herself after Her Husband's Death Temple. *See* Lienü Temple, Shanhaiguan, China
Women's Christian Temperance Union, 236
Women's Mau (Samoa), 726
Wonju, South Korea, 512
Wood, Frances, 242
World Heritage sites (UNESCO), 555, 809, 858
World War I, 9, 99, 109, 132, 156, 197, 223, 267, 386, 418, 604, 646
World War II, 13, 63, 70, 100, 116, 132, 150, 161, 189, 195, 196, 197, 203, 204, 206-207, 208, 209-210, 230, 237, 267, 298-301, 324, 331, 351, 354-355, 360-361, 365, 379-382, 418, 430, 434, 497, 499, 521, 545, 556, 558, 566, 567, 569, 592, 612, 614-615, 620, 624, 644, 647, 652, 667, 788, 792, 793, 794, 825, 830, 842, 846, 853, 861, 879, 880-882, 892
Wright, Frank Lloyd, 520
Writers Building, Calcutta, India, 172, 173, 174
Wu (Tang/Zhou empress of China), 541, 872, 884
Wu (Toba emperor of China), 893
Wu (Zhou emperor of China), 707
Wu Di (Han emperor of China), 239, 302, 871
Wu Di (Liang emperor), 616, 618
Wu Dynasties, 302, 616, 866, 868
Wu Peifu (Chinese warlord), 742, 904
Wu Sangui (Ming general), 742
Wu Ze Tian. *See* Wu (Tang/Zhou empress of China)
Wuchang, Hubei, China, 866-869
Wufenglou. *See* Wumen, Forbidden City, Beijing, China
Wuhan, China, 736, 866, 868
Wuhan Bridge, 868
Wuling (Zhao king of China), 212, 293, 294
Wumen, Forbidden City, Beijing, China, 106, 107
Wurong Zhou. *See* Quanzhou, Fujian, China
Wuting Qiao (bridge), Yangzhou, China, 886
Wuysthoff, Gerritt van, 852
Wuzhou River, 213
Wyn Harris, P., 606

Xai Fong, Laos, 851
Xanadu, 534
Xavier, Francis (saint), 288, 340, 344, 542, 544, 612, 824
Xetthathirat (king of Laos), 532, 851, 852
Xi Hu. *See* West Lake, Hangzhou, China
Xi Xia (people), 241, 244, 246, 325
Xiamafang, Nanjing, China, 619
Xiamen, China, 705, 735, 791, 813
Xian, Shaanxi, China, 109, 163, 216, 239, 461, 511, 515, 527, 538, 539, 540, 541, 621, 816, **870-873,** 874, 875, 904
Xian Di (Han emperor of China), 539
Xian Incident, 875
Xian Yang, China, 870
Xianbei (nomads), 212, 213, 214
Xianfeng (Qing emperor of China), 814
Xiang, China, 302
Xiang Fei (concubine of Qing emperor Qianlong), 458
Xiangping. *See* Liaoyang, China
Xianhe Mosque, Yangzhou, China, 887
Xianyang, China, 109
Xiao, Prince. *See* Liang Xiao Wang
Xiao Jing, 618
Xiao Jinshan, Yangzhou, China, 886
Xiao Ling (the Filial Tomb), Nanjing, China, 619-620
Xiao Xian, 741
Xiao Yan Ta, Xian, China, 872, 873
Xiao Zong (Song emperor of China), 325
Xiaopangu Garden, Yangzhou, China, 886
Xiaowen Di (Northern Wei emperor of China), 214, 539
Xie Ao (Chinese city official), 887
Xie Lingyun (poet), 616
Xieng Dong Xieng Thong. *See* Luang Prabang, Luang Prabang, Laos
Xieng Khuang, Laos, 531
Xiguanmen wall, Great Wall, China, 296
Xihao. *See* Luoyang, Henan, China
Xijing, China, 214
Xingxingxia, China, 324
Xinjiang Uighur Autonomous Region, China, 321-324, 456-459
Xinle (people), 744
Xiongnu (people), 212, 239, 293, 294, 321, 456
Xiyuan Garden, Yangzhou, China, 886
Xiyuan Si (West Garden Temple), Suzhou, China, 778
Xizang Autonomous Region, China, 526-529, 750-753
Xolo. *See* Jolo, Sulu, Philippines
Xu Da (Ming general), 214, 620, 739
Xuan Zang (Buddhist monk-pilgrim), 49, 73, 80, 81, 140, 186, 276, 279, 308, 321, 414, 435, 436, 456, 507, 522, 554, 576, 608, 657, 669, 720, 800, 805, 806, 837, 848, 872
Xuande (Ming emperor of China), 296
Xuanfu, China, 214, 215, 216, 296
Xuantu, China, 744
Xuantucheng, China, 744
Xuanwu Lake, 618

Xuanzong (Tang emperor of China), 541, 872

Yabase, Japan, 338
Yacuna Islet, Fiji, 264
Yādava Dynasty, 125, 142, 284, 572, 762
Yadus (people), 572
Yagasa Levu, Fiji, 265
Yahoué, New Caledonia, 646
Yahya Khan, Agha Muhammad, 228
Yai Chai Mongkon Temple, Ayutthaya, Thailand, 59
Yajñaśri Śātakarṇi (Sātavāhanna king of India), 626
Yaksha Malla (king of Nepal), 466
Yakub Bek (Kashgar rebel), 323, 458
Yakushi (Buddha of Healing), 429, 635, 636, 795, 808
Yakushidō, Nikkō, Japan, 636
Yale, David, 548
Yale, Elihu, 548
Yale University, New Haven, Connecticut, United States of America, 548
Yalta, Ukraine, 749
Yalu River, 509, 741, 742
Yama (god), 133, 276, 278
Yamanashi, Japan, 271, 429
Yamashina, Japan, 650
Yamato. *See* Nara, Japan
Yamato Dynasty, 377, 592
Yamato-Hime-Mikoto. *See* Himiko
Yamato History Hall, Kashihara, Japan, 462
Yamato Rekishikan, Kashihara, Japan, 462
Yamunā (goddess), 258, 660
Yamunā River, 1, 3, 4, 5, 218, 220, 222, 223, 224, 572, 576, 798
Yan, kingdom of, 109, 293, 620, 744
Yan River, 874
Yan Xishan (Chinese warlord and governor), 212, 216
Yanan, Shaanxi, China, 874-878
Yanan Period (China), 874, 876, 878
Yanan Revloutionary Memorial Hall, Yanan, China, 878
Yang (Sui emperor of China), 422
Yang Bo (Chinese war minister), 215
Yang Chaoying (poet), 325
Yang Di (Sui emperor of China), 540, 541, 875
Yang Guifei (concubine to Xuanzong), 541, 872
Yang Hsuan-chih (Chinese writer), 540
Yang Shao pottery culture, 41, 870
Yang Xiuqing (Taiping rebellion leader), 620
Yang Xuanzhi (Chinese writer), 540
Yang Yiqing, 214
Yangdi (Sui emperor of China), 325, 744
Yangon, Myanmar, 60, 61, 62, 63, 222, 558, 560, 656, **879-883**
Yangon River, 879
Yangtze River, 42, 302, 420, 424, 541, 616, 732, 735, 742, 776, 813, 866, 868, 877, 884
Yangzhou City Museum, China, 887
Yangzhou, Jiangsu, China, 704, 884-887
Yanjing. *See* Beijing, China
Yansui, China, 296
Yao Wenyuan (Gang of Four member), 738
Ya'qūb ebn Leys (founder of Ṣaffārid Dynasty), 79, 280
Ya'qūb Khān (emir of Afghanistan), 417, 418, 442
Yaquet of Dabul (architect), 127
Yar Moḥammad Khān (Bhopāl prince), 118, 119
Yarkend, China, 456, 458
Yasawa Islands, Fiji, 265
Yashima, Japan, 426
Yaśodharapura, Cambodia, 31
Yaśovarman. *See* Lakśavarman
Yāsuki (mythology), 33
Yatarō, Iwasaki, 614
Yathata Island, Fiji, 265
Yaudheya (people), 576
Yautiya (people), 506, 507
Yavanarāja Tushaspha (governor of Junāgadh), 408
Yayati (Soma king of Bhubaneswar), 123
Yayoi period (Japan), 345, 376, 462, 587, 632
Yeh-lü Ta-shih (ruler of Karakitai), 163
Yeiwene, Yeiwene, 647
Yellow Crane Tower, Wuchang, China, 866
Yellow Emperor. *See* Huang Di
Yellow Hats (Buddhist sect), 528, 750, 751
Yellow River, 40, 42, 212, 293, 294, 296, 420, 424, 538, 541, 776, 778, 870, 873, 874, 877, 901, 903, 904
Yellow Sea, 195, 197, 482, 485, 486, 813
Yellowstone National Park, Wyoming, United States of America, 832, 833
Yemen, 166
Yenan. *See* Yanan, Shaanxi, China
Yeoh (clan), 667
Yi (5th-century Chinese prince), 868
Yi (19th-century Chinese prince), 814
Yi Dynasty, 195-196
Yi He Quan. *See* Boxer Rebellion
Yi Jing (Chinese pilgrim), 872
Yi Sŏng-gye (founder of Yi Dynasty), 195-196
Yi-ai-tang (The Hall of Love Left Behind), Guangzhou, China, 305
Yifata (Sacred Hair Pagoda), Guangzhou, China, 304
Yiguan Dao (Way of Basic Unity Society), 817
Yijing (Buddhist pilgrim), 661
Yiju (people), 293
Yilu (Tuoba chief and prince of Dai), 212
Yin. *See* Anyang, Henan, China
Yin Dynasty, 901
Yinchuan, China, 296
Yingkou, China, 748
Yinshan, China, 212
Yiwu. *See* Hami, Xinjiang Uighur, China
Yizhou. *See* Hami, Xinjiang Uighur, China
YMBA. *See* Young Men's Buddhist Association
Yodo River, 648, 650, 651
Yogyakarta, Yogyakarta Special Territory, Indonesia, 888-892
Yokohama, Japan, 319, 342, 426
Yokoseura, Japan, 340
Yokosuka, Japan, 342
Yomeimon Gate, Nikkō, Japan, 637
Yongilru (Sun-greeting Pavilion), Puyŏ, South Korea, 485
Yongjia (Western Jin emperor of China), 540
Yongjizha, China, 214
Yongle (Ming emperor of China), 105, 109, 214, 296, 322, 335, 583, 584, 620, 739
Yongning Monastery, Luoyang, China, 540
Yongzheng (Qing emperor of China), 732
Yoriie (shōgun of Japan), 428
Yoritomo. *See* Minamoto Yoritomo
Yoriyoshi (ancestor of Minamoto Yoritomo), 426
York (factory), Bengkulu, Indonesia, 115
Yoshihito. *See* Taishō
Yoshijima family, 796
Yoshijima Heritage House, Takayama, Japan, 796, 797
Yoshino, Japan, 429, 518
Yoshiwara district, Tōkyō, Japan, 824
Young (*Bounty* mutineer), 675
Young, Edward, 676
Young, Sir Mark, 361
Young Men's Buddhist Association (Myanmar), 880
Young Pine (Wakamatsu), Fukushima, Japan, 10
Younghusband, Francis Edward, 529, 604, 752
Youzhou. *See* Beijing, China
Ypres, Belgium, 174
Yu (god), 868
Yu River, 214, 739
Yu Yuan, Shanghai, China, 738
Yu Zijun (Chinese military leader), 214, 296
Yuan Dynasty, 105, 109, 244, 246, 325, 327, 328, 424, 453, 541, 704, 705, 732, 739, 745, 746, 813, 866, 874, 897
Yuan Ming Yuan, Beijing, China, 708, 813
Yuan Shikai, 216, 748, 868
Yudhishtra (king of Kurukshetra), 505, 506
Yue (tribe), 358
Yue Fei (Chinese general), 325
Yue Fei (Chinese poet), 778
Yue Kang, Xiamen, China, 705
Yueh, China, 302, 304
Yüeh-Chi (people), 72, 73, 720, 859
Yuehsiu Range, China, 306
Yuen Long, Hong Kong, 358
Yuguan pass, Shanhaiguan, China, 739
Yuhua Tai (Terrace of the Rain of Flowers), Nanjing, China, 618
Yuichiro Miura, 606
Yukio Mishima, 518
Yulara, Australia, 44
Yulin. *See* Yansui, China
Yuluqiao (Bridge of the Imperial Way), Forbidden City, Beijing, China, 106
Yungang Caves, Shanxi, China, 212, 213, 214, 540, **893-896**
Yunnan, China, 52, 111, 532
Yunokawa, Japan, 317
Yunzhong. *See* Dingxiang, China
Yunzhou. *See* Datong, Shanxi, China
Yuryaku Tennō, 376
Yūsuf 'Ādil Khān (Bahmanī ruler), 125
Yusuf Has Hajip (poet), 457
Yūsufi-alī Kūkūldāsh, 335
Yūsup (king of Banten), 101-102

Zabulistan, Afghanistan, 280
Zafar Khan. *See* Muzaffar Shāh
Zahara Bāgh, Āgra, India, 1
Ẓahīr, Mohammad Shāh (king of Afghanistan), 336, 418
Ẓahīr-ud-Dīn Muḥammad. *See* Bābur
Zaida building, Kuching, Malaysia, 499
Zain-ul-Abidin Tomb, Srīnagar, India, 769
Zaiton. *See* Quanzhou, Fujian, China
Zaman Shāh (Durrāni ruler of Afghanistan), 417, 441, 671
Zamboanga Corderilla, Philippines, 900
Zamboanga, Zamboanga del Sur, Philippines, 404, **897-900**
Zanzibar, 725
Zaoyang. *See* Huailai Xian, China
Zarafshan River, 718
Zariaspa. *See* Balkh, Balkh, Afghanistan
Zeami (actor), 518
Zen Buddhism, 304, 338, 345, 349, 428, 429, 436, 518, 526
Zenana Bible and Medical Mission, 850
Zeng, China, 868
Zeniarai Benten, Kamakura, Japan, 427
Zeravshan River, 163
Zeus (god), 254
Zhang Chunqiao (Gang of Four member), 738
Zhang Ji (poet), 778
Zhang Qian, 239, 705
Zhang Xueliang, 216, 742, 748, 749
Zhang Yichao, 241
Zhang Zhidong, 866
Zhang Zuolin, 216, 742, 748
Zhao, kingdom of, 212, 293, 294
Zhao Kuangyin (Song emperor of China), 422
Zhao To (Lord of Nanyueh), 302
Zhaoxiang (king of Qin), 293
Zhejiang, China, 304, 325-328

Zheng Chenggong. *See* Koxinga
Zheng, China, 420
Zheng He (Ming admiral of China), 584, 705, 706
Zheng Naing Mu, Suzhou, China, 778
Zheng Zhenggong. *See* Koxinga
Zheng Zhilong (pirate), 790, 791
Zhengjiawazi, China, 744
Zhengtong (Ming emperor of China), 214
Zhengzhou, Henan, China, 40, **901-905**
Zhenla. *See* Chenla, Cambodia
Zhennü (Devoted Woman) Temple, Shanhaiguan, China, 741
Zhili. *See* Hebei, China
Zhob Valley, Pakistan, 491
Zhong Ziqi (legendary hermit), 868
Zhongdu (Middle Capital). *See* Beijing, China
Zhonghedian (The Hall of Complete Harmony), Forbidden City, Beijing, China, 107
Zhonghua Gate, Nanjing, China, 616, 619
Zhongnanhai, China, 108
Zhou Daguan (Chinese emissary to Cambodia), 32
Zhou Dynasty, 212, 244, 294, 302, 422, 538, 541, 707
Zhou Enlai, 111, 328, 737, 738, 876
Zhou Gong (Western Zhou regent of China), 538
Zhou Shizhong (Later Zhou emperor of China), 422
Zhou Wang (governor of Kaifeng), 424
Zhoukoudian, Beijing, China, 109
Zhu Gui (son of Ming Dynasty founder), 214
Zhu Yijun. *See* Wanli
Zhu Yuanzhang. *See* Hongwu
Zhu Zhong (mythic Chinese forefather), 40
Zhuang (Kaifeng founder), 420
Zhudi. *See* Yongle (Ming emperor of China)
Zhuhai, China, 546
Zhujiang River, 302, 305, 306, 358, 541, 542, 545
Zhuo Zheng Yuan, Suzhou, China, 779
Zia, Khaleda, 229
Zia Dynasty, 40
Zijincheng, Imperial City, Beijing, China, 105
Ziyad ibn Salih, 163
Zoffany, Johan, 173
Zōjō-ji, Shiba, Japan, 637
Zoo, Sakkar Baug, India, 413
Zoological Society of London, England, 629
Zoroaster, 72, 142, 578
Zoroastrianism, 72, 142, 163, 333, 383, 456, 578, 720, 872, 884
Zou, China, 707
Zuicho Tachibana, 244
Zuisen-ji (temple), Kamakura, Japan, 429
Zuo Zongtang (Chinese general), 323, 458

Notes on Contributors

ADSHEAD, S. A. M. Professor of History, University of Canterbury, Christchurch, New Zealand. Author of *Central Asia in World History,* 1993; and *China in World History,* 1995.

ARNOLD, David. Professor of South Asian History, School of Oriental and African Studies, University of London. Author of *Police Power and Colonial Rule: Madras 1859–1947,* 1986; and *Colonizing the Body: State Medicine and Epidemic Disease in Nineteenth-Century India,* 1993.

BEATTIE, Andrew. Teacher of geography at Eltham College, London. Author of *Visitor's Guide to Czechoslovakia,* 1991; co-author, *Visitor's Guide to Syria,* 1996.

BLOCK, Bernard A. Freelance writer. Reference and documents librarian, Ohio State University, Columbus, 1969–92.

BRICE, Elizabeth. Special Collections librarian, Miami University, Oxford, Ohio.

BROADRUP, Elizabeth E. Freelance writer and picture researcher.

BROWN, A. E. Staff Tutor in Archaeology, Department of Adult Education, University of Leicester. Editor of *Northamptonshire Archaeology,* 1974–84. Author of *Fieldwork for Archaeologists and Local Historians,* 1987.

BRUNS, Holly E. Graduate student in fiction writing, Columbia College, Chicago.

BUCH, Neville. Post-doctoral fellow, Department of History, University of Queensland, Brisbane, Australia.

CABLE, Monica. South America Manager, Wilderness Travels. Recipient of Watson Foundation fellowship for independent research in Southeast Asia, 1991–92.

CHAKRABARTI, Dilip K. University Lecturer in Indian Archaeology, Faculty of Oriental Studies, Cambridge University, Cambridge. Reader in Archaeology, Delhi University, 1977–90. Author, most recently, of *Archaeology of Eastern India: Chhotanagpur Plateau and West Bengal,* 1993; and *The Archaeology of Ancient Indian Cities,* 1995.

CHARNEY, Sappho. Technical writer, Quality Assurance Engineering, Kemet Electronics Corporation. Instructor, Clemson University, South Carolina, 1989–91; technical writer, Boeing Petroleum, 1985–87. Author of *The Secret Family,* 1991; and *Password Protected,* 1992.

CHIARA, Maria. Anthropologist and freelance researcher/writer.

CHOWDHURY, Shome. Graduate Student in the Department of South Asian Languages and Civilizations, University of Chicago.

COTÉ, Denise. Graduate Student, School of Information Technology and Library Science, University of Michigan, Dearborn.

CRIBB, Robert. Senior Lecturer, Department of History, University of Queensland, Brisbane, Australia. Research Fellow, Department of Pacific and Southeast Asian History, Australian National University, Canberra, 1987–90. Author of *Historical Dictionary of Indonesia,* 1992; co-author of *Modern Indonesia: A History Since 1945,* 1995.

DUBOVOY, Sina. Independent scholar and freelance writer specializing in history and biography.

FELSHMAN, Jeffrey. Freelance writer. Recipient of 1993 Peter Lisagor Award for exemplary journalism, from the Society of Professional Journalists, Chicago Headline Club, for "The Fall and Rise of Anita Brick," Chicago *Reader,* December 3, 1993.

FIELD, Graham. Freelance writer. Editor of *Asiamoney,* 1991–93. Author of *Economic Growth and Political Change in Asia,* 1995.

FLOOD, David. Freelance writer; editor, *Bayliner.* Copywriter, Scott Foresman, 1984–1988.

GELFAND, Lynn. Graduate student in folklore, Indiana University, Bloomington.

GOODMAN, Lawrence F. English instructor, Illinois Institute of Technology, Chicago.

GRIFFIN, Jackie. Artist and freelance writer. Freelance copy editor and researcher, St. James Press/Gale Research International, London, 1990–94.

HEENAN, Patrick. Research student, University of London. Editor of *1992*, 1989.

HOLLISTER, Pam. Freelance writer. Executive speechwriter and editorial supervisor, corporate communications department, Centerior Energy Corporation, Cleveland, 1980–93.

HOYT, Christopher A. Freelance writer.

KEAY, John. Freelance writer and historian. Author of *India Discovered,* 1981; and *The Honorable Company: A History of the English East India Company,* 1991.

KELLERMAN, Robert. English instructor, Michigan State University, East Lansing.

KINGSTON, Beverly. Associate Professor, School of History, University of New South Wales, Sydney. Member of the History Advisory Panel of the New South Wales Heritage Council, since 1985. Author of *Glad Confident Morning,* volume 3 of *The Oxford History of Australia,* 1988; and

Basket, Bag and Trolley: A History of Shopping in Australia, 1994.

KLAWINSKI, Rion. Freelance writer.

KOTTNER, Lee. Freelance writer and editor.

LAMONTAGNE, Monique. Research student, University of London. Co-editor of *The Voice of the People: Reminiscences of Early Settlers, 1866–1895,* 1984.

LEVI, Anthony. Freelance writer and independent scholar. Buchanan Professor of French Language and Literature, University of St. Andrews, Fife, Scotland, 1971–87; also lecturer at Christ Church, Oxford, and professor of French, University of Warwick, Coventry. Author of *French Moralists: The Theory of the Passions 1585–1649,* 1964; *Religion in Practice,* 1966; and *Guide to French Literature,* 1992. Editor of *Erasmus: Satires,* 1986.

LEVI, Clarissa. Freelance writer.

LEVI, Claudia. Freelance writer.

LIEW, Kit S. Senior Lecturer in History, University of Tasmania, Australia. Editorial Board member, *Australian Journal of Chinese Affairs,* 1979–82; Editor, *Chinese Studies Association of Australia Newsletter,* since 1991. Author of *Struggle for Democracy: Sung Chiao-jen and the 1911 Chinese Revolution,* 1971; and *Son Jiaoren Zhuan* (Biography of Song Jiaoren), 1990.

LONGCORE, Christine Ann. Freelance writer.

LOTUS, Jean L. Freelance writer and editor.

LUI, Adam Yuen-chung. Reader, History Department, University of Hong Kong. Editor and English Book Review Editor of *Journal of Oriental Studies,* University of Hong Kong, 1978–79 and 1986–89. Author of *Hanlin Academy: Training Ground for the Ambitious 1644–1860,* 1981; and *Two Rulers in One Reign: The Dorgon and the Shun-chih Formulae 1644–61,* 1989.

McNULTY, Mary F. Freelance writer and editor. Editor, American Association of Law Libraries newsletter, 1988–93.

MAXWELL, Caterina Mercone. Freelance writer and editor. Co-author of *A Survey of Family Literacy in the United States,* 1995.

MONTGOMERY, Sue. Freelance travel writer.

NASLUND, L. R. Freelance writer.

NEWBY, L. J. Lecturer in Chinese History, St. Hilda's College, Oxford University, Oxford.

NG LUN, Ngai-ha. Professor, Department of History, Chinese University of Hong Kong. Author of *Interactions of East and West: The Development of Public Education in Early Hong Kong,* 1984; and of *The Quest for Excellence: A History of the Chinese University of Hong Kong,* 1994. Editor of *Historical Inscriptions in Hong Kong,* 3 vols., 1982–86, and of numerous other volumes on Hong Kong and modern Chinese history.

O'LEARY, Terence Daniel. Retired British diplomat. Governor of Pitcairn Islands, 1984–87; has served in New Zealand, Australia, South Africa, Sierra Leone, and Western Samoa.

OLSSEN, Erik. Professor of History, University of Otago, New Zealand. Member of the New Zealand Historic Trust Board, 1986–93. Author of *A History of Otago,* 1984; *The Red Feds,* 1988; and *Building the New World,* 1995.

PEARSON, M. N. Professor of History, University of New South Wales, Sydney. Author of *The Portuguese in India,* 1987.

PEPPER, Tim. Freelance writer. Co-author of *Visitors Guide to Hungary,* 1994; *Visitors Guide to Syria,* 1995; and *Off the Beaten Track: Czech and Slovak Republics,* 1995.

POLLAK, Linda. Freelance writer and journalist.

REECE, Bob. Professor of History, Murdoch University, Perth, Western Australia. Author of *The Name of Brooke,* 1982; and *Exiles from Erin,* 1991.

RIJSBERMAN, Marijke. Freelance writer, editor, and translator; writer, Stanford Law School, since 1995.

RING, Trudy. Senior news reporter, Lambda Publications. Editor, *International Dictionary of Historic Places,* volumes 1–3.

SALKIN, Robert M. Commissioning Editor, Fitzroy Dearborn Publishers.

SAVILE, Charles. Freelance writer, specializing in Asia.

SAWYERS, June Skinner. Editor, Loyola University Press. Co-author of *The Chicago Arts Guide,* 1994; author of *Chicago Portraits: Biographies of 250 Famous Chicagoans,* 1991; and *Chicago Sketches: Urban Tales, Stories, and Legends from Chicago History,* 1995.

SCOTT, Paula Pyzik. Freelance writer and editor.

SHEPHERD, Kenneth R. Freelance writer and editor. Adjunct instructor in history, Henry Ford Community College, Dearborn, Michigan. Associate editor, Gale Research, 1987–94.

SINGH, Sarva Daman. Professor of History, University of Queensland, Brisbane, Australia. Author of *Ancient Indian Warfare,* 1965; *The Archaeology of the Lucknow Region,* 1972; *Polyandry in Ancient India,* 1978; and *Culture through the Ages,* 1996.

SIRACUSA, Joseph M. Reader in History, University of Queensland, Brisbane, Australia. Associate Editor, *Australian Journal of Politics and History,* 1975–90. Author of *Australian-American Relations since 1945: A Documentary History,* 1976.

STANDEN, Naomi. Junior Research Fellow in Chinese History, St. John's College, Oxford University, Oxford.

STUART-FOX, Martin. Reader in History, University of Queensland, Brisbane, Australia. Correspondent for United Press International in Laos and Vietnam, 1963–66; editor of *World Review,* 1979–82. Author of *Laos: Politics, Economics, and Society,* 1986; co-author of *Historical Dictionary of Laos,* 1992.

SULLIVAN, James. Freelance writer.

SY-QUIA, Hilary Collier. Doctoral candidate in German literature, University of California at Berkeley.

TARLING, Nicholas. Professor of History, University of Auckland, New Zealand. Author of *Britain, the Brookes, and Brunei,* 1971; *Sulu and Sabah: A Study of English Policy towards the Philippines and North Borneo from the Late Eighteenth Century,* 1978; and *The Fourth Anglo-Burman War: Britain and the Independence of Burma,* 1987; editor of *The Cambridge History of South East Asia,* 2 vols., 1992.

TERRY, Karen. Freelance writer.

TURNER, Christopher. Freelance travel writer. Author of *Visitor's Guide India: Delhi, Agra, and Rajasthan,* 1995.

VASUDEVAN, A. Editor of *Twentieth Century Romance and Historical Writers,* 1994; and *International Dictionary of Films and Filmmakers, Volume 1: Films,* 1995.

WHITE, Richard. Freelance writer and researcher.

WILKINSON, Lulu. Freelance writer.

WILOCH, Thomas. Freelance writer.

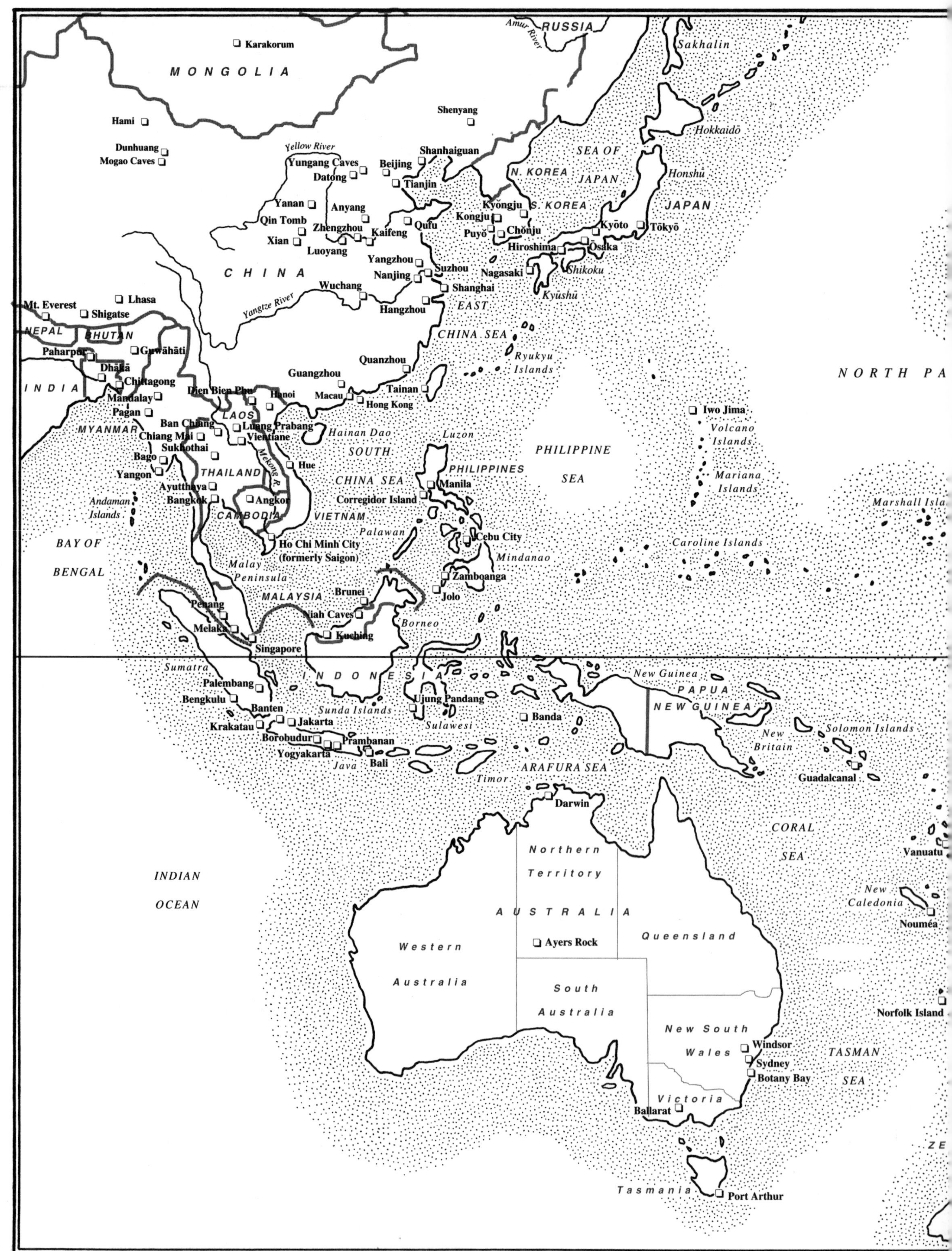

RUSSIA
Amur River
Karakorum
MONGOLIA
Sakhalin
Hami
Shenyang
Hokkaidō
Dunhuang
Mogao Caves
Yellow River
Yungang Caves
Datong
Beijing
Shanhaiguan
Tianjin
SEA OF JAPAN
N. KOREA
S. KOREA
Honshū
JAPAN
Yanan
Anyang
Qin Tomb
Xian
Zhengzhou
Kaifeng
Luoyang
Qufu
Kyŏngju
Kongju
Puyŏ
Chŏnju
Hiroshima
Kyōto
Ōsaka
Tōkyō
Shikoku
Kyūshū
Nagasaki
CHINA
Yangzhou
Nanjing
Suzhou
Shanghai
Wuchang
Hangzhou
Yangtze River
Lhasa
Mt. Everest
Shigatse
NEPAL
BHUTAN
Paharpur
Guwāhāti
Dhākā
Chittagong
INDIA
Mandalay
Pagan
MYANMAR
EAST CHINA SEA
Ryukyu Islands
Quanzhou
Guangzhou
Tainan
Macau
Hong Kong
Dien Bien Phu
Hanoi
LAOS
Ban Chiang
Luang Prabang
Chiang Mai
Vientiane
Hainan Dao
Luzon
Sukhothai
Bago
Yangon
THAILAND
Mekong R.
Hue
SOUTH CHINA SEA
PHILIPPINES
Manila
Corregidor Island
Ayutthaya
Bangkok
Angkor
CAMBODIA
VIETNAM
Andaman Islands
Palawan
Cebu City
Ho Chi Minh City (formerly Saigon)
Mindanao
BAY OF BENGAL
Malay Peninsula
Zamboanga
Jolo
MALAYSIA
Brunei
Penang
Niah Caves
Melaka
Kuching
Borneo
Singapore
PHILIPPINE SEA
NORTH PA
Iwo Jima
Volcano Islands
Mariana Islands
Marshall Isla
Caroline Islands
Sumatra
INDONESIA
Palembang
Bengkulu
Banten
Krakatau
Jakarta
Sunda Islands
Ujung Pandang
Sulawesi
Borobudur
Prambanan
Yogyakarta
Java
Bali
Timor
Banda
ARAFURA SEA
New Guinea
PAPUA NEW GUINEA
New Britain
Solomon Islands
Guadalcanal
Darwin
CORAL SEA
Vanuatu
Northern Territory
INDIAN OCEAN
AUSTRALIA
New Caledonia
Nouméa
Western Australia
Ayers Rock
Queensland
South Australia
Norfolk Island
New South Wales
Windsor
Sydney
Botany Bay
TASMAN SEA
Victoria
Ballarat
ZE
Tasmania
Port Arthur